IF FOUND, please notify and arrange return to owner. This text is important for the owner's preparation for the Uniform Certified Public Accountant Examination.

Name of CPA Candidate _____

Address   _____

City, State, Zip   _____

Telephone   ( )_____

Additional texts are available at your local bookstore

or directly from John Wiley and Sons, Inc.

Order information and order forms can be found at the front of the book

_____ _____

CPA

EXAMINATION REVIEW

VOLUME II
PROBLEMS and SOLUTIONS

17th EDITION

Irvin N. Gleim, Ph.D., CPA
University of Florida
Gainesville, Florida

&

Patrick R. Delaney, Ph.D., CPA
Northern Illinois University
DeKalb, Illinois

JOHN WILEY & SONS

New York   Chichester   Brisbane   Toronto   Singapore

WILEY

This publication is designed to provide accurate and authoritative information in regard to the subject matter covered. It is sold with the understanding that the publisher is not engaged in rendering legal, accounting, or other professional service.

If legal advice or other expert assistance is required, the services of a competent professional person should be sought.

From a declaration of principles jointly adopted by a Committee of the American Bar Association and a Committee of Publishers.

ISBN 0-471-52251-1
10 9 8 7 6 5 4 3 2 1

PREFACE

The first purpose of Volume II is to provide CPA candidates with recent examination problems/questions organized by topic, e.g., internal control, consolidations, secured transactions, etc. This text includes over 2,000 multiple choice questions. Multiple choice questions are an effective means of studying the material tested on past exams; however, it is also necessary to work with practice problems and essay questions to develop the solutions approach (the ability to solve CPA essay questions and practice problems efficiently).

The second objective of this volume is to explain the AICPA unofficial answers to the examination problems/questions included in this text. The AICPA publishes past CPA examinations and unofficial answers. No explanation is made, however, of the procedures that should have been applied to the examination problem to obtain the unofficial answers. Relatedly, the unofficial answers to multiple choice questions provide no justification and/or explanation. This text provides explanations of both how to work problems and the unofficial answers to multiple choice questions.

This text is designed to be used in conjunction with Volume I, *Outlines and Study Guides*, but may be used with or without any other study source. Both volumes are organized into 44 manageable study units (modules) to assist candidates in organizing their study programs. The multiple choice questions in this volume are grouped into topical categories which correspond to the sequencing of material as it appears in Volume I.

Multiple Choice questions from the November 1989 and May 1990 examinations have been added to this Seventeenth Edition. Also, many of the essay questions/practice problems from both 1989 exams are included. As new questions and problems are added, older ones are deleted. New problems are not added just for the sake of change. Rather, new problems emphasize more current topics, pronouncements, etc. They also illustrate the most current type and format of problems being used on the examination. Changes in the Board of Examiners, their philosophy, and most important, the AICPA examination staff, result in changing types and formats of questions and problems.

A Sample Examination for each of the four parts of the exam is included in the Appendix at the end of this volume. The questions and problems for these exams were selected on the basis of an analysis of current trends in exam coverage.

The authors are indebted to the American Institute of Certified Public Accountants and the Institute of Management Accounting of the National Association of Accountants for permission to reproduce and adapt examination materials from past certification examinations.

The authors deeply appreciate the enthusiastic and dedicated attitude of the many CPA candidates with whom the authors have had the pleasure to work. As always, the authors welcome any comments concerning materials contained in or omitted from this text. Please send these to Patrick R. Delaney, c/o CPA Examination Review, P.O. Box 886, DeKalb, Illinois 60115.

Please carefully read Chapter One, "How to Use This Book."

Good Luck on the Exam,

Irvin N. Gleim
Patrick R. Delaney
May 16, 1990

ABOUT THE AUTHORS

Patrick R. Delaney is the Arthur Andersen & Co. Alumni Professor of Accountancy at Northern Illinois University. He received his PhD in Accountancy from the University of Illinois. He has public accounting experience with Arthur Andersen & Co. and is co-author of **GAAP: Interpretation and Application** also published by John Wiley & Sons, Inc. He is a member of the Illinois CPA Society's Board of Directors currently serving as a Vice President and was Chairman of its Accounting Principles Committee; is a past president of the Rockford Chapter, National Association of Accountants; and has served on numerous other professional committees. He is a member of the American Accounting Association, American Institute of Certified Public Accountants, and National Association of Accountants. Professor Delaney has published in The Accounting Review and is a recipient of NIU's Excellence in Teaching Award and Lewis University's Distinguished Alumnus Award. He has been involved in NIU's CPA Review Course as director and instructor.

Irvin N. Gleim is Professor Emeritus at the Fisher School of Accounting at the University of Florida and is a CPA, CIA, and CMA. He received his PhD in Accountancy from the University of Illinois. He is a member of the American Institute of Certified Public Accountants, Florida Institute of Certified Public Accountants, American Accounting Association, American Business Law Association, Institute of Internal Auditors, Institute of Management Accounting, and National Association of Accountants. He has published professional articles in the Journal of Accountancy, The Accounting Review, and The American Business Law Journal. He has developed and taught both proprietary and university CPA review courses. He is author of CIA Examination Review and CMA Examination Review, both published by Accounting Publications, Inc.

ABOUT THE CONTRIBUTORS

John C. Borke, MAS, CPA, is an Associate Professor of Accounting at the University of Wisconsin-Platteville. He has worked as a staff auditor with Peat, Marwick, Mitchell & Co. Professor Borke prepared multiple choice answer explanations and solution guides for the practice problems in Financial Accounting.

John H. Engstrom, DBA, CPA, is Professor of Accountancy at Northern Illinois University. He is the author of Accounting for Governmental and Not For Profit Organizations, Richard D. Irwin, Inc. He reviewed solutions to problems in Governmental and Nonprofit Accounting.

Edward C. Foth, PhD, CPA, is an Associate Professor and Administrator of the Master of Science in Taxation Program at DePaul University. He has public accounting experience with Arthur Andersen & Co. Professor Foth is the author of Commerce Clearing House's Study Guide for Federal Tax Course, Study Guide for CCH Federal Taxation: Basic Principles, and co-author of their S Corporation Guide. Professor Foth prepared the answer explanations to the multiple choice questions in Income Taxes, selected the problem material in that area, and updated items to reflect revisions in the tax law.

Duane Lambert, JD, MBA, CPA, is Professor of Business Administration at California State University, Hayward where he teaches courses in Business Law and Accounting. He also has been a Visiting Lecturer and a Visiting Associate Professor at the University of California, Berkeley. Professor Lambert has "Big Eight" experience and has taught CPA review courses for the past several CPA examinations. He prepared answer explanations for the multiple choice questions in Business Law, Chapter 3.

Kurt Pany, PhD, CPA, is the Arthur Andersen & Co.-Don DuPont Professor of Accounting at Arizona State University. He is a member of the American Institute of Certified Public Accountants and the American Accounting Association. Prior to entering academe he worked as a staff auditor for Touche Ross & Co. Professor Pany prepared the answer explanations for the multiple choice questions and selected the problem material in Auditing, Chapter 2.

John R. Simon, PhD, CPA, is the Alumni Professor of Accountancy at Northern Illinois University and is a recipient of NIU's Excellence in Teaching Award. He has taught in NIU's CPA Review Course for the past ten years and is presently the director of the course. Professor Simon selected and updated the problem material in several modules in Financial Accounting.

Harold Wright, JD, is Coordinator and Assistant Professor of Business Law at Northern Illinois University. He has taught in NIU's CPA Review Course for the past thirteen years and is a recipient of NIU's Excellence in Teaching Award. Professor Wright prepared answer explanations for the multiple choice questions in Business Law, Chapter 3 which are retained from previous editions.

TABLE OF CONTENTS

*As explained in Chapter 1, this volume is organized into 44 modules (manageable study units). Volume I is organized in a parallel fashion. For easy reference, both Volumes I and II have numbered index tabs indicating the first page of each module.

Acknowledgements

Writing an annualized text is always a publishing event and a rejuvenating human experience. The authors are most grateful to the many users of previous editions, both instructors and students who have so generously shared with us their satisfaction with our work and their suggestions for changes and improvements. We hope that this will continue for we have benefited from those communications.

This work continues to be a "community effort." In addition to those colleagues cited as contributors, we would like to acknowledge and thank those many friends who gave us so many devoted hours to bring this 17th annualized edition to you so quickly after the May 1990 Examination: Lee Gampfer, Karen Klein, Jeanne LoCascio, Diane McCaslin, Pam Miller, Norma Rodriguez, Sara Sawyer, Barbara Stagner, and Lorrie Wildenradt.

OTHER CONTRIBUTORS AND REVIEWERS

The following individuals assisted in the preparation of this volume by drafting and reviewing answer explanations for the multiple choice questions.

Lawrence Clark, Dean of the College of Business, Louisiana State University at Shreveport.

Professor Clark assists in answering the business law multiple choice questions.

Ken Groetsema, BS, CPA.

Rebecca A. Hoger, BS, MAS, CPA, is an instructor of Accountancy at Northern Illinois University.

Carol Johnson, BS, CPA, is a candidate for the MAS degree in Acountancy at Northern Illinois University.

Jodi Latta, BS, has accepted employment with Arthur Andersen & Co.

Jeff Markert, BS, CPA, is a staff accountant at KPMG Peat Marwick.

James V. Pieper, BS, CPA, is a staff accountant at KPMG Peat Marwick.

John Pintozzi, BS, CPA, is a staff accountant with Deloitte Touche.

Catherine E. Staiger, BS, CPA, is a staff accountant at BDO Siedman.

Lori Wetzel, BS, MAS, CPA, CMA, is a senior staff accountant with Great Lake Dredge and Dock.

CHAPTER ONE
HOW TO USE THIS BOOK

This volume is a collection of recent CPA problems and solutions. The text is designed and organized to be used in conjunction with Volume I CPA EXAMINATION REVIEW: OUTLINES AND STUDY GUIDES, but may be used with or without any other study source. Each module in this volume corresponds to a module in Volume I. In this Volume, a module consists of

1. Multiple choice questions.
2. Practice problems and/or essay questions.
3. Unofficial answers for the multiple choice questions with the authors' explanations.
4. Unofficial answers for practice problems prefaced by solution guides.
5. Unofficial answers for essay questions prefaced by answer outlines.

Also included at the end of this volume is a complete sample CPA examination. It is included to enable candidates to gain experience in taking a "realistic" exam. While studying the modules, the candidate can become accustomed to concentrating on fairly narrow topics. By working through the sample examination near the end of their study program, candidates will be better prepared for taking the actual examination.

Before you begin working the recent CPA problems in this volume, peruse the table of contents and scan through the book, noting the manner in which the chapters and modules are organized. The schedule at the beginning of each chapter provides an index to the essay questions and practice problems appearing in each module. Some questions have been modified to reflect recent changes in law or practice. For a complete analysis of recent examinations and the *AICPA Content Specification Outlines* of future examinations, see Volume I, *Outlines and Study Guides*.

Multiple Choice Questions

The multiple choice questions and answer explanations can be used in many ways. First, they may be used as a diagnostic evaluation of your knowledge. For example, before beginning to review audit sampling you may wish to answer 10 to 15 multiple choice questions to determine your ability to answer CPA examination questions on audit sampling. The apparent difficulty of the questions and the correctness of your answers will allow you to determine the necessary breadth and depth of your review. Additionally, exposure to examination questions prior to review and study of the material should provide motivation. You will develop a feel for your level of proficiency and an understanding of the scope and difficulty of past examination questions. Moreover, your review materials will explain concepts encountered in the diagnostic multiple choice questions.

Second, the multiple choice questions can be used as a post-study or post-review evaluation. You should attempt to understand all concepts mentioned (even in incorrect answers) as you answer the questions. Refer to the explanation of the answer for discussion of the alternatives even though you selected the correct response. Thus, you should read the explanation of the unofficial answer unless you completely understand the question and all of the alternative answers.

Third, you may wish to use the multiple choice questions as a primary study vehicle. This is probably the quickest, but least thorough, approach. Make a sincere effort to understand the question and to select the correct reply before referring to the unofficial answer and explanation. In many cases the explanations will appear inadequate because of your unfamiliarity with the topic.

The multiple choice questions in Volume II are grouped into topical categories. These categories correspond to the sequencing of material as it appears within each of the corresponding modules in Volume I. In the answer explanations for the multiple choice questions in Volume II, we have included headings which provide cross-references to the text material in Volume I. For example, in Module 24, Fixed Assets, a heading appears above the answers to those dealing with depreciation. This heading is identified by the letter "F." To find the topical coverage of depreciation in Volume I, the candidate would refer to the Table of Contents for Financial Accounting (Chapter IV) and look under the module title (Fixed Assets) for the letter "F." Across the page on the line marked "F." would be the appropriate page number in Fixed Assets related to depreciation. As you work through the multiple choice questions in each module of this volume, you will notice that all of the questions from the latest exam (May exam preceding publication of this volume) that pertain to a given module are grouped together at the end of the module. Among these questions you will encounter some which are identified as **"identical/similar" questions**. The AICPA reuses some questions verbatim and other questions are changed slightly (e.g., the numbers in an accounting practice question that appeared in an earlier exam may all be doubled or halved). These questions and the related answer explanations are not included in this volume because they are so similar to questions appearing earlier in the respective modules that such inclusion would be redundant.

Each multiple choice question is coded as to the month, year, section, problem number, and multiple choice number. For example, (1189,A1,12) indicates the November 1989 CPA Examination, auditing section, problem number 1, and multiple choice question number 12. (Note that the 60 multiple choice questions are referred to as problem number 1 on the auditing, business law, and theory sections of the CPA examination.) Practice I is referenced with a P, Practice II is referenced with a Q,

Theory is referenced with a T, and Business Law is referenced with an L. For example, (1189,P2,21) indicates the November 1989 CPA Examination, Practice I section, problem number 2, and multiple choice question number 21, and (590,Q3,45) indicates May 1990 CPA Examination, Practice II section, problem number 3, and multiple choice question number 45. (Note that the multiple choice questions on the Practice I and Practice II section of the CPA exam are referred to as problem 1, first set of 20 multiple choice; problem 2, second set of 20 multiple choice; and problem 3, third set of 20 multiple choice. Essay questions are coded as to the month, year, section, and problem number. For example, (1189,A2) is the November 1989 CPA Examination, Auditing section, problem number 2.

The multiple choice questions outnumber the essay questions/practice problems by greater than 10 to 1 in this book. This is similar to a typical CPA exam. Recent exams have contained:

	Multiple choice	Essay/ Problem
Auditing	60	4
Business Law	60	4
Practice I	60	2
Practice II	60	2
Theory	60	4
Totals	300	16

The numbers are somewhat misleading in that many essay questions/practice problems contain multiple (and often unrelated) parts.

One difficulty with so many multiple choice questions is that you may overemphasize them. Candidates generally prefer to work multiple choice questions because they are:

1. Shorter and less time consuming,
2. Solvable with less effort, and
3. Less frustrating than essay questions and practice problems.

Essay questions require the ability to organize and compose a solution, as well as knowledge of the subject matter. Remember, working essay questions/practice problems from start to finish is just as important as, if not more important than, working multiple choice questions.

Another difficulty with the large number of multiple choice questions is that you may tend to become overly familiar with the questions. The result may be that you may begin reading the facts and assumptions of previously studied questions into the questions on your examination. Guard against this potential problem by reading each multiple choice question with **extra** care.

Although not as critical as for essay questions and practice problems, the solutions approach (a systematic problem-solving methodology) is relevant to multiple choice questions. The solutions approach for multiple choice questions consists of the following steps.

1. **Work individual questions in order.**

   a. If a question appears lengthy or difficult, skip it until you can determine that extra time is available. Put a big question mark in the margin to remind you to return to questions you have skipped or need to review.

2. **Cover the answers before reading each question.**

   a. The answers are sometimes misleading, which may cause you to misread or misinterpret the question

3. **Read each question carefully to determine the topical area.**

   a. Study the requirements first so you know which data are important
   b. Underline keywords and important data
   c. Identify pertinent information with notations in the margin of the exam
   d. Be especially careful to note when the requirement is an exception, e.g., "Which of the following is not an accounting change handled by the cumulative effect method?"
   e. If a set of data is the basis for two or more questions, read the requirements of each of the questions before beginning to work the first question (sometimes it is more efficient to work the questions out of order or simultaneously)
   f. Be alert to read questions as they are, not as you would like them to be; you may encounter a familiar looking item; don't jump to the conclusion that you know what it is
   g. For accounting practice questions, prepare intermediary solutions as you read the question

4. **Anticipate the answer before looking at the alternative answers.**

   a. Recall the applicable principle (e.g., change in estimate); the applicable model (e.g., net present value); or the applicable code section (e.g., 1245)
   b. If Accounting Practice question(s) deal with a complex area like earnings per share, set them up like full-blown problems on scratch paper, if necessary, using abbreviations that enable you to follow your work (remember these questions are machine-graded)

5. **Read the answers and select the best alternative.**

   a. For Accounting Practice questions, if the answer you have computed is not among the choices, quickly check your math and the logic of your solution. If you don't arrive at one of the given answers in the allotted time, make an educated guess.

6. **Mark the correct (or best guess) answer on the examination itself.**

7. **After completing all of the individual questions in an overall question, transfer the answers to the machine-gradable answer sheet with extreme care.**

   a. Be very careful not to fall out of sequence with the answer sheet. A mistake would cause most of your answers to be wrong. SINCE THE AICPA USES ANSWER SHEETS WITH DIFFERENT FORMATS, IT WOULD BE VERY EASY TO GO ACROSS THE SHEET INSTEAD OF DOWN OR VICE VERSA.

    b. Review to check that you have transferred the answers correctly
    c. Do not leave this step until the end of the exam as you may find your-
       self with too little time to transfer your answers to the answer sheet.
       THE PROCTORS ARE NOT PERMITTED TO GIVE YOU EXTRA TIME TO TRANSFER THEM.

Practice Problems

The solutions approach to practice problems is more critical than for multiple choice or essay questions. Many candidates have trouble with Accounting Practice due to their inability to "put a handle on" or "gain control of" practice problems. Without an efficient solutions approach, it is easy to spin your wheels and/or be overwhelmed by many of the practice problems.

To develop a solutions approach for practice problems, you have to work problems from start to finish under examination conditions. There are many possible series of solution steps. A series of solution steps is outlined below. Candidates should develop and adapt a series of specific steps to fit their individual needs. They may find that some of the steps are occasionally unnecessary, or that certain additional procedures increase their problem-solving efficiency. A solutions approach should be developed and practiced on recent CPA questions and problems prior to taking the CPA examination.

1. **Glance over the problem.** Only scan the problem. Get a feel for the type or category of problem. Do not read it. Until you understand the require- ments, you cannot discriminate important data from irrelevant data.
2. **Study the requirements.** "Study" as differentiated from "read." Candidates continually lose points due to misunderstanding the requirements. Underline key phrases and words.
2a. **Visualize the solution format.** Determine the expected format of the re- quired solution. Develop an awareness of "schedule and statement format." Put headings on the required statements and schedules. Often a single re- quirement will require two or more statements, schedules, etc. A common example is a question followed by "why" or "explain." Explicitly recognize multiple requirements by numbering or lettering them on your examination booklet, expanding on the letters already assigned to problem parts.
3. **Outline the required procedures mentally.** Interrelate any data (e.g., a trial balance or comparative balance sheets) given in the problem to the ex- pected solution format, mentally noting a "to do" list. Determine what it is you are going to do before you get started doing it. You will usually be working through the requirements in order. However, be watchful for problems with interrelated requirements (e.g., each paragraph of information given in the problem is needed to solve more than one requirement). An alternative solutions approach for these types of problems is to make all required computations for each piece of information at one time. By using this timesaving approach, you will be solving a part of each requirement as each piece of information is covered, but not necessarily in the same order as given on the exam.
3a. **Review applicable principles, knowledge.** Before immersing yourself in the details of the problem, quickly (30-60 seconds) review and organize your knowledge of the principles applicable to the problem. Jot down any acronyms, formulas, or other memory aids relevant to the topic of the ques-

tion. Otherwise, the details of the problem will confuse and overshadow your previous knowledge of the applicable principles.

4. **Study the text of the problem.** Read the problem carefully. With the requirements in mind, you now can begin to sort out relevant from irrelevant data. Underline and circle important data. The data necessary for answering each requirement may be scattered throughout the problem. As you study the text, use arrows, etc. to connect data pertaining to a common requirement. List the requirements (a, b, etc.) in the margin alongside the data to which they pertain. Use a bright colored pen to mark up the problem. Heavy colored underlining and comments are attention getting and give you confidence.

4a. **Prepare intermediary solutions as you study the problem.** E.g., calculate goodwill, reconstruct accounts, prepare time diagrams, etc. You are able to perceive these required intermediary solutions because you already understand the problem requirements. These intermediary solutions, along with your underlining and your notes in the text of the problem, will drastically decrease re-reading time.

5. **Prepare the solution.** You now are in a position to write a neat, complete, organized, labeled solution. Label computations, intermediary solutions, assumptions made, etc., on your scratch sheets and turn them in with your solution (note: not necessary for multiple choice questions).

6. **Proofread and edit.** Do not underestimate the utility of this step. Just recall all of the "silly" mistakes you made on undergraduate examinations. Corrections of errors and completion of oversights during this step can easily be the difference between passing and failing.

7. **Review the requirements.** Assure yourself that you have answered them all.

It is not recommended that candidates consult the solution guides and unofficial answers before substantially completing the practice problems.

Essay Questions

Essay questions appear on the auditing, business law, and theory portions of the examination. While multiple choice questions can often be answered by guessing or by "recognizing" a correct answer, essay questions require more extensive knowledge of the subject matter.

Such knowledge, while necessary, is not sufficient in itself to insure proper answering of essay questions. In addition, candidates must be able to organize and present a well-written answer in a limited time period. The solutions approach to essay questions will assist candidates in developing the necessary skills to successfully answer essay questions on the CPA exam. This approach must be practiced and refined by answering essay questions from previous CPA exams until you are confident of your ability to organize and present well-written answers to the graders of the CPA exam.

The major difference between the solutions approach for practice problems and essay questions is the use of a **keyword** outline. The **keyword** outline in the essay solutions approach takes the place of the intermediary solution in the problem solutions approach. Substitute the following two steps for step 4a. "Prepare intermediary solutions as you study the problem" in the practice problem "solutions approach."

     4a. Write down keywords (concepts). Jot down a list of keywords (grading concepts) in the margin of the examination. The proximity of the keywords to the text of the question will be more efficient than making notes on a separate sheet of paper which may be misplaced.

     4b. Organize the keywords into a solution outline. After you have noted all of the grading concepts which bear on the requirements, reorganize the outline for the entire answer. Make sure that you respond to each requirement and do not preempt answers to other requirements.

Next, write up your solution and edit as needed. If you have time later, review your solution again.

Plan ahead when writing your answer. You may wish to revise certain sections or add explanations if time permits you to review your answer. Writing on every other line and leaving a portion of each page blank will make it easier for you to proofread and edit. Also, your solution will be easier for the grader to read.

Note: you must write out the answers to the essay questions. Keyword outlines are not sufficient. THE AICPA EXPECTS THE GRADING CONCEPTS TO BE EXPLAINED IN CLEAR, CONCISE, WELL-ORGANIZED SENTENCES. However, you may prepare answers in list form as long as the listed items complete a sentence that begins with a lead-in phrase.

The essay questions and unofficial answers may also be used for study purposes without preparation of answers. Before turning to the unofficial answers, study the question and outline the solution (either mentally or in the margin of the book). Look at the answer outline and compare it to your own. Next, read the unofficial answer, underlining keywords and phrases. The underlining should reinforce your study of the answer content and also assist you in learning how to structure your solutions. On the next page, the unofficial answer to an auditing internal control question is underlined to illustrate the technique.

Answer outlines which summarize the major concepts contained in the unofficial answer are provided for each auditing, business law, and theory essay question. These outlines will facilitate your study of questions.

Diagnose Your Weaknesses Prior to the Exam

This volume of problems and solutions provides you with an opportunity to diagnose and correct any exam-taking weaknesses prior to your taking the examination. Continuously analyze the contributing factors to incomplete or incorrect solutions to CPA problems prepared during your study program. General categories of candidates' weaknesses include:

1. Failure to understand the requirements.
2. Misunderstanding the text of the problem.
3. Lack of knowledge of material tested.
4. Inability to apply the solutions approach.
5. Lack of an exam strategy, e.g., time budgeting.
6. Sloppiness, computational errors, etc.
7. Failure to proofread and edit.

Additional Study Aids

A more complete discussion of the solutions approach, including illustrations thereof, appears in Chapter 3 of Volume I, *Outlines and Study Guides*. Additionally, use of "note cards" as an integral part of your study program is discussed and illustrated in Chapter 1 of Volume I. Chapter 4 of Volume I includes a detailed checklist to assist candidates with their last minute preparation and to provide guidance concerning the actual taking of the exam.

Answer Outline

Problem 7   Purchasing Department Controls

a. Effective internal accounting control
   procedures
   1. Purchase requisition prepared when goods
      needed
   2. Purchase requisition copy on file in
      store's department
   3. Responsible person in store's dept. ap-
      proves requisitions
         Based on need for goods
         Clearly indicates approval on requi-
         sition
   4. Purchase orders can be issued only after
      proper approval
   5. Vendors are requested to confirm pur-
      chase orders
   6. Purchase requisitions are filed with
      purchase orders
   7. Copies of purchase orders sent to re-
      ceiving department
         But do not include quantities
         ordered
   8. Purchase orders are numbered and all
      numbers accounted for
   9. Receiving dept. only accepts goods per
      purchase orders

b. 1. The time to order is determined by
         Quantities on hand
         Expected rate of use
         Time it takes to receive goods (lead
         time)
         Cost of owning versus cost of stock-
         out
   2. The order quantity of supplies, etc., is
      based on
         Expected use
         Order costs
         Ability to receive goods
         Ability to pay for goods
         Set-up costs
         Storage costs
         Interest in investment
         Risk of obsolescence
         Quantity discounts
         Shipping costs
         Calculated by economic order quantity

Unofficial Answer

Problem 7   Purchasing Department Controls

a. Those internal accounting control procedures that Long would expect to find if
Maylou's system of internal accounting control
over purchases is effective are as follows:

• Purchase requisitions are prepared and/or
approved only after there has been a proper
determination of the need for the goods requested.

• One copy of the purchase requisition is
maintained on file in the store's department.

• Purchase requisitions are approved by a responsible person in the store's department.
Approval is given only after that person is
satisfied that a need exists and that the requisition is properly prepared. Approval is
clearly indicated on requisitions.

• Purchase orders are issued only after they
are approved by persons given the specific
responsibility to make such approval.

• Vendors are requested to confirm purchase
orders. This indicates acceptance and constitutes a contractual commitment.

• Purchase requisitions are filed with purchase orders, and both are maintained in an
orderly file in the purchase office.

• Copies of purchase orders sent to the
receiving department do not include the
quantities of merchandise ordered.

• All purchase orders are numbered, and all
numbers are accounted for. This allows control over purchase orders canceled or rejected
by vendors.

• Receiving department accepts only those
goods for which a purchase order is on hand.

b. 1 The question when to order depends primarily on quantities on hand, rate of use, and
the lead time between order placement and
receipt of goods. Other factors include the
trade-off between the cost of owning and
storing merchandise versus the risk of being
out of stock.

2 Factors considered in determining how much
to order include expected use, costs of
placing an order, receiving and paying for
what has been purchased, set-up costs, storage
costs, interest on investment, risk of obsolescence or deterioration, quantity discounts,
and shipping costs. The determination is made
judgmentally or mathematically by arriving at
an economic order quantity.

NOW IS THE TIME
TO MAKE A COMMITMENT

CHAPTER TWO
AUDITING PROBLEMS AND SOLUTIONS

Auditing is tested on Thursday morning from 8:30 to 12:00. The exam traditionally includes 60 multiple choice questions (60% of the auditing grade) and 4 essay questions (each 10% of the auditing grade).

The exam will most likely include questions on the subject matter in each of the six modules. A complete analysis of recent examinations and the AICPA *Revised Content Specification Outlines* appears in Volume I, *Outlines and Study Guides*.

Explanations to auditing answers contain references to AICPA *Professional Standards, Volume I and II*, published by Commerce Clearing House. Volume I contains the standards for Auditing (AU), Management Advisory Services (MS), Tax Practice (TX), and Accounting and Review Services (AR). Volume II contains the standards for Ethics (ET) and Quality Control (QC). Candidates are strongly urged to refer to **current** editions of these volumes.

Each question is coded as to month, year, section, problem number, and multiple choice question number. For example, (1186,A1,31) indicates November 1986, audit problem 1, and question number 31. Questions are also marked as being from the Certified Internal Auditor Examination (CIA) or the Certificate in Management Accounting Examination (CMA).

You will notice that a number of the auditing essay questions are "older" than those presented in other portions of the manual. This is because auditing includes question types that are cycled onto the exam over a relatively long period of time. Accordingly, to include a representative sample, we have included old questions.

Module 1/Professional Responsibilities (RESP)

	Exam reference	No. of minutes	Page no. Problem	Answer
60 Multiple Choice			14	24
5 Essay Questions:				
1. Planning Procedures	587,A5	15-25	22	33
2. Audit Risk & Materiality	1186,A2	15-25	22	33
3. Violations of GAAS	1176,A6	15-25	23	34
4. Errors, Irregularities, and Illegal Acts	589,A5	15-25	23	37
5. Other Auditors	1185,A2	15-25	23	37

Module 2/Internal Control (IC)

	Exam reference	No. of minutes	Page no. Problem	Answer
95 Multiple Choice			39	60
13 Essay Questions:				
1. IC Questionnaire--Purchases	1187,A2	15-25	51	76
2. Opinion on Internal Control	587,A1	15-25	51	76
3. Cash Receipts Questionnaire	586,A4	15-25	51	77
4. Purchases and Disbursements Flowchart	583,A5	15-25	52	78

Module 3/Evidence (EVID)

Module 4/Reporting (REPT)

	Exam reference	No. of minutes	Page no. Problem	Answer
3. Report Deficiencies	586,A3	15-25	148	168
4. Write Report	1184,A5	15-25	149	169
5. Report on a Review	1182,A5	15-25	150	169
6. Special Report	584,A2	15-25	150	170
7. Reports on Prospective Financial Statements	588,A2	15-25	150	171
8. Analyze Audit Report	589,A2	15-25	150	171

Module 5/Audit Sampling (AUDS)

	Exam reference	No. of minutes	Page no. Problem	Answer
44 Multiple Choice			173	181
5 Essay Questions:				
1. Attribute Sampling	1188,A3	15-25	179	189
2. Steps in a Sampling Plan	1182,A2	15-25	179	189
3. Basic Concepts	585,A5	15-25	179	189
4. Steps in a Sampling Plan	586,A5	15-25	179	191
5. Probability Proportional to Size Sampling Problem	587,A3	15-25	180	191

Module 6/Auditing EDP (EDP)

	Exam reference	No. of minutes	Page no. Problem	Answer
50 Multiple Choice			193	202
3 Essay Questions:				
1. EDP Conditions in Shipping & Billing	1186,A4	15-25	200	211
2. Payroll Input Controls	584,A4	15-25	200	211
3. Using Microcomputer Software	1187,A4	15-25	201	212

Sample Examination

	Page no.
Auditing	Appendix

Multiple Choice Questions (1-60)

1. Which of the following best describes what is meant by generally accepted auditing standards?
   a. Pronouncements issued by the Auditing Standards Board.
   b. Procedures to be used to gather evidence to support financial statements.
   c. Rules acknowledged by the accounting profession because of their universal compliance.
   d. Measures of the quality of the auditor's performance.

2. Which of the following statements best explains why the CPA profession has found it essential to promulgate ethical standards and to establish means for ensuring their observance?
   a. Vigorous enforcement of an established code of ethics is the best way to prevent unscrupulous acts.
   b. Ethical standards that emphasize excellence in performance over material rewards establish a reputation for competence and character.
   c. A distinguishing mark of a profession is its acceptance of responsibility to the public.
   d. A requirement for a profession is to establish ethical standards that stress primarily a responsibility to clients and colleagues.

3. The third general standard states that due care is to be exercised in the performance of an audit. This standard is generally interpreted to require
   a. Objective review of the adequacy of the technical training and proficiency of firm personnel.
   b. Critical review of work done at every level of supervision.
   c. Thorough review of the existing internal control structure.
   d. Periodic review of a CPA firm's quality control procedures.

4. The concept of materiality would be least important to an auditor when considering the
   a. Effects of a direct financial interest in the client upon the CPA's independence.
   b. Decision whether to use positive or negative confirmations of accounts receivable.
   c. Adequacy of disclosure of a client's illegal act.
   d. Discovery of weaknesses in a client's internal control structure.

5. An accountant who is not independent of a client is precluded from issuing a
   a. Compilation report on historical financial statements.
   b. Compilation report on prospective financial statements.
   c. Special report on compliance with contractual agreements.
   d. Report on management advisory services.

6. Hickory, Inc. is a small manufacturer. Its office building, plant, and warehouse are all located in Zena, Ohio. William Cream is the principal owner and president of Hickory.

   Hickory is not a publicly-held corporation. The primary uses of the financial statements are for its 15 shareholders and for bank credit purposes. Hickory's financial statements have never been audited or reviewed.

   On July 18, 1984, William Cream hired the CPA firm of Part & Co. to audit Hickory's financial statements for the year ended December 31, 1984. Part & Co. performed the audit field work from December 15, 1984, through March 10, 1985.

   Part & Co. has offices in Cleveland, the office that performed the Hickory audit, and Chicago.

   In order for Part & Co. to be considered independent with respect to the Hickory audit, which of the following individuals would most likely be permitted to own an immaterial direct financial interest in Hickory?
   a. Professional employees at either office.
   b. Professional employees at the Chicago office.
   c. Professional employees and partners at the Chicago office.
   d. None of the professional employees or partners at either office.

7. A CPA purchased stock in a client corporation and placed it in a trust as an educational fund for the CPA's minor child. The trust securities were not material to the CPA but were material to the child's personal net worth. Would the independence of the CPA be considered to be impaired with respect to the client?
   a. Yes, because the stock would be considered a direct financial interest and, consequently, materiality is not a factor.

b. Yes, because the stock would be considered an indirect financial interest that is material to the CPA's child.

c. No, because the CPA would not be considered to have a direct financial interest in the client.

d. No, because the CPA would not be considered to have a material indirect financial interest in the client.

8. Which of the following acts by a CPA who is not in public practice would most likely be considered a violation of the ethical standards of the profession?

a. Using the CPA designation without disclosing employment status in connection with financial statements issued for external use by the CPA's employer.

b. Distributing business cards indicating the CPA designation and the CPA's title and employer.

c. Corresponding on the CPA's employer's letterhead, which contains the CPA designation and the CPA's employment status.

d. Compiling the CPA's employer's financial statements and making reference to the CPA's lack of independence.

9. Under which of the following circumstances would the independence of a CPA be considered impaired if the CPA, who is also an attorney, serves as auditor and provides legal services to the same client?

a. When the CPA, as legal agent, consummates a business acquisition for the client.

b. When the CPA's audit fees and legal fees are not billed separately.

c. When the CPA uses legal expertise to research a question of income tax law.

d. When the legal services consist of an analysis of the terms of a lease agreement.

10. A violation of the profession's ethical standards would most likely have occurred when a CPA

a. Purchased a bookkeeping firm's practice of monthly write-ups for a percentage of fees received over a three-year period.

b. Made arrangements with a bank to collect notes issued by a client in payment of fees due.

c. Named Smith formed a partnership with two other CPAs and uses "Smith & Co." as the firm name.

d. Issued an unqualified opinion on the 1987 financial statements when fees for the 1986 audit were unpaid.

11. Which of the following legal situations would be considered to impair the auditor's independence?

a. An expressed intention by the present management to commence litigation against the auditor alleging deficiencies in audit work for the client, although the auditor considers that there is only a remote possibility that such a claim will be filed.

b. Actual litigation by the auditor against the client for an amount not material to the auditor or to the financial statements of the client arising out of disputes as to billings for management advisory services.

c. Actual litigation by the auditor against the present management alleging management fraud or deceit.

d. Actual litigation by the client against the auditor for an amount not material to the auditor or to the financial statements of the client arising out of disputes as to billings for tax services.

12. According to the profession's ethical standards, an auditor would be considered independent in which of the following instances?

a. The auditor's checking account, which is fully insured by a federal agency, is held at a client financial institution.

b. The auditor is also an attorney who advises the client as its general counsel.

c. An employee of the auditor donates service as treasurer of a charitable organization that is a client.

d. The client owes the auditor fees for two consecutive annual audits.

13. The profession's ethical standards would most likely be considered to have been violated when a CPA

a. Continued an audit engagement after the commencement of litigation against the CPA alleging excessive fees filed in a stockholders' derivative action.

b. Represented to a potential client that the CPA's fees were substantially lower than the fees charged by other CPAs for comparable services.

c. Issued a report on a financial forecast that omitted a caution regarding achievability.

d. Accepted an MAS consultation engagement concerning data processing services for which the CPA lacked independence.

14. A CPA who is seeking to sell an accounting practice must

a. Not allow a peer review team to look at working papers and tax returns without permission from the client prior to consummation of the sale.

b. Not allow a prospective purchaser to look at working papers and tax returns without permission from the client.

c. Give all working papers and tax returns to the client.

d. Retain all working papers and tax returns for a period of time sufficient to satisfy the statute of limitations.

15. Which of the following is required for a CPA partnership to designate itself "Member of the American Institute of Certified Public Accountants" on its letterhead?

a. All partners must be members.

b. The partners whose names appear in the firm name must be members.

c. At least one of the partners must be a member.

d. The firm must be a dues paying member.

16. Pursuant to the AICPA rules of conduct, if a partner in a two-member partnership dies, the surviving partner may continue to practice as an individual under the existing firm title which includes the deceased partner's name

a. For a period of time **not** to exceed five years.

b. For a period of time **not** to exceed two years.

c. Indefinitely.

d. Until the partnership pay-out to the deceased partner's estate is terminated.

17. Inclusion of which of the following statements in a CPA's advertisement is not acceptable pursuant to the AICPA Code of Professional Conduct?

a. Paul Fall
Certified Public Accountant
Fluency in Spanish and French

b. Paul Fall
Certified Public Accountant
J.D., Evans Law School 1964

c. Paul Fall
Certified Public Accountant
Free Consultation

d. Paul Fall
Certified Public Accountant
Endorsed by AICPA

18. Which of the following elements underlies the application of generally accepted auditing standards, particularly the standards of field work and reporting?

a. Internal control.

b. Corroborating evidence.

c. Quality control.

d. Materiality and relative risk.

19. When planning an examination, an auditor should

a. Consider whether the extent of substantive tests may be reduced based on the results of the internal control questionnaire.

b. Make preliminary judgments about materiality levels for audit purposes.

c. Conclude whether changes in compliance with prescribed control procedures justifies reliance on them.

d. Prepare a preliminary draft of the management representation letter.

20. The risk that an auditor's procedures will lead to the conclusion that a material error does <u>not</u> exist in an account balance when, in fact, such error does exist is referred to as

a. Audit risk.

b. Inherent risk.

c. Control risk.

d. Detection risk.

21. Which of the following audit risk components may be assessed in nonquantitative terms?

	Inherent risk	Control risk	Detection risk
a.	Yes	Yes	No
b.	Yes	No	Yes
c.	No	Yes	Yes
d.	Yes	Yes	Yes

22. The audit work performed by each assistant should be reviewed to determine whether it was adequately performed and to evaluate whether the

a. Audit procedures performed are approved in the professional standards.

b. Examination has been performed by persons having adequate technical training and proficiency as auditors.

c. Auditor's system of quality control has been maintained at a high level.

d. Results are consistent with the conclusions to be presented in the auditor's report.

23. A difference of opinion regarding the results of a sample cannot be resolved between the assistant who performed the auditing procedures and the in-charge auditor. The assistant should

a. Refuse to perform any further work on the engagement.

b. Accept the judgment of the more experienced in-charge auditor.

c. Document the disagreement and ask to be disassociated from the resolution of the matter.

d. Notify the client that a serious audit problem exists.

24. Before accepting an audit engagement, a successor auditor should make specific inquiries of the predecessor auditor regarding the predecessor's

a. Awareness of the consistency in the application of generally accepted accounting principles between periods.

b. Evaluation of all matters of continuing accounting significance.

c. Opinion of any subsequent events occurring since the predecessor's audit report was issued.

d. Understanding as to the reasons for the change of auditors.

25. A CPA may reduce the audit work on a first-time audit by reviewing the working papers of the predecessor auditor. The predecessor should permit the successor to review working papers relating to matters of continuing accounting significance such as those that relate to

a. Extent of reliance on the work of specialists.

b. Fee arrangements and summaries of payments.

c. Analysis of contingencies.

d. Staff hours required to complete the engagement.

26. A basic objective of a CPA firm is to provide professional services that conform with professional standards. Reasonable assurance of achieving this basic objective is provided through

a. Compliance with generally accepted accounting standards.

b. A system of quality control.

c. A system of peer review.

d. Continuing professional education.

27. Quality control for a CPA firm, as referred to in Statements on Quality Control Standards, applies to

a. Auditing services only.

b. Auditing and management advisory services.

c. Auditing and tax services.

d. Auditing and accounting and review services.

28. A CPA firm should establish procedures for conducting and supervising work at all organizational levels to provide reasonable assurance that the work performed meets the firm's standards of quality. To achieve this goal, the firm most likely would establish procedures for

a. Evaluating prospective and continuing client relationships.

b. Reviewing engagement working papers and reports.

c. Requiring personnel to adhere to the applicable independence rules.

d. Maintaining personnel files containing documentation related to the evaluation of personnel.

29. Which of the following is **not** an element of quality control?

a. Documentation.

b. Inspection.

c. Supervision.

d. Consultation.

30. A CPA firm's quality control procedures pertaining to the acceptance of a prospective audit client would most likely include

a. Inquiry of management as to whether disagreements between the predecessor auditor and the prospective client were resolved satisfactorily.

b. Consideration of whether sufficient competent evidential matter may be obtained to afford a reasonable basis for an opinion.

c. Inquiry of third parties, such as the prospective client's bankers and attorneys, about information regarding the prospective client and its management.

d. Consideration of whether the internal control structure is sufficiently effective to permit a reduction in the extent of required substantive tests.

31. With respect to errors and irregularities, the auditor should plan to
    a. Search for errors that would have a material effect and for irregularities that would have either material or immaterial effect on the financial statements.
    b. Search for irregularities that would have a material effect and for errors that would have either material or immaterial effect on the financial statements.
    c. Search for errors or irregularities that would have a material effect on the financial statements.
    d. Discover errors or irregularities that have either material or immaterial effect on the financial statements.

32. Which of the following factors is most important concerning an auditor's responsibility to detect errors and irregularities?
    a. The susceptibility of the accounting records to intentional manipulations, alterations, and the misapplication of accounting principles.
    b. The probability that unreasonable accounting estimates result from unintentional bias or intentional attempts to misstate the financial statements.
    c. The possibility that management fraud, defalcations, and the misappropriation of assets may indicate the existence of illegal acts.
    d. The risk that mistakes, falsifications, and omissions may cause the financial statements to contain material misstatements.

33. Because an examination in accordance with generally accepted auditing standards is influenced by the possibility of material errors, the auditor should conduct the examination with an attitude of
    a. Professional responsiveness.
    b. Conservative advocacy.
    c. Objective judgment.
    d. Professional skepticism.

34. Under Statements on Auditing Standards, which of the following would be classified as an error?
    a. Misappropriation of assets for the benefit of management.
    b. Misinterpretation by management of facts that existed when the financial statements were prepared.
    c. Preparation of records by employees to cover a fraudulent scheme.
    d. Intentional omission of the recording of a transaction to benefit a third party.

35. The auditor is most likely to presume that a high risk of a defalcation exists if
    a. The client is a multinational company that does business in numerous foreign countries.
    b. The client does business with several related parties.
    c. Inadequate segregation of duties places an employee in a position to perpetrate and conceal thefts.
    d. Inadequate employee training results in lengthy EDP exception reports each month.

36. The most likely explanation why the auditor's examination **cannot** reasonably be expected to bring all illegal acts by the client to the auditor's attention is that
    a. Illegal acts are perpetrated by management override of internal controls.
    b. Illegal acts by clients often relate to operating aspects rather than accounting aspects.
    c. The client's internal control structure may be so strong that the auditor performs only minimal substantive testing.
    d. Illegal acts may be perpetrated by the only person in the client's organization with access to both assets and the accounting records.

37. If specific information comes to an auditor's attention that implies the existence of possible illegal acts that could have a material, but indirect effect on the financial statements, the auditor should next
    a. Apply audit procedures specifically directed to ascertaining whether an illegal act has occurred.
    b. Seek the advice of an informed expert qualified to practice law as to possible contingent liabilities.
    c. Report the matter to an appropriate level of management at least one level above those involved.
    d. Discuss the evidence with the client's audit committee, or others with equivalent authority and responsibility.

38. A CPA should not submit unaudited financial statements of a nonpublic company to a client or others unless, as a minimum, the CPA complies with the provisions applicable to
   a. Compilation engagements.
   b. Review engagements.
   c. Statements on auditing standards.
   d. Attestation standards.

39. After an auditor had been engaged to perform the first audit for a nonpublic entity, the client requested to change the engagement to a review. In which of the following situations would there be a reasonable basis to comply with the client's request?
   a. The client's bank required an audit before committing to a loan, but the client subsequently acquired alternative financing.
   b. The auditor was prohibited by the client from corresponding with the client's legal counsel.
   c. Management refused to sign the client representation letter.
   d. The auditing procedures were substantially complete and the auditor determined that an unqualified opinion was warranted, but there was a disagreement concerning the audit fee.

40. If requested to perform a review engagement for a nonpublic entity in which an accountant has an immaterial direct financial interest, the accountant is
   a. Independent because the financial interest is immaterial and, therefore, may issue a review report.
   b. Not independent and, therefore, may not be associated with the financial statements.
   c. Not independent and, therefore, may not issue a review report.
   d. Not independent and, therefore, may issue a review report, but may not issue an auditor's opinion.

41. A management advisory service engagement, as opposed to a management advisory service consultation, generally involves advice or information given by a CPA that is based upon
   a. An analytical approach and process.
   b. Existing personal knowledge about the client.
   c. An incidental effort devoted to a combination of activities.
   d. The CPA's ability to implement management's recommendations.

42. An audit independence issue might be raised by the auditor's participation in management advisory services engagements. Which of the following statements is most consistent with the profession's attitude toward this issue?
   a. Information obtained as a result of a management advisory services engagement is confidential to that specific engagement and should not influence performance of the attest function.
   b. The decision as to loss of independence must be made by the client based upon the facts of the particular case.
   c. The auditor should not make management decisions for an audit client.
   d. The auditor who is asked to review management decisions is also competent to make these decisions and can do so without loss of independence.

43. The technical standards that apply to MAS engagements require the MAS practitioner to do all of the following except
   a. Maintain independence from the client.
   b. Give support for and clearly identify as estimates any quantifiable results that are based on estimates.
   c. Obtain an understanding concerning the nature, scope, and limitations of the MAS engagement to be performed.
   d. Take no position which might impair the practitioner's objectivity.

44. In performing MAS engagements, CPAs should not take any positions that might
   a. Constitute advice and assistance.
   b. Provide technical assistance in implementation.
   c. Result in new organizational policies and procedures.
   d. Impair their objectivity.

45. The form of communication with a client in a management advisory services consultation should be
   a. Either oral or written.
   b. Oral with appropriate documentation in the workpapers.
   c. Written and copies should be sent to both management and the board of directors.
   d. Written and a copy should be sent to management alone.

46. Where a reasonable basis exists for omission of an answer to an applicable question on a tax return
    a. The question may be ignored.
    b. A brief explanation of the reason for the omission should be provided.
    c. The question should be marked as nonapplicable.
    d. A note should be provided which states that the answer will be provided if the information is requested.

47. A CPA who is engaged to prepare an income tax return has a duty to prepare it in such a manner that the tax is
    a. The legal minimum.
    b. Computed in conformity with generally accepted accounting principles.
    c. Supported by the client's audited financial statements.
    d. Not subject to change upon audit.

48. In accordance with the AICPA Statements On Responsibilities In Tax Practice, if after having provided tax advice to a client there are legislative changes which affect the advice provided, the CPA
    a. Is obligated to notify the client of the change and the effect thereof.
    b. Is obligated to notify the client of the change and the effect thereof if the client was not advised that the advice was based on existing laws which are subject to change.
    c. Cannot be expected to notify the client of the change unless the obligation is specifically undertaken by agreement.
    d. Cannot be expected to have knowledge of the change.

May 1990 Questions

49. As the acceptable level of detection risk decreases, an auditor may change the
    a. Timing of substantive tests by performing them at an interim date rather than at year end.
    b. Nature of substantive tests from a less effective to a more effective procedure.
    c. Timing of tests of controls by performing them at several dates rather than at one time.
    d. Assessed level of inherent risk to a higher amount.

50. The first general standard requires that an audit of financial statements is to be performed by a person or persons having
    a. Seasoned judgment in varying degrees of supervision and review.
    b. Adequate technical training and proficiency.
    c. Knowledge of the standards of field work and reporting.
    d. Independence with respect to the financial statements and supplementary disclosures.

51. The exercise of due professional care requires that an auditor
    a. Examine all available corroborating evidence.
    b. Critically review the judgment exercised at every level of supervision.
    c. Reduce control risk below the maximum.
    d. Attain the proper balance of professional experience and formal education.

52. On completing an audit, Larkin, CPA, was asked by the client to provide technical assistance in the implementation of a new EDP system. The set of pronouncements designed to guide Larkin in this engagement is the Statements on
    a. Auditing Standards.
    b. Standards for Management Advisory Services.
    c. Quality Control Standards.
    d. Standards for Accountants' EDP Services.

53. Which of the following is the authoritative body designated to promulgate attestation standards?
    a. Auditing Standards Board.
    b. Governmental Accounting Standards Board.
    c. Financial Accounting Standards Board.
    d. General Accounting Office.

54. The element of the audit planning process most likely to be agreed upon with the client before implementation of the audit strategy is the determination of the
    a. Timing of inventory observation procedures to be performed.
    b. Evidence to be gathered to provide a sufficient basis for the auditor's opinion.
    c. Procedures to be undertaken to discover litigation, claims, and assessments.
    d. Pending legal matters to be included in the inquiry of the client's attorney.

55. Which of the following are elements of a CPA firm's quality control that should be considered in establishing its quality control policies and procedures?

	Advancement	Inspection	Consultation
a.	Yes	Yes	No
b.	Yes	Yes	Yes
c.	No	Yes	Yes
d.	Yes	No	Yes

56. Disclosure of irregularities to parties other than a client's senior management and its audit committee or board of directors ordinarily is not part of an auditor's responsibility. However, to which of the following outside parties may a duty to disclose irregularities exist?

	To the SEC when the client reports an auditor change	To a successor auditor when the successor makes appropriate inquiries	To a government funding agency from which the client receives financial assistance
a.	Yes	Yes	No
b.	Yes	No	Yes
c.	No	Yes	Yes
d.	Yes	Yes	Yes

57. Which of the following statements best describes an auditor's responsibility to detect errors and irregularities?

a. The auditor should study and evaluate the client's internal control structure, and design the audit to provide reasonable assurance of detecting all errors and irregularities.

b. The auditor should assess the risk that errors and irregularities may cause the financial statements to contain material misstatements, and determine whether the necessary internal control procedures are prescribed and are being followed satisfactorily.

c. The auditor should consider the types of errors and irregularities that could occur, and determine whether the necessary internal control procedures are prescribed and are being followed.

d. The auditor should assess the risk that errors and irregularities may cause the financial statements to contain material misstatements, and design the audit to provide reasonable assurance of detecting material errors and irregularities.

58. Morris, CPA, suspects that a pervasive scheme of illegal bribes exists throughout the operations of Worldwide Import-Export, Inc., a new audit client. Morris notified the audit committee and Worldwide's legal counsel, but neither could assist Morris in determining whether the amounts involved were material to the financial statements or whether senior management was involved in the scheme. Under these circumstances, Morris should

a. Express an unqualified opinion with a separate explanatory paragraph.

b. Disclaim an opinion on the financial statements.

c. Express an adverse opinion on the financial statements.

d. Issue a special report regarding the illegal bribes.

59. Which of the following statements concerning illegal acts by clients is correct?

a. An auditor's responsibility to detect illegal acts that have a direct and material effect on the financial statements is the same as that for errors and irregularities.

b. An audit in accordance with generally accepted auditing standards normally includes audit procedures specifically designed to detect illegal acts that have an indirect but material effect on the financial statements.

c. An auditor considers illegal acts from the perspective of the reliability of management's representations rather than their relation to audit objectives derived from financial statement assertions.

d. An auditor has no responsibility to detect illegal acts by clients that have an indirect effect on the financial statements.

60. A CPA in public practice must be independent in fact and appearance when providing which of the following services?

	Preparation of a tax return	Compilation of a financial forecast	Compilation of personal financial statements
a.	Yes	No	No
b.	No	Yes	No
c.	No	No	Yes
d.	No	No	No

Problems

Problem 1   (587,A5)

(15 to 25 minutes)

Parker is the in-charge auditor with administrative responsibilities for the upcoming annual audit of FGH Company, a continuing audit client. Parker will supervise two assistants on the engagement and will visit the client before the field work begins.

Parker has started the planning process by preparing a list of procedures to be performed prior to the beginning of field work. The list includes:

1. Review correspondence and permanent files.
2. Review prior years' audit working papers, financial statements, and auditor's reports.
3. Discuss with CPA firm personnel responsible for audit and non-audit services to the client, matters that may affect the examination.
4. Discuss with management current business developments affecting the client.

Required:

Complete Parker's list of procedures to be performed prior to the beginning of field work.

Problem 2   (1186,A2)

(15 to 25 minutes)

Audit risk and materiality should be considered when planning and performing an examination of financial statements in accordance with generally accepted auditing standards. Audit risk and materiality should also be considered together in determining the nature, timing, and extent of auditing procedures and in evaluating the results of those procedures.

Required:

a.
1. Define audit risk.
2. Describe its components of inherent risk, control risk, and detection risk.
3. Explain how these components are interrelated.

b.
1. Define materiality.
2. Discuss the factors affecting its determination.

3. Describe the relationship between materiality for planning purposes and materiality for evaluation purposes.

Problem 3   (1176,A6)

(15 to 25 minutes)

Ray, the owner of a small company, asked Holmes, CPA, to conduct an audit of the company's records. Ray told Holmes that an audit is to be completed in time to submit audited financial statements to a bank as part of a loan application. Holmes immediately accepted the engagement and agreed to provide an auditor's report within three weeks. Ray agreed to pay Holmes a fixed fee plus a bonus if the loan was granted.

Holmes hired two accounting students to conduct the audit and spent several hours telling them exactly what to do. Holmes told the students not to spend time reviewing the controls, but instead to concentrate on proving the mathematical accuracy of the ledger accounts, and summarizing the data in the accounting records that support Ray's financial statements. The students followed Holmes' instructions and after two weeks gave Holmes the financial statements which did not include footnotes. Holmes reviewed the statements and prepared an unqualified auditor's report. The report, however, did not refer to generally accepted accounting principles nor to the year-to-year application of such principles.

Required:

Briefly describe each of the generally accepted auditing standards and indicate how the action(s) of Holmes resulted in a failure to comply with each standard.

Organize your answer as follows:

Brief Description of Generally Accepted Auditing Standards	Holmes' Actions Resulting in Failure to Comply with Generally Accepted Auditing Standards

Problem 4   (589,A5)

(15 to 25 minutes)

Reed, CPA, accepted an engagement to audit the financial statements of Smith Company. Reed's discussions with Smith's new management and the predecessor auditor indicated the possibility that Smith's financial statements may be misstated due to the possible occurrence of errors, irregularities, and illegal acts.

Required:

a. Identify and describe Reed's responsibilities to detect Smith's errors and irregularities. Do not identify specific audit procedures.
b. Identify and describe Reed's responsibilities to report Smith's errors and irregularities.
c. Describe Reed's responsibilities to detect Smith's material illegal acts. Do not identify specific audit procedures.
d. Describe Reed's additional responsibilities to report on errors, irregularities, and illegal acts if this audit were one to which the requirements of Government Auditing Standards apply.

Problem 5   (1185,A2)

(15 to 25 minutes)

The CPA firm of May & Marty has audited the consolidated financial statements of BGI Corporation. May & Marty performed the examination of the parent company and all subsidiaries except for BGI-Western Corporation, which was audited by the CPA firm of Dey & Dee. BGI-Western constituted approximately 10% of the consolidated assets and 6% of the consolidated revenue.

Dey & Dee issued an unqualified opinion on the financial statements of BGI-Western. May & Marty will be issuing an unqualified opinion on the consolidated financial statements of BGI.

Required:

a. What procedures should May & Marty consider performing with respect to Dey & Dee's examination of BGI-Western's financial statements that will be appropriate whether or not reference is to be made to the other auditors?

b. Describe the various circumstances under which May & Marty could take responsibility for the work of Dey & Dee and make no reference to Dey & Dee's examination of BGI-Western in May & Marty's auditor's report on the consolidated financial statements of BGI.

Multiple Choice Answers

1. d	13. c	25. c	37. a	49. b
2. c	14. b	26. b	38. a	50. b
3. b	15. a	27. d	39. a	51. b
4. a	16. b	28. b	40. c	52. b
5. c	17. d	29. a	41. a	53. a
6. b	18. d	30. c	42. c	54. a
7. a	19. b	31. c	43. a	55. b
8. a	20. d	32. d	44. d	56. d
9. a	21. d	33. d	45. a	57. d
10. d	22. d	34. b	46. b	58. b
11. c	23. c	35. c	47. a	59. a
12. a	24. d	36. b	48. c	60. d

Multiple Choice Answer Explanations

A. General Standards and Code of Professional Conduct

A.1. GAAS--General Standards

1. (586,A1,17) (d) The requirement is to identify the statement which best describes the meaning of generally accepted auditing standards. Answer (d) is correct because generally accepted auditing standards deal with measures of the quality of the performance of auditing procedures. Answer (a) is incorrect because generally accepted auditing standards have been issued by predecessor groups as well as by the Auditing Standards Board. Answer (b) is incorrect because procedures relate to acts to be performed, not directly to the standards. Answer (c) is incorrect because there may or may not be universal compliance with the standards.

2. (1188,A1,5) (c) The requirement is to identify the statement which best explains why the CPA professional has found it essential to promulgate ethical standards and to establish means of ensuring their observation. Answer (c) is correct because, as indicated in the second article of the AICPA Code of Professional Conduct, a distinguishing mark of a profession is acceptance of its responsibility to the public as documented in an ethical code. Answer (a) is incorrect because the Code depends primarily on members' understanding and voluntary actions, and only finally upon such enforcement. Answer (b) is incorrect because material rewards need not be sacrificed because of excellence in performance. Answer (d) is incorrect because in addition to a responsibility to clients and colleagues, the preamble of the Code of Professional Conduct stresses the profession's responsibilities to the public.

3. (1189,A1,49) (b) The requirement is to determine what is implied by the third general standard which states that due care is to be exercised in the performance of an audit. Answer (b) is correct because the exercise of due care requires critical review at every level of supervision of the work done and the judgment exercised by those assisting in the audit (AU 230.02). Answer (a) is incorrect because the first general standard which addresses the adequacy of training deals more precisely with technical training and proficiency of firm personnel (AU 210). Answer (c) is incorrect because the second field work standard directly addresses the internal control structure (AU 319). Answer (d) is incorrect because the quality control standards require the periodic review of the firm's quality control procedures (QC 90).

A.2. Code of Professional Conduct

A.2.a. Code--Independence, Integrity and Objectivity

4. (589,A1,26) (a) The requirement is to identify the situation in which the concept of materiality would be least important. Answer (a) is correct because the auditor may not have any direct financial interest in a client, regardless of materiality (Interpretation 101-1). Answer (b) is incorrect because auditors generally consider the size (materiality) of account balances when choosing between the use of positive or negative confirmation (AU 331.05). Answer (c) is incorrect because materiality is considered when evaluating the adequacy of disclosures of illegal acts (AU 317.18). Answer (d) is incorrect because the materiality of internal control weaknesses should be considered by the auditor (e.g., AU 325).

5. (1188,A1,1) (c) The requirement is to identify the type of report that an accountant who is not independent is precluded from issuing. Article III of the Code of Professional Conduct requires that a CPA be independent when providing attestation services; independence is not required for accounting services. Answer (c) is correct because providing special reports is an attestation service, and therefore requires accountant independence (AU 621 discusses special reports). Answers (a) and (b) are incorrect because compilations are considered accounting, not attestation, services (AU 2100.21, AR 100.22). Answer (d) is incorrect because while objectivity is required when performing MAS services, independence is not (MS 11.06).

6.   (1185,A1,26) (b) The requirement is to identify the individuals most likely to be permitted to own an immaterial direct financial interest in an audit client. Answer (b) is correct because Interpretation 101-9 prohibits only professional employees either (1) in the office doing the audit, or (2) involved with the audit from owning any direct financial interest. Answer (a) is incorrect because professionals in the Cleveland office, which performs the audit, cannot hold any direct financial interest. Answer (c) is incorrect because all partners of the firm are prohibited from maintaining any direct financial interest (Interpretation 101-9). Answer (d) is incorrect because, as indicated, the rule does not prohibit all professional employees from maintaining any direct financial interest.

7.   (586,A1,16) (a) The requirement is to determine the effect of a CPA's minor child holding stock in a client corporation on audit independence. Answer (a) is correct because a stock investment is considered a direct financial interest and because the independence standards state that such investments by spouses and dependent persons also impair independence (Interpretation 101-9). The fact that the stock is in a trust is not relevant. Answer (b) is incorrect because such an investment is considered direct, not indirect. Answers (c) and (d) are incorrect because the CPA would not be considered independent since s/he was considered to have a direct financial interest in the client.

8.   (1188,A1,3) (a) The requirement is to identify the act performed by a CPA not in public practice which is most likely to be considered a violation of the ethical standards of the profession. Answer (a) is correct because failure to disclose a lack of independence on such statements prepared for either internal or external use is considered a knowing misrepresentation of fact (ET 191.131). Answer (b) is incorrect because a CPA who is not in public practice may indicate the CPA designation on business cards when he or she indicates his/her title and employer (ET 191.131). Answer (c) is incorrect because corresponding on the CPA's employer's letterhead, which contains the CPA designation and employment status, is considered acceptable (ET 191.131). Answer (d) is incorrect because compilations are considered accounting services and thus do not require independence (ET 191.131, AR 100.22).

9.   (588,A1,52) (a) The requirement is to identify the circumstance in which the independence of a CPA, who serves as both the auditor and as an attorney for the same client, would be impaired. Answer (a) is correct because performing management functions such as consummating business acquisitions impairs the CPA's independence (ET 191.101-.102). Answers (b), (c), and (d) are all incorrect because they are not prohibited by the AICPA Code of Professional Conduct, or by any other Professional Standards.

10. (588,A1,53) (d) The requirement is to identify the situation in which it is most likely that a violation of the profession's ethical standards may have occurred. Answer (d) is correct because independence of a CPA firm may be impaired if, at the time a CPA issues a report on a client's financial statements, the client is indebted to the member for more than one year's fees (ET 191.104). Answer (a) is incorrect because a CPA may purchase a bookkeeping firm's practice for a percentage of fees received (ET 591.221-.222). Answer (b) is incorrect because a CPA may make arrangements with a bank to collect notes issued by a client in payment of fees due (ET 591.003-.004). Answer (c) is incorrect because designations such as "and company," "and Associations," or "& Co." may be used by partnerships (AU 591.293-.294).

11. (586,A1,6) (c) The requirement is to identify the situation which would impair the auditor's independence. Answer (c) is correct because Interpretation 101-6 states that actual litigation by the auditor against the present management alleging management fraud or deceit impairs independence. That interpretation also addresses the other replies. Answer (a) is incorrect because the expressed intention by present management to commence litigation impairs independence only if the auditor concludes that a strong possibility of such a claim being filed exists. Answer (b) is incorrect because immaterial litigation by the auditor does not necessarily impair independence. Answer (d) is incorrect because non-audit related litigation does not necessarily impair audit independence.

12. (589,A1,3) (a) The requirement is to identify the situation in which an auditor would be considered independent. Answer (a) is correct because an auditor's independence would not be considered to be impaired with respect to a financial institution in which the auditor maintains a checking account which is fully insured (ET 191.141). Answer (b) is

incorrect because an auditor may not advise an audit client as its general counsel without impairing independence (ET 191.102). Answer (c) is incorrect because Interpretation 101-1 states that the performance of such services impairs independence. Answer (d) is incorrect because at the time an auditor issues a report on a client's financial statements, the client should not be indebted to the auditor for more than one year's fees (ET 191.104).

A.2.b. Code--General Standards Accounting Principles

13. (1189,A1,56) (c) The requirement is to identify the situation in which it is most likely that the profession's ethical standards have been violated. Answer (c) is correct because the professional standards on forecasts require the inclusion of a caution statement as to achievability (AT 200.32). Omission of such a caution statement would be a violation of the Code of Professional Conduct which requires that CPAs comply with the appropriate professional standards (Ethics Rule 202). Answer (a) is incorrect because stockholder commencement of litigation against the CPA will not always be deemed to have an adverse impact on independence (Ethics Interpretation 101-6). Answer (b) is incorrect because a representation as to fees does not violate the ethical standards if it is based on verifiable facts and is not false, misleading, or deceptive (Ethics Rule 502, Interpretation 502-2). Answer (d) is incorrect because independence is not required for MAS engagements (ET 55.03).

A.2.c. Code--Responsibility to Clients

14. (582,A1,25) (b) The requirement is to determine the proper treatment of working papers when a CPA is selling an accounting practice. Permission must be obtained for both audit working papers and tax returns. Answer (a) is incorrect because the confidential client information rule does not apply to peer reviews (Rule 301). Answer (c) is incorrect because working papers are the property of the CPA and need not be provided to a client. Answer (d) is incorrect because if the practice is sold, the working papers and tax returns for which permission has been obtained may be given to the CPA who has purchased the practice.

A.2.e. Code--Other Responsibilities

15. (585,A1,8) (a) The requirement is to determine the circumstances in which a CPA partnership may designate itself "Member of the American Institute of Certified Public Accountants" on its letterhead. Answer (a) is correct because a firm may designate itself as "Member of the AICPA" when all of its partners or shareholders are members of the Institute (Rule 505). Answers (b) and (c) are incorrect because all partners or shareholders must be members. Answer (d) is incorrect because individuals pay dues rather than the firm itself.

16. (1184,A1,37) (b) The requirement is to determine how long a surviving partner may continue to practice under the existing firm title after the death of the only other partner. Answer (b) is correct because Rule 505 allows the surviving partner to practice under the partnership name for a period of time not to exceed two years. Answers (a), (c), and (d) all represent incorrect time periods. Be aware that the problem is not simply that a partner in a partnership has died. The problem is that, since there were only two partners, the surviving firm is now a sole proprietorship. It would be misleading to indicate that a partnership exists when this is no longer the case.

17. (1181,A1,43) (d) The requirement is to identify the advertisement which is not acceptable under the AICPA's Code of Professional Conduct. Rule 502 prohibits advertising which is false, misleading, or deceptive. Foreign language competence [answer (a)], schools attended [answer (b)], and fees charged [answer (c)] are all acceptable (see Rule 502). Answer (d) is correct because the AICPA has no formal endorsement procedures.

B. Control of the Audit

B.1. Planning and Supervision

B.1.a. Overall Planning, Including Materiality and Audit Risk

18. (1188,A1,2) (d) The requirement is to identify the elements which underlie the application of generally accepted auditing standards, particularly the standards of field work and reporting. Answer (d) is correct because AU 150.03 states that materiality and relative risk underlie the application of all the standards. Answer (a) is incorrect because a consideration of internal control is one of the field standards, not an element underlying the standards (see AU 319). Answer (b) is incorrect because the second field work standard, on evidence, relates most directly to corroborating evidence (see AU 326). Answer (c) is incorrect because while it is accurate that quality control

standards encompass the firm's policies and procedures to provide reasonable assurance of conforming with professional standards, the standards are not related more directly to the field work and reporting standards than to the general group of generally accepted auditing standards.

19. (588,A1,55) (b) The requirement is to identify a matter which should be considered by the auditor when planning an examination. Answer (b) is correct because AU 311.03 requires that in planning, among other matters, the auditor makes a preliminary judgment about materiality levels for audit purposes. Answer (a) is incorrect because during planning, the results of the internal control questionnaire are not known. Answer (c) is incorrect because no information has generally been obtained about control procedures at the planning stage. Answer (d) is incorrect because the management represen-tation letter is normally developed subsequent to the audit planning stage.

20. (1187,A1,23) (d) The requirement is to identify the type of risk described by the likelihood that an auditor's procedures will lead to the conclusion that a material error does <u>not</u> exist when, in fact, such error does exist. Answer (d) is correct because detec-tion risk is the risk that an auditor's pro-cedures will lead him to conclude that a material error does not exist, when in fact such error does exist (AU 312.20c). An-swer (a) is incorrect because audit risk is the risk that the auditor may unknowingly fail to appropriately modify his opinion on financial statements that are materially misstated (AU 312.02). Answer (b) is incor-rect because inherent risk refers to the susceptibility of an account (or class of transactions) to error that could be material (AU 312.20a). Answer (c) is incorrect because control risk is the risk that material error could occur and not be detected by the internal control structure (AU 312.20b).

21. (589,A1,5) (d) The requirement is to determine whether inherent risk, control risk, and detection risk may be assessed in nonquan-titative terms. Answer (d) is correct because all of these risks may be assessed in quanti-tative terms such as percentages. They may also be assessed in nonquantitative terms such as a range from a minimum to a maximum (AU 312.21). Answers (a), (b), and (c) are all incorrect because they suggest that one of the risks may not be assessed in nonquantita-tive terms.

B.1.b. Supervision

22. (1188,A1,7) (d) The requirement is to identify a reason why work performed by each assistant should be reviewed. Answer (d) is correct because AU 311.13 states that the work performed by each assistant should be reviewed to determine whether it was adequately planned and to determine whether the results are con-sistent with the conclusions to be presented in the auditor's report. Answer (a) is incorrect because the professional standards do not in general indicate approval for most audit procedures. Answer (b) is incorrect because determining whether the work was adequately performed (which was provided) addresses the training and proficiency of auditors. Answer (c) is incorrect because such supervision is only one element of the overall system of quality control.

23. (588,A1,56) (c) The requirement is to determine the proper approach for handling a difference of opinion between an assistant and an in-charge auditor regarding the results of a sample. Answer (c) is correct because the quality control standards require that a firm have procedures for resolving differences of professional judgment and documentation of the considerations involved in the resolution of a difference of opinion (QC 90.14). Answer (a) is incorrect because the assistant may perform further work on the engagement. Answer (b) is incorrect because the assistant should docu-ment the disagreement and not simply accept the judgment of the more experienced in-charge auditor. Answer (d) is incorrect because the situation may <u>not</u> be a serious audit problem and because the client generally need not be so notified.

B.1.c. Communications between Prede-cessor and Successor Auditors

24. (588,A1,54) (d) The requirement is to identify the correct statement regarding a successor auditor's inquiries of the predeces-sor auditor. Answer (d) is correct because the successor should request information such as (1) facts that might bear on the integrity of management, (2) disagreements with manage-ment as to accounting principles, auditing procedures, or other significant matters, and (3) the predecessor's understanding as to the reasons for the change of auditors (AU 315.06). Answers (a), (b), and (c) all relate to matters not required to be discussed prior to accepting an audit engagement.

25. (578,A1,33) (c) AU 315.09 provides two examples of matters of continuing accounting significance which are usually provided to successor auditors by predecessor auditors. The two examples are working paper analyses of

balance sheet accounts and matters surrounding contingencies. These are items which would facilitate the predecessor's audit. Answers (a), (b), and (d) relate to the predecessor firm's auditing philosophy rather than to data underlying the client's financial statements as indicated in answer (c), i.e., analysis of contingencies.

B.2. Quality Control

26. (1188,A1,33) (b) The requirement is to determine the means by which a CPA firm obtains reasonable assurance that its professional services conform with professional standards. Answer (b) is correct because a system of quality control encompasses the firm's organizational structure, the policies adopted, and procedures established to provide the firm with reasonable assurance of conforming with professional standards (QC 10.03). Answer (a) is incorrect because complying with the reporting standards relates to only a portion of the overall professional standards. Answer (c) is incorrect because while it is true that a system of peer review helps to assure that the quality control standards are being met, such review is not relied upon to provide reasonable assurance that professional services conform with professional standards. Answer (d) is incorrect because continuing professional education relates to only a portion of the overall professional standards.

27. (1185,A1,3) (d) The requirement is to determine the types of services to which Statements on Quality Control Standards apply. Answer (d) is correct because QC 10.01 explicitly limits application to auditing and accounting and review services. Although the quality control standards may be applied to other segments of a firm's practice (e.g., management advisory services and tax), the standards do not require it. Therefore, answers (a), (b), and (c) are incorrect.

28. (1188,A1,11) (b) The requirement is to determine a procedure which a CPA firm should establish for conducting and supervising work at all organizational levels for purposes of providing reasonable assurance that the work performed meets the firm's quality standards. Answer (b) is correct because establishing procedures for reviewing engagement working papers and reports is among the suggestions made in the standards for supervising policies and procedures (QC 90.16). Answer (a) is incorrect because evaluating prospective and continuing client relationships is related more directly to the acceptance and continuance of client's quality control standard

(QC 90.24). Answer (c) is incorrect because requiring personnel to adhere to the applicable independence rules is a procedure related to the independence quality control standard (QC 90.10). Answer (d) is incorrect because maintaining personnel files documenting the evaluation of personnel is directly related to the advancement quality control standard (QC 90.22).

29. (583,A1,57) (a) The requirement is to determine which answer is _not_ an element of quality control. Answer (a), documentation, is not one of the nine elements of quality control (QC 10.07). Answers (b), (c), and (d) [inspection, supervision, and consultation] are all quality control elements.

30. (589,A1,4) (c) The requirement is to determine the most likely quality control procedure with respect to a CPA firm's acceptance of a prospective audit client. Answer (c) is correct because QC 90.24 suggests that inquiry of third parties, such as bankers and attorneys, about information regarding the prospective client and its management, is appropriate. Answer (a) is incorrect because while inquiry of management concerning disagreements is possible, QC 90.24 suggests that such inquiries be directed at the predecessor auditor. Answers (b) and (d) are incorrect because consideration of the availability of sufficient competent evidential matter as well as the effectiveness of internal control is more directly related to the planning stage of the audit.

C. Other Responsibilities
C.1. Client Errors, Management Fraud, and Defalcations

31. (1187,A1,25) (c) The requirement is to identify the CPA responsibilities with respect to errors or irregularities. Answer (c) is correct because AU 327.05 states that under generally accepted auditing standards, the independent auditor must plan the examination to search for errors _and_ irregularities that would have a _material_ effect on the financial statements. Answers (a), (b), and (d) are incorrect because each includes searching for either an immaterial error or an immaterial irregularity.

32. (1189,A1,59) (d) The requirement is to identify the most important factor concerning an auditor's responsibility to detect errors and irregularities. Answer (d) is correct because the auditor should assess the risk that errors and irregularities (which include mistakes, falsifications, and omissions) may

cause the financial statements to contain material misstatements (AU 316.05). Answers (a), (b), and (c) are all incorrect because they are less complete than is (d).

33. (1187,A1,24) (d) The requirement is to identify the proper attitude of an auditor who is performing an examination in accordance with generally accepted auditing standards. Answer (d) is correct because the auditor should plan and perform the examination with an attitude of professional skepticism, recognizing that the application of the auditing procedures may produce evidential matter indicating the possibility of errors or irregularities (AU 508.21). Answer (a) is incorrect because while a CPA must be responsive, this is not the overall attitude when conducting an examination. Answer (b) is incorrect because the CPA must be independent, and advocacy is not consistent with independence. Answer (c) is incorrect because even though the CPA must exhibit objective judgment, "professional skepticism" more accurately summarizes the proper attitude during an audit.

34. (1186,A1,3) (b) Answer (b) is correct because errors refer to unintentional mistakes in financial statements such as misinterpretation of facts (AU 316.02). Answers (a), (c), and (d) all represent irregularities which are defined as intentional distortions of financial statements (AU 316.03).

35. (1183,A1,50) (c) The requirement is to determine the situation which will cause an auditor to presume that a high risk of a defalcation exists. Incompatible functions for internal control purposes are those that place any person in a position to perpetrate and to conceal errors or irregularities (e.g., thefts) in his/her normal course of duties (AU 319.11). Answer (a) is incorrect because the mere operation in numerous foreign countries is not necessarily an indication of potential defalcations. Answer (b) is incorrect because doing business with related parties may be entirely proper. Answer (d) is incorrect because lengthy exception reports do not necessarily indicate that defalcations probably exist.

C.2. Client Illegal Acts

36. (1187,A1,28) (b) The requirement is to identify a reason why audits cannot reasonably be expected to bring all illegal acts to the auditor's attention. Answer (b) is correct because illegal acts relating to the operating aspects of an entity are often highly specialized and complex and often are far removed from the events and transactions reflected in

financial statements (AU 317.06). Answer (a) is partially correct since management override represents a limitation of the effectiveness of internal control (AU 319.15). Yet, auditors are more likely to identify such transactions because they relate to events and transactions reflected in the financial statements. Answer (c) is incorrect because many illegal acts are not subject to the client's internal control structure. Answer (d) is incorrect because illegal acts may be perpetrated without access to both assets and accounting records.

37. (1189,A1,60) (a) The requirement is to determine an auditor's responsibility when information comes to his/her attention that implies the existence of possible illegal acts with a material, but indirect effect on the financial statements. Answer (a) is correct because AU 317.07 requires the auditor to apply audit procedures specifically designed to determine whether an illegal act has occurred when such information comes to his/her attention. Answers (b), (c), and (d) are all incorrect because they represent procedures the auditor would perform after initial procedures had confirmed the existence of the possible illegal act(s).

C.3. Responsibilities in Review and Compilation

38. (1187,A1,29) (a) The requirement is to identify the CPA's minimum responsibility when submitting unaudited financial statements of a nonpublic company to a client or others. Answer (a) is correct because an accountant should not submit such information unless he/she has, at a minimum, compiled the financial statements (AR 100.07). Answer (b) is incorrect because reviews represent attestation services with procedures and responsibilities in excess of compilations (AR 100.23-.31). Answer (c) is incorrect because Statements on Auditing Standards relate primarily to audits and not to compilations or reviews. Answer (d) is incorrect because the CPA can perform a compilation, an accounting service, and thereby not comply with the provisions of the attestation standards (AU 2010.02d).

39. (586,A1,37) (a) The requirement is to identify the situation in which an auditor has a reasonable basis for complying with a client's request to change an audit engagement to a review. Answer (a) is correct because AR 100.46 states that a change in circumstances (here the client's obtaining of alternate financing) is an acceptable reason for changing the form of auditor association. Answers (b) and (c) are incorrect because scope

restrictions relating to legal counsel and the representation letter ordinarily preclude the CPA from changing an audit engagement to a review engagement (AR 100.47). Answer (d) is incorrect because in circumstances in which the auditing procedures are substantially complete, the auditor should consider the propriety of accepting a change in the engagement (AR 100.48).

40. (1189,A1,57) (c) The requirement is to determine the effect of an immaterial direct financial interest on accountant independence. Answer (c) is correct. Reviews are a form of attestation service, and an accountant may not maintain independence when an immaterial direct financial interest is held in a client when performing attestation services (ET 55.05, Interpretation 101-1). Answer (a) is incorrect because such a financial interest does impair independence. Answer (b) is incorrect because independence is not required for compilation services, and therefore, an accountant may be so associated with the financial statements (AR 100.22). Answer (d) is incorrect because neither a review report nor an auditor's opinion may be issued.

C.4. Responsibilities in Management Advisory Services

41. (1185,A1,6) (a) The requirement is to identify the statement that describes the nature of a management advisory service engagement. Answer (a) is correct because in a MAS engagement, an analytical approach and process is applied in a study or project (MS 11.04). Answer (b) is incorrect because a MAS consultation is based primarily, if not entirely, on existing personal knowledge about the client (MS 11.04). Answer (c) is incorrect because an engagement is not an "incidental effort." Answer (d) is incorrect because the CPA's role does not include implementing management's recommendations.

42. (1182,A1,2) (c) The requirement is to determine the statement which is most consistent with the profession's attitudes toward management advisory services. A MAS practitioner should not assume the role of management (make management decisions); see MS 11.06. Answer (a) is incorrect because information obtained as a result of a management advisory services engagement may influence the performance of an audit. Answer (b) is incomplete because the client is only one party which must consider the possible loss of auditor independence. Answer (d) is incorrect because the profession does not believe that auditors should make management decisions for their clients.

43. (1185,A1,12) (a) The requirement is to identify the condition which is <u>not</u> necessary in MAS engagements. Answer (a) is correct because independence is not required (MS 11.06). Answer (b) is incorrect because estimates are to be supported and clearly identified (MS 11.06). Answer (c) is incorrect because an understanding of the nature of the engagement must be obtained (MS 11.06). Answer (d) is incorrect because an accountant is to maintain objectivity (MS 11.06).

44. (585,A1,59) (d) The requirement is to determine the type of position a CPA should <u>not</u> take when performing a MAS engagement. Answer (d) is correct since MS 11.06 states that a MAS practitioner is not to take any positions that might impair objectivity. Providing advice and assistance [answer (a)], providing implementation assistance [answer (b)], and assisting in organizational policies [answer (c)] are all acceptable MAS activities.

45. (586,A1,28) (a) The requirement is to determine the form of communication with a client in a management advisory service consultation. Answer (a) is correct because MAS consultations may occur in a variety of situations including during telephone conversations, in nonbusiness settings, at periodic meetings, and through written inquiries and responses (MS 31.03-.04). Answers (b), (c), and (d) are incorrect because the form of communication may be oral <u>or</u> written.

C.5. Responsibilities in Tax Practice

46. (585,A1,43) (b) The requirement is to determine the proper procedure to be followed when a reasonable basis exists for omission of an answer to an applicable question on a tax return. Answer (b) is correct because TX 131.02 requires that the CPA provide a brief explanation of the reason for the omission. Answers (a), (c), and (d) all specify incorrect procedures.

47. (1184,A1,43) (a) The requirement is to determine a CPA's responsibility with respect to the preparation of an income tax return. Answer (a) is correct because tax minimization, not tax evasion, is desired. Answer (b) is incorrect because the various tax codes, regulations, revenue rulings, and court decisions (not generally accepted accounting principles) are followed when preparing tax returns. Answer (c) is incorrect because no audit need be performed for a CPA to prepare a tax return. Answer (d) is incorrect because tax returns are subject to change upon the discovery of errors (TX 161).

48. (580,A1,22) (c) After providing tax advice to a client, the CPA cannot be expected to notify the client of any subsequent legislative changes which affect the advice previously provided per TX 181.05. If, however, the obligation for the subsequent notification is specifically undertaken by the CPA, the CPA is obviously expected to notify the client of any such changes. Answer (a) is incorrect because the obligation does not exist unless the CPA specifically undertakes the obligation. Answer (b) is incorrect because the CPA is not required to disclaim responsibility for subsequent notification of any changes affecting the advice. Answer (d) is incorrect because the CPA should be expected to have knowledge of all changes if the CPA maintains competence in the area of taxes.

May 1990 Answers

49. (590,A1,1) (b) The requirement is to determine a likely effect on an audit of decreasing the acceptable level of detection risk. Answer (b) is correct because AU 312.17 indicates that the level of detection risk may be decreased by selecting a more effective auditing procedure. In addition, detection risk also may be decreased by performing auditing procedures closer to the balance-sheet date, or by increasing the extent of a particular auditing procedure. Answer (a) is incorrect because to decrease detection risk more tests would be performed at year end, rather than at an interim date. Answer (c) is incorrect because performing the tests at year end will generally result in performing tests at fewer dates. Answer (d) is incorrect because the auditor's assessment of detection risk should not affect the assessed level of inherent risk. See AU 312.20 for a discussion of inherent risk, control risk, and detection risk as they relate to audit risk.

50. (590,A1,46) (b) The requirement is to determine the requirements of the first general standard. Answer (b) is correct because the first general standard requires that the audit be performed by a person or persons having adequate technical training and professional proficiency as an auditor (AU 150.02). Answer (a) is incorrect because while seasoned judgment is necessary, the concept of varying degrees of supervision and review relates more directly to the first standard of field work. Answer (c) is incorrect because while it is important that an auditor have knowledge of the standards of field work and reporting, this requirement does not arise directly from the first general standard. Answer (d) is incorrect because independence requirements relate directly to the second general standard.

51. (590,A1,47) (b) The requirement is to identify the requirement relating to the exercise of due professional care on an audit. Answer (b) is correct because the exercise of due professional care (the third general standard) requires critical review at every level of supervision of the work done and the judgment exercised by those assisting in the audit (AU 230.02). Answer (a) is incorrect because auditors generally sample from the available corroborating evidence and do not examine all available corroborating evidence. Answer (c) is incorrect because control risk may be assessed at the maximum level (see AU 319.27-.38). Answer (d) is incorrect because a proper balance of professional experience and formal education relates more directly to the first general standard concerning technical training and proficiency as an auditor.

52. (590,A1,48) (b) The requirement is to identify the pronouncements that are designed to guide a CPA who is involved in providing a client with technical assistance in the implementation of a new EDP system. Answer (b) is correct because **Statements on Standards for Management Advisory Services** are designed to provide such guidance (MS 11). Answer (a) is incorrect because **Statements on Auditing Standards** provide guidance on auditing matters (AU 100). Answer (c) is incorrect because **Statements on Quality Control Standards** apply to CPA firm requirements when performing auditing, accounting, and review services for which professional standards have been established (QC 10.01). Answer (d) is incorrect because no authoritative standards known as **Standards for Accountants' EDP Services** have been promulgated.

53. (590,A1,49) (a) The requirement is to identify the listed authoritative body designated to promulgate attestation standards. Answer (a) is correct because only the Auditing Standards Board, the Accounting and Review Services Committee, and the Management Advisory Services Executive Committee have been authorized to promulgate attestation standards. Answers (b), (c), and (d) all represent organizations that have **not** been authorized to promulgate attestation standards.

54. (590,A1,52) (a) The requirement is to identify the element of the audit planning process most likely to be agreed upon with the client before implementation of the audit strategy. Answer (a) is correct because the auditor will normally wish to observe the counting of inventory (AU 310.04, 331.09-.13) and there is therefore a need for coordination of timing between the auditor and the client. Answer (b) is incorrect because the client

will not determine the evidence to be gathered
to provide a sufficient basis for the auditor's opinion. Answers (c) and (d) are incorrect because procedures relating to discovery
of litigation, claims, and assessments and
pending legal matters will be determined subsequent to implementation of the audit
strategy (see AU 337 for the auditor's responsibilities).

55. (590,A1,54) (b) The requirement is to
determine the combination of listed concepts
which are elements of a CPA firm's quality
control policies and procedures. Answer (b)
is correct because advancement, inspection,
and consultation all represent quality control
elements. Answers (a), (c), and (d) are all
incorrect because they improperly exclude one
or more of the elements. See QC 90.05 for
information on the quality control elements.

56. (590,A1,55) (d) The requirement is to
identify the circumstances in which an auditor
may have a responsibility to disclose irregularities to parties other than a client's
senior management and its audit committee or
board of directors. Answer (d) is correct
because AU 316.29 states that such a responsibility may exist to the SEC when there has
been an auditor change to a successor auditor,
when the successor auditor makes inquiries,
and to a government agency from which the
client receives financial assistance. In
addition, that section states that an auditor
may have such a disclosure responsibility in
response to a subpoena, a circumstance not
considered in this question. Answers (a), (b),
and (c) are all incorrect because they omit
one of the responsibilities listed in the
question.

57. (590,A1,56) (d) The requirement is to
identify the reply that best describes an
auditor's responsibility to detect errors and
irregularities. Answer (d) is correct because
AU 316.05 requires the auditor to assess the
risk that errors and irregularities may cause
the financial statements to contain material
misstatements, and to design that audit to
provide reasonable assurance of detecting material errors and irregularities. Answer (a)
is incorrect because the auditor is designing
the audit to detect material errors and irregularities, and not all errors and irregularities. Answers (b) and (c) are incorrect because the auditor may choose to test controls,
but it is not required (see AU 319).

58. (590,A1,57) (b) The requirement is to
determine the auditor's reporting responsibility when s/he suspects pervasive illegal
bribes, but has been unable to determine
whether the amounts involved are material or

whether senior management was involved with
the scheme. Answer (b) is correct because the
inability to obtain sufficient competent evidential matter will lead to a situation in
which the auditor generally should disclaim an
opinion on the financial statements
(AU 317.19). Answer (a) is incorrect because
the auditor is uncertain as to whether misstatements are involved, and therefore an unqualified opinion may not be appropriate. Answer (c) is incorrect since the misstatements
may not be material and therefore, an adverse
opinion may be inappropriate. Answer (d) is
incorrect because special reports do not relate to illegal bribes (see AU 623 for information on special reports).

59. (590,A1,58) (a) The requirement is to
identify the statement that most accurately
summarizes an auditor's responsibility concerning illegal acts. Answer (a) is correct
because an auditor's responsibility with
respect to illegal acts that have a direct and
material effect on the financial statements is
the same as that for errors and irregularities
(AU 317.05). That responsibility is to assess
the risk that errors and irregularities may
cause the financial statements to contain
material misstatements, and to design the
audit to provide reasonable assurance of detecting material errors and irregularities
(AU 316.05). Answer (b) is incorrect because
only when the auditor is aware of the possibility of illegal acts with an indirect but
material effect on the financial statements is
there a responsibility to perform such audit
procedures (AU 317.07). Answer (c) is incorrect because illegal acts may affect audit objectives derived from the financial statements
and should be considered from that perspective. Answer (d) is incorrect because an
auditor does not have a responsibility with
respect to illegal acts with an indirect
effect since it is required that the auditor
be aware of the possibility of such illegal
acts.

60. (590,A1,60) (d) The requirement is to
determine the circumstances in which an
auditor must be independent in providing
services. Answer (d) is correct because an
auditor need only be independent when
providing attestation services (ET 55.03).
Preparing tax returns and compiling forecasts
or financial statements are not considered
attestation services, therefore the CPA need
not be independent. Answers (a), (b), and (c)
are incorrect because they all suggest that
independence is required on one of the listed
services.

Unofficial Answer*

Problem 1   Planning Procedures
            (587,A5)

Additional procedures to be performed
prior to the beginning of field work are:

5. Read the current year's interim
   financial statements.
6. Discuss the scope of the examination
   with management of the client.
7. Establish the timing of the audit
   work.
8. Arrange with the client for adequate
   working space.
9. Coordinate the assistance of client
   personnel in data preparation.
10. Establish and coordinate staffing
    requirements including time budget.
11. Hold a planning conference with
    assistants assigned to the engagement.
12. Determine the extent of involvement,
    if any, of consultants, specialists,
    and internal auditors.
13. Consider the effects of applicable
    accounting and auditing pronounce-
    ments, particularly recent ones.
14. Consider the need for an appropriate
    engagement letter.
15. Prepare documentation setting forth
    the preliminary audit plan.
16. Make preliminary judgment about
    materiality levels.
17. Make preliminary judgment about
    reliance to be placed on internal
    controls.
18. Update the prior year's written audit
    program.

Answer Outline

Problem 2   Audit Risk and Materiality
            (1186,A2)

a. 1. Audit risk relates to auditor's opinion
      on F/Ss
      Risk auditor may unknowingly fail to
      modify opinion on materially mis-
      stated F/Ss
   2. Inherent risk concerns susceptibility
      of account balance or class of trans-
      actions to error
      Could be material when aggregated
      with errors in other balances or
      classes
      Assumes no IC
      Control risk involves effectiveness of
      IC

*Because the requirements of this question
could be answered by lists of items we have
not included an outline of the solution.

Risk that error that could occur in
account balance or class of transactions will not be prevented or detected on timely basis by IC
Could be material when aggregated
with errors in other balances or
classes
Detection risk relates to auditor's
procedures
Auditor concludes error does not
exist when error in account balance
or class of transactions does exist
Could be material when aggregated
with errors in other balances or
classes
3. Interrelationships of risk components
   Inherent and control risk differ from
   detection risk
   They exist independently of an
   audit
   Detection risk
   Relates to audit procedures
   Can be changed by discretion of
   auditor
   Bears inverse relationship to inherent and control risk
   Less inherent and control risk,
   greater acceptable detection
   risk
   Greater inherent and control
   risk, less acceptable detection
   risk
b. 1. Definition of materiality
      Magnitude of omission/misstatement
      that would likely alter judgment of
      reasonable person
      Recognizes
      Some matters individually or aggre-
      gate are important for fair pre-
      sentation in conformity with GAAP
      Other matters may not be as im-
      portant
   2. Factors affecting materiality
      Nature and amount of item in relation
      to F/Ss
      Auditor's judgment as influenced by
      perception of needs of reasonable
      person who places reliance on F/Ss
   3. Relationship of uses of materiality in
      auditing
      Planning purposes
      Different from evaluation purposes
      Cannot anticipate all circum-
      stances that may ultimately in-
      fluence judgment
      Evaluation purposes
      If lower materiality levels become
      appropriate when evaluating
      findings
      Reevaluate sufficiency of audit
      procedures already performed

Unofficial Answer

Problem 2   Audit Risk and Materiality
             (1186,A2)

a.   1.   Audit risk is the risk that the auditor may unknowingly fail to appropriately modify the auditor's opinion on financial statements that are materially misstated.

2.   Inherent risk is the susceptibility of an account balance or class of transactions to error that could be material, when aggregated with error in other balances or classes, assuming that there were no related internal controls.

Control risk is the risk that error could occur in an account balance or class of transactions and that could be material, when aggregated with error in other balances or classes, will not be prevented or detected on a timely basis by the internal control structure.

Detection risk is the risk that an auditor's procedures will lead the auditor to conclude that error in an account balance or class of transactions that could be material, when aggregated with error in other balances or classes, does not exist when in fact such error does exist.

3.   Inherent risk and control risk differ from detection risk in that they exist independently of the audit of financial statements, whereas detection risk relates to the auditor's procedures and can be changed at the auditor's discretion. Detection risk should bear an inverse relationship to inherent and control risk. The less the inherent and control risk the auditor believes exists, the greater the acceptable detection risk. Conversely, the greater the inherent and control risk the auditor believes exists, the less the acceptable detection risk.

b.   1.   Materiality is the magnitude of an omission or misstatement of accounting information that, in the light of surrounding circumstances, makes it probable that the judgment of a reasonable person relying on the information would have been changed or influenced by the omission or misstatement. This concept recognizes that some matters, either individually or in the aggregate, are important for the fair presentation of financial statements in conformity with generally accepted accounting principles, while other matters are not important.

2.   Materiality is affected by the nature and amount of an item in relation to the nature and amount of items in the financial statements under examination, and the auditor's judgment as influenced by the auditor's perception of the needs of a reasonable person who will rely on the financial statements.

3.   The auditor's judgment about materiality for planning purposes is ordinarily different from materiality for evaluation purposes because the auditor, when planning an audit, cannot anticipate all of the circumstances that may ultimately influence judgment about materiality in evaluating the audit findings at the completion of the audit. If significantly lower materiality levels become appropriate in evaluating the audit findings, the auditor should reevaluate the sufficiency of the audit procedures already performed.

Answer Outline

Problem 3   Violations of GAAS (1176,A6)

1.   Adequate technical training and auditing
       proficiency
         Students had neither
2.   Independence
         Contingent fee nullifies
3.   Due professional care
         Lack of review and supervision
         Failure to comply with GAAS
4.   Adequate planning and supervision
         Inadequate planning and no supervision
5.   Proper consideration of internal control
         None undertaken
6.   Sufficient competent evidential matter
         None obtained
7.   In accordance with GAAP
         No reference in report
         No basis for assertion
8.   GAAP consistently applied
         No reference in report may or may not
           be proper
         No basis for assertion
9.   Adequate informative disclosure
         No statement footnotes
         No exception in report
10. Expression of opinion on statements as a
       whole
         Given but not on basis of proper audit

Unofficial Answer

Problem 3   Violations of GAAS (1176,A6)

Brief Description of Generally Accepted Auditing Standards	Holmes's Actions Resulting in Failure to Comply With Generally Accepted Auditing Standards
General Standards	
(1) The examination is to be performed by a person or persons having adequate technical training and proficiency as an auditor.	(1) It was inappropriate for Holmes to hire two students to conduct the audit. The examination must be conducted by persons with proper education and experience in the field of auditing. Although a junior assistant has not completed his formal education he may help in the conduct of the examination as long as there is proper supervision and review.
(2) In all matters relating to the assignment, an independence in mental attitude is to be maintained by the auditor or auditors.	(2) To satisfy the second general standard, Holmes must be without bias with respect to the client under audit. Holmes has an obligation for fairness to the owners, management, and creditors who may rely on the report. Because of the financial interest in whether the bank loan is granted to Ray, Holmes is independent in neither fact nor appearance with respect to the assignment undertaken.
(3) Due professional care is to be exercised in the performance of the examination and the preparation of the report.	(3) This standard requires Holmes to perform the audit with due care, which imposes on Holmes and everyone in Holmes's organization a responsibility to observe the standards of field work and reporting. Exercise of due care requires critical review at every level of supervision of the work done and the judgments exercised by those assisting in the examination. Holmes did not review the work or the judgments of the assistants and clearly failed to adhere to this standard.
Standards of Field Work	
(1) The work is to be adequately planned and assistants, if any, are to be properly supervised.	(1) This standard recognizes that early appointment of the auditor has advantages for the auditor and the client. Holmes accepted the engagement without considering the availability of competent staff. In addition, Holmes failed to supervise the assistants. The work performed was not adequately planned.

Brief Description of Generally Accepted Auditing Standards	Holmes's Actions Resulting in Failure to Comply With Generally Accepted Auditing Standards
(2) A sufficient understanding of the Internal Control Structure is to be obtained to plan the audit and to determine the nature, timing, and extent of tests to be performed.	(2) Holmes did not study the system of internal control nor did the assistants conduct such a study. There appears to have been no audit examination at all. The work performed was more an accounting service than it was an auditing service.
(3) Sufficient, competent evidential matter is to be obtained through inspection, observation, inquiries, and confirmations to afford a reasonable basis for an opinion regarding the financial statements under examination.	(3) Holmes acquired no evidence that would support the financial statements. Holmes merely checked the mathematical accuracy of the records and summarized the accounts. Standard audit procedures and techniques were not performed.

Standards of Reporting

(1) The report shall state whether the financial statements are presented in accordance with generally accepted accounting principles.	(1) Holmes's report made no reference to generally accepted accounting principles. Because Holmes did not conduct a proper examination, the report should state that no opinion can be expressed as to the fair presentation of the financial statements in accordance with generally accepted accounting principles.
(2) The report shall identify those circumstances in which such principles have not been consistently observed in the current period in relation to the preceding period.	(2) Holmes's report correctly makes no reference to the consistent application of accounting principles. This assumes Holmes has gathered enough evidence to know that principles have been applied consistently.
(3) Informative disclosures in the financial statements are to be regarded as reasonably adequate unless otherwise stated in the report.	(3) Management is primarily responsible for adequate disclosure in the financial statements, but when the statements do not contain adequate disclosures the auditor should make such disclosures in the auditor's report. In this case both the statements and the auditor's report lack adequate disclosures.
(4) The report shall either contain an expression of opinion regarding the financial statements taken as a whole or an assertion to the effect that an opinion cannot be expressed. When an overall opinion cannot be expressed, the reasons therefor should be stated. In all cases where an auditor's name is associated with financial statements, the report should contain a clear-cut indication of the character of the auditor's examination, if any, and the degree of responsibility he is taking.	(4) Although the Holmes report contains an expression of opinion, such opinion is not based on the results of a proper audit examination. Holmes should disclaim an opinion because he failed to conduct an examination in accordance with generally accepted auditing standards.

Answer Outline

Problem 4   Errors, Irregularities, and
             Illegal Acts (589,A5)

a. Auditor's responsibility to detect errors
    and irregularities
        Assess risk that errors and irregulari-
        ties may cause FSs to be materially
        misstated
        Design audit to provide reasonable
        assurance of detecting errors and
        irregularities
        Exercise due care
b. Auditor's responsibility to report errors
    and irregularities
        Inform audit committee or others of
        equivalent authority and responsibility
        about material irregularities
        Qualified or adverse opinion if FSs
        materially affected and are not revised
        Disclaimer or qualified opinion if scope
        of audit has been restricted
        Consider notifying outside parties
c. Auditor's responsibility to detect illegal
    acts
        Same as for errors and irregularities
        If illegal acts are suspected, specific
        audit procedures should be performed to
        ascertain whether an illegal act has
        occurred
d. Auditor's responsibility to report on
    errors, irregularities and illegal acts
    in a GAO audit
        Determine that any illegal act indica-
        tions reported to appropriate agency
        Express positive assurance on whether
        items tested were in compliance with
        applicable laws
        Express negative assurance that untested
        items were not in compliance with
        applicable laws

Unofficial Answer

Problem 4   Errors, Irregularities, and
             Illegal Acts (589,A5)

a. To satisfy an auditor's responsibilities
    to detect Smith's errors and irregularities,
    Reed should

    •   Assess the risk that Smith's errors
    and irregularities may cause its financial
    statements to contain a material misstatement.
    •   Design the audit to provide reasonable
    assurance of detecting errors and irregulari-
    ties that are material to the financial state-
    ments.
    •   Exercise due care in planning, per-
    forming, and evaluating the results of audit

procedures, and the proper degree of professional skepticism to achieve reasonable assurance that material errors or irregularities
will be detected.

b. To satisy an auditor's responsibilities to
    report Smith's errors and irregularities, Reed
    should

    •   Inform Smith's audit committee, or
    others having equivalent authority and respon-
    sibility, about material irregularities of
    which Reed becomes aware.
    •   Express a qualified or an adverse
    opinion on the financial statements if they
    are materially affected by an error or irregu-
    larity and are not revised.
    •   Disclaim or qualify an opinion on the
    finanical statements and communicate the
    findings to the audit committee or the board
    of directors if the scope of the audit has
    been restricted concerning a possible
    irregularity.
    •   Consider notification of outside
    parties concerning irregularities in certain
    circumstances.

c. Reed's responsibilities to detect Smith's
    illegal acts that have a material and direct
    effect on Smith's financial statements are the
    same as that for errors and irregularities.
    Reed's responsibilities to detect Smith's
    illegal acts that have a material and indirect
    effect on the financial statements are to be
    aware of the possibility that such illegal
    acts may have occurred. If specific informa-
    tion comes to Reed's attention that provides
    evidence concerning the existence of such
    possible illegal acts, Reed should apply audit
    procedures specifically directed to ascer-
    taining whether an illegal act has occurred.

d. In an audit to which GAO standards apply,
    Reed should additionally

    •   Determine that instances or apparent
    indications of illegal acts are reported to
    the funding agency or other specified agency.
    •   Express positive assurance on whether
    the items tested were in compliance with ap-
    plicable laws and regulations.
    •   Express negative assurance that, ex-
    cept as otherwise noted, nothing came to
    Reed's attention that caused Reed to believe
    that the untested items were not in compliance
    with applicable laws and regulations.

Answer Outline

Problem 5 Other Auditors (1185,A2)

a. Appropriate procedures to be performed
    whether or not May & Marty reference
    other auditors

Inquire as to professional reputation
    AICPA, state society and/or local
      chapter of CPAs
    Other appropriate sources
  Obtain representation from Dey & Dee
    regarding independence
  Ascertain by communication that
    Dey & Dee is aware that BGI-Western FSs
      will be included in consolidated FSs
    Dey & Dee is familiar with GAAP and GAAS
    Dey & Dee is knowledgeable of financial
      reporting requirements with regulatory
      agencies
    Dey & Dee will review matters affecting
      intercompany eliminations and
    Uniformity of accounting practices among
      components included in FSs
b. Not necessary to make reference if
    May & Marty able to satisfy itself con-
      cerning independence and professional
      reputation and
    One of following exists:
      Dey & Dee work acceptable based on
        knowledge of professional standards
        and competence
      May & Marty hire Dey & Dee and guide
        and control the work performed
      May & Marty discuss audit procedures,
        review audit programs and/or working
        papers and is satisfied with Dey &
        Dee's audit
        Reasonableness of FSs of BGI
    BGI-Western's FSs not material part of
      consolidated FSs

Unofficial Answer

Problem 5   Other Auditors (1185,A2)

a. In order for May & Marty to satisfy itself
about the independence and professional reputation of Dey & Dee and assure itself that
there has been coordination of activities between the two auditors in order to achieve a
proper review of matters affecting consolidation, May & Marty, whether or not it makes
reference to Dey & Dee's examination, should
consider performing the following procedures:

• Make inquiries about the professional
reputation and standing of Dey & Dee to one or
more of the following:

    • AICPA, applicable state society of
CPAs, and/or local chapter.
    • Other appropriate sources such as
other practitioners, bankers, and other credit
grantors.

    • Obtain a representation from Dey & Dee
that it is independent under the requirements
of the AICPA and, if appropriate, the requirements of the SEC.

• Ascertain through communication with
Dey & Dee that

    • Dey & Dee is aware that the BGI-
Western financial statements are to be included in the BGI consolidated financial
statements on which May & Marty will report,
and that Dey & Dee's report will be relied
upon by May & Marty.
    • Dey & Dee is familiar with GAAP
and GAAS and will conduct its examination in
accordance therewith.
    • Dey & Dee has knowledge of the
relevant financial reporting requirements for
statements and schedules to be filed with
regulatory agencies such as the SEC, if appropriate.
    • A review will be made of matters
affecting elimination of intercompany transactions and accounts and, if appropriate in
the circumstances, the uniformity of accounting practices among components included in the
financial statements.

b. May & Marty could adopt the position of
not making reference to Dey & Dee's examination of BGI-Western if May & Marty is able to
satisfy itself about the independence and professional reputation of Dey & Dee and takes
steps it considers appropriate to satisfy
itself as to Dey & Dee's examination of BGI-
Western. Ordinarily, May & Marty would be
able to adopt the position of not making
reference to Dey & Dee's examination when any
one of the following conditions exists:

    • Dey & Dee is an associate or corre-
spondent firm and its work is acceptable to
May & Marty based on May & Marty's knowledge
of the professional standards and competence
of Dey & Dee; or
    • Dey & Dee is retained by May & Marty
and the work is performed under May & Marty's
guidance and control; or
    • May & Marty takes steps it considers
necessary to satisfy itself as to Dey & Dee's
examination. Such steps may include a visit
to Dey & Dee to discuss Dey & Dee's audit procedures or a review of Dey and Dee's audit
programs and/or working papers. In addition,
May & Marty is satisfied as to the reasonableness of the statements of BGI-Western for purposes of inclusion in BGI's consolidated financial statements; or
    • BGI-Western's financial statements are
not a material part of BGI's consolidated financial statements.

Multiple Choice Questions (1-95)

1. When considering internal control, an auditor should be aware of the concept of reasonable assurance, which recognizes that the
   a. Segregation of incompatible functions is necessary to ascertain that internal control is effective.
   b. Employment of competent personnel provides assurance that the objectives of internal control will be achieved.
   c. Establishment and maintenance of an internal control structure is an important responsibility of the management and not of the auditor.
   d. Cost of internal control should not exceed the benefits expected to be derived from internal control.

2. Proper segregation of functional responsibilities in an effective structure of internal control calls for separation of the functions of
   a. Authorization, execution, and payment.
   b. Authorization, recording, and custody.
   c. Custody, execution, and reporting.
   d. Authorization, payment, and recording.

3. For good internal control, which of the following functions should not be the responsibility of the treasurer's department?
   a. Data processing.
   b. Handling of cash.
   c. Custody of securities.
   d. Establishing credit policies.

4. Internal controls are not designed to provide reasonable assurance that
   a. Transactions are executed in accordance with management's authorization.
   b. Irregularities will be eliminated.
   c. Access to assets is permitted only in accordance with management's authorization.
   d. The recorded accountability for assets is compared with the existing assets at reasonable intervals.

5. Which of the following is not an element of an entity's internal control structure?
   a. Control risk.
   b. Control procedures.
   c. The accounting system.
   d. The control environment.

6. Which of the following is a provision of the Foreign Corrupt Practices Act?
   a. It is a criminal offense for an auditor to fail to detect and report a bribe paid by an American business entity to a foreign official for the purpose of obtaining business.
   b. The auditor's detection of illegal acts committed by officials of the auditor's publicly held client in conjunction with foreign officials should be reported to the Enforcement Division of the Securities and Exchange Commission.
   c. If the auditor of a publicly held company concludes that the effects on the financial statements of a bribe given to a foreign official are not susceptible of reasonable estimation, the auditor's report should be modified.
   d. Every publicly held company must devise, document, and maintain an internal control structure sufficient to provide reasonable assurances that internal control objectives are met.

7. Which of the following statements regarding auditor documentation of the client's internal control structure is correct?
   a. Documentation must include flow charts.
   b. Documentation must include procedural write-ups.
   c. No documentation is necessary although it is desirable.
   d. No one particular form of documentation is necessary, and the extent of documentation may vary.

8. In considering the internal control structure, the completion of a questionnaire is most closely associated with which of the following?
   a. Tests of controls.
   b. Substantive tests.
   c. Analytical procedures.
   d. Obtaining and documenting an understanding of the structure design.

9. Which of the following is not a reason an auditor should obtain an understanding of the elements of an entity's internal control structure in planning an audit?
   a. Identify the types of potential misstatements that can occur.
   b. Design substantive tests.
   c. Consider the operating effectiveness of the internal control structure.
   d. Consider factors that affect the risk of material misstatements.

10. When obtaining an understanding of an entity's control environment, an auditor should concentrate on the substance of management's policies and procedures rather than their form because
    a. The auditor may believe that the policies and procedures are inappropriate for that particular entity.
    b. The board of directors may not be aware of management's attitude toward the control environment.
    c. Management may establish appropriate policies and procedures but not act on them.
    d. The policies and procedures may be so weak that no reliance is contemplated by the auditor.

11. After obtaining an understanding of an entity's internal control structure and assessing control risk, an auditor may next
    a. Perform tests of controls to verify management's assertions that are embodied in the financial statements.
    b. Consider whether evidential matter is available to support a further reduction in the assessed level of control risk.
    c. Apply analytical procedures as substantive tests to validate the assessed level of control risk.
    d. Evaluate whether the internal control structure policies and procedures detected material misstatements in the financial statements.

12. Which of the following procedures most likely would be included as part of an auditor's tests of controls?
    a. Inspection.
    b. Reconciliation.
    c. Confirmation.
    d. Analytical procedures.

13. An auditor is least likely to test the internal controls that provide for
    a. Approval of the purchase and sale of marketable securities.
    b. Classification of revenue and expense transactions by product line.
    c. Segregation of the functions of recording disbursements and reconciling the bank account.
    d. Comparison of receiving reports and vendors' invoices with purchase orders.

14. Evidential matter concerning proper segregation of duties ordinarily is best obtained by
    a. Inspection of third-party documents containing the initials of who applied control procedures.
    b. Direct personal observation of the employee who applies control procedures.
    c. Preparation of a flowchart of duties performed and available personnel.
    d. Making inquiries of co-workers about the employee who applies control procedures.

15. Which of the following is least likely to be evidence the auditor examines to determine whether operations are in compliance with the internal control structure?
    a. Records documenting usage of EDP programs.
    b. Canceled supporting documents.
    c. Confirmations of accounts receivable.
    d. Signatures on authorization forms.

16. An auditor uses the knowledge provided by the understanding of the internal control structure and the assessed level of control risk primarily to
    a. Determine whether procedures and records concerning the safeguarding of assets are reliable.
    b. Ascertain whether the opportunities to allow any person to both perpetrate and conceal irregularities are minimized.
    c. Modify the initial assessments of inherent risk and preliminary judgments about materiality levels.
    d. Determine the nature, timing, and extent of substantive tests for financial statement assertions.

17. In considering internal control, the auditor is basically concerned that the structure provides reasonable assurance that
    a. Operational efficiency has been achieved in accordance with management plans.
    b. Errors and irregularities have been prevented or detected.
    c. Controls have not been circumvented by collusion.
    d. Management can not override the system.

18. After considering a client's internal control structure, an auditor has concluded that it is well designed and is functioning as intended. Under these circumstances the auditor would most likely

a. Perform tests of controls to the extent outlined in the audit program.

b. Determine the control procedures that should prevent or detect errors and irregularities.

c. Not increase the extent of predetermined substantive tests.

d. Determine whether transactions are recorded to permit preparation of financial statements in conformity with generally accepted accounting principles.

19. An auditor may compensate for a weakness in the internal control structure by increasing the
a. Level of detection risk.
b. Extent of tests of controls.
c. Preliminary judgment about audit risk.
d. Extent of analytical procedures.

20. The reliance placed on substantive tests in relation to the reliance placed on internal control varies in a relationship that is ordinarily
a. Parallel.
b. Inverse.
c. Direct.
d. Equal.

21. At which point in an ordinary sales transaction of a wholesaling business would a lack of specific authorization least concern the auditor conducting an audit?
a. Determining discounts.
b. Selling goods for cash.
c. Granting credit.
d. Shipping goods.

22. An auditor selects a sample from the file of shipping documents to determine whether invoices were prepared. This test is performed to satisfy the audit objective of
a. Accuracy.
b. Completeness.
c. Control.
d. Existence.

23. To determine whether the internal control structure operated effectively to minimize errors of failure to invoice a shipment, the auditor would select a sample of transactions from the population represented by the
a. Customer order file.
b. Bill of lading file.
c. Open invoice file.
d. Sales invoice file.

24. To achieve good internal control, which department should perform the activities of

matching shipping documents with sales orders and preparing daily sales summaries?
a. Billing.
b. Shipping.
c. Credit.
d. Sales order.

25. Which of the following would be the best protection for a company that wishes to prevent the "lapping" of trade accounts receivable?
a. Segregate duties so that the bookkeeper in charge of the general ledger has no access to incoming mail.
b. Segregate duties so that no employee has access to both checks from customers and currency from daily cash receipts.
c. Have customers send payments directly to the company's depository bank.
d. Request that customers' payment checks be made payable to the company and addressed to the treasurer.

26. Cash receipts from sales on account have been misappropriated. Which of the following acts would conceal this defalcation and be least likely to be detected by an auditor?
a. Understating the sales journal.
b. Overstating the accounts receivable control account.
c. Overstating the accounts receivable subsidiary ledger.
d. Understating the cash receipts journal.

27. When a customer fails to include a remittance advice with a payment, it is common practice for the person opening the mail to prepare one. Consequently, mail should be opened by which of the following four company employees?
a. Credit manager.
b. Receptionist.
c. Sales manager.
d. Accounts receivable clerk.

28. The most likely result of ineffective internal controls in the revenue cycle is that
a. Fictitious transactions could be recorded, causing an understatement of revenues and overstatement of receivables.
b. Irregularities in recording transactions in the subsidiary accounts could result in a delay in goods shipped.
c. Omission of shipping documents could go undetected, causing an understatement of inventory.

d. Final authorization of credit memos by personnel in the sales department could permit an employee defalcation scheme.

29. During the review of a small business client's internal control structure, the auditor discovered that the accounts receivable clerk approves credit memos and has access to cash. Which of the following controls would be most effective in offsetting this weakness?

a. The owner reviews errors in billings to customers and postings to the subsidiary ledger.

b. The controller receives the monthly bank statement directly and reconciles the checking accounts.

c. The owner reviews credit memos after they are recorded.

d. The controller reconciles the total of the detail accounts receivable accounts to the amount shown in the ledger.

30. For effective internal control, employees maintaining the accounts receivable subsidiary ledger should not also approve

a. Employee overtime wages.

b. Credit granted to customers.

c. Write-offs of customer accounts.

d. Cash disbursements.

31. Which of the following internal control procedures will most likely prevent the concealment of a cash shortage resulting from the improper write-off of a trade account receivable?

a. Write-offs must be approved by a responsible officer after review of credit department recommendations and supporting evidence.

b. Write-offs must be supported by an aging schedule showing that only receivables overdue several months have been written off.

c. Write-offs must be approved by the cashier who is in a position to know if the receivables have, in fact, been collected.

d. Write-offs must be authorized by company field sales employees who are in a position to determine the financial standing of the customers.

32. For effective internal control purposes, the vouchers payable department generally should

a. Stamp, perforate, or otherwise cancel supporting documentation after payment is mailed.

b. Ascertain that each requisition is approved as to price, quantity, and quality by an authorized employee.

c. Obliterate the quantity ordered on the receiving department copy of the purchase order.

d. Establish the agreement of the vendor's invoice with the receiving report and purchase order.

33. Internal control is strengthened when the quantity of merchandise ordered is omitted from the copy of the purchase order sent to the

a. Department that initiated the requisition.

b. Receiving department.

c. Purchasing agent.

d. Accounts payable department.

34. Which of the following procedures in the cash disbursements cycle should not be performed by the accounts payable department?

a. Comparing the vendor's invoice with the receiving report.

b. Canceling supporting documentation after payment.

c. Verifying the mathematical accuracy of the vendor's invoice.

d. Signing the voucher for payment by an authorized person.

35. When goods are received, the receiving clerk should match the goods with the

a. Purchase order and the requisition form.

b. Vendor's invoice and the receiving report.

c. Vendor's shipping document and the purchase order.

d. Receiving report and the vendor's shipping document.

36. A client erroneously recorded a large purchase twice. Which of the following internal control measures would be most likely to detect this error in a timely and efficient manner?

a. Footing the purchases journal.

b. Reconciling vendors' monthly statements with subsidiary payable ledger accounts.

c. Tracing totals from the purchases journal to the ledger accounts.

d. Sending written quarterly confirmations to all vendors.

37. The mailing of disbursement checks and remittance advices should be controlled by the employee who

a. Signed the checks last.

b.   Approved the vouchers for payment.
c.   Matched the receiving reports, purchase orders, and vendors' invoices.
d.   Verified the mathematical accuracy of the vouchers and remittance advices.

38.   The accounts payable department receives the purchase order form to accomplish all of the following except
a.   Compare invoice price to purchase order price.
b.   Ensure the purchase had been properly authorized.
c.   Ensure the goods had been received by the party requesting the goods.
d.   Compare quantity ordered to quantity purchased.

39.   An auditor performs a test to determine whether all merchandise for which the client was billed was received.   The population for this test consists of all
a.   Merchandise received.
b.   Vendors' invoices.
c.   Canceled checks.
d.   Receiving reports.

40.   An internal control narrative indicates that an approved voucher is required to support every check request for payment of merchandise. Which of the following procedures provides the greatest assurance that this control is operating effectively?
a.   Select and examine vouchers and ascertain that the related canceled checks are dated no later than the vouchers.
b.   Select and examine vouchers and ascertain that the related canceled checks are dated no earlier than the vouchers.
c.   Select and examine canceled checks and ascertain that the related vouchers are dated no earlier than the checks.
d.   Select and examine canceled checks and ascertain that the related vouchers are dated no later than the checks.

41.   Independent internal verification of inventory occurs when employees who
a.   Issue raw materials obtain material requisitions for each issue and prepare daily totals of materials issued.
b.   Compare records of goods on hand with physical quantities do not maintain the records or have custody of the inventory.

c.   Obtain receipts for the transfer of completed work to finished goods prepare a completed production report.
d.   Are independent of issuing production orders update records from completed job cost sheets and production cost reports on a timely basis.

42.   Sound internal control procedures dictate that defective merchandise returned by customers should be presented to the
a.   Inventory control clerk.
b.   Sales clerk.
c.   Purchasing clerk.
d.   Receiving clerk.

43.   Alpha Company uses its sales invoices for posting perpetual inventory records. Inadequate internal controls over the invoicing function allow goods to be shipped that are not invoiced. The inadequate controls could cause an
a.   Understatement of revenues, receivables, and inventory.
b.   Overstatement of revenues and receivables, and an understatement of inventory.
c.   Understatement of revenues and receivables, and an overstatement of inventory.
d.   Overstatement of revenues, receivables, and inventory.

44.   The physical count of inventory of a retailer was higher than shown by the perpetual records. Which of the following could explain the difference?
a.   Inventory items had been counted but the tags placed on the items had not been taken off the items and added to the inventory accumulation sheets.
b.   Credit memos for several items returned by customers had not been recorded.
c.   No journal entry had been made on the retailer's books for several items returned to its suppliers.
d.   An item purchased "FOB shipping point" had not arrived at the date of the inventory count and had not been reflected in the perpetual records.

45.   A client's physical count of inventories was higher than the inventory quantities per the perpetual records. This situation could be the result of the failure to record
a.   Sales.
b.   Sales discounts.

c.   Purchases.
d.   Purchase returns.

46. An auditor's tests of controls over the issuance of raw materials to production would most likely include

a.   Reconciling raw materials and work in process perpetual inventory records to general ledger balances.
b.   Inquiring of the custodian about the procedures followed when defective materials are received from vendors.
c.   Observing that raw materials are stored in secure areas and that storeroom security is supervised by a responsible individual.
d.   Examining material requisitions and reperforming client controls designed to process and record issuances.

47. Which of the following is a question that the auditor would expect to find on the production cycle section of an internal control questionnaire?

a.   Are vendors' invoices for raw materials approved for payment by an employee who is independent of the cash disbursements function?
b.   Are signed checks for the purchase of raw materials mailed directly after signing without being returned to the person who authorized the invoice processing?
c.   Are all releases by storekeepers of raw materials from storage based on approved requisition documents?
d.   Are details of individual disbursements for raw materials balanced with the total to be posted to the appropriate general ledger account?

48. Effective internal control over the payroll function would include

a.   Verification of agreement of job time tickets with employee clock card hours by a payroll department employee.
b.   Reconciliation of totals on job time tickets with job reports by employees responsible for those specific jobs.
c.   Custody of rate authorization records by the supervisor of the payroll department.
d.   Preparation of payroll transaction journal entries by an employee who reports to the supervisor of the personnel department.

49. Proper internal control over the cash payroll function would mandate which of the following?

a.   The payroll clerk should fill the envelopes with cash and a computation of the net wages.
b.   Unclaimed pay envelopes should be retained by the paymaster.
c.   Each employee should be asked to sign a receipt.
d.   A separate checking account for payroll be maintained.

50. The use of fidelity bonds may indemnify a company from embezzlement losses. The use also

a.   Reduces the company's need to obtain expensive business interruption insurance.
b.   Protects employees who made unintentional errors from possible monetary damages resulting from such errors.
c.   Allows the company to substitute the fidelity bonds for various parts of internal control.
d.   Reduces the possibility of employing persons with dubious records in positions of trust.

51. The purpose of segregating the duties of hiring personnel and distributing payroll checks is to separate the

a.   Administrative controls from the internal accounting controls.
b.   Human resources function from the controllership function.
c.   Operational responsibility from the record keeping responsibility.
d.   Authorization of transactions from the custody of related assets.

52. To minimize the opportunities for fraud, unclaimed cash payroll should be

a.   Deposited in a safe deposit box.
b.   Held by the payroll custodian.
c.   Deposited in a special bank account.
d.   Held by the controller.

53. An auditor would consider internal control over a client's payroll procedures to be ineffective if the payroll department supervisor is responsible for

a.   Hiring subordinate payroll department employees.
b.   Having custody over unclaimed paychecks.
c.   Updating employee earnings records.
d.   Applying pay rates to time tickets.

54. Tracing selected items from the payroll register to employee time cards that have been approved by supervisory personnel provides evidence that
   a. Internal controls relating to payroll disbursements were operating effectively.
   b. Payroll checks were signed by an appropriate officer independent of the payroll preparation process.
   c. Only bona fide employees worked and their pay was properly computed.
   d. Employees worked the number of hours for which their pay was computed.

55. The auditor may observe the distribution of paychecks to ascertain whether
   a. Payrate authorization is properly separated from the operating function.
   b. Deductions from gross pay are calculated correctly and are properly authorized.
   c. Employees of record actually exist and are employed by the client.
   d. Paychecks agree with the payroll register and the time cards.

56. Which of the following procedures is most likely to prevent the improper disposition of equipment?
   a. A separation of duties between those authorized to dispose of equipment and those authorized to approve removal work orders.
   b. The use of serial numbers to identify equipment that could be sold.
   c. Periodic comparison of removal work orders to authorizing documentation.
   d. A periodic analysis of the scrap sales and the repairs and maintenance accounts.

57. Property acquisitions that are mis-classified as maintenance expense would most likely be detected by an internal control structure that provides for
   a. Investigation of variances within a formal budgeting system.
   b. Review and approval of the monthly depreciation entry by the plant supervisor.
   c. Segregation of duties of employees in the accounts payable department.
   d. Examination by the internal auditor of vendor invoices and canceled checks for property acquisitions.

58. A weakness in internal control over recording retirements of equipment may cause an auditor to
   a. Trace additions to the "other assets" account to search for equipment that is still on hand but no longer being used.
   b. Select certain items of equipment from the accounting records and locate them in the plant.
   c. Inspect certain items of equipment in the plant and trace those items to the accounting records.
   d. Review the subsidiary ledger to ascertain whether depreciation was taken on each item of equipment during the year.

59. When there are numerous property and equipment transactions during the year, an auditor planning to assess control risk at the minimum level usually plans to obtain an understanding of the internal control structure and to perform
   a. Tests of controls and extensive tests of property and equipment balances at the end of the year.
   b. Extensive tests of current year property and equipment transactions.
   c. Tests of controls and limited tests of current year property and equipment transactions.
   d. Analytical procedures for property and equipment balances at the end of the year.

60. Which of the following internal control procedures would most likely allow for a reduction in the scope of the auditor's tests of depreciation expense?
   a. Review and approval of the periodic equipment depreciation entry by a supervisor who does not actively participate in its preparation.
   b. Comparison of equipment account balances for the current year with the current-year budget and prior-year actual balances.
   c. Review of the miscellaneous income account for salvage credits and scrap sales of partially depreciated equipment.
   d. Authorization of payment of vendors' invoices by a designated employee who is independent of the equipment receiving function.

61. Where no independent stock transfer agents are employed and the corporation issues its own stocks and maintains stock records, canceled stock certificates should

a. Be defaced to prevent reissuance and attached to their corresponding stubs.

b. Not be defaced but segregated from other stock certificates and retained in a canceled certificates file.

c. Be destroyed to prevent fraudulent reissuance.

d. Be defaced and sent to the secretary of state.

62. A company holds bearer bonds as a short-term investment. Responsibility for custody of these bonds and submission of coupons for periodic interest collections probably should be delegated to the

a. Chief Accountant.
b. Internal Auditor.
c. Cashier.
d. Treasurer.

63. In general, material irregularities perpetrated by which of the following are most difficult to detect?

a. Cashier.
b. Key-punch operator.
c. Internal auditor.
d. Controller.

64. The auditor would be __least__ likely to be concerned about internal control as it relates to

a. Land and buildings.
b. Common stock.
c. Shareholder meetings.
d. Minutes of board of directors' meetings.

65. Reportable conditions are matters that come to an auditor's attention, which should be communicated to an entity's audit committee because they represent

a. Material irregularities or illegal acts perpetrated by high-level management.

b. Significant deficiencies in the design or operation of the internal control structure.

c. Flagrant violations of the entity's documented conflict-of-interest policies.

d. Intentional attempts by client personnel to limit the scope of the auditor's field work.

66. What is the continuing auditor's obligation concerning the discovery at an interim date of a reportable condition related to internal control?

a. The auditor should communicate this condition to the client immediately because the discovery of such condition in internal control is the purpose of a review of interim financial information.

b. The auditor need __not__ communicate this condition to the client.

c. The auditor should communicate this condition to the client following completion of the examination unless the auditor decides to communicate it to the client at the interim date.

d. The auditor should extend the audit procedures to investigate whether this condition had any effect on the prior year's financial statements.

67. Which of the following statements is correct concerning the auditor's required communication of internal control reportable conditions?

a. If the auditor does __not__ become aware of any reportable conditions during the examination, that fact must be communicated.

b. Reportable conditions reported at interim dates should be tested for correction before completion of the engagement.

c. Although written communication is preferable, the auditor may communicate the findings orally.

d. Reportable conditions reported at interim dates must be repeated in the communication at the completion of the engagement.

68. During the audit the independent auditor identified the existence of a weakness in the client's internal controls and orally communicated this finding to the client's senior management and audit committee. The auditor should

a. Consider the weakness a scope limitation and therefore disclaim an opinion.

b. Document the matter in the working papers and consider the effects of the condition on the audit.

c. Suspend all audit activities pending directions from the client's audit committee.

d. Withdraw from the engagement.

69. Which of the following statements is correct concerning an auditor's communication of internal control structure related matters (reportable conditions) noted in an audit?

a. The auditor may issue a written report to the audit committee representing that <u>no</u> reportable conditions were noted during the audit.

b. Reportable conditions should be re-communicated each year even if the audit committee has acknowledged its understanding of such deficiencies.

c. Reportable conditions may <u>not</u> be communicated in a document that contains suggestions regarding activities that concern other topics such as business strategies or administrative efficiencies.

d. The auditor may choose to communicate significant internal control structure related matters either during the course of the audit or after the audit is concluded.

70. An accountant's report expressing an opinion on an entity's internal controls should

a. Briefly explain the broad objectives and inherent limitations of internal control.

b. State that the study and evaluation of the internal controls was conducted in accordance with generally accepted auditing standards.

c. Clearly disclaim responsibility for the establishment and maintenance of the internal controls.

d. Include an opinion concerning management's assertions about whether the cost of correcting any material weaknesses would exceed the benefits of reducing the risk of errors and irregularities.

71. When an auditor issues an unqualified opinion on an entity's internal control, it is implied that the

a. Entity has <u>not</u> violated provisions of the Foreign Corrupt Practices Act.

b. Likelihood of management fraud is minimal.

c. Financial records are sufficiently reliable to permit the preparation of financial statements.

d. Entity's system of internal control is in conformity with criteria established by its audit committee.

72. An accountant has been engaged to report on an entity's internal controls without performing an audit of the financial statements. What restrictions, if any, should

the accountant place on the use of this report?

a. This report should be restricted for use by management.

b. This report should be restricted for use by the audit committee.

c. This report should be restricted for use by a specified regulatory agency.

d. The accountant does <u>not</u> need to place any restrictions on the use of this report.

73. When an independent auditor reports on internal control based on criteria established by governmental agencies, the report should

a. Not include the agency's name in the report.

b. Indicate matters covered by the study and whether the auditor's study included tests of controls with the procedures covered by the study.

c. Not express a conclusion based on the agency's criteria.

d. Assume responsibility for the comprehensiveness of the criteria established by the agency and include recommendations for corrective action.

74. A CPA's report expressing an opinion on an entity's internal control identified several material weaknesses and will be published in the entity's annual report to shareholders. Management intends to include a statement asserting that the cost of correcting the weaknesses would exceed the benefits of reducing the risk of errors and irregularities. The CPA should

a. Insist that management's statement <u>not</u> appear in the same document as the CPA's report.

b. Investigate whether the cost of correcting the weaknesses would, in fact, exceed the benefits.

c. Insist that management correct the weaknesses if cost is the only consideration.

d. Not express any opinion as to management's statement.

75. An independent accountant, without auditing an entity's financial statements, may accept an engagement to express an opinion on the entity's internal controls in effect

	As of a specified date	During a specified period of time
a.	Yes	Yes
b.	Yes	No
c.	No	Yes
d.	No	No

76. If the independent auditors decide that the work performed by the internal auditor may have a bearing on their own procedures, they should consider the internal auditor's
   a. Competence and objectivity.
   b. Efficiency and experience.
   c. Independence and review skills.
   d. Training and supervisory skills.

77. When considering the objectivity of internal auditors, an independent auditor should
   a. Evaluate the quality control program in effect for the internal auditors.
   b. Examine documentary evidence of the work performed by the internal auditors.
   c. Test a sample of the transactions and balances that the internal auditors examined.
   d. Determine the organizational level to which the internal auditors report.

78. To provide for the greatest degree of independence in performing internal auditing functions, an internal auditor most likely should report to the
   a. Financial vice-president.
   b. Corporate controller.
   c. Board of directors.
   d. Corporate stockholders.

79. In connection with the examination of financial statements by an independent auditor, the client suggests that members of the internal audit staff be utilized to minimize audit costs. Which of the following tasks could most appropriately be delegated to the internal audit staff?
   a. Selection of accounts receivable for confirmation, based upon the internal auditor's judgment as to how many accounts and which accounts will provide sufficient coverage.
   b. Preparation of schedules for negative accounts receivable responses.
   c. Evaluation of the internal control for accounts receivable and sales.
   d. Determination of the adequacy of the allowance for doubtful accounts.

80. Which of the following statements best describes how a detailed audit program of a CPA who is engaged to audit the financial statements of a large publicly held company compares with the audit client's comprehensive internal audit program?
   a. The comprehensive internal audit program is substantially identical to the audit program used by the CPA

because both cover substantially identical areas.
   b. The comprehensive internal audit program is less detailed and covers fewer areas than would normally be covered by the CPA.
   c. The comprehensive internal audit program is more detailed and covers areas that would normally **not** be covered by the CPA.
   d. The comprehensive internal audit program is more detailed although it covers fewer areas than would normally be covered by the CPA.

May 1990 Questions

81. Which of the following computer documentation would an auditor most likely utilize in obtaining an understanding of the internal control structure?
   a. Systems flowcharts.
   b. Record counts.
   c. Program listings.
   d. Record layouts.

82. Miller Retailing, Inc. maintains a staff of three full-time internal auditors who report directly to the controller. In planning to use the internal auditors to provide assistance in performing the audit, the independent auditor most likely will
   a. Place limited reliance on the work performed by the internal auditors.
   b. Decrease the extent of the tests of controls needed to support the assessed level of detection risk.
   c. Increase the extent of the procedures needed to reduce control risk to an acceptable level.
   d. Avoid using the work performed by the internal auditors.

83. Which of the following elements of an entity's internal control structure includes the development of personnel manuals documenting employee promotion and training policies?
   a. Control procedures.
   b. Control environment.
   c. Accounting system.
   d. Quality control system.

84. Which of the following statements about internal control structure is correct?
   a. A properly maintained internal control structure reasonably ensures that collusion among employees cannot occur.

b.   The establishment and maintenance of the internal control structure is an important responsibility of the internal auditor.

c.   An exceptionally strong internal control structure is enough for the auditor to eliminate substantive tests on a significant account balance.

d.   The cost-benefit relationship is a primary criterion that should be considered in designing an internal control structure.

85. After obtaining an understanding of an entity's internal control structure, an auditor may assess control risk at the maximum level for some assertions because the auditor

a.   Believes the internal control policies and procedures are unlikely to be effective.

b.   Determines that the pertinent internal control structure elements are **not** well documented.

c.   Performs tests of controls to restrict detection risk to an acceptable level.

d.   Identifies internal control policies and procedures that are likely to prevent material misstatements.

86. The primary objective of procedures performed to obtain an understanding of the internal control structure is to provide an auditor with

a.   Evidential matter to use in reducing detection risk.

b.   Knowledge necessary to plan the audit.

c.   A basis from which to modify tests of controls.

d.   Information necessary to prepare flowcharts.

87. Which of the following audit techniques most likely would provide an auditor with the most assurance about the effectiveness of the operation of an internal control procedure?

a.   Inquiry of client personnel.

b.   Recomputation of account balance amounts.

c.   Observation of client personnel.

d.   Confirmation with outside parties.

88. Tracing bills of lading to sales invoices provides evidence that

a.   Shipments to customers were invoiced.

b.   Shipments to customers were recorded as sales.

c.   Recorded sales were shipped.

d.   Invoiced sales were shipped.

89. Employers bond employees who handle cash receipts because fidelity bonds reduce the possibility of employing dishonest individuals and

a.   Protect employees who make unintentional errors from possible monetary damages resulting from their errors.

b.   Deter dishonesty by making employees aware that insurance companies may investigate and prosecute dishonest acts.

c.   Facilitate an independent monitoring of the receiving and depositing of cash receipts.

d.   Force employees in positions of trust to take periodic vacations and rotate their assigned duties.

90. To determine whether accounts payable are complete, an auditor performs a test to verify that all merchandise received is recorded. The population of documents for this test consists of all

a.   Vendor's invoices.

b.   Purchase orders.

c.   Receiving reports.

d.   Canceled checks.

91. Which of the following control procedures is **not** usually performed in the vouchers payable department?

a.   Determining the mathematical accuracy of the vendor's invoice.

b.   Having an authorized person approve the voucher.

c.   Controlling the mailing of the check and remittance advice.

d.   Matching the receiving report with the purchase order.

92. Which of the following internal control procedures most likely addresses the completeness assertion for inventory?

a.   Work in process account is periodically reconciled with subsidiary records.

b.   Employees responsible for custody of finished goods do **not** perform the receiving function.

c.   Receiving reports are prenumbered and periodically reconciled.

d.   There is a separation of duties between payroll department and inventory accounting personnel.

93. The sampling unit in a test of controls pertaining to the existence of payroll transactions ordinarily is a(an)

a.   Clock card or time ticket.

b.   Employee Form W-2.

c.   Employee personnel record.

d.   Payroll register entry.

94. How do the scope, procedures, and purpose of an engagement to express an opinion on an entity's sytem of internal accounting control compare to those for obtaining an understanding of the internal control structure and assessing control risk as part of an audit?

	Scope	Procedures	Purpose
a.	Similar	Different	Similar
b.	Different	Similar	Similar
c.	Different	Different	Different
d.	Different	Similar	Different

95. When engaged to express an opinion on an entity's system of internal accounting control, an accountant should
   a. Obtain management's written representations acknowledging responsibility for establishing and maintaining the system.
   b. Qualify any opinion concerning management's assertion that the cost of correcting any weaknesses exceeds the benefits.
   c. Keep informed of events subsequent to the date of the report that might have affected the accountant's opinion.
   d. Disclaim an opinion on whether the system taken as a whole is sufficient to prevent or detect material errors or irregularities.

Problems

Problem 1   (1187,A2)

(15 to 25 minutes)

Green, CPA, has been engaged to audit the financial statements of Star Manufacturing, Inc. Star is a medium-sized entity that produces a wide variety of household goods. All acquisitions of materials are processed through the purchasing, receiving, accounts payable, and treasury functions.

Required:

Prepare the "Purchases" segment of the internal control questionnaire to be used in the evaluation of Star's internal control structure. Each question should elicit either a yes or no response.

Do **not** prepare the receiving, accounts payable, or treasury segments of the internal control questionnaire.

Do **not** discuss the internal controls over purchases.

Problem 2   (587,A4)

(15 to 25 minutes)

Martin, CPA, has been engaged to express an opinion on Beta Manufacturing Company's system of internal accounting control in effect as of June 1, 1987.

Required:

a. Compare Martin's examination of the system of internal accounting control for the purpose of expressing an opinion on it with the consideration of internal control made as part of an examination of the financial statements in accordance with generally accepted auditing standards. The comparison should be made as to the 1) scope, 2) purpose, and 3) timing of the engagements, and 4) users of the reports.

b. Identify the major contents of Martin's report expressing an opinion on Beta's system of internal accounting control. Do **not** draft the report.

Problem 3   (586,A4)

(15 to 25 minutes)

Harris, CPA, has been engaged to audit the financial statements of the Spartan Drug Store, Inc. Spartan is a medium sized retail outlet that sells a wide variety of consumer goods. All sales are for cash or check. Cashiers utilize cash registers to process these transactions. There are no receipts by mail and there are no credit card or charge sales.

Required:

Construct the "Processing Cash Collections" segment of the internal control questionnaire on "Cash Receipts" to be used in the consideration of the internal control structure for the Spartan Drug Store, Inc. Each question should elicit either a yes or no response. Do **not** discuss the internal controls over cash sales.

Problem 4 appears on the following page.

Problem 5   (1184,A3)

(15 to 25 minutes)

Cassandra Corporation, a manufacturing company, periodically invests large sums in marketable equity securities. The investment policy is established by the Investment Committee of the Board of Directors, and the treasurer is responsible for carrying out the Investment Committee's directives. All securities are stored in a bank safe deposit vault.

The independent auditor's internal control questionnaire with respect to Cassandra's investments in marketable equity securities contains the following three questions:

• Is investment policy established by the Investment Committee of the Board of Directors?

• Is the treasurer solely responsible for carrying out the Investment Committee's directives?

• Are all securities stored in a bank safe deposit vault?

Required:

In addition to the above three questions, what questions should the auditor's internal control questionnaire include with respect to the company's investments in marketable equity securities?

Problem 4 (583,A5)

The following illustrates a Manual System for Executing Purchases and Cash Disbursements Transactions.

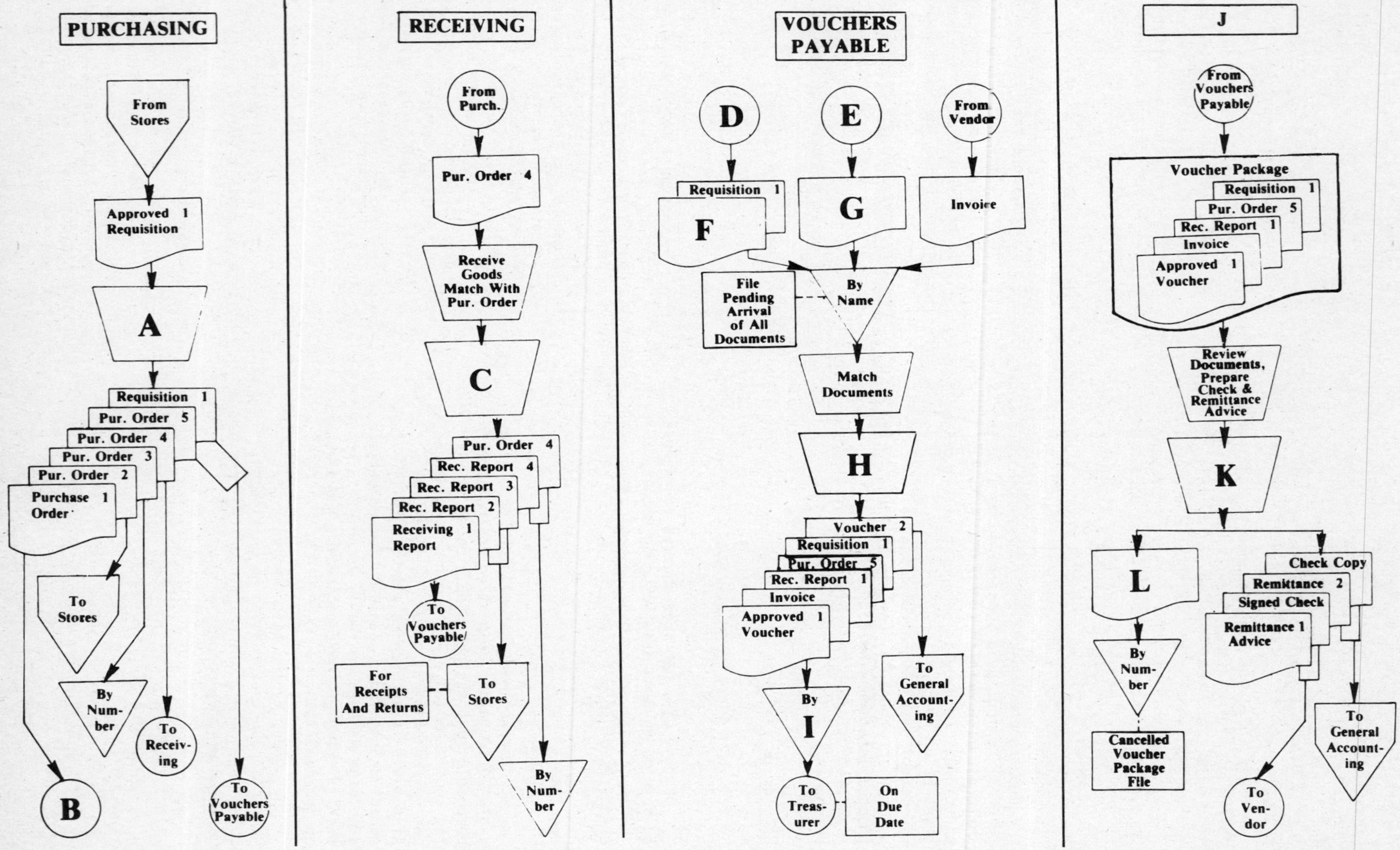

(15 to 25 minutes)

PURCHASING

From Stores → Approved 1 Requisition → A → Requisition 1 / Pur. Order 5 / Pur. Order 4 / Pur. Order 3 / Pur. Order 2 / Purchase 1 Order → To Stores / By Number → To Receiving → To Vouchers Payable / B

RECEIVING

From Purch. → Pur. Order 4 → Receive Goods Match With Pur. Order → C → Pur. Order 4 / Rec. Report 4 / Rec. Report 3 / Rec. Report 2 / Receiving 1 Report → To Vouchers Payable / To Stores → By Number / For Receipts And Returns

VOUCHERS PAYABLE

D → Requisition 1 / F
E → G
From Vendor → Invoice
By Name / File Pending Arrival of All Documents → Match Documents → H → Voucher 2 / Requisition 1 / Pur. Order 5 / Rec. Report 1 / Invoice / Approved 1 Voucher → To General Accounting / By I → To Treasurer / On Due Date

J → From Vouchers Payable → Voucher Package: Requisition 1 / Pur. Order 5 / Rec. Report 1 / Invoice / Approved Voucher → Review Documents, Prepare Check & Remittance Advice → K → Check Copy / Remittance 2 / Signed Check / Remittance 1 Advice → To General Accounting / To Vendor ; L → By Number → Cancelled Voucher Package File

Required: Indicate what each of the letters (A) through (L) represent. Do not discuss adequacies or inadequacies in the internal control structure.

Problem 6   (581,A4)

(15 to 25 minutes)

Taylor, a CPA, has been engaged to audit the financial statements of University Books, Incorporated. University Books maintains a large revolving cash fund exclusively for the purpose of buying used books from students for cash. The cash fund is active all year because the nearby university offers a large variety of courses with varying starting and completion dates throughout the year.

Receipts are prepared for each purchase and reimbursement vouchers are periodically submitted.

Required:

Construct an internal control questionnaire to be used in the consideration of the internal control structure of University Book's buying segments revolving cash fund. The internal control questionnaire should elicit a yes or no response. Do not discuss the internal controls over books that are purchased.

Problem 7   (580,A5)

(15 to 25 minutes)

A CPA's audit working papers contain a narrative description of a segment of the Croyden Factory, Inc. payroll system and an accompanying flowchart as follows:

NARRATIVE

The internal control structure with respect to the personnel department is well-functioning and is not included in the accompanying flowchart.

At the beginning of each work week payroll clerk No. 1 reviews the payroll department files to determine the employment status of factory employees and then prepares time cards and distributes them as each individual arrives at work. This payroll clerk, who is also responsible for custody of the signature stamp machine, verifies the identity of each payee before delivering signed checks to the foreman.

At the end of each work week the foreman distributes payroll checks for the preceding work week. Concurrent with this activity, the foreman reviews the current week's employee time cards, notes the regular and overtime hours worked on a summary form, and initials the aforementioned time cards. The foreman then delivers all time cards and unclaimed payroll checks to payroll clerk No. 2.

Required:

a. Based upon the narrative and accompanying flowchart, what are the weaknesses in the internal control structure?

b. Based upon the narrative and accompanying flowchart, what inquiries should be made with respect to clarifying the existence of possible additional weaknesses in the internal control structure?

Note: Do not discuss the internal control structure of the personnel department.

Flowchart appears on following page.

Problem 8   (1180,A4)

(15 to 25 minutes)

The Art Appreciation Society operates a museum for the benefit and enjoyment of the community. During hours when the museum is open to the public, two clerks who are positioned at the entrance collect a five dollar admission fee from each nonmember patron. Members of the Art Appreciation Society are permitted to enter free of charge upon presentation of their membership cards.

At the end of each day one of the clerks delivers the proceeds to the treasurer. The treasurer counts the cash in the presence of the clerk and places it in a safe. Each Friday afternoon the treasurer and one of the clerks deliver all cash held in the safe to the bank, and receive an authenticated deposit slip which provides the basis for the weekly entry in the cash receipts journal.

The board of directors of the Art Appreciation Society has identified a need to improve their internal control structure over cash admission fees. The board has determined that the cost of installing turnstiles, sales booths or otherwise altering the physical layout of the museum will greatly exceed any benefits which may be derived. However, the board has agreed that the sale of admission tickets must be an integral part of its improvement efforts.

Smith has been asked by the board of directors of the Art Appreciation Society to review the internal control over cash admission fees and provide suggestions for improvement.

Required:

Indicate weaknesses in the existing internal control structure over cash admission fees, which Smith should identify, and recommend one improvement for each of the weaknesses identified.

Problem 7 (continued)

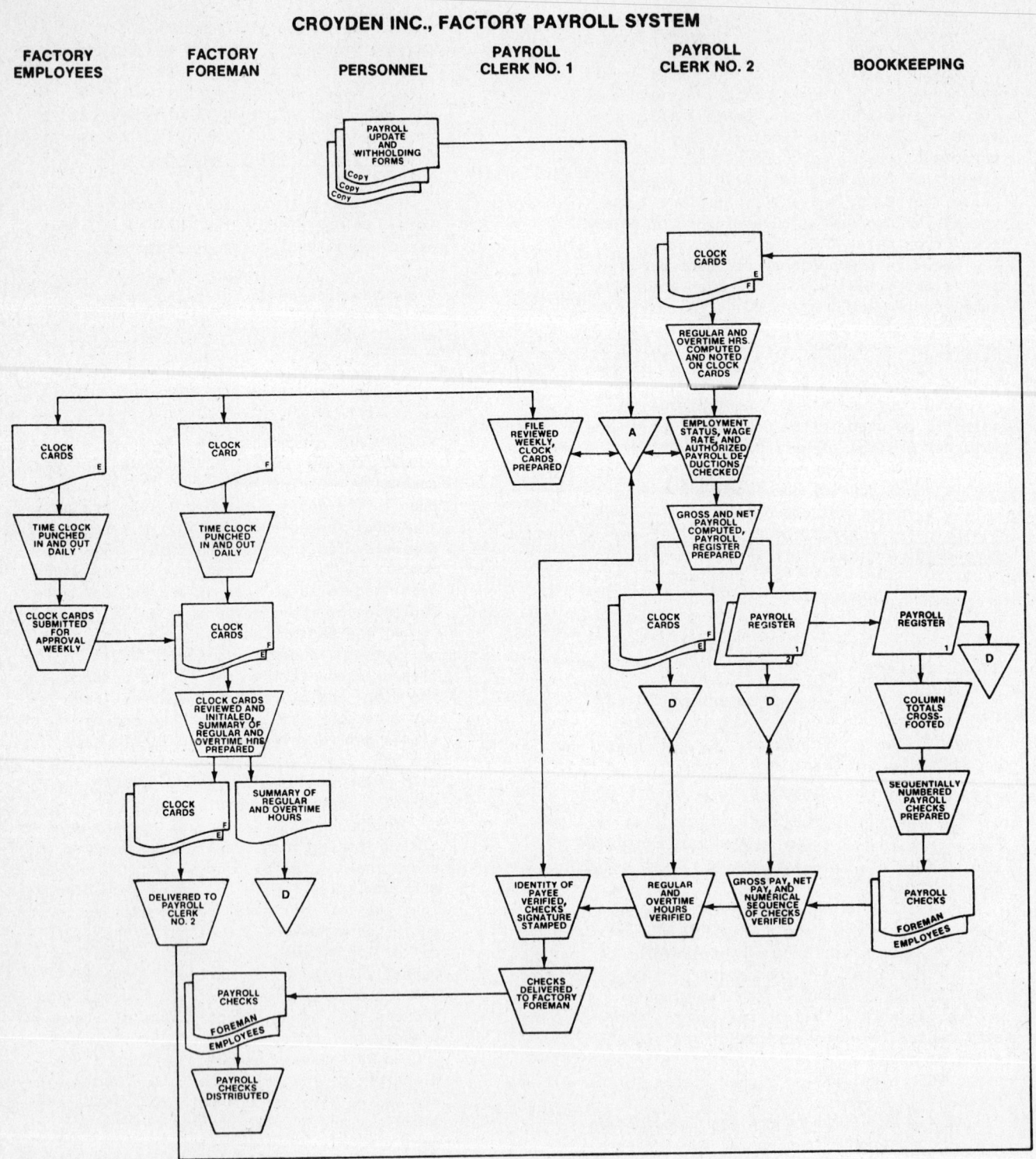

CROYDEN INC., FACTORY PAYROLL SYSTEM

Organize the answer as indicated in the following illustrative example:

Weaknesses	Recommendation
1. There is no basis for establishing the documentation of the number of paying patrons.	1. Prenumbered admission tickets should be issued upon payment of the admission fee.

Problem 9   (1175,A6)

(20 to 25 minutes)

Anthony, CPA, prepared the flowchart on the following page which portrays the raw materials purchasing function of one of Anthony's clients, a medium-sized manufacturing company, from the preparation of initial documents through the vouching of invoices for payment in accounts payable. The flowchart was a portion of the work performed on the audit engagement to consider internal control.

Required:

Identify and explain the structure and control weaknesses evident from the flowchart on the following page. Include the internal control weaknesses resulting from activities performed or not performed. All documents are prenumbered.

Flowchart appears on following page.

Problem 10   (579,A2)

(15 to 25 minutes)

A partially-completed charge sales systems flowchart follows. The flowchart depicts the charge sales activities of the Bottom Manufacturing Corporation.

A customer's purchase order is received and a six-part sales order is prepared, therefrom. The six copies are initially distributed as follows:

Copy No. 1 – Billing copy--to billing department.
Copy No. 2 – Shipping copy--to shipping department.
Copy No. 3 – Credit copy--to credit department.
Copy No. 4 – Stock request copy--to credit department.
Copy No. 5 – Customer copy--to customer.
Copy No. 6 – Sales order copy--file in sales order department.

When each copy of the sales order reaches the applicable department or destination it calls for specific internal control procedures and related documents. Some of the procedures and related documents are indicated on the

flowchart. Other procedures and documents are labeled letters a to r.

Required:

List the procedures or the internal documents that are labeled letters c to r in the flowchart of Bottom Manufacturing Corporation's charge sales system.
Organize your answer as follows (note that explanations of the letters a and b which appear in the flowchart are entered as examples):

Flowchart Symbol Letter	Procedures or Internal Document
a.	Prepare six-part sales order.
b.	File by order number.

Problem 9 (continued)

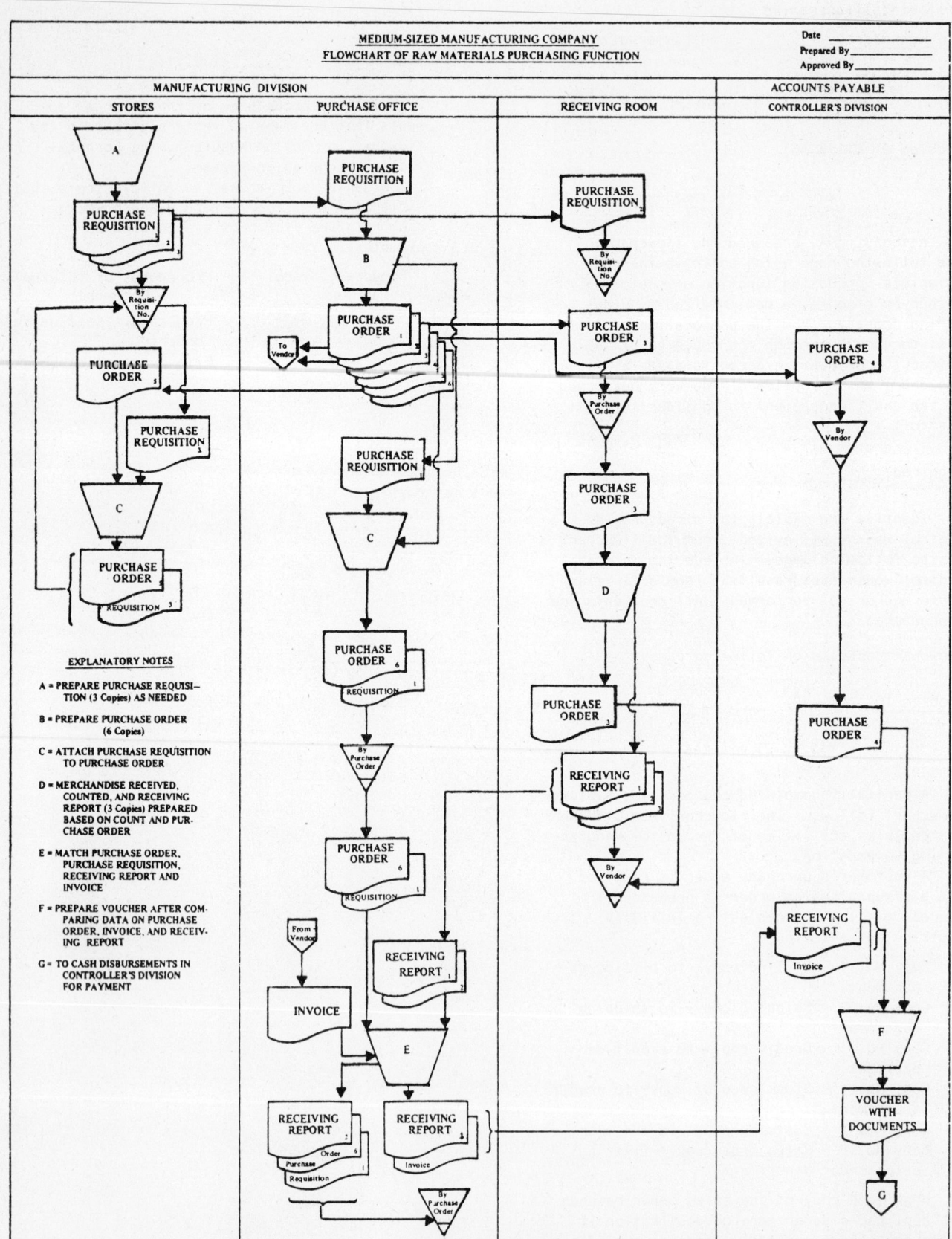

MEDIUM-SIZED MANUFACTURING COMPANY
FLOWCHART OF RAW MATERIALS PURCHASING FUNCTION

Date _____
Prepared By _____
Approved By _____

MANUFACTURING DIVISION — STORES | PURCHASE OFFICE | RECEIVING ROOM | **ACCOUNTS PAYABLE** — CONTROLLER'S DIVISION

EXPLANATORY NOTES

A = PREPARE PURCHASE REQUISI-
TION (3 Copies) AS NEEDED

B = PREPARE PURCHASE ORDER
(6 Copies)

C = ATTACH PURCHASE REQUISITION
TO PURCHASE ORDER

D = MERCHANDISE RECEIVED,
COUNTED, AND RECEIVING
REPORT (3 Copies) PREPARED
BASED ON COUNT AND PUR-
CHASE ORDER

E = MATCH PURCHASE ORDER,
PURCHASE REQUISITION,
RECEIVING REPORT AND
INVOICE

F = PREPARE VOUCHER AFTER COM-
PARING DATA ON PURCHASE
ORDER, INVOICE, AND RECEIV-
ING REPORT

G = TO CASH DISBURSEMENTS IN
CONTROLLER'S DIVISION
FOR PAYMENT

Problem 10   (continued)

BOTTOM MANUFACTURING CORPORATION
Flowchart of Credit Sales Activities

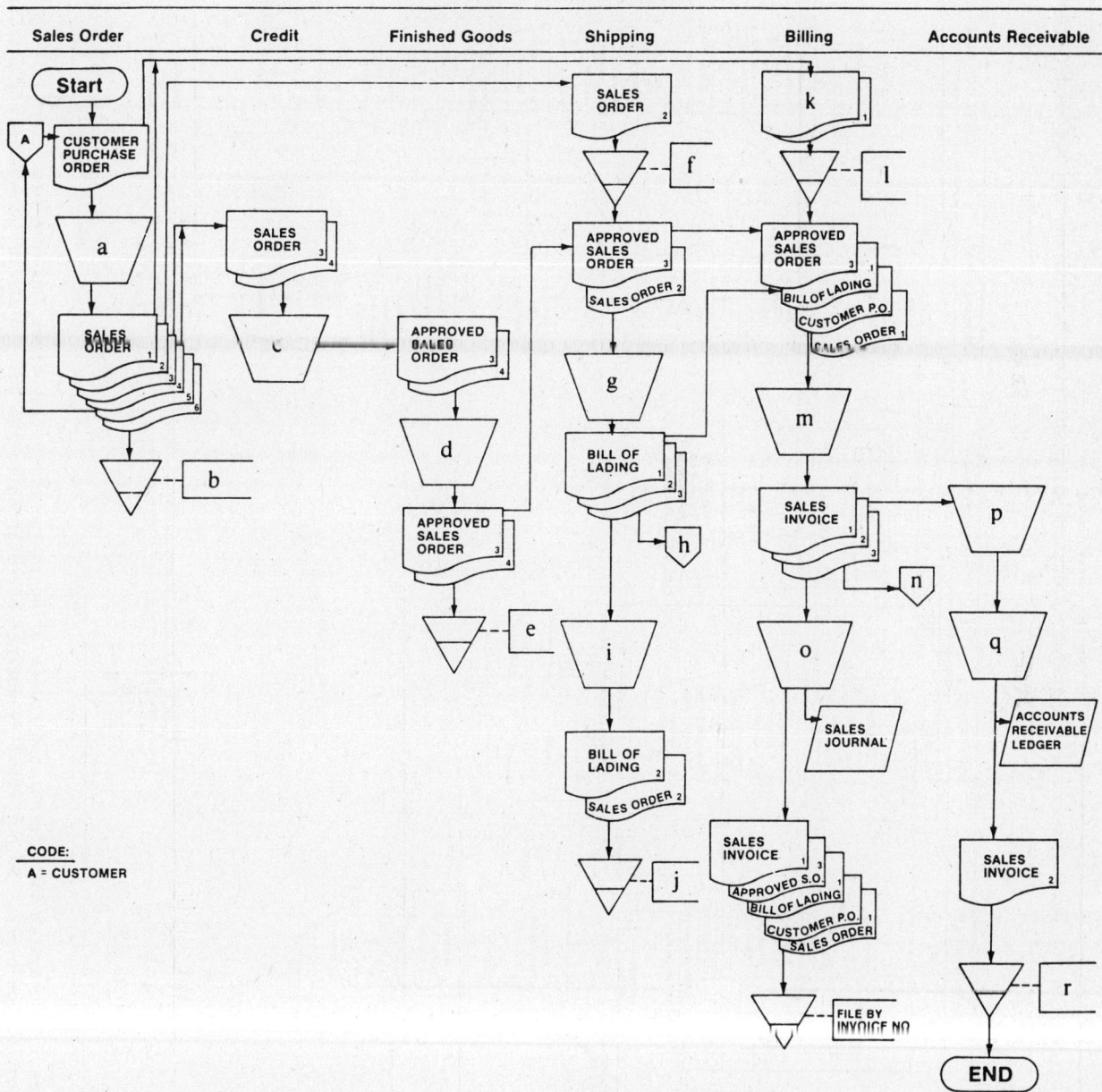

CODE:
A = CUSTOMER

Problem 11   (588,A4)   (15 to 25 minutes)

The following flowchart depicts the activities relating to the sales, shipping, billing, and collecting processes used by Newton Hardware, Inc.

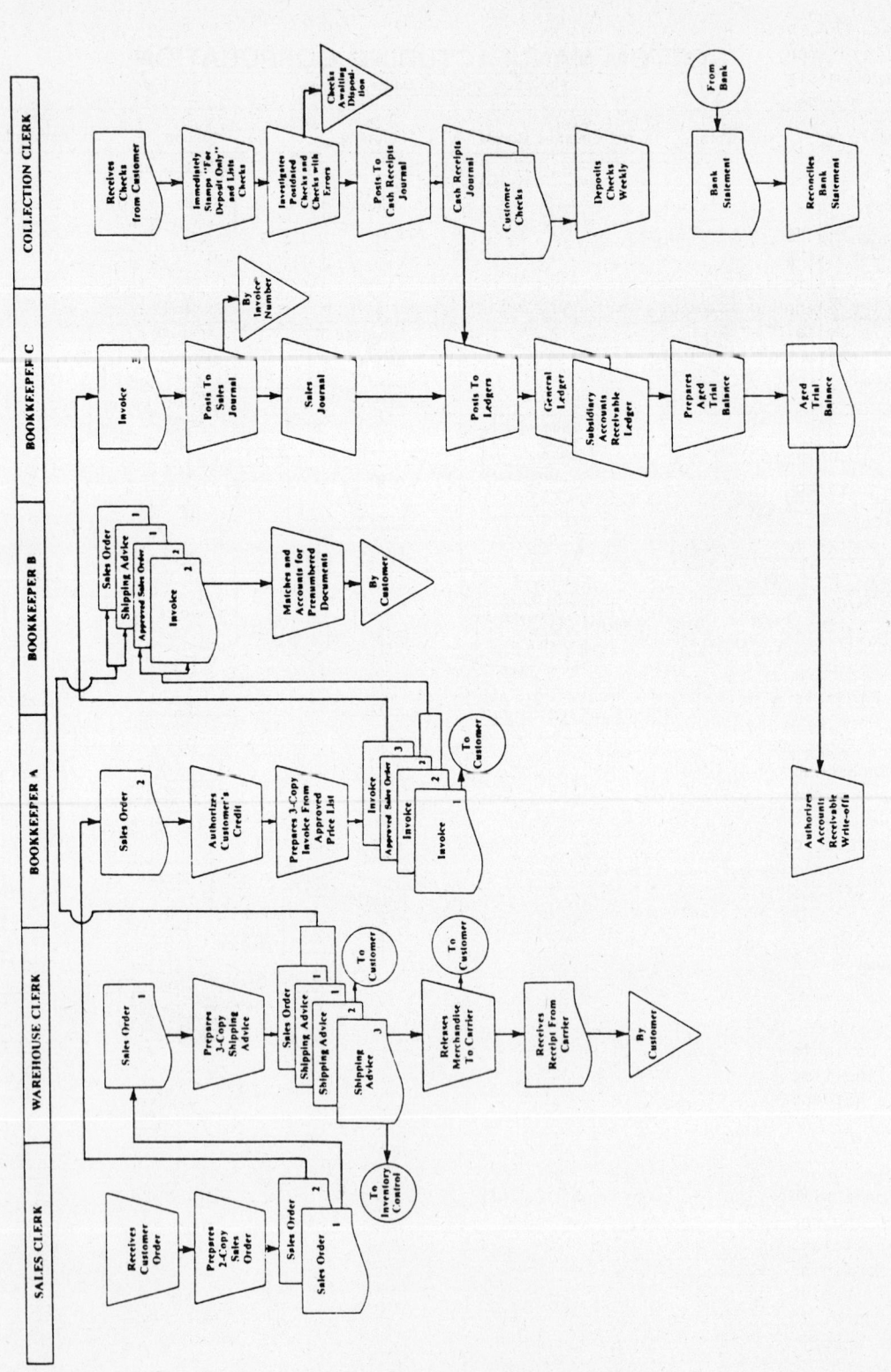

Required:
Identify the weaknesses in the system of internal control relating to the activities of a) the warehouse clerk, b) book-keeper A, and c) the collection clerk. Do not identify weaknesses relating to the sales clerk or bookkeepers B and C. Do not discuss recommendations concerning the correction of these weaknesses.

Problem 12   (589,A3)

(15 to 25 minutes)

Taylor, CPA, has been engaged to audit the financial statements of Johnson's Coat Outlet, Inc., a medium-sized mail-order retail store that sells a wide variety of coats to the public.

Required:

Prepare the "Shipment" segment of Taylor's internal control questionnaire. Each question should elicit either a yes or no response.

Do not prepare questions relating to the cash receipts, sales returns and allowances, billing, inventory control, or other segments.

Use the following format:

Question	Yes	No

Problem 13   (1189,A5)

(15 to 25 minutes)

A CPA's audit working papers include the narrative description below of the cash receipts and billing portions of the internal control structure of Parktown Medical Center, Inc. Parktown is a small health care provider that is owned by a publicly held corporation. It employs seven salaried physicians, ten nurses, three support staff in a common laboratory, and three clerical workers. The clerical workers perform such tasks as reception, correspondence, cash receipts, billing, and appointment scheduling and are adequately bonded. They are referred to in the narrative as "office manager," "clerk #1," and "clerk #2."

NARRATIVE

Most patients pay for services by cash or check at the time services are rendered. Credit is not approved by the clerical staff. The physician who is to perform the respective services approves credit based on an interview. When credit is approved, the physician files a memo with the billing clerk (clerk #2) to set up the receivable from data generated by the physician.

The servicing physician prepares a charge slip that is given to clerk #1 for pricing and preparation of the patient's bill. Clerk #1 transmits a copy of the bill to clerk #2 for preparation of the revenue summary and for posting in the accounts receivable subsidiary ledger.

The cash receipts functions are performed by clerk #1, who receives cash and checks directly from patients and gives each patient a prenumbered cash receipt. Clerk #1 opens the mail and immediately stamps all checks "for deposit only" and lists cash and checks for deposit. The cash and checks are deposited daily by the office manager. The list of cash and checks together with the related remittance advices are forwarded by clerk #1 to clerk #2. Clerk #1 also serves as receptionist and performs general correspondence duties.

Clerk #2 prepares and sends monthly statements to patients with unpaid balances. Clerk #2 also prepares the cash receipts journal and is responsible for the accounts receivable subsidiary ledger. No other clerical employee is permitted access to the accounts receivable subsidiary ledger. Uncollectible accounts are written off by clerk #2 only after the physician who performed the respective services believes the account to be uncollectible and communicates the write-off approval to the office manager. The office manager then issues a write-off memo that clerk #2 processes.

The office manager supervises the clerks, issues write-off memos, schedules appointments for the doctors, makes bank deposits, reconciles bank statements, and performs general correspondence duties.

Additional services are performed monthly by a local accountant who posts summaries prepared by the clerks to the general ledger, prepares income statements, and files the appropriate payroll forms and tax returns. The accountant reports directly to the parent corporation.

Required:

Based only on the information in the narrative, describe the reportable conditions and one resulting misstatement that could occur and not be prevented or detected by Parktown's internal control structure concerning the cash receipts and billing function. Do not describe how to correct the reportable conditions and potential misstatements. Use the format illustrated below.

Reportable condition	Potential misstatement
There is no control to verify that fees are recorded and billed at authorized rates and terms.	Accounts receivable could be overstated and uncollectible accounts understated because of the lack of controls.

Multiple Choice Answers

1. d	20. b	39. b	58. b	77. d
2. b	21. b	40. d	59. c	78. c
3. a	22. b	41. b	60. a	79. b
4. b	23. b	42. d	61. a	80. c
5. a	24. a	43. c	62. d	81. a
6. d	25. c	44. b	63. d	82. a
7. d	26. a	45. c	64. c	83. b
8. d	27. b	46. d	65. b	84. d
9. c	28. d	47. c	66. c	85. a
10. c	29. c	48. a	67. c	86. b
11. b	30. c	49. c	68. b	87. c
12. a	31. a	50. d	69. b	88. a
13. b	32. d	51. d	70. a	89. b
14. b	33. b	52. c	71. c	90. c
15. c	34. b	53. b	72. d	91. c
16. d	35. c	54. d	73. b	92. c
17. b	36. b	55. c	74. d	93. d
18. c	37. a	56. a	75. a	94. d
19. d	38. c	57. a	76. a	95. a

Multiple Choice Answer Explanations

A. The Nature of Internal Control

A.1. The Internal Control Structure-- Overall

1. (587,A1,2) (d) The requirement is to identify the meaning of the concept of reasonable assurance. Reasonable assurance recognizes that the cost of internal control should not exceed the benefits expected to be derived (AU 319.14). Answers (a), (b), and (c) all represent statements which are not part of the definition of the concept of reasonable assurance.

2. (1188,A1,32) (b) The requirement is to identify the functions that should be segregated in an effective internal control structure. Answer (b) is correct because authorizing transactions, recording transactions, and maintaining custody of assets should be segregated (AU 319.11) Answers (a), (c), and (d) are all incorrect because they suggest a less fundamental separation of functions.

3. (1183,A1,15) (a) The requirement is to determine the function which should not be the responsibility of the treasurer's department. Data processing should not be a responsibility of the treasurer's department because it is a recordkeeping function which is incompatible with the treasurer's department's custodial responsibility. Answers (b) and (c) are incorrect because under a good internal control structure, the treasurer's department is typically responsible for the custody over cash and securities. Answer (d) is incorrect because the treasurer, as an officer, will often be involved in establishing credit policies.

4. (585,A1,7) (b) The requirement is to determine the area for which internal controls are not designed to provide reasonable assurance. Answer (b) is correct because no internal control structure can provide reasonable assurance that irregularities will be eliminated; AU 319.15 describes the limitations of internal control.

A.2. Major Elements of the Internal Control Structure

5. (589,A1,11) (a) The requirement is to identify the reply that is not an element of an entity's internal control structure. Answer (a) is correct because while auditors assess control risk as a part of their consideration of internal control, it is not an element of an entity's internal control structure. Answers (b), (c), and (d) are incorrect because control procedures, the accounting system, and the control environment are the three elements of an entity's internal control structure (AU 319.08).

A.3. Related Topics

6. (1186,A1,18) (d) Answer (d) is correct because the Foreign Corrupt Practices Act makes payment of bribes to foreign officials illegal and requires publicly held companies to maintain systems of internal control sufficient to provide reasonable assurances that internal control objectives are met (AU 642.12). Answers (a), (b) and (c) are incorrect because they represent requirements not included in the Act.

B. The Auditor's Consideration of Internal Control

B.1. Obtaining an Understanding to Plan the Audit

7. (1183,A1,52) (d) The requirement is to determine the correct statement with respect to the auditor's required documentation of the client's internal control structure. An auditor may document his/her understanding of the structure and his/her conclusions about the design of that structure in the form of answers to a questionnaire, narrative memorandums, flowcharts, decision tables, or any other form that the auditor considers appropriate in the circumstances (AU 319.26). Answers (a) and (b) are, thus, incorrect because they suggest restrictions which do not exist in practice. Answer (c) is incorrect since at a minimum a list of reasons for nonreliance must be provided.

8. (586,A1,25) (d) The requirement is to determine the time at which a questionnaire is most associated during a consideration of internal control. Answer (d) is correct because questionnaires may be used to document the auditor's understanding of the internal control structure (AU 319.26). Answer (a) is incorrect because the purpose of tests of controls is to provide reasonable assurance that the accounting control procedures (as summarized in a questionnaire, for example) are being applied as prescribed. Answer (b) is incorrect because substantive tests generally follow the consideration of the internal control structure. Answer (c) is incorrect because analytical procedures do not normally include preparation of a questionnaire (see AU 329).

9. (589,A1,10) (c) The requirement is to identify the statement which is **not** a reason an auditor should obtain an understanding of the elements of an entity's internal control structure in planning an audit. Answer (c) is correct because auditors consider the oper-ating effectiveness of the internal control structure to assess control risk, not to plan the audit (AU 319.27-.38). Answers (a), (b), and (d) are incorrect because in planning the audit, auditors need to obtain an adequate understanding of an entity's internal control structure in order to identify types of poten-tial misstatements, design substantive tests, and consider factors that affect the risk of material misstatements (AU 319.16).

10. (1189,A1,39) (c) The requirement is to determine why an auditor who is obtaining an understanding of an entity's control environ-ment should concentrate on the substance of management's policies and procedures rather than their form. Answer (c) is correct be-cause management may establish appropriate policies and procedures but not act on them (AU 319.20). Answer (a) is less accurate than (c) because an auditor's primary emphasis is on evaluating the operating effectiveness of policies, not their propriety. Answer (b) is incorrect because while it is a true statement that the board of directors may not be aware of management's attitude, this is not the pri-mary reason why auditors emphasize substance over form. Answer (d) is incorrect because while it may sometimes be true that weak poli-cies and procedures may lead to a situation in which control risk is assessed at the maximum level, (i.e., no reliance is placed on them) this is not necessarily the case and is not the reason why an auditor emphasizes substance over form.

B.2. Assessing Control Risk

11. (1189,A1,40) (b) The requirement is to determine the next audit stage when an auditor has obtained an understanding of an entity's internal control structure and has assessed control risk. Answer (b) is correct because the auditor next will consider whether evidential matter is available to support a further reduction in the assessed level of control risk (AU 319.43). Answer (a) is incorrect because tests of controls may or may not be performed depending upon whether the auditor believes a further reduction in the assessed level of control risk is both possible and cost justified. Answer (c) is incorrect because analytical procedures are not used to validate the assessed level of control risk; they are substantive in nature. Answer (d) is incorrect because while an auditor may investigate the misstatements that have been detected by an internal control structure, it is likely that this will be done while obtaining an understanding of the system.

B.3. Tests of Controls

12. (588,A1,12) (a) The requirement is to identify the procedure most likely to be in-cluded as part of an auditor's tests of con-trols. Answer (a) is correct because tests of controls include inspection of written docu-mentation (AU 319.47). Answers (b), (c), and (d) are incorrect because reconciliation, con-firmation, and analytical procedures all relate more directly to substantive testing. See AU 326 for a discussion of evidential matter.

13. (1189,A1,41) (b) The requirement is to identify the area in which it is **least** likely that tests of controls will be performed. An-swer (b) is correct because, while the client may use revenue and expense information by product line, the auditor is concerned with the reporting of revenue and expense informa-tion in total. Answer (a) is incorrect be-cause when a high volume of marketable securi-ties exists, auditors will generally perform tests of controls on approval of purchases and sales of those securities. Answer (c) is in-correct because auditors will observe the se-gregation of responsibilities--a control which often may provide no documentary trail (AU 319.50). Answer (d) is incorrect because auditors will perform tests of controls com-paring receiving reports and vendors' invoices with purchase orders to determine whether the internal control structure is likely to record transactions completely and in the proper period.

14. (1189,A1,44) (b) The requirement is to identify the manner in which evidential matter concerning proper segregation of duties is ordinarily best obtained. Answer (b) is correct because the segregation of duties will often provide no documentary trail and thus observation of the employee who applies the control procedure is best (AU 319.49-.50). Answer (a) is incorrect because in many circumstances third-party documents containing the initials of those who applied the control procedures may not be present. Answer (c) is incorrect because the preparation of a flowchart provides only limited evidential matter as to the operating effectiveness of the control; flowcharts are normally used to document an understanding of an internal control system, not to obtain evidential matter regarding any of the specific controls being used. Answer (d) is incorrect because auditors will not, in general, make inquiries of co-workers concerning the employee who applies the control procedures.

15. (587,A1,7) (c) The requirement is to identify the _least_ likely type of evidence the auditor will examine to determine whether operations are in compliance with the internal control structure. Answer (c) is correct because confirmation of accounts receivable is a substantive test, not a test of a control. Answer (a) is incorrect because records documenting the usage of EDP programs may be tested to determine whether access is appropriately controlled. Answer (b) is incorrect because examining canceled supporting documents may help the auditor to determine that the structure will not allow duplicate billing to result in multiple payments. Answer (d) is incorrect because proper signatures will help the auditor to determine whether the authorization controls are functioning adequately.

16. (1189,A1,36) (d) The requirement is to determine the primary purpose for which an auditor uses the knowledge provided by the understanding of the internal control structure and the assessed level of control risk. Answer (d) is correct because the auditor uses such knowledge in determining the nature, timing, and extent of substantive tests for financial statement assertions (AU 319.05). Answer (a) is incorrect because it is incomplete. For example, while auditors are concerned with the safeguarding of assets, they also need to determine whether the financial statement information is accurate. Answer (b) is incorrect for reasons similar to (a) in that determining whether opportunities are available for committing and concealing irregularities is incomplete since this knowledge is also used to ascertain whether

the chance of errors is minimized. Answer (c) is incorrect because knowledge provided by the understanding of the internal control structure and the assessed level of control risk is not used to modify initial assessments of inherent risk and preliminary judgments about materiality levels. This knowledge is unrelated to those processes.

B.4. General Questions

17. (1188,A1,31) (b) The requirement is to determine the nature of the auditor's concern related to considering internal control. Answer (b) is correct because, when considering internal control, the auditor obtains knowledge of the types of misstatements that could occur, the risk that such misstatements may occur, and the factors that influence the design of substantive tests (AU 508.19). Answer (a) is incorrect because financial statement audits are not directed at client operational efficiency as much as detecting errors and irregularities. Answers (c) and (d) are incorrect because the effectiveness of internal control is limited in that collusion and management override may not be detected (see AU 319.15 for information on the limitations of internal control).

18. (588,A1,1) (c) The requirement is to identify the correct statement regarding a likely result when an auditor has concluded that the client's internal control structure is functioning as intended. Answer (c) is correct because when the auditor has determined that the internal control structure functions as intended, there will be either (1) a reduction of substantive tests, or (2) no change in substantive tests. An increase would only be expected when the controls are _not_ functioning as intended. AU 319.61-.64 discusses the relationship between the risks which are involved. Answers (a), (b), and (d) are all incorrect because once the auditor has concluded that the controls are functioning as intended, tests of controls, determination of control procedures that would prevent or detect errors and irregularities, and consideration of whether transactions are properly recorded will already have been performed.

19. (588,A1,8) (d) The requirement is to identify a way that an auditor may compensate for a weakness in internal control. Answer (d) is correct because increasing analytical procedures decreases detection risk in a manner which may counterbalance the condition in internal control. In effect, the condition in control is compensated for by increased substantive testing. See AU 312 for

the relationships among audit risk and its components risks--inherent risk, control risk, and detection risk. Answer (a) is incorrect because increasing both control risk (through a condition in internal control) and detection risk increases audit risks. In addition, control risk and detection risk do not compensate for one another. Answer (b) is incorrect because increasing the extent of tests of controls is unlikely to be effective since the condition is known to exist. Answer (c) is incorrect because it is not generally appropriate to increase the judgment as to audit risk based on the results obtained.

20. (1182,A1,27) (b) The requirement is to determine the relationship between reliance on internal control and reliance on substantive tests. Inverse (AU 319.63) is correct because as internal control is relied upon to a lesser extent substantive tests are relied upon to a greater extent. Answer (c) is incorrect because it describes the opposite relationship. Answers (a) and (d) appear to be nonsense answers.

21. (1188,A1,40) (b) The requirement is to identify the point in an ordinary sales transaction in which a lack of specific authorization would be of least concern to an auditor. Answer (b) is correct because the selling of ordinary goods for cash is not likely to require a specific authorization. Answers (a), (c), and (d) are all of concern because discount, credit, and shipping decisions will directly affect both short-term and long-term profits of the client.

22. (1187,A1,56) (b) The requirement is to determine the auditor's overall objective in selecting a sample from the file of shipping documents to determine whether invoices were prepared. Answer (b) is correct because the test will provide information on whether all items shipped (generally the firm's sales) have been completely invoiced. Answers (a) and (c) are incorrect because accuracy and control, while related to a number of the audit objectives, are not themselves audit objectives. Answer (d) is incorrect because existence pertains more directly to determining whether recorded transactions have occurred. This test assumes the transactions have occurred and addresses whether or not all of these transactions are included in the financial statements. The information on the objectives of auditors is presented in AU 326.

23. (1186,A1,22) (b) The requirement is to identify the population an auditor would sample from to determine whether the internal control structure operated effectively to minimize errors of failing to invoice a shipment. Answer (b) is correct because the bill of lading file will represent shipments and will allow the auditor to determine whether an invoice was present for each shipment in his/her sample. Answer (a), while a possibility, is not as complete as (b) because customer orders might not have been approved (and therefore, not shipped) or be in process at year end. Answer (c) is incorrect because the open invoice file will generally be composed of orders not shipped. Answer (d) is incorrect because the sales invoice file will only include shipments that have been invoiced.

24. (586,A1,45) (a) The requirement is to determine which department should match shipping documents with sales orders and daily sales summaries. Answer (a) is correct because billing, upon receiving the shipping documents, will match sales orders and sales summaries to ensure that all shipments have been billed and begin the recordkeeping process. Answer (b) is incorrect because the shipping department has custody of the goods and should not be responsible for determining that billing (recordkeeping) is initiated. Answer (c) is incorrect because the credit department serves an authorization function, not recordkeeping. Answer (d) is incorrect because the sales order department will secure sales, but not control the detailed recordkeeping for them.

25. (578,A1,9) (c) Lapping of trade accounts receivable is an abstraction of funds and subsequent delay in crediting receipts to accounts receivable. If the customers sent payments directly to a depository bank, there is no opportunity for abstractions or subsequent misapplication. Answer (a) is incorrect because lapping involves incorrect entries in the subsidiary ledgers, not the general ledger. Answers (b) and (d) are incorrect because lapping can occur by forging checks, i.e., there is no requirement that abstraction be made directly from cash.

26. (1188,A1,41) (a) The requirement is to identify the method of concealing a misappropriation of cash receipts from credit sales which would least likely be detected by the auditor. Answer (a) is correct because understating the sales journal (e.g., not recording the sale) and subsequent unrecorded collection of the cash would be very difficult to detect since none of the information would have been recorded in the accounting records; this will result in a situation in which the

records balance, yet are incomplete. Answers (b) and (c) are incorrect because misstatements of either the control or subsidiary receivable ledger will be easy to detect since they will be out of balance. Answer (d) is incorrect because understating cash receipts will result in overstated receivables, a situation which a number of audit procedures will detect (e.g., turnover ratios, examination of details of bank deposit tickets, confirmations).

27. (1182,A1,19) (b) The requirement is to determine who should prepare a remittance advice when the customer fails to include one with a remittance. Remittances should be opened by an individual such as a receptionist who is independent of the sales function. That individual will prepare any needed remittance advices. The credit manager [answer (a)], the sales manager [answer (c)], and the accounts receivable clerk [answer (d)] are all incorrect because all of these individuals perform functions related to sales.

28. (1187,A1,47) (d) The requirement is to identify the most likely result of ineffective internal control in the revenue cycle. Answer (d) is correct because authorization of credit memos by personnel in sales would not detect any collusion between the sales people and customers, or the manipulation of income between periods by recording fictitious sales in one period that are reversed by credit memos in the following period. Authorization of credit memos should be done by a department independent of sales, such as the credit department. Answer (a) is incorrect because fictitious transactions would be expected to overstate both revenues and receivables. Answer (b) is incorrect because the recording of an entry in a subsidiary account will not in general affect the shipping of goods. Answer (c) is incorrect because omission of shipping documents would result in an understatement of receivables, not an overstatement of inventory.

C. Accounting Cycles
C.1. Sales, Receivables, and Cash Receipts

29. (1188,A1,39) (c) The requirement is to identify the control which would offset a weakness that allowed the accounts receivable clerk to approve credit memos and to have access to cash. Note that such a weakness may lead to an irregularity in which the accounts receivable clerk receives and keeps cash payments while issuing a fraudulent credit memo as the basis for a credit to the

customer's account. Answer (c) is correct because the owner's review of credit memos could help establish that fraudulent memos had not been issued for receivables which had in actuality been collected by the clerk; for example, when reviewing credit memos the owner would expect to see a receiving report for sales returns for which credit memos have been generated. Answer (a) is incorrect because the bookkeeper may be able to maintain the records in such a manner as to avoid billing errors related to the irregularity, and therefore a review of billings and postings may not reveal such an irregularity. Answer (b) is incorrect because month-end reconciliation of checking accounts with the monthly bank statement will not reflect cash that has been improperly diverted by the accounts receivable clerk. Answer (d) is incorrect because the accounts receivable clerk should be able to maintain the detail and ledger amount in balance and thereby avoid detection.

30. (587,A1,12) (c) The requirement is to determine the approval function that should not be performed by the individual who maintains the accounts receivable subsidiary ledger. Answer (c) is correct because the recordkeeping ledger maintenance function should not be combined with a related authorization function, here write offs of customer accounts. Answer (a) is incorrect because the function of approving employee overtime wages is independent of the receivable function. Answer (b) is incorrect because the combination of the credit approval function and the accounts receivable subsidiary ledger maintenance function would not result in a possible weakness in internal control. Answer (d) is incorrect because the cash disbursements function is not directly related to accounts receivable (a cash receipts function).

31. (578,A1,32) (a) If A/R write offs must be approved by an officer on the basis of credit department recommendations including supporting evidence, there is very little likelihood of improper write offs to conceal cash shortages. Answer (b) is incorrect because receivables overdue by several months is not a basis for writing off an account; uncollectibility is. Answer (c) is incorrect because the cashier could conceal cash shortages by approving A/R write offs. Answer (d) is incorrect because sales employees could accept payments from customers and then authorize the accounts to be written off.

C.2. Purchases, Payables, and Cash Disbursements

32. (1189,A1,46) (d) The requirement is to determine the proper internal control responsibility for the vouchers payable department. Answer (d) is correct because the agreement of the documents will indicate that the goods were ordered (purchase order), received (receiving report), and the company has been billed (vendor's invoice). Answer (a) is incorrect because the individual signing the checks should stamp, perforate, or otherwise cancel supporting documentation. The vouchers payable department should not be responsible for these tasks. Answer (b) is incorrect because the purchasing department is involved with the approval of purchase requisitions, not the vouchers payable department. Answer (c) is incorrect because the purchasing department will obliterate the quantity ordered on the receiving department copy of the purchase order, not the vouchers payable department.

33. (588,A1,9) (b) The requirement is to determine which copy of the purchase order should omit indication of the quantity of merchandise ordered. Answer (b) is correct because if the receiving department personnel are unaware of the quantities ordered, they will provide an independent count of quantities received. Answer (a) is incorrect because the department that initiated the requisition needs the merchandise, and therefore, should know what has been ordered. Answer (c) is incorrect because the purchasing agent is involved with purchasing the items and therefore must be aware of the quantity involved. Answer (d) is incorrect because the accounts payable department must reconcile the quantity received and the quantity billed to the quantity that was authorized to be purchased per the purchase order.

34. (588,A1,20) (b) The requirement is to determine the procedure in the cash disbursements cycle which should not be performed by the accounts payable department. Answer (b) is correct because the individual disbursing the cash (generally the treasurer), not the accounts payable department, should cancel the supporting document to avoid duplicate payment of bills. Answer (a) is incorrect because the accounts payable department should compare the vendor's invoice with the receiving report to determine that the quantities which have been billed have been received. Answer (c) is incorrect because the accounts payable department will verify mathematical accuracy of the invoice to avoid payment of an incorrect amount. Answer (d) is incorrect because the

accounts payable department may sign the voucher to authorize payment.

35. (589,A1,14) (c) The requirement is to identify the documents that should be matched with the goods received by the receiving clerk. Answer (c) is correct because the receiving clerk should verify that the goods received have been approved for purchase (purchase order) and that all the goods ordered have been properly shipped (shipping document). Answer (a) is incorrect because the requisition form is the initial document generated within the company asking for an item to be purchased. Only after an approved purchase order has been issued in response to the requisition should the item actually be purchased. In addition, the receiving clerk will need to consider the shipping document as well. Answer (b) is incorrect because the vendor's invoice will not in general accompany the goods and thus will not be available to the receiving clerk. Also, the receiving clerk prepares the receiving report. Answer (d) is incorrect because the receiving clerk will prepare the receiving report, and because the reply does not include the purchase order.

36. (585,A1,51) (b) The requirement is to identify the audit procedure which would most likely detect a client error in recording a large purchase. Answer (b) is correct because reconciling the vendors' monthly statements with the subsidiary ledger for payables should disclose a difference in the month following the error. Answer (a), footing the purchases journal, is unlikely to detect the error since the journal's totals will have been mathematically accumulated properly. Answer (c) is incorrect because the incorrect total will be reflected in both the purchases journal and in the ledger accounts. Answer (d) is incorrect because such confirmations will only detect the error quarterly which is neither timely nor efficient.

37. (589,A1,15) (a) The requirement is to identify the employee who should control the mailing of disbursement checks and remittance advices. Answer (a) is correct because the individual who signed the checks should determine that they are properly delivered directly to the mailroom or post office. The principle involved is that duties should be segregated to reduce the opportunities for any person to be in a position to both perpetrate and conceal errors or irregularities. Accordingly, when possible, different people should be assigned responsibilities for authorizing transactions, recording

transactions, and maintaining custody of assets (AU 319.11). In this case, the employee signing the checks has the duty of custody and should be responsible for the custody of the checks until they are mailed. Answer (b) is incorrect because the individual who approved or authorized the vouchers for payment should not also have custody of the assets, in this case the checks. Answers (c) and (d) are incorrect because both are steps required in the approval process, and should not be combined with duties related to the custody of the assets (i.e., mailing of the checks).

38. (585,A1,38) (c) The requirement is to identify the statement which does not represent a purpose of providing the accounts payable department with a copy of purchase order forms. Answer (c) is correct because, although various parties may requisition goods, the goods are normally received and placed in stores. Therefore, accounts payable will be unable to determine whether the requisitioner actually received the goods. Answer (a) is incorrect because the accounts payable department will compare the invoice price with the purchase order price to determine that the invoice price is proper. Answer (b) is incorrect because the purchase order will provide evidence that the purchase was properly authorized. Answer (d) is incorrect because a comparison will be necessary to determine that the proper quantity has been received.

39. (588,A1,6) (b) The requirement is to determine the population to test for determining whether all merchandise for which the client was billed was received. Answer (b) is correct because the vendors' invoices represent the items billed to the client; the auditor would compare the vendors' invoices with the receiving reports to determine whether items billed had been received. Answer (a) is incorrect because sampling from the merchandise received would not detect items not received. Answer (c) is incorrect because canceled checks represent the population of items for which the company has paid, and would not necessarily represent all items billed to the company. Answer (d) is incorrect because receiving reports represent items received, and are thus unlikely to result in discovery of items not received.

40. (1189,A1,45) (d) The requirement is to determine the appropriate audit procedures for testing whether approved vouchers support every check request. Answer (d) is correct because vouchers should have been prepared and

approved prior to issuance of the check (otherwise the voucher was not present when the check was issued). In addition, the auditor must begin his/her test with the canceled checks to determine whether all checks are supported by an approved voucher. Answer (a) is incorrect because the checks must be issued after the approved voucher has been prepared. Answer (b) is incorrect since the direction of the test (i.e. from vouchers to canceled checks) would not detect any checks which had been prepared without the support of an approved voucher. Answer (c) is incorrect because the vouchers should be dated prior to the checks.

41. (589,A1,18) (b) The requirement is to identify an example of independent internal verification of inventory. In order to achieve an independent internal verification, the individual performing the verification must be independent of the recordkeeping and custody functions. Answer (b) is correct because the individual who makes the comparison of records of goods on hand with physical quantities and who does not maintain the records or have custody of the inventory is independent. Answers (a), (c), and (d) are all incorrect because they include individuals who are not independent of the inventory authorization, custody, or recordkeeping functions.

C.3. Inventories and Production

42. (588,A1,11) (d) The requirement is to determine the proper internal control for handling customer returns of defective merchandise. Answer (d) is correct because the receiving department can count the goods, and list them on a sales return notice to determine that all such returns are properly recorded. This serves as a control because the normal procedures of the receiving function include establishing the original accountability and recordkeeping for items received. Answers (a), (b), and (c) all represent functions not typically involved in the receiving function and thus involve a higher risk relating to establishing accountability.

43. (586,A1,38) (c) The requirement is to identify the effect on revenues, receivables, and inventory of an inadequate control over the invoicing function that allows goods to be shipped without being invoiced. Items shipped without invoicing will result in a situation in which the accounting department is unaware of the sale. Therefore, debits to accounts receivable and credits to sales will not be recorded, resulting in an understatement of both revenues and receivables. Similarly, be-

cause accounting is unaware of the sale, no entry to reduce inventory will be made, resulting in an overstatement of inventory. Therefore, answer (c) is correct. Answers (a), (b), and (d) all include errors inconsistent with the above.

44. (583,A1,36) (b) The requirement is to determine why the physical count of inventory might be higher than that shown by the perpetual records. If credit memos for items had not been recorded they would be included in the count and not in the perpetual records. Answer (a) is incorrect because if the tags had not been taken off the items, the count would be less than the perpetual records. Answer (c) is incorrect because items returned to suppliers would not be counted, and therefore, if no book entries had been made, the books would exceed the count. Answer (d) is incorrect because items which had not been received would not be included in either the count or the perpetual records; therefore, both totals would be understated by the same amount.

45. (583,A1,50) (c) The requirement is to determine the situation which could cause a client's physical count of inventories to be higher than the inventory quantities per the perpetual records. Failure to record purchases will result in a situation in which the item will be included in the count yet the perpetual records will not reflect the item. Answer (a) is incorrect because the failure to record sales (and therefore, cost of goods sold) will result in a situation in which the physical count is lower than the perpetual records. Answer (b) is incorrect because sales discounts relate to the selling price and not to the quantity of items in inventory. Answer (d) is incorrect because unrecorded returns of a firm's purchases to its suppliers will result in a lower physical count than is reflected in the perpetual records.

46. (1189,A1,47) (d) The requirement is to identify the most likely test of a control over the issuance of raw materials to production. Answer (d) is correct because examining material requisitions and reperforming client controls related to issuances will provide evidence on operating effectiveness related to issuance of raw materials to production. Answer (a) is incorrect because reconciling raw materials and work-in-process records to the general ledger balances does not directly test the controls over the issuance of raw materials to production. Answer (b) is incorrect because the handling of defective materials only

addresses a very limited portion of the issuance of raw materials to production. Answer (c) is incorrect because these procedures test the safeguard controls over raw materials, not the controls over issuance to production.

47. (1186,A1,24) (c) The requirement is to identify the question that an auditor would expect to find on the production cycle section of an internal control questionnaire. Answer (c) is correct because approved requisitions will help maintain control over raw materials released to be used in the production cycle. Answers (a), (b), and (d) are all incorrect because approval of vendors' invoices for payment, mailing of checks after signing, and comparing individual disbursements to totals all pertain more directly to the disbursement cycle.

48. (588,A1,13) (a) The requirement is to identify a control over the payroll function. Answer (a) is correct because the verification of agreement of job time tickets with employee clock card hours by an independent payroll department employee provides assurance that all labor incurred (time cards) reconciles to the appropriate projects (job time tickets). Answer (b) is incorrect because reconciling job tickets to job reports by those employees involved on the jobs is unlikely to result in discovery of such errors. Answer (c) is incorrect because the payroll department, which prepares the payroll, should not have control over the rate authorization forms. Answer (d) is incorrect because the payroll function should be independent of the personnel department.

49. (1179,A1,54) (c) If payment of wages were to be in cash, each employee receiving payment should be required to sign a receipt for the amount of pay received. Thus, there would be control over the total amount disbursed as well as amounts disbursed to each individual employee. Answer (a) is incorrect because if a signed receipt is not received from each employee paid, there would be no proof of payment. Even though the pay envelopes include both cash and a computation of net wages, the employees should have the opportunity to count the cash received before signing a payroll receipt. Answer (b) is incorrect because unclaimed pay envelopes should not be retained by the paymaster, but rather deposited in a bank account by the cashier. Answer (d) is incorrect because the wage payment will be made in cash and not by check. Accordingly, a receipt must be obtained for each cash payment.

50. (1187,A1,42) (d) The requirement is to identify a benefit of fidelity bonds in addition to indemnifying a company against embezzlement losses. Answer (d) is correct because bonding companies conduct background checks of new employees, thereby reducing the possibility of employing persons with dubious records. Answer (a) is incorrect because business interruption insurance, which covers a company in the event of work stoppages, has no relationship to the use of fidelity bonds. Answer (b) is incorrect because liability insurance, not fidelity bonds, protects employees from possible monetary damages from unintentional errors. Answer (c) is incorrect because the bonding company does not assume responsibility for internal controls.

51. (589,A1,17) (d) The requirement is to identify the purpose of segregating the duties of hiring personnel and of distributing payroll checks. Answer (d) is correct because the hiring of personnel is an authorization function while the distribution of checks is a custody function. Thus, in order to properly segregate authorization from custody, these duties should not be performed by the same individual. The combination of these two functions in the same position would create the possibility of the addition of a fictitious employee to the payroll and subsequent misappropriation of paychecks. Answer (a) is incorrect because segregation of duties does not directly address administrative vs. accounting controls. Answer (b) is incorrect because the treasury function, and not the controllership function, will normally be responsible for distributing payroll checks. Answer (c) is incorrect because the functions involved are not primarily operational or recordkeeping.

52. (582,A1,32) (c) The requirement is to determine the best method to minimize the opportunities for fraud for unclaimed cash in a cash payroll system. For a cash payroll the best control is to get the unclaimed cash out of the firm's physical control and into the bank. Answer (a) is incorrect because maintaining the accountability for cash which is in a safe deposit box is difficult. Answers (b) and (d) are incorrect because the cash need not be kept by the firm.

53. (1187,A1,54) (b) The requirement is to identify the inappropriate responsibility for the payroll department supervisor. Answer (b) is correct because the payroll supervisor is involved with the recordkeeping for payroll and therefore should not have custody over the related asset, unclaimed paychecks. The

payroll supervisor's custody over unclaimed payroll checks could result, for example, in a situation in which the supervisor continued to collect the checks of a departed employee. Answer (a) is incorrect because the payroll department supervisor will often have authority pertaining to the hiring of subordinates. Note, however, that the personnel department will also be involved with the hiring decision. Answers (c) and (d), updating employee earnings records and applying pay rates to time tickets, represent normal responsibilities of the payroll department and are therefore incorrect replies.

C.4. Personnel and Payroll

54. (589,A1,33) (d) The requirement is to determine the specific type of evidence provided when an auditor traces selected items from the payroll register to employee time cards that have been approved by supervisory personnel. Answer (d) is correct because approval by the supervisory personnel provides evidence that the hours on the time card have actually been worked and that this total is included in the payroll register. Answer (a) is incorrect because the procedure provides only limited information as to the effectiveness of controls over actual payroll disbursements, since this procedure has only tested a portion of this process. Answer (b) is incorrect because the test does not address the signing of the payroll checks. Answer (c) is partially correct in that the supervisory personnel provide evidence related to bona fide employees. However, it is less accurate than answer (d) because it suggests that pay was properly computed. This procedure does not verify that pay was properly computed.

55. (587,A1,20) (c) The requirement is to identify a reason why an auditor may observe the distribution of paychecks. Answer (c) is correct because an employee's presence to collect the paycheck provides evidence that the employee actually exists and is currently employed by the client. Answer (a) is incorrect because the distributions of payroll checks would not reveal whether payrate authorization is properly separated from the operating function. Answer (b) is incorrect because the paycheck distribution does not provide information on whether deductions from gross pay have been calculated properly. Answer (d) is incorrect because observation of the paycheck distribution process does not of itself provide assurance that the paychecks agree with the related payroll register and time cards.

C.5. Property, Plant, and Equipment

56. (1188,A1,46) (a) The requirement is to identify the best procedure for preventing the improper disposition of equipment. Answer (a) is correct because separation of those individuals with custody over the equipment to be disposed, from those individuals authorized to approve removal work orders segregates the custodial and authorization responsibilities for the equipment. As indicated in AU 319.11, the proper segregation of functional responsibilities calls for separation of the functions of authorization, recordkeeping, and custody. Answer (b) is incorrect because the mere existence of serial numbers is unlikely to prevent improper disposition of equipment. Answer (c) is incorrect because the periodic comparison of removal work orders to authorizing documentation will at best detect, and only to a lesser extent prevent, the improper disposition of equipment. Answer (d) is incorrect because analyses of scrap sales and repairs and maintenance will only detect equipment sales and transactions which have been expensed.

57. (588,A1,10) (a) The requirement is to determine the most effective procedure for identifying property acquisitions that are misclassified as maintenance expense. Answer (a) is correct because property acquisitions are generally for large dollar amounts, and their misclassification is likely to result in large, obvious variances from standards. Answer (b) is incorrect because depreciation will only be recorded on capitalized property and is thus unlikely to result in discovery of misclassified acquisitions. Answer (c) is incorrect because segregation of duties of employees is unlikely to result in detection of the misclassification. Answer (d) is incorrect because the examination of vendors, invoices, and canceled checks for recorded property acquisitions is unlikely to result in discovery of acquisitions which were not so recorded.

58. (1189,A1,48) (b) The requirement is to determine the effect on an audit of a weakness in internal control over recording retirements of equipment. Answer (b) is correct because evidence on the completeness of the recording of retirements may be obtained by selecting items from the accounting records and determining whether they are still in the plant. Answer (a) is incorrect because the question addresses situations with unrecorded retirements, not retirements of assets still on hand that have been recorded as reclassifications to "other assets." Answer (c) is incorrect because beginning with items on hand and tracing to the accounting records does not test whether all equipment retired has been recorded. Answer (d) is incorrect because whether the client is depreciating these items does not directly address the question of unrecorded retirements.

59. (589,A1,19) (c) The requirement is to determine the proper approach for an auditor who is planning to assess control risk for property and equipment transactions at the minimum level. Answer (c) is correct because tests of controls are required when an auditor wishes to assess control risk at the minimum level. In addition, when such tests indicate that controls are designed and operating effectively, limited substantive tests may be performed (AU 319.62). Answer (a) is incorrect because extensive tests of property and equipment balances will not be necessary. Answer (b) is incorrect because extensive tests of transactions will not be necessary and because tests of controls will be necessary. Answer (d) is incorrect because although analytical procedures may be performed the response does not refer to tests of controls which are necessary for assessment of control risk.

60. (1187,A1,50) (a) The requirement is to identify the internal control which would most likely allow for a reduction in the scope of the auditor's tests of depreciation expense. Answer (a) is correct because supervisory review and approval of the entry will allow for the discovery of a variety of possible errors. Answers (b) and (c) are incorrect because comparing current-year account balances with current-year budgets and prior year actual balance, or examination of income from salvage credits and scrap sales are less complete than answer (a). They represent procedures that might be performed by an independent supervisor during a review. Answer (d) is incorrect because such authorization of payment of vendors' invoices is an internal control that has no apparent direct relationship to depreciation expense.

61. (1179,A1,42) (a) Canceled stock certificates should be defaced and attached to corresponding stubs as is done with voided checks. The objective of the control is to prevent reissuance. Answer (b) is incorrect because failure to deface permits reissuance. Answer (c) is incorrect because destruction of the certificates would preclude their control, i.e., their existence after defacing provides assurance that they cannot be reissued. If the certificates were destroyed, one or more might be reissued without any proof that such

occurred. Answer (d) is incorrect because the Secretary of State has no interest in receiving defaced and canceled stock certificates.

62. (1182,A1,30) (d) The requirement is to determine who should have responsibility for custody of short-term bearer bond investments and the submission of coupons for periodic collections of interest. The treasurer authorizes such transactions. Answer (a) is incorrect because the chief accountant, who is in charge of the recordkeeping function, should not also maintain custody of the bonds. Answer (b) is incorrect because the internal auditor should not be directly involved as such involvement would make an independent review of the system impossible. Answer (c) is incorrect because the cashier function is more directly involved with details such as endorsing, depositing, and maintaining records of cash receipts.

C.6. Other Control Oriented Questions

63. (1184,A1,3) (d) The requirement is to determine the type of irregularity which is most difficult to detect. Answer (d), an irregularity committed by the controller, is most difficult to detect because the controller is in control of the recordkeeping function and thus may be able to commit an irregularity and then manipulate the accounting records so as to make its discovery unlikely. Answer (a) is incorrect because while a cashier may be able to embezzle funds, s/he will not have access to the accounting records and thus discovery of the embezzlement will be likely. Answer (b) is incorrect because a keypunch operator will not in general have access to assets. Answer (c) is incorrect because an internal auditor will not generally be able to manipulate the accounting records and generally has limited access to assets.

64.   (584,A1,5) (c) The requirement is to determine the area in which the auditor would consider internal control least important. A client's internal control structure will not relate as directly to shareholder meetings as to the other answers. CPAs will often attend the shareholder meetings and be aware of what has transpired, but important matters at such meetings are generally publicly available. Answers (a) and (b) are incorrect because land, buildings, and common stock all relate to a firm's double entry bookkeeping system which attempts to safeguard assets and the reliability of financial records. Answer (d) is incorrect because the minutes of board of directors must be received in their complete form by the auditor so the auditor may be aware of matters such as contractual agreements.

D. Other Considerations

D.1. Communicating with the Audit Committee

65. (1189,A1,58) (b) The requirement is to determine which conditions would be considered to be "reportable conditions" and should therefore be communicated to an entity's audit committee. Answer (b) is correct because reportable conditions are by definition significant deficiencies in the design or operation of the internal control structure which could adversely affect the organization's ability to record, process, summarize, and report financial data consistent with the assertions of management in the financial statements (AU 325.02). Answers (a), (c), and (d) are all incorrect because while they all describe conditions which the auditor would communicate to an entity's audit committee, the professional standards use the term "reportable conditions" to specifically describe significant deficiencies in the design or operation of internal control structures. None of these answers describe such deficiencies.

66. (586,A1,46) (c) The requirement is to determine an auditor's obligation when it is determined at an interim date that an internal control reportable condition which was previously communicated to the client has not been corrected. AU 325 discusses such communications. Answer (c) is correct because while the auditor might consider communicating the condition at an interim date, the fact that it was previously communicated makes it more likely that it will either be repeated or referred to in the current year's communication to the client. Answer (a) is incorrect because the purpose of a review of interim information is to provide a basis for the reporting of whether material modifications are needed for such information to conform with generally accepted accounting principles, not to search for reportable conditions in the internal controls (AU 722.03). Answer (b) is incorrect because, as indicated above, communication is necessary. Answer (d) is incorrect because the auditor had, in the previous year, already discovered the condition and had presumably considered it.

67. (1187,A1,51) (c) The requirement is to identify the correct statement concerning the auditor's required communication of internal control reportable conditions. Answer (c) is correct because while a written communication is considered preferable, an oral communication is acceptable (AU 325.09). Answer (a) is incorrect because when the auditor is unaware of any reportable conditions he may communicate that fact orally, but is required not to do so in writing (AU 325.05). An-

swer (b) is incorrect because while conditions
should be communicated at the earliest practi-
cable date, there is no requirement that the
auditor test for correction of the condition
before completion of the engagement. Answer (d) is incorrect because when there is
interim communication of the examination's
findings, the auditor is not obligated in the
final communication to repeat conditions
reported at interim dates, provided that
reference is made to the interim communications. AU 325 discusses reportable
conditions in detail.

68. (585,A1,54) (b) The requirement is to
determine an auditor's responsibility after
s/he has discovered and orally communicated
information on a weakness in internal control
to the client's senior management and its
audit committee. Note that AU 325.09 suggests
that the form of the communication to
management and the board of directors or its
audit committee is optional; it may be written or oral. Answer (b) is correct because the
auditor, as outlined throughout AU 319,
considers and documents his/her understanding
of internal control to assist in planning and
determining the proper nature, timing, and
extent of substantive tests. Answer (a) is
incorrect because no scope limitation is
indicated although an internal control
condition does exist. Similarly, answers (c)
and (d) are incorrect because audit activities
need not be suspended and the auditor need not
withdraw from the engagement.

69. (589,A1,20) (d) The requirement is to
identify the correct statement with respect to
an auditor's communication of internal control
structure related matters (most frequently
referred to as "reportable conditions") noted
during an audit. Answer (d) is correct because, depending upon the circumstances, the
auditor may choose to communicate such matters
either during the course of the audit or after
the audit is concluded (AU 325.18). Answer (a) is incorrect because a written report
is <u>not</u> to be issued when <u>no</u> reportable conditions were noted during the audit (AU 325.17).
Answer (b) is incorrect because reportable
conditions of which the audit committee is
aware need not be communicated (AU 325.06).
Answer (c) is incorrect because reportable
conditions may be included in a document that
includes suggestions regarding activities such
as business strategies or administrative efficiencies (AU 325.19).

70. (1187,A1,50) (a) The requirement is to
identify the reply that includes information
which should be included in an accountant's

report expressing an opinion on an entity's
internal controls. Answer (a) is correct
because AU 642.38 requires a brief explanation
of the broad objectives and inherent
limitations of internal control. Answers (b),
(c), and (d) are all incorrect because they
represent information which should not be
included in an accountant's report expressing
an opinion on an entity's internal controls.

71. (1182,A1,59) (c) The requirement is to
determine what an unqualified opinion on an
entity's system of internal control implies.
The broad objectives of internal control
(AU 642.04) are to render reasonable assurance
that assets are safeguarded from unauthorized
use or disposition and that financial records
are sufficiently reliable to permit the preparation of financial statements. Answer (a)
is incorrect because compliance with the
Foreign Corrupt Practices Act is a legal question not addressed by such an opinion. Answer
(b) is incorrect since the likelihood of management fraud may be at a higher than minimal
level. Answer (d) is incorrect because typically auditors do not address whether audit
committee criteria have been met.

72. (1189,A1,51) (d) The requirement is to
determine what restriction need be placed on
an accountant's report on an entity's system
of internal controls. Answer (d) is correct
because an auditor need not place any restrictions on the use of a report applied to an
engagement to express an opinion on an entity's system of internal accounting control
(AU 642.03). Answers (a), (b), and (c) are
incorrect because they all place restrictions
on the report which the professional standards
do not require.

73. (1185,A1,30) (b) The requirement is to
describe the contents of a report on the study
of internal control that is based on criteria
established by governmental agencies. Answer (b) is correct because the report should
indicate matters covered by the consideration
and whether the auditor's consideration included tests of controls with the procedures
covered by his/her consideration (AU 642.56).
Additionally, the report should describe the
objectives and limitations of internal control
and the accountant's evaluation thereof; state
the accountant's conclusion, based on the
agency's criteria; and describe the purpose of
the report and state that it should not be
used for any other purpose. Answer (a) is
incorrect because the agency's name should be
included (AU 642.59). Answer (c) is incorrect
because a conclusion may be made relative to
the agency's criteria (AU 642.56). Answer (d)

is incorrect because the accountant should not assume responsibility for the comprehensiveness of the criteria (AU 642.58).

74. (588,A1,15) (d) The requirement is to determine the responsibility of a CPA whose opinion on an entity's internal control is to be included in a document in which management intends to include a statement asserting that the costs of correcting material weaknesses would exceed the expected benefits. Answer (d) is correct because AU 642.41 states that the accountant should not express any opinion as to management's statement. Additionally, the accountant is not precluded from disclaiming an opinion on any such statement. Answer (a) is incorrect because the CPA need not insist that management's statement <u>not</u> appear in the document. Answer (b) is incorrect because there is no requirement relating to the CPA's cost of correction of the weaknesses. Answer (c) is incorrect because it is not within the role of the CPA to insist on correction of weaknesses.

75. (589,A1,22) (a) The requirement is to determine whether an independent accountant, without auditing an entity's financial statements, may accept an engagement to express an opinion on the entity's internal controls in effect as of a specified date and/or during a specified period of time. Answer (a) is correct because AU 642.02 states that an independent accountant may express an opinion on the entity's system of internal control as of a specified date, or in effect during a specified period of time. Answers (b), (c), and (d) all are incorrect because they inappropriately restrict the report.

76. (1185,A1,37) (a) The requirement is to identify the characteristics of an internal auditor which must be considered by an independent auditor who decides that the internal auditor's work might have a bearing on his/her procedures. Answer (a) is correct because the <u>AICPA's Professional Standards</u> require independent auditors to consider internal auditor competence, objectivity, and work performance (AU 322.04). Answer (b) is incorrect because an independent auditor is less concerned about internal auditor efficiency, although internal auditor experience will be considered in the assessment of competence. Answers (c) and (d), while partially correct, are less complete than answer (a).

D.3. Effects of an Internal Audit Function

77. (588,A1,2) (d) The requirement is to identify how an independent auditor may consider the objectivity of internal auditors. Answer (d) is correct because the objectivity of internal auditors will generally increase with increases in the organizational level to which they report the results of their work and the organizational level to which they report administratively (AU 322.07). Answer (a) is incorrect because no professional standard addresses evaluation of the quality control program for internal auditors. Answer (b) is incorrect because the purpose of examining the work performed by internal auditors relates to evaluating the work performance of internal auditors (AU 322.08). Answer (c) is incorrect because while independent auditors may test a sample of the work of internal auditors, they do this primarily to evaluate work performance (AU 322.08).

78. (585,A1,22) (c) The requirement is to identify the reporting relationship for internal auditors which will achieve the greatest degree of independence in performing their function. Answer (c) is correct because reporting to the board of directors increases the likelihood that the internal auditors will be able to act independently of those they are auditing (AU 322.07). Answers (a) and (b) are incorrect because the internal auditor who reports to the financial vice-president or the controller cannot objectively review their work. Answer (d) is incorrect because it is generally not practical for the internal auditor to report to stockholders on a timely basis.

79. (583,A1,41) (b) The requirement is to determine the most appropriate task for internal auditors to perform to assist CPAs. Because decision making responsibility is not involved, the CPA may review the work of the internal auditor relating to the preparation of schedules for negative accounts receivable responses. Answer (a) is incorrect because the CPA must make decisions pertaining to the scope of receivable confirmations. Answer (c) is incorrect because the CPA is responsible for making an evaluation of internal control. Similarly, answer (d) is incorrect because a CPA may not delegate the responsibility for the determination of the adequacy of the allowance for doubtful accounts (or, for that matter, other accounts).

80.   (589,A1,7)   (c) The requirement is to
determine how the CPA's detailed audit program
compares with the audit client's comprehensive
internal audit program. Answer (c) is correct
because the internal audit function involves
performing a broad variety of services for
management including, but not limited to,
studying and evaluating internal control,
reviewing operating practices to promote
increased efficiency and economy, and making
special inquiries at management's direction
(AU 322.02). Therefore, the comprehensive
internal audit program is often more detailed
and covers areas normally not covered by the
CPA. Answer (a) is incorrect because the
scope difference of the internal audit function (for example, emphasis on efficiency and
economy) creates differences in the internal
audit program as compared to a CPA's audit
program. Answer (b) is incorrect because the
internal audit program will not in general be
less detailed and cover fewer areas than that
of the CPA. Answer (d) is incorrect because
the comprehensive internal audit program normally covers more areas than would be covered
by the CPA.

May 1990 Answers

81.   (590,A1,27)   (a) The requirement is to
identify the form of computer documentation an
auditor would most likely utilize in obtaining
an understanding of the internal control
structure. Answer (a) is correct because a
systems flowchart provides a graphic representation of the internal control structure and
therefore may help the auditor to obtain an
understanding of the structure (AU 319.26).
Answer (b) is incorrect because record counts
provide the auditor with information of how
many transactions have been processed, but
will not provide the auditor with an understanding of the overall internal control
structure. Answer (c) is incorrect because a
program listing will provide the auditor with
a listing of program steps, but will not provide evidence relating to the overall internal
control structure. Answer (d) is incorrect
because a record layout will aid in the understanding of the detailed design of records,
but will not provide evidence relating to the
overall internal control structure.

82.   (590,A1,28)   (a) The requirement is to
identify the correct statement concerning the
independent auditor's use of internal auditors
to provide assistance in performing the
audit. Answer (a) is correct because when
internal auditors only report to a relatively
low level in the organization (here the
controller and not, for example, the audit
committee), the independent auditor will

question the internal auditors' ability to
remain objective and this will result in
limited reliance being placed upon their work
(AU 322.07). Answer (b) is incorrect because
tests of controls do not relate directly to
detection risk and because the independent
auditors do not assess detection risk (they
perform substantive tests to restrict it).
Answer (c) is incorrect because auditors
assess control risk, they do not reduce
control risk--control risk is a function of
the client's internal control structure.
Also, answer (c) has only an indirect relationship to the topic of the question, that of
using internal auditors to provide assistance
in performing the audit. Answer (d) is incorrect because with proper supervision, the independent auditors may choose to use the work
of internal auditors. See AU 322 for a discussion of the manner in which independent
auditors consider the competence, objectivity,
and work performance of internal auditors.

83.   (590,A1,29)   (b) The requirement is to
identify the element of an internal control
structure that includes the development of
personnel manuals documenting employee promotion and training policies. Answer (b) is
correct because personnel policies and practices are considered a part of the entity's
control environment and include an entity's
treatment of promotions and training
(AU 319.09,.66). Answer (a) is incorrect
because control procedures are more detailed
than control environment factors; for example,
a control procedure might detail relatively
specific policies for promotion and training
(AU 319.11). Answer (c) is incorrect because
the accounting system consists of methods and
records established for an entity's transactions, and accounts for an entity's assets and
liabilities. Answer (d) is incorrect because
quality control systems apply to the auditing,
accounting, and review services of a CPA firm,
not an entity's internal control structure
(QC 10.01).

84.   (590,A1,30)   (d) The requirement is to
identify the correct statement about an internal control structure. Answer (d) is correct
because the internal control concept of reasonable assurance recognizes that the costs of
internal controls should not exceed their expected benefits (AU 319.06). Answer (a) is
incorrect because collusion among employees
may still occur even in a properly maintained
internal control structure (AU 319.15). Answer (b) is incorrect because while an internal auditor may be involved in designing an
internal control structure, the responsibility
for establishing and maintaining it is that of
management (AU 642.35). Answer (c) is incor-

rect because while a strong internal control structure may lead to reduced substantive testing, ordinarily the assessed level of control risk cannot be sufficiently low to eliminate the need to perform any substantive tests to restrict detection risk (AU 319.63).

85. (590,A1,31) (a) The requirement is to determine why an auditor might assess control risk at the maximum level for some assertions. Answer (a) is correct because after obtaining an understanding of the internal control structure, an auditor may assess control risk at the maximum level because of the belief that the internal control policies and procedures are unlikely to be effective (AU 319.29). Answer (b) is incorrect because while documentation of the internal control procedures is important, documentation alone will not affect the auditor's evaluation of the effectiveness of the internal control procedure. Answer (c) is incorrect because detection risk is a function of the effectiveness of an auditor's substantive tests, and not of the tests of controls. Answer (d) is incorrect because, when the auditor identifies controls that appear to be strong, a decision will often be made to perform tests of controls to allow a lower assessed level of control risk.

86. (590,A1,32) (b) The requirement is to identify the primary objective of obtaining an understanding of the internal control structure. Answer (b) is correct because the auditor must obtain a sufficient understanding of an entity's control structure to plan the audit of the entity's financial statements (AU 319.16). Answer (a) is incorrect because evidential matter collected through tests of controls performed while obtaining an understanding of the internal control structure will affect the auditor's assessment of control risk more directly than detection risk. Answer (c) is incorrect because while tests of controls may be modified during the consideration of the internal control structure, modification is not a primary objective. Answer (d) is incorrect because while flowcharts may be used to document the auditor's understanding of the internal control structure, this is not a primary objective (AU 319.26).

87. (590,A1,33) (c) The requirement is to identify the audit technique that would provide an auditor with the most assurance about the effectiveness of the operation of an internal control procedure. Answer (c) is correct because an auditor may observe the application of an internal control procedure to help evaluate the effectiveness of its

operation (AU 319.35). Observation is an especially useful technique when documentation of performance of a control is not available (AU 319.49) Answer (a) is incorrect because although inquiry may provide evidence as to the operation of an internal control procedure, it alone will not in general provide sufficient competent evidential matter to support a conclusion as to the effectiveness of a control (AU 319.51). Answers (b) and (d) are incorrect because they relate to substantive tests and only indirectly relate to providing assurance about the effectiveness of the operation of an internal control procedure.

88. (590,A1,34) (a) The requirement is to identify the type of evidence provided by tracing bills of lading to sales invoices. Answer (a) is correct because by tracing bills of lading to sales invoices, the auditor obtains evidence that merchandise which has been shipped (as evidenced by a bill of lading) has been invoiced. Answer (b) is incorrect because the sales invoices do not provide sufficient evidence that the sale was recorded. Answer (c) is incorrect because to determine whether recorded sales were shipped the auditor would trace from the population of recorded sales in the sales journal to bills of lading. Answer (d) is incorrect because to determine whether invoiced sales were shipped the auditor would trace from sales invoices to bills of lading (the opposite of this question).

89. (590,A1,35) (b) The requirement is to identify a reason that employers bond employees who handle cash receipts. Answer (b) is correct because employee knowledge that bonding companies often prosecute those accused of dishonest acts may deter employees' dishonest acts. Answer (a) is incorrect because bonding protects the employer from dishonest acts, not the employee from unintentional errors. Answer (c) is incorrect because the bonding company does not serve the role of independently monitoring of cash. Answer (d) is incorrect because while rotation of positions and forcing employees to take periodic vacations are effective controls for preventing certain irregularities, they are not accomplished through bonding.

90. (590,A1,36) (c) The requirement is to identify the population of documents from which an auditor will perform tests to verify that all merchandise received is recorded. Answer (c) is correct because the auditor must choose to sample from a population of documents which represents the merchandise that

has been received--this document is the receiving report which is prepared by the receiving department when merchandise arrives. Answer (a) is incorrect because sampling from vendors' invoices only addresses items for which the client has received an invoice. Answer (d) is incorrect because canceled checks only address accounts payable that have been paid.

91. (590,A1,37) (c) The requirement is to determine the control procedure that is <u>not</u> usually performed in the vouchers payable department. Answer (c) is correct because the individual disbursing the cash, generally the treasurer, should mail the check and remittance advice so as to not allow vouchers payable to provide both recordkeeping and custody of cash (signed checks) functions. Answer (a) is incorrect because vouchers payable should verify the mathematical accuracy of the invoice to avoid payment of an incorrect amount. Answer (b) is incorrect because vouchers payable may approve the voucher, with the treasurer reviewing the available support before signing the check. Answer (d) is incorrect because matching the receiving report with the purchase order (and the vendor's invoice) is a normal function of the vouchers payable department.

92. (590,A1,38) (c) The requirement is to identify the control procedure which is most likely to address the completeness assertion for inventory. Answer (c) is correct because by prenumbering receiving reports and by reconciling them with inventory records, one is able to test completeness by determining whether all receipts have been recorded. Answer (a) is incorrect because reconciling the subsidiary records with the work in process will only identify discrepancies between the records, it will not identify whether all transactions that should be in the inventory records are represented in the records. Answer (b) is incorrect because while the segregation of receiving from custody of finished goods is important, it less directly addresses completeness than does answer (a). Answer (d) is incorrect because separating the duties between the payroll department and inventory accounting personnel does not directly address completeness of inventory.

93. (590,A1,39) (d) The requirement is to identify the sampling unit in a test of controls pertaining to the existence of payroll transactions. Answer (d) is correct because the existence assertion for payroll transactions deals with whether the recorded transactions have occurred during a given period and,

accordingly, one would use the payroll register entries (the recorded transactions) as the sampling unit. Answer (a) is incorrect because by starting with the time cards as the sampling unit and tracing to the payroll register entries the auditor is establishing completeness, rather than existence. Answers (b) and (c) are incorrect because a Form W-2 and a personnel record would provide evidence that a person had been employed by the company, but do not serve as the sampling unit in testing the existence assertion as it relates to payroll transactions. Note that to test the existence assertion the auditor might choose to select transactions from the sampling unit entries in the payroll register and trace to clock cards, Form W-2s and personnel records. See the AICPA <u>Audit Sampling Guide</u> (pp. 26-27) for more on sampling units and AU 326 for information on financial statement assertions.

94. (590,A1,40) (d) The requirement is to identify the relationship between an engagement to express an opinion on an entity's system of internal accounting control and obtaining an understanding of the internal control structure and assessing control risk as part of an audit. Answer (d) is correct because, as indicated in AU 642.10-.11, while the scope and purpose differ between the two types of engagements, the procedures followed are similar. Answers (a), (b), and (c) are all incorrect because they include differing, incorrect, combinations of the replies.

95. (590,A1,41) (a) The requirement is to determine the appropriate response with respect to an accountant who is expressing an opinion on an entity's system of internal accounting control. Answer (a) is correct because AU 642.35 requires that the accountant must obtain written representations acknowledging responsibility for establishing and maintaining the system. Answer (b) is incorrect because the accountant should not express an opinion on management's assertion that the cost of correcting any weaknesses exceeds the benefits (AU 642.41). Answer (c) is incorrect because the accountant has no responsibility to keep informed of events subsequent to the date of the report (AU 642.46). Answer (d) is incorrect because a disclaimer of an opinion on the system's ability to prevent or detect material errors or irregularities is not included in the accountant's report on the internal accounting control system (AU 642.39).

Unofficial Answer*

Problem 1   IC Questionnaire - Purchases
            (1187,A2)

            STAR MANUFACTURING, INC.
                  Purchases
        Internal Control Questionnaire

Question	Yes	No

1. Are there written purchasing
policies and procedures?

2. Are purchase requisitions
approved in accordance with
management's authorization?

3. Are purchases made from
approved vendors?

4. Are price quotations
requested for purchases over an
established amount?

5. Are purchase commitments
documented on written purchase
order forms?

6. Do purchase orders include
adequate descriptions, terms, and
instructions?

7. Are purchase orders approved
by authorized personnel before
issuance?

8. Are prenumbered purchase
order forms periodically accounted
for?

9. Is a detailed listing of
purchase orders maintained?

10. Is the purchasing function
independent of receiving,
shipping, invoice processing, and
treasury functions?

11. Are there adequate safeguards
over unissued purchase order
forms?

12. Are old items in the open
purchase order file periodically
investigated?

13. Are vendors notified of
conflict of interest policies?

*Because the requirements of this question
could be answered by lists of items, we have
not included an outline of the solution.

Answer Outline

Problem 2   Opinion on Internal Control
            (587,A4)

a. Compare engagement to express opinion to a
    consideration of internal control as part
    of an examination
    1) Scope
        Can be made in conjunction with
        each
        Consideration as part of examina-
        tion more limited
    2) Purpose
        Consideration as part of examina-
        tion used to help form an opinion
        on financial statements
        Engagement to express opinion
        provides assurance about broad
        objectives
    3) Timing of engagements
        Can be any date for opinion
        Must be early audit stages for
        consideration
    4) Users of the reports
        Users of opinion are client's
        management and third parties
        Consideration used by auditor

b. Contents of report expressing opinion of
    internal control
    Description of engagement scope
    Date of opinion
    Statement on responsibility of
     management
    Explanation of broad objectives and
     limitations
    Opinion on system as to objectives
    Description of weaknesses

Unofficial Answer

Problem 2   Opinion on Internal Control
            (587,A4)

a. 1. An engagement to express an opinion on
an entity's system of internal accounting
control and a consideration of internal
control made as part of an examination of
financial statements in accordance with
generally accepted auditing standards
generally differ in scope. While the engagement to express an opinion on an entity's
system can be made in conjunction with the
consideration made as part of an examination,
the consideration made as part of an
examination is more limited in scope.
    2. The engagements also differ in pur-
pose. The auditor's consideration of internal
control is an intermediate step in forming an
opinion on the financial statements. It

establishes a basis for reliance on the control structure and for determining the nature, extent, and timing of the auditing procedures. The purpose of the accountant's engagement to express an opinion on the system of internal accounting control is to provide assurance about whether the broad objectives of internal control are being achieved.

3. An engagement to express an opinion on an entity's system of internal accounting control can be made as of any date, while the auditor's consideration of internal control is made in the early stages of an audit with review to determine the effectiveness throughout the period.

4. Ordinarily, the users of an opinion on an entity's system of internal accounting control are the client's management or third parties, such as regulatory agencies. The primary user of a consideration of internal control made as part of an audit is the auditor who makes the consideration.

b. The accountant's report expressing an opinion on an entity's system of internal accounting control should contain
   a. A description of the scope of the engagement.
   b. The date to which the opinion relates.
   c. A statement that the establishment and maintenance of the structure is the responsibility of management.
   d. A brief explanation of the broad objectives and inherent limitations of internal control.
   e. The accountant's opinion on whether the system meets the broad objectives of internal control insofar as those objectives pertain to the prevention or detection of material errors or irregularities.
   f. The description of any weaknesses.

Unofficial Answer*

Problem 3 Cash Receipts Questionnaire
            (586,A4)

SPARTAN DRUG STORE, INC.
Processing Cash Collections
Internal Control Questionnaire

Question	Yes	No
Are customers who pay by check identified via store I.D. card or other means?		
Does company policy prohibit accepting checks for anything except merchandise sales plus a nominal cash amount?		
Is a receipt produced by the cash register given to each customer?		
Is the reading of each cash register taken periodically by an employee who is independent of the handling of cash receipts?		
Are cash counts made on a surprise basis by an individual who is independent of the handling of cash receipts?		
Is the reading of each cash register compared regularly to the cash received?		
Is a summary listing of cash register readings prepared by an employee who is independent of physically handling cash receipts?		
Are receipts forwarded to an independent employee who makes the bank deposits?		
Are each day's receipts deposited intact daily?		
Is the summary listing of cash register receipts reconciled to the duplicate deposit slips authenticated by the bank?		
Are entries to the cash receipts journal prepared from duplicate deposit slips or the summary listing of cash register readings?		
Are the entries to the cash receipts journal compared to the deposits per bank statement?		
Are areas involving the physical handling of cash reasonably safeguarded?		
Are employees who handle receipts bonded?		

*Because the requirements of this question could be answered by lists of items we have not included an outline of the solution.

Are charged back items (NSF checks, etc.) directed to an employee who does not physically handle receipts or have access to the books?

Unofficial Answer*

Problem 4   Purchases and Disbursements
            Flowchart (583,A5)

A.   Prepare purchase order
B.   To vendor
C.   Prepare receiving report
D.   From purchasing
E.   From receiving
F.   Purchase order No. 5
G.   Receiving report No. 1
H.   Prepare and approve voucher
I.   Unpaid voucher file, filed by due date
J.   Treasurer
K.   Sign checks and cancel voucher package documents
L.   Cancelled voucher package

Unofficial Answer*

Problem 5   IC Questionnaire – Marketable
            Securities (1184,A3)

The auditor's internal control questionnaire should include the following additional questions:

• Does access to the bank safe deposit vault require the signature or presence of two designated persons?
• Are all individuals who have access to marketable securities bonded?
• Are those who have access to the securities denied access to the accounting records?
• Does the accounting department keep detailed records of:
    • Purchases and sales?
    • Securities (including number of shares) owned?
    • Stock certificate numbers?
    • Dividend income?
    • Gains and losses?

• Are all securities registered in the name of the company?
• Are all securities periodically inspected?
• Is the inspection performed on a surprise basis?

• Is the physical inventory of securities reconciled with the accounting records?
• Are all purchases and sales of securities executed by the treasurer within the directives of the investment committee?
• Is the amount of dividends received on individual investments periodically reconciled to published public records?
• Does the investment committee periodically review compliance with its established policy?

Answer Outline

Problem 6   IC Questionnaire (581,A4)

Internal control questionnaire for revolving fund
Custody
    Is fund responsibility vested in one person?
    Is physical access to the fund denied to others?
    Is custodian independent of others who handle cash?
    Is custodian bonded?
    Is custodian denied access to other cash funds?
Receipts
    Are receipts unalterable?
    Are receipts prenumbered?
    Is the integrity of the prenumbered sequence periodically verified?
    Are receipts signed by the book seller?
Reimbursement Vouchers
    Are receipts attached to reimbursement vouchers?
    Are vouchers submitted for reimbursement approved by someone other than the custodian?
    Are reimbursement vouchers cancelled after payment?
Disbursements from Fund
    Is fund used only for the repurchase of books?
Non-Custodian Control
    Is fund periodically reconciled by someone other than the custodian?
    Is fund maintained on an imprest basis?
    Is size of the fund suitable for the purpose intended?

*Because the requirements of this question could be answered by lists of items we have not included an outline of the solution.

Unofficial Answer

Problem 6   IC Questionnaire (581,A4)

University Books Incorporated
Revolving Cash Fund
Internal Control Questionnaire

Question	Yes	No
Is responsibility for the fund vested in one person?		
Is physical access to the fund denied to all others?		
Is the custodian independent of other employees who handle cash?		
Is the custodian bonded?		
Is the custodian denied access to other cash funds?		
Are receipts unalterable?		
Are receipts prenumbered?		
Is the integrity of the prenumbered sequence periodically accounted for?		
Does the seller sign receipts?		
Are receipts attached to reimbursement vouchers?		
Are vouchers that are submitted for reimbursement approved by someone other than the custodian?		
Are reimbursement vouchers and attachments (receipts) cancelled after reimbursement?		
Is the fund used exclusively for the acquisition of books?		
Is the fund periodically counted and reconciled by someone other than the custodian?		
Is the fund maintained on an imprest basis?		
Is the size of the fund appropriate for the purpose intended?		

Answer Outline

Problem 7   Payroll IC Weaknesses (580,A5)

a.   Weaknesses of internal control structure
a1.   Lack of approval of foreman's clock card
a2.   Computation of regular and overtime hours by payroll clerk no. 2 not compared with foreman's summary
a3.   Computations and rates of pay not checked by independent person
a4.   Payroll checks not reconciled to payroll register
a5.   Payroll clerk should not have custody of signature-stamp machine and blank checks
a6.   Payroll not approved by officer
a7.   Payroll checks should not be distributed by foreman

a8.   Unclaimed checks not held by independent employee
a9.   Comparison of hours on check with hours on clock card should not be done by clerk who did original computation
a10.   Comparison of payroll on check with register should not be done by clerk who prepared register
b.   Inquiries concerning possible additional conditions
b1.   Are clock cards checked for foreman's approval?
b2.   Is overtime on clock cards approved?
b3.   Is data in payroll files checked with personnel files?
b4.   Is clock card punching observed by timekeeper?
b5.   Are other mitigating internal controls in existence, e.g., bonding, required vacations?

Unofficial Answer

Problem 7   Payroll IC Weaknesses (580,A5)

a.   Weaknesses of internal control structure are the following:

1.   Lack of approval of the foreman's clock card by an appropriate supervisor is an unsound practice. Employees should not be permitted to maintain their own time records and submit them without approval.

2.   The computation of regular and overtime hours prepared by payroll clerk no. 2 that is used in the preparation of the payroll register is not compared with the summary of regular and overtime hours prepared by the foreman.

3.   Arithmetic computations and rates of pay used in the preparation of the payroll register are not checked by a person who is independent of their preparation and payroll register columns are not verified (re-added) by a person other than the preparer of the payroll register.

4.   Payroll checks are not reconciled to the payroll register in order to prevent improper disbursements.

5.   A signature-stamp machine should not be in the custody of any payroll clerk who has access to unsigned checks.

6.   Payroll is not approved by an officer of the company.

7.   Since the paymaster should be independent of the payroll process, signed payroll checks should not be distributed by the foreman.

8.   Unclaimed payroll checks should be in the custody of an employee who is independent of the payroll process.

9.   The comparison of (regular and overtime) hours indicated on payroll check (or attachments) with (regular and overtime) hours indicated on clock cards should not be per-

formed by the clerk who is responsible for the original computation of (regular and overtime) hours indicated on clock cards.

10.   The comparison of gross and net payroll indicated on payroll check (or attachments) with gross and net payroll indicated in the payroll register should not be performed by the clerk who is responsible for preparing the payroll register.

b.   One should inquire whether:

1.   Payroll clerk no. 2 checks clock cards for the foreman's written approval.

2.   Approved overtime is indicated on clock cards.

3.   Employment, wage, and related data in payroll files are periodically crosschecked with personnel files for agreement.

4.   The punching of clock cards is observed by a timekeeper.

5.   Other mitigating internal control measures (for example, bonding, required vacations, and so forth) are in existence.

Answer Outline

Problem 8   Cash Receipts IC Weaknesses
              (1180,A4)

Weaknesses in and Recommended Improvements for Internal Control
1.   No segregation of duties between persons collecting admission fees and persons authorizing admission
     One clerk (collection clerk) should collect admission fees and issue prenumbered tickets
     Another clerk (admission clerk) should authorize admission upon receipt of ticket or proof of membership
2.   No independent count made of paying patrons
     Admission clerk should retain a portion of the prenumbered admission ticket
3.   No proof of accuracy of amounts collected by the clerks
     Each day treasurer should reconcile admission ticket stubs with cash collected by treasurer
4.   Cash receipts records not promptly prepared
     Collection clerk should record cash collections daily
     Recording should be a permanent record to serve as first record of accountability
5.   Cash receipts are not promptly deposited
     Deposit cash at least once a day
6.   No proof of accuracy of amounts deposited
     Compare authenticated deposit slips with daily cash collections

Investigate and resolve discrepancies promptly
     Treasurer should establish policy including analytical procedures of cash collections
7.   No record of internal accountability for cash
     Treasurer should issue signed receipt for all proceeds received from collection clerk
     Maintain receipts and periodically check against cash collection and deposit records

Unofficial Answer

Problem 8 Cash Receipts IC Weaknesses (1180,A4)

Weaknesses	Recommendation
1. There is no segregation of duties between persons responsible for collecting admission fees and persons responsible for authorizing admission.	1. One clerk (hereafter referred to as the collection clerk) should collect admission fees and issue prenumbered tickets. The other clerk (hereafter referred to as the admission clerk) should authorize admission upon receipt of the ticket or proof of membership.
2. An independent count of paying patrons is not made.	2. The admission clerk should retain a portion of the prenumbered admission ticket (admission ticket stub).
3. There is no proof of accuracy of amounts collected by the clerks.	3. Admission ticket stubs should be reconciled with cash collected by the treasurer each day.
4. Cash receipts records are not promptly prepared.	4. The cash collections should be recorded by the collection clerk daily on a permanent record that will serve as the first record of accountability.
5. Cash receipts are not promptly deposited. Cash should not be left undeposited for a week.	5. Cash should be deposited at least once each day.
6. There is no proof of accuracy of amounts deposited.	6. Authenticated deposit slips should be compared with daily cash collection records. Discrepancies should be promptly investigated and resolved. In addition, the treasurer should establish policy that includes an analytical procedures of cash collections.
7. There is no record of the internal accountability for cash.	7. The treasurer should issue a signed receipt for all proceeds received from the collection clerk. These receipts should be maintained and should be periodically checked against cash collection and deposit records.

Answer Outline

Problem 9 Purchasing Function Flowchart
(1175,A6)

Question requires identification and explanation of control problems. Only improvements are listed below.

Require proper approval of purchase requisitions

Delete purchase requisition copy sent to receiving room

Compare purchase requisitions and purchase orders

Separate file for unmatched purchase requisitions

Review need prior to preparing purchase order

Negotiate with different vendors for best price

Purchase office to review invoice prior to approving for payment

Do not show quantities on purchase orders sent to receiving room

Establish procedures for vendors' misshipments

Send copy of receiving report to stores department

Establish control over number of vouchers
  submitted for payment
Establish control over dollars of vouchers
  submitted for payment
Examine documents prior to voucher prepara-
  tion
Treasurer, not controller, should be
  responsible for cash disbursements
Establish procedures for purchase returns
Establish procedures for reconciling dis-
  crepancies
Establish control over prenumbered forms

Unofficial Answer

Problem 9   Purchasing Function Flowchart
             (1175,A6)

The identification and explanation of the
structure and control problems are as follows:

1. The purchase requisition is not
approved. The purchase requisition should be
approved by a responsible person in the stores
department. The approval should be indicated
on the purchase requisition after the approver
is satisfied that it was properly prepared
based on a need to replace stores or the proper request from a user department.

2. Purchase requisition number two is not
required. Purchase requisitions are unneces-
sarily sent from the stores department to the
receiving room. The receiving room does not
make any use of the purchase requisitions and
no purpose seems to exist for the receiving
room to obtain a copy. A copy of the requisition might be sent from stores directly to
accounts payable where it can be compared to
the purchase order to verify that the merchandise requisitioned by an authorized employee
has been properly ordered.

3. Purchase requisitions and purchase
orders are not compared in the stores department. Although purchase orders are attached
to purchase requisitions in the stores department, there is no indication that any comparison is made of the two documents. Prior to
attaching the purchase order to the purchase
requisition the requisitioner's function
should include a check that
   a. Prices are reasonable.
   b. The quality of the materials ordered
       is acceptable.
   c. Delivery dates are in accordance with
       company needs.
   d. All pertinent data on the purchase
       order and purchase requisition (e.g.,
       quantities, specifications, delivery
       dates, etc.) are in agreement.
Since the requisitioner will be charged for
the materials ordered, the requisitioner is
the logical person to perform the steps.

4. Purchase orders and purchase requisitions should not be combined and filed with
the unmatched purchase requisitions, in the
stores department. A separate file should be
maintained for the combined and matched documents. The unmatched purchase requisitions
file can serve as a control over merchandise
requisitioned but not yet ordered.

5. Preliminary review should be made
before preparing purchase orders. Prior to
preparation of the purchase order the purchase
office should review the company's need for
the specific materials requisitioned and
approve the request.

6. The purchase office should attempt to
obtain the highest quality merchandise at the
lowest possible price, and the procedures that
are followed to achieve this should be included on the flowchart. There is no indication that the purchase office submits purchase
orders to competitive bidding when appropriate. That office should be directly involved with vendors in determining the cost of
materials ordered and should be primarily
responsible for deciding at what price
materials should be ordered and which vendor
should be used.

7. The purchase office does not review
the invoice prior to processing approval. The
purchase office should review the vendor's invoice for overall accuracy and completeness,
verifying quantity, prices, specifications,
terms, dates, etc., and if the invoice is in
agreement with the purchase order, receiving
report, and purchase requisition, the purchase
office should clearly indicate on the invoice
that it is approved for payment processing.
The approval invoice should be sent to the
accounts payable department.

8. The copy of the purchase order sent to
the receiving room generally should not show
quantities ordered, thus forcing the department to count goods received. In addition to
counting the merchandise received from the
vendor, the receiving department personnel
should examine the condition and quality of
the merchandise upon receipt.

9. There is no indication of the procedures in effect when the quantity of merchandise received differs from what was ordered.
Procedures for handling over-shipments and
short-shipments should be clearly outlined and
included on the flowchart.

10. The receiving report is not sent to
the stores department. A copy of the receiving report should be sent from the receiving room directly to the stores department
with the materials received. The stores department, after verifying the accuracy of the
receiving report, should indicate approval on
that copy and send it to the accounts payable
department. The copy sent to accounts payable
will serve as proof that the materials ordered

were received by the company and are in the user department.

11. There is no indication of control over vouchers in the accounts payable department. In the accounts payable department a record of all vouchers submitted to the cashier should be maintained, and a copy of the vouchers should be filed in an alphabetical vendor reference file.

12. There is no indication of control over dollar amounts on vouchers. Accounts payable personnel should prepare and maintain control sheets on the dollar amounts of vouchers. Such sheets should be sent to departments posting transactions to general and subsidiary ledgers.

13. There is no examination of documents prior to voucher preparation. In addition to the matching procedures, the mathematical accuracy of all documents should be verified prior to preparation of vouchers.

14. The controller should not be responsible for cash disbursements. The cash disbursement function should be the responsibility of the treasurer, not the controller so as to provide proper division of responsibility between the custody of assets and the recording of transactions.

15. There is no indication of the company's procedures for handling purchase returns. Although separate return procedures may be in effect and included on a separate flowchart, some indications of this should be included as part of the purchases flowchart.

16. Discrepancy procedures are not indicated. The flowchart should indicate what procedures are followed whenever matching reveals a difference between the information on the documents compared.

17. There is no indication of any control over prenumbered forms. All prenumbered documents should be accounted for.

Unofficial Answer*

Problem 10 Sales System Flowchart (579,A2)

Flowchart symbol letter	Internal control procedure or internal document
c.	Approve customer credit and terms.
d.	Release merchandise to shipping department.
e.	File by sales order number.
f.	File pending receipt of merchandise.
g.	Prepare bill of lading.
h.	Copy of bill of lading to customer.
i.	Ship merchandise to customer.

j. File by sales order number.
k. Customer purchase order and sales order.
l. File pending notice of shipment.
m. Prepare three-part sales invoice.
n. Copy of invoice to customer.
o. Post to (or enter in) sales journal.
p. Account for numerical sequence.
q. Post to customer accounts.
r. File by (payment due) date.

Unofficial Answer*

Problem 11 Sales Flow Chart (588,A4)

The weaknesses in Newton Hardware's internal controls include these:

Warehouse Clerk

- Initiates posting to inventory records by preparation of shipping advice.
- Releases merchandise to customers before proper approvals of customers' credit.
- Does not retain a copy of the shipping advice for comparison with receipt from carrier.

Bookkeeper A

- Authorizes customers' credit and prepares source documents for posting to customers' accounts.
- Prepares invoices without notice that the merchandise was actually shipped and the date it was shipped.
- Authorizes write-offs of customer accounts receivable and authorizes customers' credit.

Collection Clerk

- Receives directly and records customers' checks.
- Does not deliver checks excluded from the deposit to an employee independent of the bank deposit for review and disposition.
- Initiates posting of receipts to subsidiary accounts receivable ledger and has initial access to cash receipts.
- Does not deposit cash receipts promptly.
- Reconciles bank statement and has initial access to cash receipts.

*Because the requirements of this question could be answered by lists of items we have not included an outline of the solution.

Unofficial Answer*

Problem 12   IC Questionnaire-Shipments
             (589,A3)

JOHNSON'S COAT OUTLET, INC.
Shipments
Internal Control Questionnaire

Question	Yes	No

1. Are shipping documents prepared from sales orders approved
in accordance with management's
authorization?

2. Are shipping documents prenumbered?

3. Are shipping documents periodically accounted for?

4. Are shipping documents recorded
in a register, log, or file?

5. Are copies of shipping documents
forwarded to the
          Billing department?
          Inventory control department?

6. Do shipping documents include
cross reference to sales orders; customer identity and address; description
and quantities of goods shipped; date;
and other details?

7. Is the shipping function independent of
          Sales orders?
          Credit approval?
          Billing and accounts receiv-
            able?
          Cash receipts?
          Warehouse?
          Receiving?
          Inventory control?

8. Is access to merchandise restricted and controlled within the
shipping department?

9. Are type and quantities of goods
withdrawn and packed for shipping verified by independent counts?

10. Are receipts from carriers obtained and filed?

*Because the requirements of this question
could be answered by lists of items we have
not included an outline of the solution.

Answer Outline

Problem 13   Cash Receipts; Reportable Conditions (1189,A5)

Reportable condition	Potential misstatement
Employees who perform services also permitted to approve credit without external credit check	U/A expense (-) and A/R (+) Because of lack of appropriate credit check
No independent verification of billing process	Fees earned and A/R (-) Because all services performed might not be reported for billing <center>or</center>Fees earned and A/R either (+) or (-) Because incorrect price or service data used or Because of mathematical errors
Employees who approve credit also approve write-offs of U/A	A/R (-) and U/A expense (+) Because W/O of A/R could be approved for accounts that are, in fact, collectible <center>or</center>A/R (+) and U/A expense (-) Because W/O of A/R might not be initiated for accounts that are uncollectible
Credit not granted based on established limits	U/A expense either (-) or (+) Because lack of established credit limits may make it more difficult to identify U/A
Employee who initially handles cash receipts also prepares billings	Fees earned and cash receipts or A/R (-) Because of omitted or inaccurate billing
Employee making bank deposits also reconciles bank statements	Cash balance per books may be (+) Because not all cash is deposited
U/A not based on established criteria	Uncollectible accounts expense either (-) or (+) Because no W/O criteria
T/B of A/R S/L not prepared independently of, or verified and reconciled to, A/R control account in G/L	Any of fees earned, cash receipts, and U/A expense either (-) or (+) Because undetected differences between S/L and G/L <center>or</center>Fees earned and cash receipts or A/R (-) Because failure to record billings, cash receipts, or W/O accurately

Unofficial Answer

Problem 13   Cash Receipts; Reportable Conditions (1189,A5)

The reportable conditions and resulting misstatements, in addition to the example, that could occur and not be prevented or detected by Parktown's internal control structure concerning the cash receipts and billing functions include the following:

Reportable condition	Potential misstatement
The employees who perform services also are permitted to approve credit without an external credit check.	Uncollectible accounts expense could be understated and accounts receivable could be overstated because of the lack of an appropriate credit check.
There is no independent verification of the billing process.	Fees earned and accounts receivable may be understated because not all services performed might be reported for billing. or Fees earned and accounts receivable may be either overstated or understated because of the use of incorrect price or service data or because of mathematical errors.
The employees who approve credit also approve write-offs of uncollectible accounts.	Accounts receivable could be understated and uncollectible accounts expense overstated because write-offs of accounts receivable could be approved for accounts that are, in fact, collectible. or Accounts receivable could be overstated and uncollectible accounts expense understated because write-offs of accounts receivable might not be initiated for accounts that are uncollectible.
Credit is not granted on the basis of established limits.	Uncollectible accounts expense could be either understated or overstated because the lack of established credit limits may make it more difficult to identify uncollectible amounts.
The employee who initially handles cash receipts also prepares billings.	Fees earned and cash receipts or accounts receivable could be understated because of omitted or inaccurate billing.
The employee who makes bank deposits also reconciles bank statements.	The cash balance per books may be overstated because not all cash is deposited.
Uncollectible accounts are not determined on the basis of established criteria.	Uncollectible accounts expense could be either understated or overstated because of the lack of established write-off criteria.
Trial balances of the accounts receivable subsidiary ledger are not prepared independently of, or verified and reconciled to, the accounts receivable control account in the general ledger.	Any of fees earned, cash receipts, and uncollectible accounts expense could be either understated or overstated because of undetected differences between the subsidiary ledger and the general ledger. or Fees earned and cash receipts or accounts receivable could be understated because of failure to record billings, cash receipts, or write-offs accurately.

3

Multiple Choice Questions (1-112)

1. Which of the following statements relating to the competence of evidential matter is always true?
   a. Evidential matter gathered by an auditor from outside an enterprise is reliable.
   b. Accounting data developed under satisfactory conditions of internal control are more relevant than data developed under unsatisfactory internal control conditions.
   c. Oral representations made by management are not valid evidence.
   d. Evidence gathered by auditors must be both valid and relevant to be considered competent.

2. Which of the following statements is generally correct about the competence of evidential matter?
   a. The auditor's direct personal knowledge, obtained through observation and inspection, is more persuasive than information obtained indirectly from independent outside sources.
   b. To be competent, evidential matter must be either valid or relevant, but need not be both.
   c. Accounting data alone may be considered sufficient competent evidential matter to issue an unqualified opinion on financial statements.
   d. Competence of evidential matter refers to the amount of corroborative evidence to be obtained.

3. Each of the following might, by itself, form a valid basis for an auditor to decide to omit a test except for the
   a. Difficulty and expense involved in testing a particular item.
   b. Degree of reliance on the relevant internal controls.
   c. Relative risk involved.
   d. Relationship between the cost of obtaining evidence and its usefulness.

4. Audit evidence can come in different forms with different degrees of persuasiveness. Which of the following is the least persuasive type of evidence?
   a. Bank statement obtained from the client.
   b. Computations made by the auditor.
   c. Prenumbered client sales invoices.
   d. Vendor's invoice.

5. An entity's financial statements were misstated over a period of years due to large amounts of revenue being recorded in journal entries that involved debits and credits to an illogical combination of accounts. The auditor could most likely have been alerted to this irregularity by
   a. Scanning the general journal for unusual entries.
   b. Performing a revenue cut-off test at year end.
   c. Tracing a sample of journal entries to the general ledger.
   d. Examining documentary evidence of sales returns and allowances recorded after year end.

6. While substantive tests may support the accuracy of underlying records, these tests frequently provide no affirmative evidence of segregation of duties because
   a. Substantive tests rarely guarantee the accuracy of the records if only a sample of the transactions has been tested.
   b. The records may be accurate even though they are maintained by persons having incompatible functions.
   c. Substantive tests relate to the entire period under audit, but tests of controls ordinarily are confined to the period during which the auditor is on the client's premises.
   d. Many computerized procedures leave no audit trail of who performed them, so substantive tests may necessarily be limited to inquiries and observation of office personnel.

7. A basic premise underlying analytical procedures is that
   a. These procedures can not replace tests of balances and transactions.
   b. Statistical tests of financial information may lead to the discovery of material errors in the financial statements.
   c. The study of financial ratios is an acceptable alternative to the investigation of unusual fluctuations.
   d. Relationships among data may reasonably be expected to exist and continue in the absence of known conditions to the contrary.

8.   An example of an analytical procedure is the comparison of

   a.   Financial information with similar information regarding the industry in which the entity operates.
   b.   Recorded amounts of major disbursements with appropriate invoices.
   c.   Results of a statistical sample with the expected characteristics of the actual population.
   d.   EDP generated data with similar data generated by a manual accounting system.

9.   The auditor's analytical procedures will be facilitated if the client

   a.   Uses a standard cost system that produces variance reports.
   b.   Segregates obsolete inventory before the physical inventory count.
   c.   Corrects reportable conditions in internal control before the beginning of the audit.
   d.   Reduces inventory balances to the lower of cost or market.

10.   To help plan the nature, timing, and extent of substantive auditing procedures, preliminary analytical procedures should focus on

   a.   Enhancing the auditor's understanding of the client's business and events that have occurred since the last audit date.
   b.   Developing plausible relationships that corroborate anticipated results with a measurable amount of precision.
   c.   Applying ratio analysis to externally generated data such as published industry statistics or price indices.
   d.   Comparing recorded financial information to the results of other tests of transactions and balances.

11.   An auditor compares 1985 revenues and expenses with those of the prior year and investigates all changes exceeding 10%. By this procedure the auditor would be most likely to learn that

   a.   Fourth quarter payroll taxes were **not** paid.
   b.   The client changed its capitalization policy for small tools in 1985.
   c.   An increase in property tax rates has **not** been recognized in the client's accrual.
   d.   The 1985 provision for uncollectible accounts is inadequate because of worsening economic conditions.

12.   The primary objective of analytical procedures used in the final review stage of an audit is to

   a.   Obtain evidence from details tested to corroborate particular assertions.
   b.   Identify areas that represent specific risks relevant to the audit.
   c.   Assist the auditor in assessing the validity of the conclusions reached.
   d.   Satisfy doubts when questions arise about a client's ability to continue in existence.

13.   In the context of an audit of financial statements, substantive tests are audit procedures that

   a.   May be eliminated under certain conditions.
   b.   Are designed to discover significant subsequent events.
   c.   May be either tests of transactions, direct tests of financial balances, or analytical tests.
   d.   Will increase proportionately with the auditor's reliance on internal control.

14.   The auditor will most likely perform extensive tests for possible understatement of

   a.   Revenues.
   b.   Assets.
   c.   Liabilities.
   d.   Capital.

15.   To test for unsupported entries in the ledger, the direction of audit testing should be from the

   a.   Journal entries.
   b.   Ledger entries.
   c.   Original source documents.
   d.   Externally generated documents.

16.   For which of the following account balances are substantive tests of details **least** likely to be performed unless analytical procedures indicate the need to extend detail testing?

   a.   Payroll expense.
   b.   Marketable securities.
   c.   Research and development costs.
   d.   Legal expense.

17.   Which of the following statements concerning working papers is incorrect?

   a.   An auditor may support an opinion by other means in addition to working papers.
   b.   The form of working papers should be designed to meet the circumstances of a particular engagement.

c. An auditor's working papers may **not** serve as a reference source for the client.

d. Working papers should show that the internal control structure has been considered to the degree necessary.

18. The permanent file section of the working papers that is kept for each audit client most likely contains

a. Review notes pertaining to questions and comments regarding the audit work performed.

b. A schedule of time spent on the engagement by each individual auditor.

c. Correspondence with the client's legal counsel concerning pending litigation.

d. Narrative descriptions of the client's accounting procedures and internal controls.

19. Working papers ordinarily would **not** include

a. Initials of the in-charge auditor indicating review of the staff assistants' work.

b. Cutoff bank statements received directly from the banks.

c. A memo describing the internal control structure.

d. Copies of client inventory count sheets.

20. The current file of the auditor's working papers generally should include

a. A flowchart of the internal controls.

b. Organization charts.

c. A copy of the financial statements.

d. Copies of bond and note indentures.

21. An audit working paper that reflects the major components of an amount reported in the financial statements is referred to as a(an)

a. Lead schedule.

b. Supporting schedule.

c. Audit control account.

d. Working trial balance.

22. To gather evidence regarding the balance per bank in a bank reconciliation, an auditor would examine all of the following **except**

a. Cutoff bank statement.

b. Year-end bank statement.

c. Bank confirmation.

d. General ledger.

23. Which of the following cash transfers results in a misstatement of cash at December 31, 1987?

| | Bank Transfer Schedule | | | |
| | Disbursement | | Receipt | |
Transfer	Recorded in books	Paid by bank	Recorded in books	Received by bank
a.	12/31/87	1/4/88	12/31/87	12/31/87
b.	1/4/88	1/5/88	12/31/87	1/4/88
c.	12/31/87	1/5/88	12/31/87	1/4/88
d.	1/4/88	1/11/88	1/4/88	1/4/88

Items 24 and 25 are based on the following:

Miles Company
Bank Transfer Schedule
December 31, 1988

Check Number	Bank Accounts From	To	Amount	Date disbursed per Books	Bank	Date deposited per Books	Bank
2020	1st Natl.	Suburban	$32,000	12/31	1/5 ◆	12/31	1/3 ▲
2021	1st Natl.	Capital	21,000	12/31	1/4 ◆	12/31	1/3 ▲
3217	2nd State	Suburban	6,700	1/3	1/5	1/3	1/6
0659	Midtown	Suburban	5,500	12/30	1/5 ◆	12/30	1/3 ▲

24. The tick mark ◆ most likely indicates that the amount was traced to the

a. December cash disbursements journal.

b. Outstanding check list of the applicable bank reconciliation.

c. January cash disbursements journal.

d. Year-end bank confirmations.

25. The tick mark ▲ most likely indicates that the amount was traced to the

a. Deposits in transit of the applicable bank reconciliation.

b. December cash receipts journal.

c. January cash receipts journal.

d. Year-end bank confirmations.

26. A cash shortage may be concealed by transporting funds from one location to another or by converting negotiable assets to cash. Because of this, which of the following is vital?

a. Simultaneous confirmations.
b. Simultaneous bank reconciliations.
c. Simultaneous verification.
d. Simultaneous surprise cash count.

27. Confirmation is most likely to be a relevant form of evidence with regard to assertions about accounts receivable when the auditor has concerns about the receivables'

a. Valuation.
b. Classification.
c. Existence.
d. Completeness.

28. Which of the following procedures would an auditor most likely rely on to verify management's assertion of completeness?

a. Review standard bank confirmations for indications of kiting.
b. Compare a sample of shipping documents to related sales invoices.
c. Observe the client's distribution of payroll checks.
d. Confirm a sample of recorded receivables by direct communication with the debtors.

29. Which of the following circumstances would most likely cause an auditor to suspect that material irregularities exist in a client's financial statements?

a. Property and equipment are usually sold at a loss before being fully depreciated.
b. Significantly fewer responses to confirmation requests are received than expected.
c. Monthly bank reconciliations usually include several in-transit items.
d. Clerical errors are listed on an EDP-generated exception report.

30. Cooper, CPA, is auditing the financial statements of a small rural municipality. The receivable balances represent residents' delinquent real estate taxes. The internal control structure at the municipality is weak. To determine the existence of the accounts receivable balances at the balance sheet date, Cooper would most likely

a. Send positive confirmation requests.
b. Send negative confirmation requests.
c. Examine evidence of subsequent cash receipts.
d. Inspect the internal records such as copies of the tax invoices that were mailed to the residents.

31. An auditor should perform alternative procedures to substantiate the existence of accounts receivable when

a. No reply to a positive confirmation request is received.
b. No reply to a negative confirmation request is received.
c. Collectibility of the receivables is in doubt.
d. Pledging of the receivables is probable.

32. Negative confirmation of accounts receivable is less effective than positive confirmation of accounts receivable because

a. A majority of recipients usually lack the willingness to respond objectively.
b. Some recipients may report incorrect balances that require extensive follow-up.
c. The auditor can not infer that all nonrespondents have verified their account information.
d. Negative confirmations do not produce evidential matter that is statistically quantifiable.

33. If a client maintains perpetual inventory records in quantities and in dollars, and its internal control over inventory is weak, an auditor would probably

a. Apply gross profit tests to ascertain the reasonableness of the physical counts.
b. Increase the extent of tests of controls of the inventory cycle.
c. Request the client to schedule the physical inventory count at the end of the year.
d. Insist that the client perform physical counts of inventory items several times during the year.

34. After accounting for a sequence of inventory tags, an auditor traces a sample of tags to the physical inventory listing to obtain evidence that all items

a. Included in the listing have been counted.
b. Represented by inventory tags are included in the listing.
c. Included in the listing are represented by inventory tags.
d. Represented by inventory tags are bona fide.

35. Which of the following is not one of the independent auditor's objectives regarding the examination of inventories?

a. Verifying that inventory counted is owned by the client.

b. Verifying that the client has used
proper inventory pricing.
c. Ascertaining the physical quantities
of inventory on hand.
d. Verifying that all inventory owned
by the client is on hand at the time
of the count.

36. An auditor usually examines receiving
reports to support entries in the
a. Voucher register and sales returns
journal.
b. Sales journal and sales returns
journal.
c. Voucher register and sales journal.
d. Check register and sales journal.

37. The auditor tests the quantity of
materials charged to work in process by
tracing these quantities to
a. Cost ledgers.
b. Perpetual inventory records.
c. Receiving reports.
d. Material requisitions.

38. When auditing a public warehouse, which
of the following is the most important audit
procedure with respect to disclosing unrecorded liabilities?
a. Confirmation of negotiable receipts
with holders.
b. Review of outstanding receipts.
c. Inspection of receiving and issuing
procedures.
d. Observation of inventory.

39. Which of the following is the most
effective audit procedure for verification of
dividends earned on the investments in
marketable equity securities?
a. Tracing deposit of dividend checks
to the cash receipts book.
b. Reconciling amounts received with
published dividend records.
c. Comparing the amounts received with
preceding year dividends received.
d. Recomputing selected extensions and
footings of dividend schedules and
comparing totals to the general
ledger.

40. When an auditor is unable to inspect and
count a client's investment securities until
after the balance-sheet date, the bank where
the securities are held in a safe deposit box
should be asked to
a. Verify any differences between the
contents of the box and the balances
in the client's subsidiary ledger.

b. Provide a list of securities added
and removed from the box between the
balance-sheet date and the security-
count date.
c. Confirm that there has been no
access to the box between the
balance-sheet date and the security-
count date.
d. Count the securities in the box so
the auditor will have an independent
direct verification.

41. Which of the following would provide the
best form of evidential matter pertaining to
the annual valuation of a long-term investment
in which the independent auditor's client owns
a 30% voting interest?
a. Market quotations of the investee
company's stock.
b. Current fair value of the investee
company's assets.
c. Historical cost of the investee
company's assets.
d. Audited financial statements of the
investee company.

42. An auditor would most likely verify the
interest earned on bond investments by
a. Vouching the receipt and deposit of
interest checks.
b. Confirming the bond interest rate
with the issuer of the bonds.
c. Recomputing the interest earned on
the basis of face amount, interest
rate, and period held.
d. Testing the internal controls over
cash receipts.

43. An auditor analyzes repairs and
maintenance accounts primarily to obtain
evidence in support of the audit assertion
that all
a. Noncapitalizable expenditures for
repairs and maintenance have been
properly charged to expense.
b. Expenditures for property and
equipment have not been charged to
expense.
c. Noncapitalizable expenditures for
repairs and maintenance have been
recorded in the proper period.
d. Expenditures for property and
equipment have been recorded in the
proper period.

44. The auditor may conclude that depreciation charges are insufficient by noting
a. Large amounts of fully depreciated
assets.
b. Continuous trade-ins of relatively
new assets.

c.   Excessive recurring losses on assets
     retired.
d.   Insured values greatly in excess of
     book values.

45. The auditor is most likely to seek information from the plant manager with respect to
the
a.   Adequacy of the provision for uncol-
     lectible accounts.
b.   Appropriateness of physical inven-
     tory observation procedures.
c.   Existence of obsolete machinery.
d.   Deferral of procurement of certain
     necessary insurance coverage.

46. Treetop Corporation acquired a building
and arranged mortgage financing during the
year. Verification of the related mortgage
acquisition costs would be least likely to
include an examination of the related
a.   Deed.
b.   Canceled checks.
c.   Closing statement.
d.   Interest expense.

47. Auditor confirmation of accounts payable
balances at the balance sheet date may be
unnecessary because
a.   This is a duplication of cutoff
     tests.
b.   Accounts payable balances at the
     balance sheet date may not be paid
     before the audit is completed.
c.   Correspondence with the audit
     client's attorney will reveal all
     legal action by vendors for nonpay-
     ment.
d.   There is likely to be other reliable
     external evidence to support the
     balances.

48. Unrecorded liabilities are most likely to
be found during the review of which of the
following documents?
a.   Unpaid bills.
b.   Shipping records.
c.   Bills of lading.
d.   Unmatched sales invoices.

49. The auditor can best verify a client's
bond sinking fund transactions and year-end
balance by
a.   Confirmation with individual holders
     of retired bonds.
b.   Confirmation with the bond trustee.
c.   Recomputation of interest expense,
     interest payable, and amortization
     of bond discount or premium.
d.   Examination and count of the bonds
     retired during the year.

50. To establish the existence and ownership
of a long-term investment in the common stock
of a publicly-traded company, an auditor
ordinarily performs a security count or
a.   Relies on the client's internal
     controls if the auditor has
     reasonable assurance that the
     control procedures are being applied
     as prescribed.
b.   Confirms the number of shares owned
     that are held by an independent
     custodian.
c.   Determines the market price per
     share at the balance sheet date from
     published quotations.
d.   Confirms the number of shares owned
     with the issuing company.

51. An auditor should trace corporate stock
issuances and treasury stock transactions to
the
a.   Numbered stock certificates.
b.   Articles of incorporation.
c.   Transfer agent's records.
d.   Minutes of the board of directors.

52. An audit program for the examination of
the retained earnings account should include a
step that requires verification of the
a.   Market value used to charge retained
     earnings to account for a two-for-
     one stock split.
b.   Approval of the adjustment to the
     beginning balance as a result of a
     write down of an account receivable.
c.   Authorization for both cash and
     stock dividends.
d.   Gain or loss resulting from disposi-
     tion of treasury shares.

53. Which of the following documentation is
required for an audit in accordance with
generally accepted auditing standards?
a.   An internal control questionnaire.
b.   A client engagement letter.
c.   A planning memorandum or checklist.
d.   A client representation letter.

54. "Provision has been made for any material
loss that might be sustained as a result of
purchase commitments for inventory quantities
in excess of normal requirements or at prices
in excess of the prevailing market prices."
The foregoing passage is most likely from
a.   A management representation letter.
b.   The explanatory paragraph of an
     "except for" qualified auditor's
     report.
c.   A vendor representation letter.
d.   The explanatory paragraph of a
     qualified auditor's report.

55. When considering the use of management's written representations as audit evidence about the completeness assertion, an auditor should understand that such representations

    a. Complement, but do not replace, substantive tests designed to support the assertion.

    b. Constitute sufficient evidence to support the assertion when considered in combination with reliance on internal controls.

    c. Are not part of the evidential matter considered to support the assertion.

    d. Replace reliance on internal controls as evidence to support the assertion.

56. A written representation from a client's management which, among other matters, acknowledges responsibility for the fair presentation of financial statements, should normally be signed by the

    a. Chief executive officer and the chief financial officer.

    b. Chief financial officer and the chairman of the board of directors.

    c. Chairman of the audit committee of the board of directors.

    d. Chief executive officer, the chairman of the board of directors, and the client's lawyer.

57. A limitation on the scope of the auditor's examination sufficient to preclude an unqualified opinion will always result when management

    a. Prevents the auditor from reviewing the working papers of the predecessor auditor.

    b. Engages the auditor after the year-end physical inventory count is completed.

    c. Fails to correct a reportable condition of internal control that had been identified during the prior year's audit.

    d. Refuses to furnish a management representation letter to the auditor.

58. Hall accepted an engagement to audit the 1985 financial statements of XYZ Company. XYZ completed the preparation of the 1985 financial statements on February 13, 1986, and Hall began the field work on February 17, 1986. Hall completed the field work on March 24, 1986, and completed the report on March 28, 1986. The client's representation letter normally would be dated

    a. February 13, 1986.

    b. February 17, 1986.

    c. March 24, 1986.

    d. March 28, 1986.

59. Which of the following statements concerning the auditor's use of the work of a specialist is correct?

    a. If the specialist is related to the client, the auditor is not permitted to use the specialist's findings as corroborative evidence.

    b. The specialist may be identified in the auditor's report only when the auditor issues a qualified opinion.

    c. The specialist should have an understanding of the auditor's corroborative use of the specialist's findings.

    d. If the auditor believes that the determinations made by the specialist are unreasonable, only an adverse opinion may be issued.

60. Which of the following is not a specialist upon whose work an auditor may rely?

    a. Actuary.

    b. Appraiser.

    c. Internal auditor.

    d. Engineer.

61. When using the work of a specialist, an auditor may refer to and identify the specialist in the auditor's report if the

    a. Auditor wishes to indicate a division of responsibility.

    b. Specialist's work provides the auditor greater assurance of reliability.

    c. Auditor expresses an adverse opinion as a result of the specialist's findings.

    d. Specialist is not independent of the client.

62. Auditors should request that an audit client send a letter of inquiry to those attorneys who have been consulted concerning litigation, claims, or assessments. The primary reason for this request is to provide

    a. Information concerning the progress of cases to date.

    b. Corroborative evidential matter.

    c. An estimate of the dollar amount of the probable loss.

    d. An expert opinion as to whether a loss is possible, probable, or remote.

63. An attorney responding to an auditor as a result of the client's letter of audit inquiry may appropriately limit the response to
    a. Items which have high probability of being resolved to the client's detriment.
    b. Asserted claims and pending or threatened litigation.
    c. Legal matters subject to unsettled points of law, uncorroborated information, or other complex judgments.
    d. Matters to which the attorney has given substantive attention in the form of legal consultation or representation.

64. Which of the following is not an audit procedure which the independent auditor would perform with respect to litigation, claims, and assessments?
    a. Inquire of and discuss with management the policies and procedures adopted for identifying, evaluating, and accounting for litigation, claims, and assessments.
    b. Obtain from management a description and evaluation of litigation, claims, and assessments that existed at the balance sheet date.
    c. Obtain assurance from management that it has disclosed all unasserted claims that the lawyer has advised are probable of assertion and must be disclosed.
    d. Confirm directly with the client's lawyer that all claims have been recorded in the financial statements.

65. A CPA has received an attorney's letter in which no significant disagreements with the client's assessments of contingent liabilities were noted. The resignation of the client's lawyer shortly after receipt of the letter should alert the auditor that
    a. Undisclosed unasserted claims may have arisen.
    b. The attorney was unable to form a conclusion with respect to the significance of litigation, claims, and assessments.
    c. The auditor must begin a completely new examination of contingent liabilities.
    d. An adverse opinion will be necessary.

66. The refusal of a client's attorney to provide a representation on the legality of a particular act committed by the client is generally

    a. Sufficient reason to issue a "subject to" qualified opinion.
    b. Considered to be a scope limitation.
    c. Insufficient reason to modify the auditor's report due to the attorney's obligation of confidentiality.
    d. Proper grounds to withdraw from the engagement.

67. Which of the following statements is correct concerning related party transactions?
    a. In the absence of evidence to the contrary, related party transactions should be assumed to be outside the ordinary course of business.
    b. An auditor should determine whether a particular transaction would have occurred if the parties had not been related.
    c. An auditor should substantiate that related party transactions were consummated on terms equivalent to those that prevail in arm's length transactions.
    d. The audit procedures directed toward identifying related party transactions should include considering whether transactions are occurring, but are not being given proper accounting recognition.

68. An auditor who is determining the scope of work to be performed concerning possible related party transactions should
    a. Assume that transactions with related parties are outside the ordinary course of business.
    b. Determine whether transactions with related parties would have taken place if the parties had not been related.
    c. Obtain an understanding of management responsibilities and the relationship of each of the parties to the total entity.
    d. Establish a basis of accounting principles different from that which would have been appropriate had the parties not been related.

69. The existence of a related party transaction may be indicated when another entity
    a. Sells real estate to the corporation at a price that is comparable to its appraised value.
    b. Absorbs expenses of the corporation.
    c. Borrows from the corporation at a rate of interest which equals the current market rate.
    d. Lends to the corporation at a rate of interest which equals the current market rate.

70. An auditor searching for related party transactions should obtain an understanding of each subsidiary's relationship to the total entity because
   a. This may permit the audit of intercompany account balances to be performed as of concurrent dates.
   b. Intercompany transactions may have been consummated on terms equivalent to arm's length transactions.
   c. This may reveal whether particular transactions would have taken place if the parties had not been related.
   d. The business structure may be deliberately designed to obscure related party transactions.

71. Which of the following audit procedures would most likely assist an auditor in identifying conditions and events that may indicate there could be substantial doubt about an entity's ability to continue as a going concern?
   a. Review compliance with the terms of debt agreements.
   b. Confirmation of accounts receivable from principal customers.
   c. Reconciliation of interest expense with debt outstanding.
   d. Confirmation of bank balances.

72. Which of the following procedures would an auditor ordinarily perform during the review of subsequent events?
   a. An analysis of related party transactions for the discovery of possible irregularities.
   b. A review of the cutoff bank statements for the period after the year end.
   c. An inquiry of the client's legal counsel concerning litigation.
   d. An investigation of material weaknesses in internal control previously communicated to the client.

73. Which of the following procedures would an auditor most likely perform to obtain evidence about an entity's subsequent events?
   a. Reconcile bank activity for the month after the balance sheet date with cash activity reflected in the accounting records.
   b. Examine on a test basis the purchase invoices and receiving reports for several days after the inventory date.
   c. Review the treasurer's monthly reports on temporary investments owned, purchased, and sold.

   d. Obtain a letter from the entity's attorney describing any pending litigation, unasserted claims, or loss contingencies.

74. After an audit report containing an unqualified opinion on a non-public client's financial statements was issued, the client decided to sell the shares of a subsidiary that accounts for 30% of its revenue and 25% of its net income. The auditor should
   a. Determine whether the information is reliable and, if determined to be reliable, request that revised financial statements be issued.
   b. Notify the entity that the auditor's report may no longer be associated with the financial statements.
   c. Describe the effects of this subsequently discovered information in a communication with persons known to be relying on the financial statements.
   d. Take no action because the auditor has no obligation to make any further inquiries.

75. A client acquired 25% of its outstanding capital stock after year end and prior to completion of the auditor's field work. The auditor should
   a. Advise management to adjust the balance sheet to reflect the acquisition.
   b. Issue pro forma financial statements giving effect to the acquisition as if it had occurred at year end.
   c. Advise management to disclose the acquisition in the notes to the financial statements.
   d. Disclose the acquisition in the opinion paragraph of the auditor's report.

76. Which of the following subsequent events will be least likely to result in an adjustment to the financial statements?
   a. Culmination of events affecting the realization of accounts receivable owned as of the balance sheet date.
   b. Culmination of events affecting the realization of inventories owned as of the balance sheet date.
   c. Material changes in the settlement of liabilities which were estimated as of the balance sheet date.
   d. Material changes in the quoted market prices of listed investment securities since the balance sheet date.

77. Soon after Boyd's audit report was issued, Boyd learned of certain related party transactions that occurred during the year under audit. These transactions were not disclosed in the notes to the financial statements. Boyd should
   a.   Plan to audit the transactions during the next engagement.
   b.   Recall all copies of the audited financial statements.
   c.   Determine whether the lack of disclosure would affect the auditor's report.
   d.   Ask the client to disclose the transactions in subsequent interim statements.

78. An auditor concludes that an audit procedure considered necessary at the time of the examination had been omitted. The auditor should assess the importance of the omitted procedure to the ability to support the previously expressed opinion. Which of the following would be least helpful in making that assessment?
   a.   A discussion with the client about whether there are persons relying on the auditor's report.
   b.   A reevaluation of the overall scope of the examination.
   c.   A discussion of the circumstances with engagement personnel.
   d.   A review of the other audit procedures that were applied that might compensate for the one omitted.

79. Ajax Company's auditor concludes that the omission of an audit procedure considered necessary at the time of the prior examination impairs the auditor's present ability to support the previously expressed unqualified opinion. If the auditor believes there are stockholders currently relying on the opinion, the auditor should promptly
   a.   Notify the stockholders currently relying on the previously expressed unqualified opinion that they should not rely on it.
   b.   Advise management to disclose this development in its next interim report to the stockholders.
   c.   Advise management to revise the financial statements with full disclosure of the auditor's inability to support the unqualified opinion.
   d.   Undertake to apply the omitted procedure or alternate procedures that would provide a satisfactory basis for the opinion.

80. An auditor concludes that the omission of a substantive procedure considered necessary at the time of the examination may impair the auditor's present ability to support the previously expressed opinion. The auditor need not apply the omitted procedure if
   a.   The risk of adverse publicity or litigation is low.
   b.   The results of other procedures that were applied tend to compensate for the procedure omitted.
   c.   The auditor's opinion was qualified because of a departure from generally accepted accounting principles.
   d.   The results of the subsequent period's tests of controls make the omitted procedure less important.

81. In the course of the examination of financial statements for the purpose of expressing an opinion thereon, the auditor will normally prepare a schedule of unadjusted differences for which the auditor did not propose adjustment when they were uncovered. What is the primary purpose served by this schedule?
   a.   To point out to the responsible client officials the errors made by various company personnel.
   b.   To summarize the adjustments that must be made before the company can prepare and submit its federal tax return.
   c.   To identify the potential financial statement effects of errors or disputed items that were considered immaterial when discovered.
   d.   To summarize the errors made by the company so that corrections can be made after the audited financial statements are released.

82. Which of the following auditing procedures is ordinarily performed last?
   a.   Obtaining a management representation letter.
   b.   Testing the purchasing function.
   c.   Reading the minutes of directors' meetings.
   d.   Confirming accounts payable.

83. Which of the following most likely would be detected by an auditor's review of a client's sales cutoff?
   a.   Unrecorded sales for the year.
   b.   Lapping of year-end accounts receivable.
   c.   Excessive sales discounts.
   d.   Unauthorized goods returned for credit.

84. The auditor is <u>most</u> likely to verify accrued commissions payable in conjunction with the
   a. Sales cutoff review.
   b. Verification of contingent liabilities.
   c. Review of post balance sheet date disbursements.
   d. Examination of trade accounts payable.

85. In an audit of contingent liabilities, which of the following procedures would be <u>least</u> effective?
   a. Reviewing a bank confirmation letter.
   b. Examining customer confirmation replies.
   c. Examining invoices for professional services.
   d. Reading the minutes of the board of directors.

86. An auditor would be most likely to identify a contingent liability by mailing a(an)
   a. Standard bank confirmation.
   b. Related party transaction confirmation.
   c. Accounts payable confirmation.
   d. Transfer agent confirmation.

87. Prior to commencing the compilation of financial statements of a nonpublic entity, the accountant should
   a. Perform analytical procedures sufficient to determine whether fluctuations among account balances appear reasonable.
   b. Complete the preliminary phase of the study and evaluation of the entity's internal control.
   c. Verify that the financial information supplied by the entity agrees with the books of original entry.
   d. Acquire a knowledge of any specialized accounting principles and practices used in the entity's industry.

88. One of the conditions required for an accountant to submit a written personal financial plan containing unaudited financial statements to a client without complying with the requirements of SSARS 1 (Compilation and Review of Financial Statements) is that the
   a. Client agrees that the financial statements will <u>not</u> be used to obtain credit.
   b. Accountant compiled or reviewed the client's financial statements for the immediate prior year.

   c. Engagement letter acknowledges that the financial statements will contain departures from generally accepted accounting principles.
   d. Accountant expresses limited assurance that the financial statements are free of any material misstatements.

89. Performing inquiry and analytical procedures is the primary basis for an accountant to issue a(an)
   a. Compilation report on financial statements for a nonpublic entity in its first year of operations.
   b. Review report on comparative financial statements for a nonpublic entity in its second year of operations.
   c. Management advisory report prepared at the request of a client's audit committee.
   d. Internal control report for a governmental agency in accordance with GAO standards.

90. Before performing a review of a nonpublic entity's financial statements, an accountant should
   a. Complete a series of inquiries concerning the entity's procedures for recording, classifying, and summarizing transactions.
   b. Apply analytical procedures to provide limited assurance that <u>no</u> material modifications should be made to the financial statements.
   c. Obtain a sufficient level of knowledge of the accounting principles and practices of the industry in which the entity operates.
   d. Inquire whether management has omitted substantially all of the disclosures required by generally accepted accounting principles.

91. Which of the following procedures is usually included in a review engagement of a nonpublic entity?
   a. The confirmation of accounts receivable.
   b. A consideration of internal control.
   c. An inquiry concerning subsequent events.
   d. The observation of physical inventory counts.

92. Which of the following would the accountant most likely investigate during the review of financial statements of a nonpublic entity if accounts receivable did not conform to a predictable pattern during the year?
    a. Sales returns and allowances.
    b. Credit sales.
    c. Sales of consigned goods.
    d. Cash sales.

93. Which of the following procedures is not usually performed by the accountant in a review engagement of a nonpublic entity?
    a. Communicating any material weaknesses discovered during the study and evaluation of internal control.
    b. Reading the financial statements to consider whether they conform with generally accepted accounting principles.
    c. Writing an engagement letter to establish an understanding regarding the services to be performed.
    d. Issuing a report stating that the review was performed in accordance with standards established by the AICPA.

94. Which of the following bodies promulgates standards for audits of federal financial assistance recipients?
    a. Governmental Accounting Standards Board.
    b. Financial Accounting Standards Board.
    c. General Accounting Office.
    d. Governmental Auditing Standards Board.

95. A governmental audit may extend beyond an examination leading to the expression of an opinion on the fairness of financial presentation to include

	Program results	Compliance	Economy & efficiency
a.	Yes	Yes	No
b.	Yes	Yes	Yes
c.	No	Yes	Yes
d.	Yes	No	Yes

96. When performing an audit of a city that is subject to the requirements of the Uniform Single Audit Act of 1984, an auditor should adhere to
    a. Governmental Accounting Standards Board General Standards.
    b. Governmental Finance Officers Association Governmental Accounting, Auditing, and Financial Reporting Principles.

    c. General Accounting Office Standards for Audit of Governmental organizations, Programs, Activities, and Functions.
    d. Securities and Exchange commission Regulation S-X.

97. Governmental auditing often extends beyond examinations leading to the expression of opinion on the fairness of financial presentation and includes audits of efficiency, effectiveness, and
    a. Internal control.
    b. Evaluation.
    c. Accuracy.
    d. Compliance.

98. Audits of certain governmental entities are required to be performed in accordance with generally accepted government auditing standards (GAGAS). These standards do not require, as part of an auditor's report, the identification of
    a. Significant internal and administration controls designed to provide reasonable assurance that federal programs are being administered in compliance with applicable laws and regulations.
    b. Weaknesses discovered as a result of the consideration of the internal control structure.
    c. Sampling methods used to test the internal controls designed to detect errors and irregularities.
    d. Significant internal controls that were not evaluated, and the reasons why they were not evaluated.

99. A CPA has performed an examination of the general purpose financial statements of Big City. The examination scope included the additional requirements of the Single Audit Act. When reporting on Big City's internal accounting and administrative controls used in administering a federal financial assistance program, the CPA should
    a. Communicate those weaknesses that are material in relation to the general purpose financial statements.
    b. Express an opinion on the systems used to administer major federal financial assistance programs and express negative assurance on the systems used to administer nonmajor federal financial assistance programs.
    c. Communicate those weaknesses that are material in relation to the federal financial assistance program.

d. Express negative assurance on the systems used to administer major federal financial assistance programs and express no opinion on the systems used to administer nonmajor federal financial assistance programs.

100. Operational auditing is primarily oriented toward
- a. Future improvements to accomplish the goals of management.
- b. The accuracy of data reflected in management's financial records.
- c. The verification that a company's financial statements are fairly presented.
- d. Past protection provided by existing internal control.

101. A typical objective of an operational audit is to determine whether an entity's
- a. Internal control structure is adequately operating as designed.
- b. Operational information is in accordance with generally accepted governmental auditing standards.
- c. Financial statements present fairly the results of operations.
- d. Specific operating units are functioning efficiently and effectively.

May 1990 Questions

102. Which of the following factors would least influence an auditor's consideration of the reliability of data for purposes of analytical procedures?
- a. Whether the data were processed in an EDP system or in a manual accounting system.
- b. Whether sources within the entity were independent of those who are responsible for the amount being audited.
- c. Whether the data were subjected to audit testing in the current or prior year.
- d. Whether the data were obtained from independent sources outside the entity or from sources within the entity.

103. Analytical procedures used in planning an audit should focus on identifying
- a. Material weaknesses in the internal control structure.
- b. The predictability of financial data from individual transactions.
- c. The various assertions that are embodied in the financial statements.

d. Areas that may represent specific risks relevant to the audit.

104. Inquiry and analytical procedures ordinarily performed during a review of a nonpublic entity's financial statements include
- a. Inquiries concerning actions taken at meetings of the stockholders and the board of directors.
- b. Analytical procedures designed to test the accounting records by obtaining corroborating evidential matter.
- c. Inquiries designed to identify reportable conditions in the internal control structure.
- d. Analytical procedures concerning management's assertions regarding continued existence.

105. An auditor testing long-term investments would ordinarily use analytical procedures to ascertain the reasonableness of the
- a. Existence of unrealized gains or losses in the portfolio.
- b. Completeness of recorded investment income.
- c. Classification between current and non-current portfolios.
- d. Valuation of marketable equity securities.

106. An auditor would be most likely to identify a contingent liability by obtaining a(an)
- a. Accounts payable confirmation.
- b. Transfer agent confirmation.
- c. Standard bank confirmation.
- d. Related party transaction confirmation.

107. An auditor's working papers should
- a. Not be permitted to serve as a reference source for the client.
- b. Not contain critical comments concerning management.
- c. Show that the accounting records agree or reconcile with the financial statements.
- d. Be considered the primary support for the financial statements being audited.

108. An auditor would be most likely to consider modifying an otherwise unqualified opinion if the client's financial statements include a footnote on related party transactions
- a. Representing that certain related party transactions were consummated on terms equivalent to those

obtainable in transactions with unrelated parties.

b. Presenting the dollar volume of related party transactions and the effects of any change in the method of establishing terms from that used in the prior period.

c. Explaining the business purpose of the sale of real property to a related party.

d. Disclosing compensating balance arrangements maintained for the benefit of related parties.

109. When a client company does **not** maintain its own stock records, the auditor should obtain written confirmation from the transfer agent and registrar concerning

a. Restrictions on the payment of dividends.

b. The number of shares issued and outstanding.

c. Guarantees of preferred stock liquidation value.

d. The number of shares subject to agreements to repurchase.

110. Before issuing a report on the compilation of financial statements of a nonpublic entity, the accountant should

a. Apply analytical procedures to selected financial data to discover any material misstatements.

b. Corroborate at least a sample of the assertions management has embodied In the financial statements.

c. Inquire of the client's personnel whether the financial statements omit substantially all disclosures.

d. Read the financial statements to consider whether the financial statements are free from obvious material errors.

111. In planning a new engagement, which of the following is **not** a factor that affects the auditor's judgment as to the quantity, type, and content of working papers?

a. The type of report to be issued by the auditor.

b. The content of the client's representation letter.

c. The auditor's estimated occurrence rate of attributes.

d. The auditor's preliminary evaluations of risk based on discussions with the client.

112. The scope and nature of an auditor's contractual obligation to a client ordinarily is set forth in the

a. Management letter.

b. Scope paragraph of the auditor's report.

c. Engagement letter.

d. Introductory paragraph of the auditor's report.

Problems

Problem 1   (1188,A2)

(15 to 25 minutes)

Temple, CPA, is auditing the financial statements of Ford Lumber Yards, Inc., a privately-held corporation with 300 employees and five stockholders, three of whom are active in management. Ford has been in business for many years, but has never had its financial statements audited. Temple suspects that the substance of some of Ford's business transactions differs from their form because of the pervasiveness of related party relationships and transactions in the local building supplies industry.

Required:

Describe the audit procedures Temple should apply to identify party relationships and transactions.

Problem 2   (1188,A5)

(15 to 25 minutes)

The purpose of all auditing procedures is to gather sufficient competent evidence for an auditor to form an opinion regarding the financial statements taken as a whole.

Required:

a. In addition to the example below, identify and describe five means or techniques of gathering audit evidence used to evaluate a client's inventory balance.

Technique	Description
Observation	An auditor watches the performance of some function, such as a client's annual inventory count.

b. Identify the five general assertions regarding a client's inventory balance and describe one **different** substantive auditing procedure for each assertion. Use the format illustrated below.

Assertion	Substantive Auditing Procedure

Problem 3   (586,A2)

(15 to 25 minutes)

Jones, CPA, the continuing auditor of Sussex, Inc., is beginning the audit of the common stock and treasury stock accounts. Jones has decided to design substantive tests without reliance on internal control.

Sussex has no par, no stated value common stock and acts as its own registrar and transfer agent. During the past year Sussex both issued and reacquired shares of its own common stock, some of which the company still owned at year end. Additional common stock transactions occurred among the shareholders during the year.

Common stock transactions can be traced to individual shareholders' accounts in a subsidiary ledger and to a stock certificate book. The company has not paid any cash or stock dividends. There are no other classes of stock, stock rights, warrants, or option plans.

Required:

What substantive audit procedures should Jones apply in examining the common stock and treasury stock accounts?

Problem 4   (1184,A2)

(15 to 20 minutes)

Pierce, an independent auditor, was engaged to examine the financial statements of Mayfair Construction, Incorporated for the year ended December 31, 1983. Mayfair's financial statements reflect a substantial amount of mobile construction equipment used in the firm's operations. The equipment is accounted for in a subsidiary ledger. Pierce performed a consideration of internal control and found it satisfactory.

Required:

Identify the substantive audit procedures which Pierce should utilize in examining mobile construction equipment and related depreciation in Mayfair's financial statements.

Problem 5   (1183,A4)

(15 to 25 minutes)

Taylor, CPA, is engaged in the audit of Rex Wholesaling for the year ended December 31, 1982. Taylor performed a proper study of the system of internal control relating to the purchasing, receiving, trade accounts payable and cash disbursement cycles and has decided not to proceed with compliance testing. Based upon analytical procedures Taylor believes that the trade accounts payable balance on the balance sheet as of December 31, 1982 may be understated.

Taylor requested and obtained a client-prepared trade accounts payable schedule listing the total amount owed to each vendor.

Required:

What additional substantive audit procedures should Taylor apply in examining the trade accounts payable?

Problem 6   (583,A4)

(15 to 25 minutes)

The following client-prepared bank reconciliation is being examined by Kautz, CPA, during an examination of the financial statements of Cynthia Company:

Cynthia Company
Bank Reconciliation
Village Bank Account 2
December 31, 1982

Balance per bank (a)		$18,375.91
Deposits in Transit (b)		
12/30	1,471.10	
12/31	2,840.69	4,311.79
Subtotal		22,687.70
Outstanding checks (c)		
837	6,000.00	
1941	671.80	
1966	320.00	
1984	1,855.42	
1985	3,621.22	
1987	2,576.89	
1991	4,420.88	(19,466.21)
Subtotal		3,221.49
NSF check returned		
12/29 (d)		200.00
Bank charges		5.50
Error Check No. 1932		148.10
Customer note collected		
by the bank ($2,750		
plus $275 interest) (e)		(3,025.00)
Balance per books (f)		$ 550.09

Required:

Indicate one or more audit procedures that should be performed by Kautz in gathering evidence in support of each of the items (a) through (f) above.

Problem 7   (582,A4)

(15 to 25 minutes)

The following schedule was prepared by the controller of World Manufacturing, Inc. for use by the independent auditors during their examination of World's year-end financial statements. All procedures performed by the audit assistant were noted at the bottom "Legend" section, and it was properly initialed, dated, and indexed, and then submitted to a senior member of the audit staff for review. Internal control was reviewed and is considered to be satisfactory.

World Manufacturing, Inc.
Marketable Securities
Year Ended December 31, 1981

Description of security			Serial no.	Face value of bonds	Gen. ledger 1/1	Purch. in 1981	Sold in 1981	Cost	Gen. ledger 12/31	12/31 market	Dividend & interest		
											Pay date(s)	Amt. rec.	Accruals 12/31
Corp. bonds	%	Yr. due											
											1/15	300 b,d	
A	6	91	21-7	10000	9400a				9400	9100	7/15	300 b,d	275
D	4	83	73-0	30000	27500a				27500	26220	12/1	1200 b,d	100
G	9	98	16-4	5000	4000a				4000	5080	8/1	450 b,d	188
Rc	5	85	08-2	70000	66000a		57000b	66000					
Sc	10	99	07-4	100000		100000e			100000	101250	7/1	5000 b,d	5000
					106900	100000	57000	66000	140900	141650		7250	5563
					a,f	f	f	f	f,g	f		f	f

Stocks

							3/1	750 b,d
P 1,000 shs.	1044		7500a		7500	7600	6/1	750 b,d
Common							9/1	750 b,d
							12/1	750 b,d	250
U 50 shs.	8530		9700a		9700	9800	2/1	800 b,d
Common							8/1	800 b,d	667
			17200		17200	17400		4600	917
			a,f		f,g	f		f	f

Legends and comments relative to above

a = Beginning balances agreed to 1980 working papers
b = Traced to cash receipts
c = Minutes examined (purchase and sales approved by the board of directors)
d = Agreed to 1099
e = Confirmed by tracing to broker's advice
f = Totals footed
g = Agreed to general ledger

Required:

a. What information that is essential to the audit of marketable securities is missing from this schedule?

b. What are the essential audit procedures that were not noted as having been performed by the audit assistant?

Problem 8   (1187,A3)

(15 to 25 minutes)

MLG Company's auditor received directly from the banks, confirmations and cutoff statements with related checks and deposit tickets for MLG's three general-purpose bank accounts. The auditor determined that internal control over cash was satisfactory and will be relied upon. The proper cutoff of external cash receipts and disbursements was established. No bank accounts were opened or closed during the year.

Required:

Prepare the audit program of substantive procedures to verify MLG's bank balances. Ignore any other cash accounts.

Problem 9   (588,A3)

(15 to 25 minutes)

Young, CPA, is considering the procedures to be applied concerning a client's loss contingencies relating to litigation, claims, and assessments.

Required:

What substantive audit procedures should Young apply when testing for loss contingencies relating to litigation, claims, and assessments?

Problem 10   (1176,A4)

(15 to 25 minutes)

Ace Corporation does not conduct a complete annual physical count of purchased parts and supplies in its principal warehouse but uses statistical sampling instead to estimate the year-end inventory. Ace maintains a perpetual inventory record of parts and supplies and believes that statistical sampling is highly effective in determining inventory values and is sufficiently reliable to make a physical count of each item of inventory unnecessary.

Required:

a. Identify the audit procedures that should be used by the independent auditor that change or are in addition to normal required

audit procedures when a client utilizes statistical sampling to determine inventory value and does not conduct a 100 percent annual physical count of inventory items.
b. List at least ten normal audit procedures that should be performed to verify physical quantities whenever a client conducts a periodic physical count of all or part of its inventory.

Problem 11   (589,A4)

(15 to 25 minutes)

Edwards, CPA, is engaged to audit the financial statements of Matthews Wholesaling for the year ended December 31, 1988. Edwards obtained and documented an understanding of the internal control structure relating to the accounts receivable and assessed control risk relating to accounts receivable at the maximum level. Edwards requested and obtained from Matthews an aged accounts receivable schedule listing the total amount owed by each customer as of December 31, 1988, and sent positive confirmation requests to a sample of the customers.

Required:

What additional substantive audit procedures should Edwards consider applying in auditing the accounts receivable?

Problem 12   (1189,A3)

(15 to 25 minutes)

Analytical procedures consist of evaluations of financial information made by a study of plausible relationships among both financial and nonfinancial data. They range from simple comparisons to the use of complex models involving many relationships and elements of data. They involve comparisons of recorded amounts, or ratios developed from recorded amounts, to expectations developed by the auditors.

Required:

a. Describe the broad purposes of analytical procedures.
b. Identify the sources of information from which an auditor develops expectations.
c. Describe the factors that influence an auditor's consideration of the reliability of data for purposes of achieving audit objectives.

Problem 13   (1189,A4) (15 to 25 minutes)

The following long-term debt working paper (indexed K-1) was prepared by client personnel and audited by AA, an audit assistant, during the calendar year 1988 audit of American Widgets, Inc., a continuing audit client. The engagement supervisor is reviewing the working papers thoroughly.

American Widgets, Inc.
WORKING PAPERS
December 31, 1988

Lender	Interest Rate	Payment Terms	Collateral	Balance 12/31/87	1988 Borrowings	1988 Reductions	Balance 12/31/88	Interest paid to	Accrued Interest Payable 12/31/88	Comments
Φ First Commercial Bank	12%	Interest only on 25th of month, principal due in full 1/1/92; no prepayment penalty	Inventories	$ 50,000 √	$300,000 A 1/31/88	$100,000 ⊕ 6/30/88	$ 250,000 CX	12/25/88	$2,500 NR	Dividend of $80,000 paid 9/2/88 (W/P N-3) violates a provision of the debt agreement, which thereby permits lender to demand immediate payment; lender has refused to waive this violation
Φ Lender's Capital Corp.	Prime plus 1%	Interest only on last day of month, principal due in full 3/5/90	2nd Mortgage on Park St. Building	100,000 √	50,000 A 2/29/88	-	200,000 C	12/31/88		Prime rate was 8% to 9% during the year
Φ Gigantic Building & Loan Assoc.	12%	$5,000 principal plus interest due on 5th of month, due in full 12/31/99	1st Mortgage on Park St. Building	720,000 √	-	60,000 ⊕	660,000 C	12/5/88	5,642 R	Reclassification entry for current portion proposed (See RJE-3)
Φ J. Lott, majority stockholder	0%	Due in full 12/31/91	Unsecured	300,000 √	-	100,000 N 12/31/88	200,000 C	-	-	Borrowed additional $100,000 from J. Lott on 1/7/89
				$1,170,000 √ F	$350,000 F	$260,000 F	$1,310,000 T/B F		$8,142 T/B F	

Interest costs from long-term debt

Interest expense for year $ 281,333 T/B
Average loan balance outstanding $1,406,667 R

Five year maturities (for disclosure purposes)
Year end		
12/31/89	$	60,000
12/31/90		260,000
12/31/91		260,000
12/31/92		310,000
12/31/93		60,000
Thereafter		360,000
		$1,310,000

Tickmark Legend

F   Readded, foots correctly
C   Confirmed without exception, W/P K-2
CX Confirmed with exception, W/P K-3
NR Does not recompute correctly
A   Agreed to loan agreement, validated bank deposit ticket, and board of directors authorization, W/P W-7
Φ   Agreed to canceled checks and lender's monthly statements
N   Agreed to cash disbursements journal and canceled check dated 12/31/88, clearing 1/8/89
T/B Traced to working trial balance
√   Agreed to 12/31/87 working papers
⊕   Agreed interest rate, term, and collateral to copy of note and loan agreement
⊕   Agreed to canceled check and board of directors' authorization, W/P W-7

Overall conclusions

Long-term debt, accrued interest payable, and interest expense are correct and complete at 12/1/88

Required: Identify the deficiencies in the working paper that the engagement supervisor should discover.

Problem 14   (1189,A2)

(15 to 25 minutes)

Bell, CPA, was engaged to audit the financial statements of Kent Company, a continuing audit client. Bell is about to audit Kent's payroll transactions. Kent uses an in-house payroll department to compute payroll data, and prepare and distribute payroll checks.

During the planning process, Bell determined that the inherent risk of overstatement of payroll expense is high. In addition, Bell obtained an understanding of the internal control structure and assessed control risk at the maximum level for payroll-related assertions.

Required:

Describe the audit procedures Bell should consider performing in the audit of Kent's payroll transactions to address the risk of overstatement. Do not discuss Kent's internal control structure.

Multiple Choice Answers

1. d	24. b	47. d	69. b	91. c
2. a	25. a	48. a	70. d	92. b
3. a	26. c	49. b	71. a	93. a
4. c	27. c	50. b	72. c	94. c
5. a	28. b	51. d	73. d	95. b
6. b	29. b	52. c	74. d	96. c
7. d	30. a	53. d	75. c	97. d
8. a	31. a	54. a	76. d	98. c
9. a	32. c	55. a	77. c	99. c
10. a	33. c	56. a	78. a	100. a
11. b	34. b	57. d	79. d	101. d
12. c	35. d	58. c	80. b	102. a
13. c	36. a	59. c	81. c	103. d
14. c	37. d	60. c	82. a	104. a
15. b	38. c	61. c	83. a	105. b
16. a	39. b	62. b	84. a	106. c
17. c	40. c	63. d	85. b	107. c
18. d	41. d	64. d	86. a	108. a
19. b	42. c	65. a	87. d	109. b
20. c	43. b	66. b	88. a	110. d
21. a	44. c	67. d	89. b	111. b
22. d	45. c	68. a	90. c	112. c
23. b	46. a			

Multiple Choice Answer Explanations
A. Evidence--General (Including Assertions, Attest Engagements)

A.1. Competent and Sufficient Evidential Matter

1. (582,A1,6) (d) The requirement is to determine the correct statement with respect to the competence of evidential matter. To be competent, evidence must be both valid and relevant (AU 326.18). Answer (a) is incorrect because while externally generated evidence is generally considered to provide greater assurance of reliability, there are important exceptions, e.g., the confirmation erroneously returned with no exception when one actually exists. Answer (b) is incorrect because while evidence so gathered is typically considered to provide greater assurance concerning reliability (AU 326.18), no similar generalization can be made about its relevance. Answer (c) is incorrect because oral representations from management, when corroborated by other forms of evidence, are considered valid evidence.

2. (588,A1,21) (a) The requirement is to identify the correct statement with respect to the competence of evidential matter. Answer (a) is correct because AU 326.19 states that the auditor's direct personal knowledge, obtained by physical examination, observation, computation, and inspection, is more persuasive than information obtained indirectly. Answer (b) is incorrect because, to be competent, evidence must be both valid and relevant (AU 326.19). Answer (c) is incorrect because in addition to the accounting data, the auditor must obtain corroborating evidential

matter (AU 326.16). Answer (d) is incorrect because the amount of corroborative evidence to be obtained refers to the sufficiency of evidential matter, not the competence of evidential matter (AU 326.20-.22).

3. (589,A1,1) (a) The requirement is to determine the reply which is not a valid basis for an auditor to decide to omit a test. Answer (a) is correct, because the professional standards state that an auditor should not rule out a test simply because of difficulty and expense involved (AU 326.22). Answer (b) is incorrect because the degree of reliance on the relevant internal control and substantive testing necessary vary inversely (AU 319.61-.64); accordingly, reliance upon internal control will affect the scope of other audit procedures. Answers (c) and (d) are incorrect because relative risk involved and the relationship between the cost of obtaining evidence and its usefulness are to be considered (AU 326.21-.22).

4. (587,A1,27) (c) The requirement is to identify the least persuasive type of evidence. Answer (c) is correct because prenumbered client sales invoices are secured from within the entity being audited, and not from independent sources, and therefore are considered to be less persuasive (AU 326.19). Answers (a) and (d) are incorrect because a bank statement (even though received from the client) and a vendor's invoice are both externally created types of evidence and therefore are more persuasive than evidential matter secured solely from within the entity. Answer (b) is incorrect because evidence obtained directly by the auditor through such computation is more persuasive than information obtained indirectly (AU 326.19).

A.2. General Types of Evidence

5. (588,A1,58) (a) The requirement is to determine which audit procedure is most likely to identify large amounts of revenues being recorded through use of journal entries that involve illogical combinations of accounts. Answer (a) is correct because a scanning of the general journal might identify those transactions which appear illogical. Answer (b) is incorrect because the transactions are occurring throughout the period, and not just at year end. Answer (c) is incorrect because simply tracing journal entries to the general ledger will only reveal whether post-

ings are consistent with entries. Answer (d) is incorrect because nothing in the problem indicates that the transactions have any relationship to sales returns and allowances.

6. (1187,A1,39) (b) The requirement is to determine why substantive tests may support the accuracy of underlying records, and yet provide no affirmative evidence of segregation of duties. Answer (b) is correct because while records may be accurate, information about maintenance of records by persons having incompatible functions may not be obtained. Answer (a) is incorrect because while it is true that substantive tests of sampled trans-actions cannot guarantee accuracy of the entire population, it is not a reason why substantive tests do not address the segre-gation of duties. Answer (c) is incorrect because tests of controls are not ordinarily confined to the period during which the auditor is on the client's premises (AU 319.52-.55). Answer (d) is incorrect because the fact that no audit trail exists for many computerized procedures does not restrict the auditor from applying analytical procedures or other substantive tests on the resultant computerized information.

B. Evidence--Specific (Substantive Tests)

B.1. Types of Substantive Tests
B.1.a. Analytical Procedures

7. (1188,A1,51) (d) The requirement is to identify a basic premise underlying analytical procedures. Answer (d) is correct because analytical procedures are based on the premise that plausible relationships among data may reasonably be expected to exist and continue in the absence of known conditions to the contrary (AU 329.02). Answer (a) is incorrect because analytical procedures can be used as substantive tests to replace some tests of balances and transactions (AU 329.09-.11). Answer (b) is incorrect because while the use of statistical tests for analytical procedures is possible, it is not required and is there-fore not a basic premise. Answer (c) is in-correct because the study of ratios may in-clude an investigation of unusual fluctuations and is therefore not considered an alternative approach.

8. (587,A1,28) (a) The requirement is to identify an analytical procedure. Answer (a) is correct because the professional standards suggest that the comparison of financial in-formation with similar information regarding the industry in which the entity operates is considered to be an analytical procedure

(AU 319.05). Answers (b), (c), and (d) are all incorrect because the procedures are generally done either as tests of controls or as substantive tests of detail transactions and balances.

9. (1186,A1,28) (a) The requirement is to determine the factor that will facilitate the auditor's analytical procedures. Answer (a) is correct because use of a standard cost system (a form of budgeting) that produces variance reports will allow the auditor to compare the financial information with the standard cost system data to identify unusual fluctuations (see AU 329.06 for the approach used). Answer (b) is incorrect because segregating obsolete inventory before the inventory count is related to the auditor's physical inventory observation and will not necessarily affect analytical procedures. An-swer (c) is incorrect because correcting a reportable condition in internal control before the beginning of the audit will have minimal, if any, effect on the historical information used for analytical procedures. Answer (d) is incorrect because reducing inventory balances to market might or might not lead to the identification of unusual fluctuations; therefore, answer (d) is not as accurate as answer (a).

10. (589,A1,28) (a) The requirement is to determine the appropriate focus for prelimi-nary analytical procedures that are being used to help plan the nature, timing, and extent of substantive auditing procedures. Answer (a) is correct because analytical procedures used in planning the audit should focus on en-hancing the auditor's understanding of the client's business and events that have oc-curred since the last audit date, and on iden-tifying areas that may represent specific risks relevant to the audit (AU 329.06). An-swer (b) is incorrect because while the re-sults of analytical procedures should be com-pared to the results anticipated by the audi-tor, any unanticipated results should serve as indicators that further testing is necessary to determine why the results attained are different than expected. Answer (c) is incor-rect because while it lists valid analytical procedures to be employed, the question does not ask which procedures should be employed. The question asks what the focus of these procedures should be, i.e., the enhancement of the auditor's understanding of the client's business and events which have occurred since the last audit date. Answer (d) is incorrect since preliminary analytical procedures are performed during the planning stage of an audit. Thus, no other tests would have yet been performed with which to make comparisons.

11. (586,A1,33) (b) The requirement is to determine the error which an auditor most likely would discover when investigating all revenue and expense changes of more than 10% compared with the prior year. Answer (b) is correct because a change in the capitalization policy for small tools would affect an expense account (e.g., "used tools"). Thus, depending upon the nature of the change, one would expect a large difference in the current year's total when compared to the prior year. Answer (a) is incorrect because the lack of **payment** of fourth quarter payroll taxes would affect the payroll tax liability account, not the payroll tax expense account. Answer (c) is incorrect because if an increase in property tax rates had **not** been recognized, one would expect the two years' expenses to approximate one another; a 10% change would not be recorded on the books and therefore no investigation would occur. Similarly, answer (d) is incorrect because the lack of a provision for the increased uncollectible accounts will cause the two years' uncollectible accounts expense to approximate one another.

12. (589,A1,27) (c) The requirement is to identify the primary objective of analytical procedures used in the **final review** stage of an audit. Answer (c) is correct because AU 329.22 states that the purpose of applying analytical procedures during the final review is to assist the auditor in assessing the conclusions reached during the audit and in the evaluation of the overall financial statement presentation. Answer (a) is incorrect because analytical procedures do not obtain evidence from details tested in order to corroborate particular assertions. Answer (b) is incorrect because analytical procedures performed to identify areas that represent specific risks relevant to the audit are performed in the **planning** stages of the audit (AU 329.06). Answer (d) is incorrect because while analytical procedures may identify doubts about a client's ability to continue in existence, it is not the **primary** objective of such procedures. AU 341 discusses the auditor's consideration of an entity's ability to continue as a going concern.

B.1.b. Tests of Details of Transactions and Balances

13. (1181,A1,27) (c) The requirement is to find the statement which describes substantive audit tests. Answer (c) is correct because substantive tests are defined as tests of transactions, direct tests of financial balances, or analytical procedures. Answer (a) is incorrect because substantive tests may not be eliminated due to the limitations of internal control. Answer (b) is incorrect since substantive tests primarily directly test

ending financial statement balances, not subsequent events. Answer (d) is incorrect because substantive tests **decrease** with increased reliance on internal control. AU 312 and 319 discuss in detail the various interrelationships among audit tests.

14. (1184,A1,47) (c) The requirement is to determine the account for which the auditor is most likely to perform extensive tests for possible understatement. An analysis of past audits, in which existing financial statement errors were not discovered prior to the issuance of the financial statements, reveals that the great majority of the errors resulted in overstated profits. Therefore, the risk to a CPA is that the client is overstating profits. Answer (c) is correct because it is the only item whose understatement results in overstated profits. Answers (a), (b), and (d) are incorrect because understatement of these items would result in understated profits.

15. (1185,A1,42) (b) The requirement is to determine the appropriate direction when the auditor wishes to test for unsupported entries in the ledger. Answer (b) is correct because by starting with the ledger entries, the auditor will determine whether each entry has the proper support. Answer (a) is incorrect because tracing from the journal entries to the ledger will indicate whether the journal entries have been properly posted. Answers (c) and (d) are incorrect because tracing from source documents or externally generated documents to the ledger will indicate whether such documents have been properly recorded. There still exists the risk that unsupported entries exist in the ledger.

16. (1188,A1,55) (a) The requirement is to identify the account for which it is **least** likely that substantive tests of details will be performed, unless analytical procedures indicate the need to extend detail testing. Answer (a) is correct because most payroll systems are relatively well controlled and deal with routine transactions. This makes approaches which emphasize testing of controls and analytical procedures more likely to be efficient for this type of an account than for the accounts listed. Answer (b) is incorrect because the highly liquid nature of most marketable securities requires the auditor to test details of the account. Answer (c) is incorrect because research and development costs are often not controlled in the routine manner as are payroll expenses and therefore generally require testing of details. Such testing will also provide the auditors with a better understanding of the client's operations. Answer (d) is incorrect because a legal expense account normally requires sepa-

rate analysis because it may reveal contingent and actual liabilities. Also, see the AICPA Accounting and Audit Manual, para 6500.690 for accounts which generally require separate analysis.

B.2. Substantive Test Audit Programs—See Essay Questions

B.3. Documentation

17. (1188,A1,56) (c) The requirement is to identify the incorrect statement concerning an auditor's working papers. Answer (c) is the proper reply since an auditor's working papers **may** serve as a reference source for the client (AU 339.07). Answer (a) is incorrect because while the working papers are the principal support for an opinion, other means may also be used (AU 339.02). Answers (b) and (d) are incorrect because the working papers should be designed to meet the circumstances of a particular engagement (AU 339.04) and because they show that internal control has been studied (AU 339.05b).

18. (586,A1,42) (d) The requirement is to determine the information which is most likely to be contained in the permanent file section of the working papers. Answer (d) is correct because the permanent files contain information (such as internal control information) which is expected to be used on many future audits of the client. Answers (a) and (b) are incorrect because review notes and time budgets would pertain most directly to the year currently being audited and because review notes are disposed of at the end of each audit. Answer (c), although possible, is less likely than (d) because much of the litigation in question would bear most directly on the year currently being audited.

19. (588,A1,29) (b) The requirement is to identify the response which will normally **not** be included in the working papers. Answer (b) is correct because cutoff bank statements belong to the client, and when the necessary audit procedures have been completed, the auditor should provide the cutoff statements to the client. Answer (a) is incorrect because the in-charge auditor will normally initial working papers to document performance of the review. Answer (c) is incorrect because a memo on the internal controls will often be included. Answer (d) is incorrect because copies of client inventory count sheets will be included to provide support for the inventory. AU 339 provides information on the overall content of working papers.

20. (588,A1,39) (c) The requirement is to identify the item which would normally be included in the auditor's current file. Answer (c) is correct because the working papers should be sufficient to show that the accounting records agree or reconcile with the financial statements; since this must be done annually, the financial statements are normally included in the current file. Answers (b), (c), and (d) are all types of evidence that bear on a number of years and will appropriately be included in the permanent file of working papers.

21. (1187,A1,31) (a) The requirement is to identify the type of audit working paper that reflects the major components of an amount reported in the financial statements. Answer (a) is correct because lead schedules aggregate the major components to be reported in the financial statements. For example, total cash in the financial statements will include components such as: total cash in banks, total cash in transit, total cash equivalents, etc. Answer (b) is incorrect because supporting schedules present the details supporting the information on a lead schedule. For example, a detailed bank reconciliation for a bank account on the cash lead schedule would be a supporting schedule. Answer (c) is incorrect because a control account is a general ledger account which aggregates a total account balance for which there is a subsidiary ledger, such as accounts receivable. Therefore, this term describes a general ledger account rather than an audit working paper. Answer (d) is incorrect because a working trial balance includes amounts that have already been summarized or combined on lead schedules.

C. Other Specific Evidence Topics
C.1. Evidence—Cash

22. (585,A1,29) (d) The requirement is to determine the source of evidence which does **not** contain information on the balance per bank in a bank reconciliation. Answer (d) is correct because the general ledger contains only the client's cash balance, not the balance per bank. Answer (a) is incorrect because the beginning balance on a cutoff statement represents the year-end bank balance. Answer (b) is incorrect because the primary purpose of a year-end bank statement is to present information on the balance per bank. Answer (c) is incorrect because the first question on a standard bank confirmation form requests information on the year-end balance per bank.

23. (588,A1,26) (b) The requirement is to identify the cash transfer which will result

in a misstatement of year-end cash. Answer (b) is correct because the receipt is recorded on the books prior to year end, while the disbursement is recorded subsequent to year end. Therefore, the cash on the books is overstated. Answers (a), (c), and (d) are incorrect because they do not reveal a cutoff error. Answer (a) is incorrect because both the disbursement and receipt are recorded on the books prior to year end; note that one would expect to see an outstanding check on the disbursing bank reconciliation as of year end. Answer (c) is incorrect because both the disbursement and receipt are recorded on the books prior to year end; one would expect the disbursing bank reconciliation to show an outstanding check and the receiving bank to show a deposit in transit as of year end. Answer (d) is incorrect because the entire transaction is recorded after year end.

24. (589,A1,36) (b) The requirement is to determine the most likely audit step summarized by the tick mark placed under "date disbursed per bank." Answer (b) is correct because the checks were written in December but cleared in January and should therefore be listed as outstanding on the year-end outstanding check list of the applicable bank reconciliation. Answer (a) is incorrect because the tick marks are beside the date per bank, and not per books. Answer (c) is incorrect because the December cash disbursements journal, and not the January cash disbursements journal, will include these disbursements. Answer (d) is incorrect because the year-end bank confirmations do not include information on outstanding checks.

25. (589,A1,37) (a) The requirement is to determine the most likely audit step summarized by the tick mark placed under "date deposited per bank." Answer (a) is correct because deposits recorded on the books as of 12/31 should be included as deposits in transit on the applicable bank reconciliation. Answer (b) is incorrect because the tick mark is placed beside the "bank" column, and not the books column. Answer (c) is incorrect because the December cash receipts journal, and not the January cash receipts journal should include the deposit. Answer (d) is incorrect because the year-end bank confirmations will not include deposits in transit.

26. (1181,A1,46) (c) The requirement is to determine an approach for detecting the concealing of a cash shortage by transporting funds from one location to another or by converting negotiable assets to cash. Answer (c) is correct because the timing of the performance of auditing procedures involves the proper synchronizing of their application and

thus comprehends the possible need for simultaneous examination of, for example, cash on hand and in banks, securities owned, bank loans, and other related items (AU 310.08). Simultaneous confirmations [answer (a)], bank reconciliations [answer (b)], and cash count [answer (d)], while all are desirable, are incomplete in and of themselves.

C.2. Evidence--Receivables

27. (1186,A1,43) (c) The requirement is to identify the assertion most directly addressed by accounts receivable confirmations. Section 326 presents information on financial statement assertions. Answer (c) is correct because a confirmation addresses whether the entity replying to the confirmation believes that a debt exists. Answer (a) is incorrect because while confirmations provide limited information on valuation, they do not directly address whether the entity replying will pay the debt (or whether the account has been factored). Answer (b) is incorrect because limited classification information is received via confirmations. Answer (d) is incorrect because confirmations are generally sent to recorded receivables, and are of limited assistance in assisting in the determination of whether all accounts are recorded (completeness).

28. (588,A1,28) (b) The requirement is to identify the audit procedure an auditor most likely would rely upon to verify management's assertion of completeness. Answer (b) is correct because comparing a sample of shipping documents to related sales invoices provides evidence that all items shipped have been properly invoiced. This is, in effect, a test of related populations (AU 9326.20). Answer (a) is incorrect because a standard bank confirmation is not effective at detecting kiting--a cash transfer schedule is generally prepared for that purpose. Answer (c) is incorrect because the observation of the client's distribution of payroll checks addresses the existence of employees who are being paid rather than completeness. Answer (d) is incorrect because confirmation of recorded receivables would not detect unrecorded receivables. However, confirmations of receivables may provide some assistance in detecting understated accounts.

29. (1188,A1,9) (b) The requirement is to identify the procedure which would most likely cause an auditor to suspect that material irregularities exist in a client's financial statements. Answer (b) is correct because receiving significantly fewer responses to confirmation requests than were expected is considered a circumstance that should cause

the auditor to consider whether material misstatements exist (AU 316.21). Answer (a) is incorrect because selling property and equipment at a loss before it is fully depreciated may simply reveal inadequate depreciation policies, as contrasted to material irregularities. Answer (c) is incorrect because for many clients the existence of in-transit items is expected and proper. Answer (d) is incorrect because the EDP generated report provides assurance to the auditor that internal controls are in place, since it provides a means of detecting errors. The existence of good controls decreases the probability of misstated financials.

30. (589,A1,29) (a) The requirement is to determine the best approach to determine the existence of the accounts receivable of a small rural municipality with a weak internal control structure. Answer (a) is correct because the positive confirmation approach is considered preferable when there may be a substantial number of accounts with inaccuracies or irregularities, or in dispute (AU 331.05). In this instance, a weak internal control structure might be indicative of many inaccuracies or irregularities. Answer (b) is incorrect because negative confirmations are suggested when there is strong internal control and when the balances involved are low (AU 331.05). Answer (c) is incorrect because evidence obtained from third parties provides the strongest evidence to substantiate the asset balance (AU 326). Also, as the balances represent delinquent taxes, confirmations may provide evidence in a more timely manner than review of subsequent receipts. As the primary risk relates to overstatement of balances, confirmation of recorded balances adequately addresses this risk. Answer (d) is incorrect because internal records in general provide weaker evidence than that which has been obtained externally (AU 326).

31. (1184,A1,24) (a) The requirement is to determine when alternative procedures should be performed in order to substantiate the existence of accounts receivable. Answer (a) is correct because the auditor should employ alternative procedures for nonresponses to positive confirmations to satisfy himself/ herself as to the existence of accounts receivable. Those procedures may include examination of evidence of subsequent cash receipts, cash remittance advices, sales and shipping documents, and other records (AU 331.08). Answer (b) is incorrect because with negative confirmations the debtor is asked to respond only if s/he disagrees with the information on the confirmation; thus, no

reply is assumed to indicate agreement (AU 331.05). Answers (c) and (d) are incorrect because while <u>additional</u> procedures may be required when collectibility is questionable, <u>alternative</u> procedures are those used in lieu of confirmation.

32. (1189,A1,27) (c) The requirement is to determine the reason why negative confirmation of accounts receivable is less effective than positive confirmation. Answer (c) is correct because for negative confirmations the debtor is asked to respond only if s/he disagrees with the information given. The auditor is therefore unable to identify circumstances in which nonrespondents have not verified their account information (AU 331.04-.05). Answer (a) is incorrect because there is no support to the assertion that a majority of recipients usually lack the willingness to respond objectively. Answer (b) is incorrect because the reporting of incorrect balances is likely to occur with either positive or negative confirmations. Answer (d) is incorrect because the evidential matter obtained with negative confirmations may be statistically quantified.

C.3. Evidence—Inventory

33. (588,A1,23) (c) The requirement is to identify the correct statement with respect to an auditor's responsibility for a client with weak perpetual inventory records. Answer (c) is correct because the lack of good internal control is likely to require a year-end inventory count so as to allow an accurate determination of both year-end inventory and cost of goods sold. Answer (a) is incorrect because the auditor will need to observe the counting of inventory. In addition, gross profit tests are unlikely to be adequate in such circumstances. Answer (b) is incorrect because weak controls will not in general be tested. Answer (d) is incorrect because physical counts throughout the year are normally used by clients with good internal control. AU 331.09-.13 discusses auditor responsibility with respect to inventory.

34. (1187,A1,34) (b) The requirement is to determine why an auditor might trace a sample of inventory tags to the physical inventory listing after accounting for a sequence of inventory tags. Answer (b) is correct because tracing from inventory tags to the listing will reveal whether the tags have been properly included on the listing. Answer (a) is incorrect because the tags represent only the items that have been counted, and reveal little about whether all items have been counted. Answer (c) is incorrect because one

would need to sample <u>from</u> the listing <u>to</u> the inventory tags to determine whether items included in the listing are represented by inventory tags. Answer (d) is incorrect because one would need to examine the actual inventory items to determine whether the items are bona fide.

35. (1185,A1,35) (d) The requirement is to identify the response which does <u>not</u> represent one of the independent auditor's objectives regarding the examination of inventory. Answer (d) is correct because verifying that all inventory owned by the client is on hand at the time of the count is not an objective. For example, purchased items in transit at year end, for which title has passed, should be included in inventory. Similarly, inventory out on consignment should be included. Answer (a) is incorrect because ownership pertains to the rights assertion (AU 326.06). Answer (b) is incorrect because pricing pertains to the valuation assertion (AU 326.07). Answer (c) is incorrect because the physical quantities of inventory pertain to the existence assertion (AU 326.04).

36. (1184,A1,23) (a) The requirement is to determine which types of entries will be supported when the auditor examines receiving reports. Answer (a) is correct because receiving reports will be prepared when goods are received through purchase (as recorded in the voucher register) and when goods are received through sales returns (as recorded in the sales returns journal). Answers (b), (c), and (d) are incorrect because entries in sales journals result in items being shipped, not received. Note, however, that answers (b), (c), and (d) are partially correct because the sales returns journal, voucher register, and check register all result from transactions related to the receipt of goods.

37. (1179,A1,4) (d) The requirement is supporting documentation for quantities of materials charged to work in process. Material requisitions by production departments would be the basis for charging materials to work in process. Answer (a) is incorrect because cost ledgers include the work-in-process account, and therefore are not a source of supporting information to initiate transactions which would be recorded later in the cost ledger. Answer (b) is incorrect because perpetual inventory records are maintained based upon supporting or initiating documentation such as material requisitions. Answer (c) is incorrect because receiving reports are generally prepared by the receiving department when received from third

parties at the plant itself. Generally, receiving reports are not prepared in addition to the material requisitions for movement.

38. (1179,A1,51) (c) The requirement is the most important audit procedure for disclosing unrecorded liabilities of a public warehouse. Warehouse receipts are issued upon storage of goods. They may be negotiable or nonnegotiable and are regulated by either UCC or the Uniform Warehouse Receipts Act. Goods represented by negotiable warehouse receipts can be released only by surrender of the receipt, but goods represented by nonnegotiable receipt may be released upon valid instructions of the holder of the receipt. Inspection of receiving and issuing procedures will permit the auditor to thoroughly evaluate the internal control structure over the custodial responsibilities of the warehousemen. If the custodial responsibilities are not properly discharged, there may be significant unrecorded liabilities (para 901.18). Answer (a) is incorrect because confirmation of negotiable instruments may be impractical due to nonidentifiability of the holder of the negotiable receipt. Answer (b) is incorrect because a review of outstanding receipts cannot be made because the auditor has no knowledge of who may hold "unrecorded" receipts. Answer (d) is incorrect because an observation of inventory will only determine what is on hand. The amount of inventories on hand must be coupled with a review of outstanding warehouse receipts to determine any unrecorded liabilities.

C.4. Evidence--Marketable Securities

39. (587,A1,31) (b) The requirement is to identify the most effective audit procedure for the verification of dividends earned on investments in marketable equity securities. Answer (b) is correct because published dividend records represent strong externally generated evidence. Answer (a) is incorrect because tracing dividend checks to the cash receipts book provides evidence with respect to whether dividend checks received were included in the cash receipts but does not test the completeness with which dividends have been recorded, nor does it test whether the earnings were recorded during the proper period. Answer (c) is incorrect because the comparison of dividends between years provides a weaker form of evidence than answer (b) since the dividends of many companies may vary greatly from year to year. Answer (d) is incorrect because recomputing extensions and footings and comparing totals to the general ledger address the clerical and mathematical accuracy of the recordation of dividends but do not verify the amount of dividends earned.

40. (1186,A1,31) (c) The requirement is to determine the best procedure when an auditor has been unable to inspect and count a client's investment securities (held in a safe deposit box) until after the balance sheet date. Answer (c) is correct because banks maintain records on access to safe deposit boxes. Thus, the confirmation of no access during the period will provide the auditor with evidence that the securities in the safe deposit box at the time of the count were those available at year end. Answers (a) and (b) are incorrect because the bank will not generally be able to provide a list of securities added and removed from the box (typically, only records on access are maintained by the bank). Therefore, the bank will have no information on reconciling items between the subsidiary ledger and the securities on hand. Answer (d) is incorrect because it is the responsibility of the auditor and the client, not the bank, to count the securities maintained in a safe deposit box.

41. (1185,A1,47) (d) The requirement is to identify the best form of evidence pertaining to the annual valuation of a long-term investment in which a client holds a 30% voting interest. Answer (d) is correct because under GAAP (APB 18), such investments are carried using the equity method which is the investor's cost of the investment adjusted for the investor's share of income and dividends. The investee's total income and dividends would, of course, be found in the investee's audited financial statements (AU 332.05). Answer (a) is incorrect because market quotations will be relevant only in situations in which the investee's market value is significantly lower than the amount arrived at when using the equity method of accounting for the investment and such decline is deemed to be other than temporary in light of other factors affecting the investment. Answer (b) is incorrect because the fair value of the investee's assets would have relevance only if the investee is not a going concern. Answer (c) is incorrect because the historical cost of the investee's assets is not the appropriate basis to use in determining the carrying amount of the investment; rather, the investor's cost should be used as the starting point.

42. (589,A1,30) (c) The requirement is to determine the best approach for verifying the <u>interest earned</u> on bond investments. Answer (c) is correct because recomputing the interest earned on the basis of face amount, interest rate, and period held will provide a good estimate of interest earned. Answer (a) is incorrect because vouching the receipt and deposit of interest checks will not address accrued interest or interest received and not yet deposited. Answer (b) is incorrect because the existence of a note agreement generally makes confirmation of the bond interest rate with the issuer unnecessary. Confirming the <u>rate itself</u> does not verify the <u>amount</u> of interest income earned. Answer (d) is incorrect because testing internal controls over cash receipts is unlikely to result in verification of the interest earned on bond investments. The reason for this is it does not consider the interest receivable accrued at the beginning or at the end of the period being audited. In addition, substantively verifying interest earned by relatively straightforward recalculations verifies the balance in a more efficient and effective manner.

C.5. Evidence--Property, Plant, and Equipment

43. (1188,A1,54) (b) The requirement is to identify a primary purpose of analyzing the repairs and maintenance accounts. Answer (b) is correct because such an examination may disclose expenditures for fixed assets which have been improperly expensed. Answer (a) is incorrect because to determine that <u>all</u> noncapitalizable expenditures for repairs and maintenance have been properly charged to expense the auditor would analyze other accounts (e.g., property and equipment) to investigate whether such items might have been improperly capitalized. Answer (c) is incorrect because while achieving a proper cutoff of repairs and maintenance into the proper period is necessary, the large dollar effect of improperly expensing property and equipment items makes (b) a better reply. Answer (d) is incorrect because the auditor would emphasize the analysis of the asset accounts for property and equipment to determine that they have been recorded in the proper period.

44. (586,A1,34) (c) The requirement is to identify the situation which is consistent with insufficient depreciation charges. Answer (c) is correct because excessive recurring losses on retired assets indicate that an inadequate portion of the cost of the asset has been charged to expense during the asset's life. This results in a NBV which is far above the asset's market value and, in turn, a loss on the retired asset. Answer (a) is incorrect because large amounts of fully depreciated assets which are still being used could indicate excess past depreciation charges. Answer (b) is incorrect because continuous trade-ins of relatively new assets does not directly indicate whether an adequate amount of depreciation has been recorded. Answer (d) is incorrect because inflation may cause firms to insure assets for amounts greatly in excess of book values.

45. (584,A1,34) (c) The requirement is to determine the information an auditor is most likely to seek from the plant manager. The plant manager comes into day-to-day contact with the machinery when producing a product; that contact is likely to provide information on its condition and usefulness. Answers (a) and (d) are incorrect because the plant manager will generally not have detailed knowledge as to the adequacy of the provision for uncollectible accounts or the amount of insurance which is desirable. Answer (b) is incorrect because the plant manager will have limited knowledge concerning physical inventory observation procedures and their appropriateness.

46. (580,A1,28) (a) The requirement is the document least likely to provide evidence regarding mortgage acquisition costs. Deeds generally consist of a legal conveyance of rights to use real property. Frequently the sales price is not even specified and the related mortgage acquisition costs are much less likely to be stated in a deed. Answer (b) is incorrect because cancelled checks would provide verification of mortgage acquisition costs. Answer (c) is incorrect because the closing statement would provide a detailed listing of the costs of acquiring the real property, including possible mortgage acquisition costs. Answer (d) is incorrect because examination of interest expense would also relate to the mortgage acquisition costs.

C.7. Evidence--Payables (Current)

47. (580,A1,52) (d) The requirement is why confirmation of accounts payable is unnecessary. Accounts payable are usually not confirmed because there is better evidence available to the auditor, i.e., examination of cash payments subsequent to the balance sheet date. If the auditor reviews all cash payments for a sufficient time after the balance sheet date for items pertaining to the period under audit and finds no such payments which were not recorded as liabilities at year end, the auditor is reasonably assured that accounts payable were not understated. Answer (a) is a nonsense answer. Answer (b) is incorrect because A/P balances could be paid during year-end audit work after the balance sheet date. Answer (c) is incorrect because whether or not legal action has been taken against the client is irrelevant to the confirmation procedure.

48. (1183,A1,20) (a) The requirement is to determine the situation in which unrecorded liabilities are most likely to be found. When an auditor reviews unpaid bills, items which should have been recorded as of year end, but were not, are often discovered. Answers (b), (c), and (d) all relate to a firm's sales, and therefore, to receivable and inventory cutoffs.

C.8. Evidence--Long-Term Debt

49. (1184,A1,40) (b) The requirement is to determine how an auditor can best verify a client's bond sinking fund transactions and year-end balance. Answer (b) is correct because confirmation with the bond trustee represents externally generated evidence received directly by the auditor. Such evidence is considered very reliable. Answer (a) is incorrect because individual holders of retired bonds will have no information on actual bond sinking fund transactions or year-end balances. Answer (c) is incorrect because while recomputing interest expense, interest payable, and amortization of bond discount or premiums are desirable procedures, they do not directly address bond sinking fund transactions and year-end balances. Answer (d) is similar to answer (c) in that it is desirable but does not address the actual bond sinking fund transactions and year-end balance.

C.9. Evidence--Owners' Equity, Other Revenues and Expenses

50. (588,A1,22) (b) The requirement is to identify the correct statement with respect to establishing the existence and ownership of a long-term investment in a publicly-traded company's stock. Answer (b) is correct because the evidential matter should include inspection of the securities, and in appropriate circumstances, the written confirmation from an independent custodian (AU 332.04). Answer (a) is incorrect because the auditor will require corroborative evidential matter in addition to the reliance upon internal control. Answer (c) is incorrect because information on market price relates more directly to the valuation of the common stock. Answer (d) is incorrect because auditors will not in general confirm the number of shares owned with the issuing company.

51. (588,A1,27) (d) The requirement is to identify a proper procedure for corporate stock issuances and treasury stock transactions. Answer (d) is correct because all changes in capital stock accounts should receive formal advance approval by the board of directors. Answer (a) is incorrect because

the shareholders retain possession of stock certificates, making it difficult or impossible to audit the certificates. Answer (b) is incorrect because the articles of incorporation will not provide information on details of specific stock issuances and treasury stock transactions. Answer (c) is incorrect because, while it may be possible under some circumstances to confirm this information with the transfer agent, it is unlikely that the auditor will be able to obtain access to the transfer agent's records.

52. (581,A1,14) (c) The requirement is to determine a likely step in the audit program for retained earnings. The legality of a dividend depends in part on whether it has been properly authorized (state laws differ on specific requirements). Thus, the auditor must determine that proper authorization exists, as both cash and stock dividends affect retained earnings. Answer (a) is incorrect since only a memo entry is required for a stock split. Answer (b) is incorrect because the write-down of an account receivable will not, in general, be recorded in retained earnings. Answer (d) is incorrect because gains from the disposition of treasury shares are recorded in paid-in capital accounts.

53. (1189,A1,30) (d) The requirement is to identify the documentation that is required for an audit to be in accordance with generally accepted auditing standards. Answer (d) is correct because AU 333.01 requires that the independent auditor obtain written representations from management as a part of an audit performed in accordance with generally accepted auditing standards. Answer (a) is incorrect because preparation of an internal control questionnaire is not required since other methods of documentation of an auditor's understanding of internal control are acceptable (e.g., memoranda, flowcharts--see AU 319.26). Answer (b) is incorrect because while obtaining an engagement letter normally represents good business practice, the professional standards do not require the auditor to obtain such a letter. Answer (c) is incorrect because completion of a planning memorandum or checklist is not required.

C.11. Client Representation Letters

54. (588,A1,46) (a) The requirement is to identify the likely source of a statement regarding the adequacy of a provision for a material loss on purchase commitments. Answer (a) is correct because AU 333.05 outlines the fact that such information may be included in a representation letter. Answer (b) is in-

correct because if the provision is adequate, no qualification is necessary. Answer (c) is incorrect because representation letters are not obtained from vendors. Answer (d) is incorrect because "subject to" qualifications are not appropriate under any circumstances under the standards passed in 1988 (AU 508.39).

55. (1187,A1,32) (a) The requirement is to determine the correct statement with respect to the use of a management representation letter as audit evidence about the completeness assertion. Answer (a) is correct because such written representations are meant to complement, but not replace, substantive tests (AU 333.03). Answer (b) is incorrect because the complementary nature of such representations is not considered sufficient, even when combined with reliance upon internal control. The inherent limitations of internal controls do not permit the auditor to replace substantive tests with complete reliance on internal controls (AU 319.15). Answer (c) is incorrect because the written representations are considered complementary evidence in support of various assertions. Answer (d) is incorrect because such written representations are not considered to be replacements for reliance upon internal controls.

56. (1184,A1,17) (a) The requirement is to determine who should sign a letter of representation. Answer (a) is correct because AU 333.09 states that, normally, the chief executive officer and the chief financial officers should sign the letter of representation. Answers (b), (c), and (d) are incorrect because a letter of representation should be signed by client management, not by the client's lawyer or members of the board of directors.

57. (587,A1,40) (d) The requirement is to identify the scope limitation which in all cases is sufficient to preclude an unqualified opinion. Answer (d) is correct because the professional standards state that management refusal to furnish written representations constitutes a limitation on the scope of the auditor's examination sufficient to preclude an unqualified opinion (AU 333.11). Answer (a) is incorrect because management's refusal to allow the auditor to review the predecessor's work may not necessarily result in report modification (AU 315.05). Answer (b) is incorrect because alternate procedures may be available that will make report modification unnecessary when the auditor has been engaged after completion of the year-end physical count. Answer (c) is

incorrect because management may choose not to
correct reportable condition of internal
control without a resulting limitation on the
scope of the audit.

58. (1186,A1,32) (c) The requirement is to
determine the proper date for a client's representation letter. AU 333.09 states that the
representation letter should be dated as of
the date of the auditor's report. Answer (c)
is correct because the auditor's report is
dated the last day of significant field work,
March 24, 1986, in this case. Answers (a),
(b), and (d) all represent alternative, incorrect, dates.

C.12. Using the Work of a Specialist

59. (587,A1,46) (c) The requirement is to
identify the correct statement with respect to
the auditor's use of the work of a specialist.
Answer (c) is correct because the specialist
should understand the auditor's corroborative
use of his/her findings in relation to the
representations in the financial statements
(AU 336.07). Answer (a) is incorrect because
while ordinarily the auditor should attempt to
obtain a specialist who is unrelated to the
client, when the circumstances so warrant,
work of a specialist having a relationship to
the client may be acceptable (AU 336.06,
.08). Answer (b) is incorrect because the
specialist may be identified in the auditor's
report whenever the auditor decides to modify
his/her opinion (whether it be to a disclaimer, qualified opinion, or adverse
opinion) as a result of the report or findings
of the specialist (AU 336.12). Answer (d) is
incorrect because only when the specialist
leads the auditor to believe that the client's
information is unreasonable would an adverse
opinion be issued, not when the specialist's
findings are unreasonable, in which case a
qualified opinion or a disclaimer of opinion
may be issued, should the auditor be unable to
resolve the difference (AU 336.09-.10).

60. (584,A1,35) (c) The requirement is to
determine which individual is not considered a
specialist upon whose work an independent
auditor may rely. The professional standards
relating to using the work of a specialist do
not apply to using the work of an internal
auditor (AU 336.01-footnote 2). Answers (a),
(b), and (d), actuary, appraiser, and
engineer, respectively, are all examples of
specialists per the professional standards
(AU 336.01). Note here that the question and
its reply do not imply that a CPA cannot use
the work of an internal auditor. What is
being suggested is that an internal auditor is
not considered a specialist under the professional standards.

61. (1189,A1,26) (c) The requirement is to
determine when an auditor should make reference to and identify the work of a specialist
in an audit report. Answer (c) is correct
because a specialist is only referred to when
the auditor decides to modify his/her report
from an unqualified opinion (e.g., to an
adverse opinion) as a result of the report or
findings of the specialist (AU 336.09-.12).
Answer (a) is incorrect because division of
responsibility refers to situations in which
other auditors have examined some portion of
the financial statements, not when a specialist has been used (see AU 543.07). Answer (b) is incorrect because, as indicated
above, the specialist is only referred to when
the audit opinion is modified as a result of
the specialist's findings. Answer (d) is
incorrect because while auditors will normally
attempt to obtain a specialist who is unrelated to the client, circumstances may warrant
the use of a specialist who is not independent. In such cases the specialist would not
be referred to in the report unless the auditor decided to modify his/her opinion
(AU 336.06,.09).

C.13. Inquiry of a Client's Lawyer

62. (589,A1,32) (b) The requirement is to
determine the primary reason auditors request
that an audit client send a letter of inquiry
to those attorneys who have been consulted
concerning litigation, claims, and assessments. Answer (b) is correct because
AU 337.08 states that a letter of audit inquiry to the client's lawyer is the auditor's
primary means of obtaining corroboration of
the information furnished by management
concerning litigation, claims, and assessments. Answer (a) is incorrect because the
client, and not the attorney, is the primary
source of information concerning the progress
of cases to date (AU 337.05). Answers (c) and
(d) are incorrect because often it will not be
possible for the attorney to estimate the
dollar amount or the likelihood of loss
(AU 337.14).

63. (1187,A1,36) (d) The requirement is to
identify the appropriate limitation for an
attorney's response to a client's letter of
audit inquiry. Answer (d) is correct because
AU 337.12 states that an attorney may
appropriately limit his response to matters to
which he has given substantive attention in
the form of legal consultation or representation. Answer (a) is incorrect because the
attorney must reply to matters, regardless of
whether the probable resolution will be
detrimental to the client (AU 337.09d(2)).
Answer (b) is incorrect because, in addition
to replying to asserted claims and pending

litigation, the attorney is obligated to reply to questions about unasserted claims and assessments (AU 337.09c). Answer (c) is incorrect because, similar to answer (b), the attorney is not exempt from responding to legal matters subject to unsettled points of law, uncorroborated information, or other complex judgments (AU 337.10).

64. (1185,A1,45) (d) The requirement is to determine the response which is not an audit procedure that the independent auditor would perform with respect to litigation, claims, and assessments. Answer (d) is correct because one would not expect all claims to be reflected in the financial statements (e.g., those for which the likelihood of loss is remote). Answers (a), (b), and (c) are required procedures under AU 337.05.

65. (580,A1,11) (a) If a client's lawyer resigned shortly after the receipt of an attorney's letter which indicated no significant disagreements with the client's assessment of contingent liabilities, the auditor should inquire why the attorney resigned. The auditor's concern is whether any undisclosed unasserted claims have arisen. Per AU 337.11 a lawyer may be required to resign if his advice concerning reporting for litigation, claims, and assessments is disregarded by the client. Accordingly, the resignation shortly after issuance of an attorney's letter may indicate a problem. Answer (b) is incorrect because the attorney issued a letter indicating no significant disagreement with the client's assessment of contingent liabilities. Answers (c) and (d) are incorrect because AU 337.11 only suggests that the auditor should consider the need for inquiries, i.e., AU 337.11 does not require a complete new exam of contingent liabilities or an adverse opinion.

66. (588,A1,59) (b) The requirement is to determine the likely effect of the refusal of a client's attorney to provide a representation on the legality of a particular act committed by the client. Answer (b) is correct because the refusal to provide the information may be considered a scope limitation (AU 328.14, 337.12.-.14). Answer (a) is incorrect because "subject to" qualified reports are no longer issued. Answer (c) is incorrect because, depending upon the circumstances, the refusal may result in report modification. Answer (d) is incorrect because the auditor may or may not choose to withdraw from the engagement (AU 328.18).

C.14. Related Party Transactions

67. (588,A1,35) (d) The requirement is to identify the correct statement concerning related party transactions. Answer (d) is correct because AU 334.04 requires that procedures directed toward identifying related party transactions should be performed, even if the auditor has no reason to suspect their existence. Answer (a) is incorrect because, in the absence of evidence to the contrary, related party transactions need not be assumed to be outside the ordinary course of business (AU 334.06). Answer (b) is incorrect because the auditor will not in general be able to determine whether a particular transaction would have occurred if the parties had not been related (AU 334.12). Answer (c) is incorrect because if proper disclosures are made, the related-party transactions are not required to be recorded on terms equivalent to arm's-length transactions.

68. (1187,A1,6) (c) The requirement is to identify the correct statement about the scope of work to be performed concerning possible related party transactions. Answer (c) is correct because the Professional Standards require the auditor to obtain such an understanding of management responsibilities (AU 334.05). Answer (a) is incorrect because while an auditor must obtain an understanding of the business purpose of such transactions, no such assumption is made that the transactions are outside the ordinary course of business (AU 334.09). Absent any evidence to the contrary, transactions with related parties should not be assumed to be outside the ordinary course of business (AU 334.06). Answer (b) is incorrect because it will generally not be possible to determine whether a particular transaction would have taken place if the parties had not been related (AU 334.12). Answer (d) is incorrect because it is not necessary to establish a basis of accounting principles different from that which would have been appropriate had the parties not been related. Although it may be impossible to determine whether a transaction was consummated on terms equivalent to those that prevail in arm's-length transactions, the principles to be applied remain the same (see AU 334.11-.12 for disclosure requirements).

69. (1185,A1,40) (b) The requirement is to identify the situation which might indicate the existence of a related party transaction. Answer (b) is correct because one would not expect an unrelated entity to absorb the expenses of the corporation (AU 334.03). Answers (a), (c), and (d) represent normal business transactions into which unrelated parties would normally enter.

70. (589,A1,42) (d) The requirement is to determine why an auditor searching for related party transactions should obtain an understanding of each subsidiary's relationship to the total entity. Answer (d) is correct because experience has shown that business structure and operating style are occasionally deliberately designed to obscure related party transactions (AU 334.05). Answer (a) is incorrect because performing the audit of intercompany account balances concurrently with the search for related party transactions in general is not necessary. Answer (b) is incorrect because entering into intercompany transactions on terms equivalent to arm's-length transactions is not considered a problem. The auditor should obtain such an understanding so that he may determine whether related party transactions may have been consummated on terms not equivalent to arm's-length transactions. Answer (c) is incorrect because the auditor in general will not be able to determine whether particular transactions would have taken place if the parties had not been related (AU 334.12).

C.15. Going Concern Considerations

71. (1189,A1,29) (a) The requirement is to identify the audit procedure most likely to assist an auditor in identifying conditions and events that may indicate there could be substantial doubt about an entity's ability to continue as a going concern. Answer (a) is correct because a review of compliance with terms of debt and loan agreements may reveal conditions of non-compliance due to poor financial condition. See AU 341.05 for a list of procedures that may identify such conditions and events. Answers (b), (c), and (d) are all incorrect because, while they might in some circumstances reveal a question concerning the company's ability to continue as a going concern, they are not considered to be as effective as answer (a).

C.16. Subsequent Events

72. (1188,A1,8) (c) The requirement is to identify the audit procedure that an auditor ordinarily would perform during the review of subsequent events. Answer (c) is correct because an inquiry of the client's legal counsel concerning litigation is completed near the end of the audit. The inquiry is completed at this time because loss contingencies may be involved and the auditor will consider the evidence available through the completion of the audit. See AU 560.12 which lists additional procedures performed during the review of subsequent events. Answer (a) is incorrect because the analysis of related party transactions occurs throughout the audit

(see AU 334), and not necessarily as a part of the review of subsequent events. Answer (b) is incorrect because the primary purpose of examining bank cut-off statements is to verify reconciling items on the year-end bank reconciliation. Answer (d) is incorrect because any investigation of material weaknesses may be done throughout the audit and is not considered a subsequent event procedure (see AU 325).

73. (588,A1,38) (d) The requirement is to identify the procedure an auditor would most likely perform to obtain evidence about an entity's subsequent events. AU 560.12 provides a detailed list of audit procedures that auditors perform to ascertain whether subsequent events require adjustment or disclosure in the financial statements. Answer (d) is correct because it is one of those procedures presented. The remaining answers are more related to routine cutoff testing rather than procedures to seek out unusual subsequent events requiring adjustment or disclosure. Answer (a) is incorrect because reconciliation of bank activity for the month after year end is normally the responsibility of the client and is not included in AU 560.12. Answer (b) is incorrect because examining purchase invoices and receiving reports for several days after the inventory date is primarily a cutoff test (AU 560.11). Answer (c) is incorect because, while it represents a possible procedure, it first assumes the existence of such a report and it also is not included as one of those presented in AU 560.12.

74. (1188,A1,28) (d) The requirement is to determine an auditor's responsibility when subsequent to issuance of an audit report a client sells the shares of a major subsidiary. Answer (d) is correct because no action need be taken since the event arose after the issuance of the auditor's report (AU 561.03). Answers (a), (b), and (c) are all incorrect because they outline responsibilities which are not appropriate in this circumstance. See AU 561 for a discussion of auditor responsibility when subsequent to the issuance of the auditor's report the auditor becomes aware of a fact that existed at the date of the auditor's report.

75. (587,A1,48) (c) The requirement is to determine the auditor's responsibility with respect to a client acquisition of 25% of its outstanding capital stock after year end and prior to the completion of the auditor's field work. Answer (c) is correct because the transaction described is a type 2 subsequent

event (since the acquisition provided evidence of a condition which came into existence after year end) and therefore the proper accounting approach would be note disclosure rather than adjustment (AU 560). Answer (a) is incorrect because adjustments are only appropriate for type 1 subsequent events (events which provide evidence that the condition was in existence at year end). Answer (b) is incorrect because the auditor does not issue financial statements for the client. Answer (d) is incorrect because the opinion paragraph of the report need not be modified; if any report modification were considered necessary, it would be an explanatory middle paragraph emphasizing the matter (AU 509.27).

76. (1184,A1,38) (d) The requirement is to determine the subsequent event least likely to result in an adjustment to the financial statements. Answer (d) is correct (least likely) to result in an adjustment to the financial statements because the condition came into effect after year end--a type 2 subsequent event which will lead to footnote disclosure. Answer (a) is incorrect because the events affecting the realization of accounts receivable owned as of the balance sheet date will generally be used in valuing accounts receivable at the balance sheet date --a type 1 subsequent event which will lead to an adjustment of the financial statements. Answer (b) is incorrect because for reasons similar to answer (a), it is a type 1 subsequent event. Answer (c) is incorrect because such information pertinent to year-end liabilities should be used to estimate the balance due at year end. See AU 560 for information on subsequent events.

77. (1189,A1,22) (c) The requirement is to identify an auditor's responsibility when, after an audit report has been issued, s/he becomes aware of a related party transaction that occurred during the year under audit. Answer (c) is correct because AU 561.05 requires that the auditor determine whether the lack of disclosure would affect the auditor's report. Answer (a) is incorrect because the auditor cannot simply plan to audit the transactions during the next engagement. Answer (b) is incorrect because any decisions concerning the recalling of the audited financial statements are to be made by the client. Answer (d) is incorrect because such disclosure of the transactions in subsequent interim statements is only appropriate when issuance of financial statements accompanied by the auditor's report for a subsequent period is imminent (AU 561.06).

78. (587,A1,47) (a) The requirement is to determine the procedure that would be least helpful to the auditor in making an assessment of the importance of an omitted procedure to the ability to support a previously expressed opinion. Answer (a) is correct because a discussion with the client about whether there are persons relying on the auditor's report relates more directly to the action to be taken after such a procedure has been omitted, and not to an assessment of the importance of the procedure (AU 390.05). Answers (b), (c), and (d) are all incorrect because the professional standards suggest that a reevaluation of the overall scope of the examination, discussion of the circumstances with engagement personnel, and a review of other possible compensating procedures are all ways for the auditor to assess the importance of the omitted procedure (AU 390.04).

C.17. Omitted Procedures Discovered After the Report Date

79. (588,A1,36) (d) The requirement is to determine the auditor's responsibility when she/he has concluded that (1) a necessary audit procedure has been omitted at the time of a prior examination, (2) it impairs the ability to support the previous opinion, and (3) there are stockholders relying upon the statements. Answer (d) is correct because AU 390.05 requires that the auditor promptly undertake to apply the omitted procedure or alternative procedures that would provide a satisfactory basis for the audit opinion. Answer (a) is incorrect because the auditor would only notify persons relying on the financial statements in a circumstance such as this when his/her attorney determines it to be an appropriate course of action. As a matter of practicality, this may be difficult if stockholders are numerous. Answer (b) is incorrect because action needs to be taken immediately, and the auditor should not wait until release of interim financial statements. Answer (c) is incorrect because there may or may not be a need to revise financial statements. However, the necessary information for this judgment is not available at this point.

80. (589,A1,44) (b) The requirement is to identify the circumstance in which an auditor need not apply an omitted procedure that was considered necessary, but not performed, at the time of the audit. Answer (b) is correct because AU 390.04 states that when the results of other procedures compensate for the procedure, it need not be performed. Answer (a) is incorrect because a low risk of adverse publicity or litigation is not a reasonable ap-

proach for justification of the omission of the procedure. Answer (c) is incorrect because the qualification may not directly relate to the omitted procedure. In addition, the procedure was considered necessary and should be performed if compensating procedures were not performed. Answer (d) is incorrect because the procedure may still be of importance after the subsequent period's tests (e.g., in the event that comparative statements are presented).

D. Completing the Audit

D.1. Overall Procedures While Completing the Audit

81. (1181,A1,2) (c) The requirement is to determine the primary purpose of a schedule of unadjusted differences for which the auditor did not propose adjustment when discovered. Answer (c) is correct because the auditor uses such a schedule to aggregate the effects of individually immaterial items for the purpose of determining whether the total effect on the financial statements is material. Answer (a) is incorrect because, depending upon their perceived importance, these immaterial errors may or may not be pointed out to client officials. Answer (b) is incorrect because there is no requirement that such immaterial adjustments be reflected on the federal tax return. Answer (d) is incorrect because the immaterial nature of the errors or disputed items made their posting at year end unnecessary.

82. (587,A1,32) (a) The requirement is to identify the listed audit procedure that is ordinarily performed last. Answer (a) is correct because, when obtaining a representation letter from the client, the auditor is concerned with events occurring through the date of his report that may require adjustment to or disclosure in the financial statements; it therefore is dated as of the date of the audit report and should be obtained at the completion of the audit (AU 333.09). Answers (b), (c), and (d) are all incorrect since they are procedures which should be performed prior to the issuance of a report. Thus, they would be completed prior to the audit report date.

D.2. General Questions on Cutoff Tests

83. (589,A1,31) (a) The requirement is to determine the type of transaction that most likely would be detected by an auditor's review of a client's sales cut off. Answer (a) is correct because the auditor's review will include a study of sales recorded late in December and early in January. This will be accomplished by reviewing the period when the revenue was earned by shipment of goods or performance of services, as compared to the period in which the revenue was recorded to determine that they have been recorded in the appropriate period. Accordingly, the review of sales recorded in January may reveal unrecorded sales for the preceding year. Answer (b) is incorrect because it is unlikely that lapping in the application of cash receipts will be detected by sales cutoff testing. More frequently, procedures such as confirmations, analytical procedures, and an analysis of deposit tickets reveal lapping. Answer (c) is incorrect because a sales cutoff test does not address the discounts issued on sales, it only addresses the period in which the sale should be recorded. Excessive discounts are normally revealed in the testing of accounts receivable valuation. Answer (d) is incorrect because while unauthorized returned goods may be detected at year end, this will normally be detected during purchases (receiving) cutoff tests.

84. (1180,A1,19) (a) Commissions are directly related to sales in verifying accrued commission payable; the auditor seeks to determine that both are recorded in the proper period. Answer (b) is incorrect because contingent liabilities generally have little to do with commissions; in most cases, the liability exists when the sale occurs. Answer (c) is incorrect because the overall general nature of the post balance sheet review makes discovery difficult, although certainly possible. Answer (d) is incorrect because the examination trade accounts payable will be of assistance in verifying accrued commissions only in those cases in which there are classification errors.

D.3. General Questions on Contingent Liabilities

85. (589,A1,35) (b) The requirement is to identify the procedure that is least likely to be effective in identifying contingent liabilities. Answer (b) is correct because while customer confirmation replies may reveal contingent liabilities (as evidenced by customer dissatisfaction), they are less likely to reveal contingent liabilities than the other replies. The AICPA Audit and Accounting Manual (AAM 6500.650) suggests that the primary sources related to contingent liabilities include a review of minutes, standard bank confirmations, agreements and contracts, legal fees, inquiries of management, and lawyers' letters. Answer (a) is incorrect because confirmations explicitly include questions pertaining to contingent liabilities. Answer (c) is incorrect because examination of invoices for professional services, such as those from attorneys, may reveal contingent liabilities.

Answer (d) is incorrect because the board of directors' minutes may reveal discussions of contingent liabilities facing the firm.

86. (1184,A1,28) (a) The requirement is to determine the procedure which is most likely to identify a contingent liability. Answer (a) is correct because a standard bank confirmation explicitly requests information relating to contingent liabilities. Answer (b) is incorrect because there is no reason to believe that a related party transaction is more likely to identify a contingent liability than a nonrelated party transaction. In fact, the related party transaction may be less likely since the parties are not independent of one another. Answer (c) is incorrect because accounts payable confirmations are generally sent to known creditors, and information on actual, not contingent, liabilities is most likely to be obtained. Answer (d) is incorrect because a transfer agent confirmation will provide information on outstanding stock.

E. Compilation and Review Procedures
E.1. Compilation Procedures

87. (587,A1,34) (d) The requirement is to determine an accountant's responsibility prior to commencing the compilation of financial statements of a nonpublic entity. Answer (d) is correct because the accountant should possess a level of knowledge of the accounting principles and practices of the industry in which the entity operates that will enable him/her to compile financial statements that are appropriate in form for an entity operating in that industry (AR 100.10). Answers (a), (b), and (c) are incorrect because the accountant is not required to make inquiries or perform other procedures to verify, corroborate, or review information supplied by the entity, either before or during the compilation (AR 100.12). Thus, no analytical procedures, consideration of internal control, or verification of information is required.

88. (589,A1,45) (a) The requirement is to identify a condition required for an accountant to submit a written personal financial plan containing unaudited financial statements to a client without complying with the compilation and review requirements presented in SSARS 1. Answer (a) is correct because AR 600.03 allows such an exception when the plan (1) is to be used to assist the client and the client's advisors in developing financial goals and objectives, (2) will not be used to obtain credit, and (3) when nothing comes to the accountant's attention that would lead him/her to believe that the statements

will be used for credit or for any other purposes. Answer (b) is incorrect because any work performed on the prior year statements is not applicable to the statements of the current year. Answer (c) is incorrect because the engagement letter need not acknowledge departures from GAAP. Answer (d) is incorrect because no assurance is provided in such reports.

E.2. Review Procedures

89. (588,A1,42) (b) The requirement is to determine the type of report which is based primarily on the performance of inquiry and analytical procedures. Answer (b) is correct because AR 100.23 -.31 outlines the various types of inquiry and analytical procedures appropriate to a review. Answer (a) is incorrect because accountants performing compilations are not required to make inquiries or to perform other procedures to verify, corroborate, or review information supplied by the client (AR 100.12). Answer (c) is incorrect because the term management advisory report has no established meaning in the standards. Answer (d) is incorrect because, as outlined in the General Accounting Office "Yellow Book," audits are based on numerous procedures beyond inquiry and analytical procedures.

90. (1189,A1,35) (c) The requirement is to identify an accountant's responsibility prior to performing a review of a non-public entity's financial statements. Answer (c) is correct because an accountant should possess a level of knowledge of the accounting principles and practices of the industry in which the entity operates, and possess an understanding of the entity's business that will allow him/her to perform the inquiry and analytical procedures of a review (AR 100.24). Answers (a), (b), and (d) are incorrect because such inquiries and procedures are to be performed during the review, not before it.

91. (1186,A1,26) (c) The requirement is to identify the procedure usually included in a review engagement of a non-public entity. Answer (c) is correct because an inquiry concerning subsequent events is a procedure required for reviews (AR 100.27 presents the various required procedures). Answers (a), (b), and (d), all represent procedures normally performed during audits, which are not required for reviews.

92. (587,A1,35) (b) The requirement is to determine the type of transaction the accountant is most likely to investigate during a review when the year's accounts receivable did

not conform to a predictable pattern. Answer (b) is correct because accounts receivable are generated from credit sales and an
accountant would therefore investigate them.
Answer (a) is incorrect because sales returns
and allowances would be less likely to cause
large shifts in accounts receivable than
credit sales. Answer (c) is incorrect because
it is less complete than answer (b) since
sales of consigned goods represent only one
possible type of sale that might impact
accounts receivable. Answer (d) is incorrect
because cash sales do not affect accounts
receivable.

93. (588,A1,40) (a) The requirement is to
identify the correct statement regarding the
procedure not usually performed by the
accountant in a review engagement of a nonpublic entity. Answer (a) is correct because
reviews do not include a study and evaluation
of internal control (AR 100.27). Answer (b)
is incorrect because reading of the financial
statements is required (AR 100.27e). Answer (c) is incorrect because the accountant
should establish an understanding regarding
the services to be performed in an engagement
letter. Answer (d) is incorrect because the
report issued does state that a review was
performed in accordance with standards
established by the AICPA (AR 100.32).

F. Other Related Topics
F.1. Compliance Audits

94. (589,A1,2) (c) The requirement is to
identify the body authorized to promulgate
standards for audits of federal financial
assistance recipients. Answer (c) is correct
because, as indicated in Governmental Auditing
Standards (the "yellow book"), the General
Accounting Office promulgates such standards.
Answers (a) and (b) are incorrect because
neither the Governmental Accounting Standards
Board nor the Financial Accounting Standards
Board promulgates auditing standards. Answer (d) is incorrect because there is no
Governmental Auditing Standards Board.

95. (588,A1,37) (b) The requirement is to
determine the proper scope of a governmental
audit. Answer (b) is correct because the
General Accounting Office's "Yellow Book" suggests that in addition to financial statements, such an audit may include consideration
of (1) program results, (2) compliance with
laws and regulations, and (3) economy and
efficiency (1981, page 3). Therefore, answers (a), (c), and (d) are all incorrect.

96. (587,A1,1) (c) The requirement is to
identify the source of authoritative guidance
for performing audits of a city that is subject to the requirements of the Uniform Single
Audit Act of 1984. Answer (c) is correct
because while the AICPA's generally accepted
auditing standards must be followed to the
extent they are pertinent, the General
Accounting Office Standards for Audit of
Governmental Organizations, Programs,
Activities, and Functions must also be adhered
to. The other replies all relate to standards
not directly related to the Uniform Single
Audit Act.

97. (583,A1,53) (d) The requirement is to
determine the scope of governmental auditing
in addition to audits of efficiency and effectiveness. Compliance audits are frequently
performed by governmental auditors (e.g., compliance with legislative restrictions on the
use of funds). Answer (a) is incorrect
because governmental auditors infrequently
directly examine internal control (although
CPAs sometimes perform such analyses--see
AU 642). Answers (b) and (c), evaluation and
accuracy, are terms which are not typically
used to describe types of audits.

98. (1187,A1,17) (c) The requirement is to
identify the type of information not required
as a part of an auditor's report performed in
accordance with generally accepted government
auditing standards. Answer (c) is correct
because such audit reports do not mention the
sampling methods used (AU 9642.24). Answers (a), (b), and (d) are all incorrect because they present information that is included in such a report. Reporting requirements for these audits is presented in
AU 9642.18-.25. The overall requirements are
presented in the United States General Accounting Office's (GAO) "Standards for Audit
of Governmental Organizations, Programs, Activities and Functions," 1981 revision (often
referred to as the "Yellow Book").

99. (1188,A1,48) (c) The requirement is to
identify the correct statement which would
communicate weaknesses in internal control
used in administering a federal financial
assistance program when a CPA has examined the
general purpose financial statements of a
municipality. Answer (c) is correct because
the AICPA Accounting and Audit Guide, Audits
of State and Local Governmental Units
(pp. 216-220), requires the communication of
weaknesses that are material in relation to
the federal financial assistance program.
Answers (a), (b), and (d) are all incorrect
because they all suggest communications not
required by the Guide.

F.2. Operational Auditing

100. (587,A1,39) (a) The requirement is to identify the correct statement with respect to the primary orientation of operational auditing. Answer (a) is correct because operational audits deal primarily with evaluating the efficiency and effectiveness with which operations function, often with the intention of making improvements to accomplish the goals of management. Answers (b) and (c) are incorrect because financial statement audits are oriented toward such determinations, not operational audits. Answer (d) is incorrect because examinations of internal controls are not performed on operational audits.

101. (589,A1,43) (d) The requirement is to identify a typical objective of an operational audit. Answer (d) is correct because operational audits typically address efficiency and effectiveness. Answer (a) is incorrect because while the adequacy of an internal control structure's design may be addressed during an operational audit, this is less complete than answer (d). Answer (b) is incorrect because operational audits may or may not be related to compliance with generally accepted governmental auditing standards. Answer (c) is incorrect because financial statement audits, not operational audits, address whether results of operations are fairly presented.

May 1990 Answers

102. (590,A1,2) (a) The requirement is to identify the factor that would <u>least</u> influence an auditor's consideration of the reliability of data for purposes of analytical procedures. Answer (a) is correct because whether the data were processed in an EDP system or in a manual accounting system will not in and of itself influence reliability--either type of system may provide reliable (or unreliable) information. AU 329.16 states that the following factors do influence the auditor's consideration of the reliability of data for purposes of achieving audit objectives: whether sources within the entity were independent of those who are responsible for the amount being audited (answer [b]), whether the data were subjected to audit testing (answer [c]), whether the data were obtained from independent sources (answer [d]), whether the data was developed under a reliable system, and whether the expectations were developed using data from a variety of sources.

103. (590,A1,3) (d) The requirement is to determine the proper focus of analytical procedures used in planning the audit. Answer (d) is correct because the objectives of analytical procedures during planning are (1) to enhance the auditor's understanding of the client, and (2) to identify areas that may represent specific risks relevant to the audit. Answer (a) is incorrect because while analytical procedures may identify material weaknesses in the internal control structure, this is not a primary objective. Answer (b) is incorrect because the predictability of financial data from individual transactions is a factor that would be taken into consideration when determining the extent of transaction testing. Answer (c) is incorrect because AU 326 clearly identifies the assertions embodied in the financial statements, and analytical procedures perform no such role.

104. (590,A1,4) (a) The requirement is to identify the reply which represents a procedure normally performed during a review of a nonpublic entity's financial statements. Answer (a) is correct because AR 100.27d recommends inquiries concerning actions taken at meetings of the stockholders and board of directors. Answer (b) is incorrect because analytical procedures designed to provide corroborating evidential matter relate more directly to performing substantive tests during audits (see AU 329.09-.21). Answer (c) is incorrect because the emphasis during a review is not primarily one of identifying reportable conditions. Answer (d) is incorrect because reviews do not emphasize consideration of management's assertions regarding an entity's continued existence.

105. (590,A1,5) (b) The requirement is to identify the reply which represents an analytical procedure that an auditor testing long-term investments would ordinarily use to ascertain reasonableness. Answer (b) is correct because analytically calculating an expected investment income based on the total of long-term investments will provide the auditor with a relatively precise expectation for the auditor to compare to recorded investment income. Answer (a) is incorrect because unrealized gains or losses in a portfolio of long-term investments will generally be directly recomputed since it is difficult to estimate the balance analytically. (This is because the unrealized gain or loss is determined based upon the market values of the individual securities which are contained in the portfolio.) Answer (c) is incorrect because the classification between current and non-current portfolios relies upon management's intent, and not upon plausible and predictable relationships. Answer (d) is incorrect because the valuation of marketable equity securities will be computed based upon the lower of cost or market rule, using market

values at year end. See AU 329 for information on analytical procedures.

106. (590,A1,6) (c) The requirement is to
identify the procedure most likely to identify
a contingent liability. Answer (c) is correct
because the standard bank confirmation being
used at the time of this exam directly requests information on contingent liabilities. Answer (a) is incorrect because while
it is possible that an accounts payable confirmation might identify a contingent liability, the information requested is generally
related to the actual liability as of year
end. Answer (b) is incorrect because a confirmation sent to a transfer agent provides
more evidence on the number of shares issued
and outstanding. Answer (d) is incorrect
because auditors do not in general send "related party transaction" confirmations.

107. (590,A1,7) (c) The requirement is to
identify the correct statement regarding an
auditor's working papers. Answer (c) is correct because AU 339.05 requires that working
papers show that the accounting records agree
or reconcile with the financial statements.
Answer (a) is incorrect because certain
working papers may sometimes serve as a useful
reference source for a client (AU 339.07).
Answer (b) is incorrect because while it may
not in general be desirable to include
critical comments concerning management in the
working papers, it is not restricted. Answer (d) is incorrect because working papers
are the principal record of the work performed
by the auditor and the conclusions reached,
rather than primary support for the financial
statements (AU 339.01).

108. (590,A1,9) (a) The requirement is to
identify the financial statement footnote
disclosure about a related party transaction
that would be most likely to result in the
auditor modifying an otherwise unqualified
opinion. Answer (a) is correct because it
generally will not be possible to determine
whether a particular transaction was consummated on terms equivalent to those with unrelated parties; therefore, the auditor may be
required to express a qualified or adverse
opinion when such an unsubstantiated disclosure is included (AU 334.12). Answers (b), (c), and (d) are all incorrect
because they represent information which might
be expected to be included in related party
transaction disclosures.

109. (590,A1,10) (b) The requirement is to
identify the information an auditor should

confirm with a client's transfer agent and
registrar. Answer (b) is correct because when
a client employs a transfer agent and registrar, there will be no stock certificate book
to examine, and accordingly, information on
shares issued and outstanding should be
confirmed. Answers (a), (c), and (d) are
incorrect because the transfer agent and
registrar often will not have information on
dividend restrictions, guarantees of preferred
stock liquidation values, and the number of
shares subject to agreements to repurchase.

110. (590,A1,20) (d) The requirement is to
identify the procedure an accountant should
perform before issuing a report on the compilation of financial statements of a nonpublic
entity. Answer (d) is correct because the
accountant is required, at a minimum, to read
the financial statements to consider whether
they are free from obvious material errors
(AR 100.13). Answer (a) is incorrect because
the accountant is not required to apply
analytical procedures. Answer (b) is
incorrect because the accountant need not corroborate financial statements assertions (see
AU 326 for information on financial statement
assertions). Answer (c) is incorrect because
while reading the financial statements, the
accountant will become aware of whether they
omit substantially all disclosures. (When
such disclosures are omitted, the accountant
may modify the compilation report to so
indicate--see AR 100.19-.21.)

111. (590,A1,50) (b) The requirement is to
identify the reply which is <u>not</u> a factor that
affects the auditor's judgment as to the quantity, type, and content of working papers.
Answer (b) is correct because the purpose of
the client's representation letter is to
complement, and not to replace, other auditing
procedures; accordingly, the representation
letter will not affect the quantity, type, and
content of working papers. (AU 333 presents
guidance on representation letters.) Answers (a), (c), and (d) are incorrect because
the type of report to be issued, the estimated
occurrence rate of attributes, and the
auditor's preliminary evaluation of risk all
will affect the quantity, type, and content of
working papers. See AU 339.04 for further
guidance on factors affecting the auditor's
judgment about the quality, type, and content
of working papers.

112. (590,A1,53) (c) The requirement is to
determine where information on the auditor's
contractual obligation with respect to the
scope and nature of the audit is presented.

Answer (c) is correct because the engagement
letter, sent by the auditor to the client,
serves as such a contract. Answer (a) is
incorrect because a "management letter" generally includes recommendations for improvement
to the client from the auditor. Answer (b) is
incorrect because the scope paragraph of the
auditor's report describes the nature of the
audit. Answer (d) is incorrect because the
introductory paragraph of the audit report
identifies the financial statements audited,
and only briefly summarizes management and
auditor responsibility.

Unofficial Answer*

Problem 1   Related Party Transactions
         (1188,A2)

The audit procedures Temple should apply to identify Ford's related party relationships and transactions include the following:

• Evaluate the company's procedures for identifying and properly reporting related party relationships and transactions.
• Request from management the names of all related parties and inquire whether there were any transactions with these parties during the period.
• Review tax returns and filings with other regulatory agencies for the names of related parties.
• Determine the names of all pension plans and other trusts and the names of their officers and trustees.
• Review stock certificate book to identify the stockholders.
• Review material investment transactions to determine whether the investments created related party relationships.
• Review the minutes of board of directors' meetings.
• Review conflict-of-interest statements obtained by the company from its management.
• Review the extent and nature of business transacted with major customers, suppliers, borrowers, and lenders.
• Consider whether transactions are occurring, but are not being given proper accounting recognition, e.g., personal use of company vehicles, interest-free loans, etc.
• Review accounting records for large, unusual, or nonrecurring transactions or balances, paying particular attention to transactions recognized at or near the end of the reporting period.
• Review confirmations of compensating balance arrangements for indications that balances are or were maintained for or by related parties.
• Review invoices from law firms that have performed services for the company for indications of the existence of related party relationships or transactions.
• Review confirmations of loans receivable and payable for indications of guarantees, and determine their nature and the relationships, if any, of the guarantors to the reporting entity.

*Because the requirements of this question could be answered by lists of items, we have not included an outline of the solution.

Unofficial Answer*

Problem 2   Techniques for Inventory
         (1188,A5)

a. The means or techniques of gathering audit evidence, in addition to the example, are as follows:

Technique	Description
Inquiry	An auditor questions client personnel about events and conditions, such as obsolete inventory.
Confirmation	An auditor obtains acknowledgements in writing from third parties of transactions or balances, such as inventory in public warehouses or on consignment.
Calculation or Recomputation	An auditor recomputes certain amounts, such as the multiplication of quantity times price to determine inventory amounts.
Analysis	An auditor combines amounts in meaningful ways to allow the application of audit judgment, such as the determination of whether a proper inventory cutoff was performed.
Inspection	An auditor examines documents relating to transactions and balances, such as shipping and receiving records to establish ownership of inventory.
Comparison	An auditor relates two or more amounts, such as inventory cost in perpetual inventory records to costs as shown on vendor invoices as part of the evaluation of whether inventory is priced at the lower of cost or market.

b. Substantive auditing procedures that would satisfy the five general assertions regarding a client's inventory balance include the following:

(one different procedure required for each assertion)

Assertion	Substantive Auditing Procedure
1. Existence or Occurence	•Observe physical inventory counts. •Obtain confirmation of inventories at locations outside the entity. •Test inventory transactions between a preliminary physical inventory date and the balance sheet date. •Review perpetual inventory records, production records, and purchasing records for indications of current activity. •Compare inventories with a current sales catalog and subsequent sales and delivery reports. •Use the work of specialists to corroborate the nature of specialized products.
2. Completeness	•Observe physical inventory counts. •Perform analytical procedures the relationship of inventory balances to recent purchasing, production, and sales activities. •Test shipping and receiving cutoff procedures. •Obtain confirmation of inventories at locations outside the entity. •Trace test counts recorded during the physical inventory observation to the inventory listing. •Account for all inventory tags and count sheets used in recording the physical inventory listing. •Test the clerical accuracy of inventory listings. •Reconcile physical counts to perpetual records and general ledger balances and investigate significant fluctuations.

Assertion	Substantive Auditing Procedure
3. Rights and Obligations	•Observe physical inventory counts. •Obtain confirmation of inventories at locations outside the entity. •Examine paid vendors' invoices, consignment agreements, and contracts. •Test shipping and receiving cutoff procedures.
4. Valuation or Allocation	•Examine paid vendors' invoices. •Review direct labor rates. •Test the computation of standard overhead rates. •Examine analyses of purchasing and manufacturing standard cost variances. •Examine an analysis of inventory turnover. •Review industry experience and trends. •Perform analytical procedures the relationship of inventory balances to anticipated sales volume. •Tour the plant. •Inquire of production and sales personnel concerning possible excess or obsolete inventory items. •Obtain current market value quotations. •Review current production costs. •Examine sales after year-end and open purchase order commitments.
5. Presentation and Disclosures	•Review drafts of the financial statements. •Compare the disclosures made in the financial statements to the requirements of generally accepted accounting principles. •Obtain confirmation of inventories pledged under loan agreements.

Unofficial Answer*

Problem 3   Procedures for Common and
                     Treasury Stock (586,A2)

The substantive audit procedures that Jones should apply in examining the common stock and treasury stock accounts are as follows:

• Review the corporate charter to verify details of the common stock such as authorized shares, par value, etc.
• Obtain or prepare an analysis of changes in common stock and treasury stock accounts.
• Compare opening balances with prior year's working papers.
• Foot the total shares outstanding in the stockholders' ledger and stock certificate book.
• Determine authorization for common stock issuances and treasury stock transactions by inspecting the minutes of the board of directors' meetings.
• Verify capital stock issuances by examining supporting documentation and tracing entries into the records.
• Verify treasury stock transactions by examining supporting documentation and tracing entries into the records.
• Examine all certificates canceled during the year.
• Inspect all treasury stock certificates owned by the client.
• Reconcile the details of the individual certificates in the stock certificate book with the individual shareholders' accounts in the stockholders' ledger.
• Compare the totals in the stockholders' ledger and the stock certificate book to the balance sheet presentation.
• Recompute the weighted average number of shares outstanding.
• Compare the financial statement presentation and disclosure with generally accepted accounting principles.
• Determine the existence of and proper accounting for common stock and treasury stock transactions occurring since year end.
• Obtain written representations concerning common and treasury stock in the client representation letter.

Unofficial Answer*

Problem 4   Equipment Audit Program (1184,A2)

Substantive audit procedures that Pierce should use in examining Mayfair's mobile construction equipment and related depreciation would include the following:

• Determine that the equipment account is properly footed.
• Determine that the subsidiary accounts agree with controlling accounts.
• Obtain or prepare an analysis of changes in the account during the year.
• Determine that beginning-of-year balances agree with prior year's ending balances.
• Inspect documents in support of additions during the year.
• Inspect documents in support of retirements during the year.
• Analyze repairs and maintenance for possible reclassifications.
• Determine the propriety of accounting for equipment not in current use.
• Test the accuracy of equipment and accounting records by:

   • Selecting items from the accounting records and verifying their physical existence.
   • Selecting items of equipment and locating them in the accounting records.

• Evaluate the reasonableness of estimated lives and methods of depreciation used.
• Test the calculation of depreciation expense and accumulated depreciation balance.
• Perform analytical review procedures such as comparing depreciation expense to balance sheet accounts for proper relationship and comparing the current year's depreciation expense with prior year's depreciation expense.
• Evaluate the financial statement presentation and disclosures for conformity with generally accepted accounting principles.
• Review insurance coverage.

*Because the requirements of this question could be answered by lists of items, we have not included an outline of the solution.

Unofficial Answer*
(Author Modified)

Problem 5   Audit Program for Accounts Payable
            (1183,A4)

Taylor should perform the following additional substantive audit procedures.

• Foot the client-prepared schedule.
• Tie the general ledger accounts payable control account to the client-prepared accounts payable schedule.
• Examine vendors' statements in support of items on the client-prepared schedule.
• Examine other documents (such as approved vouchers) in support of items on the client-prepared schedule.
• Review the general ledger control account for noncash debits or unusual items, and investigate them.
• Confirm, with positive confirmation requests, account balances from vendors with account balances and vendors with zero account balances.
• Examine unpaid invoices on hand (to ascertain whether any were erroneously omitted from the client-prepared schedule of accounts payable).
• Examine documents in support of invoices paid subsequent to the year end (to ascertain whether the payable was recorded in the appropriate year).
• Inspect receiving reports (to test the accuracy of the year-end cutoff).
• Ascertain whether year-end outstanding checks to vendors were returned with the cutoff bank statement.
• Review correspondence files with respect to disputed items.
• Review open purchase orders for unusual or old items that may have been received but not recorded.
• Examine unmatched receiving reports.
• Make certain that the client representation letter includes the proper assertions concerning accounts payable.
• Investigate and resolve confirmation exceptions and other matters requiring follow-up.

Unofficial Answer*

Problem 6   Cash Audit Procedures (583,A4)

Basic audit procedures that should be performed by Kautz in gathering evidence in support of each of the items (a) through (f) are as follows:

Balance per bank (item a)

1. Confirm by direct written communication with bank.
2. Obtain and inspect a January 1983 cutoff bank statement directly from the bank (examine opening balance).

Deposit in transit (item b)

1. Verify that the deposit was listed in the January 1983 cutoff bank statement on a timely basis.
2. Trace to the cash receipts journal.
3. Inspect the client's copy of the deposit slip for the date of deposit.

Outstanding checks (item c)

1. Trace to the cash disbursements journal.
2. Examine all supporting documents for those outstanding checks that were not returned with the cutoff bank statement.
3. Examine checks accompanying the January 1983 cutoff bank statement and trace all 1982, or prior, checks to the outstanding check list.
4. Ascertain why check number 837 is still outstanding, if possible.

NSF check returned (item d)

1. Follow up on the ultimate disposition of the NSF check.
2. Examine all supporting documents.

Note collected (item e)

1. Examine bank credit memo.

Balance per books (item f)

1. Foot this total and compare this balance with the general ledger balance.

Unofficial Answer*
(Author Modified)

Problem 7   Audit Procedures for Marketable
            Securities (582,A4)

a. Missing information that is essential to the audit of marketable securities includes:

1. General ledger account numbers.
2. Dates securities acquired and sold.

*Because the requirements of this question could be answered by lists of items, we have not included an outline of the solution.

3. Interest earned (accrual/receipt) on R prior to the date of sale.
4. Interest due (accrual/payment) on S to the date of purchase.
5. Support for accrual of dividends.
6. Data related to income accruals, 12/31/80.
7. Handling of bond discount.
8. Data necessary to determine classification of securities.

b. Essential audit procedures that were not noted as having been performed are:

1. Physically examine and count securities on hand. Compare data on securities such as name registered, maturity dates, interest rates, and serial numbers to similar data listed on schedule for agreement. Compare such data for current year to last year's work papers noting any exceptions. Follow up any exceptions.
2. Confirm securities held by others.
3. Inquire whether any securities are pledged.
4. Compare proceeds for bonds sold with broker's advice.
5. Recalculate gain (loss) on the sale of securities by verifying original cost and trace amount of gain (loss) to general ledger account.
6. Trace disbursement for bonds purchased to cash disbursements.
7. Trace dollar amount of each security held to the general ledger balance.
8. Trace the accruals to receivable accounts.
9. Trace the total interest and dividends to income accounts.
10. Cross foot the 12/31 general ledger column.
11. Check extension of the amounts in the 12/31 general ledger columns.
12. Compare market prices of bonds and common stock with a published source.
13. Check the extension of amounts in 12/31 market column.
14. Compare dividends received/accrued and interest received/accrued to published record such as Moody's.
15. Recompute bond interest received and accrued.
16. Recompute dividends received and accrued.
17. Perform analytical procedures for income and accrued receivable amounts.
18. Determine if the Allowance for the Excess of Cost over Market of Marketable Securities needs adjustment to zero since market value of securities is greater than cost.
19. Make inquiries of management concerning classification of securities.

Unofficial Answer*

Problem 8   Cash Audit Program
(1187,A3)

• Review answers to questions on confirmation requests to determine proper recognition in accounting records and the necessity for financial statement disclosure.
• Make inquiries as to compensating balances and restrictions.

• Obtain copies of the bank reconciliations as of the balance sheet date, and

• Trace the adjusted book balances to the general ledger balances.
• Compare the bank balances to the opening balances on the cut-off bank statements.
• Compare the bank balances to the balances on the confirmations.
• Trace amounts of deposits in transit to the cut-off bank statements and ascertain whether the time lags are reasonable.
• Verify the clerical accuracy of the reconciliations.
• Obtain explanation for unusual reconciling items, including checks drawn to "bearer," "cash," and related parties.
• Trace checks dated prior to the end of the period that were returned with the cut-off statements to the list of outstanding checks.
• Investigate outstanding checks that did not clear with the cut-off bank statements.
• Examine a sample of checks for payee, amount, date, authorized signatures, and endorsements to determine any irregularities from company policy or accounting records.

• Prepare a bank transfer schedule from a review of the cash receipts and disbursements journals, bank statements, and related paid checks for the last few days before and the first few days after the year end, and

• Review the schedule to determine that the deposit and disbursement of each transfer is recorded in the proper period.
• Trace incomplete transfers to the schedule of outstanding checks and deposits in transit.

*Because the requirements of this question could be answered by lists of items, we have not included an outline of the solution.

Unofficial Answer*

Problem 9   Loss Contingency Audit Procedures
             (588,A3)

The substantive audit procedures that Young should apply when testing for loss contingencies relating to litigation, claims, and assessments include the following:

- Read minutes of meetings of stockholders, directors, and committees.
- Read contracts, loan agreements, leases, and other documents.
- Read correspondence with taxing and other governmental agencies.
- Read correspondence with insurance and bonding companies.
- Read confirmation replies for information concerning guarantees.
- Discuss with management the entity's policies and procedures for identifying, evaluating, and accounting for litigation, claims, and assessments.
- Obtain from management or inside general counsel a description and evaluation of litigation, claims, and assessments.
- Obtain written assurance from management that the financial statements include all accruals and disclosures required by Statement on Financial Accounting Standards No. 5.
- Examine documents in the client's possession concerning litigation, claims, and assessments, including correspondence from lawyers.
- Obtain an analysis of professional fee expenses and review supporting invoices for indications of contingencies.
- Request the client's management to prepare for transmittal a letter of inquiry to those lawyers consulted by the client concerning litigation, claims, and assessments.
- Compare the lawyer's response to the items in the letter of inquiry to the description and evaluation of litigation, claims, and assessments obtained from management.
- Determine that the financial statements include proper accruals and disclosures of the contingencies.

*Because the requirements of this question could be answered by lists of items, we have not included an outline of the solution.

Answer Outline

Problem 10   Inventory Audit Procedures
             (1176,A4)

a. Audit procedures peculiar to statistical sampling
    Review client procedures to ascertain reliability
    Become satisfied that the sampling plan has statistical validity
      It will be properly applied
      Precision and reliability are reasonable
    Ensure all parts are included in the perpetual inventory record
    Observe drawing of sample
    Observe actual physical counts and client counting procedures
    Review the statistical evaluation

b. Audit procedures for physical inventory count
    Review client inventory procedures
    Observe physical count
    Make test counts
    Trace count data to inventory records
    Trace items from inventory records to count data
    Trace random items from the warehouse to perpetual records
    Verify footings of inventory records
    Compare physical inventory records with subsidiary ledger records
    Ascertain proper purchase and sales cutoff
    Review merchandise in transit and consigned goods
    Confirm inventory in warehouses
    Perform overall analytical procedures for inventories
    Account for all inventory count sheeets
    Review classification of inventory items
    Review for obsolete merchandise

Unofficial Answer

Problem 10 Inventory Audit Procedures
            (1176,A4)

a. When a client uses statistical sampling to estimate inventories, the auditor should perform procedures similar to the following:
    (1) The auditor should review the client's procedures and methods for determining inventories to ascertain that they are sufficiently reliable to produce results substantially the same as those that would be obtained by a 100% inventory count.

(2) The auditor should be satisfied that the statistical sampling plan to be used by the client has statistical validity, that it will be properly applied, and the planned precision and reliability, as defined statistically, will be reasonable in the circumstance.

(3) The auditor should ascertain that proper steps have been taken to ensure that all parts and supplies in the warehouse are included in the perpetual inventory record. This would normally be checked in advance of the physical count.

(4) The auditor should be present when the sample is drawn to make sure that the requirements for random selection are properly observed and that all items in the inventory have an equal or determinable probability of selection.

(5) The auditor must be present to observe counts and must be satisfied with the client's counting procedures. The inventory observation can be made either during or after the year end of the period under audit if well-kept perpetual records are maintained and the client makes periodic comparison of physical counts with such records.

(6) The auditor should review the statistical evaluation and be satisfied that the estimated value of the precision at a given level of reliability meets the materiality requirements set for the audit.

b. In addition to the above, the following standard audit procedures for verification of physical quantities should be performed whether the client conducts a periodic physical count for all or part of its inventory:

(1) Review and be satisfied with the client's physical inventory-taking procedures.

(2) Observe the physical count.

(3) Make test counts where appropriate.

(4) Trace selected count data to the inventory compilation.

(5) Select items from compilation and trace them to original count data.

(6) Select items from the warehouse at random and trace these items to the perpetual inventory record.

(7) Verify footings.

(8) Compare inventory compilation amounts to the subsidiary ledger control and investigate significant differences.

(9) Ascertain that there was a proper purchases and sales cutoff.

(10) Review the treatment of merchandise in transit and consigned merchandise.

(11) Confirm merchandise in warehouses.

(12) Perform overall analytical procedures for inventories.

(13) Account for all client inventory count sheets.

(14) Be sure inventory items are properly classified, in good condition, and of proper quality.

Unofficial Answer*

Problem 11 Audit Program--Accounts Receivable (589,A4)

Edwards should consider applying the following additional substantive audit procedures:

• Test the accuracy of the aged accounts receivable schedule.

• Send second requests for all unanswered positive confirmation requests.

• Perform alternative auditing procedures for unanswered second confirmation requests.

• Reconcile and investigate exceptions reported on the confirmations.

• Project the results of the sample confirmation procedures to the population and evaluate the confirmation results.

• Determine whether any accounts receivable are owed by employees or related parties.

• Test the cutoff of sales, cash receipts, and sales returns and allowances.

• Evaluate the reasonableness of the allowance for doubtful accounts.

• Perform analytical procedures for accounts receivable (e.g., accounts receivable to credit sales, allowance for doubtful accounts to accounts receivable, sales to returns and allowances, doubtful accounts expense to net credit sales.)

• Identify differences, if any, between the book and tax basis for the allowance for doubtful accounts and related expense.

• Review activity after the balance sheet date for unusual transactions.

• Determine that the presentation and disclosure of accounts receivable is in conformity with generally accepted accounting principles consistently applied.

*Because the requirements of this question could be answered by lists of items, we have not included an outline of the solution.

Unofficial Answer*

Problem 12   Analytical Procedures (1189,A3)

a. Analytical procedures are used for these broad purposes:
- To assist the auditor in planning the nature, timing, and extent of other auditing procedures.
- As a substantive test to obtain evidential matter about particular assertions related to account balances or classes of transactions.
- As an overall review of the financial information in the final review stage of the audit.

b. An auditor's expectations are developed from the following sources of information:

- Financial information for comparable prior periods giving consideration to known changes.
- Anticipated results--for example, budgets, forecasts, and extrapolations.
- Relationships among elements of financial information within the period.
- Information regarding the industry in which the client operates.
- Relationships of financial information with relevant nonfinancial information.

c. The factors that influence an auditor's consideration of the reliability of data for purposes of achieving audit objectives are whether the

- Data were obtained from independent sources outside the entity or from sources within the entity.
- Sources within the entity were independent of those who are responsible for the amount being audited.
- Data were developed under a reliable system with adequate controls.
- Data were subjected to audit testing in the current or prior year.
- Expectations were developed using data from a variety of sources.

Unofficial Answer*

Problem 13   Long-term Debt Working Paper Deficiencies (1189,A4)

The working paper contains the following deficiencies:

1. The subject matter of the working paper is not properly indicated in the title.

2. There is no indication of any follow-up on the identified error in the accrued interest payable computation.

3. There is no indication whether the confirmation exception was resolved.

4. The loan with the unwaived violation of a provision of the debt agreement is misclassified as long-term.

5. The liability activities of Lender's Capital Corp. and the working paper totals do not crossfoot.

6. There is no indication of cross-referencing of the stockholder loan to the related party transactions working papers.

7. There is no investigation of the payment on the stockholder loan that was reborrowed soon after year end.

8. There is no consideration of the need to impute interest expense on the 0% stockholder loan.

9. There is no indication that the dates under "interest paid to" were audited.

10. There is no indication that the unusually high average interest rate ($281,333/$1,406,667 =20%) was noted and investigated.

11. The working paper does not support the overall conclusions expressed.

12. The tickmark "R" is used but not explained in the tickmark legend.

13. There is no indication that the working paper was prepared by client personnel.

Unofficial Answer*

Problem 14   Audit Procedures for Payroll Over-statement (1189,A2)

Bell should consider performing the following procedures in the audit of Kent's payroll transactions:

Select a sample of payments to employees from the payroll register and compare each selected transaction to the related documents and records examining

- Evidence in support of authorization of rate of pay.
- Evidence in support of time on which compensation was based, such as approved time cards or attendance records.

*Because the requirements of this question could be answered by lists of items, we have not included an outline of the solution.

- Evidence in support of proper authorization of payroll withholdings.
- Evidence in support of payment, such as canceled payroll checks.
- Evidence in support of account distribution.
- The clerical accuracy of the transaction.
- The entry to the employee's records used to summarize employee compensation for payroll reporting purposes.

Obtain the payroll register for a selected period and

- Test the arithmetical accuracy of the payroll register.
- Determine whether payroll was approved in accordance with management's prescribed procedures.
- Trace. totals per the register to postings in the general ledger.

Observe the distribution of payroll checks.
Review the accounting for unclaimed wages.
Observe a sample of employees in the performance of their duties.
Perform analytical procedures.

Multiple Choice Questions (1-93)

1. When an accountant performs more than one level of service (for example, a compilation and a review, or a compilation and an audit) concerning the financial statements of a nonpublic entity, the accountant generally should issue the report that is appropriate for
    a. The lowest level of service rendered.
    b. The highest level of service rendered.
    c. A compilation engagement.
    d. A review engagement.

2. The statement that "nothing came to our attention which would indicate that these statements are not fairly presented" expresses which of the following?
    a. Disclaimer of an opinion.
    b. Negative assurance.
    c. Negative confirmation.
    d. Piecemeal opinion.

3. Negative assurance may be expressed when an accountant is requested to report on the
    a. Compilation of prospective financial statements.
    b. Compliance with the provisions of the Foreign Corrupt Practices Act.
    c. Results of applying agreed-upon procedures to an account within unaudited financial statements.
    d. Audit of historical financial statements.

4. Does an auditor make the following representations explicitly or implicitly when issuing the standard auditor's report on comparative financial statements?

	Consistent application of accounting principles	Examination of evidence on a test basis
a.	Explicitly	Explicitly
b.	Implicitly	Implicitly
c.	Implicitly	Explicitly
d.	Explicitly	Implicitly

5. An auditor should disclose the substantive reasons for expressing an adverse opinion in an explanatory paragraph
    a. Preceding the scope paragraph.
    b. Preceding the opinion paragraph.
    c. Following the opinion paragraph.
    d. Within the notes to the financial statements.

6. The fourth standard of reporting requires the auditor's report to contain either an expression of opinion regarding the financial statements taken as a whole or an assertion to the effect that an opinion cannot be expressed. The objective of the fourth standard is to prevent
    a. An auditor from expressing different opinions on each of the basic financial statements.
    b. Restrictions on the scope of the examination, whether imposed by the client or by the inability to obtain evidence.
    c. Misinterpretations regarding the degree of responsibility the auditor is assuming.
    d. An auditor from reporting on one basic financial statement and **not** the others.

7. Which of the following **best** describes the reference to the expression "taken as a whole" in the fourth generally accepted auditing standard of reporting?
    a. It applies equally to a complete set of financial statements and to each individual financial statement.
    b. It applies only to a complete set of financial statements.
    c. It applies equally to each item in each financial statement.
    d. It applies equally to each material item in each financial statement.

8. An auditor's decision concerning whether or not to "dual date" the audit report is based upon the auditor's willingness to
    a. Extend auditing procedures.
    b. Accept responsibility for subsequent events.
    c. Permit inclusion of a footnote captioned: event (unaudited) subsequent to the date of the auditor's report.
    d. Assume responsibility for events subsequent to the issuance of the auditor's report.

9. An auditor issued an audit report that was dual dated for a subsequent event occurring after the completion of field work but before issuance of the auditor's report. The auditor's responsibility for events occurring subsequent to the completion of field work was
    a. Limited to the specific event referenced.
    b. Limited to include only events occurring before the date of the last subsequent event referenced.

c. Extended to subsequent events occurring through the date of issuance of
the report.
d. Extended to include all events occurring since the completion of
field work.

10. On September 30, 1988, Miller was asked
to reissue an auditor's report, dated
March 31, 1988, on a client's financial
statements for the year ended December 31,
1987. Miller will submit the reissued report
to the client in a document that contains
information in addition to the client's basic
financial statements. However, Miller
discovered that the client suffered
substantial losses on receivables resulting
from conditions that occurred since March 31,
1988. Miller should
a. Request the client to disclose the
event in a separate, appropriately
labeled note to the financial
statements and reissue the original
report with its original date.
b. Request the client to restate the
financial statements and reissue the
original report with a dual date.
c. Reissue the original report with its
original date without regard to
whether the event is disclosed in a
separate note to the financial
statements.
d. Not reissue the original report but
issue a "subject to" qualified
opinion that discloses the event in
a separate explanatory paragraph.

11. A former client requests a predecessor
auditor to reissue an audit report on a prior
period's financial statements. The financial
statements are not restated and the report is
not revised. What date(s) should the
predecessor auditor use in the reissued
report?
a. The date of the prior-period report.
b. The date of the client's request.
c. The date of reissue.
d. The dual dates.

12. An auditor may issue the standard audit
report when the
a. Auditor refers to the findings of a
specialist.
b. Financial statements are derived and
condensed from complete audited
financial statements that are filed
with a regulatory agency.
c. Financial statements are prepared on
the cash receipts and disbursements
basis of accounting.
d. Principal auditor assumes
responsibility for the work of
another auditor.

13. When a principal auditor decides to make
reference to another auditor's examination,
the principal auditor's report should always
indicate clearly, in the introductory, scope,
and opinion paragraphs, the
a. Magnitude of the portion of the
financial statements examined by the
other auditor.
b. Disclaimer of responsibility
concerning the portion of the
financial statements examined by the
other auditor.
c. Name of the other auditor.
d. Division of responsibility.

14. Management of Hill Company has decided
not to account for a material transaction in
accordance with the provisions of an FASB
Standard. In setting forth its reasons in a
note to the financial statements, management
has clearly demonstrated that due to unusual
circumstances the financial statements
presented in accordance with the FASB Standard
would be misleading. The auditor's report
should include a separate explanatory
paragraph and contain a(an)
a. "Except for" qualified opinion.
b. "Subject to" qualified opinion.
c. Adverse opinion.
d. Unqualified opinion.

15. Grant Company's financial statements
adequately disclose uncertainties that concern
future events, the outcome of which are **not**
susceptible of reasonable estimation. The
auditor's report should include a(an)
a. Unqualified opinion.
b. "Subject to" qualified opinion.
c. "Except for" qualified opinion.
d. Adverse opinion.

16. An auditor may issue a qualified opinion
under which of the following circumstances?

	Lack of sufficient competent evidential matter	Restrictions on the scope of the audit
a.	Yes	Yes
b.	Yes	No
c.	No	Yes
d.	No	No

17. The auditor should consider adding an
explanatory paragraph to an unqualified report
when
a. The auditor is prevented from completing a procedure required by
generally accepted auditing standards.
b. The financial statements fail to
disclose information required by
generally accepted accounting principles.

c. The auditor decides to make refer-
    ence to the report of another
    auditor.
d. A question arises about the entity's
    continued existence.

18. An auditor concludes that there is
substantial doubt about an entity's ability to
continue as a going concern for a reasonable
period of time. If the entity's disclosures
concerning this matter are adequate, the audit
report may include a(an)

	Disclaimer of opinion	"Except for" qualified opinion
a.	Yes	Yes
b.	No	No
c.	No	Yes
d.	Yes	No

19. When there is a significant change in
accounting principle, an auditor's report
should refer to the lack of consistency in
a. The scope paragraph.
b. An explanatory paragraph between the
    second paragraph and the opinion
    paragraph.
c. The opinion paragraph.
d. An explanatory paragraph following
    the opinion paragraph.

20. Which of the following requires recognition in the auditor's opinion as to consistency?
a. The correction of an error in the
    prior year's financial statements
    resulting from a mathematical mis-
    take in capitalizing interest.
b. The change from the cost method to
    the equity method of accounting for
    investments in common stock.
c. A change in the estimate of provi-
    sions for warranty costs.
d. A change in depreciation method
    which has no effect on current
    year's financial statements but is
    certain to affect future years.

21. If an accounting change has no material
effect on the financial statements in the
current year, but the change is reasonably
certain to have a material effect in later
years, the change should be
a. Referred to in the auditor's report
    for the current year.
b. Disclosed in the notes to the
    financial statements of the current
    year.
c. Disclosed in the notes to the
    financial statements and referred to
    in the auditor's report for the
    current year.
d. Treated as a subsequent event.

22. When management does not provide
reasonable justification that a change in
accounting principle is preferable and it
presents comparative financial statements, the
auditor should express a qualified opinion
a. Only in the year of the accounting
    principle change.
b. Each year that the financial
    statements initially reflecting the
    change are presented.
c. Each year until management changes
    back to the accounting principle
    formerly used.
d. Only if the change is to an
    accounting principle that is not
    generally accepted.

23. Unaudited financial statements for the
prior year presented in comparative form with
audited financial statements for the current
year should be clearly marked to indicate
their status and

I. The report on the prior period
should be reissued to accompany the current
period report.
II. The report on the current period
should include as a separate paragraph a
description of the responsibility assumed for
the prior period's financial statements.

a. I only.
b. II only.
c. Both I and II.
d. Either I or II.

24. When reporting on comparative financial
statements where the financial statements of
the prior period have been examined by a
predecessor auditor whose report is not
presented, the successor auditor should
indicate in the introductory paragraph
a. The reasons why the predecessor
    auditor's report is not presented.
b. The identity of the predecessor
    auditor who examined the financial
    statements of the prior year.
c. Whether the predecessor auditor's
    review of the current year's
    financial statements revealed any
    matters that might have a material
    effect on the successor auditor's
    opinion.
d. The type of opinion expressed by the
    predecessor auditor.

25. When financial statements of a prior
period are presented on a comparative basis
with financial statements of the current
period, the continuing auditor is responsible
for
a. Expressing dual dated opinions.
b. Updating the report on the pre-
    vious financial statements only if

there has **not** been a change in the opinion.

c. Updating the report on the previous financial statements only if the previous report was qualified and the reasons for the qualification no longer exist.

d. Updating the report on the previous financial statements regardless of the opinion previously issued.

26. When reporting on comparative financial statements, an auditor ordinarily should change the previously issued opinion on the prior year's financial statements if

a. The prior year's opinion was unqualified and the opinion on the current year's financial statements is modified due to a lack of consistency.

b. The prior year's financial statements are restated following a pooling of interests in the current year.

c. The prior year's financial statements are restated to conform with generally accepted accounting principles.

d. The auditor is a predecessor auditor who has been requested by a former client to reissue the previously issued report.

27. Which of the following statements is correct regarding the auditor's responsibilities for supplementary information required by the FASB?

a. Because the supplementary information is a required part of the basic financial statements, the auditor should apply normal auditing procedures.

b. The omission of, but **not** deficiencies in, supplementary information should be disclosed in the opinion paragraph of the auditor's report.

c. Because the supplementary information is **not** a required part of the basic financial statements, the auditor should apply only certain limited procedures.

d. The omission of supplementary information ordinarily requires the auditor to issue an adverse opinion, but mere deficiencies require an "except for" qualified opinion.

28. When financial statements examined by the independent auditor contain notes which are captioned "unaudited" or "not covered by the auditor's report," the auditor

a. May refer to these notes in the auditor's report.

b. Has **no** responsibility with respect to information contained in these notes.

c. Must refer to these notes in the auditor's report.

d. Is precluded from referring to these notes in the auditor's report.

29. Which of the following best describes the auditor's responsibility for "other information" included in the annual report to stockholders which contains financial statements and the auditor's report?

a. The auditor has **no** obligation to read the "other information."

b. The auditor has **no** obligation to corroborate the "other information," but should read the "other information" to determine whether it is materially inconsistent with the financial statements.

c. The auditor should extend the examination to the extent necessary to verify the "other information."

d. The auditor must modify the auditor's report to state that the "other information is unaudited" or "**not** covered by the auditor's report."

30. An auditor concludes that there is a material inconsistency in the other information in an annual report to shareholders containing audited financial statements. If the auditor concludes that the financial statements do **not** require revision, but the client refuses to revise or eliminate the material inconsistency, the auditor may

a. Issue an "except for" qualified opinion after discussing the matter with the client's board of directors.

b. Consider the matter closed since the other information is not in the audited financial statements.

c. Disclaim an opinion on the financial statements after explaining the material inconsistency in a separate explanatory paragraph.

d. Revise the auditor's report to include a separate explanatory paragraph describing the material inconsistency.

31. Which of the following best describes the auditor's reporting responsibility concerning information accompanying the basic financial statements in an auditor-submitted document?
   a. The auditor should report on all the information included in the document.
   b. The auditor should report on the basic financial statements but may not issue a report covering the accompanying information.
   c. The auditor should report on the information accompanying the basic financial statements only if the auditor participated in the preparation of the accompanying information.
   d. The auditor should report on the information accompanying the basic financial statements only if the document is being distributed to public shareholders.

32. An auditor includes an explanatory paragraph in an otherwise unqualified report to emphasize that the financial statements are not comparable to those of prior years due to a court-ordered divestiture that is already fully explained in the notes to the financial statements. The inclusion of this paragraph
   a. Should be followed by an "except for" consistency modification in the opinion paragraph.
   b. Requires a revision of the opinion paragraph to include the phrase "with the foregoing explanation."
   c. Is not appropriate and may confuse the readers or lead them to believe the report was qualified.
   d. Is appropriate and would not negate the unqualified opinion.

33. An auditor may reasonably issue an "except for" qualified opinion for

	Inadequate disclosure	Scope limitation
a.	Yes	Yes
b.	Yes	No
c.	No	Yes
d.	No	No

34. The management of a client company believes that the statement of cash flows is not a useful document and refuses to include one in the annual report to stockholders. As a result of this circumstance, the auditor's opinion should be
   a. Adverse.
   b. Unqualified.
   c. Qualified due to inadequate disclosure.
   d. Qualified due to a scope limitation.

35. In which of the following circumstances would an auditor be most likely to express an adverse opinion?
   a. The statements are not in conformity with the FASB Statements regarding the capitalization of leases.
   b. Information comes to the auditor's attention that raises substantial doubt about the entity's ability to continue in existence.
   c. The chief executive officer refuses the auditor access to minutes of board of directors' meetings.
   d. Tests of controls show that the entity's internal control structure is so poor that it can not be relied upon.

36. Late in December, Tech Products Company sold its marketable securities which had appreciated in value and then repurchased them the same day. The sale and purchase transactions resulted in a large gain. Without the gain the company would have reported a loss for the year. Which of the following statements with respect to the auditor is correct?
   a. If the sale and repurchase are disclosed, an unqualified opinion should be rendered.
   b. The repurchase transaction is a sham and the auditor should insist upon a reversal or issue an adverse opinion.
   c. The auditor should withdraw from the engagement and refuse to be associated with the company.
   d. A disclaimer of opinion should be issued.

37. A CPA engaged to examine financial statements observes that the accounting for a certain material item is not in conformity with generally accepted accounting principles, and that this fact is prominently disclosed in a footnote to the financial statements. The CPA should
   a. Express an unqualified opinion and insert an explanatory paragraph emphasizing the matter by reference to the footnote.
   b. Disclaim an opinion.
   c. Not allow the accounting treatment for this item to affect the type of opinion because the deviation from generally accepted accounting principles was disclosed.
   d. Qualify the opinion because of the deviation from generally accepted accounting principles.

38. When a publicly-held company refuses to include in its audited financial statements any of the segment information that the auditor believes is required, the auditor should issue a(an)

a. Unqualified opinion with a separate explanatory paragraph emphasizing the matter.
b. "Except for" qualified opinion because of inadequate disclosure.
c. Adverse opinion because of the lack of conformity with generally accepted accounting principles.
d. Disclaimer of opinion because of the significant scope limitation.

39. An auditor who qualifies an opinion because of an insufficiency of evidential matter should describe the limitations in an explanatory paragraph. The auditor should also refer to the limitation in the

	Scope paragraph	Opinion paragraph	Notes to the financial statements
a.	Yes	No	Yes
b.	No	Yes	No
c.	Yes	Yes	No
d.	Yes	Yes	Yes

40. When unable to obtain sufficient competent evidential matter to determine whether certain client acts are illegal, the auditor would most likely issue

a. An unqualified opinion with a separate explanatory paragraph.
b. Either a qualified opinion or an adverse opinion.
c. Either a disclaimer of opinion or a qualified opinion.
d. Either an adverse opinion or a disclaimer of opinion.

41. The auditor would most likely issue a disclaimer of opinion because of

a. The client's failure to present supplementary information required by the FASB.
b. Inadequate disclosure of material information.
c. A client imposed scope limitation.
d. The qualification of an opinion by the other auditor of a subsidiary where there is a division of responsbility.

42. Restrictions imposed by a client prohibit the observation of physical inventories, which account for 35% of all assets. Alternative audit procedures cannot be applied, although the auditor was able to examine satisfactory evidence for all other items in the financial statements. The auditor should issue a(an)

a. "Except for" qualified opinion.
b. Disclaimer of opinion.
c. Unqualified opinion with a separate explanatory paragraph.
d. Unqualified opinion with an explanation in the scope paragraph.

43. A limitation on the scope of an auditor's examination sufficient to preclude an unqualified opinion will usually result when management

a. Presents financial statements that are prepared in accordance with the cash receipts and disbursements basis of accounting.
b. States that the financial statements are **not** intended to be presented in conformity with generally accepted accounting principles.
c. Does **not** make the minutes of the Board of Directors' meetings available to the auditor.
d. Asks the auditor to report on the balance sheet and **not** on the other basic financial statements.

44. An auditor did not observe a client's taking of beginning physical inventory and was unable to become satisfied about the inventory by means of other auditing procedures. Assuming **no** other scope limitations or reporting problems, the auditor could issue an unqualified opinion on the current year's financial statements for

a. The balance sheet only.
b. The income statement only.
c. The income and retained earnings statements only.
d. All of the financial statements.

45. An auditor has been asked to report on the balance sheet of Kane Company but not on the other basic financial statements. The auditor will have access to all information underlying the basic financial statements. Under these circumstances, the auditor

a. May accept the engagement because such engagements merely involve limited reporting objectives.
b. May accept the engagement but should disclaim an opinion because of an inability to apply the procedures considered necessary.
c. Should refuse the engagement because there is a client-imposed scope limitation.
d. Should refuse the engagement because of a departure from generally accepted auditing standards.

46. An auditor may **not** issue a qualified opinion when

    a.   A scope limitation prevents the auditor from completing an important audit procedure.

    b.   The auditor's report refers to the work of a specialist.

    c.   An accounting principle at variance with generally accepted accounting principles is used.

    d.   The auditor lacks independence with respect to the audited entity.

47. When an independent CPA is associated with the financial statements of a publicly held entity but has **not** audited or reviewed such statements, the appropriate form of report to be issued must include a(an)

    a.   Compilation report.

    b.   Disclaimer of opinion.

    c.   Unaudited association report.

    d.   Qualified opinion.

48. If an accountant concludes that unaudited financial statements on which the accountant is disclaiming an opinion also lack adequate disclosure, the accountant should suggest appropriate revision. If the client does **not** accept the accountant's suggestion, the accountant should

    a.   Issue an adverse opinion and describe the appropriate revision in the report.

    b.   Make reference to the appropriate revision and issue a modified report expressing limited assurance.

    c.   Describe the appropriate revision to the financial statements in the accountant's disclaimer of opinion.

    d.   Accept the client's inaction because the statements are unaudited and the accountant has disclaimed an opinion.

49. During a compilation of a nonpublic entity's financial statements, an accountant would be **least** likely to

    a.   Omit substantially all of the disclosures required by generally accepted accounting principles.

    b.   Issue a compilation report on one or more, but **not** all of the basic financial statements.

    c.   Perform analytical procedures designed to identify relationships that appear to be unusual.

    d.   Read the compiled financial statements and consider whether they appear to include adequate disclosure.

50. Compiled financial statements should be accompanied by a report stating all the following **except**

    a.   The accountant does **not** express an opinion or any other form of assurance on the financial statements.

    b.   A compilation is substantially less in scope than an examination in accordance with generally accepted accounting standards.

    c.   The accountant compiled the financial statements in accordance with standards established by the AICPA.

    d.   A compilation is limited to presenting in the form of financial statements information that is the representation of management.

51. In which of the following reports should a CPA **not** express negative or limited assurance?

    a.   A standard compilation report on financial statements of a nonpublic entity.

    b.   A standard review report on financial statements of a nonpublic entity.

    c.   A standard review report on interim financial statements of a public entity.

    d.   A standard comfort letter on financial information included in a registration statement of a public entity.

52. If compiled financial statements presented in conformity with the cash receipts and disbursements basis of accounting do **not** disclose the basis of accounting used, the accountant should

    a.   Disclose the basis in the notes to the financial statements.

    b.   Clearly label each page "Unaudited."

    c.   Disclose the basis of accounting in the accountant's report.

    d.   Recompile the financial statements using generally accepted accounting principles.

53. Each page of the financial statements compiled by an accountant should include a reference such as

    a.   See accompanying accountant's footnotes.

    b.   Unaudited, see accountant's disclaimer.

    c.   See accountant's compilation report.

    d.   Subject to compilation restrictions.

54. An accountant's compilation report should be dated as of the date of
   a. Completion of field work.
   b. Completion of the compilation.
   c. Transmittal of the compilation report.
   d. The latest subsequent event referred to in the notes to the financial statements.

55. When an accountant compiles a nonpublic entity's financial statements that omit substantially all disclosures required by generally accepted accounting principles, the accountant should indicate in the compilation report that the financial statements are
   a. Restricted for internal use only by the entity's management.
   b. Not to be given to financial institutions for the purpose of obtaining credit.
   c. Compiled in conformity with a comprehensive basis of accounting other than generally accepted accounting principles.
   d. Not designed for those who are uninformed about the omitted disclosures.

56. An accountant has been asked to compile the financial statements of a nonpublic company on a prescribed form that omits substantially all the disclosures required by generally accepted accounting principles. If the prescribed form is a standard preprinted form adopted by the company's industry trade association, and is to be transmitted only to such association, the accountant
   a. Need **not** advise the industry trade association of the omission of all disclosures.
   b. Should disclose the details of the omissions in separate paragraphs of the compilation report.
   c. Is precluded from issuing a compilation report when all disclosures are omitted.
   d. Should express limited assurance that the financial statements are free of material misstatements.

57. Each page of a nonpublic entity's financial statements reviewed by an accountant should include the following reference:
   a. See Accountant's Review Report.
   b. Reviewed, **No** Accountant's Assurance Expressed.
   c. See Accompanying Accountant's Footnotes.
   d. Reviewed, **No** Material Modifications Required.

58. An accountant who reviews the financial statements of a nonpublic entity should issue a report stating that a review
   a. Is substantially less in scope than an audit.
   b. Provides negative assurance that the internal control structure is functioning as designed.
   c. Provides only limited assurance that the financial statements are fairly presented.
   d. Is substantially more in scope than a compilation.

59. During a review of the financial statements of a nonpublic entity, the CPA finds that the financial statements contain a material departure from generally accepted accounting principles. If management refuses to correct the financial statement presentations, the CPA should
   a. Attach a footnote explaining the effects of the departure.
   b. Disclose the departure in a separate paragraph of the report.
   c. Issue a compilation report.
   d. Issue an adverse opinion.

60. A modification of the CPA's report on a review of the interim financial statements of a publicly-held company would be necessitated by which of the following?
   a. An uncertainty.
   b. Lack of consistency.
   c. Reference to another accountant.
   d. Inadequate disclosure.

61. The objective of a review of interim financial information is to provide the accountant with a basis for reporting whether
   a. A reasonable basis exists for expressing an updated opinion regarding the financial statements that were previously audited.
   b. Material modifications should be made to conform with generally accepted accounting principles.
   c. The financial statements are presented fairly in accordance with standards of interim reporting.
   d. The financial statements are presented fairly in accordance with generally accepted accounting principles.

62. An auditor who conducts an examination in accordance with generally accepted auditing standards and concludes that the financial statements are fairly presented in accordance with a comprehensive basis of accounting other than generally accepted accounting principles,

such as the cash basis of accounting, should
issue a
   a.   Special report.
   b.   Disclaimer of opinion.
   c.   Review report.
   d.   Qualified opinion.

63.   An auditor's report on financial statements prepared in accordance with a comprehensive basis of accounting other than generally
accepted accounting principles should include
all of the following except
   a.   Reference to the note to the
        financial statements that describes
        how the basis of preparation differs
        from generally accepted accounting
        principles.
   b.   Disclosure of the fact that the
        financial statements are presented
        using a comprehensive basis of
        accounting other than generally
        accepted accounting principles.
   c.   An opinion as to whether the basis
        of accounting used is appropriate
        under the circumstances.
   d.   An opinion as to whether the finan-
        cial statements are presented fairly
        in conformity with the basis of
        accounting described.

64.   When an auditor is requested to express
an opinion on the rental and royalty income of
an entity, the auditor may
   a.   Not accept the engagement because to
        do so would be tantamount to
        agreeing to issue a piecemeal
        opinion.
   b.   Not accept the engagement unless
        also engaged to audit the full
        financial statements of the entity.
   c.   Accept the engagement provided the
        auditor's opinion is expressed in a
        special report.
   d.   Accept the engagement provided
        distribution of the auditor's report
        is limited to the entity's
        management.

65.   An accountant may accept an engagement to
apply agreed-upon procedures that are not
sufficient to express an opinion on one or
more specified accounts or items of a
financial statement provided that
   a.   The accountant's report does not
        enumerate the procedures performed.
   b.   The financial statements are
        prepared in accordance with a
        comprehensive basis of accounting
        other than generally accepted
        accounting principles.
   c.   Distribution of the accountant's
        report is restricted.
   d.   The accountant is also the entity's
        continuing auditor.

66.   The term "special reports" may include
all of the following, except reports on
financial statements
   a.   Of an organization that has limited
        the scope of the auditor's examina-
        tion.
   b.   Prepared for limited purposes such
        as a report that relates to only
        certain aspects of financial
        statements.
   c.   Of a not-for-profit organization
        which follows accounting practices
        differing in some respects from
        those followed by business enter-
        prises organized for profit.
   d.   Prepared in accordance with his-
        torical cost/constant dollar
        accounting.

67.   Comfort letters are ordinarily signed by
the
   a.   Client.
   b.   Client's lawyer.
   c.   Independent auditor.
   d.   Internal auditor.

68.   Comfort letters ordinarily are addressed
to
   a.   The Securities and Exchange
        Commission.
   b.   Underwriters of securities.
   c.   Creditor financial institutions.
   d.   The client's audit committee.

69.   When an accountant issues to an underwriter a comfort letter containing comments on
data that have not been audited, the underwriter most likely will receive
   a.   Positive assurance on supplementary
        disclosures.
   b.   Negative assurance on capsule
        information.
   c.   A disclaimer on prospective
        financial statements.
   d.   A limited opinion on "pro forma"
        financial statements.

70.   When an independent audit report is
incorporated by reference in a SEC registration statement, a prospectus that includes a
statement about the independent accountant's
involvement should refer to the independent
accountant as
   a.   Auditor of the financial reports.
   b.   Management's designate before the
        SEC.
   c.   Certified preparer of the report.
   d.   Expert in auditing and accounting.

71. The Securities and Exchange Commission has authority to
    a. Prescribe specific auditing procedures to detect fraud concerning inventories and accounts receivable of companies engaged in interstate commerce.
    b. Deny lack of privity as a defense in third-party actions for gross negligence against the auditors of public companies.
    c. Determine accounting principles for the purpose of financial reporting by companies offering securities to the public.
    d. Require a change of auditors of governmental entities after a given period of years as a means of ensuring auditor independence.

72. Which of the following is a prospective financial statement for general use upon which an accountant may appropriately report?
    a. Financial projection.
    b. Partial presentation.
    c. Pro forma financial statement.
    d. Financial forecast.

73. When third party use of prospective financial statements is expected, an accountant may not accept an engagement to
    a. Perform a review.
    b. Perform a compilation.
    c. Perform an examination.
    d. Apply agreed-upon procedures.

74. The party responsible for assumptions identified in the preparation of prospective financial statements is usually
    a. A third-party lending institution.
    b. The client's management.
    c. The reporting accountant.
    d. The client's independent auditor.

75. Given one or more hypothetical assumptions, a responsible party may prepare, to the best of its knowledge and belief, an entity's expected financial position, results of operations, and changes in financial position. Such prospective financial statements are known as
    a. Pro forma financial statements.
    b. Financial projections.
    c. Partial presentations.
    d. Financial forecasts.

76. An accountant's standard report on a compilation of a projection should not include
    a. A separate paragraph that describes limitations on the presentation's usefulness.

    b. A statement that a compilation of a projection is limited in scope.
    c. A disclaimer of responsibility to update the report for events occurring after the report's date.
    d. A statement that the accountant expresses only limited assurance that the results may be achieved.

77. An accountant may accept an engagement to apply agreed-upon procedures to prospective financial statements provided that
    a. Distribution of the report is to be restricted to the specified users involved.
    b. The prospective financial statements are also examined.
    c. Responsibility for the adequacy of the procedures performed is taken by the accountant.
    d. Negative assurance is expressed on the prospective financial statements taken as a whole.

78. When an accountant compiles projected financial statements, the accountant's report should include a separate paragraph that
    a. Describes the differences between a projection and a forecast.
    b. Identifies the accounting principles used by management.
    c. Expresses limited assurance that the actual results may be within the projection's range.
    d. Describes the limitations on the projection's usefulness.

79. When an accountant examines a financial forecast that fails to disclose several significant assumptions used to prepare the forecast, the accountant should describe the assumptions in the accountant's report and issue a(an)
    a. "Except for" qualified opinion.
    b. "Subject to" qualified opinion.
    c. Unqualified opinion with a separate explanatory paragraph.
    d. Adverse opinion.

80. Green, CPA, is requested to render an opinion on the application of accounting principles by an entity that is audited by another CPA. Green may
    a. Not accept such an engagement because to do so would be considered unethical.
    b. Not accept such an engagement because Green would lack the necessary information on which to base an opinion without conducting an audit.

c.   Accept the engagement but should form an independent opinion without consulting with the continuing CPA.

d.   Accept the engagement but should consult with the continuing CPA to ascertain all the available facts relevant to forming a professional judgment.

May 1990 Questions

81. An auditor's report would be designated a special report when it is issued in connection with

a.   Interim financial information of a publicly held company that is subject to a limited review.

b.   Compliance with aspects of regulatory requirements related to audited financial statements.

c.   Application of accounting principles to specified transactions.

d.   Limited use prospective financial statements such as a financial projection.

82. An explanatory paragraph following the opinion paragraph of an auditor's report describes an uncertainty as follows:

As discussed in Note X to the financial statements, the Company is a defendant in a lawsuit alleging infringement of certain patent rights and claiming damages. Discovery proceedings are in progress. The ultimate outcome of the litigation cannot presently be determined. Accordingly, no provision for any liability that may result upon adjudication has been made in the accompanying financial statements.

What type of opinion should the auditor express under these circumstances?

a.   Unqualified.

b.   "Subject to" qualified.

c.   "Except for" qualified.

d.   Disclaimer.

83. The predecessor auditor, who is satisfied after properly communicating with the successor auditor, has reissued a report because the audit client desires comparative financial statements. The predecessor auditor's report should make

a.   Reference to the report of the successor auditor only in the scope paragraph.

b.   Reference to the work of the successor auditor in the scope and opinion paragraphs.

c.   Reference to both the work and the report of the successor auditor only in the opinion paragraph.

d.   No reference to the report or the work of the successor auditor.

84. An auditor's report that refers to the use of an accounting principle at variance with generally accepted accounting principles contains the words, "In our opinion, with the foregoing explanation, the financial statements referred to above present fairly..." This is considered an

a.   Adverse opinion.

b.   "Except for" qualified opinion.

c.   Unqualified opinion with an explanatory paragraph.

d.   Example of inappropriate reporting.

85. In which of the following circumstances would an auditor choose between issuing a qualified opinion or a disclaimer of opinion?

a.   Departure from generally accepted accounting principles.

b.   Inadequate disclosure of accounting policies.

c.   Inability to obtain sufficient competent evidential matter.

d.   Unreasonable justification for a change in accounting principle.

86. An auditor has previously expressed a qualified opinion on the financial statements of a prior period because of a departure from generally accepted accounting principles. The prior-period financial statements are restated in the current period to conform with generally accepted accounting principles. The auditor's updated report on the prior-period financial statements should

a.   Express an unqualified opinion concerning the restated financial statements.

b.   Be accompanied by the original auditor's report on the prior period.

c.   Bear the same date as the original auditor's report on the prior period.

d.   Qualify the opinion concerning the restated financial statements because of a change in accounting principle.

87. Under which of the following circumstances would a disclaimer of opinion **not** be appropriate?

a.   The auditor is engaged after fiscal year-end and is unable to observe physical inventories or apply alternative procedures to verify their balances.

b. The auditor is unable to determine the amounts associated with illegal acts committed by the client's management.

c. The financial statements fail to contain adequate disclosure concerning related party transactions.

d. The client refuses to permit its attorney to furnish information requested in a letter of audit inquiry.

88. During a review of the financial statements of a non-public entity, an accountant becomes aware of a lack of adequate disclosure that is material to the financial statements. If management refuses to correct the financial statement presentations, the accountant should

a. Issue an adverse opinion.

b. Issue an "except for" qualified opinion.

c. Disclose this departure from generally accepted accounting principles in a separate paragraph of the report.

d. Express only limited assurance on the financial statement presentations.

89. When reporting on financial statements prepared on the same basis of accounting used for income tax purposes, the auditor should include in the report a paragraph that

a. Emphasizes that the financial statements are **not** intended to have been examined in accordance with generally accepted auditing standards.

b. Refers to the authoritative pronouncements that explain the income tax basis of accounting being used.

c. States that the income tax basis of accounting is a comprehensive basis of accounting other than generally accepted accounting principles.

d. Justifies the use of the income tax basis of accounting.

90. When a qualified opinion results from a limitation on the scope of the audit, the situation should be described in an explanatory paragraph

a. Preceding the opinion paragraph and referred to only in the scope paragraph of the auditor's report.

b. Following the opinion paragraph and referred to in both the scope and opinion paragraphs of the auditor's report.

c. Following the opinion paragraph and referred to only in the scope paragraph of the auditor's report.

d. Preceding the opinion paragraph and referred to in both the scope and opinion paragraphs of the auditor's report.

91. Which of the following statements concerning prospective financial statements is correct?

a. Only a financial forecast would normally be appropriate for limited use.

b. Only a financial projection would normally be appropriate for general use.

c. Any type of prospective financial statements would normally be appropriate for limited use.

d. Any type of prospective financial statements would normally be appropriate for general use.

92. When an independent accountant's report based on a review of interim financial information is presented in a registration statement, a prospectus should include a statement about the accountant's involvement. This statement should clarify that the

a. Accountant is **not** an "expert" within the meaning of the Securities Act of 1933.

b. Accountant's review report is **not** a "part" of the registration statement within the meaning of the Securities Act of 1933.

c. Accountant performed only limited auditing procedures on the interim financial statements.

d. Accountant's review was performed in accordance with standards established by the American Institute of CPAs.

93. If management declines to present supplementary information required by the Governmental Accounting Standards Board (GASB), the auditor should issue a(an)

a. Adverse opinion.

b. Qualified opinion with an explanatory paragraph.

c. Unqualified opinion.

d. Unqualified opinion with an additional explanatory paragraph.

Repeat Questions

(590,A1,14) Identical/similar to item 34 above
(590,A1,59) Identical/similar to item 52 above

Problems

Problem 1   (1188,A4)

(15 to 25 minutes)

(15 to 25 minutes)

On September 30, 19X5, White & Co., CPAs, was engaged to audit the consolidated financial statements of National Motors, Inc. for the year ended December 31, 19X5. The consolidated financial statements of National had not been audited the prior year. National's inadequate inventory records precluded White from forming an opinion as to the proper application of generally accepted accounting principles to inventory balances on January 1, 19X5. Therefore, White decided not to express an opinion on the results of operations for the year ended December 31, 19X5. National decided not to present comparative financial statements.

Rapid Parts Company, a consolidated subsidiary of National, was audited for the year ended December 31, 19X5, by Green & Co., CPAs. Green completed its field work on February 28, 19X6, and submitted an unqualified opinion on Rapid's financial statements on March 7, 19X6. Rapid's statements reflect total assets and revenues constituting $700,000 and $2,000,000, respectively, of the consolidated totals of National. White decided not to assume responsibility for the work of Green. Green's report on Rapid does not accompany National's consolidated statements.

White completed its field work on March 28, 19X6, and submitted its auditor's report to National on April 4, 19X6.

The following report on the basic financial statements was drafted by a staff assistant at the completion of the review engagement of GLM Company, a continuing client, for the year ended September 30, 1988. The 1987 basic financial statements for the year ended September 30, 1987, which were also reviewed, contained a departure from generally accepted accounting principles that was properly referred to in the 1987 review report dated October 26, 1987. The 1987 financial statements have been restated.

To the Board of Directors of GLM Company:

We have reviewed the accompanying balance sheets of GLM Company as of September 30, 1988 and 1987, and the related statements of income and retained earnings for the years then ended, in accordance with generally accepted auditing standards. Our review included such tests of the accounting records as we considered necessary in the circumstances.

A review consists principally of inquiries of company personnel. It is substantially less in scope than an audit, but more in scope than a compilation. Accordingly, we express only limited assurance on the accompanying financial statements.

Based on our reviews, with the exception of the matter described in the following paragraph, we are not aware of any material modifications that should be made to the accompanying financial statements in order for them to be in conformity with generally accepted accounting principles applied on a consistent basis.

In its 1987 financial statements the company stated its land at appraised values. However, as disclosed in note X, the company has restated its 1987 financial statements to reflect land at cost.

November 2, 1988

Required:

Required:

Prepare White and Company's auditor's report on the consolidated financial statements of National Motors, Inc.

Problem 3   (586,A3)

(15 to 25 minutes)

Brown & Brown, CPAs, was engaged by the board of directors of Cook Industries, Inc. to audit Cook's calendar year 19X5 financial statements. The following report was drafted by an audit assistant at the completion of the engagement. It was submitted to Brown, the partner with client responsibility for review on March 7, 19X6, the date of the completion of field work. Brown has reviewed matters thoroughly and properly concluded that an adverse opinion was appropriate.

Brown also became aware of a March 14, 19X6 subsequent event which the client has properly disclosed in the notes to the finan-

Identify the deficiencies in the draft of the proposed report on the comparative financial statements. Group the deficiencies by paragraph. Do **not** redraft the report.

cial statements. Brown wants responsibility for subsequent events to be limited to the specific event referred to in the applicable note to the client's financial statements.

The financial statements of Cook Industries, Inc. for the calendar year 19X4 were examined by predecessor auditors who also expressed an adverse opinion and have not reissued their report. The financial statements for 19X4 and 19X5 are presented in comparative form.

Independent Auditor's Report

To the President of Cook Industry, Inc.

We have audited the financial statements of Cook Industries, Inc., for the year ended December 31, 19X5. These financial statements, in which, as discussed in Note K, the Company has properly disclosed a subsequent event dated March 14, 19X6, are the responsibility of the Company's management. Our responsibility is to express an opinion on these financial statements based on our audits.

We conducted our audits in accordance with generally accepted auditing standards. Those standards require that we plan and perform the audit to obtain reasonable assurance about whether the financial statements are free of material misstatement. An audit includes examining, on a test basis, evidence supporting the amounts and disclosures in the financial statements. An audit also includes assessing the accounting principles used and significant estimates made by management, as well as evaluating the overall financial statement presentation. We believe that our audits provide a reasonable basis for our opinion.

As discussed in Note G to the financial statements, the Company carries its property and equipment at appraisal values, and provides depreciation on the basis of such values. Further, the company does not provide for income taxes with respect to differences between financial income and taxable income arising because of the use, for income tax purposes, of the installment method of reporting gross profit from certain types of sales.

In our opinion, the financial statements referred to above do not present fairly, in all material respects, the financial position of Cook Industries, Inc. as of December 31, 19X7 and 19X6, and the results of its operations and its cash flows for the years then ended, applied on a basis consistent with that of the preceding year.

Brown & Brown, CPAs
March 7, 1986

Required:

Identify the deficiencies in the draft of the proposed report. Do <u>not</u> redraft the report or discuss corrections.

Problem 4 (1184,A5)

(15 to 25 minutes)

Devon Incorporated engaged Smith to examine its financial statements for the year ended December 31, 19X3. The financial statements of Devon Incorporated for the year ended December 31, 19X2, were examined by Jones whose March 31, 19X3, auditor's report expressed an unqualified opinion. This report of Jones is not presented with the 19X3-19X2 comparative financial statements.

Smith's working papers contain the following information that does not appear in footnotes to the 19X3 financial statements as prepared by Devon Incorporated:

- One director appointed in 19X3 was formerly a partner in Jones' accounting firm. Jones' firm provided financial consulting services to Devon during 1979 and 1978, for which Devon paid approximately $1,600 and $9,000, respectively.

- The company refused to capitalize certain lease obligations for equipment acquired in 19X3. Capitalization of the leases in conformity with generally accepted accounting principles would have increased assets and liabilities by $312,000 and $387,000 respectively, and decreased retained earnings as of December 31, 19X3 by $75,000, and would have decreased net income and earnings per share by $75,000 and $.75 respectively for the year then ended. Smith has concluded that the leases should have been capitalized.

- During the year, Devon changed its method of valuing inventory from the first-in, first-out method to the last-in, first-out method. This change was made because management believes LIFO more clearly reflects net income by providing a closer matching of current costs and current revenues. The change had the effect of reducing inventory at December 31, 19X3, by $65,000 and net income and earnings per share by $38,000 and $.38 respectively for the year then ended. The effect of the change on prior years was immaterial; accordingly, there was no cumulative effect of the change. Smith firmly supports the company's position.

After completion of the field work decision on February 29, 19X4, Smith concludes that the expression of an adverse opinion is not warranted.

Required:

Prepare the body of Smith's report dated February 29, 19X4, and addressed to the Board of Directors to accompany the 19X3-19X2 comparative financial statements.

Problem 5   (1182,A5)

(15 to 25 minutes)

For the year ended December 31, 1980, Novak & Co., CPAs, audited the financial statements of Tillis Ltd., and expressed an unqualified opinion dated February 27, 1981.

For the year ended December 31, 1981, Novak & Co., were engaged by Tillis Ltd. to review Tillis Ltd.'s financial statements, i.e., "look into the company's financial statements and determine whether there are any obvious modifications that should be made to the financial statements in order for them to be in conformity with generally accepted accounting principles."

Novak made the necessary inquiries, performed the necessary analytical procedures, and performed certain additional procedures that were deemed necessary to achieve the requisite limited assurance. Novak's work was completed on March 3, 1982, and the financial statements appeared to be in conformity with generally accepted accounting principles which were consistently applied. The report was prepared on March 5, 1982. It was delivered to Jones, the controller of Tillis Ltd., on March 9, 1982.

Required:

Prepare the properly addressed and dated report on the comparative financial statements of Tillis Ltd. for the years ended December 31, 1980 and 1981.

Problem 6   (584,A2)

(15 to 25 minutes)

Young and Young, CPAs, completed an examination of the financial statements of XYZ Company, Inc. for the year ended June 30, 1983, and issued a standard unqualified auditor's report dated August 15, 1983. At the time of the engagement, the Board of Directors of XYZ requested a special report attesting to the adequacy of the provision for federal and state income taxes and the related accruals and deferred income taxes as presented in the June 30, 1983 financial statements.

Young and Young submitted the appropriate special report on August 22, 1983.

Required:

Prepare the special report that Young and Young should have submitted to XYZ Company, Inc.

Problem 7   (588,A2)

(15 to 25 minutes)

An accountant is sometimes called on by clients to report on or assemble prospective financial statements for use by third parties.

Required:

a. 1. Identify the types of engagements that an accountant may perform under these circumstances.
    2. Explain the difference between "general use" of and "limited use" of prospective financial statements.
    3. Explain what types of prospective financial statements are appropriate for "general use" and what types are appropriate for "limited use."

b. Describe the contents of the accountant's standard report on a compilation of a financial projection.

Problem 8   (589,A2)

(15 to 25 minutes)

The auditors' report below was drafted by a staff accountant of Turner & Turner, CPAs, at the completion of the audit of the financial statements of Lyon Computers, Inc. for the year ended March 31, 1989. It was submitted to the engagement partner who reviewed matters thoroughly and properly concluded that Lyon's disclosures concerning its ability to continue as a going concern for a reasonable period of time were adequate. Early application of Statement on Auditing Standards No. 59, The Auditor's Consideration of an Entity's Ability to Continue as a Going Concern, was chosen by Turner & Turner.

To the Board of Directors of Lyon Computers, Inc.:

We have audited the accompanying balance sheet of Lyon Computers, Inc. as of March 31, 1989, and the other related financial statements for the year then ended. Our responsibility is to express an opinion on these financial statements based on our audit.

We conducted our audit in accordance with standards that require that we plan and per-

form the audit to obtain reasonable assurance
about whether the financial statements are in
conformity with generally accepted accounting
principles. An audit includes examining, on a
test basis, evidence supporting the amounts
and disclosures in the financial statements.
An audit also includes assessing the accounting principles used and significant estimates made by management.

The accompanying financial statements have
been prepared assuming that the Company will
continue as a going concern. As discussed in
Note X to the financial statements, the
Company has suffered recurring losses from
operations and has a net capital deficiency
that raises substantial doubt about its
ability to continue as a going concern. We
believe that management's plans in regard to
these matters, which are also described in
Note X, will permit the Company to continue as
a going concern beyond a reasonable period of
time. The financial statements do not include
any adjustments that might result from the
outcome of this uncertainty.

In our opinion, subject to the effects on
the financial statements of such adjustments,
if any, as might have been required had the
outcome of the uncertainty referred to in the
preceding paragraph been known, the financial
statements referred to above present fairly,
in all material respects, the financial position of Lyon Computers, Inc., and the results
of its operations and its cash flows in conformity with generally accepted accounting
principles applied on a basis consistent with
that of the preceding year.

Turner & Turner, CPAs
April 28, 1989

Required:

Identify the deficiencies contained in the
auditor's report as drafted by the staff
accountant. Group the deficiencies by
paragraph. Do not redraft the report.

Multiple Choice Answers

1. b	20. b	39. c	58. a	76. d
2. b	21. b	40. c	59. b	77. a
3. c	22. b	41. c	60. d	78. d
4. c	23. d	42. b	61. b	79. d
5. b	24. d	43. c	62. a	80. d
6. c	25. d	44. a	63. c	81. b
7. a	26. c	45. a	64. c	82. a
8. a	27. c	46. d	65. c	83. d
9. a	28. a	47. b	66. a	84. d
10. a	29. b	48. c	67. c	85. c
11. a	30. d	49. c	68. b	86. a
12. d	31. a	50. b	69. b	87. c
13. d	32. d	51. a	70. d	88. c
14. d	33. a	52. c	71. c	89. c
15. a	34. c	53. c	72. d	90. d
16. a	35. a	54. b	73. a	91. c
17. d	36. a	55. d	74. b	92. b
18. d	37. d	56. a	75. b	93. d
19. d	38. b	57. a		

Multiple Choice Answer Explanations
A. Reports—General
A.1. Overall Issues

1. (1189,A1,5) (b) The requirement is to determine an accountant's reporting responsibility when more than one level of service concerning the financial statements of a non-public entity has been performed. Answer (b) is correct because AR 100.05 requires that the accountant report on the highest level of service rendered. Answer (a) is incorrect because the highest, and not the lowest, level is reported on. Answer (c) is incorrect because regardless of the other type of service performed, the compilation level is always the lowest level and therefore should not be the basis of the report. Answer (d) is incorrect because in circumstances in which an audit has been performed, an audit report, not a review report, is appropriate.

2. (1184,A1,5) (b) The requirement is to determine what the statement "nothing came to our attention" expresses. Answer (b) is correct because such a statement is made in a letter to an underwriter in which negative assurance is provided (AU 634.02, footnote 2). Answer (a) is incorrect because in a disclaimer no assurances, positive or negative, are given (AU 508.70-.72). Answer (c) is incorrect because a negative confirmation asks the debtor to respond only if the account is incorrect; it contains no statement such as "nothing came to our attention." Answer (d) is incorrect because a piecemeal opinion (now not allowed) contained the expression of an opinion on certain identified items in financial statements which were to receive either a disclaimer of opinion or an adverse opinion (AU 508.70-.72).

3. (1189,A1,19) (c) The requirement is to identify the circumstance in which negative assurance may be expressed by an accountant. Answer (c) is correct because the results of applying agreed-upon procedures to an account within unaudited financial statements will result in such negative assurance (see AU 622). Answer (a) is incorrect because a compilation of prospective financial statements results in no assurance, not negative assurance (AT 200). Answer (b) is incorrect because an auditor should not issue a report that provides assurance on compliance with the Foreign Corrupt Practices Act (AU 9642.12). Answer (d) is incorrect because an audit of historical financial statements results in positive assurance (an opinion), not in negative assurance.

A.2. Financial Statement Audit Reports
A.2.a. Content of Audit Report

4. (1189,A1,12) (c) The requirement is to determine the representations made explicitly and implicitly when issuing the standard auditor's report on comparative financial statements. Answer (c) is correct because the standard audit report implicitly assumes consistent application of accounting principles and explicitly states that the examination of evidence is made on a test basis. Answer (a) is incorrect because consistency of application of accounting principles is not made explicitly. Answer (b) is incorrect because examination of evidence on a test basis is referred to explicitly. Answer (d) is incorrect because consistent application of accounting principles is not referred to explicitly, and because examination of evidence on a test basis is explicitly referred to.

5. (1189,A1,13) (b) The requirement is to determine the proper placement of an explanatory paragraph disclosing the substantive reasons for expressing an adverse opinion. Answer (b) is correct because AU 508.68 requires that such paragraphs precede the opinion paragraph. Answers (a), (c), and (d) are all incorrect because they suggest alternate, improper placement of the explanatory paragraph.

A.2.b. Reporting Standards and Meaning of GAAP

6. (588,A1,44) (c) The requirement is to determine the objective of the fourth reporting standard which requires either an opinion or an assertion to the effect that an opinion cannot be expressed. Answer (c) is correct because the standard states that the objective is to prevent misinterpretation of

the degree of responsibility the auditor is assuming when his/her name is associated with financial statements (AU 508.05). Answer (a) is incorrect because differing opinions may be issued on each of the financial statements (e.g., if the beginning inventory has not been counted, an auditor may disclaim an opinion on the income statement and yet express an unqualified opinion on the balance sheet). Answer (b) is incorrect because the objective does not relate directly to scope restrictions. Answer (d) is incorrect because an auditor may report on only one statement (AU 509.13).

7. (1182,A1,58) (a) The requirement is to determine the meaning of the expression "taken as a whole" in the fourth generally accepted auditing standard of reporting. AU 508.05 states that "taken as a whole" applies equally to a complete set of financial statements and to an individual financial statement.

A.2.c. Dating the Report, Including Consideration of Subsequent Events

8. (1181,A1,59) (a) The requirement is to determine the basis for deciding whether to dual date an audit report. Answer (a) is correct because if the auditor does not wish to dual date, certain audit procedures must be extended (AU 560.12). Answer (b) is incorrect since the auditor must accept responsibility for the known subsequent event regardless of whether dual dating is used. Answer (c) is incorrect because such known subsequent events are to be audited. Answer (d) is incorrect because the auditor, with or without dual dating, need not assume responsibility for events subsequent to the issuance of the auditor's report.

9. (1186,A1,40) (a) The requirement is to determine an auditor's responsibility for subsequent events when an audit report has been dual dated for a subsequent event. Answer (a) is correct because, when dual dating is used, auditor responsibility for events subsequent to the completion of field work is limited to the specific event referred to in the note (AU 530.05). Answers (b), (c), and (d) are all incorrect because they establish more responsibility than do the professional standards. Note, however, that if the auditor chooses to date the report as of the date of the subsequent event, his/her responsibility for other subsequent events extends to the date of the audit report. AU 530 discusses dating of the audit report.

10. (589,A1,48) (a) The requirement is to identify an auditor's reporting responsibility when reissuing an audit report for a client that has incurred substantial losses on receivables resulting from conditions that occurred subsequent to the report's issuance. Answer (a) is correct because this represents information which should be disclosed in a note to the financial statements and because the reissued audit report should be dated as of its original date. AU 530.08 requires that the separate note include a caption such as "Event (Unaudited) Subsequent to the Date of the Report of Independent Auditor." Answer (b) is incorrect because the financial statements should not be restated since the event is due to conditions arising subsequent to the report issuance; see AU 560 for accounting requirements relating to subsequent events. Answer (c) is incorrect because the event needs to be disclosed in a separate note to the financial statements. Answer (d) is incorrect because "subject to" qualified reports are no longer issued (AU 508.31), and because such reports were never appropriate in this situation.

11. (1189,A1,23) (a) The requirement is to determine the proper report date when a previously issued report is being reissued without revision. Answer (a) is correct because when a predecessor auditor is issuing a report on prior period financial statements that have not been restated, s/he should use the date of his previous report (AU 508.82). This date is used to avoid any implication that the auditor has examined any records after that date. Answers (b), (c), and (d) are all incorrect dates.

B. Financial Statement Audit Reports—Detailed

B.1. Circumstances Resulting in Departure From the Auditor's Standard Report

B.1.a. Opinion Based, in part, on Report of Another Auditor

12. (589,A1,60) (d) The requirement is to identify the situation in which an auditor may issue the standard audit report. Answer (d) is correct because a standard report may be issued in circumstances in which the principal auditor assumes responsibility for the work of another auditor (AU 543.04). Answer (a) is incorrect because the standard report does not include reference to a specialist. Thus, reference to a specialist within a report by definition causes modification of the standard report. Answer (b) is incorrect because the auditor is required to issue a modified report

on condensed financial statements per AU 552. Answer (c) is incorrect because audit reports on financial statements prepared on a comprehensive basis other than GAAP are considered to be "special reports" which require departures from the standard form (see AU 623).

13.   (1189,A1,1)   (d)   The requirement is to identify the information that a principal auditor who makes reference to another auditor's examination should indicate in the introductory, scope, and opinion paragraphs of the audit report. Answer (d) is correct because AU 508.12 and AU 543.07 require that information on the division of responsibility be included in all three paragraphs. Answer (a) is incorrect because the magnitude of the portion of the financial statements examined is only referred to in the scope paragraph (AU 508.13). Answer (b) is incorrect because no disclaimer is included since the opinion paragraph states the opinion is based on the work of both the principal and the other auditors (AU 508.13). Answer (c) is incorrect because the auditor will choose whether to name the other auditor (AU 543.08).

B.1.b. Unusual Circumstances Requiring a Departure From Promulgated GAAP

14.   (1189,A1,24)   (d)   The requirement is to determine the type of opinion to be issued when financial statements depart from GAAP due to the existence of unusual circumstances which would cause the financial statements to be misleading had GAAP been followed. Answer (d) is correct because the auditor should issue an unqualified opinion in this circumstance and should include a separate explanatory paragraph explaining the departure from the standard (AU 508.14-.15). Answers (a) and (c) are incorrect because when the auditor believes that the departure is justified, an "except for" or an adverse opinion is inappropriate. Answer (b) is incorrect because a "subject to " opinion is not to be used in any circumstance.

B.1.c. Uncertainties

15.   (1189,A1,8)   (a)   The requirement is to determine the appropriate type of opinion to be issued when financial statements adequately disclose uncertainties that concern future events, the outcome of which is not susceptible to reasonable estimation. Answer (a) is correct because uncertainties lead the auditor to consider adding an explanatory paragraph to what remains an unqualified opinion (AU 508.23-.26). Answer (b) is incorrect because "subject to" qualified opinions are no longer issued (AU 508.31, note 13). An-

swers (c) and (d) are incorrect because the proper treatment of uncertainties will not result in either an "except for" qualified opinion or an adverse opinion.

16.   (1189,A1,10)   (a)   The requirement is to determine the appropriate listed circumstance(s) in which a qualified opinion may be issued. Answer (a) is correct because both the lack of sufficient competent evidential matter, and scope restrictions lead to qualified opinions (AU 508.38). Answer (b) is incorrect because scope restrictions lead to qualified opinions. Answer (c) is incorrect because lack of sufficient competent evidential matter leads to qualified opinions. Answer (d) is incorrect because both the lack of sufficient competent evidential matter and restrictions on scope of the audit lead to qualified opinions.

B.1.d. Substantial Doubt About Ability to Remain a Going Concern

17.   (1186,A1,46)   (d)   The requirement is to identify the situation in which an explanatory paragraph may be added to an unqualified report. Answer (d) is correct because questions over continued existence may lead to explanatory paragraphs (AU 341). Answer (a) is incorrect because preventing an auditor from completing an audit procedure is a scope limitation that may lead to either a qualified "except for" opinion or a disclaimer (AU 508.40). Answer (b) is incorrect because the failure to disclose required information is a departure from GAAP that may lead to either a qualified "except for" opinion or an adverse opinion (AU 508.49). Answer (c) is incorrect because a report making reference to the report of another auditor is considered to be unqualified (AU 508.12-.13).

18.   (1189,A1,9)   (d)   The requirement is to identify the appropriate type of opinion(s) to be issued when the auditor has concluded that there is substantial doubt about an entity's ability to continue as a going concern, and that the client's disclosures concerning this matter are adequate. Answer (d) is correct because a disclaimer of opinion is appropriate, but an "except for" qualified opinion is not appropriate (AU 341.12). Also, such substantial doubt may lead to an unqualified opinion with an explanatory paragraph (see AU 341). Answer (a) is incorrect because an "except for" qualified opinion is not appropriate when substantial doubt has been adequately disclosed. Answer (b) is incorrect because a disclaimer of opinion is appropriate. Answer (c) is incorrect because a

disclaimer of opinion is appropriate and an "except for" qualified opinion is not appropriate.

B.1.e. Inconsistency in Application of GAAP

19. (1189,A1,2) (d) The requirement is to determine the manner in which an auditor's report should refer to a lack of consistency in application of accounting principles. Answer (d) is correct because the standard report is normally supplemented with a fourth paragraph following the opinion paragraph (AU 508.34-.36). Answer (a) is incorrect because the scope paragraph is not modified. Answer (b) is incorrect because the explanatory paragraph <u>follows</u> the opinion paragraph. Answer (c) is incorrect because the opinion paragraph is not modified.

20. (586,A1,50) (b) The requirement is to identify the circumstance which requires recognition in the auditor's report as to consistency. Answer (b) is correct because changing among the cost, equity, and consolidation methods of accounting for subsidiaries or other investments in common stock requires such recognition (AU 420.07). Answer (a) is incorrect because an error not involving a principle will not result in modification of the audit report (AU 420.13). Answer (c) is incorrect because changes in estimates (here, warranty costs) do not affect consistency (AU 420.12). Answer (d) is incorrect because changes in methods that have no material effect on the financial statements of the current year, but which are reasonably certain to have substantial effects in later years, do not affect consistency (AU 420.17).

21. (584,A1,52) (b) The requirement is to determine the proper accounting and audit report effects of a change in accounting principle which is immaterial during the year of change but is expected to have a material effect in later years. AU 420.17 suggests that in such circumstances the change should be disclosed in the notes to the financial statements in the year of change and that an unqualified audit report should be issued. Answers (a) and (c) are incorrect because no consistency explanatory language is necessary. Answer (d) is incorrect because this is not an example of a subsequent event (see AU 560 for information on subsequent events).

22. (1189,A1,14) (b) The requirement is to determine auditor reporting responsibility when management does not provide reasonable justification for a change in accounting principle and presents comparative financial statements. Answer (b) is correct because the

auditor should continue to express his/her exception with the financial statements for the year of change as long as they are presented and reported on (AU 508.66). Answer (a) is incorrect because the auditor must express his/her exception for as long as the financial statements for the year of change are presented and reported on. Answer (c) is incorrect because the auditor need not qualify the report until management changes back to the accounting principle formerly used. Answer (d) is incorrect because the qualification is necessary despite the fact that the principle is generally accepted (AU 508.66).

B.1.f. Certain Circumstances Affecting Comparative Statements

23. (589,A1,54) (d) The requirement is to determine the proper reporting procedure for comparative financial statements for which the prior year is unaudited, and the current year is audited. Answer (d) is correct because AU 504.15 states that when unaudited financial statements are presented in comparative form with audited financial statements, the report on the prior period may be reissued to accompany the current period report. In addition, the report on the current period may include a separate paragraph describing responsibility assumed for the prior period financial statements. Therefore, answers (a), (b), and (c) are incorrect. If these statements are filed with the SEC, the statements should be clearly marked as "unaudited" but should not be referred to in the auditor's report (AU 504.14).

24. (587,A1,54) (d) The requirement is to determine the necessary disclosure by a successor auditor relating to comparative financial statements when the prior period statements have been examined by a predecessor auditor whose report is not presented. Answer (d) is correct because AU 508.83 requires that when the predecessor auditor's report is not presented, the successor must indicate in the introductory paragraph that (1) the financial statements of the prior period were examined by other auditors, (2) the date of their report, (3) the type of opinion expressed by the predecessor auditor, and (4) the substantive reasons therefor, if it was other than unqualified (AU 508.83). Answers (a), (b), and (c) are all incorrect because they suggest other disclosures that are not required.

25. (1182,A1,36) (d) The requirement is to determine the continuing auditor's responsibility with respect to an audit report based on comparative statements. The report on the previous statements must be updated regardless

of the opinion previously issued (AU 508.74).
Answer (a) is incorrect because such an
opinion is not dual dated; it should be dated
as of the completion of this year's field
work. Answers (b) and (c) are both incorrect
due to the need to update regardless of the
previously issued report.

26. (1189,A1,11) (c) The requirement is to
identify the circumstance in which an auditor
who is reporting on comparative financial
statements would change the previously issued
opinion on the prior year's financial statements. Answer (c) is correct because when the
prior year's financial statements which departed from GAAP have been changed to conform
with GAAP, the auditor would change the report
from qualified (or adverse) to unqualified
(AU 508.77). Answer (a) is incorrect because
the modification of the current year's opinion
due to a lack of consistency (presumably because the client has not justified the change)
will not lead to modification of the prior
year's opinion. Answer (b) is incorrect because restatement for a pooling of interests
will not result in a change in the previously
issued opinion. Answer (d) is incorrect because the simple reissuance of an audit report
will not result in a change in the previously
issued opinion.

B.1.h. Supplementary Information Required by FASB or GASB

27. (1187,A1,15) (c) The requirement is to
identify the correct statement regarding the
auditor's responsibilities for supplementary
information required by the FASB. Answer (c)
is correct because the auditor is to apply
certain limited procedures to the supplementary information and to report deficiencies
in, or the omission of, such information
(AU 558.06). Answer (a) is incorrect because
only limited procedures, not normal auditing
procedures are performed; AU 558.07 presents
the procedures. Answer (b) is incorrect
because the Professional Standards require
that the auditor only expands his/her standard
report through an explanatory paragraph when
it is necessary to call attention to the
omission, or the departure of the supplementary information from FASB guidelines, or when
the auditor has been unable to complete the
appropriate procedures (AU 558.11). Answer (d) is incorrect because the information
is not audited, and therefore its omission
will lead to an explanatory report paragraph,
but not to an adverse or "except for" qualified opinion (AU 558.08).

28. (1181,A1,42) (a) The requirement is to
determine the audit report treatment of
"unaudited" footnotes in audited financial

statements. Answer (a) is correct since an
auditor may refer to these notes if supplementary information required by the FASB is
omitted, if the auditor has concluded that the
reported supplementary information departs
materially from FASB guidelines, or if the
auditor is unable to complete required procedures on these disclosures (para 558.08).
Answer (b) is incorrect since an auditor does
have responsibility with respect to the disclosures as noted above (see also the required
procedures outlined in para 558.07). Answer (c) is incorrect because the auditor is
not required in all cases to refer to the
notes. Answer (d) is incorrect since the circumstances cited above outline situations in
which the auditor's report does include
mention of these notes.

B.1.i. Other Information in Documents Containing Audited Financial Statements

B.1.i.(1) Client Prepared Documents

29. (1184,A1,4) (b) The requirement is to
determine an auditor's responsibility with
respect to "other information" included in a
document containing audited financial statements. Answer (b) is correct because
AU 550.04 requires that an auditor read the
"other information" to determine whether it is
inconsistent with the financial statements.
Answer (a) is incorrect because the auditor is
required to read the other information. Answer (c) is incorrect because the auditor is
not required to extend the examination to
verify the "other information." Answer (d) is
incorrect because the auditor's report is not
to be modified in such circumstances.

30. (589,A1,51) (d) The requirement is to
identify an auditor's reporting responsibility
for a material inconsistency between the
audited financial statements and the other information in an annual report to shareholders
when the financial statements do not require
revision. Answer (d) is correct because
AU 550.04 suggests inclusion of a separate explanatory paragraph describing the material
inconsistency. Answer (a) is incorrect. A
qualified opinion is not appropriate because
the financial statements are not misstated and
no scope limitation is involved. Answer (b)
is incorrect because, as indicated, an explanatory paragraph is considered necessary. Answer (c) is incorrect because no disclaimer of
opinion is required.

B.1.i.(2) Auditor Submitted Documents

31. (587,A1,59) (a) The requirement is to
identify the auditor's reporting responsi-

bility concerning information accompanying the basic financial statements in an auditor-submitted document. Answer (a) is correct because the auditor should report on all the information included in the document (AU 551.04). Answer (b) is incorrect because the auditor may issue a report covering the accompanying information (AU 551.06e). Answer (c) is incorrect because it is not necessary that the auditor participate in preparation of the accompanying information. Answer (d) is incorrect because it is not necessary that the document be distributed to public shareholders.

B.1.j. Emphasis of a Matter

32. (1188,A1,17) (d) The requirement is to identify the correct statement with respect to an audit report which includes an explanatory paragraph to emphasize the fact that the statements are not comparable to those of prior years due to a court-ordered divestiture. Answer (d) is correct because such emphasis of a matter is considered appropriate and does not negate the unqualified opinion (AU 508.37). Answers (a) and (b) are incorrect because modification of the opinion paragraph is not appropriate (AU 508.37). Answer (c) is incorrect because such a modification, as indicated, is considered appropriate and does not negate the unqualified opinion.

B.1.k. Departure from GAAP (Qualified and Adverse Opinions)

33. (1188,A1,19) (a) The requirement is to identify the circumstances in which an "except for" qualified opinion is appropriate. Answer (a) is correct because inadequate disclosure and scope limitations both lead to such reports (AU 508.38-.66). Answers (b), (c), and (d) are all incorrect because they suggest that an "except for" qualified opinion is inappropriate in either or both of those circumstances.

34. (587,A1,51) (c) The requirement is to determine the type of report modification that results when the management of a client company believes that the statement of cash flows is not a useful document and refuses to include it in the annual report to stockholders. Answer (c) is correct because the professional standards require qualification due to inadequate disclosure (AU 545.04-.05). Answer (a) is incorrect because the cited standards, in this particular inadequate disclosure situation, do not suggest an adverse opinion. Answer (b) is incorrect because an unqualified opinion can not be issued when there is inadequate disclosure. Answer (d) is incorrect

because no scope limitation is involved--the client has simply chosen not to present information that is required under generally accepted accounting standards.

35. (1186,A1,56) (a) The requirement is to identify the circumstances that would lead the auditor to express an adverse opinion. Answer (a) is correct because statements departing from GAAP (here a FASB Statement on the capitalization of leases) result in either a qualified (except for) or adverse opinion (AU 509.15-.16). Answer (b) is incorrect because questions about continued existence lead to either an explanatory paragraph being added to an unqualified opinion or a disclaimer (AU 341). Answer (c) is incorrect because scope limitations (here restriction of access to board of directors' minutes) result in either a qualified (except for) opinion or a disclaimer (AU 508.40-.44). Answer (d) is incorrect because weaknesses in internal control will cause the auditor to perform additional substantive procedures to obtain the required evidential matter. If the substantive procedures also cannot provide the required evidential matter, a disclaimer is required (AU 508.70-.72).

36. (582,A1,56) (a) The requirement is to determine the effect of a sale and subsequent repurchase of marketable securities. The accounting treatment described for these transactions is in conformity with GAAP (note that disclosure of these transactions is also necessary). Answer (b) is incorrect since transactions have occurred. Answer (c) is incorrect since there is no information provided suggesting the need to withdraw--GAAP has been followed. Answer (d) is incorrect because the transaction is in accordance with GAAP.

37. (1181,A1,31) (d) The requirement is to determine the effect of a departure from generally accepted accounting principles on an auditor's opinion. Answer (d) is correct because when financial statements are materially affected by a departure from generally accepted accounting principles an auditor should issue either a qualified or an adverse opinion (AU 508.49). Therefore, answers (a) and (b) are wrong since they suggest other types of reports. Answer (c) is incorrect because auditors do not make decisions on the types of accounting principles to be followed by their clients.

38. (589,A1,55) (b) The requirement is to identify an auditor's reporting responsibility when a publicly-held company refuses to include in its audited financial statements any

of the segment information that the auditor believes is required. Answer (b) is correct because AU 435.10 states that the auditor should modify the opinion on the financial statements because of inadequate disclosure. Answer (a) is incorrect because an explanatory paragraph is not adequate when such inadequate disclosure exists (AU 508.49-.69) Answer (c) is incorrect since AU 435.10 states that a qualified, "except for" report be issued under such circumstances. Answer (d) is incorrect because a disclaimer of opinion is not appropriate when disclosure is inadequate (AU 508.70-.72).

B.1.1. Scope Limitations (Qualified and Disclaimer of Opinions)

39. (589,A1,49) (c) The requirement is to determine whether the scope paragraph, opinion paragraph, and/or notes to the financial statements should refer to an audit scope limitation. Answer (c) is correct because the suggested report presented for a scope limitation (AU 508.44) includes modification of both the scope and opinion paragraphs. In addition, it is not appropriate for the scope of the audit to be explained in a note to the financial statements (AU 508.43). Therefore, answers (a), (b), and (d) are all incorrect.

40. (587,A1,5) (c) The requirement is to determine the appropriate type of opinion when an auditor has been unable to obtain sufficient competent evidential matter relating to acts which may be illegal. Answer (c) is correct because a scope limitation is involved and in such circumstances the professional standards require either a disclaimer of opinion or a qualified opinion (AU 317.19). Answer (a) is incorrect because a separate explanatory paragraph, by itself, is only appropriate when the auditor wishes to emphasize a matter pertaining to financial statements that are in conformity with generally accepted accounting principles (AU 508.37). Answers (b) and (d) are incorrect because an adverse opinion is considered only when the effects of the illegal act are known and are improperly reported (AU 317.18). The facts in this question indicate the auditor has uncertainty as to whether the acts are illegal.

41. (587,A1,53) (c) The requirement is to identify the situation in which the auditor would be most likely to issue a disclaimer of opinion. Answer (c) is correct because auditors are generally required to disclaim an opinion for client imposed scope limitations (AU 508.42). Answer (a) is incorrect because failure to present supplementary information does not affect the auditor's opinion, but

does result in inclusion of an explanatory paragraph to the report (AU 558.08). Answer (b) is incorrect because inadequate disclosure of material information will result in qualified opinion or an adverse opinion (AU 508.55-.58). Answer (d) is incorrect because, depending upon the circumstances involved, a qualification in the other auditor's report may or may not lead to overall report modification (AU 543.15).

42. (1189,A1,4) (b) The requirement is to identify the most appropriate audit report when the client has imposed a significant scope limitation (prohibiting the observation of physical inventories which account for 35% of all assets) and alternative audit procedures cannot be applied. Answer (b) is correct because auditors are generally required to disclaim an opinion for significant client imposed scope limitations (AU 508.42). Answer (a) is incorrect because a qualified report is not appropriate due to the significant nature of the limitation. Answers (c) and (d) are incorrect because an unqualified opinion with either an explanatory paragraph or a modified scope paragraph are not considered appropriate for significant scope limitations.

43. (1189,A1,7) (c) The requirement is to identify the circumstance which will usually preclude the issuance of an unqualified opinion. Answer (c) is correct because auditors will generally issue a disclaimer of opinion for a client imposed scope limitation such as management's failure to make minutes of the Board of Directors' meetings available (AU 508.42). Answer (a) is incorrect because a "special report" unqualified opinion may be issued for cash basis accounting statements (AU 623.02-.10). Answer (b) is incorrect because management should state that the financial statements are not intended to be presented in conformity with GAAP when another comprehensive basis of accounting is being followed (AU 623.10). In addition, this situation will not preclude an unqualified "special report." Answer (d) is incorrect because an auditor may issue an unqualified report on the balance sheet and not on the other basic financial statements (AU 508.47-.48).

44. (588,A1,41) (a) The requirement is to identify the financial statement(s) on which an auditor may issue an unqualified opinion when he or she did not observe a client's taking of the beginning physical inventory and was unable to become satisfied about the inventory by using other auditing procedures. Answer (a) is correct because the scope limitation will not affect the year-end balance sheet account balances. However, because evidence with respect to the beginning inventory is lacking, verification of cost of goods sold, an income statement element, is impossible. Although year-end retained earnings will not be affected, both the current and prior years' retained earnings statements will be affected (by an offsetting amount) by the cost of goods sold misstatement. If no other problems arise, the auditor will be able to issue an unqualified opinion on the balance sheet and a disclaimer on the income statement and on the retained earnings statement. Answers (b), (c), and (d) are all incorrect because lack of evidence on cost of goods sold affects the income statement, and retained earnings statement.

45. (1187,A1,1) (a) The requirement is to determine the auditor's responsibility when asked to report on only one financial statement, but yet provided with access to all information underlying the basic financial statements. Answer (a) is correct because the auditor may accept the engagement because the situation involves limited reporting objectives, not a limitation on the scope of audit procedures (AU 508.47-.48). Answers (b) and (c) are incorrect because the auditor is able to apply the procedures considered necessary, and therefore the scope of auditing procedures has not been restricted. Answer (d) is incorrect because there is no departure from generally accepted auditing standards.

B.1.m. Lack of Independence

46. (589,A1,52) (d) The requirement is to identify the situation in which an auditor may **not** issue a qualified opinion. Answer (d) is correct because the auditor who lacks independence must <u>disclaim</u> an opinion, not qualify an opinion (AU 504.08-.10). Answer (a) is incorrect because scope limitations result in either a qualified opinion or a disclaimer of opinion (AU 508.40-.48). Answer (b) is incorrect because a specialist may be referred to when an auditor is issuing a qualified opinion, an adverse opinion, or a disclaimer of opinion (AU 336.00-.12). Answer (c) is incorrect because a departure from GAAP will result in either a qualified opinion or an adverse opinion (AU 508.49-.69).

B.2. Audit Reports—See Essay Questions

C. Accountant Association Other than Audits

C.1. Other Forms of Accountant Association with Historical Financial Statements

C.1.a. Unaudited Statements

47. (1189,A1,16) (b) The requirement is to identify the appropriate type of report when a CPA is associated with the financial statements of a publicly held entity but has not audited or reviewed such statements. Answer (b) is correct because AU 504.05 requires a disclaimer of opinion in such circumstances. Answer (a) is incorrect because compilation reports relate to nonpublic companies (see AU 100). Answer (c) is incorrect because an unaudited association report does not exist. Answer (d) is incorrect because when an audit has not been performed, a qualified opinion is not considered appropriate.

48. (1186,A1,52) (c) The requirement is to determine an accountant's responsibility when unaudited financial statements do not include adequate disclosures. Answer (c) is correct because the necessary revisions should be described in the accountant's disclaimer of opinion (AU 504.11). Answer (a) is incorrect because no audit has been performed and therefore the accountant can not issue any opinion. Answer (b) is incorrect because no revision has been made in the financial statements and because unaudited financial statements are accompanied by a disclaimer that provides no assurance (AU 504.05). Answer (d) is incorrect because, as indicated above, the accountant must add to the disclaimer a description of necessary revisions.

C.1.b. Compiled or Reviewed Statements

C.1.b.(1) Compiled Statements

49. (1188,A1,50) (c) The requirement is to identify the procedure that is least likely to be performed during a compilation. Answer (c), perform analytical procedures, is correct (least likely) because an accountant is not required to make any inquiries or to perform any procedures to verify, corroborate, or review information supplied by the entity (AR 100.12). Answer (a) is incorrect because an accountant may be associated with financial statements that omit the disclosures required by generally accepted accounting principles (AR 100.19-.21). Answer (b) is incorrect because a compilation may relate to one or more, but not all basic financial statements (AR 100.18). Answer (d) is incorrect because the accountant must read the compiled financial statements and consider whether they appear to include adequate disclosure (AR 100.13).

50. (1188,A1,58) (b) The requirement is to determine which reply includes information that is not included in a compilation report. Answer (b) is correct because a compilation report does not state that a compilation is substantially less in scope than an examination in accordance with generally accepted auditing standards (AR 100.17). Answers (a), (c), and (d) are all incorrect because the compilation report does include the information suggested. AR 100.17 presents an illustrative compilation report.

51. (585,A1,4) (a) The requirement is to determine the type of report in which a CPA should not express negative or limited assurance. Answer (a) is correct because no assurance is expressed in a standard compilation report (AR 100.14c). Answers (b) and (c) are incorrect because in a review report, an accountant provides limited assurance by stating that s/he is not aware of any modifications necessary for the financial statements to be in conformity with GAAP (AR 100.32e and AU 722.17). Answer (d) is incorrect because negative assurance may be provided in a comfort letter (AU 631.02).

52. (588,A1,60) (c) The requirement is to determine an accountant's obligation when compiled financial statements are presented in conformity with the cash receipts and disbursements basis of accounting but do not disclose that basis. Answer (c) is correct because AR 100.20 requires that when financial statements compiled in conformity with a comprehensive basis of accounting other than generally accepted accounting principles do not include disclosure of that basis, it should be disclosed in the accountant's report. Answer (a) is incorrect because it is the responsibility of management, and not that of the accountant, to disclose the basis in the notes. Answer (b) is incorrect because each page should be marked with a reference such as "see accountant's compilation report"; also, as indicated, the basis should be included in the accountant's report. Answer (d) is incorrect because there is no requirement to recompile the financial statements using generally accepted accounting principles.

53. (584,A1,9) (c) The requirement is to determine the statement which must appear on each page of financial statements which have been compiled by an accountant. Answer (c) is correct as per the requirements of AR 100.16. Answer (a) is incorrect because the footnotes are not those of the accountant who performed the compilation. Answer (b) is incorrect because the statements are not considered

"unaudited"--see AU 504 for unaudited statements of a public company. Answer (d) is incorrect because the phrase "subject to compilation restrictions" is not recommended in AR 100.

54. (1182,A1,41) (b) The requirement is to determine the appropriate date for an auditor's compilation report. AR 100.5 requires that the date of completion of the compilation should be used. Accordingly, answers (a), (c), and (d) are incorrect.

55. (1189,A1,15) (d) The requirement is to identify the information that should be included in an accountant's compilation report when a client has omitted substantially all disclosures required by GAAP. Answer (d) is correct because AR 100.21 requires that the report indicate that the financial statements are not designed for those who are uninformed about the omitted disclosures. Answers (a) and (b) are incorrect because such restrictions are not required. Answer (c) is incorrect because the lack of such disclosures is not considered a comprehensive basis of accounting other than GAAP. See AU 623 for information on comprehensive basis financial statements.

56. (589,A1,47) (a) The requirement is to determine an auditor's responsibility when compiling the financial statements of a nonpublic company on a prescribed form which omits substantially all disclosures required by GAAP and is to be used by the company's industry trade association. Answer (a) is correct because AR 300.03 states that there is a presumption that the information required by a prescribed form is sufficient to meet the needs of the body that designed or adopted it; accordingly, there is no need for that body to be advised of departures from GAAP. Answer (b) is incorrect because per AR 300.03, details of the omissions need not be provided. Answer (c) is incorrect because a compilation report may be issued in such circumstances. Answer (d) is incorrect because compilation reports provide no assurance that the financial statements are free of material misstatement (AR 300.03).

C.1.b.(2) Reviewed Statements

57. (1188,A1,22) (a) The requirement is to identify the reference that should be included on each page of a nonpublic entity's reviewed financial statements. Answer (a) is correct because AR 100.34 indicates that each page should include a reference such as, "See Accountant's Review Report." Answer (b) is incorrect because it suggests that no

accountant's assurance is expressed, when review reports do provide limited assurance (AU 100.32). Answer (c) is incorrect because the footnotes are those of management, not the accountant. Answer (d) is incorrect because no indication as to the need for material modifications is to accompany each page of the financial statements.

58. (1189,A1,6) (a) The requirement is to identify the reply which is correct concerning the content of a review report. Answer (a) is correct because a review report indicates that a review is substantially less in scope than an audit (AR 100.32-.35). Answer (b) is incorrect because a review report provides no information on the internal control structure. Answer (c) is incorrect because while a review report states that the accountant is not aware of any material modifications that should be made to the financial statements, it does not provide limited assurance that the financial statements are fairly presented. Answer (d) is incorrect because while a review report does not state that a review is substantially less in scope than an audit, it does not refer to a compilation.

59. (586,A1,23) (b) The requirement is to determine an accountant's reporting responsibility when associated with reviewed statements of a nonpublic entity which contain a material departure from generally accepted accounting principles. Answer (b) is correct because AR 100.39-.41 requires the inclusion of a separate paragraph describing the departure. Answer (a) is incorrect because the financial statements are the representation of management and therefore the CPA does not add footnotes describing such departures from generally accepted accounting principles. Answer (c) is incorrect because a review, not a compilation, has been performed. Answer (d) is incorrect because an adverse opinion may only be issued when an audit has been performed (AU 509.41-.44).

60. (581,A1,53) (d) The requirement is to determine the circumstances which will lead to a modification of an interim report. Departures from generally accepted accounting principles, which include adequate disclosure, require modification of the accountant's report (AU 722.20). Normally neither an uncertainty [answer (a)] nor a lack of consistency [answer (b)] would cause a report modification (AU 722.20). Reference to another accountant [answer (c)] is not considered a modification (AU 722.19).

C.1.c. Reviewed Quarterly Statements

61. (1186,A1,57) (b) The requirement is to identify the objective of a review of interim financial information. AU 722.03 details the objective of a review of interim financial information. Answer (b) is correct because a review provides the accountant with a reasonable basis for reporting on whether material modifications should be made to make the financial statements conform with GAAP. Answer (a) is incorrect because an interim review does not involve updating a previously issued audit opinion. Answers (c) and (d) are incorrect because a review is more limited than an audit and does not allow the auditor to form an opinion and because the term "standards of interim reporting" is not used.

C.2. Other Reports
C.2.a. Special Reports

62. (589,A1,50) (a) The requirement is to identify the type of report to be issued when an auditor conducts an examination in accordance with generally accepted auditing standards, and concludes that the financial statements are fairly presented in accordance with a comprehensive basis of accounting other than GAAP. Answer (a) is correct because reports on financial statements presented in accordance with a basis of accounting other than GAAP are considered "special reports"--see AU 623.02-.10. Answer (b) is incorrect because it is not necessary to issue a disclaimer of opinion. Answer (c) is incorrect because an examination (audit), and not a review, has been performed. Answer (d) is incorrect because an unqualified special report may be issued on financial statements presented in accordance with a comprehensive basis of accounting other than GAAP (623.08). Only in the event that the financial statements include departures from the comprehensive basis, or if scope limitations have occurred, would the report require qualification.

63. (1187,A1,9) (c) The requirement is to identify the information **not** presented in an auditor's report on financial statements prepared in accordance with a comprehensive basis of accounting other than generally accepted accounting principles. Answer (c) is correct because the report issued does not address whether the use of the basis is appropriate (AU 623.08). Answers (a), (b), and (d) are all incorrect because they refer to information required to be disclosed in such a report. See AU 623.05 for reporting requirements on comprehensive basis statements.

64. (1189,A1,18)   (c) The requirement is to determine an auditor's appropriate response when requested to express an opinion on the rental and royalty income of an entity. Answer (c) is correct because AU 623.11-.18 outlines appropriate requirements which allow an auditor to accept such an engagement and to issue a special report. Answer (a) is incorrect because such engagements may be accepted. Answer (b) is incorrect because the auditor need not audit the full financial statements of the entity. Answer (d) is incorrect because the distribution of a report need not be limited.

65. (1188,A1,24)   (c) The requirement is to identify the correct statement with respect to an engagement in which an accountant is to apply agreed upon procedures that are **not** sufficient to express an opinion on one or more specified accounts or items of a financial statement. Answer (c) is correct because distribution of such a special report is to be restricted (AU 622.01). Answer (a) is incorrect because the accountant's report should enumerate the procedures performed (AU 622.04). Answer (b) is incorrect because such reports may be based on financial statements prepared in accordance with a comprehensive basis of accounting other than GAAP (AU 621.03). Answer (d) is incorrect because the accountant need not be the client's continuing auditor.

66. (1182,A1,20)   (a) The requirement is to determine the situation in which a special report will **not** be issued. Scope limitation situations are not a form of special report. Special reports only include financial information based on (1) a comprehensive basis of accounting other than GAAP, (2) specified elements, (3) compliance with various agreements, and (4) prescribed forms (see AU 621). Answer (b) is incorrect because such limited purpose reports are included under the "specified elements" category of special reports. Answer (c) is incorrect because not-for-profit statements are a form of comprehensive basis of accounting other than GAAP. Answer (d) is incorrect because historical cost/constant dollar reports are also an alternate comprehensive basis of accounting.

C.2.b. Letters for Underwriters, and SEC Filings

67. (1186,A1,60)   (c) The requirement is to determine who ordinarily signs a comfort letter. Answer (c) is correct because a comfort letter (also known as a letter to an underwriter) is sent by the independent auditor to the underwriter (AU 634). Answers (a), (b), and (d) are all incorrect because the client, client's lawyer, and the internal auditor do not sign the letter.

68. (589,A1,53)   (b) The requirement is to identify to whom comfort letters are ordinarily addressed. Answer (b) is correct because comfort letters, also referred to as letters for underwriters, are ordinarily addressed to underwriters (AU 634). Answers (a), (c), and (d) are all incorrect because comfort letters are not ordinarily addressed to the Securities and Exchange Commission, creditor financial institutions, or to the client's audit committee.

69. (1188,A1,26)   (b) The requirement is to determine the type of opinion or assurance provided by an accountant who issues a comfort letter containing comments on data that have **not** been audited. Answer (b) is correct because when procedures short of an audit are applied to information such as capsule information, a comfort letter will generally provide negative assurance (AU 634.02, .22-.24). Answer (a) is incorrect because positive assurance will not be provided on supplementary disclosures. Answer (c) is incorrect because no disclaimer will be included on the prospective financial statements. Answer (d) is incorrect because no "limited opinion" is issued, on "pro forma" or other information. See AU 634 for more information on comfort letters.

70. (585,A1,55)   (d) The requirement is to determine the appropriate reference to an independent accountant in a prospectus (relating to an SEC registration statement) that includes a statement about his/her involvement with an independent audit report. Answer (d) is correct since AU 711.09 indicates that the independent accountant is an expert in auditing and accounting. Answers (a), (b), and (c) all describe inappropriate references.

71. (1188,A1,14)   (c) The requirement is to identify the correct statement with respect to the authority of the Securities and Exchange Commission (SEC). Answer (c) is correct because the SEC has statutory authority to establish the accounting principles which are to be used to prepare financial statements of companies that sell securities to the public. Answers (a), (b), and (d) are all incorrect because they describe types of authority which have not explicitly been provided to the SEC.

C.2.c. Financial Forecasts and Projections

72. (1187,A1,11)   (d) The requirement is to identify the type of general use prospective financial statement on which the accountant

may appropriately report. Answer (d) is
correct because financial forecasts are
considered prospective financial statements,
and they are appropriate for general use
(AU 2100.07). Answer (a) is incorrect because
financial projections are only appropriate for
the party responsible for preparing them or
for third parties with whom the responsible
party is negotiating directly (AU 2100.08).
Answers (b) and (c) are incorrect because
partial presentations and pro forma financial
statements are not considered prospective
financial statements (AU 2100.06).

73. (1187,A1,10) (a) The requirement is to
determine the form of accountant association
that is not appropriate when third party use
of prospective financial statements is
expected. Answer (a) is correct because
AU 2100, which presents the standards with
respect to the accountant's obligations for
financial forecasts and projections, does not
allow for the review form of association under
any circumstances. Answers (b) and (c) are
incorrect because AU 2100 allows the results
of compilations and examinations to be provided to third parties. Answer (d) is
incorrect because an accountant may accept an
engagement to apply agreed-upon procedure when
third-party use of prospective financial
statements is restricted to specified third-
party users who have participated in
establishing the nature and scope of the
engagement and who take responsibility for the
adequacy of the procedures (AU 2100.49).

74. (1187,A1,12) (b) The requirement is to
identify the party that is usually responsible
for the assumptions identified in the preparation of prospective financial statements. Answer (b) is correct because the Professional
Standards state that the responsible party is
usually management, although in limited
circumstances it can be persons outside of the
entity (such as a situation in which a person
is considering acquiring the entity)--
AU 2100.06. Answers (a), (c), and (d) are all
incorrect because they all represent other
parties that are not normally considered
responsible for the assumptions identified in
the prospective financial statements.

75. (587,A1,57) (b) The requirement is to
identify the type of prospective financial
statement that includes one or more hypothetical ("what if?") assumptions. Answer (b)
is correct because financial projections
include one or more hypothetical assumptions
(AU 2100.06). Answer (a) is incorrect because
pro forma financial presentations are designed
to demonstrate the effect of a future or

hypothetical transaction by showing how it
might have affected the historical financial
statements if it had been consummated during
the period covered by those statements
(AU 2100.06, note 4). Answer (c) is incorrect
because partial presentations are presentations that do not meet the minimum presentation guidelines of AU 2100 (see AU 2100.06,
note 5). Answer (d) is incorrect because
financial forecasts present, to the best of
the responsible party's knowledge and belief,
an entity's expected financial position,
results of operations, and changes in financial information (AU 2100.06).

76. (589,A1,57) (d) The requirement is to
identify the statement which would not be
included in an accountant's standard report on
a compilation of a projection. Answer (d) is
correct because limited assurance that the
projected results may be achieved is not
provided in a compilation report (AT 200.18,
previously codified as AU 2100.18). Answers (a), (b), and (c) are all incorrect
because they represent information included in
a compilation report for a projection. See
AT 200.16 (previously codified as AU 2100.16)
for information included in such a report.

77. (589,A1,58) (a) The requirement is to
identify the correct statement with respect to
an accountant's ability to accept an engagement to apply agreed-upon procedures to prospective financial statements. Answer (a) is
correct because the application of agreed-upon
procedures results in a report with distribution restricted to the specified users
involved (AT 200.49, previously codified as
AU 2100.49). Answer (b) is incorrect because
the auditor is not required to examine the
prospective financial statements. Answer (c)
is incorrect because the specified users, not
the accountant, must take responsibility for
the adequacy of the procedures (AT 200.52,
previously codified as AU 2100.52). Answer (d) is incorrect because the accountant
will not provide negative assurance on the
prospective financial statements taken as a
whole (AT 200.57, previously codified as
AU 2100.57).

78. (1189,A1,20) (d) The requirement is to
determine the information to be included in an
accountant's compilation report on projected
financial statements. Answer (d) is correct
because compilation reports on projected financial statements must describe the limitations on the projection's usefulness
(AT 200.18). Answers (a), (b), and (c) are
all incorrect because they present information
not included in a compilation report.

79. (1189,A1,21) (d) The requirement is to
determine the appropriate type of audit report
to be issued when an accountant examines a financial forecast that fails to disclose
several significant assumptions used to prepare the forecast. Answer (d) is correct because AT 200.40 states that an adverse opinion
is appropriate when significant assumptions
are not disclosed. Answers (a), (b), and (c)
are all incorrect because they suggest reports
not recommended by AT 200.40.

C.2.d. Application of Accounting
Principles

80. (1188,A1,18) (d) The requirement is to
identify the correct statement concerning a
CPA's responsibility when asked to issue an
opinion on the application of an accounting
principle by an entity that is audited by
another CPA. Answer (d) is correct because
AU 625.07 allows the CPA to accept such an
engagement, but states that the CPA should
consult with the continuing auditor to make
certain that he or she has all of the relevant
available facts to form a professional
judgment. Answers (a) and (b) are incorrect
because they suggest that the CPA cannot
accept such an engagement. Answer (c) is
incorrect because the CPA should consult with
the continuing CPA.

May 1990 Answers

81. (590,A1,11) (b) The requirement is to
identify the example of a "special report."
Answer (b) is correct because AU 621.01 defines reports on compliance with aspects of
regulatory requirements related to audited
financial statements as special reports. (The
other types of special reports include
(1) other comprehensive basis financial
statements, (2) specified elements, (3) financial presentations to comply with contracts,
and (4) financial information presented in
prescribed forms.) Answers (a), (c), and (d)
all relate to accountant involvement with
information that is not categorized as a
special report.

82. (590,A1,12) (a) The requirement is to
determine the appropriate opinion relating to
a report which includes an explanatory paragraph, following the opinion paragraph, which
describes an uncertainty related to litigation. Answer (a) is correct because uncertainties generally lead to an unqualified
opinion with an explanatory paragraph following the opinion paragraph (AU 508.31-
.33). Answer (b) is incorrect because the
term "subject to" used to qualify an opinion
because of an uncertainty is no longer permis-

sible (AU 508.31, note 13). Answer (c) is
incorrect because scope limitations and departures from generally accepted accounting principles, but not uncertainties, lead to qualified opinions (AU 508.38). Answer (d) is incorrect because, while a disclaimer may result
from an uncertainty, it occurs less frequently
than does an unqualified opinion with an explanatory paragraph, and because when an
opinion is disclaimed, the auditor must give
all the substantive reasons for the disclaimer
in the explanatory paragraph.

83. (590,A1,13) (d) The requirement is to
determine the manner in which a predecessor
auditor who has reissued a report for comparative financial statements should refer to the
successor auditor. Answer (d) is correct
because AU 508.80 indicates that the predecessor auditor should not refer in the reissued
report to the report or work of the successor
auditor. Answers (a), (b), and (c) are all
incorrect because they indicate that the predecessor should, in some manner, refer to the
successor.

84. (590,A1,15) (d) The requirement is to
determine the correct response with respect to
an audit report which describes a departure
from generally accepted accounting principles
with "In our opinion, with the foregoing explanation, the financial statements referred
to above present fairly..." Answer (d) is
correct because AU 508.39 states that such a
statement is not clear or forceful enough and
therefore should not be used. Answers (a)
and (b) are incorrect because, as indicated,
the statement is not considered adequate.
Answer (c) is incorrect because an unqualified
opinion with a separate explanatory paragraph
includes no modification of the opinion paragraph.

85. (590,A1,16) (c) The requirement is to
identify the circumstance in which an auditor
usually is choosing between issuing a qualified opinion or a disclaimer of opinion.
Answer (c) is correct because the standards
state that inability to obtain sufficient
competent evidential matter leads to either a
qualified opinion or a disclaimer of opinion
(AU 508.40). Answer (a) is incorrect because
a departure from generally accepted accounting
principles generally results in a qualified
opinion or an adverse opinion (AU 508.49).
Answer (b) is incorrect because inadequate
disclosure of accounting policies results in
either a qualified opinion or an adverse
opinion (AU 508.55). Answer (d) is incorrect
because unreasonable justification for a
change in accounting principle is in essence a

departure from generally accepted accounting principles and results in either a qualified opinion or an adverse opinion (AU 508.60).

86. (590,A1,17) (a) The requirement is to identify the appropriate updated auditor's report on prior-period financial statements that previously led to a qualified opinion, but have now been restated. Answer (a) is correct because the auditor should indicate that the statements have been restated and should express an unqualified opinion with respect to the restated financial statements (AU 508.77). An explanatory paragraph to the report should disclose (1) the date of the auditor's previous report, (2) the type of opinion previously expressed, (3) the circumstances or events that caused the auditor to express a different opinion, and (4) that the updated opinion differs from the previous opinion. Answer (b) is incorrect because the original auditor's report has been modified. Answer (c) is incorrect because the date of the comparative statement audit report is the last day of field work for the current year audit. Answer (d) is incorrect because a change in accounting principle results in an unqualified opinion with an explanatory paragraph, not a qualified opinion (AU 508.34-.36).

87. (590,A1,18) (c) The requirement is to identify the circumstance in which a disclaimer of opinion would **not** be appropriate. Answer (c) is correct because the lack of adequate disclosure concerning related party transactions is a departure from generally accepted accounting principles that will normally lead to either a qualified or adverse opinion, but not to a disclaimer of opinion (AU 508.70). Answers (a), (b), and (d) are incorrect because inability to observe physical inventories, inability to determine the amounts of illegal acts, and refusal to permit an attorney to furnish information all represent scope limitations which result in either a qualified opinion or a disclaimer of opinion (AU 508.40-.44).

88. (590,A1,19) (c) The requirement is to determine an accountant's reporting responsibility when associated with a nonpublic entity's reviewed statements which contain a material departure from generally accepted accounting principles. Answer (c) is correct because AR 100.40 requires the inclusion of a separate paragraph describing the departure. Answers (a) and (b) are incorrect because an adverse opinion or an "except for" qualified opinion may only be issued when an audit has been performed (AU 508.38-.39, .67-.69). An-

swer (d) is incorrect because expressing limited assurance (as is normally provided in reviews) on the financial statements is not adequate to disclose the departure.

89. (590,A1,21) (c) The requirement is to determine the information that must be included in an audit report explanatory paragraph when a client uses the income tax basis of accounting for reporting financial purposes. Answer (c) is correct because the report must state that the income tax basis of accounting is a comprehensive basis other than generally accepted accounting principles (AU 623.05d). AU 623.05 provides further detail on such reports. Answer (a) is incorrect because the financial statements will have been examined in accordance with generally accepted auditing standards. Answer (b) is incorrect because the authoritative tax pronouncements are not referred to in the audit report. Answer (d) is incorrect because no such justification of the use of the income tax basis is necessary.

90. (590,A1,22) (d) The requirement is to determine the proper disclosure of a scope limitation in an audit report. Answer (d) is correct because an explanatory paragraph must precede the opinion paragraph, and must be referred to in both the scope and opinion paragraphs of the auditor's report (AU 508.43). Answer (a) is incorrect because the scope limitation is referred to in both the scope and opinion paragraphs. Answer (b) is incorrect because the explanatory paragraph precedes the opinion paragraph. Answer (c) is incorrect because the explanatory paragraph precedes the opinion paragraph and because the scope limitation is referred to in both the scope and opinion paragraphs.

91. (590,A1,23) (c) The requirement is to identify the correct statement about prospective financial statements. Answer (c) is correct because AT 200.08 states that any type of prospective financial statement would normally be appropriate for limited use. Answer (a) is incorrect because a forecast would normally be appropriate for general or limited use. Answer (b) is incorrect because a financial projection is normally appropriate only for limited, not general, use. Answer (d) is incorrect because financial projections, a type of prospective financial statement, are not appropriate for general use (AT 200.08). See AT 200 for information on financial forecasts and projections.

92. (590,A1,24) (b) The requirement is to identify the correct statement with respect to

an independent accountant's review report on
interim financial information presented in a
registration statement. Answer (b) is correct
because an accountant's review report is <u>not</u> a
part of the registration statement within the
meaning of Section 11 of the Securities Act
of 1933 (AU 711.06). Answer (a) is incorrect
because an accountant <u>is</u> an "expert within the
meaning of the Securities Act of 1933"
(AU 711.03). Answers (c) and (d) are incorrect because the accountant is not described
as having performed limited auditing procedures or as having followed AICPA standards
(AU 711.09).

93. (590,A1,25) (d) The requirement is to
determine the proper audit report when management declines to present supplementary information required by the Governmental Accounting
Standards Board. Answer (d) is correct
because omission of required supplementary
information, which when presented is not
considered audited, leads to an unqualified
opinion with an explanatory paragraph
(AU 558.08). Answers (a) and (b) are incorrect because neither an adverse opinion nor a
qualified opinion is appropriate since the
supplementary information is not audited.
Answer (c) is incorrect because it is incomplete since an unqualified opinion with an
additional explanatory paragraph is required.

Unofficial Answer*

Problem 1   Analyze a Review Report (1188,A4)

Deficiencies in the staff assistant's draft
are as follows:

Within the first paragraph

   • The statement of cash flow is not
identified.
   • Standards established by the AICPA,
not generally accepted auditing standards,
should be referred to.
   • The financial statements are not
stated to be the representations of management.
   • The phrase "our review included such
tests of the accounting records as we considered necessary in the circumstances" is
inappropriate.

Within the second paragraph

   • The phrase "analytical procedures
applied to financial data" is omitted.
   • The phrase "more in scope than a
compilation" is inappropriate.
   • An opinion should be disclaimed.
   • "Limited assurance" should not be
expressed.

Within the third paragraph

   • Reference to the "exception" in the
third paragraph when it has been restated is
inappropriate.
   • Reference to consistency is inappropriate.

Within the fourth paragraph

   • There should be reference to the prior
years' review report.
   • There should be reference to generally
accepted accounting principles.

*Because the requirements of this question
could be answered by lists of items, we have
not included an outline of the solution.

Answer Outline

Problem 2   Prepare a Report (1186,A5)
           (Differences from standard report)

Introductory Paragraph
   State that firm did not audit Rapid Parts
   Company
   List portions audited by other auditor
   Report based on other auditors

Scope Paragraph
   Add "except as discussed in the following
   paragraph" to beginning of first sentence

Explanatory Paragraph
   Did not observe taking of inventory
   Affects net income and cash flows

Disclaimer Paragraph
   Disclaims opinion on results of operations
   and cash flows

Opinion paragraph
   Unqualified opinion on balance sheet

Unofficial Answer
(Author Modified)

Problem 2 Prepare a Report (1186,A5)

Independent Auditor's Report

To the Board of Directors of National Motors,
Inc.:

   We have audited the accompanying balance
sheet of National Motors, Inc. as of December 31, 19X5, and the related consolidated
statements of income, retained earnings, and
cash flows for the year then ended. These
financial statements are the responsibility of
the company's management. Our responsibility
is to express an opinion on these financial
statements based on our audit. We did not
audit the financial statements of Rapid Parts
Company, a consolidated subsidiary, which
statements reflect total assets of $700,000 as
of December 31, 19X5, and total revenues of
$2,000,000 for the year then ended. Those
statements were audited by other auditors
whose report has been furnished to us, and our
opinion, insofar as it relates to the amounts
included for Rapid Parts Company, is based
solely on the report of the other auditors.
   Except as explained in the following
paragraph, we conducted our audits in
accordance with generally accepted auditing
standards. Those standards require that we
plan and perform the audit to obtain
reasonable assurance about whether the
financial statements are free of material
misstatement. An audit includes examining, on

a test basis, evidence supporting the amounts and disclosures in the financial statements. An audit also includes assessing the accounting principles used and significant estimates made by management, as well as evaluating the overall financial statement presentation. We believe that our audits and the report of other auditors provide a reasonable basis for our opinion.

We did not observe the taking of the physical inventory as of December 31, 19X4, since that date was prior to our appointment as auditors for the company, and we were unable to satisfy ourselves regarding inventory quantities by means of other auditing procedures. Inventory amounts as of December 31, 19X4 enter into the determination of net income and cash flows for the year ended December 31, 19X5.

Because of the matter discussed in the preceding paragraph, the scope of our work was not sufficient to enable us to express, and we do not express an opinion on the results of operations and cash flows for the year ended December 31, 19X5.

In our opinion, based on our audit and the report of other auditors, the consolidated balance sheet as of December 31, 19X5 presents fairly, in all material respects, the financial position of National Motors, Inc. as of December 31, 19X5 for the year then ended in conformity with generally accepted accounting principles.

March 28, 19X6   White and Company

Answer Outline

Problem 3   Report Deficiencies (586,A3)

Report deficiencies include

1. Report improperly addressed
      Should be to Board of Directors

Introductory paragraph

2. FSs not listed
3. Reference to Note K should be in an additional separate ¶
4. Reference to predecessor auditors needed
5. Reference to adverse opinion of predecessor auditors needed

Separate explanatory paragraph

6. Need reference to GAAP
7. Need explanation of monetary effect of GAAP violations

Opinion paragraph

8. Should refer to separate explanatory ¶
9. Need reference to GAAP
10. Should **not** refer to consistency
11. **Need dual dating**

Unofficial Answer

Problem 3   Report Deficiencies (586,A3), (Modified)

Deficiencies in the audit assistant's draft include the following:

1. The report is improperly addressed to the president.

2. The introductory paragraph does not identify the financial statements examined, i.e., balance sheet, and statements of income, retained earnings, and cash flows.

3. Reference to "Note K" pertaining to a subsequent event is inappropriate in the introductory paragraph. If the auditor wishes to emphasize this matter, such explanatory information should be presented in a separate paragraph of the auditor's report.

4. There is no reference to the predecessor auditors in the introductory paragraph as required when the statements are in comparative form.

5. There is no reference that an adverse opinion was expressed by the predecessor auditors.

6. The separate explanatory paragraph does not make reference to the requirements of generally accepted accounting principles, i.e., property and equipment should be stated at an amount not in excess of cost, and deferred income taxes should be provided. Therefore, all of the substantive reasons for the adverse opinion have not been disclosed.

7. The separate explanatory paragraph does not disclose either the monetary effects of the violations of generally accepted accounting principles or that the effects are not reasonably determinable.

8. The opinion paragraph does not include a direct reference to the separate explanatory paragraph that discloses the basis for the adverse opinion.

9. The opinion paragraph does not make reference to "conformity with generally accepted accounting principles."

10. No reference to consistency should be made.

11. The auditor's report is not properly dual dated.

Answer Outline

Problem 4   Write Report (1184,A5)
     (Differences from standard report)

Introductory Paragraph
  Final sentence refers to other auditors
    Name of subsidiary
    Date of report
    Type of opinion

Scope Paragraph
  No changes

First Explanatory Paragraph
  (Paragraph is necessary because financial
   statements do not describe inconsistency)
  Describe inconsistency and its effects

Second Explanatory Paragraph
  Describe departure from GAAP and its effects

Opinion Paragraph
  Two "except for's" added following "In our
  opinion,"

Author's note: The related party relationship
between the client and a former partner of the
predecessor auditor need not be mentioned in
the audit report.

Unofficial Answer
(Author Modified)

Problem 4   Write Report (1184,A5)

Independent Auditor's Report

To the Board of Directors of Devon
Incorporated:

We have audited the accompanying balance
sheet of Devon Incorporated as of December 31,
19X3, and the related statements of income,
retained earnings, and cash flows for the year
then ended. These financial statements are
the responsibility of the company's management. Our responsibility is to express an
opinion on these financial statements based on
our audit. The financial statements of Devon
Incorporated as of December 31, 19X2 were
audited by other auditors whose report dated
March 31, 19X2 expressed an unqualified
opinion on those statements.
We conducted our audit in accordance with
generally accepted auditing standards. Those
standards require that we plan and perform the
audit to obtain reasonable assurance about
whether the financial statements are free of
material misstatement. An audit includes
examining, on a test basis, evidence
supporting the amounts and disclosures in the
financial statements. An audit also includes
assessing the accounting principles used and

significant estimates made by management, as
well as evaluating the overall financial
statement presentation. We believe that our
audit provides a reasonable basis for our
opinion.
During the year, Devon changed its method of
valuing inventory from the first-in, first-out
method to the last-in, first-out method. This
change was made because management believes
LIFO more clearly reflects net income by
providing a closer matching of current costs
and current revenues. The change had the
effect of reducing inventory at December 31,
19X3 by $65,000 and net income and earnings
per share by $38,000 and $.38 respectively for
the year then ended. The effect of the change
on prior years was immaterial; accordingly,
there was no cumulative effect of the change.
The company has excluded from property
and debt in the accompanying balance sheet
certain lease obligations, which in our
opinion, should be capitalized in order to
conform with generally accepted accounting
principles. If these lease obligations were
capitalized, assets would be increased by
$312,000, liabilities by $387,000, and
retained earnings decreased by $75,000 as of
December 31, 19X3; net income and earnings per
share would be decreased by $75,000 and $.75
respectively for the year then ended.
In our opinion, except for the effects of
not disclosing the change in inventory methods
and except for the effects of not capitalizing
lease obligations as discussed in the preceding paragraphs, the financial statements
referred to above present fairly, in all
material respects, the financial position of
Devon Incorporated as of December 31, 19X3,
and the results of its operations and its cash
flows for the year then ended in conformity
with generally accepted accounting principles.

February 29, 19X4   Smith, CPA

Answer Outline

Problem 5   Report on a Review (1182,A5)

Report (dated March 3, 1982, and addressed to
  the Board of Directors) setting forth the
  following
Paragraph 1
  Review performed in accordance with AICPA
    standards
  Financial statements are representations of
    management
Paragraph 2
  Review procedures consist of inquiry and
    analytical procedures
  Review less in scope than audit
  No opinion is expressed

Paragraph 3
  Not aware of material modifications needed
    to be in conformity with GAAP
Paragraph 4
  Prior years' statements were examined
  Expressed unqualified opinion
  Date of previous report
  No procedures performed after date of pre-
    vious report

Unofficial Answer

Problem 5   Report on a Review (1182,A5)

To: The Board of Directors of Tillis Ltd.

  We have reviewed the accompanying balance
sheet of Tillis Ltd. as of December 31, 1981;
and the related statements of income, retained
earnings, and cash flows for the year then
ended, in accordance with standards
established by the American Institute of
Certified Public Accountants. All information
included in these financial statements is the
representation of the management of Tillis
Ltd.

  A review consists principally of inquiries
of company personnel and analytical procedures
applied to financial data. It is substantially less in scope than an examination in
accordance with generally accepted auditing
standards, the objective of which is the
expression of an opinion regarding the financial statements taken as a whole. Accordingly, we do not express such an opinion.

  Based on our review, we are not aware of any
material modifications that should be made to
the accompanying 1981 financial statements in
order for them to be in conformity with
generally accepted accounting principles.

  The financial statements for the year ended
December 31, 1980 were examined by us, and we
expressed an unqualified opinion on them in
our report dated February 27, 1981, but we
have not performed any auditing procedures
since that date.

                              Novak & Co.

March 3, 1982

Answer Outline

Problem 6 Special Report (584,A2)

Address to board of directors
Financial statements examined for year ended
  6/30/83
Report thereon issued (dated 8/15/83)
Reference to GAAS
Reference to tests of accounting records

Reference to other auditing procedures as considered necessary
During examination, examined provision for
  federal and state income taxes for year ended
  6/30/83
Examined related accruals and deferred income
  taxes
  Reviewed federal and state income tax re-
    turns as required to be filed
Opinion should refer to adequate provision by
  company for all federal and state income
  taxes
Opinion should refer to proper reflection of
  related accruals and deferred income taxes
Opinion applicable to fiscal 1983 and prior
  fiscal years reasonably estimated at time of
  exam
No reference to GAAP
Report dated 8/15/83
Signed in firm name

Unofficial Answer

Problem 6   Special Report (584,A2)

Board of Directors
XYZ Company, Inc.

  We have examined the financial statements
of XYZ Company, Inc. for the year ended
June 30, 1983, and have issued our report
thereon dated August 15, 1983. Our examination was made in accordance with generally
accepted auditing standards and, accordingly,
included such tests of the accounting records
and such other auditing procedures as we
considered necessary in the circumstances.

  In the course of our examination, we examined the provision for federal and state
income taxes for the year ended June 30, 1983
and the related accruals and deferred income
taxes included in XYZ Company's financial
statements referred to in the preceding paragraph. We also reviewed the federal and state
income tax returns filed by XYZ Company that
are subject to examination by the respective
taxing authorities.

  In our opinion, XYZ Company has made
adequate provision for all federal and state
income taxes and has properly reflected the
related accruals and deferred income taxes
applicable to fiscal 1983 and prior fiscal
years that could be reasonably estimated at
the time of our examination of the financial
statements of XYZ Company, Inc. for the year
ended June 30, 1983.

                        Young and Young
                  Certified Public Accountants

August 15, 1983

Answer Outline

Problem 7   Reports on Prospective Financial
             Statements (588,A2)

a1. Types of prospective F/S engagements
         Compilation
         Examination
         Agreed-upon procedures
a2. General use of prospective FSs
         For use by persons not negotiating
           directly with responsible party
           (management)
     Limited use of prospective FSs
         For use by responsible party alone
         For use by responsbile party and a
           third party in direct negotiations
a3. Prospective FSs appropriate for general
       use
         Financial forecast
     Prospective FSs appropriate for limited
       use
         Financial forecast
         Financial projection

b.   *no outline

Unofficial Answer

Problem 7   Reports on Prospective Financial
             Statements (588,A2)

a. 1. An accountant who reports on or
assembles prospective financial statements for
use by third parties should perform any one of
three engagements. The accountant may
compile, examine, or apply agreed-upon
procedures to the prospective financial
statements.
    2. "General use" of prospective financial
statements refers to use of the statements by
persons (creditors, stockholders, etc.) with
whom the responsible party (management) is not
negotiating directly. "Limited use" of
prospective financial statements refers to the
use of prospective financial statements by the
responsible party alone or by the responsible
party and third parties with whom the responsible party is negotiating directly.
    3. Only a financial forecast is appropri-
ate for general use, but any type of prospective financial statements (either a financial
forecast or a financial projection) would
normally be appropriate for limited use.

b.   The accountant's standard report on a
compilation of a financial projection should
include

•   An identification of the projection pre-
     sented by the responsible party.

•   A statement that the accountant has com-
     piled the projection in accordance with
     standards established by the AICPA.
•   A separate paragraph that describes the
     limitations on the use of the presenta-
     tion.
•   A statement that a compilation is limited
     in scope and does not enable the accoun-
     tant to express an opinion or any other
     form of assurance on the projection or the
     assumptions.
•   A caveat that the prospective results may
     not be achieved.
•   A statement that the accountant assumes no
     responsibility to update the report for
     events and circumstances occurring after
     the date of the report.

Unofficial Answer*

Problem 8   Analyze Audit Report (589,A2)

The auditor's report contains the following
deficiencies:

Opening (introductory) paragraph

 1. All the financial statements audited are
not identified.

 2. Management's responsibility for the
financial statements is omitted.

Scope paragraph

 3. Reference to "generally accepted auditing
standards" is omitted.

 4. An auditor obtains reasonable assurance
about whether the financial statements are
"free of material misstatement," not "in
conformity with generally accepted accounting
principles."

 5. The statement that an audit includes
"evaluating the overall financial statement
presentation" is omitted.

 6. The statement that the auditors "believe
that our audit provides a reasonable basis for
our opinion" is omitted.

*Because the requirements of this question
could be answered by lists of items, we have
not included an outline of the solution.

Explanatory paragraph

7. The explanatory paragraph should follow the opinion paragraph.

8. The auditors should not give an opinion concerning the entity's survival "beyond a reasonable period of time."

Opinion paragraph

9. A qualified ("subject to") opinion is inappropriate.

10. The date of the financial statements audited is omitted.

11. There should be no reference to consistency unless the accounting principles have not been applied consistently.

Multiple Choice Questions (1-44)

1. An underlying feature of random-based selection of items is that each
   a. Stratum of the accounting population be given equal representation in the sample.
   b. Item in the accounting population be randomly ordered.
   c. Item in the accounting population should have an opportunity to be selected.
   d. Item must be systematically selected using replacement.

2. An advantage of using statistical sampling techniques is that such techniques
   a. Mathematically measure risk.
   b. Eliminate the need for judgmental decisions.
   c. Define the values of precision and reliability required to provide audit satisfaction.
   d. Have been established in the courts to be superior to judgmental sampling.

3. Which of the following is an element of sampling risk?
   a. Choosing an audit procedure that is inconsistent with the audit objective.
   b. Choosing a sample size that is too small to achieve the sampling objective.
   c. Failing to detect an error on a document that has been inspected by the auditor.
   d. Failing to perform audit procedures that are required by the sampling plan.

4. Which of the following best illustrates the concept of sampling risk?
   a. A randomly chosen sample may **not** be representative of the population as a whole on the characteristic of interest.
   b. An auditor may select audit procedures that are **not** appropriate to achieve the specific objective.
   c. An auditor may fail to recognize errors in the documents examined for the chosen sample.
   d. The documents related to the chosen sample may **not** be available for inspection.

5. The risk of incorrect acceptance and the risk of assessing control risk too low for internal control relate to the

   a. Preliminary estimates of materiality levels.
   b. Allowable risk of tolerable mis-statement.
   c. Efficiency of the audit.
   d. Effectiveness of the audit.

6. In assessing sampling risk, the risk of incorrect rejection and the risk of assessing control risk too high (underreliance) relate to the
   a. Efficiency of the audit.
   b. Effectiveness of the audit.
   c. Selection of the sample.
   d. Audit quality controls.

7. Which of the following statistical selection techniques is **least** desirable for use by an auditor?
   a. Systematic selection.
   b. Stratified selection.
   c. Block selection.
   d. Sequential selection.

8. The size of a sample designed for dual purpose testing should be
   a. The larger of the samples that would otherwise have been designed for the two separate purposes.
   b. The smaller of the samples that would otherwise have been designed for the two separate purposes.
   c. The combined total of the samples that would otherwise have been designed for the two separate purposes.
   d. More than the larger of the samples that would otherwise have been designated for the two separate purposes, but less than the combined total of the samples that would otherwise have been designed for the two separate purposes.

9. The expected population deviation rate of client billing errors is 3%. The auditor has established a tolerable rate of 5%. In the review of client invoices the auditor should use
   a. Stratified sampling.
   b. Variable sampling.
   c. Discovery sampling.
   d. Attribute sampling.

10. Which of the following would be designed to estimate a numerical measurement of a population, such as a dollar value?
    a. Sampling for variables.
    b. Sampling for attributes.
    c. Discovery sampling.
    d. Numerical sampling.

11. Which of the following statistical sampling plans does **not** use a fixed sample size for tests of controls?
    a. Dollar-unit sampling.
    b. Sequential sampling.
    c. PPS sampling.
    d. Variables sampling.

12. If certain forms are not consecutively numbered
    a. Selection of a random sample probably is not possible.
    b. Systematic sampling may be appropriate.
    c. Stratified sampling should be used.
    d. Random number tables cannot be used.

13. Which of the following factors does an auditor generally need to consider in planning a particular audit sample for a test of control?
    a. Number of items in the population.
    b. Total dollar amount of the items to be sampled.
    c. Acceptable level of risk of assessing control risk too low.
    d. Tolerable misstatement.

14. When performing a test of a control with respect to control over cash receipts, an auditor may use a systematic sampling technique with a start at any randomly selected item. The biggest disadvantage of this type of sampling is that the items in the population
    a. Must be systematically replaced in the population after sampling.
    b. May systematically occur more than once in the sample.
    c. Must be recorded in a systematic pattern before the sample can be drawn.
    d. May occur in a systematic pattern, thus destroying the sample randomness.

15. Which of the following combinations results in a decrease in sample size in a sample for attributes?

	Risk of assessing control risk too low	Tolerable rate	Expected population deviation rate
a.	Increase	Decrease	Increase
b.	Decrease	Increase	Decrease
c.	Increase	Increase	Decrease
d.	Increase	Increase	Increase

16. An auditor plans to examine a sample of 20 purchase orders for proper approvals as prescribed by the client's internal control procedures. One of the purchase orders in the chosen sample of 20 cannot be found, and the auditor is unable to use alternative procedures to test whether that purchase order was properly approved. The auditor should
    a. Choose another purchase order to replace the missing purchase order in the sample.
    b. Consider this test of control invalid and proceed with substantive tests since internal control can **not** be relied upon.
    c. Treat the missing purchase order as a deviation for the purpose of evaluating the sample.
    d. Select a completely new set of 20 purchase orders.

17. When assessing the tolerable rate, the auditor should consider that, while deviations from control procedures increase the risk of material errors, such deviations do not necessarily result in errors. This explains why
    a. A recorded disbursement that does **not** show evidence of required approval may nevertheless be a transaction that is properly authorized and recorded.
    b. Deviations would result in errors in the accounting records only if the deviations and the errors occurred on different transactions.
    c. Deviations from pertinent control procedures at a given rate ordinarily would be expected to result in errors at a higher rate.
    d. A recorded disbursement that is properly authorized may nevertheless be a transaction that contains a material error.

Items 18 and 19 are based on the following information:

The diagram below depicts the auditor's estimated deviation rate compared with the tolerable rate, and also depicts the true population deviation rate compared with the tolerable rate.

	True State of Population	
	Deviation Rate Exceeds Tolerable Rate	Deviation Rate is Less Than Tolerable Rate
Auditor's Estimate Based On Sample Results Deviation Rate Exceeds Tolerable Rate	I.	II.
Deviation Rate is Less Than Tolerable Rate	III.	IV.

18. In which of the situations would the auditor have properly concluded that control risk is at or below the planned assessed level?
    a. I.
    b. II.
    c. III.
    d. IV.

19. As a result of tests of controls, the auditor assesses control risk too high and thereby increases substantive testing. This is illustrated by situation
    a. I.
    b. II.
    c. III.
    d. IV.

20. The objective of the tolerable rate in sampling for tests of controls of an internal control structure is to
    a. Determine the probability of the auditor's conclusion based upon reliance factors.
    b. Determine that financial statements taken as a whole are not materially in error.
    c. Estimate the reliability of substantive tests.
    d. Estimate the range of procedural deviations in the population.

21. The tolerable rate of deviations for a test of a control is generally
    a. Lower than the expected rate of errors in the related accounting records.
    b. Higher than the expected rate of errors in the related accounting records.
    c. Identical to the expected rate of errors in related accounting records.
    d. Unrelated to the expected rate of errors in the related accounting records.

22. As a result of tests of controls, an auditor assessed control risk too low and decreased substantive testing. This occurred because the true deviation rate in the population was
    a. Less than the risk of assessing control risk too low based on the auditor's sample.
    b. Less than the deviation rate in the auditor's sample.
    c. More than the risk of assessing control risk too low based on the auditor's sample.
    d. More than the deviation rate in the auditor's sample.

23. A principal advantage of statistical methods of attribute sampling over nonstatistical methods is that they provide a scientific basis for planning the
    a. Risk of assessing control risk too low.
    b. Tolerable rate.
    c. Expected population deviation rate.
    d. Sample size.

24. Which of the following statements is correct concerning statistical sampling in tests of controls?
    a. The population size has little or **no** effect on determining sample size except for very small populations.
    b. The expected population deviation rate has little or no effect on determining sample size except for very small populations.
    c. As the population size doubles, the sample size also should double.
    d. For a given tolerable rate, a larger sample size should be selected as the expected population deviation rate decreases.

25. An auditor who uses statistical sampling for attributes in testing internal controls should increase the assessed level of control risk when the
   a. Sample rate of deviation is less than the expected rate of deviation used in planning the sample.
   b. Tolerable rate less the allowance for sampling risk exceeds the sample rate of deviation.
   c. Sample rate of deviation plus the allowance for sampling risk exceeds the tolerable rate.
   d. Sample rate of deviation plus the allowance for sampling risk equals the tolerable rate.

26. What is an auditor's evaluation of a statistical sample for attributes when a test of 100 documents results in 4 deviations if the tolerable rate is 5%, the expected population deviation rate is 3%, and the allowance for sampling risk is 2%?
   a. Accept the sample results as support for planned reliance on the control because the tolerable rate less the allowance for sampling risk equals the expected population deviation rate.
   b. Modify planned reliance on the control because the sample deviation rate plus the allowance for sampling risk exceeds the tolerable rate.
   c. Modify planned reliance on the control because the tolerable rate plus the allowance for sampling risk exceeds the expected population deviation rate.
   d. Accept the sample results as support for planned reliance on the control because the sample deviation rate plus the allowance for sampling risk exceeds the tolerable rate.

27. Which of the following statistical sampling methods is most useful to auditors when testing control operating effectiveness?
   a. Ratio estimation.
   b. Variable sampling.
   c. Difference estimation.
   d. Discovery sampling.

28. If the auditor is concerned that a population may contain exceptions, the determination of a sample size sufficient to include at <u>least</u> one such exception is a characteristic of
   a. Discovery sampling.
   b. Variables sampling.
   c. Random sampling.
   d. Dollar-unit sampling.

29. An auditor initially planned to use unrestricted random sampling with replacement in the examination of accounts receivable. Later, the auditor decided to use unrestricted random sampling without replacement. As a result only of this decision, the sample size should
   a. Increase.
   b. Remain the same.
   c. Decrease.
   d. Be recalculated using a binomial distribution.

30. What is the primary objective of using stratification as a sampling method in auditing?
   a. To increase the confidence level at which a decision will be reached from the results of the sample selected.
   b. To determine the occurrence rate for a given characteristic in the population being studied.
   c. To decrease the effect of variance in the total population.
   d. To determine the precision range of the sample selected.

31. A number of factors influences the sample size for a substantive test of details of an account balance. All other factors being equal, which of the following would lead to a larger sample size?
   a. Greater reliance on internal controls.
   b. Greater reliance on analytical procedures.
   c. Smaller expected frequency of errors.
   d. Smaller measure of tolerable misstatement.

32. In estimation sampling for variables, which of the following must be known in order to estimate the appropriate sample size required to meet the auditor's needs in a given situation?
   a. The qualitative aspects of errors.
   b. The total dollar amount of the population.
   c. The acceptable level of risk.
   d. The estimated rate of misstatements in the population.

33. While performing a substantive test of details during an audit, the auditor determined that the sample results supported the conclusion that the recorded account balance was materially misstated. It was, in fact, not materially misstated. This situation illustrates the risk of
   a. Incorrect rejection.
   b. Incorrect acceptance.

c.   Assessing control risk too low.

d.   Assessing control risk too high.

34. Hill has decided to use Probability
Proportional to Size (PPS) sampling, sometimes
called dollar-unit sampling, in the audit of a
client's accounts receivable balances. Hill
plans to use the following PPS sampling table:

TABLE

Reliability Factors for Overstatements

Number of over-statements	Risk of Incorrect Acceptance				
	1%	5%	10%	15%	20%
0	4.61	3.00	2.31	1.90	1.61
1	6.64	4.75	3.89	3.38	3.00
2	8.41	6.30	5.33	4.72	4.28
3	10.05	7.76	6.69	6.02	5.52
4	11.61	9.16	8.00	7.27	6.73

Additional Information

Tolerable misstatements

 (net of effect of expected misstatements).. $ 24,000

Risk of incorrect acceptance 20%

Number of misstatements 1

Recorded amount of accounts receivable $240,000

Number of accounts 360

What sample size should Hill use?

    a.   120
    b.   108
    c.   60
    d.   30

35. In a probability-proportional-to-size
sample with a sampling interval of $10,000, an
auditor discovered that a selected account
receivable with a recorded amount of $5,000
had an audit amount of $2,000. The projected
error of this sample was

    a. $3,000
    b. $4,000
    c. $6,000
    d. $8,000

36. In the application of statistical techniques to the estimation of dollar amounts, a
preliminary sample is usually taken primarily
for the purpose of estimating the population

    a.   Variability.
    b.   Mode.
    c.   Range.
    d.   Median.

37. Using statistical sampling to assist in
verifying the year-end accounts payable
balance, an auditor has accumulated the
following data:

	Number of accounts	Book balance	Balance determined by the auditor
Population	4,100	$5,000,000	?
Sample	200	$ 250,000	$300,000

Using the ratio estimation technique, the
auditor's estimate of year-end accounts
payable balance would be

    a. $6,150,000
    b. $6,000,000
    c. $5,125,000
    d. $5,050,000

38. Use of the ratio estimation sampling
technique to estimated dollar amounts is
inappropriate when

    a.   The total book value is known and
          corresponds to the sum of all the
          individual book values.
    b.   A book value for each sample item is
          unknown.
    c.   There are some observed differences
          between audited values and book
          values.
    d.   The audited values are nearly
          proportional to the book values.

39. An auditor is performing substantive
tests of pricing and extensions of perpetual
inventory balances consisting of a large
number of items. Past experience indicates
numerous pricing and extension errors. Which
of the following statistical sampling
approaches is most appropriate?

    a.   Unstratified mean-per-unit.
    b.   Probability-proportional-to-size.
    c.   Stop or go.
    d.   Ratio estimation.

40. The major reason that the difference and
ratio estimation methods would be expected to
produce audit efficiency is that the

    a.   Number of members of the populations
          of differences or ratios is smaller
          than the number of members of the
          population of book values.
    b.   Beta risk may be completely ignored.
    c.   Calculations required in using
          difference or ratio estimation are
          less arduous and fewer than those
          required when using direct
          estimation.
    d.   Variability of the populations of
          differences or ratios is less than
          that of the populations of book
          values or audited values.

41. Which of the following statements is correct concerning the auditor's use of statistical sampling?
    a. An auditor needs to estimate the dollar amount of the standard deviation of the population to use classical variables sampling.
    b. An assumption of PPS sampling is that the underlying accounting population is normally distributed.
    c. A classical variables sample needs to be designed with special considerations to include negative balances in the sample.
    d. The selection of zero balances usually does **not** require special sample design considerations when using PPS sampling.

May 1990 Questions

42. The likelihood of assessing control risk too high is the risk that the sample selected to test controls
    a. Does **not** support the tolerable error for some or all of management's assertions.
    b. Does **not** support the auditor's planned assessed level of control risk when the true operating effectiveness of the control structure justifies such an assessment.
    c. Contains misstatements that could be material to the financial statements when aggregated with misstatements in other account balances or transaction classes.
    d. Contains proportionately fewer monetary errors or deviations from prescribed internal control structure policies or procedures than exist in the balance or class as a whole.

43. An auditor is testing internal control procedures that are evidenced on an entity's vouchers by matching random numbers with voucher numbers. If a random number matches the number of a voided voucher, that voucher ordinarily should be replaced by another voucher in the random sample if the voucher
    a. Constitutes a deviation.
    b. Has been properly voided.
    c. Cannot be located.
    d. Represents an immaterial dollar amount.

44. When planning a sample for a substantive test of details, an auditor should consider tolerable misstatement for the sample. This consideration should

    a. Be related to the auditor's business risk.
    b. Not be adjusted for qualitative factors.
    c. Be related to preliminary judgments about materiality levels.
    d. Not be changed during the audit process.

Repeat Question

(590,A1,44) Identical/similar to item 5 above

Problems

Problem 1   (1188,A3)

(15 to 25 minutes)

Sampling for attributes is often used to allow an auditor to reach a conclusion concerning a rate of occurrence in a population. A common use in auditing is to test the rate of deviation from a prescribed internal control procedure to determine whether planned assessed level of control risk is appropriate.

Required:

a. When an auditor samples for attributes, identify the factors that should influence the auditor's judgment concerning the determination of
1. Acceptable level of risk assessing control risk too low,
2. Tolerable deviation rate, and
3. Expected population deviation rate.

b. State the effect on sample size of an increase in each of the following factors, assuming all other factors are held constant:
1. Acceptable level of the risk of assessing control risk too low,
2. Tolerable deviation rate, and
3. Expected population deviation rate.

c. Evaluate the sample results of a test for attributes if authorizations are found to be missing on 7 check requests out of a sample of 100 tested. The population consists of 2500 check requests, the tolerable deviation rate is 8%, and the acceptable level of risk of assessing control risk too low is considered to be low.

d. How may the use of statistical sampling assist the auditor in evaluating the sample results described in c, above?

Problem 2   (1182,A2)

(15 to 25 minutes)

Jiblum, CPA, is planning to use attribute sampling in order to determine the degree of reliance to be placed on an audit client's system of internal control over sales. Jiblum has begun to develop an outline of the main steps in the sampling plan as follows:
1. State the objective(s) of the audit test (e.g., to test the reliability of internal controls over sales).

2. Define the population (define the period covered by the test; define the sampling unit, define the completeness of the population).
3. Define the sampling unit (e.g., client copies of sales invoices).

Required:

a. What are the remaining steps in the above outline which Jiblum should include in the statistical test of sales invoices? Do not present a detailed analysis of tasks which must be performed to carry out the objectives of each step. Parenthetical examples need not be provided.
b. How does statistical methodology help the auditor to develop a satisfactory sampling plan?

Problem 3   (585,A5)

(15 to 25 minutes)

One of the generally accepted auditing standards states that sufficient competent evidential matter is to be obtained through inspection, observation, inquiries, and confirmation to afford a reasonable basis for an opinion regarding the financial statements under examination. Some degree of uncertainty is implicit in the concept of "a reasonable basis for an opinion," because the concept of sampling is well established in auditing practice.

Required:

a. Explain the auditor's justification for accepting the uncertainties that are inherent in the sampling process.
b. Discuss the uncertainties which collectively embody the concept of audit risk.
c. Discuss the nature of the sampling risk and nonsampling risk. Include the effect of sampling risk on substantive tests of details and on tests of controls of internal control.

Problem 4   (586,A5)

(15 to 25 minutes)

Smith, CPA, has decided to rely on an audit client's internal controls affecting receivables. Smith plans to use sampling to obtain substantive evidence concerning the reasonableness of the client's accounts receivable balances. Smith has identified the first few steps in an outline of the sampling plan as follows.

1. Determine the audit objectives of the test.
2. Define the population.
3. Define the sampling unit.
4. Consider the completeness of the population.
5. Identify individually significant items.

Required:

Identify the remaining steps which Smith should include in the outline of the sampling plan. Illustrations and examples need not be provided.

Problem 5   (587,A3)

(15 to 25 minutes)

Edwards has decided to use Probability Proportional to Size (PPS) sampling, sometimes called dollar-unit sampling, in the audit of a client's accounts receivable balance. Few, if any, misstatements of account balance overstatement are expected.

Edwards plans to use the following PPS sampling table:

TABLE
Reliability Factors for Overstatements

Number of Overstatements	Risk of Incorrect Acceptance				
	1%	5%	10%	15%	20%
0	4.61	3.00	2.31	1.90	1.61
1	6.64	4.75	3.89	3.38	3.00
2	8.41	6.30	5.33	4.72	4.28
3	10.05	7.76	6.69	6.02	5.52
4	11.61	9.16	8.00	7.27	6.73

Required:

a. Identify the advantages of using PPS sampling over classical variables sampling.

Note: Requirements b and c are not related.

b. Calculate the sampling interval and the sample size Edwards should use given the following information:

Tolerable misstatements................$15,000
Risk of incorrect acceptance.................5%
Number of misstatements allowed..............0
Recorded amount of
  accounts receivable..................$300,000

Note: Requirements b and c are not related.

c. Calculate the total projected misstatement if the following three misstatements were discovered in a PPS sample:

	Recorded Amount	Audit Amount	Sampling Interval
1st misstatement	$ 400	$ 320	$1,000
2nd misstatement	500	0	1,000
3rd misstatement	3,000	2,500	1,000

Multiple Choice Answers

1. c	10. a	19. b	28. a	37. b
2. a	11. b	20. d	29. c	38. b
3. b	12. b	21. b	30. c	39. d
4. a	13. c	22. d	31. d	40. d
5. d	14. d	23. d	32. c	41. a
6. a	15. c	24. a	33. a	42. b
7. c	16. c	25. c	34. d	43. b
8. a	17. a	26. b	35. c	44. c
9. d	18. d	27. d	36. a	

Multiple Choice Answer Explanations

A. Basic Audit Sampling Concepts
A.1. Definition of Sampling

1.   (585,A1,23) (c) The requirement is to determine the correct statement with respect to random sampling. Answer (c) is correct because every item in the accounting population should have an opportunity to be selected. The 1983 AICPA Audit Sampling Guide discusses random sampling in detail. Answer (a) is incorrect because with stratified random sampling, each stratum need not be given equal representation. Answer (b) is incorrect because while sample units should be randomly selected, there is no requirement that the accounting population be randomly ordered. Answer (d) is incorrect because random sampling, by its very nature, is not systematic. Additionally, random sampling may be performed without replacement.

A.2. General Approaches to Audit Sampling—Nonstatistical and Statistical

2.   (581,A1,11) (a) The requirement is to determine an advantage of statistical sampling. The distinguishing feature of statistical sampling is that it provides a means for measuring mathematically the degree of uncertainty that results from examining only a part of the data (AU 350.45). Answer (b) is incorrect since statistical sampling still requires the auditor to make judgmental decisions (e.g., set appropriate precision and reliability levels). While answer (c) is a correct statement insofar as it relates to auditor responsibility, it cannot be considered an advantage of statistical sampling. The courts have not definitely ruled on the merits of statistical vs. judgmental sampling; thus, answer (d) is incorrect.

A.3. Uncertainty and Audit Sampling

3.   (1183,A1,7) (b) The requirement is to determine an element of sampling risk. Sampling risk arises from the possibility that, when a test of control or a substantive test is restricted to a sample, the auditor's conclusions may be different from the con-

clusions s/he would reach if the test were applied in the same way to all items in the account balance or class of transactions (AU 350.10). For example, the items in the selected sample might not disclose an error. Answers (a), (c), and (d) are all incorrect because they represent nonsampling risk examples which are unrelated to the mathematics of the sampling process (AU 350.11).

4.   (583,A1,6) (a) The requirement is to determine which answer represents the concept of sampling risk. Sampling risk arises from the possibility that an auditor's conclusions based upon a sample would differ from the conclusions which would be drawn from examining the entire population, i.e., the risk that the sample examined is not representative of the population. Answers (b), (c), and (d) are all incorrect because they relate to errors which could occur even if 100% of the population were examined, i.e., nonsampling risk (see AU 350.11 for a discussion of nonsampling risk).

5.   (1187,A1,59) (d) The requirement is to determine the nature of the risk of incorrect acceptance and the risk of assessing control risk too low for internal control. Answer (d) is correct because the risks of incorrect acceptance and assessing control risk too low relate to the effectiveness of an audit in detecting an existing material misstatement (AU 350.14). Answer (a) is incorrect because preliminary estimates of materiality levels relate most directly to the risk of incorrect acceptance, and only indirectly to the risk of assessing control risk too low. The answer is thus less accurate than answer (d). Answer (b) is incorrect because the term allowable risk of tolerable misstatement is ambiguous, and not used in the profesional literature. Answer (c) is incorrect because the risk of incorrect rejection and the risk of assessing control risk too high relate to the efficiency of the audit (AU 350.13).

6.   (1184,A1,32) (a) The requirement is to determine what is related to the risk of incorrect rejection and the risk of assessing control risk too high. Answer (a) is correct because AU 350.13 states that the risk of incorrect rejection and the risk of assessing control risk too high relate to the efficiency of the audit. These two errors generally result in an auditor performing unnecessary additional procedures. Answer (b) is incorrect because the risk of incorrect acceptance and the risk of assessing control risk too low relate to the effectiveness of an audit (AU 350.14). Answer (c) is incorrect because the risks do not relate directly to the actual selection of the sample. Answer (d) is

incorrect because the audit quality controls do not directly mention either of these risks.

7.   (1181,A1,12) (c) The requirement is to determine the least desirable statistical selection technique. Answer (c), block selection, is correct because, ideally, a sample should be selected from the entire set of data to which the resulting conclusions are to be applied. When block sampling is used the selection of blocks often precludes items from being so selected. In most cases, systematic [answer (a)], stratified [answer (b)], and sequential [answer (d)] selection techniques all provide a better representation of the entire population than does block selection.

A.4. Categories of Audit Tests in Which Sampling May Be Used

8.   (1185,A1,48) (a) The requirement is to identify the correct statement with respect to the size of a sample required for dual purpose testing. Answer (a) is correct because the auditor should select the larger of the required sample sizes (AU 350.43). Therefore, answers (b), (c), and (d) are incorrect.

A.5. Categories of Statistical Sampling Plans

9.   (1187,A1,58) (d) The requirement is to identify the type of sampling involved in a review of client invoices in which an expected population deviation rate and an established tolerable rate are provided. Both AU 350 and Audit Sampling (AICPA, 1983) provide information on sampling. Answer (d) is correct because attribute sampling is used to reach a conclusion about a population in terms of a rate of occurrence (see Audit Sampling, pages 15-16). Answer (a) is incorrect because stratified sampling is generally used to reach a dollar based conclusion in variables sampling approaches. Answer (b) is incorrect because, as indicated, variables sampling deals with a dollar amount conclusion, not deviation rates. Answer (c) is incorrect because discovery sampling is only used in cases in which the auditor expects deviation rates to be extremely low (approaching zero).

10. (1189,A1,34) (a) The requirement is to determine the type of sampling to be used when estimating a numerical measurement of a population. Answer (a) is correct because variables sampling is used if the auditor wishes to reach a conclusion about a population in terms of a dollar amount (Audit and Accounting Guide Audit Sampling, p. 16). Answer (b) is incorrect because attributes sampling is used to reach a conclusion about a

population in terms of a rate of occurrence. Answer (c) is incorrect because discovery sampling is used to determine the sample size required to have a stipulated probability of observing at least one occurrence in a population. Answer (d) is incorrect because numerical sampling is a nonsensical answer.

B. Sampling in Tests of Controls
B.1. Overall Issues
B.1.a. Attribute Sample Selection Technique

11. (588,A1,18) (b) The requirement is to identify the type of sampling plan that does not use a fixed sample size for tests of controls. Answer (b) is correct because sequential sampling results in the selection of a sample in several steps, with each step conditional on the result of the previous steps. Therefore, sample size will vary depending upon the number of stages that prove necessary. Answers (a), (c), and (d) are all incorrect because dollar-unit sampling, PPS sampling, and variables sampling all use a fixed sample size.

12. (580,A1,5) (b) The requirement is the correct statement concerning a statistical sampling application where the population consists of forms which are not consecutively numbered. Answer (b) is correct because it is not incorrect, i.e., all the other answers are incorrect. Systematic sampling is a procedure where a random start is obtained and then every n^{th} item is selected. For example, a sample of forty from a population of a thousand would require selecting every 25th item after obtaining a random start between items 1 through 25. Answer (a) is incorrect because selection of a random sample is possible even though the population is not consecutively numbered. Answer (c) is incorrect because there is no special reason for using stratified sampling. Stratified sampling breaks down the population into subpopulations and applies different selection methods to each subpopulation. This selection method is used when the population consists of different types of items, e.g., large balances and small balances. Answer (d) is incorrect because random number tables can be used even though the forms are not consecutively numbered. If random numbers are selected for which there are no forms, they are ignored. This is the same as if there were 86,000 items in a consecutively numbered population and random numbers selected between 86,000 and 99,999 are ignored.

13. (588,A1,19) (c) The requirement is to determine the factor an auditor generally needs to consider in planning a particular audit sample for a test of a control. Answer (c) is correct because attribute sampling formulas and tables used in auditing generally require the auditor to specify an acceptable level of the risk of assessing control risk too low. Answer (a), while partially correct, is not the best answer because the number of items in the population only affects sample size to a small extent. Answer (b) is incorrect because the dollar amount of items to be sampled is not considered in most tests of controls. Answer (d) is incorrect because tolerable misstatement is used for substantive tests, not for tests of controls.

14. (1186,A1,20) `(d) Answer (d) is correct because systematic items occurrence in a population **may** destroy a sample's randomness. Answer (a) is incorrect because items need not be replaced in the population, and therefore is not a disadvantage of systematic sampling. Answer (b) is incorrect because an individual item will not occur more than once in a sample when systematic sampling is being used (because the auditor selects every n^{th} item). Answer (c) is incorrect because systematic sampling refers to the type of sampling selection plan used and not the manner in which items in the population are recorded. Also, as indicated in (d) above, a systematic pattern in the population is a hinderance to systematic sampling.

15. (1189,A1,52) (c) The requirement is to determine when a sample size would be decreased when sampling for attributes. Answer (c) is correct because the sample size will decrease when the risk of assessing control risk too low is increased, the tolerable rate is increased, and the expected population deviation rate is decreased. See the Audit and Accounting Guide Audit Sampling (p. 105) for a discussion of how these factors affect sample size. Answers (a), (b), and (d) are all incorrect because they include combinations of changes that would not necessarily decrease sample size.

B.1.b. Attribute Sampling Evaluation Techniques

16. (586,A1,13) (c) The requirement is to determine the proper method of handling a sample item which cannot be located for evaluation purposes. Answer (c) is correct because an auditor would ordinarily consider the selected item to be a deviation (AU 350.39). Answers (a) and (d) are incorrect since a possible cause for the missing purchase order could be a breakdown in one of the controls of the system. Thus, in selecting a new sample item(s) the auditor may be ignoring a portion of the population which is in error and may be artificially skewing the results of the tests performed on the sample. Answer (b) is incorrect because there is no reason to believe that the entire test is invalid and cannot be relied upon.

17. (1187,A1,57) (a) The requirement is to determine why deviations from control procedures do not necessarily result in errors. Answer (a) is correct because it provides an example of a situation in which a deviation from a control procedure exists (lack of documentation of transaction approval), although the entry was authorized and proper. Thus, such a deviation does not necessarily result in an error in the financial statements (AU 350.34). Answer (b) is incorrect because a deviation from control procedure and an error may occur in the same transaction. Answer (c) is incorrect since the fact that all deviations do not lead to errors will result in a lower error rate. Answer (d) is incorrect because while it represents a correct statement, it does not follow from the point of the question which is based on the idea that deviations do not directly result in errors.

18. (1185,A1,38) (d) The requirement is to determine the situation in which an auditor has properly concluded that control risk is at or below the planned assessed level. Answer (d) is correct because to support the planned level, the deviation rate must be less than the tolerable rate and the auditor must conclude that the deviation rate is less than the tolerable rate (AU 350.12-.14). Answer (a) is incorrect because it represents a situation in which the auditor appropriately decides that the deviation rate exceeds the tolerable rate. Answer (b) is incorrect because it represents a situation in which an auditor erroneously concludes that the deviation rate exceeds the tolerable rate when it actually does not. Answer (c) is incorrect because the auditor erroneously concludes that the deviation rate is less than the tolerable rate when it actually exceeds it.

19. (1185,A1,39) (b) The requirement is to determine the situation in which the auditor assesses control risk too high and thereby increases substantive testing. Answer (b) is correct because to assess control risk too high, an auditor must estimate that the deviation rate exceeds the tolerable rate when it actually is less than the tolerable rate

(AU 350.12). Answer (a) is incorrect because it represents a situation in which the auditor appropriately decides that the deviation rate exceeds the tolerable rate. Answer (c) is incorrect because the auditor erroneously concludes that the deviation rate is less than the tolerable rate when it actually exceeds the tolerable rate. Answer (d) is incorrect because to properly rely on internal control, the deviation rate must be less than the tolerable rate and the auditor must conclude that the deviation rate is less than the tolerable rate (AU 350.12-.14).

20. (581,A1,60) (d) The requirement is to determine the objective of the tolerable rate in sampling. Tolerable rate is calculated to determine the range of procedural deviations in the population (AU 350.33). Answer (a) is incorrect because probabilities relate more directly to reliability. Answer (b) is incorrect because errors on financial statements in materiality terms relate to variables sampling. Answer (c) is incorrect because the tolerable rate does not relate directly to substantive tests.

21. (583,A1,2) (b) The requirement is to determine the correct relationship between the tolerable rate of deviations and the expected rate of deviations for a test of a control. The tolerable rate of deviations is the maximum rate of deviations from a prescribed control procedure that an auditor would be willing to accept and, unless the expected error rate is lower, reliance on internal control is not justified. Answer (a) is incorrect because if the tolerable rate of deviations is less than the expected rate, the auditor would not plan to rely on internal control and would therefore omit tests of controls. Answer (c) is incorrect because testing of controls is inappropriate if the expected rate of errors equals the tolerable rate of deviations (mathematically, the precision of zero makes the sample size equal to population size). Answer (d) is incorrect because, as indicated above, to perform tests of controls one must assume that the tolerable rate of deviations is more than the expected error rate.

22. (589,A1,8) (d) The requirement is to identify the relationship between the true deviation rate in a population, the deviation rate in an auditor's sample, and the risk of assessing control risk too low. Answer (d) is correct because when the auditor's sample deviation rate is lower than that of the population, the auditor may erroneously assess control risk too low (AU 350.12-.14, .39-.42).

This is because the low deviation rate in the sample may mislead the auditor into believing that a similarly low deviation rate exists in the population. Answers (a) and (c) are incorrect because there is no relationship between the true deviation in the population and the risk of assessing control risk too low. Thus, for example, the true deviation rate may be 10%, while the risk of assessing control risk too low based upon a sample may be at either a higher or lower level. Answer (b) is incorrect because the auditor may assess control risk too high when the deviation rate in the population is less than the deviation rate in the auditor's sample (AU 350.12). Also see the Audit and Accounting Guide, Audit Sampling for additional sampling information.

B.1.c. Other Attribute Sampling Over all Issues

23. (1189,A1,54) (d) The requirement is to identify for which item statistical sampling methods provide a scientific basis. Answer (d) is correct because when using statistical sampling, the auditor calculates the sample size using objectively verifiable formulas or tables. Accordingly, statistical methods provide a scientific basis for the sample size. Answers (a), (b), and (c) are incorrect because the risk of assessing control risk too low, the tolerable rate, and the expected population deviation rate are all established judgmentally by the auditor in order to calculate the sample size.

B.2. Statistical Sampling in Tests of Controls

24. (588,A1,32) (a) The requirement is to identify the correct statement concerning statistical sampling for tests of controls. Answer (a) is correct because population size has little or no effect on sample size. Answer (b) is incorrect because the population deviation rate has a significant effect on sample size. Answer (c) is incorrect because sample size increases to a much lesser extent than doubling as the population size doubles. Answer (d) is incorrect because for a given tolerable rate, a smaller, and not a larger, sample size should be selected as the expected population deviation rate decreases.

25. (589,A1,23) (c) The requirement is to determine the situation that will cause an auditor who uses statistical sampling for attributes to increase the assessed level of control risk. Answer (c) is correct because when the sample rate of deviation plus the allowance for sampling risk exceeds the tolerable rate, the auditor has achieved a higher level of control risk than designed in

the sample. Accordingly, the assessment of control risk on a prescribed procedure must be increased. Answer (a) is incorrect because when the sample rate of deviation is less than expected in a statistical sample, the auditor will not need to increase the assessed level of control risk. Answer (b) is incorrect because when the tolerable rate less the allowance for sampling risk exceeds the sample rate of deviation, the auditor need not increase assessed control risk. This will occur when the sample rate of deviation is less than expected in planning the sample. Answer (d) is incorrect because when the sample rate of deviation plus the allowance for sampling risk equals the tolerable rate, the risk of assessing control risk too low is at its planned level. Thus, no adjustment of the assessed level of control risk is necessary. For more information on sampling see the Audit and Accounting Guide, **Audit Sampling**.

26. (1189,A1,53) (b) The requirement is to determine the appropriate decision concerning evaluation of the results of a statistical sample. Answer (b) is correct because when an auditor is evaluating the results of a statistical sample, s/he needs to consider both the sample deviation rate and the allowance for sampling risk. The sample deviation rate in this case is 4% (4 deviations/100 documents) and the allowance for sampling risk is 2%. Since the total of these two items (6%) exceeds the tolerable rate (5%), the assessed control risk must be increased (i.e., the planned reliance on the control must be modified). Answers (a) and (d) are incorrect because the auditor would not accept the sample results. Answer (c) is incorrect because the sample deviation rate and the allowance for sampling risk should be compared to the tolerable rate. The tolerable rate and the allowance for sampling risk should not be compared to the expected population deviation rate.

27. (586,A1,30) (d) The requirement is to determine the most useful sampling method when testing control operating effectiveness. When testing controls, auditors most frequently use attribute sampling. Answer (d) is correct because discovery sampling is a form of attribute sampling. Answers (a), (b), and (c) are incorrect because ratio estimation [answer (a)] and difference estimation [answer (c)] are forms of variable sampling [answer (b)] and are used primarily for substantive tests.

28. (583,A1,5) (a) The requirement is to determine the type of sampling which is most directly related to finding at least one exception. Discovery sample sizes and related discovery sampling tables are constructed to measure the probability of at least one error occurring in a sample if the error rate in the population exceeds the tolerable rate. Answer (b) is incorrect because variables sampling need not include at least one exception (mean per unit sampling, for example, needs no errors). Answer (c) is incorrect since random sampling only deals with the technique used to select items to be included in the sample. Answer (d) is incorrect because dollar-unit sampling results are not directly related to finding at least one exception.

C. Sampling Substantive Tests of Details

C.1. Overall

29. (502,A1,2) (a) The requirement is to determine the effect on sample size of a change from unrestricted random sampling with replacement to unrestricted random sampling without replacement. When sampling without replacement, a finite correction factor will be used which will decrease sample size. Answers (a) and (b) are therefore incorrect. Answer (d) is incorrect because a binomial distribution will not generally be used.

30. (575,A1,18) (c) Stratified sampling is a technique of breaking the population down into subpopulations and applying different sample selection methods to the subpopulations. Stratified sampling is used to minimize the variance within the overall population [answer (c)]. Recall that as variance increases, so does the required sample size (because of the extreme values). Thus, stratification allows the selection of subpopulations to reduce the effect of dispersion in the population. Accordingly, answers (a), (b), and (d) are incorrect.

31. (588,A1,33) (d) The requirement is to determine the factor that would lead to larger sample size in a substantive test of details. Answer (d) is correct because the sample size required to achieve the auditor's objective at a given risk of incorrect acceptance increases as the auditor's assessment of tolerable misstatement for the balance or class decreases (AU 350.47). Answer (a) is incorrect because a greater reliance on internal controls will lead to smaller sample size in a substantive test of details (AU 350.47). Answer (b) is incorrect because greater reliance upon analytical procedures will result in a need for less reliance on substantive tests of details and therefore will result in a smaller

sample (AU 350.47). Answer (c) is incorrect because a smaller expected frequency of errors will generally include properly functioning internal controls and will therefore result in a smaller sample for substantive tests of details (AU 350.47).

32. (1185,A1,29) (c) The requirement is to identify the factor which must be known in order to estimate the appropriate sample size when using variables sampling. Answer (c) is correct because the auditor must set an acceptable level of risk for both variables sampling and attribute sampling (AU 350.16). Answer (a) is incorrect because while the auditor will consider the qualitative aspects of errors when evaluating the sample, they need not be considered in determining an appropriate sample size. Answer (b) is incorrect because a primary objective of variables sampling is to estimate the audited dollar amount of the population. Also, in some forms of variables sampling, knowledge of book values is not necessary (e.g., mean per unit). Answer (d) is incorrect because a rate of error in the population relates to attribute sampling.

33. (1189,A1,33) (a) The requirement is to determine the type of risk demonstrated by concluding an account balance was misstated when in fact it was not. Answer (a) is correct because the risk of incorrect rejection is the risk that the sample supports the conclusion that the recorded account balance is materially misstated when it is not misstated (AU 350.12). Answer (b) is incorrect because the risk of incorrect acceptance is the risk that the sample supports the conclusion that the account is not misstated when it is misstated. Answers (c) and (d) are incorrect because the risk of assessing control risk too low (overreliance) and the risk of assessing control risk too high (underreliance) relate to tests of controls and not to substantive tests of details.

C.2. Probability-Proportional-to-Size (PPS) Sampling

34. (1187,A1,38) (d) The requirement is to determine the sample size that should be used in a probability-proportional-to-size (PPS) sample. Information on PPS sampling is presented in Audit Sampling (an audit and accounting guide published by the AICPA in 1983) as well as in a variety of texts, articles, and other sources. These references present a number of ways to calculate a PPS sample size. The sampling guide presents one in which a sampling interval is first calculated and used to determine an appropriate sample

size (see page 84 of the Guide for an example). Using that approach, when provided with the tolerable misstatement already adjusted for expected misstatements (as is the situation in this problem), one divides that total by the number of expected misstatements column for the appropriate risk of incorrect acceptance (the fact that some overstatements are expected is not used). Here that computation is $24,000/1.61 = $14906.83. Sample size is computed by dividing the recorded amount by the sampling interval, here $240,000/14906.83, for a sample size of 16. An alternate approach is to use the reliability factor for the expected number of overstatements. In that case the computations become $24,000/3.00 = $8,000. Sample size is $240,000/$8,000 = 30. In either case answer (d) is the closest and therefore the correct reply. Answers (a), (b), and (c) are incorrect because they all represent incorrect sample sizes.

35. (589,A1,40) (c) The requirement is to determine the projected error of a PPS sample with a sampling interval of $10,000 when an auditor has discovered an account receivable with a recorded amount of $5,000 and an audit amount of $2,000. The Audit and Accounting Guide, Audit Sampling provides guidance on calculating projected error (see page 85 of Audit Sampling). For accounts with a book value less than the sampling interval, one must first calculate a tainting percentage which is equal to: (Recorded amount – Audit amount)/Recorded amount. The tainting percentage is multiplied by the sampling interval to determine projected error. In this question the tainting percentage is 60% [($5,000 – $2,000)/$5,000]. The projected error is calculated as 60% times the sampling interval, or .60 x $10,000 = $6,000. Therefore, answer (c) is correct.

C.3. Classical Variables Sampling

36. (1183,A1,13) (a) The requirement is to determine the purpose of taking a preliminary sample when one uses statistical techniques. It is necessary to obtain an estimate of a population's standard deviation (variability) when calculating the required sample size and when using sampling techniques. Answers (b), (c), and (d) are incorrect because, in most statistical techniques used by auditors, the mode (most frequent balance), the median (middle balance) and the range (difference between the highest and lowest values) are not used.

37. (1184,A1,14) (b) The requirement is to determine the estimated audited accounts payable balance using the ratio estimation tech-

nique. Answer (b) is correct because the
ratio estimation technique estimates the
audited value by multiplying the audited
value/book value of the sample times the population book value. In this case,
($300,000/$250,000) x $5,000,000 = $6,000,000.

38. (1180,A1,41) (b) The ratio estimation
sampling technique is based on comparing the
ratio of the book value to the audited value
of the sampled items. Answer (b) is correct
because this method cannot be used when there
is no book value to make the comparison. The
circumstances described in answers (a) and (c)
are necessary for ratio point and interval
estimation. Answer (d) describes the circumstances in which the use of ratio estimation
will be efficient in terms of required sample
size.

39. (589,A1,41) (d) The requirement is to
determine the most appropriate sampling approach for substantive tests of pricing and
extensions of perpetual inventory balances
consisting of a large number of items for
which past experience indicates numerous expected pricing and extension errors. Answer (d) is correct because ratio estimation
is appropriate when testing a population for
which a large number of errors of this nature
is expected. Answer (a) is incorrect because
the unstratified mean-per-unit method will
typically provide a larger sample size than
the ratio estimation method to achieve the
same level of sampling risk. Thus, the ratio
estimation method would be more appropriate.
Answer (b) is incorrect because probability-
proportional-to-size sampling is most efficient for testing populations with relatively
low expected error rates. Answer (c) is
incorrect because "stop or go" or "sequential"
sampling is most frequently used in attribute
sampling. See the Audit and Accounting Guide,
Audit Sampling (pp. 88-90) for additional
sampling information.

40. (580,A1,43) (d) Difference and ratio
estimation methods are statistical sampling
methods. They measure the difference between
audit and book values or the ratio of audit to
book values. As these differences should not
be great, the population of these differences
will have little variance. In statistical
sampling the less variation in a population,
the smaller the required sample to provide an
estimate of the population. In other words,
difference and ratio estimation methods are
more efficient because the differences between
audit and book values are expected to vary
less than the actual items in the population.
Answer (a) is incorrect because the number of
members in the population for differences or
ratio methods would be the same as the number

of items in the population for a direct
estimation method. In difference sampling,
many items would be zero because audit and
book are the same, and in ratio sampling, many
of the members would be 1 for the same reason.
Answer (b) is incorrect because beta risk can
never be ignored, as beta risk is the risk of
accepting an incorrect (unacceptable) population. Answer (c) is incorrect because the
calculations required in difference and ratio
sampling are similar to those used in direct
estimation sampling.

C.4. Comparison of PPS Sampling to Classical Variables Sampling

41. (588,A1,34) (a) The requirement is to
identify the correct statement concerning the
auditor's use of statistical sampling. Answer (a) is correct because an estimate of the
variation of the population, the standard
deviation, is needed to use classical variables sampling (see Audit Sampling, an AICPA
Audit and Accounting Guide, pages 45-47). Answer (b) is incorrect because PPS sampling
does not make an assumption that the underlying population is normally distributed.
Answers (c) and (d) are incorrect because
classical variables sample selected accounts
and therefore need not include special
considerations to those with a negative
balance.

May 1990 Answers

42. (590,A1,42) (b) The requirement is to
determine the meaning of the likelihood of
assessing control risk too high. Answer (b)
is correct because the risk of assessing control risk too high is the risk that the assessed level of control risk based on the sample
is greater than the true operating effectiveness of the control. Accordingly, the risk of
assessing control risk too high is the risk
that the sample results do not support the
auditor's planned assessed level of control
risk when the control does justify such an
assessment. Answers (a), (c), and (d) are all
incorrect because the concepts of tolerable
error (now tolerable misstatement), material
misstatements, and monetary errors relate to
substantive tests and variables sampling, not
to tests of controls.

43. (590,A1,43) (b) The requirement is to
identify the correct statement with respect to
treatment of a voided voucher that has been
selected in a sample. Answer (b) is correct
because the AICPA Audit Sampling Guide (p. 36)
states that the auditor should obtain
reasonable assurance that the voucher has been
properly voided, and should then replace it
with another voucher. Answer (a) is incorrect

because the voided voucher is not normally
considered to be a deviation. Answer (c) is
incorrect because the auditor must obtain
reasonable assurance that the misplaced
voucher has been voided. Answer (d) is
incorrect because the level of materiality
normally does not directly affect the
decision.

44. (590,A1,51) (c) The requirement is to
determine the correct statement concerning the
auditor's consideration of tolerable misstatement. Answer (c) is correct because the consideration of tolerable misstatement is
related to preliminary judgments in a manner
such that when the auditor's preliminary judgments about tolerable misstatement levels for
accounts or transaction types are combined for
the entire audit plan, the preliminary judgments about materiality levels for the financial statements are not exceeded (AU 350.18).
Answer (a) is incorrect because the auditor's
judgment of business risk related to a client
is not directly related to tolerable misstatement. Answer (b) is incorrect because tolerable misstatement may be adjusted for qualitative factors. Answer (d) is incorrect because
tolerable misstatement may be changed during
the audit process, especially as misstatements
are identified and the auditor considers the
nature of the misstatements.

Unofficial Answer*

Problem 1   Attribute Sampling (1188,A3)

a. 1. In determining an acceptable level of the risk of assessing control risk too low, an auditor should consider the importance of the control to be tested in determining the extent to which substantive tests will be restricted and the planned assessed level of control risk.

2. In determining the tolerable deviation rate, an auditor should consider the planned assessed level of control risk and how materially the financial statements would be affected if the control does not function properly. For example, how likely is the control to prevent or detect material errors.

3. In determining the expected population deviation rate, an auditor should consider the results of prior years' tests, the overall control environment, or utilize a preliminary sample.

b. 1. There is a decrease in sample size if the acceptable level of the risk of assessing control risk too low is increased.

2. There is a decrease in sample size if the tolerable deviation rate is increased.

3. There is an increase in sample size if the population deviation rate is increased.

c. For a low risk of assessing control risk too low it is generally appropriate to reconsider the planned risk as the calculated estimate of the population deviation rate identified in the sample (7%) approaches the tolerable deviation rate (8%). This is because there may be an unacceptably high sampling risk that these sample results could have occurred with an actual population deviation rate higher than the tolerable deviation rate.

d. If statistical sampling is used, an allowance for sampling risk can be calculated. If the calculated estimate of the population deviation rate plus the allowance for sampling risk is greater than the tolerable deviation rate, the sample results should be interpreted as not supporting the planned level of assessed control risk.

Unofficial Answer*

Problem 2   Steps in a Test of Controls
             Sampling Plan (1182,A2)

a.   The remaining steps are as follows:

4. Define the attributes (characteristics) of interest to be tested (including the criteria for establishing the existence of errors or deviant conditions).
5. Set the maximum rate of deviations from a prescribed control procedure that would support the planned reliance on the control (tolerable rate).
6. Select a risk of assessing control risk too low (overreliance).
7. Estimate the population error rate (deviation rate).
8. Determine the sample size.
9. Choose a method for randomly selecting a sample.
10. Perform the tests of controls
11. Perform misstatement analysis (calculate the deviation rate and consider the qualitative aspects of the deviations).
12. Interpret sample results (calculate a population deviation rate).
13. Decide on the acceptability of the results of the sample.

b.   Statistical sampling methodology helps the auditor (a) to design an efficient sample, (b) to measure the sufficiency of the evidential matter obtained, and (c) to evaluate the sample results. By using a statistical sampling methodology the auditor can quantify sampling risk to assist in limiting it to an acceptable level.

Answer Outline

Problem 3   Basic Concepts (585,A5)

a. Justification for accepting sampling uncertainties
    Costs Benefits of 100% examination
    Need for timely audit report precludes 100% examination

---

*Because the requirements of this question could be answered by lists of items, we have not included an outline of the solution.

b. Ultimate audit risk
    Definition: risk of failing to find
    monetary errors that exceed toler-
    able error in account balance or
    class of transactions
    Combination of three types of risks
    •   Inherent risk: risk that errors
        will occur in accounting system
    •   Control risk: risk that material
        errors won't be detected by
        internal control
    •   Detection risk: risk that material
        errors won't be detected by the
        auditor
    Includes sampling and nonsampling
    risk
c. Nature of sampling risk
    Conclusions drawn from sample might
    differ from those reached as
    result of examining entire popu-
    lation
    Nature of nonsampling risk
    Includes all aspects of ultimate risk
    not due to sampling
    •   Selection of audit procedures
        inappropriate for specific
        objective
    •   Failure to recognize errors in
        items sampled
    Effect of sampling risk on substantive
    tests
    •   Risk of incorrect acceptance:
        concludes balance is not
        materially misstated when it is
    •   Risk of incorrect rejection:
        concludes balance is materially
        misstated when it isn't
    Effect of sampling risk on test of
    control (IC)
    •   Risk of assessing control risk too
        low (overreliance): risk that
        sample supports reliance on IC when
        it should not
    •   Risk of assessing control risk to
        high (underreliance): risk that
        sample does not support reliance on
        IC when it should
    Relationship of sampling and nonsampling
    risk on effectiveness and efficiency of
    audit

Effectiveness impacted by	Efficiency impacted by
• Risk of incorrect acceptance	• Risk of incorrect rejection
• Risk of assessing control risk too low (overreliance)	• Risk of assessing control risk too high (underreliance)

Unofficial Answer

Problem 3   Basic Concepts (585,A5)

a. The auditor's justification for accepting
the uncertainties that are inherent in the
sampling process are based upon the premise
that the
    •   Cost of examining all of the financial
data would usually outweigh the benefit of the
added reliability of a complete (100%) examination.
    •   Time required to examine all of the
financial data would usually preclude issuance
of a timely auditor's report.

b. The uncertainties inherent in applying
auditing procedures are collectively referred
to as audit risk. Audit risk, with respect to
a particular account balance or class of
transactions, is the risk that there is a
monetary error greater than tolerable
misstatement in the balance or class that the
auditor fails to detect. Audit risk is a
combination of three types of risks as
follows:
    •   Inherent risk is the risk that mis-
statements will occur in the accounting
system.
    •   Control risk is the risk that material
misstatements will not be detected by the
client's structure of internal control.
    •   Detection risk is the risk that any
material misstatements that occur will not be
detected by the auditor.

    Audit risk includes both uncertainties due
to sampling and uncertainties due to factors
other than sampling. These aspects of audit
risk are referred to as sampling risk and nonsampling risk, respectively.

c. Sampling risk arises from the possibility
that, when a test of control or a substantive
test is restricted to a sample, the auditor's
conclusions may be different from the conclusions that might be reached if the test
were applied in the same way to all items in
the account balance or class of transactions. That is, a particular sample may
contain proportionately more or less monetary
errors or compliance deviations than exist in
the balance or class as a whole.
    Nonsampling risk includes all the aspects
of audit risk that are not due to sampling.
An auditor may apply a procedure to all
transactions or balances and still fail to
detect a material misstatement or an internal
control reportable condition. Nonsampling
risk includes the possibility of selecting
audit procedures that are not appropriate to
achieve the specific objective, or failing to

recognize misstatements in documents examined, which would render the procedure ineffective even if all items were examined.

The auditor should apply professional judgment in assessing sampling risk. In performing substantive tests of details the auditor is concerned with two aspects of sampling risk:

• **The risk of incorrect acceptance** is the risk that the sample supports the conclusion that the recorded account balance is not materially misstated when it is materially misstated.

• **The risk of incorrect rejection** is the risk that the sample supports the conclusion that the recorded account balance is materially misstated when it is not materially misstated.

The auditor is also concerned with two aspects of sampling risk in performing tests of controls:

• **The risk of assessing control risk too low (overreliance)** on internal control is the risk that the sample supports the auditor's planned level of assessed control risk when the true compliance rate does not justify such reliance.

• **The risk of assessing control risk too high (underreliance)** on internal control is the risk that the sample does not support the auditor's planned level of assessed control risk when the true compliance rate supports such reliance.

The risk of incorrect acceptance and the risk of assessing control risk too low, relate to the effectiveness of an audit in detecting an existing material misstatement. The risk of incorrect rejection and the risk of assessing control risk too high (underreliance) relate to the efficiency of the audit.

Unofficial Answer*

Problem 4   Steps in a Substantive Sampling
             Plan (586,A5)

The remaining steps are as follows:

6. Treat the individually significant items as a separate population.

7. Choose an audit sampling technique.

8. Determine the sample size, giving consideration for

a. Variations within the population.
b. Acceptable level of risk.
c. Tolerable misstatement.
d. Expected amount of misstatement.
e. Population size.

9. Determine the method of selecting a representative sample.

10. Select the sample items.

11. Apply appropriate audit procedures to the sample items.

12. Evaluate the sample results.

a. Project the misstatement to the population and consider sampling risk.

b. Consider the qualitative aspects of misstatements and reach an overall conclusion.

13. Document the sampling procedure.

Unofficial Answer*

Problem 5   PPS Problem (587,A3)

a. The advantages of PPS sampling over classical variables sampling are as follows:

• PPS sampling is generally easier to use than classical variables sampling.
• Size of a PPS sample is not based on the estimated variation of audited amounts.
• PPS sampling automatically results in a stratified sample.
• Individually significant items are automatically identified.
• If no misstatements are expected, PPS sampling will usually result in a smaller sample size than classical variables sampling.
• A PPS sample can be easily designed and sample selection can begin before the complete population is available.

b.

$$\text{Sampling Interval} = \frac{\text{Tolerable Misstatements}}{\text{Reliability Factor for Overstatements}}$$

$$= \frac{\$15,000}{\$3.000}$$

$$= \$5,000$$

$$\text{Sample Size} = \frac{\text{Recorded Amount}}{\text{Sampling Interval}}$$

$$= \frac{\$300,000}{\$5,000}$$

$$= 60$$

*Because the requirements of this question could be answered by lists of items, we have not included an outline of the solution.

c.

	Recorded Amount	Audit Amount	Tainting	Sampling Interval	Projected Misstatements
1st misstatement	$ 400	$ 320	20%	$1,000	$ 200
2nd misstatement	500	0	100%	1,000	1,000
3rd misstatement	3,000	2,500	*	1,000	500
Total Projected Misstatement					$1,700

* The recorded amount is greater than the sampling interval; therefore, the projected misstatement equals the actual misstatement.

Multiple Choice Questions (1-50)

1.   Which of the following symbolic representations indicates that new payroll transactions and the old payroll file have been used to prepare payroll checks, prepare a printed payroll journal, and generate a new payroll file?

a.

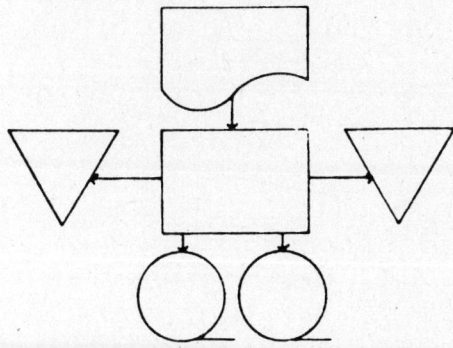

b.

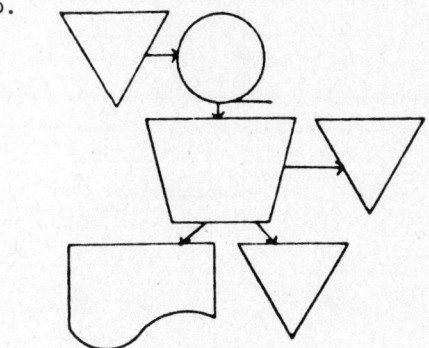

c.

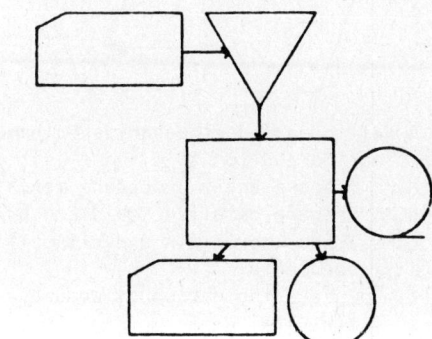

d.

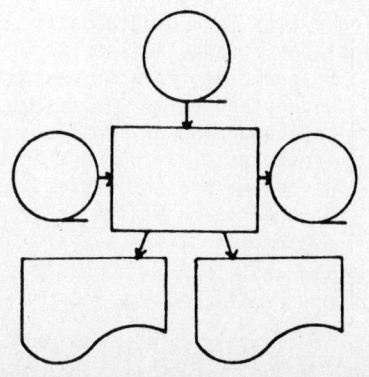

Item 2 is based on the following flowchart:

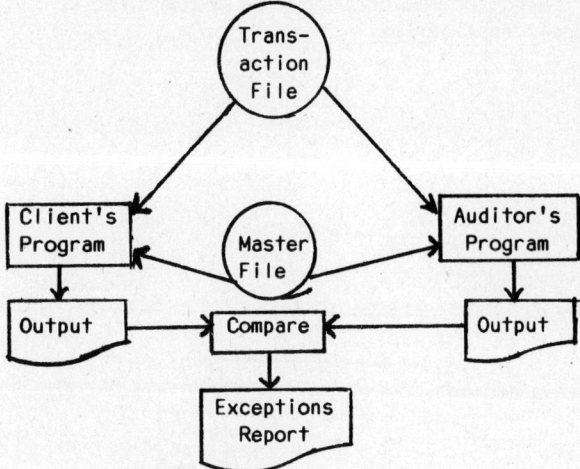

2.   The above flowchart depicts
a.   Program code checking.
b.   Parallel simulation.
c.   Integrated test facility.
d.   Controlled reprocessing.

Item 3 is based on the following flowchart:

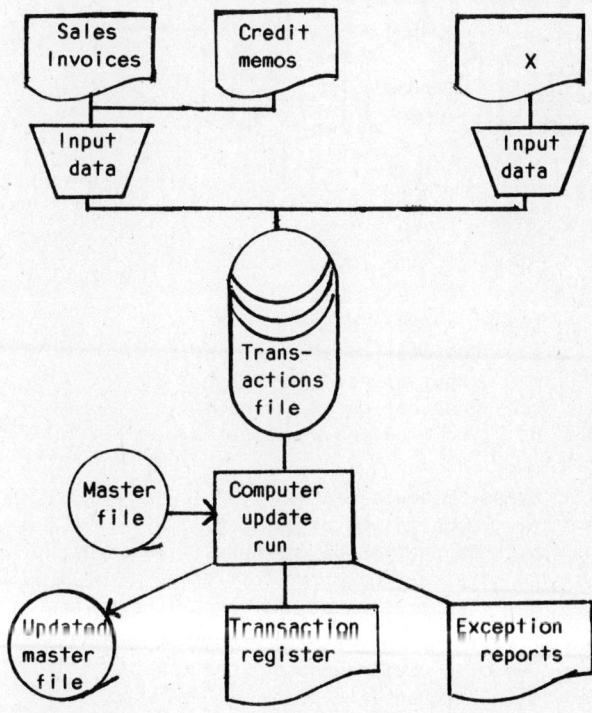

3.   In a credit sales and cash receipts system flowchart, symbol X could represent
a.   Auditor's test data.
b.   Remittance advices.
c.   Error reports.
d.   Credit authorization forms.

Items 4 through 6 are based on the following section of a system flowchart for a payroll application.

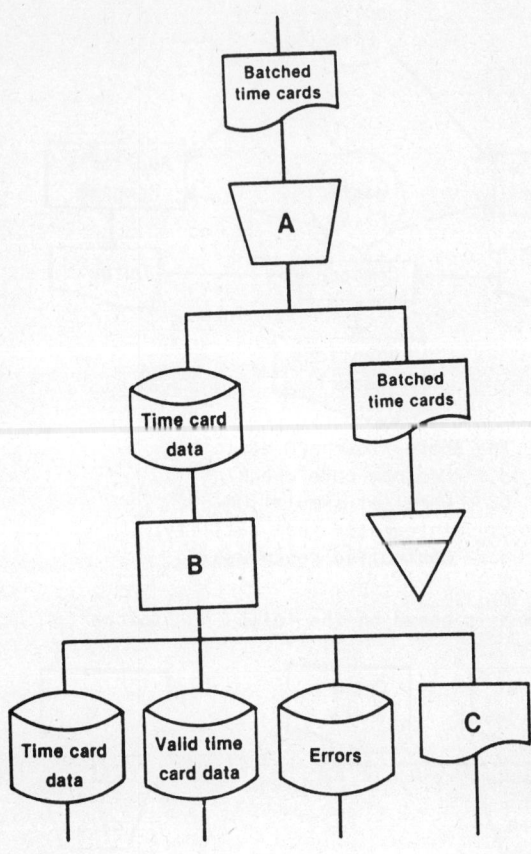

4.   Symbol A could represent
    a.   Computation of gross pay.
    b.   Input of payroll data.
    c.   Preparation of paychecks.
    d.   Verification of payrates.

5.   Symbol B could represent
    a.   Computation of net pay.
    b.   Separation of erroneous time cards.
    c.   Validation of payroll data.
    d.   Preparation of the payroll register.

6.   Symbol C could represent
    a.   Batched time cards.
    b.   Unclaimed payroll checks.
    c.   Erroneous time cards.
    d.   An error report.

7.   Which of the following flowchart symbols represents online storage?

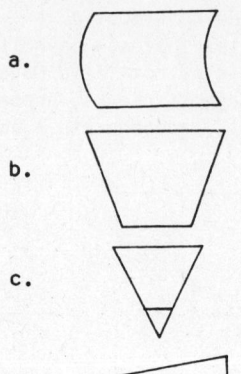

    a.
    b.
    c.
    d.

8.   Which of the following symbolic representations indicate that a file has been consulted?

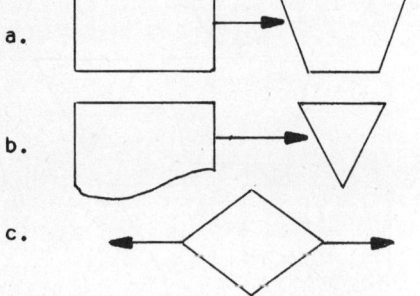

    a.
    b.
    c.

    d.

9.   A well prepared flowchart should make it easier for the auditor to
    a.   Prepare audit procedure manuals.
    b.   Prepare detailed job descriptions.
    c.   Trace the origin and disposition of documents.
    d.   Assess the degree of accuracy of financial data.

10.   An auditor's flowchart of a client's accounting system is a diagrammatic representation that depicts the auditor's
    a.   Program for tests of controls.
    b.   Understanding of the system.
    c.   Understanding of the types of irregularities that are probable, given the present system.
    d.   Documentation of the study and evaluation of the system.

11. A flowchart is most frequently used by an auditor in connection with the
    a. Preparation of generalized computer audit programs.
    b. Review of the client's internal controls.
    c. Use of statistical sampling in performing an audit.
    d. Performance of analytical procedures of account balances.

12. Which of the following characteristics distinguishes computer processing from manual processing?
    a. Computer processing virtually eliminates the occurrence of computational error normally associated with manual processing.
    b. Errors or irregularities in computer processing will be detected soon after their occurrences.
    c. The potential for systematic error is ordinarily greater in manual processing than in computerized processing.
    d. Most computer systems are designed so that transaction trails useful for audit purposes do not exist.

13. After the preliminary phase of the review of a client's EDP controls, an auditor may decide not to perform tests of controls (compliance tests) related to the control procedures within the EDP portion of the client's internal control structure. Which of the following would not be a valid reason for choosing to omit such tests?
    a. The controls duplicate operative controls existing elsewhere in the structure.
    b. There appear to be major weaknesses that would preclude reliance on the stated procedure.
    c. The time and dollar costs of testing exceed the time and dollar savings in substantive testing if the tests of controls show the controls to be operative.
    d. The controls appear adequate.

14. Internal control is ineffective when computer department personnel
    a. Participate in computer software acquisition decisions.
    b. Design documentation for computerized systems.
    c. Originate changes in master files.
    d. Provide physical security for program files.

15. Which of the following most likely represents a weakness in the internal control structure of an EDP system?
    a. The systems analyst reviews output and controls the distribution of output from the EDP department.
    b. The accounts payable clerk prepares data for computer processing and enters the data into the computer.
    c. The systems programmer designs the operating and control functions of programs and participates in testing operating systems.
    d. The control clerk establishes control over data received by the EDP department and reconciles control totals after processing.

16. Which of the following activities would most likely be performed in the EDP department?
    a. Initiation of changes to master records.
    b. Conversion of information to machine-readable form.
    c. Correction of transactional errors.
    d. Initiation of changes to existing applications.

17. For control purposes, which of the following should be organizationally segregated from the computer operations function?
    a. Data conversion.
    b. Surveillance of CRT messages.
    c. Systems development.
    d. Minor maintenance according to a schedule.

18. Which of the following is not a major reason why an accounting audit trail should be maintained for a computer system?
    a. Monitoring purposes.
    b. Analytical procedures.
    c. Query answering.
    d. Deterrent to irregularities.

19. First Federal S & L has an online real-time system, with terminals installed in all of its branches. This system will not accept a customer's cash withdrawal instructions in excess of $1,000 without the use of a "terminal audit key." After the transaction is authorized by a supervisor, the bank teller then processes the transaction with the audit key. This control can be strengthened by
    a. Online recording of the transaction on an audit override sheet.
    b. Increasing the dollar amount to $1,500.
    c. Requiring manual, rather than online, recording of all such transactions.
    d. Using parallel simulation.

20. The use of a header label in conjunction with magnetic tape is <u>most</u> likely to prevent errors by the
   a. Computer operator.
   b. Keypunch operator.
   c. Computer programmer.
   d. Maintenance technician.

21. If a control total were to be computed on each of the following data items, which would best be identified as a hash total for a payroll EDP application?
   a. Hours worked.
   b. Total debits and total credits.
   c. Net pay.
   d. Department numbers.

22. For the accounting system of Acme Company, the amounts of cash disbursements entered into an EDP terminal are transmitted to the computer that immediately transmits the amounts back to the terminal for display on the terminal screen. This display enables the operator to
   a. Establish the validity of the account number.
   b. Verify the amount was entered accurately.
   c. Verify the authorization of the disbursement.
   d. Prevent the overpayment of the account.

23. When EDP programs or files can be accessed from terminals, users should be required to enter a(an)
   a. Parity check.
   b. Personal identification code.
   c. Self-diagnosis test.
   d. Echo check.

24. Computer systems are typically supported by a variety of utility software packages that are important to an auditor because they
   a. May enable unauthorized changes to data files if <u>not</u> properly controlled.
   b. Are very versatile programs that can be used on hardware of many manufacturers.
   c. May be significant components of a client's application programs.
   d. Are written specifically to enable auditors to extract and sort data.

25. The possibility of earning a large amount of information stored on magnetic tape most likely would be reduced by the use of
   a. File protection rings.
   b. Check digits.
   c. Completeness tests.
   d. Conversion verification.

26. Auditing by testing the input and output of an EDP system instead of the computer program itself will
   a. Not detect program errors which do <u>not</u> show up in the output sampled.
   b. Detect all program errors, regardless of the nature of the output.
   c. Provide the auditor with the same type of evidence.
   d. Not provide the auditor with confidence in the results of the auditing procedures.

27. Which of the following client electronic data processing (EDP) systems generally can be audited without examining or directly testing the EDP computer programs of the system?
   a. A system that performs relatively uncomplicated processes and produces detailed output.
   b. A system that affects a number of essential master files and produces a limited output.
   c. A system that updates a few essential master files and produces no printed output other than final balances.
   d. A system that performs relatively complicated processing and produces very little detailed output.

28. When an accounting application is processed by computer, an auditor can <u>not</u> verify the reliable operation of programmed control procedures by
   a. Manually comparing detail transaction files used by an edit program to the program's generated error listings to determine that errors were properly identified by the edit program.
   b. Constructing a processing system for accounting applications and processing actual data from throughout the period through both the client's program and the auditor's program.
   c. Manually reperforming, as of a point in time, the processing of input data and comparing the simulated results to the actual results.
   d. Periodically submitting auditor-prepared test data to the same computer process and evaluating the results.

29. A primary advantage of using generalized audit software packages in auditing the financial statements of a client that uses an EDP system is that the auditor may
   a. Substantiate the accuracy of data through self-checking digits and hash totals.

b. Access information stored on computer files without a complete understanding of the client's hardware and software features.

c. Reduce the level of required tests of controls to a relatively small amount.

d. Gather and permanently store large quantities of supportive evidential matter in machine readable form.

30. Auditors often make use of computer programs that perform routine processing functions such as sorting and merging. These programs are made available by electronic data processing companies and others and are specifically referred to as

a. Compiler programs.
b. Supervisory programs.
c. Utility programs.
d. User programs.

31. Smith Corporation has numerous customers. A customer file is kept on disk storage. Each customer file contains name, address, credit limit, and account balance. The auditor wishes to test this file to determine whether credit limits are being exceeded. The best procedure for the auditor to follow would be to

a. Develop test data that would cause some account balances to exceed the credit limit and determine if the system properly detects such situations.

b. Develop a program to compare credit limits with account balances and print out the details of any account with a balance exceeding its credit limit.

c. Requires a printout of all account balances so they can be manually checked against the credit limits.

d. Request a printout of a sample of account balances so they can be individually checked against the credit limits.

32 Which of the following statements is not true to the test data approach when testing a computerized accounting system?

a. The test need consist of only those valid and invalid conditions which interest the auditor.

b. Only one transaction of each type need be tested.

c. The test data must consist of all possible valid and invalid conditions.

d. Test data are processed by the client's computer programs under the auditor's control.

33. Which of the following is not among the errors that an auditor might include in the test data when auditing a client's EDP system?

a. Numeric characters in alphanumeric fields.

b. Authorized code.

c. Differences in description of units of measure.

d. Illogical entries in fields whose logic is tested by programmed consistency checks.

34. An auditor who is testing EDP controls in a payroll system would most likely use test data that contain conditions such as

a. Deductions not authorized by employees.

b. Overtime not approved by supervisors.

c. Time tickets with invalid job numbers.

d. Payroll checks with unauthorized signatures.

35. To obtain evidence that user identification and password controls are functioning as designed, an auditor would most likely

a. Attempt to sign on to the system using invalid user identifications and passwords.

b. Write a computer program that simulates the logic of the client's access control software.

c. Extract a random sample of processed transactions and ensure that the transactions were appropriately authorized.

d. Examine statements signed by employees stating that they have not divulged their user identifications and passwords to any other person.

36. Which of the following computer-assisted auditing techniques allows fictitious and real transactions to be processed together without client operating personnel being aware of the testing process?

a. Parallel simulation.
b. Generalized audit software programming.
c. Integrated test facility.
d. Test data approach.

37. Which of the following methods of testing application controls utilizes a generalized audit software package prepared by the auditors?

a. Parallel simulation.
b. Integrated testing facility approach.
c. Test data approach.
d. Exception report tests.

38. Which of the following is <u>not</u> a characteristic of a batch processed computer system?
    a. The collection of like transactions which are sorted and processed sequentially against a master file.
    b. Keypunching of transactions, followed by machine processing.
    c. The production of numerous printouts.
    d. The posting of a transaction, as it occurs, to several files, without intermediate printouts.

39. Errors in data processed in a batch computer system may <u>not</u> be detected immediately because
    a. Transaction trails in a batch system are available only for a limited period of time.
    b. There are time delays in processing transactions in a batch system.
    c. Errors in some transactions cause rejection of other transactions in the batch.
    d. Random errors are more likely in a batch system than in an on-line system.

40. Matthews Corp. has changed from a system of recording time worked on clock cards to a computerized payroll system in which employees record time in and out with magnetic cards. The EDP system automatically updates all payroll records. Because of this change
    a. A generalized computer audit program must be used.
    b. Part of the audit trail is altered.
    c. The potential for payroll related fraud is diminished.
    d. Transactions must be processed in batches.

41. Where disk files are used, the grandfather-father-son updating backup concept is relatively difficult to implement because the
    a. Location of information points on disks is an extremely time consuming task.
    b. Magnetic fields and other environmental factors cause off-site storage to be impractical.
    c. Information must be dumped in the form of hard copy if it is to be reviewed before used in updating.
    d. Process of updating old records is destructive.

42. Using microcomputers in auditing may affect the methods used to review the work of staff assistants because
    a. Supervisory personnel may <u>not</u> have an understanding of the capabilities and limitations of microcomputers.
    b. Working paper documentation may <u>not</u> contain readily observable details of calculations.
    c. The audit field work standards for supervision may differ.
    d. Documenting the supervisory review may require assistance of management services personnel.

43. Which of the following would most likely be a weakness in the internal control structure of a client that utilizes microcomputers rather than a larger computer system?
    a. Employee collusion possibilities are increased because microcomputers from one vendor can process the programs of a system from a different vendor.
    b. The microcomputer operators may be able to remove hardware and software components and modify them at home.
    c. Programming errors results in all similar transactions being processed incorrectly when those transactions are processed under the same conditions.
    d. Certain transactions may be automatically initiated by the microcomputers and management's authorization of these transactions may be implicit in its acceptance of the system design.

44. Which of the following is a computer test made to ascertain whether a given characteristic belongs to the group?
    a. Parity check.
    b. Validity check.
    c. Echo check.
    d. Limit check.

45. A control feature in an electronic data processing system requires the central processing unit (CPU) to send signals to the printer to activate the print mechanism for each character. The print mechanism, just prior to printing, sends a signal back to the CPU verifying that the proper print position has been activated. This type of hardware control is referred to as
    a. Echo control.
    b. Validity control.
    c. Signal control.
    d. Check digit control.

46. Which of the following is an example of
check digit?
   a.   An agreement of the total number of
        employees to the total number of
        checks printed by the computer.
   b.   An algebraically determined number
        produced by the other digits of the
        employee number.
   c.   A logic test that ensures all
        employee numbers are nine digits.
   d.   A limit check that an employee's
        hours do <u>not</u> exceed 50 hours per
        work week.

47. In a computerized system, procedure or
problem-oriented language is converted to
machine language through a(an)
   a.   Interpreter.
   b.   Verifier.
   c.   Compiler.
   d.   Converter.

48. What type of EDP system is characterized
by data that are assembled from more than one
location and records that are updated immediately?
   a.   Microcomputer system.
   b.   Minicomputer system.
   c.   Batch processing system.
   d.   Online real-time system.

May 1990 Questions

49. Processing data through the use of
simulated files provides an auditor with
information about the operating effectiveness
of control policies and procedures. One of
the techniques involved in this approach makes
use of
   a.   Input validation.
   b.   Program code checking.
   c.   Controlled reprocessing.
   d.   Integrated test facility.

50. Which of the following statements most
likely represents a disadvantage for an entity
that keeps microcomputer-prepared data files
rather than manually prepared files?
   a.   It is usually more difficult to
        detect transposition errors.
   b.   Transactions are usually authorized
        before they are executed and
        recorded.
   c.   It is usually easier for
        unauthorized persons to access and
        alter the files.
   d.   Random error associated with
        processing similar transactions in
        different ways is usually greater.

Repeat Question

(590,A1,45) Identical/similar to item 6 above

Problems

<u>Problem 1</u>   (1186,A4)

(15 to 25 minutes)

Ajax Inc., an audit client, recently installed a new EDP system to process more efficiently the shipping, billing, and accounts receivable records. During interim work, an assistant completed the review of the accounting system and the internal controls. The assistant determined the following information concerning the new EDP system and the processing and control of shipping notices and customer invoices.

Each major computerized function, i.e., shipping billing, accounts receivable, etc., is permanently assigned to a specific computer operator who is responsible for making program changes, running the program, and reconciling the computer log. Responsibility for the custody and control over the magnetic tapes and system documentation is randomly rotated among the computer operators on a monthly basis to prevent any one person from having access to the tapes and documentation at all times. Each computer programmer and computer operator has access to the computer room via a magnetic card and a digital code that is different for each card. The systems analyst and the supervisor of the computer operators do not have access to the computer room.

The EDP system documentation consists of the following items: program listing, error listing, logs, and record layout. To increase efficiency, batch totals and processing controls are omitted from the system.

Ajax ships its products directly from two warehouses which forward shipping notices to general accounting. There, the billing clerk enters the price of the item and accounts for the numerical sequence of the shipping notices. The billing clerk also prepares daily adding machine tapes of the units shipped and the sales amount. Shipping notices and adding machine tapes are forwarded to the computer department for processing. The computer output consists of:

• A three-copy invoice that is forwarded to the billing clerk, and

• A daily sales register showing the aggregate totals of units shipped and sales amounts that the computer operator compares to the adding machine tapes.

The billing clerk mails two copies of each invoice to the customer and retains the third copy in an open invoice file that serves as a detail accounts receivable record.

Required:

Describe one specific recommendation for correcting each condition in internal controls in the new EDP system and for correcting each condition or inefficiency in the procedures for processing and controlling shipping notices and customer invoices.

<u>Problem 2</u>   (584,A4)

(15 to 25 minutes)

Talbert Corporation hired an independent computer programmer to develop a simplified payroll application for its newly purchased computer. The programmer developed an online, data-based micro-computer system that minimized the level of knowledge required by the operator. It was based upon typing answers to input cues that appeared on the terminal's viewing screen, examples of which follow:

A. Access routine:
    1. Operator access number to payroll file?
    2. Are there new employees?
B. New employees routine:
    1. Employee name?
    2. Employee number?
    3. Social security number?
    4. Rate per hour?
    5. Single or married?
    6. Number of dependents?
    7. Account distribution?
C. Current payroll routine:
    1. Employee number?
    2. Regular hours worked?
    3. Overtime hours worked?
    4. Total employees this payroll period?

The independent auditor is attempting to verify that certain input validation (edit) checks exist to ensure that errors resulting from omissions, invalid entries, or other inaccuracies will be detected during the typing of answers to the input cues.

Required:

Identify the various types of input validation (edit) checks the independent auditor would expect to find in the EDP system. Describe the assurances provided by each identified validation check. Do not discuss the review and evaluation of these controls.

Problem 3   (1187,A4)

(15 to 25 minutes)

Microcomputer software has been developed
to improve the efficiency and effectiveness of
the audit. Electronic spreadsheets and other
software packages are available to aid in the
performance of audit procedures otherwise
performed manually.

Required:

Describe the potential benefits to an
auditor of using microcomputer software in an
audit as compared to performing an audit
without the use of a computer.

Multiple Choice Answers

1. d	11. b	21. d	31. b	41. d
2. b	12. a	22. b	32. c	42. b
3. b	13. d	23. b	33. a	43. b
4. b	14. c	24. a	34. c	44. b
5. c	15. a	25. a	35. a	45. a
6. d	16. b	26. a	36. c	46. b
7. a	17. c	27. a	37. a	47. c
8. d	18. b	28. c	38. d	48. d
9. c	19. a	29. b	39. b	49. d
10. b	20. a	30. c	40. b	50. c

Multiple Choice Answer Explanations

A. Flowcharting

A.1. Flowcharting Symbols

1. (1189,A1,55) (d) The requirement is to determine the sequence of flowchart symbols which indicate that new payroll transactions and the old payroll file have been used to prepare checks, prepare a printed payroll journal, and generate a new payroll file. Answer (d) is correct because it presents two magnetic tape files (the new payroll transactions and the old payroll file) being processed by a computer (the rectangle) with three resulting outputs--two documents (the payroll checks and the printed payroll) and a magnetic tape file (the new payroll file) result. Answer (a) is incorrect because it indicates that two magnetic tape files and two offline storage files result, and that no printed payroll journal or payroll checks would be produced. Answer (b) is incorrect for similar reasons to (a) because only one printed document results; also, the flowchart indicates that an offline storage file becomes a magnetic tape file, which is manually processed with no resulting magnetic tape file. Answer (c) is incorrect because it indicates that two tape files are produced, and no payroll checks or payroll journal is produced.

2. (1188,A1,59) (b) The requirement is to determine the approach illustrated in the flowchart. Answer (b) is correct because parallel simulation involves processing actual client data through an auditor's program. Answer (a) is incorrect because program code checking involves an analysis of the client's actual program. Answer (c) is incorrect because an integrated test facility approach introduces dummy transactions into a system in the midst of live transaction processing and is usually built into the system during the original design. Answer (d) is incorrect because controlled reprocessing often includes using the auditor's copy of a client program, rather than the auditor's program.

3. (1188,A1,60) (b) The requirement is to identify the item represented by the "X" on the flowchart. Answer (b) is correct because the existence of a credit memo, in addition to a sales invoice, would indicate that this portion of the flowchart deals with cash receipts; therefore, the "X" would represent the remittance advices. Thus, the receipt transactions are credited to the accounts receivable master file, and an updated master file, a register of receipts, and exception reports are generated. Answer (a) is incorrect because an auditor's test data will not result in an input into the transactions file. Answer (c) is incorrect because since no processing has occurred at the point in question--an error report is unlikely. Answer (d) is incorrect because credit authorization will generally occur prior to the preparation of credit memos.

4. (587,A1,24) (b) The requirement is to identify the operation being performed in the trapezoid symbol labeled A. The trapezoid symbol indicates the performance of a manual operation. Answer (b) is correct because the manual operation results in creation of a disk containing time card data which will serve as input into a subsequent processing operation (a rectangle). Answer (a) is incorrect because there is no indication that gross pay has been computed. Answer (c) is incorrect because no paychecks are shown to emerge from the operation. Answer (d) is incorrect because no information on payrates is shown to emerge from the operation.

5. (587,A1,25) (c) The requirement is to identify the operation being performed in the rectangle symbol labeled B. Rectangles indicate a processing function. Answer (c) is correct because the outputs of this processing function operation are valid time card data, errors, and a report. Therefore, validation of payroll data is occurring. Answer (a) is incorrect because there is no indication that a computation of net pay has occurred. Answer (b) is incorrect because time cards have been filed prior to this step and are not being separated at this stage. Answer (d) is incorrect because no information on withholdings, etc., has been involved and, therefore, it is extremely unlikely that a payroll register has been prepared.

6. (587,A1,26) (d) The requirement is to identify the meaning of the symbol labeled C. This flowchart symbol is for a document. Therefore, a document has been prepared. The disks that have been prepared at the level of the document all relate to time card data,

both valid and erroneous. Answer (d) is correct because the report must be related to either the valid, or more likely, the erroneous data. Answers (a) and (c) are incorrect because the time cards have already been filed and are not involved in this portion of the processing. Answer (b) is incorrect because no payroll checks are shown to have been prepared.

7. (586,A1,47) (a) The requirement is to identify the symbol which represents online storage. Answer (a) is correct. Answer (b) is incorrect because it represents a manual operation. Answer (c) is incorrect because it represents offline storage. Answer (d) is incorrect because it represents manual input.

8. (583,A1,54) (d) The requirement is to determine the symbolic representations that indicate that a file has been consulted. Answer (d) indicates that a manual operation (the trapezoid symbol) is accessing data from a file and returning the data to the file, i.e., "consulting" the file. Answer (a) is incorrect because it represents a processing step (the rectangle) being followed by a manual operation. Answer (b) is incorrect because it represents a document being filed. Answer (c) is incorrect because the diamond symbol represents a decision process.

A.2. Types and Definitions

9. (584,A1,55) (c) The requirement is to determine a benefit of a well-prepared flow-chart. A flowchart may be used to document the auditor's understanding of the flow of transactions and documents (AU 320.51-.58). Answer (a) is incorrect because while an audit procedures manual may suggest the use of flow-charts, flowcharts will not in general be used to prepare such a manual. Answer (b) is less accurate than (c) because while it may be possible to obtain general information on various jobs, the flowchart will not allow one to obtain a detailed job description. Answer (d) is incorrect because a flowchart does not directly address actual accuracy of financial data within a system.

10. (1189,A1,37) (b) The requirement is to identify the correct statement concerning an auditor's flowchart of a client's accounting system. Answer (b) is correct because auditors may use flowcharts to document their understanding of the internal control structure, including the accounting system (AU 319.26). Answer (a) is incorrect because a flowchart is not a program for tests of controls. Answer (c) is incorrect because the flowchart in and of itself does not depict the

types of irregularities that are probable. Answer (d) is incorrect because a flowchart does not "depict the auditor's documentation;" it is the documentation of his/her understanding of the system. Additionally, a flow-chart does not document an evaluation of a system; it merely shows the flow of information through an accounting system without addressing the effectiveness of that system.

B. Principles of Auditing EDP Systems
B.1. The Auditor's Consideration of Internal Control with EDP

11. (1187,A1,16) (b) The requirement is to determine when a flowchart is most frequently used by an auditor. Answer (b) is correct because flowcharts are suggested as being appropriate for documenting the auditor's review of internal controls. Answer (a) is incorrect because auditors do not frequently write their own generalized computer audit programs, the most likely time a flowchart would be used with respect to such software. Answers (c) and (d) are incorrect because statistical sampling and analytical procedures do not in general require the use of flowcharts.

12. (1188,A1,36) (a) The requirement is to identify a characteristic that distinguishes computer processing from manual processing. Answer (a) is correct because the high degree of accuracy of computer computation virtually eliminates the occurrence of computational errors. Answer (b) is incorrect because errors or irregularities in computer processing may or may not be detected, depending upon the effectiveness of an entity's internal control structure. Answer (c) is incorrect because a programming error will result in a high level of systematic error in a computerized system and therefore, such errors may occur in either a manual or a computerized system. Answer (d) is incorrect because most computer systems are designed to include transaction trails.

13. (588,A1,4) (d) The requirement is to determine an inappropriate reason for omitting tests of controls related to EDP control procedures. Answer (d) is correct because the fact that the controls appear adequate is not sufficient justification for reliance; tests of controls must be performed before the auditor can actually rely upon a control procedure to reduce control risk (AU 319.41). Answer (a) is incorrect because when controls duplicate other controls the auditor who wishes to rely upon the structure need not test both sets. Answer (b) is incorrect

because if weak controls are not to be relied upon, the auditor need not test their effectiveness. Answer (c) is incorrect because tests of controls may be omitted if their cost exceeds the savings from reduced substantive testing resulting from reliance upon the controls.

B.2. General Controls

14. (588,A1,7) (c) The requirement is to identify the condition in internal control relating to a function performed by computer department personnel. Answer (c) is correct because individuals outside of the computer department should originate changes in master files; this separates the authorization of changes from the actual processing of records. Answer (a) is incorrect because participation of computer department personnel in making computer software acquisition decisions is often appropriate and desirable given their expertise in the area. Answer (b) is incorrect for similar reasons as (a). In addition, computer department personnel will often be able to effectively design the required documentation for computerized systems. Answer (d) is incorrect because the physical security for program files may appropriately be assigned to a library function within the computer department.

15. (1189,A1,43) (a) The requirement is to identify the situation which is most likely to constitute a weakness in the internal control of an EDP system. Answer (a) is correct because the systems analyst is responsible for designing the EDP system and therefore should not review and control the distribution of output (which is properly the role of the control group). Answer (b) is incorrect because the accounts payable clerk provides a recordkeeping function and will often prepare data for processing and will enter the data into the computer. Answer (c) is incorrect because the program designer will normally participate in testing the operating system. Answer (d) is incorrect because the control clerk will generally establish control over data received by the EDP department and reconcile control totals after processing.

16. (585,A1,25) (b) The requirement is to identify the activity most likely to be performed in the EDP department. Answer (b) is correct because the conversion of information into machine-readable form is essential to the inputting of data; EDP equipment is generally used to perform this function. Answer (a) is incorrect because under good internal control, the initiation of changes to master records should be authorized by functions independent

of those which process the records. Answer (c) is incorrect because a separate function should exist to correct transactional errors. Answer (d) is incorrect because changes to EDP applications should be initiated by the appropriate user group.

17. (585,A1,26) (c) The requirement is to identify the function which should be segregated from computer operations. Answer (c) is correct because individuals who develop the system should be restricted from operating the system. Answer (a) is incorrect because operators must deal with data conversion as part of the data entry process. Answer (b) is incorrect because operators must be aware of CRT messages in order to properly execute their function. Answer (d) is incorrect because it is generally practical and cost justifiable to have __minor__ maintenance performed by operators.

18. (589,A1,38) (b) The requirement is to identify the response which is __not__ a major reason why an accounting audit trail should be maintained for a computer. Answer (b) is correct because analytical procedures involve comparisons of recorded amounts or ratios developed from recorded amounts to expectations developed by the auditor. These procedures are performed using summary data (e.g., total sales or cost of goods sold) rather than detail transaction-level data. Since an audit trail provides a method of tracing accounting data on a detail transaction level, it would be of little use while performing analytical procedures. Answer (a) is incorrect because an audit trail makes it possible to monitor both users and the computer system. Answer (c) is incorrect because an audit trail provides the detail necessary to allow the research and answering of queries. Answer (d) is incorrect because irregularities may be deterred when the perpetrator realizes that evidence (i.e., an audit trail) relating to the irregularity will be in the computer system.

B.3. Application Controls

19. (584,A1,15) (a) The requirement is to determine a control which will strengthen an online real-time cash withdrawal system. Answer (a) is correct because documentation of all situations in which the "terminal audit key" has been used will improve the audit trail. Answer (b) is incorrect because increasing the dollar amount required for use of the key will simply reduce the number of times it is used (and allow larger withdrawals to be made without any required special authorization). Answer (c) is incorrect because there is no reason to believe that a manual system

will be more effective than an online system. Answer (d) is incorrect because parallel simulation, running the data through alternate software, would seem to have no particular advantage for processing these large withdrawals.

20. (581,A1,35) (a) The requirement is to determine the errors which a header label is likely to prevent. Since the header label is actually on the magnetic tape, it is the computer operator whose errors will be prevented. Answer (b) is incorrect because the keypunch operator deals with punch cards. Answer (c) is incorrect because the programmer will write the programs and not run them under a good internal control structure. Answer (d) is incorrect because the maintenance technician will not run the magnetic tape.

21. (1188,A1,45) (d) The requirement is to determine the total which would most likely be considered a hash total. A hash total is a meaningless sum which normally has no use other than to prove the completeness with which a batch has been processed. Answer (d) is correct because the summation of department numbers has no apparent use other than to help determine that an entire batch has been processed. Answer (a) is incorrect because a company may use the total of hours worked for various purposes. Answer (b) is incorrect because the totals of debits and credits help the auditor (and management) to determine that all transactions have been properly recorded and processed. Answer (c) is incorrect because the total of net pay normally has a meaning, such as equaling the credit to cash based on the payroll.

22. (1186,A1,23) (b) Answer (b) is correct because the entry of disbursement amounts and the subsequent display of the amounts on the terminal screen will allow the operator to visually verify that the data provided to be input was entered accurately. Answer (a) is incorrect because displaying on the screen the data entered does not ensure the validity of the data, only that the data was entered correctly. Answer (c) is incorrect because no evidence has been provided as to whether the disbursement was authorized. Answer (d) is incorrect because the display of the amount will not be compared to a "correct" amount--only to the amount that was to be input.

23. (589,A1,13) (b) The requirement is to identify a useful control when EDP programs or files can be accessed from terminals. Answer (b) is correct because use of personal identification codes (passwords) will limit access to the programs or files on the terminal to those who know the codes. Answers (a), (c), and (d) are all incorrect because while they list valid controls used in EDP systems, none of them require entry of data by the user. A parity check control is a special bit added to each character stored in memory to help detect whether the hardware has lost a bit during the internal movement of that character. A self-diagnosis test is run on a computer to check the internal operations and devices within the computer system. An echo check is primarily used in telecommunications transmissions to determine whether the receiving hardware has received the information sent by the sending hardware.

24. (1189,A1,38) (a) The requirement is to identify a reason that utility software packages are important to an auditor. Answer (a) is correct because client use of such packages requires that the auditor include tests to determine that no unplanned interventions using utility routines have taken place during processing (see Audit and Accounting Guide, Computer Assisted Audit Techniques, p. 66). Answer (b) is incorrect because a client's use of such programs implies that they are useful on his/her computer hardware, and thereby any flexibility is not of immediate relevance to the auditor. Answer (c) is incorrect because the primary purpose of utility programs is to support the computer user's applications (Computer Assisted Audit Techniques, p. 64). Answer (d) is incorrect because utility software programs have a variety of uses in addition to enabling auditors to extract and sort data (Computer Assisted Audit Techniques, p. 64-66).

25. (1189,A1,42) (a) The requirement is to identify the item which would reduce the possibility of erasing a large amount of information stored on magnetic tape. Answer (a) is correct because a file protection ring is a control that ensures that an operator does not erase important information on a magnetic tape. Answer (b) is incorrect because a check digit is a digit added to an identification number to detect entry errors. Answer (c) is incorrect because a completeness test would generally be used to test whether all data were processed. Answer (d) is incorrect because conversion verification would address whether the conversion of data from one form to another (e.g., disk to magnetic tape) was complete.

B.4. Audit Techniques Using EDP

26. (1183,A1,27) (a) The requirement is to determine the correct statement with respect to testing inputs and outputs of an EDP system instead of testing the actual computer program itself. Answer (a) is correct because portions of the program which have errors not reflected on the output will be missed. Thus, if a "loop" in a program is not used in one application, it is not tested. Answer (b) is incorrect because the lack of an understanding of the entire program precludes the detection of all errors. Answer (c) is incorrect because while auditing inputs and outputs can provide valuable evidence, it will often be different than the evidence obtained by testing the program itself. Answer (d) is incorrect because such auditing of inputs and outputs may well satisfy the auditor.

27. (579,A1,46) (a) The requirement is the type of EDP system that can be audited without examining or directly testing EDP computer programs, i.e., auditing around the system. Auditing around the system is possible if the system performs uncomplicated processes and produces detailed output, i.e., is a fancy bookkeeping machine. Answers (b), (c), and (d) all describe more complicated EDP systems that produce only limited output. In these more complicated systems, the data and related controls are within the system, and thus the auditor must examine the system itself. Auditors must identify and evaluate the accounting controls in all EDP systems. Further, complex EDP systems require auditor specialized expertise to perform the necessary procedures.

28. (1189,A1,31) (c) The requirement is to identify the procedure which will not allow the auditor to verify the reliable operation of programmed control procedures. Answer (c) is correct because manually reperforming at a point in time will only test the effectiveness of the controls at that point, and will not adequately test operating effectiveness throughout the year (AU 319.52). Answer (a) is incorrect because manually comparing detail transaction files to error listings will help an auditor to determine whether errors have been properly identified. Answer (b) is incorrect because the technique of processing data through both auditor and client programs, referred to as parallel simulation, may be used effectively to test controls. Answer (d) is incorrect because periodically using test data and evaluating the results will also help the auditor to verify the operating effectiveness of programmed control procedures.

B.4.a. Audit Software

29. (586,A1,44) (b) The requirement is to identify a primary advantage of generalized audit software packages. Answer (b) is correct because the packages may be run without a complete understanding of client hardware and software features. Answer (a) is incorrect because self-checking digits and hash totals are controls in the client's EDP system, not generally in the audit software. Answer (c) is incorrect because no relationship necessarily exists between the amount of tests of controls and the use of generalized audit software packages. Answer (d) is incorrect because the auditor wishes to obtain the evidential matter for use in this year's audit and not necessarily to permanently store large quantities of evidential matter in machine readable form.

30. (1181,A1,38) (c) The requirement is to determine the type of computer programs which auditors use to assist them in functions such as sorting and merging. Answer (c) is correct because a utility program is a standard routine for performing commonly required processing such as sorting, merging, editing, and mathematical routines. Answer (a) is incorrect because compiler programs translate programming languages such as COBOL or FORTRAN to machine-language. Answer (b) is incorrect because supervisory programs or "operating systems" consist of a series of programs that perform functions such as scheduling and supervising the application programs, allocating storage, controlling peripheral devices, and handling errors and restarts. Answer (d) is incorrect because user or "application programs" perform specific data processing tasks such as general ledger, accounts payable, accounts receivable, and payroll. Application programs make use of utility routines.

31. (585,A1,1) (b) The requirement is to determine the best approach for determining whether credit limits are being exceeded when accounts receivable information is stored on disk. Answer (b) is correct because a program to compare actual account balances with the predetermined credit limit and thereby prepare a report on whether any actual credit limits are being exceeded will accomplish the stated objective. Answer (a) is incorrect because while test data will indicate whether the client's program allows credit limits to be exceeded, it will not indicate whether credit limits are actually being exceeded. Answer (c) is incorrect because a manual check of all account balances will be very time consuming. Answer (d) is incorrect because a

sample will provide less complete information than the audit of the entire population which is indicated in answer (b).

B.4.b. Test Data

32. (588,A1,3) (c) The requirement is to identify the statement which is not true of the test data approach. Answer (c) is correct (not true) because it is impossible or not cost beneficial to test all possible valid and invalid conditions. Answer (a) is incorrect because the auditor should test those valid and invalid conditions in which s/he is interested. Answer (b) is incorrect because only one transaction of each type need be tested in a computer control system in which the controls either work or do not work. Answer (d) is incorrect because test data is run using the client's computer programs under the auditor's control.

33. (1184,A1,19) (a) The requirement is to determine which reply is not among the errors which are generally detected by test data. An auditor uses test data to determine whether purported controls are actually functioning. Answer (a) is correct because one would not use test data to test numeric characters in alphanumeric fields; numeric characters are accepted in alphanumeric fields and thus do not represent error conditions. Answer (b) is incorrect because authorization codes may be tested by inputting inappropriate codes. Answer (c) is incorrect because differing descriptions of units of measure may be inputted to test whether they are accepted. Answer (d) is incorrect because illogical combinations may be inputted to test whether they are detected by the system.

34. (589,A1,16) (c) The requirement is to identify the most likely use of test data to test EDP controls in a payroll system. Answer (c) is correct because valid job numbers are included often in files within an EDP system, and may be compared by the computer to job numbers listed on tickets to ensure that employees are reporting time worked on valid job numbers. Thus, test data including invalid job numbers could be entered to determine whether the control is functioning effectively. Answers (a) and (b) are incorrect because determining whether authorization or approval processes have been handled properly normally requires review of actual forms signed by the authorizing personnel, and could not therefore be tested using test data. Answer (d) is incorrect because an examination of actual payroll checks will in general be necessary to identify unauthorized signatures. Thus, this control could not be tested using test data.

35. (1189,A1,32) (a) The requirement is to determine which test an auditor would perform in order to determine if password controls are functioning. Answer (a) is correct because the purpose of a user identification password is to limit access to data to authorized personnel. An employee should have a password to sign on to a system or to access confidential information. The control should also provide for feedback of unauthorized attempts to access the data. In order to test this control, the auditor should attempt to access the system by using invalid user identifications and passwords. Answer (b) is incorrect because writing a program that simulates the logic of the client's access control software will not directly address the actual functioning of the client's system. Answer (c) is incorrect because testing for authorization of transactions will not identify if users were accessing the system for uses other than initiation of transactions. Answer (d) is incorrect because determining if employees have not divulged their passwords does not test whether or not the password control on the system is functioning as designed.

B.4.c. Integrated Test Facility

36. (589,A1,39) (c) The requirement is to identify the computer-assisted auditing technique which allows fictitious and real transactions to be processed together without client operating personnel being aware of the testing process. Answer (c) is correct because the integrated test facility approach introduces dummy transactions into a system in the midst of live transactions. Accordingly, client operating personnel may not be aware of the testing process. Answer (a) is incorrect because the parallel simulation technique requires the processing of actual client data through an auditor's software program. In this case, the client would be aware of the testing process since the auditor would need to request copies of data run on the actual system so that the data could then be run on the auditor's software program. Additionally, only valid transactions would be tested under parallel simulation. Answer (b) is incorrect because generalized audit software does not involve use of fictitious transactions. Answer (d) is incorrect because the test data approach generally uses only dummy transactions to test various program controls.

B.4.d. Parallel Simulation

37. (1184,A1,11) (a) The requirement is to determine the EDP auditing technique which utilizes generalized audit software. Answer (a) is correct because the parallel simulation method processes the client's data

using the CPA's software. Answers (b) and (c) are incorrect because the client's hardware and software are tested using test data designed by the CPA. Answer (d) is incorrect because although a CPA may test a client's exception reports in various manners, generalized software is unlikely to be used. Exception reports are generally tested via CPA-prepared test data containing all the possible error conditions. The test data are then run on the client's hardware and software to ascertain whether the exception reports are "picking up" the CPA's test data.

C. Unique Characteristics of Specific EDP Systems

C.1. Batch Processing

38. (1182,A1,38) (d) The requirement is to determine which answer is not a characteristic of a batch processed computer system. Simultaneous posting to several files is most frequently related to an online real-time system, not a batch system. Answer (a) is incorrect since a batch system may process sequentially against a master file. Answer (b) is incorrect because keypunching is followed by machine processing in batch systems. Answer (c) is incorrect because the numerous batches ordinarily result in numerous printouts.

39. (589,A1,12) (b) The requirement is to determine why errors in data processed in a batch computer system may not be detected immediately. Answer (b) is correct because in a batch system, transactions are grouped by type and periodically processed. Accordingly, delays in processing data will result in delays in detection of errors. Answer (a) is incorrect because transaction trails in a batch system are generally available for long periods of time. Additionally, the fact that transaction trails are not available would not in itself delay detection of errors. Answer (c) is incorrect because errors in some transactions need not cause the rejection of other transactions in the batch. Answer (d) is incorrect because random errors are not, all other things being equal, considered to be more likely in a batch system than in an online system.

C.2. Direct or Random Access Processing

40. (586,A1,1) (b) The requirement is to identify the correct statement with respect to a computerized, automatically updating payroll system in which magnetic cards are used instead of a manual payroll system with clock cards. Answer (b) is correct because the automatic updating of payroll records alters

the audit trail which, in the past, included steps pertaining to manual updating. Answer (a) is incorrect because although an auditor may choose to use a generalized computer audit program, it is not required. Answer (c) is incorrect because no information is presented that would necessarily indicate a change in the likelihood of fraud. Answer (d) is incorrect because given automatic updating, a large portion of the transactions are not processed in batches.

41. (1181,A1,8) (d) The requirement is to determine why the grandfather-father-son updating backup concept is relatively difficult to implement for disk files. Answer (d) is correct because updating destroys the old records. Answer (a) is incorrect because the location of information points on disks is not an extremely time consuming task if the disks have been properly organized and maintained. Answer (b) is incorrect because off-site storage through disks is possible, though costly. Answer (c) is incorrect because information need not be dumped in the form of hard copy.

C.4. Small Computer Environment

42. (588,A1,17) (b) The requirement is to determine an effect on methods of review caused by using microcomputers in auditing. Answer (b) is correct because when a computer performs the calculations there are often no readily observable details. Answer (a) is incorrect because to meet the professional planning and supervision standards such knowledge of microcomputer capabilities and limitations may often be necessary. Answer (c) is incorrect because the field work standard for adequate supervision does not differ based on whether or not a computer is involved. Answer (d) is incorrect because the supervisory review should be able to be performed without the assistance of management services personnel.

43. (1188,A1,38) (b) The requirement is to identify a weakness in internal control that is associated more with microcomputers than with larger computer systems. Answer (b) is correct because microcomputers create a situation in which the segregation of functions is difficult and therefore hardware and software components may easily be modified. Answer (a) is incorrect because collusion possibilities are not necessarily increased in a microcomputer environment. Answer (c) is incorrect because programming errors will generally result in improper processing of transactions under both micro-

computer and under larger computer systems.
Answer (d) is incorrect because while automatic initiation of transactions is possible
in either type of system, it is more frequent
in large computer systems.

D. EDP Definitions

44. (1179,A1,2) (b) A validity check determines whether a character is legitimate per
the given character set. Note the validity
check determines whether a given character is
within the desired group. Answer (a) is incorrect because a parity check is a summation
check in which the binary digits of a character are added to determine whether the sum
is odd or even. Another bit, the parity bit,
is turned on or off so the total number of
bits will be odd or even as required. Answer (c) is incorrect because an echo check is
a hardware control wherein data is transmitted
back to its source and compared to the original data to verify the transmission correctness. Answer (d) is incorrect because a limit
or reasonableness check is a programmed control based on specified limits. For example,
a calendar month cannot be numbered higher
than 12, or a week cannot have more than 168
hours.

45. (1178,A1,18) (a) An echo check or control consists of transmitting data back to the
source unit for comparison with the original
data that were transmitted. In this case, the
print command is sent to the printer and then
returned to the CPU to verify that the proper
command was received. A validity check [an-
swer (b)] consists of the examination of a bit
pattern to determine that the combination is
legitimate for the system character set, i.e.,
that the character represented by the bit combination is valid per the system. Answer (c),
a signal control or signal check, appears to
be a nonsense term. Answer (d), check digit
control, is a programmed control wherein the
last character or digit can be calculated from
the previous digits.

46. (585,A1,24) (b) The requirement is to
identify an example of a check digit. Answer (b) is correct because a check digit is
an extra digit in an identification number,
algebraically determined, that detects specified types of data input, transmission, or
conversion errors. Answer (a) is incorrect
because the agreement of the total number of
employees to the checks printed is an example
of a control total. Answer (c) is incorrect
because ensuring that all employee numbers are
nine digits could be considered a logic check,
a field size check, or a missing data check.
Answer (d) is incorrect because determining

that no employee has more than 50 hours per
work week is a limit check.

47. (582,A1,53) (c) The requirement is to
determine the item which converts problem
oriented language to machine language. A compiler produces a machine-language object program from a source-program (i.e., problem
oriented) language. Answer (a) is incorrect
because an interpreter is used to make punched
cards easily readable to people. Answer (b)
is incorrect because a verifier is used to
test whether key punching errors exist on
punched cards. Answer (d) is incorrect
because a converter changes a program from one
form of problem oriented language to another,
related form (e.g., from one form of COBOL to
another form of COBOL).

48. (1185,A1,52) (d) The requirement is to
determine the type of EDP system characterized
by more than one location and records that are
updated immediately. Answer (d) is correct
because online real-time systems typically
allow access from multiple locations, and
always have the immediate update of records.
Answers (a) and (b) are incorrect because
small computers often are limited to one
location, and they may or may not allow immediate updating for particular applications.
Answer (c) is incorrect because batch processing is a method which does not update
records immediately (e.g., processing the
"batch" of the firm's daily sales each
evening, not at the moment they occur).

May 1990 Answers

49. (590,A1,8) (d) The requirement is to
identify the technique that provides an
auditor with information about the operating
effectiveness of control policies and procedures through the use of simulated files.
Answer (d) is correct because the use of an
integrated test facility introduces files of
simulated transactions into a system in order
to test the effectiveness of control policies. Answer (a) is incorrect because an
input validation is a procedure used to check
that only valid data are entered into the
system and is not a test used by an auditor to
test the operating effectiveness of a control
procedure. Answer (b) is incorrect because
program code checking establishes that the
programs used by the client are properly
written and coded. Answer (c) is incorrect
because controlled reprocessing processes
actual client data, not simulated files
through the auditor's software.

50. (590,A1,26) (c) The requirement is to
identify a disadvantage of microcomputer-

prepared data files compared to manually
prepared files. Answer (c) is correct because
microcomputer usage is difficult to control
and the risk that unauthorized users will
alter files becomes greater than if the files
had been prepared manually and stored in a
controlled environment. Answer (a) is incorrect because when using a microcomputer, it is
no more difficult to detect transposition errors than if files had been prepared manually. Answer (b) is incorrect because in both
a microcomputer system and in a manual system
transactions should be authorized <u>before</u> they
are executed and recorded. Answer (d) is incorrect because the threat of a random error
is decreased by the use of a microcomputer because of the reduction of a chance for human
error.

Unofficial Answer*

Problem 1   EDP Conditions in Shipping and
             Billing (1186,A4)

Recommendations for correcting conditions in
the internal controls in the new EDP system
and conditions and inefficiencies in the procedures for processing and controlling shipping notices and customer invoices:

• The functions of programming, machine
operations, and control should be assigned to
different employees.

• Computer log should be reconciled by
the computer operations supervisor or other
independent employee.

• Access to tapes and documentation
should be controlled by an independent employee or through the use of restricted
authorization code.

• Programmers' access to computers
should be limited to testing and debugging.

• The supervisor of the computer operators should have access to the computer room.

• The EDP system's documentation should
also include flowcharts, computer programs,
and operator instructions.

• Batch totals (control totals, hash
totals, record counts) should be utilized to
assure that data have been properly authorized
and not lost or otherwise improperly changed.

• Processing controls should be put in
place to assure that errors in the input records will be detected when processing occurs.
Among the possible processing controls are
completeness tests, validation tests, sequence
tests, and limit or reasonableness tests.

• The price list should be placed on a
master file in the computer and matched with
product numbers on the shipping notices to
obtain appropriate prices.

• The computer should be programmed to
review the numerical sequence of shipping
notices and list missing numbers.

• The billing clerk or other designated
control clerk should retain the adding machine
tapes or a copy of them to compare the total
with the daily sales register.

• Copies of invoices should be forwarded
by the computer department to the mailroom
clerk for mailing to the customers.

• An individual who is independent of
billing and cash collections should maintain
the accounts receivable records; or if the
records are updated by the computer department, there should be an independent review by
general accounting.

• The accounts receivable records maintained manually in an open file should be more
efficiently maintained on magnetic tape.

Unofficial Answer*

Problem 2   Payroll Input Controls (584,A4)

The following edit checks might be used to
detect errors during the typing of answers to
the input cues:

• Password--ensures that the operator is
authorized to access computer programs and
files.

• Numeric check--ensures that numbers
are entered into and accepted by the system
where only numbers are required to be entered,
e.g., numbers 0-9 in social security number.

• Alphabetic check--ensures that letters
are entered into and accepted by the system
where only letters are required to be entered
e.g., letters A-Z in employee name.

• Special character check--ensures that
only specific special characters are entered
into and accepted by the system where only
these special characters are required to be
entered, e.g., dashes between numbers in
social security number.

• Sign checks--ensures that positive or
negative signs are entered into and accepted
by the system where only such signs are
required to be entered or that the absence of
a positive or negative sign appears where such
an absence is required, e.g., hours worked.

• Arithmetic checks--ensures the validity of the result of a mathematical computation, e.g., total employees for period equals
number of employee numbers in system.

• Validity checks--ensures that only
authorized data codes will be entered into and
accepted by the system where only such authorized data codes are required, e.g., authorized
employee account numbers.

• Limit (reasonableness) checks--ensures
that only data within predetermined limits
will be entered into and accepted by the
system, e.g., rate per hour cannot be lower
than the minimum set by law or higher than the
maximum set by management.

• Self checking digit--ensures that only
specific code numbers prepared by using a
specific arithmetic operation will be entered
into and accepted by the system, e.g., employee numbers generated by the modulus 11
method with prime number weighting.

• Size check--ensures that only data
using fixed or defined field lengths will be
entered into and accepted by the system, e.g.,

---

*Because the requirements of this question could be answered by lists of items, we have not included an
outline of the solution.

number of dependents requires exactly two digits.

    • Missing data check--ensures that no blanks will be entered into and accepted by the system when data should be present, e.g., an "S" or "M" is entered in response to, single or married.

    • Overflow check--ensures that no digits are dropped if a number becomes too large for a variable during processing, e.g., hourly rate "on size errors" are detected.

    • Control total checks--ensures that no unauthorized changes are made to specified data or data fields and all data have been entered.

    • Logic check--ensures that spurious data are rejected, e.g., no negative regular hours.

Unofficial Answer*

Problem 3   Using Microcomputer Software
           (1187,A4)

The potential benefits to an auditor of using micro-computor software in an audit as compared to performing an audit without the use of a computer include the following:

1. Time may be saved by eliminating manual footing, cross-footing, and other routine calculations.
2. Calculations, comparisons, and other data manipulations are more accurately performed.
3. Analytical procedures calculations may be more efficiently performed.
4. The scope of analytical procedures may be broadened.
5. Audit sampling may be facilitated.
6. Potential conditions in a client's internal control system may be more readily identified.
7. Preparation and revision of flowcharts depicting the flow of financial transactions in a client's system may be facilitated.
8. Working papers may be easily stored and accessed.
9. Graphics capabilities may allow the auditor to generate, display, and evaluate various financial and nonfinancial relationships graphically.
10. Engagement-management information such as time budgets and the monitoring of actual time vs. budgeted amounts may be more easily generated and analyzed.
11. Customized working papers may be developed with greater ease.
12. Standardized audit correspondence such as engagement letters, client representation letters, and attorney letters may be stored and easily modified.
13. Supervisory-review time may be reduced.
14. Staff morale and productivity may be improved by reducing the time spent on clerical tasks.
15. Client's personnel may not need to manually prepare as many schedules and otherwise spend as much time assisting the auditor.
16. Computer-generated working papers are generally more legible and consistent.

*Because the requirements of this question could be answered by lists of items, we have not included an outline of the solution.

CHAPTER THREE

BUSINESS LAW PROBLEMS AND SOLUTIONS

Business law is tested on Friday morning from 8:30 to 12:00. Recent business law exams have consisted of 60 multiple choice questions (60% of the business law grade) and 4 essay questions (each 10% of the business law grade). Essay questions generally contain 2 to 4 parts, frequently unrelated, even to the point of testing unrelated topics, e.g., part "a" tests corporations and part "b" tests bankruptcy.

Recent business law exams have covered subject matter from almost all of the 16 business law modules. A complete analysis of recent examinations and the *Revised AICPA Content Specification Outlines* appears in Volume I, *Outlines and Study Guides*.

CPA candidates tend to overemphasize multiple choice questions in business law, even more so than in other sections of the examination, due to unfamiliarity with business law topics relative to accounting topics. Special attention should be directed to law essay questions because they often require yes-no type decisions at the beginning of the answers in addition to a well-organized, complete answer presentation as in auditing and theory.

Each question is coded as to month, year, section, problem number, and multiple choice question number, e.g., (1185,L1,43): where 1185 is November 1985; L1 is law problem 1; and 43 is the multiple choice question number. Some questions were altered to make them applicable due to changes in the law.

Module 7/Contracts (CONT)

	Exam reference	No. of minutes	Page no. Problem	Page no. Answer
68 Multiple Choice			218	230
3 Essay Questions:				
1. Consideration; Effectiveness of Acceptance and Revocation; Rejection of Option	1187,L4	15-20	228	242
2. Substantial Performance; Effectiveness of Acceptance	580,L3a&b	15-20	228	242
3. Firm Offer; Revocation and Attempted Acceptance; Option Contract; Acceptance of an Offer	1189,L4	15-20	229	244

Module 8/Sales (SALE)

	Exam reference	No. of minutes	Page no. Problem	Page no. Answer
42 Multiple Choice			245	254
3 Essay Questions:				
1. Passage of Title and Risk of Loss	1188,L2	15-20	252	262
2. Product Liability; Disclaimer of Warranties	1185,L4	15-20	252	262
3. Statute of Frauds; Modification of UCC Contract; Seller's Compensatory Damages	1187,L2	15-20	253	263

Module 9/Commercial Paper (CPAP)

	Exam reference	No. of minutes	Problem	Answer
49 Multiple Choice			265	276
3 Essay Questions:				
1. Rights of a Holder in Due Course; Unauthorized Signatures; Liability of Drawee Bank	581,L2	15-20	274	284
2. Shelter Rule; Secondary Liability	583,L5a	7-10	274	285
3. Fictitious Payee; Drawee Bank's Acceptance of Check with Forgery of Drawer's Signature	587,L2	15-25	274	285

Module 10/Secured Transactions (SECU)

	Exam reference	No. of minutes	Problem	Answer
27 Multiple Choice			287	295
5 Essay Questions:				
1. Purchase Money Security Interest in Consumer Goods; Equipment	1183,L2a	7-10	292	300
2. Perfection of True Consignment Priority of Conflicting Security Interests	581,L3	15-20	292	300
3. Attachment; Perfection; Good Faith Purchaser of Consumer Goods	1184,L4a&b	15-25	293	302
4. Purchase Money Security Interest; Priority of Bankruptcy Trustee; Purchase Money Secured Party in Equipment and Buyer in Ordinary Course of Business	588,L4	15-20	293	302
5. Risk of Loss; Rights Under Entrusting of Possession of Goods; Attachment of Security Interest; Perfection of Security Interests	589,L5	15-20	293	303

Module 11/Bankruptcy (BANK)

	Exam reference	No. of minutes	Problem	Answer
23 Multiple Choice			305	311
3 Essay Questions:				
1. Involuntary Bankruptcy; Debtor's Estate; Priority of Claims	1187,L3	15-20	309	316
2. Voidable Preference; Contemporaneous Exchange	585,L5	15-20	309	316
3. Requirements for Involuntary Bankruptcy; Claims and Preferences; Discharge of Debt in Bankruptcy	589,L2	15-20	309	317

Module 12/Suretyship (SURE)

	Exam reference	No. of minutes	Page no. Problem	Answer
17 Multiple Choice			319	323
1 Essay Questions:				
1. Minority; Reasonable Covenant not to Compete; Surety's Defenses	1184,L3	15-20	322	327

Module 13/Agency (AGEN)

	Exam reference	No. of minutes	Page no. Problem	Answer
30 Multiple Choice			328	334
2 Essay Questions:				
1. Principal's Power and Right to Terminate Agency	1185,L3b	7-10	333	339
2. Ratification; Agency Coupled with an Interest	580,L5a	10-15	333	339

Module 14/Partnerships and Joint Ventures (PTJV)

	Exam reference	No. of minutes	Page no. Problem	Answer
26 Multiple Choice			340	347
4 Essay Questions:				
1. Differences Between General and Limited Partnership	1186,L2	15-20	345	351
2. Partner's Property Rights	1185,L3a	7-10	345	351
3. Partner as Agent of Partnership; Apparent Authority; Partner's Obligations under Partnership Agreement; Liability of Newly Admitted Partner; Liability of Withdrawing Partner	1188,L4	15-20	345	352
4. Withdrawal and Admission of Partner	584,L5a	7-10	346	353

Module 15/Corporations (CORP)

	Exam reference	No. of minutes	Page no. Problem	Answer
33 Multiple Choice			354	362
3 Essay Questions:				
1. Comparisons of Limited Partnership with Corporation; Formation; Transfer of Interests; Liability; Participation in Management; Share of Profits	588,L3	15-20	360	368

	Exam reference	No. of minutes	Page no. Problem	Answer
2. Promoter's Preincorporation Contracts; Cash Dividends; Director's Liability	1184,L5	15-25	360	369
3. Stated Capital; Treasury Stock; Cash Dividends	1187,L5	15-20	360	370

Module 16/Federal Securities Acts (FEDE)

	Exam reference	No. of minutes	Page no. Problem	Answer
29 Multiple Choice			371	376
1 Essay Question:				
1. Registration Requirements Under 1933 Act	582,L2	15 20	375	381

Module 17/Accountant's Legal Liability (ACLL)

	Exam reference	No. of minutes	Page no. Problem	Answer
21 Multiple Choice			383	389
5 Essay Questions:				
1. Engagement Letter; CPA's Duty to Inquire; Parties That May Sue CPA	1185,L2	15-20	386	393
2. CPA's Federal Statutory Liability; CPA's State Common Law Liability	585,L4	15-20	386	393
3. Accountant-Client Privilege; CPA's Negligence; CPA's Fraud	587,L3	15-20	386	394
4. Statute of Frauds; Restraint of Trade; Accountant's Liability for Negligence	588,L5	15-20	387	395
5. Anti-Fraud Provisions under Rule 10b-5 of the 1934 Act; Liability to Third Parties Based on Negligence	1188,L5	15-20	388	396

Module 18/Regulation of Employment (REMP)

	Exam reference	No. of minutes	Page no. Problem	Answer
19 Multiple Choice			398	403
1 Essay Question:				
1. Worker's Compensation; Definition of Employee; Strict Liability; Limited Liability of Shareholders	1188,L3	15-20	402	407

Module 19/Property (PROP)

	Exam reference	No. of minutes	Page no. Problem	Answer
32 Multiple Choice			408	415
3 Essay Questions:				
1. Purchase of Property with Existing Mortgage; Assignment and Sublease of Lease	1184,L2	15-20	413	421
2. Trade Fixtures	1182,L5b	7-10	413	421
3. Liability on Assumption of Mortgage; Subletting; Property Interests; Rights of Joint Tenants and Tenants in Common	589,L3	15-20	413	423

Module 20/Insurance (INSU)

	Exam reference	No. of minutes	Page no. Problem	Answer
15 Multiple Choice			425	430
2 Essay Questions:				
1. Coinsurance, Standard Mortgagee, and Pro Rata Clauses	1182,L5a	10-15	428	433
2. Insurable Interests	1188,L2	15-20	428	434

Module 21/Trusts and Estates (TRUS)

	Exam reference	No. of minutes	Page no. Problem	Answer
21 Multiple Choice			436	441
2 Essay Questions:				
1. Concurrent Ownership; Trust Requirements; Trustee's Duties; Termination of Trust	584,L4	15-20	440	445
2. Creation of Inter Vivos Trust; Allocation of Receipts and Disbursements between Principal and Income Beneficiaries	587,L5	15-20	440	445

Sample Examination

	Page no.
Business Law	Appendix

Multiple Choice Questions (1-68)

1. In order for an offer to confer the power to form a contract by acceptance, it must have all of the following elements **except**
   a. Be communicated to the offeree and the communication must be made or authorized by the offeror.
   b. Be sufficiently definite and certain.
   c. Be communicated by words to the offeree by the offeror.
   d. Manifest an intent to enter into a contract.

2. To announce the grand opening of a new retail business, Hudson placed an advertisement in a local newspaper quoting sales prices on certain items in stock. The grand opening was so successful that Hudson was unable to totally satisfy customer demands. Which of the following statements is correct?
   a. Hudson made an invitation seeking offers.
   b. Hudson made an offer to the people who read the advertisement.
   c. Anyone who tendered money for the items advertised was entitled to buy them.
   d. The offer by Hudson was partially revocable as to an item once it was sold out.

3. Dye sent Hill a written offer to sell a tract of land located in Newtown for $60,000. The parties were engaged in a separate dispute. The offer stated that it would be irrevocable for 60 days if Hill would promise to refrain from suing Dye during this time. Hill promptly delivered a promise not to sue during the term of the offer and to forego suit if Hill accepted the offer. Dye subsequently decided that the possible suit by Hill was groundless and therefore phoned Hill and revoked the offer 15 days after making it. Hill mailed an acceptance on the 20th day. Dye did not reply. Under the circumstances,
   a. Dye's offer was supported by consideration and was **not** revocable when accepted.
   b. Dye's written offer would be irrevocable even without consideration.
   c. Dye's silence was an acceptance of Hill's promise.
   d. Dye's revocation, **not** being in writing, was invalid.

4. The following conversation took place between Mary and Ed. Mary: "Ed, if you wanted to sell your table, what would you ask for it?" Ed: "I suppose $400 would be a fair price." Mary: "I'll take it, if you will have it refinished." Ed: "Sold." Thus,
   a. Ed's statement: "I suppose $400 would be a fair price" constituted an offer.
   b. Mary's reply: "I'll take it, if you will have it refinished" was a conditional acceptance, terminating Ed's offer.
   c. No contract resulted since Ed never stated he would actually sell the table for $400.
   d. A contract was formed when Ed said: "Sold."

5. Harris wrote Douglas a letter which might be construed alternatively as an offer to sell land, an invitation to commence negotiations, or merely an invitation to Douglas to make an offer. Douglas claims that the communication was a bona fide offer which he has unequivocally accepted according to the terms set forth therein. In deciding the dispute in question, the court will
   a. Look to the subjective intent of Harris.
   b. Use an objective standard based on how a reasonably prudent businessman would have interpreted the letter to Douglas.
   c. Decide that an offer had **not** been made if any of the usual terms were omitted.
   d. Decide on the basis of what Douglas considered the writing to be.

6. Martin wrote Dall and offered to sell Dall a building for $200,000. The offer stated it would expire 30 days from April 1. Martin changed his mind and does not wish to be bound by his offer. If a legal dispute arises between the parties regarding whether there has been a valid acceptance of the offer, which one of the following is correct?
   a. The offer cannot be legally withdrawn for the stated period of time.
   b. The offer will **not** expire before the 30 days even if Martin sells the property to a third person and notifies Dall.
   c. If Dall categorically rejects the offer on April 10, Dall cannot validly accept within the remaining stated period of time.
   d. If Dall phoned Martin on May 3, and unequivocally accepted the offer, a contract would be created, provided that Dall had **no** notice of withdrawal of the offer.

7. Which of the following statements concerning the effectiveness of an offeree's rejection and an offeror's revocation of an offer is generally correct?

	An offeree's rejection is effective when	An offeror's revocation is effective when
a.	Received by offeror	Sent by offeror
b.	Sent by offeree	Received by offeree
c.	Sent by offeree	Sent by offeror
d.	Received by offeror	Received by offeree

8. An offer is not terminated by operation of law solely because the
   a. Offeror dies.
   b. Offeree is adjudicated insane.
   c. Subject matter is destroyed.
   d. Subject matter is sold to a third party.

9. On April 2, Jet Co. wrote to Ard, offering to buy Ard's building for $350,000. The offer contained all of the essential terms to form a binding contract and was duly signed by Jet's president. It further provided that the offer would remain open until May 30 and an acceptance would not be effective until received by Jet. On April 10, Ard accepted Jet's offer by mail. The acceptance was received by Jet on April 14. Assume that on April 11 Jet sent a telegram to Ard revoking its offer and that Ard received the telegram on April 12. Under the circumstances,
   a. A contract was formed on April 10.
   b. A contract was formed on April 14.
   c. Jet's revocation effectively terminated its offer on April 12.
   d. Jet's revocation effectively terminated its offer on April 11.

10. The mailbox rule generally makes acceptance of an offer effective at the time the acceptance is dispatched. The mailbox rule does not apply if
   a. Both the offeror and offeree are merchants.
   b. The offer proposes a sale of real estate.
   c. The offer provides that an acceptance shall not be effective until actually received.
   d. The duration of the offer is not in excess of three months.

11. Stable Corp. offered in a signed writing to sell Mix an office building for $350,000. The offer, which was sent by Stable on April 1, indicated that it would remain open until July 9. On July 5, Mix mailed a letter rejecting Stable's offer. On July 6, Mix sent a telegram to Stable accepting the original offer. The letter of rejection was received by Stable on July 8 and the telegram of acceptance was received by Stable on July 7. Which of the following is correct?
   a. Mix's telegram resulted in the formation of a valid contract.
   b. Mix's letter of July 5 terminated Stable's offer when mailed.
   c. Stable was not entitled to withdraw its offer until after July 9.
   d. Although Stable's offer on April 1 was a firm offer under the UCC it will only remain open for three months.

12. Quick Corp. mailed a letter to Blue Co. on May 1, 1986, offering a three-year franchise dealership. The offer stated the terms in detail and at the bottom stated that the offer would not be withdrawn prior to June 5, 1986. Which of the following is correct?
   a. The offer can not be assigned to another party by Blue if Blue chooses not to accept.
   b. A letter of acceptance from Blue to Quick sent on June 5, 1986, and which was received by Quick on June 6, 1986, does not create a valid contract.
   c. The offer is an irrevocable option which can not be withdrawn prior to June 5, 1986.
   d. The Statute of Frauds does not apply to the proposed contract.

13. On April 1, Knox signed and mailed a letter containing an offer to sell Wax a warehouse for $75,000. The letter also indicated that the offer would expire on May 3. Which of the following is correct?
   a. The offer is a firm offer under the UCC and can not be withdrawn by Knox prior to May 3.
   b. Wax can benefit from the early acceptance rule no matter what means of communication he uses as long as the acceptance is sent on or before May 3.
   c. If Wax purports to accept the offer on April 15 at $50,000 and Knox refuses to sell at that price, Wax nevertheless has the right to accept at $75,000 by May 3.
   d. A telephone call by Wax to Knox on May 3, accepting the offer at $75,000, will effectively bind Knox.

14. Water Works had a long-standing policy of offering employees $100 for suggestions actually used. Due to inflation and a decline

in the level and quality of suggestions received, Water Works decided to increase the award to $500. Several suggestions were under consideration at that time. Two days prior to the public announcement of the increase to $500, a suggestion by Farber was accepted and put into use. Farber is seeking to collect $500. Farber is entitled to

a. $500 because Water Works had decided to pay that amount.
b. $500 because the suggestion submitted will be used during the period that Water Works indicated it would pay $500.
c. $100 in accordance with the original offer.
d. Nothing if Water Works chooses not to pay since the offer was gratuitous.

15. Wilcox mailed Norriss an unsigned contract for the purchase of a tract of real property. The contract represented the oral understanding of the parties as to the purchase price, closing date, type of deed, and other details. It called for payment in full in cash or certified check at the closing. Norriss signed the contract, but added above his signature the following:

This contract is subject to my (Norriss) being able to obtain conventional mortgage financing of $100,000 at 13% or less interest for a period of not less than 25 years.

Which of the following is correct?
a. The parties had already made an enforceable contract prior to Wilcox's mailing of the formalized contract.
b. Norriss would not be liable on the contract under the circumstances even if he had not added the "conventional mortgage" language since Wilcox had not signed it.
c. By adding the "conventional mortgage" language above his signature, Norriss created a condition precedent to his contractual obligation and made a counteroffer.
d. The addition of the "conventional mortgage" language has no legal effect upon the contractual relationship of the parties since it was an implied condition in any event.

16. In deciding whether consideration necessary to form a contract exists, a court must determine whether
a. The consideration given by each party is of roughly equal value.
b. There is mutuality of consideration.

c. The consideration has sufficient monetary value.
d. The consideration conforms to the subjective intent of the parties.

17. Baker and Able signed a contract which required Able to purchase 600 books from Baker at 90¢ per book. Subsequently, Able, in good faith, requested that the price of the books be reduced to 80¢ per book. Baker orally agreed to reduce the price to 80¢. Under the circumstances, the oral agreement is
a. Unenforceable, because Able failed to give consideration, but proof of it will be otherwise admissible into evidence.
b. Unenforceable, due to the Statute of Frauds, and proof of it will be inadmissible into evidence.
c. Enforceable, but proof of it will be inadmissible into evidence.
d. Enforceable, and proof of it will be admissible into evidence.

18. For there to be consideration for a contract, there must be
a. A bargained-for detriment to the promisor(ee) or a benefit to the promissee(or).
b. A manifestation of mutual assent.
c. Genuineness of assent.
d. Substantially equal economic benefits to both parties.

19. Polk is seeking to avoid performing a promise to pay Lake $800. Polk is relying upon lack of consideration on Lake's part sufficient to support his promise. Polk will prevail if he can establish that
a. Lake's only claim of consideration was the relinquishment of a legal right.
b. Prior to Polk's promise, Lake had already performed the requested act.
c. The contract is executory.
d. Lake's asserted consideration is worth only $250.

20. Marblehead Manufacturing, Inc. contracted with Wellfleet Oil Company in June to provide its regular supply of fuel oil from November 1 through March 31. The written contract required Marblehead to take all of its oil requirements exclusively from Wellfleet at a fixed price subject to an additional amount not to exceed 10% of the contract price and only if the market price increases during the term of the contract. By the time performance was due on the contract, the market price had

already risen 20%. Wellfleet seeks to avoid
performance. Which of the following will be
Wellfleet's best argument?

a. There is no contract since Marblehead was not required to take any
oil.

b. The contract fails because of lack
of definiteness and certainty.

c. The contract is unconscionable.

d. Marblehead has ordered amounts of
oil unreasonably disproportionate to
its normal requirements.

21. Meed entered into a written agreement to
sell a parcel of land to Beel for $80,000. At
the time the agreement was executed, Meed had
consumed a large amount of alcoholic beverages
which significantly impaired Meed's ability to
understand the nature and terms of the contract. Beel knew Meed was very intoxicated
and that the land had been appraised at
$125,000. Meed wishes to avoid the contract.
The contract is

a. Void.

b. Legally binding on both parties in
the absence of fraud or undue
influence.

c. Voidable at Meed's option.

d. Voidable at Meed's option only if
the intoxication was involuntary.

22. Kent, a 16-year old, purchased a used car
from Mint Motors, Inc. Ten months later, the
car was stolen and never recovered. Which of
the following statements is correct?

a. The car's theft is a <u>de facto</u>
ratification of the purchase because
it is impossible to return the car.

b. Kent may disaffirm the purchase
because Kent is a minor.

c. Kent effectively ratified the
purchase because Kent used the car
for an unreasonable period of time.

d. Kent may disaffirm the purchase
because Mint, a merchant, is subject
to the UCC.

23. Tell, an Ohio real estate broker, misrepresented to Allen that Tell was licensed in
Michigan under Michigan's statute regulating
real estate brokers. Allen signed a standard
form listing contract agreeing to pay Tell a
6% commission for selling Allen's home in
Michigan. Tell sold Allen's home. Under the
circumstances, Allen is

a. Not liable to Tell for any amount
because Allen signed a standard form
contract.

b. Not liable to Tell for any amount
because Tell violated the Michigan
licensing requirements.

c. Liable to Tell only for the value of
services rendered under a quasi-
contract theory.

d. Liable to Tell for the full
commission under a promissory
estoppel theory.

24. Parr is a CPA licensed to practice in
State A. Parr entered into a contract with
Jet, Inc. to perform an audit in State B for
$50,000 (including expenses). After Parr had
satisfactorily performed the audit, Jet discovered that Parr had violated State B's
licensing statute by failing to obtain a CPA
license in State B. Parr incurred $10,000 in
expenses in connection with the audit. Jet
refuses to pay any fee to Parr, arguing that
it could have engaged a local CPA licensed in
State B to perform the same services for
$35,000 (including expenses). If Parr sues
Jet based on breach of contract, Parr will be
entitled to recover a maximum of

a. $0

b. $10,000

c. $35,000

d. $50,000

25. Mix entered into a contract with Small
which provided that Small would receive
$10,000 if he stole trade secrets from Mix's
competition. Small performed his part of the
contract by delivering the trade secrets to
Mix. Mix refuses to pay Small for his
services. Under what theory may Small
recover?

a. Quasi contract, in order to prevent
the unjust enrichment of Mix.

b. Promissory estoppel, since Small has
changed his position to his detriment.

c. None, due to the illegal nature of
the contract.

d. Express contract, since both parties
bargained for and exchanged promises
in forming the contract.

26. Bradford sold a parcel of land to Jones
who promptly recorded the deed. Bradford then
resold the land to Wallace. In a suit against
Bradford by Wallace, recovery will be based on
the theory of

a. Bilateral mistake.

b. Ignorance of the facts.

c. Unilateral mistake.

d. Fraud.

27. A party to a contract who seeks to
rescind the contract because of that party's
reliance on the unintentional but materially
false statements of the other party will
assert

a. Reformation.
b. Actual fraud.
c. Misrepresentation.
d. Constructive fraud.

28. Which of the following remedies is available to a party who has entered into a contract in reliance upon the other contracting party's innocent misrepresentations as to material facts?

	Compensatory damages	Punitive damages	Rescission
a.	No	No	No
b.	Yes	No	Yes
c.	No	No	Yes
d.	Yes	Yes	No

29. Sisk contracted to sell Bleu a building for $470,000. If Sisk wishes to avoid the contract based on undue influence, one element that Sisk must prove is that Bleu
a. Induced Sisk to sell the building by unfair persuasion.
b. Was in a fiduciary relationship with Sisk.
c. Misrepresented material facts to Sisk.
d. Made improper threats to Sisk.

30. On April 6, Apple entered into a signed contract with Bean, by which Apple was to sell Bean an antique automobile having a fair market value of $150,000, for $75,000. Apple believed the auto was worth only $75,000. Unknown to either party the auto had been destroyed by fire on April 4. If Bean sues Apple for breach of contract, Apple's best defense is
a. Unconscionability.
b. Risk of loss had passed to Bean.
c. Lack of adequate consideration.
d. Mutual mistake.

31. King had several outstanding unsecured loans with National Bank. In addition, King had a separate loan with National that was secured by a mortgage on a farm owned by King. King was delinquent on the mortgage loan but not on the unsecured loans. National asked King to sign renewal notes for the unsecured loans at substantially higher interest rates. When King refused, National informed King that it would foreclose on the farm's mortgage if King did not sign. King signed but later disaffirmed the new unsecured notes and National sued. King's best defense is
a. Undue influence.
b. Unconscionability.
c. Duress.
d. Fraud in the inducement.

32. Sting, Corp., a general contractor, obtained bids from several plumbers to install piping. Lite, a licensed plumber, submitted a bid for $60,000 which was $20,000 less than the next lowest bid. Lite made an obvious and substantial arithmetic error in his bid. Sting did not have actual knowledge of Lite's mistake. If Sting accepts Lite's bid, Lite
a. Must perform the contract for $60,000 since Sting did <u>not</u> have actual knowledge of the error.
b. Must perform the contract for $60,000 unless he can show that Sting caused the error.
c. Can avoid liability for refusing to install the piping for $60,000 since Sting should have known of Lite's error.
d. Can avoid liability for refusing to install the piping for $60,000 only if the error was <u>not</u> due to his negligence.

33. The Statute of Frauds
a. Prevents the use of oral evidence to contradict the terms of a written contract.
b. Applies to all contracts having consideration valued at $500 or more.
c. Requires the independent promise to pay the debt of another to be in writing.
d. Applies to all real estate leases.

34. On May 1, Dix and Wilk entered into an oral agreement by which Dix agreed to purchase a small parcel of land from Wilk for $450. Dix paid Wilk $100 as a deposit. The following day, Wilk received another offer to purchase the land for $650, the fair market value. Wilk immediately notifed Dix that Wilk would not sell the land for $450. If Dix sues Wilk for specific performance, Dix will
a. Prevail, because the amount of the contract was less than $500.
b. Prevail, because there was part performance.
c. Lose, because the fair market value of the land is over $500.
d. Lose, because the agreement was <u>not</u> in writing and signed by Wilk.

35. With regard to an agreement for the sale of real estate, the Statute of Frauds
a. Requires that the entire agreement be in a single writing.
b. Requires that the purchase price be fair and adequate in relation to the value of the real estate.

c.   Does not require that the agreement
be signed by all parties.

d.   Does not apply if the value of the
real estate is less than $500.

36.   Able hired Carr to restore Able's antique
car for $800. The terms of their oral agree-
ment provided that Carr was to complete the
work within 18 months. Actually, the work
could be completed within one year. The
agreement is

a.   Unenforceable because it covers
services with a value in excess of
$500.

b.   Unenforceable because it covers a
time period in excess of one year.

c.   Enforceable because personal service
contracts are exempt from the
Statute of Frauds.

d.   Enforceable because the work could
be completed within one year.

37.   To satisfy the UCC Statute of Frauds, a
written agreement for the sale of goods must

a.   Contain payment terms.

b.   Be signed by both buyer and seller.

c.   Indicate that a contract for sale
has been made.

d.   Refer to the time and place of
delivery.

38.   Glass Co. telephoned Hourly Company and
ordered 2,000 watches at $2 each. Glass
agreed to pay 10% immediately and the balance
within ten days after receipt of the entire
shipment. Glass forwarded a check for $400
and Hourly shipped 1,000 watches the next day,
intending to ship the balance by the end of
the week. Glass decided that the contract was
a bad bargain and repudiated it, asserting the
Statute of Frauds. Hourly sued Glass. Which
of the following will allow Hourly to enforce
the contract in its entirety despite the
Statute of Frauds?

a.   Glass admitted in court that it made
the contract in question.

b.   Hourly shipped 1,000 watches.

c.   Glass paid 10% down.

d.   The contract is not within the
requirements of the Statute.

39.   Ward is attempting to introduce oral
evidence in an action relating to a written
contract between Ward and Weaver. Weaver has
pleaded the parol evidence rule. Ward will be
prohibited from introducing parol evidence if
it relates to

a.   A modification made several days
after the contract was executed.

b.   A change in the meaning of an
unambiguous provision in the
contract.

c.   Fraud in the inducement.

d.   An obvious error in drafting.

40.   Moss entered into a contract to purchase
certain real property from Shinn. Which of
the following statements is not correct?

a.   If Shinn fails to perform the
contract, Moss can obtain specific
performance.

b.   The contract is nonassignable as a
matter of law.

c.   The Statute of Frauds applies to the
contract.

d.   Any amendment to the contract must
be agreed to by both Moss and Shinn.

41.   Generally, which one of the following
transfers will be valid without the consent of
the other parties?

a.   The assignment by the lessee of a
lease contract where rent is a
percentage of sales.

b.   The assignment by a purchaser of
goods of the right to buy on credit
without giving security.

c.   The assignment by an architect of a
contract to design a building.

d.   The assignment by a patent holder of
the right to receive royalties.

42.   Krieg was the owner of an office building
encumbered by a mortgage securing Krieg's
promissory note to Muni Bank. Park purchased
the building subject to Muni's mortgage. As a
result of the sale to Park,

a.   Muni is not a third party creditor
beneficiary.

b.   Krieg is a third party creditor
beneficiary.

c.   Park is liable for any deficiency
resulting from a default on the
note.

d.   Krieg was automatically released
from any liability on the note.

43.   Ace contracted with Big City to train and
employ handicapped, unemployed veterans residing in Big City. Ace breached the contract
and Bell, a resident of Big City, who is a
handicapped, unemployed veteran, sues Ace for
damages. Under the circumstances, Bell will

a.   Lose, because Bell is merely an
incidental beneficiary of the
contract.

b.   Win, because Bell is a third-party
beneficiary entitled to enforce the
contract.

c.   Lose, because Big City did not
assign its contract rights to Bell.

d.   Win, because the intent of the
contract was to confer a benefit on
all handicapped, unemployed veterans
residing in Big City.

44. Jones owned an insurance policy on her
life, on which she paid all the premiums.
Smith was named the beneficiary. Jones died
and the insurance company refused to pay the
insurance proceeds to Smith. An action by
Smith against the insurance company for the
insurance proceeds will be
    a. Successful because Smith is a third
        party donee beneficiary.
    b. Successful because Smith is a proper
        assignee of Jones' rights under the
        insurance policy.
    c. Unsuccessful because Smith was not
        the owner of the policy.
    d. Unsuccessful because Smith did not
        pay any of the premiums.

45. Kent Construction Company contracted to
construct four garages for Magnum, Inc.,
according to specifications provided by
Magnum. Kent deliberately substituted 2 x 4s
for the more expensive 2 x 6s called for in
the contract in all places where the 2 x 4s
would not be readily detected. Magnum's
inspection revealed the variance and Magnum is
now withholding the final payment on the contract. The contract was for $100,000, and the
final payment would be $25,000. Damages were
estimated to be $15,000. In a lawsuit for the
balance due, Kent will
    a. Prevail on the contract, less
        damages of $15,000, because it has
        substantially performed.
    b. Prevail because the damages in ques-
        tion were not substantial in
        relation to the contract amount.
    c. Lose because the law unqualifiedly
        requires literal performance of such
        contracts.
    d. Lose all rights under the contract
        because it has intentionally
        breached it.

46. Dell owed Stark $9,000. As the result of
an unrelated transaction, Stark owed Ball that
same amount. The three parties signed an
agreement that Dell would pay Ball instead of
Stark, and Stark would be discharged from all
liability. The agreement among the parties is
    a. A novation.
    b. An executed accord and satisfaction.
    c. Voidable at Ball's option.
    d. Unenforceable for lack of
        consideration.

47. On June 1, 1986, Nord Corp. engaged Milo
& Co., CPAs, to perform certain management
advisory services for nine months for a
$45,000 fee. The terms of their oral
agreement required Milo to commence performance any time before October 1, 1986. On

June 30, 1987, after Milo completed the work
to Nord's satisfaction, Nord paid Milo $30,000
by check. Nord conspicuously marked on the
check that it constituted payment in full for
all services rendered. Nord has refused to
pay the remaining $15,000 arguing that,
although it believes the $45,000 fee is
reasonable, it had received bids of $30,000
and $38,000 from other firms to perform the
same services as Milo. Milo endorsed and
deposited the check. If Milo commences an
action against Nord for the remaining $15,000,
Milo will be entitled to recover
    a. $0 because there has been an en-
        forceable accord and satisfaction.
    b. $0 because the Statute of Frauds has
        not been satisfied.
    c. $8,000 because $38,000 was the
        highest other bid.
    d. $15,000 because it is the balance
        due under the agreement.

48. Meek & Co., CPAs, was engaged by Reed,
the president of Sulk Corp., to issue by
June 15, 1986, an opinion on Sulk's financial
statements for the fiscal year ended March 31,
1986. Meek's engagement and its fee of
$20,000 were approved by Sulk's board of
directors. Meek did not issue its opinion
until June 30 because of Sulk's failure to
supply Meek with the necessary information to
complete the audit. Sulk refuses to pay
Meek. If Meek sues Sulk, Meek will
    a. Prevail based on the contract.
    b. Prevail based on the quasi contract.
    c. Lose, since it breached the con-
        tract.
    d. Lose, since the June 15 deadline was
        a condition precedent to Sulk's per-
        formance.

49. Foster Co. and Rice executed a contract
by which Foster was to sell a warehouse to
Rice for $270,000. The contract required Rice
to pay the entire $270,000 at the closing.
Foster has refused to close the sale of the
warehouse to Rice. If Rice commences a
lawsuit against Foster, what relief would Rice
likely be entitled to?
    a. Specific performance or compensatory
        damages.
    b. Specific performance and compensa-
        tory damages.
    c. Compensatory damages or punitive
        damages.
    d. Compensatory damages and punitive
        damages.

50. A clause in a contract for the purchase
of real estate which provides that the seller
shall be entitled to retain the purchaser's

downpayment as liquidated damages should the purchaser fail to close the transaction will generally be enforceable

    a.   In addition to the seller's right to recover compensatory damages.

    b.   As a penalty if the purchaser has intentionally defaulted.

    c.   If the amount of the downpayment bears a reasonable relationship to the probable loss.

    d.   In all cases provided the parties have agreed in a signed writing.

51. Jones, CPA, entered into a signed contract with Foster Corp. to perform accounting and review services. If Jones repudiates the contract prior to the date performance is due to begin, which of the following is **not** correct?

    a.   Foster could successfully maintain an action for breach of contract after the date performance was due to begin.

    b.   Foster can obtain a judgment ordering Jones to perform.

    c.   Foster could successfully maintain an action for breach of contract prior to the date performance is due to begin.

    d.   Foster can obtain a judgment for the monetary damages it incurred as a result of the repudiation.

52. Nagel and Fields entered into a contract in which Nagel was obligated to deliver certain goods to Fields by September 10. On September 3, Nagel told Fields that Nagel had no intention of delivering the goods required by the contract. Prior to September 10, Fields may successfully sue Nagel under the doctrine of

    a.   Promissory estoppel.

    b.   Accord and satisfaction.

    c.   Anticipatory repudiation.

    d.   Substantial performance.

53. In September 1988, Cobb Company contracted with Thrifty Oil Company for the delivery of 100,000 gallons of heating oil at the price of 75¢ per gallon at regular specified intervals during the forthcoming winter. Due to an unseasonably warm winter, Cobb took delivery on only 70,000 gallons. In a suit against Cobb for breach of contract, Thrifty will

    a.   Lose, because Cobb acted in good faith.

    b.   Lose, because both parties are merchants and the UCC recognizes commerical impracticability.

    c.   Win, because this is a requirements contract.

    d.   Win, because the change of circumstances could have been contemplated by the parties.

54. Unless the parties have otherwise agreed, an action for the breach of a contract within the UCC Sales Article must be commenced within

    a.   Four years after the cause of action has accrued.

    b.   Six years after the cause of action has accrued.

    c.   Four years after the effective date of the contract.

    d.   Six years after the effective date of the contract.

May 1990 Questions

55. To satisfy the consideration requirement for a valid contract, the consideration exchanged by the parties must be

    a.   Legally sufficient.

    b.   Payable in legal tender.

    c.   Simultaneously paid and received.

    d.   Of the same economic value.

56. On September 27, Summers sent Fox a letter offering to sell Fox a vacation home for $150,000. On October 2, Fox replied by mail agreeing to buy the home for $145,000. Summers did not reply to Fox. Do Fox and Summers have a binding contract?

    a.   No, because Fox failed to sign and return Summers' letter.

    b.   No, because Fox's letter was a counteroffer.

    c.   Yes, because Summers' offer was validly accepted.

    d.   Yes, because Summers' silence is an implied acceptance of Fox's letter.

57. On November 1, Yost sent a telegram to Zen offering to sell a rare vase. The offer required that Zen's acceptance telegram be sent on or before 5:00 P.M. on November 2. On November 2, at 3:00 P.M., Zen sent an acceptance by overnight mail. It did not reach Yost until November 5. Yost refused to complete the sale to Zen. Is there an enforceable contract?

    a.   Yes, because the acceptance was made within the time specified.

    b.   Yes, because the acceptance was effective when sent.

    c.   No, because Zen did **not** accept by telegram.

    d.   No, because the offer required receipt of the acceptance within the time specified.

58. Opal offered, in writing, to sell Larkin a parcel of land for $300,000. If Opal dies, the offer will
   a. Terminate prior to Larkin's acceptance only if Larkin received notice of Opal's death.
   b. Remain open for a reasonable period of time after Opal's death.
   c. Automatically terminate despite Larkin's prior acceptance.
   d. Automatically terminate prior to Larkin's acceptance.

59. King sent Foster, a real estate developer, a signed offer to sell a specified parcel of land to Foster for $200,000. King, an engineer, had inherited the land. On the same day that King's letter was received, Foster telephoned King and accepted the offer. Which of the following statements is correct under the Statute of Frauds?
   a. No contract was formed because Foster did not sign the offer.
   b. No contract was formed because King is not a merchant and, therefore, King's letter is not binding on Foster.
   c. A contract was formed, although it would be enforceable only against King.
   d. A contract was formed and would be enforceable against both King and Foster because Foster is a merchant.

60. Which of the following will be legally binding on all parties despite lack of consideration?
   a. An irrevocable oral promise by a merchant to keep an offer open for 60 days.
   b. A promise to donate money to a charity which the charity relied upon in incurring large expenditures.
   c. A promise to pay for the college education of the child of a person who saved the promisor's life.
   d. A signed modification to a contract to purchase a parcel of land.

61. Payne entered into a written agreement to sell a parcel of land to Stevens. At the time the agreement was executed, Payne had consumed alcoholic beverages. Payne's ability to understand the nature and terms of the contract was not impaired. Stevens did not believe that Payne was intoxicated. The contract is
   a. Void as a matter of law.
   b. Legally binding on both parties.
   c. Voidable at Payne's option.
   d. Voidable at Steven's option.

62. Sand orally promised Frost a $10,000 bonus, in addition to a monthly salary, if Frost would work two years for Sand. If Frost works for the two years, will the Statute of Frauds prevent Frost from collecting the bonus?
   a. No, because Frost fully performed.
   b. No, because the contract did not involve an interest in real estate.
   c. Yes, because the contract could not be performed within one year.
   d. Yes, because the monthly salary was the consideration for the contract.

63. Union Bank lent $200,000 to Wagner. Union required Wagner to obtain a life insurance policy naming Union as beneficiary. While the loan was outstanding, Wagner stopped paying the premiums on the policy. Union paid the premiums, adding the amounts paid to Wagner's loan. Wagner died and the insurance company refused to pay the policy proceeds to Union. Union may
   a. Recover the policy proceeds because it is a creditor beneficiary.
   b. Recover the policy proceeds because it is a donee beneficiary.
   c. Not recover the policy proceeds because it is not in privity of contract with the insurance company.
   d. Not recover the policy proceeds because it is only an incidental beneficiary.

64. Steele, Inc. wanted to purchase Kalp's distribution business. On March 15, 1990, Kalp provided Steele with copies of audited financial statements for the period ended December 31, 1989. The financial statements reflected inventory in the amount of $1,200,000. On March 29, 1990, Kalp discovered that the December 31 inventory was overstated by at least $400,000. On April 3, 1990, Steele, relying on the financial statements, purchased all of Kalp's business. On April 29, 1990, Steele discovered the inventory overstatement. Steele sued Kalp for fraud. Which of the following statements is correct?
   a. Steele will lose because it should not have relied on the inventory valuation in the financial statements.
   b. Steele will lose because Kalp was unaware that the inventory valuation was incorrect at the time the financial statements were provided to Steele.
   c. Steele will prevail because Kalp had a duty to disclose the fact that the inventory value was overstated.
   d. Steele will prevail but will not be able to sue for damages.

65. On August 1, Neptune Fisheries contracted in writing with West Markets to deliver to West 3,000 pounds of lobsters at $4.00 a pound. Delivery of the lobsters was due October 1 with payment due November 1. On August 4, Neptune entered into a contract with Deep Sea Lobster Farms which provided as follows: "Neptune Fisheries assigns all the rights under the contract with West Markets dated August 1 to Deep Sea Lobster Farms." The best interpretation of the August 4 contract would be that it was

   a. Only an assignment of rights by Neptune.
   b. Only a delegation of duties by Neptune.
   c. An assignment of rights and a delegation of duties by Neptune.
   d. An unenforceable third-party beneficiary contract.

66. Paco Corp., a building contractor, offered to sell Preston several pieces of used construction equipment. Preston was engaged in the business of buying and selling equipment. Paco's written offer had been prepared by a secretary who typed the total price as $10,900, rather than $109,000, which was the approximate fair market value of the equipment. Preston, on receipt of the offer, immediately accepted it. Paco learned of the error in the offer and refused to deliver the equipment to Preston unless Preston agreed to pay $109,000. Preston has sued Paco for breach of contract. Which of the following statements is correct?

   a. Paco will <u>not</u> be liable because there has been a mutual mistake of fact.
   b. Paco will be able to rescind the contract because Preston should have known that the price was erroneous.
   c. Preston will prevail because Paco is a merchant.
   d. The contract between Paco and Preston is void because the price set forth in the offer is substantially less than the equipment's fair market value.

67. Rice contracted with Locke to build an oil refinery for Locke. The contract provided that Rice was to use United pipe fittings. Rice did not do so. United learned of the contract and, anticipating the order, manufactured additional fittings. United sued Locke and Rice. United is

   a. Entitled to recover from Rice only, because Rice breached the contract.
   b. Entitled to recover from either Locke or Rice because it detrimentally relied on the contract.
   c. Not entitled to recover because it

is a donee beneficiary.
   d. Not entitled to recover because it is an incidental beneficiary.

68. Wren purchased a factory from First Federal Realty. Wren paid 20% at the closing and gave a note for the balance secured by a 20-year mortgage. Five years later, Wren found it increasingly difficult to make payments on the note and defaulted. First Federal threatened to accelerate the loan and foreclose if Wren continued in default. First Federal told Wren to make payment or obtain an acceptable third party to assume the obligation. Wren offered the land to Moss, Inc. for $10,000 less than the equity Wren had in the property. This was acceptable to First Federal and at the closing Moss paid the arrearage, assumed the mortgage and note, and had title transferred to its name. First Federal released Wren. The transaction in question is a(an)

   a. Purchase of land subject to a mortgage.
   b. Assignment and delegation.
   c. Third party beneficiary contract.
   d. Novation.

Repeat Question

(590,L1,20) Identical/similar to item 35 above

Problems

Problem 1   (1187,L4)

(15 to 20 minutes)

On April 1, Sam Stieb signed and mailed to Bold Corp. an offer to sell Bold a parcel of land for $175,000. On April 5, Bold called Stieb and requested that Stieb keep the offer open until June 1, by which time Bold would be able to determine whether financing for the purchase was available. That same day, Stieb signed and mailed a letter indicating that he would hold the offer open until June 1 if Bold mailed Stieb $100 by April 20.

On April 17, Stieb sent Bold a signed letter revoking his offers dated April 1 and April 5. Bold received that letter on April 19. However, Bold had already signed and mailed on April 18 its acceptance of Stieb's offer of April 5 along with a check for $100. Stieb received the check and letter of acceptance on April 20.

On May 15, Bold wrote Stieb stating that the $175,000 purchase price was too high but that it would be willing to purchase the land for $160,000. Upon receipt, Stieb immediately sent a telegram to Bold indicating that he had already revoked his offer and that even if his revocation was not effective he considered Bold's offer a counteroffer which he would not accept. Otherwise, Stieb did nothing as a result of Bold's May 15 letter.

On May 25, Bold executed and delivered the original contract of April 1 to Stieb without any variation of the original terms.

Stieb does not wish to sell the land to Bold because he has received another offer for $200,000. In order to avoid the sale to Bold for $175,000, Stieb asserts the following:

• Bold could not validly accept Stieb's offer dated April 5 because $100 was inadequate consideration to hold the offer open until April 20.

• Stieb's offer dated April 5 had terminated because he had revoked the offer prior to Bold's acceptance.

• Even if his revocation was not effective, Bold's letter of May 15 was a counteroffer, which automatically terminated Bold's right to accept Stieb's offer of April 1.

Required:

Discuss Stieb's assertions, indicating whether such assertions are correct or incorrect and setting forth the reasons for any conclusions stated.

Problem 2   (580,L3a&b)

(15 to 20 minutes)

Part a.   Smithers contracted with the Silverwater Construction Corporation to build a home. The contract contained a detailed set of specifications including the type, quality, and manufacturers' names of the building materials that were to be used. After construction was completed, a rigid inspection was made of the house and the following defects were discovered.

1. Some of the roofing shingles were improperly laid.

2. The ceramic tile in the kitchen and three bathrooms was not manufactured by Disco Tile Company as called for in the specifications. The price of the alternate tile was $325 less than the Disco but was of approximately equal quality.

3. The sewerage pipes that were imbedded in concrete in the basement were also not manufactured by the specified manufacturer. It could not be shown that there was any difference in quality and the price was the same.

4. Various minor defects such as improperly hung doors.

Silverwater has corrected defects 1 and 4 but has refused to correct 2 and 3 because the cost would be substantial. Silverwater claims it is entitled to recover under the contract and demands full payment. Smithers is adamant and is demanding literal performance of the contract or he will not pay.

Required:

Answer the following, setting forth reasons for any conclusions stated.

1. If the dispute goes to court, who will prevail, assuming Silverwater's breach of contract was intentional?

2. If the dispute goes to court, who will prevail, assuming Silverwater's breach of contract was unintentional?

Part b.   Jane Anderson offered to sell Richard Heinz a ten acre tract of commercial property. Anderson's letter indicated the offer would expire on March 1, 1980, at 3:00 p.m. and that any acceptance must be received in her office by that time. On February 29, 1980, Heinz decided to accept the offer and posted an acceptance at 4:00 p.m. Heinz indicated that in the event the acceptance did not arrive on time, he would assume there was a contract if he did not hear anything from Anderson in five days. The letter arrived on March 2, 1980. Anderson never responded to Heinz's letter. Heinz claims a contract was entered into and is suing thereon.

Required:

Answer the following, setting forth reasons for any conclusions stated.
Is there a contract?

Problem 3   (1189,L4)

(15 to 20 minutes)

Anker, Corp., a furniture retailer, engaged Best & Co., CPAs, to audit Anker's financial statements for the year ended December 31, 1988. While reviewing certain transactions entered into by Anker during 1988, Best became concerned with the proper reporting of the following transactions:

• On September 8, 1988, Crisp Corp., a furniture manufacturer, signed and mailed a letter offering to sell Anker 50 pieces of furniture for $9,500. The offer stated it would remain open until December 20, 1988. On December 5, 1988 Crisp mailed a letter revoking this offer. Anker received Crisp's revocation the following day. On December 12, 1988, Anker mailed its acceptance to Crisp, and Crisp received it on December 13, 1988.

• On December 6, 1988, Dix Corp. signed and mailed a letter offering to sell Anker a building for $75,000. The offer stated that acceptance could only be made by certified mail, return receipt requested. On December 10, 1988, Anker telephoned Dix requesting that Dix keep the offer open until December 20, 1988 because it was reviewing Dix's offer. On December 12, 1988, Dix signed and mailed a letter to Anker indicating that it would hold the offer open until December 20, 1988. On December 19, 1988, Anker sent its acceptance to Dix by a private express mail courier. Anker's acceptance was received by Dix on December 20, 1988.

After reviewing the documents concerning the foregoing transactions, Best spoke with Anker's president who made the following assertions:

• The September 8, 1988 offer by Crisp was irrevocable until December 20, 1988, and therefore a contract was formed by Anker's acceptance on December 12, 1988.

• Dix's letter dated December 12, 1988 formed an option contract with Anker.

• Anker's acceptance on December 19, 1988 formed a contract with Dix.

Required:

In separate paragraphs, discuss the assertions made by Anker's president. Indicate whether the assertions are correct and the reasons therefor.

Multiple Choice Answers

1. c	15. c	29. a	43. a	56. b
2. a	16. b	30. d	44. a	57. c
3. a	17. d	31. c	45. d	58. d
4. d	18. a	32. c	46. a	59. c
5. b	19. b	33. c	47. d	60. b
6. c	20. d	34. d	48. a	61. b
7. d	21. c	35. c	49. a	62. a
8. d	22. b	36. d	50. c	63. a
9. c	23. b	37. c	51. b	64. c
10. c	24. a	38. a	52. c	65. c
11. a	25. c	39. b	53. d	66. b
12. a	26. d	40. b	54. a	67. d
13. d	27. c	41. d	55. a	68. d
14. c	28. c	42. a		

Multiple Choice Answer Explanations

B.1. Offer

1. (588,L1,16) (c) When entering into a contract, the offeror must convey a clear and definite intent to enter into a binding agreement. However, there is no requirement that the offer be communicated in words to the offeree by the offeror. An offer to enter an "implied in fact" contract occurs when the actions of the offeror convey a clear intent to contract. As long as the actions are such that a reasonable person in the offeree's position would construe them as an offer, the offer is considered valid. Answers (a), (b), and (d) are incorrect because they describe elements that must be present in order for an offer to be valid. An offer must be communicated to the offeree by the offeror, it must be sufficiently definite and certain, and it must manifest an intent to enter into a contract.

2. (589,L1,25) (a) Published price quotes of products in advertisements are merely invitations for interested parties to make an offer. Thus, Hudson has not made an offer but is seeking offers through the use of the advertisement. Answers (b) and (d) are incorrect since Hudson has not made an offer. Answer (c) is incorrect because anyone who tenders money for items advertised is making an offer to Hudson and Hudson has the option to either accept or reject that offer.

3. (589,L1,24) (a) An offer that is supported by consideration is called an option, and it cannot be revoked before the stated period of time. In this situation, it must be determined whether Hill's promise to refrain from suing Dye constitutes consideration. Consideration must be legally sufficient to satisfy the consideration requirement. That is, a party binds him/herself to do something s/he is not legally obligated to do or sur-

renders a legal right. Since Hill had a legal right to sue Dye based on their dispute, Hill's promise not to sue is valid consideration. Thus, Dye's offer was irrevocable for 60 days and Hill's acceptance on the 20th day formed a valid contract. Answer (b) is incorrect because consideration is needed to form an option contract (i.e., an irrevocable offer). Answer (c) is incorrect because normally silence is not acceptance unless it was specifically indicated that silence would constitute acceptance and Dye had intended his/her silence as acceptance. Answer (d) is incorrect because a revocation need not be in writing to be valid; it must only be communicated to the offeree.

4. (1184,L1,18) (d) Mary's statement, "I'll take it if you will have it refinished," constituted a valid offer. An offer must contain a serious proposal, be definite and complete, and be communicated to the offeree. Ed's statement, "Sold," is a valid acceptance in absolute accord with Mary's offer. A contract was formed at the moment Ed communicated his acceptance to Mary's offer. Answer (a) is incorrect because Ed's statement fails to communicate a serious intent to be legally bound, constituting merely an invitation to make an offer. Answer (b) is incorrect since Ed did not make an offer to Mary; therefore, she did not have the power to accept. Answer (c) is incorrect because Ed did not have to specify the price since prior negotiations would be incorporated into Mary's offer.

5. (1182,L1,2) (b) In determining whether a communication qualifies as an offer, the law uses an objective standard based on how a reasonably prudent businessman would have interpreted the communication. The subjective intent of Harris would be immaterial, as would Douglas' opinion, in deciding whether this letter constitutes an offer. Therefore, answers (a) and (d) are incorrect. Answer (c) is incorrect because only the essential terms must be present in the communication, and even if some of these are missing, the needed terms can be added in later negotiations.

B.1.h. Termination of Offer

6. (589,L1,21) (c) In general, an offer remains effective until it is withdrawn, rejected, accepted, or either a stated period of time or a reasonable period of time lapses. In this situation, Dall's rejection of the offer on April 10 automatically terminates the original offer on that day and thereby ends Dall's right to accept the original offer. Note that if consideration had been paid by Dall to keep the contract open (i.e., option contract), the contract would have remained

open for the full 30-day period despite Dall's rejection on April 10. Answer (a) is incorrect because an offeror can always withdraw his/her offer unless prohibited from doing so because of the existence of an option or the firm offer rule. An option is not present because Dall did not give consideration for the opportunity to purchase the building. The firm offer rule does not apply because the contract does not involve the sale of goods. Answer (b) is incorrect because Martin is not obligated to keep the offer open for the 30-day period. Once Martin notifies Dall that the property has been sold to a third party, the offer is considered to be revoked. Answer (d) is incorrect because the offeree's opportunity to accept the offer was terminated by a lapse of the stated period of time. Since the offer expired prior to May 3, Dall could no longer accept the original offer.

7.   (589,L1,22) (d) Normally, an offeree's rejection is effective when received by the offeror. The same is true in regard to an offeror's revocation; the revocation must be received by the offeree for it to be effective. Therefore, answers (a), (b), and (c) are incorrect.

8.   (589,L1,23) (d) An offer terminates automatically upon the occurrence of the following events: (1) death or insanity of the offeror, (2) death or insanity of the offeree, (3) bankruptcy or insolvency of either the offeror or offeree, (4) destruction of the specific, identified subject matter. Where an offer is for the sale of goods, the offer is revoked upon the offeree learning the goods have been sold to a third party; consequently, the offer was revoked, not terminated by operation of law.

B.2. Acceptance

9.   (1188,L1,11) (c) Normally, an acceptance is considered to be effective when sent by the offeree as long as the acceptance was sent by a means specified in the offer or by the same means used to communicate the offer. However, the offeror may stipulate that acceptance is effective only when received by the offeror. Therefore, although Ard sent an acceptance on April 10, it would not become effective until the date it was received by Jet, April 14. In this situation, Jet's revocation was received by Ard prior to the time that Ard's acceptance reached Jet. Since a revocation is effective when received, Jet's revocation effectively terminated its offer on April 12 and, thus, answers (a), (b), and (d) are incorrect.

10. (1189,L1,9) (c) Under the mailbox rule, an acceptance is ordinarily effective when sent if transmitted by the means authorized by the offeror, or by the same means used to transmit the offer if no means was authorized. However, the offeror may stipulate that acceptance is effective only when received by the offeror. If the offeror does stipulate this, the mailbox rule does not apply. Answer (a) is incorrect because the fact that both the offeror and offeree are merchants would not be relevant in determining when the acceptance becomes effective. Answers (b) and (d) are incorrect because neither the type of offer nor length of the offer would have an effect on when the acceptance of the offer is effective (i.e., the mailbox rule would apply).

11. (1186,L1,12) (a) In general, an offer remains effective until it is withdrawn, rejected, or accepted. An acceptance is ordinarily effective when sent if transmitted by the means authorized by the offeror, or by the same means used to transmit the offer if no means was authorized. However, in the instance in which the offeree sends a rejection first and then an acceptance, the acceptance is not effective until received. In this case a contract was created because the July 6 telegram accepting the offer was received before the July 5 rejection letter. Answer (b) is incorrect because while an effective rejection does terminate an offer, a rejection is never effective until communicated. Answer (c) is incorrect because an offeror can always withdraw his offer unless prohibited from doing so because of the existence of an option or the firm offer rule. An option is not present because Mix did not give consideration for the opportunity to purchase the building. The firm offer rule does not apply because this contract does not involve the sale of goods. Answer (d) is incorrect because as described above the firm offer rule is not applicable to the sale of real property.

12. (1186,L1,24) (a) An offer cannot be assigned to another party. A valid acceptance may only come from the person to whom the offer was directed. Answer (b) is incorrect because the letter of acceptance mailed on June 5, 1986, does create a valid contract. Because the acceptance was made by the same means used by the offeror (a mailed letter) the acceptance is valid on the date sent, not when received. Answer (c) is incorrect because the offer is not an irrevocable option. An option is an offer that is supported by consideration and cannot be revoked. This offer was not an option because no consideration was given by the offeree to keep the

offer open. A similar concept to the irrevocable option is the firm offer rule. The firm offer rule does not apply in this case because even though there was a written and signed offer from a merchant, sale of a franchise dealership would not be considered the sale of goods. Answer (d) is incorrect because the Statute of Frauds applies to contracts which cannot be performed within one year of entering into the agreement. The fact that it is a three-year contract precludes performance within the one-year requirement.

13. (1185,L1,11) (d) Since Wax's acceptance is received by Knox before the offer has expired, a valid contract is formed. It is not necessary that Wax accept in writing to satisfy the Statute of Frauds because Knox's written offer is sufficient to meet the Statute of Frauds requirements. It states all material terms and is signed by the party to be charged. Answer (a) is incorrect because under the provisions of the UCC, a firm offer is a written offer by a merchant offeror for the purchase or sale of goods, not real property. Answer (b) is incorrect because Wax can benefit from the early acceptance rule-- meaning that acceptance is effective upon dispatch--only if he uses the specified means of communication, or absent any such specification, the same means used to communicate the offer. Answer (c) is incorrect because such an action by Wax would constitute a rejection and counteroffer. In the absence of any consideration paid by Wax to keep the offer open (i.e., option contract), a rejection or counteroffer automatically terminates the original offer and thereby ends the right of the offeree to accept the original offer.

14. (1181,L1,7) (c) An offeree cannot accept an offer unless the offeree knows of the existence of the offer; otherwise there is no objective meeting of the minds. Farber does not know of the increase of the monetary award to $500, and submitted his suggestion as an acceptance to the terms of the offer of which he knew, i.e., the $100. Even though Water Works later raised the amount and will use the suggestion in the later period, Farber only has a right to receive $100. Thus, answers (a) and (b) are incorrect. Answer (d) is incorrect because Water Works' offer was not gratuitous; it was a manifestation of an intent to enter a contract. The offer was definite and certain and possessed the requisite essentials to make it operative; therefore, Water Works must perform its promise of remuneration for Farber's accepted and used suggestion.

15. (581,L1,13) (c) The acceptance of an offer must conform exactly to the terms of the offer. If a party intends to accept an offer, but includes additional or different terms which are intended to become part of the contract, this constitutes a counteroffer and not an acceptance (a possible exception to this exists with contracts made between two merchants concerning the sale of goods). Norriss' additional term is a condition precedent and constitutes a counteroffer. Answer (a) is incorrect because a contract for the sale of real property must be in writing (under the Statute of Frauds) to be enforceable unless the doctrine of partial performance applies. Answer (b) is incorrect since a valid contract need only be signed by the party to be charged with performance. Answer (d) is untrue because the addition of a condition precedent has a significant effect on the contractual relationship since it prevents a contract from being formed unless Wilcox accepts the new term.

B.3. Consideration

16. (588,L1,18) (b) The existence of consideration requires that there be mutuality of consideration, i.e., that each party is bound to give consideration in exchange for the consideration being given by the other party to the contract. Answers (a) and (c) are incorrect because the courts generally do not look into the adequacy of consideration (sufficient monetary value) so long as the consideration is legally sufficient. Answer (d) is incorrect because the courts do not look to whether the consideration conforms to the subjective intent of the parties. The agreement is viewed objectively, not subjectively.

17. (588,L1,21) (d) Under the UCC, a contract for the sale of goods may be modified orally or in writing without consideration if such modification is done in good faith. Additionally, the parol evidence rule prohibits the presentation of evidence of any prior or contemporaneous oral or written statements for the purpose of modifying or changing a written agreement intended by the payor to be the final and complete expression of their contract. However, it does not bar from evidence any oral or written agreements entered into by the parties subsequent to the written contract. Therefore, the agreement between Baker and Able is enforceable as modified, and evidence of the modification is admissible into evidence. Thus, answers (a), (b), and (c) are incorrect.

18. (1189,L1,10) (a) Consideration must be legally sufficient to satisfy the consideration requirement to form a contract. Consideration is legally sufficient if it is

either a legal benefit to the promisor or a legal detriment to the promisee, for example, a party binds him/herself to do something s/he is not legally obligated to do. Answers (b) and (c) are incorrect because although both a manifestation of mutual assent and a genuineness of assent are important in the formation of a contract; they are not requirements of consideration. Answer (d) is incorrect because generally the courts do not look into the adequacy of consideration (monetary value) as long as the consideration is legally sufficient.

19. (586,L1,3) (b) Past consideration is not valid consideration. Past consideration is present when something done in the past is given for a present promise. This type of consideration lacks the bargained for element. Thus, if Lake had performed the act prior to Polk's promise to pay, Polk's promise was made in exchange for past consideration and Polk will prevail. Answer (a) is incorrect because the relinquishment of a legal right is sufficient to act as consideration. Consideration is legally sufficient if it is either a legal benefit to the promisor or a legal detriment to the promisee. The promisee suffers a legal detriment if s/he promises to refrain from doing something s/he has a legal right to do. Answer (c) is incorrect because the fact that a contract is executory does not allow a party to avoid performance of the agreement; an executory contract is still a binding agreement. Answer (d) is incorrect because the value of the consideration is not considered by the court in determining whether the agreement has sufficient consideration. The court looks merely for the presence of consideration and not for its adequacy.

20. (580,L1,29) (d) The agreement involved is a requirements contract; thus, Marblehead's ordering of unreasonably disproportionate amounts of oil would be a breach by them. A requirements contract is considered definite and both parties are viewed as having provided consideration; thus, answers (a), (b), and (c) are incorrect.

B.4. Legal Capacity

21. (1186,L1,13) (c) In order to have an enforceable contract, all of the elements of a contract must be present. One of the elements of a contract is legal capacity. An intoxicated party's legal capacity is determined by his/her ability to understand and degree of intoxication. If legal capacity is determined not to exist, the contract is voidable by the intoxicated party to the contract. The alcohol had "significantly impaired Meed's ability to understand the nature and terms of the con-

tract." Therefore, it is Meed who lacked legal capacity and thus has the power to void the agreement. Answer (a) is incorrect as the contract is not automatically void, but voidable at the option of the intoxicated party. Answer (b) is incorrect because the contract is not binding upon Meed due to the lack of legal capacity. Answer (d) is incorrect because if the intoxicated party lacked legal capacity, the transaction is voidable at the option of the intoxicated person even if the intoxication was purely voluntary.

22. (1189,L1,11) (b) A minor may disaffirm a contract at any time until the minor reaches the age of majority or a reasonable time thereafter. Answer (a) is incorrect because Kent is still allowed to disaffirm the contract despite the fact that the car has been stolen and cannot be returned. Answer (c) is incorrect because a minor cannot ratify a contract until after reaching the age of majority. Answer (d) is incorrect because the fact that Mint is a merchant is not relevant in determining whether or not Kent may disaffirm the purchase. Kent may disaffirm the purchase because he is a minor.

B.5. Legality

23. (589,L1,26) (b) In general, an agreement that violates a statute is illegal, making such agreement unenforceable. However, if the statute involved is a licensing statute, it must first be determined whether the statute is regulatory in nature (i.e., one that seeks to protect the public), in which case the contract would be unenforceable, or if it is a revenue-seeking statute (i.e., its purpose is merely to raise revenue for the government), in which case the contract would be enforceable. In this situation, Tell violated a statute regulating real estate brokers and thus, the contract is unenforceable. Therefore, Allen is not liable to Tell for any amount. Answer (a) is incorrect because the use of the standard form contract signed by Allen would not make the contract unenforceable. A standard form is used in many situations to form valid contracts. Answers (c) and (d) are incorrect because the contract is unenforceable due to Tell's violation of the regulatory licensing statute. However, had the licensing statute been revenue-seeking in nature rather than regulatory, Tell would have been entitled to receive the full commission.

24. (588,L1,19) (a) In general, an agreement which violates a statute is illegal, making such an agreement unenforceable. However, if the statute involved is a licensing statute, it must first be determined

whether the statute is regulatory in nature (i.e., one that seeks to protect the public), in which case the contract would be unenforceable, or if it is a revenue-seeking statute (i.e., its purpose is merely to raise revenue for the government), in which case the contract would be enforceable. A CPA licensing statute is regulatory in nature. Thus, the contract is unenforceable, and consequently Parr will be unable to recover any damages from Jet, Inc.

25. (584,L1,11) (c) The agreement to steal trade secrets is illegal and, therefore, unenforceable. Because both parties are guilty (pari delicto), the courts will not aid either Mix or Small in recovering the consideration exchanged. Consequently, Small will not be permitted to recover the $10,000 under any theory. Answers (a), (b), and (d) are, therefore, incorrect.

B.6. Reality of Consent

26. (1189,L1,14) (d) Wallace can recover in a suit against Bradford based on the theory of fraud. Wallace will be able to prove the four requirements of fraud: 1) there was a materially misstated fact, 2) there was intent by Bradford to mislead, 3) there was reasonable reliance, and 4) there was injury suffered as a result. Answer (a) is incorrect because Bradford knew the land was sold previously to Jones. A bilateral mistake requires that the party making the mistake not know of the mistake or have reason to know of the mistake. In this case, the fact that Bradford sold the land previously to Jones is not a mistake. Answer (b) is incorrect because Bradford knew all the facts and, therefore, was not ignorant of the facts. Wallace was ignorant of the facts, but he had no reason to believe Bradford was misleading him, and he is under no obligation to have to determine if the property can be legally sold to him. Answer (c) is incorrect because a unilateral mistake is, with some exceptions not raised in this question, not grounds for getting out of contracts.

27. (1189,L1,15) (c) Misrepresentation may involve an innocent misstatement made in good faith; i.e., there is no scienter or intent to mislead. In order to rescind a contract because of a misrepresentation, the rescinding party must prove that there was a misrepresentation of a material fact, that there was reliance on this fact, and that there was injury as a result. Answer (a) is incorrect because reformation is a remedy used to correct a mutual or unilateral mistake. Reformation allows for the contract to be rewritten so that it is in agreement with the original

intentions of the contract. In this case, the party is seeking rescission; he wants to cancel the contract and return both parties to their precontract positions. Answer (b) is incorrect because actual fraud requires scienter or intent to mislead. In this case, the materially false misstatement was unintentional. Answer (d) is incorrect because constructive fraud requires reckless disregard for the truth, i.e., more than unintentional conduct.

28. (589,L1,30) (c) Under innocent misrepresentation a contract is voidable by one party if the other party has misrepresented a material fact. Since the misrepresentation is an innocent misstatement made in good faith (i.e., no scienter), the only remedy available to the party voiding the contract is rescission. Rescission is the annulment of the contract whereby parties are placed in the position they held before the contract was formed. All benefits received from the contract must be returned by both parties. Answer (b) is incorrect because the aggrieved party is not allowed to sue for damages since the misrepresentation made was an innocent misstatement.

29. (1187,L1,4) (a) Undue influence is the unfair persuasion of a party who is under the domination of the person exercising the persuasion. Even though in many cases, undue influence results from the presence of a relationship of trust or confidence (fiduciary relationship), the presence of such a relationship is not necessary in order for undue influence to exist. All that need be shown is that one party is dominated by another even in the absence of such a relationship. Therefore, answer (b) is incorrect. Answers (c) and (d) are incorrect because misrepresentation and improper threats are not conditions necessary for the existence of undue influence.

30. (1188,L1,16) (d) A mutual mistake occurs when two parties intentionally enter into an agreement, but under an erroneous conviction. In this case, at the time of entering the contract, both parties reasonably believed that the destroyed auto was still in existence. Thus, Apple's best defense is that there was a mutual mistake of an existing fact which renders the contract voidable. Answer (a) is incorrect because unconscionability arises when there is a great disparity in the bargaining powers of the contracting parties, through which one party exploits the other. There is no evidence here that Bean was in a superior bargaining position as to Apple and therefore unconscionability is not present. Answer (b) is incorrect because it would be impossible for risk of loss to pass to Bean since the auto was destroyed on

April 4 before the contract was ever formed. Answer (c) is incorrect because the law is not concerned with the adequacy of the consideration, but rather the sufficiency of the consideration. Bean's promise to pay for the auto acts as sufficient consideration since it represents a new legal detriment to which he was not previously bound. Therefore, lack of adequate consideration would not be Apple's best defense.

31. (589,L1,28) (c) A contract entered into because of duress can be voided because of invalid consent. Although physical threats were not used, King was put into a desperate economic situation with the threat of foreclosure if he did not agree to the higher interest rates on the separate unsecured notes. Answer (a) is incorrect because undue influence is the unfair persuasion of a party who is under the domination of the person exercising the persuasion. This often occurs through the abuse of a fiduciary relationship. Answer (b) is incorrect because a contract can be ruled unconscionable when one person takes severe, unfair advantage over another in a contract based on special circumstances such as the latter's lack of education or extreme lack of choice. Answer (d) is incorrect because fraud in the inducement is based on a misrepresentation of a material fact with scienter when one is injured when reasonably relying on the misrepresentation.

32. (587,L1,22) (c) Lite's error in submitting his bid is a unilateral mistake. Generally, a mistake made by one party is not sufficient grounds for voiding a contract. However, an exception exists if a computational mistake is so great that the other party should have known of the error. Lite has made an obvious and substantial arithmetic error in his bid. Therefore, Lite's mistake is so great that Sting should have realized a mistake was made. It is not necessary that Sting actually knew of the mistake in order to void the contract. It only must be determined that Sting should have known of Lite's mistake. Thus, answer (a) is incorrect. Answer (b) is incorrect because Lite is not required to show that Sting caused the error in order to avoid liability. Answer (d) is incorrect because proving that the error was not due to his negligence will not allow Lite to avoid liability. He would still be liable unless the error is so large that Sting should have known of the mistake.

B.7. Conformity with the Statute of Frauds

33. (1189,L1,12) (c) The Statute of Frauds requires that suretyship contracts be in writing to be enforceable. A suretyship relationship is a contractual relationship resulting from the unconditional promise to pay the debt or default of another. Answer (a) is incorrect because the parol evidence rule prevents the use of oral evidence to contradict the terms of a written contract, not the Statute of Frauds. Answer (b) is incorrect because the Statute of Frauds applies to the sale of goods for $500 or more. It does not apply to all contracts having consideration valued at $500 or more. Answer (d) is incorrect because the Statute of Frauds would apply to a real estate lease only if it was for longer than one year.

34. (588,L1,20) (d) In order to conform with the Statute of Frauds, and therefore be enforceable, any contract for the sale of an interest in real property (regardless of price), must be in writing and signed by the party to be charged. Thus, in this case, Dix will lose because the agreement was not in writing and signed by Wilk. Therefore, answers (a) and (c) are incorrect. Answer (b) is incorrect because the part performance exception is not present due to the fact Dix did not take possession of the property under the oral agreement.

35. (1187,L1,3) (c) The Statute of Frauds requires only that the written contract be signed by the party to be charged, not by all parties to the contract. Answer (a) is incorrect because it is not required that the contract be formalized in a single writing. Two or more documents can be combined to create a sufficient writing to satisfy the Statute of Frauds as long as one of the documents refers to the others. Answer (b) is incorrect because the Statute of Frauds does not require consideration to be fair and adequate. Answer (d) is incorrect because while the Statute of Frauds is applicable to the sale of goods only if the purchase price is $500 or more, it is always applicable to the sale of real estate, regardless of purchase price.

36. (589,L1,27) (d) Any contract which cannot possibly be performed within one year from the making of the agreement must be in writing in order to be in conformity with the Statute of Frauds. However, if the agreement is capable of being performed within the one-year period, then it need not be in writing to be enforceable. In this situation, the oral agreement will be enforceable because the work

could be completed within one year. Therefore, answer (b) is incorrect. Answer (a) is incorrect because the Statute of Frauds requires that an agreement for the sale of goods (not the value of services) for $500 or more be in writing. Answer (c) is incorrect because the Statute of Frauds applies to any agreement which cannot be completed within one year including personal service contracts.

37. (589,L1,29) (c) Under the UCC Statute of Frauds, a written agreement for the sale of goods is adequate if it indicates a contract for the sale of goods has been made between parties and is signed by the party to be charged. The written agreement may omit material terms (i.e., price, delivery, time for performance) as long as the quantity is stated. Reasonable terms will be inferred for those terms which are missing from the written agreement. Answers (a) and (d) are incorrect because the payment terms and time and place of delivery of the goods do not have to be included in the written agreement for it to be enforceable. Answer (b) is incorrect because the agreement only needs the signature of the party sought to be bound.

38. (583,L1,11) (a) Even though a contract for the sale of goods for greater than, or equal to, $500 must be in writing under the Statute of Frauds, a contract which is oral, but has been acknowledged in court by the defendant, is legally binding to the extent of the admission. Thus, since Glass admitted in court the contract with Hourly, this agreement will be enforced in its entirety. Answer (b) is incorrect because the shipment of 1,000 watches would not cause the contract to be enforceable in its entirety, but merely to the extent that goods have been delivered and accepted, in this case to the extent of the 1,000 watches. Answer (c) is incorrect since a down payment will only cause the contract to be enforceable to the extent of the payment made and accepted by Hourly, and not in the contract's entirety. Answer (d) is incorrect because the amount of the contract is $4,000, and any contract involving the sale of goods for $500 or more is within the requirements of the Statute of Frauds.

B.7.d. Parol Evidence Rule

39. (1189,L1,16) (b) The parol evidence rule prohibits the presentation as evidence of any prior or contemporaneous oral statements for the purpose of modifying or changing a written agreement intended by the parties to be the final and complete expression of their contract. It would bar the admission of evidence which relates to a change in an <u>unambiguous</u>

provision in the contract but would not bar the admission of evidence which clarifies an ambiguous provision. Answer (a) is incorrect because under the parol evidence rule, it is only evidence of prior or contemporaneous agreements which modify the written contract that is prohibited. Any subsequent written or oral agreements may be presented as evidence. Answer (c) is incorrect because the parol evidence rule does not bar the admission of evidence which is presented to establish fraud. Answer (d) is incorrect because the parol evidence rule does not bar from admission any evidence of an obvious error in drafting.

C. Assignment and Delegation

40. (1189,L1,18) (b) Assignment is the transfer of a right under a contract by one person to another. Generally, a party's rights in a contract are assignable unless a provision of the contract prohibits assignment, the contract involves personal services, or the assignment would materially change the risk or obligations of the other party. The contract to purchase real property would <u>not</u> be nonassignable as a matter of law. Answers (a), (c), and (d) are incorrect because they are all valid statements. Since the contract is for the sale of real property, specific performance is a possible remedy due to the unique nature of the subject matter of the contract. Additionally, the Statute of Frauds would apply to this contract as it applies to any contract for the sale of real property. Also, both Moss and Shinn would need to agree to any amendment to the contract before it would be binding.

41. (589,L1,33) (d) In general, a party's rights in a contract are assignable without the consent of the other parties. However, the following are situations in which this general rule does not apply and consent of the other parties would be required for a valid transfer to occur: (1) the contract involves personal services, credit, trust or confidence, (2) a provision of the contract or statute prohibits assignment, and (3) the assignment would materially change the risk or obligations of the other party. Since the assignment by a patent holder of the right to receive royalties would not alter the rights of the other parties to the contract, a valid transfer could be made without the consent of these parties. Answers (a) and (b) are incorrect because both assignments would materially change the risk of the other parties involved and would require the other parties' consent prior to a valid transfer. Answer (c) is incorrect because it involves a personal service contract.

D. Third-Party Beneficiary Contracts

42. (587,L1,23) (a) When the buyer of mortgaged property purchases the property subject to a mortgage, the buyer accepts no liability for the mortgage and the seller is still primarily liable. A third party beneficiary contract occurs when a debtor contracts with a second party to pay the debts owed to the creditor (third party beneficiary). In this situation, Park has purchased the building subject to the mortgage and is not personally liable for payment to Muni. Thus, answer (c) is incorrect. Answer (b) is incorrect because Krieg is the debtor and not the creditor in this situation. Answer (d) is incorrect because Krieg will still remain primarily liable for the note due to Muni Bank.

43. (589,L1,32) (a) When the primary parties to a contract actually intend that third parties benefit from the contract, these intended third parties have rights to enforce the contract. If, however, the individuals receive an unintended benefit, they are called incidental beneficiaries and have no rights to enforce the contract. Since Bell is merely an incidental beneficiary, s/he cannot enforce the contract. Answer (b) is incorrect because Bell was not intended to be benefited by the primary parties, i.e., Ace and Big City. Answer (c) is incorrect because the main issue in the question is an intended third party beneficiary vs. an incidental beneficiary. Answer (d) is incorrect because the facts do not show that Ace and Big City intended to benefit all handicapped, unemployed veterans, in Big City.

44. (1189,L1,17) (a) The beneficiary of a life insurance contract is an intended third party donee beneficiary, and as such, can maintain an action against the insurance company in the event of default. In this case Smith, as the third party donee beneficiary, will be successful in an action against the insurance company. Therefore, answers (c) and (d) are incorrect. Answer (b) is incorrect because Smith is not an assignee of Jones' rights under the insurance policy. S/he is a third party beneficiary and no assignment of Jones' rights has occurred.

E. Performance of Contract

45. (583,L1,19) (d) Under the doctrine of substantial performance, a contract obligation may be discharged even though the performance tendered was not in complete conformity with the terms of the agreement. Under this doctrine, if it can be shown that the defect in performance was only minor in nature, that a good faith effort was made to conform completely with the terms of the agreement, and

if the performing party is willing to accept a decrease in compensation equivalent to the amount of the minor defect in performance, the contractual obligation will be discharged. Since Kent did not make a good faith effort to conform to the terms of the agreement, but in fact intentionally breached it, their obligation will not be discharged and they will lose all rights under the contract. Therefore, answers (a) and (b) are incorrect. Answer (c) is incorrect because the law does not demand literal performance of contracts, but will allow the discharge of an obligation to a contract when it has been substantially performed as described above under the doctrine of substantial performance.

F. Discharge of Contracts

46. (588,L1,24) (a) A novation is an agreement between three parties whereby a previous agreement is discharged by the creation of a new agreement. The new agreement substitutes one contracting party for another. In this case Dell was substituted for Stark, who was discharged from all liability. Answer (b) is incorrect because an accord and satisfaction does not involve the cancelation of a contract but is merely an agreement wherein a party with an existing duty of performance under a contract promises to do something other than perform the duty originally promised in the contract. Answer (c) is incorrect because a novation is a valid and enforceable contract to which Ball would be bound. Answer (d) is incorrect because consideration exists in Dell's promise to pay Ball and in Ball's agreeing to release Stark from all liability. Both of these promises are legally sufficient to act as consideration.

47. (1187,L1,1) (d) A payment of less than the originally agreed-upon price will serve as complete discharge of an obligation under a contract only if there is a bona fide dispute as to the amount owed, and both parties agree to the lesser sum. In this case Milo and Nord had agreed upon a fee for services of $45,000; thus, this debt was liquidated since the amount was certain. And since Milo had completed the work to Nord's satisfaction, no bona fide dispute as to the amount owed arose; thus the debt remains liquidated, and Nord will be required to pay the full $45,000. The fact that Milo had endorsed and deposited the check which Nord had conspicuously marked as constituting payment in full is of no effect since the obligation was a liquidated debt, instead of an unliquidated debt. Thus answers (a), (b), and (c) are all incorrect.

48. (1186,L1,25) (a) Meek & Co., CPAs and Sulk Corp. have entered into a valid contract which required that Meek issue an opinion by June 15, 1986. However, Meek did not breach its contract due to failure to perform by the agreed-upon date because the alleged breach was caused by Sulk's failure to provide Meek with the necessary information. In every contract there is an implied agreement that the parties to the contract will not interfere with or hinder the other party's performance. Answer (b) is incorrect because a quasi contract is an implied-in-law rather than express agreement which results when one of the parties has been unjustly enriched at the expense of the other. The law creates such a contract when there is no binding agreement present to keep the unjust enrichment from occurring. Answer (c) is incorrect because as discussed above, a breach did not occur. Answer (d) is incorrect because the condition is only effective as long as Sulk does not interfere with Meek's ability to perform. Actually Sulk's supplying the necessary information would be a condition precedent to Meek's duty to perform.

G. Remedies

49. (1188,L1,19) (a) The remedy of specific performance is used when money damages will not sufficiently compensate the afflicted party due to the unique nature of the subject matter of the contract. In a contract for the sale of land, the buyer has the right to enforce the agreement by seeking the remedy of specific performance because real property is considered unique. Another remedy for this breach of contract would be for the buyer to seek compensatory damages. If the buyer desires, s/he may seek this remedy instead of specific performance. However, in this situation, Rice could only sue for either specific performance or compensatory damages but would not be entitled to both remedies. Therefore, answer (b) is incorrect. Answers (c) and (d) are incorrect because an injured party is generally not allowed to seek punitive damages. Punitive damages are awarded only when the court is seeking to punish a party for their improper actions and are not usually granted in breach of contract actions.

50. (587,L1,24) (c) A liquidated damage clause is a contractual provision which states the amount of damages that will occur if a party breaches the contract. The liquidated damage clause is enforceable if the amount is reasonable in light of the anticipated or actual harm caused by the breach. The enumerated clause will be enforceable if the amount of the downpayment bears a reasonable relationship to the loss incurred by the seller if

a breach occurs. Answer (a) is incorrect because the liquidated damages clause states the amount of compensatory damages that the seller will receive. The seller will not be able to recover compensatory damages in addition to those stated in the liquidated damage provision. Answer (b) is incorrect because it is irrelevant whether the breach was intentional when deciding if the liquidated damages clause is enforceable. Answer (d) is incorrect because excessive liquidated damages will not be enforceable in court even if both parties have agreed in writing. A clause providing for excessive damages is a penalty and the courts will not enforce a penalty.

51. (589,L1,35) (b) The contract entered into by Jones is a personal service contract. The remedy of specific performance is not available for breach of a personal service contract. It would violate the constitutional amendment prohibiting involuntary servitude. Therefore, Foster Corp. will be unable to obtain a judgment ordering Jones to perform. Answers (a) and (c) are incorrect because they are correct statements. Jones' repudiation prior to the date of performance is an anticipatory breach which will allow Foster Corp. either to sue at once or wait until after the time performance was due. Answer (d) is also a true statement and consequently, an incorrect answer. The reward of monetary damages caused by the repudiation is a remedy available in this situation. Foster Corp. will be allowed to recover foreseeable monetary damages equal to damages incurred.

52. (1189,L1,19) (c) The doctrine of anticipatory repudiation allows a party to either sue at once or wait until after performance is due when the other party indicates s/he will not perform. This doctrine is in effect because Nagel told Fields that Nagel had no intention of delivering the goods (i.e. repudiation of the contract) prior to the date of performance. Answer (a) is incorrect because promissory estoppel acts as a substitute for consideration which is an element in the forming of a contract but is not relevant in this fact situation. Answer (b) is incorrect because accord and satisfaction is an agreement wherein a party with an existing duty or performance under a contract promises to do something other than perform the duty originally promised in the contract. Answer (d) is incorrect because the doctrine of substantial performance would allow for a contract obligation to be discharged even though the performance tendered was not in complete conformity with the terms of the agreement. In this case, Fields is suing Nagel for breach of contract.

53. (589,L1,34) (d) The contract entered into by Cobb Company with Thrifty Oil Company was a valid contract for a specified quantity of heating oil. Therefore, Cobb is obligated to purchase the entire 100,000 gallons from Thrifty as agreed upon in the contract. The fact that there was an unseasonably warm winter will not change Cobb's obligation to Thrifty since this was a change of circumstances which could be foreseen by the parties. Answer (a) is incorrect because Cobb is liable despite the fact that they acted in good faith. Answer (b) is incorrect because this is not a situation in which commercial impracticability would apply since an unseasonably warm winter is a change in circumstances which could be contemplated by Cobb. Answer (c) is incorrect because this is not a requirements contract. A requirements contract is one in which one party agrees to buy all of a specified good which that party may require for use in his/her own business. In this situation, Cobb had contracted to buy a specific amount of heating oil (100,000 gallons).

H. Statute of Limitations

54. (1189,L1,13) (a) The statute of limitations requires the plaintiff to file a lawsuit within a specified period of time after the cause of action accrues (e.g. breach). A plaintiff who fails to file suit within the period of the statute of limitations loses the right to recover on the claim. In the case of an action for the breach of contract within the UCC Sales Article, the lawsuit must normally be commenced within four years after the cause of action has accrued. Therefore, answers (b), (c), and (d) are incorrect.

May 1990 Answers

55. (590,L1,11) (a) Consideration must be legally sufficient to satisfy the consideration requirement to form a contract, e.g., a party binds him/herself to do something s/he is not legally obligated to do or surrenders a legal right. Answers (b) and (c) are incorrect because consideration need not be economic in order to form a valid contract, e.g., giving up drinking, smoking or swearing, would constitute consideration if bargained for. Answer (d) is incorrect because the court does not generally consider the adequacy of consideration, only the legal sufficiency.

56. (590,L1,12) (b) Common law applies to this contract because it involves real estate. In this situation, Fox's reply on October 2 is a counteroffer and terminates Summers' original offer made on Sep-

tember 27. The acceptance of an offer must conform exactly to the terms of the offer under common law. By agreeing to purchase the vacation home at a price different from the original offer, Fox is rejecting Summers' offer and is making a counter offer. Answer (a) is incorrect because the fact that Fox failed to return Summers' letter is irrelevant to the formation of a binding contract. Fox's reply constitutes a counteroffer as Fox did not intend to accept Summers' original offer. Answer (c) is incorrect because Summers' offer was rejected by Fox's counteroffer. Answer (d) is incorrect because with rare exceptions, silence does not constitute acceptance.

57. (590,L1,13) (c) Normally, an acceptance is considered to be effective when sent by the offeree under the UCC as long as the acceptance was sent by a reasonable method. This rule can be changed if so stated in the offer. In this situation, Zen did not accept by the means specified in the offer and, therefore, the acceptance was not effective when sent and a valid contract was not formed. Therefore, answer (b) is incorrect. Answer (a) is incorrect because although acceptance was sent within the time specified, the correct means was not used. Answer (d) is incorrect because the offer did not require receipt of the acceptance within a specified time but rather that the acceptance by telegram be sent by a specified time.

58. (590,L1,14) (d) An offer automatically terminates upon the occurrence of any of the following events: (1) the death or insanity of either the offeror or offeree, (2) bankruptcy or insolvency of either the offeror or offeree, or (3) the destruction of the specific, identified subject matter. Thus the offer automatically terminates at the date of Opal's death. Therefore, answer (b) is incorrect. Answer (a) is incorrect because the offer automatically terminated upon the death of Opal and it does not matter whether Larkin received notice of the death. Answer (c) is incorrect because if Larkin had accepted the offer prior to Opal's death, a valid contract would have been formed.

59. (590,L1,15) (c) In order to conform with the Statute of Frauds, and therefore be enforceable, any contract for the sale of an interest in real property must be in writing and signed by the party to be charged. In this situation, only King has signed the contract, and, therefore, it is only enforceable against King. Answer (a) is incorrect because a valid contract was formed despite the lack of Foster's signature. However, since Foster did not sign the offer, it is not enforceable

against him/her. Answer (b) is incorrect because there is no requirement that the offeror be a merchant in order to form a valid contract. Answer (d) is incorrect because Foster must sign the offer in order for it to be enforceable against him/her. The fact that Foster is a merchant would not be relevant.

60. (590,L1,16) (b) A promise to donate money to a charity which the charity relied upon in incurring large expenditures is a situation involving promissory estoppel. Promissory estoppel acts as a substitute for consideration and renders the promise enforceable. The elements necessary for promissory estoppel are (1) detrimental reliance on a promise, (2) reliance on the promise is reasonable and foreseeable, and (3) damage results (injustice) if the promise is not enforced. Answer (c) is incorrect because the failure to enforce a promise to pay for a child's college education will not result in damages, and therefore, promissory estoppel would not apply. Answer (a) is incorrect because an irrevocable oral promise by a merchant to keep an offer open for 60 days is an option contract that must be supported by consideration. A firm offer under the UCC requires an offer signed by the merchant. Answer (d) is incorrect because the modification of a contract requires consideration, unless the contract involves the sale of goods under the UCC.

61. (590,L1,17) (b) The legal capacity of Payne to enter into this contract is determined by (1) his/her ability to understand the nature and terms of the contract, and (2) the degree of intoxication. Answer (b) is correct because Payne's ability to understand the nature and terms of the contract was not impaired. Therefore, a binding contract existed. If a person is intoxicated to a degree that would impair his/her ability to understand the nature and terms of a contract, the contract may be voidable at the option of the intoxicated individual. Answer (a) is incorrect because intoxication is the basis for a voidable, not a void contract. Answers (c) and (d) are incorrect because Payne was able to understand the nature and terms of the contract. Note that if the contract were voidable, it would only be voidable at Payne's option.

62. (590,L1,18) (a) Contracts that cannot be performed within one year of their making must normally be in writing to be enforceable. However, if one side of the performance is complete, the contract generally may be oral even if the other side cannot be completed within one year. This is especially true if performance has been accepted and all

that remains is the payment, as in the fact pattern of this question. Therefore, answer (c) is incorrect. Answer (b) is incorrect because although there is a rule for interests in real estate, this fact pattern applies to the one-year rule. Answer (d) is incorrect because the promise included both the bonus as well as the monthly salary.

63. (590,L1,19) (a) A third-party beneficiary contract is created when two other parties enter into a contractual agreement that intentionally benefits a third party. In this case, Wagner (debtor) has contracted with an insurance company to benefit Union Bank (creditor beneficiary) upon Wagner's death. As a creditor beneficiary, Union Bank may recover the policy proceeds from the insurance company. Answer (b) is incorrect because Wagner's intent in initiating the policy with the insurance company was not to confer a gift upon Union Bank, which is a requirement for a donee beneficiary contract. Answer (c) is incorrect because Union Bank is in privity of contract with the insurance company since an enforceable third-party beneficiary contract has taken place. Answer (d) is incorrect because Union Bank is not an incidental beneficiary; i.e., a third party receiving an unintended benefit from the contract. Wagner's and the insurance company's intent in entering into the contract was specifically to benefit Union Bank upon Wagner's death.

64. (590,L1,21) (c) Fraud includes the following elements: (1) misrepresentation of a material fact, (2) scienter--intent to mislead, (3) reasonable reliance by injured party, and (4) damages. All of these elements are present in this situation and Steele will prevail. Answer (a) is incorrect because it was reasonable for Steele to rely on the inventory valuation in the financial statements in deciding whether to purchase Kalp's business. Answer (b) is incorrect because Kalp had a duty to disclose the inventory overstatement when it was discovered regardless of when Steele was provided with Kalp's financial statements. Answer (d) is incorrect because as a remedy for fraud, the defrauded party (Steele) may sue for damages.

65. (590,L1,22) (c) An assignment of a contractual agreement is taken to mean both the assignment of the rights of the contract as well as the delegation of the duties of the contract. In this case, Neptune has assigned the contract to Deep Sea Lobster, therefore, answer (c) is correct. Answers (a) and (b) are incorrect because the assignment of a contract includes both assignment of rights and delegation of duties. Answer (d) is incorrect because this situation is not a third-

party beneficiary contract, but merely an assignment of an existing contract.

66. (590,L1,23) (b) A contract based on a mistake is voidable by the party making the mistake if the mistake is so obvious that the other party should have known that a mistake was made. In this situation, Preston should have known that the $10,900 price stated in the offer was erroneous. Therefore, Paco may rescind the contract. Answer (a) is incorrect because the mistake in this situation was not mutual (i.e., made by both parties); it was a unilateral mistake made by Paco. Answer (c) is incorrect because the fact that Paco is a merchant is irrelevant when deciding if a mistake has been made. Answer (d) is incorrect because a unilateral mistake generally does not cause the contract to be void. If the mistake is obvious, as it is in this situation, the contract is voidable, not void.

67. (590,L1,24) (d) United is an incidental third-party beneficiary since it was not the intent of Locke and Rice to benefit United when they formed the contract. As such, United is not entitled to money damages since only intended beneficiaries can maintain an action against the contracting parties for nonperformance. Therefore, answers (a) and (b) are incorrect. Answer (c) is incorrect because United is an incidental beneficiary, not a donee beneficiary, since it was not the intent of the two contracting parties to confer a gift on United.

68. (590,L1,25) (d) A novation is an agreement between three parties whereby a previous agreement is discharged by the creation of a new agreement. The new agreement substitutes one contracting party for another. In this case, Moss was substituted for Wren, and Wren was discharged of all liability. Answer (a) is incorrect because in the purchase of land subject to a mortgage, the buyer accepts no liability for the mortgage and the seller remains primarily liable. Answer (b) is incorrect because in an assignment and delegation, the seller remains liable on the contract for the duties delegated. Answer (c) is incorrect because a third-party beneficiary contract would have occurred if Moss had assumed the mortgage from Wren. In this case, Wren was released from all liability by First Federal. Therefore, a novation has occurred.

Answer Outline

Problem 1   Consideration; Effectiveness of
             Acceptance and Revocation;
             Rejection of Option (1187,L4)

First assertion
  Consideration must be legally sufficient and
  bargained for
    Does not need to be adequate
  Bold's payment acts as consideration
    Makes offer irrevocable
Second assertion
  Normally revocation is effective when
  received
  Acceptance is effective when sent when
  authorized means of communication is used
  Acceptance was sent before revocation was
  received
    Therefore option contract is formed
Third assertion
  Power of acceptance under an option contract
  is not terminated by rejection or
  counteroffer unless contractual duty is
  discharged or offeror changes its position
  as a result of reliance on counteroffer
  Bold's letter does not terminate it's right
  to exercise option

Unofficial Answer

Problem 1   Consideration; Effectiveness of
             Acceptance and Revocation;
             Rejection of Option (1187,L4)

Stieb's first assertion, that Bold could
not validly accept his offer dated April 5
because $100 was inadequate consideration to
hold the offer open, is incorrect. In
general, the courts will not question the
adequacy of consideration if the consideration
has legal sufficiency and there is a bargained-for exchange. Adequacy of consideration has nothing to do with legal sufficiency. Thus, the subject matter that the
parties have exchanged need not have approximately the same value. Based upon the facts,
Bold's payment of the $100 in exchange for
Stieb's promise to keep the offer open was
both legally sufficient and bargained for.
Stieb's second assertion, that his offer
dated April 5 had terminated since he had
revoked his offer prior to Bold's acceptance,
is incorrect. An offer may be terminated by
the offeror if a revocation is communicated to
the offeree before the offeree accepts. In
the majority of states revocation is effective
upon receipt of the revocation by the offeree
or the offeree's agent. On the other hand,
acceptance will generally take effect at the
time the acceptance is sent (dispatched) by an
authorized means of communication. Bold used
an authorized means of communication, i.e.,
the mail, which was the same method used by
Stieb in making the offer. Therefore, Bold's
acceptance and payment of $100 on April 18 was
effective on that date and formed an option
contract. Thus, Stieb's letter of revocation
mailed on April 17 was not effective until
Bold received the revocation on April 19 by
which time an option contract had already been
formed and the offer could not be revoked.
Stieb's third assertion, that even if his
revocation was not effective, Bold's letter of
May 15 was a counteroffer, which automatically
terminated Bold's right to accept Stieb's
offer of April 1, is incorrect. In general,
the power of acceptance under an option contract is not terminated by a rejection or
counteroffer made by the offeree, unless the
requirements are met for the discharge of a
contractual duty or the offeror changes its
position to its detriment in reliance on such
rejection or counteroffer. Although a rejection and/or counteroffer will terminate an
offer when communicated, Bold's letter of
May 15 will not terminate its right to exercise its option on the land because there was
neither a discharge of a contractual duty nor
reliance by Stieb to its detriment on the
May 15 letter.

Answer Outline

Problem 2   Substantial Performance;
             Effectiveness of Acceptance
             (580,13a&b)

a. Result if dispute goes to court
   Common law requires literal performance;
   anything less is a breach releasing
   either party from duty to perform
   Courts have developed doctrine of substantial performance as an exception
   concerning construction contracts
   If breach is immaterial; party who
   breached may recover, less damages.
   Party who breached must prove
     1. Defect was not structural in nature
     2. Breach was minor relative to total
        job (95% is a guide courts use)
     3. Breach was not intentional
   Elements 1 and 2 appear to be met in this
   case
   Satisfaction of element 3 is not determinable from facts given
     Would be met if substitutions were due
     to mistake or mere negligence, and
     Silverwater would prevail
     If substitution was willful, no re-
     covery by Silverwater

b. No contract for sale of real property
   Offer is governed by common law of con-
   tracts
   Offer stipulations stated that acceptance
   must be received before effective
     Negated possibility of acceptance being
     effective even though sent by same
     means
   Purported acceptance was counteroffer
     Had to be accepted to create contract
     Silence does not constitute acceptance
     unless
       1. Parties intended silence as accep-
          tance
       2. Prior dealing indicates silence is
          acceptable
       3. Custom of industry recognizes
          silence as acceptance
   Above exceptions do not apply, and there
   is no contract

Unofficial Answer

Problem 2   Substantial Performance; Effec-
            tiveness of Acceptance
            (580,L3a&b)

Parts a1. and a2.

The general common-law rules require
literal performance by a party to a contract.
Failure to literally perform constitutes a
breach. Since promises are construed to be
dependent upon each other, the failure by one
party to perform releases the other. However,
a strict and literal application of this type
of implied condition often results in unfairness and hardship, particularly in cases such
as this. Therefore, the courts developed some
important exceptions to the literal performance doctrine. The applicable rule is known
as the substantial performance doctrine, which
applies to construction contracts and is a
more specific statement of the material performance rule that applies to contracts other
than construction contracts. The general rule
holds that if the breach is immaterial, the
party who breached may nevertheless recover
under the contract, less damages caused by the
breach. The substantial performance doctrine
requires the builder (party breaching) to
prove the following facts.

a. The defect was not a structural
   defect.
b. The breach was relatively minor in relation to the overall performance of
   the contract. The courts and texts
   sometimes talk in terms of a 95 percent or better performance.

c. The breach must be unintentional or,
   to state it another way, the party
   breaching must have been acting in
   good faith.

It would appear that requirements a. and
b. are clearly satisfied on the basis of the
facts. Requirement c. cannot be determined on
the facts given. If Silverwater deliberately
(with knowledge) substituted the improper and
cheaper tile or sewerage pipes, then it may
not be entitled to the benefit of the substantial performance exception. On the other
hand, if these breaches were the result of an
innocent oversight or mere negligence on its
part, recovery should be granted. The recovery must be decreased by the amount of the
damages caused by the breach. The substitution of sewer pipe of like quality and value
would be considered substantial performance.

Part b.

No. The offer for the sale of real property
is governed by the common law of contracts.

Anderson's letter constituted an offer
that stated it would expire at a given time.
In addition to stating the time, the letter
indicated that acceptance "must be received in
her (Anderson's) office" by said time. This
language is clear and unambiguous and effectively negated the rule whereby acceptance may
take place upon dispatch. Thus, despite use
of the same means of communication, acceptance
was not effective until receipt by Anderson on
March 2, 1980. This was too late. Thus, the
purported acceptance was a mere counteroffer
by Heinz and had to be accepted in order to
create a contract. Silence does not usually
constitute acceptance. In fact, the common-
law exceptions to this rule are limited in
nature and narrowly construed. The law
clearly will not permit a party to unila-
terally impose silence upon the other as
acceptance. The narrow exceptions are the
following:

1. The parties intended silence as acceptance.
2. Prior dealing indicates that silence
   is an acceptable method of acceptance.
3. The custom of the trade or industry
   recognizes silence as acceptance.

It is clear that our case is not within
any of the exceptions; hence, silence does not
constitute acceptance, and there is no contract.

Answer Outline

Problem 3   Firm Offer; Revocation and
             Attempted Acceptance; Option
             Contract; Acceptance of an Offer
             (1189,L4)

First assertion is incorrect
  UCC Sales Article applies because goods
  are involved
    Offer by merchant to buy or sell goods
    which is in signed writing and states
    that it will be held open is irrevo-
    cable for stated time not to exceed
    three months
    Crisp's offer is firm offer which can-
    not be revoked before December 8
      Crisp is merchant
      Goods offered for sale
      Offer is in writing and signed by
      Crisp
  Letter of revocation on December 5 did
  not terminate firm offer because three-
  month period not yet expired
  Revocation effective on December 8 when
  three-month period expires
  Attempted acceptance on December 12 did
  not form contract

Second assertion is incorrect
  Option contract requires that all elements necessary to form contract be met
  Consideration was not furnished by Anker
  in return for Dix's promise to keep
  offer open
  Option contract was not formed

Third assertion is incorrect
  Generally, acceptance is effective when
  sent
  Sometimes offer states method of communication required to accept
    Acceptance effective only if required
    method is used
    Acceptance by any other method is in-
    effective
  Dix stated acceptance could only be made
  by certified mail
  Anker's acceptance by private express
  mail courier is ineffective
  It is irrelevant that Dix received acceptance on December 20

Unofficial Answer

Problem 3   Firm Offer; Revocation and
             Attempted Acceptance; Option
             Contract; Acceptance of an Offer
             (1189,L4)

The president's assertion that the September 8, 1988 offer by Crisp was irrevocable
until December 20, 1988, and that, therefore,
a contract was formed by Anker's acceptance on
December 12, 1988, is incorrect. Because the
offer made by Crisp involves a transaction in
goods, i.e. furniture, the UCC Sales Article
applies. The UCC Sales Article provides that
an offer by a merchant to buy or sell goods in
a signed writing which by its terms gives assurance that it will be held open is not revocable, for lack of consideration, during the
time stated or, if no time is stated, for a
reasonable time, but in no event may such
period of irrevocability exceed three months.
Under the facts of this case, Crisp's offer
was a firm offer that could not be revoked
because the offer was made by Crisp, a merchant, concerning the kind of goods being sold
(furniture); was in writing and signed by
Crisp; and stated that it would remain open
until December 20, 1988. Despite the
provision that the offer will remain open
until Decem-ber 20, 1988, a firm offer remains
irrevocable for a three-month period.
Therefore, Crisp's letter of revocation on
December 5, 1988 did not terminate the firm
offer because the three-month period had not
yet expired. The revocation was effective on
December 8, 1988, when the three-month period
expired. Therefore, Anker's attempted
acceptance on December 12, 1988 did not form a
contract with Crisp. Instead, Anker's
attempted acceptance is likely to be treated
as an offer.

The president's assertion that Dix's
December 12, 1988 letter formed an option contract is incorrect. To form an option contract, where the subject matter is real estate, all of the elements necessary to form a
contract must be met. In this case, Anker did
not furnish any consideration in return for
Dix's promise to keep the offer open until
December 20, 1988; therefore, an option contract was not formed.

The president's assertion that Anker's
acceptance on December 19, 1988 formed a
contract with Dix is incorrect. In general,
acceptance of an offer is effective when it is
dispatched. If, however, an offer specifically stipulates the method of communication
to be utilized by the offeree, the acceptance
to be effective must conform to that method.
Thus, an acceptance by another method of
communication is ineffective and no contract
is formed. Under the facts of this case,
Anker's acceptance on December 19, 1988 by a
private express mail courier is ineffective,
despite Dix's receipt of the acceptance on
December 20, 1988, because Dix's offer specifically stipulated that acceptance could only
be made by certified mail, return receipt requested. Instead, Anker's attempted acceptance is likely to be treated as a counteroffer.

Multiple Choice Questions (1-42)

1.   In general, the UCC Sales Article applies to the sale of
   a.   Goods only if the seller is a merchant and the buyer is **not**.
   b.   Goods only if the seller and buyer are both merchants.
   c.   Consumer goods by a non-merchant.
   d.   Real estate by a merchant for $500 or more.

2.   Under the UCC Sales Article, a firm offer will be created only if the
   a.   Offeree is a merchant.
   b.   Offeree gives some form of consideration.
   c.   Offer states the time period during which it will remain open.
   d.   Offer is made by a merchant in a signed writing.

3.   An oral agreement concerning the sale of goods entered without consideration is binding if the agreement
   a.   Is a firm offer made by a merchant who promises to hold the offer open for 30 days.
   b.   Is a waiver of the non-breaching party's rights arising out of a breach of the contract.
   c.   Contradicts the terms of a subsequent written contract that is intended as the complete and exclusive agreement of the parties.
   d.   Modifies the price in an existing, enforceable contract from $525 to $475.

4.   With regard to a contract governed by the UCC Sales Article, which one of the following statements is correct?
   a.   Merchants and non-merchants are treated alike.
   b.   The contract may involve the sale of any type of personal property.
   c.   The obligations of the parties to the contract must be performed in good faith.
   d.   The contract must involve the sale of goods for a price of more than $500.

5.   Mayker, Inc. and Oylco contracted to have Oylco be the exclusive provider of Mayker's fuel oil for three months. The stated price was subject to increases of up to a total of 10% if the market price increased. The market price rose 25% and Mayker tripled its normal order. Oylco seeks to avoid performance. Oylco's best argument in support of its position is that

   a.   There was **no** meeting of the minds.
   b.   The contract was unconscionable.
   c.   The quantity was **not** definite and certain enough.
   d.   Mayker ordered amounts of oil unreasonably greater than its normal requirements.

6.   Cookie Co. offered to sell Distrib Markets 20,000 pounds of cookies at $1.00 per pound, subject to certain specified terms for delivery. Distrib replied in writing as follows:

   "We accept your offer for 20,000 pounds of cookies at $1.00 per pound, weighing scale to have valid city certificate."

Under the UCC
   a.   A contract was formed between the parties.
   b.   A contract will be formed only if Cookie agrees to the weighing scale requirement.
   c.   No contract was formed because Distrib included the weighing scale requirement in its reply.
   d.   No contract was formed because Distrib's reply was a counteroffer.

7.   Bizzy Corp. wrote Wang ordering 100 Wang radios for $2,500. Wang unequivocably accepted Bizzy's offer but in doing so Wang added a clause providing for interest on any overdue invoices pertaining to the sale, a practice which is common in the industry. If Wang and Bizzy are both merchants and there are **no** further communications between the parties, relating to the terms, then
   a.   Wang has made a counteroffer.
   b.   A contract can **not** be formed unless Bizzy expressly accepts the term added by Wang.
   c.   A contract is formed incorporating only the terms of Bizzy's offer.
   d.   A contract is formed with Wang's additional term becoming a part of the agreement.

8.   On October 1, Baker, a wholesaler, sent Clark, a retailer, a written signed offer to sell 200 pinking shears at $9 each. The terms were FOB Baker's warehouse, net 30, late payment subject to a 15% per annum interest charge. The offer indicated that it must be accepted no later than October 10, that acceptance would be effective upon receipt, and that the terms were not to be varied by the offeree. Clark sent a telegram which arrived on October 6, and accepted the offer expressly subject to a change of the payment terms to 2/10, net/30. Baker phoned Clark on

October 7, rejecting the change of payment
terms. Clark then indicated it would accept
the October 1 offer in all respects, and
expected delivery within 10 days. Baker did
not accept Clark's oral acceptance of the
original offer. Which of the following is a
correct statement?

    a. Baker's original offer is a firm
       offer, hence irrevocable.

    b. There is <u>no</u> contract since Clark's
       modifications effectively rejected
       the October 1 offer, and Baker never
       accepted either of Clark's propo-
       sals.

    c. Clark actually created a contract on
       October 6, since the modifications
       were merely proposals and did <u>not</u>
       preclude acceptance.

    d. The Statute of Frauds would preclude
       the formation of a contract in any
       event.

9. DaGama bought a used boat from Magellan
Marina, which disclaimed "any and all
warranties" in connection with the sale.
Magellan was unaware that the boat had been
stolen from Colon. DaGama surrendered it to
Colon when confronted with proof of the
theft. DaGama sued Magellan. Who is likely
to prevail and why?

    a. Magellan, because of the general
       disclaimer.

    b. Magellan, because it was unaware of
       the theft.

    c. DaGama, because the warranty of
       title has been breached.

    d. DaGama, because Magellan is a
       merchant.

10. Lazur Corp. entered into a contract with
Baker Suppliers, Inc. to purchase a used word
processor from Baker. Lazur is engaged in the
business of selling new and used word processors to the general public. The contract
required Baker to ship the goods to Lazur by
common carrier pursuant to the following
provision in the contract: "FOB-Baker
Suppliers, Inc. loading dock." Baker also
represented in the contract that the word
processor had been used for only 10 hours by
its previous owner. The contract included the
provision that the word processor was being
sold "as is" and this provision was in a
larger and different type style than the
remainder of the contract. With regard to the
contract between Lazur and Baker,

    a. An implied warranty of
       merchantability does <u>not</u> arise
       unless both Lazur and Baker are
       merchants.

    b. The "as is" provision effectively
       disclaims the implied warranty of
       title.

    c. No express warranties are created by
       the contract.

    d. The "as is" provision would <u>not</u>
       prevent Baker from being liable for
       a breach of any express warranties
       created by the contract.

11. Which of the following is necessary in
order for the warranty of merchantability to
arise where there has been a sale of goods?

  I. The seller must be a merchant with
    respect to goods of that kind.

 II. The warranty must be in writing.

III. The buyer must have relied on the
    seller's skill or judgment in selecting
    the goods.

    a. I and III only.
    b. I, II, and III.
    c. II and III only.
    d. I only.

12. Under the UCC Sales Article, which of the
following warranties requires the seller to be
a merchant with respect to the goods being
sold in order for the warranty to apply?

	Implied warranty of fitness for a particular purpose	Implied warranty of merchantability
a.	Yes	Yes
b.	No	No
c.	Yes	No
d.	No	Yes

13. Wally, a CPA and a neighbor of Rita's,
offered to sell Rita his power chain saw for
$400. Rita stated that she knew nothing about
chain saws but would buy the saw if it were
capable of cutting down the trees in her back-
yard, which had an average diameter of five
feet. Wally assured Rita that the saw "would
do the job." Relying on Wally's assurance,
Rita purchased the saw. Wally has created a
warranty that

    a. The saw is of an average fair
       quality.

    b. The saw is fit for the ordinary pur-
       poses for which it is used.

    c. The saw is capable of cutting the
       trees in Rita's backyard.

    d. Is unenforceable because it is <u>not</u>
       in writing.

14. Webster purchased a drill press for $475
from Martinson Hardware, Inc. The press has
proved to be defective and Webster wishes to
rescind the purchase based upon a breach of
implied warranty. Which of the following will
preclude Webster's recovery from Martinson?

    a. The press sold to Webster was a
       demonstration model and sold at a
       substantial discount; hence, Webster
       received no implied warranties.

b. Webster examined the press carefully, but as regards the defects, they were hidden defects which a reasonable examination would <u>not</u> have revealed.

c. Martinson informed Webster that they were closing out the model at a loss due to certain deficiencies and that it was sold "with all faults."

d. The fact that it was the negligence of the manufacturer which caused the trouble and that the defect could <u>not</u> have been discovered by Martinson without actually taking the press apart.

15. Which of the following factors is least important in determimng whether a manufacturer is strictly liable in tort for a defective product?

a. The negligence of the manufacturer.

b. The contributory negligence of the plaintiff.

c. Modifications to the product by the wholesaler.

d. Whether the product caused injuries.

16. Kent suffered an injury due to a malfunction of a chain saw he had purchased from Grey Hardware. The saw was manufactured by Dill Tool Corp. Kent has commenced an action against Grey and Dill based upon strict liability. Which of the following is a correct statement?

a. Dill will <u>not</u> be liable if it manufactured the saw in a nonnegligent manner.

b. Privity will <u>not</u> be a valid defense against Kent's suit.

c. The lawsuit will be dismissed since strict liability has <u>not</u> been applied in product liability cases in the majority of jurisdictions.

d. Kent's suit against Grey will be dismissed since Grey was <u>not</u> at fault.

17. Baker fraudulently induced Able to sell Baker a painting for $200. Subsequently, Baker sold the painting for $10,000 to Gold, a good faith purchaser. Able is entitled to

a. Rescind the contract with Baker.

b. Recover the painting from Gold.

c. Recover damages from Baker.

d. Rescind Baker's contract with Gold.

18. A claim has been made by Donnegal to certain goods in your client's possession. Donnegal will be entitled to the goods if it can be shown that Variance, the party from whom your client purchased the goods, obtained them by

a. Deceiving Donnegal as to his identity at the time of the purchase.

b. Giving Donnegal his check which was later dishonored.

c. Obtaining the goods from Donnegal by fraud, punishable as larceny under criminal law.

d. Purchasing goods which had been previously stolen from Donnegal.

19. Darrow purchased 100 sets of bookends from Benson Manufacturing, Inc. Darrow made substantial prepayments of the purchase price. Benson is insolvent and the goods have not been delivered as promised. Darrow wants the bookends. Under the circumstances, which of the following will prevent Darrow from obtaining the bookends?

a. The fact that he did <u>not</u> pay the full price at the time of the purchase even though he has made a tender of the balance and holds it available to Benson upon delivery.

b. The fact that he can obtain a judgment for damages.

c. The fact that he was <u>not</u> aware of Benson's insolvency at the time he purchased the bookends.

d. The fact that the goods have <u>not</u> been identified to his contract.

20. If goods have been delivered to a buyer pursuant to a sale or return contract, the

a. Buyer may use the goods but <u>not</u> resell them.

b. Seller is liable for the expenses incurred by the buyer in returning the goods to the seller.

c. Title to the goods remains with the seller.

d. Risk of loss for the goods passed to the buyer.

21. Lazur Corp. entered into a contract with Baker Suppliers, Inc. to purchase a used word processor from Baker. Lazur is engaged in the business of selling new and used word processors to the general public. The contract required Baker to ship the goods to Lazur by common carrier pursuant to the following provision in the contract: "FOB-Baker Suppliers, Inc. loading dock." Baker also represented in the contract that the word processor had been used for only 10 hours by its previous owner. The contract included the provision that the word processor was being sold "as is" and this provision was in a larger and different type style than the remainder of the contract.

Assume that during shipment to Lazur the word processor was seriously damaged when the carrier's truck was involved in an accident. When the carrier attempted to deliver the word processor, Lazur rejected it and has refused to pay Baker the purchase price. Under the UCC Sales Article,

    a.   Lazur rightfully rejected the damaged computer.

    b.   The risk of loss for the computer was on Lazur during shipment.

    c.   At the time of the accident, risk of loss for the computer was on Baker because title to the computer had not yet passed to Lazur.

    d.   Lazur will not be liable to Baker for the purchase price of the computer because of the FOB provision in the contract.

22. Sand Corp. sold and delivered a photo-copier to Barr for use in Barr's business. According to their agreement, Barr may return the copier within 30 days. During the 30-day period, if Barr has not returned the copier or indicated acceptance of it, which of the following statements is correct with respect to risk of loss and title?

    a.   Risk of loss and title passed to Barr.

    b.   Risk of loss and title remain with Sand.

    c.   Risk of loss passed to Barr but title remains with Sand.

    d.   Risk of loss remains with Sand but title passed to Barr.

23. If a contract for the sale of goods includes a C. & F. shipping term and the seller has fulfilled all of its obligations, the

    a.   Title to the goods will pass to the buyer when the goods are received by the buyer at the place of destination.

    b.   Risk of loss will pass to the buyer upon delivery of the goods to the carrier.

    c.   Buyer retains the right to inspect the goods prior to making payment.

    d.   Seller must obtain an insurance policy at its own expense for the buyer's benefit.

24. Which of the following factors is most important in deciding who bears the risk of loss between merchants when goods are destroyed during shipment?

    a.   The agreement of the parties.

    b.   Whether the goods are perishable.

    c.   Who has title at the time of the loss.

    d.   The terms of applicable insurance policies.

25. Bell Co. owned 20 engines which it deposited in a public warehouse on May 5, receiving a negotiable warehouse receipt in its name. Bell sold the engines to Spark Corp. On which of the following dates did the risk of loss transfer from Bell to Spark?

    a.   June 11 – Spark signed a contract to buy the engines from Bell for $19,000. Delivery was to be at the warehouse.

    b.   June 12 – Spark paid for the engines.

    c.   June 13 – Bell negotiated the warehouse receipt to Spark.

    d.   June 14 – Spark received delivery of the engines at the warehouse.

26. On Monday, Wolfe paid Aston Co., a furniture retailer, $500 for a table. On Thursday, Aston notified Wolfe that the table was ready to be picked up. On Saturday, while Aston was still in possession of the table, it was destroyed in a fire. Who bears the loss of the table?

    a.   Wolfe, because Wolfe had title to the table at the time of loss.

    b.   Aston, unless Wolfe is a merchant.

    c.   Wolfe, unless Aston breached the contract.

    d.   Aston, because Wolfe had not yet taken possession of the table.

27. Cain and Zen Corp. orally agreed that Zen would specially manufacture a machine for Cain at a price of $40,000. After Zen completed the work at a cost of $30,000, Cain notified Zen that it no longer needed the machine. Zen is holding the machine for Cain and has requested payment from Cain. Despite making reasonable efforts, Zen has been unable to resell the machine for any price. Zen has incurred warehouse fees of $500 for storing the machine. If Cain refuses to pay Zen and Zen sues Cain, the most Zen will be entitled to recover is

    a. $0

    b. $30,500

    c. $40,000

    d. $40,500

28. Under the UCC Sales Article, if a buyer wrongfully rejects goods, the aggrieved seller may

	Resell the goods and sue for damages	Cancel the agreement
a.	Yes	Yes
b.	Yes	No
c.	No	Yes
d.	No	No

29. On April 5, 1987, Anker, Inc. furnished Bold Corp. with Anker's financial statements dated March 31, 1987. The financial statements contained misrepresentations which indicated that Anker was solvent when in fact it was insolvent. Based on Anker's financial statements, Bold agreed to sell Anker 90 computers, "FOB--Bold's loading dock." On April 14, Anker received 60 of the computers. The remaining 30 computers are in the possession of the common carrier and in transit to Anker.

With respect to the remaining 30 computors in transit, which of the following statements is correct if Anker refuses to pay Bold in cash and Anker is <u>not</u> in possession of a negotiable document of title covering the computers?

    a. Bold may stop delivery of the computers to Anker since their contract is void due to Anker's furnishing of the false financial statements.

    b. Bold may stop delivery of the computers to Anker despite the fact that title had passed to Anker.

    c. Bold must deliver the computers to Anker on credit since Anker has <u>not</u> breached the contract.

    d. Bold must deliver the computers to Anker since the risk of loss had passed to Anker.

30. Lazur Corp. entered into a contract with Baker Suppliers, Inc. to purchase a used word processor from Baker. Lazur is engaged in the business of selling new and used word processors to the general public. The contract required Baker to ship the goods to Lazur by common carrier pursuant to the following provision in the contract: "FOB-Baker Suppliers, Inc. loading dock." Baker also represented in the contract that the word processor had been used for only 10 hours by its previous owner. The contract included the provision that the word processor was being sold "as is" and this provision was in a larger and different type style than the remainder of the contract.

Assume that Lazur refused to accept the word processor even though it was in all respects conforming to the contract and that the contract is otherwise silent. Under the UCC Sales Article,

    a. Baker can successfully sue for specific performance and make Lazur accept and pay for the word processor.

    b. Baker may resell the word processor to another buyer.

    c. Baker must sue for the difference between the market value of the word processor and the contract price plus its incidental damages.

    d. Baker cannot successfully sue for consequential damages unless it attempts to resell the word processor.

31. Bean ordered 40 beige refrigerators at list price from Tish Co. Immediately upon receipt of Bean's order, Tish sent Bean an acceptance which was received by Bean. The acceptance indicated that shipment would be made within ten days. On the tenth day Tish discovered that all of its supply of beige refrigerators had been sold. Instead it shipped 40 white refrigerators, stating clearly on the invoice that the shipment was sent only as an accommodation. Which of the following is correct?

    a. Bean's order is a unilateral offer, and can only be accepted by Tish's shipment of the goods ordered.

    b. Tish's shipment of white refrigerators is a counteroffer, thus <u>no</u> contract exists between Bean and Tish.

    c. Tish's note of accommodation cancels the contract between Tish and Bean.

    d. Tish's shipment of white refrigerators constitutes a breach of contract.

32. On March 7, 1988, Wax Corp. contracted with Noll Wholesalers to supply Noll with specific electrical parts. Delivery was called for on June 3, 1988. On May 2, 1988, Wax notified Noll that it would not perform and that Noll should look elsewhere. Wax had received a larger and more lucrative contract on April 21, 1988, and its capacity was such that it could not fulfill both orders. The facts

    a. Will prevent Wax from retracting its repudiation of the Noll contract.

    b. Are <u>not</u> sufficient to clearly establish an anticipatory repudiation.

    c. Will permit Noll to sue only after June 3, 1988, the latest performance date.

    d. Will permit Noll to sue immediately after May 2, 1988, even though the performance called for under the contract was <u>not</u> due until June 3, 1988.

33. Lazur Corp. entered into a contract with Baker Suppliers, Inc. to purchase a used word processor from Baker. Lazur is engaged in the business of selling new and used word processors to the general public. The contract required Baker to ship the goods to Lazur by common carrier pursuant to the following provision in the contract: "FOB-Baker Suppliers, Inc. loading dock." Baker also represented in the contract that the word

processor had been used for only 10 hours by its previous owner. The contract included the provision that the word processor was being sold "as is" and this provision was in a larger and different type style than the remainder of the contract.

Assume that the contract between Lazur and Baker is otherwise silent. Under the UCC Sales Article,

a. Lazur must pay Baker the purchase price before Baker is required to ship the word processor to Lazur.
b. Baker does <u>not</u> warrant that it owns the word processor.
c. Lazur will be entitled to inspect the word processor before it accepts or pays for it.
d. Title to the word processor passes to Lazur when it takes physical possession.

34. Cox Manufacturing repudiated its contract to sell 300 televisions to Ruddy Stores, Inc. What recourse does Ruddy Stores have?

a. It can obtain specific performance by the seller.
b. It can recover punitive damages.
c. It must await the seller's performance for a commercially reasonable time after repudiation if it wishes to recover anything.
d. It can "cover," that is, procure the goods elsewhere and recover any damages.

35. Sklar, CPA, purchased from Wiz Corp. two computers. Sklar discovered material defects in the computers 10 months after taking delivery. Three years after discovering the defects, Sklar commenced an action for breach of warranty against Wiz. Wiz has raised the statute of limitations as a defense. The original contract between Wiz and Sklar contained a conspicuous clause providing that the statute of limitations for breach of warranty actions would be limited to 18 months. Under the circumstances, Sklar will

a. Win because the action was commenced within the four-year period as measured from the date of delivery.
b. Win because the action was commenced within the four-year period as measured from the time he discovered the breach or should have discovered the breach.
c. Lose because the clause providing that the statute of limitations would be limited to 18 months is enforceable.
d. Lose because the statute of limitations is three years from the date of delivery with respect to written contracts.

May 1990 Questions

36. To satisfy the UCC Statute of Frauds regarding the sale of goods, which of the following must generally be in writing?

a. Designation of the parties as buyer and seller.
b. Delivery terms.
c. Quantity of the goods.
d. Warranties to be made.

37. Under the UCC Sales Article, the warranty of title may be excluded by

a. Merchants or non-merchants provided the exclusion is in writing.
b. Non-merchant sellers only.
c. The seller's statement that it is selling only such right or title that it has.
d. Use of an "as is" disclaimer.

38. An important factor in determining if an express warranty has been created is whether the

a. Statements made by the seller became part of the basis of the bargain.
b. Sale was made by a merchant in the regular course of business.
c. Statements made by the seller were in writing.
d. Seller intended to create a warranty.

39. Cey Corp. entered into a contract to sell parts to Deck, Ltd. The contract provided that the goods would be shipped "FOB Cey's warehouse." Cey shipped parts different from those specified in the contract. Deck rejected the parts. A few hours after Deck informed Cey that the parts were rejected, they were destroyed by fire in Deck's warehouse. Cey believed that the parts were conforming to the contract. Which of the following statements is correct?

a. Regardless of whether the parts were conforming, Deck will bear the loss because the contract was a shipment contract.
b. If the parts were nonconforming, Deck had the right to reject them, but the risk of loss remains with Deck until Cey takes possession of the parts.
c. If the parts were conforming, risk of loss does <u>not</u> pass to Deck until a reasonable period of time after they are delivered to Deck.
d. If the parts were nonconforming, Cey will bear the risk of loss, even though the contract was a shipment contract.

40. Pulse Corp. maintained a warehouse where
it stored its manufactured goods. Pulse
received an order from Star. Shortly after
Pulse identified the goods to be shipped to
Star, but before moving them to the loading
dock, a fire destroyed the warehouse and its
contents. With respect to the goods, which of
the following statements is correct?
   a.   Pulse has title but no insurable
         interest.
   b.   Star has title and an insurable
         interest.
   c.   Pulse has title and an insurable
         interest.
   d.   Star has title but no insurable
         interest.

41. On September 10, Bell Corp. entered into
a contract to purchase 50 lamps from Glow
Manufacturing. Bell prepaid 40% of the purchase price. Glow became insolvent on September 19 before segregating, in its inventory,
the lamps to be delivered to Bell. Bell will
not be able to recover the lamps because
   a.   Bell is regarded as a merchant.
   b.   The lamps were not identified to the
         contract.
   c.   Glow became insolvent fewer than 10
         days after receipt of Bell's
         prepayment.
   d.   Bell did not pay the full price at
         the time of purchase.

42. Eagle Corporation solicited bids for
various parts it uses in the manufacture of
jet engines. Eagle received six offers and
selected the offer of Sky Corporation. The
written contract specified a price for 100,000
units, delivery on June 1 at Sky's plant, with
payment on July 1. On June 1, Sky had
completed a 200,000 unit run of parts similar
to those under contract for Eagle and various
other customers. Sky had not identified the
parts to specific contracts. When Eagle's
truck arrived to pick up the parts on June 1,
Sky refused to deliver claiming the contract
price was too low. Eagle was unable to cover
in a reasonable time. Its production lines
were in danger of shutdown because the parts
were not delivered. Eagle would probably
   a.   Have as its only remedy the right of
         replevin.
   b.   Have the right of replevin only if
         Eagle tendered the purchase price on
         June 1.
   c.   Have as its only remedy the right to
         recover dollar damages.
   d.   Have the right to obtain specific
         performance.

Repeat Question

(590,L1,46) Identical/similar to item 31 above

Problems

Problem 1   (588,L2)

(15 to 20 minutes)

Mirk & Co., CPAs, has been engaged to audit Spear Corp.'s 1987 financial statements. Spear is engaged in the business of buying and selling computers. Spear has adopted a calendar year for accounting purposes. While conducting the audit, Mirk reviewed the following transactions occurring in December 1987.

• On December 20, Spear sold five computers to Pica Corp. The contract required Spear to ship the computers by common carrier. The shipping terms of the contract were "FOB--Spear's loading dock." The computers were shipped on December 30, and on January 1, 1988, while the computers were in transit, the common carrier was involved in an accident causing a fire that totally destroyed the computers. Pica discovered, upon a review of a copy of the common carrier's bill of lading, that the destroyed computers were not the models it had ordered.

• On December 21, Spear purchased and took delivery of 15 computers from Larson for $20,000. Larson had purchased the computers from Xeon Co., paying Xeon with a check that Larson's bank refused to honor because of insufficient funds. Spear was unaware that Larson's check was dishonored.

• On December 22, Spear entered into a sale on approval contract with Rusk Corp. for two computers. Rusk is engaged exclusively in the business of selling furniture. The contract required Rusk to notify Spear within 15 days after delivery if it did not want to keep the computers. Rusk took delivery of the computers on December 21, and, as of December 31, had not yet decided whether to keep the computers.

With regard to the transactions described above, Mirk wishes to resolve the following issues that were not addressed in the specific contracts:

As of December 31, 1987, which of the parties bears the risk of loss for the computers with regard to the:

• December 20 transaction with Pica?
• December 22 transaction with Rusk?

As of December 31, 1987, which of the parties has title to the computers with regard to the:

• December 21 transaction with Larson?
• December 22 transaction with Rusk?

What rights do the general creditors of Rusk have to the computers delivered to Rusk pursuant to the December 22 transaction with Spear?

Required:

Discuss the issues raised by Mirk, setting forth your conclusions and reasons therefore.

Problem 2   (1185,L4)

(15 to 20 minutes)

John Barr purchased a new forklift for use in his business from Fiber Corp. Fiber designs, manufactures, and assembles forklifts, shipping them directly to customers throughout the U.S. The contract between Barr and Fiber contained a clause in fine print disclaiming "all warranties express or implied other than the limited warranty provided for on the face of this contract." The limited warranty included in the contract provided that "the buyer's sole and exclusive remedy shall be repair or replacement of defective parts and the seller shall not be liable for damages or personal injuries." The contract was a standard form used by Fiber, and as a matter of policy Fiber does not negotiate the terms and conditions of the contract with its customers.

Within one week of the purchase date, Barr was seriously injured when the steering wheel locked causing him to lose control of the forklift. Barr brings an action against Fiber for the personal injuries that he sustained based on the following causes of action:

• Negligence
• Breach of warranty
• Strict liability in tort

Fiber has asserted that the action brought by Barr should be dismissed due to the disclaimer.

Required:

Answer the following, setting forth reasons for any conclusions stated.
a. Discuss in separate paragraphs the prerequisites necessary to sustain each of the three causes of action asserted by Barr.
b. Discuss the validity of the disclaimer with regard to the breach of warranty cause of action.

Problem 3   (1187,L2)

(15 to 20 minutes)

On May 1, Starr Corp., a manufacturer and supplier of computers, mailed a proposed contract to Magic, Inc., offering to sell 20 items of specified computer equipment for $18,000. Magic was engaged in the business of selling computers to the public. Magic accepted Starr's offer by executing and returning the contract to Starr. Starr failed to sign the contract.

On May 15, Starr advised Magic by telephone that, due to certain market conditions, the price of computer parts had increased. Therefore, in order to avoid a loss on the sale to Magic, Starr requested an increase in the sales price to $20,000, which was orally agreed to by Magic. On May 17, Starr sent to Magic a signed letter acknowledging this agreement. Magic did not respond to the letter.

On September 15, Starr notified Magic that the equipment was ready for delivery. Due to substantial changes in computer technology subsequent to May 15, Magic indicated that it no longer wanted the equipment and that it would not pay for it. Starr was unable to resell the computer equipment for any price despite its reasonable efforts to do so. Therefore, Starr commenced a breach of contract action against Magic. Magic asserted the following defenses:

• The May 1 written contract between Starr and Magic is not enforceable because of the Statute of Frauds.

• Even if the May 1 contract is enforceable, the May 15 oral agreement to change the price of the equipment is not enforceable because the agreement lacked consideration and failed to satisfy the Statute of Frauds.

• In any event, Starr is not entitled to recover the full sales price because the equipment is still in Starr's possession.

Required:

Discuss Magic's assertions, indicating whether each is correct or incorrect and setting forth the reasons for any conclusions stated.

Multiple Choice Answers

1. c	10. d	19. d	27. d	35. c
2. d	11. d	20. d	28. a	36. c
3. d	12. d	21. b	29. b	37. c
4. c	13. c	22. b	30. b	38. a
5. d	14. c	23. b	31. d	39. d
6. a	15. a	24. a	32. d	40. c
7. d	16. b	25. c	33. c	41. b
8. b	17. c	26. d	34. d	42. d
9. c	18. d			

Multiple Choice Answer Explanations

A. Contracts for Sale of Goods

1. (1188,L1,43) (c) The Sales Article of the UCC applies to the sale of goods, specially manufactured or otherwise. Although certain provisions apply only to transactions between merchants, the general scope of the Article extends to sales between nonmerchants as well. Answers (a) and (b) are incorrect since they incorrectly limit the scope of the UCC Sales Article. Answer (d) is incorrect because the UCC Sales Article never applies to the sale of real estate. Nor does it apply only to the sale of goods for $500 or more. Rather, it is the Statute of Frauds which generally requires that any sale of goods for $500 or more be in writing to be enforceable.

2. (1188,L1,44) (d) In order to have a firm offer under the UCC, the offer must be made by a merchant offeror in a signed writing which gives assurance that the offer will be held open. There is no requirement that the offeree also be a merchant. A firm offer does not need to state the period of time for which it is irrevocable. If no time period is stated, the offer will be irrevocable for a reasonable period of time, not to exceed three months. A firm offer need not be supported by consideration to be irrevocable. Thus, answers (a), (b), and (c) are incorrect.

3. (1187,L1,40) (d) An oral agreement modifying an existing contract for the sale of goods needs no new consideration to be binding. If the contract, as modified, is for the sale of goods for a price less than $500, the Statute of Frauds does not apply, and the oral modification is enforceable. Answer (a) is incorrect because a firm offer made by a merchant to hold an offer open for a stated period of time without consideration must be in writing and signed by the merchant. Answer (b) is incorrect because an oral agreement which waives a non-breaching party's rights arising out of a breach of contract requires consideration to be enforceable. Answer (c) is incorrect because the parol evidence rule stipulates that a written agreement intended to be the complete and exclusive agreement of the parties may not be contradicted by prior or contemporaneous oral evidence.

4. (589,L1,54) (c) Under all contracts, including sales contracts governed by the UCC, the parties are obligated to perform in good faith. Answer (a) is incorrect because certain provisions, such as the battle of forms provision, only apply to merchants. Answer (b) is incorrect because the Sales Article of the UCC only applies to the sale of goods. Goods are defined as all things which are moveable at the time of identification to the contract. Goods would not include money, investment securities, intangible property, contract rights, accounts receivable, or real property. Answer (d) is incorrect because the sale price does not have to exceed $500.

5. (1189,L1,51) (d) The agreement between Mayker, Inc. and Oylco is a requirements contract. Under a requirements contract, the seller cannot be required to sell amounts unreasonably disproportionate to normal requirements of the buyer. Thus, Mayker's ordering of unreasonably disproportionate amounts of oil would be a breach of the contract and would allow Oylco to avoid performance. Answer (a) is incorrect because both parties did agree to the original contract and a meeting of the minds did occur when the contract was formed. Answer (b) is incorrect because an unconscionable contract occurs when there is a great disparity in the bargaining powers of the contracting parties through which one party exploits the other. There is no evidence of this in this situation. Answer (c) is incorrect because Oylco's agreement to supply Mayker's fuel oil requirements is considered definite and certain enough to satisfy the quantity term of the contract under the UCC.

6. (1189,L1,46) (a) Under common law, an acceptance must be unequivocal and unqualified in agreeing to the precise terms specified by the offer. However, the Uniform Commercial Code alters this general rule as far as the sales of goods is concerned. Under the UCC, an acceptance containing additional terms is a valid acceptance unless the acceptance is expressly conditional upon the offeror's agreement to the additional terms. In this situation, a valid contract has been formed between Cookie Co. and Distrib Markets. Answer (b) is incorrect because Distrib Markets' acceptance was not conditional upon Cookie's agreement to the additional term and,

thus, a contract is formed regardless of Cookie's agreement or objection to the additional term. Answers (c) and (d) are incorrect because this contract was for the sale of goods and is governed by the UCC rather than by common law. Under common law, Distrib Markets' reply would have been a rejection and counteroffer; but under the UCC, a contract was formed.

A.2.c. Battle of Forms

7. (1184,L1,53) (d) Since Bizzy Corp. and Wang are both merchants, the battle of forms rule allows Wang to include an additional term in its acceptance without this additional term constituting a counteroffer. In fact, this additional term is a part of the contract unless: the offer states Wang may only accept the terms stated; or the additional term materially alters the offer; or the Bizzy Corp. refuses the term within a reasonable time. Since none of these three factors are present, a contract is formed with Wang's additional term becoming a part of the agreement. Therefore, answers (a), (b), and (c) are incorrect.

8. (1183,L1,53) (b) Clark's telegram of October 6 does not operate as an effective acceptance of Baker's offer because Clark's acceptance was expressly conditioned on the change in payment terms. Consequently, the battle of the forms exception does not apply. This telegram is actually a counter-offer which Baker expressly rejected in the October 7 telephone conversation. Clark's subsequent offer to honor the terms as originally expressed October 1 was never accepted by Baker and, therefore, there is no contract between the parties. Answer (c) is incorrect because Clark expressly conditioned his acceptance on the modifications. If, in fact, Clark's changes were mere proposals, the modifications would still not have become part of the contract since this transaction was between merchants, and Baker expressly stated that the terms in his offer were not to be varied. Answer (d) is incorrect because under the Uniform Commercial Code a writing will satisfy the Statute of Frauds as long as it indicates a contract has been made, is signed by the party to be bound, and states the quantity. Assuming Clark is seeking to enforce the contract against Baker, Baker's written signed offer of October 1 stating a quantity of 200 pinking shears complies with the Statute of Frauds. Answer (a) is incorrect because Baker's original offer does not satisfy the requirements for a firm offer. Under the Uniform Commercial Code a merchant cannot revoke a written signed offer to buy or sell goods if he gives assurances that the offer will be held open. Such an offer is irrevocable for the stated time, up to a maximum of 3 months. If no period is specified, then a reasonable time is implied. Baker's offer is not a firm offer because it does not contain assurances that it will be held open. The statement that the offer "must be accepted no later than October 10" only establishes the expiration date of the offer. Baker has determined when the offer will lapse without expressly committing himself to keeping the offer open until October 10.

B.1.a. Warranty of Title

9. (1189,L1,47) (c) Under the UCC, the seller warrants good title and rightful transfer and freedom from any security interest or lien of which the buyer has no knowledge. This warranty of title may only be disclaimed by specific language or circumstances which give the buyer reason to know s/he is receiving less than full title. The general disclaimer of "any and all warranties" made by Magellan in connection with the sale only disclaims the implied warranties of merchantability and fitness for a particular purpose, not the warranty of title. Thus, DaGama will prevail in the lawsuit because the warranty of title has been breached and Magellan's general disclaimer did not disclaim it. Answer (a) is incorrect because a general disclaimer cannot be used to disclaim the warranty of title; specific language must be used. Answer (b) is incorrect because despite the fact that the seller has no knowledge of the theft, s/he still warrants good title to the goods. Answer (d) is incorrect because the warranty of title may be disclaimed by a merchant seller. If Magellan had used specific language in disclaiming the warranty of title, s/he would have prevailed in the lawsuit.

B.1.b. Express Warranties

10. (589,L1,55) (d) A seller creates an express warranty by making an affirmation of fact or promise which forms part of the basis of the bargain. Express warranties may be made orally or in writing and will exist regardless of the seller's intent. Consequently, the use of the words "as is" would not prevent Baker from being liable for a breach of any express warranties created by the contract. Answer (a) is incorrect because the implied warranty of merchantability arises whenever the seller (Baker) is a merchant with respect to the goods being sold. The status of the buyer is irrelevant. Answer (b) is incorrect because warranty of title is not an

implied warranty. Warranty of title can only be disclaimed by specific language or circumstances which give the buyer reason to know he is receiving less than full title. A general disclaimer of all warranties or such language as "as is" is insufficient. Answer (c) is incorrect because Baker represented that the word processor had been used for only ten hours by its previous owner. An express warranty was created by this representation of fact.

B.1.c. Implied Warranties

11. (1188,L1,47) (d) The warranty of merchantability (i.e., that goods are fit for ordinary purposes and that the goods are properly packaged and labeled) is always implied if the seller is a merchant. Thus, the warranty need not be in writing to be present if the seller is a merchant. Additionally, in proving that a warranty of merchantability exists, the buyer need not show that s/he relied on the seller's skill or judgment in selecting the goods. This must be shown only when proving that the implied warranty of fitness for a particular purpose exists. Thus, answers (a), (b), and (c) are incorrect.

12. (588,L1,50) (d) Every sale of goods by a merchant seller carries with it a warranty of merchantability, unless specifically disclaimed by the merchant. The merchant seller is guaranteeing the goods are fit for the ordinary purpose for which goods of this type are used. The warranty of fitness for a particular purpose is created when the seller (both merchant and nonmerchant sellers) knows of the particular use for which the goods are required and further knows that the buyer is relying on the skill and judgment of the seller to select and furnish suitable goods for this particular use. Therefore, answers (a), (b), and (c) are incorrect.

13. (1184,L1,54) (c) Under the stated facts, Wally is creating the implied warranty of fitness for a particular purpose. This warranty is created when the seller (merchant or nonmerchant) has reason to know the buyer's particular purpose and knows the buyer is relying on the seller's judgment to provide appropriate goods. This warranty guarantees the goods are fit for the buyer's particular purpose. It is the implied warranty of merchantability that guarantees the goods are of an average fair quality and are fit for ordinary purposes, but Wally did not create this warranty since he is not a merchant-seller. Since the warranty of fitness for a particular purpose is an implied warranty,

there is no requirement that it be in writing. Therefore, answers (a), (b), and (d) are incorrect.

14. (1182,L1,47) (c) When goods are sold "as is" or "with all faults," all implied warranties are disclaimed including the implied warranty of merchantability. Normally, a disclaimer of the implied warranty of merchantability must contain some form of the word "merchantability" to be effective. However, goods sold "with all faults" is an exception to that rule. Answer (a) is incorrect because selling a demonstration model at a substantial discount would not disclaim the implied warranties. Answer (b) is incorrect because offering an inspection of the goods to a buyer only disclaims the implied warranties concerning patent defects, not concerning latent (hidden) defects in the goods. Answer (d) is incorrect because a merchant seller of goods gives an implied warranty that the goods are fit for ordinary purposes, regardless of which party caused the defect in the goods. The breach of warranty theory is not based on negligence.

B.3. Strict Liability

15. (1189,L1,45) (a) Under the theory of strict liability, the plaintiff must establish the following: 1) the seller was engaged in the business of selling the product, 2) the product was defective, 3) the defect was unreasonably dangerous to the plaintiff, and 4) the defect caused injury to the plaintiff. If the plaintiff establishes these conditions, then the seller is liable regardless of whether the seller was negligent or at fault for the defective condition of the product. Thus, the negligence of the manufacturer is not a factor in determining the outcome of a case under the theory of strict liability. Answer (b) is incorrect because if the plaintiff misuses the product, this could provide a valid defense for the seller. A buyer misuses a product when s/he uses it for some purpose other than the purpose for which the product was originally intended. Answer (c) is incorrect because modifications to the product by the wholesaler may be a factor in determining that the product was defective (an element the plaintiff must establish). Answer (d) is incorrect because the plaintiff must establish that the product caused injuries in order to hold the seller liable under the theory of strict liability.

16. (1186,L1,46) (b) Under strict liability the only defenses available to a seller are misuse and assumption of risk. A buyer misuses a product when s/he uses it for some pur-

pose other than the purpose for which the
product was originally intended. Assumption
of risk exists when an individual uses the
product without regard to an inherent danger
associated with the product. Privity of
contract is not a defense under strict liability because the suit is not based on contract
law. Answer (a) is incorrect because Dill's
only defenses are misuse and assumption of
risk. The fact Dill manufactured the saw in a
nonnegligent manner is irrelevant under strict
liability since Kent does not have to establish fault to hold Dill liable. Answer (c) is
incorrect because strict liability in product
liability cases is applied in the majority of
jurisdictions. Answer (d) is incorrect because Kent does not have to establish fault
under the strict liability theory in order to
hold Grey liable. The strict liability allows
the injured party to recover against either
the manufacturer or the merchant seller.

C.   Transfer of Property Rights

17. (587,L1,19) (c) Baker fraudulently
induced Able to sell the painting to Baker;
therefore, Baker only held a voidable title
for the painting. A person with a voidable
title may transfer good title to a good faith
purchaser. Thus, Able has no course of action
against Gold, a good faith purchaser. However, Able is entitled to recover damages from
Baker. Consequently, answers (b) and (d) are
incorrect. Answer (a) is incorrect because
rescission would involve placing both parties
in the position they occupied prior to the
contract. Able would not be able to rescind
the contract because Baker has transferred
good title to a good faith purchaser.

18. (582,L1,47) (d) Donnegal will be
entitled to return of the goods if the goods
have been stolen from him. A thief has no
power to transfer good title in goods to a
good faith purchaser. However, a person with
a voidable title may transfer good title in
the goods to a good faith purchaser. A person
has a voidable title when the goods have been
delivered under a transaction of purchase and
(1) the transferor was deceived as to the
identity of the purchaser, or (2) the delivery
was in exchange for a check which is later
dishonored, or (3) the delivery was procured
through fraud punishable as larceny under
criminal law. Therefore, answers (a), (b),
and (c) are incorrect.

19. (581,L1,20) (d) Upon identification of
the goods that relate to a contract, several
specific rights are granted to the buyer of
these goods. Among these is the right to take
delivery of goods upon insolvency of the

seller if full or partial payment was made at
the time of the purchase and any balance due
is tendered to the seller. Since the question
asks which condition will prevent recovery of
the goods, lack of identification is correct
because identification must occur before any
rights of repossession accrue to the buyer.
It is not necessary that the full price be
paid at the time of purchase (a) as long as
tender of the balance due is made to the
seller. Answers (b) and (c) are incorrect
since the fact that a buyer may obtain a
judgment for damages to the goods by third
parties or that a buyer is not aware of a
seller's insolvency will not prevent the buyer
from gaining possession of the goods.

D.   Risk of Loss and Title

20. (1188,L1,46) (d) Under the UCC, in the
case of a sale or return contract, risk of
loss and title pass to the buyer according to
the shipping terms of the contract. Thus,
generally the risk of loss and ownership will
be with the buyer while the goods are in the
buyer's possession. Therefore, answer (c) is
incorrect. Answer (a) is incorrect because
the buyer may use or resell the goods delivered pursuant to a sale or return contract.
Normally in a sale or return the buyer is
purchasing the goods for the purpose of
reselling them. Answer (b) is incorrect since
all expenses incurred in returning the goods
purchased pursuant to a sale or return
contract are the buyer's responsibility.

21. (589,L1,56) (b) Provided there is no
agreement to the contrary, risk of loss will
ordinarily pass upon tender of delivery. The
shipping terms were FOB--Baker Supplier
(shipping point); therefore, Baker tendered
delivery once the word processor was in the
possession of the carrier. Consequently, the
risk of loss for the word processor was on
Lazur during shipment. Answer (a) is
incorrect because the risk of loss was on
Lazur during the shipment; therefore, Lazur
could not rightfully reject the damaged word
processor. Answer (c) is incorrect because
unlike common law, the passage of risk of loss
does not depend upon the passage of title
under the UCC. Answer (d) is incorrect
because the risk of loss was on Lazur during
shipment; consequently, Lazur would still be
liable to Baker for the purchase price of the
word processor.

22. (1187,L1,39) (b) Provided there is no
agreement to the contrary and neither party is
in breach, both risk of loss and title to
goods being purchased on a sale on approval
basis remain with the seller until the sale is

completed. Since in this case Barr has not indicated acceptance of the copier, the sale is incomplete, and the risk of loss and title remain with Sand during the 30-day period. Thus, answers (a), (c), and (d) are all incorrect.

23. (587,L1,54) (b) The shipping term "C. & F." means that the purchase price includes both the cost of the goods and the cost of delivering the goods to the shipper. Under such agreements, the risk of loss and title to the goods pass when the seller places the goods in the appropriate carrier's hands. Thus, answer (a) is incorrect. Answer (c) is incorrect because in a C. & F. contract the buyer is not entitled to inspect the goods before payment of the price. Answer (d) is incorrect because in a C. & F. contract, unlike a C.I.F. contract, the seller need not obtain an insurance policy at its own expense for the buyer's benefit.

24. (1189,L1,48) (a) The most important factor in determining who bears the risk of loss in a sale of goods is an agreement between the contracting parties which allocates the risk that each party will bear. The UCC rules concerning risk of loss will only apply if the parties have not allocated risk of loss in the contract. Consequently, shipping terms and possession would not be relevant if the parties manifested their intent in the contract. In any situation, neither title nor whether goods are perishable is a relevant factor when allocating risk of loss. Therefore, answers (b), (c), and (d) are incorrect.

25. (1185,L1,45) (c) Provided there is no agreement to the contrary and neither party is in breach, risk of loss to goods, which are held in a warehouse for delivery without being moved, will pass at the time the negotiable document of title is properly negotiated to the buyer. If the document of title is non-negotiable, then the risk of loss passes a reasonable time after the buyer receives the document. Where there is no document of title representing the goods, risk of loss will pass once the warehouseman acknowledges the buyer's right to the goods. Answers (a), (b), and (d) are incorrect since Bell has a negotiable document of title which is properly negotiated to Spark Company on June 13.

26. (1189,L1,49) (d) Provided there is no agreement to the contrary and neither party is in breach, risk of loss will in the case of a merchant seller; pass to the buyer on physical receipt of the goods. In this situation,

Aston Co., a merchant, will bear the loss of the table since Wolfe had not yet taken possession of it. Therefore, answer (c) is incorrect. Answer (a) is incorrect because unlike common law, the passage of risk of loss does not depend upon the passage of title under UCC. Answer (b) is incorrect because risk of loss is not dependent upon whether or not the buyer, Wolfe, is a merchant. The rule is based on whether or not the seller is a merchant.

E.4. Seller's Remedies

27. (1188,L1,48) (d) When a buyer breaches the contract as it becomes due, the seller may recover the full purchase price of the goods identified to the contract plus incidental damages if the seller is unable to resell the goods at a reasonable price after making a reasonable effort. Thus, in this case, Zen would be allowed to recover the purchase price of $40,000 plus the $500 of incidental damages for storage. Thus, answers (a), (b), and (c) are incorrect.

28. (1189,L1,52) (a) Under the UCC Sales Article, if the buyer refuses to accept the goods upon delivery, the seller has the right to resell the goods. In addition, if the difference between the market value and the contract price is inadequate to place the seller in as good a position as performance would have, then the seller can sue for lost profits plus incidental damages. Also, since the buyer wrongfully rejected the goods and breached the contract, the seller may cancel the agreement. Therefore, answers (b), (c), and (d) are incorrect.

29. (587,L1,53) (b) A seller is entitled to stop the delivery of goods in the hands of a carrier if an insolvent buyer who is not in possession of the document of title refuses to pay cash. Therefore, Bold may stop delivery of the computers since Anker refuses to pay in cash and is not in possession of the document of title. Answer (a) is incorrect because the furnishing of false financial statements does not void the contract, instead it extends the time the seller has to reclaim goods already delivered to the insolvent buyer. If the buyer is willing to pay cash, the seller will still have to perform. Thus, answer (c) is incorrect. The fact that Anker has assumed risk of loss will not prevent Bold from stopping delivery of the computers; therefore, answer (d) is incorrect.

30. (589,L1,58) (b) A seller has the right to resell goods to another if the buyer refuses to accept the goods upon delivery. An-

swer (a) is incorrect because specific performance is not a remedy available to the
seller. Baker cannot force Lazur to accept
the word processor. Answer (c) is incorrect
because Baker has a couple of additional remedies available. Baker can recover the full
contract price plus incidental damages if he
is unable to resell the identified goods. Alternatively, if the difference between the
market value and contract price is inadequate
to place Baker in as good a position as performance would have, then Baker can sue for
lost profits plus incidental damages. Answer (d) is incorrect because Baker could sue
for consequential damages that Lazur had
reason to know Baker would incur as a result
of Lazur's breach.

E.5. Buyer's Remedies

31. (1188,L1,50) (d) Shipment of a different
model of refrigerators, even as an accommodation, constitutes a breach of contract because
the terms of the contract have not been complied with. Answer (a) is incorrect because
Bean's offer to Tish constitutes a bilateral
offer which was accepted by Tish's communication to Bean. This bilateral offer could have
been accepted by delivery of the goods as
well. Answer (b) is incorrect because the
shipment cannot be considered a counteroffer
since there was already a contract in
existence between Bean and Tish. Answer (c)
is incorrect because only the promised performance will discharge Tish unless Bean
accepts the accommodation.

32. (1188,L1,51) (d) Anticipatory repudiation occurs when a party renounces the duty to
perform the contract before the party's obligation to perform arises. Therefore, because
Wax notified Noll of its intent not to perform, it has engaged in anticipatory repudiation. Anticipatory repudiation discharges the
nonrepudiating party (Noll) from the contract
and allows this party to sue for breach
immediately. However, if it is commercially
reasonable, the nonrepudiating party can
ignore the repudiation and await performance
at the appointed time before it sues for
breach. Should the nonrepudiating party
choose this latter course of action, the
repudiating party may retract the renunciation
and perform as originally promised. Thus,
answers (a), (b), and (c) are incorrect.

33. (589,L1,57) (c) In the absence of an
agreement to the contrary, Lazur has the right
to inspect the word processor before it
accepts or pays for it. In the event the word
processor is nonconforming, Lazur (buyer) must
give notice to Baker (seller) in a reasonable

amount of time. Answer (a) is incorrect
because if the time and method of payment is
silent, then the UCC will assume a time and
method which is customary for the industry.
The missing terms will not cause a contract
for the sale of goods to fail if there was an
intent to contract. Answer (b) is incorrect
because a seller (Baker) warrants good title
unless there is wording or circumstances which
give the buyer reason to know he is receiving
less than full title. Answer (d) is incorrect
because in the lack of wording to the contrary, the UCC provides that the title generally passes when the seller completes his performance with respect to delivery; therefore,
title passed to Lazur when Baker placed the
word processor in the possession of the
carrier.

34. (1179,L1,1) (d) The nonbreaching party
under a contract for sale can attempt to
mitigate damages by "cover," that is, by
procuring the goods elsewhere and recovering
as damages the difference between the contract
price and the price of cover. Answer (a) is
incorrect because specific performance is
available only upon the damaged party showing
that money damages are inadequate or other
unique conditions exist which require actual
performance. There is nothing here to
indicate that the televisions are unavailable
in the market or other unique conditions
exist. Answer (b) is incorrect because
punitive damages are never recoverable for
breach of contract. Answer (c) is incorrect
since a nonbreaching party need not wait after
a breach occurs to begin proceedings to
recover.

E.6. Statute of Limitations

35. (1186,L1,17) (c) The statute of limitations for the sale of goods is generally four
years; however, the parties may agree to reduce the statute to a period of not less than
one year. Therefore, Sklar will lose because
the clause providing that the statute of limitations would be limited to 18 months is enforceable, and the action was not brought
within the required time period. Thus, answer (a) is incorrect. Answer (b) is incorrect because a breach of warranty occurs upon
the tender of delivery, not upon the discovery
of the defect, and the statute begins running
at the time the breach occurs. Answer (d) is
incorrect because the statute is 18 months as
outlined in the contract.

May 1990 Answers

36. (590,L1,40) (c) A writing under common law legally sufficient to satisfy the Statute of Frauds must identify the parties, the subject matter, the essential terms of the contract, and the consideration. It must also be signed by the party to be charged. However, under the UCC the writing only has to include the quantity term and be signed by the party to be charged. Therefore, answers (a), (b), and (d) are incorrect.

37. (590,L1,42) (c) Under the UCC, every seller warrants that the goods sold are free from any security interest or lien of which the buyer has no actual knowledge. This warranty of title may only be disclaimed by specific language or circumstances which give the buyer reason to know that s/he is receiving less than full title. A seller's statement that s/he is selling only such right or title that s/he has will exclude the warranty of title. Answer (a) is incorrect because the warranty of title may be disclaimed through a specific oral statement or through circumstances which give the buyer reason to know that full title is not being received. There is no requirement that the disclaimer be in writing. Answer (b) is incorrect because the warranty of title may be disclaimed by a merchant seller. Answer (d) is incorrect because the statement "as is" only disclaims the implied warranties of merchantability and fitness for a particular purpose, not the warranty of title.

38. (590,L1,43) (a) Any description of goods that is part of the basis of a bargain creates an express warranty that the goods shall conform to that description. Answer (b) is incorrect since it is not required that the seller be a merchant to create an express warranty. Answer (c) is incorrect because an express warranty may be oral or written. Answer (d) is incorrect since the intent of the seller is not relevant when determining whether an express warranty exists. Any affirmation of fact or promise made by the seller, regardless of intent, to the buyer which relates to the goods and becomes part of the basis of the bargain creates an express warranty.

39. (590,L1,44) (d) The UCC places risk of loss on the breaching party. Since Cey shipped nonconforming goods, it breached the contract and would have risk of loss until the nonconforming goods were accepted by the buyer or until the goods were cured by Cey. Since Deck rejected the goods and Cey did not cure the goods, risk of loss remained with Cey.

Shipping terms have no bearing on risk of loss in this situation because the goods did not conform to the contract. Answer (a) is incorrect because Deck would only bear risk of loss if the goods conformed to the contract. Answer (b) is incorrect because the risk of loss was never transferred to Deck since the goods were nonconforming. Answer (c) is incorrect because if the goods were conforming, risk of loss would pass to Deck at Cey's warehouse based on the shipping terms "FOB Cey's warehouse."

40. (590,L1,45) (c) The seller of goods usually has an insurable interest in the goods as long as s/he has title or a security interest. In the absence of an agreement between the parties as to when title passes, title will generally pass when the seller completes his/her performance with respect to delivery. In this situation, Pulse, the seller, had not yet moved the goods to the loading dock, so delivery was not complete, and Pulse still had title at the time of destruction. Therefore, Pulse also had an insurable interest, and answer (a) is incorrect. Answers (b) and (d) are incorrect because although identification of the goods gives the buyer (Star) an insurable interest, Star does not have title to the goods.

41. (590,L1,47) (b) Identification occurs when the goods that are going to be used to perform the contract are shipped, marked, or otherwise designated for the contract. Identification gives the buyer (1) an insurable interest in the goods, and (2) the right to demand goods upon offering the full contract price. In this case, Bell would not be able to recover the lamps since Glow did not identify the goods. Answer (a) is incorrect because the fact that Bell is a merchant does not effect the recovery of the merchandise. Answer (c) is incorrect because the timing of Bell's prepayment in relation to Glow's insolvency does not affect Bell's collectibility of the merchandise. Note, however, that the seller can recover goods received by an insolvent buyer if the demand is made within 10 days of receipt of the goods by the buyer. Answer (d) is incorrect because as long as the goods are not identified, the buyer cannot recover the goods, no matter what percentage of the contract price was paid by the buyer.

42. (590,L1,48) (d) Although the usual remedy against the seller for breach of contract is monetary damages, the UCC allows specific performance if the goods are unique or "in other proper circumstances." In this

case, the seller had available more than
enough of the parts agreed to in the contract
but was claiming the contract price was too
low. Since the buyer (Eagle) was unable to
cover in a reasonable time and was in danger
of a shutdown, Eagle should be allowed to
resort to specific performance. Answers (a)
and (b) are incorrect because the right of
replevin is available to recover goods that
have been identified to the contract. The
fact pattern states that the parts had not
been identified to the contract. Answer (c)
is incorrect because although Eagle could use
the remedy of monetary damages, it could also
opt to use specific performance.

Answer Outline

Problem 1   Passage of Title and Risk of Loss
             (588,L2)

Risk of Loss
    Generally passes to buyer in shipment
      contract when goods are delivered to
      carrier
    Does not pass if goods are nonconforming
    Does not pass to Pica because computers
      did not conform
    Passes in sale on approval when buyer
      accepts goods
    Does not pass to Rusk because computers
      were not yet accepted
Title
    Larson has voidable title due to insuffi-
      cient funds check
    Voidable title can be transfered to good
      faith purchaser for value
    Spear has title to the 15 computers
      purchased from Larson because Spear
      purchased in good faith
    Unless otherwise stated, title passes in
      sale on approval contract when buyer
      accepts
    Spear has title because Rusk has not yet
      accepted the computers
    General creditors of Rusk have no rights

Unofficial Answer

Problem 1   Passage of Title and Risk of Loss
             (588,L2)

As of December 31, 1987, Spear bears the
risk of loss for the computers on the December 20 contract with Pica. The shipping term
"FOB--Spear's loading dock" designates a
shipment contract. In general, risk of loss
passes to the buyer (Pica) in a shipment
contract when the goods are duly delivered to
the carrier. However, where a tender or
delivery of goods so fails to conform to the
contract as to give a right of rejection, the
risk of their loss remains on the seller until
cure or acceptance. Thus, the failure of the
shipment to conform to the contract
constitutes a breach that permits Pica to
reject the computers, thereby resulting in
Spear bearing the risk of loss for the
computers while they are in transit.

With respect to the December 22 contract,
the risk of loss as of December 31, 1987
remains with Spear. Unless otherwise agreed,
the risk of loss in a sale on approval
contract does not pass to the buyer until the
buyer accepts the goods. Under the facts of
this case, Rusk had not yet accepted the
computers as of December 31, 1987. Therefore,
the risk of loss on the computers as of
December 31, 1987, remains with Spear.

As of December 31, 1987, Spear has title
to the 15 computers purchased from Larson
under the December 21 contract because a
person with voidable title has the power to
transfer good title to a good faith purchaser
for value. Larson has voidable title because
he paid for the computers with an insufficient
funds check. Spear is a good faith purchaser
for value because it paid Larson $20,000 and
was unaware that Larson's check to Xeon was
dishonored. The UCC Sales Article provides
that when goods have been delivered under a
transaction of purchase, the purchaser has the
power to transfer good title even though the
delivery was in exchange for a check that is
later dishonored. Thus, Spear has good title
to the computers as of December 31, 1987,
despite Larson's check being dishonored,
because it purchased and received the
computers on December 21, 1987.

With respect to the December 22 sale on
approval contract, title to the two computers
remains with the seller until the buyer
accepts the computers, because the contract is
silent as to when title passes. Therefore, as
of December 31, 1987, Spear retains title to
the two computers because Rusk had not yet
notified Spear whether it would accept the
computers, and the time for such notification
had not yet passed.

Because the December 22 contract between
Spear and Rusk is a sale on approval contract,
the computers are not subject to the claims of
the creditors of the buyer (Rusk) until
acceptance.

Answer Outline

Problem 2   Product Liability; Disclaimer of
             Warranties (1185,L4)

a. Negligence
      Prerequisites:
        Legal duty owed to plaintiff
        Defendant breached duty
        Plaintiff sustained actual loss
        Breach of duty caused actual loss
      Courts consider whether defendant acted
        as reasonably prudent person
    Breach of warranty
      Sale of goods by merchant seller creates
        implied warranty of merchantability
      This warranty is breached when fork-lift
        was not fit for ordinary purposes and
        plaintiff suffered a loss
    Strict liability in tort
      Prerequisites:
        Product leaves hands of merchant
          seller in an unreasonably dangerous
          condition

Seller expected product to reach
consumer without substantial changes
Proof of fault is not required
b. Disclaimer improper to exclude the implied
warranty of merchantability
Disclaimer is not conspicuous
Disclaimer language inappropriate
Disclaimer may be unconscionable
No bargaining of terms permitted con-
cerning standardized
Limitation of damages for personal
injuries

Unofficial Answer

Problem 2   Product Liability; Disclaimer of
Warranties (1185,L4)

a. Negligence. In order to establish a cause
of action based on negligence Barr must establish the following elements:

•   That the defendant owed a legal duty
to the plaintiff.
•   That the defendant breached that duty.
•   That the plaintiff sustained an actual
loss or damages.
•   That the breach of duty was the proxi-
mate cause of the plaintiff's actual loss or
damages.

In determining if negligence is present
the court will consider whether the defendant
acted as a reasonably prudent person under the
circumstances. Included in the reasonably
prudent person test is whether the risk of
harm was foreseeable.
Breach of Warranty. Since the sale of
goods (the fork-lift) is involved in the contract, the UCC Sales Article applies. Because
the seller would be regarded as a merchant, an
implied warranty of merchantability is
created. In order to establish a breach of
this warranty, the plaintiff (Barr) must show:

•   That the fork-lift was not fit for the
ordinary purposes intended and
•   That as a result of the breach of warranty, the plaintiff sustained a loss.

Strict Liability in Tort. Generally, the
elements necessary to establish a cause of action based on strict liability in tort are as
follows:

•   That the product was in defective
condition when it left the possession or control of the seller.
•   That the product was unreasonably
dangerous to the consumer or user.
•   That the cause of the consumer's or
user's injury was the defect.
•   That the seller engaged in the
business of selling such a product.

•   That the product was one which the
seller expected to and did reach the consumer
or user without substantial changes in the
condition in which it was sold.

Proof of fault is not a requirement to
establish a cause of action in strict
liability.

b. A proper disclaimer will permit the seller
to exclude the implied warranty of merchantability. Under the facts, the disclaimer
would appear to be invalid since a written
disclaimer of the implied warranty of merchantability must be conspicuous and, argu-
ably, the language in the contract is not acceptable under the UCC. In this case the disclaimer was in fine print and therefore not
conspicuous. In addition, the disclaimer may
be considered unconscionable since the contract was standardized and no bargaining of
the terms of the contract was permitted. It
should be pointed out that although consequential damages may be limited or excluded,
in the case of consumer goods limitation of
consequential damages for personal injuries is
prima facie unconscionable. However, since
the facts do not relate to consumer goods,
such limitation of damages is not prima facie
unconscionable but may be proved to be unconscionable.

Answer Outline

Problem 3   Statute of Frauds; Modification
of UCC Contract; Seller's
Compensatory Damages (1187,L2)

First assertion
Contract is sale of goods more than $500
Statute of Frauds requires a written
contract
Magic's written contract satisfies the
Statute of Frauds since signed by party
to be charged
Second assertion
Good faith modification needs no
consideration under UCC
Contract as modified falls within Statute
of Frauds
Statute of Frauds will be satisfied
because
Magic and Starr are merchants
Written confirmation was received within
a reasonable time
Magic did not give written notice of
objection to confirmation within 10
days after it was received
Third assertion
Under UCC Starr is entitled to full
recovery of sales price because
Goods have been identified
Starr is unable to resell goods
after a reasonable effort

Unofficial Answer

Problem 3   Statute of Frauds; Modification
of UCC Contract; Seller's
Compensatory Damages (1187,L2)

Magic's first assertion, that the original
contract between Starr and itself is not
enforceable because of the Statute of Frauds,
is incorrect. The sale of computer equipment
is a transaction in goods and thus is governed
by the UCC Sales Article. This Article provides that a contract for the sale of goods
for the price of $500 or more is not enforce-
able unless there is some writing sufficient
to indicate that a contract for sale has been
made between the parties which is signed by
the party against whom enforcement is sought.
Since the sales price is $18,000, the Statute
of Frauds applies. Magic's execution of the
written contract will satisfy the Statute of
Frauds since Magic is the party against whom
enforcement of the contract is being sought.

Magic's second assertion, that the oral
agreement to change the price of the equipment
is not enforceable because the agreement
lacked consideration and failed to satisfy the
Statute of Frauds, is incorrect. Under the
UCC Sales Article, an agreement to modify a
contract for the sale of goods needs no consideration to be binding. However, the modification must meet the test of good faith, which
is defined under the UCC as "honesty in fact
in the conduct or transaction concerned and
the observance of reasonable commercial standards of fair dealing in the trade." Based
upon the facts, it appears that a shift in the
market that will result in Starr bearing a
loss on the sale to Magic will satisfy the requirement of good faith. In addition, the
agreement modifying the sales price must meet
the requirements of the Statute of Frauds if
the contract, as modified, is within its provisions. Under the facts, the contract as
modified by Magic and Starr, falls within the
provisions of the Statute of Frauds and thus
the Statute of Frauds must be satisfied.
Magic's oral agreement to the modification is
not sufficient to satisfy the Statute of
Frauds. However, the Statute of Frauds will
be satisfied if: both parties are merchants;
a writing in confirmation of the agreement
which is sufficient against the sender is
received; the recipient receives the writing
within a reasonable time; the recipient has
reason to know the contents of the writing;
and, the recipient fails to give written
notice of objection to the contents of the
writing within ten days after it is received.
As the facts clearly indicate, the mailing of
the signed letter by Starr to Magic on May 17
satisfied the aforementioned requirements and
thus the modification agreement is enforceable.

Magic's third assertion that Starr is not
entitled to recover the full sales price for
the equipment is incorrect. The UCC provides
that a seller may recover the price of goods
identified to a contract and in the possession
of the seller if the seller is unable after
reasonable effort to resell them at a reasonable price or the circumstances reasonably
indicate that such effort will be unavailing.
Under the facts of the case at hand, Starr is
entitled to recover the full sales price of
$20,000 because the equipment could not be
resold for any price.

Multiple Choice Questions (1-49)

1. Gold is holding the following instrument:

```
┌─────────────────────────────────────────┐
│  To:  Sussex National Bank               │
│       Suffolk, N.Y.                      │
│                                          │
│                        October 15, 1988  │
│                                          │
│  Pay to the order of ___Tom Gold___  $2,000.00 │
│                                          │
│  Two Thousand and xx/100_____ Dollars │
│                                          │
│     on November 1, 1988___               │
│                                          │
│                                          │
│                     Lester Davis         │
│                     Lester Davis         │
│                                          │
└─────────────────────────────────────────┘
```

This instrument is a
- a. Postdated check.
- b. Draft.
- c. Promissary note.
- d. Trade acceptance.

2. A bank issues a negotiable instrument that acknowledges receipt of $50,000. The instrument also provides that the bank will repay the $50,000 plus 8% interest per annum to the bearer 90 days from the date of the instrument. The instrument is a
- a. Certificate of deposit.
- b. Time draft.
- c. Trade or banker's acceptance.
- d. Cashier's check.

3. On April 2, 1989, Harris agreed to sell a computer to Cross for $390. At the time of delivery, Cross gave Harris $90 and a written instrument, signed by Cross, in which Cross promised to pay Harris the balance on April 20, 1989. The instrument also made a reference to the sale of the computer. Under the UCC Commercial Paper Article, the instrument is a
- a. Promissory note.
- b. Non-negotiable draft.
- c. Trade acceptance.
- d. Negotiable time draft.

4. Which of the following aspects of an otherwise negotiable promissory note will render it non-negotiable?
- a. The maker is obligated to pay a sum certain to the payee but may instead deliver to the payee goods of equal value.

- b. The maker has the right to prepay the note, subject to a prepayment penalty of 10% of the amount prepaid.
- c. The maker is obligated to pay the payee's costs of collection upon default by the maker.
- d. The maker intentionally using a rubber stamp to sign the note.

5. A secured promissory note would be nonnegotiable if it provided that
- a. Additional collateral must be tendered if there is a decline in market value of the original collateral.
- b. Upon default, the maker waives a trial by jury.
- c. The maker is entitled to a 5% discount if the note is prepaid.
- d. It is subject to the terms of the mortgage given by the maker to the payee.

6. Ard is holding the following instrument:

```
┌─────────────────────────────────────────┐
│  I, Rosemary Larkin, hereby promise      │
│  to pay to the bearer twenty thousand    │
│  dollars ($20,000).  This document is    │
│  given by me as payment of the balance   │
│  due on my purchase of a 1984 Winnebago  │
│  mobile home from Ed Dill and is pay-    │
│  able when I am able to obtain a bank     │
│  loan.                                   │
│                  Rosemary Larkin         │
│                  Rosemary Larkin         │
└─────────────────────────────────────────┘
```

This instrument is not negotiable because it
- a. Refers to the contract out of which it arose.
- b. Is payable to bearer rather than to a named payee.
- c. Is not dated on the face of the instrument.
- d. Is not payable at a definite time.

7. Which of the following is required to make an instrument negotiable?
- a. Stated date of issue.
- b. An endorsement by the payee.
- c. Stated location for payment.
- d. Payment only in legal tender.

8. Which of the following on the face of an otherwise negotiable instrument will affect the instrument's negotiability?
- a. The instrument is postdated.
- b. The instrument is payable six months after the death of the maker.

c. The instrument contains a promise to provide additional collateral if there is a decrease in value of the existing collateral.

d. The instrument is payable at a definite time subject to an acceleration clause in the event of a default.

9. The following instrument is in the possession of Bill North:

On May 30, 1989, I promise to pay Bill North, the bearer of this document, $1,800.

Joseph Peppers
Joseph Peppers

Re: Auto Purchase Contract

This instrument is
a. Non-negotiable because it is undated.
b. Non-negotiable because it is **not** payable to order or bearer.
c. Negotiable even though it makes reference to the contract out of which it arose.
d. Negotiable because it is payable at a definite time.

10. Your client has in its possession the following instrument:

No. 1625

FAIR FOOD WHOLESALERS, INC.
22 Woodrow Wilson Hayes Lane
Columbus, Ohio

Jan. 10, 1986

On demand the undersigned promises to pay to

Bearer $1,200.00

Twelve hundred & ten/100's   Dollars

Fair Food Wholesalers, Inc.

By *James Duff*
James Duff, President

For: _____

The instrument is
a. A nonnegotiable promissory note.
b. Nonnegotiable because the instrument is incomplete.

c. A negotiable time draft.
d. Negotiable despite the inconsistency between the amount in words and the amount in numbers.

11. One of the requirements necessary to qualify as a holder of a negotiable bearer check is that the transferee must
a. Take the check in good faith.
b. Give value for the check.
c. Have possession of the check.
d. Receive the check that was originally made payable to bearer.

12. The following endorsements appear on the back of a negotiable promissory note made payable "to bearer." The note is in the possession of James Mix.

Pay to John Jacobs

Mary Nash
John Jacobs

(without recourse)

Which one of the following statements is correct?
a. Mix is **not** a holder because Jacobs' qualified endorsement makes the note non-negotiable.
b. Mix can negotiate the note by delivery alone.
c. The unqualified endorsement of Mix is required in order to further negotiate the note.
d. In order for Mix to negotiate the note Mix must have given value for it.

13. Hoover is a holder in due course of a check which was originally payable to the order of Nelson or bearer and has the following endorsements on its back:

Nelson
Pay to the order of Maxwell
Duffy
Without Recourse
Maxwell
Howard

Which of the following statements about the check is correct?
a. It was originally order paper.
b. It was order paper in Howard's hands.
c. Maxwell's signature was **not** necessary for it to be negotiated.
d. Presentment for payment must be made within seven days after endorsement to hold an endorser liable.

14. Balquist sold a negotiable instrument payable to her order to Farley. In transferring the instrument to Farley, she forgot to endorse it. Accordingly
   a. Farley qualifies as a holder in due course.
   b. Farley has a specifically enforceable right to obtain Balquist's unqualified endorsement.
   c. Farley obtains a better right to payment of the instrument than Balquist had.
   d. Once the signature of Balquist is obtained, Farley's rights as a holder in due course relate back to the time of transfer.

15. A purchaser of a negotiable instrument would <u>least</u> likely be a holder in due course if, at the time of purchase, the instrument is
   a. Purchased at a discount.
   b. Collateral for a loan.
   c. Payable to bearer on demand.
   d. Overdue by three weeks.

16. The value requirement in determining whether a person is a holder in due course with respect to a check will <u>not</u> be satisfied by the taking of the check
   a. As security for an obligation to the extent of the obligation.
   b. As payment for an antecedent debt.
   c. In exchange for another negotiable instrument.
   d. In exchange for a promise to perform services in the future.

17. Frey paid Holt $2,500 by check pursuant to an agreement between them whereby Holt promised to perform in Frey's theater within the next year. Holt endorsed the check, making it payable to Len Able. Holt's status with regard to the check was one of a(n)
   a. Assignee since a payee may <u>not</u> also be a holder in due course.
   b. Holder since Holt's promise failed to satisfy the value requirement necessary to become a holder in due course.
   c. Holder in due course under the shelter rule since Able's rights as a holder in due course revert to Holt.
   d. Holder in due course since all the requirements have been satisfied.

18. Who among the following can personally qualify as a holder in due course?
   a. A payee.
   b. A reacquirer who was not initially a holder in due course.

   c. A holder to whom the instrument was negotiated as a gift.
   d. A holder who had notice of a defect but who took from a prior holder in due course.

19. To the extent that a holder of a negotiable promissory note is a holder in due course, the holder takes the note free from which of the following defenses?
   a. Non-performance of a condition precedent.
   b. Discharge of the maker in bankruptcy.
   c. Minority of the maker where it is a defense to enforcement of a contract.
   d. Forgery of the maker's signature.

20. A holder in due course of a negotiable promissory note will take the note subject to which of the following defences?
   a. Fraud in the inducement.
   b. Failure of consideration.
   c. Unauthorized signature.
   d. Breach of contract.

21. Dart induces Shorr by fraud to make a promissory note payable to Dart. Dart negotiates the note for value to Best, who was aware of the fraud. Best negotiates the note to Case, a holder in due course. Subsequently, Best repurchases the note from Case. Which of the following statements is correct?
   a. Best does <u>not</u> succeed to Case's rights as a holder in due course.
   b. Best becomes a holder in due course upon taking the note from Dart.
   c. Because of the fraud by Dart, the note is nonnegotiable.
   d. Best's knowledge of Dart's fraud is immaterial in determining Best's status as a holder in due course.

22. Hunt has in his possession a negotiable instrument which was originally payable to the order of Carr. It was transferred to Hunt by a mere delivery by Drake, who took it from Carr in good faith in satisfaction of an antecedent debt. The back of the instrument read as follows, "Pay to the order of Drake in satisfaction of my prior purchase of a new video calculator, signed Carr." Which of the following is correct?
   a. Hunt has the right to assert Drake's rights, including his standing as a holder in due course and also has the right to obtain Drake's signature.
   b. Drake's taking the instrument for an antecedent debt prevents him from

qualifying as a holder in due course.

c. Carr's endorsement was a special endorsement; thus, Drake's signature was **not** required in order to negotiate it.

d. Hunt is a holder in due course.

23. Silver Corp. sold 20 tons of steel to River Corp. with payment to be by River's check. The price of steel was fluctuating daily. Silver requested that the amount of River's check be left blank and Silver would fill in the current market price. River complied with Silver's request. Within two days, Silver received River's check. Although the market price of 20 tons of steel at the time Silver received River's check was $80,000, Silver filled in the check for $100,000 and negotiated it to Hatch Corp. Hatch took the check in good faith, without notice of Silver's act or any other defense, and in payment of an antecedent debt. River will

a. Not be liable to Hatch, because the check was materially altered by Silver.

b. Not be liable to Hatch, because Hatch failed to give value when it acquired the check from Silver.

c. Be liable to Hatch for $100,000.

d. Be liable to Hatch, but only for $80,000.

24. A holder in due course will take free of which of the following defenses?

a. A wrongful filling-in of the amount payable which was omitted from the instrument.

b. Duress of a nature which renders the obligation of the party a nullity.

c. Infancy to the extent that it is a defense to a simple contract.

d. Discharge of the maker in bankruptcy.

25. A person who endorsed a check "without recourse"

a. Has the same liability as an accommodation endorser.

b. Only negates his liability insofar as prior parties are concerned.

c. Gives the same warranty protection to his transferee as does a special or blank endorser.

d. Does **not** promise or guarantee payment of the instrument upon dishonor even if there has been a proper presentment and proper notice has been given.

26. Dodger fraudulently induced Tell to issue a check to his order for $900 in payment for some nearly worthless securities. Dodger took the check and artfully raised the amount from $900 to $1,900. He promptly negotiated the check to Bay who took in good faith and for value. Tell, upon learning of the fraud, issued a stop order to its bank. Which of the following is correct?

a. Dodger has a real defense which will prevent any of the parties from collecting anything.

b. The stop order was ineffective against Bay since it was issued after the negotiation to Bay.

c. Bay as a holder in due course will prevail against Tell but only to the extent of $900.

d. Had there been no raising of the amount by Dodger, the bank would be obligated to pay Bay despite the stop order.

27. Filmore had a negotiable instrument in its possession which it had received in payment of certain equipment it had sold to Marker Merchandising. The instrument was originally payable to the order of Charles Danforth or bearer. It was endorsed specially by Danforth to Marker which in turn negotiated it to Filmore via a blank endorsement. The instrument in question, along with some cash and other negotiable instruments, was stolen from Filmore on October 1, 1981. Which of the following is correct?

a. A holder in due course will prevail against Filmore's claim to the instrument.

b. Filmore's signature was necessary in order to further negotiate the instrument.

c. The theft constitutes a common law conversion which prevents anyone from obtaining a better title to the instrument than the owner.

d. Once an instrument is bearer paper it is always bearer paper.

28. Frank Supply Co. held the following
instrument:

```
┌─────────────────────────────────────────────┐
│                                              │
│ Clark Novelties, Inc.      April 12, 1986    │
│ 29 State Street                              │
│ Spokane, Washington                          │
│                                              │
│ Pay to the order of Frank Supply Co. on      │
│ April 30, 1986 ten thousand and 00/100       │
│ dollars ($10,000.000).                       │
│                       Smith Industries, Inc. │
│                          J.C. Kahn, President │
│ ACCEPTED: Clark Novelties, Inc.              │
│ BY:                                          │
│           Mitchell Clark                     │
│        Mitchell Clark, President             │
│                                              │
│ Date: April 20, 1986                         │
│                                              │
└─────────────────────────────────────────────┘
```

As a result of an audit examination of this
instrument which was properly endorsed by
Frank to your client, it may be correctly
concluded that
   a. Smith was primarily liable on the
       instrument prior to acceptance.
   b. The instrument is nonnegotiable and
       thus no one has rights under the
       instrument.
   c. No one was primarily liable on the
       instrument at the time of issue,
       April 12, 1986.
   d. Upon acceptance, Clark Novelties,
       Inc. became primarily liable and
       Smith was released from all lia-
       bility.

29. Blue is a holder of a check which was
originally drawn by Rush and made payable to
Silk. Silk properly endorsed the check to
Field. Field had the check certified by the
drawee bank and then endorsed the check to
Blue. As a result
   a. Field is discharged from liability.
   b. Rush alone is discharged from
       liability.
   c. The drawee bank becomes primarily
       liable and both Silk and Rush are
       discharged.
   d. Rush is secondarily liable.

30. Kirk made a check payable to Haskin's
order for a debt she owed on open account.
Haskin negotiated the check by a blank endorsement to Carlson who deposited it in his
checking account. The bank returned the check
with the notation that payment was refused due
to insufficient funds. Kirk is insolvent.
Under the circumstances
   a. Kirk has a real defense assertable
       against all parties including
       Carlson, a holder in due course.

   b. If Kirk files for bankruptcy, Haskin
       or Carlson could successfully assert
       that there had been an assignment of
       whatever funds were in Kirk's
       checking account.
   c. If there is a proper presentment,
       and notice is properly given by
       Carlson to Haskin, Carlson may
       recover the amount of the check from
       Haskin.
   d. Haskin or Carlson can correctly
       assert the standing of a secured
       creditor.

31. An otherwise valid negotiable bearer note
is signed with the forged signature of Darby.
Archer, who believed he knew Darby's signature, bought the note in good faith from
Harding, the forger. Archer transferred the
note without endorsement to Barker, in partial
payment of a debt. Barker then sold the note
to Chaco for 80% of its face amount and
delivered it without endorsement. When Chase
presented the note for payment at maturity,
Darby refused to honor it, pleading forgery.
Chase gave proper notice of dishonor to Barker
and to Archer. Which of the following statements best describes the situation from
Chase's standpoint?
   a. Chase can not qualify as a holder in
       due course for the reason that he
       did not pay face value for the note.
   b. Chase can hold Barker liable on the
       ground that Barker warranted to
       Chase that neither Darby nor Archer
       had any defense valid against
       Barker.
   c. Chase can hold Archer liable on the
       ground that Archer warranted to
       Chase that Darby's signature was
       genuine.
   d. Chase can not hold Harding, the
       forger, liable on the note because
       his signature does not appear on it
       and thus, he made no warranties to
       Chase.

32. Mask stole one of Bloom's checks. The
check was already signed by Bloom and made
payable to Duval. The check was drawn on
United Trust Company. Mask forged Duval's
signature on the back of the check and cashed
the check at the Corner Check Cashing Company
which in turn deposited it with its bank, Town
National Bank of Toka. Town National pro-
ceeded to collect on the check from United.
None of the parties mentioned was negligent.
Who will bear the loss assuming the amount
cannot be recovered from Mask?
   a. Bloom.
   b. Duval.
   c. United Trust Company.
   d. Corner Check Cashing Company.

33. Gomer developed a fraudulent system whereby he could obtain checks payable to the order of certain repairmen who serviced various large corporations. Gomer observed the delivery trucks of repairmen who did business with the corporations, and then he submitted bills on the bogus letterhead of the repairmen to the selected large corporations. The return envelope for payment indicated a local post office box. When the checks arrived, Gomer would forge the payees' signatures and cash the checks. The parties cashing the checks are holders in due course. Who will bear the loss assuming the amount cannot be recovered from Gomer?

    a.   The defrauded corporations.

    b.   The drawee banks.

    c.   Intermediate parties who endorsed the instruments for collection.

    d.   The ultimate recipients of the proceeds of the checks even though they are holders in due course.

34. Jim Bass is in possession of a negotiable promissory note made payable "to bearer." Bass acquired the note from Mary Frank for value. The maker of the note was Fred Jackson. The following endorsements appear on the back of the note:

Sam Peters
Pay Jim Bass
Mary Frank
Jim Bass
(without recourse)

Bass presented the note to Jackson, who refused to pay it because he was financially unable to do so. Which of the following statements is correct?

    a.   Peters is **not** secondarily liable on the note because his endorsement was unnecessary for negotiation.

    b.   Peters is **not** secondarily liable to Bass.

    c.   Frank will probably **not** be liable to Bass unless Bass gives notice to Frank of Jackson's refusal to pay within a reasonable time.

    d.   Bass would have had secondary liability to Peters and Frank if he had **not** qualified his endorsement.

35. A trade acceptance is an instrument drawn by a

    a.   Seller obligating the seller or designee to make payment.

    b.   Buyer obligating the buyer or designee to make payment.

    c.   Seller ordering the buyer or designee to make payment.

    d.   Buyer ordering the seller or designee to make payment.

36. In general, which of the following statements is correct concerning the priority among checks drawn on a particular account and presented to the drawee bank on a particular day?

    a.   The checks may be charged to the account in any order convenient to the bank.

    b.   The checks may be charged to the account in any order provided **no** charge creates an overdraft.

    c.   The checks must be charged to the account in the order in which the checks were dated.

    d.   The checks must be charged to the account in the order of lowest amount to highest amount to minimize the number of dishonored checks.

37. For which of the following negotiable instruments is a bank **not** an acceptor?

    a.   Cashier's check.

    b.   Certified check.

    c.   Certificate of deposit.

    d.   Bank acceptance.

38. Blare bought a house and provided the required funds in the form of a certified check from a bank. Which of the following statements correctly describes the legal liability of Blare and the bank?

    a.   The bank has accepted; therefore, Blare is without liability.

    b.   The bank has **not** accepted; therefore, Blare has primary liability.

    c.   The bank has accepted, but Blare has secondary liability.

    d.   The bank has **not** accepted, but Blare has secondary liability.

39. Which of the following is **not** a warranty made by the seller of a negotiable warehouse receipt to the purchaser of the document?

    a.   The document transfer is fully effective with respect to the goods it represents.

    b.   The warehouseman will honor the document.

    c.   The seller has **no** knowledge of any facts that would impair the document's validity.

    d.   The document is genuine.

40. Klep burglarized the premises of Apple Sales Co. He stole several negotiable warehouse receipts which were deliverable to the order of Apple. Klep endorsed Apple's name on the instruments and transferred them to Margo Wholesalers, a bona fide purchaser for value. As between Apple and Margo,
   a. Apple will prevail since the warehouseman must be notified before any negotiation is effective.
   b. Apple will prevail since the thief's endorsement prevents a due negotiation.
   c. Margo will prevail since it has taken a negotiable warehouse receipt as a bona fide purchaser for value.
   d. Margo will prevail since the warehouse receipt was converted to a bearer instrument by Klep's endorsement.

41. Under the UCC, a warehouse receipt
   a. Will not be negotiable if it contains a contractual limitation on the warehouseman's liability.
   b. May qualify as both a negotiable warehouse receipt and negotiable commercial paper if the instrument is payable either in cash or by the delivery of goods.
   c. May be issued only by a bonded and licensed warehouseman.
   d. Is negotiable if by its terms the goods are to be delivered to bearer or the order of a named person.

42. Woody Pyle, a public warehouseman, issued Merlin a negotiable warehouse receipt for fungible goods stored. Pyle
   a. May not limit the amount of his liability for his own negligence.
   b. Will be absolutely liable for any damages in the absence of a statute or a provision on the warehouse receipt to the contrary.
   c. May commingle Merlin's goods with similar fungible goods of other bailors.
   d. Is obligated to deliver the goods to Merlin despite Merlin's improper refusal to pay the storage charges due.

43. Thieves broke into the warehouse of Monogram Airways and stole a shipment of computer parts belonging to Valley Instruments. Valley had in its possession a negotiable bill of lading covering the shipment. The thieves transported the stolen parts to another state and placed the parts in a bonded warehouse. The thieves received a negotiable warehouse receipt which they used to secure a loan of $20,000 from Reliable Finance. These facts were revealed upon apprehension of the thieves. Regarding the rights of the parties
   a. Reliable is entitled to a $20,000 payment before relinquishment of the parts.
   b. Monogram will be the ultimate loser of the $20,000.
   c. Valley is entitled to recover the parts free of Reliable's $20,000 claim.
   d. Valley is not entitled to the parts but may obtain damages from Monogram.

44. Dwight Corporation purchased the following instrument in good faith from John Q. Billings:

No. 7200   •••REGISTERED••• $10,000
Magnum Cum Laude Corporation Ten year 14% Debenture, Due May 15, 1990 Magnum Cum Laude Corporation, a Delaware Corporation, for value received, hereby promises to pay the sum of TEN THOUSAND DOLLARS ($10,000) to JOHN Q. BILLINGS, or registered assigns, at the principal office or agency of the Corporation in Wilmington, Delaware.

On the reverse side of the instrument, the following appeared:

"For value received, the undersigned sells, assigns, and transfers unto DWIGHT CORPORATION, (signed) JOHN Q. BILLINGS." Billings' signature was guaranteed by Capital Trust Company.

Magnum's 14% debentures are listed on the Pacific Coast Exchange. The instrument is
   a. A registered negotiable investment security which Dwight took free of adverse title claims.
   b. Nonnegotiable since the instrument must be registered with Magnum to be validly transferred.
   c. Negotiable commercial paper.
   d. A nonnegotiable investment security since the instrument lacks the words of negotiability, "to the order of or bearer."

45. While auditing the common stock ledger of Sims Corporation, a CPA uncovers the following situation. An investor has purchased a certificate representing 500 shares of common stock of the Sims Corporation from a former clerk of the corporation. It was the duty of the clerk to prepare stock certificates from a supply of

blanks for signature of the corporate secretary. The clerk forged the corporate secretary's signature on a bearer certificate and delivered the certificate for value to the investor who did not have notice of the forgery and who now demands a reissued certificate in the investor's name from the corporation. The corporation asserts that it has no liability to reissue a certificate in the name of the investor and that the investor's bearer certificate is null and void. Which of the following is correct?

    a. The certificate is valid and the investor is entitled to a reissued certificate.

    b. The certificate issued is invalid and the corporation has <u>no</u> liability to reissue.

    c. An appropriate recourse of the investor is to sue the corporation and clerk for dollar damages and to sue the clerk for the crime of forgery.

    d. The corporation is required to reissue a certificate only if appropriately compensated by the investor.

May 1990 Questions

46. Which of the following negotiable instruments is subject to the provisions of the UCC Commercial Paper Article?

    a. Installment note payable on the first day of each month.

    b. Warehouse receipt.

    c. Bill of lading payable to order.

    d. Corporate bearer bond with a maturity date of January 1, 1999.

47. Below is a copy of a note Prestige Properties obtained from Tim Hart in connection with Hart's purchase of land located in Hunter, MT. The note was given for the balance due on the purchase and was secured by a first mortgage on the land.

$200,000.00   Hunter, MT
                      November 30, 1989

    For value received, six years after date, I promise to pay to the order of Prestige Properties TWO HUNDRED THOUSAND and 00/100 DOLLARS with interest at 11% compounded annually until fully paid. This instrument arises out of the sale of land located in MT and the law of MT is to be applied to any question which may arise. It is secured by a first mortgage on the land conveyed. It is further agreed that:

1. Maker will pay the costs of collection including attorney's fees upon default.

2. Maker may repay the amount outstanding on any anniversary date of this note.

                        Tim Hart
                      Tim Hart

This note is a

    a. Nonnegotiable promissory note because it is secured by a first mortgage.

    b. Negotiable promissory note.

    c. Nonnegotiable promissory note because it permits prepayment and requires the maker's payment of the costs of collection and attorney's fees.

    d. Negotiable investment security under the UCC.

48. Bond fraudulently induced Teal to make a note payable to Wilk, to whom Bond was indebted. Bond delivered the note to Wilk. Wilk negotiated the instrument to Monk, who purchased it with knowledge of the fraud and after it was overdue. If Wilk qualifies as a holder in due course, which of the following statements is correct?

    a. Monk has the standing of a holder in due course through Wilk.

    b. Teal can successfully assert the defense of fraud in the inducement against Monk.

    c. Monk personally qualifies as a holder in due course.

    d. Teal can successfully assert the defense of fraud in the inducement against Wilk.

49.   Fred Anchor is the holder of the following check:

```
┌─────────────────────────────────────────┐
│ Peter Mason                             │
│ Champaign, Illinois          4/30  1990 │
│                                         │
│ Pay to the order of Mary Nix or bearer  $93.00 │
│                                         │
│ Ninety-Three-------------------------Dollars │
│                                         │
│ Second Bank 0453-0978                   │
│                        Peter Mason      │
└─────────────────────────────────────────┘
```

The check is endorsed on the back as follows:

```
┌─────────────────────────────┐
│      Mary Nix                │
│    Pay to John Jacobs        │
│      Mark Harris             │
│      John Jacobs             │
│                              │
│     (without recourse)       │
└─────────────────────────────┘
```

Jacobs gave the check to his son as a gift, who transferred it to Anchor for $78.00. Which of the following statements is correct?

a.   The unqualified endorsement of Jacobs was necessary in order to negotiate the check to his son.

b.   Nix's endorsement was required to negotiate the check to any subsequent holder.

c.   Anchor does not qualify as a holder because less than full consideration was given for the check.

d.   The check is bearer paper in Jacobs' son's hands.

Repeat Question

(590,L1,39) Identical/similar to item 24 above

Problems

Problem 1   (581,L2)

(15 to 20 minutes)

Part a. Oliver gave Morton his 90-day negotiable promissory note for $10,000 as a partial payment for the purchase of Morton's business. Morton had submitted materially false unaudited financial statements to Oliver in the course of establishing the purchase price of the business. Morton also made various false statements about the business' value. For example, he materially misstated the size of the backlog of orders. Morton promptly negotiated the note to Harrison who purchased it in good faith for $9,500, giving Morton $5,000 in cash, a check for $3,500 payable to him which he endorsed in blank and an oral promise to pay the balance within 5 days. Before making the final payment to Morton, Harrison learned of the fraudulent circumstances under which the negotiable promissory note for $10,000 had been obtained. Morton has disappeared and the balance due him was never paid. Oliver refuses to pay the note.

Required:

Answer the following, setting forth reasons for any conclusions stated.
In the subsequent suit brought by Harrison against Oliver, who will prevail?

Part b. McCarthy, a holder in due course, presented a check to the First National Bank, the drawee bank named on the face of the instrument. The signature of the drawer, Williams, was forged by Nash who took the check from the bottom of Williams' check book along with a cancelled check in the course of burglarizing Williams' apartment. The bank examined the signature of the drawer carefully, but the signature was such an artful forgery of the drawer's signature that only a handwriting expert could have detected a difference. The bank therefore paid the check. The check was promptly returned to Williams, but he did not discover the forgery until thirteen months after the check was returned to him.

Required:

Answer the following, setting forth reasons for any conclusions stated.

1. Williams seeks to compel the bank to credit his account for the loss. Will he prevail?
2. The facts are the same as above, but you are to assume that the bank discovered the forgery before returning the check to Williams and credited his account. Can the bank in turn collect from McCarthy the $1,000 paid to McCarthy?
3. Would your answers to 1 and 2 above be modified if the forged signature was that of the payee or an endorser rather than the signature of the drawer?

Problem 2   (583,L5a)

(7 to 10 minutes)

Part a. Dunhill fraudulently obtained a negotiable promissory note from Beeler by misrepresentation of a material fact. Dunhill subsequently negotiated the note to Gordon, a holder in due course. Pine, a business associate of Dunhill, was aware of the fraud perpetrated by Dunhill. Pine purchased the note for value from Gordon. Upon presentment, Beeler has defaulted on the note.

Required:

Answer the following, setting forth reasons for any conclusions stated.
1. What are the rights of Pine against Beeler?
2. What are the rights of Pine against Dunhill?

Problem 3   (587,L2)

(15 to 20 minutes)

Prince, Hall, & Charming, CPAs, has been retained to examine the financial statements of Hex Manufacturing Corporation. Shortly before beginning the examination for the year ended December 31, 1986, Mr. Prince received a telephone call from Hex's president indicating that he thought some type of embezzlement was occurring because the corporation's cash position was significantly lower than in prior years. The president then requested that Prince immediately undertake a special investigation to determine the amount of embezzlement, if any.

After a month of investigation, Prince uncovered an embezzlement scheme involving collusion between the head of payroll and the assistant treasurer. The following is a summary of Prince's findings:

•   The head of payroll supplied the
assistant treasurer with punched time cards
for fictitious employees. The assistant
treasurer prepared invoices, receiving
reports, and purchase orders for fictitious
suppliers. The assistant treasurer prepared
checks for the fictitious employees and
suppliers which were signed by the
treasurer. Then, either the assistant
treasurer or the head of payroll would endorse
the checks and deposit them in various banks
where they maintained accounts in the names of
fictitious payees. All of the checks in
question have cleared Omega Bank, the drawee.

•   The embezzlement scheme had been
operating for 10 months and more than $120,000
had been embezzled by the time the scheme was
uncovered. The final series of defalcations
included checks payable directly to the head
of payroll and the assistant treasurer. These
checks included skillful forgeries of the
treasurer's signature that were almost
impossible to detect. This occurred while the
treasurer was on vacation. These checks have
also cleared Omega Bank, the drawee.

Required:

    Answer the following, setting forth
reasons for any conclusions stated.

    Will Hex or Omega bear the loss with
respect to the following categories of checks:
    a.   Those which were signed by the
treasurer but payable to fictitious payees?
    b.   Those which include the forged
signature of the treasurer?

Multiple Choice Answers

1. b	11. c	21. a	31. b	41. d
2. a	12. b	22. a	32. d	42. c
3. a	13. d	23. c	33. a	43. c
4. a	14. b	24. a	34. c	44. a
5. d	15. d	25. d	35. c	45. a
6. d	16. d	26. c	36. a	46. a
7. d	17. b	27. a	37. c	47. b
8. b	18. a	28. c	38. c	48. a
9. b	19. a	29. c	39. b	49. d
10. d	20. c	30. c	40. b	

Multiple Choice Answer Explanations

B. Types of Commercial Paper

1. (1188,L1,35) (b) This instrument is a draft because it is a three-party instrument where a drawer (Davis) orders a drawee (Sussex National Bank) to pay a sum certain in money to the payee (Gold). Answer (a) is incorrect because in order for the instrument to qualify as a check, the instrument must be payable on demand. In this situation, the instrument held by Gold is a time draft which specifies the payment date as November 1, 1988. Answer (c) is incorrect because a promissory note is a two-party instrument in which one party promises to pay a sum certain in money to the payee. Answer (d) is incorrect because a trade acceptance is a special type of draft in which a seller of goods extends credit to the buyer by drawing a draft on that buyer directing the buyer to pay a sum certain in money to the seller on a specified date. The seller is therefore both the drawer and payee in a trade acceptance.

2. (1188,L1,36) (a) This instrument is a certificate of deposit since it meets all of the requirements of a negotiable instrument (explicitly stated in the question) and is a written acknowledgement by a bank of receipt of money with a promise to repay. A certificate of deposit is a two-party instrument and is a special type of note. Answer (b) is incorrect because a time draft is a three-party instrument in which one party (drawer) orders another party (drawee) to pay a third party (payee) a sum certain in money at a specified date. Answers (c) and (d) are incorrect because they are special types of drafts.

3. (589,L1,46) (a) A promissory note is a two-party instrument in which the maker promises to pay the payee a specified sum of money. In this situation, Cross is the maker and Harris is the payee. A promissory note may make reference to the underlying transaction such as the sale of the computer with-

out destroying negotiability. Answers (b) and (d) are incorrect because a draft, whether negotiable or not, is a three-party instrument. A draft is an instrument in which one party (drawer) orders a second party (drawee) to pay a third party (payee) a sum of money. Answer (c) is incorrect because a trade acceptance is a type of draft which contains an order by a seller of goods directing the buyer to pay the seller of the goods.

C. Requirements of Negotiability

4. (589,L1,49) (a) A negotiable instrument must, among other requirements, contain an unconditional promise or order to pay a sum certain in money. Since the maker has the option of delivering goods rather than paying money this would render the note non-negotiable. Answer (b) is incorrect because although the instrument must be payable on demand or at a definite time, this may be subject to acceleration at the option of the holder without affecting negotiability. Furthermore, the 10% prepayment penalty can be calculated and does not destroy negotiability. Answer (c) is incorrect because the note is considered to have a sum certain despite providing for collection fees. Answer (d) is incorrect because the signature requirement is met by any symbol or method intended to represent a signature. Thus, the use of a rubber stamp would not affect negotiability.

5. (1188,L1,38) (d) A requirement of negotiability is that the instrument must contain an unconditional promise or order to pay a sum certain in money. An unconditional promise means that it may not be subject to any conditions. If the payment depends upon (is subject to) another agreement or transaction, then it is conditional and nonnegotiable. Thus, a secured promissory note would be nonnegotiable if it provided that it was subject to the terms of the mortgage (another transaction) given by the maker to the payee. Answer (a) is incorrect because a second promise on the face of the instrument that gives security for the instrument does not destroy the negotiability of the instrument. Answer (b) is incorrect because it is also a promise that does not affect negotiability. Answer (c) is incorrect because the requirement that a sum certain of money be paid is not affected by the possible 5% discount. The amount to be paid can still be determined from the face of the instrument.

6. (588,L1,46) (d) In order to satisfy the requirements of negotiability, an instrument must be payable at a definite time or on

demand. Since the instrument presented in this problem is payable when the maker is "able to obtain a bank loan," it is not payable at a definite time and is therefore not negotiable. Answer (a) is incorrect because a reference to the contract out of which an instrument arose will not prevent it from being negotiable. However, if the instrument stated that it was "subject to" the contract, the instrument would not be negotiable. Answer (b) is incorrect because a negotiable instrument may be payable to either a named payee (order) or to bearer. Answer (c) is incorrect because there is no requirement that an instrument be dated in order to be negotiable.

7. (1189,L1,42) (d) In order for an instrument to be negotiable, it must be in writing, signed by the maker or drawer, contain an unconditional promise or order to pay a sum certain in money, and be payable on demand at a definite time. Payment in legal tender is, therefore, one of the necessary requirements. Answer (a) is incorrect because the stated date of issue is not required unless it is needed to calculate interest, or discounts, etc., or needed to determine when the instrument is due. Answer (b) is incorrect because an endorsement is not required to make an instrument negotiable. Answer (c) is incorrect because the location for payment need not be stated.

8. (587,L1,46) (b) One of the requirements for negotiability is that the instrument be payable on demand or at a definite time. An instrument which by its terms is payable only upon an act or event uncertain as to time of occurrence is not payable at a definite time. The instrument's negotiability is affected by basing the time of payment on the maker's death. This is an event which is uncertain as to time of occurrence and causes the instrument to be nonnegotiable. Answer (a) is incorrect because an instrument may be postdated or antedated and this does not affect its negotiability. Answer (c) is incorrect because the promise to maintain collateral is not a second promise that destroys negotiability. Answer (d) is incorrect because a negotiable instrument may be made payable at a definite time subject to acceleration at the option of the holder. Because the instrument does have a definite payment date, its negotiability is not affected.

9. (589,L1,48) (b) To be negotiable, the instrument must be written and signed by the maker or drawer, contain an unconditional

promise or order to pay a sum certain in money, must be payable at a definite time or on demand, and must be payable to order or to bearer. Since this instrument is not payable to order or to bearer but is simply payable to Bill North and refers to him as the bearer, it is nonnegotiable. Answer (a) is incorrect because there is no requirement that the date the instrument was written be on the note, only that the instrument is payable at a definite time (i.e., May 30, 1989). Answer (c) is incorrect because it is not negotiable. Answer (d) is incorrect because although it is payable at a definite time, negotiability has been destroyed by the fact that the instrument is not payable to order or to bearer.

D. Interpretation of Ambiguities in Negotiable Instruments

10. (1186,L1,44) (d) Inconsistency between the amount in words and the amount in numbers will not destroy the negotiability of the instrument. The written words control over the sums denoted in figures. Consequently, the value of this instrument is $1,210.00. Answers (a) and (b) are incorrect because all the requirements of negotiability for a promissory note are present. Answer (c) is incorrect because a negotiable time draft requires an order from one party directing another to pay a third party. Since the instrument contains a promise to pay, the instrument is a note, not a draft.

E. Negotiation

11. (1187,L1,49) (c) One of the requirements for a person to qualify as a holder is that he or she must have possession of a negotiable instrument. Answers (a) and (b) are incorrect because they are requirements to qualify as a holder in due course, not a holder. Answer (d) is incorrect because a check that was originally made to order may become bearer paper through subsequent negotiations.

12. (589,L1,50) (b) Since the last endorsement did not name a specific endorsee, James Mix who has possession of the negotiable note may negotiate it by delivery alone. Answer (a) is incorrect because qualified endorsements may be used to disclaim contract liability if the instrument is dishonored, but do not destroy its negotiability. Answer (c) is incorrect because Mix need not endorse the note since the last endorsement did not name a specific endorsee. This bearer paper may be negotiated by mere delivery of the instrument. Answer (d) is incorrect because value is not required for negotiation.

13. (582,L1,40) (d) A check must be presented for payment within seven days after
endorsement to hold an endorser liable. Answer (a) is incorrect because an instrument is
bearer paper if it states it is payable to a
named person or bearer and there are no
endorsements on the back. Answer (b) is
incorrect because Maxwell's blank endorsement
converts the instrument from order paper to
bearer paper in Howard's possession. A blank
endorsement is present when the endorser does
not name a specified person in the endorsement
as the endorsee. Answer (c) is incorrect
because Duffy's endorsement is an example of a
special endorsement which creates order paper
in Maxwell's possession. Proper negotiation
of order paper demands delivery and endorsement. Consequently, Maxwell's signature was
necessary for negotiation of the check.

14. (582,L1,42) (b) When an order instrument is transferred for value without endorsement, the transferee has a specifically enforceable right to obtain the transferor's
unqualified endorsement. Although the
transferee may compel an endorsement, negotiation occurs only when the endorsement is
given. Thus, Farley's rights as a holder in
due course relate to the time the endorsement
is made and do not relate back to the time of
transfer. If Farley learns of a defense
before acquiring the endorsement, she will not
qualify as a holder in due course. Therefore,
answer (d) is incorrect. Answers (a) and (c)
are incorrect because to be a holder in due
course, a person must receive the instrument
by negotiation. Since this instrument was an
order instrument, proper negotiation would
demand delivery and endorsement. Until Farley
receives Balquist's endorsement, she is unable
to qualify as a holder in due course; instead
she is merely an assignee with no better right
to payment of the instrument than Balquist.

F. Holder in Due Course

15. (1188,L1,40) (d) For a holder of a
negotiable instrument to become a holder in
due course (HDC), the holder must take the
instrument in good faith without notice that
it is overdue, has been dishonored, or that
any person has a defense or claim to it. If
the instrument is overdue by three weeks at
the time of purchase, the purchaser would not
qualify as a HDC since the holder has notice
the instrument is overdue. Answer (a) is
incorrect because the fact the holder purchased the instrument at a discount does not
destroy his/her status as a HDC. Answer (b)
is incorrect because as long as the purchaser
has no notice that a claim exists against the
negotiable instrument, his/her right to

qualify as a HDC will not be affected. The
purchaser would not be presumed to know that
the instrument was collateral for a loan at
the time of purchase. Answer (c) is incorrect
because a negotiable instrument payable to
bearer on demand would not affect the
purchaser's ability to qualify as a HDC.

16. (588,L1,48) (d) In order to meet the
value requirement of a holder in due course, a
holder must give executed, not executory,
value. A promise to perform services in the
future is an executory promise and therefore
does not satisfy the value requirement of a
holder in due course. Answer (a) is incorrect
because taking an instrument as security for
an obligation represents executed value to the
extent of the obligation being secured.
Answer (b) is incorrect because taking an
instrument as payment for an existing debt
represents executed value. Answer (c) is
incorrect because taking an instrument in
exchange for another negotiable instrument
represents executed value even though the
negotiable instrument given in exchange is a
check that has not yet been cashed.

17. (1185,L1,42) (b) For a holder of a
negotiable instrument to become a holder in
due course, the holder must take the
instrument for executed value, in good faith,
and without knowledge of any defense or claim
on the instrument. Since Holt's promise to
perform did not constitute executed value,
Holt does not qualify as a HDC. Holt can only
be a holder. Answer (a) is incorrect because
a payee can qualify as a HDC. Answer (c) is
incorrect because the shelter rule does not
transfer the rights of a HDC to prior holders,
but to individuals who hold the instrument
after it has been held by a HDC. Answer (d)
is incorrect because all of the requirements
of a HDC (specifically giving executed value)
have not been met.

18. (1180,L1,1) (a) The correct answer
is (a) since the payee is the only holder who
can meet the requirements of a holder in due
course. A holder in due course must be a
holder who gives executed value for the instrument (cannot be a gift). The holder in
due course may have no knowledge of the fact
that the instrument (principal only) is
overdue nor knowledge of any defense on the
instrument when he or she receives it. A
holder in due course must also take the
instrument in good faith. Answer (b) is
incorrect since a holder who does not qualify
as a holder in due course cannot better his
rights by transferring the instrument through
a HDC. Answer (c) is incorrect because the

holder failed to give value. The holder in answer (d) cannot qualify as a HDC since he has knowledge of a defense, but the holder does receive the rights of a HDC since he acquired the instrument through a HDC.

G. Rights of a Holder in Due Course

19. (589,L1,51) (a) A holder in due course takes an instrument free of personal defenses but is subject to real defenses. Answer (a) is correct because it involves a breach of contract or non-performance of a condition precedent which describes a personal defense. Answer (b) is incorrect because bankruptcy is a real defense. Answer (c) is incorrect because when a minor may disaffirm a contract, it is treated as a real defense. Answer (d) is incorrect because a forgery of a maker's or drawer's signature is a real defense.

20. (1187,L1,50) (c) A holder in due course (HDC) takes a negotiable instrument free of personal defenses, but not real defenses. Forgery (unauthorized signature) is a real defense, consequently a HDC will take the note subject to this defense. Answers (a), (b), and (d) are incorrect because a HDC will take a negotiable instrument free of these personal defenses.

21. (1186,L1,40) (a) When a negotiable instrument is negotiated from a holder in due course to a second holder, the second holder usually acquires the rights of a holder in due course through the shelter provision. The shelter provision applies to holders who have not previously held the instrument with knowledge of any defenses. Since Best held the instrument with knowledge of Dart's fraud prior to the instrument being held by a holder in due course, Best does not acquire the rights of a holder in due course when he reacquires the instrument. Best cannot "wash" the instrument by passing it through a holder in due course. This is an exception to the shelter provision. Answers (b) and (d) are incorrect because Best knew of the fraud on the note, which prevents him/her from becoming a holder in due course. To qualify as a holder in due course, the holder must acquire the instrument by proper negotiation prior to learning of a defense on the instrument. Answer (c) is incorrect because fraud does not render the note nonnegotiable; the fraud only creates a personal defense on the note.

22. (1185,L1,41) (a) Transfer of an instrument vests in the transferee such rights as the transferor has in the instrument. Therefore, Hunt has the right to assert Drake's rights and his standing as a holder in due course. Also, any transfer for value of an order instrument gives the transferee the right to obtain an unqualified endorsement of the transferor. Thus, Hunt may demand Drake's signature. Answer (b) is incorrect because Drake taking the instrument for an antecedent debt constitutes taking the instrument for value, which is a requirement for qualifying as a holder in due course. Answer (c) is incorrect since Carr's endorsement was a special endorsement; it created order paper, and Drake's signature was necessary for proper negotiation. Answer (d) is incorrect because Hunt is not a holder of the instrument, much less a holder in due course, until he receives Drake's signature.

23. (1189,L1,44) (c) When a check is completed through the negligence of the drawer, the defense created on the instrument is the personal defense of unauthorized completion, not the real defense of material alteration. Since River was negligent to send an incomplete check to Silver Corp., the personal defense created was unauthorized completion. Hatch Corp., as a holder in due course (HDC) who took the check for executed value and without knowledge of the unauthorized completion, can defeat the personal defense and receive the full $100,000 from River. Therefore, answers (a) and (d) are incorrect. Answer (b) is incorrect because Hatch gave value for the check acquired from Silver in the form of payment of an antecedent debt. Payment of a antecedent debt qualifies as executed value when determining HDC status.

24. (585,L1,35) (a) An unauthorized completion of an incomplete instrument is a personal defense, and as such, will not be good against a holder in due course. Answers (b), (c), and (d) are incorrect because extreme duress, infancy (unless instrument is exchanged for necessities), and the discharge of a maker in bankruptcy are all real defenses which will be good against a holder in due course.

25. (585,L1,39) (d) A person who endorsed a negotiable instrument without recourse has engaged in a qualified endorsement. Such an endorsement destroys the endorser's contractual liability, (i.e., the endorser does not promise payment of the instrument upon dishonor). Answer (a) is incorrect because an accommodating party is liable in the position that the party signs the instrument. As an accommodating endorser, the person would have contractual liability, (i.e., guarantees payment upon dishonor). Answer (b) is incorrect because an endorser only has liability to subsequent holders and a qualified endorsement

negates this liability. Answer (c) is incorrect because a qualified endorser receiving consideration only warrants that s/he has no knowledge of any defense good against the instrument, while a special or blank endorser for consideration warrants that no defense of any party is good against the instrument. All other warranties extended by a qualified endorser are the same as those extended by a blank or special endorser.

26. (1182,L1,43) (c) Bay, as a holder in due course, took the instrument free of all personal defenses but would be unable to defeat real defenses present on the instrument. Fraud in the inducement is a personal defense which would not be good against Bay. However, Dodger materially altered the check which creates a personal defense to the extent of the original tenor of the check ($900) and a real defense to the extent the instrument was altered ($1,000). Consequently, Bay will prevail against Tell to the extent of $900. Answer (a) is incorrect because Dodger, being the party who materially altered the check, would have no defense to payment of this instrument. Answer (b) is incorrect because a customer (i.e., drawer) has the right to order his/her bank to stop payment on a check if the order is received at such time and in such manner as to afford the bank a reasonable opportunity to act on it prior to payment. Therefore, it would not matter that Tell's stop payment order was issued after the negotiation to Bay. Answer (d) is incorrect because normally a holder has no right to compel payment of a check by the drawee bank. This is true even though a stop payment order has not been issued by the drawer. Only when the bank has certified the check can the holder compel payment by the drawee bank.

27. (1181,L1,39) (a) An instrument payable to order and endorsed in blank becomes payable to bearer, i.e., bearer paper. Theft of bearer paper constitutes a personal defense and a holder in due course takes free of all personal defense of any party to the instrument with whom he has not dealt. Therefore, a holder in due course will defeat Filmore's claim to the instrument. In contrast, theft of order paper would constitute a real defense, which a holder in due course would take subject to, since proper negotiation of order paper requires delivery and endorsement, which would necessitate a forgery by the thief. Answer (b) is incorrect because since the instrument is bearer paper, delivery alone would constitute proper negotiation. Answer (c) is incorrect because a holder in due course can acquire better rights than the owner. Answer (d) is incorrect because bearer

paper can be converted to order paper by a special endorsement. A holder may convert a blank endorsement into a special endorsement by writing above the signature of the endorser any contract consistent with the character of the endorsement (e.g., "pay to the order of . . .").

H. Liability of Parties

28. (586,L1,28) (c) The instrument is a negotiable draft payable on demand and the client is a holder. Smith is the drawer, Frank Supply is the payee and Clark is the drawee. Since Clark has already accepted the draft, Clark, as the drawee, is primarily liable on the draft. Before acceptance, Clark had no liability on the draft. Smith, the payee and endorser, is secondarily liable on the instrument. No party would have primary liability until acceptance by the drawee. Therefore, answers (a), (b), and (d) are incorrect.

29. (1185,L1,43) (c) When a holder obtains certification of a check, the drawer and all prior endorsers are discharged from secondary liability and the bank alone becomes primarily liable. Since Field (a holder) had the bank certify the check, Silk (the payee) and Rush (the drawer) are discharged and the bank becomes primarily liable. Answer (a) is incorrect because the holder who had the check certified (Field) is not relieved of any liability. Answer (b) is incorrect because Silk, as the payee and a prior holder, is also discharged by the certification. Answer (d) is incorrect because certification of a check by a holder discharges the drawer (Rush) of secondary liability.

30. (1182,L1,38) (c) When Haskin negotiated the check with an unqualified endorsement, he extended contractual liability. Under the concept of contractual liability, the endorser guarantees payment of the instrument if the appropriate party for payment dishonors the instrument. Consequently, if there was proper presentment and notice given, Carlson may recover from Haskin when the bank dishonors the check. Answer (a) is incorrect because the fact that Kirk is insolvent does not create a real defense. If Kirk had been discharged from the debt in a bankruptcy proceeding, Kirk would then be able to assert a real defense that would be good against the holder in due course. The issuance of a check does not act as an assignment of the funds held in the bank, nor does it create a security interest on the part of the holder of the instrument. Therefore, answers (b) and (d) are incorrect.

31. (1180,L1,9) (b) Barker, having received value for the instrument, has warranty liability to Chase, the immediate holder. Barker grants five warranties, one of which is that no defense is good on the instrument. Answer (b) is correct since this warranty was breached. If a holder performs the full agreed upon consideration or value promised for the instrument, he is a holder in due course to the face value of the instrument. This makes answer (a) incorrect. Answer (c) is incorrect because Archer's failure to endorse the instrument only extends his warranty liability (including the warranty that states all signatures are genuine) to the immediate holder, Barker. Answer (d) is incorrect since Harding is liable for the forgery he placed on the instrument.

32. (580,L1,15) (d) Corner Check Cashing Company must bear the loss because as a holder obtaining payment, it warrants that it has good title to the instrument. However, it does not have good title because the forgery prevented good title from passing. Therefore, answers (a) and (c) are incorrect because of Corner Check Cashing Company's warranty of good title. Answer (b) is incorrect because Duval has a real defense in that his endorsement was forged. Corner Check Cashing Company's only recourse is to recover from Mask.

33. (580,L1,19) (a) Normally forgeries of the payee's signature would be sufficient to relieve the defrauded corporations of any liability on these instruments. However, a drawer who voluntarily transfers payment to an imposter (Gomer) must bear the loss if a holder in due course subsequently tries to collect. Therefore, answer (a) is correct. Forgery is usually a real defense that would be good against all subsequent holders in due course but the imposter exception would allow the banks, intermediate parties, and the recipients to avoid the loss. The rationale for such a result is the fact that the defrauded corporations were in the best position to keep the defense (forgery) from occurring.

34. (589,L1,52) (c) Endorsers of a note or draft have secondary liability in that the holder can hold them liable if the primary parties fail to pay. The holder, however, must give the endorsers timely notice of dishonor to hold them secondarily liable. Thus Bass must give Frank, a previous endorser, timely notice of dishonor in order to hold her secondarily liable. Answer (a) is incorrect because an endorsement causes liability whether the endorsement was required or not. Answer (b) is incorrect because if there are

multiple endorsers, each is liable to subsequent endorsers or holders. Answer (d) is incorrect because the liability is from previous endorsers to subsequent endorsers, not the reverse.

J. Banks

35. (1189,L1,40) (c) A trade acceptance is a special type of draft in which a seller of goods extends credit to the buyer by drawing the draft on the buyer ordering the buyer to make payment to the seller on a specified date. Answers (a), (b), and (d) are incorrect because they do not conform with this definition.

36. (1188,L1,39) (a) When the drawee bank receives several checks drawn on a particular account on the same day, the bank may charge them against the account in any order convenient to the bank. Since items against an account may reach the bank in several different ways on the same day, it would be unreasonable to require the bank to determine the order of their arrival. Answers (b), (c), and (d) are incorrect because the bank is not required to charge the checks to the account in any particular order.

37. (1189,L1,41) (c) A drawee is not liable on a draft or check until s/he accepts it. Upon acceptance, the drawee becomes primarily liable. A bank or other financial institution is frequently the drawee on drafts and is always the drawee on checks. A bank cannot be an acceptor on a certificate of deposit because it is a two-party instrument in which a bank or financial institution acknowledges receipt of money and promises to repay it. The CD has no drawee that can act as an acceptor since the bank is already primarily liable. Answer (a) is incorrect because a cashier's check is a check in which the drawer and the drawee are the same bank and the payee is a separate party. The bank as the drawee can be an acceptor. Answer (b) is incorrect because the certification of the check is accomplished by the drawee bank's acceptance. Answer (d) is incorrect because a banker's acceptance is a draft in which the drawer and drawee are a bank. Therefore, the bank can be an acceptor.

38. (1189,L1,43) (c) A certified check is a check in which the payor bank has accepted the check and has agreed in advance to pay. Thus, the bank is primarily liable. The drawer, Blare, has secondary liability on the check. Answer (a) is incorrect because the drawer retains secondary liability. Answer (b) is incorrect because the bank accepts the check

when it certifies it by accepting the check. The bank has primary liability and the drawer has secondary liability. Answer (d) is incorrect because although Blare has secondary liability, the bank has accepted.

K. Transfer of Negotiable Documents of Title

39. (1188,L1,42) (b) A person who negotiates a negotiable document of title for value extends the following warranties to the immediate purchaser: (1) negotiation by the transferor is rightful and fully effective with respect to the goods it represents; (2) the transferor has no knowledge of any facts that would impair the document's validity or worth, and (3) the document is genuine. However, the transferor of a negotiable warehouse receipt does not necessarily warrant that the warehouseman will honor the document. Thus, answers (a), (c), and (d) are incorrect.

40. (1186,L1,48) (b) The negotiable warehouse receipts are negotiable documents of title covered by Article 2 of the UCC. Since the receipts were deliverable to the order of Apple, due negotiation to any subsequent party requires delivery of the documents and endorsement by Apple. Klep's signing of Apple's signature constitutes a forgery and prevents a due negotiation of the warehouse receipts. Answer (a) is incorrect because proper negotiation of the warehouse receipts does not require that the warehouseman be notified of the transfer. Answer (c) is incorrect because with regard to the transfer of negotiable documents of title the status that is comparable to a holder in due course is a holder by due negotiation, not a bona fide purchaser for value (this status is relevant in the negotiation of investment securities). Answer (d) is incorrect because Klep's endorsement is a forgery that prevents due negotiation.

41. (589,L1,53) (d) A negotiable warehouse receipt is a document issued as evidence of receipt of goods by a person engaged in the business of storing goods for hire. The warehouse receipt is negotiable if the face of the document contains the words of negotiability (order or bearer). Answer (a) is incorrect because the negotiability of the warehouse receipt is not destroyed by the inclusion of a contractual limitation on the warehouseman's liability. Answer (b) is incorrect because to qualify as commercial paper, the instrument must be payable only in money. If an instrument is payable in money or by the delivery of goods, it is a nonnegotiable instrument. Answer (c) is incorrect because the UCC does not state that only a bonded and licensed warehouseman can issue a warehouse receipt.

42. (584,L1,46) (c) Normally a warehouseman is not allowed to commingle goods of one bailor with those of another. However, in the case of fungible goods, warehousemen may commingle similar fungible goods of different bailors. Answer (a) is incorrect because a bailee may limit his liability to a stipulated maximum. To do this the warehouseman must offer the customer a choice of full liability at one rate and limited liability at a lower rate. Answer (b) is incorrect because warehousemen are not absolutely liable for any damages. The warehousemen must exercise ordinary care and is only liable for damages that could have been avoided through the exercise of due care. Answer (d) is incorrect because in the event that a bailor refuses to pay any storage charges due, a warehouseman has a lien against the goods to the extent of storage charges due and, as a result, can refuse to deliver the goods to the bailee.

L. Transfer of Investment Securities

43. (1183,L1,47) (c) A document of title procured by a thief upon placing stolen goods in a warehouse confers no rights in the underlying goods. This defense is valid against a subsequent holder to whom the document of title has been duly negotiated. Therefore, Valley Instruments, the original owner of the goods, can assert better title to the goods than Reliable Finance. Accordingly, answers (a) and (d) are incorrect. Answer (b) is incorrect because Reliable Finance will be the ultimate loser, assuming Reliable is unable to collect from the thieves.

44. (583,L1,46) (a) The given instrument is a debenture bond that is a negotiable investment security. Dwight, as a bona fide purchaser (received through proper negotiation, gave value, took in good faith and without notice of any adverse claim), acquires the security free of adverse title claims. Answer (b) is incorrect because the registration requirement for transfer would not affect the negotiable nature of the security, nor the rights of a bona fide purchaser. Answer (c) is incorrect because the instrument is a negotiable investment security governed by Article 8 of the UCC, not a negotiable instrument governed by Article 3. Answer (d) is incorrect because the word "assigns" is an acceptable substitute for the words of negotiability.

45. (582,L1,44) (a) An unauthorized signature placed on a stock certificate is effective in favor of a purchaser for value of the certificated security, if the purchaser is without notice of the lack of authority of the signing party and the signing has been done by an employee of the issuer entrusted with the responsible handling of the stock certificate. Therefore, the certificate is valid and the investor is entitled to a reissued certificate without having to further compensate the issuer, Sims Corporation. Answer (c) is incorrect because the investor is not entitled to sue the clerk for a criminal action; the criminal prosecution for the crime of forgery must be brought by the appropriate governmental state or federal authority.

May 1990 Answers

46. (590,L1,35) (a) Article 3 of the UCC lists four types of commercial paper: a draft, a check, a note, and a certificate of deposit; therefore, an installment note is subject to the provisions of the UCC Commercial Paper Article. Answers (b) and (c) are incorrect because warehouse receipts and bills of lading are documents of title governed by Article 7 of the UCC. Answer (d) is incorrect because investment bonds, such as the corporate bearer bond stated in the response, are investment securities subject to Article 8 of the UCC.

47. (590,L1,36) (b) The promissory note contains all of the elements of negotiability. It is written and signed by the maker. It contains an unconditional promise to pay a sum certain in money with the amount of interest determinable by calculation. It is payable at a definite time and is payable to the order of Prestige Properties. Answer (a) is incorrect because the instrument may state that it is secured by a mortgage. This does not destroy negotiability but, in fact, can improve it. Answer (c) is incorrect because negotiability is not destroyed when the note permits prepayment. Furthermore, the sum certain rule is not violated by allowing for collection costs or attorney's fees. Answer (d) is incorrect because the promissory note is commercial paper not an investment security, such as stocks or bonds.

48. (590,L1,38) (a) Monk is not personally a HDC because although he was a holder of the negotiable note for which he gave value, he did not take in good faith because he had knowledge of the fraud before he purchased the note. Furthermore, he had notice that the note was overdue. Therefore, answer (c) can be ruled out. Answer (a) however, is correct because even though Monk was not a HDC, he obtained the instrument from Wilk who was a HDC. Therefore, Monk qualifies as a holder through a HDC and thus obtains all of the rights of a HDC. Answers (b) and (d) are incorrect because fraud in the inducement is a personal defense. Wilk, as a HDC, and Monk, as a holder through a HDC, both take the note free of personal defenses.

49. (590,L1,41) (d) When John Jacobs (the father) endorsed the check, he used a blank qualified endorsement in that he signed it without recourse and did not specify any endorsee. Therefore, when his son received the check, he received bearer paper. Answer (a) is incorrect because a qualified endorsement is one of the valid methods used to negotiate checks or other negotiable instruments. Answer (b) is incorrect because Nix obtained the check stating "Pay to the order of Mary Nix or bearer." This wording creates bearer, not order, paper. Therefore, although Mary Nix did endorse the check, this was not required to negotiate the check to a subsequent holder. Answer (c) is incorrect because a holder does not need to give full value to qualify as a HDC. Reasonable discounts are permitted.

Answer Outline

Problem 1   Rights of Holder in Due Course;
            Unauthorized Signatures;
            Liability of Drawee Bank (581,L2)

a. Harrison will prevail against Oliver
    Harrison is a holder in due course
        Instrument is negotiable
        Harrison holder by negotiation
        Harrison took in good faith and for
        value
        Harrison took without notice of fraudu-
        lent procurement
    Harrison is able to recover to extent of
    value given ($8,500)
        Value given to extent agreed considera-
        tion has been performed
            Includes the $5,000 cash given
            Includes the $3,500 check (i.e.,
            negotiable instrument) given
        Unperformed promise of $1,000 is execu-
        tory in nature
        Does not constitute value given
b1. Williams will not prevail against the bank
    Williams must exercise reasonable care to
    examine items returned by the bank
        So as to discover unauthorized signature
        or alterations
    Williams must notify bank promptly after
    discovery thereof
    Williams must give notice within one year
    from the time such item is available to
    him
        Or else his claim against the bank is
        absolutely barred
            Regardless of negligence of either
            party
b2. The bank cannot collect the money paid to
    McCarthy
    The bank is required to know the signa-
    tures of its customers
        Bank is in superior position to detect
        forgery
            Deemed to have such knowledge of draw-
            er's signature
    Bank is denied recovery from innocent
    holder, McCarthy, who has, in good faith,
    received proceeds of a forged instrument
b3. Answer to b1. would be changed to allow
    Williams to prevail over the bank
    A forged endorsement is ineffective to
    negotiate an order instrument
        Bank not entitled to charge drawer's
        account for payment
    Williams is able to maintain claim against
    the bank
        But must give notice of forged endorse-
        ment within three years from time item
        available to Williams
        Williams precluded from asserting claim
        if his negligence contributed to the
        forgery

But bank must be free from negligence
Answer to b2. would be changed to allow
    the bank to collect from McCarthy
A forged endorsement is ineffective to
negotiate an order instrument
    Bank is permitted to recover from
    McCarthy who took under a forged en-
    dorsement
        Bank is not deemed to know genuine-
        ness of endorser's signature
        Bank is able to recover on "breach
        of warranty" theory
            McCarthy breached warranty to the
            bank
                That he has "good title" to the
                instrument

Unofficial Answer

Problem 1   Rights of Holder in Due Course;
            Unauthorized Signatures;
            Liability of Drawee Bank (581,L2)

Part a.

    Harrison will prevail, but only to the
extent of "value," here $8,500, given for the
negotiable promissory note. The primary issue
in the case is the "value" requirement for
holding in due course. The facts reveal that
Harrison purchased the instrument in good
faith, that it was not overdue, and, at the
time the negotiation took place, Harrison had
no knowledge of the fraudulent circumstances
under which the instrument was originally
obtained from Oliver. The facts indicate that
the note was negotiable and that the negotiation requirement was satisfied.
    The Uniform Commercial Code section
dealing with "taking for value" provides that
a holder, here Harrison, takes for value to
the extent that the agreed consideration has
been performed. Certainly the payment of the
$5,000 in cash constitutes value. The Code
further provides that when a holder gives a
negotiable instrument for the instrument
received, he has given value. Although this
provision is primarily concerned with the
giving of one's negotiable instrument, it is
obvious that the negotiation of another's
negotiable instrument as payment is value.
However, the promise to pay an agreed consideration is not value even though it
constitutes consideration.

Part b.

1. No. Williams will not prevail. The Uniform Commercial Code imposes upon the depositor the responsibility for reasonable care
and promptness in discovering and reporting
his unauthorized signature. In any case, the
depositor must discover and report his un-

authorized signature within one year from the
time the items (checks) are made available to
him. The latter rule applies irrespective of
lack of care on the part of either the bank or
depositor. This absolute rule is based in
part upon the rationale that, after certain
periods of time have elapsed in respect to
commercial transactions, finality is the most
important factor to be considered. Thus,
after this amount of time has elapsed, existing expectations and relations are not to be
altered.

2. No. The bank cannot collect from
McCarthy. The Uniform Commercial Code places
the burden upon the bank to know at its peril
the signature of its drawer. Therefore, when
the bank has paid on the forged signature of a
depositor, it cannot recover the loss by
seeking collection from a party who has
received payment in good faith.

3. The first answer (b.1.) would be changed
in that the law allows the depositor a three-
year period in which to discover the forged
signature of the payee or an endorser. Thus,
if both the bank and depositor are not
negligent (as it would appear from the
excellence of the forgery), the loss rests
with the bank. However, if it can be shown
that the depositor was negligent (for example,
he disregarded a notice from the proper party
that he had not received payment), the bank
will prevail if it was in no way negligent.

    The restated circumstances also change the
second answer (b.2.). A bank is not deemed to
know the signatures of endorsers; therefore,
the bank may recover its loss from McCarthy,
the party collecting on the item. Section
3-417 of the Uniform Commercial Code provides
that a party receiving payment on the instrument warrants to the payor that he has good
title to the instrument.

Answer Outline

Problem 2   Shelter Rule; Secondary Liability
             (583,L5a)

Part a.

1. Pine would recover from Beeler
        Fraud in inducement not valid against
        holder who has acquired the rights of
        holder in due course
            This is shelter rule
2. Pine could recover against Dunhill if he
    gives notice of dishonor
        Dunhill's endorsement makes him second-
        arily liable
            I.e., he promises to pay if appropri-
            ate party does not

Unofficial Answer

Problem 2   Shelter Rule; Secondary Liability
             (583,L5a)

Part a.

1. Pine is not a holder in due course because
he has knowledge of a defense against the
note. However, Pine has the rights of a
holder in due course because he acquired the
note through Gordon, who was a holder in due
course. The rule where a transferee not a
holder in due course acquires the rights of
one by taking from a holder in due course is
known as the "shelter rule." Through these
rights, Pine is entitled to recover the proceeds of the note from Beeler. The defense of
fraud in the inducement is a personal defense
and not valid against a holder in due course
or one with the rights of a holder in due
course.

2. As one with the rights of a holder in due
course, Pine is entitled to proceed against
any person whose signature appears on the
note, provided he gives notice of dishonor.
When Dunhill negotiated the note to Gordon,
Dunhill's signature on the note made him
secondarily liable. As a result, if Pine
brings suit against Dunhill, Pine would prevail because of Dunhill's secondary liability.

Answer Outline

Problem 3   Fictitious Payee; Drawee Bank's
             Acceptance of Check with Forgery
             of Drawer's Signature (587,L2)

a. Checks paid to fictitious payees
        Hex will bear the ultimate loss on these
        items
            General Rule--forged signatures of
            drawers and forged endorsements are
            real defenses valid against holder in
            due course
        Exception--fictitious payees rule shifts
        loss to employer-drawer
            Rule states that real defense not
            created when agent or employee of the
            drawer with name of payee intending
            latter to have no such interest
b. Checks containing forged signature of
    treasurer
        Forging of treasurer's signature is an
        unauthorized signature and not valid
        Bank is obligated to know the signatures
        of its customers and will bear the loss
        unless:
            Bank proves Hex contributed to forgery
            Bank provides Hex failed to exercise
            reasonable care and promptness in
            discovering unauthorized signatures
            on returned checks

Unofficial Answer

Problem 3   Fictitious Payee; Drawee Bank's
             Acceptance of Check with Forgery
             of Drawer's Signature (587,L2)

a. __Checks paid to fictitious payees.__ Hex
will bear the ultimate loss on these items
(the fictitious or non-existent "employees"
and the fictitious suppliers). As a general
rule, forged signatures of drawers and forged
endorsements are real defenses which are valid
even against a holder in due course. However,
when some of these activities are engaged in
by the employees of an employer-drawer of the
checks, a different rule is applied. Essentially, this rule negates these real defenses
in certain cases thereby shifting the loss to
the employer-drawer. The key rule is con
tained in the Uniform Commercial Code's Article on Commercial Paper which deals with "Im-
posters; Signature of Payee." In essence,
this rule makes the endorsement or signature
of the agent or employee of the drawer (Hex)
"effective" where the agent has supplied the
drawer the name of the payee intending the
latter to have no such interest.

Insofar as Omega is concerned, it will be
treated as if it had honored valid orders to
pay and need not refund to Hex the amounts it
paid. The orders are valid since the forged
endorsements are not treated as unauthorized.

b. __Checks which contain the forged signature__
__of the treasurer.__ From the facts it is apparent that the treasurer had the authority to
sign checks and not the assistant treasurer or
head of payroll. Thus, the forging of the
treasurer's signature was an "unauthorized
signature" under the UCC.

As to these checks, the UCC provides that
such signatures are wholly inoperative since
the guilty parties had no authority to sign
the treasurer's or any other authorized
party's name as the drawer on behalf of Hex.

As between Hex and Omega, there is an
obligation on the part of the bank to know the
signatures of its drawer-depositors. Since
Omega has paid the items, it cannot recoup the
loss from Hex. However, the bank has two
possible ways to escape liability to Hex.
First, it can resort to the UCC section which
imposes upon a customer to whom items (checks)
are returned, a duty to exercise reasonable
care and promptness in discovering and reporting unauthorized signatures. Another
possibility is to establish negligence on the
part of Hex which substantially contributed to
the forgeries. Unless the bank can
demonstrate that one of these exceptions
applies, it will bear the loss.

Multiple Choice Questions (1-27)

1. Which of the following is included within the scope of the Secured Transactions Article of the Code?
   a. The outright sale of accounts receivable.
   b. A landlord's lien.
   c. The assignment of a claim for wages.
   d. The sale of chattel paper as a part of the sale of a business out of which it arose.

2. Donaldson, Inc. loaned Watson Enterprises $50,000 secured by a real estate mortgage which included the land, buildings, and "all other property which is added to the real property or which is considered as real property as a matter of law." Star Company also loaned Watson $25,000 and obtained a security interest in all of Watson's "inventory, accounts receivable, fixtures, and other tangible personal property." There is insufficient property to satisfy the two creditors. Consequently, Donaldson is attempting to include all property possible under the terms and scope of its real property mortgage. If Donaldson is successful in this regard, then Star will receive a lesser amount in satisfaction of its claim. What is the probable outcome of Donaldson's action?
   a. Donaldson will not prevail if the property in question is detachable trade fixtures.
   b. Donaldson will prevail if Star failed to file a financing statement.
   c. Donaldson will prevail if it was the first lender and duly filed its real property mortgage.
   d. The problem will be decided by taking all of Watson's property (real and personal) subject to the two secured creditors' claims and dividing it in proportion to the respective debts.

3. Under the UCC Secured Transactions Article, for a security interest to attach, the
   a. Debtor must agree to the creation of the security interest.
   b. Creditor must properly file a financing statement.
   c. Debtor must be denied all rights in the collateral.
   d. Creditor must take and hold the collateral.

4. Burn Manufacturing borrowed $500,000 from Howard Finance Co., secured by Burn's present and future inventory, accounts receivable, and the proceeds thereof. The parties signed a financing statement that described the collateral and it was filed in the appropriate state office. Burn subsequently defaulted in the repayment of the loan and Howard attempted to enforce its security interest. Burn contended that Howard's security interest was unenforceable. In addition, Green, who subsequently gave credit to Burn without knowledge of Howard's security interest, is also attempting to defeat Howard's alleged security interest. The security interest in question is valid with respect to
   a. Both Burn and Green.
   b. Neither Burn nor Green.
   c. Burn but not Green.
   d. Green but not Burn.

5. Perfection of a security interest permits the secured party to protect its interest by
   a. Avoiding the need to file a financing statement.
   b. Preventing another creditor from obtaining a security interest in the same collateral.
   c. Establishing priority over the claims of most subsequent secured creditors.
   d. Denying the debtor the right to possess the collateral.

6. The perfection of a security interest by filing a financing statement
   a. Serves to protect the secured party's interest in the collateral against most creditors who acquire a security interest in the same collateral after the filing.
   b. Is necessary to enable the secured party to enforce its security interest against the debtor.
   c. Serves to give the public actual notice.
   d. Gives the secured party priority over all other parties who acquire an interest in the collateral after the filing.

7. Roth and Dixon both claim a security interest in the same collateral. Roth's security interest attached on January 1, 1989, and was perfected by filing on March 1, 1989. Dixon's security interest attached on February 1, 1989, and was perfected on April 1, 1989, by taking possession of the collateral. Which of the following statements is correct?
   a. Roth's security interest has priority because Roth perfected before Dixon perfected.

b. Dixon's security interest has priority because Dixon's interest attached before Roth's interest was perfected.
c. Roth's security interest has priority because Roth's security interest attached before Dixon's security interest attached.
d. Dixon's security interest has priority because Dixon is in possession of the collateral.

8. Unless otherwise agreed, when collateral, covered under the Secured Transactions Article of the UCC, is in the secured party's possession
   a. The risk of accidental loss is on the debtor to the extent of any deficiency in any effective insurance coverage.
   b. The secured party will lose his security interest if he commingles fungible collateral.
   c. Reasonable expenses incurred to preserve the collateral are chargeable to the secured party.
   d. Any repledge of the collateral by the secured party will be unenforceable.

9. Tawney Manufacturing approached Worldwide Lenders for a loan of $50,000 to purchase vital components it used in its manufacturing process. Worldwide decided to grant the loan but only if Tawney would agree to a field warehousing arrangement. Pursuant to their understanding, Worldwide paid for the purchase of the components, took a negotiable bill of lading for them, and surrendered the bill of lading in exchange for negotiable warehouse receipts issued by the bonded warehouse company that had established a field warehouse in Tawney's storage facility. Worldwide did not file a financing statement. Under the circumstances, Worldwide
   a. Has a security interest in the goods which has attached and is perfected.
   b. Does not have a security interest which has attached since Tawney has not signed a security agreement.
   c. Must file an executed financing statement in order to perfect its security interest.
   d. Must not relinquish control over any of the components to Tawney for whatever purpose, unless it is paid in cash for those released.

10. The Town Bank makes collateralized loans to its customers at 1% above prime on securities owned by the customer, subject to existing margin requirements. In doing so, which of the following is correct?

a. Notification of the issuer is necessary in order to perfect a security interest.
b. Filing is a permissible method of perfecting a security interest in the securities if the circumstances dictate.
c. Any dividend or interest distributions during the term of the loan belong to the bank.
d. A perfected security interest in the securities can only be obtained by possession.

11. Mern Corp. is in the business of selling computers and computer software to the public. Mern sold and delivered a personal computer to Whyte on credit. Whyte executed and delivered to Mern a promissory note for the purchase price and a security agreement covering the computer. If Whyte purchased the computer for personal use and Mern fails to file a financing statement, which of the following statements is correct?
   a. The computer was a consumer good while in Mern's possession.
   b. Perfection of Mern's security interest occurred at the time of attachment.
   c. Mern's security interest is **not** enforceable against Whyte because Mern failed to file a financing statement.
   d. Mern does **not** have a perfected security interest because it failed to file a financing statement.

12. Wurke, Inc. manufactures and sells household appliances on credit directly to wholesalers, retailers, and consumers. Wurke can perfect its security interest in the appliances without having to file a financing statement or take possession of the appliances if the sale is made by Wurke to
   a. Retailers.
   b. Wholesalers that then sell to distributors for resale.
   c. Consumers.
   d. Wholesalers that then sell to buyers in the ordinary course of business.

13. Acorn Marina, Inc. sells and services boat motors. On April 1, 1989, Acorn financed the purchase of its entire inventory with GAC Finance Company. GAC required Acorn to execute a security agreement and financing statement covering the inventory and proceeds of sale. On April 14, 1989, GAC properly filed the financing statement pursuant to the UCC Secured Transactions Article. On April 27, 1989, Acorn sold one of the motors to Wilks

for use in his charter business. Wilks, who had once worked for Acorn, knew that Acorn regularly financed its inventory with GAC. Acorn has defaulted on its obligations to GAC. The motor purchased by Wilks is

a. Subject to the GAC security interest because Wilks should have known that GAC financed the inventory purchase by Acorn.
b. Subject to the GAC security interest because Wilks purchased the motor for a commercial use.
c. Not subject to the GAC security interest because Wilks is regarded as a buyer in the ordinary course of Acorn's business.
d. Not subject to the GAC security interest because GAC failed to file the financing statement until more than 10 days after April 1, 1989.

14. On May 8, Westar Corp. sold 20 typewriters to Saper for use in Saper's business. Saper paid for the typewriters by executing a promissory note that was secured by the typewriters. Saper also executed a security agreement. On May 9, Saper filed a petition in bankruptcy and a trustee was appointed. On May 16, Westar filed a financing statement covering the typewriters. Westar claims that it has a superior interest in the typewriters. The trustee in a bankruptcy disagrees. Which of the parties is correct?

a. The trustee, because the filing of a petition in bankruptcy cuts off Westar's rights as of the date of filing.
b. The trustee, because the petition was filed prior to Westar's filing of the financing statement.
c. Westar, because it perfected its security interest within ten days after Saper took possession of the typewriters.
d. Westar, because its security interest was automatically perfected upon attachment.

15. On May 2, Safe Bank agreed to loan Tyler Corp. $50,000. Tyler signed a security agreement and financing statement covering its existing equipment. On May 4, Safe filed the financing statement. On May 7, State Bank loaned Tyler $60,000. State had notified Safe on May 5 of its intention to make the loan. Tyler signed a security agreement and financing statement covering the same existing equipment. On May 8, State filed the financing statement. On May 10, Safe loaned Tyler $50,000. If Tyler defaults on both loans, who will have a priority security interest in the equipment?

a. State, since it was the first to perfect its security interest.
b. State, since it properly notified Safe prior to making the loan.
c. Safe, since it was the first to file.
d. Safe, since it has a purchase money security interest in the equipment which was perfected within the permissible time limits.

16. Cross has an unperfected security interest in the inventory of Safe, Inc. The unperfected security interest

a. Is superior to the interest of subsequent lenders who obtain a perfected security interest in the property.
b. Is subordinate to lien creditors of Safe who become such prior to any subsequent perfection by Cross.
c. Causes Cross to lose important rights against Safe as an entity.
d. May only be perfected by Cross filing a financing statement.

17. A typewriter, which was subject to a prior UCC security interest, was delivered to Ed Fogel for repair. Fogel is engaged in the business of repairing typewriters. Fogel repaired the typewriter. However, the owner of the typewriter now refuses to pay for the services performed by Fogel. The state in which Fogel operates his business has a statute which gives Fogel a mechanics lien on the typewriter. Fogel's mechanics lien

a. Takes priority over a prior perfected security interest under all circumstances.
b. Is subject to a prior perfected purchase money security interest under all circumstances.
c. Is subject to a prior unperfected security interest where the statute is silent as to priority.
d. Takes priority over a prior perfected security interest unless the statute expressly provides otherwise.

18. Foxx purchased a stereo for personal use from Dix Audio, a retail seller of appliances. Foxx paid 30% of the $600 sales price and agreed to pay the balance in 12 equal principal payments plus interest. Foxx executed a security agreement giving Dix a security interest in the stereo. Dix properly filed a financing statement immediately. After making six payments Foxx defaulted.

If after making the third installment payment, Foxx sold the stereo to Lutz for personal use, who would have a superior interest in the stereo assuming Lutz lacked knowledge of Dix's security interest?

    a. Dix, since it filed a financing statement.

    b. Dix, since more than 30% of the purchase price had been paid.

    c. Lutz, since title passed from Foxx to Lutz.

    d. Lutz, since he purchased without knowledge of Dix's security interest and for personal use.

19. Fogel purchased a TV set for $900 from Hamilton Appliance Store. Hamilton took a promissory note signed by Fogel and a security interest for the $800 balance due on the set. It was Hamilton's policy not to file a financing statement until the purchaser defaulted. Fogel obtained a loan of $500 from Reliable Finance which took and recorded a security interest in the set. A month later, Fogel defaulted on several loans outstanding and one of his creditors, Harp, obtained a judgment against Fogel which was properly recorded. After making several payments, Fogel defaulted on a payment due to Hamilton, who then recorded a financing statement subsequent to Reliable's filing and the entry of the Harp judgment. Subsequently, at a garage sale, Fogel sold the set for $300 to Mobray. Which of the parties has the priority claim to the set?

    a. Reliable.

    b. Hamilton.

    c. Harp.

    d. Mobray.

20. Thrush, a wholesaler of television sets, contracted to sell 100 sets to Kelly, a retailer. Kelly signed a security agreement with the 100 sets as collateral. The security agreement provided that Thrush's security interest extended to the inventory, to any proceeds therefrom, and to the after-acquired inventory of Kelly. Thrush filed his security interest centrally. Later, Kelly sold one of the sets to Haynes who purchased with knowledge of Thrush's perfected security interest. Haynes gave a note for the purchase price and signed a security agreement using the set as collateral. Kelly is now in default. Thrush can

    a. Not repossess the set from Haynes, but is entitled to any payments Haynes makes to Kelly on his note.

    b. Repossess the set from Haynes as he has a purchase money security interest.

    c. Repossess the set as his perfection is first, and first in time is first in right.

    d. Repossess the set in Haynes' possession because Haynes knew of Thrush's perfected security interest at the time of purchase.

21. Robert Cunningham owns a shop in which he repairs electrical appliances. Three months ago Electrical Supply Company sold Cunningham, on credit, a machine for testing electrical appliances and obtained a perfected security interest at the time as security for payment of the unpaid balance. Cunningham's creditors have now filed an involuntary petition in bankruptcy against him. What is the status of Electrical in the bankruptcy proceeding?

    a. Electrical is a secured creditor and has the right against the trustee if not paid to assert a claim to the electrical testing machine it sold to Cunningham.

    b. Electrical must surrender its perfected security interest to the trustee in bankruptcy and share as a general creditor of the bankrupt's estate.

    c. Electrical's perfected security interest constitutes a preference and is voidable.

    d. Electrical must elect to resort exclusively to its secured interest or to relinquish it and obtain the same share as a general creditor.

22. Bonn, a secured party, sells collateral at a private sale to a good faith purchaser for value after the debtor defaults. Which of the following statements is correct under the UCC Secured Transactions Article?

    a. In all cases, the collateral will remain subject to the security interests of subordinate lien creditors.

    b. The security interest under which the sale was made and any security interest or lien subordinate to it will be discharged.

    c. In all cases, Bonn may not buy the collateral at a private sale.

    d. Bonn will be entitled to receive a first priority in the sale proceeds.

23. Bean defaulted on a promissory note payable to Gray Co. The note was secured by a piece of equipment owned by Bean. Gray perfected its security interest on May 29, 1987. Bean had also pledged the same equipment as collateral for another loan from Smith Co. after he had given the security interest to Gray. Smith's security interest was perfected on June 30, 1987. Bean is current in his payments to Smith. Subsequently, Gray took

possession of the equipment and sold it at a private sale to Walsh, a good faith purchaser for value. Walsh will take the equipment

    a. Free of Smith's security interest because Bean is current in his payments to Smith.

    b. Free of Smith's security interest because Walsh acted in good faith and gave value.

    c. Subject to Smith's security interest because the equipment was sold at a private sale.

    d. Subject to Smith's security interest because Smith is a purchase money secured creditor.

24. Under the UCC Secured Transactions Article, if a debtor is in default under a payment obligation secured by goods, the secured party has the right to

	Reduce the claim to a judgment	Sell the goods and apply the proceeds toward the debt	Take possession of the goods without judicial process
a.	Yes	Yes	No
b.	Yes	No	Yes
c.	No	Yes	Yes
d.	Yes	Yes	Yes

25. Foxx purchased a stereo for personal use from Dix Audio, a retail seller of appliances. Foxx paid 30% of the $600 sales price and agreed to pay the balance in 12 equal principal payments plus interest. Foxx executed a security agreement giving Dix a security interest in the stereo. Dix properly filed a financing statement immediately. After making six payments Foxx defaulted.

    If Dix takes possession of the stereo, it

    a. Must dispose of the stereo at a public sale.

    b. Must dispose of the stereo within 90 days after taking possession or be liable to the debtor.

    c. May retain possession of the stereo, thereby discharging Foxx of any deficiency.

    d. May retain possession of the stereo and collect any deficiency plus costs from Foxx.

26. Cole purchased furniture for her home from Thrift Furniture. The contract required Cole to pay 10% cash and the balance in equal installments over 36 months. Cole signed a security agreement with the furniture listed as collateral. Thrift properly filed a financing statement. If Cole makes the final payment due on the contract, Thrift

    a. Must file a termination statement no later than one month after final

payment in order to avoid liability unless Cole demands earlier filing.

    b. Must file a termination statement in order to avoid liability only if Cole makes a written demand.

    c. Does not have to file a termination statement since the collateral is consumer goods.

    d. Does not have to file a termination statement since the term of the financing statement is less than five years and will automatically terminate.

May 1990 Question

27. Vista is a wholesale seller of microwave ovens. Vista sold 50 microwave ovens to Davis Appliance for $20,000. Davis paid $5,000 down and signed a promissory note for the balance. Davis also executed a security agreement giving Vista a security interest in Davis' inventory, including the ovens. Vista perfected its security interest by properly filing a financing statement in the state of Whiteacre. Six months later, Davis moved its business to the state of Blackacre, taking the ovens. On arriving in Blackacre, Davis secured a loan from Grange Bank and signed a security agreement putting up all inventory (including the ovens) as collateral. Grange perfected its security interest by properly filing a financing statement in the state of Blackacre. Two months after arriving in Blackacre, Davis went into default on both debts. Which of the following statements is correct?

    a. Grange's security interest is superior because Grange had no actual notice of Vista's security interest.

    b. Vista's security interest is superior even though at the time of Davis' default Vista had not perfected its security interest in the state of Blackacre.

    c. Grange's security interest is superior because Vista's time to file a financing statement in Blackacre had expired prior to Grange's filing.

    d. Vista's security interest is superior provided it repossesses the ovens before Grange does.

Repeat Question

(590,L1,49) Identical/similar to item 12 above

Problems

Problem 1   (1183,L2a)

(7 to 10 minutes)

Part a.   Despard Finance Company is a diverse, full-line lending institution.   Its "Problems & Potential Litigation" file revealed the following disputes involving loans extended during the year of examination.
•   Despard loaned Fish $4,500 to purchase a $5,000 video recording system for his personal use.   A note, security agreement, and financing statement, which was promptly filed, were all executed by Fish.   Unknown to Despard, Fish had already purchased the system from Zeals Department Store the previous day for $5,000.   The terms were 10% down, the balance monthly, payable in three years, and a written security interest granted to Zeals. Zeals did not file a financing statement until default.
•   Despard loaned Moderne Furniture Co. $13,000 to purchase certain woodworking equipment.   Moderne did so.   A note, security agreement, and financing statement were executed by Moderne.   As a result of an oversight the financing statement was not filed until 30 days after the loan-purchase by Moderne.   In the interim Moderne borrowed $11,000 from Apache National Bank using the newly purchased machinery as collateral for the loan.   A financing statement was filed by Apache five days prior to Despard's filing.

Required:

Answer the following, setting forth reasons for any conclusions stated.
What are the priorities among the conflicting security interests in the same collateral claimed by Despard and the other lenders?

Problem 2   (581,L3)

(15 to 20 minutes)

Part a.   Walpole Electric Products, Inc. manufactures a wide variety of electrical appliances.   Walpole uses the consignment as an integral part of its marketing plan.   The consignments are "true" consignments rather than consignments intended as security interests.   Unsold goods may be returned to the owner-consignor.   Walpole contracted with Petty Distributors, Inc., an electrical appliance wholesaler, to market its products under this consignment arrangement.   Subsequently, Petty became insolvent and made a general assignment for the benefit of creditors. Klinger, the assignee, took possession of all of Petty's inventory, including all the Walpole electrical products.   Walpole has demanded return of its appliances asserting that the relationship created by the consignment between itself and Petty was one of agency and that Petty never owned the appliances.   Furthermore, Walpole argues that under the consignment arrangement there is no obligation owing by Petty at any time, thus there is nothing to secure under the secured transactions provisions of the Uniform Commercial Code.   Klinger has denied the validity of these assertions claiming that the consignment is subject to the Code's filing provisions unless the Code has otherwise been satisfied.   Walpole sues to repossess the goods.

Required:

Answer the following, setting forth reasons for any conclusions stated.
1.   What are the requirements, if any, to perfect a true consignment such as discussed above?
2.   Will Walpole prevail?

Part b.   Lebow Woolens, Inc. sold several thousand bolts of Australian wool on credit to Fashion Plate Exclusives, Inc., a clothing manufacturer, obtaining a duly executed security agreement and a financing statement. Fashion Plate became delinquent in meeting its payments.   Lebow subsequently discovered that a miscaptioned financing statement for a $12,500 sale had been filed under the name of Fashion Styles Limited, another customer. Lebow took the following actions.   First, on August 11, 1980, it repossessed the bolts of wool which were not already altered by Fashion Plate.   This amounted to some 65% of the invoice in question.   Next on August 20, 1980, it filed a corrected financing statement covering the sale in question.   Dunbar, another creditor of Fashion Plate's, levied against Fashion Plate's inventory, work in process, and raw materials on August 13th and obtained a judgment of $14,000 against Fashion Plate, an amount in excess of the value of the Lebow bolts of wool.   The judgment was obtained and entered on August 18, 1980.   Dunbar asserts its rights as a lien judgment creditor.

Required:

Answer the following, setting forth reasons for any conclusions stated.
In a lawsuit to determine the rights of the parties, how should the competing claims of Lebow and Dunbar be decided?

Problem 3   (1184,L4a & b)

(15 to 25 minutes)

Tom Sauer purchased a computer and a stereo from Zen Sounds, Inc. for personal use. With regard to the computer, Sauer signed an installment purchase note and a security agreement. Under the terms of the note Sauer was to pay $100 down and $50 a month for 20 months. The security agreement included a description of the computer. However, Zen did not file a financing statement. Sauer paid $800 cash for the stereo.

Two months later, Sauer sold the computer to Ralph for $600 cash. Ralph purchased the computer for personal use without knowledge of Zen's security interest.

Three months later, Sauer brought the stereo back to Zen for repair. Inadvertently, one of Zen's sales persons sold the stereo to Ned, a buyer in the ordinary course of business.

Required:

Answer the following, setting forth reasons for any conclusions stated.
    a. Did Zen fulfill the requirements necessary for the attachment and perfection of its security interest in the computer?
    b. Will Ralph take the computer free of Zen's security interest?

Problem 4   (588,L4)

(15 to 20 minutes)

Dunn & Co., CPAs, is auditing the 1987 financial statements of its client, Safe Finance. While performing the audit, Dunn learned of certain transactions that occurred during 1987 that may have an adverse impact on Safe's financial statements. The following transactions are of most concern to Dunn:

• On May 5, Safe sold certain equipment to Lux, who contemporaneously executed and delivered to Safe a promissory note and security agreement covering the equipment. Lux purchased the equipment for use in its business. On May 8, City Bank loaned Lux $50,000, taking a promissory note and security agreement from Lux that covered all of Lux's existing and after-acquired equipment. On May 11, Lux was involuntarily petitioned into bankruptcy under the liquidation provisions of the Bankruptcy Code and a trustee was appointed. On May 12, City filed a financing statement covering all of Lux's equipment. On

May 14, Safe filed a financing statement covering the equipment it had sold to Lux on May 5.

• On July 10, Safe loaned $600,000 to Cam Corp., which used the funds to refinance existing debts. Cam duly executed and delivered to Safe a promissory note and a security agreement covering Cam's existing and after-acquired inventory of machine parts. On July 12, Safe filed a financing statement covering Cam's inventory of machine parts. On July 15, Best Bank loaned Cam $200,000. Contemporaneous with the loan, Cam executed and delivered to Best a promissory note and security agreement covering all of Cam's inventory of machine parts and any after-acquired inventory. Best had already filed a financing statement covering Cam's inventory on June 20, after Best agreed to make the loan to Cam. On July 14, Dix, in good faith, purchased certain machine parts from Cam's inventory and received delivery that same day.

Required:

Define a purchase money security interest. In separate paragraphs, discuss whether Safe has a priority security interest over:

• The trustee in Lux's bankruptcy with regard to the equipment sold by Safe on May 5.
• City with regard to the equipment sold by Safe on May 5.
• Best with regard to Cam's existing and after-acquired inventory of machine parts.
• Dix with regard to the machine parts purchased on July 14 by Dix.

Problem 5   (589,L5)

(15 to 20 minutes)

On February 20, 1989, Pine, Inc. ordered a specially manufactured computer system consisting of a disk drive and a central processing unit (CPU) from Xeon Corp., a seller of computers and other office equipment. A contract was signed and the total purchase price was paid to Xeon by Pine on the same date. The contract required Pine to pick up the computer system at Xeon's warehouse on March 9, 1989, but was silent as to when risk of loss passed to Pine. The computer system was completed on March 1, 1989, and set aside for Pine's contemplated pickup on March 9, 1989. On March 3, 1989, the disk drive was stolen from Xeon's warehouse. On March 9, 1989, Pine picked up

the CPU. On March 15, 1989, Pine returned the
CPU to Xeon for warranty repairs. On March 18,
1989, Xeon mistakenly sold the CPU to Meed, a
buyer in the ordinary course of business.

On April 12, 1989, Pine purchased and received delivery of five word processors from
Jensen Electronics Corp. for use in its business. The purchase price of the word processors was $15,000. Pine paid $5,000 down and
executed an installment purchase note and a
security agreement for the balance. The security agreement contained a description of
the word processors. Jensen never filed a financing statement. On April 1, 1989, Pine had
given its bank a security interest in all of
its assets. The bank had immediately perfected its security interest by filing. Pine
has defaulted on the installment purchase
note.

Required:

Discuss the following assertions, indicating whether such assertions are correct and
the reasons therefor.

- As of March 3, 1989, the risk of loss
  on the disk drive remained with Xeon.
- Meed acquired no rights in the CPU as
  a result of the March 18, 1989 transaction.
- Jensen's security interest in the word
  processors never attached and therefore Jensen's security interest is not
  enforceable against Pine.
- Jensen has superior security interest
  to Pine's bank.

Multiple Choice Answers

1. a	7. a	13. c	18. a	23. b
2. a	8. a	14. c	19. b	24. d
3. a	9. a	15. c	20. a	25. b
4. a	10. d	16. b	21. a	26. a
5. c	11. b	17. d	22. b	27. b
6. a	12. c			

Multiple Choice Answer Explanations

A.1. Article 9 of UCC

1. (1180,L1,38) (a) The only item listed that is within the scope of article 9 (secured transactions) is the outright sale of accounts receivable.

A.2.a. Types of Personal Property

2. (578,L1,29) (a) Detachable trade fixtures are considered personal property, not real property. Therefore, a real estate mortgagee will not obtain a security interest in property classified as a detachable trade fixture. Answer (b) is incorrect because Donaldson's mortgage does not cover any personal property which is the issue here. Answer (c) is incorrect because the mortgage attaches only to real property. Thus property which is classified as personal will not be included whether the mortgage is recorded or not. Answer (d) is incorrect because the court's job is to distinguish between real and personal property and it lacks authority to divide disputed property in proportion to respective claims.

B. Attachment of Security Interests

3. (1189,L1,50) (a) In order for a security interest to attach, there must be a security agreement that is in writing and signed by the debtor. It may be oral if the secured party obtains possession of the collateral. In either case, the debtor must have agreed to the security interest. The secured party must also give value and the debtor must have rights in the collateral. Answer (b) is incorrect because filing a financing statement is one of the methods used to perfect a security interest but is not required for attachment. Answer (c) is incorrect because it is not an element of attachment. In fact, the debtor normally keeps possession of the collateral and, thus, retains rights in the collateral. Answer (d) is incorrect because the creditor needs possession to get attachment only if the security agreement is oral.

4. (589,L1,60) (a) A security interest attaches when the following occur, in any order: secured creditor gives value, debtor has rights in the collateral, and a security agreement exists. In this situation attachment has occurred. Howard (creditor) gave value ($500,000 loan), Burn (debtor) has rights in the collateral (inventory and future inventory and accounts receivable and proceeds thereof), and the problem states the security interest has been created. Upon attachment, the security interest is enforceable between the debtor and the secured party; thus, Howard's security interest is effective against Burn. Howard perfected its security interest by filing the financing statement in the appropriate state office; therefore, Howard's security interest is effective against subsequent creditors (Green) claiming an interest in the collateral. Thus, answers (b), (c), and (d) are incorrect.

C.3. Perfection by Filing

5. (1189,L1,53) (c) Perfection of a security interest is important in that it establishes for a secured party priority over the claims that may be made by most subsequent secured creditors. Answer (a) is incorrect because there are three methods of obtaining perfection and one of them is filing a financing statement. Answer (b) is incorrect because subsequent creditors may still obtain security interests in the same collateral although they will normally obtain a lower priority. Answer (d) is incorrect because frequently the debtor retains possession of the collateral.

6. (1186,L1,50) (a) Perfection by filing a financing statement will not defeat all other parties who acquire an interest in the same collateral; rather, perfection by filing gives the secured party his best possible rights in the collateral. For example, purchasers from a merchant in the ordinary course of business take the collateral free from any prior perfected security interest. The only time a purchaser would take the collateral subject to a prior perfected security interest would be when the purchaser knew that the merchant was selling the goods in violation of a financing statement. Therefore, answer (d) is incorrect. Answer (b) is incorrect because a creditor need not perfect the security interest in order to enforce it against the debtor. Answer (c) is incorrect because perfection by filing a financing statement gives constructive notice, not actual notice, to the public.

7. (1189,L1,54) (a) Perfection of a security interest takes place when all of the elements for attachment have occurred as well as
one of the alternate methods of perfection.
Roth's security interest was perfected on
March 1. Dixon's security interest was perfected on April 1. Therefore, Roth's security
interest has priority over that of Dixon because Roth's was perfected first. Answer (b)
is incorrect because the comparison is between
the perfection dates. Answer (c) is incorrect
because the dates of perfection are relevant
rather than the dates of attachment. Answer (d) is incorrect because the dates of the
perfection control the priorities, not the
method of perfection.

C.4. Perfection by Possession

8. (1184,L1,60) (a) The risk of accidental
loss is on the debtor to the extent of any
deficiency in any effective insurance coverage. However, the secured party must exercise
reasonable care while possessing the collateral. The secured party has liability when
the collateral is damaged through the negligence of the secured party. Answer (b) is
incorrect because the secured party may commingle fungible collateral without destroying
his security interest. Answer (c) is incorrect because reasonable expenses to preserve
the collateral (such as insurance and taxes)
are chargeable to the debtor, not the secured
party. Answer (d) is incorrect because the
secured party may repledge the collateral upon
terms which do not impair the debtor's right
to redeem it.

9. (1182,L1,55) (a) Since documents of
title, i.e., the negotiable warehouse receipts, merely represent the goods, a perfected security interest in the warehouse
receipts (by taking possession of the documents) is also a perfected security interest
in the goods covered by the documents. Answer (b) is incorrect because the debtor,
Tawney, does not have to sign the security
agreement if the collateral is in the
possession of the secured party, Worldwide,
pursuant to agreement. When a secured party
is taking a possessory security interest, an
oral security agreement is sufficient to
create such an interest. Answer (c) is
incorrect because Worldwide does not have to
file a financing statement to perfect its
security interest, since Worldwide has already
perfected its security interest by taking
possession of the negotiable warehouse
receipts. Worldwide could have perfected its
security interest by filing a financing
statement, but this filing would not protect
Worldwide against a good faith purchaser to

whom the warehouse receipts have been duly
negotiated. Answer (d) is incorrect because
temporary and limited relinquishment of control of the goods to the debtor is acceptable.
The Uniform Commercial Code provides for a
21-day continuation of the perfected security
interest in the collateral from the date of
release to the debtor.

10. (1180,L1,34) (d) A perfected security
interest in securities can only be obtained by
possession. An exception to this rule is when
the creditor temporarily returns the security
to the debtor (for sale, exchange, etc.). In
such situations, the creditor's security interest remains perfected for 21 days. However, a bona fide purchaser of the security
will defeat the creditor's security interest.
Thus, answer (d) is correct. To perfect a
security interest in securities there is no
need to notify the issuer. Dividends and
interest earned during the secured transaction
are the property of the debtor.

C.5. Perfection by Attachment

11. (1188,L1,52) (b) Perfection occurs at
the time of attachment whenever a creditor
obtains a purchase money security interest in
consumer goods. Since Whyte purchased the
computer for personal use and all the
essential elements necessary for attachment
have occurred, Mern's security interest has
been perfected. Answer (a) is incorrect
because the computer was inventory while in
Mern's possession. Answer (c) is incorrect
because Mern does not need to file a financing
statement to obtain an enforceable security
interest against Whyte. The security interest
became enforceable between Mern, the secured
party, and Whyte, the debtor, upon attachment. Perfection is not necessary in order
for the secured party to enforce the security
interest against the debtor. Attachment
occurs when the following are present:
secured creditor gives value, debtor has
rights in the collateral, and a security
agreement exists. Answer (d) is incorrect because perfection occurs at the time of attachment whenever a creditor (Mern) obtains a purchase money security interest in consumer
goods.

12. (1187,L1,41) (c) Wurke has a purchase
money security interest in all goods sold to
consumers on credit. When a purchase money
interest is acquired in consumer goods, the
secured party's (Wurke) security interest
automatically perfects upon attachment. Thus,
Wurke does not need to file a financing statement to perfect its interest on credit sales
to consumers. Answers (a), (b), and (d) are

incorrect because goods sold to retailers and wholesalers are considered inventory; therefore, Wurke would only perfect its interest on credit sales to retailers and wholesalers by filing a financing statement or taking possession of the appliances.

E. Priorities

13. (589,L1,47) (c) Buyers in the ordinary course of business take free of any security interest whether perfected or not. In general, buying in the ordinary course of business means buying goods from the inventory of one that normally sells those goods. Answer (c) is correct because Wilks bought in the ordinary course of business from Acorn who normally sells and services boat motors. The fact that Wilks knew that Acorn normally financed its inventory does not change this rule. Answer (a) is incorrect because the rule is meant to protect buyers in the ordinary course of business over secured parties. Answer (b) is incorrect because this rule applies to purchasing for commercial as well as for consumer use. Answer (d) is incorrect because Wilks would win against perfected or imperfected security interests.

14. (1187,L1,43) (c) A purchase money security interest in collateral other than inventory will have priority if the secured party perfects his interest no later than ten days after the debtor takes possession of the collateral. Westar has a purchase money security interest in the typewriters sold to Saper. The typewriters are for use in Saper's business; therefore, the typewriters are considered equipment. Westar had ten days to file the financing statement. Since the financing statement was filed on May 16, eight days after Saper received the collateral, Westar will have superior rights in the collateral. Answer (a) is incorrect because the filing of a petition in bankruptcy has no effect on Westar's ability to perfect its interest. Answer (b) is incorrect because Westar filed within the ten-day grace period; therefore, his interest was effectively perfected on May 8, one day prior to the trustee's bankruptcy petition. Answer (d) is incorrect because Westar's interest did not automatically perfect upon attachment. Perfection by attachment only occurs when purchase money security interests are acquired in consumer goods. Saper is using the goods as equipment; therefore, Westar needed to file a financing statement to perfect its security interest.

15. (1186,L1,51) (c) Since Safe was the first to perfect its security interest, it will have a priority security interest in Tyler's equipment. Perfection may only occur after the security interest has attached. Attachment takes place when all of the following have been met, in any order: the debtor executes a security agreement, the debtor acquires rights in the collateral, and the secured party gives value. On May 2, Tyler signed the security agreement and financing statement covering its existing inventory and Safe agreed to loan Tyler $50,000; therefore, all three requirements for attachment were met (Tyler executed the agreement and had rights in its inventory and Safe gave value). Value may be broadly defined and would include a binding commitment to extend credit; thus, value was given to Tyler when Safe agreed to lend Tyler $50,000 (May 2), not when Safe actually gave Tyler the cash (May 10). Safe perfected its security interest when it filed the financing statement on May 4, four days prior to State's filing. Thus, answer (a) is incorrect. Answer (b) is incorrect because Safe had already perfected its security interest. Answer (d) is incorrect because Safe did not have a purchase money security interest in the equipment since Tyler already owned the equipment. A purchase money security interest would not have occurred unless Tyler had used the $50,000 to purchase new equipment.

16. (586,L1,39) (b) Lien creditors have priority over any unperfected security interest and any security interest perfected after the lien has attached. Answer (a) is incorrect because a perfected security interest is superior to Cross's unperfected security interest unless the perfected party had knowledge of Cross's interest prior to perfection. Answer (c) is incorrect because Cross's failure to perfect does not affect his rights against Safe. By not perfecting, Cross does not obtain the best possible rights in the collateral in relation to third parties. Answer (d) is incorrect because Cross may also perfect by taking possession of the property, Safe's inventory. This could be done under a field warehousing arrangement.

17. (1185,L1,49) (d) The UCC states that when a person in the ordinary course of business furnishes services or materials for goods subject to a security interest, a mechanics lien on such goods, which arises under state law, takes priority over prior perfected security interests unless the statute expressly provides otherwise. Therefore, answers (a), (b), and (c) are incorrect.

18. (585,L1,48) (a) A subsequent consumer buyer who purchases goods from a debtor without knowledge of a prior security interest will take them free of a prior perfected security interest where perfection occurred automatically upon attachment (i.e., a purchase money security interest in consumer goods). However, if the prior perfected secured party, which gained perfection automatically upon attachment, also files a financing statement, then this secured party has a superior interest in the collateral over the good faith consumer purchaser. Since Dix has filed a financing statement, Lutz has constructive notice of the prior security interest and will not take free of Dix's interest. Answers (b) and (c) are incorrect because payment of 30% of the purchase price and passage of title have no bearing on the issue of priority in the collateral. A creditor's security interest will continue despite a sale of the collateral subject to some exceptions (i.e., buyer in ordinary course of business). Answer (d) is incorrect because even though Lutz did not have actual knowledge of the prior security interest, he had constructive knowledge due to the filed financing statement.

19. (583,L1,51) (b) Hamilton took a purchase money security interest in the TV set which would be considered consumer goods in Fogel's possession. Consequently, Hamilton's security interest was perfected automatically upon attachment. Therefore, Hamilton can defeat Reliable because Hamilton's security interest was perfected prior to the time Reliable perfected its security interest by filing. Hamilton can also defeat Harp because Harp's judgment was subsequent to Hamilton's perfection. Normally Mobray, as a good faith purchaser for personal use, would defeat a prior perfected secured party who gained his/her perfection through automatic perfection by attachment. However, Hamilton engaged in a second method of perfection (filing a financing statement) prior to the sale of the TV set to Mobray, allowing Hamilton to defeat the good faith purchaser for personal use. Therefore, answers (a), (c), and (d) are incorrect.

20. (1182,L1,57) (a) Proceeds include whatever is received upon the sale of the collateral. The secured party, Thrush, has the ability to assert rights against the proceeds received by the debtor, Kelly, upon sale of the collateral. Thrush has a perfected security interest in the proceeds from the sale of the television sets because the security agreement states proceeds are covered. Therefore, Thrush is entitled to any payments

Haynes makes to Kelly on the note. Normally, access to the proceeds upon default by the debtor is an integral part of an inventory financing agreement. Haynes, as a purchaser in the ordinary course of business, takes free of Thrush's perfected security interest in inventory. Answers (b), (c), and (d) are incorrect because since Haynes is a buyer in the ordinary course of business, he will defeat the rights of the secured creditor, Thrush, even if he were aware of Thrush's security interest at the time of purchase. Therefore, Thrush will not be able to repossess the television set. Haynes would take subject to Thrush's security interest only when he knows that the sale of the inventory is in violation of some term in the security agreement.

21. (579,L1,22) (a) Electrical, as a secured creditor, may assert a reclamation claim against the trustee in bankruptcy for the testing machine. Answer (b) is incorrect because the secured party may enforce its perfected security interest and then proceed as a general creditor against the bankrupt's estate to the extent the collateral does not satisfy the debt. Electrical's perfected security interest does not constitute a voidable preference as stated in answer (c) since the simultaneous sale and creation of the security interest is considered a fair exchange. Answer (d) is incorrect because a secured party is not forced to make an exclusive choice of remedy but may proceed against the security until it is exhausted and may then proceed in the bankruptcy action as a general creditor for any deficiency.

F. Rights of Parties Upon Default

22. (1188,L1,55) (b) Upon default of a debtor, a secured party may sell the collateral in a private sale to a good faith purchaser. Once the collateral has been sold, the security interest under which the collateral was sold plus any subordinate security interests or liens will have no further claim to the collateral. Therefore, answer (a) is incorrect. Answer (c) is incorrect because a secured party may buy the collateral at a private sale provided the sale is conducted in a commercially reasonable manner. Answer (d) is incorrect because Bonn, the secured party, will take the proceeds subject to security interests which are senior to the interests that were discharged at the sale.

23. (1187,L1,44) (b) A good faith purchaser for value at a private sale will take the property free from any security interest or subordinate liens in the property, but remains

subject to security interests which are senior
to that being discharged at the sale. In this
case, Smith perfected his security interest
later than Gray and has a subordinate interest
in the property. Thus, Walsh takes the equipment free from this subordinate security interest. Answer (a) is incorrect because the
fact that Bean is current in his payments to
Smith would not affect Smith's interest in the
property. Answer (c) is incorrect because as
long as Walsh is a good faith purchaser for
value, it doesn't matter if the equipment is
sold at a public or private sale. Answer (d)
is incorrect because Smith is not a purchase
money secured creditor since the proceeds of
Smith's loan to Bean were not used to purchase
the equipment acting as collateral.

24. (1189,L1,55) (d) Under secured transactions law governed by the UCC, the secured
party has several rights if the debtor defaults. The secured party may take possession
of the collateral or retain possession if s/he
already has possession. The secured party may
sell the collateral and apply the proceeds
toward the debt, with certain restrictions.
Additionally, the secured party may reduce the
claim to judgment to collect it. Therefore,
answers (a), (b), and (c) are incorrect.

25. (585,L1,47) (b) A secured party cannot
retain the collateral if a purchase money
security interest has been taken in consumer
goods, and the consumer has paid 60% of the
purchase price before default. The secured
party must sell the collateral within 90 days
of obtaining possession or be held liable for
the tort of conversion. Since Foxx paid in
excess of 60% of the cash price, Dix will have
to sell the collateral in a commercially
reasonable manner, applying the proceeds to
any expenses incurred and the outstanding
balance. Answer (a) is incorrect because Dix
may sell the collateral at a private or public
sale as long as every aspect of the sale is
conducted in a commercially reasonable manner.
Answers (c) and (d) are incorrect because Dix
must sell the collateral as required under the
Uniform Commercial Code.

26. (585,L1,49) (a) When a debtor has fully
paid a creditor, and the financing statement
covers consumer goods, a termination statement
must be filed by the secured party within one
month after the debt has been paid. If the
debtor requests a termination statement in
writing, the creditor must file one no later
than ten days after the debt is paid. Therefore, Thrift must file a termination within
one month of Cole's final payment. Answers (b), (c), and (d) are incorrect because

in all cases where the collateral is consumer
goods, the secured party must file a termination statement whether or not the debtor makes
a written request or the financing statement
lapses.

May 1990 Answer

27. (590,L1,51) (b) Since Vista validly
perfected under the laws of the first state,
it has a four-month period in the second state
during which the perfection is still valid.
Therefore, answer (c) is incorrect. Answer (a) is incorrect because the filing of a
financing statement gives constructive notice,
and thus the lack of actual notice is not
relevant. Answer (d) is incorrect because
Vista's security interest was perfected by
filing and thus does not require possession to
have priority.

Answer Outline

Problem 1   Purchase Money Security Interest
in Consumer Goods; Equipment
(1183,L2a)

Part a.

Zeals will prevail over Despard
   Zeals' interest is purchase money security
    interest in consumer goods that is auto-
    matically perfected upon attachment
   Despard's interest is not protected until
    filed, which is subsequent to Zeals' per-
    fection
Filing is necessary to protect purchase money
 security interest in equipment
Despard as a purchase money lender has a ten-
 day grace period for filing
   Despard did not file for 30 days
Despard's interest was not perfected until
 filed
Apache will prevail since the interest was
 perfected before Despard's

Unofficial Answer

Problem 1   Purchase Money Security Interest
in Consumer Goods; Equipment
(1183,L2a)

Part a.

   •   Zeals has priority over Despard regarding the competing security interests of
the parties. Zeals is a purchase money
secured party involving the sale of consumer
goods. As such, the security interest is
enforceable against other creditors of the
buyer without the necessity of a filing.
Despard would also attempt to assert a
purchase money security interest in the goods,
but this is questionable at best since the
money advanced was obviously not used for the
purchase of the goods. Even if Despard
qualified as a purchase money secured party,
Despard was second in point of time. The fact
that it filed does not change the priority
since filing was not required to perfect the
interest in the consumer goods (the video
system).
   •   Apache has priority over Despard in
this instance. Although Despard was the first
to advance credit and qualified as a purchase
money lender, it was second in time to perfect
its security interest. The subject matter of
the sale was equipment and filing is required
to perfect Despard's security interest. The
purchase money lender has the benefit of a 10-

day grace period for filing. Despard's security interest was not perfected until it
filed, which was after the grace period and
five days after Apache's filing.

Answer Outline

Problem 2   Perfection of True Consignment;
Priority of Conflicting Security
Interests (581,L3)

a1.   A true consignment in a commercial sense
    implies an agency relationship
   Perfection of true consignment enables
    consignor, Walpole, to prevail against
    Petty's creditors
    Walpole must comply with applicable law
     providing for consignor's interest to
     be evidenced by posted sign, or Wal-
     pole must establish that Petty is gen-
     erally known by his creditors to be
     engaged in selling goods of others, or
     Walpole must comply with filing pro-
     vision of Article 9 of UCC
   Consignor must give written notification
    to Petty's creditors who have security
    interest in same type of goods
     But only if the creditors perfected
     their security interest before date
     of filing made by Walpole
   Notice must be received by creditors
    within five years before consignee
    receives possession of the goods
   Notification states consignor expects to
    deliver goods on consignment to the con-
    signee
     Describing the goods by item or type
a2.   Walpole will not prevail against Klinger
   Walpole was unable to perfect a true con-
    signment as outlined in a1.
   Article 2 of UCC provides that where
    goods are delivered under a consignment
    agreement for sale
     The goods are deemed to be on "sale or
     return" with respect to claims of
     consignee's creditors
      Walpole is subject to claims of
      Petty's creditors
b.   Conflicting security interests rank
   according to priority in time of filing
   or perfection
   Lebow will prevail over Dunbar with
    regard to the bolts it repossessed (65%
    of the invoice)
    Lebow's repossession of goods consti-
     tuted a perfection of security
     interest
      Security interest perfected before
      Dunbar's lien attaches has
      priority over the lien

Lebow's filing of the miscaptioned statement is ineffective to create any interests or rights in Lebow
Financing statement not relevant with
regard to priority time frame
Dunbar will prevail over Lebow with
regard to goods not repossessed by Lebow
Dunbar's levy and judicial lien occurs
prior in time to Lebow's filing of corrected financing statement
Applies to the remaining goods

Unofficial Answer

Problem 2   Perfection of True Consignment;
Priority of Conflicting Security
Interests (581,L3)

Part a.

1. In order to prevail against the creditors
of a party to whom goods have been consigned,
the consignor may do one of three things
according to the Uniform Commercial Code (section 2-326):
a. Comply with applicable state law providing for a consignor's interest to
be evidenced by a posted sign. Most
states do not have such statutes.
b. Establish that the person conducting
the business is generally known by his
creditors to be substantially engaged
in selling the goods of others. This
is either not the case or is difficult
to prove.
c. Comply with the filing provisions of
Article 9: Secured Transactions.
From a practical standpoint, this last
course of action appears to be the
most logical, if not the only, choice.
Article 9 (section 9-114) requires that a consignor comply with the general filing requirements of the Code (section 9-302) and also
give notice in writing to the creditors of the
consignee who have a perfected security interest covering the same type of goods. The
written notice must be given before the date
of filing by the consignor and received within
five years before the consignee takes possession of the goods. The notice must state that
the consignor expects to deliver goods on consignment to the consignee and must contain a
description of the goods.

2. No. Walpole will not prevail. Whether a
consignment is a "true" consignment (an agency
relationship) or is intended as a security interest, the Uniform Commercial Code requires
that notice be given to creditors of the consignee.
A consignment is governed by sections from
two articles of the Code: Article 2: Sales
and Article 9: Secured Transactions. Sec-

tion 2-326 treats a consignment as a "sale or
return" because "the goods are delivered primarily for resale." Section 2-326(3) provides
the following:

Where goods are delivered to a person
for sale and such person maintains a
place of business at which he deals in
goods of the kind involved, under a
name other than the name of the person
making delivery, then with respect to
claims of creditors of the person conducting the business, the goods are
deemed to be a sale or return. The
provisions of this subsection are applicable even though an agreement
purports to reserve title to the person making delivery until payment or
resale or uses such words as "on
consignment" or "on memorandum."

It is obvious from the facts, that Walpole's marketing arrangement is covered by the
above language. The Code further provides
that the creditors of the consignee will be
able to assert claims against goods sold on a
sale or return basis unless some form of
notice is given.

Part b.

Lebow will prevail to the extent of the 65
percent of the bolts of wool that it repossessed on August 11, 1980. Since Lebow obtained possession of 65 percent of the shipment prior to attachment or judgment by Dunbar, Lebow's security interest with respect to
those goods had been perfected as of August 11. The original erroneous filing is
invalid against the creditors of Fashion
Plate. Lebow's security interest was not
perfected by filing initially, and, therefore,
Lebow will not prevail over the rights of
Dunbar, a subsequent lien creditor of Fashion
Plate. The facts of the case indicate that
the security interest was not perfected by
filing until August 20, 1980. However, prior
to that time Dunbar levied against the goods
on August 13 and obtained a judgment against
Fashion Plate on August 18, 1980. Both dates
are prior to the August 20 filing by Lebow;
thus, the lien creditor would have priority
over Lebow's claim based exclusively on
perfection by filing. Perfection can also be
accomplished by possession, but if perfection
by either method precedes the time that the
lien creditor obtains rights against the
property, it prevails.

Answer Outline

Problem 3   Attachment; Perfection; Good Faith
             Purchaser of Consumer Goods
             (1184,L4a & b)

a. Yes. Attachment of security interest
    requires
        Valid security agreement
        Secured party gives value
        Debtor has rights in collateral
    Transaction involves purchase money
        security interest in consumer goods
        Automatic perfection by attachment
        occurs
b. Yes. Secured party with perfected secu-
    rity interest generally takes priority
        Exception in case of consumer goods
        Subsequent good faith purchaser takes
        free of prior perfected security
        interests if he purchases before
        financing statement is filed

Unofficial Answer

Problem 3   Attachment; Perfection; Good Faith
             Purchaser of Consumer Goods
             (1184,L4a & b)

    a. Yes. In order for a security interest
in collateral to attach, the following three
requirements must be met: 1. the collateral
is in the possession of the secured party pursuant to agreement, or the debtor has signed a
security agreement that contains a description
of the collateral; 2. value has been given by
the secured party; and 3. the debtor has
rights in the collateral.
    Zen, under the stated facts has fulfilled
all three requirements, thereby creating an
enforceable security interest that has
attached to the computer. Since the transaction involves a purchase money security
interest in consumer goods--that is, goods
used or bought primarily for personal, family,
or household purposes--it is not necessary for
the secured party to file a financing statement or take possession of the collateral in
order to perfect its interest. The security
interest is perfected when the three requirements set forth have been fulfilled.

b. Yes. Generally, a secured party with a
perfected security interest has priority over
all subsequent claims to the same collateral.
However, in the case of consumer goods, where
perfection is achieved solely by attachment, a
subsequent buyer will take free of such prior
perfected security interests if he buys
without knowledge of the security interest,
for value, for his own personal, family, or
household use and before a financing statement
is filed by the secured party. Since Ralph

has complied with those qualifications, he
will take the computer free of Zen's perfected
security interest.

Answer Outline

Problem 4   Purchase money security interest;
             priority of bankruptcy trustee,
             purchase money secured party in
             equipment and buyer in ordinary
             course of business (588,L4)

Purchase Money Security Interest
    Interest in personal property or fixtures
    Secures payment or performance
    Occurs when either:
    (1) Seller retains interest in item sold on
         credit, or
    (2) Creditor retains interest in item
         purchased with loaned funds
Priorities
    Safe has priority over trustee (i.e., lien
    creditor from date of filing petition)
        Generally, unperfected security interest
        is subordinate to person becoming lien
        creditor before the security interest is
        perfected
    Safe as a purchase money secured party in
    equipment has 10 day grace period for
    filing
    Safe filed within 10 day grace period
        Safe has priority over City
        A purchase money security interest in
        equipment, if perfected no later than
        the end of the 10 day grace period,
        prevails over a conflicting security
        interest
        Safe filed within 10 days of Lux's
        possession of the equipment
    Best has priority over Safe
        If both conflicting security interests
        require filing to be perfected, the
        first party to file has priority
        Best filed before Safe
    Dix has priority over Safe
        A buyer in the ordinary course of
        business takes free of prior perfected
        security interest
        Dix qualifies as a buyer in the ordinary
        course of business

Unofficial Answer

Problem 4   Purchase money security interest;
             priority of bankruptcy trustee,
             purchase money secured party in
             equipment and buyer in ordinary
             course of business (588,L4)

    A purchase money security interest is an
interest in personal property or fixtures that
secures payment or performance of an obligation and that is (1) taken or retained by the

seller of the collateral to secure all or part of its price, or (2) taken by a person who by making advances or incurring an obligation gives value to enable the debtor to acquire rights in or the use of collateral if such value is in fact so used.

Safe's security interest has priority over the rights of the trustee in bankruptcy. The UCC Article on Secured Transactions states that a lien creditor includes a trustee in bankruptcy from the date of the filing of the petition. Under the general rule, an unperfected security interest is subordinate to the rights of a person who becomes a lien creditor before the security interest is perfected. However, if the secured party files with respect to a purchase money security interest before or within 10 days after the debtor receives possession of the collateral, he takes priority over the rights of a lien creditor that arise between the time the security interest attaches and the time of filing. Under the facts of our case, Safe has a purchase money security interest in the equipment because the security interest was taken by Safe to secure the price. Therefore, because Safe filed a financing statement on May 14 (within 10 days after Lux received possession of the equipment), it has a priority security interest over the trustee in bankruptcy (lien creditor) whose claim arose between the time the security interest attached (May 5) and the time of filing (May 14).

Safe has a priority security interest in the equipment over City. A purchase money security interest in collateral other than inventory has priority over a conflicting security interest in the same collateral if the purchase money security interest is perfected at the time the debtor receives possession of the collateral or within 10 days thereafter. Because Safe has a purchase money security interest in the equipment that was perfected by filing a financing statement on May 14 (within 10 days after Lux received possession of the equipment on May 5), Safe has a priority security interest over City despite City's perfection of its security interest on May 12.

Best's security interest in the inventory has priority over Safe's security interest. In general, conflicting perfected security interests rank according to priority in time of filing or perfection. Priority dates from the time a filing is first made covering the collateral or the time the security interest is first perfected, whichever is earlier, provided that there is no period thereafter when there is neither a filing nor perfection. In this case, because both Best's and Safe's security interests were perfected by filing,

the first to file (Best) will have a priority security interest. The fact that Best filed a financing statement prior to making the loan will not affect Best's priority.

Safe will not have a priority security interest over Dix because Dix is a buyer in the ordinary course of business and will take free of Safe's perfected security interest. Dix is a buyer in the ordinary course of business because Dix acted in good faith when purchasing the machine parts in the regular course of Cam's business. The UCC Article on Secured Transactions states that a buyer in the ordinary course of business takes free of a security interest created by his seller even though the security interest is perfected and even though the buyer knows of its existence. Therefore, Dix will take the machine parts purchased from Cam's inventory on July 14, free from Safe's security interest which was perfected on July 12.

Answer Outline

Problem 5   Risk of Loss; Rights Under
            Entrusting of Possession of
            Goods; Attachment of Security
            Interests; Perfection of Security
            Interests (589,L5)

Correct, risk of loss remained with Xeon
    When agreement is silent and seller is
        merchant, risk passes to buyer when
        buyer receives goods
Incorrect, Mead did acquire rights in CPU
    Entrusting situation: merchant acquires
        power to transfer ownership and title
        Entruster (Xeon) must be rightful
            owner
        Merchant must deal in goods of like
            kind
        Buyer must be in ordinary course of
            business
Incorrect, Jensen's security interest
    attached and is enforceable
    Security interest in collateral attaches
        if:
        Secured party has security agreement,
            signed by debtor containing des-
            cription of collateral
            May be oral if collateral is in
                secured parties possession
        Secured party gave value
        Debtor has rights in collateral
Incorrect, Jensen does not have superior
    interest to bank
    Purchase money security interest is not
        in consumer goods—no automatic perfec-
        tion
    Jensen must file to perfect
    Bank has superior interest because it
        perfected; Jensen did not

Unofficial Answer

Problem 5   Risk of Loss; Rights under Entrusting of Possession of Goods;
Attachment of Security Interests;
Perfection of Security Interests
(589,L5)

The assertion that as of March 3, 1989 the risk of loss on the disk drive remained with Xeon is correct. Under the UCC Sales Article, if the agreement between the parties is otherwise silent, risk of loss passes to the buyer on the buyer's receipt of the goods if the seller is a merchant. Under the facts, Xeon is a merchant because it sells computer systems. Therefore, the risk of loss remained with Xeon because the disk drive was never received by Pine.

The assertion that Meed acquired no rights in the CPU as a result of the March 18, 1989 transaction is incorrect. Under the UCC Sales Article, any entrusting of possession of goods to a merchant who deals in goods of that kind gives the merchant power to transfer all rights of the entruster to the buyer in the ordinary course of business. Entrusting includes any delivery and any acquiescence in retention of possession regardless of any condition expressed between the parties to the delivery or acquiescence, and regardless of whether the possessor's disposition of the goods have been such as to be larcenous under the criminal law. For the merchant to acquire the power to transfer ownership and title, the entruster must be the rightful owner. Under the facts of this case, Pine had title at the time the CPU was returned to Xeon for repairs and this constituted an entrusting that gave Xeon the power to transfer all of Pine's rights in the CPU to Meed.

The assertion that Jensen's security interest in the word processors never attached and therefore Jensen's security interest is not enforceable against Pine with respect to the word processors is incorrect. A security interest in collateral will attach if: the collateral is in the possession of the secured party under an agreement, or the debtor has signed a security agreement that contains a description of the collateral; the secured party has given value; and the debtor has rights in the collateral. Based on the facts, Jensen's security interest attached on April 12, 1989, when Jensen sold and Pine received the word processors and Jensen received a security agreement executed by Pine that described the word processors. On attachment, Jensen's security interest became enforceable against Pine.

The assertion that Jensen has a superior security interest to Pine's bank is incorrect.

Although Jensen has a purchase money security interest to the extent the security interest is taken by Jensen to secure the purchase price, Jensen's security interest will not be perfected by attachment alone. Jensen must file a financing statement to perfect its security interest because the collateral involved is goods used for business purposes and not consumer goods. Therefore, Jensen has an unperfected security interest in the word processors and the bank obtained a superior security interest by perfecting.

Multiple Choice Questions (1-23)

1. Which of the following statements is correct concerning the voluntary filing of a petition in bankruptcy?
    a. The debtor must be insolvent.
    b. The petition may be filed by husband and wife jointly.
    c. If the debtor has 12 or more creditors, the debtor's unsecured claims must total at least $5,000.
    d. If the debtor has fewer than 12 creditors, the debtor's unsecured claims must total at least $5,000.

2. Filing a valid petition in bankruptcy acts as an automatic stay of actions to

	Garnish the debtor's wages	Collect alimony from the debtor
a.	Yes	Yes
b.	Yes	No
c.	No	Yes
d.	No	No

3. Wilk owes a total of $25,000 to eight unsecured creditors and one fully secured creditor. Rusk is one of the unsecured creditors and is owed $7,000. Rusk has filed a petition against Wilk under the liquidation provisions of the Bankruptcy Code. Wilk has been unable to pay Wilk's debts as they become due and Wilk's liabilities exceed Wilk's assets. Wilk has filed the papers that are required to oppose the bankruptcy petition. Which of the following statements is correct?
    a. The petition will be granted because Wilk is unable to pay Wilk's debts as they become due.
    b. The petition will be granted because Wilk's liabilities exceed Wilk's assets.
    c. The petition will be dismissed because three unsecured creditors must join in the filing of the petition.
    d. The petition will be dismissed because the secured creditor failed to join in the filing of the petition.

4. An involuntary petition in bankruptcy
    a. Will be denied if a majority of creditors in amount and in number have agreed to a common law composition agreement.
    b. Can be filed by creditors only once in a seven-year period.
    c. May be successfully opposed by the debtor by proof that the debtor is solvent in the bankruptcy sense.

    d. If not contested will result in the entry of an order for relief by the bankruptcy judge.

5. The Bankruptcy Code provides that a debtor is entitled to claim as exempt property the right to receive

	Social security benefits	Disability benefits
a.	No	No
b.	Yes	No
c.	Yes	Yes
d.	No	Yes

6. The filing of an involuntary petition in bankruptcy
    a. Allows creditors to continue their collection actions against the debtor while the bankruptcy action is pending.
    b. Terminates liens associated with exempt property.
    c. Stops the enforcement of a judgment lien against property in the bankruptcy estate.
    d. Terminates all security interests in property in the bankruptcy estate.

7. Which of the following assets would be included in a debtor's bankruptcy estate in a liquidation proceeding?
    a. Proceeds from a life insurance policy received 90 days after the petition was filed.
    b. An inheritance received 270 days after the petition was filed.
    c. Property from a divorce settlement received 365 days after the petition was filed.
    d. Wages earned by the debtor after the petition was filed.

8. Which of the following is correct with respect to an involuntary bankruptcy proceeding under the liquidation provisions of the Bankruptcy Code?
    a. It may be commenced against any debtor who is insolvent.
    b. The debtor may regain possession of property in the possession of an interim trustee if the debtor files a bond.
    c. The petitioners must automatically file a bond to indemnify the debtor for any loss caused by the filing of the petition.
    d. A trustee must be elected by the creditors immediately after the court orders relief against the debtor.

9.   Fox, a sole proprietor, has been involuntarily petitioned into bankruptcy under the
liquidation provisions of the Bankruptcy Code.
Sax, CPA, has been appointed trustee of the
debtor's estate. If Sax also wishes to act as
the tax return preparer for the estate, which
of the following statements is correct?

    a.   Sax may employ himself to prepare
tax returns if authorized by the
court and may receive a separate fee
for services rendered in each capacity.

    b.   Sax is prohibited from serving as
both trustee and preparer under any
circumstances since serving in that
dual capacity would be a conflict of
interest.

    c.   Although Sax may serve as both trus-
tee and preparer, he is entitled to
receive a fee only for the services
rendered as a preparer.

    d.   Although Sax may serve as both trus-
tee and preparer, his fee for services rendered in each capacity will
be determined solely by the size of
the estate.

10.   Knox operates an electronics store as a
sole proprietor. On April 5, 1988, Knox was
involuntarily petitioned into bankruptcy under
the liquidation provisions of the Bankruptcy
Code. On April 20, a trustee in bankruptcy
was appointed and an order for relief was
entered. Knox's non-exempt property has been
converted to cash, which is available to
satisfy the following claims and expenses as
may be appropriate:

Claims and Expenses

Claim by Dart Corp. (one of Knox's
  suppliers) for computers ordered
  on April 6, 1988 and delivered on
  credit to Knox on April 10, 1988. $20,000
Fee earned by the bankruptcy
  trustee. $15,000
Claim by Boyd for a deposit given
  to Knox on April 1, 1988, for a
  computer Boyd purchased for personal
  use but that had not yet been
  received by Boyd. $1,500
Claim by Noll Co. for the delivery
  of stereos to Knox on credit. The
  stereos were delivered on March 4, 1988,
  and a financing statement was properly
  filed on March 5, 1988. These stereos
  were sold by the trustee with Noll's
  consent for $7,500, their fair market
  value. $5,000
Fees earned by the attorneys for the
  bankruptcy estate. $10,000
Claims by unsecured general
  creditors. $1,000

    The cash available for distribution
includes the proceeds from the sale of the

stereos. If the trustee in bankruptcy wishes
to avoid Noll's March 4 transaction with Knox
as a preferential transfer, the trustee will

    a.   Lose, because the transfer was in
fact a substantially contemporaneous
exchange for new value given.

    b.   Lose, because there is <u>no</u> evidence
that Knox was insolvent on March 4.

    c.   Prevail, because the transfer
occurred within 90 days of the
filing of the bankruptcy petition.

    d.   Prevail, because the financing
statement was <u>not</u> filed on the day
of delivery.

11.   One of the elements necessary to establish that a preferential transfer has been
made under the Bankruptcy Code by the debtor
to a creditor is that the

    a.   Debtor was insolvent at the time of
the transfer.

    b.   Creditor was an insider and the
transfer occurred within 90 days of
the filing of the bankruptcy petition.

    c.   Transfer was in fact a contemporan-
eous exchange for new value given to
the debtor.

    d.   Transfer was made by the debtor with
actual intent to hinder, delay, or
defraud other creditors.

12.   The federal bankruptcy act contains
several important terms. One such term is
"insider." The term is used in connection
with preferences and preferential transfers.
Which among the following is not an "insider"?

    a.   A secured creditor having a security
interest in at least 25% or more of
the debtor's property.

    b.   A partnership in which the debtor is
a general partner.

    c.   A corporation of which the debtor is
a director.

    d.   A close blood relative of the
debtor.

13.   Which of the following unsecured debts of
$500 each would have the highest relative
priority in the distribution of a bankruptcy
estate in a liquidation proceeding?

    a.   Tax claims of state and municipal
governmental units.

    b.   Liabilities to employee benefit
plans arising from services rendered
during the month preceding the
filing of the petition.

    c.   Claims owed to customers who gave
deposits for the purchase of
undelivered consumer goods.

    d.   Wages earned by employees during the
month preceding the filing of the
petition.

Item 14 is based on the following information:

On July 15, 1988, White, a sole proprietor, was involuntarily petitioned into bankruptcy under the liquidation provisions of the Bankruptcy Code. White's non-exempt property has been converted to $13,000 cash, which is available to satisfy the following claims:

Unsecured claim for 1986
  state income tax $10,000
Fee owed to Best & Co., CPA's,
  for services rendered from
  April 1, 1988, through June 30,
  1988 $6,000
Unsecured claim by Stieb for wages
  earned as an employee of White
  during March 1988 $3,000

There are no other claims.

14. What is the maximum amount that will be distributed to Stieb?
    a. $0
    b. $1,000
    c. $2,000
    d. $3,000

Items 15 through 17 are based on the following information:

Knox operates an electronics store as a sole proprietor. On April 5, 1988, Knox was involuntarily petitioned into bankruptcy under the liquidation provisions of the Bankruptcy Code. On April 20, a trustee in bankruptcy was appointed and an order for relief was entered. Knox's non-exempt property has been converted to cash, which is available to satisfy the following claims and expenses as may be appropriate:

Claims and Expenses
Claim by Dart Corp. (one of Knox's
  suppliers) for computers ordered
  on April 6, 1988 and delivered on
  credit to Knox on April 10, 1988. $20,000
Fee earned by the bankruptcy
  trustee. $15,000
Claim by Boyd for a deposit given
  to Knox on April 1, 1988, for a
  computer Boyd purchased for personal
  use but that had not yet been
  received by Boyd. $1,500
Claim by Noll Co. for the delivery
  of stereos to Knox on credit. The
  stereos were delivered on March 4, 1988,
  and a financing statement was properly
  filed on March 5, 1988. These stereos
  were sold by the trustee with Noll's
  consent for $7,500, their fair market
  value. $5,000

Fees earned by the attorneys for the
  bankruptcy estate. $10,000
Claims by unsecured general
  creditors. $1,000

The cash available for distribution includes the proceeds from the sale of the stereos.

15. What amount will be distributed to the trustee as a fee if the cash available for distribution is $15,000?
    a. $ 6,000
    b. $ 9,000
    c. $10,000
    d. $15,000

16. What amount will be distributed to Boyd if the cash available for distribution is $50,800?
    a. $ 480
    b. $ 800
    c. $ 900
    d. $1,500

17. What amount will be distributed to Dart if the cash available for distribution is $41,000?
    a. $10,100
    b. $11,000
    c. $16,000
    d. $20,000

18. Eagle Corp. is a general creditor of Dodd. Dodd filed a petition in bankruptcy under the liquidation provisions of the Bankruptcy Code. Eagle wishes to have the bankruptcy court either deny Dodd a general discharge or not have its debt discharged. The discharge will be granted and it will include Eagle's debt even if
    a.   Dodd filed for and received a previous discharge in bankruptcy under the liquidation provisions within five years of the filing of the present petition.
    b.   Eagle's debt is unscheduled.
    c.   Eagle was a secured creditor <u>not</u> fully satisfied from the proceeds obtained in disposition of the collateral.
    d.   Dodd unjustifiably failed to preserve the records from which Dodd's financial condition might be ascertained.

19. Rolf, an individual, filed a voluntary petition in bankruptcy. A general discharge in bankruptcy will be denied if Rolf
    a.   Negligently made preferential transfers to certain creditors within 90 days of filing the petition.

b.   Unjustifiably failed to preserve
Rolf's books and records.

c.   Filed a fraudulent federal income
tax return two years prior to filing
the petition.

d.   Obtained a loan by using financial
statements that Rolf knew were
false.

20.   In general, which of the following debts
will be discharged under the voluntary
liquidation provisions of the Bankruptcy Code?

a.   Debts incurred after the order for
relief but before the debtor
receives a discharge in bankruptcy.

b.   Income taxes due as the result of
filing a fraudulent return seven
years prior to the filing of the
bankruptcy petition.

c.   A debt arising before the filing of
the bankruptcy petition due to the
debtor's negligence.

d.   Alimony payments owed to the
debtor's spouse under a separation
agreement entered into prior to the
filing of the bankruptcy question.

21.   On May 5, 1988, Bold obtained a $90,000
judgment in a malpractice action against Aker,
a physician.   On June 2, 1988, Aker obtained a
$75,000 loan from Tint Finance Co. by
knowingly making certain false representations
to Tint.   On July 7, 1988, Aker filed a
voluntary petition in bankruptcy under the
liquidation provisions of the Bankruptcy
Code.   Both Bold and Tint filed claims in
Aker's bankruptcy proceeding.   Assets in
Aker's bankruptcy estate are exempt.
Tint's claim

a.   Will be excepted from Aker's
discharge in bankruptcy.

b.   Will cause Aker to be denied a
discharge in bankruptcy.

c.   Will be set aside as a preference.

d.   Will be discharged in Aker's
bankruptcy proceeding.

22.   As an alternative to bankruptcy
liquidation, a business may reorganize under
Chapter 11 of the Bankruptcy Code.   Such a
reorganization

a.   Requires the appointment of a
trustee to administer the debtor
organization.

b.   May be commenced by filing either a
voluntary or involuntary petition.

c.   Never requires the appointment of a
creditors' committee.

d.   May not be confirmed unless all
creditors accept the plan.

23.   Which of the following statements is
correct with respect to the reorganization
provisions of the Bankruptcy Code?

a.   The commencement of a proceeding may
be voluntary or involuntary.

b.   A partnership is not eligible to be
a debtor.

c.   In all cases a trustee must be
appointed.

d.   The debtor must be insolvent if the
bankruptcy petition was filed
voluntarily.

Problems

Problem 1   (1187,L3)

(15 to 20 minutes)

On July 1, 1986, Mix was petitioned by Able into bankruptcy under the liquidation provisions of the Bankruptcy Code. Able and Baker are unsecured creditors of Mix, owed $20,000 and $40,000 respectively. Mix also owes Carr $80,000, secured by a valid perfected security interest in bankruptcy on Mix's machinery, valued at $20,000. Mix has no other debts, except for 1986 federal income taxes.

Shortly after the filing of the petition Lang was appointed trustee in Mix's bankruptcy. In Lang's capacity as trustee, Lang:

• Engaged Ring & Co., CPAs, as the accountants for the bankruptcy estate.
• Included as part of the bankruptcy estate, an inheritance that Mix became entitled to receive on December 15, 1986 and that Mix actually received on January 15, 1987.

Lang has sold the property in the estate (including the sale of Mix's machinery for $20,000, which Carr consented to) and now the sole asset of the estate is $60,000 cash. Lang wishes to distribute the $60,000 so as to satisfy the following claims and expenses of the estate:

• Unsecured claim for 1986 federal income taxes	$ 6,000
• Carr's claim	80,000
• Able's and Baker's claims	60,000
• Expenses necessary to maintain and sell the unsecured property of the estate	1,000
• Ring's fee for services rendered	3,000

There are no other claims.

Required:

Answer the following, setting forth reasons for any conclusions stated.
a. Under the facts, were the requirements necessary for the filing of a valid petition in bankruptcy met? Discuss.
b. Discuss whether Lang's actions in engaging Ring and including the inheritance in the bankruptcy estate were proper.
c. Indicate the order in which the $60,000 should be distributed to satisfy the claims and expenses of the bankruptcy estate, assuming all necessary court approvals have been obtained.

Problem 2   (585,L5)

(15 to 20 minutes)

On July 1, Sam Baker, a sole proprietor operating a drugstore, was involuntarily petitioned into bankruptcy by his creditors. At that time, and for at least 60 days prior thereto, Baker was unable to pay his current obligations and also had a negative net worth. Prior to the filing of the petition Baker made the following transfers:

• May 17--Paid Nix, an unsecured creditor, the full $7,500 outstanding on a loan obtained from Nix on April 10.
• June 6--Gave Mary Wax a mortgage on his home for a loan which Wax made to Baker on June 4 which they intended to be a secured loan.
• June 16--Paid the electric bill for the month of May which was incurred in Baker's business. The bill was received by Baker on June 4 and had a June 18 due date.

At the time the petition was filed, Baker owned a rental warehouse and was involved in a divorce proceeding. The trustee in bankruptcy has informed Baker that the debtor's (Baker's) estate will include the following nonexempt property:

• Rents received from July through November 1 on the warehouse.
• Property received on October 10 as a result of the Bakers' final divorce decree.

Required:

Answer the following, setting forth reasons for any conclusions stated.
In separate paragraphs, discuss whether the trustee in bankruptcy can properly avoid or set aside the three transfers made by Baker? Was the trustee correct by including in the debtor's estate rents on the warehouse and the property received as a result of the final divorce decree?

Problem 3   (589,L2)

(15 to 20 minutes)

On March 23, 1989, Tine, a sole proprietor, was involuntarily petitioned into bankruptcy under the liquidation provisions of the Bankruptcy Code. The petition was filed by Lux, Squire, and Rusk, who were creditors of Tine with unsecured claims of $3,000, $4,000, and $2,000, respectively. Tine also has 10 other unsecured creditors, three partially secured creditors, and two fully secured

creditors, none of whom joined in the filing
of the bankruptcy petition. For the six-month
period before the filing of the bankruptcy
petition, Tine had been unable to pay current
obligations as they became due. At the time
the petition was filed, Tine had a negative
net worth.

Before March 23, 1989, Tine entered into
the following transactions:

- On December 29, 1988, Tine borrowed
  $250,000 from Safe Finance. On
  January 31, 1989, after learning of
  Tine's financial problems, Safe
  requested that Tine execute a mortgage
  on Tine's residence naming Safe as
  mortgagee. On January 31, 1989, Tine
  executed the mortgage and delivered it
  to Safe and it was recorded that same
  day. The residence had a fair market
  value of $300,000 at all times.
- On May 5, 1988, Rich Bank loaned Tine
  $50,000 based on Tine's personal
  financial statements. Tine knew the
  financial statements submitted to Rich
  substantially overstated Tine's net
  worth because of misrepresentations
  that were difficult to detect.

Required:

Answer the following, setting forth
reasons for any conclusions stated.

a. Discuss whether the requirements
necessary for the commencement of an
involuntary bankruptcy proceeding were met.

b. Assuming that the requirements
necessary for the commencement of an
involuntary bankruptcy were met, discuss the
following:

1. What action may the court take
regarding the transactions between Tine and
Safe?

2. What action may the court take
regarding the transaction between Tine and
Rich if Rich challenges the discharge of its
debt?

Multiple Choice Answers

1. b	6. c	11. a	16. b	20. c
2. b	7. a	12. a	17. b	21. a
3. a	8. b	13. d	18. c	22. b
4. d	9. a	14. b	19. b	23. a
5. c	10. a	15. a		

Multiple Choice Answer Explanations

C. Voluntary Bankruptcy Petitions

1. (1189,L1,24) (b) Voluntary bankruptcy petition is a formal request by the debtor for an order of relief. This voluntary bankruptcy petition may be filed jointly by a husband and a wife. Answer (a) is incorrect because the debtor in a voluntary bankruptcy petition need not be insolvent but needs to state that s/he has debts. Answers (c) and (d) are incorrect because there is no requirement as to the minimum amount of the debtor's liabilities in a voluntary proceeding.

2. (1189,L1,25) (b) When a valid petition in bankruptcy is filed, it acts as an automatic stay which stops the collection of most debts and the enforcement of most legal proceedings against the debtor's estate. An automatic stay is valid against the garnishment of the debtor's wages. However, the automatic stay is not effective to prevent the collection of alimony. Therefore, answers (a), (c), and (d) are incorrect.

D. Involuntary Bankruptcy Petitions

3. (1188,L1,22) (a) Under an involuntary bankruptcy petition, if there are fewer than twelve creditors, a single creditor may file the petition as long as his/her claim is $5,000 in excess of any security s/he may hold. If the involuntary petition in bankruptcy is not contested, it will automatically result in the entry of an order for relief by the bankruptcy court. However, if the petition is contested, the creditor(s) are required to prove either that the debtor is not paying his/her debts as they mature, or that during the 120 days preceding the filing of a petition, a custodian took possession of the debtor's property. In this situation, there are less than twelve creditors which enables Rusk, as an unsecured creditor owed more than $5,000, to file a bankruptcy petition against Wilk. Even though Wilk has contested this bankruptcy petition, it will be granted since Rusk can prove Wilk is unable to pay Wilk's debts as they mature. Answer (b) is incorrect because the petition will not be granted based on the fact that Wilk is insolvent in the "bankruptcy sense" (liabilities exceed

assets). The creditor must prove that the debtor is insolvent in the equity sense (unable to pay his/her debts as they become due). Answer (c) is incorrect because only when there are 12 or more creditors is it necessary for at least 3 creditors (whose claims aggregate at least $5,000 over any security held by the creditors) to sign the petition. Answer (d) is incorrect because there is no requirement that a secured creditor join in the filing of a petition.

4. (583,L1,22) (d) An involuntary petition in bankruptcy, if not contested, will automatically result in the entry of an order for relief by the bankruptcy court. Only if the petition is contested will the creditor(s) be required to prove either that the debtor is not paying his/her debts as they mature, or that during the 120 days preceding the filing of a petition, a custodian was appointed or took possession of the debtor's property. Answer (a) is incorrect because the presence of a composition agreement will not cause denial of an involuntary petition. In many cases a creditor who is left out of such a composition agreement may wish to file an involuntary petition in order to protect his/her interest before the debtor uses a major portion of his/her assets in settling the debts owed to only the creditors involved in the composition agreement. Answer (b) is incorrect because a petition may be filed only once in a six year period, not a seven year period. Answer (c) is incorrect because a debtor need only prove that s/he is solvent in the equity sense (i.e., that s/he is paying his/her debts as they mature) and that a custodian was not appointed or did not take possession of the debtor's property within 120 days before the filing of the petition. The debtor need not prove that his/her assets exceed his/her liabilities (solvency in the bankruptcy sense).

E. Bankruptcy Proceedings

5. (1188,L1,28) (c) Under the Bankruptcy Code, the debtor has the right to receive any of the following payments as exempt property: (1) a social security benefit, unemployment compensation or other local public assistance benefit, (2) a veteran's benefit, (3) a disability, illness or unemployment benefits, (4) alimony, support or separate maintenance to the extent reasonably necessary for the support of the debtor and any dependents of the debtor, and (5) a payment under a stock bonus, pension, profit sharing, annuity or similar plan or contract on account of illness, disability, death, age or length of service to the extent reasonably necessary for

the support of the debtor and any dependents of the debtor. Thus, answers (a), (b), and (d) are all incorrect.

6. (1189,L1,23) (c) The filing of an involuntary petition in bankruptcy stops the enforcement of most collections of debts and legal proceedings against the debtor's estate. Thus, the enforcement of judgment liens against property in the bankruptcy estate would be stopped by the filing of the involuntary petition. Answer (a) is incorrect because the filing stays such collection actions so that the court can see that an orderly disposition of the debts is accomplished under bankruptcy law. Answer (b) is incorrect because liens are still enforceable against exempt property. Answer (d) is incorrect because security interests in property will still be enforced despite a bankruptcy. When distributing the assets of a debtor's estate, secured creditors have first priority to the property acting as their collateral.

7. (1189,L1,27) (a) The debtor's bankruptcy estate includes property owned by the debtor when the bankruptcy petition is filed. It also includes property owed to the debtor as of the filing as well as income from property owned by the debtor. Additionally, property received by the debtor within 180 days after the petition is filed is also part of the estate if it is received by inheritance, bequest, or devise, or from life insurance, a divorce decree, or a property settlement with one's spouse. Answers (b) and (c) are incorrect because an inheritance and property from a divorce settlement must be received within 180 days after the filing of the petition to be part of the estate. Answer (d) is incorrect because debts other than those specified above are not part of the estate if received after the filing.

8. (587,L1,32) (b) The debtor may regain possession of property in the possession of an interim trustee if the debtor files the bond requested by the court. Answer (a) is incorrect because involuntary bankruptcy proceedings cannot be commenced against all debtors. Farmers, charitable organizations, railroads, banks, and insurance companies are examples of debtors that are exempt from involuntary bankruptcy proceedings even if they are insolvent. Answer (c) is incorrect because the Bankruptcy Code does not require that petitioners file a bond to indemnify the debtors for any loss caused by the filing of the petition. However, the court may require the petitioners to file such a bond to deter

the filing of frivolous petitions. Answer (d) is incorrect because after an order of relief is granted, the court appoints an interim trustee. A trustee may be elected by creditors at the first creditors' meeting but failure to elect a trustee results in the interim trustee continuing in office. The creditors are not required to elect a trustee in order for the bankruptcy proceeding to be completed.

9. (1185,L1,27) (a) A trustee in bankruptcy has the power to employ court approved professionals, such as accountants and attorneys, to handle estate matters which require professional expertise. These professionals have the right to reimbursement for services rendered. A trustee is not deemed to have the appropriate expertise required to prepare tax returns; thus, a trustee may employ a CPA to perform this function. Sax, as trustee, has the power to employ himself to prepare tax returns if authorized by the court and may receive a separate fee for services rendered. Answer (b) is incorrect because Sax may serve as both trustee and preparer if authorized to do so by the court. Answer (c) is incorrect because Sax has the right to receive fees for services rendered as both a trustee and a preparer. Answer (d) is incorrect because the fee for services rendered in each capacity is determined on the basis of the value of the services rendered, not solely the size of the estate.

E.6.f.(3) Preferential Transfers

10. (588,L1,31) (a) Under the Bankruptcy Code, a trustee has the power to set aside preferential transfers made by the debtor to creditors. Preferential transfers are those made for antecedent debts which enable the creditor to receive more than s/he would have otherwise received under the liquidation proceedings. One exception to the trustee's power to avoid preferential transfers is when a security interest is given by the debtor to acquire property that is perfected within 10 days after such security interest attaches. This is called an enabling loan. Consequently, Noll's transaction with Knox qualifies as an enabling loan and cannot be set aside by the trustee. Answer (b) is incorrect because the Bankruptcy Act presumes that the debtor is insolvent during the 90 days prior to the date the petition was filed. Thus, on March 4 Knox would have been presumed to be insolvent and the trustee would not have to provide evidence of insolvency. Answer (c) is incorrect because not all transfers occurring within 90 days of the filing of the bankruptcy petition are preferential transfers. For example,

transfers which involve contemporaneous exchange for new value given are not preferential transfers regardless of when they occur. Answer (d) is incorrect because the financing statement need not be filed on the day of delivery but must be filed within 10 days after the security interest attaches in order to qualify as an enabling loan and not be set aside as a preference. In this case, Noll filed within the 10-day period (the day after delivery) and, thus, the transaction qualifies as an exception to the trustee's power to avoid preferential transfers.

11. (587,L1,34) (a) Under the Bankruptcy Act, one of the elements which must be established in proving that a preferential transfer was made is that the debtor was insolvent at the time of the transfer. The Bankruptcy Act presumes that the debtor is insolvent during the 90 days prior to the date the petition was filed. Answer (b) is incorrect because a preferential transfer can be made to a general creditor, as well as an inside creditor. If the transfer is made to a creditor who is an insider, the transfer may be voided by the trustee if it occurred within 12 months prior to the filing of the petition. Answer (c) is incorrect because one of the elements which must be present to prove that a preferential transfer has been made is that the transfer involved an antecedent debt. Since the transfer described in answer (c) is a contemporaneous exchange for new value given, no antecedent debt was involved and, therefore, a preference is not present. Answer (d) is incorrect because there is no need to prove that the debtor actually intended to hinder, delay, or defraud other creditors in order to prove that a preferential transfer occurred. However, the trustee must prove that the transfer allowed the creditor to receive more than s/he would have under a Chapter 7 liquidation proceeding.

12. (580,L1,3) (a) Answer (a) is correct because a secured creditor is not an "insider" for the purposes of a preferential transfer. However, a partner is an insider with regard to the partnership, a director is an insider concerning the corporation, and a close relative is an insider to the debtor.

F. Claims

13. (1189,L1,28) (d) The Bankruptcy Reform Act establishes the priorities for the satisfaction of claims against the debtor in a bankruptcy proceeding. Of those claims listed in this question, the one that has the highest priority would be the employees' wages since they were earned within three months before

the filing of the petition in bankruptcy and are for less than the $2,000 maximum allowed per employee. Answer (a) is incorrect because taxes owed to the federal, state, or local government involve the next to last priority (i.e., just above unsecured creditors). Answer (b) is incorrect because contributions to employee benefits plans within the prior 180 days receive a priority after the employees' wages. This priority has a maximum limit of $2,000 per employee reduced by the amount received under the wages priority. Answer (c) is incorrect because consumer deposits for undelivered goods or services have a lower priority than both the wages and the contributions to employee benefit plans.

14. (1188,L1,24) (b) The Bankruptcy Reform Act establishes the priority for the satisfaction of claims against the debtor in an involuntary bankruptcy proceeding under Chapter 7. Of the claims listed in this fact situation, the unpaid 1986 taxes have the highest priority (6th in the overall ranking). The fees owed to Best & Co., CPAs and the wages owed to Stieb share the lowest priority. Since unsecured claims are paid at each level of priority before the claims at any lower level are paid, $10,000 will go toward the satisfaction of the 1986 unpaid taxes. The remaining $3,000 will be pro rated among the claims at the lowest level. Stieb will therefore receive $1,000 [($3,000/$9,000) x $3,000] and Best & Co. will receive $2,000 [($6,000/$9,000) x $3,000]. Answers (a), (c), and (d) are incorrect.

15. (588,L1,28) (a) When distributing the assets of a debtor's estate, secured creditors have first priority to the property acting as their collateral. Second priority in the distribution is administrative costs which include the trustee fee and the attorneys' fees. All claims of one class are paid in full before the next class receives anything. If the assets are insufficient to pay all claims of a given class, the claimants share pro rata. In this case, the first $5,000 of the remaining assets would be paid to Noll Co. since it is the only secured creditor. Since the remaining $10,000 ($15,000 - $5,000) is insufficient to cover all of the administrative costs of the bankruptcy ($15,000 owed to trustee and $10,000 owed to attorneys), a pro rata share will be distributed to the trustee and attorneys. The trustee will receive 60% of the remaining assets since s/he is owed 60% of the total administrative fees [$15,000/($10,000 + $15,000) = 60%]. Therefore, the trustee will receive 60% of $10,000 or $6,000. Thus, answers (b), (c) and (d) are incorrect.

16. (588,L1,29) (b) When distributing the assets of the debtor's estate, the trustee must follow priorities prescribed by the Bankruptcy Reform Act of 1978. In this case the first $5,000 of the remaining assets would be paid to Noll Co. since secured creditors have first priority concerning the property acting as their collateral. The next $25,000 would be paid to the trustee ($15,000) and attorneys ($10,000) because administrative costs are first priority among unsecured creditors. Next, $20,000 of the remaining $20,800 ($50,800 - $5,000 - $25,000) would be distributed to claims arising in the ordinary course of the debtor's business after the involuntary bankruptcy petition is filed but before the order for relief is entered. Since Dart Corp. is the only remaining creditor which falls into this category, it will be paid the full $20,000 owed it, leaving $800 ($20,800 - $20,000). Of the remaining creditors, Boyd is given a higher priority since consumers' deposits for undelivered goods or services (subject to a limit of $900) is given a higher priority than general, unsecured creditors. Thus, Boyd will receive the remaining $800. Therefore, answers (a), (c), and (d) are incorrect.

17. (588,L1,30) (b) When distributing the assets of the debtor's estate, the trustee must follow the statutorily prescribed priorities. Thus, in this case, the first $5,000 of the remaining assets would be paid to Noll Co. since it is the only secured creditor. The next $25,000 would be paid to cover bankruptcy administration expenses ($15,000 to trustee + $10,000 to attorneys). Finally, the remaining $11,000 ($41,000 - 5,000 - 25,000) would be distributed to claims arising in the ordinary course of the debtor's business after the involuntary bankruptcy petition is filed but prior to the appointment of a trustee and the issuance of the order for relief. Since Dart Corp. is the only creditor that fits in this category and qualifies as an "involuntary gap" creditor, it will receive the remaining $11,000. Therefore, answers (a), (c), and (d) are incorrect.

G. Discharge of a Bankrupt

18. (1189,L1,26) (c) The fact that the debt of a secured party was not fully satisfied from the proceeds obtained from the disposition of the collateral will not result in a denial of a general discharge, nor will the remaining portion of the debt be nondischargeable. In such situations the secured party has the same priority as a general unsecured creditor concerning the unpaid portion of the debt. Answer (a) is incorrect because gener-

ally, a debtor may not get a discharge of debts if s/he has been discharged in bankruptcy within the last six years. Answer (b) is incorrect because debts that are unscheduled are not discharged in a bankruptcy proceeding. Answer (d) is incorrect because a general discharge of all debts in the bankruptcy is denied if the debtor has unjustifiably failed to preserve records and financial information to aid in the bankruptcy proceedings.

19. (1189,L1,22) (b) Under bankruptcy law, there are several acts that bar a general discharge of the debtor's debts in bankruptcy. One of these acts occurs when the debtor unjustifiably fails to preserve his/her books or records. Answer (a) is incorrect because although the trustee may set aside certain preferential transfers, these do not bar a general discharge in bankruptcy. Answer (c) is incorrect because committing fraud such as on a tax return results in that debt not being discharged in bankruptcy; however, it does not result in a denial of a discharge of the other debts. Answer (d) is incorrect because obtaining a loan by use of fraud results in only that debt not being discharged.

20. (588,L1,33) (c) Under the voluntary liquidation provisions of the Bankruptcy Code, a debt arising before the filing of the bankruptcy petition due to the debtor's negligence will be discharged in the proceedings. Note that had the debt been due to the debtor's willful and intentional torts it would not be discharged in bankruptcy. Answer (a) is incorrect because only debts which are incurred prior to the issuance of the order for relief will be discharged. Debts incurred after the order for relief are excluded from the bankruptcy proceeding and will not be discharged. Answer (b) is incorrect because income taxes which are due as the result of filing a fraudulent return will not be discharged in bankruptcy regardless of when the return was filed. However, had the taxes been due as a result of filing a return which was not fraudulent, this debt would have been discharged since only tax claims of this nature which are due within 3 years of filing a bankruptcy petition are not discharged. Answer (d) is incorrect because alimony owed to a spouse is specifically listed as a debt which cannot be discharged by bankruptcy.

H. Debts Discharged by Bankruptcy

21. (1188,L1,26) (a) When a debtor is granted a discharge in a bankruptcy proceeding, most of the debtor's debts are discharged. However, certain of the debtor's

obligations are not discharged. Tint's claim
is an example of a nondischargeable debt
because Aker obtained credit from Tint through
the use of false information. Such debts are
not dischargeable. Answer (d) is therefore
incorrect. Answer (b) is incorrect because
Aker's misrepresentations to Tint will cause
that debt to be nondischargeable, but such
action is not sufficient to bar Aker from a
general discharge. Answer (c) is incorrect
because Tint's claim is not a preference. A
preference is defined as a transfer of
property to a creditor in satisfaction of an
antecedent debt made within 90 days prior to
the filing of the bankruptcy petition while
debtor is insolvent in the bankruptcy sense.

L. Business Reorganization—Chapter 11

22. (1189,L1,29) (b) A business reorganization under Chapter 11 of the Bankruptcy
Code is an alternative to a straight bankruptcy. It may be commenced by either the
debtor filing a voluntary petition or the
creditors filing an involuntary petition.
Answer (a) is incorrect because often a
trustee is not appointed to administer the
reorganization. A trustee may be appointed
"for cause" or "in the interest of the
creditors" if a party of interest requests it.
Answer (c) is incorrect because the creditors'
committee is required and selected from the
unsecured creditors once the court grants an
order for relief. Answer (d) is incorrect
because all creditors need not agree to the
court-supervised rehabilitation plan under the
Chapter 11 reorganization.

23. (588,L1,35) (a) The purpose of a
Chapter 11 Reorganization is to restructure
the organization's finances so that it may
continue to operate and pay its creditors.
Business reorganization proceedings may be
initiated by the debtor (voluntary) or creditors (involuntary). Answer (b) is incorrect
because the reorganization provisions of the
Bankruptcy Code are available to individuals,
partnerships, or corporations. Thus, a
partnership would be eligible to be a debtor
under these provisions. Answer (c) is incorrect because a trustee will not be appointed
in all situations. A trustee may be appointed
to protect the interests of creditors but
often is not appointed. Answer (d) is incorrect because the debtor need not be insolvent
to have filed voluntarily.

Answer Outline

Problem 1   Involuntary Bankruptcy; Debtor's
             Estate; Priorities of Claims
             (1187,L3)

a. Requirements for involuntary bankruptcy
        petition have been met
        Able's unsecured claim was greater than
        $5,000
    Since there were fewer than 12 creditors
        only one creditor need file
b. Trustee may engage professional persons
        with court approval
    Any property inherited within 180 days
        after filing the petition is included in
        property of the estate
        Mix received the right to inheritance
        WITHIN 180 days after the filing of the
        petition
        Mix's inherited property is properly
        included in estate
c. The estate should be distributed in the
        following order
    1. Carr's claim to the extent of the
        sale proceeds of machinery
    2. Administrative expenses including
        selling expenses and Ring's fee
    3. Unsecured claim for federal income
        taxes
    4. The unsecured claims of Able and
        Baker and the balance of Carr's
        claim, paid proportionately out of
        remaining $30,000

Unofficial Answer

Problem 1   Involuntary Bankruptcy; Debtor's
             Estate; Priorities of Claims
             (1187,L3)

a. Yes. The requirements necessary for the
filing of a valid petition in bankruptcy have
been met. An involuntary case may be commenced against a person by the filing of a
petition where the aggregate amount of unsecured claims is at least $5,000 and a suffi-
cient number of creditors join in the filing
of the petition. Where there are fewer than
12 creditors only one creditor need file the
petition. Under the facts, the petition was
validly filed against Mix because Able's unsecured claim was more than $5,000 and because
there were fewer than 12 creditors.

b. Lang's action as trustee to appoint Ring as
the accountant for the bankruptcy estate was
proper if such action was with the bankruptcy
court's approval. The trustee, with the

court's approval, may engage professional
persons such as accountants on any reasonable
terms and conditions.

Lang's inclusion of the inheritance in the
property of the estate was also correct because property of the estate includes property
that the debtor acquires or becomes entitled
to acquire by inheritance within 180 days
after the filing of the petition. By acquiring the right to inherit the property on
December 15, 1986, which was less than 180
days after the filing of the petition on
July 1, 1986, Mix's inheritance was properly
included in the bankruptcy estate. Thus,
Mix's receipt of the inheritance more than 180
days after the filing of the petition does not
prevent the inclusion of the inheritance in
the property of the estate.

c. The $60,000 will be distributed to satisfy
the claims and expenses of the bankruptcy
estate in the following order of priority:

1. Carr's claim to the extent
of the sale proceeds of the machinery
in which Carr had a valid perfected
security interest in bankruptcy. $20,000
2. Administration expenses in-
cluding the expenses to maintain and
sell the unsecured property of the
estate ($1,000) and Ring's fee for
services rendered ($3,000).   4,000
3. Unsecured claim for federal
income taxes.   6,000
4. The unsecured claims of Able
and Baker and the balance of Carr's
claim, which have equal priority, will
be paid proportionately as follows:

Able --	$\frac{\$ 20,000}{\$120,000} \times \$30,000$	5,000
Baker --	$\frac{\$ 40,000}{\$120,000} \times \$30,000$	10,000
Carr --	$\frac{\$ 60,000}{\$120,000} \times \$30,000$	15,000
Total distributions		$ 60,000

Answer Outline

Problem 2 Voidable Preference; Contempora-
           neous Exchange (585,L5)

a. Payment to Nix constitutes a preferential
        transfer
        May be set aside by trustee
        Payment to Wax is a contemporaneous
        exchange for new value
        May not be set aside by trustee

Payment to electric company in the
ordinary course of Baker's business
within 45 days after debt arose
May not be set side by trustee
Trustee was correct. Normally property
acquired after filing of the bankruptcy
petition is not part of debtor's estate
However, exceptions exist for:
Rents earned on property of debtor's
estate
Property received pursuant to final
divorce decree within 180 days of
filing of bankruptcy petition

Unofficial Answer

Problem 2   Voidable Preference;
             Contemporaneous Exchange (585,L5)

The trustee in bankruptcy may properly
avoid or set aside the payment made by Baker
to Nix on May 17 since it meets all the requirements necessary to establish a preferential transfer. In order to establish a preference, the trustee must show that the transfer
   • Was to or for the benefit of a creditor.
   • Was made for or on account of an antecedent debt owed by the debtor before such
transfer was made.
   • Was made while the debtor was insolvent.
   • Was made within 90 days prior to the
filing of the petition (when the creditor is
not an insider).
   • Enables the creditor to receive more
than such creditor would receive in a liquidation proceeding.
There is a rebuttable presumption that the
debtor is insolvent during the ninety days
preceding the filing of the petition.
   The transfer made by Baker to Wax on
June 6 may not be avoided or set aside by the
trustee. Since the transfer was intended by
Baker and Wax to be a contemporaneous exchange
for new value given to Baker and was in fact a
substantially contemporaneous exchange, the
trustee may not avoid the transfer of the
mortgage to Wax.
   The payment made by Baker on June 16 for
the electric bill may not be avoided by the
trustee since the debt was incurred and paid
in the ordinary course of Baker's business,
within 45 days after the debt arose, and in
accordance with ordinary business terms.
   The trustee was correct by including in
the estate rents and property received as a
result of the final divorce decree. Generally, property acquired after the filing of a
bankruptcy petition is not part of the debt-

or's estate in bankruptcy but belongs to the
debtor individually. However, there are certain exceptions to this rule. One such exception is rents earned on property of the debt-
or's estate. Thus, the rents received from
July 1 through November 1 will be included in
Baker's estate. Another such exception is
property received by the debtor as a result of
a final divorce decree within 180 days of the
filing of the bankruptcy petition. Thus, the
receipt of property by Baker on October 10 as
a result of the final divorce decree falls
within the 180 days after the filing of the
bankruptcy petition of July 1 and is therefore
included in the debtor's estate.

Answer Outline

Problem 3   Requirements for Involuntary Bank-
             ruptcy; Claims and Preferences;
             Discharge of Debt in Bankruptcy
             (589,L2)

a. Requirements for involuntary bankruptcy
    have been met
      Since there were 12 or more unsecured
      creditors, at least 3 need to file
      Aggregate claims of Lux, Squire, and
      Rusk were greater than $5,000
b.1. Mortgage delivered to Safe by Tine
      constitutes a preferential transfer
        Transfer may be set aside by trustee
        Benefited Safe
        Antecedent debt owed to Safe
        Tine was insolvent
        Payment made within 90 days prior to
        filing
        Safe received more than it would in
        liquidation
  2. Tine's debt to Rich Bank can be excepted
      from discharge by the court
        Tine's financial statements were
        Materialy false
        Reasonably relied upon by Rich
        Made with intent to deceive

Unofficial Answer

Problem 3   Requirements for Involuntary Bank-
             ruptcy; Claims and Preferences;
             Discharge of Debt in Bankruptcy
             (589,L2)

a. The requirements necessary for the
commencement of an involuntary bankruptcy
proceeding were met because the petition was
filed by Lux, Squire, and Rusk, who were creditors of Tine with unsecured claims aggregating more than $5,000. To properly commence
an involuntary bankruptcy proceeding in which
the debtor has 12 or more creditors with un-

secured claims, three or more creditors with unsecured claims aggregating at least $5,000 must sign the bankruptcy petition.

b. 1. The court may declare the January 31, 1989 mortgage delivered to Safe by Tine to be void as a preference. A preference occurs if there is a transfer of the interest in property:

- To or for the benefit of a creditor;
- For or on account of an antecedent debt owed by the debtor before such transfer was made;
- Made while the debtor was insolvent;
- Made within 90 days before the date of the filing of the bankruptcy petition (when the creditor is not an insider);
- That enables the creditor to receive more than the creditor would receive in a liquidation proceeding.

Under the facts of this case, the mortgage delivered by Tine to Safe was for Safe's benefit, on account of the $250,000 owed to Safe, given while Tine was unable to pay his current obligations (was insolvent), given on January 31, 1989 (which was within 90 days before the filing of the bankruptcy petition on March 23, 1989), and enabled Safe to receive more than it would have received in a liquidation proceeding ($250,000 as a secured creditor vs. a lesser amount as an unsecured creditor in liquidation).

2. The court can except Tine's debt to Rich Bank from Tine's discharge in bankruptcy. In general, the bankruptcy court will except a debt from discharge if the debtor obtains money by use of a statement in writing respecting the debtor's financial condition that is materially false; the creditor to whom the debtor is liable for such money reasonably relied on the statement, and the debtor caused the statement to be made or published with intent to deceive.

Based on the facts of this case, Tine obtained a $50,000 loan after furnishing Rich with personal financial statements, that he knew substantially overstated his net worth. Because it was difficult to detect the overstatement, Rich's reliance on the financial statements was reasonable. Therefore, the requirements necessary to except Rich's debt from Tine's discharge have been met.

Multiple Choice Questions (1-17)

1. Which of the following transactions does not establish Samp as a surety?
   a. Samp says: "Ship goods to my son and I will pay for them."
   b. Samp signs commercial paper as an accommodation endorser for one of his suppliers.
   c. Samp guarantees a debt of a corporation he controls.
   d. Samp sells an office building to Park, and, as a part of the consideration, Park assumes Samp's mortgage on the property.

2. Burns borrowed $240,000 from Dollar Bank as additional working capital for his business. Dollar required that the loan be collateralized to the extent of 20%, and that an acceptable surety for the entire amount be obtained. Surety Co. agreed to act as surety on the loan and Burns pledged $48,000 of negotiable bearer bonds. Burns defaulted. Which of the following statements is correct?
   a. Dollar must first liquidate the collateral before it can proceed against Surety.
   b. Surety is liable in full immediately upon default by Burns, but will be entitled to the collateral upon satisfaction of the debt.
   c. Dollar must first proceed against Burns and obtain a judgment before it can proceed against the collateral.
   d. Surety may proceed against Burns for the full amount of the loan even if Surety settles with Dollar for a lower amount.

3. Knott obtained a loan of $10,000 from Charles on January 1, 1982, payable on April 15, 1982. At the time of the loan, Beck became a noncompensated surety thereon by written agreement. On April 15, 1982, Knott was unable to pay and wrote to Charles requesting an extension of time. Charles made no reply but did not take any immediate action to recover. On May 30, 1902, Charles demanded payment from Knott and, failing to collect from him, proceeded against Beck. Based upon the facts stated
   a. Charles was obligated to obtain a judgment against Knott returned unsatisfied before he could collect from Beck.
   b. Beck is released from his surety obligation because Charles granted Knott an extension of time.
   c. Charles may recover against Beck despite the fact Beck was a noncompensated surety.

   d. Beck is released because Charles delayed in proceeding against Knott.

4. Welch is a surety on Stanton's contract to build an office building for Brent. Stanton intentionally abandoned the project after it was 85% completed because of personal animosity which developed toward Brent. Which of the following is a correct statement concerning the rights or responsibilities of the various parties?
   a. Any modification of the contract, however slight and even if beneficial to Welch, will release Welch.
   b. Welch would be ordered to specifically perform the completion of the building if Brent sought this remedy.
   c. Neither Stanton's failure to give Welch prior notice of its intention to abandon the project nor its actual abandonment of the project will release Welch.
   d. Welch can not engage a contractor to finish the job and obtain from Brent the balance due on the contract.

5. If a debtor defaults and the debtor's surety satisfies the obligation, the surety acquires the right of
   a. Subrogation.
   b. Primary lien.
   c. Indemnification.
   d. Satisfaction.

6. Ford was unable to repay a loan from City Bank when due. City refused to renew the loan to Ford unless an acceptable surety could be provided. Ford asked Owens, a friend, to act as surety on the loan. To induce Owens to agree to become a surety, Ford made fraudulent representations about Ford's financial condition and promised Owens discounts on merchandise sold at Ford's store. Owens agreed to act as surety and the loan was made to Ford. Subsequently, Ford's obligation to City was discharged in Ford's bankruptcy and City wishes to hold Owens liable. Owens may avoid liability
   a. Because the arrangement was void at the inception.
   b. If Owens was an uncompensated surety.
   c. If Owens can show that City Bank was aware of the fraudulent representations.
   d. Because the discharge in bankruptcy will prevent Owens from having a right of reimbursement.

7. State Bank loaned Barr $80,000 and received securities valued at $20,000 from Barr as collateral. At the request of State, Barr entered into an agreement with Rice and Noll to act as co-sureties on the loan. The agreement provided that Rice and Noll's maximum liability would be $80,000 each.

Which of the following defenses asserted by Rice will completely release Rice from liability to State?

    a. State and Barr entered into a binding agreement to extend the time for payment that increased the sureties' risk and was agreed to without the sureties' consent.

    b. Fraud by Barr which induced Rice to enter into the surety contract and which was unknown to State.

    c. Release of Barr's obligation by State without Rice's or Noll's consent but with State's reservation of its rights against Rice.

    d. Return of the collateral to Barr by State without Rice's or Noll's consent.

8. Which of the following defenses will release a surety from liability?

    a. Insanity of the principal debtor at the time the contract was entered into.

    b. Failure by the creditor to promptly notify the surety of the principal debtor's default.

    c. Refusal by the creditor, with knowledge of the surety relationship, to accept the principal debtor's unconditional tender of payment in full.

    d. Release by the creditor of the principal debtor's obligation without the surety's consent but with the creditor's reservation of his rights against the surety.

9. Allen was the surety for the payment of rent by Lear under a lease from Rosenthal Rentals. The lease was for two years. A clause in the lease stated that at the expiration of the lease, the lessee had the privilege to renew upon thirty days' prior written notice or, if the lessee remained in possession after its expiration, it was agreed that the lease was to continue for two years more. There was a default in the payment of rent during the extended term of the lease and Rosenthal is suing Allen for the rent due based upon the guarantee. Allen contends that he is liable only for the initial term of the lease and not for the extended term. Allen is

    a. Not liable since it does **not** appear that a judgment against Lear has been returned unsatisfied.

    b. Not liable because there has been a material alteration of the surety undertaking.

    c. Not liable because there was a binding extension of time.

    d. Liable on the surety undertaking which would include the additional two years.

10. Dustin is a very cautious lender. When approached by Lanier regarding a $2,000 loan, he not only demanded an acceptable surety but also collateral equal to 50% of the loan. Lanier obtained King Surety Company as his surety and pledged rare coins worth $1,000 with Dustin. Dustin was assured by Lanier one week before the due date of the loan that he would have no difficulty in making payment. He persuaded Dustin to return the coins since they had increased in value and he had a prospective buyer. What is the legal effect of the release of the collateral upon King Surety?

    a. It totally releases King Surety.

    b. It does **not** release King Surety if the collateral was obtained after its promise.

    c. It releases King Surety to the extent of the value of the security.

    d. It does **not** release King Surety unless the collateral was given to Dustin with the express understanding that if was for the benefit of King Surety as well as Dustin.

11. Which of the following defenses by a surety will be effective to avoid liability?

    a. Lack of consideration to support the surety undertaking.

    b. Insolvency in the bankruptcy sense by the debtor.

    c. Incompetency of the debtor to make the contract in question.

    d. Fraudulent statements by the principal-debtor which induced the surety to assume the obligation and which were unknown to the creditor.

12. Ott and Bane agreed to act as co-sureties on an $80,000 loan that Cread Bank made to Dash. Ott and Bane are each liable for the entire $80,000 loan. Subsequently, Cread released Ott from liability without Bane's consent and without reserving its rights against Bane. If Dash subsequently defaults, Cread will be entitled to collect a maximum of

    a. $0 from Bane.

    b. $0 from Dash.

    c. $40,000 from Bane.

    d. $40,000 from Dash.

13. Sklar borrowed $360,000 from Rich Bank. At Rich's request, Sklar entered into an agreement with Aker, Burke, and Cey to act as co-sureties on the loan. The agreement between Sklar and the co-sureties provided that the maximum liability of each co-surety was: Aker $72,000, Burke $108,000, and Cey $180,000. After making several payments, Sklar defaulted on the loan. The balance was $240,000. If Cey pays $180,000 and Sklar subsequently pays $60,000, what amounts may Cey recover from Aker and Burke?

    a. $0 from Aker and $0 from Burke.
    b. $60,000 from Aker and $60,000 from Burke.
    c. $48,000 from Aker and $72,000 from Burke.
    d. $36,000 from Aker and $54,000 from Burke.

14. Lux Financial Corp. loaned Boe $100,000. At Lux's request, Boe entered into an agreement with Frey and Harp for them to act as co-sureties on the loan in the amount of $100,000 each. If Lux releases Harp without the consent of Frey or Boe, and Boe subsequently defaults, which of the following statements is correct?

    a. Frey will be liable for 50% of the loan balance.
    b. Lux's release of Harp will have **no** effect on Boe's and Frey's liability to Lux.
    c. Boe will be released for 50% of the loan balance.
    d. Frey will be liable for the entire loan balance.

15. A distinction between a surety and a co-surety is that only a co-surety is entitled to

    a. Contribution.
    b. Exoneration.
    c. Subrogation.
    d. Reimbursement (Indemnification).

16. West promised to make Noll a loan of $180,000 if Noll obtained sureties to secure the loan. Noll entered into an agreement with Carr, Gray, and Pine to act as co-sureties on his loan from West. The agreement between Noll and the co-sureties provided for compensation to be paid to each of the co-sureties. It further indicated that the maximum liability of each co-surety would be as follows: Carr $180,000, Gray $60,000, and Pine $120,000. West accepted the commitment of the sureties and made the loan to Noll. After paying nine installments totaling $90,000, Noll defaulted. Gray's debts (including his surety obligation to West on the Noll loan) were discharged in bankruptcy. Subsequently,

Carr properly paid the entire debt outstanding of $90,000. What amounts may Carr recover from the co-sureties?

	Gray	Pine
a.	$0	$30,000
b.	$0	$36,000
c.	$15,000	$30,000
d.	$30,000	$30,000

17. In order to establish a co-surety relationship the two or more sureties must

    a. Be aware of each other's existence at the time of their contract.
    b. Sign the same contract creating the debt and the co-surety relationship.
    c. Be bound to answer for the same debt or duty of the debtor.
    d. Be bound for the same amount and share equally in the obligation to satisfy the creditor.

Problems

Problem 1   (1184,L3)

(15 to 20 minutes)

Beach, a 17-year old minor, entered into an installment contract to purchase a travel agency from Reid. The purchase price included the fair market value of the tangible assets and an agreed upon value for goodwill. At the time the contract was entered into, Beach misrepresented his age to Reid, claiming that he was 19. The age of majority in their jurisdiction was 18. Since Reid was unsure of Beach's financial position, Reid requested that Beach obtain a surety. Therefore, Beach entered into an agreement for Abel to act as a surety on the installment contract. Beach knowingly induced Abel to become a surety by supplying Abel with false financial statements.

The contract also provided that Reid was to receive a substantial payment in consideration of his agreement not to operate a travel agency within a one mile radius of Beach's travel agency for a period of two years. After 19 months, Reid opened a new travel agency across the street from Beach's business. Within one month thereafter, Beach lost nearly all of his clients to Reid and Beach defaulted on the installment payments, causing the entire amount owed to Reid to become due. Reid has brought an action against Beach and Abel to recover all monies due him.

Beach claims he is not liable on the contract since:

• He was only 17 years old at the time the contract with Reid was signed.
• The clause prohibiting Reid from competing with him is legally valid and therefore Reid's violation of such clause constitutes a breach of the sale contract.

Abel claims that he is not liable to Reid since:

• He was induced into becoming a surety by Beach's fraud.
• Beach was 17 years old at the time the contract with Reid was entered into.
• Reid breached the sale contract by failing to comply with the express clause prohibiting competition with Beach.

Required:

Answer the following, setting forth reasons for any conclusions stated.

Assuming the contract is not divisible, discuss in separate paragraphs the assertions of Beach and Abel, indicating first whether such claims are correct.

Multiple Choice Answers

1. a	5. a	9. d	12. c	15. a
2. b	6. c	10. c	13. d	16. b
3. c	7. a	11. a	14. a	17. c
4. c	8. c			

Multiple Choice Answer Explanations

A. Nature of Suretyship

1. (1182,L1,22) (a) A suretyship relationship exists where one person agrees to be answerable for the debt of another by assuring performance upon the debtor's default. A suretyship agreement involves three parties: the principal debtor, the creditor, and the surety. Answer (a) is correct because it describes a third-party beneficiary contract, not a suretyship arrangement. Samp is not promising to pay the debt of another, but rather is engaging in an original promise to pay for the goods the creditor delivers to Samp's son. Answer (b) is incorrect because an accommodation endorser is a surety since the endorser engages to pay if the negotiable instrument is not paid by the appropriate party after proper presentment and notice. Answer (c) is incorrect because Samp is entering into a suretyship arrangement whereby he promises to pay if the principal debtor (the corporation) does not pay. Answer (d) is incorrect because when Park, the purchaser, assumed the mortgage, a surety relationship was created in which Park, the buyer, was the principal debtor and Samp, the seller, was the surety.

B. Creditor's Rights and Remedies

2. (1189,L1,20) (b) Upon default by the principal debtor, the creditor has the option of either proceeding immediately against the surety or resorting to the collateral to satisfy the debt. If the creditor chooses to proceed immediately against the surety, then the surety is entitled to the right of reimbursement from the principal debtor and has a right to any collateral the creditor is holding as satisfaction of that right. Answer (a) is incorrect because upon Burn's default Dollar Bank has the option of either proceeding immediately against the surety or resorting to the collateral to satisfy the debt. Answer (c) is incorrect because the creditor, Dollar Bank, need not first proceed against the principal debtor, Burn, and obtain a judgment for payment before proceeding against the collateral. Answer (d) is incorrect because although Surety Co. is entitled to the right of reimbursement from Burns, Surety Co. may only recover the actual amount paid to Dollar Bank.

3. (1182,L1,24) (c) If the surety's undertaking arises at the time the creditor extends the loan to the principal debtor, the surety does not need to receive independent consideration to be bound. Consequently, Beck, even as a noncompensated surety, would be bound to pay Charles. Answer (a) is incorrect because since the surety is primarily liable, the creditor may proceed immediately against the surety upon debtor's default without demand first being made upon the debtor. However, when a surety is a guarantor of collection, the guarantor's liability will be conditioned on the creditor first attempting to collect from the debtor. The creditor must exhaust his remedies against the principal debtor by reducing his claim against the debtor to judgment and showing the judgment remains unpaid before the guarantor's obligation arises. Normally, an extension of time to the debtor, without surety's consent, releases the surety due to a material increase in the surety's risk. However, answer (b) is incorrect because such a variance of terms must be legally enforceable and binding on the creditor in order for the surety to be released. In this case, the debtor only made a request for an extension of time, but the extension was not granted by the creditor. Answer (d) is incorrect because a delay in the creditor proceeding against the debtor does not discharge the surety, unless such time delay exceeds the statutory period within the statute of limitations.

4. (581,L1,37) (c) Unless the contract is a conditional guaranty, it is unnecessary for creditors to give notice of the debtor's default to the surety. With or without notice, upon default the surety is liable for the performance guaranteed under the agreement. Answer (a) is incorrect because any modifications of the contract that have the possibility of increasing the surety's risk would release the surety. Brent could sue the surety for compensatory damages, not specific performance; therefore, answer (b) is incorrect. Answer (d) is incorrect since if Welch, the surety, _did_ satisfy the obligation by engaging a contractor to finish the job, Welch could collect the balance due on the agreement.

C. Surety's Rights and Remedies

5. (1189,L1,21) (a) Where a surety pursuant to his/her contractual undertaking satisfies the obligation to the creditor, the surety, to the extent s/he has satisfied the obligation,

has the same rights the creditor had. That
is, s/he acquires the right of subrogation.
Answer (b) is incorrect because a lien arises
in the event that a debt is secured by
collateral. While the surety, through the
right of subrogation, may be entitled to take
possession of collateral, a lien does not
necessarily exist in all suretyship contracts. Answer (c) is incorrect because the
surety would not acquire the right of indemnification in the event of default. Answer (d)
is incorrect because a surety does not have a
right of satisfaction.

D. Surety's Defenses

6. (1188,L1,20) (c) Fraud by the principal
debtor on the surety to induce a suretyship
agreement will not release the surety if the
creditor extended credit in good faith. But
if the creditor (City Bank) had knowledge of
the debtor's (Ford's) fraudulent representations, then the surety (Owens) may avoid
liability. Answer (a) is incorrect because
fraud in the inducement would create a voidable, not void, surety agreement. Answer (b)
is incorrect because no separate consideration
is needed to bind the surety if the surety
agreement arises at the same time the contract
between the creditor and debtor is created.
The renewal of the loan between Ford and City
Bank constitutes a new agreement; therefore,
Owens did not need to receive consideration.
Answer (d) is incorrect because personal
defenses of the debtor, such as bankruptcy,
are not defenses available to the surety.

7. (587,L1,26) (a) A material alteration
by the principal debtor and creditor in the
terms and conditions of their original contract without the surety's consent will
automatically release the surety if the
surety's risk of loss is thereby materially
increased. The extension of time for payment
is an alteration which has increased Rice's
risk and was made without Rice's consent.
Answer (b) is incorrect because fraud enacted
by the principal debtor on the surety will not
release the surety unless the creditor was
aware of this fraud. Answer (c) is incorrect
because it describes an agreement not to sue
between the principal debtor and creditor.
The creditor may release the principal debtor
without consent of the surety, and still
proceed against the surety if the creditor
reserves his rights against the surety.
Answer (d) is incorrect because the return of
the collateral to the principal debtor by the
creditor will only reduce the surety's obligation to the extent of the value of the collateral. Rice will not be completely released
from liability by the return of the collateral
to Barr.

8. (584,L1,24) (c) The surety will be
discharged by the creditor's refusal to accept
the principal debtor's tender of full payment
on a mature debt. However, the tender of full
payment will not discharge the principal debtor but will merely stop the running of interest on the monetary obligation. Answer (a)
is incorrect because a surety may not exercise
the principal debtor's personal defenses
(i.e., insanity). Answer (b) is incorrect
because, unless the contract states otherwise,
the creditor has no duty to notify the surety
of the principal debtor's default. Although a
release of the principal debtor without the
surety's consent will usually discharge the
surety, there is no discharge if the creditor
expressly reserves his rights against the
surety. Answer (d) is, therefore, incorrect.

9. (1181,L1,29) (d) The leasing arrangement, to which Allen is a surety, remained
intact with no modifications. The lease,
itself, expressed a holdover clause which went
into existence when Lear remained in possession after the original leasing period.
The essence of a surety arrangement is that
the surety promises to perform upon default of
the principal debtor. Therefore, Allen
becomes liable when Lear defaults during the
extended term of the lease. Answer (a) is
incorrect because Allen is a surety, not a
guarantor of collection; therefore, the creditor need not reduce his claim against the
principal debtor to judgment and have execution be unsatisfied before proceeding against
the surety on his promise. Answer (b) is
incorrect because there was no alteration of
the contract which materially affected the
risks to the surety. Answer (c) is incorrect
because a binding extension of time refers to
a creditor granting additional time to the
debtor to satisfy his obligation. The holdover provision was part of the original agreement and consequently, would not be considered
an alteration.

10. (1181,L1,24) (c) Upon default, the creditor (Dustin) may resort to the collateral he
holds or may proceed against the surety on his
promise. But when the creditor surrenders the
collateral before or after the debtor's default, the surety is released to the extent of
the value of the collateral. (Thus answer (a)
is incorrect.) Answers (b) and (d) are incorrect because it does not matter when the
collateral was obtained by Dustin or if it was
expressly understood that the collateral was
to benefit King Surety. Once the collateral
is returned, this reduces the surety
obligation to the extent of the value of the
collateral.

11. (582,L1,23) (a) If the surety's undertaking is not supported by consideration, the
surety will avoid liability. However, when
the surety's and principal debtor's obligations are incurred at the same time, there is
no need for any separate consideration beyond
that supporting the principal debtor's contract. If the surety's undertaking is entered
into subsequent to the debtor's contract, it
must be supported by separate consideration.
Answers (b) and (c) are incorrect because the
debtor's insolvency in either sense (equity or
bankruptcy) or the debtor's lack of contractual capacity will not release the surety.
Answer (d) is incorrect because fraud by the
principal debtor on the surety will not release the surety unless the creditor was aware
of this fraud. However, fraud by the creditor
on the surety will release the surety.

E. Co-sureties

12. (1188,L1,21) (c) Co-sureties exist when
there is more than one surety guaranteeing the
same obligation of the principal debtor.
Unless the creditor specifically reserves
his/her rights, a release of a co-surety by
the creditor will release the other co-surety
to the extent of the released co-surety's pro
rata share of debt liability. Both Ott and
Bane agreed to act as co-sureties for the full
amount of the loan, $80,000. Their pro rata
share of the debt was $40,000 ($80,000 ÷ 2).
Since Cread did not reserve its rights against
Bane when it released Ott, Bane would only be
liable for $40,000.

13. (588,L1,26) (d) The right of contribution arises when one co-surety, in performance of the principal debtor's obligation,
pays more than his/her proportionate share of
the total liability. The right of contribution allows the performing co-surety to
receive reimbursement from the other co-
sureties for their pro rata shares of the
liability. The pro rata shares of the co-
sureties are determined as follows:

Sureties				
Pro rata Share		Remaining liability	Surety's Liability	
Cey (180,000/360,000)	x	180,000	=	90,000
Aker (72,000/360,000)	x	180,000	=	36,000
Burke (108,000/360,000)	x	180,000	=	54,000

Thus, Cey is entitled to receive $36,000 from
Aker and $54,000 from Burke. Answers (a),
(b), and (c) are therefore incorrect.

14. (588,L1,27) (a) A discharge or release
of one co-surety by a creditor results in a
reduction of liability of the remaining co-
surety. The remaining co-surety is released
to the extent of the released co-surety's pro

rata share of debt liability, unless there is
a reservation of rights by the creditor
against the remaining co-surety. Frey and
Harp each had maximum liability of $100,000.
Thus, Lux's release of Harp will result in
Frey's liability being reduced by Harp's pro
rata share of the total debt liability which
was one half. Therefore, Frey's liability has
been reduced to $50,000 (i.e., 50% of the loan
balance) due to the release of Harp as a co-
surety. Answer (d) is therefore incorrect.
Answer (b) is incorrect because as discussed
above, Frey's liability has been reduced due
to Lux's release of Harp. Answer (c) is
incorrect because the release of the co-surety
does not release the principal debtor since
the debtor's obligation is not affected in any
way by Lux's release of Harp.

15. (587,L1,29) (a) Co-sureties exist when
more than one surety is bound to answer for
the same debt or duty of a debtor, and who, as
between themselves, should proportionately
share the loss caused by the default of the
debtor. The right of contribution arises when
a co-surety, in performance of the debtor's
obligation, pays more than his proportionate
share. This entitles the co-surety to compel
the other co-sureties to compensate him/her
for the excess amount paid. Exoneration,
subrogation, and reimbursement are all
remedies available to both a surety and a co-
surety. Specifically, exoneration allows the
surety or co-surety to file a suit in equity
to compel the debtor to pay the creditor
before the surety or co-surety pays the
debt. The rule of subrogation states that the
surety or co-surety, to the extent s/he has
paid, succeeds to the creditor's rights
against the principal debtor, including the
rights to any security interests the creditor
might have in the debtor's property. Reimbursement (indemnification) is the surety's
or co-surety's right to recover the amount
paid from the principal debtor. Thus,
contribution is the right which only a co-
surety is entitled to and, therefore,
answers (b), (c), and (d) are incorrect.

16. (1185,L1,32) (b) The right of contribution arises when one co-surety, in performance of debtor's obligation, pays more than
his proportionate share of the total liability. The right of contribution entitles
the performing co-surety to reimbursement from
the other co-sureties for their pro rata
shares of the liability. Since Gray's debts
have been discharged in bankruptcy, Carr may
only exercise his right of contribution
against Pine, and may recover nothing from
Gray. Pine's pro rata share of the remaining
$90,000 would be determined as follows:

$$\left(\frac{\text{Dollar amount guaranteed by Pine}}{\substack{\text{Total amount of risk assumed by} \\ \text{remaining co-sureties}}}\right) \times \substack{\text{Remaining} \\ \text{obligation}}$$

$$\frac{120,000}{120,000 + 180,000} \times 90,000 = 36,000$$

Answers (a), (c), and (d) are therefore incorrect.

17. (1176,L2,31) (c) Co-sureties are two or more sureties bound to answer for the same debt or duty of the debtor. They need not be aware of each other's existence either at the time of their contract or later. They need not sign the same contract. The only necessary connection is that they are both bound to answer for the same debt irrespective of the time they became bound. Co-sureties also need not be bound for the same amount, e.g., one could be bound for 60% and the other for 40%.

Answer Outline

Problem 1   Minority; Reasonable Covenant
             not to Compete; Surety's
             Defenses (1184,L3)

Beach's minority defense is invalid
  Misrepresentation of age does not invalidate
    defense
  However, failure to disaffirm within
    reasonable time after reaching majority
    constitutes implied ratification
Beach's assertion that Reid's violation of
  noncompetition covenant constitutes
  breach is valid
  Noncompetition clause is reasonable in
    light of circumstances present
Abel's defense based on Beach's fraud is
  invalid
  Since Reid knew nothing of Beach's fraud he
    has no duty to inform Abel
Abel's defense based on Beach's minority is
  invalid
  Surety cannot use minority of principal
    debtor as defense to payment
Abel's defense based on Reid's violation of
  noncompetition covenant is valid
  Surety may use material breach of underlying
    contract by creditor as defense to payment
  Reid's violation of noncompetition clause
    constitutes breach

Unofficial Answer

Problem 1   Minority; Reasonable Covenant
             not to Compete; Surety's
             Defenses (1184,L3)

    Beach's minority at the time the contract
with Reid was entered into will not be a valid
defense. Despite Beach's misrepresentation of
his age, the agreement with Reid was voidable
at Beach's option while Beach was a minor.
However, Beach's use and operation of the
travel agency for at least seven months after
reaching majority constituted an implied ratification of the contract. Some states may
construe Beach's mere failure to disaffirm the
contract within a reasonable time after
reaching majority to be a ratification of the
contract. Furthermore, a small number of
states provide that minority is not a defense
where the minor has entered into a business
contract.
    Beach's assertion that he is not liable
due to Reid's violation of the contract clause
prohibiting Reid from competing with Beach is
correct because violation of the noncompetition covenant is a material breach of the contract. Since the case at issue involves the

sale of a business including its goodwill, the
legal validity of a clause prohibiting competition by the seller is determined by its
reasonableness regarding the time and geographic area covered. Each case must be considered on its own facts, with a determination
of what is reasonable under the particular
circumstances. It appears that, according to
the facts of this case, the prohibition
against Reid's operating a competing travel
agency within a one mile radius of Beach's
travel agency for two years is reasonable.
    Abel's claim that he is not liable to Reid
because of Beach's fraud in supplying him with
false financial statements is incorrect.
Although a creditor has a duty to disclose to
the surety all material facts that would
increase the surety's risk, the breach of such
duty is not a valid defense of the surety if
the creditor lacks knowledge of such facts.
Therefore, unless Abel can show that Reid knew
or had reason to know of the fraud committed
by Beach, Abel will not be relieved of his
surety undertaking.
    Abel's claim that he is not liable to Reid
because of Beach's minority is without merit.
Beach's minority is a personal defense that in
a proper case may be exercised only at Beach's
option. Therefore, whether Beach has the
power to disaffirm his contract with Reid will
have no effect on Abel's surety obligations to
Reid.
    Abel's assertion that his liability to
Reid will be discharged because of Reid's
failure to comply with the express promise not
to compete with Beach is correct. Unlike the
defense of the principal debtor's minority, a
material breach of the underlying contract
between the principal debtor and creditor may
be properly asserted by the surety. The creditor's failure to perform in accordance with
the material terms of the underlying contract
without justification will discharge the principal debtor's obligation to perform, thereby
increasing the risk of the principal debtor's
nonperformance. Thus, the surety will also be
discharged from liability due to his own
increased risk of loss on the surety contract.
It seems clear that Reid's opening of a travel
agency across the street from Beach's business
after only 19 months constituted a material
breach of the sale contract. Therefore, Abel
will be discharged from his surety obligation.

Multiple Choice Questions (1-30)

1. Anker wishes to give Mix power of attorney. In general, the power of attorney
   a. May limit Mix's authority to specific transactions.
   b. Must be signed by both Anker and Mix.
   c. Will be valid only if Mix is a licensed attorney at law.
   d. May continue in existence after Anker's death.

2. Pell is the principal and Astor is the agent in an agency coupled with an interest. In the absence of a contractual provision relating to the duration of the agency, who has the right to terminate the agency before the interest has expired?

	Pell	Astor
a.	Yes	Yes
b.	No	Yes
c.	No	No
d.	Yes	No

3. A principal and agent relationship requires a
   a. Meeting of the minds and consent to act.
   b. Specified consideration.
   c. Written agreement.
   d. Power of attorney.

4. A principal will not be liable to a third party for a tort committed by an agent
   a. Unless the principal instructed the agent to commit the tort.
   b. Unless the tort was committed within the scope of the agency relationship.
   c. If the agency agreement limits the principal's liability for the agent's tort.
   d. If the tort is also regarded as a criminal act.

5. Neal, an employee of Jordan, was delivering merchandise to a customer. On the way, Neal's negligence caused a traffic accident that resulted in damages to a third party's automobile. Who is liable to the third party?

	Neal	Jordan
a.	No	No
b.	Yes	Yes
c.	Yes	No
d.	No	Yes

6. Parc contracted with Furn Brothers Corp. to buy hotel furniture and fixtures on behalf of Global Motor House, a motel chain. Global instructed Parc to use Parc's own name and not to disclose to Furn that Parc was acting on Global's behalf. Who is liable to Furn on this contract?

	Parc	Global
a.	Yes	No
b.	No	Yes
c.	Yes	Yes
d.	No	No

7. Steel has been engaged by Lux to act as the agent for Lux, an undisclosed principal. As a result of this relationship
   a. Steel has the same implied powers as an agent engaged by a disclosed principal.
   b. Lux can not be held liable for any torts committed by Steel in the course of carrying out the engagement.
   c. Steel will be free from personal liability on authorized contracts for Lux when it is revealed that Steel was acting as an agent.
   d. Lux must file the appropriate form in the proper state office under the fictitious business name statute.

8. Able, on behalf of Pix Corp., entered into a contract with Sky Corp., by which Sky agreed to sell computer equipment to Pix. Able disclosed to Sky that she was acting on behalf of Pix. However, Able had exceeded her actual authority by entering into the contract with Sky. If Pix does not want to honor the contract, it will nonetheless be held liable if Sky can prove that
   a. Able had apparent authority to bind Pix.
   b. Able believed she was acting within the scope of her authority.
   c. Able was an employee of Pix and not an independent contractor.
   d. The agency relationship between Pix and Able was formalized in a signed writing.

9. Wok Corp. has decided to expand the scope of its business. In this connection, it contemplates engaging several agents. Which of the following agency relationships is within the Statute of Frauds and thus should be contained in a signed writing?
   a. A sales agency where the agent normally will sell goods which have a value in excess of $500.
   b. An irrevocable agency.

c. An agency which is of indefinite
    duration but which is terminable
    upon one month's notice.
d. An agency for the forthcoming cal-
    endar year which is entered into in
    mid-December of the prior year.

10. Which of the following is **not** an essential element of an agency relationship?
a. It must be created by contract.
b. The agent must be subject to the
    principal's control.
c. The agent is a fiduciary in respect
    to the principal.
d. The agent acts on behalf of another
    and **not** himself.

11. Able, on behalf of Pix Corp., entered
into a contract with Sky Corp., by which Sky
agreed to sell computer equipment to Pix.
Able disclosed to Sky that she was acting on
behalf of Pix. However, Able had exceeded her
actual authority by entering into the contract
with Sky. If Pix wishes to ratify the
contract with Sky, which of the following
statements is correct?
a. Pix must notify Sky that Pix intends
    to ratify the contract.
b. Able must have acted reasonably and
    in Pix's best interest.
c. Able must be a general agent of Pix.
d. Pix must have knowledge of all
    material facts relating to the
    contract at the time it is ratified.

12. Starr is an agent of a disclosed
principal, Maple. On May 1, Starr entered
into an agreement with King Corp. on behalf of
Maple that exceeded Starr's authority as
Maple's agent. On May 5, King learned of
Starr's lack of authority and immediately
notified Maple and Starr that it was withdrawing from the May 1 agreement. On May 7,
Maple ratified the May 1 agreement in its
entirety. If King refuses to honor the
agreement and Maple brings an action for
breach of contract, Maple will
a. Prevail since the agreement of May 1
    was ratified in its entirety.
b. Prevail since Maple's capacity as a
    principal was known to Starr.
c. Lose since the May 1 agreement is
    void due to Starr's lack of
    authority.
d. Lose since King notified Starr and
    Maple of its withdrawal prior to
    Maple's ratification.

13. Harp entered into a contract with Rex on
behalf of Gold. By doing so, Harp acted outside the scope of his authority as Gold's

agent. Gold may be held liable on the contract if
a. Gold retains the benefits of the
    contract.
b. Gold ratifies the entire contract
    after Rex withdraws from the con-
    tract.
c. Rex elects to hold Gold liable on
    the contract.
d. Rex was aware of the limitation on
    Harp's authority.

14. Simmons, an agent for Jensen, has the
express authority to sell Jensen's goods.
Simmons also has the express authority to
grant discounts of up to 5% of list price.
Simmons sold Hemple goods with a list price of
$1,000 and granted Hemple a 10% discount.
Hemple had not previously dealt with either
Simmons or Jensen. Which of the following
courses of action may Jensen properly take?
a. Seek to void the sale to Hemple.
b. Seek recovery of $50 from Hemple
    only.
c. Seek recovery of $50 from Simmons
    only.
d. Seek recovery of $50 from either
    Hemple or Simmons.

15. Ritz hired West for six months as an
assistant sales manager at $4,000 a month plus
3% of sales. Which of the following is
correct?
a. The employment agreement must be in
    writing and signed by the party to
    be charged.
b. The agreement between Ritz and West
    formed an agency coupled with an
    interest.
c. West must disclose any interests he
    has which are adverse to Ritz in
    matters concerning Ritz's business.
d. West can be dismissed by Ritz during
    the six months only for cause.

16. Borg is the vice-president of purchasing
for Crater Corp. He has authority to enter
into purchase contracts on behalf of Crater
provided that the price under a contract does
not exceed $2 million. Dent, who is the pres-
ident of Crater, is required to approve any
contract that exceeds $2 million. Borg
entered into a $2.5 million purchase contract
with Shady Corp. without Dent's approval.
Shady was unaware that Borg exceeded his
authority. Neither party substantially
changed its position in reliance on the contract. What is the most likely result of this
transaction?
a. Crater will be bound because of
    Borg's apparent authority.

b. Crater will not be bound because
    Borg exceeded his authority.
c. Crater will only be bound up to $2
    million, the amount of Borg's
    authority.
d. Crater may avoid the contract since
    Shady has not relied on the contract
    to its detriment.

17. Futterman operated a cotton factory and
employed Marra as a general purchasing agent
to travel through the southern states to purchase cotton. Futterman telegraphed Marra
instructions from day to day as to the price
to be paid for cotton. Marra entered a cotton
district in which she had not previously done
business and represented that she was purchasing cotton for Futterman. Although
directed by Futterman to pay no more than 25
cents a pound, Marra bought cotton from
Anderson at 30 cents a pound, which was the
prevailing offering price at that time.
Futterman refused to take the cotton. Under
these circumstances, which of the following is
correct?
    a. The negation of actual authority to
        make the purchase effectively elimi-
        nates any liability for Futterman.
    b. Futterman is not liable on the con-
        tract.
    c. Marra has no potential liability.
    d. Futterman is liable on the contract.

18. Cox engaged Datz as her agent. It was
mutually agreed that Datz would not disclose
that he was acting as Cox's agent. Instead he
was to deal with prospective customers as if
he were a principal acting on his own behalf.
This he did and made several contracts for
Cox. Assuming Cox, Datz or the customer seeks
to avoid liability on one of the contracts
involved, which of the following statements is
correct?
    a. Cox must ratify the Datz contracts
        in order to be held liable.
    b. Datz has no liability once he dis-
        closes that Cox was the real princi-
        pal.
    c. The third party can avoid liability
        because he believed he was dealing
        with Datz as a principal.
    d. The third party may choose to hold
        either Datz or Cox liable.

19. Wall & Co. hired Carr to work as an agent
in its collection department, reporting to the
credit manager. Which of the following is
correct?
    a. Carr does not owe a fiduciary duty
        to Wall since he does not compete
        with the company.

b. Carr will be personally liable for
    any torts he commits even though
    they are committed in the course of
    his employment and pursuant to
    Wall's directions.
c. Carr has the implied authority to
    engage counsel and commence legal
    action against Wall's debtors.
d. Carr may commingle funds collected
    by him if this is convenient as long
    as he keeps proper records.

20. Agents sometimes have liability to third
parties for their actions taken for and on
behalf of the principal. An agent will not be
personally liable in which of the following
circumstances?
    a. If he makes a contract which he had
        no authority to make but which the
        principal ratifies.
    b. If he commits a tort while engaged
        in the principal's business.
    c. If he acts for a principal which he
        knows is nonexistent and the third
        party is unaware of this.
    d. If he acts for an undisclosed prin-
        cipal as long as the principal is
        subsequently disclosed.

21. Harris is a purchasing agent for Elkin, a
sole proprietor. Harris has the express
authority to place purchase orders with
Elkin's suppliers. Harris typically conducts
business through the mail and has very little
contact with Elkin. Elkin was incapacitated
by a stroke and was declared incompetent in a
judicial proceeding. Subsequently, Harris
placed an order with Ajax, Inc. on behalf of
Elkin. Neither Ajax nor Harris were aware of
Elkin's incapacity. With regard to the
contract with Ajax, Elkin (or Elkin's legal
representative) will
    a. Not be liable because Harris was
        without authority to enter into the
        contract.
    b. Not be liable provided that Harris
        had placed orders with Ajax in the
        past.
    c. Be liable because Harris was acting
        within the scope of Harris'
        authority.
    d. Be liable because Ajax was unaware
        of Elkin's incapacity.

22. The apparent authority of a general agent
for a disclosed principal will terminate
without notice to third parties when the
    a. Principal dismisses the agent.
    b. Principal or agent dies.
    c. Purpose of the agency relationship
        has been fulfilled.
    d. Time period set forth in the agency
        agreement has expired.

23. Dart Corp. dismissed Ritz as its general sales agent. Dart notified all of Ritz's known customers by letter. Bing Corp., a retail outlet located outside of Ritz's previously assigned sales territory, had never dealt with Ritz. However, Bing knew of Ritz as a result of various business contacts. After his dismissal, Ritz sold Bing goods, to be delivered by Dart, and received from Bing a cash deposit for 20% of the purchase price. It was not unusual for an agent in Ritz's previous position to receive cash deposits. In an action by Bing against Dart on the sales contract, Bing will
    a. Win, because Dart's notice was inadequate to terminate Ritz's apparent authority.
    b. Win, because a principal is an insurer of an agent's acts.
    c. Lose, because Ritz lacked any express or implied authority to make the contract.
    d. Lose, because Ritz's conduct constituted a fraud for which Dart is **not** liable.

24. A general agent's apparent authority to bind her principal to contracts with third parties will cease without notice to those third parties when the
    a. Agent has fulfilled the purpose for which the agency relationship was created.
    b. Time set forth in the agreement creating the agency relationship has expired.
    c. Principal and agent have mutually agreed to end their relationship.
    d. Principal has received a discharge in bankruptcy under the liquidation provisions of the Bankruptcy Code.

25. An agency coupled with an interest will be created by a written agreement which provides that a(n)
    a. Borrower shall pledge securities to a lender which authorizes the lender to sell the securities and apply the proceeds to the loan in the event of default.
    b. Employee is hired for a period of two years at $40,000 per annum plus 2% of net sales.
    c. Broker is to receive a 5% sales commission out of the proceeds of the sale of a parcel of land.
    d. Attorney is to receive 25% of a plaintiff's recovery for personal injuries.

May 1990 Questions

26. Generally, an agency relationship is terminated by operation of law in all of the following situations **except** the
    a. Principal's death.
    b. Principal's incapacity.
    c. Agent's renunciation of the agency.
    d. Agent's failure to acquire a necessary business license.

27. Pine, an employee of Global Messenger Co., was hired to deliver highly secret corporate documents for Global's clients throughout the world. Unknown to Global, Pine carried a concealed pistol. While Pine was making a delivery, he suspected an attempt was being made to steal the package, drew his gun and shot Kent, an innocent passerby. Kent will **not** recover damages from Global if
    a. Global discovered that Pine carried a weapon and did nothing about it.
    b. Global instructed its messengers **not** to carry weapons.
    c. Pine was correct and an attempt was being made to steal the package.
    d. Pine's weapon was unlicensed and illegal.

28. Maco Corp. develops shopping centers and regularly engages real estate brokers to act on its behalf in acquiring parcels of land. The brokers are authorized to enter into such contracts, but are instructed to do so in their own names without disclosing Maco's identity or Maco's relationship to the transaction. If a broker enters into a contract with a seller on Maco's behalf,
    a. Maco will be bound by the contract because of the broker's apparent authority.
    b. The broker will **not** be personally bound by the contract because the broker has express authority to act.
    c. Maco will **not** be liable for any negligent acts of the broker committed while acting on Maco's behalf.
    d. The broker will have the same authority as if Maco's identity had been disclosed.

29. Able, as agent for Baker, an undisclosed principal, contracted with Safe to purchase an antique car. In payment, Able issued his personal check to Safe. Able could not cover the check but expected Baker to give him cash to deposit before the check was presented for payment. Baker did not do so and the check was dishonored. Baker's identity became known to Safe. Safe may **not** recover from
    a. Baker individually on the contract.
    b. Able individually on the contract.

c.   Baker individually on the check.
d.   Able individually on the check.

30. Ace engages Butler to manage Ace's retail
business. Butler has the implied authority to
do all of the following except
   a.   Purchase inventory for Ace's
        business.
   b.   Sell Ace's business fixtures.
   c.   Pay Ace's business debts.
   d.   Hire or discharge Ace's business
        employees.

Problems

Problem 1   (1185,L3b)

(7 to 10 minutes)

John Nolan, a partner in Nolan, Stein, & Wolf partnership, transferred his interest in the partnership to Simon and withdrew from the partnership. Although the partnership will continue, Stein and Wolf have refused to admit Simon as a partner.

Subsequently, the partnership appointed Ed Lemon as its agent to market its various product lines. Lemon entered into a two-year written agency contract with the partnership which provided that Lemon would receive a 10% sales commission. The agency contract was signed by Lemon and, on behalf of the partnership, by Stein and Wolf.

After six months, Lemon was terminated without cause. Lemon asserts that:

• He is an agent coupled with an interest.
• The agency relationship may not be terminated without cause prior to the expiration of its term.
• He is entitled to damages because of the termination of the agency relationship.

Required:

Answer the following, setting forth reasons for any conclusions stated.
Discuss the merits of Lemon's assertions.

Problem 2   (580,L5a)

(10 to 15 minutes)

Part a. Vogel, an assistant buyer for the Granite City Department Store, purchased metal art objects from Duval Reproductions. Vogel was totally without express or apparent authority to do so, but believed that his purchase was a brilliant move likely to get him a promotion. The head buyer of Granite was livid when he learned of Vogel's activities. However, after examining the merchandise and listening to Vogel's pitch, he reluctantly placed the merchandise in the storeroom and put a couple of pieces on display for a few days to see whether it was a "hot item" and a "sure thing" as Vogel claimed. The item was neither "hot" nor "sure" and when it didn't move at all, the head buyer ordered the display merchandise repacked and the entire order returned to Duval with a letter that stated the merchandise had been ordered by an assistant buyer who had absolutely no authority to make the purchase. Duval countered with a lawsuit for breach of contract.

Required:

Answer the following, setting forth reasons for any conclusions stated.
Will Duval prevail?

Multiple Choice Answers

1. a	7. a	13. a	19. b	25. a
2. b	8. a	14. c	20. a	26. c
3. a	9. d	15. c	21. a	27. d
4. b	10. a	16. a	22. b	28. d
5. b	11. d	17. d	23. a	29. c
6. c	12. d	18. d	24. d	30. b

Multiple Choice Answer Explanations

A. Characteristics

1. (1188,L1,1) (a) A power of attorney is written authority conferred to an agent. It is conferred in a formal writing. A power of attorney can be general or it can grant the agent only restricted authority. Answer (b) is incorrect because the power of attorney must be signed only by the person granting such authority. Answer (c) is incorrect because anyone with the legal capacity to enter into an agency relationship may be granted the power of attorney. Answer (d) is incorrect because the death of the principal constitutes the termination of an agency relationship by operation of law.

2. (589,L1,11) (b) An agency coupled with an interest arises when an agent acquires from the principal an interest in the subject matter of the agency. In the absence of a contractual provision relating to the term of the agency, the authority of the agent (Astor) is irrevocable by the principal (Pell). If there is no time period specified for the agency, then the agent (Astor) may terminate at any time without liability, regardless of the type of agency.

3. (1189,L1,1) (a) The relationship between a principal and agent is based upon the consent of both parties involved. Consent means that each party intended for an agency relationship to exist. Answer (b) is incorrect because specified consideration is not needed to create an agency relationship; the relationship between the principal and the agent is not contractual. Answer (c) is incorrect because although the principal and agent relationship may be written, a written agreement is not required. Answer (d) is incorrect because power of attorney is not needed to create an agency relationship.

A.2. Employer's Liability for Employee's Torts

4. (1189,L1,2) (b) Generally, a principal is not liable to a third party for torts committed by an agent. The major exception is if the agent is acting within the authority of the principal; i.e., within the scope of the agency relationship. If the agent is acting within the scope of the agency relationship, the principal is liable. Answer (a) is incorrect because the tort must be committed within the scope of the agency relationship for the principal to be liable. An agent's instructions from the principal to commit the tort is not within the scope of the agency relationship. Answer (c) is incorrect because the principal cannot limit his/her liability in the agency agreement for torts committed by the agent. Answer (d) is incorrect because the fact that the tort may also be a criminal act does not protect the principal.

5. (585,L1,12) (b) An employer is generally liable for an employee's torts if the tort was committed within the course and scope of the employment relationship. Since Neal was acting within the course and scope of his duties, Jordan would be liable for damages, caused by Neal's negligence (i.e., the traffic accident). Neal, as an individual, is liable for his own torts; therefore, he would also be liable for damages caused by the traffic accident.

A.6. Types of Principals

6. (1189,L1,3) (c) Parc, the agent in this relationship, is liable to Furn on this contract. An agent is liable on a contract when the principal is undisclosed and is only released from liability when the principal performs the contract or when the third party elects to hold the principal liable. Global, the undisclosed principal in this relationship, is also liable to Furn on this contract. An undisclosed principal is liable on a contract where the agent had actual authority to contract. Parc, the agent, had actual authority to contract with Furn, thereby making Global liable. An undisclosed principal remains liable unless the third party holds the agent responsible, the agent fully performs the contract, the undisclosed principal is expressly excluded by the contract, or the contract is a negotiable instrument.

7. (1183,L1,14) (a) Classification of a principal as disclosed, undisclosed, or partially disclosed affects the contractual liability of the agent toward third parties. The authority given the agent, however, is not affected. An agent representing an undisclosed principal has the same implied authority as an agent representing a disclosed principal. Answer (b) is incorrect because a principal's liability for his agent's torts is the same regardless of whether the principal is disclosed, undisclosed, or partially dis-

closed. Answer (c) is incorrect because once
the identity of a previously undisclosed principal is known, the third party may elect to
hold either the principal or the agent liable
on the contract. Answer (d) is incorrect because a fictitious business name statute requires a party conducting business under an
assumed name to receive the state's permission
to use that name. Such a statute has no applicability to the Lux-Steel agency relationship.

B. Methods of Creation

8.   (588,L1,4) (a) Apparent authority
exists when a third party has reason to
believe that an agent has the authority to
enter into contracts of the nature involved,
based upon a principal's representations. If
the third party is unaware of any secret
limitations on the agent's normal authority,
then the principal (Pix) will be held liable
for contracts entered into by the agent (Able)
because the agent has apparent authority.
Answer (b) is incorrect because it does not
matter whether Able believed she was acting
within the scope of her authority. The third
party (Sky) must have reason to believe that
the agent is acting within his/her authority
before the principal will be held liable for
the contract. Answer (c) is incorrect because
both employees and independent contractors can
act as agents for the principal and would have
the ability to bind the principal under apparent authority. Answer (d) is incorrect because regardless of how the agency relationship was formed, the principal will not be
held liable for a contract unless the agent
was acting within his/her authority (express,
implied, or apparent).

9.   (585,L1,1) (d) Under the Statute of
Frauds, certain contracts must be contained in
a signed writing to be enforceable. Among
these is a contract that cannot be performed
within one year. In a personal service contract, the one-year period begins running at
the time that the contract is formed, not at
the time the service is to commence. A contract creating an agency relationship for the
forthcoming year which is entered into in mid-
December of the prior year could not possibly
be performed within one year and, therefore,
must be contained in a signed writing in order
to be in compliance with the Statute of
Frauds. Answer (a) is incorrect because an
agreement creating an agency relationship
authorizing the agent to sell goods that have
a value in excess of $500 need not be in
writing, although any such contracts entered
into by that agent must be in writing in order
to be enforceable under the Statute of Frauds.

Answer (b) is incorrect because an irrevocable
agency need not be contained in a signed
writing. Answer (c) is incorrect since it
describes an agency relationship which is
capable of being performed within one year.

10. (1181,L1,12) (a) A contract is not
required to create an agency relationship.
Such relationships can be created in numerous
ways, including by agreement, operation of
law, ratification and estoppel. Answer (b) is
incorrect because an agent is subject to the
continuous general control of the principal.
Answer (c) is incorrect because an agent is a
fiduciary; he owes the principal the obligation of faithful service. Answer (d) is
incorrect because an agent must act for the
benefit of the principal; an agent acts for
and in place of the principal to effect legal
relations with third persons.

B.5. Ratification

11.   (588,L1,5) (d) Ratification occurs
when there is a subsequent approval by the
principal of an agent's unauthorized action.
In order for ratification to take place, the
principal must have knowledge of all material
facts regarding the contract. Answer (a) is
incorrect because it is not necessary that the
principal expressly communicate an intent to
be bound. If the principal acts in a manner
as to imply ratification (e.g., by taking
advantage of the benefits of the contracts),
then the principal's actions will be
interpreted as ratification. Answer (b) is
incorrect because it makes no difference
whether or not the agent acts reasonably and
in the best interest of the principal. The
principal may ratify any contract as long as
the requirements for ratification are
satisfied. Answer (c) is incorrect because a
principal may ratify a contract entered into
by any type of agent.

12.   (587,L1,6) (d) Ratification occurs
only when a disclosed principal grants
approval after the fact of an unauthorized act
done by an agent or one not yet an agent.
Ratification is not effective, however, if the
third party withdraws from the contract before
the ratification occurs. Therefore, Maple
will lose since King gave notification of
withdrawal prior to Maple's ratification. Answers (a) and (b) are incorrect because
although ratification of an agreement in its
entirety and ratification by a disclosed
principal both represent requirements of an
effective ratification, such factors will be
irrelevant if the third party withdraws from
the contract prior to ratification. Answer (c) is incorrect because although Starr,

the agent, had no authority to bind Maple, the principal, to the contract when it was created, a subsequent ratification would relate back to the date of creation of the contract (May 1) and create a binding agreement. However, for this to occur, the ratification must be effective before the third party's withdrawal.

13. (584,L1,3) (a) Although the agent's act was outside the scope of his authority, the principal may, nevertheless, ratify the contract. Retention of the benefits of the contract constitutes implied ratification. Answer (b) is incorrect because ratification must occur before the third party withdraws from the contract. Answer (c) is incorrect because when the contract is unauthorized, the third party does not have the option of electing to hold the principal liable. The third party's awareness of the limitation on the agent's authority does not change the fact that the contract is unauthorized. Answer (d) is, therefore, also incorrect.

E. Obligations and Rights

14. (589,L1,13) (c) Simmons exceeded his express authority when he granted the 10% price discount to Hemple; therefore, Simmons would be liable to Jensen for the amount of damage caused by Simmons' breach, $50 [(10% - 5%) x $1,000]. Answers (a), (b), and (d) are incorrect because Hemple had not previously dealt with Simmons or Jensen; therefore, Simmons was acting with apparent authority when he granted the 10% price discount to Hemple. Consequently, Jensen would not be able to void the sale or recover from Hemple.

15. (585,L1,5) (c) As a fiduciary to the principal, an agent must act in the best interest of the principal. Therefore, the agent has an obligation to refrain from competing with or acting adversely to the principal, unless the principal knows and approves of such activity. Answer (a) is incorrect because the Statute of Frauds would not require that the described agency relationship be contained in a signed writing since it is possible for the contract to be performed within 1 year. Answer (b) is incorrect because the mere right of the agent to receive a percentage of proceeds is not sufficient to constitute an agency coupled with an interest. In order to have an agency coupled with an interest, the agent must have either a property interest or a security interest in the subject matter of the agency relationship. Answer (d) is incorrect because in all agency relationships, except agencies coupled with an interest, the principal always has the power

to dismiss the agent. However, the principal does not necessarily have the right to terminate the relationship. In certain situations the dismissed agent could sue for breach of contract.

E.3. Principal's Liability to Third Parties

16. (586,L1,59) (a) Apparent authority exists when a third party has reason to believe that an agent has the authority to enter into contracts of the nature involved, based upon a principal's representations. Secret limitations placed on the agent's normal authority creates apparent authority. In this case, it was reasonable for Shady to believe that Borg had the authority to enter into the contract, given Borg's position in the company as vice-president of purchasing. The fact that Dent secretly limited Borg's authority has no effect, and Crater Corp. can be held liable for the full terms of the contract. Thus, answers (b) and (c) are incorrect. Answer (d) is incorrect since the fact that neither party has yet relied on the contract to their detriment is irrelevant.

17. (578,L1,10) (d) The principal, Futterman, is liable for the acts of his general agent, even though the agent violated rules which were unknown to the third party. Answer (a) is incorrect because even though Marra did not have actual authority to buy at 30 cents a pound, she had apparent authority to do so (because she was a general purchasing agent). Answer (b) is incorrect because Futterman is liable on this contract. Answer (c) is incorrect because Marra has potential liability both to third parties for violating her warranty of authority and to her principal for disregarding proper instructions.

E.4. Agent's Liability to Third Parties

18. (586,L1,60) (d) In the event that an undisclosed principal is discovered by a third party to a contract, that third party may choose to hold either the principal or the agent liable on the contract. Thus, in this case, Datz or Cox may be held liable on the contract. Answer (a) is incorrect because an undisclosed principal does not have to ratify the authorized contracts of the agent in order to be bound on such agreements. Answer (b) is incorrect since, unlike the disclosed principal relationship, an agent representing an undisclosed principal is liable on authorized contracts made on behalf of the principal. Answer (c) is incorrect because the third party is bound to the contract even though the

identity of the principal was unknown at the time of contracting.

19. (1183,L1,13) (b) An agent is personally liable for the torts he commits, whether inside or outside the scope of his employment, and regardless of whether or not the principal is also liable for the tort. The principal's authorization of the tort is no defense to the agent's liability. Answer (d) is incorrect because an agent has the duty to keep the funds and property of his principal separate from his own. Maintaining proper records is no defense to the breach of this duty. Answer (a) is incorrect because every agent owes his principal a fiduciary duty of loyalty and trust. The fact that the agent does not compete with his principal does not relieve the agent of this duty. Answer (c) is incorrect because the circumstances indicate Carr's implied authority is limited. The fact that Carr must report directly to his superior, the credit manager, infers that Carr's authority does not extend to such managerial decisions as instituting legal action.

20. (1180,L1,27) (a) Since an agent, after the principal ratifies an unauthorized act, is acting within his authority and is free of any liability on the contract. An agent is personally liable for all torts s/he commits. Therefore, answer (b) is incorrect. Answer (c) is incorrect because an agent is liable if s/he acts for a principal which s/he knows is nonexistent and knows the third party is unaware of this. Answer (d) is incorrect because if an agent contracts for an undisclosed principal, the agent remains liable to the third party even though he is acting within the scope of his/her authority. The agent, however, has recourse against the principal. The third party can sue either the principal or agent.

F. Termination of Principal–Agent Relationship

21. (1188,L1,2) (a) The declaration of Elkin's incapacity constitutes the termination of the agency relationship by operation of law. When an agency relationship is terminated by operation of law, the agent's authority to enter into a binding agreement on behalf of the principal ceases. There is no requirement that notice be given to third parties when the agency relationship is terminated by operation of law. In this case Elkin will not be liable to Ajax, regardless of the fact that Ajax was not given notice of the termination of the agency relationship, because Harris was without authority to enter into the contract. Answer (b) is incorrect

because the relationship was terminated by operation of law. Consequently, no notice need be given to Harris, even though Harris had previously dealt with Elkin. Answer (c) is incorrect because Harris' authority terminated upon the declaration of Elkin's incapacity. Answer (d) is incorrect because insanity of the principal terminates the agency relationship even though the third parties are unaware of the principal's insanity.

22. (588,L1,6) (b) If an agency relationship terminates by operation of law, there generally is no requirement that third parties be notified. Upon the death of either the principal or agent, the agency relationship is terminated by the operation of law requiring no notice to third parties. Answers (a), (c), and (d) are incorrect because these are situations that constitute termination by the acts of the parties and, therefore, would require notice to third parties to terminate the apparent authority of a general agent.

23. (1187,L1,25) (a) When the agency relationship is terminated by an act of the principal and/or agent, third parties are entitled to notice of the termination from the principal. Failure of the principal to give the required notice gives the agent apparent authority to act on behalf of the principal. Specifically, the principal must give actual notice to all parties who had prior dealings with the agent or principal. Constructive or public notice must be given to parties who knew of the existence of the agency relationship, but did not actually have business dealings with the agent or principal. Since Dart Corp. did not give proper constructive notice to Bing Corp., Ritz had apparent authority to bind the principal and, therefore, Bing Corp. will win. Accordingly, answer (c) is incorrect. Answer (b) is incorrect because a principal is not an absolute insurer of his agent's acts. A principal is liable for his agent's torts only if the principal expressly authorizes the conduct or the tort is committed within the scope of the agent's employment. Answer (d) is incorrect because Dart is liable for the torts of its authorized agent under the doctrine of respondeat superior.

24. (587,L1,4) (d) A general agent's apparent authority to bind the principal in contracts with third parties arises when the third parties hold a reasonable belief based on the principal's representations that the agent has been granted actual authority. The agency relationship and the agent's apparent authority may be terminated, however, by

operation of law such as when the principal is granted a discharge in bankruptcy. When the agency relationship is terminated in this manner, no notice need be given to third parties. Answers (a), (b), and (c) are all incorrect because they all describe situations where the agency relationship is terminated by acts of the parties. In these situations, actual notice is owed to third parties who have previously dealt with the agent and constructive notice must be given to third parties who have not previously dealt with the agent, but who were aware of the existence of the relationship.

25. (585,L1,3) (a) An agency coupled with an interest will be created any time the agent has either a property interest or a security interest in the subject matter of the agency. If a lender obtains authorization to sell pledged securities and applies the proceeds to the loan in the event of the borrower's default, that lender becomes an agent with a security interest in the subject matter of the agency relationship, and the agency is irrevocable. Answers (b), (c), and (d) are all incorrect because they describe situations in which the agent merely has rights to a percentage of proceeds to be received, but has no interest in the subject matter of the agency relationship.

May 1990 Answers

26. (590,L1,1) (c) An agency relationship is terminated by operation of law if the subject of the agreement becomes illegal or impossible, the principal or the agent dies or becomes insane, or the principal becomes bankrupt. Answers (a), (b), and (d) are incorrect because they will cause the termination of an agency relationship by operation of law. Answer (c), agent's renunciation of the agency, will not cause the termination of an agency relationship.

27. (590,L1,2) (d) In general, the employer is not responsible for the crimes of the employee unless the employer aided or permitted the illegal activity even if the activity was within the scope of the employment. Answer (a) is incorrect because if the employer did nothing to instruct the employee about the use of the weapon, this could help establish negligence on the part of the employer and would not prevent the use of the doctrine of respondeat superior which makes employers liable for the tortious acts of their employees within the scope of the employment. Answer (b) is incorrect because the employer is liable for torts of the employee committed within the course and scope of the employment even if the employee was violating the employer's instructions. An-

swer (c) is incorrect because even if the employee's suspicions were correct, the shooting of an innocent passerby should establish at least negligence for which the employer and the employee are liable.

28. (590,L1,3) (d) When the principal is undisclosed in an agency relationship, the agent generally has the same authority as if the principal were disclosed. The main difference is in the liability of the agent to third parties. Answer (a) is incorrect because the principal is liable on the contract because of the express authority given to the agent to make the contract on behalf of the principal. Apparent authority exists when the principal represents the agent to third parties to be his/her agent. In this case, the principal wished to be undisclosed. Answer (b) is incorrect because the agent can be held liable on the contract by third parties when the principal is undisclosed. Answer (c) is incorrect because principal can be held liable for negligence committed by the agent within the course and scope of the agency.

29. (590,L1,4) (c) One who issues a personal check is liable on it; however, any party or principal who is not disclosed on the check is not liable on the negotiable instrument. Answers (a) and (b) are incorrect because the third party can elect to hold either the agent or the principal liable when the agent makes a contract for an undisclosed principal. Answer (d) is incorrect because the party who signs a check is liable on it.

30. (590,L1,5) (b) While Ace is acting as Butler's agent, Ace has implied authority to the extent reasonably necessary or usual to carry out the express authority of the principal (Butler). Butler has expressly authorized Ace to act as business manager, which implies duties of purchasing inventory, (a), paying debts, (c), and hiring/discharging employees, (d). Answer (b) is correct because selling business fixtures would not be considered an implied or normal duty of a business manager.

Answer Outline*

Problem 1   Principal's Power and Right to
            Terminate Agency (1185,L3b)

b. Lemon's first assertion is incorrect
      Agency coupled with an interest requires
      agent to have an interest in property
      which is subject of agency
      Lemon's commission agreement does not
      qualify as an agency coupled with an
      interest
    Lemon's second assertion is incorrect
      Principal has the power to discharge the
      agent, although the principal may not
      have the right to do so
    Lemon's third assertion is correct
      If principal wrongfully discharges
      agent, principal is liable for damages
      under breach of contract

Unofficial Answer*

Problem 1   Principal's Power and Right to
            Terminate Agency (1185,L3b)

b. Lemon's first assertion that he is an
agent coupled with an interest is incorrect.
An agency coupled with an interest in the
subject matter arises when the agent has an
interest in the property that is the subject
of the agency. The fact that Lemon entered
into a two-year written agency agreement with
the partnership that would pay Lemon a commission clearly will not establish an interest
in the subject matter of the agency. The mere
expectation of profits to be realized or proceeds to be derived from the sale of the partnership's products is not sufficient to create
an agency coupled with an interest. As a result, the principal-agency relationship may be
terminated at any time.

Lemon's second assertion that the principal-agency relationship may not be terminated without cause prior to the expiration of
its term is incorrect. Where a principal-
agency relationship is based upon a contract
to engage the agent for a specified period of
time, the principal may discharge the agent
despite the fact such discharge is wrongful.
Although the principal does not have the right
to discharge the agent, he does have the power
to do so. Thus, Lemon may be discharged
without cause.

Lemon's third assertion that he is entitled to damages because of the termination
of the agency relationship is correct. Where
a principal wrongfully discharges its agent,
the principal is liable for damages based on
breach of contract. Under the facts, Lemon's
discharge by the partnership without cause
constitutes a breach of contract for which
Lemon may recover damages.

Answer Outline

Problem 2   Ratification (580,L5a)

a. Yes, Duval will prevail in breach of
      contract action
      Initially Vogel (agent) had no express or
      apparent authority; however, principal
      ratified unauthorized contract by
        Retaining and displaying goods
        Lack of timely notification of refusal
          of goods
      Granite would not be liable if immediate
      notification had occurred

Unofficial Answer

Problem 2   Ratification (580,L5a)

a. Yes. Despite the stated lack of express
or apparent initial authority of Vogel, Granite City Department Store's agent, there would
appear to be a ratification by the principal.

It is clear from the facts stated that
Granite would not have been liable on the
Vogel contract if the head buyer had immediately notified Duval and returned the goods.
Instead the head buyer retained the goods and
placed some on display in an attempt to sell
them. Had they proved to be a "hot" item,
undoubtedly the art objects would have been
gratefully kept by Granite. Granite wants to
reject the goods if they don't sell. Such
conduct is inconsistent with a repudiation
based upon the agent's lack of express or
apparent authority. The retention of the
goods for the time indicated, the attempted
sale of the goods, and a failure to notify
Duval in a timely way, when taken together,
constitute a ratification of the unauthorized
contract.

*The solutions approach for this question
 appears in Chapter 3, Solutions Approach.

Multiple Choice Questions (1-26)

1. Many states require partnerships to file the partnership name under laws which are generally known as fictitious name statutes. These statutes
   a. Require a proper filing as a condition precedent to the valid creation of a partnership.
   b. Are designed primarily to provide registration for tax purposes.
   c. Are designed to clarify the rights and duties of the members of the partnership.
   d. Have little effect on the creation or operation of a partnership other than the imposition of a fine for noncompliance.

2. Rivers and Lee want to form a partnership. For the partnership agreement to be enforceable, it must be in writing if
   a. Rivers and Lee reside in different states
   b. The agreement cannot be completed within one year from the date on which it will be entered into.
   c. Either Rivers or Lee is to contribute more than $500 in capital.
   d. The partnership intends to buy and sell real estate.

3. Three independent sole proprietors decided to pool their resources and form a partnership. The business assets and liabilities of each were transferred to the partnership. The partnership commenced business on September 1, 1981, but the parties did not execute a formal partnership agreement until October 15, 1981. Which of the following is correct?
   a. The existing creditors must consent to the transfer of the individual business assets to the partnership.
   b. The partnership began its existence on September 1, 1981.
   c. If the partnership's duration is indefinite, the partnership agreement must be in writing and signed.
   d. In the absence of a partnership agreement specifically covering division of losses among the partners, they will be deemed to share them in accordance with their capital contributions.

4. With respect to the following matters, which is correct if a general partnership agreement is silent?
   a. A partnership will continue indefinitely unless a majority of the partners votes to dissolve the partnership.
   b. Partnership losses are allocated in the same proportion as partnership profits.
   c. A partner may assign his interest in the partnership but only with the consent of the other partners.
   d. A partner may sell the goodwill of the partnership without the consent of the other partners when the sale is in the best interest of the partnership.

5. Ted Fein, a partner in the ABC Partnership, wishes to withdraw from the partnership and sell his interest to Gold. All of the other partners in ABC have agreed to admit Gold as a partner and to hold Fein harmless for the past, present, and future liabilities of ABC. A provision in the original partnership agreement states that the partnership will continue upon the death or withdrawal of one or more of the partners.
   As a result of Fein's withdrawal and Gold's admission to the partnership, Gold
   a. Is personally liable for partnership liabilities arising before and after his admission as a partner.
   b. Has the right to participate in the management of ABC.
   c. Acquired only the right to receive Fein's share of the profits of ABC.
   d. Must contribute cash or property to ABC in order to be admitted with the same rights as the other partners.

6. Kroll, Inc., a partner in JKL Partnership, assigns its interest in the partnership to Trell, who is not made a partner. After the assignment, Trell asserts the rights to

   I. Receive Kroll's share of JKL's profits and
   II. Inspect JKL's books and records.

   Trell is correct as to which of the rights?
   a. I only.
   b. II only.
   c. I and II.
   d. Neither I nor II.

7. Gillie, Taft, and Dall are partners in an architectural firm. The partnership agreement is silent about the payment of salaries and the division of profits and losses. Gillie works full time in the firm, and Taft and Dall

each work half time. Taft invested $120,000 in the firm, and Gillie and Dall invested $60,000 each. Dall is responsible for bringing in 50% of the business, and Gillie and Taft 25% each. How should profits of $120,000 for the year be divided?

    a.   Gillie $60,000, Taft $30,000, Dall $30,000.

    b.   Gillie $40,000, Taft $40,000, Dall $40,000.

    c.   Gillie $30,000, Taft $60,000, Dall $30,000.

    d.   Gillie $30,000, Taft $30,000, Dall $60,000.

8.   A partner's interest in specific partnership property is

	Assignable to the partner's individual creditors	Subject to attachment by the partner's individual creditors
a.	Yes	Yes
b.	Yes	No
c.	No	Yes
d.	No	No

9.   Dill was properly admitted as a partner in the ABC Partnership after purchasing Ard's partnership interest. Ard immediately withdrew from the partnership. The partnership agreement states that the partnership will continue on the withdrawal or admission of a partner. Unless the partners otherwise agree,

    a.   Dill's personal liability for partnership debts incurred before Dill was admitted will be limited to Dill's interest in partnership property.

    b.   Ard will automatically be released from personal liability for partnership debts incurred before Dill's admission.

    c.   Ard will be permitted to recover from the other partners the full amount that Ard has paid on account of partnership debts incurred before Dill's admission.

    d.   Dill will be subjected to unlimited personal liability for partnership debts incurred before being admitted.

10.   The apparent authority of a partner to bind the partnership in dealing with third parties

    a.   Would permit a partner to submit a claim against the partnership to arbitration.

    b.   Must be derived from the express powers and purposes contained in the partnership agreement.

    c.   Will be effectively limited by a formal resolution of the partners of which third parties are aware.

    d.   Will be effectively limited by a formal resolution of the partners of which third parties are unaware.

11.   Ted Fein, a partner in the ABC Partnership, wishes to withdraw from the partnership and sell his interest to Gold. All of the other partners in ABC have agreed to admit Gold as a partner and to hold Fein harmless for the past, present, and future liabilities of ABC. A provision in the original partnership agreement states that the partnership will continue upon the death or withdrawal of one or more of the partners.

    The agreement to hold Fein harmless for all past, present, and future liabilities of ABC will

    a.   Prevent partnership creditors from holding Fein personally liable only as to those liabilities of ABC existing at the time of Fein's withdrawal.

    b.   Prevent partnership creditors from holding Fein personally liable for the past, present, and future liabilities of ABC.

    c.   Not affect the rights of partnership creditors to hold Fein personally liable for those liabilities.

    d.   Permit Fein to recover from the other partners only amounts he has paid in excess of his proportionate share.

12.   A general partner of a mercantile partnership

    a.   Can by virtue of his acts, impose tort liability upon the other partners.

    b.   Has no implied authority if the partnership agreement is contained in a formal and detailed signed writing.

    c.   Can have his apparent authority effectively negated by the express limitations in the partnership agreement.

    d.   Can not be sued individually for a tort he has committed in carrying on partnership business until the partnership has been sued and a judgment returned unsatisfied.

13.   In determining the liability of a partnership for the acts of a partner purporting to act for the partnership without the authorization of fellow partners, which of the following actions will bind the partnership?

1
4

a. The renewal of an existing supply
    contract which the other partners
    had decided to terminate and which
    they had specifically voted against.
b. An assignment of the partnership
    assets in trust for the benefit of
    creditors.
c. A written admission of liability in
    a lawsuit brought against the part-
    nership.
d. Signing the partnership name as a
    surety on a note for the purchase of
    that partner's summer home.

14. One of your audit clients, Major Supply,
Inc. is seeking a judgment against Danforth on
the basis of a representation made by one
Coleman, in Danforth's presence, that they
were in partnership together doing business as
the D & C Trading Partnership. Major Supply
received an order from Coleman on behalf of
D & C and shipped $800 worth of goods to Cole-
man. Coleman has defaulted on payment of the
bill and is insolvent. Danforth denies he is
Coleman's partner and that he has any liability for the goods. Insofar as Danforth's liability is concerned, which of the following is
correct?

a. Danforth is **not** liable if he is **not**
    in fact Coleman's partner.
b. Since Danforth did **not** make the
    statement about being Coleman's
    partner, he is **not** liable.
c. If Major Supply gave credit in reli-
    ance upon the misrepresentation made
    by Coleman, Danforth is a partner by
    estoppel.
d. Since the "partnership" is operating
    under a fictitious name (the D & C
    Partnership), a filing is required,
    and Major Supply's failure to ascer-
    tain whether there was in fact such
    a partnership precludes it from
    recovering.

15. Cass is a general partner in Omega
Company general partnership. Which of the
following unauthorized acts by Cass will bind
Omega?
a. Submitting a claim against Omega to
    arbitration.
b. Confessing a judgment against Omega.
c. Selling Omega's goodwill.
d. Leasing office space for Omega.

16. Darla, Jack, and Sam have formed a partnership with each agreeing to contribute
$100,000. Jack and Sam each contributed
$100,000 cash. Darla contributed $75,000 cash
and agreed to pay an additional $25,000 two
years later. After one year of operations the

partnership is insolvent. The liabilities and
fair market value of the assets of the partnership are as follows:

Assets:

Cash	$ 40,000
Trade accounts receivable	35,000
Receivable from Darla	25,000
Equipment	100,000
	$200,000

Liabilities:

Trade accounts payable	$410,000

Both Jack and Sam are personally insolvent.
Darla has a net worth of $750,000.

If Darla is a general partner, what is
her maximum potential liability?
a. $ 95,000
b. $185,000
c. $210,000
d. $235,000

17. X, Y, and Z have capital balances of
$30,000, $15,000, and $5,000, respectively, in
the XYZ Partnership. The general partnership
agreement is silent as to the manner in which
partnership losses are to be allocated but
does provide that partnership profits are to
be allocated as follows: 40% to X, 25% to Y,
and 35% to Z. The partners have decided to
dissolve and liquidate the partnership. After
paying all creditors, the amount available for
distribution will be $20,000. X, Y, and Z are
individually solvent. Under the circumstances, Z will
a. Receive $7,000.
b. Receive $12,000.
c. Personally have to contribute an
    additional $5,500.
d. Personally have to contribute an
    additional $5,000.

18. Grey and Carr entered into a written
partnership agreement to operate a hardware
store. Their agreement was silent as to the
duration of the partnership. Grey wishes to
dissolve the partnership. Which of the
following statements is correct?
a. Unless Carr consents to a dissolu-
    tion, Grey must apply to a court and
    obtain a decree ordering the
    dissolution.
b. Grey may **not** dissolve the
    partnership unless Carr consents.
c. Grey may dissolve the partnership
    only after notice of the proposed
    dissolution is given to all partner-
    ship creditors.
d. Grey may dissolve the partnership at
    any time.

19. The partnership agreement of one of your clients provides that upon death or withdrawal, a partner shall be entitled to the book value of his or her partnership interest as of the close of the year preceding such death or withdrawal and nothing more. It also provides that the partnership shall continue. Regarding this partnership provision, which of the following is a correct statement?

    a. It is unconscionable on its face.

    b. It has the legal effect of preventing a dissolution upon the death or withdrawal of a partner.

    c. It effectively eliminates the legal necessity of a winding up of the partnership upon the death or withdrawal of a partner.

    d. It is **not** binding upon the spouse of a deceased partner if the book value figure is less than the fair market value at the date of death.

20. Perone was a member of Cass, Hack & Perone, a general trading partnership. He died on August 2, 1980. The partnership is insolvent, but Perone's estate is substantial. The creditors of the partnership are seeking to collect on their claims from Perone's estate. Which of the following statements is correct insofar as their claims are concerned?

    a. The death of Perone caused a dissolution of the firm, thereby freeing his estate from personal liability.

    b. If the existing obligations to Perone's personal creditors are all satisfied, then the remaining estate assets are available to satisfy partnership debts.

    c. The creditors must first proceed against the remaining partners before Perone's estate can be held liable for the partnership's debts.

    d. The liability of Perone's estate can **not** exceed his capital contribution plus that percentage of the deficit attributable to his capital contribution.

21. Darla, Jack, and Sam have formed a partnership with each agreeing to contribute $100,000. Jack and Sam each contributed $100,000 cash. Darla contributed $75,000 cash and agreed to pay an additional $25,000 two years later. After one year of operations the partnership is insolvent. The liabilities and fair market value of the assets of the partnership are as follows:

Assets:

Cash	$ 40,000
Trade accounts receivable	35,000
Receivable from Darla	25,000
Equipment	100,000
	$200,000

Liabilities:

Trade accounts payable	$410,000

Both Jack and Sam are personally insolvent. Darla has a net worth of $750,000. If Darla is a limited partner, what is her maximum potential liability?

    a. $0

    b. $ 25,000

    c. $210,000

    d. $235,000

22. White, Grey, and Fox formed a limited partnership. White is the general partner and Grey and Fox are the limited partners. Each agreed to contribute $200,000. Grey and Fox each contributed $200,000 in cash while White contributed $150,000 in cash and $50,000 worth of services already rendered. After two years, the partnership is insolvent. The fair market value of the assets of the partnership is $150,000 and the liabilities total $275,000. The partners have made no withdrawals.

If Fox is insolvent and White and Grey each has a net worth in excess of $300,000, what is White's maximum potential liability in the event of a dissolution of the partnership?

    a. $ 62,500

    b. $112,500

    c. $125,000

    d. $175,000

23. A limited partner

    a. May not withdraw his capital contribution unless there is sufficient limited partnership property to pay all general creditors.

    b. Must not own limited partnership interests in other competing limited partnerships.

    c. Is automatically an agent for the partnership with apparent authority to bind the limited partnership in contract.

    d. Has no liability to creditors even if he takes part in the control of the business as long as he is held out as being a limited partner.

24. A limited partner's capital contribution to the limited partnership
    a. Creates an intangible personal property right of the limited partner in the limited partnership.
    b. Can be withdrawn at the limited partner's option at any time prior to the filing of a petition in bankruptcy against the limited partnership.
    c. Can only consist of cash or marketable securities.
    d. Need not be indicated in the limited partnership's certificate.

25. Which of the following statements regarding a limited partner is(are) generally correct?

	The limited partner is subject to personal liability for partnership debts	The limited partner has the right to take part in the control of the partnership
a.	Yes	Yes
b.	Yes	No
c.	No	Yes
d.	No	No

26. A joint venture is a(an)
    a. Association limited to no more than two persons in business for profit.
    b. Enterprise of numerous co-owners in a nonprofit undertaking.
    c. Corporate enterprise for a single undertaking of limited duration.
    d. Association of persons engaged as co-owners in a single undertaking for profit.

Problems

Problem 1 (1186,L2)

(15 to 20 minutes)

Edna Slavin intends to enter into a limited partnership with three of her business associates. Slavin wishes to know the advantages and disadvantages of being a general partner as opposed to a limited partner in a limited partnership. The issues of most concern to Slavin are:

• Her right as a general or limited partner to participate in the daily management of the partnership.

• Her liability as a general or limited partner for debts incurred on behalf of or by the partnership.

• Her right as a general or limited partner to assign her partnership interest and substitute a third party as a partner.

• The effect of a clause in the certificate of limited partnership which would permit the partnership to continue after the death of one of the general or limited partners.

Required:

Answer the following, setting forth reasons for any conclusions stated.
What are the essential differences in the formation of a general partnership and a limited partnership? Discuss in separate paragraphs the issues raised by Slavin.

Problem 2 (1185,L3a)

(7 to 10 minutes)

John Nolan, a partner in Nolan, Stein, & Wolf partnership, transferred his interest in the partnership to Simon and withdrew from the partnership. Although the partnership will continue, Stein and Wolf have refused to admit Simon as a partner.

Subsequently, the partnership appointed Ed Lemon as its agent to market its various product lines. Lemon entered into a two-year written agency contract with the partnership which provided that Lemon would receive a 10% sales commission. The agency contract was signed by Lemon and, on behalf of the partnership, by Stein and Wolf.

After six months, Lemon was terminated without cause. Lemon asserts that:

• He is an agent coupled with an interest.

• The agency relationship may not be terminated without cause prior to the expiration of its term.

• He is entitled to damages because of the termination of the agency relationship.

Required:

Answer the following, setting forth reasons for any conclusions stated.
Discuss Nolan's property rights in the partnership prior to his withdrawal and the property rights acquired by Simon as a result of his transaction with Nolan.

Problem 3 (1188,L4)

(15 to 20 minutes)

On January 5, Stein, Rey, and Lusk entered into a written general partnership agreement by which they agreed to operate a stock brokerage firm. The agreement stated that the partnership would continue upon the death or withdrawal of a partner. The agreement also provided that no partner could reduce the firm's commission below 2% without the consent of all of the other partners. On March 10, Rey, without the consent of Stein and Lusk, agreed with King Corp. to reduce the commission to 1 1/2% on a large transaction by King. Rey believed this would entice King to become a regular customer of the firm. King was unaware of any of the terms of the partnership agreement.

On May 15, Stein entered into a contract conveying Stein's partnership to Park and withdrew from the partnership. That same day, all of the partners agreed to admit Park as a general partner. Notice of Stein's withdrawal and Park's admission as a partner was properly published in two newspapers. In addition, third parties who had conducted business with the partnership prior to May 15 received written notice of Stein's withdrawal.

Required:

a. In separate paragraphs, discuss whether:
1. The partnership could recover the 1/2% commission from King.
2. The partnership could recover the 1/2% commission from Rey.

b. In separate paragraphs, discuss:
1. Park's liability for partnership obligations arising both before and after being admitted to the partnership.
2. Stein's liability for partnership obligations arising both before and after withdrawing from the partnership.

Problem 4   (584,L5a)

(7 to 10 minutes)

Part a. Hart was a partner in the Hart,
Gray & Race partnership. He entered into a
contract conveying to Paul his partnership
interest. The contract, which was consented
to by Gray and Race, provided that Paul would
become a partner. All known past and present
partnership creditors were given written
notice of Hart's withdrawal. Within nine
months, the partnership became insolvent. The
parties are concerned about their liability
for the partnership obligations.

Required:

Answer the following, setting forth
reasons for any conclusions stated.
1. What effect does Hart's withdrawal
have upon his liability with respect to
existing debts of the partnership and to debts
incurred after his withdrawal?
2. Describe Paul's liability for partnership obligations entered into prior to and
after his admission to the partnership.

Multiple Choice Answers

1. d	7. b	12. a	17. c	22. c
2. b	8. d	13. a	18. d	23. a
3. b	9. a	14. c	19. c	24. a
4. b	10. c	15. d	20. b	25. d
5. b	11. c	16. d	21. b	26. d
6. a				

Multiple Choice Answer Explanations

C. Formation of Partnerships

1. (1183,L1,15) (d) The purpose of fictitious name statutes is to enable interested parties to learn the identity of the individuals who operate the business. Since the name under which the business is operating often does not include the names of the partners, these statutes provide the necessary link between the name of the business and the names of the individual partners. The typical fictitious name statute provides for the imposition of a fine in the event of noncompliance. Answer (a) is incorrect because such statutes do not affect the creation of a partnership. Answer (b) is incorrect because fictitious name statutes are not related to tax purposes. It should be kept in mind that a partnership is not a separate taxable entity. Answer (c) is incorrect because such statutes are designed for the benefit of parties outside the partnership, not for the purpose of defining the rights and duties of the partners themselves.

2. (589,L1,14) (b) A partnership agreement may be expressed or implied based upon the activities and conduct of the partners. The expressed agreement may be oral or in writing with, in general, one exception. A partnership agreement that cannot be completed within one year from the date on which it is entered into must be in writing. Answer (a) is incorrect because the partners may reside in different states without having to put the partnership agreement in writing. Answer (c) is incorrect because the $500 amount applies to the sale of goods which must be in writing, not partnerships. Answer (d) is incorrect because the purpose of the partnership is irrelevant. Agreements to buy and sell real estate must be in writing, while an agreement to form a partnership whose principal activity will involve the buying and selling of real estate normally need not be in writing unless the stated duration exceeds one year.

3. (582,L1,1) (b) The Uniform Partnership Act defines a partnership as an association of two or more persons to carry on as co-owners a business for profit. A partnership relationship can be implied by the acts of the parties, as long as it appears that the parties intended joint responsibility in the management and operation of the business, and intended to share in its profits and losses. Therefore, the partnership began its existence on September 1, 1981, when the three sole proprietors demonstrated the necessary intent to carry on a business as partners. Answer (a) is incorrect because the existing creditors do not have to consent to the transfer of the individual business assets to the partnership. However, the creditors' rights are not affected or destroyed, and the creditors can avoid the transfer of assets if proved to be a fraudulent conveyance on the part of the three sole proprietors. Answer (c) is incorrect because a written agreement is not ordinarily necessary to create a partnership, unless it falls within the provisions of the Statute of Frauds (i.e., a partnership agreement which by its terms can not be performed within a year). Therefore, this partnership agreement falls outside the Statute of Frauds, since the partnership's duration is indefinite. Answer (d) is incorrect because unless the partnership agreement provides otherwise, the law implies that profits and losses are to be shared equally by the partners.

D. Partner's Rights

4. (587,L1,10) (b) If a general partnership agreement is silent regarding the distribution of the partnership's losses, such losses are to be allocated in the same proportion as partnership profits. Answer (a) is incorrect because many events can occur (e.g., death of a partner) which will cause a dissolution of the partnership without a majority vote by the partners. Answer (c) is incorrect since an interest in a partnership is freely assignable without the other partner's consent. Answer (d) is incorrect because the only time a partner may sell the goodwill of the partnership is when such a sale has been unanimously approved by the partners.

5. (586,L1,55) (b) An incoming partner has the same rights as all of the existing partners. Thus, an incoming partner has the right to participate in the management of the partnership. Thus, answer (c) is incorrect. Answer (a) is incorrect since a person admitted as a partner into an existing partnership is only liable for existing debts of the partnership to the extent of the incoming partner's capital contribution. Answer (d) is incorrect because a partner need not make a capital contribution to be admitted with the same rights as the other partners.

6.   (589,L1,16) (a) A partner is free to assign his interest in any partnership to a third party. However, the assignee does not become a partner by virtue of this assignment, but merely succeeds to the assignor's rights as to profits and return of partner's capital contribution. The assignee does not receive the right to manage, to have an accounting, to inspect the books, or to possess or use any individual partnership property. Since Trell was not made a partner, he is entitled to Kroll's share of JKL's profits, but does not have the right to inspect JKL's books and records.

7.   (1189,L1,6) (b) If the partnership agreement is silent about the payment of salaries and the division of profits and losses, then the profits and losses shall be shared equally among all partners and no salaries are paid. In this case, the profits of $120,000 are divided equally among Gillie, Taft, and Dall so that each partner receives $40,000. Therefore, answers (a), (c), and (d) are incorrect.

8.   (1189,L1,7) (d) Specific partnership property is property owned as tenants in partnership with other partners. All partners have equal rights to the property and can possess or use the partnership property for partnership purposes. Partnership property is not assignable to a partner's individual creditors; therefore, the first statement is incorrect. Partnership property can only be assigned if all partners agree, or if the property is assigned for the apparent purpose of carrying on the business. Partnership property is not subject to attachment by the partner's individual creditors; therefore, the second statement is incorrect. Partnership property is generally only subject to attachment by a claim on the entire partnership.

E. Relationship to Third Parties

9.   (588,L1,7) (a) When a new partner is admitted into a partnership, s/he is liable for existing debts of the partnership only to the extent of his/her capital contribution. An exception to this rule exists only if the new partner assumes personal liability for existing partnership debts. Therefore, answer (d) is incorrect. Answer (b) is incorrect because a withdrawing partner continues to be liable on partnership debts arising prior to his/her withdrawal from the partnership. Answer (c) is incorrect because Ard (the withdrawing partner) is personally liable on partnership debts incurred prior to Dill's admission and, therefore, would have no right to recover the amounts representing

his/her share of the debts. Naturally if Ard paid more than his/her share of these debts, then Ard could recover this portion of the payment from the other partners.

10. (1187,L1,22) (c) A partner's apparent authority is derived from the reasonable perceptions of third parties due to the manifestations or representations of the partnership concerning the authority each partner possesses to bind the partnership. However, if third parties are aware of a formal resolution which limits the partner's actual authority to bind the partnership, then that partner's apparent authority will also be limited. Answer (a) is incorrect because third parties should be aware that in order for a partner to submit a claim against the partnership to arbitration, unanimous consent of the partners is needed. Therefore, a partner has no apparent authority to take such an action. Answer (b) is incorrect because as stated above, the apparent authority of a partner to bind the partnership is not derived from the express powers and purposes contained in the partnership agreement. Answer (d) is incorrect because if third parties are unaware of such a resolution which limits the partner's actual authority, then the partner retains apparent authority to bind the partnership.

11.   (586,L1,56) (c) Partners may agree not to hold a partner liable among themselves, but they cannot prevent that partner from being held personally liable by third parties. Thus, the agreement to hold Fein harmless for all past, present, and future liabilities will not affect the rights of partnership creditors to hold Fein personally liable. Thus, answers (a) and (b) are incorrect. Answer (d) is incorrect because Fein has a right to recover any amounts he paid to satisfy partnership creditors due to the agreement among the partners.

12. (1183,L1,16) (a) Partners are jointly and severally liable for torts committed by a copartner while carrying on partnership business. The partner who commits the tort can always be sued for his own actions regardless of whether the partnership has been sued. Thus, answer (d) is incorrect. Answer (b) is incorrect because the existence of implied authority is not inconsistent with a formal, detailed partnership agreement. While such an agreement may carefully spell out a partner's express authority, the partner still retains implied authority to do those things which are reasonably necessary to the exercise of his/her express authority. Answer (c) is

incorrect because apparent authority is based upon the reasonable belief of a third party that the partner with whom he dealt possessed authority to represent the partnership in that matter. Since the third party is not a party to the partnership agreement and does not ordinarily have access to it, the third party is not bound by the terms of the agreement unless he has actual knowledge of its terms. The partnership agreement is, of course, binding among the partners themselves.

13. (583,L1,5) (a) A partner has apparent authority to renew an existing supply contract which is apparently for the purpose of carrying on the partnership business in the usual way. In the absence of knowledge by a third party that such action was unauthorized by the other partners, the contract renewal is binding on the partnership. The matters described in answers (b), (c), and (d) are actions requiring the unanimous consent of the partners: (1) assignment of partnership assets to creditors, (2) written admission of the liability of the partnership in a lawsuit, and (3) committing partnership as surety on a partner's personal debt. Therefore, a partner does not have apparent authority to bind the partnership in these matters because third parties are supposed to be aware of the requirement of unanimity.

14. (1180,L1,22) (c) A partnership can be created by estoppel. This occurs when a third party changes his position in reliance upon a misrepresentation of the fact that a partnership exists. Danforth is a partner by estoppel. Danforth does not need to make a statement to become a partner by estoppel; his silence would be sufficient considering he is present at the time Coleman represents that they are partners. Answer (c) is correct.

15. (589,L1,15) (d) A partner is an agent of the partnership and, therefore, can bind the partnership to contracts with third parties. However, there are certain acts for which the unanimous consent of the partners is required. For example, unanimous consent is needed to (1) admit a new partner, (2) dispose of partnership goodwill, (3) submit a partnership claim to an arbitrator, and (4) admit to a claim against the partnership in court. A partner would normally have the express or apparent authority to lease office space for the partnership.

F. Termination of a Partnership

16. (1184,L1,12) (d) Darla, as a general partner, is individually liable for all obligations of the partnership which would amount to $210,000. She is also personally liable for the additional $25,000 she promised to pay; her maximum potential liability would be $235,000. Therefore, answers (a), (b), and (c) are incorrect.

17. (588,L1,13) (c) Upon the liquidation of the partnership, the claims of outside creditors are satisfied first. In this situation, the amount available for distribution after creditors are paid is $20,000. Since total capital contributions are $50,000, there is a deficit (loss) of $30,000 ($20,000 - $50,000). It is important to note that when a partnership agreement is silent regarding the allocation of the partnership losses, then losses are allocated in the same manner as partnership profits. Thus, in this case, Z's share of the loss is $10,500 (35% x $30,000). Since Z's capital contribution is only $5,000, Z will personally have to contribute an additional $5,500 toward the elimination of the deficit ($10,500 - 5,000). Therefore, answers (a), (b), and (d) are incorrect.

18. (588,L1,14) (d) A partnership is considered to be a highly personal relationship and, consequently, it is a rule of law that no person can be forced to remain a partner against his/her will. Thus, Grey has the power, but not necessarily the right to dissolve the partnership. However, since the partnership agreement did not state a specified duration, Grey may dissolve at any time without liability. Thus, answer (b) is incorrect. Answer (a) is incorrect because it is not necessary for a partner leaving a partnership to obtain a decree ordering the dissolution, regardless of whether the other partners consent to the dissolution. Answer (c) is incorrect because notice of the dissolution, while necessary to remove Grey's apparent authority to deal with third parties as an agent of the partnership, is not necessary for dissolution of the partnership.

19. (1180,L1,20) (c) Such a partnership agreement does not prevent the dissolution of the partnership upon the death or withdrawal of a partner; it merely eliminates the necessity of the second step in the termination of the partnership which is the winding up process. Such an agreement is enforceable. Answer (c) is the correct answer.

20. (1180,L1,19) (b) In a partnership, a general partner has unlimited liability for the partnership debts. Upon the death of a partner, this liability continues and is assumed by the deceased partner's estate.

Under the doctrine of marshalling of assets, personal creditors have first priority to Perone's personal assets, with any excess going to the partnership creditors. Thus, answers (a) and (d) are incorrect. Answer (c) is incorrect since each partner, including a deceased partner's estate, is individually liable for the entire amount of partnership debts. However, if a partner pays more than his share of the partnership debts, he can sue his copartners to recover the excess.

G. Limited Partnerships

21. (1184,L1,13) (b) Darla, as a limited partner, is not liable for debts of the partnership beyond the amount of her capital contribution. However, she is still liable for the $25,000 of her capital contribution that she has not yet paid. Therefore, answers (a), (c), and (d) are incorrect.

22. (587,L1,7) (c) Limited partners are liable for the debts of a limited partnership only to the extent of their contributed capital. Thus, in this case, since Grey and Fox are limited partners, they will have no liability to contribute additional capital to the partnership upon dissolution. It is of no consequence that Fox is insolvent. And, since the liabilities of the partnership exceed the fair market value of the assets by $125,000, White's maximum potential liability, as the only general partner, is the full $125,000. Thus, answers (a), (b), and (d) are incorrect.

23. (1176,L1,11) (a) Limited partners may not withdraw their capital contributions so as to impair a creditor's status. Unless there is sufficient partnership property to pay all general creditors, withdrawal of limited partner capital impairs a creditor's status. Limited partners are not restricted in owning competing interests (but general partners are), because limited partners do not participate in management, i.e., they are merely investors. Limited partners are not agents and do not have apparent authority. General partners are agents, because they participate in management. If limited partners take part in the management of a business, they become liable as general partners.

24. (1176,L1,15) (a) A limited partner's (as does a general partner's) capital contribution creates an intangible property right in the partnership. Limited partners have no right to any specific partnership property, but rather a share of the total. The capital contribution cannot be withdrawn if it will impair a creditor's status, i.e., there must be enough partnership property to satisfy all

creditors. A limited partner may contribute property just as a general partner may. A limited partner cannot contribute services if they will involve managing or operating the business. Each limited partner's capital contribution is one of the required inclusions in the Certificate of Limited Partnership (generally required to be filed).

25. (1189,L1,5) (d) A limited partner is liable only for the amount of capital contributed, therefore, the first statement is incorrect. A limited partner has no right to manage or take part in the control of the partnership; therefore, the second statement is incorrect. If a limited partner assumes some control of the partnership or gets involved in management, s/he will lose the limited nature of his/her liability and will become personally liable like a general partner but only to the third parties who know of his/her involvement in management.

H. Joint Ventures

26. (1189,L1,4) (d) The definition of a joint venture is the association of two or more persons (or entities) organized to carry out a single business undertaking (or series of related undertakings) for profit. Answer (a) is incorrect because a joint venture may be an association of more than two persons. Answer (b) is incorrect because the undertaking of a joint venture must be for profit. Answer (c) is incorrect because a joint venture is the association of two or more persons or entities.

Answer Outline

Problem 1   Differences between General and
Limited Partnership (1186,L2)

Formation of general partnership:
  Agreement can be oral, written, or implied
  No filing necessary
Formation of limited partnership:
  Only if state permits
  Must file signed certificate
  Must have at least one general and one
    limited partner
Daily management:
  Limited--no participation
  General--full participation
Liability:
  Limited--limited to amount of investment
  General--unlimited
Assignment of interest or substitution:
  Limited and general--all members (except
    assignor) must consent
Clause providing for continuation upon death
  of general partner is valid
Death of limited partner has no effect on
  partnership

Unofficial Answer

Problem 1   Differences between General and
Limited Partnership (1186,L2)

Typically, a general partnership is formed
by an agreement between or among two or more
persons, whether the agreement is written,
oral, or implied. No filing of a partnership
agreement is necessary in order to legally
create the general partnership. In contrast,
a limited partnership can only be formed where
a state statute permits such formation. In
addition, a duly signed Certificate of Limited
Partnership must be completed and filed with
the appropriate state or local agency. A
limited partnership, like a general partnership, is formed by two or more persons. However, unlike a general partnership, the
limited partnership must have as members one
or more general partners and one or more
limited partners.

As a limited partner, Slavin would not be
able to participate in the daily management of
the partnership's business if she wishes to
limit her liability to her investment in the
partnership. Thus, if Slavin intends to be
involved in the daily operations of the partnership and to participate in the control of
the partnership, she should consider becoming
a general partner since general partners have
rights in the management and conduct of the
partnership's business.

In her capacity as a limited partner,
Slavin's liability would be limited to her
investment in the partnership for partnership
debts if her interest is fully paid and non-
assessable. However, if Slavin were to become
a general partner, she would have unlimited
liability which would allow partnership creditors to satisfy the debts of the partnership
out of Slavin's personal assets.

Unless otherwise provided in the partnership agreement, Slavin has the right to assign
her limited partnership interest and may also
substitute the third party as a limited partner if all the members (except the assignor)
consent thereto. Similarly, as a general
partner, Slavin may assign her interest in the
partnership and the third party may become a
general partner if all of the partners consent.

A clause providing for the partnership to
continue after the death of a general partner
is valid, and the partnership will continue.
The clause has relatively little if any effect
where a limited partner dies since the limited
partnership continues upon the death of one of
the limited partners, whether or not the
clause is contained in the certificate.

Answer Outline

Problem 2   Partner's Property Rights
(1185,L3a)

a. Nolan's property rights in partnership
     Right to possess partnership property
       for partnership purposes
     Partnership interest is personal
       property
     Right to equal voice in management of
       partnership business
   Nolan's transfer only entitles Simon to
     Nolan's share of profits and property
     distributed by the partnership
   Simon has no right to participate in
     management or to possess specific part-
     nership property

Unofficial Answer*

Problem 2   Partner's Property Rights
(1185,L3a)

a. Nolan's property rights in the partnership
prior to the conveyance of his partnership
interest consisted of:

*The solutions approach for this question
appears in Chapter 3, Solutions Approach.

• His rights in specific partnership property. This right permitted Nolan to possess any item of partnership property for partnership purposes.

• His interest in the partnership. This interest is classified as personal property and is defined as the partner's share of the profits and surplus (including capital).

• His right to participate in the management of the partnership. This right entitles Nolan to an equal voice in the management and conduct of the partnership business.

Nolan's transfer of his partnership interest to Simon merely entitles Simon to receive Nolan's share of the profits and Nolan's interest in any property distributed by the partnership. Since Stein and Wolf have refused to admit Simon as a partner, Simon will not be entitled to participate in the management of the partnership or to acquire Nolan's right to possess specific partnership property.

Answer Outline

Problem 3   Partner as Agent of Partnership; Apparent Authority; Partner's Obligations under Partnership Agreement; Liability of Newly Admitted Partner; Liability of Withdrawing Partner (1188,L4)

The partnership cannot recover 1/2 percent commission from King
  Rey had apparent authority to reduce commission to 1 1/2 percent
  It is reasonable for King to believe that Rey had authority to perform transaction
  King lacked knowledge of the partnership restriction limiting Rey's authority to bind partnership
Partnership can recover 1/2 percent commission from Rey
  Rey violated his duty to act in accordance with partnership agreement
Park is only liable for existing debts of partnership to extent of capital contributed
  Park is personally liable for partnership obligations arising after being admitted to partnership
Stein is personally liable for partnership obligations arising prior to withdrawing from partnership, unless Stein obtains a release from existing creditors
  Stein has no liability for partnership obligations arising after actual and constructive notice of withdrawing is properly given

Unofficial Answer

Problem 3   Partner as Agent of Partnership; Apparent Authority; Partner's Obligations under Partnership Agreement; Liability of Newly Admitted Partner; Liability of Withdrawing Partner (1188,L4)

a.1. The partnership cannot recover the 1/2% commission from King because Rey had the apparent authority to reduce the commission to 1 1/2%. The Uniform Partnership Act states that every partner is an agent of the partnership for the purpose of its business, and the act of every partner for apparently carrying on in the usual way the business of the partnership, binds the partnership, unless the partner so acting has in fact no authority to act for the partnership in the particular matter, and the person with whom the partner is dealing has knowledge of the fact that the partner has no such authority. In determining whether Rey had the apparent authority to bind the partnership, one must examine the circumstances and conduct of the parties and whether King reasonably believed such authority to exist. Because brokerage commissions are generally not uniform, it would be reasonable for King to believe that Rey had the authority to perform the transaction at 1 1/2% commission. Furthermore, King lacked knowledge of the restriction in the partnership agreement that prohibited Rey from reducing a commission below 2% without the other partners' consent. Therefore, King will not be liable for the 1/2% commission.

a.2. The partnership can recover the 1/2% commission from Rey because Rey violated the partnership agreement by reducing the commission to 1 1/2% without the partners' consent. Rey owes a duty to act in accordance with the partnership agreement.

b.1. Under the Uniform Partnership Act, a person admitted as a partner into an existing partnership is liable for all the obligations of the partnership arising before being admitted as though that person had been a partner when such obligations were incurred, except that this liability may be satisfied only out of partnership property. Thus, Park will not be personally liable for the partnership obligations arising prior to being admitted as a partner but would be liable based upon the extent of partnership interests held. Park will be personally liable for partnership obligations arising after being admitted to the partnership.

b.2. Stein will continue to be personally liable for partnership obligations arising prior to withdrawing from the partnership, unless Stein obtains a release from the

existing creditors. Stein will have no
liability for partnership obligations arising
after actual and constructive notice of
withdrawing was properly given. However,
Stein may be personally liable for partnership
obligations arising after withdrawing but
prior to notice being given. Actual notice of
Stein's withdrawal was given by written
notification to partnership creditors that had
conducted business with the partnership prior
to May 15. Constructive notice of Stein's
withdrawal was given by proper publication in
two newspapers to those third parties who had
not dealt with the partnership, but may have
known of its existence.

Answer Outline

Problem 4   Withdrawal and Admission of
             Partner (584,L5a)

Part a.

1. Hart liable for partnership debts incurred
    prior to his withdrawal unless released
    by existing creditors
    Hart not liable for partnership debts
    incurred after his withdrawal if Hart
    gave actual notice to existing creditors,
    and constructive notice to other third
    parties knowing of partnership existence
      Since constructive notice not given,
      Hart may be liable to future creditors,
      and third parties not aware of Hart's
      withdrawal
2. UPA provides person admitted as partner
    into existing partnership (Paul) has no
    personal liability for partnership obli-
    gations arising prior to his admission
      However, these prior partnership obli-
      gations may be satisfied out of part-
      nership property
      Paul has personal liability for debts
      incurred subsequent to admission.

Unofficial Answer

Problem 4   Withdrawal and Admission of
             Partner (584,L5a)

Part a.

1. An outgoing partner, such as Hart, continues to have potential liability for partnership debts incurred prior to his withdrawal
unless he obtains a release from the existing
creditors. Hart has no liability for partnership obligations incurred subsequent to his
withdrawal provided that appropriate notice is
given to the partnership creditors and other

third parties. In this case, actual notice
was given to the partnership's creditors in
existence at the time of Hart's withdrawal but
constructive notice (i.e., notice by publication) was not given to those third parties who
had not dealt with the partnership but may
have known of its existence. By giving the
appropriate type of notice, Hart would have
effectively eliminated third parties' rights
to rely on Hart's membership, i.e., his apparent authority in the partnership after his
withdrawal. Because constructive notice was
not given, creditors or other third parties
who deal with the partnership after Hart's
withdrawal may not be aware of his withdrawal,
and he may be liable to them. However, Hart
will not be liable to existing creditors who,
after receiving actual notice of Hart's
withdrawal, dealt with the partnership.

2. The Uniform Partnership Act provides that
a person admitted as a partner into an existing partnership is liable for all the obligations of the partnership arising before his
admission as though he had been a partner when
such obligations were incurred. However, this
liability shall be satisfied only out of partnership property. Therefore, Paul has no personal liability as to partnership obligations
existing at the time he became a partner but
can be held personally responsible for those
debts incurred after his admission as a
partner.

Multiple Choice Questions (1-33)

1. Which of the following is a characteristic of an unincorporated association?
   a. It may only be used for not-for-profit purposes.
   b. Members who actively manage the association may be held personally liable for contracts they enter into on behalf of the association.
   c. Certificates representing ownership in the association must be distributed to the members.
   d. Its duration must be for a limited period of time **not** to exceed 12 months.

2. Golden Enterprises, Inc. entered into a contract with Hidalgo Corporation for the sale of its mineral holdings. The transaction proved to be __ultra vires__. Which of the following parties, for the reason stated, may properly assert the __ultra vires__ doctrine?
   a. Golden Enterprises to avoid performance.
   b. A shareholder of Golden Enterprises to enjoin the sale.
   c. Hidalgo Corporation to avoid performance.
   d. Golden Enterprises to rescind the consummated sale.

3. Destiny Manufacturing, Inc. is incorporated under the laws of Nevada. Its principal place of business is in California and it has permanent sales offices in several other states. Under the circumstances, which of the following is correct?
   a. California may validly demand that Destiny incorporate under the laws of the state of California.
   b. Destiny must obtain a certificate of authority to transact business in California and the other states in which it does business.
   c. Destiny is a foreign corporation in California, but not in the other states.
   d. California may prevent Destiny from operating as a corporation if the laws of California differ regarding organization and conduct of the corporation's internal affairs.

4. Hobson, Jones, Carter, and Wolff are all medical doctors who have worked together for several years. They decided to form a corporation and their attorney created a typical professional corporation for them. Which of the following is correct?
   a. Such a corporation will not be recognized for federal tax purposes if one of its goals is to save taxes.
   b. The state in which they incorporated must have enacted professional corporation statutes permitting them to do so.
   c. Upon incorporation, the doctor-shareholder is insulated from personal liability beyond his capital contribution.
   d. The majority of states prohibit the creation of professional corporations by doctors.

5. Which of the following statements is correct with respect to the differences and similarities between a corporation and a limited partnership?
   a. Directors owe fiduciary duties to the corporation and limited partners owe such duties to the partnership.
   b. A corporation and a limited partnership may be created only pursuant to a state statute and a copy of its organizational document must be filed with the proper state agency.
   c. Shareholders may be entitled to vote on corporate matters whereas limited partners are prohibited from voting on any partnership matters.
   d. Stock of a corporation may be subject to the federal securities laws registration requirements whereas limited partnership interests are automatically exempt from such requirements.

6. In general, which of the following must be contained in Articles of Incorporation?
   a. The names of states in which the corporation will be doing business.
   b. The name of the state in which the corporation will maintain its principal place of business.
   c. The names of the initial officers and their terms of office.
   d. The classes of stock authorized for issuance.

7. Rice is a promoter of a corporation to be known as Dex Corp. On January 1, 1985, Rice signed a nine-month contract with Roe, a CPA, which provided that Roe would perform certain accounting services for Dex. Rice did not disclose to Roe that Dex had not been formed. Prior to the incorporation of Dex on February 1, 1985, Roe rendered accounting services pursuant to the contract. After rendering accounting services for an additional period

of six months pursuant to the contract, Roe was discharged without cause by the board of directors of Dex. In the absence of any agreements to the contrary, who will be liable to Roe for breach of contract?

  a. Both Rice and Dex.
  b. Rice only.
  c. Dex only.
  d. Neither Rice nor Dex.

8. Generally, Articles of Incorporation must contain all of the following **except** the

  a. Names of the incorporators.
  b. Name of the corporation.
  c. Number of shares authorized.
  d. Names of initial officers and their terms of office.

9. Sandy McBride, president of the Cranston Corporation, inquired about the proper method of handling the expenditures incurred in connection with the recent incorporation of the business and sale of its shares to the public. In explaining the legal or tax treatment of these expenditures, which of the following is correct?

  a. The expenditures may be paid out of the consideration received in payment for the shares without rendering such shares not fully paid or assessable.
  b. The expenditures are comparable to goodwill and are treated accordingly for nontax and tax purposes.
  c. The expenditures must be capitalized and are nondeductible for federal income tax purposes since the life of the corporation is perpetual.
  d. The expenditures may be deducted for federal income tax purposes in the year incurred or amortized at the election of the corporation over a five-year period.

10. Bixler obtained an option on a building he believed was suitable for use by a corporation he and two other men were organizing. After the corporation was successfully promoted, Bixler met with the Board of Directors who agreed to acquire the property for $200,000. Bixler deeded the building to the corporation and the corporation began business in it. Bixler's option contract called for the payment of only $155,000 for the building and he purchased it for that price. When the directors later learned that Bixler paid only $155,000, they demanded the return of Bixler's $45,000 profit. Bixler refused, claiming the building was worth far more than $200,000 both when he secured the option and when he deeded it to the corpo-

ration. Which of the following statements correctly applies to Bixler's conduct?

  a. It was improper for Bixler to contract for the option without first having secured the assent of the Board of Directors.
  b. If, as Bixler claimed, the building was fairly worth more than $200,000, Bixler is entitled to retain the entire price.
  c. Even if, as Bixler claimed, the building was fairly worth more than $200,000, Bixler nevertheless must return the $45,000 to the corporation.
  d. In order for Bixler to be obligated to return any amount to the corporation, the Board of Directors must establish that the building was worth less than $200,000.

11. In general, which of the following statements concerning treasury stock is correct?

  a. A corporation may **not** reacquire its own stock unless specifically authorized by its Articles of Incorporation.
  b. On issuance of new stock, a corporation has preemptive rights with regard to its treasury stock.
  c. Treasury stock may be distributed as a stock dividend.
  d. A corporation is entitled to receive cash dividends on its treasury stock.

12. Which of the following statements concerning treasury stock is correct?

  a. Cash dividends paid on treasury stock are transferred to stated capital.
  b. A corporation may **not** purchase its own stock unless specifically authorized by its Articles of Incorporation.
  c. A duly appointed trustee may vote treasury stock at a properly called shareholders' meeting.
  d. Treasury stock may be resold at a price less than par value.

13. Global Trucking Corporation has in its corporate treasury a substantial block of its own common stock, which it acquired several years previously. The stock had been publicly offered at $25 a share and had been reacquired at $15. The board is considering using it in the current year for various purposes. For which of the following purposes may it validly use the treasury stock?

  a. To pay a stock dividend to its shareholders.

1
5

b. To sell it to the public without the necessity of a registration under the Securities Act of 1933, since it had been previously registered.

c. To vote it at the annual meeting of shareholders.

d. To acquire the shares of another publicly held company without the necessity of a registration under the Securities Act of 1933.

14. The Larkin Corporation is contemplating a two-for-one stock split of its common stock. Its $4 par value common stock will be reduced to $2 after the split. It has 2 million shares issued and outstanding out of a total of 3 million authorized. In considering the legal or tax consequences of such action, which of the following is a correct statement?

a. The transaction will require both authorization by the Board of Directors and approval by the shareholders.

b. The distribution of the additional shares to the shareholders will be taxed as a dividend to the recipients.

c. Surplus equal to the par value of the existing number of shares issued and outstanding must be transferred to the stated capital account.

d. The trustees of trust recipients of the additional shares must allocate them ratably between income and corpus.

15. Ambrose purchased 400 shares of $100 par value original issue common stock from Minor Corporation for $25 a share. Ambrose subsequently sold 200 of the shares to Harris at $25 a share. Harris did not have knowledge or notice that Ambrose had not paid par. Ambrose also sold 100 shares of this stock to Gable for $25 a share. At the time of this sale, Gable knew that Ambrose had not paid par for the stock. Minor Corporation became insolvent and the creditors sought to hold all the above parties liable for the $75 unpaid on each of the 400 shares. Under these circumstances

a. The creditors can hold Ambrose liable for $30,000.

b. If $25 a share was a fair value for the stock at the time of issuance, Ambrose will have no liability to the creditors.

c. Since Harris acquired the shares by purchase, he is not liable to the creditors, and his lack of knowledge or notice that Ambrose paid less than par is immaterial.

d. Since Gable acquired the shares by purchase, he is not liable to the creditors, and the fact that he knew

Ambrose paid less than par is immaterial.

16. Plimpton subscribed to 1,000 shares of $1 par value common stock of the Billiard Ball Corporation at $10 a share. Plimpton paid $1,000 upon the incorporation of Billiard and paid an additional $4,000 at a later time. The corporation subsequently became insolvent and is now in bankruptcy. The creditors of the corporation are seeking to hold Plimpton personally liable. Which of the following is a correct statement?

a. Plimpton has no liability directly or indirectly to the creditors of the corporation since he paid the corporation the full par value of the shares.

b. As a result of his failure to pay the full subscription price, Plimpton has unlimited joint and several liability for corporate debts.

c. Plimpton is liable for the remainder of the unpaid subscription price.

d. Had Plimpton transferred his shares to an innocent third party, neither he nor the third party would be liable.

Items 17 and 18 are based on the following information:

Jane Cox, a shareholder of Mix Corp., has properly commenced a derivative action against Mix's Board of Directors. Cox alleges that the Board breached its fiduciary duty and was negligent by failing to independently verify the financial statements prepared by management upon which Smart & Co., CPAs, issued an unqualified opinion. The financial statements contained inaccurate information which the Board relied upon in committing large sums of money to capital expansion. This resulted in Mix having to borrow money at extremely high interest rates to meet current cash needs. Within a short period of time, the price of Mix Corp. stock declined drastically.

17. Which of the following statements is correct?

a. The Board is strictly liable, regardless of fault, since it owes a fiduciary duty to both the corporation and the shareholders.

b. The Board is liable since any negligence of Smart is automatically imputed to the Board.

c. The Board may avoid liability if it acted in good faith and in a reasonable manner.

d. The Board may avoid liability in all cases where it can show that it lacked scienter.

18. If the court determines that the Board was negligent and the Board seeks indemnification for its legal fees from Mix, which of the following statements is correct?
   a. The Board may **not** be indemnified since a presumption that the Board failed to act in good faith arises from the judgment.
   b. The Board may **not** be indemnified unless Mix's shareholders approve such indemnification.
   c. The Board may be indemnified by Mix only if Mix provides liability insurance for its officers and directors.
   d. The Board may be indemnified by Mix only if the court deems it proper.

19. Generally, officers of a corporation
   a. Are elected by the shareholders.
   b. Are agents and fiduciaries of the corporation, having actual and apparent authority to manage the business.
   c. May be removed by the board of directors without cause only if the removal is approved by a majority vote of the shareholders.
   d. May declare dividends or other distributions to shareholders as they deem appropriate.

20. Which of the following statements is correct regarding the fiduciary duty?
   a. A majority shareholder as such may owe a fiduciary duty to fellow shareholders.
   b. A director's fiduciary duty to the corporation may be discharged by merely disclosing his self-interest.
   c. A director owes a fiduciary duty to the shareholders but **not** to the corporation.
   d. A promoter of a corporation to be formed owes no fiduciary duty to anyone, unless the contract engaging the promoter so provides.

21. At their annual meeting, shareholders of the Laurellon Corporation approved several proposals made by the Board of Directors. Among them was the ratification of the salaries of the executives of the corporation. In this connection, which of the following is correct?
   a. The shareholders can **not** legally ratify the compensation paid to director-officers.
   b. The salaries ratified are automatically valid for federal income tax purposes.

   c. Such ratification by the shareholders is required as a matter of law.
   d. The action by the shareholders serves the purpose of confirming the board's action.

22. West owns 5,000 shares of $7 cumulative preferred stock of Sky Corp. During the first year of operations, cash dividends of $7 per share were declared on Sky's preferred stock but were never paid. In the second year of operations, dividends on Sky's preferred stock were neither declared nor paid. If Sky is dissolved, which of the following statements is correct?
   a. West will have priority over the claims of Sky's debenture bond owners.
   b. West will have priority over the claims of Sky's unsecured judgment creditors.
   c. Sky will be liable to West as an unsecured creditor for $35,000.
   d. Sky will be liable to West as an unsecured creditor for $70,000.

23. The essential difference between a stock dividend and a stock split is that a
   a. Stock split will increase the amount of stockholders' equity.
   b. Stock split will increase a stockholder's percentage of ownership.
   c. Stock dividend must be paid in the same class of stock as held by the stockholder.
   d. Stock dividend of newly issued shares will result in a decrease in retained earnings.

24. The stock of Crandall Corporation is regularly traded over the counter. However, 75% is owned by the founding family and a few of the key executive officers. It has had a cash dividend record of paying out annually less than 5% of its earnings and profits over the past 10 years. It has, however, declared a 10% stock dividend during each of these years. Its accumulated earnings and profits are beyond the reasonable current and anticipated needs of the business. Which of the following is correct?
   a. The shareholders can compel the declaration of a dividend only if the directors' dividend policy is fraudulent.
   b. The Internal Revenue Service can **not** attack the accumulation of earnings and profits since the Code exempts publicly held corporations from the accumulations provisions.

c.   The fact that the corporation was paying a 10% stock dividend, apparently in lieu of a cash distribution, is irrelevant insofar as the ability of the Internal Revenue Service to successfully attack the accumulation.

d.   Either the Internal Revenue Service or the shareholders could successfully obtain a court order to compel the distribution of earnings and profits unreasonably accumulated.

25. The limited liability of the shareholders of a closely-held corporation will most likely be disregarded if the shareholders

     a.   Lend money to the corporation.

     b.   Are also corporate officers, directors, or employees.

     c.   Undercapitalized the corporation when it was formed.

     d.   Formed the corporation solely to limit their personal liability.

26. The corporate veil is most likely to be pierced and the shareholders held personally liable if

     a.   An **ultra vires** act has been committed.

     b.   The corporation has elected S corporation status under the Internal Revenue Code.

     c.   A partnership incorporates its business solely to limit the liability of its partners.

     d.   The shareholders have commingled their personal funds with those of the corporation.

27. Able and Baker are two corporations, the shares of which are publicly traded. Baker plans to merge into Able. Which of the following is a requirement of the merger?

     a.   The IRS must approve the merger.

     b.   The common stockholders of Baker must receive common stock of Able.

     c.   The creditors of Baker must approve the merger.

     d.   The boards of directors of both Able and Baker must approve the merger.

28. Universal Joint Corporation has approached Minor Enterprises, Inc. about a tax-free statutory merger of Minor into Universal. The stock of both corporations is listed on the NYSE. Which of the following requirements or procedures need **not** be complied with in order to qualify as a statutory merger pursuant to state and federal law?

     a.   The boards of directors of both corporations must approve the plan of merger.

b.   Universal, the surviving corporation, must apply for and obtain a favorable revenue ruling from the Treasury Department.

c.   The boards of both corporations must submit the plan of merger to their respective shareholders for approval.

d.   The securities issued and exchanged by Universal for the shares of Minor must be registered since they are considered to be "offered" and "sold" for purposes of the Securities Act of 1933.

29. Barton Corporation and Clagg Corporation have decided to combine their separate companies pursuant to the provisions of their state corporation laws. After much discussion and negotiation, they decided that a consolidation was the appropriate procedure to be followed. Which of the following is an incorrect statement with respect to the contemplated statutory consolidation?

     a.   A statutory consolidation pursuant to state law is recognized by the Internal Revenue Code as a type of tax-free reorganization.

     b.   The larger of the two corporations will emerge as the surviving corporation.

     c.   Creditors of Barton and Clagg will have their claims protected despite the consolidation.

     d.   The shareholders of both Barton and Clagg must approve the plan of consolidation.

30. Which of the following would be grounds for the judicial dissolution of a corporation on the petition of a shareholder?

     a.   Refusal of the board of directors to declare a dividend.

     b.   Waste of corporate assets by the board of directors.

     c.   Loss operations of the corporation for three years.

     d.   Failure by the corporation to file its federal income tax returns.

May 1990 Questions

31. Absent a specific provision in its articles of incorporation, a corporation's board of directors has the power to do all of the following, **except**

     a.   Repeal the bylaws.

     b.   Declare dividends.

     c.   Fix compensation of directors.

     d.   Amend the articles of incorporation.

32. An owner of common stock will **not** have any liability beyond actual investment if the owner

    a. Paid less than par value for stock purchased in connection with an original issue of shares.

    b. Agreed to perform future services for the corporation in exchange for original issue par value shares.

    c. Purchased treasury shares for less than par value.

    d. Failed to pay the full amount owed on a subscription contract for no-par shares.

33. Johns owns 400 shares of Abco Corp. cumulative preferred stock. In the absence of any specific contrary provisions in Abco's articles of incorporation, which of the following statements is correct?

    a. Johns is entitled to convert the 400 shares of preferred stock to a like number of shares of common stock.

    b. If Abco declares a cash dividend on its preferred stock, Johns becomes an unsecured creditor of Abco.

    c. If Abco declares a dividend on its common stock, Johns will be entitled to participate with the common stock shareholders in any dividend distribution made after preferred dividends are paid.

    d. Johns will be entitled to vote if dividend payments are in arrears.

Repeat Question

(590,L1,6) Identical/similar to item 6 above

Problems

Problem 1   (588,L3)

(15 to 20 minutes)

Walsh is evaluating two different invest-ment opportunities. One requires an invest-ment of $100,000 to become a limited partner in a limited partnership that owns a shopping center. The other requires an investment of $100,000 to purchase 3% of the voting common stock of a corporation engaged in manufactur-ing. Walsh is uncertain about the advantages and disadvantages of being a limited partner versus being a shareholder. The issues of most concern to Walsh are:

* The right to transfer a limited partner-ship interest versus shares of stock.

* The liability as a limited partner versus that of a shareholder for debts incurred by a limited partnership or a corporation.

* The right of a limited partner versus that of a shareholder to participate in daily management.

* The right of a limited partner to receive partnership profits versus the right of a shareholder to receive dividends from a corporation.

Required:

Briefly identify and discuss the basic differ-ences and similarities in the formation of a limited partnership and a corporation. Dis-cuss in separate paragraphs the issues raised by Walsh. (Ignore tax and securities laws.)

Problem 2   (1184,L5)

(15 to 25 minutes)

Jim Bold is a promoter for a corporation to be formed and known as Wonda Corp. Bold entered into several supply and service agree-ments with Servco. These agreements were executed in Wonda's name, expressly contingent upon adoption by Wonda, when formed, and were based solely on Wonda's anticipated financial strength. Within two weeks after the signing of the agreements, Wonda was duly formed and operating. Shortly thereafter, Wonda, by its Board of Directors, rejected the preincorpora-tion agreements entered into by Bold and Servco, stating that it could obtain more beneficial contracts elsewhere.

During the first year of Wonda's opera-tions certain members of its Board of Direc-tors were accused of negligence in the per-formance of their duties. In addition, there were allegations made that these same direc-tors failed to exercise due care by paying cash dividends to shareholders that exceeded the profits and paid in capital. These directors based their decision upon negli-gently prepared reports issued by the Vice-President of Finance indicating that there were sufficient funds to pay cash dividends to shareholders. These incidents caused Wonda severe liquidity problems and huge losses in the following year of operation. White, a shareholder in Wonda, has properly commenced a suit against these directors.

Required:

Answer the following, setting forth reasons for any conclusions stated.
a. Discuss Wonda's and Bold's liability to Servco on the preincorporation agreements.
b. What are the necessary requirements to properly declare and pay cash dividends?
c. What defense(s) are available to the directors regarding the charges of negligence in the performance of their duties and the failure to exercise due care in declaring cash dividends?

Problem 3   (1187,L5)

(15 to 20 minutes)

Mace, Inc. wishes to acquire Creme Corp., a highly profitable company with substantial retained earnings. Creme is incorporated in a state that recognizes the concepts of stated capital (legal capital) and capital surplus.

In conjunction with the proposed acquisi-tion, Mace engaged Gold & Co., CPAs, to audit Creme's financial statements. Gold began analyzing Creme's stated capital account and was provided the following data:

* Creme was initially capitalized in 1980 by issuing 40,000 shares of common stock, 50¢ par value, at $15 per share. The total number of authorized shares was fixed at 100,000 shares.
* Costs to organize Creme were $15,000.
* During 1982, Creme's board of directors declared and distributed a 5% common stock dividend. The fair market value of the stock at that time was $20 per share.
* On June 1, 1983, the president of Creme exercised a stock option to purchase 1,000 shares of common stock at $21 per share when the market price was $25 per share.

• During 1984, Creme's board of directors declared and distributed a 2-for-1 stock split on its common stock when the market price was $28 per share.

• During 1985, Creme acquired as treasury stock 5,000 shares of its common stock at a market price of $30 per share. Creme uses the cost method of accounting and reporting for treasury stock.

• During 1986, Creme reissued 3,000 shares of the treasury stock at the market price of $32 per share.

Required:

Answer the following, setting forth reasons for any conclusions stated.

a. Discuss what effect each of the transactions described above would have on stated capital (legal capital), indicating the dollar amount of change.

b. Discuss the requirements necessary to properly declare and pay cash dividends.

Multiple Choice Answers

1. b	8. d	15. a	22. c	28. b
2. b	9. a	16. c	23. d	29. b
3. b	10. c	17. c	24. c	30. b
4. b	11. c	18. d	25. c	31. d
5. b	12. d	19. b	26. d	32. c
6. d	13. a	20. a	27. d	33. b
7. a	14. a	21. d		

Multiple Choice Answer Explanations

A. Characteristics and Advantages of Corporate Form

1. (1185,L1,1) (b) An unincorporated association is a partnership-like entity that has characteristics very similar to a partnership. Managing members of the association may be held personally liable for the contracts they or their agents enter into on behalf of the association and for the torts they or their agents may commit during their operation of association activities. Answer (a) is incorrect because an unincorporated association is not limited to not-for-profit purposes. Answer (c) is incorrect because certificates representing ownership need not be distributed, in contrast to corporations. Answer (d) is incorrect because unincorporated associations are not limited to durations of 12 months or less.

2. (580,L1,12) (b) An ultra vires doctrine applies when a corporation enters a contract outside the scope of its express or implied authority granted by its Articles of Incorporation. Answer (b) is correct because since the state or shareholder has the right to object to an ultra vires act, a competitor could not object. A shareholder can institute a derivative action against directors and officers to recover damages for such acts. Answers (a) and (c) are incorrect because when an ultra vires contract has been executed on one side, most state courts hold the nonperforming party may not raise the defense of ultra vires. Answer (d) is incorrect because when both parties have performed, neither party may sue to rescind an ultra vires contract.

C. Types of Corporations

3. (580,L1,14) (b) A corporation "doing business" in a state other than that of incorporation must comply with that state's license requirements. This usually requires filing a certificate of authority. The concept of doing business involves something more than isolated transactions. Answer (a) is incor-

rect because a corporation is not required to incorporate in a state in which it does business. Answer (c) is incorrect because Destiny is a foreign corporation in any state in which it does business other than that state in which it is incorporated. Answer (d) is incorrect because Destiny needs to comply only with the incorporation laws in its state of incorporation, in this case, Nevada.

4. (1178,L1,22) (b) Professional corporations are only allowed in states which have enacted statutes permitting their incorporation. They are not normally allowed under the general corporation statutes. Answer (a) is incorrect because such a corporation will be recognized for federal tax purposes even if its goal is to save taxes. Answer (c) is incorrect because the typical statute provides that the professional being incorporated remains personally liable for his professional acts. His liability will only be limited for ordinary business debts of the corporation. Answer (d) is incorrect because most states now permit the creation of professional corporations by doctors and similar professional persons.

D. Formation of Corporation

5. (1188,L1,5) (b) Corporations and limited partnerships may only be created pursuant to state statutes. Normally, both the Articles of Incorporation and a Certificate of Limited Partnership must be filed with the Secretary of State. Answer (a) is incorrect since limited partners do not owe fiduciary duties to the partnership. Answer (c) is incorrect since limited partners have the right to vote on partnership matters such as the dissolution or winding up of the partnership, loans of the partnership, a change in the nature of the business of a partnership, and the removal of a general partner without jeopardizing their limited partner status. Answer (d) is incorrect since sale of limited partnership interests is not automatically exempted from the federal securities laws' registration requirements.

6. (587,L1,3) (d) In addition to the corporation's proposed name, purpose, powers, and other important information, the Articles of Incorporation must contain the amount and types of capital stock authorized for issuance. Answers (a), (b), and (c) are incorrect since they describe information not required to be contained in the Articles of Incorporation.

7. (1185,L1,5) (a) When a promoter enters into contracts on behalf of a corporation yet

to be formed, the promoter is personally liable on the contracts unless the promoter explicitly states that s/he is contracting for the corporation. After the corporation is formed, the promoter remains liable on the contracts until a novation occurs substituting the corporation for the promoter in the contracts. The corporation's adoption, either explicit or implicit, of the contracts does not relieve the promoter of liability. Dex implicitly adopted the contract with Roe by continuing to accept the accounting services, thus making Dex liable on the contract. Since a novation did not occur, Rice remains liable on the contract to Roe. Answers (b), (c), and (d) are incorrect because both parties (Rice and Dex) are liable on the contract.

8. (584,L1,10) (d) The Articles of Incorporation are not required to contain the names of initial officers and their terms of office. This is true because the initial officers are not elected until the first board of directors' meeting which cannot be held until after the Articles of Incorporation have been filed. Answers (a), (b), and (c) are all incorrect since the Articles of Incorporation must contain each of these items.

9. (582,L1,11) (a) The expenditures incurred in connection with the incorporation of the business and sale of its shares to the public may be treated as an offset against the proceeds from the stock issuance and are chargeable against the paid-in capital, as long as it does not impair the amount of legal capital. This treatment is based on the premise that issue costs are unrelated to corporate operations and thus are not properly chargeable against earnings from operations; rather, they are viewed as a reduction of proceeds of the financing activity. Answer (b) is incorrect because goodwill is an intangible asset, which is recorded only when an entire business is purchased. Goodwill is a "going concern" valuation and cannot be separated from a business as a whole. The amount of goodwill is capitalized and amortized over the business' useful life not to exceed a period of 40 years. Answers (c) and (d) are incorrect because expenses of issuing shares of stock, such as commissions, professional fees, printing costs, and listing the stock on the exchange are not to be capitalized and amortized over the life of the corporation, and thus would not be capitalized and amortized under the organizational expenditure provision.

10. (581,L1,23) (c) Promoters are persons who originate and organize the formation of a corporation. They have a fiduciary duty to act for the corporation and its shareholders. For Bixler to retain the profits made from the sale of property to the corporation, he must make full disclosure to and receive approval from either the board of directors or existing shareholders. Since Bixler did not comply with these procedures, the $45,000 would be considered secret profits and must be returned to the corporation even though the building might have a market value of $200,000. Thus, answers (b) and (d) are incorrect. Answer (a) is incorrect since the promoter may enter into preincorporation contracts (e.g., employment contracts, options on property) on behalf of the corporation. The corporation is not liable on these contracts until it adopts such agreements or enters a novation (a second agreement whereby corporation replaces the promoter under the same terms as the preincorporation contract). The corporation cannot ratify the agreement since the corporate entity was not in existence when the promoter entered the contract.

E. Corporate Financial Structure

11. (588,L1,15) (c) Treasury stock is stock that is issued and then subsequently repurchased by the corporation. Treasury stock may be distributed as part of a stock dividend. Answer (a) is incorrect because a corporation has inherent authority to reacquire its own stock and therefore needs no specific authorization by its Articles of Incorporation. Answer (b) is incorrect because a corporation does not have preemptive rights with regard to its treasury stock. Answer (d) is incorrect because treasury shares do not receive dividends.

12. (584,L1,9) (d) Treasury stock may be resold at a price less than par value. Answer (a) is incorrect because cash dividends are not paid on treasury stock. Answer (b) is incorrect because a corporation need not have specific authorization from its Articles of Incorporation to purchase its own stock; all corporations have the inherent authority to do so if not denied such right by state law. Answer (c) is incorrect because treasury stock cannot be voted.

13. (581,L1,26) (a) Treasury stock may be disposed of at the discretion of the board of directors through a sale or through the declaration of dividends to shareholders. Answer (b) is incorrect since the original public offering was sufficiently long ago to require the filing of a new registration statement before selling these treasury shares. Answer (c) is incorrect because

treasury shares cannot be voted. Answer (d) is incorrect because treasury shares exchanged for the stock of another publicly held corporation are considered to be "offered" and "sold" for the purposes of the Securities Act of 1933. Therefore, a registration statement would have to be filed and approved before the transaction could be completed.

14. (581,L1,27) (a) Both the board of directors and the shareholders of a corporation must approve a fundamental change in the corporate structure. Examples of fundamental corporate changes would be: dissolution of corporation, amendment of corporate charter, increase of capital stock, etc. Larkin would need to amend its corporate charter to increase the number of authorized shares before engaging in the stock split. Answer (b) is incorrect because stock splits are normally exempt from income tax because the shareholder-recipient maintains the same proportionate interest of ownership. Answer (c) is incorrect because a stock split decreases the par value in proportion to the increase in the number of shares. Therefore, total par value is unchanged. Answer (d) is incorrect because trustees are to include shares received through a stock split or stock dividend in the principal (corpus) of the trust. Cash dividends are considered income when allocating trust items between principal (corpus) and income beneficiaries.

E.3. Marketing of Stock

15. (1183,L1,24) (a) A corporation cannot legally reduce the price of par value stock below the established par value, without amending the Articles of Incorporation. Since Ambrose purchased original issue stock for less than par value, he can be held liable to the creditors for the $30,000 difference between the par value of the stock and the price he actually paid. Answer (b) is, therefore, incorrect. A transferee of shares, for which full consideration has not been paid, can be held liable to the corporation or its creditors for the unpaid portion of the consideration, unless the transferee took the shares in good faith and without knowledge or notice that full consideration has not been paid. Harris is, therefore, not liable to creditors. Answer (c), however, is incorrect because it states that Harris' lack of knowledge is immaterial. Likewise, answer (d) is incorrect. Gable is liable to the creditors because of his knowledge that full consideration for the shares had not been paid.

16. (580,L1,16) (c) Plimpton has breached his subscription contract with the Billiard

Ball Corporation, and is therefore liable for the remainder of the unpaid subscription price. Shares may be purchased for money, services already rendered, and property. Promissory notes are not proper consideration for the purchase of shares. Plimpton is liable to creditors for the balance due on the subscription price. This is true even if Plimpton transfers the shares to an innocent third party. The issuing corporation has a lien on those shares that have not been paid for fully. However, this lien would not be effective against an innocent third party purchaser unless the lien was conspicuously noted on the stock certificate. Plimpton's failure to pay the full purchase price of the shares would not change his limited liability concerning corporate debts.

H. Officers and Directors of Corporations

17. (1185,L1,3) (c) The board of directors of a corporation owes the corporation a fiduciary duty: the board must exercise ordinary care and due diligence (i.e., in good faith and in a reasonable manner) in performing its duties in order to avoid liability. Mix's Board of Directors exercised good faith and acted in a reasonable manner by relying upon the audited financial statements prepared by management. Thus, the Board was not liable. Answer (a) is incorrect because the Board does not have strict liability, even though it owes a fiduciary duty to the corporation. This duty only requires the Board to act in good faith and in a reasonable manner. Answer (b) is incorrect because any negligence of the auditor (Smart) is not automatically imputed to the Board. Answer (d) is incorrect because the Board cannot avoid liability in all cases where scienter is missing. The Board cannot avoid liability where it did not act in good faith or in a reasonable manner.

18. (1185,L1,4) (d) Corporations have the power to indemnify their boards of directors for legal fees incurred in defending suits against the boards for normal or expected duties. Normally, in a suit brought by a shareholder, no idemnification is permitted where the board has been found liable for negligence in carrying out its duties, unless the court in which the suit was brought determines that the board is fairly and reasonably entitled to indemnification. Answer (a) is incorrect because a presumption of lack of good faith does not arise from the judgement. Answer (b) is incorrect because indemnification of the board does not require shareholder approval. Answer (c) is incorrect because the carrying of liability insurance is not a

deciding factor in an indemnification decision.

19. (585,L1,14) (b) Officers of a corporation are agents of that corporation having actual and apparent authority to manage the business; consequently, officers occupy a fiduciary relationship with the corporation. Answer (a) is incorrect since officers are appointed by the directors of a corporation who are in turn elected by the shareholders. Answer (c) is incorrect since officers may be removed by the board of directors without cause and without any form of approval from the shareholders whenever, in the board's judgment, the best interests of the corporation are served. In such a case, the officer removed may have an action for breach of contract. Answer (d) is incorrect since the directors of a corporation, and not the officers, have the power to declare dividends or other distributions to shareholders.

20. (1183,L1,23) (a) Since a majority shareholder is able to exercise substantial control over the corporation, courts have recognized that there is a fiduciary duty owed to minority shareholders. If, for instance, a majority shareholder sells controlling interest in the corporation to a party whom he should know will plunder the company, the duty owed to fellow shareholders has been breached. A director also owes a fiduciary duty to the corporation. Answer (c) is, therefore, incorrect. The duty is not discharged by disclosure alone. The director who has a conflict of interest must refrain from voting on that matter. Thus, answer (b) is incorrect. Answer (d) is incorrect because a promoter owes a fiduciary duty to subscribers, shareholders, and the corporation itself.

21. (581,L1,28) (d) The compensation of corporate officers is fixed by a resolution of the board of directors. If none is fixed, the law implies that the officer is paid a reasonable sum for his services. Any action by the shareholders serves merely to confirm the board's action concerning the officers' salaries. It is not needed as a matter of law, therefore, answer (c) is incorrect. Answer (a) is incorrect because the directors can confirm the officers' salaries even though not legally needed. Answer (b) is incorrect because the IRS has the power to attack any officer's salary as unreasonable. If the compensation is deemed unreasonable, the IRS treats the excessive amount as a constructive dividend.

I.5. Right to Dividends

22. (587,L1,2) (c) Upon declaration, a cash dividend on preferred stock becomes a legal debt of the corporation, and the preferred shareholders become unsecured creditors of the corporation. However, any dividends not paid in any year concerning cumulative preferred stock are not a liability of the corporation until they are declared. Therefore, Sky will be liable to West as an unsecured creditor for $35,000 which is the amount of the declared dividends. Answers (a) and (b) are incorrect because West has become a general unsecured creditor for the declared dividends and will have the same priority as the debenture (unsecured) bond owners and the unsecured judgment creditors. Answer (d) is incorrect because the undeclared dividends did not become a legal liability to Sky.

23. (585,L1,15) (d) A stock dividend of newly issued shares will result in a transfer of the market value of the shares issued in the dividend from Retained Earnings to the paid-in capital accounts. A stock split does not result in a transfer of Retained Earnings to the paid-in capital accounts, but merely results in a decrease in the par value of the stock proportionate to the number of new shares issued as compared to the number issued and outstanding prior to the split. Answer (a) is incorrect because a stock split or dividend will never result in an increase in the amount of stockholder's equity. An increase in equity may only be caused by an additional contribution of capital by the shareholders or the earning of income by the corporation. Answer (b) is incorrect because a stock split will not change a stockholder's percentage of ownership. A stock split increases the number of shares held by each shareholder proportionately. Answer (c) is incorrect because a stock dividend may be paid in a different class of stock than the class being held by the stockholder.

24. (581,L1,25) (c) The fact that the corporation was paying a 10% stock dividend instead of a cash distribution would not hinder the IRS from attacking the accumulation of earnings. Answer (a) is incorrect because stockholders can compel the declaration of a dividend when withholding dividends would be a clear abuse of the board of directors' discretion, even when such a dividend policy is not fraudulent. The Code does not exempt publicly held corporations from the accumulation provisions, therefore, answer (b) is incorrect. Answer (d) is incorrect because the IRS cannot compel the corporation to distribute earnings and profits that have unreasonably accumu-

lated. However, the corporation is subject to an additional tax on earnings retained in excess of $150,000 if such retention is unreasonable.

J. Stockholder's Liability

25. (1188,L1,7) (c) Normally, the liability of shareholders of corporations is limited to their capital contribution. However, the court will "pierce the corporate veil" and hold the shareholders personally liable for the debts of the corporation if the corporate entity is being used to defraud people or to achieve other injustices. Thus, if the shareholders establish a corporation, knowing that it would have less capital than required for it to pay its debts, then the court will "pierce the corporate veil" and hold the shareholders personally liable. Answer (a) is incorrect because a shareholder may loan money to the corporation without becoming personally liable for the debts of the corporation. Answer (b) is incorrect because shareholders may also be corporate officers, directors or employees without jeopardizing their limited liability status. Answer (d) is incorrect because the formation of a corporation solely to limit personal liability is a valid purpose so long as it is done without intent to defraud.

26. (587,L1,1) (d) The court will disregard the corporate entity and hold the shareholders individually liable when the corporate form is used to perpetrate a fraud or is found to be merely an agent or instrument of its owners. An example of when the corporate veil is likely to be pierced is if the corporation and its shareholders commingle assets and financial records. In such a situation, the shareholders lose their limited liability and will be held personally liable for the corporation's legal obligations. Answer (b) is incorrect because the election of S corporation status is allowable under the law and is not in itself, grounds for piercing the corporate veil. Answer (c) is incorrect because the desire of shareholders to limit their personal liability is a valid reason to form a corporation. Limited personal liability is one advantage of the corporate entity. Answer (a) is incorrect since the court will hold personally liable only those corporate officers responsible for the commission of an <u>ultra vires</u> act. The court will not pierce the corporate veil and hold the shareholders personally liable for such an act.

K. Substantial Change in Corporate Structure

27. (584,L1,7) (d) The merger of two corporations requires the approval from the boards of directors of both merging corporations. Also, normally a majority of the shareholders of each corporation must approve the merger. Answer (a) is incorrect since the merger of two corporations is not subject to the approval of the IRS. Answer (b) is incorrect because a merger can be accomplished in several different ways besides the issuance of stock to the shareholders of the merged corporation. Answer (c) is incorrect because the approval of the merging corporations' creditors is not required for a valid merger to occur. The merging corporations' creditors merely become creditors of the existing corporation upon completion of the merger.

28. (581,L1,21) (b) There is no provision requiring the surviving corporation of a tax-free statutory merger to apply for and obtain a favorable revenue ruling from the Treasury Department. Answers (a) and (c) are incorrect because the board of directors and shareholders of both corporations must approve the merger. Answer (d) is incorrect since only securities issued in conjunction with a court supervised reorganization are exempt from the registration requirements of the Securities Act of 1933. For purposes of the Act, the shares exchanged between Minor and Universal would be "offered" and "sold".

29. (580,L1,6) (b) A consolidation is the unifying of two or more corporations into one new corporation, extinguishing both existing corporations. Therefore, answer (b) is the correct answer since neither corporation will survive the consolidation. Answer (a) is incorrect because under the Internal Revenue Code reorganizations, including statutory mergers or consolidations, receive nonrecognition treatment for tax purposes. Answer (c) is incorrect because the rights of the creditors of the consolidating corporations are in no way impaired by the consolidation. Answer (d) is incorrect because before a corporation can engage in a consolidation or merger, shareholder approval must be obtained. Approval by a majority is normally sufficient but some states demand approval by two-thirds of the shareholders.

L. Dissolution

30. (584,L1,6) (b) A judicial dissolution may be brought by a shareholder in the event that there has been a waste of the corporate assets by the board of directors. The following reasons would also constitute proper grounds for judicial dissolution:

• Directors are deadlocked in the management of the corporate affairs.
• Acts of the directors are illegal or oppressive.
• Shareholders are deadlocked and have not been able to elect directors for two consecutive annual meetings.

Answers (a), (c), and (d) are all incorrect because none of them states sufficient grounds for the judicial dissolution of a corporation on the petition of a shareholder.

May 1990 Answers

31. (590,L1,7) (d) Normally, the board of directors of a corporation has the power to adopt, amend, and repeal the bylaws. It also has the power to declare dividends and fix the compensation of the directors. However, it does not have the power to amend the articles of incorporation. Therefore, answers (a), (b), and (c) are incorrect.

32. (590,L1,8) (c) A corporation may resell treasury shares without regard to par value. Therefore, an owner of common stock who purchased treasury shares for less than par value will not have any liability beyond actual investment. Answer (a) is incorrect because an owner of common stock who paid less than par value for stock purchased in connection with an original issue of shares is contingently liable in many states to creditors for the difference between the amount paid and par value. Answer (b) is incorrect because a promise to perform future services in exchange for original issue par value shares is an executory promise which is not considered valid consideration for shares. An owner of common stock who agreed to perform future services for the corporation in exchange for original issue par value shares is liable to creditors for the difference between any valid consideration (i.e., cash, property, or services performed) given and par value. Answer (d) is incorrect because once the corporation accepts an offer to buy stock subscriptions, the subscriber becomes liable for the purchase. Therefore, an owner of common stock who failed to pay the full amount owed on a subscription contract for no-par shares is liable for the difference between any amounts already paid and the full amount owed according to the contract.

33. (590,L1,9) (b) The articles of incorporation must include, among other things, the amount of capital stock authorized and the types of stock to be issued. Specific provisions applicable to stock must also be stated. Examples of stock provisions which must be authorized by the articles of incorporation include number of authorized shares, whether the stock is to be par value or no-par value, and classes of stock, including voting rights and dividend provisions. Preferred stock is given preferred status as to liquidations and dividends. This is part of the definition of preferred stock and need not be specifically included in the articles of incorporation in order to be enforceable. Therefore, Johns becomes an unsecured creditor upon Abco's declaration of preferred stock dividend. Answers (a), (c), and (d) are incorrect because in order for Johns to be entitled to convert his preferred shares to common shares, to participate with common shareholders in any dividend distribution made after preferred dividends are paid, or to be entitled to vote if dividend payments are in arrears, it must be stated in the articles of incorporation.

Answer Outline

Problem 1   Comparisons of Limited Partnership
with Corporation; Formation;
Transfer of Interests; Liability;
Participation in Management;
Share of Profits (588,L3)

Formation
    Limited Partnership
- Two or more persons
- Governed by state limited partner-
ship statute
- One or more general partners
required
- File certificate of limited
partnership with the state

    Corporation
- May only be formed under state
incorporation statute
- Must file Articles of Incorporation
with the state
- One or more incorporators must sign
Articles of Incorporation

Liability
    Limited Partner liable to extent of
capital contribution unless participates
in daily management
    Shareholder generally liable to extent of
capital contribution

Rights
    Transfer
- Limited Partnership interest assignable unless otherwise agreed
- Shares of Stock freely transferable
unless otherwise agreed

    Management Participation
- Limited Partner cannot participate
without losing limited liability
status
- Shareholders may not participate
unless they are an officer or
director
- Shareholders owning voting stock
may vote for board of directors

    Profits
- Limited Partner entitled to share
of profits based on the partnership agreement
- Shareholders generally not entitled
to dividends until declared by the
board of directors

Unofficial Answer

Problem 1   Comparisons of Limited Partnership
with Corporation; Formation;
Transfer of Interests; Liability;
Participation in Management;
Share of Profits (588,L3)

A limited partnership is formed by two or
more persons under a state's limited partnership statute, having as members one or more
general partners and one or more limited
partners. Two or more persons desiring to
form a limited partnership must execute a
certificate of limited partnership that must
be filed in the office of the secretary of
state, or other appropriate state or local
office. A corporation may be formed only
under a state incorporation statute that
requires that one or more incorporators sign
Articles of Incorporation which must be filed
with the secretary of state.

Unless otherwise provided in the
partnership agreement, or other agreements
among the partners, a limited partnership
interest is assignable in whole or in part.
Similarly, in the absence of a restriction in
the corporation's organizational documents or
other agreements among the shareholders,
shares of stock are freely transferable.

A limited partner's liability for
partnership debts is generally limited to the
partner's investment (capital contribution) in
the partnership if the interest is fully paid
and non-assessable and the partner does not
participate in the daily management of the
business. Likewise, a shareholder's liability
for a corporation's debts is generally limited
to the shareholder's investment (capital
contribution) in the corporation.

A limited partner cannot participate in
the daily operations of the partnership's
business without losing limited liability. A
shareholder who is not also an officer or a
director cannot participate in the daily
operations of the corporation's business.
However, a shareholder owning voting stock has
the right to vote for a board of directors,
which will manage the business affairs of the
corporation. The board of directors elects
officers to run the daily operations of the
corporation.

A limited partner is entitled to receive a
share of the partnership's profits in the
manner provided in the partnership
agreement. On the other hand, whether a
shareholder receives dividends is generally
within the discretion of the board of
directors.

Answer Outline

Problem 2   Promoter's Preincorporation Contracts; Cash Dividends; Direc-
tor's Liability (1184,L5)

a. Wonda not liable to Servco
      Corporation is not bound on promoter's
      preincorporation contracts until cor-
      poration adopts agreements
      Bold not liable to Servco
      Bold clearly manifested his intent not
        to be bound
      Promoter is liable only if such intent
        is not manifested
      This preincorporation agreement is not
      contract but revocable offer
b. Corporation must be solvent
      Dividends must come from unrestricted
        retained earnings
      Total assets must be maintained at level
        above total liabilities
c. Charges of negligence are without merit
      Directors are usually jointly and sever-
        ally liable for assenting to unlawful
        payment of dividends
      Exception occurs if directors act in
        good faith and in reliance upon infor-
        mation prepared by management
      No liability for honest mistakes in
        business judgment

Unofficial Answer

Problem 2   Promoter's Preincorporation
Contracts; Cash Dividends;
Director's Liability (1184,L5)

a. Wonda is not liable to Servco on the
preincorporation agreements. A preincorporation agreement made by a promoter does not
bind the corporation even though it is made in
the corporation's name. The corporation prior
to its formation lacks the capacity to enter
into contracts or to employ agents since it is
nonexistent. Furthermore, unless after being
formed the corporation adopts or knowingly
accepts the benefits under the contract, it
will not be held liable. Therefore, Wonda's
express rejection of the preincorporation
agreement will allow it to avoid liability.

Bold's liability to Servco depends on
whether Bold clearly manifested his intent not
to be personally bound on the preincorporation
agreements. Such manifestation of intent can
be shown by the express language or acts of
the parties. The facts of the case at hand
clearly show that Bold did not intend to be
held personally liable on the agreements with
Servco, since the contracts were executed in
the name of Wonda, contingent upon adoption by

Wonda, and were based solely on Wonda's anticipated credit. Therefore, Bold will not be
held liable on the agreement with Servco.

Furthermore, a preincorporation agreement
that is entered into by a promoter on behalf
of a corporation to be formed and that is intended not to bind the promoter is not a contract but is merely a revocable offer to be
communicated to the proposed corporation after
its formation. Thus, under the facts, neither
Bold nor Wonda will enjoy rights or suffer
liabilities under the agreement.

b. Cash dividends may be declared and paid
if the corporation is solvent and payment of
the dividends would not render the corporation
insolvent. Furthermore, each state imposes
additional restrictions on what funds are
legally available to pay dividends. One of
the more restrictive tests adopted by many
states permits the payment of dividends only
out of unrestricted and unreserved earned surplus (retained earnings). The Model Business
Corporation Act as recently amended prohibits
distributions if, after giving effect to the
distribution, the corporation's total assets
would be less than the sum of its total liabilities.

c. The charge of negligence will fail if
the directors can establish that they acted in
good faith, in a manner reasonably believed to
be in the best interests of the corporation
and with such care as an ordinary prudent person in a like position would use under similar
circumstances. Furthermore, under the business judgment rule, the court will not substitute its judgment for that of the board of
directors as long as the directors acted in
good faith and with due care.

The allegation that the directors failed
to exercise due care by declaring cash dividends to shareholders that exceeded Wonda's
profits and paid-in capital is without merit.
Generally, if a director votes for or assents
to the unlawful payment of dividends, that
director will be jointly and severally liable,
along with all other directors so voting or
assenting. However, directors will be relieved of liability if in voting or assenting
to the payment of cash dividends they acted in
good faith and in reliance upon information,
opinions, reports or statements prepared or
presented by an officer or employee of the
corporation whom the directors reasonably
believe to be reliable and competent in the
matters presented. Thus, the directors'
reliance on the reports prepared and issued by
Wonda's vice-president of finance was proper
so long as the directors exercised due care,
acted in good faith, and acted without knowledge that would cause reliance on the reports
to be unwarranted. The reason for such a rule

is to allow directors to use their best business judgment without incurring liability for honest mistakes.

Answer Outline

Problem 3   Stated Capital; Treasury Stock; Cash Dividends (1187,L5)

a. Stated capital is the number of shares issued, valued at par value
Organization costs do not affect stated capital
Stock dividend would increase stated capital by the number of shares issued, valued at par value
Stock option would increase stated capital by the number of shares issued, valued at par value
Stock split does not affect stated capital
Instead the par value of the stock is decreased and the number of shares is increased
The acquisition of treasury stock under cost method has no effect on stated capital
The reissuance of treasury stock has no effect on stated capital
b. Cash dividends may be declared and paid if the corporation is solvent and payment of dividends would not cause insolvency. Some states permit payment of dividends only out of retained earnings.

Unofficial Answer

Problem 3   Stated Capital; Treasury Stock; Cash Dividends (1187,L5)

a. The initial capitalization of Creme in 1980 would result in $20,000 being allocated to stated capital. Stated capital includes the par value of all shares of the corporation having a par value that have been issued. Therefore, the $20,000 is calculated as follows: 40,000 shares issued x 50¢ par value = $20,000.

The $15,000 of expenses incurred in organizing Creme would not affect stated capital. The Model Business Corporation Act permits payment of organization expenses out of the consideration received by it in payment for its shares if the payment does not render such shares assessable or unpaid. Thus, stated capital remains at $20,000.

The 5% stock dividend would increase stated capital by $1,000 calculated as follows: 40,000 shares x 5% stock dividend = 2,000 shares x 50¢ par value = $1,000. The market price of the shares would have no effect on stated capital. Thus, stated capital is $21,000.

The exercise of the stock option by Creme's president would increase stated capital by $500 calculated as follows: 1,000 shares x 50¢ par value = $500. Neither the price paid by Creme's president nor the market price of the shares on the date the option was exercised would affect stated capital. Thus, stated capital is $21,500.

The 2-for-1 stock split would not affect stated capital. Instead the par value of 50¢ per share would be reduced to 25¢ per share and the 43,000 shares of stock issued would be increased to 86,000 shares. Thus, stated capital remains at $21,500.

The acquisition of 5,000 shares as treasury stock at $30 per share by Creme would have no effect on stated capital under the cost method. Thus, stated capital remains at $21,500.

The reissuance of the 3,000 shares of treasury stock at $32 per share would also have no effect on stated capital under the cost method. Thus, stated capital remains at $21,500.

b. Cash dividends may be declared and paid if the corporation is solvent and payment of the dividends would not render the corporation insolvent. Furthermore, each state imposes additional restrictions on what funds are legally available to pay dividends. One of the more restrictive tests adopted by many states permits the payment of dividends only out of unrestricted and unreserved earned surplus (retained earnings). The Model Business Corporation Act prohibits dividend distributions if, after giving effect to the distribution, the corporation's total assets would be less than its total liabilities.

Multiple Choice Questions (1-29)

1. One of the elements necessary to recover damages if there has been a material misstatement in a registration statement filed pursuant to the Securities Act of 1933 is that the
   a. Plaintiff suffered a loss.
   b. Plaintiff gave value for the security.
   c. Issuer and plaintiff were in privity of contract with each other.
   d. Issuer failed to exercise due care in connection with the sale of the securities.

2. Which of the following is a security that is exempt from the registration requirements of the Securities Act of 1933?
   a. Convertible, subordinated debentures issued by a manufacturing company.
   b. Warrants to purchase preferred stock.
   c. Bonds issued by a charitable foundation.
   d. Common stock with a par value of less than $1.00.

3. The principal purpose of the registration requirements of the Securities Act of 1933 is to
   a. Prevent public offerings of securities in which management fraud or unethical conduct is suspected.
   b. Provide the SEC with the information necessary to determine the accuracy of the facts presented in the financial statements.
   c. Assure that investors have adequate information upon which to base investment decisions.
   d. Provide the SEC with the information necessary to evaluate the financial merits of the securities being offered.

4. With regard to an offering of common stock requiring registration under the Securities Act of 1933
   a. The SEC will attempt to pass on the investment value of the common stock before approving the offering.
   b. The registration statement is automatically effective when filed with the SEC.
   c. The issuer may make sales 10 days after filing the registration statement.
   d. The issuer would act unlawfully if it were to sell the common stock without providing the investor with a prospectus.

5. Which of the following are exempt from the registration requirements of the Securities Act of 1933?
   a. All industrial development bonds issued by municipalities.
   b. Stock of a corporation offered and sold only to residents of the state in which the issuer was incorporated and doing all of its business.
   c. Bankers' acceptances with maturities at the time of issue ranging from one to two years.
   d. Participation interests in a money market fund that consists wholly of short-term commercial paper.

6. Acme Corp. intends to make a public offering in several states of 250,000 shares of its common stock. Under the Securities Act of 1933,
   a. Acme must sell the common stock through licensed securities dealers.
   b. Acme must, in all events, file a registration statement with the SEC because the offering will be made in several states.
   c. Acme's use of any prospectus delivered to an unsophisticated investor must be accompanied by a simplified explanation of the offering.
   d. Acme may make an oral offer to sell the common stock to a prospective investor after a registration statement has been filed but before it becomes effective.

7. In general, which of the following is **least** likely to be considered a security under the Securities Act of 1933?
   a. General partnership interests.
   b. Warrants.
   c. Limited partnership interests.
   d. Treasury stock.

8. To be successful in a civil action under Section 11 of the Securities Act of 1933 concerning liability for a misleading registration statement, the plaintiff must prove

	Defendant's intent to deceive	Plaintiff's reliance on the registration statement
a.	Yes	Yes
b.	Yes	No
c.	No	Yes
d.	No	No

9. After the filing of the registration statement with the SEC but prior to the effective date, the underwriter is allowed to do which of the following?

1
6

I.   Make oral offers to sell the
     security
II. Issue a preliminary prospectus
     ("red herring")

  a.   I only.
  b.   II only.
  c.   I and II.
  d.   Neither I nor II.

10. Which of the following types of securities are generally exempt from registration under the Securities Act of 1933?

	Securities of nonprofit charitable organizations	Securities of savings and loan associations
a.	Yes	Yes
b.	Yes	No
c.	No	Yes
d.	No	No

Items 11 and 12 are based on the following:

Maco Limited Partnership intends to sell
$6,000,000 of its limited partnership inter-
ests. The state in which Maco was organized
is also the state in which it carries on all
of its business activities.

11. If Maco intends to offer the limited
partnership interests in reliance on Rule 147,
the intrastate registration exception under
the Securities Act of 1933, which one of the
following statements is correct?
  a. Maco may make up to five offers to
nonresidents without the offering
being ineligible for the Rule 147
exemption.
  b. The offering is not exempt under
Rule 147 because it exceeds
$5,000,000.
  c. Under Rule 147, certain restrictions
apply to resales of the limited
partnership interests by purchasers.
  d. Rule 147 limits to 100 the number of
purchasers of the limited
partnership interests.

12. If Maco intends to offer the limited
partnership interests in reliance on Rule 506
of Regulation D under the Securities Act of
1933 to prospective investors residing in
several states, which of the following
statements is correct?
  a. The offering will be exempt from the
anti-fraud provisions of the
Securities Exchange Act of 1934.
  b. Any subsequent resale of a limited
partnership interest by a purchaser
will be exempt from registration.
  c. Maco may make an unlimited number of
offers to sell the limited
partnership interests.

  d. No more than 35 purchasers may
acquire the limited partnership
interests.

13. Rule 504 of Regulation D of the Securities Act of 1933 provides issuers with an
exemption from registration for certain small
issues. Which of the following statements is
correct?
  a. The rule allows sales to an
unlimited number of investors.
  b. The rule requires certain financial
information to be furnished to the
investors.
  c. The issuer must offer the securities
through general public advertising.
  d. The issuer is not required to file
anything with the SEC.

14. An issuer making an offering under the
provisions of Regulation A of the Securities
Act of 1933 must file a(an)
  a. Prospectus.
  b. Offering statement.
  c. Shelf registration.
  d. Proxy.

15. Securities available under a private
placement made pursuant to Regulation D of the
Securities Act of 1933
  a. Cannot be subject to the payment of
commissions.
  b. Must be sold to accredited institutional investors.
  c. Must be sold to fewer than 20 nonaccredited investors.
  d. Cannot be the subject of an
immediate unregistered reoffering to
the public.

16. Which of the following securities is
exempt from registration under the Securities
Act of 1933?
  a. A class of shares of stock given in
exchange for another class by the
issuer to its existing shareholders
without payment of a commission.
  b. Limited partnership interests sold
for the purpose of acquiring funds
to invest in bonds issued by the
United States.
  c. Corporate debentures that were
previously subject to an effective
registration statement, provided
they are convertible into shares of
common stock.
  d. Shares of common stock, provided
their par value is less than $1.00
and they are nonvoting.

17. Rice, Inc. is a reporting company under the Securities Exchange Act of 1934. The only security it has issued is its voting common stock. Which one of the following statements is correct?

    a. Any person who owns more than 5% of Rice's common stock must file a report with the SEC.

    b. Rice need not file its proxy statements with the SEC because it has only one class of stock outstanding.

    c. It is unnecessary for the required annual report (Form 10-K) to include audited financial statements.

    d. Because Rice is a reporting company, it is not required to file a registration statement under the Securities Act of 1933 for any future offerings of its common stock.

18. Which of the following statements is correct with respect to the Securities Exchange Act of 1934?

    a. Issuers whose securities are registered under the Act are required to comply with its reporting requirements.

    b. The Act applies only to issuers whose securities are traded on a national securities exchange.

    c. The Act subjects all issuers of securities to its registration requirements if the issuer has more than $2.5 million of assets or more than 250 shareholders.

    d. The antifraud provisions of the Act do not apply to issuers of securities that are exempt from the Act's registration requirements.

19. Pace Corp. previously issued 300,000 shares of its common stock. The shares are now actively traded on a national securities exchange. The original offering was exempt from registration under the Securities Act of 1933. Pace has $2,500,000 in assets and 425 shareholders. With regard to the Securities Exchange Act of 1934, Pace is

    a. Required to file a registration statement because its assets exceed $2,000,000 in value.

    b. Required to file a registration statement even though it has fewer than 500 shareholders.

    c. Not required to file a registration statement because the original offering of its stock was exempt from registration.

    d. Not required to file a registration statement unless insiders own at least 5% of its outstanding shares of stock.

20. Rey Corp.'s management intends to solicit proxies relating to its annual meeting at which directors will be elected. Rey is subject to the registration and reporting requirements of the Securities Exchange Act of 1934. As a result, Rey must furnish its shareholders with

    a. A copy of its registration statement and bylaws.

    b. A preliminary copy of its proxy statement at the same time it is filed with the SEC.

    c. An annual report containing its audited statements of income for the five most recent years.

    d. An annual report containing its audited balance sheets for the two most recent years.

21. Which of the following statements is correct with respect to the registration requirements of the Securities Exchange Act of 1934?

    a. They require issuers of non-exempt securities traded on a national securities exchange to register with the SEC.

    b. They permit issuers who comply with the Securities Act of 1933 to avoid the registration requirements of the Securities Exchange Act of 1934.

    c. They permit issuers who comply with those requirements to avoid state registration requirements.

    d. They permit issuers who comply with those requirements to avoid the registration requirements of the Securities Act of 1933.

22. Under the provisions of the Securities Exchange Act of 1934, a corporation whose common stock is listed on a national stock exchange

    a. Is prohibited from making private placement offerings.

    b. Must submit Form 10-K to the SEC except in those years in which the corporation has made a public offering.

    c. Must distribute copies of Form 10-K to its shareholders.

    d. Is subject to having the registration of its securities suspended or revoked.

23. Which of the following persons is not an insider of a corporation subject to the Securities Exchange Act of 1934 registration and reporting requirements?

    a. The president.

    b. A member of the board of directors.

c. A shareholder who owns 8% of the outstanding common stock and whose wife owns 4% of the outstanding common stock.

d. An owner of 15% of the total face value of the corporation's outstanding debentures.

May 1990 Questions

24. Under the Securities Act of 1933, the registration of an interstate securities offering is
   a. Required only in transactions involving more than $500,000.
   b. Mandatory, unless the cost to the issuer is prohibitive.
   c. Required, unless there is an applicable exemption.
   d. Intended to prevent the marketing of securities which pose serious financial risks.

25. Dice, Inc. is a reporting company under the Securities Exchange Act of 1934. The only security Dice issued is voting common stock. With regard to Dice's proxy solicitation requirements, which of the following statements is correct?
   a. Dice must file its proxy statements with the SEC even though it has only one class of stock outstanding.
   b. Dice's current unaudited financial statements must be sent to each shareholder with every proxy solicitation.
   c. Shareholder proposals need not be included in the proxy statements unless consented to by a majority of Dice's board of directors.
   d. Dice need not provide any particular information to its shareholders unless Dice is soliciting proxies from them.

26. Under the Securities Exchange Act of 1934, which of the following individuals would not be subject to the insider reporting provisions?
   a. An owner of ten percent of a corporation's stock.
   b. An owner of five percent of a corporation's voting stock.
   c. The vice-president of marketing.
   d. A member of the board of directors.

27. Pate Corp. is offering $3 million of its securities solely to accredited investors. Under Regulation D of the Securities Act of 1933, Pate is

a. Not required to provide any specified information to the accredited investors.
b. Permitted to make a general solicitation.
c. Not allowed to sell to investors using purchaser representatives.
d. Required to provide accredited investors with audited financial statements for the three most recent fiscal years.

28. Regulation D of the Securities Act of 1933
   a. Is limited to offers and sales of common stock that do not exceed $1.5 million.
   b. Is exclusively available to small business corporations as defined by Regulation D.
   c. Permits an exempt offering to be sold to both accredited and nonaccredited investors.
   d. Restricts the number of purchasers of an offering to 35.

29. Zack Limited Partnership intends to sell $6,000,000 of its limited partnership interests. Zack conducts all of its business activities in the state in which it was organized. Zack intends to use the offering proceeds to acquire municipal bonds. Which of the following statements is correct concerning the offering and the registration exemptions that might be available to Zack under the Securities Act of 1933?
   a. The offering is exempt from registration because of the intended use of the offering proceeds.
   b. Under Rule 147 (regarding intrastate offerings), Zack may make up to five offers to non-residents without jeopardizing the Rule 147 exemption.
   c. If Zack complies with the requirements of Regulation D, any subsequent resale of a limited partnership interest by a purchaser is automatically exempt from registration.
   d. If Zack complies with the requirements of Regulation D, Zack may make an unlimited number of offers to sell the limited partnership interests.

Repeat Questions

(590,L1,28) Identical/similar to item 7 above
(590,L1,32) Identical/similar to item 5 above

Problem

Problem 1   (582,L2)

(15 to 20 minutes)

Various Enterprises Corporation is a
medium sized conglomerate listed on the
American Stock Exchange. It is constantly in
the process of acquiring smaller corporations
and is invariably in need of additional money.
Among its diversified holdings is a citrus
grove which it purchased eight years ago as an
investment. The grove's current fair market
value is in excess of $2 million. Various
also owns 800,000 shares of Resistance Corporation which it acquired in the open market
over a period of years. These shares represent a 17% minority interest in Resistance and
are worth approximately $2½ million. Various
does its short-term financing with a consor-
tium of banking institutions. Several of
these loans are maturing; in addition to
renewing these loans, it wishes to increase
its short-term debt from $3 to $4 million.

In light of the above, Various is considering resorting to one or all of the
following alternatives in order to raise
additional working capital.

• An offering of 500 citrus grove units
at $5,000 per unit. Each unit would give the
purchaser a 0.2% ownership interest in the
citrus grove development. Various would
furnish management and operation services for
a fee under a management contract and net
proceeds would be paid to the unit purchasers.
The offering would be confined almost exclusively to the state in which the groves are
located or in the adjacent state in which
Various is incorporated.

• An increase in the short-term
borrowing by $1 million from the banking
institution which currently provides short-
term funds. The existing debt would be
consolidated, extended, and increased to $4
million and would mature over a nine-month
period. This would be evidenced by a short-
term note.

• Sale of the 17% minority interest in
Resistance Corporation in the open market
through its brokers over a period of time and
in such a way as to minimize decreasing the
value of the stock. The stock is to be sold
in an orderly manner in the ordinary course of
the broker's business.

Required:

Answer the following, setting forth
reasons for any conclusions stated.

In separate paragraphs discuss the impact
of the registration requirements of the
Securities Act of 1933 on each of the above
proposed alternatives.

Multiple Choice Answers

1. a	7. a	13. a	19. b	25. a
2. c	8. d	14. b	20. d	26. b
3. c	9. c	15. d	21. a	27. a
4. d	10. a	16. a	22. d	28. c
5. b	11. c	17. a	23. d	29. d
6. d	12. c	18. a	24. c	

Multiple Choice Answer Explanations

A. Securities Act of 1933

1. (1189,L1,33) (a) In order to recover damages under a civil action under the Securities Act of 1933, the purchaser must establish that s/he purchased securities which had been issued under a registration statement containing a misleading statement or an omission of a material fact and that s/he suffered an economic loss. Answer (b) is incorrect because it does not as clearly state a necessary element as does answer (a). The emphasis is not on proving that the plaintiff gave value for the security, rather it's on proving that a loss was suffered. Answer (c) is incorrect because privity of contract is not an element needed in order to recover in the cause of action. Answer (d) is incorrect because failure to exercise due care need not be established to recover under the 1933 Act.

2. (1188,L1,34) (c) The Securities Act of 1933 requires a registration statement to be filed with and approved by the Securities and Exchange Commission before either a public sale of securities or an offer to sell securities in interstate commerce. Certain types of securities, including securities of non-profit religious, educational, or charitable organizations, are specifically exempted from the registration requirements of the 1933 Act. These exempt securities are still subject to the antifraud provisions of the 1933 Act. Answers (a), (b), and (d) are all incorrect because they do not describe classes of securities specifically exempted from the registration requirements of the 1933 Act.

3. (588,L1,36) (c) The primary purpose of the Securities Act of 1933 is to assure that securities issuers provide potential investors with full and fair disclosure of all material information needed to make a prudent investment decision. Answer (a) is incorrect because the Securities Act of 1933 does not purport to prevent offerings in which management fraud or unethical conduct is suspected. Answers (b) and (d) are incorrect because an offering approved by the SEC pursuant to registration requirements of the Securities Act of 1933 does not imply that the SEC has determined the accuracy of the facts presented in the financial statements or evaluated the financial merits of the securities offered.

4. (589,L1,39) (d) In order to provide the public with important information about securities, issuers are required under the Securities Act of 1933 to provide investors with a prospectus before or with the sale of securities. The Act provides for criminal penalties as well as civil liability if the issuer fails to provide the prospectus. Answer (a) is incorrect because the purpose of the Act is to provide the investors with full and fair disclosure. An offering approved by the SEC does not imply that the SEC has evaluated the financial merits of the securities offered. Answer (b) is incorrect because the registration becomes effective 20 days after filing but the SEC may issue a stop order if the registration statement appears incomplete or misleading. Answer (c) is incorrect because the issuer cannot sell the securities prior to the effective registration date which is at least 20 days after the filing.

5. (588,L1,41) (b) Under the Securities Act of 1933, a registration statement and prospectus must be filed with and approved by the SEC if securities are to be offered, sold, or delivered in interstate commerce. However, there are several exemptions to this requirement. One of the exemptions is the intrastate offering which occurs when the stock of a corporation is offered and sold only to residents of the state in which the issuer is a resident and doing 80% of its business. Answer (a) is incorrect because securities issued by municipalities must be for government purposes to be exempt. Industrial development bonds are therefore not exempt. Answer (c) is incorrect because commercial paper is exempt only if it has a maturity of nine months or less. Answer (d) is incorrect because although the sale of the actual short-term commercial paper could be exempt under the 1933 Act, no exemption is provided for the sale of shares of a fund that consists of short-term commercial paper.

6. (589,L1,40) (d) After the registration statement has been filed but before it becomes effective, the issuer is allowed to make certain oral offers and written offers that are preliminary prospectuses. Answer (a) is incorrect because there is no requirement that the issuer sell securities through a licensed security dealer. Answer (b) is incorrect because a registration statement need not be filed if the securities are exempt or if the

transaction is exempt. Although the issue won't qualify for exemption based on an intrastate offering, it could qualify for a different exemption. Answer (c) is incorrect because there is no such requirement to accompany a prospectus with a simplified explanation to any investors.

7. (1187,L1,6) (a) Securities are considered to be investments whereby the investor intends to make a profit through the efforts of others. Of the securities listed, a general partnership interest would be least likely to be considered a security since a general partner is normally involved in the business decision making process of the partnership. Answers (b), (c), and (d) are all incorrect since all of them are investments made with the intention of making a profit through the efforts of others.

8. (1189,L1,34) (d) To recover under a civil action under Section 11 of the Securities Act of 1933, the plaintiff must prove that s/he was a purchaser of a security issued under a registration statement that contains a misleading statement or an omission of a material fact. S/he also must prove that s/he suffered an economic loss. The plaintiff need not prove that the defendant intended to deceive or even that negligence existed. The plaintiff also need not prove that s/he relied on the registration statement. Therefore, answers (a), (b), and (c) are incorrect.

9. (1187,L1,8) (c) While the Securities Act prohibits any offers to sell or to buy securities before the registration statement is filed, the Act permits offers, but not sales, during the period between filing and effectiveness. There are no restrictions on oral offers made during this period, and written offers may be made through a preliminary prospectus ("red herring"). Thus, answers (a), (b), and (d) are all incorrect.

10. (1189,L1,39) (a) Several types of securities are exempt from registration under the Securities Act of 1933. These include securities of nonprofit religious, educational, and charitable organizations, as well as securities of governments, banks, and savings and loan associations. Therefore, answers (b), (c), and (d) are incorrect.

A.5. Exempt Transactions

11. (589,L1,44) (c) When the intrastate exemption applies, resales of the securities can only be made to residents of the same state for 9 months after the last sale by the issuer. Therefore, answer (c) is correct. Answer (a) is incorrect because all offerees must be residents of the state. Answer (b) is incorrect because the rule does not involve a dollar amount. Answer (d) is incorrect because the sale is restricted to residents of the same state with no limit to the number of purchasers.

12. (589,L1,45) (c) Rule 506 of Regulation D under the 1933 Act allows placement of an unlimited amount of securities to an unlimited number of accredited investors and up to 35 unaccredited investors that are sophisticated investors within a 12-month period. Therefore, an unlimited number of offers to sell the limited partnership interests, which are securities, will be allowed. Answer (a) is incorrect because the antifraud provisions apply even if the securities or transactions are exempt from registration under the 1933 Act. Answer (b) is incorrect because the resale of the securities must be restricted in general for two years or else the exemption is lost. Answer (d) is incorrect because an unlimited number of accredited investors may purchase the securities.

13. (1189,L1,37) (a) Rule 504 of Regulation D of the Securities Act of 1933 exempts an issuance to any number of investors of securities of up to $500,000 sold in a 12-month period or up to $1,000,000 if at least $500,000 is registered at the state level. Answer (b) is incorrect because Rule 504 does not require the furnishing of any financial information to the investors. Answer (c) is incorrect because no general offering or solicitation is allowed under Rule 504. Answer (d) is incorrect because the issuer is required to send a notice of such an offering to the SEC.

14. (1189,L1,35) (b) Issuances of securities of up to $1,500,000 are exempt from the registration requirements of the Securities Act of 1933 when they are issued under Regulation A. Although a prospectus is thus not required, an offering circular (statement) must be provided to the offerees that contains financial information about the corporation and descriptive information about the securities. Answer (a) is incorrect because Regulation A provides an exemption from the prospectus. Answer (c) is incorrect because shelf registration is not required to make an offering under Regulation A. Answer (d) is incorrect because a proxy is the granting of authority by a shareholder to someone else to vote his/her shares. Thus, it is unrelated to the issuance or securities and is not a requirement under Regulation A.

15. (1189,L1,38) (d) Securities sold through a private placement under Regulation D of the Securities Act of 1933 must, in general, restrict the purchaser's right to resell for two years. Answer (a) is incorrect because commissions may still be paid on such offerings without hindering their exempt status. Answer (b) is incorrect because unaccredited investors (within certain restrictions) may purchase securities issued under a private placement made pursuant to Regulation D. Answer (c) is incorrect because Rule 506 of Regulation D allows sales to up to 35 unaccredited, sophisticated investors within 12 months.

16. (589,L1,43) (a) Under the Securities Act of 1933, a registration statement and prospectus must be filed with and approved by the SEC if securities are to be offered, sold, or delivered in interstate commerce. However, there are several securities exempt from this requirement. Exempt securities include securities exchanged by the issuer for another class of stock to existing stockholders without commissions. Answer (b) is incorrect because limited partnership interests investing in U.S. bonds are not exempt. Answer (c) is incorrect because there is no such exemption. Answer (d) is incorrect because low par values and nonvoting characteristics do not exempt securities from registration under the Securities Act of 1933.

B. Securities Exchange Act of 1934

17. (589,L1,42) (a) Under Section 13(d) of the Securities Exchange Act of 1934, any purchaser of more than 5 percent of a class of equity securities must file a report with the SEC, the issuer, and the national securities exchange concerning the purpose of the acquisition. Answer (b) is incorrect because the need to file a proxy statement is not removed because only one class of stock is outstanding. Answer (c) is incorrect because the required annual report (Form 10-K) must include audited financial statements. Answer (d) is incorrect because reporting under the 1934 Act does not eliminate the need to comply with the 1933 Act. The purpose of the 1933 Act is generally to regulate initial offerings of securities. The 1934 Act, on the other hand, is generally intended to regulate the subsequent trading of securities. Therefore, satisfying the requirements of either Act does not exempt an issuer from the requirements of the other Act.

18. (588,L1,38) (a) Issuers of securities registered with the SEC under the Securities Exchange Act of 1934 must fulfill certain reporting requirements with the SEC. These requirements include the filing of annual reports (Form 10-K), quarterly reports (Form 10-Q), and current reports of certain material events (Form 8-K). Answer (b) is incorrect because the Act not only applies to all issuers whose securities are traded on national exchanges, but also to some issuers who trade over-the-counter. Answer (c) is incorrect because the Act covers all issuers who trade over-the-counter and have assets of 3 million or more and a class of stock that has 500 or more shareholders. Answer (d) is incorrect because the antifraud provisions of the Act are broader in scope in that they apply to any issuer whose securities are sold in interstate commerce.

19. (589,L1,41) (b) Under the Securities Exchange Act of 1934, issuers of securities that are traded on a national securities exchange are required to register with the SEC unless specifically exempted. This is true even if the entity has fewer than 500 stockholders. Answer (a) is incorrect because the securities are required to be registered because they are traded on a national securities exchange. Furthermore, even if they were over-the-counter stock traded in interstate commerce, the rule requires 500 or more stockholders and corporate assets of more than $3 million. Answer (c) is incorrect because the 1934 Act may still regulate securities even though they were exempted under the 1933 Act. Answer (d) is incorrect because the securities had to be registered because they were sold on a national securities exchange.

20. (1187,L1,9) (d) A company that is subject to SEC registration and continuing disclosure requirements must furnish its shareholders with audited financial statements for the last two years when soliciting proxies on behalf of management for an annual meeting at which directors are to be elected. Thus, Rey Corp. must furnish its shareholders with an annual report containing audited balance sheets for the two most recent years. Therefore answer (c) is incorrect. Answer (a) is incorrect because a company that is subject to SEC registration and continuing disclosure requirements is not required to furnish its shareholders with a copy of its registration statement and bylaws. Answer (b) is incorrect because preliminary copies of the proxy statement must be filed with the SEC at least 10 days before they are to be sent to the shareholders.

21. (587,L1,39) (a) Under the Securities Exchange Act of 1934 issuers of securities traded on a national securities exchange are required to register with the SEC unless specifically exempted. Answers (b) and (d) are incorrect because the registration requirements of the 1933 and 1934 Acts are not mutually exclusive. The purpose of the 1933 Act is generally to regulate initial offerings of securities. The 1934 Act, on the other hand, is generally intended to regulate the subsequent trading of securities. Therefore, satisfying the requirements of either act does not exempt an issuer from the requirements of the other act. Answer (c) is incorrect because compliance with the Securities Exchange Act of 1934 does not permit an issuer to avoid compliance with applicable state registration requirements.

22. (1189,L1,36) (d) A corporation whose stock is listed on a national stock exchange is regulated under the provisions of the Securities Exchange Act of 1934. Under the 1934 Act, one of the sanctions available to the SEC is the revocation or suspension of the registration of the securities of any registrant. Answer (a) is incorrect because the corporation may still make private placement offerings, even though it has made a public offering. Answer (b) is incorrect because the Form 10-K must be filed with the SEC each year, regardless of whether the corporation has made a public offering during that year. Answer (c) is incorrect because the Form 10-K is not required to be distributed to the shareholders but must only be filed with the SEC.

23. (587,L1,42) (d) Under the Securities Exchange Act of 1934, insiders include officers, directors, and beneficial owners of more than 10% of any class of the issuer's equity securities. An owner of 15% of the total face value of the corporation's outstanding debentures therefore does not qualify as an insider. Answers (a) and (b) are incorrect because they describe an officer and a director, respectively. Answer (c) is incorrect because it describes a beneficial owner of more than 10% of the common stock. Beneficial ownership includes ownership of securities owned by oneself, securities in a spouse's name, minor child's name or relative's name who shares the same home. Beneficial ownership also includes ownership of securities held in a trust of which an insider is a beneficiary.

May 1990 Answers

24. (590,L1,29) (c) Securities that are offered, sold, or delivered in interstate commerce must be registered under the Securities Act of 1933, unless the security has a specific exemption or unless the transaction is exempted. Answer (a) is incorrect because although there is an exemption for "small issues," the applicable amount is greater than the $500,000. Furthermore, under Regulation D, transactions greater than $500,000 can be exempted if certain requirements are met. Answer (b) is incorrect because the law does not provide exemptions from registration based on whether the cost to the issuer is prohibitive. Answer (d) is incorrect because the 1933 Act is meant to provide investors with full and fair disclosure and to prevent fraud. The SEC does not evaluate the risk of the securities. That function is left to the potential investors.

25. (590,L1,30) (a) Under the Securities Exchange Act of 1934, a reporting company that is soliciting proxies must file its proxy statement with the SEC. There is no exemption if the company has only one class of stock. Answer (b) is incorrect because if management is soliciting proxies for the meeting to elect the directors, audited financial statements for the last two years must be included. Answer (c) is incorrect because shareholder proposals that are a proper subject for shareholders to vote on should be included. Answer (d) is incorrect because there is no such provision.

26. (590,L1,31) (b) Under the Securities Exchange Act of 1934, an insider includes officers, directors, and owners of at least 10 percent of any class of the issuer's equity securities. Therefore, an owner of less than 10 percent of the corporation's stock, even if it is voting stock such as in answer (b), is not subject to the insider reporting provisions. Answer (a) is incorrect because the individual owns at least 10 percent of an equity security. Answer (c) is incorrect because the vice president of marketing is an officer. Answer (d) is incorrect because a director is an insider whether or not s/he owns stock.

27. (590,L1,33) (a) Under Regulation D of the Securities Act of 1933, the corporation may issue up to $5,000,000 of securities within a twelve-month period. If the offer is made solely to accredited investors, then there is no requirement to provide any specified information. Sales are permitted to up

to 35 unaccredited investors, in which case audited financial statements must be supplied. Answer (b) is incorrect because no general offering or solicitation is permitted under Regulation D. Answer (c) is incorrect because purchaser representatives are allowed as long as the requirements of Regulation D are met. Answer (d) is incorrect because if the sale is to only accredited investors, such as in this question, then no audited financial statements need be supplied.

28. (590,L1,34) (c) Regulation D of the Securities Act of 1933 has three important exemptions in Rules 504, 505, and 506. Rule 504 exempts an issuance of up to $500,000 of securities sold within a twelve-month period to any number of investors whether they are accredited or nonaccredited. Rule 505 increases the exemption to $5,000,000 but restricts the sale to 35 nonaccredited investors. Sale to an unlimited number of accredited investors is permitted. Rule 506 is similar to rule 505 except that the dollar amount is now unlimited, and the sale to up to 35 nonaccredited investors requires that they also be sophisticated investors with knowledge and experience in financial matters. A sale can still be made to an unlimited number of accredited investors. Answer (a) is therefore incorrect. Answer (b) is incorrect because there is no requirement that the company be a small business. Answer (d) is incorrect because in Rule 504, there is no restriction on the number of investors but on the dollar amount of the issuance. Rules 505 and 506 have a 35 person limit on nonaccredited and "sophisticated" nonaccredited investors respectively, but do not have a limit on accredited investors.

29. (590,L1,37) (d) Regulation D under the Securities Act of 1933 allows an unlimited number of offers and sales to accredited investors. If sales are made to nonaccredited investors, then under Rule 506, the nonaccredited investors must be sophisticated investors with knowledge and experience in financial matters. These sophisticated, nonaccredited investors must be limited to 35. Note that limited partnerships are generally securities under the 1933 Act. Answer (a) is incorrect because although there are exemptions for issuances of municipal bonds themselves, the mere fact that the intended use of the proceeds of the issuance of securities is to buy municipal bonds does not bring in an exemption. Answer (b) is incorrect because all offerees must be residents of the state to get the intrastate exemption. Answer (c) is incorrect because Regulation D only causes the individual transaction to be exempt. Each transaction must meet the exemption on its own.

Answer Outline

Problem 1   Registration Requirements Under
             1933 Act (582,L2)

Since sale of interest in citrus groves meets
 definition of security, must comply with registration requirement of 1933 Act
  Unless one of the three exemptions are present
    Small offering exemption
    Intrastate offering exemption
    Private offering exemption
  None met; therefore, Various must comply
Short-term note qualifies as exempt security
 under 1933 Act
  Since it is commercial paper with maturity
  of nine months or less
    And proceeds to be used for current opera-
    tions
  Also qualifies as exempt transaction as private offering
Issue is whether Various is a controlling
 person of Resistance Corporation
  If not controlling person, sale of these
   shares exempted from registration requirements
    Under casual sales exemption
  If controlling person, Various must meet
   registration requirements of 1933 Act
    Unless sale of shares meets requirements
    of Rule 144

Unofficial Answer
(Author Modified)

Problem 1   Registration Requirements Under
             1933 Act (582,L2)

•   The sale of the ownership interests in
the citrus groves qualifies as a security
under the 1933 Act. A security is the sale of
any interest in a scheme where a person invests money in a common enterprise and is led
to expect profits solely from the endeavors of
others. The purchasers of the citrus grove
units would be expecting profits from the operation and management of these units by
Various. Consequently, unless an exemption
can be found under the 1933 Act, Various must
file a registration statement with the SEC,
and such statement must be approved before the
issuance of these interests. The only possible exemptions would be an intrastate offering, a small offering and a private offering. The sale of citrus grove interests would
not constitute an intrastate offering because
interests are offered to persons residing in
more than one state. This offering would not
qualify as a small offering in that the aggregate value would exceed $1,500,000. Also, it
does not appear that it is a private offering,
since the offering is not limited to a small
number of sophisticated investors.

•   The issuance of a short-term note by
Various would not require the filing of a
registration statement with the SEC. Commercial paper having a maturity date not exceeding nine months is exempt from the registration requirements of the 1933 Act. This is
only true if the proceeds gained from the
issuance of this paper have been or are to be
used for current operations. However, if the
proceeds are to be used for long-term capital
investments, this exemption would not apply.
Since the problem states the instrument would
be used to finance current operations, it
appears that the note would qualify as an
exemption to the 1933 Securities Act requirement for filing. It appears that the requirements for a private placement would be met in
this situation. The offering is limited to
one sophisticated investor, since institutional investors such as banks and insurance
companies are considered to be sophisticated
in nature.

•   Concerning Various' sale of the
Resistance shares, the important fact is to
determine whether Various qualifies as a
controlling person of Resistance Corporation.
If Various does not qualify as a controlling
person, the sale of these shares would be
exempted from the registration requirements of
the 1933 Act under the casual sales exemption.
The casual sales exemption states that a
transaction by any person other than an
issuer, underwriter or dealer is exempt from
registration. A controlling person in a
corporation has been construed to mean anyone
with direct or indirect power to determine the
policies of the business. Obviously, ownership of a majority share of existing stock in
a company would constitute control. However,
in past court decisions, as little as 10%
ownership of outstanding shares has been determined to constitute control when combined
with such other factors as being a member of
the board of directors; an officer of the
corporation; or the fact that the remaining
shares are distributed over a large number of
shareholders. Thus, the fact that Various
only owns 17% would not keep it from being a
controlling person. If held to be a controlling person, Various' sale of shares would
not fall within the casual sales exemption of
the 1933 Act. Since this exemption is not
met, Various would have to file a registration
statement when selling these shares even
though the sale is accomplished through a
broker. However, the SEC does permit controlling persons to sell limited quantities of

their securities without registration of their
security if their sale complies with requirements of Rule 144. Rule 144 requires: adequate information concerning the company be
publicly available; sale of no more than 1% of
all outstanding shares of that class during
any three month period; that all sales take
place in broker's transactions, with the
broker receiving only the ordinary brokerage
commission and the broker not engaging in any
solicitations of offers to buy from prospective purchasers. Thus, even if Various was
considered to be a controlling person, upon
compliance with the above requirements,
Various would still be able to sell a limited
number of its shares without registration.

Multiple Choice Questions (1-21)

1. Nast Corp. orally engaged Baker & Co., CPAs, to audit its financial statements. The management of Nast informed Baker that it suspected the accounts receivable were materially overstated. Although the financial statements audited by Baker did, in fact, include a materially overstated accounts receivable balance, Baker issued an unqualified opinion. Nast relied on the financial statements in deciding to obtain a loan from Century Bank to expand its operations. Nast has defaulted on the loan and has incurred a substantial loss.

If Nast sues Baker for negligence in failing to discover the overstatement, Baker's best defense would be that
- a. Baker did **not** perform the audit recklessly or with an intent to deceive.
- b. Baker was **not** in privity of contract with Nast.
- c. The audit was performed by Baker in accordance with generally accepted auditing standards.
- d. No engagement letter had been signed by Baker.

2. If a stockholder sues a CPA for common law fraud based on false statements contained in the financial statements audited by the CPA, which of the following, if present, would be the CPA's best defense?
- a. The stockholder lacks privity to sue.
- b. The false statements were immaterial.
- c. The CPA did **not** financially benefit from the alleged fraud.
- d. The contributory negligence of the client.

3. One of the elements necessary to hold a CPA liable to a client for conducting an audit negligently is that the CPA
- a. Acted with scienter or guilty knowledge.
- b. Was a fiduciary of the client.
- c. Failed to exercise due care.
- d. Executed an engagement letter.

4. When CPAs fail in their duty to carry out their contracts for services, liability to clients may be based on

	Breach of contract	Strict liability
a.	Yes	Yes
b.	Yes	No
c.	No	No
d.	No	Yes

5. Which one of the following, if present, would support a finding of constructive fraud on the part of a CPA?
- a. Privity of contract.
- b. Intent to deceive.
- c. Reckless disregard.
- d. Ordinary negligence.

6. Krim, President and CEO of United Co., engaged Smith, CPA, to audit United's financial statements so that United could secure a loan from First Bank. Smith issued an unqualified opinion on May 20, 1988, but the loan was delayed. On August 5, 1988, on inquiry to Smith by First Bank, Smith, relying on Krim's representation, made assurances that there was no material change in United's financial status. Krim's representation was untrue because of a material change which took place after May 20, 1988. First relied on Smith's assurances of no change. Shortly thereafter, United became insolvent. If First sues Smith for negligent misrepresentation, Smith will be found
- a. Not liable, because Krim misled Smith, and a CPA is **not** responsible for a client's untrue representations.
- b. Liable, because Smith should have undertaken sufficient auditing procedures to verify the status of United.
- c. Not liable, because Smith's opinion only covers the period up to May 20.
- d. Liable, because Smith should have contacted the chief financial officer rather than the chief executive officer.

Items 7 and 8 are based on the following information:

Brown & Co., CPAs, issued an unqualified opinion on the financial statements of its client, King Corp. Based on the strength of King's financial statements, Safe Bank loaned King $500,000. Brown was unaware that Safe would receive a copy of the financial statements or that they would be used in obtaining a loan by King. King defaulted on the loan.

7. If Safe commences an action for negligence against Brown, and Brown is able to prove that it conducted the audit in conformity with GAAS, Brown will
- a. Be liable to Safe because Safe relied on the financial statements.
- b. Be liable to Safe because the Statute of Frauds has been satisfied.

c. Not be liable to Safe because there is a conclusive presumption that following GAAS is the equivalent of acting reasonably and with due care.

d. Not be liable to Safe because there was a lack of privity of contract.

8. If Safe commences an action for common law fraud against Brown, then to be successful, Safe must prove in addition to other elements that it

a. Was in privity of contract with Brown.

b. Was not contributorily negligent.

c. Was in privity of contract with King.

d. Justifiably relied on the financial statements.

9. In general, the third party (primary) beneficiary rule as applied to a CPA's legal liability in conducting an audit is relevant to which of the following causes of action against a CPA?

	Fraud	Constructive fraud	Negligence
a.	Yes	Yes	No
b.	Yes	No	No
c.	No	Yes	Yes
d.	No	No	Yes

10. If a CPA recklessly departs from the standards of due care when conducting an audit, the CPA will be liable to third parties who were unknown to the CPA based on

a. Strict liability.

b. Gross negligence.

c. Negligence.

d. Breach of contract.

Items 11 and 12 are based on the following information:

West & Co., CPAs, rendered an unqualified opinion on the financial statements of Pride Corp., which were included in Pride's registration statement filed with the SEC. Subsequently, Hex purchased 500 shares of Pride's preferred stock, which were acquired as part of a public offering subject to the Securities Act of 1933. Hex has commenced an action against West based on the Securities Act of 1933 for losses resulting from misstatements of facts in the financial statements included in the registration statement.

11. Which of the following elements must Hex prove to hold West liable?

a. West rendered its opinion with knowledge of material misstatements.

b. West performed the audit negligently.

c. Hex relied on the financial statements included in the registration statement.

d. The misstatements were material.

12. Which of the following defenses would be least helpful to West in avoiding liability to Hex?

a. West was not in privity of contract with Hex.

b. West conducted the audit in accordance with GAAS.

c. Hex's losses were caused by factors other than the misstatements.

d. Hex knew of the misstatements when Hex acquired the preferred stock.

13. Lewis & Clark, CPAs, rendered an unqualified opinion on the financial statements of a company that sold common stock in a public offering subject to the Securities Act of 1933. Based on a false statement in the financial statements, Lewis & Clark are being sued by an investor who purchased shares of this public offering. Which of the following represents a viable defense?

a. The investor has not met the burden of proving fraud or negligence by Lewis & Clark.

b. The investor did not actually rely upon the false statement.

c. Detection of the false statement by Lewis & Clark occurred after their examination date.

d. The false statement is immaterial in the overall context of the financial statements.

14. A CPA firm is being sued by a third-party purchaser of securities sold in interstate commerce to the public. The third party is relying upon the Securities Act of 1933. The CPA firm had issued an unqualified opinion on incorrect financial statements. Which of the following represents the best defense available to the CPA firm?

a. The securities sold had not been registered with the SEC.

b. The CPA firm had returned the entire fee it charged for the engagement to the corporation.

c. The third party was not in privity of contract with the CPA firm.

d. The action had not been commenced within one year after the discovery of the material misrepresentation.

15. Burt, CPA, issued an unqualified opinion on the financial statements of Midwest Corp. These financial statements were included in Midwest's annual report and Form 10-K filed with the SEC. As a result of Burt's reckless disregard for GAAS, material misstatements in the financial statements were not detected. Subsequently, Davis purchased stock in Midwest in the secondary market without ever seeing Midwest's annual report or Form 10-K. Shortly thereafter, Midwest became insolvent and the price of the stock declined drastically. Davis sued Burt for damages based on Section 10(b) and Rule 10b-5 of the Securities Exchange Act of 1934. Burt's best defense is that

    a.   There has been **no** subsequent sale for which a loss can be computed.
    b.   Davis did **not** purchase the stock as part of an initial offering.
    c.   Davis did **not** rely on the financial statements or Form 10-K.
    d.   Davis was **not** in privity with Burt.

16. Gold, CPA, rendered an unqualified opinion on the 1987 financial statements of Eastern Power Co. Egan purchased Eastern bonds in a public offering subject to the Securities Act of 1933. The registration statement filed with the SEC included the financial statements. Gold is being sued by Egan under Section 11 of the Securities Act of 1933 for the misstatements contained in the financial statements. To prevail, Egan must prove

	Scienter	Reliance
a.	No	No
b.	No	Yes
c.	Yes	No
d.	Yes	Yes

17. Mead Corp. orally engaged Dex & Co., CPAs, to audit its financial statements. The management of Mead informed Dex that it suspected that the accounts receivable were materially overstated. Although the financial statements audited by Dex did, in fact, include a materially overstated accounts receivable balance, Dex issued an unqualified opinion. Mead relied on the financial statements in deciding to obtain a loan from City Bank to expand its operations. City relied on the financial statements in making the loan to Mead. As a result of the overstated accounts receivable balance, Mead has defaulted on the loan and has incurred a substantial loss. If City sues Dex for fraud, could Dex be compelled to furnish City with the audit working papers?

    a.   No, because of the privileged communication rule, which is recognized in a majority of jurisdictions.
    b.   No, because City was **not** in privity of contract with Dex.
    c.   Yes, if the working papers are relevant to the action.
    d.   Yes, provided that Mead does **not** object.

18. A CPA is permitted to disclose confidential client information without the consent of the client to

    I.   Another CPA who has purchased the CPA's tax practice.
    II.   A successor CPA firm if the information concerns suspected tax return irregularities.
    III.   A voluntary quality control review board.

    a.   I and III only.
    b.   II and III only.
    c.   II only.
    d.   III only.

19. Tax preparers who aid and abet federal tax evasion are subject to

	Injunction to be prohibited from acting as tax preparers	General federal criminal prosecution
a.	No	No
b.	Yes	No
c.	No	Yes
d.	Yes	Yes

20. Brown, CPA, helped Cook organize a partnership that was actually an abusive tax shelter. Brown induced clients to participate by making false statements concerning the allowability of deductions and tax credits. As a result of these activities, Cook derived $100,000 gross income and Brown derived $50,000 gross income. What is Brown's federal statutory liability under the provision of the Internal Revenue Code specifically relating to promoting abusive tax shelters?

    a. $ 10,000
    b. $ 30,000
    c. $ 50,000
    d. $150,000

21. In general, if the IRS issues a 30-day letter to an individual taxpayer who wishes to dispute the assessment, the taxpayer

    a.   May, without paying any tax, immediately file a petition that would properly commence an action in Tax Court.
    b.   May ignore the 30-day letter and wait to receive a 90-day letter.
    c.   Must file a written protest within 10 days of receiving the letter.
    d.   Must pay the taxes and then commence an action in federal district court.

Problems

Problem 1   (1185,L2)

(15 to 20 minutes)

Mason & Dilworth, CPAs, were the accountants for Monrad Corporation, a closely held corporation. Mason & Dilworth had been previously engaged by Monrad to perform certain compilation and tax return work. Crass, Monrad's president, indicated he needed something more than the previous type of services rendered. He advised Walker, the partner in charge, that the financial statements would be used internally, primarily for management purposes, and also to obtain short-term loans from financial institutions. Walker recommended that a review of the financial statements be performed. Walker did not prepare an engagement letter.

In the course of the review, Walker indicated some reservations about the financial statements. Walker indicated at various stages that "he was uneasy about certain figures and conclusions" but that "he would take the client's word about the validity of certain entries since the review was primarily for internal use in any event and was not an audit."

Mason & Dilworth did not discover a material act of fraud committed by management. The fraud would have been detected had Walker not relied wholly on the representations of management concerning the validity of certain entries about which he had felt uneasy.

Required:

Answer the following, setting forth reasons for any conclusions stated.

a. What is the role of the engagement letter when a CPA has agreed to perform a review of a closely held company? What points should be covered in a typical engagement letter which would be relevant to the parties under the facts set forth above?

b. What is the duty of the CPA in the event suspicious circumstances are revealed as a result of the review?

c. What potential liability does Mason & Dilworth face and who may assert claims against the firm?

Problem 2   (585,L4)

(15 to 20 minutes)

Arthur & Doyle, CPAs, served as auditors for Dunbar Corp. and Wolfe Corp., publicly held corporations listed on the American Stock Exchange. Dunbar recently acquired Wolfe Corp. pursuant to a statutory merger by issuing its shares in exchange for shares of Wolfe. In connection with that merger, Arthur & Doyle rendered an unqualified opinion on the financial statements and participated in the preparation of the pro forma unaudited financial statements contained in the combined prospectus and proxy statement circulated to obtain shareholder approval of the merger and to register the shares to be issued in connection with the merger. Dunbar prepared a form 8-K (the current report with unaudited financial statements) and form 10-K (the annual report with audited financial statements) in connection with the merger. Shortly thereafter, financial disaster beset the merged company which resulted in large losses to the shareholders and creditors. A class action suit on behalf of the shareholders and creditors has been filed against Dunbar and its management. In addition, it names Arthur & Doyle as co-defendants, challenging the fairness, accuracy, and truthfulness of the financial statements.

Required:

Answer the following, setting forth reasons for any conclusions stated.

As a result of the CPAs having expressed an unqualified opinion on the audited financial statements of Dunbar and Wolfe and as a result of having participated in the preparation of the unaudited financial statements required in connection with the merger, indicate and briefly discuss the various bases of the CPAs' potential civil liability to the shareholders and creditors of Dunbar under:

a. The federal securities acts.
b. State common law.

Problem 3   (587,L3)

(15 to 20 minutes)

Dill Corp. was one of three major suppliers who sold raw materials to Fogg & Co. on credit. Dill became concerned over Fogg's ability to pay its debts. Payments had been consistently late and some checks had been returned, marked "insufficient funds". In addition, there were rumors concerning Fogg's solvency. Dill decided it would make no further sales to Fogg on credit unless it received a copy of Fogg's current, audited financial statements. It also required Fogg to assign its accounts receivable to Dill to provide security for the sales to Fogg on credit.

Clark & Wall, CPAs, was engaged by Fogg to perform an examination of Fogg's financial statements upon which they subsequently issued an unqualified opinion. Several months later, Fogg defaulted on its obligations to Dill. At this point Dill was owed $240,000 by Fogg. Subsequently, Dill discovered that only $60,000 of the accounts receivable that Fogg had assigned to Dill as collateral was collectible.

Dill has commenced a lawsuit against Clark & Wall. The complaint alleges that Dill has incurred a $180,000 loss as a result of negligent or fraudulent misrepresentations contained in the audited financial statements of Fogg. Specifically, it alleges negligence, gross negligence, and actual and/or constructive fraud on the part of Clark & Wall in the conduct of the audit and the issuance of an unqualified opinion.

State law applicable to this action follows the majority rule with respect to the accountant's liability to third parties for negligence. In addition, there is no applicable state statute which creates an accountant-client privilege. Dill demanded to be provided a copy of the Fogg workpapers from Clark & Wall who refused to comply with the request claiming that they are privileged documents. Clark & Wall has asserted that the entire action should be dismissed because Dill has no standing to sue the firm because of the absence of any contractual relationship with it, i.e., a lack of privity.

Required:

Answer the following, setting forth reasons for any conclusions stated.

a. Will Clark & Wall be able to avoid production of the Fogg workpapers based upon the assertion that they represent privileged communications?

b. What elements must be established by Dill to show negligence on the part of Clark & Wall?

c. What is the significance of compliance with GAAS in determining whether the audit was performed negligently?

d. What elements must be established by Dill to show actual or constructive fraud on the part of Clark & Wall?

Problem 4   (588,L5)

(15 to 20 minutes)

Birk Corp. is interested in acquiring Apple & Co. Birk engaged Kaye & Co., CPAs, to audit the 1987 financial statements of Apple. Both Birk and Apple are engaged in the business of providing management consulting services. While reviewing certain contracts entered into by Apple, Kaye became concerned with the proper reporting of the following matters:

- On December 5, 1987, Apple entered into an oral agreement with Cream Inc., to perform certain management advisory services for Cream for a fee of $150,000 per month. The services were to have commenced on February 15, 1988 and to have ended on December 20, 1988. Apple reported all of the revenues related to the contract on its 1987 financial statements. This constituted 30% of Apple's income for 1987.

- On February 8, 1987, Apple purchased the assets of Nestar & Co., a small management consulting firm. Apple and Nestar entered into a written agreement with regard to the transaction that required Apple to pay Nestar $80,000 a year for five years. The agreement required Nestar to transfer all of its assets and goodwill to Apple. Further, the agreement required Nestar not to compete with Apple or Apple's successors for a period of three years within the city where the majority of Nestar's clients were located. Nestar's office was also located in this city. Other Nestar clients were located throughout the state.

On February 1, 1988, Birk acquired all of Apple's outstanding stock. Birk's decision was based on the unqualified opinion issued by Kaye on Apple's 1987 financial statements. Within 10 days after the merger, Cream decided not to honor the agreement with Apple and gave notice that it had selected another management consulting firm. This caused the market value of the Apple stock acquired by Birk to decrease drastically.

On May 2, 1987, Birk learned that Nestar opened a management consulting firm three blocks from where Nestar's office had been located on February 8, 1987.

Based on the foregoing, Birk has commenced an action against Kaye alleging negligence in performing the audit of Apple's financial statements.

Required:

Answer the following, setting forth reasons for any conclusions stated.

a. Discuss whether the December 5, 1987 agreement between Cream and Apple is enforceable.

b. Discuss whether the agreement of Nestar not to compete with Apple is enforceable against Nestar.

c. Discuss whether Birk will prevail in its action against Kaye & Co., CPAs.

Problem 5   (1188,L5)

(15 to 20 minutes)

In order to expand its operations, Dark Corp. raised $4 million by making a private interstate offering of $2 million in common stock and negotiating a $2 million loan from Safe Bank. The common stock was properly offered pursuant to Rule 505 of Regulation D.

In connection with this financing, Dark engaged Crea & Co., CPAs, to audit Dark's financial statements. Crea knew that the sole purpose for the audit was so that Dark would have audited financial statements to provide to Safe and the purchasers of the common stock. Although Crea conducted the audit in conformity with its audit program, Crea failed to detect material acts of embezzlement committed by Dark's president. Crea did not detect the embezzlement because of its inadvertent failure to exercise due care in designing its audit program for this engagement.

After completing the audit, Crea rendered an unqualified opinion on Dark's financial statements. The financial statements were relied upon by the purchasers of the common stock in deciding to purchase the shares. In addition, Safe approved the loan to Dark based on the audited financial statements.

Within 60 days after the sale of the common stock and the making of the loan by Safe, Dark was involuntarily petitioned into bankruptcy. Because of the president's embezzlement, Dark became insolvent and defaulted on its loan to Safe. Its common stock became virtually worthless. Actions have been commenced against Crea by:

• The purchasers of the common stock who have asserted that Crea is liable for damages under Section 10(b) and rule 10b-5 of the Securities Exchange Act of 1934.

• Safe, based upon Crea's negligence.

Required:

In separate paragraphs, discuss the merits of the actions commenced against Crea, indicating the likely outcomes and the reasons therefore.

Multiple Choice Answers

1. c	6. b	10. b	14. d	18. d
2. b	7. d	11. d	15. c	19. d
3. c	8. d	12. a	16. a	20. a
4. b	9. d	13. d	17. c	21. b
5. c				

Multiple Choice Answer Explanations

A. Common Law Liability to Clients

1.   (589,L1,9) (c) The final objective of an external financial audit is to express an opinion as to the fairness of the financial statements. In meeting this objective, the CPA must adhere to GAAS. At no time during the audit does the CPA assure that all material errors or irregularities will be detected. Therefore, if Baker and Co. prove that the audit was performed in accordance with GAAS, this will be their best defense against Nast Corp. Note that although following GAAS does not automatically preclude negligence, it is strong evidence towards showing the presence of due care. Answer (a) is incorrect because Baker would be liable to Nast it the audit was performed in a negligent manner. Proving that Baker did not perform the audit recklessly or with an intent to deceive would preclude a finding of fraud but would be irrelevant when deciding whether Baker was negligent. Answer (b) is incorrect because a client is always in privity of contract with the accountant based upon the contractual relationship. Answer (d) is incorrect because although the use of an engagement letter is a normal procedure, it is not required to establish a contract between Nast and Baker. The oral agreement between the two parties is enforceable and requires that Baker and Co. perform the audit in a non-negligent manner.

2.   (589,L1,2) (b) Proof of common law fraud requires the following elements: (1) material misstatement or omission on financial statements, (2) scienter, (3) reasonable reliance by the injured party, and (4) damages. If the false statements were immaterial, the first element will not be met and this is a viable defense for the CPA. Answer (a) is incorrect because proof of privity of contract between an accountant and the suing party is not required to hold the accountant liable for fraud. Answer (c) is incorrect because it is not necessary to prove that the one committing fraud did benefit. Answer (d) is incorrect because contributory negligence of the client would have no effect on an action for fraud brought against a CPA. The stockholder would

only have to establish the CPA's fraudulent action, and the client's contributory negligence would not bar recovery.

3.   (1187,L1,28) (c) Failure to exercise due care is one of the elements necessary to hold a CPA liable to a client for conducting an audit negligently. Answer (a) is incorrect because scienter or guilty knowledge is a necessary element for proving that an audit was conducted fraudulently but not negligently. Answer (b) is incorrect because a CPA is normally a fiduciary of the client; thus the presence of such a relationship is not an indication of a negligent audit. Answer (d) is incorrect because the execution of an engagement letter is a normal procedure performed during an audit, and is therefore not an indication of a negligent audit.

4.   (589,L1,6) (b) When a CPA fails to carry out his/her obligations under a contract for services, the CPA may be held liable based on breach of contract but not strict liability. The theory of strict liability is used in some product liability cases but is not applicable when deciding the liability of the CPA. Therefore, answers (a), (c), and (d) are incorrect.

5.   (589,L1,7) (c) Constructive fraud requires the following elements: (1) misrepresentation of a material fact, (2) reckless disregard for the truth, (3) reasonable reliance by the injured party, and (4) injury. Therefore, if reckless disregard is present, it would support a finding of constructive fraud on the part of a CPA. Answer (a) is incorrect because constructive fraud does not require privity of contract. Answer (b) is incorrect because the presence of the intent to deceive is needed to satisfy the scienter requirement for fraud. However, even in the absence of the intent to deceive, the CPA can be liable for constructive fraud based on reckless disregard of the truth. Answer (d) is incorrect because ordinary negligence is not sufficient to support a finding of constructive fraud.

6.   (589,L1,1) (b) Generally, a CPA is not liable for the effects of events subsequent to the last day of the field work or the date of the report, if later. However, in this case, Smith made an affirmative assurance to the bank that there was no material change in United's financial status. In making such an assurance, Smith should have undertaken audit procedures sufficient to verify such an assurance. Answer (a) is incorrect because a CPA should make his/her independent investiga-

tion. Answer (c) is incorrect because Smith made assurances to the bank that covered the period subsequent to May 20 and, therefore, assumed liability for the additional period of time. Answer (d) is incorrect because Smith should not rely solely on either the chief financial officer or the chief executive officer but should undertake further audit procedures.

B. Common Law Liability to Third Parties (Nonclients)

7. (1187,L1,26) (d) In determining a CPA's liability to third parties with whom the CPA is not in privity of contract, distinctions are made between third-party beneficiaries, foreseen parties, and foreseeable parties. Safe Bank is a foreseeable third party in this case because Brown & Co. is unaware that Safe would receive a copy of the financial statements. Although a CPA is liable to foreseeable third parties for gross negligence or fraud, the CPA can successfully use lack of privity as a defense against a negligence suit by a foreseeable third party. Answer (a) is incorrect because although Safe relied on the financial statements, Brown & Co. was unaware of this reliance. This makes Safe a foreseeable third party to which Brown is not liable for negligence. Answer (b) is incorrect because the Statute of Frauds would have no bearing on an action for negligence brought by any third party against a CPA. Answer (c) is incorrect because following GAAS is persuasive, not conclusive, evidence that the accountant acted with due care.

8. (1187,L1,27) (d) A CPA is liable to foreseeable third-party users of audited financial statements for gross negligence or fraud. In this case, Safe is a foreseeable third party. In an action by Safe against Brown for common law fraud it must be established that Brown was responsible for a material misstatement of a fact, upon which Safe justifiably relied to its detriment. Answer (a) is incorrect because proof of privity of contract between an accountant and the suing party is not required to hold the accountant liable for fraud. Answer (b) is incorrect because the contributory negligence of a foreseeable third party would have no effect on an action for fraud brought against a CPA. The foreseeable third party must only establish the CPA's fraudulent action, and the third party's contributory negligence will not bar recovery. Answer (c) is incorrect because a foreseeable third party does not need to prove privity of contract with the client to recover against the accountant for fraud.

9. (1187,L1,29) (d) A third-party (primary) beneficiary of audited financial statements is one specifically intended by the CPA and the client to be the primary user of the financial statements. The CPA will be liable for negligence to a third party only if it can be established that the party was intended to be the primary beneficiary. Since a CPA is generally liable to all third parties, including foreseen and foreseeable third parties, for fraud and constructive fraud, the third-party (primary) beneficiary rule is relevant only in those cases based on negligence. Answers (a), (b), and (c) are therefore incorrect.

10. (1187,L1,30) (b) "Foreseeable third parties" is the phrase used to describe third-party users of the financial statements who are unknown to the CPA. If it can be established that a CPA recklessly departed from the standards of due care while performing an audit, then the CPA can be held liable to foreseeable third parties for gross negligence. Answer (a) is incorrect because the theory of strict liability is not applicable when deciding the liability of the CPA. Answer (c) is incorrect because negligence on the part of a CPA arises from his mere failure to comply with the standards of due care while conducting an audit. This is distinguished from gross negligence which is a reckless departure from the standards of due care. A CPA is generally not liable to foreseeable third parties for ordinary negligence. Answer (d) is incorrect because a CPA is liable for breach of contract only to clients. Third parties may not sue a CPA for breach of contract since there is no privity of contract between the CPA and the third parties.

C. Statutory Liability to Third Parties--Securities Act of 1933

11. (1187,L1,31) (d) Under the Securities Act of 1933, a CPA is liable to any third-party purchaser of registered securities for losses resulting from misstatements in the financial statements included in the registration statement. The plaintiff (purchaser) must establish that damages were incurred, and that the misstatements were material misstatement of facts. Answer (a) is incorrect because under the 1933 Act it is not necessary for the purchaser of securities to prove "scienter," or knowledge of material misstatement, on the part of the CPA. Answers (b) and (c) are incorrect because under the 1933 Act, the plaintiff need not prove negligence on the part of the CPA or that there was reliance by the plaintiff on the financial statements included in the registration statement.

12. (1187,L1,32) (a) Under the 1933 Act, a CPA can be held liable to a purchaser of registered securities if damages are incurred by the purchaser and if the financial statements contained in the registration statement contain a material misstatement of a fact or omit a material fact. The fact that the purchaser is not in privity of contract with the CPA is not a valid defense for the CPA. Answers (b), (c), and (d) are incorrect because they all describe defenses that would be helpful to West in avoiding liability to Hex.

13. (1183,L1,5) (d) Section II of the Securities Act of 1933 makes it unlawful for a registration statement to contain an untrue material fact or to omit a material fact. Under the 1933 Act, the plaintiff must prove damages were incurred and that there was a **material** misstatement or omission in the financials included in the registration statement. Thus, proving that the false statement is **immaterial** is a viable defense. Other viable defenses are the due diligence defense, proving that the plaintiff knew the financials were incorrect when the investment was made, and proving the loss was caused by factors other than the misstatement or omission. Answer (a) is incorrect because the plaintiff need not prove fraud or negligence. Answer (b) is incorrect because the plaintiff need not prove reliance on the financials (unless the securities were purchased after the CPA firm issued an income statement covering at least 12 months subsequent to the effective date of the registration statement). Answer (c) is incorrect because Lewis & Clark's unqualified opinion, included in the registration statement, is a certification of the financials as of the time the registration statement becomes effective. Thus, it extends Lewis & Clark's legal liability from the examination date to the effective date. They would have a duty to disclose the detection of the false statement.

14. (1178,L1,11) (d) The best defense for the CPA firm is that the third-party purchaser failed to commence his action within one year after discovery of the untrue statement or omission, or after such discovery should have been made by the exercise of reasonable diligence. This is the statute of limitations under the Securities Act of 1933. Answer (a) is not the best defense, because these securities should have been registered with the SEC and therefore the CPA firm can be held liable under the 1933 Act whether or not the securities were registered. Answer (b) is not the best defense because an accountant can be held liable whether or not he was paid. Answer (c) is not the best defense because the Securities

Act of 1933 eliminates the necessity for privity of contract.

D. Statutory Liability to Third Parties—Securities Exchange Act of 1934

15. (589,L1,8) (c) A suit for damages based on Section 10(b) and Rule 10b-5 of the Securities Exchange Act of 1934 requires proof (1) that plaintiff suffered damages, (2) there was a material misstatement or omission in information released by the firm, (3) that the plaintiff relied on financial information, and (4) existence of scienter. Thus, proving that Davis did not rely on the financial statement or Form 10-K will be the CPA's best defense. Answer (a) is incorrect because the damages can be based on the difference between the amount paid and the market value at the time of the suit. Thus, a subsequent sale is not necessary to compute the loss. Answer (b) is incorrect because this law comes under the Securities Exchange Act of 1934 which applies to subsequent sales of stock, not the initial offering. Answer (d) is incorrect because privity is not required under this type of suit.

16. (589,L1,10) (a) For a purchaser of stock to successfully sue under Section 11 of the Securities Act of 1933, s/he must prove that damages were incurred and that there was a material misstatement or omission in the financial statements included in the registration statement. The plaintiff does not need to prove negligence or scienter. Also, the plaintiff need not prove reliance on the financials (unless the securities were purchased after the CPA firm issued an income statement covering at least 12 months subsequent to the effective date of the registration statement). Therefore, answers (b), (c), and (d) are incorrect.

F.1. Accountant's Workpapers

17. (588,L1,3) (c) Working papers may be obtained by third parties where they appear to be relevant to issues raised in litigation. In this situation, City may compel (through the use of a subpoena) Dex to furnish them with working papers which relate to their lawsuit. Answer (a) is incorrect because the privileged communications rule does not exist at common law and has only been enacted by a few states. Additionally, the privileged communications rule only applies to communications which were intended to be privileged at the time of communication. Answer (b) is incorrect because City would not be required to be in privity of contract with Dex in order to receive working papers which are relevant

to the lawsuit. Answer (d) is incorrect
because it does not matter if Mead objects to
City receiving the working papers from Dex.
If City has an enforceable subpoena, Dex will
be forced to furnish the working papers
regardless of Mead's lack of consent.

F.2. Privileged Communications Between Accountant and Client

18.   (589,L1,5)   (d) The Code of Professional Conduct allows disclosure of confidential client information without the client's
consent in only certain limited situations.
Disclosure of this information to a voluntary
quality control review board under AICPA
authorization is one of these situations. Answers (a), (b), and (c) are incorrect because
they include situations which require consent
of the client to disclose confidential information.

H. Liability of Income Tax Return Preparers

19.   (589,L1,3)   (d) Tax preparers who aid
and abet federal tax evasion are subject to
both injunctions prohibiting them from acting
as tax preparers and general federal criminal
prosecution. Therefore, answers (a), (b), and
(c) are incorrect.

20.   (589,L1,4)   (a) One who derives income
from an abusive tax shelter is subject to
federal statutory liability under the Internal
Revenue Code of the greater of $1,000 or 20%
of the derived gross income. In this case,
Brown derived $50,000 in gross income and will
be liable for 20% of this amount, which is
$10,000.

I. Assessments by IRS

21.   (588,L1,9)   (b) The Internal Revenue
Service must send a 90-day letter before an
individual taxpayer is considered to have
received official notice of the assessment
against him/her. Once the taxpayer receives
the 90-day letter s/he then has 90 days to
file a Petition of Redetermination of Deficiency in the Tax Court. Thus, a 30-day
letter is not a valid notice to the taxpayer
and may be ignored until a 90-day letter is
received. Answer (a) is incorrect because the
filing of a petition will not necessarily
commence an action in Tax Court. The
individual taxpayer's petition may be settled
prior to actually reaching the Tax Court.
Answer (c) is incorrect because taxpayers have
90 days to file a written protest. Answer (d)
is incorrect because taxpayers are not
required to pay the taxes prior to commencing
an action in federal district court. The
federal district court will determine if the
disputed taxes are to be paid by the taxpayer
after hearing the case.

Answer Outline

Problem 1 Engagement Letter; CPA's Duty to
Inquire; Parties That May Sue CPA
(1185,L2)

a. Points covered in the engagement letter
Type of engagement
Procedures and tests to be performed
Letter should state that engagement
cannot be relied upon to disclose:
errors, irregularities, illegal acts,
fraud or defalcation
However, CPA will inform client of any
such matter that comes to his attention
Signed by client
b. CPA has duty to inquire into suspicious
circumstances
CPA cannot rely solely upon management's
statements
c. If right to sue based on negligently performed review
Suing parties must be of a class intended to benefit from the review and
this benefit was foreseeable by the CPA
Monrad or shareholders suing on behalf
of corporation in derivative action may
sue
If right to sue is based on constructive
fraud
No need for privity of contract
Lending institutions and shareholder in
own right could sue CPA

Unofficial Answer

Problem 1 Engagement Letter; CPA's Duty to
Inquire; Parties That May Sue CPA
(1185,L2)

a. The role of the engagement letter is to
set forth in writing the nature and limitations of the engagement and define the
arrangement between the CPA and his client.
The engagement letter should clearly and
precisely state the type of engagement contemplated and the scope of such an undertaking. It should indicate the procedures and
steps to be taken in the review and indicate
the tests that will be performed. It should
also state that the engagement cannot be
relied upon to disclose errors; irregularities, or illegal acts, including fraud or
defalcation, but the CPA will inform his
client of any such matters that come to his
attention. The engagement letter or an acknowledgement should be signed by the client.
If the engagement letter is carefully prepared
and if it spells out the engagement clearly,
it will play an important role if a dispute

arises between the CPA and his client. The engagement letter will also help the courts to
avoid any misunderstanding as to the scope of
the engagement.

b. Under such circumstances, the courts that
have considered the question and SSARS No. 1
promulgated by the AICPA both impose a duty of
inquiry when the CPA becomes aware of suspicious circumstances. Certainly, the mere reliance upon management's word is not sufficient. The facts indicated that Walker was
"uneasy about certain figures and conclusions." The CPA has an obvious duty to the
client, Monrad, to inquire into any suspicious
circumstances of which he becomes aware.

c. Depending on the circumstances about who
in management was involved and their ownership
of stock, Monrad in its own right may bring an
action or the shareholders may bring a derivative action against Mason & Dilworth on behalf of the corporation for negligently failing to detect the fraud. It is possible that
an action based upon constructive fraud might
also be asserted against the firm because the
conduct might be categorized as gross negligence or a reckless disregard for the truth.
Certainly, a shareholder in his own right and
any of the lending institutions will assert
this and privity of contract will not be a
valid defense.

There is authority supporting the rights
of third party plaintiffs to sue and to
recover from the accountants based upon a
negligently performed review. As a general
rule, third parties, even though not parties
to the contract, may successfully assert
negligence if they can show that they are
members of a class of persons intended to
benefit from the services performed by the CPA
and that this was reasonably foreseeable by
the CPA.

Answer Outline

Problem 2 CPA's Federal Statutory Liability;
CPA's State Common Law Liability
(585,L4)

a. Bases for third-party suits under federal
securities acts:
• Misstatements or omissions in the
registration statement in violation
of 1933 Act
• Fraudulent misstatements or
omissions in violation of antifraud
provisions of 1933 and 1934 Acts and
Rule 10b-5
• Misstatements or omissions included
in forms 8-K and 10-K in violation
of reporting provisions of 1934 Act

- Misstatements or omissions included in proxy statement circulated to gain approval of merger in violation of proxy solicitation rules of 1934 Act

b. Bases for third-party suits under state common law:
- Breach of contract; shareholders and creditors, as third-party beneficiaries, are in privity of contract with CPAs and therefore may claim breach of contract
- Negligence is present when CPAs fail to exercise reasonable care; shareholders and creditors, if considered reasonably foreseen third parties, can assert negligence
- Actual or constructive fraud; actual fraud if CPAs intentionally deceived third parties, constructive fraud if CPA's work was so deficient that it constituted gross negligence

Unofficial Answer

Problem 2   CPA's Federal Statutory Liability; CPA's State Common Law Liability (585,L4)

a. The basis for shareholders' and creditors' suits against Arthur & Doyle under federal securities acts include

- That a violation of the 1933 Act has occurred as a result of misstatements or omissions in the prospectus or elsewhere in the registration statement required in order to "sell" the securities. The Securities and Exchange Commission has ruled that the issuance and exchange of stock pursuant to a merger constitutes a "sale" within the meaning of the Securities Act of 1933.
- That a violation of the anti-fraud provisions of the 1934 Act and of Rule 10b-5 issued pursuant thereto has occurred since misstatements and omissions of material facts may be fraudulent. Additionally, the anti-fraud provision (Sec. 17) of the 1933 Act could be asserted.
- That a violation of the reporting requirements of the Securities Exchange Act of 1934 has occurred to the extent that false or misleading statements were included or material facts were omitted in the reports or other documents relating to the merger and which were filed with the SEC.
- That a violation of the proxy rules of the Securities Exchange Act of 1934 resulted from misstatements in or omissions from the merger proxy statement used in soliciting shareholder approval.

b. The bases for shareholders' and creditors' suits against Arthur & Doyle under state common law include

- Breach of contract. The relationship between Arthur & Doyle, and Dunbar is contractual and requires that the CPAs' performance be rendered in a competent manner. The shareholders and creditors may claim breach of contract as third-party beneficiaries of the contract between the CPAs and Dunbar, since it could be held that the contract was entered into for their benefit and therefore they are in privity with the CPAs.
- Negligence. The shareholders and creditors could assert an independent claim of negligence in addition to the action for breach of contract. Negligence will be established when the CPAs fail to exercise reasonable care, taking into account such superior skill and knowledge the CPAs have or hold themselves out as having. Despite their lack of contractual privity, the shareholders and creditors will probably be able to successfully assert this action if they can show that they are members of a class of persons intended to benefit from the services performed by the CPAs and that this was reasonably foreseen by the CPAs.
- Actual fraud or constructive fraud. Recent court decisions have substantially eroded the privity barrier faced by third parties. Arthur & Doyle may be held liable for actual fraud if it can be shown that they intentionally deceived the shareholders and creditors. Arthur & Doyle may be held liable for constructive fraud if there are deficiencies or lapses in their professional work of such a magnitude that they constitute gross negligence or a reckless disregard for the truth.

Answer Outline

Problem 3   Accountant-Client Privilege; CPA's Negligence; CPA's Fraud (587,L3)

a. No accountant-client privilege recognized at common law and no applicable state statute
   Right to assert privilege rests with client not accountant

b. Elements necessary to establish CPA's negligence
- Legal duty to protect plaintiff from unreasonable risk
- Failure of CPA to perform with due care or competence
- Failure to exercise due care caused plaintiff's loss
- Actual damage resulted from failure to exercise due care
- Plaintiff was within a known and intended class of third-party beneficiaries

c. Significance of compliance with GAAS
- Primary standard against which CPA's conduct tested
- Considered "the custom of the industry"
- Failure to meet GAAS will result in finding of CPA's negligence
- Meeting GAAS not conclusive evidence of CPA's not being negligent

d. Elements necessary to establish CPA's actual or constructive fraud
- False representation of fact by CPA
- Actual fraud requires knowledge by CPA that statement was false (scienter). Constructive fraud inferred from gross negligence or reckless disregard for truth
- Intention to have plaintiff rely on false statement
- Reasonable reliance on false statement
- Damage results from reliance

Unofficial Answer

Problem 3   Accountant-Client Privilege; CPA's Negligence; CPA's Fraud (587,L3)

a. No. Since there is no accountant-client privilege recognized at common law and there is no applicable state statute which creates an accountant-client privilege, Clark & Wall will be required to produce its workpapers. Furthermore, the right to assert the accountant-client privilege generally rests with the client and not with the accountant.

b. The elements necessary to establish a cause of action for negligence against Clark & Wall are:

- A legal duty to protect the plaintiff (Dill) from unreasonable risk.
- A failure by the defendant (Clark & Wall) to perform or report on an engagement with the due care or competence expected of members of its profession.
- A casual relationship, i.e., that the failure to exercise due care resulted in the plaintiff's loss.
- Actual damage or loss resulting from the failure to exercise due care.

In addition to the foregoing, Dill must be able to establish that it is within a known and intended class of third-party beneficiaries in order to recover damages from Clark & Wall for negligence. This is necessary because Clark & Wall has asserted that it is not in privity of contract with Dill.

c. The primary standards against which the accountant's conduct will be tested are GAAS. Such standards are generally known as "the custom of the industry." Failure by Clark & Wall to meet the standards of the profession will undoubtedly result in a finding of negligence. However, meeting the standard of the profession will not be conclusive evidence that Clark & Wall was not negligent, although it is of significant evidentiary value.

d. The requirements to establish actual or constructive fraud on the part of Clark & Wall are:

1. A false representation of fact by the defendant (Clark & Wall).
2. For actual fraud, knowledge by the defendant (Clark & Wall) that the statement is false (scienter) or that the statement is made without belief that it is truthful. Constructive fraud may be inferred from gross negligence or a reckless disregard for the truth.
3. An intention to have the plaintiff (Dill) rely upon the false statement.
4. "Justifiable" reliance upon the false statement.
5. Damage resulting from said reliance.

Answer Outline

Problem 4   Statute of Frauds; Restraint of Trade; Accountant's Liability for Negligence (588,L5)

The agreement between Cream and Apple is unenforceable
  Statute of Frauds requires an agreement that cannot possibly be performed within one year of its creation to be in writing
The agreement between Apple and Nestar is likely to be enforceable
  An agreement not to compete will be enforceable if it protects legitimate property interests and is reasonable with respect to both time and geographic area
  The agreement protects goodwill which a buyer of a business has a right to protect
Birk will prevail against Kaye
  Kaye was required to perform the audit with due care
  Kaye was negligent in issuing an unqualified opinion on financial statements that contained material misstatements

Unofficial Answer

Problem 4   Statute of Frauds; Restraint of
             Trade; Accountant's Liability for
             Negligence (588,L5)

a. The December 5 oral agreement between
Cream and Apple is unenforceable because the
agreement failed to comply with the
requirements of the Statute of Frauds. A
contract that cannot possibly be performed
within one year from the making of the
contract falls within the provisions of the
statute of frauds. As the facts clearly
indicate, the December 5 oral agreement could
not possibly be performed within one year of
the making of the agreement (December 5, 1987)
since the agreement required Apple to continue
to perform until December 20, 1988. Therefore, the oral agreement is unenforceable.

b. The agreement between Nestar and Apple
restricting Nestar from competing with Apple
for three years within the city where Nestar's
office and the majority of Nestar's clients
were located is likely to be enforceable. An
agreement not to compete will be enforceable
if there has been a sale of a business
including goodwill and the purpose of the
restraint is to protect a property interest of
the purchaser; the restraint is reasonable as
to the geographic area covered; and the
restraint is reasonable as to the time
period. Under the facts of this case, the
agreement not to compete is likely to be
enforceable. The transaction involves the
sale of Nestar's management consulting
business and goodwill. The purpose of the
restraint is to protect the goodwill. The
three year time period is reasonable. The
limitation on the geographic area covered by
the restraint to only the city where Nestar's
office and the majority of Nestar's clients
are located appears to be reasonable.

c. Birk will prevail in its action against
Kaye based on negligence. Kaye owed a duty to
Birk to conduct the audit with due care. Kaye
failed to conduct the audit with due care by
issuing an unqualified opinion on Apple's 1987
financial statements when, in fact, Apple had
made a material error by reporting all of the
revenues related to the unenforceable December 5 agreement on its 1987 financial statements. Kaye's issuance of an unqualified
opinion despite the material error caused Birk
to suffer damages as evidenced by the drastic
decrease in the market value of Apple stock.

Answer Outline

Problem 5   Anti-fraud Provisions under Rule
             10b-5 of the 1934 Act; Liability
             to Third Parties Based on Negli-
             gence (1188,L5)

Crea will not be liable to purchasers of the
common stock
  Regulation D exempts offering from registration requirements but anti-fraud
  provisions of federal securities acts
  continue to apply
  Under Section 10(b) and rule 10b-5 of 1934
  Act the purchaser must show:
    1. Material misrepresentation or
        omission
    2. Scienter (intentional or willful
        conduct)
    3. Reliance on wrongful conduct
    4. Causal connection between pur-
        chaser's loss and wrongful conduct
  Crea is not liable due to lack of scienter
Crea is probably liable to Safe Bank based
on negligence
  A CPA is generally liable for ordinary
  negligence to third parties if audit
  report is for the identified third
  party's primary benefit
  In order to establish Crea's negligence,
  Safe must show:
    1. Crea had legal duty to protect Safe
        from unreasonable risk
    2. Crea failed to exercise due care
    3. There was a causal relationship
        between Safe's loss and Crea's
        failure to exercise due care
    4. Actual damage or loss resulting
        from Crea's failure to exercise
        due care

Unofficial Answer

Problem 5   Anti-fraud Provisions under Rule
             10b-5 of the 1934 Act; Liability
             to Third Parties Based on Negli-
             gence (1188,L5)

    Crea will not be liable to the purchasers
of the common stock. Although an offering of
securities made pursuant to Regulation D is
exempt from the registration requirements of
the Securities Act of 1933, the anti-fraud
provisions of the federal securities acts
continue to apply. In order to establish a
cause of action under Section 10(b) and rule
10b-5 of the Securities Exchange Act of 1934,
the purchasers generally must show that: Crea
made a material misrepresentation or omission
in connection with the purchase or sale of a
security; Crea acted with some element of

scienter (intentional or willful conduct);
Crea's wrongful conduct was material; the
purchasers relied on Crea's wrongful conduct;
and, that there was a sufficient causal
connection between the purchasers' loss and
Crea's wrongful conduct.

Under the facts of this case, Crea's
inadvertent failure to exercise due care,
which resulted in Crea's not detecting the
president's embezzlement, will not be
sufficient to satisfy the scienter element
because such conduct amounts merely to
negligence. Therefore, Crea will not be
liable for damages under Section 10(b) and
rule 10b-5 of the Securities Exchange Act of
1934.

Crea is likely to be held liable to Safe
Bank based on Crea's negligence despite the
fact that Safe is not in privity of contract
with Crea. In general, a CPA will not be
liable for negligence to creditors if its
auditor's report was primarily for the benefit
of the client, for use in the development of
the client's business, and only incidentally
or collaterally for the use of those to whom
the client might show the financial statements. However, a CPA is generally liable for
ordinary negligence to third parties if the
audit report is for the identified third
party's primary benefit.

In order to establish Crea's negligence,
Safe must show that: Crea had a legal duty to
protect Safe from unreasonable risk; Crea
failed to perform the audit with the due care
or competence expected of members of its
professions; there was a causal relationship
between Safe's loss and Crea's failure to
exercise due care; actual damage or loss
resulting from Crea's failure to exercise due
care. On the facts of this case, Crea will be
liable based on negligence since the audited
financial statement reports were for the primary benefit of Safe, an identified third
party, and Crea failed to exercise due care in
detecting the president's embezzlement, which
resulted in Safe's loss, i.e., Dark's default
in repaying the loan to Safe.

Multiple Choice Questions (1-19)

1. Under the Federal Insurance Contributions Act (FICA) and the Social Securities Act (SSA),

    a. Persons who are self-employed are **not** required to make FICA contributions.

    b. Employees who participate in private retirement plans are **not** required to make FICA contributions.

    c. Death benefits are payable to an employee's survivors only if the employee dies before reaching the age of retirement.

    d. The receipt of earned income by a person who is also receiving social security retirement benefits may result in a reduction of such benefits.

2. Which of the following statements is **not** correct concerning federal unemployment insurance?

    a. Federal law provides general guidelines, standards, and requirements for the program.

    b. The states administer the benefit payments under the program.

    c. The program is funded by taxes imposed on employers and employees.

    d. The federal unemployment tax is calculated as a fixed percentage of each covered employee's salary up to a stated maximum.

3. In general, which of the following statements is correct with respect to unemployment compensation?

    a. An employee who is unable to work because of a disability is entitled to unemployment compensation.

    b. An individual who has been discharged from employment because of work-connected misconduct is ineligible for unemployment compensation.

    c. The maximum period during which unemployment compensation may be collected is uniform throughout the United States.

    d. The maximum amount of weekly unemployment compensation payments made by a state is determined by federal law.

4. The social security tax base is calculated on

    a. A self-employed person's net profit from self-employment.

    b. A self-employed person's gross income from self-employment.

    c. An employee's gross wages less the deduction permitted for contributions to an individual retirement account.

    d. An employee's taxable income.

5. The Federal Unemployment Tax Act

    a. Imposes a tax on all employers doing business in the U.S.

    b. Requires contributions to be made by the employer and employee equally.

    c. Allows an employer to take a credit against the federal unemployment tax if contributions are made to a state unemployment fund.

    d. Permits an employee to receive unemployment benefits that are limited to the contributions made to that employee's account.

6. Social security benefits may be obtained by

    a. Qualifying individuals who are also receiving benefits from a private pension plan.

    b. Qualifying individuals or their families only upon such individual's disability or retirement.

    c. Children of a deceased worker who was entitled to benefits until such children reach age 25 or complete their education, whichever occurs first.

    d. Only those individuals who have made payments while employed,

7. Which of the following statements is correct regarding social security benefits?

    a. Retirement benefits paid in excess of the recipient's contributions will be included in the determination of the recipient's federal taxable income regardless of his gross income.

    b. Upon the death of the recipient, immediate family members within certain age limits are entitled to a death benefit equal to the unpaid portion of the deceased recipient's contributions.

    c. Retirement benefits are fully includable in the determination of the recipient's federal taxable income if his gross income exceeds certain maximum limitations.

    d. Individuals who have made **no** contributions may be eligible for some benefits.

8.   Jay White, an engineer, entered into a contract with Sky, Inc., agreeing to provide Sky with certain specified consulting services. After performing the services, White was paid pursuant to the contract but social security taxes were not withheld from his check since Sky considered White an independent contractor. The IRS has asserted that White was an employee and claims that a deficiency exists due to Sky's failure to withhold and pay social security taxes. Which of the following factors is most likely to support the IRS's position that White is an employee?

   a.   White was paid in one lump sum after all the services were performed.
   b.   White provided his own office and supplies.
   c.   Sky supervised and controlled the manner in which White performed the services.
   d.   Sky reserved the right to inspect White's work.

9.   Which of the following statements is correct regarding social security taxes?

   a.   An individual who received net earnings from self-employment of $40,000 and wages of $40,000 in 1989 will be subject to social security taxes on $80,000.
   b.   Part of an employee's social security tax contribution qualifies for federal income tax purposes as a deduction from the employee's gross income.
   c.   A self-employed person is subject to social security taxes based on that person's gross earnings from self-employment.
   d.   An employer who fails to withhold and pay the employee's portion of social security taxes remains primarily liable for the employee's share.

10.   Bing was employed as a taxi driver by Speedy, Inc. While acting in the scope and course of his employment with Speedy, Bing collided with a van driven by Hart. Hart was an independent contractor making a delivery for Troy Corp. The collision was caused solely by Bing's negligence. As a result of the collision, both Bing and Hart suffered permanent injuries. Speedy and Troy were both in compliance with the state's workers' compensation statute. If Hart commences an action against Bing and Speedy for negligence, which of the following statements is correct?

   a.   Hart is entitled to recover damages from Bing or Speedy.
   b.   Bing will either be denied workers' compensation benefits or have his

benefits reduced because of his negligence.
   c.   Hart's action for negligence will be dismissed because Hart is an independent contractor.
   d.   Hart is entitled to recover damages from Speedy's workers' compensation carrier to the extent <u>no</u> duplicate payment has been received by Hart.

11.   Nix, an employee of Fern, Inc., was injured in the course of employment while operating a drill press manufactured and sold to Fern by Jet Corp. It has been determined that Fern was negligent in supervising the operation of the drill press and that the drill press was defectively designed by Jet. If Fern has complied with the state's mandatory workers' compensation statute, Nix may

   a.   Not properly commence a products liability action against Jet.
   b.   Not obtain workers' compensation benefits.
   c.   Obtain workers' compensation benefits and properly maintain a products liability action against Jet.
   d.   Obtain workers' compensation benefits and properly maintain separate causes of action against Jet and Fern for negligence.

12.   An employee will generally be precluded from collecting full worker's compensation benefits when the injury is caused by

	Noncompliance with the employer's rules	An intentional, self-inflicted action
a.	No	No
b.	Yes	Yes
c.	No	Yes
d.	Yes	No

13.   Farr, an employee of Sand Corp., was involved in an accident with Wohl, an independent contractor. Wohl was making a delivery for Byrd Corp. when Farr negligently passed through a red light resulting in the accident and injuries to Wohl and Farr. The accident occurred during Farr's regular working hours and in the course of Farr's employment. If Sand and Byrd have complied with the state's workers' compensation laws, which of the following is correct?

   a.   Farr will either be denied workers' compensation benefits or have his benefits reduced due to his negligence.
   b.   Farr will be denied workers' compensation benefits since Sand was free from any wrongdoing.

c. Wohl will be denied workers' compensation benefits under Sand's or Byrd's workers' compensation policy.

d. Wohl will be denied workers' compensation benefits due to the fellow-servant rule.

14. Which one of the following statements concerning workers' compensation laws is generally correct?

a. Workers' compensation laws are very narrowly construed against employees.

b. The amount of damages recoverable is based on comparative negligence.

c. Employers are strictly liable without regard to whether or not they are at fault.

d. Workers' compensation benefits are not available if the employee is grossly negligent.

15. Silk was employed at Rosco Corp. as a chauffeur. While in the course of employment, Silk was involved in an automobile accident with Lake who was employed by Stone Corp. as a truck driver. While making a delivery for Stone, Lake negligently drove through a red light causing the accident with Silk. Both Silk and Lake have received workers' compensation benefits as a result of the accident. Silk

a. Is precluded from suing Lake since both are covered under workers' compensation laws.

b. Is precluded from suing Stone if Stone complied fully with the state's workers' compensation laws.

c. Can recover in full against Lake only, but must reimburse the workers' compensation carrier to the extent the recovery duplicates benefits already obtained under workers' compensation laws.

d. Can recover in full against Lake or Stone, but must reimburse the workers' compensation carrier to the extent the recovery duplicates benefits already obtained under workers' compensation laws.

16. Wilk, an employee of Young Corp., was injured by the negligence of Quick, an independent contractor. The accident occurred during regular working hours and in the course of employment. If Young has complied with the state's workers' compensation laws, which of the following is correct?

a. Wilk is barred from suing Young or Quick for negligence.

b. Wilk will be denied workers' compensation if he was negligent in failing to adhere to the written safety procedures.

c. The amount of damages Wilk will be allowed to recover from Young will be based on comparative fault.

d. Wilk may obtain workers' compensation benefits and also properly maintain an action against Quick.

17. Musgrove Manufacturing Enterprises is subject to compulsory workers' compensation laws in the state in which it does business. It has complied with the state's workers' compensation provisions. State law provides that where there has been compliance, workers' compensation is normally an exclusive remedy. However, the remedy will not be exclusive if

a. The employee has been intentionally injured by the employer personally.

b. The employee dies as a result of his injuries.

c. The accident was entirely the fault of a fellow-servant of the employee.

d. The employer was only slightly negligent and the employee's conduct was grossly negligent.

May 1990 Questions

18. Tower drives a truck for Musgrove Produce, Inc. The truck is owned by Musgrove. Tower is paid on the basis of a formula that takes into consideration the length of the trip, cargo, and fuel consumed. Tower is responsible for repairing or replacing all flat tires. Musgrove is responsible for all other truck maintenance. Tower drives only for Musgrove. If Tower is a common law employee and not an independent contractor, which of the following statements is correct?

a. All social security retirement benefits are fully includible in the determination of Tower's federal taxable income if certain gross income limitations are exceeded.

b. Musgrove remains primarily liable for Tower's share of FICA taxes if it fails to withhold and pay the taxes on Tower's wages.

c. Musgrove would not have to withhold FICA taxes if Tower elected to make FICA contributions as a self-employed person.

d. Bonuses or vacation pay that are paid to Tower by Musgrove are not subject to FICA taxes because they are not regarded as regular compensation.

19. Taxes payable under the Federal
Unemployment Tax Act (FUTA) are
   a.   Partially deductible by the covered
         employee for federal income tax
         purposes.
   b.   Calculated as a fixed percentage of
         all compensation paid to an
         employee.
   c.   Payable by all employers regardless
         of the total amount of compensation
         paid to individual employees.
   d.   Deductible by the employer as a
         business expense for federal income
         tax purposes.

Problem

Problem 1   (1188,L3)

(15 to 20 minutes)

Maple owns 75% of the common stock of Salam Exterminating, Inc. Maple is not an officer or employee of the corporation, and does not serve on its board of directors. Salam is in the business of providing exterminating services to residential and commercial customers.

Dodd performed exterminating services on behalf of Salam. Dodd suffered permanent injuries as a result of inhaling one of the chemicals used by Salam. This occurred after Dodd sprayed the chemical in a restaurant that Salam regularly services. Dodd was under the supervision of one of Salam's district managers and was trained by Salam to perform exterminating services following certain procedures, which he did. Later that day several patrons who ate at the restaurant also suffered permanent injuries as a result of inhaling the chemical. The chemical was manufactured by Ace Chemical Corp. and sold and delivered to Salam in a closed container. It was not altered by Salam. It has now been determined that the chemical was defectively manufactured and the injuries suffered by Dodd and the restaurant patrons were a direct result of the defect.

Salam has complied with an applicable compulsory workers' compensation statute by obtaining an insurance policy from Spear Insurance Co.

As a result of the foregoing, the following actions have been commenced:

•   Dodd sued Spear to recover workers' compensation benefits.

•   Dodd sued Salam based on negligence in training him.

•   Dodd sued Ace based on strict liability in tort.

•   The restaurant patrons sued Maple claiming negligence in not preventing Salam from using the chemical purchased from Ace.

Required:

Discuss the merits of the actions commenced by Dodd and the restaurant patrons, indicating the likely outcomes and your reasons therefor.

Multiple Choice Answers

1. d	5. c	9. d	13. c	17. a
2. c	6. a	10. a	14. c	18. b
3. b	7. d	11. c	15. d	19. d
4. a	8. c	12. c	16. d	

Multiple Choice Answer Explanations

A. Federal Social Security Act

1.   (589,L1,37) (d) Returning to work after retirement can affect an individual's social security benefits. Earned income, after retirement, which exceeds an annual limitation results in reduced benefits of $1 in benefits for each $2 of earnings above a specified amount of annual earned income. Answer (a) is incorrect because self-employed persons are required to make FICA contributions based on their net earnings from self-employment. Answer (b) is incorrect because neither pension plans nor any other programs may be substituted for FICA coverage. Employees are still required to make FICA contributions even though the individual is covered by a private pension plan. Answer (c) is incorrect because death benefits are payable to an employee's survivors even if the employee dies after reaching the age of retirement.

2.   (1189,L1,31) (c) The federal unemployment insurance program is funded by taxes imposed on employers who employ one or more persons covered by the Federal Unemployment Tax Act. Thus, only employers are required to pay federal unemployment taxes. Answers (a), (b), and (d) are incorrect because they are all accurate statements regarding federal unemployment insurance.

3.   (588,L1,45) (b) Unemployment compensation is generally available only to persons unemployed through no fault of their own. Answer (a) is incorrect because an employee who is unable to work because of a disability may be entitled to workers' compensation or social security disability benefits but will not be entitled to unemployment compensation. Answers (c) and (d) are incorrect because although unemployment insurance is provided for under the Federal Unemployment Tax Act, the eligibility requirements, amount of payments, and the maximum collection period are governed by state law.

4.   (587,L1,37) (a) A self-employed person's social security liability is calculated based upon his/her net profit from self-employment. Thus, answer (b) is incorrect.

Answer (c) is incorrect because an employee's social security liability is calculated based upon his/her gross wages before the deduction permitted for contributions to an individual retirement account. Answer (d) is incorrect since an employee's taxable income may also include forms of income other than wages, such as interest or dividend income, which are not subject to social security tax.

5.   (589,L1,36) (c) The Federal Unemployment Tax Act allows an employer to take a credit against the federal unemployment tax if the employer contributions are made to a state unemployment fund. Answer (a) is incorrect since the tax is imposed only on employers having in any year as few as one employee for some portion of a day in each of twenty weeks or who have a payroll of at least $1,500 in any calendar quarter. Answer (b) is incorrect since employees are not required to pay any tax under this Act. Answer (d) is incorrect because there are no accounts established for specific employees under the Act.

6. (1186,L1,39) (a) Under the Federal Social Security Act, qualifying individuals may receive benefits even if receiving other benefits from a private pension plan as long as they have worked for the statutory period of time and/or earned the specified amount of wages. Answer (b) is incorrect because qualifying individuals or their families may receive benefits upon death of the individual in addition to retirement or disability. Answer (c) is incorrect because benefits may be received by dependents of a qualifying deceased worker until reaching the age of 18 (not 25) or completing their education, whichever comes first. Answer (d) is incorrect because benefits are not limited to individuals who have made payments while employed. The children and spouses of such individuals are also entitled to benefits.

7.   (586,L1,18) (d) Since children may receive death benefits because of the death of a parent, it is possible for some individuals who have made no contributions to be eligible to receive social security benefits. Answers (a) and (c) are incorrect because the amount of social security benefits included in gross income is computed on the following basis: if modified AGI plus one half of the social security benefits received exceeds a base amount ($32,000 for married filing jointly; $25,000 for all others), the amount of benefits included in gross income is the lesser of (1) one half of that excess or (2) one half of the benefits received. However, if modified AGI plus the benefits does not

exceed the base amount, none of the benefits are included in gross income and are thus not taxable. Answer (b) is incorrect because upon the death of a recipient, immediate family members within certain age limits are not entitled to a death benefit equal to the unpaid portion of the deceased recipient's contributions. The amount of survivor's benefits is not dependent upon the amount of contributions made by the deceased. Rather, the amount received by the beneficiary is dependent on both the average monthly earnings and the relationship of the beneficiary to the deceased worker.

8. (1185,L1,22) (c) When deciding whether a person is an employee or an independent contractor for the purposes of social security legislation, the most important factor is whether the person's performance is subject to the physical control of the employer. If Sky supervised and controlled the manner in which White performed the services, this factor would support the IRS's position that White is an employee. The fact that White was paid in one lump sum and provided his own office and supplies would support Sky's position that White was an independent contractor. Thus, answers (a) and (b) are incorrect. Answer (d) is incorrect because the fact that Sky reserved the right to inspect White's work would not necessarily mean that Sky was supervising and controlling the manner in which White performed the services. An employer of an independent contractor would always have the right to inspect the independent contractor's work when finished. Thus, this factor would not support the IRS's position that White is an employee.

9. (1189,L1,30) (d) It is the employer's duty to withhold the employee's share of FICA and remit both the employee's and the employer's shares to the government. If the employer fails to withhold, then the employer is liable to the government for both the employee's and employer's taxes. Answer (b) is incorrect because a self-employed individual may reduce his/her net earnings from self-employment by the amount of earned wages subject to FICA. The net effect is that the individual will only pay social security taxes on the portion of his self-employment income equal to the amount left after his $40,000 of wages have been subtracted from the base amount. Answer (b) is incorrect because an employee does not receive an income tax deduction for any of the social security taxes paid by him/her. Answer (c) is incorrect because a self-employed individual's FICA contribution is based on net earnings from self-employment, not gross income.

B. Workers' Compensation Act

10. (588,L1,44) (a) Under the doctrine of respondeat superior, an employer is generally liable for an employee's torts if committed within the course and scope of the employment relationship. In this case, since Hart's injuries were the result of Bing's negligence while acting within the scope of his/her employment with Speedy, Hart will be able to recover damages from both Bing and Speedy. Answer (b) is incorrect because under workers' compensation laws, any employee injured during the course of employment is entitled to workers' compensation benefits regardless of fault, as long as the injury is not self-inflicted, not the result of a fight, or the intoxication of the employee. Answer (c) is incorrect because as a third party injured by Bing's negligence, Hart's relationship to Troy is irrelevant in his/her action for negligence brought against Bing and/or Speedy. Answer (d) is incorrect because Hart is not Speedy's employee and is therefore not entitled to receive or recover damages from Speedy's workers' compensation carrier. As an independent contractor, Hart can recover only under his/her own accidental injury insurance policy, or in an action against Bing and Speedy for negligence.

11. (587,L1,36) (c) An employee's acceptance of workers' compensation benefits does not bar him/her from suing a third party whose negligence caused the injury. Thus, answer (a) is incorrect. Answer (b) is incorrect since Fern was injured in the course of employment. This is all that is required for an employee who is covered by a workers' compensation statute to obtain benefits. Answer (d) is incorrect because acceptance of benefits under workers' compensation laws precludes an employee from suing the employer for damages in a civil court.

12. (1189,L1,32) (c) Workers' compensation is a form of strict liability whereby the employer is liable to an employee for injuries or diseases sustained by the employee which arise out of and in the course of employment. The employee is entitled to workers' compensation benefits without regard to fault unless the injuries are caused by intentional self-infliction, participation in mutual altercation, or intoxication of employee. Thus, the employee will not be precluded from collecting workers' compensation benefits when the injury is caused by noncompliance with employer's rules but will be precluded if an intentional, self-inflicted action caused the injury. Therefore, answers (a), (b), and (d) are incorrect.

13. (586,L1,17) (c) Workers' compensation laws provide coverage for employees' injuries which occur in the course of employment. Since Wohl is an independent contractor, not an employee, s/he would not be entitled to coverage under Byrd's workers' compensation policy. Accordingly, Sand's workers' compensation policy would only apply to the injuries sustained by Farr, its employee. Wohl, however, may maintain common actions against Farr and/or Sand. Answers (a) and (b) are incorrect because workers' compensation laws eliminate the employer's defense of contributory negligence. Answer (d) is incorrect because the fellow-servant rule does not apply to this factual situation: Wohl is not an employee of Sand. Also, workers' compensation laws eliminate the fellow-servant rule as an employer's defense.

14. (589,L1,38) (c) Workers' compensation is a form of strict liability whereby the employer is liable to an employee for injuries or diseases sustained by the employee which arise out of and in the course of employment. The employee is entitled to workers' compensation benefits without regard to fault unless the injuries are caused by intentional self-infliction, participation in mutual altercation, or intoxication of the employee. Answer (a) is incorrect because workers' compensation laws are written to benefit employees by removing the employer's common law defenses. This allows the employee to recover for job-related injuries or diseases with little difficulty. Answer (b) is incorrect because the amount of damages the employee will be allowed is not based on comparative fault but on a scheme prescribed by state statute, usually a percentage of the injured employee's wages. Answer (d) is incorrect because the employee will receive workers' compensation despite the fact that s/he was grossly negligent.

15. (585,L1,30) (d) Silk may recover damages from either Lake or Stone since it appears that Lake negligently struck Silk while s/he was acting within the scope of his/her employment. Consequently, both the principal and the agent would be liable for the agent's negligence. However, in the event that Silk recovers damages from Lake or Stone, Silk must reimburse the workers' compensation carrier to the extent the recovery duplicates benefits already received under workers' compensation. Answer (a) is incorrect since Silk has the right to sue Lake regardless of whether both of them are covered under workers' compensation laws. Answer (b) is incorrect because compliance with the state's workers' compensation laws will not protect an employer from suits brought against him/her for negligent acts of his/her employees. Answer (c) is incorrect because under agency laws a party who is injured by an employee's negligent act, which occurs within the scope of his/her employment, may sue the employer, the employee, or both for recovery.

16. (584,L1,28) (d) Wilk may obtain workers' compensation benefits and also maintain an action against Quick (third party that caused injury). If Wilk recovers against third party (Quick) after obtaining workers' compensation benefits, a part of the recovery equal to the benefits received belongs to the employer (Young Corp.). Answer (a) is incorrect because although Wilk is barred from suing the employer for negligence, he can sue Quick. Answer (b) is incorrect because workers' compensation laws eliminate the employer's defense of contributory negligence. Consequently, Wilk will recover because the injury occurred in the course of employment. Answer (c) is incorrect because the amount of damages Wilk will be allowed is not based on comparative fault but on a scheme prescribed by state statute, usually a percentage of the injured employee's wages.

17. (581,L1,60) (a) If the employer intentionally injures the employee, the employee would not only have a right to proceed under workers' compensation, but could sue the employer in a civil court of law on the basis of an intentional tort. Answers (b), (c), and (d) are incorrect because they do not state grounds that would allow the injured employee to sue in a civil court of law if covered by a proper workers' compensation plan. Even though the injury was caused by contributory negligence of the employee or the act of a fellow servant, the injured employee could still recover, but recovery under workers' compensation would be the exclusive remedy.

May 1990 Answers

18. (590,L1,26) (b) Under the provisions of the Federal Insurance Contributions Act (FICA), if the employer neglects to withhold the appropriate amount of taxes the employer may be liable for both the employee's and employer's share of taxes. In this situation, if Musgrove fails to withhold and pay FICA taxes on Tower's wages, Musgrove will be primarily liable for Tower's share in addition to its own share (employer's share). Answer (a) is incorrect because only a portion of social security benefits received will be includable in the determination of Tower's federal taxable income if certain gross income limita-

tions are exceeded. Answer (c) is incorrect
because under the common law "right of control" test, Tower is classified as an employee. As Tower's employer, Musgrove is
required under FICA to withhold taxes, and
Tower may not elect to make FICA contributions
as a self-employed person. Answer (d) is
incorrect because under FICA, employers are
required to withhold taxes from their employee's wages, including bonuses and commissions, up to a certain fixed amount.

19. (590,L1,27) (d) Taxes payable under the
Federal Unemployment Tax Act (FUTA) are used
to provide unemployment compensation benefits
to workers who lose jobs and cannot find replacement work. These taxes paid are deductible by the employer as a business expense for
federal income tax purposes, but they are not
deductible by the employee because the
employee does not pay them. Therefore, answer (a) is incorrect. Answer (b) is incorrect because the taxes payable under the FUTA
are calculated as a fixed percentage of only
the first $6,000 of wages of each employee.
Answer (c) is incorrect because only those
employers who paid wages of $1,500 or more
during any calendar quarter or who employed at
least one employee for at least one day a week
for 20 weeks must pay FUTA taxes.

Answer Outline

Problem 1   Workers' Compensation; De-
             finition of Employee; Strict
             Liability; Limited Liability of
             Shareholders (1188,L3)

Dodd is entitled to workers' compensation
from Spear
  Dodd is considered an employee because
  Salam had control over details of Dodd's
  work and Dodd was subject to Salam's
  supervision
Dodd will be unsuccessful in his negligence
suit
  An employee who receives workers' compensation benefits cannot successfully
  maintain an action for negligence against
  his employer seeking additional
  compensation
Dodd will be successful in his action
against Ace based on strict liability in
tort
  Elements needed to prove strict tort
  liability are:
    1. Product was unreasonably dangerous
       when it left the seller's hands
    2. Defect caused the injury
    3. Seller normally sells the product
    4. Product was not substantially
       changed before reaching the buyer
Maple is not liable to restaurant patrons
based on negligence
  Shareholders of corporation are insulated
  from personal liability for negligence of
  corporation or corporation's employees

Unofficial Answer

Problem 1   Workers' Compensation; De-
             finition of Employee; Strict
             Liability; Limited Liability of
             Shareholders (1188,L3)

Dodd is entitled to recover workers'
compensation benefits from Spear because Dodd
was an employee of Salam, the injury was
accidental, and the injury occurred out of and
in the course of his employment with Salam.
Based on the facts of this case, Dodd would be
considered an employee and not an independent
contractor because Salam had control over the
details of Dodd's work by training Dodd to
perform the services in a specified manner and
Dodd was subject to Salam's supervision.
    Dodd will be unsuccessful in his action
against Salam based on negligence in training
him because Dodd is an employee of Salam and
Salam has complied with the applicable
compulsory workers' compensation statute by
obtaining workers' compensation insurance.
Under workers' compensation, an employee who
receives workers' compensation benefits cannot
successfully maintain an action for negligence
against his employer seeking additional
compensation. Therefore, whether Salam was
negligent in training Dodd is irrelevant.
    Dodd's action against Ace based on strict
liability in tort will be successful.
Generally, in order to establish a cause of
action based on strict liability in tort, it
must be shown that: the product was in
defective condition when it left the
possession or control of the seller; the
product was unreasonably dangerous to the
consumer or user; the cause of the consumer's
or user's injury was the defect; the seller
engaged in the business of selling such a
product; the product was one which the seller
expected to, and, did reach the consumer or
user without substantial changes in the
condition in which it was sold. Under the
facts of this case, Ace will be liable based
on strict liability in tort because all of the
elements necessary to state such a cause of
action have been met. The fact that Dodd is
entitled to workers' compensation benefits
does not preclude Dodd from recovering based
on strict liability in tort from a third party
(Ace).
    Maple will not be liable to the restaurant
patrons based on negligence, because shareholders of a corporation are insulated from
personal liability for the negligence of the
corporation or the corporation's employees.
This rule would apply even though Maple owned
a controlling interest in the common stock of
Salam. Therefore, whether Salam or Dodd was
negligent is irrelevant.

Multiple Choice Questions (1-32)

1.   Which of the following factors is <u>least</u> significant in determining whether an item of personal property has become a fixture?
   a.   The extent of injury that would be caused to the real property by the removal of the item.
   b.   The value of the item.
   c.   The manner of attachment.
   d.   The adaptability of the item to the real estate.

2.   Green and Nunn own a 40-acre parcel of land as joint tenants with the right of survivorship. Nunn wishes to sell the land to Ink. If Nunn alone executes and delivers a deed to Ink, what will be the result?
   a.   Green will retain a ½ undivided interest in the 40-acre parcel, and will be unable to set aside Nunn's conveyance to Ink.
   b.   Ink will obtain an interest in ½ of the parcel, or 20 acres.
   c.   Ink will share ownership of the 40 acres with Green as a joint tenant with a right of survivorship.
   d.   The conveyance will be invalid because Green did <u>not</u> sign the deed.

   Items 3 and 4 are based on the following information:

   Boch and Kent are equal owners of a warehouse. Boch died leaving a will that gave his wife all of his right, title, and interest in his real estate.

3.   If Boch and Kent owned the warehouse at all times as joint tenants with the right of survivorship, Boch's interest
   a.   Will pass to his wife after the will is probated.
   b.   Will <u>not</u> be included in his gross estate for federal estate tax purposes.
   c.   Could <u>not</u> be transferred before Boch's death without Kent's consent.
   d.   Passed to Kent upon Boch's death.

4.   If Boch and Kent owned the warehouse at all times as tenants in common, which of the following statements is correct?
   a.   Boch's interest will pass to his wife after the will is probated.
   b.   Upon Boch's death, all tenancies in common terminated.
   c.   Boch's interest will <u>not</u> be included in his gross estate for federal estate tax purposes.
   d.   Upon Boch's death, his interest passed to Kent.

5.   Hill, Knox, and Lark own a building as joint tenants with the right of survivorship. Hill donated her interest in the building to Care Charity by executing and delivering a deed to Care. Both Knox and Lark refused to consent to Hill's transfer to Care. Subsequently, Hill and Knox died. As a result of Hill's transfer to Care, Care acquired
   a.   A 1/3 interest in the building as a joint tenant.
   b.   A 1/3 interest in the building as a tenant in common.
   c.   No interest in the building because Knox and Lark refused to consent to the transfer.
   d.   No interest in the building because it failed to qualify as a bona fide purchaser for value.

6.   A condition in a contract for the purchase of real property which makes the purchaser's obligation dependent upon his obtaining a given dollar amount of conventional mortgage financing
   a.   Can be satisfied by the seller if the seller offers the buyer a demand loan for the amount.
   b.   Is a condition subsequent.
   c.   Is implied as a matter of law.
   d.   Requires the purchaser to use reasonable efforts to obtain the financing.

7.   Fulcrum Enterprises, Inc. contracted to purchase a four acre tract of land from Devlin as a site for its proposed factory. The contract of sale is silent on the type of deed to be received by Fulcrum and does not contain any title exceptions. The title search revealed that there are 51 zoning laws which affect Fulcrum's use of the land and that back taxes are due. A survey revealed a stone wall encroaching upon a portion of the land Devlin is purporting to convey. A survey made 23 years ago also had revealed the wall. Regarding the rights and duties of Fulcrum, which of the following is correct?
   a.   Fulcrum is entitled to a warranty deed with full covenants from Devlin at the closing.
   b.   The existence of the zoning laws above will permit Fulcrum to avoid the contract.
   c.   Fulcrum must take the land subject to the back taxes.
   d.   The wall results in a potential breach of the implied warranty of marketability.

8. Which of the following deeds gives the grantee the <u>least</u> amount of protection?
    a. Bargain and sale deed.
    b. Grant deed.
    c. Quitclaim deed.
    d. Warranty deed.

9. A purchaser of real property who wishes to receive the broadest protection with respect to the property being conveyed should obtain a
    a. Bargain and sale deed.
    b. General warranty deed.
    c. Quitclaim deed.
    d. Grant deed.

10. On July 1, Bean deeded her home to Park. The deed was never recorded. On July 5, Bean deeded the same home to Noll. On July 9, Noll executed a deed, conveying his title to the same home to Baxter. On July 10, Noll and Baxter duly recorded their respective deeds.

    In order for Noll's deed from Bean to be effective it must
    a. Contain the actual purchase price paid by Noll.
    b. Be signed by Noll.
    c. Include a satisfactory description of the property.
    d. Be recorded with Bean's seal affixed to the deed.

11. In order for a deed to be effective between the purchaser and seller of real estate, the deed must be
    a. Delivered by the seller with an intent to transfer title.
    b. Recorded within the permissible statutory time limits.
    c. In writing and signed by the seller and purchaser.
    d. Essentially in the same form as the contract for purchase and sale and include the actual sales price.

12. On July 1, Bean deeded her home to Park. The deed was never recorded. On July 5, Bean deeded the same home to Noll. On July 9, Noll executed a deed, conveying his title to the same home to Baxter. On July 10, Noll and Baxter duly recorded their respective deeds.

    If Noll and Baxter are bona fide purchasers for value, which of the following statements is correct?
    a. Baxter's interest is superior to Park's.
    b. Bean's deed to Park was void as between Bean and Park because it was <u>not</u> recorded.
    c. Bean's deed to Noll was void because she had <u>no</u> interest to convey.

    d. Baxter can recover the purchase price from Noll.

13. A buyer of real estate who receives a title insurance policy will
    a. Take title free of all defects.
    b. Be able to transfer the policy to a subsequent buyer of the real estate.
    c. Not have coverage for title exceptions listed in the insurance policy.
    d. Not have coverage greater than the amount of any first mortgage.

14. Bond purchased from Spear Corp. an apartment building that was encumbered by a mortgage securing Spear's promissory note to Fale Finance Co. Bond assumed Spear's note and mortgage. Subsequently, Bond defaulted on the note payable to Fale and, as a result, the building was sold at a foreclosure sale. If the proceeds of the foreclosure sale are less than the balance due on the note, which of the following statements is correct?
    a. Fale must sue both Spear and Bond to collect the deficiency because they are jointly and severally liable.
    b. Spear will be liable for the deficiency.
    c. Fale must attempt to collect the deficiency from Bond before suing Spear.
    d. Spear will <u>not</u> be liable for the deficiency because Bond assumed the note and mortgage.

15. If a borrower is in default under a purchase money mortgage loan, the
    a. Lender can file suit to have the borrower declared insolvent.
    b. Person who sold the real estate to the borrower can be forced to assume the mortgage debt.
    c. Lender may file suit for foreclosure.
    d. Lender may unilaterally obtain title without a foreclosure suit.

16. In 1982, Smith gave a mortgage to State Bank to secure a $100,000 loan. The mortgage was silent as to whether it would secure any other loans made by State to Smith. In 1984 Smith gave a second mortgage to Penn Bank to secure an $80,000 loan. Both mortgages described the same land and were properly recorded shortly after being executed by Smith. By 1988 Smith had repaid State Bank $40,000 of the $100,000 debt. State Bank then loaned Smith an additional $20,000 without taking any new security. Within a few days, Smith defaulted on the loans from both banks

and the first and second mortgages were foreclosed. The balance on the Penn loan was $20,000. The net proceeds of the foreclosure sale were $70,000. State is entitled to receive from the proceeds a maximum of

    a. $52,500
    b. $56,000
    c. $60,000
    d. $70,000

17. In general, which of the following statements is correct with respect to a real estate mortgage?

    a.   The mortgage must be in writing and signed by both the mortgagor (borrower) and mortgagee (lender).
    b.   The mortgagee may assign the mortgage to a third party without the mortgagor's consent.
    c.   The mortgage need <u>not</u> contain a description of the real estate covered by the mortgage.
    d.   The mortgage must contain the actual amount of the underlying debt and the rate of interest.

18. Bell obtained a $30,000 loan from Arco Bank, executing a promissory note and mortgage. The loan was secured by a building that Bell purchased from Marx for $50,000. Arco's recording of the mortgage

    a.   Generally does <u>not</u> affect the rights of Bell and Arco against each other under the promissory note.
    b.   Generally creates a possessory security interest in Arco.
    c.   Cuts off the rights of all prior and subsequent lessees of the building.
    d.   Transfers legal title to the building to Arco.

19. On April 6, 1988, Walsh purchased a warehouse from Bock for $150,000. Best Title Co. had performed a title search of the property. The results of the title search indicated that a mortgage given to Stone by Bock was duly recorded against the warehouse on March 9, 1988. However, the title search failed to detect a purchase money mortgage dated March 2, 1988, given by Bock to Todd. This mortgage was never recorded. Walsh was unaware of the mortgage to Todd. Under the circumstances,

    a.   Walsh will take title to the warehouse subject to Todd's mortgage because it is a purchase money mortgage.
    b.   Walsh will take title to the warehouse free of Todd's mortgage.
    c.   Todd's mortgage is superior to Stone's mortgage.
    d.   Best will be liable to Walsh because of its failure to detect the Todd mortgage.

20. Ram Corp. owns a warehouse that has a fair market value of $280,000. Area Bank holds a first mortgage and Public Finance holds a second mortgage on the warehouse. Ram has discontinued payments to Area and Public. As a result, Area, which has an outstanding mortgage of $240,000, and Public, which has an outstanding mortgage of $60,000, have foreclosed on their respective mortgages. If the warehouse is properly sold to Quincy at a judicial sale for $280,000, after expenses,

    a.   Public will receive $40,000 out of the proceeds.
    b.   Area will receive $224,000 out of the proceeds.
    c.   Public has a right of redemption after the judicial sale.
    d.   Quincy will take the warehouse subject to the unsatisfied portion of any mortgage.

21. On June 1, 1985, Byrd Corp. purchased a high-rise building from Slade Corp. for $375,000. The building was encumbered by a mortgage and note dated May 1, 1980, executed by Slade. The mortgage had been duly recorded by the mortgagee, Fale Bank. The outstanding balance on the mortgage at the time of Byrd's purchase was $300,000. Byrd acquired the property subject to the mortgage held by Fale and, in addition, gave a mortgage on the building to Foxx Finance to secure a non-purchase money promissory note in the sum of $50,000. Prior to any payments being made on either loan, Byrd defaulted. As a result, the building was properly sold at a foreclosure sale for $280,000.

Which of the following statements is correct regarding Byrd's and Slade's liability to Fale?

    a.   Byrd is liable to Fale for any deficiency.
    b.   Byrd is secondarily liable to Fale as a surety.
    c.   Slade was automatically released from all liability to Fale upon Byrd's acquisition of the building subject to the mortgage.
    d.   Slade is liable to Fale for any resulting deficiency.

22. A mortgagor who defaults on his mortgage payments will <u>not</u> be successful if he attempts to

    a.   Assert the equitable right to redeem.
    b.   Redeem the property after a judicial foreclosure sale has taken place.
    c.   Obtain any excess resulting from a judicial foreclosure sale.

d. Contest the validity of the price received at a judicial foreclosure sale by asserting that a higher price could have been received at a later date.

23. Tell, Inc. leased a building from Lott Corp. Tell paid monthly rent of $500 and was also responsible for paying the building's real estate taxes. On January 1, 1987, Vorn Co. and Tell entered into an agreement by which Vorn was entitled to occupy the building for the remainder of the term of Tell's lease in exchange for monthly payments of $600 to Tell. For the year 1987, neither Tell nor Vorn paid the building's real estate taxes and the taxes are delinquent. Learning this, Lott demanded that either Tell or Vorn pay the delinquent taxes. Both refused to do so and Lott has commenced an action against them. Lott will most likely prevail against

a. Vorn because the lease was assigned to it.
b. Tell and Vorn because both are jointly and severally liable for the delinquent taxes.
c. Tell without Vorn because their January 1 agreement constituted a sublease.
d. Vorn but only to the extent of $100 for each month that it occupied the building during 1987.

24. Sisk is a tenant of Met Co. and has two years remaining on a six-year lease executed by Sisk and Met. The lease prohibits sub-letting but is silent as to Sisk's right to assign the lease. Sisk assigned the lease to Kern Corp. which assumed all of Sisk's obligations under the lease. Met objects to the assignment. Which of the following statements is correct?

a. The assignment to Kern is voidable at Met's option.
b. Sisk would have been relieved from liability on the lease with Met if Sisk obtained Met's consent to the assignment.
c. Sisk will remain liable to Met for the rent provided for in the lease.
d. With respect to the rent provided for in the lease, Kern is liable to Sisk but not to Met.

25. Mini, Inc. entered into a five-year lease with Rein Realtors. The lease was signed by both parties and immediately recorded. The leased building was to be used by Mini in connection with its business operations. To make it suitable for that purpose, Mini attached a piece of equipment to the wall of the building.

Which of the following statements is correct regarding Mini's rights and liabilities?

a. Mini is prohibited from assigning the lease if it is silent in this regard.
b. Mini has a possessory interest in the building.
c. Mini is strictly liable for all injuries sustained by any person in the building during the term of the lease.
d. Mini's rights under the lease are automatically terminated by Rein's sale of the building to a third party.

May 1990 Questions

26. A person may own property as a joint tenant with the right of survivorship with any of the following except a(an)

a. Divorced spouse.
b. Related minor child.
c. Unaffiliated corporation.
d. Unrelated adult.

27. A tenant renting an apartment under a three-year written lease that does not contain any specific restrictions may be evicted for

a. Counterfeiting money in the apartment.
b. Keeping a dog in the apartment.
c. Failing to maintain a liability insurance policy on the apartment.
d. Making structural repairs to the apartment.

28. Delta Corp. leased 60,000 square feet in an office building from Tanner under a written 25-year lease. Which of the following statements is correct?

a. Tanner's death will terminate the lease and Delta will be able to recover any resulting damages from Tanner's estate.
b. Tanner's sale of the office building will terminate the lease unless both Delta and the buyer consented to the assumption of the lease by the buyer.
c. In the absence of a provision in the lease to the contrary, Delta does not need Tanner's consent to assign the lease to another party.
d. In the absence of a provision in the lease to the contrary, Delta would need Tanner's consent to enter into a sublease with another party.

29. On February 2, Mazo deeded a warehouse to Parko for $450,000. Parko did not record the deed. On February 12, Mazo deeded the same warehouse to Nexis for $430,000. Nexis was aware of the prior conveyance to Parko. Nexis recorded its deed before Parko recorded. Who would prevail under the following recording statutes?

	Notice statute	Race statute	Race-Notice statute
a.	Nexis	Parko	Parko
b.	Parko	Nexis	Parko
c.	Parko	Nexis	Nexis
d.	Parko	Parko	Nexis

30. On April 6, Ford purchased a warehouse from Atwood for $150,000. Atwood had executed two mortgages on the property: a purchase money mortgage given to Lang on March 2, which was not recorded; and a mortgage given to Young on March 9, which was recorded the same day. Ford was unaware of the mortgage to Lang. Under the circumstances,
   a. Ford will take title to the warehouse subject only to Lang's mortgage.
   b. Ford will take title to the warehouse free of Lang's mortgage.
   c. Lang's mortgage is superior to Young's mortgage because Lang's mortgage is a purchase money mortgage.
   d. Lang's mortgage is superior to Young's mortgage because Lang's mortgage was given first in time.

31. Sussex, Inc. had given a first mortgage when it purchased its plant and warehouse. Sussex needed additional working capital. It decided to obtain financing by giving a second mortgage on the plant and warehouse. Which of the following statements is true with respect to the mortgages?
   a. Default on payment of the second mortgage will constitute default on the first mortgage.
   b. The second mortgage may not be prepaid without the consent of the first mortgagee.
   c. The second mortgagee may not pay off the first mortgage to protect its security.
   d. If both mortgages are foreclosed, the first mortgage must be fully paid before paying the second mortgage.

32. If a mortgagor defaults in the payment of a purchase money mortgage, and the mortgagee forecloses, the mortgagor may do any of the following except

   a. Obtain any excess monies resulting from a judicial sale after payment of the mortgagee.
   b. Remain in possession of the property after a foreclosure sale if the equity in the property exceeds the balance due on the mortgage.
   c. Refinance the mortgage with another lender and repay the original mortgage.
   d. Assert the equitable right of redemption by paying the mortgagee.

Repeat Question

(590,L1,52) Identical/similar to item 5 above

Problems

Problem 1   (1184,L2)

(15 to 25 minutes)

Joe Fine, a clothing manufacturer for the past 30 years, owns a plant on which Muni Bank holds a mortgage. He also leases a warehouse from Jay Co. in which he stores the clothing manufactured in the plant. There are 10 years remaining on the lease term. Fine plans to move his operations to another location and has decided to sell to Bean his interests in the plant and lease.

Fine is contemplating selling the plant to Bean under one of the following conditions:

- Bean taking the plant subject to the mortgage.
- Bean assuming the mortgage on the plant.
- Fine obtaining a duly executed novation from Muni and Bean.

The lease contains a clause prohibiting assignment to third parties. Fine is concerned with this clause as well as his continuing liability to Jay upon the transfer of his interests in the lease to Bean. In this regard, Fine asserts that:

- The clause prohibiting the assignment of the lease is void.
- The prohibition against assignment will not affect his right to sublease.
- He will be released from liability to pay rent upon obtaining Jay's consent either to sublet or to assign.

Required:

Answer the following, setting forth reasons for any conclusions stated.

a. In separate paragraphs, discuss Fine's and Bean's liability to Muni under each of the three aforementioned conditions relating to the mortgage, if Bean after purchasing the plant defaults on the mortgage payments, thereby creating a deficiency after a foreclosure sale.

b. In separate paragraphs, comment on Fine's assertions regarding the lease, indicating whether such assertions are correct and the reasons therefor.

Problem 2   (1182,L5b)

(7 to 10 minutes)

Part b. Darby Corporation, a manufacturer of power tools, leased a building for 20 years from Grayson Corporation commencing January 1, 1981. During January 1981, Darby affixed to the building a central air conditioning system and certain heavy manufacturing machinery, each with an estimated useful life of 30 years.

While auditing Darby's financial statements for the year ended December 31, 1981, the auditor noted that Darby was depreciating the air conditioning equipment and machinery, for financial accounting purposes, over their estimated useful lives of 30 years. In reading the lease, the auditor further noted that there was no provision with respect to the removal by the lessee of the central air conditioning system or machinery upon expiration of the lease. To verify that the appropriate estimated useful lives are being utilized for recording depreciation, the auditor is interested in establishing the rightful ownership of these assets upon the expiration of the lease. The auditor knows that in order to determine ownership of the assets at the expiration of the lease, one must first determine whether the assets would be considered personalty or realty.

Required:

Answer the following, setting forth reasons for any conclusions stated.

What major factors would likely be considered by a court in determining whether the air conditioning system and the machinery are to be regarded as personalty or realty, and what would be the likely determination with respect to each?

Problem 3   (589,L3)

(15 to 20 minutes)

On March 2, 1988, Ash, Bale, and Rangel purchased an office building from Park Corp. as joint tenants with right of survivorship. There was an outstanding note and mortgage on the building, which they assumed. The note and mortgage named Park as the mortgagor (borrower) and Vista Bank as the mortgagee (lender). Vista has consented to the assumption.

Wein, Inc., a tenant in the office building, had entered into a 10-year lease

dated May 8, 1985. The lease was silent
regarding Wein's right to sublet. The lease
provided for Wein to take occupancy on June 1,
1985, and that the monthly rent would be
$5,000 for the entire 10-year term. On
March 10, 1989, Wein informed Ash, Bale, and
Rangel that it had agreed to sublet its office
to Nord Corp. On March 17, 1989, Ash, Bale,
and Rangel notified Wein of their refusal to
consent to the sublet. The following assertions have been made:

- The sublet from Wein to Nord is void
  because Ash, Bale, and Rangel did not
  consent.
- If the sublet is not void, Ash, Bale,
  and Rangel have the right to hold
  either Wein or Nord liable for payment
  of the rent.

On April 4, 1989, Ash transferred his
interest in the building to his spouse.

Required:

Answer the following, setting forth
reasons for any conclusions stated.

a. For this item only, assume that Ash,
Bale, and Rangel default on the mortgage note,
that Vista forecloses, and a deficiency
results. Discuss the personal liability of
Ash, Bale, and Rangel to Vista and the personal liability of Park to Vista.

b. Discuss the assertions as to the sublet, indicating whether such assertions are
correct and the reasons therefor.

c. For this item only, assume that Ash
and Rangel died on April 20, 1989. Discuss
the ownership interest(s) in the office
building as of April 5, 1989, and April 21,
1989.

Multiple Choice Answers

1. b	8. c	15. c	21. d	27. a
2. a	9. b	16. c	22. d	28. c
3. d	10. c	17. b	23. c	29. b
4. a	11. a	18. a	24. c	30. b
5. b	12. a	19. b	25. b	31. d
6. d	13. c	20. a	26. c	32. b
7. d	14. b			

Multiple Choice Answer Explanations

A. Distinctions between Real and Personal Property

1. (1187,L1,53) (b) A fixture is an item that was originally personal property and has been affixed to real property in a relatively permanent fashion such that it is considered to be part of the real property. Many factors must be considered when determining whether an item of personal property has become a fixture. Of the listed factors, the value of the item is the least significant. Answers (a), (c), and (d) are all significant factors used to determine whether an item of personal property has become a fixture, thus, they are all incorrect answers.

B.3. Concurrent Interest

2. (1188,L1,56) (a) In a joint tenancy, each joint tenant has an equal and undivided interest in the property. The joint tenancy may only be severed by an inter vivos conveyance. Each joint tenant can sell his/her interest in the property without the prior consent of the other joint tenants. When this occurs, the conveyance destroys the joint tenancy and creates a tenancy in common between the remaining joint tenants and the third party. When Nunn conveyed his interest in the parcel of land to Ink, Green and Ink became owners as tenants in common. Each, as tenants in common, has a nonexclusive right to use and possess the property (undivided interests). Answer (b) is incorrect because each tenant in common has the nonexclusive right to use and possess the whole property (40 acres). Answer (c) is incorrect because Nunn did not have the consent of Green; therefore, Ink becomes a tenant in common rather than a joint tenant. Tenants in common do not have the right of survivorship. Answer (d) is incorrect because a joint tenant may convey rights in property without the consent of other joint tenants.

3. (588,L1,53) (d) In a joint tenancy each joint tenant has the right of survivorship. Under the right of survivorship, the interest of a deceased joint tenant transfers to the remaining joint tenant(s) upon his/her

death. Therefore, Boch's interest will transfer to Kent upon Boch's death. Answer (a) is incorrect because the right of survivorship defeats the effects of a will; Boch's interest would not pass to his wife. Answer (b) is incorrect because Boch's interests would be included in his gross estate for federal estate tax purposes. Answer (c) is incorrect because Boch could have transferred his interest to a third party prior to his death without Kent's consent. When this occurs, the new owner becomes a tenant in common rather than a joint tenant.

4. (588,L1,54) (a) In a tenancy in common, each tenant essentially owns an undivided fractional share of the property. Each tenant has the right to convey his/her interest in the property. When one of the tenants dies, that tenant's interest passes to his/her heirs. Consequently, upon Boch's death, his interest passes to his wife after the will is probated. Answer (b) is incorrect because Kent remains as a tenant in common with Boch's wife. Answer (c) is incorrect because Boch's interest will be included in his gross estate for federal estate tax purposes. Answer (d) is incorrect because tenants in common do not have the right of survivorship; therefore, Boch's interest would not pass to Kent.

5. (1187,L1,54) (b) When rights in property held in joint tenancy are conveyed without the consent of the other joint tenants, the new owner becomes a tenant in common with the remaining joint tenants rather than a joint tenant. Thus, Care acquired a 1/3 interest as a tenant in common. Therefore, answer (a) is incorrect. Answer (c) is incorrect because a joint tenancy interest in property may be sold or transferred without consent of the remaining joint tenants. Answer (d) is incorrect because Care does not have to qualify as a bona fide purchaser for value in order to acquire an interest in the building. Hill is entitled to transfer her interest in the property through a sale or as a charitable contribution.

C. Contracts for Sale of Land

6. (582,L1,51) (d) When a "subject of financing" clause is in a contract for the purchase of real property, there must be good faith on the part of the buyer to use reasonable efforts to search out and obtain the requisite financing amount. Answer (a) is incorrect because a demand loan offered by the seller is inconsistent with the parties' intent of obtaining conventional mortgage financing and therefore does not satisfy the financing condition of the sales contract.

Answer (b) is incorrect because a "subject to financing" clause is a condition precedent to the buyer's performance of the contract. Answer (c) is incorrect because a "subject to financing" clause is not implied as a matter of law, but must appear as part of the contract for purchase of real property. The rule in construing a "subject to financing" clause is that the court will infer the intent of the parties in light of the contract and all the circumstances surrounding the making of the contract, including customary community practices in financing of similar transactions. Unless the "subject to financing" clause is definite enough so as to determine the necessary financing requirements, the contract may become illusory in nature and not be enforceable.

7. (582,L1,53) (d) Unless there is a provision in the contract to the contrary, it is implied in a contract of sale that the seller must furnish the buyer with good and marketable title at closing (implied warranty of marketability). Marketable title is title which is reasonably free from doubt, one which a prudent purchaser would accept. The title should be free from all encumbrances, encroachments and other such defects. Therefore, the stone wall encroaching upon the land results in a potential breach of the implied warranty of marketability. Answer (a) is incorrect because when the contract is silent on the type of deed to be given, the buyer is not entitled to a warranty deed with full covenants, but rather a special warranty deed which does not contain full covenants. Answer (b) is incorrect because zoning law restrictions will not render a title unmarketable. Therefore, Fulcrum would not be permitted to avoid the contract. Answer (c) is incorrect because Fulcrum does not have to take the land subject to back taxes unless it appears as a reservation on the face of the deed.

D. Types of Deeds

8. (1188,L1,58) (c) A quitclaim deed gives the grantee the least amount of protection. The grantor conveys whatever title he/she has, if any. No warranty of title is made by the grantor. Answer (a) is incorrect because with a bargain and sale deed the grantor warrants that s/he has done nothing during his/her term of ownership that would impair the title. Answer (b) is incorrect because a grant deed contains all the covenants of a warranty deed but limits its coverage to defects arising while the grantor owned the property. Answer (d) is incorrect because a warranty deed provides a grantee the best possible pro-

tection. In general, a warranty deed states the grantor's title is valid and free from any encumbrances.

9. (588,L1,51) (b) A general warranty deed warrants the greatest number of things and thus provides a purchaser with the most extensive protection against defects of title. A general warranty deed warrants that (1) the seller has title and the power to convey the property described in the deed, (2) the property is free from any encumbrances, except as disclosed in the deed, and (3) the grantee (purchaser) will not be disturbed in his/her possession of the property by the grantor (seller) or some third party's lawful claim of ownership. Answer (c) is incorrect because a quitclaim deed only conveys to the grantee whatever interest the grantor has in the property. If the grantor has no interest, then the grantee receives nothing. Bargain and sale deeds and grant deeds are essentially the same type of deed. With such deeds, the grantor only warrants that s/he has done nothing to impair the title. However, the grantor does not warrant against prior encumbrances (liens that occurred before grantor's ownership). Therefore, answers (a) and (d) are incorrect.

10. (585,L1,52) (c) The necessary requirements for a valid deed are (1) the names of the buyer (grantee) and the seller (grantor), (2) words evidencing an intent to convey, (3) a legally sufficient description of the land, (4) the grantor's (and usually the spouse's) signature, and (5) delivery of the deed. Answer (a) is incorrect since the purchase price need not be stated on the deed in order for it to be valid. Answer (b) is incorrect since a deed need not be signed by the buyer (grantee), but only by the seller (grantor) in order to be valid. Answer (d) is incorrect since the seller's (grantor's) seal need not be affixed to a deed in order for it to be effective, nor does it have to be recorded to be effective between the buyer and seller. Recordation of the deed merely protects the buyer from third parties claiming an interest in the property.

F. Recording a Deed

11. (586,L1,42) (a) In order for a deed to be effective between the purchaser and seller of real estate, the deed must be delivered by the seller with an intent to transfer title. Even though a deed may be executed it does not become effective until delivery is made with the proper intent. Answer (b) is incorrect because a deed need not be recorded in order for it to be valid between the seller and pur-

chaser. Recordation of a deed is important because it gives constructive notice to all third parties of the grantee's ownership; however, it does not affect the resolution of any disputes between the grantor and the grantee. Answer (c) is incorrect since a deed need be signed by only the seller in order for it to be effective; it does not have to be signed by the purchaser. Answer (d) is incorrect since the form of a deed is very different from a contract for the sale of real property. There is no requirement that the deed must contain the actual sales price.

12. (585,L1,53) (a) Ordinarily, priorities as to titles are governed by a first in time, first in right rule. In this case, this would mean that Park would be the legal owner of the property since the property was deeded to him/her first. However, if a subsequent bona fide purchaser for value (i.e., a person who pays valuable consideration for the land, who acts in good faith and without knowledge of any previous conveyance or sale) records his/her deed before the party to whom the property was first deeded (Park), this subsequent bona fide purchaser will have legal title which will prevail over that of the party originally granted the deed. In this case, since Noll and Baxter were bona fide purchasers and since they recorded their deeds before Park recorded his/hers, Baxter's interest in the property is superior to Park's. Answer (b) is incorrect since recordation of a deed is not necessary for it to be effective between the buyer and seller; recordation merely protects the deed holder from third parties claiming an interest in the property. Answer (c) is incorrect since, as discussed above, Noll and Baxter had legal title to the property. Answer (d) is incorrect because Baxter has received legal title to the property; thus, Noll did not breach the contract.

G. Title Insurance

13. (1189,L1,56) (c) Title insurance insures against all defects of records; however, it does not insure against those defects which would be disclosed by physical inspection of the property or those defects listed as exceptions on the face of the policy. Thus, the real estate title insurance would not cover for the title exceptions listed in the policy. Answer (a) is incorrect because the face of the title insurance policy will often state existing exceptions (e.g., taxes and easements) that are not cleared prior to the purchaser taking possession of the property and which the policy will not insure against. Answer (b) is incorrect because even though the property may be transferred to a subse-

quent owner, the title insurance does not run with the property and cannot be transferred to the purchaser. Answer (d) is incorrect because the amount of the first mortgage would not be relevant in determining the amount of coverage allowed.

I. Mortgages

14. (1188,L1,17) (b) When the buyer (Bond) assumes a mortgage s/he becomes personally liable for the mortgage debt. The seller/ mortgagor (Spear) remains personally liable as a surety, unless the mortgagee (Fale Finance) releases the seller. If the proceeds from the foreclosure sale are less than the balance due on the note, then Bond would be liable for the deficiency as the principal debtor and Spear would be liable as a surety. Answer (a) is incorrect because Fale would not have to sue both Spear and Bond to collect the deficiency. Fale could sue either party individually. Answer (c) is incorrect because Fale could proceed immediately against either Bond or Spear. Answer (d) is incorrect because Spear is liable as a surety for the deficiency even when Bond assumes the note and mortgage.

15. (1189,L1,57) (c) A purchase-money mortgage is created when a lender furnishes the money with which the property is purchased. Upon default by the borrower, the lender may file suit for foreclosure on the property. Answer (a) is incorrect because although the lender has a right to foreclosure on the property related to the mortgage, the lender would not be entitled to file suit to have the borrower declared insolvent. Answer (b) is incorrect because the seller would not be required to assume the mortgage debt since the buyer did not take the property subject to the seller's mortgage. In this situation, the seller would have no obligation related to the mortgage. Answer (d) is incorrect because the lender must first file suit for foreclosure and then a judicial foreclosure sale occurs. The lender will receive the proceeds from this sale as satisfaction of the outstanding mortgage but does not receive the title to the property.

16. (1188,L1,60) (c) When there is more than one mortgage on the same property, all properly executed and duly recorded, then the first mortgagee will have priority over subsequent mortgagees. Upon foreclosure, the first mortgage must be fully satisfied before any payment is allocated to subsequent mortgagees.

In this question, State Bank holds a first mortgage for $60,000, Penn Bank holds a second mortgage for $20,000, and State Bank is an unsecured creditor for $20,000. Mortgages may be given to secure future advances, but there is no evidence presented to indicate that the mortgage State Bank received was intended to secure future advances. Upon foreclosure, State Bank would receive the first $60,000 of proceeds and Penn Bank would receive the remaining $10,000. After all the proceeds from the foreclosure are distributed, State Bank and Penn Bank would be unsecured creditors for $20,000 and $10,000, respectively. Therefore, answers (a), (b), and (d) are incorrect.

17. (588,L1,52) (b) A mortgagee has the right to assign a mortgage to a third person without the consent of the mortgagor. Answer (a) is incorrect because the mortgage only needs to be signed by the mortgagor. Answer (c) is incorrect because the mortgage must contain a complete description of the property mortgaged. Answer (d) is incorrect because there is no legal requirement that the mortgage contain the amount of indebtedness and the rate of interest payable thereon; however, these are included in most mortgages.

18. (588,L1,56) (a) The purpose of recording a mortgage is to provide constructive notice to third parties acquiring an interest in the property that the property is subject to an existing mortgage. The recording of a mortgage has no effect on the rights of the mortgagor (Bell) or mortgagee (Arco). Answer (b) is incorrect because a mortgage generally gives the mortgagee (Arco) a non-possessory security interest in the property. The mortgagor generally wants possession of the property during the period the indebtedness is being repaid. Answer (c) is incorrect because the recording of a mortgage has no impact on lessees of mortgaged property. The new owner cannot rightfully terminate a lease unless the old owner had the same right. Answer (d) is incorrect because the recording of the mortgage has no relationship to title transfer. A mortgagee merely has a lien against the title of the property and recording the mortgage assures the mortgagee that his/her claim is superior to subsequent claimants.

19. (588,L1,57) (b) A mortgage must be recorded to be effective against subsequent third parties who acquire an interest in property with no knowledge of the prior mortgage. Since Todd did not record his/her mortgage and Walsh did not have knowledge of Todd's mortgage, Walsh will take title to the warehouse free of Todd's mortgage. Answer (a) is incorrect because all mortgages must be recorded to obtain the best possible rights, regardless of whether they are purchase money mortgages. Answer (c) is incorrect because, if a first mortgagee does not record, then a subsequent mortgagee who records will have priority if s/he did not have knowledge of the first mortgage. Since Stone did not have knowledge of Todd's mortgage, Stone will have a superior mortgage. Answer (d) is incorrect because Walsh did not suffer any damages; therefore, Walsh has no claim against Best. Also the standard title policy only insures against defects of record, and since the mortgage is unrecorded, it is not a defect of record.

20. (1189,L1,58) (a) Upon foreclosure, a first mortgage holder has priority and must be paid in full before payments are made to any subsequent mortgagees. In this example, Area Bank would have the right to the first $240,000, and Public Finance would have the right to the remaining $40,000. Public would become an unsecured creditor for the $20,000 deficiency. Therefore, answer (b) is incorrect. Answer (c) is incorrect because the mortgagor (Ram), not the mortgagee (Public), has a right of redemption after the judicial sale. Answer (d) is incorrect because Quincy, as a purchaser at a judicial sale, will take the property free of any claims.

21. (1185,L1,55) (d) When a buyer purchases property "subject to" a mortgage the buyer has no personal liability on the seller's mortgage. The seller remains personally liable on the mortgage. In a "subject to sale" the mortgagee may foreclose on the property in the hands of the purchaser. In the event the foreclosure sale yields an amount less than the unpaid balance, the original mortgagor is personally liable for the unpaid balance. Since Fale, the mortgagee, only received $280,000 from the foreclosure sale, Slade, the original mortgagor, is liable to Fale for the $20,000 unpaid balance. Answers (a) and (b) are incorrect because a buyer assumes no personal liability for a seller's mortgage when property is taken "subject to" a mortgage. Answer (c) is incorrect because in a "subject to" sale the seller remains personally liable to the mortgagee.

22. (585,L1,57) (d) A judicial foreclosure sale of the debtor's real property is conducted generally at the direction of a court official (county sheriff) and confirmed by the court. A court will not refuse to confirm a

sale merely because a higher price might have been received at a later time. The court will refuse to confirm a sale if the price is so low as to raise a presumption of unfairness or lack of protection for the mortgagor. Answer (a) is incorrect because a mortgagor has an equitable right to redeem the property up until foreclosure on the property. Answer (b) is incorrect because in a majority of states, a mortgagor has a statutory right of redemption following a foreclosure sale for a stipulated period of time. Under both an equity and a statutory redemption, the mortgagor must pay the sales price plus reasonable cost and expenses to redeem the property. Answer (c) is incorrect because a mortgagor is entitled to any excess resulting from a judicial foreclosure sale after all costs and expenses have been paid along with the amount outstanding on the mortgagor note.

J. Lessor - Lessee

23. (1188,L1,57) (c) Because the agreement between Tell and Vorn constituted a sublease, the lessor (Lott) has no privity of contract with the sublessee (Vorn). Thus, Lott cannot successfully take action against Vorn for the deliquent taxes. However, the lessee (Tell) remains liable on the lease and will be held responsible for payment of the delinquent taxes. Therefore, answers (a), (b), and (d) are incorrect. Note that if the agreement between Tell and Vorn had been an assignment, Tell and Vorn would be jointly and severally liable for the taxes.

24. (588,L1,55) (c) An assignment is the transfer by the lessee (assignor) of all his/her interests in a lease to an assignee. The lessee has the right to assign his/her interest provided there is no restriction to the contrary in the lease. A clause in the lease prohibiting a sublease does not prohibit an assignment. The assignor (lessee) is still liable to the lessor unless there is a novation or a release. Therefore, Sisk would still be liable to Met for the rent provided for in the lease. Answer (a) is incorrect because the lease was silent as to Sisk's right to assign the lease; therefore, the assignment is not voidable at Met's option. Answer (b) is incorrect because Sisk would still be liable to Met regardless of whether Met consented to the assignment. Sisk would only be relieved from liability if s/he received a novation or a release. Answer (d) is incorrect because under an assignment the assignee is in privity with the lessor (Met); therefore Kern would be liable to Met for the rent provided for in the lease.

25. (1185,L1,52) (b) A lease creates a possessory interest in real property. Mini has the right to occupy the building for the term of the lease regardless of whether the owner, Rein, sells the property to a third party. Answer (a) is incorrect because lessee may engage in an assignment unless expressly prohibited by the lease; thus, Mini may engage in an assignment if the lease is silent in this regard. Answer (c) is incorrect because Mini is only liable for those injuries that arise out of Mini's negligence. Answer (d) is incorrect because Mini's rights under the lease are not affected by a sale of the building.

May 1990 Answers

26. (590,L1,50) (c) In most jurisdictions, corporations may not be joint tenants because they do not die. Answers (a), (b), and (d) are incorrect because individuals, including minors, can be joint tenants.

27. (590,L1,53) (a) A tenant may be evicted from an apartment if s/he uses it for illegal purposes. Answer (b) is incorrect because although the lease may contain enforceable rules, such as no pets, the question stated that the lease did not contain these restrictions. Answer (c) is incorrect because the tenant does not have the duty to maintain a liability insurance policy on an apartment. Answer (d) is incorrect because although the landlord may have the duty to make certain structural repairs, the tenant may choose to make them.

28. (590,L1,54) (c) The lessee may sublease or assign the lease unless the lease agreement prohibits these. Therefore answer (c) is correct and answer (d) is incorrect. Answer (a) is incorrect because the duties and benefits of the lease pass to the heirs of the lessor upon the lessor's death. Answer (b) is incorrect because the obligations and benefits under the 25-year lease pass to the purchaser from the lessor unless the purchaser, former lessor, and tenant agree otherwise.

29. (590,L1,55) (b) Under a notice statute, a subsequent good faith purchaser, whether s/he records or not, wins over the previous purchaser who did not record before that subsequent purchase. Under a race-notice statute, the subsequent good faith purchaser wins only if s/he also records first. Therefore, Parko wins under both of these statutes because Nexis was aware of Parko's purchase, and thus, Nexis was not a good faith purchaser. Under the race statute, however,

Nexis wins because s/he was the first to record. Thus, (a), (c), and (d) are incorrect.

30. (590,L1,56) (b) A purchaser of real
estate takes title subject to any mortgage he
was aware of or any mortgage that was recorded
before the purchase. Ford, therefore, takes
title to the warehouse subject to Young's
mortgage, but free of Lang's mortgage. Therefore answer (b) is correct and answer (a) is
incorrect. Answer (c) is incorrect because
there is no such provision. Answer (d) is
incorrect because the recording statutes
change the first in time concept to encourage
the recording of mortgages.

31. (590,L1,57) (d) When two mortgages are
foreclosed, the first mortgage is paid before
paying the second mortgage. Answer (a) is incorrect because a default on a second mortgage
does not constitute a default on the first.
Answer (b) is incorrect because consent of the
first mortgagee is not needed to pay off the
second. Answer (c) is incorrect because the
second mortgagee is paid after the first, and
thus, the second mortgagee may opt to pay off
the first mortgage to protect its interest.

32. (590,L1,58) (b) After foreclosure of
the mortgage, the mortgagor has several options. The mortgagor may redeem the property
until the foreclosure sale by use of the equitable right of redemption. After the foreclosure sale, the mortgagor may pay off the
loan within a statutory period. If these
remedies are not used, the mortgagee must
return any excess proceeds from the sale. The
mortagor, however, does not otherwise have the
right to keep possession of the property after
a foreclosure sale whether or not the equity
exceeds the amount due on the mortgage.
Therefore, answers (a), (c) and (d) are
incorrect.

Answer Outline

Problem 1   Purchase of Property with Existing
               Mortgage; Assignment and Sublease
               of Lease (1184,L2)

a. If Bean takes plant subject to mortgage
    Fine remains liable to Muni for any
       deficiency after foreclosure sale
    Bean avoids liability for any deficiency
       Bean's liability limited to his equity
       in plant
    If Bean assumes mortgage
    Fine remains liable to Muni for any
       deficiency after foreclosure sale
    Bean also liable to Muni for any defi-
       ciency
    If parties execute novation
    Fine completely released from liability
       to Muni
    Bean liable to Muni for any deficiency
       after foreclosure sale
    This novation must be in writing
b. Incorrect assertion
    Clause prohibiting assignment is valid
       since Fine consented to it
    Correct assertion
    Prohibition against assignment does not
       constitute prohibition against sub-
       letting premises
    Incorrect assertion
    Original tenant remains fully liable
       for stipulated rent under sublease or
       assignment unless specifically released
       by landlord

Unofficial Answer

Problem 1   Purchase of Property with Existing
               Mortgage; Assignment and Sublease
               of Lease (1184,L2)

a. If Bean purchases the plant subject to
the mortgage, Fine will remain liable to Muni
on the note and the underlying mortgage.
Thus, Fine will be liable to Muni for any deficiency which may exist after a foreclosure
sale. By taking the plant subject to the
mortgage, Bean avoids liability for any
deficiency. Therefore, Bean's potential
liability is limited to any equity he may have
built up in the plant.

    If Bean assumes the mortgage, Fine will
continue to be liable to Muni despite the
agreement permitting Bean to assume the
mortgage. Therefore, any resulting deficiency
from a foreclosure sale will be Fine's
responsibility. In addition, since Bean
assumed the mortgage, he would also be held
liable to Muni.

    The execution of a novation would release
Fine from his liability to Muni on the mortgage and would substitute Bean in his place.
In order to have a valid novation involving
real property, Muni must agree to it in
writing.

    b. Fine is incorrect in his assertion
that the clause prohibiting the assignment of
the lease is void. A clause prohibiting the
assignment of a lease will not constitute a
disabling restraint sufficient to prevent the
free alienation of property and is therefore
valid. Fine is bound by the restrictive
clause since he consented to it when entering
into the lease.

    Fine's assertion that the prohibition
against assignment will not affect his right
to sublease is correct. In the absence of a
provision in the lease to the contrary, a
tenant has the right to assign the lease or
sublet the premises. A prohibition against
either will not be a prohibition against both.
Therefore, Fine may sublease the warehouse to
Bean despite the clause forbidding the assignment of the lease.

    Fine's assertion that he will be released
from liability under the lease upon obtaining
Jay's consent to either sublet or assign is
incorrect. Under a sublease or assignment,
the original tenant will remain fully liable
for the stipulated rent unless the landlord
releases the original tenant from that obligation. The fact that the landlord consents
to the sublease or assignment will not automatically relieve the original tenant from his
obligation to pay rent. Therefore, any rent
due pursuant to the lease will continue to be
Fine's legal responsibility.

Answer Outline

Problem 2   Trade Fixtures (1182,L5b)

Part b.

To establish rightful ownership of air
   conditioning and machinery
   Auditor must determine whether these items
      are personalty or realty
      If personalty, then Darby has ownership
      rights
      If realty, then Grayson has ownership
      rights
Issue is whether these items have become
   realty by virtue of being fixtures
   Several factors must be considered in
      determining whether personal property
      attached to real property is a fixture
      Affixer's objective intent as to whether
         property is to be regarded as personalty
         or realty

Method and permanence of physical attach-
ment
Adaptability of personal property use for
the purpose for which real property is
used
Personal property affixed by tenant for pur-
pose of conducting business is a trade
fixture
Trade fixtures remain personal property
Tenant has right to remove upon expiration
of lease
Manufacturing machinery is a trade fixture
Since integral part of Darby's business
Darby has right to remove upon expiration of
lease
Therefore, should be depreciated over
machinery's useful life, i.e., 30 years
Air conditioning system is a fixture
Does not appear to be used by Darby for
conducting business
Would result in material damage to realty
if removed
Darby does not have right to remove upon
expiration of lease
Therefore, should be depreciated over life
of lease, i.e., 20 years

Unofficial Answer
(Author Modified)

Problem 2   Trade Fixtures (1182,L5b)

Part b.

In order for the auditor to establish the
rightful ownership of the central air conditioning system and the manufacturing machinery
upon the expiration of the lease, s/he must
determine whether these items would be
considered personalty or realty. If these
assets are considered **personalty**, then upon
expiration of the lease Darby Corporation
retains ownership. But if these assets are
considered **realty**, then upon expiration of the
lease they remain with the leased building
(real property) and Grayson Corporation has
ownership rights. Therefore, the issue is
whether the air conditioning system and the
machinery have become realty, as a result of
being fixtures.

A fixture is an item that was originally
personal property, and has been affixed to
real property in a relatively permanent
fashion such that it is considered to be part
of the real property. There are several
factors which must be applied in determining
whether personal property which has been
attached to real property is a fixture
(realty).

1. **Affixer's objective intent as to
whether property is to be regarded as personalty or realty.** In general, a court will hold
that an item is a fixture if it was the intention of the parties that it becomes part of
the real property. If the intent is clear,
then this becomes the controlling factor in
the determination of whether an item is a fixture or not.

This intent can be determined from various
factors:
• The intention of the parties as expressed in the agreement.
• The nature of the article affixed.
• The relationship of the parties (i.e.,
the affixer and the owner of the real property).

2. **The method and permanence with which
the item is physically attached (annexed) to
the real property.** If the item cannot be
removed without material injury to the real
property, it is generally held that the item
has become part of the realty (i.e., a
fixture).

3. **Adaptability of use of the personal
property for the purpose for which the real
property is used.** If the personal property is
necessary or beneficial to the use of the real
property, the more likely the item is a fixture. But if the use or purpose of the item
is unusual for the type of realty involved, it
might be reasonable to conclude that it is
personalty, and the affixer intends to remove
the item when s/he leaves.

4. **The property interest of that person
in the real property at the time of the
attachment of the item.**

An item installed (affixed) by a tenant in
connection with a business s/he is conducting
on the leased premises is called a trade fixture. The personal property must be brought
onto the leased business premises for the purpose of conducting and engaging in the trade
or business for which the tenant occupies the
premises.

Trade fixtures remain personal property,
giving the tenant the right to remove these
items upon expiration of the lease. But the
tenant's right is limited to the extent that
his/her action of removing the fixture may not
materially damage the realty. If the item is
so affixed onto the real property that removing it would cause substantial damage, then
it is considered part of the realty.

Based upon the aforementioned analysis,
the manufacturing machinery qualifies as a
trade fixture. Since Darby Corporation is a
manufacturer, this asset is integral to the
conduct of business for which Darby occupies
the premises. As a trade fixture, Darby
retains rightful ownership of the machinery,
giving Darby the right to remove the machinery

upon expiration of the lease. However, Darby would be required to compensate Grayson for any damage caused by removal of the machinery. Therefore, Darby was correct to depreciate the machinery over its estimated useful life (i.e., 30 years).

However, the air conditioning system would not appear to qualify as a trade fixture. It does not appear to be employed by Darby in the furtherance of business operations for which the premises are leased. The air conditioning system would also be considered part of the realty, since it is probably so attached to the building that it would result in permanent structural damage to the building upon removal. Therefore, the air conditioning system would be considered a fixture (realty). As such, Darby would not have the right to remove it upon expiration of the lease. Thus, Darby should depreciate the air conditioning system over the life of the lease, (i.e., 20 years).

Answer Outline

Problem 3   Liability on Assumption of
            Mortgage; Subletting; Property
            Interests; Rights of Joint
            Tenants and Tenants in Common
            (589,L3)

a. Ash, Bale, and Rangel are personally
   liable to Vista
     They assumed the mortgage
   Park is also personally liable to Vista
     Assumption by third party does not
       relieve Park
b. Assertion that the sublet is void is false
     A tenant may sublet unless stated
       otherwise in the lease
   Assertion that Wein or Nord is liable for
     rent is false
     Sublessee (Nord) is only liable to
       tenant (Wein)
       Tenant (Wein) is solely liable to
         landlord (Ash, Bale, and Rangel)
c. Ash's spouse becomes 1/3 tenant in common
   on April 4, 1989
     Transfer of joint tenant's interest
       without consent of other joint
       tenants precludes transferee from
       becoming a joint tenant
     Rangel's death transfers his 1/3 inter-
       est to Bale through right of survivor-
       ship
       Bale has 2/3 interest and is now
         tenant in common since he was the
         only joint tenant remaining
         Ash's spouse remains 1/3 tenant in
           common

Unofficial Answer

Problem 3   Liability on Assumption of Mort-
            gage; Subletting; Property Inter-
            ests; Rights of Joint Tenants and
            Tenants in Common (589,L3)

a. Ash, Bale, and Rangel will be personally liable to Vista for the deficiency resulting from the foreclosure sale because they became the principal debtors when they assumed the mortgage. Park will remain liable for the deficiency. Although Vista consented to the assumption of the mortgage by Ash, Bale, and Rangel, such assumption does not relieve Park from its obligation to Vista unless Park obtains a release from Vista or there is a novation.

b. The assertion that the sublet from Wein to Nord is void because Ash, Bale, and Rangel must consent to the sublet is incorrect. Unless the lease provides otherwise, a tenant may sublet the premises without the landlord's consent. Since the lease was silent regarding Wein's right to sublet, Wein may sublet to Nord without the consent of Ash, Bale, and Rangel.

The assertion that if the sublet was not void Ash, Bale, and Rangel have the right to hold either Wein or Nord liable for payment of rent is incorrect. In a sublease, the sub-lessee/subtenant (Nord) has no obligation to pay rent to the landlord (Ash, Bale, and Rangel).

The subtenant (Nord) is liable to the tenant (Wein), but the tenant (Wein) remains solely liable to the landlord (Ash, Bale, and Rangel) for the rent stipulated in the lease.

c. Ash's inter vivos transfer of his 1/3 interest in the office building to his spouse on April 4, 1989 resulted in his spouse obtaining a 1/3 interest in the office building as a tenant in common. Ash's wife did not become a joint tenant with Bale and Rangel because the transfer of a joint tenant's interest to an outside party destroys the joint tenancy nature of the particular interest transferred. Bale and Rangel will remain as joint tenants with each other.

As of April 21, 1989, the office building was owned by Ash's spouse who had a 1/3 interest as tenant in common and Bale who had a 2/3 interest as tenant in common.

Ash's death on April 20, 1989 will have no effect on the ownership of the office building because Ash had already transferred all of his interest to his wife on April 4, 1989.

Rangel's death on April 20, 1989 resulted in his interest being acquired by Bale because of the right of survivorship feature in a joint tenancy. Because there are no surviving joint tenants, Bale will become a tenant in common who owns 2/3 of the office building. Ash's spouse will not acquire any additional interest due to Rangel's death because she was a tenant in common with Rangel.

Multiple Choice Questions (1-15)

1. Fuller Corporation insured its factory and warehouse against fire with the Safety First Insurance Company. As a part of the bargaining process, in connection with obtaining the policy Fuller was required by Safety First to give in writing certain warranties regarding the insured risk. Fuller did so, and they were incorporated into the policy. Which of the following correctly describes the law applicable to such warranties?
   a. The warranties given by Fuller will be treated as representations.
   b. It was not necessary that the warranties given by Fuller be in writing to be effective.
   c. In the event that Fuller does not strictly comply with the warranties it has given, it will be denied recovery in a substantial number of states.
   d. In deciding whether the language contained in a policy constitutes a warranty, the courts usually construe ambiguous language in a way which favors the insurance company.

2. Beal occupies an office building as a tenant under a 25-year lease. Beal also has a mortgagee's (lender's) interest in an office building owned by Hill Corp. In which capacity does Beal have an insurable interest?

	Tenant	Mortgagee
a.	Yes	Yes
b.	Yes	No
c.	No	Yes
d.	No	No

3. The earliest time a purchaser of existing goods will acquire an insurable interest in those goods is when
   a. The purchaser obtains possession.
   b. Title passes to the purchaser.
   c. Performance of the contract has been completed or substantially completed.
   d. The goods are identified to the contract.

4. To recover under a property insurance policy, an insurable interest must exist

	When the policy is purchased	At the time of loss
a.	Yes	Yes
b.	Yes	No
c.	No	Yes
d.	No	No

5. A fire insurance policy is one common type of contract. As such it must meet the general requirements necessary to establish a binding contract. In a dispute between the insured and the insurance company, which of the following is correct?
   a. The contract is always unilateral.
   b. Insurance contracts are specifically included within the general Statute of Frauds.
   c. The insured must satisfy the insurable interest requirement.
   d. The actual delivery of the policy to the insured is a prerequisite to the creation of the insurance contract.

6. Burt owns an office building which is leased to Hansen Corporation under the terms of a long-term lease. Both Burt and Hansen have procured fire insurance covering the building. Which of the following is correct?
   a. Both Burt and Hansen have separate insurable interests.
   b. Burt's insurable interest is limited to the book value of the property.
   c. Hansen has an insurable interest in the building, but only to the extent of the value of any additions or modifications it has made.
   d. Since Burt has legal title to the building, he is the only party who can insure the building.

7. Bernard Manufacturing, Inc. owns a three-story building which it recently purchased. The purchase price was $200,000 of which $160,000 was financed by the proceeds of a mortgage loan from the Cattleman Savings and Loan Association. Bernard immediately procured a standard fire insurance policy on the premises for $200,000 from the Magnificent Insurance Company. Cattleman also took out fire insurance of $160,000 on the property from the Reliable Insurance Company of America. The property was subsequently totally destroyed as a result of a fire which started in an adjacent loft and spread to Bernard's building. Insofar as the rights and duties of Bernard, Cattleman, and the insurers are concerned, which of the following is a correct statement?
   a. Cattleman Savings and Loan lacks the requisite insurable interest to collect on its policy.
   b. Bernard Manufacturing can only collect $40,000.
   c. Reliable Insurance Company is subrogated to Cattleman's rights against Bernard upon payment of Cattleman's insurance claim.
   d. The maximum amount that Bernard Manufacturing can collect from

Magnificent is $40,000, the value of its insurable interest.

8.   Alphonse, a sole CPA practitioner, obtained a malpractice insurance policy from the Friendly Casualty Company. In regard to this coverage
  a.   Issuance of an unqualified opinion by Alphonse when he knows the statements are false does not give Friendly a defense.
  b.   The policy would automatically cover the work of a new partnership formed by Alphonse and Borne.
  c.   Friendly will not be subrogated to rights against Alphonse for his negligent conduct of an audit.
  d.   Coverage includes injury to a client resulting from a slip on a rug negligently left loose in Alphonse's office.

9.   On May 15, Sly purchased a warehouse for $100,000. Sly immediately insured the warehouse in the amount of $40,000 with Riff Insurance Co. Six months later, Sly obtained additional fire insurance on the warehouse in the amount of $10,000 from Beek Insurance Co. Both policies contained an 80% coinsurance clause. Sly failed to notify Riff of the policy with Beek. Two years later, while both policies were still in effect, a fire caused by Sly's negligence resulted in $20,000 of damage to the warehouse. At the time of the loss, the warehouse had a fair market value of $50,000. Which of the following will prevent Sly from obtaining the full $20,000 from Riff?
  a.   Sly's negligence in causing the fire.
  b.   Sly's failure to satisfy the coinsurance clause.
  c.   Sly's failure to notify Riff of the policy with Beek.
  d.   Sly's purchase of insurance from Beek.

10.   Adams Company purchased a factory and warehouse from Martinson for $150,000. Adams obtained a $100,000 real estate mortgage loan from a local bank and was required by the lender to pay for the cost of title insurance covering the bank's interest in the property. In addition, Adams was required to obtain fire insurance sufficient to protect the bank against loss due to fire. The coinsurance factor has been satisfied. Under these circumstances, which of the following is correct?
  a.   Adams can purchase only $50,000 of title insurance since it already obtained a $100,000 title policy for the bank equal to the bank loan.

  b.   The bank could not have independently obtained a fire insurance policy on the property because Adams has legal title.
  c.   If Adams obtained a $150,000 fire insurance policy which covered its interest and the bank's interest in the property and there is an estimated $50,000 of fire loss, the insurer will typically be obligated to pay the owner and the bank the amounts equal to their respective interests as they may appear.
  d.   If Adams obtained a $100,000 fire insurance policy covering the bank's interest and $150,000 covering his own interest, each would obtain these amounts upon total destruction of the property.

11.   McArthur purchased a house for $60,000. The house is insured for $64,000 and the insurance policy has an 80% coinsurance provision. Storms caused $12,000 worth of damage when the house had a fair market value of $120,000. What maximum amount will McArthur recover from the insurance company?
  a. $ 8,000
  b. $ 9,000
  c. $ 9,600
  d. $12,000

12.   In general, the coinsurance feature of property insurance
  a.   Is fixed at a minimum of 80% by law.
  b.   Is an additional refinement of the insurable interest requirement.
  c.   Precludes the insured from insuring for less than the coinsurance percentage.
  d.   Prevents the insured from insuring for a minimal amount and recovering the full amount of losses.

13.   Long Co. owns a warehouse which is insured in the amount of $60,000 against loss by fire. The policy contains an 80% coinsurance clause. A fire totally destroyed the warehouse which was valued at the time of the loss at $150,000. Long is entitled to receive
  a. $0, since it failed to meet the coin-surance requirements.
  b. $48,000.
  c. $60,000.
  d. $75,000.

May 1990 Questions

14.   Lawfo Corp. maintains a $200,000 standard fire insurance policy on one of its warehouses. The policy includes an 80% coinsur-

ance clause. At the time the warehouse was
originally insured, its value was $250,000.
The warehouse now has a value of $300,000. If
the warehouse sustains $30,000 of fire damage,
Lawfo's insurance recovery will be a maximum
of
    a. $20,000
    b. $24,000
    c. $25,000
    d. $30,000

15. Orr is an employee of Vick Corp. Vick
relies heavily on Orr's ability to market
Vick's products and, for that reason, has
acquired a $50,000 insurance policy on Orr's
life. Half of the face value of the policy is
payable to Vick and the other half is payable
to Orr's spouse. Orr dies shortly after the
policy is taken out but after leaving Vick's
employ. Which of the following statements is
correct?
    a.   Orr's spouse does <u>not</u> have an insur-
        able interest because the policy is
        owned by Vick.
    b.   Orr's spouse will be entitled to all
        of the proceeds of the policy.
    c.   Vick will <u>not</u> be entitled to any of
        the proceeds of the policy because
        Vick is <u>not</u> a creditor or relative
        of Orr.
    d.   Vick will be entitled to its shares
        of the proceeds of the policy re-
        gardless of whether Orr is employed
        by Vick at the time of death.

Problems

Problem 1   (1182,L5a)

(10 to 15 minutes)

Part a. While auditing the financial statements of Jackson Corporation for the year ended December 31, 1981, Harvey Draper, CPA, desired to verify the balance in the insurance claims receivable account. Draper obtained the following information:

• On November 4, 1981, Jackson's Parksdale plant was damaged by fire. The fire caused $200,000 damage to the plant, which was purchased in 1970 for $600,000. When the plant was purchased, Jackson obtained a loan secured by a mortgage from Second National Bank of Parksdale. At the time of the fire the loan balance, including accrued interest, was $106,000. The plant was insured against fire with Eagle Insurance Company. The policy contained a "standard mortgagee" clause and an 80% coinsurance clause. The face value of the policy was $600,000 and the value of the plant was $1,000,000 at the time of the fire.

• On December 10, 1981, Jackson's Yuma warehouse was totally destroyed by fire. The warehouse was acquired in 1960 for $300,000. At the time of the fire, the warehouse was unencumbered by any mortgage; it was insured against fire with Eagle for $300,000; and it had a value of $500,000. The policy contained an 80% coinsurance clause.

• On December 26, 1981, Jackson's Rye City garage was damaged by fire. At the time of the fire, the garage had a value of $250,000 and was unencumbered by any mortgage. The fire caused $60,000 damage to the garage, which was constructed in 1965 at a cost of $50,000. In 1975 Jackson expanded the capacity of the garage at an additional cost of $50,000. When the garage was constructed in 1965, Jackson insured the garage against fire for $50,000 with Eagle, and this policy was still in force on the date of the fire. When the garage was expanded in 1975, Jackson obtained $100,000 of additional fire insurance coverage from Queen Insurance Company. Each policy contains an 80% coinsurance clause and a standard pro-rata clause.

Required:

Answer the following, setting forth reasons for any conclusions stated.
1. How much of the fire loss relating to the Parksdale plant will be recovered from Eagle?

2. How will such recovery be distributed between Second National and Jackson?
3. How much of the fire loss relating to the Yuma warehouse will be recovered from Eagle?
4. How much of the fire loss relating to the Rye City garage will be recovered from the insurance companies?
5. What portion of the amount recoverable in connection with the Rye City garage loss will Queen be obligated to pay?

Problem 2   (1188,L2)

(15 to 20 minutes)

Dunn & Co., CPAs, while performing the 1987 year-end audit of Starr Corp.'s financial statements, discovered that certain events during 1987 had resulted in litigation.

Starr had purchased the warehouse on March 1, 1987. The contract between Birk and Starr provided for a closing on September 20, 1987. On July 1, 1987, Birk executed a contract to purchase the warehouse from Starr for $200,000. On September 1, 1987, Birk contacted Starr and demanded that the purchase price be reduced to $190,000 because of a sudden rise in interest rates and declining value of real estate. Starr orally agreed to change the price to $190,000. On September 2, Birk sent Starr a signed memo confirming the reduction in price to $190,000. Starr did not sign the memo or any other agreement reducing the price. On September 15, Starr, by telephone, informed Birk that it would not sell the warehouse for $190,000. Birk refused to pay Starr $200,000 and a closing never occurred.

On October 30, 1987, a fire caused $80,000 damage to the warehouse at a time when its fair market value was $200,000. Starr had obtained a $160,000 fire insurance policy on February 15, 1987, from Pica Casualty Co., covering the warehouse. On April 11, 1987, Starr obtained another fire insurance policy from Drake Insurance Co. covering the warehouse for $40,000. Each policy contained an 80% coinsurance clause and a provision limiting each company's liability to its proportion of all insurance covering the loss. Pica has refused to pay any amount on its policy.

Starr commenced actions against Birk and Pica asserting the following:

• Birk has breached the contract with Starr because Birk failed to close the transaction and buy the warehouse at a price of $200,000.

• Starr has an insurable interest in the warehouse covered under the policy with Pica.

• Starr has met the coinsurance requirement under Pica's policy.

• Starr is entitled to recover the
entire $80,000 from Pica.

Required:

Discuss Starr's assertions, indicating
whether such assertions are correct and the
reasons therefore.

Multiple Choice Answers

1. c	4. c	7. c	10. c	13. c
2. a	5. c	8. c	11. a	14. c
3. d	6. a	9. d	12. d	15. d

Multiple Choice Answer Explanations

B. Insurance Contract

1. (1181,L1,60) (c) A warranty is a statement of fact by the insured which materially relates to the insurer's risk and must be incorporated into the policy to qualify as a warranty. The warranties given by Fuller constitute condition precedents to the liability of the insurer. Therefore, if Fuller fails to comply with these warranties, the policy is voidable at the option of the insurer and Fuller will be denied recovery. Answer (a) is incorrect because representations are statements not inserted in the policy. By statute, most warranties in life insurance policies are representations but this is not true of warranties in property insurance policies. Answer (b) is incorrect because a warranty must appear on the face of, be embodied in, or be attached to the policy itself to be effective. Therefore, the warranties given by Fuller must be in writing. Answer (d) is incorrect because the courts will construe ambiguous language based upon the mutual intent of the parties.

B.6. Insurable Interest

2. (588,L1,60) (a) The insurable interest requirement with regard to property insurance is met when a person has both a legal interest in the property and a possibility of monetary loss if the property is damaged. A tenant has a legal interest in the leased property during his/her lease term and would have an insurable interest to the extent of economic loss s/he might suffer if the property was damaged. A mortgagee has an insurable interest in mortgaged property to the extent of the unpaid indebtedness. Therefore, answers (b), (c), and (d) are incorrect.

3. (1186,L1,59) (d) Identification occurs when the goods that are going to be used to perform the contract are shipped, marked, or otherwise designated as such. Identification of the goods to the contract is the earliest time at which a purchaser of existing goods will acquire an insurable interest in the goods. Answers (a), (b), and (c) are all incorrect since possession, passage of title, and substantial performance of the contract all have no bearing on when a purchaser will receive an insurable interest.

4. (1189,L1,60) (c) An important element of an insurance contract is the existence of an insurable interest. An insurable interest in property exists when there is both a legal interest in the property and a possibility of monetary loss if the property is damaged. If the insurable interest does not exist, the party will not be allowed to recover under a property insurance policy. For property insurance, this insurable interest need not be present at the time the policy is actually purchased but must be in existence when the policy is in force and also at the time of the loss. Therefore, answers (a), (b), and (d) are incorrect.

5. (1181,L1,59) (c) An essential element of an insurance contract is the existence of an insurable interest. There must be a relationship between the insured and the insured event such that, if the event occurs, the insured will suffer substantial loss. An insurable interest in property exists when there is both a legal interest in the property and a possibility of pecuniary loss if the property is destroyed. Answer (a) is incorrect because an insurance contract often is unilateral in nature, but there is no requirement that it must be. Answer (b) is incorrect because the Statute of Frauds does not require a written contract because the event insured against may occur within one year from the issuance of the insurance policy. Answer (d) is incorrect because physical delivery of the policy is not a requisite for validity. An act or words by the insurer that clearly manifests an intent to be bound will constitute constructive delivery. The insurance contract is generally binding at the time of unconditional acceptance of the application by the insurer and communication of such acceptance to the insured.

6. (581,L1,48) (a) A person has an insurable interest in property if he will benefit by its continued existence or suffer from its destruction and has a legal or equitable interest in the property (e.g., a mortgagee, mortgagor, tenant in rented property, or partner in partnership property). Both Burt (owner of legal title) and Hansen (tenant in leased property) have an insurable interest. Answer (b) is incorrect because Burt has an insurable interest to the extent of any economic loss he might suffer. Such a loss would normally be measured by market value of the property, not book value. Answer (c) is also false because the tenant has an insurable interest for the amount of economic loss he will suffer in the event the property is destroyed. This amount may be greater or less than the value of the additions or modifica-

tions. The tenants would measure their economic loss in reference to items such as the expense of finding a new office building or new business space.

C. Subrogation

7. (1180,L1,53) (c) Answer (c) is correct because under a fire insurance policy, an insurer who pays a claim is subrogated (succeeds to the rights of the insured) to any rights that the insured had against a third party. Answer (a) is incorrect since Cattleman, as mortgagee, has an insurable interest to the extent of the outstanding debt ($160,000). If the policy is a valued policy, then Bernard will collect $200,000. If it is an open policy, then Bernard will collect the market value of the building at the time of destruction up to a maximum of $200,000. Thus, answers (b) and (d) are incorrect.

8. (574,L3,53) (c) The insurance company would not be subrogated to the rights against its insured who holds a malpractice policy for negligence. The reason for a malpractice insurance policy is to protect the insured against this type of action. Malpractice insurance would not cover intentional wrongs such as fraud. A malpractice policy would not automatically cover the new partnership, because the character of the new partner is crucial to the risk that the insurance company takes. Injuries such as a slip on a rug are not covered under malpractice insurance, but under personal liability.

E. Fire Insurance

9. (1187,L1,60) (d) A person who insures with multiple policies can only collect the proportionate amount of the loss from each insurer. The limit of recovery is the value of the loss. In this situation, the purchase of insurance from Beek results in Sly obtaining the recovery from both Beek and Riff. Since the total recovery is limited to $20,000, Riff will not be required to pay the full amount but rather only its proportionate share. Answer (a) is incorrect because the insured is protected against his/her own negligence or carelessness and this is not a defense of the insurer. However, intentional acts of the insured would prevent recovery. Answer (b) is incorrect because Sly insured the warehouse for $40,000 which is 80% of the fair market value of the building at the time the damage occurred and, thus, does satisfy the coinsurance clause. Answer (c) is incorrect because Sly's failure to notify Riff of the second policy does not affect Sly's right to recovery from Riff. The amount of the recovery has been altered but not the right to a recovery.

10. (578,L1,17) (c) Where both the owner and a mortgagee are insured under a policy, typically a loss payable clause will allow the mortgagee to collect to the extent of his loss. Answer (d) is incorrect because the policy is probably open or unvalued rather than a stated value policy. Unless it is a stated value policy, the insurance company will only be liable for the smaller of the policy face value or the FMV of the loss at the time of the loss. Answer (b) is incorrect because a mortgagee has an insurable interest and can independently obtain a fire insurance policy on mortgaged property. Answer (a) is incorrect because an owner of property can purchase any amount of title insurance that the insurance company agrees to sell.

E.5. Coinsurance Clause

11. (1189,L1,59) (a) A coinsurance clause applies when there has been partial destruction of property. The coinsurance feature of property insurance requires the insured to "self-insure" part of the property when partial destruction occurs. Coinsurance prevents the insured from carrying only a minimal amount of coverage and recovering the full amount of damages each time a partial destruction occurs. Using the coinsurance formula in this situation leads to a loss recovery of $8,000 calculated as follows:

$$\frac{\text{Fair Value of Policy}}{\substack{\text{Fair value of property} \\ \text{at time of storms}} \times \text{coinsurance \%}} \times \text{Loss} = \text{Recovery}$$

$$\frac{64,000}{120,000 \times 80\%} \times 12,000 = \$8,000$$

Therefore, answers (b), (c), and (d) are incorrect.

12. (1187,L1,58) (d) In most property insurance claims, the claim is for less than the face value of the policy. The coinsurance feature of property insurance requires the insured to "self-insure" part of property when partial destruction occurs. Coinsurance prevents the insured from carrying only a minimal amount of coverage and recovering the full amount of damages each time a partial destruction occurs. Answer (a) is incorrect because the rate of coinsurance is not fixed by law at 80%. However 80% is the normal stated percentage in a coinsurance clause. Answer (b) is incorrect because the coinsurance feature has no bearing on the insurable interest requirement. Answer (c) is incorrect because the insured can insure for less than the coinsurance percentage. If a lesser amount of insurance is carried, the insured will receive less than the full amount of damages.

13. (1186,L1,60)   (c)   Under a coinsurance clause, the insured agrees to maintain insurance equal to a specified percentage value of his/her property. When a loss occurs, the insurer only pays a proportionate share if the insured has not carried the specified percentage. A coinsurance clause does not apply, however, when the property is completely destroyed. In this case, Long would be able to recover $60,000, the amount of the insurance policy because the property is totally destroyed. Thus, answers (a), (b), and (d) are all incorrect.

May 1990 Answers

14. (590,L1,59)   (c)   The recoverable loss is calculated as follows using the coinsurance formula:

$$\frac{\text{Amount of insurance policy}}{\begin{array}{c}\text{Fair value of property at}\\ \text{time of loss x coinsurance \%}\end{array}} \times \text{Actual Loss}$$

$$\frac{\$ \; 200,000}{\$300,000 \times .8} \times \$30,000 = \$25,000$$

Answers (a), (b), and (d) are therefore incorrect. Note also that in no case would the insured receive more than the amount of the insurance policy ($200,000).

15. (590,L1,60)   (d)   A business enterprise has an insurable interest in the life of key employees. In this situation, Vick has an insurable interest in Orr since Orr may be considered a key employee (Vick relies heavily on Orr's ability to market). Unlike an insurable interest in property which must be present at the time the loss occurs, an insurable interest in life must only be present at the time the policy is purchased. Vick purchased an insurance policy on Orr's life while Orr was still employed by Vick. Therefore, regardless of whether Orr is employed by Vick at the time of death, Vick will be entitled to its share of the proceeds. Answer (a) is incorrect because although Orr's spouse does have an insurable interest in Orr, it is not needed here because the spouse is a third party beneficiary under the insurance contract. Answer (b) is incorrect because Orr's spouse will be entitled to only half of the proceeds, and Vick will be entitled to the other half of the proceeds. Answer (c) is incorrect because in this situation it is irrelevant that Vick is not a creditor or relative of Orr. Note, however, that a creditor has an insurable interest in a debtor and certain relatives may have an insurable interest in each other.

Answer Outline

Problem 1   Coinsurance, Standard Mortgagee,
                  and Pro Rata Clauses (1182,L5a)

Part a.

1. Jackson will recover $150,000 from Eagle
    Fire insurance policy contains 80% coin-
      surance clause
        Jackson must carry an amount of insur-
          ance equal to 80% of FMV of Parksdale
          plant
            In order to recover full amount of
            loss
        Jackson did not insure property to
          required 80% of its value
            Becomes a coinsurer and must propor-
              tionally share with Eagle the loss
              suffered

$$\frac{\text{Amount of insurance}}{\left(\begin{array}{c}\text{Coinsurance}\\ \text{percentage x FMV}\\ \text{of property}\end{array}\right)} \times \begin{array}{c}\text{Amount}\\ \text{of loss}\end{array} = \text{Recovery}$$

2. Second National Bank will receive $106,000
      and Jackson will receive $44,000
    Insurance policy contains "standard mort-
      gagee clause"
        Proceeds applied first to mortgagee
          In satisfaction of mortgage debt
          Any surplus paid to mortgagor
3. Jackson will recover $300,000 from Eagle
    Yuma warehouse was totally destroyed
        Coinsurance provision only applies to
          partial destruction of insured property
    Amount of recovery limited to face value
      of insurance policy
4. Jackson will recover $45,000 from the
      insurance companies
    Fire insurance policies contain 80%
      coinsurance clause
        Jackson must carry an amount of
          insurance equal to 80% of FMV of Rye
          City garage
            In order to recover full amount of
            loss
        Jackson did not insure property to
          required 80% of its value
            Becomes coinsurer and must propor-
              tionally share with the insurance
              companies the loss suffered

$$\frac{\text{Amount of insurance policies}}{\left(\begin{array}{c}\text{Coinsurance}\\ \text{percentage x FMV}\\ \text{of property}\end{array}\right)} \times \begin{array}{c}\text{Amount}\\ \text{of loss}\end{array} = \text{Recovery}$$

5. Queen will be obligated to pay $30,000
    Insurance policies contain a pro rata
      clause

If insured has multiple insurance
  policies covering same property
    Loss must be apportioned among the
      insurers
    Each insurer is liable for its pro rata
      share of loss

$$\frac{\begin{array}{c}\text{Amount of}\\ \text{insurance coverage}\\ \text{from Queen}\end{array}}{\begin{array}{c}\text{Total amount}\\ \text{of insurance}\\ \text{coverage}\end{array}} \times \begin{array}{c}\text{Liability}\\ \text{due to}\\ \text{fire}\end{array} = \begin{array}{c}\text{Pro rata}\\ \text{share}\end{array}$$

Unofficial Answer
(Author Modified)

Problem 1   Coinsurance, Standard Mortgagee,
                  and Pro Rata Clauses (1182,L5a)

Part a.

1. Under a fire insurance policy that con-
    tains an 80% coinsurance clause, the insured
    must carry an amount of insurance equal to 80%
    of the value of the property insured in order
    to recover any loss in full up to the face
    amount of the policy, but if the insured
    carries an amount of insurance less than the
    80%, s/he becomes a coinsurer and must propor-
    tionally bear with the insurance company any
    loss suffered due to partial destruction of
    the property.
       Jackson did not insure its property to the
    required 80% of its value; therefore, its
    recovery would be computed on the following
    basis:

$$\frac{\text{Amount of insurance}}{\left(\begin{array}{c}\text{Coinsurance percentage x}\\ \text{FMV of property}\end{array}\right)} \times \begin{array}{c}\text{Amount}\\ \text{of loss}\end{array} = \text{Recovery}$$

$$\frac{\$600,000}{80\% \times \$1,000,000} \times \$200,000 = \$150,000$$

2. The total amount of recovery from the fire
    loss was $150,000. Second National Bank will
    receive $106,000 and Jackson will receive
    $44,000. The insurance policy contained a
    "standard mortgagee clause" which provides
    that in the event of loss, the proceeds will
    be applied first to the mortgagee (Second
    National Bank) in satisfaction of the mortgage
    debt (including accrued interest) and any sur-
    plus will be paid to the owner of the prop-
    erty, i.e., mortgagor (Jackson).

3. Jackson will recover the face value of the
    insurance policy from Eagle. The application
    of a coinsurance provision contained in a fire
    insurance policy is limited to partial de-
    struction of the insured property. When the
    property is totally destroyed, as was the Yuma
    warehouse, the coinsurance provision has no

relevance. Since the value of Jackson's Yuma warehouse, at the time of total destruction, exceeded the policy coverage, Jackson's recovery will be limited to the face value of the insurance policy ($300,000).

4. Since the insurance policy contained an 80% coinsurance clause, the insured (Jackson) must carry an amount of insurance equal to 80% of the value of the property insured in order to recover any loss in full. Jackson did not insure its property to the required 80% of its value; therefore, it becomes a coinsurer and must proportionally bear with the insurance companies any loss suffered due to partial destruction of the property.

Jackson's recovery from the insurance companies would be computed on the following basis:

$$\frac{\text{Amount of ins. policies}}{\left(\text{Coinsurance percentage x FMV of property}\right)} \times \text{Amount of loss} = \text{Recovery}$$

$$\frac{\$50,000 + \$100,000}{80\% \times \$250,000} \times \$60,000 = \$45,000$$

5. A pro rata clause provides that if the insured has multiple fire insurance policies covering the same property, any loss must be apportioned among the insurers in the ratio that the amount of insurance issued by each insurer bears to the total amount of the insurance procured, and each insurer is liable to the insured for its pro rata share of such loss.

Consequently, since the total insurance coverage on the garage was $150,000, with Queen providing $100,000 of this, Queen must pay two-thirds of the liability due to the fire loss.

$$\frac{\text{Amount of insurance issued by Queen}}{\text{Total amount of insurance coverage}} \times \text{Liability due to fire} = \text{Queen's pro rata share}$$

$$\frac{\$100,000}{\$50,000 + \$100,000} \times \$45,000 = \$30,000$$

Answer Outline

Problem 2   Insurable Interests (1188,L2)

Starr's first assertion is correct
An oral modification to existing contract is not enforceable if modification is within Statute of Frauds
A modification of contract for sale of real estate falls within provisions of Statute of Frauds
Memo sent to Starr was not effective because it was not signed by Starr, the party to be charged

The modification to reduce the purchase price is not enforceable due to lack of Birk receiving any new consideration
Birk's failure to pay full contract price constitutes breach of contract
Starr's second assertion is correct
To have insurable interest in property there must be both a legal interest and a possibility of loss
The insurable interest need only be present at time of loss
Starr had an insurable interest on date of loss
Starr's third assertion is correct
Starr met coinsurance requirement under Pica's policy
Starr's fourth assertion is incorrect
Starr is only entitled to 80% as Pica's liability is limited to amount its policy bears to total amount of insurance on warehouse

Unofficial Answer

Problem 2   Insurable Interests (1188,L2)

Starr's first assertion, that Birk has breached the contract with Starr because Birk failed to close the transaction and buy the warehouse at a price of $200,000, is correct. An oral agreement modifying an enforceable existing contract is not enforceable if the modification is within the Statute of Frauds. A contract for the sale of real estate or a modification of such a contract falls within the provisions of the Statute of Frauds and therefore a writing signed by the party to be charged is required. The fact that Birk sent a signed memo to Starr is not effective because it was not signed by Starr. Furthermore, the agreement to reduce the purchase price to $190,000 is not enforceable because Birk did not give any consideration for the modification. Birk had a pre-existing obligation to purchase the warehouse for $200,000 and gave no new consideration for the modification of the price. The fact that Birk may have acted in good faith as a result of the decline in value of real estate and rise in interest rates will not be sufficient to make the oral agreement enforceable against Starr. Therefore, Birk's failure to pay $200,000 as required by the July 1 contract constitutes a breach of that contract.

Starr's second assertion, that it has an insurable interest in the warehouse covered by the Pica policy, is correct. To constitute an insurable interest the element of financial or economic loss to the insured must be present. Furthermore, the insurable interest must be

present at the time of the loss but need not
be present at the time the policy was issued.
Under the facts of this case, Starr had an
insurable interest on the date of the loss
(October 30) since it owned the warehouse on
that date. Whether Starr had an insurable
interest on February 15 will not affect
Starr's right to recover from Pica.

Starr's third assertion, that it has met
the coinsurance requirement under Pica's
policy, is correct.

Starr's fourth assertion, that Starr is
entitled to recover the entire $80,000 from
Pica, is incorrect. Starr is only entitled to
receive $64,000 from Pica calculated as
follows:

$$\frac{\$160,000 \text{ (Amount of Insurance Coverage with Pica)}}{\$200,000 \text{ (Total Amount of Insurance on Warehouse)}} \times \$80,000 \text{ (Amount to be Paid)} = \$64,000$$

Thus, Pica's liability is limited to the
amount its policy bears to the total amount of
insurance on the warehouse.

Multiple Choice Questions (1-21)

1. The last will and testament of Jean Bond
left various specific property and sums of
money to relatives and friends. She left the
residue of her estate equally to her favorite
niece and nephew. Which of the various properties described below will become a part of
Bond's estate and be distributed in accordance
with her last will and testament?
    a. A joint savings account which listed
her sister, who is still living, as
the joint tenant.
    b. The entire family homestead which
she had owned in joint tenancy with
her older brother who predeceased
her and which was still recorded as
jointly owned.
    c. Several substantial gifts that she
made in contemplation of death to
various charities.
    d. A life insurance policy which
designated a former partner as the
beneficiary.

2. A personal representative of an estate
would breach fiduciary duties if the personal
representative
    a. Combined personal funds with funds
of the estate so that both could
purchase treasury bills.
    b. Represented the estate in a lawsuit
brought against it by a disgruntled
relative of the decedent.
    c. Distributed property in satisfaction
of the decedent's debts.
    d. Engaged a non-CPA to prepare the
records for the estate's final
accounting.

3. Generally, an estate is liable for which
debts owed by the decedent at the time of
death?
    a. All of the decedent's debts.
    b. Only debts secured by the decedent's
property.
    c. Only debts covered by the Statute of
Frauds.
    d. None of the decedent's debts.

4. Krieg's will created a trust to take
effect upon Krieg's death. The will named
Krieg's spouse as both the trustee and
personal representative (executor) of the
estate. The will provided that all of Krieg's
securities were to be transferred to the trust
and named Krieg's child as the beneficiary of
the trust. Under the circumstances,
    a. Krieg has created a testamentary
trust.

    b. Krieg's spouse may not serve as both
the trustee and personal representative because of the inherent conflict of interest.
    c. Krieg has created an inter vivos
trust.
    d. The trust is invalid because it will
not become effective until Krieg's
death.

5. To create a valid inter vivos trust to
hold personal property, the trust must be
    a. In writing and signed by the settlor
(creator).
    b. Specific concerning the property to
be held in trust.
    c. Irrevocable.
    d. In writing and signed by the
trustee.

6. Ed Roth, a retired businessman, plans to
travel extensively during the upcoming year.
Roth is concerned that he may not be able to
handle the daily activities associated with
his financial affairs. As a solution, Roth
created a trust and transferred most of his
investment assets to Long Bank, as trustee,
naming himself as the trust's sole beneficiary. Which of the following statements is
correct?
    a. The trust is invalid under the
merger doctrine since the creator
and the beneficiary are the same
person.
    b. Long has a fiduciary duty to the
trust but not to Roth as beneficiary.
    c. Roth has created a testamentary
trust.
    d. Roth has created an inter vivos
trust.

7. With respect to trusts, which of the
following states an Invalid legal conclusion?
    a. The trustee must obtain the consent
of the majority of the beneficiaries
if a major change in the investment
portfolio of the trust is to be
made.
    b. For federal income tax purposes, a
trust is entitled to an exemption
similar to that of an individual
although not equal in amount.
    c. Both the life beneficiaries of a
trust and the ultimate takers have
rights against the trustee, and the
trustee is accountable to them.
    d. A trust is a separate taxable entity
for federal income tax purposes.

8. On January 1, 1988, Dix transferred certain assets into a trust. The assets consisted of Lux Corp. bonds with a face amount of $500,000 and an interest rate of 12%. The trust instrument named Dix as trustee, Dix's child as life beneficiary, and Dix's grandchild as remainderman. Interest on the bonds is payable semi-annually on May 1 and November 1. Dix had purchased the bonds at their face amount. As of January 1, 1988, the bonds had a fair market value of $600,000. The accounting period selected for the trust is a calendar year. The trust instrument is silent as to whether Dix may revoke the trust. Which of the following statements is correct?

    a. Dix is <u>not</u> a fiduciary because Dix is also the creator (settlor).

    b. The trust is invalid under the merger doctrine because Dix is both the creator and the trustee.

    c. A duty is owed by Dix to administer the trust property for the sole benefit of the beneficiaries.

    d. Dix has the implied right to revoke the trust without the court's permission.

9. Rusk properly created an inter vivos trust naming Gold as the trustee. The sole asset of the trust is an office building that is fully rented. Rental receipts exceed expenditures. The trust instrument is silent as to the allocation of items between principal and income. Which of the following statements is correct concerning Gold's responsibility as trustee?

    a. Gold's duty of loyalty will be breached by Gold's purchasing assets from the trust despite a provision in the trust agreement permitting such a purchase.

    b. Gold owes a duty of loyalty to the trust but <u>not</u> to the beneficiaries.

    c. Gold must exercise reasonable care and skill while performing the duties of a trustee.

    d. Gold will be free from personal liability with regard to all contracts entered into by Gold on behalf of the trust absent fraud by Gold.

10. Which of the following statements is correct with respect to a trustee?

    a. The trustee is liable for losses which result from a delegation of any duty by him.

    b. The trustee can <u>not</u> purchase property from the trust even if the trust instrument authorizes it.

    c. In the absence of a provision otherwise in the trust instrument, the trustee has the responsibility to invest the trust property so as to produce income.

    d. The trustee will be free from personal liability with regard to all contracts entered into by him on behalf of the trust and on debts incurred by the trust.

11. A trust was created in 1980 to provide funds for sending the settlor's child through medical school. The trust agreement specified that the trust was to terminate in 1987. The child entered medical school in 1983, took a leave of absence in 1984, and died in 1986. This trust terminated in

    a. 1983
    b. 1984
    c. 1986
    d. 1987

12. A distinguishing feature between the making of an inter vivos gift and the creation of a trust is that

    a. A gift may be made orally whereas a trust must be in a signed writing.

    b. Generally, a gift is irrevocable whereas a trust may be revoked in certain cases.

    c. In order to create a valid trust, the creator must receive some form of consideration.

    d. The beneficiary of a trust must be notified of the trust's creation.

13. Fine wishes to establish an inter vivos trust for the benefit of his daughter Sally, naming Sally as the sole income beneficiary for 20 years and as the sole remainder beneficiary of the corpus. The intended trust will fail if the instrument creating the trust

    a. Provides for the trustee to serve without compensation, bond, or other security.

    b. Is <u>not</u> supported by any consideration.

    c. Fails to name a trustee.

    d. Names Sally as the sole trustee.

14. On January 1, 1988, Dix transferred certain assets into a trust. The assets consisted of Lux Corp. bonds with a face amount of $500,000 and an interest rate of 12%. The trust instrument named Dix as trustee, Dix's child as life beneficiary, and Dix's grandchild as remainderman. Interest on the bonds is payable semi-annually on May 1 and November 1. Dix had purchased the bonds at their face amount. As of January 1, 1988,

the bonds had a fair market value of $600,000.
The accounting period selected for the trust
is a calendar year. The trust instrument is
silent as to whether Dix may revoke the trust.
Assuming the trust is valid, how should the
amount of interest received in 1988 be allocated between principal and income if the
trust instrument is otherwise silent?

	Principal	Income
a.	$0	$60,000
b.	$0	$72,000
c.	$10,000	$50,000
d.	$12,000	$60,000

15. Rusk properly created an inter vivos
trust naming Gold as the trustee. The sole
asset of the trust is an office building that
is fully rented. Rental receipts exceed
expenditures. The trust instrument is silent
as to the allocation of items between principal and income. Among the items to be allocated by Gold during the year are insurance
proceeds received as a result of fire damage
to the building and the mortgage interest
payments made during the year. Which of the
following items is properly allocable to
principal?

	Insurance proceeds on building	Current mortgage interest payments
a.	Yes	No
b.	Yes	Yes
c.	No	Yes
d.	No	No

16. On June 16, 1987, Eble placed 800 shares
of Singh Corp.'s common stock in a trust for
the benefit of Eble's child. On June 1, 1987,
Singh's board of directors had declared a cash
dividend of $2 per share on Singh's common
stock. Payment was made on July 30, 1987 to
shareholders of record on June 30, 1987. What
amount of the dividend should be allocated to
trust income?

    a. $0
    b. $ 800
    c. $1,200
    d. $1,600

17. Ryan is the trustee of the Carr Family
Trust. The assets of the trust are various
income-producing real estate properties. The
trust instrument is silent as to the allocation of items between principal and income.
Among the items to be allocated by Ryan during
the first year were depreciation and the cost
of a new roof. Which are properly allocable
to income?

	Depreciation	Cost of a new roof
a.	No	No
b.	Yes	No
c.	Yes	Yes
d.	No	Yes

18. A trust agreement is silent on the
allocation of the following trust receipts
between principal and income:

- Cash dividends on investments in common stock $1,000
- Royalties from property
  subject to depletion $2,000

What is the total amount of the trust receipts
that should be allocated to trust income?
    a. $0
    b. $1,000
    c. $2,000
    d. $3,000

19. Shepard created an inter vivos trust for
the benefit of his children with the remainder
to his grandchildren upon the death of his
last surviving child. The trust consists of
both real and personal property. One of the
assets is an apartment building. In administering the trust and allocating the receipts
and disbursements, which of the following
would be **improper**?
    a.   The allocation of forfeited rental
         security deposits to income.
    b.   The allocation to principal of the
         annual service fee of the rental
         collection agency.
    c.   The allocation to income of the
         interest on the mortgage on the
         apartment building.
    d.   The allocation to income of the
         payment of the insurance premiums on
         the apartment building.

20. Harper transferred assets into a trust
under which Drake is entitled to receive the
income for life. Upon Drake's death, the
remaining assets are to be paid to Neal. In
1988, the trust received rent of $1,000,
royalties of $3,000, cash dividends of $5,000,
and proceeds of $7,000 from the sale of stock
previously received by the trust as a stock
dividend. Both Drake and Neal are still
alive. How much of the receipts should be
distributed to Drake?
    a. $ 4,000
    b. $ 8,000
    c. $ 9,000
    d. $16,000

21. The Marquis Trust has been properly
created and it qualifies as a real estate
investment trust (REIT) for federal income tax
purposes. As such, it will
    a.   Be taxed as any other trust for
         income tax purposes.
    b.   Have been created under the Federal
         Trust Indenture Act.
    c.   Provide limited liability for the
         parties investing in the trust.
    d.   Be exempt from the Securities Act of
         1933.

May 1990 Question

Repeat Question

(590,L1,10) Identical/similar to item 15 above

Problems

Problem 1   (584,L4)

(15 to 20 minutes)

Ted and his wife Judy own Redacre in a tenancy by the entirety. Redacre is a lot by the seaside on which they plan someday to build a summer home. Ted also owns Bigacre in a joint tenancy with Lois, Clark, and Jeff, each owning a 1/4 undivided interest. Bigacre is a large parcel of investment acreage which produces no current income. Ted and Judy have had several arguments about the raising of their son Peter, now age 18, who Judy believes has exhibited a tendency toward irresponsibility. Ted, as a result, has decided to take certain steps on his own to protect Peter's future financial security.

Ted plans to establish a trust with Guardem Trust Company and Peter as co-trustees. He plans to transfer Redacre to the trust along with $100,000 in cash. The $100,000 is to be used to purchase Ted's interest in Bigacre. Although Judy knows of the steps being taken, she has not agreed to them. Accordingly, Ted does not plan to have her participate in the establishment of the trust or in any of the transactions or paperwork involved.

The trust will provide that all income is to be paid to Peter, with final distribution of all trust assets to Peter upon his reaching age 40. The trust will also permit Peter after reaching age 21, to remove Guardem as trustee leaving himself as successor sole trustee.

Required:

Answer the following, setting forth reasons for any conclusions stated.
If Ted's plans are carried out:
1. What interest will the trust have in Redacre and Bigacre?
2. What interests will the remaining three parties have in Bigacre, if Clark dies subsequent to the transfer of Ted's interest in Bigacre to the trust?
3. Will the requirements of a valid trust be met?
4. Will the purchase of Bigacre from Ted be a proper exercise of the trustees' duties?
5. What effect would Peter's exercise of his right to remove Guardem as a trustee after he reaches 21, have on the trust and the ownership of Bigacre?

Problem 2   (587,L5)

(15 to 20 minutes)

John Reed, a wealthy businessman, established an inter vivos on January 1, 1986, to provide for the financial needs of his son and wife. The written trust agreement signed by Reed provided for income to his wife, Myrna, for her life with the remainder to his son, Rodney. Reed named Mini Bank as the sole trustee and transferred stocks, bonds, and two commercial buildings to the trust. The accounting period selected for the trust was the calendar year.

During the first year of the trust's existence, Mini made the following allocations to principal and income arising out of transactions involving the trust property:

• With regard to the sale of $25,000 of stock, $20,000 to income representing the gain on the sale of stock and $5,000 to principal representing the cost basis of the stock.
• $95,000 to income from rental receipts earned and received after the trust was created.
• $6,000 to income and $2,000 to principal as a result of a stock dividend of 400 shares of $5 par value common stock at a time when the stock was selling for $20 per share.
• $10,000 to income for bond interest received and which is payable semi-annually on April 1 and October 1.
• $35,000 to principal as a result of mortgage payments made by the trust on the commercial buildings.

The instrument creating the trust is silent as to the allocation of the trust receipts and disbursements to principal and income.

Required:

Answer the following, setting forth reasons for any conclusions stated.

a. Have the requirements been met for the creation of valid inter vivos trust?
b. Indicate the proper allocation to principal and income of the trust receipts and disbursements described above under the majority rules, ignoring the tax effect of each transaction.

Multiple Choice Answers

1. b	6. d	10. c	14. c	18. d
2. a	7. a	11. c	15. a	19. b
3. a	8. c	12. b	16. d	20. c
4. a	9. c	13. d	17. b	21. c
5. b				

Multiple Choice Answer Explanations

A. Estates

1. (581,L1,50) (b) A joint tenancy is a form of concurrent property ownership in which the joint tenants have a right of survivorship in the property concurrently held. Thus, if a joint tenant dies, that tenant's interest in the property is divided equally among the surviving joint tenants. The deceased tenant's interest in the property will not pass to his heirs. Since Jean had full ownership of the property upon her brother's death and on her death, such property is properly included in her estate. Answer (a) is incorrect because, upon Jean's death, her sister will receive full ownership of the savings account regardless of any provision to the contrary in a will. Answer (c) is incorrect since gifts made in contemplation of death are irrevocable once made. Answer (d) is incorrect since a life insurance policy will pass to the named beneficiary without regard to the will of the deceased.

B. Administration of Estates

2. (589,L1,19) (a) Personal representatives of estates owe a fiduciary duty to act in the best interests of the estate rather than in their own best interests. As part of this duty, they must keep the estate property separate from their own and be accountable for both estate assets and their own actions. Thus, the combining of personal funds with funds of the estate would be a violation of the fiduciary duty. Answer (b) is incorrect because the fiduciary should defend the estate in a lawsuit brought against it. Answer (c) is incorrect because the decedent's debts validly come out of the estate. Answer (d) is incorrect because although an accounting of the estate should be accomplished, there is no requirement that it be done by a CPA.

3. (589,L1,17) (a) An estate is a legal entity holding title to a person's property after his/her death. The estate will be liable for all debts owed by the decedent at the time of death. Answer (b) is incorrect because unsecured as well as secured debts are to be paid. Answer (c) is incorrect because all valid claims are to be paid whether or not they are covered by the Statute of Frauds. Answer (d) is incorrect because the estate is liable for all debts as described above.

C. Trusts

4. (1188,L1,6) (a) A testamentary trust is a trust that takes effect on the death of the settlor. Answer (b) is incorrect because a trustee of a testamentary trust may also serve as the executor of the estate from which the trust was formed without causing a conflict of interest. Answer (c) is incorrect since an inter vivos trust is to take effect while the settlor is still living. Answer (d) is incorrect because the fact that a testamentary trust will not become effective until Krieg's death will not invalidate the trust.

5. (588,L1,10) (b) In order to create a valid inter vivos trust, the trust must specifically identify the property to be held in trust. Answers (a) and (d) are incorrect because an inter vivos trust need only be in writing and signed by the settlor if the property to be held in trust is real property, not personal property. Answer (c) is incorrect since a settlor may reserve the right to revoke the trust when creating a valid inter vivos trust.

6. (586,L1,51) (d) A valid inter vivos trust requires the essential trust elements (settlor, trustee, trust property, and beneficiary) and, in addition, requires that the trust property be transferred to the trustee during the settlor's life. The factual situation indicates that these conditions have been met. Answer (a) is incorrect because the settlor (creator) and the beneficiary may be the same person; however, the trustee must be a separate person in this case to avoid creating an invalid trust (i.e. when settlor [creator], beneficiary, and trustee are the same person, a trust becomes invalid). Answer (b) is incorrect because the trustee owes a fiduciary duty to the beneficiaries of the trust. Answer (c) is incorrect because in a testamentary trust, the trust property is transferred to the trustee upon the death of the settlor.

7. (581,L1,49) (a) A trust is a fiduciary relationship wherein one person (trustee) holds legal title to property for the benefit of another (beneficiary). A trustee has the power to do what is necessary to fulfill the terms of the trust. A trustee cannot speculate, must diversify and can make major changes in an investment portfolio without the consent of beneficiaries. Answer (b) is not incorrect because a simple trust is entitled to a $300 per year exemption for federal tax

purposes which is similar to an individual's exemption. Answer (c) is not incorrect because a trustee is a fiduciary to the beneficiaries and can take no personal advantage from his position. All beneficiaries can sue for mismanagement, conversion, or waste by the trustee. A trustee must also keep trust assets separate from his personal assets and be accountable for both trust assets and his actions. Answer (d) is not an incorrect statement since a trust is a separate taxable entity for federal income tax purposes although it may not be subject to any tax.

D. Administration of Trusts

8. (1188,L1,8) (c) A trustee owes a fiduciary duty to the beneficiary(ies) of the trust. Thus, Dix, as trustee, owes a duty to administer the trust property for the sole benefit of the beneficiaries. Answer (a) is incorrect since Dix, as trustee, is a fiduciary. Answer (b) is incorrect because a trustee may also be the settlor without invalidating the trust. Answer (d) is incorrect since a trust may be revoked by the settlor only if the power of revocation is specifically reserved in the trust. A settlor never has the implied right to revoke the trust.

9. (588,L1,12) (c) A trustee has a fiduciary relationship with the beneficiary. Thus, the trustee is required to exercise reasonable care and skill while performing his/her duties. Answer (a) is incorrect because a trust agreement may validly include a provision whereby the trustee has the right to purchase assets from the trust. In such a case, the trustee's duty of loyalty would not be breached upon exercise of this right unless the trustee took unfair advantage of the trust in exercising this right. Answer (b) is incorrect because a trustee owes loyalty to the beneficiary since the trustee administers the trust for the benefit of the beneficiary. Answer (d) is incorrect because the trustee is personally liable on contracts made on behalf of the trust unless the contract states otherwise. However, the trustee has the right of reimbursement from trust income.

10. (586,L1,53) (c) In the absence of a provision stating otherwise in the trust instrument, the trustee has the responsibility to invest the trust property so as to produce income. Answer (a) is incorrect because a trustee is not liable for losses which result from a delegation of any duty by the trustee, as long as the delegatee acted in a reasonable and prudent manner in performing the delegated duties. However, in the event that the dele-

gatee did not act in a reasonably prudent manner, the trustee would be liable for the resulting losses. Answer (b) is incorrect because a trustee may purchase property from the trust if the trust instrument authorizes this purchase or the beneficiaries consent to such purchase. In both situations the transaction must be fair and reasonable, since the trustee has a duty of undivided loyalty to the beneficiaries. Answer (d) is incorrect since a trustee is personally liable on all contracts entered into on behalf of the trust unless otherwise stipulated in the contract. However, the trustee may be reimbursed from trust income.

E. Termination of Trusts

11. (589,L1,20) (c) A trust terminates in several ways such as at the end of the period stated in the trust, achievement of the trust purpose, or failure of the trust purpose. In this situation, the purpose of the trust was to fund medical school for the settlor's child. When the settlor's child died in 1986, the trust purpose failed. Answer (a) is incorrect because the trust's purpose was to fund the medical school education, not just the entering into medical school. Answer (b) is incorrect because a leave of absence does not cause the trust purpose to fail. Answer (d) is incorrect because although the trust stated it would terminate in 1987, it had already terminated in 1986 when the trust purpose failed.

12. (1185,L1,58) (b) Once the necessary elements of a gift are present, the gift may not be revoked. However, a trust may be legally revoked if the settlor has reserved the power to revoke the trust, or if the settlor and beneficiaries of an irrevocable trust mutually agree to terminate the trust. Answer (a) is incorrect because a trust need only be in writing if it involves real property; all other trusts may be created orally. Answer (c) is incorrect because a contract need not be present in order to create a valid trust. Answer (d) is incorrect since notification of the beneficiary is not a necessary element to create a trust.

13. (585,L1,58) (d) A trust, by definition, is a fiduciary relationship in which one person holds legal title to property for the benefit of another person. If Sally, the sole beneficiary, is named a sole trustee, then merger of the equitable and legal titles occurs, and hence there is no trust. Answer (a) is incorrect because the trust will not fail due to the fact that the trustee is not being compensated. Answer (b) is incorrect because

there is no requirement that the instrument creating the trust be supported by consideration. Answer (c) is incorrect because normally if the instrument fails to name a trustee the court will appoint one.

F. Allocation Between Principal and Income

14. (1188,L1,9) (c) As of January 1, 1988, the value of the asset transferred to the trust would include $10,000 ($500,000 x 12% x 2 months/12 months) of interest accrued from November 1, 1987 to the date of transfer of the assets to the trust. Thus, this accrued interest should be considered a portion of the principal of the trust. Accordingly, that portion of the interest received during 1988 would be allocated to principal while the remaining $50,000 ($500,000 x 12% x 10 months/12 months) would be allocated to income as the actual interest earned while the trust held the bonds. Therefore, answers (a), (b), and (d) are incorrect.

15. (588,L1,11) (a) According to the Uniform Principal and Income Act, insurance proceeds received as a result of damage to trust property are to be allocated to principal, while interest paid on a loan owed by the trust is to be allocated to income. Therefore, answers (b), (c), and (d) are incorrect.

16. (1187,L1,16) (d) In this situation, payment of the cash dividends was made on July 30, 1987 to shareholders of record on June 30, 1987. Since Eble placed the shares in the trust prior to June 30, 1987, the trust is entitled to receive the dividends. Under the Uniform Principal and Income Act a cash dividend should be allocated by a trustee exclusively to income. Thus, $1,600 (800 x $2 per share) will be properly allocated to trust income. Therefore, answers (a), (b), and (c) are incorrect.

17. (586,L1,52) (b) In allocating items between principal and income, ordinary expenses are chargeable to the trust income, and extra ordinary expenditures (e.g., improvements) are chargeable to trust principal. Depreciation is considered to be an ordinary expense and is properly allocated to income, while the cost of a new roof is considered an improvement, which is properly allocated to principal. Thus, answers (a), (c), and (d) are incorrect.

18. (589,L1,18) (d) Unless the trust agreement states otherwise, rent, interest, cash dividends, and royalties are allocated to the trust income rather than principal. Therefore, both the $1,000 and the $2,000 are allocated to trust income causing answer (d) to be correct.

19. (581,L1,51) (b) An inter vivos trust comes into existence while the settlor (grantor) is living. The allocation of trust items to principal and income is governed by the Uniform Principal and Income Act (adopted by most states). Allocations made to trust principal include: original trust property, proceeds and gains from sale of trust property, insurance received on destruction of property, new property purchased with principal or proceeds from the principal, stock dividends and splits, and a reserve for depreciation. Disbursements from trust principal are for reduction of indebtedness, litigation over trust property, permanent improvements, and costs related to purchase/sale of trust property. Income includes profits from trust principal, e.g., rent, interest, cash dividends, and royalties. Expenses from income include interest, insurance premiums, taxes, repairs, and depreciation. The annual service fee should be allocated to income because it is an expense associated with administration and management of trust property. It should not be allocated to principal. Answers (a), (c), and (d) are all proper allocations to income.

20. (1189,L1,8) (c) In the absence of specific trust terms that define income differently, any allocation between income and principal is governed by the Uniform Principal and Income Act. Under this law, income would include the rent of $1,000, the royalties of $3,000, and the cash dividends of $5,000. The receipt of stock dividends or the sale of the stock dividends is treated as principal rather than income. Answers (a), (b), and (d) are therefore incorrect.

H. Real Estate Investment Trusts (REIT)

21. (1180,L1,45) (c) The certificate holders (owners) of a real estate investment trust have limited liability. Their liability is limited to their investment in the trust similar to the limited liability of a shareholder in a corporation and a limited partner. Thus, answer (c) is correct. Answer (d) is incorrect because the sale of an interest in a real estate investment trust is the sale of a security under the Securities Act of 1933. Consequently, the seller of these interests would have to comply with the registration requirements of this Act. A real estate investment trust does not fall within the

provisions of the Federal Trust Indenture
Act. This makes answer (b) incorrect. The
normal trust, as distinguished from a real
estate investment trust, is a taxable entity
for income tax purposes, while a real estate
investment trust is not a taxable entity.
Ordinary income passes through to the investors and each investor pays income tax on
his/her share.

Answer Outline

Problem 1   Concurrent Ownership; Trust
             Requirements; Trustee's Duties;
             Termination of Trust (584,L4)

1. Trust has no interest in Redacre
     But has 1/4 interest in Bigacre as
       tenant in common
         Realty held as tenants by entirety may
           not be transferred without co-owner's
           consent
         Joint tenant may transfer interest in
           tenancy without consent of co-tenants
           Such transfer destroys joint tenancy
             of interest transferred
2. Trust acquires no further interest in
     Bigacre upon Clark's death
       No right of survivorship to tenant in
         common
       Jeff and Lois as joint tenants have right
         of survivorship
           They own 3/8 interest in Bigacre as
             joint tenants
3. Requirements of valid trust met
     Property (res) transferred to co-
       trustees for benefit of Peter
       (beneficiary)
         Intent to create for lawful purpose is
           evident
         Sole beneficiary may act as co-trustee
4. Trustees have fiduciary duty to manage
     trust for benefit of beneficiaries
       Trustees required to invest according to
         standards of prudent investor
           Purchase of Bigacre meets standard of
             prudent investor if amount paid is
             fair and future value expected to
             increase
5. Removal of Guardem as trustee terminates
     trust with interest in Bigacre vesting in
     Peter
       Trust terminates when sole beneficiary
         and sole trustee are same person
         Legal and equitable titles merge

Unofficial Answer

Problem 1   Concurrent Ownership; Trust
             Requirements; Trustee's Duties;
             Termination of Trust (584,L4)

1. The trust will have no interest in Redacre
but would have a one-quarter interest as
tenant in common in Bigacre. The attempted
transfer of realty held as tenants by the
entirety without the co-owner's consent does
not transfer the property. Therefore, Ted is
unable to transfer any portion of Redacre
since Judy has not consented to the transfer.
A joint tenant may transfer his interest in

the tenancy without the consent of the co-
tenants. However, such a transfer destroys
the joint tenancy of the interest transferred.
Therefore, the purchase of Ted's interest in
Bigacre gives the trust a one-quarter interest
in the property as tenant in common with
Clark, Lois, and Jeff remaining as joint tenants as to three-quarters of the property.

2. Despite the trust's one-quarter interest
in Bigacre, it acquires no additional interest
due to Clark's death, since there is no right
of survivorship with respect to a tenant in
common. However, Jeff and Lois will acquire
Clark's one-quarter interest by operation of
law, due to the right of survivorship feature
among joint tenants. Therefore, Jeff and Lois
will each own a three-eighths interest in Bigacre as joint tenants, whereas the trust will
retain its one-quarter interest as a tenant in
common.

3. A valid trust has been created. Ted, as
grantor or settlor, has transferred property
(res) to Guardem and Peter for the benefit of
Peter. Intent to create a trust is evident,
and the trust is established for a lawful purpose. It is proper for the sole beneficiary
to act as co-trustee.

4. The trustees have a fiduciary duty to
manage the trust for the benefit of the beneficiaries. In the absence of trust provisions
otherwise, the trustees are required to invest
in accordance with the standard of a prudent
man in the conduct of his own investments. A
trustee should ordinarily invest in income-
producing property. However, the purchase of
Bigacre by the trustees could meet this standard even though Bigacre is not currently
earning income if the amount paid is fair and
the future value may be expected to increase.

5. The trust would terminate and the interest
in Bigacre would vest in Peter if he exercises
his right to remove Guardem as trustee. As
sole trustee Peter would hold legal title, and
as sole beneficiary he would hold equitable
title. A trust terminates when the sole beneficiary and sole trustee are the same person
as legal and equitable title will be merged.

Answer Outline

Problem 2   Creation of Inter Vivos Trust;
             Allocation of Receipts and Dis-
             bursements between Principal and
             Income Beneficiaries (587,L5)

a. Requirements are met for creation of valid
     inter vivos trust
       Elements necessary:
         Creator transfers property to the
           trust with the intent to create a
           trust

Trust instrument designates a trustee
(Muni)
Trust set up for lawful purpose
Trust names income beneficiary and
remainderman (principal beneficiary)
b. Allocation of trust and disbursements to
principal and income
  • Stock rules--entire amount to princi-
     pal
  • Rental receipts--entire amount to
     income
  • Stock dividend--entire amount to prin-
     cipal
  • Bond interest received--$2,500 of
     accrued interest to principal, $7,500
     of earned interest to income
  • Mortgage payment--repayment of
     mortgage debt to principal, payments
     deemed to be interest to income

Unofficial Answer

Problem 2   Creation of Enter Vivos Trust;
            Allocation of Receipts and
            Disbursements between Principal
            and Income Beneficiaries (587,L5)

a. Yes. The elements necessary to set up a
valid inter vivos trust have been met. John
Reed as the creator (grantor or settlor)
transferred stocks, bonds, and buildings which
constituted the trust with a present intent to
create a trust. The trust instrument which
designated Mini as trustee was set up for a
lawful purpose and named Myrna as the income
beneficiary and Rodney as the remainderman.

b. Where the trust instrument is silent as to
the allocation of the trust receipts and disbursements to principal and income, the
following rules apply:

  With respect to the $25,000 proceeds on
the sale of the stock, most states require
that the entire $25,000 be allocated to
principal. Therefore, the allocation of
$20,000 to income and $5,000 to principal is
incorrect.
  The allocation of $95,000 in rental
receipts to income is correct since the entire
amount was earned and received after the
creation of the trust.
  The allocation of the stock dividend to
principal and income is incorrect in the vast
majority of states. Even under the minority
rule, an allocation of a stock dividend to
principal based on the par value of the shares
distributed is incorrect, i.e., 400 shares x
$5 par value = $2,000. Under the majority
rule, the entire stock dividend is allocated
to principal.
  The allocation of the full $10,000 bond
interest to income is incorrect since one-half
($2,500) of the semiannual payment received on

April 1, 1986, had already accrued when the
trust was created on January 1, 1986.
Therefore, the proper allocation should be
$2,500 to principal and $7,500 to income.
  The $35,000 of mortgage payments allocated
to principal is correct to the extent such
payments represent a repayment of the mortgage
debt. Any portion of such payments which are
deemed to be interest on the mortgage should
be allocated to income.

CHAPTER FOUR

FINANCIAL ACCOUNTING PROBLEMS AND SOLUTIONS

Financial accounting is the most extensively tested topic on both the accounting theory and accounting practice section of the examination.

Theory, tested from 1:30 to 5:00 Friday afternoon, consists of 60 multiple choice questions (60% of the theory grade) and 4 essay questions (40% of the theory grade). Generally 40 to 50 of the multiple choice questions concern financial accounting topics along with 2 or 3 of the essay questions. The remaining questions cover cost, managerial, and governmental accounting.

Practice, tested from 1:30 to 6:00 on Wednesday and Thursday afternoons, consists of 120 multiple choice questions (60% of the practice grade) in six problem "sets" of 20 multiple choice questions each. The practice sections also contain 4 practice problems (40% of the practice grade). The coverage of financial topics on the May 1984 examination (typical of recent exams) consisted of 60 multiple choice questions and 2½ practice problems. The remaining items cover federal taxation as well as cost, managerial, and governmental accounting. A complete analysis of recent examinations and the AICPA Revised Content Specification Outlines appear in Volume I, Outlines and Study Guides.

Each question is coded as to month, year, section, problem number, and multiple choice question number. For example, (1189,P2,31) indicates November 1989, problem 2 of the Practice I section, multiple choice question number 31. Note that P = Practice I, Q = Practice II, and T = Theory. Some questions were altered to make them applicable due to changes in GAAP.

Module 22/Basic Theory and Financial Reporting (TREP)

	Exam reference	No. of minutes	Page no. Problem	Answer
A. Basic Concepts				
42 Multiple Choice			452	461
2 Practice Problems:				
1. Cash to Accrual Basis	1184,P5	40-50	458	467
2. Prepare a Balance Sheet	587,P5	40-50	460	470
B. Error Correction				
6 Multiple Choice			474	477
1 Practice Problem:				
1. Worksheet to Prepare Corrected Financial Statements	586,P5	40-50	475	478
C. Accounting Changes				
17 Multiple Choice			482	486
1 Essay Question:				
1. Types of Accounting Changes	586,T3	15-25	485	489
D. Financial Statements				
35 Multiple Choice			490	498
1 Essay Question and				
2 Practice Problems:				
1. Discontinued Operations and X/O Items	1189,T5	15-25	495	504
2. Income Statement Preparation	588,Q4	40-50	495	504
3. Prepare I/S; Reconcile Net Income to Taxable Income	589,P4	40-50	497	508

Module 23/Inventory (INVY)

	Exam reference	No. of minutes	Page no. Problem	Answer
50 Multiple Choice			512	521
5 Essay Questions				
1. Inventory Cost and LCM	589,T3	15-25	519	530
2. Acquisition Cost, LCM,				
Retail Method	588,T2	15-25	519	530
3. Inventory Cost and LCM	587,T3	15-25	519	531
4. Various Aspects of Inventory				
Accounting	1185,T3	15-25	520	532
5. Long-Term Contracts	586,T2	15-25	520	533

Module 24/Fixed Assets (FA)

	Exam reference	No. of minutes	Page no. Problem	Answer
64 Multiple Choice			534	545
3 Essay Questions and				
2 Practice Problems:				
1. Capital vs. Revenue Expendi-				
tures: Accounting and				
Reporting	1189,T2	15-25	542	555
2. PP&E Costs	587,T2	15-25	542	555
3. Acquisition Costs, Depreciation,				
and Asset Disposal	1188,T3	15-25	542	556
4. Changes in PP&E Accounts	1187,P4	40-50	542	557
5. Comprehensive PP&E Changes	1188,P4	45-55	543	561

Module 25/Monetary Current Assets and Current Liabilities (CACL)

	Exam reference	No. of minutes	Page no. Problem	Answer
67 Multiple Choice			565	578
5 Essay Questions				
1. Bad Debts and Reporting				
Notes Receivables	1186,T2	15-25	576	589
2. Sales Discounts Under Net				
Method, Factoring A/R, and				
Interest from N/R	1188,T2	15-25	576	589
3. Notes and Accounts Receivable	585,T3	15-25	576	590
4. Contingencies	1189,T3	15-25	577	591
5. Contingencies	1187,T4	15-25	577	592

Module 26/Present Value (PV)

	Exam reference	No. of minutes	Page no. Problem	Answer
A. Fundamentals				
14 Multiple Choice			593	596
1 Practice Problem:				
1. Long-Term Notes Receivable	584,P5	40-50	595	599
B. Bonds				
42 Multiple Choice			603	610
4 Essay Questions				
1. Issuance of Bonds	589,T4	15-25	608	617
2. Issuance, Extinguishment, and				
Conversion of Bonds	1187,T5	15-25	608	617
3. Issuance of Bonds	586,T5	15-25	608	618
4. Issuance of Bonds	585,T4	15-25	609	619
C. Debt Restructure				
6 Multiple Choice			621	622
D. Pensions				
25 Multiple Choice			624	629
2 Essay Questions				
1. Pension Terms and Accrual of				
Vacation Pay	1189,T4	15-25	628	633
2. Pensions: Basic Concepts	588,T5	15-25	628	633
E. Leases				
49 Multiple Choice			635	644
4 Essay Questions and				
1 Practice Problem:				
1. Capital Leases	589,T5	15-25	642	651
2. Rationale for Lease Capital-				
ization and Lessee Accounting	585,T2	15-25	642	651
3. Description of Lease Accounting	580,T3	15-25	642	652
4. Sale-Leaseback	588,T4	15-25	642	653
5. Long-Term Liabilities Section				
of Balance Sheet	1188,Q4	45-55	643	654

Module 27/Deferred Taxes (DFTX)

	Exam reference	No. of minutes	Page no. Problem	Answer
46 Multiple Choice			658	667
1 Essay Question				
1. Recording and Classifying				
Deferred Taxes	582,T4	15-25	666	676

Module 28/Stockholders' Equity (STK)

	Exam reference	No. of minutes	Problem	Answer
57 Multiple Choice			678	688
2 Essay Questions and				
2 Practice Problems:				
1. Treasury Stock and Dividends	1185,T5	15-25	686	697
2. Stock Option Plan	1186,T5	15-25	686	697
3. Retained Earnings Statement and Stockholders' Equity Section of Balance Sheet	586,P4	45-55	686	698
4. Prepare L-T Liabilities and Stockholders' Equity Sections of Balance Sheet	588,P4	45-55	687	701

Module 29/Investments (IVES)

	Exam reference	No. of minutes	Problem	Answer
31 Multiple Choice			705	712
1 Essay Question and				
2 Practice Problems:				
1. MES: Current and Noncurrent Portfolios	589,T2	15-25	710	718
2. MES & Equity Method Investment	589,P5	40-50	710	718
3. Other Noncurrent Assets	588,P5	40-50	711	723

Module 30/Statement of Cash Flows (SCF)

	Exam reference	No. of minutes	Problem	Answer
29 Multiple Choice			727	735
1 Essay Question and				
3 Practice Problems				
1. Statement of Cash Flows	1177,T5	20-25	731	740
2. Statement of Cash Flows	1189,P5	40-50	731	741
3. Statement of Cash Flows	1182,P4	45-55	732	744
4. Statement of Cash Flows and Changes in Partners' Capital Accounts	1187,P5	45-55	733	750

Module 31/Business Combinations and Consolidations (BCC)

	Exam reference	No. of minutes	Page no. Problem	Answer
56 Multiple Choice			754	767
2 Essay Questions and				
2 Practice Problems:				
1. Business Combinations and Consolidated Financial Statements	586,T4	15-25	762	776
2. Purchase and Pooling of Interests	587,T5	15-25	762	776
3. Consolidated Financial Statement Worksheet	1183,P5	40-50	762	777
4. Pooling of Interests	1188,P5	40-50	765	781

Module 32/Changing Prices and Foreign Currency Translation (CPFC)

	Exam reference	No. of minutes	Page no. Problem	Answer
38 Multiple Choice			785	791

Module 33/Miscellaneous (MISC)

	Exam reference	No. of minutes	Page no. Problem	Answer
A. Personal Financial Statements				
13 Multiple Choice			797	799
B. Interim Reporting				
12 Multiple Choice			801	803
C. Segment Reporting				
11 Multiple Choice			805	807
D. Ratio Analysis				
24 Multiple Choice			809	812
E. Partnership Accounting				
19 Multiple Choice			810	819

Sample Examinations

Practice I Examination	Appendix
Practice II Examination	Appendix
Theory Examination	Appendix

BASIC CONCEPTS

Multiple Choice Questions (1-42)

1. Kay Company is preparing its December 31, 1985 financial statements and must determine the proper accounting treatment for the following situations:

 • On December 30, 1985, Kay received a $200,000 offer for its ROGO patent. Kay's management is considering whether or not to sell the patent. The offer expires on February 28, 1986. The patent has a carrying amount of $130,000 at December 31, 1985.
 • On December 31, 1985, Kay, as lessee under an operating lease, sublet a building for a three-year period at $150,000 annual rental. Kay's annual rental expense for the same period will be $110,000.

Assume an income tax rate of 40%. In its 1985 income statement, Kay should recognize increased net income of
   a. $0
   b. $66,000
   c. $70,000
   d. $72,000

2. According to the FASB's conceptual framework, asset valuation accounts are
   a. Assets.
   b. Neither assets <u>nor</u> liabilities.
   c. Part of stockholders' equity.
   d. Liabilities.

3. According to the FASB's conceptual framework, comprehensive income includes which of the following?

	Operating income	Investments by owners
a.	Yes	No
b.	Yes	Yes
c.	No	Yes
d.	No	No

4. The FASB's conceptual framework classifies gains and losses based on whether they are related to an entity's major ongoing or central operations. These gains or losses may be classified as

	Nonoperating	Operating
a.	Yes	No
b.	Yes	Yes
c.	No	Yes
d.	No	No

5. According to the FASB's conceptual framework, comprehensive income includes which of the following?

	Gross margin	Operating income
a.	No	Yes
b.	No	No
c.	Yes	No
d.	Yes	Yes

6. According to the FASB conceptual framework, predictive value is an ingredient of

	Relevance	Reliability
a.	Yes	No
b.	Yes	Yes
c.	No	Yes
d.	No	No

7. According to the FASB conceptual framework, earnings
   a. Are the same as comprehensive income.
   b. Exclude certain gains and losses that are included in comprehensive income.
   c. Include certain gains and losses that are excluded from comprehensive income.
   d. Include certain losses that are excluded from comprehensive income.

8. According to Statements of Financial Accounting Concepts, neutrality is an ingredient of

	Relevance	Reliability
a.	Yes	Yes
b.	Yes	No
c.	No	No
d.	No	Yes

9. Under Statements of Financial Accounting Concepts, which of the following relates to both relevance and reliability?
   a. Timeliness.
   b. Neutrality.
   c. Feedback value.
   d. Consistency.

10. Under Statement of Financial Accounting Concepts No. 2, representational faithfulness is an ingredient of

	Relevance	Reliability
a.	Yes	Yes
b.	Yes	No
c.	No	No
d.	No	Yes

11. Lin Co., a distributor of machinery, bought a machine from the manufacturer in November 1986 for $10,000. On December 30, 1986, Lin sold this machine to Zee Hardware for $15,000, under the following terms: 2% discount if paid within 30 days, 1% discount if paid after 30 days but within 60 days, or payable in full within 90 days if not paid within the discount periods. However, Zee had the right to return this machine to Lin if Zee was unable to resell the machine before expiration of the 90-day payment period, in which case Zee's obligation to Lin would be canceled. In Lin's net sales for the year ended December 31, 1986, how much should be included for the sale of this machine to Zee?

    a. $0
    b. $14,700
    c. $14,850
    d. $15,000

12. Under a royalty agreement with another enterprise, a company will receive royalties from the assignment of a patent for four years. The royalties received in advance should be reported as revenue

    a.   In the period received.
    b.   In the period earned.
    c.   Evenly over the life of the royalty agreement.
    d.   At the date of the royalty agreement.

13. At December 31, 1987, Raft Boutique had 1,000 gift certificates outstanding, which had been sold to customers during 1987 for $70 each. Raft operates on a gross margin of 60% of its sales. What amount of revenue pertaining to the 1,000 outstanding gift certificates should be deferred at December 31, 1987?

    a. $0
    b. $28,000
    c. $42,000
    d. $70,000

14. A retail store received cash and issued gift certificates that are redeemable in merchandise. The gift certificates lapse one year after they are issued. How would the deferred revenue account be affected by each of the following transactions?

	Redemption of certificates	Lapse of certificates
a.	No effect	Decrease
b.	Decrease	Decrease
c.	Decrease	No effect
d.	No effect	No effect

15. On January 2, 1987, Shaw Company sold the copyright to a book to Poe Publishers, Inc. for royalties of 20% of future sales. On the same date, Poe paid Shaw a royalty advance of $100,000 to be applied against royalties for 1988 sales. On September 30, 1987, Poe made a $42,000 royalty remittance to Shaw for sales in the six-month period ended June 30, 1987. In January 1988, before issuance of its 1987 financial statements, Shaw learned that Poe's sales of the book totaled $250,000 for the last half of 1987. How much royalty revenue should Shaw report in its 1987 income statement?

    a. $ 92,000
    b. $142,000
    c. $150,000
    d. $192,000

16. Hart Company sells subscriptions to a specialized directory that is published semiannually and shipped to subscribers on April 15 and October 15. Subscriptions received after the March 31 and September 30 cutoff dates are held for the next publication. Cash from subscribers is received evenly during the year, and is credited to deferred revenues from subscriptions. Data relating to 1987 are as follows:

Deferred revenues from
  subscriptions, balance 12/31/86 $1,500,000
Cash receipts from subscribers   7,200,000

In its December 31, 1987 balance sheet, Hart should report deferred revenues from subscriptions of

    a. $1,800,000
    b. $3,300,000
    c. $3,600,000
    d. $5,400,000

17. Zach Company assigns some of its patents to other enterprises under a variety of licensing agreements. In some instances, advance royalties are received when the agreements are signed and, in others, royalties are remitted within 60 days after each license year end. The following data are included in Zach's December 31 balance sheets:

	1987	1988
Royalties receivable	$90,000	$85,000
Unearned royalties	60,000	40,000

During 1988, Zach received royalty remittances of $200,000. In its income statement for the year ended December 31, 1988, Zach should report royalty revenue of

    a. $225,000
    b. $215,000
    c. $205,000
    d. $195,000

18. Ott Company acquired rights to a patent from Grey under a licensing agreement that required an advance royalty payment when the agreement was signed. Ott remits royalties earned and due under the agreement on October 31 each year. Additionally, on the same date, Ott pays, in advance, estimated royalties for the next year. Ott adjusts prepaid royalties at year end. Information for the year ended December 31, 1985, is as follows:

Date		Amount
1/1/85	Prepaid royalties	$ 65,000
10/31/85	Royalty payment (charged to royalty expense)	110,000
12/31/85	Year-end credit adjustment to royalty expense	25,000

In its December 31, 1985 balance sheet, Ott should report prepaid royalties of
- a. $25,000
- b. $40,000
- c. $85,000
- d. $90,000

19. On January 1, 1984, Poe Company acquired the copyright to a book owned by Roberts for royalties of 15% of future book sales. Royalties are payable on September 30 for sales in January through June of the same year, and on March 31 for sales in July through December of the preceding year. During 1984 and 1985, Poe remitted royalty checks to Roberts as follows:

	March 31	September 30
1984	$ --	$24,000
1985	22,000	27,000

Poe's sales of the Roberts book totaled $200,000 for the last half of 1985. In its 1985 income statement, Poe should report royalty expense relating to this book of
- a. $46,000
- b. $49,000
- c. $51,000
- d. $57,000

20. Lane Company acquires copyrights from authors, paying advance royalties in some cases, and in others, paying royalties within 30 days of year end. Lane reported royalty expense of $375,000 for the year ended December 31, 1985. The following data are included in Lane's December 31 balance sheets:

	1984	1985
Prepaid royalties	$60,000	$50,000
Royalties payable	75,000	90,000

During 1985 Lane made royalty payments totaling
- a. $350,000
- b. $370,000
- c. $380,000
- d. $400,000

21. Under Hart Company's accounting system, all insurance premiums paid are debited to prepaid insurance. For interim financial reports, Hart makes monthly estimated charges to insurance expenses with credits to prepaid insurance. Additional information for the year ended December 31, 1985, is as follows:

Prepaid insurance at December 31, 1984	$210,000
Charges to insurance expense during 1985 (including a year-end adjustment of $35,000)	875,000
Unexpired insurance premiums at December 31, 1985	245,000

What was the total amount of insurance premiums paid by Hart during 1985?
- a. $910,000
- b. $875,000
- c. $840,000
- d. $665,000

22. The premium on a three-year insurance policy expiring on December 31, 1988, was paid in total on January 1, 1986. The original payment was initially debited to a prepaid asset account. The appropriate journal entry has been recorded on December 31, 1986. The balance in the prepaid asset account on December 31, 1986 should be
- a. Zero.
- b. The same as it would have been if the original payment had been debited initially to an expense account.
- c. The same as the original payment.
- d. Higher than if the original payment had been debited initially to an expense account.

23. At December 31, 1987, Cobb Company had a $695,000 balance in its advertising expense account before any year-end adjustments relating to the following:

• Included in the $695,000 is $80,000 for printing sales catalogs for a January 1988 sales promotional campaign.
• Television advertising spots telecast during December 1987 were billed to Cobb on January 2, 1988. The invoice cost of $45,000 was paid on January 11, 1988.

Cobb's advertising expense for the year ended December 31, 1987 should be
- a. $740,000
- b. $660,000

c. $615,000
d. $570,000

24.   Clay Company borrows money under various loan agreements involving notes discounted and notes requiring interest payments at maturity. During the year ended December 31, 1985, Clay paid interest totaling $100,000. Clay's December 31 balance sheets included the following information:

	1984	1985
Prepaid interest	$23,500	$18,000
Interest payable	45,000	53,500

How much interest expense should Clay report for 1985?
    a. $ 86,000
    b. $ 97,000
    c. $103,000
    d. $114,000

25.   Greg Corp. reported revenue of $1,250,000 in its accrual basis income statement for the year ended June 30, 1989. Additional information was as follows:

Accounts receivable June 30, 1988	$400,000
Accounts receivable June 30, 1989	530,000
Uncollectible accounts written off during the fiscal year	15,000

Under the cash basis, Greg should report revenue of
    a. $ 835,000
    b. $ 850,000
    c. $1,105,000
    d. $1,135,000

26.   John Tracey, M.D., keeps his accounting records on the cash basis. During 1988, Dr. Tracey collected $150,000 in fees from his patients. At December 31, 1987, Dr. Tracey had accounts receivable of $20,000. At December 31, 1988, Dr. Tracey had accounts receivable of $35,000 and unearned fees of $5,000. On the accrual basis, how much was Dr. Tracey's patient service revenue for 1988?
    a. $130,000
    b. $160,000
    c. $165,000
    d. $170,000

27.   The following information is available for Bart Company for 1986:

Disbursements for purchases	$580,000
Increase in trade accounts payable	50,000
Decrease in merchandise inventory	20,000

Cost of goods sold for 1986 was
    a. $650,000
    b. $610,000

c. $550,000
d. $510,000

28.   During 1985 Kew Company, a service organization, had $200,000 in cash sales and $3,000,000 in credit sales. The accounts receivable balances were $400,000 and $485,000 at December 31, 1984 and 1985, respectively. If Kew desires to prepare a cash basis income statement, how much should be reported as sales for 1985 on a cash basis?
    a. $3,285,000
    b. $3,200,000
    c. $3,115,000
    d. $2,915,000

29.   James Lee, M.D., keeps his accounting records on a cash basis. During 1986, Dr. Lee collected $100,000 in fees from his patients. At December 31, 1985, Dr. Lee had accounts receivable of $20,000. At December 31, 1986, Dr. Lee had accounts receivable of $30,000, and unearned fees of $1,000. On an accrual basis, how much was Dr. Lee's patient service revenue for 1986?
    a. $111,000
    b. $109,000
    c. $ 90,000
    d. $ 89,000

30.   Taft Corp., which began business on January 1, 1987, appropriately uses the installment sales method of accounting. The following data are available for December 31, 1987 and 1988.

	1987	1988
Balance of deferred gross profit on sales account:		
1987	$300,000	$120,000
1988	--	440,000
Gross profit on sales	30%	40%

The installment accounts receivable balance at December 31, 1988 is
    a. $1,000,000
    b. $1,100,000
    c. $1,400,000
    d. $1,500,000

31.   Rosson Corp., which began business on January 1, 1988, appropriately uses the installment sales method of accounting for income tax reporting purposes. The following data are available for 1988:

Installment accounts receivable, 12/31/88	$200,000
Installment sales for 1988	$350,000
Gross profit on sales	40%

Under the installment sales method, what would

be Rosson's deferred gross profit at December 31, 1988?

a. $120,000
b. $ 90,000
c. $ 80,000
d. $ 60,000

32. Karr Co. began operations on January 1, 1988 and appropriately uses the installment method of accounting. The following information pertains to Karr's operations for 1988:

Installment sales	$800,000
Cost of installment sales	480,000
General and administrative expenses	80,000
Collections on installment sales	300,000

The balance in the deferred gross profit account at December 31, 1988 should be

a. $120,000
b. $150,000
c. $200,000
d. $320,000

33. Kul Co., which began operations on January 1, 1988, appropriately uses the installment sales method of accounting. The following information is available for 1988:

Installment accounts receivable, December 31, 1988	$400,000
Deferred gross profit, December 31, 1988 (before recognition of realized gross profit for 1988)	280,000
Gross profit on sales	40%

For the year ended December 31, 1988, cash collections and realized gross profit on installment sales should be

	Cash collections	Realized gross profit
a.	$300,000	$120,000
b.	$300,000	$160,000
c.	$200,000	$120,000
d.	$200,000	$160,000

34. According to the installment method of accounting, the gross profit on an installment sale is recognized in income

a. On the date of sale.
b. On the date the final cash collection is received.
c. After cash collections equal to the cost of sales have been received.
d. In proportion to the cash collections received.

35. According to the cost recovery method of accounting, gross profit on an installment sale is recognized in income

a. After cash collections equal to the cost of sales have been received.
b. In proportion to the cash collections.
c. On the date the final cash collection is received.
d. On the date of sale.

36. On October 1, 1988, Price Corp., a real estate developer, sold land to Greene Co. for $5,000,000. Greene paid $600,000 cash and signed a 10-year $4,400,000 note bearing interest at 12%. The carrying amount of the land was $4,000,000 on date of sale. The note was payable in forty quarterly principal installments of $110,000 beginning January 2, 1989. Price appropriately accounts for the sale under the cost recovery method. On January 2, 1989, Greene paid the first principal installment of $110,000 and interest of $132,000. For the year ended December 31, 1988, what total amount of income should Price recognize from the land sale and financing?

a. $0
b. $120,000
c. $132,000
d. $252,000

37. On December 31, 1986, Reed, Inc. authorized Foy to operate as a franchisee for an initial franchise fee of $75,000. Of this amount, $30,000 was received upon signing the agreement and the balance, represented by a note, is due in three annual payments of $15,000 each beginning December 31, 1987. The present value on December 31, 1986, of the three annual payments appropriately discounted is $36,000. According to the agreement, the nonrefundable down payment represents a fair measure of the services already performed by Reed; however, substantial future services are required of Reed. Collectibility of the note is reasonably certain. On December 31, 1986, Reed should record unearned franchise fees in respect of the Foy franchise of

a. $0
b. $36,000
c. $45,000
d. $75,000

38. On January 2, 1988, Rex Enterprises, Inc. authorized Adam Company to operate as a franchisee over a 20-year period for an initial franchise fee of $60,000 received on signing the agreement. Adam started operations on June 30, 1988, by which date Rex had performed all of the required initial services. In its income statement for the six months ended June 30, 1988, what amount should Rex report as revenue from franchise fees in connection with Adam's franchise?

a. $0
b. $ 1,500
c. $30,000
d. $60,000

39. Which of the following should be expensed as incurred by the franchise with an estimated useful life of ten years?
    a. Amount paid to the franchisor for the franchise.
    b. Periodic payments to a company, other than the franchisor, for that company's franchise.
    c. Legal fees paid to the franchisee's lawyers to obtain the franchise.
    d. Periodic payments to the franchisor based on the franchisee's revenues.

May 1990 Questions

40. On December 31, 1988, Mill Co. sold construction equipment to Drew, Inc. for $1,800,000. The equipment had a carrying amount of $1,200,000. Drew paid $300,000 cash on December 31, 1988 and signed a $1,500,000 note bearing interest at 10%, payable in five annual installments of $300,000. Mill appropriately accounts for the sale under the installment method. On December 31, 1989, Drew paid $300,000 principal and $150,000 interest. For the year ended December 31, 1989, what total amount of revenue should Mill recognize from the construction equipment sale and financing?
    a $250,000
    b. $150,000
    c. $120,000
    d. $100,000

41. Bird Corp.'s trademark was licensed to Brian Co. for royalties of 15% of sales of trademarked items. Royalties are payable semiannually on March 15 for sales in July through December of the prior year, and on September 15 for sales in January through June of the same year. Bird received the following royalties from Brian:

	March 15	September 15
1988	$5,000	$7,500
1989	6,000	8,500

Brian estimated that sales of the trademarked items would total $30,000 for July through December 1989.

In Bird's 1989 income statement, the royalty revenue should be
    a. $13,000
    b. $14,500
    c. $19,000
    d. $20,500

42. Compared to the accrual basis of accounting, the cash basis of accounting overstates income by the net increase during the accounting period of the

	Accounts receivable	Accrued expenses payable
a.	No	No
b.	No	Yes
c.	Yes	No
d.	Yes	Yes

Repeat Questions

(590,P3,43) Identical/similar to item 25 above
(590,Q3,49) Identical/similar to item 19 above
(590,T1,1) Identical/similar to item 6 above

BASIC CONCEPTS

Problems

Problem 1   (1184,P5)

(40 to 50 minutes)

Presented below is information pertaining to Ward Specialty Foods, a calendar-year sole proprietorship, maintaining its books on the cash basis during the year. At year end, however, Mary Ward's accountant adjusts the books to the accrual basis only for sales, purchases, and cost of sales, and records depreciation to more clearly reflect the business income for income tax purposes.

Ward Specialty Foods
Trial Balance
December 31, 1986

	Dr.	Cr.
Cash	$ 18,500	
Accounts receivable, 12/31/85	4,500	
Inventory, 12/31/85	20,000	
Equipment	35,000	
Accumulated depreciation, 12/31/85		$ 9,000
Accounts payable, 12/31/85		4,800
Payroll taxes withheld		850
Mary Ward, drawings	24,000	
Mary Ward, capital, 12/31/85		33,650
Sales		187,000
Purchases	82,700	
Salaries	29,500	
Payroll taxes	2,900	
Rent	8,400	
Miscellaneous expense	3,900	
Insurance	2,400	
Utilities	3,500	
	$235,300	$235,300

During 1986 Ward signed a new eight-year lease for the store premises and is in the process of negotiating a loan for remodeling purposes. The bank requires Ward to present financial statements for 1986 prepared on the accrual basis. During the course of a compilation engagement, Ward's accountant obtained the following additional information:

1. Amounts due from customers totaled $7,900 at December 31, 1986.

2. A review of the receivables at December 31, 1986 disclosed that an allowance for doubtful accounts of $1,100 should be provided. Ward had no bad debt losses from inception of the business through December 31, 1986.

3. The inventory amounted to $23,000 at December 31, 1986 based on physical count of goods priced at cost. No reduction to market was required.

4. On signing the new lease on October 1, 1986, Ward paid $8,400 representing one year's rent in advance for the lease year ending October 1, 1987. The $7,500 annual rental under the old lease was paid on October 1, 1985, for the lease year ended October 1, 1986.

5. On April 1, 1986, Ward paid $2,400 to renew the comprehensive insurance coverage for one year. The premium was $2,160 on the old policy which expired on April 1, 1986.

6. Depreciation on equipment was computed at $5,800 for 1986.

7. Unpaid vendors' invoices for food purchases totaled $8,800 at December 31, 1986.

8. Accrued expenses at December 31, 1985, and December 31, 1986, were as follows:

	12/31/85	12/31/86
Payroll taxes	$250	$400
Salaries	375	510
Utilities	275	450

Required:

a. Prepare a worksheet to convert the trial balance of Ward Specialty Foods to the accrual basis for the year ended December 31, 1986. Journal entries are not required to support your adjustments. (Note: This problem provided a tear-out worksheet on the actual exam. A copy of this worksheet is provided on the following page.)

b. Prepare the statement of changes in Mary Ward, capital, for the year ended December 31, 1986.

Ward Specialty Foods
WORKSHEET TO CONVERT
TRIAL BALANCE TO ACCRUAL BASIS
December 31, 1986

	Cash basis		Adjustments		Accrual basis	
	Dr.	Cr.	Dr.	Cr.	Dr.	Cr.
Cash	$ 18,500					
Accounts receivable	4,500					
Allow. for doubtful accts.	-	-				
Inventory	20,000					
Equipment	35,000					
Accum. depreciation		$ 9,000				
Prepaid rent	-	-				
Prepaid insurance	-	-				
Accounts payable		4,800				
Accrued expenses	-	-				
Payroll taxes withheld		850				
Ward, drawings	24,000					
Ward, capital		33,650				
Sales		187,000				
Purchases	82,700					
Income summary - inventory	-	-				
Salaries	29,500					
Payroll taxes	2,900					
Rent	8,400					
Miscellaneous exp.	3,900					
Insurance	2,400					
Utilities	3,500					
Depreciation	-	-				
Doubtful accounts exp.	-	-				
	$235,300	$235,300				

Problem 2   (587,P5)

(40 to 50 minutes)

Presented below is information pertaining to Cox Stationery Supply, a calendar-year sole proprietorship owned by John Cox. The business maintains its books on the cash basis except that, at year end, the closing inventory and depreciation are recorded. On December 31, 1986, after recording inventory and depreciation, and closing the nominal accounts, Cox had the following general ledger trial balance:

Cox Stationery Supply
TRIAL BALANCE
December 31, 1986

	Dr.	Cr.
Cash	$ 16,500	
Merchandise inventory	39,000	
Equipment	52,500	
Accumulated depreciation		$ 20,500
Note payable, bank		10,000
Payroll taxes withheld		1,300
Cox, capital		76,200
	$108,000	$108,000

During the last quarter of 1986, John Cox and Mary Rice, an outside investor, agreed to incorporate the business under the name of Cox Stationers, Inc. Cox will receive 1,000 shares for his business, and Rice will pay $86,000 cash for her 1,000 shares. On January 1, 1987, they received the certificate of incorporation for Cox Stationers, Inc., and the corporation issued 1,000 shares of common stock each to Cox and Rice for the above consideration. The agreement between Cox and Rice requires that the December 31, 1986 balance sheet of the proprietorship should be converted to the accrual basis, with all assets and liabilities stated at current fair values, including Cox's goodwill implicit in the terms of the common stock issuance.

Additional information:

1. Amounts due from customers totaled $23,500 at December 31, 1986. A review of collectibility disclosed that an allowance for doubtful accounts of $3,300 is required.

2. The $39,000 merchandise inventory is based on a physical count of goods priced at cost. Unsalable damaged goods costing $2,500 are included in the count. The current fair value of the total merchandise inventory is $45,000.

3. On July 1, 1986, Cox paid $3,800 to renew the comprehensive insurance coverage for one year.

4. The $10,000 note payable is dated July 1, 1986, bears interest at 12%, and is due July 1, 1987.

5. Unpaid vendors' invoices totaled $30,500 at December 31, 1986.

6. During January 1987, final payroll tax returns filed for Cox Stationery Supply required remittances totaling $2,100.

7. Not included in the trial balance is the $3,500 principal balance at December 31, 1986 of the three-year loan to purchase a delivery van on December 31, 1984. The debt was assumed by the corporation on January 1, 1987. The current fair value of the used equipment is $40,000, including the delivery van.

8. Cox Stationers, Inc., has 7,500 authorized shares of $50 par common stock.

Required:

a. Prepare a schedule to compute Cox's goodwill implicit in the issuance to him of 1,000 shares of common stock for his business.

b. Prepare a formal balance sheet of Cox's Stationers, Inc., at January 1, 1987, immediately after the issuance of common stock to Cox and Rice. Journal entries and trial balance worksheet are <u>not</u> required.

BASIC CONCEPTS

Multiple Choice Answers

1. a	10. d	19. d	27. a	35. a
2. b	11. a	20. a	28. c	36. a
3. a	12. b	21. a	29. b	37. b
4. b	13. d	22. b	30. d	38. d
5. d	14. b	23. b	31. c	39. d
6. a	15. a	24. d	32. c	40. a
7. b	16. a	25. c	33. a	41. a
8. d	17. b	26. b	34. d	42. b
9. d	18. d			

Multiple Choice Answer Explanations

A.1. Basic Accounting Theory

1. (1186,P3,51) (a) At 12/30/85 Kay received a $200,000 offer for a patent with a book value of $130,000. No income is recognized since Kay had not decided whether to accept the offer as of 12/31/85. Also at 12/31/85, Kay sublet a building for three years. The income effects of this agreement will be recognized when the rent is earned in 1986, 1987, and 1988. Therefore, these two events have no effect ($0) on 1985 net income.

2. (1188,T1,1) (b) Per SFAC 6, para 34, asset "valuation accounts" are part of the related assets and are neither assets in their own right nor liabilities. Therefore, answer (b) is correct.

3. (589,T1,1) (a) Per SFAC 6, para 77, comprehensive income consists not only of its basic components (revenues, expenses, gains, and losses) but also the various intermediate components or measures that result from combining the basic components (e.g., income from continuing operations). SFAC 6, para 73 further states that comprehensive income equals the net of its cash receipts and cash outlays, excluding cash invested by owners or distributed to owners. Therefore, answer (a) is correct.

4. (588,T1,2) (b) Per SFAC 6, para 86, gains and losses may be described or classified as "operating" or "nonoperating," depending on their relation to an entity's major ongoing or central operations. Therefore, answer (b) is correct.

5. (1189,T1,1) (d) Per SFAC 6, para 70, comprehensive income includes all changes in equity during a period except those resulting from investments by owners and distributions to owners. Also, according to para 77, comprehensive income includes both gross margin

and operating income. These intermediate components are, in effect, subtotals in the computation of comprehensive income. Therefore, answer (d) is correct.

6. (587,T1,1) (a) According to SFAC 2, predictive value is an ingredient of one of the two primary qualities of accounting information, relevance, but is not an ingredient of the other, reliability.

7. (1186,T1,1) (b) Per SFAC 5, para 42, earnings and comprehensive income have the same broad components--revenues, expenses, gains, and losses--but are not the same because certain classes of gains and losses are included in comprehensive income but are excluded from earnings. Therefore, answer (a) is incorrect because earnings are not the same as comprehensive income. Answers (c) and (d) are incorrect because, per para 44, comprehensive income consists of earnings minus cumulative accounting adjustments plus other nonowner changes in equity; therefore, comprehensive income includes all gains and losses that are included in earnings.

8. (586,T1,1) (d) The requirement is to determine whether neutrality is an ingredient of relevance and/or reliability. Neutrality is the concept that information should be free from bias towards a predetermined result. Per SFAC 2, para 33, neutrality is an ingredient of the primary accounting quality of reliability. The two other ingredients of reliability are representational faithfulness and verifiability. Neutrality is not included in the ingredients of relevance. The three ingredients of relevance are predictive value, feedback value, and timeliness. Therefore, answers (a), (b), and (c) are incorrect.

9. (1185,T1,1) (d) The requirement is to determine which of the given terms relates to both relevance and reliability. Per SFAC 2, consistency is a secondary quality which relates to both of the primary qualities of relevance and reliability. Answers (a) and (c) are incorrect because both timeliness and feedback value are described by SFAC 2 as ingredients only of the primary quality of relevance. They are not considered ingredients of the quality of reliability. Answer (b) is incorrect because neutrality is described as an ingredient only of the primary quality of reliability.

10. (585,T1,1) (d) The requirement is to determine whether representational faithfulness is an ingredient of the two primary qualities of accounting information, relevance and

reliability. Answer (d) is correct because according to SFAC 2 representational faithfulness is an ingredient of reliability, but is not an ingredient of relevance. Therefore, answers (a), (b), and (c) are incorrect.

A.2. Income Determination

11. (587,Q1,20) (a) Per SFAS 48, para 6, revenue from the sale of a product may be recognized at the time of sale only if all of the following conditions are met:

1. The seller's price is fixed or readily determinable.
2. The buyer has paid the seller or is obligated to pay the seller, the obligation not being contingent on resale of the product.
3. The buyer's obligation to the seller remains unchanged in the event of damage or destruction of the product.
4. The buyer is independent from the seller.
5. The seller does not have any significant obligations regarding resale of the product by the buyer.
6. The amount of future returns can be reasonably estimated.

Because the buyer, Zee, has the right to return the machine to the seller, Lin, condition (2) above has not been met. Therefore, the recognition of sales revenue and cost of sales is not allowable for this transaction and answer (a) is correct.

12. (589,T1,16) (b) Per SFAC 5, para 83, revenues are considered to be "earned" (and should be recognized) when the entity has substantially completed the duties entitling it to the benefits represented by the revenues. When a company assigns patents to other enterprises, it earns royalties as the sales of patented products are made. Therefore, these royalties should be reported as revenue in the period in which they are earned, and answer (b) is correct.

A.3. Accruals and Deferrals

13. (1188,P1,20) (d) Unearned revenue is recorded and reported as a liability at gross amounts before subtracting any estimated future costs. Therefore, Raft should report as a liability unearned revenue of $70,000 (1,000 x $70) at 12/31/87. During 1988, when the revenue is earned, Raft would debit unearned revenue and credit a revenue account. At that time, any related costs incurred would be expensed.

14. (587,T1,12) (b) At the time the gift certificates were issued, the following entry was made, reflecting the store's future obligation to honor the certificates:

Cash   xx
   Deferred revenue   xx

Upon redemption of the certificates, the obligation recorded in the deferred revenue account becomes satisfied and the revenue is earned. Similarly, as the certificates expire, the store is no longer under any obligation to honor the certificates and the deferred revenue should be taken into income. In both instances, the deferred revenue account must be reduced (debited) to reflect the earning of revenue [answer (b)]. This is done through the following entry:

Deferred revenue   xx
   Revenue   xx

15. (1188,P2,40) (a) Royalty revenue earned during the first six months of 1987, and received on 9/30/87, was $42,000. Royalty revenue earned during the last months of 1987 was 20% of $250,000, or $50,000. This amount would be recorded as a receivable and revenue at 12/31/87. Thus, total 1987 royalty revenue is $92,000 ($42,000 + $50,000). The royalty advance of $100,000 to be applied against 1988 royalties does not affect 1987 revenues. When received, this amount would be recorded as a liability. It will be recognized as revenue when earned in 1988.

16. (588,P2,31) (a) The year-end balance of the liability account, deferred revenues from subscriptions, should reflect the amount of subscriptions still outstanding at that time. The 12/31/86 deferred revenue ($1,500,000) would have been earned when the April 15 directory was mailed, and therefore is no longer a liability. The cash collected through the September 30 cutoff date (9/12 x $7,200,000 = $5,400,000) would also have been earned when the April 15 and October 15 directories were mailed. (Note that the problem stated that cash is received evenly through the year.) However, the cash collected after September 30 (3/12 x $7,200,000 = $1,800,000) will not be earned until the 4/15/88 catalog is mailed, and therefore must be reported as deferred revenues from subscriptions.

17. (589,P3,53) (b) Cash received from royalties was $200,000 in 1988. To compute royalty revenue, this amount must be adjusted for changes in related accounts, as follows:

1988 royalties received	$200,000
Royalties receivable, 12/31/87	(90,000)
Royalties receivable, 12/31/88	85,000
Unearned royalties, 12/31/87	60,000
Unearned royalties, 12/31/88	(40,000)
1988 royalty revenue	$215,000

The beginning receivable balance ($90,000) is subtracted because that portion of the cash received was recognized as revenue last year. The ending receivable balance ($85,000) is added because that amount has been accrued as 1988 revenue, even though it has not yet been received. The beginning balance of unearned royalties ($60,000) is added because that amount is assumed to have been earned during the year. Finally, the ending balance of unearned royalties ($40,000) is subtracted since this amount was received, but not earned, during 1988.

18. (1186,P1,1) (d) On 1/1/85, the balance of prepaid royalties was $65,000. Ott makes no entries to this account until year end, so the 12/31/85 balance before adjustment was still $65,000. On 10/31/85, Ott made a $110,000 royalty payment which included payment in advance for 1986 royalties. However, under Ott's system, all such payments are debited to royalty expense when paid, and any necessary adjustments to prepaid royalties are made at year end. At 12/31/85, Ott made a **credit** adjustment to royalty expense:

| Prepaid royalties | 25,000 | |
| Royalty expense | | 25,000 |

Therefore, the 12/31/85 balance of prepaid royalties is $90,000 ($65,000 + $25,000).

19. (1186,P3,48) (d) On 9/30/85, Poe paid $27,000 in royalties for the first half of 1985. Royalties for the second half of 1985 will not be paid until 3/31/86. However, the royalty expense for this period (15% x $200,000 = $30,000) should be accrued at 12/31/85. Therefore, 1985 royalty expense is $57,000 ($27,000 + $30,000). Note that the 3/31/85 royalty payment ($22,000) would not affect 1985 expense; that amount would have been accrued as expense at 12/31/84.

20. (586,P3,55) (a) The requirement is the amount of 1985 royalty payments. Royalty ex-pense in 1985 totalled $375,000. However, this amount must be adjusted for changes in the related accounts to determine how much cash was paid for royalties.

1985 royalty expense	$375,000
Royalties payable, 12/31/84	75,000
Royalties payable, 12/31/85	(90,000)
Prepaid royalties, 12/31/84	(60,000)
Prepaid royalties, 12/31/85	50,000
1985 royalty payments	$350,000

The beginning payable balance ($75,000) is added because this amount was paid in 1985, but **not** included in 1985 expense (it was accrued as an expense in 1984). The ending payable balance ($90,000) is subtracted because this amount was included in 1985 expense, but was **not** paid in 1985 (it will be paid in 1986). The beginning balance of prepaid interest ($60,000) is subtracted because this amount was included in 1985 expense as the prepayments expired, but it was not paid in 1985 (it was paid in 1984). Finally, the ending balance of prepaid royalties ($50,000) is added because this amount was paid in 1985, but not included in 1985 expense.

21. (586,P1,14) (a) The requirement is the total amount of insurance premiums paid during 1985. The solutions approach is to set up a T-account for prepaid insurance.

	Prepaid Insurance		
12/31/84 balance	210,000		
1985 payments	?	875,000	1985 expense
12/31/85 balance	245,000		

The beginning and ending balances are debits in the asset account. Cash payments for insurance (the unknown factor) are recorded with a **debit** to prepaid insurance and a credit to cash. Insurance expense ($875,000) is recorded with a debit to the expense account and a **credit** to prepaid insurance. The amount of payments can be computed as $910,000.

$210,000 + Payments − $875,000 = $245,000.

Payments = $910,000

A shortcut is to take the expense of $875,000 plus the **increase** in prepaid insurance of $35,000 ($245,000 − $210,000).

22. (587,T1,9) (b) When the insurance policy was initially purchased, the entire balance was debited to a prepaid asset account (i.e., prepaid insurance). The adjusting entry at December 31, 1986, to recognize the expiration of 1 year of the policy would be:

Insurance expense   (1/3 of original pymt.)
  Prepaid insurance   (1/3 of original pymt.)

After the adjusting entry, the prepaid asset account would contain 2/3 of the original payment. If the original payment had instead been debited to an expense account (i.e., insurance expense), then the adjusting entry at December 31, 1986 would be:

Prepaid insurance   (2/3 of original pymt.)
  Insurance expense   (2/3 of original pymt.)

This alternate approach would also result in 1/3 of the original payment being expensed in 1986 and 2/3 of the original payment being carried forward as a prepaid asset. Thus, answer (b) is correct. Answer (a) is incorrect because the premium paid was for a three-year policy, 2/3 of which had not yet expired and would therefore be carried forward in the prepaid asset account. Answer (c) is incorrect because 1/3 of the original payment was already expensed. Answer (d) is incorrect because the amount would be the same as it would have been if the original payment had been debited initially to an expense account (as explained for answer (b) above).

23. (588,P3,49) (b) The balance in the advertising expense account **before** adjustment is $695,000. This amount should be reduced by the $80,000 cost of printing sales catalogs for the 1988 sales campaign. The $80,000 is a prepaid expense at 12/31/87, and is properly matched against 1988 revenues. Advertising expense should be increased for December's television advertising of $45,000 which was not billed until 1/2/88. This $45,000 must be accrued as an expense and a liability at 12/31/87. Therefore, the 1987 advertising expense should be $660,000 ($695,000 - $80,000 + $45,000).

24. (586,P3,42) (d) The requirement is the amount of 1985 interest expense. Cash paid for interest is $100,000 in 1985. However, this amount must be adjusted for changes in the related accounts, as follows:

1985 cash interest paid	$100,000
Interest payable, 12/31/84	(45,000)
Interest payable, 12/31/85	53,500
Prepaid interest, 12/31/84	23,500
Prepaid interest, 12/31/85	(18,000)
1985 interest expense	$114,000

The beginning payable balance ($45,000) is subtracted because that portion of the cash paid was recognized as expense during the previous year. The ending payable balance ($53,500) is added because that amount has been accrued as 1985 expense, even though it has not yet been paid. The beginning balance of prepaid interest ($23,500) is added because that amount is assumed to have expired during the year. Finally, the ending balance of prepaid interest ($18,000) is subtracted since this amount was paid, but not incurred as an expense, by 12/31/85.

A.4. Cash to Accrual

25. (589,P3,50) (c) To determine cash basis revenue, the solutions approach is to prepare a T-account for accounts receivable

Accts. Receivable			
6/30/88	400,000		
Credit sales	1,250,000	15,000	Write offs
		?	Collections
6/30/89	530,000		

This analysis assumes all revenues were on account. If they were not, collections **on account** would be less, but **total collections** would be the same. The missing amount, $1,105,000, is cash basis revenue.

26. (1189,P2,36) (b) Cash received for fees in 1988 was $150,000. To compute patient service revenue on an accrual basis, this amount must be adjusted for changes in related accounts, as follows:

1988 fees received	$150,000
Accounts receivable, 12/31/87	(20,000)
Accounts receivable, 12/31/88	35,000
Unearned fees, 12/31/88	(5,000)
1988 patient service revenue	$160,000

The beginning receivable balance ($20,000) is subtracted because that portion of the cash received would have been recognized as revenue last year using the accrual method. The ending receivable balance ($35,000) is added because that amount would be accrued as 1988 revenue, since the work was performed prior to 12/31/88, even though it has not yet been received. The ending balance of unearned fees ($5,000) would be subtracted because this amount was received, but not earned, during 1988. Thus, it would be recorded as a liability rather than revenue using the accrual method.

27. (587,P2,31) (a) The basic cost of goods sold formula is:

Beg. inv. + Net Purchases - End. Inv. = CGS.

In order to compute cost of goods sold from the information given, cash paid for purchases must be adjusted for increases (decreases) in both accounts payable and merchandise inventory. Cash payments for purchases during 1986 were $580,000. In addition, accounts payable increased by $50,000, indicating that total purchases exceeded cash payments for purchases by $50,000. Merchandise inventory decreased by $20,000, which means beginning inventory exceeded ending inventory by $20,000. This increase would have to be added to cash payments for purchases to compute cost of goods sold of $650,000.

Cash paid for purchases	$580,000
+ increase in A/P	50,000
+ decrease in inv.	20,000
Cost of goods sold	$650,000

28. (586,P2,27) (c) The requirement is the amount to be reported as sales for 1985 on a **cash** basis. Cash sales were $200,000 and credit sales were $3,000,000. To determine how much cash was collected from credit sales,

the solutions approach is to set up a
T-account for accounts receivable.

	A/R	
12/31/84 balance	400,000	
1985 credit sales	3,000,000	2,915,000 1985 cash collections
12/31/85 balance	485,000	

The beginning and ending balances are given,
as are 1985 credit sales (debited to A/R and
credited to sales). The missing amount, 1985
cash collections, can be computed as
$2,915,000. This amount was debited to cash
and credited to A/R. Therefore, sales on a
cash basis total $3,115,000.

Cash sales	$ 200,000
Collections of credit sales	2,915,000
Total	$3,115,000

29. (587,Q1,14) (b) The following formula
is used to adjust service revenue from the
cash basis to the accrual basis:

$$\begin{array}{l}\text{Accrual basis}\\ \text{service}\\ \text{revenue}\end{array} = \begin{array}{l}\text{Cash fees}\\ \text{collected}\end{array} + \begin{array}{l}\text{End.}\\ \text{A/R}\end{array} - \begin{array}{l}\text{Beg.}\\ \text{A/R}\end{array} + \begin{array}{l}\text{Beg.}\\ \text{unearned}\\ \text{fees}\end{array} - \begin{array}{l}\text{End.}\\ \text{unearned}\\ \text{fees}\end{array}$$

Therefore, Dr. Lee's patient service revenue
for 1986 is $109,000 (100,000 + 30,000 –
20,000 + 0 – 1,000). As an alternative,
T-accounts can be used:

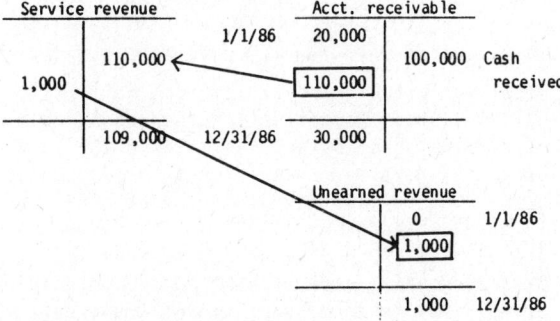

A.5. Installment Sales

30.   (589,P1,8) (d) When using the
installment sales method, the balance of the
deferred gross profit account represents the
gross profit not yet recognized because the
related receivable has not yet been collected.
The formula below expresses this relationship.

$$\left(\begin{array}{c}\text{Deferred}\\ \text{gross profit}\end{array}\right) = \left(\begin{array}{c}\text{Gross profit}\\ \text{rate}\end{array}\right) \times \left(\begin{array}{c}\text{Accounts}\\ \text{receivable}\end{array}\right)$$

This equation can be rearranged as follows:

$$\left(\begin{array}{c}\text{Deferred}\\ \text{gross profit}\end{array}\right) \div \left(\begin{array}{c}\text{Gross profit}\\ \text{rate}\end{array}\right) = \left(\begin{array}{c}\text{Accounts}\\ \text{receivable}\end{array}\right)$$

Therefore, the installment accounts receivable
balance at 12/31/88 can be computed as follows:

From 87 sales:	$120,000 ÷ 30% =	$ 400,000
From 88 sales:	440,000 ÷ 40% =	1,100,000
Total		$1,500,000

31. (589,P2,39) (c) Under the installment
method, gross profit is deferred to future
periods and is recognized by applying the
gross profit rate to subsequent cash collections. Rosson's installment sales for 1988
resulted in total deferred gross profit of
$140,000 (40% x $350,000). Because cash
collected was $150,000 ($350,000 – $200,000),
gross profit recognized is $60,000 (40% x
$150,000). This leaves a balance in deferred
gross profit of $80,000 at 12/31/88 ($140,000
– $60,000). A shortcut approach is to multi-
ply the 12/31/88 installment accounts receivable by the gross profit rate ($200,000 x 40%
= $80,000). Note that this question did not
state that the installment sales method should
be used for financial accounting purposes
(only that it is used for income tax reporting
purposes). However, if the point of sale
method (rather than the installment method)
had been used for financial reporting purposes, the deferred gross profit at December 31, 1988 would have been $0. Since $0 was
not an available answer to the question, it
must be assumed that the installment sales
method was also used for financial accounting
purposes. Determining the method used for
financial reporting purposes is important because the question was a financial accounting
question.

32. (1189,P2,23) (c) Under the installment
method, gross profit is deferred at the time
of sale and is recognized by applying the
gross profit rate to subsequent cash collections. At the time of sale, gross profit of
$320,000 is deferred ($800,000 – $480,000).
The gross profit rate is 40% ($320,000 ÷
$800,000). Since 1988 collections on install-
ment sales were $300,000, gross profit of
$120,000 is recognized in 1988 ($300,000 x
40%). This recognition of gross profit would
decrease the deferred gross profit account to
$200,000 at 12/31/88 ($320,000 – $120,000 =
$200,000).

33. (1189,Q1,8) (a) Under the installment
sales method, gross profit is deferred to
future periods and recognized proportionately
to collection of the receivables. The amount
of cash collections is computed by first
determining the amount of installment sales
made during the year. This is done by dividing deferred gross profit by the gross
profit on sales percentage ($280,000 ÷ 40% =
$700,000). The balance in the installment
accounts receivable account at 12/31/88
($400,000) is then subtracted to determine
cash collections ($700,000 – $400,000 =
$300,000). Realized gross profit is then
computed by multiplying cash collections by
the gross profit on sales percentage ($300,000
x 40% = $120,000).

34. (1188,T1,11) (d) Per APB 12, para 10, the installment method of recognizing revenue is appropriate only when "collection of the sale price is not reasonably assured." Under the installment method, gross profit is deferred to future periods and recognized proportionately to collection of the receivables. Therefore, answer (d) is correct.

A.6. Cost Recovery

35. (589,T1,14) (a) Per APB 10, para 12, installment methods of recognizing revenue are appropriate only when "collection of the sale price is not reasonably assured." Under the cost recovery method, gross profit is deferred and recognized only when the cumulative receipts exceed the cost of the asset sold. Therefore, answer (a) is correct.

36. (1189,P2,35) (a) Under the cost recovery method no profit of any type is recognized until the cumulative receipts exceed the cost of the asset sold. This means that the entire gross profit ($5,000,000 - $4,000,000 = $1,000,000) and the 1988 interest revenue ($132,000) will be deferred until cash collections exceed $4,000,000. Therefore, no income is recognized in 1988.

A.7. Franchise Agreements

37. (587,P1,14) (b) Per SFAS 45, para 5, franchise fee revenue shall be recognized when all material services have been substantially performed by the franchisor; i.e., the franchisor has no remaining obligation to refund any cash received and substantially all of the initial services of the franchisor have been performed. Of the initial fee of $75,000, the $30,000 down payment applies to the initial services already performed by Reed. Additionally, this amount is not refundable. Therefore, the $30,000 may be recognized as revenue in 1986. The three remaining $15,000 installments relate to substantial future services to be performed by Reed. The present value of these payments, $36,000, is recorded as unearned fees and recognized as revenue once substantial performance has occurred.

Cash	30,000	
Notes receivable	45,000	
Discount on N/R		9,000
Franchise revenue		30,000
Unearned franchise fees		36,000

38. (589,P3,51) (d) SFAS 45 states that the initial franchise fee shall be recognized as revenue when all the material services or conditions relating to the sale have been substantially performed or satisfied by the franchisor. Since Rex had performed all the required initial services by 6/30/88, the entire amount of the initial franchise fee ($60,000) is recognized as revenue on Rex's income statement for the six months ended 6/30/88.

39. (1185,T1,7) (d) The requirement is to determine which of the following outflows should be expensed as incurred by the franchisee. Continuing franchise fees, based on revenues [answer (d)], should be reported as expenses when incurred. Answers (a), (b), and (c) are incorrect because they represent direct franchise costs. Since these costs relate to the acquisition of the franchise, they should be capitalized and deferred, rather than expensed.

May 1990 Answers

40. (590,P3,45) (a) The plant sale is accounted for using the installment method. The gross profit percentage on the sale is 33 1/3% ($600,000 profit ÷ $1,800,000 selling price). Since $300,000 of the sales price is collected in 1989, gross profit of $100,000 is recognized (33 1/3% x $300,000). The total revenue recognized is $250,000 ($100,000 gross profit + $150,000 interest revenue).

41. (590,Q3,42) (a) On 9/15/89, Brian received $8,500 in royalties for the first half of 1989. Royalties for the second half of 1989 will not be paid until 3/15/90. However, the royalty revenue for this period (15% x $30,000 = $4,500) should be accrued at 12/31/89. Therefore, 1989 royalty revenue is $13,000 ($8,500 + $4,500). Note that the 3/15/89 royalty receipt ($6,000) would not affect 1989 revenue; that amount would have been accrued as revenue at 12/31/88.

42. (590,T1,18) (b) To determine the effect of increases in accounts receivable and accrued expenses on cash basis income, one must review the formulas to convert between the cash and accrual methods:

		Accrual		Beginning		Ending
Cash Basis Sales	=	Sales	+	A/R	−	A/R
		Accrual		Beginning		Ending
Cash Basis Expenses	=	Expenses	+	Accruals	−	Accruals

An increase in accounts receivable would result in cash sales being lower than accrual sales and understatement of cash basis income. An increase in accrued liabilities would result in cash expenses being lower than accrual expenses and overstatement of cash basis income. Therefore, answer (b) is correct.

BASIC CONCEPTS

Solution Guide

Problem 1   Cash to Accrual Basis (1184,P5)

1. Problem three consists of two related parts. Part a. requires the completion of a worksheet (provided) to convert a trial balance from the cash basis to the accrual basis. Part b. requires the preparation of a statement of changes in capital for the same proprietorship.

2. To complete the worksheet provided in part a., you must refer back to the additional information given (labeled 1 through 8). The solutions approach is to treat each of the eight items as an independent problem.

2.1 Amounts due from customers total $7,900 at 12/31/86. The balance in the accounts receivable account from the last year end is $4,500. This account must be debited for $3,400 to bring the balance up to $7,900. The corresponding credit is to Sales, since unrecorded receivables mean that there is also unrecorded sales.

2.2 An allowance for doubtful accounts of $1,100 is required at 12/31/86. Since the balance in the allowance account is $0, an adjusting entry for $1,100 is required.

Doubtful accounts expense   1,100
   Allowance for doubtful
     accounts   1,100

2.3 The 12/31/86 inventory is $23,000, but the books now reflect the 12/31/85 inventory of $20,000. The beginning inventory must be removed from the books, and the ending inventory must be recorded.

Income summary   20,000
   Inventory   20,000
Inventory   23,000
   Income summary   23,000

The net adjustment to inventory is $3,000. You may make either both of the above entries or a net entry on the worksheet. Note that the AICPA Unofficial Answer shows only a net entry.

2.4 One year's rent ($8,400) was prepaid on 10/1/86. This amount is recorded as rent expense in the trial balance. Only three months have expired; the other nine months should be reported as prepaid rent on 12/31/86. Therefore, the entry is to remove $6,300 (9/12 × $8,400) from the rent expense account and record that amount as prepaid rent.

An additional entry must be prepared to record some of the 10/1/85 rent payment as 1986 expense. The entire amount ($7,500) was expensed and closed to capital in 1985 under the cash basis. Under the accrual basis, only three months should have been expensed in 1985, nine months should have been deferred and expensed in 1986. Therefore, $5,625 (9/12 × $7,500) must be recorded as rent expense. The credit is to Ward, capital, since the 12/31/85 balance of that account was understated when the total rent payment was expensed in 1985.

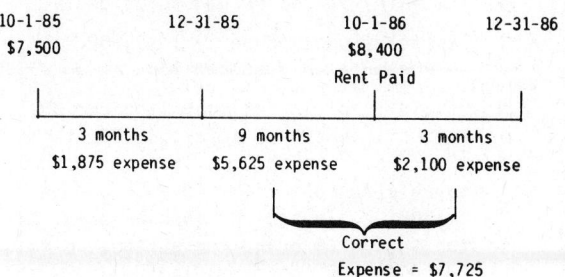

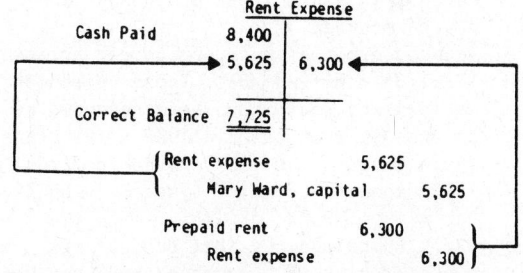

Alternatively, these entries could be netted as is done in the AICPA Unofficial Answer.

2.5 The insurance coverage is also paid one year in advance, like the rent, so the entries are similar. However, the insurance payments are every April 1. Therefore, $600 (3/12 × $2,400) must be removed from the insurance expense account and recorded as prepaid insurance.
Again, an additional entry must be made to record some of the 4/1/85 insurance premium as 1986 expense. The last three months of that payment ($2,160 × 3/12 = $540) should be expensed in 1986. Again, the credit is to Ward, capital, since the 12/31/85 balance was understated when the total premium was expensed in 1985.

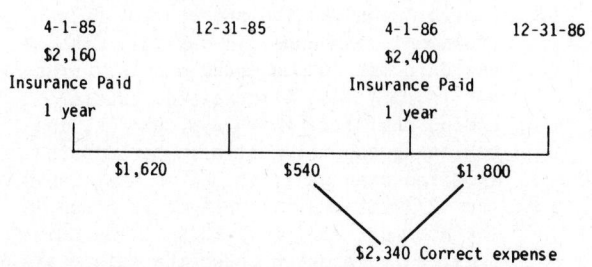

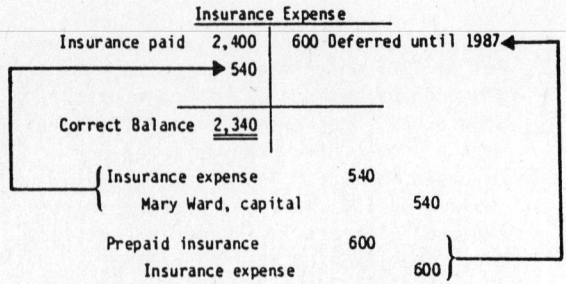

Alternatively, these entries could be netted
as is done in the AICPA Unofficial Answer.
2.6 The entry to record depreciation is:

Depreciation expense   5,800
  Accumulated depreciation   5,800

2.7 Unpaid invoices for food (the company's
product) purchases total $8,800 at
12/31/86. The balance in the accounts
payable account from the year end is
$4,800. This account must be credited
for $4,000 to bring the balance up to
$8,800. The corresponding debit is to
Purchases, since these purchases were
never recorded.

2.8 Accrued expenses were unrecorded at both
12/31/85 and 12/31/86. Those unrecorded
at 12/31/85 would have been recorded as
an expense when paid in 1986. Therefore,
those amounts must be removed from the
1986 expense accounts. The corresponding
debit is to Ward, capital, since the
12/31/85 balance of that account was
overstated when the accrued expenses were
not recorded in 1985.

Ward, capital   900
  Payroll taxes expense   250
  Salaries expense   375
  Utilities expense   275

The accrued expenses unrecorded at
12/31/86 must be recorded with an adjusting entry to debit the expenses and
credit the related liability.

Payroll taxes expense   400
Salaries expense   510
Utilities expense   450
  Accrued expenses   1,360

Alternatively, these entries could be
netted as is done in the AICPA Unofficial
Answer.

3.   Part b. requires the preparation of a
statement of changes in capital. The
basic format is beginning capital, plus
net income, less withdrawals, equals
ending capital. In this situation, the
beginning capital must also be adjusted
from the cash basis to the accrual basis.

3.1 The 12/31/85 capital balance is given in
the problem, $33,650. This is the amount
previously reported under the cash basis.

3.2 The adjustment to convert 12/31/85 capital from the cash basis to the accrual
basis can be obtained from the worksheet
of part a. 12/31/85 capital was increased by $540 (insurance adjustment)
and by $5,625 (rent adjustment). It was
decreased by $900 (accrued expenses
adjustment). These amounts net out to an
adjustment of $5,265.

3.3 Net income must be computed from the
accrual basis amounts in the worksheet.
Sales is $190,400. Cost of goods sold is
$83,700 ($20,000 beg. inv. plus $86,700
purchases less $23,000 end. inv.). This
leaves a gross margin of $106,700. The
expenses (salaries, payroll taxes, rent,
miscellaneous, insurance, utilities, depreciation, and doubtful accounts) total
$57,225. This results in a net income of
$49,475.

3.4 Withdrawals of $24,000 must be sub-
tracted, resulting in ending capital of
$64,390.

Unofficial Answer

Problem 1   Cash to Accrual Basis (1184,P5)

Ward Specialty Foods
Worksheet to Convert
Trial Balance to Accrual Basis
December 31, 1986

	Cash basis		Adjustments		Accrual basis	
	Dr.	Cr.	Dr.	Cr.	Dr.	Cr.
Cash	$ 18,500				$ 18,500	
Accounts receivable	4,500		[1] $ 3,400		7,900	
Allowance for doubtful accounts				[2] $ 1,100		$ 1,100
Inventory	20,000		[3] 3,000		23,000	
Equipment	35,000				35,000	
Accumulated depreciation		$ 9,000		[6] 5,800		14,800
Prepaid rent			[4] 6,300		6,300	
Prepaid insurance			[5] 600		600	
Accounts payable		4,800		[7] 4,000		8,800
Accrued expenses				[8] 1,360		1,360
Payroll taxes withheld		850				850
Ward, drawings	24,000				24,000	
Ward, capital		33,650	[8] 900	[4] 5,625		38,915
				[5] 540		
Sales		187,000		[1] 3,400		190,400
Purchases	82,700		[7] 4,000		86,700	
Income summary--inventory			[3] 20,000	[3] 23,000		3,000
Salaries	29,500		[8] 135		29,635	
Payroll taxes	2,900		[8] 150		3,050	
Rent	8,400			[4] 675	7,725	
Miscellaneous expense	3,900				3,900	
Insurance	2,400			[5] 60	2,340	
Utilities	3,500		[8] 175		3,675	
Depreciation			[6] 5,800		5,800	
Doubtful accounts expense			[2] 1,100		1,100	
	$235,300	$235,300	$45,560	$45,560	$259,225	$259,225

Explanations of adjustments:

[1]   To convert 1986 sales to accrual basis:

Accounts rec., 12/31/86	$ 7,900
Deduct accounts rec., 12/31/85	4,500
Increase in sales	$ 3,400

[2]   To record provision for doubtful accounts.

[3]   To record increase in inventory from 12/31/85 to 12/31/86:

Inventory, 12/31/86	$23,000
Inventory, 12/31/85	20,000
Increase	$ 3,000

[4]   To adjust rent expense for prepaid rent at 12/31/85 and 12/31/86:

Prepaid 12/31/86 ($8,400 x 9/12)	$ 6,300
Prepaid 12/31/85 ($7,500 x 9/12)	5,625
Rent expense decrease	$ 675

[5]   To adjust insurance expense for prepaid insurance at 12/31/85 and 12/31/86:

Prepaid 12/31/86 ($2,400 x 3/12)	$ 600
Prepaid 12/31/85 ($2,160 x 3/12)	540
Insurance expense decrease	$ 60

[6]   To record depreciation for 1986.

[7]   To convert 1986 purchases to accrual basis:

Accounts pay. 12/31/86	$ 8,800
Deduct accounts pay. 12/31/85	4,800
Increase in purchases	$ 4,000

[8]   To convert expenses to accrual basis:

Payroll taxes	$ 400 – $250	$150
Salaries	$ 510 – $375	135
Utilities	$ 450 – $275	175
	$1,360 $900	

Ward Specialty Foods
Statement of Changes in
Mary Ward, Capital
For the Year Ended December 31, 1986

Mary Ward, capital, 12/31/85	$38,915 [1]
Add net income for year	49,475 [2]
	88,390
Deduct drawings for year	24,000
Mary Ward, capital, 12/31/86	$64,390

Explanations of amounts:

[1]   Mary Ward, capital, 12/31/85 after adjustment to accrual basis (per worksheet).

[2]   Computation of net income on accrual basis for the year ended 12/31/86 (per worksheet).

Sales		$190,400
Purchases	$86,700	
Income summary-- inventory	(3,000)	
Salaries	29,635	
Payroll taxes	3,050	
Rent	7,725	
Miscellaneous exp.	3,900	
Insurance	2,340	
Utilities	3,675	
Depreciation	5,800	
Doubtful accounts exp.	1,100	140,925
Net income		$ 49,475

Solution Guide

Problem 2   Prepare a Balance Sheet (587,P5)

1.   Number 5 consists of two related parts requiring the computation of goodwill acquired by a corporation and the preparation of a balance sheet for the same corporation.

2.   Part a. requires the preparation of a schedule to compute the goodwill acquired by a corporation when it issues common stock for a small company. According to the agreement between the two stockholders, the books of the proprietorship are to be converted to the accrual basis, with assets and liabilities stated at current fair values at the time they are purchased by the new corporation.

2.1   The implied goodwill can be computed by subtracting Cox's adjusted interest in the proprietorship from the value of the 1,000 shares he received for his interest. Cox's 1,000 shares should be equal in value to Rice's 1,000 shares, issued for $86,000 cash at the same time.

2.2   One way of determining Cox's adjusted interest is to compute the difference between the current fair value of the assets and the current fair value of liabilities assumed.

2.3   The current fair value of cash is the amount shown on the trial balance of $16,500.

2.4   The net amount of unrecorded accounts receivable ($23,500 – $3,300 = $20,200) will be added to the fair values of the assets because the unrecorded accounts receivable are also unrecorded sales. This would _increase_ capital when recorded. The unrecorded allowance for doubtful accounts is also unrecorded bad debts expense, which would _decrease_ capital when recorded.

2.5 The $39,000 of merchandise inventory shown on the trial balance is adjusted up to its FMV of $45,000. This results in a total increase of $6,000. Note that the same effect would result from recognizing the $2,500 loss on damaged goods, then writing the inventory up by $8,500 ($45,000 − $36,500).

2.6 The unrecorded prepaid insurance is also an asset and should be included at its FMV of $1,900 ($3,800 x 6/12). The entire amount ($3,800) was expensed when paid, but only $1,900 should have been expensed in 1986. Therefore, Cox's capital was decreased by $1,900 too much ($3,800 − $1,900).

2.7 The current value of the equipment ($40,000) is given in the problem.

2.8 Total current fair value of assets equals $123,600. ($16,500 + $20,200 + $45,000 + $1,900 + $40,000).

2.9 Unpaid vendors' invoices of $30,500 are accounts payable and should be recognized as a liability.

2.10 The note payable of $10,000 is a liability also.

2.11 The $3,500 principal balance of the loan to purchase the delivery van is a liability which should be shown at its FMV as a loan payable.

2.12 Another liability is the interest payable on the $10,000 note payable. Interest of $600 ($10,000 x 12% x 6/12) should be accrued as of December 31, 1986.

2.13 The $2,100 of payroll taxes withheld and accrued as given in the additional information would be included in the liabilities.

2.14 Total current fair value of the liabilities assumed equals $46,700 ($30,500 + $10,000 + $3,500 + $600 + $2,100).

2.15 The difference between the current value of current assets of $123,600 and the current value of current liabilities of $46,700 is $76,900. This $76,900 is the net fair value of the contribution by Cox for 1,000 shares. Since the shares issued to Cox were worth $86,000, the implied goodwill was $9,100. ($86,000 − $76,900).

3.   Part b. requires the preparation of a formal balance sheet for the new corporation immediately after the issuance of stock to Cox and Rice.

3.1 Current assets include cash, accounts receivable, merchandise inventory (restated to FMV) and prepaid insurance.

3.2 Other assets include equipment (restated to FMV) and goodwill ($9,100 as computed in part a.).

3.3 Current liabilities include the note payable to the bank and the related interest payable, the loan payable on the delivery van, accounts payable, and the adjusted amount of payroll taxes payable.

3.4 Stockholder's equity consists of common stock at par value (2,000 shares at $50 par value, or a total of $100,000), and APIC of $72,000 [(2 x $86,000) − $100,000].

Unofficial Answer

Problem 2   Prepare a Balance Sheet (587,P5)

a.

Computation of Cox's Goodwill
Implicit in the Terms of the
Common Stock Issuance

Cash paid by Rice for 1,000 shares		$ 86,000
Contribution by Cox		
Current fair value of assets		
Cash	$ 16,500	
Accounts receivable	20,200	
Merchandise inventory	45,000	
Prepaid insurance	1,900	
Equipment	40,000	
	123,600	
Current fair value of liabilities assumed		
Accounts payable	30,500	
Notes payable	10,000	
Loan payable, delivery van	3,500	
Interest payable	600	
Payroll taxes withheld and accrued	2,100	
	46,700	
Net contribution by Cox for 1,000 shares		76,900
Cox's goodwill		$ 9,100

b.

Cox Stationers, Inc.
BALANCE SHEET
January 1, 1987

Assets

Current Assets:

Cash		$102,500 [1]
Accounts receivable	$23,500	
Less allowance for doubtful accounts	3,300	20,200
Merchandise inventory		45,000
Prepaid insurance		1,900 [2]
Total current assets		169,600
Equipment		40,000
Goodwill		9,100
Total assets		$218,700

Liabilities and Stockholders' Equity

Current Liabilities:

Note payable, bank	$ 10,000
Loan payable, delivery van	3,500
Accounts payable	30,500
Accrued interest	600 [3]
Payroll taxes withheld and accrued	2,100
Total current liabilities	46,700

Stockholders' Equity:

Common stock, $50 par; authorized 7,500 shares; issued an outstanding 2,000 shares	100,000
Additional paid-in capital	72,000 [4]
Total stockholders' equity	172,000
Total liabilities and stockholders' equity	$218,700

Explanations of Amounts:

[1] Cash
         Balance, 12/31/86 $ 16,500
         1/1/87, sale of common stock to Rice   86,000
         Balance, 1/1/87 $102,500

[2] Prepaid insurance
         Paid, 7/1/86 $ 3,800

         Prepaid, 12/31/86 (x ½) $ 1,900

[3] Accrued interest on note payable
         Annual interest ($10,000 x 12%) $ 1,200
         July--December 31, 1986 (x ½) $ 600

[4] Additional paid-in capital
         Total assets $218,700
         Deduct liabilities   46,700
         Total stockholders' equity   172,000
         Deduct common stock (2,000 shares x $50)   100,000
         Additional paid-in capital $ 72,000

ERROR CORRECTION

Multiple Choice Questions (1-6)

1. During 1988, Paul Company discovered that the ending inventories reported on its financial statements were incorrect by the following amounts:

1986	$60,000 understated
1987	75,000 overstated

Paul uses the periodic inventory system to ascertain year-end quantities that are converted to dollar amounts using the FIFO cost method. Prior to any adjustments for these errors and ignoring income taxes, Paul's retained earnings at January 1, 1988, would be

- a. Correct.
- b. $ 15,000 overstated.
- c. $ 75,000 overstated.
- d. $135,000 overstated.

2. On January 1, 1987, Aker Corp. acquired a machine at a cost of $200,000. It was to be depreciated on the straight-line method over a five-year period with no residual value. Because of a bookkeeping error, no depreciation was recognized in Aker's 1987 financial statements. The oversight was discovered during the preparation of Aker's 1988 financial statements. Depreciation expense on this machine for 1988 should be

- a. $0
- b. $40,000
- c. $50,000
- c. $80,000

3. The first examination of Rudd Corp.'s financial statements was made for the year ended December 31, 1988. The auditor found that Rudd had purchased another company in January 1986 and had recorded goodwill of $100,000 in connection with this purchase. It was determined that the goodwill had an estimated useful life of only five years because of obsolescence. No amortization of goodwill had ever been recorded. For the December 31, 1988 financial statements, Rudd should debit

	Amortization expense	Retained earnings
a.	$0	$100,000
b.	$20,000	$ 40,000
c.	$33,333	$0
d.	$60,000	$0

4. Terry, Inc. is a calendar-year corporation whose financial statements for 1987 and 1988 included errors as follows:

Year	Ending inventory	Depreciation expense
1987	$15,000 overstated	$12,500 overstated
1988	5,000 understated	4,000 understated

Assume that purchases were recorded correctly and that no correcting entries were made at December 31, 1987 or at December 31, 1988. Ignoring income taxes, by how much should Terry's retained earnings be retroactively adjusted at January 1, 1989?

- a. $13,500 increase.
- b. $ 3,500 decrease.
- c. $ 1,500 decrease.
- d. $ 1,000 increase.

5. After the issuance of its 1987 financial statements Terry, Inc. discovered a computational error of $150,000 in the calculation of its December 31, 1987 inventory. The error resulted in a $150,000 overstatement in the cost of goods sold for the year ended December 31, 1987. In October 1988, Terry paid $500,000 in settlement of litigation instituted against it during 1987. Ignore income taxes. In the 1988 financial statements the December 31, 1987 retained earnings balance, as previously reported, should be adjusted by a

- a. $150,000 credit.
- b. $350,000 debit.
- c. $500,000 debit.
- d. $650,000 credit.

May 1990 Question

6. On December 31, 1989, special insurance costs, incurred but unpaid, were not recorded. If these insurance costs were related to work-in-process, what is the effect of the omission on accrued liabilities and retained earnings in the December 31, 1989 balance sheet?

	Accrued liabilities	Retained earnings
a.	No effect	No effect
b.	No effect	Overstated
c.	Understated	No effect
d.	Understated	Overstated

ERROR CORRECTION

Problem

Problem 1   (586,P5)

(40 to 50 minutes)

Rand, Inc., a nonpublic enterprise, is negotiating a loan for expansion purposes and the bank requires audited financial statements. Before closing the accounting records for the year ended December 31, 1985, Rand's controller prepared the following comparative financial statements for 1985 and 1984:

Rand, Inc.
BALANCE SHEETS
December 31, 1985 and 1984

	1985	1984
Assets		
Cash	$ 275,000	$150,000
Marketable securities, at cost	78,000	78,000
Accounts receivable	487,000	392,000
Allowance for doubtful accounts	(50,000)	(32,000)
Inventories	425,000	307,000
Property and equipment	310,000	217,000
Accumulated depreciation	(150,000)	(121,000)
Total assets	$1,375,000	$991,000
Liabilities & Stockholders' Equity		
Accounts payable & accrued liabilities	$ 420,000	$347,000
Estimated liability from lawsuit	100,000	–
Common stock, $10 par	260,000	260,000
Additional paid-in capital	130,000	130,000
Retained earnings	465,000	254,000
Total liabilities & stockholders' equity	$1,375,000	$991,000

Rand, Inc.
INCOME STATEMENTS
For the Years Ended December 31, 1985 and 1984

	1985	1984
Net sales	$1,580,000	$1,250,000
Operating expenses:		
Cost of sales	755,000	690,000
Selling & administrative	485,000	365,000
Depreciation	29,000	18,000
Estimated loss from lawsuit	100,000	–
	1,369,000	1,073,000
Net income	$ 211,000	$ 177,000

During the course of the audit, the following additional information was obtained:

1. The investment portfolio consists of short-term investments with a total market valuation of $81,000 at December 31, 1984, and $67,000 at December 31, 1985.

2. In discussion with company officials, it was determined that the doubtful accounts expense rate based on net sales should be reduced to 2% from 3% effective January 1, 1985.

3. As a result of errors in physical count, inventories were overstated by $12,000 at December 31, 1984, and by $17,500 at December 31, 1985.

4. On January 1, 1984, the cost of equipment purchased for $30,000 was debited to repairs and maintenance. Rand depreciates machines of this type by the straight-line method over a five-year life, with no residual value.

5. On July 1, 1985, fully depreciated equipment purchased for $21,000, was sold as scrap for $2,500. The only entry Rand made was to debit cash and credit property and equipment for the scrap proceeds. The property and equipment (net) had a current cost of $250,000 at December 31, 1985.

6. Advertising and promotion expense for the year ended December 31, 1984, includes the $25,000 cost of printing sales catalogs for a special promotional campaign in January 1985.

7. Rand was named as a defendant in a lawsuit in October 1985. Rand's counsel is of the opinion that Rand has a good defense and does not anticipate any impairment of Rand's assets or that any significant liability will be incurred. Nevertheless, Rand's management wished to be conservative and established a loss contingency of $100,000 at December 31, 1985.

Required (Ignore income taxes):

Go to following page and remove tear-out worksheet.

Complete the tear-out worksheet to prepare a corrected balance sheet of Rand, Inc. as of December 31, 1985, and a corrected income statement for the year ended December 31, 1985. Formal statements and journal entries are not required. The worksheet adjustments should be numbered to correspond with the numbers in the additional information. Include the completed tear-out worksheet in the proper sequence with other answer sheets.

Rand, Inc.
WORKSHEET FOR BALANCE SHEET
AND INCOME STATEMENT
December 31, 1985

	Balance per books	Adjustments Debit	Adjustments Credit	Corrected balance
Balance Sheet				
Assets:	Dr. (Cr.)			
Cash	$ 275,000			
Marketable securities, at cost	78,000			
Accounts receivable	487,000			
Allowance for doubtful accounts	(50,000)			
Inventories	425,000			
Property and equipment	310,000			
Accumulated depreciation	(150,000)			
	$ 1,375,000			
Liabilities & Stockholders' Equity:	Cr.			
Accounts payable & accrued expenses	$ 420,000			
Estimated liability from lawsuit	100,000			
Common stock	260,000			
Additional paid-in capital	130,000			
Retained earnings				
Balance, 1/1/85	254,000			
Net income for 1985	211,000			
	$ 1,375,000			
Income Statement				
	Dr. (Cr.)			
Net sales	$(1,580,000)			
Cost of sales	755,000			
Selling & administrative expenses	485,000			
Depreciation expense	29,000			
Estimated loss from lawsuit	100,000			
Net income	$ (211,000)			

ERROR CORRECTION

Multiple Choice Answers

1. c   3. b   4. a   5. a   6. c
2. b

Multiple Choice Answer Explanations

B. Error Correction

1.   (587,P2,34) (c) The error in understating the 1986 ending inventory would have
reversed by 1/1/88 (1986 income understated by
$60,000; 1987 income overstated by $60,000).
The error in overstating the 1987 ending
inventory would not have been reversed by
1/1/88. This error overstates both 1987
income and the 1/1/88 retained earnings
balance by $75,000.

2.   (1189,P3,52) (b) In 1988, an error in
the 1987 income statement was discovered. No
depreciation expense was recorded in 1987; the
correct 1987 depreciation amount was $40,000
($200,000 ÷ 5). Therefore, a prior period
adjustment should be recorded to adjust the
1/1/88 balance of retained earnings down by
$40,000. The entry is:

       Retained earnings
        (prior per. adj.)   40,000
            Accumulated depreciation   40,000

In 1988, after the error is discovered,
depreciation should be recorded at the normal
rate. The entry is:

       Depreciation expense   40,000
            Accumulated depreciation   40,000

3.   (1189,Q1,15) (b) The failure to amortize
goodwill in prior years (1986 and 1987) is
considered an error. The profession requires
that a correction of an error be treated as
prior period adjustment, be recorded in the
year in which the error was discovered, and be
reported in the financial statements as an
adjustment to the beginning balance of
retained earnings. Therefore, the $40,000 of
amortization that was not expensed in 1986 and
1987 [(1/5 x $100,000) + (1/5 x $100,000)]
should be debited to retained earnings. The
$20,000 amortization expense for the current
year (1/5 x $100,000) is considered a current
year adjustment and should be expensed. The
journal entry would be:

    Amortization expense   20,000
    Retained earnings, 1/1/87 40,000
        Goodwill   60,000

4.   (585,P1,17) (a) The requirement is to
determine the retroactive adjustment which
should be made to 1/1/89 retained earnings
(ignoring income taxes) as the result of
several inventory and depreciation errors.
The error in overstating the 1987 ending
inventory would have reversed by 1/1/89 (1987
income overstated by $15,000; 1988 income
understated by $15,000). The error in under-
stating the 1988 ending inventory would not
have reversed by 1/1/89; this error understates both 1988 income and the 1/1/89 retained earnings balance by $5,000. The depre-
ciation expense errors are not reversing type
errors. The 1987 error understates 1/1/89
retained earnings by $12,500, while the 1988
error overstates 1/1/89 retained earnings by
$4,000. Therefore, 1/1/89 retained earnings
is understated by $13,500 (-$5,000 - $12,500 +
$4,000), and must be increased by $13,500.

5.   (1184,P2,29) (a) The requirement is the
adjustment which should be made to the
12/31/87 retained earnings balance in the 1988
financial statements. All corrections of
errors (such as the $150,000 computational
error) are treated as prior period adjustments. However, the $500,000 paid in settle-
ment of litigation in 1988 is not a prior
period adjustment. If we assume that the loss
had been accrued as a contingency in 1987,
there would be a debit to the liability
account established in 1987. If, in 1987, the
potential award had not met the criteria of a
contingency per SFAS 5 (i.e., probable and
reasonably estimable), then it would appropriately be considered an expense of 1988 when
paid.

May 1990 Answer

6.   (590,T1,7) (c) A liability is accrued
when an obligation to pay or perform services
has been incurred. This is the case even if
the liability will not be satisfied until a
future date. Therefore, accrued liabilities
will be understated on the December 31, 1989
balance sheet because the special insurance
costs were not recorded. However, there will
be no effect on the December 31, 1989 balance
of retained earnings because these costs relate to work in process and work in process
does not effect net income currently. Please
note that if the special insurance costs related to goods that were sold, cost of goods
sold would have been understated which would
have caused both net income and retained
earnings to be overstated.

ERROR CORRECTION

Solution Guide

Problem 1   Worksheet to Prepare Corrected
            Financial Statements (586,P5)

1.   In this problem, a worksheet to prepare
     corrected financial statements must be
     completed. Formal statements and journal
     entries are **not** required. The given in-
     formation includes tentative comparative
     financial statements, seven items of
     additional information, and the worksheet
     to be completed.

2.   The solutions approach is to first skim
     through the problem, then go through the
     additional data in detail, determining
     the necessary entries and filling in the
     worksheet as you proceed. Be sure to
     note the dates carefully.

2.1 The short-term investment portfolio of
     marketable equity securities (MES) has an
     aggregate market value of $67,000 at
     12/31/85. Since aggregate cost is
     $78,000, an unrealized loss of $11,000
     ($78,000 – $67,000) must be recorded.

     Unrealized loss on MES   11,000
       Allowance to reduce
       MES to market   11,000

     Note that the 12/31/84 market value
     ($81,000) has no effect on the entries
     since it exceeded the 12/31/84 cost
     ($78,000), and therefore was not re-
     flected in the accounts.

2.2 It was determined that the doubtful ac-
     counts expense rate based on net sales
     should be reduced to 2% from 3% effective
     1/1/85. Therefore, the expense must be
     reduced by $15,800 (1% x $1,580,000).

     Allowance for doubtful
      accounts   15,800
       Sell. and admin.
       expenses   15,800

2.3 The 12/31/84 physical inventory was over-
     stated by $12,000. Since the 1984 books
     are closed, this is a prior period ad-
     justment of 12/31/84 retained earnings.
     The overstatement of 12/31/84 inventory
     means 1984 cost of goods sold was under-
     stated, 1984 net income was overstated
     and 12/31/84 retained earnings was over-
     stated. Therefore, beginning retained
     earnings is debited. The offsetting

credit is to cost of sales. The overstatement of 12/31/84 inventory (1985
beginning inventory) overstates 1985 cost
of sales. The entry is:

Retained earnings (prior
 period adjustment)   12,000
   Cost of sales   12,000

The 12/31/85 physical inventory was overstated by $17,500. Inventory must be
credited for this amount. The offsetting
debit is to cost of sales, since the
overstatement of **ending** inventory understates cost of sales.

Cost of sales   17,500
  Inventories   17,500

Note that the AICPA Unofficial Answer
shows only a net entry of $5,500 to cost
of sales.

2.4 On 1/1/84, the $30,000 cost of equipment
     purchased was erroneously debited to ex-
     pense. The straight-line method with a
     five-year life and no residual value
     should be used. Since the 1984 books are
     closed, this is a prior period adjustment
     of 12/31/84 retained earnings. In 1984,
     $30,000 was expensed instead of $6,000
     ($30,000 x .20); therefore, 12/31/84 re-
     tained earnings is understated by
     $24,000. The correcting entry must
     record the equipment at $30,000, the
     12/31/84 accumulated depreciation of
     $6,000, and the correction of retained
     earnings.

     Equipment   30,000
       Accumulated depreci-
       ation   6,000
       Retained earnings
        (prior period adj.)   24,000

     Also, 1985 depreciation expense must be
     recorded.

     Depreciation expense   6,000
       Accumulated depreci-
       ation   6,000

     The two entries are combined in the work-
     sheet. No entry is made to reflect the
     12/31/85 current cost of property and
     equipment ($250,000). Fixed assets are
     reported at historical cost less accumu-
     lated depreciation.

2.5 On 7/1/85, fully depreciated equipment
     (cost, $21,000) was sold for $2,500. The
     entry made was:

     Cash   2,500
       Equipment   2,500

The correct entry is:

Cash	2,500	
Accumulated depreciation	21,000	
Equipment		21,000
Gain on sale		
(Other income)		2,500

The correcting entry to adjust from the entry actually made to the correct entry is:

Accumulated depreciation	21,000	
Equipment		18,500
Gain on sale		
(Other income)		2,500

The credit to equipment is the difference between the correct credit ($21,000) and the actual credit ($2,500).

2.6   **1984** expense includes the $25,000 cost of printing sales catalogs for a **1985** promotional campaign. This amount should have been reported as a prepaid expense at 12/31/84, and expensed in 1985 when the related revenue was earned. Since the 1984 books are closed, this is a prior period adjustment of 12/31/84 retained earnings, which was understated when the $25,000 was expensed rather than capitalized in 1984. Therefore, beginning retained earnings is credited. The offsetting debit is to 1985 selling and administrative expense, to reflect the expense in the proper year.

Sell. and admin. expense	25,000	
Retained earnings		
(prior period adj.)		25,000

2.7   An estimated loss and liability from a lawsuit was accrued at 12/31/85. Per SFAS 5, para 8, a contingent liability should be accrued only if information available prior to the issuance of the financial statements indicates that it is **probable** a liability existed at the balance sheet date, **and** if the amount of the liability is **reasonably estimable**. In this case, legal counsel indicates that it is **not** probable that a liability existed at the balance sheet date. Therefore, the loss and liability should **not** have been accrued, and the entry must be reversed.

Est. liability from		
lawsuit	100,000	
Est. loss from		
lawsuit		100,000

3.   The final step is to total the columns and rows in the completed worksheet. Note that the 1985 net income row in the balance sheet section must be adjusted by a $47,500 debit and a $118,300 credit. The net effect is a $70,800 credit adjustment to net income per books.

Unofficial Answer

Problem 1   Worksheet to Prepare Corrected Financial Statements (586,P5)

Rand, Inc.
**WORKSHEET FOR BALANCE SHEET
AND INCOME STATEMENT**
December 31, 1985

	Balance per books	Adjustments Debit		Adjustments Credit		Corrected balance
Balance sheet						
Assets:	Dr. (Cr.)					
Cash	$ 275,000					$ 275,000
Marketable securities, at cost	78,000					78,000
Accounts receivable	487,000					487,000
Allowance for doubtful accounts	(50,000)	[2]	$ 15,800			(34,200)
Inventories	425,000			[3]	$ 17,500	407,500
Property and equipment	310,000	[4]	30,000	[5]	18,500	321,500
Accumulated depreciation	(150,000)	[5]	21,000	[4]	12,000	(141,000)
Allowance to reduce MES to market				[1]	11,000	(11,000)
	$ 1,375,000		$ 66,800		$ 59,000	$ 1,382,800
Liabilities & Stockholders' Equity:	Cr.					
Accounts payable & accrued liabilities	$ 420,000					420,000
Estimated liability from lawsuit	100,000	[7]	100,000			-0-
Common stock	260,000					260,000
Additional paid-in capital	130,000					130,000
Retained earnings						
Balance, 1/1/85	254,000	[3]	12,000	[4]	24,000	291,000
				[6]	25,000	
Net income for 1985	211,000		47,500		118,300	281,800
	$ 1,375,000		$159,500		$167,300	$ 1,382,800
Income statement						
	Dr. (Cr.)					
Net sales	$(1,580,000)					$(1,580,000)
Cost of sales	755,000	[3]	5,500			760,500
Selling & administrative expenses	485,000	[6]	25,000	[2]	15,800	494,200
Depreciation expense	29,000	[4]	6,000			35,000
Estimated loss from lawsuit	100,000			[7]	100,000	-0-
Unrealized loss on MES		[1]	11,000			11,000
Other income				[5]	2,500	(2,500)
Net income	$ (211,000)		$ 47,500		$118,300	$ (281,800)

Problem 1 (continued)

Explanations of Corrections

[1] Decline in market valuation of marketable securities at 12/31/85
     At cost $78,000
     Market valuation   67,000
     Unrealized loss on marketable securities [Dr.] $11,000

     Allowance to reduce marketable securities to market [Cr.] $11,000

[2] Decline in doubtful accounts expense rate effective 1/1/85
     Doubtful accounts expense charged at 3% of net sales
      for 1985 [3% x $1,580,000] $47,400
     Doubtful accounts expense stated at 2% of net sales
      for 1985 [2% x $1,580,000]   31,600

     Allowance for doubtful accounts [Dr.] $15,800

     Selling & adm. expense--Doubtful accounts expense [Cr.] $15,800

[3] Inventories overstated at 12/31/84 and 12/31/85
     Retained earnings [overstatement at 12/31/84] [Dr.] $12,000
     Cost of sales for 1985 [$17,500 - $12,000] [Dr.]   5,500

     Inventories [overstatement at 12/31/85] [Cr.] $17,500

[4] Incorrect recording of equipment purchased 1/1/84
     Property and equipment [Dr.] $30,000
     Depreciation expense--1985 [20% x $30,000] [Dr.]   6,000
                                                                                                    $36,000

     Accumulated depreciation [2 x $6,000] [Cr.] $12,000
     Retained earnings (understatement at 12/31/84)[$30,000 - $6,000] [Cr.]   24,000
                                                                                                    $36,000

[5] Incorrect recording of fully depreciated equipment sold as scrap 7/1/85
     Accumulated depreciation [Dr.] $21,000
     Property and equipment [$21,000 - $2,500] [Cr.]   18,500
     Other income [Cr.] $ 2,500

[6] Incorrect recording of sales catalogs as expense in 1984
     Selling & adm. exp.--Advertising & promotion [Dr.] $25,000

     Retained earnings (understatement at 12/31/84) [Cr.] $25,000

[7] Reversal of liability from lawsuit--No probable loss 12/31/85
     Estimated liability from lawsuit [Dr.] $100,000

     Estimated loss from lawsuit [Cr.] $100,000

ACCOUNTING CHANGES

Multiple Choice Questions (1-17)

1. On January 1, 1986, Farr, Inc. changed to the straight-line method of depreciation from an accelerated method of depreciation for its machinery and equipment. The accumulated depreciation through December 31, 1985 was $600,000 higher than if the straight-line method had been used. The change was made for financial statement reporting but not for income tax reporting. Farr's income tax rate is 40% for 1985 and 1986. In Farr's 1986 income statement, the cumulative effect of this change in accounting principle should be reported at
   - a. $600,000
   - b. $360,000
   - c. $240,000
   - d. $0

2. On January 1, 1984, Bray Company purchased for $240,000 a machine with a useful life of ten years and no salvage value. The machine was depreciated by the double declining balance method and the carrying amount of the machine was $153,600 on December 31, 1985. Bray changed retroactively to the straight-line method on January 1, 1986. Bray can justify the change. What should be the depreciation expense on this machine for the year ended December 31, 1986?
   - a. $15,360
   - b. $19,200
   - c. $24,000
   - d. $30,720

3. On December 31, 1988, Kerr, Inc. appropriately changed its inventory valuation method to FIFO cost from weighted-average cost for financial statement and income tax purposes. The change will result in a $700,000 increase in the beginning inventory at January 1, 1988. Assume a 30% income tax rate. The cumulative effect of this accounting change reported for the year ended December 31, 1988 is
   - a. $0
   - b. $210,000
   - c. $490,000
   - d. $700,000

4. On January 1, 1988, Roem Corp. changed its inventory method to FIFO from LIFO for both financial and income tax reporting purposes. The change resulted in a $500,000 increase in the January 1, 1988 inventory. Assume that the income tax rate for all years is 30%. The cumulative effect of the ac-

counting change should be reported by Roem in its 1988
   - a.   Retained earnings statement as a $350,000 addition to the beginning balance.
   - b.   Income statement as a $350,000 cumulative effect of accounting change.
   - c.   Retained earnings statement as a $500,000 addition to the beginning balance.
   - d.   Income statement as a $500,000 cumulative effect of accounting change.

5. On January 1, 1985, Poe Construction, Inc. changed to the percentage-of-completion method of income recognition for financial statement reporting but not for income tax reporting. Poe can justify this change in accounting principle. As of December 31, 1984, Poe compiled data showing that income under the completed-contract method aggregated $700,000. If the percentage-of-completion method had been used, the accumulated income through December 31, 1984 would have been $880,000. Assuming an income tax rate of 40% for all years, the cumulative effect of this accounting change should be reported by Poe in the 1985
   - a.   Retained earnings statement as a $180,000 credit adjustment to the beginning balance.
   - b.   Income statement as a $180,000 credit.
   - c.   Retained earnings statement as a $108,000 credit adjustment to the beginning balance.
   - d.   Income statement as a $108,000 credit.

6. The cumulative effect of changing to a new accounting principle on the amount of retained earnings at the beginning of the period in which the change is made should be included in net income of

	Future periods	The period of change
a.	No	No
b.	Yes	No
c.	Yes	Yes
d.	No	Yes

7. A company changes from an accounting principle that is not generally accepted to one that is generally accepted. The effect of the change should be reported, net of applicable income taxes, in the current
   - a.   Income statement after income from continuing operations and before extraordinary items.
   - b.   Income statement after extraordinary items.

c.   Retained earnings statement as an adjustment of the opening balance.

d.   Retained earnings statement after net income but before dividends.

8.   The cumulative effect of changing to a new accounting principle should be recorded separately as a component of income after continuing operations for a change from the

a.   Straight-line method of depreciation for previously recorded assets to the sum-of-the-years'-digits method.

b.   LIFO method of inventory pricing to the FIFO method.

c.   Percentage-of-completion method of accounting for long-term construction-type contracts to the completed-contract method.

d.   Cash basis of accounting for vacation pay to the accrual basis.

9.   The effect of a change in accounting principle which is inseparable from the effect of a change in accounting estimate should be reported

a.   In the period of change and future periods if the change affects both.

b.   By restating the financial statements of all prior periods presented.

c.   By showing the pro forma effects of retroactive application.

d.   As a correction of an error.

10.   When a company changes from the straight-line method of depreciation for previously recorded assets to the double-declining balance method, which of the following should be reported?

	Cumulative effects of change in accounting principle	Pro forma effects of retroactive application
a.	No	No
b.	No	Yes
c.	Yes	Yes
d.	Yes	No

11.   When a cumulative effect type change in accounting principle is made during the year, the cumulative effect on retained earnings is determined

a.   During the year using the weighted-average method.

b.   As of the date of the change.

c.   As of the beginning of the year in which the change is made.

d.   As of the end of the year in which the change is made.

12.   Kemp Company purchased a patent on January 1, 1984 for $357,000. The patent was being amortized over its remaining legal life of 15 years expiring on January 1, 1999. During 1987 Kemp determined that the economic benefits of the patent would not last longer than ten years from the date of acquisition. What amount should be reported in the balance sheet as patent, net of accumulated amortization, at December 31, 1987?

a. $261,800
b. $252,000
c. $244,800
d. $214,200

13.   During 1985 Kerr Company determined that machinery previously depreciated over a seven-year life had a total estimated useful life of only five years. An accounting change was made in 1985 to reflect the change in estimate. If the change had been made in 1984, accumulated depreciation would have been $800,000 at December 31, 1984 instead of $600,000. As a result of this change, the 1985 depreciation expense was $50,000 greater. The income tax rate was 40% in both years. What should be reported in Kerr's income statement for the year ended December 31, 1985, as the cumulative effect on prior years of changing the estimated useful life of the machinery?

a. $0
b. $120,000
c. $150,000
d. $200,000

14.   A change in the periods benefited by a deferred cost because additional information has been obtained is

a.   A correction of an error.

b.   An accounting change that should be reported by restating the financial statements of all prior periods presented.

c.   An accounting change that should be reported in the period of change and future periods if the change affects both.

d.   Not an accounting change.

15.   When a company changes the expected service life of an asset because additional information has been obtained, which of the following should be reported?

	Cumulative effect of a change in accounting principle	Pro forma effects of retroactive application
a.	No	Yes
b.	Yes	No
c.	Yes	Yes
d.	No	No

16. During 1983 a textbook written by Burr
Company personnel was sold to Fox Publishing,
Inc. for royalties of 10% on sales. Royalties
are receivable semiannually on March 31 for
sales in July through December of the prior
year, and on September 30 for sales in January
through June of the same year.

   •   Royalty income of $18,000 was
accrued at 12/31/83 for the period July -
December 1983.
   •   Royalty income of $20,000 was
received on 3/31/84, and $26,000 on 9/30/84.
   •   Burr learned from Fox that sales
subject to royalty were estimated at $270,000
for the last half of 1984.

In its income statement for 1984, Burr should
report royalty income at
   a. $46,000
   b. $48,000
   c. $53,000
   d. $55,000

17. A company has included in its consolidated financial statements this year a subsidiary acquired several years ago that was
appropriately excluded from consolidation last
year. This results in
   a.   An accounting change that should be
        reported prospectively.
   b.   An accounting change that should be
        reported by restating the financial
        statements of all prior periods
        presented.
   c.   A correction of an error.
   d.   Neither an accounting change nor a
        correction of an error.

May 1990 Question

Repeat Question

(590,P1,20) Identical/similar to item 12 above

ACCOUNTING CHANGES
Problem

Problem 1   (588,T3)

(15 to 25 minutes)

There are various types of accounting changes, each of which is required to be reported differently.

Required:

a.   What type of accounting change is a change from the sum-of-the-years'-digits method of depreciation to the straight-line method for previously recorded assets? Under what circumstances does this type of accounting change occur?

b.   What type of accounting change is a change in the expected service life of an asset arising because of more experience with the asset? Under what circumstances does this type of accounting change occur?

c.   With respect to a change in accounting principle,
   1.   How should a company calculate the effect?
   2.   How should a company report the effect?

Do not discuss earnings per share requirements.

d.1.   Why are accounting principles, once adopted, normally continued?

   2.   What is the rationale for disclosure of a change from one accounting principle to another accounting principle?

ACCOUNTING CHANGES

Multiple Choice Answers

1. b	5. c	9. a	12. c	15. d
2. c	6. d	10. c	13. a	16. d
3. c	7. c	11. c	14. c	17. b
4. a	8. a			

Multiple Choice Answer Explanations

C.1. Changes in Accounting Principles

1. (1187,P3,51) (b) Per APB 20, a change in depreciation methods is a change in accounting principle in which the cumulative effect is only reported in the current year. The cumulative effect ($600,000) is reported as a separate component of income in the current year's income statement, net of the tax effect. The tax effect is $240,000 ($600,000 x 40%) which means that the net amount is $360,000 ($600,000 - $240,000).

2. (587,P3,47) (c) Per APB 20, when a change in principle is made, generally the current or catch-up approach is used. The cumulative effect of the adjustment of prior years is reported in the current income statement, and the new method is used in the current year. Do not be misled by the statement in the question that says Bray changed retroactively. The term retroactive is being used in this question to refer to the way in which the catch-up or cumulative amount is computed, not the manner of reporting it. In comparative financial statements, no changes are made to the previously published financial statements for catch-up adjustments as an accounted for catch-up or cumulative type change. In this case the cumulative effect is $38,400 ($86,400 double declining balance accumulated depreciation - $48,000 straight-line accumulated depreciation). The journal entry to reflect this cumulative effect would be:

Accumulated depreciation   38,400
    Cumulative effect   38,400

In 1986, depreciation expense would be computed using straight-line depreciation, computed as follows:

Depreciation exp. is $24,000 ($240,000 ÷ 10).

Depreciation expense   24,000
    Accumulated depreciation   24,000

3. (1189,P3,51) (c) The change in accounting principle from weighted-average to FIFO results in a $700,000 increase in inventory valuation, which means the before-tax effect on income is also $700,000. Since a

cumulative effect must be reported net of tax, the tax effect of $210,000 (30% x $700,000) is subtracted to leave a net cumulative effect of $490,000.

4. (589,P3,52) (a) APB 20 states that a change in inventory methods from LIFO is one of the exceptions requiring the use of the retroactive approach rather than the current approach. The cumulative effect at the beginning of the period of change is entered directly to retained earnings as a prior period adjustment, and the prior year statements are retroactively restated. The cumulative effect is recorded net of the related tax effect. In this case, the cumulative effect is $350,000 [$500,000 - (30% x $500,000)]

The journal entry is:

Inventory   500,000
    Retained earnings   350,000
    Deferred tax liability   150,000

Answer (c) is incorrect because the amount is not net of tax. Answers (b) and (d) are incorrect because the current approach is used [and (d) is not net of tax].

5. (586,P3,58) (c) The requirement is to indicate how a change in accounting principle from the completed-contract method to the percentage-of-completion method should be reported. Per para 27 of APB 20, a change in the method of accounting for long-term contracts is one of the exceptions requiring the use of the retroactive, rather than the current, approach. The cumulative effect at the beginning of the period of change is entered directly to retained earnings as a prior period adjustment, and prior year statements are retroactively restated. The cumulative effect is recorded net of the related tax effect. In this case, the cumulative effect is $108,000 [($880,000 - $700,000) x (1 - .40)]. The journal entry is as follows:

Construction-in-progress   180,000
    Deferred taxes   72,000
    Retained earnings   108,000

Answer (a) is incorrect because the effect is not shown net of tax. Answers (b) and (d) are incorrect because they apply the current approach instead of the retroactive approach.

6. (1188,T1,32) (d) Per APB 20, para 22c, the cumulative effect of changing to a new accounting principle on the amount of retained earnings at the beginning of the period should be included (entirely) in the income statement of the period in which the change is made. In

future periods, the newly adopted principle will be used, so there is no additional cumulative effect to report. Therefore, answer (d) is correct.

7. (1187,T1,14) (c) APB 20, para 13 states that a change from an accounting principle that is not generally accepted to one that is generally accepted should be treated in the same manner as a correction of an error. A correction of an error should be reported as a prior period adjustment (APB 20, para 36). This means that the cumulative effect at the beginning of the period of change is entered directly as an adjustment to the opening balance of retained earnings (SFAS 16, para 16a). When comparative statements are presented, prior year's statements are retroactively restated (APB 9, para 18). Therefore, answer (c) is correct and answer (d) is incorrect. Answers (a) and (b) are incorrect because no special presentation is needed in the current period's income statement for the correction of an error. The correction is integrated into the statement. Note that answer (b) would have been correct if the question asked about the change from acceptable GAAP to acceptable GAAP.

8. (589,T1,24) (a) APB 20, para 20 states that generally, the cumulative effect of changes in accounting principle or methods of application from one generally accepted accounting principle to another should be reported separately as a component of income from continuing operations. Answer (a) is such a change, and therefore, is correct. Answers (b) and (c) are incorrect because each of these answers is a "special" change as described in APB 20, para 27 and SFAS 73, para 2. These special changes are reported by retroactively applying the new method in restatements of prior periods. Answer (d) is incorrect because a change from an accounting principle that is not generally accepted to a principle that is generally accepted is a correction of an error as per APB 20, para 13, and would accordingly be accounted for as a prior period adjustment to beginning retained earnings, not as a change in accounting principle.

9. (1187,T1,26) (a) Per APB 20, para 11, the effect of a change in accounting principle which is inseparable from the effect of a change in accounting estimate should be accounted for as a change in accounting estimate. Answer (a) is correct because changes in estimate should be accounted for in the period of change and also in any affected future periods (APB 20, para 31). Answer (b) is incorrect because financial statements are restated for "special" changes in accounting principle, changes in entity, and changes due

to an error. Answer (c) is incorrect because the pro forma effects of retroactive application are shown for all changes in accounting principle other than those designated as "special" changes. Answer (d) is incorrect because errors would include mathematical mistakes, mistakes in applying principles, oversights or misuse of available facts, and changes from unacceptable to acceptable GAAP (APB 20, para 13). The situation described in this question does not meet the description of an error.

10. (585,T1,28) (c) The requirement is to determine if a change in depreciation methods, from straight-line to double-declining balance, should be reported as a cumulative effect of a change in accounting principle and if the pro forma effects of retroactive application should also be reported. Answer (c) is correct because APB 20, paras 20 and 21 requires the presentation of the cumulative effect of the change and the pro forma effects of retroactive application (for a change in accounting principle). Additionally, the pro forma effects of retroactive application are to be shown on the face of the income statement in a separate section, below earnings per share. Answers (a), (b), and (d) are incorrect.

11. (583,T1,36) (c) When a cumulative effect type change in accounting principle is made during the year, the cumulative effect on retained earnings is determined as of the beginning of the year in which the change is made (APB 20, para 19b). It is determined at the beginning of the year because the new principle is used throughout the current year. Answer (a) is nonsensical and answers (b) and (d) are incorrect because the effect of the change is determined at the beginning of the year.

C.2. Changes in Accounting Estimates

12. (1188,P2,24) (c) From 1/1/84 to 12/31/86, patent amortization was recorded using a 15-year life. Yearly amortization was $23,800 ($357,000 ÷ 15); accumulated amortization at 12/31/86 was $71,400 ($23,800 x 3); and the book value of the patent at 12/31/86 was $285,600 ($357,000 - $71,400). Beginning in 1987 this book value must be amortized over its remaining useful life of 7 years (10 years - 3 years). Therefore, 1987 amortization is $40,800 ($285,600 ÷ 7) and the book value of the patent is $244,800 ($285,600 - $40,800).

13. (586,P3,57) (a) The requirement is the amount to be reported in the 1985 income statement as the cumulative effect on prior years of changing the estimated useful life of

machinery. Per APB 20, changes in estimate
are handled prospectively. No cumulative
effect on prior years is reported; the effect
is spread out over the current and future
periods through a revised depreciation rate.
Therefore, the cumulative effect is $0.

14. (589,T1,29) (c) APB 20, para 10 states
that a change in the periods benefited by a
deferred cost should be treated as a change in
accounting estimate. Changes in accounting
estimates are accounted for in the period of
change and future periods if the change
affects both (para 31). Therefore, answer (c)
is correct.

15. (1189,T1,31) (d) Per APB 20, para 10, a
change in the expected service life of an
asset is a change in accounting estimate. Per
APB 20, para 31, changes in accounting
estimate should be accounted for in the period
of change and future periods (if the change
affects both). A change in an estimate should
not be accounted for by restating amounts
reported in financial statements of prior
periods or by reporting pro forma amounts for
prior periods. Therefore, answer (d) is
correct.

16. (1185,P2,33) (d) The requirement is the
amount of royalty income to be recognized in
1984. At 12/31/83, royalty income of $18,000
was accrued for the last six months of 1983.
This estimate was not correct, since $20,000
was received in 1984 for the last six months
of 1983. Per APB 20, changes in estimate are
handled prospectively, i.e., the effects are
accounted for in the period of change if only
that period is affected, or in the period of
change and future periods if future periods
are also affected. Thus, when the $20,000 is
received in 1984, $18,000 would be credited to
royalties receivable and $2,000 to royalty
income. Total 1984 royalty income would be
$55,000, as indicated below.

Change in estimate ($20,000 – $18,000)	$ 2,000
Income for first six months of 1984 (received on 9/30/84)	26,000
Income to be accrued for last six months of 1984 ($270,000 x 10%)	27,000
Total 1984 royalty income recognized	$55,000

C.3. Changes in Reporting Entity

17. (1183,T1,32) (b) The requirement is the
determination of the consequences of including
a subsidiary in the current year's statements
when it was appropriately excluded in last
year's. Per APB 20, para 12, when (1) consolidated or combined statements are presented in
place of individual statements; (2) there is a
change in the group of subsidiaries for which
consolidated statements are prepared [an-
swer (b)]; (3) there is a change in companies
included in combined statements; or (4) there
is a business combination accounted for as a
pooling of interests, then a change in the
reporting entity has occurred. Such changes
should be reported by restating the financial
statements of all prior periods presented in
order to show financial information for the
new reporting entity for all periods (APB 20,
para 34). Answer (a) is incorrect because
retroactive restatement is required. Answer (c) is incorrect since errors consist of
correcting mathematical mistakes, mistakes in
applying principles, oversights or misuse of
available facts, and changes from unacceptable
to acceptable GAAP. Answer (d) is incorrect
since a change in reporting entity is an accounting change.

ACCOUNTING CHANGES

Answer Outline

Problem 1   Types of Accounting Changes
(588,T3)

a. Change from SYD to S/L for previously
recorded assets
   Is Δ in accounting principle
   Results from adoption of generally
   accepted accounting principle different
   from one used previously
b. Change in expected service life of asset
   Is Δ in accounting estimate
   Occurs when experience shows original
   estimates need revision as result of
   events and their effects
c1. Cumulative effect of Δ in accounting
principle
   Difference between
      R/E at beginning of period, and
      R/E if new principle had been used in
      prior periods
c2. Reporting cumulative effect of   in
accounting principle
   Separate item on I/S between X/O items
   and N/I
   Disclose pro-forma effects of retroactive restatement on face of I/S
d1. Accounting principles normally continued
   Consistency enhances utility of FSs to
   users of comparative data
d2. Disclosure of change in accounting
principle
   Avoids misleading F/S users
   Presumption exists that once adopted
   accounting principle should not be
   changed
      For events and transactions of similar
      type

Unofficial Answer

Problem 1   Types of Accounting Changes
(588,T3)

a. A change from the sum-of-the-years'-digits
method of depreciation to the straight-line
method for previously recorded assets is a
change in accounting principle. Both the sum-
of-the-years'-digits method and the straight-
line method are generally accepted. A change
in accounting principle results from adoption
of a generally accepted accounting principle
different from the generally accepted accounting principle used previously for reporting
purposes.

b. A change in the expected service life of
an asset arising because of more experience
with the asset is a change in accounting estimate. A change in accounting estimate occurs
because future events and their effects cannot
be perceived with certainty. Estimates are an
inherent part of the accounting process.
Therefore, accounting and reporting for certain financial statement elements requires the
exercise of judgment, subject to revision
based on experience.

c. 1. The cumulative effect of a change in
accounting principle is the difference between
(1) the amount of retained earnings at the
beginning of the period of change and (2) the
amount of retained earnings that would have
been reported at that date if the new accounting principle had been used in prior
periods.
   2. The cumulative effect, net of income
taxes, should be shown as a separate item in
the income statement for the period of change
between the captions "extraordinary items" and
"net income". Pro-forma disclosure of the
effects of retroactive restatement should be
shown on the face of the income statement.

d. 1. Consistent use of accounting principles from one accounting period to another
enhances the utility of financial statements
to users of comparative accounting data.
   2. If a change in accounting principle
occurs, the nature and effect of a change in
accounting principle should be disclosed to
avoid misleading financial statement users.
There is a presumption that an accounting
principle once adopted should not be changed
in accounting for events and transactions of a
similar type.

FINANCIAL STATEMENTS

Multiple Choice Questions (1-35)

Items 1 and 2 are based on the following information:

Coffey Corp.'s trial balance of income statement accounts for the year ended December 31, 1988 was as follows:

	Debit	Credit
Net sales		$1,600,000
Cost of goods sold	$ 960,000	
Selling expenses	235,000	
Administrative expenses	150,000	
Interest expense	25,000	
Adjustment due to accounting change in depreciation method	40,000	
Gain on debt extinguishment		10,000
	$1,410,000	$1,610,000

Coffey's income tax rate is 30%. Coffey prepares a multiple-step income statement for 1988.

1. Income from operations before income tax is
   a. $190,000
   b. $200,000
   c. $230,000
   d. $240,000

2. Net income is
   a. $140,000
   b. $161,000
   c. $168,000
   d. $200,000

Items 3 through 5 are based on the following:

Karl Corp.'s trial balance of income statement accounts for the year ended December 31, 1987 included the following:

	Debit	Credit
Sales		$150,000
Cost of sales	$ 60,000	
Administrative expenses	15,000	
Loss on sale of equipment	9,000	
Commissions to salespersons	10,000	
Interest revenue		5,000
Freight out	3,000	
Loss on early retirement of long-term debt	10,000	
Bad debt expense	3,000	
Totals	$110,000	$155,000

Other information:

Finished goods inventory:	
January 1, 1987	$100,000
December 31, 1987	$ 90,000

Karl's income tax rate is 30%.

On Karl's multiple-step income statement for 1987,

3. Cost of goods manufactured is
   a. $73,000
   b. $70,000
   c. $53,000
   d. $50,000

4. Income before extraordinary item is
   a. $55,000
   b. $45,000
   c. $38,500
   d. $31,500

5. Extraordinary loss is
   a. $ 7,000
   b. $10,000
   c. $13,300
   d. $19,000

6. On January 2, 1987, Troast Co. purchased as a long-term investment 10,000 shares of Lawton Corp. common stock for $70 per share, which represents a 1% interest. On December 31, 1987, the market price of the stock was $75 per share. On December 20, 1988, Troast needed additional cash for operations and sold all 10,000 shares of Lawton's stock for $100 per share. Troast's income tax rate was 30% for 1988. For the year ended December 31, 1988, Troast should report on its income statement a gain on disposal of
   a. $300,000
   b. $250,000
   c. $210,000
   d. $175,000

7. Burl Company incurred the following loss and realized the following gain during 1987:

   • $50,000 loss as the result of an unanticipated strike by its employees.
   • $25,000 gain as the result of the early extinguishment of bonds payable.

Burl's income tax rate for 1987 was 30%. Burl's 1987 income statement should report an extraordinary loss and an extraordinary gain of

Authors' note: In the companion Volume I, 17th Edition, page 704 there is an error in footnote (b) to the Table. The error can be corrected by deleting the following phrase: "and tax benefits of loss carryforwards."

	Extraordinary loss	Extraordinary gain
a.	$0	$0
b.	$0	$17,500
c.	$35,000	$0
d.	$35,000	$17,500

8.   Ball Corporation had the following infrequent gains during 1986:

• A $240,000 gain on sale of a plant facility; Ball continues similar operations at another location.

• A $90,000 gain on repayment of a long-term note denominated in a foreign currency.

• A $190,000 gain on reacquisition and retirement of bonds.

In its 1986 income statement, how much should Ball report as total infrequent gains which are not considered extraordinary?
   a. $520,000
   b. $430,000
   c. $330,000
   d. $280,000

9.   On October 1, 1986, Poe Corporation's operating plant, located in Kansas, was destroyed by an earthquake. The portion of the resultant loss not covered by insurance was $1,400,000. Poe's income tax rate for 1986 is 40%. In Poe's income statement for the year ended December 31, 1986, this event should be reported as an extraordinary loss of
   a. $0
   b. $ 560,000
   c. $ 840,000
   d. $1,400,000

10.   Purl Corporation's income statement for the year ended December 31, 1986 shows the following:

Income before income tax and extraordinary item	$900,000
Gain on life insurance coverage-- included in the above $900,000 income amount	100,000
Extraordinary item--loss due to earthquake damage	300,000

Purl's tax rate for 1986 is 40%. How much should be reported as the provision for income tax in Purl's 1986 income statement?
   a. $200,000
   b. $240,000
   c. $320,000
   d. $360,000

11.   Jason Company incurred the following infrequent losses during 1986:

• A major strike by employees shut down one of Jason's factories. Shutdown losses totaled $180,000.

• A loss of $100,000 from writedown of plant and equipment to estimated realizable value.

• A loss of $150,000 on disposal of one of three similar factories.

In its 1986 income statement, how much should Jason report as total infrequent losses which are not considered extraordinary?
   a. $250,000
   b. $280,000
   c. $330,000
   d. $430,000

12.   Rice, Inc. incurred the following losses, net of applicable taxes, for the year ended December 31, 1984:

Loss on disposal of a segment of Rice's business	$350,000
Foreign currency transaction loss due to major devaluation	450,000

How much should Rice report as extraordinary losses in its 1984 income statement?
   a. $0
   b. $350,000
   c. $450,000
   d. $800,000

13.   The following expenses were recognized by Rex Company, a retailer, during 1984:

Accounting and legal fees	$240,000
Loss on sale of long-term investment	110,000
Property taxes and insurance	150,000
Interest	90,000

How much of these expenses should be included in Rex's general and administrative expenses for 1984?
   a. $390,000
   b. $440,000
   c. $480,000
   d. $500,000

Items 14 and 15 are based on the following information:

Parker Corporation reports operating expenses in two categories: (1) selling, and (2) general and administrative. The adjusted trial balance at December 31, 1983 included the following expense accounts:

Accounting and legal fees	$175,000
Advertising	150,000
Freight-out	75,000
Interest	60,000
Loss on sale of long-term investment	30,000
Officers' salaries	225,000
Rent for office space	180,000
Sales salaries and commissions	140,000

One half of the rented premises is occupied by the sales department.

14. How much of the expenses listed above should be included in Parker's selling expenses for 1983?

    a. $290,000
    b. $365,000
    c. $380,000
    d. $455,000

15. How much of the expenses listed above should be included in Parker's general and administrative expenses for 1983?

    a. $490,000
    b. $520,000
    c. $550,000
    d. $580,000

16. A gain or loss from a transaction that is unusual in nature and infrequent in occurrence should be reported separately as a component of income

    a.   Before cumulative effect of accounting changes and after discontinued operations of a segment of a business.
    b.   After cumulative effect of accounting changes and before discontinued operations of a segment of a business.
    c.   Before cumulative effect of accounting changes and before discontinued operations of a segment of a business.
    d.   After cumulative effect of accounting changes and before discontinued operations of a segment of a business.

17. An extraordinary item should be reported separately on the income statement as a component of income

	Before discontinued operations of a segment of a business	Net of income taxes
a.	No	No
b.	No	Yes
c.	Yes	Yes
d.	Yes	No

18. The effect of a material transaction that is unusual in nature but **not** infrequent in occurrence should be presented separately as a component of income from continuing operations when the transaction results in a

	Gain	Loss
a.	Yes	No
b.	Yes	Yes
c.	No	Yes
d.	No	No

19. The correction of an error in the financial statements of a prior period should be reflected, net of applicable income taxes, in the current

    a.   Income statement after income from continuing operations and before extraordinary items.
    b.   Income statement after income from continuing operations and after extraordinary items.
    c.   Retained earnings statement as an adjustment of the opening balance.
    d.   Retained earnings statement after net income but before dividends.

20. On April 30, 1988, Wall Corp. approved a plan to dispose of a segment of its business. For the period January 1 through April 30, 1988, the segment had revenues of $600,000 and expenses of $750,000. The assets of the segment were sold on October 15, 1988 at a loss, from which no tax benefit is available. In its income statement for the year ended December 31, 1888, how should Wall report the segment's operations from January 1 to April 30, 1988?

    a. $600,000 and $750,000 should be included with revenues and expenses, respectively, as part of continuing operations.
    b. $150,000 should be reported as part of the loss on disposal of a segment.
    c. $150,000 should be reported as an extraordinary loss.
    d. $150,000 should be reported as a loss from operations of a discontinued segment.

21. On October 1, 1987, Burns Corp. approved a formal plan to sell Hall Division, a business segment. The sale was scheduled to take place on March 31, 1988. Hall had operating income of $100,000 for the quarter ended December 31, 1987, and expected to incur an operating loss of $50,000 for the first quarter of 1988. Burns estimated that it would incur a $375,000 loss on the sale of Hall's assets. Burns' income tax rate for 1987 was 30%. In its 1987 income statement, Burns should report a loss on the disposal of Hall division of

    a. $325,000
    b. $297,500
    c. $262,500
    d. $227,500

22. On January 1, 1988, Dart, Inc. entered into an agreement to sell the assets and product line of its Jay Division, considered a segment of the business. The sale was consum-

mated on December 31, 1988 and resulted in a gain on disposition of $400,000. The division's operations resulted in losses before income tax of $225,000 in 1988 and $125,000 in 1987. Dart's income tax rate is 30% for both years. In a comparative statement of income for 1988 and 1987, as components under the caption Discontinued Operations, Dart should report a gain (loss) amounting to

	1988	1987
a.	$122,500	($87,500)
b.	$122,500	$0
c.	($157,500)	($87,500)
d.	($157,500)	$0

23. Trent Company had net income of $700,000 for the year ended December 31, 1984, after giving effect to the following events which occurred during the year:

• The decision was made January 2 to discontinue the plastics manufacturing segment.
• The plastics manufacturing segment was sold June 30.
• Operating loss from January 1 to June 30 for the plastics manufacturing segment amounted to $60,000 before tax benefit.
• Plastics manufacturing equipment with a book value of $350,000 was sold for $200,000.

Trent's tax rate was 40% for 1984. For the year ended December 31, 1984, Trent's after-tax income from continuing operations was
- a. $574,000
- b. $700,000
- c. $784,000
- d. $826,000

24. On July 1, 1983, Tyler Corporation approved a formal plan to sell its plastics division, considered a segment of the business. The sale will occur in the first three months of 1984. The division had an operating loss of $400,000 for the six months ended December 31, 1983, and expects to incur a loss of $200,000 for the first quarter of 1984. The sales price is $22,000,000 and the carrying value at the date of sale should be $20,000,000. Tyler's effective tax rate for 1983 is 40%. For the year ended December 31, 1983, how much gain should Tyler report on disposal of the plastics division?
- a. $0
- b. $ 840,000
- c. $1,080,000
- d. $1,200,000

25. Gulliver Company is disposing of a segment of its business. At the measurement date the net loss from the disposal is esti-

mated to be $475,000. Included in this $475,000 are severance pay of $50,000 and employee relocation costs of $25,000, both of which are directly associated with the decision to dispose of the segment, and estimated net operating losses of the segment from the measurement date to the disposal date of $100,000. Net losses of $75,000 from operations from the beginning of the year to the measurement date are not included in the $475,000 estimated disposal loss. Ignoring income taxes, how much should be reported on Gulliver's income statement as the total loss under the heading "Discontinued operations"?
- a. $175,000
- b. $425,000
- c. $450,000
- d. $550,000

26. When a segment of a business has been discontinued during the year, the loss on disposal should
- a. Exclude operating losses of the current period up to the measurement date.
- b. Exclude operating losses during the phase-out period.
- c. Be an extraordinary item.
- d. Be an operating item.

27. A segment of a business has been discontinued during the year. The loss on disposal should
- a. Include operating losses of the current period up to the measurement date.
- b. Include employee relocation costs associated with the decision to dispose.
- c. Exclude severance pay associated with the decision to dispose.
- d. Exclude operating losses during the phase-out period.

28. When a segment of a business has been discontinued during the year, this segment's operating losses of the current period up to the measurement date should be included in the
- a. Income statement as part of the income (loss) from operations of the discontinued segment.
- b. Income statement as part of the loss on disposal of the discontinued segment.
- c. Income statement as part of the income (loss) from continuing operations.
- d. Retained earnings statement as a direct decrease in retained earnings.

29. During 1987, Jones Company engaged in the following transactions:

- Salary expense to key employees who are also principal owners $100,000
- Sales to affiliated enter- prises   250,000

Which of the two transactions would be disclosed as related party transactions in Jones' 1987 financial statements?

a.   Neither transaction.
b.   The $100,000 transaction only.
c.   The $250,000 transaction only.
d.   Both transactions.

30. Which of the following should be disclosed in the summary of significant accounting policies?

	Composition of plant assets	Inventory pricing
a.	Yes	Yes
b.	No	Yes
c.	No	No
d.	Yes	No

31. Which of the following should be disclosed in the Summary of Significant Accounting Policies?

	Composition of inventories	Depreciation expense
a.	No	No
b.	No	Yes
c.	Yes	Yes
d.	Yes	No

32. Which of the following should be disclosed in the Summary of Significant Accounting Policies?

	Basis of consolidation	Composition of plant assets
a.	No	No
b.	No	Yes
c.	Yes	No
d.	Yes	Yes

May 1990 Questions

33. Dodd Corp. is preparing its December 31, 1989 financial statements and must determine the proper accounting treatment for the following situations:

- For the year ended December 31, 1989, Dodd has a loss carryforward of $180,000 available to offset future taxable income. However, there are no temporary differences.
- On December 30, 1989, Dodd received a $200,000 offer for its patent. Dodd's management is considering whether to sell the patent. The offer expires on February 28, 1990. The patent has a carrying amount of $100,000 at December 31, 1989.

Assume a current and future income tax rate of 30%. In its 1989 income statement, Dodd should recognize an increase in net income of
a. $0
b. $ 54,000
c. $ 70,000
d. $124,000

34. On September 30, 1989, a commitment was made to dispose of a business segment in early 1990. The segment operating loss for the period October 1 to December 31, 1989 should be included in the 1989 income statement as part of

a.   Loss on disposal of the discontinued segment.
b.   Operating loss of the discontinued segment.
c.   Income or loss from continuing operations.
d.   Extraordinary gains or losses.

35. Which of the following facts concerning fixed assets should be included in the summary of significant accounting policies?

	Depreciation method	Composition
a.	No	Yes
b.	Yes	Yes
c.	Yes	No
d.	No	No

Repeat Questions

(590,P3,58) Identical/similar to item 7 above
(590,Q3,45) Identical/similar to item 8 above
(590,Q3,47) Identical/similar to item 25 above
(590,Q3,48) Identical/similar to item 14 above

FINANCIAL STATEMENTS

Problems

Problem 1   (1189,T5)

(15 to 25 minutes)

Hillside Company had a loss during the year ended December 31, 1988 that is properly reported as an extraordinary item.

On July 1, 1988, Hillside committed itself to a formal plan for sale of a business segment. A loss is expected from the proposed sale. Segment operating losses were incurred continuously throughout 1988, and were expected to continue until final disposition in 1989. Costs were incurred in 1988 to relocate segment employees.

Required:

a. How should Hillside report the extraordinary item in its income statement? Why?

b. How should Hillside report the effect of the discontinued operations in its 1988 income statement?

c. How should Hillside report the costs that were incurred to relocate employees of the discontinued segment? Why?

Do not discuss earnings per share requirements.

Problem 2   (588,Q4)

(45 to 55 minutes)

The following information pertains to Arlon Corporation:

TRIAL BALANCE
December 31, 1987

	Debit	Credit
Cash	$ 25,000	
Accounts receivable, net	75,000	
Inventory	125,000	
Property, plant, and equipment	755,000	
Accumulated depreciation		$ 239,000
Accounts payable		70,000
Income tax payable		6,000
Rental revenue received in advance		5,000
Notes payable		55,000
Common stock, $.05 par		50,000
Additional paid-in capital		305,000
Retained earnings, 1/1/87		150,000
Sales--regular		500,000
Sales--Mem Division		100,000
Proceeds from term life insurance policy		10,000
Cost of sales--regular	310,000	
Cost of sales--Mem Division	45,000	
Administrative expenses --regular	103,000	
Administrative expenses --Mem Division	15,000	
Interest expense-- regular	10,500	
Interest expense--Mem Division	7,000	
Loss on disposal of Mem Division	12,500	
Gain on acquisition of bonds payable		13,000
Income tax expense	20,000	
Totals	$1,503,000	$1,503,000

Other Information

Income Tax

Paid with Federal Tax Deposit Forms	$14,000
Accrued	6,000
Total charged to income tax expense	$20,000*

*Does not reflect current or deferred income tax expense or intraperiod income tax allocation for income statement purposes.

Income per income tax return	$99,000

| Tax rate on all types of taxable income for all affected years | 22% |

Temporary differences

Depreciation per financial statements--regular	$30,000	
Depreciation per income tax return	46,000	$16,000
Rental revenue received in advance		5,000

Reversal of the depreciation temporary difference will result in future taxable amounts of $8,000 in each of the next two years (1988 and 1989). Reversal of the unearned rent temporary difference will occur in 1988.

Permanent difference

Proceeds from term life insurance policy	10,000

Discontinued operations

On July 30, 1987, Arlon sold its Mem Division for $200,000. The carrying amount of this business segment was $212,500 at that date. This sale was considered as a disposal of a segment of a business for financial statement purposes. Since there was no phaseout period, the measurement date was June 30, 1987.

Liabilities

On June 30, 1987, Arlon acquired $100,000 carrying amount of its long-term bonds for $87,000. All other liabilities mature in 1988.

Capital structure

Common stock, $.05 par, traded over-the-counter; 1,000,000 shares issued and outstanding at 1/1/87 and 12/31/87.

Required:

Using the multiple-step format, prepare a formal income statement for Arlon for the year ended December 31, 1987, together with supporting computations of current and deferred income taxes and of income from discontinued operations.

Problem 3   (589,P4)   (45 to 55 minutes)

Before closing the books for the year ended December 31, 1988, Pitt Corp. prepared the following condensed trial balance:

Condensed Trial Balance
December 31, 1988

	Debit	Credit
Total assets	$ 7,082,500	
Total liabilities		$ 1,700,000
Common stock		1,250,000
Additional paid-in capital		2,097,500
Donated capital		90,000
Retained earnings, 1/1/88		1,650,000
Net sales		6,250,000
Cost of sales	3,750,000	
Selling and administrative expenses	1,212,500	
Interest expense	122,500	
Gain on sale of long-term investments		130,000
Income tax expense	300,000	
Loss on disposition of plant assets	225,000	
Loss due to earthquake damage	475,000	
	$13,167,500	$13,167,500

Other financial data for the year ended December 31, 1988:

Federal income tax

Estimated tax payments	$200,000
Accrued	100,000
Total charged to income tax expense (Does not properly reflect current or deferred income tax expense or interperiod income tax allocation for income statement purposes.)	$300,000

Pitt elected to apply the provisions of FASB Statement No. 96, Accounting for Income Taxes, in its financial statements for the year ended December 31, 1988. The enacted tax rate on all types of taxable income for the current and future years is 30%. The alternative minimum tax is less than the regular income tax.

Temporary difference

Excess of book basis over tax basis in depreciable assets (arising from equipment donated as a capital contribution on December 31, 1988 and expected to be depreciated over five years beginning in 1989). There were no temporary differences prior to 1988.	$90,000

Non-deductible expenditure

Officers' life insurance expense	$70,000

Earthquake damage

This damage is considered unusual and infrequent.

Capital structure

Common stock, par value $5 per share, traded on a national exchange:

Number of shares:	
Outstanding at 1/1/88	200,000
Issued on 3/30/88 as a 10% stock dividend	20,000
Sold for $25 per share on 6/30/88	30,000
Outstanding at 12/31/88	250,000

Required:

   a. Using the multiple-step format, prepare a formal income statement for Pitt for the year ended December 31, 1988.
   b. Prepare a schedule to reconcile net income to taxable reportable on Pitt's tax return for 1988.

FINANCIAL STATEMENTS
Multiple Choice Answers

1. c	8. c	15. a	22. a	29. c
2. a	9. c	16. a	23. d	30. b
3. d	10. c	17. b	24. a	31. a
4. c	11. d	18. b	25. d	32. c
5. a	12. a	19. c	26. a	33. a
6. a	13. a	20. d	27. b	34. a
7. b	14. d	21. d	28. a	35. c

Multiple Choice Answer Explanations

D.1. Income and Retained Earnings Statements

1.   (1189,P1,1) (c) All of the accounts given in the trial balance are components of income from operations before income tax except for the adjustment due to accounting change in depreciation method (cumulative effect) and the gain on debt extinguishment. The cumulative effect ($40,000) is reported, net of tax, as a separate component of income after income from operations, in accordance with APB 20. Per SFAS 4, the gain on debt extinguishment should be reported net of tax as an extraordinary item even if it does not meet the criteria of infrequent and unusual. Therefore, income from operations before income tax is $230,000, as computed below:

Net sales	$1,600,000
Less expenses ($960,000 + $235,000 +	
$150,000 + $25,000)	1,370,000
	$ 230,000

2.   (1189,P1,2) (a) As shown in the explanation of the previous question, income from operations before income tax is $230,000. Income tax expense, the extraordinary gain on debt extinguishment (net of taxes) and the cumulative effect adjustment (net of taxes) must be included in the computation of net income, as illustrated below:

Income from ops. before taxes		$230,000
Income tax exp. (30% x $230,000)		(69,000)
Income before extraordinary items		
and cum. effect		161,000
Extraordinary gain	$10,000	
Tax effect (30% x $10,000)	(3,000)	7,000
Cum. effect	$(40,000)	
Tax effect (30% x $40,000)	12,000	(28,000)
Net income		$140,000

A short-cut approach is to subtract the income statement debits ($1,410,000) from the income statement credits ($1,610,000), giving a result of $200,000. From this amount, the tax effect of $60,000 (30% x $200,000) must be subtracted, resulting in net income of $140,000.

3.   (1188,P1,7) (d) To directly compute cost of goods manufactured, the formula is:

	Beginning work in process
+	Direct materials used
+	Direct labor
+	Factory overhead
−	Ending work in process
	Cost of goods manufactured

However, none of these elements are given in this problem, so cost of goods manufactured must be computed indirectly, using the cost of goods sold formula.

Beginning finished goods	$100,000	
+ Cost of goods manufactured	+	CGM
− Ending finished goods	−	90,000
Cost of goods sold		$60,000

Solving for the missing amount, CGM is $50,000.

4.   (1188,P1,8) (c) All the revenues, gains, expenses, and losses given in this problem are components of income from continuing operations before income taxes except for the loss on early retirement of long-term debt, which is an extraordinary item. Per SFAS 4, material gains and losses from extinguishment of debt should be reported as an extraordinary item even if these gains or losses do not meet the criteria of infrequent and unusual. Income before income taxes is $55,000, as computed below:

Revenues ($150,000 + $5,000)	$155,000
Expenses and losses ($60,000	
+ $15,000 + $9,000 + $10,000	
+ $3,000 + $3,000)	(100,000)
Income from continuing	
operations before taxes	$ 55,000

To compute income before extraordinary item, income taxes (30% x $55,000 = $16,500) must be deducted from income from continuing operations before taxes ($55,000 − $16,500 = $38,500).

5.   (1188,P1,9) (a) Per SFAS 4, material gains and losses from extinguishment of debt should be reported as extraordinary items even if these gains or losses do not meet the criteria of unusual and infrequent. As with all extraordinary items, the gain or loss should be reported net of its related tax effect. Therefore, the extraordinary loss is $7,000 [$10,000 − (30% x $10,000)].

6.   (1189,P3,44) (a) A gain on the disposal of a long-term investment is the excess of the proceeds (10,000 x $100 = $1,000,000) over the cost of the investment (10,000 x $70 =

$700,000). Therefore, the gain is $300,000 ($1,000,000 - $700,000). Changes in the market price of the investment before sale do not affect the computation of the gain. Even if the market price of the stock had fallen below cost and a valuation allowance was established, the gain or loss on disposal would still have been based on the investment's original cost; the adjustment to the valuation allowance at year end would not affect the gain on disposal. Note that the tax rate (30%) is not used; components of income from continuing operations are reported gross with income tax expense deducted from the total income from continuing operations.

7. (1188,P3,47) (b) Per APB 30, extraordinary items are material items which are both unusual in nature and infrequent in occurrence. APB 30, para 23 states that the effect of a strike is not an extraordinary item. Therefore, the $50,000 loss is not extraordinary. However, SFAS 4, para 8 states that gains and losses from extinguishment of debt are to be classified as extraordinary whether or not they meet the unusual and infrequent criteria. Therefore, the $25,000 gain should be reported, net of the related tax effect, as an extraordinary item [$25,000 - (30% x $25,000) = $17,500].

8. (1187,P2,30) (c) Per APB 30, para 30, extraordinary items are material items which are both unusual in nature and infrequent in occurrence. Neither a sale of plant facility nor a foreign currency transaction is unusual in nature. Therefore, these two items would be reported as infrequent but not extraordinary ($240,000 + $90,000 = $330,000). The gain from retirement of bonds ($190,000) is classified as extraordinary per SFAS 4, para 8, which states that gains and losses from extinguishment of debt are to be classified as extraordinary. Note that the sale of the plant facility is not classified as discontinued operations because similar operations are carried on at another location (APB 30, para 13).

9. (1187,P3,11) (a) Per APB 30, para 30, extraordinary items are material items which are both unusual in nature and infrequent in occurrence. This loss meets the criteria of unusual and infrequent because earthquake losses in Kansas are very rare (note that if this loss took place in California, it might not meet the extraordinary criteria). The extraordinary loss is reported net of income taxes in a separate section of the income statement in accordance with paras 10 and 11 of APB 30. The tax effect is $560,000 ($1,400,000 x 40%), and the net-of-tax amount is $840,000 ($1,400,000 - $560,000).

10. (587,P3,46) (c) In this situation, the provision for income tax (income tax expense) will be the amount of the tax liability to the government determined without including the extraordinary loss. This amount is determined by applying the 40% tax rate to pretax accounting income before extraordinary items adjusted for any permanent differences. Accounting income before taxes is $900,000, but that amount includes a gain on life insurance coverage ($100,000). A gain on life insurance coverage is a permanent difference because it is included in accounting income but will never be included in taxable income. Therefore, the amount of accounting income which will be subject to taxes is $800,000 ($900,000 - $100,000), and the provision for income taxes is $320,000 ($800,000 x 40%). The tax savings from the extraordinary loss ($300,000 x 40% = $120,000) will not affect the provision for income taxes because the extraordinary item must be reported together with its tax effect (extraordinary loss of $180,000; net of tax).

11. (587,P3,52) (d) Per APB 30, extraordinary items are material items which are both unusual in nature and infrequent in occurrence. Para 23 specifies six items which are not considered extraordinary, including the effects of a strike ($180,000), the writedown of plant and equipment ($100,000), and the loss on disposal of plant and equipment ($150,000). Therefore, the infrequent (but not extraordinary) losses total $430,000.

12. (1185,P3,48) (a) The requirement is the amount to be reported as extraordinary losses in 1984. Neither of the two items meet all the criteria for recognition as an extraordinary item (material, unusual, and infrequent in occurrence). Per APB 30, a loss on disposal of a segment of the business ($350,000) is reported in a separate section of the income statement as discontinued operations, but not as an extraordinary item. APB 30 also indicates that foreign currency losses ($450,000), even due to a major devaluation, are not considered extraordinary. Such losses are not unusual for a company which has foreign operations even though major devaluations are not an everyday occurrence.

13. (585,P2,35) (a) The requirement is to determine the amount of expenses which should be included in general and administrative expenses for 1984. The accounting and legal fees ($240,000) and property taxes and insurance ($150,000) are all considered general and administrative expenses. Therefore, general and administrative expenses total $390,000 ($240,000 + $150,000). The interest expense ($90,000) should be included

with financing expenses or other expenses and losses. The $110,000 loss on sale of long-term investments should be included in other expenses and losses.

14. (1184,P3,44) (d) The requirement is the amount of expenses to be included in selling expenses for 1983. Advertising ($150,000) and sales salaries and commissions ($140,000) are clearly selling expenses, as is the rent for the office space occupied by the sales department ($180,000 x ½ = $90,000). Additionally, freight-out ($75,000) is a selling expense because shipping the goods from the point of sale to the customer is the final effort in the selling process. The total selling expense is, therefore, $455,000 ($150,000 + $140,000 + $90,000 + $75,000). Of the remaining items, accounting and legal fees, officers' salaries, and the remaining office rent are general and administrative expenses. Interest expense and the loss on the sale of the long-term investment are considered nonoperating items.

15. (1184,P3,45) (a) The requirement is the amount of expenses to be included in general and administrative (G and A) expenses. Accounting and legal fees ($175,000), officers' salaries ($225,000), and the rent for the office space not occupied by the sales department ($180,000 x ½ = $90,000) are all G and A expenses, for a total of $490,000 ($175,000 + $225,000 + $90,000). Of the remaining items, advertising, freight-out, the remaining office rent, and the sales salaries and commissions are all selling expenses. Interest expense and the loss on the sale of the long-term investment are nonoperating items.

16. (588,T1,28) (a) Per APB 30, para 20, such a transaction is considered an extraordinary item. An extraordinary item is reported after discontinued operations but before cumulative effect of accounting changes, answer (a).

17. (589,T1,23) (b) Per APB 30, para 8, "operations of a segment that has or will be discontinued should be reported separately as a component of income before extraordinary items and the cumulative effect of accounting changes." As a result, an extraordinary item should be reported separately on the income statement as a component of income after discontinued operations of a segment of a business. Additionally, an extraordinary item should be reported net of income taxes as described in APB 9, para 20. Therefore, answer (b) is correct.

18. (589,T1,21) (b) APB 30, para 26 states that a material event or transaction that results in either a gain or loss and is unusual in nature or infrequent in occurrence, but not both, should be presented as a separate component of income from continuing operations. Therefore, answer (b) is correct.

19. (1186,T1,21) (c) Per APB 20, para 36, the correction of an error in a prior period is treated as a prior period adjustment. Per SFAS 16, para 16a, prior period adjustments (net of tax) should be charged or credited to the opening balance of retained earnings and, thus, excluded from the determination of net income for the current period. Therefore, answers (a) and (b) are incorrect. Answer (d) is incorrect because the adjustment is made to the opening balance of retained earnings.

D.2. Discontinued Operations

20. (589,P3,60) (d) The discontinued operations section of the income statement consists of two parts: income (loss) from operations of a discontinued segment and gain (loss) on disposal. The results of operations from the beginning of the year to the measurement date is labeled the income (loss) from operation of a discontinued segment. The measurement date is the date the decision is made to discontinue a segment's operations. In this problem, the measurement date is April 30, so the loss incurred from January 1 through April 30 [$600,000 - $750,000 = ($150,000)] is reported as a loss from operations of a discontinued segment.

21. (1188,P3,45) (d) The discontinued operations section of the income statement consists of two parts: income (loss) from operation of discontinued segment and gain (loss) on disposal. This question is concerned only with the second part. The gain (loss) on disposal consists of all results from the measurement date (October 1) to the disposal date (March 31), reported net of the related tax effect, as computed below:

Income (10/1/87 to 12/31/87)	$100,000
Expected loss (1/1/88 - 3/31/88)	(50,000)
Estimated loss on sale	(375,000)
Loss on disposal before taxes	(325,000)
Tax effect (30% x $325,000)	97,500
Loss on disposal	$(227,500)

Note that even though this loss will be realized in 1988, it is recognized in 1987 because the commitment was made to dispose of the segment during that year. If any gains were expected in 1988, they would also be accrued in 1987 to the extent they are offset by either realized 1987 losses or estimated 1988 losses.

22. (1189,P3,46) (a) APB 30 requires that "financial statements of <u>current</u> and <u>prior</u> periods... should disclose the results of the operations of the disposed segment, less applicable taxes, as a separate component of income..." Therefore, the discontinued operations should be reported separately, net of taxes, for both 1988 and 1987. The computations are:

	1988	1987
Discontinued operations:		
Loss from operating		
discontinued segment	-0-	$(87,500)**
Gain on disposal of		
discontinued segment	$122,500*	-0-
	$122,500	$(87,500)

*Since the measurement date is 1/1/88, the loss from operations for the entire year is combined with the gain on disposition [($400,000 - $225,000) - 30% ($400,000 - $225,000)].

**[$125,000 - (30% x $125,000)]

Authors' note: The income statement presentation above is presented for the candidate's review of this topic.

23. (585,P3,48) (d) The requirement is to determine the 1984 after-tax income from continuing operations. Net income (after taxes) is $700,000 including losses from discontinued operations. The discontinued operations loss is computed as follows:

Loss during phase-out period	$ 60,000
Loss on sale ($200,000 - $350,000)	150,000
Total loss, before taxes	$210,000
Tax effect (40% x $210,000)	(84,000)
Total loss, after taxes	$126,000

Therefore, the after-tax income from continuing operations must be $826,000, since $826,000 less the discontinued operations loss of $126,000 results in the net income amount of $700,000.

24. (584,P3,44) (a) The requirement is the reported gain on the disposal of a discontinued segment for the year ended 12/31/83. The problem can be diagrammed as follows:

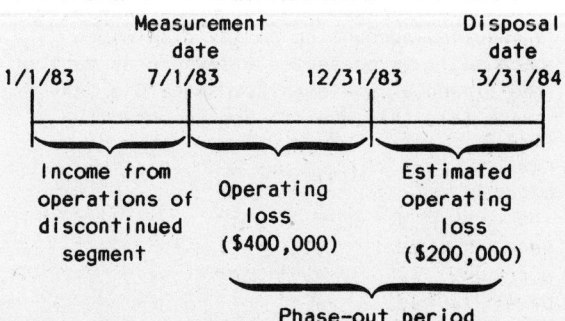

The gain (loss) on the disposal of a segment is composed of two parts: (1) the income (loss) from operations during the phase-out period, and (2) the gain (loss) from the disposal of segment assets. If the phase-out period extends over more than one reporting period, APB 30 requires that the realized loss from operations of the discontinued segment during the phase-out period included in the current reporting period be reduced by any combined gain on disposal (from both operations and the sale of the assets) estimated for the following period. Thus, the $400,000 loss from operations in 1983 would be reduced to $0 by the net gain of $1,800,000 estimated for 1984 ($2,000,000 gain from the sale of assets less $200,000 expected loss from operations). Since APB 30 also requires that any estimated net gain which is not used to offset the loss from operations incurred during the current period ($1,800,000 - $400,000 = $1,400,000 gain not used to offset losses) not be recognized until they are realized, the gain on disposal to be reported by Tyler for the year ended 12/31/83 should be $0.

25. (1182,Q1,19) (d) The requirement is the amount of total loss to appear under the heading "Discontinued operations." APB 30, para 8 states that the results of discontinued operations should be reported separately from continuing operations and that both the "Gain (Loss) from Disposal of a Segment of a Business" and the related "Income (Loss) From Operations of Discontinued Operations" should be reported under the heading "Discontinued operations." APB 30, para 15 states that the determination of a gain (loss) resulting from the disposal of a business segment should be made at the measurement date based on estimates at that date. The amount of gain (loss) should include an estimate of income (loss) from operations between the measurement date and the disposal date if the disposal plan is to be carried out over a period of time. In this case, the estimated net operating losses from the measurement date to disposal date, $100,000, are already included in the $475,000 estimated disposal loss at the measurement date. Also, inclusion of the $50,000 of severance pay and the $25,000 of employee relocation costs is appropriate because APB 30, paras 16 and 17 state that costs directly associated with the decision to dispose, including items such as severance pay and employee relocation expenses, should be included in determining the gain (loss) on disposal. The amount of net operating loss from the beginning of the year to the measurement date, $75,000, should be disclosed as a separate component under the heading "Discontinued operations." Therefore, the total loss to be

reported is $475,000 + $75,000 or $550,000. Note that in this case, since a net loss on disposal results, it is not necessary to know if the phase out period (measurement date to disposal date) overlaps accounting periods.

26. (1188,T1,31) (a) Per APB 30, para 13, gains or losses from the operation of a discontinued business segment realized from the beginning of the year to the measurement date are separately disclosed, net of tax, in the Discontinued Operations section of the income statement under the heading "Income (loss) from operations of discounted division." Thus, answer (a) is correct. Answer (b) is incorrect because operating losses during the phase-out period are included in the loss on disposal of business segment. Answers (c) and (d) are incorrect because the loss on disposal of a business segment should be shown separately on the income statement in the Discontinued Operations section, after Income from continuing operations and before Extraordinary items.

27. (1187,T1,24) (b) APB 30, para 17 states that costs and expenses directly associated with the decision to dispose of a segment, including employee relocation expenses, are to be included in the loss on disposal of a segment of a business. Therefore, answer (b) is correct. Answer (a) is incorrect because operating losses of the current period up to the measurement date are included in "Income (loss) from operations of discontinued segment." Answer (c) is incorrect because per APB 30, para 17, severance pay directly associated with the decision to dispose is included in the loss on disposal of a segment of a business. Answer (d) is incorrect because per APB 30, para 15, operating losses during the phase-out period are combined with the gain (loss) from the disposal of segment assets to determine loss on disposal of a segment of a business.

28. (585,T1,24) (a) The requirement is to determine how a discontinued segment's operating losses for the current period up to the measurement date should be classified in the financial statements. Answer (a) is correct because according to APB 30, the "income (loss) from operations" is calculated from the beginning of the period to the measurement date. The income (loss) from operations is shown as a separate line item under discontinued operations on the income statement. Answer (b) is incorrect because it is not combined with the loss on disposal. Answer (c) is incorrect because discontinued operations is shown separately from income (loss) from continuing operations. Answer (d) is incorrect because discontinued operations

is included on the income statement, not on the retained earnings statement.

D.4. Disclosure of Accounting Policies

29. (1188,P3,51) (c) SFAS 57, para 2 requires that financial statements include disclosures of material transactions between related parties. Compensation arrangements in the ordinary course of business, however, are specifically excluded from this disclosure requirement. Therefore, only the $250,000 sale to affiliated enterprises must be disclosed, and answer (c) is correct.

30. (588,T1,32) (b) Per APB 22, para 13, inventory pricing is commonly required in the disclosure of significant accounting policies. Para 14 of APB 22 specifically states composition of plant assets is not a required accounting policy disclosure because this information is presented elsewhere in the financial statements. Therefore, answer (b) is correct.

31. (1187,T1,25) (a) Per APB 22, para 12, disclosure of accounting policies should identify and describe the accounting principles followed by the reporting entity and the methods of applying those principles. Para 14 further states that financial statement disclosure of accounting policies should not duplicate details (specifically composition of inventories or of plant assets) presented elsewhere as a part of the financial statements. Also, depreciation expense should not be disclosed in the summary of significant accounting policies because this information is detailed elsewhere in the financial statements. Therefore, answer (a) is correct.

32. (1185,T1,30) (c) The requirement is to determine whether basis of consolidation and/or composition of plant assets should be disclosed in the Summary of Significant Accounting Policies. Per APB 22, para 13, basis of consolidation is a commonly required disclosure with respect to accounting policies. Para 14 of APB 22 specifically states that composition of plant assets is not a required accounting policy disclosure because it is presented elsewhere as part of the financial statements. Therefore, answers (a), (b), and (d) are incorrect.

May 1990 Answers

33. (590,Q3,60) (a) Per SFAS 96, para 17, a net operating carryforward may not be recognized except to the extent to offset a deferred tax liability. In this case no temporary differences exist and a deferred tax asset can not be recognized. In the case of the $200,000 offer for the patent, realization has not occurred and no transaction has taken place. This is an executory contract because management has not acted upon the offer. Therefore, Dodd should not recognize an increase in income for 1989, and answer (a) is correct.

34. (590,T1,26) (a) APB 30, para 14 defines the date on which a commitment is made to dispose of a business segment as the measurement date. If a loss is expected on the disposal, para 15 requires the estimated loss to be provided for at the measurement date. This loss should include the anticipated income or loss from operations of the segment during the period of time between the measurement date and the disposal date. Therefore answer (a) is correct. Answer (b) is incorrect because the operating loss of the discontinued segment would include the results of its operations for the period ending on the measurement date (in this case, from January 1, 1989 to September 30, 1989). Answer (c) is incorrect because APB 30, para 8 requires the operations of a segment that has been or will be discontinued to be reported separately as a component of income before extraordinary items and the cumulative effect of accounting changes (if applicable). Answer (d) is incorrect because APB 30, para 11 specifically excludes discontinued operations from events and transactions which are to be reported as extraordinary items.

35. (590,T1,30) (c) Per APB 22, para 12, disclosure of accounting policies should identify and describe the accounting principles followed by the reporting entity and the methods of applying those principles. Para 14 further states that financial statement disclosure of accounting policies should not duplicate details presented elsewhere as a part of the financial statements. Para 13 provides depreciation methods as an example of a commonly required accounting policy disclosure, while para 14 excludes the composition of fixed assets from required disclosure. Therefore answer (c) is correct.

FINANCIAL STATEMENTS

Answer Outline

Problem 1   Discontinued Operations and X/O
             Items (1189,T5)

a. Report X/O item after continuing opera-
       tions and discontinued operations
         Net of tax
       Presentation required to enable users to
       assess future cash flows

b. Report D/Os in separate section after C/Os
       Present as 2 components
         Loss from operations of discontinued
         segment (net of tax)
           Beg. of yr. ───────────► Meas. date

         Loss on disposal of discontinued seg-
         ment (net of tax)
           Includes
             Operating losses:
               Meas. date ──────► Disposal date
             Loss on sale of assets plus direct
             costs associated with disposal

c. Report relocation costs as part of "loss
       on disposal" component
       Reason for treating as part of "loss on
       disposal" component is that they directly
       relate to decision to dispose

Unofficial Answer

Problem 1   Discontinued Operations and X/O
             Items (1189,T5)

a. Hillside should report the extraordinary
item separately, net of applicable income
taxes, below the continuing operations section
in the income statement. Exclusion of extraordinary items from the results of continuing
operations is intended to produce a measure of
income from continuing operations that is useful in projecting future operating cash flows.

b. Hillside should report the discontinued
operations separately in the 1988 income
statement immediately below income from continuing operations. Discontinued operations
should be comprised of two categories, with
each category reported net of income taxes:

•   Loss from operations of the discontinued segment from the beginning of the year
to the measurement date.
•   Loss on disposal of the discontinued
segment, including the provision for operating
losses during the phase-out period.

c. Hillside should include the costs incurred
to relocate employees in the loss on disposal
of the discontinued segment in its 1988 income
statement. These costs are a direct result of
the commitment to dispose of its segment.

Solution Guide

Problem 2   Income Statement Preparation
             (588,Q4)

1. The requirement is to prepare a multiple-
    step income statement with all components
    of income tax appropriately shown.

2. The basic outline for a formal multiple-
    step income statement is presented below:

      Net sales
    - Cost of sales
      Gross profit
    - Operating expenses
      Income from operations
    + Other income or expense
      Income before unusual or infrequent
       items and income taxes
    ± Unusual/infrequent items
      Income from continuing operations
       before income taxes
    - Income taxes
      Income from continuing operations
    + Discontinued operations (net of tax)
      Income before extraordinary items and
       cumulative effect of accounting change
    ± Extraordinary items (net of tax)
    ± Cumulative effect of change in
       accounting principle (net of tax)
      Net income
      Per share data

3. APB 30 states that income (loss) from the
    operations of a discontinued division and
    the gain (loss) from the disposal of a
    division should be reported as a separate
    item, net of the applicable tax effect.
    It should be placed on the income state-
    ment after income from continuing opera-
    tions and before extraordinary items.

3.1 The income from the operations of the
    discontinued division is found by sub-
    tracting the division's expenses from its
    revenues (Explanation 3).

3.2 The loss on disposal of the discontinued
    division is computed by comparing the
    book value of the division with its sales
    price (Explanation 4).

4. The gain on acquisition of bonds payable
    ($13,000) must be reported as a separate
    item after discontinued operations. This
    type of gain is considered an extraordi-
    nary item per SFAS 4 without respect to
    whether both the criteria for extraordi-

nary items are met. It is reported net of applicable tax effect, as computed in Explanation 5.

5.   Once the special items have been identified, the top half of income statement can be prepared.

5.1   The sales, cost of sales, and expense figures are given in the problem. Remember, however, that these figures for the Mem Division should not be included with figures denoted as "regular."

5.2   The interest expense is not related to the main operations of the firm and should be reported as other expense. The same is true for the proceeds from term life insurance policy. Note that the entire proceeds represent a gain because term insurance does not generate a cash surrender value. It is reported as other income in the AICPA Unofficial Answer. An acceptable alternative would be to assume it is an infrequent item and show it under a section created for that item.

5.3   The current portion of income tax expense deducted from "income from continuing operations before taxes" should be 22% of that income amount adjusted for both **permanent** differences (Explanation 1). Notice that the information provided under the **income tax** heading dealing with tax payments and accruals is not used. The information under the heading **temporary differences** is needed to determine the deferred portion of the income tax expense applicable to income from continuing operations. The deferred income tax amount is computed by multiplying the $11,000 ($46,000 − $30,000 − $5,000) by the applicable tax rate of 22% (Explanation 2). Note that a schedule of future temporary difference is not needed because there is a net taxable amount in both years and the tax rate is 22% for both years.

6.   Earnings per share data must be presented on the face of the income statement because Arlon Corporation is publicly held as evidenced by the fact that their stock is traded over-the-counter.

6.1   Common shares outstanding at the beginning and at the end of the year were 1,000,000 shares.

6.2   Recall that earnings per share information must be shown on the face of the income statement for the following items:

• Income from continuing operations
• Income before extraordinary items
• Cumulative effect of change in accounting principle, and
• Net income

Since there were no cumulative effect type changes in this problem, the third category will not apply. The other three earnings amounts are simply divided by the 1,000,000 shares outstanding. As noted in the solution, an EPS amount **may** be shown for the discontinued operation.

Unofficial Answer
(Author Modified)

Problem 2   Income Statement Preparation (588,Q4)

Arlon Corporation
Income Statement
For the Year Ended December 31, 1987

Sales		$500,000
Cost of sales		310,000
Gross profit		190,000
Administrative expenses		103,000
Operating income		87,000
Other income and expense		
Proceeds from term life insurance policy	$ 10,000	
Interest expense	(10,500)	(500)
Income from continuing operations before income tax		86,500
Income tax		
Current	14,410 [1]	
Deferred	2,420 [2]	16,830
Income from continuing operations		69,670
Discontinued operations		
Income from discontinued Mem Division		
(less applicable income tax of $7,260)	25,740 [3]	
Loss on disposal of Mem Division (less applicable		
income tax savings of $2,750)	(9,750) [4]	15,990
Income before extraordinary item		85,660
Extraordinary item--Gain on acquisition of bonds		
payable (less applicable income tax of $2,860)		10,140 [5]
Net income		$95,800
Earnings per share		
Income from continuing operations		$0.070 [6]
Discontinued operations		0.016 [7]
Total before extraordinary item		0.086
Extraordinary item		0.010 [8]
Net income		$0.096

Explanation of Amounts

[1]	Current portion of income tax expense on 1987 income excluding discontinued operations and extraordianry item	
	Income from continuing operations before income tax and permanent difference	$86,500
	Less: Permanent difference resulting from proceeds from term life insurance policy	(10,000)
		76,500
	Less: Temporary differences from:	
	Depreciation per tax return	$46,000	
	Less: Depreciation per books	30,000	
	Temporary difference resulting from depreciation	16,000	
	Less: Rental revenue received in advance	5,000	
	Total temporary differences		(11,000)
	Taxable income on continuing operations		$ 65,500
	Income tax rate		$ x 22%
	Current income tax expense		$ 14,410

Author's Note:

*The $99,000 of income per income tax return given
in the problem is comprised of the following elements:*

Continuing operations	*$65,500*
Income from discontinued Mem Division	*33,000*
Loss on disposal of Mem Division	*(12,500)*
Extraordinary Gain	*13,000*
Taxable income	*$99,000*

[2]   Deferred portion of income tax expense for 1987

Depreciation per tax return	$46,000
Less: Depreciation per books	30,000
Temporary difference resulting from depreciation	16,000
Less: Rental revenue received in advance	5,000
Total temporary differences	$11,000
Income tax rate	x .22
Deferred income tax expense	$ 2,420

[3]   Discontinued operation--Operating gain from
       Mem Division

Sales		$100,000
Cost of sales	$ 45,000	
Administrative expenses	15,000	
Interest expense	7,000	67,000
Income		33,000
Income tax (22% x $33,000)		7,260
Net of income tax		$25,740

[4]   Discontinued operations--Loss on disposal of Mem Division

Loss on disposal	($12,500)
Income tax savings (22% x $12,500)	2,750
Net of income tax	($ 9,750)

[5]   Extraordinary item

Gain on acquisition of bonds payable	$13,000
Income tax (25% x $13,000)	2,860
Net of income tax	$10,140

[6]   Earnings per share--Income from continuing operations

Income from continuing operations	$69,670
Number of shares	1,000,000
Earnings per share ($69,670 ÷ 1,000,000)	$0.070

[7]   Earnings per share--Discontinued operations

Discontinued operations	$15,990
Number of shares	1,000,000
Earnings per share ($15,990 ÷ 1,000,000)	$0.016

[8]   Earnings per share--Extraordinary item

Extraordinary item	$10,140
Number of shares	1,000,000
Earnings per share ($10,140 ÷ 1,000,000)	$0.010

Solution Guide

**Problem 3   Prepare I/S; Reconcile Net Income
to Taxable Income (589,P4)**

1. This problem consists of two related
    parts requiring a multiple-step income
    statement and a schedule reconciling net
    income and taxable income.

2. Part a. requires preparation of a
    multiple-step income statement. The
    basic outline for a formal multiple-step
    income statement is presented below:

    Sales
    - Cost of sales
    Gross profit
    - Operating expenses
    Income from operations
    + Other income or expense
    Income before unusual or infrequent
      items and income tax
    + Unusual or infrequent items
    Income before income tax and extraordi-
      nary item
    - Income taxes
    Income from continuing operations
    + Discontinued operations (net of tax)
    Income before extraordinary item
    + Extraordinary item (net of tax)
    + Cumulative effect of change in ac-
      counting principle (net of tax)
    Net income

    Per share data

2.1 The first six items listed in the con-
    densed trial balance are balance sheet
    accounts. The remaining items (all
    accounts after retained earnings) are
    income statement accounts.

2.2 The operating section of the income
    statement includes net sales less cost of
    sales to compute gross profit, less
    selling and administrative expenses to
    compute operating income.

2.3 Interest expense is substracted from
    operating income to compute income before
    unusual or infrequent items and income
    tax.

2.4 Two items in this problem qualify as un-
    usual or infrequent items; loss on dispo-
    sition of plant assets and gain on sale
    of long-term investments. Note that
    neither of these items meets the criteria
    for classification as an extraordinary
    item. Also note that items which are
    either infrequent in occurrence or un-
    usual in nature, but not both, are not
    shown net-of-tax.

2.5 Income tax must be computed, since the
    amount reported in the trial balance
    ($300,000) is an estimated amount which
    does not properly reflect current or de-
    ferred income tax expense, or intraperiod
    tax allocation. Do not spend valuable
    time trying to determine how the $300,000
    was calculated.

2.6 Total income tax expense consists of
    current tax expense (payable) and
    deferred tax expense. The current
    portion is based on book income before
    taxes and extraordinary items
    ($1,070,000), adjusted for any permanent
    difference. The only permanent
    difference is the officers' life insur-
    ance expense, which is a legitimate book
    expense, but is not deductible for tax
    purposes. The premiums are added back to
    give a total of $1,140,000 of book income
    subject to a 30% tax rate. Therefore,
    the current tax provision is $342,000.

2.7 The deferred portion of income tax
    expense is the net change for the year in
    deferred tax assets or liabilities.
    Changes are due to temporary differences
    which, according to SFAS 96, can arise
    when the tax basis of assets or
    liabilities differ from their reported
    book basis. The only change is the
    temporary difference from the contributed
    asset. The excess of book basis over tax
    basis is $90,000, multiplied by the 30%
    tax rate gives the change in deferred
    tax. Since there were no temporary
    differences prior to 1988, the $27,000
    equals the deferred portion. Total
    income tax is therefore $342,000
    (current) + $27,000 (deferred) =
    $369,000.

2.8 The earthquake loss meets the criteria of
    an extraordinary item (unusual nature and
    infrequent occurrence). Per APB 30,
    extraordinary items must be reported sep-
    arately and net of their tax effect.
    Since the $475,000 loss is tax-
    deductible, a tax savings of $142,500
    will result (30% x $475,000). The net-
    of-tax loss is $332,500 ($475,000 -
    $142,500).

2.9 Earnings per share must be reported on
    income before extraordinary items and net
    income (APB 15).* Earnings per share is
    computed by dividing these amounts by the
    weighted-average number of common shares
    outstanding for the year. There were
    200,000 shares outstanding at 1/1/88.

    *EPS on the extraordinary loss may also
    be shown but it is not required.

An additional 20,000 shares (10% x 200,000) were issued as a stock dividend. These are added to the beginning balance without applying a weighting factor, since stock dividends are given retroactive treatment for weighted-average computations. An additional 30,000 shares were issued for cash on 6/30/88. These shares were outstanding for only six months during 1988, so 30,000 is multiplied by 6/12 to give a weighted-average for the year of 15,000 shares for this issuance. The total weighted-average is 235,000 shares (200,000 + 20,000 + 15,000).

3.   Part b. requires the preparation of a schedule reconciling net income to taxable income.

3.1   Net income from part a. is $368,500. This must be adjusted for any items which affect net income but not taxable income, or affect taxable income but not net income.

3.2   The provision for income taxes ($369,000) reduces net income, but is not deductible when computing taxable income. Therefore, it is added back to net income when preparing the reconciliation.

3.3   The officers' life insurance expense also reduces net income, but is not deductible for tax purposes. Therefore, the $70,000 is also added back to net income.

3.4   The tax benefit from earthquake loss ($142,500) has the effect of increasing net income, but is not included when computing taxable income. Therefore, it must be deducted in the reconciliation.

3.5   The resulting taxable income ($665,000) can be computed directly to check its correctness as follows:

Revenues and gains		
Sales revenues		$6,250,000
Gain on sale of investments		130,000
Gross income		6,380,000
Expenses and losses		
Cost of sales	$3,750,000	
Sell. and admin. expenses ($1,212,500 - $70,000)	1,142,500	
Interest expense	122,500	
Loss on disposition of plant assets	225,000	
Earthquake loss	475,000	
Total expenses and losses		5,715,000
Taxable income		$ 665,000

Unofficial Answer

Problem 3   Prepare I/S; Reconcile Net Income to Taxable Income (589,P4)

Pitt Corp.
INCOME STATEMENT
For the Year Ended December 31, 1988

Net sales		$6,250,000
Cost of sales		3,750,000
Gross profit		2,500,000
Selling and administrative expenses		1,212,500
Operating income		1,287,500
Other expenses		
Interest expense		122,500
Income before unusual or infrequent items and income tax		1,165,000
Unusual or infrequent items		
Loss on disposition of plant assets	$(225,000)	
Gain on sale of long-term investments	130,000	(95,000)
Income before income tax and extraordinary item		1,070,000
Income tax		
Current	342,000 [1]	
Deferred	27,000 [2]	369,000
Income before extraordinary item		701,000
Extraordinary item - loss from earthquake (net of applicable income tax benefit of $142,500)		332,500 [3]
Net income		$ 368,500
Earnings per share		
Income before extraordinary item		$2.98 [4]
Extraordinary loss		(1.41) *
Net income		$1.57 [5]

*Optional

b.

Pitt Corp.
RECONCILIATION OF NET INCOME TO
TAXABLE INCOME PER TAX RETURN
For the Year Ended December 31, 1988

Net income	$368,500
Add: Income tax on continuing operations	369,000
Officers' life insurance expense	70,000
	807,500
Deduct: Income tax benefit - extraordinary loss	142,500
Taxable income per tax return	$665,000

Explanation of amounts

[1] Total income tax excluding extraordinary item for 1988

Income before income tax and extraordinary item	$1,070,000
Officers' life insurance expense	70,000
Income subject to tax	1,140,000
Income tax rate	x 30%
Income tax excluding extraordinary item	$ 342,000

[2] Deferred income tax for 1988

Excess of book basis over tax basis in depreciable assets (Expected to reverse equally over next 5 years)	$90,000
Deferred income tax liability, 12/31/88 ($90,000 x 30%)	$27,000
Less beginning balance, 1/1/88	-0-
Net change in deferred tax liability for 1988	$27,000

[3] Extraordinary item – Loss from earthquake damage (net of income tax) for 1988

Loss from earthquake damage	$475,000
Income tax benefit (30% x $475,000)	142,500
Net of income tax effect	$332,500

[4] Earnings per share on income before extraordinary item for 1988

Income before extraordinary item	$701,000
Weighted average number of shares outstanding for 1988 [200,000 + 20,000 + 15,000 (1/2 x 30,000)]	235,000
Earnings per share ($701,000 ÷ 235,000)	$2.98

[5] Earnings per share on net income for 1988

Net income	$368,500
Weighted-average number of shares	235,000
Earnings per share ($368,500 ÷ 235,000)	$1.57

Multiple Choice Questions (1-50)

1. The following information is available for Mason Corp. for 1987:

Sales	$100,000
Beginning inventory	36,000
Ending inventory	19,000
Freight out	9,000
Purchases	43,000

Mason's cost of goods sold for 1987 is
   a. $52,000
   b. $60,000
   c. $69,000
   d. $88,000

2. The following data were available from Mith Co.'s records on December 31, 1988:

Finished goods inventory, 1/1/88	$120,000
Finished goods inventory, 12/31/88	110,000
Cost of goods manufactured	520,000
Loss on sale of plant equipment	50,000

The cost of goods sold for 1988 was
   a. $510,000
   b. $520,000
   c. $530,000
   d. $580,000

3. Zeno Menswear, Inc. maintains a markup of 60% based on cost. The company's selling and administrative expenses average 30% of sales. For 1984, sales amounted to $960,000. Zeno's cost of goods sold and operating profit for 1984 are

	Cost of goods sold	Operating profit
a.	$576,000	$ 96,000
b.	$576,000	$288,000
c.	$600,000	$ 72,000
d.	$600,000	$288,000

4. Grey Corp. purchased merchandise with a list price of $20,000, subject to trade discounts of 10% and 5%. What amount should Grey record as the cost of this merchandise?
   a. $17,000
   b. $17,100
   c. $17,900
   d. $20,000

5. The following costs were among those incurred by Woodcroft Corporation during 1981:

Merchandise purchased for resale	$500,000
Salesmen's commissions	40,000
Interest on notes payable to vendors	5,000

How much should be charged to the cost of the merchandise purchases?

   a. $500,000
   b. $505,000
   c. $540,000
   d. $545,000

6. According to the net method, which of the following items should be included in the cost of inventory?

	Freight costs	Purchase discounts not taken
a.	Yes	No
b.	Yes	Yes
c.	No	Yes
d.	No	No

7. A company records inventory at the gross invoice price. Theoretically, how should the following affect the costs in inventory?

	Warehousing costs	Cash discounts available
a.	Increase	Decrease
b.	No effect	Decrease
c.	No effect	No effect
d.	Increase	No effect

8. Theoretically, how should the following affect the costs to be included in a manufacturer's inventory?

	Insurance on raw materials while in transit	Cash discounts taken on purchased raw materials
a.	Increase	No effect
b.	Increase	Decrease
c.	No effect	Decrease
d.	No effect	No effect

9. Caba Co. recorded the following data pertaining to raw material Z during March 1989:

Date 1989	Units Received	Cost	Issued	On Hand
March 1 inventory		$1.00		400
March 6 issue			200	200
March 30 purchase	600	$1.20		800

The moving-weighted-average unit cost of Z inventory at March 31, 1989 is
   a. $1.20
   b. $1.15
   c. $1.12
   d. $1.10

10. In a periodic inventory system that uses the weighted average cost flow method, the beginning inventory is the
   a. Net purchases minus the ending inventory.
   b. Net purchases minus the cost of goods sold.
   c. Total goods available for sale minus the net purchases.
   d. Total goods available for sale minus the cost of goods sold.

11. The weighted average for the year inventory cost flow method is applicable to which of the following inventory systems?

	Periodic	Perpetual
a.	Yes	Yes
b.	Yes	No
c.	No	Yes
d.	No	No

12. Ward Distribution Company has determined its December 31, 1987 inventory on a FIFO basis at $200,000. Information pertaining to that inventory follows:

Estimated selling price	$204,000
Estimated cost of disposal	10,000
Normal profit margin	30,000
Current replacement cost	180,000

Ward records losses that result from applying the lower of cost or market rule. At December 31, 1987, the loss that Ward should recognize is
   a. $0
   b. $ 6,000
   c. $14,000
   d. $20,000

13. Under the lower of cost or market method, the replacement cost of an inventory item would be used as the designated market value
   a. When it is below the net realizable value less the normal profit margin.
   b. When it is below the net realizable value and above the net realizable value less the normal profit margin.
   c. When it is above the net realizable value.
   d. Regardless of net realizable value.

14. The original cost of an inventory item is above the replacement cost. The replacement cost is above the net realizable value. Under the lower of cost or market method, the inventory item should be reported at its
   a. Original cost.
   b. Replacement cost.
   c. Net realizable value.
   d. Net realizable value less the normal profit margin.

15. The original cost of an inventory item is above the replacement cost and the net realizable value. The replacement cost is below the net realizable value less the normal profit margin. As a result, under the lower of cost or market method, the inventory item should be reported at the
   a. Net realizable value.
   b. Net realizable value less the normal profit margin.
   c. Replacement cost.
   d. Original cost.

16. On December 31, 1987, the New Bite Company had capitalized costs for a new computer software product with an economic life of four years. Sales for 1988 were ten percent of expected total sales of the software. At December 31, 1988, the software had a net realizable value equal to eighty percent of the capitalized cost. The unamortized cost reported on the December 31, 1988, balance sheet should be
   a. Net realizable value.
   b. Ninety percent of net realizable value.
   c. Seventy-five percent of capitalized cost.
   d. Ninety percent of capitalized cost.

17. Dart Company's accounting records indicated the following information:

Inventory, 1/1/86	$ 500,000
Purchases during 1986	2,500,000
Sales during 1986	3,200,000

A physical inventory taken on December 31, 1986, resulted in an ending inventory of $575,000. Dart's gross profit on sales has remained constant at 25% in recent years. Dart suspects some inventory may have been taken by a new employee. At December 31, 1986, what is the estimated cost of missing inventory?
   a. $ 25,000
   b. $100,000
   c. $175,000
   d. $225,000

18. Lin Co. sells its merchandise at a gross profit of 30%. The following figures are among those pertaining to Lin's operations for the six months ended June 30, 1986:

Sales	$200,000
Beginning inventory	50,000
Purchases	130,000

On June 30, 1986, all of Lin's inventory was destroyed by fire. The estimated cost of this destroyed inventory was
   a. $120,000
   b. $ 70,000
   c. $ 40,000
   d. $ 20,000

19. Dean Company uses the retail inventory method to estimate its inventory for interim statement purposes. Data relating to the computation of the inventory at July 31, 1987, are as follows:

	Cost	Retail
Inventory, 2/1/87	$ 180,000	$250,000
Purchases	1,020,000	1,575,000
Markups, net		175,000
Sales		1,705,000
Estimated normal shoplifting losses		20,000
Markdowns, net		125,000

Under the approximate lower of average cost or market retail method, Dean's estimated inventory at July 31, 1987 is

    a. $ 90,000
    b. $ 96,000
    c. $102,000
    d. $150,000

20. At December 31, 1988, the following information was available from Huff Co.'s accounting records:

	Cost	Retail
Inventory, 1/1/88	$147,000	$ 203,000
Purchases	833,000	1,155,000
Additional markups	--	42,000
Available for sale	$980,000	$1,400,000

Sales for the year totaled $1,106,000. Markdowns amounted to $14,000. Under the approximate lower of average cost or market retail method, Huff's inventory at December 31, 1988 was

    a. $308,000
    b. $280,000
    c. $215,600
    d. $196,000

21. Marsh Company had 150 units of product A on hand at January 1, 1985, costing $21 each. Purchases of product A during the month of January were as follows:

	Units	Unit cost
Jan. 10	200	$22
18	250	23
28	100	24

A physical count on January 31, 1985, shows 250 units of product A on hand. The cost of the inventory at January 31, 1985, under the LIFO method is

    a. $5,850
    b. $5,550
    c. $5,350
    d. $5,250

22. During periods of rising prices, a perpetual inventory system would result in the same dollar amount of ending inventory as a periodic inventory system under which of the following inventory cost flow methods?

	FIFO	LIFO
a.	Yes	No
b.	Yes	Yes
c.	No	Yes
d.	No	No

23. The UNO Company was formed on January 2, 1987, to sell a single product. Over a two-year period, UNO's acquisition costs have increased steadily. Physical quantities held in inventory were equal to three months sales at December 31, 1987, and zero at December 31, 1900. Assuming the periodic inventory system, the inventory cost method which reports the highest amount for each of the following is

	Inventory December 31, 1987	Cost of sales 1988
a.	LIFO	FIFO
b.	LIFO	LIFO
c.	FIFO	FIFO
d.	FIFO	LIFO

24. On January 1, 1986, Poe Company adopted the dollar-value LIFO inventory method. Poe's entire inventory constitutes a single pool. Inventory data for 1986 and 1987 are as follows:

Date	Inventory at current year cost	Inventory at base year cost	Relevant price index
1/1/86	$150,000	$150,000	1.00
12/31/86	220,000	200,000	1.10
12/31/87	276,000	230,000	1.20

Poe's LIFO inventory value at December 31, 1987 is

    a. $230,000
    b. $236,000
    c. $241,000
    d. $246,000

25. Evan Company adopted the dollar value LIFO inventory method on December 31, 1985. Evan's entire inventory constitutes a single pool. On December 31, 1985, the inventory was $300,000 under the dollar value LIFO method. Inventory data for 1986 are as follows:

12/31/86 inventory at year-end prices	$390,000
Relevant price index at year end (base year 1985)	120

Using dollar value LIFO, Evan's inventory at December 31, 1986, is

    a. $325,000
    b. $330,000
    c. $360,000
    d. $390,000

26. On December 31, 1984, Jason Company adopted the dollar value LIFO retail inventory method. Inventory data for 1985 are as follows:

	LIFO cost	Retail
Inventory, 12/31/84	$360,000	$500,000
Inventory, 12/31/85	?	660,000
Increase in price level for 1985		10%
Cost to retail ratio for 1985		70%

Under the LIFO retail method, Jason's inventory at December 31, 1985, should be
   a. $437,000
   b. $462,000
   c. $472,000
   d. $483,200

27. When the double extension approach to the dollar value LIFO inventory cost flow method is used, the inventory layer added in the current year is multiplied by an index number. How would the following be used in the calculation of this index number?

	Ending inventory at current year cost	Ending inventory at base year cost
a.	Numerator	Denominator
b.	Numerator	Not Used
c.	Denominator	Numerator
d.	Not Used	Denominator

28. On July 1, 1986, Link Development Company purchased a tract of land for $900,000. Additional costs of $150,000 were incurred in subdividing the land during July through December 1986. Of the tract acreage, 70% was subdivided into residential lots as shown below and 30% was conveyed to the city for roads and a park.

Lot class	Number of lots	Sales price per lot
A	100	$12,000
B	100	8,000
C	200	5,000

Under the relative sales value method, the cost allocated to each Class A lot should be
   a. $2,625
   b. $2,940
   c. $3,600
   d. $4,200

29. Lake Construction Company has consistently used the percentage-of-completion method of recognizing income. During 1985 Lake entered into a fixed-price contract to construct an office building for $10,000,000. Information relating to the contract is as follows:

	At December 31,	
	1985	1986
Percentage of completion	20%	60%
Estimated total cost at completion	$7,500,000	$8,000,000
Income recognized (cumulative)	500,000	1,200,000

Contract costs incurred during 1986 were
   a. $3,200,000
   b. $3,300,000
   c. $3,500,000
   d. $4,800,000

30. Cord Builders, Inc. has consistently used the percentage-of-completion method of accounting for construction-type contracts. During 1984 Cord started work on a $9,000,000 fixed-price construction contract that was completed in 1986. Cord's accounting records disclosed the following:

	December 31,	
	1984	1985
Cumulative contract costs incurred	$3,900,000	$6,300,000
Estimated total cost at completion	7,800,000	8,100,000

How much income would Cord have recognized on this contract for the year ended December 31, 1985?
   a. $100,000
   b. $300,000
   c. $600,000
   d. $700,000

31. Hansen Construction, Inc. has consistently used the percentage-of-completion method of recognizing income. During 1984 Hansen started work on a $3,000,000 fixed-price construction contract. The accounting records disclosed the following data for the year ended December 31, 1984:

Costs incurred	$ 930,000
Estimated cost to complete	2,170,000
Progress billings	1,100,000
Collections	700,000

How much loss should Hansen have recognized in 1984?
   a. $230,000
   b. $100,000
   c. $ 30,000
   d. $0

Items 32 and 33 are based on the following data relating to a construction job started by Syl Co. during 1986:

Total contract price	$100,000
Actual costs during 1986	20,000
Estimated remaining costs	40,000
Billed to customer during 1986	30,000
Received from customer during 1986	10,000

32. Under the completed-contract method, how much should Syl recognize as gross profit for 1986?

    a. $0
    b. $ 4,000
    c. $10,000
    d. $12,000

33. Under the percentage-of-completion method, how much should Syl recognize as gross profit for 1986?

    a. $0
    b. $13,333
    c. $26,667
    d. $33,333

34. A company uses the completed-contract method to account for a four-year construction contract which is presently in its third year. Progress billings were recorded and collected in the third year. Based on events occurring in the third year, there is now an anticipated loss on the contract. When would the effect of each of the following be reported in the company's income statement?

	Third year progress billings	Anticipated loss
a.	Not third year	Third year
b.	Not third year	Fourth year
c.	Third year	Third year
d.	Third year	Fourth year

35. Which of the following would be used in the calculation of the income recognized in the fourth and final year of a contract accounted for by the percentage-of-completion method?

	Actual total costs	Income previously recognized
a.	Yes	Yes
b.	Yes	No
c.	No	Yes
d.	No	No

36. When should an anticipated loss on a long-term contract be recognized under the percentage-of-completion method and the completed-contract method, respectively?

	Percentage-of-Completion	Completed-Contract
a.	Over life of project	Contract complete
b.	Immediately	Contract complete
c.	Over life of project	Immediately
d.	Immediately	Immediately

37. In accounting for a long-term construction contract using the percentage-of-completion method, the progress billings on contracts account is a

    a.   Contra current asset account.
    b.   Contra noncurrent asset account.
    c.   Noncurrent liability account.
    d.   Revenue account.

38. Dean Company's accounts payable balance at December 31, 1987 was $1,800,000 before considering the following transactions:

   • Goods were in transit from a vendor to Dean on December 31, 1987. The invoice price was $100,000, and the goods were shipped FOB shipping point on December 29, 1987. The goods were received on January 4, 1988.

   • Goods shipped to Dean, FOB shipping point on December 20, 1987, from a vendor were lost in transit. The invoice price was $50,000. On January 5, 1988, Dean filed a $50,000 claim against the common carrier.

In its December 31, 1987 balance sheet, Dean should report accounts payable of

    a. $1,950,000
    b. $1,900,000
    c. $1,850,000
    d. $1,800,000

39. Dell Company's inventory at December 31, 1987 was $1,200,000 based on a physical count of goods priced at cost, and before any necessary year-end adjustments relating to the following:

   • Included in the physical count were goods billed to a customer FOB shipping point on December 30, 1987. These goods had a cost of $25,000 and were picked up by the carrier on January 7, 1988.

   • Goods shipped FOB shipping point on December 28, 1987, from a vendor to Dell were received on January 4, 1988. The invoice cost was $60,000.

What amount should Dell report as inventory in its December 31, 1987 balance sheet?

    a. $1,175,000
    b. $1,200,000
    c. $1,235,000
    d. $1,260,000

40. Lewis Company's usual sales terms are net 60 days, FOB shipping point. Sales, net of returns and allowances, totaled $2,300,000 for the year ended December 31, 1987, before year-end adjustments. Additional data are as follows:

   • On December 27, 1987, Lewis authorized a customer to return, for full credit, goods shipped and billed at $50,000 on

December 15, 1987. The returned goods were received by Lewis on January 4, 1988, and a $50,000 credit memo was issued and recorded on the same date.

• Goods with an invoice amount of $80,000 were billed and recorded on January 3, 1988. The goods were shipped on December 30, 1987.

• Goods with an invoice amount of $100,000 were billed and recorded on December 30, 1987. The goods were shipped on January 3, 1988.

Lewis' adjusted net sales for 1987 should be
   a. $2,330,000
   b. $2,280,000
   c. $2,250,000
   d. $2,230,000

41. Kemp Company had the following consignment transactions during December 1986:

Inventory shipped on consignment to Ashe Company	$9,000
Freight paid by Kemp	450
Inventory received on consignment from Fenn Company	6,000
Freight paid by Fenn	250

No sales of consigned goods were made through December 31, 1986. Kemp's December 31, 1986 balance sheet should include consigned inventory at
   a. $9,450
   b. $9,000
   c. $6,250
   d. $6,000

42. On November 30, 1985, North Company consigned 30 freezers to West Company for sale at $800 each and paid $600 in transportation costs. An account sales was received on December 30, 1985, from West reporting the sale of 10 freezers, together with a remittance of the $6,800 balance due. The remittance was net of the agreed 15% commission. How much, and in what month, should North recognize as consignment sales revenue?

	November 1985	December 1985
a.	$0	$8,000
b.	$0	$7,800
c.	$23,100	$0
d.	$24,000	$0

43. Shipping costs incurred by a consignor on transfer of goods to a consignee should be considered as
   a. Expense to the consignee.
   b. Expense to the consignor.
   c. Inventory cost to the consignee.
   d. Inventory cost to the consignor.

May 1990 Questions

44. On June 1, 1989, Pitt Corp. sold merchandise with a list price of $5,000 to Burr on account. Pitt allowed trade discounts of 30% and 20%. Credit terms were 2/15, n/40 and the sale was made FOB shipping point. Pitt prepaid $200 of delivery costs for Burr as an accommodation. On June 12, 1989, Pitt received from Burr a remittance in full payment amounting to
   a. $2,744
   b. $2,940
   c. $2,944
   d. $3,140

45. Union Corp. uses the first-in, first-out retail method of inventory valuation. The following information is available:

	Cost	Retail
Beginning inventory	$12,000	$ 30,000
Purchases	60,000	110,000
Net additional markups		10,000
Net markdowns		20,000
Sales revenue		90,000

If the lower of cost or market rule is disregarded, what would be the estimated cost of the ending inventory?
   a. $24,000
   b. $20,800
   c. $20,000
   d. $19,200

46. The balance in Kemp Corp.'s accounts payable account at December 31, 1989 was $900,000 before any necessary year-end adjustment relating to the following:

• Goods were in transit to Kemp from a vendor on December 31, 1989. The invoice cost was $50,000. The goods were shipped FOB shipping point on December 29, 1989 and were received on January 4, 1990.

• Goods shipped FOB destination on December 21, 1989 from a vendor to Kemp were received on January 6, 1990. The invoice cost was $25,000.

• On December 27, 1989, Kemp wrote and recorded checks to creditors totaling $10,000 that were mailed on January 10, 1990.

In Kemp's December 31, 1989 balance sheet, the accounts payable should be
   a. $940,000
   b. $950,000
   c. $975,000
   d. $990,000

47. The following information was taken from Cody Co.'s accounting records for the year ended December 31, 1989:

Decrease in raw materials inventory	$ 15,000
Increase in finished goods inventory	35,000
Raw material purchased	430,000
Direct labor payroll	200,000
Factory overhead	300,000
Freight-out	45,000

There was no work-in-process inventory at the beginning or end of the year. Cody's 1989 cost of goods sold is

    a. $895,000
    b. $910,000
    c. $950,000
    d. $955,000

48. During 1988, Mitchell Corp. started a construction job with a total contract price of $600,000. The job was completed on December 15, 1989. Additional data are as follows:

	1988	1989
Actual costs incurred	$225,000	$255,000
Estimated remaining costs	225,000	----
Billed to customer	240,000	360,000
Received from customer	200,000	400,000

Under the completed contract method, what amount should Mitchell recognize as gross profit for 1989?

    a. $ 45,000
    b. $ 72,000
    c. $ 80,000
    d. $120,000

49. Mill Construction Co. uses the percentage-of-completion method of accounting. During 1989, Mill contracted to build an apartment complex for Drew for $20,000,000. Mill estimated that total costs would amount to $16,000,000 over the period of construction. In connection with this contract, Mill incurred $2,000,000 of construction costs during 1989. Mill billed and collected $3,000,000 from Drew in 1989. What amount should Mill recognize as gross profit for 1989?

    a. $250,000
    b. $375,000
    c. $500,000
    d. $600,000

50. A company used the percentage-of-completion method of accounting for a four-year construction contract. Which of the following items would be used to calculate the income recognized in the second year?

	Income previously recognized	Progress billings to date
a.	Yes	Yes
b.	No	Yes
c.	Yes	No
d.	No	No

Repeat Questions

(590,P1,14) Identical/similar to item 4 above
(590,P3,44) Identical/similar to item 42 above

Problems

Problem 1   (589,T3)

(15 to 25 minutes)

Steel Company, a wholesaler that has been in business for two years, purchases its inventories from various suppliers. During the two years, each purchase has been at a lower price than the previous purchase.

Steel uses the lower of FIFO cost or market method to value inventories. The original cost of the inventories is above replacement cost and below the net realizable value. The net realizable value less the normal profit margin is below the replacement cost.

Required:

a. In general, what criteria should be used to determine which costs should be included in inventory?

b. In general, why is the lower of cost or market rule used to report inventory?

c. At what amount should Steel's inventories be reported on the balance sheet? Explain the application of the lower of cost or market rule in this situation.

d. What would have been the effect on ending inventories and net income for the second year had Steel used the lower of average cost or market inventory method instead of the lower of FIFO cost or market inventory method? Why?

Problem 2   (588,T2)

(15 to 25 minutes)

Hudson Company, which is both a wholesaler and a retailer, purchases its inventories from various suppliers.

Additional facts for Hudson's wholesale operations are as follows:

• Hudson incurs substantial warehousing costs.

• Hudson uses the lower of cost or market method.

• The replacement cost of the inventories is below the net realizable value and above the net realizable value less the normal profit margin. The original cost of the inventories is above the replacement cost and below the net realizable value.

Additional facts for Hudson's retail operations are as follows:

• Hudson determines the estimated cost of its ending inventories held for sale at retail using the conventional retail inventory method, which approximates lower of average cost or market.

• Hudson incurs markups and net markdowns.

Required:

a. Theoretically, how should Hudson account for the warehousing costs related to its wholesale inventories? Why?

b. 1. In general, why is the lower of cost or market method used to report inventory?

2. At which amount should Hudson's wholesale inventories be reported on the balance sheet? Explain the application of the lower of cost or market method in this situation.

c. In the calculation of the cost to retail percentage used to determine the estimated cost of its ending retail inventories, how should Hudson treat

1. Freight-in costs?
2. Net markups?
3. Net markdowns?

d. Why does Hudson's retail inventory method approximate lower of average cost or market?

Problem 3   (587,T3)

(15 to 25 minutes)

Hanlon Company purchased a significant amount of raw materials inventory for a new product that it is manufacturing. Hanlon purchased insurance on these raw materials while they were in transit from the supplier.

Hanlon uses the lower of cost or market rule for these raw materials. The replacement cost of the raw materials is above the net realizable value and both are below the original cost.

Hanlon uses the average cost inventory method for these raw materials. In the last two years, each purchase has been at a lower price than the previous purchase, and the ending inventory quantity for each period has been higher than the beginning inventory quantity for that period.

Required:

a. What is the theoretically appropriate method that Hanlon should use to account for the insurance costs on the raw materials while they were in transit from the supplier? Why?

b. 1. At which amount should Hanlon's raw materials inventory be reported on the balance sheet? Why?

2. In general, why is the lower of cost or market rule used to report inventory?

c. What would have been the effect on ending inventory and cost of goods sold had Hanlon used the LIFO inventory method instead of the average cost inventory method for the raw materials? Why?

Problem 4   (1185,T3)

(15 to 25 minutes)

Caddell Company, a wholesaler, purchases its inventories from various suppliers FOB destination; it incurs substantial warehousing costs. Caddell uses the dollar value LIFO inventory cost flow method. Caddell also consigns some of its inventories to Reed Company.

Reed also has items for sale that it purchases from other wholesalers. Reed uses the lower of FIFO cost or market inventory method.

Required:

a. When should the purchases from various suppliers generally be included in Caddell's inventory? Why?

b. Theoretically, how should Caddell account for the warehousing costs? Why?

c. 1. What are the advantages of using the dollar value LIFO inventory cost flow method as opposed to the conventional quantity of goods LIFO method?

     2. How does the calculation of dollar value LIFO differ from the conventional quantity of goods method?

d. How should Caddell account for the inventories consigned to Reed Company? Why?

e. When Reed applies the lower of cost or market method, what are the ceiling and floor limits?

Problem 5   (586,T2)

(15 to 25 minutes)

Village Company is accounting for a long-term construction contract using the percentage-of-completion method. It is a three-year fixed-fee contract that is presently in its first year. The latest reasonable estimates of total contract costs indicate that the contract will be completed at a profit. Village will submit progress billings to the customer and has reasonable assurance that collections on these billings will be received in each year of the contract.

Required:

a. 1. What is the justification for the percentage-of-completion method for long-term construction contracts?

     2. What facts in the situation above indicate that Village should account for this long-term construction contract using the percentage-of-completion method?

b. How would the income recognized in each year of this long-term construction contact be determined using the cost-to-cost method of determining percentage of completion?

c. What is the effect on income, if any, of the progress billings and the collections on these billings?

Multiple Choice Answers

1. b	11. b	21. c	31. b	41. a
2. c	12. d	22. a	32. a	42. a
3. c	13. b	23. c	33. b	43. d
4. b	14. c	24. c	34. a	44. c
5. a	15. b	25. b	35. a	45. a
6. a	16. c	26. a	36. d	46. d
7. a	17. a	27. a	37. a	47. b
8. b	18. c	28. d	38. a	48. d
9. b	19. a	29. b	39. d	49. c
10. c	20. d	30. a	40. d	50. c

Multiple Choice Answer Explanations

A. Determining Inventory and Cost of Goods Sold

1. (1188,P3,43) (b) Cost of goods sold equals beginning inventory ($36,000) plus the cost of goods purchased ($43,000) less ending inventory ($19,000), or $60,000. Note that the cost of goods purchased could be affected not only by purchases, but also by freight-in, purchase discounts, and purchase returns and allowances, none of which apply to this problem. While freight-in would have been used, freight-out ($9,000) is not. Cost of goods purchased includes only those costs associated with bringing the goods to the point of sale. Freight-out is the cost of transporting the goods from the point of sale to the customer, and is properly classified as a selling expense.

2. (1189,P3,45) (c) For a manufacturing company, cost of goods sold is computed as follows:

Finished goods inv., 1/1/88	$120,000
Cost of goods manufactured	520,000
Cost of goods available for sales	640,000
Less finished goods inv., 12/31/88	110,000
Cost of goods sold	$530,000

Note that the above computation is very similar to the computation of cost of goods sold for a merchandising firm. For a merchandising firm, merchandise inventory is used instead of finished goods inventory and cost of goods purchased is used instead of cost of goods manufactured. In either case, a loss on sale of equipment ($50,000) would not affect the computation.

3. (1185,P2,37) (c) The requirement is 1984 cost of goods sold and operating profit. In 1984, sales are $960,000, and the markup is 60%, based on cost. The formula for converting a markup on cost to a markup on selling price is:

$$\left(\begin{array}{c} \% \text{ markup on} \\ \text{selling price} \end{array}\right) = \frac{\% \text{ markup on cost}}{100\% + \% \text{ markup on cost}}$$

In this case, the % markup on sales is 37.5% [60% ÷ (100% + 60%)]. Therefore, gross profit is $360,000 (37.5% x $960,000) and cost of goods sold is $600,000 ($960,000 − $360,000). Note that the markup on cost can be verified ($600,000 x 60% = $360,000). Operating profit can now be computed as shown below:

Sales	$960,000
Cost of goods sold	(600,000)
Gross profit	360,000
S and A expenses (30% x 960,000)	(288,000)
Operating profit	$ 72,000

4. (589,P2,21) (b) Purchases are always recorded net of trade discounts. When more than one trade discount is applied to a list price, it is called a chain discount. Chain discounts are applied in steps; each discount applies to the previously discounted price. Therefore the cost of this merchandise is $17,100, as computed below:

List price	$20,000
Less 10% discount	2,000
Discounted list price	18,000
Less 5% discount	900
Gross billing price	$17,100

Note if a purchase discount, or cash discount (such as 2/10, n/30) is available, it is applied to the gross billing price and is generally recorded in a separate purchase discounts account.

5. (582,Q1,14) (a) The requirement is the amount of the costs to be included in merchandise purchases. The salesmen's commissions are a selling expense not related to the acquisition of the merchandise and are, therefore, treated as a period cost rather than as a product cost. Further, interest costs incurred in acquiring inventory are expensed as incurred. They are financing expenses. Per para 10 of SFAS 34, interest costs are not capitalized for assets that are in use or ready for their intended use (e.g. merchandise held for resale). Thus, only the $500,000 should be included in the cost of the purchases.

6. (1188,T1,6) (a) Per ARB 43, Chapter 4, para 4, the cost of inventory should include all expenditures (direct and indirect) incurred to bring an item to its existing condition and location. Freight charges are thus appropriately included in inventory costs. Under the net purchase method,

purchase discounts not taken are recorded in a Purchase Discounts Lost account. When this method is used, purchase discounts lost are considered a financial (i.e., "other") expense, and are thus excluded from the cost of inventory. Therefore, answer (a) is correct, and answers (b), (c), and (d) are incorrect.

7.   (1187,T1,1)   (a)   Per ARB 43, cost is defined as the sum of applicable expenditures and charges directly or indirectly incurred in bringing an article to its existing condition or location. Warehousing costs would, therefore, increase inventory. Theoretically, inventory should be shown net of cash discounts whether taken or not because the net method allows for a more correct reporting of the asset. Thus, cash discounts available will decrease the costs in inventory. Note that the company's use of the gross method of recording invoices does not change the effect of the available cash discounts because, from a theoretical viewpoint, inventory should be recorded net of cash discounts.

8.   (1184,T1,10)   (b)   The requirement is to determine how insurance on, and cash discounts taken on raw materials will affect the cost of the raw materials inventory. From a theoretical viewpoint, all costs incurred to acquire goods and prepare them for market are inventoriable. Insurance while in transit is a cost incurred to acquire goods and would increase the cost of the inventory. Cash discounts are accounted for as reductions of purchase price and would reduce the cost of the inventory.

B.2. Weighted Average

9.   (1189,Q1,9)   (b)   The moving average method requires that a new unit cost be computed each time goods are purchased; thereafter it must be used with perpetual records. A recomputation of unit cost is not performed when goods are sold because the inventory account is simply credited at the average price. After the 3/6/89 issue, Caba has on hand 200 units (400 − 200) at a cost of $1.00 each. After the 3/30/89 purchase, Kew has on hand 800 units at a total cost of $920 (see computation below).

Units		Cost		Extension
200	x	$1.00	=	$200
600		$1.20	=	720
800				$920

Therefore, the moving average unit cost is $1.15 ($920 ÷ 800). Note that since 1/4 of the units cost $1.00 and 3/4 cost $1.20, a shortcut approach is: (1/4 x $1.00) + (3/4 x $1.20) = $1.15.

10.   (1188,T1,26)   (c)   In a periodic inventory system (regardless of the cost flow method assumed) beginning inventory equals net goods available for sale minus net purchases. Answers (a) and (b) are nonsensical answers and answer (d) is incorrect because it is the formula for determining ending inventory.

11.   (586,T1,11)   (b)   The requirement is whether the weighted average inventory method is applicable to a periodic and/or a perpetual inventory system. The weighted average method computes a weighted average unit cost of inventory for the entire period and is used with periodic records. The moving average method requires that a new unit of cost be computed each time new goods are purchased and is used with perpetual records. Therefore, answers (a), (c), and (d) are incorrect.

B.5. Lower of Cost or Market

12.   (588,P2,21)   (d)   ARB 43, Chapter 4, para 8 requires the use of the lower of cost or market (LCM) approach for the financial reporting of inventories. The market value of inventory is defined as the replacement cost, as long as it is less than the ceiling (net realizable value) and more than the floor (net realizable value less a normal profit). In this case, the amounts are:

Ceiling	
$204,000 est. sell. price −	
$10,000 disposal cost	$194,000
Replacement cost	$180,000

Floor	
$194,000 NRV − $30,000	
normal profit	$164,000

Therefore, the designated market value is the replacement cost of $180,000 because it falls between the floor and the ceiling. Once the market value is chosen, the LCM can be determined ($180,000, since the $180,000 market value is less than the $200,000 cost). Since market is less than cost, a loss must be recognized ($200,000 cost less $180,000 market value = $20,000 loss).

13.   (1188,T1,8)   (b)   Per ARB 43, Chapter 4, para 8, "market" is equal to current replacement cost, subject to the following constraints: 1) market cannot exceed the net realizable value (NRV) of an item, and 2) market cannot be below NRV less the normal profit margin. Therefore, answer (b) is correct and answer (d) is incorrect. Answer (a) is incorrect because under these circumstances, the designated market value would be the NRV less the normal profit margin. Answer (c) is incorrect because under these circumstances the designated market value would be the NRV.

14. (1187,T1,3) (c) ARB 43, Chapter 4 requires inventory to be carried at market when market value is less than cost. Market value is defined as replacement cost, subject to ceiling and floor limitations. The ceiling is the net realizable value of the item (selling price less selling costs and costs to complete). The floor is net realizable value less a normal profit. Since replacement cost is above the ceiling, net realizable value will be used as the market value to determine lower of cost or market. Since market is below original cost, market will be used to price the inventory, and answer (c) is correct. Answer (a) is incorrect because original cost is greater than market. Answer (b) is incorrect because replacement cost is greater than NRV, which is the ceiling for market price. Answer (d) is incorrect because NRV less the normal profit margin is the floor for the market price. Since replacement cost was greater than the market ceiling, the floor would not be used in determination of market.

15. (1189,T1,10) (b) ARB 43, Chapter 4 requires the pricing of inventory at market when market value is less than cost. Market value is defined as current replacement cost, subject to a ceiling of net realizable value (NRV) and a floor of net realizable value minus a normal profit margin.

> ┌─ Original Cost
> ├─ Net Realizable Value (NRV)
> ├─ NRV - Normal Profit
> └─ Replacement Cost

In this situation, replacement cost lies outside of (below) the floor and ceiling limitations. Therefore, NRV less a normal profit margin, (the floor) will be used as the market to determine LCM. Since original cost is greater than market, market will be used to price the inventory for the period. Therefore, answer (b) is correct.

16. (1189,T1,12) (c) Per SFAS 86, para 8, the annual amortization of capitalized software costs shall be the greater of:

1) The ratio of the software's current sales to its expected total sales, or
2) The straight-line method over the economic life of the product.

In this case, the ratio of current to expected total sales is 10% (given). The annual straight-line rate is 25% per year (1 ÷ economic life of four years). The straight-line amortization should be used in 1988, since it is the higher of the two. The unamortized cost on the 12/31/88 balance sheet should, therefore, be 75% (100% - 25%

amortization), which is answer (c). Note that para 10 of SFAS 86 requires that the unamortized cost of capitalized software products must be compared to the net realizable value of those assets at each balance sheet date. Any excess of the amortized cost over the net realizable value must be written off. In this case, the net realizable value (80%) was <u>above</u> the unamortized cost (75%), so no additional write-off was required.

B.6. Gross Profit

17. (1187,P1,9) (a) The gross profit method can be used to estimate the cost of missing inventory. The first step is to compute the cost of goods available for sale.

Beginning inventory	$ 500,000
Purchases	2,500,000
Cost of goods available for sale	$3,000,000

The second step is to estimate cost of goods sold based on the gross profit percentage.

Sales	$3,200,000
Estimated gross profit ($3,200,000 x 25%)	(800,000)
Cost of goods sold ($3,200,000 x 75%)	$2,400,000

Note that a shortcut is to realize that if gross profit is 25% of sales, cost of goods sold must be 75% of sales. The third step is to compute estimated ending inventory.

Cost of goods available for sale	$3,000,000
Estimated cost of goods sold	(2,400,000)
Estimated ending inventory	$ 600,000

Since the actual count of ending inventory at December 31 was only $575,000, the estimated shortage in inventory is $25,000 ($600,000 - $575,000).

18. (1186,Q2,28) (c) Ending inventory for Lin Co. can be estimated by using the gross profit percentage to convert sales to cost of goods sold (estimated). If gross profit is 30% of sales, then cost of goods sold is 70% (1-30%) of sales. In this case, estimated cost of goods sold is 140,000 (200,000 sales x 70%). Estimated cost of goods sold is then subtracted from actual goods available for sale to determine estimated ending inventory.

Beginning inventory	$ 50,000
Purchases	130,000
Goods available for sale	180,000
Less estimated cost of goods sold	(140,000)
Estimated ending inventory	$ 40,000

B.7. Retail Method

19. (1187,P3,53) (a) Under the retail method, inventory is determined at retail and then reduced to cost by a cost-to-retail ratio. To approximate lower of cost or market, markups are included in the denominator of the cost/retail ratio, while markdowns are not. Beginning inventory is included in the computations of the ratio because the average cost basis is being used. The first step is to construct a cost and retail table.

	Cost	Retail
2/1/87 inventory	$ 180,000	$ 250,000
Purchases	1,020,000	1,575,000
Net markups		175,000
Cost/retail ratio totals	$1,200,000	2,000,000
Sales		(1,705,000)
Net markdowns		(125,000)
Estimated normal shoplifting losses		(20,000)
Ending inventory at retail		$ 150,000

Normal shoplifting losses are deducted because the goods shoplifted are no longer in inventory. If the shoplifting losses were abnormal, they would be subtracted from both the cost and retail columns before the cost/retail totals so the cost/retail ratio would not be distorted. The second step is to compute the cost/retail ratio.

$$\$1,200,000/\$2,000,000 = \underline{60\%}$$

The final step is to determine the ending inventory at cost by multiplying the cost/retail ratio by the ending inventory at retail.

$$\$150,000 \times 60\% = \underline{\$90,000}$$

20. (589,P2,22) (d) Under the conventional retail method, inventory is counted at retail and then converted to cost using a cost-to-retail ratio. The first step in the solutions approach is to review the fundamentals of the conventional retail method. To approximate lower of cost or market, markups are included in the denominator of the cost-to-retail ratio, while markdowns are not. Beginning inventory is included in the ratio because the computation is being made on an average cost basis. The computation begins as follows:

	Cost	Retail
1/1/88 inventory	$147,000	$ 203,000
Purchases	833,000	1,155,000
Markups		42,000
	$980,000	$ 1,400,000
Sales		(1,106,000)
Markdowns		(14,000)
Ending inventory at retail		$ 280,000

The cost-to-retail ratio is 70% ($980,000 ÷ $1,400,000). The ending inventory at retail is then multiplied by that ratio to determine the ending inventory at cost ($280,000 x 70% = $196,000).

B.8. & B.9. First-in, First-out (FIFO), and Last-in, First-out (LIFO)

21. (585,P1,10) (c) The requirement is to determine the cost of the 1/31/85 inventory, using the LIFO method. LIFO stands for last-in, first-out; this means that the cost of the units purchased most recently are included in cost of goods sold. Therefore, the 1/31/85 inventory consists of the 250 units which were purchased at the earliest date(s). Thus, the 1/31/85 inventory would consist of the 150 units on hand at 1/1/85 (150 x $21 = $3,150) plus an additional 100 units purchased at the earliest purchase date in January (January 10; 100 x $22 = $2,200). The total value of the inventory at 1/31/85 would be $5,350 ($3,150 + $2,200).

22. (1188,T1,7) (a) Under the FIFO method, the first goods purchased are considered to be the first goods used or sold. Ending inventory is thus made up of the latest (most recent) purchases. Whenever the FIFO method is used, the ending inventory is the same whether a perpetual or periodic system is used. This is true even during periods of rising or falling prices because the inventory flow is always in chronological order. Under the LIFO method, the latest (most recent) purchases are considered to be the first goods used or sold. Ending inventory is thus made up of the first (oldest) purchases. When a periodic method is used, the first/last purchase determination is made only at the end of the year, based upon the actual chronological order of all purchases. When a perpetual method is used, however, the first/last purchase determination is made continuously throughout the year. When inventory levels get low under the perpetual method, early purchase costs will often be assigned to goods sold, a situation which is much less likely to occur in a periodic system. Therefore, in times of either rising or falling prices, LIFO ending inventory is usually different under a periodic system than under a perpetual system, and answer (a) is correct.

23. (1189,T1,9) (c) In a period of rising prices, the FIFO inventory cost method will result in the highest balance in ending inventory. This is because the cost of the highest-priced (most recent) purchases are assigned to the ending inventory. In

contrast, the LIFO inventory cost method will result in the lowest balance in ending inventory. This is because the higher costs of the most recent purchases flow to cost of sales, and the lower (earlier) costs remain in ending inventory.

To simplify the second half of the problem, it is helpful to assign values to the 12/31/87 ending inventory balances. Since the FIFO balance is the higher of the two, let's assume that the FIFO balance is $100 and the LIFO balance is $80. To determine the cost of sales for 1988, the following formula is used (regardless of cost flow assumption):

$$\frac{Beginning}{Inventory} + \frac{Net}{Purchases} - \frac{Ending}{Inventory} = \frac{Cost\ of}{Sales}$$

Since the problem states that there is no ending inventory at 12/31/88, the cost of sales for 1988 will be the sum of beginning inventory and net purchases. Assuming net purchases of $50 during 1988, the cost of sales for the year under the two cost flow assumptions are as follows:

	Beg. Inv.	+	Net Pur.	=	Cost of Sales
FIFO	$100	+	$50	=	$150
LIFO	$ 80	+	$50	=	$130

Thus, the cost of sales for 1988 are higher under FIFO, and answer (c) is correct. Overall, the higher 12/31/87 ending inventory costs under the FIFO method result in a higher cost of sales in 1988, due to the fact that there is no ending inventory at 12/31/88.

B.10. Dollar Value LIFO

24. (588,P2,22) (c) When using dollar value LIFO, the ending inventory at current year cost must first be converted to base year cost. This amount is given at 12/31/87 ($230,000), but it could be computed as follows: $276,000 ÷ 1.20 = $230,000. The next step is to determine the incremental LIFO layers at base year cost. The 1/1/86 (base year) layer is $150,000, the 1986 layer is $50,000 ($200,000 - $150,000), and the 1987 layer is $30,000 ($230,000 - $200,000). Finally, the LIFO layers are restated using the price index in effect at the time each layer was added:

	Base Cost		Ending inventory at DV LIFO cost
1/1/86 layer	$150,000 x 1.00	=	$150,000
1986 layer	50,000 x 1.10	=	55,000
1987 layer	30,000 x 1.20	=	36,000
	$230,000		$241,000

25. (587,P1,16) (b) When using dollar value LIFO, the ending inventory at current year cost ($390,000) must first be converted to

base-year cost by dividing by the relevant price index at year end (120%). This results in ending inventory stated in base-year dollars ($390,000 ÷ 1.20 = $325,000). If this amount is greater than the base-year amount at the end of the previous year, a layer has been added. Since this question deals with the first year on the dollar value method, this will be the first LIFO layer added. As layers are added, the increase at base-year prices is restated using the price index in effect at the time each layer was added. Therefore, the 12/31/86 inventory is $330,000, computed as follows:

	Cost at base year x prices	Appropriate year-end index	=	Dollar value LIFO end. inv.
12/31/85 layer	$300,000 x	1.00	=	$300,000
12/31/86 increment	25,000 x	1.20	=	30,000
				$330,000

26. (586,P1,12) (a) The requirement is the 12/31/85 inventory using the LIFO retail method. The 12/31/85 inventory at retail is $660,000. This amount at base-year prices is $600,000 ($660,000 ÷ 1.10). This means that ending inventory at retail, in terms of base-year prices, increased by $100,000 ($600,000 - $500,000). Thus, the 12/31/85 inventory consists of two layers: the 12/31/84 LIFO-base layer ($500,000) and the 1985 layer ($100,000 at base-year prices). These two layers must be priced out using the appropriate price indexes and cost-to-retail ratios, resulting in a 12/31/85 inventory at cost of $437,000, as indicated below.

	Base-year retail	Index	Retail	Cost-to-retail ratio	LIFO cost
12/31/84 layer	$500,000 x 1.00 =		$500,000 x	72% =	$360,000
1985 layer	100,000 x 1.10 =		110,000 x	70% =	77,000
					$437,000

27. (585,T1,7) (a) The requirement is to determine the appropriate use of ending inventory at current year cost and ending inventory at base-year cost in calculating the dollar value LIFO index. Answer (a) is correct because according to ARB 43, Chapter 4, the index number used to convert the current year's inventory layer is calculated as follows:

$$Index = \frac{Ending\ inventory\ at\ current\ cost}{Ending\ inventory\ at\ base-year\ cost}$$

This index indicates the relationship between current and base-year prices as a percentage, and when multiplied by the new layer (which is in base-year dollars), it will convert the layer to current dollars. Therefore, answers (b), (c), and (d) are incorrect.

B.15 Cost Apportionment by Relative Sales Value

28. (587,P1,17) (d) Per SFAS 67, para 14, real estate donated to municipalities or other governmental agencies for uses that will benefit the project shall be allocated as a common cost of the project. None of the cost should be allocated to land donated to the city, since that land will not directly generate revenue (and therefore has no sales value). Therefore, the total cost of acquiring the land ($900,000 + $150,000 = $1,050,000) should be allocated to the lots which will generate revenue. The $1,050,000 cost is allocated based on the relative sales value of the lots, as computed below:

Lot class	# of lots		Sales price		Total sales value
A	100	x	$12,000	=	$1,200,000
B	100	x	8,000	=	800,000
C	200	x	5,000	=	1,000,000
					$3,000,000

Total cost		Fraction allocated to Class A		Allocated cost		# of lots		Cost per lot in Class A
$1,050,000	x	($1,200/$3,000)	=	$420,000	÷	100	=	$4,200

B.16. Long-Term Construction Contracts

29. (1187,P2,21) (b) Based on the information given, it must be assumed that costs incurred are used to measure the extent of progress toward project completion. At 12/31/85, the project was 20% complete and total estimated costs were $7,500,000. Therefore, costs incurred as of 12/31/85 were 20% of $7,500,000, or $1,500,000. At 12/31/86, the project was 60% complete and total estimated costs were $8,000,000. Therefore, costs incurred as of 12/31/86 are 60% of $8,000,000 or $4,800,000. The costs incurred during 1986 were $4,800,000 less $1,500,000, or $3,300,000.

30. (1186,P2,30) (a) The total expected income on the contract at 12/31/85 is $900,000 ($9,000,000 - $8,100,000). The formula for recognizing profit under the percentage-of-completion method is:

$$\frac{\text{Costs to date}}{\text{Total expected costs}} \times \text{Expected profit} = \text{Profit recognized to date}$$

$$\frac{\$6,300,000}{\$8,100,000} \times \$900,000 = \underline{\$700,000}$$

This result is the total profit on the contract in 1984 and 1985. The 1984 profit recognized must be subtracted from $700,000 to determine the 1985 profit. At 12/31/84, the total expected income on the contract was $1,200,000 ($9,000,000 - $7,800,000). The income recognized in 1984 was $600,000, as computed below:

$$\frac{\$3,900,000}{\$7,800,000} \times \$1,200,000 = \underline{\$600,000}$$

Therefore, 1985 income is $700,000 less $600,000, or $100,000.

31. (585,P2,23) (b) The requirement is to determine the amount of loss to recognize in 1984 on a long-term, fixed-price construction contract. Under both the percentage-of-completion method and the completed contract method, an expected loss on a contract must be recognized in full in the period in which the expected loss is discovered. Therefore, Hanson must recognize a loss of $100,000 in 1984.

Expected contract revenue	$3,000,000
Expected contract costs	
($930,000 + $2,170,000)	3,100,000
Expected loss	$ (100,000)

32. (587,Q1,1) (a) When a company uses the completed-contract method of accounting for construction projects, all revenue and expense recognition is deferred until the project is complete or substantially complete (ARB 45, para 9). Because there is an estimated $40,000 of remaining costs, the contract can not be considered to be substantially complete. Thus, no revenue, expenses, or gross profit would be recognized by Syl Co. in 1986 using this method [answer (a)]. Note that all costs incurred during the project would be recorded in an asset account "construction in progress" which is netted against the "billings on long-term contracts" account for balance sheet presentation purposes until the project's completion. Also note that neither customer billings nor payments on account are used to determine the revenue recognized under either the completed contract method or the percentage-of-completion method.

33. (587,Q1,2) (b) Construction companies that use the percentage of completion method in accounting for long-term construction contracts usually recognize gross profit on a periodic basis according to the cost-to-cost method:

$$\frac{\text{Costs to date}}{\text{Total estimated costs}} \times \text{Estimated profit} = \text{Gross profit to date}$$

Given the facts in this problem, Syl Co. would recognize $13,333 of gross profit in 1986:

$$\frac{\$20,000}{\$20,000 + \$40,000} \times [\$100,000 - (\$20,000 + \$40,000)] = \$13,333$$

Note that in future years, the gross profit to date (a cumulative amount) must be reduced by the amount of gross profit previously recognized to arrive at the gross profit earned in each year.

34. (589,T1,13) (a) Per ARB 45, para 9, the completed-contract method of accounting for long-term construction-type contracts recognizes income only when the contract has been completed. Accordingly, progress billings may be accumulated but there are no interim charges or credits to income in the income statement. Therefore, the effect of third year progress billings would <u>not</u> be reported in the company's income statement in the third year. However, per ARB 45, para 11, regardless of which method of accounting for long-term construction contracts is used, provisions for expected losses should be made during the year in which the expected losses become apparent. Therefore, the anticipated loss should be reported in the company's income statement in the third year, and accordingly, answer (a) is correct.

35. (1189,T1,25) (a) ARB 45, para 4 suggests the use of a cost-to-cost method to calculate the amount of income to be recognized under the percentage-of-completion method. This method is based upon the ratio of costs incurred to date versus the total expected cost of the contract. The formula used to calculate current income is:

$$\left(\frac{\text{Costs to date}}{\text{Total expected costs}} \times \begin{array}{c}\text{Expected}\\\text{profit}\end{array} \right) - \begin{array}{c}\text{Profit recognized}\\\text{in prior}\\\text{periods}\end{array}$$

In the final year of the contract (i.e., after completion), estimates no longer need to be used because total costs and actual profit are determinable. To calculate the income to be recognized in the final year, the following formulas are used: (Total revenue - Actual costs) = Actual profit; (Actual profit income previously recognized) = Income recognized in the final year. Thus, both actual total costs and income previously recognized are used in the calculation, and answer (a) is correct.

36. (1187,T1,16) (d) Per ARB 45, paras 6 and 11, an anticipated loss on a long-term contract should be recognized immediately under <u>both</u> the percentage-of-completion and the completed-contract methods. Therefore, answer (d) is correct.

37. (1185,T1,28) (a) The requirement is to determine the proper classification for the progress billings on contracts account under the percentage-of-completion method. In the construction industry, operating cycles for construction contracts generally exceed one year. Therefore, the predominant practice is to classify all contract-related assets and liabilities as current. On the balance sheet, the Construction in Progress (CIP) account is netted with the contra account, progress billings. If CIP exceeds billings, the excess is reported as a current asset [answer (a)]. If billings exceed CIP, the excess is reported as a current liability. Answers (b) and (c) are incorrect because the accounts related to construction contracts are classified as current. Answer (d) is incorrect because progress billings is not used as a basis for recognizing revenues.

D. & E. Items to Include in Inventory and Consignments

38. (1188,P1,13) (a) Before adjustment, the balance in the accounts payable account is $1,800,000. The goods in transit ($100,000) should be included in accounts payable because the terms were FOB <u>shipping point</u>. This means the buyer owns the goods while they are in transit and the $100,000 cost should be included in Dean's 12/31/87 inventory and accounts payable. The $50,000 of goods lost in transit from a vendor were also shipped FOB shipping point. Therefore, title passes to Dean when the goods are delivered to the carrier, and the purchase and payable should be recorded in 1987. Dean, not the vendor, is ultimately responsible for the lost goods; note that Dean is suing the common carrier, not the vendor. Thus, the corrected accounts payable balance is $1,950,000 ($1,800,000 + $100,000 + $50,000).

39. (1188,P1,17) (d) Before adjustment, the physical count of inventory resulted in a valuation of $1,200,000. No adjustment is necessary for the $25,000 of goods shipped on 1/7/88. When the sales terms are FOB shipping point, inventory is typically not considered sold until it is shipped (or received by the customer if the terms are FOB destination). Therefore, no sale should have been recorded until 1/7/88, and these goods were properly included in ending inventory. An adjustment is necessary for the $60,000 of goods in transit to Dell from a vendor on 12/31/87. These goods were shipped FOB <u>shipping point</u>, which means they are owned by the buyer while in transit. Because Dell did not have physical possession at 12/31/87, the $60,000 was not included in the physical count. There-

fore, the corrected inventory balance is
$1,260,000 ($1,200,000 + $60,000).

40. (1188,P2,34) (d) Net sales is
$2,300,000, subject to three possible adjust-
ments. The goods returned ($50,000) should be
recorded as a return in 1987, when Lewis
authorized the return. Since this return was
not recorded until 1988, 1987 sales must be
adjusted downward. The goods shipped on
12/30/87 ($80,000) were recorded as a sale in
1988. Since the terms were FOB shipping
point, the sale must be recorded in 1987 when
the goods were shipped; therefore 1987 sales
must be adjusted upwards. The goods shipped on
1/3/88 ($100,000) should not be recorded as a
sale until 1988. Since the sale was recorded
in 1987, 1987 sales must be adjusted downward.
Therefore, adjusted net sales for 1987 should
be $2,230,000 ($2,300,000 - $50,000 + $80,000
- $100,000).

41. (1187,P1,5) (a) Inventory out on consignment is owned by the consignor and is
included in the consignor's inventory. Therefore, the $9,000 of inventory is owned by
Kemp, while the $6,000 of inventory is owned
by Fenn. The consigned inventory owned by
Kemp is reported in its balance sheet at its
total cost: the purchase price ($9,000) plus
the cost of bringing the goods to the point of
sale ($450), for a total of $9,450. Note that
the point of sale is the consignee's place of
business.

42. (586,P2,32) (a) The requirement is to
determine how much consignment sales revenue
should be recognized by the consignor, and in
what month it should be recognized. In a
consignment, the consignor recognizes sales
revenue from consignments when the consignee
sells the consigned goods to the ultimate
customer. No revenue is recognized at the
time the consignor ships the goods to the
consignee. Therefore, in December the consignor would recognize sales revenue of $8,000
(10 x $800). The transportation costs ($600)
would not affect sales; one third would be
reflected in cost of sales and two thirds in
ending inventory. The sales commission (15% x
$8,000 = $1,200) also would not affect sales;
it would be reported as a selling expense.

43. (1189,T1,8) (d) Goods held by a consignee for a consignor are included in the
consignor's inventory until the goods are
ultimately sold to the customer. Shipping
costs incurred by the consignor are a cost of
getting the goods to their point of resale
and, thus, are considered an element of inventory cost to the consignor. Therefore, an-

swer (d) is correct. Please note that these
shipping costs will be expensed through the
consignor's cost of goods sold when the goods
are sold to the ultimate customer by the consignee.

May 1990 Answers

44. (590,P1,10) (c) Purchases are always
recorded net of trade discounts. When more
than one trade discount is applied to a list
price, it is called a chain discount. Chain
discounts are applied in steps; each discount
applies to the previously discounted price.
The cost, net of trade discounts, is $2,800
[$5,000 - (30% x $5,000) = $3,500; and $3,500
- (20% x $3,500) = $2,800]. Payment was made
within the discount period, so the net
purchase price is $2,744 [$2,800 - (2% x
$2,800)]. The remittance from Burr would also
include reimbursement of the $200 of delivery
costs. Since the terms were FOB shipping
point, Burr is responsible for paying this
amount, and must reimburse Pitt who prepaid
the freight. Thus, the total remittance is
$2,944 ($2,744 + $200).

45. (590,P1,13) (a) Under the retail
method, ending inventory is determined at
retail and then reduced to cost, or lower of
cost or market, using a cost-to-retail
ratio. To apply FIFO, beginning inventory is
excluded from the ratio. To use cost, rather
than lower of cost or market, both markups and
markdowns are included in the ratio. The
retail method schedule is as follows:

	Cost	Retail
Beg. inventory (BI)	$12,000	$30,000
Purchases	$60,000	$110,000
Markups		10,000
Markdowns		(20,000)
Cost-retail totals	$60,000	$100,000
Total including BI		$130,000
Sales		(90,000)
End. inventory at retail		$40,000

The cost-to-retail ratio is 60% ($60,000 ÷
$100,000), so ending inventory at FIFO cost is
$24,000 (60% x $40,000).

46. (590,P2,27) (d) Before adjustment,
12/31/89 accounts payable is $900,000. The
goods in transit of $50,000 should be recorded
as a purchase and as an increase in 12/31/89
accounts payable because the goods were shipped to Kemp FOB shipping point on 12/29/89.
This means the goods are owned by the buyer
(Kemp) while in transit. No adjustment is
necessary for the $25,000 of goods in transit;
they were shipped FOB destination, which means

they were owned by the seller, not Kemp, while in transit. A correcting entry must be prepared for the 12/27/89 transaction. Kemp Corp. recorded a payment of $40,000 to its creditors on that date. However, they did not give up control of the cash until 1/10/90. Therefore, the 12/27/89 payment entry must be reversed (increasing accounts payable) and rerecorded on 1/10/90. Thus, 12/31/89 accounts payable balance is $990,000 ($900,000 + $50,000 + $40,000).

47. (590,P3,49) (b) Three computations must be performed: raw materials used, cost of goods manufactured, and cost of goods sold.

(1) Raw materials purchased $430,000
    Decrease in RM inventory   15,000
      Raw materials used $445,000

(2) Beginning WIP $ -0-
    RM used (from above)   445,000
    Direct labor   200,000
    Factory overhead   300,000
      Cost to account for   945,000
    Ending WIP   -0-
      Cost of goods manuf. $945,000

(3) Cost of goods manuf. $945,000
    Increase in FG inventory   35,000
      Cost of goods sold $910,000

The decrease in RM inventory is added when computing RM used because RM were used in excess of those purchased. The increase in FG inventory is deducted when computing cost of goods sold because it represents the portion of goods manufactured which were not sold. The freight out is irrelevant for this question because freight out is a selling expense and therefore does not affect cost of goods sold.

48. (590,Q3,41) (d) When a company uses the completed-contract method of accounting for construction projects, all revenue and expense recognition is deferred until the project is complete or substantially complete (ARB 45, para 9). Also, note that neither customer billings nor payments on account are used to determine the revenue recognized under the completed-contract method (or under the percentage-of-completion method). Since the project was complete in 1989, Mitchell should recognize 120,000 ($600,000 - $480,000) in gross profit for 1989.

49. (590,Q3,57) (c) ARB 45, para 4 suggests the use of a cost-to-cost method to calculate the amount of income to be recognized under the percentage-of-completion method. This method is based upon the ratio of costs incurred to date versus the total expected

cost of the contract. The formula used to calculate current income is:

$$\left(\frac{\text{Costs to date}}{\text{Total expected costs}} \times \text{Expected profit} \right) - \text{Profit recognized in prior periods}$$

Thus, Mill should recognize $500,000 [($2,000,000/$16,000,000 x $4,000,000) - 0] as gross profit for 1989. Note that neither customer billings nor payments on account are used to determine the revenue recognized under the percentage-of-completion method (or the completed-contract method).

50. (590,T1,19) (c) Under the percentage-of-completion method of accounting for long-term contracts, the cost-to-cost formula is used to compute the amount of income to be recognized in a particular year. The formula to calculate current income is as follows:

$$\left(\frac{\text{Costs to date}}{\text{Total expected costs}} \times \text{Expected profit} \right) - \text{Profit recognized in prior periods}$$

Therefore, answer (c) is correct.

Answer Outline

Problem 1   Inventory Cost and LCM (589,T3)

a. Costs inventoried if reasonable and
     necessary costs of preparing inventory
     for sale
b. LCM rule produces realistic estimate of
     future cash flows to be realized from
     sale of inventories
       Conservatism principle
       Matching principle
         Price decline reported in period it
         occurs
c. Steels' inventories should be reported at
     market value
       Market value for Steel is replacement
       cost
       Market value cannot exceed NRV (ceiling)
       Market value cannot be less than NRV
       less normal profit margin (floor)
       Replacement cost is between ceiling and
       floor so it is designated market value
       Market < than original cost and is,
       thus, the figure reported
d. Effects would have been same
     When prices are declining, results in
       write-down to market under both methods
     Net income is same under either method

Unofficial Answer

Problem 1   Inventory Cost and LCM (589,T3)

a. Inventory cost should include all
reasonable and necessary costs of preparing
inventory for sale. These costs include not
only the purchase price of the inventories,
but also other costs associated with readying
inventories for sale.

b. The lower of cost or market rule produces
a realistic estimate of future cash flows to
be realized from the sale of inventories.
This is consistent with the principle of conservatism, and recognizes (matches) the anticipated loss in the income statement in the
period in which the price decline occurs.

c. Steel's inventories should be reported on
the balance sheet at market. According to the
lower of cost or market rule, market is defined as replacement cost. Market cannot
exceed net realizable value and cannot be less
than net realizable value less the normal
profit margin. In this instance, replacement
cost is between net realizable value and net
realizable value less the normal profit
margin. Therefore, market is established as

replacement cost. Since market is less than
original cost, inventory should be reported at
market.

d. Ending inventories and net income would
have been the same under either lower of
average cost or market or lower of FIFO cost
or market. In periods of declining prices,
the lower of cost or market rule results in a
write-down of inventory cost to market under
both methods, resulting in the same inventory
cost. Therefore, net income using either
inventory method is the same.

Answer Outline

Problem 2   Acquisition Cost, LCM, Retail
            Method (588,T2)

a. Include warehousing costs of wholesale
     inventories in inventory
     Matches warehousing costs with revenue
     when inventory sold
b1. LCM rule
     Conservative
       More realistic estimate of future cash
       flows
       Recognizes (matches) loss in period
       decline occurs
b2. Report wholesale inventory at replacement
     cost under lower of cost or market
     Market defined as replacement cost
     Market cannot exceed NRV
     Market cannot be less than NRV less
     normal profit margin
     In this case NRV > RC < (NRV – NP)
     RC < OC
       ∴ Report at RC
c. Calculation of cost to retail precentage

		Cost	Retail
1.	Freight-in	$xxx	
2.	Net markups	—	$xxx
	Cost to retail		
	amounts*	$xxx	$xxx
3.	Net markdowns		($xxx)

     *Used to compute cost to retail %
d. Conventional retail inventory method does
     not deduct net markdowns
       Results in a lower cost to retail %
       applied to ending inventory
       Inventory is reported below cost approx-
       imating LCM

Unofficial Answer

Problem 2   Acquisition Cost, LCM, Retail
             Method (588,T2)

a. Hudson should account for the warehousing
costs related to its wholesale inventories as
part of inventory. All reasonable and
necessary costs of preparing inventory for
sale should be recorded as inventory cost.
This approach results in proper matching of
the warehousing costs with revenue when the
wholesale inventories are sold.

b. 1. The lower of cost or market method
produces a more realistic estimate of future
cash flows to be realized from assets, which
is consistent with the principle of conservatism, and recognizes (matches) the anticipated
loss in the income statement in the period in
which the price decline occurs.

   2. Hudson's wholesale inventories should
be reported on the balance sheet at replacement cost. According to the lower of cost or
market method, replacement cost is defined as
market. However, market cannot exceed net
realizable value and cannot be less than net
realizable value less the normal profit margin. In this instance, replacement cost is
below original cost, below net realizable
value, and above net realizable value less the
normal profit margin. Therefore, Hudson's
wholesale inventories should be reported at
replacement cost.

c. 1. Hudson's freight-in costs should be
included only in the cost amounts to determine
the cost of retail percentage.

   2. Hudson's net markups should be
included only in the retail amounts to determine the cost to retail percentage.

   3. Hudson's net markdowns should not be
deducted from the retail amounts to determine
the cost to retail percentage.

d. By not deducting net markdowns from the
retail amounts to determine the cost to retail
percentage, Hudson produces a lower cost to
retail percentage than would result if net
markdowns were deducted. By applying this
lower percentage to ending inventory at
retail, the inventory is reported at an amount
below cost, which approximates lower of
average cost or market.

Answer Outline

Problem 3   Inventory Cost and LCM
             (587,T3)

a. Insurance costs on raw materials while in
    transit
       Accounted for as part of inventory
       Theoretically, cost associated with
       readying the goods for sale

b.1. Raw materials inventory
       Reported at net realizable value (NRV)
      Lower of cost or market value
       Market defined as replacement cost
       Market cannot exceed net realizable
       value
      In this instance, NRV below original cost

   2. Lower of cost or market rule
       Report at its future utility value
       Recognizes a decline in utility in
         period decline occurs

c. Effect of LIFO inventory method when
       prices decreasing
       EI generally higher
       CGS generally lower
       Associates oldest purchase prices with
         inventory
      LIFO in this instance
       Inventory quantities increased
       No effect on EI or CGS because EI
       reported at NRV
      NRV is less than either average cost or
      LIFO cost

Unofficial Answer

Problem 3   Inventory Cost and LCM
             (587,T3)

a. The insurance costs on the raw materials
while they were in transit from the supplier
should be accounted for as part of
inventory. Theoretically, insurance cost on
raw materials in transit is a cost associated
with readying the goods for sale.

b. 1. Hanlon's inventory should be reported
at net realizable value. According to the
lower of cost or market rule, market is
defined as replacement cost. However, market
cannot exceed net realizable value. In this
instance, net realizable value is below
original cost.

   2. The lower of cost or market rule is
used to report the inventory in the balance
sheet at its future utility value. It also
recognizes a decline in the utility of inven-

tory in the income statement in the period in
which the decline occurs.
c. Generally, ending inventory would have
been higher and cost of goods sold would have
been lower had Hanlon used the LIFO inventory
method. Inventory quantities increased and
LIFO associates the oldest purchase prices
with inventory. However, in this instance,
there would have been no effect on ending
inventory or cost of goods sold had Hanlon
used the LIFO inventory method, because
Hanlon's ending inventory would have been
reported at net realizable value according to
the lower of cost or market rule. Net realizable value of the inventory is less than
either its average cost or LIFO cost.

Answer Outline

Problem 4   Various Aspects of Inventory
            Accounting (1185,T3)

a. Purchases included in inventory when goods
    received
    Because title assumed to pass when goods
    received (FOB destination)
b. Warehousing costs are an inventory cost
    Because warehousing is cost of preparing
    goods for sale
c1. Advantages of dollar value vs. conven-
    tional LIFO
      Less clerical cost than conventional
      LIFO
      Minimize probability of unintentional
      liquidation
2. Calculation of dollar value vs. conven-
    tional LIFO
      Dollar value LIFO based on
        Dollars of inventory
        Specific price index by year for add-
        ing layers
        Broad inventory pools
      Conventional LIFO based on
        Individual units of each separate
        product
        Unit costs applicable to specific
        items in each layer
d. Consigned inventories are Caddell's inven-
    tory
    Because Caddell retains title
    ∴Earnings process not complete
e. LCM limits
      Ceiling (NRV) = SP - Disposal costs
      Floor = NRV - Normal profit margin

Unofficial Answer

Problem 4   Various Aspects of Inventory
            Accounting (1185,T3)

a. Purchases from various suppliers should
generally be included in Caddell's inventory
when Caddell receives the goods. For accounting purposes, in the absence of other
information, title to goods purchased FOB
destination is assumed to pass when the goods
are received.

b. Caddell should account for the warehousing
costs as additional cost of inventory. Theoretically, warehousing is a cost of readying
the goods for sale and should be included in
inventory cost.

c. 1. The advantages of using the dollar
value LIFO inventory cost flow method are to
reduce the cost of accounting for inventory
according to the LIFO method and to minimize
the probability of unintentional liquidation
of LIFO inventory.

    2. The calculation of dollar value LIFO
is based on dollars of inventory, a specific
price index for each year, and broad inventory
pools, whereas the conventional quantity of
goods method is applied to individual units of
each separate product. The inventory layers
are identified with the price index for the
year in which the layer was added.

d. Caddell should account for the inventories
consigned to Reed Company as part of inventory. Caddell retains title to the goods
until their sale by Reed; therefore, the
earnings process has not been completed.

e. In applying the lower of cost or market
method, market should not exceed the ceiling
or fall below the floor. The ceiling is equal
to the net realizable value, i.e., estimated
selling price in the ordinary course of
business less reasonably predictable costs of
completion and disposal. The floor is equal
to the net realizable value reduced by an
allowance for an approximately normal profit
margin.

Answer Outline

Problem 5   LT Contracts (586,T2)

a1. Justification for percentage-of-completion
    Revenue earned as worked performed
        provides more relevant information
    Revenues represent actual/expected cash
        inflows from ongoing operations
  2. Facts given that support percentage-of-
     completion
    Ability to estimate
        Costs to complete
        Extent of progress toward completion
    Billings are collectible
    Right to revenue established
b. Cost-to-cost method of determining income
    Contract price - (Estimated costs* to
    complete + Actual costs to date*) =
    Estimated total income*
        Year 1
    Estimated total income x (Actual
    costs to date ÷ Estimated total
    costs) = Year 1 income
        Year 2 (3)
    Estimated total income x (Actual
    costs to date ÷ Estimated total
    costs) - Year 1 (1 and 2) income =
    Year 2 (3) income
    *would typically change each year
c. Income effects
    Billings - no effect
    Collection of billings - no effect

Unofficial Answer

Problem 5   LT Contracts (586,T2)

a. 1. The percentage-of-completion method is
justified because revenue is earned as work is
performed under the long-term construction
contract. As a result, it provides more relevant information. Revenues represent actual
or expected cash inflows (or the equivalent)
that have occurred or will eventuate as a
result of the enterprise's ongoing major or
central operations during the period.

    2. Village Company should account for
this long-term construction contract using the
percentage-of-completion method because this
method is preferable when estimates of costs
to complete and extent of progress toward completion are reasonably dependable. The facts
in the situation also indicate that the right
to revenue is established and collectibility
is reasonably assured.

b. The income recognized in each year of this
long-term construction contract would be
determined using the cost-to-cost method of
determining percentage of completion as
follows:

• The contract price is the first part of
the determination of the total estimated income for each year. The total actual costs
(the second part of the determination of the
total estimated income for each year) represent all costs incurred from the inception of
the project to the end of the current year.
• The estimated total costs (the third part
of the determination of the total estimated
income for each year) are subtracted from the
contract price to arrive at the estimated
total income. The estimated total costs
consist of the actual costs to date and the
estimated costs to complete the contract and
would generally change each year.
• The income recognized in the first year
would be the percentage of the actual costs to
date to the estimated total costs multiplied
by the estimated total income. The income
recognized in the second (third) year would be
the percentage of the actual costs to date to
the estimated total costs multiplied by the
estimated total income less the income already
recognized in the first (first and second)
year.

c. Progress billings sent and collections on
these billings would not affect the income
recognized in each year of this long-term
contract.

Multiple Choice Questions (1-64)

1. On March 1, 1987, Kay Company purchased for $450,000 a tract of land as a factory site. An existing building on the property was razed and construction was begun on a new factory building in April 1987. Additional data are available as follows:

Cost of razing old building	$ 60,000
Title insurance and legal fees to purchase land	30,000
Architect's fees	95,000
New building construction cost	1,850,000

The capitalized cost of the completed factory building should be
   a. $2,005,000
   b. $1,975,000
   c. $1,945,000
   d. $1,910,000

2. On July 1, 1985, Town Company purchased for $540,000 a warehouse building and the land on which it is located. The following data were available concerning the property:

	Current appraised value	Seller's original cost
Land	$200,000	$140,000
Warehouse building	300,000	280,000
	$500,000	$420,000

Town should record the land at
   a. $140,000
   b. $180,000
   c. $200,000
   d. $216,000

3. On May 5, 1989, Feda Corp. exchanged 2,000 shares of its $25 par value treasury common stock for a patent owned by Crue Co. The treasury shares were acquired in 1988 for $40,000. At May 5, 1989, Feda's common stock was quoted at $27 per share, and the patent had a carrying value of $45,000 on Crue's books. Feda should record the patent at
   a. $40,000
   b. $45,000
   c. $50,000
   d. $54,000

4. Saba Co. bought a tract of land, paying $800,000 in cash and assuming an existing mortgage of $200,000. The municipal tax bill disclosed an assessed valuation of $700,000. How much should Saba record as an asset for this land acquisition?
   a. $ 600,000
   b. $ 700,000
   c. $ 800,000
   d. $1,000,000

5. A company purchased land to be used as the site for the construction of a plant. Timber was cut from the building site so that construction of the plant could begin. The proceeds from the sale of the timber should be
   a. Classified as other income.
   b. Netted against the costs to clear the land and expensed as incurred.
   c. Deducted from the cost of the plant.
   d. Deducted from the cost of the land.

6. On January 2, 1989, Parke Corp. replaced its boiler with a more efficient one. The following information was available on that date:

Purchase price of new boiler	$60,000
Carrying amount of old boiler	5,000
Fair value of old boiler	2,000
Installation cost of new boiler	8,000

The old boiler was sold for $2,000. What amount should Parke capitalize as the cost of the new boiler?
   a. $68,000
   b. $66,000
   c. $63,000
   d. $60,000

7. Clay Company started construction of a new office building on January 1, 1984, and moved into the finished building on July 1, 1985. Of the building's $2,500,000 total cost, $2,000,000 was incurred in 1984 evenly throughout the year. Clay's incremental borrowing rate was 12% throughout 1984, and the total amount of interest incurred by Clay during 1984 was $102,000. What amount should Clay report as capitalized interest at December 31, 1984?
   a. $102,000
   b. $120,000
   c. $150,000
   d. $240,000

8. A company is constructing an asset for its own use. Construction began in 1985. The asset is being financed entirely with a specific new borrowing. Construction expenditures were made in 1985 and 1986 at the end of each quarter. The total amount of interest cost capitalized in 1986 should be determined by applying the interest rate on the specific new borrowing to the
   a. Total accumulated expenditures for the asset in 1985 and 1986.
   b. Average accumulated expenditures for the asset in 1985 and 1986.
   c. Average expenditures for the asset in 1986.
   d. Total expenditures for the asset in 1986.

9. On March 31, 1988, Winn Company traded in an old machine having a carrying amount of $16,800, and paid a cash difference of $6,000 for a new machine having a total cash price of $20,500. On March 31, 1988, what amount of loss should Winn recognize on this exchange?

    a. $0
    b. $2,300
    c. $3,700
    d. $6,000

10. Pine Football Company had a player contract with Duff that is recorded in its books at $500,000 on July 1, 1988. Ace Football Company had a player contract with Terry that is recorded in its books at $600,000 on July 1, 1988. On this date, Pine traded Duff to Ace for Terry and paid a cash difference of $50,000. The fair value of the Terry contract was $700,000 on the exchange date. After the exchange, the Terry contract should be recorded in Pine's books at

    a. $550,000
    b. $600,000
    c. $650,000
    d. $700,000

11. Caine Motor Sales exchanged a car from its inventory for a computer to be used as a long-term asset. The following information relates to this exchange that took place on July 31, 1986:

Carrying amount of the car	$30,000
Listed selling price of the car	45,000
Fair value of the computer	43,000
Cash difference paid by Caine	5,000

On July 31, 1986, what amount of profit should Caine recognize on this exchange?

    a. $0
    b. $ 8,000
    c. $10,000
    d. $13,000

12. On September 1, 1982, Bertz, Inc. exchanged a delivery truck for a parcel of land. Bertz bought this truck in 1980 for $10,000. At September 1, 1982, the truck had a book value of $6,500 and a fair market value of $5,000. Bertz gave $6,000 in cash in addition to the truck as part of this transaction. The previous owner of the land had listed the land for sale at $12,000. At what amount should Bertz record the land?

    a. $11,000
    b. $11,500
    c. $12,000
    d. $12,500

13. An entity disposes of a nonmonetary asset in a nonreciprocal transfer. A gain or loss should be recognized on the disposition of the asset when the fair value of the asset transferred is determinable and the nonreciprocal transfer is to

	Another entity	A stockholder of the entity
a.	No	Yes
b.	No	No
c.	Yes	No
d.	Yes	Yes

14. Company S and Company T exchanged nonmonetary assets. The exchange did not culminate in an earnings process for either Company S or Company T. Company S paid cash to Company T in connection with the exchange. Realized gain on the exchange, to the extent that the amount of cash exceeds a proportionate share of the carrying amount of the asset surrendered, should be recognized by

	Company S	Company T
a.	No	No
b.	No	Yes
c.	Yes	Yes
d.	Yes	No

15. Clay Township owned an idle parcel of real estate consisting of land and a factory building. Clay gave title to this realty to Wolf Co. as an incentive for Wolf to establish manufacturing operations in the Township. Wolf paid nothing for this realty, which had a fair market value of $200,000 at the date of the grant. Wolf should record this nonmonetary transaction as a

    a. Memo entry only.
    b. Credit to retained earnings for $200,000.
    c. Credit to extraordinary income for $200,000.
    d. Credit to additional paid-in capital for $200,000.

16. Company N donated computer equipment to a university (a nonreciprocal transfer). The fair value of the computer equipment was determinable. The difference between the fair value of the nonmonetary asset transferred and its recorded amount at the date of donation should be recognized in Company N's income statement when the difference results in a

	Gain	Loss
a.	Yes	No
b.	Yes	Yes
c.	No	Yes
d.	No	No

17. During 1987, Fox Company made the following expenditures relating to plant machinery and equipment:

• Renovation of a group of machines at a cost of $50,000 to secure greater efficiency in production over their remaining five-year useful lives. The project was completed on December 31, 1987.
• Continuing, frequent, and low cost repairs at a cost of $35,000.
• A broken gear on a machine was replaced at a cost of $5,000.

What total amount should be charged to repairs and maintenance in 1987?
  a. $35,000
  b. $40,000
  c. $85,000
  d. $90,000

18. On June 30, 1986, Kent Company completed the rearrangement of a group of factory machines to secure greater efficiency in production. Kent estimated that benefits from the rearrangement would extend over the remaining five-year useful lives of the machines. The following costs were incurred:

Moving	$35,000
Reinstallation	75,000
Annual maintenance (performed at this time for convenience)	10,000

How much of the costs incurred should be capitalized on June 30, 1986?
  a. $0
  b. $ 75,000
  c. $110,000
  d. $120,000

19. During 1985 King Company made the following expenditures relating to its plant building:

Continuing and frequent repairs	$40,000
Repainted the plant building	10,000
Major improvements to the electrical wiring system	32,000
Partial replacement of roof tiles	14,000

How much should be charged to repair and maintenance expense in 1985?
  a. $96,000
  b. $82,000
  c. $64,000
  d. $54,000

20. On September 10, 1985, Landy Company incurred the following costs for one of its printing presses:

Purchase of stapling attachment	$45,000
Installation of attachment	10,000
Replacement parts for renovation of press	30,000
Labor and overhead in connection with renovation of press	14,000

Neither the attachment nor the renovation increased the estimated useful life of the press. However, the renovation resulted in significantly increased productivity. What amount of the costs should be capitalized?
  a. $0
  b. $44,000
  c. $55,000
  d. $99,000

21. An expenditure to install an improved electrical system is a

	Capital expenditure	Revenue expenditure
a.	No	Yes
b.	No	No
c.	Yes	No
d.	Yes	Yes

22. Which type of expenditure occurs when a company installs a higher capacity boiler to heat its plant?
  a. Rearrangement.
  b. Ordinary repair and maintenance.
  c. Addition.
  d. Betterment.

23. Rapp Company purchased a machine on July 1, 1985, for $600,000. The machine has an estimated useful life of five years and a salvage value of $80,000. The machine is being depreciated from the date of acquisition by the 150% declining balance method. For the year ended December 31, 1985, Rapp should record depreciation expense on this machine of
  a. $180,000
  b. $120,000
  c. $ 90,000
  d. $ 78,000

24. Rago Company takes a full year's depreciation expense in the year of an asset's acquisition, and no depreciation expense in the year of disposition. Data relating to one of Rago's depreciable assets at December 31, 1984 are as follows:

Acquisition year	1982
Cost	$110,000
Residual value	20,000
Accumulated depreciation	72,000
Estimated useful life	5 years

Using the same depreciation method as used in 1982, 1983, and 1984, how much depreciation expense should Rago record in 1985 for this asset?

- a. $12,000
- b. $18,000
- c. $22,000
- d. $24,000

25. A machine with a four-year estimated useful life and an estimated 15% salvage value was acquired on January 1. Would depreciation expense using the sum-of-the-years'-digits method of depreciation be higher or lower than depreciation expense using the double-declining-balance method of depreciation in the first and second years?

	First year	Second year
a.	Higher	Higher
b.	Higher	Lower
c.	Lower	Higher
d.	Lower	Lower

26. Depreciation is computed on the original cost less estimated salvage value under which of the following depreciation methods?

	Double-declining balance	Productive output
a.	No	No
b.	No	Yes
c.	Yes	Yes
d.	Yes	No

27. A depreciable asset has an estimated 15% salvage value. At the end of its estimated useful life, the accumulated depreciation would equal the original cost of the asset under which of the following depreciation methods?

	Straight-line	Productive output
a.	Yes	No
b.	Yes	Yes
c.	No	Yes
d.	No	No

28. A machine with a four-year estimated useful life and an estimated 10% salvage value was acquired on January 1, 1986. The depreciation expense for 1988 using the double-declining-balance method would be original cost multiplied by

- a. 90% x 50% x 50% x 50%.
- b. 50% x 50% x 50%.
- c. 90% x 50% x 50%.
- d. 50% x 50%.

29. Which of the following utilizes the straight-line depreciation method?

	Composite depreciation	Group depreciation
a.	Yes	Yes
b.	Yes	No
c.	No	Yes
d.	No	No

30. When equipment is retired, accumulated depreciation is debited for the original cost less any residual recovery under which of the following depreciation methods?

	Composite depreciation	Group depreciation
a.	No	No
b.	No	Yes
c.	Yes	No
d.	Yes	Yes

31. A company using the composite depreciation method for its fleet of trucks, cars, and campers retired one of its trucks and received cash from a salvage company. The net carrying amount of these composite asset accounts would be decreased by the

- a. Cash proceeds received and original cost of the truck.
- b. Cash proceeds received.
- c. Original cost of the truck less the cash proceeds.
- d. Original cost of the truck.

32. On January 1, 1985, Evan Company purchased a machine for $400,000 and established an annual depreciation charge of $50,000 over an eight-year life. During 1988, after issuing its 1987 financial statements, Evan concluded that: (1) the machine suffered permanent impairment of its operational value, and (2) $100,000 is a reasonable estimate of the amount expected to be recovered through use of the machine for the period January 1, 1988 to December 31, 1992. In Evan's December 31, 1988 balance sheet, the machine should be reported at a carrying amount of

- a. $200,000
- b. $ 80,000
- c. $ 50,000
- d. $0

33. On January 1, 1986, Huff Company owned a machine having a carrying amount of $240,000. The machine was purchased four years earlier for $400,000. Huff uses straight-line depreciation. During December 1986 Huff determined that the machine suffered permanent impairment of its operational value and will not be economically useful in its production process after December 31, 1986. Huff sold the machine for $65,000 on January 5, 1987. In its income statement for the year ended December 31, 1986, Huff should recognize a loss of

a. $200,000
b. $175,000
c. $135,000
d. $0

34. On June 30, 1986, a fire in Pine
Company's plant caused a total loss to a
production machine. The machine was being
depreciated at $20,000 annually and had a
carrying amount of $160,000 at December 31,
1985. On the date of the fire the fair value
of the machine was $220,000, and Pine received
insurance proceeds of $200,000 in Octo-
ber 1986. In its income statement for the
year ended December 31, 1986, what amount
should Pine recognize as a gain or loss on
disposition?
a. $0.
b. $20,000 loss.
c. $40,000 gain.
d. $50,000 gain.

35. On October 31, 1983, West Company
received a condemnation award of $450,000 as
compensation for the forced sale of a warehouse. On this date the warehouse, including
the land on which it was situated, had a book
value of $275,000. During December 1983, West
purchased a parcel of land for a new warehouse
site at a cost of $125,000. West should
report on its income statement for the year
ended December 31, 1983, a gain on condemnation of property at
a. $0
b. $ 50,000
c. $175,000
d. $325,000

36. In January 1984, Huff Mining Corporation
purchased a mineral mine for $3,600,000 with
removable ore estimated by geological surveys
at 2,160,000 tons. The property has an estimated value of $360,000 after the ore has been
extracted. Huff incurred $1,080,000 of devel-
opment costs preparing the property for the
extraction of ore. During 1984, 270,000 tons
were removed and 240,000 tons were sold. For
the year ended December 31, 1984, Huff should
include what amount of depletion in its cost
of goods sold?
a. $360,000
b. $405,000
c. $480,000
d. $540,000

37. Wall Company bought a trademark from
Black Corporation on January 1, 1986 for
$112,000. An independent consultant retained
by Wall estimated that the remaining useful
life is 50 years. Its unamortized cost on
Black's accounting records was $56,000. Wall

decided to write off the trademark over the
maximum period allowed. How much should be
amortized for the year ended December 31,
1986?
a. $1,120
b. $1,400
c. $2,240
d. $2,800

38. On January 1, 1981, Vick Company purchased a trademark for $400,000, having an
estimated useful life of 16 years. In January
1985, Vick paid $60,000 for legal fees in a
successful defense of the trademark. Trademark amortization expense for the year ended
December 31, 1985, should be
a. $0
b. $25,000
c. $20,750
d. $30,000

39. Which of the following legal fees should
be capitalized?

	Legal fees to obtain a franchise	Legal fees to successfully defend a trademark
a.	No	No
b.	No	Yes
c.	Yes	Yes
d.	Yes	No

40. Which of the following costs of goodwill
should be capitalized and amortized over their
estimated useful lives?

	Costs of goodwill from a business combination accounted for as a purchase	Costs of developing goodwill internally
a.	No	No
b.	No	Yes
c.	Yes	Yes
d.	Yes	No

41. Which of the following costs of goodwill
should be capitalized and amortized?

	Developing goodwill	Restoring goodwill
a.	Yes	Yes
b.	Yes	No
c.	No	No
d.	No	Yes

42. Legal fees incurred by a company in defending its patent rights should be capitalized when the outcome of the litigation is

	Successful	Unsuccessful
a.	Yes	Yes
b.	Yes	No
c.	No	No
d.	No	Yes

43. On January 1, 1980, an intangible asset with a fifty-year estimated useful life was acquired. On January 1, 1985, a review was made of the estimated useful life, and it was determined that the intangible asset had an estimated useful life of thirty more years. As a result of the review, the amount to be amortized should be
- a. The original cost at January 1, 1980, allocated equally over a thirty-five-year life.
- b. The original cost at January 1, 1980, allocated equally over a fifty-year life.
- c. The unamortized cost on January 1, 1985, allocated equally over a forty-year life.
- d. The unamortized cost on January 1, 1985, allocated equally over a thirty-year life.

44. Mark Co. bought a franchise from Fred Co. on January 1, 1988 for $204,000. An independent consultant retained by Mark estimated that the remaining useful life of the franchise was 50 years. Its unamortized cost on Fred's books at January 1, 1988 was $68,000. Mark has decided to amortize the franchise over the maximum period allowed. What amount should be amortized for the year ended December 31, 1988?
- a. $5,100
- b. $4,080
- c. $4,000
- d. $1,700

45. On January 1, 1987, Kew Corp. incurred organization costs of $24,000. For financial accounting purposes, Kew is amortizing these costs on the same basis as the maximum allowable for Federal income tax purposes. What portion of the organization costs will Kew defer to years subsequent to 1987?
- a. $23,400
- b. $19,200
- c. $ 4,800
- d. $0

46. Tobin Corp. incurred $160,000 of research and development costs to develop a product for which a patent was granted on January 2, 1983. Legal fees and other costs associated with registration of the patent totaled $30,000. On March 31, 1988, Tobin paid $45,000 for legal fees in a successful defense of the patent. The total amount capitalized for this patent through March 31, 1988 should be
- a. $ 75,000
- b. $190,000
- c. $205,000
- d. $235,000

47. Korn Company incurred the following costs during 1986:

Modification to the formulation of a chemical product	$135,000
Trouble-shooting in connection with breakdowns during commercial production	150,000
Design of tools, jigs, molds and dies involving new technology	170,000
Seasonal or other periodic design changes to existing products	185,000
Laboratory research aimed at discovery of new technology	215,000

In its income statement for the year ended December 31, 1986, Korn should report research and development expense of
- a. $520,000
- b. $470,000
- c. $385,000
- d. $335,000

48. During 1988, Rine Company incurred the following costs:

Research and development services performed by Lee Corp. for Rine	$300,000
Testing for evaluation of new products	250,000
Laboratory research aimed at discovery of new knowledge	370,000
Routine design of tools, jigs, molds, and dies	100,000

In its income statement for the year ended December 31, 1988, Rine should report research and development expense of
- a. $1,020,000
- b. $ 920,000
- c. $ 720,000
- d. $ 670,000

49. Ward Company incurred research and development costs in 1985 as follows:

Equipment acquired for use in various research and development projects	$975,000
Depreciation on the above equipment	135,000
Materials used	200,000
Compensation costs of personnel	500,000
Outside consulting fees	150,000
Indirect costs appropriately allocated	250,000

The total research and development costs charged in Ward's 1985 income statement should be
- a. $ 850,000
- b. $1,085,000

c. $1,235,000
d. $1,825,000

50.   A research and development activity for which the cost would be expensed as incurred is

a.   Engineering follow-through in an early phase of commercial production.

b.   Design, construction, and testing of preproduction prototypes and models.

c.   Troubleshooting in connection with breakdowns during commercial production.

d.   Periodic design changes to existing products.

Items 51 and 52 are based on the following information:

Towne Systems Corp. was a development stage enterprise from October 10, 1985 (inception) to December 31, 1986. The year ended December 31, 1987 is the first year in which Towne is an established operating enterprise. The following are among the costs incurred by Towne:

	For the period 10/10/85 to 12/31/86	For the year ended 12/31/87
Leasehold improvements, equipment, and furniture	$1,000,000	$150,000
Security deposits	60,000	15,000
Research and development	750,000	450,000
Laboratory operations	175,000	275,000
General and administrative	250,000	400,000

51.   For the period ended December 31, 1986, what total amount of the costs incurred should Towne have capitalized?
a. $1,060,000
b. $1,810,000
c. $1,985,000
d. $2,235,000

52.   For the year ended December 31, 1987, what total amount of the costs incurred should Towne have capitalized?
a. $875,000
b. $615,000
c. $165,000
d. $150,000

53.   A development stage enterprise should use the same generally accepted accounting principles that apply to established operating enterprises for

	Capitalization of costs	Recognition of revenue
a.	No	No
b.	No	Yes
c.	Yes	Yes
d.	Yes	No

54.   A development stage enterprise
a.   Issues an income statement that shows only cumulative amounts from the enterprise's inception.
b.   Issues an income statement that is the same as an established operating enterprise, but does **not** show cumulative amounts from the enterprise's inception as additional information.
c.   Issues an income statement that is the same as an established operating enterprise, and shows cumulative amounts from the enterprise's inception as additional information.
d.   Does **not** issue an income statement.

May 1990 Questions

55.   On December 1, 1989, East Co. purchased a tract of land as a factory site for $300,000. The old building on the property was razed, and salvaged materials resulting from demolition were sold. Additional costs incurred and salvage proceeds realized during December 1989 were as follows:

Cost to raze old building	$25,000
Legal fees for purchase contract and to record ownership	5,000
Title guarantee insurance	6,000
Proceeds from sale of salvaged materials	4,000

In East's December 31, 1989 balance sheet, what amount should be reported as land?
a. $311,000
b. $321,000
c. $332,000
d. $336,000

56.   On April 1, 1988, Kew Co. purchased new machinery for $300,000. The machinery has an estimated useful life of five years, and depreciation is computed by the sum-of-the-years'-digits method. The accumulated depreciation on this machinery at March 31, 1990 should be
a. $192,000
b. $180,000
c. $120,000
d. $100,000

57.   On December 31, 1989, a building owned by Pine Corp. was totally destroyed by fire. The building had fire insurance coverage up to $500,000. Other pertinent information as of

December 31, 1989 follows:

Building, carrying amount	$520,000
Building, fair market value	550,000
Removal and clean-up cost	10,000

During January 1990, before the 1989 financial statements were issued, Pine received insurance proceeds of $500,000. On what amount should Pine base the determination of its loss on involuntary conversion?

    a. $520,000
    b. $530,000
    c. $550,000
    d. $560,000

58. During 1989, Vest Co. incurred the following costs:

Testing in search for process alternatives	$280,000
Routine design of tools, jigs, molds, and dies	250,000
Modification of the formulation of a process	410,000
Research and development services performed by Acme Corp. for Vest	325,000

In Vest's 1989 income statement, research and development expense should be

    a. $ 410,000
    b. $ 735,000
    c. $1,015,000
    d. $1,265,000

59. On June 30, 1989, Finn, Inc. exchanged 2,000 shares of Edlow Corp. $30 par value common stock for a patent owned by Bisk Co. The Edlow stock was acquired in 1987 at a cost of $50,000. At the exchange date, Edlow common stock had a fair value of $40 per share, and the patent had a net carrying amount of $100,000 on Bisk's books. Finn should record the patent at

    a. $ 50,000
    b. $ 60,000
    c. $ 80,000
    d. $100,000

60. Land was purchased to be used as the site for the construction of a plant. A building on the property was sold and removed by the buyer so that construction on the plant could begin. The proceeds from the sale of the building should be

    a.   Classified as other income.
    b.   Deducted from the cost of the land.
    c.   Netted against the costs to clear the land and expensed as incurred.
    d.   Netted against the costs to clear the land and amortized over the life of the plant.

61. A fixed asset with a five-year estimated useful life and no residual value is sold at the end of the second year of its useful life. How would using the sum-of-the-years'-digits method of depreciation instead of the double declining balance method of depreciation affect a gain or loss on the sale of the fixed asset?

	Gain	Loss
a.	Decrease	Decrease
b.	Decrease	Increase
c.	Increase	Decrease
d.	Increase	Increase

62. Net income is understated if, in the first year, estimated salvage value is excluded from the depreciation computation when using the

	Straight-line method	Production or use method
a.	Yes	No
b.	Yes	Yes
c.	No	No
d.	No	Yes

63. Scott Co. exchanged similar nonmonetary assets with Dale Co. No cash was exchanged. The carrying amount of the asset surrendered by Scott exceeded both the fair value of the asset received and Dale's carrying amount of that asset. Scott should recognize the difference between the carrying amount of the asset it surrendered and

    a.   The fair value of the asset it received as a loss.
    b.   The fair value of the asset it received as a gain.
    c.   Dale's carrying amount of the asset it received as a loss.
    d.   Dale's carrying amount of the asset it received as a gain.

64. ABC Co. was organized on July 15, 1987, and earned no significant revenues until the first quarter of 1990. During the period 1987-1989, ABC acquired plant and equipment, raised capital, obtained financing, trained employees, and developed markets. In its financial statements as of December 31, 1989, ABC should defer all costs incurred during 1987-89,

    a.   Net of revenues earned, which are recoverable in future periods.
    b.   Net of revenues earned.
    c.   Which are recoverable in future periods.
    d.   Without regard to net revenues earned or recoverability in future periods.

Repeat Questions

(590,P1,16) Identical/similar to item 20 above
(590,Q3,52) Identical/similar to item 51 above

Problems

Required:

Problem 1   (1189,T2)

(15 to 25 minutes)

Bristol Company purchased land as a site for construction of a factory. Outside contractors were engaged to:

• Construct the factory.

• Grade and pave a parking lot adjacent to the factory for the exclusive use of the factory workers.

Operations at the new location began during the year and normal factory maintenance costs were incurred after production began.

Required:

a. Distinguish between capital and revenue expenditures.

b. Indicate how expenditures for each of the following should be accounted for and reported by Bristol at the time incurred and in subsequent accounting periods.
  1. Purchase of land.
  2. Construction of factory.
  3. Grading and paving parking lot.
  4. Payment of normal factory maintenance costs.

Do not discuss capitalization of interest during construction in your response.

Problem 2   (587,T2)

(15 to 25 minutes)

Deskin Company purchased a new machine to be used in its operations. The new machine was delivered by the supplier, installed by Deskin, and placed into operation. It was purchased under a long-term payment plan for which the interest charges approximated the prevailing market rates. The estimated useful life of the new machine is ten years, and its estimated residual (salvage) value is significant. Normal maintenance was performed to keep the new machine in usable condition.

Deskin also added a wing to the manufacturing building that it owns. The addition is an integral part of the building. Furthermore, Deskin made significant leasehold improvements to office space used as corporate headquarters.

Required:

a. What costs should Deskin capitalize for the new machine? How should the machine be depreciated? **Do not discuss specific methods of depreciation.**

b. How should Deskin account for the normal maintenance performed on the new machine? Why?

c. How should Deskin account for the wing added to the manufacturing building? Where should the added wing be reported on Deskin's financial statements?

d. How should Deskin account for the leasehold improvements made to its office space? Where should the leasehold improvements be reported on Deskin's financial statements?

Problem 3   (1188,T3)

(15 to 25 minutes)

At the beginning of the year, Patrick Company acquired a computer to be used in its operations. The computer was delivered by the supplier, installed by Patrick, and placed into operation. The estimated useful life of the computer is five years, and its estimated residual (salvage) value is significant.

During the year, Patrick received cash in exchange for an automobile that was purchased in a prior year.

Required:

a.1.   What costs should Patrick capitalize for the computer?

2.   What is the objective of depreciation accounting? **Do not discuss specific methods of depreciation.**

b.   What is the rationale for using accelerated depreciation methods?

c.   How should Patrick account for and report the disposal of the automobile?

Problem 4   (1187,P4)

(40 to 50 minutes)

The plant asset and accumulated depreciation accounts of Pell Corporation had the following balances at December 31, 1985:

	Plant asset	Accumulated depreciation
Land	$ 350,000	$ --
Land improvements	180,000	45,000
Building	1,500,000	350,000
Machinery and equipment	1,158,000	405,000
Automobiles	150,000	112,000

Depreciation methods and useful lives

Land improvements—Straight-line; 15 years.
Building—150% declining balance; 20 years.
Machinery and equipment—Straight-line; 10 years.
Automobiles—150% declining balance; 3 years.
Depreciation is computed to the nearest month.
No salvage values are recognized.

Transactions during 1986

• On January 2, 1986, machinery and equipment were purchased at a total invoice cost of $260,000, which included a $5,500 charge for freight. Installation costs of $27,000 were incurred.

• On March 31, 1986, a machine purchased for $58,000 on January 2, 1982 was sold for $36,500.

• On May 1, 1986, expenditures of $50,000 were made to repave parking lots at Pell's plant location. The work was necessitated by damage caused by severe winter weather.

• On November 1, 1986, Pell acquired a tract of land with an existing building in exchange for 10,000 shares of Pell's $20 par common stock that had a market price of $38 a share on this date. Pell paid legal fees and title insurance totaling $23,000. The last property tax bill indicated assessed values of $240,000 for land and $60,000 for building. Shortly after acquisition, the building was razed at a cost of $35,000 in anticipation of new building construction in 1987.

• On December 31, 1986, Pell purchased a new automobile for $15,250 cash and trade-in of an automobile purchased for $18,000 on January 2, 1985. The new automobile has a cash value of $19,000.

Required:

a. Prepare a schedule analyzing the changes in each of the plant assets during 1986 with detailed supporting computations. **Disregard the related accumulated depreciation accounts.**

b. For each asset classification, prepare a schedule showing depreciation expense for the year ended December 31, 1986.

c. Prepare a schedule showing the gain or loss from each asset disposal that would be recognized in Pell's income statement for the year ended December 31, 1986.

Problem 5   (1188,P4)

(45 to 55 minutes)

At December 31, 1986, Cord Company's plant asset and accumulated depreciation and amortization accounts had balances as follows:

Category	Plant asset	Accumulated depreciation and amortization
Land	$ 175,000	$ --
Building	1,500,000	328,900
Machinery and equipment	1,125,000	317,500
Automobiles and trucks	172,000	100,325
Leasehold improvements	216,000	108,000
Land improvements	--	--

Depreciation methods and useful lives

Buildings—150% declining balance; 25 years.
Machinery and equipment—Straight-line; 10 years
Automobiles and trucks—150% declining balance; 5 years, all acquired after 1983.
Leasehold improvements—Straight-line.
Land improvements—Straight-line.
Depreciation is computed to the nearest month. The salvage values of the depreciable assets are immaterial.

Transactions during 1987 and other information

• On January 6, 1987, a plant facility consisting of land and building was acquired from King Corp. in exchange for 25,000 shares of Cord's common stock. On this date, Cord's stock has a market price of $50 a share. Current assessed values of land and building for property tax purposes are $187,500 and $562,500, respectively.

• On March 25, 1987, new parking lots, streets, and sidewalks at the acquired plant facility were completed at a total cost of $192,000. These expenditures had an estimated useful life of 12 years.

• The leasehold improvements were completed on December 31, 1983 and had an estimated useful life of eight years. The related lease, which would have terminated on December 31, 1989, was renewable for an additional four-year term. On April 29, 1987, Cord exercised the renewal option.

• On July 1, 1987, machinery and equipment were purchased at a total invoice cost of $325,000. Additional costs of $10,000 for delivery and $50,000 for installation were incurred.

• On August 30, 1987, Cord purchased a new automobile for $12,500.

• On September 30, 1987, a truck with a
cost of $24,000 and a carrying amount of
$9,100 on date of sale was sold for $11,500.
Depreciation for the 9 months ended September 30, 1987 was $2,650.

• On November 4, 1987, Cord purchased
for $350,000 a tract of land as a potential
future building site.

• On December 20, 1987, a machine with a
cost of $17,000 and a carrying amount of
$2,975 at date of disposition was scrapped
without cash recovery.

Required:

a.   Prepare a schedule analyzing the
changes in each of the plant asset accounts
during 1987. This schedule should include
columns for beginning balances, increase,
decrease and ending balance for each of the
plant asset accounts. <u>Do not analyze changes
in accumulated depreciation and amortization
accounts</u>.

b.   For each asset category, prepare a
schedule showing depreciation or amortization
expense for the year ended December 31,
1987. <u>Round computations to the nearest whole
dollar</u>.

Problem 6   (1189,P4)

                (45 to 55 minutes)

[See section in Chapter 3 (Volume I of the two
volume set) entitled "Practice Problem
Solutions Approach Example."]

Multiple Choice Answers

1. c	14. b	27. d	40. d	53. c
2. d	15. d	28. b	41. c	54. c
3. d	16. b	29. a	42. b	55. c
4. d	17. b	30. d	43. d	56. b
5. d	18. c	31. b	44. a	57. b
6. a	19. b	32. b	45. b	58. c
7. a	20. d	33. c	46. a	59. c
8. b	21. c	34. d	47. a	60. b
9. b	22. d	35. c	48. b	61. b
10. a	23. c	36. c	49. c	62. b
11. b	24. a	37. d	50. b	63. a
12. a	25. c	38. d	51. a	64. c
13. d	26. b	39. c	52. c	

Multiple Choice Answer Explanations

A. Acquisition Cost

1. (588,P2,25) (c) Generally, any cost involved in preparing land for its ultimate use (as a factory site) is considered part of the cost of the land. Before the land can be used as a building site, it must be purchased and the old building must be razed. Therefore, the cost of the land is $540,000:

Purchase price of the land	$450,000
Title insurance and legal fees	30,000
Cost of razing old building	60,000
Total cost of land	$540,000

The other costs given in the problem are properly considered costs of completing the factory building.

Architect's fees	$ 95,000
Construction costs	1,850,000
Total cost of building	$1,945,000

2. (1185,P1,12) (d) The requirement is the amount at which land acquired in a group purchase of fixed assets should be recorded. The total cost ($540,000) of the land and building should be allocated based on their relative fair market value (FMV). Current appraised value is a better indicator of FMV than the seller's original cost. Therefore, the land should be recorded at $216,000:

$$\frac{\text{FMV land}}{\text{Total FMV of assets purchased}} \times \frac{\text{Purchase price}}{\text{of group assets}}$$

$$\frac{200,000}{500,000} \times 540,000 = \$216,000$$

There is no problem in recording the land at more than its appraised value since value is only an estimate of FMV.

3. (589,Q1,11) (d) Generally, property or other noncurrent assets acquired in a noncash transaction should be recorded at the FMV of the consideration given (common stock), unless the FMV of the asset acquired (patent) is more clearly determinable. In this case, there is no evidence that the FMV of the patent is a better measure of its value than the FMV of the stock given. The FMV of the stock given is therefore the correct value to assign to the patent received (2,000 shares x $27/share = $54,000), and answer (d) is correct.

4. (1186,Q1,2) (d) The cost principle requires that assets be recorded at historical cost. The purchased cost is deemed to be an objective measure of fair market value. Therefore, the assessed valuation has no impact on the recorded cost. Historical cost includes all costs incident to the acquisition of the asset. In this case, Saba Co. gave up $800,000 of cash and assumed liabilities of $200,000. The assumption of a liability is the equivalent of a payment of cash. The correct answer is (d) because the total amount incurred in acquiring the land was $1,000,000 ($800,000 + $200,000).

5. (1184,T1,13) (d) The requirement is to determine how the proceeds from the sale of the timber should be treated. The cost of land should include all expenditures made to acquire the land and to ready it for use. When land has been purchased for the purpose of constructing a plant, all costs incurred up to the point when the site is ready for construction of the plant are to be treated as part of the cost of land. Answer (d) is correct because any proceeds obtained in the process of readying the land for its intended use, such as the sale of timber that has been cleared, is treated as a reduction in the cost of the land. Answers (a) and (b) are incorrect because the proceeds or costs resulting from the readying of the land are not revenue or expense items. Answer (c) is incorrect because the accounting for the cost of the plant will begin only after the site is ready for plant construction.

6. (589,P2,25) (a) Generally, fixed assets are recorded at the cost of acquiring the asset and getting it ready for its intended use. In this case, the total cost of the new boiler is $68,000 ($60,000 purchase price + $8,000 installation costs). The information concerning the old boiler does not affect the cost of the new boiler. The only situation where information concerning the old boiler would affect the amount recorded for the new boiler would be if an exchange had taken place. The journal entries are:

Cash	2,000	
Loss on sale	3,000	
Old boiler (net)		5,000
New boiler	68,000	
Cash		68,000

B. Capitalization of Interest

7. (1185,P1,11) (a) The requirement is the amount of capitalized interest at 12/31/84. The requirements of SFAS 34, para 17 for capitalization of interest are met: (1) expenditures for the asset have been made, (2) activities that are necessary to get the asset ready for its intended use are in progress, and (3) interest cost is being incurred. The amount to be capitalized is the lower of avoidable interest or actual interest. Avoidable interest is the average accumulated expenditures multiplied by the appropriate interest rate or rates. Since $2,000,000 was spent on the building evenly throughout the year, the average accumulated expenditures were $1,000,000 ($2,000,000 ÷ 2) and the avoidable interest was $120,000 ($1,000,000 x 12%). Since actual interest ($102,000) is less than avoidable interest, the actual interest cost is capitalized.

8. (1187,T1,4) (b) Per SFAS 34, para 13, the amount of interest to be capitalized during the period equals the average accumulated expenditures for the asset during the period multiplied by the interest rate for the specific borrowing. Answer (b) is correct since the following conditions for interest capitalization were met in 1985 and continued through 1986: (1) activities necessary to get the asset ready for its intended use were in progress, (2) expenditures were made, and (3) interest costs were being incurred. Answers (a) and (d) are incorrect because the average accumulated expenditures are used to give a more accurate indication of available interest. Answer (c) is incorrect because average accumulated expenditures over the time period of the project must be used in the calculation, not just the expenditures for the current period.

C. Nonmonetary Transactions

9. (588,P3,50) (b) The cash price of the new machine represents its fair market value (FMV). The FMV of the old machine can be determined by subtracting the cash portion of the purchase price ($6,000) from the total cost of the new machine: $20,500 - $6,000 = $14,500. Since the book value of the machine ($16,800) exceeds its FMV on the date of the trade-in ($14,500), the difference of $2,300 must be recognized as a loss. Note, however, that if the FMV of the old machine had exceeded its book value that the gain would not be recognized. In accordance with APB 29, gains on nonmonetary transactions involving similar productive assets are not recognized when boot is given.

10. (589,P2,28) (a) Per para 21 of APB 29, exchanges of similar productive assets do not result in the culmination of an earnings process. Therefore, gains on these exchanges are recognized only to the extent that boot is received. Since boot is not received by Pine, the gain realized on the transaction [($700,000 - $50,000) - $500,000 = $150,000 gain] is not recognized. The asset acquired is recorded at its FMV less the gain not recognized ($700,000 - $150,000 = $550,000). This amount can also be computed as the book value of the assets surrendered ($500,000 + $50,000 = $550,000). The journal entry is:

Contract (Terry)	550,000	
Contract (Duff)		500,000
Cash		50,000

11. (1186,P3,53) (b) Per APB 29, nonmonetary exchanges of dissimilar assets are accounted for on the basis of fair values (both gains and losses recognized in full). The car exchanged was carried in Caine's books at $30,000. It was traded, with an additional cash payment of $5,000, for a computer worth $43,000. Therefore, the car had a FMV of $38,000 ($43,000 - $5,000). Caine should recognize a profit of $8,000 ($38,000 - $30,000). The entries are:

Computer	43,000	
Sales		38,000
Cash		5,000
Cost of goods sold	30,000	
Inventory of cars		30,000

Note that the list price of an asset ($45,000 for the car in this case) is not always representative of the FMV of the asset. An asset can often be purchased for less than its list price.

12. (583,Q1,2) (a) The requirement is the amount at which to record land acquired in exchange for a delivery truck. Per APB 20, para 18, both gains and losses are recognized in exchanges involving dissimilar assets and fair values reasonably determinable. The solutions approach is to prepare the journal entry to record the trade of the delivery truck for the land.

Land	11,000	
Accumulated deprec.	3,500	
Loss on exchange	1,500	
Delivery truck		10,000
Cash		6,000

The loss on the exchange of the delivery truck for the land is $1,500 ($6,500 book value - $5,000 fair market value). The value assigned to the land is the fair value of the asset(s) given up, i.e., the delivery truck ($5,000) plus cash paid ($6,000), or $11,000.

13. (1188,T1,36) (d) Per APB 29, para 18, a transfer of a nonmonetary asset in a nonreciprocal transfer should be recorded at the fair value of the asset transferred, with a gain or loss recognized on the disposition, whether the transfer is made to a stockholder or to another entity. Therefore, answer (d) is correct.

14. (588,T1,33) (b) Per APB 29, para 22, when the exchange of nonmonetary assets includes an amount of monetary consideration, the Board believes that the receiver of monetary consideration has realized a partial gain on the exchange. To determine the partial gain to be recognized, first compute the total gain which is the difference between the fair market value of the nonmonetary asset given up and its book value. Then multiply the ratio of the monetary consideration received to the total consideration received (i.e., monetary consideration plus the estimated fair market value of the asset received) times the total gain. The result is the realized gain to be recognized. The Board further believes that the entity paying the monetary consideration should not recognize any gain until the earnings process is culminated. Therefore, answer (b) is correct. Note, however, that all losses on sales or exchanges are recognized immediately.

15. (586,Q1,11) (d) The requirement is to determine the proper recording of a nonmonetary donated asset. The solutions approach is to recall applicable principles. Per APB 29, para 13, nonreciprocal receipts of nonmonetary assets should be recorded at fair value because this is the only value relevant to the recipient enterprise. Therefore, the $200,000 would be the recorded amount. The journal entry to record the receipt of the donated asset is

Land and Building	200,000	
Additional paid-in capital		200,000

Donated assets are recorded as contributed capital. Since an entry is made to record donated capital, answer (a) is incorrect. Donated assets would not be credited to retained earnings, answer (b), because the donated asset does not represent earnings of the corporation. Answer (c) is incorrect because the donation of an asset is not an unusual or infrequent transaction.

16. (1187,T1,27) (b) APB 29 states that both gains and losses on nonmonetary, nonreciprocal transfers (donations) are to be recorded. The gain or loss is calculated as the difference between the fair value of the nonmonetary asset transferred and its recorded amount at the date of donation. Gains or losses related to the nonreciprocal transfer of nonmonetary assets are recognized because they have been earned or incurred by the entity at the date of transfer.

E. Capital Versus Revenue Expenditures

17. (588,P2,23) (b) Generally, a cost should be capitalized if it improves the efficiency of the asset or extends its useful life, and expensed if it merely maintains the asset at its current level. The renovation cost ($50,000) improves the production efficiency of the machines and therefore should be capitalized. However, the continuing, frequent, and low-cost repairs ($35,000) and the replacement of a broken gear ($5,000) merely maintain the assets at their current level, and therefore $40,000 should be charged to repairs and maintenance expense.

18. (1186,P1,3) (c) The cost of moving ($35,000) and reinstalling ($75,000) machines to secure greater efficiency in production benefits future periods and therefore should be capitalized as an asset and amortized over the five-year period benefited. Annual maintenance costs ($10,000) are expenditures which merely maintain the machines in current operating condition; since they do not provide any additional future benefits, they are expensed as incurred rather than capitalized. Therefore, the total amount to be capitalized is $110,000 ($35,000 + $75,000).

19. (586,P1,16) (c) The requirement is the amount to be charged to repair and maintenance expense in 1985. Generally, a cost should be capitalized if it improves the asset, and expensed if it merely maintains the asset at its current level. Continuing and frequent repairs ($40,000) should be expensed. Similarly, the cost of repainting the plant building ($10,000) and the cost of partially replacing the roof tiles ($14,000) should be expensed. These are ordinary, regularly occurring expenditures which maintain, rather than improve, the plant building. The work on the electrical wiring system ($32,000) is capitalized instead of expensed since it is a major improvement. Therefore, the total amount expensed is $64,000 ($40,000 + $10,000 + $14,000).

20. (586,P1,19) (d) The requirement is the amount of various costs to be capitalized. The cost of the attachment ($45,000) would be capitalized since it represents an addition. The cost of installing the attachment ($10,000) is also capitalized because this

expenditure was required to get the attachment ready for its intended use. The renovation costs ($30,000 and $14,000) should also be capitalized, even though the useful life was not extended, because productivity has been significantly increased as a result of the renovation. The total amount to be capitalized is $99,000 ($45,000 + $10,000 + $30,000 + $14,000).

21. (588,T1,8) (c) Capital expenditures are **not** normal, recurring expenses, and they benefit the operations of more than one period. Examples of capital expenditures include additions, replacements, betterments, and extraordinary repairs and maintenance. Revenue expenditures are normal, recurring expenditures such as normal repairs and maintenance. The installation of an **improved** electrical system (a betterment) is a capital expenditure because it would benefit more than one period. Therefore, answer (c) is correct.

22. (1184,T1,14) (d) The requirement is to determine which type of expenditure occurs when a company installs a higher capacity boiler to heat its plant. Answer (d) is correct because a betterment is the replacement of a major part or component of an existing asset with a significantly better or improved part or component. Answer (a) is incorrect because a rearrangement deals with moving existing assets to provide greater efficiency or reduce production costs. Answer (b) is incorrect because ordinary repairs and maintenance are for recurring, relatively small expenditures that maintain normal operating condition. Answer (c) is incorrect because an addition is an extension, enlargement, or expansion made to an existing asset.

F. Depreciation

23. (1186,P3,46) (c) Salvage value is ignored when using a DB approach. The formula for 150% DB depreciation is the DB rate (150% x the straight-line rate) multiplied by the beginning-of-the-year book value. In this case the straight-line rate is 1/5 or 20% per year over the five-year life, so the DB rate is 30% (20% x 150%). The book value when the asset was purchased on 7/1/85 was its original cost ($600,000). In 1985, a half-year's depreciation should be recorded (7/1/85 to 12/31/85). Therefore, 1985 depreciation expense is $90,000 ($600,000 x 30% x 1/2).

24. (586,P3,54) (a) The requirement is the amount of depreciation expense to be recorded in 1985. After 3 years (1982-1984), accumulated depreciation is $72,000. Therefore, the method which was used was the sum-of-the-

years'-digits (SYD) method. Using this method, after 3 years the balance in accumulated depreciation would be 12/15 of the depreciable base (5/15 + 4/15 + 3/15). The depreciable base is the cost ($110,000) less the residual value ($20,000), or $90,000. Thus, using the SYD method, accumulated depreciation at 12/31/84 would be $72,000 ($90,000 x 12/15), which matches the amount given in the problem. 1985 depreciation expense, using the SYD method is $12,000 ($90,000 x 2/15).

25. (584,T1,10) (c) The equation for calculating sum-of-the-years'-digits (SYD) depreciation is:

$$\frac{\text{Years remaining}}{\text{SYD}} \times \frac{\text{Cost minus}}{\text{salvage value}}$$

Year 1: 4/10(1.00 - .15) = 34.0%
Year 2: 3/10(1.00 - .15) = 25.5%

The equation for calculating double-declining-balance (DDB) depreciation is:

$$\frac{200\%}{\text{Useful life}} \times \frac{\text{Book}}{\text{value}}$$

Year 1: 200%/4(1.00)   = 50.0%
Year 2: 200%/4(1.00 - .50) = 25.0%

Therefore:

Year 1: SYD is lower than DDB
(i.e., 34.0% < 50.0%)
Year 2: SYD is higher than DDB
(i.e., 25.5% > 25.0%)

Recall that salvage value is included in the SYD calculation and not in the DDB calculation.

26. (588,T1,25) (b) The formula to compute double-declining-balance (DDB) depreciation is:

$$\left(\begin{array}{c}\text{Twice the straight-line}\\ \text{depreciation rate}\end{array}\right) \times \left(\begin{array}{c}\text{The beginning of}\\ \text{the period book value}\end{array}\right)$$

Salvage value is ignored when using the DDB method. The formula to determine depreciation using the productive output method is:

$$\left(\frac{\text{Current activity (output)}}{\text{Total expected activity}}\right) \times \left(\begin{array}{c}\text{Original cost less}\\ \text{salvage value}\end{array}\right)$$

Therefore, answer (b) is correct.

27. (589,T1,4) (d) The formula to compute straight-line depreciation is:

$$\frac{\text{Original cost less salvage value}}{\text{Estimated useful life}}$$

The formula to determine depreciation using the productive output method is:

$$\left(\frac{\text{Current activity (output)}}{\text{Total expected activity}}\right) \times \left(\begin{array}{c}\text{Original cost less}\\ \text{salvage value}\end{array}\right)$$

Note that both of these methods use cost minus salvage value as the depreciable base of the asset. This means that after all depreciation has been recorded using either method, the net asset will be recorded at salvage value, and accumulated depreciation will be equal to the original cost minus salvage value. Therefore, answer (d) is correct.

28. (589,T1,17) (b) The equation for calculating DDB depreciation is:

$$\text{Book value} \quad \times \quad \frac{200\%}{\text{Useful life}}$$

The percentage used for DDB is always twice the straight-line rate. Note that salvage value is not used in determining depreciation expense under this method. In this case depreciation will be calculated as follows:

In 1986: Original Cost x 50% (200%/4)
In 1987: (Original Cost x 50%) x 50%
In 1988: (Original Cost x 50% x 50%) x 50%

Therefore, answer (b) is correct.

29. (1186,T1,27) (a) Composite (group) depreciation averages the service life of a number of property units and depreciates the group as if it were a single unit. The term "group" is used when the assets are similar; the term "composite" is used when they are dissimilar. The mechanical application of both of these methods is identical. The depreciation rate is the following ratio:

$$\frac{\text{Sum of annual SL depreciation of individual assets}}{\text{Total asset cost}}$$

Thus, both group and composite depreciation utilize the straight-line depreciation method. Therefore, answer (a) is correct, and answers (b), (c), and (d) are incorrect.

30. (1184,T1,15) (d) The requirement is to determine if accumulated depreciation is debited for the original cost less any residual recovery under composite depreciation or group depreciation. Composite depreciation is the term given to depreciation on a group of heterogeneous assets. Group depreciation is the term given to depreciation on a group of homogeneous assets. The mechanical application of both these methods is similar. All of the assets are recorded in a single asset account and depreciated using a single accumulated depreciation account. The depreciation rate used is an average based on the assets in the group. When an asset is retired, the asset account is credited for the original cost of the item, and the accumulated depreciation account is debited for the original cost less any residual recovery. This procedure is the same for both methods; thus answer (d) is correct.

31. (588,T1,9) (b) The solutions approach is to prepare the journal entry that would be made when an asset is retired under the composite depreciation method:

Cash   (cash proceeds)
Accum. dep.   (plug)
    Truck   (original cost)

The net decrease in the carrying amount of the assets is the credit to the asset account less the plug to accumulated depreciation. This amount would be equal to the cash proceeds received. Therefore, answer (b) is correct and answers (a), (c), and (d) are incorrect.

G. Other Disposals and Impairment of Value

32. (589,P1,27) (b) When a permanent impairment of value occurs on a plant asset, a loss should be recognized with a corresponding decrease in the carrying amount of the asset. The loss should be recognized as soon as evidence exists that such a loss has been sustained. The carrying amount of this asset at 12/31/87 is $250,000 [$400,000 - (3 x $50,000)]. In 1988, a loss of $150,000 is recognized, to bring the carrying amount down to $100,000. This carrying amount is then depreciated over the remaining life of 5 years (1/1/88 to 12/31/92), resulting in yearly depreciation of $20,000 ($100,000 ÷ 5). Therefore, the carrying amount at 12/31/88 is $80,000 ($100,000 - $20,000).

33. (587,P1,8) (c) The situation in this question is known as a permanent impairment of value. Before the loss on the machine can be determined, depreciation for 1986 must be calculated. Since the machine was used until 12/31/86, a full year's depreciation should be recorded. During the first four years, Huff recorded $160,000 of depreciation ($400,000 - $240,000). Therefore, yearly depreciation under the straight-line method is $40,000 ($160,000 ÷ 4). At the end of 1986, before recognizing a loss, the carrying amount of the machine is $200,000 ($240,000 - $40,000). A loss should be recognized in 1986 when the permanent impairment is identified, even though the actual disposal takes place in 1987. The disposal proceeds of $65,000 on 1/5/87 can be used as an estimate of the 12/31/86 value of the machine; this amount would be known well before the 1986 financial statements are issued. Thus, a loss of $135,000 ($200,000 - $65,000) should be recognized in 1986.

34. (587,P1,9) (d) The gain on the disposition of the machine is the excess of the insurance proceeds ($200,000) over the carrying amount of the machine on 6/30/86. The carrying amount on 6/30/86 is determined by

subtracting depreciation for January 1, 1986
through June 30, 1986 (6/12 x 20,000) from the
carrying amount on 12/31/85. Thus, the carrying amount on June 30, 1986 is $150,000
($160,000 - 10,000). Therefore, the gain on
the disposition of the machine is $50,000
($200,000 - 150,000).

35. (1184,P1,12) (c) The requirement is to
determine the amount to be reported on the
1983 income statement as a gain on the condemnation of property. FASB Interpretation 30
requires that a gain (loss) be recognized when
a nonmonetary asset is involuntarily converted
into monetary assets even though an enterprise
reinvests the monetary assets in replacement
nonmonetary assets. The gain or loss is the
difference between the consideration received
and that given up. In this case, the condemnation award is $450,000 and the property has
a book value of $275,000, resulting in a gain
of $175,000 ($450,000 - $275,000).

H. Depletion

36. (1185,P2,40) (c) The requirement is the
amount of depletion to be included in cost of
goods sold. The depletion charge per unit is
the net cost of the resource divided by the
estimated units of the resource. The net cost
of the resource is $4,320,000.

Cost of mine	$3,600,000
Development costs	1,080,000
Residual value	(360,000)
Net Cost	$4,320,000

Therefore the depletion charge is $2.00 per
ton ($4,320,000 ÷ 2,160,000 tons). Since
240,000 tons were sold, $480,000 of depletion
(240,000 x $2.00) is included in cost of goods
sold. Note that $60,000 [(270,000 tons -
240,000 tons) x $2.00] of depletion would be
included in inventory. Total depletion on
both the cost of goods sold and inventory
would be $540,000.

J. Intangible Assets (APB 17)

37. (1187,P1,10) (d) Wall Company would
record the trademark at its cost of
$112,000. The unamortized cost on the
seller's books ($56,000) is irrelevant to the
buyer. Although the trademark has a remaining
useful life of 50 years, intangible assets
must be amortized over no more than 40 years
per APB 17, para 29. Therefore, 1986
amortization is $2,800 ($112,000 ÷ 40 years).

38. (586,P1,18) (d) The requirement is the
amount of trademark amortization expense for
1985. The trademark was purchased at a cost
of $400,000 on 1/1/81. With an estimated use-

ful life of 16 years, amortization expense was
established as $25,000 per year ($400,000 ÷
16). At 12/31/84, the trademark had a book
value of $300,000 [$400,000 - (4 x $25,000)].
In January of 1985, $60,000 was spent success-
fully defending the patent. This amount is
properly capitalized, resulting in a book
value of $360,000 ($300,000 + $60,000) for the
trademark. This new book value is then amortized over the remaining useful life of 12
years (16 years - 4 years). Therefore, 1985
amortization expense is $30,000 ($360,000 ÷ 12
years).

39. (1188,T1,9) (c) Per APB 17, para 25,
acquired intangible assets should be recorded
at cost on the acquisition date. The legal
fees paid to obtain a franchise are properly
capitalized as part of the acquisition cost.
Legal fees and other costs incurred in successfully defending a trademark suit are also
capitalized because such a suit establishes
the legal rights of the trademark holder.
Therefore, answer (c) is correct.

40. (588,T1,10) (d) APB 17, para 24 states
that a company should record as assets the
costs of intangible assets (goodwill) acquired
from other enterprises or individuals. APB 17
further states that the cost of goodwill
should be allocated (amortized) over the useful life of the asset. Goodwill generated
internally is **not** capitalized in the accounts
because it is **not** specifically identifiable,
has an indeterminate life, and is not
separable from the enterprise. Therefore,
answer (d) is correct.

41. (589,T1,6) (c) Per APB 17, para 24,
the "costs of developing, maintaining, or re-
storing intangible assets which are not specifically identifiable, have indeterminate
lives, or are inherent in a continuing business and related to an enterprise as a whole
(such as goodwill) should be deducted from income when incurred." Therefore, answer (c) is
correct.

42. (1187,T1,9) (b) Per SFAS 2, para 10,
legal work in connection with patent litigation is **not** a research and development
activity. Therefore, the test to determine if
the legal fees incurred should be capitalized
would be based upon whether future periods
will be benefited. Legal fees incurred in
successfully defending a patent should
properly be capitalized because such litigation establishes the legal rights of the
holder and future benefits will be derived
from the patent. Costs incurred in the unsuccessful defense of a patent should not be

capitalized, however, because the unsuccessful party possesses questionable, if any, rights to the patents, and thus will derive no future benefit from the legal fees incurred.

43. (585,T1,12) (d) The requirement is to determine the amount of an intangible asset which should be amortized when a change in estimated life is made. Answer (d) is correct because APB 17 states that periodic review of amortization policies should be undertaken and required changes should be made prospectively but should not exceed a life of 40 years from date of acquisition. When the asset was acquired on January 1, 1980, it was to be amortized over its useful life, but not to exceed 40 years notwithstanding the fact that its useful life was estimated to be 50 years. The asset was determined to have a remaining useful life of 30 years at January 1, 1985. The unamortized cost at that date should be amortized over the remaining useful life of 30 years provided the total amortization period does not exceed 40 years. Answer (a) is incorrect since it implies a retroactive restatement of amortization, and APB 20 requires that a change in estimate be treated prospectively. Answer (b) is incorrect, because under no circumstances should an intangible be amortized over a life in excess of 40 years. Answer (c) is incorrect because the useful life at 1/1/85 is 30 years, and to use a life of 40 years would violate conservatism and overstate income. Additionally, using a 40-year life from 1/1/85 would yield a total amortization period of 45 years, which would violate the provisions of APB 17.

44. (1189,P1,13) (a) Mark Co. would record the franchise at its cost of $204,000. The unamortized cost on the seller's books ($68,000) is irrelevant to the buyer. Although the trademark has a remaining useful life of 50 years, intangible assets must be amortized over no more than 40 years per para 29 of APB 17. Therefore, 1988 amortization is $5,100 ($204,000 ÷ 40 years).

K. Deferred Charges

45. (1189,P1,10) (b) Organization costs are those incurred in the formation of a corporation. Since these costs will benefit the company in future years, they are properly recorded as an intangible asset to be amortized over a designated period of time. Income tax regulations require that organization costs be amortized over a period of at least five years. Therefore, the maximum allowable deduction for tax purposes is 1/5 of cost. If Kew chooses this basis, 1/5 of the cost is expensed in 1987 while 4/5 is deferred to later years (4/5 x $24,000 = $19,200).

L. Research and Development Costs (SFAS 2)

46. (1189,P1,12) (a) SFAS 2 states that all R&D costs should be expensed because it is difficult to associate these costs with particular achievements, and because it is difficult to identify the time period over which future benefits will be realized. Therefore, the R&D costs of $160,000 should be expensed. However, patent costs which should be capitalized include costs associated with the registration of a patent ($30,000) and costs incurred in successfully defending a patent ($45,000). Thus, a total of $75,000 ($30,000 + $45,000) should be capitalized for this patent through 3/31/88.

47. (1187,P3,43) (a) Research and development costs (R&D costs) are defined in para 8 of SFAS 2. Paras 9 and 10 go on to provide detailed lists of examples of activities that typically would be _included_ in R&D costs and expensed (9) and excluded from R&D costs and possibly capitalized (10). Among those items listed in SFAS 2 as being part of R&D costs are modification of the design of a product or process ($135,000), design of tools, jigs, molds, and dies involving new technology ($170,000) and laboratory research aimed at discovery of a new knowledge ($215,000). These three R&D expenses total $520,000. Included in the items listed in SFAS 2 as _not_ being part of R&D costs are trouble-shooting breakdowns during production ($150,000) and periodic design changes to existing products ($185,000).

48. (589,P1,19) (b) Per SFAS 2, all costs defined as research and development (R&D) must be expensed, due to the difficulty of associating these costs with particular achievements and identifying the amount of future benefits and the time period over which those benefits will be realized. To help differentiate R&D costs from other similar costs, paras 9 and 10 of SFAS 2 provide examples of R&D activities and of activities which are not considered R&D. All of the items listed in this problem were included in the SFAS 2 list of R&D activities except routine design of tools, jigs, molds, and dies ($100,000), which is specifically _excluded_ from R&D activities in para 10 of SFAS 2. Therefore, total R&D expense is $920,000 ($300,000 + $250,000 + $370,000).

49. (586,P3,46) (c) The requirement is the total research and development (R&D) costs to be expensed in 1985. Per SFAS 2, all R&D costs are to be charged to expense when incurred. R&D expenditures for items such as materials, equipment, and purchased intangi-

bles shall be capitalized if they have alternative future uses in R&D projects or other
areas. Therefore, the full cost ($975,000) of
the equipment acquired for use in R&D projects
is capitalized, and the depreciation
($135,000) on the equipment is expensed along
with the other R&D costs incurred (SFAS 2,
para 11).

Depreciation	$ 135,000
Materials	200,000
Compensation	500,000
Consulting fees	150,000
Indirect costs	250,000
R&D expense	$1,235,000

50. (1188,T1,27) (b) Per SFAS 2, para 12,
all costs associated with research and
development (R&D) activities enumerated in
SFAS 2, para 9, are to be expensed as incurred. Answer (b) is correct because it is
one of the para 9 R&D activities. SFAS 2,
para 10 identifies certain activities which
are __excluded__ from research and development.
Answers (a), (c), and (d) are incorrect because they are all listed in para 10 as non-
R&D activities.

M. Development Stage Enterprises

51. (588,P3,58) (a) Per SFAS 7, para 10,
financial statements issued by a development
stage enterprise shall conform with the
generally accepted accounting principles that
apply to established operating enterprises.
Leasehold improvements, equipment, furniture,
and security deposits are generally capitalized because these costs benefit future
periods ($1,000,000 + $60,000 = $1,060,000).
Research and development costs and laboratory
operations costs are expensed as incurred, in
accordance with SFAS 2. General and Administrative costs are period costs which are also
expensed as incurred.

52. (588,P3,59) (c) Leasehold improvements,
equipment, furniture, and security deposits
are generally capitalized because these costs
benefit future periods ($150,000 + $15,000 =
$165,000). Research and development costs and
laboratory operations costs are expensed as
incurred, in accordance with SFAS 2. General
and Administrative costs are period costs
which are also expensed as incurred. Note
that this answer would be the same even if the
company were in the development stage, because
SFAS 7 requires development stage companies to
follow the same GAAP as established companies.

53. (588,T1,39) (c) Per SFAS 7, para 30, a
development stage company shall use the same
GAAP that applies to established operating

enterprises to govern the recognition of
revenue and to determine whether a cost is to
be capitalized or expensed as incurred.
Therefore, answer (c) is correct.

54. (589,T1,38) (c) Per SFAS 7, para 11b, a
development stage enterprise shall issue the
same basic financial statements as an
established operating enterprise, but shall
disclose certain additional information. An
income statement, in addition to showing
amounts of revenues and expenses for each
period covered by the income statement, shall
include the cumulative amounts from the
enterprise's inception. Therefore, answer (c)
is correct.

May 1990 Answers

55. (590,P1,15) (c) Any cost involved in
preparing land for its ultimate use (such as a
factory site) is considered part of the cost
of the land. Before the land can be used as a
building site, it must be purchased and the
old building must be razed. Legal fees and
title insurance are also necessary costs of
acquiring land. Therefore, the cost of the
land is $332,000.

Purchase price	$300,000
Cost to raze old building	25,000
Legal fees	5,000
Title insurance	6,000
Proceeds from sale of scrap	(4,000)
Total net cost of land	$332,000

Note that the proceeds from the sale of scrap
is a reduction of the cost of the land because
it reduces the net cost of razing the old
building.

56. (590,P1,17) (b) When computing sum-of-
the-years'-digits (SYD) depreciation, the
depreciable cost (cost-salvage value) is
multiplied by the SYD fraction. The SYD
fraction is:

$$\frac{\text{Number of years left as of beginning of year}}{\text{Sum of the years of useful life}}$$

In this case, the depreciable cost is $300,000
(no salvage value given). The sum of the
years in useful life is 15 (1 + 2 + 3 +
4 + 5). Note that a formula can also be used
to determine the sum:

$$\frac{n(n + 1)}{2} = \frac{5 \times 6}{2} = \underline{\underline{15}}$$

The fraction for the first year is 5/15 and
for the second year is 4/15, so the acumulated
depreciation at 3/31/90 is 9/15 x $300,000, or
$180,000.

57. (590,P1,19) (b) The loss on involuntary conversion is the excess of the insurance proceeds ($500,000) over the carrying amount of assets destroyed or used up as a result of the fire. The building (carrying amount or book value, $520,000) was destroyed, and cash of $10,000 was used to cover removal and cleanup costs. Therefore, the loss is based on the $500,000 proceeds and the $530,000 ($520,000 + $10,000) book value and cleanup costs, resulting in a loss of $30,000.

58. (590,P3,53) (c) Per SFAS 2, all costs defined as research and development (R&D) must be expensed in the period in which they are incurred. This is because it is difficult to associate these costs with particular achievements and identifying the amount of future benefits and the time period over which those benefits will be realized. To help differentiate R & D costs from other similar costs, paras 9 and 10 of SFAS 2 provide examples of R & D activities, and of activities not considered R & D. All of the items in this problem are specifically identified as being R & D costs in SFAS 2, except routine design of tools, jigs, etc, ($250,000). Thus, total R & D expense is $1,015,000 ($280,000 + $410,000 + $325,000).

59. (590,Q3,58) (c) Generally, noncurrent assets acquired in a noncash transaction should be recorded at the FMV of the consideration given (common stock), unless the FMV of the asset acquired (patent) is more clearly determinable. The FMV of the stock given is therefore the correct value to assign to the patent received (2,000 shares x $40 per share = $80,000).

60. (590,T1,5) (b) Generally, any cost involved in preparing land for its ultimate use is considered a cost of the land. In this case, the cost assigned to the land should be the purchase price plus any costs associated with clearing the land and removal of the building (if any) less the proceeds from the sale of the building. Therefore answer (b) is correct. Since both the costs to clear the land and the proceeds from the sale are capitalized as part of the net cost of the land, answers (a) and (c) are incorrect. Answer (d) is incorrect because land is not subject to amortization.

61. (590,T1,20) (b) The solutions approach to solving this problem is to compute the first two years' depreciation expense under both the sum-of-the-years'-digits (SYD) and double declining balance (DDB) methods. Assuming a $100 cost and no salvage value, de-

preciation expense would be calculated as follows:

DDB Method
Depreciation expense is computed as twice the straight-line rate times the net book value at the beginning of each year. The straight line rate for an asset with a useful life of five years is 20% (1/5).

Depreciation
Yr 1:   100 x 40% = 40
Yr 2: (100 - 40) x 40% = 24
Total   64

SYD Method
Depreciation expense is computed by applying declining fractions to the depreciable cost of the asset. The denominator is the sum of the years in the life of the asset (1 + 2 + 3 + 4 + 5 = 15 in this case).

Depreciation
Yr 1: 100 x (5/15) = 33
Yr 2: 100 x (4/15) = 27
Total   60

Depreciation expense and accumulated depreciation are higher under the DDB method than under the SYD method. Note that the SYD depreciation would have been lower if the asset had an estimated salvage value greater than zero, while the DDB depreciation would not have changed. Thus, the DDB depreciation at the end of the second year would always be higher than under the SYD method. The gain or loss on the sale of the fixed asset is computed as follows:

Proceeds from		Net Book		Gain
Sale	-	Value of	=	
		Asset		<Loss>

Since the net book value (cost less accumulated depreciation) is higher under the SYD method, use of this method instead of DDB would decrease the gain or increase the loss on the sale. Therefore answer (b) is correct.

62. (590,T1,21) (b) The depreciable base used to compute depreciation expense under both the straight line and production methods is equal to the cost less estimated salvage value of the asset. Depreciation expense is overstated and net income is, therefore, understated when the estimated salvage value is excluded from the depreciation computation under both of these methods. Therefore, answer (b) is correct.

63. (590,T1,31) (a) Per APB 29, para 21, exchanges of similar nonmonetary assets do not culminate an earning process. These transactions are therefore accounted for based on the recorded amount of the asset relinquished. Although APB 29 prohibits recognition of a

gain on these exchanges, para 22 requires the
recognition of any loss. Since the carrying
value of the asset surrendered by Scott exceeds the fair market value of the asset received, Scott realized a loss on this exchange. In accordance with para 18, Scott
should value the asset received at its fair
market value. The difference between the
carrying amount of the asset surrendered and
its fair market value (measured by the fair
market value of the asset received in this
case) should be recognized as a loss. Therefore, answer (a) is correct and answer (b) is
incorrect. Dale Co.'s carrying value of the
asset would not be considered (nor typically
known) by Scott Co., therefore, answers (c)
and (d) are incorrect.

64. (590,T1,39) (c) SFAS 7, para 10 requires development stage enterprises to follow
the same generally accepted accounting principles that apply to established operating enterprises. Accordingly, ABC Co. should only
defer as assets those costs which will benefit
future periods, in accordance with SFAC 6.
Therefore, answer (c) is correct and answer (d) is incorrect. Answers (a) and (b)
are incorrect because the revenues earned
during the development stage would not be
considered when determining which costs are
appropriately deferred.

Answer Outline

Problem 1   Cap. vs. Rev. Expendit.:   Acctg.
             and Reporting (1189,T2)

a.   Expenditures
      Capital--benefit future periods
      Revenue--benefit current period only

b.   Treatment of expenditures

		Accounting	Reporting		
Land	Cap. E.	No depreciation	B/S NCA PPE	I/S --	
Factory const. costs	Cap. E.	Depreciate over expected life; include in product cost as ovhd.	C/A invent. until sold NCA PPE (net of A/D)	CGS expense as goods sold	
Grading and paving costs		(same as factory construction costs, except depreciation period shorter of life of parking lot or factory)			
Normal factory maintenance costs	Rev. E.	Include in product cost as ovhd.	C/A invent. until sold	CGS expense as goods sold	

Unofficial Answer

Problem 1   Cap. vs. Rev. Expendit.:   Acctg.
             and Reporting (1189,T2)

   a. Capital expenditures benefit future
periods. Revenue expenditures benefit the
current period only.

   b. 1. The purchase price of the land
should be capitalized. The land should be
shown as a noncurrent asset on the balance
sheet at its original cost and it is not subject to depreciation.

   2. The cost of constructing the factory should be capitalized and depreciated
over the expected life of the factory. The
depreciation should be added to cost of inventory, via factory overhead, as goods are produced, and is expensed as cost of sales as
goods are sold. The factory expenditures, net
of accumulated depreciation, should be shown
as a noncurrent asset on the balance sheet.
Inventory should be reported as a current
asset on the balance sheet, and cost of sales

should be reported as an expense on the income
statement.

   3. The cost of grading and paving the
parking lot should be capitalized and depreciated over the expected life of either the
factory or parking lot, whichever is shorter.
The depreciation should be added to cost of
inventory, via factory overhead, as goods are
produced, and is expensed as cost of sales as
goods are sold. The land improvement expenditures, net of accumulated depreciation, should
be shown as a noncurrent asset on the balance
sheet. Inventory should be reported as a current asset on the balance sheet, and cost of
sales should be reported as an expense on the
income statement.

   4. The cost of maintaining the factory once production has begun is a "revenue
type" expenditure. However, since it is a
factory cost, it should be added to cost of
inventory, via factory overhead, as goods are
produced, and is expensed as cost of sales as
goods are sold. Inventory should be reported
as a current asset on the balance sheet, and
cost of sales should be reported as an expense
on the income statement.

Answer Outline

Problem 2   PP & E Costs (587,T2)

a.   Capitalizable cost
      All cost relating to purchase or
        preparation for use
      Includes delivery and installation costs
      Represents cash equivalent price
      Would not include interest charges

     Depreciable cost
      Allocated over estimated useful life
      Systematic and rational manner
      Equal to capitalizable cost less
        estimated residual (salvage) value

b.   Normal maintenance
      Not capitalized
      Expensed as incurred if machine is not
        used in manufacturing process
      Inventoried as factory overhead if
        machine used in manufacturing process
      Does not enhance service potential of
        machine

c.   Wing addition
      Capitalized
      Depreciated over estimated useful life
        or remaining useful life of building,
        whichever shorter
      Included in property, plant, and equip-
        ment section of balance sheet

d. Leasehold improvements
    Capitalized
    Depreciated over estimated useful lives
      or the term of the lease, whichever is
      shorter
    Unamortized portion included as a
      separate caption in property, plant,
      and equipment section or intangible
      asset section
    Amortized portion shown as expense in
      income statement

Unofficial Answer

Problem 2   PP & E Costs (587,T2)

a. The capitalizable cost includes all costs
relating to purchase or preparation for use.
Such cost may include delivery and installation. The capitalizable cost represents the
cash equivalent price and accordingly would
not include interest charges.

The depreciable cost of the new machine
should be allocated over its estimated useful
life in a systematic and rational manner.
Depreciable cost is the capitalizable cost
less its estimated residual (salvage) value.

b. Normal maintenance performed on the new
machine should not be capitalized as part of
the machine's cost. It should be expensed as
incurred if the machine is not used in the
manufacturing process or should be inventoried
as part of factory overhead if the machine is
used in the manufacturing process. Normal
maintenance does not enhance the service
potential of the machine.

c. The wind added to the manufacturing
building should be capitalized. The addition
should be depreciated over its estimated
useful life or the remaining useful life of
the building of which it is an integral part,
whichever is shorter. The addition should be
included in the property, plant, and equipment
section of the balance sheet.

d. The leasehold improvements made to the
office space should be capitalized. The
leasehold improvements should be depreciated
(amortized) over their estimated useful lives
or the term of the lease, whichever is
shorter. The unamortized portion of the
leasehold improvements could be included as a
separate caption in the property, plant, and
equipment section or the intangible assets
section of the balance sheet. The amortized
portion of the leasehold improvements would be
shown as an expense in the income statement.

Answer Outline

Problem 3   Acquisition Costs, Depreciation,
             and Asset Disposal (1188,T3)

a.1. Costs to be capitalized
        All costs reasonable and necessary to
          prepare asset for intended use
          E.g., cash purchase price, delivery,
            installation, testing, set up

  2. Objective of depreciation accounting
        Allocate depreciable cost of asset
          over estimated useful life in system-
          atic and rational manner
        Matches depreciable cost of asset with
          revenues generated from use
        Depreciable cost = capitalized cost -
          estimated residual (salvage) value

b.   Rationale for using accelerated depre-
      ciation
        Asset more productive in earlier years
          of life
          Thus, larger depreciation charges
            matched against larger revenues
        Accelerated depreciation recognizes
          that asset may become technologically
          obsolete
          Risk with long-term cash flows
            greater than near-term cash flows

c.   Accounting and recording disposal of
      auto
        Record depreciation expense to
          disposal date
          Updates carrying amount
        Record gain (loss) if carrying amount
          differs from cash proceeds
          Report as income from continuing
            operations

Unofficial Answer

Problem 3   Acquisition Costs, Depreciation,
             and Asset Disposal (1188,T3)

a.1. The capitalized cost for the computer
includes all costs reasonable and necessary to
prepare it for its intended use. Examples of
such costs are the cash purchase price,
delivery, installation, testing, and set up.

  2. The objective of depreciation accounting
is to allocate the depreciable cost of an
asset over its estimated useful life in a
systematic and rational manner. This process
matches the depreciable cost of the asset with
revenues generated from its use. Depreciable
cost is the capitalized cost less its
estimated residual (salvage) value.

b. The rationale for using accelerated depreciation methods is based on the following
assumptions:

• An asset is more productive in the earlier years of its estimated useful life. Therefore, larger depreciation charges in the earlier years would be matched against the larger revenues generated in the earlier years.

• An asset may become technologically obsolete prior to the end of its originally estimated useful life. The risk associated with estimated long-term cash flows is greater than the risk associated with near-term cash flows. Accelerated depreciation recognizes this condition.

c. Patrick should record depreciation expense to the date of disposal. Recording depreciation updates the carrying amount of the automobile (capitalized cost less accumulated depreciation) differs from the cash proceeds from the disposal, a gain or loss results. Patrick should report gain or loss on disposal as part of income from continuing operations.

Solution Guide

Problem 4   Changes in PP&E Accounts
                      (1187,P4)

1. Part a. requires a schedule analyzing the changes in each of the plant assets during 1986; part b. requires a schedule of depreciation expense for each asset classification; and part c. requires a schedule showing the gain or loss from each asset disposal. The solutions approach for problems of this type in which the requirements are interrelated is to prepare time lines for each depreciable asset, make all required computations for each asset at one time, and label each computation according to the requirement to which it relates. For example, if a number or computation relates to requirement b., it can be labeled "(b)." Using this approach, the candidate will be solving a part of each requirement as each asset is covered, but not necessarily in the same order as given on the exam.

2. The only transactions affecting the land account involved the purchase of land in November. All the costs of the land and the old building are considered to be costs of the land because the land was purchased for the purpose of constructing a new building.

Therefore, the market value of the stock issued for the land and building (10,000 x $38 = $380,000), the legal fees and title insurance ($23,000), and the cost of razing the old building ($35,000) are all considered part of the cost of obtaining

the land and preparing it for its intended use. The **market value** of the stock is used because it indicates the cash equivalent price of the land. Note that the assessed values are not used because they are not as reliable as the cash equivalent price implied in the purchase transaction.

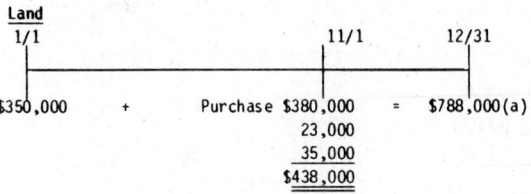

3. None of the transactions affect the land improvements account. The $50,000 spent to repair damage to parking lots caused by severe winter weather should be charged to a loss or expense account. This expenditure merely restores the parking lots to their condition before the damage and is a measure of the loss caused by the severe weather.

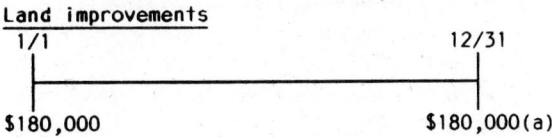

3.1 Depreciation expense on land improvements is computed on a straight-line basis over 15 years with no salvage value ($180,000 ÷ 15 = $12,000) for part b.

4. None of the transactions affected the building account during 1986.

Buildings

1/1	12/31
$1,500,000	$1,500,000(a)

4.1 Depreciation expense on the building is computed on a 150% declining balance basis over 20 years. Using this method, depreciation expense is computed by multiplying the beginning-of-year book value ($1,500,000 − $350,000 = $1,150,000) by 150% of the straight-line rate (1/20 x 150% = 7½%). This results in 1986 depreciation expense of $86,250 (part b).

5. The machinery and equipment account was increased by $287,000 on January 2 by a purchase. This cost includes all expenditures necessary to acquire the

equipment and prepare it for use:
invoice cost ($260,000 including $5,500
freight) and installation costs
($27,000), for a total of $287,000. The
machinery and equipment account was
decreased on March 31 when a machine
which originally cost $58,000 was sold.

Machine and equipment

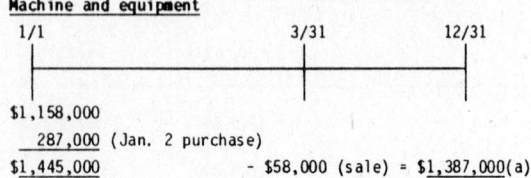

$1,158,000
 287,000 (Jan. 2 purchase)
$1,445,000   - $58,000 (sale) = $1,387,000(a)

5.1 Depreciation expense on the machinery and
equipment must be computed in two
parts: on the machine sold ($58,000 ÷ 10
years x 3/12 = $1,450) and on the
machinery owned the entire year. The
beginning balance of machinery and
equipment was $1,158,000, and machinery
was purchased on 1/2/86 for $287,000 to
bring the balance up to $1,445,000 (see
para 5. of this solution guide). The
sale of machinery which originally cost
$58,000 brought the balance down to
$1,387,000. This is the amount of
machinery that was owned the entire
year. Depreciation on this amount is
$138,700 ($1,387,000 ÷ 10 years). Thus,
total depreciation on machinery and
equipment is $140,150 ($138,700 +
$1,450).

Depreciation expense - machinery and equipment

$1,158,000
 287,000 ⌐ $1,387,000 ÷ 10   = $138,700 ⌐
$1,445,000 {   } $140,150(b)
         ⌐ $ 58,000 ÷ 10 x 3/12 = 1,450 ⌐

5.2 The sale of the machinery on 3/31
resulted in a gain on disposal. The gain
or loss on disposal is computed by
comparing the proceeds from the sale
($36,500) and the book value of the asset
sold. The asset sold cost $58,000 and
had been depreciated for 4 years prior to
1986 (1982 to 1985) and 3 months in 1986.
Therefore, accumulated depreciation at
the time of sale was $24,650 [($58,000 ÷
10) x 4 3/12 years], and the book value
was $33,350 ($58,000 - $24,650),
resulting in a gain of $3,150 ($36,500 -
$33,350).

Proceeds	Book value		Gain
	$ 58,000	Cost	
	(24,650)	A.D.[($58,000 ÷ 10) x 4 3/12]	
$36,500 -	$ 33,350	=	$3,150 (c)

6. The automobile account was increased by
$19,000 on 12/31/86 when a new auto was
obtained in an exchange. On the same
date, the automobile account was
decreased by the removal of the old auto
(cost, $18,000) which was exchanged for
the new auto.

Automobiles

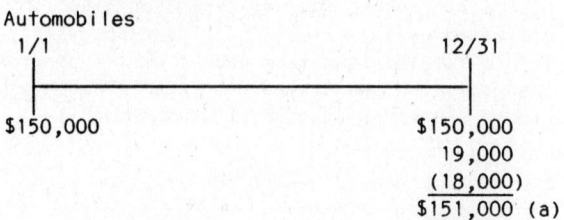

$150,000 $150,000
                       19,000
                      (18,000)
                     $151,000 (a)

6.1 Depreciation expense on the automobiles
is computed on the beginning-of-year
balance of $150,000. All of these
automobiles were owned the entire year
(even the one disposed of on 12/31). No
depreciation is recorded on the auto
obtained on 12/31 ($19,000) because it
was only owned for one day in 1986. The
depreciation method used for the automobiles is 150% declining basis over 3
years. Using this method, depreciation
is computed by multiplying the beginning-
of-year book value ($150,000 - $112,000 =
$38,000) by 150% of the straight-line
rate (1/3 x 150% = 50%). This results in
1986 depreciation expense of $19,000
(part b).

6.2 The exchange of automobiles on 12/31
resulted in a loss on disposal. Per
APB 29, this loss should be recognized
even though the exchange involves similar
productive assets. The gain or loss is
the difference between the FMV of the old
auto and its BV. The old auto was traded
with $15,250 cash for a new auto with a
cash value of $19,000, so the FMV of the
old auto is $3,750 ($19,000 - $15,250).
The old auto was purchased on 1/2/85, so
it has been depreciated for two years.
1985 depreciation was $9,000 ($18,000 x
50%), and 1986 depreciation was $4,500
[($18,000 - 9,000) x 50%]. Therefore,
the BV of the old auto is $4,500 [$18,000
- ($9,000 + $4,500)], resulting in a loss
on disposal of $750.

FMV	BV	Gain (loss)
$ 19,000	$ 18,000	
(15,250)	(13,500)	
$ 3,750 -	$ 4,500	= $(750) (c)

The journal entry would have been:

Loss on disposal	750	
Auto (new)	19,000	
Accumulated depreciation	13,500	
Auto (old)		18,000
Cash		15,250

Unofficial Answer
Problem 4   Changes in PP&E Accounts
            (1187,P4)

a.

Pell Corporation
ANALYSIS OF CHANGES IN PLANT ASSETS
For the Year Ended December 31, 1986

	Balance 12/31/85	Increase	Decrease	Balance 12/31/86
Land	$ 350,000	$438,000 [1]	$ --	$ 788,000
Land improvements	180,000	--	--	180,000
Building	1,500,000	--	--	1,500,000
Machinery and equipment	1,158,000	287,000 [2]	58,000	1,387,000
Automobiles	150,000	19,000 [3]	18,000	151,000
Total	$3,338,000	$744,000	$76,000	$4,006,000

Explanation of Amounts:

[1]	Cost of land acquired 11/1/86	
	Pell stock exchanged (10,000 x $38)	$380,000
	Legal fees and title insurance	23,000
	Razing existing building	35,000
		$438,000

[2]	Cost of machinery and equipment purchased 1/2/86	
	Invoice cost	$260,000
	Installation cost	27,000
		$287,000

[3]	Cost recorded for new automobile 12/31/86	
	Carrying amount of trade-in	
	[$18,000 - $13,500 (depreciation 150% declining	
	balance at rate of 50% for 2 years)]	$ 4,500
	Cash paid	15,250
	Subtotal	$19,750
	Loss on trade-in	750
	Cost recorded for new automobile	$19,000

Problem 4 (continued)

b.

Pell Corporation
DEPRECIATION EXPENSE
For the Year Ended December 31, 1986

Land improvements			
Cost		$ 180,000	
Straight-line rate [100% ÷ 15]		x 6 2/3%	
Total depreciation on land improvements			$ 12,000
Building			
Carrying amount 12/31/85 ($1,500,000 – $350,000)		$1,150,000	
150% declining balance rate [(100% ÷ 20) x 1½]		x 7 1/2%	
Total depreciation on building			86,250
Machinery and equipment			
Balance, 12/31/85	$1,158,000		
Deduct machine sold 3/31/86	58,000	$1,100,000	
Depreciation straight-line rate		x 10%	110,000
Purchased 1/2/86		287,000	
Depreciation		x 10%	28,700
Machine sold 3/31/86		58,000	
Depreciation from 1/1/ to 3/31/86 (10% x ¼)		x 2.5%	1,450
Total depreciation on machinery and equipment			140,150
Automobiles			
Carrying amount 12/31/85 ($150,000 – $112,000)		$ 38,000	
150% declining balance rate [100% ÷ 3 x 1½]		x 50%	
Total depreciation on automobiles			19,000
Total depreciation expense for 1986			$257,400

c.

Pell Corporation
GAIN OR LOSS FROM PLANT ASSET DISPOSALS
THAT WOULD BE RECOGNIZED IN INCOME STATEMENT
For the Year Ended December 31, 1986

	Gain or (loss)
Sale of machine 3/31/86	
Selling price	$36,500
Carrying amount of machine sold	
[$58,000 – $24,650 (Depreciation 4¼ years x 10%)]	33,350
Gain on sale	3,150
Trade-in of automobile 12/31/86	
Carrying amount of trade-in	$ 4,500 [3]
Trade-in allowed ($19,000 – $15,250)	3,750
Loss on trade-in	$ (750)
Gain from asset disposals	$ 2,400

Solution Guide

Problem 5   Comprehensive PP & E Changes
(1188,P4)

1. Part (a) requires a schedule analyzing the changes in each of the plant asset accounts during 1987, and part (b) requires a schedule of depreciation or amortization expense for each asset category. The solutions approach for problems of this type in which the requirements are interrelated is to prepare time lines for each asset, make all required computations for each asset at one time, and label each computation according to the requirement [(a) or (b)] to which it relates.

2. The only transaction affecting the land account was the basket purchase of land and building on 1/6/87 at a total cost of $1,250,000 (25,000 shares issued x $50 per share). In a basket purchase, total cost should be allocated based on the relative market value of the assets acquired. If market values are not available, appraisal or assessed values may be used. There-fore, the $1,250,000 is allocated as follows:

$1,250,000 x ($187,500/$750,000) = $312,500   Land

$1,250,000 x ($562,500/$750,000) = $937,500   Building

The change in the land account is illustrated below:

Land

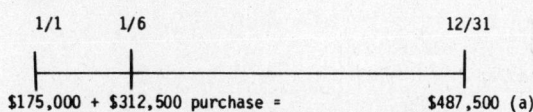

$175,000 + $312,500 purchase = $487,500 (a)

2.1 On 11/4/87, Cord purchased for $350,000 a tract of land as a potential future building site. Real estate held for future use is generally reported as a long-term investment. It does not affect the plant asset account land because it is not going to be currently used in normal operations.

3. The buildings account is affected only by the basket purchase (see item 2 above).

Buildings

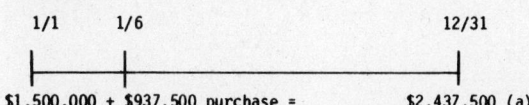

$1,500,000 + $937,500 purchase = $2,437,500 (a)

3.1 Depreciation expense on the buildings is computed on a 150% declining balance basis over 25 years. Using this method, depre-ciation expense is the beginning-of-year book value multiplied by 150% of the straight-line rate (1/25 x 150% = 6%).

The old buildings had a book value of $1,171,100 ($1,500,000 - $328,900) at 1/1/87. Total depreciation expense on the buildings is $126,516, as computed below:

Old: $1,171,000 x 6% = $70,266

$126,516 (b)

New: $ 937,500 x 6% = 56,250

Note that for the new building, the carrying amount equals the cost, since no depreciation has yet been recorded. A full year's depreciation is recorded since the new building was used for nearly 12 months.

4. The machinery and equipment account was increased by $385,000 on 7/1/87 by a purchase. This cost includes all expenditures necessary to acquire the assets and prepare them for use: invoice cost ($325,000), delivery cost ($10,000), and installation cost ($50,000), for a total of $385,000. The machinery and equipment account was decreased on 12/20/87 when a machine which originally cost $17,000 was scrapped.

Machinery and equipment

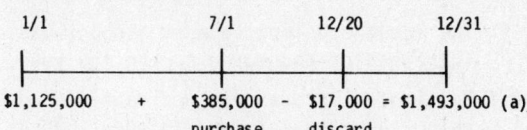

$1,125,000   + $385,000 - $17,000 = $1,493,000 (a)
                   purchase   discard

4.1 Depreciation expense on the machinery and equipment must be computed in two parts: on the machinery owned the entire year (including the machinery scrapped on 12/20 which is considered used for 12 months), and on the machinery purchased on 7/1 (six months depreciation). Depreciation is computed on a straight-line basis over 10 years. Total depreciation expense is $131,750, as shown below:

Depreciation expense - machinery and equipment

Old: $1,125,000 ÷ 10   = $112,500

$131,750 (b)

New: $385,000 ÷ 10 x 6/12 =   19,250

5. The automobiles and trucks account was increased by $12,500 on 8/30/87 when a new automobile was purchased. On 9/30/87, the account was decreased when a truck which originally cost $24,000 was sold.

Automobiles and trucks

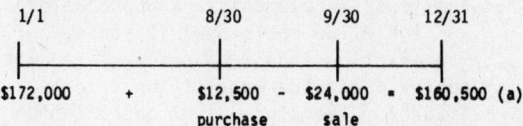

$172,000   + $12,500 - $24,000 = $160,500 (a)
                 purchase   sale

5.1 Depreciation expense on automobiles and trucks is computed on a 150% declining balance basis over five years. Using this method, depreciation expense is the beginning-of-year book value multiplied by <u>150% of the straight-line rate</u> (1/5 x 150% = 30%). Depreciation on this asset must be computed in three parts: on the assets owned the entire year, on the truck sold on 9/30/87 (9 months), and on the auto purchased on 8/30/87 (4 months). The beginning-of-the-year book value for automobiles and trucks is $71,675 ($172,000 - $100,325). This amount includes the beginning-of-year book value of the truck sold ($9,100 book value at time of sale, plus $2,650 1987 depreciation, equals $11,750 beginning-of-year book value), which must be subtracted to determine the beginning-of-year book value of the assets owned the entire year ($71,675 - $11,750 = $59,925). Total depreciation on automobiles and trucks is $21,878, as computed below.

<u>Depreciation expense - automobiles and trucks</u>

	Book value	Depreciation
Old:	$71,675	
	<u>(11,750)</u> Amount given = $ 2,650	
	<u>$59,925</u> x 30% = $17,978	$21,878 (b)
New:	$12,500 x 30% x 4/12 = $ 1,250	

6. The leasehold improvements account was not increased or decreased during the year.

6.1 Leasehold improvements are depreciated using the straight-line method. Depreciation should be recorded over the remaining life of the lease, or the useful life of the improvements, whichever is shorter. Prior to 1987, Cord had depreciated the improvements over the lease term excluding the option (6 years) which was less than the useful life (8 years). Note that at 12/31/86, accumulated depreciation is 3/6 of original cost. In 1987, the renewal option was exercised, so the remaining book value ($216,000 - $108,000 = $108,000) should be depreciated over the remaining useful life (8 years - 3 years = 5 years), which is less than the remaining lease term including option period (6 years - 3 years + 4 years = 7 years). Therefore, 1987 depreciation expense is $21,600 ($108,000 ÷ 5 = $21,600).

7. The only activity in the land improvements was the $192,000 cost of improvements completed on 3/25/87.

7.1 The land improvements are depreciated on a straight-line basis over 12 years. Depreciation should be recorded for nine months since the acquisition date is 3/25/87. Therefore, 1987 depreciation is $12,000 ($192,000 ÷ 12 x 9/12).

Unofficial Answer

Problem 5   Comprehensive PP & E Changes (1188,P4)

a.

Cord Company
ANALYSIS OF CHANGES IN PLANT ASSETS
For the Year Ended December 31, 1987

	Balance 12/31/86	Increase	Decrease	Balance 12/31/87
Land	$ 175,000	$ 312,500 [1]	$ --	$ 487,500
Land improvements	--	192,000	--	192,000
Buildings	1,500,000	937,500 [1]	--	2,437,500
Machinery and equipment	1,125,000	385,000 [2]	17,000	1,493,000
Automobiles and trucks	172,000	12,500	24,000	160,500
Leasehold improvements	216,000	--	--	216,000
	$3,188,000	$1,839,500	$41,000	$4,986,500

Explanations of Amounts:

[1] Plant facility acquired from King 1/6/87--
        allocation to Land and Building
          Fair value--25,000 shares of Cord
          common stock at $50 market price $1,250,000

        Allocation in proportion to appraised
        values at the exchange date

	Amount	% to Total
Land	$187,500	25
Building	562,500	75
	$750,000	100

Land	($1,250,000 x 25%)	$ 312,500
Building	($1,250,000 x 75%)	937,500
		$1,250,000

[2] Machinery and equipment purchased 7/1/87
        Invoice cost $ 325,000
        Delivery cost   10,000
        Installation cost   50,000
          Total acquisition cost $ 385,000

b.

Cord Company
DEPRECIATION AND AMORTIZATION EXPENSE
For the Year Ended December 31, 1987

Land improvements		
Cost	$ 192,000	
Straight-line rate (100% ÷ 12)	x 8 1/3%	
Annual depreciation	16,000	
Depreciation on land improvements for 1987		
(3/25 to 12/31/87)	x 3/4	$ 12,000
Buildings		
Carrying amount, 1/1/87 ($1,500,000 − $328,900)	$1,171,100	
Building acquired 1/6/87	937,500	
Total amount subject to depreciation	2,108,600	
150% declining balance rate [(100% ÷ 25) x 1.5]	x 6%	
Depreciation on buildings for 1987		126,516
Machinery and equipment		
Balance, 1/1/87	$1,125,000	
Straight-line rate (100% ÷ 10)	x 10%	112,500
Purchased 7/1/87	385,000	
Depreciation for 1987 (10% x 6/12)	x 5%	19,250
Depreciation on machinery and equipment for 1987		131,750
Automobiles and trucks		
Carrying amount, 1/1/87 ($172,000 − $100,325)	$ 71,675	
Deduct carrying amount, 1/1/87 on		
truck sold 9/30/87 ($9,100 + $2,650)	11,750	
Amount subject to depreciation	59,925	
150% declining balance rate [(100% ÷ 5) x 1.5]	x 30%	17,978
Automobile purchased 8/30/87	12,500	
Depreciation for 1987 (30% x 4/12)	x 10%	1,250
Truck sold 9/30/87--depreciation		
for 1987 (1/1 to 9/30/87)		2,650
Depreciation on automobiles and trucks for 1987		21,878
Leasehold improvements		
Carrying amount, 1/1/87 ($216,000 − $108,000)	$ 108,000	
Amortization period (1/1/87 to 12/31/91)	÷ 5 years	
Amortization in leasehold improvements for 1987		21,600
Total depreciation and amortization expense for 1987		$213,744

Multiple Choice Questions (1-67)

1. Burr Company had the following account balances at December 31, 1987:

Cash in banks	$2,250,000
Cash on hand	125,000
Cash legally restricted for additions to plant (expected to be disbursed in 1988)	1,600,000

Cash in banks includes $600,000 of compensating balances against short-term borrowing arrangements. The compensating balances are not legally restricted as to withdrawal by Burr. In the current assets section of Burr's December 31, 1987 balance sheet, total cash should be reported at

    a. $1,775,000
    b. $2,250,000
    c. $2,375,000
    d. $3,975,000

2. Ral Corp.'s checkbook balance on December 31, 1988 was $5,000. In addition, Ral held the following items in its safe on that date:

Check payable to Ral Corp., dated January 2, 1989, in payment of a sale made in December 1988, not included in December 31 checkbook balance	$2,000
Check payable to Ral Corp., deposited December 15 and included in December 31 checkbook balance, but returned by Bank on December 30 stamped "NSF." The check was redeposited on January 2, 1989 and cleared on January 9	500
Check drawn on Ral Corp.'s account, payable to a vendor, dated and recorded in Ral's books on December 31 but not mailed until January 10, 1989	300

The proper amount to be shown as Cash on Ral's balance sheet at December 31, 1988 is

    a. $4,800
    b. $5,300
    c. $6,500
    d. $6,800

3. In preparing its bank reconciliation at December 31, 1987, Case Company has available the following data:

Balance per bank statement, 12/31/87	$38,075
Deposit in transit, 12/31/87	5,200
Outstanding checks, 12/31/87	6,750
Amount erroneously credited by bank to Case's account, 12/28/87	400
Bank service charges for December	75

Case's adjusted cash in bank balance at December 31, 1987 is

    a. $36,525
    b. $36,450
    c. $36,125
    d. $36,050

4. Orr Company had the following bank reconciliation at March 31, 1986:

Balance per bank statement, 3/31/86	$46,500
Add: Deposit in transit	10,300
	56,800
Less: Outstanding checks	12,600
Balance per books, 3/31/86	$44,200

Data per bank statement for the month of April 1986 follow:

Deposits	$58,400
Disbursements	49,700

All reconciliation items at March 31, 1986, cleared through the bank in April. Outstanding checks at April 30, 1986 totaled $7,500. What is the amount of cash disbursements per books in April?

    a. $44,600
    b. $49,700
    c. $54,800
    d. $57,200

5. Lewis Company began operations on January 1, 1983. The following information is available for the year ended December 31, 1983:

Total merchandise purchases	$700,000
Merchandise inventory at 12/31/83	140,000
Collections from customers	400,000

All merchandise is marked to sell at 40% above cost. Assume that all sales are credit sales and all receivables are collectible. The balance in accounts receivable at December 31, 1983 should be

    a. $160,000
    b. $244,000
    c. $300,000
    d. $384,000

6. Bowy Company had the following information relating to its accounts receivable:

Accounts receivable at 12/31/86	$1,300,000
Credit sales for 1987	5,400,000
Collections from customers for 1987	4,750,000
Accounts written off 9/30/87	125,000
Collection of accounts written off in prior years (customer credit was not reestablished)	25,000
Estimated uncollectible receivables per aging of receivables at 12/31/87	165,000

At December 31, 1987, Roxy's accounts receivable, before allowance for uncollectible accounts, should be

   a. $1,825,000
   b. $1,850,000
   c. $1,950,000
   d. $1,990,000

7.   The following information pertains to Oro Corp:

Credit sales for the year ended December 31, 1988	$450,000
Credit balance in allowance for uncollectible accounts at January 1, 1988	10,800
Bad debts written off during 1988	18,000

According to past experience, 3% of Oro's credit sales have been uncollectible. After provision is made for bad debt expense for the year ended December 31, 1988, the allowance for uncollectible accounts balance would be

   a. $ 6,300
   b. $13,500
   c. $24,300
   d. $31,500

8.   Clark Company's allowance for doubtful accounts had a credit balance of $12,000 at December 31, 1985. Clark accrues doubtful accounts expense at 4% of credit sales. During 1986 Clark's credit sales amounted to $1,500,000, and uncollectible accounts totaling $48,000 were written off. The aging of accounts receivable indicated that a $50,000 allowance for doubtful accounts was required at December 31, 1986. Clark's doubtful accounts expense for 1986 would be

   a. $48,000
   b. $50,000
   c. $60,000
   d. $86,000

Items 9 and 10 are based on the following data:

Rex Company had the following information relating to its accounts receivable at December 31, 1984, and for the year ended December 31, 1985:

Accounts receivable at 12/31/84	$1,200,000
Allowance for doubtful accounts at 12/31/84	60,000
Credit sales for 1985	5,300,000
Collections from customers for 1985	4,650,000
Accounts written off 9/30/85	75,000
Estimated uncollectible receivables per aging of receivables at 12/31/85	110,000

9.   At December 31, 1985, Rex's allowance for doubtful accounts should be

   a. $135,000
   b. $125,000
   c. $110,000
   d. $ 95,000

10.   At December 31, 1985, Rex's accounts receivable, before the allowance for doubtful accounts, should be

   a. $1,850,000
   b. $1,835,000
   c. $1,815,000
   d. $1,775,000

11.   Based on the aging of its accounts receivable at December 31, 1985, Terry Company determined that the net realizable value of the receivables at that date is $190,000. Additional information is as follows:

Accounts receivable at 12/31/85	$220,000
Allowance for doubtful accounts at 1/1/85--credit balance	32,000
Accounts written off as uncollectible at 9/30/85	24,000

Terry's doubtful accounts expense for the year ended December 31, 1985 is

   a. $38,000
   b. $30,000
   c. $26,000
   d. $22,000

12.   All of Ladd Co.'s sales are on a credit basis. The following information is available for 1985:

Allowance for doubtful accounts, 1/1/85	$ 9,000
Sales	475,000
Sales returns	40,000
Accounts written off as uncollectible	10,000

Ladd provides for doubtful accounts expense at the rate of 3% of net sales. At December 31, 1985, the allowance for doubtful accounts balance should be

   a. $14,050
   b. $13,250
   c. $13,050
   d. $12,050

13.   A company uses the allowance method to recognize uncollectible accounts expense. What is the effect at the time of the collection of an account previously written off on each of the following accounts?

	Allowance for uncollectible accounts	Uncollectible accounts expense
a.	No effect	Decrease
b.	Increase	Decrease
c.	Increase	No effect
d.	No effect	No effect

14. A method of estimating uncollectible accounts that emphasizes asset valuation rather than income measurement is the allowance method based on
   a. Aging the receivables.
   b. Direct write off.
   c. Gross sales.
   d. Credit sales less returns and allowances.

15. Which of the following is a method to generate cash from accounts receivables?

	Assignment	Factoring
a.	Yes	No
b.	Yes	Yes
c.	No	Yes
d.	No	No

16. Fay, Inc. received a $30,000, six-month, 12% interest-bearing note from a customer. The note was discounted the same day by Carr National Bank at 15%. The amount of cash received by Fay from the bank was
   a. $30,000
   b. $29,550
   c. $29,415
   d. $27,750

17. On June 30, 1985, Ray Co. discounted at the bank a customer's $60,000, six-month, 10% note receivable dated April 30, 1985. The bank discounted the note at 12%. Ray's proceeds from this discounted note amounted to
   a. $56,400
   b. $57,600
   c. $60,480
   d. $61,740

18. A note receivable bearing a reasonable interest rate is sold to a bank with recourse. At the date of the discounting transaction, the notes receivable discounted account should be
   a. Decreased by the proceeds from the discounting transaction.
   b. Increased by the proceeds from the discounting transaction.
   c. Increased by the face amount of the note.
   d. Decreased by the face amount of the note.

19. On September 1, 1986, a company borrowed cash and signed a two-year interest-bearing note on which both the principal and interest are payable on September 1, 1988. How many months of accrued interest would be included in the liability for accrued interest at December 31, 1986, and December 31, 1987?

	At December 31, 1986	At December 31, 1987
a.	4 months	16 months
b.	4 months	4 months
c.	12 months	24 months
d.	20 months	8 months

20. On July 1, 1986, a company received a one-year note receivable bearing interest at the market rate. The face amount of the note receivable and the entire amount of the interest are due on June 30, 1987. The interest receivable account would show a balance on
   a. July 1, 1986, but not December 31, 1986.
   b. December 31, 1986, but not July 1, 1986.
   c. July 1, 1986, and December 31, 1986.
   d. Neither July 1, 1986, nor December 1, 1986.

21. A company borrowed cash from a bank and issued to the bank a short-term noninterest-bearing note payable. The bank discounted the note at 10% and remitted the proceeds to the company. The effective interest rate paid by the company in this transaction would be
   a. Equal to the stated discount rate of 10%.
   b. More than the stated discount rate of 10%.
   c. Less than the stated discount rate of 10%.
   d. Independent of the stated discount rate of 10%.

22. On July 1, 1986, Cody Company obtained a $2,000,000, 180-day bank loan at an annual rate of 12%. The loan agreement requires Cody to maintain a $400,000 compensating balance in its checking account at the lending bank. Cody would otherwise maintain a balance of only $200,000 in this account. The checking account earns interest at an annual rate of 6%. Based on a 360-day year, the effective interest rate on the borrowing is
   a. 12.00%
   b. 12.67%
   c. 13.33%
   d. 13.50%

23. Bloy Company pays all salaried employees on a biweekly basis. Overtime pay, however, is paid in the next biweekly period. Bloy accrues salaries expense only at its December 31 year end. Data relating to salaries earned in December 1986 are as follows:

• Last payroll was paid on 12/26/86, for the 2-week period ended 12/26/86.
• Overtime pay earned in the 2-week period ended 12/26/86 was $4,200.
• Remaining work days in 1986 were December 29, 30, and 31, on which days there was no overtime.
• The recurring biweekly salaries total $75,000.

Assuming a five-day work week, Bloy should record a liability at December 31, 1986 for accrued salaries of
a. $22,500
b. $26,700
c. $45,000
d. $49,200

24. On September 1, 1985, Pine Company issued a note payable to National Bank in the amount of $1,800,000, bearing interest at 12%, and payable in three equal annual principal payments of $600,000. On this date the bank's prime rate was 11%. The first interest and principal payment was made on September 1, 1986. At December 31, 1986, Pine should record accrued interest payable of
a. $44,000
b. $48,000
c. $66,000
d. $72,000

25. Arno Corp.'s liability account balances at June 30, 1988 included a 10% note payable in the amount of $1,800,000. The note is dated October 1, 1987 and is payable in three equal annual payments of $600,000 plus interest. The first interest and principal payment was made on October 1, 1988. In Arno's June 30, 1989 balance sheet, what amount should be reported as accrued interest payable for this note?
a. $135,000
b. $ 90,000
c. $ 45,000
d. $ 30,000

26. Robb Company requires advance payments with special orders from customers for machinery constructed to their specifications. Information for 1988 is as follows:

Customer advances--balance 12/31/87	$295,000
Advances received with orders in 1988	460,000
Advances applied to orders shipped in 1988	410,000
Advances applicable to orders cancelled in 1988	125,000

At December 31, 1988, what amount should Robb report as a current liability for customer deposits?
a. $0
b. $220,000
c. $345,000
d. $370,000

27. Cobb Company sells appliance service contracts agreeing to repair appliances for a two-year period. Cobb's past experience is that, of the total dollars spent for repairs on service contracts, 40% is incurred evenly during the first contract year and 60% evenly during the second contract year. Receipts from service contract sales for the two years ended December 31, 1986 are as follows:

1985	$500,000
1986	600,000

Receipts from contracts are credited to unearned service contract revenue. Assume that all contract sales are made evenly during the year. What amount should Cobb report as unearned service contract revenue at December 31, 1986?
a. $360,000
b. $470,000
c. $480,000
d. $630,000

28. Ral Corp. has an incentive compensation plan under which a branch manager receives 10% of the branch's income after deduction of the bonus but before deduction of income tax. Branch income for 1988 before the bonus and income tax was $165,000. The tax rate was 30%. The 1988 bonus amounted to
a. $12,600
b. $15,000
c. $16,500
d. $18,000

29. Bain Company salaried employees are paid biweekly. Occasionally, advances made to employees are paid back by payroll deductions. Information relating to salaries for the calendar year 1986 is as follows:

	12/31/85	12/31/86
Employee advances	$12,000	$18,000
Accrued salaries payable	65,000	?
Salaries expense during the year		815,000
Salaries paid during the year (gross)		780,000

At December 31, 1986, what amount should Bain report for accrued salaries payable?
a. $100,000
b. $ 94,000
c. $ 82,000
d. $ 35,000

30. Included in Witt Corp.'s liability account balances at December 31, 1988 were the following:

14% note payable issued October 1, 1988, maturing September 30, 1989	$500,000
16% note payable issued April 1, 1986, payable in six equal annual installments of $200,000 beginning April 1, 1987	800,000

Witt's December 31, 1988 financial statements were issued on March 31, 1989. On January 15, 1989, the entire $800,000 balance of the 16% note was refinanced by issuance of a long-term obligation payable in a lump sum. In addition, on March 10, 1989, Witt consummated a noncancelable agreement with the lender to refinance the 14%, $500,000 note on a long-term basis, on readily determinable terms that have not yet been implemented. Both parties are financially capable of honoring the agreement, and there have been no violations of the agreement's provisions. On the December 31, 1988 balance sheet, the amount of the notes payable that Witt should classify as short-term obligations is
   a. $700,000
   b. $500,000
   c. $200,000
   d. $0

31. Pam, Inc. has $1,000,000 of notes payable due June 15, 1989. At the financial statement date of December 31, 1988, Pam signed an agreement to borrow up to $1,000,000 to refinance the notes payable on a long-term basis. The financing agreement called for borrowings not to exceed 80% of the value of the collateral Pam was providing. At the date of issue of the December 31, 1988 financial statements, the value of the collateral was $1,200,000 and was not expected to fall below this amount during 1989. In its December 31, 1988 balance sheet, Pam should classify notes payable as

	Short-term obligations	Long-term obligations
a.	$0	$1,000,000
b.	$ 40,000	$ 960,000
c.	$ 200,000	$ 800,000
d.	$1,000,000	$0

32. A state requires quarterly sales tax returns to be filed with the sales tax bureau by the 20th day following the end of the calendar quarter. However, the state further requires that sales taxes collected be remitted to the sales tax bureau by the 20th day of the month following any month such collections exceed $500. These payments can be taken as credits on the quarterly sales tax return.

Taft Corp. operates a retail hardware store. All items are sold subject to a 6% state sales tax, which Taft collects and records as sales revenue. The sales taxes paid by Taft are charged against sales revenue. Taft pays the sales taxes when they are due.

Following is a monthly summary appearing in Taft's first quarter 1989 sales revenue account:

	Debit	Credit
January	$ –	$10,600
February	600	7,420
March	–	9,540
	$600	$27,560

In its financial statements for the quarter ended March 31, 1989, Taft's sales revenue and sales taxes payable would be

	Sales revenue	Sales taxes payable
a.	$27,560	$1,560
b.	$26,960	$ 600
c.	$26,000	$1,560
d.	$26,000	$ 960

33. Farr Company sells its products in reusable, expensive containers. The customer is charged a deposit for each container delivered and receives a refund for each container returned within two years after the year of delivery. Farr accounts for the containers not returned within the time limit as being retired by sale at the deposit amount. Information for 1985 is as follows:

Containers held by customers at December 31, 1984 from deliveries in:

1983	$ 75,000	
1984	215,000	$290,000
Containers delivered in 1985		390,000

Containers returned in 1985 from deliveries in:

1983	$ 45,000	
1984	125,000	
1985	143,000	313,000

What amount should Farr report as a liability for returnable containers at December 31, 1985?
   a. $247,000
   b. $322,000
   c. $337,000
   d. $367,000

34. Fay Corp. pays its outside salespersons fixed monthly salaries and commissions on net sales. Sales commissions are computed and paid on a monthly basis (in the month following the month of sale), and the fixed salaries

are treated as advances against commissions. However, if the fixed salaries for salespersons exceed their sales commissions earned for a month, such excess is not charged back to them. Pertinent data for the month of March 1988 for the three salespersons are as follows:

Salesperson	Fixed salary	Net sales	Commission rate
A	$10,000	$ 200,000	4%
B	14,000	400,000	6%
C	18,000	600,000	6%
Totals	$42,000	$1,200,000	

What amount should Fay accrue for sales commissions payable at March 31, 1988?

a. $70,000
b. $68,000
c. $28,000
d. $26,000

35. Grey operates as a retail furrier. Some customers pick out furs and place deposits with Grey to set the furs aside for future delivery. Grey records the cash receipts on these transactions as lay-away plan sales. However, title to the fur passes to the customer only when the full sales price is received by Grey. The average gross margin on the furs is 75% of sales. The following pertinent data were taken from Grey's December 31, 1988 unadjusted trial balance:

Regular sales	$2,500,000
Lay-away plan sales	$1,000,000
Deposits from customers	$0

An analysis of the lay-away plan sales revealed that $600,000 was received in full payment for furs delivered to customers during 1988. In Grey's December 31, 1988 balance sheet, deposits from customers would be

a. $1,000,000
b. $ 750,000
c. $ 600,000
d. $ 400,000

36. A retail store received cash and issued a gift certificate that is redeemable in merchandise. When the gift certificate was issued, a

a. Deferred revenue account should be decreased.
b. Deferred revenue account should be increased.
c. Revenue account should be decreased.
d. Revenue account should be increased.

37. A company receives an advance payment for special order goods that are to be manufactured and delivered within six months. The advance payment should be reported in the company's balance sheet as a

a. Deferred charge.
b. Contra asset account.
c. Current liability.
d. Noncurrent liability.

38. Which of the following is classified as an accrued liability?

	Liability for federal unemployment taxes	Liability for employer's share of FICA taxes
a.	Yes	Yes
b.	Yes	No
c.	No	No
d.	No	Yes

39. In packages of its products, Curran Co. includes coupons that may be presented at retail stores to obtain discounts on other Curran products. Retailers are reimbursed for the face amount of coupons redeemed plus 10% of that amount for handling costs. Curran honors requests for coupon redemption by retailers up to three months after the consumer expiration date. Curran estimates that 70% of all coupons issued will ultimately be redeemed. Information relating to coupons issued by Curran during 1988 is as follows:

Consumer expiration date	12/31/88
Total face amount of coupons issued	$600,000
Total payments to retailers as of 12/31/88	220,000

What amount should Curran report as a liability for unredeemed coupons at December 31, 1988?

a. $0
b. $200,000
c. $242,000
d. $308,000

40. During 1986, Ward Company introduced a new product carrying a two-year warranty against defects. The estimated warranty costs related to dollar sales are 2% within 12 months following sale and 4% in the second 12 months following sale. Sales and actual warranty expenditures for the years ended December 31, 1986 and 1987, are as follows:

	Sales	Actual warranty expenditures
1986	$300,000	$ 4,500
1987	500,000	15,000
	$800,000	$19,500

At December 31, 1987, Ward would report an estimated warranty liability of

a. $28,500
b. $22,500
c. $ 8,500
d. $ 5,000

41. On December 31, 1987, Beal Company was involved in a tax dispute with the IRS. Beal's tax counsel believed that an unfavorable outcome was probable and a reasonable estimate of additional taxes was $550,000, with a chance that the additional taxes could be as much as $850,000. After the 1987 financial statements were issued, Beal accepted the IRS settlement offer of $650,000. What amount of additional taxes should have been charged to income in 1987?

    a. $850,000
    b. $650,000
    c. $550,000
    d. $0

42. On November 5, 1986, a Dunn Corp. truck was in an accident with an auto driven by Bell. Dunn received notice on January 12, 1987 of a lawsuit for $700,000 damages for personal injuries suffered by Bell. Dunn Corp.'s counsel believes it is probable that Bell will be awarded an estimated amount in the range between $200,000 and $450,000, and that $300,000 is a better estimate of potential liability than any other amount. Dunn's accounting year ends on December 31, and the 1986 financial statements were issued on March 2, 1987. What amount of loss should Dunn accrue at December 31, 1986?

    a. $0
    b. $200,000
    c. $300,000
    d. $450,000

43. In March 1988, an explosion occurred at Nilo Co.'s plant, causing damage to area properties. By May 1988, no claims had yet been asserted against Nilo. However, Nilo's management and legal counsel concluded that it was reasonably possible that Nilo would be held responsible for negligence, and that $3,000,000 would be a reasonable estimate of the damages. Nilo's $5,000,000 comprehensive public liability policy contains a $300,000 deductible clause. In Nilo's December 31, 1987 financial statements, for which the auditor's field work was completed in April 1988, how should this casualty be reported?

    a.   As a footnote disclosing a possible liability of $3,000,000.
    b.   As an accrued liability of $300,000.
    c.   As a footnote disclosing a possible liability of $300,000.
    d.   No footnote disclosure or accrual is required for 1987 because the event occurred in 1988.

44. Tone Company is the defendant in a lawsuit filed by Witt in 1985 disputing the validity of a copyright held by Tone. At December 31, 1985, Tone determined that Witt would probably be successful against Tone for an estimated amount of $400,000. Appropriately, a $400,000 loss was accrued by a charge to income for the year ended December 31, 1985. On December 15, 1986, Tone and Witt agreed to a settlement providing for cash payment of $250,000 by Tone to Witt, and transfer of Tone's copyright to Witt. The carrying amount of the copyright on Tone's accounting records was $60,000 at December 15, 1986. What would be the effect of the settlement on Tone's income before income tax in 1986?

    a.   No effect.
    b. $ 60,000 decrease.
    c. $ 90,000 increase.
    d. $150,000 increase.

45. In May 1985, Croft Co. filed suit against Walton, Inc. seeking $950,000 damages for patent infringement. A court verdict in November 1988 awarded Croft $750,000 in damages, but Walton's appeal is not expected to be decided before 1990. Croft's counsel believes it is probable that Croft will be successful against Walton for an estimated amount in the range between $400,000 and $550,000, with $500,000 considered the most likely amount. What amount should Croft record as revenue from the lawsuit in the year ended December 31, 1988?

    a. $750,000
    b. $500,000
    c. $400,000
    d. $0

46. The following information pertains to a fire insurance policy in effect during the calendar year 1985, covering Vail Co.'s inventory:

Face amount of policy	$800,000
Deductible clause	50,000
Amount of premium	4,000
Coinsurance clause	80%

Vail's inventory averages $1,000,000 uniformly throughout the year. Vail's income tax rate is 40%. How much of a contingent liability should Vail accrue at December 31, 1985, to cover possible future fire losses?

    a. $0
    b. $ 30,000
    c. $ 46,000
    d. $120,000

47. When the occurrence of a gain contingency is reasonably possible and its amount can be reasonably estimated, the gain contingency should be

    a.   Included in net income and disclosed.
    b.   Included as an appropriation of retained earnings.

c.   Disclosed, but **not** included in net income.

d.   Neither included in net income nor disclosed.

48. A manufacturer of household appliances has potential costs due to the discovery of a possible defect in one of its products. The occurrence of the loss is reasonably possible and the costs can be reasonably estimated. This possible loss should be

	Accrued	Disclosed in footnotes
a.	No	No
b.	No	Yes
c.	Yes	Yes
d.	Yes	No

49. An expropriation of assets which is imminent and for which the amount of loss can be reasonably estimated should be

	Accrued	Disclosed
a.	No	No
b.	No	Yes
c.	Yes	Yes
d.	Yes	No

50. The following information relating to compensated absences was available from Graf Company's accounting records at December 31, 1988:

• Employees' rights to vacation pay vest and are attributable to services already rendered. Payment is probable, and Graf's obligation was reasonably estimated at $110,000.

• Employers' rights to sick pay benefits do not vest but accumulate for possible future use. The rights are attributable to services already rendered, and the total accumulated sick pay was reasonably estimated at $50,000.

What amount is Graf required to report as the liability for compensated absences in its December 31, 1988 balance sheet?
a. $160,000
b. $110,000
c. $ 50,000
d. $0

51. Ruhl Company grants all employees two weeks paid vacation for each full year of employment. Unused vacation time can be accumulated and carried forward to succeeding years, and will be paid at the salaries in effect when vacations are taken or when employment is terminated. There was no employee turnover in 1986. Additional information relating to the year ended December 31, 1986 is as follows:

Liability for accumulated vacations at 12/31/85	$25,000
Pre-1986 accrued vacations taken from 1/1/86 to 9/30/86 (the authorized period for vacations)	15,000
Vacations earned for work in 1986 (adjusted to current rates)	20,000

Ruhl granted a 10% salary increase to all employees on October 1, 1986, its annual salary increase date. For the year ended December 31, 1986, Ruhl should report vacation pay expense of
a. $21,000
b. $22,500
c. $30,000
d. $35,000

52. An employer's obligation relating to employee's rights to receive compensation for future absences is attributable to employees' services already rendered. The payment of compensation is probable and the amount of compensation can be reasonably estimated. Employees' compensation should be
a.   Accrued if the obligation relates to rights that vest or accumulate.
b.   Accrued if the obligation relates to rights that do **not** vest or accumulate.
c.   Expensed when paid.
d.   Disclosed, but **not** accrued if the obligation relates to rights that vest or accumulate.

53. Rogo Corp.'s trial balance reflected the following account balances at December 31, 1988:

Accounts receivable (net)	$16,000
Short-term investments	5,000
Accumulated depreciation on equipment and furniture	15,000
Cash	11,000
Inventory of merchandise	30,000
Equipment and furniture	25,000
Patent	4,000
Prepaid expenses	1,000
Land held for future business site	18,000

In Rogo Corp.'s December 31, 1988 balance sheet, the current assets total is
a. $81,000
b. $73,000
c. $67,000
d. $63,000

54. Lia Co.'s December 31, 1988 balance sheet reported the following current assets:

Cash	$ 35,000
Accounts receivable	60,000
Inventories	30,000
Total	$125,000

An analysis of the accounts disclosed that accounts receivable comprised the following:

Trade accounts	$48,000
Allowance for uncollectible accounts	(1,000)
Selling price of Lia's unsold goods sent to Jax Co. on consignment at 130% of cost and **not** included in Lia's ending inventory	13,000
Total	$60,000

At December 31, 1988, the correct total of Lia's current assets is

  a. $112,000
  b. $115,000
  c. $122,000
  d. $135,000

Items 55 through 57 are based on the following:

The following trial balance of Shaw Corp. at December 31, 1988 has been adjusted except for income tax expense.

Shaw Corp.
Trial Balance
December 31, 1988

	Dr.	Cr.
Cash	$ 675,000	
Accounts receivable (net)	2,695,000	
Inventory	2,185,000	
Property, plant, and equipment (net)	7,366,000	
Accounts payable and accrued liabilities		$1,801,000
Income tax payable		654,000
Deferred income tax liability		85,000
Common stock		2,300,000
Additional paid-in capital		3,680,000
Retained earnings, 1/1/88		3,350,000
Net sales and other revenues		13,360,000
Costs and expenses	11,180,000	
Income tax expense	1,129,000	
	$25,230,000	$25,230,000

Other financial data for the year ended December 31, 1988:

Included in the accounts receivable is $1,000,000 due from a customer and payable in quarterly installments of $125,000. The last payment is due December 30, 1990.

The balance in the deferred income tax liability account pertains to a temporary difference that arose in a prior year, of which $15,000 is expected to be paid in 1989. Shaw elected to apply the provisions of FASB Statement No. 96, Accounting for Income Taxes, in its

financial statements for the year ended December 31, 1988.

During the year, estimated tax payments of $475,000 were charged to income tax expense. The current and future tax rate on all types of income is 30%.

In Shaw's December 31, 1988 balance sheet,

55.   The current assets total is
  a. $6,030,000
  b. $5,555,000
  c. $5,530,000
  d. $5,055,000

56.   The current liabilities total is
  a. $1,995,000
  b. $2,065,000
  c. $2,470,000
  d. $2,540,000

57.   The final retained earnings balance is
  a. $4,401,000
  b. $4,486,000
  c. $4,876,000
  d. $5,055,000

May 1990 Questions

58.   The following accounts were abstracted from Roxy Co.'s unadjusted trial balance at December 31, 1989:

	Debit	Credit
Accounts receivable	$1,000,000	
Allowance for uncollectible accounts	8,000	
Net credit sales		$3,000,000

Roxy estimates that 3% of the gross accounts receivable will become uncollectible. After adjustment at December 31, 1989, the allowance for uncollectible accounts should have a credit balance of
  a. $90,000
  b. $82,000
  c. $38,000
  d. $30,000

59.   Rand, Inc. accepted from a customer a $40,000, 90-day, 12% interest bearing note dated August 31, 1989. On September 30, 1989, Rand discounted the note at the Apex State Bank at 15%. However, the proceeds were not received until October 1, 1989. In Rand's September 30, 1989 balance sheet, the amount receivable from the bank, based on a 360-day year, includes accrued interest revenue of
  a. $170
  b. $200
  c. $300
  d. $400

60.   For the year ended December 31, 1989, Beal Co. estimated its allowance for uncol-

lectible accounts using the year-end aging of accounts receivable. The following data are available:

Allowance for uncollectible accounts, 1/1/89	$42,000
Provision for uncollectible accounts during 1989 (2% on credit sales of $2,000,000)	40,000
Uncollectible accounts written off, 11/30/89	46,000
Estimated uncollectible accounts per aging, 12/31/89	52,000

After year-end adjustment, the uncollectible accounts expense for 1989 should be

    a. $46,000
    b. $48,000
    c. $52,000
    d. $56,000

61. On November 25, 1989, an explosion occurred at a Rex Co. plant causing extensive property damage to area buildings. By March 10, 1990, claims had been asserted against Rex. Rex's management and counsel concluded that it is probable Rex will be responsible for damages, and that $3,500,000 would be a reasonable estimate of its liability. Rex's $10,000,000 comprehensive public liability policy has a $500,000 deductible clause. Rex's December 31, 1989 financial statements, issued on March 25, 1990, should report this item as

    a. A footnote disclosure indicating the probable loss of $3,500,000.
    b. An accrued liability of $3,500,000.
    c. An accrued liability of $500,000.
    d. A footnote disclosure indicating the probable loss of $500,000.

62. Doren Co.'s officers' compensation expense account had a balance of $490,000 at December 31, 1989 before any appropriate year-end adjustment relating to the following:

    • No salary accrual was made for the week of December 25-31, 1989. Officers' salaries for this period totaled $18,000 and were paid on January 5, 1990.
    • Bonuses to officers for 1989 were paid on January 31, 1990 in the total amount of $175,000.

The adjusted balance for officers' compensation expense for the year ended December 31, 1989 should be

    a. $683,000
    b. $665,000
    c. $508,000
    d. $490,000

63. The premium on a three-year insurance policy expiring on December 31, 1991 was paid in total on January 2, 1989. If the company has a six-month operating cycle, then on

December 31, 1989, the prepaid insurance reported as a current asset would be for

    a. 6 months.
    b. 12 months.
    c. 18 months.
    d. 24 months.

64. A company issued a short-term note payable with a stated 12 percent rate of interest to a bank. The bank charged a .5% loan origination fee and remitted the balance to the company. The effective interest rate paid by the company in this transaction would be

    a. Equal to 12.5%.
    b. More than 12.5%.
    c. Less than 12.5%.
    d. Independent of 12.5%.

65. A retail store received cash and issued gift certificates that are redeemable in merchandise. The gift certificates lapse one year after they are issued. How would the deferred revenue account be affected by each of the following transactions?

	Redemption of certificates	Lapse of certificates
a.	Decrease	No effect
b.	Decrease	Decrease
c.	No effect	No effect
d.	No effect	Decrease

66. Management can estimate the amount of the loss that will occur if a foreign government expropriates some company assets. If expropriation is reasonably possible, a loss contingency should be

    a. Neither accrued as a liability **nor** disclosed.
    b. Accrued as a liability but **not** disclosed.
    c. Disclosed and accrued as a liability.
    d. Disclosed but **not** accrued as a liability.

67. Grim Corporation operates a plant in a foreign country. It is probable that the plant will be expropriated. However, the foreign government has indicated that Grim will receive a definite amount of compensation for the plant. The amount of compensation is less than the fair market value but exceeds the carrying amount of the plant. The contingency should be reported

    a. As a valuation allowance as a part of stockholders' equity.
    b. As a fixed asset valuation allowance account.
    c. In the notes to the financial statements.
    d. In the income statement.

Repeat Questions

(590,P1,1) Identical/similar to item 4 above
(590,P1,5) Identical/similar to item 17 above
(590,P2,22) Identical/similar to item 29 above
(590,P2,23) Identical/similar to item 24 above
(590,P2,30) Identical/similar to item 33 above
(590,P3,59) Identical/similar to item 41 above
(590,Q3,53) Identical/similar to item 51 above

Problems

Problem 1   (1186,T2)

(15 to 25 minutes)

Anth Company has significant amounts of trade accounts receivable. Anth uses the allowance method to estimate bad debts instead of the specific write-off method. During the year, some specific accounts were written off as uncollectible, and some that were previously written off as uncollectible were collected.

Anth also has some interest-bearing notes receivable for which the face amount plus interest at the prevailing rate of interest is due at maturity. The notes were received on July 1, 1985, and are due on June 30, 1987.

Required:

a. What are the deficiencies of the specific write-off method?

b. What are the two basic allowance methods used to estimate bad debts, and what is the theoretical justification for each?

c. How should Anth account for the collection of the specific accounts previously written off as uncollectible?

d. How should Anth report the effects of the interest-bearing notes receivable on its December 31, 1986 balance sheet and its income statement for the year ended December 31, 1986? Why?

Problem 2   (1188,T2)

(15 to 25 minutes)

Hogan Company uses the net method of accounting for sales discounts. Hogan also offers trade discounts to various groups of buyers.

On August 1, 1987, Hogan factored some accounts receivable on a without recourse basis. Hogan incurred a finance charge.

Hogan also has some notes receivable bearing an appropriate rate of interest. The principal and total interest are due at maturity. The notes were received on October 1, 1987, and mature on September 30, 1989. Hogan's operating cycle is less than one year.

Required:

a.1.   Using the net method, how should Hogan account for the sales discounts at the date of sale? What is the rationale for the amount recorded as sales under the net method?

2.   Using the net method, what is the effect on Hogan's sales revenues and net income when customers do not take the sales discounts?

b.   What is the effect of trade discounts on sales revenues and accounts receivable? Why?

c.   How should Hogan account for the accounts receivable factored on August 1, 1987? Why?

d.   How should Hogan report the effects of the interest-bearing notes receivable on its December 31, 1987, balance sheet and its income statement for the year ended December 31, 1987? Why?

Problem 3   (585,T3)

(15 to 25 minutes)

On July 1, 1986, Marie Company sold special-order merchandise on credit and received in return an interest-bearing note receivable from the customer. Marie will receive interest at the prevailing rate for a note of this type. Both the principal and interest are due in one lump sum on June 30, 1987.

On September 1, 1986, Marie sold special-order merchandise on credit and received in return a noninterest-bearing note receivable from the customer. The prevailing rate of interest for a note of this type is determinable. The note receivable is due in one lump sum on August 31, 1988.

Marie also has sufficient amounts of trade accounts receivable as a result of credit sales to its customers. On October 1, 1986, some trade accounts receivable were assigned to Daniel Finance Company on a with recourse, nonnotification basis for an advance of 75% of their amount at an interest charge of 20% on the balance outstanding.

On November 1, 1986, other trade accounts receivable were factored on a without recourse basis. The factor withheld 5% of the trade accounts receivable factored as protection against sales returns and allowances and charged a finance charge of 3%.

Required:

a.   How should Marie determine the interest income for 1986 on the

1.   Interest-bearing note receivable? Why?

2.   Noninterest-bearing note receivable? Why?

b.   How should Marie report the interest-bearing note receivable and the noninterest-bearing note receivable on its balance sheet at December 31, 1986?

c.   How should Marie account for subsequent collections on the trade accounts receivable assigned on October 1, 1986, and the payments to Daniel Finance? Why?

   d. How should Marie account for the trade accounts receivable factored on November 1, 1986? Why?

Problem 4   (1189,T3)

(15 to 25 minutes)

Chester Company has the following contingencies:

   • A threat of expropriation exists for one of its manufacturing plants located in a foreign country. Expropriation is deemed to be reasonably possible. Any compensation from the foreign government would be less than the carrying amount of the plant.

   • Potential costs exist due to the discovery of a safety hazard related to one of its products. These costs are probable and can be reasonably estimated.

   • One of its warehouses located at the base of a mountain could no longer be insured against rock-slide losses. No rock-slide losses have occurred.

Required:

   a. How should Chester report the threat of expropriation of assets? Why?
   b. How should Chester report the potential costs due to the safety hazard? Why?
   c. How should Chester report the noninsurable rock-slide risk? Why?

Problem 5   (1187,T4)

(15 to 25 minutes)

   Spackenkill Company is a manufacturer of household appliances. During the year, the following information became available:

• Potential costs due to the discovery of a safety hazard related to one of its products-- These costs are probable and can be reasonably estimated.
• Potential costs of new product warranty costs--These costs are probable but cannot be reasonably estimated.
• Potential costs due to the discovery of a possible product defect related to one of its products--These costs are reasonably possible and can be reasonably estimated.

Required:

   a. How should Spackenkill report the potential costs due to the discovery of a safety hazard? Why?
   b. How should Spackenkill report the potential costs of warranty costs? Why?
   c. How should Spackenkill report the potential costs due to the discovery of a possible product defect? Why?

Problem 6   (1189,T4)*

(15 to 25 minutes)

*Part C of this essay question deals with accruing compensation for future vocations. It can be found in Module 26, Present Value, D. Pensions.

Multiple Choice Answers

1. c	15. b	29. a	42. c	55. d
2. a	16. c	30. d	43. c	56. a
3. c	17. c	31. b	44. c	57. c
4. a	18. c	32. d	45. d	58. d
5. d	19. a	33. c	46. a	59. a
6. a	20. b	34. c	47. c	60. d
7. a	21. b	35. d	48. b	61. c
8. d	22. b	36. b	49. c	62. a
9. c	23. b	37. c	50. b	63. b
10. d	24. b	38. a	51. a	64. b
11. d	25. b	39. c	52. a	65. b
12. d	26. b	40. a	53. d	66. d
13. c	27. d	41. c	54. c	67. c
14. a	28. b			

Multiple Choice Answer Explanations

A. Cash

1.   (1188,P1,1) (c) Cash on hand ($125,000) and cash in banks ($2,250,000) are both reported as cash in the current asset section of the balance sheet because they are both unrestricted and readily available for use. Cash legally restricted for additions to plant ($1,600,000) is not available to meet current operating needs, and therefore should be excluded from current assets. Instead, it should be shown in the long-term asset section of the balance sheet as an investment. The amount to be reported as cash is $2,375,000 ($2,250,000 + $125,000).

2.   (1189,Q1,1) (a) To be classified as cash, the item must be readily available for current needs with no legal restrictions limiting its use. A postdated check is not acceptable for deposit and therefore is not considered cash. Thus, the $2,000 check was correctly excluded from the 12/31 checkbook balance and no adjustment is necessary. An NSF check should not be included in cash until it has been redeposited and has cleared the bank. At 12/31, the NSF check ($500) had not yet been redeposited, so it was incorrectly included in the 12/31 checkbook balance, and an adjustment must be made. The check which was not mailed until 1/10/89 ($300) should not be subtracted from cash until the company gives up physical control of that amount. Therefore, $300 must be added back to the checkbook balance. As a result of these adjustments, the correct cash balance is $4,800 ($5,000 - $500 + $300).

A.1. Bank Reconciliations

3.   (588,P1,12) (c) To determine the adjusted 12/31/87 cash in bank balance, a partial bank reconciliation must be prepared. The balance per the bank statement ($38,075)

must be adjusted for any items which the bank has not yet recorded and also for any bank errors.

Balance per bank statement	$38,075
Deposits in transit	5,200
Outstanding checks	(6,750)
Bank error	(400)
Adjusted balance	$36,125

The deposits in transit and the outstanding checks represent transactions which the bank has not yet recorded, so they must be considered when computing the correct cash balance. The bank error must be corrected. The bank erroneously credited (increased) Case's account, so the amount must be deducted when computing the correct cash balance. Note that the bank service charges ($75) are not used because these charges have already been recorded by the bank. The $75 would be an adjustment to the balance per books.

4.   (586,P1,1) (a) The requirement is the amount of cash disbursements per books in April. The cash disbursements per the bank statement were $49,700 in April. This amount included the 3/31/86 outstanding checks ($12,600), which cleared the bank in April, but were recorded on the books in March. Therefore, $12,600 must be deducted from the $49,700. The bank disbursement amount does not include the 4/30/86 outstanding checks ($7,500), which will not clear the bank until May, but were recorded on the books in April. Thus, the April disbursements, per the books totaled $44,600.

April bank disbursements	$49,700
3/31/86 outstanding checks	(12,600)
4/30/86 outstanding checks	7,500
April book disbursements	$44,600

B. Bad Debt Expense

5.   (1184,P1,3) (d) The requirement is the balance in accounts receivable at 12/31/83. The solutions approach is to use T-account analysis. Since this is the first year of operations, all accounts have a zero beginning balance. Inventory purchases of $700,000 less the ending inventory of $140,000 equals the cost of goods sold for the year. Since all sales are on credit, cost of goods sold ($560,000) times 140% (cost of 100% plus markup of 40%) equals the total sales ($784,000) debited to accounts receivable during the year. Total credit sales less collections ($784,000 - $400,000 or $384,000) equals the balance in accounts receivable at 12/31/83.

Inventory		
1/1/83	-0-	
Purchases	700,000	560,000 CGS
12/31/83	140,000	

	A/R		
1/1/83	-0-		
Sales	784,000	400,000	Collections
12/31/83	384,000		

6. (1188,P1,10) (a) The solutions approach is to set up a T-account for accounts receivable

	A/R		
12/31/86 balance	1,300,000		
1987 credit sales	5,400,000	4,750,000	1987 collections
		125,000	1987 write-offs
12/31/87 balance	1,825,000		

Credit sales are debited to A/R and credited to sales; collections are debited to cash and credited to A/R. Write-offs of customer accounts are debited to the allowance for uncollectible accounts, and credited to A/R. The other items (collection of accounts previously written off, $25,000, and the estimated uncollectible receivables at 12/31/87, $165,000) do not affect the accounts receivable account; they affect the allowance account.

7. (1189,Q1,7) (a) The solutions approach is to set up a T-account for the allowance for uncollectible accounts:

Allowance for Uncollectible Accounts			
		$10,800	1/1/88 balance
Bad debts written off			
during 1988	$18,000		
			Bad debts expense
			for 1988
		$13,500	($450,000 x 3%)
		$ 6,300	12/31/88 balance

When bad debts are written off, the allowance account is debited and accounts receivable is credited. When the bad debts expense provision is made, bad debts expense is debited and the allowance account is credited for the percentage of credit sales deemed to be uncollectible.

8. (1187,P3,46) (d) Clark Company estimates bad debts <u>during</u> the year for interim financial statements and use the aging of A/R approach at year end. The solutions approach is to set up a T-account for the allowance for doubtful accounts.

Allow for D.A.			
		12,000	12/31/85
1986 write-offs 48,000		60,000	D.A. expense
			recorded
			during 1986
		24,000	12/31/86
			before
			adjustment
		26,000	12/31/86
			adjustment
		50,000	12/31/86
			per aging

During 1986, doubtful accounts expense of $60,000 (4% x $1,500,000) was recorded periodically during the year (increasing the allowance account), while $48,000 of accounts were written off (decreasing the allowance account). This resulted in a 12/31/86 balance, before adjustment, of $24,000. An aging of the accounts indicates that a year-end balance of $50,000 is required in the allowance account. Therefore, the allowance account (and the previously recorded doubtful accounts expense) must be increased by $26,000 ($50,000 - $24,000). After this entry doubtful accounts expense is $86,000 ($60,000 + $26,000).

9. (586,P1,6) (c) The requirement is the correct 12/31/85 balance of the allowance for doubtful accounts. The balance in the allowance account should reflect the amount of receivables that are estimated to be uncollectible. An aging of receivables at 12/31/85 indicates that $110,000 of the receivables are estimated to be uncollectible. Therefore, the allowance account should be adjusted to a balance of $110,000 at 12/31/85.

10. (586,P1,7) (d) The requirement is the 12/31/85 balance of accounts receivable, before the allowance for doubtful accounts. The solutions approach is to set up a T-account for accounts receivable.

	A/R		
12/31/84 balance	1,200,000		
1985 credit sales	5,300,000	4,650,000	1985 collections
		75,000	1985 write-offs
12/31/85 balance	1,775,000		

Credit sales are debited to A/R and credited to sales; collections are debited to cash and credited to A/R. The journal entry to record write-offs under the allowance method is as follows:

Allowance for D.A.	75,000	
Accounts receivable		75,000

11. (586,P3,48) (d) The requirement is doubtful accounts expense for 1985. The solutions approach is to set up a T-account for the allowance for doubtful accounts.

	Allowance for D.A.		
		32,000	1/1/85 balance
1985 write-offs	24,000		
		8,000	Balance before adjustment
		?	Doubtful accounts expense
		30,000	12/31/85 balance

On 9/30/85, $24,000 of accounts were written off as uncollectible (debit the allowance account, credit A/R), leaving a balance in the allowance account of $8,000. The desired 12/31/85 balance is $30,000 ($220,000 A/R less $190,000 net realizable value of receivables). Therefore, to increase the allowance account from $8,000 to $30,000, doubtful accounts expense of $22,000 must be recorded.

12. (1186,Q1,3) (d) The balance of the allowance for doubtful accounts at December 31, 1985 will be determined by increasing the beginning balance by the amount of doubtful accounts expense for 1985 and reducing it by the accounts receivable written off during the year. Both the beginning balance and current year write-offs are provided in the problem. Ladd Co. provides for doubtful accounts on the percentage of net sales method. The doubtful accounts expense for the year is $13,050 [(475,000 - 40,000) x .03]. The correct answer is (d) because the balance of the account at December 31, 1985 is $12,050 ($9,000 + 13,050 - 10,000 = $12,050).

13. (589,T1,19) (c) When an account receivable which was previously written off is collected, two entries must be made. The first entry reverses the write-off and reestablishes the receivable:

Accounts receivable	XXX	
Allowance for Uncollectible Accounts		XXX

The second entry records the cash receipt:

Cash	XXX	
Accounts receivable		XXX

The credit to the allowance account in the first entry increases its balance. Uncollectible accounts expense, however, is not affected by this transaction. Therefore, answer (c) is correct.

14. (1189,T1,7) (a) The aging of receivables method of estimating uncollectible accounts is based on the theory that bad debts are a function of accounts receivable collections during the period. The aging of receivables method emphasizes reporting accounts receivable at their net realizable value. It is a "balance-sheet" approach, which stresses the collectibility (valuation) of the receivable balance. Once the balance of the allowance account required to reduce

net accounts receivable to their realizable value has been computed, bad debts expense is merely the amount needed to adjust the allowance account to the computed balance. Answer (b) is incorrect because under the direct write-off method, bad debts are considered expenses in the period in which they are written off; no consideration is given to the valuation of accounts receivable. Answers (c) and (d) are incorrect because both of these methods are based on the theory that bad debts are a function of sales. Thus, these methods emphasize reporting the bad debts expense amount accurately on the income statement.

B.3. Pledging, Assigning, Selling A/R

15. (589,T1,2) (b) An _assignment_ of accounts receivable is a financing arrangement whereby the owner of the receivables (assignor) obtains a loan from the lendor (assignee) by pledging the accounts receivable as collateral. A _factoring_ of accounts receivable is basically a sale of the receivables. "Factors" are intermediaries that buy receivables from companies (for a fee) and then collect payments directly from the customers. Thus, both of these are methods of generating cash from accounts receivable, and answer (b) is correct.

B.4. Discounting Notes Receivable

16. (589,P1,15) (c) The cash received from the discounting of a note receivable is equal to the _maturity value_ of the note less the _bank discount_. The maturity value of the note is the principal plus the interest [$30,000 + ($30,000 x 12% x 6/12) = $312,00]. The bank discount is computed as follows:

$$\begin{pmatrix} \text{Maturity} \\ \text{value} \end{pmatrix} \times \begin{pmatrix} \text{Discount} \\ \text{rate} \end{pmatrix} \times \begin{pmatrix} \text{Discount} \\ \text{period} \end{pmatrix} = \begin{pmatrix} \text{Bank} \\ \text{discount} \end{pmatrix}$$
$$\$31,800 \quad \times \quad 15\% \quad \times \quad 6/12 \quad = \quad \underline{\$2,385}$$

The discount period is the length of time the bank holds the note; in this case, the six-month note was discounted immediately, so the discount period is six months. The cash received is $29,415 ($31,800 maturity value less $2,385 discount).

17. (1186,Q1,4) (c) The cash proceeds received from the discounting of a note receivable will be equal to the maturity value of the note less the bank's interest charge (discount). The maturity value of the note is the principal plus interest. In this case, $60,000 + ($60,000 x 10% x 6/12 months) or $63,000. The bank's interest charge is computed as the maturity value ($63,000) multiplied by the discount rate of 12%. This amount is adjusted to reflect the time remaining to maturity. The correct answer is

(c), $60,480. The maturity value of $63,000 less a discount of $2,520 ($63,000 x 12% x 4/12 months).

18. (589,T1,3) (c) The journal entry to record the sale of a note receivable with recourse at the date of discounting would be:

Cash	XX	
Loss (gain) on sale	XX	
N/R discounted		XX
Interest revenue		XX

The cash proceeds equal the maturity value less the discount. The interest revenue is the amount of interest earned prior to discounting and equals the face value of the note times the contract interest rate for the number of days prior to discounting. The loss (gain) equals the face value plus the interest revenue as calculated above, less the cash proceeds. The notes receivable discounted account is credited for the face amount of the note. It is a contra-notes receivable account, and accordingly is increased when credited. Therefore, answer (c) is correct and answers (a), (b), and (d) are incorrect.

19. (588,T1,11) (a) To determine the amount of accrued interest, the solutions approach is to prepare a timeline.

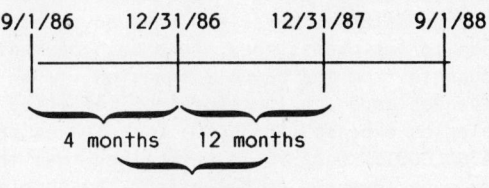

The number of months of accrued interest at December 31, 1986 is 4 months because the company issued the note on September 1, 1986. The number of months of accrued interest at December 31, 1987 is 16 months because **both** the note's **principal and interest** are payable on September 1, 1988, and 16 months of interest would accrue from September 1, 1986 to December 31, 1987. Therefore, answer (a) is correct.

20. (587,T1,3) (b) When a company receives an interest bearing note, the asset account notes receivable is debited. As time passes and interest is earned, the asset account interest receivable is debited and interest revenue is credited. The interest receivable account would have a zero balance on July 1, 1986, the date of receipt of the note, because no interest has yet been earned at that date. On December 31, 1986, 6 months of interest has been earned but not yet received, creating a debit balance in the interest account. Thus, answer (b) is correct.

21. (587,T1,10) (b) When a company discounts its own note to a bank, the bank remits proceeds to the borrower equal to the face value of the note reduced by the amount of the discount. The discount is computed by multiplying the stated discount rate times the face value of the note. From the borrower's perspective, in computing the effective interest cost, the amount of the discount will be compared to the net proceeds received from the bank. Since the discount amount is then being compared to a base which is smaller than the face value, it will effectively create an interest cost which is greater than the discount percentage. For example, if a $1,000 note were discounted at 10%, the borrower would receive $900 [1,000 face value − (10% x 1,000)]. The effective interest rate to the borrower would be

$$\frac{\$100 \text{ discount}}{\$900 \text{ net proceeds}} = 11.1\%$$

22. (587,P2,32) (b) The effective interest rate on a borrowing is the <u>net annual interest cost</u> divided by the <u>net available proceeds</u> from the borrowing. Cody's <u>gross</u> annual interest cost is $240,000 ($2,000,000 x 12%). Cody is required to maintain a compensating balance of $400,000, which is $200,000 more than their normal balance of $200,000. Therefore, Cody earns incremental annual interest revenue of $12,000 ($200,000 x 6%) on the excess compensating balance. The net annual interest cost is $228,000 ($240,000 − $12,000). The net available proceeds from the borrowing is $1,800,000 ($2,000,000 loan less $200,000 excess compensating balance). Therefore, the effective annual interest rate is 12.67% ($228,000 ÷ $1,800,000).

C.1. Examples of Current Liabilities

23. (1187,P1,8) (b) The liability for accrued salaries at 12/31/86 should include all salaries expense which has been incurred, but not yet paid. This would include the overtime pay earned by employees in the 2-week period ended 12/26/86 ($4,200), which will not be paid until the next pay period. Accrued salaries would also include the regular pay for the workdays since 12/26/86. There were three such workdays (December 29, 30, and 31). Since each biweekly pay period results in $75,000 regular pay for 10 workdays (2 five-day weeks), the accrued salaries for three workdays would be 3/10 of $75,000, or $22,500. Therefore, the total liability for accrued salaries at 12/31/86 is $26,700 ($22,500 + $4,200).

24. (1187,P1,12) (b) Accrued interest payable at 12/31/86 is interest expense which has been incurred by 12/31/86, but not yet paid. In this case, interest was last paid on

9/1/86, so the accrued interest payable includes interest expense incurred for 9/1 through 12/31 (4 months). The original balance of the note payable was $1,800,000, but the 9/1/86 principal payment of $600,000 reduced this balance to $1,200,000. There- fore, the interest payable at 12/31/86 is $48,000:

$$\$1,200,000 \times 12\% \times 4/12 = \underline{\$48,000}$$

The stated rate of 12% is used rather than the bank's prime rate of 11% because the 12% is the rate negotiated for this particular note.

25. (589,P2,33) (b) Accrued interest pay- able at 6/30/89 is interest expense which has been incurred by 6/30/89, but not yet paid. Interest was last paid on 10/1/88, so the ac- crued interest payable includes interest ex- pense incurred from 10/1/88 through 6/30/89 (9 months). The original balance of the note payable was $1,800,000, but the 10/1/88 prin- cipal payment of $600,000 reduced this balance to $1,200,000. Therefore, the interest pay- able at 6/30/89 is $90,000 ($1,200,000 x 10% x 9/12).

26. (589,P2,31) (b) To determine the 12/31/88 balance of the liability for customer advances, the solutions approach is to set up a T-account for the liability.

Customer Advances

		295,000	12/31/87
1988 advances			balance
applied	410,000	460,000	1988 advances
1988 advances			received
cancelled	125,000		
		220,000	12/31/88
			balance

When advances are received ($460,000), cash is debited and the liability account is cred- ited. When advances are applied to orders shipped ($410,000), the liability account is debited and sales is credited. When an order is cancelled ($125,000), the liability account is debited and either cash or a revenue account is credited, depending on whether or not the deposit is returned to the customer.

27. (1187,P1,19) (d) All contract sales are made evenly during the year. Therefore, the 1985 contracts range from 1 year expired (if sold on 12/31/85) to 2 years expired (if sold on 1/1/85), for an average of 1½ years expired [(2+1)/2]. Similarly, the 1986 contracts range from 0 years expired to 1 year expired, for an average of ½ year expired [(0+1)/2]. The average unearned portion of the 1985 contracts is ½ year (2 years - 1½ years), the last half of the second contract year. The amount of unearned revenue related to 1985 contracts is computed as follows:

$$\$500,000 \times 60\% \times \tfrac{1}{2} = \underline{\$150,000}$$

The average unearned portion of the 1986 contracts is 1½ years (2 years - ½ year), the last half of the first contract year and all of the second contract year. The amount of unearned revenue related to the 1986 contracts is computed as follows:

1986:	$600,000 × 40% × ½	= $120,000
	$600,000 × 60%	= 360,000
		$480,000

Therefore, the total unearned revenue is $630,000 ($150,000 + $480,000).

28. (589,Q1,19) (b) The bonus is equal to 10% of income after deducting the bonus. The solutions approach is to set up and solve an equation.

$$B = .10 \ (\$165,000 - B)$$
$$B = \$16,500 - .10B$$
$$1.10B = \$16,500$$
$$B = \$16,500 \div 1.10 = \$15,000$$

Note that the tax rate (30%) is not used. The bonus is based on income before, not after, taxes.

29. (587,P1,11) (a) A key point to under- standing this problem is that the employee advances do not affect the computation of accrued salaries payable. When advances are made to employees, they are a cash payment separate from the payroll function. The advances made are therefore not reflected in salaries expense ($815,000) or salaries paid ($780,000). Once it is determined that the employee advances do not affect the problem, the solutions approach is to set up a T- account for salaries payable and analyze the 1986 transactions.

Salaries Payable

		65,000	12/31/85
			Salaries
Salaries paid	780,000	815,000	expense
		100,000	12/31/86

Since the 12/31/85 (i.e., beginning) balance was given, the 12/31/86 balance can easily be computed. The salaries payable balance would be increased by salaries expense, but de- creased by salaries paid. In other words, Salaries Payable is increased over salaries paid during the period.

30. (589,P2,32) (d) The $500,000 note and $200,000 of the $800,000 note are due within 12 months of the balance sheet date and nor- mally the total of $700,000 ($500,000 + $200,000) would be classified as short-term. However, SFAS 6 states that a short-term obligation can be reclassified as long-term if the enterprise intends to refinance the obli- gation on a long-term basis and the intent is

supported by the ability to refinance. Witt demonstrated its intent and ability to refinance the $800,000 note when it actually refinanced the entire balance on 1/15/89, before the 1988 statements were issued. Witt demonstrated its intent and ability to refinance the $500,000 note when it entered into a noncancelable, unviolated financing agreement with a financially capable lender. Therefore, neither the $500,000 nor the $200,000 should be classified as short-term.

31. (1189,P1,14) (b) All the notes are due 6/15/89 and normally the entire amount would be classified as current. However, SFAS 6 states that a short-term obligation can be reclassified as long-term if the enterprise intends to refinance the obligation on a long-term basis <u>and</u> the intent is supported by the ability to refinance. Pam demonstrated its ability by entering into a financing agreement before the statements are issued. SFAS 6 further states that the amount to be excluded from current liabilities cannot exceed the amount available for refinancing under the agreement. Pam expects to be able to refinance at least $960,000 (80% x $1,200,000) of the notes. Therefore, that amount can be classified as long-term, while the remaining $40,000 must be classified as short-term.

32. (1189,P1,19) (d) The amount reported for sales revenue should <u>include</u> amounts charged customers when inventory is sold, but should <u>exclude</u> amounts collected for sales taxes. To determine the correct amount for sales revenue, Taft must divide the total of sales and sales taxes by 100% plus the sales tax percentage (6%), as indicated below:

Month	Total		Percentage	Sales revenue
Jan.	$10,600	÷	106%	$10,000
Feb.	$ 7,420	÷	106%	7,000
March	$ 9,540	÷	106%	9,000
Total				$26,000

Sales taxes payable would include all sales taxes collected, less any sales taxes already remitted.

January sales taxes ($10,600 - $10,000)	$600
February sales taxes ($7,420 - $7,000)	420
March sales taxes ($9,540 - $9,000)	540
Total	1,560
Less taxes remitted	(600)
Sales taxes payable	$ 960

C.1. Examples of Current Liabilities

33. (586,P2,26) (c) The requirement is the amount to be reported as a liability for returnable containers at 12/31/85. The solutions approach is to set up a T-account for the liability.

		Liability	
		290,000	12/31/84 balance
		390,000	1985 deliveries
1985 returns	313,000		
1985 sales	30,000		
		337,000	12/31/85 balance

When customers pay the deposit for a container, cash is debited and the liability is credited. Therefore, at 12/31/84, the liability consists of deposits for containers still held by customers from the last two years ($290,000). During 1985, the liability is increased for deposits on containers delivered ($390,000). When containers are returned, the deposits are returned to the customers; in 1985, the liability was debited and cash credited for $313,000. Also, at 12/31/85, some customers still held containers from 1983 ($75,000 - $45,000 = $30,000). The two-year time limit has expired on these, so the company no longer is obligated to return the deposit. The containers are considered sold to the customers, so the liability account is debited and sales credited for $30,000. This results in a 12/31/85 liability balance of $337,000.

34. (1189,P1,16) (c) No sales commission is due to salesperson A because his commissions earned ($200,000 x 4% = $8,000) are less than his fixed salary ($10,000). Note that the excess of the fixed salary over commissions earned is not charged back against A. Commissions totaling $28,000 are due to salespersons B and C as computed below:

	Commissions earned		Fixed salary paid	Commissions payable
B	(6% x $400,000)	-	$14,000	$10,000
C	(6% x $600,000)	-	$18,000	18,000
				$28,000

35. (1189,P2,21) (d) Prior to adjusting entries, Grey has balances of $1,000,000 in <u>layaway plan sales</u> and $0 in <u>deposits from customers</u>. However, of the $1,000,000 balance in the sales account, only $600,000 represents sales where payment has been made in full and title has passed to the customers. The remaining $400,000 represents collections from customers who have not yet paid in full. At 12/31/89, an adjusting entry must be prepared to remove $400,000 from the sales account and record it in the liability account, deposits from customers.

36. (588,T1,12) (b) Per SFAC 5, revenue is recognized when it is both <u>realized</u> and <u>earned</u>. The cash received upon issuance of the gift certificates is not earned until the gift certificates are redeemed. Therefore, answer (b) is correct. Answer (a) is incorrect because the deferred revenue account is decreased when the gift certificates are redeemed and the revenue is earned. Answer (c) is incorrect because the revenue account is not decreased when the gift certificates are issued. Answer (d) is incorrect because the revenue account is increased when the gift certificates are redeemed, not issued.

37. (1189,T1,13) (c) SFAC 6, para 197 specifically identifies deposits and prepayments for goods or services to be provided at a future time ("unearned revenues") as liabilities under the definition provided in para 35 of the Statement. In this case, the goods are to be manufactured and delivered within six months. Since the liability will be settled within the next year, it should be classified as current, which is answer (c).

38. (587,T1,11) (a) Accrued liabilities include expenses which have been incurred but not yet paid. Both federal unemployment tax and the employer's share of FICA taxes represent the employer's payroll tax expense which is incurred as employees earn wages, but which is only paid periodically. Therefore, both types of expense represent accrued liabilities.

C.2. Current Liabilities–
Contingencies

39. (1189,P2,33) (c) At 12/31/88, Curran should report a liability even though the coupons expired 12/31/88 because retailers may submit coupons to Curran for three months after the expiration date. Thus, Curran will still have to redeem coupons until 3/31/89. Total expected redemptions are $420,000 (70% x $600,000), and on those redemptions Curran expects to pay out $462,000 ($420,000 plus 10% of $420,000 for handling). As of 12/31/88, total payments to retailers have been $220,000, which means a liability of $242,000 should be reported ($462,000 - $220,000).

40. (1188,P2,30) (a) The solutions approach is to set up a T-account for warranty liability.

Warranty liability			
1986 payments	4,500	18,000	1986 expense (6% x $300,000)
1987 payments	15,000	30,000	1987 expense (6% x $500,000)
		28,500	12/31/87 liability

Each year, warranty expense is estimated at 6% of sales and recorded by debiting the expense account and crediting the liability. As warranty expenditures are made, the liability is debited and cash is credited. Note that the total estimated warranty cost for both years (2% + 4% = 6%) is recorded in the year

of sale in compliance with the matching principle.

41. (588,P3,41) (c) The additional taxes must be accrued as a loss contingency in accordance with SFAS 5 because an unfavorable outcome is probable and the amount of the loss is reasonably estimable. Per FASB Interpretation 14, when a range of possible losses exists, the best estimate in the range (in this case, $550,000) is accrued. Since the $650,000 settlement occurred after the statements were issued, this information was not available when the estimate was made.

42. (1187,P2,35) (c) Per SFAS 5, a loss contingency should be accrued if it is probable that a liability has been incurred at the balance sheet date and the amount of the loss is reasonably estimable. This loss must be accrued because it meets both criteria. Notice that even though the lawsuit was not initiated until 1/12/87, the liability was incurred on 11/5/86 when the accident occurred. FASB Interpretation 14 requires that when some amount within an estimated range is a better estimate than any other amount in the range, that amount is accrued. Therefore, a loss of $300,000 should be accrued. If no amount within the range is a better estimate than any other amount, the amount at the low end of the range is accrued and the amount at the high end is disclosed.

43. (589,Q1,16) (c) Per SFAS 5, a loss contingency should be accrued if it is probable that a liability has been incurred at the balance sheet date and the amount of the loss is reasonably estimable. Although this contingency is reasonably estimable, it is not probable. Therefore, no loss is accrued. However, since the contingency is reasonably possible, it will be disclosed in the footnotes to the 12/31/87 financial statements. The possible loss will be disclosed as $300,000. The additional potential liability above the deductible would be covered by the insurance policy, and would not be a loss for Nilo.

44. (587,P2,35) (c) At 12/31/85, the contingent liability from the lawsuit met SFAS 5's criteria for accrual (probable and reasonably estimable), so a loss and liability of $400,000 was recognized. In 1986, the lawsuit was settled and the actual loss was $310,000 ($60,000 copyright transfer and $250,000 cash payment). This is a change in estimate which should be accounted for in the period of change per APB 20, para 31. Therefore the $90,000 difference will be reflected

in 1986 income. The journal entry on 12/15/86
to record the settlement would be:

Lawsuit liability   400,000
   Gain from settlement
      of lawsuit   90,000
   Cash   250,000
   Copyright   60,000

45. (1189,P3,60) (d) Para 17 of SFAS 5
states that <u>gain</u> contingencies are not reflected in the accounts until realized. Since
the case is unresolved at 12/31/88, none of
this contingent gain should be recorded as
revenue in 1988.

46.   (586,Q1,7) (a) The requirement is to
determine the amount Vail should accrue as a
contingent liability at 12/31/85 to cover possible future fire losses. Answer (a) is correct because per SFAS 5, para 8, a contingent
liability shall only be accrued if the likelihood of occurrence is <u>probable</u> and the amount
of the loss can be <u>reasonably estimated</u>. An
event such as a possible future fire loss is
not considered probable at 12/31/85 based on
the information given nor can an amount of the
loss from such an event be reasonably estimated. Thus, an accrual at 12/31/85 is not
required.

47. (589,T1,33) (c) Per SFAS 5, para 17,
contingencies that might result in gains
usually are not reflected in the accounts
since to do so might result in revenue being
recognized prior to its realization. Although
adequate disclosure shall be made of contingencies that might result in gains, care shall
be exercised to avoid misleading implications
as to the likelihood of realization. Therefore, answer (c) is correct. Answer (a) is
incorrect because the gain contingency should
not be recognized in the income statement.
Answer (b) is incorrect because the gain
contingency would not be reflected in <u>any</u> of
the accounts. Answer (d) is incorrect because
the contingency should be disclosed in notes
to the statements.

48.   (589,T1,7) (b) Per SFAS 5, a loss contingency will be accrued only if its occurrence is probable and the amount can be reasonably estimated. In this case the loss is
not considered probable and, therefore, should
not be accrued. Although a contingent loss is
not accrued if it is only reasonably possible
(not probable), it will be disclosed in the
footnotes to the financial statements. Therefore, the correct answer is (b); the reasonably possible loss will not be accrued, but it
will be disclosed. Such disclosures should
indicate the nature of the contingency and

should give an estimate of the possible loss
or range of loss or state that such an estimate cannot be made.

49. (585,T1,16) (c) The requirement is to
determine the proper treatment of an expected
loss which is imminent (probable) and the
amount of which can be reasonably estimated.
Answer (c) is correct because per SFAS 5,
para 8, an estimated loss from contingencies
shall be accrued and charged to income when it
is <u>probable</u> that an asset has been impaired or
a liability incurred <u>and</u> when the amount of
the loss can be <u>reasonably estimated</u>. Both of
these requirements are met by the expropriation of assets described in this question.
Therefore, this loss contingency should be
accrued. Additionally, per para 9, the nature
of the contingency should be disclosed in a
note to the financial statements. Therefore,
answers (a), (b), and (d) are incorrect.

50. (589,P2,24) (b) SFAS 43 states that
accrual of a liability for future vacation pay
is required if all of the conditions below are
met:
   1. Obligation arises from employee
       services already performed.
   2. Obligation arises from vesting or
       accumulation of rights.
   3. Payment is probable.
   4. Amount can be reasonably estimated.

These criteria are met for the vacation pay
($110,000). Accrual for sick pay is not
required in this case, however, because the
third condition (probable payment) is not
specified in the problem. Therefore, the
proper amount of the liability to be reported
is $110,000.

51. (587,P3,50) (a) Per SFAS 43, an
employer is required to accrue a liability for
employees' rights to receive compensation for
future absences, such as vacations, when
certain conditions are met. The Statement
does <u>not</u>, however, specify how such liabilities are to be measured. Since vacation
time is paid by Ruhl Co. at the salaries in
effect when vacations are taken or when
employment is terminated, Ruhl adjusts its
vacation liability and expense to current
salary levels. Ruhl's 1986 vacation pay
expense consists of vacations earned for work
in 1986 (adjusted to current rates) of $20,000
plus the amount necessary to adjust its pre-
1986 vacation liability for the 10% salary
increase. The amount of this adjustment is
equal to ten percent of the pre-existing
liability balance at December 31, 1986
[($25,000 - 15,000) x 10% = $1,000]. Therefore, total vacation pay expense for the
period is equal to $21,000 ($20,000 + 1,000).

52. (589,T1,36) (a) SFAS 43, para 6 requires employers to accrue a liability for future absences when all of the following conditions are met:

1) The employees' services have already been rendered,
2) The obligation relates to rights which vest or accumulate,
3) Payment is probable, and
4) The amount can be reasonably estimated.

Conditions 1, 3, and 4 were met according to the given information. Condition 2 is met by answer (a), which is correct because the liability should be accrued under these conditions.

Miscellaneous

53. (589,P1,1) (d) Current assets are cash and other assets that are expected to be converted into cash, sold, or consumed either in one year or in the operating cycle, whichever is longer. Included in this category are cash, temporary investments in marketable securities, short-term receivables, inventories, and prepaid expenses. In this case, total current assets are $63,000.

Accounts receivable (net)	$16,000
Short-term investments	5,000
Cash	11,000
Inventory of merchandise	30,000
Prepaid expenses	1,000
Total	$63,000

Equipment and furniture ($25,000) and accumulated depreciation ($15,000) are reported in the property, plant, and equipment section. Patent ($4,000) is reported as an intangible asset, (always long-term), and land held for future business site ($18,000) is reported as a long-term investment.

54. (1189,Q1,5) (c) Lia Co. (the consignor) has inventory on consignment with Jax Co. (the consignee) on December 31, 1988. Consigned goods are included in the consignor's inventory until these goods are sold to the ultimate customer by the consignee. Therefore, Lia's total current assets at December 31, 1988 are:

Cash	$ 35,000
Accounts receivable, net	47,000
Inventories	30,000
Goods on consignment, which are properly part of inventory ($13,000 ÷ 130%)	10,000
Total current assets	$122,000

Note that the goods on consignment must be included in current assets at their cost. The selling price of $13,000 must therefore be reduced by dividing by 130%.

55. (589,P1,2) (d) Current assets are cash and other assets that are expected to be converted into cash, sold, or consumed either in one year, or in the operating cycle, whichever is longer. Generally included in this category are cash, temporary investments in marketable securities, short-term receivables, inventories, and prepaid expenses. The items in the trial balance which appear to fall in this category are:

Cash	$ 675,000
Accounts receivable (net)	2,695,000
Inventory	2,185,000
Total	$5,555,000

The problem indicates, however, that $500,000 of the accounts receivable (4 x $125,000) will not be collected until 1990, and therefore should **not** be included in current assets at 12/31/88. The current assets total is $5,055,000 ($5,555,000 - $500,000).

56. (589,P1,3) (a) ARB 43 states that current liabilities are obligations whose liquidation is reasonably expected to require the use of existing resources properly classified as current assets, or the creation of other current liabilities. The items in the trial balance which either fully or partially fall into this category are accounts payable and accrued liabilities, income tax payable, and deferred income tax liability. The amount shown for income tax payable ($654,000) is incorrect. Income before taxes is $2,180,000 ($13,360,000 revenues less $11,180,000 expenses), so income tax expense is $654,000 (30% x $2,180,000). Apparently, Shaw prepared these two entries:

Income tax expense	475,000	
Cash		475,000
Income tax expense	654,000	
Income tax payable		654,000

The amount in the second entry should have been $179,000 ($654,000 - $475,000), since total expense is $654,000, of which $475,000 has already been paid and recorded. Therefore, a correcting entry is necessary to reduce the expense and payable by $475,000.

Income tax payable	475,000	
Income tax expense		475,000

This entry reduces income tax payable to its correct amount ($179,000) and income tax expense to its correct amount ($654,000). The portion of the deferred income tax liability which is to be paid in 1989 ($15,000) is also a current liability. Thus, total current liabilities are $1,995,000.

A/P and accrued liabilities	$1,801,000
Income tax payable (corrected)	179,000
Deferred income tax liability	15,000
Total	$1,995,000

57. (589,P1,4) (c) The ending retained earnings balance generally is the **beginning balance** plus **net income** less **dividends**. The beginning retained earnings is $3,350,000. Net income is $1,536,000, as computed below:

Revenues	$13,360,000
Expenses	11,180,000
Income before taxes	2,180,000
Income tax expense (30% x $2,180,000)	654,000
Net income	$1,526,000

Note that the income tax expense amount in the trial balance ($1,129,000) is incorrect (see explanation for 589,P1,3 above). There were no dividends in 1988, so ending retained earnings is $4,876,000 ($3,350,000 + $1,526,000).

May 1990 Answers

58. (590,P1,9) (d) The balance in the allowance for doubtful accounts should reflect the amount of accounts receivable that are estimated to be uncollectible. Since it is estimated that 3% of the gross accounts receivable will become uncollectible, the allowance account should have a 12/31/89 balance of $30,000 (3% x $1,000,000). Note that **bad debt expense** of $38,000 would be recorded for 1989, as indicated below:

	Allowance	
Bal. before adj.	8,000	
	?	B.D. expense ($38,000)
	30,000	12/31/87 (3% x $1,000,000)

59. (590,P1,12) (a) In practice when a note is discounted, the interest accrued to date is often netted against the gain (loss), if a sale, or interest expense, if a borrowing, (due to immateriality) to determine the net interest revenue. This is the same as taking the receivable amount of $40,170 from the bank and subtracting the book value of the note of $40,000 to arrive at a net interest revenue of $170. The amount receivable from the bank is computed as follows:

Maturity value	[40,000 + (40,000 x 12%) x 1/4)]	$41,200
Discount	($41,200 x 15% x 2/12)	1,030
		$40,170

60. (590,P3,54) (d) Beal Co. estimates bad debt expense using a percentage of sales

during the year for interim reports, and uses an aging of accounts receivable to adjust previously recorded amounts at **year end**. The solutions approach is to set up a T-account for the allowance for doubtful accounts.

	Allow. for D.A.		
		42,000	1/1/89
89 write-offs	46,000	40,000	Expense recorded **during** 89
		36,000	12/31/89 before adjustment
		16,000	12/31/89 adjustment
		52,000	12/31/89 per aging

During 1989, bad debt expense of $40,000 was recorded while $46,000 of accounts were written off, leaving 12/31/89 **pre-adjustment** balance in the allowance account of $36,000. The aging schedule indicates a balance of $52,000 is required at 12/31/89. Therefore the allowance account (and the previously recorded bad debt expense) must be increased by $16,000 ($52,000 − $36,000). After this entry, bad debt expense is $56,000 ($40,000 + $16,000).

61. (590,P3,60) (c) Per SFAS 5, a loss contingency should be accrued if it is **probable** that a liability has been incurred at the balance sheet date and the amount of the loss is reasonably estimable. This contingency meets both criteria, so a liability of $500,000 is accrued. The additional potential liability above the deductible ($3,500,000 − $500,000 = $3,000,000) would be covered by the insurance policy, and therefore is not a loss or liability for Rex.

62. (590,Q3,46) (a) Accrual basis accounting requires us to record events in the periods in which the events occur, rather than when the entity receives or pays cash. Both the officers' salaries for December 25-31, 1989 and bonuses relate to 1989 and should be accrued at December 31, 1989. Thus, the compensation expense for the year ended December 31, 1989 should be $683,000 ($490,000 + $18,000 + $175,000).

63. (590,T1,6) (b) A current asset is cash and an other asset that is expected to be converted into cash, sold, or consumed either in one year or in the operating cycle, whichever is longer. Since the company only has a six-month operating cycle, the current portion of the prepaid insurance costs is 1 year or 12 months.

64. (590,T1,8) (b) The effective rate of interest paid on a note is computed as follows:

$$\text{Effective Interest Rate} = \frac{\text{Interest paid}}{\text{Cash received}}$$

In this case, let's assume the short-term note payable was in the amount of $100,000. The effective interest rate would be 12.56%.

$$\frac{(\$100,000 \times .12) + (\$100,000 \times .005)}{\$100,000 - (\$100,000 \times .005)} = 12.56$$

This is because the loan origination fee increases the interest paid on the note and reduces the net cash received from the note.

65.   (590,T1,9) (b) When a company issues gift certificates for cash, the following journal entry is made:

Cash   (amount of certificate)
   Deferred revenue   (amount of certificate)

When the gift certificates are subsequently redeemed, the following journal entry is made:

Deferred revenue (amount of certificate)
   Revenue   (amount of certificate)

However, if the gift certificates are not redeemed and lapse, the following journal entry is made:

Deferred revenue (amount of certificate)
   Gain on lapse of
   certificates   (amount of certificate)

Please note that although different accounts are credited depending on whether the certificates are redeemed or lapse, the Deferred Revenue account is decreased in both cases.

66.   (590,T1,12) (d) Per SFAS 5, when a loss contingency is reasonably possible, it is not appropriate to accrue the loss contingency as of the balance sheet date. However, a footnote disclosing the expropriation should accompany the financial statements.

67.   (590,T1,35) (c) A gain contingency results from the plant expropriation because the amount of compensation to be received from the foreign government exceeds the carrying amount of the plant. Per SFAS 5, para 17, "contingencies that might result in gains usually are not reflected in the accounts since to do so might be to recognize revenue prior to its realization." Furthermore, "adequate disclosure shall be made of contingencies that might result in gains, but care shall be exercised to avoid misleading implications as to the likelihood of realization." Therefore, answer (c) is correct.

Answer Outline

Problem 1   Bad Debts and Reporting NR
              (1186,T2)

a. Deficiencies of specific write-off method
    Overstates A/R by reporting them at more
       than NRV
    Since write-off occurs in period after
       revenues generated, matching principle
       violated
b. Allowance methods used to estimate bad
       debts
       <u>Credit sales basis</u>
          Focuses on I/S
          Attempts to match bad debts with
             revenues generated in same period
       <u>Receivable account balance basis</u>
          Focuses on balance sheet
          Attempts to value receivables at
             future collectible amounts
c. Accounting for collection of specific
       accounts previously written off
       Reinstatement of accounts previously
          written off and adjustment of
          allowance account
       Accounts receivable   xxx
          Allowance for
             doubtful accounts   xxx
       Collection of accounts previously
          written off
       Cash   xxx
          Accounts receivable   xxx
d. Presentation of interest-bearing note
       <u>Balance sheet</u>
          Face amount of note and related
             interest receivable as C/As at
             12/31/86
          Report as C/As because both due
             within one year of B/S date
       <u>Income statement</u>
          Interest income for year ended
             12/31/86 at amount equal to stated
             rate for 12 months
          Report as element of income over life
             of note, because interest accrues
             with passage of time

Unofficial Answer

Problem 1   Bad Debts and Reporting NR
              (1186,T2)

a. The specific write-off method overstates
the trade accounts receivable on the balance
sheet by reporting them at more than their net
realizable value. Furthermore, because the
write off often occurs in a period after the
revenues were generated, the specific write-
off method does not match bad debts expense
with the revenues generated by sales in the
same period.

b. One allowance method estimates bad debts
based on credit sales. The method focuses on
the income statement and attempts to match bad
debts with the revenues generated by the sales
in the same period.

   The other allowance method estimates bad
debts based on the balance in the trade
accounts receivable accounts. The method
focuses on the balance sheet and attempts to
value the accounts receivable at their future
collectible amounts.

c. Anth should account for the collection of
the specific accounts previously written off
as uncollectible as follows:

   •   Correction of allowance account by
debiting accounts receivable and crediting
allowance for doubtful accounts.
   •   Collection of specific accounts previously written off as uncollectible by
debiting cash and crediting accounts receivable.

d. Anth should report the face amount of the
interest-bearing notes receivable and the
related interest receivable for the period
July 1, 1985 through December 31, 1986, on its
December 31, 1986 balance sheet as current
assets. Both assets are due on June 30, 1987,
which is within one year of the date of the
balance sheet.

   Anth should report interest income from
the notes receivable on its income statement
for the year ended December 31, 1986. The
interest income would be equal to the amount
accrued on the notes receivable at the stated
rate for twelve months. Interest accrues with
the passage of time, and it should be accounted for as an element of income over the
life of the notes receivable.

Answer Outline

Problem 2   Sales Discounts Under Net Method,
              Factoring A/R, and Interest from
              N/R (1188,T2)

a. 1. Accounting for sales discounts using net
          method
          Record A/R and sales revenue as sales
             less sales discounts
          Rationale: Record revenues at cash
             equivalent price at date of sale
   2. Effect when customers don't take sales
          discount
          No effect on sales revenue
          Net income increased by amount of
             interest (discount) earned
b. Effect of trade discounts on sales and
       A/R

Not recorded in accounts or financial
statements
Record sales revenue and A/R net of
trade discounts
Amount recorded represents cash
equivalent price of asset sold

c.   Accounting for A/R factored
Cash   xxx
Loss   xxx
   A/R   xxx
Factoring on without recourse basis is
equivalent to a sale

d.   Presentation of interest-bearing note
Balance Sheet
   Face amount of note and related
   interest receivable as NCAs at
   12/31/87
   Report as NCAs because both due
   more than one year from B/S date

Income Statement
   Interest revenue for year ended
   12/31/87 = Face x % x 3/12
   Report as element of income over
   life of note because interest
   accrues with passage of time

Unofficial Answer

Problem 2   Sales Discounts Under Net
            Method, Factoring A/R, and
            Interest from N/R (1188,T2)

a.1. Hogan should account for the sales
discounts at the date of sale using the net
method by recording accounts receivable and
sales revenue at the amount of sales less the
sales discounts available.
     Revenues should be recorded at the cash
equivalent price at the date of sale. Under
the net method, the sale is recorded at an
amount that represents the cash equivalent
price at the date of exchange (sale).
     2. There is no effect on Hogan's sales
revenues when customers do not take the sales
discounts. Hogan's net income is increased by
the amount of interest (discount) earned when
customers do not take the sales discounts.

b.   Trade discounts are neither recorded in
the accounts nor reported in the financial
statements. Therefore, the amount recorded as
sales revenues and accounts receivable is net
of trade discounts and represents the cash
equivalent price of the asset sold.

c.   To account for the accounts receivable
factored on August 1, 1987, Hogan should
decrease accounts receivable by the amount of
accounts receivable factored, increase cash by
the amount received from the factor, and
record a loss. Factoring of accounts

receivable on a without recourse basis is
equivalent to a sale. The difference between
the cash received and the carrying amount of
the receivables is a loss.

d.   Hogan should report the face amount of the
interest-bearing notes receivable and the
related interest receivable for the period
from October 1 through December 31 on its
balance sheet as noncurrent assets. Both
assets are due on September 30, 1989, which is
more than one year from the date of the
balance sheet.
     Hogan should report interest revenue from
the notes receivable on its income statement
for the year ended December 31, 1987.
Interest revenue is equal to the amount
accrued on the notes receivable at the
appropriate rate for three months.
     Interest revenue is realized with the
passage of time. Accordingly, interest
revenue should be accounted for as an element
of income over the life of the notes
receivable.

Answer Outline

Problem 3   Notes and Accounts Receivable
            (585,T3)

a.   Determination of interest income from re-
     ceivables
     Interest-bearing note
        Interest income = Principal (face
        amount) x Stated percentage x 1/2 year
     Rationale: Interest income accrues with
        passage of time
     Noninterest-bearing note
        Interest income = Present value x
        Effective percentage x 1/3 year
     Rationale: Interest accrues with passage
        of time, even if unstated
b.   Reporting of receivables on the 12/31/86
     balance sheet
     Interest-bearing note
        Classified as a current asset at its
        face amount
     Noninterest-bearing note
        Classified as a noncurrent asset at its
        face amount minus unamortized discount
c.   Accounting for subsequent collections on
     assigned receivables and payments to
     lender
     Subsequent collections
        Debit cash and credit A/R assigned
     Payments to lender
        Debit notes payable and interest expense
        and credit cash
           Payments consist of both principal and
           interest

Interest charge is computed on balance outstanding

Rationale: A/R are assigned on a **with recourse**, nonnotification basis; there-fore, debtor responsible for collections and risk of losses

d. Accounting for factored trade A/R on 11/1/86

Debit

Cash (amount received from factor)

Receivable from factor (5% of A/R fac-tored withheld by factor)

Finance expense (3% of A/R factored)

Credit

A/R (amount factored)

Rationale: Factor is·responsible for col-lection of A/R factored on a **without recourse** basis

Unofficial Answer

Problem 3   Notes and Accounts Receivable (585,T3)

a. 1. For the interest-bearing note receiv-able, the interest income for 1986 should be determined by multiplying the principal (face) amount of the note by the note's rate of interest by one half (July 1, 1986 to December 31, 1986). Interest accrues with the pas-sage of time, and it should be ac-counted for as an element of income over the life of the note receivable.

2. For the noninterest-bearing note re-ceivable, the interest income for 1986 should be determined by multiplying the carrying value of the note by the prevailing rate of interest at the date of the note by one third (Septem-ber 1, 1986 to December 31, 1986). The carrying value of the note at Sep-tember 1, 1986 is the maturity amount discounted for two years at the pre-vailing interest rate from the matur-ity date of August 31, 1988, back to the issuance date of September 1, 1986. Interest, even if unstated, accrues with the passage of time, and it should be accounted for as an ele-ment of income over the life of the note receivable.

b. The interest-bearing note receivable should be reported at December 31, 1986 as a current asset at its principal (face) amount.

The noninterest-bearing note receivable should be reported at December 31, 1986 as a noncurrent asset at its face amount less the unamortized discount on the note at Decem-ber 31, 1986.

c. Because the trade accounts receivable are assigned on a with-recourse, nonnotification basis, Marie is responsible for collection and assumes the risks of any losses. Marie should account for the subsequent collections on the assigned trade accounts receivable by debiting cash and crediting accounts receivable as-signed. The cash collected should then be remitted to Daniel Finance until the amount advanced by Daniel Finance is settled. The payments to Daniel Finance consist of both principal and interest with interest computed at the rate of 20 percent on the balance out-standing.

d. Because the trade accounts receivable were factored on a without-recourse basis, the factor is responsible for collection. On November 1, 1986, Marie should credit accounts receivable for the amount of trade accounts receivable factored, debit cash for the amount received from the factor, debit a receivable from the factor for 5 percent of the trade accounts receivable factored, and debit finance charges (an expense) for 3 percent of the trade accounts receivable factored.

Answer Outline

Problem 4   Contingencies (1189,T3)

a. Disclose threat of expropriation in notes to F/Ss

Include estimate of possible loss or range thereof

Accrual inappropriate because threat only reasonably possible, not probable

b. Accrue loss and liability from safety hazard and report in F/Ss

Because both recognition conditions met

Probable that liability incurred

Amount of loss can be reasonably estimated

Additionally, disclose nature of hazard in notes to F/Ss

c. Do not recognize loss and liability

Because no asset impaired/liability incurred at B/S date

Disclosure of uninsured risk permitted, but not required

Unofficial Answer

Problem 4   Contingencies (1189,T3)

a. Chester should disclose the threat of expropriation of assets in the notes to the financial statements. Disclosure would in-clude an estimate of the possible loss or an estimate of the range of loss. Accrual of a loss is inappropriate because the threat of expropriation is only reasonably possible.

b. Chester should report the potential costs due to the safety hazard by accruing a loss in the income statement and a liability in the balance sheet. Accrual is required because both of the following conditions are met:

• It is considered probable that a liability has been incurred.
• The amount of the loss can be reasonably estimated.

In addition, Chester should separately disclose in the notes to the financial statements the nature of the safety hazard.

c. Chester should not accrue a loss because an asset has not been impaired nor has a liability been incurred. Disclosure of the uninsured rock-slide risk, while permitted, is not required.

Answer Outline

Problem 5   Contingencies (1187,T4)

a. Reporting potential costs from safety hazards
    Expense (loss) on I/S
    Liability on B/S
    Costs are both probable and reasonably estimable
    Disclose nature of costs in notes to FSs
b. Disclose potential costs from warranty costs in notes to FSs
    Include statement that it is not possible to reasonably estimate either single amount or range of possible loss
    No liability on B/S or expense on I/S
    Potential costs are probable but not reasonably estimable
c. Disclose potential costs from possible product defect in notes to FSs
    Include single estimate or range of possible loss
    No liability on B/S or expense on I/S
    Potential costs are reasonably estimable but not probable

Unofficial Answer

Problem 5   Contingencies (1187,T4)

a. Spackenkill should report the potential costs due to the discovery of a safety hazard as an expense or loss in the income statement and as a liability in the balance sheet because both of the following conditions for accrual are met:

• It is considered probable that a liability has been incurred.
• The amount of loss can be reasonably estimated.

In addition, Spackenkill should disclose the nature of the costs due to the discovery of a safety hazard in the notes to the financial statements.

b. Spackenkill should disclose the nature of the potential costs of warranty costs in the notes of the financial statements. The disclosure should include a statement that an estimate of the possible loss or range of loss cannot be made.

Spackenkill should not report the warranty costs as an expense in the income statement nor as a liability in the balance sheet. Although the warranty costs are probable, they cannot be reasonably estimated.

c. Spackenkill should disclose the nature of the potential costs due to the discovery of a possible product defect in the notes to the financial statements. The disclosure should include an estimate of the possible loss or range of loss.

Spackenkill should not report the costs due to the discovery of a possible product defect as an expense or loss in the income statement nor as a liability in the balance sheet. Although the costs due to the discovery of a possible product defect can be reasonably estimated, they are not probable.

FUNDAMENTALS

Multiple Choice Questions (1-14)

1.   On January 15, 1988, Carr Corp. adopted a plan to accumulate funds for environmental improvements beginning July 2, 1992, at an estimated cost of $2,000,000. Carr plans to make four equal annual deposits in a fund that will earn interest at 10% compounded annually. The first deposit was made on July 1, 1988. Future value and future amount factors are as follows:

Future value of 1 at 10% for 5 periods   1.61
Future amount of ordinary annuity of 1
  at 10% for 4 periods   4.64
Future amount of annuity in advance
  of 1 at 10% for 4 periods   5.11

Carr should make four annual deposits (rounded) of
   a. $322,000
   b. $391,400
   c. $431,000
   d. $500,000

2.   On July 1, 1984, James Rago signed an agreement to operate as a franchisee of Fast Foods, Inc. for an initial franchise fee of $60,000. Of this amount, $20,000 was paid when the agreement was signed and the balance is payable in four equal annual payments of $10,000 beginning July 1, 1985. The agreement provides that the down payment is not refundable and no future services are required of the franchisor. Rago's credit rating indicates that he can borrow money at 14% for a loan of this type. Information on present and future value factors is as follows:

Present value of $1
  at 14% for 4 periods   0.59
Future amount of $1
  at 14% for 4 periods   1.69
Present value of an
  ordinary annuity of $1
  at 14% for 4 periods   2.91

Rago should record the acquisition cost of the franchise on July 1, 1984, at
   a. $43,600
   b. $49,100
   c. $60,000
   d. $67,600

3.   On May 1, 1985, a company purchased a new machine which it does not have to pay for until May 1, 1987. The total payment on May 1, 1987 will include both principal and interest. Assuming interest at a 10% rate, the cost of the machine would be the total payment multiplied by what time value of money concept?
   a.   Future amount of annuity of 1.
   b.   Future amount of 1.

   c.   Present value of annuity of 1.
   d.   Present value of 1.

4.   For which of the following transactions would the use of the present value of an annuity due concept be appropriate in calculating the present value of the asset obtained or liability owed at the date of incurrence?
   a.   A capital lease is entered into with the initial lease payment due one month subsequent to the signing of the lease agreement.
   b.   A capital lease is entered into with the initial lease payment due upon the signing of the lease agreement.
   c.   A ten-year 8% bond is issued on January 2 with interest payable semi-annually on July 1 and January 1 yielding 7%.
   d.   A ten-year 8% bond is issued on January 2 with interest payable semi-annually on July 1 and January 1 yielding 9%.

5.   On January 1, 1986, Mill Company sold a building and received as consideration $100,000 cash and a $400,000 noninterest-bearing note due on January 1, 1989. There was no established exchange price for the building, and the note had no ready market. The prevailing rate of interest for a note of this type at January 1, 1986 was 10%. The present value of $1 at 10% for three periods is 0.75. What amount of interest revenue should be included in Mill's 1987 income statement?
   a. $44,000
   b. $40,000
   c. $33,333
   d. $33,000

6.   On January 1, 1988, Ott Company sold goods to Fox Company. Fox signed a noninterest-bearing note requiring payment of $60,000 annually for seven years. The first payment was made on January 1, 1988. The prevailing rate of interest for this type of note at date of issuance was 10%. Information on present value factors is as follows:

Periods	Present value of 1 at 10%	Present value of ordinary annuity of 1 at 10%
6	.56	4.36
7	.51	4.87

Ott should record sales revenues in January 1988 of
   a. $321,600
   b. $292,200
   c. $261,600
   d. $214,200

2
6

7.   Rex Company accepted a $10,000, 2%
interest-bearing note from Brooks Company on
December 31, 1986, in exchange for a machine
with a list price of $8,000 and a cash price
of $7,500. The note is payable on Decem-
ber 31, 1988. In its 1986 income statement,
Rex should report the sale at
   a. $ 7,500
   b. $ 8,000
   c. $10,000
   d. $10,400

8.   On July 1, 1988, a company obtained a
two-year 8% note receivable for services
rendered. At that time the market rate of
interest was 10%. The face amount of the note
and the entire amount of the interest are due
on June 30, 1990. Interest receivable at December 31, 1988, was
   a.   5% of the face value of the note.
   b.   4% of the face value of the note.
   c.   5% of the July 1, 1988, present
         value of the amount due June 30,
         1990.
   d.   4% of the July 1, 1988, present
         value of the amount due June 30,
         1990.

9.   On December 30, 1986, Case Company
purchased a machine from Pitt in exchange for
a noninterest-bearing note requiring ten
payments of $10,000. The first payment was
made on December 30, 1986, and the others are
due annually on December 30. The prevailing
rate of interest for this type of note at date
of issuance was 10%. Present value factors
are as follows:

	Present value of ordinary annuity of	Present value of annuity in advance of
Period	1 at 10%	1 at 10%
9	5.759	6.335
10	6.145	6.759

At December 31, 1986, the total note payable
to Pitt was
   a. $67,590
   b. $63,350
   c. $61,450
   d. $57,590

10.   On January 1, 1987, Tone Company exchanged equipment for a $200,000 noninterest-
bearing note due on January 1, 1990. The prevailing rate of interest for a note of this
type at January 1, 1987 was 10%. The present
value of $1 at 10% for three periods is 0.75.
What amount of interest revenue should be
included in Tone's 1988 income statement?
   a. $ 7,500
   b. $15,000
   c. $16,500
   d. $20,000

11.   On January 1, 1984, Parke Company borrowed $360,000 from a major customer evidenced
by a noninterest-bearing note due in three
years. Parke agreed to supply the customer's
inventory needs for the loan period at lower
than market price. At the 12% imputed interest rate for this type of loan, the present
value of the note is $255,000 at January 1,
1984. What amount of interest expense should
be included in Parke's 1984 income statement?
   a. $43,200
   b. $35,000
   c. $30,600
   d. $0

12.   On October 1, 1983, a company received a
one-year note receivable bearing interest at
the market rate. The face amount of the note
receivable and the entire amount of the interest are due on September 30, 1984. The interest receivable account at December 31, 1983
would consist of an amount representing
   a.   Three months of accrued interest
         income.
   b.   Nine months of accrued interest
         income.
   c.   Twelve months of accrued interest
         income.
   d.   The excess at October 1, 1983, of
         the present value of the note
         receivable over its face value.

13.   On September 1, 1982, a company borrowed
cash and signed a two-year interest-bearing
note on which both the principal and interest
are payable on September 1, 1984. At December 31, 1983, the liability for accrued
interest should be
   a.   Zero.
   b.   For 4 months of interest.
   c.   For 12 months of interest.
   d.   For 16 months of interest.

14.   On July 1, 1983, a company received a
one-year note receivable bearing interest at
the market rate. The face amount of the note
receivable and the entire amount of the
interest are due on June 30, 1984. When the
note receivable was recorded on July 1, 1983,
which of the following were debited?

	Interest receivable	Unearned discount on note receivable
a.	Yes	No
b.	Yes	Yes
c.	No	No
d.	No	Yes

May 1990 Question

Repeat Question

(590,P2,29) Identical/similar to item 9 above

FUNDAMENTALS

Problem

Problem 1   (584,P5)*

(40 to 50 minutes)

Linden, Inc. had the following long-term receivable account balances at December 31, 1985:

Note receivable from sale
 of division $1,500,000
Note receivable from officer   400,000

Transactions during 1986 and other information relating to Linden's long-term receivables were as follows:

• The $1,500,000 note receivable is dated May 1, 1985, bears interest at 9%, and represents the balance of the consideration received from the sale of Linden's electronics division to Pitt Company. Principal payments of $500,000 plus appropriate interest are due on May 1, 1986, 1987, and 1988. The first principal and interest payment was made on May 1, 1986. Collection of the note installments is reasonably assured.

• The $400,000 note receivable is dated December 31, 1983, bears interest at 8%, and is due on December 31, 1988. The note is due from Robert Finley, president of Linden, Inc., and is collateralized by 10,000 shares of Linden's common stock. Interest is payable annually on December 31 and all interest payments were paid on their due dates through December 31, 1986. The quoted market price of Linden's common stock was $45 per share on December 31, 1986.

• On April 1, 1986, Linden sold a patent to Bell Company in exchange for a $100,000 noninterest bearing note due on April 1, 1988. There was no established exchange price for the patent, and the note had no ready market. The prevailing rate of interest for a note of this type at April 1, 1986, was 15%. The present value of $1 for two periods at 15% is 0.756. The patent had a carrying value of $40,000 at January 1, 1986, and the amortization for the year ended December 31, 1986, would have been $8,000. The collection of the note receivable from Bell is reasonably assured.

• On July 1, 1986, Linden sold a parcel of land to Carr Company for $200,000 under an installment sale contract. Carr made a $60,000 cash down payment on July 1, 1986, and signed a four-year 16% note for the $140,000 balance. The equal annual payments of principal and interest on the note will be $50,000 payable on July 1, 1987, through July 1, 1990. The land could have been sold at an established cash price of $200,000. The cost of the land to Linden was $150,000. Circumstances are such that the collection of the installments on the note is reasonably assured.

Required:

1. Prepare the long-term receivables section of Linden's balance sheet at December 31, 1986.
2. Prepare a schedule showing the current portion of the long-term receivables and accrued interest receivable that would appear in Linden's balance sheet at December 31, 1986.
3. Prepare a schedule showing interest income from the long-term receivables and gains recognized on sale of assets that would appear on Linden's income statement for the year ended December 31, 1986.

*Recent Accounting Practice Exams have included two comprehensive problems that have multiple requirements related to the same problem data, similar to this one. Candidates should work all of these included in this volume so as to be prepared for them.

FUNDAMENTALS

Multiple Choice Answers

1. b	4. b	7. a	10. c	13. d
2. b	5. d	8. b	11. c	14. c
3. d	6. a	9. d	12. a	

Multiple Choice Answer Explanations

A.1. Fundamentals

1. (1188,P1,14) (b) The desired fund balance on July 2, 1992 ($2,000,000) is a future amount. The series of four equal annual deposits is an annuity in advance, as illustrated in the diagram below:

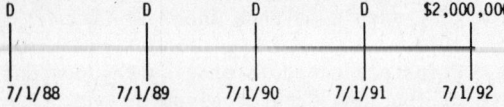

D	D	D	D	$2,000,000
7/1/88	7/1/89	7/1/90	7/1/91	7/1/92

This is an annuity in advance, rather than an ordinary annuity, because the last deposit (7/1/91) is made one year prior to the date the future amount is needed. Therefore, these are beginning-of-year payments. The deposit amount is computed by dividing the future amount by the factor for the future amount of an annuity in advance:

$$\$2,000,000 \div 5.11 = \$391,400$$

2. (1184,P1,17) (b) The requirement is to determine the acquisition cost of a franchise. The cost of this franchise is the down payment of $20,000 plus the present value of the four equal annual payments of $10,000. The annual payments represent an annuity, so the $10,000 annual payment is multiplied by the present value factor of 2.91. Therefore, the franchise cost is $49,100 ($20,000 + $29,100). The journal entry is:

Franchise	49,100	
Discount on notes payable	10,900	
Notes payable		40,000
Cash		20,000

3. (585,T1,45) (d) The requirement is to determine what time value of money concept would be used to determine the cost of a machine when a payment (principal plus interest) is to be made in two years. Answer (d) is correct because the cost of the machine is to be recorded immediately; therefore the cost of the present value of a lump-sum payment would be used. Answer (a) is incorrect because a future amount would be used in computing the payment and not the cost of the machine. Also, a lump-sum payment is involved and not an annuity. Answer (b) is incorrect because a future amount would be used in computing the payment and not the cost. Answer (c) is incorrect because a lump-sum payment is involved, not an annuity.

4. (582,T1,4) (b) The requirement is the situation which illustrates an annuity due. An annuity due (annuity in advance) is a series of payments where the first payment is made at the beginning of the first period, in contrast to an ordinary annuity (annuity in arrears), in which the first payment is made at the end of the first period. Answer (b) is correct because the initial lease payment is due immediately (at the beginning of the first period). Answers (a), (c), and (d) all illustrate situations in which the first lease or interest payment occurs at the end of the first period. Note that in answers (c) and (d), the stated rate and yield rate of the bonds differ; while this would effect the present value of the bonds, it has no effect on the classification as an annuity due or an ordinary annuity.

A.9. Notes Receivable and Payable

5. (1188,P2,36) (d) Per APB 21, para 10, property is exchanged for a note and neither the property nor the note has a known fair market value; interest is imputed using the prevailing rate of interest for a note of similar quality. Therefore, the note should be recorded at its present value of $300,000 ($400,000 x .75) by debiting notes receivable for $400,000 and crediting discount on notes receivable for $100,000 ($400,000 - $300,000). APB 21, para 15 states that the discount should be amortized and recognized as interest revenue over the life of the note using the interest method. Under the interest method, interest revenue/expense equals the carrying value of the note multiplied by the imputed interest rate. For 1986, interest revenue is $30,000 ($300,000 x 10%). Discount on notes receivable is debited for the amount of interest revenue recognized ($30,000) which increases the carrying value of the notes to $330,000. Thus, interest revenue reported in 1987 is $33,000 ($330,000 x 10%).

6. (1188,P2,38) (a) If the FMV of the goods sold and the FMV of the note received are not known, the transaction should be recorded at the PV of the note by imputing interest at the prevailing rate (10%) for this type of note. This series of seven payments is an annuity in advance, as illustrated in the diagram below:

PV = ?			
R	R	R	R
7/1/88	7/1/89	7/1/93	7/1/94

In a PV computation, one must look at the first rent to see if it is an ordinary annuity or an annuity in advance. The first rent falls on the same day as the PV computation, so these are beginning-of-year payments.

However, annuity in advance factors are not given. If the first rent is ignored, the series of the remaining six payments is an ordinary annuity. The PV of the note is equal to the first payment ($60,000) plus the PV of the remaining six payments (60,000 x 4.36 = $261,600). Thus, sales revenue of $321,600 is recorded ($60,000 + $261,600 = $321,600). Alternatively, the "6" period PV of ordinary annuity factor could be converted to an annuity in advance by adding 1.00 to obtain 5.36 which is then multiplied by $60,000 to obtain $321,600.

7.   (1187,P2,39)   (a) According to APB 21, para 12, the stated interest rate of a note exchanged for property is assumed to be fair unless no interest rate is stated, the stated interest rate is unreasonable, or the face amount is materially different from the cash sales price of the property. In this case, the last two circumstances apply. The stated rate (2%) is so low as to appear unreasonable, and the face amount ($10,000) is materially different from the cash sales price ($7,500). APB 21 states that in these circumstances, the present value of the note is measured by the fair value of the property. Therefore, this note has a present value of $7,500 and the sale should be recorded at that amount, as indicated below:

Notes receivable   10,000
   Sales   7,500
   Discount on notes receivable   2,500

Note that the list price ($8,000) is disregarded. A list price is a selling tool which generally does not reflect fair value.

8.   (1189,T1,6)   (b) When a note is issued with a stated rate (8% in this case) below the market rate (10% in this case), the note will be issued at a discount. The entry for the recipient of the note on July 1 would be as follows:

   Notes receivable   XXX
      Disc. on notes rec.   XXX
      Service revenue   XXX

On December 31, the company must accrue interest on the note. The following entry would be made:

Interest receivable   (six months at stated rate)
Disc. on notes rec.   (six months amortization)
   Interest revenue   (six months interest at market rate)

Note that interest receivable is debited for an amount based upon the stated (face) rate of the note. This is because the stated rate will determine the amount of cash interest which will be received upon maturity of the note. Since the bond was held for six months (7/1/88 to 12/31/88) as of 12/31/88, the

amount of the receivable would be determined as follows:

$$\text{Interest Receivable} = \left(\begin{array}{c}\text{Face Value}\\\text{of Note}\end{array}\right) \times \left(\begin{array}{c}\text{Stated}\\\text{Rate}\end{array}\right) \times \left(\begin{array}{c}\text{Period}\\\text{Held}\end{array}\right)$$
= Face value x 8% x (6/12 months)
= 4% x Face Value

Therefore, answer (b) is correct.

9.   (587,P1,5)   (d) Per APB 21, para 12, noninterest bearing notes are recorded at their present values. Since the first payment in this problem is due on the date of purchase, the ten annual payments represent an annuity in advance (also known as an "annuity due"). To compute the present value of this note, the $10,000 annual payment must be multiplied by 6.759, the factor for the present value of an annuity in advance of 1 at 10% for 10 periods. The present value of this note is thus $67,590 ($10,000 x 6.759). To determine the total note payable to Pitt at December 31, 1986, the first payment of $10,000 (paid on 12/30/86) must be deducted from the balance of the note. Therefore, the total note payable to Pitt at December 31, 1986 is $57,590 ($67,590 - $10,000). Alternatively, since the next payment is one year away on 12/31/86, the nine remaining payments are an ordinary annuity. The present value of the note payable at 12/31/86 is $57,590 ($10,000 x 5.759).

10.   (589,P3,59)   (c) The note should be recorded at its present value of $150,000 ($200,000 x .75) by debiting notes receivable for $200,000 and crediting discount on notes receivable for $50,000 ($200,000 - $150,000). Para 15 of APB 21 states that the discount should be amortized and recognized as interest revenue over the term of the note using the interest method. Under the interest method, interest revenue (expense) equals the carrying value of the note multiplied by the inputed interest rate. For 1987, interest revenue is $15,000 ($150,000 x 10%). Discount on note receivable is debited for the amount of interest revenue recognized, increasing the carrying value of the note to $165,000 at the beginning of 1988 ($150,000 + $15,000). Thus, 1988 interest revenue is $16,500 ($165,000 x 10%).

11.   (585,P2,38)   (c) The requirement is to determine the amount of interest expense to be recognized in 1984 from a noninterest bearing note. Parke Company is able to borrow on a noninterest basis because they agree to sell their product at less than the market price. In this type of situation, the note payable is recorded at present value, and the difference between the present value and the cash

received is recorded as <u>unearned sales revenue</u>
(to be recognized when the product is sold at
less than market value). The initial journal
entry is:

    Cash   360,000
    Discount on N.P.   105,000   ⎫
       Note payable   360,000   ⎬ 255,000
       Unearned sales revenue   105,000   ⎭

When interest expense is recognized at the end
of 1984, the effective interest method must be
used. Using this method, interest expense is
computed by multiplying the book value of the
liability ($360,000 - $105,000 = $255,000) by
the effective interest rate (12%), resulting
in interest expense of $30,600.

12. (1184,T1,8) (a) The requirement is the
amount of interest to be reported as interest
receivable on the December 31, 1983 balance
sheet in connection with interest on a note
receivable. Under the accrual basis of accounting, revenues should be recognized when
earned, regardless of when the cash is received. The portion of interest earned from
October 1 to December 31 should be accrued at
the end of the year. The journal entry made
on December 31 recording three months of
accrued income follows:

        Interest receivable   XX
           Interest revenue   XX

Since the interest applicable for the nine-
month period January 1 to September 30 has not
yet been earned [answer (b)], no revenue may
be recognized. Answer (c) is incorrect because only three months of interest income has
accrued. Since the note bears interest at the
market rate at the date of receipt, the present value of the note equals its face value
and no excess exists [answer (d)].

13. (584,T1,17) (d) The requirement is the
number of months of interest accrued as of
December 31, 1983 for a note on which the
interest is payable at maturity. In this
situation an adjusting entry would have to be
made at the end of both 1982 (4 months interest) and 1983 (12 months interest). The entries would be as follows:

        Interest expense   XXX
           Accrued interest payable   XXX

Thus, the balance in the liability account
would contain 16 months interest on December 31, 1983.

14. (1183,T1,8) (c) The requirement is to
determine the account which is debited when a
note receivable bearing interest at the market
rate is received. The journal entry to record
the receipt is:

    Notes receivable   XXX
       Sales (or cash, etc.)   XXX

Answers (a) and (b) are incorrect because no
interest has been earned on the note and,
therefore, no receivable is accrued. Answer (d) is incorrect because no discount is
recorded on a note bearing interest at the
market rate.

FUNDAMENTALS

Solution Guide

Problem 1   Long-Term Notes Receivable
                (584,P5)

1. This problem consists of three related
    requirements. The candidate is required
    to prepare a long-term receivables
    section, prepare a schedule showing the
    current portion of the receivables and
    accrued interest receivable, and prepare
    a schedule showing the interest income
    and gains recognized on the sale of
    assets. Information pertaining to four
    notes is given.

1.1 The solutions approach for problems of
    this type where the requirements are
    interrelated is to prepare time lines for
    each note, make all computations for each
    note at one time, and label each computa-
    tion according to the requirement to
    which it relates. For example, if a
    number or computation relates to re-
    quirement 1., it can be labeled "①"
    Letters can be added to designate sub-
    requirements contained in each numbered
    requirement (e.g., ②a ②b). Using
    this approach, the candidate will be
    solving a part of two to three require-
    ments as each note is covered, but not
    necessarily in the same order as given on
    the exam. After working through all the
    information given, the formal required
    schedules can be prepared.

1.2 The requirement in part one is the long-
    term receivables section of the balance
    sheet dated 12/31/86. The solutions
    approach is to determine the amount of
    each note which is due after 12/31/87.
    In preparing the receivables section, all
    relevant information must be disclosed,
    e.g., interest rates, due dates, less
    current installment (if applicable), etc.

1.3 Part two is essentially two subrequire-
    ments requiring a schedule showing the
    current portion of the long-term receiv-
    ables (requirement 2a.) and accrued
    interest receivable (requirement 2b.)
    that would appear in the balance sheet at
    12/31/86.

1.4 Part three is also essentially two subre-
    quirements requiring the preparation of a
    schedule showing interest income from
    long-term receivables (requirement 3a.)
    and gains recognized on the sale of
    assets (requirement 3b.) that would
    appear on the income statement for the
    year ending 12/31/86.

2. For the note arising from the sale of the
    electronics division, $500,000 of the
    $1,500,000 principal was received on
    5/1/86, leaving $1,000,000 to be re-
    ceived. Of this amount, $500,000 is due
    on 5/1/87 and represents the current por-
    tion. The remaining principal amount of
    $500,000 is due subsequent to 12/31/87
    and is classified as long-term (see time
    line after 2.2).

2.1 Interest has accrued on the note arising
    from the sale of the division since the
    last interest payment date, 5/1/86, in
    the amount of $60,000 ($1,000,000 x 9% x
    8/12) (see time line after 2.2).

2.2 The interest income on the note from the
    sale of the division is $105,000. This
    is equal to 9% of the note's balance out-
    standing from 1/1/86 to the date of the
    first principal payment, 5/1/86,
    ($1,500,000 x 9% x 4/12 = $45,000) plus
    the interest earned on the remaining
    balance from the payment date to 12/31/86
    ($1,000,000 x 9% x 8/12 = $60,000).

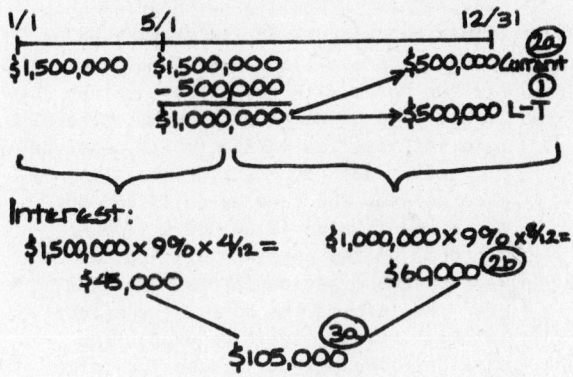

3. The $400,000 note receivable from the
    officer is due 12/31/88; therefore, the
    entire amount is classified as long-term
    (see time line after 3.3).

3.1 Since the interest is payable annually on
    12/31 and all the scheduled interest pay-
    ments have been made, no interest has
    accrued on the note received from the
    officer.

3.2 A full year's interest was earned on the
    officer's note, or $32,000 ($400,000 x
    8%) (see time line after 3.3).

3.3 Note no gain or loss is recorded on the stock acting as collateral. However, data relating to the collateral should be disclosed.

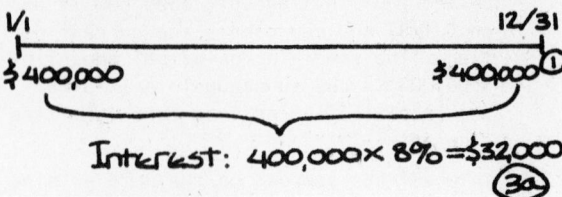

4. The carrying value of the patent is its 1/1/86 value, $40,000, less the 1986 amortization, $2,000 ($8,000 × 3/12), or $38,000. Subtracting the 4/1/86 carrying value from the present value of the note received for the patent ($75,600) equals the gain on the sale of the patent, $37,600 (see time line after 4.2).

4.1 The $100,000 note arising from the sale of the patent is due 4/1/88 and is therefore considered long-term. Per APB 21, paras 12-14, a noninterest bearing note should be recorded at its present value using the prevailing rate of interest on similar notes with any difference recorded as a discount or premium. Therefore, at the time this note was received, a discount was recorded for the difference between the face value ($100,000) and present value ($100,000 × .756 = $75,600) of the note, or $24,400, which will be amortized as interest revenue over the life of the note. The effective interest method should be used. The straight-line method is used for intraperiod allocation. Interest was earned for nine months (4/1-12/31) on the carrying value of the note; therefore, the 1986 interest revenue and discount amortization is $8,505 ($75,600 × 15% × 9/12). After the 1986 amortization ($8,505) is recorded, the unamortized discount on 12/31/86 is $15,895 ($24,400 - $8,505). The note is presented net of the discount (see time line after 4.2).

4.2 No accrued interest will be recorded in the receivable account pertaining to the note from the sale of the patent. Even though interest revenue is recorded, the interest is a direct result of amortizing the related discount on the note and is not recorded as a receivable.

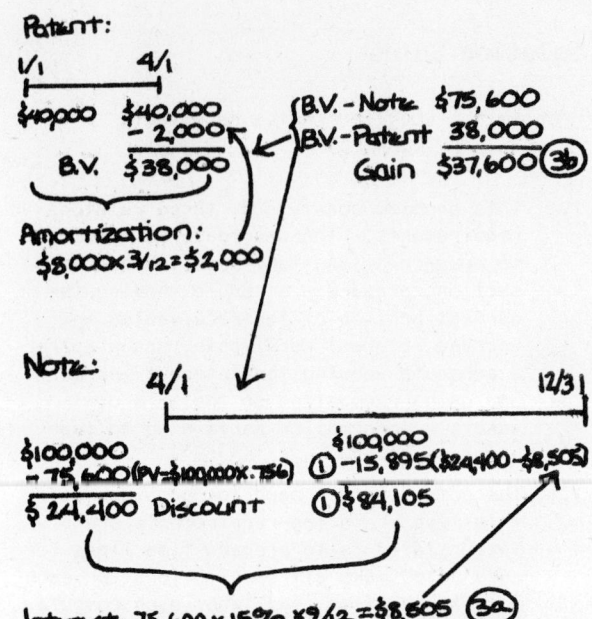

5. The gain on the land sale is the selling price, $200,000 less its cost, $150,000, or $50,000 (see time line after 5.2).

5.1 Since the principal (and interest) on the note relating to the sale of land will be paid off in four $50,000 annual installments beginning in 1987, the note must be divided between its current and long-term portions. Subtracting the first year's interest, $22,400 ($140,000 × 16%) from the $50,000 installment to be received on 7/1/87 equals $27,600, or the current portion. The remainder of the note, $112,400 ($140,000 - $27,600), is the long-term receivable (see time line after 5.2).

5.2 Six months' interest was earned and accrued in 1986 on the note arising from the sale of land, or $11,200 ($140,000 × 16% × 6/12).

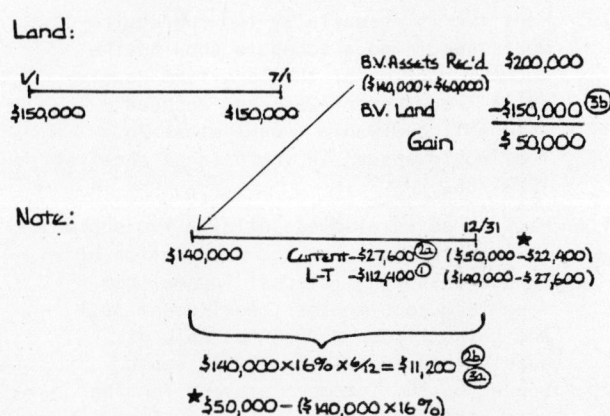

Unofficial Answer

Problem 1   Long-Term Notes Receivable
            (584,P5)

1.   Linden, Inc.
            Long-Term Receivables Section
                   of Balance Sheet
                  December 31, 1986

9% note receivable from sale of
 division, due in annual installments of $500,000 to May 1, 1988,
 less current installment
 (Schedule 1) $ 500,000
8% note receivable from officer,
 due December 31, 1988, collateralized by 10,000 shares of
 Linden, Inc. common stock with
 a fair value of $450,000   400,000
Noninterest bearing note from sale
 of patent, due April 1, 1988, less
 $15,895 discount based on 15%
 imputed interest (Schedule 2)   84,105
Installment contract receivable,
 due in annual installments of
 $50,000 to July 1, 1990, less
 current installment (Schedule 3)   112,400
Total long-term receivables $1,096,505

Schedule 1

Sale of Division

Face amount, 5/1/85 $1,500,000
Less installment received,
 5/1/86   (500,000)
Balance, 12/31/86 $1,000,000
Less current portion of
 note, due 5/1/87   (500,000)
Long-term portion of note
 receivable, 12/31/86 $ 500,000

Schedule 2

Note from Patent Sale

Face amount, 4/1/86 $100,000
Less present value of note
 ($100,000 x .756)   75,600
Unamortized discount,
 4/1/86 $ 24,400
Less interest earned,
 4/1/86-12/31/86
 ($75,600 x 15% x 9/12)   8,505
Unamortized discount,
 12/31/86 $ 15,895

Schedule 3

Sale of Land

Contract selling price,
 7/1/86 $200,000
Less down payment, 7/1/86   (60,000)
Balance, 12/31/86 $140,000
Less current portion of
 7/1/87 receipt:
  Amount to be received $50,000
  Less interest, 7/1/86-
   6/30/87, ($140,000 x
   16%)   (22,400)   (27,600)
Long-term portion of note
 receivable $112,400

2.   Linden, Inc.
      Schedule of Current Portion of Long-Term
      Receivables and Accrued Interest Receivable
                  December 31, 1986

Current portion of long-term receivables:
 Note receivable from sale of
  division (Schedule 1) $500,000
 Installment contract receivable
  (Schedule 3)   27,600
Total current portion $527,600

Accrued interest receivable:
 Note receivable from sale
  of division
  ($1,000,000 x 9% x 8/12) $60,000
 Installment contract receivable
  ($140,000 x 16% x 6/12)   11,200
Total accrued interest receivable $71,200

3.   Linden, Inc.
     Schedule of Interest Income from Long-Term
        Receivables and Gains Recognized
               on Sale of Assets
     For the Year Ending December 31, 1986

Interest income:
 Note receivable from sale
  of division (Schedule 4) $105,000
 Note receivable from
  officer ($400,000 x 8%)   32,000
 Note receivable from sale of
  patent (Schedule 2)   8,505
 Installment receivable from sale of
  land ($140,000 x 16% x 6/12)   11,200
Total interest income for 1986 $156,705

Gains from sale of assets:
 Gain on sale of patent
  (Schedule 5) $ 37,600
 Gain on sale of land
  ($200,000 - $150,000)   50,000
Total gains recognized for 1986 $ 87,600

Schedule 4

Interest from Sale of Division

Interest earned from 1/1/86 to 4/30/86 ($1,500,000 x 9% x 4/12)	$ 45,000
Interest earned from 5/1/86 to 12/31/86 ($1,000,000 x 9% x 8/12)	60,000
	$105,000

Schedule 5

Gain on Sale of Patent

Present value of note (Schedule 2)		$75,600
Carrying value of patent, 4/1/86: 1/1/86 carrying value	$40,000	
Less 1986 amortization 1/1/87 to 4/1/87 ($8,000 x 3/12)	(2,000)	(38,000)
Gain on sale		$37,600

BONDS

Multiple Choice Questions (1-42)

1.   On January 1, 1987, Colt Company issued ten-year bonds with a face amount of $1,000,000 and a stated interest rate of 8% payable annually on January 1. The bonds were priced to yield 10%. Present value factors are as follows:

	At 8%	At 10%
Present value of 1 for 10 periods	0.463	0.386
Present value of an ordinary annuity of 1 for 10 periods	6.710	6.145

The total issue price (rounded) of the bonds was
   a. $1,000,000
   b. $ 980,000
   c. $ 920,000
   d. $ 880,000

2.   An investor purchased a bond classified as a long-term investment between interest dates at a discount. At the purchase date, the carrying amount of the bond is more than the

	Cash paid to seller	Face amount of bond
a.	Yes	No
b.	Yes	Yes
c.	No	Yes
d.	No	No

3.   On April 1, 1988, Greg Corp. issued, at 99 plus accrued interest, 200 of its 8%, $1,000 bonds. The bonds are dated January 1, 1988, mature on January 1, 1998, and pay interest on July 1 and January 1. Greg paid bond issue costs of $7,000. From the bond issuance, Greg received net cash of
   a. $202,000
   b. $198,000
   c. $195,000
   d. $191,000

4.   On January 1, 1989, Bing Comp. sold 200 of its 8%, $1,000 bonds at 97 plus accrued interest. The bonds are dated October 1, 1988 and mature on October 1, 1998. Interest is payable semiannually on April 1 and October 1. Accrued interest for the period October 1, 1988 to January 1, 1989 amounted to $4,000. On January 1, 1989, Pine should report bonds payable, net of discount, at
   a. $196,000
   b. $194,150
   c. $194,000
   d. $190,150

5.   On December 31, 1988, Wall Corp. issued $100,000 maturity value, 10% bonds for $100,000 cash. The bonds are dated December 31, 1988 and mature on December 31, 1998. Interest will be paid semiannually on June 30 and December 31. In Wall's September 30, 1989 balance sheet, the amount of accrued interest expense should be
   a. $ 2,500
   b. $ 5,000
   c. $ 7,500
   d. $10,000

6.   A bond issued on June 1, 1988 has interest payment dates of April 1 and October 1. Bond interest expense for the year ended December 31, 1988 would be for a period of
   a.   Three months.
   b.   Four months.
   c.   Six months.
   d.   Seven months.

7.   During 1986 Cain Corporation incurred the following costs in connection with the issuance of bonds:

Printing and engraving	$ 15,000
Legal fees	80,000
Fees paid to independent accountants for registration information	10,000
Commissions paid to underwriter	150,000

What amount should be recorded as a deferred charge to be amortized over the term of the bonds?
   a. $ 15,000
   b. $150,000
   c. $245,000
   d. $255,000

8.   On January 1, 1989, Carrow, Inc. issued its 10% bonds in the face amount of $1,000,000 that mature on January 1, 1999. The bonds were issued for $886,000 to yield 12%, resulting in bond discount of $114,000. Carrow uses the interest method of amortizing bond discount. Interest is payable July 1 and January 1. For the six months ended June 30, 1989, Carrow should report bond interest expense at
   a. $56,840
   b. $55,700
   c. $53,160
   d. $50,000

9.   On July 1, 1987, Cobb, Inc. issued 9% bonds in the face amount of $1,000,000, which mature on July 1, 1997. The bonds were issued for $939,000 to yield 10%, resulting in a bond discount of $61,000. Cobb uses the interest method of amortizing bond discount. Interest is payable annually on June 30. At June 30,

1989, Cobb's unamortized bond discount should
be

    a. $52,810

    b. $51,000

    c. $48,800

    d. $43,000

10. On July 1, 1986, Carr, Inc. issued at
104, one thousand of its 10%, $1,000 bonds.
The bonds were issued through an underwriter
to whom Carr paid bond issue costs of $25,000.
On July 1, 1986, Carr should report the bond
liability at

    a. $ 975,000

    b. $1,015,000

    c. $1,040,000

    d. $1,065,000

11. An issuer of bonds is required by its
bond indenture agreement to use a sinking fund
for the retirement of the bonds. Cash was
transferred to the sinking fund. The sinking
fund cash was then used to purchase investments. The sinking fund

    a.   Increases when the investments are
        purchased.

    b.   Decreases when the investments are
        purchased.

    c.   Increases by revenue earned on the
        investments.

    d.   Is not affected by revenue earned on
        the investments.

12. On January 2, 1985, a company established
a sinking fund in connection with an issue of
bonds due in 1995. At December 31, 1988, the
independent trustee held cash in the sinking
fund account representing the annual deposits
to the fund and the interest earned on those
deposits. How should the sinking fund be
reported in the company's classified balance
sheet at December 31, 1988?

    a.   The entire balance in the sinking
        fund account should appear as a
        noncurrent asset.

    b.   The entire balance in the sinking
        fund account should appear as a
        current asset.

    c.   The cash in the sinking fund should
        appear as a current asset.

    d.   The accumulated deposits only should
        appear as a noncurrent asset.

13. Eller Company has outstanding at December 31, 1984, several long-term borrowings
with annual sinking fund payments and
maturities as follows:

Sinking fund		
	payments	Maturities
1985	$1,000,000	$ -
1986	1,000,000	2,500,000
1987	1,000,000	-
1988	1,500,000	3,000,000
1989	1,500,000	3,000,000
1990	2,000,000	3,000,000

Eller appropriately provides footnote
disclosures in its 1984 annual report for
long-term borrowings which include sinking
fund payments and maturities for each of the
next five years. The combined aggregate
amount for 1989, the fifth year, should be
stated as

    a. $4,500,000

    b. $5,000,000

    c. $7,500,000

    d. $9,500,000

14. Zola Corp. had the following long-term
debt:

  Bonds maturing in
    installments,
    secured by machinery $ 500,000

  Bonds maturing on a
    single date,
    secured by realty   900,000

  Collateral trust bonds   1,000,000

The debenture bonds amounted to

    a. $0

    b. $ 500,000

    c. $ 900,000

    d. $1,000,000

15. Bonds payable issued with scheduled
maturities at various dates are called

	Serial bonds	Term Bonds
a.	No	Yes
b.	No	No
c.	Yes	No
d.	Yes	Yes

16. Glen Corporation had the following long-
term debt:

Sinking fund bonds, maturing in
  installments $1,100,000

Industrial revenue bonds, maturing
  in installments   900,000

Subordinated bonds, maturing
  on a single date   1,500,000

The total of the serial bonds amounted to

    a. $1,500,000

    b. $2,000,000

    c. $2,400,000

    d. $3,500,000

17. The issue price of a bond is equal to the
present value of the future cash flows for
interest and principal when the bond is issued

	At par	At a discount	At a premium
a.	Yes	No	Yes
b.	Yes	No	No
c.	No	Yes	Yes
d.	Yes	Yes	Yes

18. An investor purchased a bond as a long-term investment on January 2. The investor's carrying value at the end of the first year would be highest if the bond was purchased at a

    a. Discount and amortized by the straight-line method.

    b. Discount and amortized by the effective interest method.

    c. Premium and amortized by the straight-line method.

    d. Premium and amortized by the effective interest method.

19. A company issued ten-year term bonds at a discount in 1986. Bond issue costs were incurred at that time. The company uses the effective interest method to amortize bond issue costs. Reporting the bond issue costs as a deferred charge would result in

    a. More of a reduction in net income in 1987 than reporting the bond issue costs as a reduction of the related debt liability.

    b. The same reduction in net income in 1987 as reporting the bond issue costs as a reduction of the related debt liability.

    c. Less of a reduction in net income in 1987 than reporting the bond issue costs as a reduction of the related debt liability.

    d. No reduction in net income in 1987.

20. For the issuer of a ten-year term bond, the amount of amortization using the interest method would increase each year if the bond was sold at a

	Discount	Premium
a.	No	No
b.	Yes	Yes
c.	No	Yes
d.	Yes	No

21. How would the carrying amount of a bond payable be affected by amortization of the following

	Discount	Premium
a.	Increase	Increase
b.	Decrease	Decrease
c.	Increase	Decrease
d.	Decrease	Increase

22. On January 1, 1987, Grey Company purchased as a long-term investment 400 of the $1,000 face amount, 8% bonds of Winn Corp. for

$369,000 to yield 10% annually. The bonds pay interest semiannually on July 1 and January 1, and mature on January 1, 1992. Grey uses the interest method of amortization. The bonds should be reported (rounded) on Grey's December 31, 1987 balance sheet at

    a. $363,980

    b. $364,100

    c. $373,900

    d. $374,020

23. On July 1, 1987, East Co. purchased as a long-term investment $500,000 face amount, 8% bonds of Rand Corp. for $461,500 to yield 10% per year. The bonds pay interest semiannually on January 1 and July 1. In its December 31, 1987 balance sheet, East should report interest receivable of

    a. $18,460

    b. $20,000

    c. $23,075

    d. $25,000

24. On January 1, 1986, Carr Company purchased Fay Corp. 9% bonds with a face amount of $400,000 for $375,600, to yield 10%. The bonds are dated January 1, 1986, mature on December 31, 1995, and pay interest annually on December 31. Carr uses the interest method of amortizing bond discount. In its income statement for the year ended December 31, 1986, what total amount should Carr report as interest revenue from the long-term bond investment?

    a. $40,000

    b. $37,560

    c. $36,000

    d. $34,440

25. An investor purchased a bond as a long-term investment on January 1. Annual interest was received on December 31. The investor's interest income for the year would be highest if the bond was purchased at

    a. Par.

    b. Face value.

    c. A discount.

    d. A premium.

26. Faber, Inc. had outstanding 10%, $1,000,000 face amount convertible bonds maturing on December 31, 1993, on which interest is paid June 30 and December 31. After amortization through June 30, 1989, the unamortized balance in the bond discount account was $30,000. On that date, all of these bonds were converted into 40,000 shares of $20 par value common stock. Faber incurred expenses of $10,000 in connection with the conversion. Recording the conversion by the book value (carrying amount) method, Faber should credit additional paid-in capital for

    a. $160,000

b. $170,000
c. $180,000
d. $230,000

27. When bonds payable are converted into
common stock, any gain or loss would be
recognized when using the

	Book value method	Market value method
a.	Yes	Yes
b.	No	Yes
c.	No	No
d.	Yes	No

28. Outstanding bonds payable are converted
into common stock. Under either the book
value or market value method, the same amount
would be debited to

	Bonds payable	Premium on bonds payable
a.	No	No
b.	No	Yes
c.	Yes	No
d.	Yes	Yes

29. On March 1, 1988, Case Corp. issued
$1,000,000 of 10% nonconvertible bonds at 103,
due on February 28, 1998. Each $1,000 bond
was issued with 30 detachable stock warrants,
each of which entitled the holder to purchase,
for $50, one share of Case common stock, par
value $25. On March 1, 1988 the quoted market
value of each warrant was $4. What amount of
the bond issue proceeds should Case record as
an increase in stockholders' equity?
a. $120,000
b. $ 90,000
c. $ 30,000
d. $0

30. On May 1, Kreal Corp. issued $1,000,000,
20-year, 10% bonds for $1,075,000. Each
$1,000 bond had a detachable warrant eligible
for the purchase of one share of Kreal's $50
par value common stock for $60. Immediately
after the bonds were issued, Kreal's securities had the following market values:

10% bond without warrant $1,050
Warrant   25
Common stock, $50 par value   65

What amount of the bond issue proceeds should
Kreal record as an increase in stockholders'
equity?
a. $50,000
b. $25,000
c. $ 5,000
d. $0

31. Wolf Company issued 1,000 of its $1,000
face amount, 20-year bonds on June 30, 1985,
for $1,020,000. Each bond carries five de-

tachable stock purchase warrants, each of
which entitles the holder to purchase for $60
one share of Wolf's common stock. On June 30,
1985, the market prices were $50 per share of
Wolf's common stock and $5 per warrant. In
its June 30, 1985 balance sheet, at what
amount should Wolf report the carrying amount
of the bonds?
a. $ 995,000
b. $1,000,000
c. $1,020,000
d. $1,045,000

32. When bonds are issued with stock purchase
warrants, a portion of the proceeds should be
allocated to paid-in capital for bonds issued
with

	Detachable stock purchase warrants	Nondetachable stock purchase warrants
a.	No	Yes
b.	No	No
c.	Yes	No
d.	Yes	Yes

33. On June 30, 1987, Town, Inc. had outstanding 10%, $1,000,000 face amount, 15-year
bonds maturing on June 30, 1995. Interest is
paid on June 30 and December 31, and bond
discount and bond issue costs are amortized on
these dates. The unamortized balances on
June 30, 1987 of bond discount and bond issue
costs were $55,000 and $20,000, respectively.
Town reacquired all of these bonds at 96 on
June 30, 1987 and retired them. Ignoring
income taxes, how much gain or loss should
Town record on the bond retirement?
a.   Loss of $15,000.
b.   Loss of $35,000.
c.   Gain of $ 5,000.
d.   Gain of $40,000.

34. On February 1, 1984, Dax Corp. issued
12%, $2,000,000 face amount, 10-year bonds for
$2,234,000 plus accrued interest. The bonds
are dated November 1, 1983, and interest is
payable on May 1 and November 1. Dax reacquired all of these bonds at 102 on May 1,
1987, and retired them. Unamortized bond
premium on that date was $156,000. Ignoring
the income tax effect, what was Dax's gain on
the bond retirement?
a. $116,000
b. $194,000
b. $234,000
d. $236,000

35. On July 1, 1982, Flax Corporation issued
2,000 of its 9%, $1,000 callable bonds for
$1,920,000. The bonds are dated July 1, 1982
and mature on July 1, 1992. Interest is payable semiannually on January 1 and July 1.
Flax uses the straight-line method of amor-

tizing bond discount. The bonds can be called
by the issuer at 101 at any time after
June 30, 1987.

On July 1, 1988, Flax called in all of
the bonds and retired them. Before income
taxes, how much loss should Flax report on
this early extinguishment of debt for the year
ended December 31, 1988?

    a. $ 20,000
    b. $ 52,000
    c. $ 68,000
    d. $100,000

36. A ten-year term bond was issued in 1985
at a discount with a call provision to retire
the bonds. When the bond issuer exercised the
call provision on an interest date in 1987,
the carrying amount of the bond was less than
the call price. The amount of bond liability
removed from the accounts in 1987 should have
equaled the

    a.   Call price.
    b.   Call price less unamortized
         discount.
    b.   Face amount less unamortized
         discount.
    d.   Face amount plus unamortized
         discount.

37. Which of the following material gains on
refunding of bonds payable should be
recognized separately as an extraordinary
gain?

	Direct exchange of old bonds for new bonds	Issuance of new bonds proceeds used to retire old bonds
a.	Yes	No
b.	Yes	Yes
c.	No	Yes
d.	No	No

May 1990 Questions

38. On January 1, 1988, Purl Corp. purchased
as a long-term investment $500,000 face value
of Shaw Inc.'s 8% bonds for $456,200. The
bonds were purchased to yield 10% interest.
The bonds mature on January 1, 1991 and pay
interest annually on January 1. Purl uses the
interest method of amortization. What amount
(rounded to nearest $100) should Purl report
on its December 31, 1989 balance sheet for
this long-term investment?

    a. $468,000
    b. $466,200
    c. $461,800
    d. $456,200

39. On July 1, 1989, Howe Corp. issued 300 of
its 10%, $1,000 bonds at 99 plus accrued in-
terest. The bonds are dated April 1, 1989 and
mature on April 1, 1999. Interest is payable

semiannually on April 1 and October 1. What
amount did Howe receive from the bond issuance?

    a. $304,500
    b. $300,000
    c. $297,000
    d. $289,500

40. On January 1, 1984, Fox Corp. issued
1,000 of its 10%, $1,000 bonds for $1,040,000.
These bonds were to mature on January 1, 1994
but were callable at 101 any time after December 31, 1987. Interest was payable semiannually on July 1 and January 1. On July 1,
1989, Fox called all of the bonds and retired
them. Bond premium was amortized on a
straight-line basis. Before income taxes,
Fox's gain or loss in 1989 on this early extinguishment of debt was

    a. $30,000 gain.
    b. $12,000 gain.
    c. $10,000 loss.
    d. $ 8,000 gain.

41. On June 30, 1989, Hamm Corp. had outstanding $2,000,000 face amount of 8% convert-
ible bonds maturing on June 30, 1994. Interest is payable on June 30 and December 31.
Each $1,000 bond is convertible into 40 shares
of Hamm's $20 par common stock. After amorti-
zation through June 30, 1989, the unamortized
balance in the premium on bonds payable account was $50,000. On June 30, 1989, all of
the bonds were converted when Hamm's common
stock had a market price of $30 per share.
Under the book value method, what amount
should Hamm credit to additional paid-in capital in recording the conversion?

    a. $350,000
    b. $400,000
    c. $450,000
    d. $800,000

42. On July 1, 1989, Pell Co. purchased Green
Corp. ten-year, 8% bonds with a face amount of
$500,000 for $420,000. The bonds mature on
June 30, 1997 and pay interest semiannually on
June 30 and December 31. Using the interest
method, Pell recorded bond discount amortization of $1,800 for the six months ended Decem-
ber 31, 1989. From this long-term investment,
Pell should report 1989 revenue of

    a. $16,800
    b. $18,200
    c. $20,000
    d. $21,800

Repeat Questions

(590,P2,37) Identical/similar to item 7 above
(590,P2,38) Identical/similar to item 8 above

BONDS

Problems

Problem 1　(589,T4)

(15 to 25 minutes)

On January 2, 1988, Druid Company issued 9% term bonds dated January 2, 1988, at an effective interest rate (yield) of 10%. Druid uses the effective interest method of amortization.

On December 1, 1988, Druid issued 8% nonconvertible bonds dated December 1, 1988 with detachable stock purchase warrants. Immediately after issuance, both the bonds and the warrants have separately determined fair market values.

Required:

    a.　How would the issue price of the 9% bonds be determined?

    b.　1.　Were the 9% bonds issued at par, at a discount, or at a premium? Why?

        2.　Using the effective interest method of amortization, would the amount of interest expense for the 9% bonds be higher in the first year or second year? Why?

    c.　How should Druid account for the proceeds from the issuance of the 8% nonconvertible bonds with detachable stock purchase warrants? Why?

Problem 2　(1187,T5)

(15 to 25 minutes)

On January 1, 1985, Brewster Company issued 2,000 of its five-year, $1,000 face value, 11% bonds dated January 1 at an effective annual interest rate (yield) of 9%. Brewster uses the effective interest method of amortization. On December 31, 1986, the 2,000 bonds were extinguished early through acquisition in the open market by Brewster for $1,980,000.

On July 1, 1985, Brewster issued 5,000 of its six-year, $1,000 face value, 10% convertible bonds dated July 1 at an effective annual interest rate (yield) of 12%. The convertible bonds are convertible at the option of the investor into Brewster's common stock at a ratio of 10 shares of common stock for each bond. Brewster uses the effective interest method of amortization. On July 1, 1986, an investor in Brewster's convertible bonds tendered 1,500 bonds for conversion into 15,000 shares of Brewster's common stock which

had a market value of $105 per share at the date of the conversion.

Required:

    a.　1.　Were the 11% bonds issued at par, at a discount, or at a premium? Why?

        2.　Would the amount of interest expense for the 11% bonds using the effective interest method of amortization be higher in the first or second year of the life of the bonds issue? Why?

    b.　1.　How should gain or loss on early extinguishment of debt be determined? Does the early extinguishment of the 11% bonds result in a gain or loss? Why?

        2.　How should Brewster report the early extinguishment of the 11% bonds on the 1986 income statement?

    c.　1.　Would recording the conversion of the 10% convertible bonds into common stock under the book value method affect net income? What is the rationale for the book value method?

        2.　Would recording the conversion of the 10% convertible bonds into common stock under the market value method affect net income? What is the rationale for the market value method?

Problem 3　(586,T5)

(15 to 25 minutes)

On November 1, 1986, Abbott Company sold its 5-year, $1,000 face value, 11% term bonds dated October 1, 1986, at a discount resulting in an effective annual interest rate (yield) of 12%. Interest is payable semiannually, and the first interest payment date is April 1, 1987. Abbott uses an acceptable method of amortizing bond discount. Bond issue costs were incurred in preparing and selling the bond issue.

On December 1, 1986, Abbott sold its 6-year, $1,000 face value, 9% nonconvertible bonds with detachable stock warrants for an amount exceeding the sum of the face value of the bonds and the fair value of the warrants.

Required:

    a.　What facts above determined that the 11% term bonds were sold at discount? Why?

    b.　How would all the items related to the 11% term bonds, except cash, be presented in a balance sheet prepared immediately after the term bond issue was sold, and in a balance sheet prepared at December 31, 1986?

c. 1. Over what period of time would the bond discount be amortized?

2. Compare the straight-line and the interest methods of amortization.

3. Which of the two methods is preferable? Why?

d. How should Abbott account for the proceeds from the sale of the 9% nonconvertible bonds with detachable stock purchase warrants? Why?

Problem 4   (585,T4)

(15 to 25 minutes)

On October 1, 1986, Janine Company sold some of its 5-year, $1,000 face value, 12% term bonds dated March 1, 1986, at an effective annual interest rate (yield) of 10%. Interest is payable semiannually and the first interest payment date is September 1, 1986. Janine uses the interest method of amortization. Bond issue costs were incurred in preparing and selling the bond issue.

On November 1, 1986, Janine sold directly to underwriters at a lump-sum price, $1,000 face value, 9% serial bonds dated November 1, 1986, at an effective annual interest rate (yield) of 11%. A total of 25% of these serial bonds are due on November 1, 1988, a total of 35% on November 1, 1989, and a total of 40% on November 1, 1990. Interest is payable semiannually and the first interest

payment date is May 2, 1987. Janine uses the interest method of amortization. Bond issue costs were incurred in preparing and selling the bond issue.

Required:

a. How would the market price of the term bonds and the serial bonds be determined?

b. 1. How would all items related to the term bonds, except for bond issue costs, be presented in a balance sheet prepared immediately after the term bond issue was sold?

2. How would all items related to the serial bonds, except for bond issue costs, be presented in a balance sheet prepared immediately after the serial bond issue was sold?

c. What alternative methods could be used to account for the bond issue costs for the term bonds in 1986?

d. How would the amount of interest expense for the term bonds and the serial bonds be determined for 1986?

Problem 5   (1188,Q4)*

This problem can be found in Section E (Leases) of this module. It is problem 5 and requires preparation of the long-term liabilities section of the balance sheet and a schedule of interest expense.

---

*Recent Accounting Practice exams have included two comprehensive problems that have multiple requirement related to the same problem data, similar to this one. Candidates should work all of these problems included in this volume so as to be prepared for them.

BONDS

Multiple Choice Answers

1. d	10. c	19. b	27. b	35. b
2. d	11. c	20. b	28. d	36. c
3. c	12. a	21. c	29. a	37. b
4. c	13. a	22. d	30. b	38. a
5. a	14. a	23. b	31. a	39. a
6. d	15. c	24. b	32. c	40. d
7. d	16. b	25. c	33. b	41. c
8. c	17. d	26. a	34. a	42. d
9. a	18. d			

Multiple Choice Answer Explanations

B.1.-4. Bonds

1. (1187,P2,26) (d) The issue price of bonds is equal to the present value (PV) of the maturity value plus the PV of the interest annuity. The PV must be computed using the yield rate. The computation is:

Amount		PV Factor		PV
$1,000,000	×	.386	=	$386,000
80,000	×	6.145	=	491,600
Total issue price				$877,600

The interest amount above ($80,000) is the principal ($1,000,000) times the stated rate (8%).

2. (587,T1,7) (d) When a bond is purchased between interest dates at a discount, the carrying value of the bond will differ from both the cash paid to the seller (for the bond and accrued interest) and its face amount. The solutions approach is to prepare the appropriate journal entry:

Investment in bonds	xxx	
Interest receivable (revenue)	xxx	
Cash		xxx

The investment in bonds account is debited for the market value of the bond, while the interest receivable or interest revenue account is debited for the amount of interest accrued from the previous interest payment date to the purchase date. The cash paid is the sum of the bond's market value (also carrying amount on the date of purchase) plus the accrued interest. Thus the carrying amount is not greater than the cash paid. The fact that the bond was purchased at a discount, by definition, means that the market value (i.e., initial carrying amount) is less than the face amount of the bond. Therefore, answers (a), (b), and (c) are incorrect.

3. (588,P2,37) (c) To determine the net cash received from the bond issuance, the solutions approach is to prepare the journal entry for the issuance.

Cash	?
Bond issue costs	7,000
Discount on bonds payable	2,000
Bonds payable	200,000
Interest expense	4,000

The bonds were issued at 99 ($200,000 × 99% = $198,000), so the discount is $2,000 ($200,000 − $198,000). The accrued interest covers the 3 months from 1/1 to 4/1 ($200,000 × 8% × 3/12 = $4,000). The net cash received includes the $198,000 for the bonds and the $4,000 for accrued interest, less the $7,000 paid for bond issue costs ($198,000 + $4,000 − $7,000 = $195,000).

4. (1189,P2,25) (c) At 1/1/89, Pine Corp. would record bonds payable at the face amount of $200,000, and discount on bonds payable of $6,000 [$200,000 − (.97 × $200,000)]. Therefore, at 1/1/89 Pine should report bonds payable, net of discount, at $194,000 ($200,000 − $6,000). Note that the accrued interest ($4,000) does not affect the net amount reported for bonds payable. The accrued interest is reported separately as a current liability at 1/1/89.

5. (1189,P1,17) (a) The bonds payable ($100,000) pay interest semiannually on June 30 and December 31. At 9/30/89, the last interest date was 6/30/89 (3 months earlier). Therefore, Wall should report 3 months accrued interest, or $2,500 ($100,000 × 10% × 3/12 = $2,500) in its 9/30/89 balance sheet.

6. (1189,T1,26) (d) The amount of interest expense for the year ended December 31, 1988 would be determined by using the time period from the date of the issuance of the bonds to the end of the year. The calculation of interest expense is not dependent on interest payment dates, but rather on the length of time the bonds are outstanding. Answer (d) is correct because interest expense would be incurred for the period from June 1, 1988 to December 31, 1988 or seven months. Thus, answers (a), (b), and (c) are incorrect.

7. (1187,P2,27) (d) Per SFAS 91, engraving and printing costs, legal and accounting fees, commissions, promotion costs, and other similar costs should be debited to a deferred charge account and amortized over the term of the bonds. All of the costs given fall into one of these categories, so a total of $255,000 ($15,000 + $80,000 + $10,000 + $150,000) should be recorded as a deferred charge (bond issue costs).

8. (1189,P2,29) (c) Under the interest method, interest expense is computed as follows:

$$\binom{BV\ of}{bonds} \times \binom{Yield}{rate} \times \binom{Time}{period} = \begin{array}{c}Interest\\expense\end{array}$$
$$\$886,000 \times 12\% \times 6/12 = \$53,160$$

The cash to be paid on 7/1/89 is $50,000 ($1,000,000 x 10% x 6/12), so the 6/30/89 entry is:

Interest expense	53,160	
Interest payable		50,000
Discount on B.P.		3,160

9. (589,P3,46) (a) Under the interest method, interest expense is computed as follows:

$$\binom{BV\ of}{bonds} \times \binom{Yield}{rate} = \binom{Interest}{expense}$$

Discount amortization is the excess of interest expense over interest paid. For the year ended 6/30/88, interest expense is $93,900 ($939,000 x 10%). Since interest paid is $90,000 ($1,000,000 x 9%), discount amortization for the first year is $3,900 ($93,900 - $90,000). This discount amortization increases the book value to $942,900 ($939,000 + $3,900). For the year ended 6/30/89, interest expense is $94,290 ($942,900 x 10%) and discount amortization is $4,290 ($94,290 - $90,000). Therefore, the unamortized bond discount at 6/30/89 is $52,810 ($61,000 - $3,900 - $4,290).

10. (1186,P1,20) (c) Bonds payable are reported as a liability on the balance sheet at their book value (the face value less a discount or plus a premium). In this case, the bonds are reported as follows:

Long-term liabilities	
Bonds payable	$1,000,000
+ Premium on B.P.	
(4% x $1,000,000)	40,000
	$1,040,000

The bond issue costs ($25,000) do not affect the presentation of the liability. Although SFAC 6 states that such costs should be treated as either an expense or a reduction of the bond liability, currently the only acceptable GAAP (APB 21) for bond issue costs is to treat them as deferred charges (assets) and amortize them on a straight-line basis over the life of the bonds.

11. (588,T1,6) (c) When revenue is earned on investments held in a bond sinking fund, the following journal entry would be made:

Bond Sinking Fund Cash   (revenue earned)
  Bond Sinking Fund Revenue (revenue earned)

The debit to the bond sinking fund increases the balance of the fund. The amount credited to bond sinking fund revenue is reported in the "Other Income (Loss)" section of the income statement. Therefore, answer (c) is correct and answer (d) is incorrect. Answers (a) and (b) are incorrect because neither of these transactions changes the total balance of the bond sinking fund. When investments are purchased by the bond sinking fund, the journal entry would be:

Bond Sinking Fund Investments   (purchase price)
  Bond Sinking Fund Cash   (purchase price)

Thus, only the composition of the bond sinking fund changes, not the total balance.

12. (1189,T1,5) (a) Companies sometimes place assets in segregated funds for special needs. These funds may become unavailable for normal operations due to debt covenants or other contractual requirements. Funds segregated for long-term needs, such as the bond sinking fund established in this problem, are reported as investments in the noncurrent section of the balance sheet. Therefore, answers (b) and (c) are incorrect. When interest is earned on investments held in a bond sinking fund, the following journal entry would be made:

Bond Sinking Fund Cash   (revenue earned)
  Bond Sinking Fund Revenue (revenue earned)

The debit to the bond sinking fund increases the balance of the fund. The amount credited to bond sinking fund revenue is reported in the "Other Income (Expense)" section of the income statement. Therefore, answer (a) is correct and answer (d) is incorrect.

13. (1185,P2,25) (a) The requirement is the combined aggregate amount to be disclosed as 1989 sinking fund payments and maturities in the 12/31/84 annual report. SFAS 47 requires disclosure at the balance sheet date of future payments for sinking fund requirements and maturity amounts of long-term debt during each of the next five years. In this case, sinking fund payments are $1,500,000 in 1989, while 1989 maturities are $3,000,000. Thus, the total amount of long-term obligations to be disclosed for 1989 is $4,500,000.

14. (586,Q1,8) (a) The requirement is to determine what amount to include as debenture bonds. A debenture bond is defined as a bond which is not secured by specifically designated collateral, but rather by the general

assets of the corporation. All of the bonds listed in this question are secured (i.e., backed up by collateral). Therefore, none of the bonds are debenture bonds and the correct answer is $0.

15. (1189,T1,18) (c) Serial bonds are bond issues that mature in installments (i.e., on the same date each year over a period of years). Term bonds, on the other hand, are bond issues that mature on a single date. Therefore, answer (c) is correct.

16. (587,P2,25) (b) Serial bonds are bond issues that mature in installments. Therefore, the total serial bonds is $2,000,000 ($1,100,000 + $900,000). The bonds which mature on a single date ($1,500,000) are called term bonds.

17. (1188,T1,14) (d) When an investor purchases a bond, s/he is entitled to receive periodic interest payments and (upon maturity) repayment of the principal or par value of the bond. The purchase price of the bond will be determined by the relationship between the face (stated) rate of interest and the market rate of interest. When the market and face rates are equal, the bond will be issued at par. When the market rate exceeds the face rate, the bond will be issued at a discount. When the market rate is below the face rate, the bond will be issued at a premium. The only constant relationship in these three situations is that the issue price of the bond is equal to the present value of the future interest and principal cash flows, discounted at the current market rate. Therefore, answer (d) is correct. Note that the use of the market rate of interest to calculate the present value of the cash flows results in the premium or discount (when the face and market interest rates are unequal).

18. (1189,T1,3) (d) At any point in time, an investor's carrying value of a bond held as a long-term investment is equal to the par value of the bond, plus the amount of the unamortized premium, or less the amount of the unamortized discount. A bond purchased at a premium, thus, has a higher carrying value at any point in time than if it had been purchased at a discount. This is logical since its initial cost is also higher when purchased at a premium. Therefore, answers (a) and (b) are incorrect.

Having determined that the bond purchased at a premium will result in the highest carrying value, we must now determine which amortization method will result in the higher carrying value at the end of the first year.

Under the straight-line method, the periodic amortization is constant; it is computed by dividing the total premium by the number of periods involved. Under the effective interest method, the periodic amortization changes over the term of the bond. A review of amortization tables for bonds issued at a premium will demonstrate that the periodic amortizaiton of the premium is lowest in the first period, but increases over subsequent periods. Therefore, the straight-line method would result in higher amortization of the premium at the end of the first year than under the effective interest method. The higher amortization would result in a smaller unamortized premium and lower, overall carrying value at the end of the first year under the straight-line method than under the effective interest method. Therefore, answer (d) is correct.

19. (1188,T1,15) (b) When bonds are issued, the issuing company often incurs printing costs, legal fees, commissions, and other similar expenses. Per APB 21, para 15, these costs should be debited to the deferred charge account Unamortized Bond Issue Costs, and amortized similarly to the bond discount. Answer (b) is correct because the amortization expense related to the bond issue costs is the same regardless of how the bond issue costs are reported (i.e., as a deferred charge or as a reduction of the liability). Answers (a) and (c) are incorrect for the same reason. Answer (d) is incorrect because the amortization of the bond issue costs will reduce net income over the ten-year life of the bonds.

20. (583,T1,24) (b) The requirement is to determine whether the amount of amortization increases each year using the interest method when a bond is sold either at a discount or premium or both. Using the interest method, interest expense for the period is based on the carrying value of the bond multiplied by the effective rate of interest. Cash interest paid for the period equals the face value of the bond multiplied by the stated rate of interest. The difference between these two resulting figures is the amortization of the discount or premium each period. The solutions approach is to prepare a table for a bond issued at a discount and at a premium and examine the direction of the successive amortization amounts. Consider $100,000 of 8% bonds issued on January 1, 1983, due on January 1, 1988, with interest payable each July 1 and January 1. Investors wish to obtain a yield of 10% on the issue. The amortization for the first two periods is as follows:

Date	Credit cash	Debit interest expense	Credit bond discount	Carrying value of bonds
1/1/83				$92,278
7/1/83	$4,000	$4,614	$614	92,892
1/1/84	4,000	4,645	645	93,537

Assume the same facts, except the investors wish to obtain a yield of only 6% on the issue:

Date	Credit cash	Debit interest expense	Debit bond premium	Carrying value of bonds
1/1/83				$108,530
7/1/83	$4,000	$3,256	$744	107,786
1/1/84	4,000	3,234	766	107,020

The above tables show that when bonds are sold at either a discount or a premium, the amount of amortization using the interest method will increase each year.

21. (1189,T1,17) (c) The carrying value of a bond payable at any point in time is equal to the par value of the bond, plus the unamortized premium or less the unamortized discount. As the premium is amortized, a smaller amount is added to the par value to determine the carrying value (CV), so the CV decreases. As the discount is amortized, a smaller amount is subtracted from the par value to determine the carrying value, so the CV increases. Therefore, answer (c) is correct.

22. (1188,P1,15) (d) When using the interest method of amortization, interest expense is computed as follows:

$$\left(\begin{array}{c}BV\ of\\bonds\end{array}\right) \times \left(\begin{array}{c}Yield\\rate\end{array}\right) \times \left(\begin{array}{c}Time\\period\end{array}\right) = \left(\begin{array}{c}Interest\\expense\end{array}\right)$$
$$\$369,000 \times 10\% \times 6/12 = \underline{\$18,450}$$

Conversely, the amount of interest payable is computed as follows:

$$\left(\begin{array}{c}FV\ of\\bonds\end{array}\right) \times \left(\begin{array}{c}Stated\\rate\end{array}\right) \times \left(\begin{array}{c}Time\\period\end{array}\right) = \left(\begin{array}{c}Interest\\payable\end{array}\right)$$
$$\$400,000 \times 8\% \times 6/12 = \underline{\$16,000}$$

At July 1, 1987, the discount amortized is $2,450 ($18,450 - $16,000). This increases the book value of the bonds to $371,450 ($369,000 + $2,450). For the second six months, interest expense is:

$$\$371,450 \times 10\% \times 6/12 = \underline{\$18,573}$$

At December 31, 1987, the discount amortized is $2,573 ($18,573 - $16,000). This increases the book value of the bonds to $374,023, (371,450 + 2,573) which can be rounded to $374,020. Please note that interest payable remains the same for each payment date.

23. (1188,P1,18) (b) Interest receivable on an investment in bonds is computed using the basic interest formula:

$$\left(\begin{array}{c}Face\\value\end{array}\right) \times \left(\begin{array}{c}Stated\\rate\end{array}\right) \times \left(\begin{array}{c}Time\\period\end{array}\right) = \left(\begin{array}{c}Interest\\receivable\end{array}\right)$$
$$\$500,000 \times 8\% \times 6/12 = \$20,000$$

Note that interest revenue is $23,075 ($461,500 x 10% x 6/12) using the interest method.

24. (587,P1,1) (b) Interest revenue from a long-term investment in bonds is equal to the stated interest, adjusted for discount or premium amortization. Carr Company uses the interest method of amortizing bond discount. Under the interest method, interest revenue is:

$$\left(\begin{array}{c}BV\\of\ bonds\end{array}\right) \times \left(\begin{array}{c}Yield\\rate\end{array}\right) \times \left(\begin{array}{c}Time\\period\end{array}\right) = \begin{array}{c}Interest\\revenue\end{array}$$
$$\$375,600 \times 10\% \times 1 = \underline{\$37,560}$$

The journal entry to record 1986 interest revenue on 12/31/86 is:

Cash ($400,000 x 9%)	36,000	
Inv. in bonds	1,560	
Int. revenue		37,560

25. (586,T1,5) (c) The requirement is the purchase price of a bond which will yield the highest interest income for the investor. If the bond's market rate of interest on the date of acquisition is different than the stated rate, the bonds will sell at a premium or discount. If the market rate of interest is higher than the bond's stated rate, the purchase price will be lower than the face value (i.e., discounted). The discount will be recognized over the life of the investment as an addition to interest income. Annual interest income will equal the cash interest received plus the discount amortization for the year. Answers (a) and (b) are incorrect because if the bonds are purchased at par (face value), the interest income will equal the cash interest received. Answer (d) is incorrect because the interest income for a bond purchased at a premium would equal the cash interest received less the premium amortization for the year.

B.5. Convertible Bonds

26. (1189,P2,30) (a) Under the book value method, the common stock is recorded at the carrying amount of the converted bonds less any conversion expenses. No gain or loss is recognized. The carrying amount of these converted bonds is $970,000 ($1,000,000 - $30,000), and conversion expenses were $10,000. Therefore, the common stock must be

recorded at $960,000 ($970,000 - $10,000).
Since the par value of the stock issued is
$800,000 (40,000 x $20), additional paid-in
capital (APIC) is credited for $160,000
($960,000 - $800,000). The entry is:

Bonds payable	1,000,000	
Discount on B.P.		30,000
Cash		10,000
Common stock		800,000
APIC		160,000

Note that additional consideration given to
bondholders to induce conversion is treated
differently than conversion expense. The
value of this additional consideration is
recorded as an expense upon conversion.

27. (1189,T1,19) (b) Under the book value
method of accounting for the conversion of
bonds payable into common stock, the common
stock is recorded at the book value of the
bonds at the date of conversion. Thus, no
gain or loss is recognized.

Under the market value method, common
stock is recorded at its fair market value at
the date of conversion. Any difference
between the stock's market value and bonds'
book value at the date of conversion is a
recognized gain or loss. Therefore, answer (b) is correct.

28. (1186,T1,19) (d) Under both the book
value and market value methods of accounting
for bond conversions, the bonds payable and
any related premium or discount must be removed from the accounting records. Also, the
stock issued and any APIC must be recorded.
Under the market value method, the stock is
recorded at the market value of the stock (or,
alternately, of the bonds) and a gain or loss
is recognized on the transaction. Under the
book value method, the stock is recorded at
the book value of the bonds, and no gain or
loss is recognized. The choice between the
two methods, however, does not affect the
removal of the bonds payable balance or the
premium balance from the accounts. The
amounts debited would be identical under
either method. Therefore, answer (d) is
correct, and answers (a), (b), and (c) are
incorrect.

B.6. Bonds Issued with Detachable
Purchase Warrants

29. (1188,P2,32) (a) APB 14, para 13 states
that the proceeds from the issuance of debt
with detachable stock warrants should be allocated between the debt and equity elements.
1,000 bonds ($1,000,000 ÷ $1,000) were issued
with 30 detachable stock warrants each, for a

total of 30,000 warrants. Paid-in capital
from stock warrants issued (30,000 x $4 =
$120,000). Note that if a FMV is given for
the bonds without warrants, APB 14 states that
the proceeds should be allocated between the
bonds and warrants based on their relative
FMVs at the time of issuance.

30. (1189,P2,28) (b) The proceeds of bonds
issued with detachable warrants are allocated
between the bonds and the warrants based upon
their relative fair market values at the time
of issuance, in accordance with para 16 of
APB 14. In this case, the portion allocated
to the warrants is $25,000 (25/1,075 x
$1,075,000). This amount is recorded as an
increase in stockholders' equity. The portion
allocated to the bonds is $1,050,000
(1,050/1,075 x $1,075,000). Therefore, the
journal entry to record the issuance is:

Cash	1,075,000		
APIC-stock warrants		25,000	
Bonds payable		1,000,000	} 1,050,000
Premium on B.P.		50,000	

31. (586,P2,37) (a) The requirement is the
6/30/85 carrying amount of bonds payable,
which were issued with detachable stock warrants on that date. APB 14, para 13 states
that the proceeds from the sale of debt with
detachable stock warrants should be allocated
between the separate debt and equity elements.
1,000 bonds were issued with 5 warrants each,
for a total of 5,000 warrants. APIC-Stock
warrants is credited for the FMV of the
warrants issued or $25,000 (5,000 x $5). The
remaining $995,000 ($1,020,000 - $25,000)
becomes the carrying value of the bonds
payable. Note that if a FMV is available for
the bonds without the warrants, APB 14,
para 15 states that the proceeds should be
allocated to the bonds and the warrants based
on the relative FMVs at the time of issuance.

32. (588,T1,16) (c) Bonds issued with stock
purchase warrants are, in substance, composed
of two elements: a debt element and a
stockholders' equity element. Per APB 14,
para 15, proceeds from bonds issued with
detachable stock purchase warrants should be
allocated between the bonds and the warrants
on the basis of their relative fair market
values. Detachable warrants trade separately
from the debt; thus, a market value is
available. The amount allocated to the
warrants should be accounted for as paid-in
capital. Bonds issued with nondetachable
stock purchase warrants must be surrendered in
order to exercise the warrants. Since this
inseparability prevents the determination of
individual market values, no allocation is
permitted under APB 14.

B.7. Extinguishment of Debt

33. (1187,P2,25) (b) $1,000,000 of bonds were retired at 96 on 6/30/87, when the unamortized balance of bond discount and bond issue costs were $55,000 and $20,000, respectively. When bonds are retired before maturity, the bonds payable, the discount or premium, and the bond issue costs must be removed from the books. Any difference between the net book value of the bonds ($1,000,000 - $55,000 - $20,000 = $925,000) and the cash paid ($1,000,000 x 96% = $960,000) is recognized immediately as an extraordinary gain or loss ($925,000 - $960,000 = $35,000 loss). The journal entry is:

Loss on retirement	35,000	
Bonds payable	1,000,000	
Discount on B.P.		55,000
Bond issue costs		20,000
Cash		960,000

34. (587,P2,38) (a) A gain or loss on the retirement of bonds is the difference between the carrying amount of the bonds and the cash paid to retire the bonds. The carrying amount of the bonds is $2,156,000 ($2,000,000 face amount + $156,000 unamortized bond premium). The cash paid to retire the bonds is $2,040,000 ($2,000,000 x 102%). Therefore, the gain on bond retirement is $116,000 ($2,156,000 - $2,040,000).

35. (589,P3,49) (b) The loss on the early extinguishment of debt is the excess of the cash paid ($2,000,000 x 101% = $2,020,000) over the book value of the bonds at the time of extinguishment. On 7/1/82, the balance in the bonds payable account is $2,000,000 and the bond discount is $80,000 ($2,000,000 - $1,920,000) at 7/1/88, the discount had been amortized for 6 years. Since the bond term was 10 years, the total discount amortized is $48,000 ($80,000 x 6/10). At 7/1/88, the unamortized discount is $32,000 ($80,000 - $48,000), so the book value of the bonds is $1,968,000 ($2,000,000 - $32,000). Note that a shortcut approach is to take the 1/1/82 book value ($1,920,000) and add the discount amortization ($48,000) to determine the 7/1/88 book value of $1,968,000. The loss is $52,000 ($2,020,000 cash paid less $1,968,000 book value).

36. (1188,T1,16) (c) When a bond issue is called early, the issuer must pay any accrued interest plus the call price of the bonds. Since the bonds were called on an interest date, there is no accrued interest. Regardless of the call price, the bond liability must be removed from the accounts at its current carrying value (i.e., par value less

the unamortized discount or plus the unamortized premium). The entry to remove the liability would be:

Bonds Payable	(Par)
Loss on Retirement	(Plug)
Unamortized Bond Disc.	(Carrying Amt)
Cash	(Call Price)

Since these bonds were issued at a discount, the amount of the liability to be removed is the face amount less unamortized discount. Thus, answer (c) is correct and answer (d) is incorrect. Answers (a) and (b) are incorrect because the call price has no effect on the amount of bond liability removed from the books.

37. (1183,T1,17) (b) The requirement is to determine whether or not material gains on refunding of debt by either direct exchange of bonds or issuance of new bonds and use of the proceeds to retire old bonds should be recognized separately as an extraordinary item. SFAS 4, as amended by SFAS 64, requires that all early extinguishments of debt prior to one year before maturity, except cash purchases to satisfy present or future sinking fund requirements, are to be separately recognized as extraordinary items, if material.

May 1990 Answers

38. (590,P1,4) (a) When using the interest method of amortization, interest revenue is computed directly as follows:

$$\left(\begin{array}{c} BV \\ \text{of bonds} \end{array} \right) \times \left(\begin{array}{c} \text{Yield} \\ \text{rate} \end{array} \right) \times \left(\begin{array}{c} \text{Time} \\ \text{period} \end{array} \right) = \left(\begin{array}{c} \text{Interest} \\ \text{revenue} \end{array} \right)$$

$$\$456,200 \times 10\% \times 1 = \$45,620$$

The amount of interest receivable (cash interest to be received on 1/1) is computed as shown below:

$$\left(\begin{array}{c} \text{FV of} \\ \text{bonds} \end{array} \right) \times \left(\begin{array}{c} \text{Stated} \\ \text{rate} \end{array} \right) \times \left(\begin{array}{c} \text{Time} \\ \text{period} \end{array} \right) = \left(\begin{array}{c} \text{Interest} \\ \text{receivable} \end{array} \right)$$

$$\$500,000 \times 8\% \times 1 = \$40,000$$

Therefore, 1988 discount amortization is computed indirectly as $5,620 ($45,620 - $40,000). This increases the book value to $461,820 at 12/31/88 ($456,200 + $5,620.) The same computations are performed for 1989. Interest revenue is $46,182 ($461,820 x 10%), and interest receivable is again $40,000, resulting in amortization of $6,182 ($46,182 - $40,000). Thus, the 12/31/89 carrying amount for the investment is $468,002 ($461,820 + $6,182).

39. (590,P2,36) (a) To determine the cash received from a bond issuance, one solutions approach is to prepare the journal entry for the issuance.

Cash	304,500	
Discount on bonds payable	3,000	
Bonds payable		300,000
Interest payable		7,500

The bonds were issued at 99 ($300,000 x 99% = $297,000), so the discount is $3,000 ($300,000 - $297,000). The accrued interest is for the three months from 4/1 to 7/1 ($300,000 x 10% x 3/12 = $7,500). Therefore, the cash received is $304,500, as computed below.

For the bonds ($300,000 x 99%)	$297,000
For accrued interest ($300,000 x 10% x 3/12)	7,500
	$304,500

40. (590,P2,40) (d) The gain on early extinguishment of debt is the excess of the book value of the bonds at the time of retirement over the cash paid ($1,000,000 x 101% = $1,010,000). On 1/1/84, the original balance in the premium account was $40,000 ($1,040,000 - $1,000,000). At 7/1/89, the premium had been amortized for 5½ years, or 11 six-month periods (1/11/84 to 7/1/89). Since the bond term was 10 years, or 20 six-month periods, the total premium amortized was $22,000 ($40,000 x 11/20). Therefore, the unamortized premium was $18,000 ($40,000 - $22,000) and the book value of the bonds was $1,018,000 ($1,000,000 + $18,000). A shortcut approach is to take the 1/1/84 book value ($1,040,000) and subtract the amortization ($22,000) to determine the 7/1/89 book value of $1,018,000. The gain is $8,000 ($1,018,000 book value less $1,010,000 cash paid).

41. (590,P3,42) (c) Under the book value method, the common stock is recorded at the carrying amount of the converted bonds, less any conversion expenses. The carrying amount of the converted bonds is $2,050,000 ($2,000,000 + $50,000). The common stock is recorded at this amount, since there are no conversion expenses in this case. Since the par value of the stock issued is $1,600,000 (80,000 shares x $20), additional paid-in capital (APIC) is credited for $450,000 ($2,050,000 - $1,600,000). The entry is:

Bonds payable	2,000,000	
Premium on B.P.	50,000	
Common stock		1,600,000
APIC		450,000

Note that when using the book value method, the market price of the stock ($30 per share is not considered, and no gain or loss is recognized.

42. (590,P3,46) (d) When the interest method of amortization is used, interest revenue is computed directly, and the amount of discount amortization is computed indirectly as follows:

$$\left(\begin{array}{c}\text{Interest}\\\text{revenue}\end{array}\right) - \left(\begin{array}{c}\text{Stated or}\\\text{cash interest}\end{array}\right) = \left(\begin{array}{c}\text{Discount}\\\text{amortization}\end{array}\right)$$

In this case, the interest revenue cannot be computed directly because the effect or yield rate is not given. However, the stated or cash interest can be computed ($500,000 x 8% x 6/12 = $20,000) and the discount amortization is given ($1,800). Thus the interest revenue can be computed indirectly as indicated below:

Interest revenue - $20,000 = $1,800
Interest revenue = $20,000 + $1,800
Interest revenue = $21,800

BONDS

Answer Outline

Problem 1   Issuance of Bonds (589,T4)

a.   Issue price = PV of all expected future
         cash outflows discounted at 10%
              Effective interest rate (yield) is used
              Issue price inludes PV of maturity
              amount plus all interest payments
b.1. The 9% bonds were issued at a discount
              Face rate of 9% < prevailing rate of
              10%
              Yield of 10% had to be provided to
              investors
    2. Interest expense would be higher in the
         second year than first year
              Carrying value of bonds increases each
              year as discount is amortized
              The 10% effective rate is applied to
              the increased carrying value each year
c.   Allocate proceeds between bonds and war-
         rants on basis of relative FMVs
              Portion allocated to bonds should be
              accounted for as long-term debt
              Portion allocated to warrants should be
              accounted for as APIC

Unofficial Answer

Problem 1   Issuance of Bonds (589,T4)

a. The issue price of the bond is determined
by calculating the present value of all
expected future cash outflows discounted at
the effective interest rate (yield) of 10%.
The issue price is the sum of the present
value of the bonds' maturity amount (face
value) plus the present value of the series of
future interest payments.

b. 1. The 9% bonds were issued at a discount
(less than face value). Although the bonds
provide for the payment of interest at 9% of
face value, 9% was less than the prevailing or
market rate. Thus, in order to provide a
yield of 10% to investors, the bonds must have
been issued at a discount.

    2. The amount of interest expense would
be higher in the second year than in the first
year. According to the effective interest
method of amortization, the 10% effective
interest rate is applied to an increasing bond
carrying amount, which results in a higher
interest expense in each successive year.

c. The proceeds from the issuance of the 8%
nonconvertible bonds with detachable stock

purchase warrants should be allocated between
the bonds and the warrants on the basis of
their relative fair market values. The
portion of the proceeds allocable to the bonds
should be accounted for as long-term debt,
while the portion allocable to the warrants
should be accounted for as paid-in capital.

Answer Outline

Problem 2   Issuance, Extinguishment, and
                  Conversion of Bonds (1187,T5)

a1. 11% bonds issued at premium
              Payment of 11% face (cash) interest is
              more than market rate for similar
              bonds
              Bonds must sell at premium to yield 9%
a2. Interest expense would be higher in first
         year than in second year
              9% effective interest rate applied to
              declining bond carrying value each
              year
              Results in lower interest expense each
              successive year
b1. Gain (loss) on early extinguishment is
         difference between net carrying value of
         bonds and reacquisition price
              Net carrying value > reacquisition
              price--gain results
              Net carrying value < reacquisition
              price--loss results
              Early extinguishment of 11% bonds
              results in gain
              Bonds issued at premium
              Carrying value at date of
              extinguishment must exceed face value
              Net carrying value exceeds
              reacquisition price
b2. Report gain on early extinguishment in
         1986 net income
              Extraordinary item, net of tax
c1. Under book value method, net income not
         affected by conversion
              Convertible bonds viewed as similar to
              equity capital
              Conversion is completion of prior
              transaction (issuance of convertible
              bonds), not culmination of earnings
              process
c2. Under market value method, gain (loss)
         results and net income is affected by
         conversion
              When market value differs from carrying
              amount
              Convertible bonds viewed as debt
              Conversion is separate transaction and
              represents culmination of earnings
              process
              Market value of common stock at date of
              conversion is proper amount to record
              as common stock

Unoffical Answer

Problem 2   Issuance, Extinguishment, and
                    Conversion of Bonds (1187,T5)

a. 1. The 11% bonds were issued at a premium
(more than face value). Although the bonds
provide for the payment of interest of 11% of
face value, this rate was more than the
prevailing or market rate for bonds of similar
quality at the time the bonds were issued.
Thus, the bonds must sell at a premium to
yield 9%.
    2. The amount of interest expense would
be higher in the first year of the life of the
bond issue than in the second year of the life
of the bond issue. According to the effective
interest method of amortization, the 9%
effective interest rate is applied to a
declining bond carrying amount, and results in
a lower interest expense in each successive
year.

b. 1. Gain or loss on early extinguishment
of debt should be determined by comparing the
net carrying amount of the bonds at the date
of extinguishment with the reacquisition
price. If the net carrying amount exceeds the
reacquisition price, a gain results. If the
net carrying amount is less than the reacquisition price, a loss results.
    In this case, a gain results. The bonds
were issued at a premium, therefore, the
carrying amount of the bonds at the date of
extinguishment must exceed face value. Thus,
the net carrying amount exceeds the reacquisition price.
    2. Brewster should report the gain on the
early extinguishment in net income for 1986,
as an extraordinary item, net of related
income tax effect.

c. 1. Net income is not affected by
conversion under the book value method. The
book value method views the convertible bonds
as possessing substantial characteristics of
equity capital. The conversion represents the
completion of a prior transaction (the
issuance of the convertible debt), not the
culmination of an earning process.
    2. A gain or loss results, and thus net
income is affected by conversion under the
market value method when market value differs
from the carrying amount of the convertible
bonds. The market value method views the
convertible bonds primarily as debt whose
conversion was a significant economic transaction. The conversion represents the
culmination of an earning process. The market
value method views the market value of the
common stock at the date of the conversion to
be the proper measurement at which to carry
the common stock.

Answer Outline

Problem 3   Issuance of Bonds (586,T5)

a. 11% term bonds sold at discount because
    effective rate (12%) > stated rate (11%)
    Cash interest (11%) < the prevailing
      rate for similar bonds (12%)
      Market value (MV) of bonds < face
        value (FV) of bonds giving investors
        effective rate (12%) over life of
        issue
b. BS presentation of items related to 11%
    term bonds
    November 1, 1986 (issue date)
      Term bonds payable
        Noncurrent liability
        Amount = FV - discount
      Bond issue costs
        Noncurrent asset as deferred charge;
        Reduction of noncurrent liability; or
        Expense as incurred
      Accrued interest payable
        Current liability
        FV x 11% x 1/12 = Interest for October
    December 31, 1986
      Term bonds payable
        Noncurrent liability
        Amount = FV - unamortized discount
          Amount increased by November and
          December discount amortization
      Bond issue costs
        If presented as noncurrent asset, Nov.
        and Dec. amortization decrease amount
        If presented as reduction of noncur-
        rent liability, Nov. and Dec. amorti-
        zation would increase amount of term
        bonds payable, net of discount
        If expensed, no effect from date of
        issuance
      Accrued interest payable
        Current liability
        FV x 11% x 3/12 = Interest for
        October, November, and December
c1. Bond discount amortized over period bonds
    outstanding
    Date of sale (11/1/86) to maturity date
    (10/1/91)
c2. Straight-line vs. interest method
    Straight-line--provides even dollar
      amount of amortization over period
      bonds are outstanding
    Interest method--provides increasing
      amount of amortization when bonds sold
      at discount
c3. Interest method preferable
    Provides constant interest rate to
      increasing carrying value
d. Accounting for proceeds of 9% nonconver-
    tible bonds with detachable stock pur-
    chase warrants

Paid-in capital = portion of proceeds
   allocable to warrants
   Because warrants are an equity
      instrument with separate fair value
Long-term debt = remainder of proceeds
   including premium on convertible bonds
   Because bonds are debt instruments

Unofficial Answer

Problem 3   Issuance of Bonds (586,T5)

a. The 11% term bonds were sold at a discount
(less than face value) because the effective
annual interest rate (yield) of 12% was higher
than the stated interest rate of 11%. The
bonds provide for the payment of interest of
11%; however, this rate was less than the prevailing or market rate for bonds of similar
quality at the time the issue was sold.
Therefore, the market value of the bonds at
the date of sale must be less than face value
so that investors may receive the effective
annual interest rate (yield) on their investments.

b. In a balance sheet prepared immediately
after the term bond issue was sold, a noncurrent liability, term bonds payable, would be
presented at an amount equal to the face value
of the bonds less the discount. At December 31, 1986, a noncurrent liability, term
bonds payable, would be presented in the
balance sheet at the face value of the bonds,
less the unamortized discount. Therefore, the
amortization of bond discount for November and
December 1986 would increase the amount of
term bonds payable, net of discount.

The bond issue costs incurred in preparing
and selling the bond issue could be presented
in one of three ways in a balance sheet prepared immediately after the term bond issue
was sold:

• Noncurrent asset, deferred charge
• Reduction of the noncurrent liability,
term bonds payable
• Not presented in balance sheet (expensed
as incurred in 1986)

At December 31, 1986, the bond issue costs
could be presented in one of three ways:

• If the bond issue costs were presented in
the balance sheet as a noncurrent asset, deferred charge, the amortization of bond issue
costs for November and December 1986 would
decrease the amount of the deferred charge.
• If the bond issue costs were presented in
the balance sheet as a reduction of the noncurrent liability, term bonds payable, the
amortization of bond issue costs for November
and December 1986 would increase the amount of
the term bonds payable, net of discount.
• If the bond issue costs were expensed as
incurred in 1986, there would be no effect

from the date the term bond issue was sold to
December 31, 1986.

A current liability, accrued interest payable, would be presented in a balance sheet
prepared immediately after the term bond issue
was sold for accrued interest received for
October 1986. At December 31, 1986, the
accrued interest payable would include accrued
interest received for October 1986 and accrued
interest for November and December 1986.

c. 1. Bond discount for bonds sold between
interest dates should be amortized over the
period the bonds will be outstanding, that is,
the period from the date of sale (November 1,
1986) to the maturity date (October 1, 1991).
    2. The straight-line method of amortiza-
tion provides an even dollar amount of amortization each year allocated over the period the
bonds are outstanding. The interest method of
amortization provides for an increasing dollar
amount of amortization each year.
    3. The interest method of amortization is
preferable to the straight-line method because
it provides a constant interest rate when
applied to the increasing carrying value.

d. The proceeds from the sale of the 9%
nonconvertible bonds with detachable stock
purchase warrants should be accounted for as
paid-in capital and long-term debt. Because
the detachable stock purchase warrants are
equity instruments which have a separate fair
value at the issue date, the portion of the
proceeds allocable to the warrants should be
accounted for as paid-in capital. Because the
bonds are debt instruments, the remainder of
the proceeds, including the premium, should be
accounted for as long-term debt.

Answer Outline

Problem 4   Issuance of Bonds (585,T4)

a. Determination of market price of bonds
    Term bonds
       Market price = Σ Present value of ex-
       pected net future cash outflows
       Net future cash outflows = Maturity
       amount (face value) + interest payments
       Discount rate = Effective annual
       interest rate (yield)
    Serial bonds
    • 2 step process
       First Step: Compute market price of
       each serial as done for term bond
          Serial market price = Σ Present value
          of expected net future cash outflows
       Second Step: Compute price of all
       serials
          Market price = Σ Each serial market
          price
b1. Presentation of term bonds in BS immedi-
    ately after issue

<u>Current assets</u>
  Cash increased by proceeds of sale
<u>Current liabilities</u>
  Accrued interest payable for accrued
  interest received
<u>Noncurrent liabilities</u>
  Term bonds payable = Face value of bonds
  + Premium

b2. Presentation of serial bonds in balance
    sheet immediately after issue
    <u>Current assets</u>
      Cash increased by proceeds of sale
    <u>Noncurrent liability</u>
      Serial bonds payable = Face value −
      Discount

c. Alternative accounting methods for bond
    issue costs
    <u>Alternative 1</u>
      Account for as noncurrent asset,
      deferred charge
      Amortize deferred charge over period
      bonds outstanding
    <u>Alternative 2</u>
      Account for as expense in year of sale
    <u>Alternative 3</u>
      Account for like bond discount
      (reduction of term bonds payable)

d. Determination of interest expense
    <u>Term bonds</u>
      Interest expense = Net carrying value of
      bonds x Effective rate x 1/4 year
    <u>Serial bonds</u>
      Interest expense = Net carrying value of
      bonds x Effective rate x 1/6 year

Unofficial Answer

Problem 4   Issuance of Bonds (585,T4)

a. The market price of the term bonds would
be the sum of the present values of all of the
expected net future cash flows discounted at
an effective annual interest rate (yield) of
10 percent. The net future cash outflows are
the maturity amount (face value) and the
series of future semiannual interest payments
adjusted for accrued interest received.

    The market price of the serial bonds would
be determined by computing the market price
for each serial separately in the same way
that a term bond would be determined and then
totaling these prices for the various serials.

b. 1. Immediately after the term bond issue
        was sold, the current asset—cash—
        would be increased by the proceeds
        from the sale of the term bond
        issue. A noncurrent liability—term
        bonds payable—would be presented in
        the balance sheet at the face value of
        the term bonds, plus the premium. In
        addition, a current liability—accrued
        interest payable—would be presented
        in the balance sheet for accrued

        interest received (September 1, 1986
        to October 1, 1986).

    2. Immediately after the serial bond
        issue was sold, the current asset—
        cash—would be increased by the pro-
        ceeds from the sale of the serial bond
        issue. A noncurrent liability—serial
        bonds payable—would be presented in
        the balance sheet at the face value of
        the serial bonds, less the discount.

c. The bond issue costs incurred in preparing
and selling the bond issue could be accounted
for as a noncurrent asset—deferred charge.
The bond issue costs would then be amortized
over the period the bonds will be outstanding,
that is, the period from the date of sale
(October 1, 1986) to the maturity date
(March 1, 1991).

    Alternately, under Statements of Financial
Accounting Concepts, the bond issue costs
incurred in preparing and selling the bond
issue could be either accounted for as an expense in 1986, or as a reduction of the noncurrent liability—term bonds payable—and
accounted for the same as debt discount.

d. To determine the amount of interest expense for the term bonds for 1986, the net
carrying value of the term bonds on October 1,
1986 would be multiplied by the effective
interest rate (yield) of 10 percent by one
fourth (October 1, 1986 to December 31, 1986).

    To determine the amount of interest ex-
pense for the serial bonds for 1986, the net
carrying value of the serial bonds on November 1, 1986 would be multiplied by the effective interest rate (yield) of 11 percent by
one sixth (November 1, 1986 to December 31,
1986).

DEBT RESTRUCTURE

Multiple Choice Questions (1-6)

1.   Grey Company holds an overdue note receivable of $800,000 plus recorded accrued interest of $64,000. As the result of a court imposed settlement on December 31, 1986, Grey agreed to the following restructuring arrangement:

   •   Reduced the principal obligation to $600,000.
   •   Forgave the $64,000 accrued interest.
   •   Extended the maturity date to December 31, 1988.
   •   Annual interest of $60,000 is to be paid to Grey on December 31, 1987 and 1988.

On December 31, 1986, Grey must recognize a loss from restructuring of
   a. $144,000
   b. $200,000
   c. $204,000
   d. $264,000

2.   Hull Company is indebted to Apex under a $500,000, 12% three-year note dated December 31, 1984. Because of Hull's financial difficulties developing in 1986, Hull owed accrued interest of $60,000 on the note at December 31, 1986. Under a troubled debt restructuring, on December 31, 1986, Apex agreed to settle the note and accrued interest for a tract of land having a fair value of $450,000. Hull's acquisition cost of the land is $360,000. Ignoring income taxes, on its 1986 income statement Hull should report as a result of the troubled debt restructuring

	Other income	Extraordinary gain
a.	$200,000	$0
b.	$140,000	$0
c.	$ 90,000	$ 50,000
d.	$ 90,000	$110,000

3.   Colt, Inc. is indebted to Kent under an $800,000, 10% four-year note dated December 31, 1982. Annual interest of $80,000 was paid on December 31, 1983 and 1984. During 1985 Colt experienced financial difficulties and is likely to default unless concessions are made. On December 31, 1985, Kent agreed to restructure the debt as follows:

   •   Interest of $80,000 for 1985, due December 31, 1985, was made payable December 31, 1986.
   •   Interest for 1986 was waived.
   •   The principal amount was reduced to $700,000.

Assuming an income tax rate of 40%, how much should Colt report as extraordinary gain in its income statement for the year ended December 31, 1985?

   a. $0
   b. $ 60,000
   c. $100,000
   d. $108,000

4.   Bricker Company is indebted to Springburn Bank under a $200,000, 16% three-year note dated January 1, 1981. Interest, payable annually on December 31, was paid on the December 31, 1981, due date. During 1982 Bricker experienced severe financial difficulties and is likely to default on the note and interest unless a concession is made by the bank. On December 31, 1982, the bank agreed to settle the note and interest for 1982 for $10,000 cash and a tract of land having a current market value of $140,000. Bricker's acquisition cost of the land is $100,000. Ignoring income taxes, what amount should Bricker report as extraordinary gain on the debt restructure in its income statement for the year ended December 31, 1982?
   a. $0
   b. $ 50,000
   c. $ 82,000
   d. $122,000

5.   On December 31, 1979, Marsh Company entered into a debt restructuring agreement with Saxe Company, which was experiencing financial difficulties. Marsh restructured a $100,000 note receivable as follows:

   •   Reduced the principal obligation to $70,000.
   •   Forgave $12,000 of accrued interest.
   •   Extended the maturity date from December 31, 1979 to December 31, 1981.
   •   Reduced the interest rate from 12% to 8%. Interest was payable annually on December 31, 1980 and 1981.

In accordance with the agreement, Saxe made payments to Marsh on December 31, 1980 and 1981. How much interest income should Marsh report for the year ended December 31, 1981?
   a. $0
   b. $ 5,600
   c. $ 8,400
   d. $11,200

6.   For a troubled debt restructuring involving only modification of terms, it is appropriate for a debtor to recognize a gain when the carrying amount of the debt
   a.   Exceeds the total future cash payments specified by the new terms.
   b.   Is less than the total future cash payments specified by the new terms.
   c.   Exceeds the present value specified by the new terms.
   d.   Is less than the present value specified by the new terms.

DEBT RESTRUCTURE
Multiple Choice Answers

1. a   3. b   4. c   5. a   6. a
2. d

Multiple Choice Answer Explanations
C. Debt Restructure

1. (587,P1,12) (a) Per SFAS 15, when a troubled debt restructure involves modification of terms, the creditor recognizes a loss (and no interest revenue in the future) if the carrying amount (principal + accrued interest) exceeds all cash payments to be received in the future. In this problem, the carrying amount is $864,000 ($800,000 note receivable plus accrued interest of $64,000). The future payments total $720,000 (principal of $600,000 plus two annual interest payments of $60,000 each). The difference of $144,000 ($864,000 − $720,000) is recognized as a loss in 1986, and no interest revenue is recognized in 1987 or 1988.

2. (587,P3,59) (d) In this restructure, the debt is retired by a transfer of land to the creditor. The extraordinary gain, per para 13 of SFAS 15, is the excess of the carrying amount of the debt over the fair value of the assets transferred. The carrying amount of this debt is $560,000 ($500,000 note payable plus $60,000 accrued interest). Since the fair value of the land transferred is $450,000, the extraordinary gain is $110,000 ($560,000 − $450,000). The excess of the fair value of the land over its acquisition cost ($450,000 − $360,000 = $90,000) is a gain on the transfer of an asset, properly included in income before taxes as other income. The journal entry is:

Notes payable	500,000	
Interest payable	60,000	
Land		360,000
Gain on transfer of land		90,000
Extraordinary gain		110,000

3. (586,P3,41) (b) The requirement is the amount of extraordinary gain to be recognized from a troubled debt restructure. According to SFAS 15, if the debt is continued with a modification of terms, an extraordinary gain is recognized by the debtor if the future cash payments on the debt are less than the carrying value of the debt. For troubled debt restructures, carrying value is defined as the principal amount ($800,000) plus accrued interest ($80,000), or $880,000. The future payments total $780,000 ($700,000 reduced principal and $80,000 interest). The $100,000

difference ($880,000 − $780,000) is recognized as an extraordinary gain, net of the related tax effect [$100,000 − (40% x $100,000) = $60,000]. The following entry would be made:

Notes Payable	800,000	
Interest Payable	80,000	
Note Payable		780,000
(restructured amt)		
X/O Gain		100,000

4. (583,P1,14) (c) The requirement is the amount to be reported as an extraordinary gain as the result of a troubled debt restructure. In this restructure, the debt is retired by transferring cash and land to the creditor. The extraordinary gain, per para 13 of SFAS 15, is the excess of the carrying amount of the debt over the fair value of the assets transferred. The carrying amount of the debt is its book value ($200,000) plus any accrued interest ($200,000 x 16%, or $32,000). The extraordinary gain is, therefore, $82,000.

Carrying amount of debt ($200,000 + $32,000)	$232,000
FV of assets transferred ($10,000 + $140,000)	150,000
X/O gain on restructure	$ 82,000

The difference between the market value ($140,000) and cost ($100,000) of the land is treated as a $40,000 gain on the transfer of the asset, which is included in income before taxes.

5. (1182,P1,18) (a) The requirement is the amount of Interest Income to be recorded by Marsh in 1981 after a modification of terms type of troubled debt restructure on 12/31/79. Per SFAS 15, when a troubled debt restructure involves modification of terms, the creditor recognizes a loss (and no interest income in the future) if the carrying amount (principal + accrued interest) exceeds all cash payments to be received in the future. In this instance, the carrying amount is $112,000 ($100,000 note receivable plus accrued interest of $12,000). The future payments total $81,200 (principal of $70,000 plus two annual 8% interest payments of $5,600 each). The difference of $30,800 ($112,000 less $81,200) is recognized as a loss by Marsh in 1979 and no interest income is recognized in 1980 or 1981.

6. (1181,T1,29) (a) SFAS 15 states that the debtor records a gain and the creditor records a loss at the date of a restructure involving only a modification of terms when the prerestructure carrying amount exceeds the total future cash flows per the modification. The

gain recognized is the difference between the
pre-restructure carrying amount and the future
cash flows. No gain or loss is recorded if
the carrying amount is less than total future
cash flows [answer (b)]. Present values of
future cash flows are not considered in determining whether a gain or loss is recognized on
a restructuring of troubled debt [answers (c)
and (d)].

PENSIONS

Multiple Choice Questions (1-25)

1.   Rice Corp. adopted a defined benefit pension plan on January 1, 1986. The plan does not provide any retroactive benefits for existing employees. The pension funding payment is made to the trustee on December 31 each year. The following information is available for 1986 and 1987:

	1986	1987
Service cost	$150,000	$165,000
Funding payment	170,000	185,000
Interest on projected		
benefit obligation	--	15,000
Actual return on plan assets	--	18,000
Experience gains or losses	--	--

In its December 31, 1987 balance sheet, Rice should report prepaid pension cost of

    a. $20,000
    b. $25,000
    c. $40,000
    d. $43,000

2.   The following information relates to the 1987 activity of the defined benefit pension plan of Lindy Corp., a company whose stock is publicly traded:

Service cost	$150,000
Return on plan assets	40,000
Interest cost on pension	
benefit obligation	82,000
Amortization of actuarial loss	15,000
Amortization of unrecognized	
net obligation	35,000

Lindy's 1987 pension cost is

    a. $322,000
    b. $287,000
    c. $242,000
    d. $158,000

3.   Jerry Corp., a company whose stock is publicly traded, provides a noncontributory defined benefit pension plan for its employees. The company's actuary has provided the following information for the year ended December 31, 1988:

Projected benefit obligation	$400,000
Accumulated benefit obligation	350,000
Plan assets (fair value)	410,000
Service cost	120,000
Interest on projected	
benefit obligation	12,000
Amortization of unrecognized	
prior service cost	30,000
Expected and actual return	
on plan assets	41,000

The market-related asset value equals the fair value of plan assets. Prior contributions to the defined benefit pension plan equaled the amount of net periodic pension cost accrued for the previous year end. No contributions have been made for 1988 pension cost. In its December 31, 1988 balance sheet, Jerry should report an accrued pension cost of

    a. $203,000
    b. $162,000
    c. $121,000
    d. $109,000

4.   West Company adopted a defined benefit pension plan on January 1, 1986. West amortizes the prior service cost over 16 years and funds prior service cost by making equal payments to the fund trustee at the end of each of the first ten years. The service (normal) cost is fully funded at the end of each year. The following data are available for 1986:

Service (normal) cost for 1986	$110,000
Prior service cost:	
Amortized	41,700
Funded	57,200

West's prepaid pension cost at December 31, 1986 is

    a. $0
    b. $15,500
    c. $41,700
    d. $57,200

5.   Cey Company has a defined benefit pension plan. Cey's policy is to fund net periodic pension cost annually, payment to an independent trustee being made two months after the end of each year. Data relating to the pension plan for 1986 are as follows:

Net pension cost for 1986	$190,000
Unrecognized prior service	
cost, 12/31/86	150,000
Accumulated benefit	
obligation, 12/31/86	480,000
Fair value of plan	
assets, 12/31/86	500,000

How much should appear on Cey's balance sheet at December 31, 1986 for pension liability?

	Current	Noncurrent
a.	$0	$480,000
b.	$0	$330,000
c.	$190,000	$150,000
d.	$190,000	$0

6.   Which of the following components should be included in the calculation of net pension cost recognized for a period by an employer sponsoring a defined benefit pension plan?

	Interest cost	Actual return on plan assets
a.	Yes	No
b.	Yes	Yes
c.	No	Yes
d.	No	No

7.   An employer sponsoring a defined benefit pension plan should
   a.   Disclose the projected benefit obligation, identifying the accumulated benefit obligation and the vested benefit obligation.
   b.   Disclose the projected benefit obligation, identifying the accumulated benefit obligation but not the vested benefit obligation.
   c.   Disclose the projected benefit obligation, identifying the vested benefit obligation but not the accumulated benefit obligation.
   d.   Not disclose the projected benefit obligation.

8.   Which of the following components should be included in the calculation of net pension cost recognized for a period by an employer sponsoring a defined benefit pension plan?

	Actual return on plan assets, if any	Amortization of unrecognized prior service cost, if any
a.	No	Yes
b.	No	No
c.	Yes	No
d.	Yes	Yes

9.   Which of the following components should be included in net pension cost by an employer sponsoring a defined benefit pension plan?

	Amortization of unregonized prior service cost	Fair value of plan assets
a.	Yes	No
b.	Yes	Yes
c.	No	Yes
d.	No	No

10.   As of December 31, 1987, the projected benefit obligation and plan assets of a non-contributory defined benefit plan sponsored by Reed, Inc. were:

Projected benefit obligation	$780,000
Plan assets at fair value	600,000
Initial unfunded obligation	$180,000

Reed elected to apply the provisions of FASB Statement No. 87, Employers' Accounting for Pensions, in its financial statements for the year ended December 31, 1988. At December 31, 1987, all amounts accrued as net periodic pension cost had been contributed to the plan.

The average remaining service period of active plan participants expected to receive benefits was estimated to be 10 years at the date of transition. Some participants' estimated service periods are 20 and 25 years. To minimize an accrual for pension cost, what amount of unrecognized net obligation should Reed amortize?
   a. $ 7,200
   b. $ 9,000
   c. $12,000
   d. $18,000

11.   An employer sponsoring a defined benefit pension plan should disclose the

	Amount of unrecognized prior service cost	Fair value of plan assets
a.	No	No
b.	No	Yes
c.	Yes	Yes
d.	Yes	No

12.   An employer sponsoring a defined benefit pension plan should disclose the

	Amount of unrecognized prior service cost	Projected benefit obligation
a.	Yes	Yes
b.	Yes	No
c.	No	No
d.	No	Yes

13.   Which of the following terms includes assumptions concerning projected changes in future compensation when the pension benefit formula is based on future compensation levels (e.g., pay related and final pay plans)?

	Service cost component	Projected benefit obligation	Accumulated benefit obligation
a.	Yes	Yes	Yes
b.	Yes	Yes	No
c.	Yes	No	No
d.	No	No	No

14.   Kent, Inc., a calendar year company, established a defined benefit pension plan in December 1987. The following data relate to this plan at December 31, 1988:

Projected benefit obligation	$4,700,000
Accumulated benefit obligation	4,000,000
Total fair value of plan assets	3,000,000

Kent elected to apply the provisions of FASB Statement No. 87, Employers' Accounting for Pensions, in its financial statements for the year ended December 31, 1988.

In its December 31, 1988 balance sheet, Kent should report a minimum liability relating to the pension plan of

a. $4,000,000
b. $1,700,000
c. $1,000,000
d. $0

15.   In which of the following pension instances would the contra equity account, net
loss not recognized as pension expense, be
reported on the balance sheet for a particular
year?

    a.   When the additional pension lia-
bility required to be recognized
exceeds the unrecognized prior
service cost.

    b.   When the unrecognized prior service
cost exceeds the additional pension
liability required to be recognized.

    c.   Only when an employer sponsors two
or more separate defined benefit
pension plans.

    d.   Only when there is an amendment to a
defined benefit pension plan.

16.   A necessary condition for the recording
of an additional pension liability is present
when

    a.   Projected benefit obligation exceeds
accumulated benefit obligation.

    b.   The market-related asset value
exceeds accumulated benefit obligation.

    c.   Accumulated benefit obligation ex-
ceeds the fair value of plan assets.

    d.   Projected benefit obligation exceeds
accrued pension cost.

17.   The funded status of John Jacob Corporation's pension plan is as follows:

Accumulated benefit obligation	1,300,000
Plan assets at fair value	1,100,000
Projected benefit obligation	1,800,000
Prepaid pension cost	30,000

What is the amount of the adjustment necessary to reflect the required pension liability?

    a. $170,000
    b. $200,000
    c. $230,000
    d. $700,000

18.   Bulls Corporation amends its pension plan
on 1/1/86. The following information is
available:

	1/1/86 before amendment	1/1/86 after amendment
Accumulated benefit obligation	$ 950,000	$1,425,000
Projected benefit obligation	1,300,000	1,900,000

The total amount of unrecognized prior service
cost to be amortized over future periods as a
result of this amendment is

    a. $950,000
    b. $600,000
    c. $475,000
    d. $125,000

19.   Jordon Corporation obtains the following
information from its actuary. All amounts
given are __as of__ 1/1/87 (beginning of the
year).

	1/1/87
Projected benefit obliga-tion	$1,530,000
Market-related asset value	1,650,000
Unrecognized net loss	235,000
Average remaining service period	5.5 years

What amount of unrecognized net loss should be
recognized as part of pension expense in 1987?

    a. $70,000
    b. $42,727
    c. $14,909
    d. $12,727

20.   An employer offered for a short period of
time special termination benefits to some employees. The employees accepted the offer,
which provided for immediate lump-sum payments
and future payments at the end of the next two
years. The amounts can be reasonably estimated. The amount of expense recognized this
year should include

    a.   One third of the lump-sum payments
and one third of the present value
of the future payments.

    b.   Only the lump-sum payments.

    c.   The lump-sum payments and the total
of the future payments.

    d.   The lump-sum payments and the pre-
sent value of the future payments.

21.   On September 1, 1987, Howe Corp. offered
special termination benefits to employees who
had reached the early retirement age specified
in the company's pension plan. The termination benefits consisted of lump-sum and
periodic future payments. Additionally, the
employees accepting the company offer receive
the usual early retirement pension benefits.
The offer expired on November 30, 1987.
Actual or reasonably estimated amounts at
December 31, 1987 relating to the employees
accepting the offer are as follows:

    •   Lump-sum payments totaling $475,000
were made on January 1, 1988.

    •   Periodic payments of $60,000
annually for three years will begin January 1,
1989. The present value at December 31, 1987
of these payments was $155,000.

•   Reduction of accrued pension costs at December 31, 1987 for the terminating employees was $45,000.

In its December 31, 1987 balance sheet, Howe should report a total liability for special termination benefits of

    a. $475,000
    b. $585,000
    c. $630,000
    d. $655,000

May 1990 Questions

Items 22 and 23 are based on the following:

Mann Industries provides retirement benefits to employees through a funded defined benefit pension plan. The company administering the plan provided the following information for the year ended December 31, 1989:

Plan assets (at fair value)	$400,000
Accumulated benefit obligation	$445,000
Pension cost	$100,000
Employer's contribution, 12/1/89	$120,000
Prior service cost not yet recognized in earnings	$ 10,000

On December 31, 1988, the accrued/prepaid pension cost account had a debit balance of $15,000. Assume that the fair value of the plan assets is equal to the market-related asset value. Prior to 1989, the fair value of plan assets exceeded the accumulated benefit obligation.

22.   In Mann's December 31, 1989 balance sheet, what is the amount of prepaid pension cost?

    a. $35,000
    b. $30,000
    c. $20,000
    d. $ 5,000

23.   In Mann's December 31, 1989 balance sheet, what is the amount of minimum liability (unfunded accumulated benefit)?

    a. $10,000
    b. $20,000
    c. $45,000
    d. $80,000

24.   Interest cost included in the net pension cost recognized for a period by an employer sponsoring a defined benefit pension plan represents the

    a.   Shortage between the expected and actual returns on plan assets.
    b.   Increase in the projected benefit obligation due to the passage of time.
    c.   Increase in the fair value of plan assets due to the passage of time.
    d.   Amortization of the discount on unrecognized prior service costs.

25.   Barrett Co. maintains a defined benefit pension plan for its employees. At each balance sheet date, Barrett should report a minimum liability at least equal to the

    a.   Accumulated benefit obligation.
    b.   Projected benefit obligation.
    c.   Unfunded accumulated benefit obligation.
    d.   Unfunded projected benefit obligation.

PENSIONS

Problems

Problem 1   (1189,T4)

(15 to 25 minutes)

Essex Company has a single-employer defined benefit pension plan, and a compensation plan for future vacations for its employees.

Required:

a. Define the interest cost component of net pension cost for a period. How should Essex determine its interest cost component of net pension cost for a period?

b. Define prior service cost. How should Essex account for prior service cost? Why?

c. What conditions must be met for Essex to accrue compensation for future vacations? What is the theoretical rationale for accruing compensation for future vacations?

Author's Note: Part C of this question is covered in Module 25.

Problem 2   (588,T5)

(15 to 25 minutes)

Carson Company sponsors a single-employer defined benefit pension plan. The plan provides that pension benefits are determined by age, years of service, and compensation. Among the components that should be included in the net pension cost recognized for a period are service cost, interest cost, and actual return on plan assets.

Required:

a. What two accounting problems result from the nature of the defined benefit pension plan? Why do these problems arise?

b. How should Carson determine the service cost component of the net pension cost?

c. How should Carson determine the interest cost component of the net pension cost?

d. How should Carson determine the actual return on plan assets component of the net pension cost?

PENSIONS

Multiple Choice Answers

1. d	6. b	11. c	16. c	21. c
2. c	7. a	12. a	17. c	22. *
3. c	8. d	13. b	18. b	23. *
4. b	9. a	14. c	19. d	24. b
5. d	10. c	15. a	20. d	25. c

Multiple Choice Answer Explanations

D. Pensions

1. (1188,P2,23) (d) Prepaid pension cost is the cumulative excess of the amount funded over the amount recorded as pension expense. In 1986, funding was $170,000 and the only element of pension expense which applied was service cost ($150,000), so prepaid pension cost was $20,000 at 12/31/86. In 1987, pension expense was $162,000 as computed below:

Service cost	$165,000
Interest on projected benefit obligation	15,000
Actual return on plan assets	(18,000)
Pension expense	$162,000

Therefore, the 1987 funding ($185,000) exceeded pension expense ($162,000) by $23,000, increasing prepaid pension cost to $43,000 ($20,000 + $23,000).

2. (1188,P3,54) (c) Pension cost is a net amount calculated by adding or subtracting six factors. The only one of the six factors not present in this problem is amortization of unrecognized prior service cost. The other factors are combined as follows:

Service cost	$150,000
Return on plan assets	(40,000)
Interest on projected benefit obligation	82,000
Amortization of actuarial loss	15,000
Amortization of unrecognized net obligation	35,000
Pension cost	$242,000

Service cost and interest on the projected benefit obligation always increase pension expense; return on plan assets almost always decreases pension expense. Amortization of actuarial loss increases pension expense, while amortization of an actuarial gain would decrease pension expense. Amortization of transition amount can either increase or decrease pension expense. If the transition amount is a net obligation, its amortization increases pension expense; if it is a net

asset, its amortization decreases pension expense.

3. (1189,P1,18) (c) Since prior contributions equaled the amount of net pension cost previously accrued, there is no prepaid/ accrued pension cost at 1/1/88. 1988 pension expense is $121,000, as computed below:

Service cost	$120,000
Interest on PBO	12,000
Amort. of unrec. PSC	30,000
Return on plan assets	(41,000)
Pension cost	$121,000

Because no 1988 contributions have been made, this amount should be reported as a liability, accrued pension cost, at 12/31/88. Note that no additional liability would be recorded, because the accumulated benefit obligation ($350,000) is less than the fair value of the plan assets ($410,000).

4. (1187,P1,11) (b) Prepaid pension cost is the excess of the amount funded over the amount recorded as pension expense. The amount funded is $167,200 ($110,000 service cost + $57,200 funding of prior service cost). Based on the incomplete information given, pension expense is $151,700 ($110,000 service cost + $41,700 amortization of prior service cost). Therefore, prepaid pension cost is $15,500 ($167,200 - $151,700). Note that the information given is incomplete. The existence of prior service cost indicates that a projected benefit obligation (PBO) existed at 1/1/86, and interest on this PBO would increase pension expense. However, the PBO and the settlement rate are not given.

5. (587,P1,15) (d) The current liability for pensions at 12/31/86 consists of the 1986 net pension cost ($190,000), which will not be paid until two months after year end. There is no noncurrent liability. A noncurrent liability would exist if the accumulated benefit obligation ($480,000) exceeds the fair value of plan assets ($500,000). SFAS 87 requires the recording of an additional liability when the accumulated benefit obligation is greater than the fair value of plan assets. The unrecognized prior service cost ($150,000) is not directly recorded as a liability. It is amortized to pension cost over future periods.

6. (1188,T1,29) (b) Per SFAS 87, para 20, both the interest cost and the actual return on plan assets (if any) should be included in the calculation of net pension cost recognized for a period by an employer sponsoring a defined benefit pension plan. Therefore, answer (b) is correct, and answers (a), (c), and (d) are incorrect.

*Any of the four answers was accepted.

7. (1187,T1,36) (a) Per SFAS 87, para 54c, employers sponsoring a defined benefit pension plan must disclose a schedule reconciling the funded status of the plan with amounts reported in the employer's statement of financial position. They must show separately the projected benefit obligation, identifying the accumulated benefit obligation and the vested benefit obligation. Therefore, answer (a) is correct, and answers (b), (c), and (d) are incorrect.

8. (587,T1,23) (d) Per SFAS 87, para 20, among the components which should be included in the net pension cost recognized for a period by an employer sponsoring a defined benefit pension plan are both actual return on plan assets, if any, and amortization of unrecognized prior service cost, if any. Therefore, answer (d) is correct, and answers (a), (b), and (c) are incorrect.

9. (589,T1,20) (a) Per SFAS 87, para 20, the six factors which an employer sponsoring a defined benefit pension plan must include in its net pension cost are:

1. Service cost
2. Interest cost
3. Actual return on plan assets (if any)
4. Amortization of unrecognized prior service cost (if any)
5. Gain or loss (if any)
6. Amortization of the unrecognized net obligation or unrecognized net asset existing at the date of initial application of SFAS 87

Answer (a) is correct because net pension cost includes amortization of unrecognized prior service cost but does not include the fair value of plan assets. The fair value of plan assets is, however, used to determine the amount of any additional liability which must be disclosed.

10. (589,P2,35) (c) SFAS 87 states that a transition adjustment should be amortized on a straight-line basis over the average remaining employee service period (10 years in this case). However, an exception is provided when the length of the computed amortization period is less than 15 years. In that case, the employer can elect to use a 15-year period. In this case, Reed desires to minimize pension cost. Use of the 15-year period would result in a smaller charge to pension cost than would use of the 10-year period. Therefore, the amortization amount is $12,000 ($180,000 ÷ 15 years).

11. (587,T1,39) (c) Per SFAS 87, para 54, an employer sponsoring a defined benefit pension plan shall disclose both of the following: the amount of unrecognized prior service cost and the fair value of plan assets. Therefore, answer (c) is correct, and answers (a), (b), and (d) are incorrect. Please note that these are only two of the disclosures required by the FASB regarding the employer's pension plan.

12. (589,T1,35) (a) SFAS 87, para 54 provides a list of disclosures which must be provided by employers sponsoring a defined benefit pension plan. Both the amount of unrecognized prior service cost and the projected benefit obligation are among the required disclosures. Therefore, answer (a) is correct.

13. (b) The requirement is to determine which of the listed pension terms includes assumptions concerning projected changes in future compensation levels if the pension benefit formula is based on future compensation levels. Answer (b) is correct because per SFAS 87, paras 46 and 47, the service cost component and the projected benefit obligation reflect projected future compensation levels while the accumulated benefit obligation is measured based on employees' history of service and compensation without an estimate of projected future compensation levels. Therefore, answers (a), (c), and (d) are incorrect.

14. (589,P2,36) (c) SFAS 87 states that a minimum liability must be reported for the excess of the accumulated benefit obligation over the fair value of the plan assets. In this case, the minimum liability to be reported is $1,000,000 ($4,000,000 – $3,000,000). Note that the amount recorded in the journal entry (the additional, not minimum, liability) is the minimum liability plus prepaid pension cost or less accrued pension cost. This is because the additional liability is combined with accrued pension cost (or netted against the prepaid pension cost), so the resulting amount reported is the minimum liability.

15. (a) The requirement is to determine when the contra equity account, net loss not recognized as pension expense, should be reported on the balance sheet for a particular year. Per SFAS 87, para 37, when the additional liability required to be recognized exceeds the unrecognized prior service cost, the excess should be reported as a separate component (that is, a reduction) of equity, net of any

tax benefits. Therefore, answer (a) is correct and answer (b) is incorrect. Answer (c)
is incorrect because an employer that sponsors
only one defined benefit pension plan may be
required to report the contra equity account
as well as an employer with two or more defined benefit pension plans. Answer (d) is
incorrect because an amendment to an existing
plan does not always cause the difference
between the fair value of the plan assets and
the accumulated benefit obligation.

16. (c) Per SFAS 87, an additional pension
liability must be considered when the accumulated benefit obligation exceeds the fair
value of plan assets. The amount of liability
to be recorded is this excess less accrued
pension cost, or this excess plus prepaid
pension cost. The additional liability recorded is then combined (netted) with accrued
(prepaid) pension cost, so the minimum liability reported on the balance sheet is equal
to the excess of accumulated benefit obligation over fair value of plan assets.

17. (c) The requirement is to determine the
amount of the adjustment necessary to reflect
the required pension liability. Per SFAS 87,
the amount of the necessary adjustment would
be as follows:

Accumulated benefit obligation	$1,300,000
Plan assets (at fair value)	(1,100,000)
Unfunded accumulated benefit	200,000
Prepaid pension cost	30,000
Additional liability required	$ 230,000

The existing balance in the prepaid pension
cost of $30,000 is combined with the addi-
tional pension liability into one amount and
reported as accrued pension cost or pension
liability in the net amount of $200,000. An-
swers (a), (b), and (d) are incorrect.

18. (b) The requirement is the total amount
of unrecognized prior service cost to be
amortized over future periods as a result of a
pension plan amendment. Prior service cost is
the present value of retroactive benefits
given to employees for years of service provided before the date of an amendment to the
plan. Per SFAS 87, the cost of these retroactive benefits is measured by the increase in
the projected benefit obligation at the date
of amendment ($1,900,000 - $1,300,000 =
$600,000). This amount will be recognized as
expense (amortized) during the service periods
of those employees who are expected to receive
benefits under the plan.

19. (d) The requirement is the amount of unrecognized net loss to be recognized as a part

of pension expense in 1987. Per SFAS 87, the
corridor approach is to be used to determine
gain or loss amortization. Under this approach, only the unrecognized net gain or loss
in excess of 10% of the greater of the projected benefit obligation (PBO) or the market-
related asset value (M-RAV) is amortized. In
this case, the M-RAV ($1,650,000) is larger
than the PBO ($1,530,000). The corridor is
$165,000 (10% x $1,650,000). The unrecognized
net loss ($235,000) exceeds the corridor by
$70,000 ($235,000 - $165,000). This excess is
amortized over the average remaining service
period of active employees expected to participate in the plan ($70,000 ÷ 5.5 = $12,727).

20. (1187,T1,21) (d) Per SFAS 88, para 15,
an employer that offers for a short period of
time special termination benefits to employees
shall recognize a liability and an expense
when the employees accept the offer and the
amount can be reasonably estimated. The
amount recognized shall include any lump-sum
payments and the present value of any expected
future payments. Answer (d) is correct
because the employees accepted the offer and
the amount can be reasonably estimated.
Answer (a) is incorrect because the entire
expense should be recognized in the current
period. Answer (b) is incorrect because the
present value of the future payments must also
be recognized in the current period. Answer (c) is incorrect because the future
payments should be recognized at their present
value.

21. (588,P2,29) (c) Per SFAS 88, when
special termination benefits are offered to
employees, a loss and liability must be
recognized when the employee accepts the offer
and the amount can be reasonably estimated.
The amount to be recognized shall include any
lump-sum payments ($475,000) and the present
value of any expected future payments
($155,000). Therefore, the total liability
for special termination benefits is $630,000
($475,000 + $155,000). Note that the
reduction of accrued pension costs ($45,000)
would reduce the amount of the loss, but would
not affect the liability. Instead it would be
recorded as a reduction of accrued pension
costs. The journal entry would be:

Loss from termination		
benefits	585,000	
Accrued pension costs	45,000	
Liability from		
termination benefits		630,000

May 1990 Answers

22. (590,P2,24) (See following explanation)
Prepaid pension cost is the cumulative excess
of the amount funded over the amount recorded
as pension expense. Because this question is
related to item 23 below and SFAS 87 requires
that the balance sheet presentation of the
minimum liability shall include accrued/
prepaid pension cost, determination of the
amount to be reported on the balance sheet
depends on whether a minimum liability is to
be recognized in item 23. At 12/31/88, the
balance in the ledger account was $15,000.
During 1989, funding was $120,000 while pen-
sion cost was $100,000, causing prepaid pen-
sion cost to increase to $35,000 [$15,000 +
($120,000 - $100,000)]. This would be the
answer if the requirement had been the "balance in the prepaid pension cost account."
However, because a minimum liability of
$45,000 including prepaid pension cost is to
be reported on the balance sheet at December 31, 1989, the answer is -0-. Since an
answer option of -0- was not one of the four
presented, the AICPA decided to accept any of
the four answers. Only the minimum liability
of $45,000 ($35,000 prepaid netted with the
$80,000 additional liability that would need
to be recorded on the books) would be reported
on Mann's 12/31/89 balance sheet.

23. (590,P2,25) (See following explanation)
Per SFAS 87, a minimum liability must be
reported for the excess of the accumulated
benefit obligation over the fair value of plan
assets. In this case, the minimum liability
to be reported is $45,000 ($445,000 -
$400,000). Note that the amount recorded in
the journal entry (the additional liability)
would be the $45,000 minimum liability plus
$35,000 prepaid pension cost. Because the
questions are related and the correct answer
for number 22 was not one of the answer
options, the AICPA decided to accept any of
the four answers.

24. (590,T1,23) (b) Net pension cost (expense) is comprised of six elements. One of
these elements is interest on the projected
benefit obligation which is defined as the increase in the amount of the projected benefit
obligation due to the passage of time. Therefore, answer (b) is correct. Candidates must
be careful so as not to confuse "interest
cost" with the "actual return" component of
net pension cost which is the earnings on the
plan assets. If the latter component is positive, it reduces the net pension cost for the
period.

25. (590,T1,37) (c) Per SFAS 87, para 36,
if the accumulated benefit obligation exceeds
the fair value of plan assets, the employer
shall recognize ... a liability that is at
least equal to the unfunded accumulated benefit obligation. Therefore, answer (c) is
correct.

PENSIONS

Answer Outline

Problem 1   Pension Terms and Accrual of
            Vacation Pay (1189,T4)

a. Interest cost component = Increase in PBO
       caused by passage of time
    Calculation
       Assumed discount rate x beginning PBO

b. PSC = increased benefits based on services
       rendered in prior periods
       Granted at adoption or amendment date
    Accounting
       Include amortization of PSC in net
        pension cost during future service
        periods of employees active at date of
        adoption/amendment
       Because PSC incurred in anticipation of
        future economic benefits to employer

c. Conditions necessary for accrual of future
       vacation compensation
       Obligation stems from services already
        performed
       Obligation relates to vested/accumulated
        rights
       Payment is probable
       Amount can reasonably be estimated
    Rationale for accrual
       Matches costs and revenues
       Recognizes measurable liability

Unofficial Answer

Problem 1   Pension Terms and Accrual
            of Vacation Pay (1189,T4)

a. The interest cost component of the net
pension cost for a period is the increase in
the projected benefit obligation due to the
passage of time. Essex would determine its
interest cost component by applying an assumed
discount rate to the beginning projected benefit obligation.

b. Prior service cost is the cost of retroactive benefits (increased benefits based on
services rendered in prior periods) granted at
the date of adoption or amendment of a pension
plan. Prior service cost should be included
in net pension cost during the future service
periods of those employees active at the date
of the pension plan adoption or amendment, as
appropriate, who are expected to receive benefits under the pension plan. Prior service
cost is incurred with the expectation that the
employer will realize economic benefits in
future periods.

c. Essex must accrue compensation for future
vacations if all of the following conditions
are met:

   • Essex's obligation relating to employees' rights to receive compensation for
future vacations is attributable to employees'
services already rendered.
   • The obligation relates to rights that
vest or accumulate.
   • Payment of the vacation benefits is
probable.
   • The amount can be reasonably estimated.

   The theoretical rationale is that accruing
compensation matches the cost of vacation
benefits to the period in which services are
rendered, and results in recognition of a measurable liability.

Answer Outline

Problem 2   Pensions: Basic Concepts
            (588,T5)

a. Two accounting problems of defined benefit
       pension plan
       Estimating or selecting assumption in
        determining amount and timing of
        payments
       Attributing cost to years of service
    Problems arise because cost recognition
     precedes benefit payment
b. Service cost component = actuarial PV of
       benefits
       Attributed to employee services for
        period based on pension benefit formula
c. Interest cost component = PBO at beginning
       of period x assumed discount %
d. Actual return on plan assets = Δ in FV of
       plan assets (End. bal. – Beg. bal.) – con-
       tributions + benefits paid

Unofficial Answer

Problem 2   Pensions: Basic Concepts (588,T5)

a. The two accounting problems resulting from
the nature of the defined benefit pension plan
are as follows:

   • Estimates or assumptions must be made
      concerning the future events that will
      determine the amount and timing of the
      benefit payments.
   • Some approach to attributing the cost of
      pension benefits to individual years of
      service must be selected.

The two problems arise because a company must
recognize pension costs before it pays pension
benefits.

b. Carson should determine the service cost
component of the net pension cost as the
actuarial present value of pension benefits
attributable to employee services during a
particular period based on the application of
the pension benefit formula.

c. Carson should determine the interest cost
component of the net pension cost as the
increase in the projected benefit obligation
due to the passage of time. Measuring the
projected benefit obligation requires accrual
of an interest cost at an assumed discount
rate.

d. Carson should determine the actual return
on plan assets component of the net pension
cost as the change in the fair value of plan
assets during the period, adjusted for (1)
contributions and (2) benefit payments.

LEASES

Multiple Choice Questions (1-49)

1.   Conn Company purchased a new machine for $480,000 on January 1, 1986, and leased it to East the same day. The machine has an esti- mated 12-year life, and will be depreciated $40,000 per year. The lease is for a three- year period expiring January 1, 1989, at an annual rental of $85,000. Additionally, East paid $30,000 to Conn as a lease bonus to obtain the three-year lease. For 1986 Conn incurred insurance expense of $8,000 for the leased machine. What is Conn's 1986 operating profit on this leased asset?

    a. $67,000
    b. $55,000
    c. $47,000
    d. $37,000

2.   On July 1, 1986, Park Company leased office space for ten years to Rudd at a monthly rental of $15,000, and received the following amounts:

    First month's rent $15,000
    Security deposit   25,000

Rudd made timely rent payments through November 1986; the December rent was paid, together with the January 1987 rent, on January 6, 1987. At December 31, 1986, Park should report rent receivable of

    a. $0
    b. $ 5,000
    c. $15,000
    d. $30,000

3.   On January 1, 1988, Post Corp. leased a warehouse to Winn under an operating lease for ten years at $60,000 per year, payable the first day of each lease year. Post paid $27,000 to a real estate broker as a finder's fee. The warehouse is depreciated $15,000 per year. For 1988, Post incurred insurance and property tax expense totaling $12,000. Post's net rental income for 1988 should be

    a. $33,000
    b. $30,300
    c. $21,000
    d. $ 6,000

4.   Grady Company purchased a machine on January 1, 1983 for $720,000. The machine is expected to have a ten-year life, no residual value, and will be depreciated by the straight-line method. On January 1, 1983, the machine was leased to Lesch Company for a three-year period, at an annual rental of $125,000. Grady could have sold the machine for $860,000 instead of leasing it. Grady incurred maintenance and other executory costs

of $15,000 in 1983 under the terms of the lease. What amount should Grady report as operating profit on this leased asset for the year ended December 31, 1983?

    a. $ 38,000
    b. $ 53,000
    c. $125,000
    d. $178,000

5.   On January 1, 1988, Mill Corp. leased a machine to Ott Corp. for a five-year term at an annual rental of $50,000. The lease is an operating lease. At the inception of the lease Mill received $100,000, covering the first year's rent of $50,000 and a security deposit of $50,000. This deposit will not be returned to Ott upon expiration of the lease, but will instead be applied to payment of rent for the last year of the lease. Mill properly reported rental revenue of $100,000 in its 1988 income tax return. Mill's tax rate was 30%. In Mill's December 31, 1988 balance sheet, what portion of the $100,000 should be reported as a liability?

    a. $50,000
    b. $40,000
    c. $35,000
    d. $28,000

6.   Rent should be reported by the lessor as revenue over the lease term as it becomes receivable according to the provisions of the lease for a

	Direct-financing lease	Operating lease	Sales-type lease
a.	Yes	Yes	Yes
b.	Yes	No	No
c.	No	Yes	No
d.	No	No	Yes

7.   Rent received in advance by the lessor for an operating lease should be recognized as revenue

    a.   When received.
    b.   At the lease's inception.
    c.   In the period specified by the lease.
    d.   At the lease's expiration.

8.   On July 1, 1987, Kemp Company leased office space for five years at $15,000 a month. On that date, Kemp paid the lessor the following amounts:

Rent security deposit	$ 35,000
First month's rent	15,000
Last month's rent	15,000
Nonrefundable reimbursement to lessor for modifications to the leased premises	90,000
	$155,000

Kemp made timely rental payments August 1 through December 1, 1987. What portion of the payments to the lessor should Kemp have recognized as deferred to years beyond 1987?

    a. $140,000
    b. $131,000
    c. $125,000
    d. $ 50,000

9.   As an inducement to enter a lease, Arts, Inc., a lessor, grants Hompson Corp., a lessee, nine months of free rent under a five-year operating lease. The lease is effective on July 1, 1988 and provides for monthly rental of $1,000 to begin April 1, 1989.

In Hompson's income statement for the year ended June 30, 1989, rent expense should be reported as

    a. $10,200
    b. $ 9,000
    c. $ 3,000
    d. $ 2,550

10.   Glen Apparel, Inc. leases and operates a retail store. The following information relates to the lease for the year ended December 31, 1985:

    •   The store lease, an operating lease, calls for fixed monthly rent of $1,500 the first day of each month, and additional rent equal to 6% of net sales over $300,000 per calendar year. Net sales for 1985 are $900,000.

    •   Additionally, Glen paid executory costs to the lessor for property taxes of $5,000 and insurance of $2,500.

For 1985, Glen's expenses relating to the store lease are

    a. $25,500
    b. $54,000
    c. $59,000
    d. $61,500

11.   When equipment held under an operating lease is subleased by the original lessee, the original lessee would account for the sublease as a(an)

    a.   Operating lease.
    b.   Sales-type lease.
    c.   Direct financing lease.
    d.   Capital lease.

12.   On August 1, 1984, Kern Company leased a machine to Day Company for a six-year period requiring payments of $10,000 at the beginning of each year. The machine cost $48,000, which is the fair value at the lease date, and has a useful life of eight years with no residual value. Kern's implicit interest rate is 10% and present value factors are as follows:

Present value of an annuity
    due of $1 at 10% for 6 periods   4.791
Present value of an annuity
    due of $1 at 10% for 8 periods   5.868

Kern appropriately recorded the lease as a direct financing lease. At the inception of the lease, the gross lease receivables account balance should be

    a. $60,000
    b. $58,680
    c. $48,000
    d. $47,910

13.   Peg Co. leased equipment from Howe Corp. on July 1, 1988 for an eight-year period expiring June 30, 1996. Equal payments under the lease are $600,000 and are due on July 1 of each year. The first payment was made on July 1, 1988. The rate of interest contemplated by Peg and Howe is 10%. The cash selling price of the equipment is $3,520,000, and the cost of the equipment on Howe's accounting records is $2,800,000. The lease is appropriately recorded as a sales-type lease. What is the amount of profit on the sale and interest revenue that Howe should record for the year ended December 31, 1988?

	Profit on sale	Interest revenue
a.	$720,000	$176,000
b.	$720,000	$146,000
c.	$ 45,000	$176,000
d.	$ 45,000	$146,000

14.   In a lease that is recorded as a sales-type lease by the lessor, interest revenue

    a.   Does not arise.
    b.   Should be recognized over the period of the lease using the interest method.
    c.   Should be recognized over the period of the lease using the straight-line method.
    d.   Should be recognized in full as revenue at the lease's inception.

15.   A lease is recorded as a sales-type lease by the lessor. The difference between the gross investment in the lease and the sum of the present values of the two components of the gross investment (the net receivable) should be

    a.   Amortized over the period of the lease as interest revenue using the interest method.
    b.   Amortized over the period of the lease as interest revenue using the straight-line method.
    c.   Recognized in full as interest revenue at the lease's inception.
    d.   Recognized in full as manufacturer's or dealer's profit at the lease's inception.

16. The excess of the fair value of leased property at the inception of the lease over its cost or carrying amount should be classified by the lessor as
   a. Unearned income from a sales-type lease.
   b. Unearned income from a direct-financing lease.
   c. Manufacturer's or dealer's profit from a sales-type lease.
   d. Manufacturer's or dealer's profit from a direct-financing lease.

17. The present value of minimum lease payments should be used by the lessee in determining the amount of a lease liability under a lease classified by the lessee as a(an)

	Capital lease	Operating lease
a.	Yes	Yes
b.	Yes	No
c.	No	No
d.	No	Yes

18. On January 2, 1989, Ashe Company entered into a ten-year noncancelable lease requiring year-end payments of $100,000. Ashe's incremental borrowing rate is 12%, while the lessor's implicit interest rate, known to Ashe, is 10%. Present value factors for an ordinary annuity for ten periods are 6.145 at 10%, and 5.650 at 12%. Ownership of the property remains with the lessor at expiration of the lease. There is no bargain purchase option. The leased property has an estimated economic life of 12 years. What amount should Ashe capitalize for this leased property on January 2, 1989?
   a. $1,000,000
   b. $ 614,500
   c. $ 565,000
   d. $0

19. Beal, Inc. intends to lease a machine from Paul Corp. Beal's incremental borrowing rate is 14%. The prime rate of interest is 8%. Paul's implicit rate in the lease is 10%, which is known to Beal. Beal computes the present value of the minimum lease payments using
   a. 8%
   b. 10%
   c. 12%
   d. 14%

20. On December 30, 1988, Haber Co. leased a new machine from Gregg Corp. The following data relate to the lease transaction at the inception of the lease:

Lease term	10 years
Annual rental payable at the end of each lease year	$100,000
Useful life of machine	12 years
Implicit interest rate	10%
Present value of an annuity of 1 in advance for 10 periods at 10%	6.76
Present value of annuity of 1 in arrears for 10 periods at 10%	6.15
Fair value of the machine	$700,000

The lease has no renewal option, and the possession of the machine reverts to Gregg when the lease terminates. At the inception of the lease, Haber should record a lease liability of
   a. $0
   b. $615,000
   c. $630,000
   d. $676,000

21. On December 30, 1986, Drew Co. leased equipment under a capital lease for a period of 10 years. It contracted to pay $90,000 annual rent on December 31, 1986 and on December 31 of each of the next 9 years. The capital lease liability was appropriately recorded at $608,400 on December 30, 1986 before the first payment. The leased equipment has a useful life of 12 years and the interest rate implicit in the lease is 10%. Drew uses the straight-line method in depreciating all equipment. In recording the December 31, 1987 payment, Drew should reduce the capital lease liability by
   a. $38,160
   b. $50,700
   c. $51,840
   d. $60,840

22. On December 31, 1986, Ott Company leased a new machine from Wolf with the following pertinent information:

Lease term	12 years
Annual rental payable at beginning of each year	$100,000
Useful life of machine	15 years
Implicit interest rate	12%
Present value of an annuity of 1 in advance for 12 periods at 12%	6.94

The lease contains no renewal options and the machine reverts to Wolf at the termination of the lease. The cost of the machine on Wolf's accounting records is $750,000. At the inception of the lease, Ott should record a lease liability of
   a. $0
   b. $100,000
   c. $694,000
   d. $750,000

23. Kew Company leased equipment for its entire nine-year useful life, agreeing to pay $100,000 at the start of the lease term on December 31, 1985, and $100,000 annually on December 31 of the next eight years. The present value on December 31, 1985 of the nine lease payments over the lease term, discounted at the lessor's implicit rate known by Kew to be 10%, was $633,000. The December 31, 1985 present value of the lease payments discounted at Kew's incremental borrowing rate of 12% was $597,000. Kew made a timely second lease payment. The total lease liability at December 31, 1986 was

 a. $0
 b. $456,640
 c. $486,300
 d. $700,000

24. On January 1, 1986, Kerr Company signed a ten-year noncancelable lease for a new machine, requiring $20,000 annual payments at the beginning of each year. The machine has a useful life of 15 years, with no salvage value. Title passes to Kerr at the lease expiration date. Kerr uses straight-line depreciation for all of its plant assets. Aggregate lease payments have a present value on January 1, 1986 of $126,000, based on an appropriate rate of interest. For 1986, Kerr should record depreciation (amortization) expense for the leased machine at

 a. $20,000
 b. $12,600
 c. $ 8,400
 d. $0

25. East Company leased a new machine from North Company on May 1, 1986, under a lease with the following information:

Lease term	10 years
Annual rental payable at beginning of each lease year	$40,000
Useful life of machine	12 years
Implicit interest rate	14%
Present value of an annuity of 1 in advance for 10 periods at 14%	5.95
Present value of 1 for 10 periods at 14%	0.27

East has the option to purchase the machine on May 1, 1996 by paying $50,000, which approximates the expected fair value of the machine on the option exercise date. On May 1, 1986, East should record a capitalized lease asset of

 a. $251,500
 b. $238,000
 c. $224,500
 d. $198,000

26. A six-year capital lease expiring on December 31 specifies equal minimum annual lease payments. Part of this payment represents interest and part represents a reduction in the net lease liability. The portion of the minimum lease payment in the fifth year applicable to the reduction of the net lease liability should be

 a. Less than in the fourth year.
 b. More than in the fourth year.
 c. The same as in the sixth year.
 d. More than in the sixth year.

27. Lease Y does not contain a bargain purchase option, but the lease term is equal to 90 percent of the estimated economic life of the leased property. Lease Z does not transfer ownership of the property to the lessee by the end of the lease term, but the lease term is equal to 75 percent of the estimated economic life of the leased property. How should the lessee classify these leases?

	Lease Y	Lease Z
a.	Capital lease	Operating lease
b.	Capital lease	Capital lease
c.	Operating lease	Capital lease
d.	Operating lease	Operating lease

28. The lessee should amortize the capitalizable cost of the leased asset in a manner consistent with the lessee's normal depreciation policy for owned assets for leases that

	Contain a bargain purchase option	Transfer ownership of the property to the lessee by the end of the lease term
a.	No	No
b.	No	Yes
c.	Yes	Yes
d.	Yes	No

29. A lease contains a bargain purchase option. In determining the lessee's capitalizable cost at the beginning of the lease term, the payment called for by the bargain purchase option would

 a. Not be capitalized.
 b. Be subtracted at its present value.
 c. Be added at its exercise price.
 d. Be added at its present value.

30. On January 1, 1987, West Co. entered into a ten-year lease for a manufacturing plant. The annual minimum lease payments are $100,000. In the notes to the December 31, 1988 financial statements, what amounts of subsequent years' lease payments should be disclosed?

	Amount for appropriate required period	Aggregate amount for the period thereafter
a.	$100,000	$0
b.	$300,000	$500,000
c.	$500,000	$300,000
d.	$500,000	$0

31. On December 31, 1987, Parke Corp. sold Edlow Corp. an airplane with an estimated remaining useful life of ten years. At the same time, Parke leased back the airplane for three years. Additional information is as follows:

Sales price	$600,000
Carrying amount of airplane at date of sale	$100,000
Monthly rental under lease	$ 6,330
Interest rate implicit in the lease as computed by Edlow and known by Parke (this rate is lower than the lessee's incremental borrowing rate)	12%
Present value of operating lease rentals ($6,330 for 36 months @ 12%)	$190,581

The leaseback is considered an operating lease In Parke's December 31, 1987 balance sheet, what amount should be included as deferred revenue on this transaction?
   a. $0
   b. $190,581
   c. $309,419
   d. $500,000

32. On December 31, 1987, Ruhl Corp. sold equipment to Dorr and simultaneously leased it back for three years. The following data pertain to the transaction at this date:

Sales price	$220,000
Carrying amount	150,000
Present value of lease rentals ($2,000 for 36 months @ 12%)	60,800
Estimated remaining useful life	10 years

At December 31, 1987, what amount should Ruhl report as deferred revenue from the sale of the equipment?
   a. $0
   b. $ 9,200
   c. $60,800
   d. $70,000

33. On December 31, 1986, Lane, Inc. sold equipment to Noll, and simultaneously leased it back for 12 years. Pertinent information at this date is as follows:

Sales price	$480,000
Carrying amount	360,000
Estimated remaining economic life	15 years

At December 31, 1986, how much should Lane report as deferred revenue from the sale of the equipment?
   a. $0
   b. $110,000
   c. $112,000
   d. $120,000

34. On January 1, 1984, Marsh Company sold an airplane with an estimated useful life of ten years. At the same time, Marsh leased back the airplane for three years under a lease classified as an operating lease. Pertinent data are:

Sales price	$500,000
Book value of airplane	100,000
Monthly rental under leaseback	5,100
Present value of lease rentals	153,000

For the year ended December 31, 1984, Marsh's rent expense for the airplane should be
   a. $0
   b. $10,200
   c. $51,000
   d. $61,200

35. The following information pertains to equipment sold by Bard Co. to Kerr Co. on December 31, 1984:

Sales price	$300,000
Book value	100,000
Estimated remaining economic life	20 years

Simultaneously with the sale, Bard leased back the equipment for a period of 16 years. How much of the profit on the sale should Bard defer at December 31, 1984?
   a. $200,000
   b. $ 12,500
   c. $ 10,000
   d. $0

36. In a sale-leaseback transaction, the seller-lessee has retained the property. The gain on the sale should be recognized at the time of the sale-leaseback when the lease is classified as a(an)

	Capital lease	Operating lease
a.	Yes	Yes
b.	No	No
c.	No	Yes
d.	Yes	No

37. On December 1, 1988, Barr Company leased office space for five years at a monthly rental of $60,000. On that date, Barr paid the lessor the following amounts:

First month's rent	$ 60,000
Last month's rent	60,000
Security deposit (refundable at lease expiration)	80,000
Installation of new walls and offices	360,000

Barr's December 1988 expense relating to its use of this office space is

- a. $ 60,000
- b. $ 66,000
- c. $126,000
- d. $200,000

38.   On January 2, 1983, Wayne, Inc. signed an eight-year lease for office space. Wayne has the option to renew the lease for an additional four-year period on or before January 2, 1990. During January 1985, two years after occupying the leased premises, Wayne made general improvements to the premises costing $360,000 and having an estimated useful life of ten years. At December 31, 1985, Wayne's intentions as to exercise of the renewal option are uncertain because they depend upon future office space requirements. A full year's amortization expense is taken for calendar year 1985. Wayne should record amortization of leasehold improvements for 1985 at

- a. $30,000
- b. $36,000
- c. $45,000
- d. $60,000

39.   A lessee incurred costs to construct office space in a leased warehouse. The estimated useful life of the office is ten years. The remaining term of the nonrenewable lease is fifteen years. The costs should be

- a.   Capitalized as leasehold improvements and depreciated over fifteen years.
- b.   Capitalized as leasehold improvements and depreciated over ten years.
- c.   Capitalized as leasehold improvements and expensed in the year in which the lease expires.
- d.   Expensed as incurred.

40.   A lessee incurred landscaping costs to improve leased property. The estimated useful life of the landscaping costs is six years. The remaining term of the nonrenewable lease is five years. The landscaping costs should be

- a.   Capitalized as leasehold improvements and depreciated over five years.

- b.   Capitalized as leasehold improvements and depreciated over six years.
- c.   Expensed as incurred and included with rent expense.
- d.   Expensed as incurred but **not** included with rent expense.

May 1990 Questions

41.   On January 2, 1989, Ames Corp. signed an eight-year lease for office space. Ames has the option to renew the lease for an additional four-year period on or before January 2, 1996. During January 1989, Ames incurred the following costs:

- • $120,000 for general improvements to the leased premises with an estimated useful life of ten years.
- • $50,000 for office furniture and equipment with an estimated useful life of ten years.

At December 31, 1989, Ames' intentions as to exercise of the renewal option are uncertain. A full year's amortization of leasehold improvements is taken for calendar year 1989. In Ames' December 31, 1989 balance sheet, accumulated amortization should be

- a. $10,000
- b. $15,000
- c. $17,000
- d. $21,250

42.   On December 31, 1989, Bain Corp. sold a machine to Ryan and simultaneously leased it back for one year. Pertinent information at this date follows:

Sales price	$360,000
Carrying amount	330,000
Present value of reasonable rentals ($3,000 for 12 months @ 12%)	34,100
Estimated remaining useful life	12 years

In Bain's December 31, 1989 balance sheet, the deferred revenue from the sale of this machine should be

- a. $34,100
- b. $30,000
- c. $ 4,100
- d. $0

43.   On January 1, 1989, Day Corp. entered into a 10-year lease agreement with Ward, Inc. for industrial equipment. Annual lease payments of $10,000 are payable at the end of each year. Day knows that the lessor expects a 10% return on the lease. Day has a 12% incremental borrowing rate. The equipment is expected to have an estimated useful life of 10 years. In addition, a third party has guaranteed to pay Ward a residual value of $5,000 at the end of the lease.

The present value of an ordinary annuity of $1 at

     12% for 10 years is 5.6502
     10% for 10 years is 6.1446

The present value of $1 at

     12% for 10 years is .3220
     10% for 10 years is .3855

In Day's October 31, 1989 balance sheet, the principal amount of the lease obligation was
- a. $63,374
- b. $61,446
- c. $58,112
- d. $56,502

44. Rapp Co. leased a new machine to Lake Co. on January 1, 1989. The lease expires on January 1, 1994. The annual rental is $90,000. Additionally, on January 1, 1989, Lake paid $50,000 to Rapp as a lease bonus and $25,000 as a security deposit to be refunded upon expiration of the lease. In Rapp's 1989 income statement, the amount of rental revenue should be

- a. $140,000
- b. $125,000
- c. $100,000
- d. $ 90,000

Items 45 and 46 are based on the following:

On January 2, 1989, Dix Machine Shops, Inc. signed a ten-year noncancellable lease for a heavy duty drill press. The lease stipulated annual payments of $30,000 starting at the end of the first year, with title passing to Dix at the expiration of the lease. Dix treated this transaction as a capital lease. The drill press has an estimated useful life of 15 years, with no salvage value. Dix uses straight-line depreciation for all of its fixed assets. Aggregate lease payments were determined to have a present value of $180,000, based on implicit interest of 10%.

45. In its 1989 income statement, what amount of interest expense should Dix report from this lease transaction?
- a. $0
- b. $12,000
- c. $15,000
- d. $18,000

46. In its 1989 income statement, what amount of depreciation expense should Dix report from this lease transaction?
- a. $30,000
- b. $20,000
- c. $18,000
- d. $12,000

47. On January 1, 1989, Park Co. signed a 10-year operating lease for office space at $96,000 per year. The lease included a provision for additional rent of 5% of annual company sales in excess of $500,000. Park's sales for the year ended December 31, 1989 were $600,000. Upon execution of the lease, Park paid $24,000 as a bonus for the lease. Park's rent expense for the year ended December 31, 1989 is
- a. $ 98,400
- b. $101,000
- c. $103,400
- d. $125,000

48. A lessee had a ten-year capital lease requiring equal annual payments. The reduction of the lease liability in year 2 should equal
- a. The current liability shown for the lease at the end of year 1.
- b. The current liability shown for the lease at the end of year 2.
- c. The reduction of the lease obligation in year 1.
- d. One-tenth of the original lease liability.

49. A twenty-year property lease, classified as an operating lease, provides for a 10% increase in annual payments every five years. In the sixth year compared to the fifth year, the lease will cause the following expenses to increase

	Rent	Interest
a.	No	Yes
b.	Yes	No
c.	Yes	Yes
d.	No	No

Repeat Question

(590,P2,33) Identical/similar to item 23 above

LEASES

Problems

Problem 1   (589,T5)

(15 to 25 minutes)

On January 1, 1988, Von Company entered into two noncancelable leases for new machines to be used in its manufacturing operations. The first lease does not contain a bargain purchase option; the lease term is equal to 80 percent of the estimated economic life of the machine. The second lease contains a bargain purchase option; the lease term is equal to 50 percent of the estimated economic life of the machine.

Required:

    a. What is the theoretical basis for requiring lessees to capitalize certain long-term leases? Do not discuss the specific criteria classifying a lease as a capital lease.
    b. How should a lessee account for a capital lease at its inception?
    c. How should a lessee record each minimum lease payment for a capital lease?
    d. How should Von classify each of the two leases? Why?

Problem 2   (585,T2)

(15 to 25 minutes)

On January 1, 1986, Lani Company entered into a noncancelable lease for a machine to be used in its manufacturing operations. The lease transfers ownership of the machine to Lani by the end of the lease term. The term of the lease is eight years. The minimum lease payment made by Lani on January 1, 1986 was one of eight equal annual payments. At the inception of the lease, the criteria established for classification as a capital lease by the lessee were met.

Required:

    a. What is the theoretical basis for the accounting standard which requires certain long-term leases to be capitalized by the lessee? Do not discuss the specific criteria for classifying a specific lease as a capital lease.
    b. How should Lani account for this lease at its inception and determine the amount to be recorded?
    c. What expenses related to this lease will Lani incur during the first year of the lease, and how will they be determined?
    d. How should Lani report the lease transaction on its December 31, 1986 balance sheet?

Problem 3   (580,T3)

(15 to 25 minutes)

    Part a. Capital leases and operating leases are the two classifications of leases described in FASB pronouncements, from the standpoint of the lessee.

Required:

    1. Describe how a capital lease would be accounted for by the lessee both at the inception of the lease and during the first year of the lease, assuming the lease transfers ownership of the property to the lessee by the end of the lease.
    2. Describe how an operating lease would be accounted for by the lessee both at the inception of the lease and during the first year of the lease, assuming equal monthly payments are made by the lessee at the beginning of each month of the lease. Describe the change in accounting, if any, when rental payments are not made on a straight-line basis.
    Do not discuss the criteria for distinguishing between capital leases and operating leases.

    Part b. Sales-type leases and direct financing leases are two of the classifications of leases described in FASB pronouncements, from the standpoint of the lessor.

Required:

    Compare and contrast a sales-type lease with a direct financing lease as follows:

    1. Gross investment in the lease.
    2. Amortization of unearned interest income.
    3. Manufacturer's or dealer's profit.

    Do not discuss the criteria for distinguishing between the leases described above and operating leases.

Problem 4   (588,T4)

(15 to 25 minutes)

On January 1, 1987, Metcalf Company sold equipment for cash and leased it back. As seller-lessee, Metcalf retained the right to substantially all of the remaining use of the equipment.

The term of the lease is eight years. There is a gain on the sale portion of the transaction. The lease portion of the transaction is classified appropriately as a capital lease.

Required:

a. What is the theoretical basis for requiring lessees to capitalize certain long-term leases? Do not discuss the specific criteria for classifying a lease as a capital lease.

b.1. How should Metcalf account for the sale portion of the sale-leaseback transaction at January 1, 1987?

2. How should Metcalf account for the leaseback portion of the sale-leaseback transaction at January 1, 1987?

c. How should Metcalf account for the gain on the sale portion of the sale-leaseback transaction during the first year of the lease? Why?

Problem 5   (1188,Q4)*

(45 to 55 minutes)

Lino Corporation's liability account balances at December 31, 1986 included the following:

Note payable to bank	$800,000
Liability under capital lease	280,000
Deferred tax liability	100,000

Additional information:

• The note payable, dated October 1, 1986, bears interest at an annual rate of 10% payable semiannually on April 1 and October 1. Principal payments are due annually on October 1 in four equal installments.

• The capital lease is for a 10-year period beginning December 31, 1981. Equal annual payments of $100,000 are due on December 31 of each year. The 16% interest rate implicit in the lease is known by Lino. At December 31, 1986, the present value of the four remaining lease payments discounted at 16% was $280,000.

• Deferred income taxes are provided in recognition of temporary differences between financial statement and income tax reporting of depreciation. For the year ended December 31, 1987, depreciation per tax return exceeded book depreciation by $50,000. Lino's income tax rate for 1987 (assume no changes have been enacted for future years) was 30%.

• On July 1, 1987, Lino issued $1,000,000 face amount of 10-year, 10% bonds for $750,000, to yield 15%. Interest is payable annually on July 1. Bond discount is amortized by the interest method.

• All required principal and interest payments were made on schedule in 1987.

Required:

a. Prepare the long-term liabilities section of Lino's balance sheet at December 31, 1987.

b. Prepare a schedule showing interest expense that should appear in Lino's income statement for the year ended December 31, 1987.

*Recent Accounting Practice Exams have included two comprehensive problems that have multiple requirements related to the same problem data, similar to this one. Candidates should work all of these problems included in this volume so as to be prepared for them.

LEASES

Multiple Choice Answers

1. c	11. a	21. a	31. b	41. b
2. c	12. a	22. c	32. c	42. d
3. b	13. b	23. c	33. d	43. b
4. a	14. b	24. c	34. b	44. c
5. a	15. a	25. b	35. a	45. d
6. c	16. c	26. b	36. b	46. d
7. c	17. b	27. b	37. b	47. c
8. b	18. b	28. c	38. d	48. a
9. a	19. b	29. d	39. b	49. b
10. d	20. b	30. c	40. a	

Multiple Choice Answer Explanations

E.1.a.(1). Operating Leases: Lessor

1. (1187,P2,37) (c) This lease is an operating lease because it does not meet any of the four criteria to be a capital lease as described in para 7, SFAS 13. The lessor should recognize as revenue the 1986 rental payment ($85,000) plus a proportionate fraction of the lease bonus ($30,000 ÷ 3-year lease term = $10,000 per year). Therefore, total revenue for 1986 is $95,000 ($85,000 + $10,000). 1986 expenses total $48,000 (depreciation of $40,000 and insurance of $8,000). Thus, operating profit on the leased asset is $47,000 ($95,000 revenues less $48,000 expenses).

2.   (587,P1,6) (c) At 12/31/86, rent receivable should consist of any rent revenue which has been earned, but has not yet been collected. Rent revenue earned through November 1986 has been collected on a timely basis. However, the December 1986 earned rent ($15,000) was not collected until 1/6/87 and should be reported as rent receivable at 12/31/86. The January 1987 rent payment is not included in 12/31/86 rent receivable because it was not earned as of 12/31/86. The security deposit ($25,000) would be reported as a long-term payable and would not affect rent receivable.

3.   (589,P3,54) (b) Net rental income on an operating lease is equal to rental revenue less related expenses, as computed below:

Rental revenue	$60,000
Depreciation expense	(15,000)
Executory costs	(12,000)
Finder's fee ($27,000 ÷ 10)	(2,700)
Net rental income	$30,300

The finder's fee ($27,000) is capitalized as a deferred charge at the inception of the lease and amortized over 10 years to match the expense to the revenues it enabled the lessor to earn.

4. (1184,P3,47) (a) The requirement is to determine the amount of operating profit recognized on the leased asset in 1983. This is an operating lease because the classification criteria are not met for a sales-type, direct, or leveraged lease (SFAS 13, paras 6-8). Therefore, lease payments are recognized as revenue in the period received or due, and costs are charged to expense as incurred. In 1983 rental revenue is $125,000, depreciation expense is $72,000 ($720,000 ÷ 10 years), and executory costs total $15,000. Therefore, the net operating profit from the lease is $38,000 ($125,000 - $72,000 - $15,000).

5. (1189,P1,20) (a) Deposits and prepayments received for services to be provided in the future are unearned revenues which should be recorded as a liability until earned. The first year's rent is recorded as rent revenue, but the $50,000 deposit is recorded as rent collected in advance (unearned rent) because Mill is required to render future services (use of the machine) to the lessee. The tax rate (30%) does not affect the amount of the liability to the lessee, although a separate deferred tax asset may be recorded in certain circumstances.

6. (1188,T1,24) (c) Per SFAS 13, para 19b, rent should be reported by the lessor as revenue over the lease term for an operating lease as it becomes receivable according to the lease provisions. Both direct-financing and sales-type leases are types of capital leases. For these lease types, the lessor reports interest income over the lease term, not rental income. Therefore, answer (c) is correct, and answers (a), (b), and (d) are incorrect.

7. (583,T1,29) (c) The requirement is to determine when rent, received in advance by the lessor for an operating lease, should be recognized as revenue. Per the revenue recognition principle, under an operating lease rental revenue is to be recognized in each accounting period on a straight-line basis unless another systematic and rational basis is more representative of the decline in the asset's service potential. Answer (a) is incorrect because when the cash is received is irrelevant since revenue recognition is on the accrual basis. Answer (b) is incorrect because the earnings process is not complete at the lease's inception. Answer (d) is incorrect because rental revenue is earned daily by the lessor as the property is being leased; therefore, deferring revenue recognition until the lease's expiration would violate the revenue recognition principle.

E.1.a.(2) Operating Leases: Lessee

8.   (588,P2,26) (b) The first month's rent and the subsequent monthly rental payments should be expensed as incurred in 1987. The rent security deposit ($35,000) is deferred and recorded as a long-term receivable, since Kemp can expect to receive the deposit back at lease end. The prepayment of the last month's rent ($15,000) is also deferred, and will be recognized as expense in the last month of the lease. The nonrefundable payment ($90,000) should be recognized as rent expense ratably over the lease term. Therefore, 6 months of the total is recorded as an expense in 1987 (6/60 x $90,000 = $9,000) and 54 months worth is deferred to years beyond 1987 (54/60 x $90,000 = $81,000). The total amount deferred is $131,000 ($35,000 + $15,000 + $81,000).

9.   (589,P1,12) (a) SFAS 13 states that rent on operating leases should be expensed on a straight-line basis unless another method is better suited to the particular benefits and costs associated with the lease. In this lease, the lessee must pay rent of $1,000 monthly for 5 years excluding the first 9 months, or 51 months (60 – 9). Therefore, total rent expense for the 5 years is $51,000 (51 x $1,000). Recognizing rent expense on a straight-line basis, rent expense for the first year is $10,200 ($51,000 ÷ 5 years).

10. (1186,P3,50) (d) The expenses relating to the store lease consist of the three items listed below:

Monthly rent (12 x $1,500)	$18,000
Addl. rent	
[6% x ($900,000 – $300,000)]	36,000
Executory costs ($5,000 + $2,500)	7,500
Total	$61,500

Monthly rent is $1,500. Additional rent is due equal to 6% of net sales over $300,000. 1985 net sales were $900,000, resulting in an excess of $600,000 and additional rent of $36,000 (6% x $600,000). Additionally, executory costs (property taxes and insurance on the leased asset) were $7,500 in 1985 ($5,000 + $2,500).

11. (583,T1,34) (a) The requirement is the treatment of a sublease of equipment held under an operating lease by the original lessee. A sublease arises when the lease agreement between the two original parties remain in effect, and the leased property is released to a third party by the original lessee. Consequently, if the original lease is an operating lease, the original lessee shall account for the sublease as an operating lease (SFAS 13, para 39).

E.1.b. Direct Financing Leases: Lessor

12. (585,P1,6) (a) The requirement is to determine the balance in the <u>gross</u> lease payments receivable account at the inception of a direct financing lease. Lease payments receivable is debited for the gross investment in the lease, which includes the minimum lease payments plus any unguaranteed residual value. Since there is no residual value in this problem, gross investment is simply the minimum lease payments (6 rentals at $10,000 each, or $60,000).

E.1.c. Sales-Type Leases: Lessor

13. (1189,P2,34) (b) This is a sales-type lease, so at the inception of the lease, the lessor would recognize sales of $3,520,000 and cost of goods sold of $2,800,000, resulting in a <u>profit on sale of $720,000</u>. In addition, interest revenue is recognized for the period July 1, 1988 to December 31, 1988. The initial net lease payments receivable on 7/1/88 is $3,520,000. The first rental payment received on 7/1/88 consists entirely of principal, reducing the net receivable to $2,920,000 ($3,520,000 – $600,000). Therefore, 1988 <u>interest revenue for the six months from 7/1/88 to 12/31/88 is $146,000</u> ($2,920,000 x 10% x 6/12).

14. (588,T1,24) (b) Per SFAS 13, para 17b, revenue is to be recognized for a sales-type lease over the lease term so as to produce a <u>constant rate</u> of return on the net investment in the lease. This requires the use of the <u>interest method</u>. Therefore, answer (b) is correct and answer (c) is incorrect. Answer (a) is incorrect because, per SFAS 13, interest revenue <u>does</u> arise in a sales-type lease. Answer (d) is incorrect because the interest is to be earned over the life of the lease, not in full at the lease's inception.

15. (587,T1,27) (a) Per SFAS 13, para 17b, the difference between the gross investment in the lease and the sum of the present values of the two components of the gross investment shall be recorded as unearned income. The unearned income shall be <u>amortized</u> to income <u>over the lease term</u> so as to provide a <u>constant periodic rate</u> of return on the net investment in the lease. Per APB 12, para 16, the objective of the interest method is to arrive at a <u>level</u> (i.e., constant) effective rate (of interest). Therefore, answers (b), (c), and (d) are incorrect.

16. (1182,T1,17) (c) Per SFAS 13, para 17, the excess of the fair value of leased property at the inception of the lease over the

lessor's cost is defined as the manufacturer's or dealer's profit. Answer (a) is incorrect because the unearned income from a sales-type lease is defined as the difference between the gross investment in the lease and the sum of the present values of the components of the gross investment. Answer (b) is incorrect because the unearned income from a direct-financing lease is defined as the excess of the gross investment over the cost (also the PV of lease payments) of the leased property. Answer (d) is incorrect because a sales-type lease involves a manufacturer's or dealer's profit while a direct-financing lease does not.

E.1.d. Capital Leases: Lessee

17. (1189,T1,16) (b) Per SFAS 13, para 15, rental on an operating lease is to be charged to expense over the lease term as it becomes payable, unless the payment pattern does not represent a systematic and rational allocation over the lease term (in which case the straight-line method is recommended). No lease liability is established for operating leases, nor is a "leased asset" recognized. The statement does, however, require the lessee in a capital leasing transaction to both establish a lease liability equal to the present value of the minimum lease payments, and recognize the leased asset for the same amount. Therefore, answer (b) is correct.

18. (589,P2,23) (b) This is a capital lease for the lessee because the lease term (10 years) covers more than 75% of the economic life of the leased asset (75% x 12 = 9 years). In a capital lease, the lessee records the PV of the minimum lease payments as an asset and a liability. The lease payments are discounted using the lesser of the lessee's incremental borrowing rate or the implicit rate used by the lessor, if known. In this case, the lessee knows the implicit rate is 10%, which is lower than the incremental rate of 12%. Thus, when the lease is signed, the PV amount recorded as an asset and liability is $614,500 ($100,000 x 6.145).

19. (589,P3,44) (b) SFAS 13 states that the lessee should compute the PV of the minimum lease payments using the lesser of the lessee's incremental borrowing rate (14% in this case) or the implicit rate used by the lessor if known, (10% in this case). The PV of the minimum lease payments should be computed using the implicit rate of 10% because it is known by the lessee and is lower than the incremental rate. The prime rate (8%) is never used unless it happens to be the same as the incremental or implicit rate.

20. (1189,P2,27) (b) This is a capital lease for the lessee because the lease term exceeds 75% of the useful life of the machine (10/12 > 75%). For a capital lease, the lessee must record an asset and a liability equal to the present value of the minimum lease payments. Since these rentals are paid at the end of each year, the present value factor for an annuity in arrears must be used to determine the present value. Therefore, at the inception of the lease, Haber should record a lease liability of $615,000 ($100,000 x 6.15).

21. (588,P2,36) (a) The initial lease liability at 12/30/86, before the first lease payment, is $608,400. The 12/31/86 payment consists entirely of principal, bringing the 12/31/86 balance down to $518,400 ($608,400 - $90,000). The 12/31/87 payment consists of both principal and the interest incurred during 1987. 1987 interest is $51,840 ($518,400 x 10%), so the principal portion of the 12/31/87 payment is $38,160 ($90,000 - $51,840).

22. (587,P2,21) (c) This is a capital lease for the lessee because the lease term exceeds 75% of the useful life of the machine (12/15 > 75%). In a capital lease, the lessee records as an asset and liability the present value (PV) of the minimum lease payments (unless the PV exceeds the asset's FMV, in which case the FMV is recorded). The minimum lease payments include rentals, a lessee-guaranteed residual value, and a bargain purchase option. Only the rentals apply in this case. Therefore, the PV of the minimum lease payments is $694,000 ($100,000 x 6.94). Note that the lessor's cost for the leased asset ($750,000) has no effect on the lessee's records.

23. (587,P2,22) (c) The initial lease liability at 12/31/85, before the 12/31/85 payment, is $633,000 (PV of the nine lease payments at 10%). The 10% rate is used because according to SFAS 13, the rate used to compute the present value shall be the lessee's incremental borrowing rate unless the lessor's implicit rate is known and is less than the incremental borrowing rate. The 12/31/85 payment consists entirely of principal, bringing the 12/31/85 balance down to $533,000 ($633,000 - $100,000). The 12/31/86 payment consists of both principal and interest incurred during 1986. 1986 interest is $53,300 ($533,000 x 10%), so the principal portion of the 12/31/86 payment is $46,700 ($100,000 - $53,300). Therefore, the 12/31/86 liability is $486,300 ($533,000 - $46,700).

Initial liability	$633,000
12/31/85 payment	(100,000)
12/31/85 liability	$533,000
12/31/86 principal	
payment ($100,000 - $53,300)	(46,700)
12/31/86 liability	$486,300

24. (587,P3,45) (c) Since title passes to the lessee at the end of the lease, this is a **capital** lease for the lessee. The lessee records the leased asset and lease liability at an amount equal to the lesser of the FMV of the leased asset or the PV of the minimum lease payments ($126,000). This asset is depreciated on a straight-line basis over its useful life of 15 years, resulting in a yearly depreciation charge of $8,400 ($126,000 ÷ 15). The asset is depreciated over its useful life rather than over the lease term because title transfers to the lessee, allowing the lessee to use the asset for 15 years.

25. (586,P1,20) (b) The requirement is the amount to be recorded as a capitalized leased asset. This is a capital lease for the lessee because the lease term exceeds 75% of the economic life of the leased asset (10/12 > 75%). In a capital lease, the lessee records as an asset and liability the present value (PV) of the minimum lease payments (unless the PV exceeds the asset's FMV, in which case the FMV is recorded). The minimum lease payments include rentals, and a lessee-guaranteed residual value or a bargain purchase option. Only rentals apply in this case. Note that the $50,000 purchase option is not a **bargain** purchase option which the lessee would be compelled to exercise. A bargain purchase option is an option to purchase the leased asset at an amount **less** than its expected fair value. Therefore, the present value of the minimum lease payments is $238,000 ($40,000 x 5.95).

26. (1188,T1,13) (b) Per SFAS 13, para 12, each minimum lease payment shall be allocated between a reduction of the obligation and interest expense so as to produce a constant periodic rate of interest on the remaining balance of the obligation. Since the interest will be computed based upon a **declining** obligation balance, the interest component of each payment will also be declining. The result will be a relatively larger portion of the minimum lease payment allocated to the reduction of the lease obligation in the latter portion of the lease term. Therefore, answer (b) is correct and answers (a), (c), and (d) are incorrect.

27. (587,T1,14) (b) Per SFAS 13, para 7, if a lease meets one or more of four criteria, the lease is classified as a capital lease by the lessee. One of these criterion is that the lease term is equal to 75 percent or more of the estimated economic life of the leased property. Therefore, **both** leases Y and Z in this problem should be classified as capital leases. Therefore, answers (a), (c), and (d) are incorrect.

28. (586,T1,19) (c) The requirement is to determine if a lessee should amortize the capitalizable cost of a leased asset in a manner consistent with the lessee's normal depreciation policy for owned assets for leases that contained a bargain purchase option and/or transferred ownership at the end of the lease term. Transfer of ownership of the property to the lessee by the end of the lease term and a lease that contains a bargain purchase option are properly classified as capital leases [SFAS 13, paras 7(a) and 7(b)]. Per SFAS 13, para 11(a), if the lease meets either of the above criteria, the asset shall be amortized in a manner consistent with the lessee's normal depreciation policy for owned assets. Therefore, answers (a), (b), and (d) are incorrect.

29. (584,T1,12) (d) The requirement is to determine whether or not a bargain purchase option should be capitalized as part of the minimum lease payments. Per SFAS 13, para 5j, minimum lease payments include the rental payments plus the amount of the bargain purchase option if it exists. Per para 10, the amount to be capitalized is the present value of the minimum lease payments. Therefore, the present value of the bargain purchase option would be added to the present value of the rental payments (assumed to be previously calculated) in determining the lessee's capitalizable cost.

30. (1189,P3,53) (c) SFAS 13, as amended and interpreted, requires the disclosure of future minimum lease payments (MLPs) for each of the next five years and the aggregate amount of MLPs due after five years. At 12/31/00, eight annual payments of $100,000 each have not yet been paid. Therefore, future MLPs are $800,000 (8 x $100,000). The amount for the appropriate required period (5 years) is $500,000, while the aggregate amount for the period thereafter is $300,000 ($800,000 - $500,000).

E.2.d. Sale-Leaseback

31. (1188,P2,21) (b) SFAS 13, para 33 generally treats a sale-leaseback as a single financing transaction in which any profit on the sale is deferred and amortized by the seller. However, SFAS 28 amends this general rule when either only a minor part of the remaining use of the leased asset is retained (case 1), or when more than a minor part but less than substantially all of the remaining use of the leased asset is retained (case 2). Case 1 occurs when the PV of the lease payments is 10% or less of the FMV of the sale-leaseback property. Case 2 occurs when the leaseback is more than minor but does not meet the criteria of a capital lease. This is an example of case 2 because while the PV of the lease payments ($190,581) is more than 10% of the FMV of the asset ($600,000), the lease falls into the operating lease category. SFAS 28 specifies that under these circum- stances the gain on sale ($600,000 - $100,000 = $500,000) is recognized to the extent that it exceeds the PV of the lease payments ($190,581). The gain reported would be $309,419 ($500,000 - $190,581). The portion of the gain represented by the $190,581 PV of the lease payments is deferred and amortized on a straight-line basis over the life of the lease.

32. (588,P2,32) (c) Para 33 of SFAS 13 generally treats a sale-leaseback as a single financing transaction in which any profit on the sale is deferred and amortized by the seller. However, SFAS 28 amends this general rule when either (1) only a minor part of the remaining use of the property is retained, or (2) more than a minor part but less than substantially all of the remaining use of the property is retained. Case 1 occurs when the PV of the lease payments is 10% or less of the FMV of the sales-leaseback property. Case 2 occurs when the leaseback is more than minor but does not meet the criteria of a capital lease. This problem is an example of case 2, because the PV of the lease payments ($60,800) is more than 10% of the FMV of the asset ($220,000), but none of the capital lease cri- teria are met. SFAS 28 specifies that under these circumstances, the profit is recognized only to the extent that it exceeds the present value of the lease payments ($70,000 - $60,800 = $9,200). The remaining gain of $60,800 would be deferred. Note that if case 1 is applied, the full gain would be recognized (none deferred).

33. (1187,P1,18) (d) According to SFAS 13, sale-leaseback arrangements are treated as though two transactions were a single financing transaction, if the lease qualifies as a capital lease. Any gain or loss on the sale is deferred and amortized over the lease term (if possession reverts to the lessor) or the economic life (if ownership transfers to the lessee). In this case, the lease qualifies as a capital lease because the lease term (12 years) is 80% of the remaining economic life of the leased property (15 years). Therefore, at 12/31/86, all of gain ($480,000 - $360,000 = $120,000) would be deferred and amortized over 12 years. Since the sale took place on 12/31/86, there is no amortization for 1986.

34. (1185,P3,43) (b) The requirement is the amount of rent expense to be recognized in 1984 on a sale-leaseback. SFAS 13, para 33 generally treats a sale-leaseback as a single financing transaction in which any profit on the sale is deferred and amortized by the seller. However, SFAS 28 amends this general rule when either only a minor part of the re- maining use is retained (case 1), or when more than a minor part but less than substantially all of the remaining use of the property is retained (case 2). Case 1 occurs when the PV of the lease payments is 10% or less of the FMV of the sale-leaseback property. Case 2 occurs when the leaseback is more than minor but does not meet the criteria of a capital lease. This is an example of case 2 because the PV of the lease payments ($153,000) is more than 10% of the FMV of the asset ($500,000), but the capital lease criteria are not met. SFAS 28 specifies that under these circumstances the gain on sale ($400,000) is recognized to the extent that it exceeds the PV of the lease payments ($153,000). There- fore, $247,000 of the gain is recognized immediately ($400,000 - $153,000), while the other $153,000 of the gain is deferred and amortized against rent expense. Net rent expense as computed below is $10,200.

Rental payments (12 x $5,100)	$61,200
Profit amortization ($153,000 x 12/36)	(51,000)
Net rent expense	$10,200

35. (585,Q1,10) (a) The requirement is to determine the amount of profit to be deferred by Bard Co., the lessee, in a sale-leaseback transaction. According to SFAS 13, sale-and- leaseback arrangements are treated as though two transactions were a single financing transaction if the lease qualifies as a capital lease. Any gain or loss on the sale is deferred and amortized over the lease term if possession remains with the lessor, or economic life if ownership transfers to the lessee. In this case, the lease qualifies as

a capital lease because the lease term is 80% of the remaining economic life of the leased property. Therefore, at December 31, 1984, all of the $200,000 ($300,000 - $100,000) gain on sale of equipment would be deferred by Bard Co. and amortized over 16 years. Since the sale was on December 31, there is no amortization for 1984.

36. (1189,T1,14) (b) Per SFAS 28, any profit related to a sale-leaseback transaction in which the seller-lessee retains the property leased (i.e., the seller-lessee retains substantially all of the benefits and risks of the ownership of the property sold), shall be deferred and amortized in proportion to the amortization of the leased asset, if a capital lease. If it is an operating lease, the profit will be deferred in proportion to the related gross rental charged to expense over the lease term. It is important to note that losses, however, are recognized immediately for either a capital or operating lease. Since the gain on the sale should be deferred in either case, no gain is recognized at the time of the sale, and answer (b) is correct.

Authors' note: an example of an operating lease in which substantially all of the remaining use of the leased asset is retained by the lessee occurs when the lease term begins within the last 25% of the asset's original useful life.

E.2.f. Leasehold Improvements

37. (1189,P3,42) (b) The first month's rent ($60,000) is expensed as incurred in December 1988. The prepayment of the last month's rent (also $60,000) is deferred and will be recognized as expense at the end of the lease. The refundable security deposit ($80,000) is recorded as a long-term receivable, since Barr can expect to receive the deposit back at year end. The cost of installing new walls and offices ($360,000) is recorded as an asset, leasehold improvements, and amortized over the lease term. The amortization for December is $6,000 ($360,000 ÷ 60 months). Therefore, total expense is $66,000 ($60,000 + $6,000).

38. (586,P1,15) (d) The requirement is the amount of 1985 amortization expense for leasehold improvements. The cost of leasehold improvements ($360,000) should be amortized over the remaining life of the lease, or the useful life of the improvements, whichever is shorter. When the lease contains a renewal option, the life of the lease does **not** include the renewal period unless it is probable that the option will be exercised. Therefore, in this case, the remaining life of the lease is six years (8-year lease term less the two

years gone by). The renewal period of four years is not considered since exercise of the option is uncertain. The useful life of the improvements is ten years, so the improvements are amortized over the remaining lease life of six years. This results in 1985 amortization of $60,000 ($360,000 ÷ 6 years).

39. (589,T1,5) (b) Leasehold improvements are properly capitalized and amortized over the remaining life of the lease, or the useful life of the improvements, whichever is shorter. Since the useful life of the office is only 10 years and the remaining term of the lease is 15 years, the cost should be depreciated over the 10-year period. Therefore, answer (b) is correct, and answers (a), (c), and (d) are incorrect.

40. (586,T1,20) (a) The requirement is the proper treatment of landscaping costs to improve leased property. The improvements should be capitalized and amortized over the lesser of the remaining lease term (five years) or the useful life of the improvements (six years). Practically speaking, the leasehold improvements will no longer be useful to this lessee after the lease expires. Therefore, answers (b), (c), and (d) are incorrect.

May 1990 Answers

41. (590,P1,18) (b) Leasehold improvements are an asset (usually shown on the balance sheet under property, plant, and equipment) which must be amortized over the remaining life of the lease, or the useful life of the improvements, whichever is shorter. Since Ames' intentions as to exercise of the renewal option are uncertain, the original lease term (8 years) is used as a basis for amortization rather than the useful life of 10 years. Therefore, accumulated amortization at 12/31/89 is $15,000 ($120,000 ÷ 8) the same amount as amortization expense for 1989 because the requirement is for the year of acquisition. Note that the problem asked for accumulated **amortization**. Therefore, the accumulated **depreciation** on furniture and equipment ($50,000 ÷ 10 = $5,000) is **not** included.

42. (590,P2,31) (d) SFAS 13, para 33 generally treats a sale-leaseback as a single financing transaction in which any profit on the sale is deferred and amortized by the seller. However, SFAS 28 amends this general rule when either **only a minor part** of the remaining use of the leased asset is retained (case 1), or when **more than a minor part but less than substantially all** of the remaining

use of the leased asset is retained (case 2).
Case 1 occurs when the PV of the lease payments is 10% or less of the FMV of the sale-
leaseback property. Case 2 occurs when the
leaseback is more than minor but does not meet
the criteria of a capital lease. This is an
example of case 1, because the PV of the lease
payments ($34,100) is equal to or less than
10% of the FMV of the asset ($360,000). SFAS
28 specifies that under these circumstances,
the full gain ($360,000 - $330,000 = $30,000)
is recognized , and none is deferred.

43. (590,P2,35) (b) This is a capital lease
since the lease term (10 years) is the same as
the useful life of the leased asset. In a
capital lease, the lessee records an asset and
a liability based on the PV of the minimum
lease payments. The minimum lease payments
includes rentals and a guaranteed residual
value, if guaranteed by the lessee. In this
case the minimum lease payments include only
the rentals, since the residual value is
guaranteed by a third party. The minimum
lease payments are discounted using the lower
of the lessee's incremental borrowing rate or
the implicit rate used by the lessor, if
known. In this case, the lessee knows the
implicit rate is 10%, which is lower than the
incremental borrowing rate of 12%. Thus, the
present value or principal amount of the lease
obligation is $61,446 ($10,000 x 6.1446)
through the first year. Although accrued interest would be recognized at 10/31/89, the
principal amount does not change until 1/1/90.

44. (590,P3,48) (c) SFAS 13 specifies that,
in an operating lease, the lessor should
recognize rental revenue on a straight-line
basis. This means that the lease bonus
($50,000) should be recorded as unearned reve-
nue on 1/1/89, and recognized as rental revenue over the 5-year lease term. Therefore,
1989 rental revenue should be $100,000
[$90,000 + ($50,000 ÷ 5)]. The security deposit ($25,000) does not affect rental reve-
nue. Since it is to be refunded to the lessee
upon expiration of the lease, it is recorded
as a deposit, a long-term liability when
received.

45. (590,P3,50) (d) This is a capital lease
since title passes to Dix, the lessee, at the
end of the lease. At the inception of the
lease on 1/2/89, the capitalized lease liability is $180,000 (the present value of the min-
imum lease payments). Since the first annual
payment is not due until the end of the first
year, 1989 interest expense is based on the
full initial liability ($180,000 x 10% =
$18,000) and is determined by using the
interest method.

46. (590,P3,51) (d) This is a capital lease
since title passes to Dix, the lessee, at the
end of the lease. At the inception of the
lease on 1/2/89, the lessee records the PV of
the lease payments ($180,000) as an asset and
a liability. The asset is depreciated on a
straight-line basis over its useful life of 15
years, resulting in a yearly depreciation
charge of $12,000 ($180,000 ÷ 15 years). The
asset is depreciated over its useful life
rather than over the lease term because title
transfers to the lessee, allowing the lessee
to use the asset for 15 years.

47. (590,P3,56) (c) SFAS 13 specifies that,
in an operating lease, the lessee should
recognize rent expense on a straight-line
basis unless another method is better suited
to the particular lease. Therefore, the lease
bonus should be recognized as rent expense on
a straight-line basis over the 10-year lease
term ($24,000 ÷ 10 = $2,400). However, the
contingent rentals, which are based on company
sales, shall be expensed in the period to
which they relate. Therefore, in 1989,
contingent rentals of $5,000 [5% x ($600,000 -
$500,000)] should be included in rent
expense. Total rent expense is $103,400, as
computed below:

Base rental	$96,000
Lease bonus ($24,000 ÷ 10)	2,400
Cont. rental [5% x ($600,000 - $500,000)]	5,000
	$103,400

48. (590,T1,11) (a) When a leasing agreement is accounted for as capital lease, the
lessee recognizes a liability on its books
equal to the present value of the minimum
lease payments. The liability should be divided between current and noncurrent based upon
when each lease payment is due. At the end of
year 1, the current lease liability should
equal the principal portion of the lease payment due in year 2. Therefore, when the lease
payment is made in year 2, the reduction of
the lease liability will equal the current
liability shown at the end of year 1.

49. (590,T1,24) (d) When a leasing agreement is accounted for as an operating lease,
the lessor and the lessee recognize rental
revenue and rental expense respectively on a
straight-line basis unless another systematic
and rational basis more clearly reflects the
time pattern in which use benefit is given
(received) by the respective parties. Per
FASB Technical Bulletin 85-3, para 1 the
straight-lining of uneven lease payments includes scheduled rent increases. Even though
the amount of the annual lease payment increases in year 6, rental expense would not
change. Interest is not an element of revenue
(expense) in operating leases. Therefore, the
correct answer is (d).

LEASES

Answer Outline

Problem 1   Capital Leases (589,T5)

a. Economic effects are similar to a purchase
       using installment debt
       Most benefits and risks of ownership of
          property are transferred to the lessee
       Obligation of lessee is similar to that
          created when funds are borrowed
    Enhances comparability between firms that
       acquire assets by purchasing and those
       that acquire assets by leasing
b. Lessee should account for lease as an
       asset and an obligation
       Amounts should equal PV of total minimum
          lease payments
       Exclude executory costs and profit
          thereon
       If PV exceeds fair value of property,
          asset and obligation should be reported
          at FMV
c. Allocate each minimum lease payment
       between reduction in obligation and
       interest expense using interest method
       Produces constant periodic rate of
          interest on remaining balance of
          obligation
d. First lease is capital lease
       Lease term is > 75% of the estimated
          economic life of the machine
    Second lease is capital lease
       Lease contains a bargain purchase option

Unofficial Answer

Problem 1   Capital Leases (589,T5)

a. The economic effects of a long-term
capital lease on the lessee are similar to
that of an equipment purchase using installment debt. Such a lease transfers substantially all of the benefits and risks incident
to the ownership of property to the lessee,
and obligates the lessee in a manner similar
to that created when funds are borrowed. To
enhance comparability between a firm that
purchases an asset on a long-term basis and a
firm that leases an asset under substantially
equivalent terms, the lease should be capitalized.

b. A lessee should account for a capital
lease at its inception as an asset and an
obligation at an amount equal to the present
value at the beginning of the lease term of
minimum lease payments during the lease term,
excluding any portion of the payments
representing executory costs, together with

any profit thereon. However, if the present
value exceeds the fair value of the leased
property at the inception of the lease, the
amount recorded for the asset and obligation
should be the fair value.

c. A lessee should allocate each minimum
lease payment between a reduction of the
obligation and interest expense so as to
produce a constant periodic rate of interest
on the remaining balance of the obligation.

d. Von should classify the first lease as a
capital lease because the lease term is 75
percent or more of the estimated economic life
of the machine. Von should classify the
second lease as a capital lease because the
lease contains a bargain purchase option.

Answer Outline

Problem 2   Rationale for Lease Capitalization
               and Lessee Accounting (585,T2)

a. Theoretical basis for capitalizing leases
       by lessee
    Lease transfers substantially all benefits
       and risks incident to ownership
       Economic effect similar to installment
          purchase
b. Accounting for lessee's capital lease at
       inception
    Record asset and obligation
       Amount = Present value of minimum lease
          payments
       Minimum lease payments exclude executory
          costs
       If amount > fair value of leased
          machine, record at fair value
c. Lessee's lease related expenses
    Interest expense = Interest rate x Carry-
       ing value of liability
    Amortization expense = Normal depreciation
       policy of lessee
       Use life of asset in this case because
          title will pass to lessee
d. Reporting lease transaction in 12/31/86
       balance sheet
    Asset and accumulated amortization
       Classified as noncurrent and identified
          separately in statement or footnotes
    Obligation
       Classified into current and noncurrent

Unofficial Answer

Problem 2   Rationale for Lease Capitalization
and Lessee Accounting (585,T2)

a. When a lease transfers substantially all
of the benefits and risks incident to the ownership of property to the lessee, it should be
capitalized by the lessee. The economic
effect of such a lease on the lessee is similar, in many respects, to that of an installment purchase.

b. Lani should account for this lease at its
inception as an asset and an obligation at an
amount equal to the present value at the
beginning of the lease term of minimum lease
payments during the lease term. Minimum lease
payments exclude executory costs, including
any profit thereon. However, if the amount so
determined exceeds the fair value of the
leased machine at the inception of the lease,
the amount recorded as the asset and
obligation should be the machine's fair value.

c. Lani will incur interest expense equal to
the interest rate used to capitalize the lease
at its inception multiplied by the appropriate
net carrying value of the liability.

In addition, Lani will incur an expense
relating to amortization of the capitalized
cost of the leased asset. This amortization
should be based on the estimated useful life
of the leased asset and amortized in a manner
consistent with Lani's normal depreciation
policy for owned assets.

d. The asset recorded under the capital lease
and the accumulated amortization should be reported on Lani's December 31, 1986 balance
sheet classified as noncurrent and should be
separately identified by Lani in its balance
sheet or footnotes thereto. The related obligation recorded under the capital lease should
be reported on Lani's December 31, 1986 balance sheet appropriately classified into current and noncurrent categories and should be
separately identified by Lani in its balance
sheet.

Answer Outline

Problem 3   Description of Lease Accounting
(580,T3)

a1. Accounting for lessee's capital lease
which transfers title to leased property
Inception of lease
Record asset and obligation
During first year
Apply lease payments to reduction of
principal and interest expense
Depreciate leased asset using lessee's
normal depreciation policy

Use life of asset in this case because
title will pass to lessee
a2. Accounting for lessee's operating lease
Inception of lease
No asset or liability recorded
During first year
Recognize rent expense on a straight-
line basis
Use other basis only if more
representative of benefit receipt
pattern (i.e., more rational)
b1. Sales-type leases versus direct financing
leases
For both gross investment in lease equals
Minimum lease payments + Unguaranteed
residual value
Minimum lease payments include guaranteed residual value but exclude executory costs
b2. Amortization of unearned interest (lease)
income for both utilizes the effective
interest method
Results in a constant rate of return per
period
Other methods of amortization acceptable
if amounts obtained not materially different
b3. Manufacturer's or dealer's profit
Sales-type
Profit = sales price - carrying amount
Direct financing
No dealer's profit
Only income is from interest

Unofficial Answer

Problem 3   Description of Lease Accounting
(580,T3)

Part a.

1. A lessee would account for a capital lease
as an asset and an obligation at the inception
of the lease. Rental payments during the year
would be allocated between a reduction in the
obligation and interest expense. The asset
would be amortized in a manner consistent with
the lessee's normal depreciation policy for
owned assets, except that in some circumstances, the period of amortization would be
the lease term.

2. No asset or obligation would be recorded
at the inception of the lease. Normally,
rental on an operating lease would be charged
to expense over the lease term as it becomes
payable. If rental payments are not made on a
straight-line basis, rental expense nevertheless would be recognized on a straight-line
basis unless another systematic or rational
basis is more representative of the time pattern in which use benefit is derived from the
leased property, in which case that basis
would be used.

Part b.

1. The gross investment in the lease is the same for both a sales-type lease and a direct-financing lease. The gross investment in the lease is the minimum lease payments (net of amounts, if any, included therein for executory costs such as maintenance, taxes, and insurance to be paid by the lessor, together with any profit thereon) plus the unguaranteed residual value accruing to the benefit of the lessor.

2. For both a sales-type lease and a direct-financing lease, the unearned interest income would be amortized to income over the lease term by use of the interest method to produce a constant periodic rate of return on the net investment in the lease. However, other methods of income recognition may be used if the results obtained are not materially different from the interest method.

3. In a sales-type lease, the excess of the sales price over the carrying amount of the leased equipment is considered manufacturer's or dealer's profit and would be included in income in the period when the lease transaction is recorded.

In a direct-financing lease, there is no manufacturer's or dealer's profit. The income on the lease transaction is composed solely of interest.

Answer Outline

Problem 4   Sale-leaseback (588,T4)

a. Theoretical basis for capitalizing leases
     Transfers substantially all risks and
        rewards of ownership to lessee
     Economic effect similar to installment
        purchase
b1. Accounting for sales portion
     Cash   xxx
     Accum. deprec.   xxx
         Equipment   xxx
         Deferred gain from
           sale-leaseback   xxx*
     *Sales price – book value
b2. Accounting for leaseback portion
     Record asset and liability
        Amount = PV of minimum lease payments
           (MLPs)
        MLPs exclude executory costs
        If PV > FV of leased equipment, record
           at FV
c. Accounting for gain on sale portion during
       first year of lease
     Amortize deferred gain over lease term
        or life of asset in proportion to
        amortization of asset

Deferral and amortization required because sale and leaseback are two components of a single transaction
Because of this interdependence, gain deferred and amortized over lease term

Unofficial Answer

Problem 4   Sale-leaseback (588,T4)

a. The economic effect of a long-term capital lease on the lessee is similar to that of an installment purchase. Such a lease transfers substantially all of the benefits and risks incident to the ownership of property to the lessee. Therefore, the lease should be capitalized.

b1. Metcalf should account for the sale portion of the sale-leaseback transaction at January 1, 1987, by recording cash for the sale price, decreasing equipment at the undepreciated cost (net carrying amount) of the equipment, and establishing a deferred gain on sale-leaseback for the excess of the sale price of the equipment over its undepreciated cost (net carrying amount).

2. Metcalf should account for the leaseback portion of the sale-leaseback transaction at January 1, 1987, by recording both an asset and a liability at an amount equal to the present value at the beginning of the lease term of minimum lease payments during the lease term, excluding any portion of the payments representing executory costs, together with any profit. However, if the present value exceeds the fair value of the leased equipment at January 1, 1987, the amount recorded for the asset and liability should be the equipment's fair value.

c. The deferred gain should be amortized over the lease term or life of asset, whichever is appropriate. During the first year of the lease, the amortization will be an amount proportionate to the amortization of the asset. This deferral and amortization method for a sale-leaseback transaction is required because the sale and the leaseback are two components of a single transaction rather than two independent transactions. Because of this interdependence of the sale and leaseback portions of the transaction, the gain should be deferred and amortized over the lease term.

Solution Guide

Problem 5   Long-Term Liabilities Section of
Balance Sheet (1188,Q4)

1. Part (a) requires the preparation of the
    long-term liabilities section of the
    12/31/87 balance sheet, while part (b)
    requires a schedule showing 1987 interest
    expense. The solutions approach for
    problems in which the requirements are
    interrelated is to make all computations
    for each item at one time. After making
    the computations, label each computation
    according to the requirement [(a) or (b)
    in this problem] to which it relates.
    Formulas, time lines, journal entries,
    etc. can be used to help the analysis of
    each item.

2. The note payable is to be paid in four
    equal annual installments ($800,000 ÷ 4 =
    $200,000) beginning 10/1/87. Therefore,
    the note payable balance was $800,000
    from 1/1/87 to 9/30/87. After the first
    principal payment, the balance is
    $600,000 from 10/1/87 until 10/1/88. The
    total liability at 12/31/87 is $600,000,
    but the next installment ($200,000 due in
    9 months) would be reclassified as a
    current liability. The remainder
    ($600,000 − $200,000 = $400,000) is
    reported as a long-term liability.

2.1 Interest expense on the note payable
    should be computed in two parts: on the
    $800,000 outstanding from 1/1/87 to
    9/30/87, and on the $600,000 outstanding
    from 10/1/87 to 12/31/87 (see item 2
    above). Total interest expense on the
    note is $75,000.

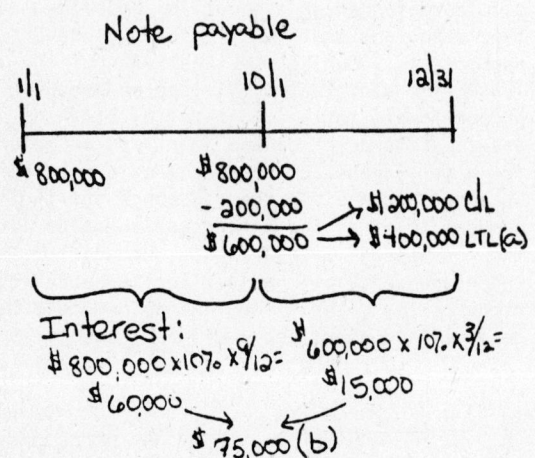

3. The capital lease liability after the
    12/31/86 payment was $280,000. During
    1987, the interest on the lease was
    $44,800 ($280,000 x 16%), so the 12/31/87
    payment reduced the principal by $55,200
    ($100,000 payment − $44,800 interest).
    The _total_ liability after the 12/31/87
    payment is $224,800 ($280,000 −
    $55,200). This liability is part current
    and part long-term. The current portion
    at 12/31/87 is the amount of principal to
    be reduced in 1988. Since 1988 interest
    will be $35,968 ($224,800 x 16%), the
    1988 principal reduction will be $64,032
    ($100,000 payment − $35,968 interest).
    Therefore, the current liability is
    $64,032 and the long-term liability is
    $160,768 ($224,800 − $64,032).

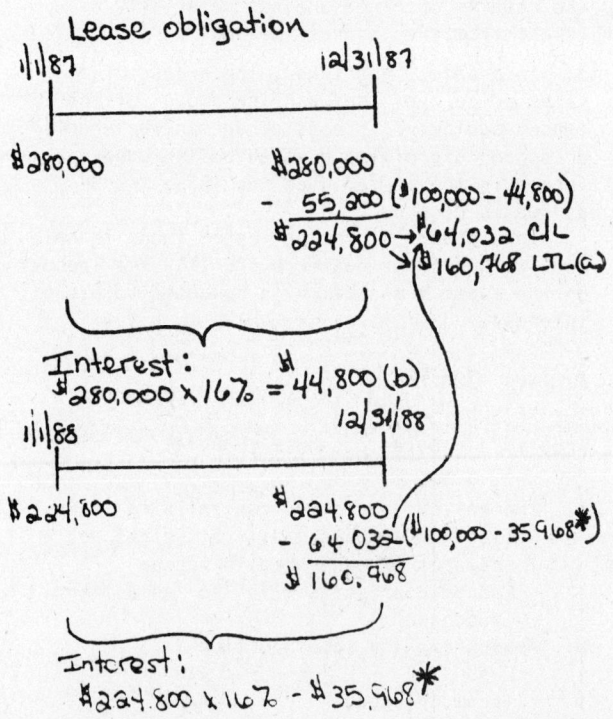

4. The deferred tax liability is increased
    in 1987 because depreciation for tax
    purposes exceeds book depreciation by
    $50,000. This temporary difference
    results in future taxable amounts, so the
    deferred tax liability must be increased
    by the tax effect of the difference (30%
    x $50,000 = $15,000).

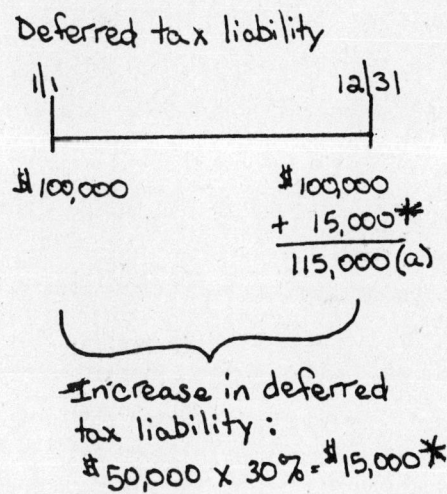

Deferred tax liability

Increase in deferred tax liability:
$50,000 × 30% = $15,000*

4.1   Interest expense is not recognized on a deferred tax liability.

5.   On 7/1/87, Lino issued $1,000,000 face amount of 10% bonds for $750,000, to yield 15%. Under the interest method, interest expense is computed as follows: Book value x Effective interest rate x Time. Interest payable is Face amount x Stated rate x Time. Therefore, at 12/31/87, Lino would make the following adjusting entry:

Interest expense	56,250	(750,000 x 15% x 6/12)
Interest payable		50,000 (1,000,000 x 10% x 6/12)
Discount on BP		6,250

This entry decreases the discount account, which increases the book value of the liability. The interest payable ($50,000) is a current liability.

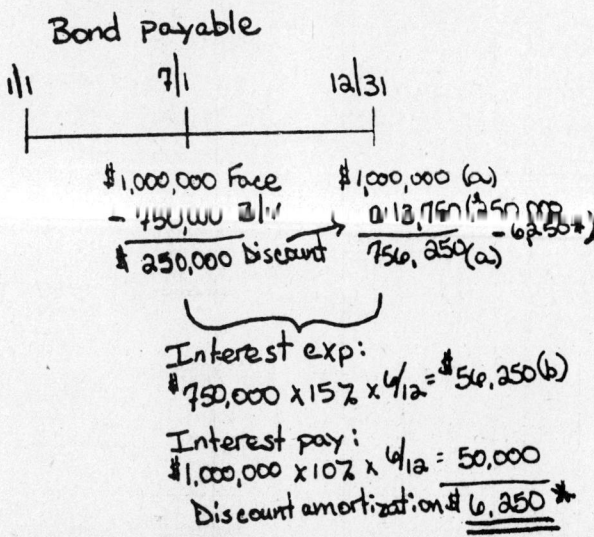

Bond payable

Interest exp:
$750,000 × 15% × 6/12 = $56,250(b)

Interest pay:
$1,000,000 × 10% × 6/12 = 50,000
Discount amortization $6,250*

Unofficial Answer

Problem 5   Long-Term Liabilities Section of
             Balance Sheet (1188,Q4)

a.

Lino Corporation
LONG-TERM LIABILITIES SECTION
OF BALANCE SHEET
December 31, 1987

10% note payable to bank, due in annual installments of $200,000, less current installment	$ 400,000	[1]
Liability under capital lease, net present value of lease payments, less current installment	160,768	[2]
10% bonds payable due July 1, 1997, less unamortized discount of $243,750	756,250	[3]
Deferred tax liability	115,000	[4]
Total long-term liabilities	$1,432,018	

b.

Lino Corporation
INTEREST EXPENSE
For the Year Ended December 31, 1987

Note payable to bank	$ 75,000	[5]
Liability under capital lease	44,800	[2]
Bonds payable	56,250	[3]
Total	$ 176,050	

Explanations of Amounts

[1] 10% Note payable to bank

Note payable, 12/31/86		$800,000
Less installment paid 10/1/87		200,000
Balance, 12/31/87		600,000
Less current installment due 10/1/88		200,000
Long-term portion, 12/31/87		$400,000

[2] Liability under capital lease

Liability under capital lease, 12/31/86		$280,000
Less principal portion of 12/31/87 payment		
Lease payment	$100,000	
Less imputed interest ($280,000 x 16%)	44,800	55,200
Balance, 12/31/87		224,800
Less current principal payment due 12/31/88		
Lease payment	100,000	
Less imputed interest ($224,800 x 16%)	35,968	64,032
Long-term portion, 12/31/87		$160,768

[3] Bonds payable

Bonds payable issued 7/1/87		$750,000
Add amortization of bond discount		
Effective interest ($750,000 x 15% x 6/12)	56,250	
Less accrued interest payable 12/31/87 ($1,000,000 x 10% x 6/12)	50,000	6,250
Balance, 12/31/87		$756,250

[4] Deferred tax liability

Deferred tax liability, 12/31/86	$100,000
Add temporary difference--excess of tax depreciation over book depreciation of $50,000 x 30%	15,000
Balance, 12/31/87	$115,000

[5] Interest expense on note payable to bank

1/1/87 to 9/30/87 ($800,000 x 10% x 9/12)	$ 60,000
10/1/87 to 12/31/87 ($600,000 x 10% x 3/12)	15,000
Interest, year ended 12/31/87	$ 75,000

Multiple Choice Questions (1-46)

1. Temporary differences arise when revenues are taxable

	After they are recognized in financial income	Before they are recognized in financial income
a.	Yes	Yes
b.	Yes	No
c.	No	No
d.	No	Yes

2. Temporary differences arise when expenses are deductible for tax purposes

	After they are recognized in financial income	Before they are recognized in financial income
a.	No	No
b.	No	Yes
c.	Yes	Yes
d.	Yes	No

3. Among the items reported on Neal Corporation's income statement for the year ended December 31, 1986 are the following:

Interest received on municipal bonds	$10,000
Amortization of goodwill	18,000

Temporary differences for measuring deferred taxes (interperiod tax allocation) amount to
- a. $28,000
- b. $18,000
- c. $10,000
- d. $0

4. Among the items reported on Cord, Inc.'s income statement for the year ended December 31, 1988 were the following:

Amortization of goodwill	$10,000
Insurance premium on life of an officer with Cord as owner and beneficiary	5,000

Temporary differences amount to
- a. $0
- b. $ 5,000
- c. $10,000
- d. $15,000

5. The Ward Corp.'s books showed income of $300,000 before provision for income tax for the year ended December 31, 1988. In the computation of taxable income for federal income tax purposes, the following items should be noted:

Income from exempt municipal bonds	$30,000
Depreciation deducted for tax purposes in excess of depreciation recorded on the books	$60,000
Proceeds received for life insurance on death of officer	$50,000
Estimated tax payments	$0
Enacted corporate income tax rate	30%

Ignore the alternate minimum tax provisions. What amount should Ward record as its current federal income tax liability at December 31, 1988?
- a. $81,000
- b. $75,000
- c. $57,000
- d. $48,000

6. The books of Apex, Inc. for the year ended December 31, 1985 showed income of $720,000 before provision for income tax. In computing the taxable income for federal income tax purposes, the following differences were taken into account:

Depreciation deducted for tax purposes in excess of depreciation recorded on the books	$32,000
Rent received in excess of rent earned	24,000

Assuming a corporate income tax rate of 40%, what should Apex record as its current federal income tax liability at December 31, 1985?
- a. $291,200
- b. $288,000
- c. $284,800
- d. $275,200

7. A temporary difference which would result in a deferred tax liability is
- a. Interest revenue on municipal bonds.
- b. Accrual of warranty expense.
- c. Excess of tax depreciation over financial accounting depreciation.
- d. Subscriptions received in advance.

8. On January 1, 1988, Lum, Inc. purchased a machine for $90,000 which will be depreciated $9,000 per year for financial statement reporting. For income tax reporting, Lum elected to expense $10,000 and to use straight-line depreciation which will allow a cost recovery deduction of $8,000 for 1988. Lum uses the liability method to account for temporary differences. Assume a present and future enacted income tax rate of 30%. What amount should be added to Lum's deferred in-

---

Authors' note: **All** questions in this module have been updated to reflect SFAS 96. We are informing you of this because the recent CPA exam questions included in this module state that the company elected early application of FASB Statement No. 96 to indicate the questions are to be answered using SFAS 96 requirements.

come tax liability for this temporary difference at December 31, 1988?
  a. $5,400
  b. $3,000
  c. $2,700
  d. $2,400

9.   Purl Company began operations on January 1, 1985. It recognizes income from
construction-type contracts under the
percentage-of-completion method for financial
reporting. However, on its income tax returns, Purl appropriately reports revenues
under the completed-contract method (assume a
small contract per IRS criteria). Information
concerning income recognition under each
method is as follows:

Year	Percentage of completion	Completed contract
1985	$450,000	$0
1986	675,000	425,000
1987	825,000	925,000

For all affected years, assume the income tax
rate is 30% and there are no other temporary
differences. For 1987 Purl should record an
increase (decrease) in the deferred taxes
liability account of
  a. $165,000
  b. $ 70,000
  c.   ($ 30,000)
  d.   ($100,000)

Items 10 and 11 are based on the following:

Bee Corp. prepared the following reconciliation between book income and taxable
income for the year ended December 31, 1988:

Pretax accounting income	$500,000
Taxable income	300,000
Difference	$200,000

Differences:
Interest on municipal bonds	$ 50,000
Lower depreciation per financial statements	150,000
Total differences	$200,000

Bee elected early application of FASB
Statement No. 96, Accounting for Income Taxes,
in its financial statements for the year ended
December 31, 1988.

Bee's enacted income tax rate for 1988 is
30%. The depreciation difference will reverse
equally over the next three years at enacted
tax rates as follows:

Years	Tax rates
1989	30%
1990	25%
1991	25%

10.   In Bee's 1988 income statement, the
current portion of its provision for income
taxes should be
  a. $150,000
  b. $125,000
  c. $ 90,000
  d. $ 75,000

11.   In Bee's 1988 income statement, the
deferred portion of its provision for income
taxes should be
  a. $60,000
  b. $50,000
  c. $45,000
  d. $40,000

Items 12 and 13 are based on the following
data:

Munn Corporation's income statement for
the year ended December 31, 1986 shows pretax
income of $300,000. The following items are
treated differently on the tax return and in
the accounting records:

	Tax return	Accounting records
Warranty expense	$170,000	$185,000
Depreciation expense	150,000	100,000
Premiums on officers' life insurance	None	60,000

Assume that the enacted tax rate for 1986 and
other affected years is 40% and temporary
differences reverse equally over the next 5
years.

12.   What is the current portion of Munn's
total income tax expense for 1986?
  a. $106,000
  b. $120,000
  c. $130,000
  d. $144,000

13.   What is the deferred portion of Munn's
total income tax expense for 1986?
  a. $ 6,000
  b. $14,000
  c. $20,000
  d. $24,000

14.   Frey Company, a construction company,
appropriately uses the completed contract
method of accounting for income tax purposes. However, Frey uses the percentage-of-
completion accounting method for financial
statement purposes. Pertinent data at
December 31, 1988, the close of Frey's first
year of operations, are:

2
7

Date contract began	Estimated completion date	Income recognized in 1988 on each contract
3/1/88	9/1/89	$600,000
6/1/88	12/1/89	300,000
9/1/88	3/1/90	200,000
12/1/88	6/1/90	100,000

Frey's enacted income tax rates are 30% for 1988, 25% for 1989, and 20% for 1990. Frey elected early application of FASB Statement No. 96, Accounting for Income Taxes, in its financial statements for the year ended December 31, 1988. What amount should be included in the deferred income tax liability at December 31, 1988 for these transactions?

    a. $360,000
    b. $330,000
    c. $285,000
    d. $240,000

15. On December 2, 1988, Huff Corp. received a condemnation award of $450,000 as compensation for the forced sale of land purchased five years earlier for $300,000. The gain was not reported as taxable income on its income tax return for the year ended December 31, 1988, because Huff elected to replace the land within the allowed replacement period for at least $450,000. Huff has an income tax rate of 25% for 1988, and there is an enacted rate of 30% for years ending after 1988. There were no other temporary differences. Huff elected early application of FASB Statement No. 96, Accounting for Income Taxes. In its December 31, 1988 balance sheet, Huff should report a deferred income tax liability of

    a. $135,000
    b. $ 45,000
    c. $ 37,500
    d. $0

16. Landwer Company had taxable income of $450,000 for 1987. During 1987, Landwer accrued a loss contingency of $100,000 (before tax) on its books. For tax purposes, Landwer will not be able to show this loss until 1990, the expected year of settlement for the lawsuit that created the loss. The appropriate income tax rates are as follows:

1987	1988	1989	1990
40%	45%	42%	35%

Assuming that the loss contingency is Landwer's only temporary difference, what should Landwer record as income tax expense for 1987?

    a. $140,000
    b. $145,000
    c. $180,000
    d. $215,000

17. For the year ended December 31, 1985, Rapp, Inc. reported royalty income of $450,000 in its income statement. Royalties received, reported as taxable income, amounted to $700,000 for 1985. Also in 1985, Rapp paid $175,000 of premiums on officers' life insurance, on which Rapp is the beneficiary. Assume a tax rate of 40% for any prior and current years affected, and that in 1984 taxable income was $450,000. By what amount would the deferred tax asset account increase for 1985?

    a. $100,000
    b. $150,000
    c. $170,000
    d. $255,000

18. Caleb Corporation has three financial statement elements for which the December 31, 1988 book value is different than the December 31, 1988 tax basis:

	Book value	Tax basis	Difference
Equipment	$200,000	$120,000	$80,000
Goodwill	75,000	0	75,000
Warranty liability	50,000	0	50,000

As a result of these differences, future taxable amounts are

    a. $ 50,000
    b. $ 80,000
    c. $155,000
    d. $205,000

Use the information below for questions 19 and 20.

Huskie Corporation has taxable income of $300,000 for 1987--its first year of operations. During 1987, two temporary differences originated for Huskie as shown below:

1987 Effect	Year(s) of expected reversal
$50,000 excess of tax depreciation over book depreciation	Equally over the years 1988 and 1989
$60,000 rent received in advance	1989

Assume a 40% tax rate for all years.

19. What is Huskie's income tax expense for 1987?

    a. $116,000
    b. $124,000
    c. $130,000
    d. $140,000

20. How much should Huskie show on the 12/31/87 balance sheet as noncurrent deferred taxes?
    a. $ 4,000 deferred tax liability.
    b. $14,000 deferred tax liability.
    c. $14,000 deferred tax asset.
    d. $24,000 deferred tax liability.

21. Wright Corporation has taxable income of $240,000 for 1987--its first year of operations. During 1987, two temporary differences originated for Wright as shown below:

1987 Effect	Year(s) of expected reversal
$90,000 contingent liability per books only	1991
$30,000 excess of tax depreciation over book depreciation	Equally over the years 1988, 1989, and 1990

Assume a 30% tax rate for all years. How much should Wright show on the 12/31/87 balance sheet as current deferred taxes?
    a. $0
    b. $ 3,000 deferred tax liability.
    c. $ 3,000 deferred tax asset.
    d. $24,000 deferred tax liability.
    e. $24,000 deferred tax asset.

22. On 1/1/86, Hearn Corporation purchased an asset. The following temporary difference was created by Hearn because it used an accelerated method of depreciation for tax purposes:

	1986	1987	1988	1989
Originating	($20,000)*	($20,000)*		
(Reversing)			$20,000	$20,000

*Brackets indicate deductible amounts.

This is Hearn's only temporary difference. Hearn correctly recorded income tax expense and income tax payable for 1986 using the appropriate current and future expected tax rate of 40%. During 1987, a new tax rate of 35% was enacted into law. This new tax rate is applicable for 1987 and all future years. If Hearn's taxable income is $150,000 for both 1986 and 1987 what is Hearn's income tax expense for 1987?
    a. $46,500
    b. $58,500
    c. $59,500
    d. $60,500

23. Which of the following differences would result in future taxable amounts?
    a. Expenses or losses that are deductible after they are recognized in financial income.
    b. Revenues or gains that are taxable before they are recognized in financial income.
    c. Expenses or losses that are deductible before they are recognized in financial income.
    d. Revenues or gains that are recognized in financial income but are never included in taxable income.

24. When a temporary difference will result in net taxable amounts in five years
    a. A deferred tax asset is recognized in the current year.
    b. A deferred tax asset may be recognized in the current year if certain conditions are met.
    c. A deferred tax liability is recognized in the current year.
    d. A deferred tax liability may be recognized in the current year if certain conditions are met.

25. A deferred tax liability is computed using
    a. The current tax laws, regardless of expected or enacted future tax laws.
    b. Expected future tax laws, regardless of whether those expected laws have been enacted.
    c. Current tax laws, unless enacted future tax laws are different.
    d. Either current or expected future tax laws, regardless of whether those expected laws have been enacted.

26. A deferred tax asset is recognized for the tax benefit of net deductible amounts
    a. In all situations.
    b. Only if the net deductible amounts could be realized by loss carryback from future years to reduce an existing deferred tax liability.
    c. Only if the net deductible amounts could be realized by loss carryback from future years to reduce taxes paid in a current or prior year.
    d. Only if the net deductible amounts could be realized by loss carryback from future years to reduce (1) an existing deferred tax liability, or (2) taxes paid in the current or a prior year.

27. North, Inc. uses the equity method of accounting for its 50% investment in Mill Corp.'s common stock. During 1987, Mill reported earnings of $600,000 and paid dividends of $200,000. Assume that: (1) all undistributed earnings of Mill will be distributed as

dividends in future periods, (2) the dividends received from Mill are eligible for the 80% dividends received deduction, and (3) North's income tax rate is 30%. The change in the amount of deferred income tax to be reported by North for 1987 is

    a. $0
    b. $12,000
    c. $24,000
    d. $60,000

28. On January 1, 1988, Lundy Corp. purchased 40% of the voting common stock of Glen, Inc. and appropriately accounts for its investment by the equity method. During 1988, Glen reported earnings of $225,000 and paid dividends of $75,000. Lundy assumes that all of Glen's undistributed earnings will be distributed as dividends in future periods when the enacted tax rate will be 30%. Ignore the dividend-received deduction. Lundy's current enacted income tax rate is 25%. Lundy uses the liability method to account for temporary differences. The increase in Lundy's deferred income tax liability for this temporary difference is

    a. $45,000
    b. $37,500
    c. $27,000
    d. $18,000

29. Dina, Inc. owns 75% of the voting common stock of its domestic subsidiary, Spruce Corp. During 1987, Spruce had earnings of $300,000, and paid dividends of $100,000. Dina assumes that Spruce's remaining earnings will be distributed as dividends in future periods. Dina's income tax rate is 40%. For 1987, how much should Dina report as deferred income tax?

    a. $90,000
    b. $13,500
    c. $12,000
    d. $0

30. Dix, Inc., a calendar-year corporation, reported the following operating income (loss) before income tax for its first three years of operations:

1984	$100,000
1985	(200,000)
1986	400,000

There are no permanent or temporary differences between operating income (loss) for financial and income tax reporting purposes. When filing its 1985 tax return, Dix did not elect to forgo the carryback of its loss for 1985. Assume a 40% tax rate for all years. What amount should Dix report as its income tax liability at December 31, 1986?

    a. $160,000
    b. $120,000

    c. $ 80,000
    d. $ 60,000

31. Town, a calendar-year corporation incorporated in January 1982, experienced a $600,000 net operating loss (NOL) in 1985. For the years 1982-1984, Town reported a taxable income in each year, and a total of $450,000 for the three years. Assume that: (1) there is no difference between pretax accounting income and taxable income for all years, (2) the income tax rate is 40% for all years, (3) the NOL will be carried back to the profit years 1982-1984 to the extent of $450,000, and $150,000 will be carried forward to future periods. In its 1985 income statement, what amount should Town report as the reduction of loss due to NOL carryback and carryforward?

    a. $240,000
    b. $180,000
    c. $270,000
    d. $360,000

32. Bishop Corporation began operations in 1985 and had operating losses of $200,000 in 1985 and $150,000 in 1986. For the year ended December 31, 1987, Bishop had pretax book income of $300,000. For the three-year period 1985 to 1987, assume an income tax rate of 40% and no permanent or temporary differences between book and taxable income. In Bishop's 1987 income statement, how much should be reported as net current income tax expense?

    a. $0
    b. $ 40,000
    c. $ 60,000
    d. $120,000

33. For the year ended December 31, 1987, Colt Corp. has a loss carryforward of $180,000 available to offset future taxable income. At December 31, 1987, realization of the tax benefit of the carryforward is probable. Assume an income tax rate of 30%. What amount of the tax benefit should be reported in Colt's 1987 income statement?

    a. $180,000
    b. $126,000
    c. $ 54,000
    d. $0

34. The amount of income tax applicable to transactions that are not reported in the continuing operations section of the income statement is computed

    a.   By multiplying the item by the effective income tax rate.
    b.   As the difference between the tax computed based on taxable income without including the item and the tax computed based on taxable income including the item.

c. As the difference between the tax
    computed on the item based on the
    amount used for financial reporting
    and the amount used in computing
    taxable income.
d. By multiplying the item by the
    difference between the effective
    income tax rate and the statutory
    income tax rate.

35. As a result of differences between depreciation for financial reporting purposes
and tax purposes, the financial reporting
basis of a company's plant assets exceeded the
tax basis. Assuming the company had no other
temporary differences, the company should report a
a. Current tax asset.
b. Current tax payable.
c. Deferred tax asset.
d. Deferred tax liability.

36. At the most recent year end, a company
had a deferred income tax liability expected
to reverse beyond the next year that exceeded
a deferred income tax asset expected to
reverse in the next year. Which of the
following should be reported in the company's
most recent year-end balance sheet?
a. The excess of the deferred income
    tax liability over the deferred
    income tax asset as a noncurrent
    liability.
b. The excess of the deferred income
    tax liability over the deferred
    income tax asset as a current
    liability.
c. The deferred income tax liability as
    a noncurrent liability.
d. The deferred income tax liability as
    a current liability.

37. At the most recent year end, a company
had a deferred tax liability expected to
reverse in the next year. The amount exceeded
a deferred tax asset also expected to reverse
in the next year, and a deferred tax liability
expected to reverse in periods subsequent to
the following year. Which of the following
should be reported in the company's most
recent year-end balance sheet?
a. The sum of the two deferred tax
    liabilities as a noncurrent
    liability.
b. The excess of the two deferred tax
    liabilities over the deferred tax
    asset as a current liability.
c. The excess of the deferred tax
    liability expected to reverse in the
    next year over the deferred tax
    asset expected to reverse in the
    next year as a current liability.
d. The deferred tax asset as a current
    asset.

May 1990 Questions

38. Black Co., organized on January 2, 1989,
had pretax accounting income of $500,000 and
taxable income of $800,000 for the year ended
December 31, 1989. The only temporary difference is accrued product warranty costs which
are expected to be paid as follows:

1990	$100,000
1991	50,000
1992	50,000
1993	100,000

The enacted income tax rates are 35% for 1989,
30% for 1990 through 1992, and 25% for 1993.
Black elected early application of FASB Statement No. 96, Accounting for Income Taxes, in
its financial statements for the year ended
December 31, 1989. In Black's December 31,
1989 balance sheet, the deferred income tax
asset should be
a. $ 60,000
b. $ 70,000
c. $ 85,000
d. $105,000

39. Graf Corp.'s 1989 income statement showed
pretax accounting income of $200,000. To com-
pute the federal income tax liability, the
following 1989 data are provided:

Income from exempt municipal bonds	$10,000
Depreciation deducted for tax pur- poses in excess of depreciation de- ducted for financial statement pur- poses	$20,000
Estimated federal income tax pay- ments made	$40,000
Enacted corporate income tax rate	30%

If the alternate minimum tax provisions are
ignored, what amount of current federal income
tax liability should be included in Graf's December 31, 1989 balance sheet?
a. $11,000
b. $20,000
c. $39,000
d. $51,000

40. Tell Corp.'s 1989 income statement had
pretax financial income of $38,000 in its
first year of operations. Tell uses an
accelerated cost recovery method on its tax
return and straight-line depreciation for
financial reporting.

The differences between the book and tax
deductions for depreciation over the five-year
life of the assets acquired in 1989, and the
enacted tax rates for 1989 to 1993 are as follows:

	Book over (under) tax	Tax rates
1989	$ (8,000)	35%
1990	(13,000)	30%
1991	(3,000)	30%
1992	10,000	25%
1993	14,000	25%

There are no other temporary differences. Tell elected early application of FASB Statement No. 96, Accounting for Income Taxes. In Tell's December 31, 1989 balance sheet, the gross noncurrent deferred income tax liability and the income taxes currently payable should be

	Gross noncurrent deferred income tax liability	Income taxes currently payable
a.	$6,000	$ 7,500
b.	$6,000	$10,500
c.	$4,800	$ 9,000
d.	$4,800	$10,500

41. Tara Corp. uses the equity method of accounting for its 40% investment in Flax, Inc.'s common stock. During 1989, Flax reported earnings of $750,000 and paid dividends of $250,000. Assume that:

• All the undistributed earnings of Flax will be distributed as dividends in future periods.
• The dividends received from Flax are eligible for the 80% dividends received deduction.
• There are no other temporary differences.
• Tara's 1989 income tax rate is 30%.
• Enacted income tax rates after 1989 are 25%.

Tara elected early application of FASB Statement No. 96, Accounting for Income Taxes. In its December 31, 1989 balance sheet, the increase in the deferred income tax liability from the above transactions would be
   a. $10,000
   b. $12,000
   c. $15,000
   d. $18,000

42. Huff Corp. began operations on January 1, 1988. Huff recognizes revenues from all sales under the accrual method for financial reporting purposes and appropriately uses the installment method for income tax purposes. Huff's gross margin on installment sales under each method was as follows:

Year	Accrual Method	Installment method
1988	$ 800,000	$300,000
1989	1,300,000	700,000

Huff elected early application of FASB Statement No. 96, Accounting for Income Taxes. Enacted income tax rates are 30% for 1989 and 25% thereafter. There are no other temporary differences. In Huff's December 31, 1989 balance sheet, the deferred income tax liability should be
   a. $150,000
   b. $180,000
   c. $275,000
   d. $330,000

43. For the year ended March 31, 1990, Dunn Corp.'s pretax financial statement income was $700,000, and its taxable income was $600,000. The difference is due to the following:

Interest on municipal bonds	$ 30,000
Lower depreciation for financial statement	70,000
Total	$100,000

Dunn elected early application of FASB Statement No. 96, Accounting for Income Taxes. Dunn's enacted income tax rate is 30%. What is Dunn's current portion of income tax expense for the year ended March 31, 1990?
   a. $210,000
   b. $189,000
   c. $180,000
   d. $159,000

44. In 1989, Lobo Corp. reported for financial statement purposes the following revenue and expenses which were not included in taxable income:

Premiums on officers' life insurance under which the corporation is the beneficiary	$ 5,000
Interest revenue on qualified state or municipal bonds	10,000
Estimated future warranty costs to be paid in 1990 and 1991	60,000

Lobo's enacted tax rate for the current and future years is 30%. Lobo has paid income taxes in the amount of $170,000 for the three-year period ended December 31, 1989. There were no temporary differences in prior years.

Lobo elected early application of FASB Statement No. 96, Accounting for Income Taxes. The deferred tax benefit to be applied against current income tax expense is
   a. $18,000
   b. $19,500
   c. $21,000
   d. $22,500

45. Cahn Co. applies straight-line amortization to its organization costs for both income taxes and financial statement reporting. However, for tax purposes a 5-year period is used and for financial statement

purposes a 10-year period is used. Cahn has
no other temporary differences, has an operating cycle of less than 1 year, and has taxable income in all years. Cahn should report
both current and noncurrent deferred income
tax liabilities at the end of

	Year 1	Year 8
a.	No	Yes
b.	No	No
c.	Yes	Yes
d.	Yes	No

46. No deferred tax asset was recognized in
the 1988 financial statements by the Chaise
Company when a loss from discontinued segments
was carried forward for tax purposes. Chaise
had no temporary differences. The tax benefit
of the loss carried forward reduced current
taxes payable on 1989 continuing operations.
In accordance with FASB Statement No. 96, the
1989 income statement would include the tax
benefit from the loss brought forward in
a.   Income from continuing operations.
b.   Gain or loss from discontinued
     segments.
c.   Extraordinary gains.
d.   Cumulative effect of accounting
     changes.

Problems

Problem 1   (573,T3, Revised for SFAS 96)

(15 to 25 minutes)

Part a.

In preparing financial statements a corporation is expected to follow the practice of comprehensive income tax allocation.

Required:

Describe the objective of accounting for income taxes on an accrual basis.

Part b.

The following differences enter into the reconciliation of financial accounting income and taxable income of A. P. Baxter Corp. for the current year.
1. Tax depreciation exceeds book depreciation by $30,000.
2. Estimated warranty costs of $6,000 applicable to the current year's sales have not been paid.
3. Percentage depletion deducted on the tax return exceeds cost depletion by $45,000.
4. Unearned rent of $25,000 was deferred on the books but appropriately included in taxable income.
5. A book expense of $2,000 for life insurance premiums on officers' lives is not allowed as a deduction on the tax return.
6. A $7,000 tax deduction resulted from expensing relocation costs for tax purposes while such costs were capitalized for financial reporting.

Required:

Consider each reconciling item independently of all others and explain whether each item would enter into the calculation of deferred taxes. For any which are included in the calculation, explain the effect of the item on the current year's income tax expense and how the amount would be reported on the balance sheet. (Calculations are not required.)

Problem 2

(45 to 55 minutes)

[See Problem 2 in Module 22 D. (Includes a permanent and temporary difference.)]

Problem 3

(45 to 55 minutes)

[See Problem 3 in Module 22 D. (Requirement b.)]

Problem 4   (1188,Q4)

[See Problem 5 in Module 26 E. (Requirement a.)]

Multiple Choice Answers

1. a	11. d	20. c	29. c	38. b
2. c	12. c	21. b	30. b	39. a
3. d	13. b	22. b	31. b	40. b
4. a	14. c	23. c	32. a	41. a
5. d	15. b	24. c	33. d	42. c
6. c	16. a	25. c	34. b	43. c
7. c	17. a	26. d	35. d	44. a
8. c	18. b	27. b	36. c	45. a
9. c	19. a	28. d	37. c	46. a
10. c				

Multiple Choice Answer Explanations

B. Permanent and Temporary Differences Defined

1. (589,T1,22) (a) SFAS 96, para 10 cites nine examples of temporary differences. Among these examples are revenues which are taxable both before and after they are recognized in financial income. Therefore, answer (a) is correct. Note that emphasis is placed on the difference between book and tax, not the chronological order of the reporting.

2. (1189,T1,27) (c) A temporary difference occurs when financial accounting rules allow an item of revenue or expense to be recognized in one period while the tax rules allow that item to be recognized in another period. An item may be recognized for tax purposes before it is recognized for financial accounting purposes and vice versa. Therefore, answer (c) is correct.

3. (1187,P2,22) (d) Temporary differences are differences between taxable income and accounting income which originate in one period and reverse in one or more subsequent periods. Interest received on municipal bonds ($10,000) and amortization of goodwill ($18,000) are not temporary differences because they never reverse. These are examples of permanent differences, which are items that either enter into accounting income but never into taxable income (such as these two items), or enter into taxable income but never into accounting income.

4. (589,P3,42) (a) Temporary differences are differences between taxable income and accounting income which originate in one period and reverse in one or more subsequent periods. Amortization of goodwill ($10,000) and insurance premiums where the corporation is the beneficiary ($5,000) are not temporary differences because they never reverse. These are examples of permanent differences, which are items that either enter into accounting income but never into taxable income (such as

these two items), or enter into taxable income but never into accounting income.

C. Deferred Tax Liability and Deferred Tax Asset

5. (589,P2,38) (d) To determine the current federal tax liability, book income ($300,000) must be adjusted for any temporary or permanent differences to determine taxable income.

Book income	$300,000
Municipal interest	(30,000)
Excess tax depreciation	(60,000)
Insurance proceeds	(50,000)
Taxable income	$160,000

Municipal interest (permanent difference) is subtracted from book income because it is excluded from taxable income. The excess tax depreciation (temporary difference) is subtracted because this excess amount is an additional tax deduction beyond the accounting depreciation. The insurance proceeds (permanent difference) are subtracted because, like the municipal interest, such proceeds are excludable from taxable income. The current tax liability is computed by multiplying taxable income by the tax rate ($160,000 x 30% = $48,000).

6. (586,P2,25) (c) The requirement is to determine the current federal income tax liability at 12/31/85. Book income of $720,000 must be adjusted for any temporary or permanent differences to determine taxable income. The solutions approach is to prepare a reconciliation of book to tax income.

Book income	$720,000
Less excess tax depreciation	(32,000)
Plus excess tax rental income	24,000
Taxable income	$712,000

The excess tax depreciation (temporary difference) must be deducted from book income when adjusting to taxable income. The excess rent received over the amount earned (also a temporary difference) must be added to book income. Once the taxable income ($712,000) is determined, the current liability for taxes can be computed as 40% of that amount ($712,000 x 40% = $284,800).

7. (Author constructed) (c) An excess of tax depreciation over financial accounting depreciation results in future taxable amounts and, therefore, a deferred tax liability. Answer (a) is an example of a permanent difference which does not result in future taxable or deductible amounts. Answers (b) and (d) are examples of temporary differences which result in future deductible amounts and a possible deferred tax asset.

8.   (589,P2,37) (c) Accounting income will exceed taxable income by $9,000 because accounting depreciation is $9,000 while the total 1988 tax deduction is $18,000 ($10,000 + $8,000). This is a temporary difference, because total expense over the life of the asset will be $90,000 for both accounting and tax purposes. The tax effect of a temporary difference is reflected in the deferred income tax liability account. The $9,000 temporary difference is a future taxable amount, so the deferred income tax liability account should increase by $2,700 (30% x $9,000).

9.   (588,P2,34) (c) For financial reporting purposes, income is recognized using the percentage-of-completion method, and 1987 income was $825,000. For tax purposes, income is recognized using the completed-contract method, under which 1987 income was $925,000. Taxable income exceeds financial reporting income by $100,000 ($925,000 - $825,000). This $100,000 taxable amount is a reversal of a prior temporary difference. In 1985 and 1986, financial reporting income exceeded taxable income, resulting in a deferred tax liability. In 1987, part of this temporary difference is reversing, so the deferred tax liability must decrease by the tax effect of $30,000 (30% x $100,000).

10. (1189,P3,47) (c) SFAS 96 states that income tax provision (expense) must be reported in two components: the amount currently payable (current portion) and the tax effects of temporary differences (deferred portion). The amount currently payable, or current portion, Is computed by multiplying taxable income by the current enacted tax rate ($300,000 x 30% = $90,000).

11. (1189,P3,48) (d) SFAS 96 states that income tax provision (expense) must be reported in two components: the amount currently payable (current portion) and the tax effects of temporary differences (deferred portion). The depreciation difference is the only temporary difference in this case, and it will result in future taxable amounts of $50,000 per year for 1989, 1990, and 1991. Bee's deferred tax liability should be based on the future enacted tax rates (30% for 1989 and 25% for 1990 and 1991). Therefore, the deferred portion of income taxes is $40,000, as computed below:

Year	Taxable amount		Rate		Deferred tax
89	$50,000	x	30%	=	$15,000
90	50,000	x	25%	=	12,500
91	50,000	x	25%	=	12,500
Total	$150,000				$40,000

The interest on municipal bonds is a permanent difference because it will never be taxable, so it does not affect deferred taxes.

12. (1187,P3,49) (c) According to SFAS 96, income tax expense must be reported in two components: the amount currently payable (current portion) and the tax effects of temporary differences (deferred portion). Since the current portion is based on <u>taxable</u> income, pretax financial <u>(accounting)</u> income must be adjusted as follows:

Pretax accounting income	$300,000
Excess accounting warranty expense	15,000
Excess tax depreciation	(50,000)
Nondeductible premium	60,000
Taxable income	$325,000

The first two items (excess warranty and excess depreciation expense) are temporary differences. In 1986, warranty expense for accounting purposes exceeded the allowable tax deduction by $15,000 ($185,000 - $170,000). Since this excess results in lower accounting income than taxable income, it must be added back to accounting income to arrive at taxable income. Also, 1986 tax depreciation exceeds 1986 accounting depreciation by $50,000 ($150,000 - $100,000). This excess must be subtracted from accounting income in computing taxable income. The life insurance premiums ($60,000) are a permanent difference which are never deductible for tax purposes. Since these are not deductible, they must be added back to accounting income in computing taxable income. Once the taxable income ($325,000) is determined, the current portion of income tax expense can be computed as $130,000 ($325,000 x 40%).

13. (1187,P3,50) (b) The deferred portion of income tax expense can be computed by taking the tax effect of the two <u>temporary</u> differences (warranty expense and depreciation expense). The excess warranty expense for accounting purposes ($185,000 - $170,000 = $15,000) results in a future <u>deductible</u> amount, while the excess tax depreciation ($150,000 - $100,000 = $50,000) results in a future <u>taxable</u> amount. Note that in this case it is not necessary to prepare a schedule of future temporary differences because there would be a net taxable amount of $7,000 in each of the five future years and the enacted rate is 40% for all affected years. Thus, the aggregate method may be used. The net taxable amount is $35,000 ($50,000 Excess deprec. - $15,000 Excess warr.), resulting in a net deferred income tax expense of $14,000 ($35,000 x 40%). Note that the life insurance

premiums are a <u>permanent</u> difference, so they do not affect deferred taxes.

14. (1189,P2,24) (c) For financial reporting purposes, Frey recognizes income using the percentage-of-completion method, and 1988 income was $1,200,000 ($600,000 + $300,000 + $200,000 + $100,000). For tax purposes, income is recognized using the completed-contract method. Since no contracts were completed the first year, income for tax purposes was $0. Financial reporting income exceeds taxable income by $1,200,000. This is a temporary difference which will result in future taxable amounts in 1989 and 1990 when the contracts are completed. Frey's deferred tax liability should be based on the future <u>enacted</u> tax rates (25% for 1989 and 20% for 1990). The deferred tax liability for the $900,000 amount which will become taxable in 1989 is $225,000 ($900,000 x 25%), while the liability for the $300,000 amount which will become taxable in 1990 is $60,000 ($300,000 x 20%). The total deferred tax liability is $285,000 ($225,000 + $60,000).

15. (1189,P2,26) (b) For financial reporting purposes, a gain of $150,000 is recognized in 1988 ($450,000 - $300,000). For tax purposes, the gain is not reported in 1988. This temporary difference of $150,000 will result in a future taxable amount of $150,000 when the gain is recognized for tax purposes. Huff's deferred tax liability should be based on the future <u>enacted</u> tax rate (30% for years ending after 1988). Therefore, the deferred tax liability at 12/31/88 is $45,000 ($150,000 x 30%).

16. (Author constructed) (a) The requirement is the <u>income tax expense</u> for 1987. The following schedule represents Landwer's future deductible or taxable amounts:

	Current Year	Future Years		
	1987	1988	1989	1990
Pretax income	350,000	--	--	
Temporary difference	100,000	--	--	(100,000)
Taxable income	450,000			
"As if" loss carryback	(100,000)			100,000
Amounts used to determine deferred tax asset	(100,000)			-0-

Note a deferred tax asset can be recognized because Landwer Company has net income in 1987 which could be used to realize a tax benefit from a loss carryback. In this case, the deferred tax asset to be recognized is $100,000 x 40% or $40,000. The appropriate rate is 40%, not the 35% because if the only

item of taxable income in 1988-90 that is different then book income (assumed to be -0-) is the $100,000 deductible amount, an operating loss of $100,000 would develop on the tax return in 1990 and be carried back to 1987 and a refund of $40,000 (40% x $100,000) would result. The following entry for the 1987 tax effects would be made:

Income tax expense	140,000	
Deferred tax asset--noncurrent (100,000 x .40)	40,000	
Taxes payable (450,000 x .4)		180,000

Note that if the $100,000 had been a deductible amount in 1987 and a taxable amount in 1990, the appropriate rate to measure the resulting deferred tax liability would have been 35%.

17. (586,P1,8) (a) The requirement is to determine the amount by which the deferred tax asset account would increase in 1985. The premiums on officers' life insurance ($175,000) are a <u>permanent</u> difference: they are an accounting expense which are never deductible for tax purposes. Permanent differences do <u>not</u> affect deferred income taxes. The difference in royalty income ($700,000 - $450,000 = $250,000) is a <u>temporary</u> difference; the same total amount of income will be recognized in different periods for financial and tax purposes. Temporary differences <u>do</u> affect deferred taxes. Taxable income will exceed accounting income by $250,000 as a result of this temporary difference; that will cause a $100,000 increase ($250,000 x 40%) in the deferred income tax asset account. The increase in the deferred tax asset can be recognized because the future deductible amount could be carried back against 1984 taxable income.

18. (Author constructed) (b) The goodwill difference ($75,000) is a permanent difference which does not result in future taxable or deductible amounts. The warranty difference ($50,000) is a temporary difference, but it results in future <u>deductible</u> amounts in future years when tax warranty expense exceeds book warranty expense. However, the equipment difference ($80,000) is a temporary difference which results in future taxable amounts in future years when tax depreciation is less than book depreciation.

19. (Author constructed) (a) The requirement is the <u>income tax expense</u> for 1987. The solutions approach is to first prepare a schedule of future taxable (deductible) amounts:

	Current Year	Future Years	
	1987	1988	1989
Pretax accounting (book)	$290,000		
Temporary differences:			
Rent	60,000		(60,000)
Depreciation	(50,000)	25,000	25,000
Taxable income	$300,000	$25,000	$(35,000)
"As if" loss carryback	(35,000)		35,000
Amounts used to determine			
deferred tax asset and/or liability	$(35,000)	$25,000	$ -0-

Once the future temporary differences have been scheduled, the journal entry to record tax expense and the assets and liabilities can be made:

Deferred tax asset--noncurrent ($35,000 x .4)	14,000	
Income tax expense ($120,000 + $10,000 - $14,000)	116,000	
Deferred tax liability--current ($25,000 x .4)		10,000
Income taxes payable ($300,000 x .4)		120,000

Note that a deferred tax asset can be recognized as Huskie Corporation has taxable income in 1987 which could be used to realize a tax benefit from a loss carryforward.

20. (Author constructed) (c) Per the journal entry in "19." above the answer is a $14,000 deferred tax asset.

21. (Author constructed) (b) The requirement is the amount of the current deferred tax liability Wright Corporation should show on the 12/31/87 balance sheet. The following schedule represents future taxable (deductible) amounts:

	Current Year		Future Years		
	1987	1988	1989	1990	1991
Pretax accounting income (book)	$180,000	--	--	--	--
Temporary differences:					
Depreciation	(30,000)	10,000	10,000	10,000	
Contingency	90,000				(90,000)
Taxable income	$240,000	10,000	10,000	10,000	<90,000>
"As if" loss carryback		<10,000>	<10,000>	<10,000>	<30,000>
		-0-	-0-	-0-	(60,000)

Based on the schedule of future temporary differences, the deferred portion of income tax expense is -0- and tax expense is equal to income taxes payable. This is because $30,000 of the $90,000 deductible amount in 1991 can be carried back to 1988, 1989, and 1990 to offset the $10,000 taxable amounts in each of those years. Additionally, the $60,000 deductible amount left after the "as is"

carryback has no effect on deferred tax expense since recognition of an asset for the possible future tax benefit of $18,000 ($60,000 x 30%) is prohibited. However, a current liability of $3,000 ($10,000 x 30%) must be shown on the 12/31/87 balance sheet since taxable income is scheduled to exceed pretax accounting (financial) income by $10,000 in 1988 which precedes the $90,000 deductible amount scheduled for 1991. The journal entry below reflects the current and noncurrent elements.

Deferred tax asset--noncurrent	9,000	
Income tax expense	72,000	
Income taxes payable		72,000
Deferred tax liability-- current		3,000
Deferred tax liability-- noncurrent		6,000

On the balance sheet, a current liability of $3,000 would be shown. Additionally, the two noncurrent elements would be netted together to give a net noncurrent asset of $3,000. Thus, the answer is (b).

22. (Author constructed) (b) The requirement is the income tax expense for 1987. Each future year needs
to be evaluated separately using the enacted tax rate in the future year. At 12/31/86, the tax rate was
40% and since the new rate was not enacted until 1987, the tax effects of temporary differences would have
been provided for using the 40% rate. At 12/31/86, deferred taxes would have been calculated as follows:

	Current Year	Future Years		
	1986	1987	1988	1989
Pretax accounting income (book)	170,000	--	--	--
(Deductible) taxable amounts	(20,000)	(20,000)	20,000	20,000
Taxable income	150,000			
"As if" loss carryback	(20,000)	20,000		
Amounts used to determine deferred tax asset and/or liability	(20,000)	-0-	20,000	20,000

The following entry would be made to record the 1986 tax effects:

Deferred tax asset--current (20,000 x .4)	8,000	
Income tax expense ($60,000 + $16,000 - $8,000)	68,000	
Deferred tax liability--noncurrent (40,000 x .4)		16,000
Income taxes payable ($150,000 x .4)		60,000

Note a deferred tax asset can be recognized as Hearn Corporation has taxable income in 1986 which could be
used to realize a tax benefit from a loss carryback. At 12/31/87, deferred taxes would be calculated as
follows:

	1987	1988	1989
Pretax income	170,000		
Taxable amounts	(20,000)	20,000	20,000
Taxable income	150,000		
Amounts used to determine deferred tax asset and/or liability		20,000	20,000

Note that a tax rate change has occurred and this change will be reflected in the journal entry amount by
recording the amounts necessary to adjust the 1/1/87 deferred tax account balances to the necessary
12/31/87 balances. The following entry would be made to record the 1987 tax effects:

Income tax expense ($52,500 + $7,000 + $8,000 - $9,000)	58,500	
Deferred tax liability--noncurrent [$16,000 - (20,000 x .35)]	9,000	
Deferred tax asset--current		8,000
Deferred tax liability--current (20,000 x .35)		7,000
Income taxes payable (150,000 x .35)		52,500

Therefore, the correct answer is (b), $58,500.

23. (Author constructed) (c) Expenses or
losses that are deductible before they are
recognized in financial income would result in
future taxable amounts. For example, the cost
of an asset may have been deducted for tax
purposes faster than it was depreciated for
financial reporting. In future years, tax
depreciation will be less than financial
accounting depreciation, meaning future
taxable income will exceed future financial
accounting income. Answers (a) and (b) are
temporary differences which would result in
future deductible amounts. Answer (d) is a
permanent difference which does not result in
either future taxable or future deductible
amounts.

24. (Author constructed) (c) If a temporary
difference results in future taxable amounts,
a deferred tax liability must be recorded in
the current year because a post event has
resulted in a present obligation which will

require a probable future sacrifice (the
payment of taxes in five years). Note that a
temporary difference which will result in net
deductible amounts in future years would
prompt the recording of a deferred tax **asset**,
if those deductible amounts can be offset
against taxable amounts through carryback or
carryforward.

25. (Author constructed) (c) Per para 14 of
SFAS 96, a deferred tax liability is
recognized for the amount of taxes payable in
future years as a result of the deferred tax
consequences (as measured by the provisions of
enacted tax laws) of events recognized in the
financial statements in the current or
preceding years.

26. (Author constructed) (d) Para 17(e) of
SFAS 96 indicates that a deferred tax asset
can be recognized only in those circumstances
expressed in answer (d).

D. Deferred Tax Related to Business Investments

27. (588,P2,33) (b) The undistributed earnings of an investee, when the equity method is used, should be accounted for as a temporary difference. Investment revenue of $300,000 (50% x $600,000) is included in accounting income, while dividends received of $100,000 could be included in taxable income. Therefore, the temporary difference, before considering the dividends received deduction, is $200,000. Using the deduction, 80% of the amount becomes a permanent difference (never included in taxable income). The other 20% of the undistributed earnings (20% x $200,000 = $40,000) is a temporary difference because it will eventually be included in taxable income when distributed as dividends in the future. The $40,000 is a future taxable amount which should be reflected as a $12,000 increase in the deferred tax account ($40,000 x 30% = $12,000).

28. (589,P2,40) (d) The increase in the deferred income tax liability is the result of undistributed earnings of an equity investee, which the investor assumes will eventually be distributed as dividends in future periods. For accounting purposes, Lundy will recognize equity earnings of $90,000 (40% x $225,000). For tax purposes, Lundy will report dividend income of $30,000 (40% x $75,000). This temporary difference of $60,000 ($90,000 - $30,000) is a future taxable amount, resulting in an increase in the deferred tax liability of $18,000 ($60,000 x 30% tax rate). The 30% tax rate is used because this is the rate which will be in effect when the dividends are distributed. Note that if the dividend-received deduction (DRD) was considered, the temporary difference would be 20% of $60,000, or $12,000, since 80% of the dividends would never be taxable (the DRD is a permanent difference).

29. (586,Q1,16) (c) The requirement is to determine the amount to be reported as deferred income tax as a result of undistributed earnings of the subsidiary. The undistributed earnings of a subsidiary included in the income of the parent company should be accounted for as a temporary difference. Note that the computation of the deferred tax liability depends on the manner in which the parent company expects to ultimately receive their share of the undistributed earnings. If the expectation of receipt is via dividends, then the temporary difference is 20% of the parent's share of the undistributed earnings because for tax purposes 80% of the expected dividends will be excluded from income when

received. The 40% tax rate is applied after expected dividends have been reduced by the dividend received deduction as follows.

Subsidiary earnings	$300,000
Dividends paid	-100,000
Undistributed subsidiary earnings	200,000
Parent's interest	x .75
Parent's share of undistributed earnings	150,000
Reciprocal of DRD	x .20
Future taxable portion	30,000
Tax rate	x .40
Deferred income tax	$ 12,000

E. Loss Carryforwards and Carrybacks

30. (1187,P1,17) (b) Dix did <u>not</u> elect to forgo the loss carryback, so $100,000 of the $200,000 loss will be carried back to offset 1984 income, resulting in a tax refund of $40,000 (40% x $100,000). The remaining $100,000 of the 1985 loss will be carried forward to offset part of 1986 income. Thus, the income tax <u>liability</u> at 12/31/86 will be $120,000 [40% x ($400,000 - $100,000)].

31. (586,P3,53) (b) The requirement is the amount to be reported in 1985 as the reduction of loss due to NOL carryback and carryforward. Per SFAS 96, the tax benefits of loss carryforwards may not be recognized unless future taxable amounts from temporary differences are scheduled to reverse in the carryforward period. In this situation, there are no differences between pretax accounting income and taxable income for all years. Thus, there would not be any scheduled reversals of temporary differences. Therefore, as shown below, only the tax benefits of the carryback can be recognized in 1985 ($450,000 x 40% = $180,000).

	1982	1983	1984	1985
Inc (loss)		450,000		($600,000)
Carryback		(450,000)		450,000
Unused NOL				$150,000
Reduction for 1985	$450,000 x 40% = $180,000			

Entry:

Tax refund receiv.	180,000	
Reduction of loss from carryback		180,000

The bottom of the income statement would appear as follows:

Loss before tax benefit	($600,000)
Reduction of loss from carryback	180,000
Net loss	($420,000)

32. (1184,P3,50) (a) The requirement is the amount of 1987 current income tax expense to be reported in the income statement. Loss carryforwards should not be recognized until they are actually realized, except where there are future reversals of temporary differences that will result in taxable amounts during the carryforward period. Since none exist in this case, this loss carryforward is not recognized until 1987.

Income or loss	($200,000)	($150,000)	$300,000
Carryforward	200,000	100,000	(300,000)
Unused Carryforward	-0-	$150,000	-0-

(As shown below) In 1987 Bishop would recognize income tax expense at the normal rate ($300,000 x 40% = $120,000), less the tax reduction due to loss carryforward ($300,000 x 40% = $120,000), or net tax expense of $0. These two components shall be shown either on the face of the income statement or in the notes thereto.

Income tax exp.:
Before NOL benefit	$120,000
Tax benefit of NOL	120,000
	-0-

33. (588,P3,56) (d) Tax loss carryforwards are not recognized until they are realized in a subsequent period (when taxable income exists). The only exception to this general rule is when future taxable amounts from temporary differences are scheduled to reverse in the carryforward period. This question is silent as to whether any future taxable amounts exist. Therefore, none of the potential tax benefit should be reported in Colt's 1987 income statement.

F. Financial Statement Presentation of Income Tax

34. (579,T1,9) (b) Per SFAS 96 income tax expense must be associated with (i.e., allocated among) income from continuing operations, discontinued operations, extraordinary items, cumulative effect of an accounting change, and prior period adjustments. The tax effect to be associated with any of the special items (other than income from continuing operations) is computed by determining the income tax on overall taxable income and comparing it with the income tax on continuing operations. If more than one special item exists, the difference between tax on ordinary operations and tax on overall taxable income must be allocated proportionately among the special items.

35. (1189,T1,15) (d) Since the financial reporting basis of the plant assets is greater than their tax basis, the cumulative tax depreciation must exceed financial reporting ("book") depreciation. In future years, the temporary difference between tax and book depreciation will begin to reverse (periodic book depreciation will be greater than tax depreciation), and the difference will be reduced to zero. Per SFAS 96, a deferred tax liability is recognized for temporary differences that will result in net taxable amounts in future years. Since the financial reporting carrying value of the plant assets exceeds their tax basis, the continued use or sale of the plant assets will result in taxable amounts in future years as the assets become fully depreciated for tax purposes, or (on a sale) when the tax gain exceeds the book gain (due to a lower tax carrying value). Therefore, this temporary difference should be reported as a deferred tax liability, making answer (d) correct and answer (c) incorrect. Answers (a) and (b) are incorrect because temporary differences result in deferred, not current, tax assets and liabilities.

36. (587,T1,15) (c) Deferred taxes should be separated and classified into two components: one for net current amounts and one for net noncurrent amounts. Therefore, the company's balance sheet should report the deferred income tax asset as a current asset and the deferred income tax liability as a noncurrent liability. Answer (d) is incorrect because the deferred tax liability expected to reverse beyond one year should be classified as a noncurrent liability, not a current liability. Current and noncurrent components should not be netted; thus, answers (a) and (b) are incorrect.

37. (1186,T1,13) (c) Proper classification of deferred assets and liabilities involves two steps. First, deferred tax assets or liabilities must be classified as current or noncurrent for presentation on the balance sheet. Second, the current assets and liabilities should be netted to give a single current asset or liability and the same would be done for the noncurrent items. Thus, the current deferred tax liability and the current deferred tax asset should be netted in this case, and the noncurrent deferred tax liability would be disclosed separately. Therefore, answer (c) is correct, and answers (a), (b), and (d) are incorrect.

May 1990 Answers

38. (590,P2,21) (b) The warranty expense accrued for accounting purposes in 1989, an estimated amount, will provide future deductible amounts in 1990-1993, because under the IRS Code a deduction for warranty cost is not permitted until such cost is incurred. A deferred tax asset can be recognized for future deductible amounts only if tax benefits are assured by offsetting future taxable amounts or by exercise of loss carryback provisions. The solutions approach is to schedule out future deductible amounts (in thousands):

	Current Year	Future Years			
	1989	1990	1991	1992	1993
Acctg income	$500				
Warranty exp.	300	$(100)	$(50)	$(50)	$(100)
Taxable income	$800				
Assumed loss carrybacks	$(200)	100	50	50	
Adj. ded. amounts	$(200)	$ 0	$ 0	$ 0	$(100)
Enacted tax rates	35%	30%	30%	30%	25%
Deferred tax asset	$ 70				

The future deductible amounts for 1990-92 can be assumed to be carried back to 1989, resulting in a deferred tax asset of $70 [($100 + $50 + $50) times the 1989 tax rate of 35%]. No deferred tax asset can be recognized for the 1993 deductible amount since it cannot be offset, carried back, or carried forward.

39. (590,P2,26) (a) The current federal income tax liability is based on taxable income, which is computed in the "book to tax reconciliation" below:

Acctg. income	$200,000
Municipal bond income	(10,000)
Excess tax depreciation	(20,000)
Taxable income	$170,000

Municipal bond income (a permanent difference) is subtracted from accounting income because it is included in accounting income but excluded from taxable income. The excess tax depreciation (a temporary difference) is subtracted from accounting income because it causes taxable income to be less than accounting income. Taxes payable before considering estimated payments is $51,000 (30% x $170,000). Since tax payments of $40,000 have already been made, the current federal income taxes payable is $11,000 ($51,000 - $40,000).

40. (590,P2,28) (b) Pretax accounting income in 1989 is $38,000. Excess tax depreciation for 1989 is $8,000, resulting in 1989 taxable income of $30,000 ($38,000 - $8,000) and income taxes currently payable of $10,500 ($30,000 x 35%). To determine the gross non-

current deferred income tax liability, the future taxable and deductible amounts can be scheduled out as follows (in thousands):

	Current Year	Future Years			
	1989	1990	1991	1992	1993
Acctg income	$38				
Excess depreciation	(8)	$(13)	$(3)	$10	$14
Taxable income	$30				
Assumed loss carrybacks	$13	13			
	3		3		
Adjusted amounts	$16	$ 0	$ 0	$10	$14
Enacted tax rates	35%	30%	30%	25%	25%
Deferred tax liab. (asset)					
Current	$(4,550)				
Noncurrent	$(1,050)			$2,500	$3,500

As the schedule indicates, the gross noncurrent liability is $6,000 ($2,500 + $3,500). Note that the net noncurrent amount shown on the balance sheet would be $5,950 [($1,050) + $6,000].

41. (590,P2,32) (a) The increase in the deferred income tax liability is the result of the undistributed earnings of an equity investee, which the investor assumes will eventually be distributed as dividends in future periods. For accounting purposes, investment revenue is $300,000 (40% x $750,000). This amount needs to be subtracted from financial (book) income to arrive at taxable income and will result in future taxable amounts. For tax purposes, dividend revenue before considering the dividends received deduction is $100,000 (40% x $250,000). This amount needs to be added to financial (book) income to arrive at taxable income and will result in future deductible amounts. The net difference of $200,000 ($300,000 - $100,000) is partially a permanent difference because of the dividends received deduction (80% x $200,000 = $160,000 permanent difference). The rest of the $200,000 net difference is a temporary difference which results in future taxable amounts of $40,000 (20% x $200,000). This amount will become taxable after 1989 when the enacted tax rate is 25%. Therefore, the increase in the deferred tax liability is $10,000 (25% x $40,000).

42. (590,P2,34) (c) The use of the installment method for tax purposes results in 1988-89 gross margin of $1,000,000 ($300,000 + $700,000), while for financial reporting purposes 1988-89 gross margin was $2,100,000 ($800,000 + $1,300,000) using the accrual or point of sale method. This temporary difference results in future taxable amounts of $1,100,000 ($2,100,000 - $1,000,000) because in future years, as the installment receivables are collected, the gross margin portion of the collections will be added to accounting income in the "book to tax reconciliation." The $1,100,000 difference will become taxable after 1989 when the enacted tax rate is 25%. Therefore, the 12/31/89 deferred tax liability is $275,000 (25% x $1,100,000).

43. (590,P2,39) (c) SFAS 96 states that income tax expense must be reported in two components: the amount of tax currently payable (current portion) and the tax effects of temporary differences (deferred portion). The amount of tax currently payable, or current portion, is computed by multiplying taxable income by the current tax rate ($600,000 x 30% = $180,000).

44. (590,P3,41) (a) The premiums on officers' life insurance ($5,000) and the municipal interest revenue ($10,000) are both permanent differences, so they do not affect deferred taxes. The estimated future warranty cost ($60,000) is a temporary difference which results in future deductible amounts in 1990 and 1991. The deferred tax benefit is $18,000 (30% x $60,000). The deferred tax asset can be recorded because the future deductible amounts can be assumed to be carried back and offset against prior years' income of $170,000.

45. (590,T1,10) (a) When a company amortizes organization costs over different periods of time for financial statement purposes and for tax purposes, a temporary difference results. A temporary difference may result in current or noncurrent deferred taxes depending on when it is expected to reverse. A temporary difference will result in current deferred taxes if it will reverse in 1 year or less. In this situation, the organization costs are being amortized over 10 years for financial statement purposes and over 5 years for tax purposes. Therefore, in years 1-5, tax amortization will exceed financial statement amortization. This will result in a deferred tax liability as taxable income will be less than financial statement income. In years 6-10 however, this situation will reverse or financial statement amortization exceeds tax amortization. This will reduce the deferred tax liability accumulated in years 1-5. Under the liability method of accounting for deferred taxes, the deferred asset/liability is recorded at the expected effective tax rate for the period in which the temporary difference reverses except in the case of an "assumed carryback" in which the carryback tax benefit is measured using the rate in effect for the year(s) to which the assumed carryback could

be carried. In year 1, the temporary difference that occurs will not reverse until year 6 and therefore should be classified as noncurrent on the year-end balance sheet. At the end of year 8, however, one half of the remaining temporary difference tax effected using the rate applicable to year 9 that will reverse in year 9 is current and the remaining portion that will reverse in year 10 is classified as noncurrent.

46. (590,T1,25) (a) Per SFAS 96, para 138, the benefit of a loss or tax credit carryforward should be based on event(s) that occurred in the current year, (i.e., the earning of income). The reasons for this are that it (a) produces understandable results, and (b) avoids the sometimes complex problem of tracing back to events of prior years. Therefore, the tax benefit of the loss is carried forward to reduce current taxes on income from continuing operations, [answer (a)].

Answer Outline

Problem 1   Accounting for Income Taxes:
Objectives and Temporary
Differences (573,T3, Revised
for SFAS 96)

Part a.

Objective of accounting for income taxes

Recognize current and deferred taxes payable
(refundable) at financial statement date
due to events and transactions

(1)   Recognized in financial statements
(2)   Measured using provisions of enacted
tax laws

Part b.

Differences entering into reconciliation of
taxable and financial (book) net income

(1)   Excess tax depreciation of $30,000

Temporary difference--results in
future taxable amounts
Tax effect reported as current
and/or long-term deferred tax
liability
Increases tax expense by amount payable when temporary difference
reverses

(2)   Accrued warranty expense of $6,000

Temporary difference--results in
future deductible amounts
Tax effect reported as current
and/or noncurrent deferred tax
asset
  Depends on when deductible amounts
  are expected to occur, and
  If deductible amounts can be
  offset by taxable amounts through
  carryback or carryforward
Decreases tax expense by amount of
benefit realized when temporary
difference reverses

(3)   Excess tax depletion of $45,000

Does not affect deferred taxes
Excess never used in determination
of financial (book) income

(4)   Unearned rent of $45,000

Temporary difference--results in
future deductible amounts
Tax effect reported as current
and/or noncurrent deferred tax
asset

Depends on when deductible amounts
are expected to occur, and
If deductible amounts can be offset by taxable amounts through
carryback or carryforward
Decreases tax expense by amount of
benefit realized when temporary
difference reverses

(5)   Financial (book) expense of $2,000
for life insurance premiums

Does not affect deferred taxes
Never used in determination of taxable income

(6)   Relocation costs of $7,000

Temporary difference--results in
future taxable amounts
Tax effect reported as current
and/or long-term deferred tax
liability
Increases tax expense by amount payable when temporary difference
reverses

Unofficial Answer

Problem 1   Accounting for Income Taxes: Objectives and Temporary Differ-
ences (573,T3, Revised for
SFAS 96)

Part a.

The objective of accounting for income
taxes is to recognize current and deferred
taxes payable or refundable at the date of the
financial statements due to events and transactions (1) that have been recognized at the
date of the financial statements, and (2) that
are measured using the provisions of enacted
tax laws.

Part b.

Following are the differences entering
into the reconciliation of taxable and
financial net income of A. P. Baxter Corp. for
the current year. Each is identified as
either affecting or not affecting the deferred
taxes calculation. The effect on the current
year's income tax expense and the method of
reporting the amount on the balance sheet are
indicated for those affecting deferred taxes.

1. Excess tax depreciation of $30,000 is a
temporary difference which results in future
taxable amounts. The tax effect will be
reported as a current and/or long-term
deferred tax liability, and will increase tax

expense by the amount payable when the temporary difference reverses.

2. The $6,000 of accrued warranty expense is a temporary difference which results in future deductible amounts. The tax effect will be reported as either a current or noncurrent asset, depending on when the deductible amounts are expected to occur and if the future deductible amounts can be offset against taxable amounts through carryback or carryforward. This tax effect will decrease tax expense by the amount of the tax benefit to be realized when reversal of the temporary difference occurs.

3. The $45,000 excess of percentage depletion over cost depletion is a difference which does not affect deferred taxes because this excess will never enter into the determination of book or financial income.

4. Unearned rent of $25,000 is a temporary difference which results in future deductible amounts. The tax effect will be reported as a current and/or noncurrent asset, depending on when the deductible amounts are expected to occur and if the future deductible amounts can be offset against taxable amounts through carryback or carryforward. This tax effect will decrease tax expense by the amount of the tax benefit to be realized when reversal of the temporary difference occurs.

5. The $2,000 life insurance expense is a difference which does not affect deferred taxes because this item will never enter into the determination of taxable income.

6. The $7,000 of relocation costs is a temporary difference which results in future taxable amounts. The tax effect will be reported as a current and/or long-term deferred tax liability, and will increase tax expense by the amount expected to be payable in the period when reversal occurs.

Multiple Choice Questions (1-57)

1.   A corporation was organized in January 1988 with authorized capital of $10 par value common stock. On February 1, 1988, shares were issued at par for cash. On March 1, 1988, the corporation's attorney accepted 5,000 shares of the common stock in settlement for legal services with a fair value of $60,000. Additional paid-in capital would increase on

	February 1, 1988	March 1, 1988
a.	Yes	No
b.	Yes	Yes
c.	No	No
d.	No	Yes

2.   The December 31, 1984 condensed balance sheet of Dunn Services, an individual proprietorship, follows:

Current assets	$140,000
Equipment (net)	130,000
	$270,000
Liabilities	$ 70,000
John Dunn, Capital	200,000
	$270,000

Fair values at December 31, 1984 are as follows:

Current assets	$160,000
Equipment	210,000
Liabilities	70,000

On January 2, 1985, Dunn Services was incorporated, with 5,000 shares of $10 par value common stock issued. How much should be credited to additional paid-in capital?
   a. $320,000
   b. $250,000
   c. $230,000
   d. $200,000

3.   On July 1, 1986, Hart Corporation issued 1,000 shares of its $10 par common and 2,000 shares of its $10 par convertible preferred stock for a lump sum of $40,000. At this date Hart's common stock was selling for $18 per share and the convertible preferred stock for $13.50 per share. The amount of proceeds allocated to Hart's preferred stock should be
   a. $22,000
   b. $24,000
   c. $27,000
   d. $30,000

4.   During 1980 Bradley Corporation issued for $110 per share, 5,000 shares of $100 par value convertible preferred stock. One share of preferred stock can be converted into three shares of Bradley's $25 par value common stock

at the option of the preferred shareholder. On December 31, 1981, all of the preferred stock was converted into common stock. The market value of the common stock at the conversion date was $40 per share. What amount should be credited to the common stock account on December 31, 1981?
   a. $375,000
   b. $500,000
   c. $550,000
   d. $600,000

5.   The issuance of shares of preferred stock to shareholders
   a.   Increases preferred stock outstanding.
   b.   Has no effect on preferred stock outstanding.
   c.   Increases preferred stock authorized.
   d.   Decreases preferred stock authorized.

6.   On December 1, 1987, shares of authorized common stock were issued on a subscription basis at a price in excess of par value. A total of 20% of the subscription price of each share was collected as a down payment on December 1, 1987, with the remaining 80% of the subscription price of each share due in 1988. Collectibility was reasonably assured. At December 31, 1987, the stockholders' equity section of the balance sheet would report additional paid-in capital for the excess of the subscription price over the par value of the shares of common stock subscribed and
   a.   Common stock issued for 20% of the par value of the shares of common stock subscribed.
   b.   Common stock issued for the par value of the shares of common stock subscribed.
   c.   Common stock subscribed for 80% of the par value of the shares of common stock subscribed.
   d.   Common stock subscribed for the par value of the shares of common stock subscribed.

7.   When collectibility is reasonably assured, the excess of the subscription price over the stated value of the no par common stock subscribed should be recorded as
   a.   Additional paid-in capital when the common stock is issued.
   b.   Additional paid-in capital when the subscription is collected.
   c.   Additional paid-in capital when the subscription is recorded.
   d.   No par common stock.

8. In 1988, Newt Corp. acquired 6,000 shares of its own $1 par value common stock at $18 per share. In 1989, Newt issued 3,000 of these shares at $25 per share. Newt uses the cost method to account for its treasury stock transactions. What accounts and amounts should Newt credit in 1989 to record the issuance of the 3,000 shares?

	Treasury stock	Additional paid-in capital	Retained earnings	Common stock
a.	$54,000		$21,000	
b.	$54,000	$21,000		
c.		$72,000		$3,000
d.		$51,000	$21,000	$3,000

9. At December 31, 1987, Rama Corp. had 20,000 shares of $1 par value treasury stock that had been acquired in 1987 at $12 per share. In May 1988, Rama issued 15,000 of these treasury shares at $10 per share. The cost method is used to record treasury stock transactions. Rama is located in a state where laws relating to acquisition of treasury stock restrict the availability of retained earnings for declaration of dividends. At December 31, 1988, what amount should Rama show in notes to financial statements as a restriction of retained earnings as a result of its treasury stock transactions?
    a. $ 5,000
    b. $10,000
    c. $60,000
    d. $90,000

10. Victor Corporation was organized on January 2, 1982 with 100,000 authorized shares of $10 par value common stock. During 1982 Victor had the following capital transactions:

January 5--issued 75,000 shares at $14 per share.
December 27--purchased 5,000 shares at $11 per share.

Victor used the par value method to record the purchase of the treasury shares. What would be the balance in the paid-in capital from treasury stock account at December 31, 1982?
    a. $0
    b. $ 5,000
    c. $15,000
    d. $20,000

11. Treasury stock was acquired for cash at a price in excess of its par value. The treasury stock was subsequently reissued for cash at a price in excess of its acquisition price. Assuming that the cost method of accounting for treasury stock transactions is used, what is the effect of the subsequent reissuance of the treasury stock on each of the following?

	Additional paid-in capital	Retained earnings	Total stockholders' equity
a.	Decrease	Decrease	No effect
b.	Increase	Increase	Increase
c.	Increase	No effect	Increase
d.	No effect	No effect	No effect

12. Treasury stock was acquired for cash at a price in excess of its original issue price. The treasury stock was subsequently reissued for cash at a price in excess of its acquisition price. Assuming that the par value method of accounting for treasury stock transactions is used, what is the effect on total stockholders' equity?

	Acquisition of treasury stock	Reissuance of treasury stock
a.	No effect	No effect
b.	Increase	Decrease
c.	Decrease	No effect
d.	Decrease	Increase

13. The par-value method of accounting for treasury stock differs from the cost method in that
    a. Any gain is recognized upon repurchase of stock but a loss is treated as an adjustment to retained earnings.
    b. No gains or losses are recognized on the issuance of treasury stock using the par-value method.
    c. It reverses the original entry to issue the common stock with any difference between carrying value and purchase price adjusted through paid-in capital and/or retained earnings and treats a subsequent reissuance like a new issuance of common stock.
    d. It reverses the original entry to issue the common stock with any difference between carrying value and purchase price being shown as an ordinary gain or loss and does not recognize any gain or loss on a subsequent resale of the stock.

14. In 1980, Rona Corp. issued 5,000 shares of $10 par value common stock for $100 per share. In 1988, Rona reacquired 2,000 of its shares at $150 per share from the estate of one of its deceased officers and immediately canceled these 2,000 shares. Rona uses the cost method in accounting for its treasury stock transactions. In connection with the retirement of these 2,000 shares, Rona should debit

	Additional paid-in capital	Retained earnings
a.	$ 20,000	$280,000
b.	$100,000	$180,000
c.	$180,000	$100,000
d.	$280,000	$0

15. Bain Corp. owned 20,000 common shares of Tell Corp. purchased in 1983 for $180,000. On December 15, 1987, Bain declared a property dividend of all of its Tell Corp. shares on the basis of one share of Tell for every 10 shares of Bain common stock held by its stockholders. The property dividend was distributed on January 15, 1988. On the declaration date, the aggregate market price of the Tell shares held by Bain was $300,000. The entry to record the declaration of the dividend would include a debit to retained earnings (or property dividends declared) of

     a. $0
     b. $120,000
     c. $180,000
     d. $300,000

16. At December 31, 1987 and 1988, Tri Corp. had outstanding 2,000 shares of $100 par value 6% cumulative preferred stock and 10,000 shares of $10 par value common stock. At December 31, 1987, dividends in arrears on the preferred stock were $6,000. Cash dividends declared in 1988 totaled $22,000. What amounts were payable on each class of stock?

	Preferred stock	Common stock
a.	$12,000	$10,000
b.	$16,000	$ 6,000
c.	$18,000	$ 4,000
d.	$22,000	$0

17. On May 1, 1989, Rhud Corp. declared and issued a 10% common stock dividend. Prior to this dividend, Rhud had 100,000 shares of $1 par value common stock issued and outstanding. The fair value of Rhud's common stock was $30 per share on May 1, 1989. As a result of this stock dividend, Rhud's total stockholders' equity

     a.   Increased by $300,000.
     b.   Decreased by $300,000.
     c.   Decreased by $10,000.
     d.   Did not change.

18. On December 31, 1984, the stockholders' equity section of Bergen, Inc., was as follows:

Common stock, par value $10; authorized 30,000 shares; issued and outstanding 9,000 shares	$ 90,000
Additional paid-in capital	116,000
Retained earnings	146,000
Total stockholders' equity	$352,000

On March 31, 1985, Bergen declared a 10% stock dividend, and accordingly 900 additional shares were issued, when the fair market value of the stock was $16 per share. For the three months ended March 31, 1985, Bergen sustained a net loss of $32,000. The balance of Bergen's retained earnings as of March 31, 1985 should be

     a. $ 99,600
     b. $105,000
     c. $108,600
     d. $114,000

19. An investment in marketable securities was accounted for by the cost method. These securities were distributed to stockholders as a property dividend in a nonreciprocal transfer. The dividend should be reported at the

     a.   Fair value of the asset transferred or the recorded amount of the asset transferred, whichever is higher.
     b.   Fair value of the asset transferred or the recorded amount of the asset transferred, whichever is lower.
     c.   Fair value of the asset transferred.
     d.   Recorded amount of the asset transferred.

20. A corporation declared a dividend, a portion of which was liquidating. How would this declaration affect each of the following?

	Additional paid-in capital	Retained earnings
a.	Decrease	No effect
b.	Decrease	Decrease
c.	No effect	Decrease
d.	No effect	No effect

21. The actual total amount of a cash dividend to be paid is determined on the date of
     a.   Record.
     b.   Declaration.
     c.   Declaration or date of record, whichever is earlier.
     d.   Payment.

22. How would total stockholders' equity be affected by the declaration of each of the following?

	Stock dividend	Stock split
a.	No effect	Increase
b.	Decrease	Decrease
c.	Decrease	No effect
d.	No effect	No effect

23. How would the declaration and subsequent issuance of a 10% stock dividend by the issuer affect each of the following when the market value of the shares exceeds the par value of the stock?

	Common stock	Additional paid-in capital
a.	No effect	No effect
b.	No effect	Increase
c.	Increase	No effect
d.	Increase	Increase

24. On July 1, 1986, Bart Corporation has 200,000 shares of $10 par common stock outstanding and the market price of the stock is $12 per share. On the same date, Bart declared a 1-for-2 reverse stock split. The par of the stock was increased from $10 to $20 and one new $20 par share was issued for each two $10 par shares outstanding. Immediately before the 1-for-2 reverse stock split, Bart's additional paid-in capital was $450,000. What should be the balance in Bart's additional paid-in capital account immediately after the reverse stock split is effected?
   a. $0
   b. $450,000
   c. $650,000
   d. $850,000

25. On July 1, 1988, Alto Corp. split its common stock 5 for 1 when the market value was $100 per share. Prior to the split, Alto had 10,000 shares of $10 par value common stock issued and outstanding. After the split, the par value of the stock
   a. Remained at $10.
   b. Was reduced to $8.
   c. Was reduced to $5.
   d. Was reduced to $2.

26. How would a stock split in which the par value per share decreases in proportion to the number of additional shares issued affect each of the following?

	Additional paid-in capital	Retained earnings
a.	Increase	No effect
b.	No effect	No effect
c.	No effect	Decrease
d.	Increase	Decrease

27. On January 1, 1987, Ward Corp. granted stock options to corporate executives for the purchase of 20,000 shares of the company's $20 par value common stock at 80% of the market price on the exercise date, December 28, 1987. All stock options were exercised on December 28, 1987. The quoted market prices of Ward's $20 par value common stock were as follows:

   January 1, 1987 $45
   December 28, 1987   60

As a result of the exercise of the stock options and the issuance of the common stock, Ward should record a credit to additional paid-in capital of
   a. $800,000
   b. $740,000
   c. $560,000
   d. $500,000

28. On January 1, 1987, Doro Corp. granted an employee an option to purchase 3,000 shares of Doro's $5 par value common stock at $20 per share. The option became exercisable on December 31, 1988, after the employee completed two years of service. The option was exercised on January 10, 1989. The market prices of Doro's stock were as follows:

   January 1, 1987 $30
   December 31, 1988   50
   January 10, 1989   45

For 1988, Doro should recognize compensation expense of
   a. $45,000
   b. $37,500
   c. $15,000
   d. $0

29. For a compensatory stock option plan for which the date of grant and the measurement date are different, the stock options outstanding account should be reduced at the
   a. Adoption date of the plan.
   b. Date of grant.
   c. Measurement date.
   d. Exercise date.

30. Compensatory stock options were granted to executives on January 1, 1983, with a measurement date of June 30, 1984, for services to be rendered during 1983, 1984, and 1985. The excess of the market value of the stock over the option price at the measurement date was reasonably estimable at the date of grant. The stock options were exercised on April 30, 1985. Compensation expense should be recognized in the income statement in which of the following years?

	1983	1984	1985
a.	No	No	Yes
b.	No	Yes	Yes
c.	Yes	Yes	Yes
d.	Yes	No	No

31. On January 2, 1986, for past services, Day Corp. granted Jan Bell, its president, 10,000 stock appreciation rights that are exercisable immediately and expire on January 2, 1989. On exercise, Bell is entitled to receive cash for the excess of the market price of the stock on the exercise date over

the market price on the grant date. Bell did not exercise any of the rights during 1986. The market price of Day's stock was $30 on January 2, 1986, and $45 on December 31, 1986. As a result of the stock appreciation rights, Day should recognize compensation expense for 1986 of

    a. $0
    b. $ 50,000
    c. $150,000
    d. $300,000

32. On December 31, 1984, Case, Inc. had 300,000 shares of common stock issued and outstanding. Case issued a 10% stock dividend on July 1, 1985. On October 1, 1985, Case purchased 24,000 shares of its common stock for treasury, and recorded the purchase by the cost method. What is the number of shares that should be used in computing earnings per share for the year ended December 31, 1985?

    a.   306,000
    b.   309,000
    c.   324,000
    d.   330,000

33. Seco Corp. was incorporated on January 2, 1988. The following information pertains to Seco's common stock transactions:

1988

January 2	Number of shares authorized	80,000
February 1	Number of shares issued	60,000
July 1	Number of shares reacquired but **not** canceled	5,000
December 1	Two-for-one stock split	

At December 31, 1988, the number of shares of Seco's common stock outstanding is

    a.   150,000
    b.   120,000
    c.   115,000
    d.   110,000

34. At December 31, 1985 and 1984, Gow Corp. had 100,000 shares of common stock and 10,000 shares of 5%, $100 par value cumulative preferred stock outstanding. No dividends were declared on either the preferred or common stock in 1985 or 1984. Net income for 1985 was $1,000,000. For 1985, earnings per common share amounted to

    a. $10.00
    b. $ 9.50
    c. $ 9.00
    d. $ 5.00

35. Earnings per share data should be reported on the face of the income statement for

	Income before extraordinary items	Cumulative effect of a change in accounting principle
a.	Yes	Yes
b.	Yes	No
c.	No	No
d.	No	Yes

36. Jones Corp.'s capital structure was as follows:

	December 31	
	1988	1987
Outstanding shares of stock:		
Common	110,000	110,000
Convertible preferred	10,000	10,000
8% convertible bonds	$1,000,000	$1,000,000

During 1988, Jones paid dividends of $3.00 per share on its preferred stock. The preferred shares are convertible into 20,000 shares of common stock and are considered common stock equivalents. The 8% bonds are convertible into 30,000 shares of common stock but are not considered common stock equivalents. Net income for 1988 is $850,000. Assume that the income tax rate is 30%.

The fully diluted earnings per share for 1988 is

    a. $5.48
    b. $5.66
    c. $5.81
    d. $6.26

37. Mann, Inc. had 300,000 shares of common stock issued and outstanding at December 31, 1983. On July 1, 1984, an additional 50,000 shares of common stock were issued for cash. Mann also had unexercised stock options to purchase 40,000 shares of common stock at $15 per share outstanding at the beginning and end of 1984. The average market price of Mann's common stock was $20 during 1984. What is the number of shares that should be used in computing primary earnings per share for the year ended December 31, 1984?

    a.   325,000
    b.   335,000
    c.   360,000
    d.   365,000

38. Cox Corporation had 1,200,000 shares of common stock outstanding on January 1 and December 31, 1983. In connection with the acquisition of a subsidiary company in June 1982, Cox is required to issue 50,000 additional shares of its common stock on July 1, 1984, to the former owners of the subsidiary. Cox paid $200,000 in preferred stock dividends in 1983, and reported net income of $3,400,000 for the year. Cox's fully diluted earnings per share for 1983 should be

a. $2.83
b. $2.72
c. $2.67
d. $2.56

39.   Newt Corp. had earnings per share of
$12.00 for 1985, before taking any dilutive
securities into consideration. No conversion
or exercise of dilutive securities took place
in 1985. However, possible conversion of convertible preferred stock, a common stock equivalent, would have reduced earnings per share
to $11.90. The effect of possible exercise of
common stock warrants would have reduced
earnings per share by an additional $0.05.
For 1985, what is the maximum amount that Newt
may report as a single presentation of
earnings per share?
      a. $12.00
      b. $11.95
      c. $11.90
      d. $11.85

40.   Dilutive stock options would generally be
used in the calculation of

	Primary earnings per share	Fully diluted earnings per share
a.	No	No
b.	No	Yes
c.	Yes	Yes
d.	Yes	No

41.   The if-converted method of computing
earnings per share data assumes conversion of
convertible securities as of the
      a.   Beginning of the earliest period
           reported (or at time of issuance,
           if later).
      b.   Beginning of the earliest period
           reported (regardless of time of
           issuance).
      c.   Middle of the earliest period
           reported (regardless of time of
           issuance).
      d.   Ending of the earliest period
           reported (regardless of time of
           issuance).

42.   In computing earnings per share, a method
of recognizing the use of proceeds that would
be obtained upon exercise of options and warrants is the
      a.   Antidilution method.
      b.   Common stock equivalents method.
      c.   Treasury stock method.
      d.   If-converted method.

43.   Antidilutive stock options would generally be used in the calculation of

	Primary earnings per share	Fully diluted earnings per share
a.	Yes	Yes
b.	Yes	No
c.	No	No
d.	No	Yes

44.   A company's convertible debt is both a
common stock equivalent and dilutive in
determining earnings per share. What would be
the effect of consideration of the convertible
debt in calculating

	Primary earnings per share	Fully diluted earnings per share
a.	Decrease	Decrease
b.	Increase	No effect
c.	No effect	Decrease
d.	Decrease	Increase

45.   In determining primary earnings per
share, dividends on nonconvertible cumulative
preferred stock should be
      a.   Disregarded.
      b.   Added back to net income whether
           declared or not.
      c.   Deducted from net income only if
           declared.
      d.   Deducted from net income whether
           declared or not.

46.   Barb Co. has been forced into bankruptcy
and liquidated. Unsecured claims will be paid
at the rate of 50¢ on the dollar. Yola Co.
holds a noninterest-bearing note receivable
from Barb in the amount of $25,000, collatera-
lized by equipment with a liquidation value of
$5,000. The total amount to be realized by
Yola on this note receivable is
      a. $ 5,000
      b. $12,500
      c. $15,000
      d. $17,500

47.   Decker Company filed a voluntary bankruptcy petition on August 15, 1984, and the
statement of affairs reflects the following
amounts:

	Book carrying amount	Estimated current value
Assets:		
Assets pledged with fully secured creditors	$150,000	$185,000
Assets pledged with partially secured creditors	90,000	60,000
Free assets	210,000	160,000
	$450,000	$405,000

Liabilities:

Liabilities with priority	$35,000
Fully secured creditors	130,000
Partially secured creditors	100,000
Unsecured creditors	270,000
	$535,000

Assume that the assets are converted into cash at the estimated current value and the business is liquidated. How much cash will be available to pay unsecured nonpriority claims?

a. $240,000
b. $180,000
c. $160,000
d. $125,000

48. A corporation issued rights to its existing stockholders to purchase unissued shares of $10 par value common stock for $25 per share. The rights were issued for no consideration. Additional paid-in capital will be credited when the rights are

	Issued	Exercised
a.	No	Yes
b.	No	No
c.	Yes	No
d.	Yes	Yes

49. A company issued rights to its existing shareholders to purchase, for $30 per share, unissued shares of $15 par value common stock. Additional paid-in capital will be credited when the

	Rights are issued	Rights lapse
a.	Yes	No
b.	No	No
c.	No	Yes
d.	Yes	Yes

Items 50 and 51 are based on the following data:

On January 1, 1986, Fay Corporation established an employee stock ownership plan (ESOP). Selected transactions relating to the ESOP during 1986 were as follows:

• On April 1, 1986, Fay contributed $30,000 cash and 3,000 shares of its $10 par common stock to the ESOP. On this date the market price of the stock was $18 a share.

• On October 1, 1986, the ESOP borrowed $100,000 from Union National Bank and acquired 5,000 shares of Fay's common stock in the open market at $17 a share. The note is for one year, bears interest at 10%, and is guaranteed by Fay.

• On December 15, 1986, the ESOP distributed 6,000 shares of Fay common stock to employees of Fay in accordance with the plan formula.

50. In its 1986 income statement, how much should Fay report as compensation expense relating to the ESOP?

a. $184,000
b. $120,000
c. $ 84,000
d. $ 60,000

51. In Fay's December 31, 1986 balance sheet, how much should be reported as a reduction of shareholders' equity and as an endorsed note payable in respect of the ESOP?

	Reduction of shareholders' equity	Endorsed note payable
a.	$0	$0
b.	$0	$100,000
c.	$100,000	$0
d.	$100,000	$100,000

52. Munn Corp.'s records included the following stockholders' equity accounts:

Preferred stock, par value $15, authorized 20,000 shares	$255,000
Additional paid-in capital, preferred stock	15,000
Common stock, no par, $5 stated value, 100,000 shares authorized	300,000

In Munn's statement of stockholders' equity, the number of issued and outstanding shares for each class of stock is

	Common stock	Preferred stock
a.	60,000	17,000
b.	60,000	18,000
c.	63,000	17,000
d.	63,000	18,000

53. Magnolia, Inc.'s December 31, 1988 unadjusted current assets section and stockholders' equity section are as follows:

Current Assets:

Cash	$ 30,000
Investments in marketable equity securities (including $150,000 of Magnolia, Inc. common stock)	200,000
Trade accounts receivable	170,000
Inventories	74,000
Total	$ 474,000

Stockholders' Equity:

Common Stock	$1,112,000
Retained earnings (deficit)	(112,000)
Total	$1,000,000

The investments and inventories are reported at their costs which approximate market values.

In its 1988 statement of changes in stockholders' equity, Magnolia's total amount of equity at December 31, 1988 is

- a. $ 850,000
- b. $ 962,000
- c. $1,000,000
- d. $1,112,000

May 1990 Questions

54. Peters Corp.'s capital structure was as follows:

	December 31	
	1988	1989
Outstanding shares of stock:		
Common	110,000	110,000
Convertible preferred	10,000	10,000
8% convertible bonds	$1,000,000	$1,000,000

During 1989, Peters paid dividends of $3.00 per share on its preferred stock. The preferred shares are convertible into 20,000 shares of common stock and are considered common stock equivalents. The 8% bonds are convertible into 30,000 shares of common stock but are not considered common stock equivalents. Net income for 1989 was $850,000. Assume that the income tax rate is 30%. The primary earnings per share for 1989 is

- a. $6.31
- b. $6.54
- c. $7.08
- d. $7.45

55. The acquisition of treasury stock will cause the number of shares outstanding to decrease if the treasury stock is accounted for by the

	Cost method	Par value method
a.	Yes	No
b.	No	No
c.	Yes	Yes
d	No	Yes

56. Pott Co. owned shares in Rose Co. On December 1, 1989, Pott declared and distributed a property dividend of Rose shares when their fair value exceeded the carrying amount. As a consequence of the dividend declaration and distribution, the accounting effects would be

	Property dividends recorded at	Retained earnings
a.	Fair value	Decreased
b.	Fair value	Increased
c.	Cost	Increased
d.	Cost	Decreased

57. Blue Co. issued preferred stock with detachable common stock warrants at a price which exceeded both the par value and the market value of the preferred stock. At the time the warrants are exercised, Blue's total stockholders' equity is increased by the

	Cash received upon exercise of the warrants	Carrying amount of warrants
a.	Yes	No
b.	Yes	Yes
c.	No	No
d.	No	Yes

Repeat Questions

(590,P3,55) Identical/similar to item 31 above
(590,T1,15) Identical/similar to item 12 above
(590,T1,29) Identical/similar to item 43 above

Problems

Problem 1   (1185,T5)

(15 to 25 minutes)

Brady Company has 30,000 shares of $10 par value common stock authorized and 20,000 shares issued and outstanding. On August 15, 1986, Brady purchased 1,000 shares of treasury stock for $12 per share. Brady uses the cost method to account for treasury stock. On September 14, 1986, Brady sold 500 shares of the treasury stock for $14 per share.

In October 1986, Brady declared and distributed 2,000 shares as a stock dividend from unissued shares when the market value of the common stock was $16 per share.

On December 20, 1986, Brady declared $1 per share cash dividend, payable on January 10, 1987, to shareholders of record on December 31, 1986.

Required:

a. How should Brady account for the purchase and sale of the treasury stock, and how should the treasury stock be presented in Brady's balance sheet at December 31, 1986?

b. How should Brady account for the stock dividend, and how would it affect Brady's stockholders' equity at December 31, 1986? Why?

c. How should Brady account for the cash dividend, and how would it affect Brady's balance sheet at December 31, 1986? Why?

Problem 2   (1186,T5)

(15 to 25 minutes)

Wesley Company granted compensatory common stock options to its executives on January 1, 1983, the measurement date, for services to be rendered during 1983 and 1984. The quoted market price of Wesley's par value common stock exceeded the option price on January 1, 1983.

The stock options were exercisable beginning on January 1, 1985, and they lapsed on December 31, 1985. Half of the stock options were exercised in 1985 and half were allowed to lapse.

Required:

a. How should Wesley determine the amount of compensation expense related to the compensatory stock options, if any, that should be recognized in its income statements for 1983, 1984, and 1985? Why?

b. How should Wesley account for the exercise of the stock options? Justify the accounting recommended.

c. How should Wesley account for the lapse of the stock options? Justify the accounting recommended.

Problem 3   (586,P4)

(45 to 55 minutes)

Carr Corporation had the following stockholders' equity account balances at December 31, 1984:

Preferred stock	$1,800,000
Additional paid-in capital from preferred stock	90,000
Common stock	5,150,000
Additional paid-in capital from common stock	3,500,000
Retained earnings	4,000,000
Net unrealized loss on noncurrent marketable equity securities	245,000
Treasury common stock	270,000

Transactions during 1985 and other information relating to the stockholders' equity accounts were as follows:

• Carr's preferred and common shares are traded on the over-the-counter market. At December 31, 1984, Carr had 100,000 authorized shares of $100 par, 10% cumulative preferred stock; and 3,000,000 authorized shares of no par common stock with a stated value of $5 per share.

• On January 10, 1985, Carr formally retired all 30,000 shares of its treasury common stock and had them revert to an unissued basis. The treasury stock had been acquired on January 20, 1984. The shares were originally issued at $10 per share.

• Carr owned 10,000 shares of Bush, Inc. common stock purchased in 1982 for $750,000. The Bush stock was included in Carr's short-term marketable securities portfolio. On February 15, 1985, Carr declared a dividend in kind of one share of Bush for every hundred shares of Carr common stock held by a stockholder of record on February 28, 1985. The market price of Bush common stock was $63 per share on February 15, 1985. The dividend in kind was distributed on March 12, 1985.

• On April 1, 1985, 250,000 stock rights were issued to the common stockholders permitting the purchase of one new share of common stock in exchange for one right and $11 cash. On April 25, 1985, 210,000 stock rights were exercised when the market price of Carr's common stock was $13 per share. Carr issued new shares to settle the transaction. The remaining 40,000 rights were not exercised and expired.

• On January 1, 1982, Carr granted stock options to employees for the purchase of 100,000 shares of the company's common stock at $8 per share which was also the market price. The options are exercisable within a three-year period beginning January 1, 1984. The measurement date is the same as the grant date. On July 1, 1985, employees exercised 80,000 options for $8 per share. On July 1, 1985, the market price of Carr's common stock was $15 per share. Carr used new shares to settle the transaction.

• On December 12, 1985, Carr declared the yearly cash dividend on preferred stock, payable on January 14, 1986, to stockholders of record on December 31, 1985.

• After year-end adjustment the Net Unrealized Loss on Noncurrent Marketable Equity Securities account had a debit balance of $135,000 at December 31, 1985.

• On January 15, 1986, before the accounting records were closed for 1985, Carr became aware that rent income for the year ended December 31, 1984, was overstated by $500,000. The after tax effect on 1984 net income was $275,000. The appropriate correcting entry was recorded the same day.

• After correcting the rent income, net income for 1985 was $2,600,000.

Required:

a. Prepare Carr's statement of retained earnings for the year ended December 31, 1985. Assume that only single-period financial statements for 1985 are presented.

b. Prepare the stockholders' equity section of Carr's balance sheet at December 31, 1985.

Problem 4   (588,P4)

(45 to 55 minutes)

Fay, Inc. finances its capital needs approximately one third from long-term debt and two-thirds from equity. At December 31, 1986, Fay had the following liability and equity account balances:

11% Debenture bonds payable,	
face amount	$5,000,000
Premium on bonds payable	352,400
Common stock	8,000,000
Additional paid-in capital	2,295,000
Retained earnings	2,465,000
Treasury stock, at cost	325,000

Transactions during 1987 and other information relating to Fay's liabilities and equity accounts were as follows:

• The debenture bonds were issued on December 31, 1984, for $5,378,000 to yield 10%. The bonds mature on December 31, 1999. Interest is payable annually on December 31. Fay uses the interest method to amortize bond premium.

• Fay's common stock shares are traded on the over-the-counter market. At December 31, 1986, Fay had 2,000,000 authorized shares of $10 par common stock.

• On January 15, 1987, Fay reissued 15,000 of its 25,000 shares of treasury stock for $225,000. The treasury stock had been acquired on February 28, 1986.

• On March 2, 1987, Fay issued a 5% stock dividend on all issued shares. The market price of Fay's common stock at time of issuance was $14 per share.

• On November 1, 1987, Fay borrowed $4,000,000 at 9%, evidenced by an unsecured note payable to United Bank. The note is payable in five equal annual principal installments of $800,000. The first principal and interest payment is due on November 1, 1988.

• On December 31, 1987, Fay owned 10,000 shares of Ryan Corp.'s common stock, which represented a 1% ownership interest. Fay accounts for this marketable equity investment as a long-term investment. The stock was purchased on May 1, 1986, at $20 per share. The market price was $21 per share on December 31, 1986, and $18 per share on December 31, 1987.

• Fay's net income for 1987 was $2,860,000.

Required:

(Include formal schedules of supporting computations with each item referenced to correspond with the items in the solution):

a. Prepare the long-term liabilities section of Fay's December 31, 1987 balance sheet, including all disclosures applicable to each obligation.

b. Prepare the stockholders' equity section of Fay's December 31, 1987 balance sheet.

c. Prepare a schedule showing interest expense for the year ended December 31, 1987.

Multiple Choice Answers

1. d	13. c	25. d	36. b	47. b
2. b	14. c	26. b	37. b	48. a
3. b	15. d	27. a	38. d	49. b
4. a	16. c	28. c	39. a	50. c
5. a	17. d	29. d	40. c	51. d
6. d	18. a	30. c	41. a	52. a
7. c	19. c	31. c	42. c	53. a
8. b	20. b	32. c	43. c	54. b
9. c	21. a	33. d	44. a	55. c
10. c	22. d	34. b	45. d	56. a
11. c	23. d	35. a	46. c	57. a
12. d	24. b			

Multiple Choice Answer Explanations

A. Common Stock

1. (1189,T1,20) (d) On February 1, 1988, when shares were issued at par for cash, the following journal entry would have been made:

```
Cash                 (cash received)
    Common Stock                     (par)
```

On March 1, 1988, however, the issuance of 5,000 shares in settlement for legal services rendered would have been recorded as follows:

```
Legal Fees                          60,000
    Common Stock ($10 x 5,000 shares)        50,000
    Add'l. Paid-in Capital                   10,000
```

Per APB 29, para 18, stock issued for services (i.e., in a nonmonetary transaction) should be recorded at the fair market value of those services (in this case $60,000). Therefore, answer (d) is correct.

2. (585,P2,21) (b) The requirement is to determine the amount that should be credited to additional paid-in capital as a result of the incorporation of an individual proprietorship. The basis for determining the value of the stock is the fair value of the net assets contributed to the corporation:

Current assets	$160,000
Equipment (net)	210,000
Liabilities	(70,000)
Fair value of net assets	$300,000

The par value of the stock issued is $50,000 (5,000 x $10). Thus, additional paid-in capital is credited for $250,000 ($300,000 − $50,000).

B. Preferred Stock

3. (1186,P2,25) (b) In a lump sum issuance of common and preferred stock, the proceeds ($40,000) are generally allocated based on the relative fair market values of the securities issued. The FMV of the preferred stock is $27,000 (2,000 x $13.50) and the FMV of the

common stock is $18,000 (1,000 x $18). The proceeds are allocated as follows:

Preferred $\dfrac{\$27,000}{\$45,000}$ x $40,000 = $24,000

Common $\dfrac{\$18,000}{\$45,000}$ x $40,000 = $16,000

4. (1182,P1,4) (a) The requirement is the amount to be credited to the common stock account as a result of the conversion of preferred stock. All 5,000 shares of the convertible preferred stock were converted to common stock at the rate of 3 shares of common for every share of preferred. Therefore, 15,000 shares of common stock were issued (5,000 x 3). The common stock account is credited for the par value of these shares: 15,000 x $25 or $375,000. Although not necessary, the journal entry to record the conversion can be prepared:

```
Preferred stock        500,000         5,000 x $100
Paid-in capital, PS  50,000         5,000 x $ 10
    Common stock               375,000 15,000 x $ 25
    Paid-in capital, CS       175,000     plugged in
```

Note that the $40 market value of the common stock is ignored. Gains and/or losses are not recognized on the conversion of preferred stock. The book value method is used and the paid-in capital, common stock account is credited for the amount necessary to balance the entry.

5. (1186,T1,20) (a) The amount of preferred stock authorized is established by the corporate charter; it is the maximum number of shares that the corporation may issue. The amount of preferred stock outstanding is the actual number of shares that have been issued and are held by stockholders. Thus, while issuances increase the number of shares outstanding, they have no effect on the number of shares authorized. Therefore, answer (a) is correct, and answers (b), (c), and (d) are incorrect.

C. Stock Subscriptions

6. (1188,T1,17) (d) When stock is sold on a subscription basis, the full price of the stock is not received initially, and the stock is not issued until the full subscription price is received. On the subscription contract date of December 1, 1987, the journal entry would be:

```
Cash                    (amount received)
Subscriptions receivable    (balance due)
    Common stock subscribed         (par)
    Additional paid-in capital      (plug)
```

Thus, answer (d) is correct, and answers (a), (b), and (c) are incorrect.

7. (588,T1,18) (c) When no par common stock is sold on a subscription basis at a price above the stock's stated value, the stock is not issued until the full subscription price is received. The journal entry on the subscription contract date would be:

Cash   (amount received-if any)
Subscription Receivable   (balance due)
  Common Stock Subscribed   (stated value)
  Additional Paid-in Capital   (plug)

The journal entry on the date the balance of the subscription is collected and the common stock is issued would be:

Cash   (balance due)
Common Stock Subscribed   (stated value)
  Common Stock   (stated value)
  Subscription Receivable   (balance due)

Thus, the additional paid-in capital account would increase on the date that the stock is <u>subscribed</u>, and answers (a), (b), and (d) are incorrect.

D. Treasury Stock Transactions

8.   (589,Q1,4) (b) When treasury stock is acquired by an entity using the cost method, the treasury stock account is debited for the full acquisition cost:

Treasury stock
  (6,000 x $18)   108,000
  Cash   108,000

Note that retained earnings is not affected by this entry. When the shares are later re-issued for an amount <u>greater</u> than cost, as in this case, the excess is credited to paid-in capital:

Cash (3,000 x $25)   75,000
  Treasury stock
    ($3,000 x $18)   54,000
  APIC--Treas. stock   21,000

Retained earnings is not affected by this entry, and would <u>never</u> be <u>credited</u> upon reissuance of treasury stock under either the cost <u>or</u> the par value method. Note, however, that had the shares been reissued for an amount <u>less than</u> cost, APIC--Treasury stock would be debited for the difference, but only to the extent that a credit balance already exists in the account. If the balance in APIC--Treasury stock is not sufficient, retained earnings would be debited to make up any difference.

9.   (589,Q1,6) (c) The entry that Rama made on acquisition of treasury stock was as follows using the <u>cost method</u>:

Treasury stock
  (20,000 x $12)   240,000
  Cash   240,000

When some of the shares are later reissued, the entry is:

Cash (15,000 x $10)   150,000
Retained earnings   30,000
  Treasury stock
    (15,000 x$12)   180,000

It is assumed there was no balance in APIC--Treasury stock prior to this entry. If the problem had stated there was a credit balance, APIC--Treasury stock would be debited before retained earnings to the extent a credit balance existed in APIC--Treasury stock. SFAS 5 requires disclosure when retained earnings are legally restricted. In this case, the net treasury stock account balance is $60,000 ($240,000 - $180,000), and this is the amount of retained earnings that must be disclosed as legally restricted.

10. (583,P1,15) (c) The requirement is the balance in the paid-in capital from treasury stock account at 12/31/82. Using the par value method, treasury stock is debited for par value (5,000 x $10, or $50,000) when purchased. Any excess over par from the original issuance (5,000 x $4, or $20,000) is removed from the appropriate paid-in capital account. In effect, the total original issuance price (5,000 x $14, or $70,000) is charged to the two accounts. Any difference between the original issuance price ($70,000) and the cost of the treasury stock (5,000 x $11, or $55,000) is credited to paid-in capital from treasury stock, as illustrated below.

Treasury stock   50,000   (5,000 x $10)
APIC   20,000   (5,000 x $ 4)
  Cash   55,000 (5,000 x $11)
  PIC-Treasury Stock   15,000   ($70,000 -
                                    $55,000)

11. (1188,T1,19) (c) When treasury stock is acquired by an entity using the cost method, the journal entry would be:

Treasury stock (acquisition price)
  Cash   (acquisition price)

When the treasury stock is subsequently reissued for cash in excess of its acquisition price, the journal entry would be:

Cash   (amount received)
  Treasury stock   (acquisition price)
  Additional paid-in capital   (plug)

These entries increase both additional paid-in capital and total stockholders' equity but have no effect on retained earnings. Therefore, answer (c) is correct, and answers (a), (b), and (d) are incorrect.

12. (588,T1,20) (d) Under the par value method of accounting for treasury stock, when treasury stock is acquired for cash at a price in excess of its original issue price, the journal entry would be:

```
Treasury stock                    (par)
APIC              (issue price over par)
Retained Earnings                 (plug)
  Cash                        (cash paid)
```

When the treasury stock is subsequently reissued for cash in excess of the acquisition price, the journal entry would be:

```
Cash               (amount received)
  Treasury stock                  (par)
  Additional paid-in capital     (plug)
```

Thus, total stockholders' equity is <u>decreased</u> when treasury stock is acquired and is <u>increased</u> when the treasury stock is subsequently reissued, and answer (d) is correct.

13. (589,T1,10) (c) Per APB 9, para 28, adjustments, charges, or credits resulting from transactions in a company's own capital stock <u>cannot</u> be included in determination of net income (i.e., gains/losses cannot be recognized). Therefore, answers (a) and (d) are incorrect. Answer (b) is incorrect because although no gains or losses are recognized using the par-value method, this is also true of the cost method--the question asks for the <u>difference</u> between the methods. Answer (c) is correct because upon repurchase of treasury shares under the par method, the original entry is reversed (treasury stock and additional paid-in capital are debited for the average issue price), while the cost method debits treasury stock for the entire reacquisition cost.

Upon reissuance, the par method treats the transaction as if it were an original issuance, while the cost method adjusts any difference between cash proceeds and treasury stock as a debit to PIC-treasury stock (or retained earnings) or as a credit to additional paid-in capital.

E. Retirement of Stock

14. (1189,Q1,12) (c) When accounting for the retirement of stock, common stock and additional paid-in-capital are removed from the books based on the original issuance of the stock. Cash is credited for the cost of the shares. Any difference is debited to <u>retained earnings</u> or credited to <u>paid-in-capital from retirement</u>. The entry in this case is:

```
Common Stock      20,000 (2,000 x $10)
APIC             180,000 (2,000 x $90)
Retained Earnings 100,000 (2,000 x $50)
  Cash                           300,000
```

Therefore, APIC should be debited for $180,000 and retained earnings should be debited for $100,000.

F. Dividends

15. (1188,P3,60) (d) Per APB 29, property dividends are recorded at the FMV of the asset transferred, with a gain (loss) recognized for the difference between the asset's FMV and BV at the time of declaration. In this case, a gain of $120,000 is recognized ($300,000 FMV - $180,000 BV).

```
Investment in stock      120,000
  Gain on appreciation           120,000
```

The dividend is then recorded at FMV ($300,000).

```
Retained earnings        300,000
  Property divs. declared        300,000
Property divs. declared  300,000
  Investment in stock            300,000
```

Therefore, the debit to retained earnings is $300,000.

16. (1189,Q1,14) (c) When a company declares a cash dividend, it must pay its preferred stockholders, including dividends in arrears, before its common stockholders. At 12/31/87, there were dividends in arrears on preferred stock of $6,000. For 1988, preferred stockholders are entitled to a cash dividend of $12,000 (2,000 shares x $100 par x 6%). Therefore, preferred stockholders will receive a total cash dividend of $18,000 ($6,000 + $12,000). The remaining $4,000 ($22,000 - $18,000) is payable to common stockholders. Thus, answer (c) is correct.

17. (589,Q1,3) (d) A stock dividend has <u>no effect</u> on total stockholders' equity. No assets are transferred to stockholders as in the case of a cash or property dividend. Stockholders merely receive more shares of stock. The journal entry to record a small stock dividend (less than 20-25%) transfers an amount equal to the fair market value of the stock to be issued from retained earnings to paid-in capital. Therefore, one part of stockholders' equity decreases while another part increases. The journal entry below summarizes the net effect of the entries to record a stock dividend.

```
Retained earnings (10,000 x $30) 300,000
  Common stock (10,000 x $1)            10,000
  Paid-in capital                      290,000
```

18. (585,P1,18) (a) The requirement is to determine the 3/31/85 balance of retained earnings. The 12/31/84 retained earnings balance of $146,000 must be decreased for both

the stock dividend and the net loss of
$32,000. 900 shares (9,000 x 10%) were issued
for the stock dividend. For a small stock
dividend (less than 20%-25% of the number of
shares), the charge to retained earnings is
the FMV of the shares to be issued. Therefore, retained earnings is decreased by
$14,400 (900 x $16) as a result of the stock
dividend. The 3/31/85 balance of retained
earnings is $99,600 ($146,000 - $32,000 -
$14,400).

19. (1189,T1,34) (c) Per APB 29, para 18, a
transfer of a nonmonetary asset to a stockholder or to another entity in a nonreciprocal
transfer should be recorded at the fair market
value of the asset transferred. The declaration date is the date that a dividend becomes
a liability of the corporation and thus is the
date to measure and record the dividend.
Therefore, answer (c) is correct. Note that a
gain or loss is recognized for the difference
between the recorded amount (i.e., book value)
and market value of the asset transferred.
Therefore, regardless of the method used to
account for the investments in this problem,
the recorded amount of the asset transferred
would not be used to value the transaction,
and answers (a), (b), and (d) are incorrect.

20. (1189,T1,21) (b) When a corporation
declares a liquidating dividend, the following
journal entry is made:

Retained Earnings   (balance)
Add'l. Paid-in Capital (plug)
   Dividends Payable   (dividend amount)

Therefore, answer (b) is correct.

21.   (589,T1,9) (a) A cash dividend becomes
a liability of a corporation, both legally and
for financial reporting purposes, on the date
of declaration. It is also on this date that
the tentative amount of the dividend is established. However, it is possible for the cash
paid to holders of record to differ from the
amount of the liability recorded on the declaration date. For example, because cash dividends are not paid on treasury stock, either
an acquisition or sale of treasury stock
between the declaration date and the date of
record would cause the amount of the dividend
paid to decrease or increase. The difference
would result in an adjustment to retained
earnings or the dividends account, if one was
used by the enterprise. Therefore, answer (a)
is correct and answers (b) and (c) are incorrect. Answer (d) is incorrect because the
payment date is merely the date when checks
are mailed to stockholders, and has no impact
on the amount of the dividend.

22. (1186,T1,22) (d) ARB 43, Chapter 7, defines a stock dividend as an issuance by a
corporation of its own common shares to its
common shareholders without consideration...
to give the recipient shareholders evidence of
a part of their respective interests in accumulated corporate earnings without distribution of cash or other property. A stock
split-up is defined as an issuance by a corporation of common shares to its common shareholders without consideration... prompted
mainly by a desire to increase the number of
outstanding shares for the purpose of
effecting a reduction in their unit market
price and, thereby, of obtaining wider distribution and improved marketability of the
shares. Thus, neither of these transactions
results in a transfer of assets among the
shareholders and the corporation. While the
allocation of stockholders' equity among the
various accounts (retained earnings, common
stock, and additional paid-in capital) will
change, the total stockholders' equity is not
affected. Therefore, answer (d) is correct,
and answers (a), (b), and (c) are incorrect.

23. (1184,T1,28) (d) The requirement is to
determine how the declaration and subsequent
issuance of a 10% stock dividend would affect
the issuer's common stock and additional paid-
in capital accounts. The issuance of a stock
dividend of 20-25% or less requires that the
market value of the stock be transferred from
retained earnings (ARB 43, Chap. 7B, paras 10-
13):

Retained earnings   (fair market value)
   Common stock   (par value)
   Additional paid-
     in capital   (excess)

Answer (a) is incorrect because it assumes a
stock split. A stock split requires no
journal entry since the dollar values of the
common stock and additional paid-in capital
accounts do not change; only the numbers of
shares change (recorded by a memorandum entry
only). Answer (c) is incorrect because it
assumes a 20-25% or larger stock dividend
which requires the par value of the stock (not
market value) to be transferred from retained
earnings to common stock (ARB 43, Chap. 7B,
paras 15-16). Answer (c) would be correct for
a 10% stock dividend if market value equaled
par value; however, the problem states that
market value exceeds par value. Answer (b) is
nonsensical and, therefore, incorrect.

G. Stock Splits

24. (1186,P2,31) (b) The requirement is the
balance of additional paid-in capital immediately after a reverse stock split. Stock

splits change the number of shares outstanding and the par value per share, but the total par value outstanding does not change. Stock splits do not affect any account balances, including additional paid-in capital. Therefore, the balance of additional paid-in capital remains at $450,000.

25. (1189,Q1,13) (d) The requirement is the par value of common stock after a 5 for 1 stock split. A stock split results in an increase or decrease in the number of shares outstanding and a corresponding decrease or increase in the par value per share. A 5 for 1 split in this case would increase the shares outstanding to 50,000 and decrease the par value per share to $2 ($10/5). Total par value is not affected by a stock split (10,000 x $10 before split; 50,000 x $2 after split).

26. (1188,T1,18) (b) A stock split does not affect either the balance of the additional paid-in capital or the retained earnings accounts. The number of shares outstanding and the par value per share merely change in proportion to each other. When this occurs, only a memorandum entry is made. Therefore, answer (b) is correct, and answers (a), (c), and (d) are incorrect.

I. Stock Options

27. (1188,P3,41) (a) For financial reporting purposes, total compensation expense related to a stock option program is computed on the measurement date--that date on which both the number of shares and the option price are known. Generally, the measurement date is the date of grant, but in this case, the option price is not known until the date of exercise. Therefore, that date is the measurement date. The compensation expense "measured" is the excess of the market value of the stock over the option price multiplied by the number of shares involved. In this case, the market value is $60, the option price is $48 (80% x $60), and the number of shares is 20,000, so total compensation expense is $240,000 [20,000 x ($60 - $48)]. The following entry is made to record compensation expense:

Compensation expense	240,000	
Paid-in capital--Stock Options		240,000

Since the options were exercised on the same date, the entry is made to record the issuance of the common stock:

Cash	960,000	(20,000 x $48)
Paid-in capital--Stock Options	240,000	(20,000 x $12)
Common stock		400,000 (20,000 x $20)
Addl. P-I capital		800,000 (excess)

Thus, Ward should record a credit to additional paid-in capital of $800,000 as a result of these transactions.

28. (589,Q1,7) (c) Employee compensation expense as the result of a stock option plan is calculated as the difference between the option price and the market price <u>at the date of grant</u> times the number of option shares.

$$\begin{array}{ccccc} \text{Option} & & \text{Market} & \text{Option} & \text{Total} \\ \text{shares} & \times & \text{price} - \text{price} & = & \text{Compensation expense} \\ 3,000 & \times & (\$30 - \$20) & = & \underline{\$30,000} \end{array}$$

The total compensation expense must be recognized over the period for which the option plan represents compensation. If not otherwise specified, the required service period (2 years) is assumed to be the period benefited. Therefore, 1988 compensation expense is $15,000 ($30,000 ÷ 2). Note that compensation expense is not affected by changes in the market value of the stock after the measurement date.

29. (1187,T1,37) (d) The stock options outstanding account is reduced when the options are exercised or when the options expire. Answer (a) is incorrect because the adoption date of the plan simply represents the date the plan is approved by the firm's board of directors, and generally no entry is recorded on this date. Answers (b) and (c) are incorrect because at both the date of grant and the measurement date <u>all</u> options are outstanding. Note that the stock options outstanding account is credited at the measurement date when this date follows the date of the grant.

30. (585,T1,23) (c) The requirement is to determine when compensation expense should be recognized under a compensatory stock option plan. Answer (c) is correct because ARB 43, Chapter 13B states that the compensation cost should be spread over the period of service covered by the option contract. The compensation expense is the excess of fair value over option price, with the fair value, in this case, being the reasonably estimated value at the date of grant. The expense is allocated over 1983, 1984, and 1985, the years for which services are to be rendered. Therefore, answers (a), (b), and (d) are incorrect.

J. Stock Appreciation Rights

31. (587,P3,43) (c) The 10,000 stock appreciation rights (SARs) each entitle the holder to receive cash equal to the excess of the market price of the stock on the exercise date over the market price on the grant date ($30). Since these SARs are payment for past services and are exercisable immediately, there is no required service period. Therefore, the expense computed at 12/31/86 does not have to be allocated to more than one period. At 12/31/86, compensation expense is measured based on the excess of the 12/31/86 market price ($45) over the predetermined price ($30), resulting in compensation expense of $150,000 [10,000 x ($45 - $30)]. Note that if Bell was required to work three years before the SARs could be exercised, the 1986 expense would be $50,000 ($150,000 x 1/3) because the expense would be allocated over the three years of required service period.

K. Earnings Per Share for Simple Capital Structures

32. (586,P3,51) (c) The requirement is the number of shares to be used in computing 1985 earnings per share (EPS). APB 15, para 48, states that for EPS purposes, shares of stock issued as a result of stock dividends or splits should be considered outstanding for the entire period in which they were issued. Therefore, both the original 300,000 shares and the additional 30,000 shares (10% x 300,000) are treated as outstanding for the entire year. The 10/1/85 purchase of 24,000 treasury shares results in a weighted average deduction of 6,000 shares (3/12 x 24,000) because the shares were not outstanding for only 3 months during 1985. Therefore, the number of shares for EPS computations is 324,000.

Outstanding 12/31/84	300,000
Stock dividend (10% x 300,000)	30,000
10/1 purchase (3/12 x 24,000)	(6,000)
	324,000

33. (1189,Q1,11) (d) Before the stock split 60,000 shares of common stock were issued, of which 5,000 shares were reacquired. Any time stock is reacquired, it is not considered outstanding. Stock is however, still considered issued unless it is formally retired. Therefore, there were 55,000 (60,000 - 5,000) shares outstanding before the two-for-one stock split and 110,000 (55,000 x 2) shares outstanding after the stock split.

34. (1186,Q1,17) (b) The formula for earnings per common share is:

$$\frac{\$1,000,000 \text{ net income} - \$50,000 \text{ preferred dividends}}{100,000 \text{ common shares outstanding}} = \$9.50$$

In calculating the numerator the claims of preferred shareholders against 1985 earnings should be deducted to arrive at the 1985 earnings attributable to common shareholders. This amount is 50,000 [(5%) ($100) (10,000 shares)]. The $50,000 preferred dividends in arrears is not deducted to compute the numerator in determining 1985 EPS. This is because the $50,000 dividends in arrears is a claim of preferred shareholders against 1984 earnings and would reduce 1984 EPS.

35. (588,T1,29) (a) Per the FASB Current Text, section E, paras 103 and 104, earnings per share data shall be shown on the face of the income statement. Earnings per share amounts shall be presented for (1) income from continuing operations, (2) income before extraordinary items, (3) the cumulative effect of a change in accounting principle, and (4) net income. Therefore, answer (a) is correct.

L. Earnings Per Share for Complex Capital Structures

36. (1189,P3,54) (b) Fully diluted EPS is based on common stock and all dilutive securities, whether they are common stock equivalents or not. To determine if a security is dilutive, EPS, including the effects of the security, must be compared to benchmark EPS. In this case, benchmark EPS is $7.45.

$$\frac{\$850,000 \text{ net income} - \$30,000 \text{ preferred dividends}}{110,000 \text{ shares}} = \$7.45$$

The effect of the convertible bonds is to increase the numerator by $56,000 [Interest of $80,000 ($1,000,000 x 8%) less $24,000 tax effect ($80,000 x 30%)], and increase the denominator by 30,000 shares. This security is dilutive because it would decrease EPS from $7.45 to $6.26.

$$\frac{\$850,000 - \$30,000 + \$56,000}{110,000 + 30,000} = \$6.26$$

The effect of the convertible preferred stock is to increase the numerator by $30,000 (dividends, 10,000 shares x $3 per share) and increase the denominator by 20,000 shares. This security is dilutive because it further decreases the EPS from $6.26 to $5.66.

$$\frac{\$850,000 - \$30,000 + \$56,000 + \$30,000}{110,000 + 30,000 + 20,000} = \$5.66$$

37. (585,P3,51) (b) The requirement is to determine the number of shares that should be used in computing 1984 primary earnings per share. Primary earnings per share is based on common stock and common stock equivalents (CSEs). The first step is to compute the weighted-average number of common shares outstanding. 300,000 shares were outstanding the entire year, and 50,000 more shares were outstanding for six months, resulting in a weighted-average of 325,000 [300,000 + (50,000 x 6/12)]. Second, since stock options are always CSEs, the denominator effect of the options must be computed. This is done using the treasury stock method, as illustrated below:

Assumed proceeds (40,000 x $15)	$600,000
Shares issued	40,000
Shares reacquired ($600,000 ÷ $20)	(30,000)
Shares issued, not reacquired	10,000

The CSEs increase the number of shares used in the computation only if they are dilutive. The stock options are dilutive because the exercise price is less than the market value. Therefore, the number of shares used for computing primary earnings per share is 335,000 (325,000 + 10,000).

38. (584,P3,49) (d) The requirement is to compute the fully diluted earnings per share (FDEPS) for 1983. The purpose of FDEPS is to show the maximum potential dilution of current earnings per share (EPS) on a prospective basis (APB 15, para 40). Therefore, all contingent issuances of common stock that reduce current EPS must be included in the computation. The formula for FDEPS is

$$\frac{\text{Net income available to common shareholders}}{\text{Weighted-average common shares outstanding}}$$

The net income available to common shareholders is $3,200,000. This is the net income of $3,400,000 less the preferred stock dividend of $200,000. The weighted-average common shares outstanding is 1,250,000. This is computed as the actual common shares outstanding for the full year of 1,200,000 plus the contingent common shares of 50,000 which were outstanding for the full year because the contingency was incurred in 1982. Thus,

$$\text{FDEPS} = \frac{\$3,200,000}{1,250,000} = \$2.56$$

39. (1186,Q1,18) (a) The capital structure of this corporation is complex because it contains dilutive securities. A complex capital structure requires a dual presentation of earnings per share, unless the potential dilution is less than 3%. If the potential dilution is less than 3%, the dilution is considered immaterial and dual presentation of EPS is not required. If the dilutive effect would reduce EPS below $11.64 ($12.00 x 97%), a presentation involving dilutive securities would be required. The diluted EPS is $11.85 ($11.90 - $.05) which is greater than $11.64. Therefore, dual presentation is not required. The single presentation of EPS is $12.00.

40. (1188,T1,33) (c) Primary earnings per share is computed based on common stock and common stock equivalents (CSEs), while fully diluted earnings per share is based on common stock and all dilutive securities, whether they are CSEs or not. Per APB 15, dilutive stock options are used in the calculation of both primary and fully diluted earnings per share. Therefore, answer (c) is correct, and answers (a), (b), and (d) are incorrect.

41. (1187,T1,33) (a) Per APB 15, para 51, the if-converted method of computing earnings per shares assumes that convertible securities are converted at the beginning of the earliest period reported or at the time of issuance, if that date is later. Therefore, answer (a) is correct and answers (b), (c), and (d) are incorrect. Note, however, that the convertible securities have to be deemed common stock equivalents for the purpose of computing primary earnings per share or are assumed to have been converted for the purpose of computing fully diluted earnings per share.

42. (1185,T1,25) (c) The requirement is the method of recognizing the use of proceeds that would be obtained upon exercise of options and warrants. The treasury stock method, according to APB 15, is used to adjust EPS on outstanding common shares for dilutive options and warrants. Under this method, options and warrants are assumed to be exercised at the beginning of the period, and the proceeds used to purchase treasury stock at the average price over the year for PEPS and the end of the year price--if higher--for FDEPS. Therefore, answer (c) is correct. The "if converted" method is used to adjust EPS on outstanding common stock for dilutive convertible securities. Therefore, answer (d) is incorrect. The common stock equivalents method, and the antidilution method, do not represent any accounting methods whatsoever. Therefore, answers (a) and (b) are incorrect.

43. (589,T1,25) (c) Per APB 15, paras 30 and 40, computations of both primary and fully diluted earnings per share should not give

effect to common stock equivalents or other contingent issuance for any period in which their inclusion would have an antidilutive effect (i.e., increase the earnings per share amount or decrease the loss per share amount otherwise computed). Therefore, answer (c) is correct.

44. (1189,T1,28) (a) Primary earnings per share is computed based on common stock and common stock equivalents (CSEs), while fully diluted earnings per share is based on common stock and all dilutive securities, whether they are CSEs or not. Per APB 15, dilutive convertible debt instruments which are common stock equivalents (as in this case) are used in the calculation of both primary and fully diluted earnings per share. Therefore, answer (a) is correct, and answers (b), (c), and (d) are incorrect.

45. (584,T1,29) (d) The requirement is to determine the treatment of nonconvertible cumulative preferred dividends in determining primary EPS. Per APB 15, para 50, dividends on nonconvertible cumulative preferred shares should be deducted from net income whether an actual liability exists or not. This is because cumulative preferred stock owners must receive any dividends in arrears before future dividend distributions can be made to common stockholders. Answer (a) is incorrect because cumulative preferred stock dividends are not disregarded in computing EPS. Answer (b) is incorrect because cumulative preferred dividends are deducted, not added, to net income in EPS calculations. Answer (c) is incorrect because it describes the treatment of dividends for noncumulative preferred stock.

M. Corporate Bankruptcy

46. (589,Q1,8) (c) Bankruptcy law requires that the claims of secured creditors be satisfied before any unsecured claims are paid. Barb is a secured creditor in the amount of $5,000 (the liquidation value of the collateral). The remainder of Barb's claim ($25,000 - $5,000 = $20,000) is an unsecured claim, because it is not secured by any collateral. Therefore, Barb will receive a total of $15,000 on this note: $5,000 received in full as a secured creditor, and $10,000 received as an unsecured creditor ($20,000 x .50).

47. (1184,P2,35) (b) The requirement is the amount of cash available to pay unsecured non-priority claims. The total cash available to pay all unsecured claims, including priority claims, is the cash obtained from free assets ($160,000) and any excess cash available from

assets pledged with fully secured creditors after they are used to satisfy those claims ($185,000 - $130,000 = $55,000). Therefore, the total cash available is $215,000 ($160,000 + $55,000). After paying priority claims ($35,000), $180,000 will remain to pay unsecured nonpriority claims.

N. Stock Rights

48. (1189,T1,23) (a) When a corporation issues rights to its stockholders, it only makes a memorandum entry. If the rights are exercised at a later date, the corporation would make the following entry for each "X" number of rights exercised:

Cash	25X	
Common stock		10X
Additional paid-in capital		15X

Additional paid-in capital (APIC) is credited when the rights are exercised, not issued. Therefore, answer (a) is correct. Note that APIC is only credited when the exercise price exceeds the par value of the stock.

49. (587,T1,34) (b) Note that the only time an entry related to the issuance and exercise of stock rights, which affects the equity accounts of a corporation, is recorded is on the date of exercise. At the date of issuance, only a memorandum entry is recorded, and on the date of the rights lapsing, no entry is recorded which would affect the company's equity accounts. Thus, the correct answer is (b): the additional paid-in capital account would not be credited at the time the rights are issued or at the date on which the rights lapse.

O. Employee Stock Ownership Plan (ESOP)

50. (1187,P3,56) (c) Per AICPA Statement of Position 76-3, para 9, the amount contributed or committed to be contributed to an employee stock ownership plan (ESOP) in a given year should be the measure of the amount to be charged to expense by the employer. Therefore, Fay should record 1986 compensation expense of $84,000 [contribution of $30,000 cash and common stock with a FMV of $54,000 (3,000 x $18)].

51. (1187,P3,57) (d) Per AICPA Statement of Position 76-3, para 5, an obligation of an Employee Stock Ownership Plan (ESOP) should be recorded as a liability in the financial statements of the employer when the obligation is covered by either a guarantee of the employer or a commitment by the employer to make future contributions to the ESOP suffi-

cient to meet the debt service requirements. Therefore, the note payable of $100,000 (which is guaranteed by Fay) should be reported in Fay's 12/31/86 balance sheet. The Statement of Position also states that the offsetting debit to the employer's liability should be reported as a reduction of stockholders' equity (para 7). Therefore, Fay should also report $100,000 as a reduction of stockholders' equity.

P. Stockholders' Equity: Comprehensive

52. (589,P1,18) (a) The balances in the common stock and preferred stock accounts equal the total par or stated value of the shares issued. Therefore, when the account balance is divided by the par or stated value per share, the result is the number of shares issued.

> Preferred stock ($225,000 ÷ $15),
>   17,000 shares issued
> Common stock ($300,000 ÷ $5),
>   60,000 shares issued

53. (1189,P1,9) (a) The unadjusted stockholders' equity section shows a total of $1,000,000. However, analysis of the current asset section of the balance sheet reveals that Magnolia has incorrectly classified $150,000 of treasury stock as a current asset. Although this account has a debit balance, it is <u>not an asset</u>. Treasury stock should be reported as a reduction of stockholders' equity. Therefore, total equity at 12/31/88 is $850,000 ($1,000,000 - $150,000).

May 1990 Answers

54. (590,Q3,51) (b) Primary earnings per share (EPS) is based on common stock and all dilutive common stock equivalents. Common stock equivalents (CSEs) are options, warrants, and convertible securities whose annual effective yield is < 2/3 of the average Aa Corporate bond yield. To determine if a security is dilutive, EPS, including the effect of the dilutive security must be compared to the bench mark EPS. In this case, benchmark EPS is 7.45.

$$\frac{850,000 \text{ (N.I.)} - 30,000 \text{ (pref. div.)}}{110,000 \text{ shares}} = 7.45$$

The effect of the convertible preferred stock is to increase the numerator by $30,000 ($3.00 dividend per share x 10,000 shares) for the amount of the preferred dividends that would not be paid (assuming conversion) and increase the denominator by 20,000 shares. This security is dilutive because it decreases the EPS from 7.45 to 6.54

$$\frac{850,000 - 30,000 + 30,000}{110,000 + 20,000} = 6.54$$

In practice, if there is more than one potentially dilutive CSE, they must first be ranked from potentially most dilutive to potentially least dilutive. Then, they must be added one at a time starting with the potentially most dilutive CSE. If the EPS increases due to the inclusion of a security, that security is anti-dilutive and should not be included.

55. (590,T1,13) (c) When treasury stock is repurchased by a company, the number of shares outstanding is decreased because the shares acquired are no longer available on the open market. The method used to account for the treasury stock acquisition is irrelevant.

56. (590,T1,14) (a) When Pott Co. declares and distributes the property dividend of Rose Co.'s shares, the following journal entry is made:

Retained earnings property dividends distributed	(FMV of Rose Co. shares)
Investment in Rose Co.	(carrying amount)
Gain on appreciation in value of inv. in Rose Co.	(plug)

Therefore, answer (a) is correct.

57. (590,T1,16) (a) When the preferred stock and detachable warrants are issued, the following journal entry is made:

Cash	(cash received)
Preferred stock	(par value)
APIC--preferred stock	(FMV of preferred stock - par value)
APIC--stock warrants	(plug)

When the stock warrants are exercised, the following journal entry is made:

Cash	(cash received)
APIC--stock warrants	(original amount credited)
Common stock	(par value)
APIC--common stock	(plug)

Therefore, stockholders' equity is increased by the cash received upon the exercise of the common stock warrants. The carrying amount of the warrants increased total stockholders' equity when the preferred stock was issued, not when the warrants were issued.

Answer Outline

Problem 1   Treasury Stock and Dividends
            (1185,T5)

a. Accounting for treasury stock
            8/15/86
    Treasury stock   (1)
      Cash   (1)
    (1) 1,000 shares x $12
            9/14/86
    Cash   (1)
      Treasury stock   (2)
      APIC   (3)
    (1) 500 shares x $14 per share
    (2) 500 shares x $12 per share
    (3) 500 shares x ($14 – $12) per share
    Balance sheet at 12/31/86
      Remaining TS (500 shares x $12) pre-
        sented as an unallocated reduction of
        total SE
      Remaining shares considered issued but
        not outstanding
b. Accounting for stock dividend in October
    1986
      RE   (1)
        CS   (2)
        APIC   (3)
    (1) 2,000 shares x $16 FMV per share
    (2) 2,000 shares x $10 par value per
        share
    (3) 2,000 shares x ($16 – $10) per
        share
    Total stockholders' equity does not change
    Because small stock dividend, capitalize
    RE at FMV of additional shares
c. Accounting for cash dividend on 12/20/86
      RE   (1)
        Cash div. payable   (1)
    (1) Outstanding shares x $1
    Dividend is distribution to corpora-
      tion's shareholders
      Liability incurred on declaration date
      CL because due within 1 year
    Balance sheet at 12/31/86
      Increase to current liabilities and de-
        crease retained earnings

Unofficial Answer

Problem 1   Treasury Stock and Dividends
            (1185,T5)

a. Brady should account for the purchase of
the treasury stock on August 15, 1986, by
debiting treasury stock and crediting cash for
the cost of the purchase (1,000 shares x $12
per share). Brady should account for the sale
of the treasury stock on September 14, 1986,

by debiting cash for the selling price (500
shares x $14 per share), crediting treasury
stock for cost (500 shares x $12 per share),
and crediting additional paid-in capital from
treasury stock transactions for the excess of
the selling price over the cost (500 shares x
$2 per share). The remaining treasury stock
(500 shares x $12 per share) should be pre-
sented separately in the stockholders' equity
section of Brady's December 31, 1986, balance
sheet as an unallocated reduction of stockholders' equity. These shares are considered
issued but not part of common stock outstanding.

b. Brady should account for the stock dividend by debiting retained earnings for $16 per
share (the market value of the stock in October 1986, the date of the stock dividend)
multiplied by the 2,000 shares distributed.
Brady should then credit common stock for the
par value of the common stock ($10 per share)
multiplied by the 2,000 shares distributed,
and credit additional paid-in capital for the
excess of the market value ($16 per share)
over the par value ($10 per share) multiplied
by the 2,000 shares distributed. Total stockholders' equity does not change, but because
this is considered a small stock dividend,
recognition has been made of a capitalization
of retained earnings equivalent to the market
value of the additional shares resulting from
the stock dividend.

c. Brady should account for the cash dividend
on December 20, 1986, the declaration date, by
debiting retained earnings and crediting cash
dividends payable for $1 per share multiplied
by the number of shares outstanding. A cash
dividend is a distribution to the corporation's stockholders. The liability for this
distribution is incurred on the declaration
date, and it is a current liability because it
is payable within one year (January 10,
1987). The effect of the cash dividend on
Brady's balance sheet at December 31, 1986, is
an increase in current liabilities and a decrease in retained earnings.

Answer Outline

Problem 2   Stock Option Plan (1186,T5)

a. Determination of compensation expense
    1983
      One half of excess of quoted market
      price over option price on 1/1/83 for
      shares on which options granted
    1984
      Same as 1983
    1985
      No compensation expense

Compensation expense in periods in which
services are rendered
  Matches compensation expense with appropriate revenues
b. Accounting for exercise of stock options

1985

Contributed capital--stock options	(1)
Cash	(2)
Common stock	(3)
Contributed capital in excess of par	(4)

(1) One half amount originally credited
    on 1/1/83
(2) Proceeds received (shares exercised
    x option price on 1/1/83)
(3) Par value of stock
(4) (1) + (2) - (3)

Objective is to assign appropriate value
  to contributed capital for common stock
  issued
    Value is sum of cash proceeds and amount
    originally assigned to "contributed
    capital--stock options" for shares
    issued
c. Accounting for lapsed stock options

Contributed capital--stock options	(1)
Contributed capital--expired stock options	(1)

(1) One half of amount originally
    credited to contributed capital--
    stock options on 1/1/83
Reclassifies expired stock options
Compensation expense **not** altered because
  some options lapsed

Unofficial Answer

Problem 2   Stock Options (1186,T5)

a. Wesley's compensation expense for 1983
should be one half of the excess of the quoted
market price over the option price on January 1, 1983, for those shares on which stock
options were granted.
  Wesley's compensation expense for 1984
should be one half of the excess of the quoted
market price over the option price on January 1, 1983, for those shares on which stock
options were granted.
  Wesley should not report compensation expense related to the compensatory stock options for 1985.
  Compensation expense should be recognized
in the income statement of each period in
which services are rendered. This procedure
relates the compensation expense with the
revenues in conformity with the matching principle.

b. Wesley should account for the exercise of
the stock options as follows:

  • Debit contributed capital--stock
options for one half of the amount originally
credited to that account on January 1, 1983.
  • Debit cash for the proceeds received,
which represents the number of shares exercised multiplied by the option price on January 1, 1983.
  • Credit common stock for the par value
of the stock, and credit contributed capital
in excess of par--common for the difference.
The objective of the accounting is to assign
the appropriate value to contributed capital
for common stock issued. That value is the
sum of the cash proceeds and the amount that
had been assigned originally to contributed
capital--stock options for those shares
issued.

c. Wesley should account for the lapse of the
stock options as follows:

  • Debit contributed capital--stock
options for one half of the amount originally
credited to that account on January 1, 1983.
  • Credit contributed capital--expired
stock options for the same amount.

  This entry reclassifies the expired stock
options to contributed capital--expired stock
options. Compensation expense is not altered
by the fact that some stock options were
allowed to lapse.

Solution Guide

Problem 3   Retained Earnings Statement and
            Stockholders' Equity Section of
            Balance Sheet (586,P4)

1. This problem consists of two related re-
    quirements. For the same company, the
    candidate must prepare a statement of
    retained earnings in part one and the
    stockholders' equity section in part two.
    Only single-period (1985) financial state-
    ments are presented.

2. The solutions approach is to analyze each
    item of information, and prepare journal
    entries where appropriate. As each item
    is analyzed, the candidate should deter-
    mine whether that item will be used in
    part one, part two, or both parts.

2.1 The information on shares authorized, par
    value, stated value, and dividend rate
    will be used primarily in the SE section.

2.2 On 1/10/85 the 30,000 treasury shares are
    retired. They are recorded at cost

($270,000 ÷ 30,000 = $9 per share). The journal entry to record the retirement under the cost method is

```
Common stock              150,000
Addl. P-I Cap from CS     150,000
   Treasury stock                      270,000
   Addl. P-I Cap from retirement        30,000
```

Common stock and addl. P-I Cap from CS are removed from the books based on the original issuance of the stock at $10 per share (30,000 shares at $5 each for both accounts). Treasury stock is also taken off the books, and the difference is credited to P-I Cap from retirement (a subsidiary account of additional paid-in capital). This entry will effect the SE section (all four accounts are SE accounts).

2.3 On 2/15/85, a property dividend was declared. One share of Bush is to be distributed for every 100 shares outstanding. At this time, 1,000,000 shares are outstanding [($5,150,000 - $150,000) ÷ $5]. Therefore, all 10,000 shares of Bush will be distributed (1,000,000 ÷ 100 = 10,000). First, the loss on the investment is recognized.

```
Loss on investment        120,000
   Temporary investment              120,000
```

The loss is the difference between the investment's cost ($750,000) and its market value (10,000 x $63 = $630,000). Then, the dividend is distributed.

```
Retained earnings         630,000
   Temporary investment              630,000
```

The loss affects RE through net income. The property dividend will go in the RE statement and reduce the RE balance.

2.4 On 4/25/85, common stock is issued. The current market price ($13) does not affect the entry; the transaction is recorded based on the actual amount of cash received per share ($11). The journal entry is

```
Cash                    2,310,000
   Common stock                     1,050,000
   Addl. P-I Cap from CS            1,260,000
```

The proceeds are $2,310,000 (210,000 x $11); the stated value of the stock is $1,050,000 (210,000 x $5). The excess is credited to additional paid-in capital. The two accounts credited are SE accounts and will affect the SE section.

2.5 On 7/1/85, options are exercised. When the options were granted, the option price was equal to the market price. Therefore,

no value was assigned to the options for accounting purposes and no entries were recorded at that time. When the options are exercised, the entry is

```
Cash                      640,000
   Common stock                      400,000
   Addl. P-I Cap from CS             240,000
```

Again, the transaction is recorded based on the actual amount of cash received (80,000 x $8 = $640,000); the current market price of the stock ($15 per share) is not considered. The stated value of the stock is $400,000 (80,000 x $5), and the excess is credited to additional paid-in capital. The two accounts credited are SE accounts and will affect the SE section.

2.6 On 12/12/85, the yearly preferred dividend ($1,800,000 x 10% = $180,000) is declared. The entry is

```
Retained earnings         180,000
   Dividends payable                 180,000
```

The dividend will appear in the RE statement and reduce the RE balance.

2.7 After year-end adjustment, the unrealized loss account has a debit balance of $135,000 at 12/31/85. Remember, for noncurrent MES, the balance in the unrealized loss account is reported as a contra-SE account. It is not reported in the income statement.

2.8 Before the books were closed for 1985, an error in recording 1984 rent income was discovered. 1984 net income, after taxes, was overstated by $275,000. This amount is reported in the RE statement as a prior period adjustment (deduction) to 1/1/85 RE.

2.9 1985 net income was $2,600,000. This amount will appear in the RE statement and increase the RE balance.

3. The RE statement begins with the previously reported 12/31/84 balance ($4,000,000), which is to agree with prior year's statements. Then the prior period adjustment is subtracted to derive the corrected beginning balance. The remainder of the RE statement shows the addition of net income and deduction of the dividends.

4. The paid-in capital section is presented first in SE.

4.1 Preferred stock and its related additional paid-in capital account did not change during 1985. Note that there are 18,000 shares issued ($1,800,000 ÷ $100).

4.2 Common stock has a balance of $6,450,000 at 12/31/85 ($5,150,000 - $150,000 + $1,050,000 + $400,000).

4.3 The control account, additional paid-in capital from common stock, increased to $4,880,000 during 1985. The beginning balance was $3,500,000. The control account had a net decrease of $120,000 when the treasury stock was issued ($150,000 - $30,000). The account increased by $1,260,000 and $240,000 when stock was issued on 4/25/85 and 7/1/85.

4.4 The 12/31/85 RE balance ($5,515,000) was computed in the RE statement in part a.

4.5 The net unrealized loss on noncurrent marketable equity securities ($135,000) is a contra-SE account, subtracted at the bottom of the SE section.

4.6 The 20,000 unexercised options are not reflected in SE, except through footnote disclosure (not required in this problem).

Unofficial Answer

Problem 3   Retained Earnings Statement and Stockholders' Equity Section of Balance Sheet (586,P4)

a.

Carr Corporation
STATEMENT OF RETAINED EARNINGS
For the Year Ended December 31, 1985

Balance, December 31, 1984			
As originally reported			$4,000,000
Deduct prior period adjustment from error overstating rent income for year ended December 31, 1984	$500,000		
Less income tax effect	225,000		275,000
As restated			3,725,000
Net income			2,600,000
			6,325,000
Deduct dividends			
Cash dividend on preferred stock	180,000	[1]	
Dividend in kind on common stock	630,000	[2]	810,000
Balance, December 31, 1985			$5,515,000

b.

Carr Corporation
STOCKHOLDERS' EQUITY SECTION OF BALANCE SHEET
December 31, 1985

Preferred stock, $100 par, 10% cumulative; 100,000 shares authorized; 18,000 shares issued and outstanding		$ 1,800,000
Common stock, $5 stated value; 3,000,000 shares authorized, 1,290,000 shares issued and outstanding		6,450,000 [3]
Additional paid-in capital		
From preferred stock	$ 90,000	
From common stock	4,880,000 [4]	
Total additional paid-in capital		4,970,000
Retained earnings		5,515,000
		18,735,000
Less net unrealized loss on noncurrent marketable equity securities		135,000
Total stockholders' equity		$18,600,000

Explanations of Amounts

[1] Cash dividend on preferred stock for 1985

Shares outstanding	18,000
Dividend per share ($100 par x 10%)	x $10
Total dividend	$ 180,000

[2] Dividend in kind on common stock for 1985

Bush, Inc., common stock shares	10,000
Market price on 2/15/85 declaration date	x $63
Total dividend	$ 630,000

[3] Common stock

	Date	Shares	Amount
Balance	12/31/84	1,030,000	$5,150,000
Deduct treasury stock retired	1/10/85	30,000	150,000
		1,000,000	5,000,000
Stock rights exercised	4/25/85	210,000	1,050,000
Employee stock options exercised	7/1/85	80,000	400,000
Balance	12/31/85	1,290,000	$6,450,000

[4] Additional paid-in capital from common stock

12/31/84, balance	$3,500,000
1/10/85, deduct treasury stock retired ($270,000 - $150,000)	120,000
	3,380,000
4/25/85, stock rights exercised [($11 - $5) x 210,000 shares]	1,260,000
7/1/85, employee stock options exercised ($8 - $5) x 80,000 shares]	240,000
12/31/85, balance	$4,880,000

Solution Guide

Problem 4   Prepare L-T Liabilities and
             Stockholders' Equity Sections of
             Balance Sheet (588,P4)

1. This problem consists of three related
    parts requiring the preparation of the
    long-term liabilities section, the
    stockholders' equity section, and a
    schedule of interest expense.

2. The solutions approach is to first
    analyze all the additional information
    given, and then organize it as required
    for parts (a), (b), and (c).

2.1 The carrying amount of the bonds at
     12/31/86 is $5,352,400 ($5,000,000 face +
     $352,400 premium). The stated interest
     rate is 11%, while the effective rate is
     10%. Since Fay uses the interest method,
     the 12/31/87 entry to record interest is:

Interest expense	535,240	($5,352,400 x 10%)
Premium on B.P.	14,760	
Cash		550,000 ($5,000,000 x 11%)

Under the interest method, interest
expense is the **carrying amount** times the
effective rate, and discount or premium
amortization is plugged in.

2.2 Treasury stock was reissued on 1/15/87
     for $225,000. Since the treasury stock
     account balance is stated at cost, the

cost method is used. The treasury shares
were purchased at a cost of $13 per share
($325,000 ÷ 25,000 shares). The journal
entry to record the sale is:

Cash	225,000	
Treasury stock		195,000 (15,000 x $13)
Paid-in capital from t.s.		30,000

Paid-in capital from treasury stock is a
subsidiary account of additional paid-in
capital.

2.3 A 5% stock dividend was issued on 3/2/87
     on all **issued** shares. While **cash**
     dividends are **not** declared and paid on
     treasury stock, **stock** dividends may be
     declared and issued on treasury stock in
     certain situations. Since the problem
     states the dividend was issued on **issued**
     stock, not on **outstanding** stock, you can
     assume that the dividend is also declared
     on treasury stock: 800,000 shares of
     stock are outstanding ($8,000,000 ÷ $10),
     so the stock dividend is 40,000 shares
     (800,000 x 5%). A small stock dividend
     is recorded at fair market value. The
     entry is:

Retained earnings	560,000 (40,000 x $14)	
Common stock		400,000 (40,000 x $10)
Paid-in capital in		
excess of par		160,000

Paid-in capital in excess of par is a
subsidiary account of additional paid-in
capital.

2.4 The note payable ($4,000,000) is reported as a current liability (the $800,000 installment due 11/1/88) and as a long-term liability (the remaining balance of $3,200,000). The interest expense on this note for 1987 is $60,000 ($4,000,000 x 9% x 2/12).

2.5 A long-term investment in marketable equity securities, when the ownership level is less than 20%, is accounted for using the lower of cost or market method. The cost of the investment is $200,000 (10,000 x $20) and at 12/31/87, the market value is $180,000 (10,000 x $18). The following entry is made:

Unrealized loss, etc.   20,000   ($200,000 - $180,000)
   Allowance, etc.   20,000

The balance in the unrealized loss account is reported as a deduction from stockholders' equity in the balance sheet. If this were a temporary investment, the loss would be reported in the income statement, but for a long-term investment, the income statement is bypassed.

2.6 1987 net income ($2,860,000) will increase retained earnings.

3. Once the information is analyzed, you can proceed to the specific requirements.

4. Part (a) requires the preparation of the 12/31/87 long-term liability section, including necessary disclosures.

4.1 The bonds payable are reported at face value ($5,000,000) plus unamortized premium. The premium balance at 12/31/86 was $352,400, and after 12/31/87 amortization of $14,760 (see 2.1), the 12/31/87 balance is $337,640 ($352,400 - $14,760).

4.2 The note payable is reported in the long-term liability section at the total face value ($4,000,000) less the current maturity ($800,000), or $3,200,000.

5. Part (b) requires the preparation of the 12/31/87 stockholders' equity section.

5.1 Common stock is reported at $8,400,000, consisting of the 12/31/86 balance of $8,000,000 plus the additional $400,000 from the stock dividend (see 2.3). Also, the number of shares authorized, issued, and outstanding must be disclosed.

5.2 The 12/31/87 balance of additional paid-in capital is $2,485,000, consisting of the 12/31/86 balance of $2,295,000, the increase of $30,000 from the treasury stock sale (see 2.2), and the increase of $160,000 from the stock dividend (see 2.3).

5.3 The 12/31/87 balance of retained earnings is $4,765,000. The 12/31/86 balance of $2,465,000 is increased by the net income of $2,860,000 and decreased by the stock dividend of $560,000 (see 2.3).

5.4 The cost of the stock still held in treasury must be deducted at the bottom of the stockholders' equity section. At 12/31/86, the balance in the treasury stock account was $325,000. On 1/15/87, treasury stock with a cost of $195,000 (see 2.2) was sold, bringing the balance down to $130,000. Note that the stock dividend on 3/2/87 increases the number of treasury shares to 10,500 [10,000 + (10,000 x 5%)], but does not increase the cost, since the additional 500 shares did not cost anything.

5.5 The unrealized loss on noncurrent marketable equity securities ($20,000) must also be deducted in the stockholders' equity section (see 2.5).

6. Part (c) requires the preparation of a schedule showing 1987 interest expense.

6.1 Interest expense on the bonds is $535,240 (see 2.1), and interest expense on the note is $60,000 (see 2.4). Total interest expense is $595,240.

Unofficial Answer
Problem 4   Prepare L-T Liabilities and Stockholders'
            Equity Section of Balance Sheet (588,P4)

a.   Fay, Inc.
                        LONG-TERM LIABILITIES SECTION
                             OF BALANCE SHEET
                            December 31, 1987

9% unsecured note payable to bank, due in annual principal
 installments of $800,000, less current portion $ 3,200,000   [1]

11% debenture bonds payable due December 31, 1999, plus
 unamortized premium of $337,640   5,337,640   [2]

Total long-term liabilities $ 8,537,640

b.   Fay, Inc.
                        STOCKHOLDERS' EQUITY SECTION
                             OF BALANCE SHEET
                            December 31, 1987

Common stock, $10 par; 2,000,000 shares
 authorized; 840,000 shares issued; 829,500 shares outstanding $ 8,400,000   [3]

Additional paid-in capital   2,485,000   [4]

Retained earnings   4,765,000   [5]
                                                                    15,650,000

Less: net unrealized loss on noncurrent
 marketable equity securities $ 20,000   [6]
 Treasury stock, at cost, 10,500 shares   130,000   [7]   (150,000)

Total stockholders' equity $15,500,000

c.   Fay, Inc.
                             INTEREST EXPENSE
                    For the Year Ended December 31, 1987

Note payable to bank $ 60,000   [8]

Debenture bonds payable   535,240   [9]

Total interest expense $ 595,240

Explanations of Amounts

[1] 9% note payable to bank
     Note payable, 11/1/87 $4,000,000
     Deduct installment due 11/1/88   800,000

     Long-term portion, 12/31/87 $3,200,000

[2] Debenture bonds payable
     Carrying amount, 12/31/86 $5,352,400
     Deduct amortization of bond premium
       Interest paid 12/31/87 ($5,000,000 x 11%) $550,000
       Less effective interest
        ($5,352,400 x 10%)   535,240   14,760

     Carrying amount, 12/31/87 $5,337,640

[3] Common stock issued	Date	Shares	Amount
Balance	12/31/86	800,000	$8,000,000
5% stock dividend issued	3/ 2/87	40,000	400,000
Balance	12/31/87	840,000	$8,400,000

[4] Additional paid-in capital
       Balance, 12/31/86 $2,295,000
       Treasury stock reissued, 1/15/87
         [$225,000 - $195,000 ($325,000 x 60%)]   30,000
       Stock dividend issued, 3/2/87
         [($14 - $10) x 40,000 shares]   160,000

       Balance, 12/31/87 $2,485,000

[5] Retained earnings
       Balance, 12/31/86 $2,465,000
       Stock dividend issued, 3/2/87
         ($14 x 40,000 shares)   (560,000)
       Net income for 1987   2,860,000

       Balance, 12/31/87 $4,765,000

[6] Net unrealized loss on noncurrent
     marketable equity securities
       Balance, 12/31/87
         [($20 - $18) x 10,000 shares] $ 20,000

[7] Treasury stock at cost
       (10,000 ÷ 25,000 x $325,000) $ 130,000

[8] Interest expense on note payable to bank
       [11/1/87 to 12/31/87 ($4,000,000 x 9% x 2/12)] $ 60,000

[9] Interest expense on debenture bonds payable
       Interest paid 12/31/87 for year ended 12/31/87 $550,000   [2]

       Deduct amortization of bond premium for year   14,760   [2]

       Interest expense year ended 12/31/87 $ 535,240

Multiple Choice Questions (1-31)

1. During 1985 Garr Company purchased marketable equity securities as a short-term investment. At December 31, 1985, the balance in the allowance to reduce marketable equity securities to market was $23,000. There were no security transactions during 1986. Pertinent information at December 31, 1986 is as follows:

Security	Cost	Market value
A	$245,000	$230,000
B	180,000	182,000
	$425,000	$412,000

In its 1986 income statement, Garr should report a(an)
   a. Recovery of unrealized loss of $8,000.
   b. Recovery of unrealized loss of $10,000.
   c. Unrealized loss of $13,000.
   d. Unrealized loss of $15,000.

2. During 1986 Rex Company purchased marketable equity securities as a short-term investment. The cost and market value at December 31, 1986 were as follows:

Security	Cost	Market value
A -- 100 shares	$ 2,800	$ 3,400
B -- 1,000 shares	17,000	15,300
C -- 2,000 shares	31,500	29,500
	$51,300	$48,200

Rex sold 1,000 shares of Company B stock on January 31, 1987 for $15 per share, incurring $1,500 in brokerage commission and taxes. On the sale, Rex should report a realized loss of
   a. $ 300
   b. $1,800
   c. $2,000
   d. $3,500

3. Ross Corp. was organized on January 1, 1988. At December 31, 1988, Ross had the following investment portfolio of marketable equity securities:

	In current assets	In non-current assets
Aggregate cost	$300,000	$450,000
Aggregate market value	240,000	370,000
Net unrealized loss	$ 60,000	$ 80,000

All of the declines are judged to be temporary. Valuation allowances at December 31, 1988 should be established with corresponding charges against

	Income	Stockholders' equity
a.	$0	$140,000
b.	$ 60,000	$ 80,000
c.	$ 80,000	$ 60,000
d.	$140,000	$0

4. The following information pertains to Plat Corp.'s long-term marketable equity securities portfolio:

	December 31,	
	1987	1988
Cost	$100,000	$100,000
Market value	90,000	120,000

Differences between cost and market values are considered to be temporary. The decline in market value was properly accounted for at December 31, 1987. By what amount should the contra account--unrealized loss in long-term marketable equity securities--decrease from December 31, 1987 to December 31, 1988?
   a. $0
   b. $10,000
   c. $20,000
   d. $30,000

5. On December 31, 1986, Wall Company purchased marketable equity securities as a temporary investment. Pertinent data are as follows:

Security	Cost	Market Value at 12/31/87
A	$39,000	$36,000
B	50,000	55,000
C	96,000	85,000

On December 31, 1987, Wall reclassified its investment in security C from current to noncurrent because Wall intends to retain security C as a long-term investment. What total amount of loss on its securities should be included in Wall's income statement for the year ended December 31, 1987?
   a. $0
   b. $ 9,000
   c. $11,000
   d. $14,000

6. The amount by which the aggregate cost of a marketable equity securities portfolio exceeds its aggregate market value should be reported as a valuation allowance when the portfolio is included

	As a current asset	In an unclassified balance sheet
a.	Yes	No
b.	Yes	Yes
c.	No	Yes
d.	No	No

2
9

7.   Robin Co. has a marketable equity securities portfolio classified as noncurrent. None of the holdings enables Robin to exercise significant influence over an investee. The aggregate cost exceeds its aggregate market value. The decline is considered temporary and should be reported as a(an)

a.   Unrealized loss in the income statement.
b.   Realized loss in the income statement.
c.   Valuation allowance in the noncurrent liability section of the balance sheet.
d.   Valuation allowance in the asset section of the balance sheet.

8.   A short-term marketable debt security was purchased on September 1, 1987 between interest dates. The next interest payment date was February 1, 1988. Because of a permanent decline in market value, the cost of the debt security substantially exceeded its market value at December 31, 1987. On the balance sheet at December 31, 1987, the debt security should be carried at

a.   Market value plus the accrued interest paid.
b.   Market value.
c.   Cost plus the accrued interest paid.
d.   Cost.

9.   When the market value of an investment in debt securities exceeds its carrying amount, how should the asset be reported at the end of the year for each of the following?

	Short-term marketable debt securities	Long-term marketable debt securities
a.	Carrying amount	Market
b.	Carrying amount	Carrying amount
c.	Market	Carrying amount
d.	Market	Market

10. On January 1, 1988, Dyer Co. acquired as a long-term investment a 20% common stock interest in Eason Co. Dyer paid $700,000 for this investment when the fair value of Eason's net assets was $3,500,000. Dyer can exercise significant influence over Eason's operating and financial policies. For the year ended December 31, 1988, Eason reported net income of $400,000 and declared and paid cash dividends of $160,000. How much revenue from this investment should Dyer report for 1988?

a. $ 32,000
b. $ 48,000
c. $ 80,000
d. $112,000

11. On January 1, 1983, Miller Company purchased 25% of Wall Corporation's common stock; no goodwill resulted from the purchase. Miller appropriately carries this investment at equity, and the balance in Miller's investment account was $190,000 at December 31, 1983. Wall reported net income of $120,000 for the year ended December 31, 1983, and paid common stock dividends totaling $48,000 during 1983. How much did Miller pay for its 25% interest in Wall?

a. $172,000
b. $202,000
c. $208,000
d. $232,000

12. An investor uses the equity method to account for an investment in common stock. After the date of acquisition, the investment account of the investor would

a.   Not be affected by its share of the earnings or losses of the investee.
b.   Not be affected by its share of the earnings of the investee, but be decreased by its share of the losses of the investee.
c.   Be increased by its share of the earnings of the investee, but not be affected by its share of the losses of the investee.
d.   Be increased by its share of the earnings of the investee, and decreased by its share of the losses of the investee.

13. An investor in common stock received dividends in excess of the investor's share of investee's earnings subsequent to the date of the investment. How will the investor's investment account be affected by those dividends under each of the following accounting methods?

	Cost method	Equity method
a.	No effect	No effect
b.	Decrease	No effect
c.	No effect	Decrease
d.	Decrease	Decrease

14. An investor uses the equity method to account for an investment in common stock. The investor's equity in the earnings of the investee would be affected by

	Cash dividends from investee	A change in market value of the investee's common stock
a.	No	Yes
b.	No	No
c.	Yes	No
d.	Yes	Yes

15. An investor uses the equity method to account for its 30% investment in common stock of an investee. Amortization of the investor's share of the excess of fair market value

over book value of depreciable assets at the date of the purchase should be reported in the investor's income statement as part of

a.   Other expense.
b.   Depreciation expense.
c.   Equity in earnings of investee.
d.   Amortization of goodwill.

16.   Cash dividends declared out of current earnings are distributed to an investor. How will the investor's investment account be affected by those dividends under each of the following accounting methods?

	Cost method	Equity method
a.	Decrease	No effect
b.	Decrease	Decrease
c.	No effect	Decrease
d.	No effect	No effect

17.   On January 2, 1986, Saxe Company purchased 20% of Lex Corporation's common stock for $150,000. This investment did not give Saxe the ability to exercise significant influence over Lex. During 1986 Lex reported net income of $175,000 and paid cash dividends of $100,000 on its common stock. The balance in Saxe's investment in Lex Corporation account at December 31, 1986 should be

a. $130,000
b. $150,000
c. $165,000
d. $185,000

18.   On January 2, 1985, Winn Company purchased as a long-term investment 5,000 shares of Pyle Corp. common stock for $70 per share, which represents a 1% interest. On December 31, 1985, the market price of the stock was $75 per share. On December 18, 1986, Winn needed additional cash for operations and sold all 5,000 shares of Pyle stock for $100 per share. Winn's income tax rate was 40% for 1986. For the year ended December 31, 1986, Winn should include in its income from continuing operations a gain on disposal of long-term investment of

a. $0
b. $ 75,000
c. $125,000
d. $150,000

19.   Albert Co. acquired 4,000 shares of Nolan, Inc. common stock on October 20, 1986 for $66,000. On November 30, 1988, Nolan distributed a 10% common stock dividend when the market price of the stock was $25 per share. On December 20, 1988, Albert sold 400 shares of its Nolan stock for $10,600. For the year ended December 31, 1988, how much should Albert report as dividend revenue?

a. $10,600
b. $10,000

c. $ 4,600
d $0

20.   Adam Company received dividends from its common stock investments during the year ended December 31, 1986, as follows:

•   A stock dividend of 200 shares from Brock Corp. was received on July 25, 1986, on which date the market price of Brock's shares was $20 per share. Adam owns less than 1% of Brock's common stock.
•   A cash dividend of $60,000 from Celt Corp., in which Adam owns a 25% interest. A majority of Celt's directors are also directors of Adam.

What amount of dividend revenue should Adam report in its 1986 income statement?

a. $0
b. $ 4,000
c. $60,000
d. $64,000

21.   On February 24, 1986, Bart Company purchased 2,000 shares of Winn Corp.'s newly issued 6% cumulative $75 par preferred stock for $152,000. Each share carried one detachable stock warrant entitling the holder to acquire at $10, one share of Winn no-par common stock. On February 25, 1986, the market price of the preferred stock ex-warrants was $72 a share and the market price of the stock warrants was $8 a warrant. On December 29, 1986, Bart sold all the stock warrants for $20,500. The gain on the sale of the stock warrants was

a. $0
b. $ 500
c. $4,500
d. $5,300

22.   On January 3, 1986, Falk Co. purchased 500 shares of Milo Corp. common stock for $36,000. On December 2, 1988, Falk received 500 stock rights from Milo. Each right entitles the holder to acquire one share of stock for $85. The market price of Milo's stock was $100 a share immediately before the rights were issued, and $90 a share immediately after the rights were issued. Falk sold its rights on December 3, 1988 for $10 a right. Falk's gain from the sale of the rights is

a. $0
b. $1,000
c. $1,400
d. $5,000

23.   On January 1, 1980, Ball Inc. purchased a $1,000,000 ordinary life insurance policy on its president. The policy year and Ball's

accounting year coincide. Additional data are available for the year ended December 31, 1985:

Cash surrender value, 1/1/85	$43,500
Cash surrender value, 12/31/85	54,000
Annual advance premium paid 1/1/85	20,000
Dividend received 7/1/85	3,000

Ball, Inc. is the beneficiary under the life insurance policy. How much should Ball report as life insurance expense for 1985?

  a. $ 6,500
  b. $ 9,500
  c. $17,000
  d. $20,000

Items 24 through 26 are based on the following data:

Lake Corporation's accounting records showed the following investments at January 1, 1986:

Common stock:	
Kar Corp. (1,000 shares)	$ 10,000
Aub Corp. (5,000 shares)	100,000
Real estate:	
Parking lot (leased to Day Co.)	300,000
Other:	
Trademark (at cost, less accumulated amortization)	25,000
Total investments	$435,000

Lake owns 1% of Kar and 30% of Aub. Lake's directors constitute a majority of Aub's directors. The Day lease, which commenced on January 1, 1984 is for ten years, at an annual rental of $48,000. In addition, on January 1, 1984, Day paid a nonrefundable deposit of $50,000, as well as a security deposit of $8,000 to be refunded upon expiration of the lease. The trademark was licensed to Barr Co. for royalties of 10% of sales of the trademarked items. Royalties are payable semi-annually on March 1 (for sales in July through December of the prior year), and on September 1 (for sales in January through June of the same year).

During the year ended December 31, 1986, Lake received cash dividends of $1,000 from Kar, and $15,000 from Aub, whose 1986 net incomes were $75,000 and $150,000, respectively. Lake also received $48,000 rent from Day in 1986, and the following royalties from Barr:

	March 1	September 1
1985	$3,000	$5,000
1986	4,000	7,000

Barr estimated that sales of the trademarked

items would total $20,000 for the last half of 1986.

24. In Lake's 1986 income statement, how much should be reported for dividend revenue?
  a. $16,000
  b. $ 2,400
  c. $ 1,000
  d. $ 150

25. In Lake's 1986 income statement, how much should be reported for royalty revenue?
  a. $14,000
  b. $13,000
  c. $11,000
  d. $ 9,000

26. In Lake's 1986 income statement, how much should be reported for rental revenue?
  a. $43,000
  b. $48,000
  c. $53,000
  d. $53,800

May 1990 Questions

27. On April 1, 1989, Saxe, Inc. purchased $200,000 face value, 9% U.S. Treasury Notes for $198,500, including accrued interest of $4,500. The notes mature July 1, 1990, and pay interest semiannually on January 1 and July 1. Saxe uses the straight-line method of amortization. The notes were sold on December 1, 1989 for $206,500, including accrued interest of $7,500. In its October 31, 1989 balance sheet, the carrying amount of this investment should be
  a. $194,000
  b. $196,800
  c. $197,200
  d. $199,000

Items 28 through 30 are based on the following:

Lee, Inc. acquired 30% of Polk Corp.'s voting stock on January 1, 1988 for $100,000. During 1988, Polk earned $40,000 and paid dividends of $25,000. Lee's 30% interest in Polk gives Lee the ability to exercise significant influence over Polk's operating and financial policies. During 1989, Polk earned $50,000 and paid dividends of $15,000 on April 1 and $15,000 on October 1. On July 1, 1989, Lee sold half of its stock in Polk for $66,000 cash.

28. Before income taxes, what amount should Lee include in its 1988 income statement as a result of the investment?
  a. $40,000
  b. $25,000

  c. $12,000
  d. $ 7,500

29. The carrying amount of this investment in Lee's December 31, 1988 balance sheet should be
  a. $100,000
  b. $104,500
  c. $112,000
  d. $115,000

30. What should be the gain on sale of this investment in Lee's 1989 income statement?
  a. $16,000
  b. $13,750
  c. $12,250
  d. $10,000

31. During 1988, Wall Co. purchased 2,000 shares of Hemp Corp. common stock for $31,500 as a short-term investment. The market value of this investment was $29,500 at December 31, 1988. Wall sold all of the Hemp common stock for $14 per share on December 15, 1989, incurring $1,400 in brokerage commissions and taxes. On the sale, Wall should report a realized loss of
  a. $4,900
  b. $3,500
  c. $2,900
  d. $1,500

Repeat Questions

(590,P1,2) Identical/similar to item 1 above
(590,P3,47) Identical/similar to item 20 above
(590,T1,4) Identical/similar to item 9 above

Problems

Problem 1   (589,T2)

(15 to 25 minutes)

Vane Company has two portfolios of marketable equity securities. One is classified as a current asset, and the other is classified as a noncurrent asset. Vane does not have the ability to exercise significant influence over any of the companies in either portfolio. Some securities from each portfolio were sold during the year. One of the securities in the current portfolio was reclassified to the noncurrent portfolio when its market value was less than cost. At the beginning and end of the year, the aggregate cost of each portfolio exceeded its aggregate market value by different amounts.

Required:

    a. How should Vane measure and report the income statement effects of the securities sold during the year from each portfolio?

    b. How should Vane account for the security which was reclassified from the current asset portfolio to the noncurrent asset portfolio?

    c. How should Vane report the effects of investments in each portfolio in its balance sheet as of the end of the year and its income statement for the year? Why? Do not discuss the securities sold.

Problem 2   (589,P5)

(40 to 50 minutes)

At December 31, 1987, Poe Corp. properly reported as current assets the following marketable equity securities:

Axe Corp., 1,000 shares, $2.40 convertible preferred stock	$ 40,000
Purl Inc., 6,000 shares of common stock	60,000
Day Co., 2,000 shares of common stock	55,000
Marketable equity securities at cost	155,000
Less valuation allowance	7,000
Marketable equity securities at market value	$148,000

On January 2, 1988, Poe purchased 100,000 shares of Scott Corp. common stock for $1,700,000, representing 30% of Scott's outstanding common stock and an underlying equity of $1,400,000 in Scott's net assets on January 2. Poe, which had no other financial transactions with Scott during 1988, amortizes goodwill over a 40-year period. As a result of Poe's 30% ownership of Scott, Poe has the ability to exercise significant influence over Scott's financial and operating policies.

During 1988, Poe disposed of the following securities:

    • January 18--sold 2,500 shares of Purl for $13 per share.

    • June 1--sold 500 shares of Day, after a 10% stock dividend was received, for $21 per share.

    • October 1--converted 500 shares of Axe's preferred stock into 1,500 shares of Axe's common stock, when the market price was $60 per share for the preferred stock and $21 per share for the common stock.

The following 1988 dividend information pertains to stock owned by Poe:

    • February 14--Day issued a 10% stock dividend, when the market price of Day's common stock was $22 per share.

    • April 5 and October 5--Axe paid dividends of $1.20 per share on its $2.40 preferred stock, to stockholders of record on March 9 and September 9, respectively. Axe did not pay dividends on its common stock during 1988.

    • June 30--Purl paid a $1.00 per share dividend on its common stock.

    • March 1, June 1, September 1, and December 1--Scott paid quarterly dividends of $0.50 per share on each of these dates. Scott's net income for the year ended December 31, 1988 was $1,200,000.

At December 31, 1988, Poe's management intended to hold Scott's stock as a long-term investment, with the remaining investments being considered as temporary. Market prices per share of the marketable equity securities were as follows:

	At December 31,	
	1988	1987
Axe Corp.--preferred	$56	$42
Axe Corp.--common	20	18
Purl, Inc.--common	11	11
Day Co.--common	22	20
Scott Corp.--common	16	18

All of the foregoing stocks are listed on major stock exchanges. Declines in market value from cost would not be considered permanent.

Required:

    a. Prepare a schedule of Poe's current marketable equity securities at December 31, 1988, including any information necessary to determine the related valuation allowance and unrealized gains and losses.

    b. Prepare a schedule to show the carrying amount of Poe's noncurrent marketable equity securities at December 31, 1988.

    c. Prepare a schedule showing all revenue, gains, and losses (realized and unrealized) relating to Poe's investments for the year ended December 31, 1988.

Problem 3   (588,P5)*

(40 to 50 minutes)

    Among the account balances of Rowe Corp. at December 31, 1986, are the following:

Patent, net of accumulated patent
  amortization $245,000
Installment contract receivable,
  including current portion   720,000

In its year-end financial statements, Rowe reports as other noncurrent assets all assets that are not classified as property, plant, and equipment or as current assets. Relevant transactions and other information for 1987 were as follows:

• The patent was purchased from Lake Co. for $315,000 on September 1, 1983. On that date the remaining legal life was 15 years, which was also determined to be the useful life.

• The installment contract receivable represents the balance of the consideration received from the sale of a factory building to Pitt Co. on March 31, 1985 for $1,200,000. Pitt made a $300,000 down payment and signed a five-year 13% note for the $900,000 balance. The first of equal annual principal payments of $180,000 was received on March 31, 1986, together with interest to that date. The note is collateralized by the factory buildings with a fair value of $1,000,000 at December 31, 1986 and December 31, 1987. The 1987 payment was received on time.

• On January 2, 1987, Rowe purchased a trademark from Kerr Corp. for $250,000. Rowe considers the life of the trademark to be indefinite. The trademark will be amortized over the maximum period allowable.

• On May 1, 1987, Rowe sold the patent to Strand Co. in exchange for a $500,000 noninterest bearing note due on May 1, 1990. There was no established exchange price for the patent, and the note had no ready market. The prevailing rate of interest for a note of this type at May 1, 1987 was 14%. The present value of 1 for three periods at 14% is 0.675. The collection of the note receivable from Strand is reasonably assured.

• On July 1, 1987, Rowe paid $1,880,000 for 75,000 shares of Black Corp.'s common stock, which represented a 25% investment in Black. The fair value of all of Black's identifiable assets net of liabilities equals their carrying amount of $6,400,000. Rowe has the ability to exercise significant influence over Black's operating and financial policies. Rowe amortizes goodwill over a 40-year period. The market price of Black's common stock on December 31, 1987 was $26.50 per share.

• Black reported net income and paid dividends of:

	Net income	Dividends per share
Six months ended 6/30/87	$576,000	None
Six months ended 12/31/87	704,000	$2.00

(Dividend was paid 11/30/87)

• Rowe and Black had no other intercompany transactions.

Required:

    a. Prepare a separate schedule of changes for each of the other noncurrent asset accounts during 1987.

    b. Prepare a schedule showing the revenues, gains, and expenses relating to Rowe's other noncurrent assets for the year ended December 31, 1987.

---

    *Author's Note: The required schedules for this problem include several accounts not included in this module (patent, installment contract receivable, and trademark). However, it does include an investment requiring accounting under the equity method. Since your review of the accounting for all the accounts found in the problem will have been completed once this module is finished, we have decided to place the problem in this module. Please note that doing comprehensive problems like this one is essential to your success on the Accounting Practice part of the CPA Exam.

Multiple Choice Answers

1. b	8. b	14. b	20. a	26. c
2. d	9. b	15. c	21. d	27. b
3. b	10. c	16. c	22. c	28. c
4. b	11. a	17. b	23. a	29. b
5. c	12. d	18. d	24. c	30. c
6. b	13. d	19. d	25. d	31. a
7. d				

Multiple Choice Answer Explanations

B.1. Marketable Equity Securities

1. (1187,P1,2) (b) Per SFAS 12, para 11, unrealized losses and recoveries of unrealized losses on current MES are recognized in the income statement in the period in which they occur. The solutions approach is to set up a T-account for the allowance account.

```
                 Allowance for MES
                        |  23,000  12/31/85
12/31/86 adj      ?     |
                        |-----------------
                        |  13,000  12/31/86
```

The 12/31/85 balance is given. The desired balance of $13,000 at 12/31/86 is the amount needed to reduce the carrying value of the investment from cost ($425,000) to lower of cost or market ($412,000). The required 12/31/86 adjustment is a $10,000 debit to the allowance account and a corresponding credit to recovery of unrealized loss. Note that the lower of cost or market determination is performed on an aggregate basis.

2. (587,P3,48) (d) A realized loss on the disposal of marketable equity securities is the excess of the original cost of the investment ($17,000) over the net proceeds from the sale [(1,000 x $15) – $1,500 = $13,500]. Therefore, the loss is $3,500 ($17,000 – $13,500). Changes in the market price of the investment before sale do not affect the computation of the realized loss. At 12/31/86, the market value of the investment was below its cost and was accounted for in the valuation allowance account established for the aggregate portfolio. At the time of sale, no regard is given to unrealized losses accumulated in the valuation allowance account because the valuation account relates to the entire portfolio and not to a specific security.

3. (1189,Q1,2) (b) Per SFAS 12, unrealized losses on current marketable equity securities (MES) are reported in the income statement, while unrealized losses on noncurrent MES are reported as a direct reduction of stockholders' equity (bypassing the income statement). The unrealized loss is computed by comparing the aggregate cost and the aggregate market value. Therefore, Ross should report an unrealized loss of $60,000 in the income statement, and should establish a contra-stockholders' equity (valuation) account for the unrealized loss of $80,000.

4. (1189,Q1,16) (b) Per SFAS 12, the amount by which a noncurrent marketable equity securities portfolio's aggregate cost exceeds its market value should be recognized as an unrealized loss and shown in the stockholders' equity section of the balance sheet. If in future years the portfolio's aggregate market value increases, the recovery is recognized only to the extent that unrealized losses were previously recognized in the contra equity account. Plat Corp's journal entries for 1987 and 1988 were:

1987:

Unrealized Loss (Contra Equity)	10,000	
Allow. for decline in MES		10,000

1988:

Allow. for decline in MES	10,000	
Unrealized loss (Contra Equity)		10,000

So, the contra account, unrealized loss, would decrease by $10,000 in 1988 for the recovery in market value of the previously recognized unrealized loss of $10,000 in 1987.

5. (588,P1,18) (c) Per SFAS 12, when a marketable equity security is moved from the current to the noncurrent portfolio (or vice versa), it is recorded at the lower of its cost or market value. When the market value is less than its cost, the security is recorded in the new portfolio at market value, and the loss is treated as a realized loss. Therefore, a loss of $11,000 on security C is reported in the income statement ($96,000 – $85,000 = $11,000). No gain or loss is recognized on the current portfolio (securities A and B) because the aggregate market value ($36,000 + $55,000 = $91,000) exceeds the aggregate cost ($39,000 + $50,000 = $89,000). The principle is lower of cost or market, and since cost is lower, no change in value is recorded. Note that since these securities were purchased on 12/31/86, this is the first year that the aggregate market value and aggregate cost value are compared and no allowance account needs to be considered. Therefore, the only loss recognized is the $11,000 loss on security C.

6. (1188,T1,2) (b) Per SFAS 12, paras 8 and 9, the amount by which the aggregate cost of a marketable equity securities portfolio exceeds its aggregate market value should be

reported as a valuation allowance. In a classified balance sheet the securities would be grouped according to current and noncurrent classifications for the purpose of comparing aggregate cost to market value. In an unclassified balance sheet marketable equity securities are considered noncurrent. The valuation allowance is used for both current and noncurrent classifications; therefore, the correct answer is (b).

7. (1189,T1,2) (d) When a company holds investments in marketable equity securities but does not exercise significant influence over its investees, the investments are valued using the lower-of-cost-or-market method. When the aggregate cost of the portfolio exceeds its aggregate market value at the balance sheet date and the decline is temporary, the difference should be reported as a valuation allowance in the asset section of the balance sheet. Therefore, answer (d) is correct and answer (c) is incorrect. Answer (a) is incorrect because any unrealized loss on noncurrent marketable equity securities is reported in the stockholders' equity section of the balance sheet. Answer (b) is incorrect because the decline in value is temporary and therefore, no loss has been realized yet.

B.2. Marketable Debt Securities

8. (1188,T1,3) (b) Answer (b) is correct because per ARB 43, Chapter 3A, para 9, when the market value of a short-term marketable security is substantially less than cost and is not due to a temporary condition, the amount to be included on the balance sheet should not exceed market value. Answer (d) is incorrect because there has been a permanent decline in the market value of the security which requires a write-down to market value. Answers (a) and (c) are incorrect because accrued interest would be recorded separately as interest receivable rather than as part of the cost of the security.

9. (587,T1,6) (b) Per ARB 43, Chapter 3, para 9, cost is the prescribed carrying value for debt securities unless two conditions which necessitate a switch to the lower of cost or market are present. The conditions are that (1) market value is less than cost by a substantial amount, and (2) it is evident that the decline in market value is not due to a mere temporary condition. Under no circumstances, however, is the carrying value allowed to exceed cost. ARB 43 does not specify differing rules for current and noncurrent marketable debt securities; therefore, answer (b) is correct, and answers (a), (c), and (d) are incorrect. It is important not to

confuse ARB 43's rules for debt securities with those of SFAS 12 regarding marketable equity securities.

C. Equity Method

10. (1189,P2,37) (c) This investment should be accounted for using the equity method since Dyer owns a 20% interest and has the ability to exercise significant influence over Eason. The cost of the investment was $700,000 and the fair value of the net assets purchased was also $700,000 (20% x $3,500,000). The book value of the net assets acquired was not given, so it must be assumed that there was no excess of cost over book value to amortize. Therefore, investment revenue consists solely of the investor's share of the investee's earnings (20% x $400,000 = $80,000). The journal entry is:

| Investment in Eason | 80,000 | |
| Income from investment | | 80,000 |

The cash dividend received (20% x $160,000 = $32,000) does not affect investment revenue using the equity method. The entry is:

| Cash | 16,000 | |
| Investment in Eason | | 16,000 |

11. (584,P1,4) (a) The requirement is to compute the amount paid for a 25% interest in an investee. The equity method is used to account for the investment, and no goodwill resulted from the acquisition. The solutions approach is to set up a T-account for the investment account remembering that under the equity method the investor debits the investment account for the cost of the investment and its share of the earnings of the investee and credits the account for its share of dividends paid by the investee.

```
               Investment in Wall
Cost            X  |            Dividends (25% x
Earnings (25% x    |  12,000     $48,000)
 $120,000)  30,000 |
12/31/83   190,000 |
```

The initial cost (purchase price) of $172,000 is computed by solving the following equation for X:

$$\begin{array}{l}\text{Beg.} \\ \text{balance} + \text{Earnings} - \text{Dividends} = \dfrac{\text{End.}}{\text{balance}} \\ \text{(cost)}\end{array}$$

$$X + \$30,000 - \$12,000 = \$190,000$$
$$X = \$172,000$$

12. (1188,T1,5) (d) When an entity uses the equity method to account for an investment in another entity's stock, the investment is recorded at cost on the date of acquisition. As the investee reports income or losses, the investor will recognize its percentage of owner-

ship share of that income or loss by increasing or decreasing the investment account.
Therefore, answer (d) is correct, and answers (a), (b), and (c) are incorrect.

13. (1189,T1,4) (d) Per APB 18, para 6a,
under the cost method, "dividends received in
excess of earnings subsequent to the date of
investment and are recorded as reductions of cost of
the investment." Additionally, per APB 18,
para 6b, under the equity method, "dividends
received from an investee reduce the carrying
amount of the investment." Therefore, answer (d) is correct.

14. (589,T1,15) (b) The key to this question is that it asks for the effect of two
occurrences on the investor's equity in the
earnings of an investee, rather than the
effect on the investment balance. The investor's equity in the earnings of the subsidiary is only affected by the investee's
income or loss for the period (i.e., the investor recognizes its proportionate share of
the investee's net income or loss). Since
neither cash dividends nor changes in the market value of the investee's common stock affect the investee's income or loss for the
period, they also do not affect the investor's
equity in earnings. Therefore, answer (b) is
correct. Note, however, that the cash dividends from the investee would reduce the investor's investment balance.

15. (1184,T1,33) (c) The requirement is to
determine how amortization of the investor's
share of the excess of fair market value over
the book value of depreciable assets at date
of purchase should be reported in the investor's income statement. When an investor uses
the equity method to account for an investee,
amortization of the investor's share of the
excess should be reported in the investor's
income statement as part of the equity in the
earnings of the investee (APB 18, para 19b).
Under the equity method, the investor accounts
for the investee as if it were a consolidated
subsidiary. To record the amortization of
this excess, the following journal entry would
be made:

Income from investment   xxx
    Investment in stock of investee   xxx

Investment income, rather than other expense
[answer (a)], is debited under the presumption
that the investee's net income is overstated
because its depreciation expense and cost of
goods sold figures are based on understated
asset values. Answer (b) is incorrect because
depreciation expense is generally recorded on
a firm's own assets, not the assets of an

entity in which it has invested. Answer (d)
is incorrect because goodwill is not specifically recorded under the equity method;
rather, it is included within the investment
account.

16. (1183,T1,6) (c) The requirement is the
effect of cash dividends declared and paid out
of current earnings upon an investor's investment account, accounted for under both the
cost and equity methods. Under the cost
method, APB 18, para 6 states that dividends
received are to be recognized as income to the
investor and the investment account is unaffected. However, if dividends were received
in excess of earnings subsequent to the investment date, they would be considered a
return of the investment and would be recorded
as a reduction in the investment account. In
this case, dividends are paid from current
earnings and are not, therefore, considered a
return of capital. Under the equity method
(APB 18, para 10), the receipt of dividends
reduces the carrying amount of the investment.

17. (587,P1,19) (b) The equity method is to
be used when the investor owns 20% or more of
the investee's voting stock, unless there is
evidence that the investor does not have the
ability to exercise significant influence over
the investee. Since this is the case, Saxe
must use the cost method. Under the cost
method, APB 18, para 6 states that dividends
received are to be recognized as income to the
investor, and the investment account is unaffected. Also, under the cost method, the investor's share of the investee's net income is
not recognized. Therefore, the investment
account would still have a balance of $150,000
at 12/31/86. Note that the dividends received
by Saxe were distributed from Lex's net accumulated earnings since the date of acquisition
by Saxe. However, if dividends received had
been in excess of earnings subsequent to the
investment date, they are considered a return
of capital and would be recorded as a reduction in the investment account.

18. (587,P2,39) (d) A gain on the disposal
of a long-term investment is the excess of the
proceeds (5,000 x $100 = $500,000) over the
cost of the investment (5,000 x $70 =
$350,000). Therefore, the gain is $150,000
($500,000 - $350,000). Changes in the market
price of the investment before sale do not
affect the computation of the gain. Even if
the market price of the stock falls below cost
and a valuation allowance is established, the
gain or loss on disposal is still based on the
investment's original cost. The adjustment to
the valuation allowance would occur at year

end and not affect the gain on the disposal of the investment. Note that the tax rate (40%) is not used; components of income from continuing operations are reported gross with income tax expense deducted from the total income from continuing operations.

E. Stock Dividends and Splits

19. (1189,P2,39) (d) No dividend revenue is recognized when an investor receives a <u>stock</u> dividend. The investor only receives additional shares of the investee's stock. These shares are not revenue to the investor because the investor continues to own the same proportion of the investee as before the stock dividend, and because the investee has not distributed any assets to the investor (ARB 43, chapter 7B, para 9). Therefore, dividend revenue is $0.

20. (1187,P2,33) (a) Since Adam's interest in Celt is greater than 20% and the companies have several common directors, Adam is presumed to have significant influence over Celt's operations and the equity method should be used. Therefore, the cash dividend received ($60,000) is recorded as a reduction of the investment account rather than as dividend revenue. The stock dividend received from Brock (200 shares) is <u>not</u> considered to be income, because Adam receives no assets and its interest in Brock remains unchanged. Therefore, Adam should <u>not</u> recognize any dividend revenue from these transactions.

21. (1187,P2,40) (d) When the preferred stock and stock warrants are purchased, the total cost ($152,000) is allocated between the stock and the warrants based on their relative fair market values, calculated below

FMV of stock	2,000 x $72 =	$144,000
FMV of warrants	2,000 x $8 =	16,000
Total FMV		$160,000

The cost allocated to the stock warrants is 10% ($16,000/$160,000) of $152,000, or $15,200. Therefore, the gain on the sale of the stock warrants was $5,300 ($20,500 proceeds less $15,200 cost)

F. Stock Rights

22. (1189,P3,41) (c) When the rights are received, the cost of the investment ($36,000) is allocated between the stock and the rights based on their relative fair market values, calculated below:

FMV of stock	500 x $90	=	$45,000
FMV of rights	500 x $10	=	5,000
Total FMV			$50,000

The cost allocated to the stock is $32,400 ($45,000/$50,000, or 90%, of $36,000) and to the rights is $3,600 ($5,000/$50,000, or 10%,

of $36,000). The net proceeds from the sale of the rights is $5,000 (500 x $10), so the gain on the sale of the rights is $1,400 ($5,000 – $3,600).

G. Cash Surrender Value of Life Insurance

23. (586,P3,47) (a) The requirement is the amount to be reported as 1985 life insurance expense. The cash surrender value (CSV) of the policy, which is an asset of the company, increased by $10,500 during 1985 ($54,000 – $43,500). Therefore, part of the premium paid is not expense, but a payment to increase the CSV. The journal entry when the premium is paid is

Cash surrender value	10,500	
Insurance expense	9,500	
Cash		20,000

The dividend received from the policy ($3,000) is not a dividend earned from a separate investment. The dividend is received only because the company owns the insurance policy. This related item should be offset against insurance expense. When the cash is received, the entry is

Cash	3,000	
Insurance expense		3,000

Therefore, 1985 insurance expense is $6,500 ($9,500 – $3,000).

Miscellaneous

24. (587,Q1,15) (c) In determining the amount which should be reported in Lake's 1986 income statement as dividend revenue, the first step is to determine what method should be used in accounting for Lake's investments. Per APB 18, para 17, the Board concluded that the equity method of accounting for an investment in common stock should be followed by an investor whose investment in common stock gives it the ability to exercise significant influence over the operating and financial policies of an investee even though the investor may hold 50% or less of the voting stock. Ability to exercise that influence may be indicated in several ways, such as representation on the board of directors. Another important consideration is the extent of ownership by an investor. The Board concluded that an investment of 20% or more of the voting stock of an investee should lead to a presumption, in the absence of evidence to the contrary, that an investor has the ability to exercise significant influence over an investee. Conversely, an investment of less than 20% of the voting stock of an investee should lead to a presumption that an investor does <u>not</u> have the ability to exercise significant influence unless such ability can be demonstrated. Lake's 30% ownership of Aub and its representation on Aub's board of directors clearly indicate that the investment in Aub should be accounted for using the equity method. Lake's 1% ownership in Kar and lack of evidence in this problem that Lake has "significant influence" over Kar indicate that this investment should be accounted for using the cost method, in accordance with SFAS 12. Per APB 18, para 6b, when the equity method is used, dividends received from an investee reduce the carrying amount of the investment (i.e., are not reported as dividend revenue). Per APB 18, para 6a, however, the investor recognizes dividends received from investees as income under the cost method. Therefore, the $1,000 of cash dividends from Kar would be reported as dividend revenue by Lake, while the $15,000 of cash dividends from Aub would reduce the carrying amount of Lake's investment in Aub. Thus, answer (c) is correct, and answers (a), (b), and (d) are incorrect.

25. (587,Q1,16) (d) Lake's royalty revenue results from the licensing of their trademark to Barr Co. Lake receives royalties of 10% of Barr's sales of trademarked items. To determine royalty revenue for 1986, it must first be realized that the royalty payment on September 1, 1986, is for sales in January through June of 1986. This royalty payment of $7,000 is the first portion of royalty revenue for 1986. The second portion of royalty revenue is for Barr's sales of trademarked items for July through December of 1986. This second portion consists of 10% of Barr's estimated sales of trademarked items for the last half of 1986. Royalty revenue for the second half of 1986 is then $2,000 (10% x $20,000). Therefore, answer (d) is correct because royalty revenue would be $9,000 for 1986 and is comprised of the $7,000 royalty payment received on September 1, 1986 plus 10% of estimated sales for months July through December.

26. (587,Q1,17) (c) Lake receives rental revenue from leasing a parking lot to Day Co. The annual rental payment made by Day Co. to Lake is $48,000. However, Day Co. also paid a nonrefundable deposit of $50,000 on January 1, 1984. This $50,000 deposit, since it is nonrefundable, is considered unearned revenue which must be recognized over the life of the lease on a straight-line basis. Therefore, in addition to the $48,000 annual rental payment, $5,000 ($50,000 ÷ 10 years) of the nonrefundable deposit will be recognized as rental revenue in 1986. Thus, answer (c) is correct because $53,000 will be recognized as rental revenue in 1986. Note that the $8,000 security deposit will not be revenue because it is to be refunded at the end of the lease period.

It is deferred in its entirety and recorded as a long-term liability. Only a nonrefundable deposit would be recognized as rental revenue over the life of the lease.

May 1990 Answers

27. (590,P1,3) (b) The investment is recorded on 4/1/89 at its cost of $194,000 ($198,500 less accrued interest of $4,500). The problem is silent as to whether this is a temporary investment (no amortization of discount) or a long-term investment (requires amortization). The key in determining whether it is temporary or long-term is management's intent when they purchased the investment. Since intent is not discussed, the fact that the investment was purchased 15 months before maturity, and the fact that straight-line amortization is mentioned in the problem, would lead toward an assumption that this is a long-term investment. Therefore, the 10/31/89 carrying amount is $196,800 [$194,000 + ($6,000 x 7/15)]. Note that if the investment was temporary, the 10/31/89 carrying amount would be the unadjusted cost of $194,000.

28. (590,P1,6) (c) This investment is accounted for using the equity method since Lee owns 30% of Polk's voting stock and has the ability to exercise significant influence. Under the equity method, investment revenue consists of the investor's share of the investee's earnings (30% x $40,000 = $12,000). The journal entry is:

```
Investment in Polk       12,000
    Income from investment        12,000
```

The cash dividends received (30% x $25,000 = $7,500) do not affect investment revenue under the equity method. The dividend is recorded as a reduction of the investment account. The entry is:

```
Cash                     7,500
    Investment in Polk            7,500
```

29. (590,P1,7) (b) This investment is accounted for using the equity method since Lee owns 30% of Polk's voting stock and has the ability to exercise significant influence. Under the equity method, the carrying amount of the investment is increased by the investor's share of the investee earnings and decreased by dividends received. Therefore at 12/31/88, the carrying amount is $104,500 [$100,000 + (30% x $40,000) - (30% x $25,000)].

30. . (590,P1,8) (c) This investment is accounted for using the equity method since Lee owns 30% of Polk's voting stock and has

the ability to exercise significant influence.
Under the equity method, the carrying amount
of the investment is increased by the invest-
or's share of investee earnings and decreased
by dividends received. Therefore at 12/31/88,
the carrying amount is $104,500 [$100,000 +
(30% x $40,000) - (30% x $25,000)]. By
7/1/89, Polk earned 1989 income of $25,000
($50,000 x 6/12) and paid dividends of
$15,000. The carrying amount at 7/1/89 is
$107,500 [$104,500 + (30% x $25,000) - (30% x
15,000)]. At 7/1/89, half of the stock is
sold for $66,000, resulting in a gain of
$12,250 [$66,000 - (1/2 x $107,500)].

31. (590,P3,57) (a) A realized loss on the
disposal of marketable equity securities (MES)
is the excess of the original cost of the investment ($31,500) over the net proceeds from
the sale [(2,000 x $14) - $1,400 = $26,600].
Therefore, the loss is $4,900 ($31,500 -
$26,600). Changes in the market value of the
MES before sale do not affect the computation
of the realized loss. At 12/31/88, the market
value of the MES was below its cost, which
affected the valuation allowance for the
aggregate portfolio. However, at the time of
sale no regard is given to the balance in the
allowance account because the balance relates
to the entire portfolio and not to a specific
security.

Answer Outline

Problem 1   MES: Current and Noncurrent
             Portfolios (589,T2)

a. I/S effects should be measured as
    difference between selling prices and
    cost of securities sold
    Differences should be reported as realized
    gains and losses
b. Reclassification of current MES to
    noncurrent portfolio
      Basis should be LCM at date of
       reclassification
         Market value of security < cost
      Difference is loss in current period
c. B/S reporting
      Each portfolio shall be reported at LCM
       on aggregate basis
      Valuation allowance reports excess of
       aggregate cost over aggregate market
       value
      Current period reporting
       Current portfolio change in valuation
        account is unrealized gain (loss) in
        current period I/S
       Noncurrent portfolio valuation account
        balance is reported in equity section
        of B/S
      Reasons portfolios are reported this way
       Conservatism--reflects realizable value
        of portfolio at end of period
       Matching
          Current portfolio
           Estimated loss is reported in period
           it occurred
           Indicates expected cash flow conse-
           quences from sale of the securities
          Noncurrent portfolio
           Realization of gains (losses) from
           sale is less certain in near term
           Market value decline
             May not be a reasonable estimate
             Not useful for cash flow projec-
              tions

Unofficial Answer

Problem 1   MES: Current and Noncurrent
             Portfolios (589,T2)

a. The differences between the selling prices
and the costs of securities sold should be reported as realized gains and losses in the
determination of net income.

b. The security in the current portfolio
should be reclassified to the noncurrent
portfolio at the lower of its cost or market

value at the date of reclassification. Since
its market value was less than cost, the
market value becomes the new cost basis. The
excess of cost over market value at the date
of reclassification should be reported as a
realized loss in the determination of net
income.

c. Each portfolio should be reported in the
balance sheet at its separately determined
lower of aggregate cost or market value.
Applying this rule, Vane would report each
portfolio at market by using a valuation allowance (contra) account for the excess of
aggregate cost over aggregate market value.

   For the current portfolio, the change in
the valuation allowance (contra) account that
occurred during the year should be reported as
an unrealized gain or loss in the income
statement. For the noncurrent portfolio, an
amount equal to the valuation allowance
(contra) account balance should be reported
separately in the equity section of the
balance sheet.

   Reporting the portfolio at market value
reflects the realizable value of the portfolio
at the end of the period and is consistent
with conservatism. For the current portfolio,
the estimated loss is reported (matched) in
the income statement in the period in which
the change in realizable value occurred.
Reporting the current portfolio at market
indicates the expected cash flow from the sale
of the securities. Inclusion of the reduction
in market value of the current portfolio in
net income assists in cash flow projections by
acknowledging the expected impairment in
future cash flows as a consequence of the investment. For the noncurrent portfolio, the
decline in market value (loss) is less certain
of realization in the near term, and may not
be a reasonable estimate of the cash flow
consequence of the investment. Therefore,
changes in market value of the noncurrent
portfolio are not considered useful for cash
flow projections.

Solution Guide

Problem 2   MES & Equity Method Invest-
             ment (589,P5)

1.   This problem consists of three related
     requirements concerning a company's
     investments in marketable equity
     securities.

1.1 In part a., a schedule of Poe's current
     marketable equity securities at 12/31/88
     must be prepared. This schedule should
     include columns for cost, market, and
     unrealized gain or loss.

1.2 A schedule to show the carrying amount of Poe's noncurrent investments at 12/31/88 is required in part b.

1.3 In part c., a schedule showing all revenues, gains, and losses for 1988 relating to Poe's investments must be prepared.

1.4 The solutions approach for problems of this type in which the requirements are interrelated is to prepare time lines for each security and proceed through the given information making computations and notations on the appropriate time line. Labeling of computations by requirement helps to organize your data. For example, if a computation or number relates to requirement c., it can be labeled "c." Using this approach, the candidate will be solving a part of two to three requirements as each security is covered, but not necessarily in the same order as given on the exam. After working through all the information given, the formal required schedules can be prepared.

2. Poe owned 1,000 shares of Axe preferred which cost $40,000 or $40 per share. Poe converted 500 shares of Axe perferred into 1,500 shares of Axe common. The 500 shares still held have a cost of $20,000 (500 x $40), and a market value of $28,000 (500 x $56). The cost of the 1,500 shares of common acquired is the book value of the preferred stock surrendered (500 x $40 = $20,000). The market value of the common at year end is $30,000 (1,500 x $20). See time line after 2.1.

2.1 Dividend revenue received on the Axe preferred stock should be included in Poe's income statement. The Axe preferred stock paid a $1.20 dividend on 1,000 shares twice during the year, for a total of $2,400. Note that the second dividend was received on October 5, after 500 shares of preferred were converted. However, the dividend was received for all 1,000 shares, since the date of record was September 9.

3. Poe owned 6,000 shares of Purl common which cost $60,000 or $10 per share. 2,500 of these shares were sold. The 3,500 still held have a cost of $35,000 (3,500 x $10), and a market value of $38,500 (3,500 x $11). See the time line after 3.2.

3.1 A $7,500 gain was realized on the sale of Purl common and should be included in Poe's income statement. The selling price was $32,500 (2,500 x $13), and the cost was $25,000 (2,500 x $10. See time line after 3.2.

3.2 Dividend income received on the Purl common stock should also be included in Poe's income statement. A $1.00 per share dividend was received on the Purl common stock (3,500 shares x $1.00 per share or $3,500).

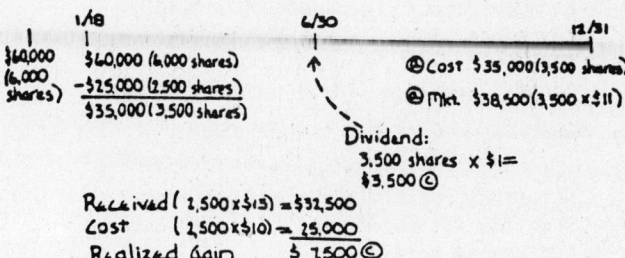

4. Poe owned 2,000 shares of Day common which cost $55,000. Day issued a 10% stock dividend on February 14 which gave Poe an additional 200 shares (2,000 x 10%) at no additional cost. Therefore, the 2,200 shares had an adjusted cost of $25 per share ($55,000 ÷ 2,200). The stock dividend is not reflected in income. Poe sold 500 shares on June 1. The 1,700 still held have a cost of $42,500 (1,700 x $25) and a market value of $37,400 (1,700 x $22). See time line after 4.1.

4.1 A $2,000 loss was realized on the sale of Day common and should be included in Poe's income statement. It was sold for $10,500 (500 x $21) and had a cost of $12,500 (500 x $25).

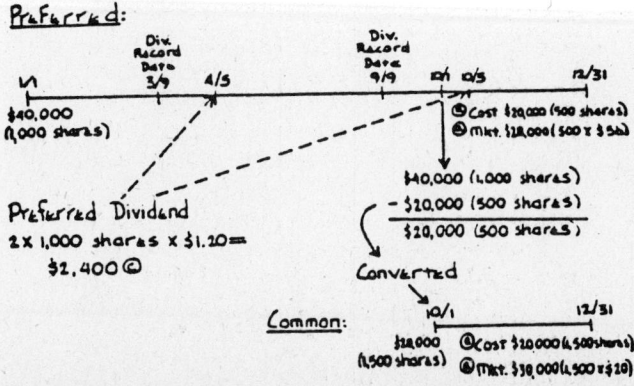

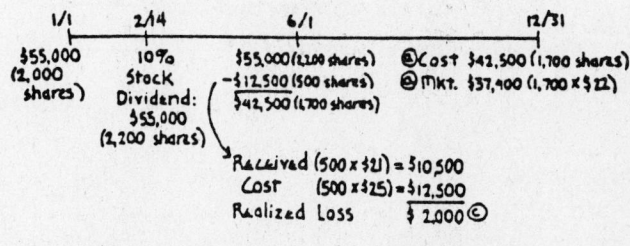

5. Poe intends to hold the Scott stock as a long-term investment. Since they own 30% of the voting stock and can exercise significant influence over Scott, the use of the equity method is appropriate.

5.1 The original cost of the investment was $1,700,000. The excess of investment cost ($1,700,000) over the book value of the net assets purchased ($1,400,000) is $300,000. This amount must be amortized over 40 years ($300,000 ÷ 40 = $7,500) and is a reduction of both investment revenue and the investment account. See time line after 5.3.

```
Investment revenue          7,500
   Investment in Scott              7,500
```

5.2 The investment account is also reduced by dividends received when the equity method is used. Scott paid quarterly dividends of $.50 a share, or a total of $50,000 each quarter to Poe (100,000 x $.50). Therefore, Poe received a total of $200,000 in dividends (4 x $50,000) from Scott. See time line after 5.3.

```
Cash                        200,000
   Investment in Scott              200,000
```

Note that the dividend received from Scott is not recognized as income under the equity method.

5.3 Using the equity method, the investment account is increased by the investor's share of investee earnings (30% x $1,200,000 = $360,000).

```
Investment in Scott         360,000
   Investment revenue               360,000
```

6. The aggregate market value of the current marketable equity securities is greater than aggregate cost. Therefore, no valuation allowance is needed and the recovery of the $7,000 unrealized loss is reflected in the 1988 income statement.

```
Valuation allowance                  7,000
   Unrealized gain on current
      marketable equity securities*        7,000
```

*Alternatively, the account title used could be "Recovery of unrealized loss."

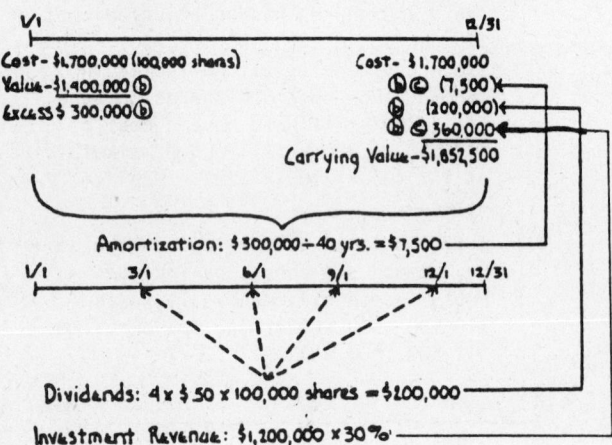

Unofficial Answer

Problem 2   MES & Equity Method Investment (589,P5)

a.

Poe Corp.
SCHEDULE OF CURRENT MARKETABLE
EQUITY SECURITIES
December 31, 1988

	Number of shares	Cost	Market price per share	Market value	Unrealized gain or (loss)
Axe – preferred	500	$ 20,000	$56	$ 28,000	$ 8,000
Axe – common	1,500	20,000	20	30,000	10,000
Purl – common	3,500	35,000	11	38,500	3,500
Day – common	1,700	42,500	22	37,400	(5,100)
		$117,500		$133,900	$16,400
Valuation allowance [1]		-0-			
Carried at cost		$117,500			

b.

Poe Corp.
SCHEDULE OF NONCURRENT MARKETABLE
EQUITY SECURITIES
December 31, 1988

Scott Corp. – 100,000 shares of common stock:

Cost:			
Acquisition price			$1,700,000
Increase in equity during 1988:			
Equity in Scott's income		$360,000	
Less:			
Amortization of excess of cost			
over underlying equity	$ 7,500 [2]		
Dividends received	200,000	207,500	
Net increase in equity			152,500
Carrying amount of Poe Corp.'s investment in Scott			$1,852,500

c.

Poe Corp.
SCHEDULE OF INVESTMENT INCOME
For the Year Ended December 31, 1988

Dividends:

Axe Corp. - preferred (1,000 shares x $2.40 per share)	$ 2,400	
Purl, Inc. - common (3,500 shares x $1.00 per share)	3,500	
Total dividend revenue		$ 5,900

Gains on marketable equity securities:

Unrealized gain on current marketable equity securities		7,000 [1]	
Realized gain/(loss) on sale of securities:			
Purl, Inc. - common ($13 - $10 = $3 x 2,500 shares)	$ 7,500		
Day Co. - common ($55,000/2,000 shares x 110%),			
or cost per share of $25 - $21 selling price			
per share = $4 loss per share x 500 shares sold	(2,000)		
Net realized gain on sale of securities		5,500	
Net gains on current marketable equity securities			12,500

Equity in income of Scott Corp.:

Poe's 30% interest in Scott's net income of			
$1,200,000		360,000	
Amortization of excess of cost over underlying equity		(7,500) [2]	
Equity in income of Scott Corp.			352,500
			$370,900

Explanation of Amounts:

[1]   The valuation allowance of $7,000 at December 31, 1987 for current marketable equity securities
should be eliminated by a debit to valuation allowance - current, and a credit to unrealized gain on
current marketable equity securities. The $7,000 unrealized gain should be included in Poe's income
statement for the year ended December 31, 1988.

[2]	Poe's acquisition price for its 30% interest	$1,700,000
	Poe's interest in the underlying equity	1,400,000
	Excess of cost over underlying equity	$ 300,000
	Amortization based on 40 years	$ 7,500

Solution Guide

Problem 3 Other Noncurrent Assets (588,P5)

1. This problem consists of two related parts. Part (a) requires schedules analyzing the changes in various noncurrent asset accounts (patent, trademark, long-term receivables, and investment in stock), while part (b) requires a schedule showing the revenues, gains, and expenses related to those same accounts.

1.1 The solutions approach for problems in which the requirements are interrelated is to make <u>all</u> computations for each asset at one time, and label each computation either (a) or (b), according to the requirement to which it relates. After working through all the information given, your work can be organized into the formal schedules required for each part.

2. The patent was held for four months in 1987, then sold. The useful life was 15 years, or 180 months (15 x 12). Since the original cost was $315,000, the amortization to be recorded in 1987 for four months is $7,000 ($315,000 x 4/180). The book value of the patent at 12/31/86 was $245,000, so the book value at the time of sale was $238,000 (see the time line after 2.1).

2.1 The patent was sold in exchange for a $500,000 noninterest bearing 3-year note. Per paras 12-14 of APB 21, a noninterest bearing note should be recorded at its present value under the prevailing rate of interest on similar notes with any difference recorded as a discount. The present value of this note is $337,500 ($500,000 x .675), and the gain on the sale of the patent is $99,500 ($337,500 - $238,000). The 5/1/87 entry is:

Note receivable 500,000
   Discount on N.R.   162,500 ($500,000 - $337,500)
   Patent   238,000
   Gain on sale   99,500

The time line below summarizes the information from 2 and 2.1:

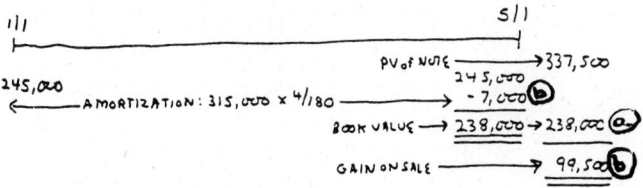

2.2 APB 21 also specifies that the effective interest method should be used to recognize interest on notes where interest has been imputed. Under the effective interest method, interest revenue is computed as follows:

$$\left(\begin{array}{c}\text{Book value}\\\text{of note}\end{array}\right) \times \left(\begin{array}{c}\text{Effective}\\\text{rate}\end{array}\right) \times \left(\text{Time}\right) = \left(\begin{array}{c}\text{Interest}\\\text{revenue}\end{array}\right)$$
$$\$337,500 \quad\times\quad 14\% \quad\times\quad 8/12 \;=\; \$31,500$$

Since there is no cash interest, this entire amount is discount amortization. The journal entry is:

Discount on N.R.   31,500
   Interest revenue   31,500

After this entry is recorded, the discount account has a balance of $131,000 ($162,500 - $31,500), so the note receivable has a 12/31/87 carrying amount of $369,000 ($500,000 - $131,000). See the time line below.

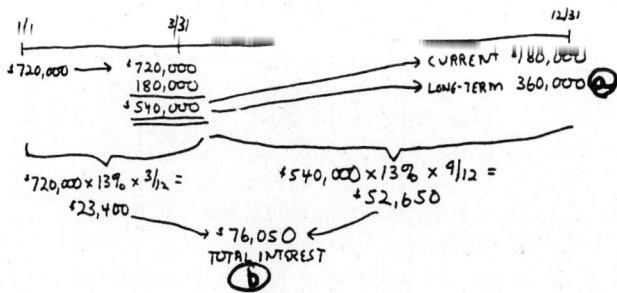

3. The 12/31/86 balance of the installment contract receivable (including the current portion) is $720,000. On 3/31/87, the $180,000 installment paid brought the balance down to $540,000. Of this total, $180,000 is current (due 3/31/88) and the remainder ($540,000 - $180,000 = $360,000) is noncurrent. See the time line after 3.1.

3.1 The interest earned on the installment contract before the 3/31/87 installment was $23,400 ($720,000 x 13% x 3/12). After the installment was received, interest earned was $52,650 ($540,000 x 13% x 9/12). See the time line below.

4. A trademark was obtained on 1/2/87 at a cost of $250,000. The trademark is to be amortized over the maximum period allowable. Para 29 of APB 17 states that intangible assets must be amortized over no more than 40 years. Therefore, 1987 amortization is $6,250 ($250,000 x 1/40) and the 12/31/87 book value of the trademark is $243,750 ($250,000 - $6,250). See the time line below:

The entry is:

Cash   150,000
    Investment in stock   150,000

At 12/31/87, the balance in the investment account is $1,902,500 ($1,880,000 + $172,500 - $150,000 = $1,902,500). See the time line below:

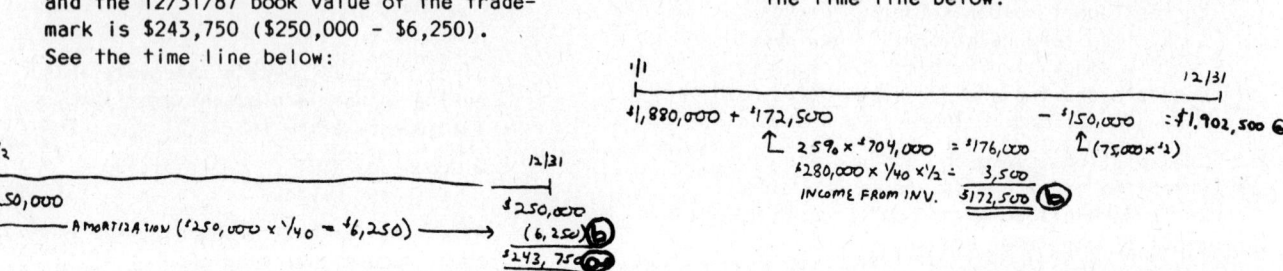

5. The investment in Black common stock should be accounted for using the equity method, because Rowe owns more than 20% of Black and can exercise significant influence over Black's operating and financial policies.

5.1 When using the equity method, the investor recognizes its share of the investee's earnings. Black's earnings for the last six months of 1987 (since Rowe made the investment on 7/1/87) were $704,000, so Rowe's share of those earnings would be $176,000 (25% x $704,000). The journal entry would be:

Investment in stock   176,000
    Income from investment   176,000

5.2 The excess of cost over book value must be amortized when using the equity method. Since the fair value of Black's net assets equals the book value, the excess is attributed to goodwill, which Rowe amortizes over 40 years. The cost of the investment is $1,880,000, the book value of the net assets purchased is $1,600,000 (25% x $6,400,000), so the excess of cost over book value is $280,000 ($1,880,000 - $1,600,000). The amortization for six months (7/1 to 12/31) is $3,500 ($280,000 x 1/40 x 1/2). The journal entry is:

Income from investment   3,500
    Investment in stock   3,500

From the entry above and the entry in 5.1, you can see that the net income from this investment is $172,500 ($176,000 - $3,500).

5.3 Under the equity method, dividends received (75,000 x $2 = $150,000) are recorded as a reduction of the investment account rather than as dividend revenue.

Unofficial Answer

Problem 3   Other Noncurrent Assets (588,P5)

a.

Rowe Corp.
SCHEDULE OF CHANGES IN NOTE
FROM SALE OF PATENT
1987

Face amount, 5/1/87 (due 5/1/90)	$500,000
Deduct imputed interest	
[$500,000 − ($500,000 x 0.675)]	162,500
Balance, 5/1/87	337,500
Add interest earned to 12/31/87	
($337,500 x 14% x 8/12)	31,500
Balance, 12/31/87, noncurrent	$369,000

Rowe Corp.
SCHEDULE OF CHANGES IN INSTALLMENT
CONTRACT RECEIVABLE
1987

Balance, 12/31/86	$720,000
Deduct payment, 3/31/87	180,000
Balance, 3/31/87 and 12/31/87	540,000
Deduct installment due 3/31/88	180,000
Balance, 12/31/87, noncurrent	$360,000

Rowe Corp.
SCHEDULE OF CHANGES IN INVESTMENT
IN BLACK CORP., AT EQUITY
1987

	Underlying equity		Goodwill		Total at equity
25% interest, 7/1/87	$1,600,000	[1]	$280,000		$1,880,000
Period 7/1/87 to 12/31/87					
Equity in earnings	176,000	[2]			176,000
Dividend, 11/30/87	(150,000)	[3]			(150,000)
Amortization of goodwill			(3,500)	[4]	(3,500)
Balance, 12/31/87	$1,626,000		$276,500		$1,902,500

Rowe Corp.
SCHEDULE OF CHANGES IN PATENT
1987

Cost, net of accumulated amortization, 12/31/86		$ 245,000
Deduct amortization, 1/1/87 to 5/1/87 ($315,000 ÷ 15 x 4/12)		(7,000)
		238,000
Cost of patent sold, 5/1/87		(238,000)
Balance, 12/31/87	$	0

Rowe Corp.
SCHEDULE OF CHANGES IN TRADEMARK
1987

Cost, 1/2/87	$250,000
Deduct amortization for 1987 ($250,000 ÷ 40)	6,250
Balance, net of accumulated amortization, 12/31/87	$243,750

Explanations of Amounts

Underlying equity ($25% x $6,400,000)	$1,600,000	[1]
Equity in earnings (25% x $704,000)	$ 176,000	[2]
Dividend, 11/30/87 ($2 x 75,000 shares)	$ 150,000	[3]
Amortization of goodwill ($280,000 ÷ 40 x 1/2)	$ 3,500	[4]

b.

Rowe Corp.
SCHEDULE OF REVENUES, GAINS, AND EXPENSES
RELATING TO OTHER NONCURRENT ASSETS
For the Year Ended December 31, 1987

Gain recognized on sale of patent	$99,500	[5]
Interest revenue		
Noninterest bearing note	$ 31,500	[Part a]
Installment contract	76,050	[6]
Total	$107,550	
Equity in earnings of Black Corp.	$172,500	[7]
Amortization expense--intangibles		
Patent	$ 7,000	[Part a]
Trademark	6,250	[Part a]
Total	$ 13,250	

Explanations of Amounts

[5] Gain recognized on sale of patent

Selling price (net of imputed interest)	$337,500	[Part a]
Carrying amount of patent at date of sale	238,000	[Part a]
Gain recognized	$ 99,500	

[6] Interest revenue--installment contract

Interest received 3/31/87 ($720,000 x 13%)	$93,600	
Interest 1/1/87 to 3/31/87	x 1/4	$ 23,400
Interest accrued 4/1/87 to 12/31/87		
($540,000 x 13% x 9/12)		52,650
Interest, year ended 12/31/87		$ 76,050

[7] Equity in earnings of Black Corp.

Equity in Black's net income for 1987	$176,000	[2]
Deduct amortization of goodwill	3,500	[4]
Equity in earnings of Black Corp.	$172,500	

Multiple Choice Questions (1-29)

1. In a statement of cash flows, receipts from sales of property, plant, and equipment and other productive assets should generally be classified as cash inflows from
   a. Operating activities.
   b. Financing activities.
   c. Investing activities.
   d. Selling activities.

2. In a statement of cash flows, interest payments to lenders and other creditors should be classified as cash outflows for
   a. Operating activities.
   b. Borrowing activities.
   c. Lending activities.
   d. Financing activities.

3. In a statement of cash flows, proceeds from issuing equity instruments should be classified as cash inflows from
   a. Lending activities.
   b. Operating activities.
   c. Investing activities.
   d. Financing activities.

4. In a statement of cash flows, payments to acquire debt instruments of other entities (other than cash equivalents) should be classified as cash outflows for
   a. Operating activities.
   b. Investing activities.
   c. Financing activities.
   d. Lending activities.

5. Which of the following should be reported when preparing a statement of cash flows?

	Conversion of long-term debt to common stock	Conversion of preferred stock to common stock
a.	No	No
b.	No	Yes
c.	Yes	Yes
d.	Yes	No

6. The following information is available from Sand Corp.'s accounting records for the year ended December 31, 1987.

Cash received from customers	$870,000
Rent received	10,000
Cash paid to suppliers and employees	510,000
Taxes paid	110,000
Cash dividends paid	30,000

Net cash flow provided by operations for 1987 was
   a. $220,000
   b. $230,000

c. $250,000
d. $260,000

Items 7 and 8 are based on the following information:

Patsy Corp. has estimated its activity for December 1986. Selected data from these estimated amounts are as follows:

- Sales $350,000
  Gross profit (based on sales)   30%
  Increase in trade accounts receivable during month $10,500
  Change in accounts payable during month $0
  Increase in inventory during month $5,000

- Variable selling, general and administrative expenses (S,G&A) includes a charge for uncollectible accounts of 1% of sales. A/R write offs were $3,000.
- Total S,G&A is $35,500 per month plus 15% of sales.
- Depreciation expense of $20,000 per month is included in fixed S,G&A.

7. On the basis of the above data, what is the cash inflow from operating activities for December?
   a. $336,500
   b. $339,500
   c. $346,500
   d. $350,000

8. On the basis of the above data, what is the cash outflow from operating activities for December?
   a. $309,500
   b. $313,000
   c. $314,500
   d. $318,000

9. A company's accounts receivable decreased from the beginning to the end of the year. In the company's statement of cash flows (operating activities shown using direct approach), the cash collected from customers would be
   a. Sales revenues plus accounts receivable at the beginning of the year.
   b. Sales revenues plus the decrease in accounts receivable from the beginning to the end of the year.
   c. Sales revenues less the decrease in accounts receivable from the beginning to the end of the year.
   d. The same as sales revenues.

10. In a statement of cash flows (operating activities shown using indirect approach), a decrease in prepaid expenses should be
   a. Reported as an inflow and outflow of cash.

b.   Reported as an outflow of cash.
c.   Deducted from net income.
d.   Added to net income.

11.   In a statement of cash flows in which the operating activities section is prepared under the indirect method, a gain on the sale of an investment should be presented as a(an)
a.   Deduction from net income.
b.   Addition to net income.
c.   Inflow and outflow of cash.
d.   Outflow of cash.

12.   A company's wages payable increased from the beginning to the end of the year. In the company's statement of cash flows in which the operating activities section is prepared under the direct method, the cash paid for wages would be
a.   Salary expense plus wages payable at the beginning of the year.
b.   Salary expense plus the increase in wages payable from the beginning to the end of the year.
c.   Salary expense less the increase in wages payable from the beginning to the end of the year.
d.   The same as salary expense.

13.   A loss on the sale of machinery in the ordinary course of business should be presented in a statement of cash flows (using indirect approach for operating activities) as a(an)
a.   Deduction from net income.
b.   Addition to net income.
c.   Inflow and outflow of cash.
d.   Outflow of cash.

14.   In a statement of cash flows (using indirect approach for operating activities) an increase in inventories should be presented as a(an)
a.   Outflow of cash.
b.   Inflow and outflow of cash.
c.   Addition to net income.
d.   Deduction from net income.

15.   Deferred income tax expense resulting from temporary differences related to depreciation of plant assets should be presented in a statement of cash flows (using indirect approach for operating activities) as a(an)
a.   Noncash financing and investing activity reported in a separate schedule.
b.   Financing activity.
c.   Deduction from net income.
d.   Addition to net income.

16.   The amortization of bond premium on long-term debt should be presented in a statement of cash flows (using indirect approach for operating activities) as a(an)
a.   Financing activity.
b.   Investing activity.
c.   Addition to net income.
d.   Deduction from net income.

Items 17 through 19 are based on the following:

Dice Corp.'s balance sheet accounts as of December 31, 1988 and 1987 and information relating to 1988 activities are presented below.

	December 31,	
	1988	1987
Assets		
Cash	$ 230,000	$ 100,000
Short-term investments	300,000	--
Accounts receivable (net)	510,000	510,000
Inventory	680,000	600,000
Long-term investments	200,000	300,000
Plant assets	1,700,000	1,000,000
Accumulated depreciation	(450,000)	(450,000)
Goodwill	90,000	100,000
Total Assets	$3,260,000	$2,160,000

Liabilities and Stockholders' Equity		
Accounts payable and accrued liabilities	$ 825,000	$ 720,000
Short-term debt	325,000	--
Common stock, $10 par	800,000	700,000
Additional paid-in capital	370,000	250,000
Retained earnings	940,000	490,000
Total liabilities and stockholders' equity	$3,260,000	$2,160,000

Information relating to 1988 activities
•   Net income for 1988 was $690,000.
•   Cash dividends of $240,000 were declared and paid in 1988.
•   Equipment costing $400,000 and having a carrying amount of $150,000 was sold in 1988 for $150,000.
•   A long-term investment was sold in 1988 for $135,000. There were no other transactions affecting long-term investments in 1988.
•   10,000 shares of common stock were issued in 1988 for $22 a share.
•   Short-term investments consist of treasury bills maturing on 6/30/89.

17. Net cash provided by Dice's 1988 operating activities was
    a. $690,000
    b. $915,000
    c. $940,000
    d. $950,000

18. Net cash used in Dice's 1988 investing
activities was
    a. $1,115,000
    b. $ 895,000
    c. $ 865,000
    d. $ 815,000

19. Net cash provided by Dice's 1988 financing activities was
    a. $305,000
    b. $440,000
    c. $455,000
    d. $545,000

Items 20 and 21 are based on the following:

Brock Corp.'s transactions for the year ended
December 31, 1988 included the following:

    • Acquired 50% of Hoag Corp.'s common
stock for $225,000 cash which was borrowed
from a bank.
    • Issued 5,000 shares of its preferred
stock for land having a fair value of
$400,000.
    • Issued 500 of its 11% debenture
bonds, due 1996, for $490,000 cash.
    • Purchased a patent for $275,000
cash.
    • Paid $150,000 toward a bank loan.
    • Sold investment securities for
$995,000.
    • Had a net increase in customer
deposits of $110,000.

20. Brock's net cash provided by investing
activities for 1988 was
    a. $370,000
    b. $495,000
    c. $595,000
    d. $770,000

21. Brock's net cash provided by financing
activities for 1988 was
    a. $565,000
    b. $675,000
    c. $715,000
    d. $825,000

Items 22 and 23 are based on the following:

Kollar Corp.'s transactions for the year ended
December 31, 1988 included the following:

    • Purchased real estate for $550,000
cash which was borrowed from a bank.
    • Sold investment securities for
$500,000.
    • Paid dividends of $600,000.
    • Issued 500 shares of common stock
for $250,000.
    • Purchased machinery and equipment
for $125,000 cash.
    • Paid $450,000 toward a bank loan.
    • Reduced accounts receivable by
$100,000.
    • Increased accounts payable by
$200,000.

22. Kollar's net cash used in investing
activities for 1988 was
    a. $675,000
    b. $375,000
    c. $175,000
    d. $ 50,000

23. Kollar's net cash used in financing
activities for 1988 was
    a. $ 50,000
    b. $250,000
    c. $450,000
    d. $500,000

Items 24 through 27 relate to data to be
reported in the statement of cash flows of
Debbie Dress Shops, Inc. based on the
following information:

Debbie Dress Shops, Inc.
Balance Sheets

	December 31,	
	1988	1987
Assets:		
Current assets:		
Cash	$ 300,000	$ 200,000
Accounts receivable		
--net	840,000	580,000
Merchandise inventory	660,000	420,000
Prepaid expenses	100,000	50,000
Total current		
assets	1,900,000	1,250,000
Long-term investments	80,000	-
Land, buildings and		
fixtures	1,130,000	600,000
Less accumulated		
depreciation	110,000	50,000
	1,020,000	550,000
Total assets	$3,000,000	$1,800,000

Equities:

Current liabilities:

Accounts payable	$ 530,000	$ 440,000
Accrued expenses	140,000	130,000
Dividends payable	70,000	-
Total current liabilities	740,000	570,000
Note payable--due 1983	500,000	-

Stockholders' equity:

Common stock	1,200,000	900,000
Retained earnings	560,000	330,000
	1,760,000	1,230,000
Total liabilities and stockholders' equity	$3,000,000	$1,800,000

Debbie Dress Shops, Inc.
Income Statements

	Year ended December 31,	
	1988	1987
Net credit sales	$6,400,000	$4,000,000
Cost of goods sold	5,000,000	3,200,000
Gross profit	1,400,000	800,000
Expenses (including income taxes)	1,000,000	520,000
Net income	$ 400,000	$ 280,000

Additional information available included the following:

• All accounts receivable and accounts payable related to trade merchandise. Accounts payable are recorded net and always are paid to take all of the discount allowed. The Allowance for doubtful accounts at the end of 1988 was the same as at the end of 1987; no receivables were charged against the Allowance during 1988.

• The proceeds from the note payable were used to finance a new store building. Capital stock was sold to provide additional working capital.

24. Cash collected during 1988 from accounts receivable amounted to
   a. $5,560,000
   b. $5,840,000
   c. $6,140,000
   d. $6,400,000

25. Cash payments during 1988 on accounts payable to suppliers amounted to
   a. $4,670,000
   b. $4,910,000
   c. $5,000,000
   d. $5,150,000

26. Net cash provided by financing activities for 1988 totaled
   a. $140,000
   b. $300,000
   c. $500,000
   d. $700,000

27. Net cash used in investing activities during 1988 was
   a. $ 80,000
   b. $530,000
   c. $610,000
   d. $660,000

May 1990 Questions

Items 28 and 29 are based on the following:

A company acquired a building, paying a portion of the purchase price in cash and issuing a mortgage note payable to the seller for the balance.

28. In a statement of cash flows, what amount is included in investing activities for the above transaction?
   a. Cash payment.
   b. Acquisition price.
   c. Zero.
   d. Mortgage amount.

29. In a statement of cash flows, what amount is included in financing activities for the above transaction?
   a. Cash payment.
   b. Acquistion price.
   c. Zero.
   d. Mortgage amount.

Problems

Problem 1   (1177,T5) (Modified)

(20 to 25 minutes)

The statement of cash flows is normally a required basic financial statement for each period for which an earnings statement is presented.

Required:

a. What are the objectives of the statement of cash flows?

b. What are two types of transactions which would be disclosed in a separate schedule in the statement of cash flows although they don't affect cash during the report period?

c. What effect, if any, would each of the following seven items have upon the preparation of a cash flow statement assuming **direct** presentation is used to present cash flows from operations?
1. Accounts receivable--trade.
2. Inventory.
3. Depreciation.
4. Deferred tax liability from inter-period allocation.
5. Issuance of long-term debt in payment for a building.
6. Payoff of current portion of debt.
7. Sale of a fixed asset resulting in a loss.

Problem 2   (1189,P5)

(40 to 50 minutes)

Presented below are the balance sheet accounts of Kerns, Inc. as of December 31, 1988 and 1987 and their net changes.

	1988	1987	Net change
Assets			
Cash	$ 471,000	$ 307,000	$ 164,000
Marketable equity securities, at cost	150,000	250,000	(100,000)
Allowance to reduce marketable equity securities to market	(10,000)	(25,000)	15,000
Accounts receivable, net	550,000	515,000	35,000
Inventories	810,000	890,000	(80,000)
Investments in Word Corp., at equity	420,000	390,000	30,000
Property, plant, and equipment	1,145,000	1,070,000	75,000
Accumulated depreciation	(345,000)	(280,000)	(65,000)
Patent, net	109,000	118,000	(9,000)
Total assets	$3,300,000	$3,235,000	$ 65,000
Liabilities and Stockholders' Equity			
Accounts payable and accrued liabilities	$ 845,000	$ 960,000	$ (115,000)
Note payable, long-term	600,000	900,000	(300,000)
Deferred income taxes	190,000	190,000	--
Common stock, $10 par value	850,000	650,000	200,000
Additional paid-in capital	230,000	170,000	60,000
Retained earnings	585,000	365,000	220,000
Total liabilities and stockholders' equity	$3,300,000	$3,235,000	$ 65,000

Additional information:
- On January 2, 1988, Kern sold equipment costing $45,000, with a carrying amount of $28,000, for $18,000 cash.

- On March 31, 1988, Kern sold one of its marketable equity security holdings for $119,000 cash. There were no other transactions involving marketable equity securities.

- On April 15, 1988, Kern issued 20,000 shares of its common stock for cash at $13 per share.

- On July 1, 1988, Kern purchased equipment for $120,000 cash.

- Kern's net income for 1988 is $305,000. Kern paid a cash dividend of $85,000 on October 26, 1988.

- Kern acquired a 20% interest in Word Corp.'s common stock during 1985. There was no goodwill attributable to the investment which is appropriately accounted for by the equity method. Word reported net income of $150,000 for the year ended December 31, 1988. No dividend was paid on Word's common stock during 1988.

Required:

Prepare a statement of cash flows for Kern, Inc. for the year ended December 31, 1988 using the indirect method. A worksheet is <u>not</u> required.

<u>Problem 3</u>   (1182,P4)

(45 to 55 minutes)

Presented below are the balance sheets of Farrell Corporation as of December 31, 1987 and 1986, and the statement of income and retained earnings for the year ended December 31, 1987.

Farrell Corporation
Balance Sheets
December 31, 1987 and 1986

	1987	1986	Increase (decrease)
Assets:			
Cash and cash equivalents	$ 275,000	$ 180,000	$ 95,000
Accounts receivable, net	295,000	305,000	(10,000)
Inventories	549,000	431,000	118,000
Investment in Hall, Inc. at equity	73,000	60,000	13,000
Land	350,000	200,000	150,000
Plant and equipment	624,000	606,000	18,000
Less accumulated depreciation	(139,000)	(107,000)	(32,000)
Goodwill	16,000	20,000	(4,000)
Total assets	$2,043,000	$1,695,000	$348,000
Liabilities and stockholders' equity:			
Accounts payable	$ 504,000	$ 453,000	$ 51,000
Accrued expenses	100,000	110,000	(10,000)
Note payable, long-term	150,000	–	150,000
Bonds payable	160,000	210,000	(50,000)
Deferred tax liability	41,000	30,000	11,000
Common stock, par value $10	430,000	400,000	30,000
Additional paid-in capital	226,000	175,000	51,000
Retained earnings	432,000	334,000	98,000
Treasury stock, at cost	–	(17,000)	17,000
Total liabilities and stockholders' equity	$2,043,000	$1,695,000	$348,000

Farrell Corporation
Statement of Income
and Retained Earnings
For the Year Ended December 31, 1987

Net sales	$1,950,000
Operating expenses:	
Cost of sales	1,150,000
Selling and administrative	
expenses	505,000
Depreciation	53,000
	1,708,000
Operating income	242,000
Other (income) expense:	
Interest expense	15,000
Equity in net income of Hall, Inc.	(13,000)
Loss on sale of equipment	5,000
Amortization of goodwill	4,000
	11,000
Income before income taxes	231,000
Income taxes:	
Current	79,000
Deferred	11,000
Provision for income taxes	90,000
Net income	141,000
Retained earnings, January 1, 1987	334,000
	475,000
Cash dividends, paid August 14, 1987	43,000
Retained earnings, December 31, 1987	$ 432,000

Additional information:

• On January 2, 1987, Farrell sold equipment costing $45,000, with a book value of $24,000, for $19,000 cash.

• On April 1, 1987, Farrell issued 1,000 shares of common stock for $23,000 cash.

• On May 15, 1987, Farrell sold all of its treasury stock for $25,000 cash.

• On June 1, 1987, individuals holding $50,000 face value of Farrell's bonds exercised their conversion privilege. Each of the 50 bonds was converted into 40 shares of Farrell's common stock.

• On July 1, 1987, Farrell purchased equipment for $63,000 cash.

• On December 31, 1987, land with a fair market value of $150,000 was purchased through the issuance of a long-term note in the amount of $150,000. The note bears interest at the rate of 15% and is due on December 31, 1992.

• Deferred income taxes represent temporary differences relating to the use of accelerated depreciation methods for income tax reporting and the straight-line method for financial statement reporting.

Required:

Prepare a statement of cash flows (operating activities section showing indirect approach) and all necessary related schedules of Farrell Corporation for the year ended December 31, 1987.

Problem 4 (1187,P5)

(45 to 55 minutes)

Presented below are the condensed statements of financial position of Public Relations Associates as of December 31, 1986 and 1985, and the condensed statement of income for the year ended December 31, 1986.

Public Relations Associates
CONDENSED STATEMENTS OF FINANCIAL POSITION
December 31, 1986 and 1985

	1986	1985	Net change increase (decrease)
Assets			
Cash and cash equivalents	$ 326,000	$ 140,000	$186,000
Accounts receivable, net	223,000	184,000	39,000
Investment in King, Inc, at equity	275,000	233,000	42,000
Property and equipment	635,000	550,000	85,000
Accumulated depreciation	(95,000)	(65,000)	(30,000)
Excess cost over book value of investment in King (net)	76,000	78,000	(2,000)
Total assets	$1,440,000	$1,120,000	$320,000
Liabilities and Partners' Equity			
Accounts payable and accrued expenses	$ 160,000	$ 135,000	$ 25,000
Mortgage payable	125,000	135,000	(10,000)
Partners' equity	1,155,000	850,000	305,000
Total liabilities and partners' equity	$1,440,000	$1,120,000	$320,000

Public Relations Associates
CONDENSED STATEMENT OF INCOME
For the Year Ended December 31, 1986

Fee revenue	$1,332,000
Operating expenses	970,000
Operating income	362,000
Equity in earnings of King, Inc. (net of $2,000 amortization of excess cost over book value)	88,000
Net income	$ 450,000

Additional information:

• On December 31, 1985, partners' capital and profit sharing percentages were as follows:

	Capital	Profit sharing %
Burr	$510,000	60%
Cox	340,000	40%
	$850,000	

• On January 1, 1986, the partners admitted Davis to the partnership for a cash payment of $170,000 to Public Relations Associates. In addition, Davis paid a $100,000 cash bonus directly to Burr and Cox. This amount was divided $60,000 to Burr and $40,000 to Cox. The new profit sharing arrangement is as follows:

Burr	50%
Cox	30%
Davis	20%

• On July 1, 1986, Public Relations Associates purchased an office computer for $85,000 which included $10,000 for sales tax, delivery, and installation. There were no dispositions of property and equipment during 1986.
• Throughout 1986, Public Relations Associates owned 25% of the common stock of King, Inc. During 1986, King paid cash dividends totaling $192,000 and reported net income of $360,000. Public's 1986 amortization of excess cost over book value in King was $2,000.
• Partners' drawings for 1986 were as follows:

Burr	$140,000
Cox	100,000
Davis	75,000
	$315,000

Required:

    a. Prepare a statement of cash flows of Public Relations Associates for the year ended December 31, 1986. Use the direct method of preparing the operating activities section of the statement.
    b. Prepare an analysis of changes in partners' capital accounts for the year ended December 31, 1986.*

*This requirement should be completed after studying Module 33E, Partnership Accounting. A cross reference from the problem material for Section E of Module 33 will refer you back to this requirement later if you don't want to review partnerships at this time.

Multiple Choice Answers

1. c	7. a	13. b	19. a	25. d
2. a	8. c	14. d	20. b	26. d
3. d	9. b	15. d	21. a or b	27. c
4. b	10. d	16. d	22. c	28. a
5. c	11. a	17. c	23. b	29. c
6. d	12. c	18. a	24. c	

Multiple Choice Answer Explanations

B. Statement of Cash Flows Classification

1. (589,T1,26) (c) Per SFAS 95, para 16, receipts from sales of property, plant, and equipment and other productive assets are categorized as cash flows from investing activities. Therefore, answer (c) is correct.

2. (589,T1,27) (a) Per SFAS 95, para 23, interest payments to lenders and other creditors are categorized as cash flows from operating activities. Therefore, answer (a) is correct.

3. (1189,T1,29) (d) Per SFAS 95, paras 18 and 19, financing activities include obtaining resources from owners and providing them with a return on, and a return of, their investment. Proceeds from issuing equity instruments are specifically identified as cash inflows from financing activities. Therefore, answer (d) is correct, and answers (a), (b), and (c) are incorrect.

4. (1189,T1,30) (b) Per SFAS 95, paras 15 and 17, investing activities include making and collecting loans and acquiring and disposing of debt or equity instruments and property, plant, and equipment. Payments to acquire debt instruments of other entities (other than cash equivalents) are specifically identified as cash outflows for investing activities. Therefore, answer (b) is correct and answers (a), (c), and (d) are incorrect.

5. (585,T1,27) (c) The requirement is to determine if a conversion of long term debt and preferred stock to common stock should be reported when preparing a statement of cash flows. Noncash transactions may not involve cash receipts or payments in the period in which they occur but may have a significant effect on prospective cash flows of a company. Therefore, both items should be reported in a separate schedule. Both conversion of long-term debt and conversion of preferred stock to common stock are considered a noncash financing and investing activity and should be disclosed in a separate schedule. Therefore, answers (a), (b), and (d) are incorrect.

C. Direct or Indirect Presentation in Reporting Operating Activities

6. (588,P1,3) (d) The net cash flow provided by operations can be computed using either the indirect approach or the direct approach. Under the indirect approach, the computation begins with net income which is then adjusted for noncash items. Under the direct approach, each of the items which are reported on the income statement (sales, cost of goods sold, etc.) are directly adjusted for changes in related balance sheet items, and these adjusted amounts are used to compute the net cash flow. In this question, the direct approach is used and the items have already been adjusted (for example, sales has been adjusted to cash received from customers), so the net cash flow can be computed as follows:

Cash received from customers	$870,000
Rent received	10,000
Cash paid to suppliers and employees	(510,000)
Taxes paid	(110,000)
Net cash flow provided by operations	$ 260,000

Cash dividends paid is not used in the computation because it is a financing activity, not an operating activity.

7. (1176,P2,35) (a) Cash provided by operating activities for December are the sales figure of $350,000 less accounts written off of $3,000 less the $10,500 increase in accounts receivable.

$350,000	Sales
- 3,000	A/R written off
- 10,500	Increase in A/R
$336,500	Cash provided by operating activities

8. (1176,P2,36) (c) The cash disbursed from operating activities for December are 70% (1.00 – GP%) of the $350,000 of sales, plus $5,000 of inventory increase, plus S,G&A of $64,500. The $64,500 of S,G&A consists of $35,500 plus 15% of sales, totaling $88,000 adjusted for noncash items of $20,000 depreciation and $3,500 of bad debts.

Cash Disbursed		S,G&A	
$350,000		$35,500	Fixed
70%		52,500	Variable
$245,000		- 20,000	Depreciation
+ 5,000	Inventory incr.	- 3,500	Bad debts
+64,500	S,G&A	$64,500	S,G&A
$314,500	Cash disbursed from operating activities		

9. (1188,T2,34) (b) In a statement of cash flows in which the operating activities section is prepared using the direct method, the cash collected from customers would be equal to the accrual-basis sales revenue, plus/minus any decrease/increase in accounts receivable account. Therefore, answer (b) is correct, and answers (a), (c), and (d) are incorrect.

10. (1188,T2,35) (d) The objective of a statement of cash flows is to provide information about a company's cash receipts and payments during a period. The first step in this process is to determine cash provided by operations. When presenting cash from operations under the indirect approach, net income must be adjusted for changes in current assets other than cash and in current liabilities. When prepaid expenses decrease during the period, reported expenses exceed cash paid. In computing cash provided by operations, the decrease in prepaid expenses must therefore be added to net income. Answers (a) and (b) are incorrect because a decrease in prepaid expenses involves neither an inflow nor an outflow of cash; it is a necessary adjustment to net income under the indirect method to reflect the fact that cash was unaffected by the accrual basis adjustment in which an expense was debited and a prepaid expense account was credited. Answer (c) is incorrect because a decrease in prepaid expenses would be an addition to net income, not a deduction.

11. (588,T1,30) (a) Net income is the starting point when preparing the operating activities section of a statement of cash flows using the indirect method. Net income is adjusted for items which affect income, but not cash. A gain on the sale of an investment is such an item. The adjustment is necessary because the cash inflow from selling the investment shall be shown in the investing activities section of the cash flow statement. The gain is deducted so as to remove the gain portion of the proceeds from the cash flow from operating activities section thereby avoiding a double counting of the gain. Therefore, answer (a) is correct, and answers (b), (c), and (d) are incorrect.

12. (588,T1,31) (c) In a statement of cash flows in which the operating activities section is prepared using the direct method, the cash paid for wages would be equal to the accrual-basis salary expense, plus/minus any decrease/increase in the wages payable account. (The logic is essentially the same as an accrual-basis to cash-basis adjustment).

Therefore, answer (c) is correct and answers (a), (b), and (d) are incorrect.

13. (1187,T1,35) (b) When preparing the statement of cash flows under the indirect approach, a loss on the sale of machinery would be an addition to net income. The loss decreases net income, but does <u>not</u> reduce cash. Therefore, the loss must be added back to net income to determine cash flows from operating activities. Thus, answer (b) is correct, and answer (a) is incorrect. Answers (c) and (d) are incorrect because a loss on the sale of machinery does not reduce or increase cash. The <u>cash proceeds</u> from the sale would, however, be shown as an inflow of cash.

14. (587,T1,28) (d) The objective of a statement of cash flows is to explain what caused the change in the cash balance. The first step in this process is to determine cash provided by operations. When presenting cash from operating activities under the indirect approach, net income must be adjusted for changes in current assets other than cash and in current liabilities. These adjustments are required because items which resulted from noncash events must be removed from accrual-based income. For example, when inventory increases during the period, inventory sold is less than inventory purchased. Considering only the increase in the inventory account, cost of goods sold on an accrual basis is less than it would have been if cash basis were being used. In converting to the cash basis, the increase in inventory must be subtracted from net income to arrive at cash from operations [answer (d)]. Answer (a) is incorrect because even though an increase in inventories requires an outflow of cash, inventories are shown as adjustments to net income under the indirect method. Answer (b) is incorrect because it describes how a noncash transaction such as the exchange of land for a note would be handled. Answer (c) is incorrect because an increase in an inventory would be a deduction from net income, not an addition.

15. (586,T1,25) (d) The requirement is the correct presentation of deferred income tax expense from timing differences related to depreciation of plant assets in the statement of cash flows. When using the indirect approach to determine cash flows from operating activities, noncash deductions from net income should be added back to determine cash flows from operating activities. Since the deferred income tax expense did not use cash but was subtracted in determining net income, it is proper to add it back to net income in cash

flows from operating activities. Answer (a) is incorrect because this item is an operating activity item which must go into the determination of net cash flows from operating activities. Even though it was a noncash transaction it must be used to adjust net income to cash flows from operating activities. Answer (b) is incorrect because it is not a cash inflow or outflow and is not a financing activity. Answer (c) is incorrect because deferred income tax expense should be added to, not deducted from, net income.

16. (1185,T1,27) (d) The requirement is to determine how the amortization of a bond premium on long-term debt should be presented in the statement of cash flows. Answer (d) is correct. If bonds are sold at a discount or premium, the interest expense for the period will differ from the change in cash resulting from payment of interest expense. When the premium is amortized, the interest expense included in income determination is not as large as the interest paid or becoming payable in the period. Because the cash outflow is larger than the deduction in arriving at net income, a deduction from net income is necessary to determine cash provided by operating activities (when using the indirect approach of presenting cash flows from operating activities). Answers (a) and (b) are incorrect because amortization of a premium does not involve direct changes to cash. Answer (c) is incorrect because amortization of a premium would be a deduction from net income.

D. Example of Statement of Cash Flows

17. (589,P1,5) (c) Cash provided by operations can be computed using either the direct or indirect approach. In this case, there is insufficient information to use the direct approach. In the indirect approach, the computation begins with net income which is then adjusted for noncash items, as indicated below:

Net income	$690,000
Increase in inventory	(80,000)
Gain on sale of investment	(35,000)
Depreciation expense	250,000
Goodwill amortization expense	10,000
Increase in A/P and accr. liabs.	105,000
Cash provided by operations	$940,000

The increase in inventory ($680,000 - $600,000 = $80,000) is deducted because cash was used to increase inventory. The gain on sale of

investment [$135,000 - ($300,000 - $200,000) = $35,000] is deducted because all cash effects of this transaction are reported as an investing activity. Depreciation expense [$450,000 - ($450,000 - $250,000) = $250,000] and goodwill amortization expense ($100,000 - $90,000 = $10,000) are added because they are noncash expenses. Finally, the increase in accounts payable and accrued liabilities ($825,000 - $720,000 = $105,000) is added because this increase means some expenses were not yet paid in cash.

18. (589,P1,6) (a) Investing activities include all cash flows involving assets other than operating items. Financing activities include all cash flows involving liabilities and equity other than operating items. In this case, the changes in the assets accounts receivable, inventory, accumulated depreciation, and goodwill are operating items. The cash flows involving the other assets, listed below, are investing activities:

Purchase of short-term investments ($300,000 - $0)	$(300,000)
Purchase of plant assets (see below)	(1,100,000)
Sale of long-term investments (given)	135,000
Sale of plant assets (given)	150,000
Net cash used in investing activities	$(1,115,000)

The purchase of plant assets can be determined from a T-account:

Plant assets			
12/31/87	1,000,000		
Purchased	?	400,000	Sold
12/31/88	1,700,000		

19. (589,P1,7) (a) Financing activities include all cash flows involving liabilities and equity other than operating items. Investing activities include all cash flows involving assets other than operating items. In this case, the change in the liability account, "accounts payable and accrued liabilities," is an operating item. The part of the change in retained earnings caused by net income is also an operating item. The cash flows involving the other liability and equity accounts, listed below, are financing activities.

Issuance of short-term debt ($325,000 - $0)	$325,000
Issuance of common stock (10,000 x $22)	220,000
Payment of cash dividends	(240,000)
	$305,000

The issuance of common stock can be computed by analyzing the increases in common stock ($100,000) and APIC ($120,000).

20.   (589,P1,9)   (b)   Investing activities include all cash flows involving assets other than operating items. The investing activities are:

Investment in Hoag Corp.	$(225,000)
Purchase of patent	(275,000)
Sale of investment securities	995,000
Net cash provided by investing activities	$495,000

The issuance of preferred stock for land ($400,000) is a noncash item. The bank borrowing ($225,000), bond issuance ($490,000) and bank loan payment ($150,000) are financing activities. The net increase in customer deposits ($110,000) is either an operating item or a financing item.

21.   (589,P1,10)   (a or b)   Financing activities include all cash flows involving liabilities and equity, other than operating items. The financing activities that net to answer (a) are:

Borrowing from bank	$225,000
Issuance of bonds	490,000
Paid bank loan	(150,000)
Net cash provided by financing activities	$565,000

The issuance of preferred stock for land ($400,000) is a noncash item. The investment in Hoag Corp. ($225,000), purchase of patent ($275,000), and sale of investment securities ($995,000) are investing activities. The net increase in customer deposits ($110,000) could be either an operating item [adjustment added to either revenue (direct method) or net income (indirect method)] as is assumed above by excluding it from the calculation or as a financing activity. If the customer deposits liability will be satisfied by providing goods or services, it would be an operating item because as the deposits are earned the "customer deposits account" would be reduced and a revenue account would be increased. However, if these deposits are to be returned to the customer as is the case with utility deposits, for example, then the deposits would be treated as a financing item and the total net cash provided by financing activities would be $675,000 [answer (b)].

22.   (589,P1,16)   (c)   Investing activities include cash flows involving assets other than operating items. The investing activities are:

Purchased real estate	$(550,000)
Sold investment securities	500,000
Purchased mach. and equip.	(125,000)
Net cash used in investing activities	$(175,000)

The bank borrowing ($550,000), dividend payment ($600,000), issuance of stock ($250,000), and bank loan payment ($450,000) are financing activities. The reduction of accounts receivable ($100,000) and the increase in accounts payable ($200,000) are operating items (both are adjustments which are added to net income under the indirect method).

23.   (589,P1,17)   (b)   Financing activities include all cash flows involving liabilities and equity other than operating items. The financing activities are:

Bank borrowing	$550,000
Dividend payment	(600,000)
Issuance of stock	250,000
Bank loan payment	(450,000)
Net cash used in financing activities	$(250,000)

The purchase of real estate ($550,000), sale of investment securities ($500,000), and purchase of machinery and equipment ($125,000) are investing activities. The reduction of accounts receivable ($100,000) and the increase in accounts payable ($200,000) are operating items (both are adjustments which are added to net income under the direct method).

24.   (581,Q2,25)   (c)   The requirement is cash collected during 1988 from accounts receivable. The solutions approach is to prepare a T-account for accounts receivable. The allowance account has no effect on this analysis, because the problem states that the balance in this account has not changed and no accounts receivable were written off. Net credit sales are the only debit to accounts receivable because all accounts receivable relate to trade merchandise. In the T-account below, you must solve for the missing credit to determine that $6,140,000 was collected on account during 1988.

	A/R--Net		
12/31/87 balance	580,000	?	1988
1988 Net Credit Sales	6,400,000		Collections
12/31/88 balance	840,000		

Authors' Note: Based on the information given in this problem, no bad debt expense was recorded during 1988. However unrealistic this assumption might be, it is important to simply work with the information as given.

25. (581,Q2,26) (d) The requirement is cash payments during 1988 on accounts payable. The solutions approach is to visualize the accounts payable T-account.

Accounts Payable

		440,000	12/31/87
Payments	?	?	Purchases
		530,000	12/31/88

It is apparent that in order to determine payments to suppliers, purchases of trade merchandise must first be computed. The cost of goods sold statement can be used to compute purchases.

Beginning Inventory	$	420,000
+ Purchases	+	?
- Ending Inventory	-	660,000
Cost of Goods Sold		$5,000,000

Purchases = $5,000,000 - ($420,000 - $660,000)
        = $5,240,000

Finally, the purchases are entered into the accounts payable T-account, and payments to suppliers of $5,150,000 can be plugged in.

Accounts Payable

		440,000	12/31/87
Payments	5,150,000	5,240,000	Purchases
		530,000	12/31/88

26. (581,Q2,27) (d) The requirement is net cash flows provided by financing activities in 1988. The solutions approach is to work through the comparative balance sheets noting increases and decreases in liability accounts other than those related to operations and increases or decreases in stockholders' equity accounts. The additional information given must be considered in connection with these changes. Cash inflows from financing activities include proceeds from long-term borrowing, and issuance of capital stock.

Proceeds from long-term note	$500,000
Proceeds from issuance of common stock	300,000
	$800,000

To determine the amount of dividends paid, it is necessary to analyze both the retained earnings and the dividends payable accounts.

Dividends Payable				Retained Earnings		
		-0-	12/31/87		330,000	12/31/87
Dividends			Dividends			
Paid	?	?	declared	?	400,000	Net income
		70,000	12/31/88		560,000	12/31/88

Dividends declared = $330,000 + 400,000 - 560,000 = $170,000

Dividends paid   = $0 + 170,000 - 70,000 = $100,000

Net cash flows provided by financing activities is $700,000 ($800,000 - $100,000).

27. (581,Q2,28) (c) The requirement is cash used in investing activities during 1988. The two assets other than those related to operations shown on the balance sheet (long-term investments and land, building, and fixtures) have increased from 12/31/87 to 12/31/88, indicating cash purchases since the additional information does not suggest any other means of acquisition. Therefore, cash outflows from investing activities include $80,000 for long-term investments and $530,000 ($1,130,000 - $600,000) for land, building, and fixtures.

May 1990 Answers

28. (590,T1,27) (a) Per SFAS 95, para 16, payments at the time of purchase or soon before or after purchase to acquire property, plant, and equipment and other productive assets are categorized as cash outflows for investing activities. Generally, these payments only include advance payments, down payments, or payments made at the time of purchase or soon before or after purchase. Therefore, only the cash payment is considered a cash outflow for investing activities and answer (a) is correct.

29. (590,T1,28) (c) Per SFAS 95, para 32, noncash investing and financing activities include acquiring assets by assuming directly related liabilities, such as purchasing a building by incurring a mortgage to the seller. This type of transaction does not involve the flow of cash. Therefore, cash flows for financing activities related to this transaction would be zero and answer (c) is correct. Note that the cash down payment would be reported as a cash outflow for investing activities.

Answer Outline

Problem 1   Statement of Cash Flows (1177,T5)

a. Objectives of statement
    Information about cash receipts and
    payments
    Information about investing and
    financing activities
    Facilitate user assessments
b. Transactions not affecting cash, but
    reported in separate schedule
    Acquisition of assets with
        Debt
        Other assets
        Equity securities
    Reduction of debt by
        Other debt
        Distribution of assets
        Issuance of equity securities
c. Effect on statement of cash flows when
    direct presentation used for operating
    activities
    Change in accounts receivable affects
        cash received from customers
    Change in inventory affects cash used
        for COGS
    Depreciation is noncash expense
        Deduct from operating expenses
    Change in deferred tax liability is
        neither inflow nor outflow of cash
    Long-term debt issued for building does
        not affect cash
        Noncash financing and investing
        transaction shown on a separate
        schedule
    Reduction of current debt is outflow of
        cash--financing activity
    Proceeds are an inflow of cash--
        investing activity

Unofficial Answer

Problem 1   Statement of Cash Flows (1177,T5)

a. The objectives of the statement of cash
flows are to provide information about cash
receipts and payments from operating, investing, and financing activities. This information helps users assess the company's
ability to generate future net cash flows and
ability to meet obligations and pay dividends.
The statement also helps users assess the
differences between income and associated cash
receipts and payments.

b.   Investing and financing activities that do
not involve cash receipts and payments during
the period should be excluded from the cash
flow statement and reported in a separate
schedule. Transactions that would be

classified as noncash financing and investing
activities would include the following:
   1. Purchase of assets by the issuance of
      capital stock or debt, or a reduction
      in another asset.
   2. Reduction of a liability by the
      issuance of capital stock or the
      incurrence of another liability, or a
      reduction in an asset.

c. The effects and procedural considerations
of the seven account balances (transactions)
upon the preparation of a statement of cash
flows are as follows:
   1. Accounts receivable--trade are gener-
      ated as a result of credit sales. A
      balance in accounts receivable--trade
      represents sales (a part of operating
      earnings) not represented by cash. An
      increase in the accounts receivable--
      trade balance indicates that the ac-
      tual cash generated is equal to sales
      as reported on the earnings statement
      less the increase in accounts receiv-
      able--trade balance. Conversely, a
      net decrease in the accounts receiv-
      able--trade balance would have to be
      added to sales as reported on the
      earnings statement to arrive at cash
      generated from sales. In the prepara-
      tion of a statement of cash flows the
      increase (decrease) in this account
      balance between two periods is sub-
      tracted from (or added to) net sales
      to arrive at cash received from
      customers for sales.
   2. Inventory is a component part of cost
      of goods sold. The net change in in-
      ventory balances affects the cash used
      for cost of goods sold. An increase
      in ending inventory over beginning
      inventory reduces the cost of goods
      sold. However, cash was presumed to
      be used to increase the inventory bal-
      ance. An increase in the inventory
      balance represents a use of cash.
      When there is an increase in inventory
      balances, the cash used for cost of
      goods sold is the cost of goods sold
      as shown in the current earnings
      statement plus the increase in inven-
      tory balance.
         A similar analysis leads to the
      conclusion that a decrease in ending
      inventory balance with respect to
      beginning inventory balance gives rise
      to a net increase in cost of goods
      sold as shown in the current earnings
      statement but a reduction in the cash
      so used.
   3. Depreciation represents a systematic
      allocation of the cost of a fixed
      asset to the accounting periods bene-

fited by the asset. The process of recognizing depreciation does not affect cash. Cash paid for operating expenses is determined by deducting depreciation expense from total operating expenses and adjusting the operating expenses for prepaid expenses.

4. Deferred income taxes are the difference between income taxes matched against earnings and the actual amount paid or payable for the period. If the balance of the deferred tax liability account, for example, increases between two periods, the amount of income taxes paid was less than the indicated income tax expense. Conversely, if deferred liability tax account decreases, the amount paid was greater than the correct income tax expense. Although the change in the deferred tax liability account is included in the indirect approach, the direct approach is not affected by the change. To determine the cash paid for taxes under the direct presentation, the <u>current</u> portion of income tax expense is adjusted for the increase or decrease in the income tax payable account.

5. The purchase of a building by issuing long-term debt obviously does not require a cash outlay. However, this noncash activity should be reported in a separate schedule as a noncash financing and investing activity.

6. The payment of the current portion of debt represents a cash outflow from financing activities.

7. The total proceeds from the sale of the fixed asset should be shown as an inflow from investing activities. This transaction would not be reflected under operating activities when the <u>direct</u> presentation is used.

Solution Guide

Problem 2   Statement of Cash Flows (1189,P5)

1. The problem requires the preparation of a statement of cash flows. The solutions approach is to analyze the net change in each account, using the additional information where applicable, and to identify the cash inflows, cash outflows, and net income adjustments. Journal entries and T-accounts can be used to facilitate the analysis.

1.1 As each item is analyzed, it can be entered into a "skeleton" statement prepared by listing the heading and main categories, such as cash flows from operating activities, investing activities, and financing activities. The individual descriptions and numbers can be filled in as you go through the problem. The first item under operating activities is net income of $305,000 which was given.

2. Cash increased by $164,000. This should be the net increase in cash reported in the reconciliation of the change in cash shown at the bottom of the statement.

2.1 The marketable equity securities (MES) account decreased by $100,000. The additional information states that the only transaction affecting this account was a sale for $119,000 cash. The journal entry to record this sale was:

Cash   119,000
  MES   100,000
  Gain on sale   19,000

The cash <u>inflow</u> of $119,000 is an investing activity. The gain on sale is <u>deducted</u> in the operating section as a net income adjustment, because the $19,000 is already included as a cash inflow as part of the $119,000.

2.2 The MES allowance account decreased by $15,000. The journal entry was

Allowance, etc.   15,000
  Recovery, etc.   15,000

The recovery increased net income, but did not involve a cash inflow. Therefore, it must be <u>deducted</u> in the operating section as a net income adjustment.

2.3 Net accounts receivable increased by $35,000. This is <u>deducted</u> as a net income adjustment in the operating section because it indicates that not all of this year's sales have been collected.

2.4 Inventories decreased by $80,000. This is <u>added</u> in the operating section as a net income adjustment. A decrease in inventory means that cash was not used to purchase all the inventory items included in cost of goods sold.

2.5 The Investment in Word account increased by $30,000. The additional information indicates that this is due to the recognition of Kern's share of Word's income (20% x $150,000 = $30,000) under the equity method. The entry was

Investment in Word   30,000
  Income from investment   30,000

This entry is similar to the recovery entry discussed in 2.2 above. The entry increases net income, but does not involve a cash inflow. Therefore, it must be <u>deducted</u> as a net income adjustment in the operating section.

2.6 Property, plant, and equipment increased by $75,000. This is the net result of two transactions described in the additional information. Equipment (cost $45,000) with a book value of $28,000 was sold for $18,000 cash:

Cash	18,000	
Loss on sale	10,000	(18,000 - 28,000)
Accum. depr.	17,000	(45,000 - 28,000)
Equipment		45,000

The cash received ($18,000) is a cash inflow from investing activities. The loss on sale ($10,000) is added as a net income adjustment in the operating section because even though it decreased net income, it did not involve an outflow of cash. The other transaction affecting this account is a purchase of equipment for $120,000, which is a cash outflow from investing activities. These two transactions explain the $75,000 net increase in the account, as the T-account below illustrates:

Prop., plant & equip.			
Purchase	120,000	45,000	Sale
Net incr.	75,000		

2.7 Accumulated depreciation increased by $65,000. This net change is the result of the sale of equipment (discussed in 2.6) and depreciation expense. The amount of depreciation expense can be determined through T-account analysis.

Accumulated depreciation			
Sale	17,000	?	Depr. expense
		65,000	Net incr.

The missing amount is depreciation expense of $82,000. Depreciation expense is added as a net income adjustment in the operating section because, although it decreased net income, it was not a cash outflow.

2.8 The patent account decreased by $9,000. Since no sale of patents was mentioned in the additional information, this decrease must be patent amortization. Patent amortization is added as a net income adjustment in the operating section because, although it decreased net income, it was not a cash outflow.

3. Accounts payable and accrued liabilities decreased by $115,000. This is deducted as a net income adjustment in the operating section because cash was spent to pay the liabilities.

3.1 The long-term note payable decreased by $300,000. The payment of the note is a cash outflow from the financing activities.

3.2 There was no change in the deferred income taxes account.

3.3 Common stock increased by $200,000, and additional paid-in capital increased by $60,000. This is the result of the issuance of 20,000 shares of $10 par stock at $13 per share, as described in the additional information. The entry was:

Cash	260,000	
Common stock		200,000 (20,000 x $10)
Add. P-I cap.		60,000 (20,000 x $3)

The $260,000 is a cash inflow from financing activities.

3.4 Retained earnings increased by a net amount of $220,000. The additional information indicates that net income was $305,000 and dividends paid were $85,000.

Retained earnings			
Divs.	85,000	305,000	NI
		220,000	Net incr.

Net income is reported in the operating section, while the dividends are a cash outflow from financing activities.

Unofficial Answer

Problem 2   Statement of Cash Flows (1189,P5)

Kern, Inc.
STATEMENT OF CASH FLOWS
For the Year Ended December 31, 1988
Increase (Decrease) in Cash

Cash flows from operating activities:		
Net income	$ 305,000	
Adjustments to reconcile net income to net		
cash provided by operating activities:		
Depreciation	82,000 [1]	
Amortization of patent	9,000	
Loss on sale of equipment	10,000	
Equity in income of Word Corp.	(30,000) [2]	
Gain on sale of marketable equity securities	(19,000)	
Decrease in allowance to reduce		
marketable equity securities to market	(15,000)	
Increase in accounts receivable	(35,000)	
Decrease in inventories	80,000	
Decrease in accounts payable		
and accrued liabilities	(115,000)	
Net cash provided by operating activities		$272,000
Cash flows from investing activities:		
Sale of marketable equity securities	$ 119,000	
Sale of equipment	18,000	
Purchase of equipment	(120,000)	
Net cash provided by investing activities		17,000
Cash flows from financing activities:		
Issuance of common stock	$260,000 [3]	
Cash dividend paid	(85,000)	
Payment on note payable	(300,000)	
Net cash used in financing activities		(125,000)
Net increase in cash		164,000
Cash at beginning of year		307,000
Cash at end of year		$471,000

Explanations of Amounts:

[1]	Depreciation	
	Net increase in accumulated depreciation	
	for year ended 12/31/88	$ 65,000
	Accumulated depreciation on equipment sold	17,000
	Depreciation for 1988	$ 82,000
[2]	Equity in income of Word Corp.	
	Reported net income for 1988	$150,000
	Kern's ownership	x 20%
	Equity in income of Word Corp. for 1988	$ 30,000
[3]	Issuance of common stock	
	4/15/88, issued 20,000 shares for cash	
	at $13 per share	$260,000

Solution Guide

Problem 3   Statement of Cash Flows
                    (1182,P4)

Authors' note: We have provided two alternatives for preparing this solution. One is the approach described below (prior to the unofficial answer) for which line items are entered on the required statement, reference to the increases or decreases is given in the problem, and use of schedules or "T-accounts" is limited. The other is the formal "T-account approach" which is illustrated after the unofficial answer. Both alternatives yield the same result; therefore, only one unofficial answer is presented.

1.   This problem requires a statement of cash flows. All of the necessary numbers are given in the problem under the increase (decrease) column.

2.   The solutions approach is to directly analyze the increases or decreases in the balance sheet accounts by relating them to the additional text information. The increase (decrease) column shown in the problem reflects the effect on total assets or total liabilities resulting from the change in each specific account balance. Supporting schedules, journal entries, and T-accounts can be used as necessary.

> Authors' note: The AICPA solution to this problem included a worksheet (not required). We (the authors) believe that such an approach is too time consuming because of the necessity to copy the accounts and numbers (increases and decreases) from the exam booklet onto a worksheet, identify (write) the source and use items on the worksheet, and finally transfer the information to the required statement. We believe that solving the problem without the worksheet enables candidates to analyze carefully the more complex transactions but avoids wasting valuable time transferring information on and off of a worksheet.

3.   As each item is analyzed it can be entered into a "skeleton" statement. This statement can be prepared first by listing the heading and main categories, such as cash flows from operations, from investing activities and from financing activities. Then the numbers are filled in as you go through the problem.

3.1   Cash and cash equivalents increased by $95,000. This should be the result obtained in the cash flow statement. The first entry in the "Operating Activities" section is for Net Income, $141,000.

3.2   Accounts receivable decreased by $10,000. This is _added_ as an adjustment to net income in the computation of cash flows from operating activities. The decrease of $10,000 means that $10,000 more cash was collected on account than the amount of sales reported in the income statement.

3.3   Inventories increased by $118,000. This is subtracted from net income in the computation of cash flows from operating activities. The increase of $118,000 means that additional cash was spent to increase inventories; this expenditure is not reflected in cost of goods sold.

3.4   Investment in Hall increased by $13,000. Note that the equity method is used, and the income statement lists $13,000 as Farrell's equity in the net income of Hall. This item should be subtracted from net income because it increased accrual net income, but did not represent a cash inflow (see entry below).

Investment in Hall	13,000	
Equity in income of		
Hall		13,000

3.5   Land increased by $150,000. The additional information states that land was purchased through issuance of a long-term interest-bearing note. The entry to record this transaction is:

Land	150,000	
Long-term note payable		150,000

Although cash is not affected by this transaction, it is included in this problem in a separate schedule as a noncash investing and financing activity. The reasoning is that this is a significant financing (issuance of note payable) and investing (purchase of land) activity, which should be pointed out to financial statement users.

3.6   Plant and equipment increased by $18,000. This is the result of two transactions described in the additional information. Equipment (cost, $45,000) with a book value of $24,000 was sold for $19,000 cash:

Cash   19,000
Loss on sale
 ($19,000 – $24,000)   5,000
Accumulated depreciation
 ($45,000 – $24,000)   21,000
        Equipment   45,000

The $19,000 cash received is a cash inflow from investing activities. The loss on the sale of the asset is used as an adjustment when using the indirect approach because even though it decreased accrual net income, it does not involve an outflow of cash. Therefore, it is added to net income to arrive at cash flows from operating activities. The other transaction is a purchase of equipment, $63,000, which is a cash outflow from investing activities. These two transactions explain the $18,000 net change in the plant and equipment account.

Plant and Equipment		
Purchase		Sale of
of equip. 63,000	45,000	equip.
18,000		

3.7   Accumulated depreciation increased by $32,000. This net change is the result of the sale of equipment (discussed in 3.6) and depreciation expense of $53,000 listed in the income statement.

Accumulated Depreciation	
Sale of equip. 21,000	53,000 Depr. exp.
	32,000

Depreciation is added as an adjustment when using the indirect approach because even though it decreased accrual net income, it does not involve an outflow of cash.

3.8   Goodwill decreased by $4,000 as a result of goodwill amortization shown in the income statement. This item is added as an adjustment when using the indirect approach because although it decreased accrual basis net income, it does not involve an outflow of cash.

3.9   Accounts payable increased by $51,000. This is added as an adjustment to net income. The increase of $51,000 means that purchases were $51,000 more than the amount paid to vendors; therefore, cost of goods sold was increased but cash was not affected.

3.10   Accrued expenses decreased by $10,000. This is subtracted from net income in computing cash flows from operating activities. The decrease means that expenses paid in cash were $10,000 more than S&A expenses on an accrual basis.

3.11   The $150,000 increase in note payable (long-term) was discussed in 3.5.

3.12   Bonds payable decreased by $50,000. This is the result of the conversion into common stock described in the additional information. The bonds were converted into 2,000 (50 x 40) shares of stock. Since no extraordinary items are shown in the income statement, the book value method of recording the conversion (no gain or loss) must have been used.

Bonds payable   50,000
 Common stock
  (2,000 x $10)   20,000
  APIC ($50,000 – $20,000)   30,000

Although cash is not affected by this transaction, it is presented in a separate schedule as a noncash financing and investing activity. Issuing stock and retiring bonds are both significant <u>financing</u> activities. Therefore, both of these transactions will be reported in a separate schedule even though they do not directly affect the cash account.

3.13   Deferred tax liability increased by $11,000. This amount is added to net income in computing cash flows from operating activities. This increase means that $11,000 of deferred income tax expense reduced net income, but was not payable in cash.

3.14   Common stock increased by $30,000. $20,000 of this change was the result of the conversion of bonds payable (item 3.12). The other $10,000 was due to the issuance of stock for cash described in the additional information.

Cash   23,000
 Common stock
  (1,000 x $10)   10,000
 Additional paid-in
  capital   13,000

The $23,000 inflow is a financing activity.

3.15   The change in additional paid-in capital ($51,000 increase) is explained in items 3.12 ($30,000), 3.14 ($13,000), and 3.17 ($8,000).

3.16 Retained earnings increased by $98,000.
      Examination of the statement of income
      and retained earnings reveals that the
      change consists of $141,000 net income
      and $43,000 of cash dividends. The
      $43,000 outflow from the cash dividends
      would be presented as a financing
      activity.

3.17 Treasury stock decreased by $17,000.
      The additional information indicates
      that this stock was sold for $25,000.
      Per the balance sheet, the cost method
      is used, resulting in the following
      entry:

      Cash   25,000
          Treasury stock   17,000
          APIC   8,000

      The $25,000 inflow is a financing
      activity.

Unofficial Answer

Problem 3 Statement of Cash Flows
           (1182,P4)

Farrell Corporation
Statement of Cash Flows
For the Year Ended December 31, 1987

Cash flows from operating activities:

Net income		$141,000
Add (or deduct) items not affecting cash:		
Loss on sale of equipment	$ 5,000	
Depreciation expense	53,000	
Goodwill amortization	4,000	
Decrease in accounts receivable	10,000	
Increase in accounts payable	51,000	
Decrease in accrued expenses	(10,000)	
Increase in deferred income taxes	11,000	
Equity in earnings of Hall, Inc.	(13,000)	
Increase in inventories	(118,000)	(7,000)
Net cash flows from operating activities		134,000

Cash flows from investing
activities:

Proceeds from disposal of property, plant, and equipment	19,000	
Purchases of property, plant, and equipment	(63,000)	
Net cash used by investing activities		(44,000)

Cash flows from financing activities:

Proceeds from issuing common stock	23,000	
Proceeds from issuing treasury stock	25,000	
Dividends paid	(43,000)	
Net cash provided by financing activities		5,000
Net increase (decrease) in cash		95,000
Cash and cash equivalents at beginning of year		180,000
Cash and cash equivalents at end of year		$275,000

Schedule of noncash investing and financing
activities:

Common stock issued to convert bonds payable	$ 50,000
Notes payable issued to purchase land	$ 150,000

Disclosure of accounting policy:

For purposes of the statement of cash flows,
the Company considers all highly liquid debt
instruments purchased with a maturity of three
months or less to be cash equivalents.

Authors' note: Other required disclosures
when the indirect method is used are only paid
for interest and income taxes. However, there
is not enough information given in this
problem to obtain these numbers.

Alternate Solution Guide

Problem 3   Statement of Cash Flows (1182,P4)

     The problem may also be solved using the
"T-account approach." This method provides a
systematic way to accumulate the information
necessary to prepare the statement. The
T-accounts appear at the end of this solution
guide.

1.   The first step would be to calculate the
     change in cash and cash equivalents;
     however, this is given as a $95,000
     increase.

2. Next, set up T-accounts for each of the accounts and enter the beginning and ending balances. Also set up four T-accounts: cash and cash equivalents; cash and cash equivalents--operations; cash and cash equivalents--investing activities; and cash and cash equivalents--financing activities.

3. After this is done, analyze the events that affect cash: distinguish the items that affect cash from operations and other items that affect cash but are not a part of normal operations. Those latter items should be classified as financing or investing activities. Begin with the effects of the additional information and then consider the Statement of Income and Retained Earnings. Lastly, examine the Balance Sheet to ascertain that all changes have been explained.

Additional information:

(a) Using the T-account approach, the journal entry would be:

Cash and cash equivalents--investing	19,000	
Cash and cash equivalents--operating	5,000	
Accum. depreciation	21,000	
Plant and equipment		45,000

The cash proceeds would be considered an inflow and therefore debited to cash and cash equivalents from investing activities. The loss would be debited to cash and cash equivalents--operations because this amount was used in the calculation of accrual-basis income but did not require an outflow of cash. The debit to accumulated depreciation and the credit to equipment remove the asset from the books.

(b) The $23,000 proceeds from the issuance of stock would be considered an inflow of cash   The $23,000 inflow is classified as a financing activity and should be debited to cash and cash equivalents--financing. The remaining credits would be to common stock for the par value ($10,000) of the stock and additional paid-in capital (APIC) for the amount received in excess of par ($13,000).

(c) The proceeds ($25,000) from the issuance of treasury stock would be considered an inflow of cash and debited to cash and cash equivalents--financing. The credits would be to treasury stock for the original purchase price ($17,000) and to

APIC for the proceeds in excess of cost ($8,000). The change in the treasury stock account is now explained.

(d) The journal entry to record the conversion of the bonds into common stock would be recorded as:

Bonds payable	50,000	
Common stock		20,000
APIC		30,000

Although this entry does not affect cash, it would be reported in a separate schedule as a noncash financing activity. The information contained in this and the previous two adjustments explains the net increase of $51,000 in additional paid-in capital. Also, the information in (b) and the current adjustment (d) explain the $30,000 increase in common stock.

(e) The purchase of equipment was an outflow of cash from investing activities of $63,000, while increasing plant and equipment by the same amount. Additionally, once this information and the entry made in (a) are entered, the net increase ($18,000) in the plant and equipment account is reconciled.

(f) Land was purchased through the issuance of notes payable, thereby increasing both the land and notes payable accounts and accounting for their changes. This transaction, although not affecting cash, would be reported in a separate schedule as a noncash financing and investing activity.

(g) Deferred tax liability increased by $11,000 and were recognized as an expense of the period. Since this expense did not require the outlay of cash during the current period, it is added to net income to arrive at cash flows from operating activities. The entry would debit cash and cash equivalents--operations and credit deferred tax liability, thus reconciling this latter account.

Statement of Income and Retained Earnings:

(h) Net income of $141,000 was reported for the year. It is treated as an inflow of cash and adjusted for items that do not affect cash flow. Net income is credited to retained earnings since it increases retained earnings for the year.

(i) Depreciation, although recognized as an expense, does not require the outlay of cash. Depreciation expense is shown as a debit to cash and cash equivalents--operations because it reduced accrual-basis income. The credit to accumulated depreciation provides the necessary credit to explain the $32,000 increase in accumulated depreciation after the sale of the asset in (a).

(j)   The equity in net income of Hall, Inc. is a reconciling item since the equity method is being used to account for this investment. The entry made <u>to record the accrual of Hall's income was:</u>

Investment in Hall   13,000
    Equity in income of Hall   13,000

This does not represent a cash inflow; however, it must be shown as a credit to cash and cash equivalents--operations because it increased accrual-basis income. The debit to the investment account explains its $13,000 increase for the year.

(k)   The next reconciling item is the amortization of goodwill. Like depreciation expense, amortization reduces net income while not affecting cash flows. Therefore, it is debited to cash and cash equivalents--operations. The corresponding credit to goodwill explains the $4,000 decrease in the account.

(l)   The payment of a cash dividend ($43,000) was an outflow of cash during the period and reduces retained earnings. The payment of cash dividends would be classified as an outflow from financing activities. This entry along with the net income for the period explains the net increase of $98,000 in retained earnings.

Balance Sheet:

(m)   The $10,000 decrease in accounts receivable must be debited to cash and cash equivalents--operations. The decrease means that $10,000 was collected in excess of sales reported in the income statement. With this entry the change in accounts receivable is explained.

(n)   The increase in inventory indicates that $118,000 was spent to increase inventories but was not included in cost of goods sold. Therefore, $118,000 should be credited to cash and cash equivalents--operations.

The increases (decreases) have now been explained for all of the asset accounts.

(o)   Accounts payable increased by $51,000. This amount is debited to cash and cash

equivalents--operations. This increase means that purchases were made on account and these purchases increased cost of goods sold but did not require cash. The accounts payable account is now reconciled.

(p)   Accrued expenses decreased by $10,000. This amount is credited to cash and cash equivalents--operations because cash was paid out, but net income was not affected by this outlay. The accrued expenses account is now reconciled.

The increases (decreases) have now been explained for all of the liability and stockholders' equity accounts.

(q)   Cash flows from operating activities can be derived by adding and subtracting the amounts in the T-account cash and cash equivalents--operations. This amount, $134,000, should be transferred to cash and cash equivalents to reconcile the net increase in cash and cash equivalents.

(r)   Net cash flows from investing activities can be derived by using the debits (inflows) and credits (outflows) in the T-account for cash and cash equivalents--investing. The inflows and outflows would each be a separate line item in the formal statement. Net cash used by investing activities is $44,000. This amount should be transferred to cash and cash equivalents to reconcile the net increase in cash and cash equivalents.

(s)   Net cash flows from financing activities can be derived by using the debits (inflows) and credits (outflows) in the T-account for cash and cash equivalents--financing. The inflows and outflows would each be a separate line item in the formal statement. Net cash provided by financing activities is $5,000. This amount should be transferred to cash and cash equivalents to reconcile the net increase in cash and cash equivalents.

4.   Once the net inflow or outflow from operating, financing, and investing is transferred to cash and cash equivalents, the net increase in cash, $95,000 is reconciled.

5.   The final step is the preparation of the statement. The unofficial answer of the statement of cash flows would appear the same as presented earlier.

Cash and Cash Equivalents

(q) OPERATIONS	134,000	44,000	INVESTING (r)
(s) FINANCING	5,000		
	139,000	44,000	
		95,000	Increase in cash
	139,000	139,000	

Cash and Cash Equivalents--OPERATIONS

(a) Loss on Sale	5,000	13,000	Equity in income	(j)
(g) Inc. in DT	11,000	118,000	Inc. in Inv.	(n)
(h) Net Income	141,000	10,000	Dec. in Acc. Exp.	(p)
(i) Depr.	53,000			
(k) Amort. Exp.	4,000			
(m) Dec. in AR	10,000			
(o) Inc. in AP	51,000			
	275,000	141,000		
		134,000	OPERATIONS	(q)
	275,000	275,000		

Cash and Cash Equivalents--FINANCING

(b) Iss. of cm. stk.	23,000	43,000	Div. Pd. (l)
(c) Iss. of tr. stk.	25,000		
	48,000	43,000	
		5,000	FINANCING (s)
	48,000	48,000	

Cash and Cash Equivalents--INVESTING

(a) Sale of FA	19,000	63,000	Pur. of FA (e)
	19,000	63,000	
(r) INVESTING	44,000		
	63,000	63,000	

Accounts Receivable

305,000	
	10,000 (m)
295,000	

Inventories

431,000	
(n) 118,000	
549,000	

Investment in Hall

60,000	
(j) 13,000	
73,000	

Land

200,000	
(f) 150,000	
350,000	

Plant & Equipment

606,000	
	45,000 (a)
(e) 63,000	
624,000	

Accum. Depreciation

	107,000	
(a) 21,000	53,000	(i)
	139,000	

Goodwill

20,000	
	4,000 (k)
16,000	

Accounts Payable

	453,000
	51,000 (o)
	504,000

Notes Payable

	-0-
	150,000 (f)
	150,000

Bonds Payable

	210,000
(d) 50,000	
	160,000

Deferred Tax Liability

	30,000
	11,000 (g)
	41,000

Common Stock

	400,000
	10,000 (b)
	20,000 (d)
	430,000

Accrued Expenses

	110,000
(p) 10,000	
	100,000

APIC

	175,000
	13,000 (b)
	8,000 (c)
	30,000 (d)
	226,000

Retained Earnings

(l) Dividends 43,000	334,000	
	141,000	Net Income (h)
	432,000	

Treasury Stock

17,000	
	17,000 (c)
-0-	

Solution Guide

Problem 4   SCF and Changes in Partners'
             Capital Accounts (1187,P5)

1. This problem consists of two related
    parts. Part a. requires a statement of
    cash flows using the direct method in the
    operating activities section of the
    statement and part b. requires an
    analysis of changes in partners' capital
    accounts. Visualize the format of the
    statement for part a: operating
    activities, investing activities, and
    financing activities.

2. Cash received from fees is an item that
    should be included under operating
    activities. Using the direct approach,
    accrual revenues must be adjusted to
    revenues on a cash basis. To do this,
    accrual sales must be increased
    (decreased) by the decrease (increase) in
    accounts receivable. Accounts receivable
    increased by $39,000, implying that some
    revenue has not yet been collected.
    Therefore, cash received from fees is
    $1,293,000 ($1,332,000 fee revenue less
    $39,000 A/R increase).

2.1 Dividends received are also an operating
    activity. Cash received from dividends,
    not equity in earnings, must be reported
    in the statement of cash flows. The
    investee paid dividends of $192,000, and
    Public Relations Associates (PRA)
    received 25% of those dividends. This
    resulted in a cash inflow of $48,000 (25%
    x $192,000). Note that the equity in
    earnings ($88,000) is not a cash inflow;
    it results in an increase in the
    investment account, not in the cash
    account.

2.2 The last item to include under operating
    activities is operating expenses. Under
    the direct approach, cash paid for
    operating expenses must be computed by
    adjusting operating expenses for noncash
    expenses, accrued expenses, and deferred
    expenses. In this case, operating
    expenses are $970,000. This amount must
    be adjusted for a noncash expense,
    depreciation (indicated by the $30,000
    increase in accumulated depreciation) and
    for the increase in accounts payable and
    accrued expenses ($25,000). This $25,000
    increase implies that operating expenses
    have been recorded for which the cash
    payment has not been made. Therefore,
    cash paid for operating expenses is
    $915,000 ($970,000 - $30,000 - $25,000).

2.3 The net cash flow from operating
    activities is $426,000. It consists of
    cash received from fees ($1,293,000) and
    cash received from dividends ($48,000),
    less cash paid for operating expenses
    ($915,000).

3. Per SFAS 95, an indirect reconciliation
    of net income to net cash flow from
    operating activities is required. When
    the direct approach is used in the body
    of the statement, this reconciliation
    should be provided in a separate
    schedule. If the indirect approach is
    used, this reconciliation is included in
    the body of the statement under operating
    activities. The same adjustments are
    made under either approach.

3.1 The reconciliation starts off with net
    income. Net income in this case is
    $450,000. Depreciation expense ($30,000)
    must be added back because it is a
    noncash expense which reduced net income
    but did not reduce cash. The excess of
    equity in earnings over the dividends
    received from the investment ($88,000 -
    $48,000 = $40,000) must be subtracted
    because $40,000 of equity earnings were
    not received in cash. The increase in
    accounts receivable ($39,000) is deducted
    because it implies that $39,000 of
    revenue was not collected in cash. The
    increase in accounts payable and accrued
    expenses ($25,000) is added back to net
    income because it implies that some
    recorded expenses were not paid in
    cash. Therefore, the net cash flow from
    operating activities under the indirect
    approach is $426,000 ($450,000 + $30,000
    - $40,000 - $39,000 + $25,000), the same
    as under the direct approach.

4. The other asset accounts must be analyzed
    to determine the cash flows from
    investing activities. All the asset
    accounts except property and equipment
    were related to operating activities.
    Property and equipment increased by
    $85,000 as the result of a July 1
    purchase of an office computer. This
    cash outflow is reported as an investing
    activity. Note that the portion of the
    $85,000 cost which was paid for sales
    tax, delivery, and installation ($10,000)
    is considered part of the cost of the
    asset acquired.

5. The other liability and equity accounts
    must be analyzed to determine the cash
    flows from financing activities. Only
    accounts payable and accrued expenses are
    solely related to operating activities.

5.1 Mortgage payable decreased by $10,000. The cash outflow to reduce the mortgage is reported as a financing activity.

5.2 Partners' equity increased by $305,000. This increase must be analyzed further to determine the related cash flows. The typical items which affect partners' equity are investments, net income, and drawings. These are summarized below.

Partners' equity, 12/31/85	$ 850,000	
1/1/86 investment by Davis	170,000	Financing
Net income	450,000	Operating
Drawings	(315,000)	Financing
Partners' equity, 12/31/86	$1,155,000	

The investment by the new partners ($170,000) is a cash inflow reported as a financing activity, similar to the issuance of common stock by a corporation. The drawings ($315,000) are a cash outflow reported as a financing activity, similar to the payment of dividends by a corporation. Note that the $100,000 cash payment from the new partner directly to the old partners is <u>not</u> a cash flow of the partnership.

5.3 Finally, the amounts within each category can be netted to arrive at net cash inflows or outflows in each of the three main sections of the statement, and the beginning and ending balances of cash and cash equivalents can be reconciled at the end of the statement.

6. Part (b) requires an analysis of changes in partners' capital accounts. The typical changes in partners' capital accounts are investments, net income, and drawings.

6.1 The beginning balances were $510,000 for Burr and $340,000 for Cox, for a total of $850,000.

6.2 The only investment during the year was the $170,000 investment by Davis, the new partner. Note that the $100,000 cash payment from Davis directly to the old partners does <u>not</u> affect the partnership accounts.

6.3 Net income was $450,000, as reported in the income statement. Net income is divided 50% Burr, 30% Cox, and 20% Davis.

6.4 The drawings (Burr, $140,000; Cox, $100,000; and Davis, $75,000) decrease the capital accounts and total partners' equity.

Unofficial Answer

Problem 4   SCF and Changes in Partners' Capital Accounts (1187,P5)

a.

Public Relations Associates
Statement of Cash Flows
For the Year Ended December 31, 1986
Increase (Decrease) in Cash and Cash Equivalents

Cash flows from operating activities:

Cash received from fees (Schedule 1)	$1,293,000	
Cash received from dividends (Schedule 2)	48,000	
Cash provided by operating activities		$1,341,000
Cash paid for operating expenses (Schedule 3)		(915,000)
Net cash flow from operating activities		426,000
Cash flows from investing activities		
Purchase of office computer		(85,000)
Cash flows from financing activities		
Reduction in mortgage payable	$ (10,000)	
Investment by partners	170,000	
Drawings by partners	(315,000)	
Net cash used by financing activities		(155,000)
Net increase in cash and cash equivalents		$186,000
Cash and cash equivalents at beginning of year		140,000
Cash and cash equivalents at end of year		$ 326,000

Reconciliation of net income to cash provided by operating activities:

Net income	$ 450,000
Depreciation expense	30,000
Excess of equity income over dividends received (Schedule 4)	(40,000)
Increase in accounts receivable	(39,000)
Increase in accounts payable and accrued expenses	25,000
Net cash flow from operating activities	$ 426,000

Disclosure of accounting policy:

For purposes of the statement of cash flows, the company considers all highly liquid debt instruments purchased with a maturity of three months or less to be cash equivalents.

Schedule 1	Cash received from fees	
Fee revenue	$1,332,000	
Increase in accounts receivable	(39,000)	
Cash received from fees	$1,293,000	

Schedule 2	Cash received from dividends	
Dividend paid by King	$ 192,000	
Public Relation Associates' ownership interest	x 25%	
Cash received from dividends	$ 48,000	

Schedule 3	Cash paid for operating expenses		
Operating expenses		$ 970,000	
Depreciation expense	$30,000		
Increase in accts. pay. and accr. exps.	25,000	(55,000)	
Cash paid for operating expenses		$ 915,000	

Schedule 4	Excess of equity income over dividends received	
Equity income	$ 88,000	
Cash dividends received (Schedule 2)	48,000	
Excess of equity income over dividends received	$ 40,000	

b.

Public Relations Associates
ANALYSIS OF CHANGES IN PARTNERS' CAPITAL ACCOUNTS
For the Year Ended December 31, 1986

	Total	Burr	Cox	Davis
Balance, December 31, 1985	$ 850,000	$510,000	$340,000	$ --
Capital investment	170,000	--	--	170,000
Distribution of net income	450,000	225,000	135,000	90,000
Balance before drawings	1,470,000	735,000	475,000	260,000
Drawings	315,000	140,000	100,000	75,000
Balance, December 31, 1986	$1,155,000	$595,000	$375,000	$185,000

Multiple Choice Questions (1-56)

Items 1 through 5 are based on the following:

On January 1, 1988, Polk Corp. and Strass Corp. had condensed balance sheets as follows:

	Polk	Strass
Current assets	$ 70,000	$20,000
Noncurrent assets	90,000	40,000
Total assets	$160,000	$60,000
Current liabilities	$ 30,000	$10,000
Long-term debt	50,000	--
Stockholder's equity	80,000	50,000
Total liabilities and stockholders' equity	$160,000	$60,000

On January 2, 1988, Polk borrowed $60,000 and used the proceeds to purchase 90% of the outstanding common shares of Strass. This debt is payable in 10 equal annual principal payments, plus interest, beginning December 30, 1988. The excess cost of the investment over Strass' book value of acquired net assets should be allocated 60% to inventory and 40% to goodwill.

On Polk's January 2, 1988 consolidated balance sheet,

1. Current assets should be
    a. $99,000
    b. $96,000
    c. $90,000
    d. $79,000

2. Noncurrent assets should be
    a. $130,000
    b. $134,000
    c. $136,000
    d. $140,000

3. Current liabilities should be
    a. $50,000
    b. $46,000
    c. $40,000
    d. $30,000

4. Noncurrent liabilities including minority interests should be
    a. $115,000
    b. $109,000
    c. $104,000
    d. $ 55,000

5. Stockholders' equity should be
    a. $ 80,000
    b. $ 85,000
    c. $ 90,000
    d. $130,000

6. On April 1, 1988, Hart, Inc. paid $1,700,000 for all the issued and outstanding common stock of Ray Corp. On that date the costs and fair values of Ray's recorded assets and liabilities were as follows:

	Cost	Fair value
Cash	$ 160,000	$ 160,000
Inventory	480,000	460,000
Property, plant, and equipment (net)	980,000	1,040,000
Liabilities	(360,000)	(360,000)
Net assets	$1,260,000	$1,300,000

Hart amortizes goodwill over 40 years. In Hart's March 31, 1989 balance sheet, what is the amount of goodwill that should be reported as a result of this business combination?
    a. $390,000
    b. $400,000
    c. $429,000
    d. $440,000

7. Key Corp. issued 1,000 shares of its nonvoting preferred stock for all of Lev Corp.'s outstanding common stock. At the date of the transaction, Key's nonvoting preferred stock had a market value of $100 per share, and Lev's tangible net assets had a book value of $60,000. In addition, Key issued 100 shares of its nonvoting preferred stock to an individual as a finder's fee for arranging the transaction. As a result of this capital transaction, Key's total net assets would increase by
    a. $0
    b. $ 60,000
    c. $100,000
    d. $110,000

Items 8 and 9 are based on the following:

On December 31, 1988, Saxe Corporation was merged into Poe Corporation. In the business combination, Poe issued 200,000 shares of its $10 par common stock, with a market price of $18 a share, for all of Saxe's common stock. The stockholders' equity section of each company's balance sheet immediately before the combination was:

	Poe	Saxe
Common stock	$3,000,000	$1,500,000
Additional paid-in capital	1,300,000	150,000
Retained earnings	2,500,000	850,000
	$6,800,000	$2,500,000

8. Assume that the merger qualifies for treatment as a purchase. In the December 31, 1988 consolidated balance sheet, additional paid-in capital should be reported at
    a. $ 950,000
    b. $1,300,000

c. $1,450,000
d. $2,900,000

9.   Assume that the merger qualifies for treatment as a pooling of interests. In the December 31, 1988 consolidated balance sheet, additional paid-in capital should be reported at

a. $ 950,000
b. $1,300,000
c. $1,450,000
d. $2,900,000

10. A business combination is accounted for appropriately as a pooling of interests. Registration fees related to effecting the business combination should be

a.   Deducted directly from retained earnings of the combined corporation.
b.   Deducted in determining net income of the combined corporation for the period in which the costs were incurred.
c.   Capitalized and subsequently amortized over a period not exceeding forty years.
d.   Capitalized but not subsequently amortized.

11. Company L acquired all of the outstanding common stock of Company M in exchange for cash. The acquisition price exceeds the fair value of net assets acquired. How should Company L determine the amounts to be reported for the plant and equipment and long-term debt acquired from Company M?

	Plant and equipment	Long-term debt
a.	Fair value	M's carrying amount
b.	Fair value	Fair value
c.	M's carrying amount	Fair value
d.	M's carrying amount	M's carrying amount

12. A business combination is accounted for properly as a pooling of interests. Which of the following expenses related to effecting the business combination should enter into the determination of net income of the combined corporation for the period in which the expenses are incurred?

	Fees of finders and consultants	Registration fees
a.	Yes	Yes
b.	Yes	No
c.	No	No
d.	No	Yes

13. In a business combination accounted for as a purchase, costs of registering equity securities to be issued by the acquiring company are a(an)

a.   Expense of the combined company for the period in which the costs were incurred.
b.   Direct addition to stockholders' equity of the combined company.
c.   Reduction of the otherwise determinable fair value of the securities.
d.   Addition to goodwill.

14. A business combination is accounted for appropriately as a purchase. Which of the following should be deducted in determining the combined corporation's net income for the current period?

	Direct costs of acquisition	General expenses related to acquisition
a.	Yes	No
b.	Yes	Yes
c.	No	Yes
d.	No	No

15. A supportive argument for the pooling of interests method of accounting for a business combination is that

a.   One company is clearly the dominant and continuing entity.
b.   Goodwill is generally a part of any acquisition.
c.   A portion of the total cost is assigned to individual assets acquired on the basis of their fair value.
d.   It was developed within the boundaries of the historical cost system and is compatible with it.

16. In order to report a business combination as a pooling of interests, the minimum amount of an investee's common stock which must be acquired during the combination period in exchange for the investor's common stock is

a.   100 percent.
b.   51 percent.
c.   80 percent.
d.   90 percent.

17. Par Corp. owns 60% of Sub Corp.'s outstanding capital stock. On May 1, 1988, Par advanced Sub $70,000 in cash, which was still outstanding at December 31, 1988. What portion of this advance should be eliminated in the preparation of the December 31, 1988 consolidated balance sheet?

a. $70,000
b. $42,000
c. $28,000
d. $0

18. Cobb, Inc. has current receivables from affiliated companies at December 31, 1985 as follows:

• A $75,000 cash advance to Hill Corporation. Cobb owns 30% of the voting stock of Hill and accounts for the investment by the equity method.

• A receivable of $260,000 from Vick Corporation for administrative and selling services. Vick is 100% owned by Cobb and is included in Cobb's consolidated financial statements.

• A receivable of $200,000 from Ward Corporation for merchandise sales on credit. Ward is a 90% owned, unconsolidated subsidiary of Cobb.

In the current assets section of its December 31, 1985 consolidated balance sheet, Cobb should report accounts receivable from investees in the total amount of

a. $180,000
b. $255,000
c. $275,000
d. $535,000

Items 19 through 26 are based on the following data:

The separate condensed balance sheets and income statements of Par Corp. and its wholly-owned subsidiary, Sub Corp., are as follows:

BALANCE SHEETS
December 31, 1986

	Par	Sub
Assets		
Current		
Cash	$ 150,000	$ 50,000
Accounts receivable (net)	190,000	60,000
Inventories	90,000	40,000
Total current assets	430,000	150,000
Property, plant, and equipment (net)	365,000	200,000
Investment in Sub (equity method)	315,000	--
Total assets	$1,110,000	$350,000
Liabilities and Stockholders' Equity		
Current liabilities		
Accounts payable	$ 100,000	$ 60,000
Accrued liabilities	30,000	20,000
Total current liabilities	130,000	80,000
Stockholders' equity		
Common stock ($10 par)	220,000	30,000
Additional paid-in capital	140,000	100,000
Retained earnings	620,000	140,000
Total stockholders' equity	980,000	270,000
Total liabilities and stockholders' equity	$1,110,000	$350,000

INCOME STATEMENTS
For the Year Ended December 31, 1986

	Par	Sub
Sales	$1,000,000	$300,000
Cost of goods sold	770,000	200,000
Gross margin	230,000	100,000
Other operating expenses	130,000	50,000
Operating income	100,000	50,000
Equity in earnings of Sub	25,000	--
Income before income taxes	125,000	50,000
Provision for income taxes	40,000	20,000
Net income	$ 85,000	$ 30,000

Additional information:

• On January 1, 1986, Par purchased for $300,000 all of Sub's $10 par, voting common stock. On January 1, 1986, the fair value of Sub's assets and liabilities equaled their carrying amount of $330,000 and $80,000, respectively. Par's policy is to amortize intangible assets over a 10-year period, unless a definite life is ascertainable.

• During 1986, Par and Sub paid cash dividends of $50,000 and $10,000, respectively. For tax purposes, Par receives the 100% exclusion for dividends received from Sub.

• There were no intercompany transactions except for Par's receipt of dividends from Sub, and Par's recording of its shares of Sub's earnings.

• On June 30, 1986, Par issued 2,000 shares of common stock for $17 per share. There were no other changes in either Par's or Sub's common stock during 1986.

• Both Par and Sub paid income taxes at the rate of 40%.

19. In the 1986 consolidated income statement of Par and its subsidiary, Sub, what amount should be reported as consolidated net income?
a. $ 60,000
b. $ 85,000
c. $ 90,000
d. $115,000

20. The consolidated balance sheet of Par and its subsidiary, Sub, should report total consolidated assets of
    a. $1,110,000
    b. $1,145,000
    c. $1,190,000
    d. $1,460,000

21. The consolidated balance sheet of Par and its subsidiary, Sub, should report total retained earnings of
    a. $620,000
    b. $640,000
    c. $650,000
    d. $760,000

22. In the consolidated income statement of Par and its subsidiary, Sub, how much expense should be reported for amortization of goodwill?
    a. $0
    b. $ 3,000
    c. $ 5,000
    d. $10,000

23. In computing the consolidated earnings per share for Par and its subsidiary, Sub, the number of shares used should be
    a. 25,000
    b. 24,000
    c. 22,000
    d. 21,000

24. In the December 31, 1986 consolidated balance sheet of Par and its subsidiary, Sub, how much should be reported as total current assets?
    a. $150,000
    b. $280,000
    c. $430,000
    d. $580,000

25. Par's January 1, 1986 inventory was $110,000. Par's (parent only) 1986 inventory turnover ratio was
    a. 11.1
    b. 10.0
    c. 7.7
    d. 7.0

26. In Par's 1986 income statement, what amount of deferred income taxes on Par's equity in Sub's earnings should be included in Par's provision for income taxes?
    a. $0
    b. $ 2,000
    c. $10,000
    d. $12,000

27. A subsidiary was acquired for cash in a business combination on January 1, 1987. The purchase price exceeded the fair value of identifiable net assets. The acquired company owned equipment with a market value in excess of the carrying amount as of the date of combination. A consolidated balance sheet prepared on December 31, 1987 would
    a. Report the unamortized portion of the excess of the market value over the carrying amount of the equipment as part of goodwill.
    b. Report the unamortized portion of the excess of the market value over the carrying amount of the equipment as part of plant and equipment.
    c. Report the excess of the market value over the carrying amount of the equipment as part of plant and equipment.
    d. Not report the excess of the market value over the carrying amount of the equipment because it would be expensed as incurred.

28. A business combination occurs in the middle of the year. Results of operations for the year of combination would include the combined results of operations of the separate companies for the entire year if the business combination is a

	Pooling of interests	Purchase
a.	Yes	No
b.	Yes	Yes
c.	No	Yes
d.	No	No

29. A subsidiary, acquired for cash in a business combination, owned inventories with a market value different than the book value as of the date of combination. A consolidated balance sheet prepared immediately after the acquisition would include this difference as part of
    a. Deferred credits.
    b. Goodwill.
    c. Inventories.
    d. Retained earnings.

30. How would the retained earnings of a subsidiary acquired in a business combination usually be treated in a consolidated balance sheet prepared immediately after the acquisition?
    a. Excluded for both a purchase and a pooling of interests.
    b. Excluded for a pooling of interests but included for a purchase.
    c. Included for both a purchase and a pooling of interests.
    d. Included for a pooling of interests but excluded for a purchase.

31. Consolidated financial statements are typically prepared when one company has
   a. Accounted for its investment in another company by the equity method.
   b. Accounted for its investment in another company by the cost method.
   c. Significant influence over the operating and financial policies of another company.
   d. The controlling financial interest in another company.

32. A subsidiary may be acquired by issuing common stock in a pooling of interests transaction or by paying cash in a purchase transaction. Which of the following items would be reported in the consolidated financial statements at the same amount regardless of the accounting method used?
   a. Minority interest.
   b. Goodwill.
   c. Retained earnings.
   d. Capital stock.

33. Ownership of 51 percent of the outstanding voting stock of a company would usually result in
   a. The use of the cost method.
   b. The use of the lower of cost or market method.
   c. A pooling of interests.
   d. A consolidation.

34. King Corp. owns 80% of Lee Corp.'s common stock. During October 1987, Lee sold merchandise to King for $100,000. At December 31, 1987, one half of the merchandise remained in King's inventory. For 1987, gross profit percentages were 30% for King and 40% for Lee. The amount of unrealized intercompany profit in ending inventory at December 31, 1987 that should be eliminated in consolidation is
   a. $40,000
   b. $20,000
   c. $16,000
   d. $15,000

35. Dunn Corp. owns 100% of Grey Corp.'s common stock. On January 2, 1986, Dunn sold to Grey for $40,000 machinery with a carrying amount of $30,000. Grey is depreciating the acquired machinery over a five-year life by the straight-line method. The net adjustments to compute 1986 and 1987 consolidated income before income tax would be an increase (decrease) of

	1986	1987
a.	($ 8,000)	$2,000
b.	($ 8,000)	$0
c.	($10,000)	$2,000
d.	($10,000)	$0

Items 36 and 37 are based on the following:

On June 30, 1988, Purl Corp. issued 150,000 shares of its $20 par common stock for which it received all of Scott Corp.'s common stock. The fair value of the common stock issued is equal to the book value of Scott Corp.'s net assets. Both corporations continued to operate as separate businesses, maintaining accounting records with years ending December 31. Net income from separate company operations and dividends paid were:

	Purl	Scott
Net income		
Six months ended 6/30/88	$750,000	$225,000
Six months ended 12/31/88	825,000	375,000
Dividends paid		
March 25, 1988	950,000	--
November 15, 1988	--	300,000

On December 31, 1988, Scott held in its inventory merchandise acquired from Purl on December 1, 1988 for $150,000, which included a $45,000 markup.

36. Assume that the business combination qualifies for treatment as a purchase. In the 1988 consolidated income statement, net income should be reported at
   a. $1,650,000
   b. $1,905,000
   c. $1,950,000
   d. $2,130,000

37. Assume that the business combination qualifies for treatment as a pooling of interests. In the 1988 consolidated income statement, net income should be reported at
   a. $1,905,000
   b. $1,950,000
   c. $2,130,000
   d. $2,175,000

Items 38 through 42 are based on the following information:

On June 30, 1987, Post, Inc. issued 630,000 shares of its $5 par common stock, for which it received 180,000 shares (90%) of Shaw Corp.'s $10 par common stock, in a business combination appropriately accounted for as a pooling of interests. The stockholders' equities immediately before the combination were:

	Post	Shaw
Common stock	$ 6,500,000	$2,000,000
Additional paid-in		
capital	4,400,000	1,600,000
Retained earnings	6,100,000	5,400,000
	$17,000,000	$9,000,000

Both corporations continued to operate as separate businesses, maintaining accounting records with years ending December 31. For 1987, net income and dividends paid from separate company operations were:

	Post	Shaw
Net income		
Six months ended		
6/30/87	$1,000,000	$300,000
Six months ended		
12/31/87	1,100,000	500,000
Dividends paid		
April 1, 1987	1,300,000	--
October 1, 1987	--	350,000

38. In the June 30, 1987 consolidated balance sheet, common stock should be reported at
   a. $9,650,000
   b. $9,450,000
   c. $8,500,000
   d. $8,300,000

39. In the June 30, 1987 consolidated balance sheet, additional paid-in capital should be reported at
   a. $4,400,000
   b. $4,490,000
   c. $5,840,000
   d. $6,000,000

40. In the June 30, 1987 consolidated balance sheet, retained earnings should be reported at
   a. $ 6,100,000
   b. $ 9,660,000
   c. $10,960,000
   d. $11,500,000

41. In the 1987 consolidated income statement, net income should be reported at
   a. $2,550,000
   b. $2,600,000
   c. $2,820,000
   d. $2,900,000

42. In the December 31, 1987 consolidated balance sheet, total minority interest should be reported at
   a. $950,000
   b. $945,000
   c. $915,000
   d. $900,000

43. Eltro Company acquired a 70% interest in the Samson Company in 1988. For the years ended December 31, 1989 and 1990, Samson reported net income of $80,000 and $90,000, respectively. During 1989, Samson sold merchandise to Eltro for $10,000 at a profit of $2,000. The merchandise was later resold by Eltro to outsiders for $15,000 during 1990. For consolidation purposes what is the minority interest's share of Samson's net income for 1989 and 1990, respectively?
   a. $23,400 and $27,600.
   b. $24,000 and $27,000.
   c. $24,600 and $26,400.
   d. $26,000 and $25,000.

Items 44 and 45 are based on the following:

On January 1, 1988, Ritt Corp. purchased 80% of Shaw Corp.'s $10 par common stock for $975,000. On this date, the carrying amount of Shaw's net assets was $1,000,000. The fair values of Shaw's identifiable assets and liabilities were the same as their carrying amounts except for plant assets (net) which were $100,000 in excess of the carrying amount. For the year ended December 31, 1988, Shaw had net income of $190,000 and paid cash dividends totaling $125,000.

44. In the January 1, 1988 consolidated balance sheet, goodwill should be reported at
   a. $0
   b. $ 75,000
   c. $ 95,000
   d. $175,000

45. In the December 31, 1988 consolidated balance sheet, minority interest should be reported at
   a. $200,000
   b. $213,000
   c. $220,000
   d. $233,000

46. At December 31, 1987, Spud Corp. owned 80% of Jenkins Corp.'s common stock and 90% of Thompson Corp.'s common stock. Jenkins' 1987 net income was $100,000 and Thompson's 1987 net income was $200,000. Thompson and Jenkins had no intercompany ownership or transactions during 1987. Combined 1987 financial statements are being prepared for Thompson and Jenkins in contemplation of their sale to an outside party. In the combined income statement, combined net income should be reported at
   a. $210,000
   b. $260,000
   c. $280,000
   d. $300,000

47. Jay Company acquired a wholly-owned foreign subsidiary on January 1, 1988. The stockholders' equity section of the December 31, 1988 consolidated balance sheet follows:

Common stock	$ 500,000
Additional paid-in capital	200,000
Retained earnings	900,000
	1,600,000
Less: Contra account	600,000
Total stockholders' equity	$1,000,000

The contra account balance appropriately represents adjustments in translating the foreign subsidiary's financial statements into U.S. dollars.

The consolidated income statement for 1988 included the excess of cost of investments in marketable equity securities over their market values, which is considered temporary, as follows:

Noncurrent investments	$200,000
Current investments	$100,000

The correct amounts for retained earnings and the contra accounts in the consolidated statement of stockholders' equity for the year ended December 31, 1988 are

	Retained earnings	Contra accounts
a.	$ 900,000	$600,000
b.	$1,000,000	$700,000
c.	$1,100,000	$800,000
d.	$1,200,000	$900,000

48. Mr. and Mrs. Gasson own 100% of the common stock of Able Corp. and 90% of the common stock of Baker Corp. Able previously paid $4,000 for the remaining 10% interest in Baker. The condensed December 31, 1987 balance sheets of Able and Baker are as follows:

	Able	Baker
Assets	$600,000	$60,000
Liabilities	$200,000	$30,000
Common stock	100,000	20,000
Retained earnings	300,000	10,000
	$600,000	$60,000

In a combined balance sheet of the two corporations at December 31, 1987, what amount should be reported as total stockholders' equity?
a. $430,000
b. $426,000
c. $403,000
d. $400,000

49. Selected data for two subsidiaries of Dunn Corp. taken from December 31, 1988 pre-closing trial balances are as follows:

	Banks Co.	Lamm Co.
	Debit	Credit
Shipments to Banks	$ -	$150,000
Shipments from Lamm	200,000	-
Intercompany inventory profit on total shipments	-	50,000

Additional data relating to the December 31, 1988 inventory are as follows:

Inventory acquired from outside parties	$175,000	$250,000
Inventory acquired from Lamm	60,000	-

At December 31, 1988, the inventory reported on the combined balance sheet of the two subsidiaries should be
a. $425,000
b. $435,000
c. $470,000
d. $485,000

50. When combined financial statements are prepared for a group of related companies, intercompany transactions and intercompany profits or losses should be eliminated when the group is composed of

	Commonly controlled companies	Unconsolidated subsidiaries
a.	No	No
b.	No	Yes
c.	Yes	Yes
d.	Yes	No

51. Which of the following items should be treated in the same manner in both combined financial statements and consolidated statements?

	Income taxes	Minority interest
a.	No	No
b.	No	Yes
c.	Yes	Yes
d.	Yes	No

52. Which of the following items should be treated in the same manner in both combined financial statements and consolidated statements?

	Different fiscal periods	Foreign operations
a.	No	No
b.	No	Yes
c.	Yes	Yes
d.	Yes	No

May 1990 Questions

53. At December 31, 1989, Grey, Inc. owned 90% of Winn Corp., a consolidated subsidiary, and 20% of Carr Corp., an investee in which Grey cannot exercise significant influence. On the same date, Grey had receivables of $300,000 from Winn and $200,000 from Carr. In its December 31, 1989 consolidated balance sheet, Grey should report accounts receivable from affiliates of
- a. $500,000
- b. $340,000
- c. $230,000
- d. $200,000

54. P Co. purchased term bonds at a premium on the open market. These bonds represented 20 percent of the outstanding class of bonds issued at a discount by S Co., P's wholly owned subsidiary. P intends to hold the bonds until maturity. In a consolidated balance sheet, the difference between the bond carrying amounts in the two companies would be
- a. Included as a decrease to retained earnings.
- b. Included as an increase to retained earnings.
- c. Reported as a deferred debit to be amortized over the remaining life of the bonds.
- d. Reported as a deferred credit to be amortized over the remaining life of the bonds.

55. In order to report a business combination as a pooling of interests, the minimum amount of an investee's common stock that must be acquired during the combination period in exchange for the investor's common stock is
- a. 51 percent.
- b. 80 percent.
- c. 90 percent.
- d. 100 percent.

56. In a business combination accounted for as a purchase, the appraisal values of the identifiable assets acquired exceeds the acquisition price. The excess appraisal value should be reported as a
- a. Deferred credit.
- b. Reduction of the values assigned to current assets and a deferred credit for any unallocated portion.
- c. Reduction of the values assigned to noncurrent assets and a deferred credit for any unallocated portion.
- d. Pro rata reduction of the values assigned to current and noncurrent assets.

Problems

Problem 1   (586,T4)

(15 to 25 minutes)

Spellman Company will acquire 90% of Moore Company in a business combination. The total consideration has been agreed upon. The nature of Spellman's payment has not been fully agreed upon. Therefore, it is possible that this business combination might be accounted for as either a purchase or a pooling of interests. It is expected that at the date the business combination is to be consummated, the fair value will exceed the book value of Moore's assets minus liabilities. Spellman desires to prepare consolidated financial statements which will include the financial statements of Moore.

Required:

a. 1. Would the method of accounting for the business combination (purchase vs. pooling of interests) affect whether or not goodwill is reported?
   2. If goodwill is reported, explain how the amount of goodwill is determined.
   3. Would the method of accounting for the business combination (purchase vs. pooling of interests) affect whether or not minority interest is reported? If the amount reported differs, explain why.
   b. 1. From a theoretical standpoint, why should consolidated financial statements be prepared?
   2. From a theoretical standpoint, what is the usual condition to be met before consolidated financial statements can be prepared?
   3. From a theoretical standpoint, does the method of accounting for the business combination (purchase vs. pooling of interests) affect the decision to prepare consolidated financial statements? Why?

Problem 2   (587,T5)

(15 to 25 minutes)

Flaherty Company entered into a business combination with Steeley Company in the middle of the year. The combination was accounted for as a pooling of interests. Both companies use the same methods of accounting. Registration fees for the equity securities involved in the combination were incurred. There were no intercompany transactions before or after the combination.

Flaherty Company acquired all of the voting common stock of Rubin Company in the middle of the year. This combination was accounted for as a purchase and resulted in goodwill. Both companies use the same methods of accounting. Registration fees for the equity securities involved in the combination were incurred. There were no intercompany transactions before or after the combination.

Required:

a. 1. In the business combination accounted for as a pooling of interests, how should the recorded assets and liabilities of the separate companies be accounted for? What is the rationale for accounting for a business combination as a pooling of interests?
   2. In the business combination accounted for as a pooling of interests, how should the registration fees and direct costs related to effecting the business combination be accounted for?
   3. In the business combination accounted for as a pooling of interests, how should the results of operations for the year in which the business combination occurred be reported?
   b. 1. In the business combination accounted for as a purchase, how should the assets acquired and liabilities assumed be recorded? What is the rationale for accounting for a business combination as a purchase?
   2. In the business combination accounted for as a purchase, how should the registration fees and direct costs related to effecting the business combination be accounted for?
   3. In the business combination accounted for as a purchase, how should the results of operations of the acquired company for the year in which the business combination occurred be reported?

Problem 3   (1183,P5)

(40 to 50 minutes)

Amboy Corporation acquired all of the outstanding $10 par voting common stock of Taft, Inc., on January 1, 1986, in exchange for 50,000 shares of its $10 par voting common stock. On December 31, 1985, Amboy's common stock had a closing market price of $15 per share on a national stock exchange. The acquisition was appropriately accounted for as a purchase. Both companies continued to operate as separate business entities maintaining separate accounting records with years ending December 31.

On December 31, 1986, after year-end adjustments but before the nominal accounts were closed, the companies had condensed general ledger trial balances as follows:

	Amboy Dr. (Cr.)	Taft Dr. (Cr.)
Net sales	$(1,900,000)	$(1,500,000)
Dividend income from Taft, Inc.	(40,000)	
Gain on sale of warehouse	(30,000)	
Cost of goods sold	1,180,000	870,000
Operating expenses (includes depreciation)	550,000	440,000
Cash	285,000	150,000
Accounts receivable (net)	430,000	350,000
Inventories	530,000	410,000
Land, plant, & equipment	660,000	680,000
Accumulated depreciation	(185,000)	(210,000)
Investment in Taft, Inc. (at cost)	750,000	
Accounts payable & accrued expenses	(670,000)	(594,000)
Common stock ($10 par)	(1,200,000)	(400,000)
Additional paid-in capital	(140,000)	(80,000)
Retained earnings (1/1/86)	(220,000)	(156,000)
Dividends paid		40,000
Total	$ 0	$ 0

Additional information is as follows:
•   There were no changes in the common stock and additional paid-in capital accounts during 1986 except the one necessitated by Amboy's acquisition of Taft.
•   At the acquisition date the current value of Taft's machinery exceeded its book value by $54,000. The excess will be amortized over the estimated average remaining life of six years. The fair values of all of Taft's other assets and liabilities were equal to their book values. Any goodwill resulting from the acquisition will be amortized over a 20-year period.
•   On July 1, 1986, Amboy sold a warehouse facility to Taft for $129,000 cash. At the date of sale Amboy's book values were $33,000 for the land and $66,000 for the undepreciated cost of the building. Taft allocated the $129,000 purchase price to the land for $43,000 and to the building for $86,000. Taft is depreciating the building over its estimated five-year remaining useful life by the straight-line method with no salvage value.
•   During 1986 Amboy purchased merchandise from Taft at an aggregate invoice price of $180,000, which included a 100% markup on Taft's cost. At December 31, 1986, Amboy owed Taft $75,000 on these purchases, and $36,000 of the merchandise purchased remained in Amboy's inventory.

Required:

Complete the tear-out worksheet to prepare a consolidated income statement and retained earnings statement for the year ended December 31, 1986, and a consolidated balance sheet as of December 31, 1986, for Amboy Corporation and its subsidiary, Taft, Inc. Formal consolidated statements and journal entries are not required. Ignore income tax considerations. Supporting computations should be in good form. Include the completed tear-out worksheet in the proper sequence and turn in with other answer sheets.

Amboy Corporation and Subsidiary
Consolidated Statement Worksheet
December 31, 1986

Income Statement	Amboy Corp.	Taft Inc.	Adjustments & eliminations Debit	Credit	Adjusted balance
Net sales	$(1,900,000)	$(1,500,000)			
Dividends from Taft	(40,000)				
Gain on sale of warehouse	(30,000)				
Cost of goods sold	1,180,000	870,000			
Operating expenses (incl. deprec.)	550,000	440,000			
Net income	$ (240,000)	$ (190,000)			
Retained Earnings Statement					
Balance, 1/1/86	$ (220,000)	$ (156,000)			
Net income	(240,000)	(190,000)			
Dividends paid		40,000			
Balance, 12/31/86	$ (460,000)	$ (306,000)			
Balance Sheet					
Assets:					
Cash	$ 285,000	$ 150,000			
Accounts receivable (net)	430,000	350,000			
Inventories	530,000	410,000			
Land, plant & equipment	660,000	680,000			
Accumulated depreciation	(185,000)	(210,000)			
Investment in Taft (at cost)	750,000				
	$ 2,470,000	$ 1,380,000			
Liabilities & stockholders' equity:					
Accounts pay. & accrued exp.	$ (670,000)	$ (594,000)			
Common stock ($10 par)	(1,200,000)	(400,000)			
Additional paid-in capital	(140,000)	(80,000)			
Retained earnings	(460,000)	(306,000)			
	$(2,470,000)	$(1,380,000)			

Problem 4   (1188,P5)

(40 to 50 minutes)

Peel, Inc., acquired all of the outstanding $25 par value common stock of Stagg, Inc., on June 30, 1987, in exchange for 40,000 shares of its $25 par value common stock. The business combination meets all conditions for a pooling of interests. On June 30, 1987, Peel's common stock closed at $65 per share on a national stock exchange. Both corporations continued to operate as separate businesses maintaining separate accounting records with years ending December 31.

On December 31, 1987, after year-end adjustments and closing nominal accounts, the companies had condensed balance sheet accounts as follows:

	Peel	Stagg
Assets:		
Cash	$ 925,000	$ 300,000
Accounts and other receivables	2,140,000	835,000
Inventories	2,310,000	1,045,000
Land	600,000	330,000
Depreciable assets, net	4,525,000	1,980,000
Investment in Stagg, Inc.	2,430,000	--
Long-term investments and other assets	865,000	385,000
	$13,795,000	$4,875,000
Liabilities and Stockholders' Equity:		
Accounts payable and other current liabilities	$ 2,465,000	$1,145,000
Long-term debt	1,900,000	1,300,000
Common stock, $25 par value	3,200,000	1,000,000
Additional paid-in capital	1,850,000	190,000
Retained earnings	4,380,000	1,240,000
	$13,795,000	$4,875,000

Additional information is as follows:

• Peel uses the equity method of accounting for its investment in Stagg. The investment in Stagg has not been adjusted for any intercompany transactions.

• On June 30, 1987, Stagg's assets and liabilities had fair values equal to the book balances with the exception of land, which had a fair value of $550,000.

• On June 15, 1987, Stagg paid a cash dividend of $4 per share on its common stock.

• On December 10, 1987, Peel paid a cash dividend totaling $256,000 on its common stock.

• On June 30, 1987, immediately before the combination, the stockholders' equities were:

	Peel	Stagg
Common stock	$2,220,000	$1,000,000
Additional paid-in capital	1,660,000	190,000
Retained earnings	3,036,000	980,000
	$6,896,000	$2,170,000

• Stagg's long-term debt consisted of 10% ten-year bonds issued at face value on March 31, 1981. Interest is payable semi-annually on March 31 and September 30. Peel had purchased Stagg's bonds at face value of $320,000 in 1981, and there was no change in ownership through December 31, 1987.

• During October 1987 Peel sold merchandise to Stagg at an aggregate invoice price of $720,000, which included a profit of $180,000. At December 31, 1987, one-half of the merchandise remained in Stagg's inventory, and Stagg had not paid Peel for the merchandise purchased.

• Stagg's 1987 net income was $580,000. Peel's 1987 income before considering equity in Stagg's net income was $890,000.

• The balances in retained earnings at December 31, 1986, were $2,506,000 and $820,000 for Peel and Stagg, respectively.

Required:

a. Complete the tear-out worksheet to prepare a consolidated balance sheet of Peel, Inc., and its subsidiary, Stagg, Inc., at December 31, 1987. A formal consolidated balance sheet and journal entries are not required. Include the completed tear-out worksheet in the proper sequence with other answer sheets.

b. Prepare a formal consolidated statement of retained earnings for the year ended December 31, 1987.

Peel, Inc. and Subsidiary
CONSOLIDATED BALANCE SHEET WORKSHEET
December 31, 1987

	Peel, Inc.	Stagg, Inc.	Adjustments & Eliminations Debit	Credit	Consolidated Balance
Assets:					
Cash	$ 925,000	$ 300,000			
Accounts & other receivables	2,140,000	835,000			
Inventories	2,310,000	1,045,000			
Land	600,000	330,000			
Depreciable assets, net	4,525,000	1,980,000			
Investment in Frey, Inc.	2,430,000				
Long-term investments & other assets	865,000	385,000			
	$13,795,000	$4,875,000			
Liabilities and stockholders' equity:					
Accounts payable & other current liabilities	$ 2,465,000	$1,145,000			
Long-term debt	1,900,000	1,300,000			
Common stock, $25 par value	3,200,000	1,000,000			
Additional paid-in capital	1,850,000	190,000			
Retained earnings	4,380,000	1,240,000			
	$13,795,000	$4,875,000			

Multiple Choice Answers

1. a	13. c	24. d	35. a	46. d
2. c	14. c	25. c	36. b	47. c
3. b	15. d	26. a	37. c	48. b
4. b	16. d	27. b	38. a	49. c
5. a	17. a	28. a	39. b	50. c
6. a	18. c	29. c	40. c	51. c
7. d	19. b	30. d	41. c	52. c
8. d	20. c	31. d	42. c	53. d
9. a	21. a	32. a	43. a	54. a
10. b	22. c	33. d	44. c	55. c
11. b	23. d	34. b	45. b	56. c
12. a				

Multiple Choice Answer Explanations

A. Accounting for the Combination, and Sections B. - E.

1.   (1188,P1,2) (a) In the consolidated balance sheet, the parent company's "investment in subsidiary" account should be eliminated and replaced by the net assets of the subsidiary. Under the purchase method, the assets of the acquired firm are recorded at their FMVs. The cost of the investment is $60,000 and the book value of the acquired net assets is $45,000 (90% x $50,000), so the excess of cost over book value is $15,000 ($60,000 - $45,000). 60% of this excess is allocated to inventory because its FMV exceeds its cost (60% x $15,000 = $9,000). Therefore, current assets should be reported at $99,000.

Current assets--Polk	$70,000
Current assets--Strass	20,000
Excess allocated to inventory	9,000
Total	$99,000

2.   (1188,P1,3) (c) In the consolidated balance sheet, the parent company's "investment in subsidiary" account should be eliminated and replaced by the net assets of the subsidiary. Under the purchase method, the assets of the acquired firm are recorded at their FMVs. The cost of the investment is $60,000 and the book value of the acquired net assets is $45,000 (90% x $50,000) the excess of cost over book value is $15,000 ($60,000 - $45,000). 40% of this excess is allocated to goodwill (40% x $15,000 = $6,000). Therefore, noncurrent assets should be reported at $136,000.

Noncurrent assets--Polk	$90,000
Noncurrent assets--Strass	40,000
Excess allocated to goodwill	6,000
Total	$136,000

3.   (1188,P1,4) (b) In the consolidated balance sheet, the parent company's "investment in subsidiary" account should be eliminated and replaced by the assets and liabilities of the subsidiary. Therefore, the consolidated balance sheet should include the current liabilities of both companies, plus the current portion of the debt incurred on 1/2/88 ($60,000 ÷ 10 = $6,000). Thus, current liabilities should be reported at $46,000 as computed below.

Current liabs.--Polk	$30,000
Current liabs.--Strass	10,000
Current portion of new debt	6,000
Total	$46,000

4.   (1188,P1,5) (b) In the consolidated balance sheet, the parent company's "investment in subsidiary" account should be eliminated and replaced by the assets and liabilities of the subsidiary. Therefore, the consolidated balance sheet should include the noncurrent liabilities of both companies, plus the noncurrent portion of the debt incurred on 1/2/88 ($60,000 - $6,000 = $54,000), plus the minority interest in the subsidiary ($50,000 x 10% = $5,000).

Noncurrent liabs.--Polk	$50,000
Noncurrent liabs.--Strass	0
Noncurrent portion of new debt	54,000
Minority interest	5,000
Total	$109,000

5.   (1188,P1,6) (a) In the consolidated balance sheet, neither the parent company's investment account nor the subsidiary's stockholders' equity is reported. These amounts are eliminated in the same journal entry that records the excess of cost over book value. The portion of the subsidiary's stockholders' equity which is <u>not</u> eliminated is reported as minority interest in the noncurrent liabilities section of the consolidated balance sheet. Therefore, the parent's stockholders' equity ($80,000) equals the consolidated stockholders' equity. Note that once the candidate has completed items 1 through 5, the answers can be checked using the balance sheet equation,

$$\left(\begin{array}{c}\text{Current}\\\text{assets}\end{array}\right) + \left(\begin{array}{c}\text{Non-}\\\text{current}\\\text{assets}\end{array}\right) = \left(\begin{array}{c}\text{Current}\\\text{liabilities}\end{array}\right) + \left(\begin{array}{c}\text{Non-}\\\text{current}\\\text{liabilities}\end{array}\right) + \left(\begin{array}{c}\text{Stock-}\\\text{holders'}\\\text{equity}\end{array}\right)$$

$$\$99,000 + \$136,000 = \$46,000 + \$109,000 + \$80,000$$

6.   (589,P2,29) (a) In a purchase, the net assets of the acquired firm are recorded at their FMVs. The excess of the cost of the investment over the FMV of the net assets acquired is allocated to goodwill. The cost of this investment is $1,700,000, and the FMV of the net assets acquired is $1,300,000; there-

fore, the amount allocated to goodwill is $400,000 ($1,700,000 - $1,300,000). Amortization for the year ended 3/31/89 is $10,000 ($400,000 x 1/40), so the amount reported in the 3/31/89 balance sheet is $390,000 ($400,000 - $10,000).

7. (1189,Q1,4) (d) The requirement is the increase in net assets to be recorded by Key as a result of acquiring all of the outstanding common stock of Lev Corporation. This acquisition is a purchase because Key issued nonvoting preferred stock in exchange for all of Lev's common stock. A purchase is accounted for under the basic historical cost principle; the net assets acquired are recorded at their fair value or the fair value of the stock issued, whichever is more objectively determinable. In this case, the fair value of the stock issued is a better measure of the value of the purchase (1,000 shares x $100 per share = $100,000). The total cost of acquiring the net assets is the fair value of the preferred stock ($100,000) plus the finder's fee of $10,000 (100 shares x $100 per share) equals $110,000. Therefore, answer (d) is correct.

8. (1189,P1,10) (d) In a business combination accounted for as a purchase, the fair market value of the net assets is used as the valuation basis for the combination. In this case, the net assets of the subsidiary have an implied fair market value of $3,600,000 which is the value of the common stock issued to Saxe's shareholders (200,000 x $18). Since $3,600,000 is the basis for recording this purchase, the common stock issued is recorded at $2,000,000 (200,000 shares x $10 par value per share) and additional paid-in capital is recorded at $1,600,000 ($3,600,000 - $2,000,000). Therefore, in the 12/31/88 consolidated balance sheet, additional paid-in capital should be reported at $2,900,000 ($1,300,000 + $1,600,000).

9. (1189,P1,11) (a) In a pooling of interests, the book values of the previous companies' assets and liabilities are carried forward, so the new company's stockholders' equity must equal the combined stockholders' equity of the preceding companies ($6,800,000 + $2,500,000 = $9,300,000). Common stock must be reported at its par value [$3,000,000 + (200,000 x $10) = $5,000,000]. The retained earnings of the preceding companies are carried forward to the extent possible ($2,500,000 + $850,000 = $3,350,000). Therefore, additional paid-in capital must be recorded at $950,000 [$9,300,000 - ($5,000,000 + $3,350,000)].

10. (589,T1,30) (b) Per APB 16, para 58, all expenses relating to effecting a business combination accounted for by the pooling of interests method should be deducted in determining the net income of the resulting combined corporation in the period in which the expenses are incurred. Thus, the registration fees should be deducted in the period incurred in determining net income of the combined corporation. Therefore, answer (b) is correct.

11. (588,T1,35) (b) Since Company M was acquired for cash, purchase accounting must be used to account for the acquisition. APB 16, paras 72 and 88 state that, in general, all assets and liabilities (including plant and equipment and long-term debt) should be reported at fair value when the purchase method is used. Answer (d) is incorrect because it describes the treatment accorded to plant and equipment when a combination is accounted for as a pooling of interests. However, since cash is used exclusively in the transaction, a pooling of interest is precluded (APB 16, 47b).

12. (1189,T1,32) (a) APB 16, para 58 states that all expenses relating to effecting a business combination accounted for by the pooling of interests method should be deducted in determining the net income of the resulting combined corporation for the period in which the expenses are incurred. Thus, both the fees of finders and consultants and the registration fees should be expensed in determining the net income of the combined corporation for the period during which they were incurred.

13. (585,T1,29) (c) The requirement is to determine the proper treatment of the costs of registering equity securities to be issued by the acquiring company when the business combination is accounted for as a purchase. Answer (c) is correct because, per APB 16, para 76, the costs of registering equity securities should be a reduction of the otherwise determinable fair value of the securities. Answer (a) is incorrect because costs of registering equity securities to be issued are not considered to be general or indirect expenses related to the acquisition. Answer (b) is incorrect because a cost will never be an addition to stockholders' equity. Answer (d) is incorrect because goodwill is the difference between the consideration given and the fair market value of the net assets obtained.

14. (589,T1,31) (c) Per APB 16, para 76, the direct costs of acquisition should be included as part of the cost of a company

acquired in a business combination accounted for by the purchase method. General expenses related to the acquisition, however, are deducted as incurred in determining the combined corporation's net income for the current period. Therefore, answer (c) is correct.

15. (1189,T1,33)   (d) Per APB 16, paras 31 and 45, the objective of the pooling of interests method of accounting for business combinations is to present as a single interest two or more common stockholder interests which were previously independent and the combined rights and risks represented by those interests. Pooling demonstrates that stockholder groups neither withdraw nor invest assets, but rather exchange voting common stock in a ratio which reflects their proportionate ownership in the combined entity. No single entity in a pooling of interests is considered to be the "acquirer." The individual assets, liabilities, equity, and income of the individual entities are merely combined. Since a pooling of interests does not involve a "purchase," there is no need to revalue the assets of any of the individual entities to their market value (as would normally take place in a purchase transaction). Proponents of pooling of interests accounting point out that, since no asset revaluation is performed, the pooling concept was developed within the boundaries of the historical cost system and is compatible with it. Therefore, answer (d) is correct. Answer (a) is incorrect because no single entity is considered dominant in a pooling of interests. Answer (b) is incorrect because goodwill cannot result from a combination under pooling of interests accounting. Goodwill cannot be recorded since there is no purchase or asset revaluation and, therefore, there can be no excess of cost over fair market value (which is the "goodwill" portion of the purchase price). Answer (c) is incorrect because no assets are recorded at their fair value in a pooling of interests.

16. (1183,T1,34)   (d) The requirement is the minimum amount of an investee's stock which must be acquired in order to report a business combination as a pooling of interests. APB 16, para 47 requires that one of the combining companies issues voting common stock in exchange for at least 90 percent of the voting stock of another combining company that is outstanding at the date the combination is consummated.

F. Consolidated Financial Statements, and Sections G. - I.

17. (1189,Q1,6)   (a) Consolidated statements are prepared as if the parent and subsidiaries

were one economic entity. From the point of view of the consolidated entity, the $70,000 is not payable to or receivable from any outside company. In other words, the consolidated entity does not have a receivable or payable. Therefore, the entire $70,000 payable on Sub's books and the entire $70,000 receivable on Par's books must be eliminated against each other. The level of ownership (60%) does not affect this elimination.

18. (586,P1,9)   (c) The requirement is the amount to be reported for accounts receivable from investees in the 12/31/85 current assets section of the consolidated balance sheet. The $260,000 receivable from the consolidated subsidiary would be eliminated on the consolidated worksheet and, therefore, is not reported on the consolidated balance sheet. The receivables from the unconsolidated subsidiaries of $275,000 ($75,000 + $200,000) would not be eliminated and, therefore, would be reported as receivables in the consolidated balance sheet. Therefore, answer (c) is correct.

19. (587,Q1,4)   (b) Under the "full" equity method of accounting, the parent company's net income will be equal to consolidated net income. In this problem, Par's net income of $85,000 will equal the consolidated net income; thus, answer (b) is correct. This relationship can be proven or reconciled as the parent company's income from independent operations plus its share of reported subsidiary income as follows:

Par's operating income less provision for taxes ($100,000 - $40,000)	$60,000
Add: Sub's net income	30,000
Less: Amortization of goodwill	(5,000)*
	$85,000

*Purchase price	$300,000
Less: FMV (same as book value) of identifiable net assets on date of purchase ($330,000 - $80,000)	(250,000)
Goodwill	$ 50,000

$50,000 ÷ 10-year life = $5,000/year

20. (587,Q1,5)   (c) In the consolidated balance sheet, the parent company's investment in subsidiary account should be eliminated and replaced with the assets of the subsidiary. Thus, the total consolidated assets are equal to Par's total assets, less the investment in Sub account (with the unamortized goodwill added back), plus the total assets of Sub. Answer (c) is correct, determined as follows:

Total assets of Par	$1,110,000
Less: Investment in Sub account	(315,000)
	795,000
Add: Unamortized goodwill	45,000*
	840,000
Add: Total assets of Sub	350,000
Total consolidated assets	$1,190,000

*Goodwill, 1/1/86

($300,000 - $250,000)	$50,000
Less: Goodwill amortized,	
1/1/86-12/31/86 ($50,000/10 years)	(5,000)
Unamortized goodwill, 12/31/86	$45,000

21.   (587,Q1,6) (a) Under the "full" equity method of accounting, consolidated retained earnings will equal the retained earnings of the parent company. This is true because consolidated retained earnings under the equity method equals beginning of the year consolidated retained earnings plus consolidated net income (which is identical to parent company net income), minus dividends declared during the year by the parent company only. Thus, answer (a) is correct.
Note: No proof of answer is presented because beginning retained earnings was not given in the problem.

22.   (587,Q1,7) (c) Since the fair market value (FMV) of the identifiable assets and liabilities equaled their book value (BV) on the date of purchase, goodwill is the excess of purchase price over FMV (BV) of the net assets. Net assets are total assets ($330,000) less liabilities ($80,000), or $250,000. Therefore, goodwill is $50,000 ($300,000 - 250,000). Since Par's policy is to amortize intangible assets over 10 years, amortization expense for 1986 is $5,000 ($50,000 ÷ 10 years). Thus, answer (c) is correct.

23.   (587,Q1,8) (d) Per APB 15, para 47, computations of earnings per share data should be based on the weighted average number of common shares and common share equivalents outstanding during each period presented. For this computation, only Par's 20,000 common stock shares which were outstanding at the beginning of the year are treated as outstanding for the entire year. The June 30, 1986, issuance of 2,000 shares results in a weighted average of 1,000 shares (6/12 x 2,000) because the shares were outstanding for six months during the year. Thus, the total number of shares for EPS computations is 21,000.

Outstanding 1/1/86	20,000
June 30 issuance (6/12 x 2,000)	1,000
	21,000

24.   (587,Q1,9) (d) In the December 31, 1986 consolidated balance sheet of Par and Sub, total current assets of $580,000 should be reported. This amount is computed simply by adding Par's total current assets of $430,000 to Sub's total current assets of $150,000. This is true because there are no intercompany transactions in this problem whose effects would have to be eliminated in preparing the consolidated statements (e.g., intercompany receivables or unrealized intercompany profits on inventory).

25.   (587,Q1,10) (c) The inventory turnover ratio for Par (parent only) is computed by dividing cost of goods sold by average inventory. Average inventory is equal to: (Beginning inventory + Ending inventory) ÷ 2. Thus, the ratio is 7.7, as determined by the following equation:

$$\frac{770,000}{[(110,000 + 90,000)/2]} = 7.7$$

26.   (587,Q1,11) (a) Since Sub Corp. is a wholly-owned subsidiary, for tax purposes it is a controlled corporation, and Par receives the 100% dividends received deduction for dividends received from Sub. Because both Par and Sub pay their own income taxes, and because of the 100% dividend received deduction, Par will __never__ pay taxes on Sub's income. Therefore, there should be __no__ deferred income taxes on Par's equity in Sub's earnings, and answer (a) is correct.

27.   (588,T1,3) (b) The purchase method is used to account for this situation because the subsidiary was acquired for cash. APB 16, paras 72 and 88 state that, in general, all assets and liabilities (including equipment) should be reported at market value. The excess of the equipment's market value over its carrying amount is allocated to the equipment and amortized over the equipment's useful life. The unamortized portion of the excess of the market value over the carrying amount of the equipment is then reported as part of plant and equipment. Consequently, answer (b) is correct and answer (c) is incorrect. Answer (a) is incorrect because the unamortized portion of the excess of the market value over the carrying amount of the equipment is reported in plant and equipment, __not__ goodwill. Only the unamortized portion of the excess of the acquisition cost over the market value of the net identifiable assets acquired is reported as goodwill. Answer (d) is incorrect because the excess of the market value over the carrying amount of the equipment is capitalized and subsequently amortized over the equipment's useful life, __not__ expensed as incurred.

28. (1187,T1,29) (a) Per APB 16, the purchase method treats a business combination as the acquisition of one company by another, and accordingly, only the results of operations of the acquired company subsequent to the combination are included in the reported income of the acquiring corporation. Conversely, the pooling of interests method treats a business combination as the uniting of the ownership interests of the combining companies by an exchange of equity securities. In essence, the companies are treated as if they had always been combined, so results of operations are combined for the entire fiscal period in which the combination occurred (in addition, the reported income of the combined companies for any prior periods presented is combined and restated as income of the combined entity).

29. (1186,T1,3) (c) Since the subsidiary was acquired for cash, purchase accounting must be used in preparing the consolidated balance sheet. Therefore, the assets acquired would be revalued to their fair market value. The inventory account would then include the difference between the market value and book value. Answer (a) is incorrect because a deferred credit represents the excess of fair market value over acquisition cost. Answer (b) is incorrect because goodwill represents the excess of cost over fair market value. Answer (d) is incorrect because the retained earnings account is not affected by this transaction when purchase accounting is used.

30. (1182,T1,2) (d) In a consolidated balance sheet prepared immediately after the acquisition, the retained earnings of a subsidiary are included for a pooling of interests (APB 16, para 53) but excluded for a purchase (ARB 51, para 9).

31. (1182,T1,4) (d) Per SFAS 94, para 13, consolidated financial statements are typically prepared when one company has the controlling financial interest in another company. This control is usually direct or indirect ownership of over 50% of the outstanding voting stock. Significant influence, [answer (c)], usually between 20% and 50% voting stock ownership, should be reported using the equity method (APB 18, para 17). The method of accounting for a subsidiary [answers (a) and (b)] is irrelevant when determining whether consolidated financial statements should or should not be prepared because consolidated subsidiaries may be accounted for using either the cost or equity method.

32. (582,T1,12) (a) The percentage of stock not owned by the parent company represents the minority interest's share of the net assets of the subsidiary. Under both purchase and pooling accounting, minority interest income will be a deduction on the consolidated income statement for its portion of the subsidiary's income. Minority interest will be shown on the consolidated balance sheet in an amount determined by multiplying the owners' equity of the subsidiary by the minority's respective ownership percentage. Answer (b) is incorrect because goodwill is only recorded under the purchase method. Answer (c) is incorrect because under purchase accounting none of the subsidiary's retained earnings is carried over in the consolidated balance sheet whereas under pooling of interest accounting all or some of the subsidiary's retained earnings will be carried over. Answer (d) is incorrect because the additional stock issued by the parent in the pooling transaction will appear in the consolidated balance sheet.

33. (582,T1,18) (d) SFAS 94, para 13 states that consolidated financial statements should generally be prepared when there is greater than 50% ownership of the outstanding voting stock of the company although there are unusual circumstances in which reporting under the equity method or even the cost method is more appropriate. (Note that consolidation may also refer to a form of business combination where two or more entities form a new entity.) The exhibit below illustrates the accounting treatment for equity investments.

Financial reporting	% owned
Cost or LCM	20
Equity	20-50
Consolidated or Equity	51-100

Answers (a) and (b) are incorrect because the ownership in voting stock is greater than 20%. Pooling of interest, [answer (c)], is incorrect because recording an acquisition of stock as a pooling requires at least 90% ownership of the voting stock.

G. Date of Combination Consolidated Balance Sheet Purchase Accounting

34. (588,P1,10) (b) Unrealized profit in ending inventory arises when intercompany sales are made at prices above cost and the merchandise not resold to third parties prior to year end. The profit is unrealized because the inventory has not yet been sold outside of the consolidated entity. In this case, $50,000 of the inventory sold to King by Lee ($100,000 x 50%) remains in ending inventory. The gross profit Lee recognized on this

inventory at the time of sale was $20,000 ($50,000 x 40%). For the consolidated entity, this $20,000 gross profit has not been earned and must be eliminated.

35. (588,P1,11) (a) When computing consolidated income, the objective is to restate the accounts as if the intercompany transactions had not occurred. In 1986, the gain on the sale of the equipment ($40,000 - $30,000 = $10,000) must be eliminated, since the consolidated entity has not realized any gain. Also in 1986, some depreciation expense must be eliminated because the subsidiary computed depreciation based on a cost of $40,000 rather than on the original carrying amount of $30,000. Additional depreciation of $2,000 [($40,000 - $30,000) ÷ 5] must be eliminated. Therefore, 1986 income must be adjusted downward by $8,000 ($10,000 - $2,000). 1987 income must also be adjusted for the additional depreciation, so it must be adjusted upward by $2,000.

36. (589,P3,57) (b) In a purchase, the consolidated financial statements reflect the combined operations of the parent and subsidiary **from the date of combination**. Earnings of the subsidiary prior to the combination are **not** included with the parent's income. The parent's 1988 income is $1,575,000 ($750,000 + $825,000), while the subsidiary's income after the combination is $375,000 for a total of $1,950,000 ($1,575,000 + $375,000). The unrealized inventory profit of $45,000 must be eliminated, because from a consolidated viewpoint, revenue cannot be recognized until these goods are sold to a third party (i.e., a sale has not yet occurred). Therefore, 1988 consolidated net income is $1,905,000 ($1,950,000 - $45,000). Note that the net income amounts given are from **separate company operations**, so no elimination of equity earnings or dividend income is necessary.

37. (589,P3,58) (c) Per para 56 of APB 16, business combinations accounted for by the pooling of interests method should report net income **as if the combination took place at the beginning of the year**. The parent's 1988 income is $1,575,000 ($750,000 + $825,000), while the subsidiary's 1988 income (including pre-combination income) is $600,000 ($225,000 + $375,000), for a total of $2,175,000 ($1,575,000 + $600,000). The unrealized inventory profit of $45,000 must be eliminated, because from a consolidated viewpoint, revenue cannot be recognized until these goods are sold to a third party (i.e., a sale has not yet occurred). Therefore, 1988 consolidated net income is $2,130,000 ($2,175,000 - $45,000). Note that the net income amounts given are from **separate company operations**, so

no elimination of equity earnings or dividend income is necessary.

L. Minority Interest

38. (588,P1,13) (a) In a pooling of interests, the book values of the previous companies' assets and liabilities are carried forward. Therefore, Post will record its investment at $8,100,000 (90% x $9,000,000) and stockholders equity accounts must be credited at the same amount. The new common stock issued must be recorded at its par value (630,000 x $5 = $3,150,000). Post's share of the subsidiary's retained earnings (90% x $5,400,000 = $4,860,000) is carried forward to the extent possible. Therefore, APIC must be recorded at $90,000 [$8,100,000 - ($3,150,000 + $4,860,000)]. The journal entry is:

Investment in stock of Shaw	8,100,000	
Common stock		3,150,000
APIC		90,000
Retained earnings		4,860,000

Thus, common stock should be reported at $9,650,000 ($6,500,000 + $3,150,000). The $900,000 of the subsidiary's equity that is not carried over ($9,000,000 - $8,100,000) will be reported as minority interest.

39. (588,P1,14) (b) The journal entry to record Post's investment is:

Investment in stock of Shaw	8,100,000	
Common stock		3,150,000
APIC		90,000
Retained earnings		4,860,000

For a discussion of this entry, see the explanation for number 35. Therefore, additional paid-in capital will be reported at $4,490,000 ($4,400,000 + $90,000).

40. (588,P1,15) (c) The journal entry to record Post's investment is:

Investment in stock of Shaw	8,100,000	
Common stock		3,150,000
APIC		90,000
Retained earnings		4,860,000

For a discussion of this entry, see the explanation for number 35. Therefore, retained earnings should be reported at $10,960,000 ($6,100,000 + $4,860,000).

41. (588,P1,16) (c) Per APB 16, para 56, business combinations accounted for by the pooling of interests method should report net income as if the combination took place at the beginning of the year. Therefore, the consolidated income would be $2,820,000.

Separate income of Post
($1,000,000 + 1,100,000) $2,100,000
Separate income of Shaw
($300,000 + $500,000) $800,000
  x Post's % of ownership   x.90   720,000
Consolidated income $2,820,000

Note that the earnings figures given are for separate company operations, so Post's earnings include no income from its investment in Shaw. If Post's earnings had included such income, the amount would have to be calculated and eliminated from Post's earnings before the earnings of the two companies were pooled.

42. (588,P1,17) (c) The percentage of the subsidiary's stockholders' equity not owned by the parent company represents the minority interest's share of the net assets of the subsidiary. At 12/31/87, the subsidiary's stockholders' equity is $9,150,000.

6/30/87 stockholders' equity $9,000,000
Income for six months
  ended 12/31/87   500,000
Dividends paid on 10/1/87   (350,000)
12/31/87 stockholders' equity $9,150,000

Since the parent's share is 90%, the minority interest is 10% of $9,150,000 or $915,000.

43. (1175,Q1,7) (a) Without the intercompany transaction, the minority interest income from Samson in 1989 would be $24,000 (30% of $80,000). In 1990, the minority interest income would be $27,000 (30% of $90,000). On the consolidated statements in 1989 the $2,000 intercompany profit will be eliminated, because from a consolidated viewpoint an arm's length transaction has not occurred with third parties. The elimination entry will be to credit inventory (which is in effect on the books of Eltro) for $2,000 and debits will be made of $1,400 to majority interest income and $600 to minority interest income. In 1990 when Eltro sells the inventory to outsiders, the $2,000 profit has effectively been earned. In 1990 an entry will be made on the consolidated books to effectively recognize this profit and allocate it to the majority and minority interest. Thus, the 1989 minority interest income will be reduced by $600 and 1990 minority interest income increased by $600.

	1989		1990
MI % of profit	$24,000	MI % of profit	$27,000
Elim. of inter-		Recognition of	
company profit	- 600	profit	+ 600
MI income	$23,400		$27,600

44. (589,P3,55) (c) The cost of this investment is $975,000. Ritt purchased 80% of

the identifiable net assets of Shaw, which have a fair value of $1,100,000 ($1,000,000 + $100,000). Thus, Ritt purchased net assets with a fair value of $880,000 (80% x $1,100,000). The excess amount paid ($975,000 - $880,000 = $95,000) is allocated to goodwill.

45. (589,P3,56) (b) The percentage of the subsidiary's stockholders' equity not owned by the parent company represents the minority interest's share of the net assets of the subsidiary. The minority interest is based on book value, to remove the minority shareholder's portion of reported equity from the financial statements (parent company concept). At 12/31/88, the subsidiary's stockholders' equity at book value is $1,065,000, as computed below:

1/1/88 net assets
  (stockholders' equity) $1,000,000
1988 net income   190,000
1988 dividends   (125,000)
12/31/88 net assets
  (stockholders' equity) $1,065,000

Since the parent's share is 80%, the minority interest is 20% of $1,065,000, or $213,000.

P. Combined Financial Statements

46. (1188,P3,58) (d) Combined financial statements are financial statements prepared for companies that are owned by the same parent company or other owner. Combined financial statements are prepared by simply combining the subsidiaries' financial statement classifications, with appropriate elimination of intercompany transactions, balances, and profit (loss). Thompson and Jenkins had no intercompany ownership or transactions during 1987, so combined net income is computed simply by adding the separate net incomes of the two companies ($100,000 + $200,000 = $300,000).

47. (1189,P1,3) (c) Per SFAS 12, unrealized losses on current marketable equity securities (MES) are reported in the income statement, while unrealized losses on noncurrent MES are reported as a direct reduction of stockholders' equity (bypassing the income statement). Thus, Jay's income statement is incorrect because it included a $200,000 unrealized loss from a noncurrent MES. This caused net income to be understated by $200,000, so retained earnings is also understated by $200,000 and should be adjusted to $1,100,000 ($900,000 + $200,000). Instead of being reported in the income statement, the $200,000 unrealized loss should be reported as a contra account to stockholders' equity. Therefore,

total contra accounts are $800,000 ($600,000 + $200,000).

48. (588,P3,53) (b) Combined financial statements is the term used to describe financial statements prepared for companies that are owned by the same parent company or individual. Combined financial statements are prepared by combining all of the subsidiaries' financial statement classifications. Intercompany transactions should be eliminated in the same way as for consolidated statements. Combining the stockholders' equity accounts of Able and Baker results in a total of $430,000 ($100,000 + $20,000 + $300,000 + $10,000). The intercompany balances (Investment in Baker, $4,000; and Common Stock, $4,000) must be eliminated, which reduces combined stockholders' equity to $426,000 ($430,000 - $4,000). If these amounts were not eliminated, the combined balance sheet would overstate both assets and equity by $4,000.

49. (1189,P3,55) (c) The inventory reported on the 12/31/88 combined balance sheet should reflect the original cost to the companies of any inventory on hand (ARB 51, para 23). The inventory on hand which was acquired from outside parties should be reported at its cost ($175,000 + $250,000 = $425,000). The Banks inventory on hand which was acquired from Lamm must be restated back to the cost Lamm originally paid when it was purchased from outside parties. This must be done to eliminate intercompany profits. During 1988, Lamm shipped inventory which originally cost $150,000 to Banks at a billing price of $200,000. Therefore, the original cost is 75% of Banks carrying amount. Therefore, the correct inventory amount is $470,000 [$175,000 + $250,000 + ($60,000 x 75%)].

50. (1187,T1,40) (c) Combined financial statements are sometimes prepared because they are likely to be more meaningful than individual statements. Per ARB 51, para 23, when combined statements are prepared for a group of related companies (e.g., a group of commonly controlled companies or a group of unconsolidated subsidiaries), intercompany transactions and intercompany profits or losses should always be eliminated. Therefore, answer (c) is correct.

51. (589,T1,40) (c) Per APB 51, para 23, where combined statements are prepared for a group of related companies, intercompany transactions and profit and losses should be eliminated. Matters such as minority interests, income taxes, foreign operations, or different fiscal periods should be treated in

the same manner for both combined financial statements and consolidated statements. Therefore, answer (c) is correct.

52. (1189,T1,40) (c) Per ARB 51, para 23, "where combined statements are prepared for a group of related companies....if there are any problems in connection with such matters as minority interests, foreign operations, different fiscal periods, or income taxes, they should be treated in the same manner as in consolidated statements." Therefore, answer (c) is correct.

May 1990 Answers

53. (590,P1,11) (d) The $300,000 receivable from the consolidated subsidiary would be eliminated on the consolidated worksheet and is not reported on the consolidated balance sheet. The purpose of this elimination is to avoid double counting. The receivable from the unconsolidated investee ($200,000) would not be eliminated and therefore would be reported as a receivable in the 12/31/89 consolidated balance sheet.

54. (590,T1,2) (a) This question is silent as to which year consolidated financial statements are being prepared. However, answer (a) is correct for either the year of acquisition or a subsequent year. If financial statements were being prepared for the current year the loss would be reported as an extraordinary loss on the income statement. P Co. acquired the 20 percent interest in S Company bonds and incurred a loss on them. This loss would be carried through to the consolidated balance sheet as a decrease in retained earnings. In subsequent years, the unamortized portion of the loss would also decrease retained earnings.

55. (590,T1,32) (c) According to APB 16, in a pooling of interests, a corporation offers and issues only common stock with rights identical to those of the majority of its outstanding voting common stock in exchange for substantially all the voting common stock interest of another company at the date the plan of combination is consummated. The term "substantially all" is defined by the APB as meaning at least 90 percent of the voting common stock of the other company outstanding on the date the combination is consummated.

56. (590,T1,33) (c) When the appraised values of the identifiable assets acquired in a purchase combination exceeds the acquisition price, the difference is referred to as negative goodwill. APB 16 requires negative good-

will to be allocated against noncurrent assets
acquired, excluding marketable securities, in
proportion to their fair values. If the noncurrent assets are reduced to zero and some
negative goodwill remains unallocated, the excess should be reported on the balance sheet
as a deferred credit. Subsequently, this
amount is amortized over a period not exceeding 40 years. Answer (a) is incorrect
because only the unallocated portion is reported as a deferred credit. Answers (b) and
(d) are incorrect because the negative goodwill is allocated only to noncurrent assets.

Answer Outline

Problem 1   Bus. Comb. & Consolid. FSs
             (586,T4)

a1. Method of accounting for business
     combination affects whether or not GW
     reported
       Pooling accounting
         GW does not arise
         Record assets and liabilities at book
         values
       Purchase accounting
         Goodwill should be reported
         Record assets at FMVs and liabilities
         at PVs
a2. Determination of GW
       Cost of Moore - (FMVs assigned to
         identifiable assets - PVs of lia-
         bilities assumed) = GW
a3. Method of accounting for business
     combination does **not** affect whether or
     not minority interest reported
       Minority interest should be reported
       for
         Pooling of interest
         Purchase
       Amount of minority interest same
       whether
         Pooling of interest
         Purchase
b1. Consolidated FSs should be prepared to
     present more meaningful FSs showing
       Financial position
       Operating results
b2. Necessary condition for
     consolidated FSs to be prepared
       Control evidenced by majority voting
         interest (> 50%, directly/indirectly)
b3. Method of accounting for business
     combination does **not** affect decision to
     prepare consolidated FSs
       Control exists independent of method of
         accounting used

Unofficial Answer

Problem 1   Bus. Comb. & Consolid. FSs
             (586,T4)

a. 1. Goodwill does not arise and, therefore,
should not be reported if the business
combination is accounted for as a pooling of
interests. The recorded assets and liabilities of the separate companies generally
become the recorded assets and liabilities of
the combined corporation.

   However, goodwill should be reported if
the business combination is accounted for as a
purchase.

2. All identifiable assets acquired,
either individually or by type, and liabilities assumed in a business combination,
whether or not shown in the financial statements of Moore, should be assigned a portion
of the cost of Moore, normally equal to their
fair values at date of acquisition. Then, the
excess of the cost of Moore over the sum of
the amounts assigned to identifiable assets
acquired less liabilities assumed should be
recorded as goodwill.

3. Minority interest should be reported
whether the business combination is accounted
for as a purchase or a pooling of interests.
The amount of minority interest reported would
be the same whether the business combination
is accounted for as a purchase or a pooling of
interests.

b. 1. Consolidated financial statements
should be prepared in order to present financial position and operating results in a
manner more meaningful than in separate statements.

2. The usual condition for consolidation
is control as evidenced by ownership of a
majority voting interest. Therefore, as a
general rule, ownership by one company,
directly or indirectly, of over fifty percent
of the outstanding voting shares of another
company is a condition necessary for
consolidation.

3. Consolidated financial statements
should be prepared whether a business
combination is accounted for as a purchase or
a pooling of interests. Control exists and is
independent of the method of accounting used.

Answer Outline

Problem 2   Purchase and Pooling of Interests
             (587,T5)

a. Pooling of interests method
     1. Accounting for assets and
         liabilities
         Book value recorded
         Existing basis of accounting
           continues
         Regarded as arrangement among
           stockholder groups
     2. Accounting for registration fees and
         direct costs
         Expense in period incurred
     3. Reporting in year of combination
         Report as if combined as of
           beginning of year
         .

b. Purchase method
   1. Accounting for assets and lia-
      bilities
        Allocate cost of acquired company
          to assets acquired and lia-
          bilities assumed
        Identifiable assets acquired and
          liabilities assumed are recorded
          at fair values at date of
          acquisition
        Excess of costs over amounts
          assigned to identifiable assets
          less liabilities is recorded as
          goodwill
        Regarded as a bargained trans-
          action
        Establishes new basis of ac-
          counting
   2. Accounting for registration fees and
      direct cost
        Registration fees are a reduction
          of determinable fair value of
          securities
        Direct costs included as part of
          acquisition cost
   3. Reporting in year of combination
        Include income of acquired company
          after date of acquisition
        Include revenues and expenses
          based on cost of acquiring
          corporation

Unofficial Answer

Problem 2 Purchase and Pooling of Interests
        (587,T5)

a. 1. In a pooling of interests, the
recorded amounts of the assets and liabilities
of the separate companies generally become the
recorded amounts of the assets and liabilities
of the combined corporation. The existing
basis of accounting continues. A pooling of
interests transaction is regarded as an
arrangement among stockholder groups.
   2. In a pooling of interests, the registration fees and direct costs related to
effecting the business combination should be
deducted in determining the net income of the
resulting combined corporation for the period
in which the expenses are incurred.
   3. In a pooling of interests, the results
of operations for the year in which the
business combination occurred should be
reported as though the companies had been
combined as of the beginning of the year.
b. 1. In a purchase, the acquiring corporation should allocate the cost of the acquired
company to the assets acquired and liabilities
assumed. All identifiable assets acquired and
liabilities assumed in the business combina-

tion should be recorded at their fair values
at date of acquisition. The excess of the
cost of the acquired company over the sum of
the amounts assigned to identifiable assets
acquired less liabilities assumed should be
recorded as goodwill. A purchase transaction
is regarded as a bargained transaction (i.e.,
a significant economic event which results
from bargaining between independent parties)
which establishes a new basis of accounting.
   2. In a purchase, the registration fees
related to effecting the business combination
are a reduction of the otherwise determinable
fair value of the securities, (usually as a
reduction of paid-in capital). The direct
costs related to effecting the business
combination are included as part of the
acquisition cost of the acquired company.
   3. In a purchase, the results of
operations for the year in which the business
combination occurred should include income of
the acquired company after the date of acquisition by including the revenues and expenses
of the acquired company based on the cost to
the acquiring corporation.

Solution Guide

Problem 3   Consolidated Financial Statement
                Worksheet (1183,P5)

1.   This problem requires the completion of a
      consolidating worksheet. The worksheet
      incorporates the income statement, the
      retained earnings statement, and the
      balance sheet. In this approach, any
      postings to the income statement section
      are totalled and carried forward to the
      retained earnings section. Similarly,
      the postings in the retained earnings
      statement section are totalled and
      carried forward to the balance sheet
      section.

2.   The solutions approach is to go through
      the information and prepare any entries
      necessary to be posted on the worksheet.

2.1   The primary elimination entry is simply
      the elimination of the investment account
      (at cost) and the subsidiary's equity
      accounts at the time of investment
      (1/1/86). Additionally, the excess of
      cost over book value must be allocated to
      the proper accounts. The investment
      account has a balance of $750,000. The
      equity purchased is 100% of the subsi-
      diary's equity accounts at the time of
      investment, or $636,000. The difference
      ($114,000) is allocated first to machi-
      nery ($54,000), and then to goodwill
      ($60,000).

Common stock (Taft)	400,000	
APIC (Taft)	80,000	
Retained earnings (Taft)	156,000	
Machinery	54,000	
Goodwill	60,000	
Investment in Taft		750,000

Note that the debit to retained earnings is entered into the beginning balance line in the retained earnings statement section of the worksheet.

2.2 The second elimination entry amortizes the excess of cost over book value. Because the parent uses the cost method rather than the equity method, this entry becomes an adjusting entry rather than a reclassifying entry. The excess allocated to machinery ($54,000) is amortized over six years ($9,000 per year). The amount allocated to goodwill ($60,000) is amortized over twenty years ($3,000 per year).

Operating expenses	12,000	
Accumulated depreciation		9,000
Goodwill		3,000

Note that the depreciation is debited to operating expenses, since the problem indicates that the account includes depreciation. However, it can be argued that depreciation of machinery should be reflected in cost of goods sold.

2.3 The third elimination entry is necessary to eliminate the parent's income from subsidiary dividends.

Dividends from Taft	40,000	
Dividends paid		40,000

Note that the credit to dividends paid is entered on the appropriate line in the retained earnings statement section.

2.4 Next the gain on the intercompany fixed asset sale must be eliminated. The gain on land is $10,000 ($43,000 - $33,000) and the gain on the warehouse is $20,000 ($86,000 - $66,000). This $30,000 gain must be eliminated, and the assets written down to original cost.

Gain on sale of warehouse	30,000	
Land, plant, and equipment		30,000

Taft has depreciated some of the extra $20,000 paid for the warehouse. Depreciation for a half-year would be $2,000 ($20,000 × 1/5 × $\frac{1}{2}$). This depreciation must also be eliminated.

Accumulated depreciation	2,000	
Operating expenses		2,000

2.5 An intercompany sale of inventory has also occurred. Taft sold $180,000 of merchandise to Amboy. The original cost of the merchandise to Taft was $90,000 [$180,000 ÷ (100% + 100%)]. Amboy sold $144,000 of this merchandise ($180,000 - $36,000) to outside customers.

```
                                    36,000
                                   End. Inv.
                                  ↗   (20%)
     Taft (90,000)——180,000→Amboy
                                  ↘  144,000
                                     → CGS
                                      (80%)
```

The intercompany sales of $180,000 must be eliminated. Additionally, cost of goods sold (CGS) and inventory must be adjusted. Since 80% of the inventory was sold, CGS should include 80% of Taft's original cost of $90,000, or $72,000. Since Taft recorded CGS of $90,000, and Amboy recorded CGS of $144,000, a total CGS of $234,000 was recorded. Therefore, CGS must be reduced by $162,000 ($234,000 - $72,000). Finally, inventory must be reduced by $18,000, from $36,000 to its original cost of $18,000 (20% × $90,000).

Net sales	180,000	
Cost of goods sold		162,000
Inventories		18,000

2.6 Since Amboy still owes Taft $75,000 on the purchases, the intercompany receivable/payable must also be eliminated.

Accounts payable	75,000	
Accounts receivable		75,000

3. The worksheet can now be totalled and completed.

3.1 The income statement adjustments total $262,000 debits and $164,000 credits. These amounts are entered on the net income lines in the retained earnings section.

3.2 The retained earnings adjustments total $418,000 debits and $204,000 credits. These amounts are entered on the retained earnings line in the balance sheet section.

3.3 The worksheet can now be totalled across.

Unofficial Answer

Problem 3   Consolidated Financial Statement Worksheet (1183,P5)

Amboy Corporation and Subsidiary
Consolidating Statement Worksheet
December 31, 1986

Income Statement	Amboy Corp.	Taft Inc.	Adjustments & eliminations Debit	Adjustments & eliminations Credit	Adjusted balance
Net sales	$(1,900,000)	$(1,500,000)	180,000 (5)		$(3,220,000)
Dividends from Taft	(40,000)		40,000 (3)		
Gain on sale of warehouse	(30,000)		30,000 (4)		
Cost of goods sold	1,180,000	870,000		162,000 (5)	1,888,000
Operating expenses (incl. deprec.)	550,000	440,000	12,000 (2)	2,000 (4)	1,000,000
Net income	$ (240,000)	$ (190,000)	262,000	164,000	$ (332,000)
Retained Earnings Statement					
Balance, 1/1/86	$ (220,000)	$ (156,000)	156,000 (1)		$ (220,000)
Net income	(240,000)	(190,000)	262,000	164,000	(332,000)
Dividends paid		40,000		40,000 (3)	
Balance, 12/31/86	$ (460,000)	$ (306,000)	418,000	204,000	$ (552,000)
Balance Sheet					
Assets:					
Cash	$ 285,000	$ 150,000			$ 435,000
Accounts receivable (net)	430,000	350,000		75,000 (6)	705,000
Inventories	530,000	410,000		18,000 (5)	922,000
Land, plant, & equipment	660,000	680,000	54,000 (1)	30,000 (4)	1,364,000
Accumulated depreciation	(185,000)	(210,000)	2,000 (4)	9,000 (2)	(402,000)
Investment in Taft (at cost)	750,000			750,000 (1)	
Goodwill			60,000 (1)	3,000 (2)	57,000
	$ 2,470,000	$ 1,380,000			$3,081,000
Liabilities & stockholders' equity:					
Accounts pay. & accrued exp.	$ (670,000)	$ (594,000)	75,000 (6)		$(1,189,000)
Common stock ($10 par)	(1,200,000)	(400,000)	400,000 (1)		(1,200,000)
Additional paid-in capital	(140,000)	(80,000)	80,000 (1)		(140,000)
Retained earnings	(460,000)	(306,000)	418,000	204,000	(552,000)
	$(2,470,000)	$(1,380,000)	1,089,000	1,089,000	$(3,081,000)

Explanations of adjustments & eliminations:

(1) To eliminate the reciprocal elements in investment, equity, and property accounts. Amboy's investment is carried at cost at December 31, 1986.

(2) To record amortization of current value in excess of book value of Taft's machinery at date of acquisition ($54,000 ÷ 6) and amortization of goodwill ($60,000 ÷ 20) for the year ended December 31, 1986.

(3) To eliminate Amboy's dividend income from Taft.

(4) To eliminate the intercompany profit on the sale of the warehouse by Amboy to Taft and to eliminate the excess depreciation on the warehouse building sold by Amboy to Taft [($86,000 − $66,000) ÷ 5] × ½.

(5) To eliminate intercompany sales from Taft to Amboy and the intercompany profit in Amboy's ending inventory as follows:

	Total	On hand
Sales	$180,000	$36,000
Gross profit	90,000	18,000

(6) To eliminate Amboy's intercompany balance for merchandise owed to Taft.

Schedule 1

Allocation of Excess of Cost
Over Book Value

Cost of investment		$750,000
Equity purchased at time of investment		
Common stock	$400,000	
Addl. paid-in capital	80,000	
Retained earnings	156,000	(636,000)
Excess of cost over book value		114,000
Amount allocated to machinery		(54,000)
Amount allocated to goodwill		$60,000

Schedule 2

Amortization of Excess of Cost
Over Book Value

Amount allocated to machinery	$ 54,000
Remaining useful life	÷ 6 years
Amortization	$9,000/year

Amount allocated to goodwill	$ 60,000
Amortization period	÷ 20 years
Amortization	$3,000/year

Schedule 3

Excess Depreciation Recorded on Warehouse

Purchase price of warehouse	$86,000
Original cost of warehouse	(66,000)
Excess cost recorded by subsidiary	$20,000
Remaining useful life	÷ 5 years
Depreciation per year	$4,000
Portion of year (July 1 - Dec. 31)	× 6/12
Excess depreciation recorded in 1986	$2,000

Schedule 4

Elimination of Cost of Goods Sold

Cost of goods sold recorded by Taft ($180,000 ÷ 200%)	$90,000
Cost of goods sold recorded by Amboy ($180,000 − $36,000)	144,000
Total cost of goods sold recorded	234,000
Consolidated cost of goods sold (80% × $90,000)	(72,000)
Cost of goods sold to be eliminated	$162,000

Schedule 5

Restatement of Inventory to Original Cost

Inventory at sales price	$36,000
Inventory restated to cost ($36,000 ÷ 200%)	$18,000

Solution Guide

Problem 4   Pooling of Interests (1188,P5)

1.   This problem consists of two related
     parts. Part (a) requires the completion
     of a consolidating worksheet, while part
     (b) requires preparation of a consoli-
     dated statement of retained earnings.
     The business combination is an <u>acquisi-
     tion</u> effected through a <u>pooling of
     interests</u>.

2.   The solutions approach for part (a) is to
     go through the information and prepare
     any entries to be posted on the work-
     sheet.

2.1 The first eliminating entry is to elimi-
     nate the investment account and the sub-
     sidiary's equity accounts at the time of
     investment (6/30/87). At that time, the
     parent issued $1,000,000 of par value
     common stock (40,000 x $25), which is
     equal to the par value of the subsi-
     diary's stock obtained. The parent's
     investment is recorded at the <u>book value</u>
     of the subsidiary's net assets
     ($2,170,000) under the pooling-of-inter-
     ests method, and the stockholders'
     equities of the combining firms are
     "united." Thus, the 6/30/87 entry was:

     Investment in Stagg   2,170,000
       Common stock   1,000,000
       Additional paid-
        in capital   190,000
       Retained earnings   980,000

     The eliminating entry is the reverse of
     the above entry:

     Retained earnings   980,000
     Additional paid-
      in capital   190,000
     Common stock   1,000,000
       Investment in Stagg   2,170,000

     In the worksheet, this entry and the
     entry discussed in 2.2 are combined and
     labeled as entry one.

2.2 The second eliminating entry eliminates
     the parent's equity in the subsidiary's
     earnings. Stagg earned income of
     $260,000 from 6/30/87 to 12/31/87
     (12/31/87 RE of $1,240,000 less 6/30/87
     RE of $980,000; no dividends were
     declared by Stagg during the last six
     months). The parent's share (100%) was
     debited to the investment account and
     credited to a revenue account, which
     ultimately was closed to retained
     earnings. Therefore, the eliminating
     entry is:

     Retained earnings   260,000
       Investment in Stagg   260,000

     In the worksheet, this entry and the
     entry discussed in 2.1 are combined and
     labeled as entry one.

2.3 The next entry is to eliminate the
     parent's investment in the subsidiary's
     bonds. $320,000 is included in the
     parent's long-term investments and also
     in the subsidiary's long-term debt, even
     though from a consolidated viewpoint the
     bonds are effectively retired. The
     eliminating entry is:

     Long-term debt   320,000
       Long-term investments
        and other assets   320,000

     Note that the interest income/expense on
     these bonds is equal, and while the
     <u>income statement</u> must be adjusted, there
     is no effect on retained earnings on the
     <u>balance sheet</u> since the expense and
     revenue off-set each other.

2.4 The interest receivable/payable on the
     intercompany bonds at 12/31/87 ($320,000
     x 10% x 3/12 = $8,000) must also be
     eliminated:

     Accounts payable and other
      current liabilities   8,000
       Accounts and other re-
        ceivables   8,000

2.5 An intercompany sale of inventory has
     also occurred. The parent sold inventory
     to the subsidiary at a profit of
     $180,000. At year end, one-half of this
     inventory remains in the subsidiary's
     inventory. This means that inventory is
     reflected on the books at $90,000 (1/2 x
     $180,000) above its cost to the consoli-
     dated entity. Also, retained earnings
     includes $90,000 of profit which was not
     earned from a consolidated viewpoint.
     Therefore, both inventory and retained
     earnings must be reduced.

     Retained earnings   90,000
       Inventory   90,000

2.6 The intercompany sale of inventory
     (discussed in 2.5) took place at an
     invoice price of $720,000. Since payment
     has not yet been made, an account
     receivable remains on the parent's books
     and an account payable remains on the
     subsidiary's book. Since there is no
     receivable or payable from a consolidated
     point of view, these amounts must also be
     eliminated.

     Accounts payable and other
      current liabilities   720,000
       Accounts and other re-
        ceivables   720,000

3.   Part (b) requires the preparation of a
        consolidated statement of retained
        earnings for 1987.

3.1   The statement should start with last
        year's ending retained earnings balance
        as previously reported. At 12/31/86,
        Peel did not own Stagg, so the previously
        reported balance was Peel's balance of
        $2,506,000.

3.2   In a pooling of interests, the financial
        statements of the acquiring company are
        restated for all prior years presented to
        include the operations and financial
        position of the pooled companies. Thus,
        the beginning retained earnings of
        $2,506,000 must be restated to include
        the subsidiary's 12/31/86 retained
        earnings of $820,000. This results in a
        12/31/86 restated balance of $3,326,000.

3.3   The consolidated net income must be added
        to the restated retained earnings
        balance. Consolidated income consists of
        the two companies' separate incomes
        ($890,000 + $580,000 = $1,470,000) less
        the eliminated intercompany profit
        ($1,470,000 - $90,000 = $1,380,000).

3.4   Finally, 1987 dividends declared must be
        subtracted in the retained earnings
        statement. Remember, the two companies
        are reported on a consolidated basis
        retroactively (as discussed in 3.2).
        Therefore, the dividends declared and
        paid by the subsidiary prior to the
        combination (on 6/15/87) are included in
        dividends declared. Thus, total consoli-
        dated 1987 dividends include the 6/15/87
        dividend (40,000 x $4 = $160,000) and the
        12/10/87 dividend paid by the parent
        ($256,000), for a total of $416,000.

3.5   As a check figure, note that the 12/31/87
        retained earnings balance in part (b)
        ($4,290,000) is equal to the 12/31/87
        consolidated retained earnings balance in
        the worksheet in part (a).

Unofficial Answer

Problem 4   Pooling of Interests (1188,P5)

a.

Peel, Inc. and Subsidiary
CONSOLIDATED BALANCE SHEET WORKSHEET
December 31, 1987

	Peel, Inc.	Stagg, Inc.	Adjustments & Eliminations Debit	Adjustments & Eliminations Credit	Consolidated Balance
Assets:					
Cash	$ 925,000	$ 300,000			$ 1,225,000
Accounts & other receivables	2,140,000	835,000		[3] $ 8,000	2,247,000
				[4] 720,000	
Inventories	2,310,000	1,045,000		[5] 90,000	3,265,000
Land	600,000	330,000			930,000
Depreciable assets, net	4,525,000	1,980,000			6,505,000
Investment in Frey, Inc.	2,430,000			[1] 2,430,000	
Long-term investments & other assets	865,000	385,000		[2] 320,000	930,000
	$13,795,000	$4,875,000			$15,102,000
Liabilities and Stockholders' Equity:					
Accounts payable & other current liabilities	$ 2,465,000	$1,145,000	[3] $ 8,000		$ 2,882,000
			[4] 720,000		
Long-term debt	1,900,000	1,300,000	[2] 320,000		2,880,000
Common stock, $25 par value	3,200,000	1,000,000	[1] 1,000,000		3,200,000
Additional paid-in capital	1,850,000	190,000	[1] 190,000		1,850,000
Retained earnings	4,380,000	1,240,000	[1] 1,240,000		4,290,000
			[5] 90,000		
	$13,795,000	$4,875,000	$3,568,000	$3,568,000	$15,102,000

b.   Peel, Inc. and Subsidiary
                CONSOLIDATED STATEMENT OF
                    RETAINED EARNINGS
           For The Year Ended December 31, 1987

Balance, December 31, 1986:
  As originally reported $2,506,000
  Adjustment for pooling of
    interests with Stagg, Inc.   820,000
As restated   3,326,000
Net income   1,380,000 [6]
                                4,706,000

Deduct cash dividends paid:
  By Stagg, Inc., prior to
    combination   160,000 [7]
  By Peel, Inc., after the
    combination   256,000
                                  416,000

Balance, December 31, 1987 $4,290,000

Explanations of Worksheet Entries & Other
Amounts

[1] To eliminate the reciprocal elements in
     investment and equity accounts

[2] To eliminate Peel's investment in Stagg's
     bonds

[3] To eliminate Peel's intercompany accrued
     interest receivable on its investment in
     Stagg's bonds for the period 10/1-
     12/31/87. ($320,000 x 10% x 1/4 =
     $8,000)

[4] To eliminate Peel's Intercompany balance
     for merchandise owed by Stagg

[5] To eliminate intercompany profit in
     ending inventory of Stagg ($180,000 x 1/2
     = $90,000)

[6] Consolidated net income for 1987
     Peel, Inc. $ 890,000
     Stagg, Inc.   580,000
                            $1,470,000

     Deduct intercompany profit
       in inventory   90,000 [5]
                            $1,380,000

[7] Dividend paid 6/15/87
       [40,000 shares x $4] $ 160,000

Multiple Choice Questions (1-38)

1. Lewis Company was formed on January 1, 1983. Selected balances from the historical cost balance sheet at December 31, 1984, were as follows:

Land (purchased in 1983)	$120,000
Investment in nonconvertible bonds (purchased in 1983, and expected to be held to maturity)	60,000
Long-term debt	80,000

The average Consumer Price Index was 100 for 1983, and 110 for 1984. In a supplementary constant dollar balance sheet (adjusted for changing prices) at December 31, 1984, these selected account balances should be shown at

	Land	Investment	Long-term debt
a.	$120,000	$60,000	$88,000
b.	$120,000	$66,000	$88,000
c.	$132,000	$60,000	$80,000
d.	$132,000	$66,000	$80,000

2. At both the beginning and end of the year, Lange Co.'s monetary assets exceeded monetary liabilities by $3,000,000. On January 1, the general price level was 125. On December 31, the general price level was 150. How much was Lange's purchasing power loss on net monetary items during the year?
   a. $0
   b. $ 600,000
   c. $ 750,000
   d. $1,125,000

3. The following items were among those that appeared on Roth Co.'s books at the beginning and end of the year:

Demand bank deposits	$500,000
Net long-term receivables	300,000
Deferred income tax asset	100,000

In preparing constant dollar financial statements, how much should Roth classify as monetary assets?
   a. $500,000
   b. $600,000
   c. $800,000
   d. $900,000

Items 4 and 5 are based on the following data:

The trial balance of Sosa Corp. at December 31, 1983, when the price index was 160, included the following accounts:

Bonds payable (due in 1988)	$200,000
Sales (made evenly throughout the year)	990,000

During 1983, the average price index was 140. The bonds were issued in 1978 when the price index was 120. Sosa wishes to present December 31, 1983, constant dollar financial statements in end-of-year dollars.

4. What fraction should be used to adjust bonds payable for price-level changes?
   a. 140/160
   b. 160/160
   c. 160/140
   d. 160/120

5. What fraction should be used to adjust sales for price-level changes?
   a. 160/160
   b. 160/150
   c. 160/140
   d. 140/160

6. The following items were among those that appeared on Rubi Co.'s books at the end of 1988:

Merchandise inventory	$600,000
Loans to employees	20,000

What amount should Rubi classify as monetary assets in preparing constant dollar financial statements?
   a. $0
   b. $ 20,000
   c. $600,000
   d. $620,000

7. During a period of inflation in which a liability account balance remains constant, which of the following occurs?
   a. A purchasing power loss if the item is a nonmonetary liability.
   b. A purchasing power gain if the item is a nonmonetary liability.
   c. A purchasing power loss if the item is a monetary liability.
   d. A purchasing power gain if the item is a monetary liability.

8. When purchasing power gains or losses are computed, how is each of the following classified?

	Patents	Unamortized premium on bonds payable
a.	Nonmonetary	Monetary
b.	Nonmonetary	Nonmonetary
c.	Monetary	Nonmonetary
d.	Monetary	Monetary

9. When computing information on a historical cost/constant dollar basis, which of the following is classified as nonmonetary?
   a. Accumulated depreciation of equipment.

b.   Advances to unconsolidated
     subsidiaries.
c.   Allowance for doubtful accounts.
d.   Unamortized premium on bonds
     payable.

10. When computing information on a historical cost/constant dollar basis, which of the
following is classified as monetary?
  a.   Goodwill arising from a business
       combination concluded last year.
  b.   Deferred investment tax credits
       related to equipment.
  c.   Obligation under warranties expiring
       in one year.
  d.   Allowance for doubtful accounts on
       long-term receivables.

11. At December 31, 1987, Jannis Corp. owned
two assets as follows:

	Equipment	Inventory
Current cost	$100,000	$80,000
Recoverable amount	$ 95,000	$90,000

Jannis voluntarily disclosed supplementary
information about current cost at December 31,
1987. In such a disclosure, at what amount
would Jannis report total assets?
  a. $175,000
  b. $180,000
  c. $185,000
  d. $190,000

12. Information with respect to Bruno Co.'s
cost of goods sold for 1988 is as follows:

	Historical cost	Units
Inventory, 1/1/88	$1,060,000	20,000
Production during 1988	5,580,000	90,000
	6,640,000	110,000
Inventory, 12/31/88	2,520,000	40,000
Cost of goods sold	$4,120,000	70,000

Bruno estimates that the current cost per unit
of inventory was $58 at January 1, 1988 and
$72 at December 31, 1988. In Bruno's supple-
mentary information restated into average
current cost, the cost of goods sold for 1988
should be
  a. $5,040,000
  b. $4,550,000
  c. $4,410,000
  d. $4,060,000

Items 13 and 14 are based on the following
data:

Rice Wholesaling Corp. accounts for
inventory on a FIFO basis. There were 8,000
units in inventory on January 1, 1986. Costs
were incurred and goods purchased as follows
during 1986:

1986	Historical costs	Units purchased	Units sold
1st quarter	$ 410,000	7,000	7,500
2nd quarter	550,000	8,500	7,300
3rd quarter	425,000	6,500	8,200
4th quarter	630,000	9,000	7,000
	$2,015,000	31,000	30,000

Rice estimates that the current cost per unit
of inventory was $57 at January 1, 1986, and
$71 at December 31, 1986.

13. In Rice's voluntary supplementary information restated into current cost, the December 31, 1986 inventory should be reported at
  a. $576,000
  b. $585,000
  c. $630,000
  d. $639,000

14. In Rice's voluntary supplementary information restated into current cost, the cost of
goods sold for 1986 would be
  a. $1,920,000
  b. $1,944,000
  c. $2,100,000
  d. $2,130,000

15. Details of Poe Corp.'s plant assets at
December 31, 1986, are as follows:

Year acquired	Percent depreciated	Historical cost	Estimated current cost
1984	30	$200,000	$280,000
1985	20	60,000	76,000
1986	10	80,000	88,000

Poe calculates depreciation at 10% per annum,
using the straight-line method. A full year's
depreciation is charged in the year of acquisition. There were no disposals of plant
assets. In Poe's voluntary supplementary
information restated into current cost, the
net current cost (after accumulated depreciation) of the plant assets at December 31,
1986, should be stated as
  a. $364,000
  b. $336,000
  c. $260,000
  d. $232,000

16. Kerr Company purchased a machine for
$115,000 on January 1, 1985, the company's
first day of operations. At the end of the
year, the current cost of the machine was
$125,000. The machine has no salvage value, a
five-year life, and is depreciated by the
straight-line method. For the year ended
December 31, 1985, the amount of the current
cost depreciation expense which would appear
in supplementary current cost financial statements is:
  a. $14,000
  b. $23,000

c. $24,000
d. $25,000

17. When measuring the current cost of inventories in accordance with FASB Statement No. 89, the date of sale is the

	Entry date	Exit date
a.	No	Yes
b.	Yes	Yes
c.	Yes	No
d.	No	No

18. A method of accounting based on measures of current cost or lower recoverable amount, without restatement into units having the same general purchasing power, is
   a.   Historical cost/constant dollar accounting.
   b.   Historical cost/nominal dollar accounting.
   c.   Current cost/constant dollar accounting.
   d.   Current cost/nominal dollar accounting.

19. When measuring the current cost of inventories in accordance with FASB Statement No. 89, the "entry" date can mean which of the following?

	Beginning of year	Date of sale
a.	Yes	No
b.	Yes	Yes
c.	No	Yes
d.	No	No

20. FASB Statement No. 89 requires that the current cost for inventories be measured as the
   a.   Recoverable amount regardless of the current cost.
   b.   Current cost regardless of the recoverable amount.
   c.   Higher of current cost or recoverable amount.
   d.   Lower of current cost or recoverable amount.

21   Certain balance sheet accounts of a foreign subsidiary of Post, Inc. at December 31, 1986, have been translated into U.S. dollars as follows:

	Translated at	
	Current rates	Historical rates
Accounts receivable, long-term	$120,000	$100,000
Prepaid insurance	55,000	50,000
Copyright	75,000	85,000
	$250,000	$235,000

The subsidiary's functional currency is the currency of the country in which it is located. What total amount should be included in Post's December 31, 1986, consolidated balance sheet for the above accounts?
   a. $225,000
   b. $235,000
   c. $240,000
   d. $250,000

22. A wholly owned subsidiary of Ward, Inc. has certain expense accounts for the year ended December 31, 1984, stated in local currency units (LCU) as follows:

	LCU
Depreciation of equipment (related assets were purchased January 1, 1982)	120,000
Provision for doubtful accounts	80,000
Rent	200,000

The exchange rates at various dates are as follows:

	Dollar equivalent of 1 LCU
December 31, 1984	$.40
Average for year ended 12/31/84	.44
January 1, 1982	.50

Assume that the LCU is the subsidiary's functional currency and that the charges to the expense accounts occurred approximately evenly during the year. What total dollar amount should be included in Ward's 1984 consolidated income statement to reflect these expenses?
   a. $160,000
   b. $168,000
   c. $176,000
   d. $183,200

23. On January 1, 1982, Kiner Company formed a foreign branch. The branch purchased merchandise at a cost of 720,000 local currency units (LCU) on February 15, 1982. The purchase price was equivalent to $180,000 on this date. The branch's inventory at December 31, 1982, consisted solely of merchandise purchased on February 15, 1982, and amounted to 240,000 LCU. The exchange rate was 6 LCU to $1 on December 31, 1982, and the average rate of exchange was 5 LCU to $1 for 1982. Assume that the LCU is the functional currency of the branch. In Kiner's December 31, 1982, balance sheet, the branch inventory balance of 240,000 LCU should be translated into United States dollars at
   a. $40,000
   b. $48,000
   c. $60,000
   d. $84,000

24. A foreign subsidiary's functional currency is its local currency, which has not experienced significant inflation. The weighted average exchange rate for the current year would be the appropriate exchange rate for translating

	Wages expense	Sales to customers
a.	Yes	No
b.	Yes	Yes
c.	No	Yes
d.	No	No

25. Gains resulting from the process of translating a foreign entity's financial statements from the functional currency, which has not experienced significant inflation, to U.S. dollars should be included as a(an)
   a. Separate component of stockholders' equity.
   b. Deferred credit.
   c. Component of income from continuing operations.
   d. Extraordinary item.

26. At what remeasurement rates should the following balance sheet accounts in foreign statements be remeasured into United States dollars? Assume the functional currency is the U.S. dollar.

	Equipment	Accumulated depreciation of equipment
a.	Current	Current
b.	Current	Average for year
c.	Historical	Current
d.	Historical	Historical

27. On September 1, 1987, Bain Corp. received an order for equipment from a foreign customer for 300,000 local currency units (LCU) when the U.S. dollar equivalent was $96,000. Bain shipped the equipment on October 15, 1987, and billed the customer for 300,000 LCU when the U.S. dollar equivalent was $100,000. Bain received the customer's remittance in full on November 16, 1987, and sold the 300,000 LCU for $105,000. In its income statement for the year ended December 31, 1987, Bain should report a foreign exchange gain of
   a. $0
   b. $4,000
   c. $5,000
   d. $9,000

28. On July 1, 1984, Clark Company borrowed 1,680,000 local currency units (LCU) from a foreign lender, evidenced by an interest bearing note due on July 1, 1985, which is denominated in the currency of the lender. The U.S. dollar equivalent of the note princi-

pal was as follows:

Date	Amount
7/1/84 (date borrowed)	$210,000
12/31/84 (Clark's year end)	240,000
7/1/85 (date repaid)	280,000

In its income statement for 1985, what amount should Clark include as a foreign exchange gain or loss?
   a. $70,000 gain.
   b. $70,000 loss.
   c. $40,000 gain.
   d. $40,000 loss.

29. Lindy, a U.S. corporation, bought inventory items from a supplier in West Germany on November 5, 1987 for 100,000 marks, when the spot rate was $.4295. At Lindy's December 31, 1987 year end, the spot rate was $.4245. On January 15, 1988, Lindy bought 100,000 marks at the spot rate of $.4345 and paid the invoice. How much should Lindy report in its income statements for 1987 and 1988 as foreign exchange gain or (loss)?

	1987	1988
a.	$ 500	($1,000)
b.	$0	($ 500)
c.	($ 500)	$0
d.	($1,000)	$ 500

30. On July 1, 1981, Stone Company lent $120,000 to a foreign supplier, evidenced by an interest bearing note due on July 1, 1982. The note is denominated in the currency of the borrower and was equivalent to 840,000 local currency units (LCU) on the loan date. The note principal was appropriately included at $140,000 in the receivables section of Stone's December 31, 1981, balance sheet. The note principal was repaid to Stone on the July 1, 1982, due date when the exchange rate was 8 LCU to $1. In its income statement for the year ended December 31, 1982, what amount should Stone include as a foreign currency transaction gain or loss?
   a. $0.
   b. $15,000 loss.
   c. $15,000 gain.
   d. $35,000 loss.

31. If one Canadian dollar can be exchanged for 90 cents of United States money, what fraction should be used to compute the indirect quotation of the exchange rate expressed in Canadian dollars?
   a. 1.10/1
   b. 1/1.10
   c. 1/.90
   d. .90/1

32. On November 30, 1980, Tyrola Publishing Company, located in Colorado, executed a

contract with Ernest Blyton, an author from Canada, providing for payment of 10% royalties on Canadian sales of Blyton's book. Payment is to be made in Canadian dollars each January 10 for the previous year's sales. Canadian sales of the book for the year ended December 31, 1981, totaled $50,000 Canadian. Tyrola paid Blyton his 1981 royalties on January 10, 1982. Tyrola's 1981 financial statements were issued on February 1, 1982. Spot rates for Canadian dollars were as follows:

November 30, 1980	$.87
January 1, 1981	$.88
December 31, 1981	$.89
January 10, 1982	$.90

How much should Tyrola accrue for royalties payable at December 31, 1981?

   a. $4,350
   b. $4,425
   c. $4,450
   d. $4,500

33. On April 8, 1987, Day Corp. purchased merchandise from an unaffiliated foreign company for 10,000 units of the foreign company's local currency. Day paid the bill in full on March 1, 1988 when the spot rate was $.45. The spot rate was $.60 on April 8, 1987 and was $.55 on December 31, 1987. For the year ended December 31, 1988, Day should report a transaction gain of

   a. $1,500
   b. $1,000
   c. $ 500
   d. $0

34. A sale of goods was denominated in a currency other than the entity's functional currency. The sale resulted in a receivable that was fixed in terms of the amount of foreign currency that would be received. The exchange rate between the functional currency and the currency in which the transaction was denominated changed. The effect of the change should be included as a

   a. Separate component of stockholders' equity whether the change results in a gain or a loss.
   b. Separate component of stockholders' equity if the change results in a gain, and as a component of income if the change results in a loss.
   c. Component of income if the change results in a gain, and as a separate component of stockholders' equity if the change results in a loss.
   d. Component of income whether the change results in a gain or a loss.

35. A December 15, 1986, purchase of goods was denominated in a currency other than the entity's functional currency. The transaction

resulted in a payable that was fixed in terms of the amount of foreign currency, and was paid on the settlement date, January 20, 1987. The exchange rates between the functional currency and the currency in which the transaction was denominated changed at December 31, 1986, resulting in a loss that should

   a. Not be reported until January 20, 1987, the settlement date.
   b. Be included as a separate component of stockholders' equity at December 31, 1986.
   c. Be included as a deferred charge at December 31, 1986.
   d. Be included as a component of income from continuing operations for 1986.

36. The balance in Bart Corp.'s foreign exchange loss account was $13,000 at December 31, 1988, before any necessary year-end adjustment relating to the following:

   • Bart had a $20,000 loss resulting from the translation of the accounts of its wholly owned foreign subsidiary for the year ended December 31, 1988.
   • Bart had an account payable to an unrelated foreign supplier payable in the local currency of the foreign supplier on January 27, 1989. The U.S. dollar equivalent of the payable was $100,000 on the November 28, 1988 invoice date, and it was $106,000 on December 31, 1988.

In Bart's 1988 consolidated income statement, what amount should be included as foreign exchange loss?

   a. $33,000
   b. $27,000
   c. $19,000
   d. $13,000

May 1990 Questions

37. During a period of inflation, the specific price of a parcel of land increased at a lower rate than the consumer price index. The accounting method that would measure the land at the highest amount is

   a. Historical cost/nominal dollar.
   b. Current cost/nominal dollar.
   c. Current cost/constant dollar.
   d. Historical cost/constant dollar.

38. A balance arising from the translation or remeasurement of a subsidiary's foreign currency financial statements is reported in the consolidated income statement when the subsidiary's functional currency is the

	Foreign currency	U.S. dollar
a.	No	No
b.	No	Yes
c.	Yes	No
d.	Yes	Yes

Repeat Questions

(590,P3,52) Identical/similar to item 36 above
(590,Q3,44) Identical/similar to item 21 above
(590,Q3,50) Identical/similar to item 3 above

Multiple Choice Answers

1. c	9. a	17. a	25. a	32. c
2. b	10. d	18. d	26. d	33. b
3. d	11. a	19. a	27. c	34. d
4. b	12. b	20. d	28. d	35. d
5. c	13. d	21. d	29. a	36. c
6. b	14. a	22. c	30. d	37. d
7. d	15. b	23. a	31. c	38. b
8. a	16. c	24. b		

Multiple Choice Answer Explanations

A. Constant Dollar Accounting

1. (1185,P3,51) (c) The requirement is the amounts to be reported for three balance sheet accounts in a supplementary <u>constant dollar</u> balance sheet. In a constant dollar balance sheet, <u>nonmonetary</u> items are restated to the current price level, while monetary items are <u>not</u> restated because they are already stated in current dollars. The investment in bonds and the long-term debt are monetary items since their amounts are fixed by contract in terms of number of dollars. Therefore these items are not restated and are reported at $60,000 and $80,000, respectively. The land, however, is a nonmonetary item and its cost ($120,000) must be restated to current dollars by using the TO/FROM ratio (110/100), resulting in an adjusted amount of $132,000 ($120,000 x 110/100). Reference to SFAS 89, paras 96-108, will provide guidance on monetary/nonmonetary classifications.

2. (586,Q1,1) (b) The requirement is the purchasing power loss on net monetary items for the year. Per SFAS 89, purchasing power gains and losses arise on monetary items during changes in the general price level. Purchasing power loss is found by restating the opening balance of net monetary assets in constant dollars and comparing it with the actual net monetary assets at the end of the period. The January 1 balance of $3,000,000 beginning net monetary assets is converted into constant dollars in year-end purchasing power by multiplying it by the TO/FROM ratio of 150/125.

$$3,000,000 \times 150/125 = 3,600,000$$

In order to keep up with inflation, net monetary assets would have to be $3,600,000 at year end. Therefore, the purchasing power loss is $600,000 ($3,600,000 - $3,000,000).

3. (586,Q1,10) (d) The requirement is to determine the amount to be classified as monetary assets in preparing constant dollar fi-

nancial statements. Per SFAS 89, para 96, demand bank deposits, net long-term receivables, and deferred income tax assets are all classified as monetary assets. Thus, Roth should classify $900,000 ($500,000 + 300,000 + 100,000) as monetary assets.

4. (1184,Q1,9) (b) The requirement is the fraction used to adjust bonds payable for price level changes for proper inclusion in Sosa Corp.'s constant dollar balance sheet. Bonds payable are classified as monetary items per SFAS 89, para 96, because the amount of dollars that will be expended to redeem them at maturity is fixed by the bond indenture. Therefore, no adjustment to this account is required. Thus, the ratio used is 160/160 (the end-of-year index divided by itself), resulting in no adjustment to the bonds payable.

5. (1184,Q1,10) (c) The requirement is the fraction used to adjust sales for price level changes for proper inclusion in Sosa Corp.'s 1983 constant dollar income statement which is to be prepared in end-of-year dollars. To adjust sales to end-of-year dollars, an assumption is made that sales take place evenly throughout the year. Therefore, the fraction used for the constant dollar adjustment must convert average-year dollars to end-of-year dollars. The adjustment is as follows:

$$\frac{\text{Index at end of year}}{\text{Average index for year}} = 160/140$$

6. (589,Q1,13) (b) According to SFAS 89, para 96, "loans to employees" is a monetary asset account since its payment amount is fixed at some point in the future. Conversely, merchandise inventory is considered a nonmonetary asset account since its value will change based on relative price levels in the future. The total value of monetary assets is the balance of the loans to employees account, or $20,000.

7. (588,T1,4) (d) Per SFAS 89, para 44, the dollar amounts of monetary assets and liabilities are fixed or determinable without reference to future prices or specific goods or services. If the general price level changes, a purchasing power gain (loss) may occur on monetary items. A monetary liability held constant during a period of inflation creates a purchasing power gain because the liability could be paid using a fixed amount of cash which is worth less than the cash borrowed earlier. Therefore, answer (d) is correct and answer (c) is incorrect. Answers (a) and (b) are incorrect because the

dollar amount of nonmonetary liabilities is not fixed; and, therefore, changes in the general price level will not result in a purchasing power gain (loss).

8. (587,T1,2) (a) SFAS 89, para 44 defines a monetary item as one that is fixed or determinable without reference to future prices. Patents are nonmonetary because their value is not fixed in terms of number of dollars. However, the unamortized premium is inseparable from the bonds payable account to which it relates, and bonds payable are a monetary item (SFAS 89, para 96).

9. (585,T1,3) (a) The requirement is to determine which item would be considered nonmonetary when preparing information on a historical cost/constant dollar basis. Answer (a) is correct because per SFAS 89, nonmonetary items include assets and liabilities whose amounts may change over time in terms of a monetary unit (e.g., the U.S. dollar). Examples of nonmonetary assets and liabilities included inventory, property, plant, equipment, and obligations under warranties. Accumulated depreciation is a nonmonetary item because it relates to equipment. Answer (b) is incorrect because the advance represents a claim to receive a fixed amount in terms of a monetary unit and is therefore a monetary item. Answer (c) is incorrect because the allowance account relates to the accounts receivable, which is a monetary item. Answer (d) is incorrect because the unamortized premium relates to the bonds payable account, which is a monetary item.

10. (1184,T1,6) (d) The requirement is to determine which of the items listed is classified as a monetary item. Per SFAS 89, para 44, the dollar amounts of monetary assets and liabilities are fixed or determinable without reference to future prices of specific goods or services. The allowance for doubtful accounts on long-term receivables is inseparable from the receivables to which it relates, and the receivables are a monetary item (SFAS 89, para 96). Answers (a) and (c) are incorrect because neither goodwill nor the obligation under warranties is fixed in terms of numbers of dollars. Answer (b) is incorrect because the deferred investment credits are not to be settled with cash and are associated with the equipment which is a nonmonetary item.

B. Current Cost Accounting

11. (1188,P3,52) (a) SFAS 89 requires that current cost for inventories and equipment be measured at the lower of current cost or recoverable amount. For equipment, recoverable amount ($95,000) is lower than current cost; for inventory, current cost ($80,000) is lower than recoverable amount. Therefore, the total amount to be reported for these assets is $175,000 ($95,000 + $80,000).

12. (1189,P3,59) (b) Per para 56 of SFAS 89, cost of goods sold is restated into average current cost by multiplying units sold (70,000) by the average current cost during the year. Average current cost is the current cost at the beginning of the year, plus the current cost at the end of the year, divided by 2:

$$(\$58 + \$72) \div 2 = \underline{\$65}$$

Therefore, cost of goods sold restated into average current cost is $4,550,000 (70,000 x $65).

13. (1187,P3,54) (d) Per SFAS 89, the amount to be reported as the current cost of inventory (voluntary supplementary information) is the current cost of purchasing or manufacturing the inventory. In this case, the ending inventory consists of 9,000 units (8,000 beginning inventory + 31,000 purchased − 30,000 sold), and management estimates that the year-end current cost is $71 per unit. Therefore, the current cost of the 12/31/86 inventory is $639,000 (9,000 units x $71 per unit).

14. (1187,P3,55) (a) Per SFAS 89, para 56, current cost of goods sold is computed by multiplying units sold (30,000) by the average current cost during the year. Average current cost is current cost at the beginning of the year plus current cost at the end of the year, divided by 2:

$$(\$57 + \$71) \div 2 = \underline{\$64}$$

Average current cost of goods sold is 30,000 units x $64, or $1,920,000.

15. (587,P3,57) (b) The net current cost of plant assets is simply the estimated current cost less the percentage of the asset depreciated to date. Thus, the net current cost is $336,000, computed as follows:

Year acquired	Estimated current cost	Current cost accumulated depreciation	Net current cost
1984	$280,000 −	.30($280,000) =	$196,000
1985	$76,000 −	.20 ($76,000) =	60,800
1986	$88,000 −	.10 ($88,000) =	79,200
			$336,000

16. (1186,P3,60) (c) The requirement is the amount of current cost depreciation expense which would appear in supplementary current cost financial statements. Per para 52b of SFAS 89, depreciation is to be measured based on the average current cost of the asset during the period of use. The average current cost of this machine during 1985 is $120,000 [($115,000 + $125,000) ÷ 2]. Therefore, 1985 depreciation expense is $24,000 ($120,000 ÷ 5 year useful life).

17. (1186,T1,4) (a) Per SFAS 89, para 34, the exit date means the end of the year or the dates of use, sale, or commitment to a specific contract, whichever is applicable. The entry date means the beginning of the year or the dates of acquisition. Therefore, when measuring the current cost of inventories in accordance with SFAS 89, the date of sale is the exit date. Consequently, answers (b), (c), and (d) are incorrect.

18. (583,T1,7) (d) Current cost/nominal dollar accounting is a method of accounting based on measures of current cost or lower recoverable amount without restatement into units, each of which has the same general purchasing power. Answers (a) and (b) are incorrect because historical cost is an alternative to current cost in which items are measured and reported at their historical prices. Answer (c) is incorrect because under constant dollar accounting, dollars are restated into units having the same general purchasing power.

19. (1182,T1,34) (a) SFAS 89, para 34 states that when measuring the current cost of inventories or property, plant, and equipment, the "entry" date means the beginning of the year or the date of acquisition, whichever is applicable. The "exit" date means the end of the year or the date of sale.

20. (1181,T1,6) (d) Para 16 of SFAS 89 requires that the current cost for inventories be measured at the lower of current cost or recoverable amount at the measurement date.

E. Translation of Foreign Currency Statements

21. (587,P2,36) (d) When the functional currency of a foreign subsidiary is the foreign currency, balance sheet accounts are translated using the current exchange rate (the rate of translation in effect at the balance sheet date). Therefore, these accounts should be included in the balance sheet at $250,000. Note that if the func-

tional currency was the U.S. dollar, balance sheet accounts would be remeasured using a combination of historical and current rates.

22. (585,P3,41) (c) The requirement is to determine the total amount of various expenses incurred by a foreign subsidiary which should be reported in the 1984 consolidated income statement. SFAS 52 states that if the foreign currency is the functional currency of the subsidiary, the current rate method should be used to translate the financial statements. In this method, revenues and expenses are translated at the rates in effect at the time these items were recognized during the period. Because translation at the date the revenues and expenses were recognized is generally deemed impractical, SFAS 52 allows that an appropriate weighted-average rate may be used to translate these items. This results in a translated expense of $176,000 [($120,000 + $80,000 + $200,000) x .44].

23. (1183,P2,37) (a) The requirement is the amount of branch inventory after translation into U.S. dollars. Per SFAS 52, if the functional currency is that of the foreign branch or subsidiary, assets and liabilities are translated using the exchange rate at the balance sheet date. This exchange rate is 6 LCU to $1. Therefore, the inventory balance of 240,000 LCU is translated to $40,000 (240,000 ÷ 6).

24. (1187,T1,17) (b) Per SFAS 52, para 12, the weighted average exchange rate is used to translate revenues, expenses, gains, and losses from the functional currency to the reporting currency. Both wages expense and sales to customers fall under this rule and should be translated using the weighted average exchange rate. Therefore, answer (b) is correct.

25. (1185,T1,21) (a) The requirement is to determine the proper classification of foreign currency translation gains for a currency which has not experienced significant inflation. Answer (a) is correct because SFAS 52, para 13 states that when an entity's functional currency is the foreign currency, that entity's financial statements are to be translated into the reporting currency using the current rate of exchange. Gains and losses from the translation process are known as translation adjustments and are to be reported as a separate component of stockholders' equity. They are not to be included in income, except in the case of a highly inflationary economy, one with a cumulative inflation rate of 100% or more over a three-

year period. If this occurs, the foreign entity's financial statements would be <u>unmeasured</u> into the reporting currency, with gains and losses from the remeasurement process included in the determination of net income.

26. (1181,T1,27) (d) When the functional currency is the U.S. dollar, SFAS 52 requires monetary assets and monetary liabilities be translated to U.S. dollars by using the current rate. Nonmonetary assets and liabilities are translated by using the exchange rates in effect when the transactions occurred which gave rise to the foreign currency balances. Historical exchange rates would be used to translate historical cost balances. Consequently, both property, plant, and equipment and accumulated depreciation should be translated by using historical rates.

F. Translation of Foreign Currency Transactions

27. (588,P3,47) (c) When the <u>sale is made</u> on 10/15/87, Bain would record a receivable and sales at $100,000, the U.S. dollar equivalent on that date.

| Accounts receivable | 100,000 | |
| Sales | | 100,000 |

On 11/16/87, Bain receives foreign currency worth $105,000. Since the receivable was recorded at $100,000, a $5,000 gain must be recorded.

Foreign currency	105,000	
Accounts receivable		100,000
Foreign exchange gain		5,000

The U.S. dollar equivalent when the order was received on 9/1/87 ($96,000) is not used to compute the gain because no entry is recorded on this date. The receipt and acceptance of a purchase order from a customer is an executory commitment which is not generally recorded.

28. (586,P3,56) (d) The requirement is the amount of 1985 foreign exchange gain or loss. Clark borrowed local currency units (LCUs) from a foreign lender. The note will be settled in LCUs. Per para 15 of SFAS 52, a transaction gain (loss) will result if the exchange rate on the settlement date is different than the rate existing on the transaction date. Para 15 also states that a provision must be made at any intervening year-end date for such rate changes. Therefore, in 1984, a $30,000 loss would be recognized, since a change in the exchange rate caused the U.S. dollar equivalent of the liability to increase from $210,000 at 7/1/84 to $240,000 at

12/31/84. In 1985, a change in the exchange rate caused the U.S. dollar equivalent of the liability to increase even further, from $240,000 at 12/31/84 to $280,000 at 7/1/85. This results in a 1985 loss of $40,000 ($280,000 - $240,000).

29. (589,P1,11) (a) A transaction has occurred in which settlement will be made in German marks. Since Lindy's functional currency is the U.S. dollar, a transaction gain (loss) will result if the spot rate on the settlement date is different than the rate on the transaction date (SFAS 52, para 15). Para 15 also states that a provision must be made at any intervening year end date if there has been a rate change. Thus, in 1987, a $500 foreign exchange gain [100,000 x ($.4295 - $.4245)] would be recognized, while in 1988 a $1,000 foreign exchange loss [100,000 x ($.4245 - $.4345)] would be recognized.

30. (1183,P1,11) (d) The requirement is the foreign currency transaction gain (loss) in Stone's 1982 income statement. Since the rate is denominated in a foreign currency at a fixed 840,000 (LCU), fluctuations in the exchange rates will produce foreign currency gains (losses). Per SFAS 52, the increase (decrease) in expected functional currency cash flows is a foreign currency transaction gain (loss) to be included in income in the period during which the exchange rate changes. At December 31, 1981 changes in the exchange rates produced a recognized gain of $20,000. At the repayment date (July 1, 1982) changes in the exchange rate resulted in a realized loss of $35,000 computed as follows:

$$\frac{\text{Received from borrower 840,000 LCU}}{\text{8 LCU for each \$1}} = \$105,000$$

Note carrying value	$140,000
Cash received	- 105,000
Translation loss	$ 35,000

31. (1186,Q1,14) (c) The direct quotation is the rate expressed in U.S. dollars. It means that $.90 can be exchanged for 1 Canadian dollar. The direct quotation is $.90/1, answer (d). The indirect quotation is the inverse of the direct quotation or 1/$.90, answer (c). The indirect quotation is the rate expressed in foreign currency.

32. (582,Q1,1) (c) The requirement is the amount which Tyrola should accrue for royalties payable, 12/31/81. This situation is a foreign currency transaction in which settlement is denominated in other than a company's functional currency (SFAS 52, para 5 and 15). In this case the functional currency is the

U.S. dollar because it is the currency of the primary economic environment in which the Colorado firm operates. Note that in this royalty agreement, 12/31/81 is the point at which the amount due to the author (50,000 Canadian dollars x 10% = 5,000 Canadian dollars) is determined. Royalty expense is measured and the related liability is denominated at 12/31/81. The year-end accrual would be:

.89 (10% x 50,000 Canadian dollars) = $4,450.

On January 10, 1982, Tyrola will have to purchase 5,000 Canadian dollars for payment to the Canadian author. The amount of U.S. dollars required to accomplish this will depend on the spot rate on January 10th ($.90 in this case). The number of U.S. dollars required to satisfy the obligation will be $50 greater [($.90 - .89) x 5,000 Canadian dollars]. This will result in a $50 transaction loss which would be included in 1982 net income.

33. (1189,P3,43) (b) On 4/8/87, Day incurs a liability which is payable in a foreign currency. Para 15 of SFAS 52 states that a transaction gain (loss) will result if the exchange rate on the settlement date is different from the rate existing on the transaction date. Para 15 further states that a gain (loss) must be recognized at any intervening year-end dates, if necessary. Therefore, Day would recognize a $500 gain in 1987, since a change in the exchange rate decreased the liability (in U.S. dollars) from $6,000 on 4/8/87 (10,000 x $.60) to $5,500 on 12/31/87 ($10,000 x $.55). In 1988, a gain of $1,000 would be recognized since the liability (in U.S. dollars) further decreased from $5,500 on 12/31/87 to $4,500 when paid on 3/1/88 (10,000 x $.45).

34. (589,T1,18) (d) Per SFAS 52, para 15, a foreign currency transaction is a transaction that is denominated in a currency other than the entity's functional currency. Such a transaction may result in a receivable or payable that is fixed in terms of the amount of foreign currency that will be received or paid. A change in the exchange rate will cause an increase or decrease in the amount of functional currency expected to be received or paid. This increase or decrease is a foreign currency transaction gain or loss, and it should be included as a component of income whether the change results in a gain or loss. Therefore, answer (d) is correct. Answers (a), (b), and (c) are incorrect because either a gain or a loss should be reported as a component of income and neither a gain nor a loss should be included separately as a component of stockholders' equity.

35. (587,T1,24) (d) Per SFAS 52, transaction gains and losses are generally reported on the income statement as a component of income from continuing operations in the period during which the change in exchange rates occurs. Thus, answer (d) is correct. Answer (a) is incorrect because the loss is reported in the year of occurrence, not at the settlement date. Answers (b) and (c) are incorrect because the loss would not be shown as a balance sheet component.

36. (589,P1,20) (c) Translation adjustments result from translating an entity's financial statements into the reporting currency. Such adjustments, which result when the entity's functional currency is the foreign currency, should not be included in net income. Instead, such adjustments should be reported in stockholders' equity. (Note that if the functional currency was the reporting currency, a remeasurement process would have been used instead of translation, with the resulting gain or loss included in income). The $20,000 translation loss is not reported on the income statement. In contrast, gains and losses which result from foreign exchange transactions (purchases/sales) are reported on the income statement. Therefore, Bart should report the $13,000 foreign exchange loss, plus the $6,000 unrealized foreign exchange loss ($106,000 year-end liability less $100,000 original liability), for a total loss of $19,000.

May 1990 Answers

37. (590,T1,3) (d) Per SFAS 89, para 44, the historical cost/constant dollar accounting method reports the original cost on the balance sheet, but measured in dollars of equal purchasing power (i.e., adjusted for the consumer price index). Both the current cost/nominal dollar and the current cost/constant dollar method report the current cost on the balance sheet. The historical cost/nominal dollar method reports the original cost. Because this is a period of inflation, the historical cost/nominal dollar amount [answer (a)] can be eliminated immediately. Because the consumer price index increased at a faster rate than did the specific price of this parcel of land, the historical cost/constant dollar method [answer (d)] would measure the land at a higher amount than would the current cost/nominal dollar or current cost/constant dollar methods [answers (b) and (c)].

38. (590,T1,22) (b) Per SFAS 12, para 13, translation adjustments result from trans-

lating an entity's financial statements into
the reporting currency. Such adjustments,
which result when the entity's functional currency is the foreign currency, should not be
included in net income. Instead, such adjustments should be reported in the stockholders'
equity section of the balance sheet. If the
functional currency is the reporting currency
(U.S. dollar), a remeasurement process takes
place, with the resulting gain or loss included in income. Therefore, answer (b) is
correct.

PERSONAL FINANCIAL STATEMENTS

Multiple Choice Questions (1-13)

1. On December 31, 1987, Shane is a fully-vested participant in a company-sponsored pension plan. According to the plan's administrator, Shane has at that date the nonforfeitable right to receive a lump sum of $100,000 on December 28, 1988. The discounted amount of $100,000 is $90,000 at December 31, 1987. The right is not contingent on Shane's life expectancy and requires no future performance on Shane's part. In Shane's December 31, 1987 personal statement of financial condition, the vested interest in the pension plan should be reported at

    a. $0
    b. $ 90,000
    c. $ 95,000
    d. $100,000

2. On December 31, 1987, Mr. and Mrs. Blake owned a parcel of land held as an investment. The land was purchased for $95,000 in 1980, and was encumbered by a mortgage with a principal balance of $60,000 at December 31, 1987. On this date the fair value of the land was $150,000. In the Blakes' December 31, 1987 personal statement of financial condition, at what amount should the land investment and mortgage payable be reported?

	Land investment	Mortgage payable
a.	$150,000	$60,000
b.	$ 95,000	$60,000
c.	$ 90,000	$0
d.	$ 35,000	$0

3. Leslie Shaw's personal statement of financial condition at December 31, 1986 shows net worth of $400,000 before consideration of employee stock options owned on that date. Information relating to the stock options is as follows:

    • Options to purchase 10,000 shares of Korn Corporation stock.
    • Option exercise price is $10 a share.
    • Options expire on June 30, 1987.
    • Market price of the stock is $25 a share on December 31, 1986.
    • Assume that exercise of the options in 1987 would result in ordinary income taxable at 35%.

After giving effect to the stock options, Shaw's net worth at December 31, 1986 would be

    a. $497,500
    b. $550,000

    c. $562,500
    d. $650,000

Items 4 and 5 are based on the following data:

Mr. & Mrs. Taft are applying for a bank loan and the bank has requested a personal statement of financial condition as of December 31, 1984. Included in their assets and liabilities at this date are the following:

Assets
Mr. Taft owns 50% of the common stock of Dee Corporation. A shareholders' agreement restricts the sale of the stock and, under certain circumstances, requires Dee to repurchase the stock based on the book value of the net assets, plus an agreed amount for goodwill. At December 31, 1984, the buyout value of Taft's stock is $675,000. Mr. Taft's stock is $675,000. Mr. Taft's tax basis for his Dee stock is $430,000.

Mrs. Taft owns jewelry appraised on December 31, 1984, at $70,000 by an independent appraiser for insurance purposes. The jewelry, acquired by purchase and gift over a ten-year period, has a total tax basis of $40,000.

Liabilities
The Taft residence is encumbered by a mortgage which is payable in monthly installments of $1,000 through December 1990. Interest at 10% a year is included in the $1,000 monthly payment. The balance of the mortgage principal is $58,000 at December 31, 1984.

Mr. Taft has guaranteed the payment of loans of Dee Corporation under a $300,000 line of credit. The loan balance is $200,000 at December 31, 1984. Dee's financial condition at December 31, 1984, is such that its repayment of the loan balance is reasonably assured.

4. In the Tafts' December 31, 1984 personal statement of financial condition, the Dee Corporation investment and the jewelry should be reported at a total amount of

    a. $470,000
    b. $500,000
    c. $715,000
    d. $745,000

5. In the Tafts' December 31, 1984 personal statement of financial condition, the liabilities listed above should be reported at a total amount of

    a. $ 58,000
    b. $ 72,000
    c. $258,000
    d. $272,000

33

6.   John Holt owns 50% of the common stock of Brett Corp. Holt paid $25,000 for this stock in 1983. At December 31, 1988, it was ascertained that Holt's 50% stock ownership in Brett had a current value of $185,000. Brett's cumulative net income and cash dividends declared for the five years ended December 31, 1988 were $300,000 and $30,000 respectively. In Holt's personal statement of financial condition at December 31, 1988, what amount should be reported as his net investment in Brett?
   a. $ 25,000
   b. $160,000
   c. $175,000
   d. $185,000

7.   Ron Alda owns 100% of Hako Corp.'s outstanding capital stock. Alda paid $60,000 for this stock in 1980. At December 31, 1988, the book value of Hako's net assets amounted to $300,000. It has been ascertained that Alda's 100% stock ownership in Hako had a current value of $500,000 at December 31, 1988. Alda has an employment contract with Hako under which Alda is to receive a salary of $100,000 annually for a ten-year period beginning in January 1988. In Alda's personal statement of financial condition at December 31, 1988, what amount should be shown as his net investment in Hako?
   a. $ 60,000
   b. $100,000
   c. $300,000
   d. $500,000

8.   In a personal statement of financial condition, which of the following should be reported at quoted market prices?

	Marketable debt securities	Marketable equity securities
a.	No	No
b.	No	Yes
c.	Yes	Yes
d.	Yes	No

9.   In a personal statement of financial condition, which of the following should be reported at estimated current values?

	Investments in closely held businesses	Investments in leaseholds
a.	Yes	Yes
b.	Yes	No
c.	No	No
d.	No	Yes

10.   Personal financial statements should report an investment in life insurance in the statement of financial condition as an
   a.   Asset for the cash value of the policy less the amount of any loans against it.
   b.   Asset for the cash value of the policy and a liability for the amount of any loans against it.
   c.   Asset for the face amount of the policy less the amount of any loans against it.
   d.   Asset for the face amount of the policy less the amount of premiums paid.

11.   Personal financial statements should include which of the following statements?

	Financial condition	Changes in net worth	Cash flows
a.	No	Yes	Yes
b.	Yes	No	No
c.	Yes	Yes	No
d.	Yes	Yes	Yes

May 1990 Questions

12.   Dale Hall's holdings at December 31, 1989 included the following:

•   5,000 shares of Arno Corp. common stock purchased in 1984 for $85,000. The market value of the stock was $120,000 at December 31, 1989.

•   A life insurance policy with a cash value of $50,000 at December 31, 1989.

In Hall's December 31, 1989 personal statement of financial condition, the above items should be reported at
   a. $170,000
   b. $135,000
   c. $120,000
   d. $ 85,000

13.   A business interest that constitutes a large part of an individual's total assets should be presented in a personal statement of financial condition as
   a.   A single amount equal to the proprietorship equity.
   b.   A single amount equal to the estimated current value of the business interest.
   c.   A separate listing of the individual assets and liabilities, at cost.
   d.   Separate line items of both total assets and total liabilities, at cost.

PERSONAL FINANCIAL STATEMENTS

Multiple Choice Answers

1. b	4. d	7. d	10. a	12. a
2. a	5. a	8. c	11. c	13. b
3. a	6. d	9. a		

Multiple Choice Answer Explanations

A. Personal Financial Statements

1. (1188,P3,59) (b) In a personal statement of financial condition, assets are generally presented at estimated current values. Depending on the nature of the asset, current value can be estimated using fair market value, net realizable value, discounted cash flow, or appraised value. AICPA Statement of Position 82-1 specifies that a future interest which is nonforfeitable should be valued using discounted cash flow. Therefore, the interest in the pension plan should be valued at $90,000.

2. (588,P3,60) (a) Per SOP 82-1, assets are generally presented at their estimated current values on personal financial statements. Therefore, the land investment should be reported at its fair value of $150,000, rather than at its cost of $95,000. SOP 82-1 also states that liabilities are presented at the lesser of the discounted amount of cash to be paid, or the current cash settlement amount. For a mortgage, both the discounted cash flow and the current settlement amount should be equal to the principal balance of $60,000.

3. (587,P3,53) (a) Per SOP 82-1, assets are generally presented at their estimated current values in a personal statement of financial condition. For stock options, market price would typically be used as estimated current value. Since no market price is given for the options, their value can be estimated as the excess of the market price of the stock over the option exercise price [10,000 options x ($25 - $10) = $150,000]. SOP 82-1 also specifies that a personal statement of financial condition should include the estimated income tax on the difference between the current value of assets and their tax bases. Since the options have a current value of $150,000 and a $0 tax basis, an estimated income tax liability of $52,500 ($150,000 x 35%) must be deducted. The net effect on Shaw's net worth is an increase of $97,500 ($150,000 - $52,500) resulting in a 12/31/86 net worth of $497,500 ($400,000 + $97,500).

4. (1185,P3,57) (d) Per SOP 82-1, assets are generally presented at their estimated current values on such statements. Since sale of the investment in common stock is restricted, the buyout value ($675,000) is the best estimate of its current value. The best estimate of the current value of the jewelry is its appraised value of $70,000. Therefore, the total estimated current value of the two assets is $745,000 ($675,000 + 70,000). Note that tax basis is not generally a reasonable estimate of current value.

5. (1185,P3,58) (a) Per SOP 82-1, liabilities are presented at the lesser of the discounted amount of cash to be paid, or the current cash settlement amount. For the mortgage, both the discounted amount and the estimated current settlement amount would be equal to the balance of the mortgage principal ($58,000). Remember, the current mortgage principal balance is the present value of the future mortgage payments discounted at the mortgage interest rate. The guarantee of the Dee Corporation's indebtedness is a contingent liability. This contingency should be disclosed in a footnote to the statement, but should not be reported in the body of the statement since it is not probable that Taft has incurred a personal liability as of 12/31/84. Thus, the total amount of liabilities is $58,000.

6. (1189,P3,58) (d) Per para 6(a) of SOP 82-1, assets should be reported at estimated current value in personal financial statements. This is the amount at which the asset could be exchanged assuming both parties are well-informed and neither party is compelled to buy or sell. The current value of Holt's investment in Brett common stock is $185,000, so this amount should be reported in Holt's personal statement of financial condition. The information given on Brett's cumulative net income ($300,000) and cumulative cash dividends declared ($30,000) would be relevant if the equity method was used, but is not relevant for personal financial statements.

7. (589,Q1,17) (d) Per SOP 82-1, investments in closely held businesses should be reported at their current values in personal financial statements. As of December 31, 1988, the current value of Alda's 100% stock ownership in Hako is $500,000. Therefore, answer (d) is correct. The employment contract does not affect the valuation of the net investment.

8. (1188,T1,40) (c) Per AICPA Statement of
Position 82-1, both marketable debt and equity
securities should be reported in the personal
statement of financial condition at their
quoted market prices on the date of the statement. Therefore, answer (c) is correct, and
answers (a), (b), and (d) are incorrect.

9. (589,T1,39) (a) Per SOP 82-1, both
investments in closely held businesses and
investments in leaseholds (like virtually all
other assets) should be reported at their
estimated current values in a personal statement of financial condition. Therefore, answer (a) is correct.

10. (588,T1,40) (a) Per SOP 82-1, an
investment in life insurance should be
reported in a statement of financial condition
at the policy's cash value less any outstanding loans against it. Therefore, answer (a)
is correct. Answer (b) is incorrect because
the loans against the policy are to be netted
against the cash value of the policy, not disclosed separately. Answers (c) and (d) are
incorrect because the investment is to be
reported at its cash value, not face value.
However, the face amount of the life insurance
policy should be disclosed in either the body
or in the notes to the personal financial
statements.

11. (1189,T1,39) (c) Per AICPA Statement of
Position 82-1, personal financial statements
consist of (1) a statement of financial
condition, and (2) a statement of changes in
net worth. A statement of cash flows is not
required. Therefore, answer (c) is correct.

May 1990 Answers

12. (590,Q3,59) (a) Per SOP 82-1, assets
are generally presented at their estimated
current values in personal financial statements. This is the amount at which the asset
could be exchanged assuming both parties are
well-informed and neither party is compelled
to buy or sell. The current value of Hall's
investment in Arno common stock is $120,000.
The current value of the life insurance policy
is the cash value of $50,000. Thus, Hall
should report $170,000 ($120,000 + $50,000) in
his personal financial statements.

13. (590,T1,40) (b) Per SOP 82-1, para 10,
business interests that constitute a large
part of a person's total assets should be
shown separately from other investments. The
estimated current value of an investment in a
separate entity, such as a closely held corporation, a partnership, or a sole proprietor-

ship, should be shown in one amount as an
investment if the entity is marketable as a
going concern. Therefore, answer (b) is
correct.

INTERIM REPORTING

Multiple Choice Questions (1-12)

1.   During the second quarter of 1988, Buzz Company sold a piece of equipment at a $12,000 gain. What portion of the gain should Buzz report in its income statement for the second quarter of 1988?
   a. $12,000
   b. $ 6,000
   c. $ 4,000
   d. $0

2.   On March 15, 1987, Rex Company paid property taxes of $180,000 on its factory building for calendar year 1987. On April 1, 1987, Rex made $300,000 in unanticipated repairs to its plant equipment. The repairs will benefit operations for the remainder of the calendar year. What total amount of these expenses should be included in Rex's quarterly income statement for the three months ended June 30, 1987?
   a. $ 75,000
   b. $145,000
   c. $195,000
   d. $345,000

3.   Harper Co. incurred an apparently permanent inventory loss from market decline of $840,000 during June 1989. What amount of the inventory loss should be recognized in Harper's quarterly income statement for the three months ended June 30, 1989?
   a. $210,000
   b. $280,000
   c. $420,000
   d. $840,000

4.   Bailey Company, a calendar year corporation, has the following income before income tax provision and estimated effective annual income tax rates for the first three quarters of 1989:

Quarter	Income before income tax provision	Estimated effective annual tax rate at end of quarter
First	300,000	10%
Second	70,000	40%
Third	40,000	45%

Bailey's income tax provision in its interim income statement for the third quarter should be
   a. $18,000
   b. $24,500
   c. $25,500
   d. $76,500

5.   On January 1, 1989, Builder Associates entered into a $1,000,000 long-term, fixed-price contract to construct a factory building for Manufacturing Company. Builder accounts for this contract under the percentage-of-completion and estimated costs at completion at the end of each quarter for 1979 were as follows:

Quarter	Estimated percentage of completion	Estimated costs at completion
1	10%	$750,000
2*	10%	$750,000
3	25%	$960,000
4*	25%	$960,000

*No work performed in the 2nd and 4th quarters.

What amounts should be reported by Builder as "Income on Construction Contract" in its quarterly income statements based on the above information?

	Gain (Loss) for the Three Months Ended		
March 31, 1989	June 30, 1989	September 30, 1989	December 31, 1989
a. $0	$0	$0	$10,000
b. $25,000	$0	$(15,000)	$0
c. $25,000	$0	$0	$0
d. $25,000	$0	$ 6,000	$0

6.   Vilo Corp. has estimated that total depreciation expense for the year ending December 31, 1989 will amount to $60,000, and that 1989 year-end bonuses to employees will total $120,000. In Vilo's interim income statement for the six months ended June 30, 1989, what is the total amount of expense relating to these two items that should be reported?
   a. $0
   b. $ 30,000
   c. $ 90,000
   d. $180,000

7.   On July 1, 1985, Dolan Corp. incurred an extraordinary loss of $300,000, net of income tax saving. Dolan's operating income for the full year ending December 31, 1985 was expected to be $500,000. In Dolan's income statement for the quarter ended September 30, 1985, how much of this extraordinary loss should be disclosed separately?
   a. $300,000
   b. $150,000
   c. $ 75,000
   d. $0

8.   For interim financial reporting, which of the following may be accrued or deferred to provide an appropriate cost in each period?

	Interest	Rent
a.	Yes	No
b.	Yes	Yes
c.	No	Yes
d.	No	No

9.   For interim financial reporting, the computation of a company's second quarter provision for income taxes uses an effective tax rate expected to be applicable for the full fiscal year. The effective tax rate should reflect anticipated

	Foreign tax rates	Available tax planning alternatives
a.	No	Yes
b.	No	No
c.	Yes	No
d.	Yes	Yes

10.   An inventory loss from a market price decline occurred in the first quarter. The loss was not expected to be restored in the fiscal year. However, in the third quarter the inventory had a market price recovery that exceeded the market decline that occurred in the first quarter. For interim financial reporting, the dollar amount of net inventory should

   a.   Decrease in the first quarter by the amount of the market price decline and increase in the third quarter by the amount of the market price recovery.

   b.   Decrease in the first quarter by the amount of the market price decline and increase in the third quarter by the amount of decrease in the first quarter.

   c.   Not be affected in the first quarter and increase in the third quarter by the amount of the market price recovery that exceeded the amount of the market price decline.

   d.   Not be affected in either the first quarter or the third quarter.

11.   For external reporting purposes, it is appropriate to use estimated gross profit rates to determine the cost of goods sold for

	Interim financial reporting	Year-end financial reporting
a.	Yes	Yes
b.	Yes	No
c.	No	Yes
d.	No	No

May 1990 Question

12.   Advertising costs may be accrued or deferred to provide an appropriate expense in each period for

	Interim financial reporting	Year-end financial reporting
a.	Yes	No
b.	Yes	Yes
c.	No	No
d.	No	Yes

Repeat Question

(590,Q3,43) Identical/similar to item 3 above

INTERIM REPORTING

Multiple Choice Answers

1. a	4. b	7. a	9. d	11. b
2. b	5. b	8. b	10. b	12. b
3. d	6. c			

Multiple Choice Answer Explanations

B. Interim Reporting

1. (1188,P3,46) (a) APB 28 states that revenues and gains should be recognized in interim reports on the same basis as used in annual reports. In annual reports, gains on the sale of equipment are recognized in the period when the sale occurs. Since this sale of equipment occurred in the second quarter, the entire gain ($12,000) should be recognized in the second quarter income statement.

2. (588,P3,54) (b) Per APB 28, a cost charged to an expense in an annual period should be allocated among the interim periods which clearly benefit from the expense through the use of accruals and/or deferrals. The annual property taxes clearly benefit all four quarters, so the $180,000 cost should be deferred and reported as $45,000 expense in each of the four quarters ($180,000 ÷ 4). The repairs made on April 1 will benefit operations for the <u>remainder of the calendar year</u>, so the $300,000 cost should be deferred and reported as $100,000 expense in each of the remaining three quarters ($300,000 ÷ 3). Therefore, the total for these expenses in the second quarter income statement is $145,000 ($45,000 + $100,000).

3. (1189,P3,49) (d) Para 14 of APB 28 states that provisions for writedowns of inventory to market should be made at interim dates on the same basis as is used at annual reporting dates. Therefore, the full $840,000 loss should be recognized when incurred in the quarter ending 6/30/89. Note that if this loss had been considered <u>temporary</u> in nature, it need not be recognized at an interim date (para 14 of APB 28).

4. (1180,P1,9) (b) The requirement is Bailey's income tax provision (expense) in its interim income statement for the third quarter. APB 28, para 19 states that the tax provision for an interim period is the tax for the year to date (estimated effective rate for the year times year-to-date income) less the total tax provisions reported for previous interim periods.

Year-to-date tax (45%)($170,000)	$76,500
Previously reported tax (40% x $130,000)	52,000
Third quarter tax provision	$24,500

5. (580,P1,8) (b) The requirement is to compute the income to be recognized in quarterly (interim) financial statements on a construction contract using the percentage-of-completion method. The solutions approach is to compute the income on the contract at the end of each quarter by (1) applying the estimated percentage of completion to the total estimated income to be recognized on the contract, and (2) subtracting the income recognized in preceding quarters to arrive at the income for the latest quarter. In the second and fourth quarters there was no work done on the contract and no change in the total estimated cost of completion. In quarter three the estimated costs of completion are revised upward. Since the cumulative income to date is less than income recognized in the first quarter, it is necessary to recognize a loss in the third quarter. The loss is handled as a change in accounting estimate rather than restating the first quarter.

Quarter 1:
  10% ($1,000,000 - $750,000) = $25,000 income recognized

Quarter 2:
  -0-

Quarter 3:
  25% ($1,000,000 - $960,000) = $10,000 income earned to date

  $10,000 income to date - $25,000 income recognized in previous periods = $(15,000) loss for quarter

Quarter 4:
  -0-

6. (589,Q1,12) (c) Per APB 28, para 15a, a cost charged to expense in an annual period should be allocated among the interim periods which clearly benefit from the expense through the use of accruals and/or deferrals. Both yearly bonuses and the use of an asset (depreciation expense) benefit the entire year. The expense for the <u>six month</u> interim statement should be ($60,000 + $120,000) ÷ 2 = $90,000.

7. (586,Q1,12) (a) The requirement is to determine the amount of the extraordinary loss which should be separately disclosed in an interim financial statement. Per APB 28, para 21, extraordinary items should be disclosed separately and included in the determination of net income for the interim period in which they occur. According to para 21,

extraordinary items should not be prorated over the balance of the fiscal year. Also, in determining materiality, extraordinary items should be related to the **estimated** income for the entire fiscal year. The extraordinary loss is considered material based on estimated 1985 income of $500,000. Therefore, Dolan should disclose the $300,000 separately for the quarter ended 9/30/85.

8. (1188,T1,37) (b) Per APB 28, para 15, costs and expenses other than product costs (i.e., interest and rent) should be charged to income as incurred or allocated among interim periods if they benefit more than one interim period. Therefore, interest and rent expenses may be accrued or deferred, and answer (b) is correct.

9. (1189,T1,35) (d) Per APB 28, para 19, "the effective tax rate should reflect anticipated investment tax credits, foreign tax rates, percentage depletion, capital gains rates, and other available tax planning alternatives. Therefore, answer (d) is correct.

10. (589,T1,32) (b) Per APB 28, a decline in inventory market price, expected to be other than temporary, should be recognized in the period of decline. A subsequent recovery of market value should be recognized as a cost recovery in the period of increase, but **never** above original cost. Thus, answer (b) is correct because the decline should be recognized when it occurs in the first quarter. The subsequent recovery should be recognized when it occurs in the third quarter. Answer (a) is incorrect because the subsequent recovery cannot exceed the amount of decline. Answers (c) and (d) are incorrect because a nontemporary decline should be shown in the quarter of price decrease.

11. (1183,T1,35) (b) The requirement is the appropriateness of estimated gross profit rates in determining cost of goods sold for interim and year-end external financial reporting purposes. The use of estimated gross profit rates to determine the cost of goods sold for an interim period is appropriate per APB 28, para 14. The method of estimation used and any significant adjustments that result from reconciliations with the annual physical inventory should be disclosed. An estimation of cost of goods sold is not allowable for year-end financial reporting per APB 43, para 4. (The actual cost of the goods sold must be determined by the use of a cost flow assumption which most clearly reflects periodic income.) Thus, an estimated cost of goods sold figure may be used for interim but not year-end statements.

May 1990 Answer

12. (590,T1,34) (b) Per APB 28, para 16, advertising costs may be deferred within a fiscal year if the benefits clearly extend beyond the interim period that the expense was paid. Also, advertising costs may be accrued and assigned to interim periods in relation to sales. Year-end accruals and deferrals of costs are also considered appropriate accounting treatment. Note, however, that deferral in year-end reporting is permitted only if the advertising has not been run in the media. Therefore, answer (b) is correct.

SEGMENT REPORTING

Multiple Choice Questions (1-11)

1.   Cord Corporation discloses supplementary
industry segment information for its two
reportable segments. Data for 1986 are
available as follows:

	Segment E	Segment W
Sales	$750,000	$250,000
Traceable operating expenses	325,000	130,000

Additional 1986 expenses are as follows:

Indirect operating expenses	$120,000
General corporate expenses	100,000

Appropriately selected common expenses are
allocated to segments based on the ratio of
each segment's sales to total sales. The 1986
operating profit for segment E was
   a. $260,000
   b. $335,000
   c. $395,000
   d. $425,000

2.   Clay Company has three lines of business,
each of which was determined to be a reportable segment. Company sales aggregated
$1,500,000 in 1986, of which Segment No. 1
contributed 40%. Traceable costs were
$350,000 for Segment No. 1 out of a total of
$1,000,000 for the company as a whole. For
internal reporting, Clay allocates common
costs of $300,000 based on the ratio of a
segment's income before common costs to the
total income before common costs. In its 1986
financial statements, how much should Clay
report as operating profit for Segment No. 1?
   a. $250,000
   b. $200,000
   c. $130,000
   d. $100,000

3.   Eller Company discloses supplemental
industry segment information. The following
data are available for 1983:

Segment	Sales	Traceable costs	Allocable costs
R	$300,000	$240,000	?
S	400,000	220,000	?
T	200,000	140,000	?
	$900,000	$600,000	$120,000

Costs are appropriately allocated based on the
ratio of a segment's income before allocable
costs to total income before allocable costs.
What is the operating profit for segment R for
1983?
   a. $20,000
   b. $24,000

   c. $36,000
   d. $48,000

4.   The following information pertains to
Aria Corp. and its divisions for the year
ended December 31, 1988:

Sales to unaffiliated customers	$2,000,000
Intersegment sales of products similar to those sold to un- affiliated customers	600,000
Interest earned on loans to other industry segments	40,000

Aria and all of its divisions are engaged
solely in manufacturing operations. Aria has
a reportable segment if that segment's revenue
exceeds
   a. $264,000
   b. $260,000
   c. $204,000
   d. $200,000

5.   In financial reporting for segments of a
business enterprise, the revenue of a segment
should include
   a.   Intersegment billings for the cost
        of shared facilities.
   b.   Intersegment sales of services
        similar to those sold to unaffili-
        ated customers.
   c.   Equity in income from unconsolidated
        subsidiaries.
   d.   Extraordinary items.

6.   In financial reporting for segments of a
business enterprise, which of the following
should be taken into account in computing the
amount of an industry segment's identifiable
assets?

	Accumulated depreciation	Marketable securities valuation allowance
a.	No	No
b.	No	Yes
c.	Yes	Yes
d.	Yes	No

7.   In financial reporting for segments of a
business enterprise, the operating profit or
loss of a segment should include

	Expenses related to revenue from intersegment sales	Portion of general corporate expenses
a.	Yes	Yes
b.	Yes	No
c.	No	No
d.	No	Yes

8.   In Logan Company's financial reporting
for segments of a business enterprise, which
of the following assets should be included as

an identifiable asset of the textile mill product industry segment?

    a.   A loan from the textile mill product segment to another industry segment.

    b.   An investment by the textile mill product segment in another industry segment.

    c.   An allocated portion of assets maintained for general corporate purposes and not used in the operations of the textile mill product segment.

    d.   An allocated portion of intangible assets used jointly by the textile mill product segment and another industry segment.

9.   In financial reporting for segments of a business enterprise, the operating profit or loss of a manufacturing segment includes

	Interest expense	Portion of general corporate expense
a.	Yes	Yes
b.	Yes	No
c.	No	No
d.	No	Yes

May 1990 Questions

10.   Correy Corp. and its divisions are engaged solely in manufacturing operations. The following data (consistent with prior years' data) pertain to the industries in which operations were conducted for the year ended December 31, 1989:

Industry	Total revenue	Operating profit	Identifiable assets at 12/31/89
A	$10,000,000	$1,750,000	$20,000,000
B	8,000,000	1,400,000	17,500,000
C	6,000,000	1,200,000	12,500,000
D	3,000,000	550,000	7,500,000
E	4,250,000	675,000	7,000,000
F	1,500,000	225,000	3,000,000
	$32,750,000	$5,800,000	$67,500,000

In its segment information for 1989, how many reportable segments does Correy have?

    a.   Three
    b.   Four
    c.   Five
    d.   Six

11.   YIV Inc. is a multidivisional corporation which has both intersegment sales and sales to unaffiliated customers. YIV should report segment financial information for each division meeting which of the following criteria?

    a.   Segment operating profit or loss is 10% or more of consolidated profit or loss.

    b.   Segment operating profit or loss is 10% or more of combined operating profit or loss of all company segments.

    c.   Segment revenue is 10% or more of combined revenue of all the company segments.

    d.   Segment revenue is 10% or more of consolidated revenue.

Repeat Question

(590,Q3,54) Identical/similar to item 2 above

SEGMENT REPORTING

Multiple Choice Answers

1. b	4. b	6. c	8. d	10. c
2. d	5. b	7. b	9. c	11. c
3. c				

Multiple Choice Answer Explanations

C. Segment Reporting

1. (1187,P3,59) (b) Per SFAS 14, operating profit for a segment is that segment's total revenues less all <u>operating</u> expenses, including both traceable operating expenses and common, or indirect, operating expenses. Items which would have to be allocated on an arbitrary basis, such as general corporate expenses, are <u>not</u> used in the computation of operating profit or loss. Therefore, segment E's operating profit would be $335,000, as computed below:

Sales	$750,000
Traceable operating expenses	(325,000)
Indirect operating expenses	
(3/4 x $120,000)	(90,000)
Operating profit	$335,000

Segment E is allocated 3/4 of indirect operating expenses because E's sales are 3/4 of total sales ($750,000/$1,000,000).

2. (587,P3,56) (d) Segment No. 1 had sales of $600,000 in 1986 ($1,500,000 x 40%), and income before common costs (i.e., Sales - traceable costs) of $250,000 ($600,000 - $350,000). Total income for the company as a whole before common costs is $500,000 ($1,500,000 - $1,000,000). Since common costs are allocated based on the ratio of a segment's income before common costs to the total income before common costs, Segment No. 1 is allocated 50% ($250,000 ÷ $500,000) of the common costs. This amounts to $150,000 ($300,000 x 50% = $150,000). Therefore, the segment's operating profit is $100,000, as indicated below.

Sales	$600,000
Less traceable costs	(350,000)
Income before common costs	$250,000
Common costs (50% x $300,000)	(150,000)
Operating profit	$100,000

3. (584,P3,53) (c) The requirement is the operating profit for segment R. The first step is to compute the segment's income before allocable costs.

Sales	$300,000
Less traceable costs	(240,000)
Income before allocable costs	$ 60,000

Allocable costs are allocated based on segment income before allocable costs to total income before allocable costs. Total income before allocable costs is $300,000 (sales of $900,000 less traceable costs of $600,000). Therefore, segment R's share of allocable costs is $24,000 [($60,000/$300,000) x $120,000], and segment R's operating profit is $36,000:

Sales	$300,000
Less traceable costs	(240,000)
Income before allocable costs	60,000
Less allocable costs	(24,000)
Operating profit	$ 36,000

4. (589,Q1,20) (b) SFAS 14, para 15 requires that selected data for a segment be reported separately if one of three criteria is met. One of these criteria is met when a segment's revenue is greater than or equal to 10% of the combined revenues of all industry segments. Para 10c states that combined revenue includes sales to unaffiliated customers and intersegment sales or transfers. Para 10c specifically excludes interest earned on loans to other industry segments. Thus, Ana has a reportable segment if that segment's revenues exceed $260,000 [($2,000,000 + $600,000) x 10%].

5. (588,T1,37) (b) Per SFAS 14, para 10c, the revenue of an industry sgement includes sales to unaffiliated customers and intersegment sales or transfers of products and services similar to those sold to unaffiliated customers. Therefore, answer (b) is correct. Answer (a) is incorrect because para 10c, footnote 5, states that intersegment billings for the cost of shared facilities or other jointly incurred costs do not represent intersegment sales or transfers as that term is used in SFAS 14. Equity in income from unconsolidated subsidiaries and extraordinary items are not considered revenues of an industry segment per SFAS 14, para 10d; therefore, answers (c) and (d) are incorrect.

6. (589,T1,34) (c) Per SFAS 14, para 10, asset valuation allowances such as accumulated depreciation, allowance for doubtful accounts, and marketable securities valuation allowance shall be taken into account in computing the amount of an industry segment's identifiable assets. Therefore, answer (c) is correct.

7. (1185,T1,33) (b) The requirement is to determine which item should be included in computing the operating profit or loss of a segment. SFAS 14, para 10d states that expenses related to revenue from intersegment sales should be included in computing operating profit or loss of a business enterprise,

while general corporate expenses shall <u>not</u> be included. Therefore, answers (a), (c), and (d) are incorrect.

8.   (585,T1,31) (d) The requirement is to determine which item would be included as an identifiable asset of a reportable segment. Answer (d) is correct because SFAS 14, para 10e states that identifiable assets are those directly associable with or used by the segment, and include an allocated portion of assets used jointly with other segments. Answers (a) and (b) are both incorrect because SFAS 14 specifically excludes investments or loans in another industry segment as identifiable assets. Answer (c) is incorrect because SFAS 14 specifically excludes assets used by central administration from identifiable assets of a segment.

9.   (1189,T1,36) (c) Per SFAS 14, the operating profit or loss of a manufacturing segment is equal to unaffiliated revenue and intersegment revenue, less all <u>operating</u> expenses, including allocated common costs. General corporate revenues and expenses are never allocated to business segments. Please note that the interest expense of a manufacturing segment is not related to its operations and, therefore, should not be included in the segment's operating profit or loss. Thus, answer (c) is correct.

May 1990 Answers

10. (590,Q3,56) (c) A division is a reportable segment if it is significant. A division is significant if it satisfies at least <u>one</u> of the three 10% tests:

1. <u>Revenue</u> is 10% or more of the combined segment revenue (including intersegment revenue).
2. <u>Operating profit</u> (loss) is 10% or more of the greater of the <u>absolute</u> combined segment profit or loss.
3. <u>Identifiable assets</u> are 10% or more of the combined segment identifiable assets.

Industry A, B, C, and E pass the revenue and operating profit tests, but A, B, C, D, and E all pass the identifiable assets test. Since a division only has to pass one of the three 10% tests to be considered a reportable segment, Corey Corp. has five reportable segments.

11. (590,T1,36) (c) Per SFAS 14, para 15, a segment is considered reportable if it is significant. A segment is significant if it satisfies at least <u>one</u> of the three 10% tests:

1. <u>Revenue</u> is 10% or more of the combined segment revenue (including intersegment revenue).

2. <u>Operating profit</u> (loss) is 10% or more of the greater of the <u>absolute</u> combined segment profit or loss.
3. <u>Identifiable assets</u> are 10% or more of the combined identifiable assets.

Therefore, answer (c) is correct.

RATIO ANALYSIS

Multiple Choice Questions (1-24)

Items 1 and 2 are based on the following:

Rey, Inc.
Selected Financial Data
December 31,

	1988	1987
Cash	$ 170,000	$ 90,000
Accounts receivable (net)	450,000	400,000
Merchandise inventory	540,000	420,000
Short-term marketable securities	80,000	40,000
Land and building (net)	1,000,000	1,000,000
Mortgage payable-- current portion	60,000	50,000
Accounts payable and accrued liabilities	240,000	220,000
Short-term notes payable	100,000	140,000

Net credit sales totaled $3,000,000 and $2,000,000 for the years ended December 31, 1988 and 1987, respectively.

1.   At December 31, 1988, Rey's quick (acid test) ratio was
   a.   1.50 to 1.
   b.   1.75 to 1.
   c.   2.06 to 1.
   d.   3.10 to 1.

2.   For 1988, Rey's accounts receivable turnover was
   a.   1.13
   b.   1.50
   c.   6.67
   d.   7.06

3.   Which of the following ratios is(are) useful in assessing a company's ability to meet currently maturing or short-term obligations?

	Acid-test ratio	Debt to equity ratio
a.	No	No
b.	No	Yes
c.	Yes	Yes
d.	Yes	No

4.   How are trade receivables used in the calculation of each of the following?

	Acid test (quick) ratio	Receivable turnover
a.	Denominator	Denominator
b.	Not used	Numerator
c.	Numerator	Numerator
d.	Numerator	Denominator

5.   If current assets exceed current liabilities, payments to creditors made on the last day of the month will
   a.   Decrease current ratio.
   b.   Increase current ratio.
   c.   Decrease net working capital.
   d.   Increase net working capital.

6.   Lind Corp. declared a cash dividend of $50,000 on March 10, 1989 to stockholders of record March 25, 1989 payable on April 5, 1989. As a result of this cash dividend, working capital
   a.   Decreased on March 10 by $50,000.
   b.   Decreased on March 25 by $50,000.
   c.   Decreased on April 5 by $50,000.
   d.   Did not change.

7.   Which of the following ratios measures short-term solvency?
   a.   Current ratio.
   b.   Age of receivables.
   c.   Creditors' equity to total assets.
   d.   Return on investment.

8.   Selected information for Cain Corp. for the year ended December 31, 1987 follows:

Average days' sales in inventories   124
Average days' sales in accounts
   receivable   48

The average number of days in the operating cycle for 1987 was
   a.   172
   b.   124
   c.   86
   d.   76

9.   During 1985, Dunn Company purchased $1,920,000 of inventory. The cost of goods sold for 1985 was $1,800,000 and the ending inventory at December 31, 1985 was $360,000. What was the inventory turnover for 1985?
   a.   5.0
   b.   5.3
   c.   6.0
   d.   6.4

10.   Utica Company's net accounts receivable were $250,000 at December 31, 1988, and $300,000 at December 31, 1989. Net cash sales for 1989 were $100,000. The accounts receivable turnover for 1989 was 5.0. What were Utica's total net sales for 1989?
   a. $1,475,000
   b. $1,500,000
   c. $1,600,000
   d. $2,750,000

11. How are each of the following used in the calculation of the receivable turnover?

	Cash sales	Credit sales
a.	Not used	Numerator
b.	Not used	Denominator
c.	Numerator	Numerator
d.	Denominator	Denominator

12. How is the average inventory used in the calculation of each of the following?

	Acid test (quick ratio)	Inventory turnover rate
a	Not used	Denominator
b.	Not used	Numerator
c.	Numerator	Numerator
d.	Numerator	Denominator

13. Which of the following ratios should be used in evaluating the effectiveness with which the company uses its assets?

	Receivables turnover	Dividend payout ratio
a.	Yes	Yes
b.	No	No
c.	Yes	No
d.	No	Yes

Items 14 and 15 are based on the following information:

Apex Corporation
Selected Financial Data
Year Ended December 31, 1985

Operating income	$900,000
Interest expense	100,000
Income before income tax	800,000
Income tax expense	320,000
Net income	480,000
Preferred stock dividends	200,000
Net income available to common stockholders	$280,000
Common stock dividends	$120,000

14. The times interest earned ratio is
   a. 2.8 to 1.
   b. 4.8 to 1.
   c. 8.0 to 1.
   d. 9.0 to 1.

15. The times preferred dividend earned ratio is
   a. 1.4 to 1.
   b. 1.7 to 1.
   c. 2.4 to 1.
   d. 4.0 to 1.

Items 16 and 17 are based on the following data:

Frey, Inc. was organized on January 2, 1984 with the following capital structure:

10% cumulative preferred stock, par value $100 and liquidation value $105; authorized, issued and outstanding 1,000 shares	$100,000
Common stock, par value $25; authorized 100,000 shares; issued and outstanding 10,000 shares	$250,000

Frey's net income for the year ended December 31, 1984, was $450,000, but no dividends were declared.

16. How much was Frey's book value per preferred share at December 31, 1984?
   a. $100
   b. $105
   c. $110
   d. $115

17. How much was Frey's book value per common share at December 31, 1984?
   a. $45.00
   b. $68.50
   c. $69.50
   d. $70.00

18. Selected information for Moore Corporation is as follows:

	December 31	
	1982	1983
Preferred stock	$180,000	$180,000
Common stock	648,000	840,000
Retained earnings	192,000	360,000
Net income for year ended	144,000	240,000

What is Moore's rate of return on average stockholders' equity for 1983?
   a. 16.0%
   b. 20.0%
   c. 23.5%
   d. 26.0%

19. Which of the following ratios are useful for evaluating the effectiveness with which the company uses its assets?

	Acid test (quick) ratio	Price earnings ratio
a.	Yes	Yes
b.	Yes	No
c.	No	No
d.	No	Yes

20. How are dividends per share for common
stock used in the calculation of the
following?

		Dividend per-share payout ratio	Earnings per share
a.		Numerator	Numerator
b.		Numerator	Not used
c.		Denominator	Not used
d.		Denominator	Denominator

21. On December 31, 1985 and 1986, Taft
Corporation had 100,000 shares of common stock
and 50,000 shares of noncumulative and
nonconvertible preferred stock issued and
outstanding. Additional information is as
follows:

Stockholders' equity at 12/31/86	$4,500,000
Net income year ended 12/31/86	1,200,000
Dividends on preferred stock year ended 12/31/86	300,000
Market price per share of common stock at 12/31/86	72

The price-earnings ratio on common stock at
December 31, 1986 was
  a. 5 to 1.
  b. 6 to 1.
  c. 8 to 1.
  d. 9 to 1.

22. Selected information for Irvington
Company is as follows:

	December 31	
	1988	1989
Preferred stock, 8%, par $100, nonconvertible, noncumulative	$125,000	$125,000
Common stock	300,000	400,000
Retained earnings	75,000	185,000
Dividends paid on preferred stock for year ended	10,000	10,000
Net income for year ended	60,000	120,000

Irvington's return on common stockholders'
equity, rounded to the nearest percentage
point, for 1989 is
  a. 17%
  b. 19%
  c. 23%
  d. 25%

23. Which of the following is an appropriate
computation for return on investment?
  a. Income divided by total assets.
  b. Income divided by sales.
  c. Sales divided by total assets.
  d. Sales divided by stockholders'
      equity.

May 1990 Question

24. How is the average inventory used in the
calculation of each of the following?

		Acid test (quick ratio)	Inventory turnover rate
a.		Numerator	Numerator
b.		Numerator	Denominator
c.		Not used	Denominator
d.		Not used	Numerator

Repeat Question

(590,Q3,55) Identical/similar to item 14 above

RATIO ANALYSIS

Multiple Choice Answers

1. b	6. a	11. a	16. d	21. c
2. d	7. a	12. a	17. b	22. c
3. d	8. a	13. c	18. b	23. a
4. d	9. c	14. d	19. c	24. c
5. b	10. a	15. c	20. b	

Multiple Choice Answer Explanations

D.1. Solvency

1.   (589,Q1,14) (b) The quick (acid-test) ratio is quick assets (cash, temporary investments in marketable equity securities, and net receivables) divided by current liabilities. The quick ratio measures the ability to pay current liabilities from cash and near-cash items. In this case, quick assets total $700,000 ($170,000 + $450,000 + $80,000) and current liabilities total $400,000 ($60,000 + $240,000 + $100,000), resulting in a quick ratio of 1.75 to 1 ($700,000 ÷ $400,000).

2.   (589,Q1,15) (d) The formula to compute accounts receivable turnover is:

$$\frac{\text{Net credit sales}}{\text{Average accounts receivable}}$$

The average receivable is the sum of the beginning and ending net accounts receivable divided by two. The 1988 beginning accounts receivable equals the 1987 ending balance in accounts receivable. Average accounts receivable is $425,000 [($450,000 + $400,000) ÷ 2]. Applying the formula, the 1988 accounts receivable turnover is 7.06 times ($3,000,000 ÷ $425,000).

3.   (589,T1,37) (d) Ratios which are useful in assessing a company's ability to meet currently maturing or short-term obligations are referred to as solvency ratios. The acid-test ratio is classified as a solvency ratio, and it measures the ability to pay current liabilities from cash and near-cash items. The acid-test ratio is:

$$\frac{\text{Cash, Net Receivables, Marketable Securities}}{\text{Current Liabilities}}$$

The debt to equity ratio is a leverage ratio which measures the relative amount of leverage or debt a company has. The debt to equity ratio is:

$$\frac{\text{Total Liabilities}}{\text{Common Stockholders' Equity}}$$

Therefore, answer (d) is correct because the acid-test ratio is useful in assessing a company's ability to meet currently maturing or short-term obligations while the debt to equity ratio is not.

4.   (1187,T1,38) (d) The formula for the acid test (quick) ratio is:

$$\frac{\text{(Cash + Net receivables + Marketable securities)}}{\text{Current liabilities}}$$

and the formula for the receivable turnover ratio is:

$$\frac{\text{Net credit sales}}{\text{Average net receivables}}$$

Therefore, net receivables is used in the numerator for the acid test ratio and in the denominator for the receivable turnover ratio, and answer (d) is correct.

5.   (580,T1,1) (b) Payments to creditors will decrease both cash (current asset) and payables (current liability). Therefore, both answers (c) and (d) are incorrect because there is no effect on net working capital. If current assets exceed current liabilities prior to this payment, the current ratio is greater than one. Subtracting equal amounts from both the numerator and the denominator of a fraction which is greater than one will increase the fraction. Note that such a payment in cases where the current ratio is less than one will decrease the ratio.

6.   (589,Q1,2) (a) Lind Corporation makes the following entry to record the dividend on the declaration date (March 10, 1989):

| Dividends declared | 50,000 | |
| Dividends payable | | 50,000 |

No entry is made on the date of record (March 25, 1989). When the dividends are paid on April 5, 1989, Lind makes the following entry:

| Dividends payable | 50,000 | |
| Cash | | 50,000 |

Working capital equals current assets minus current liabilities. On March 10, current liabilities (dividends payable) increased by $50,000, thereby reducing working capital by $50,000. On April 5, both a current asset (cash) and a current liability are decreased by the same amount ($50,000), and this therefore has no effect on total working capital.

7.   (580,T1,50) (a) Age of receivables is an activity ratio (measures how effectively assets are used). Return on investment is a profitability ratio. Both the current ratio

and creditors' equity to total assets measure
solvency, but the latter is geared more to
long-term creditors.

D.2. Operational Efficiency

8. (588,P3,57) (a) The average number of
days in the operating cycle measures the
length of time from purchase of inventory to
collection of cash. The formula is:

$$\left(\begin{array}{c}\text{Average days' sales}\\\text{in inventories}\end{array}\right) + \left(\begin{array}{c}\text{Average days' sales}\\\text{in accts. receivable}\end{array}\right) = \left(\begin{array}{c}\text{Average days in}\\\text{operating cycle}\end{array}\right)$$

$$124 \text{ days} \quad + \quad 48 \text{ days} \quad = \quad \underline{172 \text{ days}}$$

Note that the average days' sales in
inventories measures the number of days from
the purchase of inventory to the sale of
inventory, while the average days' sales in
accounts receivable measures the number of
days from the sale of inventory to the
collection of cash.

9. (1186,P3,59) (c) The requirement is the
inventory turnover for 1985. The formula for
inventory turnover is:

$$\frac{\text{Cost of goods sold}}{\text{Average inventory}}$$

Average inventory is equal to beginning inventory plus ending inventory, divided by 2.
Since beginning inventory is not given, it
must be computed using the cost of goods sold
relationship:

Cost of goods sold	$1,800,000
+ Ending inventory	360,000
Cost of goods available	
for sale	$2,160,000
- Purchases	(1,920,000)
Beginning inventory	$ 240,000

Therefore, average inventory is $300,000
[($240,000 + $360,000) ÷ 2], and inventory
turnover is 6.0 times ($1,800,000 ÷ $300,000).

10. (1180,P1,5) (a) The requirement is
Utica's total net sales for 1979. The amount
of cash sales ($100,000) was given, so only
credit sales must be computed using the
information given on accounts receivable
turnover.

$$\text{A/R turnover} = \frac{\text{Credit Sales}}{\text{Average A/R}}$$

The information given can be inserted into the
above equation:

$$5.0 = \frac{\text{Credit Sales}}{(250,000 + 300,000)/2}$$

Therefore, credit sales are $1,375,000. Total
sales are $100,000 higher, or $1,475,000.

11. (1186,T1,39) (a) Receivable turnover is
calculated using the following formula:

$$\frac{\text{Net credit sales}}{\text{Average net receivables}}$$

Thus, cash sales are not used and credit sales
are used in the numerator. Therefore, answer (a) is correct, and answers (b), (c), and
(d) are incorrect.

12. (586,T1,39) (a) The requirement is to
determine whether average inventory is used in
the calculation of the acid test (quick ratio)
and the inventory turnover rate. The solutions approach is to recall the formulas for
the acid test ratio and inventory turnover
rate. The formula for the acid test ratio is:

$$\frac{\text{Cash + Net receivables + Marketable securities}}{\text{Current liabilities}}$$

The formula for the inventory turnover rate
is:

$$\frac{\text{Cost of goods sold}}{\text{Average inventory}}$$

Thus, average inventory is not used in calculating the acid test ratio and is the
denominator of the inventory turnover rate.
Therefore, answers (b), (c), and (d) are
incorrect.

13. (1189,T1,37) (c) Financial ratios
generally relate to solvency, operational
efficiency/effectiveness, and profitability.
The receivables turnover ratio indicates how
quickly a company collects on its credit
sales; this is a measure of the effectiveness
of a company's credit and collection policies.
The dividend payout ratio, on the other hand,
is an indication of profitability as it compares the amount of cash dividends paid by a
company to its net income. Therefore, answer (c) is correct.

D.3. Leverage (Long-Term Risk)

14. (1186,P3,56) (d) The requirement is the
times interest earned ratio. Times interest
earned, a measure of the company's ability to
pay interest costs, is computed as follows:

$$\frac{\text{Net income + Interest expense + Income taxes}}{\text{Interest expense}}$$

$$\frac{\$480,000 + \$100,000 + \$320,000}{\$100,000} = \underline{9.0 \text{ to } 1}$$

D.4. Profitability

15. (1186,P3,57) (c) The requirement is the
times preferred dividend earned ratio. This
ratio, a measure of the company's ability to
pay preferred dividends, is computed as
follows:

$$\frac{\text{Net income}}{\text{Preferred dividends}} = \frac{\$480,000}{200,000} = \underline{2.4 \text{ to } 1}$$

Note that both interest and income tax expense are excluded from the numerator. This is because preferred shareholders may share in the income of the company only after senior claims to income (i.e., interest expense and taxes) have been satisfied.

16. (585,P1,14) (d) The requirement is to determine the book value per preferred share at 12/31/84. The book value per preferred share is the amount each share would receive if the company were liquidated. For preferred stock, it is equal to the liquidating value (1,000 x $105 = $105,000) plus any dividends in arrears ($100,000 x 10% = $10,000), for a total of $115,000 ($105,000 + $10,000), or $115 per share ($115,000 ÷ 1,000).

17. (585,P1,15) (b) The requirement is to determine the book value per common share at 12/13/84. The book value per common share is the amount each share would receive if the company were liquidated based on amounts reported on the balance sheet. The owners' equity must be allocated first to the preferred stockholders, then to the common stockholders. The amount of owners' equity allocated to the preferred stockholders is equal to the liquidation value (1,000 x $105 = $105,000) plus the cumulative dividends in arrears ($100,000 x 10% = $10,000), for a total of $115,000. Since total owners' equity is $800,000 ($100,000 + $250,000 + $450,000), the owners' equity allocated to the common stockholders is $800,000 less $115,000, or $685,000. Book value per common share is $685,000 divided by 10,000 shares, or $68.50.

18. (584,P3,56) (b) The requirement is the rate of return on average stockholders' equity. The formula for this ratio is:

$$\frac{\text{Net income}}{\text{Average stockholders' equity}}$$

1983 net income is $240,000. Average stockholders' equity for 1983 is computed by adding 12/31/82 and 12/31/83 stockholders' equity and dividing by 2. Stockholders' equity is computed below.

	12/31/82	12/31/83
Preferred stock	$180,000	$ 180,000
Common stock	648,000	840,000
Retained earnings	192,000	360,000
Total	$1,020,000	$1,380,000

Average stockholders' equity is $1,200,000 [($1,020,000 + $1,380,000) ÷ 2]. Therefore, the rate of return on average stockholders' equity is 20%.

$$\frac{\$240,000}{\$1,200,000} = \underline{20\%}$$

19. (588,T1,38) (c) The quick (acid-test) ratio is equal to quick assets (cash, temporary investments in marketable securities and net receivables) divided by current liabilities. The quick ratio measures the ability to pay current liabilities from cash and near-cash assets. The price-earnings ratio is the market price per share of stock divided by earnings per share. The price earnings ratio is a measure of the amount of capital available through stock issuances. Since neither of these ratios would be useful in evaluating the effectiveness with which the company uses its assets, answer (c) is correct. Ratios that would be useful in this evaluation would include inventory turnover, receivable turnover, and asset turnover.

D.5. Common Size Financial Statements

20. (587,T1,40) (b) Answer (b) is correct because dividends per share is used in the numerator of the dividend payout ratio as shown below:

$$\frac{\text{Dividend}}{\text{payout ratio}} = \frac{\text{Dividend per share}}{\text{Earnings per share}}$$

However, dividends per share are not used in the calculation of earnings per share:

$$\frac{\text{Earnings}}{\text{per share}} = \frac{\text{Net income - preferred dividends}}{\text{Weighted-average number of shares outstanding}}$$

Therefore, answers (a), (c), and (d) are incorrect.

D.6. Other

21. (1187,P3,60) (c) The formula for the price-earnings ratio is:

$$\frac{\text{Market price per share of stock}}{\text{Earnings per share}}$$

First, earnings per share (EPS) must be computed. The formula for a simple capital structure is:

$$\frac{\text{Net income - Preferred dividends}}{\text{Weighted-average common shares outstanding}}$$

Therefore, EPS is $9 per share [($1,200,000 - $300,000) ÷ 100,000 shares], and the price-earnings ratio is 8 to 1 ($72 ÷ 9).

22. (1180,P1,7) (c) The requirement is Irvington's return on common stockholders' equity for 1979, which is computed by dividing net income available to common stockholders (net income less preferred dividends) by average common stockholders' equity:

$$\frac{\$120,000 - \$10,000}{(\$375,000 + \$585,000)/2} = 23\%$$

23. (581,T1,30) (a) The requirement is the
appropriate computation for return on investment. The return on investment is the product
of two components: net income as a percentage
of sales and capital turnover as shown below:

$$\text{ROI} = \frac{\text{Net income}}{\text{Sales}} \times \frac{\text{Sales}}{\text{Total assets}}$$

Through a simple algebraic manipulation, the
"sales" in both ratios cancel each other out,
leaving ROI equal to income divided by total
assets. Answer (b) is incorrect because it
only takes into consideration the first component of the return on investment calculation.
Answer (c) is incorrect because it only takes
into consideration the second component of the
return on investment calculation. Answer (d)
is incorrect because stockholders' equity is
equivalent to total assets only if the company
has incurred no liabilities (a highly unlikely
situation), and also because sales do not
appear in the numerator of the ROI computation.

May 1990 Answer

24. (590,T1,38) (c) The acid text (quick
ratio) is equal to quick assets (cash, temporary investments in marketable equity securities, and net receivables) divided by current
liabilities. The inventory turnover rate is
equal to the cost of goods sold divided by
average inventory. Therefore, answer (c) is
correct.

PARTNERSHIP ACCOUNTING

Multiple Choice Questions (1-19)

1. On May 1, 1989, Cobb and Mott formed a partnership and agreed to share profits and losses in the ratio of 3:7, respectively. Cobb contributed a parcel of land that cost him $10,000. Mott contributed $40,000 cash. The land was sold for $18,000 on May 1, 1989 immediately after formation of the partnership. What amount should be recorded in Cobb's capital account on formation of the partnership?
   - a. $18,000
   - b. $17,400
   - c. $15,000
   - d. $10,000

2. At December 31, 1985, Reed and Quinn are partners with capital balances of $40,000 and $20,000, and they share profit and loss in the ratio of 2:1, respectively. On this date Poe invests $17,000 cash for a one fifth interest in the capital and profit of the new partnership. Assuming that goodwill is not recorded, how much should be credited to Poe's capital account on December 31, 1985?
   - a. $12,000
   - b. $15,000
   - c. $15,400
   - d. $17,000

3. On July 1, 1988, a partnership was formed by Johnson and Smith. Johnson contributed cash. Smith, previously a sole proprietor, contributed property other than cash including realty subject to a mortgage, which was assumed by the partnership. Smith's capital account at July 1, 1988 should be recorded at
   - a. Smith's book value of the property at July 1, 1988.
   - b. Smith's book value of the property less the mortgage payable at July 1, 1988.
   - c. The fair value of the property less the mortgage payable at July 1, 1988.
   - d. The fair value of the property at July 1, 1988.

4. Gow and Cubb formed a partnership on March 1, 1989 and contributed the following assets:

	Gow	Cubb
Cash	$80,000	
Equipment (market value)		$50,000

The equipment was subject to a chattel mortgage of $10,000 that was assumed by the partnership. The partners agreed to share profits and losses equally. Cubb's capital account at March 1, 1989 should be
   - a. $40,000
   - b. $45,000
   - c. $50,000
   - d. $60,000

5. The Low and Rhu partnership agreement provides special compensation to Low for managing the business. Low receives a bonus of 15 percent of partnership net income before salary and bonus, and also receives a salary of $45,000. Any remaining profit or loss is to be allocated equally. During 1988, the partnership had net income of $50,000 before the bonus and salary allowance. As a result of these distributions, Rhu's equity in the partnership would
   - a. Increase.
   - b. Not change.
   - c. Decrease the same as Low's.
   - d. Decrease.

6. Fox, Greg, and Howe are partners with average capital balances during 1986 of $120,000, $60,000, and $40,000, respectively. Partners receive 10% interest on their average capital balances. After deducting salaries of $30,000 to Fox and $20,000 to Howe, the residual profit or loss is divided equally. In 1986 the partnership sustained a $33,000 loss before interest and salaries to partners. By what amount should Fox's capital account change?
   - a. $ 7,000 increase.
   - b. $11,000 decrease.
   - c. $35,000 decrease.
   - d. $42,000 increase.

7. The partnership agreement for the partnership of Somer and Primrose provided for interest on each partner's average capital investment. Somer's average capital investment was more than Primrose's average capital investment. Profit in excess of interest was allocated equally. If during the year the partnership had profits in excess of the interest on each partner's average capital investment, the amount of Somer's partnership capital would
   - a. Increase the same as Primrose's.
   - b. Increase more than Primrose's.
   - c. Decrease the same as Primrose's.
   - d. Decrease more than Primrose's.

8. At December 31, 1984, Arno and Dey are partners with capital balances of $80,000 and $40,000, and they share profit and loss in the ratio of 2:1, respectively. On this date West invests $36,000 cash for a one fifth interest

in the capital and profit of the new partnership. The partners agree that the implied
partnership goodwill is to be recorded simultaneously with the admission of West. The
total implied goodwill of the firm is

    a. $ 4,800
    b. $ 6,000
    c. $24,000
    d. $30,000

9.   Blau and Rubi are partners who share
profits and losses in the ratio of 6:4,
respectively. On May 1, 1989, their
respective capital accounts were as follows:

      Blau $60,000
      Rubi   50,000

On that date, Lind was admitted as a partner
with a one third interest in capital and
profits for an investment of $40,000. The new
partnership began with total capital of
$150,000. Immediately after Lind's admission,
Blau's capital should be

    a. $50,000
    b. $54,000
    c. $56,667
    d. $60,000

Items 10 and 11 are based on the
following data:

The following condensed balance sheet is
presented for the partnership of Lever, Polen,
and Quint, who share profits and losses in the
ratio of 4:3:3, respectively:

Cash	$ 90,000
Other assets	830,000
Lever, loan	20,000
	$940,000
Accounts payable	$210,000
Quint, loan	30,000
Lever, capital	310,000
Polen, capital	200,000
Quint, capital	190,000
	$940,000

10.   Assume that the assets and liabilities
are fairly valued on the balance sheet and
that the partnership decides to admit Fahn as
a new partner, with a 20% interest. No goodwill or bonus is to be recorded. How much
should Fahn contribute in cash or other
assets?

    a. $140,000
    b. $142,000
    c. $175,000
    d. $177,500

11.   Assume that instead of admitting a new
partner, the partners decide to liquidate the
partnership. If the other assets are sold for

$700,000, how much of the available cash
should be distributed to Lever?

    a. $230,000
    b. $238,000
    c. $258,000
    d. $310,000

12.   The partnership of Metcalf, Petersen, and
Russell shared profits and losses equally.
When Metcalf withdrew from the partnership,
the partners agreed that there was unrecorded
goodwill in the partnership. Under the bonus
method, the capital balances of Petersen and
Russell were

    a.   Not affected.
    b.   Each reduced by one half of the
        total amount of the unrecorded
        goodwill.
    c.   Each reduced by one third of the
        total amount of the unrecorded
        goodwill.
    d.   Each reduced by one half of
        Metcalf's share of the total amount
        of the unrecorded goodwill.

Items 13 and 14 are based on the following:

On June 30, 1988, the condensed balance sheet
for the partnership of Eddy, Fox, and Grimm,
together with their respective profit and loss
sharing percentages was as follows:

Assets, net of liabilities	$320,000
Eddy, capital (50%)	$160,000
Fox, capital (30%)	96,000
Grimm, capital (20%)	64,000
	$320,000

13.   Eddy decided to retire from the
partnership and by mutual agreement is to be
paid $180,000 out of partnership funds for his
interest. Total goodwill implicit in the
agreement is to be recorded. After Eddy's
retirement, what are the capital balances of
the other partners?

	Fox	Grimm
a.	$ 84,000	$56,000
b.	$102,000	$68,000
c.	$108,000	$72,000
d.	$120,000	$80,000

14.   Assume instead that Eddy remains in the
partnership and that Hamm is admitted as a new
partner with a 25% interest in the capital of
the new partnership for a cash payment of
$140,000. Total goodwill implicit in the
transaction is to be recorded. Immediately
after admission of Hamm, Eddy's capital
account balance should be

    a. $280,000
    b. $210,000

c. $160,000
d. $140,000

15. On June 30, 1981, the balance sheet for
the partnership of Coll, Maduro, and Prieto,
together with their respective profit and loss
ratios, were as follows:

Assets, at cost	$180,000
Coll, loan	$ 9,000
Coll, capital (20%)	42,000
Maduro, capital (20%)	39,000
Prieto, capital (60%)	90,000
Total	$180,000

Coll has decided to retire from the partnership. By mutual agreement, the assets are to
be adjusted to their fair value of $216,000 at
June 30, 1981. It was agreed that the partnership would pay Coll $61,200 cash for Coll's
partnership interest, including Coll's loan
which is to be repaid in full. No goodwill is
to be recorded. After Coll's retirement, what
is the balance of Maduro's capital account?
   a. $36,450
   b. $39,000
   c. $45,450
   d. $46,200

16. When Dubke retired from the partnership
of Dubke, Logan, and Flaherty, the final
settlement of Dubke's partnership interest
exceeded Dubke's capital balance. Under the
bonus method, the excess
   a.   Was recorded as goodwill.
   b.   Was recorded as an expense.
   c.   Has no effect on the capital
        balances of Logan and Flaharty.
   d.   Reduced the capital balances of
        Logan and Flaherty.

17. On January 1, 1987, the partners of Cobb,
Davis, and Eddy, who share profits and losses
in the ratio of 5:3:2, respectively, decided
to liquidate their partnership. On this date
the partnership condensed balance sheet was as
follows:

Assets

Cash	$ 50,000
Other assets	250,000
	$300,000

Liabilities and Capital

Liabilities	$ 60,000
Cobb, capital	80,000
Davis, capital	90,000
Eddy, capital	70,000
	$300,000

On January 15, 1987, the first cash sale of
other assets with a carrying amount of
$150,000 realized $120,000. Safe installment
payments to the partners were made the same
date. How much cash should be distributed to
each partner?

	Cobb	Davis	Eddy
a.	$15,000	$51,000	$44,000
b.	$40,000	$45,000	$35,000
c.	$55,000	$33,000	$22,000
d.	$60,000	$36,000	$24,000

18. The December 31, 1988 condensed balance
sheet of Mason & Gross, a partnership,
follows:

Current assets	$125,000
Equipment (net)	15,000
Total assets	$140,000
Liabilities	$ 10,000
Mason, Capital	80,000
Gross, Capital	50,000
Total liabilities and capital	$140,000

Market values at December 31, 1988 are as
follows:

Current assets	$90,000
Equipment	30,000
Liabilities	10,000

On January 2, 1989, the partnership was
incorporated and 1,000 shares of $5 par value
common stock were issued. What amount should
be credited to additional contributed capital?
   a. $0
   b. $105,000
   c. $125,000
   d. $135,000

May 1990 Question

19. Allen retired from the partnership of
Allen, Beck, and Chale. Allen's cash settlement from the partnership was based on new
goodwill determined at the date of retirement
plus the carrying amount of the other net
assets. As a consequence of the settlement,
the capital accounts of Beck and Chale were
decreased. In accounting for Allen's withdrawal, the partnership could have used the

	Bonus method	Goodwill method
a.	No	Yes
b.	No	No
c.	Yes	Yes
d.	Yes	No

PARTNERSHIP ACCOUNTING

Multiple Choice Answers

1. a	5. d	9. b	13. c	17. a
2. c	6. a	10. c	14. b	18. b
3. c	7. b	11. b	15. c	19. d
4. a	8. c	12. d	16. d	

Multiple Choice Answer Explanations

E.1. Partnership Formation

1.   (589,Q1,9) (a) Property other than
cash that is part of the initial investment in
a partnership should be measured at the fair
market value of the assets on the date contributed. This is done to properly reflect the
value of the assets contributed to the partnership. The fair market value of the land
equals $18,000, the amount it was sold for on
May 1 (which was also the date the land was
contributed to the partnership).

2. (1186,P3,36) (c) The requirement is to
determine the amount to be credited to Poe's
capital account, assuming goodwill is not
recorded upon his admission to the partnership. If goodwill is not recorded, the bonus
method is used to record the transaction. Poe
receives credit for a 1/5 interest in the
total partnership equity of $77,000 ($40,000 +
$20,000 + $17,000). Therefore, his capital
account is credited for $15,400 (1/5 x
$77,000). The difference between his cash
contribution ($17,000) and his capital credit
($15,400) is the bonus to the old partners and
is credited to their capital accounts, as indicated in the entry below:

Cash	17,000	
Poe, capital		15,400
Reed, capital		
(1,600 x 2/3)		1,067
Quinn, capital		
(1,600 x 1/3)		533

3. (1189,T1,24) (c) All assets contributed
to a partnership are recorded by the partnership at their fair market values. Additionally, all liabilities assumed by the
partnership are recorded at their present
values. The amount credited to the partner's
capital account is the difference between the
fair value of the assets contributed and the
present value of the liabilities assumed from
that partner. Therefore, answer (c) is
correct, and answers (a), (b), and (d) are
incorrect.

E.2. Allocation of Partnership Income (Loss)

4. (1189,Q1,17) (a) The requirement is to
determine the balance in Cubb's capital ac-

count at the formation date of the partnership, March 1, 1989. Unless otherwise agreed
upon by the partners, individual capital accounts should be credited for the fair market
value (on the date of contribution) of the net
assets contributed by that partner. The fair
market value of the net assets that Cubb contributed is $40,000 (50,000 - 10,000). There-
fore, answer (a) is correct.

5.   (589,T1,12) (d) The distribution of the
partnership net income of $50,000 occurs in
three steps.
      First, the bonus of 15% of partnership
net income before salary and bonus is distributed to Low. The bonus will be $7,500
($50,000 x 15%).
      Second, Low's salary of $45,000 is dis-
tributed. These distributions result in a
deficit of $2,500 ($50,000 - $7,500 -
$45,000).
      Third, any remaining profit or loss (in
this case a loss of $2,500) is distributed
equally. The allocation of the $50,000 net
income results in a $51,250 increase in capi-
tal for Low ($7,500 bonus + $45,000 salary -
$1,250 which is one half of the deficit) and a
$1,250 decrease in capital for Rhu (equal to
one half of the $2,500 deficit). Therefore,
answer (d) is correct.

6.   (587,P2,40) (a) When dividing the
partnership loss of $33,000, first interest
and salaries are allocated to the partners,
increasing their capital balances. This
allocation of interest and salaries will also
increase the amount of loss. This increased
loss amount would then be allocated to the
partners, decreasing their capital accounts.
The computations are shown below:

	Fox	Grey	Howe
Interest allow-			
ance (10% of			
avg. cap.			
balances)	$12,000	$ 6,000	$ 4,000
Salaries	30,000		20,000
Residual*			
($105,000 ÷ 3)	(35,000)	(35,000)	(35,000)
Increase (de-			
crease) in cap.			
account	$ 7,000	$(29,000)	$(11,000)

Thus, answer (a) is correct; Fox's account
increases by $7,000.

*The residual loss of $105,000 is the loss
resulting after the interest and salary
allowances are deducted [$33,000 loss -
($12,000 + $6,000 + $4,000) - ($30,000 +
$20,000)].

7. (1187,T1,13) (b) Interest earned on a
partner's capital investment and allocated
excess profits both increase a partner's

capital account. Since Somer's average capital is greater than Primrose's, the interest earned by Somer will be greater than the interest earned by Primrose. Excess profits are allocated to each partner equally, and accordingly the excess profit credited to each account will be the same. Therefore, Somer's partnership capital would increase more than Primrose's due to the greater amount of interest earned by Somer. Therefore, answer (b) is correct.

E.3.a.1. Admission of a New Partner

8. (585,P2,26) (c) The requirement is to determine the amount of goodwill implied by West's investment. West is investing $36,000 for a 1/5 interest in the partnership. Therefore, $36,000 represents 1/5 of the value of the equity of the new partnership ($36,000 ÷ 1/5 = $180,000). The tangible portion of the equity is $156,000 ($80,000 + $40,000 + $36,000). Thus, the total implied goodwill is $24,000 ($180,000 - $156,000).

9. (1189,Q1,19) (b) The requirement is the balances in the capital accounts of a partnership after the admission of a new partner. In this case, the new partner is investing $40,000 for a 1/3 interest in the new total capital of $150,000. No goodwill is recorded because the new capital ($150,000) equals the total of the old capital ($110,000) and Carter's investment ($40,000). However, a bonus of $10,000 is being credited to the new partner's capital account because his interest (1/3 of $150,000, or $50,000) exceeds his investment ($40,000). The bonus to the new partner is charged to the old partners in their profit and loss ratios as shown below:

Blau [60,000 - 3/5 (10,000)]	$54,000
Rubi [50,000 - 2/5 (10,000)]	46,000
Lind (150,000 ÷ 3)	50,000
	$150,000

10. (1185,Q1,10) (c) The requirement is to determine the amount to be contributed by a new partner in a partnership where no goodwill or bonus is to be recorded. The formula to determine the necessary contribution is:

$$\text{Partnership interest of new partners} \times \left(\begin{array}{c} \text{Capital bal.} \\ \text{of existing} \\ \text{partners} \end{array} + \begin{array}{c} \text{Amount} \\ \text{to be} \\ \text{contributed} \end{array} \right) = \begin{array}{c} \text{Amount} \\ \text{to be} \\ \text{contributed} \end{array}$$

In this case the formula is applied as follows:

$$20\% \times (\$700,000 + x) = x$$
$$\$140,000 + .2x = x$$
$$\$140,000 = .8x$$
$$\$175,000 = x$$

11. (1185,Q1,11) (b) The requirement is to determine the amount of cash to be distributed upon the liquidation of a partnership. The solutions approach is to prepare an abbreviated statement of partnership liquidation. Recall that in a partnership liquidation, cash is distributed based on the capital balances of the partners __after__ adjusting them for any income (loss) to the date of liquidation, including the sale of partnership assets, and any loans or advances between the partnership and one or more of the partners. The abbreviated statement follows:

	Lever	Polen	Quint	Total
Beg. capital bal.	$310,000	$200,000	$190,000	$700,000
Adj. for loans	(20,000)	-	30,000	10,000
Adj. for loss on sale of other assets*	(52,000)	(39,000)	(39,000)	(130,000)
Adj. capital bal.	$238,000	$161,000	$181,000	$580,000

*($830,000 - $700,000)

Note that the payment of the partnership's liabilities to outside creditors does not affect the abbreviated statement of liquidation as only equity related items are shown and there was sufficient cash to cover all liabilities. The total adjusted capital balances is reconciled to total cash available as follows: $90,000 original cash balance + $700,000 from asset sale - $210,000 liabilities to creditors = $580,000.

12. (1188,T1,21) (d) When the bonus method is used to account for the withdrawal of a partner from a partnership with unrecorded goodwill, the withdrawing partner's (Metcalf's) capital balance is removed from the books and the remaining partners' (Peterson's and Russell's) capital accounts are reduced by the withdrawing partner's share of the partnership's total unrecorded goodwill in relation to their respective profit-loss ratios. Since the partners agreed to share profits and losses equally, remaining partners' capital accounts will each be reduced by one half of the withdrawing partner's share of the partnership's unrecorded goodwill. Therefore, answer (d) is correct, and answers (a), (b), and (c) are incorrect.

E.3.a.2. Partner Death or Withdrawal

13. (1188,P2,26) (c) Eddy is to be paid $180,000 for his 50% interest in the partnership. This implies that the net assets of the partnership are worth $360,000 ($180,000 ÷ 50%). Since the net assets are currently reported at $320,000, implied goodwill is $40,000 ($360,000 - $320,000). When goodwill is recorded, the goodwill account is debited and the partners' capital accounts are credited for their share of the goodwill.

Therefore, the capital balances of Fox and Grimm are $108,000 and $72,000, as computed below.

	Fox	Grimm
Previous capital balance	$96,000	$64,000
Share of goodwill		
Fox (30% x $40,000)	12,000	
Grimm (20% x $40,000)		8,000
New capital balance	$108,000	$72,000

14. (1188,P2,27) (b) Hamm will pay $140,000 for a 25% interest in the partnership. This implies that the net assets of the partnership, including the new investment, are worth $560,000 ($140,000 ÷ 25%). Net assets are currently reported at $320,000, and Hamm's cash payment of $140,000 brings that total up to $460,000. Therefore, implied goodwill is $100,000 [$560,000 − ($320,000 + $140,000)]. When goodwill is recorded, the goodwill account is debited and the partners' capital accounts are credited for their share of goodwill. Therefore, Eddy's capital balance ($160,000) is increased by his share of the goodwill (50% x $100,000 = $50,000), to result in a balance of $210,000 ($160,000 + $50,000).

15. (1181,Q2,25) (c) The requirement is the balance in Maduro's capital account after Coll's retirement. When a partner withdraws from a partnership a determination of the fair market value of the entity must be made. Since it is stated in the problem that the withdrawing partner is selling his interest to the partnership and that no goodwill is to be recorded, the bonus method must be employed after restatement of assets to FMV. The capital accounts after restatement to FMV would be:

Coll
  [$42,000 + 20%($216,000 − $180,000)] = $ 49,200
Maduro
  [$39,000 + 20%($216,000 − $180,000)] = $ 46,200
Prieto
  [$90,000 + 60%($216,000 − $180,000)] = $111,600

The bonus paid to Coll is the difference between the cash paid to him for his partnership interest and the balance of that interest plus his loan balance:

Bonus = [$61,200 − ($49,200 + $9,000)] = $3,000

Maduro's capital account would be reduced by his proportionate share of the bonus, based on the profit and loss ratio of the remaining partners [20%/(20% + 60%) = 25%].

Maduro's capital [$46,200 − 25% ($3,000)] = $45,450.

16. (587,T1,35) (d) Answer (d) is correct because under the bonus method, adjustments are made only between partner's capital accounts (no goodwill is recorded on the partnership books). Since Dubke's partnership interest exceeded the amount of Dubke's capital balance, the excess interest would reduce the capital balances of the remaining partners, Logan and Flaherty. Answer (a) is incorrect because only under the goodwill method can the excess interest be recorded as goodwill. Answer (b) is incorrect because under no circumstances should the excess partnership interest be recorded as an expense. Answer (c) is incorrect because the capital balances of the remaining partners were affected.

E.4. Partnership Liquidation

17. (587,P2,33) (a) A schedule of safe payments must be prepared to determine the amount of cash to be distributed to each partner at January 15, 1987. The first cash sale of other assets with a total book value of $150,000 realized $120,000 in cash, resulting in a $30,000 loss. This loss is allocated among the partners based upon their profit and loss ratios. The schedule is completed based upon the assumption that the remaining other assets are totally worthless, and their book values are distributed to the partners as losses, based upon the partners' profit and loss ratios. The cash payments to each partner can be found at the bottom of the schedule.

	Cash	O.A.	Liab.
Beginning	$ 50	$250	$ 60
Sale of Assets	+120	−150	
	170	100	60
Dist. to creditors	−60		−60
	110	100	−0−
Disposal of other assets		−100	
Dist. to partners	−110		
	−0−	−0−	−0−

	Capital		
	C	D	E
Beginning	$ 80,000	$ 90,000	$ 70,000
Sale of Assets	−15,000	− 9,000	− 6,000
	65,000	81,000	64,000
Disposal of other assets	−50,000	−30,000	−20,000
	15,000	51,000	44,000
Dist. to partners	−15,000	−51,000	−44,000
	−0−	−0−	−0−

Thus, the cash should be distributed as follows: $15,000 to Cobb, $51,000 to Davis, and $44,000 to Eddy.

E.5. Incorporation of a Partnership

18. (1189,Q1,18) (b) When a partnership incorporates, assets and liabilities must be revalued to their fair market values on the date of incorporation. In this case, the assets will have a fair market value of $120,000 (90,000 + 30,000), and the liabilities will have a fair market value of 10,000. The stockholders' equity of the new corporation will be $110,000 (120,000 - 10,000), and the journal entry to create this new corporation will be:

Current assets	90,000	
Equipment	30,000	
Liabilities		10,000
Common Stock ($5 x 1000)		5,000
Add. contributed capital (110,000 - 5,000)		105,000

May 1990 Answer

19. (590,T1,17) (d) Under both the bonus and goodwill methods, the assets of the partnership must first be restated to their fair market value. Then, the withdrawing partner's capital account must be adjusted to the amount that the withdrawing partner is expected to receive. When the bonus method is used, no new goodwill is recorded. Instead, the existing partners' capital accounts are reduced by the amount necessary to increase the withdrawing partner's capital to the amount s/he is to be paid. When the goodwill method is used, new goodwill is recorded, and each partner's capital account is increased accordingly. Therefore, answer (d) is correct since the bonus method results in a **decrease** of existing partners' capital accounts, while the goodwill method results in an **increase** of existing partners' capital accounts.

CHAPTER FIVE
COST ACCOUNTING

Cost accounting questions appear with regularity on both the practice and theory sections. In both practice and theory, you may expect either a series of multiple choice questions or a cost essay question (theory)/cost practice problem (practice). A complete analysis of recent examinations and the *Revised AICPA Content Specification Outlines* appear in Volume I, *Outlines and Study Guides*.

Each question is coded as to month, year, section, problem number, and multiple choice question number. For example, (1189,T1,27) indicates November 1989, Theory problem 1, and multiple choice question 27. Note that P = Practice I, Q = Practice II, and T = Theory.

Module 34/Costing Systems (COST)

	Exam reference	No. of minutes	Page no. Problem	Page no. Answer
52 Multiple Choice			825	833
2 Practice Problems:				
1. Cost of Goods Manufactured	584,Q4a	25-30	832	842
2. Weighted-Average and Standard				
Process Costing	1187,Q4	45-55	832	843

Module 35/Planning, Control, and Analysis (PLAN)

	Exam reference	No. of minutes	Page no. Problem	Page no. Answer
59 Multiple Choice			846	855
3 Practice Problems:				
1. C-V-P Analyses	588,Q5	40-50	853	865
2. Cash Budget	585,Q4	45-55	853	868
3. Budgeting and Standard Costs	589,Q5	40-50	854	870

Module 36/Standards and Variances (STAN)

	Exam reference	No. of minutes	Page no. Problem	Page no. Answer
27 Multiple Choice			872	877
1 Practice Problem:				
1. Budgeted Production Costs and				
Variance Analysis	584,Q5	40-50	876	882

Module 37/Nonroutine Decisions (DECI)

	Exam reference	No. of minutes	Page no. Problem	Page no. Answer
36 Multiple Choice			885	891
1 Practice Problem:				
1. Three Unrelated Decisions	1185,Q5	40-50	890	897

Sample Examination

Multiple Choice Questions (1-52)

1.   The following information was taken from Kay Company's accounting records for the year ended December 31, 1986:

Increase in raw materials inventory	$ 15,000
Decrease in finished goods inventory	35,000
Raw materials purchased	430,000
Direct-labor payroll	200,000
Factory overhead	300,000
Freight-out	45,000

There was no work-in-process inventory at the beginning or end of the year. Kay's 1986 cost of goods sold is
   a. $950,000
   b. $965,000
   c. $975,000
   d. $995,000

Items 2 through 4 are based on the following information pertaining to Arp Co.'s manufacturing operations:

Inventories	3/1/89	3/31/89
Direct materials	$36,000	$30,000
Work-in-process	18,000	12,000
Finished goods	54,000	72,000

Additional information for the month of March 1989:

Direct materials purchased	$84,000
Direct labor payroll	60,000
Direct labor rate per hour	7.50
Factory overhead rate per direct labor hour	10.00

2.   For the month of March 1989, prime cost was
   a. $ 90,000
   b. $120,000
   c. $144,000
   d. $150,000

3.   For the month of March 1989, conversion cost was
   a. $ 90,000
   b. $140,000
   c. $144,000
   d. $170,000

4.   For the month of March 1989, cost of goods manufactured was
   a. $218,000
   b. $224,000
   c. $230,000
   d. $236,000

5.   Luna Co.'s 1985 manufacturing costs were as follows:

Direct materials and direct labor	$500,000
Depreciation of manufacturing equipment	70,000
Depreciation of factory building	40,000
Janitor's wages for cleaning factory premises	15,000

How much of these costs should be inventoried for external reporting purposes?
   a. $625,000
   b. $610,000
   c. $585,000
   d. $500,000

Items 6 and 7 are based on the following data:

Blum Corp. manufactures plastic coated metal clips. The following were among Blum's 1984 manufacturing costs:

Wages

Machine operators	$200,000
Maintenance workers	30,000
Factory foreman	90,000

Materials used

Metal wire	$500,000
Lubricant for oiling machinery	10,000
Plastic coating	380,000

6.   Blum's 1984 direct labor amounted to
   a. $200,000
   b. $230,000
   c. $290,000
   d. $320,000

7.   Blum's 1984 direct materials amounted to
   a. $890,000
   b. $880,000
   c. $510,000
   d. $500,000

8.   The fixed portion of the semivariable cost of electricity for a manufacturing plant is a

	Period cost	Product cost
a.	Yes	No
b.	Yes	Yes
c.	No	Yes
d.	No	No

9.   An example of a direct labor cost is wages paid to a

	Factory machine operator	Supervisor in a factory
a.	No	No
b.	No	Yes
c.	Yes	Yes
d.	Yes	No

3
4

10. Direct materials cost is a

	Conversion cost	Prime cost
a.	No	No
b.	No	Yes
c.	Yes	Yes
d.	Yes	No

11. Direct labor cost is a

	Conversion cost	Prime cost
a.	No	No
b.	No	Yes
c.	Yes	Yes
d.	Yes	No

12. Costs are accumulated by responsibility center for control purposes when using

	Job order costing	Process costing
a.	Yes	Yes
b.	Yes	No
c.	No	No
d.	No	Yes

13. Regan Company operates its factory on a two-shift basis and pays a late-shift differential of 15%. Regan also pays a premium of 50% for overtime work. Since Regan manufactures only for stock, the cost system provides for uniform direct-labor hourly charges for production done without regard to shift worked or work done on an overtime basis. Overtime and late-shift differentials are included in Regan's factory overhead application rate. The May 1983 payroll for production workers is as follows:

Wages at base direct-labor rate	$325,000
Shift differentials	25,000
Overtime premiums	10,000

For the month of May 1983, what amount of direct labor should Regan charge to work in process?
   a. $325,000
   b. $335,000
   c. $350,000
   d. $360,000

14. Blackwood uses a job order cost system and applies factory overhead to production orders on the basis of direct-labor cost. The overhead rates for 1982 are 200% for Department A and 50% for Department B. Job 123, started and completed during 1982, was charged with the following costs:

	Department	
	A	B
Direct materials	$25,000	$ 5,000
Direct labor	?	30,000
Factory overhead	40,000	?

The total manufacturing costs associated with Job 123 should be
   a. $135,000
   b. $180,000
   c. $195,000
   d. $240,000

Items 15 and 16 are based on the following information:

Harper Company's Job 501 for the manufacture of 2,200 coats was completed during August 1982 at the following unit costs:

Direct materials	$20
Direct labor	18
Factory overhead (includes an allowance of $1 for spoiled work)	18
	$56

Final inspection of Job 501 disclosed 200 spoiled coats which were sold to a jobber for $6,000.

15. Assume that spoilage loss is charged to all production during August 1982. What would be the unit cost of the good coats produced on Job 501?
   a. $53.00
   b. $55.00
   c. $56.00
   d. $58.60

16. Assume, instead, that the spoilage loss is attributable to exacting specifications of Job 501 and is charged to this specific job. What would be the unit cost of the good coats produced on Job 501?
   a. $55.00
   b. $57.50
   c. $58.60
   d. $61.60

17. Axe Co. has a job order cost system. The following debits (credits) appeared in the work-in-process account for the month of March 1989:

March	Description	Amount
1	Balance	$ 2,000
31	Direct materials	12,000
31	Direct labor	8,000
31	Factory overhead	6,400
31	To finished goods	(24,000)

Axe applies overhead to production at a predetermined rate of 80% based on direct labor cost. Job No. 9, the only job still in process at the end of March 1989, has been charged with direct labor of $1,000. The amount of direct materials charged to Job No. 9 was

   a. $12,000
   b. $ 4,400

c. $ 2,600
d. $ 1,500

18. The completion of goods is recorded as a decrease in work-in-process control when using

	Job order costing	Process costing
a.	Yes	No
b.	Yes	Yes
c.	No	Yes
d.	No	No

19. In a job order cost system, the use of indirect materials previously purchased usually is recorded as a decrease in
   a.   Stores control.
   b.   Work-in-process control.
   c.   Factory overhead control.
   d.   Factory overhead applied.

20. In a job order cost system using predetermined factory overhead rates, indirect materials usually are recorded initially as an increase in
   a.   Work-in-process control.
   b.   Factory overhead applied.
   c.   Factory overhead control.
   d.   Stores control.

21. In a process cost system, the application of factory overhead usually would be recorded as an increase in
   a.   Cost of goods sold.
   b.   Work-in-process control.
   c.   Factory overhead control.
   d.   Finished goods control.

22. Nil Co. uses a predetermined factory overhead application rate based on direct labor cost. For the year ended December 31, 1985, Nil's budgeted factory overhead was $600,000, based on a budgeted volume of 50,000 direct labor hours, at a standard direct labor rate of $6.00 per hour. Actual factory overhead amounted to $620,000, with actual direct labor cost of $325,000. For 1985, overapplied factory overhead was
   a. $20,000
   b. $25,000
   c. $30,000
   d. $50,000

23. In developing a factory overhead application rate for use in a process costing system, which of the following could be used in the denominator?
   a.   Estimated direct labor hours.
   b.   Actual direct labor hours.
   c.   Estimated factory overhead.
   d.   Actual factory overhead.

24. Worley Company has underapplied overhead of $45,000 for the year ended December 31, 1982. Before disposition of the underapplied overhead, selected December 31, 1982, balances from Worley's accounting records are as follows:

Sales	$1,200,000
Cost of goods sold	720,000
Inventories:	
Direct materials	36,000
Work in process	54,000
Finished goods	90,000

Under Worley's cost accounting system, over- or underapplied overhead is allocated to appropriate inventories and cost of goods sold based on year-end balances. In its 1982 income statement, Worley should report cost of goods sold of
   a. $682,500
   b. $684,000
   c. $756,000
   d. $757,500

25. Barnett Company adds materials at the beginning of the process in department M. Conversion costs were 75% complete as to the 8,000 units in work in process at May 1, 1983, and 50% complete as to the 6,000 units in work in process at May 31. During May 12,000 units were completed and transferred to the next department. An analysis of the costs relating to work in process at May 1 and to production activity for May is as follows:

	Costs	
	Materials	Conversion
Work in process, 5/1	$ 9,600	$ 4,800
Costs added in May	15,600	14,400

Using the weighted-average method, the total cost per equivalent unit for May was
   a. $2.47
   b. $2.50
   c. $2.68
   d. $3.16

26. Walden Company has a process cost system using the FIFO cost flow method. All materials are introduced at the beginning of the process in Department One. The following information is available for the month of January 1983:

	Units
Work in process, 1/1/83 (40% complete as to conversion costs)	500
Started in January	2,000
Transferred to Department Two during January	2,100
Work in process, 1/31/83 (25% complete as to conversion costs)	400

What are the equivalent units of production
for the month of January 1983?

	Materials	Conversion
a.	2,500	2,200
b.	2,500	1,900
c.	2,000	2,200
d.	2,000	2,000

27. Information for the month of January 1982
concerning department A, the first stage of
Ogden Corporation's production cycle, is as
follows:

	Materials	Conversion
Work in process, beginning	$ 8,000	$ 6,000
Current costs	40,000	32,000
Total costs	$48,000	$38,000
Equivalent units using weighted-average method	100,000	95,000
Average unit costs	$ 0.48	$ 0.40
Goods completed	90,000 units	
Work in process, end	10,000 units	

Materials are added at the beginning of the
process. The ending work in process is 50%
complete as to conversion costs. How would
the total costs accounted for be distributed,
using the weighted-average method?

	Goods completed	Work in process, end
a.	$79,200	$6,800
b.	$79,200	$8,800
c.	$86,000	$0
d.	$88,000	$6,800

28. The Cutting Department is the first stage
of Mark Company's production cycle. Conversion costs for this department were 80%
complete as to the beginning work in process
and 50% complete as to the ending work in
process. Information as to conversion costs
in the Cutting Department for January 1980 is
as follows:

	Units	Conversion costs
Work in process at January 1, 1980	25,000	$ 22,000
Units started and costs incurred during January	135,000	$143,000
Units completed and transferred to next department during January	100,000	

Using the FIFO method, what was the conversion
cost of the work in process in the Cutting
Department at January 31, 1980?

a. $33,000
b. $38,100
c. $39,000
d. $45,000

29. Glo Co., a manufacturer of combs,
budgeted sales of 125,000 units for the month
of April 1987. The following additional information is provided:

	Number of units
Actual inventory at April 1	
Work in process	None
Finished goods	37,500
Budgeted inventory at April 30	
Work in process (75% processed)	8,000
Finished goods	30,000

How many equivalent units of production did
Glo budget for April 1987?

a.   126,500
b.   125,500
c.   123,500
d.   117,500

30. Dex Co. had the following production for
the month of June:

	Units
Work in process at June 1	10,000
Started during June	40,000
Completed and transferred to finished goods	33,000
Abnormal spoilage incurred	2,000
Work in process at June 30	15,000

Materials are added at the beginning of the
process. As to conversion cost, the beginning
work in process was 70% completed and the
ending work in process was 60% completed.
Spoilage is detected at the end of the process. Using the weighted-average method, the
equivalent units for June, with respect to
conversion cost, were

a.   42,000
b.   44,000
c.   45,000
d.   46,000

31. Spoilage from a manufacturing process was
discovered during an inspection of work in
process. In a process costing system, the
cost of the spoilage would be added to the
cost of the good units produced if the
spoilage is

	Abnormal	Normal
a.	No	Yes
b.	No	No
c.	Yes	Yes
d.	Yes	No

32. In manufacturing its products for the month of March 1989, Elk Co. incurred normal spoilage of $5,000 and abnormal spoilage of $9,000. How much spoilage cost should Elk charge as a period cost for the month of March 1989?
   - a. $0
   - b. $ 5,000
   - c. $ 9,000
   - d. $14,000

33. Kew Co. had 3,000 units in work in process at April 1, 1986, which were 60% complete as to conversion cost. During April, 10,000 units were completed. At April 30, 4,000 units remained in work in process which were 40% complete as to conversion cost. Direct materials are added at the beginning of the process. How many units were started during April?
   - a. 9,000
   - b. 9,800
   - c. 10,000
   - d. 11,000

34. In the computation of manufacturing cost per equivalent unit, the weighted-average method of process costing considers
   - a. Current costs only.
   - b. Current costs plus cost of ending work-in-process inventory.
   - c. Current costs plus cost of beginning work-in-process inventory.
   - d. Current costs less cost of beginning work-in-process inventory.

35. Assuming that there was no beginning work-in-process inventory, and the ending work-in-process inventory is 50% complete as to conversion costs, the number of equivalent units as to conversion costs would be
   - a. The same as the units completed.
   - b. The same as the units placed in process.
   - c. Less than the units completed.
   - d. Less than the units placed in process.

36. When using the first-in first-out method of process costing, total equivalent units of production for a given period of time is equal to the number of units
   - a. In work in process at the beginning of the period times the percent of work necessary to complete the items, plus the number of units started during the period, less the number of units remaining in work in process at the end of the period times the percent of work necessary to complete the items.

   - b. In work in process at the beginning of the period, plus the number of units started during the period, plus the number of units remaining in work in process at the end of the period times the percent of work necessary to complete the items.
   - c. Started into process during the period, plus the number of units in work in process at the beginning of the period.
   - d. Transferred out during the period, plus the number of units remaining in work in process at the end of the period times the percent of work necessary to complete the items.

37. The units transferred in from the first department to the second department should be included in the computation of the equivalent units for the second department for which of the following methods of process costing?

	First-in first-out	Weighted-average
a.	Yes	Yes
b.	Yes	No
c.	No	Yes
d.	No	No

38. Lee Co. produces two joint products, BEX and ROM. Joint production costs for June 1986 were $30,000. During June 1986 further processing costs beyond the split-off point, needed to convert the products into salable form, were $25,000 and $35,000 for 1,600 units of BEX and 800 units of ROM, respectively. BEX sells for $50 per unit, and ROM sells for $100 per unit. Lee uses the net realizable value method for allocating joint product costs. For June 1986, the joint costs allocated to product BEX were
   - a. $20,000
   - b. $16,500
   - c. $13,500
   - d. $10,000

39. Lite Co. manufactures products X and Y from a joint process that also yields a by-product, Z. Revenue from sales of Z is treated as a reduction of joint costs. Additional information is as follows:

	Products			
	X	Y	Z	Total
Units produced	20,000	20,000	10,000	50,000
Joint costs	?	?	?	$262,000
Sales value at split-off	$300,000	$150,000	$10,000	$460,000

Joint costs were allocated using the sales value at split-off approach. The joint costs allocated to product X were
  a. $ 75,000
  b. $100,800
  c. $150,000
  d. $168,000

40.   Lane Co. produces main products Kul and Wu. The process also yields by-product Zef. Net realizable value of by-product Zef is subtracted from joint production cost of Kul and Wu. The following information pertains to production in July 1985 at a joint cost of $54,000:

Product	Units produced	Market value	Additional cost after split-off
Kul	1,000	$40,000	$ 0
Wu	1,500	35,000	0
Zef	500	7,000	3,000

If Lane uses the net realizable value method for allocating joint cost, how much of the joint cost should be allocated to product Kul?
  a. $18,800
  b. $20,000
  c. $26,667
  d. $27,342

41.   Pendall Company manufactures products Dee and Eff from a joint process. Product Dee has been allocated $2,500 of total joint costs of $20,000 for the 1,000 units produced. Dee can be sold at the split-off point for $3 per unit, or it can be processed further with additional costs of $1,000 and sold for $5 per unit. If Dee is processed further and sold, the result would be
  a.   A break-even situation.
  b.   An additional gain of $1,000 from further processing.
  c.   An overall loss of $1,000.
  d.   An additional gain of $2,000 from further processing.

42.   Actual sales values at the split-off point for joint products Y and Z are not known. For purposes of allocating joint costs to products Y and Z, the relative sales value at split-off method is used. An increase in the costs beyond split-off occurs for product Z, while those of product Y remain constant. If the selling prices of finished products Y and Z remain constant, the percentage of the total joint costs allocated to Product Y and Product Z would
  a.   Decrease for Product Y and increase for Product Z.
  b.   Decrease for Product Y and Product Z.
  c.   Increase for Product Y and decrease for Product Z.
  d.   Increase for Product Y and Product Z.

43.   For the purposes of cost accumulation, which of the following are identifiable as different individual products before the split-off point?

	By-products	Joint products
a.	Yes	Yes
b.	Yes	No
c.	No	No
d.	No	Yes

44.   For purposes of allocating joint costs to joint products, the relative sales value at split off method could be used in which of the following situations?

	No costs beyond split-off	Costs beyond split-off
a.	Yes	Yes
b.	Yes	No
c.	No	Yes
d.	No	No

45.   Abel Corp. manufactures a product that yields the by-product, "Yum." The only costs associated with Yum are selling costs of $.10 for each unit sold. Abel accounts for sales of Yum by deducting Yum's separable costs from Yum's sales, and then deducting this net amount from the major product's cost of goods sold. Yum's sales were 100,000 units at $1 each. If Abel changes its method of accounting for Yum's sales of showing the net amount as additional sales revenue, then Abel's gross margin would
  a.   Increase by $ 90,000.
  b.   Increase by $100,000.
  c.   Increase by $110,000.
  d.   Be unaffected.

46.   The sale of scrap from a manufacturing process usually would be recorded as a(an)
  a.   Decrease in factory overhead control.
  b.   Increase in factory overhead control.
  c.   Decrease in finished goods control.
  d.   Increase in finished goods control.

47.   In accounting for by-products, the value of the by-product may be recognized at the time of

	Production	Sale
a.	Yes	Yes
b.	Yes	No
c.	No	No
d.	No	Yes

48. By-products could have which of the following characteristics?

	Zero costs beyond split-off	Additional costs beyond split-off
a.	No	No
b.	No	Yes
c.	Yes	Yes
d.	Yes	No

	P	Q
a.	Increases	Decreases
b.	Increases	Increases
c.	Decreases	Decreases
d.	Decreases	Increases

49. Which of the following is often subject to further processing in order to be salable?

	By-products	Scrap
a.	No	No
b.	No	Yes
c.	Yes	Yes
d.	Yes	No

May 1990 Questions

50. Indirect labor is a
a. Prime cost.
b. Conversion cost.
c. Period cost.
d. Nonmanufacturing cost.

51. In process 2, material G is added when a batch is 60 percent complete. Ending work-in-process units, which are 50 percent complete, would be included in the computation of equivalent units for

	Conversion costs	Material G
a.	Yes	No
b.	No	Yes
c.	No	No
d.	Yes	Yes

52. The diagram below represents the production and sales relationships of joint products P and Q. Joint costs are incurred until split-off, then separable costs are incurred in refining each product. Market values of P and Q at split-off are used to allocate joint costs.

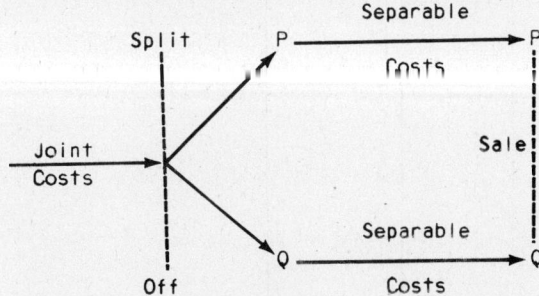

It the market value of P at split-off increases and all other costs and selling prices remain unchanged, then the gross margin of

Problems

Problem 1   (584,Q4a)

(25 to 30 minutes)

Part a. Mat Company's cost of goods sold for the month ended March 31, 1986, was $345,000. Ending work-in-process inventory was 90% of beginning work-in-process inventory. Factory overhead applied was 50% of direct labor cost. Other information pertaining to Mat Company's inventories and production for the month of March is as follows:

Beginning inventories--March 1
Direct materials	$ 20,000
Work in process	40,000
Finished goods	102,000

Purchases of direct materials during March	110,000

Ending inventories--March 31
Direct materials	26,000
Work in process	?
Finished goods	105,000

Required:

1. Prepare a schedule of cost of goods manufactured for the month of March.
2. Prepare a schedule to compute the prime cost incurred during March.
3. Prepare a schedule to compute the conversion cost charged to work in process during March.

Problem 2   (1187,Q4)

(45 to 55 minutes)

Webb & Company is engaged in the preparation of income tax returns for individuals. Webb uses the weighted average method and actual costs for financial reporting purposes. However, for internal reporting, Webb uses a standard cost system. The standards, based on equivalent performance, have been established as follows:

Labor per return	5 hrs. @ $20 per hr.
Overhead per return	5 hrs. @ $10 per hr.

For March 1987 performance, budgeted overhead is $49,000 for the standard labor hours allowed. The following additional information pertains to the month of March 1987:

Inventory data
Returns in process, March 1 (25% complete)	200
Returns started in March	825
Returns in process, March 31 (80% complete)	125

Actual cost data
Returns in process March 1:
Labor	$ 6,000
Overhead	2,500
Labor, March 1 to 31	
4,000 hours	89,000
Overhead, March 1 to 31	45,000

Required:

a. Using the weighted average method, compute the following for each cost element:

(1) Equivalent units of performance.
(2) Actual cost per equivalent unit.

b. Compute the actual cost of returns in process at March 31.
c. Compute the standard cost per return.
d. Prepare a schedule for internal reporting analyzing March performance, using the following variances, and indicating whether these variances are favorable or unfavorable:

(1) Total labor.
(2) Labor rate.
(3) Labor efficiency.
(4) Total overhead.
(5) Overhead volume.
(6) Overhead budget.

NOTE: Requirements c. and d. should be completed after studying Module 36, Standards and Variances. A cross reference from the problem material for Module 36 will refer you back to this requirement later if you don't want to review standard costs and variance analysis at this time.

Multiple Choice Answers

1. a	12. a	23. a	33. d	43. c
2. d	13. a	24. d	34. c	44. a
3. b	14. a	25. c	35. d	45. d
4. d	15. c	26. d	36. a	46. a
5. a	16. b	27. a	37. a	47. a
6. a	17. c	28. c	38. b	48. c
7. b	18. b	29. c	39. d	49. d
8. c	19. a	30. b	40. c	50. b
9. d	20. d	31. a	41. b	51. a
10. b	21. b	32. c	42. c	52. d
11. c	22. c			

Multiple Choice Answer Explanations

A. Cost of Goods Manufactured

1. (1187,P3,42) (a) Three computations must
be performed: raw materials used, cost of
goods manufactured, and cost of goods sold.

(1)	Raw materials purchased	$430,000
	Less: Increase in raw	
	materials inventory	15,000
	Raw materials used	$415,000
(2)	Beginning WIP	$ -0-
	Raw materials used	
	(from above)	415,000
	Direct labor	200,000
	Factory overhead	400,000
	Cost to account for	$915,000
	Less: Ending WIP	-0-
	Cost of goods manufactured	$915,000
(3)	Cost of goods manufactured	$915,000
	Add: Decrease in finished	
	goods inventory	35,000
	Cost of goods sold	$950,000

The increase in raw materials inventory represents the amount of inventory that was purchased but was not used. Therefore, this
increase must be subtracted from raw materials
purchased to determine the amount of raw
materials used. Work-in-process inventory is
an adjustment in arriving at cost of goods
manufactured (as shown above). For this
question no adjustment is necessary because
Kay has no work-in-process inventory. The
decrease in finished goods inventory represents the amount of inventory that was sold in
excess of the inventory manufactured during
the current period. Therefore, this amount
must be added to cost of goods manufactured to
determine cost of goods sold. The freight-out
of $45,000 is irrelevant for this question
because freight-out is a selling expense and
thus, would not be used in computing cost of
goods sold.

2. (1189,Q2,33) (d) Prime cost is the sum
of direct materials and direct labor. Direct
labor is $60,000. Direct materials used must
be computed. The solutions approach is to

enter the information given into the materials
T-account and solve for the unknown:

Direct Materials			
3/1/89 bal.	$36,000		
Purchases	84,000	?	Materials used
3/30/89	$30,000		

Using the T-account above, direct materials
used are easily computed as $90,000. Thus,
prime cost incurred was $150,000 ($90,000 +
$60,000).

3. (1189,Q2,34) (b) Conversion cost is the
sum of direct labor ($60,000, as given) and
applied factory overhead. The factory overhead rate per direct-labor hour is $10.00. To
compute the number of direct-labor hours
worked, the direct-labor payroll ($60,000) is
divided by the direct-labor rate per hour
($7.50), resulting in 8,000 direct-labor
hours. Factory overhead applied is 8,000
hours at $10 per hour, or $80,000. Thus,
conversion cost incurred was $140,000 ($60,000
of direct labor plus $80,000 of applied
factory overhead).

4. (1189,Q2,35) (d) Cost of goods manufactured (CGM) is the cost of goods completed and
transferred to finished goods. It is the sum
of direct materials used, direct labor used,
applied factory overhead, and any adjustment
for work-in-process inventories. Direct labor
used ($60,000) is given. Direct materials
used ($90,000) and applied factory overhead
($80,000) were computed in the answers to the
two previous questions. Beginning work in
process ($18,000) and and ending work in
process ($12,000) are given. Using this data,
CGM can be computed as follows:

BWIP	$ 18,000
DM used	90,000
DL	60,000
OH applied	80,000
Costs to account for	$248,000
EWIP	(12,000)
CGM	$236,000

5. (586,Q2,26) (a) The requirement is the
total amount of cost that should be inventoried for external reporting purposes. In a
manufacturing firm, all product costs are "inventoriable" costs. Product costs are all
costs that can be associated with production
of the product (i.e., "factory costs"). Product costs are inventoried because they are
expensed in the period in which the unit they
relate to is sold. Product costs include
direct materials, direct labor, and factory
(manufacturing) overhead. The $500,000 of
direct materials and direct labor is by def-

inition a product cost. The $70,000 depreciation of manufacturing equipment and $40,000 depreciation of factory building are a part of manufacturing overhead and, therefore, are product costs. The $15,000 of janitor's wages are also a part of manufacturing overhead and, thus, a product cost because the janitor cleans the factory. Therefore, the total amount of costs that should be inventoried are $625,000 ($500,000 + $70,000 + $40,000 + $15,000).

6. (1185,Q1,2) (a) The requirement is the amount of Blum's direct labor cost of 1984. Direct labor includes all labor costs that are directly traceable to the product. Other labor costs necessary for the operation of the factory are considered indirect labor. Maintenance worker labor cost is not direct labor since these workers do not work directly on the product. Factory foremen labor cost is also considered indirect. Although necessary for operation of the factory, foremen do not work directly on the product. The direct labor cost for 1984 is solely the machine operator cost of $200,000.

7. (1185,Q1,3) (b) The requirement is the amount of Blum's direct material cost for 1984. Direct materials includes all materials costs that can be traced to the finished product in an economically feasible manner. Lubricant for oiling machinery may be traceable to the metal clips, but to do so would be the result of great cost to identify the amount of lubricant associated with the production of each metal clip. Unlike lubricant, metal wire and plastic coating end up as physically observable components of the finished product, plastic coated metal clips. Therefore, the direct materials cost consists of the metal wire cost and the plastic coating cost:

$500,000 + $380,000 = $880,000

8. (1188,T1,41) (c) Product costs are costs that can be associated with the production of specific revenues. These costs attach to a physical unit and become expenses in the period in which the unit to which they attach is sold. Product costs include direct labor, direct material, and factory overhead. Period costs, on the other hand, cannot be associated with specific revenues and, therefore, become expenses as time passes. Answer (c) is correct because the cost of electricity for a manufacturing plant, whether fixed or variable, is included in factory overhead and, therefore, is a product cost.

9. (588,T1,41) (d) Direct labor costs include all costs that are directly traceable to the product. All other labor costs which are necessary for the operation of the factory are considered indirect labor. Wages of a factory supervisor would be considered indirect labor, since the supervisor would not be directly involved in production. However, the wages of a factory machine operator are directly traceable to the product, and thus would be considered a direct labor cost. Therefore, the correct answer is (d).

10. (589,T1,41) (b) The requirement is to properly classify direct materials cost. Prime cost includes direct materials and direct labor. Conversion cost is the cost of converting direct materials into a finished product which includes direct labor and manufacturing overhead. The correct answer is (b) because direct materials is included in prime cost but excluded from conversion cost.

11. (1189,T1,41) (c) Prime cost includes direct materials and direct labor. Conversion costs are those costs associated with conversion of direct materials into finished goods. Therefore, conversion costs include direct labor and overhead. The correct answer is (c) because direct labor is both a prime cost and a conversion cost.

B. Cost Flows

12. (1186,T1,42) (a) A responsibility center is any point within an organization where control exists over cost incurrence, revenue generation, and/or the use of investment funds. A responsibility center can be an operation, a department, a division, or even an individual. The key point to note for this question is that no matter what product costing method is used, the responsibility center is always used for control purposes. In job order costing, costs are accumulated by responsibility center and then assigned to specific jobs or orders through the use of a job cost sheet. Even though the job cost sheet will usually reflect the efforts of a number of responsibility centers, it will not be used for control purposes. Any needed cost control will be handled on the responsibility center level. In process costing, costs are accumulated by the responsibility center and recorded on a production cost report which will be used to develop a product's cost. Since the production cost report shows the efforts of only one responsibility center, it is used for both product costing and control purposes. Thus, for control purposes, costs are accumulated by responsibility center for both job order and process costing.

C. Job-Order Costing

13. (1183,P3,43) (a) The requirement is the amount of direct labor to be charged to work in process. The base direct-labor wages, totaling $325,000, should be debited to work in process. The shift differentials ($25,000) and overtime premiums ($10,000) should be charged to factory overhead as incurred. These costs will be spread over production throughout the year via the overhead application rate.

14. (583,P2,32) (a) The requirement is the total manufacturing costs associated with Job 123. The total cost of any manufactured job includes direct materials used, direct labor, and factory overhead applied. In Department A, the overhead rate is 200% of direct labor cost, so direct labor must be $20,000.

DL x 200% = OH applied
DL x 200% = $40,000
     DL = $40,000 ÷ 200% = $20,000

In Department B, the overhead rate is 50%, so overhead applied is 50% of $30,000, or $15,000. The cost of Job 123 totals $135,000:

DM used ($25,000 + $5,000)	$30,000
DL ($20,000 + $30,000)	50,000
OH applied ($40,000 + $15,000)	55,000
Total manufacturing cost of Job 123	$135,000

15. (1182,P2,28) (c) The requirement is the unit cost of good coats produced on Job 501, assuming that spoilage loss is charged to all of August production. Job 501 included 2,200 coats, of which 200 were spoiled and sold as inferior goods for $6,000. Note that factory overhead of $18 per unit includes an allowance of $1 per unit for spoiled work. It is through this allowance that the cost of spoiled goods is "spread" over the entire month's production. Therefore, if this spoilage is to be charged to all production during the month, the cost of good coats in Job 501 would be full unit cost of $56, which includes the normal spoilage allowance. In this case the cost of spoiled units, less the $6,000 proceeds, would be charged to factory overhead.

16. (1182,P2,29) (b) The requirement is the unit cost of good coats produced on Job 501, assuming that the spoilage is attributable to the exacting specifications of Job 501 and is, therefore, charged to this specific job. In this case, since spoilage is a function of specific job requirements rather than general factory conditions, the overhead rate should not include the $1 allowance for spoiled work.

Therefore, the cost of all coats, before adjustment for spoilage, is $55 ($56 - $1). The cost of the 2,000 good coats on Job 501 would be the total cost of all 2,200 coats, less the scrap value of bad coats.

Cost of 2,200 coats (2,200 x $55)	$121,000
Scrap value of bad coats	(6,000)
Net cost of Job 501	$115,000
Cost per good coat ($115,000 ÷ 2,000)	$57.50

Note that the net cost of spoilage [(200 x $55) - $6,000] is charged to the good coats in Job 501. In this case, the net spoilage cost is included in the charge to finished goods along with the cost of good units.

17. (1189,T1,39) (c) Per AICPA Statement of Position 82-1, personal financial statements consist of (1) a statement of financial condition, and (2) a statement of changes in net worth. A statement of cash flows is not required. Therefore, answer (c) is correct.

18. (1188,T1,42) (b) Job order costing systems are used by organizations whose products or services are readily identified by individual units or batches. Each unit or batch receives varying inputs of direct materials, direct labor, and factory overhead. These inputs are accumulated in work-in-process control as they are added to units of production. Upon completion, the accumulated cost of these goods is transferred to finished goods inventory, thus decreasing the work-in-process control account. Process costing systems are used by organizations in order to apply costs to like products that are mass-produced in a continuous fashion through a series of production steps. Costs accumulated in work in process are transferred to finished goods on the basis of costs per equivalent unit, thus decreasing the work-in-process control account. Therefore, answer (b) is correct.

19. (1189,T1,42) (a) Under job order costing, the entry to record the use of indirect materials in production is as follows:

Factory overhead control	XXX	
Stores control		XXX

As shown, the use of indirect materials would result in a decrease in stores control. Therefore, answer (a) is correct. Answer (b) is incorrect because work-in-process control is decreased only when completed units are transferred to finished goods control. Answer (c) is incorrect because factory overhead control is increased when indirect materials are placed into the production process. Answer (d) is incorrect because the account factory overhead applied is not part of the entry to record the use of indirect materials.

20. (1187,T1,41) (d) Indirect materials are initially entered into the accounting system when they are purchased. The usual entry to record the purchase of either direct or indirect materials is a debit to the stores control account and a credit to either accounts payable or cash. Since stores control is increased by this transaction, answer (d) is correct. Answer (a) is incorrect because work-in-process control is increased when direct materials are used. Answer (b) is incorrect because factory overhead applied is increased when a predetermined overhead rate is used to assign overhead to production, and the actual purchase or use of overhead items has no effect on the application of overhead. Answer (c) is incorrect because factory overhead control is increased when indirect materials are used, not purchased.

21. (589,T1,42) (b) The application of factory overhead usually would be recorded as an increase in work-in-process control, as the following entry illustrates:

Work in process   xx
   Factory overhead applied   xx

Answer (a) is incorrect because cost of goods sold would increase when a product is sold. Answer (c) is incorrect because factory overhead control would increase when actual factory overhead costs are incurred. Answer (d) is incorrect because finished goods control would increase when goods are finished and transferred from work in process to finished goods control.

D. Accounting for Overhead

22. (1186,Q2,29) (c) The first step in the solutions approach is to compute the predetermined factory overhead rate.

$$\frac{\text{Predetermined}}{\text{Overhead rate}} = \frac{\text{Est. OH cost}}{\text{Est. DL cost}}$$

Estimated or budgeted factory overhead is given as $600,000. Budgeted direct labor cost is $300,000 (50,000 x $6.00). Thus, the predetermined overhead rate is computed as follows:

$$\frac{\$600,000}{\$300,000} = 200\% \text{ or } \$2 \text{ per DL\$}$$

The next step in the solutions approach is to set up a T-account for factory overhead showing the actual and applied amounts.

Factory Overhead

Actual	Applied	
$620,000	$650,000	(200% x $325,000)
	$ 30,000	overapplied

23. (587,T1,41) (a) An overhead application rate is commonly called a predetermined overhead rate and is computed as follows:

$$\frac{\text{Estimated overhead costs}}{\text{Estimated activity level}} = \text{Predetermined rate}$$

Estimated figures are used because actual figures are not known at the beginning of a period. Therefore, estimated direct labor hours [answer (a)] is correct since this is a commonly used activity base. Answer (b) is incorrect because actual direct labor hours would not be known until the end of the period. Answers (c) and (d) are incorrect because factory overhead would not be used in the denominator.

E. Disposition of Overhead

24. (1183,P3,44) (d) The requirement is the amount of costs of goods sold to be reported on the 1982 income statement. The balance in the cost of goods sold account is $720,000. This amount must be increased by the portion of underapplied overhead allocated to cost of goods sold. The underapplied overhead is appropriately allocated to work in process, finished goods, and cost of goods sold. No overhead is allocated to direct materials inventory, since this account contains only the cost of unused materials. The other three accounts contain the cost of materials, labor, and overhead. The amounts to be allocated to work in process, finished goods, and cost of goods sold are determined by each account's relative balance as compared to the total balance in the accounts. The total balance of the three accounts is $864,000 ($720,000 + $54,000 + $90,000). Therefore, the amount allocable to cost of goods sold is [$720,000/$864,000 x ($45,000)] or $37,500. Since overhead was underapplied, not enough costs were applied to production during the year. Thus, cost of goods sold is increased to $757,500 ($720,000 + $37,500).

F. Process Costing

25. (1183,P3,46) (c) The requirement is the total cost per equivalent unit using the weighted-average method. The solutions approach is to first visualize the physical flow of the units.

BWIP 8,000 ———— 8,000 ———→12,000 Completed
                              4,000
Started 10,000* ——6,000 ———→6,000 EWIP

*12,000 + 6,000 - 8,000

Next, the equivalent units (EU) are computed.

	Materials	Conversion
Units completed and transferred	12,000	12,000
Work on EWIP	6,000	3,000
Equivalent units	18,000	15,000

Note that under the weighted-average assumption, no distinction is made between work done last period and work done in the current period on BWIP. All BWIP is "averaged" together. In EWIP, all 6,000 units are included in EU for materials, since materials are added at the beginning of the process. However, the EWIP is only 50% complete as to conversion costs so only 3,000 (6,000 x 50%) units are included in EU for conversion costs. Under the weighted-average assumption, BWIP costs and current period costs are combined. The cost per EU for materials is:

$$\frac{\$9,600 + \$15,600}{18,000} = \$1.40$$

While the cost per EU for conversion is:

$$\frac{\$4,800 + \$14,400}{15,000} = \$1.28$$

The total cost per equivalent unit is $1.40 + $1.28, or $2.68.

26. (583,P2,21) (d) The requirement is the equivalent units of production (EUP) for materials and conversion costs, using the FIFO cost flow method. First, visualize the physical flow of units.

```
BWIP       500 ── 500 ─────────→ 2,100 Transferred
                      ↗
                 ── 1,600 ──↗
Started 2,000 ── 400 ─────────→ 400 EWIP
```

Next, set up the FIFO EUP computation.

	Materials	Conversion
Work to complete, BWIP	0	300
Units started and transferred	1,600	1,600
Work to date on EWIP	400	100
EUP	2,000	2,000

Since materials are introduced at the beginning of the process, BWIP is already complete as to materials. All materials were added this month for any units started this month, whether those units were transferred or remain in EWIP. Since BWIP is 40% complete on 1/1/83 as to conversion costs, 60% of the work (60% x 500, or 300) must have been done in January. EWIP is 25% complete at 1/31/83, which means 25% of the conversion work (25% x 400, or 100) was done in January. Remember, under the FIFO assumption, EUP measures only the work done in the current period.

27. (582,P2,26) (a) The requirement is the allocation of manufacturing costs to goods completed and to ending work in process. The weighted-average method of process costing is used, which means beginning work-in-process costs are merged with those of the current month, rather than being accounted for separately. The cost of goods completed is equal to the number of units completed times the weighted average unit cost.

$$\text{Cost of goods completed} = 90,000 \times \$.88 = \$79,200$$

The cost of ending work in process must be computed separately for materials (added at the beginning of the process; 100% complete) and for conversion costs (50% complete).

Materials cost (10,000 x $.48)	$4,800
Conversion cost [(10,000 x 50%) x $.40]	2,000
Cost of EWIP	$6,800

Notice that the total cost to account for is $86,000 ($48,000 materials plus $38,000 conversion). The cost allocated to goods completed and to ending work in process must also total $86,000. Only choices (a) and (c) meet this requirement, and (c) allocates $0 to ending work in process. Therefore, choice (a) can be selected by process of elimination without even performing the preceding calculations.

28. (1180,P2,33) (c) The requirement is the conversion cost of the ending work-in-process inventory using the FIFO method. The number of units in ending work in process must be computed:

Work in Process			
BWIP	25,000	100,000	Units completed
Units started	135,000	?	EWIP
Units to account for	160,000	160,000	Units accounted for

EWIP = 160,000 units to account for - 100,000 units completed = 60,000 units.

The next step is to compute equivalent units of production under the FIFO method:

Units completed	100,000
EU in ending WIP (60,000)(50%)	30,000
	130,000
EU in beginning WIP (25,000)(80%)	(20,000)
EU of production	110,000

Conversion cost per unit for the current period is $143,000/110,000 or $1.30 per equivalent unit. The cost of the ending WIP is the equivalent units in ending WIP times the conversion cost/unit of $1.30:

$$(30,000)(\$1.30) = \$39,000$$

29. (587,Q2,39) (c) The first step in the solutions approach to this problem is to prepare a production budget:

Budgeted sales	125,000
Budgeted ending FG	30,000
Total units needed	155,000
Beginning FG	37,500
Units to be completed	117,500

Since there is no BWIP, the units started must cover both the units to be completed (117,500) and those in budgeted EWIP (8,000). Therefore, 125,500 units (117,500 + 8,000) must be started during April:

BWIP 0————0————➤117,500 Completed

         ╲117,500╱

Started 125,500 ———— 8,000 ——➤ 8,000 EWIP

EUP budgeted for April would be 117,500 units started and completed, plus 6,000 EUP (8,000 x 75%) in EWIP, for a total of 123,500 EUP. Note that the problem does not specify either the FIFO or weighted-average method. This information is not needed because there is not BWIP. FIFO and weighted-average will give identical results when there is no BWIP.

30. (1186,Q2,37) (b) It is helpful to first visualize the physical flow of units:

BWIP   10,000 ———— 10,000 ——➤35,000 Completed
                                          and
              ╲25,000╱   spoiled

Started 40,000 ———— 15,000 ——➤15,000 EWIP

In the weighted-average method, no distinction is made between work done last period on BWIP and work done in the current period on BWIP. All BWIP is "averaged" together. Therefore, the completion percentages for BWIP can be ignored. The EUP computation for conversion cost is:

Units completed	33,000
Abnormal spoilage	2,000
Work to date on	
EWIP (15,000 x 60%)	9,000
EUP	44,000

Note that abnormal spoilage is included in the EUP computation. This is because the cost assigned to abnormal spoilage would be recognized as a loss in the period of occurrence. Contrast this with the treatment of normal spoilage. Normal spoilage is a necessary cost in the production process and therefore is a product cost. Because of this, some cost textbooks advocate not including normal spoilage in the computation of EUP. One additional point should also be noted. Since spoilage is detected at the end of the process, the equivalent units for the abnormal spoilage are equal to the physical units. Had the inspection point been earlier, say at the 60% point,

only 60% of the conversion costs would have been incurred on these units.

31. (589,T1,44) (a) The requirement is to determine whether the cost of spoilage would be added to the cost of the good units produced if the spoilage is abnormal or normal. Abnormal spoilage is due to some unnecessary act, event, or condition; it is a period cost and is not added to the cost of the good units produced. Normal spoilage is due to the nature of the manufacturing process and is considered a necessary cost in the production process. Normal spoilage is a product cost and is added to the cost of the good units produced. Therefore, answers (b), (c), and (d) are incorrect.

32. (1189,Q2,32) (c) The requirement is how much spoilage cost should be charged as a period cost. Normal spoilage is a necessary cost in the production process and is, therefore, a product cost. Abnormal spoilage occurs through some unnecessary act or event. Since abnormal spoilage is not necessary to produce the product, it should be treated as a period cost and expensed in the period of occurrence (i.e., debit "loss on abnormal spoilage"). Therefore, only the $9,000 of abnormal spoilage should be treated as a period expense.

33. (586,Q2,25) (d) The requirement is to determine the number of units started in April. The solutions approach is to prepare a schedule summarizing the physical flow of units.

	Units		Units
BWIP	3,000	Completed	10,000
Started	?	EWIP	4,000
To acct. for	14,000	Acctd. for	14,000

Since 14,000 units were either completed or left in ending work in process, 14,000 must be the total of units in beginning work in process (BWIP) and units started (units to account for). BWIP consisted of 3,000 units, so 11,000 units were started during April (14,000 - 3,000).

34. (586,T1,42) (c) The requirement is the costs that are used in the computation of cost per equivalent unit under the weighted-average method of process costing. When computing equivalent units of production under the weighted-average method, the work done last period on beginning work in process (BWIP) is considered. Therefore, when computing cost per equivalent unit, the cost associated with BWIP must be added to the current costs [answer (c)]. Answer (a) would be the correct answer for the FIFO method. Answer (b) is incorrect because beginning and not ending work-in-process costs are added to current costs. Answer (d) is incorrect because the cost in BWIP is added to and not subtracted from current costs.

35. (1185,T1,39) (d) The requirement is to determine the number of equivalent units as to conversion costs. Since BWIP is zero, equivalent units of production equal:

> Units started and completed
> + Work to date on EWIP (50%)
> Equivalent units

It must be noted that all the units placed in process are either completed or left in EWIP. Because the units in EWIP are only 50% complete, these units placed in process will not be counted fully as equivalent units. Therefore, the equivalent units would be less than the units placed in process [answer (d)]. Answer (a) is incorrect because it is not only the units completed but also 50% of the units in EWIP. Answer (b) is incorrect because the units in EWIP that are not complete will not be counted fully as equivalent units although they were placed in process. Answer (c) is incorrect because equivalent units include the units completed and 50% of the units in process.

36. (585,T1,41) (a) The requirement is to determine the total equivalent units of production for a given period of time using the first-in, first-out (FIFO) method of process costing. Answer (a) is correct; the FIFO method determines equivalent units of production (EUP) based on the work done in the current period. The work done in the current period can be dichotomized as: (1) the work necessary to complete beginning work in process (BWIP), and (2) the work performed on the units started in the current period. The units started during the period are either completed or they remain as ending work in process (EWIP); thus, the EUP relative to units started consists of the number of units completed plus the work done on the EWIP. Another way of stating the EUP relative to units started is the units started in the period less the EUP based on the work necessary to complete the items in EWIP. Therefore, the EUP for FIFO can be calculated in various ways, two of which are presented below:

> Work to complete BWIP
> + Units started and completed
> + Work to date on EWIP
> Equivalent units (FIFO)

> Work to complete BWIP
> + Units started
> − Work to complete EWIP
> Equivalent units (FIFO)

Answer (b) is incorrect because it includes work done in the previous period by including the total BWIP. Additionally, by including units started and EWIP, it "double counts" the units in EWIP, since units started may or may not be finished at the end of the period. Answer (c) is incorrect since it too includes work from a previous period, total BWIP. This answer represents the physical units to be accounted for. Answer (d) is incorrect because it includes work done in a previous period. Completed and transferred would include the entire BWIP, as it would be completed before any new units. The BWIP would in turn include work from a previous period. Additionally, this answer includes work to be done in the next period by including the work necessary to complete the EWIP.

37. (581,T1,46) (a) The requirement is for the proper treatment of transferred in costs in computing equivalent units. Units transferred into the second department should be taken into account in the equivalent units computation for the second department under both FIFO and weighted-average [answer (a)]. They are treated the same as materials added at the beginning of a process.

H. Joint Products

38. (1186,Q2,30) (b) In this question, joint costs are allocated based on net realizable value (NRV). The NRV for products BEX and ROM is computed as follows:

	Sales value	−	Separable costs	=	NRV
BEX	$80,000*		$25,000		$ 55,000
ROM	$80,000**		$35,000		$ 45,000
					$100,000

*1,600 @ $ 50 = $80,000
** 800 @ $100 = $80,000

The joint cost allocated to each product is computed by taking the ratio of each product's NRV to total NRV of all joint products:

	Ratio		Joint cost	−	Allocated joint cost
BEX	55/100 = 55%		$30,000		$16,500
ROM	45/100 = 45%		$30,000		$13,500
					$30,000

Thus, the joint costs allocated to product BEX were $16,500.

39. (1186,Q2,39) (d) Total joint costs must first be adjusted before the joint costs allocated to product X can be computed. This is because the revenue from by-product Z is treated as a reduction of joint costs. Thus, total joint costs to allocate to products X

and Y are $252,000 ($262,000 - $10,000).
Joint costs are then allocated on the basis of
the sales value at split-off. The joint cost
allocated to product X is computed by taking
the ratio of X's sales value to the total
sales value of X and Y:

$$\text{Ratio} \quad \times \quad \text{Joint costs} = \frac{\text{Allocated}}{\text{joint costs}}$$

$330,000/$450,000* x $252,000 = $168,000

*$300,000 + $150,000

Thus, the joint costs allocated to product X
are $168,000. Although not part of the
question, the joint costs allocated to product Y are computed as follows:

$150,000/$450,000 x $252,000 = $84,000

40. (1185,Q1,6) (c) The requirement is to
determine how to allocate joint cost using the
net realizable value (NRV) method when a by-
product is involved. NRV is the predicted
selling price in the ordinary course of
business less reasonably predictable costs of
completion and disposal. The joint cost of
$54,000 is reduced by the NRV of the by-
product ($4,000) to get the allocable joint
cost ($50,000). The computation is:

	Sales value at split-off	Weighting	Joint costs allocated
Kul	$40,000	40,000/75,000 x 50,000	$26,667
Wu	35,000	35,000/75,000 x 50,000	23,333
	$75,000		$50,000

Therefore, $26,667 of the joint cost should be
allocated to product Kul.

41. (1182,Q2,26) (b) The requirement is to
calculate the profit effect of further
processing a product after the split-off
point. The solutions approach is to calculate
the incremental effects assuming product Dee
is further processed past split-off. If
product Dee was further processed, the sales
price per unit would increase by $2 ($5 -
$3); the $1,000 of additional processing
costs allocated over the 1000 units produced
mean that cost per unit would increase by $1
($1,000 ÷ 1,000 units). Therefore, a decision
to further process product Dee would result in
an additional gain of $1,000 [(1,000 units) x
($2 - $1)].

42. (1189,T1,44) (c) When using the relative
sales value at split-off method for joint
products, joint costs are allocated based on
the ratio of each product's sales value at
split-off to total sales value at split-off
for all joint products. If sales value at

split-off is not known, then it is necessary
to use the product's selling price at completion and subtract from it the costs incurred beyond split-off to arrive at a hypothetical sales value at split-off. In this
case, the costs beyond split-off are increasing for Product Z. This results in a
smaller hypothetical sales value for Product Z, which results in a smaller ratio of
joint costs allocated to Product Z. Since
there are only two joint products, Y's ratio
of joint costs must necessarily increase.
Therefore, the percentage of joint cost allocated will increase for Product Y and decrease for Product Z which means answer (c) is
correct.

43. (587,T1,44) (c) In a joint production
process, the split-off point is the point of
production where the joint products and any
by-products can be individually identified.
All costs incurred up to the split-off point
are common or joint costs because the individual products **are not** yet separately identifiable. Therefore, for the purposes of cost
accumulation, neither by-products nor joint
products are identifiable as different individual products before the split-off point.
After the split-off point when the products
are separately identifiable, the costs
incurred on any of the products can be easily
assigned to the individual products. These
costs after the split-off point are known as
separable costs.

44. (582,T1,44) (a) The requirement is to
determine when the relative sales value at
split-off method may be used to allocate joint
costs. The relative sales value method
allocates common costs to the joint products
based on their sales value at split-off. It
can be used whether or not there are processing costs beyond the split-off [an-
swer (a)]. When no sales value exists at the
split-off, an estimated one is derived by
subtracting the processing costs beyond the
split-off from the selling price obtainable
after additional processing. This method is
called the **hypothetical sales value** method.

I. By-Products

45. (586,Q2,36) (d) The requirement is the
effect on gross margin by reporting the sale
of a by-product as additional sales revenue
instead of as a deduction from the major product's cost of goods sold. The solutions approach is to determine what is currently being
done, then calculate the effect of the accounting change. To facilitate understanding,
assume that dollar amounts for sales and cost
of goods sold (CGS) are $300,000 and $200,000,
respectively.

	Present Method	Proposed Method
Sales	$300,000	$300,000 + $90,000*
CGS	$200,000 - $90,000*	$200,000
GM	$190,000	$190,000

*100,000 units x ($1 selling price - $.10 selling cost)

Note that the change in accounting treatment has no effect on gross margin.

46. (1188,T1,44) (a) Typically, scrap has a nominal market value so its value is not recorded as an asset in an inventory account. When the scrap is sold, however, the journal entry would be:

    Cash   (disposal value)
       Factory overhead
          control   (disposal value)

Thus, factory overhead control is decreased when scrap is sold, and answer (a) is correct.

47. (588,T1,44) (a) The value of the by-products may be recognized at two points in time: (1) at the time of production, or (2) at the time of sale. Therefore, answer (a) is correct. Under the production method, the net realizable value of the by-products **produced** is deducted from the cost of the major products **produced**. Under the sale method, net revenue from by-products **sold** (gross revenue from by-product sales minus separable costs incurred) is deducted from the cost of the major products **sold**.

48. (1186,T1,44) (c) "By-products" is a term given to joint products that generally have little market value in comparison to the over-all value of the other joint products resulting from a process. At the split-off point, all joint products become separately identifiable. By-products are often subject to additional costs beyond the split-off point. These costs can be either disposal costs or further processing costs. However, it is also possible that no additional cost incurrence is needed beyond the split-off point.

49. (586,T1,44) (d) The requirement is whether by-products and/or scrap are often subject to further processing in order to be salable. Scrap has only a relatively minor recovery value and is either sold as is or is reused. By-products are similar to scrap and the proper distinction between the two is sometimes difficult to determine. There are two general rules that are helpful to use in making the distinction. First, by-products are often subject to additional costs beyond the split-off point such as either disposal costs or further processing costs. Second, by-products have a relatively greater sales value than scrap. Therefore, answers (a), (b), and (c) are incorrect.

May 1990 Answers

50. (590,T1,41) (b) Indirect labor consists of labor costs incurred during production which cannot be traced directly to specific products. These labor costs are part of factory overhead. Conversion costs consist of direct labor and factory overhead, therefore, indirect labor is a conversion cost, [answer (b)]. Answer (a) is incorrect because prime costs are direct materials and direct labor. Answer (c) is incorrect because period costs are the selling and general and administrative expenses of a firm. These costs cannot be easily associated with specific revenues, and are expensed as incurred. Answer (d) is incorrect because period costs are also called nonmanufacturing costs.

51. (590,T1,42) (a) Conversion costs consist of direct labor and factory overhead. Because the EWIP units are 50% in process 2, some conversion costs have been incurred. These units would be included in the computation of equivalent units for conversion costs. However, because material G is added only when a batch is 60% complete, this material has not yet been added to this batch. These units would not be included in the computation of equivalent units for material G. Therefore answer (a) is correct.

52. (590,T1,44) (d) When using the relative sales value at split-off method for joint products, joint costs are allocated based on the ratio of each product's sales value at split-off to total sales value at split-off for all joint products. If the market value at split-off (sales value) of joint product P increases, then a larger proportion of the total joint costs will be allocated to that product. Because all other costs and selling prices remain unchanged, the gross margin of product P will, therefore, decrease. Product Q's gross margin will, however, increase because a smaller proportion of the total joint costs will be allocated to it. Therefore answer (d) is correct.

Solution Guide

**Problem 1   Cost of Goods Manufactured
                (584,Q4a)**

1. Part a. requires three schedules for the month of March: (1) cost of goods manufactured, (2) prime cost, and (3) conversion cost.

2. The cost of goods manufactured schedule is a summary of the work-in-process account. The solutions approach is to set up the cost of goods manufactured (COGM) schedule placing the given information in the appropriate places.

2.1 COGM ($348,000) is solved by subtracting beginning finished goods inventory ($102,000) from the cost of goods available for sale ($450,000). Place the $348,000 in the COGM schedule.

2.2 Ending work in process (EWIP) is solved as $36,000 [90% of $40,000 beginning work in process (BWIP)]. Manufacturing cost to account for ($384,000) is determined by adding COGM ($348,000) and EWIP ($36,000). Total manufacturing cost ($344,000) is then found by subtracting BWIP ($40,000) from manufacturing cost to account for ($384,000).

2.3 Direct materials used must be determined. Recall that this is computed by adding the BI of direct materials to the purchases to arrive at direct materials available. EI is subtracted from direct materials available to determine direct materials used.

2.4 Recall that total manufacturing cost is the sum of direct materials (DM) used, direct labor (DL) incurred, and overhead (OH) applied. This relationship is expressed by the equation:

   DM + DL + OH = Total mfg. cost
Given that OH is 50% of DL, solve for DL.
   $104,000 + DL + .5DL = $344,000
                    DL = $160,000
OH is, therefore, $80,000 [50% of $160,000 (DL)].

2.5 The candidate should organize his/her answer into a formal schedule of costs of goods manufactured. Preparation of the schedule requires that total manufacturing costs be added to BWIP to arrive at manufacturing costs to be accounted for. EWIP is then subtracted from this number to arrive at COGM.

3. Requirements 2 and 3 call for schedules to compute prime cost and conversion cost.

3.1 Prime cost ($264,000) is the sum of DM ($104,000) and DL ($160,000). Conversion cost ($240,000) is the sum of DL ($160,000) and OH applied ($80,000). Formal schedules with three-line headings should be prepared for each required item.

Unofficial Answer

**Problem 1   Cost of Goods Manufactured
                (584,Q4a)**

a1.   **Mat Company**
**Schedule of Cost of Goods Manufactured
For the Month Ended March 31, 1986**

Direct materials:		
Inventory, 3/1	$ 20,000	
Purchases	110,000	
Available	130,000	
Inventory, 3/31	26,000	
Direct materials used		$104,000
Direct labor		160,000
Factory overhead applied		80,000
Total manufacturing cost incurred		344,000
Add work-in-process inventory, 3/1		40,000
Manufacturing costs to account for		384,000
Deduct work-in-process inventory, 3/31		36,000
Cost of goods manufactured		$348,000

a2.   **Mat Company**
**Schedule to Compute Prime Cost
For the Month Ended March 31, 1986**

Direct materials used	$104,000
Direct labor incurred	160,000
Prime cost incurred during March	$264,000

a3.   **Mat Company**
**Schedule to Compute Conversion Cost
For the Month Ended March 31, 1986**

Direct labor incurred	$160,000
Factory overhead applied	80,000
Conversion cost incurred during March	$240,000

Solution Guide

Problem 2   WA and Standard Process
            Costing (1187,Q4)

1. This problem consists of four parts which
    are based on common information. The
    requirements include computations of
    equivalent units, actual costs, standard
    costs, and various variances.

2. Part a. requires the computation of equiv-
    alent units and actual cost per equivalent
    unit using the weighted average (WA)
    method. Note that the computation has to
    be done for each cost element (i.e., labor
    and overhead).

2.1 In order to compute equivalent units of
    performance (EUP) you need to first
    visualize the physical flow of units:

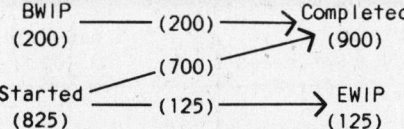

    Under the WA method, EUP are computed as
    the sum of all units completed plus the
    work to date on EWIP. The diagram above
    indicates that 900 units were completed.
    The additional information in the problem
    indicates that 125 units were in EWIP and
    that 80% of the work on these units was
    complete. Thus, for labor, the EUP are
    1,000 [900 + 80%(125)]. Since labor hours
    are used as the overhead base, the EUP for
    overhead are identical to those for labor.

2.2 Under the WA method, cost per EUP utilizes
    the sum of the previous cost in BWIP plus
    current cost. The previous cost in BWIP
    is included because the WA calculation of
    EUP included all work done on BWIP (i.e.,
    no distinction was made between work done
    last period and work done this period).
    Thus, the actual cost per EUP is $95.00
    [($6,000 + $89,000) ÷ 1,000] for labor and
    $47.50 [($2,500 + $45,000) ÷ 1,000] for
    overhead.

3. Part b. requires the computation of the
    actual cost of returns in EWIP. This
    requires the utilization of amounts
    computed in Part a.

3.1 Since 80% of the work was done on EWIP,
    100 EUP (80% x 125) are contained in
    EWIP. The actual cost per EUP was
    computed in Part a. as $95.00 and $47.50

for labor and for overhead, respectively. Thus, the actual cost of returns
in process at 3/31 is $9,500 (100 x
$95.00) for labor and $4,750 (100 x
$47.50) for overhead which is a total cost
in EWIP of $14,250.

4. Part c. requires the computation of the
    standard cost per return. This part can
    be easily computed from the given infor-
    mation.

4.1 The standards established by Webb are
    clearly indicated in the given infor-
    mation. Each return should use a standard
    5 hours of labor at a standard rate of $20
    per hour. This means that the standard
    labor cost **per return** is $100 (5 hrs. x
    $20/hr.). Labor hours are also used as
    the overhead base. Standard overhead cost
    per hour is $10. Thus, the standard
    overhead cost **per return** is $50 (5 hrs. x
    $10/hr.). Therefore, total standard cost
    per return is $150 ($100 + $50).

5. Part d. requires the computation of six
    variances. The solutions approach to this
    part involves the use of variance
    diagrams.

5.1 Standard EUP for March must first be com-
    puted before the labor efficiency and the
    overhead volume variances can be
    computed. The EUP computed in Part a.
    cannot be used. Standard EUP will only
    include equivalent units of output
    achieved during the current period. This
    is because variances are designed to
    reflect performance of only the current
    reporting period. Any variance related to
    previous work done on BWIP would have been
    analyzed in the previous period. Thus,
    standard EUP are the same as EUP computed
    under the FIFO method.

5.2 For this problem, the easiest way to com-
    pute FIFO EUP is to start with the WA EUP
    computed in Part a. and deduct from this
    amount the work done on BWIP in the
    previous period. In the additional in-
    formation, it is indicated that BWIP
    consists of 200 units that were 25%
    complete at the beginning of March. This
    indicates that 50 EUP (25% x 200) were
    completed in the previous month.
    Therefore, FIFO EUP for March are 950
    (1,000 - 50). Another way to compute this
    amount is to add up the EUP needed to
    complete BWIP during March, units started
    and completed, and the EUP done on EWIP
    during March. This calculation is as
    follows:

EUP for BWIP (75% x 200)	150
Units started and completed (825 - 125)	700
EUP for EWIP (80% x 125)	100
Total EUP - FIFO method	950

5.3 The first three variances are computed as follows:

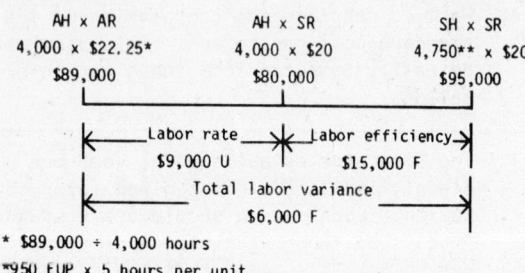

AH x AR
4,000 x $22.25*
$89,000

AH x SR
4,000 x $20
$80,000

SH x SR
4,750** x $20
$95,000

Labor rate
$9,000 U

Labor efficiency
$15,000 F

Total labor variance
$6,000 F

* $89,000 ÷ 4,000 hours

**950 EUP x 5 hours per unit

5.4 The labor rate variance is unfavorable because the actual price paid for actual input, ($89,000) is greater than the standard price allowed for actual input ($80,000). The labor efficiency variance is favorable because the standard price allowed for actual input ($80,000) is less than the standard price allowed for standard output ($95,000). The total labor variance is the sum of the labor rate and labor efficiency variances. Alternatively, it is the difference between the actual price paid for actual input and the standard price allowed for standard output.

5.5 The last three variances are computed as follows:

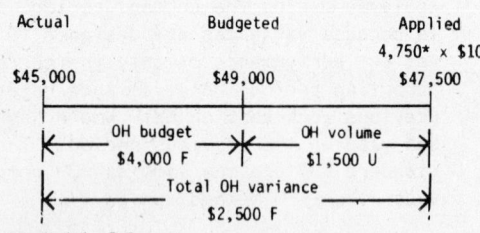

Actual
$45,000

Budgeted
$49,000

Applied
4,750* x $10
$47,500

OH budget
$4,000 F

OH volume
$1,500 U

Total OH variance
$2,500 F

*As computed in 5.3

5.6 The overhead budget variance is favorable because actual overhead ($45,000) is less than budgeted overhead ($49,000). The overhead volume variance is unfavorable because budgeted overhead ($49,000) is greater than applied overhead ($47,500). The total overhead variance is the sum of the overhead budget and overhead volume variances. Alternatively, it is the difference between actual overhead and applied overhead.

Unofficial Answer

Problem 2   WA and Standard Process Costing (1187,Q4)

Webb & Company
March 1987

a.

(1) Equivalent Units

	Labor	Overhead
Returns completed (200 + 825 - 125)	900	900
Returns in process, 3/31 (125 x 80%)	100	100
Equivalent units	1,000	1,000

(2) Actual Cost Per Equivalent Unit

	Labor	Overhead
Cost of return in process, 3/1	$ 6,000	$ 2,500
Add: March costs	89,000	45,000
Total costs	95,000	47,500
Divided by weighted average equivalent units	÷ 1,000	÷ 1,000
Actual cost per equivalent unit	$ 95.00	$ 47.50

b.   Actual Cost of Returns in Process at 3/31

Labor (125 returns x 80% x $95.00)	$ 9,500
Overhead (125 returns x 80% x $47.50)	4,750
Total	$14,250

c.   Standard Cost Per Return

Labor (5 hrs. at $20)	$100
Overhead (5 hrs at $10)	50
Total	$150

d.   Analysis of March Performance

(1) Total labor variance (actual minus standard) $89,000 - (950* x $100) = $6,000 favorable

(2) Labor rate variance [($89,000/4,000) - $20] x 4,000 = $9,000 unfavorable

(3) Labor efficiency variance [4,000 - (950* x 5)] x $20 = $15,000 favorable

(4) Total overhead variance (actual
    minus standard) $45,000 –
    (950* x $50) = $2,500
    favorable

(5) Overhead volume variance
    $49,000 – (950* x $50) =
    $1,500 unfavorable

(6) Overhead budget variance
    $45,000 – $49,000 =
    $4,000 favorable

	Labor	Overhead
*Equivalent units (weighted average method)	1,000	1,000
Less equivalent units beginning inventory (25% x 200)	50	50
Equivalent units for current production	950	950

Multiple Choice Questions (1-59)

1. Jackson, Inc. is preparing a flexible budget for 1981 and requires a breakdown of the cost of steam used in its factory into the fixed and variable elements. The following data on the cost of steam used and direct-labor hours worked are available for the last six months of 1980:

Month	Cost of steam	Direct-labor hours
July	$ 15,850	3,000
August	13,400	2,050
September	16,370	2,900
October	19,800	3,650
November	17,600	2,670
December	18,500	2,650
Total	$101,520	16,920

Assuming that Jackson uses the high-low points method of analysis, the estimated variable cost of steam per direct-labor hour should be
   a. $4.00
   b. $5.42
   c. $5.82
   d. $6.00

2. Meg Co. has developed a regression equation to analyze the behavior of its maintenance costs (Q) as a function of machine hours (Z). The following equation was developed by using 30 monthly observations with a related coefficient of determination of .90:

$$Q = \$6,000 + \$5.25Z$$

If 1,000 machine hours are worked in one month, the related point estimate of total maintenance costs would be
   a. $11,250
   b. $10,125
   c. $ 5,250
   d. $ 4,725

3. Multiple regression analysis involves the use of

	Dependent variables	Independent variables
a.	One	More than one
b.	More than one	More than one
c.	More than one	One
d.	One	One

4. Simple regression analysis involves the use of

	Dependent variables	Independent variables
a.	One	None
b.	One	One
c.	One	Two
d.	None	Two

5. Multiple regression analysis
   a. Establishes a cause and effect relationship.
   b. Is not a sampling technique.
   c. Involves the use of independent variables only.
   d. Produces measures of probable error.

6. Kent Co.'s 1985 operating percentages were as follows:

Sales		100%
Cost of sales		
Variable	50%	
Fixed	10	60
Gross profit		40
Other operating expenses		
Variable	20	
Fixed	15	35
Operating income		5%

Kent's 1985 sales totaled $2,000,000. At what 1985 sales level would Kent break even?
   a. $1,900,000
   b. $1,666,667
   c. $1,250,000
   d. $ 833,333

7. The following information pertains to Nova Co.'s cost-volume-profit relationships:

Breakeven point in units sold	1,000
Variable costs per unit	$ 500
Total fixed costs	$150,000

How much will be contributed to profit before income taxes by the 1,001st unit sold?
   a. $650
   b. $500
   c. $150
   d. $0

8. The following information pertains to Sisk Co.:

Sales (25,000 units)	$500,000
Direct materials and direct labor	150,000
Factory overhead:	
Variable	20,000
Fixed	35,000
Selling and general expenses:	
Variable	5,000
Fixed	30,000

Sisk's breakeven point in number of units is
   a. 4,924
   b. 5,000
   c. 6,250
   d. 9,286

9. The following information pertains to
Mete Co.:

Sales	$400,000
Variable costs	80,000
Fixed costs	20,000

Mete's breakeven point in sales dollars is
a. $ 20,000
b. $ 25,000
c. $ 80,000
d. $100,000

10. Koby Co. has sales of $200,000 with
variable expenses of $150,000, fixed expenses
of $60,000, and an operating loss of $10,000.
By how much would Koby have to increase its
sales in order to achieve an operating income
of 10% of sales?
a. $400,000
b. $251,000
c. $231,000
d. $200,000

11. Breakeven analysis assumes that over the
relevant range total
a.   Revenues are linear.
b.   Costs are unchanged.
c.   Variable costs are nonlinear.
d.   Fixed costs are nonlinear.

12. Breakeven analysis assumes that over the
relevant range
a.   Total costs are unchanged.
b.   Unit variable costs are unchanged.
c.   Variable costs are nonlinear.
d.   Unit fixed costs are unchanged.

13. In using cost-volume-profit analysis to
calculate expected unit sales, which of the
following should be added to fixed costs in
the numerator?
a.   Predicted operating loss.
b.   Predicted operating profit.
c.   Unit contribution margin.
d.   Variable costs.

14. If the fixed costs attendant to a product
increase while variable costs and sales price
remain constant, what will happen to (1)
contribution margin and (2) breakeven point?

	Contribution margin	Breakeven point
a.	Increase	Decrease
b.	Decrease	Increase
c.	Unchanged	Increase
d.	Unchanged	Unchanged

15. Thomas Company sells products X, Y, and
Z. Thomas sells three units of X for each
unit of Z, and two units of Y for each unit of

X. The contribution margins are $1.00 per
unit of X, $1.50 per unit of Y, and $3.00 per
unit of Z. Fixed costs are $600,000. How
many units of X would Thomas sell at the
breakeven point?
a.   40,000
b.   120,000
c.   360,000
d.   400,000

16. Gordon Company began its operations on
January 1, 1982, and produces a single product
that sells for $10 per unit. Gordon uses an
actual (historical) cost system. In 1982,
100,000 units were produced and 80,000 units
were sold. There was no work-in-process
inventory at December 31, 1982.
    Manufacturing costs and selling and
administrative expenses for 1982 were as
follows:

	Fixed costs	Variable costs
Raw materials	--	$2.00 per unit produced
Direct labor	--	1.25 per unit produced
Factory overhead	$120,000	.75 per unit produced
Selling and administrative	70,000	1.00 per unit sold

What would be Gordon's operating income for
1982 under the variable (direct) costing
method?
a. $114,000
b. $210,000
c. $234,000
d. $330,000

17. During the month of April, Vane Co.
produced and sold 10,000 units of a product.
Manufacturing and selling costs incurred
during April were as follows:

Direct materials and direct labor	$400,000
Variable manufacturing overhead	90,000
Fixed manufacturing overhead	20,000
Variable selling costs	10,000

The product's unit cost under direct
(variable) costing was
a. $49
b. $50
c. $51
d. $52

18. The following information appeared in the
accounting records of a retail store for the
year ended December 31, 1988:

Sales	$300,000
Purchases	140,000
Inventories	
January 1	70,000
December 31	100,000
Sales commissions	10,000

The gross margin was
   a. $190,000
   b. $180,000
   c. $160,000
   d. $150,000

19. West Co.'s 1988 manufacturing costs were
as follows:

Direct materials and direct labor	$700,000
Other variable manu- facturing costs	100,000
Depreciation of factory building and manu- facturing equipment	80,000
Other fixed manufacturing overhead	18,000

What amount should be considered product cost
for external reporting purposes?
   a. $700,000
   b. $800,000
   c. $880,000
   d. $898,000

20. In an income statement prepared as an internal report, total fixed costs normally
would be shown separately under

	Absorption costing	Variable costing
a.	No	No
b.	No	Yes
c.	Yes	Yes
d.	Yes	No

21. In an income statement prepared as an
internal report using the variable costing
method, variable selling and administrative
expenses would
   a.   Not be used.
   b.   Be treated the same as fixed selling
        and administrative expenses.
   c.   Be used in the computation of oper-
        ating income but not in the compu-
        tation of the contribution margin.
   d.   Be used in the computation of the
        contribution margin.

22. In an income statement prepared as an
internal report using the absorption costing
method, which of the following terms should
appear?

	Contribution margin	Gross profit (margin)
a.	No	Yes
b.	No	No
c.	Yes	No
d.	Yes	Yes

23. In an income statement prepared using the
variable costing method, fixed factory
overhead would
   a.   Not be used.
   b.   Be used in the computation of the
        contribution margin.
   c.   Be used in the computation of
        operating income but not in the
        computation of the contribution
        margin.
   d.   Be treated the same as variable
        factory overhead.

24. Operating income using direct costing as
compared to absorption costing would be higher
   a.   When the quantity of beginning
        inventory equals the quantity of
        ending inventory.
   b.   When the quantity of beginning
        inventory is more than the quantity
        of ending inventory.
   c.   When the quantity of beginning
        inventory is less than the quantity
        of ending inventory.
   d.   Under no circumstances.

25. Walman Company is budgeting sales of
42,000 units of product Y for March 1989. To
make one unit of finished product, three
pounds of raw material A are required. Actual
beginning and desired ending inventories of
raw material A and product Y are as follows:

	3/1/89	3/31/89
Raw material A	100,000 pounds	110,000 pounds
Product Y	22,000 units	24,000 units

There is no work-in-process inventory for
product Y at the beginning and end of March.
For the month of March, how many pounds of raw
material A is Walman planning to purchase?
   a.   126,000
   b.   132,000
   c.   136,000
   d.   142,000

26. In preparing its cash budget for May
1989, Ben Co. made the following projections:

Sales	$3,000,000
Gross margin (based on sales)	25%
Decrease in inventories	140,000
Decrease in accounts payable for inventories	240,000

For May 1989, the estimated cash disbursements
for inventories were
   a. $2,350,000
   b. $2,110,000
   c. $2,100,000
   d. $1,870,000

27. Reid Company is developing a forecast of March 1980 cash receipts from credit sales. Credit sales for March 1980 are estimated to be $320,000. The accounts receivable balance at February 29, 1980 is $300,000; one quarter of the balance represents January credit sales and the remainder is from February sales. All accounts receivable from months prior to January of 1980 have been collected or written off. Reid's history of accounts receivable collections is as follows:

In the month of sale	20%
In the first month after month of sale	50%
In the second month after month of sale	25%
Written off as uncollectible at the end of the second month after month of sale	5%

Based on the above information, Reid is forecasting March 1980 cash receipts from credit sales of
a. $176,500
b. $195,250
c. $253,769
d. $267,125

28. Bye Co. is considering the sale of banners at the state university football championship game. Bye could purchase these banners for $0.60 each. Unsold banners would be nonreturnable and worthless after the game. Bye would have to rent a booth at the stadium for $250. Bye estimates sales of 500 banners at $2.00 each. If Bye's prediction proves to be incorrect and only 300 banners were sold, the cost of this prediction error would be
a. $120
b. $130
c. $170
d. $280

29. Dean Company is preparing a flexible budget for 1982 and the following maximum capacity estimates for department M are available:

	At maximum capacity
Direct-labor hours	60,000
Variable factory overhead	$150,000
Fixed factory overhead	$240,000

Assume that Dean's normal capacity is 80% of maximum capacity. What would be the total factory overhead rate, based on direct-labor hours, in a flexible budget at normal capacity?
a. $6.00
b. $6.50

c. $7.50
d. $8.13

30. The flexible budget for a company may include

	Direct material costs	Variable selling costs
a.	Yes	No
b.	Yes	Yes
c.	No	Yes
d.	No	No

31. When a flexible budget is used, a decrease in production levels within a relevant range would
a. Increase total fixed costs.
b. Increase variable cost per unit.
c. Decrease variable cost per unit.
d. Decrease total costs.

32. The flexible budget for a producing department may include

	Direct labor	Factory overhead
a.	No	Yes
b.	No	No
c.	Yes	No
d.	Yes	Yes

33. A flexible budget is appropriate for a(an)

	Administrative budget	Marketing budget
a.	Yes	Yes
b.	Yes	No
c.	No	No
d.	No	Yes

34. A company is analyzing the performance of responsibility centers. Controllable costs would be included in the performance reports of which of the following types of responsibility centers?

	Investment centers	Profit centers
a.	No	No
b.	No	Yes
c.	Yes	Yes
d.	Yes	No

35. Controllable costs for responsibility accounting purposes are those costs that are directly influenced by
a. A given manager within a given period of time.
b. A change in activity.
c. Production volume.
d. Sales volume.

36. The contribution margin ratio always increases when the
    a.   Variable costs as a percentage of net sales increase.
    b.   Variable costs as a percentage of net sales decrease.
    c.   Breakeven point increases.
    d.   Breakeven point decreases.

Items 37 through 41 are based on the following data:

Oslo Co.'s industrial photo-finishing division, Rho, incurred the following costs and expenses in 1985:

	Variable	Fixed
Direct materials	$200,000	
Direct labor	150,000	
Factory overhead	70,000	$42,000
General, selling, and administrative	30,000	48,000
Totals	$450,000	$90,000

During 1985, Rho produced 300,000 units of industrial photo-prints, which were sold for $2.00 each. Oslo's investment in Rho was $500,000 and $700,000 at January 1, 1985 and December 31, 1985, respectively. Oslo normally imputes interest on investments at 15% of average invested capital.

37. For the year ended December 31, 1985, Rho's return on average investment was
    a.   15.0%
    b.   10.0%
    c.   8.6%
    d.   (5.0%)

38. For the year ended December 31, 1985, Rho's residual income (loss) was
    a. $150,000
    b. $ 60,000
    c.   ($ 45,000)
    d.   ($ 30,000)

39. How many industrial photo-print units did Rho have to sell in 1985 to break even?
    a.   180,000
    b.   120,000
    c.   90,000
    d.   60,000

40. For the year ended December 31, 1985, Rho's contribution margin was
    a. $250,000
    b. $180,000
    c. $150,000
    d. $ 60,000

41. Based on Rho's 1985 financial data, and an estimated 1986 production of 350,000 units of industrial photo-prints, Rho's estimated 1986 total costs and expenses would be
    a. $525,000
    b. $540,000
    c. $615,000
    d. $630,000

Items 42 and 43 are based on the following information pertaining to Yola Co.'s East Division for 1988:

Sales	$620,000
Variable costs	500,000
Traceable fixed costs	100,000
Average invested capital	50,000
Imputed interest rate	18%

42. The return on investment was
    a.   40.00%
    b.   29.00%
    c.   18.00%
    d.   8.33%

43. The residual income was
    a. $ 3,600
    b. $ 9,000
    c. $11,000
    d. $20,000

44. Residual income is income
    a.   To which an imputed interest charge for invested capital is added.
    b.   From which an imputed interest charge for invested capital is deducted.
    c.   From which dividends are deducted.
    d.   To which dividends are added.

45. A company's rate of return on investment is the
    a.   Percentage of profit to sales divided by the capital-employed turnover rate.
    b.   Percentage of profit to sales multiplied by the capital-employed turnover rate.
    c.   Investment capital divided by the capital-employed turnover rate.
    d.   Investment capital multiplied by the capital-employed turnover rate.

46. Assuming that sales and net income remain the same, a company's return on investment will
    a.   Increase if invested capital increases.
    b.   Decrease if invested capital decreases.
    c.   Decrease if the invested capital-employed turnover rate decreases.
    d.   Decrease if the invested capital-employed turnover rate increases.

47. Aba Caterers quotes a price of $30 per person for a dinner party. This price includes the 6% sales tax and the 15% service charge. Sales tax is computed on the food plus the service charge. The service charge is computed on the food only. At what amount does Aba price the food?
   a. $23.70
   b. $24.61
   c. $25.50
   d. $28.20

48. Diva Co. wants to establish a selling price that will yield a gross margin of 40% on sales of a product whose cost is $12.00 per unit. The selling price should be
   a. $16.80
   b. $19.20
   c. $20.00
   d. $30.00

49. Adly Corp. wishes to earn a 30% return on its $100,000 investment in equipment used to produce Product X. Based on estimated sales of 10,000 units of Product X next year, the costs per unit would be as follows:

Variable manufacturing costs	$5
Fixed selling and administrative costs	2
Fixed manufacturing costs	1

At how much per unit should Product X be priced for sale?
   a. $ 5
   b. $ 8
   c. $10
   d. $11

50. In the contribution margin approach to pricing, the price at which the income remains constant is equal to the price that covers
   a. Prime costs.
   b. Variable costs.
   c. Fixed costs.
   d. Fixed and variable costs plus the desired profit.

51. Politan Company manufactures bookcases. Set up costs are $2.00. Politan manufactures 4,000 bookcases evenly throughout the year. Using the economic-order-quantity approach the optimal production run would be 200 when the cost of carrying one bookcase in inventory for one year is
   a. $0.05
   b. $0.10
   c. $0.20
   d. $0.40

52. The Polly Company wishes to determine the amount of safety stock that it should maintain for Product D that will result in the lowest cost. The following information is available:

Stockout cost	$80 per occurrence
Carrying cost of safety stock	$2 per unit
Number of purchase orders	5 per year

The available options open to Polly are as follows:

Units of safety stock	Probability of running out of safety stock
10	50%
20	40%
30	30%
40	20%
50	10%
55	5%

The number of units of safety stock that will result in the lowest cost are
   a. 20
   b. 40
   c. 50
   d. 55

53. Ral Co. sells 20,000 radios evenly throughout the year. The cost of carrying one unit in inventory for one year is $8, and the purchase order cost per order is $32. What is the economic order quantity?
   a. 625
   b. 400
   c. 283
   d. 200

54. The following information pertains to material X which is used by Sage Co.:

Annual usage in units	20,000
Working days per year	250
Safety stock in units	800
Normal lead time in working days	30

Units of material X will be required evenly throughout the year. The order point is
   a. 800
   b. 1,600
   c. 2,400
   d. 3,200

55. How would the following be used in the economic order quantity formula?

	Inventory carrying cost	Cost per purchase order
a.	Numerator	Numerator
b.	Denominator	Numerator
c.	Denominator	Denominator
d.	Not used	Denominator

56. Which of the following is a relevant factor in the determination of an ecomomic order quantity?
   a. Physical plant insurance costs.
   b. Warehouse supervisory salaries.

c. Variable costs of processing a
    purchase order.
d. Physical plant depreciation charges.

May 1990 Questions

57. A manufacturing company prepares income
statements using both absorption and variable
costing methods. At the end of a period
actual sales revenues, total gross profit, and
total contribution margin approximated budgeted figures, whereas net income was substantially below the budgeted amount. There were
no beginning or ending inventories. The most
likely explanation of the net income shortfall
is that, compared to budget, actual
    a. Sales prices and variable costs had
        declined proportionately.
    b. Sales prices had declined
        proportionately more than variable
        costs.
    c. Manufacturing fixed costs had
        increased.
    d. Selling and administrative fixed
        expenses had increased.

     Items 58 and 59 are based on the fol-
lowing:

The diagram below is a cost-volume-profit
chart.

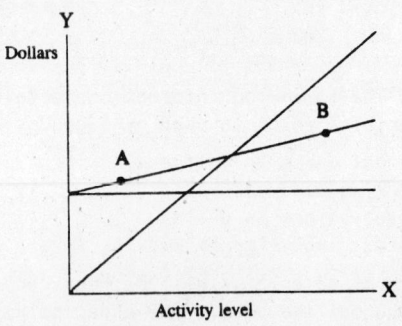

58. At point A compared to point B, as a
percentage of sales revenues

	Variable costs are	Fixed costs are
a.	Greater	Greater
b.	Greater	The same
c.	The same	The same
d.	The same	Greater

59. If sales dollars are used to measure
activity levels, total costs and total
revenues may be read from the X and Y axes as
follows:

	Total costs	Total revenues
a.	X or Y	X or Y
b.	X or Y	X only
c.	Y only	X or Y
d.	Y only	X only

Repeat Question

(590,T1,49) Identical/similar to item 45 above

Problems

Problem 1   (588,Q5)

(40 to 50 minutes)

Seco Corp., a wholesale supply company, engages independent sales agents to market the company's lines. These agents currently receive a commission of 20% of sales, but they are demanding an increase to 25% of sales made during the year ending December 31, 1989. Seco had already prepared its 1989 budget before learning of the agents' demand for an increase in commissions. The following pro forma income statement is based on this budget:

Seco Corp.
PRO FORMA INCOME STATEMENT
For the Year Ending December 31, 1989

Sales		$10,000,000
Cost of sales		6,000,000
Gross margin		4,000,000
Selling and administrative costs		
Commissions	$2,000,000	
All other costs (fixed)	100,000	2,100,000
Income before income tax		1,900,000
Income tax (30%)		570,000
Net income		$ 1,330,000

Seco is considering the possibility of employing its own salespersons. Three individuals would be required, at an estimated annual salary of $30,000 each, plus commissions of 5% of sales. In addition, a sales manager would be employed at a fixed annual salary of $160,000. All other fixed costs, as well as the variable cost percentages, would remain the same as the estimates in the 1989 pro forma income statement.

Required:

a. Compute Seco's estimated breakeven point in sales dollars for the year ending December 31, 1989 based on the pro forma income statement prepared by the company.

b. Compute Seco's estimated breakeven point in sales dollars for the year ending December 31, 1989 if the company employs its own salespersons.

c. Compute the estimated volume in sales dollars that would be required for the year ending December 31, 1989 to yield the same net income as projected in the pro forma income statement, if Seco continues to use the independent sales agents and agrees to their demand for a 25% sales commission.

d. Compute the estimated volume in sales dollars that would generate an identical net income for the year ending December 31, 1989, regardless of whether Seco employs its own salespersons or continues to use the independent sales agents and pays them a 25% commission.

Problem 2   (585,Q4)

(45 to 55 minutes)

Mayne Manufacturing Co. has incurred substantial losses for several years, and has become insolvent. On March 31, 1986, Mayne petitioned the court for protection from creditors, and submitted the following statement of financial position:

Mayne Manufacturing Co.
Statement of Financial Position
March 31, 1986

Assets:	Book value	Liquidation value
Accounts receivable	$100,000	$ 50,000
Inventories	90,000	40,000
Plant and equipment	150,000	160,000
Totals	$340,000	$250,000

Liabilities and Stockholders' Equity:	
Accounts payable--general creditors	$600,000
Common stock outstanding	60,000
Deficit	(320,000)
Total	$340,000

Mayne's management informed the court that the company has developed a new product, and that a prospective customer is willing to sign a contract for the purchase of 10,000 units of this product during the year ending March 31, 1987; 12,000 units of this product during the year ending March 31, 1988; and 15,000 units of this product during the year ending March 31, 1989, at a price of $90 per unit. This product can be manufactured using Mayne's present facilities. Monthly production with immediate delivery is expected to be uniform within each year. Receivables are expected to be collected during the calendar month following sales.

Unit production costs of the new product are expected to be as follows:

Direct materials	$20
Direct labor	30
Variable overhead	10

Fixed costs (excluding depreciation) will amount to $130,000 per year.

Purchases of direct materials will be paid during the calendar month following purchase. Fixed costs, direct labor, and variable overhead will be paid as incurred. Inventory of direct materials will be equal to 60 days' usage. After the first month of operations, 30 days' usage of direct materials will be ordered each month.

The general creditors have agreed to reduce their total claims to 60% of their March 31, 1986 balances, under the following conditions:

• Existing accounts receivable and inventories are to be liquidated immediately, with the proceeds turned over to the general creditors.

• The balance of reduced accounts payable is to be paid as cash is generated from future operations, but in no event later than March 31, 1988. No interest will be paid on these obligations.

Under this proposed plan, the general creditors would receive $110,000 more than the current liquidation value of Mayne's assets. The court has engaged you to determine the feasibility of this plan.

Required:

Ignoring any need to borrow and repay short-term funds for working capital purposes, prepare a cash budget for the years ending March 31, 1987 and 1988, showing the cash expected to be available to pay the claims of the general creditors, payments to general creditors, and the cash remaining after payment of claims.

Problem 3 (589,Q5)

(40 to 50 minutes)

The following information pertains to the pricing and delivery functions of Tapa Wholesale Company:

Number of sales made to customers in 1988	20,000
Average number of items per sale in 1988	4
Number of sales projected for 1989	24,000
Average number of items per sale projected for 1989	5

Sales invoices are priced by clerks whose wage rate is $6.00 per hour. Labor negotiations have resulted in a 10% increase in the hourly rate for 1989. It is expected that Tapa's pricing function will operate at the same level of productivity in 1989 as it did in 1988. Payroll tax rates and workers' compensation insurance rates will be the same in 1989 as in 1988. Prices for various items of supplies are expected to be the same in 1989 as in 1988.

The following costs were charged to Tapa's pricing function in 1988:

Variable:	
Wages	$40,000
Payroll taxes	4,000
Workers' compensation insurance	2,000
Supplies	1,000
Total variable	47,000
Fixed	3,400
Total costs	$50,400

Fixed costs are allocated equally to all units. Except for delivery costs, all variable costs vary directly with the number of items priced. Supplies increase in proportion to the increase in the number of items priced. Tapa sells three products: Arcil, Balo, and Cacha. Differences in size and weight among these products affect variable delivery costs. For example, truck capacity is 10 units of Arcil, or 5 units of Balo, or 4 units of Cacha. Units projected to be delivered in 1989 are as follows:

Arcil	60,000
Balo	40,000
Cacha	20,000
Total	120,000

Projected 1989 costs for the delivery function are as follows:

Variable	$228,000
Fixed	30,000

Required:

a. Prepare the 1989 budget of all costs for Tapa's pricing function.

b. Prepare a schedule showing the 1989 standard delivery cost per unit of each of the three products sold by Tapa.

Multiple Choice Answers

1. a	13. b	25. d	37. b	49. d
2. a	14. c	26. a	38. d	50. b
3. a	15. b	27. d	39. a	51. d
4. b	16. b	28. a	40. c	52. d
5. d	17. a	29. c	41. c	53. b
6. b	18. a	30. b	42. a	54. d
7. c	19. d	31. d	43. c	55. b
8. b	20. b	32. d	44. b	56. c
9. b	21. d	33. a	45. b	57. d
10. d	22. a	34. c	46. c	58. d
11. a	23. c	35. a	47. b	59. c
12. b	24. b	36. b	48. c	

Multiple Choice Answer Explanations

A. Analyzing Cost Behavior

1. (1181,P2,25) (a) The requirement is to estimate the variable cost of steam using the high-low points method of analysis. The high-low method separates a mixed cost into its variable and fixed components. The initial step in the high-low method utilizes a formula to find the variable rate. The formula used in developing the variable rate is:

$$\frac{\text{Cost at high point} - \text{Cost at low point}}{\text{High activity point} - \text{Low activity point}} = \text{Variable rate}$$

In this problem, the cost of steam is given at several levels of the designated activity, direct labor hours (DLH). Substituting into the formula gives the variable cost of steam per direct labor hour:

$$\frac{\$19,800 - \$13,400}{3650 \text{ DLH} - 2050 \text{ DLH}} = \$4.00/\text{DLH}$$

2. (587,Q2,27) (a) The formula developed by Meg Co. is for total maintenance costs (Q) where $6,000 is equal to the fixed portion per month, $5.25 represents the variable rate, and Z is the activity level. The correct answer is determined by substituting the given activity level of 1,000 machine hours for Z resulting in $11,250 [$6,000 + $5.25 (1,000)] of total maintenance costs. The coefficient of determination is irrelevant for this computation. The coefficient of determination measures how much of the variation in the dependent variable (total maintenance costs) is explained by the variation in the independent variable (machine hours). The coefficient of determination, being .90, tells us that 90% of the variation in total maintenance cost is explained by the variation in machine hours.

3. (1188,T1,50) (a) Regression analysis determines the functional relationship between variables and provides a measure of probable error. In multiple regression, two or more independent variables are used to predict one dependent variable. Therefore, answer (a) is correct.

4. (1186,T1,50) (b) Regression analysis determines the functional relationship between variables and provides a measure of probable error. In simple regression analysis, one independent variable, usually some measure of activity, is used to predict one dependent variable, usually cost. Therefore, answer (b) is correct. Contrast this with multiple regression analysis which involves the use of two or more independent variables to predict one dependent variable.

5. (585,T1,48) (d) The requirement is to determine the appropriate attribute of multiple regression analysis. Answer (d) is correct because a major advantage of regression analysis over other cost analysis techniques is the fact that it does produce measures of probable error (such as the standard error of estimate). Answer (a) is incorrect because regression analysis does not establish a cause and effect relationship but merely indicates the extent to which variables move together. Answer (b) is incorrect because multiple regression analysis __is__ by definition a formal sampling technique. Answer (c) is incorrect because multiple regression analysis involves the use of both independent __and__ dependent variables.

B. Cost-Volume-Profit (CVP) Analysis

6. (1186,Q2,34) (b) One way to compute the breakeven point in sales dollars is to divide total fixed costs by the contribution margin ratio. Total fixed costs can be computed as follows:

Cost of sales, fixed (10% x $2,000,000)	$200,000
Other operating expenses, fixed (15% x $2,000,000)	$300,000
Total fixed costs	$500,000

The contribution margin ratio can be computed as follows:

Sales		100%
- Variable expenses		
Cost of sales	50%	
Other operating expenses	20%	70%
Contribution margin ratio		30%

The breakeven point can now be computed using the following formula:

$$\frac{\text{Total fixed costs}}{\text{Contribution margin ratio}} = \text{BEP in dollars}$$

$$\frac{\$500,000}{30\%} = \$1,666,667$$

7. (586,Q2,27) (c) The requirement is the amount that will be contributed to profit before income taxes by the first unit sold after the breakeven point. At the breakeven point, all fixed costs have been covered. Thereafter, all of the contribution margin will be pretax profit. Therefore, the pretax profit on the first unit sold after the break-even point will be the unit contribution margin (i.e., sales price per unit minus variable costs per unit). The unit contribution margin can be computed by inserting the given information into the following equation.

$$\frac{\text{Total fixed costs}}{\text{Unit contribution margin}} = \text{BEP in units}$$

$$\frac{\$150,000}{\text{Unit contribution margin}} = 1,000$$

1,000 (Unit contribution margin) = $150,000
             Unit contribution margin = $150

8. (1189,Q2,27) (b) The breakeven point is calculated by dividing total fixed costs by contribution margin per unit. Total fixed costs for Sisk are $65,000 ($35,000 fixed factory overhead + $30,000 fixed selling and general expenses). The contribution margin per unit is calculated as follows:

Sales (25,000 units)		$500,000
Variable costs:		
Direct materials and		
direct labor	150,000	
Factory overhead	20,000	
S & G expenses	5,000	175,000
Contribution margin		325,000

$$\frac{\$325,000 \text{ CM}}{25,000 \text{ units}} = \$13 \text{ CM per unit}$$

The breakeven point is then computed using these figures:

$$\frac{\$65,000 \text{ total fixed cost}}{\$13 \text{ CM per unit}} = 5000 \text{ units}$$

Please note that a dollar figure divided by a dollar figure results in an answer stated in units.

9. (1189,Q2,28) (b) The breakeven point can be thought of as the amount of contribution margin (sales minus variable costs) required to cover the fixed costs. The contribution margin for Neete Company is $320,000 ($400,000 sales minus $80,000 variable costs) or 80% of sales ($320,000 ÷ $400,000). If the contribution margin was $20,000 (equal to fixed costs), net income would be zero at the break-

even point. A $20,000 contribution margin is 80% of $25,000 in sales ($20,000 ÷ .80). Thus, the breakeven point in sales is $25,000.

10. (1183,Q1,12) (d) The requirement is the increase in sales in order to achieve an operating income of 10% of sales (expressed as .10S below). The solutions approach is to use the standard breakeven formula and solve for S. Variable costs are $150,000 at a sales level of $200,000; therefore, variable costs are .75S ($150,000/$200,000).

     S = VC + FC   + Expected profit
     S = .75S + $60,000 +   .10S
 .15S = $60,000
     S = $400,000

Remember that the requirement was the increase in sales to achieve a profit of 10% of sales. The correct answer is $200,000 ($400,000 total sales needed less $200,000 present sales level).

11. (1188,T1,47) (a) Breakeven analysis is based upon several simplified assumptions. One assumption is that the selling price per unit remains constant. Thus, revenues are linear over the relevant range and answer (a) is correct. Answer (b) is incorrect because total variable costs change with production. Answers (c) and (d) are incorrect because two assumptions of breakeven analysis are (1) variable cost per unit is constant over the relevant range, and (2) total fixed costs are constant over the relevant range.

12. (589,T1,47) (b) Certain assumptions are held to be true for breakeven analysis within the relevant, or normal operating, range of activity. The assumptions include: (1) variable costs per unit are constant, and (2) total fixed costs are constant. Therefore, answer (a) is incorrect because the variable portion of total costs will change with the level of activity. Answer (c) is incorrect because variable costs are assumed to be linear. Answer (d) is incorrect because total fixed costs are unchanged, but unit fixed costs change with the level of activity.

13. (1187,T1,48) (b) Answer (b) is correct as shown by the following formula for computing unit sales.

Sales in units	=	Fixed Costs	+	Predicted operating profit or -	Predicted operating loss

Contribution margin per unit

A predicted operating profit means that sales are expected to be above the breakeven point and, thus, should be added to fixed costs. A predicted operating loss [answer (a)] means

that sales will be below the breakeven
point. This is why a predicted operating loss
is <u>subtracted</u> from fixed costs. Answer (c) is
incorrect because the unit contribution margin
is the amount used in the denominator of the
formula. Answer (d) is incorrect because
variable cost per unit is subtracted from
sales price per unit to get the unit
contribution margin.

14. (580,T1,47) (c) The requirement is to
determine the effect on contribution margin
and the breakeven point when fixed costs
increase, holding variable costs and sales
price constant. Contribution margin is
defined as sales less variable costs. An
increase in fixed costs has no effect on
contribution margin. Increasing fixed costs
would, however, cause the breakeven point to
increase. Additional units must be sold to
cover the increased fixed costs. Accordingly,
answer (c) is correct.

B.2. Breakeven: Multi-Product Firm

15. (1180,P2,29) (b) The requirement is how
many units of product X (one of three products) Thomas would sell at the breakeven
point. The solutions approach is first to
find the number of composite units to breakeven; a composite unit consists of the number
of units of each of the three products in the
mix. Since Thomas sells 3 units of X for each
unit of Z and 2 units of Y for each unit of X,
they are selling 6 units of Y for each unit of
Z; therefore, a composite unit consists of 3X,
6Y, and 1Z. The total contribution margin for
1 composite unit is

```
        X (3) ($1.00) = $ 3
        Y (6) ($1.50) = $ 9
        Z (1) ($3.00) = $ 3
                        $15
```

The breakeven point in terms of units of the
product mix group is:

        $600,000 ÷ $15 = 40,000 composite units

Since there are three units of X in each
composite unit, (40,000)(3) or 120,000 units
of X are sold at breakeven.

C. Direct (Variable) and Absorption (Full) Costing

16. (583,P2,33) (b) The requirement is
Gordon's operating income for 1982 under the
variable (direct) costing method. Under
direct costing, fixed manufacturing costs are
treated as period costs (expensed in full)
rather than as product costs. Only variable
manufacturing costs are inventoriable. Direct
costing income for 1982 is $210,000.

Sales (80,000 x $10)	$800,000
Variable expenses (80,000 x $5)	(400,000)
Contribution margin	400,000
Fixed expenses ($120,000 +	
$70,000)	(190,000)
Operating income	$210,000

The variable expense per unit ($5) is obtained
by adding together the variable costs per unit
as given ($2 + $1.25 + $.75 + $1).

17. (1189,Q2,30) (a) Under the direct
(variable) costing method, product cost
includes direct materials, direct labor, and
variable manufacturing overhead. Therefore,
product cost per unit is $49 [($400,000 +
$90,000) ÷ 10,000 units], and answer (a) is
correct.

18. (1189,Q2,25) (a) The solutions approach
is to visualize the format of an absorption
costing income statement:

                Sales
        - Cost of goods sold
          Gross margin (profit)

Cost of goods sold is calculated as follows:

                Beginning inventory
        + Net purchases
          Available for sale
        - Ending inventory
          Cost of goods sold

Using the information given in the problem,
cost of goods sold is $110,000 ($70,000
beginning inventory + $140,000 purchases −
$100,000 ending inventory). Thus, gross
margin is $190,000 ($300,000 sales − $110,000
cost of goods sold). Sales commissions are
not a product expense under absorption costing
and are ignored for these calculations.

19. (1189,Q2,29) (d) Per GAAP, only absorption costing is used for external reporting.
Absorption costing considers <u>all</u> manufacturing
related costs to be product costs. All of the
items listed in this problem are manufacturing
costs and, thus, are considered product costs.
Therefore, total product cost is $898,000 and
answer (d) is correct.

20. (1189,T1,46) (b) In an income statement
prepared as an internal report, operating
income may be measured under either absorption
costing or variable costing. The solutions
approach to this question is to visualize each
income statement shown below.

Absorption costing I/S
    Sales
  − Cost of goods sold
    Gross profit (margin)
  − Selling & admin. expenses
    Operating income

Variable costing I/S
    Sales
  − Variable expenses
    Contribution margin
  − Fixed expenses
    Operating income

Answer (b) is correct because total fixed costs are normally shown separately only under the variable costing method.

21. (588,T1,45) (d) The income statement format under variable costing is:

    Sales
  − Variable manufacturing costs
  = Manufacturing contribution margin
  − Variable selling and administrative expenses
  = Contribution margin
  − Fixed manufacturing, selling, and administrative expenses
  = Net income

Note that both variable manufacturing costs and variable selling and administrative expenses are deducted when computing contribution margin. Therefore, answer (d) is correct. Answer (a) is incorrect because variable selling and administrative expenses would be used. Answer (c) is incorrect because, under variable costing, expenses are classified by behavior. Therefore, variable selling and administrative would not be treated the same as fixed selling and administrative. Answer (c) is incorrect because all variable expenses are deducted in calculating contribution margin.

22. (587,T1,45) (a) The solutions approach to this problem is to visualize the format of the absorption costing income statement:

    Sales
  − Cost of goods sold
    Gross profit (margin)
  − Selling & admin. expenses
    Operating income

Gross profit is clearly shown in an absorption costing income statement as sales minus cost of goods sold. Contribution margin is not shown. Contribution margin is shown in a **direct (variable)** costing income statement as sales minus variable expenses.

23. (589,T1,45) (c) In a variable or direct costing income statement, costs are organized by cost behavior. This type of statement is commonly referred to as a contribution income statement. The solutions approach to this question is to visualize the format of the contribution income statement:

    Sales
  − Variable expenses
    Contribution margin
  − Fixed expenses
    Operating income

Variable expenses include both variable manufacturing expenses (i.e., direct materials, direct labor, and variable overhead) and variable selling and administrative expenses. Fixed expenses include both fixed manufacturing expenses (i.e., fixed overhead) and fixed selling and administrative expenses. Thus, as answer (c) states, fixed factory overhead is used to compute operating income but is not used to compute contribution margin. Answer (a) is incorrect because fixed factory overhead is used in the contribution income statement. Answer (b) is incorrect because fixed factory overhead is not needed to compute contribution margin. Answer (d) is incorrect because variable overhead is included with the variable expenses and fixed overhead is included with the fixed expenses. Also note that under variable costing, variable overhead is treated as a product cost while fixed overhead is treated as a period cost.

24. (583,T1,47) (b) Under direct costing, all fixed costs are expensed as incurred. Under absorption costing, fixed manufacturing costs attach to the product and become a part of inventory. If beginning inventory exceeds ending inventory, one must conclude that some of the units produced in a prior period were sold in the current period. As a result, absorption costing expenses not only the current period's fixed manufacturing costs, but also charges to expense some of the prior period's fixed manufacturing costs related to beginning inventory. Answer (a) will result in income being equal under both methods. Answer (c) will result in absorption income being higher. Answer (d) is incorrect, because per the discussion above, the operating incomes can differ.

D. Budgeting

25. (1183,P3,41) (d) The requirement is the number of pounds of raw material A that Walman is planning to purchase. The first step is to prepare a production budget for product Y.

Sales	42,000
Desired ending inventory	24,000
Total units needed	66,000
Beginning inventory	(22,000)
Units of Y to be produced	44,000

Next, a purchases budget for raw material A should be prepared.

Production needs (44,000 x 3)	132,000
Desired ending inventory	110,000
Total pounds needed	242,000
Beginning inventory	(100,000)
Pounds of A to be purchased	142,000

Note that the production needs for material A are equal to the units of Y to be produced, multiplied by 3 (number of pounds of A per unit of Y).

26. (1189,Q2,31)   (a)   The requirement is to determine cash disbursements for inventories for May.   The solutions approach is to use T-accounts to arrive at cash disbursements for the month.   Cash disbursements for inventory are found on the debit side of the accounts payable account.   This debit is found using T-accounts for inventory and accounts payable.

Inventory

(3) Purchases of inventory	$2,110	$2,250	(1) Cost of goods sold
(2) Decrease	$ 140		

Accounts Payable

(5) Cash disbursements	X	$2,110	(3) Purchases of inventory
		$ 240	(4) Decrease

Begin by finding the credit to inventory for cost of goods sold (1).   If gross profit is 25% of sales, then cost of goods sold must be 75%, or .75 x $3,000,000 = $2,250,000.   If the inventory account has decreased by $140,000 (2), purchases of inventory on accounts must have been $2,250,000 - $140,000, or $2,110,000 (3), reflected as a debit to inventory and a credit to accounts payable.   Finally, if the accounts payable account was decreased by $240,000 (4), payments on account (X) must be $2,110,000 + $240,000, or $2,350,000 (5).

27. (1180,P2,23)   (d)   The requirement is Reid's forecast of March 1980 cash receipts from credit sales; credit sales for March will be $320,000.   A/R at the end of February is $300,000, broken down as follows:

From January sales: (1/4)($300,000) = $ 75,000
From February sales: (3/4)($300,000) = $225,000

This problem must be read carefully; a key point is that the collection percentages given are **based on sales**, not on the A/R balance. The first step of the solutions approach is to compute January and February credit sales. January sales remaining in A/R are $75,000, but 70% of January sales have already been collected; therefore,

(30%) (January sales) = $ 75,000
January sales = $250,000

February sales remaining in A/R are $225,000, but 20% of February sales have already been collected; therefore,

(80%) (February sales) = $225,000
February sales = $281,250

Once the sales figures have been computed, estimated March collections can be obtained by applying the appropriate collection percentages:

Collections from	Sales	%	Cash to be collected
January sales	$250,000	25%	$ 62,500
February sales	$281,250	50%	$140,625
March sales	$320,000	20%	$ 64,000
			$267,125

28. (1185,Q1,20)   (a)   The requirement is to determine the cost of an error in predicting sales.   The cost of prediction error is the cost of failing to accurately forecast a critical parameter, in this case, demand.   The cost of prediction error is computed by taking the difference between the estimated cost and the actual cost of sales.   The computation is:

Estimated cost	500 x $.60	= $300
Actual cost	300 x .60	= 180
Cost of prediction error		$120

E. Flexible Budgets

29. (1182,P2,21)   (c)   The requirement is the total factory overhead rate, based on direct-labor hours, in a flexible budget at normal capacity.   The variable portion of the factory overhead rate can be computed by dividing variable factory overhead (at maximum capacity) by direct-labor hours (at maximum capacity).

$150,000 ÷ 60,000 = $2.50

Note that the variable overhead rate is constant over the relevant range of activity. Since **total** fixed overhead is constant over the relevant range, the budgeted fixed overhead is divided by direct-labor hours at 80% of maximum capacity, or 48,000 hours (60,000 x 80%).

$240,000 ÷ 48,000 = $5.00

The total factory overhead rate is $2.50 plus $5.00, or $7.50 per direct-labor hour.

30.   (588,T1,46)   (b)   A flexible budget is a budget which has been adjusted for changes in activity level or volume.   It allows management to compare actual costs and revenues with those budgeted based on the actual activity

level achieved during the period. The flexible budget may be used for any cost or revenue item. Therefore, answer (b) is correct.

31. (1189,T1,45) (d) When describing cost behavior, the terms "fixed" and "variable" refer to the behavior of <u>total</u> cost. Thus, when production levels decline within a relevant range, fixed costs remain constant in total but <u>increase</u> on a per unit basis because the same amount of fixed cost is spread over fewer units. Variable costs behave in the opposite manner; variable costs would <u>remain constant</u> on a per unit basis but would decrease in total as production levels declined. Answer (d) is correct because, as production levels decreased, the amount of total variable costs would decrease and the total fixed costs would remain constant. Thus, total costs (variable + fixed) would decrease. Answer (a) is incorrect because total fixed costs would not change as long as the production levels remained within the same relevant range. Answers (b) and (c) are incorrect because changes in production levels (within a relevant range) do not affect the variable cost per unit.

32. (587,T1,46) (d) The flexible budget for a producing department will include all costs associated with the manufacture of goods. These costs are called product or inventoriable costs. The three major classifications for product costs are direct materials, direct labor, and factory overhead. Thus, answer (d) is correct.

33. (589,T1,46) (a) The requirement is whether a flexible budget is appropriate for an administrative budget and/or a direct material budget. Flexible budgets are used to analyze changes in costs and revenues as changes in activity levels take place. If no changes are expected to occur, there would be no need for a flexible budget. This would happen if all amounts in the flexible budget remained constant throughout the relevant range (i.e., all costs were fixed). An administrative budget includes executives' salaries, depreciation, taxes, and other corporate expenses. Although most items in an administrative budget are generally fixed amounts, some items, such as certain clerical costs, are variable costs and would change in total with changes in the activity level. Therefore, a flexible budget would be appropriate. In addition, a marketing budget includes expenses incurred for promotion and sales. Some of these items, such as sales commissions or sample promotional products

would change with activity level. Therefore, a flexible budget would be appropriate. Since a flexible budget would be appropriate for both an administrative budget and a marketing budget, answer (a) is correct.

F. Responsibility Accounting

34. (588,T1,49) (c) Under responsibility accounting, costs, revenues, and investments are only allocated to those responsibility centers which have control over them. The manager of a profit center would have control over both costs and revenues, while the manager of an investment center would have control over costs, revenues, and investments. Therefore, answer (c) is correct.

35. (1181,T1,51) (a) Controllable costs are defined as those costs which can be directly influenced by a given manager within a given time span, answer (a). Answers (b), (c), and (d) are not directly related to responsibility accounting concepts or to the definition of controllable costs.

G. Segmented Reporting and Controllability

36. (1186,T1,48) (b) Contribution margin is equal to net sales less variable costs. The contribution margin ratio is calculated as contribution margin divided by net sales. A reduction in variable costs as a percentage of sales would increase contribution margin and thereby increase the contribution margin ratio. Answer (a) is incorrect because an increase in variable costs would cause the contribution margin ratio to decrease. Answers (c) and (d) are incorrect because a change in the breakeven point does not always imply a change in the contribution margin ratio (e.g., a change in the breakeven point may be caused by a change in fixed costs).

H. Performance Analysis

37. (1186,Q2,22) (b) Return on investment (ROI) measures the relationship between a division's profit and capital invested in the division. ROI can be computed as follows:

$$ROI = \frac{\text{Net operating income of division}}{\text{Average invested capital}}$$

The net operating income of the division is computed as follows:

Sales (300,000 units x $2.00)	$600,000
Variable costs	450,000
Contribution margin	$150,000
Fixed costs	90,000
Operating income	$ 60,000

The average invested capital is an average of the beginning and ending balances:

$$\text{Average invested capital} = \frac{\$500,000 + \$700,000}{2} = \$600,000$$

ROI can now be computed:

$$\text{ROI} = \frac{\$60,000}{\$600,000} = \underline{10\%}$$

38. (1186,Q2,23) (d) Residual income is the net operating income of a division less a minimum required return on the division's invested capital. Using the amounts computed in solving the previous question, residual income is computed as follows:

Net operating income	$60,000
Minimum return	
(15% x $600,000)	90,000
Residual income	$(30,000)

39. (1186,Q2,24) (a) The breakeven point in units can be computed by dividing total fixed costs by the contribution margin per unit. The contribution margin per unit for Rho can be computed as follows:

	Per unit
Sales	$2.00
Variable costs	
($450,000 ÷ 300,000)	1.50
Unit contribution margin	$0.50

The breakeven point can now be computed using the following formula:

$$\frac{\text{Total fixed costs}}{\text{Unit contribution margin}} = \text{BEP in units}$$

$$\frac{\$90,000}{\$0.50} = \underline{180,000 \text{ units}}$$

40. (1186,Q2,25) (c) Contribution margin is the margin after all variable costs have been covered. Rho's contribution margin for 1985 is computed as follows:

Sales (300,000 units x $2.00)	$600,000
Variable costs	450,000
Contribution margin	$150,000

41. (1186,Q2,26) (c) To answer this question, an understanding of cost behavior patterns is needed. Within a relevant range, total variable costs will vary directly with the number of units produced and sold. However, total fixed costs will remain the same. This means that at a production level of 350,000 units, total costs and expenses would be as follows:

Variable costs	
($1.50* x 350,000)	$525,000
Fixed costs	90,000
Total costs and expenses	$615,000

*($450,000 ÷ 300,000 units)

Note that the increase in total costs and expenses is solely due to variable costs.

42. (1189,Q2,37) (a) The return on investment (ROI) formula is:

$$\frac{\text{Net income of division}}{\text{Average capital invested in division}}$$

The average invested capital (denominator) is given at $50,000. The net income of the division (numerator) must be computed as follows:

Sales	$620,000
Variable expenses	(500,000)
Contribution margin	120,000
Traceable fixed costs	(100,000)
Net income	$ 20,000

The ROI for East Division is 40% ($20,000 net income divided by $50,000 average invested capital).

43. (1189,Q2,38) (c) Residual income is the net income of the division less the cost of capital on the division's assets. Net income for East Division was computed above as $20,000. The cost of capital is computed as $9,000 ($50,000 average invested capital x 18% imputed interest rate). The residual income is calculated below:

Division net income	$20,000
Cost of capital	
($50,000 x 18%)	(9,000)
Residual income	$11,000

44. (589,T1,49) (b) Residual income is the net income of a division less the cost of capital on the division's assets. The cost of capital is determined by using an imputed interest charge times the invested capital. Answer (a) is incorrect because the interest charge is subtracted not added. Answers (c) and (d) are incorrect because dividends are not considered in residual income.

45. (587,T1,49) (b) The formula to compute return on investment (ROI) is:

$$\text{ROI} = \frac{\text{Net operating income}}{\text{Sales}} \times \frac{\text{Sales}}{\text{Average invested capital}}$$

Another way of expressing this formula is:

$$ROI = \frac{Profit}{margin} \times \frac{Capital}{turnover}$$

Answer (b) is a description of the formula above. The percentage of profit to sales, or profit margin, multiplied by the capital-employed turnover rate will equal ROI. Answer (a) is incorrect because the profit margin is multiplied by, not divided by, the capital turnover rate to get ROI. Answers (c) and (d) are incorrect because they both ignore profit margin and involve needless calculations.

46. (586,T1,49) (c) The requirement is the effect on a company's return on investment (ROI) when the invested capital or the invested capital-employed turnover rate changes. The ROI formula is

$$ROI = \frac{Net\ income}{Sales} \times \frac{Sales}{Invested\ capital}$$

or

$$ROI = \frac{Profit}{margin} \times \frac{Capital}{turnover}$$

ROI will decrease when the capital turnover rate decreases and profit margin is held constant. Therefore, answer (c) is correct and answer (d) incorrect. Answer (a) is incorrect because an increase in invested capital will decrease the capital turnover rate which would <u>decrease</u> ROI. Answer (b) is incorrect because a decrease in invested capital will increase the capital turnover rate which would <u>increase</u> ROI.

I. Product Pricing

47. (587,Q2,28) (b) The solutions approach to this question is to algebraically reconstruct how Aba Caterers figured the total price per person. Three components make up the total price: the cost of the food, the service charge, and the sales tax. The service charge of 15% is computed on the food (F) only. The sales tax is computed on the food plus the service charge. The equation can be constructed as follows:

$$F + .15F + .06(F + .15\ F) = \$30$$

Where:

$$F = the\ cost\ of\ the\ food\ alone$$
$$.15\ F = the\ service\ charge$$
$$.06(F + .15\ F) = the\ sales\ tax$$

Solving algebraically:

$$1.219\ F = \$30.00$$
$$F = \underline{\$24.61}$$

48. (1189,Q2,23) (c) The selling price of a product minus the cost of a product equals the product's gross margin. If the gross margin percentage is 40%, the percentage for the cost

of the product has to be 60% (100% - 40%). This means that 60% of the selling price of a product will go to cover the cost of the product which, in this case, is $12.00 per unit. Since this $12.00 represents 60% of the selling price, the selling price should be $20.00 ($12.00 ÷ 60%).

49. (586,Q2,31) (d) The requirement is the selling price per unit for 10,000 units of product X. The price per unit has to cover all costs to produce and sell product X plus earn a 30% return on the $100,000 investment in equipment. The cost per unit to produce and sell product X is $8 ($5 + $2 + $1). Therefore, the total cost to produce and sell X is $80,000 ($8 x 10,000 units). The price that should be set for product X can be computed using the following formula.

$$\frac{Selling}{price} = \frac{Total\ cost + \left(\frac{Desired\ rate}{of\ return} \times \frac{Total}{investment}\right)}{Sales\ volume\ in\ units}$$
per unit

$$\frac{Selling}{price} = \frac{\$80,000 + (30\% \times \$100,000)}{10,000}$$
per unit

$$\frac{Selling}{price} = \frac{\$80,000 + \$30,000}{10,000}$$
per unit

$$\frac{Selling}{price} = \underline{\$11.00}$$
per unit

50. (586,T1,50) (b) The requirement is what costs are covered under the contribution approach to pricing when setting a price at which income remains constant. Prices under the contribution approach are set at variable cost plus a percentage markup. Variable cost is used because variable cost varies in total with the level of sales. The percentage markup, or contribution margin, will be used to cover fixed costs and any remainder will be profit. If the selling price is set at variable cost, no contribution margin will be generated to cover fixed costs or contribute to profit. Therefore, income will remain constant. Thus, answer (b) is correct. Answer (a) is incorrect because prime cost, direct materials plus direct labor, does not include all variable costs. Answers (c) and (d) are incorrect because fixed costs will remain the same in total no matter how many units are sold within a relevant range.

J. Inventory Models

51. (1179,P2,31) (d) The requirement is to determine the cost of carrying one bookcase in inventory for 1 year using the EOQ model. The economic order quantity (EOQ) is a formula based on an inventory cost function. The

objective of the formula is to minimize both carrying costs and total ordering costs. The formula is:

$$EOQ = \sqrt{\frac{2aD}{k}}$$

a = fixed order cost
D = annual demand
k = unit carrying cost

This problem requires you to calculate the value of k. The solutions approach is to plug the data in the problem into the formula above, as illustrated below. Squaring both sides of the equation gives 40,000k = $16,000 or k = $.40.

$$200 = \sqrt{\frac{2 \times \$2.00 \times 4,000}{k}}$$

$$40,000 = \frac{2 \times \$2.00 \times 4,000}{k}$$

$$40,000k = \$16,000$$

$$k = \$.40$$

52. (579,P2,28) (d) The requirement is the number of units of safety stock that will result in the lowest cost. The approach is to compute the total cost for each of the 4 alternative levels of safety stock as illustrated below. The carrying cost is $2 for each unit of safety stock. The stock-out cost is the probability of running out times $80 for each of the 5 reorders. The lowest total cost of both carrying safety stock and running out is $130 [(55 units x $2/unit) + ($80 x 5% x 5 reorders)]. Thus, 55 units of safety stock should be maintained.

Safety stock	Carrying cost	Stockout cost/order	Stockout cost/5 orders	Total cost
20	$40	$32	$160	$200
40	$80	$16	$80	$160
50	$100	$8	$40	$140
55	$110	$4	$20	$130

53. (587,Q2,22) (b) The requirement is the economic order quantity (EOQ). The EOQ formula is:

$$EOQ = \sqrt{\frac{2aD}{k}}$$

In the above equation a = cost of placing one order, D = annual demand in units, and k = annual cost of carrying one unit in inventory for one year. Substituting the given information, the equation becomes:

$$EOQ = \sqrt{\frac{(2)(32)(20,000)}{8}} = \sqrt{160,000} = 400 \text{ units}$$

54. (585,Q1,11) (d) The requirement is to determine the order point for material X. When safety stock is maintained, the order point is computed as follows:

$$\left(\begin{array}{c} \text{Daily} \\ \text{demand} \end{array} \times \begin{array}{c} \text{Lead Time} \\ \text{in days} \end{array}\right) + \begin{array}{c} \text{Safety} \\ \text{Stock} \end{array}$$

Daily demand is 80 units (20,000 units ÷ 250 days). Therefore, the order point is 3,200 units [(80 x 30) + 800].

55. (587,T1,50) (b) The economic order quantity formula is:

$$EOQ = \sqrt{\frac{2aD}{K}}$$

In the above equation, a = cost of placing one order, D = annual demand in units, and k = annual cost of carrying one unit in inventory for one year (i.e., inventory carrying cost). With this information it is easy to see that inventory carrying cost is used in the denominator and cost per purchase order in the numerator.

56. (578,T1,32) (c) The requirement is the factor relevant to determining EOQ. The EOQ model minimizes variable order costs and variable inventory carrying costs. Answer (c) is correct because the EOQ model minimizes variable order costs and variable inventory carrying costs. Answer (a) is incorrect because insurance on the plant extends beyond simply protecting inventory from loss, i.e., production equipment is also covered. Also, insurance is a fixed cost. Answers (b) and (d) are incorrect because supervisory salaries and depreciation are fixed costs. The EOQ model considers only variable costs.

May 1990 Answers

57. (590,T1,45) (d) The solutions approach to this question is to visualize each income statement as shown below:

Absorption costing I/S

    Sales
- Cost of goods sold
    Gross profit (margin)
- Selling & admin. expenses
    Operating income

Variable costing I/S

    Sales
- Variable expenses
    Contribution margin
- Fixed expenses
    Operating income

Because the question states that actual sales revenue, total gross profit, and total contribution margin approximated budgeted expenses, COGS, and variable expenses must have also approximated budgeted figures. Net income is substantially lower, therefore, because selling and administrative fixed

expenses had increased. If sales prices and
variable costs had declined proportionately
[answer (a)], the contribution margin would
have declined by the same percentage. If
sales prices had declined more than variable
costs [answer (b)], the contribution margin
would have again declined. If manufacturing
fixed costs had increased [answer (c)], gross
margin would have decreased.

58. (590,T1,46) (d) To answer this
question, an understanding of cost behavior
patterns and CVP charts is needed. The CVP
chart presented in the problem can be
interpreted as follows:

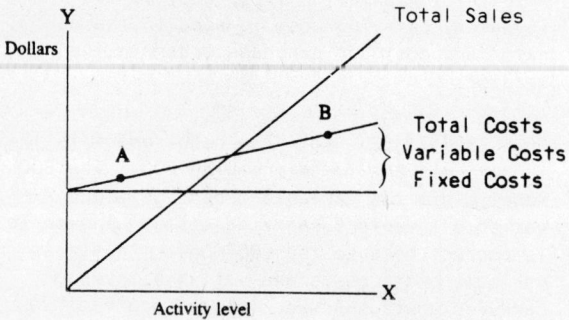

Within a relevant range, **total** variable costs
vary directly with the number of units produced and sold. Because these costs remain
constant per unit, the variable costs associated with point A and point B will be the same
percentage of total sales associated with each
point. Total fixed costs remain constant in
total at any activity level. Because these
costs are allocated evenly to units produced
and sold, they represent a higher percentage
of lower sales than of higher sales. Point A
is to the left of point B, indicating a lower
sales level for point A. The fixed costs
will, therefore, be a greater percentage of
sales at point A than at point B. Therefore,
answer (c) is correct.

59. (590,T1,47) (c) If sales dollars are
used to measure activity levels, the various
activity levels on the X axis would be expressed in terms of sales. Total costs could
be read by comparing a point on the total cost
line to the Y axis only, because total costs
are a dependent variable, which are measured
on the Y axis. Total revenues could be read
by comparing a point on the total sales line
to either the Y axis or the X axis. Therefore, answer (c) is correct.

Solution Guide

Problem 1   C-V-P Analyses

(588,Q5)

1. This problem consists of four related parts requiring cost-volume-profit analysis of various alternatives. The solutions approach is to first study the requirements; second, mentally review cost-volume-profit analysis; third, read through the information given; and fourth, make the necessary computations.

2. Part (a) requires the computation of the breakeven point in sales dollars based on the pro forma income statement. One shortcut approach is the following formula:

$$\text{Dollars to breakeven} = \frac{\text{Fixed costs}}{\text{Contribution margin percentages}}$$

2.1 The only fixed costs given in the problem were in the income statement category all other costs ($100,000).

2.2 The variable costs include cost of goods sold ($6,000,000) and commissions (20% of sales, or $2,000,000). Note that the entire cost of goods sold is assumed to be a variable cost because this is a merchandising company. For a manufacturing company, part of cost of goods sold would be fixed.

2.3 Sales ($10,000,000) less variable costs ($6,000,000 + $2,000,000 = $8,000,000) is contribution margin ($10,000,000 − $8,000,000 = $2,000,000). The contribution margin percentage is contribution margin ($2,000,000) divided by sales ($10,000,000), or 20%.

2.4 The breakeven point is computed using the formula from item 2 above:

$$\$100,000 \div 20\% = \$500,000$$

Note that income tax expense is not considered because no taxes are due at the breakeven point (zero income).

3. Part (b) requires the computation of the breakeven point in sales dollars if the company selects the alternative of employing its own salespersons. The same formula from item 2 above can be used.

3.1 Under this alternative, fixed costs include the salespersons' salaries (3 x $30,000 = $90,000), the sales manager's salary (160,000), and the other fixed costs ($100,000). Total fixed costs are $350,000 ($90,000 + $160,000 + $100,000).

3.2 The variable costs include cost of goods sold, which is 60% of sales ($6,000,000 ÷ $10,000,000), and sales commissions, which are 5% of sales. Therefore, variable expenses are 65% of sales and the contribution margin percentage is 35% of sales.

3.3 The breakeven point is computed using the formula from item two above:

$$\$350,000 \div 35\% = \underline{\$1,000,000}$$

Again, income tax expense is not considered because no taxes are due at the breakeven point (zero income).

4. Part (c) requires the computation of the sales volume required to yield the same net income as in the pro forma income statement, if sales commissions are increased to 25%. Note that to achieve the target net income of $1,330,000, Seco must achieve income before taxes of $1,900,000, as indicated in the income statement.

4.1 The basic formula discussed in item 2 must be modified when a target income is involved:

$$\text{Dollars to earn target income} = \frac{\text{Fixed costs + Target income}}{\text{Contribution margin percentage}}$$

4.2 Fixed costs remain at $100,000 (see 2.1), and the target income is $1,900,000 (see 4).

4.3 Under this plan, variable costs include cost of goods sold, which is 60% of sales ($6,000,000 ÷ $10,000,000), and sales commissions, which are 25% of sales. Therefore, variable expenses are 85% of sales and the contribution margin percentage is 15% of sales.

4.4 The required sales volume is computed using the formula from item 4.1. above:

$$(\$100,000 + \$1,900,000) \div 15\% = \underline{\$13,333,333}$$

5. Part (d) requires the computation of the estimated sales volume that would generate an identical net income for the sales agents 25% commission alternative and the hire salespersons alternative.

5.1 The solutions approach is to first determine how to compute net income under each
of these alternatives.

5.2 Under the sales agents alternative,
variable expenses are 85% of sales (cost
of goods sold, 60%; and sales commissions, 25%). Fixed costs are $100,000.
Therefore, net income can be computed
using this formula:

$$NI = X - .85 X - \$100,000$$
(where X = sales dollars)

5.3 Under the salespersons alternative,
variable expenses are 65% of sales (cost
of goods sold, 60%; and sales commissions, 5%). Fixed costs are $350,000
(see item 5.1 above). Therefore, net

income can be computed using this
formula:

$$NI = X - .65 X - \$350,000$$
(where X = sales dollars)

5.4 The goal is to determine when these two
incomes are identical (note that if the
income before tax is identical, then the
net income must be identical). Therefore, we need to determine when the two
formulas (from 5.2 and 5.3) are equal:
X - .85X - $100,000 = X - .65X -
$350,000. When this equation is alge-
braically solved, it is determined that X
= $1,250,000. In other words, at a sales
volume of $1,250,000, both alternatives
result in the same income.

Unofficial Answer

Problem 1   C-V-P Analyses (588,Q5)

Seco Corp.
Year Ending December 31, 1989

a.   Estimated Breakeven Point Based on Pro Forma Income Statement

Sales		$10,000,000
Variable costs		
Cost of sales	$6,000,000	
Commissions	2,000,000	8,000,000
Contribution margin		$ 2,000,000
Contribution margin ratio ($2,000,000 ÷ $10,000,000)		20%
Fixed costs		$ 100,000
Contribution margin ratio		÷ .20
Estimated breakeven point		$ 500,000

b.   Estimated Breakeven Point With Company Employing Its Own Salespersons

Variable cost ratios	
Cost of sales	60%
Commissions	5%
Total	65%
Contribution margin ratio (100% - 65%)	35%
Fixed costs	
Sales manager	$ 160,000
3 salespersons @ $30,000 each	90,000
Administrative	100,000
Total	$ 350,000
Fixed costs	$ 350,000
Contribution margin ratio	÷ .35
Estimated breakeven point	$ 1,000,000

c.

Estimated Sales Volume Yielding Net Income
Projected in Pro Forma Income Statement
With Independent Sales Agents Receiving 25% Commission

Target income before income tax	$ 1,900,000
Fixed costs	100,000
Total	$ 2,000,000
Variable cost ratios	
Cost of sales	60%
Commissions	25%
Total	85%
Contribution margin ratio (100% – 85%)	15%
Target income + fixed costs	$ 2,000,000
Contribution margin ratio	÷ .15
Estimated sales volume	$13,333,333

d.

Estimated Sales Volume Yielding An Identical Net Income
Regardless of Whether the Company Employs its Own Salespersons
or
Continues With Independent Sales Agents and Pays Them 25% Commission

Total costs with agents receiving 25% commission = Total costs with company's own sales force

$$X = \text{sales volume}$$

$$\frac{\$8,500,000}{\$10,000,000} X + \$100,000 = \frac{\$6,500,000}{\$10,000,000} X + \$350,000$$

$$.85X + \$100,000 = .65X + \$350,000$$

$$.20X = \$250,000$$

$$X = \$1,250,000$$

Solution Guide

Problem 2   Cash Budget (585,Q4)

1. This problem requires the preparation of a cash budget for two years. The company is undergoing a troubled debt restructuring, and the budget must indicate cash expected to be available to pay the claims of the general creditors, payments to general creditors, and cash remaining after payment of claims. The answer should not include funds needed for working capital purposes.

2. First, prepare the budget for the first year, ending 3/31/87.

2.1 There is no cash on hand at 4/1/86.

2.2 Cash will be collected from sales and from liquidation of accounts receivable and inventories. Sales during the first year are expected to be $900,000 (10,000 x $90). Receivables will be collected in the calendar month following sales. Therefore, the first 11 months of sales will be collected in the fist year; the twelth month will be collected in the second year. Thus, collections from sales will be $825,000 ($900,000 x 11/12). Cash collected from liquidating the assets will be equal to the assets' liquidation values ($50,000 + $40,000 = $90,000).

2.3 Payments will be made for direct materials, direct labor, variable overhead, and fixed costs. Direct labor, variable overhead, and fixed costs are paid when incurred. To compute payments for direct materials, you must first compute materials purchases. Mayne needs $200,000 of materials for production (10,000 x $20) and $40,000 of materials for ending inventory (60 days of next year's materials needs, or 60/360 x 12,000 x $20). There is no beginning inventory after liquidation of inventories, so $240,000 of materials must be purchased. All of these purchases will be paid for during the first month of the next year. Therefore, payments for purchases total $220,000 [$240,000 - (1/2 x $240,000)].

2.4 The total cash available ($165,000) is the excess of total cash collected ($825,000 + $90,000) over total disbursements ($750,000).

2.5 Since Mayne owes general creditors $360,000 (60% x $600,000), the entire amount available ($165,000) would accrue to them. (Note that the AICPA solution shows a distribution of only the $90,000 from the accounts receivable and inventories but acknowledges that distribution of the entire $165,000 is also acceptable.

3. Next, prepare the budget for the second year, ending 3/31/88.

3.1 If all available cash was distributed on 3/31/87, there would be no cash on hand at 4/1/87.

3.2 Cash will be collected only from sales during the second year. Sales during the second year are expected to be $1,080,000 (12,000 x $90). Collections will include the sales from the twelfth month of the first year ($900,000 x 1/12 = $75,000) and the sales from the first 11 months of the second year ($1,080,000 x 11/12 = $990,000). The total is $1,965,000 ($75,000 + $990,000).

3.3 Again, payments for direct labor, variable overhead, and fixed costs are made as incurred. Payments for direct materials must be computed. Mayne needs $240,000 of materials for production (12,000 x $20) and $50,000 of materials for ending inventory (60,360 x 15,000 x $20). The beginning inventory is $40,000 (the ending inventory from the first year). Therefore, materials purchases during the second year will be $250,000 ($240,000 + $50,000 - $40,000). All of these purchases will be paid for in the second year except the last month's (30 days) purchases, which will be paid for during the first month of the third year [$250,000 - (1/12 x $300,000) = $225,000]. Also paid for during the second year are the purchases made during the last month of the first year ($240,000 x 1/12 = $20,000). Therefore, total payments for direct materials in the second year are $245,000 ($225,000 + $20,000).

3.4 The total cash available generated in the second year ($210,000) is the excess of cash collections ($1,065,000) over total disbursements ($855,000).

3.5 Mayne owed a reduced balance of $360,000 (60% x $600,000) to general creditors. In the first year $165,000 was generated. Therefore, only $195,000 is needed in the second year. This leaves an ending cash balance of $15,000 ($210,000 - $195,000).

Unofficial Answer

Problem 2   Cash Budget (585,Q4)

Mayne Manufacturing Co.
Cash Budget
For the Years Ending March 31,

	1987		1988	
Balance of cash at beginning		$ 0		$ 75,000
Cash generated from operations				
Collections from customers – Schedule A	$825,000		$1,065,000	
Disbursemnets				
Direct materials – Schedule B	220,000		245,000	
Direct labor	300,000		360,000	
Variable overhead	100,000		120,000	
Fixed costs	130,000		130,000	
Total disbursements	750,000		855,000	
Excess of cash collections over cash disbursements from operations		75,000		210,000
Cash available from operations		75,000		285,000
Cash received from liquidation of existing accounts receivable and inventories		90,000		0
Total cash available		165,000		285,000
Payments to general creditors		90,000		270,000 [2]
Balance of cash at end		$ 75,000 [1]		$ 15,000

[1] This amount could have been used to
    pay general creditors or carried for-
    ward to the beginning of the next year
[2] ($600,00 x 60%) – ($50,000 + $40,000)

Schedule A

Mayne Manufacturing Co.
Collections From Customers
For the Years Ending March 31,

	1987	1988
Sales	$900,000	$1,080,000
Beginning accounts receivable	0	75,000
Total	900,000	1,155,000
Less ending accounts receivable	75,000	90,000
Collections from customers	$825,000	$1,065,000

Schedule B

Mayne Manufacturing Co.
Disbursements for Direct Materials
For the Years Ending March 31,

	1987	1988
Direct materials required for production	$200,000	$240,000
Required ending inventory	40,000 [3]	50,000 [4]
Total	240,000	290,000
Less beginning inventory	0	40,000
Purchases	240,000	250,000
Beginning accounts payable	0	20,000
Total	240,000	270,000
Less ending accounts payable	20,000	25,000
Disbursements for direct materials	$220,000	$245,000

[3] 12,000 units x 2/12 = 2,000; 2,000 x $20 per unit = $40,000
[4] 15,000 units x 2/12 = 2,500; 2,500 x $20 per unit = $50,000

Solution Guide

Problem 3   Budgeting and Standard
              Costs (589,Q5)

1. This problem requires the preparation of
    schedules pertaining to the pricing and
    delivery functions of a wholesale com-
    pany. Part (a) requires a budget for the
    costs involved with the pricing function,
    while part (b) requires a schedule
    showing the standard delivery cost per
    unit for each product.

2. Since variable pricing costs vary di-
    rectly with the number of items priced,
    the first step in preparing a budget of
    pricing costs is to determine the number
    of items expected to be priced in 1989.
    The number of sales is expected to be
    24,000 and the average number of items
    per sale is projected to be 5, so the
    number of items expected to be priced is
    120,000 (24,000 x 5).

2.1 In 1988, wage cost was $0.50 per item
     ($40,000/80,000). The 10% increase in
     the wage rate will increase the cost per
     item to $0.55 [$0.50 + (10% x $0.50)].
     Therefore, budgeted wage cost per item is
     $66,000 (120,000 x $0.55). An alterna-
     tive computation is shown below:

1988 units (20,000 x 4)		80,000
1988 wages	$40,000	
1988 rate	÷ 6.00	
1988 hours		÷ 6,666
Units priced per hour		12

1989 hours (120,000 units ÷ 12 units per hour)	10,000
1989 wage rate [$6.00 + ($6.00 x 10%)]	x 6.60
1989 budgeted wage cost	$66,000

2.2 Payroll tax rates and workers' compensa-
     tion insurance rates will be the same in
     1989 as in 1988. Since the 1988 payroll
     tax rate was 10% of wages ($4,000 ÷
     $40,000), 1989 payroll taxes should be
     budgeted at $6,600 (10% x $66,000).
     Since the 1988 workers' compensation in-
     surance rate was 5% of wages ($2,000 ÷
     $40,000), the 1989 amount should be bud-
     geted at $3,300 (5% x $66,000).

2.3 The supplies cost in 1988 was $0.0125 per
     item ($1,000 ÷ 80,000 units). Therefore,
     the budgeted 1989 cost is $1,500 (120,000
     x $0.0125) or [(120,0000 ÷ 80,000) x
     $1,000].

2.4 Total variable costs are $77,400 ($66,000
     + $6,600 + $3,300 + $1,500).

2.5 By definition, the fixed cost should be
     the same ($3,400) for 120,000 units in
     1989 as it was for 80,000 units in 1988.
     Total budgeted pricing costs for 1989 are
     $80,800 ($77,400 + $3,400).

3. Part (b) requires a schedule showing the
    1989 standard delivery cost per unit for
    each product.

3.1 Fixed costs are allocated equally to all
     units. Total fixed delivery costs are
     $30,000 for 120,000 units, or $0.25 per
     unit.

3.2 Variable delivery costs depends on the
     size and weight of units, which is
     reflected in the number of units per
     delivery or truckload. The number of
     deliveries or truckloads needed for each
     product is computed by taking the total
     number of units of each product and
     dividing by the the capacity for those
     units.

	Arcil	Balo	Cacha
Total # of units	60,000	40,000	20,000
÷ capacity	÷ 10	÷ 5	÷ 4
Deliveries	6,000	8,000	5,000

     Total deliveries to be made therefore is
     19,000 (6,000 + 8,000 + 5,000).

3.3 The next step is to determine the vari-
     able cost per unit. Variable costs are
     expected to be $228,000 and expected de-
     liveries are 19,000, resulting in a $12
     per truckload cost ($228,000 ÷ 19,000).
     Variable cost per unit is then calculated
     by dividing the $12 variable cost per de-
     livery by the unit capacity per truck for
     each product.

	Arcil	Balo	Cacha
V.C. per delivery	$ 12	$ 12	$ 12
÷ Capacity per truck	÷ 10	÷ 5	÷ 4
V.C. per unit	$1.20	$2.40	$3.00

3.4 The fixed cost per unit is calculated by
     dividing the fixed cost by the total num-
     ber of units expected to be delivered
     ($30,000 ÷ 120,000 units). Fixed cost
     per unit is $.25.

3.5 Total standard delivery cost per unit is
     computed by adding the fixed cost per
     unit to the variable cost per unit.

Unofficial Answer

Problem 3   Budgeting and Standard Costs
                (589,Q5)

a.

Tapa Wholesale Company
PRICING FUNCTION BUDGET
For the Year Ending
December 31, 1989

Variable costs:	
Wages	$66,000
Payroll taxes	6,600
Workers' compensation insurance	3,300
Supplies	1,500
Total variable costs	77,400
Fixed costs	3,400
Total costs	$80,800

COMPUTATIONS

Wages

Number of items priced in 1988 (20,000 x 4)	80,000
Projected number of items priced in 1989 (24,000 x 5)	120,000
Average wage cost per item in 1988 ($40,000/80,000)	$0.50
Projected wage cost in 1989 (120,000 @ $0.50 + 10%)	$66,000

Payroll taxes

$66,000 x 10%	$ 6,600

Workers' compensation insurance

$66,000 x 5%	$ 3,300

Supplies

1989 projected multiple of number of 1988 items (120,000/80,000)	1.5 times
$1,000 x 1.5	$ 1,500

b.

Tapa Wholesale Company
COMPUTATION OF STANDARD DELIVERY
COST PER UNIT OF PRODUCT
For the Year Ending December 31, 1989

Product	Units	Unit capacity per truck	Number of deliveries projected	Variable costs per delivery	Variable costs per unit delivered	Fixed costs	Total
Arcil	60,000	10	6,000	$12	$1.20	$0.25	$1.45
Balo	40,000	5	8,000	12	2.40	0.25	2.65
Cacha	20,000	4	5,000	12	3.00	0.25	3.25
Totals	120,000		19,000				

Variable costs per delivery:	
Total number of deliveries	19,000
Variable costs	$228,000
Variable costs per delivery	$12
Fixed costs per unit:	
Total number of units	120,000
Fixed costs	$30,000
Fixed costs per unit	$0.25

Multiple Choice Questions (1-27)

1. The absolute minimum cost that would be possible under the best conceivable operating conditions is a description of which type of standard cost?
    a.   Currently attainable (expected).
    b.   Theoretical.
    c.   Normal.
    d.   Practical.

2. Dahl Co. uses a standard costing system in connection with the manufacture of a "one size fits all" article of clothing. Each unit of finished product contains 2 yards of direct material. However, a 20% direct material spoilage calculated on input quantities occurs during the manufacturing process. The cost of the direct material is $3 per yard. The standard direct material cost per unit of finished product is
    a. $4.80
    b. $6.00
    c. $7.20
    d. $7.50

3. Information on Kennedy Company's direct-material costs is as follows:

Standard unit price	$3.60
Actual quantity purchased	1,600
Standard quantity allowed for actual production	1,450
Materials purchase price variance--favorable	$ 240

What was the actual purchase price per unit, rounded to the nearest penny?
    a. $3.06
    b. $3.11
    c. $3.45
    d. $3.75

4. Information on Rex Co.'s direct material costs for May 1985 is as follows:

Actual quantity of direct materials purchased and used	30,000 lbs.
Actual cost of direct materials	$84,000
Unfavorable direct materials usage variance	$ 3,000
Standard quantity of direct materials allowed for May production	29,000 lbs.

For the month of May, what was Rex's direct materials price variance?
    a. $2,800 favorable.
    b. $2,800 unfavorable.
    c. $6,000 unfavorable.
    d. $6,000 favorable.

5. If a company follows a practice of isolating variances at the earliest point in time, what would be the appropriate time to isolate and recognize a direct material price variance?
    a.   When material is issued.
    b.   When material is purchased.
    c.   When material is used in production.
    d.   When purchase order is originated.

6. The standard unit cost is used in the calculation of which of the following variances?

	Materials price variance	Materials usage variance
a.	No	No
b.	No	Yes
c.	Yes	No
d.	Yes	Yes

7. Which department is customarily held responsible for an unfavorable materials usage variance?
    a.   Quality control.
    b.   Purchasing.
    c.   Engineering.
    d.   Production.

8. Palo Corp. manufactures one product with a standard direct labor cost of 2 hours at $6.00 per hour. During March, 500 units were produced using 1,050 hours at $6.10 per hour. The unfavorable direct labor efficiency variance is
    a. $100
    b. $105
    c. $300
    d. $305

Items 9 and 10 are based on the following data:

The following processing standards have been set for Duo Co.'s clerical workers:

Number of hours per 1,000 papers processed	150
Normal number of papers processed per year	1,500,000
Wage rate per 1,000 papers	$600
Standard variable cost of processing 1,500,000 papers	$900,000
Fixed costs per year	$150,000

The following information pertains to the 1,200,000 papers that were processed during 1986:

Total cost	$915,000
Labor cost	$760,000
Labor hours	190,000

9. For 1986, Duo's expected total cost to process the 1,200,000 papers, assuming standard performance, should be
   a. $910,000
   b. $900,000
   c. $870,000
   d. $840,000

10. For 1986, Duo's labor rate variance would be
    a. $40,000 unfavorable.
    b. $32,000 favorable.
    c. $10,000 unfavorable.
    d. $0.

11. Tub Co. uses a standard cost system. The following information pertains to direct labor for product B for the month of October:

Actual rate paid	$8.40 per hour
Standard rate	$8.00 per hour
Standard hours allowed for actual production	2,000 hours
Labor efficiency variance	$1,600 unfavorable

What were the actual hours worked?
   a. 1,800
   b. 1,810
   c. 2,190
   d. 2,200

12. For the month of April, Thorp Co.'s records disclosed the following data relating to direct labor:

Actual costs	$10,000	
Rate variance	1,000	favorable
Efficiency variance	1,500	unfavorable
Standard cost	$ 9,500	

For the month of April, actual direct labor hours amounted to 2,000. In April, Thorp's standard direct labor rate per hour was
   a. $5.50
   b. $5.00
   c. $4.75
   d. $4.50

13. Which of the following is the most probable reason a company would experience an unfavorable labor rate variance and a favorable labor efficiency variance?
   a. The mix of workers assigned to the particular job was heavily weighted towards the use of higher paid experienced individuals.
   b. The mix of workers assigned to the particular job was heavily weighted towards the use of new relatively low paid unskilled workers.

c. Because of the production schedule, workers from other production areas were assigned to assist this particular process.
d. Defective materials caused more labor to be used in order to produce a standard unit.

14. A debit balance in the labor-efficiency variance indicates that
   a. Standard hours exceed actual hours.
   b. Actual hours exceed standard hours.
   c. Standard rate and standard hours exceed actual rate and actual hours.
   d. Actual rate and actual hours exceed standard rate and standard hours.

15. Universal Company uses a standard cost system and prepared the following budget at normal capacity for the month of January 1983:

Direct-labor hours	24,000
Variable factory overhead	$ 48,000
Fixed factory overhead	$108,000
Total factory overhead per direct-labor hour	$ 6.50

Actual data for January 1983 were as follows:

Direct-labor hours worked	22,000
Total factory overhead	$147,000
Standard direct-labor hours allowed for capacity attained	21,000

Using the two-way analysis of overhead variances, what is the budget (controllable) variance for January 1983?
   a. $ 3,000 favorable.
   b. $ 5,000 favorable.
   c. $ 9,000 favorable.
   d. $10,500 unfavorable.

16. Under the two-variance method for analyzing factory overhead, which of the following is used in the computation of the controllable (budget) variance?

	Budget allowance based on actual hours	Budget allowance based on standard hours
a.	Yes	Yes
b.	Yes	No
c.	No	No
d.	No	Yes

17. Under the two-variance method for analyzing overhead, which of the following variances consists of both variable and fixed overhead elements?

	Controllable (budget) variance	Volume variance
a.	Yes	Yes
b.	Yes	No
c.	No	No
d.	No	Yes

18. Under the two-variance method for analyzing factory overhead, the difference between the actual factory overhead and the budget allowance based on standard hours allowed is the
   a. Net overhead variance.
   b. Efficiency variance.
   c. Volume variance.
   d. Controllable (budget) variance.

   Items 19 and 20 are based on the following information.

   The following information relates to a given department of Herman Company for the fourth quarter 1987:

Actual total overhead (fixed
 plus variable) $178,500
Budget formula $110,000 plus $0.50/hr.
Total overhead application rate $1.50 hr.
Spending variance $8,000 unfavorable
Volume variance $5,000 favorable

The total overhead variance is divided into three variances--spending, efficiency, and volume.

19. What were the actual hours worked in this department during the quarter?
   a. 110,000
   b. 121,000
   c. 137,000
   d. 153,000

20. What were the standard hours allowed for good output in this department during the quarter?
   a. 105,000
   b. 106,667
   c. 110,000
   d. 115,000

21. Under the three-variance method for analyzing factory overhead, which of the following is used in the computation of the spending variance?

	Actual factory overhead	Budget allowance based on actual hours
a.	No	Yes
b.	No	No
c.	Yes	No
d.	Yes	Yes

22. Under the three-variance method for analyzing factory overhead, the difference between the actual factory overhead and the factory overhead applied to production is the
   a. Net overhead variance.
   b. Controllable variance.
   c. Efficiency variance.
   d. Spending variance.

   Items 23 and 24 are based on the following data:

   Based on a monthly normal volume of 50,000 units (100,000 direct labor hours), Raff Co.'s standard cost system contains the following overhead costs:

Variable	$6 per unit
Fixed	8 per unit

The following information pertains to the month of March 1986:

Units actually produced	38,000
Actual direct labor hours worked	80,000
Actual overhead incurred:	
Variable	$250,000
Fixed	384,000

23. For March 1986 the unfavorable variable overhead spending variance was
   a. $ 6,000
   b. $10,000
   c. $12,000
   d. $22,000

24. For March 1986 the fixed overhead volume variance was
   a. $96,000 unfavorable.
   b. $96,000 favorable.
   c. $80,000 unfavorable.
   d. $80,000 favorable.

25. Which of the following variances would be useful in calling attention to a possible short-term problem in the control of overhead costs?

	Spending variance	Volume variance
a.	No	No
b.	No	Yes
c.	Yes	No
d.	Yes	Yes

26. How should a usage variance that is significant in amount be treated at the end of an accounting period?
   a. Reported as a deferred charge or credit.
   b. Allocated among work-in-process inventory, finished goods inventory, and cost of goods sold.

   c.   Charged or credited to cost of goods
          manufactured.
   d.   Allocated among cost of goods
          manufactured, finished goods
          inventory, and cost of goods sold.

May 1990 Question

27. On the diagram below, the line OW
represents the standard labor cost at any
output volume expressed in direct labor
hours. Point S indicates the actual output at
standard cost, and Point A indicates the
actual hours and actual cost required to
produce S.

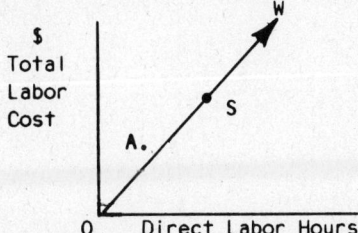

Which of the following variances are favorable
or unfavorable?

	Rate variance	Efficiency variance
a.	Favorable	Unfavorable
b.	Favorable	Favorable
c.	Unfavorable	Unfavorable
d.	Unfavorable	Favorable

Problems

Problem 1   (584,Q5)

(40 to 50 minutes)

At the beginning of 1987, Beal Company adopted the following standards:

Total	Input	
Direct materials	3 lbs. @ $2.50 per lb.	$ 7.50
Direct labor	5 hrs. @ $7.50 per hr.	37.50
Factory overhead:		
Variable	$3.00 per direct labor hour	15.00
Fixed	$4.00 per direct labor hour	20.00
Standard cost		
per unit		$80.00

Normal volume per month is 40,000 standard labor hours. Beal's January 1987 budget was based on normal volume. During January Beal produced 7,800 units, with records indicating the following:

Direct materials purchased	25,000 lbs. @ $2.60
Direct materials used	23,100 lbs.
Direct labor	40,100 hrs. @ $7.30
Factory overhead	$300,000

Required:

a. Prepare a schedule of budgeted production costs for January 1987, based on actual production of 7,800 units.

b. For the month of January 1987, compute the following variances, indicating whether each is favorable or unfavorable:
1. Direct materials price variance, based on purchases.
2. Direct materials usage variance.
3. Direct labor rate variance.
4. Direct labor efficiency variance.
5. Factory overhead spending variance.
6. Variable factory overhead efficiency variance.
7. Factory overhead volume variance.

Problem 2   (1187,Q4)

(45 to 55 minutes)

[See Problem 2 in Module 34 (Requirements c. and d.)]

Multiple Choice Answers

1. b	7. d	13. a	18. d	23. b
2. d	8. c	14. b	19. b	24. a
3. c	9. c	15. a	20. d	25. c
4. d	10. d	16. d	21. d	26. b
5. b	11. d	17. b	22. a	27. d
6. d	12. a			

Multiple Choice Answer Explanations

A. Variance Analysis

1. (1180,T1,48) (b) There are basically two types of standard costs, currently attainable [answer (a)] and theoretical [answer (b)]. A currently attainable cost is the target cost that employees are expected to achieve under efficient conditions. A theoretical standard cost is the absolute minimum cost that would be possible under the best conceivable operating conditions. Normal [answer (c)] and practical [answer (d)] are not terms used to describe the attainability of standard costs; they are alternative bases for determining budgeted fixed cost per hour or unit.

B. Material Variances

2. (1189,Q2,26) (d) Each unit of finished product contains 2 yards of direct material. However, the problem states that the 20% direct material spoilage is calculated on the quantity of direct material <u>input</u>. Although not mentioned, the facts in this question infer that the spoilage is normal and should be part of the product's standard cost. The solutions approach would be to set up the following formula:

Input quantity − spoilage = output amount
$$x - .2x = 2 \text{ yds.}$$
$$.8x = 2 \text{ yds.}$$
$$x = 2.5 \text{ yds.}$$

Thus, the standard direct material cost per unit of finished product is $7.50 (2.5 yds. × $3).

3. (1179,P2,38) (c) The requirement is the actual purchase price per unit given a standard unit price of $3.60 and a favorable price variance of $240. Dividing the actual quantity purchased of 1,600 units into the $240 favorable variance results in a $.15 per unit favorable price variance. The actual cost per unit was $3.45 ($3.60 standard less $.15 favorable variance).

4. (1185,Q1,9) (d) The requirement is to determine the direct materials price variance. The direct materials price variance is the difference between actual unit prices and standard unit prices multiplied by the actual quantity. The direct materials usage variance is the difference between the actual number of units and the standard number of units multiplied by the standard unit price. Standard unit price is necessary to measure the price variance, but it is not directly stated in the problem. The diagram below summarizes the information given and to be determined:

AQ × AP	AQ × SP	SQ × SP
$84,000	30,000 lbs. × $?	29,000 lbs. × $?
	Price, ? Usage, $3,000 unfav.	

The standard unit price can be determined from the information provided on the usage variance (UV):

$$\left(\begin{array}{c}\text{Actual} \\ \text{quantity}\end{array} - \begin{array}{c}\text{Standard} \\ \text{quantity}\end{array}\right) \times \begin{array}{c}\text{Standard} \\ \text{price}\end{array} = UV$$

$$(30,000 - 29,000) \times SP = 3,000$$
$$SP = \$3/\text{unit}$$

With this information, the price variance (PV) can be determined:

Actual cost − Standard cost = PV
$$\$84,000 - (30,000 \times \$3.00) = (\$6,000)$$

The $6,000 price variance is favorable because the actual price is lower than the standard price.

5. (1184,T1,50) (b) The requirement is to determine the earliest appropriate time for isolating and recognizing a direct materials price variance. The solutions approach is to recall the computation for the price variance. The price variance is computed as: (AP − SP) × AQ. Once all three variables are known, the price variance can be recognized. The purchase date is the earliest time that all three variables are known. Answers (a) and (c) are incorrect because both the issuance and use of materials in production occur after the material is purchased. Answer (d) is incorrect because total actual price is not known when the purchase order is originated since shipping and insurance costs may not be included in the total purchase price.

6. (1182,T1,50) (d) The requirement is to identify whether the standard unit cost is necessary to calculate the materials price and/or usage variance. The materials price variance is computed as: Actual quantity (Actual price − Standard unit cost). The materials usage variance is computed as: Standard unit cost (Actual quantity − Standard quantity). Thus, the standard unit cost is used in the calculation of both the materials price and usage variances [answer (d)].

7. (581,T1,50) (d) The requirement is to identify the department customarily held

responsible for an unfavorable materials usage
variance. The department customarily held
responsible for an unfavorable materials usage
variance is the production department [an-
swer (d)]. Although the engineering [an-
swer (c)] and quality control [answer (a)] departments may have some effect on the use of
materials, they are not usually responsible
for material usage variances. The purchasing
department [answer (b)] is usually responsible
for material price variances.

C. Labor Variances

8. (1189,Q2,24) (c) The standard direct
labor cost per unit is given (2 hours @ $6.00
per hour). Because 500 units were produced in
March, the amount that would have been applied
to work in process is $6,000 (500 units x 2
hours x $6.00 per hour). The problem states
that 1050 hours were used at $6.10 per hour.
Because we are computing the labor efficiency
variance, we do not need the actual labor
rate. The actual hours are multiplied by the
standard rate to arrive at the flexible budget
amount for actual inputs ($6.00 x 1,050 hours
= $6,300). Thus, the unfavorable labor
efficiency variance is $300 ($6,300 - $6,000)
shown in the diagram:

AH x SR	SH x SR
1050 x $6	1000 x $6
$6,300	$6,000

| Efficiency variance, $300 U |

9. (587,Q2,32) (c) Duo's total standard
cost to process 1,200,000 papers has both a
variable cost component and a fixed cost
component. The standard wage rate of $600 per
1,000 papers is needed to compute the variable
cost component. Using this rate, the total
standard variable cost for 1,200,000 papers is
$720,000 (1,200 x $600). The fixed cost
component is simply the standard fixed costs
per year of $150,000 because fixed costs do
not change within a relevant range. Thus, the
total standard cost to process 1,200,000
papers is $870,000 ($720,000 + $150,000).

10. (587,Q2,33) (d) This question can be
answered by filling in the labor rate variance
diagram:

AH x AR   AH x SR
Labor Rate Variance

Actual labor hours (AH) are given as 190,000.
The actual rate (AR) per hour is $4 and is
computed by dividing the actual labor cost of
$760,000 by the actual labor hours of 190,000.
The standard rate (SR) per hour is also $4.
The SR is computed by dividing the standard
wage rate of $600 (per 1,000 papers) by the

150 standard hours (per 1,000 papers). This
will result in a labor rate variance of $0 as
shown in the diagram below:

AH x AR	AH x SR
190,000 x $4	190,000 x $4
$760,000	$760,000

| Labor Rate Variance = 0 |

11. (1186,Q2,21) (d) The solutions approach
for a question such as this one is to set up a
diagram computing the direct-labor efficiency
variance (which is given) and fill in the
information given.

AH x SR	SH x SR
? x $8.00	2,000 x $8.00
?	$16,000

| Efficiency variance, $1,600 unfavorable |

Since the variance is unfavorable, AH x SR
must equal $16,000 plus $1,600 or $17,600.
The actual hours worked can then be computed
by dividing $17,600 by $8.00, resulting in AH
of 2,200. The diagram can be completed as
follows:

AH x SR	SH x SR
2,200 x $8.00	2,000 x $8.00
$17,600	$16,000

| Efficiency variance, $1,600 unfavorable |

12. (586,Q2,28) (a) The requirement is the
standard direct labor rate per hour (SR) for
April. The solutions approach is to set up a
diagram computing the direct-labor rate
variance (which is given) and solve for any
unknowns.

Actual	AH x SR
labor cost	2,000 x ?
$10,000	?

|←   Rate variance, $1,000 F   →|

Since the variance is favorable, AH x SR must
equal $10,000 plus $1,000, or $11,000. The SR
can then be computed by dividing $11,000 by
2,000 hours, resulting in a SR of $5.50.

13. (1178,T1,43) (a) The requirement is the
situation that would produce an unfavorable
labor rate variance and a favorable labor
efficiency variance. Unfavorable labor rate
variances will be caused by higher-paid employees. Favorable labor efficiency variances
can be caused by more experienced, better
trained employees. Thus, higher-paid,
experienced individuals would tend to produce
unfavorable labor rate variances and favorable
labor efficiency variances. Answer (b) is
incorrect because it is just the opposite of
answer (a); low-paid unskilled workers will
produce favorable labor rate variances and
unfavorable labor efficiency variances. An-

swer (c) is incorrect because workers from other areas of production will probably result in unfavorable labor efficiency variances as they are unfamiliar with the task at hand. Answer (d) is incorrect because using more labor due to defective materials to produce a standard unit results in unfavorable labor efficiency variances.

14. (1176,T2,31) (b) The labor efficiency variance relates to the number of direct labor hours incurred. A debit balance indicates inefficiency or actual hours exceeded standard hours. Answer (a) describes a favorable efficiency variance. Answer (c) describes both a favorable rate variance and a favorable efficiency variance. Answer (d) describes both an unfavorable rate variance and an unfavorable efficiency variance.

E. Overhead Analysis: 2-Way

15. (583,P2,39) (a) The requirement is the budget (controllable) variance for January 1983, using the two-way analysis of overhead variances. The controllable variance is the difference between actual overhead costs ($147,000), and overhead budgeted for the output achieved. When overhead is applied based on direct-labor hours, the budgeted amount is equal to budgeted fixed overhead ($108,000), plus standard direct-labor hours times the standard variable overhead rate (21,000 x $2 = $42,000). The standard variable rate is computed by dividing budgeted variable overhead by the budgeted activity level ($48,000 ÷ 24,000 = $2). The budget (controllable) variance is computed below.

	Budget for output achieved
Actual	$108,000 + (21,000 x $2)
$147,000	$150,000

Budget variance, $3,000 F

The variance is favorable because actual costs are less than budgeted costs.

16. (1188,T1,43) (d) The two-variance method for analyzing factory overhead is computed as follows:

	Budget for outputs achieved	Applied overhead
Actual overhead	Fixed OH + (SQ x SVR)	SQ x STR*
	Controllable (budget) variance	Volume variance

*STR = Standard variable rate (SVR) + Standard fixed rate (SFR)

As shown above, the controllable variance is the difference between actual overhead costs and the overhead budgeted for the output achieved (fixed overhead plus the budget allowance based on standard hours). A budget allowance based on actual hours is not used under the two-variance method. Therefore, answer (d) is correct.

17. (589,T1,43) (b) The requirement is to determine which of the variances given consist of both variable and fixed overhead elements under a two-variance method. As shown in the diagram below, the controllable or budget variance includes both variable and fixed overhead elements, because the actual overhead amount, the first vertical line, includes both elements as does the budgeted overhead amount, the middle vertical line.

	Budget for outputs achieved	Applied
Actual	FOH + (SQ x SVR)	SQ x STR*
	Budget var.	Volume var.

*STR = Standard variable rate (SVR) + Standard fixed rate (SFR)

The volume variance includes only the variance of fixed overhead, because the SQ x SVR is common to both amounts (i.e., it is included in the STR) used to determine the volume variance. The difference in the two amounts is the volume variance. It arises because the middle vertical line includes the total amount of budgeted fixed overhead whereas the third vertical line includes the amount of fixed overhead applied using a per unit amount based on normal volume or level of activity. Whenever the standard activity level based on good output (SQ) is different than the normal activity level, a volume variance will arise. Therefore, (b) is correct because both variable and fixed overhead elements are included in the controllable variance but not in the volume variance.

18. (1186,T1,43) (d) The two-variance method for analyzing factory overhead is computed as follows:

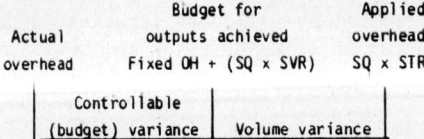

	Budget for outputs achieved	Applied overhead
Actual overhead	Fixed OH + (SQ x SVR)	SQ x STR*
	Controllable (budget) variance	Volume variance

*STR = Standard variable rate (SVR) + Standard fixed rate (SFR)

Standard hours allowed is used to compute the budget for outputs achieved. Thus, answer (d) is correct because the difference between the actual factory overhead and the budget allowance based on standard hours allowed is the controllable (budget) variance. Answer (a) is incorrect because the net overhead variance is

the difference between actual overhead and
applied overhead. Answer (b) is incorrect
because the efficiency variance is the
difference between the budget for actual
inputs and the budget for outputs achieved
under the three-variance method. Answer (c)
is incorrect because the volume variance is
the difference between the budget allowance
based on standard hours allowed and applied
overhead.

F. Overhead Analysis: 3-Way

19. (575,P2,18) (b) Note that the data set
applies to two questions and involves the
three-variance method. The requirement is the
actual hours worked. The solutions approach
is to set up the variance diagram and solve
for any unknowns.

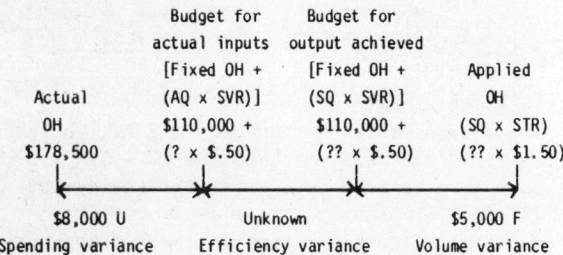

The actual hours worked are calculated as
follows:

$$\$178,500 - [\$110,000 + \$.50(?)] = \$8,000$$
$$\$68,500 - \$.50(?) = \$8,000$$
$$\$60,500 = \$.50(?)$$
$$? = \underline{121,000} \text{ hours}$$

20. (575,P2,19) (d) The requirement is the
standard hours allowed for the output
achieved. See the diagram in the previous
question. The standard hours allowed are
calculated as follows:

$$\$110,000 + \$.50(??) + \$ 5,000 = \$1.50(??)$$
$$\$115,000 = \$1 (??)$$
$$? = \underline{115,000} \text{ hours}$$

21. (1187,T1,42) (d) The three-variance
method can be illustrated as follows:

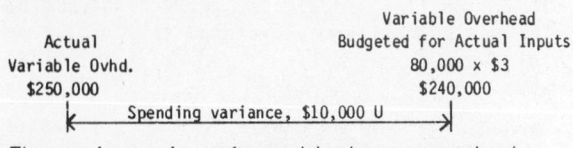

The spending variance is computed as the
difference between actual overhead and overhead budgeted for actual inputs (hours).
Therefore, answer (d) is correct.

22. (585,T1,39) (a) The requirement is to
determine which variance describes the difference between the actual factory overhead and

the factory overhead applied to production
when using the three-variance method. The
diagram for the three-variance method is as
follows:

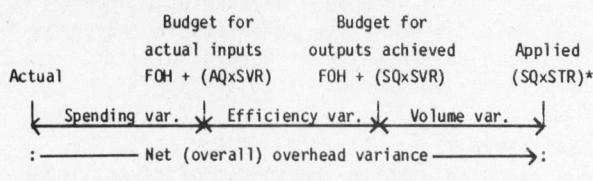

*STR = Standard variable rate (SVR) + Standard fixed rate
    (SFR)

Answer (a) is correct because the difference
between actual factory overhead applied to
production represents the total of all three
variances. This total is called the net or
overall overhead variance. Answer (b) is
incorrect since this label is used with the
two-variance method and would be the difference between actual factory overhead and
budget for outputs achieved. Answer (c) is
incorrect because the efficiency variance is
the difference between budget for actual inputs and budget for outputs achieved. Answer (d) is incorrect because the spending
variance is the difference between actual
factory overhead and budget for actual inputs.

G. Overhead Analysis by Cost Behavior

23. (586,Q2,23) (b) The requirement is the
amount of the unfavorable variable overhead
spending variance. The spending variance is
the difference between actual variable overhead incurred and variable overhead budgeted
for **actual inputs**. Actual variable overhead
incurred is $250,000. Variable overhead bud-
geted for actual inputs is actual direct labor
hours (AH) multiplied by the standard variable
rate per hour (SVR). Actual hours are 80,000.
Standard hours per unit are 2 hours (100,000
hours ÷ 50,000 units). Therefore, the standard variable rate is $3 per hour ($6 per unit
÷ 2 hours per unit). The spending variance is
computed as follows:

Actual	Variable Overhead Budgeted for Actual Inputs
Variable Ovhd.	80,000 x $3
$250,000	$240,000
Spending variance, $10,000 U	

The variance is unfavorable because actual
costs are greater than budgeted costs.

24. (586,Q2,24) (a) The requirement is the
fixed overhead volume variance. The volume
variance is the difference between budgeted
fixed overhead and fixed overhead applied to
production. Budgeted fixed overhead is
$400,000 (50,000 units x $8 per unit). Fixed
overhead applied is standard hours (SH) for
good output multiplied by the standard fixed

rate per hour (SFR). Standard hours for one
unit of output is 2 hours (100,000 hours ÷
50,000 units). Thus, standard hours for all
output of the month is 76,000 (38,000 units x
2 hours per unit) and the SFR is $4 per hour
($8 per unit ÷ 2 hours per unit). The volume
variance is computed as follows:

	Applied Fixed Ovhd.
Budgeted Fixed Ovhd.	76,000 x $4
$400,000	$304,000

Volume variance, $96,000 U

The variance is unfavorable because budgeted
cost is greater than the cost applied to production.

25. (1189,T1,43) (c) A spending variance is
caused by differences between the actual
amount spent on fixed and variable overhead
items and the amounts budgeted based on actual
inputs. A volume variance is the difference
between budgeted fixed overhead and applied
fixed overhead. It is caused by under- or
over-utilization of plant capacity. Differences between actual and budgeted amounts
(spending variances) occur often and can be
corrected by changing the accounting estimates
used in the budgeting process or the
purchasing policies used. A difference in
under- or over-utilization of plant capacity
is a complex problem not easily corrected.
Spending variances indicate short-term problems dealing with amounts spent on overhead
while volume variances indicate long-term
problems dealing with plant capacity.
Therefore, answer (c) is the correct answer.

J. Disposition of Variances

26. (579,T1,25) (b) Significant usage variances (or any other significant variance)
should be allocated to work-in-process inventory, finished goods inventory, and cost of
goods sold at year end [answer (b)]. If significant variances exist, the inventory and
cost of goods sold figures are not stated at
actual costs, i.e., they are misstated. This
may be the result of faulty standards, changed
conditions, etc. If the variance is favorable, inventory and cost of goods sold have
been overstated. If the variance is unfavorable, inventory and cost of goods sold have
been understated. An additional allocation
must be made between work-in-process and
finished goods inventories. Answers (a) and
(c) are incorrect because the variance should
be allocated to the appropriate accounts.
Answer (d) is incorrect because cost of goods
manufactured refers to the amount of goods
completed in the period and transferred from
the work-in-process account to the finished
goods (inventory) account, i.e., it represents
a flow rather than a year-end balance.

May 1990 Answer

27. (590,T1,43) (d) A labor rate variance
is the difference between budgeted wage rates
and the wage rates actually paid. The problem
states that line OW represents the standard
labor cost at any output volume. Because
point A is <u>above</u> the line, the actual cost was
higher than the standard. The rate variance
is, therefore, unfavorable. A labor efficiency variance is the difference between
actual hours worked and standard hours allowed
for output. On the diagram, point S is further on the X axis (Direct labor hours) than
point A indicating that the standard hours
allowed are higher than the actual hours
worked. Because actual hours are less than
standard hours, this variance would be favorable. Therefore answer (d) is correct.

Solution Guide*

Problem 1   Budgeted Production Costs and
            Variance Analysis (584,Q5)

1. Part a. requires a schedule of budgeted
    production costs and part b. requires the
    computation of seven variances for a
    standard costing system.

2. Budgeted production costs are calculated
    by multiplying the standard amounts
    allowed for the output achieved by the
    related standard rates as provided in the
    problem. The only exception relates to
    fixed overhead (FOH). Budgeted fixed
    overhead is simply the amount provided in
    the flexible budget, $160,000 (see 2.6).

2.1 The standard amount allowed for the
    output achieved is referred to as the
    standard quantity (SQ). The SQ for
    direct materials (DM) is calculated by
    multiplying actual output (7,800 units)
    times the standard number of DM pounds
    per finished unit (3 lbs./unit) yielding
    23,400 standard pounds. The SQ of DM
    (23,400 lbs.) is then multiplied by the
    standard price per pound of DM ($2.50/lb.
    as given) yielding the budgeted produc-
    tion cost for DM of $58,500.

2.2 The candidate must recognize from the
    data provided that overhead costs are
    being applied to production on the basis
    of direct-labor hours (DLHs) worked. In
    a standard costing system, the appli-
    cation of overhead is based on standard
    DLHs worked rather than actual DLHs. The
    SQ of direct labor (DL) is needed,
    therefore, to calculate the budgeted
    production costs for DL and variable
    overhead (VOH).

2.3 The SQ of DL is calculated by multiplying
    actual output (7,800 units) times the
    standard number of DLHs per finished unit
    (5 hrs./unit) yielding 39,000 standard
    hours. The budgeted production cost for
    DL ($292,500) is calculated as 39,000
    hours (SQ of DL) times $7.50 (standard
    rate per DLH, as given).

*Author's note: Our solution guide is struc-
tured around the use of variance diagrams as a
tool to aid the candidate in solving standard
costing problems. The AICPA Unofficial Answer
does not incorporate the diagram approach in
its answer. We believe that the diagram
approach illustrated herein is a useful
learning aid.

2.4 The budgeted production cost for VOH
    ($117,000) is calculated by multiplying
    39,000 standard hours [SQ of DL used to
    apply overhead (see 2.2)] times $3
    [standard variable rate (SVR)]. The SVR
    represents the amount of VOH applied to
    production for each standard DLH worked.

2.5 Overhead could be applied to production
    in total (i.e., not segregating VOH from
    FOH) by using the standard total rate
    (STR) for overhead. The STR comes from
    the flexible budget and represents the
    total predetermined overhead rate based
    on total estimated overhead (both vari-
    able and fixed). Therefore, the STR ($7)
    = SVR ($3) + SFR ($4) [standard fixed
    rate].

2.6 The budgeted production cost for FOH is
    $160,000. The budgeted fixed overhead is
    calculated as the budgeted activity level
    (40,000 hours) times the SFR ($4). The
    SFR represents the amount of FOH applied
    to production for each standard DLH
    worked.

2.7 Total budgeted production costs
    ($628,000) are the sum of the budgeted
    amounts for DM, DL, VOH, and FOH as
    determined above.

3. The solutions approach to part b.
    (computation of variances) involves the
    use of variance diagrams.

3.1 Note that DM purchases (25,000 lbs.)
    differ from the usage of DM in production
    (23,100 lbs.). The DM price variance
    will be based on purchases, and the DM
    usage variance will be based on usage.
    The price variance is $2,500 unfavorable
    and the usage variance is $750 favorable
    as calculated below.

```
        AQ x AP              AQ x SP
    25,000 x $2.60       25,000 x $2.50
        $65,000              $62,500

                   Price variance
                     $2,500 U

                    AQ x SP                SQ x SP
                23,100 x $2.50        23,400* x $2.50
                    $57,750               $58,500

                            Usage variance
                              $750 F
```

*As calculated in 2.1.

3.2 The direct labor diagram is essentially the same as the materials diagram except that the actual quantity (AQ) and standard quantity (SQ) of labor are expressed in labor hours. Also, the standard price (SP) for direct labor is expressed as a rate per hour of labor (i.e., $7.50 per hour).

3.3 The DL rate variance and the DL efficiency variance are $8,020 favorable and $8,250 unfavorable, respectively, as calculated below.

$$\begin{array}{ccc}
AQ \times AP & AQ \times SP & SQ \times SP \\
40,100 \times \$7.30 & 40,100 \times \$7.50 & 39,000^* \times \$7.50 \\
\$292,730 & \$300,750 & \$292,500
\end{array}$$

$$\begin{array}{cc}
\text{Rate variance} & \text{Efficiency variance} \\
\$8,020 \text{ F} & \$8,250 \text{ U}
\end{array}$$

*As calculated in 2.3.

3.4 The requirements call for three overhead variances: overhead spending, variable overhead efficiency, and (fixed) overhead volume. The candidate must conclude that the three-way analysis of overhead variances is required.

	Actual	Budget for actual inputs	Budget for outputs achieved	Applied
		$FOH + (AQ^1 \times SVR^3)$	$FOH + (SQ^2 \times SVR^3)$	$SQ^2 \times STR^4$
		$\$160,000 + (40,100 \times \$3)$	$\$160,000 + (39,000 \times \$3)$	$39,000 \times \$7$
	$300,000	$280,300	$277,000	$273,000

$$\begin{array}{ccc}
\text{Spending variance} & \text{Efficiency variance} & \text{Volume variance} \\
\$19,700 \text{ U} & \$3,300 \text{ U} & \$4,000 \text{ U}
\end{array}$$

[1] From information given in the problem
[2] As discussed in 2.3
[3] As discussed in 2.4
[4] As discussed in 2.5

3.5 The overhead spending variance is the difference between actual overhead costs incurred and the budget for overhead items based on actual inputs. The overhead efficiency variance is solely a function of variable overhead. It is calculated as the difference between the budget for overhead items based on actual inputs and the budget adjusted for output achieved. The overhead volume variance is solely a function of fixed overhead. This variance is calculated as the difference between the budgeted overhead based on outputs and the overhead applied to production.

3.6 The spending variance is $19,700 unfavorable, the efficiency variance is $3,300 unfavorable, and the volume variance is $4,000 unfavorable as calculated below. Note that the actual overhead cost incurred is expressed as a lump-sum amount of $300,000. This precludes the spending variance from being further segregated into its variable and fixed elements.

Unofficial Answer

Problem 1   Budgeted Production Costs and Variance Analysis (584,Q5)

a.

Beal Company
Schedule of Budgeted Production Costs
Based on 7,800 Units
For the Month Ended January 31, 1987

Direct materials	
(7,800 units x 3 lbs. x $2.50)	$ 58,500
Direct labor	
(7,800 units x 5 hrs. x $7.50)	292,500
Factory overhead:	
Variable (7,800 units x 5 hrs. x $3.00)	117,000
Fixed (40,000 hrs. x $4.00)	160,000
Total budgeted production costs	$628,000

b.

1. Direct materials price variance based on materials purchased: ($2.60 – $2.50) x 25,000 lbs. $ 2,500 U

2. Direct materials usage variance: [23,100 lbs. – (7,800 units x 3 lbs.)] x $2.50 $ 750 F

3. Direct labor rate variance: ($7.30 – $7.50) x 40,100 hrs. $ 8,020 F

4. Direct labor efficiency variance: [40,100 hrs. – (7,800 units x 5 hrs.)] x $7.50 $ 8,250 U

5. Factory overhead spending variance:

Actual total factory overhead	$300,000
Budgeted total factory overhead at actual hours (40,100 x $3.00) + (40,000 x $4.00)	280,300
Factory overhead spending variance	$ 19,700 U

6. Variable factory overhead efficiency variance:

Budgeted total factory overhead at actual hours	$280,300
Budgeted total factory overhead at standard hours ($117,000 + $160,000)	277,000
Variable factory overhead efficiency variance	$ 3,300 U

7. Factory overhead volume variance:

Budgeted total factory overhead at standard hours	$277,000
Applied total factory overhead (7,800 x 5 hrs. x $7.00)	273,000
Factory overhead volume variance	$ 4,000 U

Multiple Choice Questions (1-36)

1. The manufacturing capacity of Jordan Company's facilities is 30,000 units of product a year. A summary of operating results for the year ended December 31, 1982, is as follows:

Sales (18,000 units @ $100)	$1,800,000
Variable manufacturing and selling costs	990,000
Contribution margin	810,000
Fixed costs	495,000
Operating income	$ 315,000

A foreign distributor has offered to buy 15,000 units at $90 per unit during 1983. Assume that all of Jordan's costs would be at the same levels and rates in 1983 as in 1982. If Jordan accepted this offer and rejected some business from regular customers so as not to exceed capacity, what would be the total operating income for 1983?

    a. $390,000
    b. $705,000
    c. $840,000
    d. $855,000

2. Wagner Company sells product A at a selling price of $21 per unit. Wagner's cost per unit based on the full capacity of 200,000 units is as follows:

Direct materials	$ 4
Direct labor	5
Overhead (two-thirds of which is fixed)	6
	$15

A special order offering to buy 20,000 units was received from a foreign distributor. The only selling costs that would be incurred on this order would be $3 per unit for shipping. Wagner has sufficient existing capacity to manufacture the additional units. In negotiating a price for the special order, Wagner should consider that the minimum selling price per unit should be

    a. $14
    b. $15
    c. $16
    d. $18

3. Gandy Company has 5,000 obsolete desk lamps that are carried in inventory at a manufacturing cost of $50,000. If the lamps are reworked for $20,000, they could be sold for $35,000. Alternatively, the lamps could be sold for $8,000 to a jobber located in a distant city. In a decision model analyzing these alternatives, the sunk cost would be

    a. $ 8,000
    b. $15,000
    c. $20,000
    d. $50,000

4. Plainfield Company manufactures part G for use in its production cycle. The cost per unit for 10,000 units of part G are as follows:

Direct materials	$ 3
Direct labor	15
Variable overhead	6
Fixed overhead	8
	$32

Verona Company has offered to sell Plainfield 10,000 units of part G for $30 per unit. If Plainfield accepts Verona's offer, the released facilities could be used to save $45,000 in relevant costs in the manufacture of part H. In addition, $5 per unit of the fixed overhead applied to part G would be totally eliminated. What alternative is more desirable and by what amount is it more desirable?

	Alternative	Amount
a.	Manufacture	$10,000
b.	Manufacture	$15,000
c.	Buy	$35,000
d.	Buy	$65,000

5. The Blade Division of Dana Company produces hardened steel blades. One third of the Blade Division's output is sold to the Lawn Products Division of Dana; the remainder is sold to outside customers. The Blade Division's estimated sales and standard cost data for the fiscal year ending June 30, 1981, are as follows:

	Lawn products	Outsiders
Sales	$15,000	$40,000
Variable costs	(10,000)	(20,000)
Fixed costs	(3,000)	(6,000)
Gross margin	$ 2,000	$14,000
Unit sales	10,000	20,000

The Lawn Products Division has an opportunity to purchase 10,000 identical quality blades from an outside supplier at a cost of $1.25 per unit on a continuing basis. Assume that the Blade Division cannot sell any additional products to outside customers. Should Dana allow its Lawn Products Division to purchase the blades from the outside supplier, and why?

    a.   Yes, because buying the blades would save Dana Company $500.
    b.   No, because making the blades would save Dana Company $1,500.
    c.   Yes, because buying the blades would save Dana Company $2,500.
    d.   No, because making the blades would save Dana Company $2,500.

6.   The following standard costs pertain to a component part manufactured by Bor Co.:

Direct materials	$ 4
Direct labor	10
Factory overhead	40
Standard cost per unit	$54

Factory overhead is applied at $1 per standard machine hour. Fixed capacity cost is 60% of applied factory overhead, and is not affected by any "make or buy" decision. It would cost $49 per unit to buy the part from an outside supplier. In the decision to "make or buy," what is the total relevant unit manufacturing cost?

a. $54
b. $38
c. $30
d. $ 5

7.   Mili Co. plans to discontinue a division with a $20,000 contribution to overhead. Overhead allocated to the division is $50,000, of which $5,000 cannot be eliminated. The effect of this discontinuance on Mili's pretax income would be an increase of

a. $ 5,000
b. $20,000
c. $25,000
d. $30,000

8.   At December 31, 1984, Zar Co. had a machine with an original cost of $84,000, accumulated depreciation of $60,000, and an estimated salvage value of zero. On December 31, 1984, Zar was considering the purchase of a new machine having a five-year life, costing $120,000, and having an estimated salvage value of $20,000 at the end of five years. In its decision concerning the possible purchase of the new machine, how much should Zar consider as sunk cost at December 31, 1984?

a. $120,000
b. $100,000
c. $ 24,000
d. $ 4,000

9.   A company is considering exchanging an old asset for a new asset. Ignoring income tax considerations, which of the following is economically relevant to the decision?

	Original cost of old asset	Fair market value of old asset
a.	Yes	Yes
b.	Yes	No
c.	No	Yes
d.	No	No

10. The discount rate (hurdle rate of return) must be determined in advance for the
a.   Internal rate of return method.
b.   Net present value method.
c.   Payback period method.
d.   Time adjusted rate of return method.

11. Nelson Company is planning to purchase a new machine for $500,000. The new machine is expected to produce cash flow from operations, before income taxes, of $135,000 a year in each of the next five years. Depreciation of $100,000 a year will be charged to income for each of the next five years. Assume that the income tax rate is 40%. The payback period would be approximately
a.   2.2 years.
b.   3.4 years.
c.   3.7 years.
d.   4.1 years.

12. The capital budgeting technique known as payback period uses

	Depreciation expense	Time value of money
a.	Yes	Yes
b.	Yes	No
c.	No	No
d.	No	Yes

13. Which of the following is necessary in order to calculate the pay-back period for a project?
a.   Useful life.
b.   Minimum desired rate of return.
c.   Net present value.
d.   Annual cash flow.

14. Garwood Company purchased a machine which will be depreciated on the straight-line basis over an estimated useful life of seven years and no salvage value. The machine is expected to generate cash flow from operations, net of income taxes, of $80,000 in each of the seven years. Garwood's expected rate of return is 12%. Information on present value factors is as follows:

Present value of $1 at 12% for seven periods	.0452
Present value of an ordinary annuity of $1 at 12% for seven periods	4.564

Assuming a positive net present value of $12,720, what was the cost of the machine?
a. $240,400
b. $253,120
c. $352,400
d. $377,840

Items 15 and 16 are based on the following data:

Apex Corp. is planning to buy production machinery costing $100,000. This machinery's expected useful life is five years, with no residual value. Apex requires a rate of return of 20%, and has calculated the following data pertaining to the purchase and operation of this machinery:

Year	Estimated annual cash inflow	Present value of 1 at 20%
1	$ 60,000	.91
2	30,000	.76
3	20,000	.63
4	20,000	.53
5	20,000	.44
Totals	$150,000	3.27

Assuming that the cash inflow was received evenly during the year,

15. The payback period is
   a. 2.50 years.
   b. 2.75 years.
   c. 3.00 years.
   d. 5.00 years.

16. The net present value is
   a. $ 9,400
   b. $ 54,128
   c. $ 80,000
   d. $109,400

17. The capital budgeting technique known as net present value uses

	Cash flow over life of project	Time value of money
a.	No	Yes
b.	No	No
c.	Yes	No
d.	Yes	Yes

18. The capital budgeting technique known as accounting rate of return uses

	Depreciation expense	Time value of money
a.	No	No
b.	No	Yes
c.	Yes	Yes
d.	Yes	No

19. A proposed project has an expected economic life of eight years. In the calculation of the net present value of the proposed project, salvage value would be
   a. Excluded from the calculation of the net present value.
   b. Included as a cash inflow at the estimated salvage value.
   c. Included as a cash inflow at the future amount of the estimated salvage value.
   d. Included as a cash inflow at the present value of the estimated salvage value.

20. The net present value capital budgeting technique can be used when cash flows from period to period are

	Uniform	Uneven
a.	No	Yes
b.	No	No
c.	Yes	No
d.	Yes	Yes

21. Kern Co. is planning to invest in a two-year project that is expected to yield cash flows from operations, net of income taxes, of $50,000 in the first year and $80,000 in the second year. Kern requires an internal rate of return of 15%. The present value of $1 for one period at 15% is 0.870 and for two periods at 15% is 0.756. The future value of $1 for one period at 15% is 1.150 and for two periods at 15% is 1.323. The maximum that Kern should invest immediately is
   a. $ 81,670
   b. $103,980
   c. $130,000
   d. $163,340

22. The capital budgeting technique known as internal rate of return uses

	Cash flow over entire life of project	Time value of money
a.	Yes	No
b.	Yes	Yes
c.	No	Yes
d.	No	No

23. If income tax considerations are ignored, how is depreciation expense used in the following capital budgeting techniques?

	Internal rate of return	Net present value
a.	Excluded	Excluded
b.	Excluded	Included
c.	Included	Excluded
d.	Included	Included

24. It is assumed that cash flows are reinvested at the rate earned by the investment in which of the following capital budgeting techniques?

	Internal rate of return	Net present value
a.	Yes	Yes
b.	Yes	No
c.	No	No
d.	No	Yes

Items 25 through 27 are based on the following data:

Allo Foundation, a tax-exempt organization, invested $200,000 in a five-year project at the beginning of 1985. Allo estimates that the annual cash savings from this project will amount to $65,000. The $200,000 of assets will be depreciated over their five-year life on the straight-line basis. On investments of this type, Allo's desired rate of return is 12%. Information on present value factors is as follows:

	At 12%	At 14%	At 16%
Present value of 1 for 5 periods	0.57	0.52	0.48
Present value of an annuity of 1 for 5 periods	3.6	3.4	3.3

25. The net present value of the project is
   a. $ 34,000
   b. $ 36,400
   c. $ 90,000
   d. $125,000

26. Allo's internal rate of return on this project is
   a.   Less than 12%.
   b.   Less than 14%, but more than 12%.
   c.   Less than 16%, but more than 14%.
   d.   More than 16%.

27. For the project's first year, Allo's accounting rate of return, based on the project's average book value for 1985, would be
   a.   14.4%
   b.   13.9%
   c.   12.5%
   d.   12.0%

Items 28 and 29 are based on the following data:

Amaro Hospital, a nonprofit institution not subject to income taxes, is considering the purchase of new equipment costing $20,000, in order to achieve cash savings of $5,000 per year in operating costs. The equipment's estimated useful life is ten years, with no net residual value. Amaro's cost of capital is 14%. For ten periods at 14%, the present value of $1 is 0.270, while the present value of an ordinary annuity of $1 is 5.216.

28. What factor contained in or developed from the above information should be used in computing the internal rate of return for Amaro's proposed investment in the new equipment?
   a.   5.216
   b.   4.000

   c.   1.400
   d.   0.270

29. How much is the accounting rate of return based on Amaro's initial investment in the new equipment?
   a.   27%
   b.   25%
   c.   15%
   d.   14%

30. Doro Co. is considering the purchase of a $100,000 machine that is expected to result in a decrease of $25,000 per year in cash expenses after taxes. This machine, which has no residual value, has an estimated useful life of 10 years and will be depreciated on a straight-line basis. For this machine, the accounting rate of return based on initial investment would be
   a.   10%
   b.   15%
   c.   25%
   d.   35%

31. The capital budgeting technique known as accounting rate of return uses

	Revenue over life of project	Depreciation expense
a.	No	Yes
b.	No	No
c.	Yes	No
d.	Yes	Yes

32. Joe Neil, CPA, has among his clientele a charitable organization that has a legal permit to conduct games of chance for fundraising purposes. Neil's client derives its profit from admission fees and the sale of refreshments, and therefore wants to "break even" on the games of chance. In one of these games, the player draws one card from a standard deck of 52 cards. A player drawing any one of four "queens" wins $5, and a player drawing any one of 13 "hearts" wins $2. Neil is asked to compute the price that should be charged per draw, so that the total amount paid out for winning draws can be expected to equal the total amount received from all draws. Which one of the following equations should Neil use to compute the price (P)?
   a. $5 - 2 = \dfrac{35P}{52}$

   b. $\dfrac{4}{52}(5) + \dfrac{13}{52}(2) = \dfrac{35}{52}P$

   c. $\dfrac{4}{52}(5 - P) + \dfrac{13}{52}(2 - P) = P$

   d. $\dfrac{4}{52}(5) + \dfrac{13}{52}(2) = P$

33. The following information pertains to three shipping terminals operated by Krag Corp.:

Terminal	Percentage of cargo handled	Percentage of error
Land	50	2
Air	40	4
Sea	10	14

Krag's internal auditor randomly selects one set of shipping documents, ascertaining that the set selected contains an error. The probability that the error occurred in the Land Terminal is
- a. 2%
- b. 10%
- c. 25%
- d. 50%

34. During 1985, Seco Corp. experienced the following outages:

Number of outages per month	Number of months
0	3
1	2
2	4
3	3
	12

Each power outage results in out-of-pocket costs of $200. For $250 per month, Seco can lease an auxiliary generator to provide power during outages. If Seco leases an auxiliary generator in 1986, the estimated savings (or additional expenditures) for 1986 would be
- a. $ 800
- b. $ 950
- c. ($ 600)
- d. ($1,800)

35. Olex Co. is considering a proposal to introduce a new product called Vee. An outside marketing consultant prepared the following probability distribution indicating the relative likelihood of monthly sales volume levels and related income (loss) for Vee:

Monthly sales volume	Probability	Income (loss)
6,000	.10	$(70,000)
12,000	.20	10,000
18,000	.40	60,000
24,000	.20	100,000
30,000	.10	140,000

If Olex decides to market Vee, the expected value of the added monthly income will be
- a. $240,000
- b. $ 60,000
- c. $ 53,000
- d. $ 48,000

36. In statistical analysis, a weighted average using probabilities as weights is the
- a. Standard deviation.
- b. Expected value.
- c. Coefficient of variation.
- d. Objective function.

May 1990 Questions

Repeat Questions

(590,T1,48) Identical/similar to item 24 above
(590,T1,50) Identical/similar to item 36 above

Problems

Problem 1   (1185,Q5)

(40 to 50 minutes)

Leif Company is faced with the necessity of making the following three unrelated financial management decisions involving its Sigma Division:

a. **Establishment of a selling price for a new product, called Kace, developed by Sigma.** Kace's variable cost is $3 per unit. The following probabilities of reaching annual sales levels for Kace have been estimated:

Sales (in units)	If each unit is sold for		
	$6	$7	$8
70,000	10%	40%	70%
80,000	50%	30%	20%
90,000	40%	30%	10%

b. **Discontinuance of a currently produced product and acquisition of a new machine.** Sigma's manager, Baum, has recommended that an unprofitable product, called Sago, be discontinued, which would decrease Sigma's current sales volume by 10%. In addition, Baum wants to improve efficiency by investing $100,000 in a new machine. Baum believes that implementation of his two recommendations would increase the pre-tax income rate on sales to 12%.

Sigma's current rate of pre-tax income is 10% on annual sales of $2,000,000. Financing of these current annual sales requires an investment of $600,000. Leif measures Sigma's performance by the pre-tax accounting rate of return based on the initial investment.

c. **Financing of a distributor.** Cote Corp., which is one of Sigma's distributors, wants to borrow $200,000 from Leif and to repay this loan within three years. As an inducement, Cote is offering Leif a participation in Cote's income for three years. Payments by Cote at the end of each of the three years would include principal plus 5% of Cote's net income for each of these years. The estimated amounts to be remitted by Cote to Leif under this arrangement would be as follows:

At the end of year	Amount
1	$ 50,000
2	90,000
3	110,000
Total estimated remittances	$250,000

Leif would be willing to grant Cote's loan request if the annual pre-tax internal rate of return on this loan exceeds Leif's hurdle (discount) rate of 20% on investment. Present value factors yielding 20% are approximately:

Year	Factor
1	.8
2	.7
3	.6

Required:

a. As a guide to Leif Company in determining a selling price for Kace, prepare a schedule of the expected annual contribution margin for each of the sales prices proposed for Kace.

b. 1. Compute Leif Company's current pre-tax accounting rate of return on its investment in Sigma Division.

2. Compute Leif Company's expected pre-tax accounting rate of return on its proposed investment in Sigma Division if Baum's two recommendations are implemented.

c. Regarding the possible financing of Cote Corp. by Leif Company, compute the net present value of Leif Company's investment opportunity on the proposed loan to Cote Corp., and state whether the investment would earn Leif a minimum internal rate of return of 20%.

Multiple Choice Answers

1. b	9. c	16. a	23. a	30. b
2. a	10. b	17. d	24. b	31. d
3. d	11. d	18. d	25. a	32. d
4. c	12. c	19. d	26. d	33. c
5. d	13. d	20. d	27. b	34. a
6. c	14. c	21. b	28. b	35. c
7. c	15. a	22. b	29. c	36. b
8. c				

Multiple Choice Answer Explanations

A. Short-Term Differential Cost Analysis

1. (1183,P3,50) (b) The requirement is the total operating income for 1983 if a special order is accepted. Since capacity is 30,000 units, acceptance of the special order for 15,000 units leaves only 15,000 units (30,000 - 15,000) of capacity for business from regular customers. Assuming the order is accepted, revenue would consist of 15,000 units at $100 per unit ($1,500,000) and 15,000 units at $90 per unit ($1,350,000), or a total of $2,850,000. Variable costs at $55 per unit ($990,000 ÷ 18,000) would total $1,650,000 (30,000 x $55). Fixed costs would remain at $495,000. The summary below indicates operating income would be $705,000 if the order is accepted.

Sales	$2,850,000
Variable costs	(1,650,000)
Contribution margin	1,200,000
Fixed costs	(495,000)
Operating income	$ 705,000

2. (582,P2,24) (a) The requirement is the minimum selling price to be considered in negotiating for a special order. The minimum selling price, given sufficient existing capacity, should be at least equal to the incremental costs associated with the order. Fixed manufacturing costs of $4 per unit (2/3 x $6) are not incremental since they will be incurred regardless of the activity level within the relevant range. However, the selling price must at least cover the variable manufacturing costs and the variable shipping costs.

Direct materials	$ 4
Direct labor	5
Variable overhead (1/3 x $6)	2
Shipping	3
Minimum acceptable selling price	$14

3. (582,P2,30) (d) The requirement is the sunk cost in a decision involving the sale of obsolete inventory. A sunk cost is a past cost which has been previously incurred; it cannot be changed no matter what alternative is chosen. The $50,000 manufacturing cost of the inventory is a sunk cost. It was previously incurred and it cannot be changed in any alternative; thus, it is irrelevant to the decision. The other items are differential. If the lamps are reworked, it will cost $20,000 and produce revenue of $35,000. If the lamps are scrapped, it will produce $8,000 revenue.

4. (581,P2,29) (c) The requirement is to compute the alternative (make or buy) that is most desirable and the amount by which that alternative is more desirable. The solutions approach is to list the relevant costs associated with each alternative.

Buy G		Manufacture G	
Purchase price of G		Direct materials:	
10,000 x $30 = $300,000		10,000 x $3 = $ 30,000	
		Direct labor:	
		10,000 x $15 = 150,000	
Less cost savings		Variable OH:	
on Product H	(45,000)	10,000 x $6 = 60,000	
		Fixed OH:	
		10,000 x $5* = 50,000	
Total cost	$255,000	Total cost	$290,000

*The relevant (out of pocket) cost is the $5 cost which is avoided if part G is not manufactured.

Buying part G from Verona Company is the more desirable alternative; the net cost savings is $35,000.

5. (1180,P2,31) (d) The requirement is to determine whether or not Dana should let its Lawn Products Division purchase the blades required for production from an outside supplier. The solutions approach is to identify any differential costs between the two alternatives.

	Differential costs		
	Make	Buy	Difference
Variable costs	(10,000)		
Cost to buy (10,000)($1.25)		(12,500)	
	(10,000)	(12,500)	(2,500)

The cost of buying from an outside supplier is $2,500 more than making, so the Lawn Products Division should not buy the blades from the outsider. Note that fixed costs are not differential; they would be incurred under either alternative.

6.   (587,Q2,26) (c) Relevant costs are those future costs that differ between the alternatives under consideration. The direct material and direct labor are both relevant as these costs would not be incurred if a "buy" decision were made. Of the $40 of factory overhead, only 40% would be relevant since 60% is not affected by the "make or buy" decision. Therefore, total relevant unit manufacturing cost is $30 ($4 DM + $10 DL + $16 overhead avoided if the buy decision is made).

7.   (1189,Q2,22) (c) The requirement is the effect on pretax profit if a department is discontinued. The solutions approach is to isolate those revenues and costs that would differ if the department is discontinued. If the department is discontinued, $20,000 of contribution margin would be lost. The $5,000 of allocated overhead will continue regardless of the decision made. Thus, $45,000 ($50,000 - $5,000) of allocated overhead cost would be eliminated or avoided. The net effect on pre-tax profit would be an increase of $25,000 ($45,000 of cost avoided less $20,000 of con-tribution margin lost).

8.   (585,Q1,14) (c) The requirement is to determine the amount of sunk costs associated with the decision to purchase a new machine. Sunk costs are those which are not avoidable and are the result of a past decision. The original cost of the old machine, its accumu-lated depreciation, and therefore, its book value, $24,000 ($84,000 - $60,000), are con-sidered sunk costs. The costs associated with the new machine are avoidable. For example, if Zar Company decides not to buy the machine, it will not incur the costs associated with it. However, whether Zar buys the new machine or not, the book value of the old machine is $24,000.

9.   (1189,T1,50) (c) When a company is considering exchanging an old asset for a new asset, the only factors that are economically relevant to the decision are those that differ between the two alternatives. When income tax considerations are ignored, the original cost of the old asset is irrelevant because the amount is unavoidable. It is a sunk cost. Sunk costs are irrelevant because they are the result of the past decision and, thus, will not affect the decision at hand. Fair market value of the old asset is relevant because, if the company decides to exchange the old asset, its fair market value could represent a reduction of the investment or cash outlay to acquire the new asset. Therefore, answer (c) is correct.

B. Capital Budgeting

10. (1185,T1,47) (b) The requirement is to identify the capital budgeting method for which the discount rate must be determined in advance. There are two capital budgeting methods which consider time value of money: internal rate of return and net present value. Under the net present value method, all cash inflows and outflows related to a capital project are discounted to a present value and netted to arrive at a net present value for the project. In order to discount the inflows and outflows, a discount rate must be determined in advance of the analysis of the project; therefore, answer (b) is cor-rect. Internal rate of return (or time-adjusted rate of return) determines the actual rate of return earned by analyzing the ex-pected cash flows of a project. The discount rate is used after the rate of return is computed to determine the project's accept-ability (through comparison of the rates). Therefore, answers (a) and (d) are incor-rect. Payback is a capital budgeting method which evaluates investments on the length of time necessary to recover the initial invest-ment. This method does not consider the time value of money in analyzing the investment. Therefore, answer (c) is incorrect.

B. Capital Budgeting: Payback

11. (1181,P2,36) (d) The requirement is to calculate the payback period for a machine. The payback period is that period of time over which the net cash inflows will equal the ini-tial investment (cash outflow). The net cash inflows given in the problem are equal annual amounts. Therefore, the payback period can be computed by dividing the initial investment by the annual net cash inflow. The first step is to calculate the amount of each equal annual net cash inflow. The data given includes cash inflow before taxes and an income tax rate of 40%. Net cash inflow is:

Cash inflow before taxes	–	Taxes	=	Annual net cash inflow
$135,000	–	Taxes	=	x
$135,000	–	[(135,000–100,000).40]	=	x
$135,000	–	$14,000	=	x
		$121,000	=	x

Note that depreciation is deducted in order to obtain the amount of income tax. The second step is to use the calculated value of annual net cash inflow in the formula to determine payback:

$$\frac{\text{Original investment cash outflow}}{\text{Annual net cash inflow}} = \text{Payback in years}$$

$$\frac{\$500,000}{\$121,000} = 4.1 \text{ years}$$

12. (589,T1,48) (c) The payback period is computed by dividing the initial investment by the annual net cash inflow. Depreciation expense is not subtracted from cash inflow; only the income taxes which are caused by the depreciation deduction are subtracted. One of the weaknesses of the payback period is that it ignores the time value of money. Therefore, answer (c) is correct.

13. (1180,T1,33) (d) The payback method evaluates investments on the basis of the length of time until the initial investment is returned. If annual cash flows are constant, the payback period is calculated as follows:

$$\frac{\text{Initial investment}}{\text{Annual cash flow}}$$

Answer (a) is incorrect because the payback period is not a function of useful life. Answers (b) and (c) are incorrect because the payback method ignores the time value of money.

B. Capital Budgeting: Net Present Value

14. (1181,P2,39) (c) The requirement is to solve for the cost of a machine, given annual net cash inflows and a specified positive net present value. Net present value is defined as the excess of the present value of the cash inflows over the initial net investment. In this case, the net present value is positive. Therefore, the present value of the outflow must be less than the present value of the inflows.

Cash inflows x	Present value of an ordinary annuity for 7 per.	=	Present value of cash inflows
$80,000	x 4.564	=	$365,120

Present value of cash inflows	−	Initial net investment	=	Net present value
$365,120	−	X	=	$ 12,720
		Initial investment (X)	=	$352,400

15. (1185,Q1,7) (a) The requirement is to determine the payback period of an investment in machinery. The payback period measures the length of time required by the project to recover the initial outlay. The computation for the project is:

Year	Needed	Cash flow	Balance	Payback years required
1	$100,000	$60,000	$40,000	1.00
2	40,000	30,000	10,000	1.00
3	10,000	20,000	0	.50
Total payback period in years				2.50

16. (1185,Q1,8) (a) The requirement is to determine the net present value (NPV) of an investment in machinery, using a discount rate of 20%. NPV is the difference between the required investment and the present value of the future cash flows. The computation for the project is:

Year	Cash (outflow) inflow	Present value of $1 at 20%	Net present value of cash flow
0	$(100,000)	1.000	$(100,000)
1	60,000	.91	54,600
2	30,000	.76	22,800
3	20,000	.63	12,600
4	20,000	.53	10,600
5	20,000	.44	8,800
		NPV	$ 9,400

17. (1188,T1,48) (d) The net present value method of capital budgeting calculates the present value of the future cash flows of a project and compares the present value of the cash flows to the investment outlay required to implement the project. Therefore, answer (d) is correct because **both** cash flow over the life of the project **and** the time value of money are considered.

18. (1187,T1,49) (d) The accounting rate of return (ARR) is based on financial statements prepared on the accrual basis. The formula to compute the ARR is:

$$\text{ARR} = \frac{\text{Expected increase in annual net income}}{\text{Initial (or average) investment}}$$

Note that the numerator is the expected increase in **net income**, not **cash flows**. Since depreciation expense is needed to compute net income, it would be used in computing the ARR. This is a weakness of this method because depreciation expense is not a cash flow. Another weakness is that the ARR ignores the time value of money. Therefore, answer (d) is correct.

19. (587,T1,48) (d) The requirement is to determine how the salvage value of a project is used in the calculation of the project's net present value (NPV). NPV is the difference between the initial investment (outlay) and the present value of the net cash inflows. The salvage value is a cash flow; thus, it should be included in the NPV calculation at its present value. Answer (a) is incorrect because the salvage value should be treated as a cash inflow in the NVP calculation. Answer (b) is incorrect because it ignores the time value of money. Answer (c) is incorrect because the NPV calculation involves the present value of cash flows, not the future values.

20. (586,T1,48) (d) The requirement is to determine if the net present value (NPV) capital budgeting technique can be used with uniform cash flows and/or with uneven cash flows. The NPV of a project is the present value of all future cash flows minus the required investment. If the cash flows are uniform, the present value of an annuity factor can be used to simplify the NPV computation. The amount of the cash flow each period is simply multiplied by the annuity factor to get the total present value of the cash flows. If the cash flows are uneven, the NPV computation is longer but still can be done. When cash flows are uneven, the present value of each period's cash flow has to be computed separately. This is done with the present value of $1.00 factors. These amounts are then added together to get the total present value of the cash flows. Since the NPV technique can be used with both uniform and uneven cash flows, answer (d) is correct.

B. Capital Budgeting: Internal (Time-Adjusted) Rate of Return

21. (1189,Q2,36) (b) The maximum amount that Kern Co. should invest now to obtain a 15% internal rate of return is the present value of the project's total net-cash flows as computed below:

Year	Net Cash flows	x	Present value of an ord. annuity	=	Present value of net cash flows
1	$50,000	x	.870	=	$43,500
2	$80,000	x	.756	=	$60,480
	Total present value				$103,980

22. (588,T1,48) (b) The internal rate of return (IRR) of a project is the discount rate at which the present value of the project's cash flows will exactly equal its initial investments (i.e., net present value = $0). Under this method, the cash flow over the entire life of the project, as well as the time value of money as expressed in a time value of money factor (TVMF) are taken into consideration. Therefore, answer (b) is correct. The IRR of a project is determined as follows:

PV (initial investment) = TVMF x Periodic cash flow amount

TVMF = Initial investment ÷ Periodic cash flow amount

Once the TVMF is derived, the IRR is found by finding the TVMF on the "n" line in the PV of an ordinary annuity table that represents the life of the project. Finally look at the top of that column to find the rate.

23. (1186,T1,49) (a) The internal rate of return (IRR) method determines the rate of return at which the present value of the cash

flows of a project will exactly equal the investment outlay for the project. The net present value (NPV) method determines the present value of the future cash flows of a project based on some predetermined discount rate. For this question, the key point to note is that both of these capital budgeting techniques are discounted cash flow techniques. This means that only cash flows are relevant in the computations involved in both of these methods. Because depreciation expense is not a cash flow, it does not enter directly into the calculation of the IRR or NPV of a project. It should be noted, however, that depreciation expense is deducted in calculating net income and would result in reduction of income tax expense (a cash flow item). However, this is not relevant for this question because you were told to ignore income tax considerations.

24. (585,T1,46) (b) The requirement is to determine which capital budgeting techniques assume that cash flows are reinvested at the rate earned by the investment. Answer (b) is correct. The internal rate of return method determines the rate of return at which the present value of the cash flows or benefits will exactly equal the investment outlay. This method assumes that cash flows received are reinvested to earn the same internal rate of return. The net present value method requires the selection of a discount rate which represents the minimum rate of return desired. This method assumes that all cash flows received are reinvested at this minimum rate of return and not the rate earned on the investment. Therefore, answers (a), (c), and (d) are incorrect.

B. Capital Budgeting: Accounting Rate of Return

25. (1186,Q2,31) (a) The NPV is the difference between the required investment and the present value of the future cash flows. The computation of the NPV for the project in this question is:

Year(s)	Cash (outflow) inflow	12% present value factor	Present value of cash flow
0	($200,000)	1.00	($200,000)
1-5	$ 65,000	3.60	234,000
		NPV	$ 34,000

Note that because depreciation is not a cash flow, it is not used in the calculation of NPV.

26. (1186,Q2,32) (d) When annual cash inflows are equal, the first step of computing the IRR is accomplished with the following formula:

$$\frac{\text{Initial investment}}{\text{Annual cash inflow}} = \frac{\text{PV of an ordinary}}{\text{annuity factor}}$$

$$\frac{\$200,000}{\$65,000} = 3.08 \text{ (rounded)}$$

The next step is to match the annuity factor with a rate of return. Note that PV factors decrease as the rate of return increases. Therefore, since 3.08 is less than the 3.3 annuity factor for 16%, the IRR on this project must be more than 16% [answer (d)].

27. (1186,Q2,33) (b) The solutions approach is to recall the ARR formula below:

$$\text{ARR} = \frac{\text{Expected increase in annual net income}}{\text{Average investment}}$$

The expected increase in annual net income is the $65,000 annual cash savings minus the $40,000 annual depreciation ($200,000 ÷ 5 years). Note that the average investment for Allo is based on the average book value for 1985. The book value at the beginning of 1985 is $200,000. The book value at the end of 1985 is $160,000 ($200,000 - $40,000). Therefore, the average book value is $180,000 [($200,000 + $160,000) ÷ 2]. The ARR can now be computed:

$$\text{ARR} = \frac{\$65,000 - \$40,000}{\$180,000} = 13.9\%$$

28. (1183,Q1,17) (b) The requirement is to determine the factor which should be used in computing the internal rate of return for Amaro's proposed investment in new equipment. The internal rate of return (IRR) is defined as the rate of discount which will cause the present value of the benefits to exactly equal the investment outlay. This discount rate represents "true" rate of return the project will generate. The IRR is then compared with the cost of capital to determine if the investment should be made. The IRR is determined by setting the investment outlay equal to the discounted value of future net cash inflows as illustrated below. The discount factor is the unknown.

$$\begin{pmatrix} \text{PV} \\ \text{investment} \\ \text{today} \end{pmatrix} = \begin{pmatrix} \text{TVMF} \\ \text{unknown rate} \\ \text{of return} \end{pmatrix} \times \begin{pmatrix} \text{Payments} \\ \text{annual cash} \\ \text{savings} \end{pmatrix}$$

$$\$20,000 = \text{TVMF} \times \$5,000$$
$$\text{TVMF} = 4.000$$

29. (1183,Q1,18) (c) The requirement is to calculate the accounting rate of return (ARR) based on Amaro's initial investment in the new equipment. The accounting rate of return is based on financial statements prepared on the accrual basis. Gauging profitability is an objective of this method; however, consideration of the time value of money is ignored. The solutions approach is to recall the formula below.

$$\text{ARR} = \frac{\text{Expected increase in annual net income}}{\text{Initial investment}}$$

$$\text{ARR} = \frac{\overset{\$5,000}{\overbrace{\text{(annual cash savings)}}} - \overset{\$2,000}{\overbrace{\text{(annual dep.)}}}}{\$20,000}$$

ARR = 15%

The problem could have required the accounting rate of return based on average investment, in which case the denominator would have been $10,000 ($20,000 ÷ 2).

30. (1189,Q2,40) (b) The accounting rate of return (ARR) computes an approximate rate of return, but ignores the time value of money. It is computed as follows:

$$\text{ARR} = \frac{\text{Expected increase in annual net income}}{\text{Investment}}$$

Note that the numerator used for ARR is the increase in annual net income (not cash flows). This increase is equal to the $25,000 annual savings after taxes, less the annual depreciation on the equipment. Depreciation in this case would be $10,000 annually ($100,000 ÷ 10 years). The ARR for this purchase is computed as follows:

$$\frac{\$25,000 \text{ decrease in cash}}{\text{expenses} - \$10,000 \text{ depreciation}} = 15\%$$
$$\frac{}{\$100,000 \text{ initial investment}}$$

31. (1189,T1,48) (d) The accounting rate of return (ARR) is based on financial statements prepared on the accrual basis. The formula to compute the ARR is:

$$\text{ARR} = \frac{\text{Expected increase in annual net income}}{\text{Initial (or average) investment}}$$

Answer (d) is correct because both the revenue over life of project and depreciation expense are used in the calculation of ARR. Depreciation expense over the project's life and other expenses directly associated with the project under consideration including income tax effects are subtracted from revenue over life of the project to determine net income over life of project. Net income over the project's life is then divided by the economic life to determine annual net income, the numerator of the ARR formula. This is a weakness of the ARR method because it does not consider actual cash flows or the time value of money.

C. Probability Analysis

32. (587,Q2,21) (d) This question is in actuality an expected value problem. The expected value or price (P) to charge to break even is the sum of the probability of each

event occurring times the payoff of that event. There are two events to account for in this question. First, there is a 4 in 52 chance or probability of someone drawing a queen. The payoff of this event is $5. Thus, the expected value for this event would be the 4/52 probability multiplied by the $5. Second, there is a 13 in 52 probability of someone drawing a heart. The payoff of this event is $2. Thus, the expected value for this event would be the 13/52 probability multiplied by the $2. Therefore, the total expected value or price is the sum of the expected values for the two events:

$$\frac{4}{52} \; (5) \; + \; \frac{13}{52} \; (2) \; = \; P$$

Note that in order for the above equation to be correct, you have to assume that anyone that draws a queen of hearts will receive $7.

33. (1189,Q2,21) (c) A 4% error rate is present for all cargo shipped as shown by the following computation:

Terminal	Percentage of cargo shipped	x	Individual error rates	=	Error rate for all cargo
Land	50%		2%		1.0%
Air	40%		4%		1.6%
Sea	10%		14%		1.4%
				Total	4.0%

One quarter or 25% of the total error rate occurs in the land terminal (1.0% ÷ 4.0%). Thus, there is a 25% probability that a given error will occur in the land terminal. The probability that the error occurred in the air terminal is 40% (1.6% ÷ 4.0%) and in the sea terminal is 35% (1.4% ÷ 4.0%).

34. (1186,Q2,36) (a) In a given year, Seco will incur 19 power outages as shown by the following computation:

Number of outages per month	x	Number of months	=	Total number of outages
0		3		–
1		2		2
2		4		8
3		3		9
		Total		19

Each power outage costs Seco $200, or a total cost of $3,800 ($200 x 19) per year. An auxiliary generator costs $250 per month or a total cost of $3,000 ($250 x 12 months) per year. Therefore, by using an auxiliary generator, Seco can save $800 ($3,800 – $3,000) per year.

35. (585,Q1,17) (c) The requirement is to determine the expected value of the added

monthly income from the proposed product. The expected value is the sum of the probability of each event occuring times the payoff of that event. The expected value is computed as follows:

Monthly sales volume	Probability	x	Income (loss)	=	Expected value
6,000	.10		$(70,000)		$(7,000)
12,000	.20		10,000		2,000
18,000	.40		60,000		24,000
24,000	.20		100,000		20,000
30,000	.10		140,000		14,000
					$53,000

Therefore, product Vee has an expected value of $53,000.

36. (588,T1,50) (b) Of the four alternatives, only expected value uses probabilities as weights in determining the probability of outcome. Each possible outcome is multiplied by an appropriate weight (probability). These are then summed to determine the expected value. Therefore, answer (b) is correct. Answer (a) is incorrect because the standard deviation is the square root of the variance. Answer (c) is incorrect because the coefficient of variation is the standard deviation divided by the expected value. Answer (d) is incorrect because the objective function is a decision model which quantifies a goal.

Solution Guide

Problem 1   Three Unrelated Decisions
         (1185,Q5)

1.   Number 1 consists of three unrelated parts. In part a., a schedule of the expected annual contribution margin must be prepared. Two schedules computing pre-tax accounting rate of return on initial investment must be prepared in part b. Finally, in part c., the net present value of an investment opportunity must be computed.

2.   In part a., Sigma is considering three different selling prices ($6, $7, or $8) for a new product. A schedule of expected annual contribution margins for each alternative must be prepared. The expected value is a weighted average of the possible contribution margins, using the associated probabilities as weights.

2.1   The first step is to compute the expected number of units to be sold for each of the three different per unit selling prices. This is accomplished by multiplying the three possible annual sales levels by their probabilities for each per unit price. For example, if the selling price is $6, there is a 10% chance that 70,000 units will be sold, a 50% chance that 80,000 units will be sold, and a 40% chance that 90,000 units will be sold. If these are multiplied and then added together, the result is an expected sales level of 83,000 units. This process should then be repeated for the selling prices of $7 and $8.

2.2   The expected sales level expressed in units for each price must then be multiplied by the per unit price to express the expected sales level as a dollar amount.

2.3   The expected sales level expressed in units for each price must then be multiplied by the per unit variable cost ($3). This calculates the expected total variable cost for each of the different selling prices.

2.4   The expected variable cost for each different selling price must then be subtracted from the expected total sales (in dollars) for that price to determine the expected contribution margin for that selling price.

3.   In part b., Sigma is considering two recommendations. The first requirement is to compute the <u>current</u> pre-tax accounting rate of return on initial investment. The second requirement is to compute the <u>expected</u> pre-tax accounting rate of return on initial investment if the two recommendations are implemented.

3.1   The formula to compute the required ratio is:

$$\frac{\text{Pre-tax accounting income}}{\text{Initial investment}}$$

3.2   The current pre-tax accounting income is $200,000 (10% x $2,000,000). The current initial investment is $600,000, resulting in a rate of return of 33 1/3% ($200,000 ÷ $600,000).

3.3   The expected pre-tax accounting income if the recommendations are implemented is 12% of sales. However, sales will decrease by 10% to $1,800,000 ($2,000,000 x 90%). Thus, the expected income is $216,000 (12% x $1,800,000). The initial investment would be $700,000 ($600,000 + $100,000), resulting in a rate of return of 30.86% ($216,000 ÷ $700,000).

4.   Part c. requires a computation of the net present value of an investment opportunity. Sigma must invest $200,000 today to receive returns of $50,000, $90,000, and $110,000 at the end of the next three years.

4.1   The yearly returns are multiplied by the appropriate present value factor to determine their present value.

4.2   The initial investment ($200,000) is subtracted from the present value of the future inflows ($169,000) to compute the <u>negative</u> net present value of $31,000.

4.3   A <u>negative</u> NPV indicates that the rate of return is less than desired. If the NPV was 0, the rate of return would be equal to the desired return. If the NVP is <u>positive</u>, the rate of return is <u>more</u> than desired.

Unofficial Answer

Problem 1   Three Unrelated Decisions (1185,Q5)

a.

Leif Company
Sigma Division
SCHEDULE OF EXPECTED ANNUAL CONTRIBUTION MARGIN
FOR KACE AT VARIOUS SALES PRICES

Sales price	Expected sales level (units)	Expected total sales	Expected variable costs at $3	Expected contribution margin
$6	83,000 [1]	$498,000	$249,000	$249,000
7	79,000 [2]	553,000	237,000	316,000
8	74,000 [3]	592,000	222,000	370,000

[1]	70,000 x 10%	=	7,000	[2]	70,000 x 40%	=	28,000	[3]	70,000 x 70%	=	49,000
	80,000 x 50%	=	40,000		80,000 x 30%	=	24,000		80,000 x 20%	=	16,000
	90,000 x 40%	=	36,000		90,000 x 30%	=	27,000		90,000 x 10%	=	9,000
			83,000				79,000				74,000

b.

1. COMPUTATION OF CURRENT PRE-TAX ACCOUNTING RATE OF RETURN ON INVESTMENT

Sigma Division's current annual sales	$2,000,000	
Current pre-tax rate of return on sales	10%	$200,000
Investment in Sigma Division		600,000
Pre-tax accounting rate of return on investment		33 1/3%

b.

2. COMPUTATION OF EXPECTED PRE-TAX ACCOUNTING RATE OF RETURN ON IMPLEMENTATION OF RECOMMENDATIONS BY MANAGER OF SIGMA DIVISION

Sigma Division's current annual sales	$2,000,000	
Expected reduction in sales volume (10%)	200,000	
Expected sales volume after discontinuance of Sago	1,800,000	
Expected pre-tax accounting rate of return on sales	12%	$216,000
Total proposed investment in Sigma Division		700,000
Expected pre-tax accounting rate of return on investment		30.86%

c.

COMPUTATION OF NET PRESENT VALUE OF
INVESTMENT OPPORTUNITY ON PROPOSED LOAN TO COTE CORP.

Discounted cash flows for year:					
	1	.8 x $ 50,000	=	$ 40,000	
	2	.7 x 90,000	=	63,000	
	3	.6 x 110,000	=	66,000	
Total				$169,000	
Proposed loan				200,000	
Net present value				$(31,000)	

This investment will not earn an internal rate of return of 20%.

CHAPTER SIX

GOVERNMENTAL PROBLEMS AND SOLUTIONS

Governmental and not-for-profit accounting questions appear on both the theory and practice sections of the examination. A complete analysis of recent examinations and the *Revised AICPA Content Specification Outlines* appear in Volume I, *Outlines and Study Guides*.

Each question is coded as to month, year, section, problem number, and multiple choice question number. For example, (1189,T1,38) indicates November 1989, theory, problem 1, and multiple choice question number 38. Note that P = Practice I, Q = Practice II, and T = Theory.

Module 38/Governmental Accounting (GOV)

	Exam reference	No. of minutes	Page no. Problem	Answer
97 Multiple Choice			900	913
1 Essay Question and				
1 Practice Problem:				
1. Basis of Accounting: Reporting Issues	1184,T5	15-25	911	927
2. General Fund Journal Entries	1184,Q4	45-55	911	927

Module 39/Nonprofit Accounting (NPF)

	Exam reference	No. of minutes	Page no. Problem	Answer
69 Multiple Choice			931	947
5 Practice Problems:				
1. University Journal Entries and Statement of Changes in Fund Balance	1183,Q4	45-55	940	958
2. Hospital Worksheet	587,Q5	40-50	941	960
3. Voluntary Health and Welfare Organizations Journal Entries	1189,Q4	45-55	943	964
4. Journal Entries and All-Inclusive Activity Statement for Nonprofit Organization	583,Q5	40-50	945	966
5. Entries for Governmental Units vs. Nonprofit Organizations	586,Q5	40-50	945	967

Sample Examinations

Multiple Choice Questions (1-97)

Items 1 through 5 are based on the following information:

Maple Township uses encumbrance accounting, and formally integrates its budget into the accounting records for its general fund. For the year ending June 30, 1988, the Township Council adopted a budget comprising estimated revenues of $10,000,000, appropriations of $9,000,000, and an estimated transfer of $300,000 to the debt service fund. The following additional information is provided:

• For the month of April 1988, salaries and wages expense of $200,000 was incurred.

• On April 10, 1988, an approved $1,500 purchase order was issued for supplies. These supplies were received on May 1, 1988, and the $1,500 invoice was approved for payment.

• In November 1987, an unexpected state grant of $100,000 was received to finance the purchase of school buses, and an additional grant of $5,000 was received for bus maintenance and operations. Only $60,000 of the capital grant was used in the current year for the purchase of buses, but the entire operating grant of $5,000 was disbursed in the current year. The remaining $40,000 of the capital grant is expected to be expended during the year ending June 30, 1989. Maple's school bus system is appropriately accounted for in the capital projects fund.

1. On adoption of the budget, the journal entry to record the budgetary fund balance should include a
   a. Debit of $700,000.
   b. Credit of $700,000.
   c. Debit of $1,000,000.
   d. Credit of $1,000,000.

2. Budgeted revenues would be recorded by a
   a. Debit to estimated revenues control, $10,000,000.
   b. Debit to estimated revenues receivable, $10,000,000.
   c. Credit estimated revenues, $10,000,000.
   d. Credit to other financing sources control, $10,000,000.

3. Budgeted appropriations would be recorded by a
   a. Debit to estimated expenditures, $9,300,000.
   b. Credit to appropriations control, $9,300,000.
   c. Debit to estimated expenditures, $9,000,000.
   d. Credit to appropriations control, $9,000,000.

4. What journal entry should be made on April 10, 1988 to record the approved purchase order?

		Debit	Credit
a.	Expenditures control	$1,500	
	Encumbrances control		$1,500
b.	Encumbrances control	1,500	
	Expenditures control		1,500
c.	Encumbrances control	1,500	
	Fund balance reserved for encumbrances		1,500
d.	Encumbrances control	1,500	
	Appropriations control		1,500

5. What journal entries should be made on May 1, 1988 upon receipt of the supplies and approval of the invoice?

		Debit	Credit
a.	Encumbrances control	$1,500	
	Appropriations control		$1,500
	Supplies expense	1,500	
	Vouchers payable		1,500
b.	Fund balance reserved for encumbrances	1,500	
	Encumbrances control		1,500
	Expenditures control	1,500	
	Vouchers payable		1,500
c.	Appropriations control	1,500	
	Encumbrances control		1,500
	Expenditures control	1,500	
	Vouchers payable		1,500
d.	Expenditures control	1,500	
	Encumbrances control		1,500
	Supplies expense	1,500	
	Vouchers payable		1,500

6. The following balances are included in the subsidiary records of Burwood Village's Parks and Recreation Department at March 31, 1982:

Appropriations—supplies	$7,500
Expenditures—supplies	4,500
Encumbrances—supply orders	750

How much does the Department have available for additional purchases of supplies?
   a. $0
   b. $2,250
   c. $3,000
   d. $6,750

7. The budget of a governmental unit, for which the appropriations exceed the estimated revenues, was adopted and recorded in the general ledger at the beginning of the year. During the year, expenditures and encumbrances were less than appropriations; whereas revenues equaled estimated revenues. The budgetary fund balance account is
   a. Credited at the beginning of the year and not changed at the end of the year.

b.   Credited at the beginning of the
     year and debited at the end of the
     year.
c.   Debited at the beginning of the year
     and not changed at the end of the
     year.
d.   Debited at the beginning of the year
     and credited at the end of the year.

8.   The appropriations control account of a
governmental unit is debited when

	The budgetary accounts are closed	Expenditures are recorded
a.	No	Yes
b.	No	No
c.	Yes	No
d.	Yes	Yes

9.   The budgetary fund balance reserved for
encumbrances account of a governmental unit is
decreased when
     a.   Supplies previously ordered are
          received.
     b.   A purchase order is approved.
     c.   The vouchers are paid.
     d.   Appropriations are recorded.

10.   The estimated revenues control account
balance of a governmental fund type is
eliminated when
     a.   The budgetary accounts are closed.
     b.   The budget is recorded.
     c.   Property taxes are recorded.
     d.   Appropriations are closed.

11.   The encumbrances control account of a
governmental unit is increased when

	A voucher payable is recorded	The budgetary accounts are closed
a.	No	No
b.	No	Yes
c.	Yes	Yes
d.	Yes	No

12.   The budgetary fund balance reserved for
encumbrances account of a governmental fund
type is increased when
     a.   A purchase order is approved.
     b.   Supplies previously ordered are
          received.
     c.   Appropriations are recorded.
     d.   The budget is recorded.

13.   The expenditures control account of a
governmental unit is credited when
     a.   The operations accounts are closed.
     b.   The budget is recorded.
     c.   Supplies are purchased.
     d.   Supplies previously encumbered are
          received.

14.   Which of the following accounts of a
governmental unit is credited when supplies
previously ordered are received?
     a.   Budgetary fund balance reserved for
          encumbrances.
     b.   Encumbrances control.
     c.   Expenditures control.
     d.   Appropriations control.

15.   The revenues control account of a
governmental unit is debited when
     a.   The budget is recorded at the
          beginning of the year.
     b.   The account is closed out at the end
          of the year.
     c.   Property taxes are recorded.
     d.   Property taxes are collected.

16.   Which of the following requires the use
of the encumbrance system?
     a.   Special revenue fund.
     b.   Debt service fund.
     c.   General fixed assets group of
          accounts.
     d.   Enterprise fund.

17.   In connection with Albury Township's
long-term debt, the following cash
accumulations are available to cover payment
of principal and interest on

Bonds for financing on
 water treatment plant
 construction $1,000,000
General long-term obligations   400,000

The amount of these cash accumulations that
should be accounted for in Albury's debt
service funds is
     a. $0
     b. $ 400,000
     c. $1,000,000
     d. $1,400,000

Items 18 and 19 are based on the
following information:

On December 31, 1987, Vane City paid a
contractor $3,000,000 for the total cost of a
new municipal annex built in 1987 on city-
owned land. Financing was provided by a
$2,000,000 general obligation bond issue sold
at face amount on December 31, 1987 with the
remaining $1,000,000 transferred from the
general fund.

18.   What account and amount should be
reported in Vane's 1987 financial statements
for the general fund?
     a.   Other financing uses control,
          $1,000,000.
     b.   Other financing sources control,
          $2,000,000.

    c.   Expenditures control, $3,000,000.
    d.   Other financing sources control, $3,000,000.

19. What accounts and amounts should be reported in Vane's 1987 financial statements for the capital projects fund?
    a.   Other financing sources control, $2,000,000; General long-term debt, $2,000,000.
    b.   Revenues control, $2,000,000; Expenditures control, $2,000,000.
    c.   Other financing sources control, $3,000,000; Expenditures control, $3,000,000.
    d.   Revenues control, $3,000,000; Expenditures control, $3,000,000.

20. The comprehensive annual financial report (CAFR) of a governmental unit should contain a combined statement of revenues, expenditures, and changes in fund balances for

	Governmental funds	Proprietary funds
a.	Yes	No
b.	Yes	Yes
c.	No	Yes
d.	No	No

21. The comprehensive annual financial report (CAFR) of a governmental unit should contain a combined statement of revenues, expenses, and changes in retained earnings for

	Account groups	Proprietary funds
a.	Yes	Yes
b.	Yes	No
c.	No	No
d.	No	Yes

22. In the comprehensive annual financial report (CAFR) of a governmental unit, the account groups are included in
    a.   Both the combined balance sheet and the combined statement of revenues, expenditures, and changes in fund balances.
    b.   The combined statement of revenues, expenditures, and changes in fund balances, but not the combined balance sheet.
    c.   The combined balance sheet but not the combined statement of revenues, expenditures, and changes in fund balances.
    d.   Neither the combined balance sheet nor the combined statement of revenues, expenditures, and changes in fund balances.

23. The comprehensive annual financial report (CAFR) of a governmental unit should contain a combined statement of cash flows for

	Governmental funds	Account groups
a.	Yes	No
b.	Yes	Yes
c.	No	Yes
d.	No	No

24. The comprehensive annual financial report (CAFR) of a governmental unit should contain a combined balance sheet for

	Governmental funds	Proprietary funds	Account groups
a.	Yes	Yes	No
b.	Yes	Yes	Yes
c.	Yes	No	Yes
d.	No	Yes	No

25. Which of the following accounts would be included in the asset section of the combined balance sheet of a governmental unit for the general long-term debt account group?

	Amount available in debt service funds	Amount to be provided for retirement of general long-term debt
a.	Yes	Yes
b.	Yes	No
c.	No	Yes
d.	No	No

26. The following proceeds received by Grove City in 1987 are legally restricted to expenditure for specified purposes:

Donation by a benefactor mandated to an expendable trust fund to provide meals for the needy	$300,000
Sales taxes to finance the maintenance of tourist facilities in the shopping district	900,000

What amount should be accounted for in Grove's special revenue funds?
    a. $0
    b. $ 300,000
    c. $ 900,000
    d. $1,200,000

27. During its fiscal year ended June 30, 1988, Lake County financed the following projects by special assessments:

Capital improvements	$2,000,000
Service-type projects	800,000

For financial reporting purposes, what amount should appear in special assessment funds?
    a. $2,800,000
    b. $2,000,000
    c. $ 800,000
    d. $0

Items 28 and 29 are based on the following information:

Maple Township uses encumbrance accounting, and formally integrates its budget into the accounting records for its general fund. For the year ending June 30, 1988, the Township Council adopted a budget comprising estimated revenues of $10,000,000, appropriations of $9,000,000, and an estimated transfer of $300,000 to the debt service fund. The following additional information is provided:

• For the month of April 1988, salaries and wages expense of $200,000 was incurred.
• On April 10, 1988, an approved $1,500 purchase order was issued for supplies. These supplies were received on May 1, 1988, and the $1,500 invoice was approved for payment.
• In November 1987, an unexpected state grant of $100,000 was received to finance the purchase of school buses, and an additional grant of $5,000 was received for bus maintenance and operations. Only $60,000 of the capital grant was used in the current year for the purchase of buses, but the entire operating grant of $5,000 was disbursed in the current year. The remaining $40,000 of the capital grant is expected to be expended during the year ending June 30, 1989. Maple's school bus system is appropriately accounted for in the capital projects fund.

28. In connection with the grants for the purchase of school buses and bus maintenance and operations, what amount should be reported as grant revenues for the year ending June 30, 1988?

    a. $ 5,000
    b. $ 60,000
    c. $ 65,000
    d. $100,000

29. What journal entry should be made to record the salaries and wages expense incurred for April?

		Debit	Credit
a.	Salaries and wages expense	$200,000	
	Vouchers payable		$200,000
b.	Appropriations control	200,000	
	Vouchers payable		200,000
c.	Encumbrances control	200,000	
	Vouchers payable		200,000
d.	Expenditures control	200,000	
	Vouchers payable		200,000

30. Which of the following is an appropriate basis of accounting for a proprietary fund of a governmental unit?

	Cash basis	Modified accrual basis
a.	Yes	Yes
b.	Yes	No
c.	No	No
d.	No	Yes

31. In 1986, Menton City received $5,000,000 of bond proceeds to be used for capital projects. Of this amount, $1,000,000 was expended in 1986. Expenditures for the $4,000,000 balance were expected to be incurred in 1987. These bond proceeds should be recorded in capital projects funds for

    a. $5,000,000 in 1986.
    b. $5,000,000 in 1987.
    c. $1,000,000 in 1986 and $4,000,000 in 1987.
    d. $1,000,000 in 1986 and in the general fund for $4,000,000 in 1986.

32. On December 31, 1988, Park Township paid a contractor $4,000,000 for the total cost of a new police building built in 1988. Financing was by means of a $3,000,000 general obligation bond issue sold at face amount on December 31, 1988 with the remaining $1,000,000 transferred from the general fund. What amount should Park record as revenues in the capital projects fund in connection with the bond issue proceeds and the transfer?

    a. $0
    b. $1,000,000
    c. $3,000,000
    d. $4,000,000

33. Which of the following funds of a governmental unit recognizes revenues in the accounting period in which they become available and measurable?

    a.   Capital projects funds.
    b.   Nonexpendable trust funds.
    c.   Enterprise funds.
    d.   Internal service funds.

34. A local governmental unit could have funds using which of the following accounting bases?

	Accrual basis	Modified accrual basis
a.	No	Yes
b.	No	No
c.	Yes	No
d.	Yes	Yes

35. The revenues control account of a governmental unit is increased when

    a.   The budget is recorded.
    b.   Property taxes are recorded.
    c.   Appropriations are recorded.
    d.   The budgetary accounts are closed.

36. Which of the following funds of a governmental unit uses the modified accrual basis of accounting?
    a. Enterprise funds.
    b. Internal service funds.
    c. Nonexpendable trust funds.
    d. Special revenue funds.

37. Which of the following funds of a governmental unit uses the same basis of accounting as the special revenue fund?
    a. Expendable trust funds.
    b. Nonexpendable trust funds.
    c. Enterprise funds.
    d. Internal service funds.

38. Under the modified accrual basis of accounting for a governmental unit, revenues should be recognized in the accounting period in which they
    a. Are earned and become measurable.
    b. Are collected.
    c. Become available and measurable.
    d. Become available and earned.

39. The debt service fund of a governmental unit is used to account for the accumulation of resources to pay, and the payment of, general long-term debt

	Principal	Interest
a.	Yes	Yes
b.	Yes	No
c.	No	No
d.	No	Yes

40. Which one of the following funds of a governmental unit is a governmental fund?
    a. Enterprise funds.
    b. Internal service funds.
    c. Debt service funds.
    d. Nonexpendable trust funds.

41. When fixed assets purchased from general fund revenues were received, the appropriate journal entry was made in the general fixed asset account group. What account, if any, should have been debited in the general fund?
    a. No journal entry should have been made in the general fund.
    b. Fixed assets.
    c. Expenditures.
    d. Due from general fixed asset account group.

42. Under the modified accrual basis of accounting, which of the following taxes is usually recorded before it is received in cash?
    a. Property.
    b. Income.

    c. Gross receipts.
    d. Gift.

43. Interest expense on bonds payable should be recorded in a Debt Service Fund
    a. At the end of the fiscal period if the interest due date does not coincide with the end of the fiscal year.
    b. When bonds are issued.
    c. When legally payable.
    d. When paid.

44. The expenditures control account of a governmental unit is increased when

	A purchase order is approved	The budget is recorded
a.	No	No
b.	No	Yes
c.	Yes	Yes
d.	Yes	No

45. The initial transfer of cash from the general fund in order to establish an internal service fund would require the general fund to credit cash and debit
    a. Accounts receivable--internal service fund.
    b. Unreserved fund balance.
    c. Fund balance reserved for encumbrances.
    d. Operating transfers out.

46. The following information for the year ended June 30, 1988 pertains to a proprietary fund established by Burwood Village in connection with Burwood's public parking facilities:

Receipts from users of parking facilities	$400,000
Expenditures	
Parking meters	210,000
Salaries and other cash expenses	90,000
Depreciation of parking meters	70,000

For the year ended June 30, 1988, this proprietary fund should report net income of
    a. $0
    b. $ 30,000
    c. $100,000
    d. $240,000

47. Hull City has established a separate internal service (self-insurance) fund to pay claims and judgments of all of Hull's funds. In 1987, payments to the insurer fund amounted to $500,000, while the actuarially determined amount was $400,000. The payments to the insurer fund should be accounted for as

	An operating transfer of	A residual equity transfer of
a.	$0	$0
b.	$100,000	$400,000
c.	$400,000	$100,000
d.	$500,000	$0

48. During 1987, Pine City recorded the following receipts from self-sustaining activities paid for by users of the services rendered:

Municipal bus system	$1,000,000
Operation of water supply and sewerage plant	1,800,000

What amount should be accounted for in Pine's enterprise funds?

- a. $2,800,000
- b. $1,800,000
- c. $1,000,000
- d. $0

49. The following funds are among those maintained by Arlon City:

Enterprise funds	$2,000,000
Internal service funds	800,000

Arlon's proprietary funds amount to

- a. $0
- b. $ 800,000
- c. $2,000,000
- d. $2,800,000

50. The following data relates to Lely Township:

Printing and binding equipment used for servicing all of Lely's departments and agencies, on a cost-reimbursement basis	$100,000
Equipment used for supplying water to Lely's residents	900,000
Receivables for completed sidewalks to be paid for in installments by affected property owners	950,000
Cash received from federal government, dedicated to highway maintenance, which must be accounted for in a separate fund	995,000

How much could be accounted for in an internal service fund?

- a. $100,000
- b. $900,000
- c. $950,000
- d. $995,000

51. During the year ended December 31, 1981, Leyland City received a state grant of $500,000 to finance the purchase of buses, and an additional grant of $100,000 to aid in the financing of bus operations in 1981. Only $300,000 of the capital grant was used in 1981 for the purchase of buses, but the entire operating grant of $100,000 was spent in 1981.

If Leyland's bus transportation system is accounted for as an enterprise fund, how much should Leyland report as grant revenues for the year ended December 31, 1981?

- a. $100,000
- b. $300,000
- c. $400,000
- d. $500,000

52. Which of the following funds of a governmental unit would include retained earnings in its balance sheet?

- a. Expendable pension trust.
- b. Internal service.
- c. Special revenue.
- d. Capital projects.

53. Customers' security deposits that cannot be spent for normal operating purposes were collected by a governmental unit and accounted for in the enterprise fund. A portion of the amount collected was invested in marketable debt securities and a portion in marketable equity securities. How would each portion be classified in the balance sheet?

	Portion in marketable debt securities	Portion in marketable equity securities
a.	Unrestricted asset	Restricted asset
b.	Unrestricted asset	Unrestricted asset
c.	Restricted asset	Unrestricted asset
d.	Restricted asset	Restricted asset

54. Which of the following funds of a governmental unit uses the same basis of accounting as the enterprise fund?

- a. Nonexpendable trust funds.
- b. Expendable trust funds.
- c. Special revenue funds.
- d. Capital projects funds.

55. Which of the following funds of a governmental unit would account for depreciation in the accounts of the fund?

- a. General.
- b. Internal service.
- c. Capital project.
- d. Special assessment.

56. Fixed assets of an enterprise fund should be accounted for in the

- a. Enterprise fund but <u>no</u> depreciation on the fixed assets should be recorded.
- b. Enterprise fund and depreciation on the fixed assets should be recorded.

c.   General fixed asset account group but no depreciation on the fixed assets should be recorded.

d.   General fixed asset account group and depreciation on the fixed assets should be recorded.

57. Which of the following funds of a governmental unit would include contributed capital in its balance sheet?
a.   Expendable pension trust.
b.   Special revenue.
c.   Capital projects.
d.   Internal service.

58. Which of the following funds of a governmental unit would account for general long-term debt in the accounts of the fund?
a.   Special revenue.
b.   Capital projects.
c.   Internal service.
d.   General.

59. Which fund is not an expendable fund?
a.   Capital projects.
b.   General.
c.   Special revenue.
d.   Internal service.

60. "Excess of net billings to departments over cost" would appear in the financial statement of which fund?
a.   Internal service.
b.   Enterprise.
c.   Capital projects.
d.   Special revenue.

61. If a governmental unit established a data processing center to service all agencies within the unit, the data processing center should be accounted for as a(n)
a.   Capital projects fund.
b.   Internal service fund.
c.   Agency fund.
d.   Trust fund.

62. Recreational facilities run by a governmental unit and financed on a user-charge basis would be accounted for in which fund?
a.   General.
b.   Trust.
c.   Enterprise.
d.   Capital projects.

63. The following fund types used by Green Township had total assets at June 30, 1989 as follows:

Agency funds $ 300,000
Debt service funds   1,000,000

Total fiduciary fund assets amount to
a. $0
b. $ 300,000
c. $1,000,000
d. $1,300,000

64. Grove County collects property taxes levied within its boundaries and receives a 1% fee for administering these collections on behalf of the municipalities located in the county. In 1987, Grove collected $1,000,000 for its municipalities and remitted $990,000 to them after deducting fees of $10,000. In the initial recording of the 1% fee, Grove's agency fund should credit
a.   Fund balance--agency fund, $10,000.
b.   Fees earned--agency fund, $10,000.
c.   Due to Grove County general fund, $10,000.
d.   Revenues control, $10,000.

65. A local governmental unit could use which of the following types of funds?

	Fiduciary	Proprietary
a.	Yes	No
b.	Yes	Yes
c.	No	Yes
d.	No	No

66. Which type of fund can be either expendable or nonexpendable?
a.   Debt service.
b.   Enterprise.
c.   Special revenue.
d.   Trust.

67. Taxes collected and held by a municipality for a school district would be accounted for in a(n)
a.   Enterprise fund.
b.   Internal service fund.
c.   Agency fund.
d.   Special revenue fund.

68. Which of the following funds frequently does not have a fund balance?
a.   General fund.
b.   Agency fund.
c.   Special revenue fund.
d.   Capital projects fund.

69. The following information pertains to a computer that Pine Township leased from Karl Supply Co. on July 1, 1988 for general township use:

Karl's cost	$5,000
Fair value at July 1, 1988	$5,000
Estimated economic life	5 years
Fixed noncancelable term	30 months
Rental at beginning of each month	$135
Guaranteed residual value	$2,000
Present value of minimum lease payments at July 1, 1988 using Pine's incremental borrowing rate of 10.5%	$5,120
Karl's implicit interest rate of 12.04%	$5,000

On July 1, 1988, what amount should Pine capitalize in its general fixed assets account group for this leased computer?
    a. $0
    b. $3,000
    c. $5,000
    d. $5,120

70. Unmatured general obligation bonds payable of a governmental unit should be reported in the liability section of the
    a.   General fund.
    b.   Capital projects fund.
    c.   General long-term debt account group.
    d.   Debt service fund.

71. The following items were among Wood Township's expenditures from the general fund during the year ended June 30, 1987:

Furniture for Township Hall	$10,000
Minicomputer for tax collector's office	15,000

The amount that should be classified as fixed assets in Wood's general fund balance sheet at June 30, 1987 is
    a. $25,000
    b. $15,000
    c. $10,000
    d. $0

72. Kew City issued the following long-term obligations:

Revenue bonds to be paid from admission fees collected from users of the city swimming pool	$1,000,000
General obligation bonds issued for the city water and sewer fund which will service the debt	1,800,000

Although the above-mentioned bonds are expected to be paid from enterprise funds, the full faith and credit of the city has been pledged as further assurance that the obligations will be paid. What amount of these bonds should be accounted for in the general long-term debt account group?

    a. $0
    b. $1,000,000
    c. $1,800,000
    d. $2,800,000

73. Dodd Village received a gift of a new fire engine from a local resident. The fair market value of this fire engine was $200,000. The entry to be made in the general fixed assets account group for this gift is

		Debit	Credit
a.	Machinery and equipment	$200,000	
	Investment in general fixed assets from private gifts		$200,000
b.	Investment in general fixed assets	$200,000	
	Gift revenue		$200,000
c.	General fund assets	$200,000	
	Private gifts		$200,000
d.	Memorandum entry only	--	--

74. Fred Bosin donated a building to Palma City in 1983. Bosin's original cost of the property was $100,000. Accumulated depreciation at the date of the gift amounted to $60,000. Fair market value at the date of the gift was $300,000. In the general fixed assets account group, at what amount should Palma record this donated fixed asset?
    a. $300,000
    b. $100,000
    c. $ 40,000
    d. $0

75. Fixed assets should be accounted for in the general fixed assets account group for the

	Enterprise fund	Special revenue fund
a.	Yes	No
b.	Yes	Yes
c.	No	Yes
d.	No	No

76. Which of the following accounts would be included in the fund equity section of the combined balance sheet of a governmental unit for the general fixed asset account group?

	Investment in general fixed assets	Fund balance reserved for encumbrances
a.	Yes	Yes
b.	Yes	No
c.	No	No
d.	No	Yes

77. Fixed assets used by a governmental unit should be accounted for in the

	Capital projects fund	General fund
a.	Yes	Yes
b.	Yes	No
c.	No	No
d.	No	Yes

78. Which of the following funds of a governmental unit could use the general fixed assets account group to account for fixed assets?
   a. Internal service.
   b. Enterprise.
   c. Trust.
   d. Capital projects fund.

May 1990 Questions

Items 79 through 84 are based on the following:

Rock County has acquired equipment through a noncancelable lease-purchase agreement dated December 31, 1989. This agreement requires no down payment and the following minimum lease payments:

December 31	Principal	Interest	Total
1990	$50,000	$15,000	$65,000
1991	50,000	10,000	60,000
1992	50,000	5,000	55,000

79. What account should be debited for $150,000 in the general fund at inception of the lease if the equipment is a general fixed asset and Rock does **not** use a capital projects fund?
   a. Other financing uses control.
   b. Equipment.
   c. Expenditures control.
   d. Memorandum entry only.

80. What account should be credited for $150,000 in the general fixed assets account group at inception of the lease if the equipment is a general fixed asset?
   a. Fund balance from capital lease transactions.
   b. Other financing sources control--capital leases.
   c. Expenditures control--capital leases.
   d. Investment in general fixed assets--capital leases.

81. What journal entry is required for $150,000 in the general long-term debt account group at inception of the lease if the lease payments are to be financed with general government resources?

	Debit	Credit
a.	Expenditures control.	Other financing sources control.
b.	Other financing uses control.	Expenditures control.
c.	Amount to be provided for lease payments.	Capital lease payable.
d.	Capital lease payable.	Amount to be provided for lease payments.

82. If the lease payments are required to be made from a debt service fund, what account or accounts should be debited in the debt service fund for the December 31, 1990 lease payment of $65,000?

a.	Expenditures control	$65,000
b.	Other financing sources control	$50,000
	Expenditures control	15,000
c.	Amount to be provided for lease payments	$50,000
	Expenditures control	15,000
d.	Expenditures control	$50,000
	Amount to be provided for lease payments	15,000

83. If the equipment is used in enterprise fund operations and the lease payments are to be financed with enterprise fund revenues, what account should be debited for $150,000 in the enterprise fund at the inception of the lease?
   a. Expenses control.
   b. Expenditures control.
   c. Other financing sources control.
   d. Equipment.

84. If the equipment is used in internal service fund operations and the lease payments are financed with internal service fund revenues, what account or accounts should be debited in the internal service fund for the December 31, 1990 lease payment of $65,000?

a.	Expenditures control	$65,000
b.	Expenses control	$65,000
c.	Capital lease payable	$50,000
	Expenses control	15,000
d.	Expenditures control	$50,000
	Expenses control	15,000

Items 85 through 87 are based on the following:

Elm City contributes to and administers a single-employer defined benefit pension plan on behalf of its covered employees. The plan is accounted for in a pension trust fund. Actuarially determined employer contribution requirements and contributions actually made for the past three years, along with the percentage of annual covered payroll, were as follows:

	Contribution made		Actuarial requirement	
	Amount	Percent	Amount	Percent
1989	$11,000	26	$11,000	26
1988	5,000	12	10,000	24
1987	None	None	8,000	20

85. What account should be credited in the pension trust fund to record the 1989 employer contribution of $11,000?
   a. Revenues control.
   b. Other financing sources control.
   c. Due from special revenue fund.
   d. Pension benefit obligation.

86. To record the 1989 pension contribution of $11,000, what debit is required in the governmental-type fund used in connection with employer pension contributions?
   a. Other financing uses control.
   b. Expenditures control.
   c. Expenses control.
   d. Due to pension trust fund.

87. In the notes to Elm's 1989 financial statements, employer contributions expressed as percentages of annual covered payroll should be shown to the extent available for a minimum of
   a. 1 year.
   b. 2 years.
   c. 3 years.
   d. 12 years.

88. Grove Township issued $50,000 of bond anticipation notes at face amount in 1989 and placed the proceeds into its capital projects fund. All legal steps were taken to refinance the notes, but Grove was unable to consummate refinancing. In the capital projects fund, what account should be credited to record the $50,000 proceeds?
   a. Other financing sources control.
   b. Revenues control.
   c. Deferred revenues.
   d. Bond anticipation notes payable.

Items 89 through 93 are based on the following:

Todd City formally integrates budgetary accounts into its general fund. Todd uses an internal service fund to account for the operations of its data processing center, which provides services to Todd's other governmental units.

During the year ended December 31, 1989, Todd received a state grant to buy a bus, and an additional grant for bus operation in 1989. In 1989, only 90% of the capital grant was used for the bus purchase, but 100% of the operating grant was disbursed.

Todd has incurred the following long-term obligations:

   • General obligation bonds issued for the water and sewer fund which will service the debt.

   • Revenue bonds to be repaid from admission fees collected from users of the municipal recreation center.

These bonds are expected to be paid from enterprise funds, and secured by Todd's full faith, credit, and taxing power as further assurance that the obligations will be paid.

Todd's 1989 expenditures from the general fund include payments for structural alterations to a firehouse and furniture for the mayor's office.

89. To record the billing for data processing services provided to Todd's other governmental units, the internal service fund should credit
   a. Operating revenues.
   b. Data processing departmental expenses.
   c. Intergovernmental transfers.
   d. Interfund exchanges.

90. In reporting the state grants for the bus purchase and operation, what should Todd include as grant revenues for the year ended December 31, 1989?

	90% of the capital grant	100% of the capital grant	Operating grant
a.	Yes	No	No
b.	No	Yes	No
c.	No	Yes	Yes
d.	Yes	No	Yes

91. Which of Todd's long-term obligations should be accounted for in the general long-term debt account group?

	General obligation bonds	Revenue bonds
a.	Yes	Yes
b.	Yes	No
c.	No	Yes
d.	No	No

92. When Todd records its annual budget, which of the following control accounts indicates the amount of the authorized spending limitation for the year ending December 31, 1989?
   a. Reserved for appropriations.
   b. Appropriations.
   c. Reserved for encumbrances.
   d. Encumbrances.

93. In Todd's general fund balance sheet
presentation at December 31, 1989, which of
the following expenditures should be
classified as fixed assets?

	Structual alterations to firehouse	Mayor's office furniture
a.	No	No
b.	No	Yes
c.	Yes	No
d.	Yes	Yes

94. Revenues that are legally restricted to
expenditures for specified purposes should be
accounted for in special revenue funds,
including
    a.   Accumulation of resources for
          payment of general long-term debt
          principal and interest.
    b.   Pension trust fund revenues.
    c.   Gasoline taxes to finance road
          repairs.
    d.   Proprietary fund revenues.

95. The basis of accounting for a capital
projects fund is the
    a.   Cash basis.
    b.   Accrual basis.
    c.   Modified cash basis.
    d.   Modified accrual basis.

96. For state and local governmental units,
generally accepted accounting principles
require that encumbrances outstanding at year
end be reported as
    a.   Expenditures.
    b.   Reservations of fund balance.
    c.   Deferred liabilities.
    d.   Current liabilities.

97. Fixed assets donated to a governmental
unit should be recorded
    a.   As a memorandum entry only.
    b.   At the donor's carrying amount.
    c.   At estimated fair value when
          received.
    d.   At the lower of donor's carrying
          amount or estimated fair value when
          received.

Problems

Problem 1   (1184,T5)

(15 to 25 minutes)

The accounting system of the municipality of Kemp is organized and operated on a fund basis. Among the types of funds used are a general fund, a special revenue fund, and an enterprise fund.

Required:

a. Explain the basic differences in revenue recognition between the accrual basis of accounting and the modified accrual basis of accounting as it relates to governmental accounting.

b. What basis of accounting should be used for each of the following funds:
  • General fund.
  • Special revenue fund.
  • Enterprise fund.
Why?

c. How should fixed assets and long-term liabilities related to the general fund and to the enterpise fund be accounted for?

d. How should the balance sheets of the general fund, the special revenue fund, and the enterprise fund be handled when preparing the comprehensive annual financial report (CAFR)? Why?

Problem 2   (1184,Q4)

(45 to 55 minutes)

The general fund trial balance of the city of Solna at December 31, 1985 was as follows:

	Dr.	Cr.
Cash	$ 62,000	
Taxes receivable--delinquent	46,000	
Estimated uncollectible taxes--delinquent		$ 8,000
Stores inventory--program operations	18,000	
Vouchers payable		28.000
Fund balance reserved for stores inventory		18,000
Fund balance reserved for encumbrances		12,000
Unreserved undesignated fund balance		60,000
	$126,000	$126,000

Collectible delinquent taxes are expected to be collected within 60 days after the end of

the year. Solna uses the "purchases" method to account for stores inventory. The following data pertain to 1986 general fund operations:

1. Budget adopted:

Revenues and other financing sources

Taxes	$220,000
Fines, forfeits, and penalties	80,000
Miscellaneous revenues	100,000
Share of bond issue proceeds	200,000
	$600,000

Expenditures and other financing uses

Program operations	$300,000
General administration	120,000
Stores--program operations	60,000
Capital outlay	80,000
Periodic transfer to capital projects fund	20,000
	$580,000

2. Taxes were assessed at an amount that would result in revenues of $220,800, after deduction of 4% of the tax levy as uncollectible.

3. Orders placed but not received:

Program operations	$176,000
General administration	80,000
Capital outlay	60,000
	$316,000

4. The city council designated $20,000 of the unreserved undesignated fund balance for possible future appropriation for capital outlay.

5. Cash collections and transfer:

Delinquent taxes	$ 38,000
Current taxes	226,000
Refund of overpayment of invoice for purchase of equipment	4,000
Fines, forfeits, and penalties	88,000
Miscellaneous revenues	90,000
Share of bond issue proceeds	200,000
Transfer of remaining fund balance of a discontinued fund	18,000
	$664,000

6. Canceled encumbrances:

	Estimated	Actual
Program operations	$156,000	$166,000
General admin- isration	84,000	80,000
Capital outlay	62,000	62,000
	$302,000	$308,000

7. Additional vouchers:

Program operations	$188,000
General administration	38,000
Capital outlay	18,000
Transfer to capital projects fund	20,000
	$264,000

8. Albert, a taxpayer, overpaid his 1986 taxes by $2,000. He applied for a $2,000 credit against his 1987 taxes. The city council granted his request.

9. Vouchers paid amounted to $580,000.

10. Stores inventory on December 31, 1986 amounted to $12,000.

Required:

a. Prepare journal entries to record the effects of the foregoing data. Omit explanations. Assume that encumbrances lapse at the end of the year (December 31).
b. Prepare closing entries.

Problem 3

See Problem 5 (586,Q5a) in Module 39, Nonprofit Accounting. This problem requires entries for a governmental unit and a voluntary health and welfare organization from the same set of transactions.

Multiple Choice Answers

1. b	21. d	41. c	60. a	79. c
2. a	22. c	42. a	61. b	80. d
3. d	23. d	43. c	62. c	81. c
4. c	24. b	44. a	63. b	82. a
5. b	25. a	45. b	64. c	83. d
6. b	26. c	46. d	65. b	84. c
7. d	27. d	47. c	66. d	85. a
8. c	28. c	48. a	67. c	86. b
9. a	29. d	49. d	68. b	87. c
10. a	30. c	50. a	69. c	88. d
11. a	31. a	51. a	70. c	89. a
12. a	32. a	52. b	71. d	90. d
13. a	33. a	53. d	72. a	91. d
14. b	34. d	54. a	73. a	92. b
15. b	35. b	55. b	74. a	93. a
16. a	36. d	56. b	75. c	94. c
17. b	37. a	57. d	76. b	95. d
18. a	38. c	58. c	77. c	96. b
19. c	39. a	59. d	78. d	97. c
20. a	40. c			

Multiple Choice Answer Explanations

B. Budgets and Their Impact Upon the Accounting System

1.   (588,Q3,44) (b) The budget determines the nature and scope of most governmental fund fiscal operations by setting the amounts of sources of estimated revenues and transfers in, on the one hand, and the amounts and purposes of authorized expenditures and transfers out, on the other (GASB Codification, para 1700.126). The following entry is made when the budget is adopted:

Estimated revenues control	10,000,000	
Appropriations control		9,000,000
Estimated operating transfers out		300,000
Budgetary fund balance		700,000

Therefore, answer (b) is correct.

2.   (588,Q3,45) (a) The following entry is made when the budget is adopted:

Estimated revenues control	10,000,000	
Appropriations control		9,000,000
Estimated operating transfers out		300,000
Budgetary fund balance		700,000

Therefore, answer (a) is correct. Answer (b) is incorrect because receivables are not recorded when the budget is adopted. Answer (c) is incorrect because budgeted revenues are recorded by a debit. Answer (d) is incorrect because other financing sources is not a budgetary account. However, it is important to note that estimated other financing sources could be a budgetary account.

3.   (588,Q3,46) (d) The following entry is made when the budget is adopted:

Estimated revenues control	10,000,000	
Appropriations control		9,000,000
Estimated operating transfers out		300,000
Budgetary fund balance		700,000

It is important to note that the $300,000 estimated transfer to the debt service fund is recorded as an operating transfer and not as an appropriation. Therefore, the credit to Appropriations Control is $9,000,000. Therefore, answer (b) is incorrect. Estimated expenditures is not the appropriate title for a budgetary account. Therefore, answers (a) and (c) are incorrect.

4.   (588,Q3,47) (c) An encumbrance is a commitment related to an unperformed (executory) contract for goods or services (GASB Codification, para 1700.129). Upon approval of the purchase order, an encumbrance is established. The encumbrance should be recorded as follows:

Encumbrances control	$1,500
Budgetary fund balance reserved for encumbrances	1,500

Therefore, answer (c) is correct. Answers (a) and (b) are incorrect because the corresponding expenditure is not recorded until the invoice is approved. Answer (d) is incorrect because Appropriations Control is only credited when the budget is adopted.

5.   (588,Q3,48) (b) When an invoice is approved for payment before year end, the encumbrance must be eliminated. This is done by merely reversing the original encumbrance entry as follows:

Budgetary fund balance reserved for encumbrances	$1,500
Encumbrances control	1,500

Also, the liability and expenditure must be recorded as follows:

Expenditures Control	$1,500
Vouchers payable	1,500

Therefore, answer (b) is correct.

6.   (582,Q2,25) (b) The requirement is the funds available for additional purchases of supplies. GASB Codification states that appropriations constitute maximum expenditure authorizations during the fiscal year, and cannot legally be exceeded unless subsequently amended by the legislative body. An encumbrance reduces appropriation authority and is formally recorded in the accounting records.

Appropriations		$7,500
Less: Encumbrances	$ 750	
Expenditures	4,500	5,250
Unencumbered balance		$2,250

The unencumbered balance is the amount of resources that can still be obligated or expended without exceeding the legal or authorized limit.

7. (1188,T1,52) (d) The budgetary fund balance account is debited upon budget adoption when the appropriations exceed the estimated revenues. The following entry is made when the budget is adopted:

```
    Estimated Revenues Control    xx
    Budgetary Fund Balance        xx
        Appropriations Control          xx
```

At the end of the year, the budgetary accounts must be closed out. The budgetary closing entry is simply a reverse of the adoption entry:

```
    Appropriations Control        xx
        Estimated Revenues Control      xx
        Budgetary Fund Balance          xx
```

Therefore, answer (d) is correct. Answers (a) and (b) are incorrect because the budgetary fund balance is debited at the beginning of the year when appropriations exceed the estimated revenues. Answer (c) is incorrect because an entry must be made to close the budgetary fund balance account at the end of the year. Note that any differences between the budgeted revenues and appropriations and the actual revenues and expenditures and encumbrances do not affect the **budgetary** fund balance account. They would, however, affect the unreserved fund balance account when the operations accounts are closed out.

8. (1188,T1,53) (c) Entries are made to the appropriations control account of a governmental unit only upon adoption (i.e., initial recording) of the budget and at the end of the year when the budget is closed out. When the budgetary accounts are closed, appropriations control is debited as in the following entry:

```
    Appropriations Control        xx
    Budgetary Fund Balance        xx
        Estimated Revenues Control      xx
```

Assuming estimated revenues exceed appropriations, the entry to record expenditures is as follows:

```
    Expenditures Control          xx
        Vouchers payable (or cash)      xx
```

No entry is made to the appropriations control account. Therefore, answer (c) is correct and answers (a), (b), and (d) are incorrect.

9. (588,T1,52) (a) "Budgetary Fund Balance Reserved for Encumbrances" is a fund equity account. When goods or services are ordered, appropriations are encumbered (i.e., re-

stricted from expenditure) and Budgetary Fund Balance Reserved for Encumbrances is **increased** by the following entry:

```
Encumbrances Control              xxx
    Budgetary fund balance re-
        served for encumbrances             xxx
```

Note that the entry is made for the amount of the estimated cost of the goods or services ordered. When the goods are received, the encumbrance entry is reversed (i.e., Budgetary Fund Balance Reserved for Encumbrances is **decreased**) in order to correctly state unencumbered appropriations, and the corresponding expenditure is recorded in the amount of the actual resource outflow. Therefore, answer (a) is correct.

10. (1189,T1,52) (a) The estimated revenues control account of a governmental unit is established (debited) as the following entry is made to record the budget in the accounts at the beginning of the year:

```
    Estimated revenues control    XXX
        Appropriations control          XXX
        Budgetary fund balance          XXX
```

The estimated revenues control account is not debited or credited thereafter until the budget is closed out at the end of the year. The closing entry is a reversal of the adoption entry and eliminates the estimated revenues control accounts.

```
    Appropriations control        XXX
    Budgetary fund balance        XXX
        Estimated revenues control      XXX
```

Answer (b) is incorrect because the estimated revenues control account is established when the budget is recorded. Answers (c) and (d) are incorrect because those entries do not affect the estimated revenues control account.

11. (589,T1,52) (a) When goods or services are ordered, appropriations are encumbered (i.e., restricted) and encumbrances are increased with the following entry:

```
    Encumbrances control          XX
        Budgetary fund balance re-
            served for encumbrances         XX
```

When the goods or services ordered are received, the encumbrance entry is reversed (i.e., encumbrances decrease) and the expenditure is recorded for the actual cost as follows:

```
    Budgetary fund balance re-
        served for encumbrances    XX
            Encumbrances Control            XX

    Expenditures Control          XX
        Vouchers payable                    XX
```

At the end of the year, any balance in the encumbrances control account is closed out (i.e., encumbrances decrease) as follows:

Appropriations	XX	
Encumbrances Control		XX

Therefore, encumbrances control is not increased when either a voucher payable is recorded or when the budgetary accounts are closed, and answer (a) is correct.

12. (1189,T1,53) (a) "Budgetary Fund balance reserved for encumbrances" is a fund equity account. When goods or services are ordered (purchase order approved), appropriations are encumbered, or restricted from use, in the amount of the estimated purchase cost. The following entry is made which increases fund balance reserved for encumbrances:

Encumbrances	XXX
Budgetary fund balance reserved for encumbrances	XXX

Note that when the goods are received, budgetary fund balance reserved for encumbrances is decreased because the above entry must be reversed in order to correctly state unencumbered appropriations. The actual expenditure is then recorded in the amount of the actual payment. Therefore, answer (a) is correct.

13. (587,T1,53) (a) When the budgetary accounts at the end of the fiscal year are closed, the nominal accounts (expenditures, revenues, and encumbrances) must also be closed out. The following entry is made when the operations accounts are closed:

Revenues control	xx
Expenditures control	xx
Encumbrances	xx
Fund balance—unreserved	xx

Therefore, answer (a) is correct. When the budget is adopted, only the budgetary accounts are used, and therefore, nominal accounts, such as expenditures, are not debited or credited. Therefore, answer (b) is incorrect. Answers (c) and (d) are incorrect because when supplies are purchased or received, the expenditures control is debited, not credited, and vouchers payable is credited. The only difference between (c) and (d) is that (c) was an unencumbered purchase, and therefore, encumbrances need not be reversed. However, in (d), encumbrances must be reversed.

14. (586,T1,52) (b) The requirement is what account is credited when supplies previously ordered are received. Per GASB Codification, when supplies are ordered, the following entry is made for the estimated price of the supplies.

Encumbrances control	xxx
Budgetary fund balance reserved for encumbrances	xxx

When the goods previously ordered are received, the above entry is reversed for the estimated amount, and the expenditure is recorded for the actual price of the supplies.

Budgetary fund balance reserved for encumbrances	xxx
Encumbrances control	xxx

Expenditures control	xxx
Vouchers payable	xxx

Answer (a) is incorrect because when the supplies previously ordered are received, the fund balance reserved for encumbrances is debited, not credited. Answer (c) is incorrect because the Expenditures control account is debited when supplies previously ordered are received. Answer (d) is incorrect because the Appropriations control account represents the expenditure authority of a governmental unit which is created upon legally adopting the budget.

15. (586,T1,53) (b) The requirement is to determine when the revenues control account of a governmental unit is debited. The revenues control account is debited when the following entry is made to close out the budget at the end of the year.

Revenues control	xx
Expenditures control	xx
Encumbrances control	xx
Fund balance—unreserved	xx

When the budget is recorded, the following entry is made.

Estimated revenues control	xx	
Budgetary fund balance	xx	xx
Appropriations control		xx

Revenues control is not debited when the budget is recorded, but estimated revenues control is debited making answer (a) incorrect. When a property tax levy is recorded, the following entry is made.

Property taxes receivable	xx
Allowance for uncollectible taxes	xx
Revenues control	xx

Therefore, answer (c) is incorrect because revenues control is credited when property taxes are recorded. When property taxes are collected, property taxes receivable is credited and cash is debited. Therefore, answer (d) is incorrect.

16. (582,T1,58) (a) Budgeting is important in the financial planning, control, and evaluation processes of governmental units. Integration of budgetary accounts (including encumbrances) in the formal accounting system is essential in general, special revenue, and

other annually budgeted governmental funds which have numerous types of revenues, expenditures, and transfers. For example, full or partial budgetary account integration would be essential where numerous construction projects are being financed through a capital projects fund. Budgetary accounts (including encumbrances) are not necessary in controlling most debt service funds [answer (b)], where the amounts required to be received and expended are set forth in bond indentures or sinking fund provisions and only a few transactions occur each year. Encumbrance accounting is inappropriate for nonfund account groups [answer (c)] and proprietary funds [answer (d)].

C. Reporting Entity

17. (1188,Q3,45) (b) Per GASB Codification, para 1300.104, a debt service fund is used to account for the accumulation of resources for, and the payment of, general long term debt principal and interest. Long term debt related to proprietary type funds is recorded within those funds. Therefore, the $400,000 cash accumulations for payment of general long-term obligations should be accounted for in Albury's debt service fund [answer (b)]. The $1,000,000 cash accumulations for payment of bonds related to the water treatment plant construction would be accounted for in the water treatment plant enterprise fund. Therefore, answers (a), (c), and (d) are incorrect.

D. Financial Statements For State and Local Governments

18. (1188,Q3,41) (a) Per GASB Codification, transfers from the general fund to a capital projects fund are operating transfers and should be reported in the "other financing uses" section of the general fund's statement of revenues, expenditures, and changes in fund balance. Therefore, answer (a) is correct. Answers (b) and (d) are incorrect because the operating transfer to the capital projects fund is a use of funds (i.e., not a source). Answer (c) is incorrect because operating transfers are not expenditures.

19. (1188,Q3,42) (c) Per GASB Codification, proceeds from a general obligation bond and operating transfers from the general fund are classified as "other financing sources" in the financial statements of a capital projects fund. Expenditures of governmental type funds are generally recognized in the period in which the fund liability is incurred. Therefore, Vane's capital projects fund should report other financing sources of $3,000,000 and expenditures of $3,000,000 [answer (b)].

Answer (a) is incorrect because governmental type funds do not record general long term debt. Answers (b) and (d) are incorrect because operating transfers and proceeds from general obligation bonds are not classified as revenues.

20. (1188,T1,58) (a) Per GASB Codification, para 1900.113, the comprehensive annual financial report (CAFR) of a governmental unit should contain a combined statement of revenue, expenditures, and changes in fund balances for all governmental fund types. Per para 1300.102, governmental fund type groups include general, special revenue, capital projects, and debt service funds. Therefore, answer (a) is correct. Account groups and proprietary funds are not included in the comprehensive annual financial report (CAFR). Furthermore, proprietary funds are income determination funds (para 1300.102), and the primary proprietary fund operating statement is the statement of revenues, expenses, and changes in retained earnings. Therefore, answers (b), (c), and (d) are incorrect.

21. (589,T1,58) (d) Per GASB Codification, the comprehensive annual financial report (CAFR) should contain both (a) the general purpose financial statements (GPFS) by fund type and account group and (b) combining statements by fund type and individual fund statements. The CAFR should also contain introductory information, schedules necessary to demonstrate compliance with finance-related legal and contractual provisions, and statistical data. The GPFS include several combined statements, one of which is the combined statement of revenues, expenses, and changes in retained earnings for all proprietary fund types. Proprietary funds include both Enterprise Funds and Internal Service Funds. Governmental funds and account groups are not proprietary funds. Therefore, answer (d) is correct. Note that governmental funds use a modified accrual basis of accounting and do not report retained earnings or expenses (i.e., they report fund balances and expenditures).

22. (587,T1,58) (c) Per GASB Codification, para 2200.108, the accounts groups, general fixed assets and general long-term debt, are included in the comprehensive financial report of a governmental unit in the combined balance sheet but not the combined statement of revenues, expenditures, and changes in fund balances [answer (c)]. Answer (a) is incorrect because per para 2200.110, only governmental fund types are included in the combined statement of revenues, expenditures,

and changes in fund balances because account
groups are not fiscal entities and therefore
do not have revenues, expenditures, or fund
balances. Answers (b) and (d) are incorrect
because account groups are included in the
combined balance sheet along with all
governmental and proprietary fund types.

23. (1186,T1,58) (d) Per GASB Codification,
the comprehensive annual financial report
(CAFR) of a governmental unit should contain a
combined statement of changes in financial
position for all proprietary fund types. A
combined statement of changes is not required
for either governmental funds or account
groups. Therefore, answers (a), (b), and (c)
are incorrect.

24. (585,T1,58) (b) The requirement is to
determine whether the comprehensive annual
financial report (CAFR) of a governmental unit
should contain a combined balance sheet for
governmental funds, proprietary funds, and/or
account groups. Answer (b) is correct because
as per GASB Codification, the CAFR for a
governmental unit shall include a combined
balance sheet for all fund types and account
groups. As a result, answers (a), (c), and
(d) are incorrect.

25. (583,T1,58) (a) The requirement is to
determine which accounts are included in the
asset section of the combined balance sheet of
a governmental unit for the general long-term
debt account group. The general long-term
debt account group records the repayment of
long-term debt incurred by the general fund,
special revenue funds, and capital projects
funds. When long-term debt is initially
recorded, the following entry is made:

    Amount to be provided for
    retirement of general
    long-term debt   xxx
      Bonds payable   xxx

As monies are set aside in the debt service
fund for bond repayment, the following entry
is made:

Amount available in debt
  service fund   xxx
    Amount to be provided for retire-
      ment of general long-term debt   xxx

Per GASB, the accounts debited in the entries
above are to be included in the asset section
of a governmental unit's combined balance
sheet. Therefore, answer (a) is correct.

E. Governmental Funds

26. (1188,Q3,44) (c) Per GASB Codification,
para 1300.104a, special revenue funds account

for the proceeds of specific revenue sources
(other than expendable trusts or for major
capital projects) that are legally restricted
to expenditures for specified purposes.
Therefore, only the $900,000 of sales tax
proceeds received to finance the maintenance
of tourist facilities in the shopping district
would be accounted for in Grove's special
revenue funds [answer (c)]. The $300,000
donation to an expendable trust would be
accounted for by a separate trust (i.e.,
fiduciary) fund.

27. (1188,Q3,46) (d) The special assessments
fund has been eliminated per GASB Statement 6. Furthermore, per Statement 6, the
accounting for special assessments projects
depends on the liability of the governmental
unit for the special assessment debt. If the
governmental unit is not obligated in any
manner for the debt, as is the case with
levies, the special assessment activities will
be accounted for in an agency fund, not a
special revenue fund. Therefore, answer (d)
is correct.

28. (588,Q3,49) (c) Grants, entitlements,
or shared revenues recorded in governmental
funds should be recognized in the accounting
period when they become susceptible to
accrual, that is, both measurable and available (modified accrual basis criteria) (GASB
Codification, para G60.109). In the case of a
grant, failure to comply with the legal requirements for spending it will cause the
recipient to forfeit the grant. Therefore,
grants become susceptible to accrual only
after they are expended in accordance with the
prescribed regulations. The only amounts
reported as grant revenues for the year are
the $60,000 of capital grant and the $5,000
operating grant for a total of $65,000.
Therefore, answer (c) is correct.

29. (588,Q3,50) (d) The measurement focus
of governmental fund accounting is on expenditures (decreases in net financial resources)
rather than expenses (GASB Codification,
para 1600.117), so salaries and wages expense
is recorded as a debit to Expenditures Control
and a credit to Vouchers Payable. An expense
account is not used, and therefore answer (a)
is incorrect. Appropriations and encumbrances
are budgetary accounts. The appropriations account is used only when recording the adoption
of the budget and the closing of the budget.
Therefore, answer (b) is incorrect. Encumbrances are not required for regular periodic
expenditures such as salaries and wages.
Therefore, answer (c) is incorrect.

30. (1188,T1,51) (c) According to GASB Codification, proprietary fund revenues and expenses should be recognized on the accrual basis, as an objective of such funds is the maintenance of capital. The modified accrual basis of accounting is used for a governmental fund of a governmental unit. According to GAAP, cash basis accounting is not used in governmental accounting. Thus, answers (a), (b), and (d) are incorrect.

31. (1187,Q3,48) (a) Per GASB Codification, para 1300.104, the objective of a capital projects fund is to account for the financial resources to be used for the acquisition or construction of major capital facilities. The inflow of bond proceeds should be accounted for in the year received, regardless of when the bond proceeds are expended. Therefore, the $5,000,000 of bond proceeds should be recorded in the capital projects fund in 1986, the year received. They should be treated as an "Other Financing Source" in the operating statement of the fund (para 1500.108). Note that the servicing of the debt will be accounted for in the debt service fund and the general long-term debt account group.

32. (589,Q2,28) (a) Per GASB Codification, para 1300.104, the objective of a capital projects fund is to account for the financial resources to be used for the acquisition or construction of major capital facilities. Both the $3,000,000 bond proceeds and the $1,000,000 general fund transfer should be treated as "Other Financing Sources" in the operating statement of the fund (para 1500.108), not as revenues of the fund. Therefore, answer (a) is correct. Note that revenues of a capital projects fund generally tend to originate from interest earned on the financial resources being accounted for by the fund which have yet to be expended.

33. (1188,T1,54) (a) Per GASB Codification, the modified accrual basis of accounting, which is used by governmental funds, recognizes revenues when they become measurable and available to finance expenditures of the fiscal period. Answer (a) is correct because per GASB Codification, all governmental fund types (i.e., general, special revenue, capital projects, debt service) and expendable trust funds should use the modified accrual basis of accounting. Answer (b) is incorrect because nonexpendable trust funds are accounted for as proprietary funds (which use the accrual basis). Answers (c) and (d) are incorrect because they are proprietary funds and thus require the accrual basis of accounting. Note that the accrual basis of accounting recog-

nizes revenues when they are measurable and earned.

34. (589,T1,59) (d) Per GASB Codification, all governmental type funds (i.e., general, special revenue, capital projects, and debt service) and expendable trust funds should use the modified accrual basis of accounting. Also, proprietary fund types should recognize revenues and expenses on the accrual basis. Therefore, a local governmental unit could have funds using both the accrual basis and the modified accrual basis of accounting, and answer (d) is correct.

35. (588,T1,53) (b) Revenues and other increases in governmental fund financial resources that usually can and should be recorded on the modified accrual basis include property taxes, regularly billed charges for inspection or other routinely provided services, most grants from other governments, interfund transfers and other transactions, and sales and income taxes where taxpayer liability has been established and collectibility is assured or losses can be reasonably estimated (GASB Codification, para 1600.107). Therefore, answer (b) is correct. Appropriations is a budgetary account, and revenues of a governmental unit are not increased or decreased by the recording or closing of the budget. Therefore, answers (a), (c), and (d) are incorrect.

36. (588,T1,54) (d) Per GASB Codification, governmental fund revenues and expenditures should be recognized on the modified accrual basis. Governmental funds include the General Fund, Special Revenue Funds, Capital Projects Funds, and Debt Service Funds. Therefore, answer (d) is correct. Per GASB Codification, proprietary fund revenues and expenses should be recognized on the accrual basis. Proprietary funds include Enterprise Funds and Internal Service Funds. Therefore, answers (a) and (b) are incorrect. Per GASB Codification, fiduciary fund revenues and expenses or expenditures (as appropriate) should be recognized on the basis consistent with the fund's accounting measurement objective. Nonexpendable trust and pension trust funds should be accounted for on the accrual basis; expendable trust funds should be accounted for on the modified accrual basis. Agency fund assets and liabilities should be accounted for on the modified accrual basis. Therefore, answer (c) is incorrect.

37. (588,T1,55) (a) The Special Revenue Fund is a governmental fund. Per GASB Codification, governmental fund's revenues and expenditures should be recognized on the modified accrual basis. Governmental funds include the General Fund, Special Revenue Funds, Capital Projects Funds, and Debt Service Funds. In addition to governmental funds, expendible trust funds and agency fund assets and liabilities should be accounted for on the modified accrual basis. Therefore, answer (a) is correct. Proprietary funds and fiduciary funds (except for expendible trust and agency funds) should be accounted for on the accrual basis. Therefore, answers (b), (c), and (d) are incorrect.

38. (589,T1,51) (c) Per GASB Codification, para 1600.106, revenues recognized when they become measurable and available to finance expenditures of the fiscal period are accounted for under the modified accrual basis of accounting. This basis is used in accounting for governmental funds and expendable trust funds. Revenues which are recognized in the accounting period in which they are earned and become measurable are accounted for under the accrual basis of accounting. This basis is used in accounting for commercial enterprises, proprietary funds, and nonexpendable trust funds. Therefore, answer (c) is correct and answers (a), (b), and (d) are incorrect.

39. (1187,T1,55) (a) Per GASB Codification, para 1300.104, the debt service fund of a governmental unit is used to account for the accumulation of resources for, and the payment of, general long-term debt principal and interest. Therefore, answer (a) is correct and answers (b), (c), and (d) are incorrect.

40. (589,T1,54) (c) There are three types of funds used by state and local governments: governmental, proprietary, and fiduciary. Per GASB Codification, a debt service fund is a governmental fund. Other governmental funds include general fund, special revenue fund, and capital projects fund. Therefore, answer (c) is correct. Answers (a) and (b) are incorrect because enterprise funds and internal service funds are proprietary type funds. Answer (d) is incorrect because trust funds are fidiciary type funds.

41. (1183,T1,53) (c) The requirement is the treatment of a fixed asset purchase out of the general fund revenues. The fixed asset purchase results in a reduction in the fund balance or resource outflow. Resource outflows are recorded as a debit to expenditures and a credit to vouchers payable. Answer (a)

is incorrect as no journal entry would result in an overstatement of the fund balance. Answer (b) is incorrect because per GASB Codification, general fixed assets do not represent financial resources available for expenditure and, therefore, are not recorded in the general fund. Answer (d) is incorrect because transfers and the resulting "due froms" are a result of interfund transactions; the general fixed asset group is not a fund.

42. (1179,T1,42) (a) Under the modified accrual basis, property taxes are usually recorded before they are received. The rationale is that collection of property taxes is reasonably assured (as the property can be liened and even sold for taxes). Answers (b), (c), and (d), (income taxes, gross receipts taxes, and gift taxes), are not as reasonably assured as property taxes, and, therefore, are not recorded as income until received.

43. (1179,T1,45) (c) Interest on bonds payable should be recorded in the debt service fund when the interest is legally payable. The debt service fund accounts for the monies used to repay debt. Thus, there is no need to accrue the interest as suggested in answer (a). Answer (b) is incorrect because there is no interest payable upon issuance of the bonds. Answer (d) is incorrect because the payable is extinguished upon payment.

44. (589,T1,53) (a) Per GASB Codification, when a purchase order is approved and supplies are ordered, the following entry is made for the estimated price of the supplies.

Encumbrance control	XXX	
Fund balance reserved for encumbrances		XXX

When the goods previously ordered are received, the above entry is reversed for the estimated amount, and the expenditure is recorded for the actual price of the supplies.

Fund balance reserved for encumbrances	XXX	
Encumbrance control		XXX
Expenditures control	XXX	
Vouchers payable		XXX

Upon adoption and recording of the budget, the following entry is made:

Estimated Revenues	XX	
Appropriations		XX
Unreserved Fund Balance		XX

Therefore, the expenditures control account is not increased when a purchase order is approved or when the budget is recorded, and answer (a) is correct.

45. (1177,T1,23) (b) When the general fund transfers money to establish a new internal service fund, a residual equity transfer has occurred. This requires a debit to fund balance in the general fund. In the internal service fund, Cash is debited and "Contribution from general fund" is credited. Answer (c) is incorrect because "Fund balance reserved for encumbrances" is not debited for cash payments. Answer (d) is incorrect because the accounts "Operating transfers out" and "Operating transfers in" are used for interfund transfers which are not residual equity transfers.

F. Proprietary Funds

46. (1188,Q3,43) (d) A proprietary fund is created to account for goods or services the governmental unit provides to benefit the general public. It uses the accrual basis of accounting and is non-expendable; i.e., capital maintenance is an objective. Fixed assets and depreciation on them are recorded in such funds. Therefore, the $210,000 expenditure for the parking meters would be capitalized and shown net of accumulated depreciation on Burwood's June 30, 1988 balance sheet. Burwood's net income for the year ending June 30, 1988 would be $240,000 calculated as:

Receipts from users	$400,000
Expenses	
Depreciation--Parking meters	(70,000)
Salaries and other	(90,000)
Net income	$240,000

47. (1188,Q3,47) (c) Per GASB Codification, para C50.117, a governmental entity may create a separate internal service (self insurance) or other fund to pay claims and judgments of all governmental funds. Because the full faith and credit remains with the governmental unit, risk is not transferred to the separate insurer fund. Therefore, any payments to the insurer fund are accounted for as an operating transfer and are not an expenditure of the insured fund. The amount of this operating transfer shall be no greater than actuarially determined. Any additional payment to the insurer fund shall be treated as a residual equity transfer. Therefore, $400,000 (actuarially determined amount) of the payments to the insurer fund is classified as an operating transfer and the remaining $100,000 of payments is classified as a residual equity transfer [answer (c)].

48. (588,Q3,42) (a) An enterprise fund is used to account for the activities of a governmental unit to which the government provides goods and services which are: (1) rendered primarily to the general public, (2) financed substantially or entirely through user charges, and (3) intended to be self-supporting. Thus, the self-sustaining activities paid for by users of the services rendered are classified as enterprise funds, and all $2,800,000 ($1,000,000 + $1,800,000) should be accounted for in Pine's enterprise funds. Therefore, answer (a) is correct.

49. (1187,Q3,59) (d) Per GASB Codification, para 1600, proprietary funds are used to account for a governmental unit's activities in a manner similar to commercial entities. Two types of proprietary funds exist-- enterprise funds and internal service funds (para 1300.104). Therefore, the total proprietary funds maintained by Arlon City amount to $2,800,000 ($2,000,000 enterprise funds plus $800,000 internal service funds).

50. (584,Q3,49) (a) The requirement is the amount to be accounted for in an internal service fund. Internal service funds are used to account for activities in which one department in a governmental unit provides services exclusively to other departments within the governmental unit, generally on a not-for-profit (cost-reimbursement) basis. An example is a motor pool. Among the items listed, only the printing/binding service qualifies for inclusion in an internal service fund.

51. (582,Q2,33) (a) GASB Codification states that grants, entitlements, or shared revenues received for proprietary fund operating purposes, or which may be utilized for either operations or capital expenditures at the discretion of the recipient, should be recognized as "nonoperating" revenue in the accounting period in which they are earned and become measurable. Such resources restricted for the acquisition or construction of capital assets should be recorded as contributed equity. In this case $100,000 would be reported as revenue and $500,000 as contributed equity.

52. (1188,T1,55) (b) A fund of a governmental unit which would include retained earnings in its balance sheet would have capital maintenance as an objective and use the accrual basis of accounting. These funds include enterprise, internal service [answer (b)], nonexpendable trust and pension funds. Expendable pension trust [answer (a)], special revenue [answer (c)], and capital projects [answer (d)] are incorrect because they are examples of funds which lack the capital maintenance objective. Instead, their purpose is to account for the inflows and outflows (expenditures) of a governmental unit during a particular period. Only the fund balance ac-

count is carried forward into the next accounting period.

53. (1189,T1,57) (d) Per Governmental Accounting, Auditing and Financial Reporting (GAAFR), Chapter 8, customer deposits should be classified as restricted assets. Other examples of restricted assets in an enterprise fund include accounts associated with bond indentures or assets legally restricted for a specific use. Note that there is no difference in classification for deposits invested in debt versus equity securities. Therefore, answer (d) is correct.

54. (1189,T1,55) (a) Per GASB Codification, para 1600.103, proprietary funds of a governmental unit are to use the accrual basis of accounting, since one of their objectives is capital maintenance. Revenues are recognized when they are both earned and measurable, while expenses are recognized when they are incurred. Nonexpendable trust funds are a type of fiduciary fund, which also use the accrual basis of accounting. Therefore, answer (a) is correct. Governmental funds, two of which are special revenue [answer (c)] and capital projects [answer (d)], use the modified accrual basis of accounting, since the focus in accounting for these funds is determination of financial position and the changes in financial position rather than on determination of income. Revenues are recognized when they become available and measurable, while expenditures are recognized when a fund liability is incurred, if measurable. Expendable trust funds are accounted for in essentially the same manner as governmental funds (para 1300.102). Therefore, expendable trust funds [answer (b)] are also accounted for using the modified accrual basis.

55. (587,T1,55) (b) Depreciation, per GASB Codification, para 1400.105, is an important element of the income determination process. Accordingly, it is recognized in the proprietary funds and in those trust funds where expenses, net income, and/or capital maintenance are measured. Therefore, depreciation is recorded in the internal service fund and answer (b) is correct. On the other hand, depreciation, per para 1400.116, is not recorded in governmental funds, i.e., in general, capital projects, or special assessments. Expenditures, not expenses, are measured in governmental fund accounting. To record depreciation expense in governmental funds would inappropriately mix two fundamentally different measurements, expense and expenditures. Therefore, answers (a), (c), and (d) are incorrect. Note that per GASB 6, the special assessment fund no longer exists.

56. (589,T1,55) (b) According to GASB Codification, Section 1400, para .103, enterprise fund fixed assets are capitalized in the fund accounts because the fixed assets are used in the production of the goods or services provided and sold. Furthermore, para .113 states that depreciation of these fixed assets must be recorded in the enterprise fund to determine total expenses, net income, and changes in fund equity. Thus, answer (b) is correct. Answer (a) is incorrect because depreciation must be taken on fixed assets recorded in an enterprise fund. Answers (c) and (d) are incorrect because the fixed assets benefit the enterprise fund and should be recorded in that fund. On the other hand, general fixed assets are accounted for in the General Fixed Assets Account Group rather than in the governmental funds because they benefit the governmental unit as a whole, not just one specific fund.

57. (1185,T1,56) (d) The requirement is to determine which of the listed funds include contributed capital in its balance sheet. Answer (d) is correct because proprietary funds (internal service and enterprise) and nonexpendable funds have a capital maintenance objective similar to businesses in the private sector. Therefore, such funds include contributed capital as a component of the balance sheet. Answers (a), (b), and (c) are all governmental funds which do not have a capital maintenance objective and therefore do not have contributed capital (equity) in the balance sheet.

58. (584,T1,55) (c) The requirement is to determine in which fund a governmental unit would account for general long-term debt. Per GASB Codification, long-term liabilities directly related to and expected to be paid from proprietary funds and trust funds should be included in the accounts of these funds. All other unmatured long-term indebtedness is considered general long-term debt and should be accounted for in the general long-term debt group of accounts. The internal service fund [answer (c)] is a proprietary fund; therefore, long-term debt to this fund should be accounted for by the fund. Answers (a), (b), and (d) are all governmental funds.

59. (1179,T1,43) (d) The internal service fund is not an expendable fund as are the general fund, capital projects funds, and special revenue funds. The internal service fund is established to provide services to other funds. Accounting for internal service funds follows normal profit accounting except "contribution from general fund" is used in lieu of the capital stock account. Answers (a), (b), and (c) are incorrect because the capital projects, general, and special

revenue funds collect monies to be spent to provide services.

60. (1178,T1,29) (a) "Excess of net billings to departments over costs" would appear in the financial statements of internal service fund. The internal service fund provides services to other governmental funds. An excess of net billings to departments over cost would be the "income" figure of the fund. The objective of an internal service fund is not to create a profit, but rather to provide services at cost to other funds. Small profits or losses can be expected from time to time; these would be closed to a retained earnings account.

61. (578,T1,29) (b) Governmental units that provide services to other governmental units are accounted for in the internal service fund. Internal service funds use accrual accounting and have accounting systems similar to for-profit organizations. The only difference is that the internal service fund attempts to price its service at cost rather than to make a profit. Answer (a) is incorrect because the capital projects fund is used to account for capital expenditures, e.g., issuance of bonds to build buildings or federal grants to construct streets. Answers (c) and (d) are incorrect because agency and trust funds provide a fiduciary capacity, i.e., holding funds for some future use. Agency funds usually involve short-term holdings, and trust funds involve long-term holdings.

62. (1176,T1,38) (c) The enterprise fund is appropriate for recreational and similar facilities for which one half or more of the finances are obtained by user charges. If more than one half of the finances come from taxes, a special revenue fund is used. The general fund accounts for all transactions not accounted for in other funds. The trust fund accounts for assets that are going to be held on behalf of others for long periods of time, e.g., pension funds. Capital project funds account for the proceeds of bond issues, federal grants, etc., which are used to construct capital projects such as schools, libraries, etc.

G. Fiduciary Funds—Trust and Agency

63. (589,Q2,39) (b) Per GASB Codification, para 1300.104c, fiduciary funds are used to account for assets held by a governmental unit in a trustee capacity or as an agent for individuals, private organizations, other governmental units, and/or other funds. They include expendable, nonexpendable, and pension trust funds and agency funds. Therefore, the total fiduciary fund assets of Green Township at June 30, 1989 is 300,000. Therefore, an-

swer (b) is correct. The debt service fund is a governmental type fund.

64. (588,Q3,43) (c) Fiduciary Funds (i.e., Agency Funds and Trust Funds) are used to account for assets held by a governmental unit in a trustee capacity or as an agent for individuals, private organizations, other governmental units, and/or other funds (GASB Codification, para 1300.104). The entry to record the 1% fee and the disbursement to the municipalities would be as follows:

Due to various municipalities   1,000,000
   Due to Grove County   10,000
   General fund cash   990,000

Thus, answer (c) is correct. Note that the General Fund would make the following entry:

Due from agency fund   xxx
   Revenue from tax collec. ser.   xxx

Agency Funds have only assets and liabilities as accounts and do not record revenues, expenditures, or transfers. Therefore, answers (b) and (d) are incorrect. In addition, Agency Funds do not have a fund balance; therefore, answer (a) is incorrect.

65. (1187,T1,59) (b) Per GASB Codification, para 1300.102, three categories of funds are used by a local governmental unit: government funds, proprietary funds, and fiduciary funds. Governmental funds include the general, special revenue, capital projects, and debt service funds. Proprietary funds include enterprise and internal service funds. Fiduciary funds include expendable trust, nonexpendable trust, pension, and agency funds. Therefore, answer (b) is correct and answers (a), (c), and (d) are incorrect.

66. (586,T1,56) (d) The requirement is which type of fund can be either expendable or nonexpendable. Expendable funds are those whose entire resources may be expended, i.e., they are not concerned with preserving capital or measuring net income. GASB Codification states that the governmental funds (general, special revenue, capital projects, and debt service) are often called expendable funds. Expendable assets are assigned to the various governmental funds according to the purpose for which they may or must be used; current liabilities are assigned to the fund from which they are to be paid; and the difference between fund assets and liabilities is referred to as "Fund Balance." Per para 1300.102, proprietary funds (internal service and enterprise) are referred to as nonexpendable. Trust funds, according to GASB Codification, may be either expendable (entire resources may be expended) or nonexpendable principal (corpus), and perhaps the earnings

must be held intact. Enterprise funds, answer (b), are nonexpendable, while debt service and special revenue funds, answers (a) and (c), respectively, are expendable.

67. (580,T1,53) (c) Agency funds are used to account for assets held by a governmental unit as an agent for individuals, private organizations, other governmental units, or other funds. Enterprise funds, answer (a), are used to account for funds which are operated in a fashion similar to private business concerns. Internal service funds, answer (b), are used to account for operations which provide goods or services for other departments. Special revenue funds, answer (d), are used to account for proceeds that are restricted to expenditures for specified purposes, but these funds do not hold resources for another governmental unit.

68. (1177,T1,27) (b) Agency funds perform a holding operation for money, e.g., collection of union dues, employees withholding, etc. Thus, the assets are usually liquid and offset entirely by liabilities rather than a fund balance. The general, special revenue, and capital projects funds all use budgetary accounts, i.e., recording appropriations, estimated revenues, etc., which result in a fund balance account.

H. The GFA and GLTD Account Groups

69. (1188,Q3,49) (c) To determine the amount at which Pine should capitalize a leased computer in its general fixed assets account group, the lease must first be classified pursuant to the requirements of SFAS 13, Accounting for Leases, per para 1400.108 of the GASB Codification. Because the present value at the minimum lease payments ($5,120 at Pine's incremental borrowing rate) is in excess of $4,500 (90% of the computer's fair market value of $5,000), the lease is considered a capital lease to Pine. When one of the four criteria is met, a lessee ordinarily capitalizes a leased asset at the present value of the minimum lease payments using its incremental borrowing rate, unless the lessor's rate is known to the lessee and is lower. However, para 10 of SFAS 13 states that the lessee is limited to capitalizing the fair market value of the leased equipment, or $5,000. Therefore, answer (c) is correct.

70. (589,T1,56) (c) The general long-term debt account group is used to account for unmatured long-term indebtedness that is not a specific liability of any proprietary fund or trust fund. Long-term debt of a proprietary or a trust fund is a specific liability of that

fund and should be accounted for by such funds (GASB Codification, paras 1500.102 and .103), even though the full faith and credit of the governmental unit may be pledged as further assurance that the liability will be paid. The general fund, capital projects fund, and debt service fund are governmental type funds (i.e., not proprietary or trust funds). Therefore, answer (c) is correct.

71. (588,Q3,41) (d) Fixed assets other than those accounted for in proprietary funds or trust funds are general fixed assets. General fixed assets are accounted for in the General Fixed Assets Account Group (GFAAG) rather than in governmental funds (GASB Codification, para 1400.106). General fixed assets do not represent financial resources available for expenditure, but are items for which financial resources have been used and for which accountability should be maintained. Their inclusion in the financial statements of a governmental fund would increase the fund balance, which could mislead users of the fund balance sheet. Therefore, none of the items listed would be classified as fixed assets in the general fund balance sheet, so answer (d) is correct.

72. (589,Q2,40) (a) The general long-term debt account group is used to account for unmatured long-term indebtedness that is not a specific liability of any proprietary fund or trust fund. Long-term debt of a proprietary or trust fund is a specific liability of that fund and should be accounted for by such funds (GASB Codification, paras 1500.102 and .103), even though the full faith and credit of the governmental unit may be pledged as further assurance that the liability will be paid. No entries are necessary to account for the bonds in the general long-term debt account group because the mentioned bonds will be accounted for in the corresponding enterprise funds. Therefore, answer (a) is correct.

73. (1187,Q3,56) (a) Per the GASB Codification, para 1400.113, a property acquired by a governmental unit through donation should be recorded at its fair market value at the time of acquisition in the general fixed assets account group. The related journal entry to record the acquisition of the asset should indicate the asset's source:

Machinery and equipment	200,000	
Investment in fixed assets from private gifts		200,000

Note that if either a proprietary or trust fund had received the donated asset, it would be recorded directly in that fund's accounts.

74. (584,Q3,47) (a) The requirement is the amount at which Palma City should record a donated building. Gifts and donations received by governmental units are recognized at FMV (GASB Codification). Answers (b), (c), and (d) all use some other basis for recognition and are, therefore, incorrect.

75. (1189,T1,56) (c) The general fixed assets account group is used to establish accounting control and responsibility for the government's general fixed assets. Per GASB Codification, the fixed assets of a special revenue fund (governmental fund) should be included as part of this general fixed asset account group. However, the fixed assets of an enterprise fund (proprietary fund) should not be accounted for in the general fixed asset account group. The fixed assets for these funds are recorded within the individual funds themselves. Therefore, answer (c) is correct.

76. (587,T1,56) (b) The general fixed asset account group is not a fund and therefore does not reflect available financial resources and related liabilities. Per GASB Codification, para 1300.103, it is only an accounting entity, not a fiscal entity, and therefore it does not have a fund balance. Since the GFAAG does not have a fund balance, a fund balance reserved for encumbrances would not be an account of the GFAAG and would not be shown anywhere in the combined balance sheet under GFAAG. The offset to the fixed asset accounts is a set of equity accounts, investment in general fixed assets, that indicate the sources from which the fixed assets were acquired. Per Section 2200, Example 1, investment in general fixed assets is included in the fund equity section of the combined balance sheet. Answer (b) is correct and answers (a), (c), and (d) are incorrect.

77. (1189,T1,54) (c) The requirement is to determine whether fixed assets should be accounted for in the capital projects fund and/or the general fund. GASB Codification states that general fixed assets are accounted for in the general fixed asset account group rather than in the governmental funds. The fixed assets represent a use of expendable fund resources for which accountability should be maintained. However, their inclusion in the financial statements of a governmental fund would increase the fund balance. This could mislead users of the combined balance sheet to believe that the amount represents financial resources available for expenditure. Therefore, fixed assets should not be accounted for in either the capital projects fund or the general fund. Therefore, answer (c) is correct.

78. (1182,T1,58) (d) Per GASB Codification, the general fixed assets account group should be used to account for fixed assets other than those related to specific proprietary funds or trust funds. The capital projects fund, a governmental fund, should use the general fixed assets account group to account for its fixed assets.

May 1990 Answers

79. (590,Q1,1) (c) As described in the AICPA Audits of State & Local Governmental Units, the aggregate lease liability is recorded as an expenditure and an "Other Financing Source" in the general fund. Therefore, Expenditures Control is debited. Answer (b) is incorrect because the equipment is recorded in the General Fixed Asset Account Group, not the General Fund. Answer (d) is incorrect because an entry needs to be recorded and posted on the books when equipment is acquired through noncancelable lease-purchase agreement. A memorandum entry is not sufficient. Answer (a) is incorrect because "Other Financing Uses" account is only used for operating transfers out of a fund.

80. (590,Q1,2) (d) According to GASB Codification, the equipment acquired through the lease agreement should be capitalized in the General Fixed Asset Account Group by debiting Equipment and crediting Investment in General Fixed Assets--Capital Leases. Answer (b) is incorrect because Other Financing Sources Control would be the credit in the General fund when the capital lease is entered into. Answer (a) is incorrect because the General Fixed Asset Account Group does not have a Fund Balance. The GFAAG is an account group and not a fund. Answer (c) is incorrect because expenditures are not recorded in the GFAAG, but in the General Fund.

81. (590,Q1,3) (c) GASB Codification explains that the amount due for the principal portion of a capital lease should be recorded as a liability. Therefore, Capital Lease Payable needs to be credited for $150,000. Also, amount To Be Provided For Lease Payments needs to be debited for $150,000. Answer (d) is incorrect because this is the entry made to reflect payments on the capital lease obligation. Answers (a) and (b) are incorrect because the GLTDAG is not a fund and does not record expenditures.

82. (590,Q1,4) (a) According to AICPA Audits of State and Local Governmental Units, on the due date, the current installment of principal should be removed from the GLTDAG and recorded as an expenditure and a liability of the debt service fund, along with the in-

terest that is due. Therefore, Expenditures--
Control should be debited for $65,000.

83.   (590,Q1,5) (d) The enterprise fund is
a proprietary fund and according to GASB
Codification, all assets and liabilities of
proprietary funds are accounted for and reported in their respective funds. Therefore,
transactions for enterprise fund capital
leases are accounted for and reported entirely
within the enterprise fund. Equipment would
be debited for $150,000 in the enterprise fund
and not in the general fixed asset account
group.

84.   (590,Q1,6) (c) The GASB **Codification**
indicates that all assets and liabilities of
proprietary funds are accounted for and reported in their respective funds. The entry
to establish the capital lease in the internal
service fund would include a debit to Equipment for $150,000 and a credit to Capital
Lease Payable for $150,000. Using general
business accounting, the entry to make the
December 31, 1990 payment of $65,000 would
debit Capital Lease Payable for the principal
of $50,000 and Expenses Control for the inter-
est of $15,000, and credit Cash for $65,000.
Answers (a) and (d) are incorrect because the
internal service fund is nonexpendable and
expenses (**not** expenditures) are recognized on
the full accrual basis. Answer (b) is incorrect because Expenses should only be debited
for the interest of $15,000, not for the prin-
cipal of $50,000.

85.   (590,Q1,7) (a) The entry to record the
1989 employer contribution in the Pension
Trust Fund consists of a debit to Cash (or a
"Due From" account) and a credit to Revenues--
Employer Contributions, both for $11,000. The
GASB **Codification** classifies this contribution
as a quasi-external transaction that would be
treated as a revenue if it involved organizations external to the governmental unit.
Therefore, the GASB states that it should be
accounted for as a revenue for the pension
trust fund. Answer (b) is incorrect because
other financing sources include operating
transfers to a fund which are recurring,
routine transfers from one fund to another.
The employer contribution is not an operating
transfer. Answer (c) is incorrect because
"Due From" is a debit account and the question
asks for the credit account. Answer (d) is
incorrect because Pension Benefit Obligation
is the actuarial present value of credited
projected benefits. It measures the present
value of pension benefits adjusted for the
effects of projected salary increases and any
step-rate benefits estimated to be payable in

the future as a result of employer service to
date. The employer contribution is not included in this definition.

86.   (590,Q1,8) (b) As described in the
GASB **Codification**, the employer pension
contribution is a quasi-external transaction,
one that would be treated as revenue, expense,
or expenditure if it involved organizations
external to the governmental unit. This
should be accounted for as a revenue expenditure, or expense in the funds involved. In
this case, the entry for the governmental-type
fund would include a debit to Expenditures for
$11,000 and a credit to Cash (or a "Due To"
account) for $11,000. Answer (a) is incorrect
because Other Financing Uses include operating
transfers out of a fund, which are routine
recurring transfers of resources from one fund
to another. Consequently, the employer contribution does not fall under the category of
an Other Financing Use. Answer (c) is incorrect because governmental-type funds are expendable and use expenditures, not expenses.
Answer (d) is incorrect because Due To Pension
Trust Fund could be the credit entry, and not
the debit entry asked for in the question.

87.   (590,Q1,9) (c) According to GASB **Codification**, three year historical trend information is required for employer contributions
expressed as percentages of annual covered
payroll.

88.   (590,Q1,10) (d) According to GASB **Codification**, for governmental funds, if the
necessary legal steps and the ability to con-
summate refinancing criteria have **not** been
met, then the bond anticipation notes should
be reported as a fund liability in the fund
receiving the proceeds. Thus, Bond Anticipation Notes Payable should be credited for
$50,000 in the capital projects fund. An-
swer (a) is incorrect because Other Financing
Sources encompass routine and recurring operating transfers of resources between funds.
This transaction is not a routine transfer.
Answer (b) is incorrect because this transaction is not a quasi-external transaction
which allows the recognition of revenue. Answer (c) is incorrect because the liability
that must be recorded is not a potential
revenue.

89.   (590,T1,51) (a) The internal service
fund accounts for activities that produce
goods or services to be provided to other
departments or other governmental units on a
cost reimbursement basis. Internal service
fund recognizes revenues and expenses on the
full accrual basis. Therefore, as services

are rendered, the internal service fund would record operating revenues, and answer (a) is correct.

90. (590,T1,52) (d) According to GASB Codification, grants, entitlements, or shared revenues recorded in governmental funds should be recognized as revenues in the accounting period when they become susceptible to accrual, that is, both measurable and available. However, if not all of a grant is spent, the unexpended portion should be treated as deferred revenue. Therefore, since 90% of the capital grant and 100% of the operating grants were incurred in 1989, these are the amounts recognized as revenue in 1989, and answer (d) is correct. Note that the two grants relate to a governmental fund due to the term "Grant Revenues" used in the question. Had these grants been related to a proprietary fund, the term used would have been "Contributed Equity" or a similar account name.

91. (590,T1,53) (d) According to GASB Codification, bonds, notes, and other long-term liabilities directly related to and expected to be paid from proprietary funds should be included in the accounts of such funds. These are specific fund liabilities, even though the full faith and credit of the governmental unit may be pledged as further assurance that the liabilities will be paid. Therefore, neither the general obligation bonds nor the revenue bonds should be accounted for in the general long-term debt account group, but instead in the enterprise fund.

92. (590,T1,54) (b) The GASB Codification states that appropriations constitute maximum expenditure authorizations during the fiscal year, and cannot legally be exceeded unless subsequently amended by the legislative body. Answer (d) is incorrect because the Encumbrances account is for commitments related to unperformed (executory) contracts for goods or services. Answer (c) is incorrect because the Reserved for Encumbrances account indicates that a portion of the fund balance has been segregated for expenditure on vendor performance. Answer (d) is incorrect because there is no Reserved for Appropriations account. It is a nonsensical answer.

93. (590,T1,55) (a) The GASB Codification states that fixed assets other than those accounted for in the proprietary funds or trust funds are general fixed assets. General fixed assets are accounted for in the General Fixed Assets Account Group rather than in the governmental funds. Therefore, neither the

structural alterations nor the office furniture should be included as fixed assets in the general fund, but instead, both should be accounted for in the General Fixed Asset Account Group.

94. (590,T1,56) (c) Special revenue funds are needed when legal or policy considerations require that separate funds be created for current purposes other than those served by proprietary or fiduciary funds. Examples of special revenue funds include Revenue Sharing, State Motor Fuel Tax, CETA, and Library Operating. Answer (a) is incorrect because the debt service fund is used to account for the accumulation of resources for, and the payment of, general long-term debt principal and interest. Answer (b) is incorrect because the pension trust fund accounts for the pension trust fund revenues. Answer (d) is incorrect because proprietary fund revenues are accounted for in the appropriate proprietary fund.

95. (590,T1,57) (d) Per GASB Codification, governmental fund revenues and expenditures should be recognized on the modified accrual basis. Governmental funds include the General Fund, Special Revenue Funds, Capital Projects Funds, and Debt Service Funds. Therefore, since the Capital Projects Fund is a governmental fund, it uses the modified accrual basis. Answer (a) is incorrect because the cash basis of accounting is not appropriate in governmental accounting. Answer (b) is incorrect because the full accrual basis is used by proprietary funds. Answer (c) is incorrect because the modified cash basis of accounting is a method permitted for income taxes, but not used for governmental accounting.

96. (590,T1,58) (b) According to GASB Codification, encumbrances outstanding at year end should be reported as a reservation of fund balance. Encumbrances outstanding at year end represent the estimated amount of the expenditures ultimately to result if unperformed contracts in process at year end are completed. Encumbrances outstanding at year end do not constitute expenditures or liabilities. Therefore, answers (a), (c), and (d) are incorrect.

97. (590,T1,59) (c) Per GASB Codification, donated fixed assets should be recorded in the fund to which they relate or in the general fixed asset account group, as appropriate, at their estimated fair value at the time of acquisition.

Answer Outline

Problem 1   Basis of Accounting; Reporting
             Issues (1184,T5)

a. <u>Accrual basis</u> - revenues recognized when
    earned and measurable
    <u>Modified accrual basis</u> - revenues recog-
    nized in period in which they are both
    measurable and available to finance
    expenditures
       Available means collectible in current
       period or soon enough to pay liabili-
       ties of current period
b. <u>Accrual method</u> - used by capital mainte-
    nance funds (proprietary and fiduciary
    nonexpendable funds) which require
    periodic determination of income
       Enterprise fund is proprietary fund
    <u>Modified accrual method</u> - used by expend-
    able funds (governmental and expendable
    fiduciary funds) which require segrega-
    tion of financial resources
       General fund and special revenue funds
       are governmental funds
c. <u>General fund</u> - fixed assets accounted for
    in General Fixed Assets Account Group and
    long-term liabilities accounted for in
    General Long-Term Debt Account Group
    <u>Enterprise fund</u> - both fixed assets and
    long-term liabilities accounted for
    solely within fund
d. <u>CAFR</u> should contain combined balance sheet
    for all fund types and account groups
       Combined balance sheet designed to make
       governmental reports more useful to
       average voter, investor, and other
       users
    Balances of individual funds must be shown
    in combining balance sheets

Unofficial Answer

Problem 1   Basis of Accounting; Reporting
             Issues (1184,T5)

a. In the accrual basis of accounting, revenues should be recognized in the accounting
period in which they are earned and become
measurable.

   In the modified accrual basis of accounting, revenues should be recognized in the
accounting period in which they become susceptible to accrual--that is, when they become
both measurable and available to finance expenditures of the fiscal period. "Available"
means collectible within the current period or
soon enough thereafter to be used to pay
current period liabilities.

b. For the general fund, the modified accrual
basis of accounting should be used because it
is a governmental fund, which is, in essence,

an accounting segregation of financial
resources.

   For the special revenue fund, the modified
accrual basis of accounting should be used
because it is a governmental fund, which is,
in essence, an accounting segregation of
financial resources.

   For the enterprise fund, the accrual basis
of accounting should be used because it is a
proprietary fund, whose ongoing organizations
or activities are similar to the organizations
or activities found in the private sector; or
Kemp's governing body has decided that
periodic determination of revenues earned,
expenses incurred, and/or net income is
appropriate for capital maintenance, public
policy, management control, accountability, or
other purposes.

c. In the general fund, the fixed assets
should be accounted for through the general
fixed assets account group, and the unmatured
general long-term liabilities should be
accounted for through the general long-term
debt account group.

   In the enterprise fund, both the fixed
assets and the long-term liabilities should be
accounted for in the enterprise fund.

d. When preparing the comprehensive annual
financial report (CAFR), the balance sheets of
the general fund, the special revenue fund,
and the enterprise fund should be combined.
The CAFR should contain a combined balance
sheet for all fund types and account groups.

   If more than one special revenue fund or
enterprise fund exists in a governmental unit,
combining balance sheets are required to show
the balances of the individual funds.

Solution Guide

Problem 2   General Fund Journal Entries
             (1184,Q4)

1. Problem requires journal entries
    necessary for the general fund of the
    city of Solna for its calendar year,
    1986. Ten specific events are described
    for which journal entries are to be
    prepared for the general fund in
    addition to the closing entries. The
    solution format to be used is described
    in the requirement.

2. The solutions approach is to analyze
    each of the ten events that occurred in
    1986 in terms of the event's effect on
    the general fund.

2.1   The first journal entry made relates to the carryover encumbrances of Solna from the year 1985. At the end of 1985, Fund Balance Reserved for Encumbrances totals $12,000. One manner of accounting for these encumbrances from 1985 is to reestablish the encumbrances account at the beginning of 1986. This is done by debiting Encumbrances - Prior Year for $12,000 and crediting Unreserved Undesignated Fund Balance for $12,000.

2.2   In governmental funds, such as the general fund, the annual operating budget is recorded in the accounts. Thus, estimated revenues of $400,000 from taxes, from fines, forfeits, and penalties, and from miscellaneous sources, is debited. Estimated other financing sources from bond issue proceeds is also debited for $200,000. On the other hand, appropriations for program operations, general administration, and capital outlays is credited for $560,000. Estimated other financing uses from operating transfers is credited for $20,000. The difference of $20,000 is credited to Budgetary Fund Balance.

2.3   In governmental funds, such as the general fund, revenues are recorded under the modified accrual basis, that is, when they are both measurable and available. Property taxes are both measurable and available at the date they are assessed or levied. Therefore, a journal entry is needed to record the assessment. Note that $220,800 is the revenue expected to be collected. This amount represents 96% of the total assessment, which is $230,000 ($220,800 ÷ 96% = $230,000). The $9,200 difference between the Taxes Receivable--Current of $230,000 and the Revenues of $220,800 is credited to Estimated Uncollectible Taxes--Current. When accruing property taxes, the estimated uncollectible accounts are netted against revenues because the uncollectible accounts represent negative resource inflows.

2.4   When goods and services are ordered, encumbrances should be recorded in the general fund. Encumbrances are recorded by debiting Encumbrances--Current Year and by crediting Fund Balance Reserved for Encumbrances. The amount of the encumbrances, $316,000, represents an estimate of the amount that will be expended on the items ordered.

2.5   The designation of $20,000 by the city council for possible future capital outlay requires a reduction in the Unreserved Undesignated Fund Balance. This latter account is debited and the account Fund Balance Designated for Capital Outlays is credited.

2.6   The $664,000 of cash received represents many sources. The collection of delinquent taxes is credited to the account Taxes Receivable--Delinquent. The collection of current taxes is credited to the account Taxes Receivable--Current. The refund for overpayment of the invoice for equipment is credited to the account Expenditures--Capital Outlays. This account is credited because it was the account charged when the equipment was acquired. The $88,000 of fines, forfeits, and penalties and the $90,000 of miscellaneous revenues are credited to revenue accounts. Unlike property taxes, these resource inflows are recorded only when cash is received because they are not measurable and available until this point. The $200,000 of bond issue proceeds is credited to Other Financing Sources-- Proceeds of Bond Issue. This item relates to that which was budgeted from this source in the first entry. Finally, the $18,000 transfer from the discontinued fund represents a residual equity transfer. One alternative is to credit a Residual Equity Transfer In account. (See note 1).

2.7   The receipt of goods and services ordered requires reversing the encumbrances which were recorded when the orders were placed. The orders relating to the encumbrances from 1985 are assumed to be taken care of before those relating to goods and services ordered in 1986. Therefore, Encumbrances--Prior Year is credited for $12,000 and Encumbrances--Current Year is credited for $290,000. Fund Balance Reserved for Encumbrances is debited for the total, $302,000. After reversing the encumbrances, expenditures are recorded for program operations, general administration, and capital outlay. These expenditures represent the actual amount owed of $308,000.

2.8   The additional vouchers represent expenditures related to the appropriations for program operations, general administration, and capital outlay. Various expenditure accounts are debited for $244,000. Note that these expenditures were not preceded by encumbrances, as were those in the case of item 6. The $20,000 transfer to the capital projects fund represents an other financing use. This transfer relates to the operating transfer which was budgeted in the first entry.

2.9 The overpayment of property taxes is recorded by crediting Deferred Revenues. Since the $2,000 of resources is not used to finance 1986 expenditures, it must be deferred in 1986. In 1987, an entry will be made which debits Deferred Revenues and credits Revenues for $2,000. Taxes Receivable--Current is debited in 1986 because when the taxpayer paid his 1986 taxes, this account was credited in error for the $2,000 overpayment.

The second entry is needed because the balance in Estimated Uncollectible Taxes--Current is $3,200 larger than the $6,000 balance in Taxes Receivable--Current. Overstatement of the Estimated Uncollectible Taxes--Current by $3,200 means that Revenues from Taxes was understated by $3,200. After debiting Estimated Uncollectible Taxes--Current for $3,200, the balance in this account is $6,000, which equals the balance in Taxes Receivable--Current.

2.10 The vouchers paid are debited. Therefore, $580,000 is debited to Vouchers Payable.

2.11 The stores inventory at 12/31/86 of $12,000 represents a $6,000 decline from the $18,000 on hand at 12/31/85. Note that Solna uses the "purchases" method in accounting for its stores inventory. This means that expenditures is charged when stores inventory is acquired. To properly record Solna's stores inventory at 12/31/86, Fund Balance Reserved for Stores Inventory should be charged for $6,000 so as to reduce it to the $12,000 of inventory on hand. The account Stores Inventory--Program Operations is appropriately reduced also for $6,000.

3.0 In the closing process, the budgetary entry is reversed. All revenues, expenditures, encumbrances, operating transfers, and residual equity accounts are closed to Fund Balance--Unreserved, Undesignated, which is increased by $26,000.

Unofficial Answer (Author Modified)

Problem 2   General Fund Journal Entries
            (1184,Q4)

a.   City of Solna
         General Fund Journal Entries
      For the Year Ended December 31, 1986

		Dr.	Cr.
1.	To reestablish encumbrances		
	Encumbrances-prior year	$ 12,000	
	Unreserved Undesig-		
	nated Fund Balance		12,000
	Budget entry		
	Estimated Revenues	400,000	
	Estimated Other Fi-		
	nancing Sources--		
	Proceeds of Bonds	200,000	
	Appropriations		560,000
	Estimated Other Fi-		
	nancing Uses--Oper-		
	ating Transfers Out		20,000
	Budgetary Fund Balance		20,000
2.	Taxes receivable--current	230,000	
	Estimated uncollectible		
	taxes--current		9,200
	Revenues--taxes		220,800
3.	Encumbrances - current		
	year	316,000	
	Fund balance reserved		
	for encumbrances		316,000
4.	Unreserved undesignated		
	fund balance	20,000	
	Fund balance designated		
	for possible Future Appro-		
	priation for Capital Out-		
	lay		20,000
5.	Cash	664,000	
	Taxes receivable--		
	delinquent		38,000
	Taxes receivable--		
	current		226,000
	Expenditures--capital		
	outlays		4,000
	Revenues--fines, forfeits,		
	and penalties		88,000
	Revenues--misc.		90,000
	Other financing sources--		
	proceeds of bond issue		200,000
	Residual Equity Trans-		
	fers In (Unreserved Un-		
	designated Fund Bal-		
	ance)[1]		18,000

Notes

[1] A separate account has been used for Residual Equity Transfers in this solution, and this account is closed out in entry b. An alternative approach would be to credit Unreserved Undesignated Fund Balance directly in entry a.5. In either case, the amount would be shown as an addition to the beginning Fund Balance in the Statement of Revenues, Expenditures, and Changes in Fund Balances.

6. Fund balance reserved for

    encumbrances   302,000
        Encumbrances--prior
            year   12,000
        Encumbrances--
            current year   290,000
        Expenditures--program
            operations   166,000
        Expenditures--general
            administration   80,000
        Expenditures--capital
            outlays   62,000
            Vouchers payable   308,000

7. Expenditures--program
        operations   188,000
    Expenditures--general
        administration   38,000
    Expenditures--capital
        outlays   18,000
    Other financing uses--
        operating transfers out to
        capital projects fund   20,000
        Vouchers payable   264,000

8. Taxes receivable--current   2,000
        Deferred revenue--taxes   2,000

    Estimated uncollectible taxes--
        current   3,200
        Revenues--taxes   3,200

    (A net of $224,000 has been collected for current year
    taxes, **whereas only** $220,800 was recognized as Revenues
    in entry 2. This entry assumes that none of the
    remaining taxes receivable are expected to be
    collected.)

9. Vouchers payable   580,000
        Cash   580,000

10. Fund balance reserved for
        stores inventory   6,000
        Stores inventory--
            program operations   6,000

b.   City of Solna
              Closing Entries
       For the Year Ended December 31, 1986

                                          Dr.   Cr.
1. Appropriations   560,000
    Estimated Other
    Financing Uses-
    Operating Transfers
    Out   20,000
    Budgetary Fund Balance   20,000
        Estimated Revenues   400,000
        Estimated Other
            Financing Sources-
            Proceeds of Bonds   200,000

2. Revenues-Taxes   224,000
    Revenues-Fines and
        Penalties   88,000
    Revenues-Miscellaneous   90,000
    Other Financing Sources-
        Proceeds of Bond Issue   200,000
    Residual Equity Trans-
        fer In   18,000
        Expenditures-Program
            operations   354,000
        Expenditures-General
            Admin.   118,000
        Expenditures-Capital
            Outlay   76,000
        Encumbrances-Current Year   26,000
        Other Financial Uses-
            Operating Transfers Out
            to Capital Projects Fund   20,000
        Unreserved Undesignated
            Fund Balance   26,000

Multiple Choice Questions (1-69)

1. The following information pertains to interest received by Beech University from endowment fund investments for the year ended June 30, 1988:

	Received	Expended for current operations
Unrestricted	$300,000	$100,000
Restricted	500,000	75,000

What amount should be credited to endowment income for the year ended June 30, 1988?
- a. $800,000
- b. $375,000
- c. $175,000
- d. $100,000

2. On July 31, 1988, Sabio College showed the following amounts to be used for

Renewal and replacement of college properties	$200,000
Retirement of indebtedness on college properties	300,000
Purchase of physical properties for college purposes, but unexpended at 7/31/88	400,000

What total amount should be included in Sabio's plant funds at July 31, 1988?
- a. $900,000
- b. $600,000
- c. $400,000
- d. $200,000

3. For the 1987 fall semester, Brook University assessed its students $4,000,000 (net of refunds), covering tuition and fees for educational and general purposes. However, only $3,700,000 was expected to be realized because tuition remissions of $80,000 were allowed to faculty members' children attending Brook and scholarships totaling $220,000 were granted to students. What amount should Brook include in educational and general current funds revenues from student tuition and fees?
- a. $4,000,000
- b. $3,920,000
- c. $3,780,000
- d. $3,700,000

4. The following information was available from Forest College's accounting records for its current funds for the year ended March 31, 1988:

Restricted gifts received	
Expended	$100,000
Not expended	300,000
Unrestricted gifts received	
Expended	600,000
Not expended	75,000

What amount should be included in current funds revenues for the year ended March 31, 1988?
- a. $ 600,000
- b. $ 700,000
- c. $ 775,000
- d. $1,000,000

5. The following expenditures were among those incurred by Alma University during 1987:

Administrative data processing	$ 50,000
Scholarships and fellowships	100,000
Operation and maintenance of physical plant	200,000

The amount to be included in the functional classification "Institutional Support" expenditures account is
- a. $ 50,000
- b. $150,000
- c. $250,000
- d. $350,000

Items 6 and 7 are based on the following information pertaining to Cabal University as of June 30, 1989 and for the year then ended:

Unrestricted current funds comprised $7,500,000 of assets and $4,500,000 of liabilities (including deferred revenues of $150,000). Among the receipts recorded during the year were unrestricted gifts of $550,000 and restricted grants totaling $330,000, of which $220,000 was expended during the year for current operations and $110,000 remained unexpended at the close of the year.

Volunteers from the surrounding communities regularly contribute their services to Cabal and are paid nominal amounts to cover their travel costs. During the year, the total amount paid to these volunteers aggregated $18,000. The gross value of services performed by them, determined by reference to equivalent wages available in that area for similar services, amounted to $200,000.

6. At June 30, 1989, the fund balance of Cabal's unrestricted current funds was
- a. $7,500,000
- b. $3,150,000
- c. $3,000,000
- d. $2,850,000

7. For the year ended June 30, 1989, what amount should be included in Cabal's current funds revenues for the unrestricted gifts and restricted grants?
- a. $550,000
- b. $660,000
- c. $770,000
- d. $880,000

8.   This question is based on the following information pertaining to Cabal University as of June 30, 1989 and for the year then ended:

Unrestricted current funds comprised $7,500,000 of assets and $4,500,000 of liabilities (including deferred revenues of $150,000). Among the receipts recorded during the year were unrestricted gifts of $550,000 and restricted grants totaling $330,000, of which $220,000 was expended during the year for current operations and $110,000 remained unexpended at the close of the year.

Volunteers from the surrounding communities regularly contribute their services to Cabal and are paid nominal amounts to cover their travel costs. During the year, the total amount paid to these volunteers aggregated $18,000. The gross value of services performed by them, determined by reference to equivalent wages available in that area for similar services, amounted to $200,000.

For the year ended June 30, 1989, what amount should Cabal record as expenditures for the volunteers' services?

    a. $218,000
    b. $200,000
    c. $ 18,000
    d. $0

9.   During the years ended June 30, 1980 and 1981, Sonata University conducted a cancer research project financed by a $2,000,000 gift from an alumnus. This entire amount was pledged by the donor on July 10, 1979, although he paid only $500,000 at that date. The gift was restricted to the financing of this particular research project. During the two-year research period, Sonata's related gift receipts and research expenditures were as follows:

	Year ended June 30	
	1980	1981
Gift receipts	$1,200,000	$ 800,000
Cancer research expenditures	900,000	1,100,000

How much gift revenue should Sonata report in the restricted column of its statement of current funds revenues, expenditures, and other changes for the year ended June 30, 1981?

    a. $0
    b. $ 800,000
    c. $1,100,000
    d. $2,000,000

10.   On January 2, 1982, John Reynolds established a $500,000 trust, the income from which is to be paid to Mansfield University for general operating purposes. The Wyndham National Bank was appointed by Reynolds as trustee of the fund. What journal entry is required on Mansfield's books?

		Dr.	Cr.
a.	Memorandum entry only	--	--
b.	Cash	$500,000	
	Endowment fund balance		$500,000
c.	Nonexpendable endowment fund	$500,000	
	Endowment fund balance		$500,000
d.	Expendable funds	$500,000	
	Endowment fund balance		$500,000

11.   Which of the following funds are usually encountered in a not-for-profit private university?

	Current funds	Plant funds
a.	No	Yes
b.	No	No
c.	Yes	No
d.	Yes	Yes

12.   Which of the following funds are usually encountered in a not-for-profit private university?

	Loan funds	Life income funds
a.	No	Yes
b.	No	No
c.	Yes	No
d.	Yes	Yes

13.   Which of the following not-for-profit organizations would use plant funds to account for land, buildings, equipment, and other capital assets?

	Colleges and universities	Voluntary health and welfare organizations
a.	Yes	Yes
b.	Yes	No
c.	No	No
d.	No	Yes

14.   The current funds group of a not-for-profit private university includes which of the following?

	Agency funds	Plant funds
a.	No	No
b.	No	Yes
c.	Yes	Yes
d.	Yes	No

15.   Funds established at a college by donors who have stipulated that the principal is nonexpendable but that the income generated may be expended by current operating funds would be accounted for in the

    a.   Quasi-endowment fund.
    b.   Endowment fund.

c. Term endowment fund.
d. Agency fund.

16. Funds which the governing board of an institution, rather than a donor or other outside agency, has determined are to be retained and invested for other than loan or plant purposes would be accounted for in the

a. Quasi-endowment fund.
b. Endowment fund.
c. Agency fund.
d. Current fund-restricted.

17. Which of the following should be included in the current funds revenues of a not-for-profit private university?

	Tuition waivers	Unrestricted bequests
a.	Yes	No
b.	Yes	Yes
c.	No	Yes
d.	No	No

18. The current funds group of a not-for-profit private university includes which of the following subgroups?

	Term endowment funds	Life income funds
a.	No	No
b.	No	Yes
c.	Yes	Yes
d.	Yes	No

19. Tuition waivers for which there is no intention of collection from the student should be classified by a not-for-profit university as

	Revenue	Expenditures
a.	No	No
b.	No	Yes
c.	Yes	Yes
d.	Yes	No

20. Which of the following is utilized for current expenditures by a not-for-profit university?

	Unrestricted current funds	Restricted current funds
a.	No	No
b.	No	Yes
c.	Yes	No
d.	Yes	Yes

21. Which of the following receipts is properly recorded as restricted current funds on the books of a university?

a. Tuition.
b. Student laboratory fees.
c. Housing fees.
d. Research grants.

22. Under Cura Hospital's established rate structure, patient service revenues of $9,000,000 would have been earned for the year ended December 31, 1987. However, only $6,750,000 was collected because of charity allowances of $1,500,000 and discounts of $750,000 to third-party payors. For the year ended December 31, 1987, what amount should Cura record as patient service revenues?

a. $6,750,000
b. $7,500,000
c. $8,250,000
d. $9,000,000

23. An organization of high school seniors performs services for patients at Leer Hospital. These students are volunteers and perform services that the hospital would not otherwise provide, such as wheeling patients in the park and reading to patients. Leer has no employer-employee relationship with these volunteers, who donated 5,000 hours of service to Leer in 1987. At the minimum wage rate, these services would amount to $18,750, while it is estimated that the fair value of these services was $25,000. In Leer's 1987 statement of revenues and expenses, what amount should be reported as nonoperating revenue?

a. $25,000
b. $18,750
c. $ 6,250
d. $0

24. In June 1988, Park Hospital purchased medicines from Jove Pharmaceutical Co. at a cost of $2,000. However, Jove notified Park that the invoice was being canceled, and that the medicines were being donated to Park. Park should record this donation of medicines as

a. A memorandum entry only.
b. Other operating revenue of $2,000.
c. A $2,000 credit to operating expenses.
d. A $2,000 credit to nonoperating expenses.

25. On March 1, 1988, Allan Rowe established a $100,000 endowment fund, the income from which is to be paid to Elm Hospital for general operating purposes. Elm does not control the fund's principal. Rowe appointed West National Bank as trustee of this fund. What journal entry is required by Elm to record the establishment of the endowment?

		Debit	Credit
a.	Cash	$100,000	
	Nonexpendable endowment fund		$100,000
b.	Cash	100,000	
	Endowment fund balance		100,000
c.	Nonexpendable endowment fund	100,000	
	Endowment fund balance		100,000
d.	Memorandum entry only	--	--

26. In 1988, Wells Hospital received an unrestricted bequest of common stock with a fair
market value of $50,000 on the date of receipt
of the stock. The testator had paid $20,000
for this stock in 1986. Wells should record
this bequest as
   a. Nonoperating revenue of $50,000.
   b. Nonoperating revenue of $30,000.
   c. Nonoperating revenue of $20,000.
   d. A memorandum entry only.

27. Cedar Hospital has a marketable equity
securities portfolio that is appropriately
included in noncurrent assets in unrestricted
funds. The portfolio has an aggregate cost of
$300,000. It had an aggregate fair market
value of $250,000 at the end of 1987 and
$290,000 at the end of 1986. If the portfolio
was properly reported in the balance sheet at
the end of 1986, the change in the valuation
allowance at the end of 1987 should be
   a. $0.
   b. A decrease of $40,000.
   c. An increase of $40,000.
   d. An increase of $50,000.

28. Ross Hospital's accounting records
disclosed the following information:

   • Net resources invested in
plant assets $10,000,000
   • Board-designated funds
(assets whose use is limited)   2,000,000

What amount should be included as part of
general funds?
   a. $12,000,000
   b. $10,000,000
   c. $ 2,000,000
   d. $0

29. Cura Hospital's property, plant, and
equipment, net of depreciation, amounted to
$10,000,000 with related mortgage liabilities
of $1,000,000. What amount should be included
in the restricted fund grouping?
   a. $0
   b. $ 1,000,000

   c. $ 9,000,000
   d. $10,000,000

30. Palma Hospital's patient service revenues
for services provided in 1986, at established
rates, amounted to $8,000,000 on the accrual
basis. For internal reporting, Palma uses the
discharge method. Under this method, patient
service revenues are recognized only when
patients are discharged, with no recognition
given to revenues accruing for services to
patients not yet discharged. Patient service
revenues at established rates using the
discharge method amounted to $7,000,000 for
1986. According to generally accepted
accounting principles, Palma should report
patient service revenues for 1986 of
   a. Either $8,000,000 or $7,000,000, at
       the option of the hospital.
   b. $8,000,000.
   c. $7,500,000.
   d. $7,000,000.

31. In 1986, Pyle Hospital received a
$250,000 pure endowment fund grant. Also in
1986, Pyle's governing board designated, for
special uses, $300,000 which had originated
from unrestricted gifts. What amount of these
resources should be accounted for as part of
general (unrestricted) funds?
   a. $0
   b. $250,000
   c. $300,000
   d. $550,000

32. On July 1, 1981, Lilydale Hospital's
Board of Trustees designated $200,000 for
expansion of outpatient facilities. The
$200,000 is expected to be expended in the
fiscal year ending June 30, 1984. In Lilydale's balance sheet at June 30, 1982, this
cash should be classified as a $200,000
   a. Restricted current asset.
   b. Restricted noncurrent asset.
   c. General current asset.
   d. Asset whose use is limited.

33. Proceeds from sale of cafeteria meals and
guest trays to visitors operated by a hospital
would normally be included in
   a. Patient service revenue.
   b. Ancillary service revenue.
   c. Other operating revenue.
   d. Other nonoperating revenue.

34. Revenue of a hospital from grants
specified by the donor for research would
normally be included in
   a. Other nonoperating revenue.
   b. Other operating revenue.
   c. Patient service revenue.
   d. Ancillary service revenue.

35. Which of the following normally would be
included in Other Operating Revenues of a
hospital?

	Revenue from educational programs	Unrestricted gifts
a.	Yes	No
b.	Yes	Yes
c.	No	Yes
d.	No	No

36. Revenue from educational programs of a
hospital normally would be included in
   a.   Ancillary service revenue.
   b.   Patient service revenue.
   c.   Other nonoperating revenue.
   d.   Other operating revenue.

37. Which of the following would be included
in the general funds of a not-for-profit
hospital?
   a.   Permanent endowments.
   b.   Term endowments.
   c.   Board designated funds orginating
        from previously accumulated income.
   d.   Plant expansion and replacement
        funds.

38. An unrestricted pledge from an annual
contributor to a voluntary not-for-profit
hospital made in December 1981 and paid in
cash in March 1982 would generally be credited
to
   a.   Nonoperating revenue in 1981.
   b.   Nonoperating revenue in 1982.
   c.   Operating revenue in 1981.
   d.   Operating revenue in 1982.

Items 39 through 41 are based on the
following information pertaining to Lori
Hospital for the year ended May 31, 1989:

In March 1989, a $300,000 unrestricted
bequest and a $500,000 pure endowment grant
were received. In April 1989, a bank notified
Lori that the bank received $10,000 to be held
in permanent trust by the bank. Lori is to
receive the income from this donation.

39. Lori should record the $300,000
unrestricted bequest as
   a.   Nonoperating revenue.
   b.   Other operating revenue.
   c.   A direct credit to the fund balance.
   d.   A credit to operating expenses.

40. The $500,000 pure endowment grant
   a.   May be expended by the governing
        board only to the extent of the
        principal since the income from this
        fund must be accumulated.

   b.   Should be reported as nonoperating
        revenue when the full amount of
        principal is expended.
   c.   Should be recorded as a memorandum
        entry only.
   d.   Should be accounted for as
        restricted funds upon receipt.

41. The $10,000 donation being held by the
bank in permanent trust should be
   a.   Recorded in Lori's restricted
        endowment fund.
   b.   Recorded by Lori as nonoperating
        revenue.
   c.   Recorded by Lori as other operating
        revenue.
   d.   Disclosed in notes to Lori's
        financial statements.

42. During 1988, unrestricted pledges of
$600,000 were received, of which it was
estimated that $72,000 would be uncollectible.
By the end of 1988, $480,000 of the pledges
had been collected, and it was expected that
an additional $48,000 of these pledges would
be collected in 1989, with the balance to be
written off as uncollectible. Donors did **not**
specify any periods during which the donations
were to be used.

Also during 1988, Rega sold a computer
for $18,000. Its cost was $21,000 and its
book value was $15,000. Rega made the correct
entry to record the gain on sale.

What amount should Rega include under
public support in 1988 for net contributions?
   a. $480,000
   b. $528,000
   c. $531,000
   d. $600,000

Items 43 and 44 are based on the following information pertaining to Rega Foundation, a voluntary welfare organization funded
by contributions from the general public:

During 1988, unrestricted pledges of
$600,000 were received, of which it was
estimated that $72,000 would be uncollectible.
By the end of 1988, $480,000 of the pledges
had been collected, and it was supposed that
an additional $48,000 of these pledges would
be collected in 1989, with the balance to be
written off as uncollectible. Donors did **not**
specify any periods during which the donations
were to be used.

Also during 1988, Rega sold a computer
for $18,000. Its cost was $21,000 and its
book value was $15,000. Rega made the correct
entry to record the gain on sale.

43. In addition to the entry recording the
gain on sale of the computer, the other
accounts that Rega should debit and credit in
connection with this sale are

	Debit	Credit
a.	Current unrestricted funds	Fund balance-- undesignated
b.	Excess revenues control	Sale of equipment
c.	Fund balance-- unexpended	Fund balance-- expended
d.	Fund balance-- expended	Fund balance-- unexpended

44. The amount that should be debited and credited for the additional entry in connection with the sale of the computer is
   a. $ 3,000
   b. $15,000
   c. $18,000
   d. $21,000

Items 45 and 46 are based on the following data:

Community Service Center is a voluntary welfare organization funded by contributions from the general public. During 1983, unrestricted pledges of $900,000 were received, half of which were payable in 1983, with the other half payable in 1984 for use in 1984. It was estimated that 10% of these pledges would be uncollectible.

45. How much should Community report as net contribution revenue for 1983 with respect to the pledges?
   a. $0
   b. $405,000
   c. $810,000
   d. $900,000

46. How much should Community record in 1983 for contributed service expense?
   a. $8,000
   b. $4,000
   c. $ 800
   d. $0

47. Which of the following would appear in the plant fund of a voluntary health and welfare organization?

	Land	Equipment
a.	Yes	No
b.	Yes	Yes
c.	No	Yes
d.	No	No

48. In a statement of support, revenue, and expenses and changes in fund balances of a voluntary health and welfare organization, contributions to the building fund should
   a. Be included as an element of support.
   b. Be included as an element of revenue.
   c. Be included as an element of other changes in fund balances.
   d. Not be included.

49. In a statement of support, revenue, and expenses and changes in fund balances of a voluntary health and welfare organization, depreciation expense should
   a. Be included as an element of expense.
   b. Be included as an element of other changes in fund balances.
   c. Be included as an element of support.
   d. Not be included.

50. Securities donated to a voluntary health and welfare organization should be recorded at the
   a. Donor's recorded amount.
   b. Fair market value at the date of the gift.
   c. Fair market value at the date of the gift, or the donor's recorded amount, whichever is lower.
   d. Fair market value at the date of the gift, or the donor's recorded amount, whichever is higher.

51. A voluntary health and welfare organization received a cash donation in 1983 from a donor specifying that the amount donated be used in 1985. The cash donation should be accounted for as
   a. Support in 1983.
   b. Support in 1983, 1984, and 1985, and as a deferred credit in the balance sheet at the end of 1983 and 1984.
   c. Support in 1985, and no deferred credit in the balance sheet at the end of 1983 and 1984.
   d. Support in 1985, and as a deferred credit in the balance sheet at the end of 1983 and 1984.

52. Which of the following funds of a voluntary health and welfare organization does not have a counterpart fund in governmental accounting?
   a. Current unrestricted.
   b. Land, building, and equipment.
   c. Custodian.
   d. Endowment.

53. Lane Foundation received a nonexpendable endowment of $500,000 in 1986 from Gant Enterprises. The endowment assets were invested in publicly traded securities. Gant did not specify how gains and losses from dispositions of endowment assets were to be treated. No restrictions were placed on the

use of dividends received and interest earned on fund resources. In 1987, Lane realized gains of $50,000 on sales of fund investments, and received total interest and dividends of $40,000 on fund securities. The amount of these capital gains, interest, and dividends available for expenditure by Lane's unrestricted current fund is

    a. $0
    b. $40,000
    c. $50,000
    d. $90,000

54. In 1987, the Board of Trustees of Burr Foundation designated $100,000 from its current funds for college scholarships. Also in 1987, the foundation received a bequest of $200,000 from an estate of a benefactor who specified that the bequest was to be used for hiring teachers to tutor handicapped students. What amount should be accounted for as current restricted funds?

    a. $0
    b. $100,000
    c. $200,000
    d. $300,000

55. In 1987, a nonprofit trade association enrolled five new member companies, each of which was obligated to pay nonrefundable initiation fees of $1,000. These fees were receivable by the association in 1987. Three of the new members paid the initiation fees in 1987, and the other two new members paid their initiation fees in 1988. Annual dues (excluding initiation fees) received by the association from all of its members have always covered the organization's costs of services provided to its members. It can be reasonably expected that future dues will cover all costs of the organization's future services to members. Average membership duration is 10 years because of mergers, attrition, and economic factors. What amount of initiation fees from these five new members should the association recognize as revenue in 1987?

    a. $5,000
    b. $3,000
    c. $ 500
    d. $0

56. On January 2, 1987, a nonprofit botanical society received a gift of an exhaustible fixed asset with an estimated useful life of 10 years and no salvage value. The donor's cost of this asset was $20,000, and its fair market value at the date of the gift was $30,000. What amount of depreciation of this asset should the society recognize in its 1987 financial statements?

    a. $3,000
    b. $2,500

    c. $2,000
    d. $0

57. In April 1987, Alice Reed donated $100,000 cash to her church, with the stipulation that the income generated from this gift is to be paid to Alice during her lifetime. The conditions of this donation are that, after Alice dies, the principal can be used by the church for any purpose voted on by the church elders. The church received interest of $8,000 on the $100,000 for the year ended March 31, 1988, and the interest was remitted to Alice. In the church's March 31, 1988 financial statements

    a. $8,000 should be reported under support and revenue in the activity statement.
    b. $92,000 should be reported under support and revenue in the activity statement.
    c. $100,000 should be reported as deferred support in the balance sheet.
    d.   The gift and its terms should be disclosed only in notes to the financial statements.

58. The following expenditures were among those incurred by a nonprofit botanical society during 1987:

Printing of annual report	$10,000
Unsolicited merchandise sent to encourage contributions	20,000

What amount should be classified as fund-raising costs in the society's activity statement?

    a. $0
    b. $10,000
    c. $20,000
    d. $30,000

May 1990 Questions

59. In July 1988, Ross donated $200,000 cash to a church with the stipulation that the revenue generated from this gift be paid to Ross during Ross' lifetime. The conditions of this donation are that, after Ross dies, the principal may be used by the church for any purpose voted on by the church elders. The church received interest of $16,000 on the $200,000 for the year ended June 30, 1989, and the interest was remitted to Ross. In the church's June 30, 1989 annual financial statements

    a. $200,000 should be reported as deferred support in the balance sheet.
    b. $184,000 should be reported under support and revenue in the activity statement.

c. $16,000 should be reported under
support and revenue in the activity
statement.

d. The gift and its terms should be
disclosed only in notes to the
financial statements.

60. Birdlovers, a community foundation,
incurred $5,000 in management and general
expenses during 1989. In Birdlovers' statement of revenue, expense, and changes in fund
balance for the year ended December 31, 1989,
the $5,000 should be reported as

a. A contra account offsetting revenue
and support.

b. Part of program services.

c. Part of supporting services.

d. A direct reduction of fund balance.

61. Lema Fund, a voluntary welfare organization funded by contributions from the general
public, received unrestricted pledges of
$200,000 during 1989. It was estimated that
10% of these pledges would be uncollectible.
By the end of 1989, $130,000 of the pledges
had been collected. It was expected that
$50,000 more would be collected in 1990 and
that the balance of $20,000 would be written
off as uncollectible. What amount should Lema
include under public support in 1989 for net
contributions?

a. $200,000

b. $180,000

c. $150,000

d. $130,000

Items 62 through 64 are based on the following:

In 1979, Community Helpers, a voluntary health
and welfare organization, received a bequest
of a $100,000 certificate of deposit maturing
in 1989. The testator's only stipulations
were that this certificate be held until
maturity and that the interest revenue be used
to finance salaries for a preschool program.
Interest revenue for 1989 was $8,000. When
the certificate was redeemed, the board of
trustees adopted a formal resolution desig-
nating $20,000 of the proceeds for the future
purchase of equipment for the preschool program.

62. In regard to the certificate of deposit,
what should be reported in the endowment fund
column of the 1989 statement of support, revenue, and expenses and changes in fund
balances?

a. Legacies and bequests, $100,000.

b. Direct reduction in fund balance for
transfer to current unrestricted
fund, $100,000.

c. Transfer to land, building, and
equipment fund, $20,000.

d. Revenues control, $100,000.

63. What should be reported in the current
unrestricted funds column of the 1989 statement of support, revenue, and expenses and
changes in fund balances?

a. Investment income, $8,000.

b. Direct reduction of fund balance for
transfer to land, building, and
equipment fund, $20,000.

c. Direct addition to fund balance for
transfer from endowment fund,
$100,000.

d. Public support, $108,000.

64. What should be reported in the 1989 year-
end current unrestricted funds balance sheet?

a. Fund balance designated for
preschool program, $28,000;
Undesignated fund balance, $80,000.

b. Fund balance designated for purchase
of equipment, $20,000;
Undesignated fund balance, $80,000.

c. Fund balance designated for
preschool program salaries, $8,000;
Undesignated fund balance, $80,000.

d. Undesignated fund balance, $72,000.

Items 65 through 68 are based on the following:

Metro General is a municipally-owned and
operated hospital and a component unit of
Metro City. In 1989, the hospital received
$7,000 in unrestricted gifts and $4,000 in
unrestricted bequests. The hospital has
$800,000 in long-term debt and $1,200,000 in
fixed assets.

The hospital has transferred certain resources to a hospital guild. Substantially
all of the guild's resources are held for the
benefit of the hospital. The hospital controls the guild through contracts that provide
it with the authority to direct the guild's
activities, management, and policies. The
hospital has also assigned certain of its
functions to a hospital auxiliary, which
operates primarily for the benefit of the
hospital. The hospital does **not** have control
over the auxiliary. The financial statements
of the guild and the auxiliary are **not** consolidated with the hospital's financial statements. The guild and the auxiliary have total
assets of $20,000 and $30,000, respectively.

Before the hospital's financial
statements were combined with those of the
city, the city's statements included data on
one special revenue fund and one enterprise
fund. The city's statements showed $100,000
in enterprise fund long-term debt, $500,000 in

enterprise fund fixed assets, $1,000,000 in
general long-term debt, and $6,000,000 in
general fixed assets.

65. What account or accounts should be
credited for the $7,000 of unrestricted gifts
and the $4,000 of unrestricted bequests?

a.	Operating revenue	$11,000
b.	Nonoperating revenue	$11,000
c.	Operating revenue	$7,000
	Nonoperating revenue	4,000
d.	Nonoperating revenue	$7,000
	Operating revenue	4,000

66. The hospital's long-term debt should be
reported in the city's combined balance sheet
as

    a. Part of $900,000 enterprise fund
        type long-term debt in the enter-
        prise fund type column.

    b. An $800,000 contra amount against
        fixed assets.

    c. Part of the $1,800,000 general long-
        term debt account group.

    d. A separate "discrete presentation"
        of $800,000 in the hospital column.

67. In the hospital's notes to financial
statements, total assets of hospital-related
organizations required to be disclosed amount
to

    a. $0
    b. $20,000
    c. $30,000
    d. $50,000

68. The hospital's fixed assets should be
reported in the city's combined balance sheet
as

    a. Hospital fixed assets of $1,200,000
        in a separate "discrete
        presentation" hospital column.

    b. Special revenue fund type fixed as-
        sets of $1,200,000 in the general
        fixed assets account group column.

    c. Part of $1,700,000 enterprise fund
        type fixed assets in the enterprise
        fund type column.

    d. Part of $7,200,000 general fixed
        assets in the general fixed assets
        account group.

69. Which of the following should be included
in a university's current funds revenue?

	Unrestricted gifts	Expended restricted current funds	Unexpended restricted current funds
a.	Yes	Yes	Yes
b.	Yes	Yes	No
c.	Yes	No	No
d.	No	No	Yes

Problems

Problem 1   (1183,Q4)

(45 to 55 minutes)

A partial balance sheet of Rapapo State University as of the end of its fiscal year ended July 31, 1985 is presented below:

Rapapo State University
Current Funds Balance Sheet
July 31, 1985

Assets:

Unrestricted:

Cash	$200,000
Accounts receivable--	
tuition and fees, less allowance	
for doubtful accounts of $15,000	360,000
Prepaid expenses	40,000
Total unrestricted	600,000

Restricted:

Cash	10,000
Investments	210,000
Total restricted	220,000
Total current funds	$820,000

Liabilities and fund balances:

Unrestricted:

Accounts payable	$100,000
Due to other funds	40,000
Deferred revenue--tuition	
and fees	25,000
Fund balance	435,000
Total unrestricted	600,000

Restricted:

Accounts payable	5,000
Fund balance	215,000
Total restricted	220,000
Total current funds	$820,000

The following information pertains to the year ended July 31, 1986:

1. Cash collected from students' tuition totaled $3,000,000. Of this $3,000,000, $362,000 represented accounts receivable outstanding at July 31, 1985; $2,500,000 was for current year tuition; and $138,000 was for tuition applicable to the semester beginning in August 1986.

2. Deferred revenue at July 31, 1985 was earned during the year ended July 31, 1986.

3. Accounts receivable at July 31, 1985, which were not collected during the year ended July 31 1986, were determined to be uncollectible and were written off against the allowance account. At July 31, 1986, the allowance account was estimated at $10,000.

4. During the year, an unrestricted appropriation of $60,000 was made by the state. This state appropriation was to be paid to Rapapo sometime in August 1986.

5. During the year, unrestricted cash gifts of $80,000 were received from alumni. Rapapo's board of trustees allocated $30,000 of these gifts to the student loan fund.

6. During the year, investments costing $25,000 were sold for $31,000. Restricted fund investments were purchased at a cost of $40,000. Investment income of $18,000 was earned and collected during the year.

7. Unrestricted general expenses of $2,500,000 were recorded in the voucher system. At July 31, 1986, the unrestricted accounts payable balance was $75,000.

8. The restricted accounts payable balance at July 31, 1985 was paid.

9. The $40,000 due to other funds at July 31, 1985, was paid to the plant fund as required.

10. One quarter of the prepaid expenses at July 31, 1985 expired during the current year and pertained to general education expense. There was no addition to prepaid expenses during the year.

Required:

a. Prepare journal entries in summary form to record the foregoing transactions for the year ended July 31, 1986. Number each entry to correspond with the number indicated in the description of its respective transaction. Your answer sheet should be organized as follows:

		Current funds			
Entry		Unrestricted		Restricted	
no.	Accounts	Debit	Credit	Debit	Credit

b. Prepare a statement of changes in fund balances for the year ended July 31, 1986.

Problem 2   (587,Q5)

(40 to 50 minutes)

Esperanza Hospital's post-closing trial balance at December 31, 1986 appears on the tear-out worksheet on the following page.

Esperanza, which is a nonprofit hospital, did not maintain its books in conformity with the principles of hospital fund accounting. Effective January 1, 1987, Esperanza's board of trustees voted to adjust the December 31, 1986 general ledger balances, and to establish separate funds for the general (unrestricted) funds, the endowment fund, and the plant replacement and expansion fund.

Additional account information:

- Investment in corporate bonds pertains to the amount required to be accumulated under an agreement with third party payors to invest cash equal to accumulated depreciation until the funds are needed for asset replacement. The $500,000 balance at December 31, 1986 is less than the full amount required because of errors in computation of building depreciation for past years. Included in the allowance for depreciation is a correctly computed amount of $90,000 applicable to equipment.

- Endowment fund balance has been credited with the following:

Donor's bequest of cash	$300,000
Gains on sales of securities	100,000
Interest and dividends earned in 1984, 1985, and 1986	120,000
Total	$520,000

The terms of the bequest specify that the principal, plus all gains on sales of investments, are to remain fully invested in U.S. government or corporate securities. At December 31, 1986, $400,000 was invested in U.S. Treasury bills. The bequest further specifies that interest and dividends earned on investments are to be used for payment of current operating expenses.

- Land comprises the following:

Donation of land in 1970, at appraised value	$ 40,000
Appreciation in fair value of land is determined by independent appraiser in 1980	60,000
Total	$100,000

- Building comprises the following:

Hospital building completed in January 1947, when operations were started (estimated useful life 50 years), at cost	$720,000
Installation of elevator in January 1967 (estimated useful life 20 years), at cost	80,000
Total	$800,000

Required:

Turn to the tear-out worksheet on the following page, and enter the adjustments necessary to restate the general ledger account balances properly. Distribute the adjusted balances to establish the separate fund accounts, and complete the worksheet. Formal journal entries are not required, but supporting computations should be referenced to the worksheet adjustments.

Esperanza Hospital
WORKSHEET TO ADJUST GENERAL LEDGER BALANCES
AND TO ESTABLISH SEPARATE FUNDS
January 1, 1987

Account	Trial Balance December 31, 1986		Adjustments		General (Unrestricted) Funds		Endowment Fund		Plant Replacement and Expansion Fund	
	Debit	Credit	Debit	Credit	Debit	Credit	Debit	Credit	Debit	Credit
Cash	60,000									
Investment in U.S. Treasury bills	400,000									
Investment in corporate bonds	500,000									
Interest receivable	10,000									
Accounts receivable	50,000									
Inventory	30,000									
Land	100,000									
Building	800,000									
Equipment	170,000									
Allowance for depreciation		410,000								
Accounts payable		20,000								
Notes payable		70,000								
Endowment fund balance		520,000								
Other fund balances		1,100,000								
Totals	2,120,000	2,120,000								

Problem 3   (1189,Q4)

(45 to 55 minutes)

Children's Agency, a voluntary health and
welfare organization, conducts two programs:
Medical Services Program and Community Information Services Program. It had the following
transactions during the year ended June 30,
1989:

1. Received the following contributions:
   Unrestricted pledges $800,000
   Restricted cash   95,000
   Building fund pledges   50,000
   Endowment fund cash   1,000

2. Collected the following pledges:
   Unrestricted   450,000
   Building fund   20,000

3. Received the following unrestricted
   cash revenues:
   From theatre party (net of
     direct costs)   12,000
   Bequests   10,000
   Membership dues   8,000
   Interest and dividends   5,000

4. Program expenses incurred
   (processed through vouchers
   payable):
   Medical services   60,000
   Community information services 15,000

5. Services expenses incurred
   (processed through vouchers
   payable):
   General administration   150,000
   Fund raising   200,000

6. Fixed assets purchased with
   unrestricted cash   18,000

7. Depreciation of all buildings
   and equipment in the land,
   buildings, and equipment
   fund was allocated as follows:
   Medical services program   4,000
   Community information services
     program   3,000
   General administration   6,000
   Fund raising   2,000

8. Paid vouchers payable   330,000

Current Fund--Unrestricted
Current Fund--Restricted
Land, Buildings, and Equipment Fund
Endowment Fund

Number the journal entries to coincide
with the transaction numbers indicated.

Required:

On the worksheet on the following page,
record the journal entries (without explanations) for the preceding transactions. With
credit amounts placed in parentheses, insert
the amounts in the proper columns for each of
the following funds:

Children's Agency
JOURNAL ENTRIES
For the Year Ended June 30, 1989

Account Title	Current Fund		Land, Buildings, and Equipment Fund Dr. (Cr.)	Endowment Fund Dr. (Cr.)
	Unrestricted Dr. (Cr.)	Restricted Dr. (Cr.)		

Problem 4   (583,Q5)

(40 to 50 minutes)

In 1950 a group of civic-minded merchants in Albury City organized the "Committee of 100" for the purpose of establishing the Community Sports Club, a nonprofit sports organization for local youth. Each of the Committee's 100 members contributed $1,000 towards the Club's capital, and in turn received a participation certificate. In addition, each participant agreed to pay dues of $200 a year for the Club's operations. All dues have been collected in full by the end of each fiscal year ending March 31. Members who have discontinued their participation have been replaced by an equal number of new members through transfer of the participation certificates from the former members to the new ones. Following is the Club's trial balance at April 1, 1982:

	Debit	Credit
Cash	$ 9,000	
Investments (at market, equal to cost)	58,000	
Inventories	5,000	
Land	10,000	
Building	164,000	
Accumulated depreciation-- building		$130,000
Furniture and equipment	54,000	
Accumulated depreciation-- furniture and equipment		46,000
Accounts payable		12,000
Participation certificates (100 at $1,000 each)		100,000
Cumulative excess of revenue over expenses		12,000
	$300,000	$300,000

Transactions for the year ended March 31, 1983 were as follows:

(1) Collections from participants for dues $20,000
(2) Snack bar and soda fountain sales   28,000
(3) Interest and dividends received   6,000
(4) Additions to voucher register:

    House expenses   17,000
    Snack bar and soda fountain   26,000
    General and administrative   11,000

(5) Vouchers paid   55,000
(6) Assessments for capital improve- ments not yet incurred (assessed on March 20, 1983: none collected by March 31, 1983: deemed 100% collectible during year ending March 31, 1984)   10,000
(7) Unrestricted bequest received   5,000

Adjustment data:

(1) Investments are valued at market, which amounted to $65,000 at March 31, 1983. There were no investment transactions during the year.
(2) Depreciation for the year:
    Building $4,000
    Furniture and equipment   8,000
(3) Allocation of depreciation:
    House expenses   9,000
    Snack bar and soda fountain   2,000
    General and administrative   1,000
(4) Actual physical inventory at March 31, 1983 was $1,000, and pertains to the snack bar and soda fountain.

Required:

On a functional basis
    a. Record the transactions and adjustments in journal entry form for the year ended March 31, 1983. Omit explanations.
    b. Prepare the appropriate all-inclusive activity statement for the year ended March 31, 1983.

Problem 5   (586,Q5)

(40 to 50 minutes)

Listed below are four independent transac- tions or events that relate to a local govern- ment and to a voluntary health and welfare organization:

[1] $25,000 was disbursed from the general fund (or its equivalent) for the cash purchase of new equipment.

[2] An unrestricted cash gift of $100,000 was received from a donor.

[3] Listed common stocks with a total carrying value of $50,000, exclusive of any allowance, were sold by an endowment fund for $55,000, before any dividends were earned on these stocks. There were no restrictions on the gain.

[4] $1,000,000 face amount of general obligation bonds payable were sold at par, with the proceeds required to be used solely for construction of a new building. This building was com- pleted at a total cost of $1,000,000, and the total amount of bond issue proceeds was disbursed in connection therewith. Disregard interest capi- talization.

Required:

    a.   For each of the above listed trans-
actions or events, prepare journal entries,
without explanations, specifying the affected
funds and account groups, and showing how
these transactions or events should be recorded by a local government whose debt is
serviced by general tax revenues.

    b.   For each of the above listed trans-
actions or events, prepare journal entries,
without explanations, specifying the affected
funds, and showing how these transactions or
events should be recorded by a voluntary
health and welfare organization that maintains
a separate plant fund.

Multiple Choice Answers

1. b	15. b	29. a	43. d	57. c
2. a	16. a	30. b	44. b	58. c
3. a	17. b	31. c	45. b	59. a
4. c	18. a	32. d	46. a	60. c
5. a	19. c	33. c	47. b	61. b
6. c	20. d	34. b	48. a	62. b
7. c	21. d	35. a	49. c	63. c
8. b	22. d	36. d	50. b	64. b
9. c	23. d	37. c	51. d	65. b
10. a	24. b	38. a	52. b	66. a
11. d	25. d	39. a	53. b	67. b
12. d	26. a	40. d	54. c	68. c
13. a	27. c	41. d	55. a	69. b
14. a	28. a	42. b	56. a	

Multiple Choice Answer Explanations

A. College and University Accounting

1. (1188,Q3,53) (b) Chapter 5 of the AICPA Colleges and Universities Audit Guide states that endowment income includes endowment and similar funds' unrestricted income, endowment and similar funds' restricted income to the extent expended for operational purposes, and income from funds held in trust by others under irrevocable trusts. Beech University's endowment income for the year ended June 30, 1988 is therefore $300,000 unrestricted income received plus $75,000 restricted income received to the extent expended for current operations, or $375,000. Therefore, answer (b) is correct.

2. (1188,Q3,54) (a) The plant fund consists of four categories per the AICPA College and University Audit Guide: unexpended funds to be used in the acquisition of physical properties, funds for the retirement of indebtedness on these properties, funds for the renewal and replacement of the properties, and funds previously expended to acquire properties. As of July 31, 1988, all of the funds are properly includible in Sabio College's plant funds, for a total of $900,000. Therefore, answer (a) is correct.

3. (1188,Q3,55) (a) Per the AICPA Audits of Colleges and Universities, Chapter 5, student tuition and fees include all student tuition and fees assessed (net of refunds) against students for educational and general purposes. Tuition and fee remissions or exemptions should be assessed and reported as revenue even though there is no intention of collecting from the student. Therefore, the total amount assessed, $4,000,000, should be included in the educational and general current funds as revenues from student tuition and fees.

4. (588,Q3,59) (c) Per AICPA Audits of Colleges and Universities, Chapter 5, current funds revenues include (1) all unrestricted gifts and other unrestricted resources earned during the reporting period, and (2) restricted current funds to the extent that such funds were expended for current operating purposes. Current funds revenues do not include restricted current funds received but not expended, nor resources which are restricted by outside persons or agencies to loan funds, endowment or term endowment funds, annuity and life income funds, plant funds, or agency funds. Therefore, the amount that should be included in current funds revenues for the year ended March 31, 1988 is:

Unrestricted gifts received	
Expended	$600,000
Not expended	75,000
Restricted gifts received	
Expended	100,000
TOTAL	$775,000

Therefore, answer (c) is correct.

5. (588,Q3,60) (a) Per AICPA Audits of Colleges and Universities, current funds expenditures accounts should bear identifying codes and symbols that will identify functions, such as Instruction, Institutional Support, and Scholarships and Fellowships; identify organizational units, such as Department of Physics, Controller's Office, and Registrar's Office, and identify the object of expenditures, such as Personnel Compensation, Supplies and Expenses, and Capital Expenditures. The audit guide provides an extensive listing as to what constitutes Institutional Support. Of the three items in this question, only administrative data processing is included under the functional classification of Institutional Support. Therefore, answer (a) is correct. Scholarships and Fellowships and Operations and Maintenance of Plant are separate functional classifications. Therefore, answers (b), (c), and (d) are incorrect.

6. (589,Q2,32) (c) Per AICPA Audits of Colleges and Universities, Chapter 5, the fund balance of unrestricted current funds represents the difference between the assets and liabilities, including deferred revenues, of unrestricted current funds. Therefore, the fund balance is $3,000,000 ($7,500,000 − $4,500,000), and answer (c) is correct.

7. (589,Q2,33) (c) Per AICPA Audits of Colleges and Universities, Chapter 5, current funds revenues include (1) all unrestricted

gifts and other unrestricted resources earned during the reporting period and (2) restricted current funds to the extent that such funds were expended for current operating purposes. Current funds revenues do not include restricted current funds received but not expended, nor resources which are restricted by outside persons or agencies to loan funds, endowment or term endowment funds, annuity and life income funds, plant funds, or agency funds. The amount that should be included in current funds revenues is:

Unrestricted gifts	$550,000
Restricted grants	
(expended for current	
operating purposes)	220,000
TOTAL	$770,000

Therefore, answer (c) is correct.

8.   (589,Q2,34) (b) In order to provide an accurate measurement of performance, a university should recognize donated services as expenditures, with an equivalent amount recorded as revenues. In addition, the organization must have a clearly measurable basis for the amount to be recorded. Equivalent wages in the area for similar services provides a clearly measurable basis for recording the donated services. Therefore, answer (b) is correct.

9.   (582,Q2,24) (c) The requirement is the gift revenue that should be reported in the restricted column of the Statement of Current Fund Revenues, Expenditures, and Other Changes for the year ended 6/30/81. The AICPA Colleges and Universities Audit Guide states the donor-restricted resources designated for specific operating purposes should be accounted for in a restricted fund or as defined revenue in the unrestricted fund. These resources should be reported as revenue in the financial statements of the period in which expenditures are made for the purpose intended by the donor. In 1981 revenues would be recognized to the extent of the 1981 research expenditures - $1,100,000.

10.   (582,Q2,31) (a) The requirement is the journal entry required on the books of the trust fund beneficiary. Funds held in trust by others are resources neither in the possession of nor under the control of the institution. They are held and administered by outside fiscal agents, with the institution deriving income from such funds. The AICPA Colleges and Universities Audit Guide states that funds held in trust by others preferably should not be included in the balance sheet

with other funds administered by the institution, but should be disclosed parenthetically in the endowment and similar funds group in the balance sheet or in the notes to the financial statements.

11.   (588,T1,59) (d) The following funds are usually encountered in a not-for-profit university:

(1)   Current Funds
    (a)   Unrestricted
    (b)   Restricted

(2)   Loan Funds

(3)   Endowment and similar funds

(4)   Annuity and Life Income Funds

(5)   Plant Funds
    (a)   Unexpended
    (b)   Investment in Plant
    (c)   Funds for Retirement of Indebtedness
    (d)   Funds for Renewals and Replacements

(6)   Agency Funds

Both current funds and plant funds are usually encountered, and, therefore, answer (d) is correct.

12.   (589,T1,60) (d) The following funds are usually encountered in a not-for-profit university:

(1)   Current Funds
    (a)   Unrestricted
    (b)   Restricted

(2)   Loan Funds

(3)   Endowment and similar funds

(4)   Annuity and Life Income Funds

(5)   Plant Funds
    (a)   Unexpended
    (b)   Investment in Plant
    (c)   Funds for Retirement of Indebtedness
    (d)   Funds for Renewals and Replacements

(6)   Agency Funds

Both loan funds and life income funds are usually encountered, and, therefore, answer (d) is correct.

13.   (1187,T1,57) (a) Per AICPA of Voluntary Health and Welfare Organizations, voluntary health and welfare organizations record transactions involving fixed assets used in connection with their program or supporting services in a separate land, buildings, and equipment fund. Likewise, per AICPA Audits of Colleges and Universities, Chapter 9, plant funds are also used by colleges and universities to account for land, buildings, equipment, and other capital assets. Therefore, answer (a) is correct and answers (b), (c), and (d) are incorrect.

14. (1187,T1,60) (a) Per AICPA Audits of
Colleges and Universities, the current funds
group includes those economic resources of the
institution which are expendable for any purpose in performing the primary objectives of
the institution. Agency funds group consists
of funds held by an institution as custodian
or fiscal agent for others such as student organizations, individual students, or faculty
members. Transactions of agency funds represent charges or credits to the individual
asset and liability accounts and are not
transactions of unrestricted or restricted
current funds. Plant funds consist of funds
used for acquisition, renewal, or replacement
of physical properties or set aside for debt
service charges and for the retirement of
indebtedness on institutional properties.
Since the agency funds and the plant funds are
two separate and distinct fund groups and the
funds' resources are not expendable for any
purpose, they are not included within the current funds subgroup. Therefore, answer (a) is
correct and answers (b), (c), and (d) are incorrect.

15. (589,T1,57) (b) Per the AICPA Audits of
Colleges and Universities Audit Guide, endowment funds are funds with respect to which
donors or other outside agencies have stipulated, as a condition of the gift instrument,
that the principal is to be maintained invio-
late and in perpetuity and invested for the
purpose of producing present and future income
which may either be expended or added to principal. Term endowment funds are similar to
endowment funds except that, upon the passage
of a stated period of time or the happening of
a particular event, all or a part of the principal may be expended. Quasi-endowment funds
(funds functioning as endowment) are funds
which the governing board of an institution,
rather than a donor or other outside agency,
has determined are to be retained and invested. Since these funds are internally
designated rather than externally restricted,
the governing board has the right to decide at
any time to expend the principal. Agency
funds are used to account for monies held for
others. Therefore, answer (b) is correct.

16. (587,T1,57) (a) Per SOP 74-8, Financial
Accounting and Reporting by Colleges and Universities, funds which the governing board of
an institution, rather than a donor or other
outside agency, has determined are to be retained and invested for other than loan or
plant purposes would be accounted for in the
quasi-endowment fund. Endowment funds are
used to account for funds which are restricted
by outside sources, and therefore answer (b)
is incorrect. Quasi-endowment funds are
usually set aside to fulfill the same purpose

as endowment funds and therefore are accounted
for in the same manner as endowment funds.
The only significant difference is that donors
or other outside agencies require that endowment fund principal be used for the production
of income whereas principal of quasi-endowment
funds is retained and invested voluntarily by
the governing board of an institution. Agency
funds, per Industry Audit Guide for Audits of
Colleges and Universities, Chapter 10, consist
of funds held by an institution as custodian
or fiscal agent for others such as student organizations, individual students, or faculty
members. Therefore, answer (c) is incorrect.
Answer (d) is incorrect because current
funds--restricted, per Chapter 4, consists of
those funds expendable for operating purposes
but restricted by donors or other outside
agencies as to the specific purpose for which
they may be expended.

17. (585,T1,59) (b) The requirement is to
determine whether tuition waivers and unrestricted bequests should be included in the
current fund revenues of a not-for-profit
private university. Answer (b) is correct
because the AICPA Colleges and Universities
Audit Guide states that current funds revenue
includes both tuition waivers and unrestricted
bequests. Answers (a), (c), and (d) are incorrect.

18. (1183,T1,59) (a) Per the AICPA Colleges
and Universities Audit Guide, current funds
are those which are expendable for any purpose
in performing the primary objectives of the
institution. Term endowment funds are those
in which the principal is required to be kept
intact in perpetuity until a certain event or
condition (e.g., time passage) has been met,
and then all or part of the principal may be
expended. Life income funds receive gifts or
amounts from donors which constitute principal, with the principal's earnings being
paid to the donor annually while living. Upon
the donor's death, the principal may then be
transferred to the current funds group. Since
the principal amount in the term endowment and
life income funds is not readily available for
expenditures, they may not be included within
the current funds subgroups.

19. (583,T1,60) (c) Per the AICPA Colleges
and Universities Audit Guide, tuition waivers
for which there is no intention of collection
from the student should be assessed and reported as revenue. The amount of the waiver
should also be recorded as an expenditure and
appropriately classified as student aid, or as
staff benefits associated with the functional
category to which the student personnel relate.

20. (582,T1,59) (d) Per the AICPA Colleges and Universities Audit Guide, both unrestricted and restricted current funds are utilized for current expenditures.

21. (579,T1,45) (d) The requirement is the type of receipt to be accounted for in the restricted current funds of a university. Research grants are usually made with specific restrictions as to expenditure and accordingly are accounted for in current restricted funds. Tuition, laboratory fees, and housing fees are within the general operations of a university and thus are not restricted resources, i.e., they are used to fund general operations.

B. Hospital Accounting*

22. (1188,Q3,56) (d) Per the AICPA Hospital Audit Guide, Chapter 6, the patient service revenue account should show a complete summary of gross revenues earned at established rates on an accrual basis. Items such as charity allowances, courtesy allowances, policy discounts, and contractual adjustments or discounts to third-party payors should be reported (net of any related revenues) as a deduction from gross patient service revenues. Therefore, Cura Hospital should report the full $9,000,000 [answer (d)] as patient service revenues for the year ended December 31, 1987.

23. (1188,Q3,57) (d) Per Chapter 2 of the AICPA Hospital Audit Guide, donated services of individuals should be recorded at their fair market value when there is the equivalent of an employer-employee relationship and an objective basis for valuing such services. Because no employer-employee relationship exists with the volunteers, no amount should be reported as nonoperating revenue. Therefore, answer (d) is correct. Note that if such a relationship did exist, the services would be valued at their fair value of $25,000 and reported as an expense with an offsetting credit to nonoperating revenue.

24. (1188,Q3,58) (b) Per AICPA Hospital Audit Guide, Chapter 1, donation of medicines, linen, office supplies, and other materials which normally would be purchased by a hospital should be recorded at fair market value and reported as other operating revenue. Therefore, $2,000 would be shown as other operating revenue, and answer (b) is correct. Answer (a) is incorrect because a journal

entry would be required. Answers (c) and (d) are incorrect because the donated medicines are revenues (i.e., not a decrease in expenses).

25. (588,Q3,51) (d) Per the AICPA Hospital Audit Guide, funds held in a trust by outside parties should not be included in the hospital balance sheet. Because West National Bank was appointed as trustee of the fund, the fund will not appear on Elm's books. However, the AICPA Hospital Audit Guide does encourage footnote disclosure of the endowment fund's existence and terms. Therefore, Elm should make a memorandum entry [answer (d)].

26. (588,Q3,52) (a) Per the AICPA Hospital Audit Guide, nonoperating revenue includes revenue not directly related to patient care, related patient services, or the sale of related goods. Also, per the AICPA Hospital Audit Guide, donations of property should be recorded in the unrestricted fund balance at fair market value as of the date of contribution, unless designated for endowment or other restricted purposes. Therefore, the donation of common stock should be reported as nonoperating revenue at its $50,000 fair market value on the date of contribution.

27. (588,Q3,53) (c) The carrying amount of a marketable equity securities portfolio of a not-for-profit hospital must be the lower of its aggregate cost or market value, determined at the balance sheet date. The amount by which the aggregate cost of the portfolio exceeds market value should be accounted for as valuation allowance (SOP 78-1). The proper balance in the valuation allowance account on the 1986 balance sheet was $10,000, computed as the difference between the $300,000 cost and the $290,000 fair market value at the end of 1986. The proper balance in the valuation allowance account on the 1987 balance sheet should be $50,000, computed as the difference between the $300,000 cost and the $250,000 fair market value at the end of 1987. Therefore, the year-end adjustment to (change in) the valuation allowance account should reflect a $40,000 increase [answer (c)].

28. (588,Q3,54) (a) Per the AICPA Hospital Audit Guide, property, plant, and equipment and related liabilities should be accounted for as part of general funds, since segregation in a separate fund would imply the existence of restrictions on asset use. Also, per

*It is important to note that unrestricted funds has been used historically to identify those funds that are not restricted by donors or grantors; however, per Statement of Position 85-1, unrestricted funds should now be referred to as general funds.

SOP 85-1, para 7, assets set aside by the governing board for identified (designated) purposes and over which the board retains control and may, at its discretion, subsequently use for other purposes are recorded in the general (unrestricted) funds section of the balance sheet. Therefore, both plant assets and board designated assets (i.e., assets whose use is limited) should be reported as unrestricted (general) funds.

29. (1187,Q3,41) (a) Per the AICPA Hospital Audit Guide, Chapter 2, property, plant, and equipment and related liabilities should be accounted for as a part of general (unrestricted) funds, not restricted funds. Segregation in a separate fund would imply the existence of restrictions on the assets use. Therefore, the answer is $0.

30. (1187,Q3,46) (b) Per AICPA Hospital Audit Guide, Chapter 2, patient service revenues should be reported at established rates on the accrual basis in the period during which service is provided; other accounting methods, such as the "discharge method," are not acceptable. Therefore, Palma should report patient service revenues for 1986 of $8,000,000.

31. (1187,Q3,51) (c) Per SOP 85-1, para 7, assets set aside by the governing board for identified purposes and over which the board retains control and may, at its discretion, subsequently use for other purposes are recorded in the general (unrestricted) funds section of the balance sheet. Per AICPA Hospital Audit Guide, Chapter 1, endowment resources include pure endowment funds (the principal of which may not be expended by the governing board). This endowment fund should be accounted for as restricted funds. Therefore, $300,000 should be accounted for as part of general (unrestricted) funds.

32. (582,Q2,40) (d) The requirement is how the designated funds should be classified on Lilydale's balance sheet at 6/30/82. Per Statement of Position 85-1, para 7, assets set aside by the governing board for identified purposes and over which the board retains control and may, at its discretion, subsequently use for other purposes will be included in the general funds section of the balance sheet as assets whose use is limited. Therefore, answer (d) is correct.

33. (1188,T1,59) (c) Per the AICPA Hospital Audit Guide, other operating revenues [answer (c)] include revenue from nonpatient care services to patients, and sales and activities to persons other than patients. These revenues are normal to the day-to-day operations of a hospital and should be accounted for separately from patient revenues. The proceeds from sales of cafeteria meals and guest trays to visitors is an example of such a revenue. Answer (a), patient service revenues are revenues derived from the primary operations of the hospital and include daily patient services, other nursing services, and other professional services, also known as ancillary service revenue, [answer (b)]. Answer (d), other nonoperating revenue, includes revenue not directly related to patient care, related patient services, or the sale of related goods. Therefore, answers (a), (b), and (d) are incorrect.

34. (588,T1,60) (b) Per AICPA Hospital Audit Guide, Chapter 6, other operating revenue normally includes revenue from educational programs, research, and other specific purpose grants (i.e., revenue from grants, gifts, or subsidies specified by the donor for research, educational, or other programs), and other miscellaneous items. Therefore, answer (b) is correct.

35. (587,T1,59) (a) Per the AICPA's Hospital Audit Guide, Chapter 6, other operating revenues would include revenue from educational programs, but not unrestricted gifts. Other operating revenue includes revenue from nonpatient care services to patients, and sales and activities to persons other than patients. Such revenue is normal day-to-day operation of a hospital and should be accounted for separately from patient service revenue. Nonoperating revenue, on the other hand, includes revenue not directly related to patient care, related patient service, or sales of related goods. It normally includes unrestricted gifts, unrestricted income from endowment funds, donated services, gain on sale of hospital properties, income and gains from investments of unrestricted funds, and net rentals of facilities not used in hospital operations. Therefore, answers (b), (c), and (d) are incorrect.

36. (1189,T1,59) (d) Per the AICPA's Hospital Audit Guide, Chapter 6, other operating revenues would include revenue from educational programs. Other operating revenue also includes revenue from nonpatient care services to patients, and sales and activities to persons other than patients. Such revenue is normal day-to-day operation of a hospital and should be accounted for separately from patient service revenue. Ancillary service is a subcategory of patient service; therefore,

both (a) and (b) are incorrect. <u>Nonoperating revenue</u>, on the other hand, includes revenue not directly related to patient care, related patient service, or sales of related goods. It normally includes unrestricted gifts, unrestricted income from endowment funds, donated services, gain on sale of hospital properties, income and gains from investments of unrestricted funds, and net rentals of facilities not used in hospital operations. Therefore, answer (c) is incorrect.

37. (584,T1,59) (c) The requirement is to determine which of the alternatives is considered an unrestricted resource and, therefore, would be included in the general funds of a not-for-profit hospital. The <u>AICPA Hospital Audit Guide</u> states that the term <u>restricted</u> should not be used in connection with board or other internal hospital appropriations or designations of funds. The reasoning is that if the governing board can appropriate resources in such a manner, it can also rescind such action. Therefore, answer (c) is correct. The AICPA Audit Guide identifies three categories: (1) funds for specific operating purposes, (2) funds for additions to property, plant, and equipment, and (3) endowment funds. Answers (a), (b), and (d) are incorrect because all fall into one of the categories identified.

38. (1182,T1,60) (a) Per the <u>AICPA Hospital Audit Guide</u>, an <u>unrestricted</u> pledge should appear as nonoperating revenue in the financial statements of the period in which the pledge is made. Answer (b) is incorrect because unless the donor specifies that part or all of the pledge is to be applied to a future period(s) (if such a restriction were made, deferred or restricted revenue would be recorded in 1981), the entire amount should be recognized as nonoperating revenue in 1981. Answers (c) and (d) are incorrect because such pledges are not part of the revenue from operations, i.e., the revenue does not come from patients who receive care from the hospital.

39. (589,Q2,29) (a) Per <u>AICPA Hospital Audit Guide</u>, gifts, grants, and bequests that are not restricted by donors are subject to designation by the governing board and should be reported as nonoperating revenue and not credited directly to fund balance. It is deemed that such revenue is available for the same uses as patient service revenue; however, it is not operating revenue. Therefore, answer (a) is correct and answers (b), (c), and (d) are incorrect.

40. (589,Q2,30) (d) Per <u>AICPA Hospital Audit Guide</u>, Chapter 1, endowment resources

include pure endowment funds (the principal of which may be expended by the governing board). This endowment fund should be accounted for as restricted funds upon receipt. Therefore, answer (d) is correct. Answers (a) and (b) are incorrect because, by definition, the principal of a pure endowment fund may not be expended. Answer (c) is incorrect because an entry must be made upon receipt of the funds.

41. (589,Q2,31) (d) Per the <u>AICPA Hospital Audit Guide</u>, funds held in trust by outside parties should not be included in the hospital balance sheet. Therefore, the fund will not appear on Lori's books. However, the <u>AICPA Audit Guide</u> does encourage footnote disclosure of the endowment fund's existence and terms. Therefore, answer (d) is correct.

C. Voluntary Health and Welfare Organizations

42. (589,Q2,36) (b) Per the <u>AICPA Audits of Voluntary Health and Welfare Organizations Audit Guide</u>, the amount of all pledges should be recorded when the pledges are obtained, and provisions should be made for uncollectible pledges. The allowance for uncollectible pledges and the net amount of pledges receivable should be disclosed in the financial statements of the organization. Therefore, Rega should include $528,000 (i.e., $600,000 -$72,000) under public support in 1988 for net contributions, and answer (b) is correct.

43. (589,Q2,37) (d) When an asset is sold in a voluntary health and welfare organization, it is necessary to transfer the carrying amount of the asset from Fund balance—expended to Fund balancer—unexpended, in addition to recording the disposal of the asset. Note that the Fund balance in the land, building, and equipment fund is segregated into Fund balance—expended and Fund balance—unexpended. The additional entry required is as follows:

Fund balance—expended   15,000
   Fund balance—unexpended   15,000

Therefore, answer (d) is correct. Note that Fund balance—expended represents the net book value of the fixed assets and Fund balance—unexpended represents assets available for future plant expenditures.

44. (589,Q2,38) (b) When an asset is sold in a voluntary health and welfare organization, it is necessary to transfer the carrying amount of the asset from Fund balance—expended to Fund balance—unexpended, in addition to recording the disposal of the asset. Note that the Fund balance in the land, building, and equipment fund is segregated

into Fund balance--expended and Fund balance--unexpended. The additional entry required is as follows:

Fund balance--expended 15,000
    Fund balance--unexpended 15,000

Therefore, answer (b) is correct. Note that Fund balance--expended represents the net book value of the fixed assets and Fund Balance--unexpended represents assets available for future plant expenditures.

45. (584,Q3,44) (b) The requirement is the Community's net contribution revenue for 1983 with respect to the pledges. The AICPA Voluntary Health and Welfare Organizations Audit Guide requires that unless donors specify otherwise, donations and pledges should be recorded as support in the period received. Estimated uncollectible pledges should be treated as a reduction of such support, not as an expense. In this case, however, the half of the pledges receivable in 1984 are specified "for use in 1984." Therefore, the net contribution revenue for 1983 is [1/2($900,000 - .10($900,000)] or $405,000. Note that the remaining $405,000 not recognized in 1983 would be recorded as a deferred credit in the balance sheet of the appropriate fund.

46. (584,Q3,45) (a) Per the AICPA Voluntary Health and Welfare Organizations Audit Guide, the fair market value of donated services should be reported both as a contributed service revenue and contributed service expense, provided an employer-employee relationship exists. Answer (b) is incorrect because it includes only one half of the contributed services. Answer (c) is incorrect because it assumes a value less than market value. Answer (d) is incorrect because it would fail to recognize the true cost of Community's operation.

47. (1188,T1,57) (b) Per the AICPA Audits of Voluntary Health and Welfare Organizations Audit Guide, the plant fund is used to accumulate the net investment in fixed assets and to account for the unexpended resources contributed specifically for the purpose of acquiring or replacing land, buildings, or equipment for use in the operations of the organization. Therefore, answer (b) is correct.

48. (1188,T1,60) (a) Per the AICPA Audit Guide for Voluntary Health and Welfare Organizations, contributions to the building fund should be included in a statement of support, revenue, and expenses and changes in fund balance as an element of support when received

[answer (a)]. Note that if a portion of the contribution received is specified by the donor for use in a future period, that portion should be recorded as a deferred credit in the balance sheet and recorded as support in the year in which it may be used. Examples of items included as elements of revenue [answer (b)] are membership dues, investment income, and realized gains on investment transactions. Examples of items included as an element of other changes in fund balances [answer (c)] are property acquisitions from unrestricted funds and returns to donors. Answer (d) is incorrect because the contributions must be included as an element of support.

49. (1189,T1,58) (a) Per Industry Audit Guide for Audits of Voluntary Health and Welfare Organizations, Chapter 3, depreciation expense should be recognized as a cost of rendering current services and should be included as an element of expense in the statement of support, revenue, and expenses of the fund in which the assets are recorded and in the statement of functional expenditures. Therefore, answer (a) is correct and answer (d) is incorrect. Examples of elements included as other changes in fund balances [answer (b)] include fixed asset acquisitions from unrestricted funds, realized endowment fund appreciation, and returns to donors. Items generally included as elements of support include funds derived from contributions, special events, bequests, mail campaigns, and solicitations (i.e., cash inflows from the public). Expenses are excluded from such elements. Therefore, answer (c) is incorrect.

50. (586,T1,60) (b) The requirement is to determine how securities which are donated to a voluntary health and welfare organization should be recorded. Per the AICPA Audit Guide for Audits of Voluntary Health and Welfare Organizations, Chapter 2, page 5, securities donated to the organization should be recorded at their fair value at the date of the gift. The donation of investments that have been restricted as to use should be included as contributions to the endowment or other restricted funds, whereas unrestricted donations of investments should be reported as contributions in the current unrestricted fund. Since the basis of valuation is the fair market value of the donated security, answers (a), (c), and (d) are incorrect.

51. (1185,T1,59) (d) The requirement is to identify the proper period for recognizing support (revenue) received in 1983 from a donor specifying that the amount donated be

used in 1985. Per the <u>AICPA Audit Guide for</u>
<u>Voluntary Health and Welfare Organizations,</u>
Chapter 4, donations are to be recorded as
assets (here, a debit to cash). If portions
of amounts received in one year are designated
for use in subsequent years, such portions
should be reported as a deferred credit in the
balance sheet in the year of receipt and recorded as support in the year in which the
donor permitted use.

52. (579,T1,46) (b) The land, building, and
equipment fund in voluntary health and welfare
organizations is used to account for the net
investment in fixed assets and also used to
account for unexpended resources contributed
specifically for the purpose of replacing
land, building, and equipment. Mortgages or
liabilities are also included in the fund, and
depreciation is recorded on fixed assets.
Thus, there is no comparable fund in governmental accounting. Answer (a) is incorrect
because unrestricted current funds are somewhat similar to special revenue funds in governmental accounting. Answer (c) is incorrect
because custodian funds are similar to agency
funds in governmental accounting. Answer (d)
is incorrect because endowment funds in voluntary health and welfare organizations are similar to endowment funds in governmental accounting.

D. SOP 78-10 "Accounting Principles and Reporting Practices for Certain Non-profit Organizations

53. (1188,Q3,51) (b) Per SOP 78-10,
para 20, unrestricted funds are the net amount
of resources available without (outside) restriction for carrying out the organization's
objectives. Those resources include amounts
designated by the board for specific purposes,
undesignated amounts, and frequently, amounts
invested in operating plant. Only assets restricted by outside donors or grantors should
be classified as restricted. Because Gant did
not specify how gains and losses from dispositions of endowment assets were to be treated,
the $50,000 of realized gains become part of
the nonexpendable endowment fund principal.
Since no restrictions were placed on the use
of dividends received and interest earned on
fund resources, Lane should classify the
$40,000 of interest and dividends as un-
restricted current funds. Therefore, answer (b) is correct.

54. (1188,Q3,52) (c) Per SOP 78-10,
para 20, unrestricted funds are the net amount
of resources available without (outside) restriction for carrying out the organization's
objectives. Those resources include amounts

designated by the board for specific purposes,
undesignated amounts, and frequently, amounts
invested in operating plant. Only assets restricted by outside donors or grantors should
be classified as restricted. Therefore, the
$100,000 board designated funds are classified
as unrestricted current funds and the $200,000
bequest restricted by the donor (benefactor)
should be classified as current restricted
funds. As a result, answer (c) is correct.

55. (1188,Q3,59) (a) Per <u>AICPA Audits of</u>
<u>Certain Nonprofit Organizations</u>, para 84,
revenue derived from membership dues should be
recognized by the organization over the period
to which the dues relate. Nonrefundable initiation and life membership fees should be
recognized as revenue in the period the fees
are receivable, if future dues or fees can
reasonably be expected to cover the cost of
future services; otherwise, the fees should be
amortized to future periods based on average
membership duration, life expectancy, or other
appropriate methods. However, if items such
as dues, assessments, and nonrefundable initiation fees are in substance contributions
and services not to be provided to the member,
they should be recognized as revenue and support in the periods in which the organization
is entitled to them. Because the nonrefundable initiation fees (collected and/or receivables) cover all costs of future services to
be provided to members, they should be recognized as revenue when they become receivable
(1987). Therefore, all $5,000 should be
recognized as revenue in 1987 [answer (a)].

56. (1188,Q3,60) (a) Per SOP 78-10,
para 107, exhaustible fixed assets should be
depreciated over their estimated useful life.
In addition, nonprofit organizations should
capitalize purchased fixed assets at cost.
Donated fixed assets should be recorded at
their fair value at the date of the gift.
Therefore, assuming a straight line basis, the
amount of depreciation would be $3,000
($30,000 ÷ 10 years), and answer (a) is cor-
rect.

57. (588,Q3,55) (c) Per SOP 78-10, para 62,
current restricted gifts, grants, bequests,
and other income should be accounted for as
revenue and support in the statement of activity of nonprofit organizations covered by
SOP 78-10 to the extent that expenses have
been incurred for the purpose specified by the
donor or grantor during the period. The balances that remain to be recognized in the
future when expenses are incurred for the specified purposes of the donor or grantor should
be accounted for as deferred revenue or sup-

port in the balance sheet. Therefore, answers (a) and (b) are incorrect because the
church had no expenses related to the gift for
the period ended March 31, 1988, and answer (d) is incorrect because deferred revenue
recognition is required.

58. (588,Q3,56) (c) Per SOP 78-10, fund-
raising costs are incurred in inducing others
to contribute money, securities, time, materials, or facilities for which the contributor
will receive no direct economic benefit. They
normally include the costs of personnel, occupancy, maintaining mailing lists, printing,
mailing, and all direct and indirect costs of
soliciting, as well as the cost of unsolicited
merchandise sent to encourage contributions.
Only the $20,000 cost of the unsolicited mer-
chandise was incurred in inducing others to
contribute. The $10,000 cost of printing the
annual report did not encourage contributions.
Therefore, answer (c) is correct.

May 1990 Answers

59. (590,Q1,11) (a) Per AICPA Audits of
Certain Nonprofit Organizations, resources
that are restricted for specified operating
purposes should be reported as deferred
support until the restrictions of the donor
have been met. In this case, the $200,000 is
to be considered deferred support until Ross's
death. Therefore, answer (a) is correct. Answer (b) is incorrect because the $16,000 in
interest earned is income generated from the
$200,000 donation, and not a reduction of the
principal balance. Answer (c) is incorrect
because the $16,000 interest income must be
remitted to Ross based on stipulations of the
donation, and should not be presented as a
support or revenue item. Answer (d) is incorrect because the gift needs to be recorded in
the financial statements.

60. (590,Q1,12) (c) Per AICPA Audits of
Certain Nonprofit Organization, expenses of
other nonprofit organizations that receive
significant support from the general public
should be appropriately categorized between
program expenses and supporting services.
Program expenses relate directly to the primary missions of the organization. Supporting
services do not relate directly to the primary
missions of the organization, and include
items such as management and general costs, as
well as fund-raising costs. Based on this definition, answer (c) is correct and answer (b)
is incorrect. Answer (a) is incorrect because
offsetting expenses against revenue and support is not a valid financial statement presentation. Answer (d) is incorrect because

the expense must be recognized separately as
part of supporting services, and not as a
direct reduction of fund balance.

61. (590,Q1,13) (b) Per the AICPA Audit
Guide for Voluntary Health and Welfare
Organizations, amounts of all pledges should
be recorded when the pledge is obtained.
Furthermore, provisions should be made for
uncollectible pledges based on the organization's policy, past experience, as well as
other pertinent factors. Since Lema Fund has
obtained pledges of $200,000 and the related
provision for uncollectible pledges was estimated at $20,000, net contributions under
public support should be $180,000 ($200,000 -
$20,000). Answers (a), (c), and (d) are all
incorrect. Note that the $50,000 in pledges
not collected in 1989 are included as part of
net contributions since the pledge was obtained in 1989.

62. (590,Q1,14) (b) Per the AICPA Audit
Guide for Voluntary Health and Welfare Organizations, when restrictions on endowment fund
principal lapse, the resources released should
be transferred to the unrestricted fund or to
a specific restricted fund, according to the
terms of the original gift or bequest. In
this case, no stipulation was made by the
donor as to the use of the $100,000 principal
upon maturation in 1989. Therefore, the endowment fund should report a reduction in fund
balance of $100,000 for the transfer to the
current unrestricted fund. Answer (a) is incorrect because Legacies and Bequests would be
credited in the endowment fund upon receipt of
the bequest in 1979, not upon its maturation
in 1989. Answer (c) is incorrect because the
entire $100,000 that is unrestricted needs to
be transferred to the current unrestricted
fund. Answer (d) is incorrect because bequests are considered public support and not
revenue. Revenue would include items such as
investment income or realized gain on investment transactions. In addition, the bequest
would be recorded when donated and not when
matured.

63. (590,Q1,15) (c) Per the AICPA Audit
Guide for Voluntary Health and Welfare
Organizations, when restrictions on endowment
fund principal lapse, the resources released
should be transferred to the unrestricted fund
or to a specific restricted fund, according to
the terms of the original gift or bequest. In
this case, no stipulation was made by the
donor as to the use of the $100,000 principal
upon maturation in 1989. Therefore, the
current unrestricted fund should report an
addition in fund balance of $100,000 for the

transfer from the endowment fund. Answer (a)
is incorrect because the investment income
should be reported in the current restricted
fund due to the terms of the original bequest.
Answer (b) is incorrect because the designation of $20,000 for the purchase of equipment
merely changes the current unrestricted fund
balance from "undesignated" to "designated for
purchase of equipment." The $20,000 would
only be transferred to the land, building, and
equipment fund upon use by that fund. Answer (d) is incorrect because the transfer
from the endowment fund to the current unrestricted fund is reported as a change in fund
balance and is not considered a public support
item.

64. (590,Q1,16) (b) Per the AICPA Audit
Guide for Voluntary Health and Welfare Organizations, when restrictions on endowment fund
principal lapse, the resources released should
be transferred to the unrestricted fund or to
a specific restricted fund, according to the
terms of the original gift or bequest. In
this case, no stipulation was made by the
donor as to the use of the $100,000 principal
upon maturation in 1989. Therefore, the current unrestricted fund should report a total
of $100,000 in the fund balance section. Of
this $100,000, $20,000 should be reported as
"designated for purchase of equipment" because
of the designation by the board of trustees.
The $20,000 would only be transferred to the
land, building, and equipment fund upon use by
that fund. The $80,000 remaining balance is
considered undesignated fund balance. Answers (a), (c), and (d) are incorrect because
the $20,000 should be reported in the current
unrestricted fund as designated for purchase
of equipment. The $20,00 would only be trans-
ferred to the land, building, and equipment
fund upon use by that fund. Also, the $8,000
of interest revenue should be reported in the
current restricted fund due to the terms of
the original bequest.

65. (590,Q1,17) (b) Per the AICPA Hospital
Audit Guide, gifts, grants, and bequests that
are not restricted by donors are subject to
designation by the governing board and should
be reported as nonoperating revenue and not
credited directly to fund balance. Therefore,
Metro General should report $11,000 as non-
operating revenue ($7,000 in unrestricted
gifts + $4,000 in unrestricted bequests). Al-
though it is deemed that such revenue is
available for the same use as patient service
revenue, it is not considered operating revenue since the revenue does not come from
patients who receive care from the hospital.
Therefore, answers (a), (c), and (d) are incorrect.

66. (590,Q1,18) (a) Per GASB Codification,
para H50.101, if a governmental reporting entity is required to include hospitals in its
combined financial statements, these governmental hospitals can best be accomodated in
the enterprise funds column, based on the accounting recommended in the AICPA Hospital
Audit Guide. Therefore, total long-term debt
in the enterprise fund type column would be
$900,000 ($100,00 of other enterprise fund
long-term debt + $800,000 of hospital long-
term debt). Answer (b) is incorrect because
netting long-term debt against fixed assets is
not a valid financial presentation. Answer (c)
is incorrect because enterprise funds
(including hospitals in this case) record
long-term debt within their own fund and not
in the general long-term debt account group.
Answer (d) is incorrect because the hospital's
financial presentation would not be shown
separate from the enterprise fund type column.

67. (590,Q1,19) (b) Per SOP 81-2, a hospital's financial statements should disclose
information concerning related organizations
which are not consolidated or combined with
the hospital if both of the folloiwng conditions are met: 1) the hospital controls the
separate organization with authority to direct
the organization's activities, management, and
policies, and 2) for all practical purposes,
the hospital is the sole beneficiary of the
organization. The disclosures required in the
notes to the hospital's financial statements
include summarized information about the
assets, liabilities, results of operations,
and changes in fund balances of the related
organizations. In this case, neither the
guild nor the auxiliary are consolidated with
the hospital's financial statements. The
guild meets the two requirements listed above
for disclosure in the notes to the hospital's
financial statement, which the auxiliary does
not, since the hospital does not have control
over the auxiliary. Therefore, only the
guild's assets of $20,000 need to be dis-
closed, and answers (a), (c), and (d) are incorrect.

68. (590,Q1,20) (c) Per GASB Codification,
para H50.101, if a governmental reporting entity is required to include hospitals in its
combined financial statements, these governmental hospitals can best be accomodated in
the enterprise funds column, based on the
accounting recommended in the AICPA Hospital
Audit Guide. Therefore, total fixed assets in
the enterprise fund type column would be
$1,700,000 ($500,000 of other enterprise fund
fixed assets + $1,200,000 of hospital fixed
assets). Answer (a) is incorrect because the
hospital's financial presentation would not be

shown separate of the enterprise fund type column. Answer (b) is incorrect because the hospital's fixed assets would be shown as part of the enterprise fund, not the special revenue fund. Answer (d) is incorrect because enterprise funds (including hospitals in this case) record fixed assets within their own fund and <u>not</u> in the general fixed assets account group.

69. (590,T1,60) (b) Per **AICPA Audits of Colleges and Universities**, Chapter 5, current funds revenues include (1) all unrestricted gifts and other unrestricted resources earned during the reporting period, and (2) restricted current funds to the extent that such funds were expended for current operating purposes. Current funds revenues do not include restricted current funds received but not expended, nor resources which are restricted by outside persons or agencies to loan funds, endowment or term endowment funds, annuity and life income funds, plant funds, or agency funds. Therefore, answer (b) is correct.

Solution Guide

**Problem 1   University Journal Entries and
                Statement of Changes in Fund
                Balance (1183,Q4)**

1. Number 1 consists of two related parts
    requiring university journal entries and
    a financial statement.

2. Part a. requires journal entries for ten
    transactions of Rapapo State Univer-
    sity. The entries are to be recorded in
    the current unrestricted and current
    restricted funds.

3. The solutions approach is to analyze each
    of the ten transactions and determine the
    fund affected and the appropriate journal
    entry or entries. The unrestricted cur-
    rent fund is used for all transactions
    not accounted for elsewhere, similar to
    the general fund in governmental ac-
    counting. The current restricted fund
    accounts for monies which have been
    externally restricted for specified cur-
    rent operating purposes. Note that by
    using the given 7/31/85 balance sheet and
    the additional information, you can find
    many "hints" as to which fund or accounts
    are to be used.

3.1 Tuition and fees are accounted for in the
    unrestricted fund. The $3,000,000 debit
    to cash is offset by a $362,000 credit to
    accounts receivable; a $2,500,000 credit
    to revenues for the current year tuition;
    and a $138,000 credit to deferred revenue
    for the tuition paid in advance.

3.2 The deferred revenue in the 7/31/85 bal-
    ance sheet was earned during the year.
    Therefore, deferred revenue is debited
    and revenues are credited.

3.3 Accounts receivable at 7/31/85 which were
    not collected in item one are uncollect-
    ible. Note that $375,000 of receivables
    were outstanding, since the $360,000
    listed in the balance sheet was net of a
    $15,000 allowance for doubtful accounts.
    Therefore, $13,000 of receivables
    ($375,000 total less $362,000 collected)
    must be written off by debiting the
    allowance account and crediting accounts
    receivable. Additionally, at year end
    the allowance account must be increased
    from $2,000 ($15,000 balance at 7/31/85
    less $13,000 of write-offs) to $10,000.
    This results in the recording of bad
    debts of $8,000.

3.4 The unrestricted state appropriation is
    recorded as revenue in the unrestricted
    fund on the accrual basis by debiting a
    receivable and crediting a revenue
    account.

3.5 Unrestricted cash gifts received are
    recorded as revenue in the unrestricted
    fund. Monies designated by the board of
    trustees to be transferred from unre-
    stricted funds to nonoperating funds,
    such as the $30,000 transfer in this
    problem, are called nonmandatory trans-
    fers. The transfer is recorded as a
    debit to fund balance.

3.6 The investments in the 7/31/85 balance
    sheet are held in the restricted fund.
    The $6,000 ($31,000 selling price less
    $25,000 cost) is credited directly to the
    restricted fund balance account. This is
    a peculiarity of university accounting;
    the earnings of current restricted funds
    are credited to fund balance when
    received and recognized as revenue when
    expended for the specified purpose.
    Similarly, the investment income
    ($18,000) is credited to fund balance.
    Investments purchased are recorded with a
    debit to investments and a credit to
    cash.

3.7 The unrestricted expenses recorded in the
    voucher system ($2,500,000) are recorded
    in the unrestricted fund by debiting ex-
    penditures and crediting accounts pay-
    able. When a voucher system is used, all
    expenditures run through accounts or
    vouchers payable. Since the accounts
    payable totaled $75,000 at year end, cash
    payments of $2,525,000 ($100,000 begin-
    ning balance plus $2,500,000 expendi-
    tures, less $75,000 ending balance) must
    also be recorded.

3.8 The restricted accounts payable at
    7/31/85 ($5,000) were paid; this is
    recorded by debiting accounts payable and
    crediting cash.

3.9 The $40,000 due to other funds was a lia-
    bility of the unrestricted funds on the
    7/31/85 balance sheet. Payment is
    recorded by debiting the liability and
    crediting cash.

3.10 The prepaid expenses in the unrestricted
    portion of the 7/31/85 balance sheet
    amounted to $40,000. Since one quarter
    of these prepayments expired, $10,000
    (1/4 x $40,000) must be debited to expen-
    ditures and credited to prepaid expenses.

4. Part b. requires a statement of changes
    in fund balances for the year ended
    7/31/86.

4.1 The statement of changes in fund balance
    is a primary university financial state-
    ment, as it explains the activity (in-

flows and outflows) for the restricted
and unrestricted current funds.

4.2   Unrestricted revenues include $2,500,000
tuition, $25,000 in deferred revenue
earned during the current year, a $60,000
appropriation from the state, and $80,000
in gifts. These revenues total
$2,665,000. Additions to the restricted
fund balance include the $6,000 gain on
sale of investments and the $18,000 of
investment income.

4.3   Unrestricted expenditures included
$2,500,000 for general expenses, $10,000
of expired prepayments, and $8,000 of bad
debts for a total of $2,518,000. There
were no restricted expenditures.

4.4   The nonmandatory transfer is not similar
to a normal expenditure and, therefore,
is reported in a separate section near
the bottom of the statement.

4.5   Finally, the beginning fund balance is
added to the net increase during the
year, to result in the ending fund
balance.

Unofficial Answer

Problem 1   University Journal Entries and Statement of Changes in Fund Balance (1183,Q4)

Part a.   Rapapo State University
                                       General Journal

Entry no.	Accounts	Current funds			
		Unrestricted		Restricted	
		Debit	Credit	Debit	Credit
1.	Cash	3,000,000			
	Accounts receivable--Tuition and fees		362,000		
	Revenues--Tuition and fees		2,500,000		
	Deferred revenue--Tuition and fees		138,000		
2.	Deferred revenue--Tuition and fees	25,000			
	Revenues--Tuition and fees		25,000		
3.	Allowance for doubtful accounts	13,000			
	Accounts receivable--Tuition and fees		13,000		
	Provision for uncollectible tuition and fees	8,000			
	Allowance for doubtful accounts		8,000		
4.	State appropriation receivable	60,000			
	Revenues--State appropriation		60,000		
5.	Cash	80,000			
	Revenues--Private gifts, grants, and contracts		80,000		
	Fund balance	30,000			
	Cash (or due to student loan fund)		30,000		
6.	Cash			31,000	
	Investments				25,000
	Fund balance--Gain on sale of investments				6,000
	Investments			40,000	
	Cash				40,000
	Cash			18,000	
	Fund balance--Investment income				18,000
7.	Expenditures--General expenses	2,500,000			
	Accounts payable		2,500,000		
	Accounts payable	2,525,000			
	Cash		2,525,000		
8.	Accounts payable			5,000	
	Cash				5,000
9.	Due to other funds	40,000			
	Cash		40,000		
10.	Expenditures--Education and general	10,000			
	Prepaid expenses		10,000		

Part b.   Rapapo State University
           Statement of Changes in Fund Balances
                Year Ended July 31, 1985

	Current funds	
	Unrestricted	Restricted
Revenues and other additions:		
Tuition and fees	$2,525,000	
State appropriation	60,000	
Gifts	80,000	
Realized gains on investments--Restricted		6,000
Investment income--Restricted		18,000
Total revenues and other additions	$2,665,000	$ 24,000
Expenditures and other deductions:		
Unrestricted expenditures	$2,518,000	
Transfers among funds-- additions/deductions:		
Nonmandatory transfer to student loan fund	(30,000)	
Net increase (decrease) for the year	$ 117,000	$ 24,000
Fund balance at beginning of year	435,000	215,000
Fund balance at end of year	$ 552,000	$239,000

Solution Guide

Problem 2   Hospital Worksheet (587,Q5)

1.   This problem requires the completion of a worksheet for a hospital. First, adjustments must be entered into the worksheet to adjust the account balances in accordance with principles of hospital fund accounting. Then, the adjusted balances must be distributed to the appropriate worksheet columns (general fund, endowment fund, and plant replacement and expansion fund).

2.   The first step is to prepare adjustments.

2.1   The first adjustment is for the endowment fund balance. The endowment fund balance should properly include the principal ($300,000) and the gains on sales of securities ($100,000), for a total of $400,000. The interest and dividends earned, used for the payment of current operating expenses, should have been transferred as revenue to the general fund with a corresponding decrease to the endowment fund balance. Therefore, an adjustment must be made to debit the endowment fund balance and credit general

(unrestricted) funds balance for $120,000.

2.2   The next adjustment concerns the land account. Donated assets are recorded by hospitals at their FMV at the time of donation, and that FMV is treated as cost. Therefore, Experanza's writeup of the land was inappropriate. An adjustment must be made to credit the land account for $60,000, and debit general (unrestricted) funds balance for the same amount.

2.3   The third adjustment is the correction of the allowance for depreciation. The problem states that depreciation on the building has been incorrectly computed. Depreciation on the original cost of the building should be 40/50 of $720,000, or $576,000. Depreciation on the elevator should be 20/20 of $80,000, or $80,000. Depreciation on the equipment is given as $90,000, so the correct total allowance for depreciation is $746,000 ($576,000 + $80,000 + $90,000). Therefore, the allowance must be adjusted with a credit of $336,000 ($746,000 - $410,000). The debit is to general (unrestricted) funds balance, to which the unrecorded depreciation expense would have been closed and the credit is to allowance for depreciation. Note that even though the elevator is completely depreciated, it is not removed from the books because it is apparently still in use.

2.4   The next adjustment is to record the fund balance designated for plant replacement. The policy is to invest cash equal to accumulated depreciation for the purpose of asset replacement. The adjusted allowance for depreciation of $746,000 less the existing investment in corporate bonds of $500,000 is the funding needed for asset replacement. The underfunding of $246,000 should be debited to due from general (unrestricted) funds and the credit is to plant replacement and expansion fund balance. The next entry would be the reciprocal entry for the above entry to remove the amount due to the plant replacement and expansion fund from the general (unrestricted) funds balance. The entry for this would be

General (unrestricted)
  funds balance   246,000
   Due to plant replace-
   ment and expansion
   fund   246,000

2.5   The next adjustment would be to allocate the other fund balances of $1,100,000 to the plant replacement and expansion fund

balance and the general (unrestricted)
funds balance. Note the endowment fund
balance includes only the principal
($300,000) and the gains on sales of
securities ($100,000), for a total of
$400,000. Therefore, the endowment funds
balance will not be allocated any of the
$1,100,000 that exists in the other fund
balances account. The $500,000 invest-
ment in corporate bonds was initially
credited to the other fund balances
account; therefore, this amount should be
transferred to the plant replacement and
expansion funds balance. The remainder
of $600,000 should be transferred to
general (unrestricted) funds balance.
The entry would be

Other fund balances	1,100,000	
Plant replacement		
and expansion fund		
balance		500,000
General (unrestricted)		
funds balance		600,000

3. The next step is to distribute the
    adjusted balances to the appropriate
    worksheet columns.

Unofficial Answer

Problem 2   Hospital Worksheet (587,Q5)

Esperanza Hospital
**WORKSHEET TO ADJUST GENERAL LEDGER BALANCES
AND TO ESTABLISH FUNDS**
January 1, 1987

Account	Trial Balance December 31, 1986		Adjustments		General (Unrestricted) Funds		Endowment Fund		Plant Replacement and Expansion Fund	
	Debit	Credit	Debit	Credit	Debit	Credit	Debit	Credit	Debit	Credit
Cash	60,000				60,000					
Investment in U.S. Treasury bills	400,000						400,000			
Investment in corporate bonds	500,000								500,000	
Interest receivable	10,000				10,000					
Accounts receivable	50,000				50,000					
Inventory	30,000				30,000					
Land	100,000			60,000(2)	40,000					
Building	800,000				800,000					
Equipment	170,000				170,000					
Allowance for depreciation		410,000		336,000(3)		746,000				
Accounts payable		20,000				20,000				
Notes payable		70,000				70,000				
Endowment fund balance		520,000	120,000(1)					400,000		
Other fund balances		1,100,000	1,100,000(6)							
Due from general (unrestricted) funds			246,000(4)						246,000	
Due to plant replacement and expansion fund				246,000(5)		246,000				
Plant replacement and expansion fund balance				246,000(4) 500,000(6)						746,000
General (unrestricted) funds balance			60,000(2)	120,000(1)						
			336,000(3)	600,000(6)						
			246,000(5)			78,000				
Totals	2,120,000	2,120,000	2,108,000	2,108,000	1,160,000	1,160,000	400,000	400,000	746,000	746,000

Esperanza Hospital
ADJUSTING JOURNAL ENTRIES
January 1, 1987

(Not Required)

	Debit	Credit
(1)		
Endowment fund balance	120,000	
General (unrestricted) funds balance		120,000
To transfer investment income		
(2)		
General (unrestricted) funds balance	60,000	
Land		60,000
To eliminate appreciation in land value		
(3)		
General (unrestricted) funds balance	336,000	
Allowance for depreciation		336,000

To correct allowance for
depreciation account as follows:

Building--$720,000 x 2% x 40 years	$576,000
Elevator--$80,000 x 5% x 20 years	80,000
Equipment (correctly computed)	90,000
Correct allowance for depreciation	746,000
Balance per books	410,000
Understatement	$336,000

	Debit	Credit
(4)		
Due from general (unrestricted) funds	246,000	
Plant replacement and expansion fund		246,000

Adjusted allowance for depreciation	$746,000
Investment in corporate bonds	500,000
Underfunded for asset replacement	$246,000

	Debit	Credit
(5)		
General (unrestricted) funds balance	246,000	
Due to plant replacement and expansion		246,000
Reciprocal entry for (4)		
(6)		
Other fund balances	1,100,000	
Plant replacement and expansion fund balance		500,000
General (unrestricted) funds balance		600,000
To allocate other fund balances		

Solution Guide

Problem 3   Voluntary Health & Welfare
            Organizations Journal Entries
            (1189,Q4)

1. This problem requires journal entries for
   a series of transactions. The entries
   are to be recorded in the current unrestricted and restricted funds, the land,
   buildings and equipment fund, and the
   endowment fund.

1.1 The solutions approach is to analyze each
   transaction and determine the fund affected and the appropriate journal entries. The unrestricted current fund is
   used for all transactions not accounted
   for elsewhere, similar to the general
   fund in governmental accounting. The
   current restricted fund accounts for resources available for specific current
   operations per donor specifications. The
   land, buildings, and equipment fund is
   used to account for investments in fixed
   assets including unexpended resources
   contributed specifically for replacement
   of fixed assets. Also accounted for in
   this fund are related obligations, depreciation, and sales of fixed assets. The
   endowment fund is used to account for
   donated amounts where the principal is
   required, by the donor, to be kept
   intact.

2. The pledges ($800,000 unrestricted and
   $50,000 designated for the building fund)
   are debited to pledges receivable and
   credited to contributions in the appropriate funds. The cash contributions
   received ($95,000 restricted and $1,000
   designated for the endowment fund) are
   debited to cash and credited to contributions in the appropriate funds. For this
   type of organization, revenue-like inflows are recorded either as public support (contributions, special events, legacies and bequests, and indirect support)
   or as revenues (dues, investment income,
   and charges for services).

2.1 The collection of pledges ($450,000 unre-
   stricted and $20,000 for the building
   fund) is recorded as a debit to cash and
   a credit to pledges receivable in the
   appropriate fund.

2.2 The other cash received from unrestricted
   sources ($12,000 from theatre party--a
   special event, $10,000 from bequests,
   $8,000 from membership dues, and $5,000
   from interest and dividends) is recorded
   in the unrestricted current fund as a
   debit to cash and as credits to either
   public support accounts (for the special
   event and bequests) or revenue accounts
   (for the membership dues and interest and
   dividends). Note that the AICPA Unofficial Answer credits the individual ac

counts instead of these two main categories. See item 2 above for further discussion of these two categories.

2.3 The program expenses incurred ($60,000
   for medical services and $15,000 for
   community information services) are recorded in the unrestricted current fund
   as debits to the two expense accounts and
   a credit to vouchers payable. Voluntary
   health and welfare organizations record
   expenses by function in the fund which
   incurred the expense.

2.4 The services expenses incurred ($150,000
   for general administration and $200,000
   for fund-raising) are recorded similarly
   to the program expenses (see 2.3 above)
   by debiting the two expense accounts and
   crediting vouchers payable in the unrestricted current fund.

2.5 As discussed in 1.1 above, all transactions involving the purchase, depreciation, sale, etc., of fixed assets are
   recorded in the land, buildings, and
   equipment fund (LBE fund). Therefore,
   when fixed assets are purchased with
   unrestricted cash ($18,000), the payment
   is recorded by the unrestricted current
   fund as a transfer to the LBE fund. This
   is done by debiting transfer to land,
   buildings, and equipment fund and
   crediting cash. The LBE fund does not
   receive the cash, but instead receives
   the purchased equipment. This is recorded as a debit to the specific fixed
   asset accounts and a credit to the expended fund balance. In effect, the current unrestricted fund is getting smaller
   (decrease in cash and increase in transfers) that in turn decrease fund balance
   while the LBE fund is getting bigger
   (increase in fixed assets and fund
   balance).

2.6 Voluntary health and welfare organizations record depreciation expense in the
   LBE fund. As discussed in 2.3, expenses
   are recorded by function. Therefore, the
   debits are to the specific expense accounts (medical services, $4,000; commu-
   nity information services, $3,000; gen-
   eral administration, $6,000; fund rais-
   ing, $2,000), with a credit to accumu-
   lated depreciation. Additionally, it is
   necessary to decrease fund balance-
   expended and to increase fund balance-
   unexpended. Note that the AICPA Unofficial Answer has a debit to depreciation
   expense in one entry and then a credit to
   depreciation expense in a separate allocation entry. This merely reflects bookkeeping alternatives used in practice.

2.7 The payment of vouchers payable is recorded in the unrestricted current fund
   as a debit to vouchers payable and a
   credit to cash.

Unofficial Answer

Problem 3   Voluntary Health & Welfare
     Organization Journal Entries
     (1189,Q4)

Children's Agency
JOURNAL ENTRIES
For the Year Ended June 30, 1989

Account Title	Current Fund Unrestricted Dr. (Cr.)	Restricted Dr. (Cr.)	Land, Buildings, and Equipment Fund Dr. (Cr.)	Endowment Fund Dr. (Cr.)
1. Pledges receivable	$ 800,000		$ 50,000	
Cash		$ 95,000		$ 1,000
Contributions	(800,000)	(95,000)	(50,000)	(1,000)
2. Cash	450,000		20,000	
Pledges receivable	(450,000)		(20,000)	
3. Cash	35,000			
Special events support	(12,000)			
Legacies and bequests	(10,000)			
Membership dues	(8,000)			
Investment revenue	(5,000)			
4. Medical services program	60,000			
Community information services program	15,000			
Vouchers payable	(75,000)			
5. Management and general services	150,000			
Fund raising services	200,000			
Vouchers payable	(350,000)			
6. Transfer to land, buildings,				
and equipment fund	18,000			
Cash	(18,000)			
Buildings and equipment			18,000	
Fund balance--expended			(18,000)	
7. Depreciation expense			15,000	
Accumulated depreciation			(15,000)	
Fund balance--expended			15,000	
Fund balance--unexpended			(15,000)	
Medical services program			4,000	
Community information services program			3,000	
Management and general services			6,000	
Fund raising services			2,000	
Depreciation expense			(15,000)	
8. Vouchers payable	330,000			
Cash	(330,000)			

Solution Guide

Problem 4   Journal Entries and All-Inclusive Activity Statement for Nonprofit Organization (583,Q5)

1.   This problem requires (1) transaction and adjusting entries, and (2) an activity statement for a nonprofit organization. Since this is not a Voluntary Health and Welfare Organization, the provisions of <u>AICPA Statement of Position 78-10, Accounting Principles and Reporting Practices for Certain Nonprofit Organizations</u>, would apply.

2.   The solutions approach for the journal entries is to approach the transactions and adjustments consecutively, relating each situation to SOP 78-10 principles. Account titles for the balance sheet accounts are given, and revenue and expense accounts would be generated using the descriptive phrases given for each numbered item.

2.1   The $20,000 is recorded as a credit to membership dues, which is considered to be revenue for the current period and will be included on the activity statement.

2.2   The $28,000 is a revenue of the organization, and the account title used is simply: Snack bar and soda fountain sales.

2.3   The $6,000 represents another investment revenue of the organization for the period.

2.4   Under SOP 78-10 rules, expenses are recorded on the accrual basis. The titles used for the expenses listed are as given. The amounts should be credited to either vouchers payable or accounts payable.

2.5   Since accrual accounting is used, the entry to pay the vouchers simply reduces the liability.

2.6   Under SOP 78-10, "capital additions that are restricted for acquisition of plant assets should be treated as deferred capital support in the balance sheet until they are used for the indicated purposes." (para .052)

2.7   The $5,000 unrestricted bequest is considered to be a current revenue.

2.8   SOP 78-10 permits carrying certain investments at market. When investments are carried at market, increases and decreases in market value are to be recognized in the current period. The $7,000 increase is, accordingly, credited to a gain account, unrealized gain on investments.

2.9   Under SOP 78-10, depreciation of fixed assets is to be recognized and recorded. Also, the beginning trial balance includes accumulated depreciation accounts.

2.10   Nonprofit organizations report expenses by function in the statement of activity. Also, the necessity of a functional classification is suggested by the adjustment data given. This entry reclassifies depreciation expense to functional categories.

2.11   The beginning trial balance includes a $5,000 balance in the inventory account. The reduction of $4,000 would be charged to the snack bar and soda fountain expense account used in entry number 4.

3.   SOP 78-10 contains several illustrative financial statements for nonprofit organizations, one of which is directly applicable to the organization described in this problem, i.e., a country club which is shown in para 131 of the SOP.

3.1   The title of the statement should be "Statement of revenues, expenses and charges in cumulative excess of revenues over expenses."

3.2   All the revenues are grouped together.

3.3   The expenses which are supported by the revenues are listed in the same fashion as they were recorded in Part a.

3.4   The unrealized gain on investments is shown separately after the revenues and expenses.

3.5   The beginning and ending balance amounts for the account "Cumulative excess of revenues over expenses" are shown at the end of the statement in order to tie into the balance sheet.

Unofficial Answer

Problem 4   Journal Entries and All-Inclusive
             Activity Statement for Nonprofit
             Organization (583,Q5)

a.   Community Sports Club
                        Transactions
              For the Year Ended March 31, 1983

		Debit	Credit
(1)	Cash	$20,000	
	Revenue--annual dues		$20,000
(2)	Cash	28,000	
	Revenue--snack bar		
	and soda fountain		28,000
(3)	Cash	6,000	
	Investment income		6,000
(4)	Expense--house	17,000	
	Expense--snack bar and		
	soda fountain	26,000	
	Expense--general and		
	administrative	11,000	
	Accounts payable		54,000

		Debit	Credit
(5)	Accounts payable	55,000	
	Cash		55,000
(6)	Assessments receivable	10,000	
	Deferred capital support		10,000
(7)	Cash	5,000	
	Revenue--bequest		
	(unrestricted revenue)		5,000

                    Adjustments
                   March 31, 1983

		Debit	Credit
(1)	Investments	7,000	
	Unrealized gain on in-		
	vestment		7,000
(2)	Expense--house	9,000	
&	Expense--general and		
(3)	soda fountain	2,000	
	Expense--general and		
	administrative	1,000	
	Accumulated depre-		
	ciation--building		4,000
	Accumulated depre-		
	ciation furniture and		
	equipment		8,000
(4)	Expense--snack bar and		
	soda fountain	4,000	
	Inventories		4,000

b.   Community Sports Club
          Statement of Revenue, Expenses, and Changes
               in Cumulative Excess of Revenues over
                    Expenses For the Year Ended
                         March 31, 1983

Revenue

Snack bar and soda fountain sales	$28,000
Dues	20,000
Investment income	6,000
Bequest	5,000
Total revenue	59,000

Expenses

Snack bar and soda fountain	$32,000	
House	26,000	
General and Administrative	12,000	
Total expenses		70,000
Deficiency of revenue over		
expenses before unrealized		
gain on investments		(11,000)
Unrealized gain on investments		7,000
Deficiency of revenue over ex-		
penses after unrealized gain on in-		
vestments		(4,000)
Cumulative excess of revenue over ex-		
penses at April 1, 1982		12,000
Cumulative excess of revenue over		
expenses at March 31, 1983		$ 8,000

Solution Guide

Problem 5   Entries for Gov. Units vs. NFP
             Organiz. (586,Q5)

1. This problem consists of two related
    parts. Four independent transactions or
    events are given. In part a., journal
    entries must be prepared for the trans-
    actions for a local government. In part
    b., journal entries must be prepared for
    the same transactions for a voluntary
    health and welfare organization.

2. The solutions approach is to first men-
    tally review accounting for local govern-
    ments and voluntary health and welfare
    organizations. Then go through each inde-
    pendent item and determine what entries
    would have to be prepared for each type of
    organization.

3. In item one, $25,000 is disbursed from the
    general fund (or current unrestricted
    fund) for cash purchase of new equip-
    ment. For a local government, this is
    recorded as an expenditure in the general
    fund, since it is an outflow of
    resources. However, the equipment is

reflected in the general fixed assets account group.

3.1 For a voluntary health and welfare organization, when equipment is acquired with resources of the current unrestricted fund, it should be treated as a transfer from the current fund to the plant fund. Such transfers are reflected as direct reductions and additions to the respective fund balances. Therefore, the current fund records the cash payment and a decrease in fund balance--undesignated. The plant fund records the equipment and an increase in fund balance--expended. The fund balance in the plant fund is segregated into fund balance--expended and fund balance--unexpended. Since the funds are expended and are not available for future purchases, fund balance--expended should be credited.

4. In item two, an unrestricted cash gift of $100,000 is received from a donor. For both types of organizations, this is recorded with a debit to cash and a credit to a revenue account in the general operating fund (general fund and current unrestricted fund respectively).

5. In item three, investments with a carrying value of $50,000 are sold by an endowment fund for $55,000. The $5,000 gain is unrestricted. The endowment trust fund of a governmental unit would record the transaction in the normal way, recognizing the gain on sale. The trust fund would also accrue an operating transfer out to the general fund for the amount of the gain, since the gain is unrestricted. Note that often, such gains are restricted and remain as part of the endowment principal, in which case fund balance is credited for the gain and no operating transfer is made. Note that this additional entry is not in the AICPA Unofficial Answer.

5.1 A voluntary health and welfare organization recognizes unrestricted earnings from endowment funds in the appropriate revenue account of the unrestricted current fund. Therefore, the endowment fund credits **due to current unrestricted fund** instead of a gain account. The current unrestricted fund then recognizes the earnings. Note that this additional entry for the current unrestricted fund is not in the AICPA Unofficial Answer.

6. In item four, $1,000,000 of general obligation bonds are issued at face value. The proceeds are restricted, to be used solely for constructing a new building, which was then constructed. The capital projects fund of the governmental unit would debit cash and credit proceeds of bonds (other financing sources), and then debit expenditures and credit cash as the funds are disbursed. The general long-term debt account group would record the amount to be provided and bonds payable liability. When the building is completed, it is reflected in the general fixed assets account group.

6.1 For a voluntary health and welfare organization, generally all transactions related to land, building, and equipment (unexpended resources, borrowing, construction, etc.) are recorded in the plant fund. For these transactions, the plant fund would record the issuance of the bonds and the construction of the building in the normal way.

Unofficial Answer

Problem 5 Entries for Gov. Units vs. NFP Organiz. (586,Q5)

	Debit	Credit
a. Local government		
[1] General fund		
Expenditures control	$ 25,000	
Cash		$ 25,000
General fixed assets account group		
Equipment	25,000	
Investment in general fixed assets from general fund revenues		25,000
[2] General fund		
Cash	100,000	
Revenues		100,000
[3] Nonexpendable trust (endowment) fund		
Cash	55,000	
Fund balance--gain on sale		5,000
Investments		50,000
[4] Capital projects fund		
Cash	1,000,000	
Bond issue proceeds		1,000,000
Expenditures	1,000,000	
Cash		1,000,000

	Debit	Credit
General long-term debt account group		
Amount to be provided for retirement of general long-term debt	1,000,000	
General obligation bonds payable		1,000,000
General fixed assets account group		
Buildings	1,000,000	
Investments in general fixed assets capital projects funds-- general obligation bonds		1,000,000

b. Voluntary health and welfare organization

[1] **Current unrestricted fund**

	Debit	Credit
Fund balance-- undesignated	$ 25,000	
Cash		$ 25,000
Plant fund		
Equipment	25,000	
Fund balance-- expended		25,000

[2] **Current unrestricted fund**

	Debit	Credit
Cash	100,000	
Contributions		100,000

[3] **Endowment fund**

	Debit	Credit
Cash	55,000	
Due to current unrestricted fund (or investment income)		5,000
Investments		50,000

[4] **Plant fund**

	Debit	Credit
Cash	1,000,000	
Bonds payable		1,000,000
Buildings	1,000,000	
Cash		1,000,000

CHAPTER SEVEN

TAX PROBLEMS AND SOLUTIONS

Federal income taxation appears only in the practice sections. Interperiod and intraperiod tax allocation questions are presented in Chapter 4, Module 27: Deferred Taxes.

Two of the accounting practice problems will test federal income taxation. One generally tests individual taxation and the other tests corporate and partnership taxation. From May 1980 through November 1985, both tax problems consisted solely of multiple choice questions. However, on the May 1986 examination, one problem required the use of a worksheet to convert a corporation's book income to taxable income; on the November 1986 examination, one problem required the preparation of a detailed schedule to compute taxable income on a joint return; on the May 1987 examination, one problem required the preparation of a detailed schedule to compute projected taxable income for an individual taxpayer, and, on the May 1989 examination, one problem consisted of 20 multiple choice questions testing individual and estate taxation while the other problem required the detailed computation of a corporation's taxable income. Occasionally, a section of another problem will require calculation of deferred taxes. A complete analysis of recent examinations and the *AICPA Revised Content Specification Outlines* appear in Volume I, *Outlines and Study Guides*.

Since federal income taxation rules and regulations vary from year to year, some of the exam items have been changed so that the question, solution, and explanation reflect the current law for which you are responsible.

The month, year, exam section, problem number, and multiple choice question number are given for each question. For example, (1189,Q2,37) indicates November 1989, problem 2 of the Practice II section, multiple choice question number 37. Note that P = Practice I and Q = Practice II.

Module 40/Individual Taxation (ITAX)

	Exam reference	No. of minutes	Page no. Problem	Page no. Answer
114 Multiple Choice			972	991
3 Practice Problems				
1. Joint Taxable Income Schedule	1186,Q5	40-50	987	1004
2. Projected Taxable Income Schedule	587,Q4	45-55	988	1007
3. Joint Taxable Income Schedule	1189,Q5	40-50	989	1010

Module 41/Transactions in Property (TPRO)

44 Multiple Choice			1013	1018

Module 42/Partnership Taxation (PTAX)

45 Multiple Choice			1023	1030

Module 43/Corporate Taxation (CTAX)

119 Multiple Choice			1036	1053
2 Practice Problems				
1. Book to Tax Worksheet	586,Q4	45-55	1050	1060
2. Schedule of Taxable Income	589,Q4	45-55	1052	1073

Module 44/Gift and Estate Tax (GETX)

16 Multiple Choice			1075	1077

Sample Examination

Multiple Choice Questions (1-114)

1. Richard Brown, who retired on May 31, 1989, receives a monthly pension benefit of $700 payable for life. His life expectancy at the date of retirement is 10 years. The first pension check was received on June 15, 1989. During his years of employment, Brown contributed $12,000 to the cost of his company's pension plan. How much of the pension amounts received may Brown exclude from taxable income for the years 1989, 1990, and 1991?

	1989	1990	1991
a.	$0	$0	$0
b.	$4,900	$4,900	$4,900
c.	$ 700	$1,200	$1,200
d.	$4,900	$8,400	$8,400

2. Seymour Thomas named his wife, Penelope, the beneficiary of a $100,000 (face amount) insurance policy on his life. The policy provided that upon his death, the proceeds would be paid to Penelope with interest over her present life expectancy, which was calculated at 25 years. Seymour died during 1989 and Penelope received a payment of $5,200 from the insurance company. What amount should she include in her gross income for 1989?

    a. $ 200
    b. $1,200
    c. $4,200
    d. $5,200

3. David Hetnar is covered by a $90,000 group-term life insurance policy of which his wife is the beneficiary. Hetnar's employer pays the entire cost of the policy, for which the uniform annual premium is $8 per $1,000 of coverage. How much of this premium is taxable to Hetnar?

    a. $0
    b. $320
    c. $360
    d. $720

4. Howard O'Brien, an employee of Ogden Corporation, died on June 30, 1990. During July, Ogden made employee death payments of $10,000 to his widow, and $10,000 to his 15 year old son. What amounts should be included in gross income by the widow and son in their respective tax returns for 1990?

	Widow	Son
a.	$0	$0
b.	$5,000	$ 5,000
c.	$5,000	$10,000
d.	$7,500	$ 7,500

5. John Budd files a joint return with his wife. Budd's employer pays 100% of the cost of all employees' group-term life insurance under a qualified plan. Under this plan, the maximum amount of tax-free coverage that may be provided for Budd by his employer is

    a. $100,000
    b. $ 50,000
    c. $ 10,000
    d. $ 5,000

6. During the current year Hal Leff sustained a serious injury in the course of his employment. As a result of this injury, Hal received the following payments during the year

Workers' compensation	$2,400
Reimbursement from his employer's accident and health plan for medical expenses paid by Hal and not deducted by him	1,800
Damages for personal injuries	8,000

The amount to be included in Hal's gross income for the current year should be

    a. $12,200
    b. $ 8,000
    c. $ 1,800
    d. $0

7. James Martin received the following compensation and fringe benefits from his employer during 1989

Salary	$50,000
Year-end bonus	10,000
Medical insurance premiums paid by employer	1,000
Allowance paid for moving expenses	5,000

What amount of the preceding payments should be included in Martin's 1989 gross income?

    a. $60,000
    b. $61,000
    c. $65,000
    d. $66,000

8. In 1989, Gail Judd received the following dividends from

Benefit Life Insurance Co., on Gail's life insurance policy (Total dividends received have not yet exceeded accumulated premiums paid)	$100
Safe National Bank, on bank's common stock	300
Roe Mfg. Corp., a Delaware corporation, on preferred stock	500

What amount of dividend income should Gail report in her 1989 income tax return?

a. $900
b. $800
c. $500
d. $300

9.   Amy Finch had the following cash receipts during 1990

Dividend from a mutual insurance company on a life insurance policy	500
Dividend on listed corporation stock; payment date by corporation was 12/30/89, but Amy received the dividend in the mail on 1/2/90	875

Total dividends received to date on the life insurance policy do not exceed the aggregated premiums paid by Amy. How much should Amy report for dividend income for 1990?
   a. $1,375
   b. $ 875
   c. $ 500
   d. $0

10.   Jack and Joan Mitchell, married taxpayers and residents of a separate property state, elect to file a joint return for 1989 during which they received the following dividends

	Received by	
	Jack	Joan
Alert Corporation (a qualified, domestic corporation)	$400	$ 50
Canadian Mines, Inc. (a Canadian company)		300
Eternal Life Mutual Insurance Company (dividends on life insurance policy)	200	

For 1989, what amount should the Mitchells report on their joint return as dividend income?
   a. $550
   b. $600
   c. $750
   d. $800

11.   Daniel Kelly received interest income from the following sources in 1989

New York Port Authority bonds	$1,000
Puerto Rico Commonwealth bonds	1,800

What portion of such interest is tax exempt?
   a. $0
   b. $1,000
   c. $1,800
   d. $2,800

12.   In 1989 Uriah Stone received the following interest payments

   •   Interest of $400 on refund of federal income tax for 1987.

   •   Interest of $300 on award for personal injuries sustained in an automobile accident during 1987.

   •   Interest of $1,500 on municipal bonds.

   •   Interest of $1,000 on United States savings bonds (Series HH).

What amount, if any, should Stone report as interest income on his 1989 tax return?
   a. $0
   b. $ 700
   c. $1,700
   d. $3,200

13.   During 1989, Clark received the following interest income:

On Veterans Administration insurance dividends left on deposit with the V.A.	$20
On state income tax refund	30

What amount should Clark include for interest income in his 1989 return?
   a. $50
   b. $30
   c. $20
   d. $0

14.   For the year ended December 31, 1989, Don Raff earned $1,000 interest at Ridge Savings Bank on a certificate of deposit scheduled to mature in 1991. In January 1990, before filing his 1989 income tax return, Raff incurred a forfeiture penalty of $500 for premature withdrawal of the funds. Raff should treat this $500 forfeiture penalty as a
   a.   Reduction of interest earned in 1989, so that only $500 of such interest is taxable on Raff's 1989 return.
   b.   Deduction from 1990 adjusted gross income, deductible only if Raff itemizes his deductions for 1990.
   c.   Penalty not deductible for tax purposes.
   d.   Deduction from gross income in arriving at 1990 adjusted gross income.

15.   Amy Finch had the following cash receipts during 1989

Interest on Veterans Administration insurance dividends left on deposit with the V.A.	$ 10
Interest on state income tax refund	18

How much should Amy include in her 1989 taxable income for interest?
   a. $0
   b. $10

c. $18
d. $28

16. On January 1, 1990, James Davis was awarded a post-doctorate fellowship grant of $4,500 by a tax-exempt educational organization. Davis is not a candidate for a degree and was awarded the grant to continue his research. The grant was awarded for the period March 1, 1990 through July 31, 1991.

On March 1, 1990, Davis elected to receive the full amount of the grant. What amount should be included in his gross income for 1990?
   a. $0
   b. $1,500
   c. $3,000
   d. $4,500

17. In July 1975, Dan Farley leased a building to Robert Shelter for a period of fifteen years at a monthly rental of $1,000 with no option to renew. At that time the building had a remaining estimated useful life of twenty years.

Prior to taking possession of the building, Shelter made improvements at a cost of $18,000. These improvements had an estimated useful life of twenty years at the commencement of the lease period. The lease expired on June 30, 1990 at which point the improvements had a fair market value of $2,000. The amount that Farley, the landlord, should include in his gross income for 1990 is
   a. $ 6,000
   b. $ 8,000
   c. $10,000
   d. $18,500

18. The following information is available for Ann Drury for 1989

Salary	$36,000
Premiums paid by employer on group- term life insurance in excess of $50,000	500
Proceeds from state lottery	5,000

How much should Drury report as gross income on her 1989 tax return?
   a. $36,000
   b. $36,500
   c. $41,000
   d. $41,500

19. Mr. and Mrs. Alvin Charak took a foster child, Robert, into their home in 1989. A state welfare agency paid the Charaks $3,900 during the year for related expenses. Actual expenses incurred by the Charaks during 1989 in caring for Robert amounted to $3,000. The remaining $900 was spent by the Charaks in 1989 towards their own personal expenses. How much of the foster child payments is taxable income to the Charaks in 1989?
   a. $0
   b. $ 900
   c. $2,900
   d. $3,900

20. Pierre, a headwaiter, received tips totaling $2,000 in December 1989. On January 5, 1990, Pierre reported this tip income to his employer in the required written statement. At what amount, and in which year, should this tip income be included in Pierre's gross income?
   a. $2,000 in 1989.
   b. $2,000 in 1990.
   c. $1,000 in 1989, and $1,000 in 1990.
   d. $ 167 In 1989, and $1,833 In 1990.

21. With regard to the alimony deduction in connection with a 1990 divorce, which one of the following statements is correct?
   a.   Alimony is deductible by the payor spouse, and includible by the payee spouse, to the extent that payment is contingent on the status of the divorced couple's children.
   b.   The divorced couple may be members of the same household at the time alimony is paid, provided that the persons do not live as husband and wife.
   c.   Alimony payments must terminate on the death of the payee spouse.
   d.   Alimony may be paid either in cash or in property.

22. In 1990, Joan accepted and received a $10,000 award for outstanding civic achievement. Joan was selected without any action on her part, and no future services are expected of her as a condition of receiving the award. What amount should Joan include in her 1990 adjusted gross income in connection with this award?
   a. $0
   b. $ 4,000
   c. $ 5,000
   d. $10,000

23. In 1989, Emil Gow won $5,000 in a state lottery. Also in 1989, Emil spent $400 for the purchase of lottery tickets. Emil elected the standard deduction on his 1989 income tax return. The amount of lottery winnings that should be included in Emil's 1989 taxable income is
   a. $0
   b. $2,000
   c. $4,600
   d. $5,000

24. Paul Bristol, a cash basis taxpayer, owns an apartment building. The following information was available for 1989

- An analysis of the 1989 bank deposit slips showed recurring monthly rents received totaling $50,000.
- On March 1, 1989, the tenant in apartment 2B paid Bristol $2,000 to cancel the lease expiring on December 31, 1989.
- The lease of the tenant in apartment 3A expired on December 31, 1989, and the tenant left improvements valued at $1,000. The improvements were not in lieu of any rent required to have been paid.

In computing net rental income for 1989, Bristol should report gross rents of

 a. $50,000
 b. $51,000
 c. $52,000
 d. $53,000

25. Emil Gow owns a two-family house which has two identical apartments. Gow lives in one apartment and rents out the other. In 1989, the rental apartment was fully occupied and Gow received $7,200 in rent. During the year ended December 31, 1989, Gow paid the following:

Real estate taxes	$6,400
Painting of rental apartment	800
Annual fire insurance premium	600

In 1989, depreciation for the entire house was determined to be $5,000. What amount should Gow include in his adjusted gross income for 1989?

 a. $2,900
 b. $ 800
 c. $ 400
 d. $ 100

26. Amy Finch had the following cash receipts during 1989

Net rent on vacant lot used by a car dealer (lessee pays all taxes, insurance, and other expenses on the lot)	6,000
Advance rent from lessee of above vacant lot, such advance to be applied against rent for the last two months of the 5-year lease in 1993	1,000

How much should Amy include in her 1989 taxable income for rent?

 a. $7,000
 b. $6,800
 c. $6,200
 d. $6,000

27. John Budd is single, with no dependents. During 1989, John received wages of $11,000 and state unemployment compensation benefits of $2,000. He had no other source of income. The amount of state unemployment compensation benefits that should be included in John's 1989 adjusted gross income is

 a. $2,000
 b. $1,000
 c. $ 500
 d. $0

28. Blair, CPA, uses the cash receipts and disbursements method of reporting. In 1989, a client gave Blair 100 shares of a listed corporation's stock in full satisfaction of a $5,000 accounting fee the client owed Blair. This stock had a fair market value of $4,000 on the date it was given to Blair. The client's basis for this stock was $3,000. Blair sold the stock for cash in January 1990. In Blair's 1989 return, what amount of income should be reported in connection with the receipt of the stock?

 a. $0
 b. $3,000
 c. $4,000
 d. $5,000

29. Under the cash method of reporting, an individual should report gross income
 a. Only for the year in which income is actually received in cash.
 b. Only for the year in which income is actually received either in cash or in property.
 c. For the year in which income is either actually or constructively received in cash only.
 d. For the year in which income is either actually or constructively received either in cash or in property.

30. Alex Burg, a cash-basis taxpayer, earned an annual salary of $80,000 at Ace Corp. in 1989, but elected to take only $50,000. Ace, which was financially able to pay Burg's full salary, credited the unpaid balance of $30,000 to Burg's account on the corporate books in 1989, and actually paid this $30,000 to Burg on April 30, 1990. How much of the salary is taxable to Burg in 1989?
 a. $50,000
 b. $60,000
 c. $65,000
 d. $80,000

31. Dr. Berger, a physician, reports on the cash basis. The following items pertain to Dr. Berger's medical practice in 1989

Cash received from patients in 1989 $200,000
Cash received in 1989 from third-
  party reimbursers for services
  provided by Dr. Berger in 1988   30,000
Salaries paid to employees in 1989   20,000
Year-end 1989 bonuses paid to em-
  ployees in 1990   1,000
Other expenses paid in 1989   24,000

What is Dr. Berger's net income for 1988 from his medical practice?

  a. $155,000
  b. $156,000
  c. $185,000
  d. $186,000

32. With regard to the deduction for bad debts in 1990, corporations that are not financial institutions

  a.   May take a deduction for a reasonable addition to a "reserve" for bad debts, if the reserve method was consistently used in prior years.
  b.   May change from the direct charge-off method to the reserve method, if approval is requested from the IRS.
  c.   Must use the direct charge-off method rather than the reserve method.
  d.   May elect either the reserve method or the direct charge-off method, if the election is made in the corporation's first taxable year.

33. Ram Corp.'s operating income for the year ended December 31, 1989 amounted to $100,000. Included in Ram's 1989 operating expenses is a $6,000 insurance premium on a policy insuring the life of Ram's president. Ram is beneficiary of this policy. In Ram's 1989 tax return, what amount should be deducted for the $6,000 life insurance premium?

  a. $6,000
  b. $5,000
  c. $1,000
  d. $0

34. Jason Budd, CPA, reports on the cash basis. In April 1988, Budd billed a client $3,500 for the following professional services

Personal estate planning $2,000
Personal tax return preparation   1,000
Compilation of business financial
  statements   500

No part of the $3,500 was ever paid. In April 1990, the client declared bankruptcy, and the $3,500 obligation became totally uncollectible. What loss can Budd deduct on his 1990 tax return for this bad debt?

  a. $0
  b. $ 500

  c. $1,500
  d. $3,500

35. Earl Cook, who worked as a machinist for Precision Corp., loaned Precision $1,000 in 1986. Cook did not own any of Precision's stock, and the loan was not a condition of Cook's employment by Precision. In 1990, Precision declared bankruptcy, and Cook's note receivable from Precision became worthless. What loss can Cook claim on his 1990 income tax return?

  a. $0.
  b. $ 500 long-term capital loss.
  c. $1,000 short-term capital loss.
  d. $1,000 business bad debt.

36. During the 1989 holiday season, Palo Corp. gave business gifts to 17 customers. These gifts, which were not of an advertising nature, had the following fair market values

      4 at $ 10
      4 at   25
      4 at   50
      5 at 100

How much of these gifts was deductible as a business expense for 1989?

  a. $840
  b. $365
  c. $140
  d. $0

37. With regard to the passive loss rules involving rental real estate activities, which one of the following statements is correct?

  a.   The term "passive activity" includes any rental activity without regard as to whether or not the taxpayer materially participates in the activity.
  b.   Gross investment income from interest and dividends not derived in the ordinary course of a trade or business is treated as passive activity income that can be offset by passive rental activity losses when the "active participation" requirement is not met.
  c.   Passive rental activity losses may be deducted only against passive income, but passive rental activity credits may be used against tax attributable to nonpassive activities.
  d.   The passive activity rules do not apply to taxpayers whose adjusted gross income is $300,000 or less.

38. If an individual taxpayer's passive losses and credits relating to rental real

estate activities cannot be used in the current year, then they may be carried
  a. Back three years, but they cannot be carried forward.
  b. Forward up to a maximum period of 15 years, but they cannot be carried back.
  c. Back three years or forward up to 15 years, at the taxpayer's election.
  d. Forward indefinitely or until the property is disposed of in a taxable transaction.

39. In 1989, Roe Corp. purchased and placed in service a machine to be used in its manufacturing operations. This machine cost $201,000. What portion of the cost may Roe elect to treat as an expense rather than as a capital expenditure?
  a. $0
  b. $ 9,000
  c. $10,000
  d. $20,100

40. On March 1, 1989, Milford Corporation purchased for $70,000 machinery that was installed in its factory on April 1, 1989. The machinery was estimated to have a salvage value of $7,000 at the end of its estimated useful life which was 8 years. What is Milford's maximum depreciation allowance for 1989?
  a. $ 9,450
  b. $15,750
  c. $10,000
  d. $17,500

41. Charles Gilbert, a corporate executive, incurred business-related, unreimbursed expenses in 1989 as follows

Entertainment	$900
Travel	700
Education	400

Assuming that Gilbert does not itemize deductions, how much of these expenses should he deduct on his 1989 tax return?
  a. $0
  b. $ 700
  c. $1,300
  d. $1,600

42. Ronald Birch, who is single, earned a salary of $30,000 in 1989 as a plumber employed by Lupo Company. Birch was covered for the entire year 1989 under Lupo's qualified pension plan for employees. In addition, Birch had a net income of $10,000 from self-employment in 1989. What is the maximum amount that Birch can deduct in 1989 for contributions to an individual retirement account (IRA)?

  a. $4,500
  b. $2,000
  c. $1,500
  d. $0

43. Sol and Julia Crane are married, and filed a joint return for 1989. Sol earned a salary of $80,000 in 1989 from his job at Troy Corp., where Sol is covered by his employer's pension plan. In addition, Sol and Julia earned interest of $3,000 in 1989 on their joint savings account. Julia is not employed, and the couple had no other income. On January 15, 1990, Sol contributed $2,000 to an IRA for himself, and $250 to an IRA for his spouse. The allowable IRA deduction in the Cranes' 1989 joint return is
  a. $0
  b. $ 250
  c. $2,000
  d. $2,250

44. Paul and Lois Lee, both age 50, are married and filed a joint return for 1989. Their 1989 adjusted gross income was $80,000, including Paul's $75,000 salary. Lois had no income of her own. Neither spouse was covered by an employer-sponsored pension plan. What amount could the Lees contribute to IRAs for 1989 to take advantage of their maximum allowable IRA deduction in their 1989 return?
  a. $0
  b. $2,000
  c. $2,250
  d. $4,000

45. Ida Korb, who is divorced, received taxable alimony of $25,000 in 1989. In addition, she received $900 in earnings from a part-time job in 1989. Ida is not covered by a qualified pension plan. What was the maximum IRA contribution that Ida could have made for 1989, which she could have deducted on her 1989 individual tax return, assuming that everything was done on a timely basis?
  a. $ 250
  b. $ 900
  c. $1,125
  d. $2,000

46. In 1989, deductible contributions to a qualified retirement plan on behalf of a self-employed individual whose income from self-employment is $20,000 are limited to
  a. $2,000
  b. $4,000
  c. $5,000
  d. $7,500

47. For the year 1989 Fred and Wilma Todd reported the following items of income

	Fred	Wilma
Salary	$40,000	--
Interest income	1,000	$ 200
Cash prize won on TV game show	--	8,800
	$41,000	$9,000

Fred is not covered by any qualified retirement plan and he and Wilma established individual retirement accounts during the year. Assuming a joint return was filed for 1989, what is the maximum amount that they can be allowed for the contributions to their individual retirement accounts?

    a. $2,000
    b. $2,250
    c. $6,000
    d. $7,500

48. Which one of the following types of allowable deductions can be claimed as a deduction in arriving at an individual's 1990 adjusted gross income?

    a.   Unreimbursed business expenses of an outside salesman-employee.
    b.   Personal casualty losses.
    c.   Charitable contributions.
    d.   Alimony payments.

49. Jill Nolan's filing status for 1990 was that of a single individual. If Jill does not itemize deductions, what will be the amount of Jill's standard deduction for 1990?

    a. $1,880
    b. $2,540
    c. $3,100
    d. $3,250

50. Jon Stenger, a cash basis taxpayer, had adjusted gross income of $35,000 in 1989. During the year he incurred and paid the following medical expenses

Drugs and medicines prescribed by doctors	$ 300
Health insurance premiums	750
Doctors' fees	2,550
Eyeglasses	75
	$3,675

Stenger received $900 in 1989 as reimbursement for a portion of the doctors' fees. If Stenger were to itemize his deductions, what would be his allowable net medical expense deduction?

    a. $0
    b. $ 150
    c. $1,050
    d. $2,475

51. During 1989 Mr. and Mrs. Benson provided substantially all the support, in their own home, for their son John, age 26, and for Mrs. Benson's cousin Nancy, age 17. John had $2,100 of income for 1989, and Nancy's income was $500. The Bensons paid the following medical expenses during the year

Medicines and drugs:	
For themselves	$400
For John	500
For Nancy	100
Doctors:	
For themselves	600
For John	900
For Nancy	200

What is the total amount of medical expenses (before application of any limitation rules), that would enter into the calculation of itemized deductions on the Benson's 1989 tax return?

    a. $1,000
    b. $1,300
    c. $2,400
    d. $2,700

52. Gail and Jeff Payne are married and filed a joint return for 1989. In 1989 they paid the following doctors' bills for

Gail's mother, who received over half of her support from Gail and Jeff, but who does not live in the Payne household, and who earned $2,100 in 1989 for baby-sitting. $700

Their unmarried 26-year old son, who earned $4,000 in 1989, but was fully supported by his parents. He is not a full-time student.   500

Disregarding the adjusted gross income percentage test, how much of these doctors' bills may be included on the Paynes' joint return in 1989 as qualifying medical expenses?

    a. $0
    b. $ 500
    c. $ 700
    d. $1,200

53. Henry Warren did not itemize his deductions on his 1988 and 1987 federal income tax returns. However, Warren plans to itemize his deductions for 1989. The following information relating to his state income taxes is available

Taxes withheld in 1989	$2,000
Refund received in 1989 of 1988 tax	300
Assessment paid in 1989 of 1987 tax	200

What amount should Warren utilize as state and local income taxes in calculating itemized deductions for his 1989 federal income tax return?

    a. $1,700
    b. $1,900
    c. $2,000
    d. $2,200

54. Sara Harding is a cash basis taxpayer who itemized her deductions. The following information pertains to Sara's state income taxes for the taxable year 1989

Withheld by employer in 1989		$2,000
Payments on 1989 estimate:		
4/15/89	$300	
6/15/89	300	
9/15/89	300	
1/15/90	300	1,200
Total paid and withheld		$3,200
Actual tax, per state return		3,000
Overpayment		$ 200

There was no balance of tax or refund due on Sara's 1988 state tax return. How much is deductible for state income taxes on Sara's 1989 federal income tax return?

    a. $2,800
    b. $2,900
    c. $3,000
    d. $3,200

55. During 1989 Jack and Mary Bronson paid the following taxes

Taxes on residence (for period January 1 to September 30, 1989)	$2,700
State motor vehicle tax on value of the car	360

The Bronsons sold their house on June 30, 1989, under an agreement in which the real estate taxes were not prorated between the buyer and sellers. What amount should the Bronsons deduct as taxes in calculating itemized deductions for 1989?

    a. $1,800
    b. $2,160
    c. $2,700
    d. $3,060

56. In 1989, Lyons paid $3,000 to the tax collector of Maple Township for realty taxes on a two-family house owned by Lyons' mother. Of this amount, $1,400 covered back taxes for 1988, and $1,600 was in payment of 1989 taxes. Lyons resides on the second floor of the house, and his mother resides on the first floor. In Lyons' itemized deductions on his 1989 return, what amount may Lyons claim for realty taxes?

    a. $0

    b. $1,500
    c. $1,600
    d. $3,000

57. George Granger sold a plot of land to Albert King on July 1, 1989. Granger had not paid any realty taxes on the land since 1987. Delinquent 1988 taxes amounted to $600, and 1989 taxes amounted to $700. King paid the 1988 and 1989 taxes in full in 1989, when he bought the land. What portion of the $1,300 is deductible by King in 1989?

    a. $ 353
    b. $ 700
    c. $ 953
    d. $1,300

58. During 1989 Mr. and Mrs. West paid the following taxes

Property taxes on residence	$1,800
Special assessment for installation of a sewer system in their town	1,000
State personal property tax on their automobile	600
Property taxes on land held for long-term appreciation	300

What amount can the Wests deduct as property taxes in calculating itemized deductions for 1989?

    a. $2,100
    b. $2,700
    c. $3,100
    d. $3,700

59. Robert and Judy Parker made the following payments during 1990

Interest on a life insurance policy loan (the loan proceeds were used for personal use)	$1,200
Interest on home mortgage for period January 1 to October 4, 1990	3,600
Penalty payment for prepayment of home mortgage on October 4, 1990	900

How much can the Parkers utilize as interest expense in calculating itemized deductions for 1990?

    a. $5,700
    b. $4,740
    c. $4,620
    d. $3,600

60. Charles Wolfe purchased the following long-term investments at par during 1990

    $20,000 general obligation bonds of Burlington County (wholly tax exempt)
    $10,000 debentures of Arrow Corporation

Wolfe financed these purchases by obtaining a $30,000 loan from the Union National Bank.

For the year 1990, Wolfe made the following
interest payments

Union National Bank	$3,600
Interest on home mortgage	3,000
Interest on credit card charges	500

What amount can Wolfe utilize as interest expense in calculating itemized deductions for
1990?

a. $3,170
b. $3,340
c. $5,400
d. $7,100

61. For the year ended December 31, 1990,
David Roth, a married taxpayer filing a joint
return, reported the following

Investment income from dividends and interest	$24,000
Long-term capital gains	25,000
Investment expenses	4,000
Interest expense on funds borrowed in 1990 to purchase investment property	70,000

What amount can Roth deduct in 1990 as investment interest expense?

a. $20,000
b. $46,000
c. $47,000
d. $70,000

62. During 1990, William Clark was assessed a
deficiency on his 1988 federal income tax return. As a result of this assessment he was
required to pay $1,120 determined as follows

Additional tax	$900
Late filing penalty	60
Negligence penalty	90
Interest	70

What portion of the $1,120 would qualify as
itemized deductions for 1990?

a. $ 7
b. $ 14
c. $150
d. $220

63. Ruth Lewis has adjusted gross income of
$100,000 for 1989 and itemizes her deduc-
tions. On September 1, 1989, she made a contribution to her church of stock held for investment for two years which cost $10,000 and
had a fair market value of $70,000. The
church sold the stock for $70,000 on the same
date. Assume that Lewis made no other contributions during 1989 and made no special election in regard to this contribution on her
1989 tax return. How much should Lewis claim
as a charitable contribution deduction for
1989?

a. $50,000
b. $30,000

c. $20,000
d. $10,000

64. On December 15, 1989, Donald Calder made
a contribution of $500 to a qualified charita-
ble organization, by charging the contribution
on his bank credit card. Calder paid the $500
on January 20, 1990 upon receipt of the bill
from the bank. In addition, Calder issued and
delivered a promissory note for $1,000 to
another qualified charitable organization on
November 1, 1989, which he paid upon maturity
six months later. If Calder itemizes his deductions, what portion of these contributions
is deductible in 1989?

a. $0
b. $ 500
c. $1,000
d. $1,500

65. Dan Barlow, who itemizes his deductions,
had an adjusted gross income of $70,000 in
1989. The following additional information is
available for 1989

Cash contribution to church	$5,000
Purchase of art object at church bazaar (with a fair market value of $1,000 on the date of purchase)	1,600
Donation of used clothing to Salva-tion Army (fair value evidenced by receipt received)	800

What is the maximum amount Barlow can claim as
a deduction for charitable contributions in
1989?

a. $5,600
b. $6,400
c. $6,600
d. $6,800

66. Under a written agreement between Mrs.
Norma Lowe and an approved religious exempt
organization, a ten year old girl from Vietnam
came to live in Mrs. Lowe's home on August 1,
1989, in order to be able to start school in
the U.S. on September 3, 1989. Mrs. Lowe
actually spent $500 for food, clothing, and
school supplies for the student during 1989,
without receiving any compensation or reimbursement of costs. What portion of the $500
may Mrs. Lowe deduct on her 1989 income tax
return as a charitable contribution?

a. $0
b. $200
c. $250
d. $500

67. During 1989 Vincent Tally gave to the municipal art museum title to his private collection of rare books that was assessed and
valued at $60,000. However, he reserved the

right to the collection's use and possession during his lifetime. For 1989 he reported an adjusted gross income of $100,000. Assuming that this was his only contribution during the year, and that there were no carryovers from prior years, what amount can he deduct as contributions for 1989?

- a. $0
- b. $30,000
- c. $50,000
- d. $60,000

Items 68 and 69 are based on the following selected 1989 information pertaining to Sam and Ann Hoyt, who filed a joint federal income tax return for the calendar year 1989. The Hoyts had adjusted gross income of $34,000 and itemized their deductions for 1989. Among the Hoyts' cash expenditures during 1989 were the following:

$2,500 repairs in connection with 1989 fire damage to the Hoyt residence. This property has a basis of $50,000. Fair market value was $60,000 before the fire and $55,000 after the fire. Insurance on the property had lapsed in 1988 for nonpayment of premium. $800 appraisal fee to determine amount of fire loss.

68. What amount of fire loss were the Hoyts entitled to deduct as an itemized deduction on their 1989 return?

- a. $5,000
- b. $2,500
- c. $1,600
- d. $1,500

69. The appraisal fee to determine the amount of Hoyts' fire loss was

- a.   Deductible from gross income in arriving at adjusted gross income.
- b.   Subject to the 2% of adjusted gross income floor for miscellaneous itemized deductions.
- c.   Deductible after reducing the amount by $100.
- d.   Not deductible.

70. The following information pertains to Cole's personal residence, which sustained casualty fire damage in 1990:

Adjusted basis	$150,000
Fair market value immediately before the fire	200,000
Fair market value immediately after the fire	180,000
Fire damage repairs paid for by Cole in 1990	10,000

The house was uninsured. Before consideration of any "floor" or other limitation on tax

deductibility, the amount of this 1990 casualty loss was

- a. $30,000
- b. $20,000
- c. $10,000
- d. $0

71. Martin Dawson, who resided in Detroit, was unemployed for the last six months of 1989. In January 1990, he moved to Houston to seek employment, and obtained a full-time job there in February. He kept this job for the balance of the year. Martin paid the following expenses in 1990 in connection with his move

Rental of truck to move his personal belongings to Houston	$ 800
Penalty for breaking the lease on his Detroit apartment	300
Total	$1,100

How much can Martin deduct in 1990 for moving expenses?

- a. $0
- b. $ 300
- c. $ 800
- d. $1,100

72. The unreimbursed moving expenses of an employee who takes a new job 100 miles away from a previous residence and place of employment are

- a.   Fully deductible from gross income in arriving at adjusted gross income.
- b.   Deductible only as miscellaneous itemized deductions subject to a 2% floor.
- c.   Fully deductible only as miscellaneous itemized deductions.
- d.   Not deductible.

73. Richard Putney, who lived in Idaho for five years, moved to Texas in 1990 to accept a new position. His employer reimbursed him in full for all direct moving costs, but did not pay for any part of the following indirect moving expenses incurred by Putney

Househunting trips to Texas	$800
Temporary housing in Texas	$900

How much of the indirect expenses can be deducted by Putney as moving expenses?

- a. $0
- b. $ 900
- c. $1,500
- d. $1,700

74. Which one of the following types of itemized deductions is included in the category of unreimbursed expenses that is deductible only if the aggregate amount of such

expenses exceeds 2% of the taxpayer's adjusted gross income?
- a.   Employee moving expenses.
- b.   Tax return preparation fees.
- c.   Medical expenses.
- d.   Interest expense.

75. Joel Rich is an outside salesman, deriving his income solely from commissions, and personally bearing all expenses without reimbursement of any kind. During 1989, Joel paid the following expenses pertaining directly to his activities as an outside salesman:

Travel	$10,000
Secretarial	7,000
Telephone	1,000

How should these expenses be deducted in Joel's 1989 return?

	From gross income, in arriving at adjusted gross income	As itemized deductions
a.	$18,000	$0
b.	$11,000	$ 7,000
c.	$10,000	$ 8,000
d.	$0	$18,000

76. During 1989 Burt Knox made the following unreimbursed personal expenditures

Legal fee for preparation of will	100
Education expenses to qualify for occupation	975

How much should be included in Burt's 1989 itemized deductions for miscellaneous deductions?
- a. $1,075
- b. $ 975
- c. $ 100
- d. $0

77. Magda Micale, a public school teacher with adjusted gross income of $10,000, paid the following items in 1989 for which she received no reimbursement

Initiation fee for membership in teachers' union	$100
Dues to teachers' union	180
Voluntary unemployment benefit fund contributions to union --established fund	72

How much can Magda claim in 1989 as allowable miscellaneous deductions on Schedule A of Form 1040?
- a. $ 80
- b. $280
- c. $252
- d. $352

78. Harold Brodsky is an electrician employed by a contracting firm. His adjusted gross income is $25,000. During the current year he incurred and paid the following expenses

Use of personal auto for company business (reimbursed by employer for $200)	$300
Specialized work clothes	550
Union dues	600
Cost of income tax preparation	150
Preparation of will	100

If Brodsky were to itemize his personal deductions, what amount should he claim as miscellaneous deductible expenses?
- a. $ 800
- b. $ 900
- c. $1,500
- d. $1,700

79. During 1989 Robert Moore, who is 50 years old and unmarried, maintained his home in which he and his widower father, age 75, resided. His father had $2,000 interest income from a savings account and also received $2,400 from social security during 1989. Robert provided 60% of his father's total support for 1989. What is Robert's filing status for 1989, and how many exemptions should he claim on his tax return?
- a.   Head of household and 2 exemptions.
- b.   Single and 2 exemptions.
- c.   Head of household and 1 exemption.
- d.   Single and 1 exemption.

80. During 1989 Mary Dunn provided 20% of her own support; the remaining 80% was provided by her three sons as follows

Bill	15%
Jon	25%
Tom	40%
	80%

Assume that a multiple support agreement exists and that the brothers will sign multiple support declarations as required. Which of the brothers is eligible to claim the mother as a dependent for 1989?
- a.   None of the brothers.
- b.   Tom only.
- c.   Jon or Tom only.
- d.   Bill, Jon, or Tom.

81. John and Mary Arnold are a childless, married couple who lived apart (alone in homes maintained by each) the entire year 1989. On December 31, 1989, they were legally separated under a decree of separate maintenance. Which of the following is the only filing status choice available to them when filing for 1989?
- a.   Single.
- b.   Head of household.
- c.   Married filing separate return.
- d.   Married filing joint return.

82. Mark Erikson, age 46, filed a joint
return for 1989 with his wife Helen, age 24.
Their son John was born on December 16, 1989.
Mark provided 60% of the support for his 72
year old widowed mother until April 10, 1989,
when she died. His mother's only income was
from social security benefits totaling $2,100
during 1989. How many exemptions should the
Eriksons claim on their 1989 tax return?

    a. 2
    b. 3
    c. 4
    d. 5

83. Albert and Lois Stoner, age 66 and 64,
respectively, filed a joint tax return for
1989. They provided all of the support for
their blind 19 year old son, who has no gross
income. Their 23 year old daughter, a full-
time student until her graduation on June 14,
1989, earned $3,000, which was 40% of her
total support during 1989. Her parents provided the remaining support. The Stoners also
provided the total support of Lois' father,
who is a citizen and life-long resident of
Peru. How many exemptions can the Stoners
claim on their 1989 income tax return?

    a. 4
    b. 5
    c. 6
    d. 7

84. Jim Planter, who reached age 65 on January 1, 1990, filed a joint return for 1989
with his wife Rita, age 50. Mary, their 21
year old daughter, was a full-time student at
a college until her graduation on June 2,
1989. The daughter had $6,500 of income and
provided 25% of her own support during 1989.
In addition, during 1989 the Planters were the
sole support for Rita's niece, who had no income. How many exemptions should the Planters
claim on their 1989 tax return?

    a. 2
    b. 3
    c. 4
    d. 5

85. In 1989, Sam Dunn provided more than half
the support for his wife, his father's
brother, and his cousin. Sam's wife was the
only relative who was a member of Sam's
household. None of the relatives had any
income, nor did any of them file an individual
or a joint return. All of these relatives are
U.S. citizens. Which of these relatives
should be claimed as a dependent or dependents
on Sam's 1989 return?

    a. Only his wife.
    b. Only his father's brother.
    c. Only his cousin.

    d. His wife, his father's brother, and
       his cousin.

86. In Mona Lux's 1989 income tax return,
Mona validly claimed the $1,950 personal
exemption for her dependent 17 year old son,
Brett. Since Brett earned $5,000 in 1989
selling novelties at the college he attended
full time, Brett was also required to file a
1989 income tax return. How much should Brett
claim as a personal exemption in his 1989 individual income tax return?

    a. $0
    b. $ 500
    c. $1,000
    d. $1,950

87. In 1989 Alan Kott provided more than half
the support for his following relatives, none
of whom qualified as a member of Alan's household

            Cousin
            Niece
            Foster parent

None of these relatives had any income, nor
did any of these relatives file an individual
or joint return. All of these relatives are
U.S. citizens. Which of these relatives could
be claimed as a dependent on Alan's 1989
return?

    a. No one.
    b. Niece.
    c. Cousin.
    d. Foster parent.

88. Sara Hance, who is single and lives alone
in Idaho, has no income of her own and is supported in full by the following persons

	Amount of support	Percent of total
Alma (an unrelated friend)	$2,400	48
Ben (Sara's brother)	2,150	43
Carl (Sara's son)	450	9
	$5,000	100

Under a multiple support agreement, Sara's dependency exemption can be claimed by

    a. No one.
    b. Alma.
    c. Ben.
    d. Carl.

89. Mr. and Mrs. Vonce, both age 62, filed a
joint return for 1989. They provided all the
support for their daughter, who is 19, legally
blind, and who has no income. Their son, age
21 and a full-time student at a university,
had $4,200 of income and provided 70% of his
own support during 1989. How many exemptions
should Mr. and Mrs. Vonce have claimed on
their 1989 joint income tax return?

a.   2
b.   3
c.   4
d.   5

90. William Dalton, who is not covered by a qualified retirement plan and is age 30 and single, provided the following information for his 1989 income tax return

Salary	$30,000
Payment to an Individual Retirement Account	$ 2,000
Total itemized deductions	$ 3,400
Number of exemptions claimed	1

Dalton should report taxable income for 1989 of
a. $22,600
b. $22,650
c. $26,900
d. $27,900

91. During 1989 Howard Thomson maintained his home in which he and his sixteen year old son resided. The son qualifies as a dependent. Thomson's wife died in 1988, for which year a joint return was appropriately filed. Thomson remarried on March 15, 1990. What is Thomson's filing status for 1989?
a.   Single.
b.   Head of household.
c.   Surviving spouse.
d.   Married filing jointly.

92. Emil Gow's wife died in 1987. Emil did not remarry, and he continued to maintain a home for himself and his dependent infant child during 1988 and 1989, providing full support for himself and his child during these years. For 1987, Emil properly filed a joint return. For 1989, Emil's filing status is
a.   Single.
b.   Head of household.
c.   Qualifying widower with dependent child.
d.   Married filing joint return.

93. Nell Brown's husband died in 1986. Nell did not remarry, and continued to maintain a home for herself and her dependent infant child during 1987, 1988, and 1989, providing full support for herself and her child during these three years. For 1986, Nell properly filed a joint return. For 1989, Nell's filing status is
a.   Single.
b.   Married filing joint return.
c.   Head of household.
d.   Qualifying widow with dependent child.

94. Martin Dale, single, paid the entire cost of maintaining his dependent mother in a home for the aged, for the whole year 1989. How much is Martin's standard deduction amount for 1989?
a. $0
b. $3,100
c. $4,550
d. $5,200

95. Mrs. Irma Felton, by herself, maintains her home in which she and her unmarried son reside. Her son, however, does not qualify as her dependent. Mrs. Felton's husband died in 1988. What is Mrs. Felton's filing status for 1989?
a.   Single.
b.   Surviving spouse.
c.   Head of household.
d.   Married filing jointly.

96. Alex Berger, a retired building contractor, earned the following income during 1989

Director's fee received from Keith Realty Corp.	$ 600
Executor's fee received from the estate of his deceased sister	7,000

Berger's self-employment income for 1989 is
a. $0
b. $ 600
c. $7,000
d. $7,600

97. Smith, a retired corporate executive, earned consulting fees of $8,000 and director's fees of $2,000 in 1989. Smith's gross income from self-employment in 1989 was
a. $0
b. $ 2,000
c. $ 8,000
d. $10,000

98. An employee who has had social security tax withheld in an amount greater than the maximum for a particular year, may claim
a.   The excess as a credit against income tax, if that excess was withheld by one employer.
b.   The excess as a credit against income tax, if that excess resulted from correct withholding by two or more employers.
c.   Reimbursement of such excess from his employers if that excess resulted from correct withholding by two or more employers.

d.   Such excess as either a credit or an
      itemized deduction, at the election
      of the employee, if that excess
      resulted from correct withholding by
      two or more employers.

99. Kirk Kory, a cash basis sole proprietor,
had the following cash receipts and disbursements for 1989

Net sales	$120,000
Dividend income (on personal in-
vestment)	800
Cost of sales	60,000
Other operating expenses	12,000
State business tax	1,200
Federal self-employment tax	3,200

What amount should Kory report as net earnings
from self-employment for 1989?
    a. $43,600
    b. $46,800
    c. $47,600
    d. $48,000

100. On July 1, 1985, Pemberton Corporation
bought a new drill press for $20,000, which
was placed in service the same day. The drill
press qualifies as five-year accelerated cost
recovery system property, for which an investment credit of $2,000 was claimed. If Pember-
ton disposes of this drill press on May 31,
1990, how much of the investment credit must
be recaptured in 1990?
    a. $0
    b. $ 400
    c. $ 800
    d. $1,200

101. Melvin Crane is 66 years old, and his
wife, Matilda, is 65. They filed a joint income tax return for 1989, reporting an adjusted gross income of $7,500, on which they
paid a tax of $60. They received $1,250 from
social security benefits in 1989. How much
can they claim on Form 1040 in 1989, as a
credit for the elderly?
    a. $0
    b. $ 60
    c. $315
    d. $938

102. Nora Hayes, a widow, maintains a home for
herself and her two dependent preschool children. In 1989, Nora's earned income and adjusted gross income was $29,000. During 1989,
Nora paid work-related expenses of $3,000 for
a housekeeper to care for her children. How
much can Nora claim for child care credit in
1989?
    a. $0
    b. $480

    c. $600
    d. $900

103. Robert and Mary Jason, filing a joint tax
return for 1989, had a tax liability of $9,000
based on their tax table income and three exemptions. Robert and Mary had earned income
of $20,000 and $12,000, respectively, during
1989. In order for Mary to be gainfully employed, the Jasons incurred the following
employment-related expenses for their four
year old son John in 1989

Payee	Amount
Union Day Care Center	$1,500
Acme Home Cleaning Service	500
Wilma Jason, babysitter
(Robert Jason's mother)	1,000

Assuming that the Jasons do not claim any
other credits against their tax, what is the
amount of the child care tax credit they
should report on their tax return for 1989?
    a. $300
    b. $480
    c. $500
    d. $600

104. During 1989 Bell Corporation had worldwide taxable income of $675,000 and a tenta-
tive United States income tax of $270,000.
Bell's taxable income from business operations
in Country A was $300,000, and foreign income
taxes imposed were $135,000 stated in United
States dollars. How much should Bell claim as
a credit for foreign income taxes on its
United States income tax return for 1989?
    a. $0
    b. $ 75,000
    c. $120,000
    d. $135,000

105. A corporation may reduce its income tax
by taking a tax credit for
    a.   Accelerated depreciation.
    b.   State income taxes.
    c.   Foreign income taxes.
    d.   Dividends-received exclusion.

106. If a taxpayer qualifies for the earned
income credit, such credit may
    a.   Be carried back or forward if
          unused.
    b.   Be subtracted from adjusted gross
          income to arrive at taxable income.
    c.   Result in a refund even if the
          taxpayer had no tax withheld from
          wages.
    d.   Result in a refund only if the tax-
          payer had tax withheld from wages.

107. If a taxpayer qualifies for the earned income credit, such credit can be subtracted from

 a. Gross income to arrive at adjusted gross income.

 b. Adjusted gross income to arrive at taxable income after personal exemptions.

 c. The tax owed, or can result in a refund, but only if the taxpayer had tax withheld from wages.

 d. The tax owed, or can result in a refund, even if the taxpayer had <u>no</u> tax withheld from wages.

108. In 1989, Alex Burgos paid $600 to Rita, his ex-wife, for child support. Under the terms of the divorce decree, Alex claims the exemption for his five year old son, William, who lived with Rita for the entire year. Alex's only income in 1989 was from wages of $5,500, resulting in an income tax of $75. How much is Alex's earned income credit for 1989?

 a. $0
 b. $328
 c. $378
 d. $500

109. Ray Birch, age 60, is single with no dependents. Birch's only income is from his occupation as a self-employed plumber. Birch must file a return for 1989 if his net earnings from self-employment are at least

 a. $ 400
 b. $1,950
 c. $3,000
 d. $4,950

110. A married couple filed their joint 1988 calendar-year return on March 15, 1989 and attached a check for the balance of tax due as shown on the return. On June 15, 1989, the couple discovered that they had failed to include $2,000 of home mortgage interest in their itemized deductions. In order for the couple to recover the tax that they would have saved by using the $2,000 deduction, they must file an amended return no later than

 a. December 31, 1991.
 b. March 15, 1992.
 c. April 15, 1992.
 d. June 15, 1992.

111. Richard Baker filed his 1988 individual income tax return on April 15, 1989. On December 31, 1989, he learned that 100 shares of stock that he owned had become worthless in 1988. Since he did not deduct this loss on his 1988 return, Baker intends to file a claim for refund. This refund claim must be filed not later than April 15,

 a. 1990
 b. 1992
 c. 1995
 d. 1996

112. On April 15, 1989, a married couple filed their joint 1988 calendar-year return showing gross income of $80,000. Their return had been prepared by a professional tax preparer who mistakenly omitted $30,000 of income which, in good faith, the preparer considered to be nontaxable. No information with regard to this omitted income was disclosed on the return or attached statements. By what date must the Internal Revenue Service assert a notice of deficiency before the statute of limitations expires?

 a. December 31, 1991.
 b. April 15, 1992.
 c. December 31, 1994.
 d. April 15, 1995.

113. Harold Thompson, a self-employed individual, had income transactions for 1988 (duly reported on his return filed in April 1989) as follows

Gross receipts	$400,000
Less cost of goods sold and deductions	320,000
Net business income	$ 80,000
Capital gains	36,000
Gross income	$116,000

In March 1990 Thompson discovers that he had inadvertently omitted some income on his 1988 return and retains Mann, CPA, to determine his position under the statute of limitations. Mann should advise Thompson that the six-year statute of limitations would apply to his 1988 return only if he omitted from gross income an amount in excess of

 a. $ 20,000
 b. $ 29,000
 c. $100,000
 d. $109,000

114. If a taxpayer omits from his or her income tax return an amount that exceeds 25% of the gross income reported on the return, the Internal Revenue Service can issue a notice of deficiency within a maximum period of

 a. 3 years from the date the return was filed, if filed before the due date.

 b. 3 years from the date the return was due, if filed by the due date.

 c. 6 years from the date the return was filed, if filed before the due date.

 d. 6 years from the date the return was due, if filed by the due date.

Problem

Problem 1   (1186,Q5)

(40 to 50 minutes)

The following information pertains to Alex and Myra Cole, a married couple filing a joint federal income tax return for the calendar year 1989

Alex, age 72—cash received in 1989

Social security benefits	
Gross amount	$ 9,900
Less voluntary premiums under Medicare Part B	190
Net amount received	$ 9,710
Proceeds of life insurance policy on death of friend	5,000
Proceeds from sales of stock	
Bought in May 1980— basis $2,000	3,000
Bought in October 1989— basis $900	700
Dividends	
From taxable domestic corporations	500
On life insurance policy (accumulated premiums not exceeded)	131

Myra, age 60—cash received in 1989

Salary—employed as actuary			
Gross amount		$62,000	
Amount withheld			
Federal income tax	$10,000		
State income tax	3,349		
FICA taxes	3,380		
United Fund pledge	240	16,969	45,031
Total cash received			$64,072

Cash paid in 1989

Rent, household, and other personal expenses		$40,000
Estimated 1989 federal income tax		3,000
Business travel away from home overnight		800
Continuing professional education courses required by Society of Actuaries		400
Medical and dental expenses		
Doctors	$ 3,000	
Dentures	800	
Travel to doctors	100	3,900
Contribution to a national political party		500
Total cash paid		$48,600

Additional information:

• The 1988 joint federal income tax return showed a tax overpayment of $900, which was refunded to the Coles in 1989.

• The 1988 joint state income tax return showed a tax overpayment of $110, which was refunded to the Coles in 1989.

• The Coles itemized their deductions on their 1988 return.

• In March 1989, Alex donated 100 shares of stock of a listed corporation to a recognized charitable organization. Alex's basis for this stock, which was bought in 1960, was $1,000. Fair market value of this stock on the date of the donation was $7,000.

• Included in the Coles' personal expenses was $1,100 for state sales taxes, substantiated by receipts.

• The Coles supported their son, Ben, who had been disabled since birth, and who lived in the Cole household. Ben had no income. He died January 1989 at the age of 34.

• In June 1989, Myra received a watch as a gift from her employer, as a token of the employer's appreciation for Myra's efforts in recruiting new clients. This watch had a fair market value of $1,500. The recruiting of new clients was not part of Myra's prescribed duties.

• In 1980, Alex established a reversionary ("Clifford") trust for the benefit of a destitute friend who lives alone. Trust income amounted to $2,200 in 1989, which constituted more than 50% of the friend's support for the year. A local bank is trustee.

• Personal exemptions and exemptions for dependents are $2,000 each.

• The standard deduction is $5,200.

Required:

a. Prepare a detailed schedule computing Alex and Myra Cole's joint taxable income for 1989. Show each appropriate item separately in the schedule, and classify each item properly. Any possible alternative treatment should be resolved in a manner that will minimize 1989 taxable income.

b. Assume that Alex and Myra Cole's 1989 federal income tax on their 1989 joint taxable income is $12,957 before tax credits and payments. Compute the net amount of tax payable or net overpayment of tax.

Problem 2   (587,Q4)   (45 to 55 minutes)

In December 1988, John Ford (age 40) died, leaving a wife (Ann, age 35) and a dependent son (Earl, age 3). A 1988 joint return was filed in April 1989 for John and Ann. Ann now consults you, as a CPA, for advice as to her 1989 tax status. She furnishes you with the following projections pertaining to her expected cash receipts and expenditures for the year ending December 31, 1989:

Employment as an outside salesperson:

Gross salary and commissions	$50,000
Ordinary and necessary employee business expenses	
Allowable transportation	4,000
Stationery, postage, telephone	1,000

Payroll taxes

Federal income tax withheld	9,000
FICA tax withheld ($3,604.80 rounded to nearest dollar)	3,605
State income tax withheld	1,800

Employment as part-time teacher:

Gross salary	3,000
Payroll taxes	
Federal income tax withheld	300
FICA tax withheld	225

Other cash expected to be received in 1989:

Bequest under husband's will	25,000
Life insurance proceeds on husband's death	15,000
Dividends from taxable domestic corporations	500
Gross lottery winnings in January 1989	2,000

Security transaction in 1989:

Net proceeds from sale of 500 shares of stock	10,000

(This stock was inherited from Ann's father, Sam, in 1980; Sam had paid $2,500 for this stock, which had a fair market value of $6,000 on the date of Sam's death; Sam's estate did not elect to use the alternate valuation date.)

In addition, John had provided in his will for the establishment of a simple trust, under which all of the trust's income was required to be distributed currently to Ann, as beneficiary of this trust. The entire trust principal was invested in bank certificates of deposit. Trust income is expected to be $12,000 in 1989. However, Ann wants to draw only $7,000 of this income in 1989.

During 1989, Ann expects to have the following cash expenditures in addition to those indicated previously:

Food, clothing, household, and miscellaneous personal expenses for both Ann and Earl	$20,000
Estimated income tax--federal	5,000
Estimated income tax--state	1,200
State inheritance tax on John's taxable estate	2,100
Realty taxes on residence	3,600
City and state sales taxes	1,100
Auto license and registration fees	50
Contribution to church	600
Political contribution	100
Lottery tickets	420
Pari-mutuel gambling	480

Required:

    a. Prepare a schedule listing all items of projected receipts and expenditures that have <u>no</u> effect on Ann Ford's 1989 federal taxable income.

    b. Prepare a schedule computing Ann Ford's projected 1989 federal taxable income, in the following sequence:

> Adjusted gross income
> Itemized deductions
> Personal exemptions ($2,000 per exemption)
> Taxable income

    c. Assume that Ann Ford's projected 1989 federal income tax on her federal income will be $12,421 before credits and prepayments of tax. Compute the projected balance of tax payable or net overpayment.

<u>Problem 3</u>   (1189,Q5)   (40 to 50 minutes)

    The following information pertains to Fred and Laura Shaw, a married couple filing a joint federal income tax return for the calendar year 1989:

<u>Fred, age 73 – cash received in 1989</u>

Salary--employed as an industrial engineer		
Gross amount		$80,000
Amounts withheld		
Federal income tax	$17,000	
State income tax	4,000	
FICA taxes	3,605	
Medical insurance premiums	1,200	25,805
Net amount received		$54,195
Social security benefits		12,000
Dividends on life insurance policy		
(accumulated net premiums not exceeded)		400

<u>Laura, age 61 – cash received in 1989</u>

Salary--from part-time employment		
Gross amount		$15,000
Amounts withheld		
Federal income tax	$ 2,800	
State income tax	120	
FICA taxes	1,127	4,047
Net amount received		10,953
Unemployment compensation benefits		600

<u>Cash received jointly in 1989</u>

Proceeds from sale of stock	
(Bought in 1970--basis $9,000)	2,500
Dividends from taxable domestic corporations	527
Interest on U.S. Government Savings Bonds	100
Total cash received	$81,275

Problem 3 (continued)

Cash disbursed in 1989

Household and miscellaneous personal expenses	$50,000
State sales taxes substantiated by receipts	1,900
Estimated 1989 federal income tax payments	2,000
Fee paid to CPA for tax return preparation	250
Unreimbursed business travel away from home overnight	900
Continuing prefessional education courses required to maintain job skills	700
Membership dues to Society of Industrial Engineers	150
Contribution to a national political party	200
Realty taxes on primary residence	3,000
Realty taxes on summer cottage	800
Mortgage interest on primary residence	2,300
Mortgage principal on primary residence	500
Mortgage interest on summer cottage (no payments on principal)	1,800
Total cash disbursed	$64,500

Additional information:

• The 1988 joint federal income tax return showed a tax overpayment of $43, which the Shaws elected to credit to their 1989 estimated tax.

• The 1988 joint state income tax return showed no balance of tax due or overpayment.

• In June 1989, Fred donated 500 shares of stock to a listed corporation to a recognized charitable organization. Fred's basis for this stock, which was bought in 1975, was $1,100. Fair market value of this stock on the date of the donation was $1,400.

• In July 1989, the summer cottage, which was not insured, sustained fire damage. Information pertaining to this property is as follows:

Basis	$40,000
Fair market value immediately before the fire	66,000
Fair market value immediately after the fire	50,000

• The Shaws supported their daughter, Doris, who had been disabled since infancy, and who lived in the Shaw household. Doris had no income. She died on January 2, 1989.

• Personal exemptions and dependency exemptions are $2,000 each for 1989.

• The basic standard deduction is $5,000 and the additional standard deduction is $600 for 1989.

Required:

a. Prepare a detailed schedule computing Fred and Laura Shaw's joint taxable income for 1989. Show each appropriate item separately in the schedule, and classify each item properly. Any possible alternative treatment should be resolved in a manner that will minimize 1989 taxable income. Round to the nearest dollar.

b. Assume that Fred and Laura Shaw's 1989 federal income tax on their 1989 joint taxable income is $16,946 before tax credits and payments. Compute the net amount of tax payable or net overpayment of tax.

Multiple Choice Answers

1. c	24. c	47. b	70. b	93. c
2. b	25. c	48. d	71. d	94. c
3. b	26. a	49. d	72. c	95. c
4. d	27. a	50. b	73. c	96. b
5. b	28. d	51. d	74. b	97. d
6. d	29. d	52. d	75. d	98. b
7. c	30. d	53. d	76. d	99. b
8. b	31. d	54. b	77. a	100. b
9. b	32. c	55. b	78. b	101. b
10. c	33. d	56. a	79. d	102. c
11. d	34. a	57. a	80. d	103. b
12. c	35. c	58. b	81. a	104. c
13. a	36. b	59. c	82. c	105. c
14. d	37. a	60. a	83. a	106. c
15. d	38. d	61. b	84. c	107. d
16. d	39. b	62. a	85. b	108. a
17. a	40. c	63. b	86. a	109. a
18. d	41. a	64. b	87. b	110. c
19. b	42. d	65. b	88. c	111. d
20. b	43. a	66. b	89. b	112. d
21. c	44. c	67. a	90. b	113. d
22. d	45. d	68. d	91. c	114. d
23. d	46. b	69. b	92. c	

Multiple Choice Answer Explanations

I.B.3. Annuities

1. (580,P3,57) (c) The requirement is to determine the pension (annuity) amounts excluded from income during 1989, 1990, and 1991. Brown's contribution of $12,000 will be recovered pro rata over the life of the annuity. Under this rule, $100 per month (12,000 ÷ 120 months) is excluded from income.

	Received	Excluded	Included
1989	$4,900	$ 700	$4,200
1990	8,400	1,200	7,200
1991	8,400	1,200	7,200

I.B.4. Life Insurance Proceeds

2. (1180,Q2,28) (b) The requirement is to determine the amount of life insurance payments to be included in a widow's gross income. Life insurance proceeds paid by reason of death are excluded from income if paid in a lump sum or in installments. If the payments are received in installments, the principal amount of the policy divided by the number of payments is excluded each year. Therefore, $1,200 of the $5,200 insurance payment is included in Penelope's gross income:

Annual installment	$ 5,200
Principal amount	
($100,000 ÷ 25)	- 4,000
	$ 1,200

The exclusion of the first $1,000 in excess of the pro rata portion of the death benefit for a surviving spouse was repealed for deaths occurring after 10/22/86.

I.B.5. Employee Benefits

3. (1182,P3,47) (b) The requirement is to determine the amount of group-term life insurance premium that is taxable to Hetnar. The cost of group-term life insurance provided by an employer must be included in an employee's income to the extent of the cost of the life insurance coverage in excess of $50,000. The excess coverage is $90,000 – $50,000 = $40,000. At a cost of $8 per thousand, the amount taxable to Hetnar is $8 x 40 = $320.

4. (582,P3,47) (d) The requirement is to determine the amount of employee death payments to be included in gross income by the widow and the son. Up to $5,000 of an employee's death benefits is excluded from income. Note that there is only one $5,000 exclusion allowed. Since $10,000 was received by each beneficiary, the $5,000 exclusion is allocated proportionately to each beneficiary. Thus, each includes $10,000 – $2,500 = $7,500 in gross income.

5. (1187,Q1,1) (b) The requirement is to determine the maximum amount of tax-free group-term life insurance coverage that can be provided to an employee by an employer. The cost of the first $50,000 of group-term life insurance coverage provided by an employer will be excluded from an employee's income.

6. (586,Q3,49) (d) The requirement is to determine the amount to be included in Hal's gross income for the current year. All three amounts that Hal received as a result of his injury are excluded from gross income. Benefits received as workers' compensation and compensation for damages for personal injuries are always excluded from gross income. Amounts received from an employer's accident and health plan as reimbursement for medical expenses are excluded so long as the medical expenses are not deducted as itemized deductions.

7. (579,Q2,26) (c) James Martin's gross income is:

Salary	$50,000
Bonus	10,000
Allowance for moving expenses	5,000
	$65,000

Although the moving expense allowance must be included in income, Martin may deduct amounts spent on qualified moving expenditures. Medical insurance premiums paid by an employer are excluded from the employee's income.

I.B.9. Dividends

8. (1187,Q1,9) (b) The requirement is to
determine the amount of dividend income that
should be reported by Gail Judd. The $100
dividend on Gail's life insurance policy is
treated as a reduction of the cost of
insurance (because total dividends have not
yet exceeded accumulated premiums paid) and is
excluded from gross income. Thus, Gail will
report the $300 common stock dividend and the
$500 preferred stock dividend, a total of $800
as dividend income for 1989.

9. (1185,Q2,26) (b) The requirement is to
determine the amount of dividend income to be
reported on Amy's 1990 return. Dividends are
included in income at earlier of actual or
constructive receipt. When corporate dividends are paid by mail, they are included in
income for the year in which received. Thus,
the $875 dividend received 1/2/90 is included
in income for 1990. The $500 dividend on a
life insurance policy from a mutual insurance
company is treated as a reduction of the cost
of insurance and is excluded from gross
income.

10. (579,Q2,23) (c) The requirement is to
determine the amount of dividends to be
reported by the Mitchells on a joint return.
The amount of dividends would be ($400 + $50
+ $300) = $750. The $200 dividend on the life
insurance policy is not gross income, but is
considered a reduction of the cost of the
policy.

I.B.11. Interest Income

11. (1182,P3,44) (d) The requirement is to
determine the amount of tax-exempt interest.
Interest on obligations of a state or one of
its political subdivisions (e.g., New York
Port Authority bonds), or a possession of the
U.S. (e.g., Puerto Rico Commonwealth bonds) is
tax-exempt.

12. (580,P3,48) (c) Stone will report
$1,700 of interest income. Interest on FIT
refunds, personal injury awards, U.S. savings
bonds, and most other sources is fully taxable. However, interest on state or municipal
bonds is generally not taxable.

13. (1188,Q1,4) (a) The requirement is to
determine the amount of interest income to be
included in Clark's gross income for 1989.
Both the $20 of interest on insurance
dividends left on deposit with the Veterans
Administration and the $30 of interest on the
state income tax refund must be included in
Clark's gross income for 1989.

14. (1187,Q1,5) (d) The requirement is to
determine how Don Raff's $500 interest for-
feiture penalty should be reported. An
interest forfeiture penalty for making a
premature withdrawal from a certificate of
deposit should be deducted from gross income
in arriving at adjusted gross income in the
year in which the penalty is incurred, which
in this case is 1990.

15. (1185,Q2,24) (d) The requirement is to
determine the amount of interest income to be
reported on Amy's 1989 return. Both the $10
of interest on insurance dividends left on deposit and the $18 of interest on state income
tax refund must be reported on Amy's return, a
total of $28. Note that the exclusion for in-
terest income on state and municipal bonds
does not apply to interest received on a state
tax refund.

I.B.12. Scholarships

16. (1180,Q2,21) (d) The requirement is to
determine the amount to be included in Davis'
gross income for 1990 from the fellowship
grant. Scholarships and fellowships may be
excludable for degree candidates. But if the
recipient is not a candidate for a degree, the
grant is not excludable. Therefore, $4,500 is
included in Davis' gross income for 1990.

I.B.16. Lease Improvements

17. (1179,Q2,31) (a) The requirement is to
determine a lessor's 1990 gross income. A
lessor excludes from income any increase in
the value of property caused by improvements
made by the lessee, unless the improvements
were made in lieu of rent. In this case,
there is no indication that the improvements
were made in lieu of rent. Therefore, for
1990, Farley should only include the six rent
payments in income: 6 x $1,000 = $6,000.

I.C. Items to be Included in Gross Income

18. (583,P3,45) (d) The requirement is to
determine the amount of gross income. Drury's
gross income includes the $36,000 salary, the
$500 of premiums paid by her employer for
group-term life insurance coverage in excess
of $50,000, and the $5,000 proceeds received
from a state lottery.

19. (1182,P3,46) (b) The requirement is to
determine the amount of foster child payments
to be included in income by the Charaks. Foster child payments are excluded from income to
the extent they represent reimbursement for
expenses incurred for care of the foster
child. Since the payments ($3,900) exceeded

the expenses ($3,000), the $900 excess used for the Charaks' personal expenses must be included in their gross income.

20. (1188,Q1,3) (b) The requirement is to determine the amount and the year in which the tip income should be included in Pierre's gross income. If an individual receives less than $20 in tips during one month while working for one employer, the tips do not have to be reported to the employer and the tips are included in the individual's gross income when received. However, if an individual receives $20 or more in tips during one month while working for one employer, the individual must report the total amount of tips to that employer by the 10th day of the next month. Then the tips are included in gross income for the month in which they are reported to the employer. Here, Pierre received $2,000 in tips during December 1989 which he reported to his employer in January 1990. Thus, the $2,000 of tips will be included in Pierre's gross income for 1990.

21. (1188,Q1,7) (c) The requirement is to determine the correct statement regarding the alimony deduction in connection with a 1990 divorce. To be considered alimony, cash payments must terminate on the death of the payee spouse. Answer (a) is incorrect because alimony payments cannot be contingent on the status of the divorced couple's children. Answer (b) is incorrect because the divorced couple cannot be members of the same household at the time the alimony is paid. Answer (d) is incorrect because only cash payments can be considered alimony.

22. (1188,Q1,9) (d) The requirement is to determine the amount of a $10,000 award for outstanding civic achievement that Joan should include in her 1990 adjusted gross income. An award for civic achievement can be excluded from gross income only if the recipient was selected without any action on his/her part, is not required to render substantial future services as a condition of receiving the award, and designated that the award is to be directly transferred by the payor to a governmental unit or a tax-exempt charitable, educational, or religious organization. Here, since Joan accepted and actually received the award, the $10,000 must be included in her adjusted gross income.

23. (588,Q1,2) (d) The requirement is to determine the amount of lottery winnings that should be included in Gow's taxable income. Lottery winnings are gambling winnings and must be included in gross income. Gambling losses are deductible from AGI as a miscellaneous deduction (to the extent of winnings) not subject to the 2% of AGI floor if a taxpayer itemizes deductions. Since Gow elected the standard deduction for 1989, the $400 spent on lottery tickets is not deductible. Thus, all $5,000 of Gow's lottery winnings are included in his taxable income.

I.C.6. Rents and Royalties

24. (583,P3,42) (c) The requirement is to determine the amount to be reported as gross rents. Gross rents include the $50,000 of recurring rents plus the $2,000 lease cancellation payment. The $1,000 of lease improvements are excluded from income since they were not required in lieu of rent.

25. (1187,Q1,3) (c) The requirement is to determine the amount of net rental income that Gow should include in his adjusted gross income. Since Gow lives in one of two identical apartments, only 50% of the expenses relating to both apartments can be allocated to the rental unit.

Rent	$7,200
Less:	
Real estate taxes (50% x $6,400)	(3,200)
Painting of rental apartment	(800)
Fire insurance (50% x $600)	(300)
Depreciation (50% x $5,000)	(2,500)
Net rental income	$ 400

26. (1185,Q2,25) (a) The requirement is to determine the amount of rent income to be reported on Amy's 1989 return. Both the $6,000 of rent received for 1989, as well as the $1,000 of advance rent received in 1989 for the last two months of the lease must be included in income for 1989. Advance rent must be included in income in the year received regardless of the period covered or the accounting method used.

I.C.19. Unemployment Compensation

27. (588,Q1,1) (a) The requirement is to determine the amount of state unemployment benefits that should be included in adjusted gross income. All unemployment compensation benefits received after 1986 must be included in gross income.

I.D.1. Cash Method or Accrual Method

28. (1188,Q1,1) (c) The requirement is to determine the amount of income to be reported

in Blair's 1989 return for the stock received in satisfaction of a client fee owed to Blair. Since Blair is a cash method taxpayer, the amount of income to be recognized equals the $4,000 fair market value of the stock on date of receipt. Note that the $4,000 of income is reported by Blair in 1989 when the stock is received; not in 1990 when the stock is sold.

29. (1187,Q1,6) (d) The requirement is to determine the correct statement with regard to the cash method of reporting income. Under the cash method of tax accounting, income is reported (i.e., recognized) when first actually received or constructively received either in cash or in property. In the case of property, the FMV of the property received is the amount to be reported. Constructive receipt means that an item of income is unqualifiedly available without restriction (e.g., interest resulting from a savings account is reported as income for the year in which the interest is credited to the account).

30. (1184,Q2,37) (d) The requirement is to determine the amount of salary taxable to Burg in 1989. Since Burg is a cash-basis taxpayer, salary is taxable to Burg when actually or constructively received, whichever is earlier. Since the $30,000 of unpaid salary was unqualifiedly available to Burg during 1989, Burg is considered to have constructively received it. Thus, Burg must report a total of $80,000 of salary for 1989; the $50,000 actually received plus $30,000 constructively received.

31. (1183,Q2,36) (d) The requirement is to determine the 1989 medical practice net income for a cash basis physician. Dr. Berger's income consists of the $200,000 received from patients and the $30,000 received from third-party reimbursers during 1989. His 1989 deductions include the $20,000 of salaries and $24,000 of other expenses paid in 1989. The year-end bonuses will be deductible for 1990.

I.E. Business Income and Deductions

32. (588,Q2,25) (c) The requirement is to determine the correct statement regarding a corporation's deduction for bad debts in 1990. Except for certain financial institutions, the 1986 TRA repealed the reserve method of accounting for bad debts. Taxpayers who previously used the reserve method are required to switch to the direct (i.e., specific) charge-off method for taxable years after 1986.

33. (587,Q3,48) (d) The requirement is to determine the amount of life insurance premium that can be deducted in Ram Corp.'s income tax return. Generally, no deduction is allowed for expenditures which produce tax-exempt income. Here, no deduction is allowed for the $6,000 life insurance premium because Ram is the beneficiary of the policy, and the proceeds of the policy will be excluded from Ram's income when the officer dies.

34. (586,Q3,52) (a) The requirement is to determine the amount of bad debt deduction for a cash basis taxpayer. Accounts receivable resulting from services rendered by a cash basis taxpayer have a zero tax basis, because the income has not yet been reported. Thus, failure to collect the receivable results in a nondeductible loss.

35. (584,Q2,21) (c) The requirement is to determine the loss that Cook can claim as a result of the worthless note receivable in 1990. Cook's $1,000 loss will be treated as a nonbusiness bad debt, deductible as a short-term capital loss. The loss is not a business bad debt because Cook was not in the business of lending money, nor was the loan required as a condition of Cook's employment. Since Cook owned no stock in Precision, the loss could not be deemed to be a loss from worthless stock, deductible as a long-term capital loss.

36. (1183,Q3,59) (b) The requirement is to determine the amount of gifts deductible as a business expense. The deduction for business gifts is limited to $25 per recipient each year. Thus, Palo Corporation's deduction for business gifts would be [(4 x $10) + (13 x $25)] = $365.

I.E.6. Passive Activity Losses

37. (589,Q3,54) (a) The requirement is to determine the correct statement regarding the passive loss rules involving rental real estate activities. By definition, any rental activity is a passive activity without regard as to whether or not the taxpayer materially participates in the activity. Answer (b) is incorrect because interest and dividend income not derived in the ordinary course of business is treated as portfolio income, and cannot be offset by passive rental activity losses when the "active participation" requirement is not met. Answer (c) is incorrect because passive rental activity credits cannot be used to offset the tax attributable to nonpassive activities. Answer (d) is incorrect because the passive activity rules contain no provision that excludes taxpayers below a certain income level from the limitations imposed by the passive activity rules.

38. (1188,Q1,5) **(d)** The requirement is to determine the correct statement regarding an individual taxpayer's passive losses and credits relating to rental real estate activities that cannot be currently deducted. Generally, losses and credits from passive activities can only be used to offset income from (or tax allocable to) passive activities. If there is insufficient passive-activity income (or tax) to absorb passive activity losses and credits, the unused losses and credits are carried forward indefinitely or until the property is disposed of in a taxable transaction. Answers (a) and (c) are incorrect because unused passive losses and credits are never carried back to prior taxable years. Answer (b) is incorrect because there is no maximum carryforward period.

I.F.2. Depreciation

39. (588,Q2,26) **(b)** The requirement is to determine the portion of the $201,000 cost of the machine that can be treated as an expense. Sec. 179 permits a taxpayer to annually elect to treat up to $10,000 of the cost of qualifying depreciable personal property as an expense rather than as a capital expenditure. However, the $10,000 maximum is reduced dollar-for-dollar by the cost of qualifying property placed in service during the taxable year that exceeds $200,000. Here, the maximum amount that can be expensed is [$10,000 – ($201,000 – $200,000)] = $9,000.

40. (580,Q2,40) **(c)** The requirement is to determine the depreciation allowance for 1989. The salvage value of $7,000 is irrelevant since salvage value is disregarded in computing the depreciation allowance. The machinery is classified as 7-year property subject to 200% declining balance and a midyear convention:

$$($70,000 \times 1/7) = $10,000$$

II.A.1. Reimbursed Expenses

41. (583,P3,46) **(a)** The requirement is to determine the amount of unreimbursed employee expenses that can be deducted by Gilbert if he does not itemize deductions. Since only reimbursed employee expenses can be deducted for AGI, Gilbert cannot deduct any of the expenses listed if he does not itemize deductions. The unreimbursed employee business expenses are deductible only as itemized deductions.

II.D. Contributions to Certain Retirement Plans

42. (1182,P3,58) **(d)** A single individual with AGI over $35,000 for 1989 would only be entitled to an IRA deduction if the taxpayer is not covered by a qualified employee pension plan.

43. (1188,Q1,11) **(a)** The requirement is to determine the allowable IRA deduction on the Cranes' 1989 joint return. Since Sol is covered by his employer's pension plan, the Cranes' contribution of $2,250 is proportionately phased-out as a deduction by their adjusted gross income in the bracket between $40,000 and $50,000. Thus, since their adjusted gross income exceeds $50,000, they are not allowed any deduction for their 1989 IRA contribution.

44. (588,Q1,15) **(c)** The requirement is to determine the Lees' maximum IRA contribution and deduction on a joint return for 1989. Since neither taxpayer was covered by an employer-sponsored pension plan, there is no phase-out of the maximum deduction due to the level of their adjusted gross income. The contribution and deduction limit on a joint return when there is a nonworking spouse is the lesser of $2,250, or 100% of compensation. Thus, the Lees may contribute and deduct a maximum of $2,250 to their individual retirement accounts for 1989.

45. (586,Q3,50) **(d)** The requirement is to determine Ida's maximum IRA contribution and deduction for 1989. If an individual is not covered by a qualified pension plan, the maximum contribution and deduction for an IRA is limited to the lesser of (1) $2,000, or (2) 100% of compensation (including alimony). Since Ida received $25,000 of alimony and had earnings of $900 from a part-time job, Ida's maximum contribution and deduction for an IRA is $2,000.

46. (1179,Q2,34) **(b)** The maximum deduction for contributions to a self-employed retirement plan is limited to the lesser of $30,000, or 25% of earned income. Since "earned income" includes the retirement plan deduction, the maximum deduction is the lesser of $30,000, or 20% of income from self-employment. Since 20% of $20,000 ($4,000) is less than $30,000, the deduction is limited to $4,000.

47. (579,Q2,25) **(b)** Since neither spouse is covered by a qualified employee pension plan, the Todds may contribute and deduct a total of

$2,250 to their individual retirement ac-
counts. The contribution limit when there is
a nonworking spouse is the lesser of 100% of
compensation or $2,250. In this case, $2,250
is less than 100% of $40,000. The prize won
on the TV game show does not qualify Wilma as
a working spouse, nor is it compensation for
purposes of computing the 100% limit.

II.F. Alimony

48. (1188,Q1,10) (d) The requirement is to
determine which allowable deduction can be
claimed as a deduction in arriving at an
individual's 1990 adjusted gross income. Of
the deductions listed, only alimony payments
can be deducted in arriving at an individual's
adjusted gross income. Personal casualty
losses and charitable contributions are
deductible only as itemized deductions. The
unreimbursed business expenses of an outside
salesman-employee are deductible only as a
miscellaneous itemized deduction (subject to a
2% floor).

III. Itemized Deductions from Adjusted Gross Income

49. (1183,Q2,24) (d) The requirement is to
determine Jill's standard deduction for 1990.
Since Jill is a single individual, her
standard deduction amount is $3,250.

III.A. Medical and Dental Expenses

50. (582,P3,50) (b) The requirement is to
determine Stenger's net medical expense deduction for 1989. It would be computed as
follows

Prescription drugs	$ 300
Medical insurance premiums	750
Doctors	1,650
Eyeglasses	75
	$2,775
Less 7.5% of AGI ($35,000)	2,625
Medical expense deduction for 1989	$ 150

51. (580,P3,53) (d) The requirement is to
determine the total amount of deductible
medical expenses for the Bensons before the
application of any limitation rules. Deductible medical expenses include those incurred
by a taxpayer, taxpayer's spouse, dependents
of the taxpayer, or any person for whom the
taxpayer could claim a dependency exemption
except that the person had income of $2,000 or
more, or filed a joint return. Thus, the
Bensons may deduct medical expenses incurred
for themselves, for John (i.e., no dependency
exemption only because his income is $2,000 or
more), and for Nancy (i.e., a dependent of the
Bensons).

52. (586,Q3,56) (d) The requirement is to
determine the amount of qualifying medical expenses to be included on the Paynes' return
for 1989 before the adjusted gross income percentage test. The Paynes' return can include
medical expenses that the Paynes pay for
themselves, as well as the medical expenses
they pay for an individual qualifying as a
dependent, even though a dependency exemption
cannot be claimed because the individual has
gross income of $2,000 or more or files a
joint return. An individual qualifies as a
taxpayer's dependent for purpose of the
medical deduction if the individual is of
specified relationship or a member of the
taxpayer's household, is a U.S. citizen or
resident, and the taxpayer provides more than
half of the individual's support. Thus, the
Paynes can include the $700 of medical ex-
penses paid for Gail's mother, as well as the
$500 of medical expenses paid for their son,
who does not qualify as a dependency exemption
only because he has gross income of $2,000 or
more.

III.B. Taxes

53. (583,P3,51) (d) The requirement is to
determine the amount of state income taxes
deductible as an itemized deduction for 1989.
The amount deductible includes the $2,000 of
taxes withheld during 1989, plus the $200
assessment of 1987 tax paid in 1989. Note
that the 1988 refund is **not** netted against the
taxes paid in 1989.

54. (1182,P3,51) (b) The requirement is to
determine Sara's deduction for state income
taxes in 1989. Sara's deduction would consist
of the $2,000 withheld by her employer in
1989, plus the three estimated payments (3 x
$300 = $900) actually paid during 1989, a total of $2,900. Note that the 1/15/90 esti-
mated payment would be deductible for 1990.

55. (582,P3,52) (b) The requirement is to
determine the amount of **taxes** deductible as an
itemized deduction. The $360 vehicle tax
based on value is deductible. The real property tax of $2,700 must be apportioned between
the Bronsons and the buyer for tax purposes
even though they did not actually make an
apportionment. Since the house was sold
June 30, while the taxes were paid to September 30, the Bronsons would deduct 6/9 x $2,700
= $1,800. The buyer would deduct the remain-
ing $900.

56. (1188,Q1,13) (a) The requirement is to
determine Lyons' itemized deduction for real
estate taxes on his 1989 return. Generally,
an individual's payment of state, local, or
foreign real estate taxes is deductible as an

itemized deduction if the individual is the owner of the property on which the taxes are imposed. Since the $3,000 that Lyons paid was for real estate taxes on a two-family house owned by Lyons' mother, Lyons cannot deduct the payment because he did not own the property.

57. (1181,Q3,56) (a) The requirement is to determine what portion of the $1,300 of realty taxes is deductible by King in 1989. The $600 of delinquent taxes charged to the seller and paid by King are not deductible, but are added to the cost of the property. The $700 of taxes for 1989 are apportioned between the seller and King according to the number of days that each held the property during the year. King's deduction would be:

$$\frac{184}{365} \times \$700 = \underline{\underline{\$353}}$$

58. (581,P3,57) (b) The requirement is to determine the amount of property taxes deductible as itemized deductions. The property taxes on the residence and the land held for appreciation, together with the personal property taxes on the auto are deductible. The special assessment is not deductible, but would be added to the basis of the residence.

III.C. Interest Expense

59. (583,P3,50) (c) The requirement is to determine the amount of interest expense deductible as an itemized deduction. The $3,600 of home mortgage interest, and the $900 mortgage prepayment penalty are fully deductible as interest expense in computing itemized deductions. The $1,200 interest on the life insurance policy is limited to $120 ($1,200 x 10%) since it is classified as personal interest.

60. (582,P3,51) (a) The requirement is to determine the amount of interest deductible as an itemized deduction. Since 2/3 of the loan proceeds were used to purchase tax-exempt bonds, 2/3 of the bank interest is nondeductible. The remaining 1/3 of the bank interest ($1,200) is related to the purchase of the Arrow debentures and is classified as investment interest deductible to the extent of net investment income ($0). However, under a phase-in rule, $120 (10% x $1,200) would be deductible for 1990. The $3,000 of home mortgage interest is fully deductible as qualified residence interest. The interest on credit card charges is personal interest and is deductible to the extent of $50 (10% x $500).

61. (1180,Q2,30) (b) The requirement is to determine the amount deductible as investment interest expense. The deduction for invest-

ment interest is generally limited to the amount of net investment income. The net investment income is $45,000 (dividends and interest of $24,000, plus long-term capital gains of $25,000, less investment expense of $4,000). Under a phase-in rule, 10% of up to an additional $10,000 of investment interest is also allowed as a deduction for 1990. Thus, the amount deductible as investment interest expense is $46,000 ($45,000 + $1,000).

62. (1180,Q2,39) (a) Of the items listed relating to the tax deficiency for 1988, only the interest is deductible. The portion of this interest which is deductible in 1990 is limited to $7 (10% x $70). The additional federal income tax, the late filing penalty, and the negligence penalty are not deductible. Therefore, only $7 relating to the tax deficiency is deductible as an itemized deduction for 1990.

III.D. Charitable Contributions

63. (583,P3,52) (b) The requirement is to determine Lewis' charitable contribution deduction. The donation of appreciated stock held more than twelve months is a contribution of intangible, long-term captial gain appreciated property. The amount of contribution is the stock's FMV of $70,000, but is limited in deductibility for 1989 to 30% of AGI. Thus, the 1989 deduction is $100,000 x 30% = $30,000. The amount of contribution in excess of the 30% limitation ($70,000 - $30,000 = $40,000) can be carried forward for up to 5 years, subject to the 30% limitation in the carryforward years.

64. (1182,P3,52) (b) The requirement is to determine the amount of contributions deductible in 1989. Charitable contributions are generally deductible in the year actually paid. The 12/15/89 $500 charge to his bank credit card is considered a payment, and is deductible for 1989. The $1,000 promissory note delivered 11/1/89 is not considered a contribution until payment of the note upon maturity in 1990.

65. (1184,Q2,28) (b) The requirement is to determine Barlow's charitable contribution deduction for 1989. The cash contribution of $5,000 and the $800 FMV of used clothing are fully deductible. The deduction for the art object is limited to the $600 excess of its cost ($1,600) over its FMV ($1,000).

66. (1181,Q3,45) (b) The requirement is to determine the amount of student expenses deductible as a charitable contribution. A taxpayer may deduct as a charitable contribu-

tion up to $50 per <u>school</u> <u>month</u> of unreim-
bursed expenses incurred to maintain a student
(in the 12th or lower grade) in the taxpayer's
home pursuant to a written agreement with a
qualified organization. Since the student
started school in September, the amount deductible as a charitable contribution is $50 x
4 = $200.

67. (1179,Q2,37) (a) Vincent Tally is not
entitled to a deduction for contributions in
1989 because he did not give up his entire interest in the book collection. By reserving
the right to use and possess the book collection for his lifetime, Vincent Tally has made
a gift of a future interest. Therefore, no
deduction is available. The contribution will
be deductible when his entire interest in the
books is transferred to the art museum.

III.E. Casualty and Theft Losses

68. (589,Q3,48) (d) The requirement is to
determine the amount of the fire loss damage
to their personal residence that the Hoyts can
deduct as an itemized deduction. The amount
of a nonbusiness casualty loss is computed as
the lesser of (1) the adjusted basis of the
property, or (2) the property's decline in
FMV; reduced by any insurance recovery, and a
$100 floor. If an individual has a net
casualty loss for the year, it is then
deductible as an itemized deduction to the
extent that it exceeds 10% of adjusted gross
income.

Lesser of:			
Adjusted basis	=	$50,000	
Decline in FMV			
($60,000 –			
$55,000)	=	$ 5,000	$5,000
Reduce by:			
Insurance recovery		(0)	
$100 floor		(100)	
10% of $34,000 AGI		(3,400)	
Casualty loss			
itemized deduction		$1,500	

Note that the $2,500 spent for repairs is not
included in the computation of the loss.

69. (589,Q3,51) (b) The requirement is to
determine the proper treatment for the $800
appraisal fee that was incurred to determine
the amount of the Hoyts' fire loss. The appraisal fee is considered an expense of determining the Hoyts' tax liability; it is not a
part of the casualty loss itself. Thus, the
appraisal fee is deductible as a miscellaneous
itemized deduction subject to a 2% of adjusted
gross income floor.

70. (1188,Q1,15) (b) The requirement is to
determine the amount of a casualty loss
sustained on Cole's uninsured personal

residence before consideration of any "floor"
or other limitation on tax deductibility. The
amount of a personal casualty loss is the
lessor of (1) the adjusted basis of the
property ($150,000), or (2) the decline in the
property's fair market value resulting from
the casualty ($200,000 – $180,000 =
$20,000). Thus, Cole's casualty loss before
consideration of the "$100 floor" or the 10%
of adjusted gross income limitation is
$20,000.

III.F. Moving Expenses

71. (1182,P3,45) (d) The requirement is to
determine Martin's deductible moving expenses. Moving expenses are deductible if
closely related to the start of work at a new
location and a distance (i.e., new job must be
at least 35 miles from former residence) and
time (i.e., employed at least 39 weeks out of
12 months following move) tests are met.
Since the two tests are met, Martin's deductible moving expenses include both the $800
truck rental and the $300 penalty for breaking
his apartment lease.

72. (588,Q1,13) (c) The requirement is to
determine the correct statement regarding unreimbursed employee moving expenses. Answer (a) is incorrect because the 1986 TRA
changed the moving expense deduction to an
itemized deduction for taxable years beginning
after 1986. Answer (b) is incorrect because
the moving expense deduction is not subject to
a 2% of AGI floor. Answer (d) is incorrect
because moving expenses are deductible if a
distance test (i.e., distance between former
residence and new job must be at least 35
miles further than from the former residence
to the former job) and the time test (i.e.,
must be employed at least 39 weeks out of the
12 months following the move) are met. Answer (c), "Fully deductible only as miscellaneous itemized deductions," is the best
answer. However, note that although moving
expenses are deductible as an itemized
deduction for calendar-year 1989, they appear
on Form 1040 as a separate category of
itemized deduction and are not grouped with
"miscellaneous itemized deductions."

73. (1181,Q3,46) (c) The requirement is to
determine the amount deductible as indirect
moving expenses. The expenses of temporary
housing (limited to a 30-day period) and
househunting trips are deductible up to a
maximum of $1,500.

III.G. Miscellaneous Deductions

74. (1188,Q1,14) (b) The requirement is to determine the itemized deduction included in the category of miscellaneous itemized deductions subject to a 2% of adjusted gross income floor. Tax return preparation fees are deductible only as miscellaneous itemized deductions to the extent that the aggregate amount of expenses in that category exceeds 2% of the taxpayer's adjusted gross income. Employee moving expenses, medical expenses, and interest expense are deductible as separate categories of itemized deductions.

75. (586,Q3,51) (d) The requirement is to determine how expenses pertaining to business activities should be deducted by an outside salesman. An outside salesman is an employee who principally solicits business for his employer while away from the employer's place of business. All unreimbursed business expenses of an outside salesman are deducted as miscellaneous itemized deductions, subject to a 2% of AGI floor. Deductible expenses include business travel, secretarial help, and telephone expenses.

76. (1185,Q2,36) (d) The requirement is to determine the amount deductible as miscellaneous itemized deductions. The legal fee for preparation of a will is considered a personal expense and is not deductible. Similarly, the education expenses to qualify for a new occupation are not deductible. Education expenses are deductible only if they are incurred to maintain or improve skills in an employee's present occupation.

77. (1181,Q3,52) (a) The requirement is to determine the amount that can be claimed as miscellaneous itemized deductions. Both the initiation fee and the union dues are fully deductible. The voluntary benefit fund contribution is not deductible. Miscellaneous itemized deductions are generally deductible only to the extent they exceed 2% of AGI. In this case the deductible amount is $80 [$280 - (.02 x $10,000)].

78. (1180,Q2,38) (b) The requirement is to compute the amount of miscellaneous itemized deductions. The cost of uniforms not adaptable to general use (specialized work clothes), union dues, unreimbursed auto expenses, and the cost of income tax preparation are all miscellaneous itemized deductions. The preparation of a will is personal in nature, and is not deductible. Thus, the computation of Brodsky's miscellaneous itemized deductions in excess of the 2% of AGI floor is as follows

Unreimbursed auto expenses	$ 100
Specialized work clothes	550
Union dues	600
Cost of income tax preparation	150
	$1,400
Less (2% x $25,000)	(500)
Deduction allowed	$ 900

IV. Exemptions

79. (583,P3,56) (d) The requirement is to determine Robert's filing status and the number of exemptions that he should claim. Robert's father does not qualify as Robert's dependent because his father's gross income (interest income of $2,200) was not less than $2,000. Social security is not included in the gross income test. Since his father does not qualify as his dependent, Robert does not qualify for head-of-household filing status. Thus, Robert will file as single with one exemption.

80. (583,P3,57) (d) The requirement is to determine which of the brothers is eligible to claim the mother as a dependent through the use of a multiple support agreement. In the event no one person provides more than 50% of a dependent's support, any individual who contributes more than 10% is entitled to claim the exemption if each other person contributing more than 10% of the support signs a written consent not to claim the exemption. Thus, either Bill, Jon, or Tom may claim the mother as a dependent.

81. (583,P3,58) (a) The requirement is to determine the filing status of the Arnolds. Since they were legally separated under a decree of separate maintenance on the last day of the taxable year and do not qualify for head-of-household status, they must each file as single.

82. (582,P3,60) (c) The requirement is to determine the number of exemptions that can be claimed by the Ericksons. There is one exemption for Mr. Erickson and one exemption for his spouse. There is a dependency exemption for their son, and a dependency exemption for Mr. Erickson's mother. Note that a full exemption is allowed in the year of birth or death.

83. (581,P3,55) (a) Mr. and Mrs. Stoner are entitled to one exemption each. They are entitled to one exemption for their daughter since they provided over 50% of her support, and she was a full-time student not subject to the $2,000 gross income test. An exemption can be claimed for their son because they supported him, and he made less than $2,000 in gross income. No exemption is allowable for Mrs. Stoner's father since he was neither a U.S. citizen nor resident of U.S., Canada, or Mexico. Beginning in 1987, there is no additional exemption for being age 65 or older.

84. (580,P3,60) (c) The requirement is to determine the number of exemptions the Planters may claim on their joint tax return. There is one exemption for Mr. Planter, and one exemption for his spouse. In addition there is one dependency exemption for their daughter, and one dependency exemption for the niece. The dependency gross income test does not apply to their daughter since she was a full-time student for at least some part of at least 5 calendar months. There is no additional exemption for being age 65 or older.

85. (1187,Q1,17) (b) The requirement is to determine which of the relatives can be claimed as a dependent (or dependents) on Sam's 1989 return. A taxpayer's own spouse is never a dependent of the taxpayer. Although a personal exemption is generally available for a taxpayer's spouse on the taxpayer's return, it is not a "dependency exemption." Generally, a dependency exemption is available for a dependent if (1) the taxpayer furnishes more than 50% of the dependent's support, (2) the dependent's gross income is less than $2,000, (3) the dependent is of specified relationship to the taxpayer or lives in the taxpayer's household for the entire year, (4) the dependent is a U.S. citizen or resident of the U.S., Canada, or Mexico, and, (5) the dependent does not file a joint return. Here, the support, gross income, U.S. citizen, and joint return tests are met with repect to both Sam's cousin and his father's brother (i.e., Sam's uncle). However, Sam's cousin is not of specified relationship to Sam as defined in the IRC, and could only be claimed as a dependent if the cousin lived in Sam's household for the entire year. Since Sam's cousin did not live in Sam's household, Sam cannot claim a dependency exemption for his cousin. On the other hand, Sam's uncle is of specified relationship to Sam as defined in the IRC and can be claimed as a dependency exemption by Sam.

86. (586,Q3,46) (a) The requirement is to determine the amount of personal exemption that Brett can claim on his income tax return for 1989, when he is being claimed as a dependent by his mother. No personal exemption is allowed for an individual on the individual's income tax return if the individual can be claimed as a dependent by another taxpayer.

87. (1185,Q2,40) (b) The requirement is to determine which relative could be claimed as a dependent. One of the requirements that must be satisfied to claim a person as a dependent is that the person must be (1) of specified relationship to the taxpayer, or (2) a member of the taxpayer's household. Cousins and foster parents are not of specified relationship and only qualify if a member of the taxpayer's household. Since Alan's cousin and foster parent do not qualify as members of Alan's household, only Alan's niece can be claimed as a dependent.

88. (585,Q2,30) (c) The requirement is to determine who can claim Sara's dependency exemption under a multiple support agreement. A multiple support agreement can be used if (1) no single taxpayer furnishes more than 50% of a dependent's support, and (2) two or more persons, each of whom would be able to take the exemption but for the support test, together provide more than 50% of the dependent's support. Then, any taxpayer who provides more than 10% of the dependent's support can claim the dependent if (1) the other persons furnishing more than 10% agree not to claim the dependent as an exemption, and (2) the other requirements for a dependency exemption are met. One of the other requirements that must be met is that the dependent be related to the taxpayer or live in the taxpayer's household. Alma is not eligible for the exemption because Sara is unrelated to Alma and did not live in Alma's household. Carl is not eligible for the exemption because he provided only 9% of Sara's support. Ben is eligible to claim the exemption for Sara under a multiple support agreement because Ben is related to Sara and has provided more than 10% of her support.

89. (1179,Q2,22) (b) The requirement is to determine the number of exemptions allowable in 1989. Mr. and Mrs. Vonce are entitled to one exemption each. They are also entitled to one exemption for their dependent daughter since they provided over one half of her support and she had less than $2,000 of income. An exemption is not available for their son because he provided over one half of his own support.

V. Tax Computation

90. (583,P3,49) (b) Dalton's 1989 taxable income would be computed as follows:

Salary	$30,000
Less IRA contribution	(2,000)
Adjusted gross income	$28,000
Less larger of:	
Itemized deductions ($3,400), or	
standard deduction ($3,100)	(3,400)
Personal exemption	(2,000)
Taxable income	$22,600

V.B. Tax Rate Schedules

91. (581,P3,44) (c) Thomson should file as a surviving spouse. A surviving spouse is taxed at the same rate as married taxpayers filing a joint return. Surviving spouse filing status is available for two taxable years after a spouse's death if a dependent child lives with the surviving spouse, the surviving spouse pays more than 50% of the costs of maintaining a household, and the surviving spouse does not marry before year end.

92. (1188,Q1,16) (c) The requirement is to determine Emil Gow's filing status for 1989. Emil should file as a "Qualifying widower with dependent child" (i.e., surviving spouse) which will entitle him to use the joint return tax rates. Surviving spouse filing status is available for the two taxable years following the year of a spouse's death if (1) the surviving spouse was eligible to file a joint return in the year of the spouse's death, (2) does not remarry before the end of the current tax year, and (3) the surviving spouse pays over 50% of the cost of maintaining a household that is the principal home for the entire year of the surviving spouse's dependent child.

93. (586,Q3,59) (c) The requirement is to determine Nell's filing status for 1989. Nell qualifies as a head of household because she is unmarried and maintains a household for her infant child. Answer (a) is incorrect because although Nell is single, head of household filing status provides for lower tax rates. Answer (b) is incorrect because Nell is unmarried at the end of 1989. Since Nell's spouse died in 1986, answer (d) is incorrect because the filing status of a "qualifying widow" is only available for the two years following the year of the spouse's death.

94. (1181,Q3,53) (c) For 1989, the standard deduction amount for a taxpayer who is a head of household is $4,550.

95. (579,Q2,21) (c) Mrs. Felton qualifies as a head of household because she is both unmarried and maintains a household for her

unmarried child. The unmarried child for whom she maintains a household need not qualify as her dependent in order for Mrs. Felton to claim the head-of-household status. Answer (b) is incorrect because in order for Mrs. Felton to qualify as a surviving spouse, her son must qualify as a dependent, which he does not. Although Mrs. Felton would have qualified as married filing jointly, answer (d), in 1988 (the year of her husband's death), the problem requirement is her 1989 status. Answer (a), single, is incorrect because although the widow is single, her circumstances make head of household her proper filing status.

V.E. Other Taxes

96. (1182,P3,43) (b) The requirement is to determine Berger's self-employment income for 1989. Self-employment income represents the net earnings of an individual from a trade or business carried on as a proprietor or partner, or from rendering services as an independent contractor. The director's fee is self-employment income since it is related to a trade or business, and Berger is not an employee. Fees received by a fiduciary (e.g., executor) are generally not related to a trade or business and not self-employment income. However, executor's fees may constitute self-employment if the executor is a professional fiduciary or carries on a trade or business in the administration of an estate.

97. (1188,Q1,2) (d) The requirement is to determine Smith's gross income from self-employment. Self-employment income represents the net earnings of an individual from a trade or business carried on as a sole proprietor or partner, or from rendering services as an independent contractor (i.e., not an employee). The $8,000 consulting fee and the $2,000 of director's fees are self-employment income because they are related to a trade or business and Smith is not an employee.

98. (588,Q1,10) (b) The requirement is to determine the correct treatment when an amount of social security tax withheld from an employee exceeds the maximum for a particular year. The maximum amount of social security tax (FICA) to be withheld from an employee's wages is 7.51% x $48,000 = $3,604.80 for 1989. If an amount in excess of the maximum is withheld, the correct treatment depends upon the cause of the excess withholding. If one employer incorrectly withholds more than the maximum, the employer should adjust the withholding or refund the excess to the employee. However, if an employee works for two or more employers and the amount withheld in excess of

the maximum was the result of correct withholding, the employee may claim the excess as
a tax credit to be deducted in computing the
employee's federal income tax liability or
refund. Answer (d) is incorrect because the
excess can never be deducted as an itemized
deduction.

99. (586,Q3,45) (b) The requirement is to
compute the net earnings from self-employment
for a sole proprietor. The net sales of
$120,000 would be reduced by the cost of sales
($60,000), other operating expenses ($12,000),
and the state business taxes ($1,200). The
dividend income from personal investments is
not included in earnings from self-employment,
and the federal self-employment tax is not
deductible. Thus, the computation of Kory's
net earnings from self-employment is as follows

Net sales	$120,000
Cost of sales	(60,000)
Gross profit	$ 60,000
Other operating expenses	(12,000)
State business tax	(1,200)
Net self-employment earnings	$ 46,800

100. (582,Q3,60) (b) The requirement is to
determine the amount of investment credit recapture. Each full year that ACRS property is
held earns 1/5 of the ITC for 5, 10, and 15-
year property. Since the drill press was 5-
year property and was only held for four full
years, only 4/5 of the ITC was earned, and 1/5
x $2,000 = $400 is recaptured.

VI.E. Credit for the Elderly

101.(1181,Q3,58) (b) The requirement is to
determine the amount that can be claimed as a
credit for the elderly. The credit is the
lesser of (1) taxpayer's tax liability of $60,
or (2) 15% ($7,500 - $1,250 social security) =
$937.50.

VI.F. Child Care Credit

102.(1182,P3,57) (c) The requirement is to
compute Nora's child care credit for 1989.
Since she has two dependent preschool children, all $3,000 paid for child care qualifies
for the credit. The credit is 30% of
qualified expenses, but is reduced by 1 percentage point for each $2,000 (or fraction
thereof) of AGI over $10,000 down to a minimum
of 20%. Since Nora's AGI is $29,000, her
credit is 20% x $3,000 = $600.

103. (581,P3,59) (b) The requirement is to
determine the amount of the child care credit
allowable to the Jasons. The credit is from

20% to 30% of certain dependent care expenses
limited to the lesser of (1) $2,400 for one
qualifying individual, $4,800 for two or more;
(2) taxpayer's earned income, or spouse's if
smaller; or (3) actual expenses. The $1,500
paid to the Union Day Care Center qualifies,
as does the $1,000 paid to Wilma Jason. Pay-
ments to relatives qualify if the relative is
not a dependent of the taxpayer. Since Robert
and Mary Jason only claimed three exemptions,
Wilma was not their dependent. The $500 paid
to Acme Home Cleaning Service does not qualify
since it is completely unrelated to the care
of their child. To qualify, expenses must be
at least partly for the care of a qualifying
individual. Since qualifying expenses exceed
$2,400, the Jason's credit is 20% x $2,400 =
$480.

VI.G. Foreign Tax Credit

104.(1181,P3,55) (c) The requirement is to
determine the amount of foreign tax credit
that may be claimed by Bell Corporation for
1989. The deduction of a credit for foreign
income taxes is subject to an overall limit
of:

$$\frac{\text{Foreign TI}}{\text{World-wide TI}} \times (\text{U.S. tax})$$

Thus, the $135,000 of foreign taxes are de-
ductible as a credit for 1989 to the extent
of:

$$\frac{\$300,000}{\$675,000} \times (\$270,000) = \underline{\$120,000}$$

105. (587,Q3,51) (c) The requirement is to
determine the tax credit available to a
corporation. A corporation may reduce its
income tax by taking a tax credit for foreign
income taxes. There is no tax credit
available for accelerated depreciation, state
income taxes, and the dividends-received
exclusion [sic].

VI.I. Earned Income Credit

106. (589,Q3,53) (c) The requirement is to
determine the correct statement regarding the
earned income credit. The earned income
credit is a refundable credit and can result
in a refund even if the taxpayer had no tax
withheld from wages. Answer (a) is incorrect
because the credit is refundable and will
never be "unused." Answer (b) is incorrect
because the credit is a direct subtraction
from the computed tax.

107. (586,Q3,43) (d) The requirement is to
determine the correct statement concerning the
earned income credit. The earned income
credit for 1989 is 14% of the first $6,500 of
earned income reduced by (1) 10% of earned

income (or AGI if larger) that exceeds $10,240, and (2) the amount of the taxpayer's alternative minimum tax liability. Answers (a) and (b) are incorrect because the credit is a direct subtraction from the computed tax. Answer (c) is incorrect because if the credit exceeds a taxpayer's tax liability, the excess will be refunded even if the taxpayer had no tax withheld from wages.

108.(1181,Q3,57) (a) The requirement is to determine Alex's earned income credit for 1989. Alex is not eligible for the earned income credit because his dependent child did not live with him.

VII. Filing Requirements

109. (585,Q2,23) (a) The requirement is to determine Birch's filing requirement. A self-employed individual must file an income tax return if net earnings from self-employment are $400 or more.

VIII.A. Claims for Refund

110. (589,Q3,55) (c) The requirement is to determine the date by which a taxpayer must file an amended return to claim a refund of tax paid on a calendar-year 1988 return. A taxpayer must file an amended return to claim a refund within 3 years from the date a return was filed, or 2 years from the date of payment of tax, whichever is later. If a return is filed before its due date, it is treated as filed on its due date. Thus, the taxpayer's 1988 calendar-year return that was filed on March 15, 1989 is treated as filed on April 15, 1989. Therefore, an amended return to claim a refund must be filed not later than April 15, 1992.

111.(1184,Q2,39) (d) The requirement is to determine the date by which a refund claim due to worthless security must be filed. The normal three-year statute of limitations is extended to seven years for refund claims resulting from bad debts or worthless securities. Since the securities became worthless during 1988, and Baker's 1988 return was filed on April 15, 1989, Baker's refund claim must be filed no later than April 15, 1996.

VIII.B. Assessments

112. (589,Q3,56) (d) The requirement is to determine the date by which the IRS must assert a notice of tax deficiency for a 1988 calendar-year return. The normal period for assessment is 3 years after the return is filed, or 3 years after the due date, whichever is later. However, since the $30,000 of gross income omitted from the

return exceeds 25% of the $80,000 of gross income stated on the return, the normal 3-year period is extended to 6 years. Here, the IRS may assess a tax deficiency on or before April 15, 1995.

113. (583,P3,55) (d) A six-year statute of limitations applies if gross income omitted from the return exceeds 25% of the gross income reported on the return. For this purpose, gross income of a business includes total gross receipts before subtracting cost of goods sold and deductions. Thus, a six-year statute of limitations will apply to Thompson if he omitted from gross income an amount in excess of ($400,000 + $36,000) x 25% = $109,000.

114.(1187,Q1,15) (d) The requirement is to determine the maximum period during which the IRS can issue a notice of deficiency if the gross income omitted from a taxpayer's return exceeds 25% of the gross income reported on the return. A 6-year statute of limitations applies if gross income omitted from the return exceeds 25% of the gross income reported on the return. Additionally, a tax return filed before its due date is treated as filed on its due date. Thus, if a return is filed before its due date, and the gross income omitted from the return exceeds 25% of the gross income reported on the return, the IRS has 6 years from the due date of the return to issue a notice of deficiency.

Solution Guide

Problem 1   Joint Taxable Income Schedule
            (1186,Q5)

1. This problem has two requirements: a detailed schedule computing taxable income and a computation of net tax payable or overpaid. Recall the formula for computing taxable income:

> Gross income
> -Deductions for A.G.I.
> =Adjusted Gross Income
> -Itemized deductions (or
> standard deduction)
> -Exemptions
> =Taxable income

2. Identify the items to be included in gross income for this couple. Salary will be included at its gross amount, $62,000.

2.1 Dividends from taxable domestic corporations of $500 are included in gross income. Dividends on the life insurance policy are not included in income unless they exceed the accumulated net premiums paid on the policy. The problem states that this amount was not exceeded.

2.2 The two stock sales transactions need to be classified as long-term or short-term. The first sale listed is long-term because the stock was held more than 12 months. This transaction resulted in a gain of $1,000 ($3,000 proceeds - $2,000 basis). The second transaction listed is short-term because the stock was not held more than 12 months. This transaction resulted in a loss of $200 ($700 proceeds - $900 basis). The excess of the LTCG of $1,000 over the STCL of 200 is $800 and is included in income.

2.3 Proceeds from a life insurance policy are excluded from gross income.

2.4 The state income tax refund received in 1989 is included in income to the extent a tax benefit was received for the deduction of state income tax in the previous year. The problem states that the taxpayers itemized deductions in 1988; therefore, there was a prior tax benefit. The federal tax refund is excluded from gross income.

2.5 The $1,500 watch from Myra's employer is included in income because it was compensation for recruiting new clients.

2.6 Social security received may be includable, depending on the level of the taxpayer's other income. Recall the formula to compute the amount of social security to be included in income:

A.G.I. without social security	$63,430
+1/2 of social security received (A)	4,950
=Combined income	$68,380
-Base amount	32,000
Excess over base amount	$36,380
x1/2	x 1/2
1/2 of excess over base amount (B)	$18,190

Include the lesser of (A) or (B) in income. $ 4,950

2.7 The income resulting from a transfer to a "Clifford" trust after March 1, 1986 is taxable to the grantor. Since this trust was established in 1980, the $2,200 of trust income is taxable to Alex's destitute friend.

3. Expenses for rent, household, and other personal expenses are not deductible. Federal income tax payments are also not deductible in computing taxable income.

3.1 The $800 of unreimbursed business travel and the $400 cost of the required professional education courses are deductible as miscellaneous itemized deductions to the extent that their total ($1,200) exceeds 2% of adjusted gross income.

3.2 Medical and dental expenses are allowed as itemized deductions only to the extent that they exceed 7.5% of A.G.I. Remember to include the $190 of medicare premiums paid during the year as a medical expense, as well as travel to doctors.

3.3 A charitable contribution deduction is allowed for the donated stock. The amount deductible is the fair market value $7,000. This amount is not required to be reduced by the appreciation since the donation was not made to a private foundation and was not tangible personal property. Remember to also include in charitable contributions the $240 United Fund pledge withheld from Myra's salary. The payment to a political party is not considered a charitable contribution, and is not deductible.

3.4 The deduction for state and local taxes is the $3,349 state income tax withheld from Myra's salary.

3.5 The total of all the itemized deductions must be compared to the standard deduction. Since the Cole's itemized deductions exceed the available standard deduction, the Coles will itemize for 1989.

3.6 The Coles are entitled to two personal exemptions and one dependency exemption. Myra and Alex are each entitled to one personal exemption. Their son, Ben, qualifies as their dependent. The support

test, gross income test, and relationship
test are met. Ben's death before year end
does not disqualify him as a dependent.
The friend who is supported through the
trust does not qualify as a dependent because the friend does not meet the relationship test. A nonrelative will qualify
as a dependent only if the individual
lives with the taxpayer throughout the
year.

4. The second requirement is to determine the
    net tax payable or overpaid assuming that
    the federal income tax computed is $12,957
    before credits and payments. From this
    amount should be subtracted the federal
    tax withheld from Myra's salary ($10,000)
    and the federal estimated tax payments
    ($3,000).

Unofficial Answer

Problem 1   Joint Taxable Income Schedule
             (1186,Q5)

Alex and Myra Cole
Taxable Income
For the Year Ended December 31, 1989

Income
Salary		$62,000
Nonmonetary remuneration (watch)		1,500
Dividends		500
Refund of state income tax		110
Capital gain (loss)		
Long-term ($3,000 minus $2,000)	$1,000	
Short-term ($700 minus $900)	(200)	
Net capital gain		800
Social security benefits		
Gross amount	$9,900	
Taxable portion	50%	4,950
Adjusted Gross Income		$69,860

Itemized Deductions
Medical and dental expenses			
Doctors	$3,000		
Dentures	800		
Travel to doctors	100		
Medicare premiums	190		
Total	$4,090		
Less: 7.5% x 69,860	5,240	$0	
Taxes			
State income tax		3,349	
Contributions			
United Fund	$ 240		
Other charitable organizations	7,000	7,240	
Miscellaneous			
Travel expense	$ 800		
Education expense	400		
	$1,200		
Less: 2% of $69,860	1,397	0	
Total Itemized Deductions			-10,589

Exemptions
Alex	1		
Myra	1		
Ben	1	3 x $2,000	-6,000
Taxable income			$53,271

b.

Alex and Myra Cole
Computation Of Federal Income Tax Overpayment
For The Year Ended December 31, 1989

Tax before credit and payments		$12,957
Payments		
Tax withheld	$10,000	
Estimated tax	3,000	13,000
Net overpayment of tax		$ 43

Solution Guide

Problem 2   Projected Taxable Income Schedule
                (587,Q4)

1.   This problem consists of three related
     parts concerning the federal income
     taxation of an individual.

2.   Part a. requires a schedule listing all
     items of projected receipts and expendi-
     tures that have no effect on the determi-
     nation of federal taxable income. Note
     that items included in part a. may also
     be used in the determination of part c.

3.   Part b. requires a schedule computing
     federal taxable income in the sequence of
     adjusted gross income (AGI), itemized
     deductions, personal exemptions, and
     taxable income. Items included in part
     b. will not be the same as the items in
     part a.

4.   Part c. requires the computation of tax
     payable or net overpayment based on
     federal income tax of $12,421.

5.   The solutions approach is to analyze each
     receipt and expenditure to determine
     first, whether the item is excluded
     (part a.) or included (part b.) in the
     determination of federal taxable income,
     and then whether the item is included in
     the computation of AGI (part b.),
     itemized deductions (part b.), or tax
     payable or net overpayment (part c.).

5.1 Gross salary and commissions of $50,000
     from employment as an outside sales-
     person, and gross salary of $3,000 from
     employment as a part-time teacher are
     included in the determination of AGI in
     part b.

5.2 The ordinary and necessary employee
     business expenses of $5,000 are included
     as a miscellaneous itemized deduction in
     part b. Note that total miscellaneous
     itemized deductions are subject to a 2-
     percent-of-AGI floor. Therefore, the
     itemized deductions for this particular
     item will be [$5,000 - (2% x AGI)].

5.3 Under payroll taxes, the federal income
     tax withheld and FICA tax withheld are
     nondeductible expenditures that are
     excluded from the determination of
     taxable income (part a.). Both of these
     items, however, will be used to determine

the balance of tax payable or net
overpayment in part c. On the other
hand, the state income tax withheld of
$1,800 is deductible as an itemized
deduction in part b.

5.4 Under the other cash expected to be
     received in 1989, the bequest under her
     husband's will of $25,000 and the life
     insurance proceeds on her husband's death
     of $15,000 are items excluded from the
     determination of taxable income
     (part a.). The dividends from taxable
     domestic corporations of $500 and the
     lottery winnings of $2,000 are included
     in AGI in part b.

5.5 The net proceeds of $10,000 from the sale
     of 500 shares of stock is used in the
     determination of the capital gain to be
     included in AGI in part b. The fair
     market value on the date of death is used
     as the basis for the stock. The capital
     gain equals the proceeds of $10,000 minus
     Ann's basis of $6,000. The $4,000 is a
     long-term capital gain included in AGI
     under part b.

5.6 The trust income of $12,000 is included
     in AGI in part b. Note that the income
     of a simple trust is taxed to beneficia-
     ries even though not distributed.

5.7 The food, clothing, household, and
     miscellaneous personal expenses of
     $20,000 are nondeductible expenses that
     are excluded from the determination of
     taxable income (part a.).

5.8 The estimated federal income tax,
     inheritance tax, city and state sales
     taxes, auto license and registration
     fees, and the political contribution are
     nondeductible expenditures that are
     excluded from the determination of
     taxable income (part a.). The estimated
     federal income tax is also used to
     determine the balance of tax payable or
     net overpayment in part c.

5.9 The estimated state income tax of $1,200,
     the realty tax of $3,600, the charitable
     contribution of $600, and the gambling
     losses of $900 are included as itemized
     deductions in part b.

6. The next step after analyzing each item is to prepare each of the required schedules.

7. In part b. adjusted gross income equals $71,500, and total itemized deductions equals $11,670. There are two exemptions (one for Ann and one for her dependent son, Earl) totaling $4,000 (2 x $2,000). Since Ann's husband, John, died in 1988, there will be no exemption for him on Ann's 1989 tax return. Taxable income of $55,830 is computed by subtracting itemized deductions of $11,670 and the exemptions of $4,000 from AGI of $71,500.

8. In part c. the federal income tax of $12,421 is used to determine tax payable or net overpayment. From that amount, federal income tax withheld of $9,300, excess FICA tax paid of $225, and estimated federal income tax paid of $5,000 are subtracted to determine the net overpayment of tax of $2,104. Note that for 1989, the maximum FICA tax is $48,000 x 7.51% = $3,379.50. If an employee works for more than one employer, and more than $3,604.80 of FICA tax is withheld, the excess ($225) is deducted in computing the net federal income tax payable or overpayment.

Unofficial Answer

Problem 2   Projected Taxable Income Schedule (587,Q4)

a.

Ann Ford
PROJECTED RECEIPTS AND EXPENDITURES
WITH NO EFFECT ON TAXABLE INCOME
1989

	Receipts	Expenditures
Federal income tax ($9,000 + $300 + $5,000)		$14,300
FICA tax ($3,605 + $225)		3,830
Bequest under husband's will	$25,000	
Life insurance proceeds on husband's death	15,000	
Food, clothing, household, and miscellaneous		20,000
State inheritance tax		2,100
City and state sales taxes		1,100
Auto license and registration		50
Political contribution		100

b.
                              Ann Ford
                COMPUTATION OF PROJECTED TAXABLE INCOME
                                1989

<u>Adjusted Gross Income</u>
   Salary and commissions--outside salesperson $50,000
   Salary--part-time teacher   3,000
   Dividends   500
   Long-term capital gain ($10,000 less $6,000)   4,000
   Simple trust   12,000
   Lottery winnings   2,000
      Total $71,500

<u>Itemized Deductions</u>
   Taxes
   State income taxes ($1,800 + $1,200) $ 3,000
   Realty taxes   3,600
      Total taxes $ 6,600

   Contribution to church   600
   Gambling losses ($420 + $480)   900
   Employee business expenses
      ($5,000 less 2% of $71,500)   3,570
         Total itemized deductions $11,670

<u>Personal Exemptions</u> ($2,000 x 2)   4,000   15,670

<u>Taxable income</u> $55,830

c.   Ann Ford
                       COMPUTATION OF PROJECTED
                    FEDERAL INCOME TAX OVERPAYMENT
                                1989

Tax before prepayments $12,421
Prepayments
   Federal income tax withheld $9,300
   Estimated tax payments   5,000
   Excess FICA tax   225   14,525
Amount overpaid $ 2,104

Solution Guide

Problem 3   Joint Taxable Income Schedule
             (1189,Q5)

1. This problem has two related require-
    ments: a detailed schedule computing
    joint taxable income and a computation of
    net tax payable or net overpayment of
    tax. Recall the tax formula for com-
    puting taxable income for individuals:

        Gross income
        - Deductions for AGI
        = Adjusted Gross Income
        - Itemized deductions (or
          standard deduction)
        - Personal exemptions
        = Taxable Income

2. The solution approach is to analyze each
    receipt and disbursement and the addi-
    tional information to determine whether
    each item should be included in the de-
    termination of taxable income (part a.),
    or net tax payable or overpayment
    (part b.).

3. First, review the cash received to ident-
    ify the items to be included in gross in-
    come for this couple. The gross salary
    of $80,000 from employment as an engi-
    neer, and the gross salary from part-time
    employment of $15,000 should be included
    in gross income.

3.1 Under amounts withheld, the federal in-
    come tax and FICA taxes are not deduct-
    ible in computing taxable income. How-
    ever, the federal income tax withheld
    will be used to determine the net amount
    of tax payable or overpayment in part b.

3.2 The state income taxes withheld of $4,000
    and $120 are deductible as an itemized
    deduction. The medical insurance pre-
    miums withheld will be used to determine
    the itemized deduction for medical ex-
    penses.

3.3 The $400 of dividends on the life insur-
    ance policy are treated as a reduction of
    the cost of insurance and are excluded
    from gross income unless they exceed the
    accumulated net premiums paid on the
    policy. The problem states that the net
    premiums have not been exceeded.

3.4 The $527 of dividends from taxable domes-
    tic corporations, $100 of interest on
    U.S. Savings Bonds, and $600 of unemploy-
    ment compensation benefits are fully in-
    cluded in gross income.

3.5 The $2,500 of proceeds from the sale of
    stock with a basis of $9,000 results in a
    $6,500 long-term capital loss since the
    stock was purchased in 1970. However,
    the allowable deduction for a net capital
    loss is limited to $3,000. The remaining
    net capital loss ($6,500 - $3,000 =
    $3,500) would be carried forward.

3.6 Up to 50% of social security benefits may
    have to be included in gross income.
    Recall the formula to compute the amount
    to be included:

AGI before social security	$93,227
+ 1/2 of social security benefits (A)	6,000
= Combined income	$99,227
- Base amount	32,000
= Excess over base amount	$67,227
x 1/2	x 1/2
= 1/2 of excess over base amount (B)	$33,614

    Include the lesser of A or B in gross income: $ 6,000

4. Next, analyze the cash disbursements to
    determine which items are deductible in
    computing taxable income. The household
    and miscellaneous expenses, state sales
    taxes, estimated federal income tax pay-
    ments, and the political contribution are
    not deductible in computing taxable
    income. However, the estimated federal
    income tax payments will be used to com-
    pute the net tax payable or overpayment
    in part b.

4.1 The $250 fee for tax return preparation,
    $900 of unreimbursed business travel
    expenses, $700 cost of continuing educa-
    tion courses, and the $150 of profes-
    sional society dues are deductible as
    miscellaneous itemized deductions to the
    extent that their total exceeds 2% of
    AGI. $2,000 - (2% x $99,227) = $15.

4.2 The itemized deduction for taxes includes
    the state income taxes of $4,000 and $120
    that were withheld from their salaries.
    Also included are the real estate taxes
    of $3,000 on their primary residence, and
    the $800 of real estate taxes on their
    cottage.

4.3 The mortgage interest on their primary
    residence ($2,300) as well as the mort-
    gage interest on their summer cottage
    ($1,800) is qualified residence interest
    and is fully deductible as an itemized
    deduction. The $500 mortgage principal
    payment on their primary residence is not
    deductible.

4.4   A charitable contribution deduction is allowed for the donated stock. Since the stock was appreciated in value and had been held long-term, the contribution of stock is classified as a contribution of long-term capital gain appreciated property. As a result, the amount of contribution is the stock's fair market value of $1,400. Although potentially subject to a 30% of AGI limitation, the limitation does not apply in this case.

4.5   An itemized casualty loss deduction is allowed for the fire damage sustained by their summer cottage. The amount of loss is the lesser of (a) the cottage's basis of $40,000, or (b) the decline in market value resulting from the fire [$66,000 – $50,000 = $16,000]. The loss of $16,000 must then be reduced by a $100 "floor" and 10% of AGI.

4.6   There will be no deduction for medical and dental expenses because the only medical expense incurred ($1,200 of medical insurance premiums withheld from Mr. Shaw's salary) did not exceed 7.5% of AGI.

4.7   The total of all itemized deductions must be compared to the standard deduction. Since the Shaw's itemized deductions ($19,412) exceed the available basic ($5,200) and additional ($600) standard deductions, the Shaws will itemize for 1989.

5.   The Shaws are entitled to two personal exemptions and one dependency exemption. Fred and Laura are each entitled to one personal exemption on their joint return. Their daughter, Doris, qualifies as a dependency exemption since the dependency tests (e.g., support, gross income, relationship) were met at the time of her death. Note that a full $2,000 exemption is allowed for Doris, and is not prorated because of her death during the year.

6.   Part b. requires the computation of the net amount of tax payable or net overpayment of tax assuming that the Shaw's federal income tax is $16,946 before tax credits and payments. From the tax of $16,946, subtract (a) the federal income tax withheld from their salaries [$17,000 + $2,800], (b) the estimated tax payments of $2,000, and (c) the 1988 federal income tax overpayment of $43 which had been credited to their 1989 estimated tax. This results in a net overpayment of $4,897.

Unofficial Answer

Problem 3   Joint Taxable Income Schedule (1189,Q5)

a.

Fred and Laura Shaw
COMPUTATION OF TAXABLE INCOME
For the Year Ended December 31, 1989

Income

Salary--Fred			$80,000
Salary--Laura			15,000
Interest			100
Dividends			527
Social security benefits (1/2 of $12,000)			6,000
Unemployment compensation			600
Long-term capital loss			
(Basis $9,000; sales price $2,500;			
allowable loss limited to $3,000)			(3,000)
Adjusted gross income			$99,227

Itemized deductions

Taxes			
State income taxes ($4,000 + $120)	$ 4,120		
Real estate taxes ($3,000 + $800)	3,800	$ 7,920	
Interest ($2,300 + $1,800)		4,100	
Contributions (fair market value)		1,400	
Casualty loss			
Decline in market value after fire	$16,000		
Less 10% of $99,227	$9,923		
"Floor"	100	10,023	5,977
Miscellaneous deductions			
Business travel	$ 900		
Professional education	700		
Professional dues	150		
Tax return preparation fee	250		
Total	$ 2,000		
Less 2% of $99,227	1,985	15	
Total itemized deductions			19,412
Balance			79,815
Exemptions (3 x $2,000)			6,000
TAXABLE INCOME			$73,815

b.   COMPUTATION OF FEDERAL INCOME TAX OVERPAYMENT

Tax before payments on account		$16,946
Payments on account		
Tax withheld ($17,000 + $2,800)	$19,800	
Estimated tax ($2,000 + $43)	2,043	21,843
AMOUNT OVERPAID		$ 4,897

Multiple Choice Questions (1-44)

Items 1 and 2 are based on the following data:

In 1988, Iris King bought a diamond necklace for her own use, at a cost of $10,000. In 1990, when the fair market value was $12,000, Iris gave this necklace to her daughter, Ruth. No gift tax was due.

1. Ruth's holding period for this gift
    a. Starts in 1990.
    b. Starts in 1988.
    c. Depends on whether the necklace is sold by Ruth at a gain or at a loss.
    d. Is irrelevant because Ruth received the necklace for no consideration of money or money's worth.

2. If Ruth sells this diamond necklace in 1990 for $13,000, Ruth's recognized gain would be
    a. $3,000
    b. $2,000
    c. $1,000
    d. $0

Items 3 through 5 are based on the following data:

Laura's father, Albert, gave Laura a gift of 500 shares of Liba Corporation common stock in 1990. Albert's basis for the Liba stock was $4,000. At the date of this gift, the fair market value of the Liba stock was $3,000.

3. If Laura sells the 500 shares of Liba stock in 1990 for $5,000, her basis is
    a. $5,000
    b. $4,000
    c. $3,000
    d. $0

4. If Laura sells the 500 shares of Liba stock in 1990 for $2,000, her basis is
    a. $4,000
    b. $3,000
    c. $2,000
    d. $0

5. If Laura sells the 500 shares of Liba stock in 1990 for $3,500, what is the reportable gain or loss in 1990?
    a. $3,500 gain.
    b. $ 500 gain.
    c. $ 500 loss.
    d. $0.

6. On June 1, 1989, Ben Rork sold 500 shares of Kul Corp. stock. Rork had received this stock on May 1, 1989 as a bequest from the estate of his uncle, who died on March 1, 1989. Rork's basis was determined by reference to the stock's fair market value on March 1, 1989. Rork's holding period for this stock was
    a. Short-term.
    b. Long-term.
    c. Short-term if sold at a gain; long-term if sold at a loss.
    d. Long-term if sold at a gain; short-term if sold at a loss.

7. Fred Zorn died on January 5, 1990, bequeathing his entire $2,000,000 estate to his sister, Ida. The alternate valuation date was validly elected by the executor of Fred's estate. Fred's estate included 2,000 shares of listed stock for which Fred's basis was $380,000. This stock was distributed to Ida nine months after Fred's death. Fair market values of this stock were:

At the date of Fred's death	$400,000
Six months after Fred's death	450,000
Nine months after Fred's death	480,000

Ida's basis for this stock is
    a. $380,000
    b. $400,000
    c. $450,000
    d. $480,000

Items 8 and 9 are based on the following data:

On March 1, 1990, Lois Rice learned that she was bequeathed 1,000 shares of Elin Corp. common stock under the will of her uncle, Pat Prevor. Pat had paid $5,000 for the Elin stock in 1985. Fair market value of the Elin stock on March 1, 1990, the date of Pat's death, was $8,000 and had increased to $11,000 six months later. The executor of Pat's estate elected the alternative valuation date for estate tax purposes. Lois sold the Elin stock for $9,000 on May 1, 1990, the date that the executor distributed the stock to her.

8. Lois' basis for gain or loss on sale of the 1,000 shares of Elin stock is
    a. $ 5,000
    b. $ 8,000
    c. $ 9,000
    d. $11,000

9. Lois should treat the 1,000 shares of Elin stock as a
    a. Short-term Section 1231 asset.
    b. Long-term Section 1231 asset.
    c. Short-term capital asset.
    d. Long-term capital asset.

Items 10 and 11 are based on the following data:

In January 1990, Joan Hill bought one share of Orban Corp. stock for $300. On March 1, 1990, Orban distributed one share of preferred stock for each share of common stock held. This distribution was nontaxable. On March 1, 1990, Joan's one share of common stock had a fair market value of $450, while the preferred stock had a fair market value of $150.

10. After the distribution of the preferred stock, Joan's bases for her Orban stocks are

	Common	Preferred
a.	$300	$0
b.	$225	$ 75
c.	$200	$100
d.	$150	$150

11. The holding period for the preferred stock starts in
   a.   January 1990.
   b.   March 1990.
   c.   September 1990.
   d.   December 1990.

12. On July 1, 1986, Lila Perl paid $90,000 for 450 shares of Janis Corp. common stock. Lila received a nontaxable stock dividend of 50 new common shares in August 1989. On December 20, 1989, Lila sold the 50 new shares for $11,000. How much should Lila report in her 1989 return as long-term capital gain?
   a. $0
   b. $ 1,000
   c. $ 2,000
   d. $11,000

13. Pat Leif owned an apartment house that he bought in 1970. Depreciation was taken on a straight-line basis. In 1990, when Pat's adjusted basis for this property was $200,000, he traded it for an office building having a fair market value of $600,000. The apartment house has 100 dwelling units, while the office building has 40 units rented to business enterprises. The properties are not located in the same city. What is Pat's reportable gain on this exchange?
   a. $400,000 Section 1250 gain.
   b. $400,000 Section 1231 gain.
   c. $400,000 long-term capital gain.
   d. $0.

14. On July 1, 1989, Riley exchanged investment real property, with an adjusted basis of $160,000 and subject to a mortgage of $70,000, and received from Wilson $30,000 cash and other investment real property having a fair market value of $250,000. Wilson assumed the mortgage. What is Riley's recognized gain in 1989 on the exchange?
   a. $ 30,000
   b. $ 70,000
   c. $ 90,000
   d. $100,000

15. On October 1, 1989, Donald Anderson exchanged an apartment building, having an adjusted basis of $375,000 and subject to a mortgage of $100,000, for $25,000 cash and another apartment building with a fair market value of $550,000 and subject to a mortgage of $125,000. The property transfers were made subject to the outstanding mortgages. What amount of gain should Anderson recognize in his tax return for 1989?
   a. $0
   b. $ 25,000
   c. $125,000
   d. $175,000

16. James Harper, a self-employed individual, owned a truck driven exclusively for business use. The truck had an original cost of $8,000 and had an adjusted basis on December 31, 1989, of $3,600. On January 2, 1990, he traded it in for a new truck costing $10,000 and was given a trade-in allowance of $2,000. The new truck will also be used exclusively for business purposes and will be depreciated with no salvage value. The basis of the new truck is
   a. $ 8,000
   b. $ 8,400
   c. $10,000
   d. $11,600

17. The following information pertains to the acquisition of a six-wheel truck by Sol Barr, a self-employed contractor:

Cost of original truck traded in	$20,000
Book value of original truck at trade-in date	4,000
List price of new truck	25,000
Trade-in allowance for old truck	6,000
Business use of both trucks	100%

The basis of the new truck is
   a. $27,000
   b. $25,000
   c. $23,000
   d. $19,000

18. An office building owned by Elmer Bass was condemned by the state on January 2, 1988. Bass received the condemnation award on March 1, 1989. In order to qualify for non-recognition of gain on this involuntary conversion, what is the last date for Bass to acquire qualified replacement property?

a.   August 1, 1990.
b.   January 2, 1991.
c.   March 1, 1992.
d.   December 31, 1992.

19. The following information pertains to the sale of Al Oran's principal residence:

Date of sale	May 1989
Date of purchase	May 1979
Net sales price	$260,000
Adjusted basis	$ 70,000

In June 1989, Oran (age 70) bought a smaller residence for $90,000. Oran elected to avail himself of the exclusion of realized gain available to taxpayers age 55 and over. What amount of gain should Oran recognize in 1989 on the sale of his residence?
a. $45,000
b. $65,000
c. $70,000
d. $90,000

Items 20 and 21 are based on the following data:

Gary Barth, who is unmarried, owns a house which has been his principal residence for the past ten years. Gary wants to sell his house and move to a rental apartment. He has no intention of buying another residence at any time in the future, but wishes to avail himself of the one-time exclusion of gain on the sale of his house.

20. What is the minimum age Gary must attain in order to avail himself of the one-time exclusion of gain on the sale of his house?
a.   55
b.   65
c.   70
d.   72

21. Assume that Gary has attained the required age to qualify for the one-time exclusion of gain on the sale of his house. What is the maximum amount allowable for this type of exclusion?
a.   40% of long-term gain.
b.   60% of long-term gain.
c. $100,000.
d. $125,000.

22. On March 10, 1989, James Rogers sold 300 shares of Red Company common stock for $4,200. Rogers acquired the stock in 1986 at a cost of $5,000.
On April 4, 1989, he repurchased 300 shares of Red Company common stock for $3,600 and held them until July 18, 1989, when he sold them for $6,000.

How should Rogers report the above transactions for 1989?
a.   A long-term capital loss of $800.
b.   A long-term capital gain of $1,000.
c.   A long-term capital gain of $1,600.
d.   A long-term capital loss of $800 and a short-term capital gain of $2,400.

23. Murd Corporation, a domestic corporation, acquired a 90% interest in the Drum Company in 1985 for $30,000. During 1990, the stock of Drum was declared worthless. What type and amount of deduction should Murd take for 1990?
a.   Long-term capital loss of $1,000.
b.   Long-term capital loss of $15,000.
c.   Ordinary loss of $30,000.
d.   Long-term capital loss of $30,000.

24. On July 1, 1989, Daniel Wright owned stock (held for investment) purchased two years earlier at a cost of $10,000 and having a fair market value of $7,000. On this date he sold the stock to his son, William, for $7,000. William sold the stock for $6,000 to an unrelated person on November 1, 1989. How should William report the stock sale on his 1989 tax return?
a.   As a short-term capital loss of $1,000.
b.   As a long-term capital loss of $1,000.
c.   As a short-term capital loss of $4,000.
d.   As a long-term capital loss of $4,000.

25. Al Eng owns 55% of the outstanding stock of Rego Corp. During 1989, Rego sold a trailer to Eng for $10,000. The trailer had an adjusted tax basis of $12,000, and had been owned by Rego for three years. In its 1989 income tax return, what is the allowable loss that Rego can claim on the sale of this trailer?
a. $0.
b. $2,000 ordinary loss.
c. $2,000 Section 1231 loss.
d. $2,000 Section 1245 loss.

26. For the year 1989 Diana Clark had salary income of $38,000. In addition, she had the following capital transactions during the year:

Long-term capital gain	$14,000
Short-term capital gain	6,000
Long-term capital loss	(4,000)
Short-term capital loss	(8,000)

There were no other items includible in her gross income. What is her adjusted gross income for 1989?

a. $38,000
b. $41,200
c. $42,800
d. $46,000

27. For the year ended December 31, 1989, Sol Corp. had an operating income of $20,000. In addition, Sol had capital gains and losses resulting in a net short-term capital gain of $2,000 and a net long-term capital loss of $7,000. How much of the excess of net long-term capital loss over net short-term capital gain could Sol offset against ordinary income for 1989?

a. $5,000
b. $3,000
c. $1,500
d. $0

28. In 1989, Nam Corp., which is not a dealer in securities, realized taxable income of $160,000 from its business operations. Also, in 1989, Nam sustained a long-term capital loss of $24,000 from the sale of marketable securities. Nam did not realize any other capital gains or losses since it began operations. In Nam's income tax returns, what is the proper treatment for the $24,000 long-term capital loss?

a. Use $3,000 of the loss to reduce 1989 taxable income, and carry $21,000 of the long-term capital loss forward for five years.
b. Use $6,000 of the loss to reduce 1989 taxable income by $3,000, and carry $18,000 of the long-term capital loss forward for five taxes.
c. Use $24,000 of the long-term capital loss to reduce 1989 taxable income by $12,000.
d. Carry the $24,000 long-term capital loss forward for five years, treating it as a short-term capital loss.

29. For assets acquired in 1989, the holding period for determining long-term capital gains and losses is more than

a. 18 months.
b. 12 months.
c. 9 months.
d. 6 months.

30. On July 1, 1989, Kim Wald sold an antique for $15,000 that she had bought for her personal use in 1985 at a cost of $12,000. In her 1989 return, Kim should treat the sale of the antique as a transaction resulting in

a. No taxable gain.
b. Ordinary income.

c. Short-term capital gain.
d. Long-term capital gain.

31. Paul Beyer, who is unmarried, has taxable income of $30,000 exclusive of capital gains and losses and his personal exemption. In 1989, Paul incurred a $1,000 net short-term capital loss and a $5,000 net long-term capital loss. His capital loss carryover to 1990 is

a. $0
b. $1,000
c. $3,000
d. $5,000

32. In 1989, Ruth Lee sold a painting for $25,000 that she had bought for her personal use in 1979 at a cost of $10,000. In her 1989 return, Lee should treat the sale of the painting as a transaction resulting in

a. Ordinary income.
b. Long-term capital gain.
c. Section 1231 gain.
d. No taxable gain.

33. A 1989 capital loss incurred by a married couple filing a joint return

a. Will be allowed only to the extent of capital gains.
b. Will be allowed to the extent of capital gains, plus up to $3,000 of ordinary income.
c. May be carried forward up to a maximum of five years.
d. Is not an allowable loss.

34. For a married couple filing a joint return, the excess of net long-term capital loss over net short-term capital gain is

a. Reduced by 50% before being deducted from ordinary income.
b. Limited to a maximum deduction of $3,000 from ordinary income.
c. Allowed as a carryover against future capital gains up to a maximum period of five years.
d. Not deductible from ordinary income.

35. In 1990, Al Oran bought a paved vacant lot adjacent to his retail store for use as a customers' parking lot at a cost of $15,000. In addition, Oran bought new store fixtures costing $8,000. What portion of these assets constitutes capital assets?

a. $0
b. $ 8,000
c. $15,000
d. $23,000

36. In 1987, Iris King bought a diamond necklace for her own use, at a cost of $10,000. In 1990, when the fair market value was $12,000, Iris gave this necklace to her daughter, Ruth. No gift tax was due. This diamond necklace is a
   a. Capital asset.
   b. Section 1231 asset.
   c. Section 1245 asset.
   d. Section 1250 asset.

37. Which of the following is a capital asset?
   a. Delivery truck.
   b. Goodwill.
   c. Land used as a parking lot for customers.
   d. Treasury stock, at cost.

38. Mike Karp owns machinery, with an adjusted basis of $50,000, for use in his car-washing business. In addition, Karp owns his personal residence and furniture, which together cost him $100,000. The capital assets amount to
   a. $0
   b. $ 50,000
   c. $100,000
   d. $150,000

39. Don Mott was the sole proprietor of a high-volume drug store which he owned for 15 years before he sold it to Dale Drug Stores, Inc. in 1989. Besides the $900,000 selling price for the store's tangible assets and goodwill, Mott received a lump sum of $30,000 in 1989 for his agreement not to operate a competing enterprise within ten miles of the store's location for a period of six years. The $30,000 will be taxed to Mott as
   a. $30,000 ordinary income in 1989.
   b. $30,000 short-term capital gain in 1989.
   c. $30,000 long-term capital gain in 1989.
   d. Ordinary income of $5,000 a year for six years.

40. In June 1990, Olive Bell bought a house for use partially as a residence and partially for operation of a retail gift shop. In addition, Olive bought the following furniture:

Kitchen set and living room pieces
  for the residential portion $ 8,000
Showcases and tables for the business portion   12,000

How much of this furniture comprises capital assets?
   a. $0
   b. $ 8,000

   c. $12,000
   d. $20,000

41. Thayer Corporation purchased an apartment building on January 1, 1983, for $200,000. The building was depreciated on the straight-line basis. On December 31, 1989, the building was sold for $220,000, when the asset balance net of accumulated depreciation was $170,000. On its 1989 tax return, Thayer should report
   a. Section 1231 gain of $42,500 and ordinary income of $7,500.
   b. Section 1231 gain of $44,000 and ordinary income of $6,000.
   c. Ordinary income of $50,000.
   d. Section 1231 gain of $50,000.

42. Arch Corp. sold machinery for $80,000 on December 31, 1989. This machinery was purchased on January 2, 1987, for $68,000 and had an adjusted basis of $40,000 at the date of sale. For 1989 Arch should report
   a. Ordinary income of $12,000 and Section 1231 gain of $28,000.
   b. Ordinary income of $28,000 and Section 1231 gain of $12,000.
   c. Ordinary income of $40,000.
   d. Section 1231 gain of $40,000.

43. For the year ended December 31, 1989, Murray Corporation, a calendar-year corporation, reported book income before income taxes of $120,000. Included in the determination of this amount were the following items:

Loss on sale of building depreciated
  on the straight-line method   ($12,000)
Gain on sale of land used in business   7,000
Loss on sale of investments in marketable securities (long-term)   (8,000)

For the year ended December 31, 1989, Murray's taxable income was
   a. $113,000
   b. $120,000
   c. $125,000
   d. $128,000

44. David Price owned machinery which he had acquired in 1986 at a cost of $100,000. During 1989, the machinery was destroyed by fire. At that time it had an adjusted basis of $86,000. The insurance proceeds awarded to Price amounted to $125,000, and he immediately acquired a similar machine for $110,000.
   What should Price report as ordinary income resulting from the involuntary conversion for 1989?
   a. $14,000
   b. $15,000
   c. $25,000
   d. $39,000

Multiple Choice Answers

1. b		10. b		19. a		28. d		37. b
2. a		11. a		20. a		29. b		38. c
3. b		12. c		21. d		30. d		39. a
4. b		13. d		22. c		31. c		40. b
5. d		14. d		23. c		32. b		41. b
6. b		15. b		24. a		33. b		42. b
7. c		16. d		25. a		34. b		43. d
8. c		17. c		26. d		35. a		44. a
9. d		18. d		27. d		36. a		

Multiple Choice Answer Explanations

A.1.b. Gift

1. (1187,Q1,18)   (b) The requirement is to determine Ruth's holding period for a diamond necklace received as a gift. If property is received as a gift and the donee's basis is determined by using the donor's basis, the donee's holding period includes the donor's holding period. On the other hand, if the gift property's FMV on date of gift is used to determine a loss, the donee's holding period begins on the date of gift.

  Here, the necklace was purchased by Ruth's mother in 1988 and had a cost basis of $10,000, while its FMV at date of gift was $12,000. Since the necklace was appreciated in value, Ruth's basis for determining gain or loss would be determined by using her mother's cost basis of $10,000. Thus, Ruth's holding period starts when the necklace was acquired by her mother in 1988.

2. (1187,Q1,20)   (a) The requirement is to determine Ruth's recognized gain if she sells the necklace received as a gift for $13,000. Since the necklace's FMV ($12,000) exceeded its basis ($10,000) at the date of gift, and no gift tax was paid, Ruth's basis for computing gain or loss is the same as her mother's basis of $10,000. Thus, Ruth's recognized gain is $13,000 - $10,000 = $3,000.

3. (584,Q2,26)   (b) The requirement is to determine the basis of the Liba stock if it is sold for $5,000. If property acquired by gift is sold at a gain, its basis is the donor's basis ($4,000), increased by any gift tax paid attributable to the net appreciation in value of the gift ($0).

4. (584,Q2,27)   (b) The requirement is to determine the basis of the Liba stock if it is sold for $2,000. If property acquired by gift is sold at a loss, its basis is the lesser of (1) its gain basis ($4,000 above), or (2) its FMV at date of gift ($3,000).

5. (584,Q2,28)   (d) The requirement is to determine the amount of reportable gain or loss if the Liba stock is sold for $3,500. No gain or loss is recognized on the sale of property acquired by gift if the basis for loss ($3,000 above) results in a gain and the basis for gain ($4,000 above) results in a loss.

A.1.c. Acquired from Decedent

6. (589,Q3,52)   (b) The requirement is to determine the holding period for stock received as a bequest from the estate of a deceased uncle. Property received from a decedent is deemed to be held long-term regardless of the actual period of time that the decedent or beneficiary actually held the property.

7. (1185,Q2,29)   (c) The requirement is to determine Ida's basis for stock inherited from a decedent. The basis of property received from a decedent is generally the property's FMV at date of the decedent's death, or FMV on the alternate valuation date (six months after death). Since the executor of Zorn's estate elected to use the alternate valuation date for estate tax purposes, the stock's basis to Ida is its $450,000 FMV six months after Zorn's death.

Note: If the stock had been distributed to Ida between the date of Zorn's death and the alternate valuation date, the stock's basis would be its FMV on date of distribution.

8. (1184,Q2,35)   (c) The requirement is to determine Lois' basis for gain or loss on the sale of Elin stock acquired from a decedent. Since the alternate valuation date (9/1/90) was elected for Prevor's estate but the stock was distributed to Lois before that date, Lois' basis is the $9,000 FMV of the stock on date of distribution (5/1/90).

9. (1184,Q2,36)   (d) The requirement is to determine how Lois should treat the shares of Elin stock. The stock should be treated as a capital asset held long-term since (1) property acquired from a decedent is always considered to be held long-term regardless of its actual holding period, and (2) the stock is an investment asset in Lois' hands. The stock is not a Sec. 1231 asset because it was not held for use in Lois' trade or business.

A.1.d. Stock Received as a Dividend

10. (586,Q3,54)   (b) The requirement is to determine the basis for the common stock and the preferred stock after the receipt of a nontaxable preferred stock dividend. Joan's original common stock basis must be allocated

between the common stock and the preferred stock according to their relative fair market value.

Common stock (FMV)	$450
Preferred stock (FMV)	150
Total value	$600

The ratio of the common stock to total value is $450/$600 or 3/4. This ratio multiplied by the original common stock basis of $300 results in a basis for the common stock of $225. The basis of the preferred stock would be ($150/$600 x $300) = $75.

11. (586,Q3,55) (a) The requirement is to determine the holding period for preferred stock that was received in a nontaxable distribution on common stock. Since the tax basis of the preferred stock is determined in part by the basis of the common stock, the holding period of the preferred stock includes the holding period of the common stock (i.e., the holding period of the common stock tacks on to the preferred stock). Thus, the holding period of the preferred stock starts when the common stock was acquired, January 1990.

12. (585,Q2,37) (c) The requirement is to determine the amount of long-term capital gain to be reported on the sale of 50 shares of stock received as a nontaxable stock dividend. After the stock dividend, the basis of each share would be determined as follows:

$$\frac{\$90,000}{450 + 50} = \$180 \text{ per share}$$

Since the holding period of the new shares includes the holding period of the old shares, the sale of the 50 new shares for $11,000 results in a LTCG of $2,000 [$11,000 - (50 shares x $180)].

A.4.a. Like-Kind Exchange

13. (586,Q3,58) (d) The requirement is to determine the reportable gain resulting from the exchange of an apartment building for an office building. No gain or loss is recognized on the exchange of business or investment property for property of a like-kind. The term "like-kind" means the same class of property (i.e., real estate must be exchanged for real estate, personal property exchanged for personal property). Thus, the exchange of an apartment building for an office building qualifies as a like-kind exchange. Since no boot (money or un-like property) was received, the realized gain of $600,000 - $200,000 = $400,000 is not recognized.

14. (583,P3,47) (d) The requirement is to determine the amount of recognized gain re-

sulting from a like-kind exchange of investment property. In a like-kind exchange, gain is recognized to the extent of the lesser of (1) "boot" received, or (2) gain realized.

FMV of property received	$250,000
Cash received	30,000
Mortgage assumed	70,000
Amount realized	$350,000
Basis of property exchanged	(160,000)
Gain realized	$190,000

Since the "boot" received includes both the cash and the assumption of the mortgage, gain is recognized to the extent of the $100,000 of "boot" received.

15. (582,P3,56) (b) The requirement is to determine the amount of gain recognized to Anderson on the like-kind exchange of apartment buildings. Anderson's realized gain is computed as follows:

FMV of building received		$550,000
Mortgage on old building		100,000
Cash received		25,000
Total consideration received		$675,000
Less:		
Basis of old building	$375,000	
Mortgage on new building	125,000	
		500,000
Realized gain		$175,000

Since the boot received in the form of cash cannot be offset against boot given in the form of an assumption of a mortgage, the realized gain is recognized to the extent of the $25,000 cash received.

16. (582,P3,41) (d) The requirement is to determine the basis of a truck acquired in a like-kind exchange. The basis of the new truck is the adjusted basis of the old truck of $3,600 plus the additional cash paid of $8,000 ($10,000 - $2,000), a total of $11,600.

17. (585,Q2,32) (c) The requirement is to determine the basis of a new truck acquired in a like-kind exchange. The basis of the new truck is the book value (i.e., adjusted basis) of the old truck of $4,000 plus the additional cash paid of $19,000 (i.e., the list price of the new truck of $25,000 less the trade-in allowance of $6,000).

18. (1183,Q2,39) (d) The requirement is to determine the end of the replacement period for nonrecognition of gain following the condemnation of real property. For a condemnation of real property held for productive use in a trade or business or for investment, the

replacement period ends three years after the close of the taxable year in which the gain is first realized. Since the gain was realized in 1989, the replacement period ends December 31, 1992.

A.4.c. Sale or Exchange of Residence

19. (589,Q3,42) (a) The requirement is to determine the amount of gain to be recognized by Oran in 1989 on the sale of his principal residence. A taxpayer age 55 or older may make a once-in-a-lifetime election to exclude up to $125,000 of the realized gain on the sale of principal residence, if the taxpayer owned and occupied the home as a principal residence for at least 3 years out of the 5-year period ending on date of sale. Any remaining realized gain will be recognized to the extent that the adjusted sales price of the old residence exceeds the cost of the new residence.

Oran realized a gain of $260,000 - $70,000 = $190,000, which is then reduced by the $125,000 of excluded gain to $65,000. The $125,000 of excluded gain is also subtracted from the net sales price of $260,000 resulting in an adjusted sales prices of $135,000. Oran's remaining realized gain of $65,000 is then recognized to the extent that the adjusted sales price of $135,000 exceeds the $90,000 cost of the replacement residence ($135,000 - $90,000 = $45,000).

20. (1185,Q2,21) (a) The requirement is to determine the minimum age that a taxpayer must obtain in order to elect to make the one-time exclusion of gain on sale of a principal residence. A taxpayer must be age 55 or older on the date of sale or exchange of a principal residence in order to be eligible to exclude gain. Additionally, the taxpayer must have owned and occupied the home as a principal residence for at least 3 of the 5 years ending on date of sale.

21. (1185,Q2,22) (d) The maximum amount of gain that can be excluded on the sale or exchange of a principal residence is $125,000. For a married taxpayer filing a separate return, the maximum exclusion is $62,500.

A.5. Sales and Exchanges of Securities

22. (576,Q2,16) (c) The purchase of substantially identical stock within 30 days of the sale of stock at a loss is known as a wash sale. The $800 loss incurred in the wash sale ($5,000 basis less $4,200 amount realized) is disallowed. The basis of the replacement (substantially identical) stock is its cost

($3,600) plus the disallowed wash sale loss ($800). The holding period of the replacement stock includes the holding period of the wash sale stock. The amount realized ($6,000) less the basis ($4,400) results in a long-term gain of $1,600.

23. (1175,Q2,19) (c) Worthless securities generally receive capital loss treatment. However, if the loss is incurred by a corporation on its investment in an affiliated corporation (80% or more ownership), the loss is treated as an ordinary loss.

A.6. Losses, Expenses, and Interest Between Related Taxpayers

24. (583,P3,48) (a) Losses are disallowed on sales between related parties, including family members. Thus, Daniel's loss of $3,000 is disallowed on the sale of stock to his son, William. William's basis for the stock is his $7,000 cost. Since William's stock basis is determined by his cost (not by reference to Daniel's cost), there is no "tack-on" of Daniel's holding period. Thus, a later sale of the stock for $6,000 on November 1 generates a $1,000 STCL for William.

25. (1186,Q3,41) (a) The requirement is to determine the amount of loss that Rega Corp. can deduct on a sale of its property to a 55% shareholder. Losses are disallowed on transactions between related taxpayers, including a corporation and a shareholder owning more than 50% of its stock. Since Al Eng owns 55%, no loss is allowable to Rega Corp.

B. Capital Gains and Losses

26. (583,P3,44) (d) Clark's adjusted gross income would be computed as follows:

Salary income		$38,000
LTCG	$14,000	
LTCL	(4,000)	
NLTCG		$10,000
STCG	$6,000	
STCL	(8,000)	
NSTCL		(2,000)
NLTCG-NSTCL		8,000
Adjusted gross income		$46,000

27. (587,Q3,42) (d) The requirement is to determine the amount of excess of net long-term capital loss over net short-term capital gain that Sol Corp. can offset against ordinary income. A corporation's net capital loss cannot be offset against ordinary income. Instead, a net capital loss is generally carried back 3 years and forward 5 years to offset capital gains in those years.

28. (1186,Q3,42) (d) The requirement is to determine the proper treatment for a $24,000 NLTCL for Nam Corp. A corporation's capital losses can only be used to offset capital gains. If a corporation has a net capital loss, the net capital loss cannot be currently deducted, but must be carried back 3 years and forward 5 years as a STCL to offset capital gains in those years. Since Nam had not realized any capital gains since it began operations, the $24,000 LTCL can only be carried forward for 5 years as a STCL.

29. (1185,Q2,33) (b) The requirement is to determine the holding period for determining long-term capital gains and losses. For property acquired after 1987, long-term capital gain or loss results if the property is held more than 12 months.

30. (585,Q2,38) (d) The requirement is to determine the treatment for the sale of the antique by Wald. The definition of capital assets includes investment property and property held for personal use (if sold at a gain). Since Wald bought the antique for personal use in 1985, a sale of the antique at a gain in 1989 will be treated as long-term capital gain.

31. (1181,Q3,41) (c) The requirement is to determine the capital loss carryover to 1990. The NSTCL and the NLTCL result in a net capital loss of $6,000. LTCLs are deductible dollar-for-dollar, the same as STCLs. Since an individual can deduct a net capital loss up to a maximum of $3,000, the net capital loss of $6,000 results in a capital loss deduction of $3,000 for 1989, and a capital loss carry-over to 1990 of $3,000.

B.1. Capital Assets

32. (589,Q3,41) (b) The requirement is to determine the proper treatment for the gain recognized on the sale of a painting that was purchased in 1979 and held for personal use. The definition of "capital assets" includes investment property and property held for personal use (if sold at a gain). Because the painting was held for more than 1 year, the gain of sale on the painting must be reported as a long-term capital gain. Note that if personal-use property is sold at a loss, the loss is not deductible.

33. (1188,Q1,8) (b) The requirement is to determine the correct treatment for a capital loss incurred by a married couple filing a joint return for 1989. Capital losses first offset capital gains, and then are allowed as a deduction of up to $3,000 against ordinary income, with any unused capital loss carried forward indefinitely. Note that a married taxpayer filing separately can only offset up to $1,500 of net capital loss against ordinary income.

34. (588,Q1,4) (b) The requirement is to determine the treatment of an excess of net long-term capital loss over net short-term capital gain for a married couple filing a joint return. Both a NLTCL and a NSTCL are used dollar-for-dollar in computing an individual's capital loss deduction. A net capital loss deduction is limited to $3,000 ($1,500 if married filing separately). Any unused net capital loss is carried forward for an unlimited period of time retaining its identity as long-term or short-term in the years to which carried.

35. (1187,Q1,2) (a) The requirement is to determine the amount of capital assets owned by Oran. The definition of capital assets includes investment property and property held for personal use, but excludes property <u>used</u> in a trade or business. Thus, the vacant lot used as a customers' parking lot and the store fixtures do not constitute capital assets.

36. (1187,Q1,19) (a) The requirement is to determine the classification of Ruth's diamond necklace. The diamond necklace is classified as a capital asset because the definition of "capital asset" includes investment property and <u>property held for personal use</u>. Answers (b), (c), and (d) are incorrect because Sec. 1231 generally includes only assets used in a trade or business, while Sections 1245 and 1250 only include depreciable assets.

37. (587,Q3,46) (b) The requirement is to determine which asset is a capital asset. The definition of capital assets includes goodwill, but excludes property used in a trade or business (e.g., delivery truck, land used as a parking lot). Treasury stock is not considered an asset, but instead is treated as a reduction of stockholder's equity.

38. (1184,Q2,21) (c) The requirement is to determine the amount of capital assets owned by Karp. The definition of capital assets includes investment property and property held for personal use (e.g., personal residence and furniture), but excludes property used in a trade or business (e.g., car wash machinery).

39. (1183,Q2,21) (a) The requirement is to determine how a lump sum of $30,000 received in 1989, for an agreement not to operate a

competing enterprise, should be treated. A
<u>covenant not to compete</u> is not a capital
asset. Thus, the $30,000 received as con-
sideration for such an agreement must be
reported as ordinary income in the year received.

40. (1183,Q2,33) (b) The requirement is to
determine the amount of furniture classified
as capital assets. The definition of capital
assets includes investment property and property held for personal use (e.g., kitchen and
living room pieces), but excludes property
used in a trade or business (e.g., showcases
and tables).

C. Gains and Losses on Business Property

41. (1180,P3,44) (b) The requirement is to
determine the proper treatment of the $50,000
gain on the sale of the building, which is
Sec. 1250 property. Sec. 1250 recaptures gain
as ordinary income to the extent of "excess"
depreciation (i.e., depreciation deducted in
excess of straight-line). The total gain less
any depreciation recapture is Sec. 1231 gain.
Since straight-line depreciation was used,
there is no Sec. 1250 recapture. However,
Sec. 291 requires that the ordinary income
element on the disposition of Sec. 1250
property by corporations be increased by 20%
of the additional amount that would have been
ordinary income if the property had been
Sec. 1245 property. If the building had been
Sec. 1245 property the amount of recapture
would have been $30,000 ($200,000 -
$170,000). Thus, the Sec. 291 ordinary income
is $30,000 x 20% = $6,000. The remaining
$44,000 is Sec. 1231 gain.

42. (584,Q1,5) (b) The requirement is to
determine the proper treatment of the $40,000
gain on the sale of the machinery. Since the
machinery is subject to Sec. 1245 recapture,
gain will be treated as ordinary income to the
extent of all depreciation deducted.

Selling price		$80,000
Cost	$68,000	
Depreciation	-28,000	
Adjusted basis		40,000
Recognized gain		$40,000
Sec. 1245 ordinary income		-28,000
Sec. 1231 gain		$12,000

43. (580,Q2,32) (d) The requirement is to
determine Murray Corporation's TI given book
income plus additional information. The gain
on sale of land ($7,000) and loss on sale of
building ($12,000) are Sec. 1231 gains and
losses. The resulting Sec. 1231 net loss of

$5,000 is an ordinary tax deduction which has
already been deducted in computing book income
of $120,000. The loss on sale of investments
results in a net capital loss which is not deductible for 1989 (carry back 3 and forward 5
years to offset capital gains in other years).

Book income before taxes	$120,000
Add back net capital loss	+ 8,000
Taxable income	$128,000

44. (576,Q2,26) (a) The realized gain resulting from the involuntary conversion
($125,000 insurance proceeds - $86,000 adjusted basis = $39,000) is recognized only to
the extent that the insurance proceeds are not
reinvested in similar property ($125,000 -
$110,000 = $15,000). Since the machinery was
Sec. 1245 property, the recognized gain of
$15,000 is recaptured as ordinary income to
the extent of the $14,000 of depreciation pre-
viously deducted. The remaining $1,000 is
Sec. 1231 gain.

Multiple Choice Questions (1-45)

1.   On June 1, 1989, Don Kerr received a 10%
interest in the capital of Rev Company, a
partnership, for services rendered. Rev's net
assets at June 1 had a basis of $35,000 and a
fair market value of $50,000. What income
must Kerr include in his 1989 tax return for
the partnership interest transferred to him by
the other partners?
   a. $5,000 capital gain.
   b. $5,000 ordinary income.
   c. $3,500 capital gain.
   d. $3,500 ordinary income.

2.   The following information pertains to
Carr's admission to the Smith & Jones
partnership on July 1, 1989:

   Carr's contribution of capital:
   800 shares of Ed Corp. stock
   bought in 1975 for $30,000; fair
   market value $150,000 on July 1,
   1989.

   Carr's interest in capital and
   profits of Smith & Jones: 25%.

   Fair market value of net assets
   of Smith & Jones on July 1, 1989
   after Carr's admission:
   $600,000.

Carr's gain in 1989 on the exchange of the Ed
stock for Carr's partnership interest was
   a. $120,000 ordinary income.
   b. $120,000 long-term capital gain.
   c. $120,000 Section 1231 gain.
   d. $0.

3.   The following information pertains to
land contributed by Pink for a 50% interest in
a new partnership:

Adjusted basis to Pink	$100,000
Fair market value	300,000
Mortgage assumed by partnership	30,000

The basis for Pink's partnership interest is
   a. $ 70,000
   b. $ 85,000
   c. $100,000
   d. $300,000

4.   The holding period of property acquired
by a partnership as a contribution to the
contributing partner's capital account
   a.   Begins with the date of contribution
        to the partnership.
   b.   Includes the period during which the
        property was held by the contrib-
        uting partner.
   c.   Is equal to the contributing
        partner's holding period prior to
        contribution to the partnership.

   d.   Depends on the character of the
        property transferred.

5.   In 1990, Dave Burr acquired a 20%
interest in a partnership by contributing a
parcel of land. At the time of Burr's contribution, the land had a fair market value of
$35,000, an adjusted basis to Burr of $8,000,
and was subject to a mortgage of $12,000.
Payment of the mortgage was assumed by the
partnership. Burr's basis for his interest in
the partnership is
   a. $0
   b. $ 5,600
   c. $ 8,000
   d. $23,000

6.   On May 1, 1990, John Alda was admitted to
partnership in the firm of Bartok & Benson.
Alda's contribution to capital consisted of
500 shares of stock in Asch Corp., purchased
in 1983 for $20,000, which had a fair market
value of $100,000 on May 1, 1990. Alda's
interest in the partnership's capital and
profits is 25%. On May 1, 1990, the fair
market value of the partnership's net assets
(after Alda was admitted) was $400,000. What
was Alda's gain in 1990 on the exchange of the
Asch stock for Alda's partnership interest?
   a. $0.
   b. $80,000 ordinary income.
   c. $80,000 long-term capital gain.
   d. $80,000 Section 1231 gain.

7.   On September 1, 1989, James Elton received a 25% capital interest in Bredbo Associates, a partnership, in return for services
rendered plus a contribution of assets with a
basis to Elton of $25,000 and a fair market
value of $40,000. The fair market value of
Elton's 25% interest was $50,000. How much is
Elton's basis for his interest in Bredbo?
   a. $25,000
   b. $35,000
   c. $40,000
   d. $50,000

8.   In the computation of the ordinary income
of a partnership, a deduction is allowed for
   a.   Contributions to qualified
        charities.
   b.   The net operating loss deduction.
   c.   Guaranteed payments to partners.
   d.   Short-term and long-term capital
        losses.

9.   Dunn and Shaw are partners who share
profits and losses equally. In the computation of the partnership's 1989 book income
of $100,000, guaranteed payments to partners
totaling $60,000 and charitable contributions

totaling $1,000 were treated as expenses.
What amount should be reported as ordinary
income on the partnership's 1989 return?

    a. $100,000
    b. $101,000
    c. $160,000
    d. $161,000

10. The partnership of Martin & Clark sustained an ordinary loss of $84,000 in 1989.
The partnership, as well as the two partners,
are on a calendar-year basis. The partners
share profits and losses equally. At December 31, 1989, Clark, who materially participates in the partnership's business, had an
adjusted basis of $36,000 for his partnership
interest, before consideration of the 1989
loss. On his individual income tax return for
1989, Clark should deduct a(n)

    a.   Ordinary loss of $36,000.
    b.   Ordinary loss of $42,000.
    c.   Ordinary loss of $36,000 and a
        capital loss of $6,000.
    d.   Capital loss of $42,000.

11. The partnership of Felix and Oscar had
the following items of income during the
taxable year ended December 31, 1989.

Income from operations	$156,000
Tax-exempt interest income	8,000
Dividends from foreign	
corporations	6,000
Net rental income	12,000

What is the total ordinary income of the
partnership for 1989?

    a. $156,000
    b. $174,000
    c. $176,000
    d. $182,000

12. At December 31, 1988, Burns and Cooper
were equal partners in a partnership with net
assets having a tax basis and fair market
value of $100,000. On January 1, 1989, Todd
contributed securities with a fair market
value of $50,000 (purchased in 1978 at a cost
of $35,000) to become an equal partner in the
new firm of Burns, Cooper, and Todd. The
securities were sold on December 15, 1989, for
$65,000. How much of the partnership's
capital gain from the sale of these securities
should be allocated to Todd?

    a. $ 5,000
    b. $10,000
    c. $15,000
    d. $20,000

13. Gilroy, a calendar-year taxpayer, is a
partner in the firm of Adams and Company which
has a fiscal year ending June 30. The part-

nership agreement provides for Gilroy to receive 25% of the ordinary income of the partnership. Gilroy also receives a guaranteed
payment of $1,000 monthly which is deductible
by the partnership. The partnership reported
ordinary income of $88,000 for the year ended
June 30, 1989, and $132,000 for the year ended
June 30, 1990. How much should Gilroy report
on his 1989 return as total income from the
partnership?

    a. $25,000
    b. $30,500
    c. $34,000
    d. $39,000

14. A partner's taxable income, arising from
the partner's interest in a partnership,
includes

    a.   Only the partner's share of partner-
        ship income actually distributed to
        the partner during the year.
    b.   The partner's share of partnership
        income, whether or not distributed
        to the partner during the year.
    c.   Only the partner's salary actually
        paid to the partner during the year.
    d.   Only the partner's salary and inter-
        est paid to the partner during the
        year, and deducted by the partner-
        ship during that year.

15. On December 31, 1988, Edward Baker gave
his son, Allan, a gift of a 50% interest in a
partnership in which capital is a material
income-producing factor. For the year ended
December 31, 1989, the partnership's ordinary
income was $100,000. Edward and Allan were
the only partners in 1989. There were no
guaranteed payments to partners. Edward's
services performed for the partnership were
worth a reasonable compensation of $40,000 for
1989. Allan has never performed any services
for the partnership. What is Allan's distributive share of partnership income for 1989?

    a. $20,000
    b. $30,000
    c. $40,000
    d. $50,000

16. Clark and Lewis are partners who share
profits and losses 60% and 40%, respectively. The tax basis of each partner's
interest in the partnership as of December 31,
1988, was as follows:

Clark	$24,000
Lewis	$18,000

During 1989, the partnership had ordinary income of $50,000 and a long-term capital loss
of $10,000 from the sale of securities. There
were no distributions to the partners during
1989. What is the amount of Lewis' tax basis
as of December 31, 1989?

a. $33,000
b. $34,000
c. $38,000
d. $42,000

17. Hall and Haig are equal partners in the firm of Arosa Associates. On January 1, 1989, each partner's adjusted basis in Arosa was $40,000. During 1989 Arosa borrowed $60,000, for which Hall and Haig are personally liable. Arosa sustained an operating loss of $10,000 for the year ended December 31, 1989. The basis of each partner's interest in Arosa at December 31, 1989, was
   a. $35,000
   b. $40,000
   c. $65,000
   d. $70,000

18. Doris and Lydia are equal partners in the capital and profits of Agee & Nolan, but are otherwise unrelated. The following information pertains to 300 shares of Mast Corp. stock sold by Lydia to Agee & Nolan:

   Year of purchase   1980
   Year of sale   1989
   Basis (cost) $9,000
   Sales price (equal to
     fair market value) $4,000

The amount of long-term capital loss that Lydia realized in 1989 on the sale of this stock was
   a. $5,000
   b. $3,000
   c. $2,500
   d. $0

19. In March 1989, Lou Cole bought 100 shares of a listed stock for $10,000. In May 1989, Cole sold this stock for its fair market value of $16,000 to the partnership of Rook, Cole & Clive. Cole owned a one-third interest in this partnership. In Cole's 1989 tax return, what amount should be reported as short-term capital gain as a result of this transaction?
   a. $6,000
   b. $4,000
   c. $2,000
   d. $0

20. Kay Shea owns a 55% interest in the capital and profits of Admor Antiques, a partnership. In 1989 Kay sold an oriental lamp to Admor for $5,000. Kay bought this lamp in 1970 for her personal use at a cost of $1,000 and had used the lamp continuously in her home until the lamp was sold to Admor. Admor purchased the lamp as inventory for sale to customers in the ordinary course of business. What is Kay's reportable gain in 1989 on the sale of the lamp to Admor?

a. $4,000 ordinary income.
b. $4,000 long-term capital gain.
c. $3,400 ordinary income.
d. $3,400 long-term capital gain.

21. Gladys Peel owns an 80% interest in the capital and profits of the partnership of Peel and Poe. On July 1, 1989, Peel bought surplus land from the partnership at the land's fair market value of $10,000. The partnership's basis in the land was $16,000. For the year ended December 31, 1989, the partnership's net income was $94,000 after recording the $6,000 loss on the sale of land. Peel's distributive share of ordinary income from the partnership for 1989 was
   a. $70,400
   b. $75,200
   c. $78,200
   d. $80,000

22. Without obtaining prior approval from the IRS, a newly formed partnership may adopt
   a. A taxable year which is the same as that used by one or more of its partners owning an aggregate interest of more than 50% in profits and capital.
   b. A calendar year, only if it comprises a 12-month period.
   c. A January 31 year end if it is a retail enterprise, and all of its principal partners are on a calendar year.
   d. Any taxable year that it deems advisable to select.

23. Irving Aster, Dennis Brill, and Robert Clark were partners who shared profits and losses equally. On February 28, 1989, Aster sold his interest to Phil Dexter. On March 31, 1989, Brill died, and his estate held his interest for the remainder of the year. The partnership continued to operate and for the fiscal year ending June 30, 1989, it had a profit of $45,000. Assuming that partnership income was earned on a pro rata monthly basis and that all partners were calendar-year taxpayers, the distributive shares to be included in 1989 gross income should be
   a. Aster $10,000, Brill $0, Estate of Brill $15,000, Clark $15,000, and Dexter $5,000.
   b. Aster $10,000, Brill $11,250, Estate of Brill $3,750, Clark $15,000, and Dexter $5,000.
   c. Aster $0, Brill $11,250, Estate of Brill $3,750, Clark $15,000, and Dexter $15,000.
   d. Aster $0, Brill $0, Estate of Brill $15,000, Clark $15,000, and Dexter $15,000.

24. On November 1, 1989, Kerry and Payne, each of whom was a 20% partner in the calendar-year partnership of Roe Co., sold their partnership interests to Reed, who was a 60% partner. For tax purposes, the Roe Co. partnership

    a. Was terminated as of November 1, 1989.

    b. Was terminated as of December 31, 1989.

    c. Continues in effect until a formal partnership dissolution notice is filed with the IRS.

    d. Continues in effect until a formal partnership dissolution resolution is filed in the office of the county clerk where Roe Co. had been doing business.

25. A partnership is terminated for tax purposes

    a. Only when it has terminated under applicable local partnership law.

    b. When at least 50% of the total interest in partnership capital and profits changes hands by sale or exchange within 12 consecutive months.

    c. When the sale of partnership assets is made only to an outsider, and <u>not</u> to an existing partner.

    d. When the partnership return of income (Form 1065) ceases to be filed by the partnership.

26. David Beck and Walter Crocker were equal partners in the calendar-year partnership of Beck & Crocker. On July 1, 1989, Beck died. Beck's estate became the successor in interest and continued to share in Beck & Crocker's profits until Beck's entire partnership interest was liquidated on April 30, 1990. At what date was the partnership considered terminated for tax purposes?

    a. April 30, 1990.

    b. December 31, 1989.

    c. July 31, 1989.

    d. July 1, 1989.

27. On April 1, 1989, George Hart, Jr. acquired a 25% interest in the Wilson, Hart and Company partnership by gift from his father. The partnership interest had been acquired by a $50,000 cash investment by Hart, Sr. on July 1, 1985. The tax basis of Hart, Sr.'s partnership interest was $60,000 at the time of the gift. Hart, Jr. sold the 25% partnership interest for $85,000 on December 17, 1989. What type and amount of capital gain should Hart, Jr. report on his 1989 tax return?

    a. A long-term capital gain of $25,000.

    b. A short-term capital gain of $25,000.

    c. A long-term capital gain of $35,000.

    d. A short-term capital gain of $35,000.

28. Dave Cole's adjusted basis for his interest in Marb Associates, a partnership, was $50,000. This amount included $20,000 of partnership liabilities for which Cole was personally liable. Marb had no unrealized receivables or substantially appreciated inventory. After having been paid his share of partnership income for the tax year, Cole sold his entire interest in Marb for $40,000 cash and a release from all partnership liabilities. Cole's recognized gain or loss on the sale of his interest in Marb was

    a. $0.

    b. $10,000 ordinary income.

    c. $10,000 capital gain.

    d. $10,000 capital loss.

Items 29 and 30 are based on the following data:

The partnership of Hager, Mazer & Slagle had the following cash basis balance sheet at December 31, 1989:

Assets:

	Adjusted basis per books	Fair market value
Cash	$51,000	$ 51,000
Accounts receivable	--	210,000
Totals	$51,000	$261,000

Liabilities and Capital:

Note payable	$30,000	$ 30,000
Capital accounts:		
Hager	7,000	77,000
Mazer	7,000	77,000
Slagle	7,000	77,000
Totals	$51,000	$261,000

Slagle, an equal partner, sold his partnership interest to Burns, an outsider, for $77,000 cash on January 1, 1990. In addition, Burns assumed Slagle's share of partnership liabilities.

29. How much ordinary income should Slagle report in his 1990 income tax return on the sale of his partnership interest?

    a. $0

    b. $10,000

    c. $70,000

    d. $77,000

30. What was the total amount realized by Slagle on the sale of his partnership interest?

a. $67,000
b. $70,000
c. $77,000
d. $87,000

31. On June 30, 1989, James Roe sold his interest in the calendar-year partnership of Roe
& Doe for $30,000. Roe's adjusted basis in
Roe & Doe at June 30, 1989, was $7,500 before
apportionment of any 1989 partnership income. Roe's distributive share of partnership
income up to June 30, 1989, was $22,500. Roe
acquired his interest in the partnership in
1980. How much long-term capital gain should
Roe report in 1989 on the sale of his partnership interest?
   a. $0
   b. $15,000
   c. $22,500
   d. $30,000

32. The basis of property (other than money)
distributed by a partnership to a partner, in
complete liquidation of the partner's
interest, shall be an amount equal to the
   a.   Fair market value of the property.
   b.   Book value of the property.
   c.   Adjusted basis of such partner's
        interest in the partnership, reduced
        by any money distributed in the same
        transaction.
   d.   Adjusted basis of such partner's
        interest in the partnership,
        increased by any money distributed
        in the same transaction.

Items 33 and 34 are based on the following
data:

   Mike Reed, a partner in Post Co.,
received the following distribution from Post:

	Post's basis	Fair market value
Cash	$11,000	$11,000
Land	5,000	12,500

Before this distribution, Reed's basis in Post
was $25,000.

33. If this distribution were nonliquidating,
Reed's recognized gain or loss on the distribution would be
   a. $11,000 gain.
   b. $ 9,000 loss.
   c. $ 1,500 loss.
   d. $0.

34. If this distribution were in complete
liquidation of Reed's interest in Post, Reed's
basis for the land would be

a. $14,000
b. $12,500
c. $ 5,000
d. $ 1,500

35. In 1985, Lisa Bara acquired a one-third
interest in Dee Associates, a partnership. In
1989, when Lisa's entire interest in the partnership was liquidated, Dee's assets consisted
of the following: cash, $20,000 and tangible
property with a basis of $46,000 and a fair
market value of $40,000. Dee has no liabili-
ties. Lisa's adjusted basis for her one-third
interest was $22,000. Lisa received cash of
$20,000 in liquidation of her entire inter-
est. What was Lisa's recognized loss in 1989
on the liquidation of her interest in Dee?
   a. $0.
   b. $2,000 short-term capital loss.
   c. $2,000 long-term capital loss.
   d. $2,000 ordinary loss.

36. For tax purposes, a retiring partner who
receives retirement payments ceases to be regarded as a partner
   a.   On the last day of the taxable year
        in which the partner retires.
   b.   On the last day of the particular
        month in which the partner retires.
   c.   The day on which the partner
        retires.
   d.   Only after the partner's entire in-
        terest in the partnership is liqui-
        dated.

37. Ted King's adjusted basis for his partnership interest in Troy Company was $24,000.
In complete liquidation of his interest in
Troy, King received cash of $4,000 and realty
having a fair market value of $40,000. Troy's
adjusted basis for this realty was $15,000.
King's basis for the realty is
   a. $ 9,000
   b. $15,000
   c. $16,000
   d. $20,000

38. Magda Shaw's adjusted basis for her partnership interest in Shaw & Zack was $60,000.
In complete liquidation of her interest in
Shaw & Zack, Shaw received cash of $44,000
plus the following assets:

	Adjusted basis to Shaw & Zack
Land-Tract "A"	$24,000
Land-Tract "B"	8,000

How much is Shaw's basis for Tract "B"?
   a. $16,000
   b. $15,000
   c. $ 8,000
   d. $ 4,000

39. John Albin is a retired partner of Brill & Crum, a personal service partnership. Albin has not rendered any services to Brill & Crum since his retirement in 1985. Under the provisions of Albin's retirement agreement, Brill & Crum is obligated to pay Albin 10% of the partnership's net income each year. In compliance with this agreement, Brill & Crum paid Albin $25,000 in 1989. How should Albin treat this $25,000?

    a.   Not taxable.
    b.   Ordinary income.
    c.   Short-term capital gain.
    d.   Long-term capital gain.

May 1990 Questions

40. Partnership Abel, Benz, Clark & Day is in the real estate and insurance business. Abel owns a 40% interest in the capital and profits of the partnership, while Benz, Clark, and Day each owns a 20% interest. All use a calendar year. At November 1, 1989, the real estate and insurance business is separated, and two partnerships are formed: Partnership Abel & Benz takes over the real estate business, and Partnership Clark & Day takes over the insurance business. Which one of the following statements is correct for tax purposes?

    a.   Partnership Abel & Benz is considered to be a continuation of Partnership Abel, Benz, Clark & Day.
    b.   In forming Partnership Clark & Day, partners Clark and Day are subject to a penalty surtax if they contribute their entire distributions from Partnership Abel, Benz, Clark & Day.
    c.   Before separating the two businesses into two distinct entities, the partners must obtain approval from the IRS.
    d.   Before separating the two businesses into two distinct entities, Partnership Abel, Benz, Clark & Day must file a formal dissolution with the IRS on the prescribed form.

Items 41 and 42 are based on the following:

The personal service partnership of Allen, Baker & Carr had the following cash basis balance sheet at December 31, 1989:

Assets

	Adjusted basis per books	Market value
Cash	$102,000	$102,000
Unrealized accounts receivable	--	420,000
Totals	$102,000	$522,000

Liability and Capital

Note payable	$ 60,000	$ 60,000
Capital accounts:		
Allen	14,000	154,000
Baker	14,000	154,000
Carr	14,000	154,000
Totals	$102,000	$522,000

Carr, an equal partner, sold his partnership interest to Dole, an outsider, for $154,000 cash on January 1, 1990. In addition, Dole assumed Carr's share of the partnership's liability.

41. What was the total amount realized by Carr on the sale of his partnership interest?

    a. $174,000
    b. $154,000
    c. $140,000
    d. $134,000

42. What amount of ordinary income should Carr report in his 1990 income tax return on the sale of his partnership interest?

    a. $0
    b. $ 20,000
    c. $ 34,000
    d. $140,000

43. Dale's distributive share of income from the calendar-year partnership of Dale & Eck was $50,000 in 1989. On December 15, 1989, Dale, who is a cash-basis taxpayer, received a $27,000 distribution of the partnership's 1989 income, with the $23,000 balance paid to Dale in May 1990. In addition, Dale received a $10,000 interest-free loan from the partnership in 1989. This $10,000 is to be offset against Dale's share of 1990 partnership income. What total amount of partnership income is taxable to Dale in 1989?

    a. $27,000
    b. $37,000
    c. $50,000
    d. $60,000

44. Which one of the following statements regarding a partnership's tax year is correct?

    a.   A partnership formed on July 1 is required to adopt a tax year ending on June 30.
    b.   A partnership may elect to have a tax year other than the generally required tax year if the deferral period for the tax year elected does **not** exceed three months.
    c.   A "valid business purpose" can **no** longer be claimed as a reason for adoption of a tax year other than the generally required tax year.

    d.   Within 30 days after a partnership
           has established a tax year, a form
           must be filed with the IRS as noti-
           fication of the tax year adopted.

45. Hart's adjusted basis of his interest in
a partnership was $30,000. He received a non-
liquidating distribution of $24,000 cash plus
a parcel of land with a fair market value and
partnership basis of $9,000. Hart's basis for
the land is
    a. $9,000
    b. $6,000
    c. $3,000
    d. $0

Multiple Choice Answers

1. b	10. a	19. a	28. c	37. d
2. d	11. a	20. a	29. c	38. d
3. b	12. d	21. d	30. d	39. b
4. b	13. c	22. a	31. a	40. a
5. a	14. b	23. a	32. c	41. a
6. a	15. b	24. a	33. d	42. d
7. b	16. b	25. b	34. a	43. c
8. c	17. c	26. a	35. c	44. b
9. b	18. a	27. a	36. d	45. b

Multiple Choice Answer Explanations

A.   Partnership Formation

1.   (1189,Q3,54)   (b)   The requirement is to determine the amount of income to be included in Kerr's 1989 tax return for the 10% partnership interest received in exchange for services rendered. An individual must recognize ordinary income when a capital interest in a partnership is received for services rendered. The amount of ordinary income to be included in Kerr's 1989 return is the fair market value of the partnership interest received ($50,000 x 10% = $5,000).

2.   (1189,Q3,55)   (d)   The requirement is to determine the amount of gain recognized on the exchange of stock for a partnership interest. Generally no gain or loss is recognized on the transfer of property to a partnership in exchange for a partnership interest. Since Carr's gain is not recognized, there will be a carryover basis of $30,000 for the stock to the partnership, and Carr will have a $30,000 basis for the 25% partnership interest received.

3.   (1188,Q2,34)   (b)   The requirement is to determine the basis of Pink's 50% partnership interest. Pink's basis consists of the $100,000 basis of the land contributed to the partnership, less the reduction in Pink's individual liability resulting from the partnership's assumption of the mortgage ($30,000 x 50% = $15,000). Thus, Pink's basis for the partnership interest is $100,000 - $15,000 = $85,000.

4.   (1188,Q2,36)   (b)   The requirement is to determine the holding period for property acquired by a partnership as a contribution to the contributing partner's capital account. Generally no gain or loss is recognized on the contribution of property to a partnership in exchange for a capital interest. Since the partnership's basis for the contributed property is determined by reference to the contributing partner's former basis for the property (i.e., a carryover basis), the partnership's holding period includes the period during which the property was held by the contributing partner.

5.   (588,Q2,33)   (a)   The requirement is to determine the basis of a 20% partnership interest that was acquired through a contribution of land subject to a liability that was assumed by the partnership. Burr's basis is the $8,000 adjusted basis of the land contributed reduced (but not below zero) by the decrease in his individual liability resulting from the assumption by the partnership of his liability (80% x $12,000 = $9,600). Thus, Burr's basis for the partnership interest is zero. Note that Burr would have to recognize a gain of $9,600 - $8,000 = $1,600.

6.   (1184,Q3,45)   (a)   The requirement is to determine the amount of gain recognized on the exchange of stock for a partnership interest. Generally no gain or loss is recognized on the contribution of property in exchange for a partnership interest.

7.   (582,Q3,58)   (b)   The requirement is to determine Elton's basis for his 25% interest in the Bredbo partnership. Since Elton received a capital interest with a FMV of $50,000 in exchange for property worth $40,000 and services, Elton must recognize compensation income of $10,000 ($50,000 - $40,000) on the transfer of services for a capital interest. Thus, Elton's basis for his partnership interest consists of the $25,000 basis of assets transferred plus the $10,000 of income recognized on the transfer of services, a total of $35,000.

B.   Partnership Income and Loss

8.   (1188,Q2,37)   (c)   The requirement is to determine the item that is deductible in the computation of the ordinary income of a partnership. Guaranteed payments to partners are always deductible in arriving at a partnership's ordinary income. Contributions to qualified charities and short-term and long-term capital losses cannot be deducted in computing a partnership's ordinary income because they are subject to special limitations and must be separately allocated to partners. Answer (b) is incorrect because a partnership is not allowed a net operating loss deduction since its expenses and losses flow through to partners each year.

9.   (588,Q2,36)   (b)   The requirement is to determine the amount to be reported as ordinary income on the partnership's return

given partnership book income of $100,000. The $60,000 of guaranteed payments to partners were deducted in computing partnership book income and are also deductible in computing partnership ordinary income. However, the $1,000 charitable contribution deducted in arriving at partnership book income must be separately passed through to partners on Schedule K-1 and can not be deducted in computing partnership ordinary income. Thus, the partnership's ordinary income is $100,000 + $1,000 = $101,000.

10. (1184,Q3,54) (a) The requirement is to determine the amount and type of partnership loss to be deducted on Clark's individual return. Since a partnership functions as a conduit or pass-through entity, the nature of a loss as an ordinary loss is maintained when passed through to partners. However, the amount of partnership loss that can be deducted by a partner is limited to a partner's tax basis in the partnership at the end of the partnership taxable year. Thus, Clark's distributive share of the ordinary loss ($42,000) is only deductible to the extent of $36,000. The remaining $6,000 of loss would be carried forward by Clark and could be deducted after his partnership basis has been increased.

11. (581,Q3,49) (a) The requirement is to determine the ordinary income of the partnership. Income from operations is considered ordinary income. The net rental income and the dividends from foreign corporations are separately allocated to partners and must be excluded from the computation of the partnership's ordinary income. Tax-exempt income remains tax-exempt and must also be excluded from the computation of ordinary income. Thus, ordinary income only consists of the income from operations of $156,000.

C.   Partnership Agreements

12. (1181,P3,53) (d) The requirement is to determine the amount of the partnership's capital gain from the sale of securities to be allocated to Todd. The partnership's gain from the sale of securities was $65,000 - $35,000 = $30,000. The pre-contribution gain ($50,000 - $35,000) plus 1/3 of the post-contribution gain ($65,000 - $50,000) must be allocated to Todd, a total of $20,000.

13. (1181,P3,58) (c) The requirement is to determine the amount that Gilroy should report for 1989 as total income from the partnership. Gilroy's income will consist of his share of the partnership's ordinary income for the fiscal year ending June 30, 1989 (the

partnership year that ends within his year), plus the 12 monthly guaranteed payments that he received for that period of time.

$$25\% \times \$88,000 = \$22,000$$
$$12 \times \$1,000 = \underline{12,000}$$
$$\text{Total income} = \underline{\$34,000}$$

14. (1185,Q3,57) (b) A partnership functions as a conduit and its items of income are passed through and reported by partners as income, whether or not the income is actually distributed to partners during the year.

15. (1183,Q3,42) (b) The requirement is to determine Allan's distributive share of the partnership income. In a family partnership, services performed by family members must first be reasonably compensated before income is allocated according to the capital interests of the partners. Since Edward's services were worth $40,000, Allan's distributive share of partnership income is ($100,000 - $40,000) x 50% = $30,000.

D.   Partner's Basis in Partnership

16. (1180,P3,60) (b) The requirement is to determine the tax basis of Lewis' partnership interest as of December 31, 1989. Since Lewis' share of profits and losses is 40%, Lewis' December 31, 1988 basis of $18,000 is increased by $20,000 (40% of $50,000) and decreased by $4,000 (40% of $10,000) resulting in a basis of $34,000 at December 31, 1989.

17. (585,Q3,57) (c) The requirement is to determine the basis of each partner's interest in Arosa at December 31, 1989. Since there are two equal partners, each partner's adjusted basis in Arosa of $40,000 on January 1, 1989, would be increased by 50% of the $60,000 loan and would be decreased by 50% of the $10,000 operating loss. Thus, each partner's basis in Arosa at December 31, 1989, would be $40,000 + $30,000 liability - $5,000 loss = $65,000.

E.   Transaction Between Partnership and Partners

18. (1189,Q3,56) (a) The requirement is to determine the amount of long-term capital loss realized by Lydia from the sale of stock to a partnership in which she has a 50% capital and profits interest. Although gains and losses incurred in sale transactions between a partnership and its partners are generally recognized, a loss is disallowed if incurred in a transaction between a partnership and a partner owning (directly or constructively) more than a 50% capital or profits interest.

Since Lydia's partnership interest does not exceed 50%, she realizes and recognizes a long-term capital loss of $9,000 - $4,000 = $5,000 from the sale of stock.

19. (587,Q3,55) (a) The requirement is to determine the amount to be reported as short-term capital gain on Cole's sale of stock to the partnership. If a person engages in a transaction with a partnership other than as a partner of such partnership, any resulting gain or loss is generally recognized just as if the transaction had occurred with a non-partner. Here, Cole's gain of $16,000 - $10,000 = $6,000 is fully recognized. Since the stock was not held for more than 12 months, Cole's $6,000 gain is treated as a short-term capital gain.

20. (585,Q3,59) (a) The requirement is to determine the amount and nature of Kay's gain on the sale of the lamp to Admor. A gain recognized on a sale of property between a partnership and a more than 50% partner is treated as ordinary income if the property is not a capital asset in the hands of the transferee. Since Kay has a 55% partnership interest and the lamp was purchased as inventory (not a capital asset) by Admor, Kay's gain of $5,000 - $1,000 = $4,000 will be reported as ordinary income.

21. (584,Q1,14) (d) The requirement is to determine Peel's distributive share of ordinary income from the partnership. Since a loss is disallowed on a sale or exchange between a partnership and a more than 50% partner, the $6,000 loss on the sale of land to Peel must be added back to the partnership's net income of $94,000. Peel's distributive share of partnership ordinary income is then ($94,000 + $6,000) x 80% = $80,000.

F. Taxable Year of Partnership and Partners

22. (1186,Q3,52) (a) A newly formed partnership must adopt the same taxable year as is used by its partners owning a more than 50% interest in profits and capital. If partners owning more than 50% do not have the same taxable year, a partnership must adopt the same taxable year as used by all of its principal partners (i.e., a partner with a 5% or more interest in capital and profits). If its principal partners have different taxable years, a partnership must adopt a calender year, unless IRS permission is received to do otherwise.

23. (574,Q2,31) (a) Brill received nothing due to his death, but his estate is entitled to his 1/3 share ($15,000). Clark was a partner for the full year and receives his 1/3 share ($15,000). Aster was a partner for 2/3 of the year, and, therefore, 2/3 of the 1/3 partnership income is includable by him ($10,000). Dexter must report the remaining 1/3 of the 1/3 partnership income ($5,000). The split between Aster and Dexter is based on the assumption that income was earned on a pro rata monthly basis.

H. Termination or Continuation of Partnership

24. (588,Q2,37) (a) The requirement is to determine the date on which the partnership was terminated for tax purposes. The partnership was terminated on November 1, 1989, the date on which Kerry and Payne sold their interests to Reed. On that date, the business ceased to operate as a partnership because the operation of a partnership requires two or more partners.

25. (1185,Q3,59) (b) A partnership is terminated for tax purposes when there is a sale or exchange of 50% or more of the total interest in partnership capital and profits within a 12-month period. Termination under local partnership law, a sale of partnership assets to an outsider, and the partnership's failure to file Form 1065 will not terminate a partnership for federal income tax purposes.

26. (583,Q3,57) (a) The requirement is to determine the date on which the partnership was terminated. A partnership generally does not terminate for tax purposes upon the death of a partner, since the deceased partner's estate or successor in interest continues to share in partnership profits and losses. Here, the partnership was terminated on April 30, 1990, when Beck's entire partnership interest was liquidated, and the business ceased to exist as a partnership.

I. Sale of Partnership Interest

27. (1181,P3,56) (a) The requirement is to determine the amount and type of capital gain to be reported by Hart, Jr. from the sale of his partnership interest. Since the partnership interest was acquired by gift from Hart, Sr., Jr.'s basis would be the same as Sr.'s basis at date of gift, $60,000. Since Jr.'s basis is determined from Sr.'s basis, Jr.'s holding period includes the period the partnership interest was held by Sr. Thus, Hart, Jr. will report a LTCG of $85,000 - $60,000 = $25,000.

28. (1187,Q2,37) (c) The requirement is to determine the amount and type of gain or loss recognized by Dave Cole from the sale of his partnership interest. A sale of a partnership interest generally results in capital gain or loss. There is no ordinary income to be recognized here because Marb Associates had no unrealized receivables or substantially appreciated inventory. In this case, the amount realized by Cole consists of the cash received of $40,000 plus the buyer's assumption of Cole's share of partnership liabilities of $20,000, a total of $60,000. Since the basis of Cole's partnership interest (including his share of liabilities) was $50,000, Cole's recognized capital gain is $60,000 - $50,000 = $10,000.

29. (1184,Q3,42) (c) The requirement is to determine the amount of ordinary income to be reported on the sale of a partnership interest. Although the sale of a partnership interest generally results in capital gain or loss, ordinary income must be recognized to the extent of the selling partner's share of unrealized receivables and substantially appreciated inventory. Here, Slagle must report ordinary income to the extent of his 1/3 share of the unrealized accounts receivable of $210,000, or $70,000.

30. (1184,Q3,43) (d) The requirement is to determine the amount realized by Slagle from the sale of his partnership interest. The amount realized consists of the cash received plus the buyer's assumption of Slagle's share of partnership liabilities. Thus, the amount realized is $77,000 + ($30,000 x 1/3) = $87,000.

31. (583,Q3,53) (a) The requirement is to determine the amount of LTCG to be reported by Roe on the sale of his partnership interest. Roe's basis for his partnership interest of $7,500 must first be increased by his $22,500 distributive share of partnership income, to $30,000. Since the selling price also was $30,000, Roe will report no gain or loss on the sale of his partnership interest.

J.   Pro Rata Distributions from Partnership

32. (1189,Q3,57) (c) The requirement is to determine the basis of property (other than money) distributed by a partnership to a partner in complete liquidation of the partner's interest. In a complete liquidation of a partner's interest in a partnership, the property distributed will have a basis equal to the adjusted basis of the partner's partnership interest reduced by any money received in the same distribution. Generally, in a liquidating distribution, the basis for a partnership interest is (1) first reduced by the amount of money received, (2) then reduced by the partnership's basis for any unrealized receivables and inventory received, (3) with any remaining basis for the partnership interest allocated to the other property received in proportion to their adjusted bases (not FMV) to the partnership.

33. (1187,Q2,38) (d) The requirement is to determine Mike Reed's recognized gain or loss resulting from a nonliquidating distribution of cash and land. No loss can ever be recognized as a result of a pro rata nonliquidating partnership distribution and gain will only be recognized if the amount of cash received exceeds the basis for the partner's partnership interest. If both cash and non-cash property are received in a single distribution, the cash reduces the basis of the partner's interest before the non-cash property. Here, no gain is recognized because the cash distribution of $11,000 does not exceed the $25,000 basis of Reed's partnership interest before the distribution.

34. (1187,Q2,39) (a) The requirement is to determine the basis of land received if a distribution of cash and land were in complete liquidation of Reed's partnership interest. In a liquidating distribution, the basis for a partnership interest is (1) first reduced by the amount of money received; (2) then reduced by the partnership's basis for any unrealized receivables and inventory received; with (3) any remaining basis for the partnership interest allocated to other property received. Here, the basis for Reed's partnership interest of $25,000 is first reduced by the $11,000 of cash received, with the remaining basis of $14,000 becoming the basis for the land received.

35. (1185,Q3,58) (c) The requirement is to determine the amount of loss recognized by Lisa on the complete liquidation of her one-third partnership interest. A distributee partner can recognize loss only upon the complete liquidation of the partner's interest through receipt of only money, unrealized receivables, or inventory. Since Lisa only received cash, the amount of recognized loss is the $2,000 difference between the $22,000 adjusted basis of her partnership interest and the $20,000 of cash received. Since a partnership interest is a capital asset and Lisa acquired her one-third interest in 1985, Lisa has a $2,000 long-term capital loss.

36. (1185,Q3,60)   (d) The requirement is to determine when a retiring partner who receives retirement payments ceases to be regarded as a partner. A retiring partner continues to be a partner for income tax purposes until the partner's entire interest has been completely liquidated through distributions or payments.

37. (585,Q3,60) (d) The requirement is to determine the basis of realty received in complete liquidation of a partnership interest. In a liquidating distribution, a partner's basis for a partnership interest is first reduced by the amount of money and the partnership's basis for any unrealized receivables and inventory received. Any remaining basis is then allocated to other property received. Here, King's partnership basis of $24,000 is first reduced by the $4,000 cash, to $20,000. This $20,000 becomes the basis of the distributed realty. Note that even though the FMV of the realty is $40,000, King recognizes no gain, since gain is only recognized on a distribution if the money received exceeds basis.

38. (1183,Q3,58) (d) The requirement is to determine the basis of the Tract "B" land received in complete liquidation of Shaw's partnership interest. Shaw's basis for her partnership interest of $60,000 is first reduced by the $44,000 of cash received, to $16,000. This remaining basis of $16,000 is then allocated to Tracts "A" and "B" according to their relative adjusted bases. Thus, the basis of the Tract "B" land to Shaw is (8/32 x $16,000) = $4,000.

39. (583,Q3,60) (b) The requirement is to determine the treatment for the payments received by Albin. Payments to a retired partner that are determined by partnership income are distributive shares of partnership income, regardless of the period over which they are paid. Thus, they are taxable to Albin as ordinary income.

May 1990 Answers

40. (590,Q2,21) (a) The requirement is to determine the correct statement concerning the division of Partnership Abel, Benz, Clark, & Day into two partnerships. Following the division of a partnership, a resulting partnership is deemed to be a continuation of the prior partnership if the resulting partnership's partners had a more than 50% interest in the prior partnership. Here, as a result of the division, Partnership Abel & Benz is considered to be a continuation of the prior partnership because its partners (Abel and Benz) owned more than 50% of the interests in

the prior partnership (i.e., Abel 40% and Benz 20%).

41. (590,Q2,22) (a) The requirement is to determine the total amount realized by Carr on the sale of his partnership interest. The total amount realized consists of the amount of cash received plus the buyer's assumption of Carr's share of partnership liabilities. Thus, the total amount realized is $154,000 + ($60,000 x 1/3) = $174,000.

42. (590,Q2,23) (d) The requirement is to determine the amount of ordinary income that Carr should report on the sale of his partnership interest. Although the sale of a partnership interest generally results in capital gain or loss, ordinary income must be recognized to the extent of the selling partner's share of unrealized receivables and substantially appreciated inventory. Here, Carr must report ordinary income to the extent of his 1/3 share of the unrealized accounts receivable of $420,000, or $140,000.

43. (590,Q2,24) (c) The requirement is to determine the total amount of partnership income that is taxable to Dale in 1989. A partnership functions as a pass-through entity and its items of income and deduction are passed through to partners on the last day of the partnership's taxable year. Income and deduction items pass through to be reported by partners even though not actually distributed during the year. Here, Dale is taxed on his $50,000 distributive share of partnership income for 1989, even though $23,000 was not received until 1990. The $10,000 interest-free loan does not effect the pass-through of income for 1989, and the $10,000 offset against Dale's distributive share of partnership income for 1990 will not effect the pass-through of that income in 1990.

44. (590,Q2,25) (b) The requirement is to determine the correct statement regarding a partnership's tax year. A partnership must generally determine its taxable year in the following order: (1) it must adopt the taxable year used by its one or more partners owning an aggregate interest of more than 50% in profits and capital; (2) if partners owning a more than 50% interest in profits and capital do not have the same year end, the partnership must adopt the same taxable year as used by all of its principal partners; and, (3) if principal partners have different taxable years, the partnership must adopt a calendar year.
     A different taxable year other than the year determined above can be used by a partnership if a valid business purpose can be

established and IRS permission is received.
Alternatively, a partnership can elect to use
a fiscal year (other than one required under
the general rules in the first paragraph), if
the election does not result in a deferral of
income of more than three months. The deferral period is the number of months between the
close of the elected fiscal year and the close
of the year that would otherwise be required
under the general rules. Thus, a partnership
that would otherwise be required to adopt a
tax year ending December 31, could elect to
adopt a fiscal year ending September 30
(three-month deferral), October 31 (two-month
deferral), or November 30 (one-month deferral). Note that a partnership that makes
this election must make "required payments"
which are in the nature of refundable, noninterest bearing deposits which are intended
to compensate the Treasury for the revenue
lost as a result of the deferral period.

45. (590,Q2,26). (b) The requirement is to
determine the basis for a parcel of land received in a nonliquidating partnership distribution. If both cash and non-cash property
are received in a single distribution, the
basis for the partner's partnership interest
is first reduced by the cash, before the noncash property. Although a partner's basis for
distributed property is generally the same as
the partnership's former basis for the property is generally the same as the partnership's former basis for the property (a carryover basis), the distributed property's basis
will be limited to the partner's basis for the
partnership interest reduced by any money received in the same distribution. Here, the
basis of Hart's partnership interest of
$30,000 is first reduced by the $24,000 of
cash received, with the remaining basis of
$6,000 allocated as the basis for the parcel
of land received.

Multiple Choice Questions (1-119)

1. Rela Associates, a partnership, transferred all of its assets, with a basis of $300,000, subject to liabilities of $50,000, to a newly formed corporation in return for all of the corporation's stock. Rela then distributed this stock to the partners in liquidation. In connection with this incorporation of the partnership, Rela recognizes

    a. No gain or loss on the transfer of its assets nor on the assumption of Rela's liabilities by the corporation.

    b. Gain on the assumption of Rela's liabilities by the corporation.

    c. Gain or loss on the transfer of its assets to the corporation.

    d. Gain, but not loss, on the transfer of its assets to the corporation.

2. Roberta Warner and Sally Rogers formed the Acme Corporation on October 1, 1989. On the same date Warner paid $75,000 cash to Acme for 750 shares of its common stock. Simultaneously, Rogers received 100 shares of Acme's common stock for services rendered. How much should Rogers include as taxable income for 1989, and what will be the basis of her stock?

	Taxable income	Basis of stock
a.	$0	$0
b.	$0	$10,000
c.	$10,000	$0
d.	$10,000	$10,000

3. On July 1, 1990, Mr. Grey formed Dover Corporation. The same date Grey paid $100,000 cash and transferred property with an adjusted basis of $50,000 to Dover in exchange for 3,000 shares of its common stock. The property had a fair market value of $85,000 on the date of the exchange. Dover had no other shares of common stock outstanding on July 1, 1990. As a result of the above transaction, Grey's basis in his stock and Dover's basis in the property, respectively, are:

    a. $150,000 and $50,000.
    b. $150,000 and $85,000.
    c. $185,000 and $50,000.
    d. $185,000 and $85,000.

4. In 1990, Dr. James Pyle, a cash basis taxpayer, incorporated his dental practice. No liabilities were transferred. The following assets were transferred to the corporation:

Cash (checking account)	$1,000
Equipment	
Adjusted basis	60,000
Fair market value	68,000

Immediately after the transfer, Pyle owned 100% of the corporation's stock. The corporation's total basis for the transferred assets is

    a. $69,000
    b. $68,000
    c. $61,000
    d. $60,000

5. To qualify for tax-free incorporation, a sole proprietor must be in control of the transferee corporation immediately after the exchange of the proprietorship's assets for the corporation's stock. "Control" for this purpose means ownership of stock amounting to at least

    a. 80.00%
    b. 66.67%
    c. 51.00%
    d. 50.00%

6. A corporation's tax preference items that must be taken into account for 1989 alternative minimum tax purposes include

    a. Use of the percentage-of-completion method of accounting for long-term contracts.

    b. Casualty losses.

    c. Accelerated depreciation on pre-1987 real property to the extent of the excess over straight-line depreciation.

    d. Capital gains.

7. In computing its 1989 alternative minimum tax, a corporation must include as a tax preference

    a. The dividends received deduction.

    b. ACRS excess deduction on 18-year real property.

    c. Charitable contributions.

    d. Interest expense on investment property.

8. Finbury Corporation's taxable income for the year ended December 31, 1989 was $2,000,000 on which its tax liability was $680,000. In order for Finbury to escape the estimated tax underpayment penalty for the year ending December 31, 1990, Finbury's 1990 estimated tax payments must equal at least

    a. 60% of the 1990 tax liability.
    b. 75% of the 1990 tax liability.
    c. 90% of the 1990 tax liability.
    d. The 1989 tax liability of $680,000.

9. If a corporation's tentative minimum tax exceeds the regular tax, the excess amount is

    a. Carried back to the preceding taxable year.

    b. Carried back to the third preceding taxable year.

c.   Payable in addition to the regular
     tax.
d.   Subtracted from the regular tax.

10.   Reproduced below are the 1989 corporate
tax rates:

If the amount on
Form 1120, Line 30,   Enter on Form 1120,
Page 1 is: Schedule J, Line 3:

Over –	But not over –		Of the amount over–
0	$ 50,000	15%	0
50,000	75,000	7,500 + 25%	50,000
75,000		13,750 + 34%	75,000

Mason Corporation's 1989 taxable income was
$80,000. Mason's 1989 tax would be
   a. $13,750
   b. $15,450
   c. $18,750
   d. $27,200

11.   The following information pertains to
treasury stock sold by Lee Corp. to an
unrelated broker in 1990:

Proceeds received $50,000
Cost   30,000
Par value   9,000

What amount of capital gain should Lee
recognize in 1990 on the sale of this treasury
stock?
   a. $0
   b. $ 8,000
   c. $20,000
   d. $30,500

12.   During 1989, Ral Corp. exchanged 5,000
shares of its own $10 par common stock for
land with a fair market value of $75,000. As
a result of this exchange, Ral should report
in its 1989 tax return
   a. $25,000 Section 1245 gain.
   b. $25,000 Section 1231 gain.
   c. $25,000 ordinary income.
   d.   No gain.

13.   Pym, Inc., which had earnings and profits
of $100,000, distributed land to Kile Corpor-
ation, a stockholder, as a dividend in kind.
Pym's adjusted basis for this land was
$3,000. The land had a fair market value of
$12,000 and was subject to a mortgage
liability of $5,000, which was assumed by Kile
Corporation. The dividend was declared and
paid during November 1989.
     How much of the distribution would be
reportable by Kile as a dividend, before the
dividends-received deduction?

   a. $0
   b. $ 3,000
   c. $ 7,000
   d. $12,000

14.   Yuki Corp., which began business in 1990,
incurred the following costs in 1990 in connection with organizing the corporation:

Printing of stock certificates $ 5,000
Underwriters' commissions on
   sale of stock   100,000

What portion of these costs qualifies as
amortizable organization expenses deductible
ratably over a period of not less than 60
months?
   a. $105,000
   b. $100,000
   c. $ 5,000
   d. $0

15.   Filo, Inc. began business on July 1,
1989, and elected to file its income tax returns on a calendar-year basis. The following
expenditures were incurred in organizing the
corporation:

August 1, 1989 $300
September 3, 1989 $600

The maximum allowable deduction for amortization of organization expense in 1989 is
   a. $60
   b. $65
   c. $81
   d. $90

16.   Gero Corp. had operating income of
$160,000, after deducting $10,000 for
contributions to State University, but not
including dividends of $2,000 received from
nonaffiliated taxable domestic corporations.
     In computing the maximum allowable
deduction for contributions, Gero should apply
the percentage limitation to a base amount of
   a. $172,000
   b. $170,400
   c. $170,000
   d. $162,000

17.   If a corporation's charitable contributions exceed the limitation for deductibility in a particular year, the excess
   a.   May be carried back to the third
        preceding year.
   b.   May be carried forward to a maximum
        of five succeeding years.
   c.   May be carried back or forward for
        one year at the corporation's
        election.
   d.   Is not deductible in any future or
        prior year.

4
3

18. Thor Corporation's operating income for
1989 was $300,000, after consideration of
$50,000 for charitable contributions. What
was the maximum allowable deduction for contributions in Thor's 1989 return?
  a. $35,000
  b. $30,000
  c. $17,500
  d. $15,000

19. Norwood Corporation is an accrual-basis
taxpayer. For the year ended December 31,
1989, it had book income before tax of
$500,000 after deducting a charitable contri-
bution of $100,000. The contribution was
authorized by the Board of Directors in December 1989, but was not actually paid until
March 1, 1990. How should Norwood treat this
charitable contribution for tax purposes to
minimize its 1989 taxable income?
  a.   It cannot claim a deduction in 1989,
        but must apply the payment against
        1990 income.
  b.   Make an election claiming a deduc-
        tion for 1989 of $50,000 and carry
        the remainder over a maximum of five
        succeeding tax years.
  c.   Make an election claiming a deduc-
        tion for 1989 of $60,000 and carry
        the remainder over a maximum of five
        succeeding tax years.
  d.   Make an election claiming a 1989
        deduction of $100,000.

20. In 1989, Ryan Corp. had the following
income:

Income from operations $300,000
Dividends from unrelated taxable
  domestic corporations less
  than 20% owned   2,000

Ryan had no portfolio indebtedness. In Ryan's
1989 taxable income, what amount should be
included for the dividends received?
  a. $ 400
  b. $ 600
  c. $1,400
  d. $1,600

21. In 1989, Daly Corp. had the following income:

Profit from operations $100,000
Dividends from 20%-owned
  taxable domestic corporation   1,000

In Daly's 1989 taxable income, how much should
be included for the dividends received?
  a. $0
  b. $ 200
  c. $ 800
  d. $1,000

22. Cava Corp., which has no portfolio indebtedness, received the following dividends
in 1989:

From a mutual savings bank $1,500
From a 20%-owned unaffiliated
  domestic taxable corporation   7,500

How much of these dividends qualifies for the
80% dividends-received deduction?
  a. $9,000
  b. $7,500
  c. $1,500
  d. $0

23. For the year ended December 31, 1989,
Atkinson, Inc. had gross business income of
$160,000 and dividend income of $100,000 from
unaffiliated domestic corporations that are at
least 20%-owned. Business deductions for 1989
amounted to $170,000. What is Atkinson's
dividends received deduction for 1989?
  a. $0
  b. $72,000
  c. $80,000
  d. $90,000

24. In the computation of a corporation's
taxable income for a particular year, a net
capital loss sustained in that year is
  a.   Limited to a maximum deduction of
        $3,000.
  b.   Deductible in full.
  c.   Deductible to a maximum extent of
        50%.
  d.   Not deductible.

25. For the year ended December 31, 1989,
Haya Corp. had gross business income of
$600,000 and expenses of $800,000. Contributions of $5,000 to qualified charities were
included in expenses. In addition to the
expenses, Haya had a net operating loss carryover of $9,000. What was Haya's net operating
loss for 1989?
  a. $209,000
  b. $204,000
  c. $200,000
  d. $195,000

26. Dorsett Corporation's income tax return
for 1989 shows deductions exceeding gross
income by $56,800. Included in the tax return
are the following items:

Net operating loss deduc-
  tion (carryover from 1988) $15,000
Dividends received deduction   6,800

What is Dorsett's net operating loss for 1989?
  a. $56,800
  b. $50,000
  c. $41,800
  d. $35,000

27. Ram Corp.'s operating income for the year ended December 31, 1989 amounted to $100,000. Also in 1989, a machine owned by Ram was completely destroyed in an accident. This machine's adjusted basis immediately before the casualty was $15,000. The machine was not insured and had no salvage value.

In Ram's 1989 tax return, what amount should be deducted for the casualty loss?
- a. $ 5,000
- b. $ 5,400
- c. $14,900
- d. $15,000

28. For the first taxable year in which a corporation has qualifying research and experimental expenditures, the corporation
- a. Has a choice of either deducting such expenditures as current business expenses, or capitalizing these expenditures.
- b. Has to treat such expenditures in the same manner as they are accounted for in the corporation's financial statements.
- c. Is required to deduct such expenditures currently as business expenses or lose the deductions.
- d. Is required to capitalize such expenditures and amortize them ratably over a period of not less than 60 months.

29. For the year ended December 31, 1989, Dodd Corp. had net income per books of $100,000. Included in the computation of net income were the following items:

Provision for federal income tax	$27,000
Net long-term capital loss	5,000
Keyman life insurance premiums (corporation is beneficiary)	3,000

Dodd's 1989 taxable income was
- a. $127,000
- b. $130,000
- c. $132,000
- d. $135,000

30. For the year ended December 31, 1989, Bard Corp.'s income per accounting records, before federal income taxes, was $450,000 and included the following:

State corporate income tax refunds	$ 4,000
Life insurance proceeds on officer's death	15,000
Net loss on sale of securities bought for investment in 1987	20,000

Bard's 1989 taxable income was
- a. $435,000
- b. $451,000
- c. $455,000
- d. $470,000

31. For the year ended December 31, 1989, Kork Corp.'s book income, before federal income taxes, was $300,000. Included in this $300,000 were the following items:

Provision for state corporation income tax	$3,000
Interest income on United States obligations	8,000
Interest paid on loan to carry United States obligations	2,000

How much was Kork's 1989 taxable income?
- a. $292,000
- b. $294,000
- c. $300,000
- d. $303,000

32. Dale Corporation's book income before federal income taxes was $520,000 for the year ended December 31, 1989. Dale was organized three years earlier. Organization costs of $260,000 are being written off over a ten-year period for financial statement purposes. For tax purposes these costs are being written off over the minimum allowable period. For the year ended December 31, 1989, Dale's taxable income was
- a. $468,000
- b. $494,000
- c. $520,000
- d. $546,000

33. Bishop Corporation reported taxable income of $700,000 on its federal income tax return for calendar year 1989. Selected information for 1989 is available from Bishop's records as follows:

Provision for federal income tax per books	$280,000
Depreciation claimed on the tax return	130,000
Depreciation recorded in the books	75,000
Life insurance proceeds on death of corporate officer	100,000

Bishop reported net income per books for 1989 of
- a. $855,000
- b. $595,000
- c. $575,000
- d. $475,000

34. For the year ended December 31, 1989, Apollo Corporation had net income per books of $1,200,000. Included in the determination of net income were the following items:

Interest income on municipal bonds	$ 40,000
Gain on settlement of life insurance policy (death of officer)	200,000
Interest paid on loan to purchase municipal bonds	8,000
Provision for federal income tax	524,000

What should Apollo report as its taxable income for 1989?

   a. $1,492,000
   b. $1,524,000
   c. $1,684,000
   d. $1,692,000

35. In the reconciliation of income per books with income per return

   a.   Only temporary differences are considered.
   b.   Only permanent differences are considered.
   c.   Both temporary and permanent differences are considered.
   d.   Neither temporary nor permanent differences are considered.

36. Barbaro Corporation's retained earnings at January 1, 1989 was $600,000. During 1989 Barbaro paid cash dividends of $150,000 and received a federal income tax refund of $26,000 as a result of an IRS audit of Barbaro's 1986 tax return. Barbaro's net income per books for the year ended December 31, 1989 was $274,900 after deducting federal income tax of $183,300. How much should be shown in the reconciliation Schedule M-2, of Form 1120, as Barbaro's retained earnings at December 31, 1989?

   a. $443,600
   b. $600,900
   c. $626,900
   d. $750,900

37. Olex Corporation's books disclosed the following data for the calendar year 1989:

Retained earnings at beginning of year	$50,000
Net income for year	70,000
Contingency reserve established at end of year	10,000
Cash dividends paid during year	8,000

What amount should appear on the last line of reconciliation Schedule M-2 of Form 1120?

   a. $102,000
   b. $120,000
   c. $128,000
   d. $138,000

38. With regard to consolidated returns, which one of the following statements is correct?

   a.   The common parent must directly own 51% or more of the total voting power of all corporations included in the consolidated return.
   b.   Of all intercompany dividends paid by the subsidiaries to the parent, 70% are excludible from taxable income on the consolidated return.
   c.   Only corporations that issue their audited financial statements on a consolidated basis may file consolidated tax returns.
   d.   Operating losses of one group member may be used to offset operating profits of the other members included in the consolidated return.

39. Dana Corp. owns stock in Seco Corp. For Dana and Seco to qualify for the filing of consolidated returns, at least what percentage of Seco's total voting power and total value of stock must be directly owned by Dana?

	Total voting power	Total value of stock
a.	51%	51%
b.	51%	80%
c.	80%	51%
d.	80%	80%

40. Consolidated returns may be filed

   a.   Either by parent-subsidiary corporations or by brother-sister corporations.
   b.   Only by corporations that formally request advance permission from the IRS.
   c.   Only by parent-subsidiary affiliated groups.
   d.   Only by corporations that issue their financial statements on a consolidated basis.

41. In the filing of a consolidated income tax return for a corporation and its wholly-owned subsidiaries, intercompany dividends between the parent and subsidiary corporation are

   a.   Fully taxable.
   b.   Included in taxable income to the extent of 80%.
   c.   Included in taxable income to the extent of 20%.
   d.   Not taxable.

42. Parent Corporation and Subsidiary Corporation file consolidated returns on a calendar-year basis. In January 1988, Subsidiary sold land, which it had used in its business, to Parent for $50,000. Immediately

before this sale, Subsidiary's basis for the land was $30,000. Parent held the land primarily for sale to customers in the ordinary course of business. In July 1989, Parent sold the land to Adams, an unrelated individual. In determining the consolidated Section 1231 net gain for 1989, how much should Subsidiary take into account as a result of the 1988 sale of the land from Subsidiary to Parent?

    a. $0
    b. $20,000
    c. $30,000
    d. $50,000

43. The following information pertains to Ral Corp.:

Accumulated earnings and profits at January 1, 1989	$30,000
Earnings and profits for the year ended December 31, 1989	40,000
Cash distributions to individual stockholders in 1989	90,000

What is the total amount of distributions taxable as dividend income to Ral's stockholders in 1989?

    a. $0
    b. $40,000
    c. $70,000
    d. $90,000

44. Mem Corp., which had earnings and profits of $500,000, made a nonliquidating distribution of property to its stockholders in 1989, as a dividend in kind. This property, which had an adjusted basis of $10,000 and a fair market value of $15,000 at the date of distribution, did not constitute assets used in the active conduct of Mem's business. How much gain did Mem have to recognize on this distribution?

    a. $0
    b. $ 5,000
    c. $10,000
    d. $15,000

45. Pym, Inc. which had earnings and profits of $100,000, distributed land to Alex Rowe, a stockholder, as a dividend in kind. Pym's adjusted basis for this land was $3,000. The land had a fair market value of $12,000 and was subject to a mortgage liability of $5,000, which was assumed by Rowe. The dividend was declared and paid during November 1989. How much of the distribution was taxable to Rowe as a dividend?

    a. $9,000
    b. $7,000
    c. $4,000
    d. $3,000

46. On June 30, 1989, Ral Corporation had retained earnings of $100,000. On that date, it sold a plot of land to a noncorporate stockholder for $50,000. Ral had paid $40,000 for the land in 1980, and it had a fair market value of $80,000 when the stockholder bought it. The amount of dividend income taxable to the stockholder in 1989 is

    a. $0
    b. $10,000
    c. $20,000
    d. $30,000

47. On December 1, 1989, Gelt Corporation declared a dividend and distributed to its sole shareholder, as a dividend in kind, a parcel of land that was not an inventory asset. On the date of the distribution, the following data were available.

Adjusted basis of land	$ 6,500
Fair market value of land	14,000
Mortgage on land	5,000

For the year ended December 31, 1989, Gelt had earnings and profits of $30,000 without regard to the dividend distribution. By how much should the dividend distribution reduce the earnings and profits for 1989?

    a. $ 1,500
    b. $ 6,500
    c. $ 9,000
    d. $14,000

48. How does a noncorporate shareholder treat the gain on a redemption of stock that qualifies as a partial liquidation of the distributing corporation?

    a. Entirely as capital gain.
    b. Entirely as a dividend.
    c. Partly as capital gain and partly as a dividend.
    d. As a tax-free transaction.

49. In 1990, Kara Corp. incurred the following expenditures in connection with the repurchase of its stock from shareholders to avert a hostile takeover:

Interest on borrowings used to repurchase stock	$100,000
Legal and accounting fees in connection with the repurchase	400,000

The total of the above expenditures deductible in 1990 is

    a. $0
    b. $100,000
    c. $400,000
    d. $500,000

50. In 1990, Aca Corp. adopted a plan of complete liquidation. Distributions to stockholders in 1990, under this plan of complete

liquidation, included marketable securities purchased in 1988 with a basis of $100,000 and a fair market value of $120,000 at the date of distribution. In Aca's 1990 return, what amount should be reported as long-term capital gain?

- a. $20,000
- b. $10,000
- c. $ 8,000
- d. $0

51. When a parent corporation completely liquidates its 80%-owned subsidiary, the parent (as stockholder) will ordinarily

- a. Be subject to capital gains tax on 80% of the long-term gain.
- b. Be subject to capital gains tax on 100% of the long-term gain.
- c. Have to report any gain on liquidation as ordinary income.
- d. Not recognize gain or loss on the liquidating distributions.

52. Lark Corp. and its wholly-owned subsidiary, Day Corp., both operated on a calendar year. In January 1990 Day adopted a plan of complete liquidation. Two months later, Day paid all of its liabilities and distributed its remaining assets to Lark. These assets consisted of the following:

Cash $50,000
Land (at cost)   10,000

Fair market value of the land was $30,000. Upon distribution of Day's assets to Lark, all of Day's capital stock was cancelled. Lark's basis for the Day stock was $7,000. Lark's recognized gain in 1990 on receipt of Day's assets in liquidation was

- a. $0
- b. $50,000
- c. $53,000
- d. $73,000

53. On June 1, 1990, Green Corp. adopted a plan of complete liquidation. The liquidation was completed within a 12-month period. On August 1, 1990, Green distributed to its stockholders installment notes receivable that Green had acquired in connection with the sale of land in 1989. The following information pertains to these notes:

Green's basis $ 90,000
Present value   162,000
Face amount   185,000

How much gain must Green recognize in 1990 as a result of this distribution?

- a. $0
- b. $23,000
- c. $72,000
- d. $95,000

54. Carmela Corporation had the following assets on January 2, 1989, the date on which it adopted a plan of complete liquidation:

	Adjusted basis	Fair market value
Land	$ 75,000	$150,000
Inventory	43,500	66,000
Totals	$118,500	$216,000

The land was sold on June 30, 1989, to an unrelated party at a gain of $75,000. The inventory was sold to various customers during 1989 at an aggregate gain of $22,500. On December 10, 1989, the remaining asset (cash) was distributed to Carmela's stockholders, and the corporation was liquidated. What is Carmela's recognized gain in 1989?

- a. $0
- b. $22,500
- c. $75,000
- d. $97,500

55. For the collapsible corporation provisions to be imposed, the holding period of the corporation's stock

- a. Must be a minimum of six months.
- b. Must be a minimum of 12 months.
- c. Depends on the stockholder's basis for gain or loss.
- d. Is irrelevant.

56. Will Benton owned all of the stock of a corporation that has been determined to be collapsible. The basis of the stock to Benton was $25,000, and the corporation had accumulated earnings and profits of $1,000. Benton sold his stock for $40,000. As a result of the sale, Benton must report

- a. $15,000 ordinary gain.
- b. $1,000 ordinary income and $14,000 capital gain.
- c. $14,000 capital gain.
- d. $15,000 capital gain.

57. Ati Corp. has two common stockholders. Ati derives all of its income from investments in stocks and securities, and it regularly distributes 51% of its taxable income as dividends to its stockholders. Ati is a

- a. Personal holding company.
- b. Regulated investment company.
- c. Corporation subject to the accumulated earnings tax.
- d. Corporation subject to tax only on income not distributed to stockholders.

58. Benson, a singer, owns 100% of the outstanding capital stock of Lund Corp. Lund contracted with Benson, specifying that Benson was to perform personal services for Magda

Productions, Inc., in consideration of which
Benson was to receive $50,000 a year from
Lund. Lund contracted with Magda, specifying
that Benson was to perform personal services
for Magda, in consideration of which Magda was
to pay Lund $1,000,000 a year. Personal
holding company income will be attributable to

    a. Benson only.
    b. Lund only.
    c. Magda only.
    d. All three contracting parties.

59. The accumulated earnings tax can be
imposed
    a. On both partnerships and corpora-
       tions.
    b. On companies that make distributions
       in excess of accumulated earnings.
    c. On personal holding companies.
    d. Regardless of the number of
       stockholders of a corporation.

60. The personal holding company tax
    a. Qualifies as a tax credit that may
       be used by partners or stockholders
       to reduce their individual income
       taxes.
    b. May be imposed on both corporations
       and partnerships.
    c. Should be self-assessed by filing a
       separate schedule with the regular
       tax return.
    d. May be imposed regardless of the
       number of equal stockholders in a
       corporation.

61. The accumulated earnings tax does not
apply to
    a. Corporations that have more than 100
       stockholders.
    b. Personal holding companies.
    c. Corporations filing consolidated
       returns.
    d. Corporations that have more than one
       class of stock.

62. The personal holding company tax may be
imposed
    a. As an alternative tax in place of
       the corporation's regularly computed
       tax.
    b. If more than 50% of the corpora-
       tion's stock is owned, directly or
       indirectly, by more than ten
       stockholders.
    c. If at least 60% of the corporation's
       adjusted ordinary gross income for
       the taxable year is personal holding
       company income, and the stock owner-
       ship test is satisfied.
    d. In conjunction with the accumulated
       earnings tax.

63. The accumulated earnings tax
    a. Should be self-assessed by filing a
       separate schedule along with the
       regular tax return.
    b. Applies only to closely held
       corporations.
    c. Can be imposed on S corporations
       that do not regularly distribute
       their earnings.
    d. Can not be imposed on a corporation
       that has undistributed earnings and
       profits of less than $150,000.

64. The accumulated earnings tax is not
imposed on corporations that
    a. Are personal holding companies.
    b. Are subsidiary corporations.
    c. Have assets with an aggregate book
       value of less than $1,000,000.
    d. Have more than 100 stockholders.

65. Kee Holding Corp. has 80 unrelated equal
stockholders. For the year ended December 31,
1989, Kee's income comprised the following:

Net rental income	$ 1,000
Commissions earned on sales of franchises	3,000
Dividends from taxable domestic corporations	90,000

Deductible expenses for 1989 totaled $10,000.
Kee paid no dividends for the past three
years. Kee's liability for personal holding
company tax for 1989 will be based on
    a. $12,000
    b. $11,000
    c. $ 9,000
    d. $0

66. The accumulated earnings tax
    a. Depends on a stock ownership test
       based on the number of stockholders.
    b. Can be avoided by sufficient
       dividend distributions.
    c. Is computed by the filing of a
       separate schedule along with the
       corporation's regular tax return.
    d. Is imposed when the entity is
       classified as a personal holding
       company.

67. Where passive investment income is involved, the personal holding company tax may
be imposed
    a. On both partnerships and corpor-
       ations.
    b. On companies whose gross income
       arises solely from rentals, if the
       lessors render no services to the
       lessees.
    c. If more than 50% of the company is
       owned by five or fewer individuals.

d. On small business investment companies licensed by the Small Business Administration.

68. In determining accumulated taxable income
for the purpose of the accumulated earnings
tax, which one of the following is allowed as
a deduction?
   a. Capital loss carryover from prior
       year.
   b. Dividends received deduction.
   c. Net operating loss deduction.
   d. Net capital loss for current year.

69. The minimum accumulated earnings credit
is
   a. $150,000 for all corporations.
   b. $150,000 for nonservice corporations
       only.
   c. $250,000 for all corporations.
   d. $250,000 for nonservice corporations
       only.

70. Daystar Corp. which is not a mere holding
or investment company, derives its income from
consulting services. Daystar had accumulated
earnings and profits of $45,000 at Decem-
ber 31, 1988. For the year ended December 31,
1989, it had earnings and profits of $115,000
and a dividends-paid deduction of $15,000. It
has been determined that $20,000 of the
accumulated earnings and profits for 1989 is
required for the reasonable needs of the
business. How much is the allowable
accumulated earnings credit at December 31,
1989?
   a. $105,000
   b. $205,000
   c. $150,000
   d. $250,000

71. With regard to S corporations and their
stockholders, the "at risk" rules applicable
to losses
   a. Depend on the type of income
       reported by the S corporation.
   b. Are subject to the elections made by
       the S corporation's stockholders.
   c. Take into consideration the S
       corporation's ratio of debt to
       equity.
   d. Apply at the shareholder level
       rather than at the corporate level.

72. An S corporation may deduct
   a. Charitable contributions within the
       percentage of income limitation
       applicable to corporations.
   b. Net operating loss carryovers.
   c. Foreign income taxes.
   d. Compensation of officers.

73. An S corporation's accumulated adjustments account, which measures the amount of
earnings that may be distributed tax-free,
   a. Must be adjusted downward for the
       full amount of federal income taxes
       attributable to any taxable year in
       which the corporation was a C
       corporation.
   b. Must be adjusted upward for the full
       amount of federal income taxes
       attributable to any taxable year in
       which the corporation was a C
       corporation.
   c. Must be adjusted upward or downward
       for only the federal income taxes
       affected by capital gains or losses,
       respectively, for any taxable year
       in which the corporation was a C
       corporation.
   d. Is not adjusted for federal income
       taxes attributable to a taxable year
       in which the corporation was a C
       corporation.

74. To be eligible for S corporation status,
a corporation can
   a. Not have a decedent's estate as a
       stockholder.
   b. Not have a bankruptcy estate as a
       stockholder.
   c. Have both voting and nonvoting
       common stock issued and outstanding.
   d. Not have more than 25 stockholders.

75. Tau Corp. which has been operating since
1980, has an October 31 year end, which coin-
cides with its natural business year. On
May 15, 1990, Tau filed the required form to
elect S corporation status. All of Tau's
stockholders consented to the election, and
all other requirements were met. The earliest
date that Tau can be recognized as an S corporation is
   a. November 1, 1989.
   b. May 15, 1990.
   c. November 1, 1990.
   d. November 1, 1991.

76. Bow, Inc., an S corporation, has three
equal stockholders. For the year ended December 31, 1989, Bow had taxable income of
$300,000. Bow made cash distributions
totaling $120,000 during 1989. For 1989, what
amount from Bow should be included in each
stockholder's gross income?
   a. $140,000
   b. $100,000
   c. $ 60,000
   d. $ 40,000

77. If a calendar-year S corporation does **not** request an automatic six-month extension of time to file its income tax return, the return is due by
    a. January 31.
    b. March 15.
    c. April 15.
    d. June 30.

78. An S corporation is **not** permitted to take a deduction for
    a. Compensation of officers.
    b. Interest paid to individuals who are **not** stockholders of the S corporation.
    c. Charitable contributions.
    d. Employee benefit programs established for individuals who are **not** stockholders of the S corporation.

79. An S corporation may
    a. Have both common and preferred stock.
    b. Have a corporation as a shareholder.
    c. Be a member of an affiliated group.
    d. Have as many as 35 shareholders.

80. Lindal Corp., organized in 1989, immediately filed an election for S corporation status under the rules of Subchapter S. What is the maximum amount of passive investment income that Lindal will be allowed to earn and still qualify as an S corporation (Subchapter S)?
    a. 80% of gross receipts.
    b. 50% of gross receipts.
    c. 20% of gross receipts.
    d. No limit on passive investment income.

81. Which of the following is **not** a requirement for a corporation to elect S corporation status (Subchapter S)?
    a. Must be a member of a controlled group.
    b. Must confine stockholders to individuals, estates, and certain qualifying trusts.
    c. Must be a domestic corporation.
    d. Must have only one class of stock.

82. Brooke, Inc., an S corporation, was organized on January 2, 1989, with two equal stockholders who materially participate in the S corporation's business. Each stockholder invested $5,000 in Brooke's capital stock, and each loaned $15,000 to the corporation. Brooke then borrowed $60,000 from a bank for working capital. Brooke sustained an operating loss of $90,000 for the year ended December 31, 1989. How much of this loss can

each stockholder claim on his 1989 income tax return?
    a. $ 5,000
    b. $20,000
    c. $45,000
    d. $50,000

83. Which one of the following is a corporate reorganization as defined in the Internal Revenue Code?
    a. Mere change in place of organization of one corporation.
    b. Stock redemption.
    c. Change in depreciation method from accelerated to straight-line.
    d. Change in inventory costing method from FIFO to LIFO.

84. Pursuant to a plan of corporate reorganization adopted in June 1990, Lois Pell exchanged 100 shares of Ral Corp. common stock that she had purchased in March 1988 at a cost of $10,000 for 150 shares of Lars Corp. common stock having a fair market value of $12,000. Pell's recognized gain on this exchange was
    a. $0.
    b. $2,000 ordinary income.
    c. $2,000 short-term capital gain.
    d. $2,000 long-term capital gain.

85. With regard to corporate reorganizations, which one of the following statements is correct?
    a. A mere change in identity, form, or place of organization of one corporation does **not** qualify as a reorganization.
    b. The reorganization provisions can **not** be used to provide tax-free treatment for corporate transactions.
    c. Securities in corporations **not** parties to a reorganization are always "boot."
    d. A "party to the reorganization" does **not** include the consolidated company.

86. Which one of the following is **not** a corporate reorganization as defined in the Internal Revenue Code?
    a. Stock redemption.
    b. Recapitalization.
    c. Mere change in identity.
    d. Statutory merger.

87. Claudio Corporation and Stellar Corporation both report on a calendar-year basis. Claudio merged into Stellar on June 30, 1989. Claudio had an allowable net operating loss carryover of $270,000. Stellar's taxable income for the year ended December 31, 1989,

was $360,000 before consideration of Claudio's net operating loss carryover. Claudio's fair market value before the merger was $1,500,000. The federal long-term tax-exempt rate is 8%. How much of Claudio's net operating loss carryover can be used to offset Stellar's 1989 taxable income?

a. $ 60,493
b. $120,000
c. $180,000
d. $181,479

88. In 1987, Celia Mueller bought a $1,000 bond issued by Disco Corporation, for $1,100. Instead of paying off the bondholders in cash, Disco issued 100 shares of preferred stock in 1990 for each bond outstanding. The preferred stock had a fair market value of $15 per share. What is the recognized gain to be reported by Mueller in 1990?

a. $0.
b. $400 dividend.
c. $400 long-term capital gain.
d. $500 long-term capital gain.

89. On July 1, 1990, in connection with a recapitalization of Yorktown Corporation, Robert Moore exchanged 1,000 shares of stock which cost him $95,000 for 1,000 shares of new stock worth $108,000 and bonds in the principal amount of $10,000 with a fair market value of $10,500. What is the amount of Moore's recognized gain during 1990?

a. $0
b. $10,500
c. $23,000
d. $23,500

90. Which one of the following types of organizations qualifies as an organization exempt from income tax?

a. An "action" organization established for the purpose of influencing legislation pertaining to protection of animal rights.
b. All "feeder" organizations, primarily conducting businesses for profit, but distributing 100% of their profits to organizations exempt from income tax.
c. A social club organized and operated exclusively for the pleasure and recreation of its members, supported solely by membership fees, dues, and assessments.
d. An organization whose purpose is to foster national or international amateur sports competition by providing athletic facilities and equipment.

91. To qualify as an exempt organization other than an employees' qualified pension or profit-sharing trust, the applicant

a. Is barred from incorporating and issuing capital stock.
b. Must file a written application with the Internal Revenue Service.
c. Cannot operate under the "lodge system" under which payments are made to its members for sick benefits.
d. Need not be specifically identified as one of the classes on which exemption is conferred by the Internal Revenue Code, provided that the organization's purposes and activities are of a nonprofit nature.

92. Carita Fund, organized and operated exclusively for charitable purposes, provides insurance coverage, at amounts substantially below cost, to exempt organizations involved in the prevention of cruelty to children. Carita's insurance activities are

a. Exempt from tax.
b. Treated as unrelated business income.
c. Subject to the same tax provisions as those applicable to insurance companies.
d. Considered "commercial-type" as defined by the Internal Revenue Code.

93. Annual information returns of exempt organizations must be filed by

a. Churches.
b. Internally supported auxiliaries of churches.
c. Private foundations.
d. All exempt organizations whose gross receipts in each taxable year are less than $5,000.

94. The filing of a return covering unrelated business income

a. Is required of all exempt organizations having at least $1,000 of unrelated business taxable income for the year.
b. Relieves the organization of having to file a separate annual information return.
c. Is not necessary if all of the organization's income is used exclusively for charitable purposes.
d. Must be accompanied by a minimum payment of 50% of the tax due as shown on the return, with the balance of tax payable six months later.

95. An exempt organization subject to tax on its 1989 unrelated business income
    a. Must comply with the Code provisions regarding installment payments of estimated income tax by corporations.
    b. Must pay at least 50% of the tax due as shown on the return when filed, with the balance of tax payable six months later.
    c. May defer payment of the tax for up to nine months following the due date of the return.
    d. May elect to make installment payments of estimated tax but is **not** required to do so.

96. A condominium management association wishing to be treated as a homeowners association and to qualify as an exempt organization for a particular year
    a. Need **not** file a formal election.
    b. Must file an election as of the date the association was organized.
    c. Must file an election at the beginning of the association's first taxable year.
    d. Must file a separate election for each taxable year no later than the due date of the return for which the election is to apply.

97. An organization wishing to qualify as an exempt organization
    a. Is prohibited from issuing capital stock.
    b. Is limited to three prohibited transactions a year.
    c. Must **not** have non-U.S. citizens on its governing board.
    d. Must be of a type specifically identified as one of the classes on which exemption is conferred by the Code.

98. Which one of the following statements is correct with regard to exempt organizations?
    a. An organization is automatically exempt from tax merely by meeting the statutory requirements for exemptions.
    b. Exempt organizations that are required to file annual information returns must disclose the identity of all substantial contributors, in addition to the amount of contributions received.
    c. An organization will automatically forfeit its exempt status if any executive or other employee of the organization is paid compensation in excess of $150,000 per year, even if such compensation is reasonable.

    d. Exempt status of an organization may **not** be retroactively revoked.

99. To qualify as an exempt organization, the applicant
    a. Must fall into one of the specific classes upon which exemption is conferred by the Internal Revenue Code.
    b. Can **not**, under any circumstances, be a foreign corporation.
    c. Can **not**, under any circumstances, engage in lobbying activities.
    d. Can **not** be exclusively a social club.

100. The private foundation status of an exempt organization will terminate if it
    a. Does **not** distribute all of its net assets to one or more public charities.
    b. Qualifies as an exempt operating foundation.
    c. Becomes a public charity.
    d. Is governed by a charter that limits the organization's exempt purposes.

101. To qualify as an exempt organization,
    a. A written application need **not** be filed if no applicable official form is provided.
    b. No employee of the organization is permitted to receive compensation in excess of $100,000 per year.
    c. The applicant must be of a type specifically identified as one of the classes upon which exemption is conferred by the Code.
    d. The organization is prohibited from issuing capital stock.

102. With regard to unrelated business income of an exempt organization, which one of the following statements is correct?
    a. An unrelated trade or business activity that results in a loss is excluded from the definition of unrelated business.
    b. The tax on unrelated business income can be imposed even if the unrelated business activity is intermittent and is carried on once a year.
    c. An exempt organization is **not** taxed on unrelated business income of less than $1,000.
    d. An exempt organization that earns any unrelated business income in excess of $100,000 during a particular year will lose its exempt status for that particular year.

103. If an exempt organization is a charitable trust, then unrelated business income is
   a.   Not subject to tax.
   b.   Taxed at rates applicable to corporations.
   c.   Subject to tax even if such income is less than $1,000.
   d.   Subject to tax only for the amount of such income in excess of $1,000.

104. If an exempt organization is a corporation, the tax on unrelated business taxable income is
   a.   Computed at corporate income tax rates.
   b.   Computed at rates applicable to trusts.
   c.   Treated as a credit against the tax on recognized capital gains.
   d.   Abated.

105. With regard to unrelated business income of an exempt organization, which one of the following statements is true?
   a.   If an exempt organization has any unrelated business income, such organization automatically forfeits its exempt status for the particular year in which such income was earned.
   b.   When an unrelated trade or business activity results in a loss, such activity is excluded from the definition of unrelated business.
   c.   If an exempt organization derives income from conducting games of chance, in a locality where such activity is legal, and in a state that confines such activity to nonprofit organizations, then such income is exempt from the tax on unrelated business income.
   d.   Dividends and interest earned by all exempt organizations always are excluded from the definition of unrelated business income.

May 1990 Questions

106. Which one of the following will render a corporation ineligible for S corporation status?
   a.   One of the stockholders is a decedent's estate.
   b.   One of the stockholders is a bankruptcy estate.
   c.   The corporation has both voting and nonvoting common stock issued and outstanding.
   d.   The corporation has 50 stockholders.

107. Krol Corp. distributed marketable securities in redemption of its stock in a complete liquidation. On the date of distribution, these securities had a basis of $100,000 and a fair market value of $150,000. What gain does Krol have as a result of the distribution?
   a. $0.
   b. $50,000 capital gain.
   c. $50,000 Section 1231 gain.
   d. $50,000 ordinary gain.

Items 108 through 113 are based on the following:

John Budd is the sole stockholder of Ral Corp., an accrual basis taxpayer engaged in wholesaling operations. Ral's retained earnings at January 1, 1989 amounted to $1,000,000. For the year ended December 31, 1989, Ral's book income, before federal income tax, was $300,000. Included in the computation of this $300,000 were the following:

Dividends received on 500 shares of stock of a taxable domestic corporation that had 1,000,000 shares of stock outstanding (Ral had no portfolio indebtedness)	$ 1,000
Loss on sale of investment in stock of unaffiliated corporation (this stock had been held for two years; Ral had no other capital gains or losses)	(5,000)
Keyman insurance premiums paid on Budd's life (Ral is the beneficiary of this policy)	3,000
Group term insurance premiums paid on $10,000 life insurance policies for each of Ral's four employees (the employees' spouses are the beneficiaries)	4,000
Amortization of cost of acquiring a perpetual dealer's franchise (Ral paid $48,000 for this franchise on July 1, 1989, and is amortizing it over a 48-month period)	6,000
Contribution to a recognized, qualified charity (this contribution was authorized by Ral's board of directors in December 1989, to be paid on January 31, 1990)	75,000

On December 1, 1989, Ral received advance rental of $27,000 from a tenant for a three-year lease commencing January 1, 1990 to cover rents for the years 1990, 1991, and 1992. In conformity with GAAP, Ral did not include any part of this rental in its income statement for the year ended December 31, 1989.

108. What portion of the dividend revenue should be included in Ral's 1989 taxable income?
   a. $150
   b. $200
   c. $300
   d. $900

109. In computing taxable income for 1989, Ral should deduct a capital loss of
   a. $0
   b. $2,500
   c. $3,000
   d. $5,000

110. What amount should Ral include in its 1989 taxable income for rent revenue?
   a. $0
   b. $ 750
   c. $ 9,000
   d. $27,000

111. What amount should Ral deduct for keyman and group life insurance premiums in computing taxable income for 1989?
   a. $0
   b. $3,000
   c. $4,000
   d. $7,000

112. What amount is deductible in Ral's 1989 return for purchase of the dealer's franchise?
   a. $0
   b. $ 600
   c. $1,200
   d. $6,000

113. With regard to Ral's contribution to the recognized, qualified charity, Ral
   a.   Can elect to deduct in its 1989 return any portion of the $75,000 that does **not** exceed the deduction ceiling for 1989.
   b.   Cannot deduct any portion of the $75,000 in 1989 because the contribution was **not** paid in 1989.
   c.   Can deduct the entire $75,000 in its 1989 return because Ral reports on the accrual basis.
   d.   Can elect to carry forward indefinitely any portion of the $75,000 **not** deducted in 1989 or 1990.

114. For the year ended December 31, 1989, Maple Corp.'s book income, before federal income tax, was $100,000. Included in this $100,000 were the following:

Provision for state income tax $1,000
Interest earned on U.S. Treasury
   Bonds   6,000
Interest expense on bank loan to
   purchase U.S. Treasury Bonds   2,000

Maple's taxable income for 1989 was
   a. $ 96,000
   b. $ 97,000
   c. $100,000
   d. $101,000

115. In the consolidated income tax return of a corporation and its wholly-owned subsidiary, what percentage of cash dividends paid by the subsidiary to the parent is tax-free?

   a.   0%.
   b.   70%.
   c.   80%.
   d.   100%.

116. If a corporation's tentative minimum tax exceeds the regular tax, the excess amount is
   a.   Subtracted from the regular tax.
   b.   Payable in addition to the regular tax.
   c.   Carried back to the third preceding taxable year.
   d.   Carried back to the first preceding taxable year.

117. An incorporated exempt organization subject to tax on its 1989 unrelated business income
   a.   Must make estimated tax payments if its tax can reasonably be expected to be $100 or more.
   b.   Must comply with the Code provisions regarding installment payments of estimated income tax by corporations.
   c.   Must pay at least 70% of the tax due as shown on the return when filed, with the balance of tax payable in the following quarter.
   d.   May defer payment of the tax for up to nine months following the due date of the return.

118. The private foundation status of an exempt organization will terminate if it
   a.   Is governed by a charter that limits the organization's exempt purposes.
   b.   Does **not** distribute all of its net assets to one or more public charities.
   c.   Is a foreign corporation.
   d.   Becomes a public charity.

119. To qualify as an exempt organization, the applicant
   a.   May be organized and operated for the primary purpose of carrying on a business for profit, provided that all of the organization's net earnings are turned over to one or more tax exempt organizations.
   b.   Need **not** be specifically identified as one of the classes upon which exemption is conferred by the Internal Revenue Code, provided that the organization's purposes and activities are of a nonprofit nature.
   c.   Must **not** be classified as a social club.
   d.   Must **not** be a private foundation organized and operated exclusively to influence legislation pertaining to protection of the environment.

Problem

Problem 1   (586,Q4)

(45 to 55 minutes)

The following adjusted revenue and expense accounts appeared in the accounting records of Wolf, Inc., an accrual basis taxpayer, for the year ended December 31, 1989:

Revenues

Net sales	$3,000,000	[1]
Equity in earnings of F & W Partnership	60,000	[2]
Dividends	8,000	[3]
Interest	18,000	[4]
Gains on sale of stock	5,000	[5]
Key-man life Insurance proceeds	100,000	[6]
Total	$3,191,000	

Costs and expenses

Cost of goods sold	$2,000,000	[7]
Salaries and wages	500,000	
Bad debts	13,000	[8]
Taxes, other than federal income	62,000	[9]
Interest	12,000	[10]
Contributions	50,000	[11]
Depreciation	60,000	[12]
Other	40,000	[13]
Federal income taxes	120,000	[14]
Total	$2,857,000	
Net income	$ 334,000	

The following additional information is provided:

[1] Trade accounts receivable at December 31, 1988, and at December 31, 1989, amounted to $200,000 and $250,000, respectively.

[2] Wolf, Inc. owns 60% of F & W Partnership. The other 40% of F & W is owned by an unrelated individual. F & W reported the following tax information to Wolf, Inc.:

Wolf, Inc.'s share of:

Partnership ordinary income	$58,000
Dividends qualifying for deduction	10,000
Net long-term capital gain (loss)	(8,000)
Equity in earnings	$60,000

The $10,000 dividends were from a 20%-owned domestic corporation, Jel Corp., whose securities are traded on a major stock exchange.

[3] The $8,000 dividends were from Meg, Inc., a 20%-owned taxable domestic corporation, whose securities are traded on a major stock exchange.

[4] Interest revenue consists of interest on:

Corporate bonds	$15,000
Municipal bonds	3,000

[5] Gains on sale of stock of the following unrelated corporations:

Ral Corp. (bought in May 1989; sold in June 1989)	$ 1,000
Blu, Inc. (bought in November 1988; sold in September 1989)	4,000

[6] Wolf, Inc. owned the key-man life insurance policy, paid the premiums, and was the direct beneficiary. The proceeds were collected on the death of the corporation's treasurer.

[7] Accounts payable for merchandise at December 31, 1988, and at December 31, 1989, amounted to $75,000 and $100,000, respectively.

[8] Bad debts expense represents the actual accounts written off in 1989.

[9] Taxes, other than federal income, consist of:

Payroll taxes	$40,000
Property taxes	20,000
Penalty for late payment of taxes	2,000

[10] Interest expense consists of: $11,000 interest on funds borrowed for working capital, and $1,000 interest on funds borrowed to buy the municipal bonds.

[11] Contributions were all paid in 1989 to State University, specifically designated for the purchase of laboratory equipment.

[12] Depreciation per books is straight-line. For tax purposes, depreciation amounted to $85,000.

[13] Other expenses include premiums of $5,000 on the key-man life insurance policy covering the treasurer, who died in December 1989.

[14] Federal income tax paid in 1989 amounted to $105,000. The difference between the income tax provision and income tax paid is the result of interperiod tax allocation.

Required:

Go to following page and complete the worksheet by making the necessary adjustments to convert Wolf, Inc.'s 1989 book income to federal taxable income.

Any possible alternative treatment should be resolved in a manner that will minimize 1989 taxable income for Wolf, Inc.

Wolf, Inc.
WORKSHEET TO CONVERT BOOK INCOME TO TAXABLE INCOME
For the Year Ended December 31, 1989

	Per books and GAAP	Increases	Decreases	Per tax return
Revenues				
Net sales	3,000,000			
Equity in earnings of F & W Partnership	60,000			
Dividends	8,000			
Interest	18,000			
Gains on sale of stock	5,000			
Key-man life insurance proceeds	100,000			
Totals	3,191,000			
Costs and expenses				
Cost of goods sold	2,000,000			
Salaries and wages	500,000			
Bad Debts	13,000			
Taxes, other than federal income	62,000			
Interest	12,000			
Contributions	50,000			
Depreciation	60,000			
Other	40,000			
Federal income taxes	120,000			
Totals	2,857,000			
Net income	334,000			

Problem 2   (589,Q4)

(45 to 55 minutes)

The following adjusted accounts appeared in the records of Elm Corp., an accrual basis corporation, for the year ended December 31, 1989. Numbers in brackets refer to the items in Additional information.

Revenues and gains

Net sales	$5,500,000	[1]
Dividends	10,000	[2]
Interest	4,000	[3]
Gain on sale of stock	6,000	[4]
Equity in earnings of Luz Partnership	50,000	[5]
Key-man life insurance proceeds	200,000	[6]
Tax refund	3,000	[7]
Total	5,773,000	

Costs and expenses

Cost of goods sold	3,900,000	[8]
Salaries and wages	571,000	[9]
Doubtful accounts	15,000	[10]
Taxes	100,000	[11]
Interest	20,000	[12]
Contributions	175,000	[13]
Depreciation	90,000	[14]
Other	30,000	[15]
Federal income tax	193,000	[16]
Total	5,094,000	
Net income	$ 679,000	

Additional information:

[1] Trade accounts receivable at December 31, 1989 and at December 31, 1988 amounted to $300,000 and $180,000, respectively.

[2] Dividends were declared and paid in 1989 by an unrelated taxable domestic corporation whose securities are traded on a major stock exchange.

[3] Interest revenue comprises interest on municipal bonds issued in 1982 and purchased by Elm in the open market in 1989.

[4] Gain on sale of stock arose from the following purchase and sale of stock in an unrelated corporation listed on a major stock exchange:

Bought in 1980	Cost	$12,000
Sold in 1989	Proceeds of sale	18,000

[5] Elm owns 50% of Luz Partnership. The other 50% is owned by an unrelated individual. Luz reported the following tax information to Elm:

Elm's share of:

Partnership ordinary income	$63,000
Net long-term capital loss	(13,000)

[6] Elm owned the key-man life insurance policy, paid the premiums, and was the direct beneficiary. The proceeds were collected on the death of Elm's controller.

[7] The tax refund arose from Elm's overpayment of federal income tax on the 1987 return.

[8] Cost of goods sold relates to Elm's net sales.

[9] Salaries and wages includes officers' compensation of $125,000.

[10] Doubtful accounts expense represents an addition to Elm's allowance for doubtful accounts based on an aging schedule whereby Elm "reserves" all accounts receivable over 120 days for book purposes. The balance in Elm's allowance for doubtful accounts was $142,000 at December 31, 1989. Actual bad debts written off in 1989 amounted to $9,000. Elm's allowance for doubtful accounts at December 31, 1986 (at the beginning of the first year of the tax law change) was $120,000.

[11] Taxes comprise payroll taxes and property taxes.

[12] Interest expense resulted from borrowing for working capital purposes.

[13] Contributions were all paid in 1989 to State University, specifically designated for the purchase of computers.

[14] Elm has always used straight-line depreciation for both book and tax purposes.

[15] Other expenses include premiums of $12,000 on the key-man life insurance policy covering the controller.

[16] Federal income tax is the amount estimated and accrued before preparation of the return.

Required:

Prepare a schedule of taxable income as it should appear on Elm's 1989 federal income tax return. Show all items required to be included in the return. Assume that the alternative minimum tax is less than the regular tax. Any possible optional treatment should be resolved in a manner that will minimize Elm's 1989 taxable income.

Multiple Choice Answers

1. a	25. d	49. b	73. d	97. d
2. d	26. c	50. a	74. c	98. b
3. a	27. d	51. d	75. c	99. a
4. c	28. a	52. a	76. b	100. c
5. a	29. d	53. c	77. b	101. c
6. c	30. c	54. d	78. c	102. c
7. b	31. c	55. d	79. d	103. d
8. c	32. b	56. a	80. d	104. a
9. c	33. c	57. a	81. a	105. c
10. b	34. a	58. b	82. b	106. d
11. a	35. c	59. d	83. a	107. b
12. d	36. d	60. c	84. a	108. c
13. c	37. a	61. b	85. c	109. a
14. d	38. d	62. c	86. a	110. d
15. d	39. d	63. d	87. a	111. c
16. a	40. c	64. a	88. a	112. a
17. b	41. d	65. d	89. b	113. a
18. a	42. b	66. b	90. c	114. c
19. c	43. c	67. c	91. b	115. d
20. b	44. b	68. d	92. a	116. b
21. b	45. b	69. d	93. c	117. b
22. b	46. d	70. a	94. a	118. d
23. b	47. a	71. d	95. a	119. d
24. d	48. a	72. d	96. d	

Multiple Choice Answer Explanations

A. Transfers to a Controlled Corporation

1. (1189,Q3,53) (a) The requirement is to determine whether gain or loss is recognized on the incorporation of Rela Associates (a partnership). No gain or loss is recognized if property is transferred to a corporation solely in exchange for stock, if immediately after the transfer, the transferor is in control of the corporation. For purposes of determining whether consideration other than stock (boot) has been received, the assumption of liabilities or acquisition of property subject to liabilities by the transferee corporation is not to be treated as the receipt of money or other property by the transferor. Thus, Rela Associates recognizes no gain or loss on the transfer of its assets, subject to its liabilities, to a newly formed corporation in return for all of the corporation's stock.

Also note that no gain or loss will be recognized by Rela Associates on the distribution of the corporation's stock to its partners in liquidation, and no gain or loss will be recognized by the partners when they receive the corporation's stock in liquidation of their partnership interests.

2. (1181,P3,46) (d) The requirement is to determine the taxable income to Rogers and the basis of her stock. Since services are excluded from the definition of "property," Rogers' transfer does not fall under the non-

recognition provision of Sec. 351, but instead is a taxable exchange. Rogers reports $10,000 of income and the basis for the stock is $10,000, the amount reported as income.

3. (1180,P3,43) (a) The requirement is to determine Grey's basis for his stock and Dover's basis for the property following a nontaxable transfer to a controlled corporation. Grey's basis in the stock equals the $50,000 adjusted basis of property plus the $100,000 cash transferred, a total of $150,000. Dover's basis for the property equals Grey's adjusted basis plus any gain recognized on the transfer. Since no gain was recognized by Grey, the basis of the property to Dover is $50,000.

4. (588,Q2,34) (c) The requirement is to determine the corporation's total basis for the transferred assets. The cash and equipment were transferred by Pyle in a nontaxable Sec. 351 transfer to a controlled corporation because Pyle owned at least 80% of the corporation's stock immediately after the transfer. The corporation's basis for the transferred assets would be the same as Pyle's adjusted basis, increased by any gain recognized by Pyle on the transfer. Since Pyle did not receive any boot, no gain was recognized. Thus, the corporation's total basis for the transferred assets would be $1,000 + $60,000 = $61,000.

5. (587,Q3,45) (a) The requirement is to determine the percentage of stock ownership necessary to satisfy the "control test" for a tax-free incorporation. For this purpose, the definition of control means the ownership of at least 80% of the combined voting power of stock entitled to vote, and at least 80% of each class of nonvoting stock.

C.1. Payment of Tax

6. (1188,Q2,23) (c) The requirement is to determine which item is a tax preference that must be included in the computation of a corporation's alternative minimum tax (AMT) for 1989. Accelerated depreciation on pre-1987 real property to the extent of the excess over straight-line depreciation is a tax preference item. Answer (a) is incorrect because it is the excess of income under the percentage of completion method over the amount reported using the completed contract method that is a positive adjustment in computing the AMT. Answer (b) is incorrect because a deduction for casualty losses is allowed in the computation of AMT. Answer (d) is incorrect because capital gains are no longer given preferential treatment in the computation of regular taxable income and thus are not a preference item in computing the AMT for 1989.

7. (1184,Q3,59) (b) In computing its 1989 alternative minimum tax, a corporation must include as a tax preference item the ACRS excess deductions on 18-year real property. The dividends received deduction, charitable contributions, and investment interest expense are not tax preference items.

8. (583,Q3,45) (c) The requirement is to determine the minimum estimated tax payments that must be made by Finbury Corporation to avoid the estimated tax underpayment penalty for 1990. Since Finbury is a large corporation (i.e., a corporation with TI of $1,000,000 or more in any of its three preceding tax years), its estimated tax payments must be at least equal to 90% of its 1990 tax liability.

C.2 Corporate Tax Rates

9. (1187,Q2,30) (c) The requirement is to determine the correct statement regarding the excess of a corporation's tentative minimum tax over its regular tax. Answer (c) is correct because a corporation is subject to the alternative minimum tax to the extent that its tentative minimum tax exceeds its regular tax liability. Answers (a) and (b) are incorrect because the excess is not carried back to a previous year, but instead is payable currently. Answer (d) is incorrect because the excess is not a subtraction from regular tax, but instead is an __addition__ to a corporation's regular tax.

10. (1185,Q3,55) (b) The requirement is to determine the amount of federal income tax on Mason Corporation's 1989 taxable income of $80,000. The amount of tax determined from the table is $13,750 plus 34% of the excess of the $80,000 of TI over $75,000. $13,750 + 34% ($80,000 - $75,000) = $15,450.

C.3. Gross Income

11. (1188,Q2,22) (a) The requirement is to determine the amount of capital gain recognized by Lee Corp. on the sale of its treasury stock. A corporation will never recognize gain or loss on the receipt of money or other property in exchange for its stock, including treasury stock.

12. (588,Q2,22) (d) The requirement is to determine the amount of gain to be recognized by Ral Corp. when it issues its stock in exchange for land. No gain or loss is ever recognized by a corporation on the receipt of money or other property in exchange for its own stock (including treasury stock).

13. (584,Q1,10) (c) The requirement is to determine the amount of dividend reportable by a corporate distributee on a property distribution. The amount of dividend to be reported by a corporate distributee is the FMV of the property less any liability assumed. Kile's dividend would be $12,000, reduced by the liability of $5,000 = $7,000.

C.4.b. Organization Expenditures

14. (1183,Q3,44) (d) The requirement is to determine the amount qualifying as amortizable organization expenses. Expenses incurred for printing and selling stock certificates are neither deductible, nor amortizable as organization expenses. These expenses of issuing stock are treated as a reduction of paid-in capital.

15. (581,Q3,55) (d) The requirement is to determine the maximum deduction for amortization of organization expense for 1989. A corporation's organizational expenditures can be amortized ratably over a period of not less than 60 months, beginning with the month in which a corporation begins business. Thus, the maximum deduction for 1989 is $900 x 6/60 = $90.

C.4.c. Charitable Contributions

16. (1188,Q2,26) (a) The requirement is to determine the contribution base for purposes of computing Gero Corp.'s charitable contributions deduction. A corporation's contribution base is its taxable income before the charitable contributions deduction, the dividends received deduction, and before deductions for NOL and capital loss carrybacks. Since Gero had operating income of $160,000 after deducting $10,000 of contributions, its contribution base would be $160,000 + $10,000 + $2,000 dividends = $172,000.

17. (588,Q2,24) (b) The requirement is to determine the proper treatment of a corporation's charitable contributions that exceed the amount deductible for a particular year. Charitable contributions in excess of the 10% limitation are carried forward to a maximum of five succeeding years. The contributions actually made during a later year plus any carryforwards are also subject to a 10% limitation. Contributions actually made during a later year are deducted before carryforwards.

18. (1185,Q3,47) (a) The requirement is to determine the maximum allowable deduction for charitable contributions in Thor Corporation's

1989 return. A corporation's charitable contribution deduction is limited to 10% of taxable income before the charitable contribution
deduction. Thus, the maximum deduction is
computed as follows:

Operating income	$300,000
+ Charitable contributions	50,000
TI before CC deduction	$350,000
	x 10%
Maximum CC deduction	$ 35,000

19. (581,Q3,48) (c) The requirement is to determine the maximum charitable contribution
deduction for 1989. An accrual-basis corporation can elect to deduct a charitable contribution paid within 2-1/2 months of the close
of its taxable year if its board of directors
authorizes the contribution during the taxable
year. Thus, the $100,000 charitable contri-
bution is deductible in 1989, but is limited
to 10% of taxable income before the charitable
contribution deduction. The maximum amount
deductible in 1989 is:

Book income	$500,000
+ Charitable contribution	100,000
TI before CC deduction	$600,000
	x 10%
Maximum CC deduction	$ 60,000

The remaining $40,000 can be carried over a
maximum of 5 years.

C.4.e. Dividend Received Deduction

20. (1188,Q2,21) (b) The requirement is to
determine the amount of dividends to be
included in Ryan Corp.'s taxable income.
Since the dividends were received from less
than 20% owned taxable domestic corporations,
they are eligible for a 70% dividends received
deduction. Thus, the amount of dividends to
be included in taxable income is $2,000 - (70%
x $2,000) = $600.

21. (1186,Q3,44) (b) The requirement is to
determine the amount of dividends to be included in Daly Corp.'s taxable income for
1989. Since the dividends were received from
20%-owned taxable domestic corporations, they
are eligible for an 80% dividends received deduction. Thus, the amount of dividends to be
included in taxable income is $1,000 - (80% x
$1,000) = $200.

22. (1185,Q3,44) (b) The requirement is to
determine the amount of dividends that qualifies for the 80% dividends-received deduction.
Only dividends received from taxable domestic
unaffiliated corporations that are at least
20%-owned qualify for the 80% dividends-
received deduction ($7,500). So-called

"dividends" paid by mutual savings banks are
reported as interest, and are not eligible for
the dividends-received deduction.

23. (1182,Q3,50) (b) The requirement is to
determine Atkinson's DRD for dividends received from unaffiliated domestic corporations
that are at least 20%-owned. The DRD
(normally 80% of dividends) may be limited to
80% of TI before the DRD.

Gross business income	$160,000
Dividend income	100,000
	$260,000
Less business deductions	(170,000)
TI before DRD	$ 90,000
DRD ($90,000 x 80%)	(72,000)
TI	$ 18,000

Since the full deduction (80% x $100,000 =
$80,000) would not create a NOL, the limi-
tation applies.

C.4.j. Losses

24. (1189,Q3,47) (d) The requirement is to
determine the deductibility of a corporation's
net capital loss in the year that it is
sustained. A corporation is not allowed to
deduct a net capital loss in computing its
taxable income. Instead, a net capital loss
is generally carried back 3 years and forward
5 years as a short-term capital loss to offset
capital gains in the carryback and carryforward years.

25. (1183,Q3,47) (d) The requirement is to
determine Haya Corporation's net operating
loss (NOL) for 1989. A deduction for a net
operating loss carryover is not allowed in
computing a NOL. Furthermore, a deduction for
charitable contributions is generally not
allowed, since the charitable contributions
deduction is limited to 10% of taxable income
before the charitable contributions and dividends-received deductions. Thus, Haya's NOL
for 1989 would be computed as follows:

Gross income	$ 600,000
Less expenses	(800,000)
	$(200,000)
Add back contributions	
included in expenses	5,000
NOL for 1989	$(195,000)

26. (1182,Q3,48) (c) The requirement is to
determine the NOL for 1989 given that deductions in the tax return exceed gross income by
$56,800. In computing the NOL for 1989, the
DRD of $6,800 would be fully allowed, but the
$15,000 NOL deduction (carryover from 1988)
would not be allowed. $56,800 - $15,000 =
$41,800.

27. (587,Q3,49) (d) The requirement is to determine the amount of casualty loss deduction available to Ram Corp. due to the complete destruction of its machine. If business property is completely destroyed, the amount of casualty loss deduction is the property's adjusted basis immediately before the casualty. Note that the "$100 floor" and "10% of adjusted gross income" limitations that apply to personal casualty losses, do not apply to business casualty losses.

C.4.1. R & D Expenditures

28. (587,Q3,50) (a) The requirement is to determine the proper treatment for qualifying research and experimentation expenditures. A taxpayer can elect to deduct qualifying research and experimentation expenditures as a current expense if the taxpayer so elects for the first taxable year in which the expenditures are incurred. Otherwise, the taxpayer must capitalize the expenditures. Then, if the capitalized costs are not subject to depreciation (because there is no determinable life), the taxpayer can amortize them over a period of 60 months or longer.

C.6. Reconcile Book and Taxable Income

29. (588,Q2,27) (d) The requirement is to determine Dodd Corp.'s taxable income given net income per books of $100,000. The $27,000 provision for federal income tax deducted per books is not deductible in computing taxable income. The $5,000 net capital loss deducted per books is not deductible in computing taxable income because a corporation can only use capital losses to offset capital gains. The life insurance premiums of $3,000 deducted per books are not deductible in computing taxable income because life insurance proceeds are excluded from gross income. Thus, Dodd Corp.'s taxable income is $100,000 + $27,000 + $5,000 + $3,000 = $135,000.

30. (1187,Q2,28) (c) The requirement is to determine Bard Corp.'s taxable income given book income of $450,000. No adjustment is necessary for the $4,000 of state corporate income tax refunds since they were included in book income and would also be included in taxable income due to the "tax benefit rule" (i.e., an item of deduction that reduces a taxpayer's income tax must be included in gross income if later recovered). The life insurance proceeds of $15,000 must be subtracted from book income because they were included in book income, but would be excluded from taxable income. The net capital loss of $20,000 which was subtracted in computing book income must be added back to book income

because a net capital loss is not deductible in computing taxable income. Thus, Bard Corp.'s taxable income would be $450,000 − $15,000 + $20,000 = $455,000.

31. (1186,Q3,49) (c) The requirement is to determine taxable income given book income before federal income taxes. The provision for state income taxes deducted per books is an allowable deduction in computing taxable income. The interest income on U.S. obligations that was included per books, is taxable for federal income tax purposes. The interest expense incurred to carry U.S. obligations was deducted per books and is also deductible in computing taxable income, because the interest income from the obligations is taxable. Interest incurred to carry investments is nondeductible when the interest income from the investments is tax-exempt (e.g., interest on state and municipal bonds). Since there were no differences between book and tax treatment, taxable income is the same as book income before federal income taxes, $300,000.

32. (584,Q1,1) (b) The requirement is to determine Dale Corporation's taxable income, given book income of $520,000. Organization expenditures may be amortized over a minimum period of 60 months. Adding back the book amortization of organization costs of $26,000 ($260,000 ÷ 10 years), and then deducting the maximum amount of $52,000 ($260,000 × 12/60) results in taxable income of $494,000 ($520,000 + $26,000 − $52,000) for the Dale Corporation.

33. (1182,Q3,53) (c) The requirement is to determine net income per books given TI of $700,000.

Taxable income	$700,000
Provision for federal income tax	−280,000
Depreciation on tax return	+130,000
Depreciation per books	− 75,000
Life insurance proceeds	+100,000
Net income per books	**$575,000**

The provision for federal income is not deductible in computing TI but must be deducted per books. The life insurance proceeds are tax exempt, but must be included per books.

34. (581,Q3,42) (a) The requirement is to compute Apollo's taxable income for 1989. None of the income/expense items listed are includable in the computation of taxable income. Taxable income is computed as follows:

Book income	$1,200,000
- Municipal bond interest	(40,000)
- Proceeds of life insurance	(200,000)
+ Nondeductible interest expense (to produce tax-exempt interest income)	8,000
+ Provision for federal income tax	524,000
Taxable income	$1,492,000

C.6.c.   Schedule M-1

35. (1185,Q3,49) (c) The reconciliation of income per books with income per return is accomplished on Schedule M-1 of Form 1120. Both temporary differences (e.g., accelerated depreciation on tax return and straight-line on books) and permanent differences (e.g., tax-exempt interest) must be considered to convert book income to taxable income.

C.6.d. Schedule M-2

36. (583,Q3,49) (d) The requirement is to determine the amount to be shown on Schedule M-2 of Form 1120 as Barbaro's retained earnings at December 31, 1989. Beginning with the balance at January 1, 1989, the end of year balance would be computed as follows:

Balance, 1/1/89	$600,000
Net income for year	+ 274,900
Federal income tax refund	+ 26,000
Cash dividends	- 150,000
Balance, 12/31/89	$750,900

37. (582,Q3,50) (a) The requirement is to determine the amount that should appear on the last line of Schedule M-2 of Form 1120. Schedule M-2 is an "Analysis of Unappropriated Retained Earnings Per Books." Its first line is the balance at the beginning of the year and its last line is the balance at the end of the year. The end-of-year balance would be computed as follows:

Retained earnings, beginning	$ 50,000
Net income for year	+70,000
Contingency reserve	-10,000
Cash dividends	- 8,000
Retained earnings, end of year	$102,000

D. Affiliated and Controlled Corporations

38. (1189,Q3,48) (d) The requirement is to determine the correct statement regarding a consolidated tax return. One of the advantages of filing a consolidated tax return is that operating losses of one group member may be used to offset operating profits of the other members included in the consolidated return. Answer (a) is incorrect because the common parent corporation must directly own at least 80% of the combined voting power and

value of all stock (except nonvoting preferred stock) in at least one other includible corporation. Answer (b) is incorrect because intercompany dividends are completely eliminated by worksheet entries and are not included in the computation of consolidated taxable income. Answer (c) is incorrect because an affiliated group's election to file a consolidated tax return is independent of its issuing financial statements on a consolidated basis.

39. (1188,Q2,28) (d) The requirement is to determine the stock ownership requirement that must be satisfied to enable Dana Corp. to elect to file a consolidated tax return that includes Seco Corp. For Dana and Seco to qualify for filing a consolidated tax return, Dana must directly own stock possessing at least 80% of the total voting power, and at least 80% of the total value of Seco stock.

40. (588,Q2,28) (c) The requirement is to determine the correct statement regarding the filing of consolidated returns. The election to file consolidated returns is limited to affiliated corporations. Affiliated corporations are parent-subsidiary corporations that are connected through stock ownership wherein at least 80% of the combined voting power and value of all stock (except the common parent's) is directly owned by other includable corporations. Answer (a) is incorrect because brother-sister corporations are not affiliated corporations. Answer (b) is incorrect because no advance permission is required. Answer (d) is incorrect because an affiliated group's election to file consolidated returns is independent of its issuing financial statements on a consolidated basis.

41. (1187,Q2,29) (d) The requirement is to determine the taxability of an intercompany dividend between affiliated corporations filing a consolidated return. A dividend distribution between members of an affiliated group during a consolidated return year is eliminated in determining the consolidated taxable income of the affiliated group, and therefore is not taxable.

Note that if a consolidated return is not filed, members of an affiliated group (80% or more ownership) may elect a 100% dividends received deduction for dividends received from other members of the affiliated group.

42. (1184,Q3,56) (b) The requirement is to determine the amount of Sec. 1231 gain for 1989 that Subsidiary should take into account as a result of the 1988 sale of land to Parent. Since Parent and Subsidiary are filing consolidated tax returns, the $20,000

of gain to Subsidiary in <u>1988</u> is not recognized, but instead is deferred and recognized
when the land is sold outside the affiliated
group in <u>1989</u>.

E. Dividends and Distributions

43. (1188,Q2,31) (c) The requirement is to
determine the amount of distributions taxable
as dividend income to Ral Corp.'s shareholders. A dividend is a corporate distribution to shareholders from the earnings and
profits of the corporation's current taxable
year (CEP), or from the earnings and profits
of the corporation accumulated at the
beginning of the current taxable year (AEP).
Here, Ral Corp. had $40,000 of CEP and $30,000
of AEP. Thus, of the $90,000 distributed
during the year, a total of $70,000 will be
taxable as dividend income to Ral's
shareholders.

44. (587,Q3,57) (b) The requirement is to
determine the amount of gain that Mem Corp.
must recognize on the nonliquidating distribution of appreciated property. If a corporation makes a nonliquidating distribution of
appreciated property to a shareholder, the
corporation must recognize gain just as if the
property were sold at its fair market value.
Here, Mem must recognize a gain of $15,000 -
$10,000 = $5,000. Note that it makes no
difference whether the property was used in
the active conduct of its business.

45. (584,Q1,9) (b) The requirement is to
determine the amount of the taxable dividend
for an individual shareholder on a property
distribution. A noncorporate distributee is
considered to have received a dividend equal
to the fair market value of the property distributed less any liabilities assumed. In
this case, Rowe received a taxable dividend of
$7,000 ($12,000 - $5,000).

46. (581,Q3,57) (d) The requirement is to
determine the amount of dividend income taxable to the shareholder. If a corporation
sells property to a shareholder for less than
fair market value, the shareholder is considered to have received a constructive
dividend to the extent of the difference
between the fair market value of the property
and the price paid. Thus, the shareholder's
dividend income is $80,000 - $50,000 =
$30,000.

47. (1177,Q2,31) (a) Distributions of property to shareholders reduce earnings and profits (E & P) by the greater of the property's
adjusted basis, or its FMV at date of distri-

bution. E & P must be adjusted by any gain
recognized to the distributing corporation,
and any liabilities to which the property
being distributed is subject. Gelt Corporation would recognize a gain of $7,500 on the
distribution (i.e., $14,000 FMV - $6,500
basis). The adjustments to E & P (before tax)
would be:

		E & P
Gain recognized		$ 7,500
Distribution of property		
(FMV)		(14,000)
Distribution of liability		5,000
Net decrease in E & P (before tax)		$ (1,500)

E.4. Stock Redemptions

48. (1189,Q3,52) (a) The requirement is to
determine how the gain resulting from a stock
redemption should be treated by a noncorporate
shareholder if the redemption qualifies as a
partial liquidation of the distributing corporation. A corporate stock redemption is
treated as an exchange, generally resulting in
capital gain or loss treatment to a shareholder if the redemption meets any one of five
tests. Redemptions qualifying for exchange
treatment include (1) a redemption that is not
essentially equivalent to a dividend, (2) a
redemption that is substantially disproportionate, (3) a redemption that completely
terminates a shareholder's interest, (4) a
redemption of a noncorporate shareholder in a
partial liquidation, and (5) a redemption to
pay death taxes. If none of the above five
tests are met, the redemption proceeds are
generally treated as a dividend.

49. (1188,Q2,24) (b) The requirement is to
determine the amount of interest and legal and
accounting fees that were incurred in connection with Kara Corp.'s stock repurchase that
is deductible for 1990. No deduction is
allowed for any amount paid or incurred by a
corporation in connection with the redemption
of its stock, except for interest expense on
loans to repurchase stock. Thus, the $100,000
of interest expense on loans used to repurchase stock is deductible, while the $400,000
of legal and accounting fees incurred in
connection with the repurchase of stock is not
deductible.

E.5. Complete Liquidations

50. (587,Q3,59) (a) The requirement is to
determine the amount of long-term capital gain
to be reported on the distribution of marketable securities in complete liquidation of Aca
Corp. Generally, a corporation will recognize
gain or loss on the distribution of its property in liquidation just as if the property

were sold to the distributee at its fair
market value. Since the marketable securities
were held more than twelve months, their distribution results in a long-term capital gain
of $120,000 - $100,000 = $20,000.

51. (1185,Q3,54) (d) When a parent corporation liquidates its 80% or more owned subsidiary, the parent corporation (as stockholder)
will ordinarily not recognize any gain or loss
on the receipt of liquidating distributions
from its subsidiary.

52. (585,Q3,42) (a) The requirement is to
determine the recognized gain to Lark Corp. on
the complete liquidation of its wholly-owned
subsidiary, Day Corp. No gain or loss will be
recognized by a parent corporation (Lark
Corp.) on the receipt of property in complete
liquidation of an 80% or more owned subsidiary
(Day Corp.).

53. (1184,Q3,57) (c) The requirement is to
determine the amount of gain to be recognized
by Green Corp. as a result of the distribution
of installment notes in the process of liquidation. A corporation generally recognizes
gain on the distribution of appreciated
property in the process of liquidation. Thus,
Green Corp. must recognize gain on the
distribution of the notes to the extent that
the FMV of the notes ($162,000) exceeds the
basis of the notes ($90,000), or $72,000.

54. (583,Q3,48) (d) The requirement is to
determine Carmela's recognized gain from the
sale of assets during a complete liquidation.
Gain or loss is generally recognized by a
corporation on the sale of **property** following
the adoption of a plan of complete liquidation
even if the corporation then distributes all
of its assets within 12 months after the plan
of liquidation is adopted. Carmela would
recognize gain on the land of $75,000
($150,000 - $75,000) and on the inventory of
$22,500 ($66,000 - $43,500).

F. Collapsible Corporations

55. (1188,Q2,33) (d) The requirement is to
determine the necessary holding period for a
corporation's stock in order for the collapsible corporation provisions to be imposed.
The 1986 TRA amended the collapsible corporation provisions of Sec. 341 by deleting the
requirement that stock be "held for more than
six months." Thus, for sales, exchanges, and
distributions after 9/27/85, the holding
period of a corporation's stock is irrelevant. If a corporation is collapsible,
Sec. 341 may apply and require a shareholder

to report ordinary income instead of capital
gain regardless of how long the shareholder
has held the corporation's stock.

56. (1172,P1,6) (a) A shareholder owning
more than 5% of the stock of a corporation
which has been determined to be collapsible is
generally denied capital gain treatment on a
sale of stock or on the liquidation of the
corporation. Instead, the shareholder must
report all gain as ordinary income.

Sale price	$40,000
Basis	-25,000
Ordinary income	$15,000

G. Personal Holding Company and Accumulated Earnings Tax

57. (1189,Q3,49) (a) The requirement is to
determine the status of Ati Corporation. A
corporation is a personal holding company
(PHC) if (1) 5 or fewer individuals own more
than 50% of its stock during the last half of
the taxable year, and (2) at least 60% of its
adjusted ordinary gross income is derived from
passive sources (e.g., dividends, interest,
rents, etc.). Although the amount of dividends paid to its shareholders may affect the
computation of the PHC tax, the amount of dividends paid has no effect on the determination
of PHC status. Answer (b) is incorrect because a regulated investment company is a
status obtained by registering under the Investment Company Act of 1940, and is not determined by the facts and circumstances present for any given year. Answer (c) is incorrect because the accumulated earnings tax does
not apply to a personal holding company. Answer (d) is incorrect because all of Ati's
taxable income is subject to federal income
tax.

58. (1188,Q2,29) (b) The requirement is to
determine the taxpayer to whom the personal
holding company (PHC) income will be attributed. A corporation will be classified as a
personal holding company if (1) it is more
than 50% owned by five or fewer individuals,
and (2) at least 60% of the corporation's
adjusted ordinary gross income is PHC income.
PHC income is generally passive income and
includes dividends, interest, adjusted rents,
adjusted royalties, compensation for the use
of corporate property by a 25% or more shareholder, and certain personal service contracts
involving a 25% or more shareholder. An
amount received from a personal service contract is classified PHC income if 1) some person other than the corporation has as the
right to designate, by name or by description,
the individual who is to perform the services,

and (2) the person so designated is (directly or constructively) a 25% or more shareholder. Here, since Benson owns 100% of Lund Corp. and Lund Corp. contracted with Magda specifying that Benson is to perform personal services for Madga, the income from the personal service contract will be personal holding company income to Lund Corp.

59. (1188,Q2,30) (d) The requirement is to determine the correct statement concerning the accumulated earnings tax (AET). The AET can be imposed on a corporation if it accumulates earnings in excess of reasonable business needs regardless of the number of shareholders that the corporation has. Answer (a) is incorrect because the AET cannot be imposed on partnerships. Answer (b) is incorrect because a corporation that distributes all of its accumulated earnings cannot be subject to the tax. Answer (c) is incorrect because the AET cannot be imposed on a corporation that is a personal holding company.

60. (588,Q2,31) (c) The requirement is to determine the correct statement regarding the personal holding company (PHC) tax. The PHC tax should be self-assessed by filing a separate schedule 1120-PH along with the regular tax return Form 1120. Answer (a) is incorrect because the PHC tax is a penalty tax imposed in addition to regular federal income taxes. Answer (b) is incorrect because the PHC tax can only be imposed on corporations. Answer (d) is incorrect because the PHC tax can only be imposed if five or fewer individuals own more than 50% of the value of a corporation's stock. Thus, if a corporation's stock is owned by ten or more equal unrelated shareholders, the corporation cannot be a PHC.

61. (588,Q2,32) (b) The requirement is to determine the correct statement regarding the accumulated earnings tax (AET). The AET does not apply to corporations that are personal holding companies. Answer (a) is incorrect because the AET can apply regardless of the number of shareholders that a corporation has. Answers (c) and (d) are incorrect because the AET applies to corporations that accumulate earnings is excess of their reasonable business needs and is not dependent upon whether a corporation files a consolidated return or the number of classes of stock that a corporation has.

62. (1187,Q2,34) (c) The requirement is to determine the correct statement concerning the personal holding company (PHC) tax. The personal holding company tax may be imposed if at least 60% of the corporation's adjusted

ordinary gross income for the taxable year is personal holding company income, and the stock ownership test is satisfied. Answer (b) is incorrect because the stock ownership test is met if more than 50% of the corporation's stock is owned, directly or indirectly, by five or fewer stockholders. Answer (a) is incorrect because the PHC tax is a penalty tax imposed in addition to the regular corporate income tax. Answer (d) is incorrect because the PHC tax takes precedent over the accumulated earnings tax. The accumulated earnings tax does not apply to a personal holding company.

63. (1187,Q2,35) (d) The requirement is to determine the correct statement concerning the accumulated earnings tax (AET). Answer (d), "The accumulated earnings tax can not be imposed on a corporation that has undistributed earnings and profits of less than $150,000" is correct because every corporation (even a personal service corporation) is eligible for an accumulated earnings credit of at least $150,000. Answer (a) is incorrect because the AET is not self-assessing, but instead is assessed by the IRS after finding a tax avoidance intent on the part of the taxpayer. Answer (b) is incorrect because the AET may be imposed regardless of the number of shareholders that a corporation has. Answer (c) is incorrect because the AET cannot be imposed on a corporation for any year in which an S corporation election is in effect because an S corporation's earnings pass through and are taxed to shareholders regardless of whether the earnings are actually distributed.

64. (587,Q3,41) (a) The requirement is to determine the applicability of the accumulated earnings tax (AET). The AET is a penalty tax assessed on corporations that accumulate earnings in excess of reasonable business needs. The AET is applicable to all corporations except personal holding companies, foreign personal holding companies, and tax-exempt corporations. The number of stockholders that a corporation has, the aggregate dollar amount of its assets, or whether a corporation is a subsidiary does not affect the imposition of the AET.

65. (587,Q3,44) (d) The requirement is to determine the amount on which Kee Holding Corp.'s liability for personal holding company (PHC) tax will be based. To be classified as a personal holding company, a corporation must meet both a "stock ownership test" and an "income test." The "stock ownership test" requires that more than 50% of the stock must

be owned (directly or indirectly) by five or fewer individuals. Since Kee has 80 unrelated equal shareholders, the stock ownership test is not met. Thus, Kee is not a personal holding company and has no liability for the PHC tax.

66. (585,Q3,43) (b) The accumulated earnings tax (AET) can be avoided by sufficient dividend distributions. The imposition of the AET does not depend on a stock ownership test, nor is it self-assessing requiring the filing of a separate schedule attached to the regular tax return. The AET cannot be imposed on personal holding companies.

67. (585,Q3,44) (c) The personal holding company (PHC) tax may be imposed if more than 50% of a corporation's stock is owned by five or fewer individuals. The PHC tax cannot be imposed on partnerships. Additionally, small business investment companies licensed by the Small Business Administration are excluded from the tax. If a corporation's gross income arises solely from rents, the rents will not be PHC income (even though no services are rendered to lessees) and thus, the PHC tax cannot be imposed.

68. (1184,Q3,53) (d) A net capital loss for the current year is allowed as a deduction in determining accumulated taxable income for purposes of the accumulated earnings tax. A capital loss carryover from a prior year, a dividends received deduction, and a net operating loss deduction would all be added back to taxable income in arriving at accumulated taxable income.

69. (583,Q3,42) (d) The minimum accumulated earnings credit is $250,000 for nonservice corporations; $150,000 for service corporations.

70. (582,Q3,44) (a) The requirement is to determine Daystar's allowable accumulated earnings credit for 1989. The credit is the greater of (1) the earnings and profits of the tax year retained for reasonable business needs of $20,000; or, (2) $150,000 less the accumulated earnings and profits at the end of the preceding year of $45,000. Thus, the credit is $150,000 - $45,000 = $105,000.

H. S Corporations

71. (1189,Q3,50) (d) The requirement is to determine the correct statement with regard to the application of the "at-risk" rules to S corporations and their shareholders. The at-risk rules limit a taxpayer's deduction of losses to the amount that the taxpayer can actually lose (i.e., generally the amount of cash and the adjusted basis of property invested by the taxpayer, plus any liabilities for which the taxpayer is personally liable). The at-risk rules apply to S corporation shareholders rather than at the corporate level, with the result that the deduction of S corporation losses is limited to the amount of a shareholder's at-risk investment. The application of the at-risk rules does not depend on the type of income reported by the S corporation, are not subject to any elections made by S corporation shareholders, and are applied without regard to the S corporation's ratio of debt to equity.

72. (1189,Q3,51) (d) The requirement is to determine the item that may be deducted by an S corporation. An S corporation is a passthru entity--the character of any item of income, expense, gain, loss, or credit is determined at the corporate level and is passed through to shareholders. Items having special characteristics or whose separate treatment could effect the tax liability of any shareholder must be passed through separately so that any special characteristics or treatment is maintained. On the other hand, items having no special characteristics can be netted together in the computation of the S corporation's nonseparately computed income or loss, with only the net amount of the S corporation's ordinary income or loss passed through to shareholders. Thus, only ordinary items (e.g., compensation of officers) can be deducted by an S corporation.

Answer (a) is incorrect because the 10% limitation on charitable contributions does not apply at the corporate level. Instead, all charitable contributions are separately passed through so that the percentage limitations can be applied at the shareholder level. Answer (b) is incorrect because an S corporation never has a net operating loss carryover. If an S corporation's netting of ordinary income and deductions results in a loss, it is currently passed through to shareholders in the year sustained. Answer (c) is incorrect because foreign taxes must be separately passed through to shareholders so that they can individually elect to treat the payment of foreign taxes as a deduction or as a credit.

73. (1188,Q2,25) (d) The requirement is to determine the correct statement regarding an S corporation's Accumulated Adjustments Account (AAA). An S corporation that has accumulated earnings and profits must maintain an AAA. The AAA represents the cumulative balance of all items of the undistributed net income and

deductions for S corporation years beginning after 1982. The AAA is generally increased by all income items and is decreased by distributions and all loss and deduction items except no adjustment is made for tax-exempt income and related expenses, and no adjustment is made for Federal income taxes attributable to a taxable year in which the corporation was a C corporation. The payment of Federal income taxes attributable to a C corporation year would decrease an S corporation's accumulated earnings and profits (AEP). Note that the amounts represented in the AAA differ from AEP. A positive AEP balance generally represents earnings and profits accumulated in C corporation years that have never been taxed to shareholders. A positive AAA balance represents income from S corporation years that has already been taxed to shareholders but not yet distributed. An S corporation will not generate any AEP for taxable years beginning after 1982.

74. (588,Q2,30) (c) The requirement is to determine the correct statement regarding eligibility for S corporation status. Although an S corporation is generally limited to one class of stock issued and outstanding, an S corporation will not be treated as having more than one class of stock solely because of differences in voting rights among the common shares. Thus, having both voting and non-voting common stock outstanding meets the "one class of stock" requirement. Answers (a) and (b) are incorrect because a decedent's estate (including a bankruptcy estate) is eligible to be an S corporation shareholder. Answer (d) is incorrect because an S corporation may have as many as 35 shareholders.

75. (1187,Q2,27) (c) The requirement is to determine the earliest date on which Tau Corp. will be recognized as an S corporation. A subchapter S election that is filed on or before the 15th day of the third month of a corporation's taxable year is generally effective as of the beginning of the taxable year in which filed. If the S election is filed after the 15th day of the third month, the election is generally effective as of the first day of the corporation's next taxable year. Tau Corp. uses a fiscal year which begins November 1 and ends October 31 of each year. Here, its S election was filed on May 15, 1990, which is beyond the 15th day of the third month of its taxable year (January 15th). Therefore, Tau Corp's subchapter S election will become effective as of the first day of its next taxable year, November 1, 1990.

76. (587,Q3,43) (b) The requirement is to determine the amount from Bow, Inc. (an S corporation) to be included in each shareholder's gross income. A shareholder of an S corporation must include in gross income the shareholder's pro rata daily share of the S corporation's income, regardless of whether the income is distributed. Thus, each shareholder must include $100,000 in gross income ($300,000/3). This income would be reported for the shareholder's taxable year in which the taxable year of the S corporation ends. Note that the cash distribution of $120,000 (i.e., $40,000 per shareholder) is nontaxable because it represents a partial distribution of the $100,000 that is already being included in each shareholder's income.

77. (1185,Q3,42) (b) The requirement is to determine the due date of a calendar-year S corporation's tax return. An S corporation must file its federal income tax return (Form 1120-S) by the 15th day of the third month following the close of its taxable year. Thus, a calendar-year S corporation must file its tax return by March 15, if an automatic six-month extension of time is not requested.

78. (1185,Q3,43) (c) The requirement is to determine the item for which an S corporation is not permitted a deduction. Compensation of officers, interest paid to nonshareholders, and employee benefits for nonshareholders are deductible by an S corporation in computing its ordinary income or loss. However, charitable contributions, since they are subject to percentage limitations at the shareholder level, must be separately stated and are not deductible in computing an S corporation's ordinary income or loss.

79. (1184,Q3,41) (d) An S corporation may have as many as 35 shareholders. However, an S corporation cannot have both common and preferred stock outstanding because an S corporation is limited to a single class of stock. Similarly, a corporation is not permitted to be a shareholder in an S corporation because all S corporation shareholders must be individuals, estates, or certain trusts. Additionally, an S corporation cannot generally be a member of an affiliated group of corporations.

80. (584,Q1,16) (d) Since this S corporation was organized in 1989, there is no limit on the amount of passive investment income that can be earned and still qualify as an S corporation. If a corporation was in existence prior to 1983 and has Subchapter C earn-

ings and profits, an S corporation election will be terminated if passive investment income exceeds 25% of gross receipts for three consecutive taxable years. Subchapter C earnings and profits are earnings and profits accumulated during a taxable year for which a Subchapter S election was not in effect.

81. (1183,Q3,46) (a) The requirement is to determine which is **not** a requirement for a corporation to elect S corporation status. An S corporation must generally have only one class of stock, be a domestic corporation, and confine shareholders to individuals, estates, and certain trusts. An S corporation need **not** be a member of a controlled group.

82. (582,Q3,52) (b) The requirement is to determine the amount of loss from an S corporation that can be deducted by each of two equal shareholders. An S corporation loss is passed through to shareholders and is deductible to the extent of a shareholder's basis for stock plus the basis for any debt owed the shareholder by the corporation. Here, each shareholder's allocated loss of $45,000 ($90,000 ÷ 2) is deductible to the extent of stock basis of $5,000 plus debt basis of $15,000, or $20,000. The remainder of the loss ($25,000 for each shareholder) can be carried forward indefinitely by each shareholder and deducted when there is basis to absorb it.

I. Corporate Reorganizations

83. (1188,Q2,32) (a) The requirement is to determine the item that is defined in the Internal Revenue Code as a corporate reorganization. Corporate reorganizations generally receive nonrecognition treatment. Sec. 368 of the Internal Revenue Code defines seven types of reorganization, one of which is listed. An "F" reorganization is one corporation, however effected;..."A stock redemption is not a reorganization but instead results in dividend treatment or qualifies for exchange treatment." A change of depreciation method or inventory method is a change of an accounting method.

84. (1187,Q2,36) (a) The requirement is to determine the amount of Lois Pell's recognized gain resulting from her exchange of Ral Corp. stock for Lars Corp. stock pursuant to a plan of corporate reorganization. No gain or loss is recognized to a shareholder if stock in one party to a reorganization (Ral Corp.) is exchanged **solely** for stock in another corporation (Lars Corp.) that is a party to the reorganization.

85. (587,Q3,58) (c) The requirement is to determine the correct statement concerning corporate reorganizations. Answer (b) is incorrect because the reorganization provisions do provide for tax-free treatment for certain corporate transactions. Specifically, shareholders will not recognize gain or loss when they exchange stock or securities in a corporation that is a party to a reorganization solely for stock or securities in such corporation, or in another corporation that is also a party to the reorganization. Thus, securities in corporations not parties to the reorganization are always treated as "boot." Answer (d) is incorrect because the term "a party to the reorganization" includes a corporation resulting from the reorganization (i.e., the consolidated company). Answer (a) is incorrect because a mere change in identity, form, or place of organization of one corporation qualifies as a type-F reorganization.

86. (1186,Q3,45) (a) The requirement is to determine which is not a corporate reorganization. A corporate reorganization is specifically defined in Sec. 368 of the Internal Revenue Code. Sec. 368 defines seven types of reorganization, of which three are present in this item: Type A, a statutory merger; Type E, a recapitalization; and, Type F, a mere change in identity, form, or place of organization. Answer (a), a stock redemption, is the correct answer because it is not a reorganization as defined by Sec. 368 of the Code.

87. (583,Q3,52) (a) The requirement is to determine the amount of Claudio's net operating loss (NOL) carryover that can be used to offset Stellar's 1989 taxable income. The amount of Claudio's NOL ($270,000) that can be utilized by Stellar for 1989 is limited by Sec. 381 to the taxable income of Stellar for its full taxable year (before a NOL deduction) multiplied by the fraction:

$$\frac{\text{Days after acquisition date}}{\text{Total days in the taxable year}}$$

This limitation is 184/365 days x $360,000 = $181,479. Additionally, since there was a more than 50% change of ownership in Claudio, Sec. 382 limits the amount of Claudio's NOL carryover that can be utilized by Stellar to the fair market value of Claudio multiplied by the federal long-term tax-exempt rate.

$$\$1,500,000 \times 8\% = \$120,000$$

However, for purposes of applying this limitation for the year of acquisition, the limitation amount is only available to the extent allocable to the days in Stellar's taxable year after the acquisition date.

$$\$120,000 \times 184/365 \text{ days} = \$60,493$$

Note: The remainder of Claudio's NOL ($270,000 − $60,493 = $209,507) can be carried forward and used to offset Stellar's taxable income (subject to the Sec. 382 limitation) in carryforward years.

88. (582,Q3,53) (a) The requirement is to determine the recognized gain to be reported by Mueller on the exchange of her Disco bond for Disco preferred stock. The issuance by Disco Corporation of its preferred stock in exchange for its bonds is a nontaxable "Type E" reorganization (i.e., a recapitalization). Since Mueller did not receive any boot, no part of her $400 realized gain is recognized.

89. (1181,P3,41) (b) The requirement is to determine the amount of recognized gain in a recapitalization. Since a recapitalization is a reorganization, a realized gain is recognized only to the extent that consideration other than stock or securities is received, including the FMV of an excess of the principal amount of securities received over the principal amount of securities surrendered. Since no securities were surrendered, the excess principal amount of securities received is $10,000, and Moore's realized gain of $23,500 is recognized to the extent of the $10,500 FMV of the excess principal amount of securities received.

J.1.   Tax Exempt Organizations

90. (1189,Q3,58) (c) The requirement is to determine which organization qualifies as an organization exempt from income tax. Organizations that can qualify as exempt organizations are listed in Sec. 501 of the Internal Revenue Code. Answer (a) is incorrect because an "action" organization established for the purpose of influencing legislation will not qualify for exemption. Answer (b) is incorrect because no exemption is provided for "feeder" organizations. An organization must have an exempt purpose, not merely remit its profits to exempt organizations. Answer (d) is incorrect because an organization will not qualify for exempt status if it solely provides athletic facilities and equipment. To qualify, the organization must be organized and operated primarily to conduct national or international competition in sports or to support and develop amateur athletes for national or international competition in sports.

91. (1189,Q3,59) (b) Organizations that can qualify as exempt organizations are listed in Sec. 501 of the Internal Revenue Code, and can take the form of a trust or corporation. To receive exempt status, the organization must

file a written application with the IRS. In no event will exempt status be conferred upon an organization unless the organization is one of those types of organizations specifically listed in the Code. An organization operating under the "lodge system" means an organization carrying on its activities under a form of organization that comprises local branches chartered by a parent organization, if it is established to pay for its members' sick or accident benefits.

92. (1188,Q2,38) (a) The requirement is to determine the proper tax treatment of Carita Fund's insurance activities. An otherwise qualifying exempt organization will instead be subject to tax if a substantial part of its activities consists of providing commercial-type insurance. Sec. 501(m)(3) provides that "commercial-type insurance" does not include insurance provided at substantially below cost to a class of charitable recipients. Since Carita Fund was organized and operated exclusively for charitable purposes, and provided below cost insurance coverage to exempt organizations involved in the prevention of cruelty to children, its insurance activities are exempt from tax. The insurance activities do not constitute unrelated business income because the insurance activities were substantially related to the performance of the fund's exempt purpose. Answer (c) is incorrect because Carita Fund qualifies as an exempt organization.

93. (1188,Q2,39) (c) Private foundations must file annual information returns specifically stating items of gross income, receipts and disbursements, and such other information as may be required. In contrast, churches, religious groups, and exempt organizations other than private foundations are only required to file an information return if their gross receipts are normally more than $25,000.

94. (1188,Q2,40) (a) The filing of a return covering unrelated business income (Form 990-T) is required of all exempt organizations having at least $1,000 of unrelated business taxable income for the year. However, this does not realize the organization of having to file a separate information return (Form 990) if it is otherwise required to file. Answer (c) is incorrect because in determining whether income is unrelated business income, the exempt organization's need for the income or the use it makes of the profits is irrelevant. Answer (d) is incorrect because the tax on unrelated business income of exempt organizations must be paid in full with the return.

95. (588,Q2,38) (a) The requirement is to determine the correct statement regarding an exempt organization's payment of estimated taxes on its unrelated business income. An exempt organization subject to tax on its unrelated business income must comply with the Code provisions regarding installment payments of estimated income tax by corporations. This means that an exempt organization must make quarterly estimated tax payments if it expects its estimated tax on its unrelated business income to be $40 or more. Answers (b) and (c) are incorrect because any tax on unrelated business income must be paid in full by the due date of the exempt organization's return. Answer (d) is incorrect because estimated tax payments are required if the $40 threshold is expected to be met.

96. (588,Q2,39) (d) A condominium management association wishing to be treated as a homeowners association and thereby qualify as an exempt organization for a particular year must file a separate election for each taxable year no later than the due date of the tax return for which the election is to apply.

97. (588,Q2,40) (d) An organization wishing to qualify as an exempt organization must be of a type specifically identified as one of the classes on which exemption is conferred by the Code. In no event will exempt status be conferred upon an organization unless the organization is one of those listed. Furthermore, in order to receive exempt status, the organization must file an application with the Internal Revenue Service. Answer (a) is incorrect since an exempt organization may be organized as a corporation. Answer (b) is incorrect because an exempt organization may lose its exempt status by engaging in any prohibited transaction. Answer (c) is incorrect because non-U.S. citizens may be on an exempt organization's governing board.

98. (1187,Q2,32) (b) The requirement is to determine the correct statement regarding exempt organizations. With the exception chiefly of churches, an exempt organization (other than a private foundation) must nevertheless file an annual information return specifically stating items of gross income, receipts, and disbursements unless its gross receipts are normally not more than $25,000. An exempt organization required to file a return must annually report the total amount of contributions received as well as the identity of substantial contributors.
    Answer (a) is incorrect because an organization can only achieve exempt status by filing an application for exemption with the

Internal Revenue Service. Answer (c) is incorrect because there is no limitation on the amount of compensation that can be paid to an employee if the compensation is reasonable. Answer (d) is incorrect because exempt status can be retroactively revoked if an organization's character, purposes, or methods of operation are other than as stated in the application for exemption.

99. (1187,Q2,33) (a) The requirement is to determine the correct statement regarding qualification as an exempt organization. To qualify as an exempt organization, the applicant for exemption must fall into one of the specified classes of organizations that are listed in Sec. 501 as being exempt from tax. Answer (d) is incorrect because a social club can be an exempt organization as long as substantially all its activities are for such purposes and no part of its net earnings inures to the benefit of any private shareholder. Answer (c) is incorrect because most exempt organizations are permitted specified levels of lobbying expenditures, and can even elect to be subject to a tax equal to 25% of their excess lobbying expenditures to prevent loss of exempt status. Answer (b) is incorrect because foreign corporations can qualify as exempt organizations.

100. (587,Q3,60) (c) The requirement is to determine what will terminate an exempt organization's status as a private foundation. The private foundation status of an exempt organization will terminate if it becomes a public charity. Answer (a) is incorrect because private foundations are not required to distribute their assets to public charities. Answer (b) is incorrect because an exempt operating foundation is still classified as a private foundation. Answer (d) is incorrect because the activities of private foundations are already severely restricted by the Internal Revenue Code.

101. (1186,Q3,56) (c) Organizations that can qualify as exempt organizations are listed in Sec. 501 of the Internal Revenue Code. An exempt organization can take the form of a trust or a corporation. In order to receive exempt status, the organization must file an application with the Internal Revenue Service. In no event will exempt status be conferred upon an organization unless the organization is one of those listed in the Code. Answer (b) is incorrect because there is no limitation on the amount of salary that can be paid an employee.

J.2.   Determination of UBI

102.(1189,Q3,60) (c) The requirement is to determine the correct statement with regard to the unrelated business income (UBI) of an exempt organization. An exempt organization is not taxed on its UBI if its UBI is less than $1,000. Answer (a) is incorrect because an unrelated trade or business activity that results in a loss is still considered an unrelated business. Answer (b) is incorrect because the tax will not apply to a business activity that is not regularly carried on. Answer (d) is incorrect because unrelated business income will not cause a loss of exempt status if the organization is otherwise qualified.

103.(1187,Q2,31) (d) The requirement is to determine the correct statement regarding the taxability of unrelated business income (UBI) to an exempt organization that is a charitable trust. Answer (c) is incorrect because an exempt organization that is a charitable trust is subject to tax on its UBI only to the extent that its UBI exceeds $1,000. Answers (a) and (b) are incorrect because an exempt organization with UBI in excess of $1,000 is subject to tax at rates applicable to trusts if it is organized as a charitable trust.

104. (587,Q3,56) (a) The requirement is to determine how the tax on unrelated business income (UBI) is computed for a corporation that is an exempt organization. If an exempt organization is a corporation, the tax on UBI is computed at corporate income tax rates. Similarly, if an exempt organization is a trust, its tax on UBI is computed using the income tax rates pertaining to trusts. Answer (c) is incorrect because an exempt organization's capital gains are generally not subject to tax and are not included in figuring UBI. Answer (d) is incorrect because an exempt organization's tax on UBI is not abated.

105.(1186,Q3,57) (c) Unrelated business income (UBI) is gross income derived from any trade or business the conduct of which is not substantially related to the exercise or performance of an organization's exempt purpose. Although dividends and interest are generally excluded from UBI, they will be included if they result from debt-financed investments. Answer (d) is incorrect because it states that dividends and interest are always **excluded** from UBI. Answer (a) is incorrect because the Code only imposes a tax on UBI, it does not revoke an organization's exempt status. An-

swer (b) is incorrect because a net operating loss is allowed in computing unrelated business taxable income. Answer (c) is correct because this exact situation is now found in a footnote to Code Sec. 513(a).

May 1990 Answers

106. (590,Q2,27) (d) The requirement is to determine which will render a corporation ineligible for S corporation status. Answer (d) is correct because an S corporation is limited to 35 shareholders. Answers (a) and (b) are incorrect because a decedent's estate and a bankruptcy estate are allowed as S corporation shareholders. Although an S corporation may only have one class of stock issued and outstanding, answer (c) is incorrect because a difference in voting rights among outstanding common shares is not treated as having more than one class of stock outstanding.

107. (590,Q2,28) (b) The requirement is to determine the amount of Krol Corp.'s gain resulting from the distribution of marketable securities in complete liquidation. Generally, a corporation will recognize gain or loss on the distribution of its property in complete liquidation just as if the property were sold to the distributee for its fair market value. Since the marketable securities were a capital asset to Krol Corp., the distribution results in a capital gain of $150,000 - $100,000 = $50,000.

108. (590,Q2,29) (c) The requirement is to determine the amount of dividends to be included in Ral Corp.'s taxable income. Since the dividends were received from a less-than-20%-owned taxable domestic corporation, the dividends are eligible for a 70% dividends received deduction. Thus, the amount of dividends to be included in taxable income is $1,000 - (70% x $1,000) = $300.

109. (590,Q2,30) (a) The requirement is to determine the amount of capital loss that can be deducted by Ral Corporation. A corporation's capital losses can only be used to offset capital gains. If a corporation has a net capital loss, the net capital loss cannot be currently deducted, but instead must be carried back 3 years and forward 5 years as a STCL to offset capital gains in those years.

110. (590,Q2,31) (d) The requirement is to determine the amount of the $27,000 advance rent revenue to be included in taxable income for 1989. The advance rent payment was received on December 1, 1989 from a tenant for a three-year lease beginning January 1, 1990.

For federal income tax purposes, rents received in advance must be included in gross income in the year received under both the cash and accrual methods. Thus, even though Ral Corp. is an accrual method taxpayer, the $27,000 of advance rent must be included in taxable income for 1989.

111. (590,Q2,32) (c) The requirement is to determine the amount of keyman and group life insurance premiums that Ral Corp. can deduct in computing its taxable income. Generally, no deduction is allowed for expenditures which produce tax-exempt income. Here, no deduction is allowed for the $3,000 of keyman insurance premiums because Ral Corp. is the beneficiary of the policy and the proceeds of the policy will be excluded from Ral's income when Budd dies. On the other hand, Ral Corp. can deduct the $4,000 of group term insurance premiums on employees' lives because the employees' spouses are the beneficiaries of the policies.

112. (590,Q2,33) (a) The requirement is to determine the amount deductible in Ral's 1989 return for the purchase of the dealer's perpetual franchise. Generally, the transfer of a franchise is not treated as a sale or exchange of a capital asset because the transferor retains a significant power, right, or interest with respect to the franchise (e.g., a right to terminate, prescribe standards for service, require the transferee to purchase substantially all supplies and equipment from transferor, a right to payments contingent on productivity). Any contingent franchise payments are then treated as ordinary income to the transferor and result in an ordinary deduction for the transferee. The payment of a noncontingent lump-sum of up to $100,000 made by a transferee may be amortized over the shorter of the franchise period or 10 years; while a noncontingent lump-sum payment exceeding $100,000 may be amortized over 25 years.

On the other hand, a transfer of a franchise will be treated as the sale or exchange of a capital asset if the seller retains no significant powers, rights, or continuing interest with respect to the franchise. Then any noncontingent lump-sum payment results in capital gain to the transferor and must be capitalized by the transferee and cannot be deducted. In this case, since Ral's lump-sum payment resulted in the acquisition of a perpetual dealer's franchise, the transfer is treated as the sale of a capital asset and Ral's $48,000 lump-sum payment must be capitalized and cannot be deducted.

113. (590,Q2,34) (a) The requirement is to determine the correct statement regarding Ral Corp.'s contribution to a qualified charity. Although charitable contributions are generally deductible only when paid, an accrual-method corporation may elect to deduct a charitable contribution in the year in which it is authorized by its board of directors (subject to the 10% of taxable income limitation) if the contribution is paid within 2-1/2 months of the close of the taxable year. Here, since the contribution is to be paid on January 31, 1990, Ral Corp. can elect to deduct in its 1989 return any portion of the $75,000 that does not exceed the 10% deduction ceiling for 1989.

114. (590,Q2,35) (c) The requirement is to determine Maple Corp.'s taxable income given book income before federal income taxes of $100,000. The provision for state income taxes of $1,000 that was deducted per books is also an allowable deduction in computing taxable income. The interest earned on U.S. Treasury Bonds of $6,000 that was included in book income must also be included in computing taxable income. The $2,000 of interest expense on the bank loan to purchase the U.S. Treasury Bonds was deducted per books and is also an allowable deduction in computing taxable income, because the interest income from the obligations is taxable. Since there are no differences between the book and tax treatment of these items, taxable income is the same as book income before federal income taxes, $100,000.

115. (590,Q2,36) (d) The requirement is to determine the percentage of cash dividends received from a wholly-owned subsidiary that are tax-free in the consolidated income tax return filed by the parent corporation. A dividend distribution from a subsidiary corporation to a parent corporation during a consolidated return year is eliminated in determining the consolidated taxable income of the affiliated group, and therefore is 100% tax-free.

116. (590,Q2,37) (b) The requirement is to determine the correct statement regarding the amount of excess of a corporation's tentative minimum tax over regular tax. If a corporation's tentative minimum tax exceeds its regular tax, the excess represents the corporation's alternative minimum tax and is payable in addition to its regular tax liability.

117. (590,Q2,38) (b) The requirement is to determine the correct statement regarding an exempt organization's payment of estimated

taxes on its unrelated business income. An
exempt organization subject to tax on its unrelated business income must comply with the
Code provisions regarding installment payments
of estimated income tax by corporations. This
means that an exempt organization must make
quarterly estimated tax payments if it expects
its estimated tax on its unrelated business
income to be $500 or more. Answers (c) and
(d) are incorrect because any tax on unrelated
business income must be paid in full by the
due date of the exempt organization's return.

118. (590,Q2,39) (d) The requirement is to
determine what will terminate an exempt organization's status as a private foundation.
The private foundation status of an exempt
organization will terminate if it becomes a
public charity. Answer (a) is incorrect
because a private foundation's activities are
already severely restricted by the Code.
Answer (b) is incorrect because private
foundations are not required to distribute
their assets to public charities. Answer (c)
is incorrect because a private foundation can
be organized as a foreign corporation.

119. (590,Q2,40) (d) The requirement is to
determine the correct statement regarding
qualification as an exempt organization. To
qualify as an exempt organization, the applicant must not be a private foundation organized and operated exclusively to influence
legislation pertaining to protection of the
environment. Exempt status is specifically
denied to organizations if a substantial part
of their activities consists of "carrying on
propaganda, or otherwise attempting, to influence legislation," if expenditures exceed certain amounts. Answer (a) is incorrect because
an exempt organization cannot be organized for
the primary purpose of carrying on a business
for profit. Answer (b) is incorrect because
an organization must be one of those classes
upon which exemption is specifically conferred
by the Internal Revenue Code. Answer (c) is
incorrect because a social club organized for
recreation will qualify for exemption if substantially all of the activities of the club
are for such purposes and none of the profits
inure to the benefit of any shareholder.

Solution Guide

Problem 1   Book to Tax Worksheet (586,Q4)

1.   The problem states that Wolf, Inc. is an accrual basis taxpayer. Since the sales data given is already stated on an accrual basis, no adjustment for the tax return is necessary.

2.   Portions of the partnership income which have special characteristics must be segregated from ordinary partnership income.

2.1   The portion of the partnership income which represents dividend income ($10,000) should be reclassified from partnership income to dividend income so that the dividends received deduction will be correctly computed. Note that another alternative would be to show these dividends separately on another line as done in the AICPA unofficial answer.

2.2   The portion of the partnership income which represents a capital loss ($8,000) should be reclassified to be included with the capital gains. Once again note that another alternative would be to show this capital loss separately on another line as done in the AICPA unofficial answer.

3.   The corporation can deduct 80% of its dividends received. $8,000 x .80 = $6,400 plus $10,000 x .80 = $8,000 for a total of $14,400. The deduction is limited to 80% of taxable income before the dividends received deduction. This limitation can only be checked after adjustments have been made to all of the other elements of taxable income.

4.   Municipal bond interest ($3,000) is not included in taxable income.

5   After reclassifying the $8,000 LTCL from F & W, the corporation has a net capital loss of $3,000. A corporation may deduct capital losses only up to the amount of capital gains. Any excess of capital losses over gains is carried back.

6.   Life insurance proceeds received are not included in taxable income.

7.   The problem states that Wolf, Inc. is an accrual basis taxpayer. Since the COGS data given is already stated on an accrual basis, no adjustment for the tax return is necessary.

8.   The TRA of 1986 generally eliminated the reserve method for bad debts. Since the bad debts expense of $13,000 per books represents the actual accounts written off during the year, no adjustment is needed for the tax return.

9.   Payments of penalties ($2,000) are not deductible on the tax return.

10.   Interest expense on debt to acquire or carry municipal bonds is not deductible.

11.   Charitable contributions are limited to 10% of taxable income before deducting the dividends received deduction and the charitable contribution. Before computing this limitation it is necessary to complete the remaining adjustments to other deductions.

12.   Depreciation is to be increased from $60,000 per books to $85,000 per tax return. The $85,000 is given.

13.   Insurance premiums on a life insurance policy for which the company is the beneficiary are not deductible for the tax return.

14.   The federal income tax provision is not deductible for the tax return. The actual federal income tax payments also are not deductible.

15.   Having made all the necessary adjustments to the other items, the limitations on the charitable contributions deduction and the dividends received deduction can be computed.

15.1 The contribution limitation needs to be computed based on the adjusted income and expense data:

Net sales	$3,000,000
Partnership income	58,000
Dividends	18,000
Interest	15,000
Capital gains	--
Life insurance	--
COGS	(2,000,000)
Salaries	(500,000)
Bad debts	(13,000)
Taxes	(60,000)
Interest	(11,000)
Depreciation	(85,000)
Other	(35,000)
Taxable income before contributions and DRD	$ 387,000
	x 10%
Contribution deductible	$ 38,700

15.2 After the allowable contribution deduction has been determined, the dividends received deduction limit can be checked. The DRD may be limited to 80% of taxable income before DRD.

Taxable income before contribution	$387,000
Contribution deduction	(38,700)
Taxable income before DRD	$348,300

Since the dividends received ($18,000) are less than taxable income before the DRD ($348,300), the DRD computed in step 3 ($14,400) is fully deductible.

UNOFFICIAL ANSWER
Problem 1 Book to Tax Worksheet (586,Q4)

Wolf, Inc.
WORKSHEET TO CONVERT BOOK INCOME TO TAXABLE INCOME
For the Year Ended December 31, 1989

	Per books and GAAP	Increases	Decreases	Per tax return
Revenues				
Net sales	3,000,000			3,000,000
Equity in earnings of F & W Partnership	60,000		2,000[a]	58,000
Dividends	8,000		6,400[b]	1,600
Interest	18,000		3,000[c]	15,000
Gains on sale of stock	5,000		[d]	5,000
Key-man life insurance proceeds	100,000		100,000[e]	---
Share of dividends from F & W Partnership		10,000	8,000[f]	2,000
Net long-term capital loss		3,000	8,000[d]	(5,000)
Totals	3,191,000	13,000	127,400	3,076,600
Costs and expenses				
Cost of goods sold	2,000,000			2,000,000
Salaries and wages	500,000			500,000
Bad debts	13,000			13,000
Taxes, other than federal income	62,000		2,000[g]	60,000
Interest	12,000		1,000[h]	11,000
Contributions	50,000		11,300[i]	38,700
Depreciation	60,000	25,000		85,000
Other	40,000		5,000[J]	35,000
Federal income taxes	120,000		120,000[k]	---
Totals	2,857,000	25,000	139,300	2,742,700
Net income	334,000	(12,000)	(11,900)	333,900

Problem 1 (continued)

Explanation of adjustments to convert book income to taxable income:

[a] Decrease in equity in earnings of F & W Partnership:

Dividends qualifying for exclusion	$10,000
Less net long-term capital loss	(8,000)
Decrease	$ 2,000

[b] Dividends-received deduction:

$8,000 x .80	$6,400

[c] Interest earned on municipal bonds is excludible from taxable income.

[d] Capital loss is limited to capital gains.

Capital gains from sale of	
Ral Corp. stock	$1,000
Blu, Inc. stock	4,000
Total	$5,000
Share of net long-term capital loss from F & W Partnership	(8,000)
Amount available for carryback or carryover against capital gains	($3,000)

[e] Proceeds of life insurance policies, if paid by reason of the death of the insured, are excluded from taxable income of the recipient.

[f] Dividends-received deduction:

$10,000 x .80	$8,000

[g] Tax penalty is not an allowable deduction.

[h] Interest on debt incurred to carry tax-free obligations is not an allowable deduction.

[i] Decrease in deduction for contributions:

Taxable income before contributions		
Revenues	$3,076,600	
Deductions	2,704,000	
Balance	$ 372,600	
Plus dividends-received deductions	14,400	
Total	$ 387,000	
10% allowable deduction	$ 38,700	
Actual contributions	50,000	
Excess not deductible in current year	$ 11,300	

[j] Life insurance premiums are not allowable as a deduction if the corporation is the beneficiary.

[k] Federal income tax expense is not an allowable deduction.

SOLUTION GUIDE

Problem 2   Schedule of Taxable Income
              (589.Q4)

1.   The problem states that Elm Corp. is an accrual basis corporation. Since the net sales are already stated on an accrual basis, no adjustment is necessary for beginning and ending trade accounts receivables.

2.   The $10,000 of dividends received from an unrelated taxable domestic corporation are eligible for a dividends received deduction. Since the stock was traded on a "major stock exchange," it should be assumed that Elm owned less than 20% of the dividend-paying corporation and that the dividends qualify for a 70% DRD ($10,000 x 70% = $7,000). The $7,000 DRD will be deducted last, after the charitable contribution limitation is computed.

3.   The $4,000 of interest income from municipal bonds is excluded from Elm's gross income.

4.   Elm's $6,000 of LTCG is offset by Elm's share of the partnership's LTCL.

5.   The $50,000 of earnings from the Luz Partnership represents the netting of Elm's share of the partnership's ordinary income of $63,000 and LTCL of $13,000.

5.1 Since the $13,000 LTCL is a special loss item, it cannot be netted against ordinary income but instead must be reported as LTCL and be combined with Elm's $6,000 of LTCG.

5.2 The resulting net LTCL of $7,000 ($13,000 LTCL − $6,000 LTCG) is not currently deductible, but instead can be carried back three years and forward five years to offset capital gains in the carryback and carryforward years.

6.   The $200,000 of life insurance proceeds resulting from the death of Elm's controller are excluded from Elm's gross income.

7.   The $3,000 refund of Elm's 1987 federal income tax is excluded from Elm's gross income because Elm's payment of federal income tax was not deductible.

8.   The cost of goods sold is already stated on the accrual basis and no adjustment is necessary.

9.   Since officers' compensation must be separately stated on Elm's tax return, the $125,000 of officers' compensation must be subtracted from salaries and wages, and separately deducted.

10.   Since the 1986 TRA generally eliminated the reserve method for bad debts, Elm's deduction for bad debts is limited to the $9,000 of accounts receivable actually written off during the year.

10.1 The December 31, 1986 $120,000 balance in Elm's Allowance for Doubtful Accounts must be included in gross income over a four-year period beginning with 1987. Thus, for 1989, $120,000 x 25% = $30,000 must be included in Elm's gross income.

11.   The payroll taxes and property taxes are fully deductible and no adjustment is necessary.

12.   The interest expense incurred for working capital purposes is fully deductible and no adjustment is necessary.

13.   The deduction for the $175,000 of charitable contributions is limited to 10% of Elm's taxable income before the charitable contributions and dividends received deductions. Before computing this limitation, it is necessary to first consider any remaining adjustments.

14.   Since straight-line depreciation is used for both book and tax purposes, no adjustment is necessary.

15.   The $30,000 of Other expenses must be reduced by the $12,000 of premiums paid on the key-man life insurance policy covering Elm's controller. No deduction is allowed for life insurance premiums on a policy for which Elm is the beneficiary.

16.   The provision for federal income tax is not deductible in computing taxable income.

17.   Having made the necessary adjustments for the other items, the charitable contributions deduction and the dividends received deduction can now be computed. Note that no limitation applies to the dividends received deduction.

UNOFFICIAL ANSWER

Problem 2   Schedule of Taxable Income
(589.Q4)

Elm Corp.
FEDERAL TAXABLE INCOME
For the Year Ended December 31, 1989

Sales (net)	$5,500,000	[1]
Cost of goods sold	3,900,000	[8]
Gross profit	$1,600,000	
Dividends	10,000	
Other income		
From partnership $63,000 [5]		
Recapture of		
bad debt reserve 30,000 [10]	93,000	
Total income	$1,703,000	
Compensation of officers	$ 125,000	[9]
Salaries and wages	446,000	[9]
Bad debts	9,000	[10]
Taxes	100,000	[11]
Interest	20,000	[12]
Contributions	89,500	[13]
Depreciation	90,000	[14]
Other deductions	18,000	[15]
Total deductions	$ 897,500	
Taxable income before		
special deduction	$ 805,500	
Special deduction	7,000	[2]
Taxable income	$ 798,500	

EXPLANATIONS AND COMPUTATIONS

[1]   Net sales – no adjustment.

[2]   Dividends – $10,000 x 70% dividends-received deduction = $7,000.

[3]   Interest – not taxable.

[4]   Gain on sale of stock – offset by share of partnership long-term capital loss. Excess capital loss not deductible.

[5]   Equity in earnings of Luz Partnership – $50,000 + $13,000 = $63,000.

[6]   Key-man life insurance proceeds – not taxable.

[7]   Tax refund – not taxable.

[8]   Cost of goods sold – no adjustment.

[9]   Salaries and wages – separate $125,000 officers' compensation.

[10]   Doubtful accounts – limited to $9,000 actual bad debts. One-fourth of $120,000 "reserve" at December 31, 1986 = $30,000 income.

[11]   Taxes – no adjustment.

[12]   Interest – no adjustment.

[13]   Contributions:

Taxable income	$798,500
Dividends-received deduction	7,000
Contributions deduction	89,500
Total	$895,000
Allowable – 10%	$ 89,500

[14]   Depreciation – no adjustment.

[15]   Other – $30,000 less $12,000 life insurance premiums = $18,000.

[16]   Federal income tax – not deductible.

Multiple Choice Questions (1-16)

1.   If an individual donor makes a gift of future interest whereby the donee is to receive possession of the gift at some future time, the annual exclusion for gift tax purposes is
    a. $0
    b. $ 3,000
    c. $ 5,000
    d. $10,000

2.   Raff created a joint bank account for himself and his friend's son, Dave. There is a gift to Dave when
    a.   Raff creates the account.
    b.   Raff dies.
    c.   Dave draws on the account for his own benefit.
    d.   Dave is notified by Raff that the account has been created.

3.   In 1989, Blum, who is single, gave an outright gift of $50,000 to a friend, Gould, who needed the money to pay medical expenses. In filing the 1989 gift tax return, Blum was entitled to a maximum exclusion of
    a. $20,000
    b. $10,000
    c. $ 3,000
    d. $0

4.   Mr. & Mrs. John Hance jointly gave a $100,000 outright gift in 1989 to an unrelated friend, Fred Green, who needed the money to pay medical expenses. In filing their gift tax returns for 1989, Mr. & Mrs. Hance were entitled to annual exclusions aggregating
    a. $0
    b. $ 6,000
    c. $10,000
    d. $20,000

5.   Eng and Lew, both U.S. citizens, died in 1989. Eng made taxable lifetime gifts of $100,000 that are not included in Eng's gross estate. Lew made no lifetime gifts. At the dates of death, Eng's gross estate was $300,000, and Lew's gross estate was $400,000. A federal estate tax return must be filed for

	Eng	Lew
a.	No	No
b.	No	Yes
c.	Yes	No
d.	Yes	Yes

6.   With regard to the federal estate tax, the alternate valuation date
    a.   Is required to be used if the fair market value of the estate's assets has increased since the decedent's date of death.
    b.   If elected on the first return filed for the estate, may be revoked in an amended return provided that the first return was filed on time.
    c.   Must be used for valuation of the estate's liabilities if such date is used for valuation of the estate's assets.
    d.   Can be elected only if its use decreases both the value of the gross estate and the estate tax liability.

7.   Proceeds of a life insurance policy payable to the estate's executor, as the estate's representative, are
    a.   Includible in the decedent's gross estate only if the premiums had been paid by the insured.
    b.   Includible in the decedent's gross estate only if the policy was taken out within three years of the insured's death under the "contemplation of death" rule.
    c.   Always includible in the decedent's gross estate.
    d.   Never includible in the decedent's gross estate.

8.   Ross, a calendar-year, cash basis taxpayer who died in June 1990, was entitled to receive a $10,000 accounting fee that had not been collected before the date of death. The executor of Ross' estate collected the full $10,000 in July 1990. This $10,000 should appear in
    a.   Only the decedent's final individual income tax return.
    b.   Only the estate's fiduciary income tax return.
    c.   Only the estate tax return.
    d.   Both the fiduciary income tax return and the estate tax return.

Items 9 through 11 are based on the following data:

Alan Curtis, a U.S. citizen, died on March 1, 1989, leaving an adjusted gross estate with a fair market value of $1,400,000 at the date of death. Under the terms of Alan's will, $375,000 was bequeathed outright to his widow, free of all estate and inheritance taxes. The remainder of Alan's estate was left to his mother. Alan made no taxable gifts during his lifetime.

9.   Disregarding extensions of time for filing, within how many months after the date of Alan's death is the federal estate tax return due?

    a. $2\frac{1}{2}$
    b. $3\frac{1}{2}$
    c.   9
    d.   12

10. In computing the taxable estate, the executor of Alan's estate should claim a marital deduction of
    a. $ 250,000
    b. $ 375,000
    c. $ 700,000
    d. $1,025,000

11. If the executor of Alan's estate elects the alternate valuation method, all remaining undistributed property included in the gross estate must be valued as of how many months after Alan's death?
    a.   12
    b.   9
    c.   6
    d.   3

12. In 1986, Edwin Ryan bought 100 shares of a listed stock for $5,000. In June 1989, when the stock's fair market value was $7,000, Edwin gave this stock to his sister, Lynn. No gift tax was paid. Lynn died in October 1989, bequeathing this stock to Edwin, when the stock's fair market value was $9,000. Lynn's executor did not elect the alternate valuation. What is Edwin's basis for this stock after he inherits it from Lynn's estate?
    a. $0
    b. $5,000
    c. $7,000
    d. $9,000

13. All trusts, except tax exempt trusts,
    a.   Must adopt a calendar year, except for existing trusts with fiscal years ended in 1987.
    b.   May adopt a calendar year or any fiscal year.
    c.   Must adopt calendar year regardless of the year the trust was established.
    d.   Must use the same taxable year as that of its principal beneficiary.

14. For income tax purposes, all estates
    a.   Must adopt a calendar year, except for existing estates with fiscal years ended in 1987.
    b.   May adopt a calendar year or any fiscal year.
    c.   Must adopt a calendar year regardless of the year the estate was established.
    d.   Must use the same taxable year as that of its principal beneficiary.

15. With regard to estimated income tax, estates
    a.   Must make quarterly estimated tax payments starting no later than the second quarter following the one in which the estate was established.
    b.   Are exempt from paying estimated tax during the estate's first two taxable years.
    c.   Must make quarterly estimated tax payments only if the estate's income is required to be distributed currently.
    d.   Are **not** required to make payments of estimated tax.

16. A complex trust is a trust that
    a.   Must distribute income currently, but is prohibited from distributing principal during the taxable year.
    b.   Invests only in corporate securities and is prohibited from engaging in short-term transactions.
    c.   Permits accumulation of current income, provides for charitable contributions, or distributes principal during the taxable year.
    d.   Is exempt from payment of income tax since the tax is paid by the beneficiaries.

Multiple Choice Answers

1. a	5. a	8. d	11. c	14. b
2. c	6. d	9. c	12. b	15. b
3. b	7. c	10. b	13. c	16. c
4. d				

Multiple Choice Answer Explanations

I.A. Gift Tax

1. (589,Q3,58) (a) The requirement is to determine the amount of annual gift tax exclusion when the donor makes a gift whereby the donee is to receive possession of the gift at some future time. A donor receives a $10,000 annual exclusion per donee for gifts that constitute a present interest. A present interest is an unrestricted right to the immediate use, possession, or enjoyment of property, or the income from property. In contrast, no annual gift tax exclusion is available for those gifts that constitute a future interest. A future interest is a legal term that includes reversions, remainders, and other interests which are limited to commence in use, possession, or enjoyment at some future date or time.

2. (1188,Q1,17) (c) The requirement is to determine when a gift occurs in conjunction with Raff's creation of a joint bank account for himself and his friend's son, Dave. A gift does not occur when Raff opens the joint account and deposits money into it. Instead, a gift results when the noncontributing tenant (Dave) withdraws money from the account for his own benefit.

3. (1188,Q1,20) (b) The requirement is to determine the maximum gift tax exclusion for Blum's $50,000 gift to a friend who needed the money to pay medical expenses. The first $10,000 of gifts made to a donee during the calendar year (except gifts of future interests) is excluded in determining the amount of the donor's taxable gifts for the year. Note that Blum does not qualify for the unlimited exclusion for medical expenses paid on behalf of a donee, because Blum did not pay the $50,000 to a medical care provider on Gould's behalf.

4. (1187,Q2,25) (d) The requirement is to determine the amount of gift tax exclusions allowable to the Hances for 1989. In computing a donor's gift tax, there is an annual exclusion of $10,000 per donee. Since the $100,000 gift was jointly made by Mr. & Mrs. Hance, each would be entitled to a $10,000 exclusion, a total of $20,000.

I.B. Estate Tax

5. (589,Q3,59) (a) The requirement is to determine whether federal estate tax returns must be filed for the estates of Eng and Lew. An executor must file a federal estate tax return (Form 706) if the decedent's gross estate exceeds $600,000. If a decedent made taxable lifetime gifts such that the decedent's unified transfer tax credit was used to offset the gift tax, the $600,000 exemption amount must be reduced by the amount of taxable lifetime gifts to determine whether a return is required to be filed.

Since Lew made no lifetime gifts and the value of Lew's gross estate was only $400,000, no federal estate tax return is required to be filed for Lew's estate. In Eng's case, the $600,000 exemption is reduced by Eng's $100,000 of taxable lifetime gifts to $500,000. However, since Eng's gross estate totaled only $300,000, no federal estate tax return is required to be filed for Eng's estate.

6. (589,Q3,60) (d) The requirement is to determine the correct statement regarding the use of the alternate valuation date in computing the federal estate tax. An executor of an estate can elect to use the alternate valuation date (the date 6 months after the decedent's death) to value the assets included in a decedent's gross estate only if its use decreases both the value of the gross estate and the amount of estate tax liability. Answer (a) is incorrect because the alternate valuation date cannot be used if its use increases the value of the gross estate. Answer (b) is incorrect because the use of the alternate valuation date is an irrevocable election. Answer (c) is incorrect because the alternate valuation date is only used to value an estate's assets, not its liabilities.

7. (1188,Q1,18) (c) The requirement is to determine when the proceeds of life insurance payable to the estate's executor, as the estate's representative, are includible in the decedent's gross estate. The proceeds of life insurance on the decedent's life are always included in the decedent's gross estate if (1) they are receivable by the estate, (2) the decedent possessed any incident of ownership in the policy, or (3) they are receivable by another (e.g., the estate's executor) for the benefit of the estate.

8. (1188,Q1,19) (d) The requirement is to determine the proper income and estate tax treatment of an accounting fee earned by Ross before death, that was subsequently collected by the executor of Ross' estate. Since Ross was a calendar-year, cash method taxpayer, the

income would not be included on Ross' final individual income tax return because payment had not been received. Since the accounting fee would not be included in Ross' final income tax return because of Ross' cash method of accounting, the accounting fee would be "income in respect of a decedent." For estate tax purposes, income in respect of a decedent will be included in the decedent's gross estate at its fair market value on the appropriate valuation date. For income tax purposes, the income tax basis of the decedent (zero) transfers over to the estate or beneficiary who collects the fee. The recipient of the income must classify it in the same manner (i.e., ordinary income) as would have the decedent. Thus, the accounting fee must be included in Ross' gross estate and must also be included in the estate's fiduciary income tax return (Form 1041) because the fee was collected by the executor of Ross' estate.

9. (1187,Q1,11) (c) The requirement is to determine within how many months after the date of Alan's death his federal estate tax return should be filed. The federal estate tax return (Form 706) must be filed and the tax paid within 9 months of the decedent's death, unless an extension of time has been granted.

10. (1187,Q1,12) (b) The requirement is to determine the amount of marital deduction that can be claimed in computing Alan's taxable estate. In computing the taxable estate of a decedent, an unlimited marital deduction is allowed for the portion of the decedent's estate that passes to the decedent's surviving spouse. Since $375,000 was bequeathed outright to Alan's widow, Alan's estate will receive a marital deduction of $375,000.

11. (1187,Q1,13) (c) The requirement is to determine the number of months after Alan's death that is to be used for valuing undistributed property included in the gross estate if the alternate valuation method is used for federal estate tax purposes. An executor of a decedent's estate may elect to use an alternate valuation method if such election will reduce both the gross estate and the federal estate tax liability. Under the alternate valuation method, <u>undistributed</u> property included in the decedent's gross estate is valued at its FMV as of 6 months after the decedent's death.
   Note that if the alternate valuation method is elected, and property is distributed or otherwise disposed of within 6 months of the decedent's death, the distributed (or

disposed) property is included in the decedent's gross estate at its FMV on the date of its distribution (or disposal).

12. (1183,Q2,26) (b) The requirement is to determine Edwin's basis for the stock inherited from Lynn's estate. A special rule applies if a decedent (Lynn) acquires appreciated property as a gift within one year of death, and this property passes to the donor (Edwin) or donor's spouse. Then the donor's (Edwin's) basis is the basis of the property in the hands of the decedent (Lynn) before death. Since Lynn had received the stock as a gift, Lynn's basis before death ($5,000) becomes the basis of the stock to Edwin.

II. Income Taxation of Estates and Trusts

13. (588,Q1,17) (c) The requirement is to determine the correct statement regarding a trust's taxable year. The 1986 TRA requires that for taxable years beginning after 1986, both existing and newly created trusts (except tax-exempt trusts) must adopt the calendar year as their taxable year.

14. (588,Q1,18) (b) The requirement is to determine the correct statement regarding an estate's taxable year. Although the 1986 TRA required trusts to use the calendar year, estates continue to be able to adopt a calendar year or any fiscal year.

15. (588,Q1,19) (b) The requirement is to determine the correct statement regarding an estate's estimated income taxes. The 1986 TRA requires new and existing trusts and estates to make quarterly estimated tax payments, except that an estate is exempt from making estimated tax payments for taxable years ending within two years of the decedent's death.

16. (588,Q1,20) (c) The requirement is to determine the correct statement regarding a complex trust. A simple trust is one that (1) is required to distribute all of its income to designated beneficiaries every year, (2) has no beneficiaries that are qualifying charitable organizations, and (3) makes no distributions of trust corpus (i.e., principal) during the year. A complex trust is any trust that is not a simple trust. Answer (a) is incorrect because a complex trust is not required to distribute income currently, nor is it prohibited from distributing trust principal. Answer (b) is incorrect because there are no investment restrictions imposed on a complex trust. Answer (d) is incorrect because an income tax is imposed on a trust's taxable income.

EXAMINATION IN AUDITING

NOTE TO CANDIDATES: Suggested time allotments are as follows:

All questions are required:

	Point Value	Estimated Minutes	
		Minimum	Maximum
No. 1	60	90	110
No. 2	10	15	25
No. 3	10	15	25
No. 4	10	15	25
No. 5	10	15	25
Total	100	150	210

Number 1 (Estimated time--90 to 110 minutes)

1.   A CPA firm's personnel partner periodically studies the CPA firm's personnel advancement experience to ascertain whether individuals meeting stated criteria are assigned increased degrees of responsibility. This is evidence of the CPA firm's adherence to prescribed standards of
    a.   Quality control.
    b.   Due professional care.
    c.   Supervision and review.
    d.   Field work.

2.   Due professional care requires
    a.   A critical review of the work done at every level of supervision.
    b.   The examination of all corroborating evidence available.
    c.   The exercise of error-free judgment.
    d.   A consideration of internal control that includes tests of controls.

3.   Which of the following, if material, would be an irregularity?
    a.   Mistakes in the application of accounting principles.
    b.   Clerical mistakes in the accounting data underlying the financial statements.
    c.   Misappropriation of an asset or groups of assets.
    d.   Misinterpretations of facts that existed when the financial state-ments were prepared.

4.   An auditor ordinarily should send a standard confirmation request to all banks with which the client has done business during the year under audit, regardless of the year-end balance, because this procedure
    a.   Provides for confirmation regarding compensating balance arrangements.

    b.   Detects kiting activities that may otherwise **not** be discovered.
    c.   Seeks information about indebtedness to the bank.
    d.   Verifies securities held by the bank in safekeeping.

5.   In verifying the amount of goodwill recorded by a client, the most convincing evidence which an auditor can obtain is by comparing the recorded value of assets acquired with the
    a.   Assessed value as evidenced by tax bills.
    b.   Seller's book value as evidenced by financial statements.
    c.   Insured value as evidenced by insur-ance policies.
    d.   Appraised value as evidenced by independent appraisals.

6.   Which of the following procedures is **least** likely to be performed before the balance sheet date?
    a.   Observation of inventory.
    b.   Review of internal control over cash disbursements.
    c.   Search for unrecorded liabilities.
    d.   Confirmation of receivables.

7.   As one of the year-end audit procedures, the auditor instructed the client's personnel to prepare a standard bank confirmation request for a bank account that had been closed during the year. After the client's treasurer had signed the request, it was mailed by the assistant treasurer. What is the major flaw in this audit procedure?
    a.   The confirmation request was signed by the treasurer.
    b.   Sending the request was meaningless because the account was closed before the year ended.

c. The request was mailed by the assistant treasurer.

-d. The CPA did **not** sign the confirmation request before it was mailed.

8. When performing a test of a control with respect to cash disbursements, a CPA may use a systematic sampling technique with a start at any randomly selected item. The biggest disadvantage of this type of sampling is that the items in the population

a. Must be recorded in a systematic pattern before the sample can be drawn.

b. May occur in a systematic pattern, thus destroying the sample randomness.

c. May systematically occur more than once in the sample.

d. Must be systematically replaced in the population after sampling.

9. The auditor concludes that there is a material inconsistency in the other information in an annual report to shareholders containing audited financial statements. If the client refuses to revise or eliminate the material inconsistency, the auditor should

a. Revise the auditor's report to include a separate explanatory paragraph describing the material inconsistency.

b. Consult with a party whose advice might influence the client, such as the client's legal counsel.

c. Issue a qualified opinion after discussing the matter with the client's board of directors.

d. Consider the matter closed since the other information is **not** in the audited financial statements.

10. When an independent accountant issues a letter for an underwriter containing comments on data that have **not** been audited, the underwriter most likely will receive

a. A disclaimer on prospective financial statements.

b. A limited opinion on "pro forma" financial statements.

c. Positive assurance on supplementary disclosures.

d. Negative assurance on capsule information.

11. Which of the following would lessen internal control in an electronic data processing system?

a. The computer librarian maintains custody of computer program instructions and detailed listings.

b. Computer operators have access to operator instructions and detailed program listings.

c. The control group is solely responsible for the distribution of all computer output.

d. Computer programmers write and debug programs which perform routines designed by the systems analyst.

12. In auditing through a computer, the test data method is used by auditors to test the

a. Accuracy of input data.

b. Validity of the output.

c. Procedures contained within the program.

d. Normalcy of distribution of test data.

13. Which of the following should **not** be included in an accountant's standard report based upon the compilation of an entity's financial statements?

a. A statement that a compilation is limited to presenting in the form of financial statements information that is the representation of management.

b. A statement that the compilation was performed in accordance with standards established by the American Institute of CPAs.

c. A statement that the accountant has **not** audited or reviewed the financial statements.

d. A statement that the accountant does **not** express an opinion but expresses only limited assurance on the financial statements.

14. Which of the following is intended to detect deviations from prescribed Accounting Department procedures?

a. Substantive tests specified by a standardized audit program.

b. Tests of controls designed specifically for the client.

c. Analytical procedures as designed in the industry audit guide.

d. Computerized analytical procedures tailored for the configuration of EDP equipment in use.

15. An auditor's consideration of the internal control structure made in connection with an annual audit is usually **not** sufficient to express an opinion on an entity's internal controls because

a. The evaluation of weaknesses is subjective enough that an auditor should **not** express an opinion.

b.   The audit cost-benefit relationship permits an auditor to express only reasonable assurance that the internal controls operates as designed.

c.   Management may change the internal controls to correct weaknesses.

d.   Only those controls on which an auditor intends to rely are reviewed, tested, and evaluated.

16.   In a properly designed accounts payable system, a voucher is prepared after the invoice, purchase order, requisition, and receiving report are verified. The next step in the system is to

a.   Cancel the supporting documents.

b.   Enter the check amount in the check register.

c.   Approve the voucher for payment.

d.   Post the voucher amount to the expense ledger.

17.   Which of the following is an effective internal control measure that encourages receiving department personnel to count and inspect all merchandise received?

a.   Quantities ordered are excluded from the receiving department copy of the purchase order.

b.   Vouchers are prepared by accounts payable department personnel only after they match item counts on the receiving report with the purchase order.

c.   Receiving department personnel are expected to match and reconcile the receiving report with the purchase order.

d.   Internal auditors periodically examine, on a surprise basis, the receiving department copies of receiving reports.

18.   Which of the following requires recognition in the auditor's opinion as to consistency?

a.   Changing the salvage value of an asset.

b.   Changing the presentation of prepaid insurance from inclusion in "other assets" to disclosing it as a separate line item.

c.   Division of the consolidated subsidiary into two subsidiaries which are both consolidated.

d.   Changing from consolidating a subsidiary to carrying it on the equity basis.

19.   When the auditor is unable to determine the amounts associated with the illegal acts of client personnel because of an inability to obtain adequate evidence, the auditor should issue a(an)

a.   "Subject to" qualified opinion.

b.   Disclaimer of opinion.

c.   Adverse opinion.

d.   Unqualified opinion with a separate explanatory paragraph.

20.   When there are a large number of relatively small account balances, negative confirmation of accounts receivable is feasible if internal control is

a.   Strong, and the individuals receiving the confirmation requests are unlikely to give them adequate consideration.

b.   Weak, and the individuals receiving the confirmation requests are likely to give them adequate consideration.

c.   Weak, and the individuals receiving the confirmation requests are unlikely to give them adequate consideration.

d.   Strong, and the individuals receiving the confirmation requests are likely to give them adequate consideration.

21.   With respect to the auditor's planning of a year-end examination, which of the following statements is always true?

a.   An engagement should **not** be accepted after the fiscal year end.

b.   An inventory count must be observed at the balance sheet date.

c.   The client's audit committee should **not** be told of the specific audit procedures which will be performed.

d.   It is an acceptable practice to carry out substantial parts of the examination at interim dates.

22.   An auditor who accepts an audit engagement and does not possess the industry expertise of the business entity, should

a.   Engage financial experts familiar with the nature of the business entity.

b.   Obtain a knowledge of matters that relate to the nature of the entity's business.

c.   Refer a substantial portion of the audit to another CPA who will act as the principal auditor.

d.   First inform management that an unqualified opinion cannot be issued.

23. The CPA who undertakes the performance of a management advisory service engagement should bear in mind that the results should

    a. Increase the client's earnings capabilities.

    b. Be communicated in quantitative terms.

    c. Not be set forth as quantitative estimates.

    d. Not be explicitly or implicitly guaranteed.

24. Which of the following underlies the application of generally accepted auditing standards, particularly the standards of field work and reporting?

    a. The elements of materiality and relative risk.

    b. The element of internal control.

    c. The element of corroborating evidence.

    d. The element of reasonable assurance.

25. To strengthen internal control over the custody of heavy mobile equipment, the client would most likely institute a policy requiring a periodic

    a. Increase in insurance coverage.

    b. Inspection of equipment and reconciliation with accounting records.

    c. Verification of liens, pledges, and collateralizations.

    d. Accounting for work orders.

26. With respect to an internal control measure that will assure accountability for fixed asset retirements, management should implement a system that includes

    a. Continuous analysis of miscellaneous revenue to locate any cash proceeds from sale of plant assets.

    b. Periodic inquiry of plant executives by internal auditors as to whether any plant assets have been retired.

    c. Continuous utilization of serially numbered retirement work orders.

    d. Periodic observation of plant assets by the internal auditors.

27. In the consideration of internal control, the auditor is basically concerned that the structure provides reasonable assurance that

    a. Management can not override the system.

    b. Operational efficiency has been achieved in accordance with management plans.

    c. Errors have been prevented or detected.

    d. Controls have not been circumvented by collusion.

28. Comparative financial statements include the financial statements of a prior period which were examined by a predecessor auditor, whose report is not presented. If the predecessor auditor's report was qualified, the successor auditor must

    a. Express an opinion on the current year statements alone and make no reference to the prior year statements.

    b. Issue a standard short-form comparative report indicating the division of responsibility.

    c. Obtain written approval from the predecessor auditor to include the prior year's financial statements.

    d. Disclose the reasons for any qualification included in the predecessor auditor's opinion.

29. The auditor who wishes to point out that the entity has sufficient transactions with related parties should disclose this fact in

    a. An explanatory paragraph to the auditor's report.

    b. An explanatory footnote to the financial statements.

    c. The body of the financial statements.

    d. The "Summary of significant accounting policies" section of the financial statements.

30. A CPA examines a sample of copies of December and January sales invoices for the initials of the person who verified the quantitative data. This is an example of a

    a. Test of a control.

    b. Substantive test.

    c. Cutoff test.

    d. Statistical test.

31. Tracing bills of lading to sales invoices will provide evidence that

    a. Recorded sales were shipped.

    b. Invoiced sales were shipped.

    c. Shipments to customers were invoiced.

    d. Shipments to customers were recorded as sales.

32. The auditor should design the audit to provide reasonable assurance of detecting

    a. Errors or irregularities that would have a material or immaterial effect on the financial statements.

    b. Errors or irregularities that would have a material effect on the financial statements.

c. Errors that would have a material effect on the financial statements, but the auditor need not plan to search for irregularities.

d. Irregularities that would have a material effect on the financial statements, but the auditor need not plan to search for errors.

33. As guidance for measuring the quality of the performance of an auditor, the auditor should refer to

a. Statements of the Financial Accounting Standards Board.

b. Generally accepted auditing standards.

c. Interpretations of the Statements on Auditing Standards.

d. Statements on Quality Control Standards.

34. A violation of the Code of Professional Conduct would least likely have occurred when a CPA in public practice

a. Used a records-retention agency to store the CPA's working papers and client records.

b. Served as an expert witness in a damage suit and received compensation based on the amount awarded to the plaintiff.

c. Referred life insurance assignments to the CPA's spouse, who is a life insurance agent.

d. Served simultaneously as state director of revenues and practiced public accounting in the same state.

35. Which of the following would be least likely to suggest to an auditor that the client's management may have overridden the internal control structure?

a. There are numerous delays in preparing timely internal financial reports.

b. Management does not correct internal control weaknesses that it knows about.

c. Differences are always disclosed on a computer exception report.

d. There have been two new controllers this year.

36. Which of the following statements concerning the independent auditor's communication of internal control reportable conditions is correct?

a. Reportable conditions reported at interim dates must be repeated in the final communication.

b. If the auditor does not become aware of any reportable conditions during the examination, that fact must be communicated.

c. Reportable conditions that had been reported in prior years' communications and have not been corrected need be repeated in the current year's communication.

d. Although written communication is preferable, the auditor may communicate the findings orally.

37. Effective internal control over the payroll function would include which of the following?

a. Total time recorded on time-clock punch cards should be reconciled to job reports by employees responsible for those specific jobs.

b. Payroll department employees should be supervised by the management of the personnel department.

c. Payroll department employees should be responsible for maintaining employee personnel records.

d. Total time spent on jobs should be compared with total time indicated on time-clock punch cards.

38. If the auditor obtains satisfaction with respect to the accounts receivable balance by alternative procedures because it is impracticable to confirm accounts receivable, the auditor's report should be unqualified and could be expected to

a. Disclose that alternative procedures were used due to a client-imposed scope limitation.

b. Disclose that confirmation of accounts receivable was impracticable in the opinion paragraph.

c. Not mention the alternative procedures.

d. Refer to a footnote that discloses the alternative procedures.

39. When financial statements are prepared on the basis of a going concern and the auditor believes that the client may not continue as a going concern, the auditor should issue

a. An unqualified opinion with an explanatory paragraph.

b. A standard unqualified opinion.

c. An "except for" opinion.

d. An adverse opinion.

40. Which of the following is not usually performed by the accountant in a review engagement of a nonpublic entity?

a. Writing an engagement letter to

establish an understanding regarding the services to be performed.

b. Issuing a report stating that the review was performed in accordance with standards established by the AICPA.

c. Communicating any material weaknesses discovered during the consideration of internal control.

d. Reading the financial statements to consider whether they conform with generally accepted accounting principles.

41. Which of the following material events occurring subsequent to the December 31, 1988 balance sheet would **not** ordinarily result in an adjustment to the financial statements before they are issued on March 2, 1989?

a. Write-off of a receivable from a debtor who had suffered from deteriorating financial condition for the past 6 years. The debtor filed for bankruptcy on January 23, 1989.

b. Acquisition of a subsidiary on January 23, 1989. Negotiations had begun in December of 1988.

c. Settlement of extended litigation on January 23, 1989, in excess of the recorded year-end liability.

d. A 3 for 5 reverse stock split consummated on January 23, 1989.

42. The proper use of prenumbered termination notice forms by the payroll department should provide assurance that all

a. Uncashed payroll checks were issued to employees who have **not** been terminated.

b. Personnel files are kept up to date.

c. Employees who have **not** been terminated receive their payroll checks.

d. Terminated employees are removed from the payroll.

43. The purpose of segregating the duties of distributing payroll checks and hiring personnel is to separate the

a. Duties within the accounting function.

b. Custody of assets from the accounting for those assets.

c. Authorization of transactions from the custody of related assets.

d. Operational responsibility from record keeping responsibility.

44. When the financial statements contain a departure from generally accepted accounting principles, the effect of which is material, the auditor should

a. Qualify the opinion and explain the effect of the departure from generally accepted accounting principles in a separate paragraph.

b. Qualify the opinion and describe the departure from generally accepted accounting principles within the opinion paragraph.

c. Disclaim an opinion and explain the effect of the departure from generally accepted accounting principles in a separate paragraph.

d. Disclaim an opinion and describe the departure from generally accepted accounting principles within the opinion paragraph.

45. The prior year's financial statements of YZ, Inc., which were audited by Pate, CPA, are presented for comparative purposes without Pate's audit report. Jennings, CPA, the successor auditor, should indicate in the current year audit report that the prior year's financial statements were examined by another auditor

a. Only if Pate's opinion was other than unqualified.

b. But should **not** indicate the type of opinion expressed by Pate.

c. Only if the prior year's financial statements have been restated.

d. But should **not** name Pate as the predecessor auditor.

46. Which of the following expressions is **least** likely to be included in a client's representation letter?

a. No events have occurred subsequent to the balance sheet date that require adjustment to, or disclosure in, the financial statements.

b. The company has complied with all aspects of contractual agreements that would have a material effect on the financial statements in the event of noncompliance.

c. Management acknowledges responsibility for illegal actions committed by employees.

d. Management has made available all financial statements and related data.

47. An auditor should perform tests of control on

a. Those controls that have a material effect upon the financial statement balances.

b.   A random sample of the controls that were reviewed.

c.   Those controls that the auditor plans to depend upon to assess control risk below the maximum level.

d.   Those controls in which material weaknesses were identified.

48.   In order to avoid the misappropriation of company-owned marketable securities, which of the following is the best course of action that can be taken by the management of a company with a large portfolio of marketable securities?

a.   Require that one trustworthy and bonded employee be responsible for access to the safekeeping area, where securities are kept.

b.   Require that employees who enter and leave the safekeeping area sign and record in a log the exact reason for their access.

c.   Require that employees involved in the safekeeping function maintain a subsidiary control ledger for securities on a current basis.

d.   Require that the safekeeping function for securities be assigned to a bank that will act as a custodial agent.

49.   The Code of Professional Conduct would most likely be considered to have been violated when the CPA represents that specific consulting services will be performed for a stated fee and it is apparent at the time of the representation that the

a.   CPA would not be independent.

b.   Fee was a competitive bid.

c.   Actual fee would be substantially higher.

d.   Actual fee would be substantially lower than the fees charged by other CPAs for comparable services.

50.   Which of the following is implied when a CPA signs the preparer's declaration on a federal income tax return?

a.   The tax return is not misleading based on all information of which the CPA has knowledge.

b.   The tax return and supporting schedules were prepared in accordance with generally accepted accounting principles.

c.   The tax return was examined in accordance with standards established by the AICPA's Federal Tax Division.

d.   The tax return was prepared by a CPA who maintained an impartial attitude.

51.   Below are the names of four CPA firms and pertinent facts relating to each firm. Unless otherwise indicated, the individuals named are CPAs and partners, and there are no other partners. Which firm name and related facts indicates a violation of the AICPA Code of Professional Conduct?

a.   Arthur, Barry, and Clark, CPAs, (Clark died about five years ago; Arthur and Barry are continuing the firm).

b.   Dave and Edwards, CPAs (The name of Fredricks, CPA, a third active partner, is omitted from the firm name).

c.   Jones & Co., CPAs, P.C. (The firm is a professional corporation and has ten other stockholders who are all CPAs).

d.   George and Howard, CPAs (Howard died three years ago; George is continuing the firm as a sole proprietorship).

52.   An auditor's report includes a statement that, "the financial statements do not present fairly the financial position, results of operations or changes in financial position in conformity with generally accepted accounting principles." This auditor's report was probably issued in connection with finanical statements that were

a.   Prepared on a comprehensive basis of accounting other than generally accepted accounting principles.

b.   Restricted for use of management.

c.   Misleading.

d.   Condensed.

53.   Thomas, CPA, has examined the consolidated financial statements of Kass Corporation. Jones, CPA, has examined the financial statements of the sole subsidiary which is material in relation to the total examined by Thomas. It would be appropriate for Thomas to serve as the principal auditor, but it is impractical for Thomas to review the work of Jones. Assuming an unqualified opinion is expressed by Jones, one would expect Thomas to

a.   Refuse to express an opinion on the consolidated financial statements.

b.   Express an unqualified opinion on the consolidated financial statements and not refer to the work of Jones.

c.   Express an unqualified opinion on the consolidated financial statements and refer to the work of Jones.

d.   Express an "except for" opinion on the consolidated financial statements and refer to the work of Jones.

54. Sound internal control procedures dictate that defective merchandise returned by customers should be presented to the
    a. Purchasing clerk.
    b. Receiving clerk.
    c. Inventory control clerk.
    d. Sales clerk.

55. When considering an internal control structure to determine whether the necessary procedures are designed and operating effectively, an auditor must
    a. Develop questionnaires and checklists.
    b. Perform tests of controls.
    c. Perform analytical procedures.
    d. Evaluate administrative policies.

56. Which of the following best describes what is meant by generally accepted auditing standards?
    a. Audit objectives generally determined on audit engagements.
    b. Acts to be performed by the auditor.
    c. Measures of the quality of the auditor's performance.
    d. Procedures to be used to gather evidence to support financial statements.

57. A client company has not paid its 19X3 audit fees. According to the AICPA Code of Professional Conduct, for the auditor to be considered independent with respect to the 19X4 audit, the 19X3 audit fees must be paid before the
    a. 19X3 report is issued.
    b. 19X4 field work is started.
    c. 19X4 report is issued.
    d. 19X5 field work is started.

58. The first general standard recognizes that regardless of how capable an individual may be in other fields, the individual can not meet the requirements of the auditing standards without the proper
    a. Business and finance courses.
    b. Quality control and peer review.
    c. Education and experience in auditing.
    d. Supervision and review skills.

59. When auditing a public entity's financial statements that include segment information, the auditor should
    a. Make certain the segment information is labeled unaudited and determine that the information is consistent with audited information.
    b. Make certain the segment information is labeled unaudited and perform

only analytical review procedures on the segment information.
    c. Audit the segment information, and, if the information is adequate and in conformity with GAAP, do not make reference to the segment information in the auditor's report.
    d. Audit the segment information and, if the information is adequate and in conformity with GAAP, refer to the segment information in the auditor's report.

60. Which of the following should be included in an accountant's standard report based upon the review of a nonpublic entity's financial statements?
    a. A statement that the review was performed in accordance with generally accepted review standards.
    b. A statement that a review consists principally of inquiries and analytical procedures.
    c. A statement that the accountant is independent with respect to the entity.
    d. A statement that a review is substantially greater in scope than a compilation.

Number 2 (Estimated time--15 to 25 minutes)

Andrews, CPA, has been engaged to examine the financial statements of Broadwall Corporation for the year ended December 31, 1981. During the year, Broadwall obtained a long-term loan from a local bank pursuant to a financing agreement which provided that the:

1. Loan was to be secured by the company's inventory and accounts receivable.
2. Company was to maintain a debt to equity ratio not to exceed two to one.
3. Company was not to pay dividends without permission from the bank.
4. Monthly installment payments were to commence July 1, 1981.

In addition, during the year the company also borrowed, on a short-term basis, from the president of the company, including substantial amounts just prior to the year end.

Required:

a. For purposes of Andrews' audit of the financial statements of Broadwall Corporation, what procedures should Andrews employ in examining the described loans? **Do not discuss internal control.**

b. What are the financial statement disclsoures that Andrews should expect to find with respect to the loans from the president?

Number 3 (Estimated time--15 to 25 minutes)

George Beemster, CPA, is examining the financial statements of the Louisville Sales Corporation, which recently installed an off-line electronic computer. The following comments have been extracted from Mr. Beemster's notes on computer operations and the processing and control of shipping notices and customer invoices:

To minimize inconvenience Louisville converted without change its existing data processing system, which utilized tabulating equipment. The computer company supervised the conversion and has provided training to all computer department employees (except key punch operators) in systems design, operations and programming.

Each computer run is assigned to a specific employee, who is responsible for making program changes, running the program and answering questions. This procedure has the advantage of eliminating the need for records of computer operations because each employee is responsible for his own computer runs.

At least one computer department employee remains in the computer room during office hours, and only computer department employees have keys to the computer room.

System documentation consists of those materials furnished by the computer company--a set of record formats and program listings. These and the tape library are kept in a corner of the computer department.

The company considered the desirability of programmed controls but decided to retain the manual controls from its existing system.

Company products are shipped directly from public warehouses which forward shipping notices to general accounting. There a billing clerk enters the price of the item and accounts for the numerical sequence of shipping notices from each warehouse. The billing clerk also prepares daily adding machine tapes ("control tapes") of the units shipped and the unit prices.

Shipping notices and control tapes are forwarded to the computer department for key punching and processing. Extensions are made on the computer. Output consists of invoices (in six copies) and a daily sales register. The daily sales register shows the aggregate totals of units shipped and unit prices which the computer operator compares to the control tapes.

All copies of the invoice are returned to the billing clerk. The clerk mails three copies to the customer, forwards one copy to the warehouse, maintains one copy in a numerical file and retains one copy in an open invoice file that serves as a detailed accounts receivable record.

Required:

Describe weaknesses in internal control over information and data flows and the procedures for processing shipping notices and customer invoices and recommend improvements in these controls and processing procedures. Organize your answer sheets as follows:

Weaknesses	Recommended Improvements

Number 4 (Estimated time--15 to 25 minutes)

The CPA firm of Wright & Co. is in the process of examining William Corporation's 1989 financial statements. The following open matters must be resolved before the audit can be completed:

(1) No audit work has been performed on non-responses to customer accounts receivable confirmation requests. Both positive and negative confirmations were used. A second re-

tive confirmations were used. A second request was sent to debtors who did not respond to the initial positive request.

(2) The client representation letter has not been completed and signed by William's management. Wright has started to outline the content of the representation letter and believes the following matters should be included in the letter: Management should acknowledge whether or not

- All material transactions have been properly reflected in the financial statements.

- It is aware of irregularities that could have a material effect on the financial statements or that involve management or employees.

- Events have occurred subsequent to the balance sheet date that would require adjustment to, or disclosure in, the financial statements.

- There are any communications from regulatory agencies concerning noncompliance with, or deficiencies in, financial reporting practices.

- The company has complied with all aspects of contractual agreements that would have a material effect on the financial statements in the event of noncompliance.

- There are any plans or intentions that may materially affect the carrying value or classification of assets or liabilities.

- There are any losses from sales commitments.

- There are any losses from purchase commitments for inventory quantities in excess of requirements or at prices in excess of market.

- There are any agreements to repurchase assets previously sold.

- There are any violations or possible violations of laws or regulations whose effects should be considered for disclosure in the financial statements or as a basis for recording a loss contingency.

- There are any capital stock repurchase options or agreements or capital stock reserved for options, warrants, conversions, or other requirements.

Required:

a. What alternative audit procedures should Wright consider performing on the nonresponses to customer accounts receivable confirmation requests?

b. Identify the other matters that Wright would expect to be included in William's management representation letter.

Number 5 (Estimated time--15 to 25 minutes)

Sturdy Corporation owns and operates a large office building in a desirable section of New York City's financial center. For many years the management of Sturdy Corporation has modified the presentation of their financial statements by:

1. Reflecting a write-up to appraisal values in the building accounts.
2. Accounting for depreciation expense on the basis of such valuations.

Wyley, a successor CPA, was asked to examine the financial statements of Sturdy Corporation, for the year ended December 31, 19X0. After completing the examination Wyley concluded that, consistent with prior years, an adverse opinion would have to be expressed because of the materiality of the apparent deviation from the historical-cost principle.

Required:

a. <u>Describe</u> in detail the form of presentation of the explanatory paragraph of the auditor's report on the financial statements of Sturdy Corporation for the year ended December 31, 19X0, clearly identifying the information contained in the paragraph. <u>Do not discuss deferred taxes.</u>

b. <u>Write a draft</u> of the opinion paragraph of the auditor's report on the financial statements of Sturdy Corporation for the year ended December 31, 19X0.

ANSWERS TO SAMPLE EXAMINATION
AUDITING ANSWER KEY

Answer 1

1. a	11. b	21. d	31. c	41. b	51. d
2. a	12. c	22. b	32. b	42. d	52. c
3. c	13. d	23. d	33. b	43. c	53. c
4. c	14. b	24. a	34. a	44. a	54. b
5. d	15. d	25. b	35. c	45. d	55. b
6. c	16. c	26. c	36. d	46. c	56. c
7. c	17. a	27. c	37. d	47. c	57. c
8. b	18. d	28. d	38. c	48. d	58. c
9. a	19. b	29. a	39. a	49. c	59. c
10. d	20. d	30. a	40. c	50. a	60. b

Answer 2

a.   Andrews should use following procedures
  • Send standard bank confirmation
      Direct liabilities
      Security agreements
  • Examine notes for terms, provisions, etc.
  • Review board meeting minutes
      Authority for transactions
      Dividends declared
  • Determine compliance with bank loan provisions
  • Consider effects of president's loans on debt/equity
  • Investigate business purpose of loan
  • Trace loan proceeds to cash receipts records
  • Trace interest and principal payments to cash disbursements records
  • Recompute and verify interest expense and accrual computations
  • Consider balance sheet presentation/disclosure
      Current/noncurrent portions
      Assets pledged as collateral
      Related party
  • Obtain management representation letter

b.   Broadwall's financials should include following related party disclosures
  • Nature of party's relationship
  • Description of the transaction
  • Dollar volume of the loans
  • Amounts due to president and terms of settlement

Answer 3

	Weakness		Recommended Improvements
1.	Computer department functions have not been properly separated. Under existing procedures one employee completely controls programming and operations.	1.	The functions of systems analysis and design, programming, machine operation and control should be assigned to different employees. This also should improve efficiency since different levels of skill are involved.
2.	Records of computer operations have not been maintained.	2.	In order to properly control usage of the computer, a usage log should be kept and reconciled with running times by the supervisor. The system also should provide for preparation of error lists on the console typewriter. These should be removable only by the supervisor or a control clerk independent of the computer operators.
3.	Physical control over computer operations is not adequate. All computer department employees have access to the computer.	3.	Only operating employees should have access to the computer room. Programmers' usage should be limited to program testing and debugging.
4.	System operations have not been adequately documented. No record has been kept of adaptations made by the programmer or new programs.	4.	The company should maintain up-to-date system and program flow charts, record layouts program listings and operator instructions. All changes in the system should be documented.
5.	Physical control over tape files and systems documentation is not adequate. Materials are unguarded and readily available in the computer department. Environmental control may not be satisfactory.	5.	Programs and tape libraries should be carefully controlled in a separate location. Preferably a librarian who does not have access to the computer should control these materials and keep a record of usage. The company should consult with the computer company about necessary environment controls.
6.	The company has not made use of programmed controls. Some of the procedures and controls used in the tabulating system may be unnecessary or ineffective in the computerized system.	6.	Programmed controls should be used to supplement existing manual controls, and an independent review should be made of manual controls and tabulating system procedures to determine their applicability. Examples of computer checks that might be programmed include data validity tests, check digits, limit and reasonableness tests, sequence checks and error routines for unmatched items, erroneous data and violations of limits.
7.	Insertion of prices on shipping notices by the billing clerk is inefficient and subject to error.	7.	The company's price list should be placed on a master file in the computer and matched with product numbers on the shipping notices to obtain appropriate prices.

Weakness	Recommended Improvements
8. Manual checking of the numerical sequence of shipping notices also is inefficient.	8. The computer should be programmed to check the numerical sequence of shipping notices and list missing numbers.
9. Control over computer input is not effective. The computer operator has been given responsibility for checking agreement of output with the control tapes. This is not an independent check.	9. The billing clerk (or another designated control clerk), should retain the control tapes and check them against the daily sales register. This independent check should be supplemented by programming the computer to check control totals and print error messages where appropriate.
10. The billing clerk should not maintain accounts-receivable detail records.	10. If receivable records are to be maintained manually, a receivable clerk who is independent of billing and cash collections should be designated. If the records are updated by the computer department, as recommended below, there still should be an independent check by the general accounting department.
11. Accounts-receivable records are maintained manually in an open invoice file.	11. These records could be maintained more efficiently on magnetic tape.
12. The billing clerk should not receive or mail invoices.	12. Copies of invoices should be forwarded by the computer department to the customer (or to the mailroom) and distributed to other recipients in accordance with established procedures.
13. Maintaining a chronological file of invoices appears to be unnecessary.	13. This file's purpose may be fulfilled by the daily sales register.
14. Sending duplicate copies of invoices to the warehouse is inefficient.	14. The computer can be programmed to print a daily listing of invoices applicable to individual warehouses. This will eliminate the sorting of invoices.

Answer 4

a. Since recipients of negative accounts
receivable confirmations are requested to
respond only if they disagree with the information in the confirmation, no additional
audit procedures are necessary on nonresponses
to negative accounts receivable confirmations.

For nonresponses to positive confirmations,
Wright should consider performing the following alternative audit procedures:

  • The use of other means, e.g., telephone inquiry, of directly communicating with
the debtor.
  • Examination of evidence of subsequent
cash receipts.
  • Examination of evidence of customer
orders, duplicate sales invoices, and shipping
documents.
  • Examination of William's files involving correspondence with the customers.

b. The other matters that Wright would expect
to be included in William's management representation letter are whether or not

  • Management acknowledges responsibility
for the fair presentation in the financial
statements of financial position, results of
operations, and changes in financial position
in conformity with generally accepted accounting principles (or other comprehensive basis
of accounting).
  • All financial records and data were
made available.
  • The accountant has been furnished with
copies of all minutes of meetings of stockholders, board of directors, and committees of
the board of directors (or other similar
bodies).
  • The company has satisfactory title to
all owned assets, and whether there are liens
or encumbrances on such assets or any pledging
of assets.
  • Provision, when material, has been
made to reduce excess or obsolete inventories
to their estimated net realizable value.
  • There are related party transactions
or related party receivables or payables that
have not been properly disclosed in the financial statements.
  • There are compensating balance or
other arrangements involving restrictions on
cash balances.

  • Unasserted claims or assessments that
management's counsel has advised are probable
of assertion have been disclosed in accordance
with Statement of Financial Accounting Standards No. 5.
  • There are other material liabilities
or gain or loss contingencies that are required to be accrued or disclosed.

Answer 5

a. A separate paragraph (preceding the
opinion paragraph) should set forth reasons
for the expression of an adverse opinion and
the principal effects of the subject matter of
the adverse opinion. The separate paragraph
should state the following, providing dollar
amounts where praticable:
  • The company carries its building
accounts at appraisal values and provides for
depreciation on the basis of such values.
  • Buildings, accumulated depreciation,
and equity (attributed to appraisals) are
overstated.
  • Net income is understated.
  • Depreciation expense is overstated.

b. The opinion paragraph should contain a
reference to the separate paragraph and state
that the financial statements do not present
fairly the financial position, results of
operations, and changes in financial position.
It should be worded as follows:

  In our opinion, because of the effects of
  the matters discussed in the preceding
  paragraph, the financial statements
  referred to above do not present fairly,
  in conformity with generally accepted
  accounting principles, the financial
  position of Sturdy Corporation as of
  December 31, 19X0, or the results of its
  operations or its cash flows for the year
  then ended.

EXAMINATION IN BUSINESS LAW
(Commercial Law)

NOTE TO CANDIDATES: Suggested time allotments are as follows:

	Point Value	Estimated Minutes* Minimum	Maximum
All questions are required:			
No. 1	60	110	130
No. 2	10	15	20
No. 3	10	15	20
No. 4	10	15	20
No. 5	10	15	20
Total	100	170	210

*   The time allocated to essay questions on recent business law exams has been 15 - 20 minutes per essay. In the past, however, longer essay questions were given. Some of these older questions are used in this sample examination in order to obtain a representative exam. Therefore, you may not be able to finish this exam in $3\frac{1}{2}$ hours. When you sit for the "real" exam, however, remember that you have only $3\frac{1}{2}$ hours to complete the Business Law Examination.

Number 1 (Estimated time--110 to 130 minutes)

Select the <u>best</u> answer for each of the following items.

1.   Fine Tuning, Inc. sent Watson a letter offering to sell Watson a custom made automobile for $75,000. Watson immediately sent a telegram to Fine purporting to accept the offer. However, the telegraph company erroneously delivered the telegram to Pine Tuna, Inc. Three days later, Fine mailed a letter of revocation to Watson which was received by Watson. Fine refused to sell Watson the automobile. Watson sued Fine for breach of contract. Fine
   a.   Will be liable for breach of contract.
   b.   Will avoid liability due to the telegraph company's error.
   c.   Will avoid liability since it revoked its offer prior to receiving Watson's acceptance.
   d.   Would have been liable under the deposited acceptance rule only if Watson had accepted by mail.

2.   A salesman for A & C Company called upon the purchasing agent for Major Enterprises, Inc., and offered to sell Major 1,500 screwdriver sets at $1.60 each. Major's purchasing agent accepted, and the following day sent A & C a purchase order which bore Major's name and address at the top and also had the purchasing agent's name and title stamped at the bottom with his initials. The purchase order recited the agreement reached orally the prior day. Subsequently, Major decided it did not want the screwdriver sets since it was overstocked in that item. Major thereupon repudiated the contract and asserted the Statute of Frauds as a defense. Under the circumstances, which of the following is correct?
   a.   The Statute of Frauds does not apply to this transaction since performance is to be completed within one year from the date of the making of the contract.
   b.   Major will lose but only if its purchasing agent's authority to make the contract was in writing.
   c.   The fact that an authorized agent of A & C did not sign the purchase order prevents its use by A & C against Major to satisfy the Statute of Frauds.
   d.   The purchase order is sufficient to satisfy the Statute of Frauds even though the purchasing agent never signed it in full.

3.   Montbanks' son, Charles, was seeking an account executive position with Dobbs, Smith, and Fogarty, Inc., the largest brokerage firm in the United States. Charles was very independent and wished no interference by his father. The firm, after several weeks deliberation, decided to hire Charles. They made him an offer on April 12, 1979, and Charles readily accepted. Montbanks feared that his son would not be hired. Being unaware of the fact that his son had been hired, Montbanks mailed a letter to Dobbs on April 13 in which he promised to give the brokerage firm $50,000 in commission business if the firm would hire

his son. The letter was duly received by Dobbs, and they wish to enforce it against Montbanks. Which of the following statements is correct?

   a. Past consideration is no consid-
       eration, hence, there is no
       contract.
   b. The pre-existing legal duty rule
       applies and makes the promise unen-
       forceable.
   c. Dobbs will prevail since the promise
       is contained in a signed writing.
   d. Dobbs will prevail based upon pro-
       missory estoppel.

4. Martin, a wholesale distributor, made a contract for the purchase of 10,000 gallons of gasoline from the Wilberforce Oil Company. The price was to be determined in accordance with the refinery price as of the close of business on the delivery date. Credit terms were net/30 after delivery. Under these circumstances, which of the following is true?

   a. If Martin pays upon delivery, he is
       entitled to a 2% discount.
   b. The contract being silent on the
       place of delivery, Martin has the
       right to expect delivery at his
       place of business.
   c. Although the price has some degree
       of uncertainty, the contract is en-
       forceable.
   d. Because the goods involved are tan-
       gible, specific performance is a
       remedy available to Martin.

5. Major Steel Manufacturing, Inc., signed a contract on October 2, 1978, with the Hard Coal & Coke Company for its annual supply of coal for three years commencing on June 1, 1979, at a price to be determined by taking the average monthly retail price per ton, less a ten cent per ton quantity discount. On March 15, 1979, Major discovered that it had made a bad bargain and that it could readily fulfill its requirements elsewhere at a much greater discount. Major is seeking to avoid its obligation. Which of the following is correct?

   a. The pricing term is too indefinite
       and uncertain, hence, there is no
       contract.
   b. Since the amount of coal required is
       unknown at the time of the making of
       the contract, the contract is too
       indefinite and uncertain to be
       valid.
   c. Major is obligated to take its
       normal annual coal requirements from
       Hard or respond in damages.
   d. There is no contract since Major
       could conceivably require no coal
       during the years in question.

6. Potter orally engaged Arthur as a salesman on April 5, 1978, for exactly one year commencing on May 1, 1978. Which of the following is correct insofar as the parties are concerned?

   a. If Arthur refuses to perform and
       takes another job on April 14, 1978,
       he will not be liable if he pleads
       the Statute of Frauds.
   b. The contract need not be in writing
       since its duration is exactly one
       year.
   c. Potter may obtain the remedy of
       specific performance if Arthur
       refuses to perform.
   d. The parol evidence rule applies.

7. Milbank undertook to stage a production of a well-known play. He wired Lucia, a famous actress, offering her the lead in the play at $2,000 per week for six weeks from the specified opening night plus $1,000 for a week of rehearsal prior to opening. The telegram also said, "offer ends in three days." Lucia wired an acceptance the same day she received it. The telegram acceptance was temporarily misplaced by the telegraph company and did not arrive until five days after its dispatch. Milbank, not hearing from Lucia, assumed she had declined and abandoned the production. Which of the following is correct if Lucia sues Milbank?

   a. The contract was automatically ter-
       minated when Milbank decided not to
       proceed.
   b. Lucia has entered into a valid con-
       tract and is entitled to recover
       damages if Milbank fails to honor
       it.
   c. Lucia may not take any other engage-
       ment for the period involved if she
       wishes to recover.
   d. Milbank is excused from any lia-
       bility since his action was reason-
       able under the circumstances.

8. Which of the following offers for the sale of the Lazy L Ranch is enforceable?

   a. Owner tells buyer she will sell the
       ranch for $35,000 and that the offer
       will be irrevocable for ten days.
   b. Owner writes buyer offering to sell
       the ranch for $35,000 and stating
       that the offer will remain open for
       ten days.
   c. Owner telegraphs buyer offering to
       sell the ranch for $35,000 and
       promises to hold the offer open for
       ten days.
   d. Owner writes buyer offering to sell
       the ranch for $35,000 and stating
       that the offer will be irrevocable
       for ten days if buyer will pay
       $1.00. Buyer pays.

9. The parol evidence rule prohibits contra-
diction of a written contract through the
proof of
    a. A previous oral contract.
    b. A subsequent written contract.
    c. The meaning or clarification of the
        contract's terms.
    d. A subsequent oral contract.

10. Higgins orally contracted to pay $3,500
to Clark for $4,000 of thirty-day accounts
receivable that arose in the course of Clark's
office equipment leasing business. Higgins
subsequently paid the $3,500. What is the
legal status of this contract?
    a. The contract is unenforceable by
        Higgins since the Statute of Frauds
        requirement has not been satisfied.
    b. If Higgins failed to notify the
        debtors whose accounts were pur-
        chased, they will, upon payment in
        good faith to Clark, have no lia-
        bility to Higgins.
    c. The contract in question is illegal
        because it violates the usury laws.
    d. Higgins will be able to collect
        against the debtors free of the
        usual defenses which would be as-
        sertable against Clark.

11. Duval Manufacturing Industries, Inc.
orally engaged Harris as one of its district
sales managers for an 18-month period commencing April 1, 1980. Harris commenced work
on that date and performed his duties in a
highly competent manner for several months.
On October 1, 1980, the company gave Harris a
notice of termination as of November 1, 1980,
citing a downturn in the market for its products. Harris sues seeking either specific
performance or damages for breach of contract. Duval pleads the Statute of Frauds
and/or a justified dismissal due to the
economic situation. What is the probable
outcome of the lawsuit?
    a. Harris will prevail because he has
        partially performed under the terms
        of the contract.
    b. Harris will lose because his termi-
        nation was caused by economic
        factors beyond Duval's control.
    c. Harris will lose because such a
        contract must be in writing and
        signed by a proper agent of Duval.
    d. Harris will prevail because the
        Statute of Frauds does not apply to
        contracts such as his.

12. Mathews is an agent for Sears with the
express authority to solicit orders from
customers in a geographic area assigned by
Sears. Mathews has no authority to grant
discounts nor to collect payment on orders

solicited. Mathews secured an order from
Davidson for $1,000 less a 10% discount if
Davidson makes immediate payment. Davidson
had previously done business with Sears
through Mathews but this was the first time
that a discount-payment offer had been made.
Davidson gave Mathew a check for $900 and,
thereafter, Mathews turned in both the check
and the order to Sears. The order clearly
indicated that a 10% discount had been given
by Mathews. Sears shipped the order and
cashed the check. Later, Sears attempted to
collect $100 as the balance owed on the order
from Davidson. Which of the following is
correct?
    a. Sears can collect the $100 from
        Davidson because Mathews contracted
        outside the scope of his express or
        implied authority.
    b. Sears can not collect the $100 from
        Davidson because Mathews as an agent
        with express authority to solicit
        orders had implied authority to give
        discounts and collect.
    c. Sears can not collect the $100 from
        Davidson as Sears has ratified the
        discount granted and made to
        Mathews.
    d. Sears can not collect the $100 from
        Davidson because although Mathews
        had no express or implied authority
        to grant a discount and collect,
        Mathews had apparent authority to do
        so.

13. For which of the following reasons would
the corporate veil most likely be pierced and
the shareholders held personally liable?
    a. The corporation is a personal
        holding company.
    b. The corporation was organized
        because the shareholders wanted to
        limit their personal liability.
    c. The corporation and its shareholders
        do not maintain separate bank ac-
        counts and records.
    d. The corporation's sole shareholder
        is another domestic corporation.

14. Phillips was the principal promoter of
the Waterloo Corporation, a corporation which
was to been incorporated not later than
July 31, 1981. Among the many things to be
accomplished prior to incorporation were the
obtaining of capital, the hiring of key
executives and the securing of adequate office
space. In this connection, Phillips obtained
written subscriptions for $1.4 million of
common stock from 17 individuals. He hired
himself as the chief executive officer of
Waterloo at $200,000 for five years and leased
three floors of office space from Downtown

Office Space, Inc. The contract with Downtown was made in the name of the corporation. Phillips had indicated orally that the corporation would be coming into existence shortly. The corporation did not come into existence through no fault of Phillips. Which of the following is correct?

a. The subscribers have a recognized right to sue for and recover damages.

b. Phillips is personally liable on the lease with Downtown.

c. Phillips has the right to recover the fair value of his services rendered to the proposed corporation.

d. The subscribers were <u>not</u> bound by their subscriptions until the corporation came into existence.

15. A corporation may not redeem its own shares when it

a. Is currently solvent but has been insolvent within the past five years.

b. Is insolvent or would be rendered insolvent if the redemption were made.

c. Has convertible debt that is publicly traded.

d. Has mortgages and other secured obligations equal to 50 percent of its stated capital.

16. Hapless is a bankrupt. In connection with a debt owed to the Suburban Finance Company, he used a false financial statement to induce it to loan him $500. Hapless is seeking a discharge in bankruptcy. Which of the following is a correct statement?

a. Hapless will be denied a discharge of any of his debts.

b. Even if it can be proved that Suburban did not rely upon the financial statement, Hapless will be denied a discharge either in whole or part.

c. Hapless will be denied a discharge of the Suburban debt.

d. Hapless will be totally discharged despite the false financial statement.

17. Hard Times, Inc. is insolvent. Its liabilities exceed its assets by $13 million. Hard Times is owned by its president, Waters, and members of his family. Waters, whose assets are estimated at less than a million dollars, guaranteed the loans of the corporation. A consortium of banks is the principal creditor of Hard Times having loaned it $8 million, the bulk of which is unsecured. The banks decided to seek reorganization of Hard

Times, and Waters has agreed to cooperate. Regarding the proposed reorganization

a. Waters' cooperation is necessary since he must sign the petition for a reorganization.

b. If a petition in bankruptcy is filed against Hard Times, Waters will also have his personal bankruptcy status resolved and relief granted.

c. Only a duly constituted creditors committee may file a plan of reorganization of Hard Times.

d. Hard Times will remain in possession unless a request is made to the court for the appointment of a trustee.

18. A bankrupt who has voluntarily filed for and received a discharge in bankruptcy

a. Will receive a discharge of any and all debts owed by him as long as he has <u>not</u> committed a bankruptcy offense.

b. Can obtain another voluntary discharge in bankruptcy after five years have elapsed from the date of the prior discharge.

c. Must surrender for distribution to the creditors amounts received as an inheritance if the receipt occurs within 180 days after filing of the petition.

d. Is precluded from owning or operating a similar business for two years.

19. Hack Company owned 100 tires which it deposited in a public warehouse on April 25, receiving a negotiable warehouse receipt in its name. Hack sold the tires to Fast Freight Co. On which of the following dates did the risk of loss transfer from Hack to Fast?

a. May 1—Fast signed a contract to buy the tires from Hack for $15,000. Delivery was to be at the warehouse.

b. May 2—Fast paid for the tires.

c. May 3—Hack negotiated the warehouse receipt to Fast.

d. May 4—Fast received delivery of the tires at the warehouse

20. Sample has in his possession a negotiable instrument which was originally payable to the order of Block. It was transferred to Sample by a mere delivery by Cox, who took it from Block in good faith in satisfaction of an antecedent debt. The back of the instrument read as follows, "Pay to the order of Cox in satisfaction of my prior purchase of a desk, signed Block." Which of the following is correct?

a. Sample has the right to assert Cox's rights, including his standing as a

holder in due course and also has
the right to obtain Cox's signature.
  b. Block's endorsement was a special
      endorsement, thus, Cox's signature
      was **not** required in order to negoti-
      ate it.
  c. Sample is a holder in due course.
  d. Cox's taking the instrument for an
      antecedent debt prevents him from
      qualifying as a holder in due
      course.

21. Which of the following will **not** constitute value in determining whether a person is
a holder in due course?
  a. The taking of a negotiable instru-
      ment for a future consideraton.
  b. The taking of a negotiable instru-
      ment as security for a loan.
  c. The giving of one's own negotiable
      instument in connection with the
      purchase of another negotiable in-
      strument.
  d. The performance of services rendered
      the payee of a negotiable instrument
      who endorses it in payment for ser-
      vices.

22. Nat purchased a typewriter from Rob. Rob
is not in the business of selling typewriters.
Rob tendered delivery of the typewriter after
receiving payment in full from Nat. Nat informed Rob that he was unable to take possession of the typewriter at that time, but would
return later that day. Before Nat returned,
the typewriter was destroyed by a fire. The
risk of loss
  a. Passed to Nat upon Rob's tender of
      delivery.
  b. Remained with Rob, since Nat had **not**
      yet received the typewriter.
  c. Passed to Nat at the time the con-
      tract was formed and payment was
      made.
  d. Remained with Rob, since title had
      not yet passed to Nat.

23. Kent, a wholesale distributor of cameras,
entered into a contract with Williams.
Williams agreed to purchase 100 cameras with
certain optional attachments. The contract
was made on October 1, 1976, for delivery by
October 15, 1976; terms: 2/10, net 30. Kent
shipped the cameras on October 6, and they
were delivered on October 10. The shipment
did not conform to the contract, in that one
of the attachments was not included. Williams
immediately notified Kent that he was rejecting the goods. For maximum legal advantage Kent's most appropriate action is to
  a. Bring an action for the price less
      an allowance for the missing attach-
      ment.

  b. Notify Williams promptly of his in-
      tention to cure the defect and make
      a conforming delivery by October 15.
  c. Terminate his contract with Williams
      and recover for breach of contract.
  d. Sue Williams for specific perform-
      ance.

24. Your client has in its possession the
following instrument

$700.000   Provo, Utah   June 1, 1983

Thirty days after date I promise to pay
to the order of
_____
              Cash
              Seven hundred   Dollars
at   Boise, Idaho

Value received with interest at the rate
of ten percent per annum.
This instrument is secured by a conditional sales contract.

No. 20   Due July 1, 1983   *Len Bowie*

This instrument is
  a. A negotiable time draft.
  b. A nonnegotiable note since it states
      that it is secured by a conditional
      sales contract.
  c. Not negotiable until July 1, 1983.
  d. A negotiable bearer note.

25. Which of the following on the face of an
otherwise negotiable instrument will affect
the instrument's negotiability?
  a. The instrument contains a promise to
      provide additional collateral if
      there is a decrease in value of the
      existing collateral.
  b. The instrument is payable six months
      after the death of the maker.
  c. The instrument is payable at a defi-
      nite time subject to an acceleration
      clause in the event of a default.
  d. The instrument is postdated.

26. Regarding certification of a check,
  a. Certification by a bank constitutes
      an acceptance of the check.
  b. Certification of a check obtained by
      the drawer releases the drawer.
  c. A bank is obligated to certify a
      customer's check if a holder demands
      certification and there are suffi-
      cient funds in the drawer's account.
  d. If a holder obtains certification of
      a check, all prior endorsers are
      discharged, but the drawer remains
      liable.

27. Which of the following is a valid defense against a holder in due course of a negotiable instrument?
   a.   Execution of the instrument by one without authority to sign the instrument.
   b.   Fraudulent statements made to the drawer as to the value of the consideration given for the instrument.
   c.   Duress on the drawer which renders the instrument voidable at the drawer's option.
   d.   Delivery of the instrument subject to a condition precedent which has yet to be performed.

28. Dilworth, an employee of Excelsior Super Market, Inc., stole his payroll check from the cashier before it was completed. The check was properly made out to his order, but the amount payable had not been filled in because Dilworth's final time sheet had not yet been received. Dilworth filled in an amount which was $300 in excess of his proper pay and cashed it at the Good Luck Tavern. Good Luck took the check in good faith and without suspecting that the instrument had been improperly completed. Excelsior's bank paid the instrument in due course. Excelsior is demanding that the bank credit its account for the $300 or that it be paid by Good Luck. Which of the following is correct?
   a.   Good Luck has <u>no</u> liability for the return of the $300.
   b.   Excelsior's bank must credit Excelsior's account for the $300.
   c.   A theft defense would be good against all parties including Good Luck.
   d.   Only in the event that negligence on Excelsior's part can be shown will Excelsior bear the loss.

29. Assuming each of the following is negotiable, which qualifies as a draft?
   a.   A bearer bond.
   b.   A trade acceptance.
   c.   A certificate of deposit.
   d.   A demand promissory note.

30. Wilmont owned a tract of waterfront property on Big Lake. During Wilmont's ownership of the land, several frame bungalows were placed on the land by tenants who rented the land from Wilmont. In addition to paying rent, the tenants paid for the maintenance and insurance of the bungalows, repaired, altered and sold them, without permission or hindrance from Wilmont. The bungalows rested on surface cinderblock and were not bolted to the ground. The buildings could be removed without injury to either the buildings or the land. Wilmont sold the land to Marsh. The deed to Marsh recited that Wilmont sold the land, with buildings thereon, "subject to the rights of tenants, if any,..." When the tenants attempted to remove the bungalows, Marsh claimed ownership of them. In deciding who owns the bungalows, which of the following is <u>least</u> significant?
   a.   The leasehold agreement itself, to the extent it manifested the intent of the parties.
   b.   The mode and degree of annexation of the buildings to the land.
   c.   The degree to which removal would cause injury to the buildings or the land.
   d.   The fact that the deed included a general clause relating to the buildings.

31. Marcross and two business associates own real property as tenants in common that they have invested in as a speculation. The speculation proved to be highly successful, and the land is now worth substantially more than their investment. Which of the following is a correct legal incident of ownership of the property?
   a.   Upon the death of any of the other tenants, the deceased's interest passes to the survivor(s) unless there is a will.
   b.   Each of the co-tenants owns an undivided interest in the whole.
   c.   A co-tenant cannot sell his interest in the property without the consent of the other tenants.
   d.   Upon the death of a co-tenant, his estate is entitled to the amount of the original investment, but not the appreciation.

32. Purdy purchased real property from Hart and received a warranty deed with full covenants. Recordation of this deed is
   a.   Not necessary if the deed provides that recordation is <u>not</u> required.
   b.   Necessary to vest the purchaser's legal title to the property conveyed.
   c.   Required primarily for the purpose of providing the local taxing authorities with the information necessary to assess taxes.
   d.   Irrelevant if the subsequent party claiming superior title had actual notice of the unrecorded deed.

33. Smith purchased a tract of land. To protect himself, he ordered title insurance from Valor Title Insurance Company. The policy was the usual one issued by title companies. Accordingly

a. Valor will **not** be permitted to take
    exceptions to its coverage if it
    agreed to insure and prepared the
    title abstract.

b. The title policy is assignable in
    the event Smith subsequently sells
    the property.

c. The title policy provides protection
    against defects in record title
    only.

d. Valor will be liable for any title
    defect which arises, even though the
    defect could **not** have been dis-
    covered through the exercise of
    reasonable care.

34. Moch sold her farm to Watkins and took
back a purchase money mortgage on the farm.
Moch failed to record the mortgage. Moch's
mortgage will be valid against all of the
following parties **except**

a. The heirs or estate of Watkins.

b. A subsequent mortgagee who took a
    second mortgage since he had heard
    there was a prior mortgage.

c. A subsequent bona fide purchaser
    from Watkins.

d. A friend of Watkins to whom the farm
    was given as a gift and who took
    without knowledge of the mortgage.

35. Peters defaulted on a purchase money
mortgage held by Fairmont Realty. Fairmont's
attempts to obtain payment have been futile
and the mortgage payments are several months
in arrears. Consequently, Fairmont decided to
resort to its rights against the property.
Fairmont foreclosed on the mortgage. Peters
has all of the following rights **except**

a. To remain in possession as long as
    his equity in the property exceeds
    the amount of debt.

b. An equity of redemption.

c. To refinance the mortgage with
    another lender and repay the ori-
    ginal mortgage.

d. A statutory right of redemption.

36. Tremont Enterprises, Inc. needed some
additional working capital to develop a new
product line. It decided to obtain intermediate term financing by giving a second mortgage
on its plant and warehouse. Which of the
following is true with respect to the mortgages?

a. If Tremont defaults on both mort-
    gages and a bankruptcy proceeding is
    initiated, the second mortgagee has
    the status of general creditor.

b. If the second mortgagee proceeds to
    foreclose on its mortgage, the first

mortgagee must be satisfied completely before the second mortgagee
is entitled to repayment.

c. Default on payment to the second
    mortgagee will constitute default on
    the first mortgage.

d. Tremont can **not** prepay the second
    mortgage prior to its maturity
    without the consent of the first
    mortgagee.

37. Lake purchased a home from Walsh for
$95,000. Lake obtained a $60,000 loan from
Safe Bank to finance the purchase, executing a
promissory note and mortgage. The recording
of the mortgage by Safe

a. Gives the world actual notice of
    Safe's interest.

b. Protects Safe's interest against the
    claims of subsequent bona fide pur-
    chasers for value.

c. Is necessary in order that Safe have
    rights against Lake under the pro-
    missory note.

d. Is necessary in order to protect
    Safe's interest against the claim of
    a subsequent transferee who does **not**
    give value.

38. The underlying rationale which justifies
the use of the coinsurance clause in fire
insurance is

a. It provides an insurable interest in
    the insured if this is **not** already
    present.

b. To require certain minimum coverage
    in order to obtain full recovery on
    losses.

c. It prevents arson by the owner.

d. It makes the insured more careful in
    preventing fires since the insured
    is partially at risk in the event of
    loss.

39. Overall, Inc. owns 100% of the stock of
Controlled Corporation, each being a separate
entity. Overall telephoned the Factory Supply
Company and ordered $400 of miscellaneous mer-
chandise. Overall told Factory to ship the
supplies to Controlled, and Overall would pay
for them. Factory did so and now seeks
recovery of the price or damages. Which of
the following is correct?

a. Overall is a surety.

b. The Statute of Frauds will **not** bar
    Factory from recovering from
    Overall.

c. Controlled is the principal debtor.

d. Overall and Controlled are jointly
    and severally liable on the
    contract.

40. Anthony is a surety on a debt owed by Victor to Day.
   a. Day must satisfy the Uniform Commercial Code's filing requirements in order to perfect his security interest.
   b. The surety undertaking need not be in writing if the surety is obtained by Victor at Day's request.
   c. The extension of credit by Day to Victor, contingent upon Anthony's agreeing to act as surety, provides the consideration for Anthony's promise.
   d. Upon default, Anthony would be allowed to deduct a personal claim that he has against Victor from his required payment to Day.

41. Dunlop loaned Barkum $20,000 which was secured by a security agreement covering Barkum's machinery and equipment. A financing statement was properly filed covering the machinery and equipment. In addition, Delson was a surety on the Barkum loan. Barkum is now insolvent, and a petition in bankruptcy has been filed against him. Delson paid the amount owed ($17,000) to Dunlop. The property was sold for $12,000. Which of the following is correct?
   a. Delson has the right of a secured creditor to the $12,000 via subrogation to Dunlop's rights and the standing of general creditor for the balance.
   b. To the extent Delson is not fully satisfied for the $17,000 he paid Dunlop, his claim against Barkum will not be discharged in bankruptcy.
   c. Delson's best strategy would have been to proceed against Barkum in his own right for reimbursement.
   d. Delson should have asserted his right of exoneration.

42. Alfred Matz negotiated with Basic Construction Company, Inc., to construct an apartment house. Desiring additional assurance of completion or payment of damages in the event of default, Matz insisted that a performance bond be posted. Basic obtained First Fidelity Surety Bonding Company as the surety on the undertaking. In addition to the normal terms of such contracts, First Fidelity insisted upon the right to complete the building in the event of default by Basic. The contract was drafted and signed by all the parties involved. Under the circumstances
   a. Basic Construction is the third-party beneficiary of the contract.
   b. If Basic Construction refuses to perform, Matz can obtain a court order obligating First Fidelity to complete construction.
   c. First Fidelity has assumed the primary obligation to perform.
   d. First Fidelity would be entitled to any and all rights that Matz would have against Basic in the event Basic defaults and First Fidelity pays.

43. Dilworth provided collateral to Maxim to secure Dilworth's performance of an obligation owed to Maxim. Maxim also obtained the Protection Surety Company as a surety for Dilworth's performance. Dilworth has defaulted, and Protection has discharged the obligation in full. Which of the following is the correct legal basis for Protection's assertion of rights to the collateral?
   a. Promissory estoppel.
   b. Exoneration.
   c. Indemnification.
   d. Subrogation.

44. A debtor will be denied a discharge in bankruptcy if the debtor
   a. Failed to timely list a portion of his debts.
   b. Unjustifiably failed to preserve his books and records which could have been used to ascertain the debtor's financial condition.
   c. Has negligently made preferential transfers to favored creditors within 90 days of the filing of the bankruptcy petition.
   d. Has committed several willful and malicious acts which resulted in bodily injury to others.

45. Chapter 11 of the Bankruptcy Reform Act of 1978 deals with reorganizations. This Chapter
   a. Is exclusively available to corporations.
   b. Permits the debtor-in-possession to continue to operate the business in the same manner as a Chapter 11 trustee.
   c. Provides for filing of voluntary petitions but prohibits the filing of involuntary petitions.
   d. Provides separate procedures for corporations with publicly-held securities.

46. Which of the following regarding workers' compensation is correct?
   a. A purpose of workers' compensation is for the employer to assume a definite liability in exchange for

the employee giving up his common law rights.

b. It applies to workers engaged in or affecting interstate commerce only.

c. It is optional in most jurisdictions.

d. Once workers' compensation has been adopted by the employer, the amount of damages recoverable is based upon comparative negligence.

47. Which of the following is a part of the social security law?

a. A self-employed person must contribute an annual amount which is less than the combined contributions of an employee and his or her employer.

b. Upon the death of an employee prior to his retirement, his estate is entitled to receive the amount attributable to his contributions as a death benefit.

c. Social security benefits must be fully funded and payments, current and future, must constitutionally come only from social security taxes.

d. Social security benefits are taxable as income when they exceed the individual's total contributions.

48. Issuer, Inc., a New York corporation engaged in retail sales within New York City, was interested in raising $1,600,000 in capital. In this connection it approached through personal letters eighty-eight people in New York, New Jersey, and Connecticut, and then followed up with face-to-face negotiations where it seemed promising to do so. After extensive efforts in which Issuer disclosed all the information that these people requested, nineteen people from these areas purchased Issuer's securities. Issuer did not limit its offers to insiders, their relatives, or wealthy or sophisticated investors. In regard to this securities issuance

a. The offering is probably exempt from registration under federal securities law as a private placement.

b. The offering is probably exempt from registration under federal securities law as a small offering.

c. The offering is probably exempt from registration under federal securities law as an intrastate offering.

d. The offering probably is not exempt from registration under federal securites law.

49. Securities available under a private placement made pursuant to Regulation D of the Securities Act of 1933

a. Must be sold to accredited institutional investors.

b. Must be sold to less than 25 nonaccredited investors.

c. Can **not** be the subject of an immediate reoffering to the public.

d. Can **not** be subject to the payment of commissions.

50. The Securities Act of 1933, in general, exempts certain small stock offerings from full registration. What is the maximum dollar amount which would qualify for this exemption?

a. $ 300,000

b. $1,500,000

c. $ 750,000

d. $1,000,000

51. The Securities Act of 1933 applies to the

a. Sale in interstate commerce of insurance and regular annuity contracts.

b. Sale by a dealer of securities issued by a bank.

c. Sale through a broker of a controlling person's investment in a public corporation.

d. Sale in interstate commerce of bonds issued by a charitable foundation.

52. The partnership of Maxim & Rose, CPAs, has been engaged by their largest client, a limited partnership, to examine the financial statements in connection with the offering of 2,000 limited-partnership interests to the public at $5,000 per subscription. Under these circumstances, which of the following is true?

a. Maxim & Rose may disclaim any liability under the Federal Securities Acts by an unambiguous, bold-faced disclaimer of liability on its audit report.

b. Under the Securities Act of 1933, Maxim & Rose has responsibility only for the financial statements as of the close of the fiscal year in question.

c. The dollar amount in question is sufficiently small so as to provide an exemption from the Securities Act of 1933.

d. The Securities Act of 1933 requires a registration despite the fact that the client is not selling stock or another traditional "security."

53. One of the major purposes of federal security regulation is to

a. Establish the qualifications for accountants who are members of the profession.

b.   Eliminate incompetent attorneys and accountants who participate in the registration of securities to be offered to the public.

c.   Provide a set of uniform standards and tests for accountants, attorneys and others who practice before the Securities and Exchange Commission.

d.   Provide sufficient information to the investing public who purchases securities in the marketplace.

54. In which of the following situations would an oral agreement without any consideration be binding under the Uniform Commercial Code?

a.   A renunciation of a claim or right arising out of an alleged breach.

b.   A firm offer by a merchant to sell or buy goods which gives assurance that it will be held open.

c.   An agreement which is a requirements contract.

d.   An agreement which modifies an existing sales contract.

55. Keats Publishing Company shipped textbooks and other books for sale at retail to Campus Bookstore. An honest dispute arose over Campus's right to return certain books. Keats maintained that the books in question could not be returned and demanded payment of the full amount. Campus relied upon trade custom which indicated that many publishers accepted the return of such books. Campus returned the books in question and paid for the balance with a check marked "Account Paid in Full to Date." Keats cashed the check. Which of the following is a correct statement?

a.   Keats is entitled to recover damages.

b.   Keats' cashing of the check constituted an accord and satisfaction.

c.   The pre-exisiting legal duty rule applies and Keats is entitled to full payment for all the books.

d.   The custom of the industry argument would have no merit in a court of law.

56. Marco Auto Inc., made many untrue statements in the course of inducing Rockford to purchase a used auto for $3,500. The car in question turned out to have some serious faults. Which of the following untrue statements made by Marco should Rockford use in seeking recovery from Marco for breach of warranty?

a.   "I refused a $3,800 offer for this very same auto from another buyer last week."

b.   "This auto is one of the best autos we have for sale."

c.   "At this price the auto is a real steal."

d.   "I can guarantee that you will never regret this purchase."

57. If a seller repudiates his contract with a buyer for the sale of 100 radios, what recourse does the buyer have?

a.   He can "cover," i.e., procure the goods elsewhere and recover the difference.

b.   He must await the seller's performance for a commercially reasonable time after repudiation.

c.   He can obtain specific performance by the seller.

d.   He can recover punitive damages.

58. A dispute has arisen between two merchants over the question of who has the risk of loss in a given sales transaction. The contract does not specifically cover the point. The goods were shipped to the buyer who rightfully rejected them. Which of the following factors will be the most important factor in resolving their dispute?

a.   Who has title to the goods.

b.   The shipping terms.

c.   The credit terms.

d.   The fact that a breach has occurred.

59. On July 14, 1976, Seeley Corp. entered into a written agreement to sell to Boone Corp. 1,200 cartons of certain goods at $.40 per carton, delivery within 30 days. The agreement contained no other terms. On July 15, 1976, Boone and Seeley orally agreed to modify their July 14 agreement so that the new quantity specified was 1,500 cartons, same price and delivery terms. What is the status of this modification?

a.   Enforceable.

b.   Unenforceable under the statute of frauds.

c.   Unenforceable for lack of consideration.

d.   Unenforceable because the change is substantial.

60. Allgood is a trustee of a trust in which Lance is the life beneficiary and Ronald is the remainderman who is entitled to the corpus (principal) upon the death of Lance. Five thousand shares of stock in Parkard Company make up a portion of the trust. In September 1977, Parkard declared a 10% stock dividend out of the earnings accumulated after the trust was created. Parkard also issued rights to subscribe to new stock, and the trustee sold these stock rights for $5,000. Regarding Allgood's duties as the trustee, which of the following is correct, assuming there is no

express provision covering the point in the trust indenture?

    a.   The proceeds from the subsequent sale of the 10% stock dividend must be divided proportionately between the beneficiaries.

    b.   The proceeds from the sale of the stock rights must be added to the corpus (principal) of the trust.

    c.   Allgood has discretion insofar as determining the proper share the beneficiaries are to receive in connection with the $5,000.

    d.   Allgood was obligated to obtain the consent of the beneficiaries prior to selling the stock rights.

Number 2 (Estimated time—15 to 20 minutes)

During the course of your year-end audit for a new client, Otis Corporation, you discover the following facts. Otis was incorporated in 1974 and is owned 94% by James T. Parker, President; 1% by his wife; and 5% by Wilbur Chumley. These three individuals were incorporators and are officers and directors of the corporation.

Otis manufactures and sells telephone equipment. In 1974, it sold approximately $350,000 of its various products almost exclusively in the state of its incorporation. In 1975, it began to branch out and sold $550,000 of its products throughout that state and $50,000 of its products in a neighboring state. Otis expanded rapidly, and 1976 was a banner year with sales of $1,250,000 and profits of $175,000. Otis constructed a small office building on a tract of land it had purchased for expansion purposes in the neighboring state and used the top floor to establish a regional sales office and rented the balance of the building.

During the course of your audit for the year 1976, you discover that Parker commingles his personal funds with those of the corporation, keeps very few records of board and shareholder meetings, and at his convenience disregards corporate law regarding separateness of personal and corporate affairs. The corporation had 1976 sales in excess of $300,000 in the neighboring state. The corporation has not filed any papers with the Secretary of State of that state in connection with these operations.

In light of the above discoveries, it was deemed prudent to examine the original incorporation papers which were filed by Parker in 1974. The following irregularities were discovered. The powers and purposes clause states that the geographical territory in which the newly created corporation was to do business was solely the state of incorporation. Next, a certified copy of the corporate charter was not obtained and filed in the county in which the corporation's principal place of business is located, as required by state law. Additionally, Mr. Chumley and Mrs. Parker did not sign the articles of incorporation, and prior to the effective date of incorporation, a lease was taken out and a car purchased in the corporate name.

Required:

Answer the following, setting forth reasons for any conclusions stated.

Discuss the legal problems which Otis may face as a result of the above facts. <u>Do not consider any tax implications</u>.

Number 3 (Estimated time—15 to 20 minutes)

Part a. The CPA firm of Martinson, Brinks & Sutherland, a partnership, was the auditor for Masco Corporation, a medium-sized wholesaler. Masco leased warehouse facilities and sought financing for leasehold improvements to these facilities. Masco assured its bank that the leasehold improvements would result in a more efficient and profitable operation. Based on these assurances, the bank granted Masco a line of credit.

The loan agreement required annual audited financial statements. Masco submitted its 1975 audited financial statements to the bank which showed an operating profit of $75,000, leasehold improvements of $250,000, and net worth of $350,000. In reliance thereon, the bank loaned Masco $200,000. The audit report which accompanied the financial statements disclaimed an opinion because the cost of the leasehold improvements could not be determined from the company's records. The part of the audit report dealing with leasehold improvements reads as follows

> Additions to fixed assets in 1975 were found to include principally warehouse improvements. Practically all of this work was done by company employees and the cost of materials and overhead were paid by Masco. Unfortunately, fully complete detailed cost records were not kept of these leasehold improvements and no exact determination could be made as to the actual cost of said improvements. The total amount capitalized is set forth in note 4.

In late 1976 Masco went out of business, at which time it was learned that the claimed leasehold improvements were totally fictitious. The labor expenses charged as leasehold improvements proved to be operating expenses. No item of building material cost had been recorded. No independent investiga-

tion of the existence of the leasehold improvements was made by the auditors.

If the $250,000 had not been capitalized,
the income statement would have reflected a
substantial loss from operations, and the net
worth would have been correspondingly decreased.

The bank has sustained a loss on its loan
to Masco of $200,000 and now seeks to recover
damages from the CPA firm, alleging that the
accountants negligently audited the financial
statements.

Required:

Answer the following, setting forth reasons
for any conclusions stated.

    1.   Will the disclaimer of opinion ab-
solve the CPA firm from liability?
    2.   Are the individual partners of
Martinson, Brinks, & Sutherland, who did not
take part in the audit, liable?

Part b. A CPA firm has been named as a
defendant in a class action by purchasers of
the shares of stock of the Newly Corporation.
The offering was a public offering of securities within the meaning of the Securities
Act of 1933. The plaintiffs alleged that the
firm was either negligent or fraudulent in
connection with the preparation of the audited
financial statements filed with the SEC.
Specifically, they alleged that the CPA firm
either intentionally disregarded, or failed to
exercise reasonable care to discover, material
facts which occurred subsequent to January 31,
1978, the date of the auditor's report. The
securities were sold to the public on
March 16, 1978. The plaintiffs have sub-
poenaed copies of the CPA firm's working
papers. The CPA firm is considering refusing
to relinquish the papers, asserting that they
contain privileged communication between the
CPA firm and its client. The CPA firm will,
of course, defend on the merits irrespective
of the questions regarding the working papers.

Required:

Answer the following, setting forth reasons for any conclusions stated.
    1.   Can the CPA firm rightfully refuse
to surrender its working papers?
    2.   Discuss the liability of the CPA
firm in respect to events which occur in the
period between the date of the auditor's
report and the effective date of the public
offering of the securities.

Number 4 (Estimated time--15 to 20 minutes)
    Number 4 consists of 2 unrelated parts

Part a. Davidson was one of Fenner Corporation's chief stock clerks. His net weekly
salary was $125. Unfortunately, he lost a
substantial sum of money betting on sports
events, and he owed $2,000 to the loan sharks.
Under these circumstances, he decided to raise
the amount of his paychecks to $725 per week.
His strategem was to wait until the assistant
treasurer, in whose office the paymaster check
imprinting machine was located, was away from
his desk. He would then go into the office
and artfully strike the number 7 over the
number 1 and raise the paycheck amount from
$125 to $725. The checks were promptly negotiated to Smith, a holder in due course, who
cashed them at his own bank, and the checks
were subsequently paid by Fenner's bank,
Beacon National. The fraudulent scheme was
discovered within a week after Beacon returned
Fenner's canceled checks for the month. By
that time five weekly paychecks had been
raised by Davidson and cashed by Smith.
Fenner promptly notified Beacon of the fraud.

Required:

Answer the following, setting forth
reasons for any conclusions stated.
    1.   To whom is Davidson liable?
    2.   What are the rights and liabilities
        of Fenner?
    3.   What are the rights and liabilities
        of Beacon?
    4.   What are the rights and liabilities
        of Smith?

Part b. Sill Corporation operates a retail appliance store. About a year ago, Sill
borrowed $3,000 from Castle to supplement its
working capital. At that time it granted to
Castle a security interest in its present and
future inventory pursuant to a written security agreement signed by both parties. Castle
duly filed a properly executed financing
statement a few days later. In the ordinary
course of business, a customer purchased a
$500 television set from Sill. The customer
knew of the existence of Castle's security
interest.

Required:

What rights does Castle have against
Sill's customer? Explain.

Number 5 (Estimated time--15 to 20 minutes)
(Number 5 consists of 2 unrelated parts)

Part a. Granville Motors, Inc. wished to acquire a 4-acre tract of land owned by Bonanza Realty Developers in an industrial city. Granville did not want to waste time and money considering the suitability of the property unless assured that the plant site would be available if studies indicated that the proposed purchase would be desirable. Granville did not discuss this concern with Bonanza but proposed to Bonanza that an option be drafted granting Granville 30 days in which to purchase the plant site for $62,950. Bonanza agreed and mailed to Granville the following written option

> For ONE DOLLAR ($1.00) and other valuable consideration, Bonanza Realty Developers hereby grants to Granville Motors, Inc., the exclusive option to purchase for SIXTY-TWO THOUSAND NINE HUNDRED FIFTY DOLLARS ($62,950) the 4-acre tract of land known as the N.E. corner site...(assume legal description included) for THIRTY (30) days. This option is exclusive and irrevocable and will automatically expire on September 15, 1977.

Joseph T. Verona
Joseph T. Verona, President
Bonanza Realty Developers

The letter containing the option was mailed on August 14, but due to a delay in the mails, did not reach Granville until August 18. Upon receipt Granville promptly engaged an expert to do a feasibility study with respect to the location and began to solicit bids on the construction of the proposed plant. Bonanza had no knowledge of these facts. Granville had no further correspondence with Bonanza after the receipt of the option, and Granville neither paid the $1.00 nor gave any other bargained for consideration.

On September 15, Jordan, Granville's President, telephoned Verona intending to accept the offer for Granville. However, before Jordan could accept, Verona stated that the property had already been sold at a higher price. The purchaser had no actual knowledge of the above facts. Jordan nevertheless accepted on Granville's behalf. The next day Jordan sent a written confirmation which stated that Granville expected performance by Bonanza, and that if Bonanza failed to perform, Granville would be forced to sue to protect its interests. Jordan also reminded Verona that the offer was irrevocable and that

substantial time, money, and effort had been expended in a feasibility study. In addition, Jordan noted the adverse effect which a refusal would have on Granville's future profits in that plans had been finalized calling for the plant to be on line by April 1978 to supply the increased demand of its customers.

Required:

Answer the following, setting forth reasons for any conclusions stated.
1.   Is the option legally binding on Bonanza?
2.   Assuming Granville will prevail, is specific performance available to Granville?
3.   Assuming Granville will prevail, what would Granville be entitled to recover if it seeks damages as a form of relief?

Part b. The Minlow, Richard, and Jones partnership agreement is silent on whether the partners may assign or otherwise transfer all or part of their partnership interests to an outsider. Richard has assigned his partnership interest to Smith, a personal creditor, and as a result the other partners are furious. They have threatened to remove Richard as a partner, not admit Smith as a partner, and bar Smith from access to the firm's books and records.

Required:

Answer the following, setting forth reasons for any conclusions stated.
Can Minlow and Jones successfully implement their threats? Discuss the rights of Richard and Smith and the effects of the assignment on the partnership.

ANSWERS TO SAMPLE EXAMINATION
BUSINESS LAW

Answer 1

1. a	11. c	21. a	31. b	41. a	51. c
2. d	12. c	22. a	32. d	42. d	52. d
3. a	13. c	23. b	33. d	43. d	53. d
4. c	14. b	24. d	34. c	44. b	54. d
5. c	15. b	25. b	35. a	45. b	55. b
6. a	16. c	26. a	36. b	46. a	56. a
7. b	17. d	27. a	37. b	47. a	57. a
8. d	18. c	28. a	38. b	48. d	58. d
9. a	19. c	29. b	39. b	49. c	59. b
10. b	20. a	30. d	40. c	50. b	60. b

Answer 2

The facts pose the following legal problems.

(1) Is there a valid corporate entity? There are two separate aspects of this problem. First, the incorporation was irregular. Second, there is a question whether the corporation is a mere sham.

It is possible that the irregularities in the original incorporation procedures would be of sufficient gravity to result in a finding that Otis was neither a corporation de jure nor de facto. This issue would not arise unless Otis encountered financial difficulty and it became necessary for a party to try to impose personal liability against Parker or others associated with him, such as directors, owners, and managers of Otis. When deciding the problem of de jure, de facto, or no corporation, the key legal factor that often is not clearly articulated by the courts is the question of deciding on what basis the plaintiff dealt with the corporation. Obviously, from a practical standpoint, all of the irregularities should be remedied by the corporation's attorney. Any existing contracts which were made prior to incorporation should be adopted by or re-executed in the corporate name.

By and large, courts are reluctant to disregard the corporate entity. This is so because the very purpose of incorporation is to permit the avoidance of personal liability. However, Parker has treated the corporation as his alter ego and has ignored its existence; consequently, a court may not respect the corporate entity in view of the fact that Parker himself has not. Certainly the commingling of funds and near total disregard for the formalities required by law would create problems for the corporation and Mr. Parker.

(2) What is the effect of doing business in the neighboring state without having first qualified to do business in that state?

The volume of business, the frequency of contact, and, most important, the fact that it has established a facility in the neighboring state is conclusive that Otis is doing business in that state. Under the circumstances, Otis was obligated to file the appropriate papers necessary to qualify for doing business in the neighboring state. Failure to do so can have serious legal consequences. Although the law varies from jurisdiction, the corporation may be subject to fines, penalties, or injunction proceedings to prohibit its carrying on business in the state. Furthermore, the corporation may be denied the right of access to the courts of the neighboring state. This has the effect of making its contracts legally unenforceable.

(3) What is the effect of doing business outside the state of incorporation, where the corporate charter is narrowly drafted and does not permit engaging in business outside of that state?

This question has not been adjudicated frequently by the courts in recent times. Current practice is to draft purposes and powers clauses in such a manner that virtually anything can be done at any time and anywhere by the corporation. Consequently, the charter under which Otis is operating, in this fact situation, raises the question of ultra vires. Currently, the courts by and large take a practical and sensible view of the matter. Although the contracts made in the neighboring state exceed the corporate purposes and powers as stated in the charter they are a fait accompli; therefore, they should be recognized as valid except in extraordinary circumstances which would not appear to be present in the facts given. From a practical standpoint, it is obvious that the corporate charter should be amended immediately to permit the corporation to do business anywhere and everywhere.

Answer 3

Part a.

1. No. The disclaimer of opinion will not absolve the CPA firm from liability. The auditor was negligent by failing either to take adequate measures to determine whether the leasehold improvements existed or to give notice that their existence had not been verified. As a result of such negligence and the bank's reliance upon the report, the CPA firm would be liable to the bank.

    An auditor generally will not be held responsible for limitations on the audit if the auditor's report gives adequate notice of them. A disclaimer of opinion is the means used by the auditor to give adequate notice of limitations. Although the CPA firm attempted to disclaim an opinion on the financial statements, the wording in the auditor's report was sufficiently unclear that it is doubtful a court would find the report accomplished its intended purpose. The disclaimer said only that the "actual cost" of the improvements could not be determined, and the explanation strongly implied that the improvements actually existed and had substantial value (by use of such phrases as "were found" and "work was done") when in fact they did not exist. Consequently, the report was misleading.

2. Yes. The individual partners of the CPA firm are liable even though they did not take part in the audit. A partnership is an entity that is an association of two or more persons as co-owners to carry on a business for profit. All partners are jointly and severally liable and therefore personally responsible for the firm's liability to the bank. The individual partners may have to satisfy the bank's claim from their personal assets, even though they did not personally take part in the audit.

Part b.

1. No. Neither federal nor common law recognizes the validity of the privilege rule insofar as accountants are concerned. Furthermore, even where the privilege rule is applicable, it can only be claimed by the client. Only a limited number of jurisdictions recognize the rule, and these jurisdictions have by statute overridden the common law rule which does not consider such communications to be within the privilege rule. The privilege rule applies principally to the attorney-client and doctor-patient relationships.

2. The Securities Act of 1933 requires a review by the auditor who reported on the financial statements accompanying the registration statement of events in the period between the date of the auditor's report and the date of the public sale of the securities. The auditors must show that they made a reasonable investigation, had a reasonable basis for their belief, and they did believe the financial statements were true as of the time the registration statement became effective. The auditor defendants have the burden of proving that the requisite standard was met. Therefore, unless the auditors can satisfy the foregoing tests, they will be liable.

Answer 4

Part a.

1. The embezzler, Davidson, is liable to whichever party bears the ultimate loss.

2. Fenner Corporation would normally be able to recover $600 per check from Beacon National because it has a real defense (material alteration), which is valid even against a holder in due course. However, Beacon National has a possible defense of contributory negligence by Fenner on the basis that Fenner did not exercise proper safeguards to prevent improper use of the check-imprinting machine. The Uniform Commercial Code provides that any person who by his negligence substantially contributes to a material alteration of the instrument is precluded from asserting the alteration against a holder in due course or against a drawee or other payor who pays the instrument in good faith and in accordance with the reasonable commercial standards of the drawee's or payor's business. In any event, Fenner is still liable to the extent of the original amount of $125 per check.

3. Normally, Beacon National must credit Fenner's account for the overpayments. It in turn has an action against the parties endorsing the instruments based upon a breach of their warranty that there were no material alterations. However, as discussed above, the possible defense of contributory negligence would be equally applicable here.

4. Smith, as a holder in due course, has the same rights and liabilities as Beacon National as they are given above.

Part b.

None. The Uniform Commercial Code provides that a retail customer in the ordinary course of business takes free of a security interest created by his seller even though the security interest is perfected and even though the buyer knows of its existence. A buyer in the ordinary course of business is, generally, a person who, in good faith and without knowledge that the sale to him is in violation of the ownership rights or security interest of a third party in the goods, buys goods from someone in the business of selling them.

By duly filing a financing statement, Castle permits security interest in then-existing as well as after-acquired inventory. Even though Castle held a perfected security interest in Sill's inventory, the customer who purchased the television set from Sill in the ordinary course of business took the property free of Castle's security interest.

Answer 5

Part a.

1. The option is not legally binding on Bonanza. The issue is whether the option fails for want of legal consideration. The option involved here must meet the necessary common law requirements to establish a legally enforceable contract. Since land is the subject matter of the option, it is tested under the common law rules as contrasted with the more liberal Uniform Commercial Code rule on options. The main pitfall is the lack of consideration. Despite the facts that the promise was written and was signed by the offeror, and that it recited consideration, and manifested a clear intent that it be irrevocable for 30 days, it is not legally binding. It is not supported by actual consideration and, therefore, fails to meet the requirements necessary to establish a valid contract under common law principles.

Neither the signed written offer, nor the expenditures made by Granville constitute consideration. With respect to the feasibility study, the parties did not bargain for the performance of such acts and expenditures by Granville in exchange for the promise contained in the option. The facts indicate that Bonanza had no knowledge that Granville was incurring the expense of a feasibility study prior to reaching a decision whether to exercise the option.

Although the courts generally are receptive to a formal satisfaction of the consideration requirement by the actual payment of $1.00 or some other bargained for token consideration, they do not accept fictional statements of receipt of consideration. If the option were valid, the acceptance would of course be timely even if made orally on September 15, provided the fact of acceptance could be established. One need not use the same means of communication in order to have a valid acceptance, provided it is received prior to the termination of the offer.

2. No. Although specific performance generally is not available as a remedy for breach of contract, there is a notable exception with respect to contracts for the sale of real property. Real property is deemed to be unique, and therefore, specific performance usually is available. However, when there has been a subsequent sale to a good faith third-party purchaser, the courts will let the title rest where they find it. Thus, Granville would fail unless the third party had actual or constructive notice of the option granted by Bonanza to Granville. If this option agreement had been recorded, the third party would be deemed to have constructive notice.

3. Granville would be limited to recovery of the typical contract measure of damages, that is, the difference between the fair market value and the contract price at the date the contract was to be performed. The sale at the higher price to the third party will have strong evidentiary value as to the fair market value. Recovery for the expenditures made it possible but not probable unless these facts were known to the seller and thus was within the contemplation of the parties at the time the contract was made. Such does not appear to be the case. This would also apply to the lost future profits. In addition, the lost future profits are at best speculative and would appear to be unattainable as damages.

Part b.

Unless there is an express prohibition against
the assignment of a partner's partnership
interest stated in the partnership agreement,
it is assignable. This rule applies whether
all or part of the partnership interest is
assigned. Probably the most common situation
in which a partner assigns his partnership
interest is in connection with collateralizing
a personal loan. Therefore, barring an express prohibition or a clause requiring the
consent of the other partners, Richard may
assign his interest.

 As a result of the above assignment,
Richard remains a partner. Although Richard
has assigned his partnership interest, he
still remains a partner and retains all of the
rights, privileges, perquisites, duties, and
liabilities he formerly had vis-a-vis the
partnership and his fellow partners. The
assignee (Smith) has only the right to
Richard's share of the profits in the event of
a default. He would succeed to Richard's
rights, in whole or in part, upon the dissolution and winding up of the partnership or upon
its bankruptcy. Smith does not, however,
succeed to Richard's right to access to the
partnership's books and records.

EXAMINATION IN ACCOUNTING PRACTICE - PART 1

NOTE TO CANDIDATES: Suggested time allotments are as follows:

All questions are required:	Point Value	Estimated Minutes Minimum	Maximum
No. 1	10	45	55
No. 2	10	45	55
No. 3	10	45	55
No. 4	10	40	50
No. 5	10	45	55
Total	50	220	270

Number 1 (Estimated time--45 to 55 minutes)

Select the best answer for each of the following items relating to a variety of financial accounting problems.

1.   On January 1, 1990, Platt Company issued 200,000 additional shares of $5 par value voting common stock in exchange for all of Drew Company's voting common stock in a business combination appropriately accounted for by the pooling of interests method. Immediately before the business combination the total stockholders' equity of Platt was $16,000,000 and of Drew was $4,000,000. Net income for the year ended December 31, 1990, was $1,500,000 for Platt, exclusive of any consideration of Drew, and $450,000 for Drew. During 1990, Platt paid $750,000 in dividends to stockholders. The consolidated stockholders' equity at December 31, 1990, should be
   a. $17,750,000
   b. $19,250,000
   c. $21,200,000
   d. $21,950,000

Items 2 and 3 are based on the following data:

On January 1, 1990, Rolan Corporation issued 10,000 shares of common stock in exchange for all of Sandin Corporation's outstanding stock. Condensed balance sheets of Rolan and Sandin immediately prior to the combination are as follows

	Rolan	Sandin
Total assets	$1,000,000	$500,000
Liabilities	$ 300,000	$150,000
Common stock		
($10 par)	200,000	100,000
Retained earnings	500,000	250,000
Total equities	$1,000,000	$500,000

Rolan's common stock had a market price of $60 per share on January 1, 1990. The market price of Sandin's stock was not readily ascertainable.

2.   Assuming that the combination of Rolan and Sandin qualifies as a purchase, Rolan's investment in Sandin's stock will be stated in Rolan's balance sheet immediately after the combination in the amount of
   a. $100,000
   b. $350,000
   c. $500,000
   d. $600,000

3.   Assuming that the combination of Rolan and Sandin qualifies as a pooling of interests, rather than as a purchase, what should be reported as retained earnings in the consolidated balance sheet immediately after the combination?
   a. $500,000
   b. $600,000
   c. $750,000
   d. $850,000

4.   On April 1, 1990, Union Company paid $1,600,000 for all the issued and outstanding common stock of Cable Corporation in a transaction properly accounted for as a purchase. The recorded assets and liabilities of Cable on April 1, 1990, were as follows

Cash	$160,000
Inventory	480,000
Property, plant, and equipment (net)	960,000
Liabilities	(360,000)

On April 1, 1990, it was determined that Cable's inventory had a fair value of $460,000 and the property, plant and equipment (net) had a fair value of $1,040,000. What is the amount of goodwill resulting from the business combination?
   a. $0
   b. $ 20,000
   c. $300,000
   d. $360,000

5.   Greenfield Company had the following cash balances at December 31, 1990.

Cash in banks $1,500,000
Petty cash funds (all funds were
  reimbursed on December 31, 1990)   20,000
Cash legally restricted for addi-
  tions to plant (expected to be
  disbursed in 1992)   2,000,000

Cash in banks includes $500,000 of compen-
sating balances against short-term borrowing
arrangements at December 31, 1990. The compensating balances are not legally restricted
as to withdrawal by Greenfield. In the current assets section of Greenfield's December 31, 1990 balance, what total amount should
be reported as cash?

    a. $1,020,000
    b. $1,520,000
    c. $3,020,000
    d. $3,520,000

6.   On January 1, 1990, Rey Corporation paid
$150,000 for 10,000 shares of Rio Corpora-
tion's common stock, representing a 15% investment in Rio. Rio declared and paid a
dividend of $1 a share to its common stock-
holders during 1990. Rio's net income was
$130,000 for the year ended December 31, 1990.
At what amount should Rey's investment in Rio
appear on Rey's balance sheet as of December 31, 1990?

    a. $140,000
    b. $150,000
    c. $159,500
    d. $169,500

7.   All of Glenn's sales are on a credit
basis. The following information is available
for 1990.

Allowance for doubtful accounts,
  1/1/90 $ 18,000
Sales   950,000
Sales returns   80,000
Accounts written off as uncol-
  lectible, 11/30/90   20,000

Glenn provides for doubtful accounts expense
at the rate of 3% of net sales. At December 31, 1990, the allowance for doubtful accounts balance should be

    a. $28,100
    h $26,500
    c. $26,100
    d. $24,100

8.   Q Co. prepares monthly income statements.
A physical inventory is taken only at year
end; hence, month-end inventories must be
estimated. All sales are made on account.
The rate of mark-up on cost is 50%. The following information relates to the month of
June 1990

Accounts receivable, June 1, 1990 $10,000
Accounts receivable, June 30, 1990   15,000
Collection of accounts receivable
  during June 1990   25,000
Inventory, June 1, 1990   18,000
Purchases of inventory during
  June 1990   16,000

    The estimated cost of the June 30, 1990
inventory would be

    a. $12,000
    b. $14,000
    c. $19,000
    d. $22,000

9.   On December 31, 1989, Kern Company
adopted the dollar value LIFO inventory
method. All of Kern's inventories constitute
a single pool. The inventory on December 31,
1989, using the dollar value LIFO inventory
method was $600,000. Inventory data for 1990
are as follows

12/31/90 inventory at year-end
  prices $780,000
Relevant price index at year end
  (base year 1989)   120

Under the dollar value LIFO inventory method,
Kern's inventory at December 31, 1990, would
be

    a. $650,000
    b. $655,000
    c. $660,000
    d. $720,000

10.   On January 1, 1990, Ward Corporation purchased a press for $90,000, which will be de-
preciated $9,000 per year for financial state-
ment reporting. For income tax reporting,
Ward uses the ACRS and will be allowed a cost
recovery deduction of $13,500 for 1990.
Assuming an income tax rate of 40%, how much
deferred income tax should be added to Ward's
deferred tax liability at December 31, 1990?

    a. $0
    b. $1,800
    c. $2,700
    d. $5,400

11.   On June 30, 1990, Eddy Corp. had outstanding 8%, $2,000,000 face amount conver-
tible bonds maturing on June 30, 2000. Interest is payable on June 30 and December 31.
Each $1,000 bond is convertible into 40 shares
of Eddy's $20 par common stock. After amorti-
zation through June 30, 1990, the unamortized
balance in the premium on bonds payable
account was $50,000. On June 30, 1990, 1,000
bonds were converted when Eddy's common stock
had a market price of $30 per share. Under
the book value method, what amount should Eddy
credit to additional paid-in capital in

recording the conversion?
a. $425,000
b. $400,000
c. $225,000
d. $200,000

12.   Farr Company pays its outside salespersons fixed monthly salaries and commissions
on net sales. Sales commissions are computed
and paid on a monthly basis (in the month
following the month of sale), and the fixed
salaries are treated as advances against commissions for this purpose. However, if the
fixed salaries for salespersons exceed their
sales commissions earned for a month, such excess is not charged back to them. Pertinent
data for the month of March 1990 for the three
salespersons in sales region 101 are as follows

Salesperson	Fixed salary	Net sales	Commission rate
A	$ 2,500	$100,000	2%
B	3,500	200,000	3%
C	4,500	300,000	3%
	$10,500	$600,000	

In respect of sales region 101, what total
amount should Farr accrue for sales commissions payable at March 31, 1990?
a. $ 6,500
b. $ 7,000
c. $17,000
d. $17,500

13.   Starr Trading Stamp Company records stamp
service revenue and provides for the cost of
redemptions in the year stamps are furnished
to licensees. Starr's past experience indicates that only 90% of the stamps sold to
licensees will be redeemed. Starr's liability
for stamp redemptions was $18,000,000 at
December 31, 1989. Additional information for
1990 is as follows

Stamp service revenue from stamps furnished to licensees	$10,000,000
Cost of redemptions	$ 8,500,000
Estimated cost of future re- demptions as a percentage of stamps redeemable	60%

What amount should Starr report as a liability
for stamp redemptions at December 31, 1990?
a. $ 9,500,000
b. $14,900,000
c. $18,500,000
d. $19,500,000

14.   On June 1, 1990, Ichor Company entered
into a ten-year noncancellable lease with
Gillie, Inc., for a machine owned by Gillie.
The machine had a fair value of $180,000 at

the inception of the lease. Ownership of the
machine is transferred to Ichor upon expiration of the lease. The present value of the
ten $30,000 annual lease payments, based on
Ichor's incremental borrowing rate of 12%, is
$190,000. The lease agreement specifies that
all executory costs are assumed by Ichor. How
much should Ichor record as an asset and corresponding liability at the inception of the
lease?
a. $0
b. $180,000
c. $190,000
d. $300,000

15.   Day Company carries a $10,000,000 compre-
hensive public liability policy which has a
$100,000 deductible clause. A personal injury
liability suit was brought against Day in
1990. Day's counsel believes it is probable
that the suit will be settled out of court for
an estimated amount of $150,000. In its De-
cember 31, 1990, balance sheet, Day should report an accrued liability of
a. $0
b. $ 50,000
c. $100,000
d. $150,000

16.   Following is the condensed balance sheet
of Fine Products, an individual proprietorship, at December 31, 1989

Current assets	$100,000
Equipment	200,000
Accumulated depreciation	(120,000)
	$180,000
Liabilities	$ 40,000
Silvia Fine, Capital	140,000
	$180,000

Fair market values of assets at December 31,
1989, were as follows

Current assets	$110,000
Equipment	290,000

The liabilities were fairly stated at book
values. On January 2, 1990, the proprietorship was incorporated, with 2,000 shares of
$20 par value common stock issued. How much
should be credited to additional paid-in
capital?
a. $100,000
b. $140,000
c. $320,000
d. $360,000

17.   The following information pertains to a
property dividend of marketable securities,
declared by Tyson Corp.

	Fair value
Declaration date--December 20, 1989	$300,000
Record date--January 10, 1990	310,000
Distribution date--January 28, 1990	305,000

Carrying value of the securities on Tyson's books was $200,000. How much gain should Tyson recognize in 1989 as a result of this property dividend?

    a. $0
    b. $100,000
    c. $105,000
    d. $110,000

18. On June 30, 1990, Gilman, Inc., declared and issued a 10% common stock dividend. Prior to this dividend Gilman had 20,000 shares of $10 par value common stock issued and out-standing. The market price of Gilman's common stock on June 30, 1990, was $24 per share. As a result of this stock dividend, by what amount should Gilman's total stockholders' equity increase (decrease)?

    a. $0
    b. $ 20,000
    c. $ 28,000
    d. $(48,000)

19. The stockholders' equity balances of Rice Corporation as of December 31, 1989, are as follows

Common stock, $10 par; 50,000 shares authorized; 25,000 shares issued	$250,000
Paid-in capital in excess of par	50,000
Retained earnings	100,000
Less treasury stock, 2,000 shares at cost	(32,000)
Total stockholders' equity	$368,000

On January 4, 1990, Rice sold the treasury shares on the open market at $20 per share. The entry to record this sale on Rice's books should include a credit to

    a.   Gain from sale of treasury stock of $8,000.
    b.   Paid-in capital from treasury stock of $8,000.
    c.   Retained earnings of $8,000.
    d.   Paid-in capital from treasury stock of $12,000.

20. Jordon Corporation has 80,000 shares of $50 par value common stock authorized, issued and outstanding. All 80,000 shares were issued at $55 per share. Retained earnings of the company amounts to $160,000. If 1,000 shares of Jordon common stock are reacquired at $62 and the par value method of accounting for treasury stock is used, stockholders' equity would decrease by

    a. $0
    b. $50,000
    c. $55,000
    d. $62,000

Number 2 (Estimated time--45 to 55 minutes)

    Select the best answer for each of the following items relating to a variety of financial accounting problems.

21. For the year ended December 31, 1990, Hurd, Inc. reported book income of $900,000 before income taxes. Selected information for 1990 is available from Hurd's records as follows:

Interest income on municipal bonds	$ 70,000
Depreciation claimed on tax return in excess of depreciation per books	130,000
Warranty expense on the accrual basis	60,000
Actual warranty expenditures	35,000

Hurd's income tax rate is 40% for 1990. Hurd's current liability for 1990 income taxes (before reduction for estimated taxes paid) should be

    a. $280,000
    b. $290,000
    c. $332,000
    d. $360,000

22. Hadley Construction Company has consistently used the percentage-of-completion method of recognizing income. During 1989 Hadley started work on a $3,000,000 construction contract which was completed in 1990. The accounting records provided the following data

	1989	1990
Progress billings	$1,100,000	$1,900,000
Costs incurred	900,000	1,800,000
Collections	700,000	2,300,000
Estimated cost to complete	1,800,000	

How much income should Hadley have recognized in 1989?

    a. $100,000
    b. $110,000
    c. $150,000
    d. $200,000

23. Anderson Company accepted a $20,000, 90-day, 12% interest-bearing note dated September 15, 1990, from a customer. On October 15, 1990, Anderson discounted the note without recourse at Provident National Bank at a 15% discount rate. The customer paid the note at

maturity. Based on a 360-day year, what amount should Anderson report as the loss on sale from the note transaction?

    a. $ 85
    b. $515
    c. $115
    d. $200

24. On January 2, 1990, Kiner Company sold the copyright to a book to Western Publishers, Inc., for royalties of 20% of future sales. The same date Western paid Kiner a royalty advance of $50,000 to be applied against royalties for 1991 sales. On September 30, 1990, Western made a $21,000 royalties remittance to Kiner for sales in the six-month period ended June 30, 1990. In January 1991, before issuance of its 1990 financial statements, Kiner learned that Western's sales of the book totaled $125,000 for the last half of 1990. How much royalty income should Kiner report in its 1990 income statement?

    a. $21,000
    b. $46,000
    c. $71,000
    d. $75,000

25. Hall Company owns an office building and leases the offices under a variety of rental agreements involving rent paid monthly in advance and rent paid annually in advance. Not all tenants make timely payments of their rent. Hall's balance sheets contained the following data

	1989	1990
Rentals receivable	$ 4,800	$ 6,200
Unearned rentals	16,000	12,000

During 1990 Hall received $40,000 cash from tenants. How much rental revenue should Hall record for 1990?

    a. $34,600
    b. $37,400
    c. $42,600
    d. $45,400

26. On December 27, 1990, Holden Company sold a building, receiving as consideration a $400,000 noninterest bearing note due in three years. The building cost $380,000, and the accumulated depreciation was $160,000 at the date of sale. The prevailing rate of interest for a note of this type was 12%. The present value of $1 for three periods at 12% is 0.71. In its 1990 income statement, how much gain or loss should Holden report on the sale?

    a. $ 20,000 gain.
    b. $ 64,000 gain.
    c. $ 96,000 loss.
    d. $180,000 gain.

27. The following information is available for The Gant Company for 1990

Freight-in	$ 20,000
Purchase returns	80,000
Selling expenses	200,000
Ending inventory	90,000

The cost of goods sold is equal to 700% of selling expenses.

What is the cost of goods available for sale?

    a. $1,390,000
    b. $1,490,000
    c. $1,500,000
    d. $1,590,000

28. The following expenses were among those incurred by Sayre Company during 1990

Accounting and legal fees	$160,000
Interest	60,000
Loss on sale of office equipment	25,000
Rent for office space	200,000

One-quarter of the rented premises is occupied by the sales department. How much of the expenses listed above should be included in Sayre's general and administrative expenses for 1990?

    a. $310,000
    b. $335,000
    c. $360,000
    d. $370,000

29. On July 1, 1990, Lundy Company issued for $438,000, five hundred of its 8%, $1,000 bonds. The bonds were issued to yield 10%. The bonds are dated July 1, 1990, and mature on July 1, 2000. Interest is payable semi-annually on January 1 and July 1. Using the interest method, how much of the bond discount should be amortized for the six months ended December 31, 1990?

    a. $3,800
    b. $3,100
    c. $2,480
    d. $1,900

30. Wayne, Inc., incurred the following costs during the year ended December 31, 1990

Laboratory research aimed at discovery of new knowledge	$150,000
Radical modification to the formulation of a chemical product	125,000
Research and development costs reimbursable under a contract to perform research and development for Apex Chemicals, Inc.	350,000
Testing for evaluation of new products	250,000

The total amount to be classified and expensed as research and development for 1990 is

- a. $150,000
- b. $275,000
- c. $525,000
- d. $625,000

31. On January 1, 1990, Stoner Corporation granted stock options to key employees for the purchase of 10,000 shares of the company's common stock at $25 per share. The options are intended to compensate employees for the next two years. The options are exercisable within a four-year period beginning January 1, 1992, by grantees still in the employ of the company. The market price of Stoner's common stock was $32 per share at the date of grant. Stoner plans to distribute up to 10,000 shares of treasury stock when options are exercised. The treasury stock was acquired by Stoner during 1989 at a cost of $28 per share and was recorded under the cost method. Assume that no stock options were terminated during the year. How much should Stoner charge to compensation expense for the year ended December 31, 1990?

- a. $70,000
- b. $35,000
- c. $30,000
- d. $15,000

32. On December 1, 1990, Studley Company leased office space for ten years at a monthly rental of $25,000. On the same date Studley paid the lessor the following amounts

Security deposit (refundable upon expiration of the lease)	$ 20,000
First month's rent	25,000
Last month's rent	25,000
Installation of new walls and offices	120,000

For the year ended December 31, 1990, Studley should record expense of

- a. $25,000
- b. $26,000
- c. $45,000
- d. $51,000

33. On December 31, 1989, Clark Company purchased marketable equity securities as a temporary investment. Pertinent data are as follows

Security	Cost	Market value at 12/31/90
W	$24,000	$26,000
X	36,000	33,000
Y	72,000	65,000

On December 31, 1990, Clark reclassified its investment in security Y from current to non-current because Clark intends to retain se-

curity Y as a long-term investment. What total amount of loss on these securities should be included in Clark's income statement for the year ended December 31, 1990?

- a. $0
- b. $1,000
- c. $7,000
- d. $8,000

34. Kipling Company does not carry insurance on its office typewriters. On December 28, 1989, one of its typewriters was stolen. The book value of the typewriter at the date of the burglary was $500. On January 15, 1990, another typewriter was vandalized. The book value of that typewriter, depreciated to the date of the vandalism, was $600. On February 1, 1990, before the issuance of the 1989 financial statements, the vandalized typewriter was repaired for $120. The total amount of losses that should be charged to income in 1989 is

- a. $0
- b. $ 500
- c. $ 620
- d. $1,100

35. The Standard Company leased a piece of equipment to the Piping Company on July 1, 1989, for a one-year period expiring June 30, 1990, for $90,000 a month. On July 1, 1990, Standard leased this piece of equipment to the Tacking Company for a three-year period expiring June 30, 1993, for $100,000 a month. The original cost of the piece of equipment was $6,000,000. The piece of equipment which has been continually on lease since July 1, 1985, is being depreciated on a straight-line basis over an eight-year period with no salvage value. Assuming that both the lease to Piping and the lease to Tacking are appropriately recorded as operating leases for accounting purposes, what is the amount of income (expense) before income taxes that each would record as a result of the above facts for the year ended December 31, 1990?

	Standard	Piping	Tacking
a.	$ 390,000	($540,000)	($600,000)
b.	$ 390,000	($540,000)	($975,000)
c.	$1,140,000	($165,000)	($225,000)
d.	$1,140,000	($915,000)	($600,000)

36. Art, Inc., decided on January 1, 1990, to discontinue its cinder block manufacturing division. The division, considered a reportable segment of the business, was sold on July 1, 1990. Division assets with a carrying value of $450,000 were sold for $300,000. Operating income from January 1 to June 30, 1990, for the division amounted to $90,000. Ignoring income taxes, what amount should be

reported on Art's income statement for the year ended December 31, 1990, under the caption "discontinued operations?"

a. $ 60,000
b. $ 90,000
c. $150,000
d. $240,000

37. Martin Company had the following account balances for the year ended December 31, 1990

Interest expense	$120,000
Loss on disposal of noncurrent investment	80,000
Write-down of plant and equipment to estimated realizable value	60,000

In its income statement for 1990, how much should Martin report as total extraordinary items?

a. $0
b. $140,000
c. $180,000
d. $200,000

38. During 1990, Olsen Company discovered that the ending inventories reported on its financial statements were understated as follows

Year	Understatement
1987	$50,000
1988	$60,000
1989	$0

Olsen ascertains year-end quantities on a periodic inventory system. These quantities are converted to dollar amounts using the FIFO cost flow method. Assuming no other accounting errors, Olsen's retained earnings at December 31, 1989, will be

a. Correct.
b. $ 60,000 understated.
c. $ 60,000 overstated.
d. $110,000 understated.

39. On December 31, 1990, King Company appropriately changed to the FIFO cost method from the weighted-average cost method for financial statement and income tax purposes. The change will result in a $350,000 increase in the beginning inventory at January 1, 1990. Assuming a 40% income tax rate, the cumulative effect of the accounting change reported for the year ended December 31, 1990, is

a $350,000
b. $210,000
c. $140,000
d. $0

40. In October 1990 Ewing Company exchanged

an old packaging machine, which cost $120,000 and was 50% depreciated, for a dissimilar used machine and paid a cash difference of $16,000. The market value of the old packaging machine was determined to be $70,000. For the year ended December 31, 1990, what amount of gain or loss should Ewing recognize on this exchange?

a. $0.
b. $ 6,000 loss.
c. $10,000 loss.
d. $10,000 gain.

Number 3 (Estimated time--45 to 55 minutes)

Select the best answer for each of the following items relating to a variety of financial accounting problems.

41. On January 15, 1990, Forrester Company paid property taxes on its factory building for the calendar year 1990 in the amount of $60,000. The first week of April 1990 Forrester made unanticipated major repairs to its plant equipment at a cost of $240,000. These repairs will benefit operations for the remainder of the calendar year. How should these expenses be reflected in Forrester's quarterly income statements?

	Three months ended			
	March 31, 1990	June 30, 1990	September 30, 1990	December 31, 1990
a.	$15,000	$ 95,000	$95,000	$95,000
b.	$15,000	$255,000	$15,000	$15,000
c.	$60,000	$240,000	$0	$0
d.	$75,000	$ 75,000	$75,000	$75,000

42. Information with respect to Roundtree Company's cost of goods sold for 1990 is as follows

	Units	Historical cost
Inventory, January 1, 1990	10,000	$ 530,000
Production during 1990	45,000	2,790,000
	55,000	3,320,000
Inventory, December 31, 1990	15,000	945,000
Cost of goods sold	40,000	$2,375,000

Roundtree estimates that the current cost per unit of inventory was $58 at January 1, 1990, and $72 at December 31, 1990. In Roundtree's supplementary information restated into average current cost, the cost of goods sold for the year ended December 31, 1990, should be

a. $2,290,000
b. $2,520,000
c. $2,600,000
d. $2,880,000

43. Hines Corporation reports operating profit as to industry segments in its supplementary financial information annually. The following information is available for 1990

	Sales	Traceable costs
Segment A	$ 750,000	$450,000
Segment B	500,000	225,000
Segment C	250,000	125,000
	$1,500,000	$800,000

Additional expenses not included above are as
follows

Indirect operating expenses	$240,000
General corporate expenses	180,000
Interest expense	96,000

Hines allocates common costs based on the
ratio of a segment's sales to total sales.
What should be the operating profit for
segment B for 1990?
   a. $103,000
   b. $135,000
   c. $163,000
   d. $195,000

44. The following information pertains to
Bass Co. for 1990

Merchandise purchased	$1,800,000
Cost of goods sold	2,000,000
Inventory at December 31, 1990	400,000

The inventory turnover for 1990 was
   a.   10.0
   b.   5.0
   c.   4.0
   d.   3.6

45. Bretton Corporation's books disclosed the
following information as of and for the year
ended December 31, 1990

Net credit sales	$2,000,000
Net cash sales	500,000
Merchandise purchase	1,000,000
Inventory at beginning	600,000
Inventory at end	200,000
Accounts receivable at beginning	300,000
Accounts receivable at end	700,000
Net income	100,000

Bretton's account receivable turnover is
   a.   2.9 times.
   b.   3.6 times.
   c.   4.0 times.
   d.   5.0 times.

46. Georgia, Inc., has an authorized capital
of 1,000 shares of $100 par, 8% cumulative
preferred stock and 100,000 shares of $10 par
common stock. The equity account balances at
December 31, 1990, are as follows

Cumulative preferred stock	$ 50,000
Common stock	90,000
Additional paid-in capital	9,000
Retained earnings	13,000
Treasury stock, common-- 100 shares at cost	(2,000)
	$160,000

Dividends on preferred stock are in arrears
for the year 1990. The book value of a share
of common stock, at December 31, 1990, should
be
   a. $11.78
   b. $11.91
   c. $12.22
   d. $12.36

47. Dale, Inc., a U.S. corporation, bought
machine parts from Kluger Company of West
Germany on March 1, 1989, for 30,000 marks,
when the spot rate for marks was $.4895.
Dale's year end was March 31, 1989, when the
spot rate for marks was $.4845. Dale bought
30,000 marks and paid the invoice on April 20,
1989, when the spot rate was $.4945. How much
should be shown in Dale's income statements as
foreign exchange gain or loss for the years
ended March 31, 1989 and 1990?

	1989	1990
a.	$0	$0
b.	$0	$150 loss
c.	$150 loss	$0
d.	$150 gain	$300 loss

48. Certain balance sheet accounts in a
foreign subsidiary of Rose Company at December 31, 1990, have been remeasured into United
States dollars as follows

	Remeasured at	
	Current rates	Historical rates
Accounts receivable, current	$200,000	$220,000
Accounts receivable, long-term	100,000	110,000
Prepaid insurance	50,000	55,000
Goodwill	80,000	85,000
	$430,000	$470,000

What total should be included in Rose's balance sheet at December 31, 1990, for the above
items? Assume the U.S. dollar is the functional currency.
   a. $430,000
   b. $435,000
   c. $440,000
   d. $450,000

Items 49 through 51 relate to data to be reported in the statement of cash flows of Pipe Company based on the following information:

Pipe Company
Balance Sheets

	December 31	
	1990	1989
Current Assets		
Cash	$631,000	$100,000
Accounts Receivable –net	750,000	575,000
Prepaid Expenses	15,000	25,000
Merchandise Inventory	350,000	400,000
Total Current Assets	$1,746,000	$1,100,000
Investment in Stage (equity method)	$ 99,000	$ 0
Property, Plant, and Equipment	800,000	1,000,000
Less Accumulated Depreciation	(275,000)	(300,000)
Total Assets	$2,370,000	$1,800,000
Liabilities		
Accounts Payable	$415,000	$320,000
Dividends Payable	15,000	10,000
Total Liabilities	$430,000	$330,000
Stockholder's Equity		
Common Stock	$1,000,000	$1,000,000
Retained Earnings	940,000	470,000
Total Liabilities and Stockholders Equity	$2,370,000	$1,800,000

Additional information available included the following:

• Net income for 1990 was $500,000.

• On January 1, 1990, Pipe Company purchased 30% of the net assets of Stage Company. The book value of Stage's net assets equaled $300,000 on January 1, 1990 which reflected their fair market value on this date. Stage reported net income of $40,000 for 1990 and paid total cash dividends of $10,000 during the year.

• During 1990, Pipe Company sold at a $20,000 gain equipment with a book value of $50,000. This was the only transaction affecting the Property, Plant, and Equipment account.

• Throughout 1990, Pipe Company declared a total of $30,000 in cash dividends.

49. Cash provided by Pipe's operations for 1990 was

a. $576,000
b. $573,000
c. $548,000
d. $448,000

50. Pipe's net cash used by investing activities during 1990 was
a. $90,000
b. $87,000
c. $20,000
d. $17,000

51. The net cash change from financing activities during 1990 was
a. 3,000 increase.
b. 25,000 decrease.
c. 5,000 increase.
d. 30,000 decrease.

52. Aprile Company had the following information for its noncontributory defined pension plan on December 31, 1990

Long-Term Expected Rate of Return	.08
Settlement-Basis Discount Rate	.08
Service Cost	$ 75,000
Projected Benefit Obligation	$700,000
Fair Value of Plan Assets	$300,000
Actual Return on Plan Assets	$ 60,000
Unamortized Prior Service Cost	$350,000
Average Remaining Service Period from Date Benefits Amended	16 years

What is pension expense for December 31, 1990?
a. $ 92,875
b. $109,875
c. $128,875
d. $176,875

53. At December 31, 1990, the following information is provided by the Mack Corporation after the corporation amends its pension plan giving retroactive benefits to its employees

Unrecognized prior Service Cost	$ 1,700,000
Plan Assets (at fair value)	$ 9,500,000
Accrued Pension Cost	$ 300,000
Market-related asset value	$ 5,800,000
Accumulated benefit obligation	$ 9,000,000
Projected benefit obligation	$10,000,000

What is the additional pension liability that must be recorded as of December 31, 1990?
a. $3,000,000
b. $2,700,000
c. $3,300,000
d. $0

54. An analysis and aging of the accounts receivable of Grey Company at December 31, 1990, revealed the following data

Accounts receivable	$900,000
Allowance for uncollectible accounts per books	50,000
Amounts deemed uncollectible	64,000

The net realizable value of the accounts receivable at December 31, 1990, should be
- a. $886,000
- b. $850,000
- c. $836,000
- d. $786,000

55. During 1990, the Commander Corporation acquired 3 pieces of machinery at an auction for a lump sum price of $240,000. In addition, Commander paid $12,000 to have the machines installed. An appraisal disclosed the following values

Machine A	$ 50,000
Machine B	$150,000
Machine C	$100,000

What costs should be assigned to Machines A, B, and C, respectively?
- a. $40,000, $120,000, and $ 80,000.
- b. $42,000, $126,000, and $ 84,000.
- c. $50,000, $150,000, and $100,000.
- d. $84,000, $ 84,000, and $ 84,000.

56. During 1989 Waldron Company introduced a new line of machines that carry a two-year warranty against manufacturer's defects. Based on industry experience, the estimated warranty costs related to dollar sales are as follows

Year of sale	4%
Year after sale	6%

Sales and actual warranty expenditures for the years ended December 31, 1989 and 1990, were as follows

	Sale	Actual warranty expenditures
1989	$ 500,000	$15,000
1990	700,000	47,000
	$1,200,000	$62,000

What amount should Waldron report as its estimated warranty liability at December 31, 1990?
- a. $0
- b. $16,000
- c. $42,000
- d. $58,000

57. Morgan Company determined that: (1) it has a material obligation relating to employees' rights to receive compensation for future absences attributable to employees' services already rendered, (2) the obligation

relates to rights that vest, and (3) payment of the compensation is probable. The amount of Morgan's obligation as of December 31, 1990, is reasonably estimated for the following employee benefits

Vacation pay	$100,000
Holiday pay	25,000

What total amount should Morgan report as its liability for compensated absences in its December 31, 1990, balance sheet?
- a. $0
- b. $ 25,000
- c. $100,000
- d. $125,000

58. On December 31, 1989, Kern Company leased a machine from Woods Company for a ten-year period expiring December 30, 1999. Equal annual payments under the lease are $50,000 and are due on December 31 of each year. The first payment was made on December 31, 1989, and the second payment was made on December 31, 1990. The present value at December 31, 1989, or the ten lease payments over the lease term discounted at 10% was $338,000. The lease is appropriately accounted for as a capital lease by Kern. In its December 31, 1990, balance sheet Kern should report the capitalized lease liability at
- a. $243,000
- b. $259,200
- c. $266,800
- d. $400,000

59. Ott Company began operations on January 1, 1989, and appropriately uses the installment sales method of accounting. The following data are available for 1989 and 1990

	1989	1990
Installment sales	$1,500,000	$1,800,000
Gross profit on sales	30%	40%
Cash collections from:		
1989 sales	500,000	600,000
1990 sales	--	700,000

The realized gross profit for 1990 is
- a. $720,000
- b. $520,000
- c. $460,000
- d. $280,000

60. Marsh, Inc., has an incentive compensation plan under which the president is paid a bonus of 10% of corporate income in excess of $100,000 before income tax but after deducting the bonus. The 1990 income before income tax and bonus is $430,000. The bonus should be
- a. $39,091
- b. $36,667
- c. $33,000
- d. $30,000

Number 4 (Estimated time--40 to 50 minutes)

The following information pertains to Woodbine Circle Corporation

Adjusted Trial Balance
December 31, 1990

	Dr	Cr.
Cash	$ 500,000	
Accounts receivable net	1,500,000	
Inventory	2,500,000	
Property, plant, and equipment	15,100,000	
Accumulated depreciation		$ 4,900,000
Accounts payable		1,400,000
Income taxes payable		100,000
Notes payable		1,000,000
Common stock ($1 par value)		1,100,000
Additional paid-in capital		6,100,000
Retained earnings, 1/1/86		3,000,000
Sales--regular		10,000,000
Sales--AL Division		2,000,000
Interest on municipal bonds		100,000
Cost of sales--regular	6,200,000	
Cost of sales--AL Division	900,000	
Administrative expenses--regular	2,000,000	
Administrative expenses--AL Division	300,000	
Interest expense--regular	210,000	
Interest expense--AL Division	140,000	
Loss on proposal of AL Division	250,000	
Gain on repurchase of bonds payable		300,000
Income tax expense	400,000	
	$30,000,000	$30,000,000

Other financial data for the year ended December 31, 1990:

Federal income taxes

Paid on Federal Tax Deposit Forms 503	$ 300,000
Accrued	100,000
Total charged to income tax expense (estimated)	$ 400,000*

*Does not properly reflect current or deferred income tax expense or distribution of income taxes among income statement sections

Income per tax return	$2,150,000
Tax rate on all types of taxable income	40%

Temporary difference

Depreciation, per financial statements	$ 600,000
Depreciation, per tax return	750,000

Permanent difference

Interest on municipal bonds	100,000

Discontinued operations

On September 30, 1990, Woodbine sold its Auto Leasing (AL) Division for $4,000,000. Book value of this business segment was $4,250,000 at that date. For financial statement purposes, this sale was considered as discontinued operations of a segment of a business. Since there was no phase-out period, the measurement date was September 30, 1990.

Liabilities

On June 30, 1990, Woodbine repurchased $1,000,000 carrying value of its long-term bonds for $700,000. All other liabilities mature in 1991.

Capital structure

Common stock, par value $1 per share, traded on the New York Stock Exchange:

Number of shares outstanding at 1/1/90	900,000
Number of shares sold for $8 per share on 6/30/90	200,000
Number of shares outstanding at 12/31/90	1,100,000

Required:

Using the multiple-step format, prepare a formal income statement for Woodbine for the year ended December 31, 1990, together with the appropriate supporting schedules. Recurring and nonrecurring items in the income statement should be properly separated. All income taxes should be appropriately shown.

Number 5 (Estimated time--40 to 50 minutes)

This problem consists of two unrelated parts.

Part a. Information concerning Tully Corporation's assets is a follows:

• On January 1, 1990, Tully signed an agreement to operate as a franchisee of Rapid Copy Service, Inc., for an initial franchise fee of $85,000. Of this amount, $25,000 was paid when the agreement was signed and the balance is payable in four annual payments of $15,000 each beginning January 1, 1991. The agreement provides that the down payment is not refundable and no future services are required of the franchisor. The present value at January 1, 1990, of the four annual payments discounted at 14% (the implicit rate for a loan of this type) is $43,700. The agreement also provides that 5% of the revenue from the franchise must be paid to the franchisor annually. Tully's revenue from the franchise for 1990 was $900,000. Tully estimates the useful life of the franchise to be ten years.

• Tully incurred $78,000 of experimental and development costs in its laboratory to develop a patent which was granted on January 2, 1990. Legal fees and other costs associated with registration of the patent totaled $16,400. Tully estimates that the useful life of the patent will be eight years.

• A trademark was purchased from Walton Company for $40,000 on July 1, 1987. Expenditures for successful litigation in defense of the trademark totaling $10,000 were paid on July 1, 1990. Tully estimates that the useful life of the trademark will be 20 years from the date of acquisition.

Required:

1. Prepare a schedule showing the intangibles section of Tully's balance sheet at December 31, 1990. Show supporting computations in good form.

2. Prepare a schedule showing all expenses resulting from the transactions that would appear on Tully's income statement for the year ended December 31, 1990. Show supporting computations in good form.

Part b. On January 1, 1990, Brock Corporation purchased a tract of land (site number 101) with a building for $600,000. Additionally, Brock paid a real estate broker's commission of $36,000, legal fees of $6,000, and title guarantee insurance of $18,000. The closing statement indicated that the land value was $500,000 and the building value was $100,000. Shortly after acquisition, the building was razed at a cost of $75,000.

Brock entered into a $3,000,000 fixed-price contract with Barnett Builders, Inc., on March 1, 1989, for the construction of an office building on land site number 101. The building was completed and occupied on September 30, 1990. Additional construction costs were incurred as follows:

Plans, specifications and blueprints	$ 12,000
Architects' fees for design and supervision	95,000

The building is estimated to have a forty-year life from date of completion and will be depreciated using the 150% declining balance method.

To finance the construction cost, Brock borrowed $3,000,000 on March 1, 1989. The loan is payable in ten annual installments of $300,000 plus interest of 14%. Brock's average amounts of accumulated building construction expenditures were as follows:

For the period March 1 to December 31, 1989	$ 900,000
For the period January 1 to September 30, 1990	2,300,000

Required:

1. Prepare a schedule which discloses the individual costs making up the balance in the land account in respect of land site number 101 as of September 30, 1990.

2. Prepare a schedule which discloses the individual costs that should be capitalized in the office building account as of September 30, 1990. Show supporting computation in good form.

3. Prepare a schedule showing the depreciation expense computation of the office building for the year ended December 31, 1990.

ANSWERS TO SAMPLE EXAMINATION
PRACTICE I

Answer 1		Answer 2		Answer 3	
1. c	11. c	21. b	31. b	41. a	51. b
2. d	12. b	22. a	32. b	42. c	52. c
3. c	13. b	23. c	33. d	43. d	53. d
4. c	14. b	24. b	34. b	44. c	54. c
5. b	15. c	25. d	35. a	45. c	55. b
6. b	16. c	26. b	36. a	46. b	56. d
7. d	17. b	27. b	37. a	47. d	57. d
8. b	18. a	28. a	38. a	48. c	58. c
9. c	19. b	29. d	39. b	49. a	59. c
10. b	20. d	30. c	40. d	50. c	60. d

Answer 4

Woodbine Circle Corporation
Income Statement
For the Year Ended December 31, 1990

Sales		$10,000,000
Cost of sales		6,200,000
Gross profit		$ 3,800,000
Less operating expenses:		
Administrative expense		2,000,000
Income from operations		$ 1,800,000
Other income:		
Interest income	100,000	
Other expense:		
Interest expense	(210,000)	(110,000)
Income from continuing operations before taxes		$ 1,690,000
Income taxes (Schedule 1)		
Current	576,000	
Deferred	60,000	636,000
Income from continuing operations		$ 1,054,000
Discontinued operations:		
(Schedules 2 and 3)		
Income from operations of Auto Leasing Division, less applicable income taxes of 264,000	396,000	
Loss on disposal of Auto Leasing Division, less applicable income of 100,000	(150,000)	246,000
Income before extraordinary item		$1,300,000

Extraordinary item:		
Gain on the redemption of bonds, net of income taxes of $120,000 (Schedule 4)		180,000
Net income		$1,480,000

Earnings per share of common stock (Schedules 5 and 6)

Income from continuing operations	$1.05
*Discontinued operations	.25
Income before extraordinary item	1.30
*Extraordinary item, net of tax	.18
Net Income	$1.48

*Not required by APBs 9, 15, or 30.

Schedule 1

Income Tax Expense on Continuing Operations

Income from continuing operations, before taxes	$1,690,000
Less interest on municipal bonds	100,000
Taxable income	$1,590,000
Tax rate	x 40%
Current income taxes on continuing operations	$ 636,000
Depreciation temporary difference	$ 150,000
Tax rate	x 40%
Deferred income taxes on continuing operations	$ 60,000

Schedule 2

Income from Discontinued AL Division

Sales	$2,000,000
Cost of Sales	900,000
Gross Profit	$1,100,000
Less operating expenses:	
Administrative expense	300,000

Operating income	$ 800,000
Other expense:	
Interest expense	140,000
Income from AL Division	
before taxes	$ 660,000
Income taxes ($660,000	
x 40%)	264,000
Income from discontinued	
AL Division	$ 396,000

Schedule 3

Loss on Disposal of Discontinued AL Division

Sales price of AL Division	$4,000,000
Book value of AL Division	4,250,000
Loss on sale of AL Division	
before tax benefit	($ 250,000)
Tax effect of loss ($250,000 x 40%)	100,000
Loss on disposal of discontinued AL Division (net of tax)	($ 150,000)

Schedule 4

Extraordinary Gain

Book value of bonds redeemed	$1,000,000
Repurchase cost	700,000
Gain on redemption of bonds	$ 300,000
Less income taxes ($300,000 x 40%)	(120,000)
Gain on redemption of bonds (net of tax)	$ 180,000

Schedule 5

Weighted Average Number of Shares Outstanding

Number of Shares outstanding, 1/1/90		900,000
Issued on 6/30/90	200,000	
x 6 months/year	x 6/12	100,000
Weighted average number of shares		1,000,000

Schedule 6

Per Share Data

	Income figure		Weighted average		Per share
Income from cont. ops.	$1,054,000	÷	1,000,000	=	$1.05
Discontinued operations	246,000	÷	1,000,000	=	.25
Income before X/O item	$1,300,000	÷	1,000,000	=	$1.30
Extraordinary item	180,000	÷	1,000,000	=	.18
Net income	$1,480,000	÷	1,000,000	=	$1.48

Answer 5

Part a.

1.

**Tully Corporation
Intangible Assets
December 31, 1990**

Franchise, net of accumulated amortization of $6,870 (Schedule 1)	$ 61,830
Patent, net of accumulated amortization of $2,050 (Schedule 2)	14,350
Trademark, net of accumulated amortization of $7,294 (Schedule 3)	42,706
Total intangible assets	$118,886

Schedule 1

Franchise

Cost of franchise on 1/1/90 ($25,000 + $43,700)	$68,700
1990 amortization ($68,700 x 1/10)	(6,870)
Cost of franchise, net of amortization	$61,830

Schedule 2

Patent

Cost of securing patent on 1/2/90	$16,400
1990 amortization ($16,400 x 1/8)	(2,050)
Cost of patent, net of amortization	$14,350

Schedule 3

Trademark

Cost of trademark on 7/1/87	$40,000
Amortization, 7/1/87 to 12/31/89 ($40,000 x 5/40)	(5,000)
Amortization, 1/1/90 to 7/1/90 (40,000 x 1/10)	(1,000)
Book value on 7/1/90	$34,000
Cost of successful legal defense on 7/1/90	10,000
Book value after legal defense	$44,000
Amortization, 7/1/90 to 12/31/90 ($44,000 x 1/17 x 6/12)	(1,294)
Cost of trademark, net of amortization	$42,706

2.   Tully Corporation
          Expense Resulting from Selected
                Intangibles Transactions
          For the Year Ended December 31, 1990

Interest expense ($43,700 x 14%)	$ 6,118
Franchise amortization (Schedule 1)	6,870
Franchise fee ($900,000 x 5%)	45,000
Patent amortization (Schedule 2)	2,050
Trademark amortization (Schedule 4)	2,294
Total expenses	$62,332

Note: The $78,000 of research and development
costs incurred in developing the patent would
have been expensed per SFAS 2 prior to 1990.

Schedule 4

Trademark Amortization

Amortization of original cost	
($40,000 x 1/20)	$ 2,000
Amortization of legal fees	
($10,000 x 1/17 x 6/12)	294
Total trademark amortization	$ 2,294

Part b.

1.   Brock Corporation
              Cost of Land (Site #101)
              As of September 30, 1990

Cost of land and old building	$600,000
Real estate broker's commission	36,000
Legal fees	6,000
Title insurance	18,000
Removal of old building	75,000
Cost of land	$735,000

2.   Brock Corporation
                  Cost of Building
              As of September 30, 1990

Fixed construction contract price	$3,000,000
Plans, specifications, and	
blueprints	12,000
Architects' fees	95,000
Interest capitalized during 1989	
(Schedule 1)	105,000
Interest capitalized during 1990	
(Schedule 1)	241,500
Cost of building	$3,453,500

Schedule 1

Interest Capitalized During 1989

Avg. accumulated construction expenditures	x	Interest rate for portion of year	=	Interest to be capitalized
1989:				
$ 900,000		x (14% x 10/12) =		$105,000
1990:				
$2,300,000		x (14% x 9/12) =		$241,500

3.   Brock Corporation
              Depreciation Expense on
                  Office Building
          For Year Ended December 31, 1990

Cost	$3,453,500
150% declining balance rate	
[(100% ÷ 40 years)	
x 1.5 = 3.75%]	x 3.75%
First full year's depreciation	$ 129,506
1990 (10/1 to 12/31) depre-	
ciation ($129,506 x 3/12)	$ 32,377

EXAMINATION IN ACCOUNTING PRACTICE - PART II

NOTE TO CANDIDATES: Suggested time allotments are as follows

	Point Value	Estimated Minutes	
All questions are required:		Minimum	Maximum
No. 1	10	45	55
No. 2	10	45	55
No. 3	10	45	55
No. 4	10	45	55
No. 5	10	40	50
Total	50	220	270

Number 1   (Estimated time - 45 to 55 minutes)

Select the best answer for each of the following items relating to a variety of financial accounting problems.

1.   Lee Company's current liabilities at December 31, 1990, totaled $1,500,000 before any necessary year-end adjustment relating to the following:

• On December 23, 1990, a vendor authorized Lee to return, for full credit, goods shipped and billed at $45,000 on December 10, 1990. The returned goods were shipped by Lee on December 29, 1990. A $45,000 credit memo was received and recorded by Lee on January 7, 1991.

• During December 1990, Lee received $75,000 from Marr, a customer, as an advance payment for a bottling machine which Lee will construct to Marr's specifications. From this transaction Lee has a $75,000 credit balance in its account receivable from Marr at December 31, 1990.

At December 31, 1990, what amount should Lee report as total current liabilities?

a. $1,455,000
b. $1,470,000
c. $1,530,000
d. $1,575,000

2.   Included in King Corporation's liability account balances at December 31, 1989, was a note payable in the amount of $2,400,000. The note is dated October 1, 1989, bears interest at 15%, and is payable in three equal annual payments of $800,000. The first interest and principal payment was made on October 1, 1990. In its December 31, 1990 balance sheet, what amount should King report as accrued interest payable for this note?

a. $ 60,000
b. $ 90,000

c. $180,000
d. $270,000

3.   Dean, Inc. has $2,000,000 of notes payable due June 15, 1990. At the financial statement date of December 31, 1989, Dean signed an agreement to borrow up to $2,000,000 to refinance the notes payable on a long-term basis. The financing agreement called for borrowings not to exceed 80% of the value of the collateral Dean was providing. At the date of issue of the December 31, 1989 financial statements, the value of the collateral was $2,400,000 and was not expected to fall below this amount during 1990. In its December 31, 1989 balance sheet, Dean should classify notes payable as

	Short-term obligations	Long-term obligations
a.	$2,000,000	$0
b.	$ 400,000	$1,600,000
c.	$ 80,000	$1,920,000
d.	$0	$2,000,000

4.   In its accrual basis income statement for the year ended December 31, 1990, Glen Corp. reported revenue of $1,550,000. Additional information was as follows:

Accounts receivable--December 31, 1989	$350,000
Accounts receivable--December 31, 1990	$550,000

Under the cash basis, how much should Glen report as revenue for 1990?

a. $1,000,000
b. $1,200,000
c. $1,350,000
d. $1,750,000

5.   On April 1, 1990, Fox, Inc. issued 400 of its 10%, $1,000 bonds at 97 plus accrued interest. The bonds are dated January 1, 1990

and mature on January 1, 2000. Interest is payable semiannually on January 1 and July 1. What amount of cash would Fox receive from the bond issuance?

    a. $378,000
    b. $388,000
    c. $393,000
    d. $398,000

6.   On July 1, 1990, Day Company purchased Parr Corp. ten-year, 8% bonds with a face amount of $400,000 for $358,000, which included $8,000 of accrued interest. The bonds, which mature on April 1, 1998, pay interest semiannually on April 1 and October 1. Using the interest method, Day recorded bond discount amortization of $1,500 for the six months ended December 31, 1990. From this long-term investment, Day should report 1990 revenue of

    a. $14,000
    b. $14,500
    c. $16,000
    d. $17,500

7.   On January 1, 1990, Wolf, Inc. issued its 10% bonds in the face amount of $500,000, that mature on January 1, 2000. The bonds were issued for $443,000 to yield 12%, resulting in bond discount of $57,000. Wolf uses the interest method of amortizing bond discount. Interest is payable July 1 and January 1. For the six months ended June 30, 1990, Wolf should report bond interest expense at

    a. $25,000
    b. $26,580
    c. $27,850
    d. $28,420

8.   Burg, Inc. issued $500,000 face amount of 10% bonds with interest payable on January 1 and July 1. The bonds were called in at 103 on July 1, 1990, and retired. Unamortized bond discount amounted to $40,000 at July 1, 1990. Burg's income tax rate is 40% for 1990. How much loss should Burg report on this early extinguishment of debt?

    a. $15,000
    b. $22,000
    c $33,000
    d. $55,000

9.   On May 1, 1990, Hill Corp. issued $2,000,000, 20-year, 10% bonds for $2,120,000. Each $1,000 bond had a detachable warrant eligible for the purchase of one share of Hill's $50 par common stock for $60. Immediately after bonds were issued, Hill's securities had the following market values:

10% bond without warrant	$1,040
Warrant	20
Common stock, $50 par	56

What amount should Hill credit to premium on bonds payable?

    a. $120,000
    b. $ 80,000
    c. $ 40,000
    d. $0

10.   Jay Dunn owns 50% of the common stock of Nolan Corp. Jay paid $10,000 for this stock in 1985. At December 31, 1990, it was ascertained that Jay's 50% stock ownership in Nolan had a current value of $90,000. Nolan's cumulative net income and cash dividends declared for the five years ended December 31, 1990, were $150,000 and $20,000 respectively. In Jay's personal statement of financial condition at December 31, 1990, how much should be shown as his net investment in Nolan?

    a. $90,000
    b. $85,000
    c. $75,000
    d. $10,000

11.   Luca and Mira formed a partnership on July 1, 1990, and contributed the following assets:

	Luca	Mira
Cash	$65,000	$100,000
Realty		300,000

The realty was subject to a mortgage of $25,000, which was assumed by the partnership. The partnership agreement provides that Luca and Mira will share profits and losses in the ratio of one-third and two-thirds respectively. Mira's capital account at July 1, 1990 should be

    a. $400,000
    b. $391,667
    c. $375,000
    d. $310,000

12.   Presented below is the condensed balance sheet of the partnership of Kane, Clark, and Lane who share profits and losses in the ratio of 6:3:1, respectively.

Cash	$ 85,000
Other assets	415,000
	$500,000
Liabilities	$ 80,000
Kane, capital	252,000
Clark, capital	126,000
Lane, capital	42,000
	$500,000

The assets and liabilities on the above balance sheet are fairly valued and the partnership wishes to admit Bayer with a 25% interest in the capital and profits/losses without recording goodwill or bonus. How much should Bayer contribute in cash or other assets?

    a. $ 70,000
    b. $105,000
    c. $125,000
    d. $140,000

13. James Dixon, a partner in an accounting firm, decided to withdraw from the partnership. Dixon's share of the partnership profits and losses was 20%. Upon withdrawing from the partnership he was paid $74,000 in final settlement for his interest. The total of the partners' capital accounts before recognition of partnership goodwill prior to Dixon's withdrawal was $210,000. After his withdrawal the remaining partners' capital accounts, excluding their share of goodwill, totaled $160,000. The total agreed upon goodwill of the firm was

    a. $120,000
    b. $140,000
    c. $160,000
    d. $250,000

14. The following condensed balance sheet is presented for the partnership of Alexander, Bell, and Graham, who share profits and losses in the ratio of 6:2:2, respectively.

Cash	$ 80,000
Other assets	280,000
Total	$360,000
Liabilities	$140,000
Alexander, capital	100,000
Bell, capital	100,000
Graham, capital	20,000
Total	$360,000

The partners agreed to liquidate the partnership after selling the other assets. If the other assets are sold for $160,000, how much should Alexander receive upon liquidation?

    a. $ 25,000
    b. $ 26,000
    c. $ 28,000
    d. $100,000

15. Kew Company leased equipment to Pitt on January 1, 1990, for an eight-year period expiring December 31, 1997. Equal payments under the lease of $300,000 are due on January 1 of each year. The first payment was made on January 1, 1990. The rate of interest contemplated by Kew and Pitt is 10%. The cash selling price of the equipment is $1,760,000, and the cost of the equipment on Kew's accounting records is $1,400,000. Kew appropriately recorded the lease as a sales-type

lease. For the year ended December 31, 1990, what amount of profits on the sale and interest income should Kew record?

    a. $0 and $0.
    b. $0 and $80,000.
    c. $360,000 and $146,000.
    d. $360,000 and $176,000.

16. Frey Company bought a building at auction on June 30, 1990 for $2,000,000. On July 15, 1990, before occupying the building, Frey sold it to a creditworthy company for $2,400,000. Frey received a cash down payment of $600,000 and a first mortgage note at the market rate of interest, for the balance. No additional payments were required of the buyer until July 1991. How much gain should Frey recognize on July 15, 1990 from the sale of the building?

    a. $0
    b. $100,000
    c. $400,000
    d. $600,000

17. In January 1990, the Under Mine Corporation purchased a mineral mine for $3,400,000 with removable ore estimated by geological surveys at 4,000,000 tons. The property has an estimated value of $200,000 after the ore has been extracted. The company incurred $800,000 of development costs preparing the mine for production. During 1990, 400,000 tons were removed and 375,000 tons were sold. What is the amount of depletion that Under Mine should record for 1990?

    a. $375,000
    b. $393,750
    c. $400,000
    d. $420,000

Items 18 and 19 are based on the following data:

At December 31, 1990 and 1989, Gravin Corporation had 90,000 shares of common stock and 20,000 shares of convertible preferred stock outstanding, in addition to 9% convertible bonds payable in the face amount of $2,000,000. During 1990, Gravin paid dividends of $2.50 per share on the preferred stock. The preferred stock is convertible into 20,000 shares of common stock and is considered a common stock equivalent. The 9% convertible bonds are convertible into 30,000 shares of common stock, but are not considered common stock equivalents. Net income for 1990 was $970,000. Assume an income tax rate of 40%.

18. How much is the primary earnings per share for the year ended December 31, 1990?

    a. $ 7.70
    b. $ 8.36

c. $ 8.82
d. $10.78

19. How much is the fully diluted earnings
per share for the year ended December 31,
1990?
  a. $ 7.70
  b. $ 8.21
  c. $ 9.35
  d. $10.22

20. An inventory loss from market decline of
$720,000 occurred in May 1990. King Company
appropriately recorded this loss in May 1990
after its March 31, 1990 quarterly report was
issued. How much of the inventory loss should
be reflected in King's quarterly income statement for the three months ended June 30, 1990?
  a. $720,000
  b. $360,000
  c. $180,000
  d. $0

Number 2 (Estimated time - 45 to 55 minutes)

     Select the best answer for each of the
following items relating to the federal income
taxation of individuals.

21. Ronald Raff filed his 1988 individual income tax return on January 15, 1989. There
was no understatement of income on the return,
and the return was properly signed and filed.
The statute of limitations for Raff's 1988
return expires on
  a.   January 15, 1991.
  b.   April 15, 1991.
  c.   January 15, 1992.
  d.   April 15, 1992.

     Items 22 through 26 are based on the
following data:

     Emil and Judy Ryan are married and file a
joint return. They have no children. Emil is
68 and Judy is 60. They contribute over half
of the support for Judy's mother, Cora, age
85, who earned $800 from baby-sitting jobs and
received $1,900 in social security benefits
during 1989. Cora lives alone in her own
apartment.

     Emil earned a salary of $60,000 in 1989
from his job at Korma Corp., where Emil is
covered by his employer's pension plan. Judy,
who worked part-time in 1989 and earned
$1,000, is not covered by an employer's pen-
sion plan. Other items received jointly by
Emil and Judy in 1989 were as follows:

Life insurance proceeds on the death of an unrelated friend	$8,000
Interest on income tax refund	100
Interest on life insurance policy's accumulated dividends	300
Dividends on stock of a Swiss cor- poration	500
Dividend on life insurance policy	200

22. How many exemptions should be claimed by
the Ryans for 1989?
  a.   Two.
  b.   Three.
  c.   Four.
  d.   Five.

23. The Ryans do not itemize their deductions. How much can they contribute and
deduct for contributions to their IRAs in
their 1989 return?
  a. $0
  b. $1,000
  c. $2,250
  d. $3,000

24. How much of the life insurance proceeds
should be reported by the Ryans in their 1989
return?
  a. $0
  b. $3,000
  c. $5,000
  d. $8,000

25. How much interest income should be
reported by the Ryans in their 1989 return?
  a. $0
  b. $100
  c. $300
  d. $400

26. How much of the dividends are reportable
by the Ryans in their 1989 return?
  a. $0
  b. $200
  c. $500
  d. $700

     Items 27 through 29 are based on the
following data:

     Bart Sheen, who is single, itemized his
deductions. Bart has investment income for
1989 of $1,200. The following were among
Bart's cash expenditures during 1989:

Interest on bank loan to purchase taxable securities	$1,000
Finance charges on a revolving charge account at a department store, based on monthly unpaid balances	400
Fourth quarter 1988 estimated state income tax	1,200

City real estate taxes on property owned by Bart and leased
to a tenant   3,000
Charitable contributions   5,000
Contribution to candidate for
public office   200

27. How much interest expense should Bart
include in his schedule of itemized deductions
for 1989?
    a. $0
    b. $ 280
    c. $1,080
    d. $1,400

28. How much should Bart include as taxes in
his schedule of itemized deductions for 1989?
    a. $0
    b. $1,200
    c. $3,000
    d. $4,200

29. How much should Bart include for
political contributions in his schedule of
itemized deductions for 1989?
    a. $0
    b. $ 50
    c. $100
    d. $200

Items 30 through 32 are based on the
following data:

During 1989 Burt Knox, who had adjusted
gross income of $60,000, made the following
unreimbursed personal expenditures:

Interest on note payable to a bank;
proceeds of loan were used to buy
municipal bonds $1,000
Payments pertaining to condominium
apartment occupied by Burt:
Interest ($3,000) and principal
($2,200) on mortgage   5,200
Realty taxes   1,800
State and city gasoline taxes   150
State hunting license fee   25
Legal fee for preparation of will   100
Education expenses to qualify for
new job in same occupation   975

30. What is Burt's deduction for miscellaneous itemized deductions for 1989?
    a. $0
    b. $ 975
    c. $1,075
    d. $1,150

31. How much interest expense should be included in Burt's 1989 itemized deductions?
    a. $6,200
    b. $5,200
    c. $4,000
    d. $3,000

32. How much should be included in Burt's
1989 itemized deductions for taxes?
    a. $1,800
    b. $1,825
    c. $1,950
    d. $1,975

Items 33 and 34 are based on the following data:

Gene Blake, who is single, had an adjusted gross income of $40,000 in 1989. Dur-
ing 1989 Gene paid the following unreimbursed
medical and dental expenses

Medical insurance premiums $ 300
Dental surgery   5,000

Also in 1989, Gene suffered a $8,000 loss due
to vandalism, for which Gene had no insurance.
Gene itemized his deductions for 1989.

33. How much was deductible in Gene's 1989
return for medical and dental expenses?
    a. $1,250
    b. $1,550
    c. $2,500
    d. $2,800

34. How much was deductible in Gene's 1989
return as a casualty loss?
    a. $0
    b. $ 100
    c. $3,900
    d. $4,000

35. On January 8, 1990, Sam Meyer, age 62
sold for $210,000 his personal residence which
had an adjusted basis of $60,000. On May 1,
1990, he purchased a new residence for
$80,000. Meyer elected the exclusion of real-
ized gain available to taxpayers over age 55.
For 1990, Meyer should recognize a gain
on the sale of his residence of
    a. $0
    b. $ 5,000
    c. $ 30,000
    d. $130,000

36. On July 1, 1987, William Greene paid
$45,000 for 450 shares of Acme Corporation
common stock. Greene received a nontaxable
stock dividend of 50 new common shares in
February 1989. On February 15, 1989, Greene
sold the 50 new shares of common stock for
$5,500. In respect of this sale Greene should
report on his 1989 tax return
    a.   No gain or loss since the stock div-
         idend was nontaxable.
    b. $500 of long-term capital gain.
    c. $1,000 of long-term capital gain.
    d. $5,500 of long-term capital gain.

37. Ray Birch, age 60, is single with no dependents. Birch's only income is from his occupation as a self-employed plumber. Birch owns the following assets used in his plumbing business

	Adjusted basis
Land on which a storage shack is erected	$ 3,000
Shack for storage of plumbing supplies	12,000

The capital assets used by Birch in his business amount to
   a. $0
   b. $ 3,000
   c. $12,000
   d. $15,000

Items 38 and 39 are based on the following data:

On April 1, 1989, Kim sold 100 shares of Ral Corp. stock. Kim had received this stock on March 1, 1989 as a bequest from the estate of John Wolf who died on January 2, 1989, when this stock had a fair market value of $8,000. The executor of John's estate did not elect the alternate valuation. John had bought this stock in 1986 for $1,000.

38. Kim's basis for the 100 shares of Ral stock was
   a. $0
   b. $ 1,000
   c. $ 8,000
   d. $10,000

39. Kim's holding period for the 100 shares of Ral stock was
   a. Long-term.
   b. Short-term.
   c. Long-term if sold at a gain; short-term if sold at a loss.
   d. Short-term if sold at a gain; long-term if sold at a loss.

40. In January 1987, Kirk Kelly bought 100 shares of a listed stock for $8,000. In March 1988, when the fair market value was $6,000, Kirk gave this stock to his cousin, Clara. No gift tax was paid. Clara sold this stock in January 1989 for $7,000. How much is Clara's reportable gain or loss in 1989 on the sale of this stock?
   a. $0.
   b. $1,000 loss.
   c. $1,000 gain.
   d. $7,000 gain.

Number 3   (Estimated time – 45 to 55 minutes)

Select the best answer for each of the following items relating to the federal income taxation of corporations, partnerships, and tax exempt organizations.

41. The holding period of property acquired by a partnership as a contribution to the contributing partner's capital account
   a. Includes the period during which the property was held by the contributing partner.
   b. Is subtracted from the period during which the property was held by the contributing partner.
   c. Begins with the date of contribution to the partnership.
   d. Depends on whether the transfer to the partnership results in a gain or a loss to the contributing partner.

42. On October 1, 1989, Adam Krol received a 10% interest in the capital of Fine & Co., a partnership, for past services rendered. Fine's net assets at October 1 had a basis of $140,000 and a fair market value of $200,000. How much ordinary income should Adam include in his 1989 return for the partnership interest transferred to him by the other partners?
   a. $20,000
   b. $14,000
   c. $ 6,000
   d. $0

43. The following information pertains to land contributed by Earl Mott for a 50% interest in a new partnership:

Adjusted basis to Mott	$50,000
Fair market value	90,000
Mortgage assumed by partnership	10,000

Mott's basis for his partnership interest is
   a. $40,000
   b. $45,000
   c. $55,000
   d. $80,000

44. In computing the ordinary income of a partnership, a deduction is allowed for
   a. Guaranteed payments to partners.
   b. Short-term capital losses.
   c. Investment interest expense.
   d. Contributions to recognized charities.

45. Fred Elk's adjusted basis of his partnership interest in Arias & Nido was $30,000. Elk received a current nonliquidating distribution of $12,000 cash, plus property with a

fair market value of $26,000 and an adjusted basis to the partnership of $24,000. How much is Elk's basis for the distributed property?
- a. $18,000
- b. $24,000
- c. $26,000
- d. $30,000

46. At December 31, 1989, Max Curcio's adjusted basis in the partnership of Maduro & Motta was $36,000. On December 31, 1989, Maduro & Motta distributed cash of $6,000 and a parcel of land to Curcio in liquidation of Curcio's entire interest in the partnership. The land had an adjusted basis of $18,000 to the partnership and a fair market value of $42,000 at December 31, 1989. How much is Curcio's basis in the land?
- a. $0
- b. $12,000
- c. $30,000
- d. $36,000

47. Axel, Banner & Carr, a calendar-year partnership, had the following partners since 1970:

	Partnership interest (%)
Axel	20
Banner	20
Carr	60

On October 20, 1989, Axel and Banner sold their partnership interests to Carr and withdrew from participation in the partnership's affairs. At what date was the partnership terminated for tax purposes?
- a. October 1, 1989.
- b. October 20, 1989.
- c. October 31, 1989.
- d. December 31, 1989.

48. James Bell, CPA, a sole practitioner reporting on the cash basis, incorporated his accounting practice in 1989, transferring the following assets to the newly formed corporation:

Cash	$ 5,000
Office furniture and equipment:	
Adjusted basis	35,000
Fair market value	45,000

No liabilities were transferred, and there were no other stockholders. The corporation's total basis for the transferred assets is
- a. $35,000
- b. $40,000
- c. $45,000
- d. $50,000

49. During 1989 Wyld Corp., in need of additional factory space, exchanged 10,000 shares of its common stock with a par value of $50,000 for a building with a fair market value of $60,000. On the date of the exchange the stock had a fair market value of $65,000. For 1989, how much and what type of gain or loss should Wyld report on this transaction?
- a. $10,000 section 1231 gain.
- b. $10,000 capital gain.
- c. $ 5,000 capital loss.
- d. No gain or loss.

50. At January 1, 1989, Pearl Corp. owned 90% of the outstanding stock of Seso Corp. Both companies were domestic corporations. Pursuant to a plan of liquidation adopted by Seso in March 1989, Seso distributed all of its property in April 1989, in complete redemption of all its stock, when Seso's accumulated earnings equalled $18,000. Seso had never been insolvent. Pursuant to the liquidation, Seso transferred to Pearl a parcel of land with a basis of $10,000 and a fair market value of $40,000. How much gain must Seso recognize in 1989 on the transfer of this land to Pearl?
- a. $0
- b. $18,000
- c. $27,000
- d. $30,000

51. If a corporation's charitable contributions exceed the limitation for deductibility in a particular year, such excess
- a. Is not deductible in any future year.
- b. Becomes a carryover to a maximum of 5 succeeding years.
- c. May be carried back to the third preceding year.
- d. Reduces the corporation's capital loss carryback for that year.

52. Ram Corp.'s operating income for the year ended December 31, 1989 amounted to $100,000. In addition, Ram received $2,000 in dividends from a 20%-owned taxable domestic corporation in 1989. In Ram's 1989 tax return, what amount should be included in taxable income for the dividends?
- a. $ 300
- b. $ 400
- c. $1,600
- d. $1,700

53. The filing of consolidated returns is available
- a. Only to parent-subsidiary corporations.

b.   Only to brother-sister corporations.
c.   Either to parent-subsidiary corporations or to brother-sister corporations.
d.   Neither to parent-subsidiary corporations nor to brother-sister corporations.

54. Pursuant to a plan of corporate reorganization adopted in 1989, Emil Gow exchanged 2,000 shares of Bly Corp. common stock for 3,600 shares of Rolf Corp. common stock. Gow had paid $75,000 for the Bly stock. The fair market value of the Rolf stock was $86,000 on the date of the exchange. As a result of this exchange, how much was Gow's recognized gain and his basis in the Rolf stock?

	Recognized gain	Basis
a.	$11,000	$86,000
b.	$11,000	$75,000
c.	$0	$86,000
d.	$0	$75,000

55. The accumulated earnings tax can be imposed
a.   Regardless of the number of stockholders of a corporation.
b.   On both partnerships and corporations.
c.   On companies that make distributions in excess of accumulated earnings.
d.   Only on parent-subsidiary affiliated groups.

56. The accumulated earnings tax does not apply to
a.   Corporations filing consolidated returns.
b.   Corporations that have preferred stock outstanding.
c.   Personal holding companies.
d.   Corporations that have more than 35 stockholders.

57. The personal holding company tax
a.   May be imposed regardless of the number of equal stockholders in a corporation.
b.   Should be self-assessed by filing a separate schedule with the regular tax return.
c.   May be imposed on both corporations and partnerships.
d.   Qualifies as a tax credit which may be used by partners or stockholders to reduce their individual income taxes.

58. With regard to S corporations and their stockholders, the "at-risk" rules applicable to losses

a.   Apply at the shareholder level rather than at the corporate level.
b.   Depend on the number of persons owning the S corporation's stock.
c.   Take into consideration the character of the S corporation's income.
d.   Are subject to the elections made by the S corporation's stockholders.

59. To qualify as an exempt organization, the applicant
a.   Need not be specifically identified as one of the classes upon which exemption is conferred by the Internal Revenue Code, provided that the organization's purposes and activities are of a nonprofit nature.
b.   Must not be classified as a social club.
c.   Must file a written application with the Internal Revenue Service, even where no official forms are provided.
d.   Must meet the tests that permit donors to deduct their contributions on their individual or corporate tax returns.

60. Which one of the following types of organizations qualifies as an organization exempt from income tax?
a.   All "feeder" organizations, primarily conducting businesses for profit, but distributing 100% of their profits to organizations exempt from taxation.
b.   A social club, supported solely by members' dues and members' purchases of food and drink for consumption on club premises with 100% of the club's profits used for its recreational facilities.
c.   A private foundation organized to influence legislation pertaining to protection of the environment.
d.   A business league operated primarily to publish a yearbook comprised of members' paid advertisements, solicited by paid employees.

Number 4 (Estimated time--45 to 55 minutes)

Melford Hospital operates a general hospital, but rents space and beds to separately owned entities rendering specialized services such as pediatrics and psychiatric. Melford charges each separate entity for common services such as patients' meals and laundry, and for administrative services such as billings and collections. Space and bed rentals are fixed charges for the year, based on bed capacity rented to each entity.

Melford charged the following costs to pediatrics for the year ended June 30, 1990:

	Patient days (variable)	Bed capacity (fixed)
Dietary	$ 600,000	--
Janitorial	--	$ 70,000
Laundry	300,000	--
Laboratory	450,000	--
Pharmacy	350,000	--
Repairs and main- tenance	--	30,000
General and admin- istrative	--	1,300,000
Rent	--	1,500,000
Billings and col- lections	300,000	--
Totals	$2,000,000	$2,900,000

During the year ended June 30, 1990, pediatrics charged each patient an average of $300 per day, had a capacity of 60 beds, and had revenue of $6,000,000 for 365 days.

In addition, pediatrics directly employed the following personnel:

	Annual salaries
Supervising nurses	$25,000
Nurses	20,000
Aides	9,000

Melford has the following minimum departmental personnel requirements based on total annual patient days:

Annual patient days	Aides	Nurses	Supervising nurses
Up to 21,900	20	10	4
21,901 to 26,000	26	13	4
26,001 to 29,200	30	15	4

These staffing levels represent full-time equivalents. Pediatrics always employs only the minimum number of required full-time equivalent personnel. Salaries of supervising nurses, nurses, and aides are therefore fixed within ranges of annual patient days.

Pediatrics operated at 100% capacity on 90 days during the year ended June 30, 1990. It is estimated that during these 90 days the demand exceeded 20 patients more than capacity. Melford has an additional 20 beds available for rent for the year ending June 30, 1991. Such additional rental would increase pediatrics' fixed charges based on bed capacity.

Required:

a. Calculate the minimum number of patient days required for pediatrics to break even for the year ending June 30, 1991, if the additional 20 beds are not rented. Patient demand is unknown, but assume that revenue per patient day, cost per patient day, cost per bed, and salary rates will remain the same as for the year ended June 30, 1990.

b. Assume that patient demand, revenue per patient day, cost per patient day, cost per bed, and salary rates for the year ending June 30, 1991 remain the same as for the year ended June 30, 1990. Prepare a schedule of increase in revenue and increase in costs for the year ending June 30, 1991, in order to determine the net increase or decrease in earnings from the additional 20 beds if pediatrics rents this extra capacity from Melford.

Number 5 (Estimated time – 45 to 55 minutes)

Presented below is the current funds balance sheet of Burnsville University as of the end of its fiscal year ended June 30, 1989.

Burnsville University
Current Funds Balance Sheet
June 30, 1989

Assets:

Current funds:
Unrestricted:

Cash	$210,000	
Accounts receivable-- student tuition and fees, less allowance for doubtful accounts of $9,000	341,000	
State appropriations receivable	75,000	$626,000

Restricted:

Cash	7,000	
Investments	60,000	67,000
Total current funds		$693,000

Liabilities and fund balances:

Current funds:
Unrestricted:

Accounts payable	$45,000	
Deferred revenues	66,000	
Fund balances	515,000	$626,000

Restricted:

Fund balances	67,000
Total current funds	$693,000

The following transactions presented below occurred during the fiscal year ended June 30, 1990:

1. On July 1, 1989, a gift of $100,000 was received from an alumnus. The alumnus requested that one-half of the gift be used for the purchase of books for the university library and the remainder be used for the establishment of a scholarship fund. The alumnus further requested that the income generated by the scholarship fund be used annually to award a scholarship to a qualified disadvantaged student. On July 20, 1989, the board of trustees resolved that the funds of the newly established scholarship fund would be invested in savings certificates. On July 21, 1989, the savings certificates were purchased.

2. Revenue from student tuition and fees applicable to the year ended June 30, 1990, amounted to $1,900,000. Of this amount, $66,000 was collected in the prior year and $1,686,000 was collected during the year ended June 30, 1990. In addition, at June 30, 1990, the university had received cash of $158,000 representing fees for the session beginning July 1, 1990.

3. During the year ended June 30, 1990, the university had collected $349,000 of the outstanding accounts receivable at the beginning of the year. The balance was determined to be uncollected and was written off against the allowance account. At June 30, 1990, the allowance acount was increased by $3,000.

4. During the year, interest charges of $6,000 were earned and collected on late student fee payments.

5. During the year, the state appropria-

tion was received. An additional unrestricted appropriation of $50,000 was made by the state, but had not been paid to the university as of June 30, 1990.

6. An unrestricted gift of $25,000 cash was received from alumni of the university.

7. During the year, investments of $21,000 were sold for $26,000. Investment income amounting to $1,900 was received.

8. During the year, unrestricted operating expenses of $1,777,000 were recorded. At June 30, 1990, $59,000 of these expenses remained unpaid.

9. Restricted current funds of $13,000 were spent for authorized purposes during the year.

10. The accounts payable at June 30, 1989, were paid during the year.

11. During the year, $7,000 interest was earned and received on the savings certificates purchased in accordance with the board of trustees resolution, as discussed in item 1.

Required:

a. Prepare journal entries to record in summary the above transactions for the year ended June 30, 1990. Each journal entry should be numbered to correspond with the transaction described above.

Your answer sheet should be organized as follows:

	Current funds				Endowment	
	Unrestricted		Restricted		fund	
Accounts	Dr.	Cr.	Dr.	Cr.	Dr.	Cr.

b. Prepare a statement of changes in fund balances for the year ended June 30, 1990.

ANSWERS TO SAMPLE EXAMINATION

Practice II

Answer 1		Answer 2		Answer 3	
1. c	11. c	21. d	31. d	41. a	51. b
2. a	12. d	22. b	32. a	42. a	52. b
3. c	13. a	23. a	33. b	43. b	53. a
4. c	14. a	24. a	34. c	44. a	54. d
5. d	15. c	25. d	35. b	45. a	55. a
6. d	16. c	26. c	36. c	46. c	56. c
7. b	17. c	27. c	37. a	47. b	57. b
8. c	18. c	28. b	38. c	48. b	58. a
9. b	19. a	29. a	39. a	49. d	59. c
10. a	20. a	30. a	40. a	50. a	60. b

Answer 4

a. The breakeven point in patient days equals total fixed costs divided by contribution margin per patient day.

Pediatrics
Computation of Breakeven Point
in Patient Days
For the Year Ending June 30, 1991

Total fixed costs (Schedule 1)	$3,380,000
Divided by contribution margin per patient day (Schedule 2)	$ 200
Breakeven point in patient days	16,900

Schedule 1

Total Fixed Costs

Melford Hospital charges	$2,900,000
Supervising nurses ($25,000 x 4)	100,000
Nurses ($20,000 x 10)	200,000
Aides ($9,000 x 20)	180,000
Total fixed costs	$3,380,000

Schedule 2

Contribution Margin Per Patient Day

Revenue per patient day	$300
Variable costs per patient day ($6,000,000/$300 = 20,000 patient days) ($2,000,000/20,000 patient days)	100
Contribution margin per patient day	$200

b.
Pediatrics
Computation of
Loss from Rental of Additional 20 Beds
For the Year Ending June 30, 1991

Increase in revenue (20 additional beds x 90 days x $300 charge per day)	$ 540,000
Increase in expenses Variable charges by Melford hospital (20 addi- (tional beds x 90 days x $100 per day)	180,000
Fixed charges by Melford Hospital ($2,900,000/60 beds = $48,333 per bed x 20 beds) (or, $2,900,000 x 20/60)	966,667
Salaries expense (20,000 patient days before addi- tional 20 beds, + 20 additional beds x 90 days = 21,800, which does not exceed 21,900 patient days; there- fore, no additional personnel are required)	--
Total increase in expenses	1,146,667
Net decrease in earnings from rental of additional 20 beds	$ 606,667

Answer 5

Part a.

Burnsville University
TRANSACTIONS FOR THE YEAR ENDED JUNE 30, 1990

Accounts	Current Funds Unrestricted Debit	Unrestricted Credit	Restricted Debit	Restricted Credit	Endowment Fund Debit	Endowment Fund Credit
1. Cash			$50,000			
Fund balance				$50,000		
To record receipt of cash gift to purchase of books						
Cash					$50,000	
Endowment fund balance						$50,000
To record receipt of cash gift to establish scholarship fund						
Investment in savings certificates					$50,000	
Cash						$50,000
To record purchase of savings certificates						
2. Cash	$1,686,000					
Deferred revenue	66,000					
Accounts receivable--student tuition and fees	148,000					
Revenue		$1,900,000				
To record revenue on tuition and fees						
Cash	158,000					
Deferred revenue		158,000				
To record deferred revenue at June 30, 1990						
3. Cash	349,000					
Allowance for uncollectible accounts	1,000					
Accounts receivable-- tuition and fees		350,000				
To record collection and write-off of accounts receivable						
Expense	3,000					
Allowance for uncollect-ible accounts		3,000				
To record increase in allow-ance account						
4. Cash	6,000					
Revenue		6,000				
To record interest earned on late student fee payments						
5. Cash	75,000					
State appropriation receivable	50,000					
Revenue		50,000				
State appropriation receivable		75,000				
To record receipt of regular appropriation and to record additional appropriation						

Burnsville University
TRANSACTIONS FOR THE YEAR ENDED JUNE 30, 1990

| | Current Funds | | | | Endowment Fund | |
| | Unrestricted | | Restricted | | | |
Accounts	Debit	Credit	Debit	Credit	Debit	Credit
6. Cash	25,000					
Revenue		25,000				
To record receipt of unrestricted gift						
7. Cash			$26,000			
Investments				$21,000		
Fund balance				5,000		
To record sale of investments						
Cash			1,900			
Fund balance				1,900		
To record income earned on investments						
8. Expenses	1,777,000					
Accounts payable		59,000				
Cash		1,718,000				
To record expenses for year						
9. Expenditures			13,000			
Cash				13,000		
To record payment of author- ized expenditures						
Fund balance			13,000			
Revenue				13,000		
To record as revenue amounts expended for restricted purposes						
10. Accounts payable	45,000					
Cash		45,000				
To record payment of accounts payable at June 30, 1989						
11. Cash					7,000	
Fund balance						7,000
To record receipt of interest income on savings certificates purchased by Endowment Fund						

Part b.

Burnsville University
STATEMENT OF CHANGES IN FUNDS BALANCES
For the year ended June 30, 1990

| | Current Funds | | Endowment |
	Unrestricted	Restricted	Fund
Revenues and other additions			
Establishment of scholarship fund			$50,000
Revenue from student tuition and fees	$1,900,000		
Revenue from additional state appropriation	50,000		
Interest income on deferred payments	6,000		
Receipt of gift for library books		$ 50,000	
Investment income		1,900	
Interest income on savings certificates		7,000	
Unrestricted gift received	25,000		
Increase in fund balance on sale of investments		5,000	
Total revenues and other additions	$1,981,000	$ 63,900	$50,000
Expenditures and other deductions			
Operating and authorized expenses	$1,777,000	$ 13,000	
Increase in provision for uncollectible accounts receivable	3,000		
Total expenditures and other deductions	$1,780,000	$ 13,000	--
Net increase (decrease)	201,000	50,900	50,000
Current funds balances, July 1, 1989	515,000	67,000	--
Current funds balances, June 30, 1990	$ 716,000	$117,900	$50,000

EXAMINATION IN ACCOUNTING THEORY

NOTE TO CANDIDATES: Suggested time allotments are as follows:

All questions are required:	Point Value	Estimated Minutes	
		Minimum	Maximum
No. 1	60	90	110
No. 2	10	15	25
No. 3	10	15	25
No. 4	10	15	25
No. 5	10	15	25
Total	110	150	210

Number 1 (Estimated time--90 to 110 minutes)

Select the best answer for each of the following items relating to a variety of issues in accounting.

1.   Under Statement of Financial Accounting Concepts No. 2, which of the following relates to both relevance and reliability?
   a.   Timeliness.
   b.   Materiality.
   c.   Verifiability.
   d.   Neutrality.

2.   Under Statement of Financial Accounting Concepts No. 6, comprehensive income includes which of the following?

	Losses	Contribution margin
a.	No	No
b.	No	Yes
c.	Yes	Yes
d.	Yes	No

3.   When computing information on a historical cost/constant dollar basis, which of the following is classified as nonmonetary?
   a.   Allowance for doubtful accounts.
   b.   Accumulated depreciation of equipment.
   c.   Unamortized premium on bonds payable.
   d.   Advances to unconsolidated subsidiaries.

4.   The effect of a material transaction that is infrequent in occurrence but not unusual in nature should be presented separately as a component of income from continuing operations when the transaction results in a

	Gain	Loss
a.	No	Yes
b.	No	No
c.	Yes	No
d.	Yes	Yes

5.   When the allowance method of recognizing bad debt expense is used, the entries at the time of collection of a small account previously written off would
   a.   Increase net income.
   b.   Have no effect on total current assets.
   c.   Increase working capital.
   d.   Decrease total current liabilities.

6.   The premium on a four-year insurance policy expiring on December 31, 1992, was paid in total on January 1, 1989. Assuming that the original payment was recorded as a prepaid asset, the balance in the prepaid asset account on December 31, 1990, would be
   a.   Lower than the balance on December 31, 1989.
   b.   Lower than the balance on December 31, 1991.
   c.   The same as the balance on December 31, 1992.
   d.   The same as the original payment.

7.   A purchased patent has a remaining legal life of 15 years. It should be
   a.   Expensed in the year of acquisition.
   b.   Amortized over 15 years regardless of its useful life.
   c.   Amortized over its useful life if less than 15 years.
   d.   Amortized over 40 years.

8.   Which of the following should be disclosed in the summary of significant accounting policies?

	Composition of inventories	Maturity dates of long-term debt
a.	Yes	Yes
b.	Yes	No
c.	No	No
d.	No	Yes

9. When the allowance method of recognizing bad debt expense is used, the entry to record the specific write-off of an uncollectible account would decrease
    a. Net accounts receivable.
    b. Allowance for doubtful accounts.
    c. Net income.
    d. Working capital.

10. Temporary differences arise when expenses are deductible

	Before they are recognized in financial income	After they are recognized in financial income
a.	Yes	No
b.	No	No
c.	No	Yes
d.	Yes	Yes

11. Which of the following are generally associated with payables classified as accounts payable?

	Periodic payment of interest	Secured by collateral
a.	No	No
b.	No	Yes
c.	Yes	No
d.	Yes	Yes

12. At its inception, the lease term of Lease D is 80% of the estimated remaining economic life of the leased property. However, the lease term falls within the last 40% of the total estimated economic life of the leased property. The lessee should record Lease D as a(an)
    a. Asset and a liability.
    b. Asset but not a liability.
    c. Neither an asset nor a liability.
    d. Expense.

13. At the time progress billings are sent on a long-term contract, income is recognized under the

	Completed-contract method	Percentage-of-completion method
a.	Yes	Yes
b	Yes	No
c.	No	No
d.	No	Yes

14. Theoretically, freight costs incurred in the transfer of consigned goods from the consignor to the consignee should be considered
    a. An expense by the consignee.
    b. An expense by the consignor.
    c. Inventoriable by the consignee.
    d. Inventoriable by the consignor.

15. An activity that would be expensed currently as research and development costs is the
    a. Adaptation of an existing capability to a particular requirement or customer's need as a part of continuing commercial activity.
    b. Legal work in connection with patent applications or litigation, and the sale or licensing of patents.
    c. Engineering follow-through in an early phase of commercial production.
    d. Testing in search for or evaluation of product or process alternatives.

16. Antidilutive common stock equivalents would generally be used in the calculation of

	Primary earnings per share	Fully diluted earnings per share
a.	Yes	Yes
b.	No	Yes
c.	No	No
d.	Yes	No

17. A loss from early extinguishment of debt, if material, should be reported as a component of income
    a. After cumulative effect of accounting changes and after discontinued operations of a segment of a business.
    b. After cumulative effect of accounting changes and before discontinued operations of a segment of a business.
    c. Before cumulative effect of accounting changes and after discontinued operations of a segment of a business.
    d. Before cumulative effect of accounting changes and before discontinued operations of a segment of a business.

18. The amortization of bond discount on long-term debt should be presented in a statement of cash flows using the indirect method for operating activities as a(an)
    a. Addition to net income.
    b. Deduction from net income.
    c. Financing activity.
    d. Investing activity.

19. A temporary difference which could result in a deferred tax asset is
    a. Interest revenue on municipal bonds.
    b. Accrual of warranty expense.
    c. Excess of tax depreciation over financial accounting depreciation.
    d. Goodwill amortization.

20. A deferred tax liability is computed using
   a. The current tax laws, regardless of expected or enacted future tax laws.
   b. Expected future tax laws, regardless of whether those expected laws have been enacted.
   c. Current tax laws, unless enacted future tax laws are different.
   d. Either current or expected future tax laws, regardless of whether those expected laws have been enacted.

21. Under which of the following conditions would flood damage be considered an extraordinary item for financial reporting purposes?
   a. Only if floods in the geographical area are unusual in nature and occur infrequently.
   b. Only if floods are normal in the geographical area but do not occur frequently.
   c. Only if floods occur frequently in the geographical area but have been insured against.
   d. Under any circumstances flood damage should be classified as an extraordinary item.

22. In accounting for a long-term construction-type contract using the percentage-of-completion method, the gross profit recognized during the first year would be the estimated total gross profit from the contract multiplied by the percentage of the costs incurred during the year to the
   a. Total cost incurred to date.
   b. Total estimated cost.
   c. Unbilled portion of the contract price.
   d. Total contract price.

23. For a compensatory stock option plan for which the date of the grant and the measurement date are the same, what account is credited at the date of the grant?
   a. Retained earnings.
   b. Stock options outstanding.
   c. Deferred compensation cost.
   d. Compensation expense.

24. Q, R, S, and T are partners sharing profits and losses equally. The partnership is insolvent and is to be liquidated; the status of the partnership and each partner is as follows

	Partnership Capital Balance	Personal Assets (Exclusive of Partnership Interest)	Personal Liabilities (Exclusive of Partnership Interest
Q	$ 15,000	$100,000	$40,000
R	$ 10,000	30,000	60,000
S	(20,000)	80,000	5,000
T	(30,000)	1,000	28,000
Total	$(25,000)		

Assuming the Uniform Partnership Act applies, the partnership creditors
   a. Must first seek recovery against S because he is solvent personally, and he has a negative capital balance.
   b. Will not be paid in full regardless of how they proceed legally because the partnership assets _are_ less than the partnership liabilities.
   c. Will have to share R's interest in the partnership on a pro rata basis with R's personal creditors.
   d. Have first claim to the partnership assets before any partner's personal creditors have rights to the partnership assets.

25. The original cost of an inventory item is above the replacement cost and above the net realizable value. The replacement cost is below the net realizable value less the normal profit margin. Under the lower-of-cost-or-market method the inventory item should be priced at its
   a. Original cost.
   b. Replacement cost.
   c. Net realizable value.
   d. Net realizable value less the normal profit margin.

26. A change in accounting entity is actually a change in accounting
   a. Principle.
   b. Estimate.
   c. Method.
   d. Concept.

27. A six-year capital lease specifies equal minimum annual lease payments. Part of this payment represents interest and part represents a reduction in the net lease liability. The portion of the minimum lease payment in the fourth year applicable to the reduction of the net lease liability should be
   a. The same as in the third year.
   b. Less than in the third year.
   c. Less than in the fifth year.
   d. More than in the fifth year.

28. When the interest payment dates of a bond are May 1 and November 1, and the bond is

issued on June 1, 1990, the amount of interest expense for the year ended December 31, 1990, would be for
- a. Two months.
- b. Six months.
- c. Seven months.
- d. Eight months.

29. In a business combination what is the appropriate method of accounting for an excess of fair value assigned to net assets over the cost paid for them?
- a. Record as negative goodwill.
- b. Record as additional paid-in capital from combination on the books of the combined company.
- c. Proportionately reduce values assigned to nonmonetary assets and record any remaining excess as a deferred credit.
- d. Proportionately reduce values assigned to noncurrent assets and record any remaining excess as a deferred credit.

30. An example of a special change in accounting principle that should be reported by restating the financial statements of prior periods is the change from the
- a. Straight-line method of depreciating plant equipment to the sum-of-the-years-digits method.
- b. Sum-of-the-years-digits method of depreciating plant equipment to the straight-line method.
- c. LIFO method of inventory pricing to the FIFO method.
- d. FIFO method of inventory pricing to the LIFO method.

31. Gilbert Corporation issued a 40% stock split-up of its common stock which had a par value of $10 before and after the split-up. At what amount should retained earnings be capitalized for the additional shares issued?
- a. There should be no capitalization of retained earnings.
- b. Par value.
- c. Market value on the declaration date.
- d. Market value on the payment date.

32. Which of the following terms includes assumptions concerning projected changes in future compensation when the pension benefit formula is based on future compensation levels (e.g., pay related and final pay plans)?

	Service cost component	Projected benefit obligation	Accumulated benefit obligation
a.	Yes	Yes	Yes
b.	Yes	Yes	No
c.	Yes	No	No
d.	No	No	No

33. In the calculation of pension expense recognized for a period by an employer sponsoring a defined benefit pension plan, which component will not be included?
- a. Interest cost on the projected benefit obligation.
- b. Actuarial present value of benefits attributed by the pension benefit formula to employee service during that period.
- c. Amortization of the unrecognized net obligation (and loss or cost) or unrecognized net asset (and gain) existing at the date of transition.
- d. Excess of accumulated benefit obligation over the fair value of the plan assets.

34. An investor purchased a bond as a long-term investment between interest dates at a premium. At the purchase date, the cash paid to the seller is
- a. The same as the face amount of the bond.
- b. The same as the face amount of the bond plus accrued interest.
- c. More than the face amount of the bond.
- d. Less than the face amount of the bond.

35. An increase in the inventory balance would be reported in a statement of cash flows using the indirect method for operating activities as a
- a. Financing activity.
- b. Investing activity.
- c. Addition to net income.
- d. Deduction from net income.

36. A development stage enterprise
- a. Issues an income statement that is the same as an established operating enterprise, and shows cumulative amounts from the enterprise's inception as additional information.
- b. Issues an income statement that is the same as an established operating enterprise, but does not show cumulative amounts from the enterprise's inception as additional information.
- c. Issues an income statement that only shows cumulative amounts from the enterprise's inception.
- d. Does not issue an income statement.

37. The granting by a company to its shareholders of the opportunity to buy additional
shares of stock within a specified future time
at a specified price is an example of a
    a. Dividend reinvestment plan.
    b. Stock right.
    c. Stock dividend.
    d. Stock option.

38. A company that has no temporary differences suffers an operating loss that exceeds
taxable income for the previous three years.
In the year of loss, the tax benefit from this
loss that may be recognized as an asset on the
balance sheet and as a reduction of the loss
on the income statement is
    a. The tax benefit from applying carry-
        back provisions only.
    b. The tax benefit from applying carry-
        back provisions and the future tax
        benefit from applying carryforward
        provisions.
    c. The tax benefit of applying carry-
        back provisions, and if realization
        is likely, also the future tax
        benefit of applying carryforward
        provisions.
    d. The future tax benefit of applying
        carryforward provisions only.

39. If the conventional (lower of cost or
market) retail inventory method is used, which
of the following calculations would include
(exclude) net markdowns?

	Cost ratio (percentage)	Ending inventory at retail
a.	Include	Include
b.	Include	Exclude
c.	Exclude	Include
d.	Exclude	Exclude

40. Which of the following is a potential
abuse that can arise when a business combination is accounted for as a pooling of
interests?
    a. Assets of the investee may be over-
        valued when the price paid by the
        investor is allocated among specific
        assets.
    b. Liabilities may be undervalued when
        the price paid by the investor is
        allocated to the specific liabili-
        ties.
    c. An undue amount of cost may be as-
        signed to goodwill, thus,
        potentially allowing for an
        overstatement of pooled earnings.
    d. Earnings of the pooled entity may be
        increased because of the combination
        only and not as a result of effi-
        cient operations.

41. The fixed portion of the semivariable
cost of electricity for a manufacturing plant
is a

	Conversion cost	Product cost
a.	No	No
b.	No	Yes
c.	Yes	Yes
d.	Yes	No

42. In developing a factory overhead
application rate for use in a process costing
system, which of the following could be used
in the denominator?
    a. Actual factory overhead.
    b. Estimated factory overhead.
    c. Actual direct labor hours.
    d. Estimated direct labor hours.

43. Under the three-variance method for
analyzing factory overhead, the difference
between the actual factory overhead and the
budget allowance based on actual hours is the
    a. Efficiency variance.
    b. Spending variance.
    c. Volume variance.
    d. Idle capacity variance.

44. A basic tenet of direct costing is that
period costs should be currently expensed.
What is the basic rationale behind this
procedure?
    a. Period costs are uncontrollable and
        should not be charged to a specific
        product.
    b. Period costs are generally imma-
        terial in amount and the cost of
        assigning the amounts to specific
        products would outweigh the bene-
        fits.
    c. Allocation of period costs is arbi-
        trary at best and could lead to
        erroneous decisions by management.
    d. Period costs will occur whether or
        not production occurs and so it is
        improper to allocate these costs to
        production and defer a current cost
        of doing business.

45. When production levels are expected to
decline within a relevant range, and a
flexible budget is used, what effects would be
anticipated with respect to each of the
following?

	Fixed costs per unit	Variable costs per unit
a.	Increase	Increase
b.	Increase	No change
c.	No change	No change
d.	No change	Increase

46. In using cost-volume-profit analysis to calculate the expected sales level expressed in units, a predicted operating loss would be
  a. Added to fixed costs in the numerator.
  b. Added to fixed costs in the denominator.
  c. Subtracted from fixed costs in the numerator.
  d. Subtracted from fixed costs in the denominator.

47. Under the internal rate of return capital budgeting technique, it is assumed that cash flows are reinvested at the
  a. Cost of capital.
  b. Hurdle rate of return.
  c. Rate earned by the investment.
  d. Payback rate.

48. A company's return on investment is affected by a change in

	Capital turnover	Profit margin on sales
a	Yes	Yes
b.	Yes	No
c.	No	No
d.	No	Yes

49. A company is deciding whether to exchange an old asset for a new asset. Within the context of the exchange decision, and ignoring income tax considerations, the undepreciated book balance of the old asset would be considered a(an)

	Sunk cost	Irrelevant cost
a.	No	No
b.	Yes	No
c.	No	Yes
d.	Yes	Yes

50. A company buys a certain part for its manufacturing process. In order to determine the optimum size of a normal purchase order, the formula for the economic order quantity (EOQ) is used. In addition to the annual demand, what other information is necessary to complete the formula?
  a. Cost of placing an order, and annual cost of carrying a unit in stock.
  b. Cost of the part, and annual cost of carrying a unit in stock.
  c. Cost of placing an order.
  d. Cost of the part.

51. When the budget of a governmental unit is adopted and the estimated revenues exceed the appropriations, the excess is
  a. Debited to reserve for encumbrances.
  b. Credited to reserve for encumbrances.
  c. Debited to budgetary fund balance.
  d. Credited to budgetary fund balance.

52. Which of the following funds should use the modified accrual basis of accounting?
  a. Capital projects.
  b. Internal service.
  c. Enterprise.
  d. Nonexpendable trust.

53. What is not a major concern of governmental units?
  a. Budgets.
  b. Funds.
  c. Legal requirements.
  d. Consolidated statements.

54. A reason for a voluntary health and welfare organization to adopt fund accounting is that
  a. Restrictions have been placed on certain of its assets by donors.
  b. It provides more than one type of program service.
  c. Fixed assets are significant.
  d. Donated services are significant.

55. When a truck is received by a governmental unit, it should be recorded in the General Fund as a(an)
  a. Appropriation.
  b. Encumbrance.
  c. Expenditure.
  d. Fixed asset.

56. Within a governmental unit, three funds that are accounted for in a manner similar to a for-profit entity are
  a. General, Debt Service, Special Revenue.
  b. Special Revenue, Enterprise, Internal Service.
  c. Internal Service, Enterprise, Nonexpendable Trust.
  d. Enterprise, General, Debt Service.

57. What is the recommended method of accounting to be used by colleges and universities?
  a. Cash.
  b. Modified cash.
  c. Restricted accrual.
  d. Accrual.

58. Under the modified accrual method of accounting used by a local governmental unit, which of the following would be a revenue susceptible to accrual?
  a. Income taxes.
  b. Business licenses.
  c. Property taxes.
  d. Sales taxes.

59. The accounting for special revenue funds is most similar to which type of fund?
   a. Capital projects.
   b. General.
   c. Enterprise.
   d. Agency.

60. Which governmental fund would account for fixed assets in a manner similar to a "for-profit" organization?
   a. Enterprise.
   b. Capital projects.
   c. General fixed asset group of accounts.
   d. General.

Number 2 (Estimated time--15 to 25 minutes)

Walker Company has a noncurrent marketable equity securities portfolio. Walker does not own more than five percent of the outstanding voting stock for any of the securities in the portfolio. At the beginning of the year, the aggregate market value of the portfolio exceeded its cost. Cash dividends on these securities were received during the year. None of the securities in the portfolio were sold during the year. At the end of the year, the aggregate cost of the portfolio exceeded its market value. The decline in the market price of the securities in the portfolio is attributable to general market decline.

During the year, Walker purchased for cash thirty-five percent of the outstanding voting stock of Sipe Company. Cash dividends on this investment were received from Sipe during the year, and the earnings of Sipe after the acquisition date were reported by Sipe to Walker.

Required:

   a. How should Walker report on its balance sheet and income statement the effects of its investment in the noncurrent marketable equity securities portfolio for the year? Why?
   b. How should Walker report on its balance sheet and income statement the effects of its investment in Sipe for the year? Why?

Number 3 (Estimated time--15 to 25 minutes)

Incurring long-term debt with an arrangement whereby lenders receive an option to buy common stock during all or a portion of the time the debt is outstanding is a frequently used corporate financing practice. In some situations the result is achieved through the issuance of convertible bonds; in others the debt instruments and the warrants to buy stock are separate.

Required:

   a. 1. Describe the differences that exist in current accounting for original proceeds of the issuance of convertible bonds and of debt instruments with separate warrants to purchase common stock.
      2. Discuss the underlying rationale for the differences described in a.1. above.
      3. Summarize the arguments which have been presented for the alternative accounting treatment.

b. At the start of the year AB Company issued $6,000,000 of 7% notes along with warrants to buy 400,000 shares of its $10 par value common stock at $18 per share. The notes mature over the next ten years starting one year from date of issuance with annual maturities of $600,000. At the time, AB had 3,200,000 shares of common stock outstanding, and the market price was $23 per share. The company received $6,680,000 for the notes and the warrants. For AB Company, 7% was a relatively low borrowing rate. If offered alone, at this time, the notes would have been issued at a 20 to 24 percent discount. Prepare journal entries for the issuance of the notes and warrants for the cash consideration received.

Number 4 (Estimated time--15 to 25 minutes)

Part a. Property, plant, and equipment (plant assets) generally represent a material portion of the total assets of most companies. Accounting for the acquisition and usage of such assets is, therefore, an important part of the financial reporting process.

Required:

1. Distinguish between revenue and capital expenditures and explain why this distinction is important.
2. Briefly define depreciation as used in accounting.
3. Identify the factors that are relevant in determining the annual depreciation and explain whether these factors are determined objectively or whether they are based on judgment.
4. Explain why depreciation is not a source or use of cash.

Part b. A company may acquire plant assets (among other ways) for cash, on a deferred-payment plan, by exchanging other assets, or by a combination of these ways.

Required:

1. Identify six costs that should be capitalized as the cost of land. For your answer, assume that land with an existing building is acquired for cash and that the existing building is to be removed in the immediate future in order that a new building can be constructed on that site.
2. At what amount should a company record a plant asset acquired on a deferred-payment plan?
3. In general, at what amount should plant assets received in exchange for other nonmonetary assets be recorded? Specifically, at what amount should a company record a new machine acquired by exchanging an older, similar machine and paying cash?

Number 5 (Estimated time--15 to 25 minutes)

Cope Company is a manufacturer of household appliances. During the year, the following information became available:

• Probable warranty costs on its household appliances are estimated to be 1% of sales.
• One of its manufacturing plants is located in a foreign country. There is a threat of expropriation of this plant. The threat of expropriation is deemed to be reasonably possible. Any compensation from the foreign government would be less than the carrying amount of the plant.
• It is probable that damages will be received by Cope next year as a result of a lawsuit filed this year against another household appliances manufacturer.

Required:

In answering the following, do not discuss deferred income tax implications.

a. How should Cope report the probable warranty costs? Why?
b. How should Cope report the threat of expropriation of assets? Why?
c. How should Cope report this year the probable damages that may be received next year? Why?

ANSWERS TO SAMPLE EXAMINATION

THEORY

Answer 1

1. b	11. a	21. a	31. b	41. c	51. d
2. c	12. a	22. b	32. b	42. d	52. a
3. b	13. c	23. b	33. d	43. b	53. d
4. d	14. d	24. d	34. c	44. d	54. a
5. b	15. d	25. d	35. d	45. b	55. c
6. a	16. c	26. a	36. a	46. c	56. c
7. c	17. c	27. c	37. b	47. c	57. d
8. c	18. a	28. c	38. a	48. a	58. c
9. b	19. b	29. d	39. c	49. d	59. b
10. d	20. c	30. c	40. d	50. a	60. a

Answer 2

a. A noncurrent marketable equity securities portfolio should be accounted for at cost or market, whichever is lower. Therefore, at the end of the year Walker should report the non-current marketable equity securities portfolio as a noncurrent asset at market. It is conservative to carry the portfolio at market value when it is below cost because of the uncertainty of future recovery of the market decline. The amount by which the aggregate cost of the portfolio exceeded the market value at the end of the year should be accounted for as a valuation allowance to the portfolio. The offsetting portion of the entry is included in the equity section of the balance sheet and shown separately. The rationale for this treatment is that a decline in market value of an equity security classified as a noncurrent asset can be viewed as temporary and thus is not reflected in net income because the probability of realization of the loss is small.

Walker should report the cash dividends received during the year on the securities in the noncurrent marketable equity securities portfolio as dividend income.

b. Due to the size of its investment, i.e., over twenty percent of the outstanding voting stock of Sipe, Walker is presumed to be able to exercise significant influence over Sipe. Therefore, Walker should use the equity method of accounting for its investment in Sipe.

Walker should report the purchase of the stock of Sipe as a long-term investment, and initially account for it at cost, which is the amount of cash paid. The cash dividends received during the year by Walker on the investment in the stock of Sipe should be deducted from the carrying amount of the investment and have no effect on Walker's income statement.

Subsequent to the acquisition, Walker should report thirty-five percent of Sipe's earnings after the acquisition date as revenue in its income statement and add the same amount to the carrying amount of its investment on the balance sheet. This amount should be modified by adjustments similar to those made in preparing consolidated statements, including adjustments to eliminate intercompany gains and losses, and to amortize, if appropriate, any difference between Walker's cost and the underlying equity in net assets of Sipe on the acquisition date.

Answer 3

a. 1. When the debt instrument and the option to acquire common stock are inseparable, as in the case of convertible bonds, the entire proceeds of the bond issue should be allocated to the debt and the related premium or discount accounts.

When the debt and the warrants are separable, the proceeds of their sale should be allocated between them. The basis of allocation is their relative fair values. As a practical matter, these relative values are usually determined by reference to the price at which the respective instruments are traded in the open market. Thus, if the debt alone would bring six times as much as would the stock purchase warrants, if sold separately, one-seventh of the total proceeds should be apportioned to the warrants and six-sevenths to the debt securities. That portion of the proceeds assigned to the warrants should be accounted for as paid-in capital. The result may be that the debt is issued at a reduced premium or at a discount.

2. In the case of convertible debt there are two principal reasons why all the proceeds should be ascribed to the

debt. First, the option is inseparable from the debt. The investor in
such securities has two mutually
exclusive choices: he may be a
creditor and later receive cash for
his security; or, he may give up his
right as a creditor and become a
stockholder. There is no way to
retain one right while selling the
other. Second, the valuation of the
conversion option presents practical
problems. For example, in the absence
of separate transferability, no
separate market values are established
and the only values which could be
assigned to each would be subjective.

Separability of the debt and the
warrants and the establishment of a
market value for each results in an
objective basis for allocating proceeds to the two different equities--
creditors' and stockholders'--
involved.

3. Arguments have been advanced that
accounting for convertible debt should
be the same as for debt issued with
detachable stock purchase warrants.
Convertible debt has features of debt
and stockholders' equity, and separate
recognition should be given to those
characteristics at the time of
issuance. Difficulties encountered in
separating the relative values of the
features are not insurmountable and,
in any case, should not result in a
solution which ignores the problem.
In effect, the company is selling a
debt instrument and a call on its
stock. Coexistence of the two features in one instrument is no reason
why each cannot receive its proper
accounting recognition. The practical
difficulties of estimation of the
relative values may be overcome with
reliable professional advice. Allocation is a well recognized accounting
technique and could be applied in this
case once reliable estimates of the
relative values are known. If the
convertible feature was added in order
to sell the security at an acceptable
price, the value of the convertible
option is obviously material and
recognition is essential. The
question of whether or not the
purchaser will exercise his option is
not relevant to reflecting the
separate elements at the time of
issuance.

b.

	Debit	Credit
Cash	$6,680,000	
Discount on notes payable	1,320,000	
Notes payable		$6,000,000
Paid-in capital (option to buy common stock)		2,000,000

To record issuance of notes at 22%
discount with options to buy 400,000
shares of the company's no-par common
stock at a price of $5 a share below the
current market value. Debt matures in ten
years in equal annual installments of
$600,000 and options, if not exercised,
lapse as notes mature.

Answer 4

a. 1. Relative to plant assets, a cost
incurred or an expenditure made, that
is assumed to benefit only the current
accounting period is called a revenue
expenditure and is charged to expense
in the period believed to benefit. A
capital expenditure is similarly a
cost incurred or an expenditure made
but is expected to yield benefits
either in all future accounting
periods (acquisition of land) or in a
limited number of accounting
periods. Capital expenditures (if
material in amount) are capitalized,
that is, recorded as assets, and, if
related to assets of limited life,
amortized over the periods believed to
benefit.

The distinction between capital
and revenue expenditures is of significance because it involves the timing
of the recognition of expense, and
consequently, the determination of
periodic earnings. It also affects the
amounts reported as assets whose costs
generally have to be recouped from
future periods' revenues.

If a revenue expenditure is improperly capitalized, current earnings
are overstated, assets are overstated,
and future earnings are understated
for all the periods to which the
improperly capitalized cost is
amortized. If the cost is not
amortized, future earnings will not be
affected but assets and retained
earnings will continue to be overstated for as long as the cost remains
on the books. If a nonamortizable
capital expenditure is improperly
expensed, current earnings are
understated and assets and retained

earnings are understated for all foreseeable periods in the future. If an
amortizable capital expenditure is
improperly expensed, current earnings
are understated, assets and retained
earnings are understated, and future
earnings are overstated for all
periods to which the cost should have
been amortized.

2. Depreciation is the accounting process
of allocating an asset's historical
cost (recorded amount) to the accounting periods benefitted by the use
of the asset. It is a process of cost
allocation, not valuation. Depreciation is not intended to provide funds
for an asset's replacement; it is
merely an application of the matching
concept.

3. The factors relevant in determining
the annual depreciation for a depreciable asset are the initial recorded
amount (cost), estimated salvage
value, estimated useful life, and
depreciation method.

      Assets are typically recorded at
their acquisition cost, which is in
most cases objectively determinable.
But cost assignments in other cases--
"basket purchases" and the selection
of an implicit interest rate in asset
acquisition under deferred-payment
plans--may be quite subjective
involving considerable judgment.

      The salvage value is an estimate
of an amount potentially realizable
when the asset is retired from
service. It is initially a judgment
factor and is affected by the length
of its useful life to the enterprise.

      The useful life is also a judgment
factor. It involves selecting the
"unit" of measure of service life and
estimating the number of such units
embodied in the asset. Such units may
be measured in terms of time periods
or in terms of activity (for example,
years or machine hours). When
selecting the life, one should select
the lower (shorter) of the physical
life or the economic life to this
user. Physical life involves wear and
tear and casualties; economic life involves such things as technological
obsolescence and inadequacy.

      Selecting the depreciation method
is generally a judgment decision; but,
a method may be inherent in the definition adopted for the units of service life, as discussed earlier. For
example, if such units are machine
hours, the method is a function of the
number of machine hours used during
each period. A method should be selected that will best measure the portion of services expiring each period.
Once a method is selected, it may be
objectively applied by using a predetermined, objectively derived formula.

4. When an asset is purchased, the payment for the asset and the allocation
of the cost of the asset are separate
transactions. The effect on cash
occurs when payment for the asset is
made. Depreciation is the allocation
of the asset's cost to the accounting
periods benefitted as charges to expense. Therefore, depreciation will
reduce reported net earnings, but will
not involve an outflow of cash. Note,
however, that although depreciation is
not a source or use of cash, there is
an income tax savings from including
depreciation as an expense.

b. 1. The following costs, if applicable,
should be capitalized as a cost of
land

(a) Negotiated purchase price
(b) Brokers' commission
(c) Legal fees
(d) Title fee
(e) Recording fee
(f) Escrow fees
(g) Surveying fees
(h) Existing unpaid taxes, inter-
        est, or liens assumed by the
        buyer
(i) Clearing, grading, landscaping,
        and subdividing
(j) Cost of removing old building
        (less salvage)
(k) Special assessments such as
        lighting or sewers if they are
        permanent in nature.

2   A plant asset acquired on a deferred-
payment plan should be recorded at an
equivalent cash price excluding interest. If interest is not stated in the
sales contract, an imputed interest
should be determined. The asset
should then be recorded at its present
value, which is computed by discounting the payments at the stated or
imputed interest rate. The interest
portion (stated or imputed) of the
contract price should be charged to
interest expense over the life of the
contract.

3. In general, plant assets should be recorded at the fair value of the consideration given or the fair value of the asset received, whichever is more clearly evident. This general theoretical preference is somewhat constrained by the requirements of APB Opinion No. 29.

Specifically when exchanging an old machine and paying cash for a new machine, the new machine should be recorded at the amount of monetary consideration (cash) paid plus the undepreciated cost of the nonmonetary asset (old machine) surrendered if there is no indicated loss. An indicated loss should be recognized; this would reduce the recorded amount of the new machine. No indicated gain, however, should be recognized by the party paying monetary consideration.

Answer 5

a. Cope should report the probable warranty costs as an expense in the income statement and a liability in the balance sheet because both of the following required conditions for accrual were met:

- It is considered probable that liabilities have been incurred.
- The amount of loss can be reasonably estimated.

In addition, it may be necessary for Cope to disclose the nature of the probable warranty costs in the notes to the financial statements.

b. Cope should disclose the nature of the threat of expropriation of assets in the notes to the financial statements. In addition, an estimate of the possible loss or range of loss should be disclosed in the notes to the financial statements.

Cope should not report the threat of expropriation of assets as an expense in the income statement nor as a liability in the balance sheet because it does not meet both required conditions for accrual. The actual expropriation of assets is only reasonably possible instead of probable.

c. Adequate disclosure should be made of contingencies that result in gains, but care should be exercised to avoid misleading implications as to the likelihood of realization.

Cope should not report this year the probable damages that may be received next year as a gain in the income statement nor as an asset in the balance sheet. Gain contingencies usually are not recorded in the accounts until the gains are realized.